15 reasons why you should be part of the Cr...

– as well as the fact that we work with Imray to produce th...
we do the words, they do the pictures...

A wealth of information – the world's best cruising llibrary and a member-only web site wiith thousands of web pages

Friends afloat and ashore – 20 local and sea-area groups meeting regularly

The chance to learn – lectures, seminars, training around the UK

Make your budget go further – a long list of suppliers offer you significant discounts: many members save more than the cost of membership every year

A London home – affordable guest cabins at CA House when you're visiting the UK capital

Crew finding – our crewing service puts skippers in touch with crew, and crew in touch with skippers

In-port help – you'll be able to call on almost 250 CA special representatives in ports around the UK, Europe and the world

Rallies – from in-port meets to extended cruises in company

Exclusive publicati... guides, lay-up directories and a quar...

Online advice – general, specialist and geographical forums, with help offered by known, named and trusted contributors

Influence – we're invited by the authorities to consult widely on matters ranging from windfarms to colregs

Classified advertising – buy and sell between members: everything from charts to boats

Paperwork – advice on what you need to take when you go foreign

Cruise planning – all the latest planning and navigation software available on PCs in our library

Don't just join, join in – we're volunteer-run; there's always the opportunity for you to contribute to the wider cruising community

CAptain's Mate – that's the app you see below. Absolutely up-to-date member-generated information from just about anywhere you can take a small boat

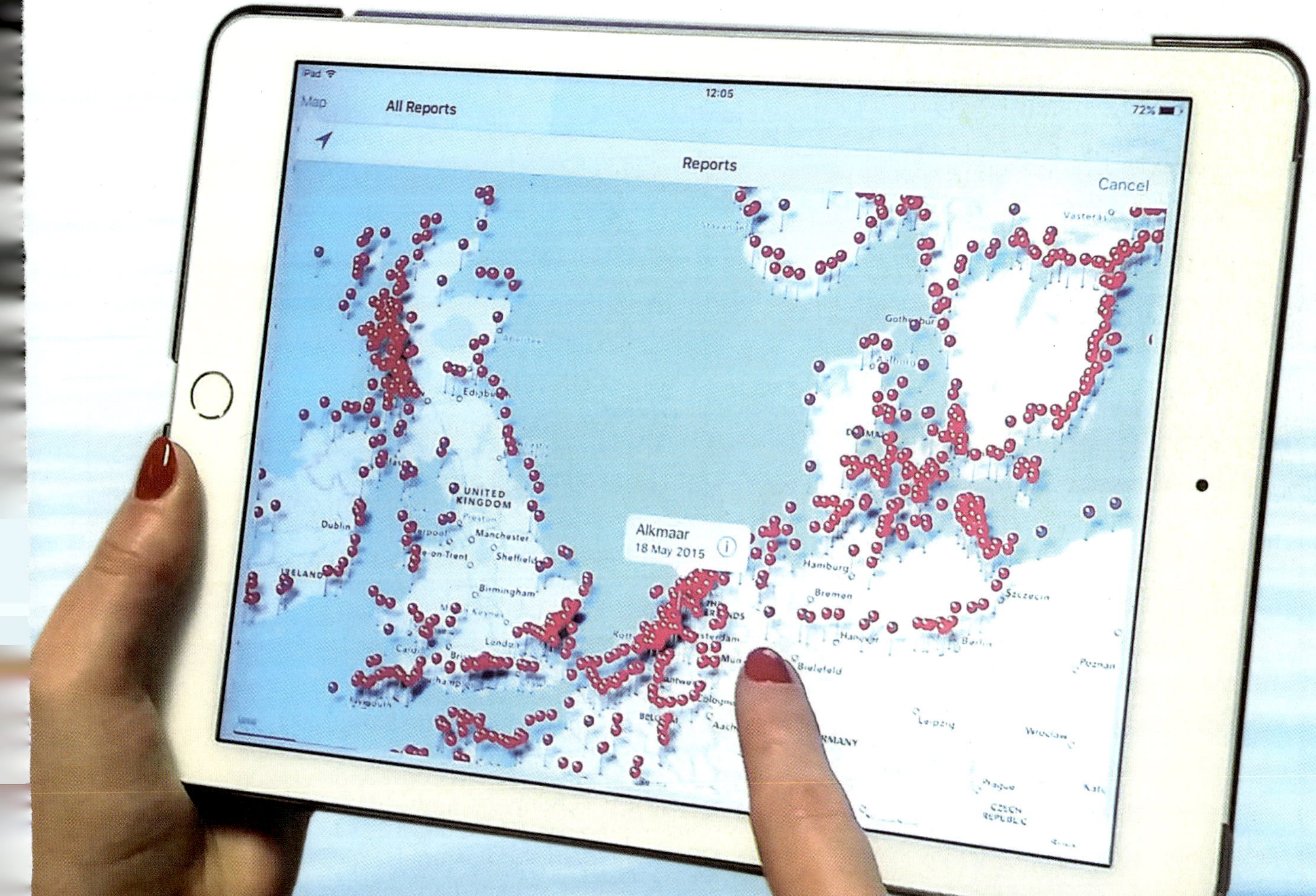

The Cruising Association
CA House, 1 Northey Street, Limehouse Basin, London E14 8BT, UK
0207 537 2828
office@theca.org.uk
www.theca.org.uk

The Cruising Almanac 2018

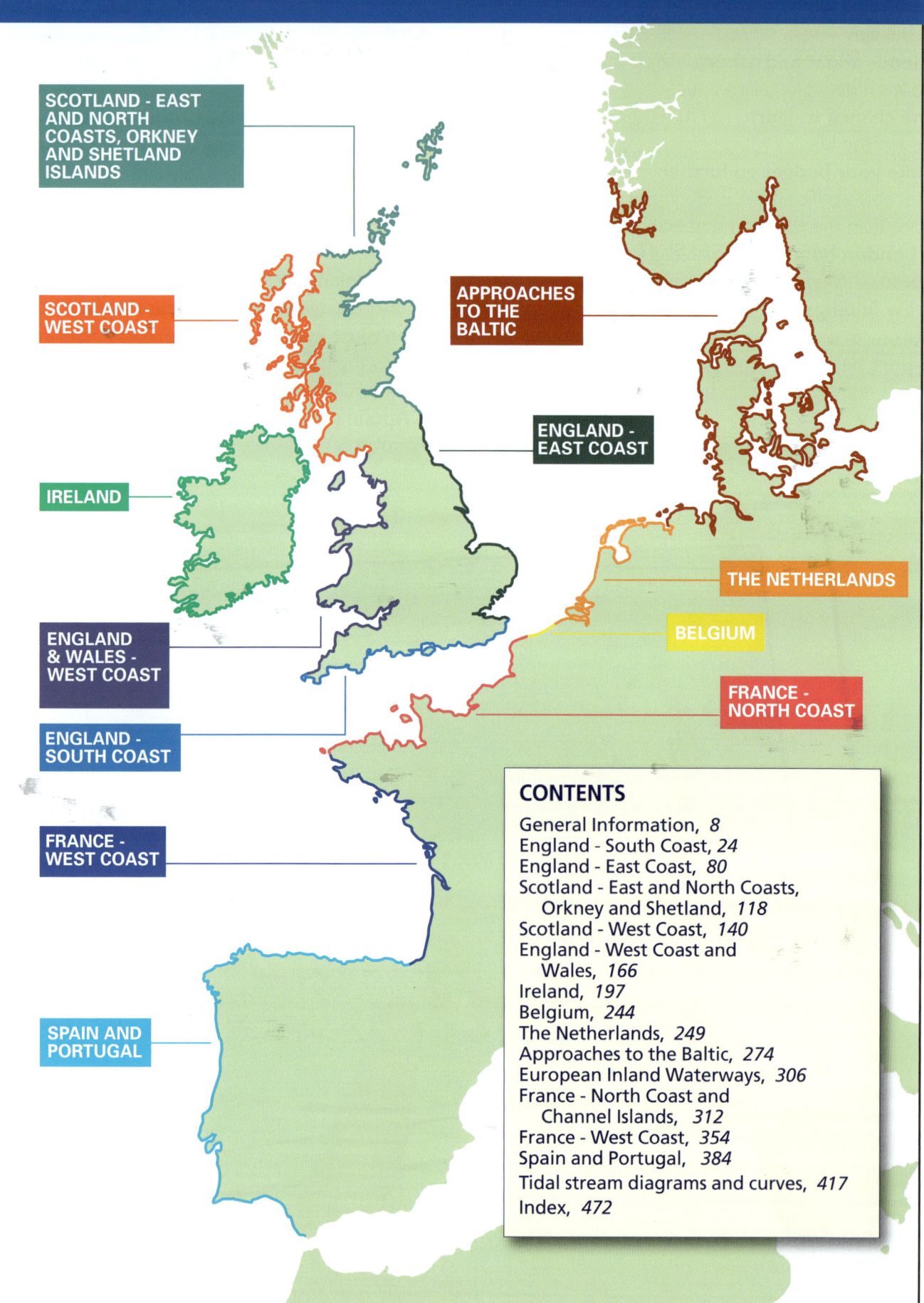

- SCOTLAND - EAST AND NORTH COASTS, ORKNEY AND SHETLAND ISLANDS
- SCOTLAND - WEST COAST
- APPROACHES TO THE BALTIC
- ENGLAND - EAST COAST
- IRELAND
- THE NETHERLANDS
- BELGIUM
- ENGLAND & WALES - WEST COAST
- FRANCE - NORTH COAST
- ENGLAND - SOUTH COAST
- FRANCE - WEST COAST
- SPAIN AND PORTUGAL

CONTENTS

General Information, 8
England - South Coast, 24
England - East Coast, 80
Scotland - East and North Coasts, Orkney and Shetland, 118
Scotland - West Coast, 140
England - West Coast and Wales, 166
Ireland, 197
Belgium, 244
The Netherlands, 249
Approaches to the Baltic, 274
European Inland Waterways, 306
France - North Coast and Channel Islands, 312
France - West Coast, 354
Spain and Portugal, 384
Tidal stream diagrams and curves, 417
Index, 472

The Cruising Almanac 2018

Imray Laurie Norie & Wilson Ltd
and The Cruising Association

Published by
Imray, Laurie, Norie & Wilson Ltd
Wych House, The Broadway, St Ives,
Cambridgeshire PE27 5BT England
☎ +44 (0)1480 462114
www.imray.com
2017

The Cruising Association
CA House, 1 Northey Street, Limehouse Basin,
London E14 8BT
☎ +44 (0)20 7537 2828
www.theca.org.uk

All rights reserved. No part of this publication may be reproduced, transmitted or used in any form by any means – graphic, electronic or mechanical, including photocopying, recording, taping or information storage and retrieval systems or otherwise – without the prior permission of the publishers.

© The Cruising Association 2017

© Cartography Imray, Laurie, Norie & Wilson Ltd 2017

This product has been derived in part from material obtained from the UK Hydrographic Office with the permission of the UK Hydrographic Office, Her Majesty's Stationery Office and Vlaamse Hydrografie (Belgium), Dienst Der Hydrographie (Netherlands), Armada Española (Spain) and Instituto Hidrográfico da Marinha Portuguesa (Portugal).

THIS PRODUCT IS NOT TO BE USED FOR NAVIGATION.

The UK Hydrographic Office (UKHO) and its licensors make no warranties or representations, express or implied, with respect to this product. The UKHO and its licensors have not verified the information within this product or quality assured it.

© British Crown Copyright 2017. All rights reserved. Licence number GB AA - 005 - Imrays

© Data reproduced with permission of SHOM – Service Hydrographique et Oceanographique de la Marine, France. Licence no.44/2013.

© Data reproduced with permission of the Bundesamt für Seeschifffahrt und Hydrographie, Hamburg Licence no. 11123/2012-15.

First edition 2002
Second edition 2004
Third edition 2006
Fourth edition 2008
Fifth edition 2010
Sixth edition 2011
Seventh edition 2012
Eighth edition 2013
Ninth edition 2014
Tenth edition 2015
Eleventh edition 2016
Twelfth edition 2017

British Library Cataloguing in Publication Data. A catalogue record for this book is available from the British Library.

ISBN 978 184623 870 3

Originally published as Sailing Directions within the *Cruising Association Handbook 1909*
Editions 1920, 1928
Fifth edition 1971
Sixth edition 1981
Seventh edition 1990
Seventh edition revised 1992
Eighth edition 1996

CAUTION

The plans in this almanac should not be used for navigation except in conjunction with the proper up-to-date charts of appropriate scale, together with the latest *Notices to Mariners*.

The Cruising Association, its officers, members, the editor and individual authors make no warranty as to the accuracy or reliability of any information contained in this publication and accept no liability for any loss, injury or damage occasioned to any person acting or refraining from action as a result of the use of such information or any decision made or action taken in reliance or partial reliance on it save that nothing contained in this publication in any way limits or excludes liability for negligence causing death or personal injury or for anything which may not legally be excluded or limited.

This book contains selected information and thus is not definitive and does not include all known information on the subject in hand; this is particularly relevant to the plans, which should not be used for navigation. The publisher and author believe that its selection is a useful aid to prudent navigation, but the safety of a vessel depends ultimately on the judgement of the navigator, who should assess all information, published or unpublished, available to him/her.

The last input of technical information was May 2017

Printed and bound in Croatia by Zrinski

CORRECTIONS

Cumulative corrections are published on the CA website at approximately two monthly intervals.

www.theca.org.uk/almanac/corrections

These take into account *Notices to Mariners*, information received from Harbourmasters, changes to buoyage and lights as well as new developments that have taken place during the life of the Almanac. These may also be obtained as printed copies from:

The Cruising Association, CA House, 1 Northey Street, Limehouse Basin, London E14 8BT at a nominal charge.

The editor would be glad to receive any corrections, information or suggestions which readers may consider would improve the book, as new impressions will be required from time to time. Letters should be addressed to the Editor, care of the publishers or *Email* almanac@theca.org.uk. The more precise the information the better, but even partial or doubtful information is helpful, if the nature of the doubt is made clear.

Foreword

Don't do what I did last summer. I thought it would be interesting, for a change, to cruise abroad using local charts and pilot books, buying them en route as I bumbled along.

I'd also resolved to jolt my Luddite brain into the 21st century, so I stuffed my phone full of navigation and pilotage apps, bought a bunch of spare batteries and chargers and set off downwind with only a vague idea of where I wanted to go.

I learned a few things. Chandlers are fewer and further between than they used to be and you can't assume they'll have a useful range of charts in stock, let alone the pilot book you're after. Nowhere between Chichester and Cuxhaven could I find a decent chart of the Elbe, nor a pilot for the Dutch Delta until I'd passed through it.

Cruising through Holland, I was half way to Amsterdam before I managed to buy a copy of the important – and mandatory – ANWB *Wateralmanak*, which tells you when the bridges open and how to communicate with the people who operate them. Unsurprisingly I spent several nights stuck between bridges, tied to a siding and exposed to heavy wash from passing barges.

You can, in theory, find a lot of that information online, but I can't recommend it. Despite paying £5 a day on top of my phone contract for 'unlimited super-fast roaming broadband', I found that access to Google was blocked in The Netherlands and Germany and the local met office websites were unavailable. Eventually, I learned that my mobile phone carrier was 'shaping traffic' to give its customers lightning-quick access to Facebook and Twitter, at the expense of normal web browsing.

I also discovered, twice in fact, how easily a mobile phone SIM card can escape the clutches of cold-numbed fingers in a gentle breeze, slip between cabin sole boards and drown in the bilge sump.

I was glad of that phone, though, when I sailed off the edge of my plotter chart on a foggy day in the shoal waters of southern Denmark. I hate to admit it, but five years of using a reliable chartplotter have blunted my old-school pilotage skills. It's worth knowing that most chandlers don't keep plotter charts in stock, as I found after backtracking forty-odd miles. It can take several days after you've paid for them to download the data.

No matter. I sailed on for a few hundred miles with an excellent German chart folio in one hand and an identical chart on my phone in the other. There are lots of chartplotter apps and some are even quite good, although I soon learned that it pays to have two of them running simultaneously when you're on passage.

The thing I missed most, in all six countries I visited, was an up-to-date, printed, English-language almanac. If you've ever had to try using Google Translate to make sense of a foreign pilot book or app while approaching a tricky harbour entrance in a rising wind, you'll know what I mean.

The way we navigate may have changed, but *The Cruising Almanac* remains invaluable. Don't go sailing without it.

Kieran Flatt
Editor Yachting Monthly

Dunstaffnage Bay *M J Richards in memory of G C Betts*

Preface

This is the twelfth edition of the *Cruising Almanac* in its present form. Its origins can be traced back to the *Sailing Directions*, published in 1909, by the Cruising Association. Its contents included port information, facilities, tides, passage notes and rudimentary sketch plans. By 1914 it was covering Great Britain and Ireland, and on the continent, ports from Dunkerque to Penerf in southern Brittany. It was edited, almost singlehandedly by H J Hanson, one of the founder members of the CA. Today we have some eighteen Regional Editors who have wide cruising experience, especially in their own areas. Imray, the well established nautical publishers, use their expertise in drawing the plans, laying out the text, and finally preparing it for sale.

I never cease to be amazed by the number of changes and updates which are necessary each year. Regional Editors meet in October to discuss ways in which the Almanac can be improved. The main work now starts; no editor can be expected to have visited every port in their area, so we rely on and are grateful for help and information from other members of the Cruising Association, harbourmasters, marina managers, and many others. Ultimately it goes to print during June and is published in early September.

In this edition the General Information chapter has been revised with the help of those with specialist knowledge; in particular the First Aid section has been completely re-written. Throughout the Almanac, both the text and plans have been thoroughly reviewed; well over twenty plans have been redrawn and there are four new plans for Ireland and Spain. Inevitably by the time you use this Almanac further changes will have taken place.

Brexit, whatever form it ultimately takes, will affect the cruising sailor who enters or leaves UK waters but at this point none of us know how. Updates on all Almanac matters can be viewed and freely downloaded from
www.theca.org.uk/almanac/corrections

If a reader wishes to report anything which has changed or simply wishes to make a comment please contact
almanac@theca.org.uk

In some 500 pages, inevitably some ports have to be omitted; however we remain committed to the original objective of including enough information to enable the mariner to reach a safe haven. Also our Editors strive to make it a good read. We hope you find it so.

Acknowledgements

The key contributors to this 2018 edition are:

GENERAL INFORMATION
Robin Baron

S ENGLAND
John Robinson, Judi and Stuart King, and John Parsons

SE ENGLAND
David Sadler

E ENGLAND AND E SCOTLAND
John Calver

W AND N SCOTLAND
Mike Henderson

NW ENGLAND AND ISLE OF MAN
Richard Collier

N AND W WALES
Paul Bond

S WALES AND BRISTOL CHANNEL
Roger Lloyd

IRELAND
Daria Blackwell and Paul Bond

APPROACHES TO THE BALTIC
Frances Wensley and Hans Jakob Valderhaug

HOLLAND AND BELGIUM
Peter Gibbs

EUROPEAN INLAND WATERWAYS
Roger Edgar

NE FRANCE AND CHANNEL ISLANDS
Tony Truin

NW FRANCE
Robin Baron

W FRANCE
Judith Grimwade

ATLANTIC COAST OF SPAIN AND PORTUGAL
Tony Montgomery-Smith

METEOROLOGY
Frank Singleton

John Calver
Honorary Editor

General Information

CONVENTIONS

Passage notes are easily identified in the text by their distinctive blue background.

Courses and bearings are given TRUE unless stated otherwise. Bearings of lights, etc. are as seen from the position of the observer.

Depths are in metres below Lowest Astronomical Tide which usually coincides with Chart Datum.

Chart datum Drying heights are given as such in the text but on plans the number is underlined. On the plans depths more than 2m are coloured dark blue and depths less than this are coloured light blue. On many of the plans on the continent the light blue extends out to the 5m contour. Drying heights are coloured brown and land is green. No distinction is made in dredged areas although the depth may be reduced by silting.

Bridges and lights have their height in metres above HAT. On old continental charts this may be related to Mean Tidal Level.

Power lines Safe vertical clearance may be less than that on the plan.

Distances are given in Nautical Miles (M), equal to a minute of latitude. Lesser distances are tenths of this, called a cable (ca) which is equal to 185·2m.

Winds are given as the compass point from which they blow unless they are described as off or onshore.

Times of HW and LW, together with their heights, are given in relation to the 47 standard ports in the attached Tide Tables booklet. For most other (secondary) ports the differences of times and heights are given at the beginning of the text for virtually every port included in this Almanac. The rule of twelfths gives a useful estimation of the height at times between HW and LW; the main exception to this being the area between Poole and the Solent where reference should be made to the tidal curves on pp 454 and 456. These are only predictions: in particular, the actual tidal heights may vary considerably due to the effects of barometric pressure and wind.

Tidal streams are described by the direction in which they are running, for example south means a south-flowing stream. The timing of the change of direction of the stream is usually referred to HW Dover, unless stated otherwise. For example DS +0200 NE, –0345 SW, means that the tide is slack 2 hours after High Water Dover and about to run in a NE'ly direction; the tide is slack at 3 hours and 45 minutes before HW Dover and about to run SW'ly. If a speed is quoted this will be the maximum speed which is usually about 3 hours after slack water.

Direction of Stream (DS) in the Offing In the approaches to some harbours or rivers a vessel may encounter a strong tidal set in what has traditionally been called 'the Offing'. When this is significant it is noted under the title of the harbour as DS.

Recommended entry times eg 'HW –0200 to HW +0130' assume a draught of 1·5m and no significant swell or sea.

Other navigational information The prudent navigator must not rely on the Cruising Almanac alone. It is essential to use up-to-date British Admiralty, Imray or official foreign charts and refer to *Notices to Mariners*.

BA charts are best updated by using UKHO *Notices to Mariners* available at www.ukho.gov.uk/nmwebsearch

For Imray charts go to www.imray.com/corrections

For this *Cruising Almanac* go to www.theca.org.uk/almanac/corrections

Electronic charts Note that symbols, depths, contours and other matters of navigational significance may not be visible on electronic charts where layering of the display may remove them.

Passage lights Only selected principal lights are included.

Telephones The area code is given with the first telephone number but not repeated.

International dialing codes

UK	+44	Norway	+47
Republic of Ireland	+353	Sweden	+46
Belgium	+32	France	+33
Netherlands	+31	Spain	+34
Germany	+49	Portugal	+351
Denmark	+45	Gibraltar	+350

ABBREVIATIONS

These are additional to many standard abbreviations.

Tides
DS	Direction of Stream
HW	High Water
kn	Knot(s)
HAT	Highest Astronomical Tide
LAT	Lowest Astronomical Tide
LW	Low Water
CD	Chart Datum
MHWS	Mean High Water Springs
MHWN	Mean High Water Neaps
MLWN	Mean Low Water Neaps
MLWS	Mean Low Water Springs
HWD	High Water Dover
np	Neap
sp	Spring

Direction
N, Nly	North, Northerly
E, S, W	East, South, West

Lights
Lt, lt	Light
Al	Alternating
Dir	Directional
F	Fixed
Fl	Flashing
Fl(3)	Group Flashing
Intens	Intensified sector
IPTS	International Port Traffic Signals
Iso	Isophase
IQ	Interrupted Quick Flashing
Ldg Lts	Leading Lights
LtF	Light Float
LtHo	Light House
LtV	Light Vessel
LFl	Long Flashing
Mo	Morse
Oc	Occulting
Oc(2)	Group Occulting
Occas	Occasional
Q	Continuous Quick Flashing
VQ	Very Quick Flashing

Colours
W	White (Lts assumed White unless coloured)
R	Red
G	Green
Y	Yellow
Vi	Violet
Bu	Blue
B	Black

Miscellaneous
AIS	Automatic Indentification of Ships
ATT	Admiralty Tide Tables
bn	Beacon
br(s)	Bridge(s)
ca	Cable
con	Conical
CG	Coastguard
CGOC	Coastguard Operations Centre
conspic	Conspicuous
Dn	Dolphin
EC	Early closing
F5	Beaufort wind scale Force 5
FS	Flagstaff
HM	Harbourmaster
hbr(s)	Harbour(s)
hPA	Hectopascal (=millibar)
h or H	Hour(s)
ht	Height
I, Is	Island
kn	Knot(s)
LB	Lifeboat station
ldg ln	Leading line
LT	Local time
M	Miles (nautical)
m	Metre(s)
mkt	Market
MSI	Marine Safety Information
NCI	National Coastwatch Institution
NMOC	National Maritime Operations Centre
PH	Public House
PO	Post Office
Pt	Point
rk	Rock(s)
Rly	Railway
s	Second
SAR	Search and Rescue
SC	Sailing Club
sph	Spherical
stb	Starboard
t	tonne
tel	Telephone
tr	Tower
TSS	Traffic Separation Scheme
VHF	VHF channel
VTS	Vessel Traffic Service
wk	Wreck(s)
YC	Yacht Club

Charts
BA	British Admiralty
SC	Small Craft
I	Imray
B	Belgian
D	Danish
F	French
G	German
N	Netherlands
N	Norwegian
P	Portuguese
S	Spanish, Swedish

SYMBOLS

- ⚓ Marina
- ⚓ Yacht berthing, few facilities
- Ⓥ Visitors' mooring
- Harbourmaster/Reception
- Customs office
- Slip
- Fuel
- Yacht club
- Pump out
- Laundry
- Boat hoist
- Lifeboat

IALA BUOYAGE SYSTEM REGION A

Lateral marks
Port hand
All red
Topmark (if any): can
Light (if any): red

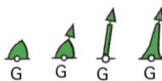

Starboard hand
All green
Topmark (if any): cone
Light (if any): green

Preferred channel to port
Green/red/green
Light (if any): Fl(2+1)G

Preferred channel to starboard
Red/green/red
Light (if any): Fl(2+1)R

Isolated danger marks
(stationed over a danger with navigable water around)
Black with red band
Topmark: 2 black balls
Light (if any): Fl(2) (white)

Special mark
Body shape optional, yellow
Topmark (if any): Yellow X
Light (if any): Fl.Y etc

Safe water marks
(mid-channel and landfall)
Red and white vertical stripes
Topmark (if any): red ball
Light (if any): Iso, Oc, LFl.10s or Mo(A) (white)

Emergency Wreck Marking buoy
Yellow and blue vertical stripes
Topmark: upright yellow cross
Light (if any): Fl.Bu/Y.3s

Cardinal marks

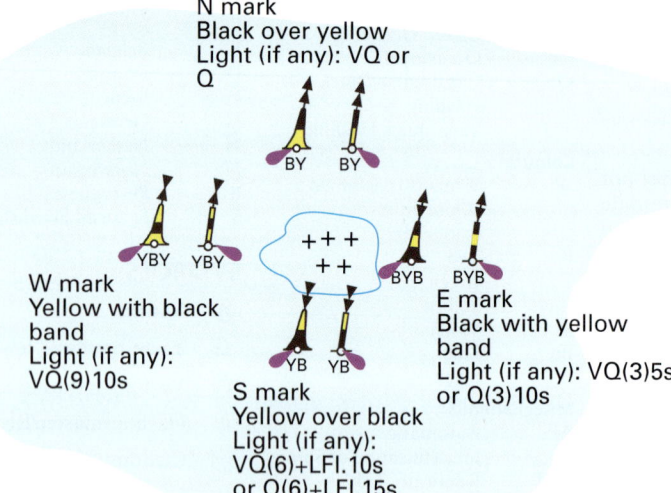

N mark
Black over yellow
Light (if any): VQ or Q

W mark
Yellow with black band
Light (if any): VQ(9)10s

E mark
Black with yellow band
Light (if any): VQ(3)5s or Q(3)10s

S mark
Yellow over black
Light (if any): VQ(6)+LFl.10s or Q(6)+LFl.15s

INTERNATIONAL PORT TRAFFIC SIGNALS (IPTS)

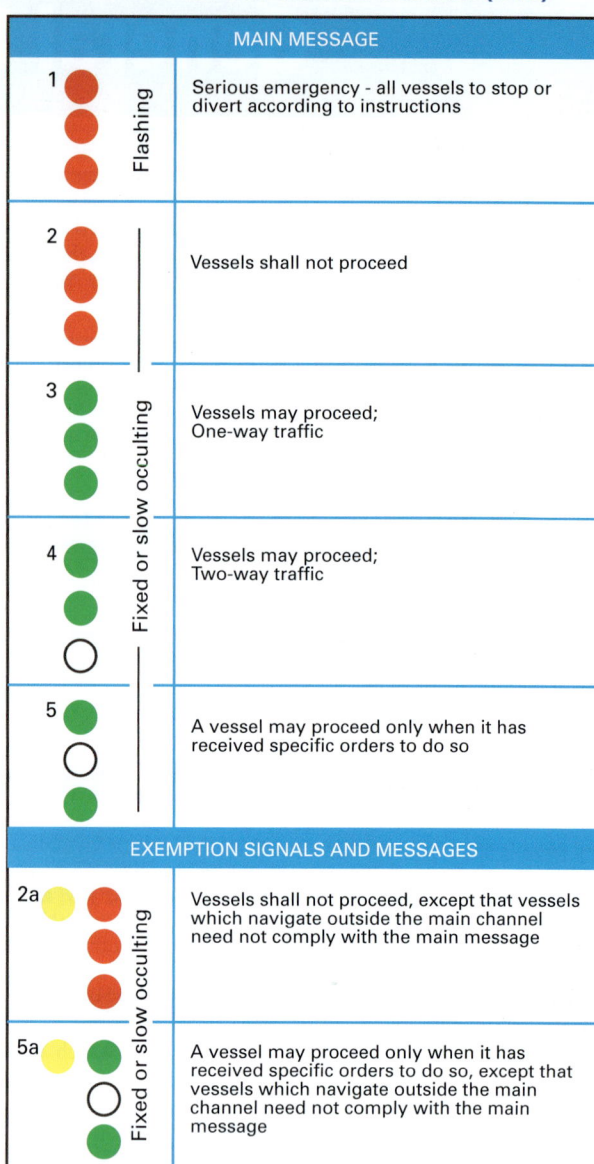

Spar buoys that are unlit have distinctive colouring, but may lack a topmark, particularly in the Baltic and the Netherlands.

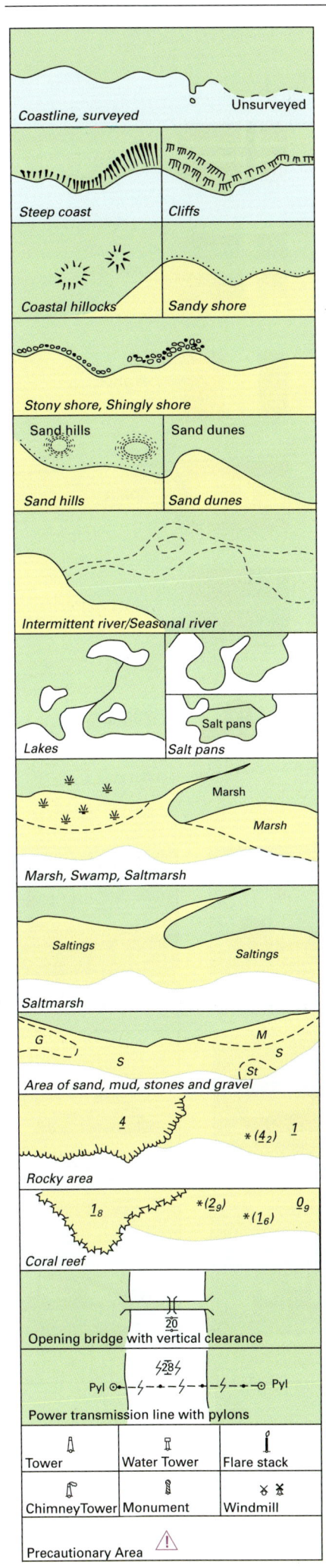
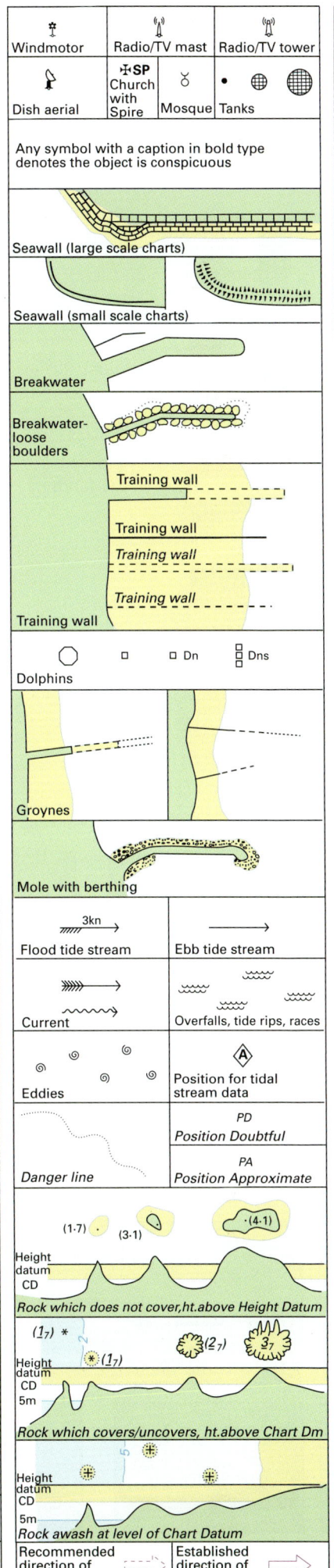
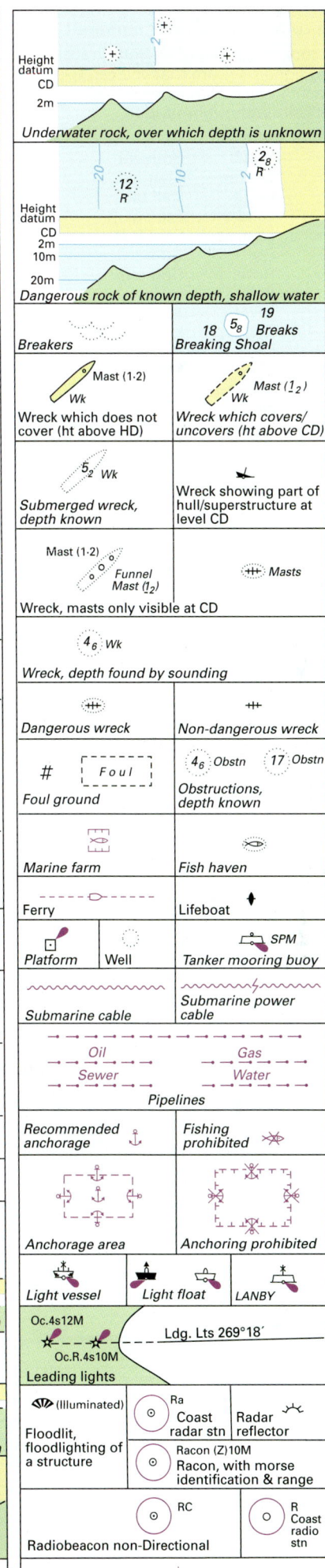

Morse code and phonetic alphabet

Morse code may be used on lights, racons, and fog signals. Ensure that you can spell your yacht's name and radio call sign phonetically without hesitation.

A	·—	Alfa	Al fah
B	—···	Bravo	Brah voh
C	—·—·	Charlie	Char lee
D	—··	Delta	Dell tah
E	·	Echo	Eck oh
F	··—·	Foxtrot	Foks trot
G	——·	Golf	Golf
H	····	Hotel	Hoh tell
I	··	India	In dee ah
J	·———	Juliet	Jew lee ett
K	—·—	Kilo	Key Loh
L	·—··	Lima	Lee mah
M	——	Mike	Mike
N	—·	November	No vem ber
O	———	Oscar	Oss Cah
P	·——·	Papa	Pah pah
Q	——·—	Quebec	Keh beck
R	·—·	Romeo	Roh me oh
S	···	Sierra	See air rah
T	—	Tango	Tang go
U	··—	Uniform	You nee form
V	···—	Victor	Vik tah
W	·——	Whiskey	Wiss key
X	—··—	X-Ray	Ecks ray
Y	—·——	Yankee	Yang key
Z	——··	Zulu	Zoo loo

Numbers

1	·————	Wun	6	—····	Six
2	··———	Too	7	——···	Sev en
3	···——	Tree	8	———··	Ait
4	····—	Fow er	9	————·	Nin er
5	·····	Fife	0	—————	Zero

National flags

United Kingdom, Norway, Ireland, Sweden, Belgium, France, Netherlands, Spain, Germany, Portugal, Denmark, Gibraltar

Navigational lights and shapes

Rule 25 Motor Sailing Cone point down, forward

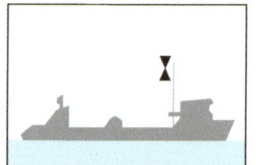
Rule 26 Fishing/Trawling A shape consisting of two cones point to point in a vertical line one above the other

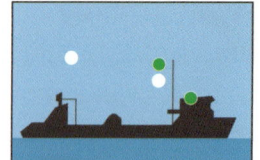
Rule 26 Vessel Trawling All round green light over all-round white, plus side-lights and sternlight when making way

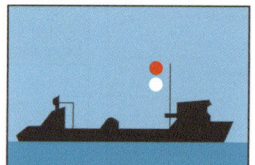
Rule 26 Vessel Fishing All-round red light over all-round white, plus side-lights and sternlight when making way

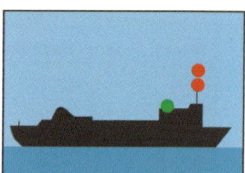
Rule 27 Not under command Two all-round red lights, plus sidelights and stern-light when making way

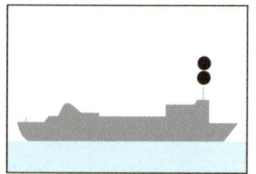
Rule 27 Not under command Two black balls vertically

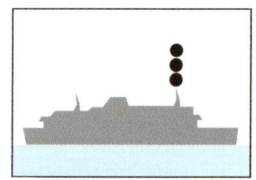
Rule 30 Vessel aground Three black balls in a vertical line

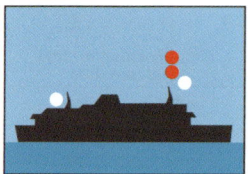
Rule 30 Vessel aground Anchor light(s), plus two all-round red lights in a vertical line

Rule 30 Vessel at anchor All-round white light: if over 50m, a second light aft and lower

Rule 30 Vessel at anchor Black ball forward

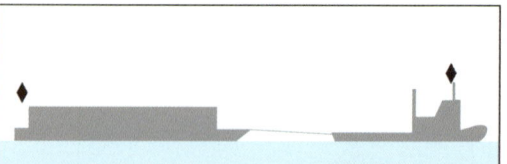
Rule 24 Towing by day - Length of tow more than 200m Towing vessel and tow display diamond shapes

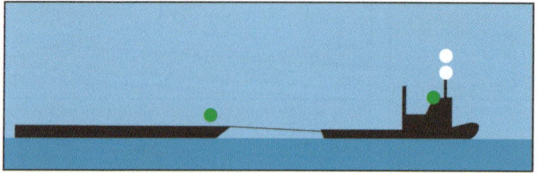
Rule 24 Vessels being towed and towing Vessel towed shows side - lights (forward) and sternlight Tug shows two masthead lights, sidelights, stern-light, yellow towing light

Rule 27 Dredger

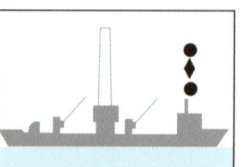
Rule 27 Vessel restricted in her ability to manoeuvre Three shapes in a vertical line - ball, diamond, ball

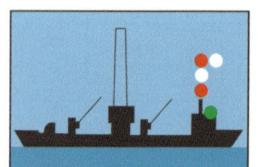
Rule 27 Vessel restricted in her ability to manoeuvre All-round red, white, red lights vertically; plus normal steaming lights

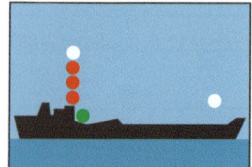
Rule 28 Constrained by draught Three all round red lights in a vertical line, plus normal steaming lights. By day-a cylinder

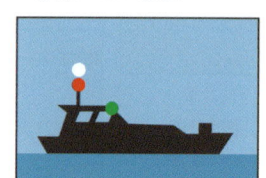
Rule 29 Pilot boat All-round white light over all-round red; plus side-lights and sternlight when underway or anchor light

Rule 27 Divers down Letter 'A' International Code

Safety

REGULATIONS

Yachts are regulated under **SOLAS V** (The International Convention for the Safety of Life at Sea). Although most of the regulations only apply to large ships, parts of Chapter V apply to small, privately owned, pleasure craft. These regulations are mostly those which any prudent skipper would take anyway but it may be prudent to record in the Ship's Log that you have complied for legal and insurance purposes in case you have an accident.

V/34 Passage Planning

Weather Before departure obtain forecasts and get regular weather updates, including warnings, whilst on passage. Texts of these are available from Public Service Radio, CGOC (VHF and MF/SSB), NAVTEX, INMARSAT-C and the internet. Other GMDSS services can be received by HF/SSB radio using voice, Radio Fax or Radio Teletype. With a receive only set the long range certificate is not necessary.

Forecasts broadcast as MSI are necessarily brief and general in nature. However, they are produced by professional meteorologists on the basis of output from their weather prediction computer models. They benefit from human experience and judgement. Sailing decisions for the next 24 to 48 hours should always be made with these forecasts in mind whatever other information is being used.

Maritime forecast details for the UK and the near continent are given later in this chapter. For the Approaches to the Baltic see p.277. The MyCA website, (CA Members only), Frank Singleton's site http://weather.mailasail.com/Franks-Weather and *Le Guide Marine de Météo France* are also useful reference sources.

Tides Check the time of HW, tidal gates and other predictions.

Craft Is your boat seaworthy for the intended trip? Do you have the right safety equipment: flares, harnesses, life jackets, radio, fire extinguishers, liferaft, tools, bilge pumps, first aid kit, charts and other navigation equipment?

Crew Is your crew fit and warm? Have you enough food? Are they sufficiently experienced and briefed to relieve you? Are they liable to be seasick?

Dangers Are there any hazards such as shoals, rocks, tidal races or overfalls or are you likely to meet large vessels in traffic lanes or constrained by their draught?

Ports of Refuge On any long trip when the weather may deteriorate, it is wise to have an alternative plan to allow you to take shelter. You should consider what action you might take if someone is ill or injured.

System Failure Are you able to navigate if the electrical system goes down or the GPS fails? Can you cope with engine failure, a major leak or a defect in the steering? We can all get a rope or a piece of fishing gear round the propeller; have you the means to disentangle yourself?

Overdue It is important that someone ashore knows your plans and that you complete a CG66 so that Search and Rescue Services (SAR) know who they are looking for. Reporting your departure on a long trip means that the CG have logged this but will not monitor your trip unless alerted.

V/19 Radar

Large ships rely a great deal on radar. All small craft are required to fit a radar reflector if practical. Boats longer than 15m are required to fit a reflector to IMO standards of 10cm^2. The reflector should be fitted as recommended and be as high as possible. (Some vessels have an active radar transponder which shows up clearly on a radar screen).

V/29 Lifesaving signals
A copy of the lifesaving signals should be kept accessible to the helmsman.

V/31/32/33
Report any hazards to navigation to the coastguard and to any vessels in the vicinity. You must respond to any distress signal and render assistance if you can.

V/35 Misuse of Distress Signals
It is prohibited to misuse distress signals as it places lives at risk and severe penalties are imposed on those who fire flares without a distress situation or send malicious radio messages.

Out of date pyrotechnics

Out of date pyrotechnics should be landed ashore as soon as possible after the date of expiry, for safe disposal. It is an offence to fire them at sea or on land for practice or as fireworks, nor may they be disposed of as household waste. Possible methods of disposal are:

a. through your supplier
b. liferaft service station
c. harbour or marina where your vessel is berthed (a charge may be made)
d. coastguard, your MRCC may accept them but they have limited storage facilities. Contact them in advance

Briefing The prudent skipper will explain the trip to his crew. The briefing should include the location of safety equipment, fire extinguishers/blankets; the procedures for use in emergency; and the use of the grab-bag to take in the life raft (with spare water, flares and a torch) should be described. Each member of the crew should have his own harness and life-jacket and know how to put them on and adjust them. They should be told the rules for wearing them and clipping on. Finally, they should each know how to make a distress call on the radio. A distress procedure card should be displayed near the radio.

MARINE COMMUNICATIONS

Most yachts engaged in coastal cruising or short offshore passages will only have a VHF radio, preferably one fitted with DSC.

Usage is intended to be brief, clear and to allow other vessels to use VHF in turn. You may send a message to another vessel, a water-taxi or an authorised shore station such as the CG, hbr control or marina. You must not call an individual person by name but must use a vessel's name or call-sign and your boat name. Low power (1watt) should be used in harbours and is compulsory on European inland waterways.

All radios must be licensed; OFCOM issues free lifetime licences for ship's radios online (with an alternative hard copy for a fee). These must be carried on board but not displayed and list all the radio and radar equipment. A fixed penalty of £100 will be payable for not being registered. Details at
http://licensing.ofcom.org.uk/radiocommunicationlicences/ships-radio/

MAYDAY Distress Call

If the radio is fitted with Digital Selective Calling it will have a red distress button on the front of the set. Carry out the following procedure

1. Make sure the set is turned on and, if a separate GPS is connected, make sure that is turned on as well.
2. Lift or slide open the cover over the RED distress button.
3. Press the RED button momentarily once.
4. If time allows scroll down on the screen and select the nature of the distress.
5. Press and hold the RED button for 10 seconds. This will send your boat identity and GPS position to the CG and all ships within range.
   The screen will show that the alert has been sent.
6. Wait no more than 15 seconds and send a voice MAYDAY as below.

The set will now automatically be on Channel 16 on HIGH POWER. If time does not allow you to carry out item 4 above, the automatic distress call will still be sent, but without giving the nature of the distress.

MAYDAY voice procedure

Make sure you are on Channel 16, High Power, adjust the SQUELCH, lift the microphone, press the transmit button firmly and say, for example:

'MAYDAY, MAYDAY, MAYDAY
This is SAILING YACHT BOAT NAME, BOAT NAME, BOAT NAME
CALL SIGN 2GBH4   MMSI 235899982
MAYDAY BOAT NAME
THREE persons on board
My position is 50°13'.20N 002°44'.30W
(or give bearing and distance from headland etc)
Serious engine fire. I require immediate assistance.
OVER'

Release the transmission button. Listen.

If your set does not have a RED distress button, just carry out the voice procedure as given above but without the MMSI number. The minimum information required is your vessel's name and position.

- VHF 16 is for Calling and Distress only. Call on a working channel if you can.
- Monitor VHF 16 for Distress calls and port channels when in harbour areas.
- Boats with a DSC radio should enter the MMSI number of the coastguard station for the area in which they are sailing. Mayday calls made using the RED button alert all DSC radios within range.
- Intership channels are VHF 06, 08, 72, 77. If sailing in company, arrange the VHF in advance (usually VHF 77 for yachts).
- The Global Maritime Distress and Safety System (GMDSS) includes INMARSAT, Search and Rescue Transponders, EPIRBs and Navtex (see Meteorology section). It provides for a worldwide co-ordinated Search and Rescue Service of coastguards, lifeboats and helicopters. In Europe there are Centres every 100M with VHF aerials every 25M. Once in contact with CG they will co-ordinate all SAR action.

EMERGENCY

In an emergency, VHF is preferred to mobile phones for summoning assistance because the latter:
- only have a range of about 10M,
- cannot be located by direction finding equipment.
- do not alert nearby vessels.

All radio-operators must be licensed although a VHF radio can be operated by a non-licensed person under the supervision of a radio-operator or in an emergency.

MAYDAY is the International Distress Call on VHF 16 using high power (25 watt). All other radio traffic must cease until the emergency is over unless related to distress working. It may only be used when a person or a vessel is in grave and imminent danger needing immediate assistance. All vessels are required to monitor VHF 16 and, if practical, proceed to the casualty to render assistance. The dangers could be fire, sinking or drifting onto a lee shore without control. Heart attack, haemorrhage and man overboard would be similar life-threatening emergencies.

- DSC sets send repeated distress messages once the Red button has been pressed. These include the vessel's identity and GPS position, to the coastguard. This transmission has a slightly better range than normal VHF and should carry 50M. It will also switch all DSC radios to VHF16 on all stations within range and turn on an alarm.

MAN OVERBOARD

Much has been written on this topic. Every boat is different, there is not one method which will suit every vessel and crew, but your man overboard drill should be part of the skipper's initial briefing and practised regularly, especially if a new crew member is aboard. The following points need consideration.

If someone goes over, shout for help, watch the casualty all the time, press the MOB buttons on the GPS, throw a lifebelt and release the Danbuoy. Take all way off the boat, if under sail heave-to, if under engine go astern and then to neutral. Drop the sails.

Do not run the casualty down, try to drift down on him across wind. A boat without power or sails may still make 1–2 knots through the water.

The person will be very heavy to lift, the boarding ladder with a scoop stern may be attractive in calm water but it is close to the propeller and in a seaway, as the stern rises and falls it may inflict a head injury. There is least movement at the shrouds and there may be a halyard and a winch to assist with the lifting. Commercial aids provide either a sling or a raft but these are not easy to get under the casualty. Do not send a second person into the water to help unless absolutely necessary; it will mean two people to be rescued. A person in the water rapidly becomes hypothermic. Ideally the casualty should be lifted horizontally and kept flat until warm. Treat the casualty for hypothermia, and drowning (if necessary): see First Aid. If a casualty is lifted in the upright position, then, without the support of the water, blood can pool in the legs and the brain is starved leading to rapid death.

The Rescue Services are keen that you put out a distress call (MAYDAY) before manoeuvring.

It is a good test of boat manoeuvrability and often humbling to attempt to retrieve a bucket tied to a fender. It is so difficult to get someone back on board that it is worth preventing it by the proper use and maintenance of lifejackets, harnesses and jackstays.

- During emergency working the following prowords are in use:
  SEELONCE MAYDAY is a sharp rebuke from the controlling rescue centre to remind all stations not to transmit.
  PRUDONCE MAYDAY Some emergencies take considerable time and to permit safety of navigation, the controlling coastguard may announce PRUDONCE MAYDAY. This means that although the emergency is continuing, priority VHF calls concerned with the safety of navigation may be made.
  SEELONCE FEENEE means that normal transmissions may resume.
- The MAYDAY call may only be used if the vessel, or a person, is in grave and imminent danger and needs immediate assistance. It is not justified for engine breakdown, running out of fuel or seasickness. In these circumstances send an urgency message with the words PANPAN replacing MAYDAY in the message. On DSC sets this is an Urgency call. Do not use the red button.
- Urgency messages are prefaced by PANPAN repeated three times on VHF 16. These go straight to the Rescue Centre. These calls are made when a vessel is in urgent need of assistance or there is a major casualty on board. Such emergencies could include loss of power or steering, or a medical emergency. The Rescue Centre will arrange lifeboats, helicopters or advice as necessary, in some cases they will make an ALL SHIPS call asking any vessel in the vicinity of the casualty to render assistance.

ALL SHIPS SECURITAY messages are usually used by the CG to indicate hazards to navigation. They may also be used by tugs, seismic ships and similar vessels. Small craft seldom have cause to use this type of call but it would be justified if for example you found a floating container which was a hazard to shipping. It would also be correct to report this hazard to the coastguard who have a greater VHF range and would investigate and log it.

LIFEBOAT OR HELICOPTER EVACUATION

When control over a vessel is lost at sea for any reason, or a crew member is dangerously incapacitated, then help has to be summoned to prevent serious loss. How best to make this decision?

Remaining on the vessel is the best course of action if at all feasible: resorting to a liferaft is a fallback, not a prime option e.g. if sea water ingress is uncontrollable and the level is rising fast in the cabin the vessel will soon founder and evacuation is essential. But in a case where steerage is lost or the engine has failed and the vessel is drifting into danger, launching the liferaft may not improve the prospects for survival.

Where control cannot be re-established, a distress call issued early has the best prospects of saving vessel and crew; holding on in hope is bound to reduce the odds of a satisfactory outcome.

In coastal waters, following a MAYDAY, the CG or similar organisation will coordinate assistance. Most rescues in coastal waters will be by lifeboat. Prepare by clearing the foredeck for a tow to be established. Lash down all loose items immediately and get all sail off the moment the vessel is secured and before the lifeboat approaches. The lifeboat may put a crew member on board; he will know more than you do; do as he says.

A helicopter evacuation requires precise co-ordination with the pilot. Your helm must be able to hear the pilot's instructions, and cannot be distracted as he follows them. Helicopters are very noisy. It may be necessary to get a crew member to relay messages if the VHF is down below and your helm cannot hear directly. Generally the vessel will be instructed to remove sail if the engine is capable of maintaining steerage: all lines and gear likely to be dislodged by the downdraft must be secured or ditched. The boom is normally secured to starboard. The vessel will usually be instructed to make way to windward – this is the best angle for helicopter control. The downdraft and noise from an approaching helicopter are unnerving, especially if the crew is already in a state of apprehension: keeping the crew well directed is essential to the operation.

As it approaches, the helicopter will lower a line that must touch the sea to ground the static that builds up during the flight. It can be seized by your crew only when so discharged, and then taken aboard to guide the descending rescue crewman to the deck. The lifeline must be hand held and should not, under any circumstances, be attached to the vessel; if the helicopter has to sheer off and remake contact, the line could be severed and the operation set back.

Helicopters only have a limited fuel range – speed of evacuation will be essential so control of the whole operation will be assumed by the crewman, once on deck.

COASTGUARD OPERATIONS CENTRE

Station	MMSI	Telephone
United Kingdom		
NMOC (Fareham)	002320011	+44 2392 552100
Falmouth	002320014	+44 1326 317575
Dover	002320010	+44 1304 210008
London	002320063	+44 2083 127380
Humber	002320007	+44 1262 672317
Aberdeen	002320004	+44 1224 592324
Shetland	002320001	+44 1595 692976
Stornoway	002320024	+44 1851 702013
Holyhead	002320018	+44 1407 762051
Milford Hn	002320017	+44 1646 690909
Belfast	002320021	+44 2891 463933
Channel Islands		
Alderney	002320196	+44 1481 822620
Guernsey	002320064	+44 1481 720672
Jersey	002320060	+44 1534 447705
Republic of Ireland		
Dublin	002500300	+353 1 620922
Malin Hd	002500100	+353 74930103
Valentia	002500200	+353 669476109
Belgium		
Oostende	002050480	+32 59 701100
Netherlands		
Den Helder	002442000	+31 223 542300
Norway		
Rogaland	002570300	+47 51517000 / +47 120
Tjøme	002570100	+47 120
Germany		
Bremen	002111240	+49 42 15 36 8714
Denmark		
Lyngby	002191000	+45 66 63 48 00
Sweden		
Göteborg	002653000	+46 31 64 80 20

France There are four marine operations centres known as CROSS (Centres régionaux opérationnels de surveillance et de sauvetage)

Gris-Nez	002275100	+33 3 21 87 21 87
Jobourg	002275200	+33 2 33 52 16 16
Corsen	002275300	+33 2 98 89 31 31
Étel	002275000	+33 2 97 55 35 35
Spain		
Bilbao	002241021	+34 94 483 9286
Gijon	002240997	+34 985 326 050
Finisterre	002241022	+34 981 967 320

UK COASTGUARD

Under the NMOC at Fareham, there are 10 other Coastguard Operation Centres. They work as an integrated network managing workload on a national basis.

On land, if you call 999 and ask for the Coastguard or at sea you issue a Mayday broadcast, there will be someone there to help. When making a routine call at sea, DSC calls are preferred, however VHF 16 will still be monitored. If you are uncertain of your Coastguard Operations Centre area, a call on VHF 16 to *UK Coastguard* will bring a reply.

NATIONAL COASTWATCH INSTITUTION

The NCI is a voluntary organization which provides a visual lookout by day along many parts of the UK coastline. They call themselves the 'Eyes along the coast' and have over 50 stations, often in recently closed coastguard lookouts. Their working channel is VHF 65; stations will be able to respond to requests from passing, as well as local craft, for radio checks, and for local weather and sea state conditions. They will also be able to provide information on a range of local facilities including, for example, local moorings, charted anchorages, water taxi contact details and local hazards. For further details contact www.nci.org.uk.

Search and rescue remains the responsibility of the Coastguard. In the event of an emergency, distress and urgency messages should be broadcast on VHF 16 or be reported by dialing 999 and asking for the Coastguard.

NCI Station	Tel	NCI Station	Tel
Gwennap Hd	01736 871351	Whitstable	07758 671422
Penzance	01736 367063	Herne Bay	01227 744454
Bass Pt	01326 290212	Southend	07815 945210
Portscatho	01872 580180	Holehaven	01268 696971
Nare Point	01326 231113	Felixstowe	01394 670808
Charlestown	01726 817068	Gorleston	01493 440384
Polruan	01726 870291	Caister	07257 977613
Rame Hd	01752 823706	Mundesley	01263 722399
Froward Pt	07976 505649	Runton	01263 513725
Prawle Pt	01548 511259	Wells	01328 710587
Torbay	01803 411145	Mablethorpe	07958 038564
Teignmouth	01626 772377	Skegness	01754 610900
Exmouth	01395 222492	Sunderland	01915 672579
Lyme Bay	07745 756872	Rossall Point	01253 681378
Portland Bill	01305 860178	Rhoscolyn	07935 822171
St Albans Hd	01929 439220	Porthdinllaen	07814 823430
Swanage	01929422596	Wooltack Pt	07817 871549
Needles	01983 754231	Worms Hd	01792 390167
Calshot Tr	02380 893562	Nells Pt	01446 420746
Lee on Solent	02392 556758	Boscastle	01840 250965
Gosport	02392 765194	Stepper Pt	07810 898041
Shoreham	01273 463292	St Agnes Hd	01872 552073
Newhaven	01273 516464	St Ives	01736 799398
Folkestone	01303 227132	Cape Cornwall	01736 787890

THE INTERNATIONAL REGULATIONS FOR PREVENTING COLLISION AT SEA

COLREGS are mandatory for all vessels on tidal waters and are contained in RYA booklet G2. The following notes are only explanatory but emphasize points of particular relevance to all small vessels under sail or power. They apply to vessels within sight of each other by day and night and to vessels detected by radar. Special rules apply in reduced visibility. You should refer to a copy of the full Regulations.

It should be noted that no-one at sea has right-of-way. In some situations some vessels are designated stand-on vessels and others give-way vessels, however this is relative and even stand-on vessels should be prepared to make an early and substantial alteration of course to avoid a collision.

All vessels should be navigated with prudence and at a safe speed for the prevailing conditions. As a rule of thumb, all powered vessels pass port to port, vessels crossing or in a nearly head-on situation make an early and substantial turn to stb to avoid collision. When vessels are crossing, a risk of collision exists when the other vessel is on a constant bearing, the vessel on your stb bow stands on and your vessel is the give-way vessel which turns to stb and passes astern of it.

Vessels in a narrow channel keep to the stb side as far as their draught allows.

Overtaking vessels give way to the overtaken until safely past and clear.

An all-round watch should be kept at all times but attention should be particularly paid to ships on the stb bow or to port-hand navigation lights. There is a moral and legal difficulty about keeping watch if the vessel is single-handed and the helmsman needs to go below.

Give a wide berth to:
- fishing vessels (two cones points together, R over W or G over W),
- sailing boats,
- vessels restricted in their ability to manoeuvre (ball-diamond-ball vert, RWR vert), vessels not under command (two balls vert),
- tugs (diamond, two or three W vert and Y stern Lt) and tows, dive boats showing an 'A' flag (W Bu chevron),
- minesweepers (three balls in a triangle, three green Lts at night)
- vessels flying 'Romeo Yankee' (Y cross on R and RY oblique stripes).

In some countries dive boats are marked by a red flag with a white stripe from upper left to lower right corners.

If your craft creates wash, slow down for moored boats and in crowded waters.

Avoid yacht races unless you are participating.

Sail

A yacht which is motor-sailing is classed as a powered craft and should display a cone point down and obey the rules for powered vessels above. In some places in the UK and abroad spot fines are imposed for not displaying this cone correctly.

Sailing vessels should stand on and powered craft should give way. There are problems with this. In shallow water a ship is often constrained by its draught and has to maintain speed for steerage way. Five short blasts warn you that you are in the way. At sea there may be single-man bridge-manning and the watch-keeper may be very busy. His vision may be obscured by deck cargo or the forecastle. He may be travelling at 25kn and you are making 5kn. He may have been used to the Baltic where leisure traffic always gives way to all commercial ships. The motto 'Discretion is the better part of Valour' springs to mind and a significant turn away from the ship will usually put you behind him and indicate your intentions.

Sailing vessels which meet other sailing vessels have special rules:

- A yacht on the port tack – with the wind coming over the port side) gives way to a yacht on the stb tack. Usually it will bear off the wind and pass astern.
- Yachts on the same tack, the yacht to windward gives way to the leeward boat.
- Unless racing, a yacht with a spinnaker should be cleared; in theory a spinnaker set on a pole to stb is on a stb tack, whether it has the mainsail set or not.
- In German territorial waters a sailing vessel tacking up a fairway has to give way to a vessel (even a motor yacht) travelling along the fairway.

In reduced visibility

In fog, snow and heavy rain according to the rules, a vessel should reduce speed, post a lookout in the bows to listen and if under power give a 4–6 second blast on the foghorn not less frequently than every two minutes.

Under sail the signal is a long and two short blasts every two minutes. In practice one suspects that a yacht horn cannot be heard on a ship but it could on another yacht. Stay in port but if caught outside, get out of the shipping lanes and if accessible make for shallow water where a large ship cannot follow and consider anchoring.

Traffic Separation Schemes (TSS)

Ships are obliged to use these where they are shown on the chart. They must keep in the stb lane and enter or leave at an oblique angle. No-one may anchor in a lane.

Vessels less than 20m should use the Inshore Traffic Zone when navigating along the coast and should keep well clear of the TSS. Off N Germany it is an offence to sail within 1M of a TSS except at designated crossing places.

When crossing a TSS, cross on a HEADING at right angles to the lane and do so as fast as possible, keeping a good lookout and give way to vessels using the lane. Rule 10 states 'A vessel of less than 20m in length or a sailing vessel shall not impede the safe passage of a power-driven vessel following a traffic lane.' As many TSS are monitored by radar or patrol craft infringements could be expensive.

Sound signals

A short blast is 1 second; a long blast is 4–6 seconds.

•	I am turning to stb
• •	I am turning to port
• • •	My engines are going astern
• • • • •	I am uncertain of your intentions
–	I am coming round the bend
– – •	I am overtaking on stb
– – • •	I am overtaking on port
– • – •	I agree you can overtake

In restricted visibility, at intervals of not more than 2 minutes

–	I am making way through the water
—	I am underway, but stopped
– • •	I am restricted in my ability to manoeuvre or sailing

Vessels at anchor or aground ring bells, sound gongs or sound
• – • for five seconds every minute.

RENEWABLE ENERGY GENERATION

All EU nations are committed to development of renewable sources of energy from marine areas: wind-farms, tidal stream generators and tidal height generators. More and more of these will be found around all coasts of the British Isles, in the North Sea and in the Baltic. The positions of completed schemes are shown on the latest large-scale charts and details of those under construction normally appear in the latest *Notices to Mariners*.

Wind farms

The air-draught under blades is 22m at MHWS. During construction and maintenance operations a moving exclusion area of 500m applies around all work vessels including the cable layers and this must be observed. When operational with no work vessels present, sailing through a UK wind-farm between the towers is normally permitted but anchoring or sailing within 50m of any fixed structure such as a turbine tower, substation or met mast is not advised. Sailing through a wind farm is not recommended at night or poor visibility: due notice should be taken of tidal stream. The law is still under discussion in some other EU countries and it is essential to obtain local information before sailing through.

All wind farm towers are painted yellow to a height of 15m and have illuminated identification letters. Peripheral towers are also lit by Fl.Y. lights at intervals according to a standard pattern which applies throughout Europe. Some towers have F.R. or Fl.R. lights on top. These are aero lights not intended for marine navigation but are often the first lights seen on approach. Wind-farms do not cause problems with compasses, GPS, VHF, wind or AIS but may interfere with radar reception when very close to.

Tidal generators

These are all experimental at present with no standard design. Sailing through them is not possible and a comfortable clearance all round is strongly advised, particularly near the turbine structures where some turbulence in the sea may occur. They are marked generally with standard cardinal buoys with some having additional Fl.Y. lights.

Oil rigs, gas rigs and gas storage

A 500m exclusion zone applies to all these structures which are still being built in all areas. They are usually well lit with work lights and Fl.Y and Fl.Morse lights.

AIDS TO ELECTRONIC NAVIGATION

GPS

The Global Positioning System has revolutionised navigation and can give an accuracy of less than 20m. Differential GPS using land-based corrections can improve this to 1m. It is provided free by the United States government and is based on timed radio-signals from geostatic satellites. In spite of reassurances, it could be turned off and the fairly weak radio signals can be blocked electronically or by strong electromagnetic radiation experienced near warships. Alternative systems are proposed but not yet available.

On any boat the receiver may develop a fault or there may be an electrical power failure.

Old surveys, old charts and outdated chart datum may mean that the accuracy of the GPS may be greater than the chart in use. It is not sensible to rely on GPS in narrow channels or near the shore.

Horizontal Chart Datum and GPS

All plans and geographical positions in this Almanac refer to WGS 84 (effectively the same as ETRS 89). Most new charts refer to WGS 84, however some charts of the West coast of Ireland refer to Ordnance Survey Ireland and a few European charts refer to ED50. Mariners are advised to look at the small print on the chart under the title, especially if using old charts, since there could well be a 100m error. GPS sets can be adjusted to the appropriate datum, otherwise a correction using data on the chart can be applied.

PRECAUTIONS

- **Accuracy** Even though you may be using a modern up to date chart the survey in parts of it may have been carried out many years ago and may not be as accurate as your GPS position. This applies particularly to areas which have little commercial traffic.
- **Waypoint lists** These should be treated with caution as they can lead to serious error. They are subject to editorial, printer's and reader's error and should always be plotted on the chart as a precaution. It is prudent to record waypoints in the logbook

by number, lat and long, and written description such as '1M N of Cherbourg W Entrance'.
- **Choice of waypoints** A ruler or straight edge should always be laid between adjoining waypoints to ensure that the course does not cross rocks or other hazards, making due allowance for tidal drift and leeway. It is a mistake to position waypoints at buoys as the accuracy is such that collision with the buoy is a possibility. This is particularly likely in poor visibility, when there is the additional hazard of collision with another vessel using the same mark. Care should be taken on approach lines and at geographical features.
- **Electronic charts** Symbols for individual wind turbines are often indistinct and may disappear altogether at some levels of zoom.
- **Cross track error** The GPS has no feeling for leeway or tidal set. Allowance must always be made for these, both in advance and by monitoring progress and correcting cross track error when appropriate to avoid the boat being set into a hazard. In a close-quarters situation it is often more accurate to rely on visual transits than GPS. In some circumstances, such as crossing the English Channel, it may be counterproductive to use crosstrack error as allowing the tides to cancel out makes the journey shorter rather than using an off-set first one way and then the other.
- **Geographical features** Although radar and GPS are a great assistance if caught in a fog at sea, they require experience and skill to interpret. The prudent mariner will avoid going to sea in a fog even if he has a dedicated, skilled operator to assist him.

Internet
Internet access is of increasing importance for the cruising yachtsman and many marinas provide WiFi, sometimes at no extra cost. In some countries, if a long stay is envisaged, it may be more practical to either buy a dongle or subscribe to an individual provider. A WiFi booster will increase the strength of the signal but not its bandwidth, which will also limit the WiFi traffic. If using a USB cable greater than 5m, it must be an active cable (i.e. taking a little power from the computer to avoid signal losses in the cable). Non-directional and directional aerials are available. If you know the direction of the transmitter a directional aerial, when correctly orientated, will offer the greater boost.

AIS Automatic Identification of Ships
All ships over 300 tonnes are required to carry an AIS transponder which transmits data about its name, MMSI number, position, speed and course over the ground, and heading. AIS receivers are already common on leisure vessels and transmitters are becoming increasingly so. They all require a VHF aerial and connection to GPS. Best results are obtained if they can be linked to the yacht's radar or chart plotter. Stand alone sets are also available. They display the data received from ships within line of sight and can calculate the closest distance of approach. It is not a foolproof system, it depends on ships having their set switched on, and it should be regarded as another useful aid to safe navigation.

Increasingly AIS is being fitted to lights, buoys, and other aids to navigation. A recent development is the **Virtual AIS** aid to navigation which is a mark that does not physically exist. There is no structure or light to be seen at the given position of the mark and it does not have a transmitter; it is operated by shore stations. It is likely to be used as a temporary mark e.g. marking a wreck until a buoy can be deployed. It is depicted on a chart by a magenta circle showing that a radio transmission is involved and the words V-AIS. Inside, it contains the description of the physical mark if it were actually at that place. Many AIS receivers used on pleasure craft cannot receive virtual targets.

BREXIT
In a referendum held on 23 June 2016 a majority of those voting expressed the view that the UK should leave the EU. On 29 March 2017 the government gave notice that the UK intended to leave the EU and embarked upon a period of negotiation with the EU in order to disentangle UK commitments to the EU and vice versa. This is unlikely to be completed before September 2019. When it happens, Brexit is likely to affect border entry and immigration rules, VAT and import duties on vessels, parts and spares and fuel and, possibly, technical regulations. The value of the £ could well change. At the time of going to press (May 2017) it is impossible to predict what effect Brexit will have on leisure cruising. Skippers and crew members are advised to check for the latest information when setting out for or arriving from an EU country. For non-UK citizens entering the UK: www.gov.uk/guidance/immigration-rules, for leisure vessels entering or leaving the UK: www.gov.uk/government/publications/notice-8-sailing-your-pleasure-craft-to-and-from-the-uk, and for non-EU citizens entering the EU: http://ec.europa.eu/immigration/.

If there are significant changes during the lifetime of this Almanac we shall promulgate them on the public pages of the CA at www.theca.org.uk/almanac/corrections.

CUSTOMS
Every skipper travelling across borders should be familiar with the customs and immigration regulations of the state which he is entering. In general, documents to be carried should include:

Ship's papers
Registration document for the boat
Proof of ownership, such as a Bill of Sale
Proof of VAT status
Ship radio licence
Details of insurance cover, including a current receipt.

Personal papers
Passports for all crew members with appropriate visa(s) if necessary
Proof of Authority to operate maritime radio
EHIC - European Health Insurance Card
List of Medication, e.g. copy of prescription, and short medical history if appropriate
Certificate of competence such as the International Certificate of Competence (ICC) – valid for inland waters, if planning to use the inland waterways.

Proof of VAT status
An original receipt for VAT paid within the EU on first purchase is required or, for older vessels, evidence that the vessel was in use in the EU before 1992 and was built before 1985. Evidence for the former could be mooring/harbour dues receipt and for the latter Part 1 registry, builder's receipt.

Schengen
With the exception of the UK and Ireland, all countries covered in this Almanac are signatories to the Schengen Agreement. Passage between the EU countries should be reasonably free from formalities for EU/EEA citizens on EU flagged vessels. There are in general no restrictions on individuals who are citizens of the EU who are carrying goods between EU countries on which tax has been paid. Norway is a member of the EEA but not the EU, there are restrictions on alcohol and tobacco which may be imported, currently one litre of spirits or three litres of wine. Holders of non EU/EEA passports should establish beforehand whether there are any visa requirements: they will normally be required to report to immigration or the police. Yachts arriving from a non Schengen country may be required to complete an entry procedure. Skippers may be asked for a crew list with dates of birth and passport numbers. If intending to sail from the UK to either Belgium or the Netherlands a special form is required to be presented on arrival. It is easiest to download this from www.rya.org.uk before departure. Many states have reduced their customs facilities, an enquiry to the harbourmaster or marina will usually reveal local procedure.

Individuals travelling on non-EU passports should always report to the police or immigration.

Individuals living in the EU but only having visas should check that they will be readmitted before crossing borders.

Prohibited imports
All countries have strict laws prohibiting the import of addictive drugs, pornography and firearms. The UK prohibits handguns except for licensed signal pistols. Other countries may prohibit various types of miniflares and pyrotechnics. Many countries prohibit the carrying of out of date flares: on the spot fines may be demanded. Many countries have regulations on the transport of animals, meat, dairy produce, fruit and vegetables. These may be very strictly enforced particularly in the UK and Ireland. A ham sandwich, milk, a potato, an apple, a dog or budgerigar may be confiscated. See Customs Notice No.8 of December 2002.

UK Customs allow private users to use red diesel for yacht propulsion within UK waters provided that they make a simple declaration to the supplier and pay tax at the appropriate rate. If going abroad, the regulations of the appropriate country must be obeyed. Keep receipts, do not carry red diesel in cans. It is advisable to record fuel purchases in the yacht's log.

If carrying duty-free goods, be prepared to demonstrate that the stock on board does not exceed EU allowances. In the event of having a large quantity of dutiable goods on board it is a requirement to report to Customs.

Boats entering the EU from a non-EU country should always fly a yellow flag and contact the Customs when entering territorial waters. (In the UK Yachtline ☎ 0845 723 1110.) They should follow instructions carefully.

For Customs purposes the Channel Islands and Gibraltar are outside the EU and very limited quantities of goods may be imported duty-free. For a comprehensive explanation of British Customs regulations go to www.hmrc.gov.uk and then search for *Notice 8*.

UK Customs www.hmrc.gov.uk

National Yachtline (to report arrival or departure)
☎ 0845 723 1110
Helpline service ☎ 0845 010 900
or +44(0)208 929 0152 from abroad.

UK Customs Confidential Hotline
If you see any suspicious activity (drugs, smuggling, etc) around the UK coastline, don't ignore it, report it to
☎ 0800 595 000

PETS FROM ABROAD

Any dog, cat, or other animal on a vessel arriving from abroad must at all times be restrained and securely confined within a totally enclosed part of the vessel. It must not land nor come into contact with animals ashore. The UK Pet Passport Scheme does not apply to dogs or cats landed from private vessels, and is only intended to include animals being imported via certain commercial sea or air routes. There are no requirements for pets travelling directly between the UK and the Republic of Ireland or the Channel Islands since they are currently both free of rabies. Failure to observe the rules is a criminal offence. Penalties include heavy fines and destruction of the animal. It is not an offence to have a pet aboard a UK-based yacht or vessel, provided it is not taken outside the UK waters. This regulation is found under the Rabies Importation Order. Further information can be found at: www.gov.uk/take-pet-abroad

CONSERVATION AND POLLUTION

By law it is illegal to throw any refuse over the side of your vessel whether it is biodegradable or not and however far you are out to sea. Heavy fines may be enforced. In most harbours and inland waterways, it is illegal to discharge marine toilets. There are no restrictions on the discharge of washing up water. Avoid the use of bleach; choose environmentally favourable detergents. To reduce oily discharge in bilge water, install in-line bilge filters, drip tray or bilge sock. The Helcom Convention prohibited any discharges into the Baltic. Individual countries are implementing this. Take recent advice from the CA or RYA.

In the absence of discharge facilities, holding tanks should be pumped out and flushed at least two miles off the coast. In the Netherlands and Denmark there is a ban on the application of antifouling paint of any sort. Visiting vessels are exempt but new coats must not be applied. Paints based on organic tin compounds are illegal on vessels throughout the world and an increasing number of countries are considering banning copper.

Bird and seal preservation areas are marked on new charts. Usually rights of navigation are preserved but landing near nesting sites is usually prohibited. Care should be taken in the Waddensee and in the Baltic to observe the local regulations which are obtainable from harbourmasters. Grounding is usually forbidden.

Marine conservation areas or parks may contain corals, sea grass or other delicate natural features. Anchoring may be forbidden but buoys may be provided. Fishing is usually prohibited in these areas.

Underwater archaeology and wrecks are often protected and local or national law must be respected. On some wrecks diving is completely forbidden; these are usually marked on charts.

First aid

PERSONAL RECOMMENDATIONS

Every crew member should ensure they have on board their own supplies to deal with minor injuries or illness. These should include:

- Own prescribed medication with enough to last longer than the planned voyage
- Pain relief medicine
- Sea sickness medication
- Sickness and diarrhoea medication
- Copy of their prescription, medical history and emergency contacts
- Dressings for minor injuries
- Sun block SPF 50+.

In addition every vessel should carry a full first aid box with the addition of a tourniquet and emergency trauma dressing.

Any crew member with a long standing medical condition should seek advice from their own GP before each voyage and discuss such advice with the skipper. It is important that the skipper is aware of illnesses which may need help while at sea e.g. asthma, diabetes, epilepsy, allergies. These are NOT a contra-indication to sailing. It is recommended that each adult crew member have an up-to-date First Aid certificate. Remember it may be the skipper needing help.

ASSESSMENT

In the event of any illness or injury the casualty should be treated following the basic principles of **DR ABCE**

D – Danger Ensure that you do not put yourself in danger; if the casualty is in danger, r move them to a safe place without putting yourself at risk

R – Response Gently shake the casualty and shout in each ear

A – Airways If the casualty is unresponsive, remove anything you can see in their mouth and open their airway by putting one hand on the forehead and lifting their chin with the other hand. (Children <1 year should have a less extended tilt – see CPR panel).

B – Breathing Put your ear to the casualty's mouth and look down their chest. Look for the chest rising and falling and feel for breath for 10 seconds. If the casualty is not breathing, start CPR; if the casualty is breathing, place them in the recovery position and monitor their breathing.

C – Circulation and Catastrophic Bleeding Check the casualty for any major bleeding and presence of a pulse. If there are no signs of life or no pulse (feel neck behind the angle of the jaw) start CPR immediately and call the CG. If you do not want to do mouth to mouth, chest compression is better than nothing at all.

If major bleeding is present, try to control it urgently by applying direct pressure with an emergency trauma dressing as per the manufacturer's instruction. Any object in a wound should be left and pressure applied either side to minimise bleeding. If you do not suspect a fracture you may also elevate a limb above the level of the heart to minimize further bleeding If the casualty bleeds through the trauma dressing , apply a tourniquet (if available) as per manufacturer's instructions. Do not remove dressing but apply an extra one on top and continue to apply pressure.

E – Examine Examine the casualty's body from head to toe looking for any bruises, wounds, deformities or bleeding – treat appropriately.

Reassess DR ABCE every 2 minutes.

Always remember that if someone is involved in a traumatic injury, opening the airway is more important than supporting the spine.

CPR (Cardio pulmonary resuscitation)

CPR - Adults

1. Place the heel of your hand on the centre of the person's chest, then place the other hand on top and press down by 5-6cm (2-2.5 inches) at a steady rate of 100 to 120 compressions per minute.
2. After every 30 chest compressions, give two rescue breaths.
3. Tilt the casualty's head gently and lift the chin up with two fingers. Remove any visible obstructions from the mouth and nose. Pinch the person's nose. Seal your mouth over their mouth and blow steadily and firmly into their mouth for about one second. Check that their chest rises. Give two rescue breaths.
4. Continue with cycles of 30 chest compressions and two rescue breaths until they begin to recover or emergency help arrives.

CPR - Children over one year old

1. Open the child's airway by placing one hand on the child's forehead and gently tilting their head back and lifting the chin. Remove any visible obstructions from the mouth and nose.
2. Pinch their nose. Seal your mouth over their mouth and blow steadily and firmly into their mouth, checking that their chest rises. Give five initial rescue breaths.
3. Place the heel of one hand on the centre of their chest and push down by 5cm (about two inches), which is approximately one-third of the chest diameter. The quality (depth) of chest compressions is very important. Use two hands if you can't achieve a depth of 5cm using one hand.
4. After every 30 chest compressions at a rate of 100 to 120 per minute, give two breaths.
5. Continue with cycles of 30 chest compressions and two rescue breaths until they begin to recover or emergency help arrives.

CPR - Infants under one year old

1. Open the infant's airway by placing one hand on their forehead and gently tilting the head back and lifting the chin. Remove any visible obstructions from the mouth and nose.
2. Place your mouth over the mouth and nose of the infant and blow steadily and firmly into their mouth, checking that their chest rises. Give five initial rescue breaths.
3. Place two fingers in the middle of the chest and push down by 4cm (about 1.5 inches), which is approximately one-third of the chest diameter. The quality (depth) of chest compressions is very important. Use the heel of one hand if you can't achieve a depth of 4cm using the tips of two fingers.
4. After 30 chest compressions at a rate of 100 to 120 per minute, give two rescue breaths.
5. Continue with cycles of 30 chest compressions and two rescue breaths until they begin to recover or emergency help arrives.

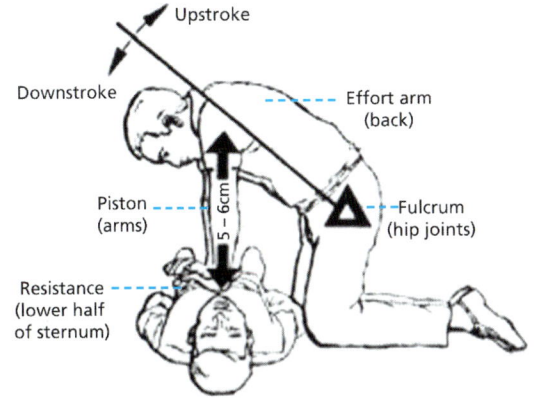

In the case of any of the following, call MAYDAY as soon as possible
- chest pain
- difficulty in breathing
- unconsciousness
- severe loss of blood
- severe burns or scalds
- choking
- fitting or concussion
- drowning
- severe allergic reactions.
- broken/amputated limbs
- No pulse, CPR started

They should be treated as follows:

Chest pain Encourage the casualty to slow down their breathing, get them into a comfortable position and take own medication if available. If it persists or becomes worse, becoming tight across the chest or down either arm, give 300mg of aspirin unless the subject is on tablets to thin the blood.

Difficulty in breathing Encourage the casualty to slow down their breathing, get them in a comfortable position and take own medication if available.

Unconsciousness Follow the DR ABCE assessment.

Diabetic coma This may be due to too much or too little sugar. If diabetes is known, ensure they eat regularly or take glucose gel. They may deriorate rapidly and need evacuation.

Stroke Facial weakness, arm weakness, or speech problems, are an emergency as clot busting drugs may make a difference.

Severe loss of blood Follow the DR ABCE assessment.

Burns (not involving chemicals) Cool with cold water for at least 10 minutes then cover with loosely applied clingfilm or burns dressing and cool for a further 10 minutes (only cool down for 10 minutes for children).

Burns (involving chemicals) Rinse with cold water for 20 minutes (unless COSHH states otherwise), do not cover injury site and contact CG for advice.

Choking Encourage the casualty to cough. If still choking give up to 5 back slaps. If unsuccessful and over 12 month give up to 5 abdominal thrusts; if under 12 month give up to 5 chest thrusts. Repeat if needed. If patient goes unconscious, follow the DR ABCE assessment.

Fitting or convulsions Move all dangers out of the way and protect the casualty's head. Do not put anything into the casualty's mouth. Once the fitting or convulsion stops, follow the DR ABCE assessment.

Drowning Get the casualty out the water by any means possible. Follow the DR ABCE assessment. Be aware of the complications of drowning and, if the casualty has inhaled or swallowed any water, get urgent assistance.

Severe allergic reactions (Wheeze, rash, swelling particularly around face, feeling faint) remove trigger if known. Encourage the patient to slow down their breathing, get them in a comfortable position and take own medication if available. Intra-muscular adrenaline may save their life.

Broken bones Support the casualty in the position they were found

Amputated limb Wrap the limb in clingfilm and place in a bag of ice. Dress the stump to stop bleeding.

Record in the log book the sequence and timing of the event and of any treatment given.

Remember, if in doubt call the CG for advice. IF in any doubt, call MAYDAY instead of PANPAN

Following first aid send a PANPAN call, as extensive burns, fractured bones or any multiple injury may result in fluid loss. If there is a possibility of needing surgical intervention do not give anything to eat, drink or smoke. Keep the patient warm to minimize shock.

HYPOTHERMIA

Suspect this in anyone exposed for long periods to cold, wind, wet or immersion (as in drowning, see Man Overboard box p.12). Although shivering may occur in the early stages, it tends to be followed by apathy, disorientation or irrational behaviour, this is followed by a progressive diminishing level of response, eventually descending into unconsciousness, with slow shallow breathing, a slow pulse, and finally cardiac arrest. The casualty will lack insight and not appreciate they are in any danger. To prevent this wear several layers of clothing with an outer wind and waterproof layer. Short watches with ample hot drinks and warm dry conditions below. Single handers are particularly at risk. Manage this condition by ensuring the casualty is in dry clothing, and put them in a warm sleeping bag with a hat on their head. Also cover with an overblanket. Give warm drinks. Do not give alcohol or use hot water bottles. It is stressed that gradual re warming is safer.

Do not leave the casualty alone as may deteriorate rapidly.

SEASICKNESS

Seasickness is caused by a combination of motion, cold, hunger, fumes and fear. It is often worse in young people. A heavy meal and/or alcohol is not recommended on the evening before setting sail. It is relieved by fresh air, work, a view of the horizon, and some tablets. Stugeron, or perhaps hyoscine is better still, is normally given to prevent motion sickness rather than after nausea or vomiting develops. Stugeron can be absorbed from the mucosa of the mouth without swallowing if nausea or sickness has started. For children over 10 years a transdermal hyoscine patch provides prolonged activity but it needs to be applied several hours before travelling. Other sedating type antihistamines are generally held to be less effective, although some individuals may tolerate these well, and in some cases find them effective. Most will need to be taken two hours in advance of boarding – follow directions on packet.

MINOR INJURIES

Sunburn is common, and as with other burns the area should be cooled for at least 10 minutes with cool water; wear cotton next to the skin. Do not burst blisters, as this is a route for infection; if they do burst, treat as an open wound and cover with a sterile dressing. Check daily for signs of infection, worsening pain, swelling, pus or any sign of fever. Wounds should be kept clean and dry.

Sunburn of the conjunctiva may prevent the wearing of contact lenses, so bring a spare pair of glasses.

Contact lens injuries and corneal abrasions are common on boats. The casualty says he/she has something in their eye. Careful inspection with a bright torch will usually reveal nothing. Close the eye and keep it closed with a sterile pad. Inspect daily for any worsening signs particularly infection. Healing may be assisted with the use of an antibacterial eye ointment Chloramphenical (available over the counter for those over two years). Contact lenses should not be worn for 10 days after healing appears to have taken place.

Sprains, bruises, and other soft tissue injuries are treated with Ibuprofen, follow the packet instructions carefully and take after food. This medication is not advised for those who have asthma, kidney problems, gastric ulcer, indigestion or are taking some other medications. (It may also relieve gout).

Rope burns should be kept clean and dry; if open cover with a sterile dressing and inspect daily for infection.

Diarrhoea and vomiting is usually self-limiting; keep drinking fluids, since the body is losing them, there is advantage in replacing lost fluids with sachets of Dioralyte or rehydration mix (1 litre water, 6 level teaspoons sugar and ½ level teaspoon salt flavoured with fruit squash if desired), although the casualty should not be kept on this alone for more than 24 hours. Diarrhoea may commonly last for up to a week and relief may be obtained by using Loperamide, again follow the packet instructions carefully. Of utmost importance is the maintenance of good hygiene, especially HANDWASHING, and those experiencing this condition should not prepare food for others. If severe abdominal pain develops with breathlessness, dizziness or fever, urgent medical assistance should be sought.

Dehydration is common on some small boats, it can result in constipation and bladder infections. It is important to keep fresh tap water in readily available plastic bottles. Generally an adult needs two litres of fluid a day to remain healthy; more if they have a fever or in hot weather.

Any condition likely to last more than 48 hours is not suitable for nursing on a small boat and the casualty should be landed and be either admitted to a medical facility or sent home.

Meteorology

UK Sea Area (Shipping) Forecasts

These are broadcast by the BBC on Radio 4 LW, 198kHz at 0048*, 0520*, 1201 and 1754 LT. Those marked with * are also on FM and MW. All broadcasts comprise a gale warning summary (when appropriate), synopsis and area forecasts of wind, weather and visibility. Areas are shown on the chart below. Parts of the Shipping Forecast are broadcast by CGOC on VHF, MF/SSB and on NAVTEX 518 kHz. (See p.21).

In common with many other countries the UK uses the Beaufort scale to describe wind force. The table shows equivalent wind speeds at a standard 10m (33ft) above sea level and an indication of sea state. Other terms having specific meanings in UK Shipping and NAVTEX broadcasts are as follows.

In the synopsis, speeds of movement of lows and highs are given as:

Slowly	<15kn	Steadily	15–25kn
Rather quickly	25–35kn	Rapidly	35–45kn
Very rapidly	>45kn		

In the area forecasts, visibility is described as:

Fog	< 1000m	Poor	1000m–2M
Moderate	2–5M	Good	>5M

Gale and strong wind warnings

Gale warnings are issued when the average wind is currently or is forecast to be Force 8 or above. The UK also warns of gales if the average wind is Force 7 but gusts are expected to exceed 41kn. Warnings are broadcast as soon as possible after receipt by the BBC on 198kHz and by HMCG via VHF, MF and NAVTEX.

Coastguards issue Strong Wind warnings if Force 6 or more is expected in inshore waters but are not included in the latest Inshore Waters Forecast.

The terminology and wind speeds in knots are as in the Beaufort Force table below. Gusts may be stronger than the average by 10kn or more.

A gale warning is described as:

Imminent	Within the next six hours
Soon	Within 6–12 hours
Later	Within 12–24 hours

In case of uncertainty the term 'perhaps … later' can be used in forecasts but with no warnings issued. HOWEVER, a gale warning MUST be issued if it may occur within the next 12 hours, even if the forecast uses words like 'perhaps locally' or 'perhaps at times'.

HM Coastguard forecasts on VHF, MF/SSB and the BBC LW

HMCG broadcasts parts of the shipping forecast on VHF and MF/SSB – twice a day, at the times shown in the table on p.20. Inshore Waters forecasts are broadcast on VHF every three hours. There are 18 Inshore Waters areas including Shetland and the Isle of Man. New Inshore Waters forecasts for this purpose are issued at about 0600, 1200, 1800 and 0000 LT.

VHF broadcasts are preceded by a brief announcement on Channel 16 and then transmitted on one of Channels 62, 63 or 64, except for the Western Isles of Scotland and Southwest England where Channel 10 is also used. MF/SSB broadcasts are announced on 2182 kHz.

Inshore Waters forecasts including the Channel Islands are broadcast on the national NAVTEX frequency, 490kHz. See p.23 for details. Inshore Waters forecasts are broadcast after the 0048 and 0521 shipping forecasts on Radio 4. They cover up to 12 miles offshore starting from Cape Wrath clockwise around the UK in 18 sections. They are valid for 24 hours.

Coastal station reports

The 0520 forecast on Radio 4 is followed by reports of actual wind, weather, visibility, barometric pressure and tendency from coastal stations and light vessels. Reports are from Tiree, Stornoway, Lerwick, Leuchars, Bridlington, Sandettie LV, Greenwich LV, Jersey, Channel LV, Scilly, Valentia, Ronaldsway and Malin Head. Locations are shown on the UK sea area chartlet. Some of the stations are automatic and measure visibility but not 'weather' ie there are no reports of rain, drizzle, showers etc.

The 0048 forecast on Radio 4 is followed by an extended list. These lists may change from time to time.

In coastal reports, pressures are given in hectoPascals (hPa) the scientifically correct unit. One hPa = one millibar (mb). Pressure changes relate to the three hours previous to the time of the report and are described as:

Steady	<0·1 hPa
Rising or falling slowly	0·1 to 1·5 hPa
Rising or falling	1·6 to 3·5 hPa
Rising or falling quickly	3·6 to 6·0 hPa
Rising or falling very rapidly	>6·0 hPa

Now falling (rising) means that the pressure has changed from rising (falling) within the last three hours.

Other terms used in the coastal reports are self evident. Some coastal reports are broadcast on NAVTEX 490kHz, see p.23.

GMDSS services from other countries

All the countries in the area of this almanac broadcast Inshore Waters and Sea Area forecasts on VHF and/or MF/SSB. Varying from country to country, there are usually between two and eight forecasts a day.

NAVTEX weather broadcasts are available throughout except for local areas of poor reception.

Some information will be found in the various sections of this almanac and fuller details can be found in *Admiralty Marine Communications manuals*, *Votre Livre de Bord (Bloc Marine)*, *Le Guide Marine of Météo France*.

Bulletins for open sea areas will usually be in English, the international maritime language. Some Inshore Waters forecasts will be in English but meteorological terms in other languages are usually fairly recognisable with some practice. Useful multi-language glossaries are found in the *Yachtsman's 10 Language Dictionary* (Adlard Coles Nautical) and *RYA G5*.

Sea areas

A common set of sea areas is used by countries bordering the North Sea although the names may differ slightly from the English. Note that French broadcasts covering METAREA I (north of 48°27'N) use the same areas as the UK except that the names of Channel Sea areas are Tamise, Pas-de-Calais, Antifer, Casquets and Ouessant, for Thames, Dover, Wight, Portland and Plymouth. Similarly, France, Spain and Portugal use common areas in METAREA II (south of 48°27'N). Spain adds an area known as Gran Sol, effectively Plymouth, Lundy, Fastnet, and east Sole. Countries surrounding the Baltic also use common sea areas.

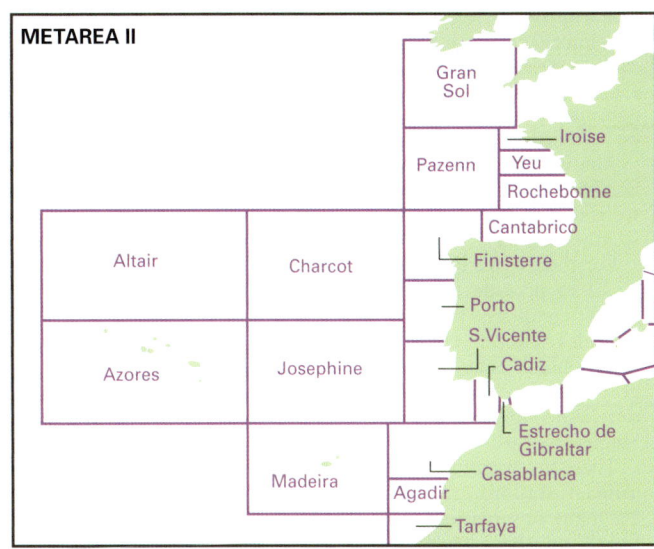

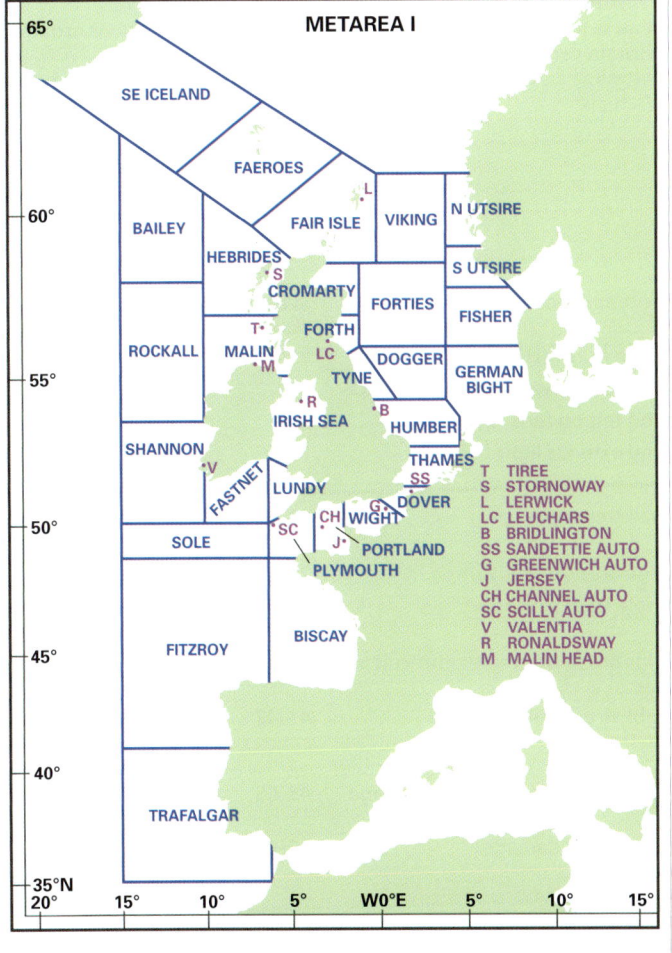

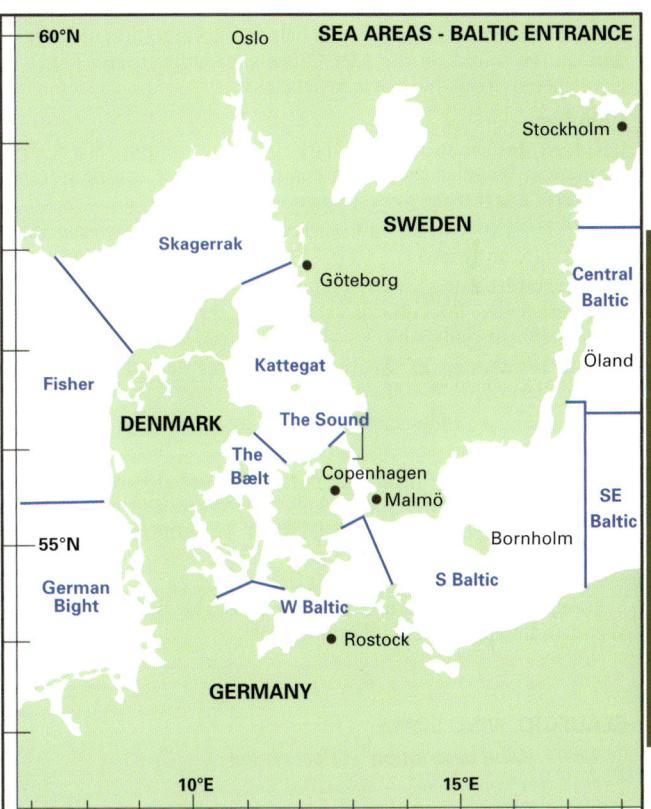

GMDSS HF/SSB radio broadcasts

Voice broadcasts from Monaco Radio, in slow, clear French and English, include the NAVTEX areas used by France to the south of 48°27'N (METAREA II).

Analyses, forecast charts and sea state charts can be received on Radio Fax from the DWD (Hamburg/Pinnenburg) and from the Royal Navy, Northwood. However, note that the latter are not part of the GMDSS and transmissions may cease from time to time.

Inshore waters forecasts for the Northern North Sea and Southern Baltic (Ostsee) and open sea area forecasts can be received in text from Hamburg on Radio Teletype. Hamburg also broadcasts forecasts of wind at specific points for up to five days ahead. For schedules and broadcast content see the DWD website www.dwd.de, *Admiralty Marine Communications* manuals, or Frank Singleton's website.

Other sources of forecasts

All the countries in the area of this almanac broadcast weather forecasts on their Public Service FM and MF frequencies. Schedules and content vary greatly and the latest available details are in Admiralty manuals.

The internet

The internet is a valuable source of weather information. Access to mobile data networks and WiFi hotspots has made the internet easily accessible to all using smartphones, tablets or laptop computers. Even without dedicated aerials the internet can often be accessed several miles out to sea.

The internet is an additional source of GMDSS MSI forecasts and synoptic charts. MyCA weather pages and Frank Singleton's website give fast direct links to information provided by national weather services.

For those with limited bandwidth the free Saildocs service uses email to provide text, of GMDSS forecasts. For details send a blank email to info@saildocs.com. A free MailASail service provides synoptic charts as small email attachments. For details, send a blank email to weather@mailasail.com with subject 'help-graphic'. For forecasts from Météo France, try the somewhat unreliable Navimail email service. Details are on MyCA and Frank Singleton's site.

There are many sources of actual weather reports. Those from 'official' stations are often rather sparse geographically but there are many observations from 'unofficial' sites. Links to both can be found on the MyCA 'Weather Actuals' page and on Frank Singleton's site.

Radar and satellite images can help in interpretation of forecasts and can be found on the Met Office site. Other useful pages are www.meteox.com and www.meteociel.fr.

GRIB files

GRidded Information in Binary files are output direct from Numerical Weather Prediction computers. These can be obtained at no cost apart from communications, in four ways:

- Direct transfer to an on-board computer using free zyagrib.org software and viewer.
- On a tablet using low cost Apps for an iPad (eg Weathertrack, Weather4D, PocketGrib, iGrib) or Android (mobileGRIB, PocketGrib, SailGrib)
- Web browser eg XCWeather, Passageweather, Magic Seaweed, Weatheronline, Windfinder etc
- By email via Saildocs or MailASail. See Frank Singleton's website.

The data are usually from the US NOAA Global Forecast System. The only differences in the various services are in the parameters available and the presentation. Wind vectors and isobars are always available. Other parameters include precipitation, air and sea temperatures, cloud cover, sea state and swell.

Forecasts in GRIB form are usually available up to 8 or 10 days ahead and provide useful planning tools.

Suggestions for using GRIB files

For planning purposes, receive and save the forecasts starting at 00 and/or 12 UTC to at least 8 days ahead. Compare each forecast with preceding forecasts. Use consistency as a guide to reliability. Inconsistency in forecasts is a good guide that the weather situation is unstable and that it is not sensible to make firm plans ahead.

For day to day use, GRIB data can help in the interpretation of GMDSS texts. But remember that the data is straight from a computer and not vetted or modified by a forecaster. It may well under-predict strong winds by one or even two Beaufort forces.

Other automatically produced forecasts

There are many other forecasts on the internet and sometimes seen as printouts in marinas. The majority are derived directly from the NOAA GFS or use the GFS as a starting point. For most cruising purposes, they cannot be consistently better than the GFS. Most are free.

Although forecasts may be given in text there is unlikely to be any human input. All should be used in the same way as GRIB files, whether from national weather services or other sources.

Actual weather information

For those with Internet access, useful data can be obtained from:
www.metoffice.gov.uk/weather/marine/observations/index.html
This gives the latest Marine hourly observations around UK coasts and including open ocean buoys to the west pf the British Isles and Biscay. Updated hourly.

www.met.ie/latest/buoy.asp for a very handy collection of data buoys around Ireland and coastal stations.

For the latest three-hourly reports from useful locations around German coasts go to the MyCA Scandinavian Weather Forecast page. Alternatively, go to www.dwd.de look for Wetter, Seewetter, Aktuell or Stationmeldungen.

The most comprehensive source of actual wind data for weather observing sites over the British Isles and France is www.xcweather.co.uk. This gives latest wind data from airfields, data buoys, light vessels etc.

Latest actual reports around Brittany are at
www.meteo-bretagne.fr/observation-vent-rafale.php

Latest reports from 'unofficial' automatic weather stations around Britain can be found at
http://weather.mailasail.com/Franks-Weather/Unofficial-Weather-Actuals

BEAUFORT WIND SCALE

No.	Wind description	Effect on sea	Effect on land	Wind speed (knots)	Av / max Wave Ht (m)
0	Calm	Sea like a mirror	Smoke rises vertically	<1	–
1	Light air	Ripples like scales, no crests	Direction of wind shown by smoke	1–3	0·1
2	Light breeze	Small wavelets, crests do not break	Wind felt on face, leaves rustle	4–6	0·2/0·3
3	Gentle breeze	Large wavelets, some crests break	Wind extends light flags	7–10	0·6/1·0
4	Moderate breeze	Small waves, frequent white horses	Small branches move	11–16	1·0/1·5
5	Fresh breeze	Moderate waves, many white horses	Small trees sway	17–21	2·0/2·5
6	Strong breeze	Large waves form, white crests	Large branches move	22–27	3·0/4·0
7	Near gale	Sea heaps up, white foam from breaking waves	Whole trees in motion	28–33	4·0/5·5
8	Gale	Moderately high waves some spindrift. Foam blown with wind	Twigs break from trees, difficult to walk	34–40	5·5/7·5
9	Strong gale	High waves, dense foam, wave creststopple, spray may affect visibility	Slight structural damage	41–47	7·0/10·0
10	Storm	Very high waves, sea appears white, visibility affected	Trees uprooted, structural damage	48–55	9·0/12·5
11	Violent storm	Exceptionally high waves, long white patches of foam, crests blown into froth	Widespread damage	56–63	11·5/16·0
12	Hurricane	The air is filled with foam, visibility very seriously affected	Widespread structural damage	64+	>14

Note – to get m/sec divide knots by two ie 5m/sec =10kn.

VHF SCHEDULES FOR WESTERN EUROPE
Times are in UTC unless otherwise stated

France
French, CROSS, stations broadcasting Inshore waters forecasts (in French). Forecasts cover up to 20M offshore. Transmissions are pre-recorded and broadcast from each transmitter in sequence.

Area	Transmitter	VHF	Times (LT)
The Belgian frontier to Baie de Somme (Gris-Nez)	Dunkerque	79	0720, 1603, 1920
	Gris-Nez	79	0710, 1545, 1910
The Baie de Somme to Cap de la Hague (Gris-Nez)	Ailly	79	0703, 1533, 1903
Cap de la Hague to Pointe de Penmarc'h (Jobourg)	Antifer	80	0803, 1633, 2003
	Port-en-Bessin	80	0745, 1615, 1945
	Jobourg	80	0733, 1603, 1933
Warning for sea areas Antifer to Casquets	Jobourg	80	on receipt, at every half hour H+20 and H+50 (in English)
Cap de la Hague to Pointe de Penmarc'h (Jobourg)	Jobourg	80	0715, 1545, 1915
	Granville	80	0703, 1533, 1903
Cap de la Hague to Pointe de Penmarc'h (Etel)	Raz	79	0445, 0703, 1103*, 1533, 1903
	Stiff	79	0503, 0715, 1115* 1545, 1915
	Batz	79	0515, 0733, 1133*, 1603, 1933
	Bodic	79	0533, 0745, 1145*, 1615, 1945
	Fréhel	79	0545, 0803, 1203*, 1633, 2003

from 1 May to 30 September

Area	Transmitter	VHF	Times (LT)
Pointe de Penmarc'h to Anse de l'Aiguillon (Etel)	Penmarc'h	80	0703, 1533, 1903
	Groix	80	0715, 1545, 1915
	Etel	63	Continuously
	Belle-Ile	80	0733, 1603, 1933
	Saint-Nazaire	80	0745, 1615, 1945
	Yeu	80	0803, 1633, 2003
	Les Sables d'Olonne	80	0815, 1645, 2015
Anse de l'Aiguillon to the Spanish Frontier (Etel)	Chassiron	63	Continuously
	Chassiron	79	0703, 1533, 1903
	Soulac	79	0715, 1545, 1915
	Cap-Ferret	79	0733, 1603, 1933
	Contis	79	0745, 1615, 1945
	Biarritz	79	0803, 1633, 2003

Note Danmarks Radio broadcasts marine forecasts for Skaggerak, Fisher, and German Bight at 0545, 0845, 1145 and 1745 on 243kHz. Strong winds and gale warnings are broadcast on VHF 16 and 2182 kHz. Portugal broadcasts weather forecasts on MF although there are some port forecasts on VHF 11 and Radionaval may be heard on VHF 11 from Monsanto, (try 0805 and 2005 UTC), or Sagres, (try 0835 and 2035 UTC.) If you do not hear them, then call on VHF.

Talk to a forecaster
There is a Met Office service, call ☎ 0378 900 0100 or *Fax* 0370 900 5050 for details. Alternatively, use Simon Keeling weatherweb.net ☎ 0906 515 0046, Jersey Met Office ☎ 01534 448770, or weatherquest.co.uk, University of East Anglia, call ☎ 09065 77 76 75. If you think that you may use these services, it might be wise to check availability and charges in advance.

Spain
Spanish stations broadcasting Sea Area forecast in English and Inshore waters forecasts, sometimes in English

Station	VHF Ch	Times
Bilbao	16, 10, 74	Even hours +0015
Santander	11, 72	0245, 0445, 0645, 0845, 1045, 1445, 1845, 2245
Gijón	10, 06	Even hours +0015
A Coruña	10, 06	0005, 0405, 0805, 1605, 2005
Finisterre	11, 06, 74, 72	0233, 0633, 1033, 1433, 1833, 2233
Vigo	10, 06	0015, 0415, 0815, 1215, 1615, 2015
Cádiz	15	0315, 0715, 1115, 1515, 1915, 2315
Tarifa	10, 06, 74, 72	Even hours +0015
Huelva	10, 06	0415, 0815, 1215, 1615, 2015
Algeciras	15, 06	Odd hours +0015

Spanish stations broadcasting Inshore Waters forecasts, in Spanish only.

Station	VHF Ch	Times
Pasajes	27	0300, 1215, 1733
Bilbão	26	0300, 1215, 1733
Santander	24	0300, 1215, 1733
Cabo Peñas	27	0300, 1215, 1733
Navia	60	0300, 1215, 1733
Cabo Ortegal	2	0300, 1215, 1733
A Coruña	26	0300, 1215, 1733
Finisterre	22	0300, 1215, 1733
Vigo	20	0300, 1215, 1733
La Guardia	82	0300, 1215, 1733
Huelva	26	0340, 1340, 1903
Cádiz	28	0340, 1340, 1903
Tarifa	83	0340, 1340, 1903

Channel Isles, Ireland, Belgium, Netherlands, Germany
Most coast coastguard stations will broadcast warnings. Routine forecasts are as in the table below.

Station	VHF Ch and Times	Areas
Jersey Coastguard	82 at 0645, 0745, 0845 (all LT) and 1245, 1845, 2245 (all UTC)	Area bounded by 50°N, 3°W and the French Coast. 24 hour forecast and 24 hour outlook
Irish Coastguard	02, 04, 23, 24, 26, 28, 83 (3 hourly LT from 0103)	24 hour forecast for coastal waters to 30M and Irish Sea
Oostende Radio	27 0720, LT, 0820, 1720 UTC	Thames, Dover
Dutch Coastguard	23, 25, 27, 83, 84, 87 0805 & 1305, (12h forecast) 1905 & 2305, (24h forecast), LT	Dutch waters, the Waddenzee and the IJsselmeer,
German Coastguard	24, 25, 26, 28, 61, 83 0745, 0945, 1245, 1645 and 1945	North Sea and Baltic Sea

German Traffic Centres give regular and frequent updates of weather conditions in the approaches to ports and harbours.
To find a comprehensive list of German, Danish, and Dutch marine broadcasts on VHF, MF, and other channels, search for a PDF file, Wetter- und Warnfunk.

UK COASTAL FORECASTS AND MSI ON VHF

The working channel is given after an initial announcement on VHF 16

Coastguard Operations Centre Area	Coastal Forecast Areas	Broadcast times (in local time) and schedules				
		B	C	A	C	Shipping Forecast Areas
ABERDEEN Cape Wrath to Berwick	Cape Wrath to Rattray Head, Rattray Head to Berwick	0130 1330	0430 1630	0730 1930	1030 2230	Fair Isle, Viking, Cromarty, Forties, Forth, South Utsire
HUMBER Berwick to Southwold	Berwick to Whitby, Whitby to Gibraltar Point, Gibraltar Point to N Foreland	0150 1350	0450 1650	0750 1950	1050 2250	Forties, Forth, Tyne, Dogger, Fisher, Humber, German Bight
DOVER Southwold to Beachy Head	Gibraltar Point to N Foreland, N Foreland to Selsey Bill	0110 1310	0410 1610	0710 1910	1010 2210	Humber, Thames, Dover, German Bight
SOLENT (operated from NMOC Fareham) Beachy Head to Exmouth	N Foreland to Selsey Bill, Selsey Bill to Lyme Regis, Lyme Regis to Land's End inc. Isles of Scilly	0130 1330	0430 1630	0730 1930	1030 2230	Portland, Wight
FALMOUTH Exmouth to Cornwall/Devon border inc Isles of Scilly	Lyme Regis to Land's End inc. Isles of Scilly, Land's End to St David's Hd inc. Bristol Channel	0110 1310	0410 1610	0710 1910	1010 2210	Portland, Plymouth, Sole, Shannon, Lundy, Fastnet, Biscay, Fitzroy
MILFORD HAVEN Cornwall/Devon border to Barmouth	Land's End to St David's Hd inc. Bristol Channel, St David's Hd to the Great Orme Hd inc. St George's Channel	0150 1350	0450 1650	0750 1950	1050 2250	Lundy, Fastnet, Irish Sea, Shannon
HOLYHEAD Barmouth to Mull of Galloway inc Isle of Man	St David's Hd to the Great Orme Hd inc. St George's Channel, Isle of Man, Great Orme Hd to Mull of Galloway	0130 1330	0430 1630	0730 1930	1030 2230	Irish Sea
BELFAST Mull of Galloway and Carlingford Lough to Jura and Lough Foyle inc Firth of Clyde	Mull of Galloway to Mull of Kintyre inc Firth of Clyde and North Channel, Carlingford Lough to Lough Foyle, Mull of Kintyre to Ardnamurchan	0210 1410	0510 1710	0810 2010	1110 2310	Irish Sea, Rockall, Malin
STORNOWAY Jura to Cape Wrath inc Mull, Skye, and the Hebrides	Mull of Kintyre to Ardnamurchan, The Minch, Ardnamurchan to Cape Wrath	0110 1310	0410 1610	0710 1910	1010 2210	Rockall, Malin, Hebrides, Bailey, Fair Is, Faroes, SE Iceland
SHETLAND Shetland, Orkney and North coast of Scotland	Shetland Isles and 60M offshore, Cape Wrath to Rattray Head inc Orkney	0110 1310	0410 1610	0710 1910	1010 2210	Viking, Fair Isle, Faroes, N Utsire

Note – The CG areas are approximate. If on a boundary, in hilly areas such as West Scotland, it may be advantageous to listen to the neighbouring transmission as well.

Schedule A
Full maritime safety information broadcast, including new inshore forecast and outlook, gale warnings, general synopsis and shipping forecast for appropriate sea areas, WZ navigation warnings, SUBFACTS and GUNFACTS where appropriate, three-day fisherman's forecast (October to March).

Schedule B
New inshore forecast, new outlook, gale warnings.

Schedule C
Repetition of inshore forecast and gale warnings as per previous Schedule A or B broadcast plus new strong wind warning.

UK COASTGUARD FORECASTS AND MSI ON MF

Aerial	Frequency/KHz	Times (UTC)	
Aberdeen	2226	0730	1930
Cullercoats	1925	0730	1930
Scillies	1880	0710	1910
Tiree	1833	0810	2010
Butt of Lewis	1743	0710	1910
Shetland	1770	0710	1910

NAVTEX Broadcast content and schedules (Times in UT)
Stations broadcasting weather forecasts on the International Frequency 518 kHz, in English

Station	Times	Content	Areas
Niton (E)	0840, 2040	Warning summary, 24h forecast and brief outlook	Thames, Dover, Wight, Portland, Plymouth, Biscay, Fitzroy, Sole, Lundy, Fastnet
	0040	Extended outlook	Thames, Dover, Wight, Portland, Plymouth, Biscay, Sole, Lundy
Portpatrick (O)	0620, 1820	Warning summary, 24h forecast and brief outlook	Lundy, Fastnet, Irish Sea, Rockall, Malin, Hebrides, Bailey, Fair Isle, Faeroes and SE Iceland
	0220	Extended outlook	Fair Isle, Viking, North Utsire, South Utsire, Forties, Cromarty, Forth, Tyne, Dogger, Fisher, German Bight, Humber, Thames, Dover and Wight
Cullercoats (G)	0900, 2100	Warning summary, 24h forecast and brief outlook	Viking, Forties, Cromarty, Forth, Tyne, Dogger, Humber, Thames and Fair Isle
	0100	Extended outlook	Fair Isle, Viking, North Utsire, South Utsire, Forties, Cromarty, Forth, Tyne, Dogger, Fisher, German Bight, Humber, Thames, Dover and Wight
Valentia (W)	0740, 1940	24h forecast and brief outlook	Sole, Fastnet and Shannon
	1140, 2340	High seas bulletin	East Central section of METAREA I, High Seas
Malin Head (Q) see Note 1	0640, 1840	24h forecast, brief outlook and high seas bulletin	Shannon, Rockall, Malin Hebrides and Bailey, East Northern & East Central sections of METAREA I, High Seas
Thorshavn (D)	Every 4 hours from 0030	24h forecast and brief outlook	Outer Banks, The Munk, Fugloy Banks, Iceland Ridge
Rogaland (L)	0150 and 1350	36h forecast	North Utsire, South Utsire, Fisher, Forties, German Bight, Shetlands banks, East and West Tampen
Jeløy (M)	0200, 1400	24h forecast	Skagerrak
Grimeton (I)	0520, 1720	24h forecast	Kattegat and The Belts
Ørlandet (N)	0210, 1410	24h forecast	Norwegian Sea Areas to the north of 61°N
Oostende (T)	0710, 1910	24h forecast	Coasts of Belgium and Sea Areas Thames and Dover
Hamburg (S)	Every 4h from 0300	24h forecast	German Bight
IJmuiden (P)	0230, 1430	Warning summary. Forecasts for next 12h and 12h outlook	German Bight, Fisher, Humber, Thames and Dogger
Corsen (A)	0000, 1200	Warning summary. Forecasts for next 24h and brief outlook	Iroise, Yeu, Rochebonne, Cantabrico, Finisterre and Pazenn
A Coruña (D)	0030, 1230	Sea area forecasts for next 24h (in English and Spanish)	Gran Sol, Pazenn, Iroise, Yeu, Rochebonne, Altair, Charcot, Finisterre, Cantabrico, Azores, Josephine, Porto, São Vicente, Cádiz, Estrecho, Madeira, Casablanca & Agadir
Monsanto (R)	0030, 1230	Sea area forecasts for next 24h (in English and Spanish)	Charcot, Josephine, Finisterre, Porto, São Vicente and Cádiz, (There is a second separate forecast for Madeira, Casablanca, and Agadir)
Tarifa (G)	0030, 1230	Sea area forecasts for next 24h (in English and Spanish)	São Vicente, Cádiz, Casablanca, Agadir, Gibraltar, Strait / Estrecho

Stations broadcasting weather forecasts on the national frequency of 490 kHz

Station	Times	Content	Areas
Niton (I)	0120, 0520, 1320, 1720	Inshore waters forecast and 24h outlook	Gibraltar Point to St David's Head including the Channel Islands, the Isles of Scilly and the Bristol Channel
	0920, 2120	Latest observations	South coast
Niton (T)	0710, 1910	Warning summary and sea area forecasts for next 24h and a brief outlook (in French)	Humber, Tamise, Pas de Calais and Antifer
Portpatrick (C)	0200, 0820, 1220, 2020	Inshore waters forecast and 24h outlook	From Lands End to Cape Wrath, including Northern Ireland
	0420, 1620	Latest observations	West coast
Malin Head (A)	Every 4h from 0000	Inshore waters forecast and 24h outlook	Lough Foyle to Carlingford Lough, Mull of Galloway to Mull of Kintyre including the Firth of Clyde and North Channel, Mull of Kintyre to Ardnamurchan Point, The Minch, Ardnaurchan Pt to Cape Wrath, Isle of Man
Cullercoats (U)	0720, 1120, 1920, 2320	Inshore waters forecast and 24h outlook	Shetland Isles, coastal waters from Cape Wrath to Duncansby Hd and the east coast to North Foreland
	0320, 1520		East coast
Hamburg (L)	0150, 0950, 1750	24h forecast (In German)	German Bight and S Baltic German waters
Oostende (B)	0810, 1210, 1610, 2010	24h forecast (in French)	Thames, Dover
Corsen (E)	0840, 2040	Warning summary. 24h forecast and brief outlook (in French)	Casquets, Ouessant, Iroise, Yeu, Rochebonne, Cantabrico, Finisterre, Pazenn, Sole, Shannon, Fastnet, Lundy and Irish Sea
A Coruña (W)	1140, 1940	Sea area forecasts for next 24h (in Spanish)	Gran Sol, Pazenn, Iroise, Yeu, Rochebonne, Charcot, Finisterre, Cantabrico, Josephine, Porto, São Vicente, Cádiz, Estrecho
Monsanto (G)	0500, 1700	Sea area forecasts for next 24h (in Portuguese)	Charcot, Josephine, Finisterre, Porto, São Vicente and Cádiz

Note 1 On W coast of Scotland, Malin Head may give better reception.

The Cruising Almanac

ENGLAND – SOUTH COAST

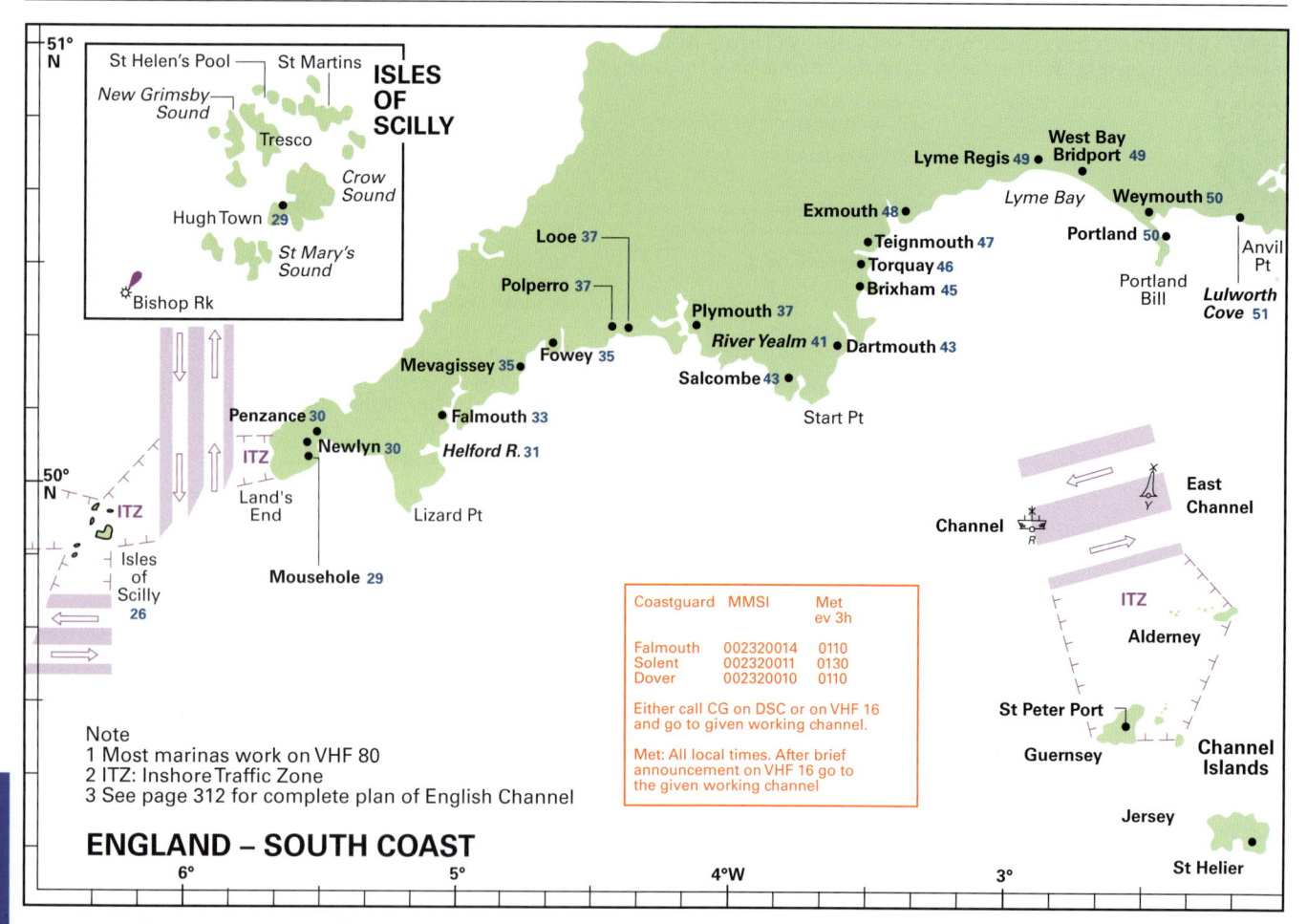

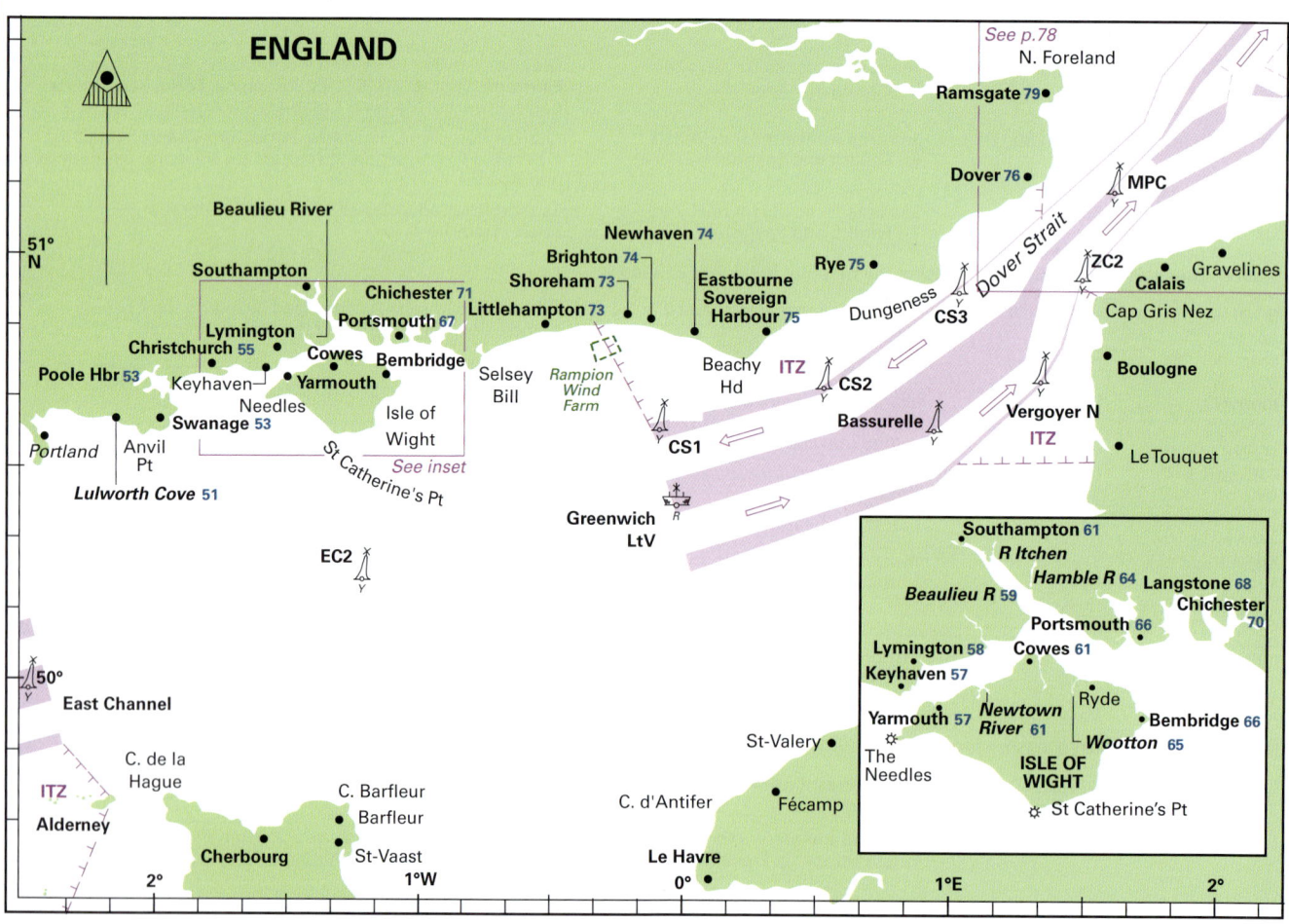

Isles of Scilly
- St Helen's Pool
- St Martins
- *New Grimsby Sound*
- Tresco
- *Crow Sound*
- Hugh Town **29**
- *St Mary's Sound*
- Bishop Rk

South Cornwall / Devon / Dorset
- Isles of Scilly **26**
- Mousehole **29**
- Penzance **30**
- Newlyn **30**
- Land's End
- Lizard Pt
- *Helford R.* **31**
- Falmouth **33**
- Mevagissey **35**
- Fowey **35**
- Polperro **37**
- Looe **37**
- Plymouth **37**
- *River Yealm* **41**
- Salcombe **43**
- Start Pt
- Dartmouth **43**
- Brixham **45**
- Torquay **46**
- Teignmouth **47**
- Exmouth **48**
- Lyme Regis **49**
- *Lyme Bay*
- West Bay Bridport **49**
- Weymouth **50**
- Portland **50**
- Portland Bill
- Anvil Pt
- **Lulworth Cove** **51**

Channel Islands
- Channel
- East Channel
- Alderney
- St Peter Port
- Guernsey
- Jersey
- St Helier

Coastguard	MMSI	Met ev 3h
Falmouth	002320014	0110
Solent	002320011	0130
Dover	002320010	0110

Either call CG on DSC or on VHF 16 and go to given working channel.

Met: All local times. After brief announcement on VHF 16 go to the given working channel

Note
1 Most marinas work on VHF 80
2 ITZ: Inshore Traffic Zone
3 See page 312 for complete plan of English Channel

ENGLAND

- Poole Hbr **53**
- Portland
- Anvil Pt
- *Lulworth Cove* **51**
- Swanage **53**
- Christchurch **55**
- Lymington
- Keyhaven
- Needles
- Yarmouth
- Cowes
- Bembridge
- *Beaulieu River*
- Southampton
- Chichester **71**
- Portsmouth **67**
- *Isle of Wight*
- *St Catherine's Pt*
- Selsey Bill
- Littlehampton **73**
- Shoreham **73**
- Brighton **74**
- Newhaven **74**
- Eastbourne Sovereign Harbour **75**
- Beachy Hd
- Rampion Wind Farm
- CS1
- Greenwich LtV
- EC2
- Dungeness
- Rye **75**
- CS3
- Dover **76**
- N. Foreland (See p.78)
- Ramsgate **79**
- MPC
- ZC2
- Calais
- Gravelines
- Cap Gris Nez
- CS2
- Bassurelle
- Boulogne
- Vergoyer N
- ITZ
- Le Touquet
- St-Valery
- Fécamp
- C. d'Antifer
- Le Havre
- St-Vaast
- Barfleur
- C. Barfleur
- Cherbourg
- C. de la Hague
- Alderney
- East Channel
- ITZ

Isle of Wight inset
- Southampton **61**
- *R Itchen*
- *Hamble R* **64**
- Langstone **68**
- *Beaulieu R* **59**
- Portsmouth **66**
- Chichester **70**
- Lymington **58**
- Cowes **61**
- Keyhaven **57**
- Ryde
- Bembridge **66**
- Yarmouth **57**
- *Newtown River* **61**
- *Wootton* **65**
- The Needles
- ISLE OF WIGHT
- St Catherine's Pt

Page references are shown after locations, for example:
Falmouth 33. Bold type indicates that it is accompanied by a plan.
Italics are used for rivers, lochs, bays, seas etc.

24

England – South Coast
Isles of Scilly to Ramsgate

The S coast of England has a great variety of beautiful sailing areas varying from the exposed and rugged W parts with their sheltered and extensive rivers and relatively little commercial traffic to the very popular and attractive Solent, busy with ships, cruising boats and yacht racing. Here, though the waters are more sheltered, there are strong tidal streams. Care has to be taken when negotiating unfamiliar port entrances as the Solent has interesting tidal stands in parts. There are many yacht havens, some of which can become overcrowded at weekends at the height of the season. E of the Solent the ports are well spaced, there are fewer boats and east of Brighton the chalk cliff scenery is spectacular. The prevailing winds are from the SW and the Channel generates its own particular sort of choppy seas in strong winds. Careful plans need to be made to negotiate the headlands with their tidal gates and take advantage of the tidal streams which can run fast, bearing in mind that the sea may become treacherous in wind over tide conditions.

For reference or more details refer to:
The Shell Channel Pilot Tom Cunliffe (Imray)
Isles of Scilly RCC Pilotage Foundation (Imray)
The West Country Carlos Rojas & Susan Kemp-Wheeler (Imray)
West Country Cruising Mark Fishwick (Wiley Nautical)
Inshore along the Dorset Coast Peter Bruce (Boldre Marine)

PASSAGES AROUND LAND'S END

Pedn an Laaz means the end of the earth and is appropriate to this inhospitable but beautiful, most westerly point of mainland England. There are many rocks in addition to the Longships. Weather forecasts are less reliable here than elsewhere in the UK, and SE winds can quickly veer to the W and freshen, making this a lee shore. There is also a tidal gate, especially if southbound, so use the tidal streams, which run at up to 4kn and are modified by strong winds. Close to the coast, there are counter-stream currents during much of the tidal cycle. All the headlands, and Carn Base shoal, have heavy overfalls in wind against tide conditions, particularly at springs.

The passage inside the **Runnel Stone** is safe near high water in fine weather. All of the shoals are now on the latest editions of plotter software. However, the inshore passage is best avoided in any swell, and near local LW. Tides here run to the west from Newlyn HW+0230 to HW-0200; and to the east from Newlyn HW-0100 to HW+0200. Near the Runnel Stone the E-going stream begins HW Newlyn-0120 (Dover-0600) and runs for 3 hours only, but the NW-going stream begins at Newlyn+0140 (Dover-0300) and runs for 9½ hours.

Carn Bras, the most westerly of the **Longships** rocks on which the LtHo stands, is fairly steep to on its seaward side and the TSS lies 3M offshore. Tides around the Longships are complex. **Kettle's Bottom** (dr 5.2m) is awash at HW, usually has swell breaking on it, and lies halfway between the LtHo and the shore. There is an inshore passage ½M wide between Kettle's Bottom and Land's End, with Peel Rocks and the Armed Knight (with their spits) being close to the shore. This inshore passage is deep and safe in fine weather and daylight. Do not attempt in bad weather, and never at night. If fitted with radar put 0.25 ring on and keep it on the cliff, because the channel is 0.5 miles wide. N Brison (higher) just open W of S Brison (lower) on 001° also leads through. Inshore tides run 1-2 hours earlier than to W of the Longships. Inshore N'ly flood runs from Newlyn LW-0100 to Newlyn HW-0200; S'ly ebb from Newlyn HW-0100 to Newlyn LW-0200, but getting later further W. These are strong streams, particularly S-going spring ebb.

Between Longships, Kettle's Bottom and Shark's Fin there is no safe passage, but shoals and many tidal eddies. There is no safe passage inside **The Brisons**. Give them a wide berth to seaward. There is a very strong tidal race just W of **Pendeen** with no inshore passage. Give this a 1M berth.

Northbound. This is the easier direction. W of Longships the tide turns N at HW Dover +0100 (HW Plymouth 0500 approx). However, close inshore it turns much earlier. If off Runnel Stone S card Lt buoy HW Dover -0300 one has a fair tide through the Longships Passage up to the Brisons in time to catch the NE going stream along the N Cornwall coast. 10h of fair tide can be achieved. If late, the tide inshore of Longships will be contrary. When passing W of Longships on a N-going tide at night, stay in the white sector, but one may be carried towards Longships LtHo, in an area where neither Tater Du nor Pendeen LtHo's are visible for a cross bearing, which can be disconcerting.

By locking out of Penzance up to HW +0100, one can reach Padstow to lock in at local HW. Alternatively, if bound further NE the contrary tide can be dodged in Widemouth Bay to catch the next fair tide at Hartland Pt. From Falmouth it is more difficult as slack water off Lizard Pt is at HW Dover ±0300 and it is 18M to Runnel Stone S card buoy, although tides in Mount's Bay are weak.

Southbound. Timing is more critical, and there is less help from the tidal stream. Tides are weak off the N Cornwall coast but strengthen W of St Ives. If one leaves St Ives on the first of the offshore SW stream (HW Dover -0430) the tidal gate will start closing against you a few hours later off Gwennap Hd. Here the ebb starts at HW Newlyn+0230 inside the Runnel Stone, and Newlyn+0300 outside the Runnel Stone. One needs to be here before about HW Newlyn to have 2h of fair tide to get into Mount's Bay. Therefore leave St Ives at HW Dover, initially against the stream, so keep well inshore. Later, stay inshore to take advantage of favourable eddies, but keep to seaward of the near-shore rocks, especially the Vyneck (off Cape Cornwall and its chimney), the Wra (close N of Pendeen LtHo), the Brisons, and if necessary the overfalls off Pendeen. Then, if possible, use the inshore Longships Passage where the stream will now be favourable, but adverse offshore of Longships. If bound from Milford Haven to W Brittany the timing is less critical.

England South Coast: Isles of Scilly to Ramsgate distances (miles)

	Hugh Town	Newlyn	Lizard (2M S)	Falmouth	Fowey	Plymouth BW	Salcombe	Start Point	Dartmouth	Portland Hbr	Poole	Yarmouth	Portsmouth	St Catherine's	Nab Tower	Chichester	Brighton	Beachy Head	Dungeness	Dover	Ramsgate
Hugh Town	0																				
Newlyn	37	0																			
Lizard (2M S)	44	18	0																		
Falmouth	63	35	18	0																	
Fowey	51	49	34	20	0																
Plymouth BW	85	68	47	38	22	0															
Salcombe	104	77	60	50	36	20	0														
Start Point	108	81	63	55	41	25	7	0													
Dartmouth	117	90	73	65	50	35	16	9	0												
Portland Hbr	164	137	103	111	97	81	63	56	53	0											
Poole	185	157	140	131	117	102	79	77	72	32	0										
Yarmouth	202	169	148	144	129	114	95	88	84	38	20	0									
Portsmouth	219	186	165	161	146	131	112	105	101	55	37	17	0								
St Catherine's	200	171	155	147	132	117	99	92	88	42	26	19	20	0							
Nab Tower	215	188	170	162	148	132	114	107	103	57	42	35	10	15	0						
Chichester	221	192	171	167	152	137	118	112	108	62	43	24	10	22	7	0					
Brighton	248	220	204	196	181	166	147	140	137	91	75	64	41	49	33	41	0				
Beachy Head	260	232	215	208	193	178	159	152	149	102	87	69	54	60	46	48	15	0			
Dungeness	290	261	245	237	223	208	190	183	179	133	117	100	84	90	77	79	46	31	0		
Dover	308	279	263	255	241	226	208	201	197	151	135	118	102	108	95	97	64	49	18	0	
Ramsgate	325	296	280	272	257	242	224	217	213	167	151	134	118	125	111	113	80	65	33	15	0

The Cruising Almanac

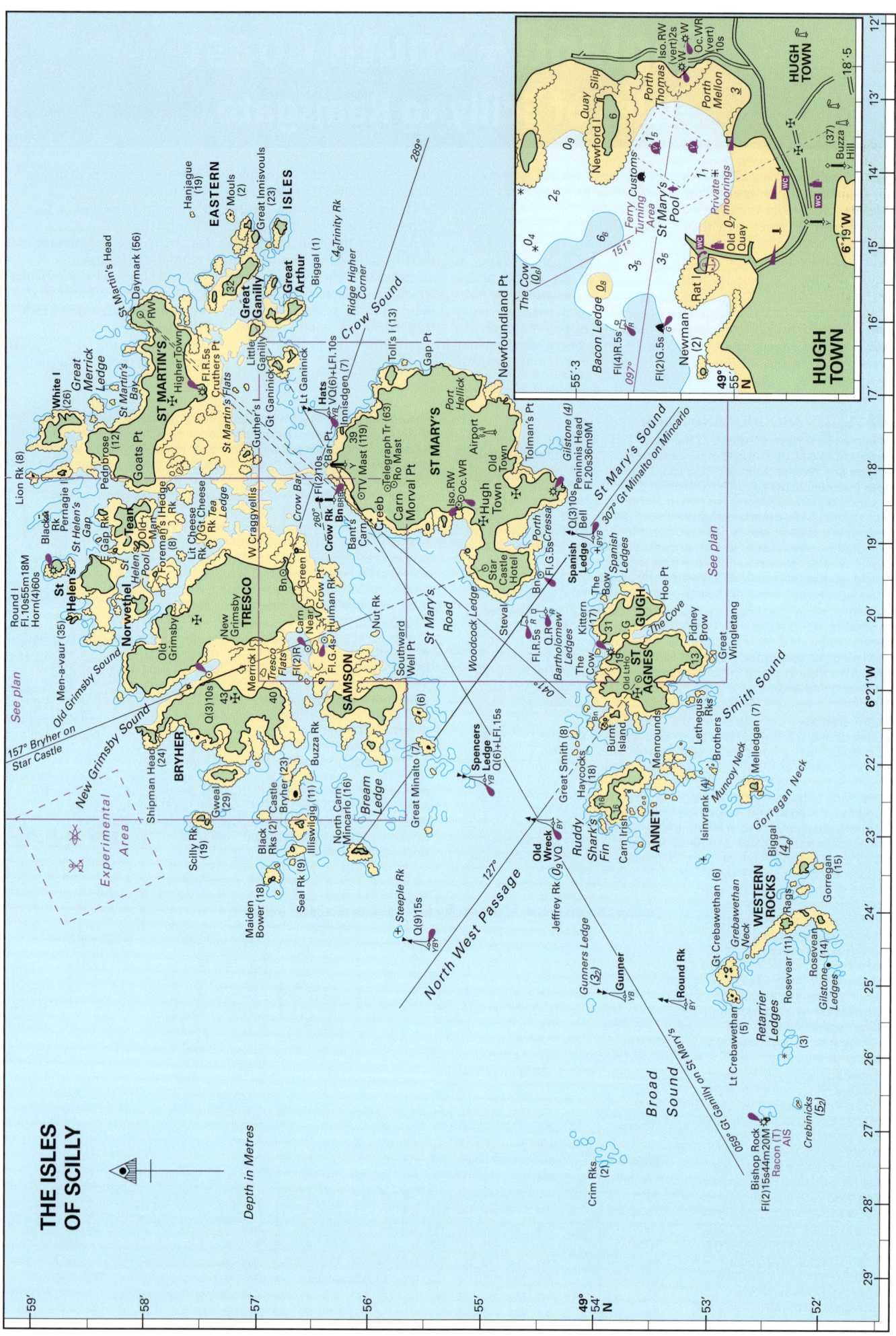

The Cruising Almanac

ISLES OF SCILLY

Standard Port Plymouth

St Mary's
HW (sp) –0105 (np) –0052
LW (sp) –0048 (np) –0045

MHWS MHWN MLWN MLWS
+0·2m –0·1m –0·2m –0·1m

The Isles of Scilly are made up of five inhabited islands and many smaller islets and rocky outcrops. They are exposed, low lying, the highest land being 46m, and are situated about 28M SW of the Cornish mainland. Their rotary tidal streams and exposure to Atlantic swell mean they are liable to rough seas in strong winds. The weather can change quickly so boats need to be prepared to change their anchorage fast, as none of the anchorages are protected from all directions. However, they are well worth a visit for their beauty and wild life.

The Isles of Scilly are most easily approached in light weather when there is good visibility in daylight so that Ldg marks and lobster pots are more obvious. The intricacies of navigating all the islands are well covered in the pilot books mentioned above.

The tidal streams are rotary clockwise ¾ to 1½kn but more at various points. Off St Martin's Head there is a tide rip to S and SE for 3M.

DS off Gilstone: Dover +0245 NE 1·8kn; –0415 SW 2·5kn.

St Mary's Road: Dover +0145E –0545W (varies between SW and NW), both about 1kn.

St Mary's Sound: Dover +0245SE; –0400NW, both 2kn.

ISLES OF SCILLY TO PENZANCE

Passage lights   BA No
Bishop Rock   0002
Fl(2)15s44m20M AIS
Round Is   0018
Fl.10s55m18M Horn(4)60s
Peninnis Head   0006
Fl.20s36m9M
Seven Stones LtV   0020
Fl(3)30s15M Horn(3)60s
Racon(O) (---) AIS
Longships   0028
Fl(2)WR.10s35m15/11M
Horn 10s
Wolf Rk   0030
Fl.15s34m16M Horn 30s
Racon(T) (–) AIS
Tater-Du   0032
Fl(3)15s34m20M+F.R (over Runnel Stone)

Streams related to HW Dover

Scilly Is to Land's End +0100NW, +0300N; +0500NE; –0400SSE; –0100SSW

Runnelstone –0600 to –0300E; –0300 to +0600NW

Land's End HWD N; –0500S

When going E from the Scillies to Penzance make for the Wolf Rock LtHo, deep water up to ½M off on all sides. Then pass well S of the Runnel Stone, S card Lt buoy liable to drift, and follow the coast at least 1M offshore.

Crow Sound: weak and irregular except from Dover –0145 to +0515 when it runs SE at first, changing through E to N; max 1·4kn at 0245 NE.

New Grimsby Harbour: Dover –0400N; +0040S, both 1kn. Off the entrance: +0115E; –0515W, both 2½kn.

N of Round Is, streams are up to 4kn ½M off.

Approaches Principal landmarks are:

St Mary's Is – TV mast 118m, radio masts and telegraph tr 63m, and Peninnis Head LtHo (W circular iron 36m with a black cupola).

St Agnes Is – disused LtHo (W stone 23m). Bishop Rock LtHo (grey circular 44m). Round Is LtHo (W circular 55m).

St Martin's Is – daymark (R & W horizontal bands 56m).

From E, St Martin's daymark comes up first; from S, St Mary's TV mast.

Main approaches arranged in clockwise order:

From SE – St Mary's Sound.
From S – Smith's Sound W of St Agnes. Not recommended because of unmarked dangers, distant Ldg marks and difficulty in identifying recognisable points for fixing a position.
From SW – Broad Sound close N of Bishop Rock.
From W – North Channel between Annet and Mincarlo.
From NNW
• to New Grimsby Harbour, between Bryher and Tresco.
• to Old Grimsby Harbour on NE side of Tresco.
From N – E of Round Is to St Helen's Pool and Old Grimsby.
From E – Crow Sound.

Approach and Entrance

• **St Mary's Sound** Easiest, buoyed but beware of set to stb and unlit lobster pot markers. Exposed in any SW swell. Round S of St Mary's keeping ½M off Tolman Point to clear Gilstone; close round Peninnis Head Fl.20s leaving Spanish Ledge (E card) Lt buoy and N Bartholomew R can buoy Fl.R.5s to port with N Carn of Mincarlo in line with W extreme of Gt Minalto 307° until NW corner of St Mary's is in line with St Martin's RW daymark; follow this line (040°) and enter St Mary's Pool on line 097° of Lt bns, front white topmark, rear orange X.

• **Broad Sound** Buoyed, unlit. Enter 4ca N of Bishop Rock LtHo and S of Flemings Ledge. Ldg line 059° Gt Gannilly summit (8½M off) just open N of Bants Carn.

• **North Channel** Cross tide, outlying rks. Keep on approach Ldg line, 127° keeping St Agnes old LtHo in line with Tins Walbert bn until on Ldg line for Broad Sound (*see above*).

• **New Grimsby Sound** Beware cross stream in approach. Round Is Lt is 1½M to port (Ro Bn), otherwise unlit. Keep the W side of Hangman Is (conspic pinnacle 19m) in line with Star Castle on St Mary's 157°.

• **Old Grimsby Sound** Overfalls exist over Kettle Bottom off the point between Old and New Grimsby Sounds and there are strong cross streams in approach, unbuoyed and unlit. From N of Tresco steer 124° for mid-pt between Norwethel and Merchants Point. Beware the Little Kittern (dries 1·9m). Past Merchants Point beware Tide Rock.

• **St Helen's Gap** Beware cross stream in approach. Leave Round Is 1¼ca to W and keep Star Castle in line with E Gap Rock (2m) 182° until past E extreme of St Helen's Is whence steer 201° between E and W Gap Rks into St Helen's Pool.

• **Crow Bar** Bar dries 0·7m 2ca N of Bar Pt, but has 1m to S, unlit. Leave Hats S card buoy close to stb and clear Bar Pt by 1ca; pass 50m either side of Crow bn Fl(2)10s. Follow island round to pass between Bacon and Cow ledges (latter dries 0·6m) by keeping B vert strip on white shelter on promenade in line with Buzza Tr on skyline 151°. This approach is sheltered from the W, with a good anchorage at Watermill Cove to await the tide to get round to Hugh Town.

Interior channels

• St Mary's to New Grimsby. Leave 2hrs after LW for 1·3m draught and at half flood for 1·8m. Leave Nut Rock to port and Hulman Bn 50m to stb until Merrick Is is in line with right-hand edge of Hangman Is. On this transit keep Little Rag Ledge Bn (E of Great Rag Ledge) to port, Chink Rks to stb, Gt Crabs Ledge to port, Plump Rocks to stb, Merrick Is to port and Plumb Is to stb, direction generally 340° but varies.

• To Old Grimsby. At half tide steer on back bearing of Crow Bn in line with middle TV tr on St Mary's (160°) to Lizard Pt whence steer for middle of gap between Tresco and Norwethel.

• To St Helen's Pool. At half tide from Hats anchorage, N of St Mary's, steer on the centre islet of Men-a-vaur in line with the landing cairn on SW corner of St Helen's, 322°. As the anchorage nears, the islet will be obscured by the cairn.

Anchorages and Moorings

None of the following anchorages offer all round shelter, so it is important to consider wind direction, probable wind shift and direction of swell.

• **St Mary's, Hugh Town** No resident customs here but occasional visits by patrol boats. Busy in season. No anchoring is allowed in the hbr. Uncomfortable in winds SW to N. 28+10 Y visitors' moorings, (charged). Dinghy pontoon near stairs on S side of St Mary's Pool. Yachts may lie alongside St Mary's Quay, the harbourmaster will give directions. The ferry *Scillonian* comes in at 1200 and leaves at 1630 weekdays (two calls on summer Saturdays).

• **St Mary's, Porth Cressa**, W side of bay only, V mooring buoys (charged). Untenable in strong winds from SE to SW, sheltered from W through N to E, but swell possible from W or ESE. Markers indicate submarine power cable.

• **St Mary's, Watermill Cove** Sheltered from S through W to NW.

• **New Grimsby Harbour** Best and most sheltered anchorage. Sheltered SSW through W to NW and from NNE through E to SSE. Submarine cables. 22 visitors' moorings (charged) are encroaching on the anchorage. Beware weed when anchoring.

• **Old Grimsby** Sheltered from SSW to W. Subject to swell, even from W. Strong spring tidal streams. Six visitors' moorings.

• **St Helen's Pool** Anchor astride line joining centre of Men-a-vaur to landing cairn on SW tip of St Helen's Is. Comparatively sheltered; some scend at HW.

• **St Agnes/Gugh** These two islands are connected by a bar drying 4·6m, providing anchorages to the S in the Cove for winds from WSW through N to NNE, and to the N in Porth Conger for winds from E by S to W. Bar covers at HW springs when anchorages may be uncomfortable for HW ±0130.

• Visitors' buoys opposite the hotel in Tean Sound, W of St Martins. No charge if visiting the hotel. Beware rocky bottom if anchoring. If going ashore to St Martin's take the dinghy on to the beach leaving the quay clear.

Facilities Fuel, water and showers on quay at Hugh Town. Water also on quays at Bryher and Tresco. Toilets, showers, and community meeting room above beach at Porth Cressa. Shops at Hugh Town and stores at St Agnes, Bryher and Tresco. Pubs or hotels at Hugh Town, Tresco, Bryher, St Martin's and St Agnes.

☏/VHF HM 01720 422768. VHF 14 in working hours.

Transport By ferry from Penzance. By air from Exeter, Newquay, and Land's End to St Mary's.

Interest Exotic Tresco Abbey Gardens. Exciting gig races off St Mary's on Wednesdays and Fridays.

MOUSEHOLE

See plan p.30

Tidal data as Newlyn but dries LW

A small drying hbr S of Newlyn, 4m springs, 2·6m neaps, access HW±0300. 3F.R(vert) indicates hbr closed. Sand and rock. Entrance closed in S gales. Good anchorage S of entrance. Water, shops. A very picturesque hbr with an RSPB bird sanctuary close by.

☏ HM (01736) 731644.

NEWLYN

Standard Port Plymouth
HW (sp) –0108   (np) –0053
LW (sp) –0035   (np) –0036

MHWS	MHWN	MLWN	MLWS
0·0m	–0·1m	–0·2m	0·0m

From last quarter flood to first quarter ebb the tide flows NE in the N part of Mount's Bay.

For those coming from the Bristol Channel going S this is a useful port of refuge in the event of a bad weather forecast, affording protection in gales from S through W to NE. SE winds may bring in a heavy swell.

Approach From Penzance leave Gear Rock to stb and steer for pier heads. From S, leave St Clement's Is ½M to port, steer N with Low Lee E card Lt buoy, to port until LtHo on S

The Cruising Almanac

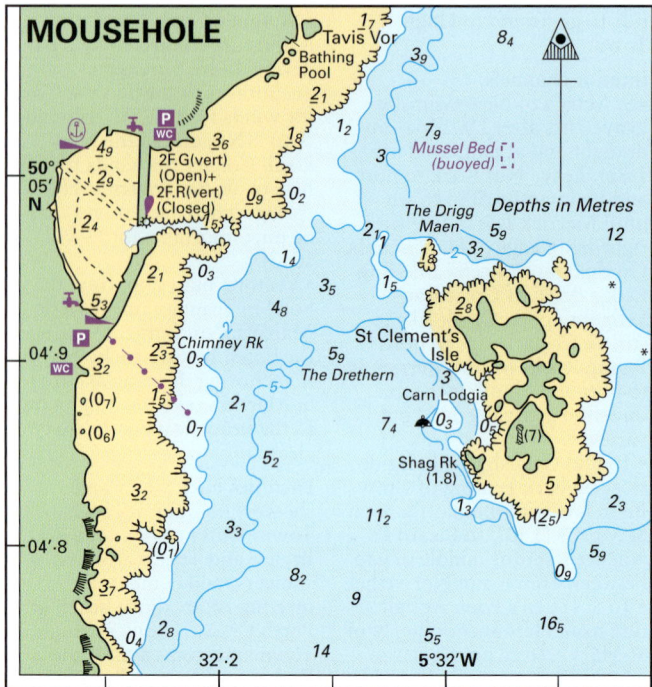

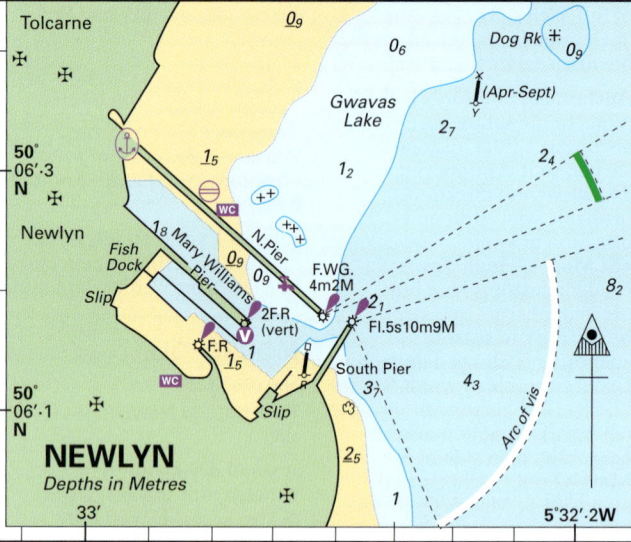

arm of hbr bears 305°, which course clears Carn Base Rks. By night, keep in W sector of Penzance LtHo (Fl.WR.5s 268°-W-345°) until Newlyn Lt (Fl.5s) bears 305°.

Note W sectors of Penzance and Newlyn are Fl.5s.

Entrance Beware of emerging fishing boats and L.B. Turn to stb, leaving to port R spar buoy at end of slipway.

Berthing
• Anchor outside in Gwavas Lake, N of end of North Pier; good holding and sheltered in W winds.
• Berth on the two outer fingers, or on the hammerhead, of the pontoon to the SW of the Mary Williams pier. Yachts <9m usually berth on SW side of pontoon. Crowded in summer.

Facilities Fuel from tanker; water on quays. Shops. Showers; key from Harbour Office near shore or from watchman's cabin out of hours.

☎/VHF HM 01736 362523. After 1700, mobile 07818 415871. VHF 12.

PENZANCE
Tidal data as Newlyn

Tide flows NE in N part of Mount's Bay from last quarter flood to first quarter ebb.

There is a wet dock with sheltered berths open HW–0200 to HW+0100 (yachts welcome), an outer drying hbr and outside anchorage. Entrance to drying hbr dangerous in strong S or SE winds.

Approach From the E leave Mountamopus S card buoy to stb. From W clear Low Lee E card Lt buoy and Carn Base Rks off Penlee Pt, the Gear Rock (bn) and the Battery Rocks to SW of South Pier. At night keep in W sector (268°-345°) of Lt Fl.WR.5s on S pier head. Do not confuse with Lt Fl.5s on S pier at Newlyn.

Signals
3F.G(vert) Lts – gates open.
3F.R(vert) Lts – gates closed.
Signal mast on N side of dock entrance.

Entrance Keep clear of Cressar Rocks to N of approach and be prepared to stand off if ship arrival or departure is imminent. When waiting for dock opening either anchor (in fair weather) E of end of Albert Pier, or wait in tidal hbr, or alongside LtHo pier if not required by the *Scillonian*. In bad weather and at weekends the ship may use the Albert Pier, but her normal berth is alongside the LtHo pier and she occupies this only from 1900–0930 and on Saturdays in summer from 1230–1400. The berth is therefore usually available while awaiting the opening of the dock gates between 1000 and 1830. There is 1·8m alongside between the LtHo and the ladder halfway along the pier. The S wall is swept by seas in S and SE gales and it may not be possible to open the dock gates in winds of storm force from those directions. Otherwise they open HW–0200 to HW+0100. 10 R visitors' waiting buoys on the S side of the S pier (seasonal).

Berthing
• Anchor in fair weather, with winds SW–W–N, 2ca or more off the LtHo pier, clear of fairway but not E of LtHo because of swell.
• Drying moorings may be available in tidal hbr.
• Visitors alongside berths in wet dock.
• 10 Y visitors' moorings on S side of pier.

Facilities Diesel from hbr staff day or night when dock gates are open. Water on quay. Chandlery and 10-ton crane. All facilities, incl cycle hire. Electricity near hbr building. Showers.

Transport Rly, buses to Land's End, St Ives. Ferry to Isles of Scilly.

☎/VHF HM 01736 366113. VHF 12 *Penzance Harbour*, during office hours and HW–0200 to HW+0100.

ST MICHAEL'S MOUNT
Tidal data as Newlyn

The outline of St Michael's Mount, a drying hbr, is a distinctive landmark in Mount's Bay.

Approach The E and N sides are foul with shoals so the approach should be made either from the S or SW. Give the Mount an offing of 1½ca to clear Maltman Rock, (dr 0·9m), Guthen Rock and the obstruction to its N, until E side of Chapel Rock is in line

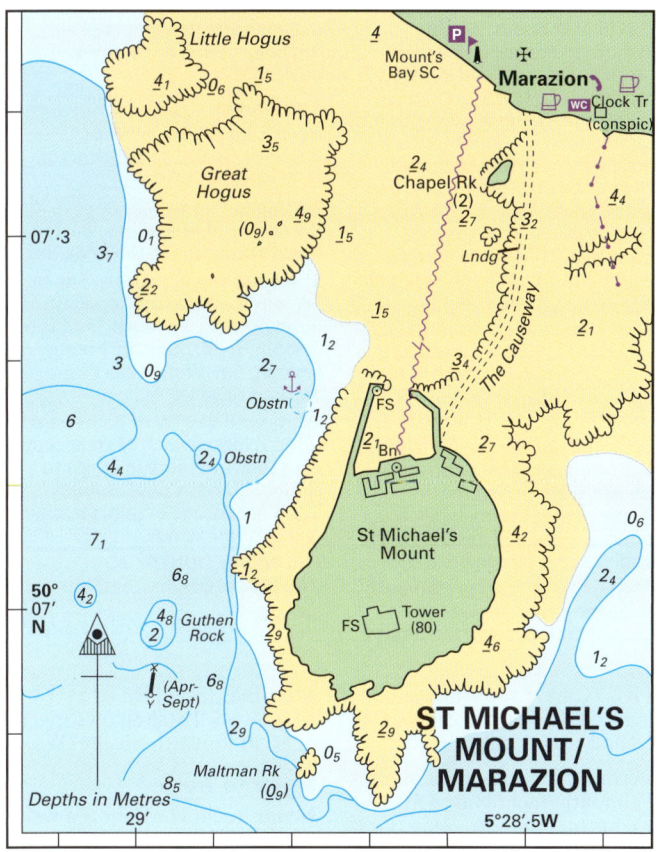

PENZANCE TO FALMOUTH

Passage Lights	BA No
Lizard	0060

Fl.3s70m26M Horn 30s

St Anthony Hd	0062

Iso.WR.15s22m16/14M Horn 30s

Streams related to HW Dover

Mount's Bay (middle): rotary clockwise. –0600E; +0030W (weak)

Lizard –0330W; +0200E

Lizard to Falmouth –0300 SW; +0300 to –0400 NE

Bound to Falmouth from Mount's Bay it is desirable to reach the Lizard at the turn of the tide to the E because the ebb stream out of Falmouth makes progress slow. Avoid the Boa, an 11m shoal 3½M W of the Lizard LtHo, in strong SW winds because of breaking seas. Off the Lizard dangers extend ½M to seaward, and a race extends to the S and SE for 3M. The violence of the seas varies with the tide and wind, but it is particularly bad in strong westerlies against an ebb tide. In bad weather keep at least 3–4M offshore. Otherwise, to clear Lizard dangers keep Godolphin Hill open of Rill Head, 337°, until Lowland Point opens E of Black Head, 036°. Black Head should be cleared by ½M and the Manacles E card Lt buoy given a wide berth to seaward. In E winds a confused sea builds up between Black Head and the Manacles; with the flood tide a race may develop, dangerous at springs.

HELFORD RIVER

Standard Port Plymouth

At entrance
HW (sp) –0035 (np) –0030
LW (sp) –0015 (np) –0010

MHWS	MHWN	MLWN	MLWS
–0·2m	–0·2m	–0·3m	–0·2m

A sheltered river, except in E winds, with several creeks, navigable to Gweek at the top of the tide, 4½M within entrance.

In such conditions if heading for Falmouth it is best to keep about 4M off Black Head and then steer N, not steering for Falmouth until due S of St Anthony Lt.

From the Manacles to Helford River and Falmouth the passage is straightforward.

Anchorages

Loe Pool Good anchorage ¾M SSW of Pool. There is no navigable water between the sea and the Pool.

Mullion Good anchorage in E wind N of the island.

Housel Bay between Lizard Pt and Bass Pt, 6ca ENE. Large hotel conspic at head. Two RW striped bns on Bass Pt bear 292°.

Parn Voose Balk Bn RW mast, W diamond top, at head of cove in line with a W patch 4½ca SSE bears 325°. This transit's intersection with 292° transit of Bass Point bns marks Vrogue Rk.

Cadgwith Cove SW of lifeboat station at Kilcobben Cove. (N.B. It is imperative to get out to sea from the above three anchorages if onshore wind is expected.)

Coverack Cove has a small drying harbour protected by a pier extending NW from Dolor Point. Anchorage possible in offshore winds ENE of the pier.

Porthoustock Cove midway between Manacle Pt and Pencra Hd, ½M N with conspic RW radar tr. Beware rks awash on N side of entrance for 1ca offshore.

Approach from NE: to clear the Gedges keep Pennance Point well open of Rosemullion Head until Bosahan Point on S side of the entrance is well open of Mawnan Shear on N side. From S, bring N extremity of the point, ¼M NNW of Helford Point, just open of Bosahan Point, 270°.

---

with the Marazion clock tr on 053°. From the W, avoid Outer Penzeath Rk (awash at LAT) ½M to W, and the Great Hogus (dr 4·9m) 1ca NW of the W pier head.

Entrance The ferries berth alongside to the E of the hbr mouth in the deepest water. There are many small fishing boat moorings in the hbr.

Berthing Good anchorage in offshore wind 1–1½ca W of W arm of hbr (or, with permission, visitors berth alongside the N end of the W arm to dry out.

☎ HM 01736 710265.

Interest Beautiful NT property and garden with café.

PORTHLEVEN

Standard Port Plymouth
HW (sp) –0105 (np) –0045
LW (sp) –0030 (np) –0025

MHWS	MHWN	MLWN	MLWS
0·0m	–0·1m	–0·2m	0·0m

A drying hbr 8M NW of Lizard. Entrance closed in bad weather. Used mainly by small fishing boats but room for a few yachts. 3·6m on sill at springs, 2·7m at neaps. Visitors' berth is along E quay immediately to stb. Access HW±0300. Water, shops, boat and engine repairs.

☎ HM 01326 574270.

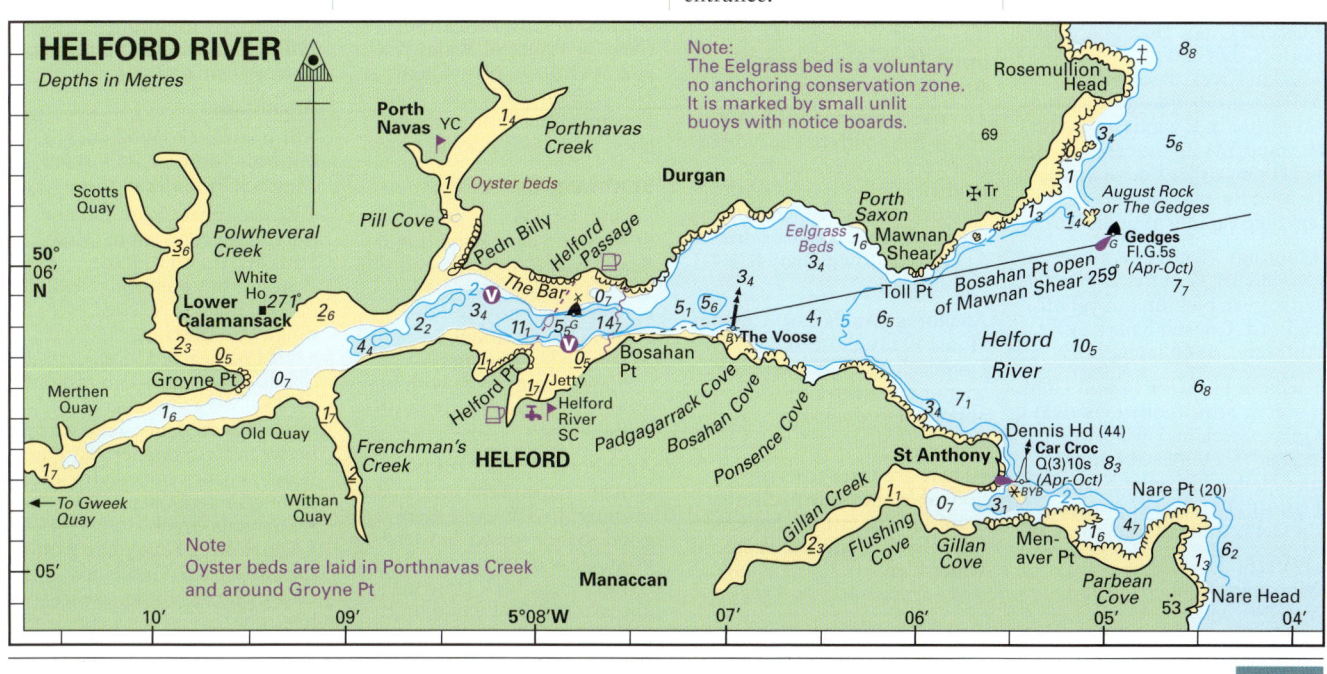

Entrance is between Rosemullion Head in N and Nare Point in S. G con buoy (seasonal) lies about 1ca SE of the Gedges (August Rock). Give Nare Pt a wide berth at all states of the tide. Keep Helford Pt open of Bosahan Pt to clear a reef off the E end of the latter. To port an unlit N card buoy marks the Voose, a drying ledge. Beware of oyster storage area, marked by Y special buoys to W of the Voose. NW of the Bosahan Narrows the G con buoy on the edge of the N bank is difficult to see among moored craft.

The river may be explored at HW to Gweek, Mawgan and Polwheveral.

Gillan Creek is entered S of Dennis Head. Enter to N of E card buoy, midway between the buoy and Dennis Hd. The buoy marks a rock (dries 1m) almost in the centre of the entrance. The passage S of the buoy is not recommended without local knowledge, due to off-lying rks.

Anchorages
- Off Durgan or Grebe Rocks, 2½–3½m, to W of restricted eelgrass conservation area, disturbed in S to E winds.
- Off Helford, 5½–11m, among or at W end of moorings; very limited room, strong tide. Edge of mud across Penarvon Cove (W of Helford Point) is steep-to.
- On S side, in offshore weather, in Ponsence or Boshanan coves.
- Near entrance to Navas Creek along the N shore out of the tide, if space allows, 1¾m or more. Uncomfortable if far out in the stream in fresh E or W winds. Holding poor W of the entrance, better to E, inshore of moorings.
- Quiet anchorage inside Navas Creek, among moorings, in Abraham's Bosom pool, 2m, but space very limited. NB 0·9m bar at entrance. Land at Oyster Fisheries Quay. No anchoring in River W of Navas Creek because of oyster beds.
- Gweek Quay. Dries; hard level bottom (beyond plan).
- Gillan Creek. Pool with 1½–2m inside the entrance but no shelter in E winds unless on the mud 1M up the creek. There is 1½–3m either side of and just beyond the mid-channel rk, shoaling rapidly to under 1m.

Moorings Visitors' moorings in two blocks, G buoys (some with green pick-up buoys) off Helford. Consult Sailaway, St Anthony, for Gillan Creek.

Facilities Fuel (not in bulk) and water at St Anthony (Sailaway), Gillan Creek and at Porth Navas YC. Water at Durgan and Helford River SC. Stores at Helford. Landing at pontoon on Helford Pt (charge) or at SC.

☎/VHF
Moorings 07808 071485, VHF 80, M.

FALMOUTH TO PLYMOUTH

Passage Lights	BA No
St Anthony Hd	0062

Iso.WR.15s22m16/14M
(R over Manacles) Horn30s

Eddystone 0098
Fl(2)10s41m17M+Iso.R.10s 110°-vis-133° Horn(1)30s AIS

Streams related to HW Dover
Rectilinear in W, rotary clockwise in E

5M E of St Anthony Head: Dover +0300NE; –0330SW

Plymouth +0400E –0200W

Leaving Falmouth bound E, keep at least 1M offshore to clear the Bizzies, a shoal patch off Greeb Point, and the Whelps off Nare Head. In bad weather keep at least 2M off Dodman Pt (conspic stone cross) because of overfalls. There is a naval firing range off Dodman Point and Gribbin Head VHF FOST OPS Ch 74. It is 2·5M S of the point, marked by three special Y Lt buoys. If going inshore to Fowey, give a wide berth to Gwineas and Yaw Rks (E card Lt buoy) ¾M S of Chapel Point, and Cannis Rock (S card Lt buoy) 4ca SE of Gribbin Head. E-bound from Fowey keep well clear of Udder Rock (S card, bell) 3M to E, and Ranneys Rocks off Looe Is. Rame Head appears conical and has a small chapel on its summit. No off-lying dangers. Bound up-channel offshore give a wide berth to Eddystone Lt Ho, especially in bad weather; also avoid Hand Deeps, 3¾M to NW (in F.R sector), dangerous overfalls, (W card Lt buoy).

With light winds along the shore it is often possible to carry a breeze close inshore by the Dodman and Fowey, while a direct course to Plymouth might end in being becalmed.

Bound from Fowey or Plymouth to Falmouth, there is a considerable set into the bight E of Falmouth. Remember St Anthony Lt first appears when bearing NW.

Anchorages
Gorran Haven 1M WSW of Gwineas Rock. Good anchorage in W winds in 6m.

Portmellon a small sandy cove in SW corner of Mevagissey Bay. Good anchorage in W winds, 5m.

St Austell Bay in S corner, 5m. In SW winds anchor off Ropehaven, good holding. Polkerris 1½M N of Gribbin Head: good anchorage in E winds, 5m. Water skiers; harbour dries.

Whitesand Bay (W of Rame Head) offers a long stretch of clear coast with shelving shore in which to close the land in poor visibility. Good anchorage in calm weather and offshore winds.

THE WEST COUNTRY TO L'ABERWRAC'H
See p.353.

FALMOUTH AND TRURO RIVER

DS Dover –0300SW +0300NE
Standard Port Plymouth
Falmouth Docks
HW (sp) –0043 (np) –0025
LW (sp) –0009 (np) –0009
MHWS MHWN MLWN MLWS
–0·4m –0·3m –0·4m –0·3m
Truro
HW (sp) –0024 (np) –0021
MHWS MHWN MLWN MLWS
–2·0m –2·0m n/a n/a

The Fal estuary provides excellent shelter and beautiful anchorages, with several drying creeks and navigation at HW via Truro River to Truro.

Approach From E, St Anthony Lt is not visible until it bears NW. From SW, coast between Pennance and Pendennis Pts has drying rks up to 1ca from shore.

Entrance is divided into two channels by Black Rock conspic B bn and red can Lt buoy. When this rock is covered there is 2·7m over the banks inside the river as far as Trelissick.

Inner Harbour, Falmouth And Penryn River

The river continues 1M to W above Falmouth to Penryn but there are moorings on the mudflats on both sides of the channel. Above the wharf at Boyer's Cellars the river dries. At Penryn, Town Quay has 4·3 to 3·0m at HW.

Anchorage Anchor off Custom House Quay, close SE of Falmouth Yacht Haven (buoy anchor and keep clear of approach to docks).

Moorings
- There are three trots of bookable Harbour Authority moorings for visitors between Greenbank Quay and Prince of Wales Pier.
- RCYC have some buoys marked for visitors; others may be had from local yards.

Berthing Marinas at Falmouth: **Falmouth Yacht Haven** 40 yachts on pontoons, 1·5–2·5m; best for shopping in town, water and short stays, but exposed in strong E winds. **Port Pendennis** marina has pontoons in 3m outside a locked basin, access HW±0300. No fuel available in marina. **Falmouth Marina** North Parade, ½M above Greenbank Quay: 30 pontoon berths for visitors; leave E card bn to stb for dredged access channel 2m. Pipeline and cill (dries 1·8m) with tide gauges across middle of basin. Call Falmouth Marina, if no reply, arrivals go to end of fuel pontoon (J).

Landing places at Custom House Quay or Falmouth Yacht Haven, Fish Strand Quay, Prince of Wales Pier, R Cornwall YC and Greenbank Quay all on S side of the channel (do not leave dinghies moored at Custom House Quay or Prince of Wales Pier); and at Old and New Quays at Flushing on the N side. Hard at Flushing Quay and several good ones both sides of hbr.

St Mawes Creek

From Castle G con buoy, leave St Mawes S card buoy (Lugo Rock) well to port. At half tide there is not less than 1·8m between the buoy and the Point. There is about 1·2m up to Percuil but channel is tortuous, unmarked, with many moorings and oyster beds off both banks.

Anchorage Anchor off two beaches beyond the pier, in 2m or more. In SW wind there is good shelter round Amsterdam Point clear of moorings, dries. Avoid Black Rock close inshore abreast N end of wood on E side.

Moorings from HM or St Mawes SC. Landing on slipway at SC at Polvarth except LWS.

Mylor to Truro

Mylor Yacht Harbour is a well appointed marina with 30 moorings and 4 pontoon berths for visitors. The creek is navigable to Mylor Br by dinghy.

Truro River There is plenty of water up to Malpas, the limit of LW navigation, except at Maggoty Bank (G con buoy). Concrete mooring clumps, drying, are reported near the W bank 3ca S of the ferry at King Harry Passage. They are marked by a W post. With a draught of less than 3m (springs) or 2m (neaps), Truro can be reached on the tide following the lit buoyed channel.

Flood Barrier in the approaches to Truro closes (2F.R Lts) when very high tides (5·6m Falmouth datum) are accompanied by a tidal surge or heavy river flood water. Gates will then be closed to all traffic for about HW±0230; waiting pontoon on downstream end of gate.

Anchorages
- St Just Creek Good anchorage but little room in 3m inside Messack Pt under N shore
- Restronguet Creek Anchor off entrance; no room inside. Landing at Ferry Ho or Pandora Inn pontoon. Devoran (1½M) may be reached by dinghy on the tide.
- Off Loe beach. Good, clean, quiet anchorage in 2m inshore off Loe Vean. Summer moorings are laid all the way between Restronguet and Loe Beach: anchor outside these. Riding Lt necessary.
- Channals Creek.
- Above King Harry Ferry off the entrance to Cowlands Creek on the N side, use trip line.

The Cruising Almanac

ENGLAND – SOUTH COAST

- Off the mouth of the River Fal (Ruan Creek) where it joins River Truro near Tregothnan. Beware of drying concrete blocks close inshore off ruined cottage on N side of entrance to Ruan Creek.
- On Maggoty Bank according to tide.

Moorings off thatched restaurant at Tolverne, opposite entrance to Cowlands Creek; four Carrick visitors' buoys off Malpas Point; and at Malpas Marine. Visitors' pontoons on W side of channel N of Turnaware Pt at (50°12'N), and off E bank just N of entrance to Ruan Creek. Also at W of channel at Woodbury Point and Malpas.

Mooring possible alongside Town and Worths quays and Garras Wharf at Truro; dries, soft mud.

Facilities Fuel and water at Falmouth Yacht Haven and Marina, Mylor Yacht Hbr.

33

The Cruising Almanac

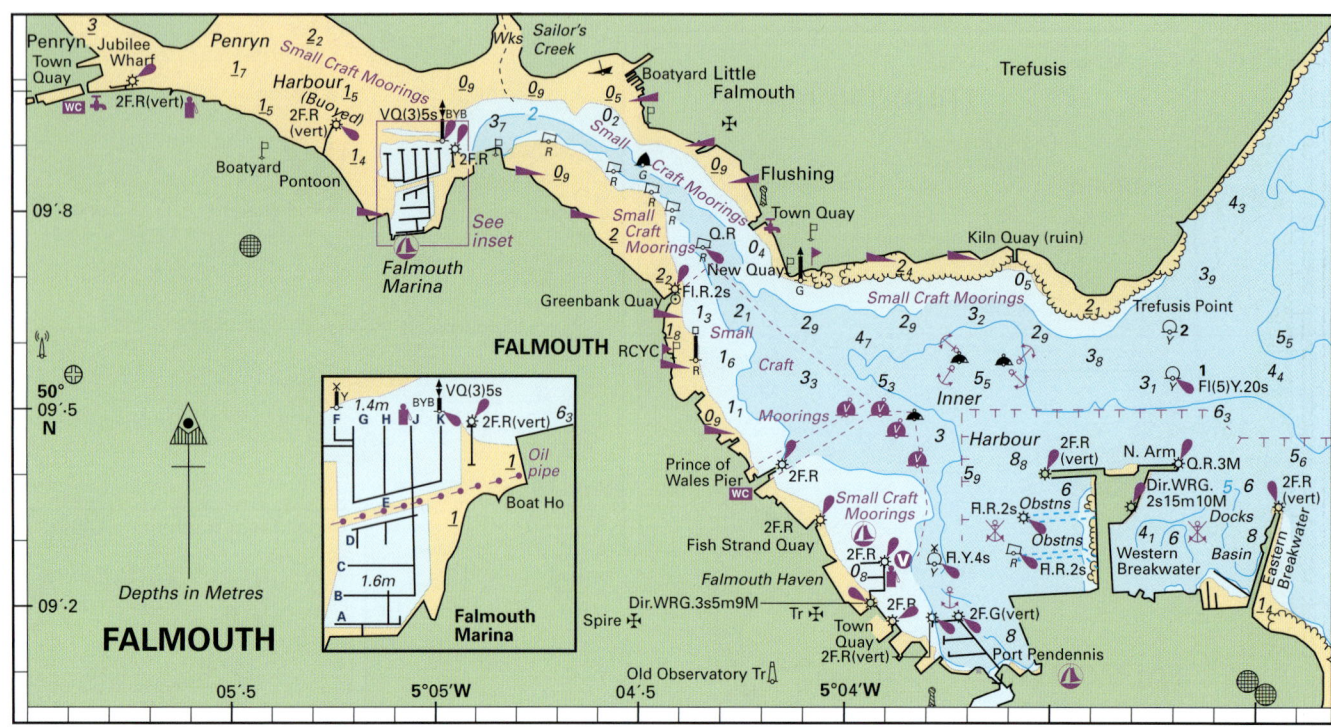

ENGLAND – SOUTH COAST

Water at RCYC, St Mawes (tap opposite hbr steps), Porthcuel, King Harry Ferry W pontoon, Truro and Malpas Marine. Sailmaker and chandler at Falmouth. Repairs at Falmouth Boat Const Co. When Falmouth is crowded in the season it is interesting to go to Truro at HW for water and supermarket.

☏/VHF Falmouth Yacht Haven (Berthing master) 01326 310991, (Main Office) 310990 *Falmouth Haven* VHF 12. HM Launch VHF 12.

Port Pendennis Marina 211211. Falmouth Marina 316620, VHF 80, 37. Falmouth Boat Const Co 374309. RCYC 311105, VHF 37 (for boatman). St Mawes SC 270686 or 270808 for moorings. Mylor Yacht Hbr 372121, VHF 37, 80. Truro hbr office 01872 272130, 224231. VHF 12 *Carrick*. Fal River patrol VHF 16, 12 *Carrick 3*. Penryn HM 01326 373352. Malpas Marine 01872 271260.

Transport Rly to main line at Truro. National Express coaches. Hire cars at Falmouth Yacht Haven.

Interest National Maritime Museum Cornwall on Discovery Quay at Falmouth close by Port Pendennis. Trelissick Gardens (NT).

MEVAGISSEY
Standard Port Plymouth
HW (sp) –0020 (np) –0015
LW (sp) –0010 (np) –0005
MHWS MHWN MLWN MLWS
–0·1m –0·1m –0·2m –0·1m

Mevagissey is a fishing hbr which can accept only a few visiting yachts. It provides good shelter except in strong E winds when it is dangerous to approach.

Entrance Beware of Black Rk (dries 0·3m) to N of entrance 20m wide and 2·1m depth.

Outer Harbour has 2m alongside S pier with drying rocks along S and N sides. Inner Harbour dries and is reserved for fishing boats except when taking on fuel or water.

Berthing Call HM on VHF before berthing. If unable to contact moor alongside S Pier, clear of steps, and report to HM (or car park attendant in hut at root of quay). There are two sets of fore and aft moorings for visitors. Do not pick up a vacant buoy without HM's consent. There is a good anchorage in offshore winds off Porthmellon ½M S of hbr.

Supplies Fuel and water at W side of Inner Harbour. Diesel delivery to S pier. Boatyard and slip.

☏/VHF HM (01726) 843305. VHF 16, 14 (working hours); Harbourmaster out of hours 842496.

Interest Visit The Eden Project close by.

FOWEY
Standard Port Plymouth
HW (sp) –0015 (np) –0010
LW (sp) –0010 (np) –0005
MHWS MHWN MLWN MLWS
–0·1m –0·1m –0·2m –0·2m

Fowey has many sheltered moorings for yachts but is also a commercial port used by large ships for the export of china clay. Gales from the S cause swell in the hbr especially on the ebb.

Approach from E: keep RWHS tr on Gribbin Hd bearing more than 273° to clear the Udder Rock 3M E of Fowey (S card bell buoy). To pass between the Udder and the mainland keep Looe Is shut in by Nealand Pt. From SW to clear the Cannis Rock, ¼M SE from Gribbin Hd daymark RWHS, keep Dodman Pt open to seaward of Gwineas until tower of Fowey Parish church is open of St Catherine Point. To pass between Cannis and the mainland (1·2m) keep the old castle on Polruan Point in line with conspic memorial on Penleath Point (048°).

At night from E keep a mile offshore and alter course N when in G sector of Whitehouse Point Lt (Iso.WRG.3s) and bring W Lt ahead steering 025°. From SW bring W Lt bearing 025° and keep in W sector.

Entrance Fowey church tr in line with Whitehouse Point, 028°, leads in mid-channel. To clear Lamp Rk on E side, keep the houses in Bodinnick shut in by Fowey town quay. To clear Mundy Rk on W side, keep the FS at the YC open of the end of Whitehouse Point breakwater.

The River is often crowded with shipping and it is inadvisable to attempt to reach Wiseman's Pt without reliable power. The upper reaches can be explored by dinghy to Lostwithiel and Lerryn. Overhead cable (9m) crosses river ½M S of Lostwithiel.

Berthing Anchoring is allowed only with permission of HM. Anchoring off Polruan, clear of the swinging area, is normally allowed only when pontoons or moorings are full or with no shipping movements. Give 90m berth to large can mooring buoy, used for swinging, off Pont Pill. Avoid anchoring between Penleath Point and Wiseman's Point as large ships swing in channel. There are no floating anchorages in upper reaches. Anchoring is permitted above Wiseman's Point (charged as for mooring).

Moorings Pontoon at Albert Quay is short-stay (max 2hrs) and for water only. There are blue visitors' buoys, without strops, for craft up to 12m, and a 120ft pontoon just N of Penleath Point; pontoon and buoys are uncomfortable in SW winds above Force 4 (and removed in winter). There is

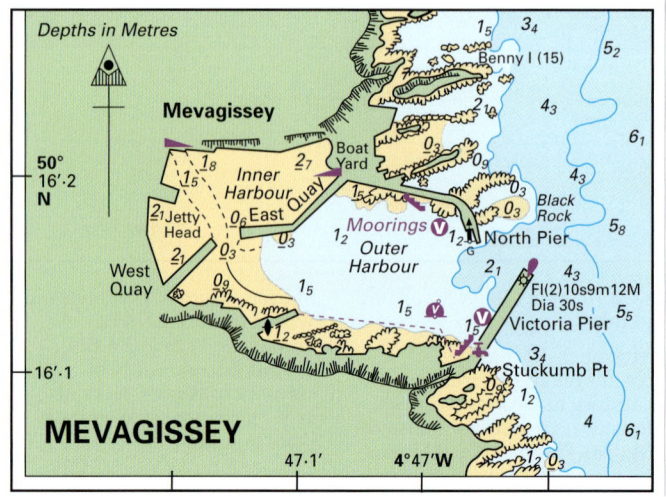

34

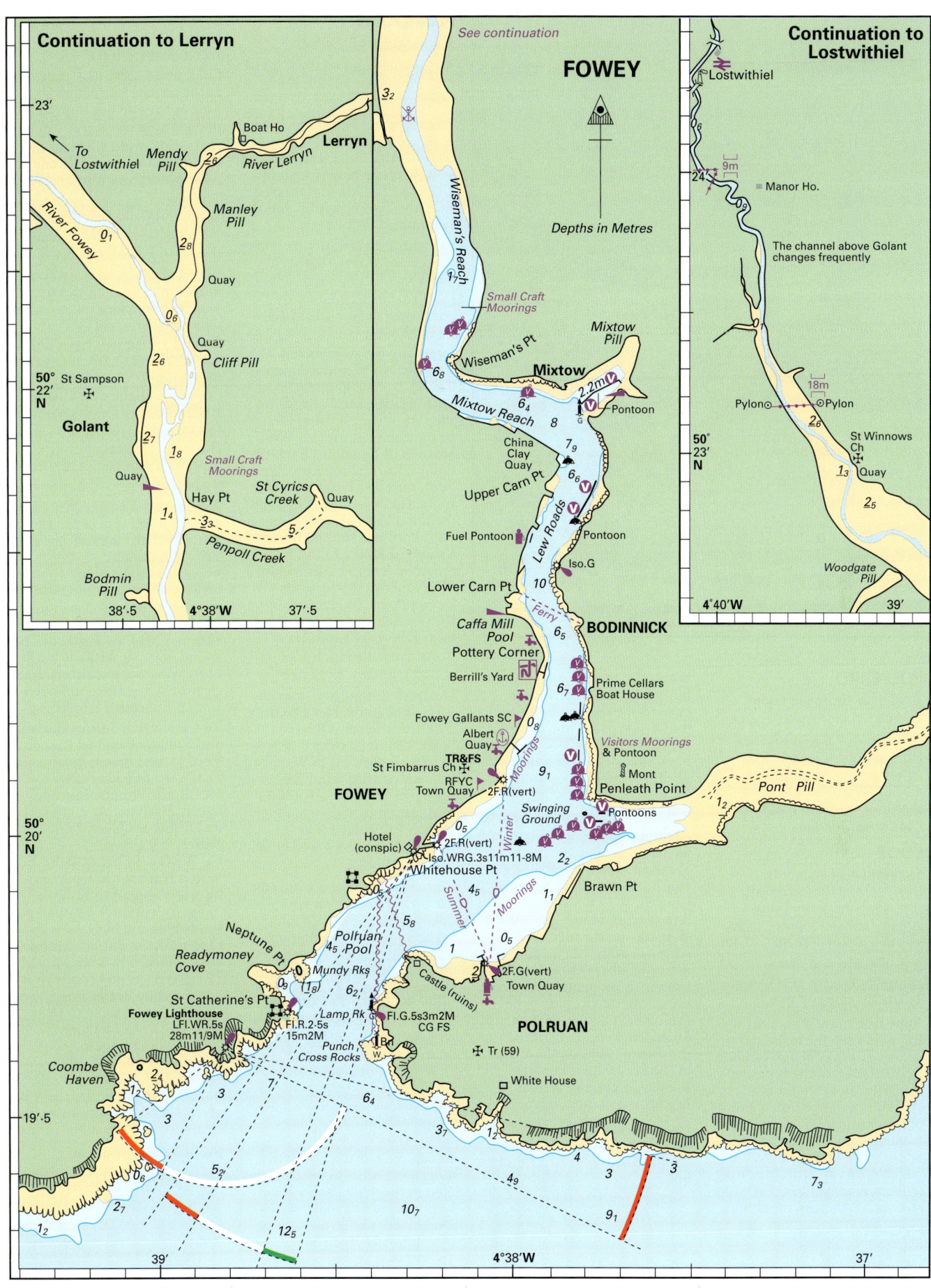

more shelter in Pont Pill on trots of fore and aft moorings (each taking two boats) and another 120ft pontoon. Beyond Bodinnick, visitors berth on the W side of the pontoon, and at Mixtow Pill, where there are showers and a café, berth on the S side of the walk-ashore pontoon. There are three V buoys off Wiseman's Pt, very sheltered in SW gales.

Facilities Fuel at deep water pontoon just above Boddinick ferry, 24/7 self service, and on Polruan Quay; Water on pontoons at Albert Quay (max 2h) and S of Pottery Corner, and Polruan Quay. All stores. Showers at RFYC, Toms boatyard Polruan Quay, and Fowey Gallants YC, 24/7. Secure stowage for visitors' lifejackets in RNLI lockers at shore end of Town Pontoon.

☎/VHF HM 01726 832471/2, VHF 12, 11. Hbr Patrol Boat (Apr–Sept) VHF 12. Water taxi VHF 6.

Interest Visits to The Eden Project can be arranged via the tourist information office.

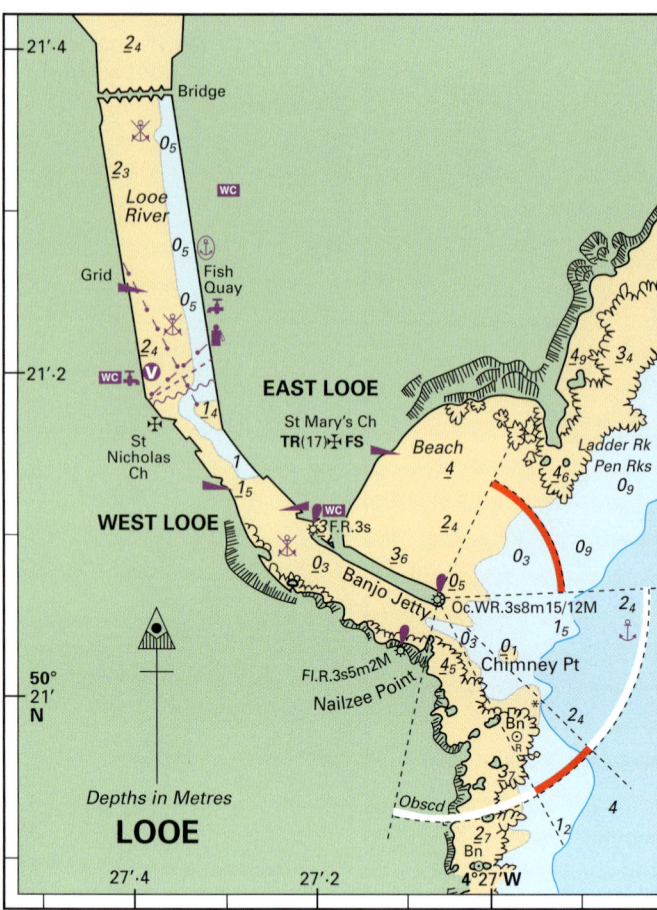

Depths in Metres
LOOE

POLPERRO

Tidal data approx as Looe

An attractive small drying hbr with visitors' buoys for four. Uncomfortable in onshore winds and swell. A fair weather anchorage outside the pier. Entrance closed in bad weather. Fuel, water, shops.

LOOE

Standard Port Plymouth

HW (sp) –0010 (np) –0010
LW (sp) –0005 (np) –0005

MHWS	MHWN	MLWN	MLWS
–0·1m	–0·2m	–0·2m	–0·2m

A drying hbr with 3·4m alongside E quay at HW and 1·2m–3m along W one.

Approach from W to clear the Ranneys keep the mainland showing above the top of Looe Is; overfalls S of the Is on the ebb. Steer in when E Looe church is well open of W point of the entrance. At night, coming from W, keep in W sector of pier head Lt Oc.WR which opens at 313°. If beating in from E, remember that rocks run out 1½ca from the shore NE of the entrance. Passage between the Is and the mainland should not be attempted except at HW with local knowledge. Dangerous half-tide rock (Dunker) ½ca off NW corner of Is.

Entrance Stream runs at 3kn through the narrows on both flood and ebb. On the flood there is an out-going eddy on both sides of the river from the inner end of the narrows to beyond the visitors' berth on the W side of the hbr, causing problems coming alongside. A bank runs down the centre of hbr from the br to opposite St Nicholas Church giving ½m less water.

Berthing Anchorage outside. Sheltered in W winds, open to SE and E, and S by W. Bring pier head on with St Nicholas Church, W Looe, and anchor in 3m, sand and mud, abreast the W marks on the rock at W entrance of the hbr. Inside mooring: hbr is crowded when fishermen are in and yachts are not allowed to lie alongside fishing boats. Visitors' berth is immediately up-river of the third set of steps on the W side of the hbr by a fishermen's shelter. 2–3 berths abreast. Fender board essential.

Facilities Water and showers on quays; fuel in cans at E Looe. Shops. Rly to Liskeard for main line.

☎ HM 01503 262839.

PLYMOUTH

Standard Port Plymouth

At Cotehele Quay HW is up to HW Plymouth +0020; LW is LW Plymouth +0045.

Plymouth is a Naval Dockyard Port, under a QHM, with considerable commercial traffic as well as extensive yachting facilities. The hbr is protected by a breakwater with E and W entrances.

In E entrance streams are rotary clockwise, Dover +0500 N; –0330 S.

In W entrance, streams are rectilinear, Dover +0215 NE; –0430 SE.

Internally the streams run strongly NNW and SSE across The Br. In Asia Pass the flood (1kn springs) sets towards the shoal running NE from Drake's Is; the ebb sets towards Winter Shoal. S of Vanguard Bank the flood (2kn) sets towards Barn Pool, the ebb SE towards The Br. In The Narrows at the S end the flood (2¾kn) sets NE out of Barn Pool and the ebb towards Vanguard Bank. At the N end the flood sets towards Mount Wise and the ebb towards Devil's Point. In Hamoaze S of Rubble Bank the ebb starts local HW+0030 and sets towards Millbrook Lake.

Approach From E, round the Great Mewstone and steer on summit of Rame Head bearing 290° until Tinker Q(3)10s bears 325° then steer to leave it a cable to port. From W, in bad weather or with wind against tide, give Rame Head at least ½M clearance and steer to leave breakwater LtHo (Fl.WR.10s+Iso.4s) well clear to stb.

Entrance In strong S winds the sea breaks heavily on Knap and Panther shoals, to SSW of breakwater LtHo, and on the ebb in the E entrance, which also has a dangerous sea in strong W winds. E entrance: bring the Lt bn, LFl.WR.10s, on E arm of breakwater in line with Smeaton's tr (RW bands) on the Hoe, 355° (at night keep in W sector of breakwater East Head Lt). Give breakwater end 1ca clearance. W entrance: leave the breakwater West Head LtHo well clear to stb.

Signals Signals to control the movement of ships longer than 20m in the main channels may be displayed at a mast on Drake's Is or at FS at Devonport N Dockyard:

3R Fl – Emergency. All unauthorised movements stopped.

1R Oc over 2G Oc – Outgoing traffic only may proceed on recommended track.

2G Oc over 1R Oc – Incoming traffic only may proceed on recommended track.

2G Oc over 1W Oc – Give wide berth to HM vessels on recommended track.

Craft under 20m may proceed in the contrary direction so long as they do not impede the main channels.

In daytime wind warning signal Lts are shown from Drake's Is mast when there is no traffic Lt signal:

1 Lt Oc – Wind Force 5–7

2 Lts Oc(vert) – Wind greater than Force 7.

North of the breakwater, craft longer than 45m have right of way over smaller craft whether under power or sail.

The main channels have W bns 9m high with Or/W day marks, mostly lit: W on course; Al.WR or Al.WG slightly off channel; F.R or F.G further off channel.

Lt QY is displayed at all major Dir Lts when main power supplies are interrupted.

The Sound

Anchorages Yachts can approach to 1½ca of the shore, apart from the area of The Br, SW of Drake's Is.

• **Cawsand Bay**, W of breakwater, except in E and SE winds. Anchor close inshore on S side of bay.

• **Jenny Cliff Bay**, E side of The Sound, near to Withyhedge dir Lt to avoid off-lying reefs. Keep clear of skiing area. Sheltered from NE through E to SE.

To Cattewater, Sutton Harbour and Cobbler Channel Pass ½ca W of Mount Batten breakwater 2F.G(vert) to Fisher's Nose Fl(3)R.10s W of entrance to Sutton Harbour. At night pick up Dir Lts at Queen Anne's Battery F.R (front) Oc.WRG.7·5s (rear), 049°. For Sutton Harbour Marina steer N, when abreast of Fisher's Nose, for entrance between pier heads Fl.R and Fl.G.3s, with Queen Anne's Battery Marina to stb marked by four pairs of 2F.G(vert) Lts on breakwater and pontoon heads. For Cattewater continue to steer 049° on Dir Lt on Queen Anne's Marina, then Cattedown Ldg bns 102° followed by Turnchapel Ldg bns 129°, depth 4·9m. Laira Br, at the N end of Cattewater, has clearance of 4·9m in the centre.

Berthing Anchoring in Cattewater is difficult: space may be found in Clovelly Bay. There are Cattewater Harbour Commissioners visitors' buoys S of Sutton Harbour entrance (exposed to S and SW winds; wash) and four belonging to RWYC (Or with W tops) S of QAB breakwater; moorings may also be available from Turnchapel yacht yards. Two marinas at Sutton: Sutton Harbour Marina in N (lock 24hrs; free flow HW±0200; boats up to 45ft) and Queen

The Cruising Almanac

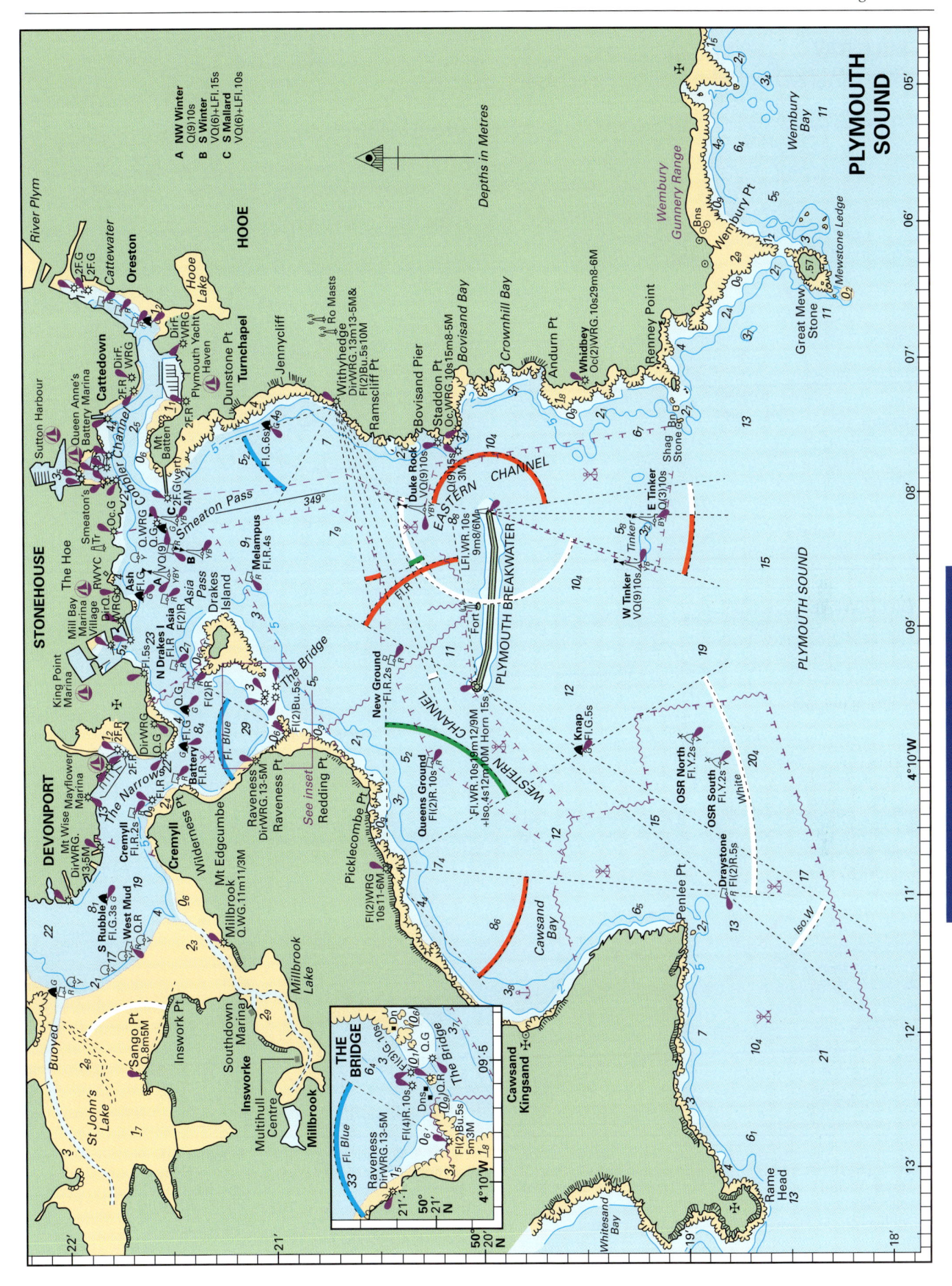

ENGLAND – SOUTH COAST

37

The Cruising Almanac

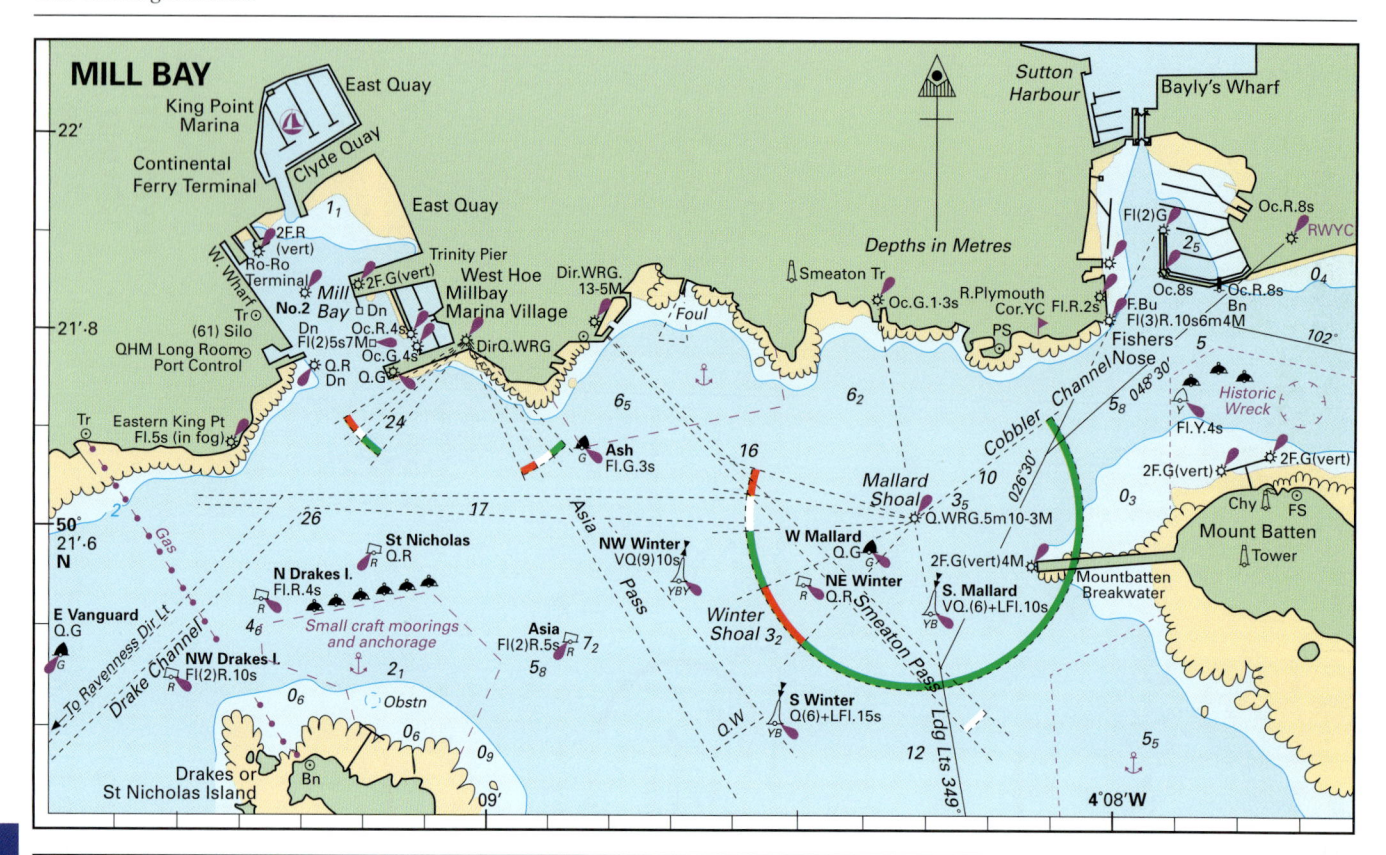

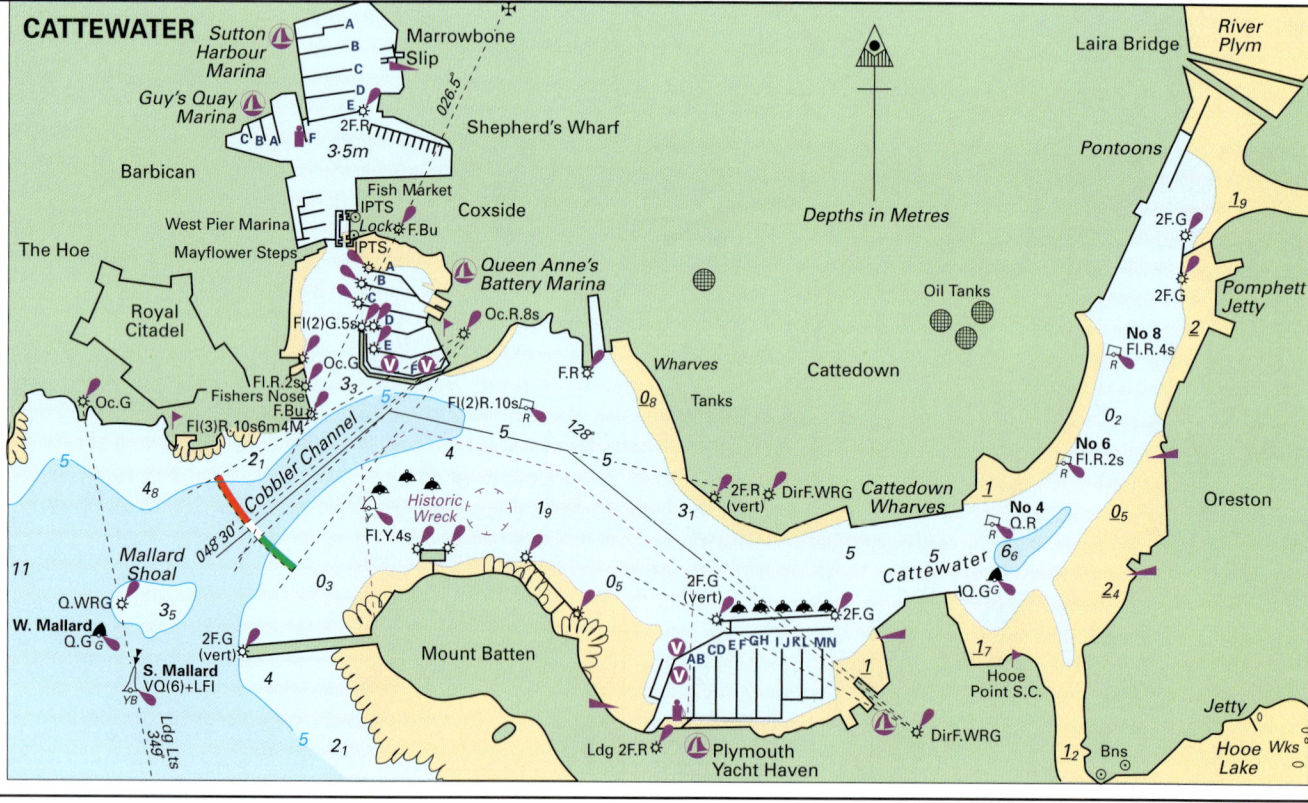

ENGLAND – SOUTH COAST

Anne's Battery Marina (visitors' berths, up to 100ft), and Plymouth Yacht Haven in Clovelly Bay.

To Millbay Docks From Melampus R can Lt buoy either steer NNW over Asia Knoll shoal, 5·5m, or follow Asia Pass round Asia buoy (Fl(2)5s). By night approach from The Sound with Millbay dir Lt (DirQ.WRG) bearing 326°, within W sector to Asia Lt buoy and NW Winter (W card Lt buoy) and thence to entrance between pier heads. King Point Marina free flow access 24/7, wave protector gate used in bad weather, beware of ferries using RoRo terminal.

Anchorage Off W Hoe, 3½–7½m, in all but S winds, very uncomfortable in SE wind. Bottom foul, buoy anchor. Steamer wash day and night.

Hamoaze and Mayflower Marina From Melampus R can buoy make for Asia Pass buoys and follow buoyed channel round to the Narrows where Mayflower Marina is to stb. By night follow Dir Lts (all F) from Asia Pass: Western King 271°, Ravenness 225°, Mount Wise 343°.

Another route by day is via The Br to SW of Drake's Is. The passage is marked by four Lt bns and has only 1·5m. There are obstructions on the bottom close to the channel either side of the bns and in bad weather the sea breaks heavily in the approach. Across The Br the streams run strongly NNW and SSE. There are depth gauges on the NW and SE bns showing ht above CD.

St John's Lake dries but a narrow channel, buoys and bns, has 0·4 to 1·8m to Trevol Point, jetty with 1·9m at head.

Anchorage
- In NW corner of Barn Pool at W end of Drake Channel, bottom very steep-to; good shelter from W winds. Beware fouling anchor on wreck (*see plan*).
- N of Drake's Is to E of private pier – buoy anchor.
- Millbrook Lake, 3ca W of Mashford's Yard at Cremyll.

38

The Cruising Almanac

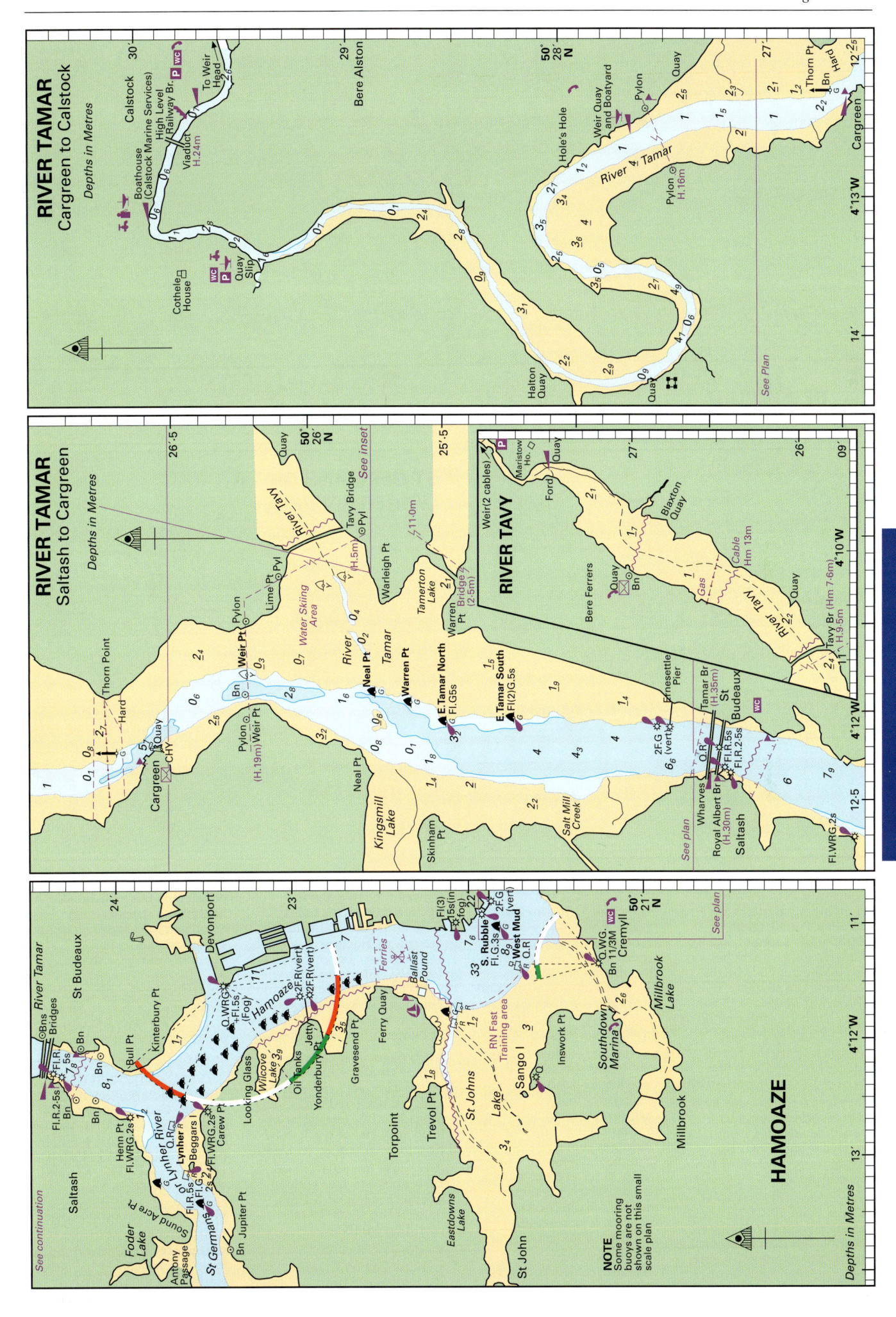

ENGLAND – SOUTH COAST

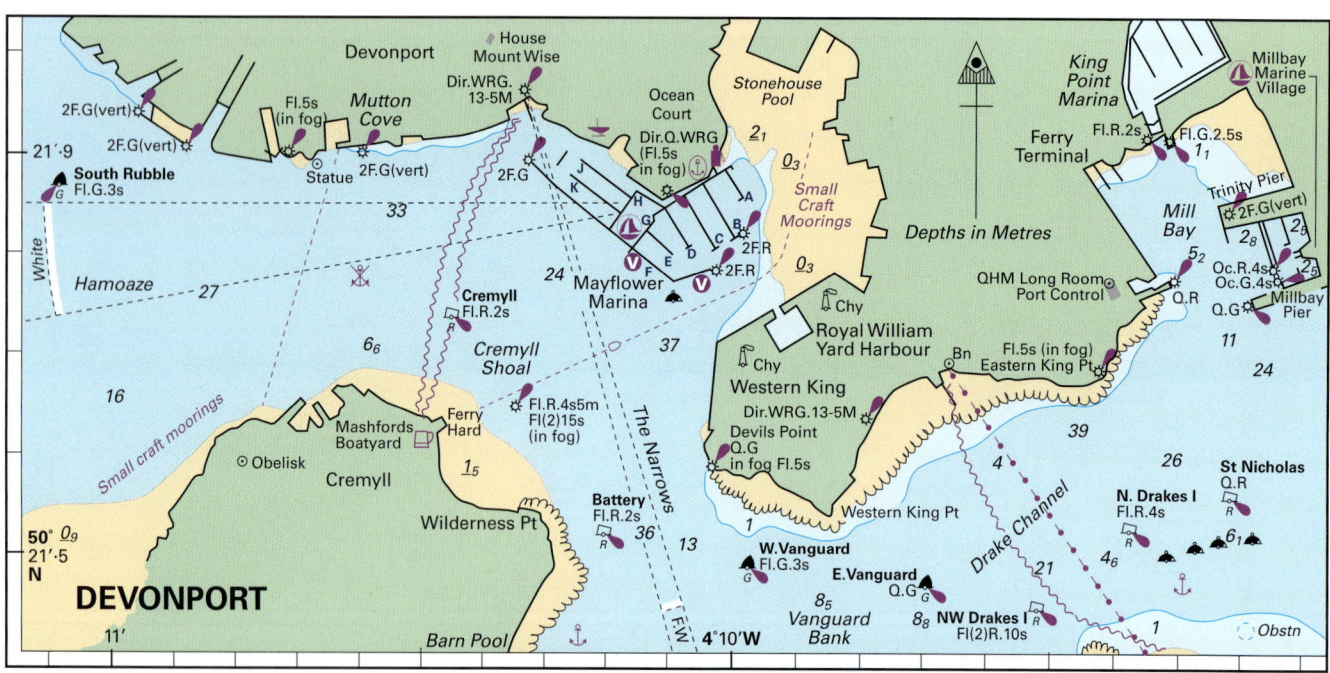

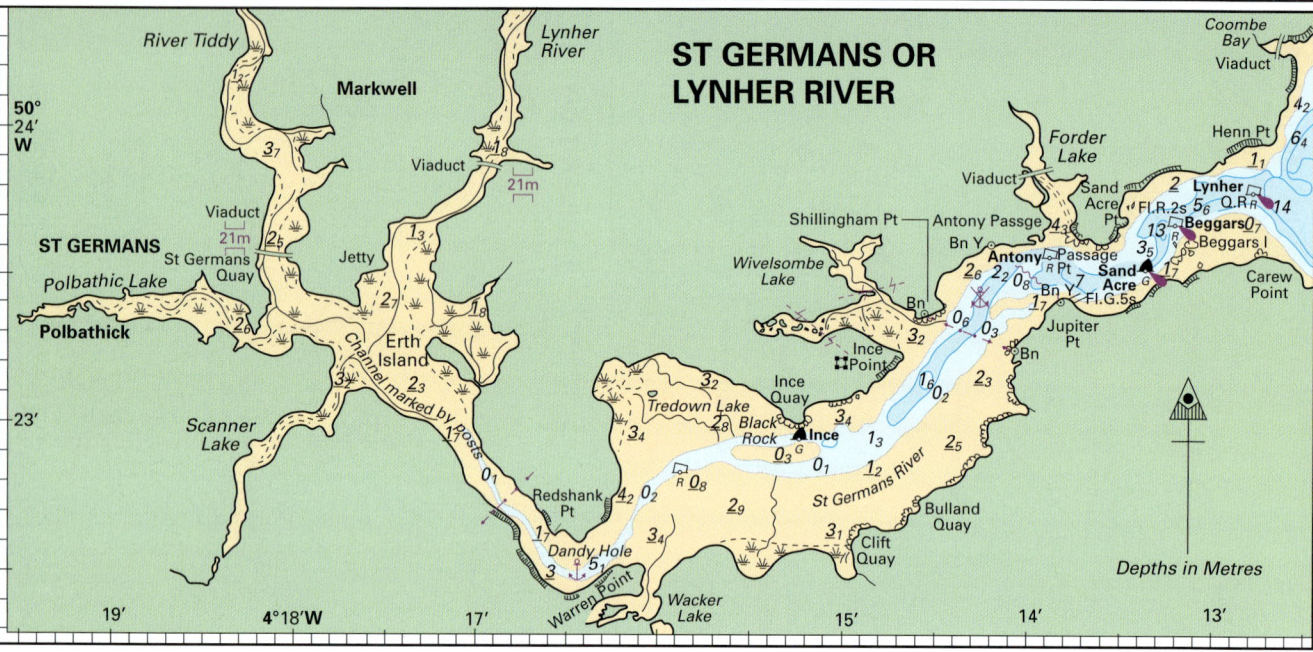

Moorings available in Stonehouse Pool from yard adjoining Admiral's Hard; and at Ballast Pound Yacht Harbour off Torpoint, 2ca S of chain ferry. This yacht hbr has also drying quayside berths accessible HW±0200. Mayflower Marina at Ocean Quay has berths for craft up to 19·8m long, 3m draught

Passage beneath the Tamar bridges (50°24'·5N) is best taken at LW Devonport +0100.

The Hamoaze has many large unlit mooring buoys for warships extending from Cremyll to the Tamar Br. Passage in poor visibility is not recommended.

The Tamar has Lt bns as far as Warren Point 50°25'N. Above Skinham Point LW depths are generally less than 2m but some stretches have more (*see notes below on mooring*). Calstock can be reached at HW and craft with 1·5m draught can reach ¼M off the head of navigation at Weir Head at HWS. Navigation in this area at LW (even LWN) is not recommended owing to debris (water-logged tree trunks) and the unreliability of charts. Channel winds through mudbanks and is unmarked.

Although the Torpoint chain ferry between Torpoint and Devonport is required to give way, yachts should avoid impeding its passage. The ferries carry four Lts, one at each corner, showing W ahead or astern, and R on the beam. Underway they show a VQ Or Lt at the leading end. When in use by the emergency services they also show VQ Bu below the Or Lt in direction of progress. In transit in fog they sound a bell for five seconds each 30 seconds.

Overhead cables cross 4ca below Cargreen with 19m clearance and 1¼M above Cargreen, 16m.

St German's or Lynher River is buoyed for 2¼M and is navigable by yachts to St German's Quay and with 2m draught to Tideford at MHWS; also to Notter Br on River Lynher. Cables cross each route with clearance to Tideford of 20m 1ca S of Morvah Quay and 3m at the quay; and 26m S of Notter.

Anchorages in St German's River: Off Antony Village or Dandy Hole off S tip of Erth Hill, 3m, sheltered but landing difficult at LW. Keep clear of bend at W end of reach, used by salmon fishermen with nets.

River Tavy has an overhead cable at its entrance with 5m clearance. Craft with 1·5m draught can reach the falls (2½M) at MHWS.

Berthing
- Saltash Bay on W side below the bridges in 3½m.
- Cargreen. Good holding in 3–3½m except opposite quays.

Several deep-water holes may be found in this area, good holding but stream strong.
- Cotehele ¼M above quay but spring streams strong.
- In pools above Calstock.

Facilities Alongside fuel and water at the marinas and Calstock Boatyard; water at St Germans SC. All facilities in Plymouth; PO and shop at Cargreen.

☎/VHF (all 01752). *Longroom Port Control* 836528, VHF 14 (private and commercial craft), VHF 13 (military). Cattewater Harbour Commissioners 665934, VHF 14 (Monday–Friday). Marinas VHF 80. Plymouth Yacht Haven 404231. Mayflower Marina 556633, *Mobile* 07840 116853. Millbay Marina Village 226785. Queen Anne Battery Marina 671142. Sutton Harbour Marina 204737, *Mobile* 07785 986921, King Point Marina 204702/424297,

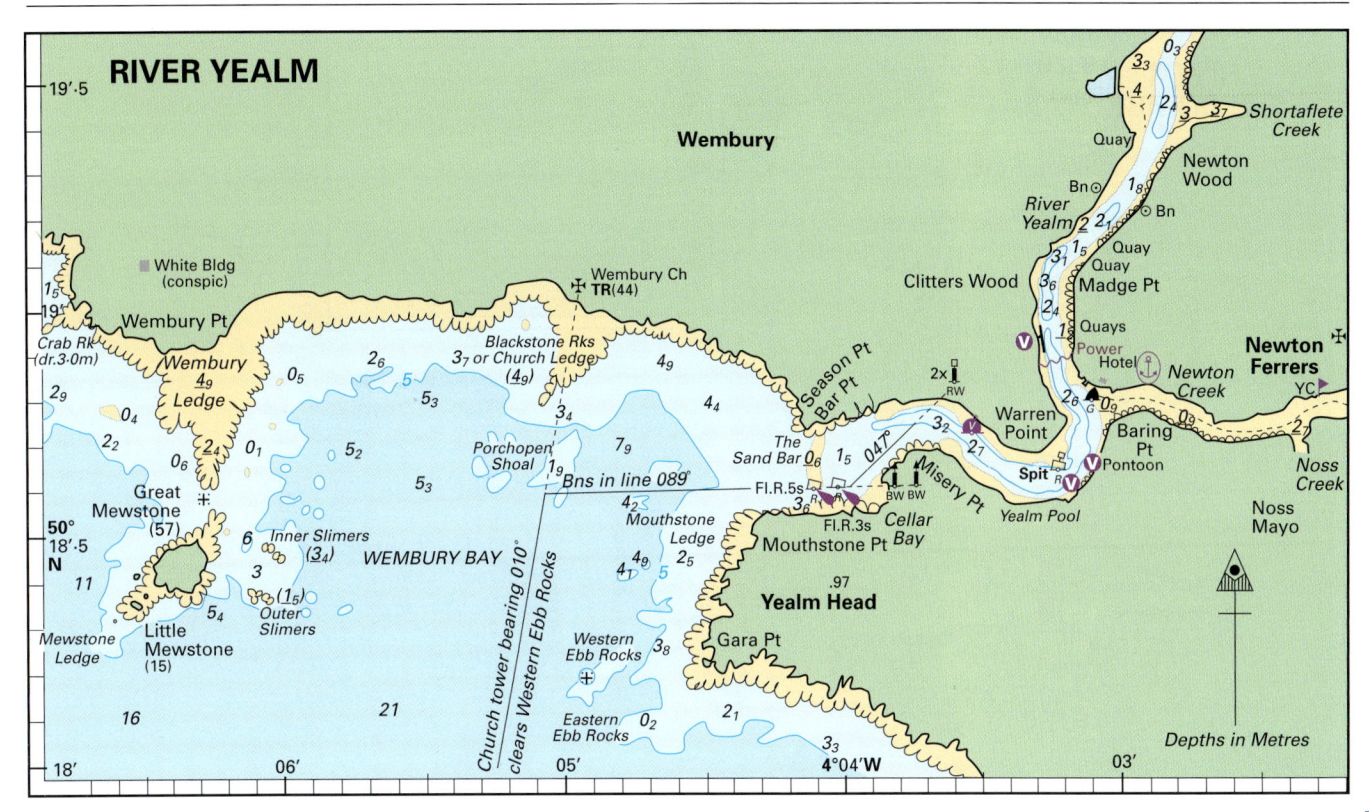

Lock VHF 12. River Plymouth Corinthian YC 664327. RWYC 660077.

Interest Particularly National Marine Aquarium, Plymouth, and Cotehele House (NT). Morwellham Quay living museum.

RIVER YEALM

Standard Port Plymouth
HW (sp) +0006 (np) +0006
LW (sp) +0002 (np) +0002
MHWS MHWN MLWN MLWS
−0·1m −0·1m −0·1m −0·1m

In the river the flood starts at Plymouth −0545 (1kn) and the ebb at +0015 (2kn but 4½kn off Warren Point).

Approach To clear outlying rks on E and W of approach, keep Cawsand open of the Mewstone 298° until, coming from W, Wembury church (St Werburgh's on BA charts) bears 030° which clears Slimers Rocks on W of approach; or, coming from E, Wembury church bearing 006° clears Ebb Rocks on the E of the approach. Stand in between these limits until the outer marks are identified. Entry should not be attempted in strong SW winds.

Entrance A sand bar runs S from Season Point leaving a narrow channel close along the S shore (least depth 1m). The outer ldg bns, W rectangular topmarks with vertical black line, well up wooded hill-side , lead 089° into Cellar Bay. To avoid the S end of the bar which dries 0.6m, once past Mouthstone Pt, head towards the Bar buoy, R can Fl.R.5s. Leave it close to port and then once well past the small second R buoy, which marks the inner edge of the bar, follow the transit of the two bns on the N shore which have W rectangular top marks with vert

PLYMOUTH TO TORBAY

Passage Lights	BA No
Start Point	0228

Fl(3)10s62m25M+F.R (over Skerries) Horn 60s

Berry Head 0244
Fl(2)15s 58m19M

Streams related to HW Dover
Bolt Tail to Bolt Head +0500E −0200W
3M S of Start Point +0500ENE −0115WSW 2kn
Start Point inshore +0430E −0145W 4kn
Start Bay: +0415NE −0115SW
Berry Head: +0545N −0100S

Between Plymouth and Bolt Tail keep at least ½M offshore in fine weather to clear rocky ledges. In strong onshore winds keep well out to sea.

From Bolt Tail to Bolt Head there are cliffs up to 120m; conspic radio masts 1¼M E of Bolt Tail. Heavy swell possible, keep at least ½M offshore.

In strong winds the race off Start Point may be severe for 1M or more SE, and up to 2M with strong SW wind against tide. There is a set into West Bay especially in S winds. Bound for Dartmouth either pass outside the Skerries (Berry Head bearing 021° between Scabbacombe Hd (Downend Pt), 50°21′N, 3°31′W and E Blackstone Rock to the S, clears Skerries to SE) or take the inner passage, usually smoother, between Start Pt and Skerries, ¾M wide. Keep at least 4ca off LtHo until it bears 320°, at least 2ca S of Start Rocks, thence pass close to the Pt. Southernmost white ho (conspic) at Beesands bearing 320° leads through.

In fog do not try to make the land between Bolt Tail and Start Pt: aim for Start Bay or Torbay.

Start Bay may be entered in a calm with no swell if position known within 2M. From SE aim for Torcross, sounding continuously. 40+m depth up to 5ca off Skerries, 2·3m on its SW end, 5m in the middle and over 4½m on its NE end. Start Point fog signal often inaudible here. When soundings reach 14m you are over the bank: steer WNW and anchor in 8·9m. Sand, good holding, little traffic and sheltered between SSW and N. If shallow soundings not met when expected, stand off to E and wait for it to clear, N of shipping lane. With any swell keep away from the Skerries.

E-bound from Dartmouth keep ¾M offshore to clear E Blackstone and Nimble Rock and keep 1M offshore of Hope's Nose to clear Ore Stone. Coast is then free of dangers to Exmouth apart from Dawlish Rock, 3·5m, ¼M off the town.

Anchorages

R Erme Keep close to port on entry to avoid reef off Fernycombe Point on starboard. Anchor off cove W of pine-clad hill. Keep clear of historic wreck restricted area.

Burgh Is Pool N of Murrays Rock (R beacon, cross top) 2m, sand. Exposed at HW, otherwise protected from W to N. Keep well to E in approach as there is an underwater rock E of Murrays.

River Avon 1ca E of Murray Rocks head 060° towards two most E'ly houses on Mount Folly hilltop. These lie conveniently above one another. A W mark is painted on the cliffs just to the N of the houses mentioned above. When this point is reached turn onto 030° and head towards point of Lower Cellars Bank steep to on starboard. Once past boat houses keep close under cliff to find the deepest water. Anchor 1½ca W of thatched boat house for flat bottom. Breaking waves add interest and diversion to the entrance to this beautiful anchorage.

Hope Cove Anchor in offshore winds only. Poor holding. Beware rock drying 2·7m ¼ca offshore.

Start Bay in offshore winds off Hall Sands or Torcross close inshore. Run for Dartmouth if wind backs S.

Torbay Elberry Cove in SW corner of bay in 5m, 3ca offshore.

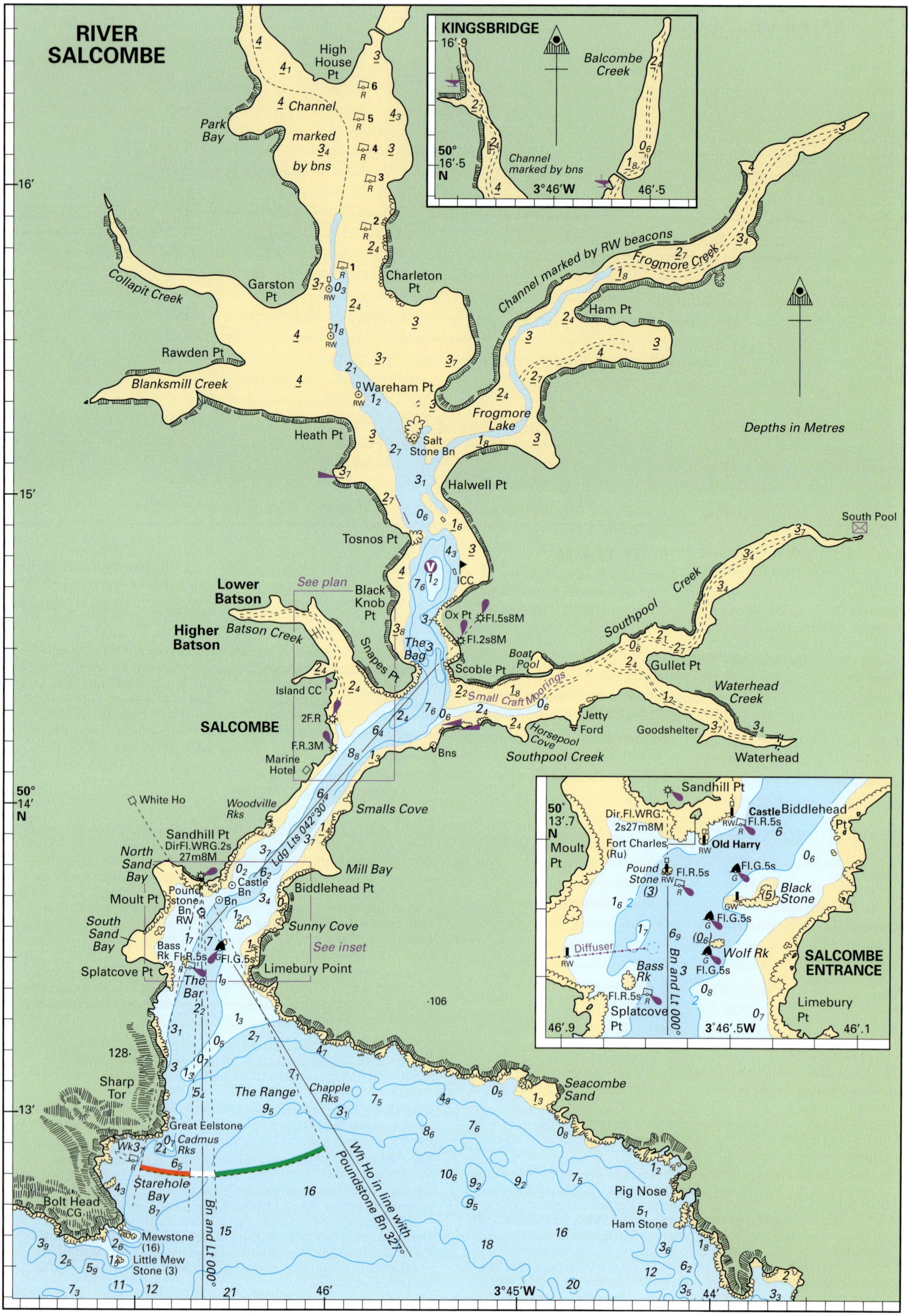
RIVER SALCOMBE
KINGSBRIDGE
Balcombe Creek
Channel marked by bns
3°46′W
46′·5
50° 16′·5 N
High House Pt
Channel marked by bns
Park Bay
Collapit Creek
Garston Pt
Charleton Pt
Rawden Pt
Blanksmill Creek
Wareham Pt
Heath Pt
Salt Stone Bn
Frogmore Lake
Channel marked by RW beacons
Frogmore Creek
Ham Pt
Depths in Metres
Halwell Pt
Tosnos Pt
ICC
See plan
Lower Batson
Black Knob Pt
Higher Batson
Batson Creek
Ox Pt
Fl.5s8M
Fl.2s8M
Snapes Pt
The Bag
Scoble Pt
Boat Pool
Small Craft Moorings
Island CC
2F.R
F.R.3M
SALCOMBE
Marine Hotel
Bns
Jetty
Ford
Horsepool Cove
Southpool Creek
Southpool Creek
Gullet Pt
Waterhead Creek
Goodshelter
Waterhead
South Pool
White Ho
Woodville Rks
Smalls Cove
Sandhill Pt
DirFl.WRG.2s
27m8M
North Sand Bay
Ldg Lts 042°30′
Mill Bay
Castle Bn
Biddlehead Pt
Moult Pt
Poundstone Bn RW
Bn
Sunny Cove
South Sand Bay
See inset
Bass Rk
Fl.R.5s
Fl.G.5s
Limebury Point
Splatcove Pt
The Bar
128
Sharp Tor
The Range
Chapple Rks
Great Eelstone
Wk
Cadmus Rks
Starehole Bay
Bolt Head
CG
Mewstone (16)
Little Mew Stone (3)
Bn and Lt 000°
Wh Ho in line with Poundstone Bn 327°
Seacombe Sand
Pig Nose
Ham Stone
3°45′W
46′
44′
16′
15′
50° 14′ N
13′
SALCOMBE ENTRANCE
Sandhill Pt
Dir.Fl.WRG.
2s27m8M
Castle
Biddlehead Pt
Fl.R.5s
Old Harry
Fort Charles (Ru)
Moult Pt
50° 13′.7 N
Pound Stone
Fl.R.5s
Fl.G.5s
Black Stone
Diffuser
Bass Rk
Fl.G.5s
Wolf Rk
Fl.R.5s
Splatcove Pt
Bn and Lt 000°
Limebury Pt
46′.9
3°46′.5W
46′.1

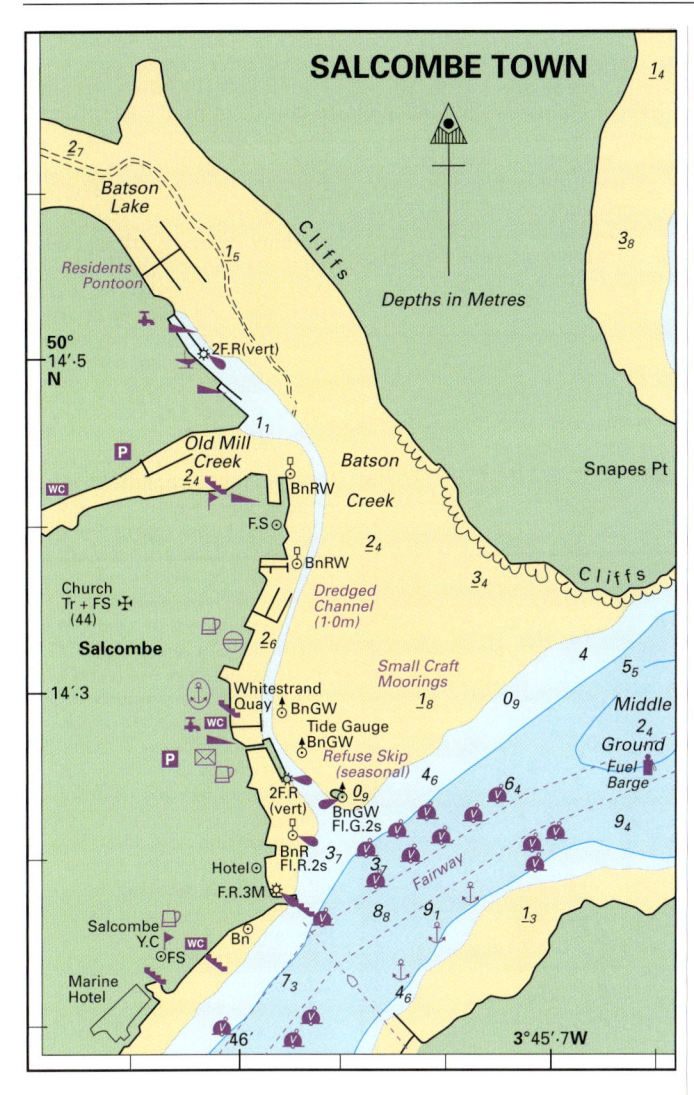

R line. Once well N of Misery Pt keep mid-channel. NB; Spit R can buoy, marking drying spit SE of Warren Pt, is often hidden behind yachts on moorings.

Berthing Anchor in fine weather in Cellar Bay (open from W to NW). The river is crowded with moorings. No anchoring east or north of Misery Point. For visitors there is a mooring for craft up to 60ft off Misery Point, further in are three moorings each taking three craft or 25 tonnes. There is a line of pontoons in the Pool with some 25 berths and a further pontoon on the W shore providing 20 berths; and a trot of fore and aft moorings (yachts may moor up to five abreast) on W side N of Yealm Hotel. Residents' moorings may be picked up if they are vacant but do not leave unattended without HM's approval.

Facilities Water at slip near Yealm Hotel; toilets, rubbish disposal, showers (0800–1800 only), no fuel. Newton: PO/Store, butcher, chemist, pub, YC. Noss: pubs. EC Thursday. Bus to Plymouth.

✆/VHF HM 01752 872533, VHF 10 (not 24hr). Water taxi 07817 132757.

SALCOMBE

Standard Port Plymouth

HW (sp) –0010 (np) +0000
LW (sp) +0005 (np) –0005
MHWS MHWN MLWN MLWS
–0·2m –0·3m –0·1m –0·1m

Salcombe is a very attractive hbr, but The Bar is very dangerous in strong onshore winds with the ebb tide. With a swell of 1m, crossing should not be attempted until there is a considerable rise in tide, HW – 0200 is recommended. Inside the stream can reach 3kn below the ferry landing. If in doubt contact the HM. The wind is fluky off the cliffs and as cruising yachts are prohibited from sailing inside the hbr in July and August, it is best to be under engine with the sails stowed before crossing The Bar. Yachts may not sail in the fairway during July and August.

Approach From W give the Mewstone and Cadmus Rocks clearances of 2ca and 1ca respectively. Starehole Bay provides temporary anchorage in W winds to wait for a suitable time to cross the bar. From E give Prawle Point clearance of 2ca and steer 298° for the pinewood S of Bar Lodge, a tall narrow building with a red roof. (Note also Ldg line on plan for clearing Chapple Rock, 3·1m). From 2ca off Mewstone steer N for about 4ca to a position about 1ca off the Eelstones and follow entry directions.

Entrance At the N end of the gradually shoaling range is The Bar (0·7m), extending SW from Limebury Point. The deepest water is ¾ca W of the Ldg line, Poundstone Bn (RW with R can top) in line with Sandhill Point bn (RWHS, diamond top) to W of red-roofed house, 000°. Leave Bass Rocks to port, and follow the buoyed channel. Round up to 042° with Ox Point Lts in line once Blackstone Rk is abeam.

By night enter in W sector (358°-003°) of Sandhill Point Dir Lt, Fl.WRG.2s. Follow the buoyed channel leaving Bass Rock R. can, Fl.R.5s to port, and then bring Ox Point Ldg Lts front Fl.2s (may be obscured by anchored vessels), rear Fl.5s, in line 042°.

The river is marked by bns to Kingsbridge where Squares Quay dries 3·4m and has 1·3m HWS and 0·2 HWN.

Berthing Anchorages
• In settled weather with modest draught, off Sunny Cove and Mill Bay on the E side. If anchoring in Smalls Cove, give the YC racing start line a wide berth.
• In settled weather, in deep water to E of fairway off the town.
• N of Halwell Point.
• W of Salt Stone bn.
• Frogmore Lake: Narrow pool (2m) just before bay on S side.
• For Kingsbridge by dinghy, anchor off junction to Balcombe Lake.

Moorings Visitors' pontoon at Whitestrand allows short-stay (30 minutes) for shopping; no double banking. Overnight stays incur charges.

Visitors' moorings mostly R (up to 30ft) and Y (over 30ft), marked 'V', off the town, N of the fairway, and off entrance to Southpool Creek.

With strong winds from SE to W, it is well worth going beyond The Bag where there is complete shelter. No anchoring in The Bag.

Alongside: two berths, overnight only (depart by 0800) on northern pontoon at Whitestrand; pre-booking essential; also visitors' pontoon on W side of Bag, not connected to shore. Half-tide pontoon in Frogmore Creek.

Drying berths at Kingsbridge alongside car park on W bank or pontoon on E. Check availability with the HM. Navigable HW±0230.

Facilities Landing at Ferry Pier (dinghies cannot be left), at Whitestrand pontoon and at Creek Boat Park Slip (1m). Boatyards at Salcombe and Lyncombe. Water from Whitestrand pontoon. Refuse barge off Whitestrand (April–October). Showers at Salcombe YC and Whitestrand. Water taxi (VHF 12), but from Oct–Apr limited service, weekdays only, at 0900, 1100, 1400 and 1600. Sailmaker at Kingsbridge.

✆/VHF HM 01548 843791, VHF 14. Hbr water taxi VHF 12. Salcombe YC 842872.

DARTMOUTH

Standard Port Plymouth

Dartmouth
HW (sp) +0025 (np) +0015
LW (sp) 0000   (np) –0005
MHWS MHWN MLWN MLWS
–0·6m –0·6m –0·2m –0·2m

Dittisham
HW (sp) +0045 (np) +0030
LW (sp) +0025 (np) +0005
MHWS MHWN MLWN MLWS
–0·6m –0·6m –0·2m –0·2m

Approaches SW set may be experienced on the flood and NE on the ebb, except near the ends of both. To the E above Froward Pt there is a truncated stone pyramid bn 24m (177m above HW).

From E, give Mewstone Rock (35m) a clear berth to stb (crab pots) leaving West Rock S card buoy to stb. After this make for Castle Ledge G con buoy (Fl.G.5s). From W, keep outside the Homestone buoy (R can) and keep E of W Blackstone Rock (2·4m). Keep away from Coombe Pt at all times. From S, Skerries R buoy, 3½M from the entrance, is a good guide.

At night, from E keep Lts of Berry Head and Start Pt both just visible until Castle Ledge buoy, G con (Fl.G 5s), is visible. Steer for this until in W sector of Kingswear (see below). From W, keep both Berry Head and Start Point lights visible until in Kingswear W sector.

Entrance is easy under power but squalls off the high land either side of the entrance may make sailing difficult, particularly with winds from SW through W to NW. Checkstone buoy is just E of a rocky ledge and must be left well to port. At springs localised streams up to 3kn may be experienced off Battery and Castle Pts with associated heavy swell in the entrance. The swell and fast tides disappear inside the estuary.

At night keep in W sector of Kingswear Lt (Iso.WRG.3s9m8M; 325°-W-331°) until within W sector of Bayards Cove Lt, Fl.WRG.2s, 289°-W-297°. (There is a F Lt NNW of Kettle Point for vessels leaving; it is useful to keep it astern on this leg). Keep in the Bayards Cove W sector until the G Lts on Kingswear pontoon are well open, when course should be altered to pass through the fairway to the anchorage E of the main hbr buoys.

The River Dart is navigable to Dittisham at any state of the tide and to Totnes after half-flood. It is controlled all the way by the Harbour Authority; dues are levied on all vessels. The S-most ferry has right of way and the cable ferry should be given a clear berth as under strong wind or tide the cables can be very close to the surface. Do not pass between the ferry and the shore unless the ferry is at least one third of the river's width clear of the side in question. Between Noss Point and the Anchor Stone the channel hugs the E bank. Dittisham Lake, ½M wide, has two navigable channels separated by Flat Owers (dries 2m). Large vessels use the W channel. Above this the channel is winding, marked to Totnes by buoys and bns. Keep High Gurrow and Blackness Pts close to port, Pighole and Mill Points close to stb; alter course to port to cross the river, pass close N of White Rock and make for buoys off Langham Wood Pt, leaving latter close to port. Then follow the buoys, keeping to outside of bends. At springs the river dries for 2M below Totnes but yachts of 1m draught can proceed there at LW+0130.

Berthing During working hours the River Officers (VHF 11, *Dart Nav*) are on duty near the town jetty and up-river at Dittisham. Dinghies may be left at pontoons adjacent to Dartmouth YC and at pontoons N of Lee Court Flats.
• Anchor E of the town and of the ships' buoys in 4½m. Good holding but beware the chains of large moorings.
• Visitors' buoys marked with a blue flag or blue with a V, and pontoons between buoys: enquire of river officers.
• Visitors' pontoons adjacent to Dartmouth YC (max 30ft) W bank; yachts may use S end of inshore side of town jetty for 1hr free; also for craft under 26ft at pontoons on W bank N of Court Flats.
• Darthaven Marina pontoons (E side).
• Dart Marina pontoons (W side, just above cable ferry).
• Fore and aft moorings sometimes available at River Dart YC on E bank.
• Noss-on-Dart Marina on E side of river.
• Anchor on W side of river below Anchor Stone (R can) off Parson's Mud clear of moorings and out of main channel.
• Visitors' moorings off Dittisham, clearly marked with holding capacity which must be observed.
• Above Dittisham, including Totnes, consult river officer, VHF 11 *Dart Nav*, waiting for him at Dittisham if necessary.

Facilities Diesel and petrol from Dartmouth Fuel Barge, VHF 06, call sign *Dart Crusader* or *Dart Fuel Barge*. Water at North Embankment (by WCs) and South Embankment, Dartmouth YC, Dittisham, Galmpton. Water and stores at Dittisham, Galmpton and Totnes. Dittisham–Greenbanks ferry will also serve Dittisham moorings, VHF 10. Dittisham–Dartmouth ferry will also serve moorings below Ned's Point, VHF 10.

☎/VHF (all 01803). HM 832337, VHF 11 (callsign *Dartnav*). Dartmouth YC 832305. R Dart YC 752496; Dart Marina 833351. VHF 80, 37. Darthaven Marina 752545, VHF 80. Noss-on-Dart Marina 833351. Dartside Quay, Galmpton 845445, VHF 37, 80. Yacht Taxi 833727, 07970 346571 (summer 0800–2300, winter 1000–1600), VHF 8, 69. Fuel Barge 07801 798861, VHF 06. Greenway Ferries 882811, VHF 10.

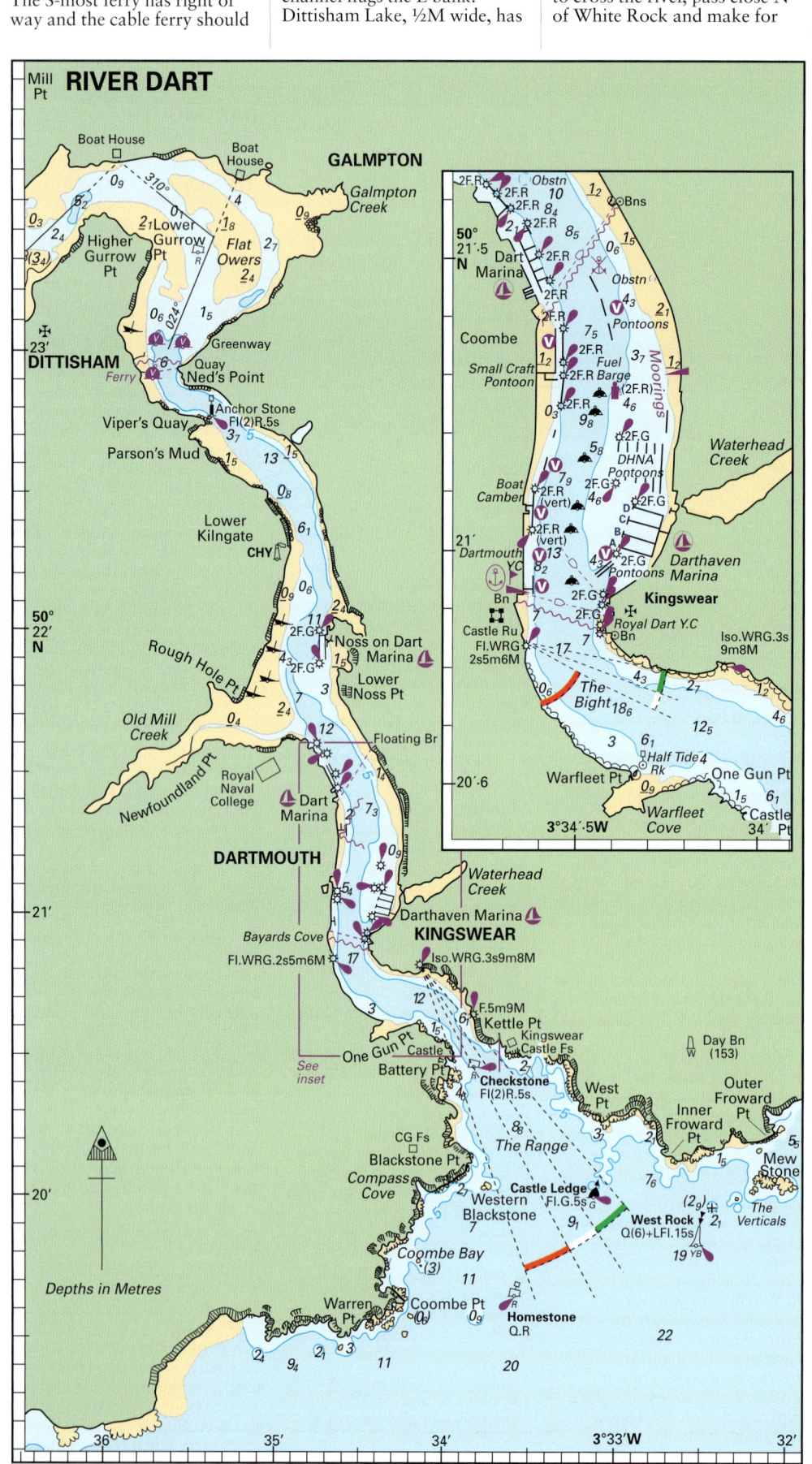

BRIXHAM

Tidal data as Torquay

Brixham is a busy fishing port with marina accommodation for yachts. In N–NE winds there is considerable scend in outer hbr.

Approach Steer for safe water sph Lt buoy, Mo(A)10s (· −), bearing 308°, 1·2ca, from Victoria Breakwater LtHo.

From N, clear rocks off Hope's Nose by keeping W edge of Cod Rock, off Berry Head, bearing more than 195° and open E of Berry Head. From S, clear dangers S of Berry Head by keeping Hope's Nose open E of Berry Hd, 359°. From Berry Head (25m depth close inshore) steer 284° for Safewater Buoy.

Signals 3R balls or Lts at the inner harbour entrance indicate hbr is closed.

Entrance Give the breakwater end a wide berth, as large beam trawlers can often emerge from behind it: you should then keep to the stb side of the Main Fairway, marked by two pairs of lateral Lt buoys. Give way to

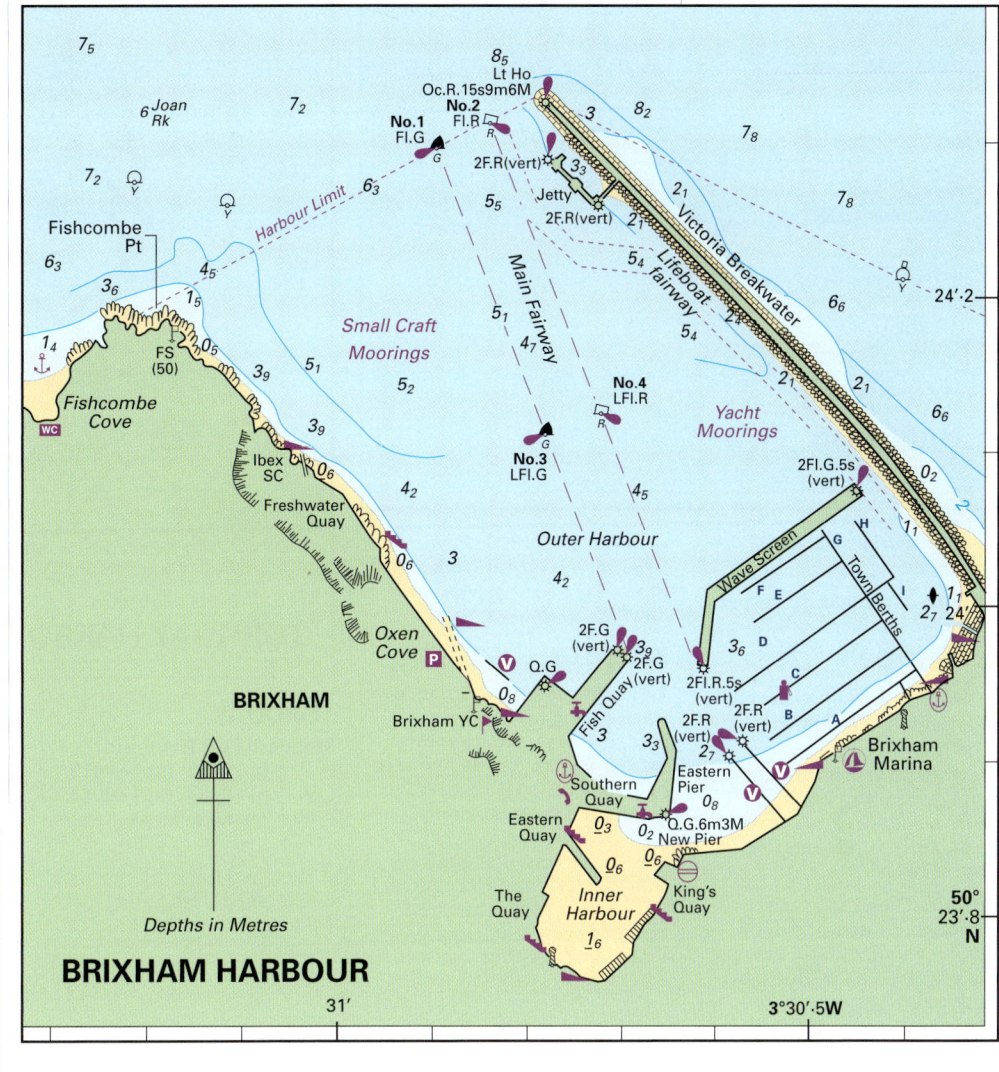

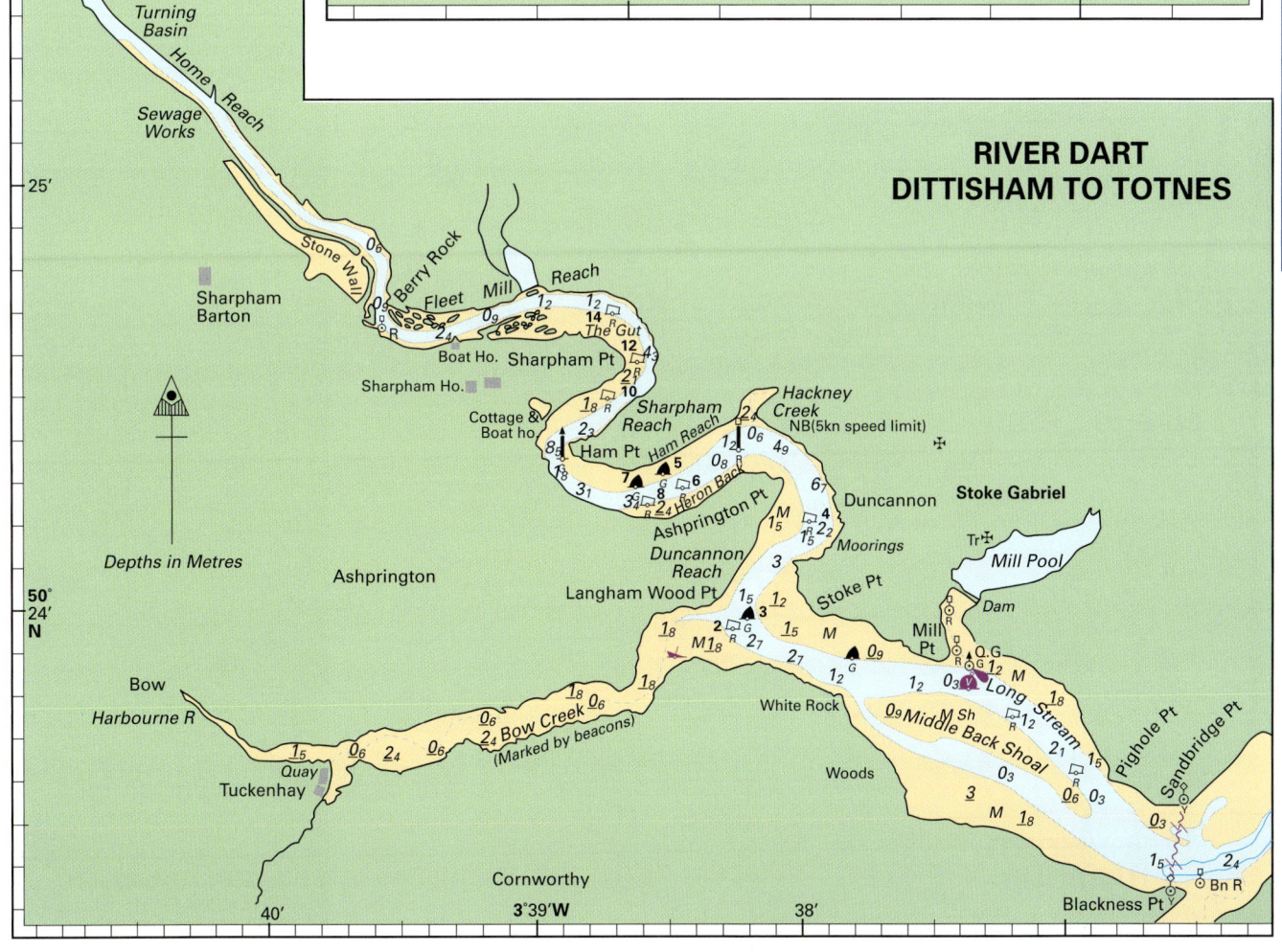

BRIXHAM HARBOUR

RIVER DART DITTISHAM TO TOTNES

ENGLAND – SOUTH COAST

45

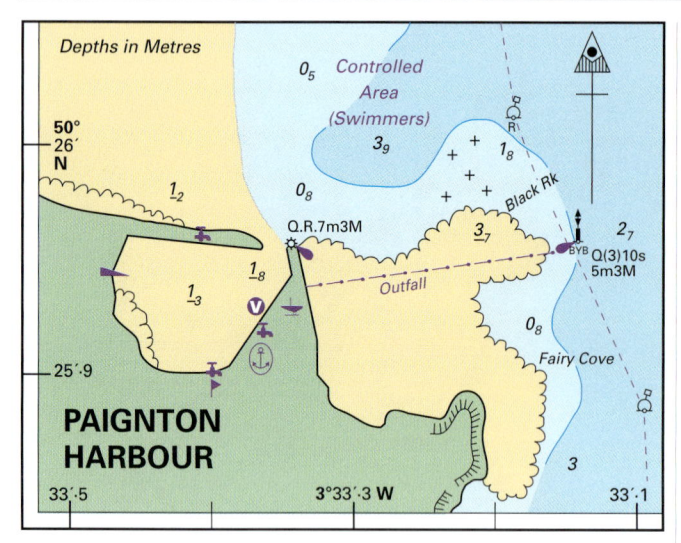

the LB when showing emergency signals.

Berthing Marina in SE corner of hbr. In summer a pontoon is moored off Brixham YC, subject to MFV wash. There is no room to anchor in the hbr and holding in Fishcombe Cove is very poor.

Leaving the marina, give way to fishing vessels leaving the MFV basin or manoeuvring off fuel berth, and to craft entering hbr from seaward.

Facilities Diesel at marina, pontoon C; water at end of pier, breakwater hard, new pier and oil jetty. All facilities. EC Wednesday.

☎/VHF (all 01803) HM 853321, VHF 14, (*Brixham Port*). YC 853332. Marina 882929, VHF 80.

PAIGNTON

Tidal data as for Torquay. A small drying hbr with very limited accommodation for smaller yachts. Visiting vessels may secure alongside East Quay for a short stay only. Alongside berthing is very limited, so vessels should contact Harbour Office on VHF 14 for permission and specific berthing instructions. Water, fuel at garage, shops.

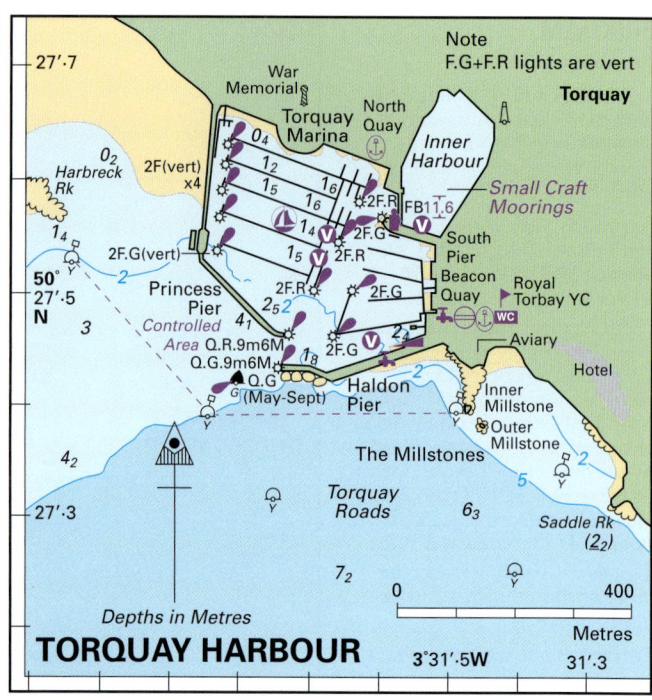

TORQUAY

Standard Port Plymouth
HW (sp) +0035 (np) +0015
LW (sp) +0031 (np) +0014
MHWS MHWN MLWN MLWS
−0·6m −0·7m −0·2m −0·1m

A sheltered hbr with marina, commercial traffic and passenger launches. Busy in summer.

Approach From E a church tr and a spire stand out on the skyline above Babbacombe. There is a safe passage between the Orestone and the Flat Rock off Hope's Nose. It is not safe for strangers to pass inside the Thatcher even at HW. The Orestone with its own length open of the Thatcher will clear all shoals along the N shore of Torbay.

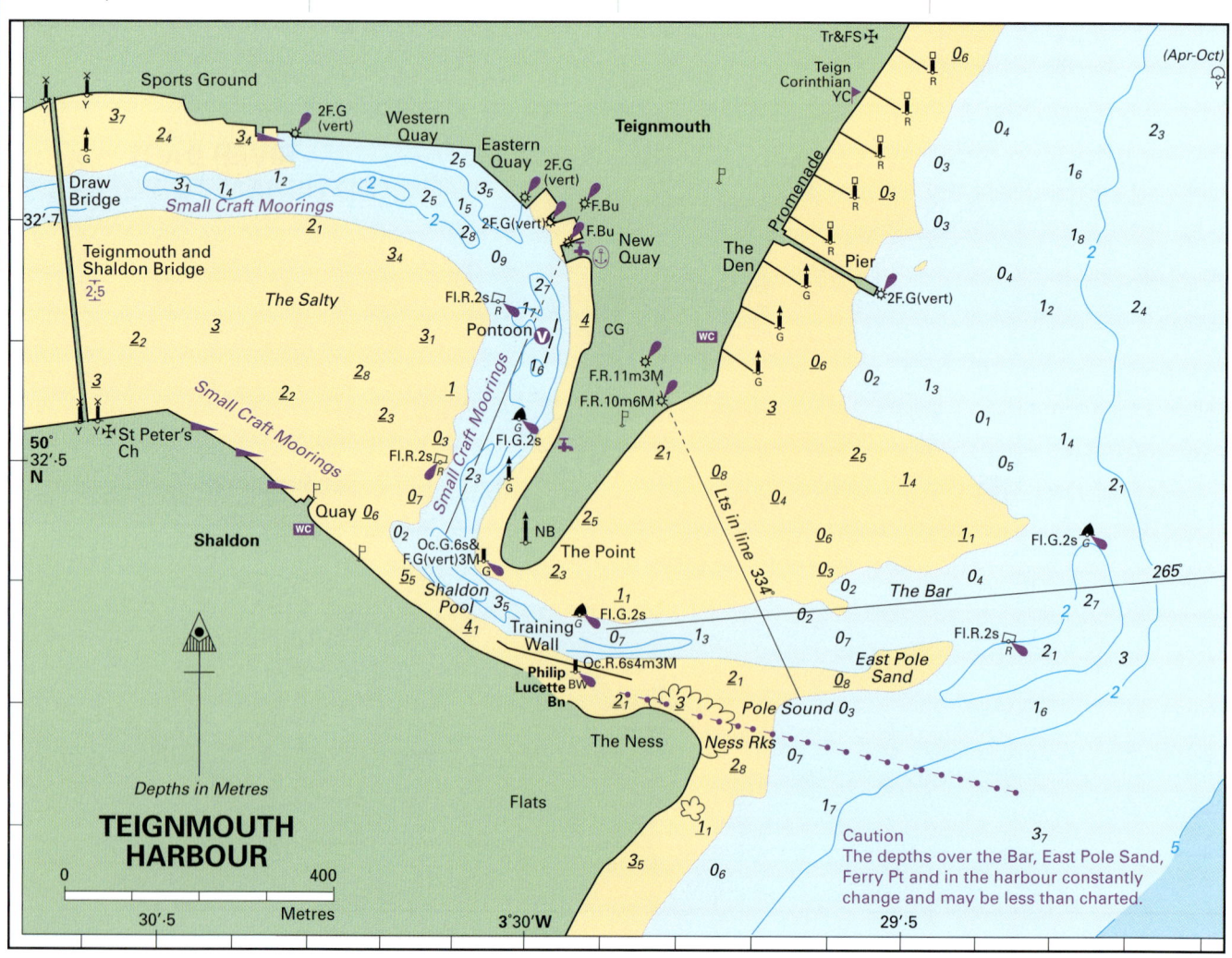

LYME BAY (TORBAY) TO WEYMOUTH

There is a Firing Practice Area extending from Exmouth to Chesil Beach.

Caution In Lyme Bay if S–SW gales blow up there is no refuge in onshore winds.

From Exmouth to Portland Bill there are two conspic features: Beer Head 130m, the W-most chalk cliff on S coast; and 3M before Bridport is Golden Cap 187m.

Passage Lights	BA No
Portland Bill	0294

Fl(4)20s43m25M+
Dia 30s (From 221° to 244° gradually changes 1 Fl to 4 Fl, then 4 Fl to 117°, gradually changing from 4 Fl to 1 Fl by 141°) + F.R.13M (over Shambles)

W Shambles W card buoy
Q(9)15s Bell

E Shambles
E card buoy   0300
Q(3)10s Bell

Portland Harbour
A Pier head   0314
Fl.2·5s22m10M

Streams related to HW Dover
Inshore off Bridport: +0600E; HWD W.

On W-going stream Portland Bill produces an eddy in West Bay with a N set felt up to 10M off the Bill and a S set felt as far as 6M S of the Bill.

Portland Bill Streams
(*Caveat* Yachtsmen approaching Portland Bill from E may be using BA Charts with streams related to HW Portsmouth or Dover; but for the Bill they are shown on charts *2615* and *3315* related to HW Plymouth. See p.420 for tidal stream chart related to Plymouth. Those below are related to Dover).

W of the Bill
From +0200 to –0345 (about 9½hrs) S, 3kn
From –0015 to +0200N, 1·1kn

Off the Bill
From +0500E to SE (max 6kn at –0500)
From –0100SW to W (max 7+kn at +0100)

E of the Bill
From –0515 to +0500 (about 10¼hrs) S, 4½kn
From +0500 to –0515N, 1·8kn

Portland Bill
The strong S streams either side of the Bill, running for nine or 10hrs, meet the main Channel streams causing violent turbulence on Portland Ledge. The resultant race is dangerous for yachts and should be avoided either by passing at least 5M S of the Bill and outside E Shambles E card buoy; or in good conditions with accurate timing, by the 5ca-wide passage between the Bill and the Race. Timing is important or the yacht may be set out of the channel into the Race.

For passing inshore the best time E-bound is at Dover +0500 and is possible to –0500. Between these times the S stream is running out of W Bay and the land must be closed to 1·2ca well N of Is of Portland: keep close to Chesil Beach in the approach and round the Bill at 1·2ca off.

W-bound the best time is Dover –0100 (earlier risks being set in to the last of the E-going Race) and is possible until +0200. During this period the yacht will have a strong fair stream down the E side of the peninsula; the land should be kept within 1·2ca down to the pitch of the Bill. If the tide has turned to the W when the pitch is reached, steer NW into West Bay to avoid being set into the Race.

Caution
- In winds of Force 6+, and in weaker E winds, the inshore passage ceases to be relatively smooth.
- Lobster pots and their buoys are a hazard in the passage and along the E coast as are divers and their support boats.

The Shambles
The passage between the Race and the Shambles needs extreme care. Strong tidal streams may cause heavy seas; allow for strong set into the race or onto the Shambles. Ldg marks are Portland Harbour 'A' pier head Lt in line with Grove Point 358°, leading 3ca W of The Shambles.

Anchorages
Babbacombe (close N of Long Quarry Point) clear of local moorings in offshore winds.

Exmouth, outside anchorage near Fairway buoy if waiting for the tide in fair weather.

Littleham Cove just N of Straight Point.

Beer Roads E of Beer Head, good anchorage in offshore winds through W to SW in Bay of Beer.

Signals 3R balls or Lts vert: hbr closed, or incoming traffic must wait until entrance is clear.

Entrance faces W. G con buoy Q.G is moored (May–September) off W end of Haldon Pier. Much traffic in summer: keep well to stb in entrance.

Berthing 500-berth marina occupies W half of outer harbour with some 50 berths for visitors (signposted). Harbour Authority pontoons northwards of Haldon Pier. Call *Torquay Harbour* on VHF 14.

Haldon Pier is used by commercial vessels. Tidal gate HW±3hrs approx to inner harbour for small local craft. Good anchorage outside the hbr: keep clear of buoyed fairway. Landing inside Haldon and Princess piers. Short stay visitors may remain on visitors' pontoons for up to two hours free of charge.

Facilities Fuel at South Pier. Small to medium craft may dry against wall in inner harbour. All facilities.

✆/VHF HM 01803 292429, VHF 16, 14.
Marina 200210, VHF 80.
Royal Torbay YC 292006.

TEIGNMOUTH
Standard Port Plymouth
Bar
HW (sp) +0050 (np) +0020
LW (sp) +0025 (np) 0000
MHWS MHWN MLWN MLWS
–0·9m –0·8m –0·2m –0·1m

A commercial port with limited accommodation for yachts. Entrance difficult and not accessible in strong onshore winds from NE to S.

Approach River Teign is N of the Ness, a red sandstone headland with pines at summit.

Entrance The bar is dangerous in onshore winds and with a swell. It is wise to seek local guidance to approach even when there are offshore winds at the last quarter of the flood. The bar is constantly changing. It extends from the Ness, a distinctive red sandstone cliff, to Teignmouth Pier. Tides scour channels which are marked by buoys for the use of pilots but because of constant changes in the channel, should not be used by visitors for navigation. There is a dredged channel, (least depth 1m above CD) marked by a Ldg line (Lucette Lt Oc.R.6s on the training wall on the left of the entrance with W black W stripes on the hbr wall behind) on approx 270°.

Note The 2F.R Lts on the shore bearing 334° are not Ldg Lts but show the dangers off the Ness and visitors should keep E of this line.

Past The Point steer 021° for New Quay leaving R can buoys well to port. Beware of set along the Shaldon shore and unmarked shoals above the quay on stb side. The stream off The Point runs at 4kn and is strong throughout the hbr especially for last half of the ebb.

Inadvisable to attempt entrance at night or to leave when ebb is running strongly.

Berthing In settled weather anchor outside 2ca E of end of pier, 2m. Fore and aft mooring for visitors 1ca N of The Point and also on pontoon (2·5m at chart datum) 2 ca N of the Point. Quiet anchorage above the br, clearance 3m. Drawbridge section has 2m depth at MHWS.

Facilities Water at quays. Fuel by tanker. Scrubbing hard on S side of New Quay. Shops: EC Thursday.

✆/VHF HM 01626 773165, VHF 12 (office hours).

ENGLAND – SOUTH COAST

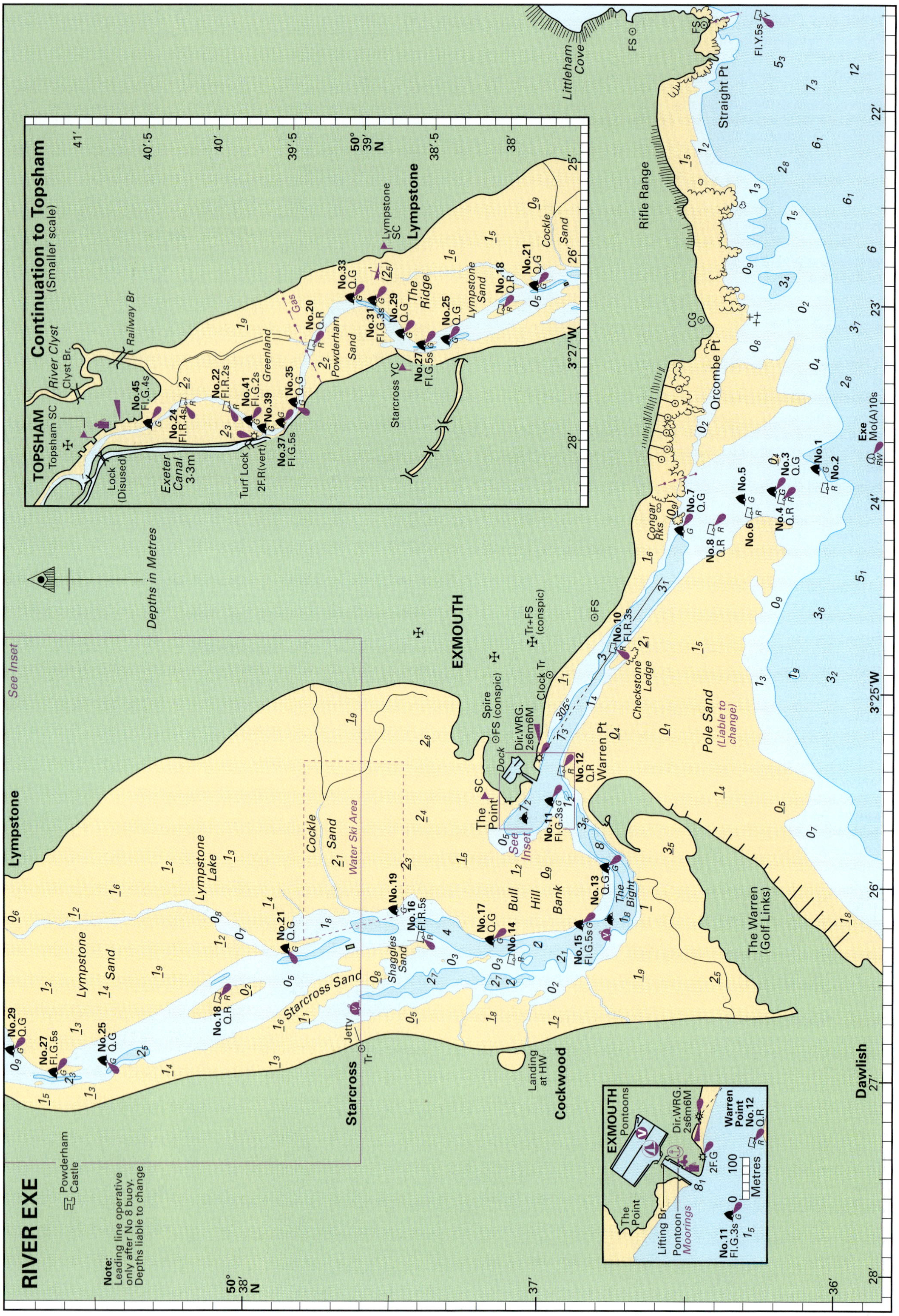

RIVER EXE
Standard Port Plymouth
Bar
HW (sp) +0050 (np) +0030
LW (sp) +0015 (np) +0005
MHWS MHWN MLWN MLWS
−0·9m −1·0m −0·5m −0·3m

Turf Lock
HW (sp) +0100 (np) +0045
MHWS MHWN MLWN MLWS
−1·6m −1·6m n/a   n/a
DS Dover +0445E HWD W

A pleasant estuary with many moorings (few for visitors) but still places to anchor. Exmouth Dock now closed to commercial traffic. Approach dangerous in strong onshore winds.

Approach and Entrance Make for Exe RW safewater buoy Mo(A)10s, at 50°35'·9N 3°23'·7W, then follow buoyed channel, on approx 340°. Turn to port at R can buoy Q.R. No.8. After passing buoy No.10, head for a point just S of the pierhead. At night, after passing No.7, follow W sector of DirWRG.2s. For an assessment of current weather and sea conditions at river entrance, call duty watchkeeper at National Coastwatch Institution, Exmouth, ☎ 01395 222492 (daylight hours).

River Exe Proceeding up-river follow the curves of the centre of the channel rather than straight lines between the buoys. Bull Head obtrudes between 13 and 15 buoys. The channel is buoyed to Topsham. Turf lock gives access to a canal leading to Exeter, used by commercial craft. Daily convoy to Exeter (max headroom 11m under M5), lock opening HW Exmouth −0100.

Berthing
- In the Bight, 3–5½m, sand.
- 4 moorings near No.15 buoy, see plan.
- Off Starcross S of pier, but many moorings.
- In Lympstone Lake.
- Off Turf lock, clear of fairway and entrance (strong ebb).
- Marina in Exmouth Dock – contact Dock Master for update on depths in entrance.

There are yellow visitors' buoys near No.15 buoy, one to E of line between Nos.17 and 19 buoys, and two S of Starcross Pier. (Ferry service from yachts in river to the Dock.) Limited mooring in Exmouth Dock and in canal via Turf Lock (opens HW Exmouth −0100). Limited buoys and pontoon berths for visitors (shallow at springs, sand/mud) at Topsham (Trout's boatyard). Land at dock entrance pontoon, Starcross or on the beach S or N of hbr entrance. It is dangerous to anchor off the point especially with spring tides or SE wind against tide as streams may reach 5kn.

Facilities Water from Dock and Topsham. Shops at Exmouth and Topsham. Water taxi VHF 37 Mobile 07970 918418.

☎/VHF Marina 01395 269314. Exmouth Docks VHF 14; HM 274 306; NCI Exmouth 222492.

HM River and Canal 01392 274306, VHF 12 (*Port of Exeter*). Trout's Boatyard Topsham 01392 873044.

AXMOUTH
Tidal data as Lyme Regis

A small drying hbr in mouth of River Axe. Enter HW±0030, dangerous in more than moderate onshore wind. Bar dries 1m; entrance channel 2m. Spring ebb 6kn. Moorings from Axe YC ☎ 01297 20043, bilge keels, max 8·5m LOA and 1·2m draught. Anchorage offshore 2ca W of entrance.

LYME REGIS
Standard Port Plymouth
HW (sp) +0100 (np) +0040
LW (sp) +0005 (np) −0005
MHWS MHWN MLWN MLWS
−1·2m −1·3m −0·5m −0·2m

Approach Lyme lies 22M NW of Portland Bill. The approach is straightforward. Comfortable in offshore winds but bad in heavy weather from S to E as swell enters the hbr.

Entrance The hbr is protected from the W by a stone pier, the Cobb, surrounded by rocks, with a R bn marking the extension of rocks at the E end which cover at ½ tide. The inner arm of the hbr and its entrance are to the NW. The leading line 284°, is Lt with a sectored RW Lt. It is safest to keep just inside the W sector until the hbr begins to open.

Berthing The hbr dries (0·3m to 1·3m, hard sand) with limited accommodation for visitors in boats under 9m alongside the Victoria Pier. HM may reserve moorings for intending visitors. *Mobile* 07870 240645. Enter HW±0230. Anchor to the N of the Ldg line opposite the Victoria Pier. R visitors' buoys lie to the NW of the anchorage.

There are many moorings for local boats. There are three pontoons (May–September), check depth with HM, usually 1m at outer end.

Facilities Fuel, water, shops.

☎/VHF HM 01297 442137, VHF 14 (*Lyme Regis Harbour Radio*).

Interest A very attractive town famous for the fossils to be found on the beaches under the cliffs.

WEST BAY (BRIDPORT)
Standard Port Plymouth
HW (sp) +0040 (np) +0025
LW (sp) +0000 (np) −0000
MHWS MHWN MLWN MLWS
−1·4m −1·4m −0·6m −0·1m

A small artificial hbr, recently extended to improve shelter and provide 200m of berthing for visitors (approx. 1·5m). Dredging is frequently necessary. Enter HW±0200. Pontoon access to new quay.

Facilities Water, electricity. Showers in nearby campsite.

☎/VHF HM 01308 423222, *Mobile* 07870 240636, VHF 11.

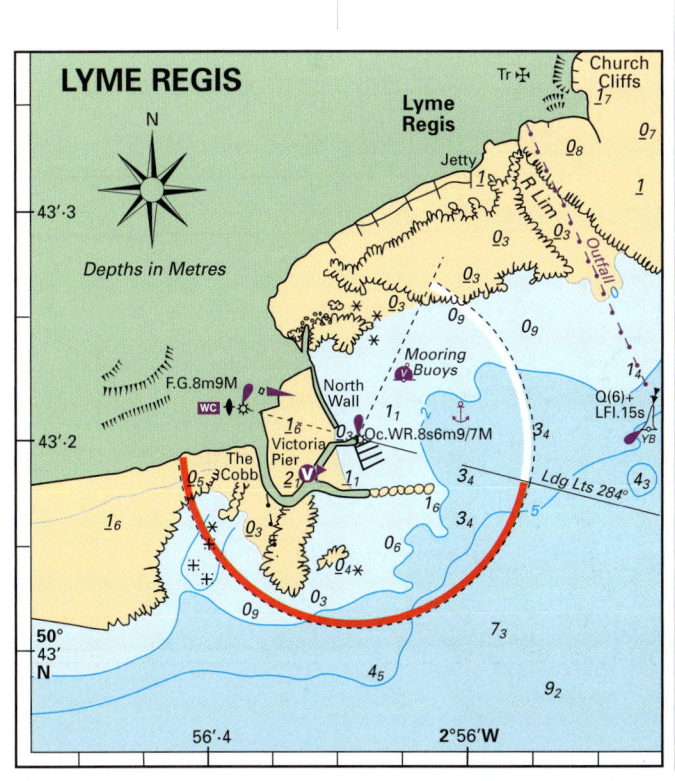

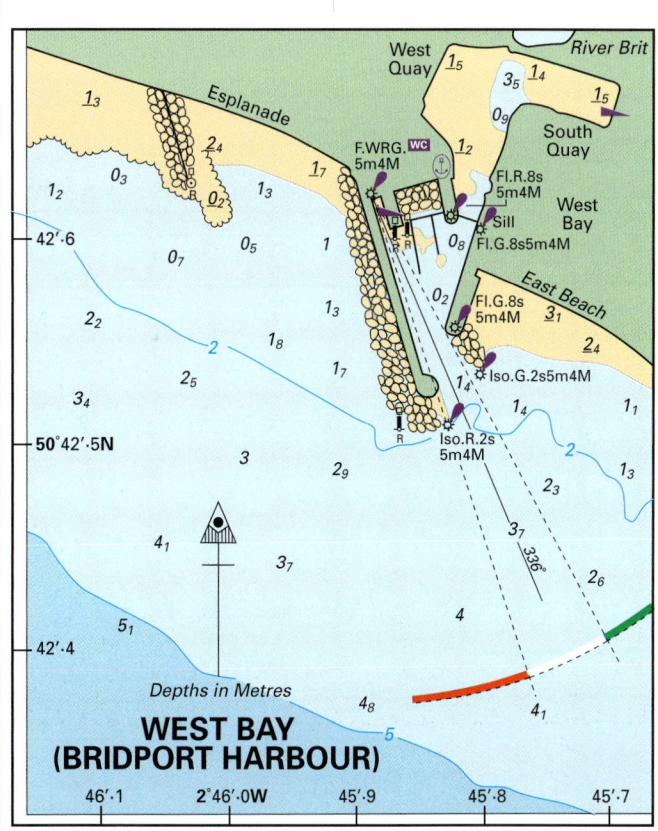

PORTLAND HARBOUR
Standard Port Portland
See tidal curves, p.454

A spacious hbr but not well sheltered now has good facilities for visiting yachts.

Streams are imperceptible in the hbr but run up to 1kn in the entrances, with eddies.

Approach The hbr is on the E side of Portland peninsula. From the W the main hazard is Portland Race; from S the Shambles and from E, Lulworth gunnery ranges. *Study Passage Notes Lyme Bay to Weymouth (above) and Weymouth to Poole (p.51).*

Entrance The South Ship Channel is closed. Yachts must use the North Channel and follow the buoyed safety fairway. Observe 6kn speed limit at S end of the fairway. Use engine. Monitor *Portland Harbour Radio* VHF 74 while entering. Observe Port Traffic Signals (IPTS) when shown from North and East Ship Channels.

Berthing Ferrybridge Marine Service moorings, marked FMS, in vicinity of New Channel bn, or anchor nearby, clear of moorings. Visitors' moorings may also be obtainable from Royal Dorset YC or Castle Cove SC. Uncomfortable in southerlies. Portland Marina at southern end of Safety Fairway. All facilities. Call *Marina Control* on VHF 80.

Facilities Fuel from garages. Water from SC dinghy park. Shops.

☏ HM (01305) 824 044; Royal Dorset YC 786 258; Castle Cove SC 783 708; Ferrybridge Marine Services *Mobile* 07780 610 997. Portland Marina 0845 430 2012.
www.portland-port.co.uk

WEYMOUTH
Tidal data as Portland Harbour
DS Dover +0545E HWD W
Tides 4hrs flood, 4hrs ebb, 4hrs slack

Owing to an eddy, stream in Weymouth Roads is W-going (not more than ½kn) at all times except Dover −0515 to −0315.

Weymouth is busy with fishing boats and a few commercial craft. Yachts in transit are normally given a berth in the main hbr with friendly accommodation and good facilities for yachts.

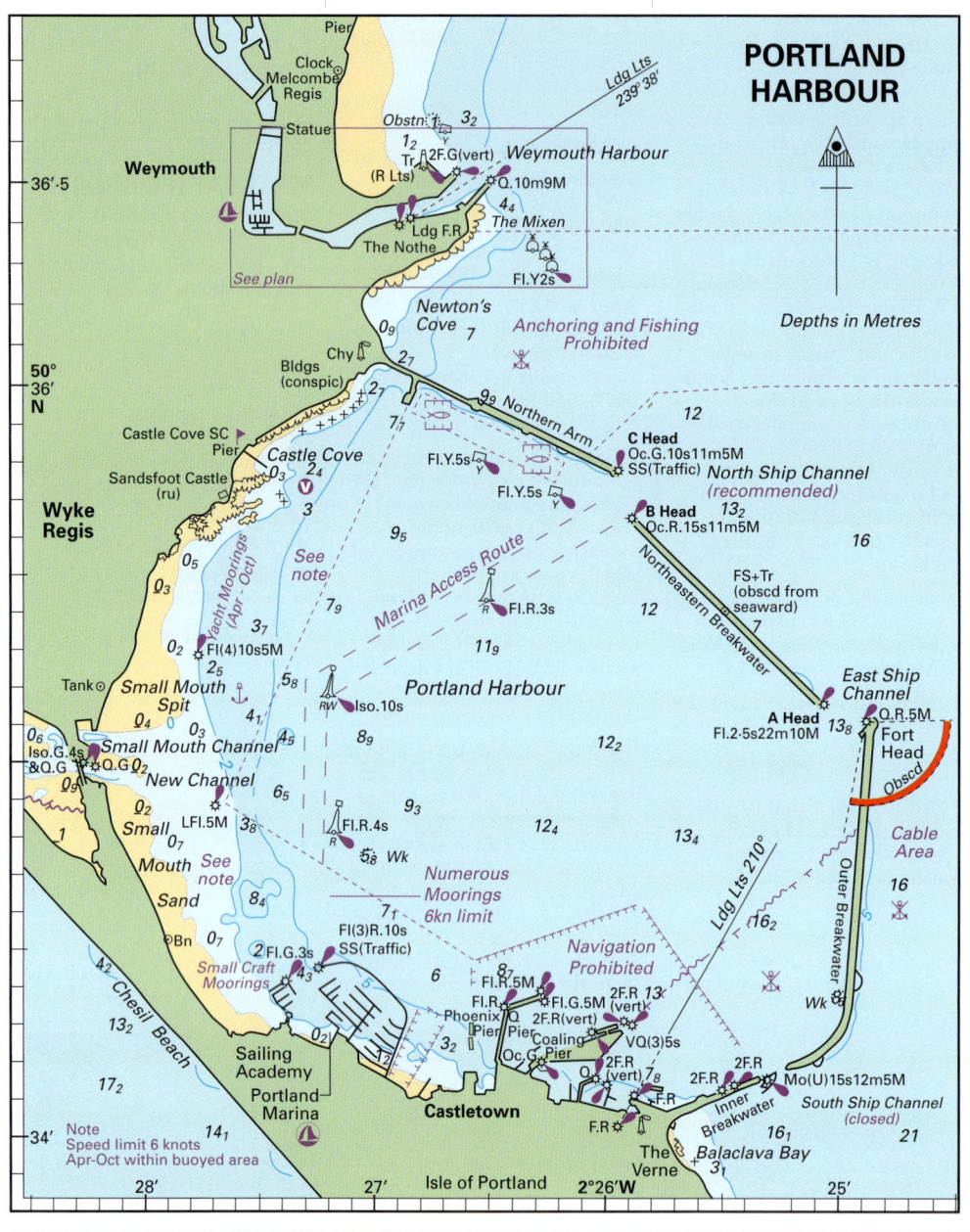

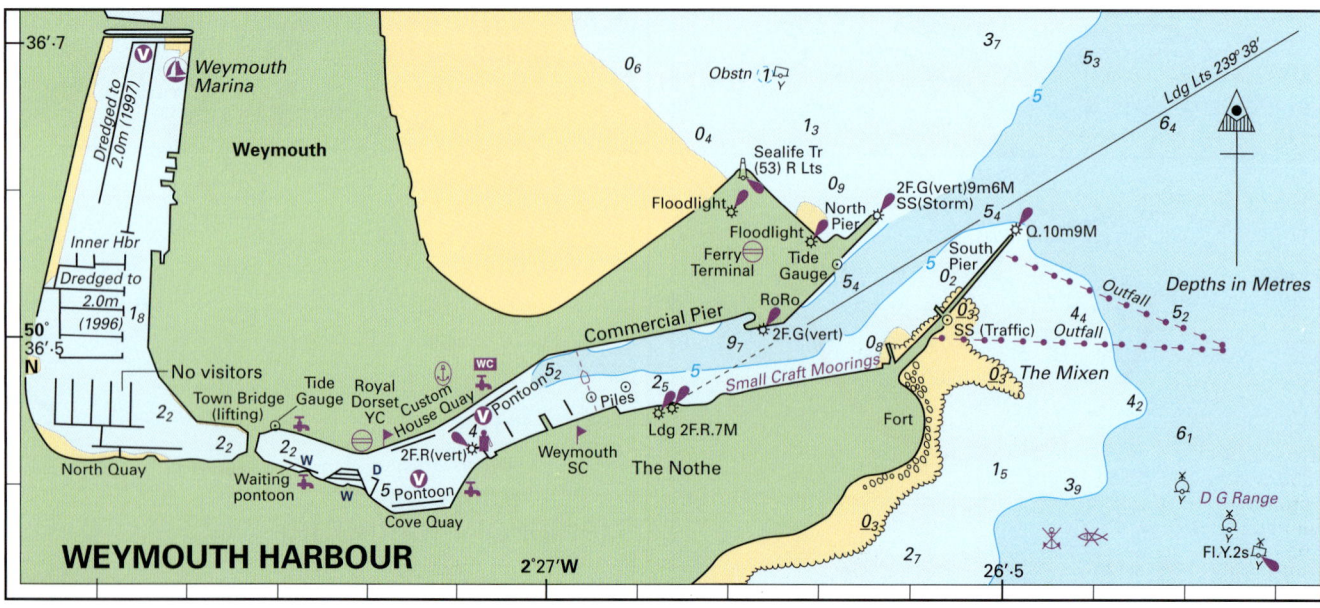

Approach As for Portland. From the east, The Sealife Tower, approx 200m west of the harbour entrance, is a very good landmark. It is a pencil-like structure, height 55m with flashing red light at the top. Before closing entrance, call *Weymouth Harbour* VHF 12 (not 24hrs). IPTS may be shown.

Entrance Keep to N of transit through the ends of hbr piers and steer in as soon as entrance is wide open. Two R diamonds (R Lts at night) on S side of hbr in line 240° lead between the piers.

Berthing Visitors' berths on pontoon in The Cove and, for craft over 10m, off Custom House Quay opposite LBS. Anchoring in the hbr is forbidden. Swell runs up the hbr with winds from E–NE. Pontoon berths for local yachts above the br; beyond them, Weymouth Marina may have some visitors' berths. Depth 2·5m, check berth availability before asking for a transit of the bridge. Br opens every 2hrs between 0800 and 1800 with later openings in summer (consult HM); R and G traffic Lts.

In fine weather there is a good anchorage outside the hbr 3 or 4ca N of S pier-head, 2½–3½m.

Facilities All facilities.

☎/**VHF** Berthing officer 01305 838 423; HM 838 386, VHF 12 (working day or when vessels expected), Royal Dorset YC 786 258; Weymouth Marina 767 576.
www.harbour.weymouth.gov.uk

LULWORTH COVE

Standard Port Portland
HW (sp) +0015 (np) +0005
LW (sp) −0005 (np) 0000
MHWS MHWN MLWN MLWS
+0·1m +0·1m +0·2m +0·1m

A popular tourist spot comprising a circular basin with a narrow entrance. In S winds a heavy swell rolls in, dangerous with strong winds; and in NE winds katabatic effects reported in E part of the cove. Otherwise a yacht with good ground tackle may ride out bad W weather safely but uncomfortably.

Approach From W keep ½M offshore to clear Ringstead Ledge. Lulworth lies 3M E of White Nothe where the cliffs change from clay to chalk. Near the hbr the shore is steep-to. From E, Arish Mell Gap open of Worbarrow Head clears Kimmeridge Ledges.

Entrance Channel is 80m wide with 4·8m depth. The wind may be fluky or squally in the entrance. Rocky ledges extend into the hbr NNW and ENE from each side of the entrance. The W ledge obtrudes more into the entrance and a yacht should therefore keep a third of the way over from the E cliff and head for the junction of green and white cliffs on N side of hbr. Do not deviate to port or stb until fully halfway across the cove.

Anchorage in NE corner of Cove in 3m, good holding (but dragging reported in E part, SE of Y MoD mooring). Avoid obstructing the fairway to NW corner of the bay, used by tourist boats to land passengers. Mooring buoy in NE part is for MoD vessels. If there is any suggestion of the wind going into S, get out.

Facilities Garage, hotel, stores, PO. Water at car park.

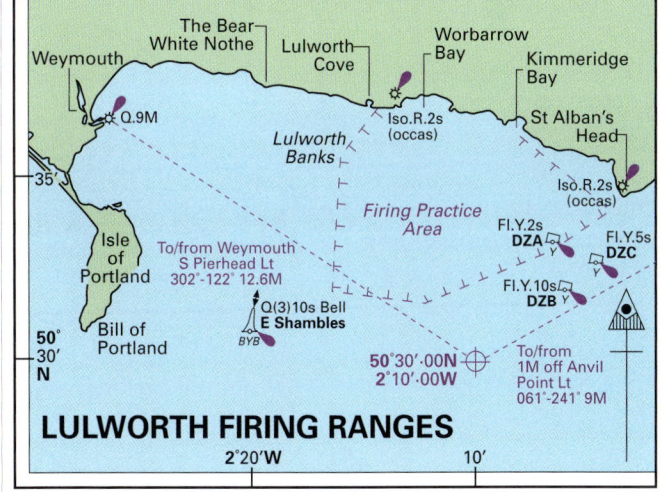

WEYMOUTH TO POOLE

Hazards are Lulworth Gunnery Ranges and St Alban's Race.

Passage Light	BA No
Anvil Point	0496
Fl.10s45m9M	

Streams related to HW Dover
Lulworth to St Alban's Head, close inshore: +0500E −0200 W
W side of St Alban's Head SE almost continuously.
3½M S of St Alban's Head +0545E −0015W, 4·5kn
Durlston Head +0530NE −0030, 3kn
Peveril buoy: +0500NNE, (1½kn) −0215SSW, (3kn)
Old Harry: +0500E; −0115W

When coming from S or W of Portland Race study Passage Notes – Lyme Bay to Weymouth (p.47).

Inshore E of Weymouth there is an obstruction, least depth 4m, 3ca SE of Redcliffe Point, and rocks running out 3ca from Ringstead Point with wreck dries 2·5m. There are no dangers outside 2ca as far as Lulworth Cove. E of that avoid Kimmeridge Ledge extending seaward more than ½M.

Lulworth Gunnery Range for army firing extends from St Albans Head to a point 5M S of Lulworth Cove. In addition there is a naval gunnery range, firing from 2°17'·5W (approx) at targets marked by three DZ Lt buoys (Fl.Y, from W to E, 2s, 10s, 5s) 2½M S to SW of St Alban's Head.

Army firing is mainly in the daytime, Monday–Friday, but occasionally there is night and weekend firing. No firing in August. Information obtainable from ☎ 01929 404819 (recording) or 404700.

Naval firing is less regular. Warships patrol S of Lulworth Banks and fly R flags during firing.

When firing is in progress, range safety boats, VHF Ch 08 and 16, are stationed at the edges of the danger area. Firing times are broadcast by both the Coastguard and Radio Solent; 24h pre-recorded message on firing times ☎ 01929 404819. Legally yachts may pass through the firing area; some do. The range officer is responsible for ceasing fire, but as this disrupts the firing schedule, yachtsmen may find themselves under very considerable pressure from the safety boats to pass clear of the area on the recommended tracks: from Weymouth Pierhead 121° to a turning point at 50°30'N 2°09'W, thence 062° to clear Anvil Point, a course which clears St Alban's Race.

St Alban's Head is easily identified with chapel and CG hut on top. Off the head the dangerous race varies in position and severity. It extends 3M seaward, less in S winds. Overfalls extend 2½M further SW on the ebb than on the flood and are much more dangerous. Either avoid the race by giving the head a berth of 3½M or in good weather and offshore winds use the ½M-wide passage between the head and the race (passage can narrow to 50m in some conditions).

Close inshore the E-going stream starts at Dover +0500, offshore at Dover +0600. The W-going stream starts at Dover – 0020.

There is deep water to close inshore between the hd and Anvil Point (W LtHo). From Anvil Point to Peveril Point rough water is frequent. Durlston Head has a castellated building on top; Peveril Point (CG and FS) has a rocky ledge running ¼M to seaward with R can buoy at end. Stream sets towards the ledge. In bad weather a dangerous race runs seaward of the buoy especially to SE with W-going stream. Between Swanage and Poole lobster-pot buoys are frequent.

On sp ebb tides the tidal streams around Anvil and Peveril Points are stronger close inshore than further out.

Anchorages

Worbarrow Bay 1M E of Lulworth Cove, sheltered from WNW·ESE. Approach on line of W ldg beacons on high ground in NE corner, front ▲, rear ♦, 043°. Anchor in E half of the bay to avoid pipe-line running SSE from Arish Mell Gap: inshore end marked by BY bn, can top. This is in the Gunnery Range area and mooring is forbidden when firing is in progress.

Chapman's Pool W of St Alban's Head. 1·6m in centre of Pool; depths inshore unreliable due to cliff falls. Open from S to SW and swell from SE. If becalmed, W of Kimmeridge Ledge, clear of rocky bottom, may be preferable.

See also separate entries for Lulworth, Swanage and Studland.

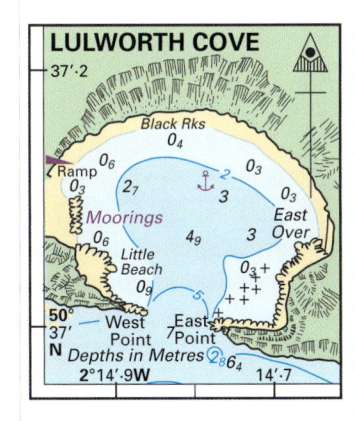

ENGLAND – SOUTH COAST

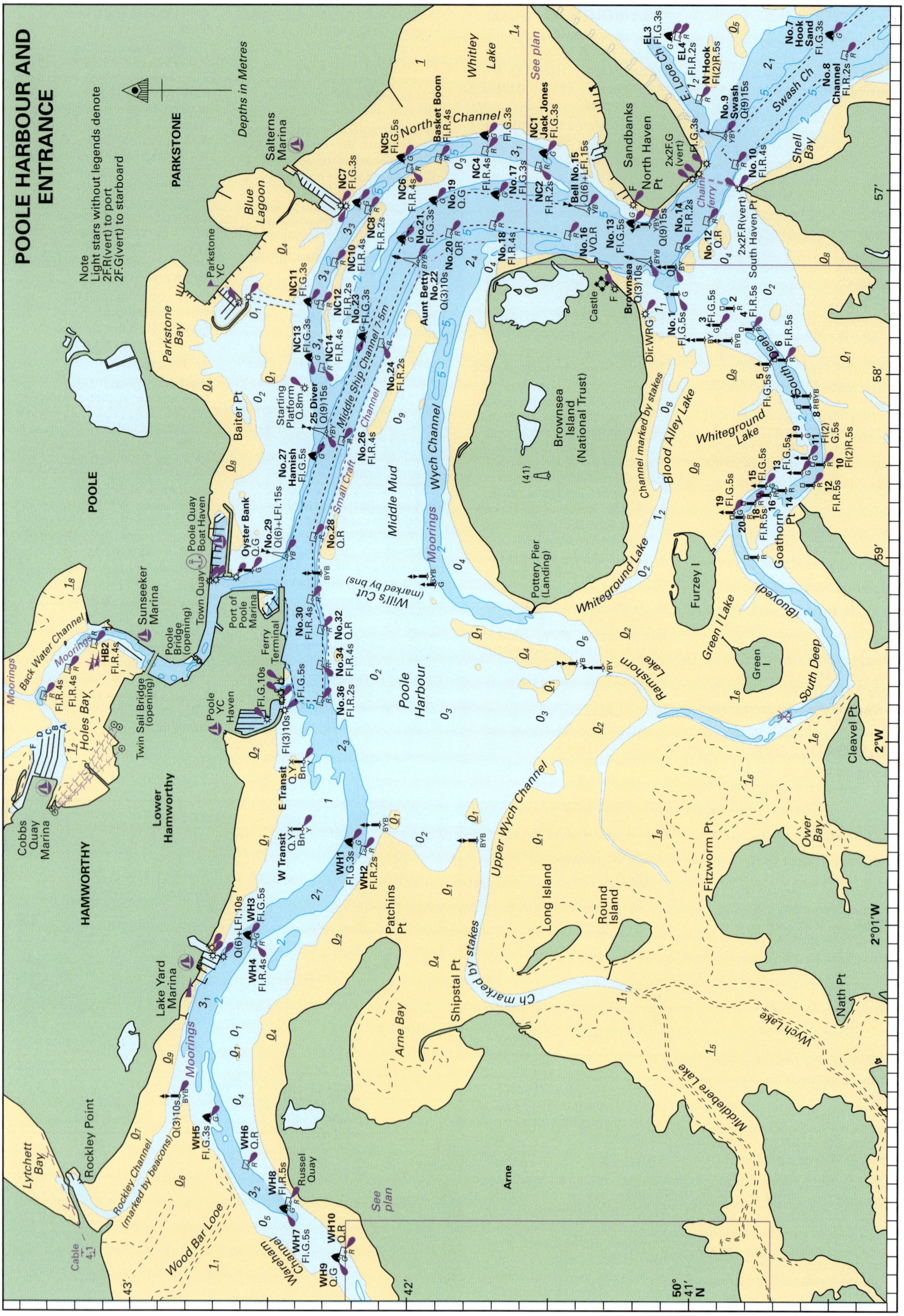
POOLE HARBOUR AND ENTRANCE
Note
Light stars without legends denote
2F.R(vert) to port
2F.G(vert) to starboard
Depths in Metres
PARKSTONE
POOLE
HAMWORTHY
Lower Hamworthy
Parkstone Bay
Parkstone YC
Blue Lagoon
Salterns Marina
Baiter Pt
Poole Quay Boat Haven
Town Quay
Poole Bridge (opening)
Sunseeker Marina
Port of Poole Marina
Ferry Terminal
Poole YC Haven
Twin Sail Bridge (opening)
Cobbs Quay Marina
Holes Bay
Back Water Channel
Moorings
Lake Yard Marina
Rockley Point
Lytchett Bay
Rockley Channel (marked by beacons)
Wood Bar Looe
Wareham Channel
Russel Quay
Arne
Arne Bay
Shipstal Pt
Patchins Pt
Long Island
Round Island
Upper Wych Channel
Ch marked by stakes
Fitzworm Pt
Ower Bay
Cleavel Pt
Nath Pt
Wych Lake
Middlebere Lake
Poole Harbour
Middle Mud
Wych Channel
Will's Cut (marked by bns)
Ramshorn Lake
Green I
Green I Lake
Furzey I
South Deep
(Buoyed)
Goathorn Pt
Whiteground Lake
Blood Alley Lake
Channel marked by stakes
Brownsea Island (National Trust)
Pottery Pier (Landing)
Castle
Middle Ship Channel 7.5m
Small Craft Channel
North Channel
Whitley Lake
Sandbanks
North Haven Pt
Chain ferry
South Haven Pt
Shell Bay
Swash Ch
E Looe Ch
See plan
2°W
2°01'W
50° 41' N

SWANAGE

Standard Port Poole
LW (sp) −0045 (np) −0050
Double HW at springs

MHWS	MHWN	MLWN	MLWS
−0·1m	+0·1m	+0·2m	+0·2m

Approach From W give Peveril Ledge buoy a good berth as tide sets across the ledge. There can be a sharp race off the Pt extending beyond the buoy.

Anchorage There is good shelter from W winds. Anchor 1ca WNW of head of pier, good holding but foul in places. Land on beach.

Facilities Water at pier. Shops, EC Thursday.

STUDLAND BAY

Tidal data as Swanage. A popular, very pleasant anchorage, sheltered from S through W to WNW. Good holding except on visible weed patches. Anchor about 2ca off the beach, 2½m abreast the Yards, three prominent projections in the cliff. In sounding to find suitable depth, be aware of abnormal tide heights; see tidal curves for Poole, p.454. Riding Lts desirable but many yachts do not hoist them – care needed if entering at night. Water skiers in E half of Bay.

Supplies Shops up steep hill. Pub nearer at hand.

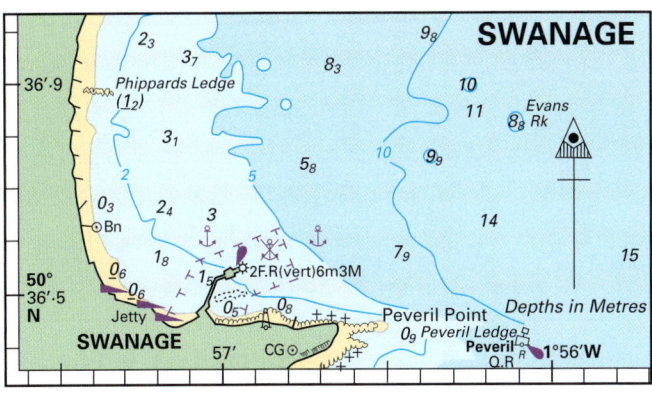

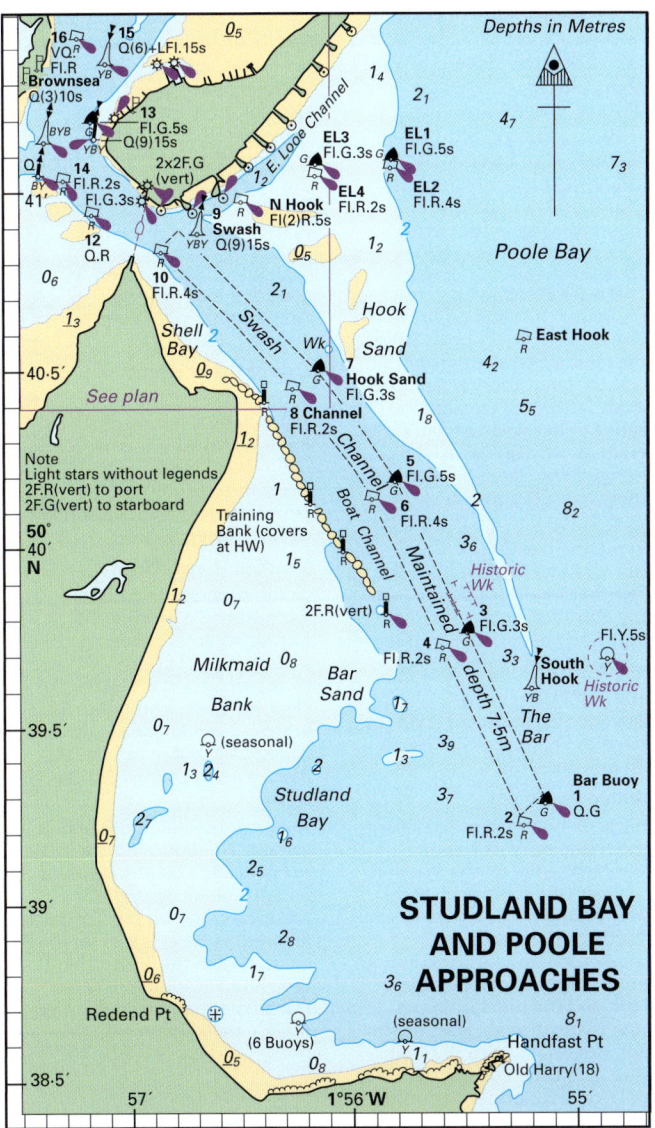

POOLE HARBOUR

Standard Port Poole
See tidal curves, p.454

An extensive natural hbr with quays at the town, many channels and islands, several marinas and anchorages. There is considerable commercial traffic, including that from the oil-field base at Furzey Is. Monitor VHF 16/14.

LW (Town Quay) Poole LW. See tidal curves, p.454.

HW sp (when LW is between 0230 and 0830 or 1430 and 2030) is about 5hrs after LW; a second, lesser, HW is 4hrs after that, 3hrs before next LW.

HW np (LW between 2030 and 0230 or 0830 and 1430) is just over 3hrs before the next LW. There may also be a first, lesser, HW at nps or there may be a rise, a stand for 2hrs and then another rise to main HW. Range only 0·5m.

HW related to Town Quay is: Entrance −0030, Russel Quay +0015, Wareham Quay +0030.

Variations in tide levels above CD in different parts of the area are small and levels can be taken as:

MHWS	MHWN	MLWN	MLWS
2·2m	1·7m	1·2m	0·6m

but Wareham:

MHWS	MHWN	MLWN	MLWS
2·2m	1·7m	1·2m	0·9m

These heights are subject to a variation of ±0·3m according to barometric pressure and wind direction.

Streams in entrance are ingoing Dover −0600 3kn; outgoing −0115, 4¾kn. Outgoing stream is weak for first 3hrs.

Approach From W, to clear shoals off Handfast Point, keep Anvil Point LtHo open until you pick up the Poole Lts, then head up the Swash Channel. Avoid Handfast Point tide-rip on the ebb or in a breeze. From the E, in reasonable conditions, small craft need not round Bar Buoy but should join the Swash Channel well S of No.3 buoy, Fl.G.3s, according to draft and rise of tide.

Strong winds between S and E cause a heavy sea.

Entrance Swash Channel, buoyed and lighted and dredged to 7·5m, leads to the entrance between Sandbanks and S Haven Pt. A chain ferry, that has right of way, runs between these two points and it must be given a clear berth as the chains are near the surface at each end of the ferry. Use engine.

W of Swash Channel is a training bank which covers at half tide and is marked by five bns, R can tops. A subsidiary Boat Channel, 3m, for small craft, between the training bank and Swash Channel, runs from the port-hand bn, 2F.R(vert), to rejoin Swash Channel just before the entrance.

East Looe is another subsidiary channel for small craft from E parallel to the shore close to S side of Sandbanks. Outer end, marked by EL1 and EL2 buoys (see plan), may have less than 1m. Only use with sufficient rise of tide and do not attempt in swell or onshore winds.

For commercial shipping entering the hbr the centre of the channel may occasionally be shown by a DirWRG sectored light, the W sector bearing 299°.

Signal Orange flashing warning light at South Haven Pt when large vessel navigating between Swash Channel and Aunt Betty buoy in Middle Ship Channel.

Interior Channels It is advisable to keep to the marked channels: outside them the water is generally shallow. However recreational craft are advised to avoid using the main channel when leaving hbr and keep close to Brownsea and No.14 buoys.

South Deep Channel is to port after No.14 buoy, Fl.R.5s, and leads to the network of channels S of Brownsea Is and the oil base on Furzey Is, to which pt there are Lt bns (mainly stb).

Anchoring Avoid oyster beds, marked by YW buoys and stakes, and mussel beds at W end of Blood Alley Lake. Otherwise anchor:
• Between Brownsea E Cardinal and first green beacon at entrance of South Deep. Keep out of channel.
• In South Deep W of Goathorn Pt or W of Green Is; tripper boats, keep out of fairway.
• For shallow bilge-keel craft, Blood Alley Lake, 0·3m, mud.

Middle Ship, Small Craft, Northern and Little Channels The main channel bears NNE round N Haven W card Lt bn after which the array of buoys, bns and moored yachts may appear confusing. At No.15 Middle Ground S card Lt buoy the Northern Channel (marked as Main Channel on some charts) is to stb, NE; and Middle Ship Channel (used by large vessels) to port, due N. Both are buoyed and lit and bear round to W to Poole, joining again at No.25 (Diver) W card Lt bn.

Small craft are advised to take the Northern, rather than Middle Ship, Channel; but if following the latter there is on SW side, from No.18 R can buoy, a Small Craft Channel running alongside Middle Ship Channel. It is marked on its south side by R stakes with R can tops and on its north side by the Middle Ship Channel port-hand buoys, mostly Fl.R.4s.

WAREHAM CHANNEL

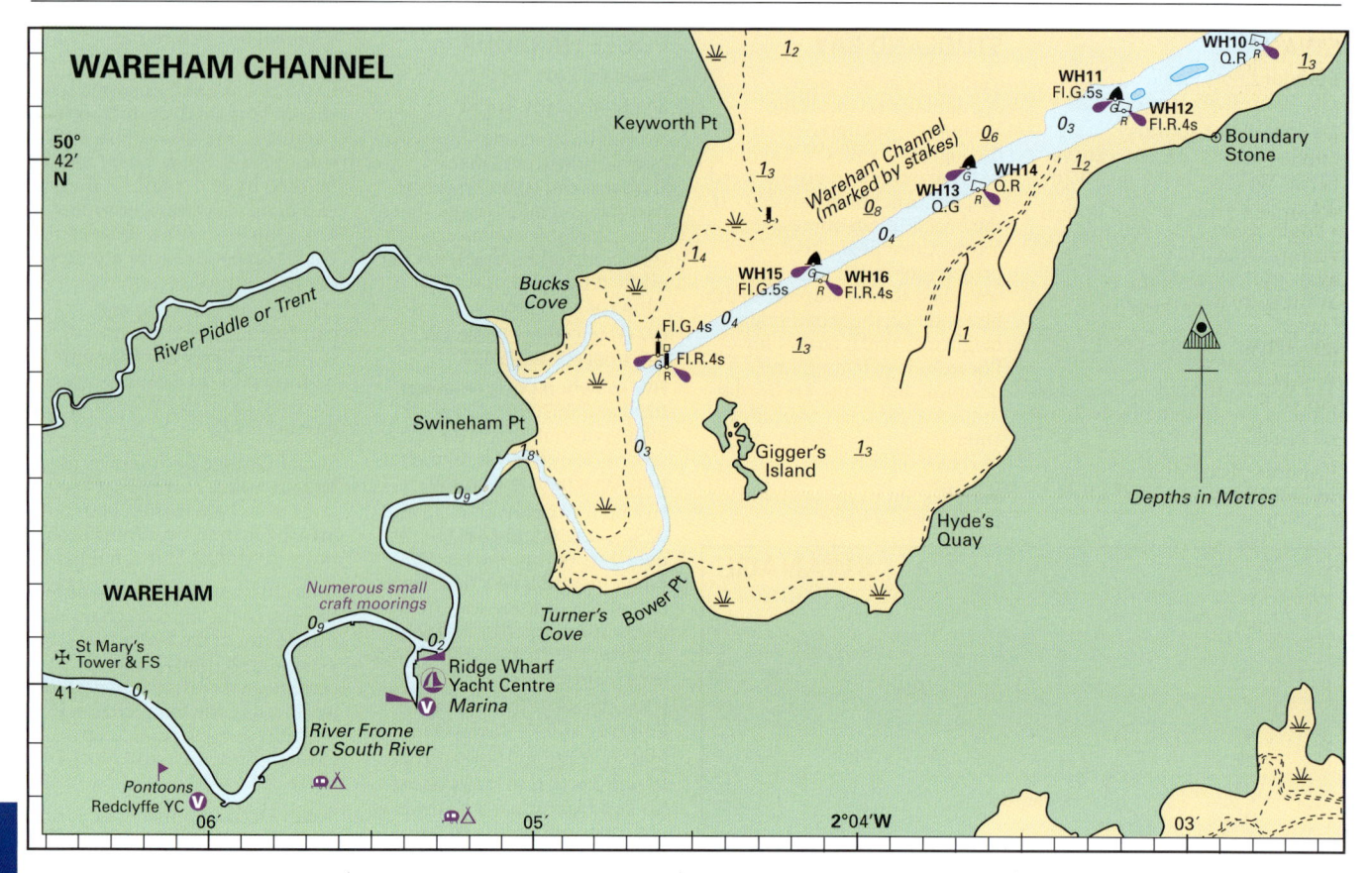

It is 30m wide, for craft with up to 1·5m draught, and goes as far as No.28 R can buoy.

Entrance to Poole Quays is via Little Channel after No.29 (Stakes) S card Lt buoy. Little Channel is buoyed N of the lifting br.

Poole Bridge and Twin Sail Bridge Call *Poole Bridge* on VHF 12 for opening times. IPTS Traffic Lts. Only 2m clearance when closed.

Berthing Anchoring is forbidden in Middle Ship, Northern and Little Channels. Moorings are sometimes available from yards.
• Salterns Marina, entered from NC7 buoy in North Channel, may have visitors' berths.
• Parkstone Haven (part of Parkstone YC), entered via a channel dredged to 1·5m from NC11 buoy in North Channel, welcomes visitors. Call Parkstone Haven on VHF 80 or 37.
• Port of Poole Marina.
• Town Quay entered via Little Channel. Can be crowded and difficult to clear on ebb with several craft outside; very uncomfortable with strong winds from S to E. Berth in vacant space or alongside another vessel of similar size to yours. Vessels under 15m should use Poole Quay Boat Haven below if space is available.
• Poole Quay Boat Haven, immediately E of Town Quay. For both Port of Poole Marina and Poole Quay Boat Haven call *Poole Quay Boat Haven* on VHF 80. You will then be

POOLE TO CHICHESTER

The main hazards are Christchurch Ledge and the Shingles Bank on NW side of the Needles Channel. Studland Bay and Poole approaches are frequently used for military parachute exercises when voluntary exclusions zones are set up. Call *Poole Harbour Control* on VHF 14 for information.

Passage Lts	BA No
Bridge Lt buoy	0527.6

VQ(9)10s5M, Racon(T) (–)

The Needles 0528
Oc(2)WRG.20s24m17/13M
Horn(2)30s (R sector over Shingles) and dangers to S of Island

Hurst Point 0538.1
Fl(4)WR.15s23m13/11M
DirIso.WRG.4s19m21–17M
(W sector 041° over Needles Channel)

St Catherine's Point 0774
Fl.5s41m25M
(+F.R.13M 099°·vis-116°)

Nab Tower 0780
Fl.10s17m12M, Horn(2)30s AIS

Tides
From Christchurch to Southampton there is a stand around the time of HW Portsmouth during which some places have a small fall followed by a second HW; others have a second HW only at sps.

Streams related to HW Dover
Poole Bay,
offshore +0530NE –0030SW, inshore +0500E –0115W, 1kn

Needles entrance
+0530E; –0030W

North Channel to Hurst approx +0500E –0100W

Ryde Pier, N of +0415E –0130W

S of Isle of Wight +0530ENE –0045WSW, 5kn between St Catherine's Point and Dunnose.

Nab Tower HWD W +0100SW +0615E –0400ENE –0245NE –0030N

The E stream sets towards Christchurch ledge and across the Shingles. The W stream sets well S of Durlston Head and Anvil Point. Streams are weak inside the line Handfast Point to Hengistbury Head and in Christchurch Bay but are strong across Christchurch Ledge and the Shingles. Between Poole and Wight the flood sets strongly into Poole Bay.

Hengistbury Head is prominent with dark red cliffs, 18m high and a lookout, conspic, with FS 4½ca to W. There are overfalls on Christchurch Ledge on the ebb. Christchurch Priory open SW of the lookout on Warren Hill (W side of Hengistbury Head), 333° leads SW of it. If crossing the Ledge in fair weather aim for a point about 1½M SE of Hengistbury Head. Close inshore there are rocks, awash at LW, ½ca off the head of the groyne.

In fog the position of Needles Lt can often be gauged from the fact that fog lies lightly to W of the entrance, but hangs in a dark and heavy patch on the cliff overlooking the Lt.

The Solent
Entrance to the Solent is via the Needles Channel or the North Channel.

Within the Solent
Hazards are the mud flats along the N side of West Solent, Gurnard Ledge on the S side W of West Cowes, Bramble Bank (dries 1·1m) in the entrance to Southampton Water, the submerged obstruction running inshore from N of Horse Sand Fort, and the remains of the submerged barrier, least depth 2m, extending 3·5ca SW from No Man's Land Fort. Movements of large ships present another Hazard – see *Shipping Movements* under *Central Solent, p.59.*

East of Isle of Wight
Note that the Nab Channel, N of Nab Tower, is for deeply-laden inbound tankers; further south, deep draft vessels manoeuvre to enter the channel and there are pilot boarding areas SE and SW of Nab Tower.

South of Isle of Wight
At night, rounding St Catherine's Point from NW, keep in Needles W sector until St Catherine's Lt bears 064° and keep S of latter's F.R sector. To clear the worst of the race (bad in strong wind against tide conditions, severe to SE of the Point with W gales) keep 2M offshore.

Anchorages are to be found in suitable conditions off the coast in Poole and Christchurch Bays, and off the Isle of Wight in Freshwater Bay on the SW coast and N of St Helen's Fort on the E coast. Within the Solent there are good anchorages NW of Hurst Point (see *Keyhaven plan, p.57*), and in Osborne Bay.

directed to an available berth. Call Poole Quay Boat Haven before entering from N end of Little Channel. 100 berths, all for visitors, but at peak times phone in advance to reserve berth. W half has 3·5m, E half 2·5m.

• **Poole Yacht Club** welcomes visitors when berths are available. Visitors must check availability before entering the Haven. Call *Pike* on VHF 37/80 or ☎ 01202 672687.

Wych Channel Adjacent to No.18 R can buoy a bn marks the S edge of the entrance to Wych Channel, rounding Brownsea Is to N, marked with stakes. There are two shallow (1m) short-cuts across the mud linking Wych to the main channel: Ball's Lake, near the NE tip of Arne peninsula, and Wills Cut from NW corner of Brownsea Is. Each is marked by stakes.

Berthing Anchor
• Clear of moorings (e.g. to NW of Brownsea Is) clear of oyster beds or off Pottery Pier.
• Shipstal Point 1m.

Wareham Channel is the continuation of the main channel after the entrance to Poole Quay and leads to the entrance to River Frome and thence to Wareham. It is buoyed and staked and is lit at the main turning pts as far Gigger's Island; it is navigable at HW to Wareham for craft up to 1·5m draught. Channel subject to silting.

Berthing Anchor off Russel Quay or elsewhere according to draft and oyster beds S of Hamworthy. Alongside berths:
• Ridge Wharf in River Frome.
• Redclyffe YC welcomes visitors ☎ 01929 551227, VHF 80.
• Wareham Town Quay is not recommended except for very short stay as tourist launches are liable to berth alongside.

Supplies
• Diesel in Parkstone Haven;
• Fuel at Corals, oposite Town Quay, just below br;
• Fuel at Ridge Wharf on River Frome, and at most yards. Shops at Poole and Wareham. Visitors to Parkstone Haven are temporary members of Parkstone YC, with bar and restaurant.

☎/VHF HM 01202 440 230, VHF 16, 14 (24hrs); Salterns Marina 709 971, VHF 80, 37; Parkstone Haven 743 610, VHF 80, 37 *(Parkstone Haven)*; Poole Quay Boat Haven 649488, VHF 80 *(Poole Quay Boat Haven)*; Cobb's Quay 674299, VHF 80, 37 *(CQ Base)*; Ridge Wharf 01929 554434; for moorings: Sandbanks Boatyard and Marina (01202) 708068; Poole Moorings and Jetties 695 336 or 07976 238857; Dorset Yacht Co (Hamworthy) 674531
www.phc.co.uk

CHRISTCHURCH
Standard Port Portsmouth
HW (sp) –0230 (np) +0030
LW (sp) –0035 (np) –0035
MHWS MHWN MLWN MLWS
–2·9m –2·4m –1·2m –0·2m

At sps there is 5hrs rise, 3½hrs stand, 4hrs ebb. At nps there is 5½hrs flood, 2¾hrs stand and 4¼hrs ebb. The ebb in the entrance is fierce after the second HW. In the hbr, tide height can be critical – see Poole tidal curves.

Entry safe during HW stand for draughts up to 1·1m (1·3m at sps) except in fresh winds between S and E.

Approach Entrance lies about ¾M NE of Hengistbury Head. From E, leave the Solent via North Channel. From W give groyne off Hengistbury Head ¾M berth to clear Beerpan Rocks. Beware of Clarendon Rocks, a groyne of stones running 1½ca offshore, 3ca SSW of entrance. Keep offshore to make approach from SE.

Bar has normally 0·3 to 0·6m but varies in depth and position.

Entrance over the bar is marked in season by two lateral buoys and about four pairs of sph buoys. There is a Lt Fl.G.2s at NE end of Mudeford Quay. Best times to enter: sps from 2hrs before first HW to second HW; nps at or between the two HWs. Streams in The Run are strong. The ebb there and in the hbr continues until 1½hrs after LW. Beware fishermen shooting nets in The Run.

Inside, after Mudeford Quay bear sharply to port and give first G sph buoy a wide berth to stb. The channel is well buoyed to Grimsbury Pt after which moorings indicate it. Leave moored boats to stb until the pontoon jetty, after which leave them to port. Depths in the two rivers vary from 0·6m to 1·3m.

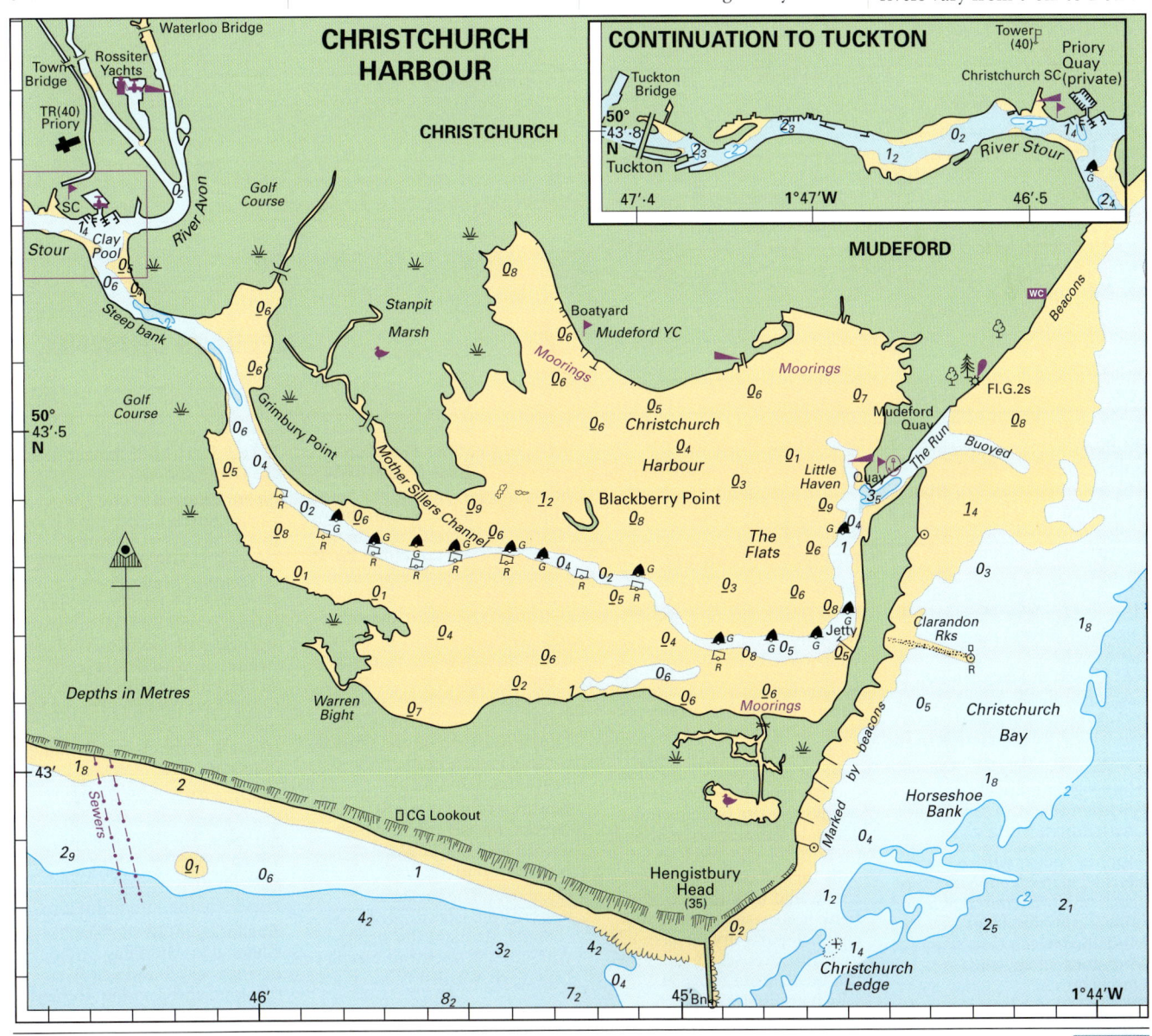

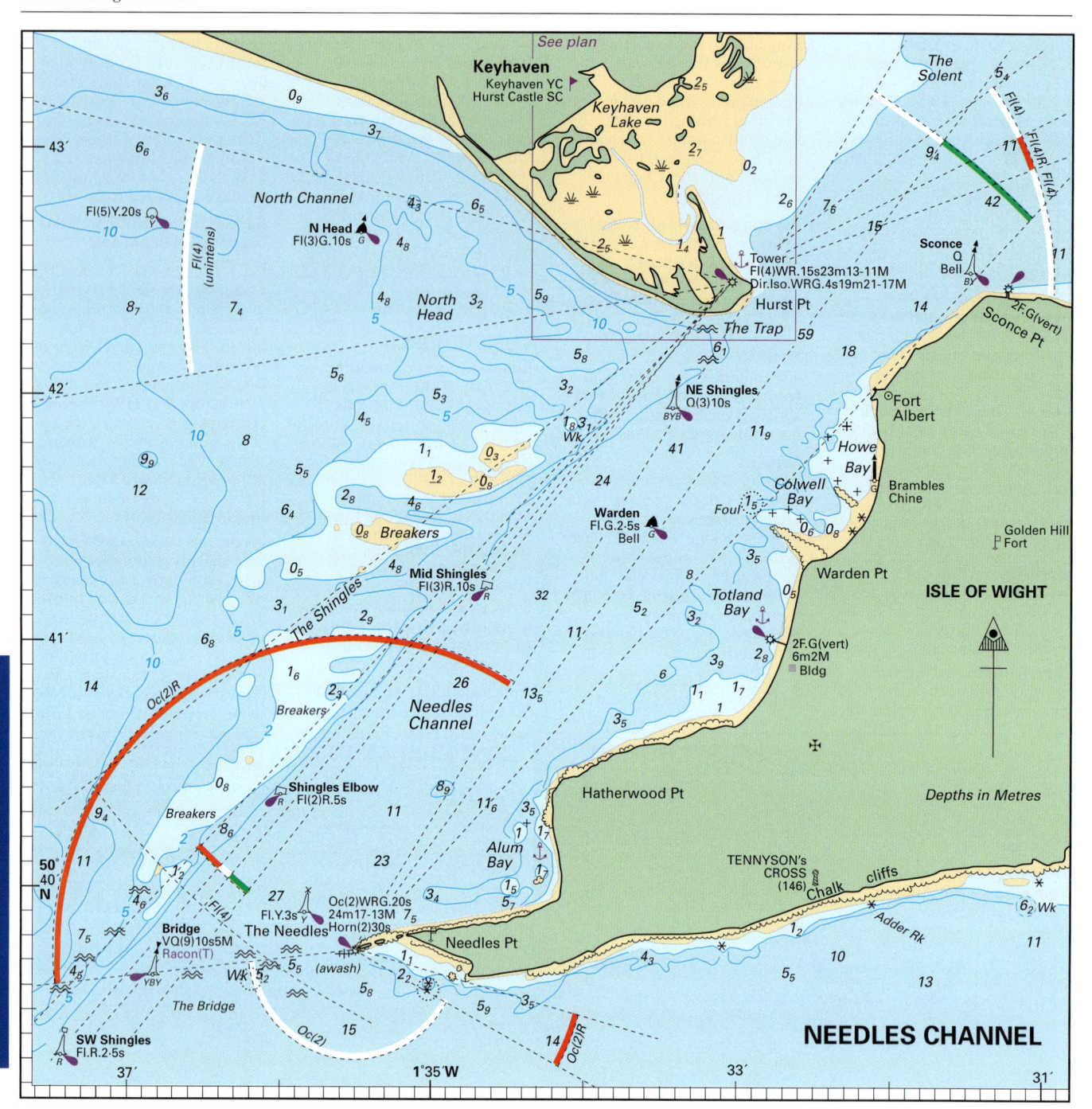

Berthing Anchoring room is limited but possibilities are:
- In reach running SSW from Mudeford Quay between Black House and pontoon jetty; restrict swing with two anchors.
- In unmarked pool (0·6m) close to N side of Hengistbury Hd, entered from reach above pontoon jetty.
- At SE end of Steepbank on W side immediately below moorings in approach to rivers.
- In Clay Pool at junction of the rivers.

Moorings enquire at Christchurch SC, G Elkins or Christchurch Marine.

Supplies Fuel at Christchurch Marine; water from Mudeford beach or Christchurch SC. Limited supplies from Mudeford beach café. Shops at Mudeford village and Christchurch.

☏ Harbour Authority Christchurch Borough Council 01202 486 321; Christchurch SC 483 150; Christchurch Marine 483 250.

NEEDLES CHANNEL

DS (Needles entrance) Portsmouth +0520E; –0045W

For lights see Poole to Chichester Passage Notes.

With wind against the ebb, the entrance is uncomfortable, at times dangerous, and N Channel is then to be preferred. Even at other times conditions can be difficult for small craft when there are strong winds. The tide sets across the Shingles on both the ebb and flood; this calls for extreme care when SW-bound with the ebb. The Bank is encroaching into the channel, parts drying as much as 1·2m; after severe gales there can be deposits above HW level which gradually disperse.

Needles Channel The main entrance is made between SW Shingles port-hand pillar buoy, Fl.R.2·5s, and Br W card buoy, VQ(9)10s Racon(T) (–), in the W sector (041°) of Hurst Point Lt Iso.WRG.4s. The Br can be very turbulent and small craft will generally find it smoother to cross 3ca E of the Br buoy, about a third of the distance to Needles LtHo, just E of the Iso.G sector of Hurst Point Lt. (Note that a W sector of the Fl(4)WR.15s Lt on the same tr is visible when Hurst Point bears less than 053°).

Beware of the Goose Rock and wrecks, awash at LW, which extend nearly 2ca W from Needles LtHo.

Once over The Br, steer towards the Island side of the channel. At night this brings you into a W sector of Needles Lt, Ldg to Warden G con buoy, Fl.G.2·5s, clear of dangers off the Island shore.

North Channel From Christchurch Ledge make good to NE (flood setting onto Shingles to stb) in the northern W sector of Hurst Point Lt (Fl(4)WR.15s) to North Head buoy, G con Fl(3)G.10s, then steer SE with Golden Hill Fort (white) on with Brambles Chine, parallel with Hurst Spit to leave NE Shingles E card Lt buoy to stb. Streams run strongly in the channel, mainly in its direction.

Caution There are nearly always overfalls in Hurst narrows. The Trap is a spit which runs S from Hurst Point with 0·2m at its inshore end which the tide sets onto.

Anchorages: Off the Needles Channel in Alum Bay (mind drying rocks 1 and 2ca W of coloured cliffs) and in Totland

The Cruising Almanac

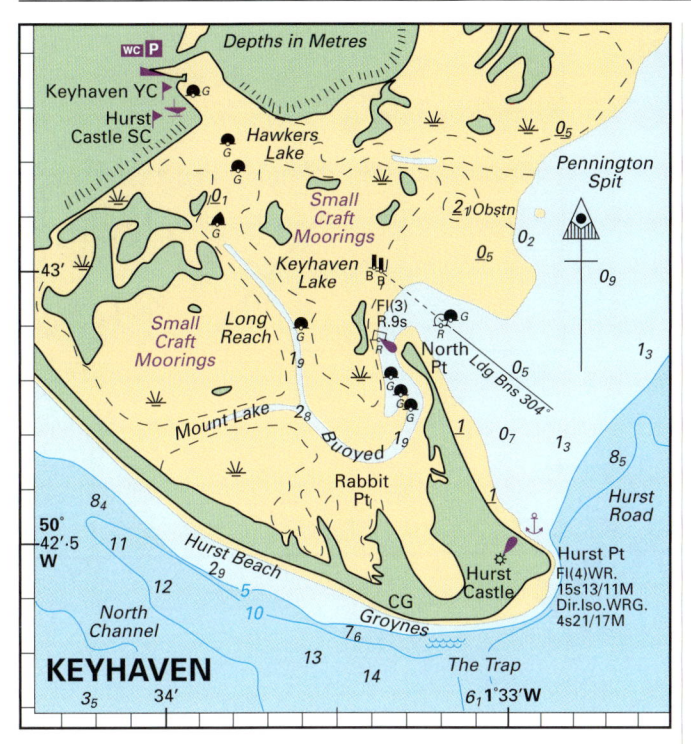

Bay where the 2F.G(vert) Lts on the pier provide a guide at night; also a good anchorage NW of Hurst Pt (*see Keyhaven plan*). These anchorages are useful when waiting for a fair stream through the channel.

KEYHAVEN

Standard Port Portsmouth
At Hurst Point
HW (sp) −0115 (np) +0005
LW (sp) −0030 (np) −0025
MHWS MHWN MLWN MLWS
−2·0m −1·5m −0·5m −0·1m
See tidal curves, p.457

Sps: rise for 6½hrs to 1st HW, fall for 1hr, stand and small rise to 2nd HW for 1½hrs, fall for 3½hrs. Nps: Rise for 7½hrs, followed by fall, with no stand or 2nd HW.

DS (Hurst Narrows) Portsmouth +0515NE −0100SW, 4kn

A small attractive creek with limited room for anchoring.

Approach From E, keep Hurst Point Lt tr bearing not less than 225°. From W, give The Trap off S side of Hurst Castle a berth of 1½ca.

Entrance The bar changes. Do not attempt entrance in strong E winds. The leading line, marked by two small RW horizontally striped boards (inconspic) which are moved from time to time, is generally about 300°. The entrance is marked by two small buoys, G and R. Inside, the channel is marked by a few stb buoys, one port buoy just inside the entrance and the line of private moorings. Pass round the bows of all moored craft as the areas astern are shallow.

Berthing The river is congested with private moorings but space to anchor may be found in the bay just inside the entrance. The heavy mooring there is used by the tender for maintenance at the castle. Land on the spit or at Keyhaven hard. Short-term mooring is generally possible at HW at Keyhaven Quay.

In favourable conditions it may be preferable to anchor outside the entrance where there is more room. Sound to find a suitable depth with Hurst Lt tr bearing about 220°. Land on beach near ferry pier. Riding Lt essential at night.

Facilities Fuel at W Solent Boat Builders in emergency only; otherwise by can from Milford. Water at Keyhaven YC and at River Warden's Office. Inn at Keyhaven; shops at Milford. EC Wednesday.

ⓘ Harbour Authority New Forest DC, 023 80285 000; River Warden 01590 645 695; Keyhaven YC 01590 642 165.

YARMOUTH (ISLE OF WIGHT)

Standard Port Portsmouth
HW (sp) −0105 (np) +0005
LW (sp) −0025 (np) −0030
MHWS MHWN MLWN MLWS
−1·7m −1·2m −0·3m 0·0
See tidal curves, p.457

DS Portsmouth +0500E −0100W. Stream runs hard across the outer half of pier but weaker near the entrance where hbr stream takes over.

A very popular hbr, likely to be full early on Saturday afternoons in season.

Approach From W keep 2ca offshore to clear Black Rock (dries) until abreast Y buoy, Fl.Y.5s, then aim for the pier, about a third of its length from the head, until Ldg marks in line. From E beware anglers' lines in rounding pier.

Entrance Ldg Lts F.G front and rear, W diamonds black band on W posts, 188°. There are 2F.R(vert) each side of the ferry ramp and Fl.G.5s on dolphin at W side of entrance. Illuminated notice 'Harbour Full' or R flag by day at end of ferry jetty (R flag also at Pierhead) mean no spare berths inside, but there is usually room outside on the visitors' moorings N of breakwater. Failing that, anchor N of moorings, but stream is strong. It is inadvisable to enter under sail because of ferry movements and, in season, congestion. At the dolphin beware of traffic emerging on stb hand from outer line of piles.

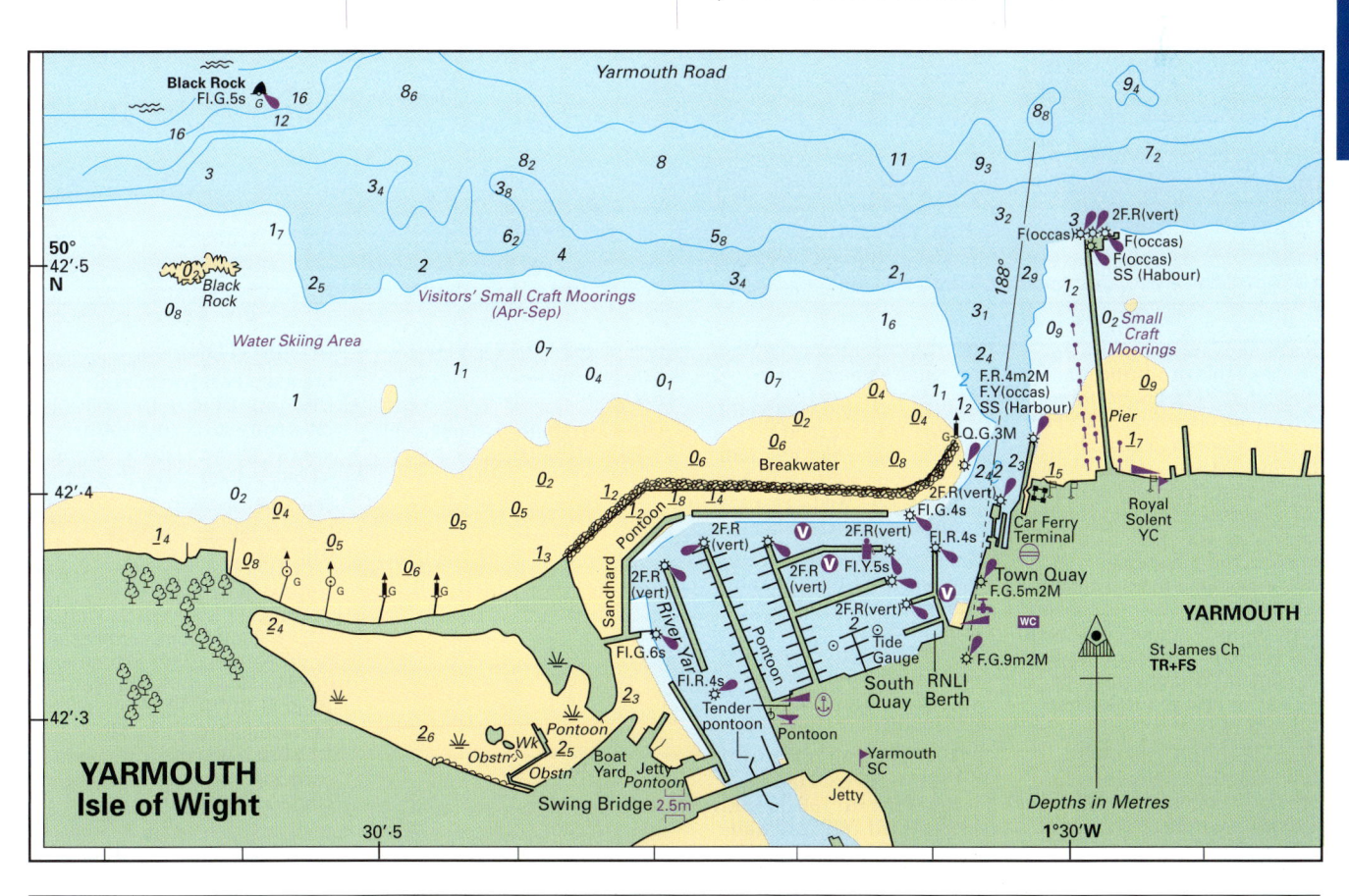

ENGLAND – SOUTH COAST

57

The Cruising Almanac

LYMINGTON

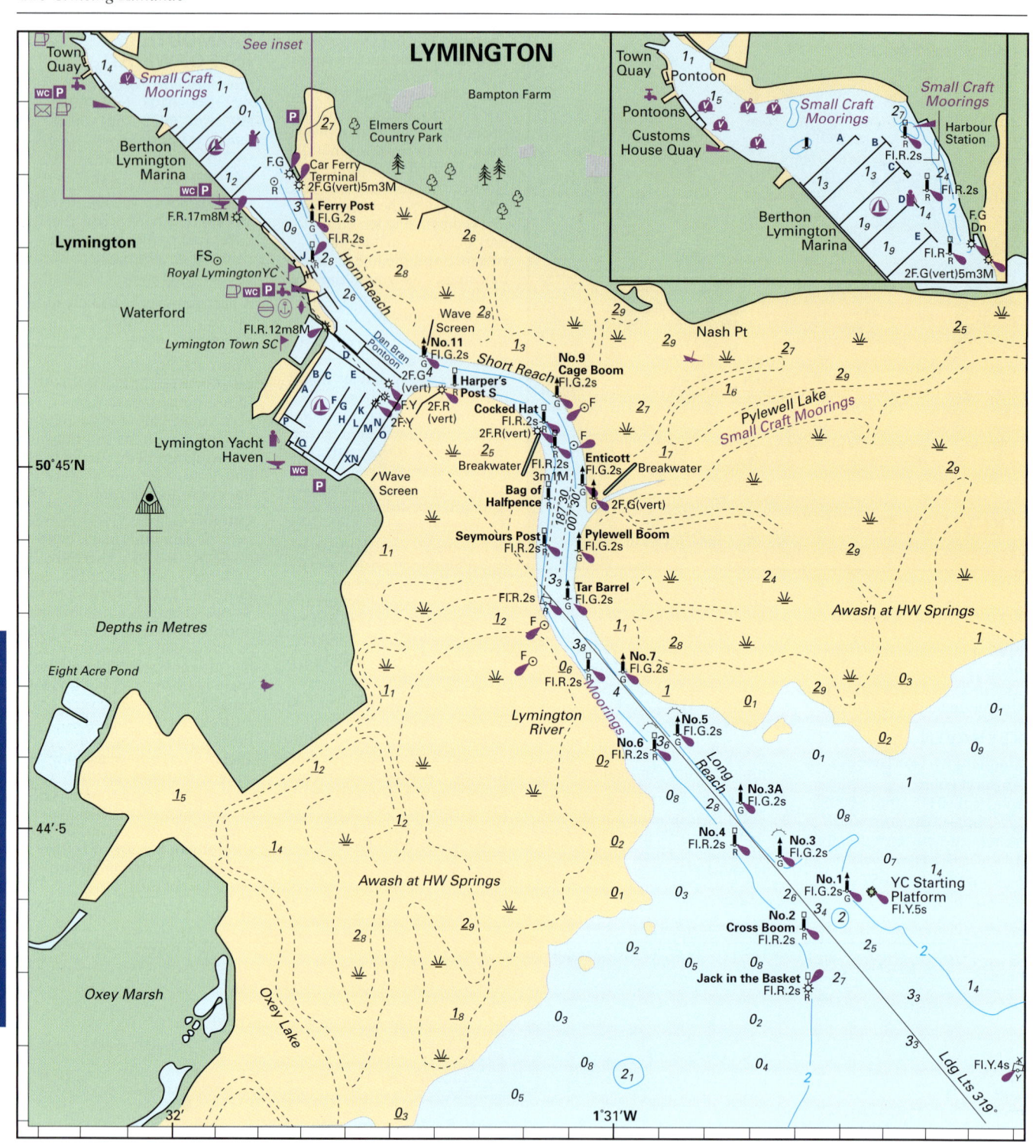

Berthing Walk-ashore berths are bookable in advance through the Harbour Office. Otherwise on arrival call VHF 68 and moor as directed by Berthing Master or find space on a visitors' pontoon, rafting up if necessary. Berthing on S quay only, with permission, for loading and unloading. Moorings sometimes available from the two yards for a longer stay. Br opens about every two hrs in summer; by arrangement in winter. River navigable by dinghy at HW to Freshwater Causeway.

Outside visitors' moorings following 3m contour except two at W end in 2m. Anchor outside according to height of tide, clear of entrance to W of pier. Sand, shingle.

Facilities Fuel and pumpout facilities at E end central pontoon, water also at South Quay. Good shops, including chandlers (EC Wed), also at Freshwater (EC Thurs).

Water taxi serves all moorings, including those outside and anchored craft. Scrubbing berths alongside breakwater – *see plan*. Buses to Freshwater and Newport. Ferry to Lymington. Showers, toilets and laundry on S quay.

☎/**VHF** Harbour office 01983 760 321. VHF 68; Harold Hayles Boatyard 760 373; River Yar Boatyard 760 521; Water taxi 07969 840173, VHF 15; Bridge requests VHF 68, *Yar Bridge*.

www.yarmouth-harbour.co.uk

LYMINGTON

Standard Port Portsmouth
HW (sp) –0110 (np) +0005
LW (sp) –0020 (np) –0020

MHWS	MHWN	MLWN	MLWS
–1·6m	–1·2m	–0·4m	–0·1m

See tidal curves, p.457

DS Portsmouth +0430NE –0130SW

Approach Keep Hurst Lt tr bearing not less than 225° to clear the mud banks either side of the entrance; at night do not go N of W sector of Hurst Point Fl(4)WR.15s until on line of F.R Ldg Lts, 319°. The RLYC starting platform on E corner of entrance is conspic landmark by day.

SOLENT – CHERBOURG PASSAGE NOTES

Cherbourg Passe de l'Ouest is 59M from the Needles, 65M from Nab Tower, so the open water passage will typically take 10 to 15 hours. There are no traffic separation zones on either route but you will cross fairly busy shipping lanes just N and S of 50°N lat.

Starting from Cowes or Southampton Water, the course via the Needles is usually the better choice because it is shorter and, with the prevailing SW'ly wind, you are more likely to complete the crossing in a single reach. In deciding your departure time, it is important to ensure that you get through the Needles channel before the end of the ebb (HW Dover +0400). Also, you will probably want to aim to reach Cherbourg before dusk or after dawn.

In setting a course to steer across the channel, it is best to start by estimating what the direction of the tidal stream will be when you reach the French coast and to set a course to arrive a couple of miles upstream of your destination, taking account of the net tidal vector for the whole crossing. You will need to correct the course as you close the French coast.

Additional considerations apply to the return crossing, from Cherbourg to the Solent. If heading for the Needles it is important to arrive on the flood, with at least an hour in hand to get through Hurst Narrows before the stream turns foul. With strong W or SW winds it may be better to avoid the Needles and enter the Solent through the North Channel (see above) or even via the Nab.

Entrance All craft must give way to Wightlink ferries which take up much of the channel. They pass abreast between Cocked Hat pile and Seymours Post on parallel Ldg lines 008° and 188°. Keep well to stb but remember that in passing they lower the water level and the mud flats are steep-to. The channel is marked by Lt bns as far as ferry terminal opposite Berthon Lymington Marina. The bns are on the edge of the drying mud flats. It is important to follow the natural curves of the river rather than going in a straight line from bn to bn, especially above Cage Boom and Cocked Hat bns. The final stretch to Town Quay is not lit but is navigable at night with care by following lines of moored boats. Entrance to Lymington Yacht Haven is marked by Harper's Post E card Lt bn and 2F.G(vert) on S end of breakwater. Leave both to stb on Ldg Lts F.Y 244°.

Berthing Anchoring in hbr is prohibited. Visitors' berths at Lymington Yacht Haven, Berthon Lymington Marina and at Town Quay (pontoons alongside and fore and aft buoys). Hbr very busy. Seek advice from HM if berthing near Town Quay.

Facilities Fuel at marinas, water but no electricity at Town Quay; all facilities. Chandlers and good shops. Rly.

☎/VHF HM 01590 672 014; R Lymington YC 672 677; Lymington Yacht Haven 677 071, VHF 80, 37; Lymington Marina 647 405, VHF 80, 37. No VHF for Town Quay.

BEAULIEU RIVER

Standard Port Portsmouth
Entrance
Rise for 7h(sp), 7½h(np)
LW   (sp) –0100   (np) –0100

MHWS	MHWN	MLWN	MLWS
–0.8	–0.5	–0.4	+0.1

See tidal curves, p.457

Bucklers Hard
HW (sp) -0040   (np) -0010
LW (sp) +0010   (np) -0010

MHWS	MHWN	MLWN	MLWS
–1.0m	–0.8m	–0.2m	–0.3m

See tidal curves, p.457
DS Portsmouth –0115W +0500E

A beautiful, natural river, winding its way down through wooded countryside, past Buckler's Hard, a historic village with maritime museum, hotel and marina, past Gull Island and mud flats to emerge into the West Solent at Lepe.

Approach From the SW, keep well off the Beaulieu Spit mudbanks until abreast of East Lepe R can buoy, Fl(2)R.5s, to stb and the conspicuous boathouse to port. By day, this boathouse on with the W-most cottage beyond it, heads towards the entrance, intercepting the Ldg line Lepe House in line with No.2 bn, 324°. By night follow in the W sector, 334°, of the DirOc.WRG.4s Lt on the Millennium Bn. From the NE, leave Lepe Spit S card Lt buoy to stb and head SW to intercept one or other Ldg line.

Entrance with 5ft draught should not be attempted 1½h either side of MLWS. The entrance is well marked by closely spaced bns and the outermost mark is a port-hand dolphin with directional Lt Fl.R.5s, visible from seaward.

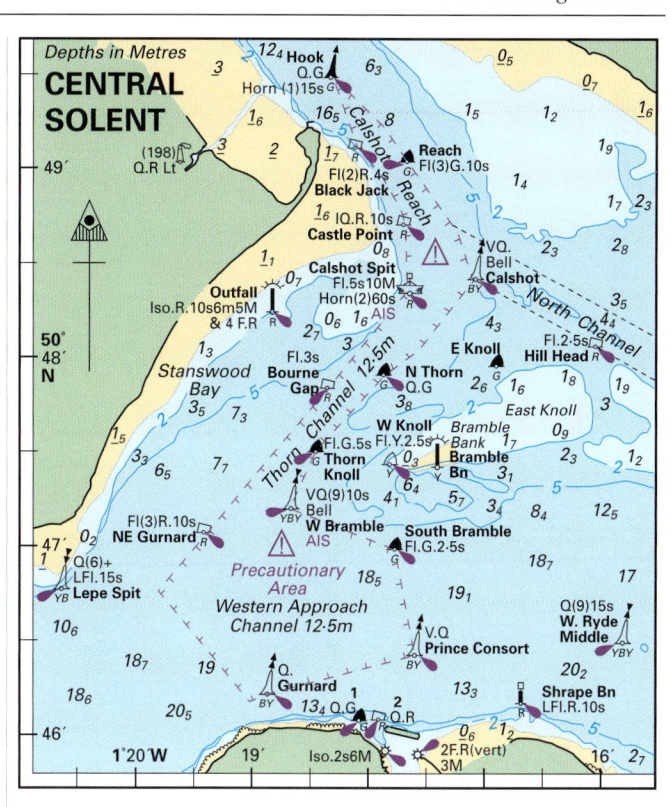

CENTRAL SOLENT

HW (Calshot Castle) Southampton +0015
DS W app Ch Portsmouth +0500E –0115W

Shipping movements Large vessels navigating between Spithead and Southampton invariably use the Western Approach Channel (SW of Bramble Bank), Thorn Channel (W of the Bank) and Calshot Reach (N of the Bank) and have to make two turns, one of them through 120°. These channels are designated a **Precautionary Area** (see plan). Within the area, vessels over 150m in length display a black cylinder by day, 3 F.R(vert) Lts by night, and may be preceded by a patrol launch showing a Fl.Bu Lt. Such vessels are deemed to be enclosed by a Moving Prohibited Zone (MPZ), 200m wide and extending 1000m ahead. Small craft are required to remain outside the MPZ.

Small craft skippers are advised to monitor Southampton VTS, VHF Ch 12, to keep informed of shipping movements. They can also hear warnings of large vessel movements and other information broadcast on VHF Ch 14 on the hour between 0600 and 2200 Fridays to Sundays and Bank Holidays from Easter Good Friday to end of October, and daily between 1 June and 30 September.

The North Channel connects Calshot Reach with the East Solent and is used by smaller commercial shipping.

High Speed Craft mainly plying between Southampton and Cowes, generally use the recognised main channels but may navigate outside them to avoid risk of collision. In good visibility during daylight in the summer they may take a more direct route across the Bramble Bank area. They are not allowed to pass inshore of Calshot Reach and Thorn Channel between Black Jack and Bourne Gap Lt buoys.

Cowes – Southampton Water
The three mile crossing between Cowes and Southampton Water deserves careful planning to take account of shipping movements, Bramble Bank (dries 1·2m), East Knoll (least depth 0·6m) and strong tidal streams, especially between Cowes and the Bramble where the spring rate can reach nearly 4kn. It is best to keep out of the Precautionary Area as far as possible, particularly the Western Approach Channel where large vessels may turn through 120° and the stream can exceed 2·5kn. The Bramble beacon, Y, unlit, can be hard to see but once spotted is an invaluable guide both to the position of the drying bank and to how one is being set by the stream.

Racing buoys There are several Y racing buoys (not shown in plan) in the area, many of which are lit Fl.Y.4s.

Go to www.scra.org.uk for full details.

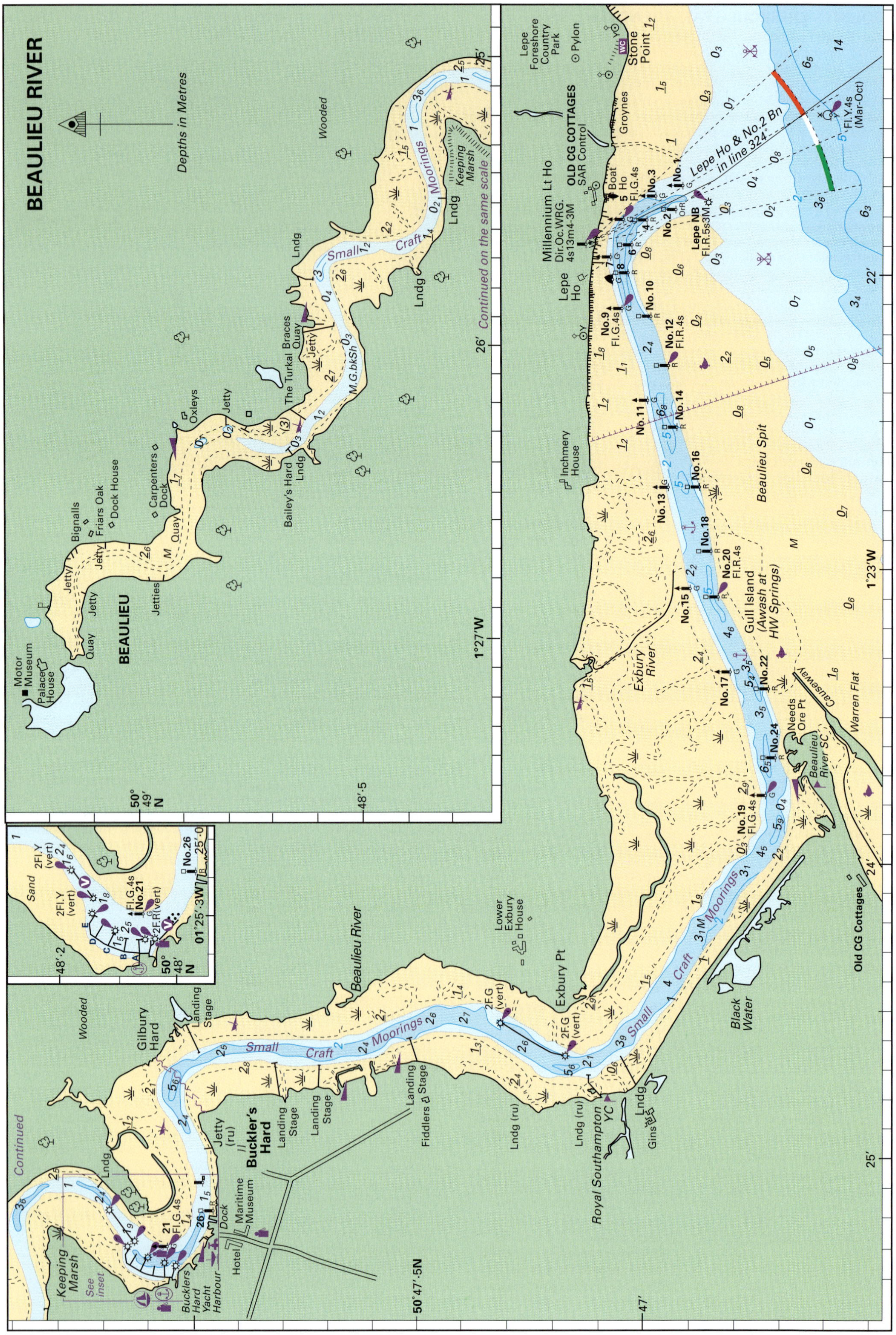
BEAULIEU RIVER
Depths in Metres
Continued on the same scale
BEAULIEU
Motor Museum
Palace House
Bignalls
Friars Oak
Dock House
Carpenters Dock
Oxleys
The Turkal Braces Quay
Bailey's Hard
Wooded
Keeping Marsh
Small Craft Moorings
M.G.bkSh
Millennium Lt Ho
Dir.Oc.WRG.4s13m4-3M
OLD CG COTTAGES
SAR Control
Lepe Foreshore Country Park
Pylon
Stone Point
Groynes
Boat Ho
Lepe Ho
Lepe Ho & No.2 Bn in line 324°
Lepe NB
Fl.R.5s3M
Fl.Y.4s (Mar-Oct)
Inchmery House
Exbury River
Beaulieu Spit
Gull Island (Awash at HW Springs)
Needs Ore Pt
Beaulieu River SC
Causeway
Warren Flat
Black Water
Old CG Cottages
Lower Exbury House
Exbury Pt
Royal Southampton YC
Gins
Fiddlers
Landing Stage
Beaulieu River
Buckler's Hard
Maritime Museum
Hotel
Bucklers Hard Yacht Harbour
Gilbury Hard
See inset
Sand
50°47'·5N
1°27'W
1°23'W
01°25'·3W

Channel is well marked, initially by bns with R and G reflectors, of which three stb and two port are lit; after the bns there are perches. Least depth 1·5m to Buckler's Hard.

Berthing Anchor in first reach up to Needs Oar Point clear of fairway; strong stream. Anchoring prohibited within 1M either side of Buckler's Hard. Marina (2m) and pile moorings at Buckler's Hard. At marina, visitors berth on outer pontoons above marina; beware of stream setting across pontoons. Visitors also at fuel berth pontoon. Report to HM within 24hrs of arrival.

Facilities Water, fuel, gas and limited food supplies from HM, well stocked chandlery, hotel, shop and Maritime Museum at Buckler's Hard. Boat-lift, scrubbing and storage ashore by arrangement with HM. Shops at Beaulieu, 2M by footpath or, depending on tide, by dinghy.

☎ HM and Yacht Harbour 01590 616 200 or 616 234.

NEWTOWN RIVER (ISLE OF WIGHT)

LW Portsmouth –0015. Rise for 6¾hrs (sp), 7¼hrs (np).

An unspoilt sheltered natural hbr renowned for its bird life, especially in winter. Owned by the National Trust; fees for mooring buoys, none for anchoring but donations welcome.

Approach The entrance lies ¾M E of Hamstead Ledge G con buoy Fl(2)G.5s. From E, Yarmouth Pierhead open of Hamstead Pt skirts the edge of Newtown Gravel Banks (3½m).

Entrance Ldg bns (130°): front RW, Y-shaped top, rear W bn, W circle with black surround at top, off Fishhouse Point lead over the bar (1·1m) with a W card buoy Q(9)15s to port in approach. Within, channels are marked by stakes and buoys. Beware of overhead power lines near the head of Clamerkin Lake, clearance 9m.

Berthing W visitors' buoys on both sides of entrance. HM allows double rafting if first occupant agrees. HM may also allocate vacant R buoys to visitors. Anchorage in main channel before the moorings or in Clamerkin Lake as far as the two 'Anchorage Prohibited' notice boards (oyster beds). Poor holding on clay unless anchor well dug in. Anchoring possible E or W of entrance, clear of banks. Landing on Fishhouse Point is prohibited (nature reserve). Land at Shalfleet Quay, Newtown Quay (both dry) or Lower Hamstead on W side of entrance.

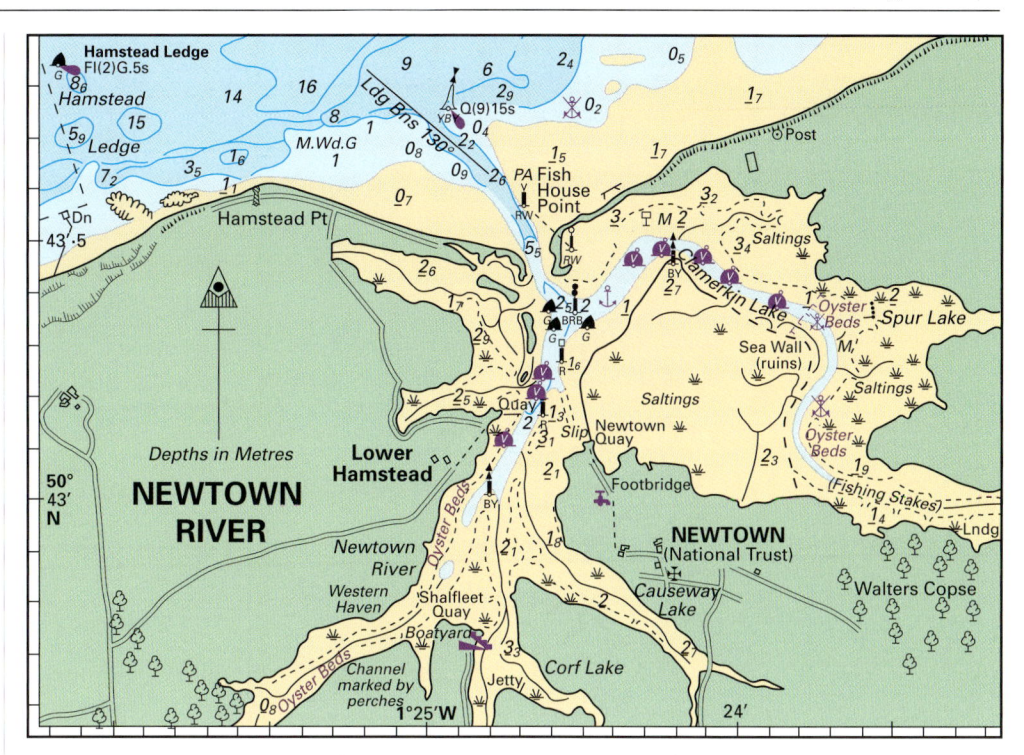

Facilities Fuel and bottled gas at Shalfleet Garage. Food at Shalfleet PO/shop and New Inn, or farm produce at Coleman's Farm; bus to Yarmouth or Newport. Water at Newtown and Shalfleet Quays and Lower Hamstead. Small yard at Shalfleet Quay.

☎ HM 01983 531 424, no VHF. Shalfleet Garage 531 315. New Inn 531 314.

COWES AND RIVER MEDINA (ISLE OF WIGHT)

Standard Port Portsmouth
Cowes
HW (sp) –0014 (np) +0013
LW (sp) –0001 (np) –0016
MHWS   MHWN   MLWN   MLWS
–0·5m   –0·3m   –0·1m   0·0m
Folly Inn
HW (sp) –0015 (np) +0015
LW (sp) 0000   (np) –0020
MHWS   MHWN   MLWN   MLWS
–0·6m   –0·4m   –0·1m   +0·2m

DS Portsmouth +0430E –0115W
In R Medina, Portsmouth +0515 flood, +0015 ebb

A busy port and yachting centre with car ferry and fast cat to Southampton. Accessible at all states of tide and with good all-round shelter in upper reaches.

The new Outer Breakwater and new buoyage is complete. Go to www.cowesharbourcommission.co.uk/ for latest news and local notices to mariners. A new marina inside the east breakwater is planned (2017/8).

Approach Restrictions apply in the area N of line Gurnard buoy to Prince Consort buoy. See Shipping Movements entry for Southampton.

E side of entrance is occupied by Shrape Mud, covered at half-flood. From E, keep 2ca off Old Castle Point.

Entrance This is a 'Narrow Channel' and Col Reg 9 must be obeyed. Enter between the first G (No.1 Q.G) and R (No.2 Q.R) buoys. From HW Cowes –0130 to +0300 there is a strong W-going set in the entrance extending as far as No.4 buoy, Fl(3)R.5s. The channel is straight and well marked by lit port-hand buoys as far as Red Funnel Car Ferry Terminal on the E Cowes side.

For vessels arriving from the east a small craft channel allows passage from the Shrape Bn, LFl.R.10s, through the moorings to the end of the E breakwater. It is marked by three pairs of lit lateral buoys. Note limited depth of 0·2m at CD and for the last 2½h before local HW there is a strong west going tide flowing into and across the Inner Fairway. Auxiliary sailing craft must have engine running if sailing within the harbour.

Beware of the chain ferry which has right of way and exhibits VQ.Y light when moving. Here the sp ebb can reach 4kn – special care needed if heading N past the ferry under these conditions. Below the ferry the ebb runs hardest on E side, above it hardest on the W side.

Cowes

Berthing Anchoring in Cowes Roads. Contact Harbourmaster for swinging moorings in hbr and in Cowes Roads E. Visitors' pontoons on E side ¼M S of chain ferry. No shore access. Marinas on stb, Cowes Yacht Haven and Shepards Wharf Marina, and port, East Cowes Marina. Short stop allowed at Trinity Landing.

Supplies Fuel from Lallows yard ½ca S of Cowes Yacht Haven, and from fuel berth 1ca S of chain ferry. All facilities in Cowes. Water at Trinity Landing. EC Wednesday. Sewage pump out at Shepards Wharf Marina.

River Medina

Above Cowes there are open rural surroundings to Newport. River is navigable for boats up to 2m draught to Folly Inn and boats can reach Newport at –0130 HW Portsmouth to +0230 with 2m draught. Max length 40ft. Channel is buoyed but not lit above Folly Inn. ½M above the inn is Island Harbour Marina entrance lock. Enter alongside jetty.

Berthing Visitors' pontoons opposite Folly Inn; pontoons at Island Harbour Marina, lock open HW±0330, 1·8m draught. At Newport twin-keeled boats tie to a pontoon, fin keels to the quay. Bottom soft mud. Showers and toilets for yachtsmen on quay.

Supplies Island Harbour Marina: Large chandlery, full boatyard facilities. Newport: Water at Town Quay, shops in town.

☎/VHF HM 01983 293 952, VHF 16, 69; for Ferry movements monitor VHF 69; Cowes Yacht Haven 299 975, VHF 80; East Cowes Marina 293 983, VHF 80; Cowes Water Taxi 07551 431 993, VHF 06. Folly Berthing 07884 400 046, VHF 72; Folly Water Bus 07974 864 627, VHF 77. Island Harbour Marina 539 994, VHF 80.

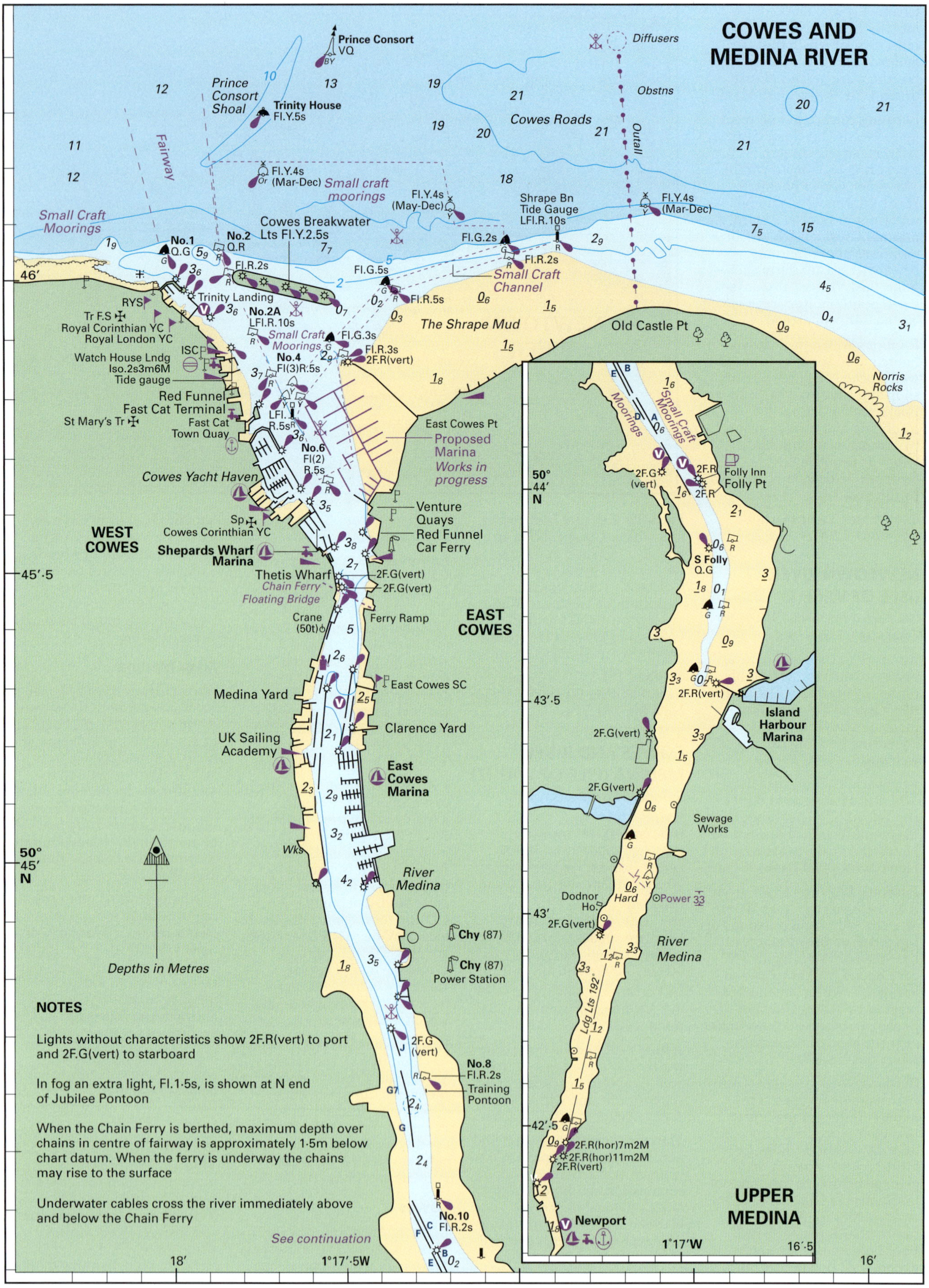

ENGLAND – SOUTH COAST

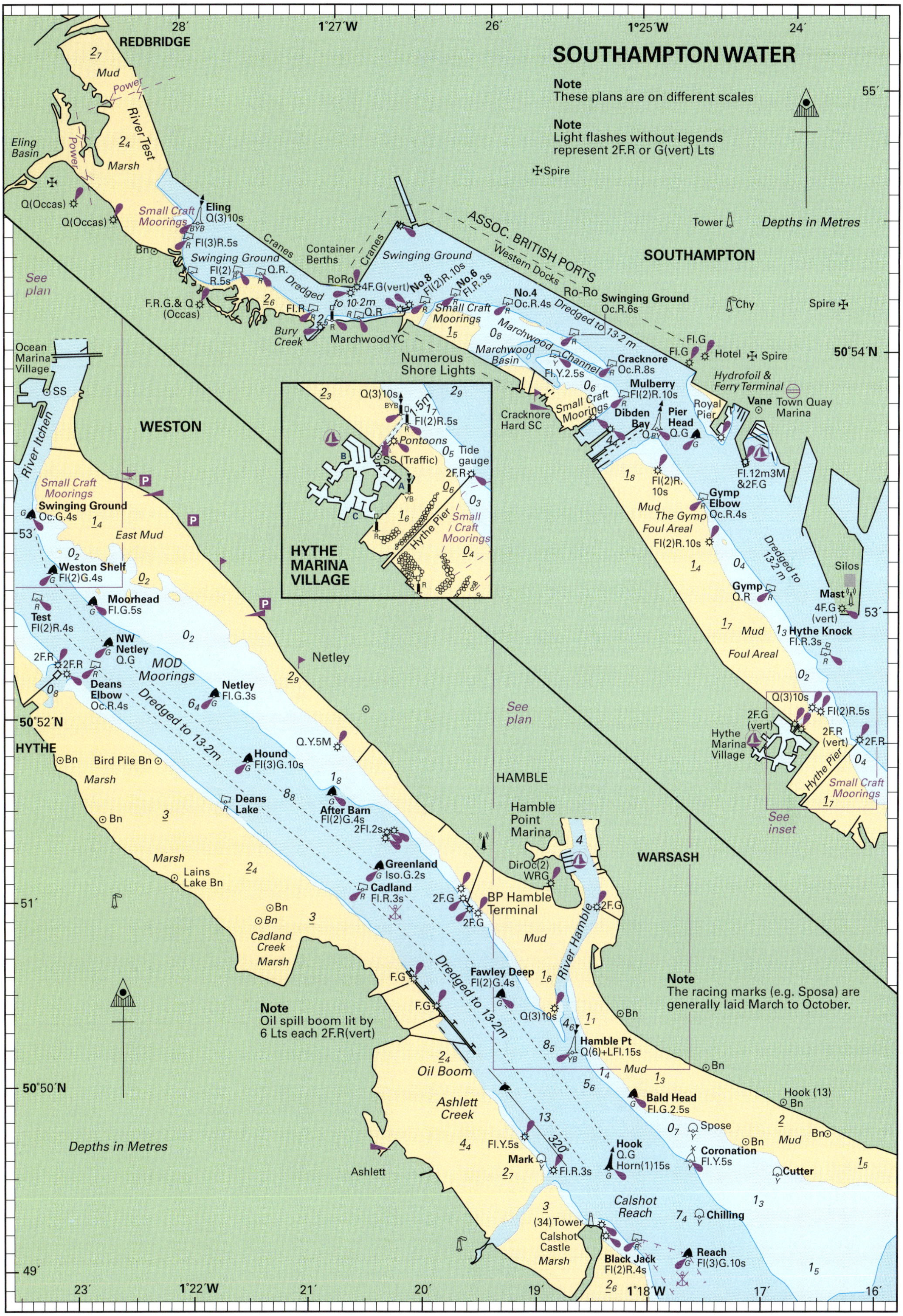

ENGLAND – SOUTH COAST

SOUTHAMPTON WATER

Standard Port Southampton
DS (Calshot) Portsmouth –0100 to +0400 mainly SW, +0500 to –0100 mainly NE
See tidal curves p.456

A very busy commercial hbr and oil terminal with good facilities for yachts.

Approach From E take North Channel, buoyed and lit, entered from E Bramble E card Lt buoy. Coming from Cowes beware Bramble Bank, dries 1·1m. Depending on wind, draft and tidal stream, either keep W of the bank, passing near W Bramble W card Lt buoy and Thorn Knoll G con buoy, Fl.G.5s, or head NE to join the North Channel.

Channel is clearly marked. For River Itchen, head N after passing Weston Shelf G con buoy, Fl(3)G.15s. The entrance to Hythe Marina Village is immediately opposite, just above Hythe Pier. Town Quay Marina is 1M further on, to stb.

Going up River Itchen, Ocean Village Marina is on W side, below Itchen Br which has 24·4m clearance; Ocean Quay and Shamrock Quay about a mile further up, also on W side, and Kemps Marina ½ mile beyond on N bank.

Anchorages
- Calshot Castle inshore near Activities Centre. Shallow.
- Ashlett Creek (just SE of Fawley oil wharf), below the notice board. (Chart BA 2022) The creek itself dries and is full of private moorings. Land at Public Quay near HW or at LW hard, 0·3m. All stores, EC Wednesday.
- Netley, outside moorings in 2m.
- Hythe Pier, N of pierhead, 2m, clear of ferry. (These four anchorages are exposed to wash from commercial traffic).
- Marchwood near former power intake at top of permanently navigable water; local YC.
- Clear of moorings in former power station basin.

Marinas Visitors are accommodated in vacant berths as available. Call VHF 80 before entering.
- **Hythe Marina Village.** Entrance, 1·5m, marked by piles, some lit. IPTS. Lock manned 24hrs, waiting pontoon outside. Free flow during HW. Fuel 24hrs. All facilities. Passenger ferries from Hythe Pier to Southampton.
- **Town Quay Marina.** Enter leaving outer wave screen to stb, inner screen to port. Few facilities but shops nearby.
- **Ocean Village Marina.** Few facilities but shops nearby and bus to town centre.
- **Shamrock Quay.** Stream strong on outer pontoons. No fuel but chandlers and all boatyard services. Visitors' pontoon D.
- Berths for shallow draught boats, and those capable of taking the ground, at Kemp's Shipyard above Shamrock Quay to stb.

Supplies Fuel at Hythe Marina Village (through lock, no charge for fuelling stop), Itchen Marine at American wharf (diesel only) and at Kemp's Shipyard.

☎/**VHF** HM 023 8033 0022. VHF 16, 12; Hythe Marina Village 8020 7073. VHF 80. Town Quay Marina 8023 4397. VHF 80; Ocean Village Marina 8022 9385. VHF 80. Shamrock Quay 8022 9461. VHF 80. WiFi; Itchen Marine 8063 1500; Kemps Quay 8063 2323; R Southampton YC 8022 3352; Ocean Quay Marina 8023 5089.

HAMBLE

Standard Port Southampton

Warsash
HW (sp) –0010 (np) +0020
LW (sp) 0000 (np) –0010
MHWS MHWN MLWN MLWS
0·0m +0·1m –0·1m +0·3m

Burlesdon
HW (sp) +0020 (np) +0020
LW (sp) +0010 (np) +0010
MHWS MHWN MLWN MLWS
+0·1m +0·1m +0·2m +0·2m

The River Hamble is perfect for access to the Solent or to destinations further afield and is often used as a base for competing in the various regattas, National, European and World Championships, that are run by the yacht clubs based on the river. Traffic at weekends is heavy, engines should be used.

Regulations VHF 68 should be monitored at all times. Speed limit 6kn, no wash, starting at pile No1.

Vessels should keep to stb side of fairway. When crossing the fairway give way to other vessels. Anchoring is prohibited between No.1 bn and M27 br (50°53′·33N).

Approach Steer for Hamble Point S card Lt buoy, then head 352° (W sector of Oc(2)WRG.12s dir Lt) up channel marked by lit bns. After bn 5, steer 028° (W sector of Iso.WRG.6s dir Lt), as far as Warsash Jetty, 2F.G(vert), then head up the river, marked by piles. Some of them are lit, all have R or G reflectors. Do not cut corners, which are shallow, particularly on E side opposite Mercury Y Harbour and on W side approaching Swanwick.

Bridges at Burlsedon have 3·5m headroom HAT.

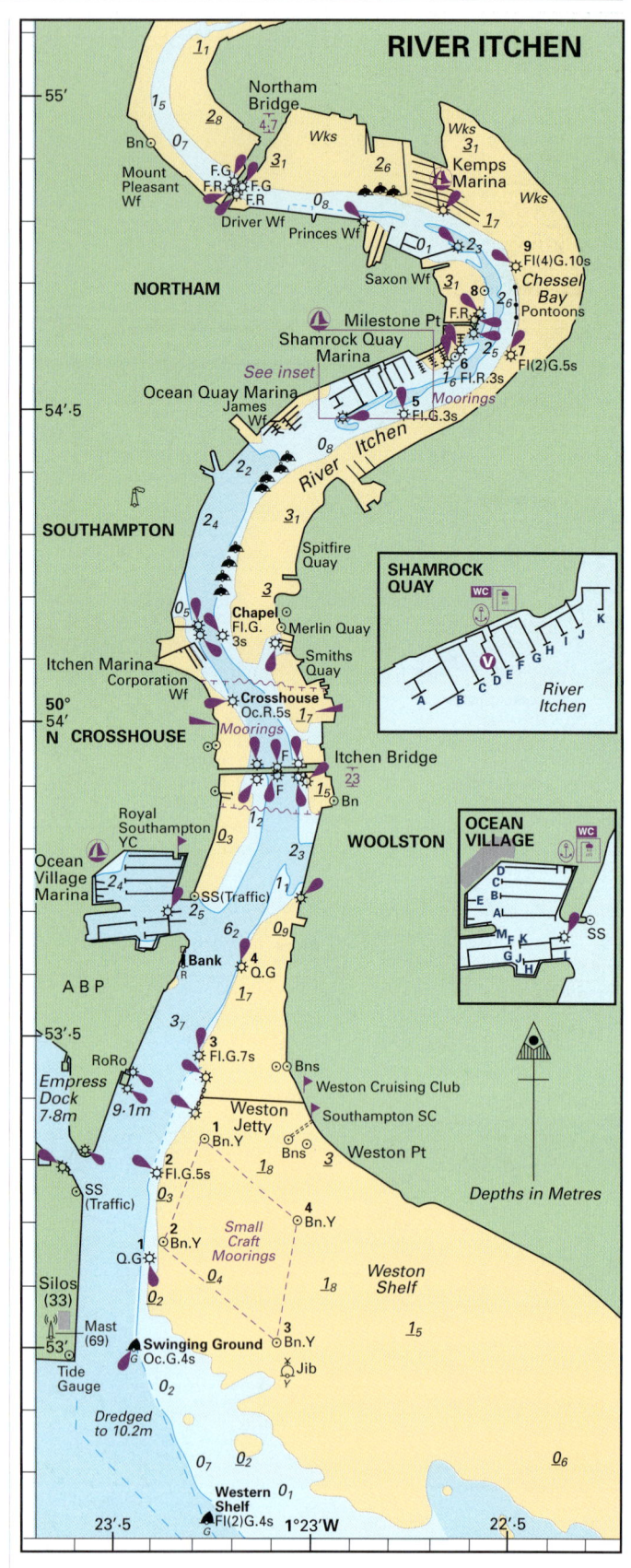

Berthing Short stay and overnight, walk-ashore berthing at HM's jetty off HM's office (conspic round tr), Warsash and at Hamble-le-Rice Jetty. Harbour Authority visitors' moorings on midstream pontoons between piles B1 and B6. No advance booking on Harbour Authority V moorings except for rallies. Marinas (call on VHF to check availability). Numerous boatyards and marinas offer visitor berthing by arrangement.

Landing on public hards at Warsash, Hamble-le-Rice, Swanwick Shore; on pontoons at HM's jetty, Hamble-le-Rice Quay, and at Jolly Sailor Inn at Burlsedon; or at jetty at Hamble.

Supplies Fuel and water at fuelling berth, Hamble Point Marina. Water at HM's jetty and at all marinas. Provisions

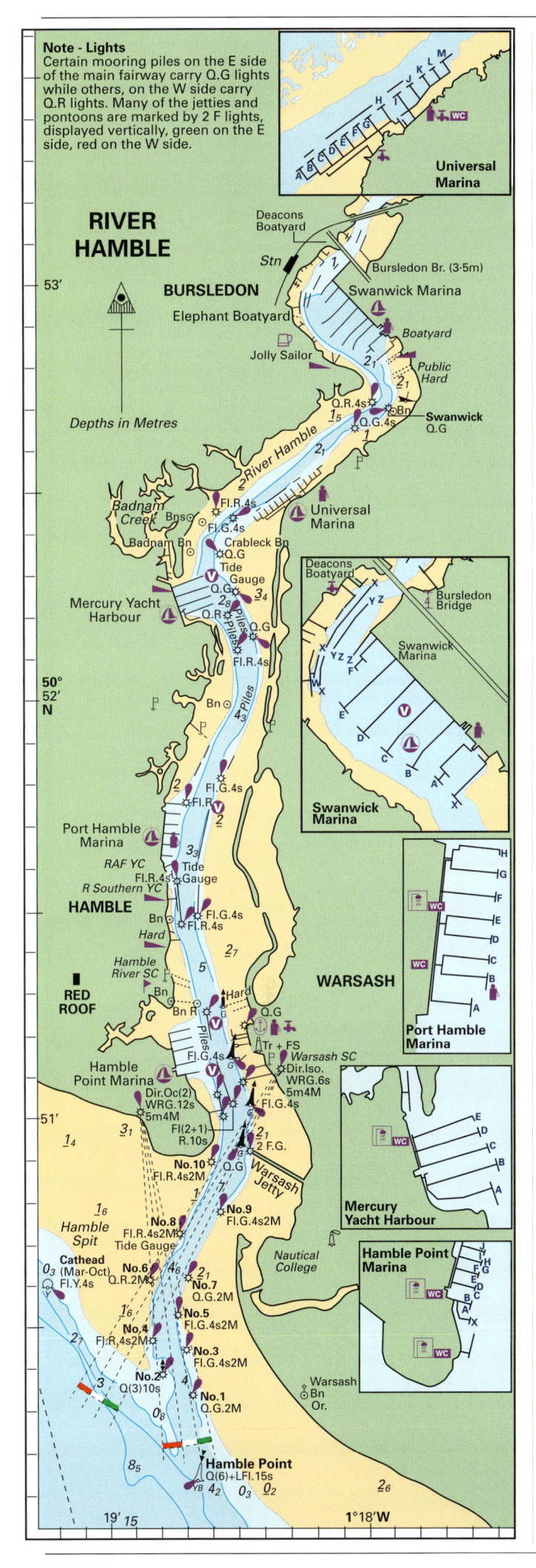

The Cruising Almanac

Note - Lights
Certain mooring piles on the E side of the main fairway carry Q.G lights while others, on the W side carry Q.R lights. Many of the jetties and pontoons are marked by 2 F lights, displayed vertically, green on the E side, red on the W side.

and chandlery at Warsash, Hamble and Swanwick.

Facilities Sewage pump out at HM's jetty. All boatyard facilities available on the river.

☎/VHF Warsash HM 01489 576 387, *Hamble Harbour Radio* VHF 68; Hamble Point Marina 023 8045 2464, VHF 80i; Port Hamble 023 8045 2741, VHF 80; Hamble Yacht Services 023 8045 4111, VHF 80. Mercury Y Harbour 023 8045 5994, VHF 80; Universal Marina 01489 574 272, *Universal Marina* VHF 80; Swanwick Marina 01489 884081. VHF 80; RAF YC 023 8045 2208; R Southern YC 023 8045 0300.

WOOTTON (ISLE OF WIGHT)

Tidal data as Portsmouth

An attractive winding creek, most of which dries. No room for single keel boats except during HW.

Approach From W keep N of Peel Wreck, R can, and Y RVYC racing platform. From E keep 5ca off shore. Make for Wootton N card Lt bn or, with sufficient rise of tide, for No.1 bn, Fl(2)G.5s, and turn into the channel, 224°.

Beware of inbound ferries which may at times approach ferry terminal to west (outside) of marked channel.

Entrance Channel, dredged 3m is marked both sides by lit bns and W sector of the dir Lt, Oc.WRG.10s at the terminal for the Portsmouth vehicle ferry. Wootton Br (impassable) can be reached by shallow draught vessels near HW but the fairway is generally not marked after R and G buoys and piles at the N end.

Berthing Visitors' berths are available on RVYC walk ashore pontoon which is southern section of pontoon. Northern section of pontoon is privately owned. Pontoon dries to mud at LW and can be used with care by keel boats. Boats may raft up. Mooring can be uncomfortable in strong winds from NW to NE. Drying pontoons for local yachts at Fishbourne Quay.

Anchoring Forbidden in fairway, not recommended in any areas of Wootton Creek south of RVYC and all moorings are privately owned.

Facilities Bar, restaurant, showers at RVYC; inn/restaurant, PO and shops at Wootton Br.

☎ RVYC 01983 882 325.
www.wcfa.co.uk

RYDE (ISLE OF WIGHT)

Ryde Harbour is a small craft drying hbr (sand/mud) 300m E of Ryde Pier and Pavilion (conspic). Pontoon berths and quay for fin keels. Max recommended draught 1m, though depth at HW is approx 2m. Accessible HW–0230 to +0200 by buoyed drying approach across Ryde Sands, 197°. Contact Hbr for latest information. Call *Ryde Harbour* on approach. Entrance Lts 2F.R(vert) and Fl.G.3s7m1M. Look out for fast catamaran and hovercraft ferries.

Visitors welcome. Visitors' pontoon is Pontoon A unless directed elsewhere.

Supplies Water; fuel 200m.

☎/VHF HM (01983) 613 879, *Mob* 07970 009899 VHF 80 *Ryde Harbour*.

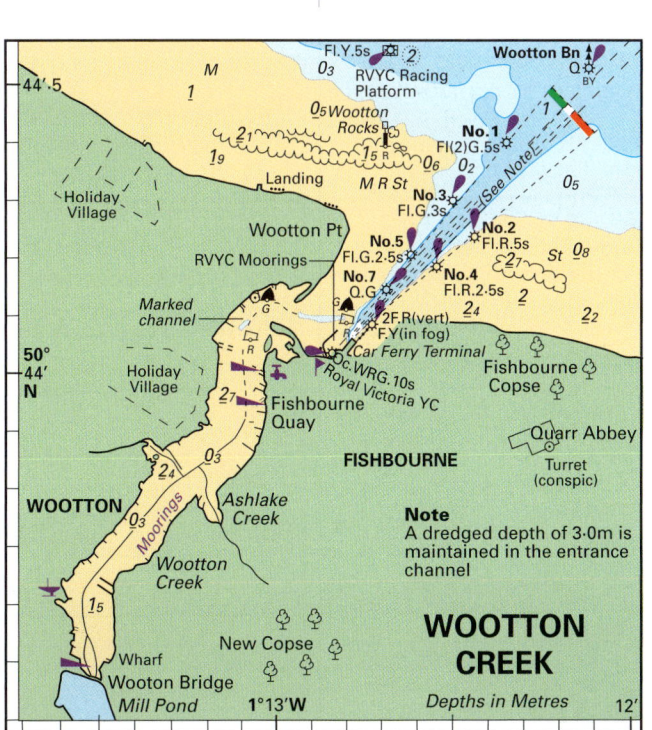

ENGLAND – SOUTH COAST

65

BEMBRIDGE (ISLE OF WIGHT)

Standard Port Portsmouth

Approaches
HW (sp) –0010 (np) –0005
LW (sp) 0000 (np) +0005
MHWS MHWN MLWN MLWS
+0·1m +0·1m 0·0 +0·1m

A natural hbr, much of it drying, dries 0·9m in entrance. Electronic tidal gauge showing depth of water in the entrance channel available at www.bembridgeharbour.co.uk/ The tidal gauge just north of St Helens' Fort is non-usable.

Approach Aim for N side of St Helen's Fort, making sure the tide has risen enough.

Entrance The channel starts at the tide gauge 2ca N of the fort and is buoyed and lit. With sp or medium tides vessels with up to 2m draught can enter from HW–0300 to +0200. There is a minimum depth of 1m between No.10 buoy and the marina. Max flow across the entrance is 1½kn.

Berthing Anchoring is forbidden except for boats that can dry out, anchored fore and aft, in sandy bay on E side by Bembridge SC. Visitors berth at the Duver pontoon on the N side of the channel, shown by V symbol on plan. Bottom is soft and 2m draught can be accommodated. Resident berth holders use Bembridge Marina. Buoys are private.

Facilities Water at marina and quay. Shops up the hill in Bembridge or at St Helens. Restaurants, including good seafood near hbr.

☎/VHF Harbour Office 01983 872828, VHF 80 *Bembridge Harbour*; Water Taxi 07932 459 389.

VENTNOR (ISLE OF WIGHT)

HW Portsmouth –0025

Position 50°35'·6N 1°12'·13W

A small drying haven, exposed to the SE. Limited mooring space for small twin keelers.

☎/VHF Supervisor 07976 009260, VHF 80 in season.

PORTSMOUTH

Standard Port Portsmouth

A busy naval and commercial port with ferry terminal and marinas, under control of Queen's HM. The town has much to offer in maritime history.

Regulations Small craft under 20m must enter and leave by the Small Boat Channel and vessels with engines must proceed under power. No loitering in Small Boat Channel and no overtaking if that means straying into the main channel. Small craft may continue to use the Small Boat Channel when the main channel is closed for the passage of a large vessel. Prior permission to cross between Ballast bn and Gunwharf Quay must be obtained from QHM VHF 11. Observe mandatory 50m exclusion zone around all warships and berths in HM Naval Base. Also, when directed by QHM on VHF 11, observe 500m exclusion zone around underway warships. Such warships display two diamond shapes (vert) by day and two Fl.R Lts (hor) by night. Craft fitted with engines must use them between the Southsea War Memorial and Ballast Bn. Listen on VHF 11 for information on large ship movements but do not transmit on that frequency except in emergency or to request permission from QHM to cross the main channel.

Do not stop or linger in the area of Tipner Range in the approach to Port Solent (*see under Portchester Lake, below*).

During busy periods, the Small Boat Channel and other parts of the port are patrolled by the Queen's HM Harbour Patrol, QHP, a 6m white hulled launch, VHF 11 call *Harbour Patrol Launch*. The QHP is tasked with assisting recreational users and, where necessary, enforcing regulations.

Approach A submerged barrier nearly 2M long runs S from the shore 8ca E of Southsea Castle to Horse Sand Fort. From Langstone and Chichester Harbours there is an inshore passage for small craft (0·6m), 12m wide, 1ca from shore, marked to N and S by a stb and port bn respectively. A better passage (1·2m) 8ca offshore is marked by a G pile to N and a dolphin, QR, to S; pass close N of the dolphin. Otherwise pass S of Horse Sand Fort. In all cases cross to W side of main channel and follow port-hand buoys to the Small Boat Channel.

From W either
• Steer towards Outer Spit S card Lt buoy, turning to port when S of Spit Sand Fort, Fl.R.5s. Follow the main channel port-hand buoys and enter the Small Boat Channel at No.4, Q.R; or

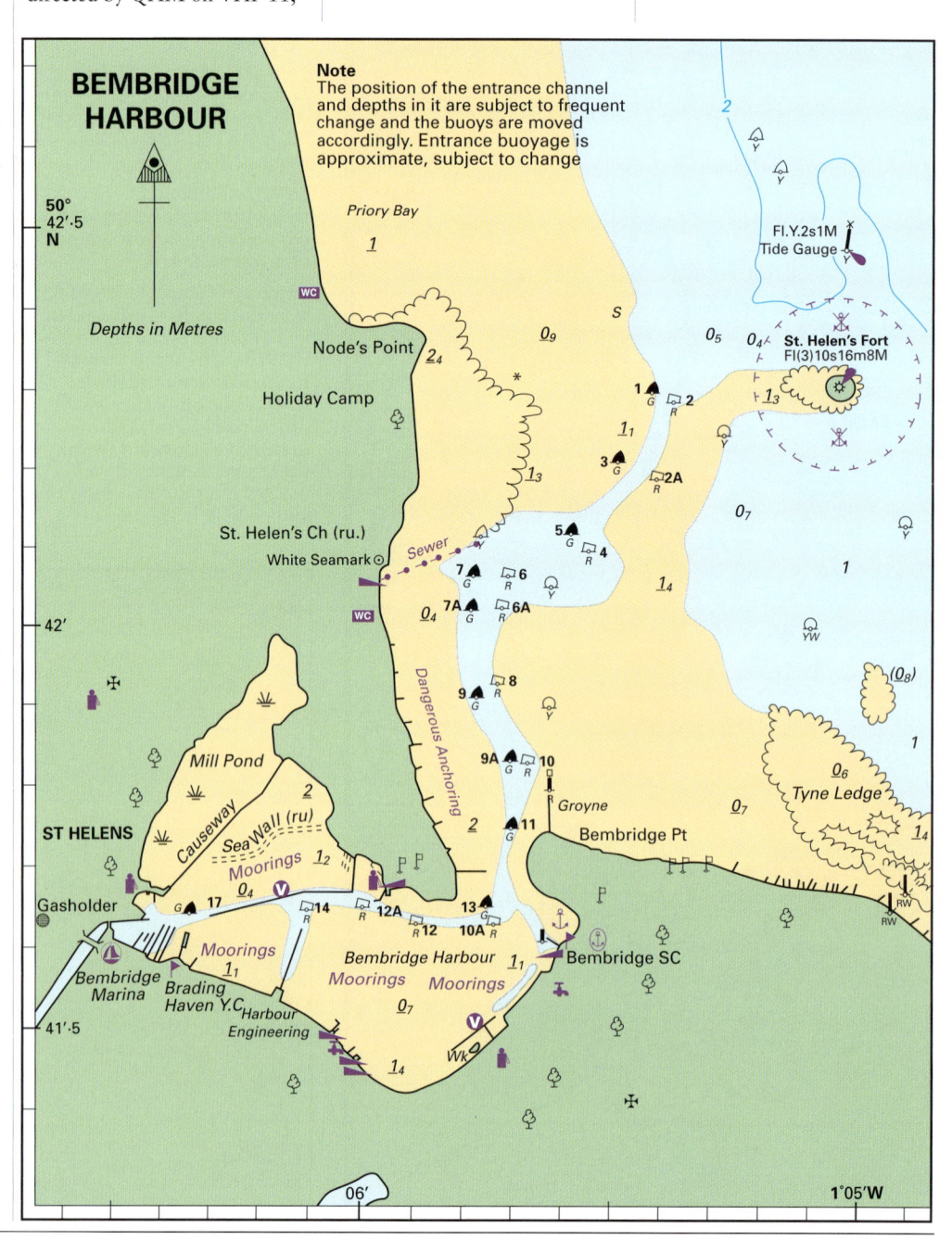

PORTSMOUTH HARBOUR AND APPROACHES

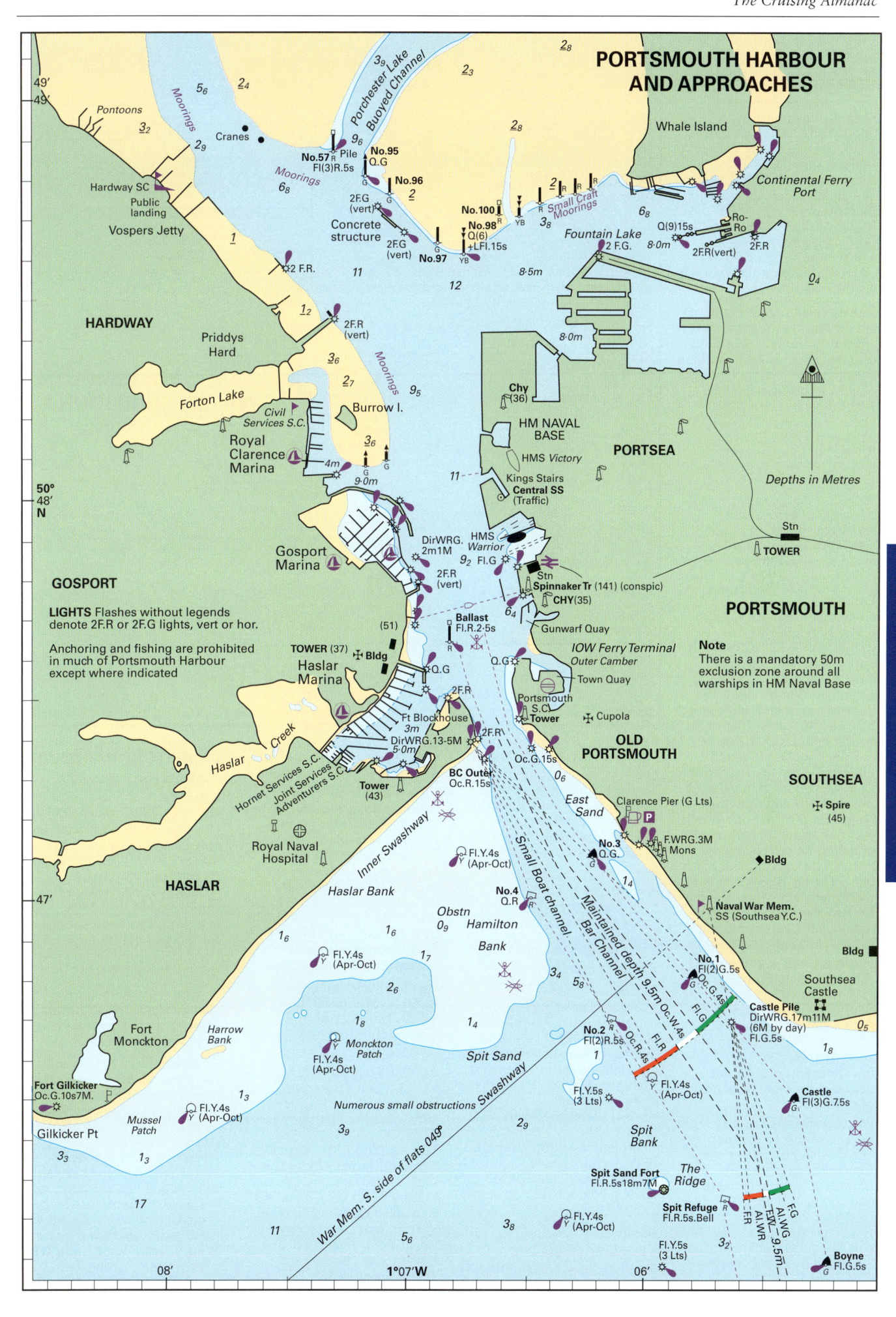

England – South Coast

- Take the Swashway over Spit Bank (1·8m), with War Memorial (unlit) bearing 049°, turning to port when you have come into deep water: or
- Use the Inner Swashway (0·5m, forbidden to craft over 20m), steering on the W edge of round tr (unlit) 029°. This course passes close to the N tip of a drying shoal 2ca S of Fort Blockhouse. The N end of the Inner Swashway is marked by BC Outer, a R Bn, Oc.R.15s, which must be left to port on entering the hbr or on leaving it via the Inner Swashway.

Signals These signals, displayed at Fort Blockhouse, do not apply to craft under 20m long using the small boat channel but should be watched for warnings of movements of large ships which must be given a clear berth. Instructions from QHM will be on VHF 11 or 13.
R/G/G Lts – Large vessel underway; other vessels may be ordered to wait
W/G Lts – Large vessel leaving. Vessels may leave; those entering will be kept clear
G/W Lts – Large vessel entering. Vessels may enter; those leaving will be kept clear.

Entrance
Small Boat Channel Vessels under 20m must use this channel in the hbr entrance. It is 50m wide and runs from No.4 Bar buoy, Q.R, close along Fort Blockhouse wall (leaving two unlit R stick bns, BC2 and BC4 close to port) to Ballast bn, Fl.R.2·5s, which must be left close to port. Likewise, when leaving the hbr, all vessels under 20m must use this channel, again leaving Ballast bn close to port. Vessels may only cross the entrance N of Ballast bn with permission from QHM or S of No.4 Bar buoy. The Oc.R sector of Fort Blockhouse Lt (24hrs) and the Iso.R sector of the Lt on dolphin off Gosport Marina show over Small Boat Channel.
Hbr is difficult to enter on the ebb which runs strongest (5+kn) in third and fourth hours. Flood runs strongest in last two hours (3¼kn) but an eddy runs along E side of hbr during part of the flood. There is slack in entrance for ¾hr during second and third hours of the flood.

Portchester Lake has 4·4m at its lower end and 1·8m near Portchester. Firing from the Tipner Range crosses the channel between piles 63/67 and 70/80. You are not allowed to stop or linger in this area. If R flags are flying, you may still pass but do so quickly. Channel is marked by R and G posts, nine lighted. The channel to Port Solent (dredged 2m, Lt piles) starts just E of Portchester Castle.

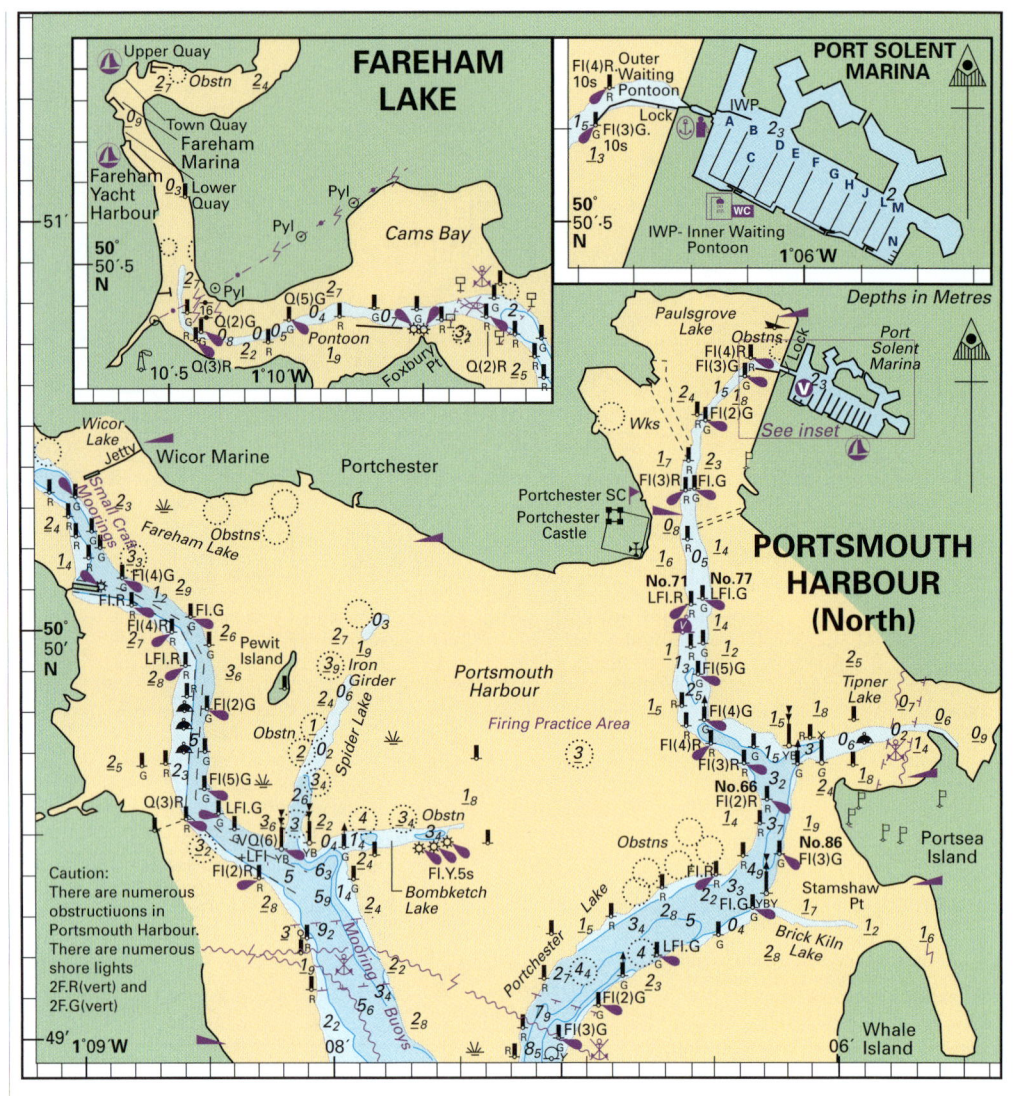

Fareham Lake is marked by R and G poles, some are lit. There is a least depth of 5·0m to Bedenham Pier but it dries out ½M below Fareham town. There is also an overhead cable in the same area with clearance of 16m.

Anchorages
- Off Portchester Castle near top of Portchester Lake, 1·8m. Land at hard.
- ¾M below Fareham, 1·5m. Riding Lt necessary.

Marinas
- **Haslar Marina**, just inside entrance to port. Visitors berth alongside in NE corner of marina, beware of through tide especially on the flood. No fuel.
- **Gosport Marina**, 4ca further N; fuel available.
- **Royal Clarence Marina**, 2ca further NW.
- **Port Solent Marina** ½M NE of Portchester Castle, call ahead at Bn 78, lock 24/7; waiting pontoon, lit Fl(3)G.10s.

Berthing
- **Hardway SC** has long pontoon, fin keels sink into soft mud.
- **WicorMarine**, Fareham. Near R pile No27. Deepwater moorings and pontoon (not walk ashore) may be available. Advisable to phone in advance.
- **The Camber** Short term berthing alongside dock wall, 1ca inside entrance to stb. Pontoon berthing 1ca further N at Gunwharf Quays by prior arrangement; expensive and exposed to wash. For either of these, call QHM, VHF 11, for permission before crossing hbr from Ballast Buoy at top of Boat Channel, also before leaving.

Supplies Fuel at Gosport marina (self-service), Port Solent, Hardway Marine, Wicormarine, Fareham Yacht Harbour.

☏/VHF QHM 023 9272 3124. VHF 11, or 13 if so instructed; Harbour Control 023 9272 3694; Camber Berthing Master 9285 5902, VHF 14. Haslar Marina 9260 1201, VHF 80; Gosport Marina 9252 4811, VHF 80; Royal Clarence Marina 9252 3523, VHF 80; Gunwharf Quays 9283 6700, VHF 80 Gunwharf Quays; Port Solent 9221 0765, VHF 80; Hardway SC 9258 1875; Wicormarine 01329 237 112, VHF 80; Fareham Yacht Harbour 01329 232 854, VHF 80; Fareham Marine 01329 822 445.

LANGSTONE HARBOUR

Standard Port Portsmouth
Entrance
HW (sp) –0015 (np) 0000
LW (sp) –0010 (np) 0000

MHWS	MHWN	MLWN	MLWS
+0·1m	+0·1m	0·0m	0·0m

DS (Winner) Portsmouth –0300N; +0230S, rotary anti-clockwise, less than 1kn

In entrance stream is strongest for fourth and fifth hours of the flood (3·4kn) and second and third of the ebb (3·1kn).

A natural hbr with narrow channels lacking anchorages convenient to shore. Has a large water-skiing area.

Approach From Portsmouth there are two inshore passages in the submerged barrier between the shore and Horse Sand Fort. See Portsmouth Approach for details. Otherwise from W pass S of Horse Sand Fort and keep No Man's Land Fort open to S of the latter until entrance is open. From Chichester, steer S for 4ca past Bar Bn and then steer for Winner S card buoy, unlit. With a heavy sea or strong S wind the shallows can be dangerous for 1½M offshore.

The Cruising Almanac

LANGSTONE HARBOUR

Entrance is bounded on either side by gravel banks, steep to on E side of fairway. These may move in gales and their height varies. The connecting bar has a least depth of 1·8m and is dangerous in onshore winds especially near LW on the ebb. Bring Fairway bn, R sph on RW pile, LFl.10s, on with centre of hbr entrance, 354°. Alternatively, concrete dolphin off Eastney Pt, Q.R, in line with outfall jetty to N, 2F.R(vert), 353° has 1·7m on the bar. Inside, Langstone Channel is buoyed, lit and dredged 1·8m at its N end and leads to Havant Quay used mainly by gravel dredgers. The drying channel leading to Chichester Harbour round the N of Hayling Is has 3·7m at MHWS with a br clearance of 1·7m and cables 1·8m.

Channel through Lock and Eastney Lakes to Southsea Marina has lit and unlit piles and is dredged 0·5m.

Berthing All visiting vessels should report to Harbour Office just inside the entrance to stb, on the Hayling Island side. Go alongside pontoon, leaving NW berth clear for ferry.

- **Moorings** Contact HM prior to arrival. Y visitors' buoys to stb off Ferry Boat Inn, max LOA 10m; no doubling up, not for use in S'ly gales.
- **Anchorages** With HM's approval in upper reaches of Broom and Langstone Channels, but both are in use by gravel dredgers day and night; the latter channel is a water-skiing area (April–September); mooring may be uncomfortable.
- **Southsea Marina** See plan p.70. Access via automatic sill gate, minimum depth 1·6m when open, giving free flow HW±0300; waiting pontoon (2·5m) with pedestrian access to marina.

Supplies Fuel outside marina; petrol on wall (tidal). Chandlery. Provisions in West Town, Hayling Island (1½M).

☎/VHF HM 023 9246 3419, VHF 12 *Langstone Harbour Radio*. Southsea Marina 9282 2719, VHF 80 *Southsea Marina* (24hrs).

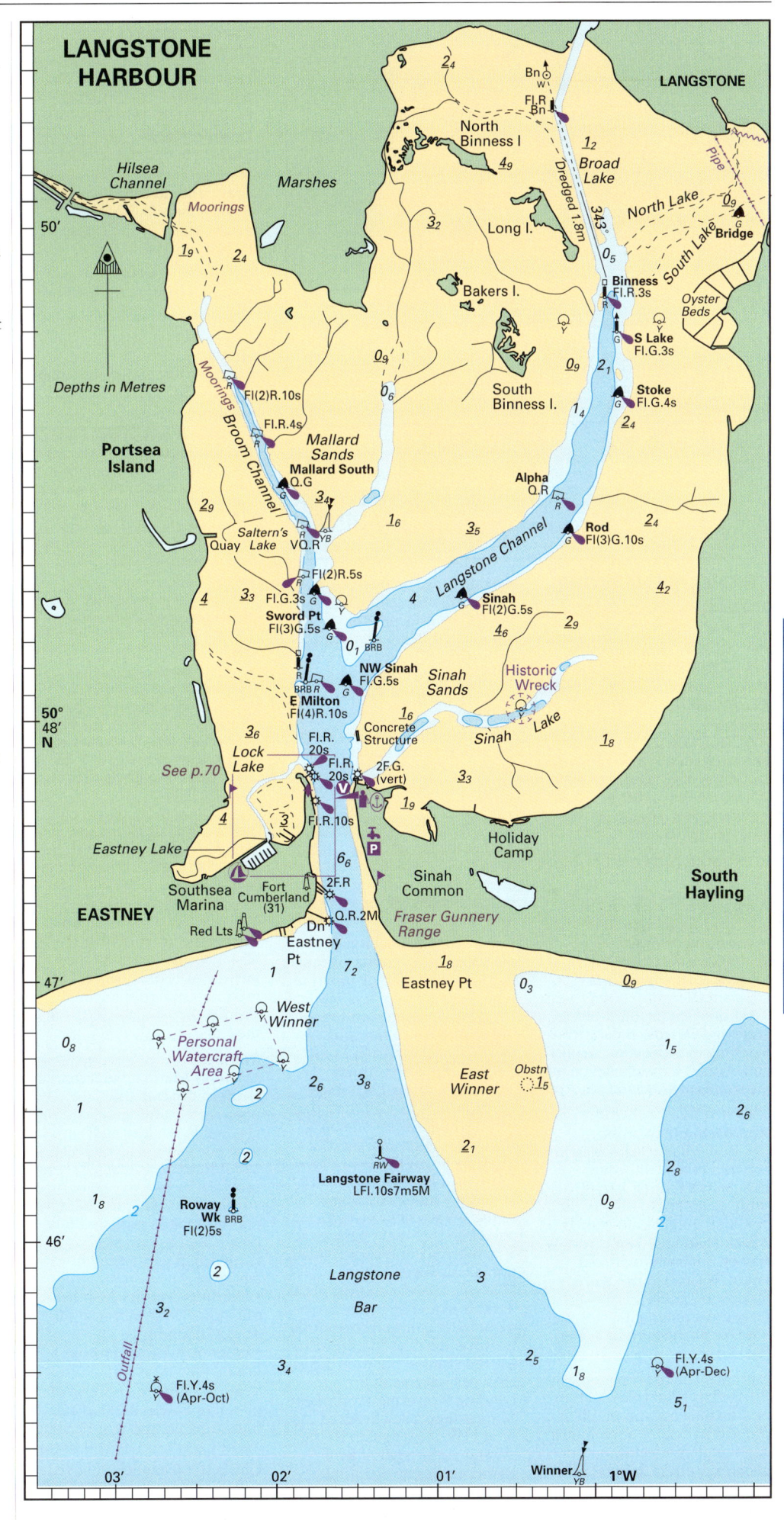

ENGLAND – SOUTH COAST

69

The Cruising Almanac

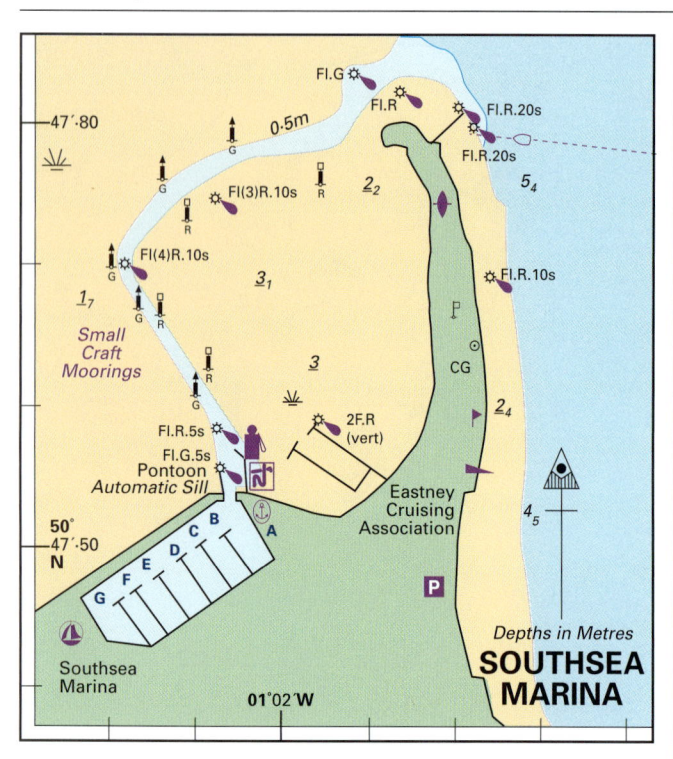

CHICHESTER HARBOUR
Standard Port Portsmouth
Entrance
HW (sp) −0010 (np) +0005
LW (sp) +0015 (np) +0020

MHWS	MHWN	MLWN	MLWS
+0·2m	+0·2m	0·0m	+0·1m

Itchenor
HW (sp) −0005 (np) +0005
LW (sp) +0005 (np) +0025

MHWS	MHWN	MLWN	MLWS
+0·1m	0·0m	−0·2m	−0·2m

DS (off bar) Portsmouth
+0500SE −0130NW

In entrance flood reaches 2·8kn, ebb 6·4kn

A major yachting centre in largely unspoilt natural hbr with marinas, moorings and anchorages near pleasant villages. Virtually no commercial traffic except tourist and fishing boats. Bar restricts entry and exit and is dangerous in strong onshore wind against an ebb tide. www.chimet.co.uk gives current wind and sea conditions at W Pole bn.

Approach Aim to cross Chichester Bar at slack water or between HW−0300 and HW+0100. From E keep 2M offshore (in poor visibility the 5m line); from S keep Nab Tr on a back bearing of 186°; from W stay on 5m line or with old target (N card) in line with Cakeham Tr, 064°. From all three directions get Bar Bn and Eastoke Bn, open to E of West Pole Bn.

Entrance The bar is periodically dredged to 1·5m below datum but shoaling may occur and it is prudent to assume a minimum depth of 0·75m below datum giving a depth of 1·4m at MLWS (0·7m). For the deepest water, leave West Pole tripod Bn and Bar Bn about ½ca to port and follow a course of 013° to the centre of the entrance. Note that the tide gauge on the West Pole bn, like all other tide gauges in the hbr, reads depth above datum, NOT depth on the bar. Follow the W shore until abreast of Hayling Is SC after which channel divides at Fishery S card Lt buoy.

Chichester Channel goes to stb with three G con buoys in an arc marking NW edge of the Winner. Channel to Emsworth and Northney Marina continues to N, buoyed and lit.

Within the hbr anchored yachts must hoist a B ball, and an anchor Lt at night, and must not be left unattended for more than four hours.

Emsworth Channel is free of moorings between the entrance to Mill Rythe and the junction with Sweare Deep. It is marked by half-tide perches and three Lt bns (two port, one stb). Sweare Deep is also lit as far as the entrance to Northney Marina (but near LW follow the moorings to stb rather than going straight from one bn to the other). Although there is a Lt bn, Echo, at the head of the Emsworth branch, the stretch between it and Fisherman's Bn to the S is so congested with moorings that night passage for a stranger is not recommended, nor is Emsworth Yacht Harbour easily accessible in the dark. It would be better at night to tie alongside one of the boats on the piles to port or to use the visitors' pontoon 1·5ca SSW of Fisherman's bn. Landing is possible at Sparkes Marina (approach dredged 2m) or at HW at Mengham Rythe SC and at the head of Mill Rythe; each is navigable at MHWS for draughts up to 1·5m. *For passage through Sweare Deep to Langstone Harbour see entry for that hbr.*

CHICHESTER TO NEWHAVEN
Passage lights BA No
Nab Tower 0780
Fl.10s17m12M, Horn(2)30s AIS
Owers Lt buoy
S card Lt buoy Bell Racon(O) (−−−)
W entrance to Looe Channel
Boulder buoy Fl.G.2·5s
Beachy Hd 0840
Fl(2)20s31m8M

Streams Related to HW Dover
The Looe +0445E −0115W 2kn
S of Owers +0545E −0045W 2kn
E-going stream sets onto Outer Owers
Selsey Bill HW Portsmouth −0005
There are three ways of passing Selsey Bill:

• S of the Owers S card Lt buoy, the best route in strong winds when the sea is breaking heavily on the shallows of the Owers, at night, or in poor visibility

• Through the Looe, passing 1½M S of the Bill; for use by day and in good visibility

• Close inshore; only by day around HW in good visibility with light or offshore winds. Beware crab pots in this whole area.

E-bound through the Looe, steer about 097° between the two entrance Lt buoys, R can QR and G con Fl.G.2·5s; when the Mixon S card bn Q(6)+LFl.15s2M bears N 2ca, alter course to 077° to clear East Borough Head (E card Lt buoy, Bell).

The inshore route should be made within 0230hrs either side of HW. From E approach LB Ho, ½M NE of the Bill, on a bearing of not less than 280° and follow round the line of the Bill, keeping about 40m off the ends of the groynes until windmill (conspic 1M NW of Bill) is abeam; then head out for Nab Tower 238°. Shallowest water will be between the end of the High Street and coastguard tower. When ¾M clear of the shore, course may be set for West Pole bn leaving the unlit S card beacon S of East Pole Sands close to starboard.

For the inshore passage from W, head for the windmill with Nab astern and follow the line of beaconed groynes. The direction of the stream changes considerably earlier than in the Looe; on the early spring ebb there may be a current of 6·7kn just to the E and round the Bill. If going E, the effect may be reduced by a wider sweep offshore.

Pagham Harbour is only a basin of mudflats. Access is difficult, and as it is a nature reserve, landing and anchoring are forbidden.

Between Selsey Bill and Beachy Hd the effect of a foul tide may be escaped by keeping close inshore, where the tide may turn 1½–2hrs before the main offshore stream. But be careful between Littlehampton and Shoreham where shallows extend a considerable way offshore.

Anchorages In W and N weather, in The Run N and S of Selsey LB Ho, clear of moorings (2m).

In offshore winds, on NE side of Bognor Rocks, between them and the shore. SE winds bring in a heavy sea.

Anchorage in Emsworth Channel: anchor out of the fairway to N of Hayling Is SC moorings (use tripping line). Visitors' buoys available from the club.

Marinas
• **Sparkes Marina.** Enter marked channel, dredged 2m, immediately after outer end of Hayling Is SC, leaving E card bn with tide gauge and stb bn close S of it to stb. Ldg line, 277°, is provided by two dayglo orange crosses. After 3ca turn S, leaving pile mooring to port, and follow port-hand bns into hbr. Crowded in season, call in advance.
• **Northney Marina** Near head of Sweare Deep; entrance sill dries at datum.
• **Emsworth Yacht Harbour** Sill dries 2·4m.

Visitors' pontoon at N end of piles E of Fowley Is. Half-tide buoys and pontoons at Hayling Yacht Co at head of Mill Rythe.

Chichester Channel is buoyed and lit as far as entrance to Chichester Marina. Landing at East Head, Itchenor Hard, hard on Bosham side of Itchenor ferry (dries out for 2ca) and Dell Quay. At entrance junction with Bosham Channel leave Fairway G con buoy, Fl(3)G.10s, (not readily distinguishable against background of moorings) to stb for fairway through the trots.

Anchorage Anchor N and NE of East Head (uncomfortable with winds from NW to NE; swimming dangerous) or W of the Fairway buoy on S side of channel. Anchoring is forbidden in Itchenor Reach. Six Conservancy visitors' buoys, white marked V, off Itchenor take up to six vessels each (depending on size); visitors' pontoon (first two lengths only) on S side above Itchenor SC, at W end of Conservancy fore and aft moorings.

Marinas
• **Birdham Pool** (1·6m draught, lock HW±0300).
• **Chichester Marina** (lock HW±0400). Visitors berth temporarily at waiting pontoon and report to reception.

Thorney Channel Entrance is in gap, marked by port-hand bn in line of broken piles which runs NE from S tip of Pilsey Is. 2ca to N, the channel passes through a gap in a second line of broken piles running E from S tip of Thorney, this gap being marked by an unlit port bn and a stb bn Fl.G.5s. Rest of channel is marked by perches, some well above LW mark. Pilsey Is is a nature reserve and access above HW mark is not allowed. Thorney Is is MoD controlled but the public are allowed to use the foreshore path all round the island. Land at stage by the channel just beyond Thorney Is SC.

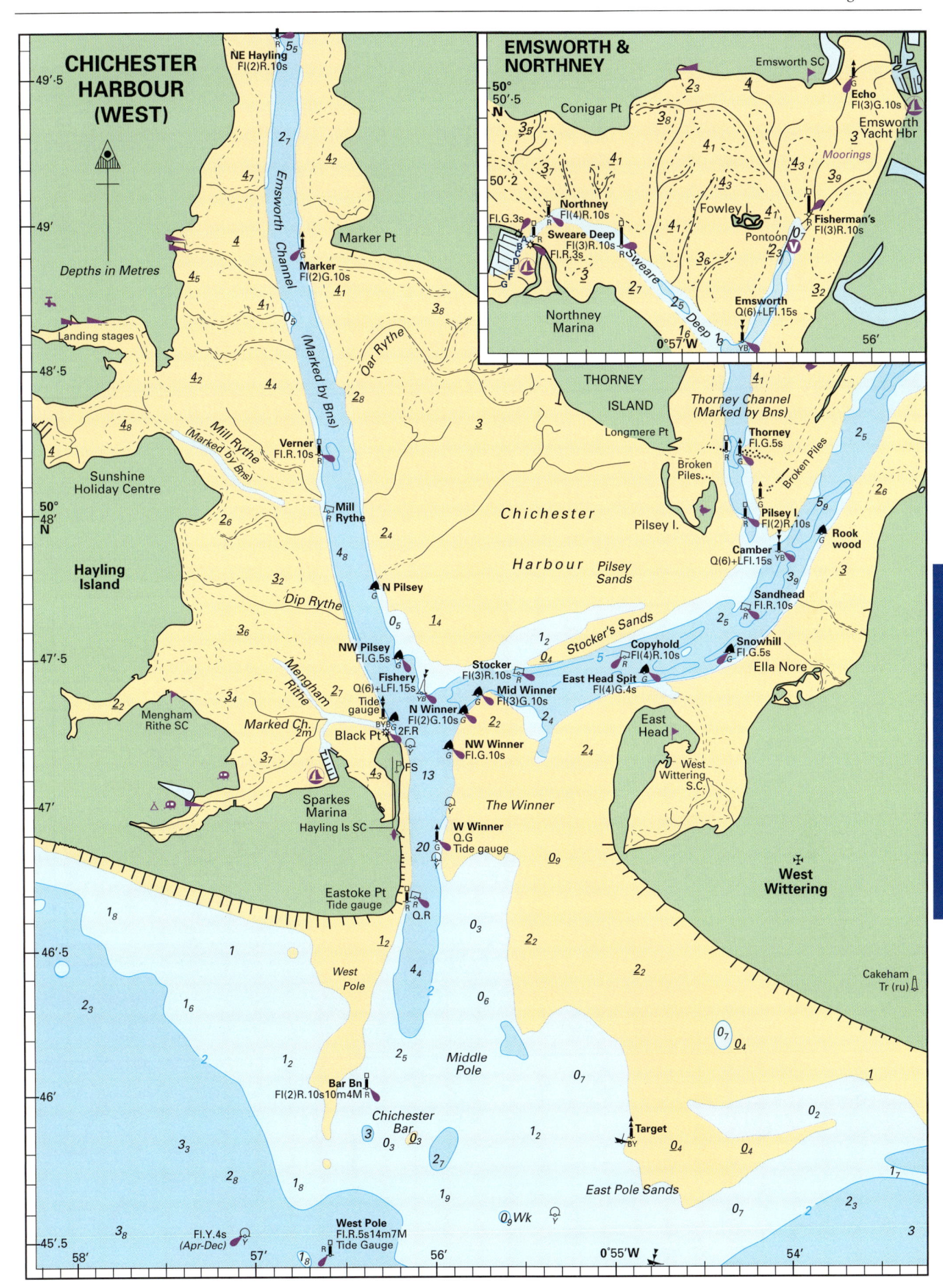

Anchorage Anchor off Pilsey in the stretch between the two lines of broken piles. Shore is steep-to and current strong. Sheltered from strong NW winds when East Head is untenable. Anchoring also possible further up the channel clear of moorings.

Visitors' buoy available from SC near channel. Drying berths (jetty and buoy) at Thornham Marina (about HW±0100) at head of channel.

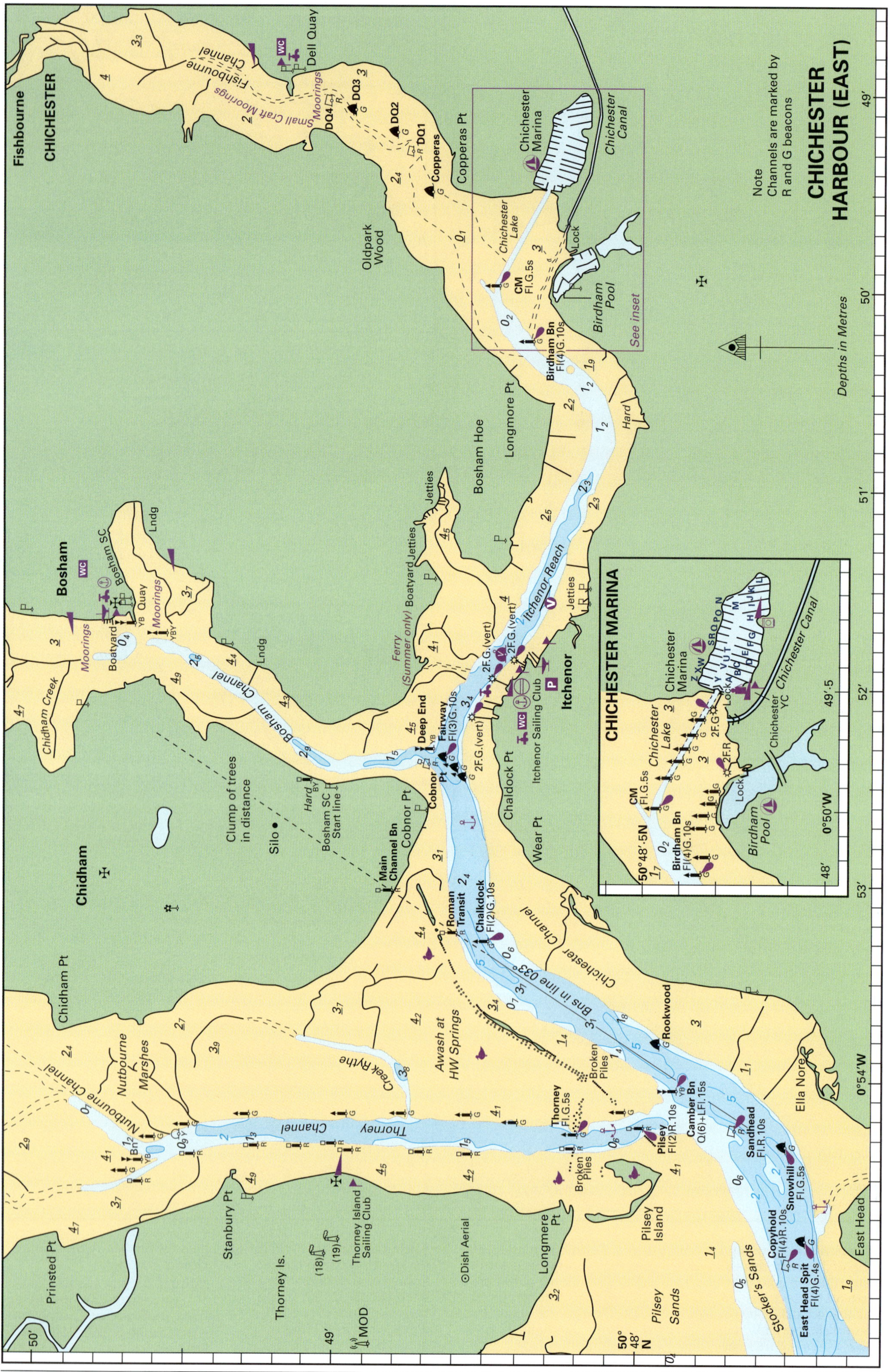
CHICHESTER HARBOUR (EAST)
Note
Channels are marked by
R and G beacons
Depths in Metres
Fishbourne
CHICHESTER
Dell Quay
Fishbourne Channel
Small Craft Moorings
Moorings
DQ4
DQ3
DQ2
DQ1
Copperas
Copperas Pt
Oldpark Wood
Chichester Marina
Chichester Canal
Chichester Lake
CM Fl.G.5s
Lock
Birdham Pool
See inset
Birdham Bn Fl(4)G.10s
Longmore Pt
Bosham Hoe
Hard
Jetties
Boatyard Jetties
Ferry (Summer only)
Itchenor Reach
2F.G.(vert)
Itchenor Sailing Club
Itchenor
Chaldock Pt
Wear Pt
Deep End
Fairway Fl(3)G.10s
Cobnor Pt
Bosham
Bosham SC
Quay
Boatyard
Moorings
Lndg
Bosham Channel
Chidham Creek
Clump of trees in distance
Silo
Bosham SC Start line
Main Channel Bn
Chidham
Roman Transit
Chalkdock Fl(2)G.10s
Chichester Channel
Bns in line 033°
Rookwood
Chidham Pt
Nutbourne Marshes
Nutbourne Channel
Thorney Channel
Creek Rythe
Awash at HW Springs
Broken Piles
Thorney Fl.G.5s
Camber Bn Q(6)+LFl.15s
Pilsey Fl(2)R.10s
Sandhead Fl.R.10s
Snowhill Fl.G.5s
Ella Nore
East Head
Copyhold Fl(4)R.10s
East Head Spit Fl(4)G.4s
Stocker's Sands
Pilsey Sands
Pilsey Island
Longmere Pt
Dish Aerial
Thorney Island Sailing Club
Thorney Is.
MOD
Stanbury Pt
Prinsted Pt
CHICHESTER MARINA
Chichester YC
2F.R
2F.G
50°48'·5N
0°50'W
49'·5
0°54'W
50°48'N

Bosham Channel is unlit and dries near the quay. There are no visitors' buoys (all moorings are private) but it is possible to dry out alongside the quay – charges. Alternatively Bosham, an attractive village, can be reached by dinghy with the tide or, in the season, by the ferry from Itchenor.

Facilities Fuel at Sparkes Marina, Hayling Yacht Co, Northney Marina, Emsworth Yacht Harbour, Birdham Pool (at HW to stb outside lock, diesel only), Chichester Marina (lock dues). Water also at pontoon off HM office (Itchenor), Emsworth landing pontoon and Bosham Quay. Provisions at Emsworth, Mengham, West Wittering, Chichester Marina, Birdham and Bosham (EC Wednesday). None at Itchenor. Chichester (EC Thursday) best reached by train from Emsworth or bus from Bosham, Birdham or Itchenor cross-roads.

☎/VHF HM 01243 512 301. VHF 14 *Chichester Harbour Radio*; Patrol Launch (when manned) VHF 16, 14 *Chichester Harbour Patrol*; Coastguard 023 9255 2100; Sparkes Marina 023 9246 3572, VHF 80; Hayling Y Co 023 9246 3592; Northney Marina 023 9246 6321, VHF 80; Hayling Is SC 023 9246 3768, VHF 37, M *Hayling Club*; Emsworth Yacht Harbour 01243 377 727, VHF 80, 37; Thornham Marina 01243 375 335; Birdham Pool 01243 512 310; Chichester Marina 01243 512 731, VHF 80.

LITTLEHAMPTON

Standard Port Shoreham

HW	(sp) 0000	(np) +0010
LW	(sp) –0010	(np) +0005

MHWS	MHWN	MLWN	MLWS
–0·4m	–0·4m	–0·2m	–0·2m

This commercial port is the estuary of River Arun; navigation is limited by a bar ¾M from the entrance. The bar dries 0·9m.

Approach Leaving Looe Channel at E Borough Head E Card Lt buoy, make good 049° towards the Y pile bn, Fl(5)Y.20s9m5M, SSE of entrance. Call HM on VHF 71 before entering. Do not attempt entrance in strong onshore winds.

Entrance Littlehampton Bar extends 600m southwards from the end of West Pier and is 0·9m above chart datum. From approx HW-0230 to +0300 there will be 2·5m over the bar. The approach should be made on a bearing of 346°. Tide boards on West Pierhead show height of tide above CD marked in units of 20cm. Ldg Lts on East Pier Head are Oc.WY.7·5s9m10M and F.G.6m7M. From abeam the West Pierhead, keep to E centre of fairway to allow for W going set.

The swing footbridge has 3·6m closed; requests for opening must be made before 1600 the preceding day (not Sundays or Bank Holidays). 4ca upstream is a fixed br, clearance also 3·6m. Littlehampton Marina to port above the footbridge. River is navigable to Arundel for 1·2m draught and dinghies can get to Amberley.

Berthing Report to HM on Town Quay where there are marked berths alongside pontoon with depths varying between 1·4m and 1·9m. Aruncraft and Arun YC have berths on port side below foot br.

Facilities Water and electricity on pontoon. Fuel at Littlehampton Marina.

☎/VHF HM 01903 721215, Mobile 07775 743078 VHF 71. Aruncraft 713327. Arun YC 714533, VHF 37, M. Littlehampton Marina 713553, VHF 80, 37.
www.littlehampton.org.uk

SHOREHAM

Standard Port Shoreham
DS Dover –0145W +0530E

Comprises the estuary of River Adur (dries) and a non-tidal basin, approached through locks, with busy commercial wharves and a small marina which may have a visitors' berth.

Approach High Lt is Fl.10s13m15M. Avoid from W, Church Rocks, 0·9m, over ¼M offshore and 1½M W of entrance; from E, Jenny Ground 1½m, 3ca offshore, and 1¾M E of entrance, and S card Lt sewer buoy 3ca ESE of entrance. Shallows in approach can be very rough in strong onshore winds particularly on the ebb, when Newhaven is a better refuge. Keep front Ldg Lt on Middle Pier watch house (Oc.3s) in line with High Light Fl.10s, 355°. If vessel is over 10m call *Shoreham Harbour Radio* before entering.

Signals

Traffic signals, shown as below, do not apply to small craft provided they do not impede ship movements. Beware turbulence from ships.

Middle pier control station, Lt Oc.Amber.3s showing seaward: Major vessel manoeuvring or leaving port. Entry forbidden.

LB Ho Oc.R.3s showing over E arm: Major vessel entering port or leaving W arm. Navigation in E arm forbidden.

LB Ho Oc.R.3s showing over W arm: Major vessel entering port or leaving E arm for sea or to W arm. Navigation in W arm forbidden.

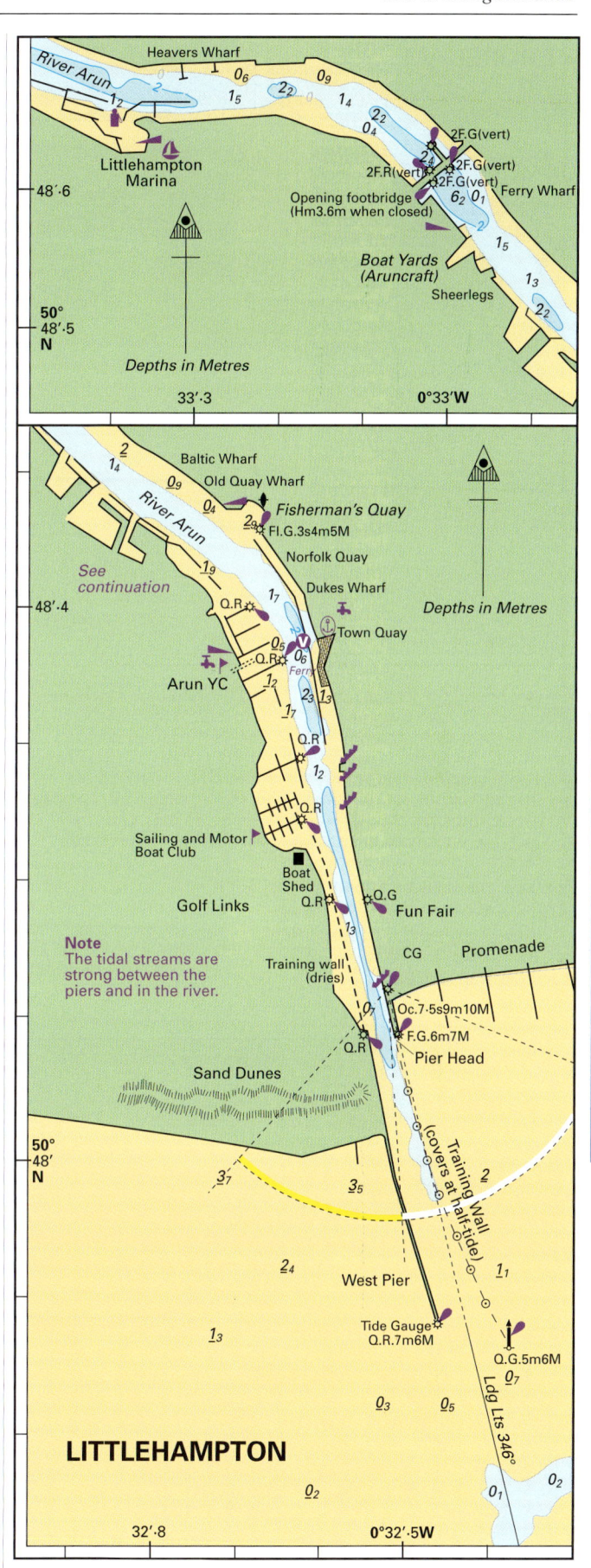

IPTS signals for lock opening.

Entrance Keep to middle and avoid eddies along the piers. Turn to port for Adur; beware training wall extending N from W pier, awash at half-tide, marked with port perches. Tide sets against E end of Kingston Wharf. Turn to stb for locks and Lady Bee Marina.

Berthing Yachts, small commercial vessels and fishing boats use E arm and the smaller, northern, Prince

SHOREHAM

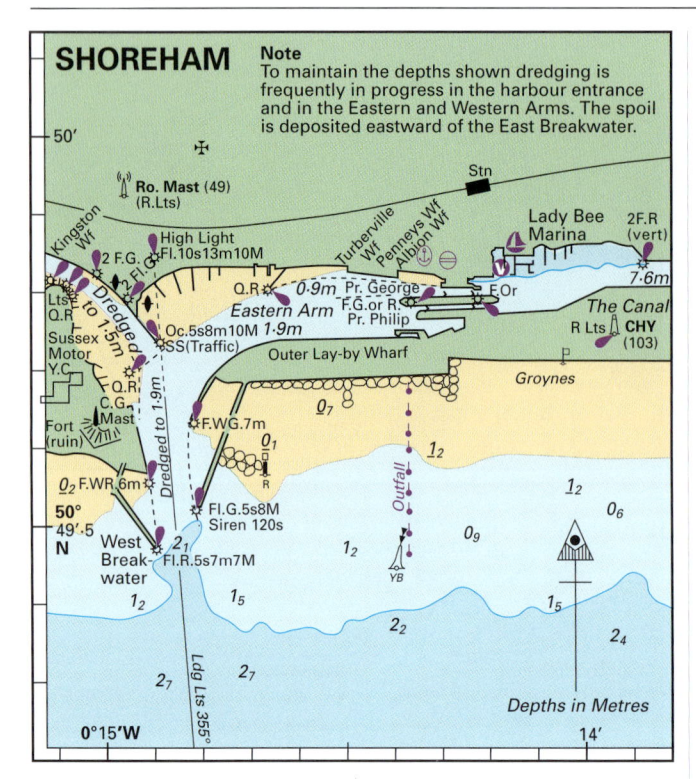

Note To maintain the depths shown dredging is frequently in progress in the harbour entrance and in the Eastern and Western Arms. The spoil is deposited eastward of the East Breakwater.

George Lock. The lock is open 24h except at LWS ± about 0100 as the lock sill 0·26m below CD. Incoming boats 0030 and outgoing on the hr. Small craft waiting for the lock may wait in the approaches to the lock but must remain manned and ready to move.

Visitors' moorings by prior arrangement from Lady Bee Marina (to port after lock). Few facilities for visitors.

Facilities Rail service.

☏/VHF Shoreham Harbour Radio 01273 592366, VHF 14. Vessel Notification Form (if over 10m) Fax 01273 592492 or Email HarbourRadio@shoreham-port.co.uk. Lady Bee Marina 591705, VHF 14.
www.shoreham-port.co.uk

BRIGHTON

Standard Port Shoreham
HW (sp) –0002 (np) –0002
LW (sp) 0000 (np) 0000
MHWS MHWN MLWN MLWS
+0·2m +0·2m +0·1m +0·1m
DS –0130W +0430E

A man-made marina with 1200 berths in tidal hbr; and inner harbour through lock with yard and domestic moorings. Entry not advised in SE gales or at LW springs.

Approach No outlying dangers. Landmarks are Roedean School on cliffs to E and tall hospital block with W vert stripe to W.

Entrance Avoid shoal obstruction adjacent S and N of E breakwater hd. If approaching from W beware blind corner with much small craft traffic. Channel is very close to W breakwater until well in. Channel turns to E, marked by Lt buoys. Entrance to marina marked by 2F.R(vert) port and 2F.G(vert) stb Lts. Breakwater and channel lights are difficult to distinguish against the clutter of shore lights. Entrance is dredged to 1.7m below CD. Vessels with draught >1m should not enter or leave LW±0200; call Brighton Marina for advice. Depths may be less than shown on plan due to silting. Bottom is hard chalk. Room to lower sails when in hbr.

Berthing Three unlit G buoys mark shallows of inside of E breakwater. Reception pontoon (No.10) is immediately inside hbr. Max. 30m LOA +2m draught. Beware W/E cross currents on ebb and flood. Depths within the marina fairways and berths may be 0.5m or less than CD.

Facilities Good rail service to London. Large supermarket nearby.

☏/VHF HM 01273 819919, VHF 80/37 Brighton Marina.

NEWHAVEN

Standard Port Shoreham
HW (sp) –0005 (np) –0003
LW (sp) +0005 (np) 0000
MHWS MHWN MLWN MLWS
+0·5m +0·4m +0·1m +0·1m
DS –0530E –0130W

The estuary of River Ouse. A busy commercial and ferry port with a marina. It is accessible with care in all weathers. Call VHF 12 before entering or leaving.

Approach The hbr lies immediately E of the line of cliffs running from Brighton to Newhaven. To its E the coastline is low. From W at night the lights of Seaford make a good mark to steer on. From E in heavy weather keep breakwater LtHo Oc(2)10s to stb until E pier Lts are open to clear shallows E of entrance.

Signals Entry signals on mast at base of LtHo do not conform to the International System but are as follows:

3Fl.R(vert) Serious emergency. All vessels stop, follow instructions from HM.

3F.R(vert) Vessels may not proceed.

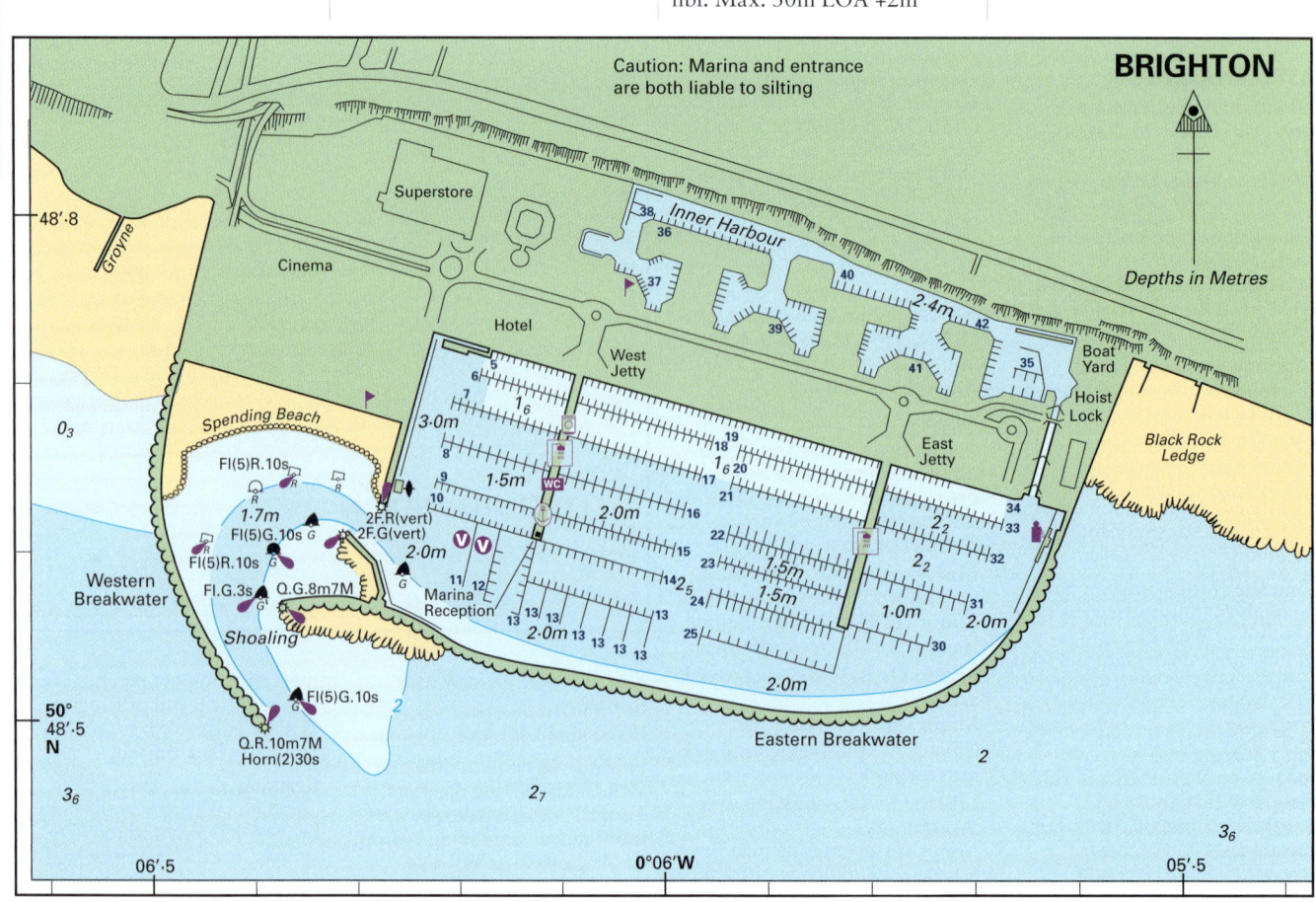

F.GGW(vert). Small vessels may proceed. Two-way traffic.
FGWG(vert) Proceed as instructed. All other vessels keep clear.
Swing br Fl.G – Operating.
F.G pass S to N.
F.R pass N to S.

When R Lts showing on signal mast at N end of marina no vessel may leave.

Entrance Within the breakwater keep in main channel to clear the mud on W side between it and the W pier. Inside, 2½ca N, Newhaven Marina is to port. Swing br opens on demand through Port Radio. Above the br to port is Cantell's Yard. At HW river is navigable to Lewes, 3m headroom.

Berthing
• Newhaven Marina moor to visitors' pontoon, accessible for 1·5m HW ±0230.
• Cantell's drying pontoons, accessible HW±0200.

Supplies Fuel N of Marina. Shops. Chandlery.

Facilities Rail services. Ferry to Dieppe.

☎/VHF HM 01273 612868, Port Radio VHF 12. Marina 513881, VHF 80. Cantell 514118. Bridge Control VHF 12 ☎ 612926 (min 3h notice for bridge opening).
www.newhavenportauthority.co.uk

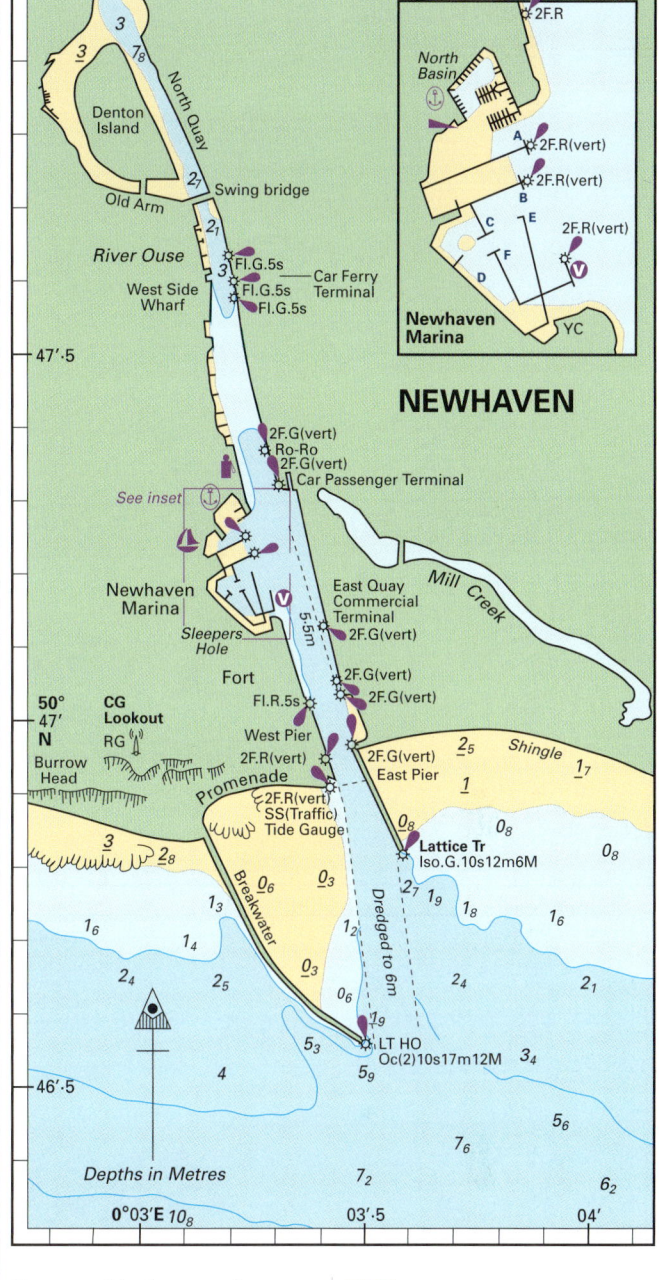

EASTBOURNE – SOVEREIGN HARBOUR

Standard Port Shoreham
HW (sp) –0005 (np) –0010
LW (sp) –0020 (np) –0015
MHWS MHWN MLWN MLWS
+1·1m +0·6m +0·2m +0·1m
DS 2M S of Beachy Head –0500E 0000W

A purpose-built yacht hbr with inner non-tidal basin with twin entrance locks and an outer tidal basin, shallow, not used.

Approach From the W clear Beachy Head by 1½M and head NE past Eastbourne for Langney Point. From the E, approach N of Royal Sovereign shoals. The coast is low, main features being blocks of flats, 1M NW of Langney Point and a line of five Martello towers NE of the point. The entrance is not easy to see against a setting sun and may be found most easily with the aid of GPS. The entrance channel is liable to silting so it is prudent to check the depth with the HM before entering at LW.

Entrance Lies between Langney Point, identified by the most SW Martello tr, lit Fl(3)15s12m7M, high intensity strobe flash, and a wreck on the shore. Call VHF 17 on arrival at Safewater buoy, SH LFl.10s, keep in W sector of Dir Lt (visible by day and night) Fl.WRG.5s4m1M, 260.5°, between port and stb bns, Fl(4)R.12s3m6M and Fl.G.5s3m6M. Wreck visible at LW Springs. Buoyed channel, lit, dredged 2·0m. Locks work 24h; traffic signals. Locks operate on hour and half hour only. Wait in open lock.

Berthing At pontoons, 4m depth. Berthing instructions from Lock-keeper.

Facilities Shops, cafés, boatyard, launderette. Cinema.

☎/VHF HM 01323 470099, VHF 17 (locks and bridges).

NEWHAVEN TO RAMSGATE

Passage Lights	BA No
Beachy Head	0840

Fl(2)20s31m8M

Royal Sovereign 0843
Fl.20s28m12M Horn(2)30s

Dungeness 0876
Fl.10s40m21M+F.RG.37m10M
(057°-R-073°-G-078°, 196°-R-216°)
Horn(3)60s

Lydd Range
F.R 2·5M W of Dungeness when firing is taking place

Dover Admiralty Pier 0900
Fl.7·5s21m20M Horn 10s

N Foreland 0966
Fl(5)WR.20s57m19/15M.
(R over N approach)

Streams Related to HW Dover

Beachy Head (2M S) +0015W – 0515E

Dungeness (2M SE) +0430SW –0200NE

Gull Stream +0430SSW –0030NNE

N Foreland (3M SE) +0445SSW – 0115NE

Inshore

S Foreland to Deal and Ramsgate to N Foreland +0415S –0145N

Streams run at 2½kn off Beachy Head, Royal Sovereign and Dungeness but at only 1½kn between the latter. Passing Dungeness at the beginning of the W stream, one has only 2hrs of fair tide. It is better to pass with the last of a fair stream, fight the weak foul stream between Rye and Hastings and take the next fair stream off Eastbourne. If faced with foul tide when W-bound at Beachy Head consider anchoring off Eastbourne or staying at Sovereign Harbour Marina to await the next tide.

E-bound with adequate speed a fair tide can be carried for 10hrs to N Foreland.

Anchorages

Seaford Road ¼M offshore abreast the channel. Sheltered from ESE to NNW, little stream, good holding.

Eastbourne E of pier; sheltered from W by N to NE.

Rye In N winds, anchor 1M·1¼M (according to draught) NNE of Rye Fairway buoy, LFl.10s.

Dungeness W Road In NE winds anchor inside the Ness out of stream, but the best anchorages, 1·3M W of the light, are now in Lydd Range danger area, which extends E to within 8ca from the Ness. Reported uncomfortable scend from E winds. Range control launches may be encountered W or E of the Ness; VHF 73, 13. 24h pre-recorded message on firing times, ☎ 01303 225467.

E Road Good anchorage NE off the Ness in 5·6m E of water tower (conspic) and Dungeness new LtHo bearing 197°, on W edge of R sector of the Lt. Sheltered with wind from SW through W to N.

Small Downs 1M N of Deal Pier off Sandown Castle, less than ½M offshore. Sheltered from SSW through W to N. Good holding, some stream. Beware wreck 4·4m ¾M NNE of Deal Pier.

Anchoring in Pegwell Bay is not recommended as the fetch from W is too great when flats are covered.

RYE

Standard Port Dover
Approaches
HW (sp) +0005 (np) –0010
MHWS MHWN MLWN MLWS
+1·0m +0·7m n/a n/a
DS –0400E +0300W

The approach dries and is liable to shifts in depth but generally 7·8m can be found at MHWS, about 6·0m at MHWN.

The Port of Rye dries completely and entry should only be made between HW – 0200 and HW + 0100. It should not be attempted in strong onshore winds.

Approach From Dungeness to the east, or from Fairlight to the west, follow the coast keeping at least two miles off shore in a depth of 6m until Rye Fairway RW Sph Lt buoy LFl.10s, *AIS*, in 50°55'·58N, 0°46'·56E is sighted, 1·8M from entrance.

The Cruising Almanac

NEWHAVEN

ENGLAND – SOUTH COAST

75

The Cruising Almanac

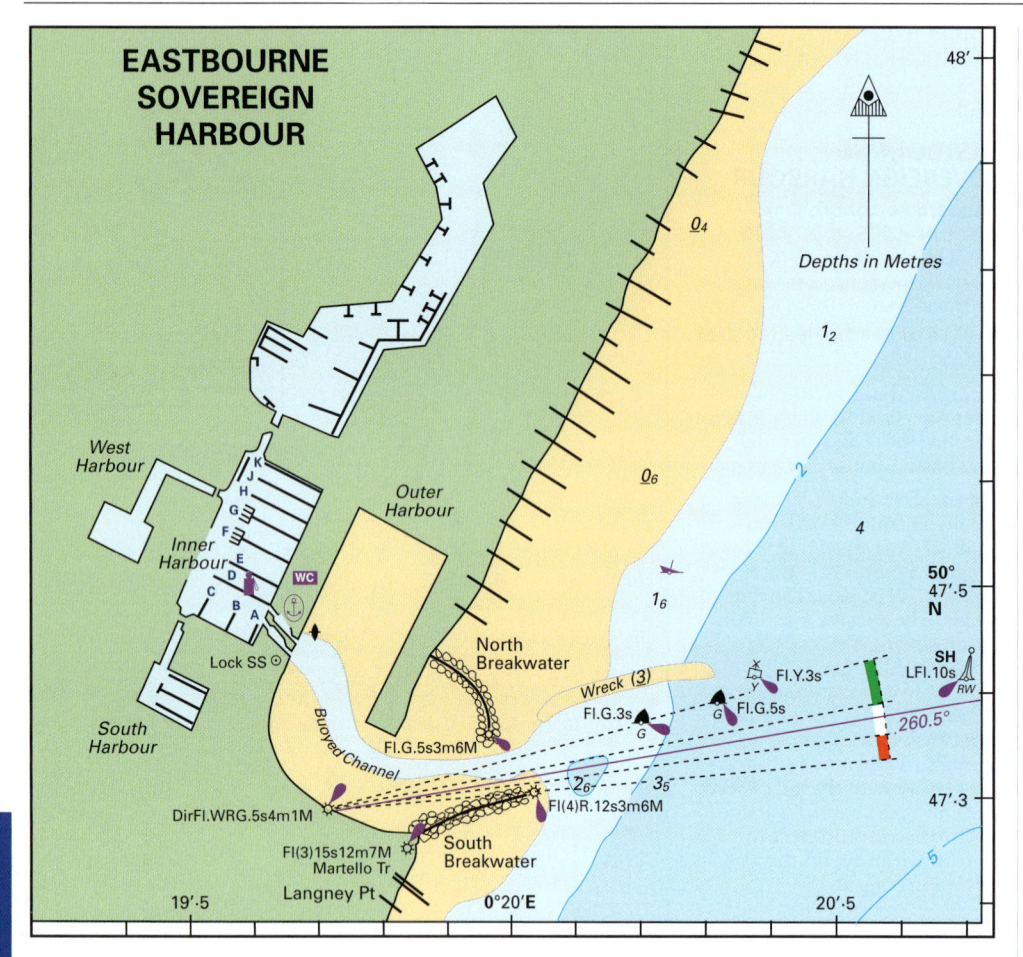

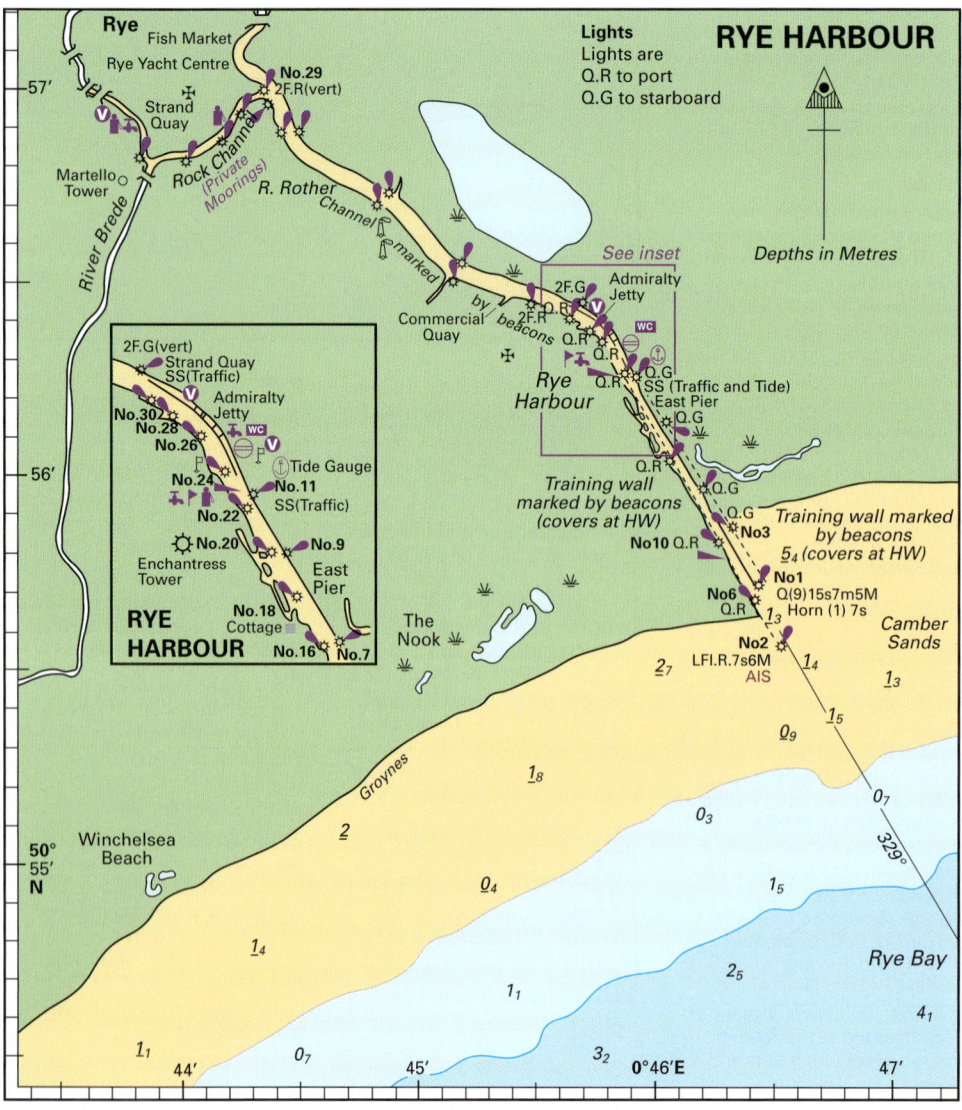

ENGLAND – SOUTH COAST

Signals near HM office. IPTS. Contact Port Control on VHF 14.

Entrance From Fairway Buoy steer 329° for R tripod bn Fl.R.5s and G square bn Q(9)15s Horn(1)7s. Floodlit. Follow buoyed channel and report to HM.

Berthing Boats up to 15m berth at Strand Quay upstream in soft mud. Boats over 15m and up to 25m berth near Harbour Office on hard ground. All berths dry. Facilities at both sites.

Facilities Water, shops and yards at Rye. Water, store, inn and PO at Rye Harbour village.

☎/**VHF** HM 01797 225225. VHF 14; Lydd and Hythe Firing Ranges VHF 73, 13.

DOVER

Standard Port Dover
DS –0200E +0500W

A very busy ferry port, but with good accommodation for yachts.

Major works in progress 2016-2019 in vicinity of Prince of Wales pier:

• marina NE of pier (to open 2018)
• commercial development of area to SW of Prince of Wales Pier and, after opening of new marina, closure of Granville and Tidal Basins.

Latest information from www.doverport.co.uk/dwdr

Approach From E observe Separation Zone regulations.

Signals International traffic signals (no exemptions) are displayed day and night on the port side of the western entrance and the stb side of the eastern entrance.

Entrance Permission to enter when two miles from entrance or leave **must** be obtained from port control on VHF 74. State which entrance you propose to use, and if you intend to anchor.

Report again on VHF 74 when 200m off entrance and follow instructions (all very clear and helpful). Continue to listen on VHF 74, until you approach the marina area where VHF 80 is used. (See plan.)

When leaving, report to marina VHF 80 before leaving berth, Port Control VHF 74 on entering harbour area and follow instructions, which are likely to refer to 'The Knuckle', which is near the bend in the Southern Breakwater.

Both the W and E entrances have strong streams setting across them with overfalls and confused seas. Keep up-tide and clear of entrance until entry is permitted. Enter under power at all times.

76

The Cruising Almanac

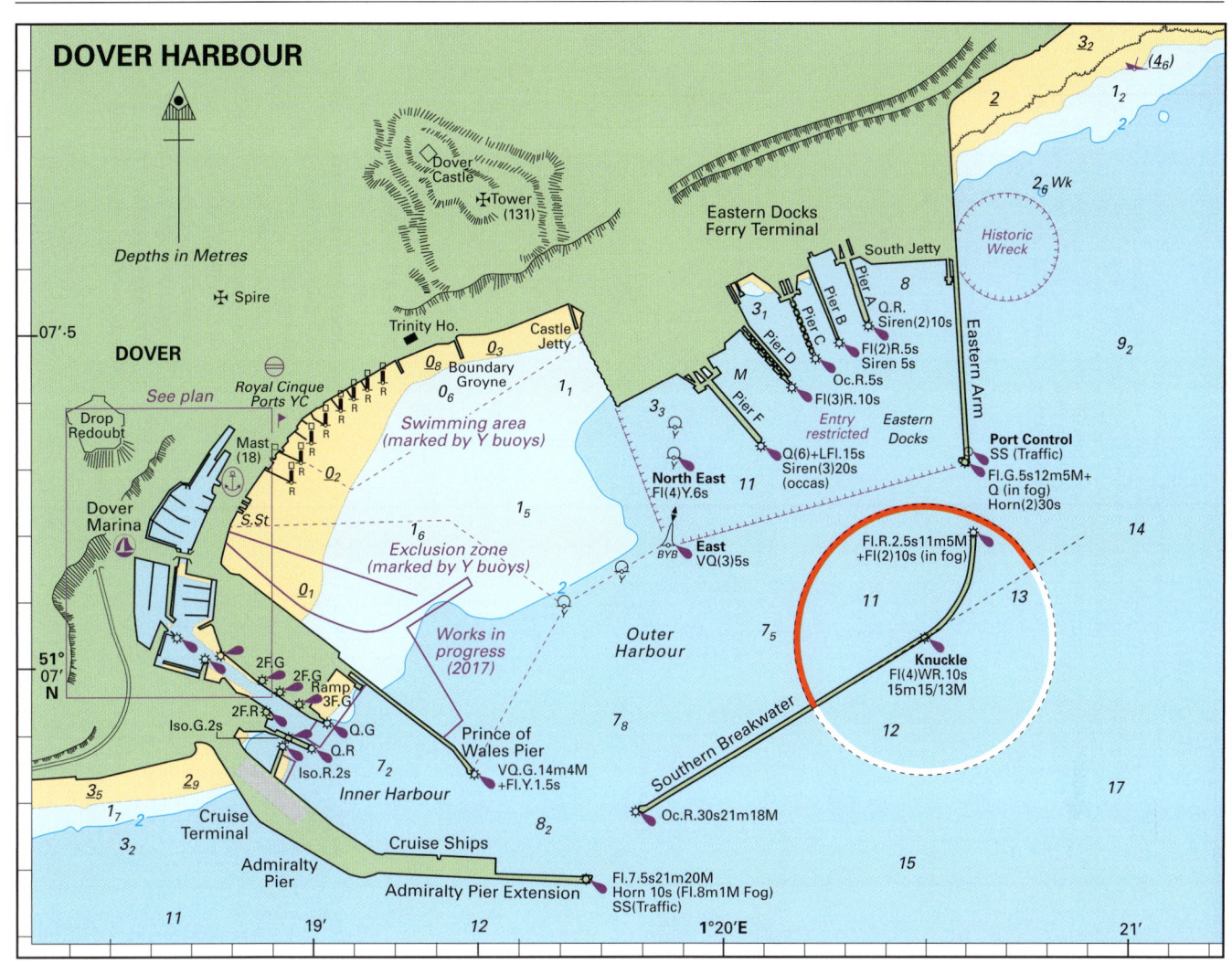

DOVER HARBOUR

Berthing Tidal harbour for short-stay with access 24hrs. Wellington Dock (gates open HW±0130). Granville Dock (gates open HW−3·5 to +4·5). Approaching the marina area, keep in the main channel until the Ldg Lt F 324°-333° opens, especially near LW.

Anchorage NE of Prince of Wales Pier, inshore of Y buoys; may be restricted during works. Exposed from NE through S to SW; in gales a heavy sea builds up. Yachts must not be left here unattended.

Facilities 24hr fuel, LPG, pump-out, scrubbing grid and 50-ton boat hoist. Launderette.

☎/VHF Port Control 01304 240400 VHF 74, 12. Dover Marina 241663, VHF 80. Channel Navigation Information Service VHF 11, h +40. Royal Cinque Ports YC 206262.

www.doverport.co.uk

RIVER STOUR AND SANDWICH

Standard Port Dover
Richborough
HW +0015

MHWS	MHWN	MLWN	MLWS
−3·4m	−2·6m	n/a	n/a

DS (offing): Dover −0215NE +0400SW

Flood in entrance probably starts about Dover −0445; ebb +0200

Sandwich ebb runs for 9hrs, flood for 3hrs

Approach at HW±0200 to avoid berthing with flood. From Ramsgate, steer 255° for RWVS buoy at 51°18′·9N 1°23′·6E (approx) then follow the channel marked with seasonal lateral buoys, entering the river at Shellness Pt. See plan at
www.sandwichphc.uk/page12.html

Entrance Channel buoyed at entrance to R Stour after which buoys mark channel to Sandwich. 3m at springs, 1·9m at neaps. Br at Sandwich has only 1m clearance at HW but opens with 1hrs notice. Above br river is navigable for some miles with 1·8m draught and 3·1m headroom.

Berthing Richborough Quay is used by commercial vessels and is private. Berth at Town Quay. Limited room to turn, difficult with flood. Sloping bottom is mud on chalk.

☎/VHF HM 07958 376183, VHF 8; Lifting bridge 01304 826236.

www.sandwichphc.uk

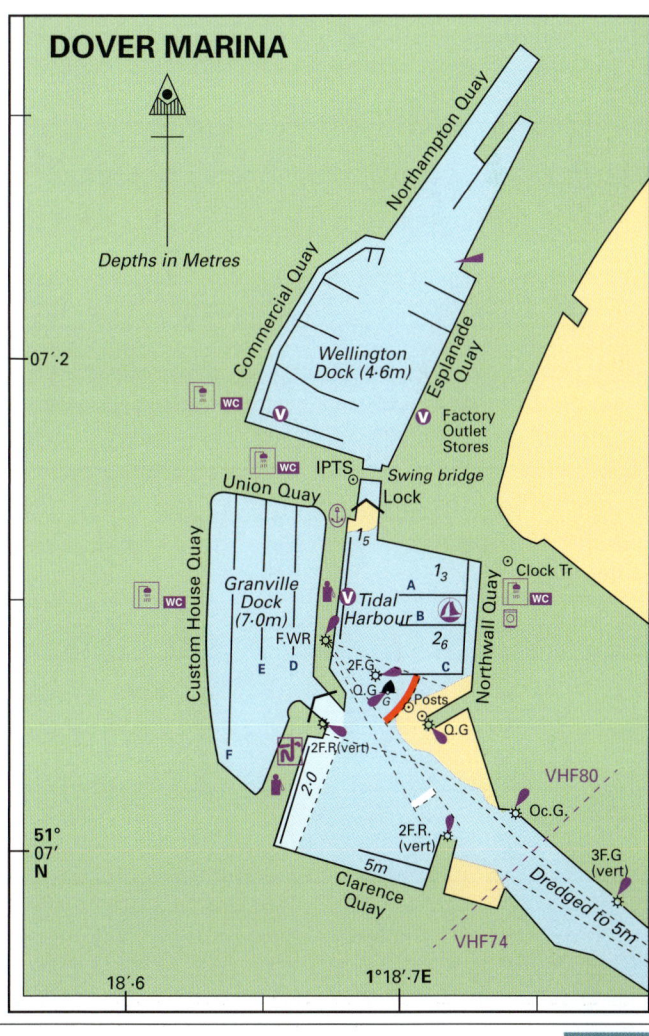

DOVER MARINA

ENGLAND – SOUTH COAST

77

NORTH FORELAND TO OOSTENDE

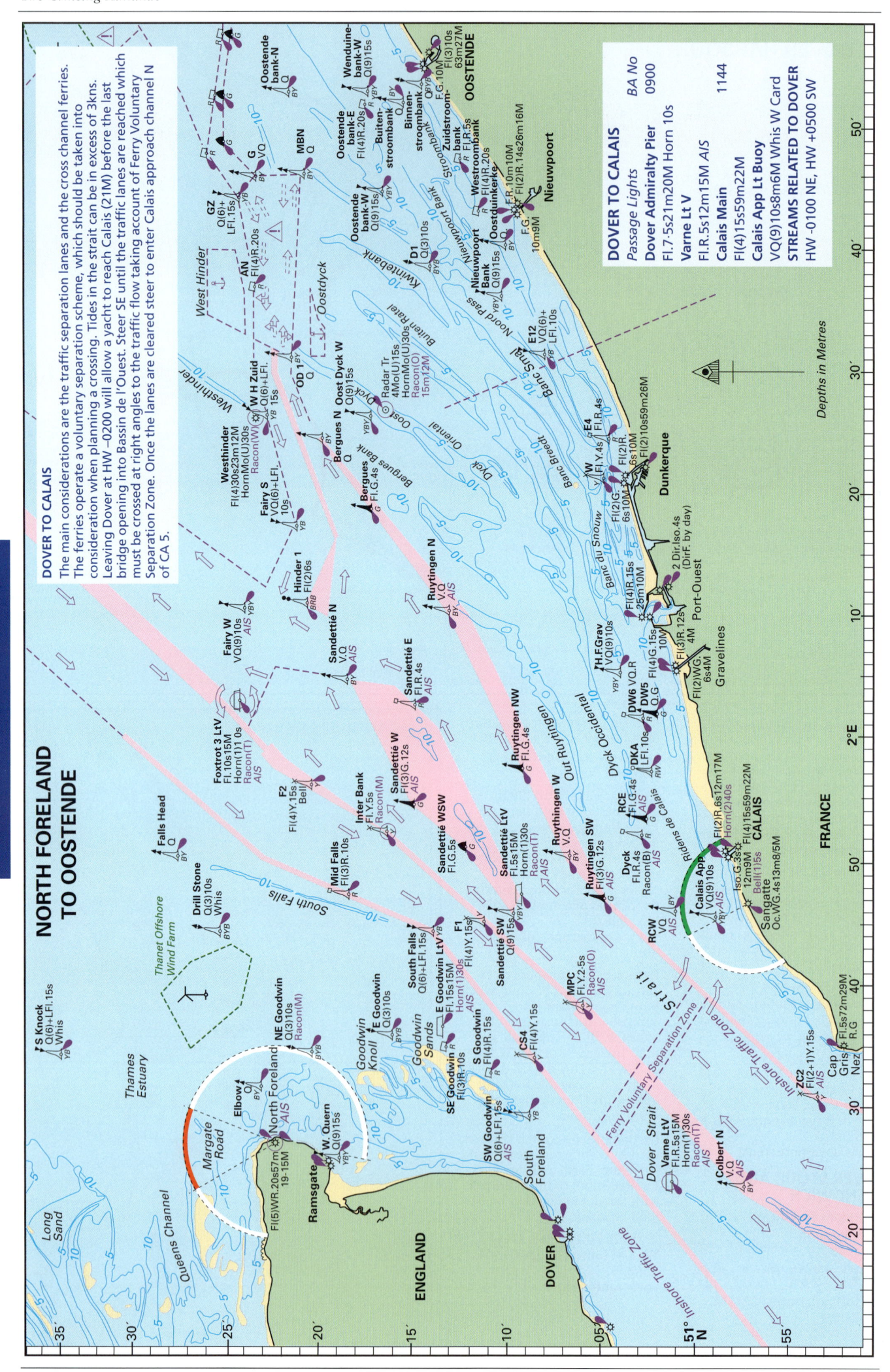

DOVER TO CALAIS

The main considerations are the traffic separation lanes and the cross channel ferries. The ferries operate a voluntary separation scheme, which should be taken into consideration when planning a crossing. Tides in the strait can be in excess of 3kns. Leaving Dover at HW −0200 will allow a yacht to reach Calais (21M) before the last bridge opening into Bassin de l'Ouest. Steer SE until the traffic lanes are reached which must be crossed at right angles to the traffic flow taking account of Ferry Voluntary Separation Zone. Once the lanes are cleared steer to enter Calais approach channel N of CA 5.

DOVER TO CALAIS

Passage Lights	BA No
	0900
Dover Admiralty Pier	
Fl.7.5s21m20M Horn 10s	
	1144
Varne Lt V	
Fl.R.5s12m15M AIS	
Calais Main	
Fl(4)15s59m22M	
Calais App Lt Buoy	
VQ(9)10s8m6M Whis W Card	

STREAMS RELATED TO DOVER
HW −0100 NE, HW +0500 SW

Depths in Metres

RAMSGATE

Standard Port Dover
HW (sp) +0030 (np) +0030
LW (sp) +0007 (np) +0017
MHWS MHWN MLWN MLWS
−1·6m −1·3m −0·7m −0·2m
DS (inshore) Dover −0100N +0500S

Ramsgate Harbour consists of the outer hbr, known as the Turning Basin, to S and the inner, Royal Harbour, to the N, sharing the same approach channel. Hbr busy with fishing boat and wind farm traffic.

Approach Yachts must report to *Ramsgate Port Control* on VHF 14 and remain listening, before entering the recommended yacht track (*see plans*) to enter.

There are small craft holding areas to N of No.3 buoy and to S of the South breakwater to which yachts may be directed to keep the hbr entrance clear during ship movements. The recommended crossing track is at right angles to the channel on the W side of No.3 and 4 buoys.

Signals IPTS on E pier control movement in and out of Royal Harbour. A Fl.O Lt indicates that a ship is on the move. At this time no vessel may move from the Royal Harbour or enter from the sea.

Entrance There is a dredged approach channel, used by commercial shipping, before the entrance between N and S breakwaters. At night steer 270° on dir Oc.WRG.10s. After clearing the breakwaters steer to stb for the Royal Harbour whose entrance is 3m or less, variable, giving the hbr G con buoy, Q.G, a wide berth to stb and keeping close to the W Pier as the entrance dries 1m on the E side. Yachts should pass quickly under power through the area between the outer breakwaters and Royal Harbour; Beware fishing boat and wind farm traffic.

Berthing With winds from WNW to NNE small craft can anchor near hbr entrance S of breakwater and entrance channel, 2½–3½m. There are three marinas in Royal Harbour, outer marina E mainly used by fishing boats at **B** (2m) and outer marina W for yachts at **A**, as well as a locked inner harbour (3m) open approx HW ±0200. A red and yellow flag by day and single green light at night indicate the gate is open.

Facilities Boatyard, sail loft, chandlery and launderette.

☎/VHF HM 01843 572100, Marina Office 572110. Port radio VHF 14. Berthing and Lock control VHF 80. Royal Temple YC 591766.
www.portoframsgate.co.uk

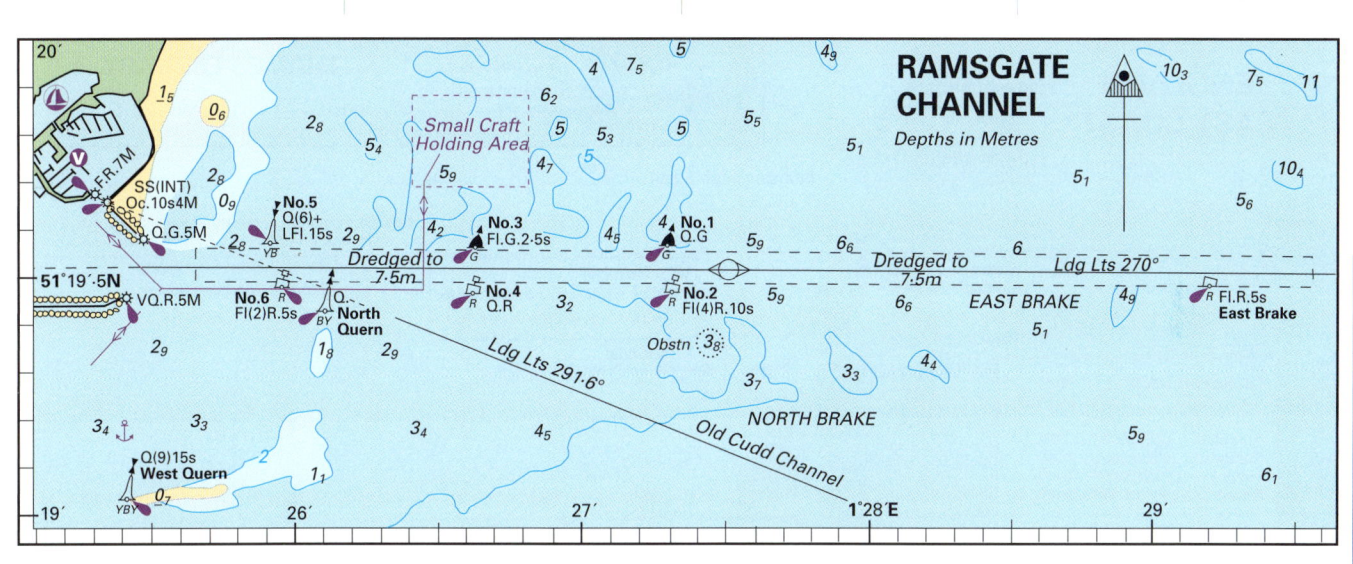

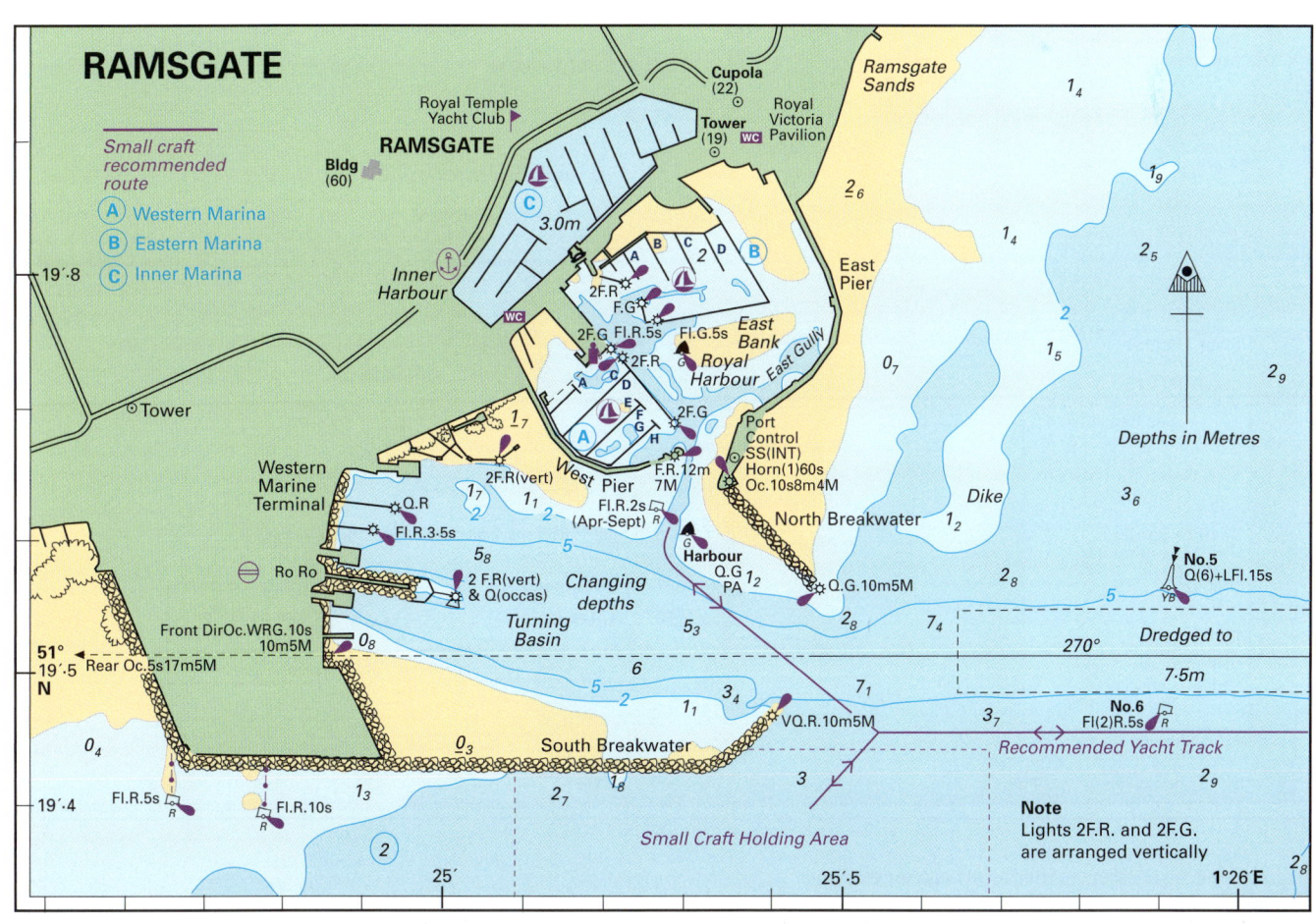

ENGLAND – EAST COAST

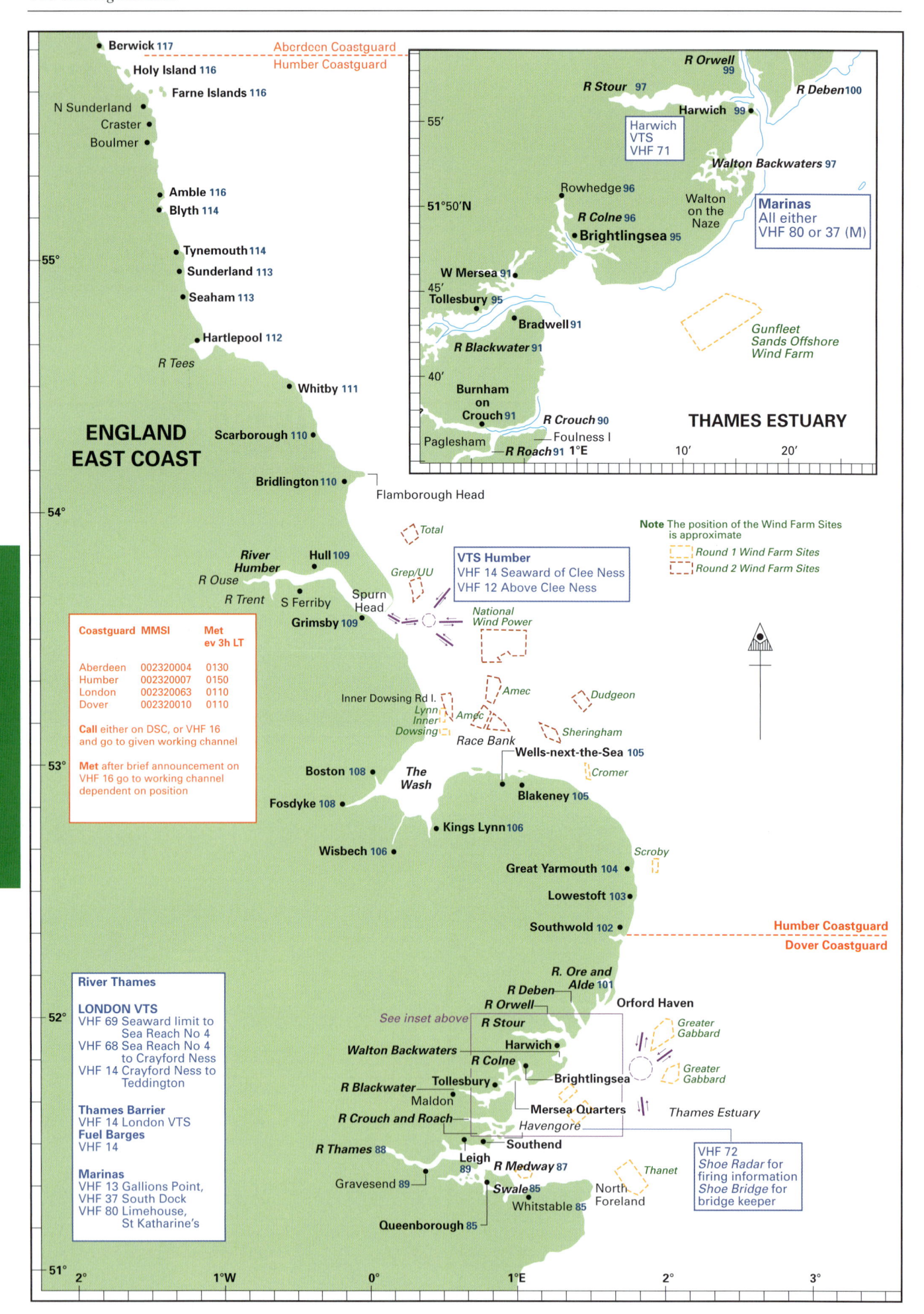

The Cruising Almanac

Map Labels

England East Coast:
- Berwick 117
- Holy Island 116
- Farne Islands 116
- N Sunderland
- Craster
- Boulmer
- Amble 116
- Blyth 114
- Tynemouth 114
- Sunderland 113
- Seaham 113
- Hartlepool 112
- *R Tees*
- Whitby 111
- Scarborough 110
- Bridlington 110
- Flamborough Head
- *River Humber*
- Hull 109
- *R Ouse*
- *R Trent*
- S Ferriby
- Spurn Head
- Grimsby 109
- Inner Dowsing Rd I.
- Boston 108
- Fosdyke 108
- *The Wash*
- Wells-next-the-Sea 105
- Blakeney 105
- Kings Lynn 106
- Wisbech 106
- Great Yarmouth 104
- Lowestoft 103
- Southwold 102
- *R. Ore and Alde* 101
- *R Deben*
- *R Orwell*
- *R Stour*
- Orford Haven
- Walton Backwaters
- Harwich
- *R Colne*
- *R Blackwater*
- Tollesbury
- Maldon
- Brightlingsea
- Mersea Quarters
- *R Crouch and Roach*
- Havengore
- *R Thames* 88
- Gravesend 89
- Leigh 89
- Southend
- *R Medway* 87
- *Swale* 85
- Whitstable 85
- Queenborough 85
- North Foreland
- *Thanet*
- *Thames Estuary*
- Greater Gabbard

Thames Estuary inset:
- *R Orwell* 99
- *R Stour* 97
- Harwich 99
- *R Deben* 100
- Harwich VTS VHF 71
- Walton Backwaters 97
- Walton on the Naze
- Rowhedge 96
- *R Colne* 96
- Brightlingsea 95
- Marinas All either VHF 80 or 37 (M)
- W Mersea 91
- Tollesbury 95
- Bradwell 91
- *R Blackwater* 91
- Gunfleet Sands Offshore Wind Farm
- Burnham on Crouch 91
- Paglesham
- *R Crouch* 90
- Foulness I
- *R Roach* 91

Coastguard information

Coastguard	MMSI	Met ev 3h LT
Aberdeen	002320004	0130
Humber	002320007	0150
London	002320063	0110
Dover	002320010	0110

Call either on DSC, or VHF 16 and go to given working channel

Met after brief announcement on VHF 16 go to working channel dependent on position

VTS Humber
VHF 14 Seaward of Clee Ness
VHF 12 Above Clee Ness

River Thames
LONDON VTS
VHF 69 Seaward limit to Sea Reach No 4
VHF 68 Sea Reach No 4 to Crayford Ness
VHF 14 Crayford Ness to Teddington

Thames Barrier
VHF 14 London VTS
Fuel Barges
VHF 14

Marinas
VHF 13 Gallions Point,
VHF 37 South Dock
VHF 80 Limehouse, St Katharine's

VHF 72 *Shoe Radar* for firing information *Shoe Bridge* for bridge keeper

Note The position of the Wind Farm Sites is approximate
- Round 1 Wind Farm Sites
- Round 2 Wind Farm Sites

Wind Farms labelled: Total, Grep/UU, National Wind Power, Amec, Lynn Inner Dowsing, Race Bank, Dudgeon, Sheringham, Cromer, Scroby, Greater Gabbard, Thanet

Page references are shown after locations, for example:
Lowestoft 103. Bold type indicates that it is accompanied by a plan. *Italics* are used for rivers, lochs, bays, seas etc.

England – East Coast
North Foreland to Berwick

The Thames Estuary, from North Foreland to Orfordness with its rich tradition of commercial shipping, is a cruising area in itself. It has many quiet, secluded anchorages, especially in the Essex and Suffolk rivers, but at the same time there is a good selection of marinas. The chart, with its many sandbanks may look daunting, but the buoyage is good. Much of the area is reasonably sheltered but tides are strong and should be used to advantage, however wind against tide rapidly sets up a steep short sea, especially with a NE'ly wind. There is often considerable commercial shipping in the Princes Channel, about five miles north of the Kent coast, and also in the approaches to Harwich/Felixstowe where due attention must be paid to the TSS. Wind farms continue to grow. The N Kent coast has chalk cliffs as far as Westgate and is backed by hills; there are low cliffs on the Isle of Sheppey. If time allows, a visit to London is well worthwhile. The Essex coast is low apart from the sandy cliffs near Walton-on-the-Naze. Major yachting areas include the R. Medway, and the Suffolk and Essex Rivers; they provide excellent sailing in virtually all weathers. Harwich Harbour and its rivers provide a very safe port of refuge. The coastal marshes of Kent, Essex and Suffolk are important for the breeding and overwintering of water birds. There are RSPB sites on the Stour (one mile east of Wrabness), the Ore (Havergate Island), at Elmley Marshes and Cliffe Pools, the latter two both in North Kent. The estuaries of the Stour, Colne, Blackwater, Crouch and Thames have many Sites of Special Scientific Interest which support plants and animals that find it more difficult to survive in the wider countryside.

Between Orfordness and Flamborough Head many yachts tend to be on longer passages. Bound north, Lowestoft is a convenient port of departure for say Scarborough or Whitby. With the exception of the sandy cliffs between Happisburgh and Cromer much of the coastline is low. It is particularly difficult to identify the shore between the Wash and the Humber. Both Lowestoft and Gt Yarmouth provide access to the Broads for sea-going craft. The Wash and the R. Humber provide access to the inland waterways. To enjoy the north Norfolk coast one needs shallow draught, it is dangerous in fresh onshore winds.

Flamborough Head with its high chalk cliffs is very conspicuous. From here to Berwick there are few convenient anchorages, with the exception of Holy Island and the Farnes in suitable conditions. On passage, distances between harbours are such that overnight passages are rarely necessary; there are pontoon berths at Scarborough, Whitby, Hartlepool, Sunderland, Newcastle, Royal Quays marina (River Tyne), Blyth and Amble. The Yorkshire coast with its superb cliff scenery, bays, and ports is delightful in offshore winds, but beware of the swell which may build up after N'ly weather making many harbour entrances dangerous. Tees Bay is an industrial area and there are usually several ships at anchor. Blyth is a safe port in heavy weather, except from the SE. The Northumberland coast with its sandy beaches and views towards the Cheviots is very attractive.

North Foreland to Harwich

Off North Foreland the tidal streams are complex. Within the Thames Estuary the tide runs W or SW during the flood and E or NE during the ebb. In the approaches to the Dover Strait, eg the Gull Stream, the change in direction of the tidal stream does not occur at local HW or LW. The best advice is to consult tidal stream charts: see p.434 to p.440. Times of HW and LW, and also tidal heights may differ significantly from predictions, owing to meteorological conditions. Beware, most tidal stream charts for Dover Strait are related to HW Dover, and those for Thames Estuary are related to HW Sheerness.

Passage lights	BA No
N Foreland LtHo	0966
Fl(5)WR.20s57m19/15M	AIS
Sunk Inner RW Lt Float	2172
Fl(5)15s12M *AIS* Horn(1)30s Racon T (–)	
Sunk Centre LtV	2170
Fl(2)20s12m16M Horn(2)60s Racon C (– · · ·) *AIS*	

THAMES ESTUARY PASSAGES

Tides should be used to their best advantage. From the S, depending upon destination, it may be best to stem an adverse tide in the Downs to make the first of the flood at N Foreland. A careful analysis of the tidal streams and depths may permit straight line passages but for most boats it is necessary to navigate a way through the sand banks. Alternatively one can pass to seaward of the sand banks, but beware of the Sunk Precautionary Area. Three TSSs lead traffic into and out of the Outer Area. Traffic within the Outer Area flows in a counter-clockwise direction around an area to be avoided, one nautical mile in diameter, centred on the Sunk Centre LtF Fl(2)20s16M in position 51°50'·10N 1°46'·02E. See plan on pp.82–83. There are many ways to pass through the maze of channels and swatchways. Some are indicated on the passage plan (see pp.82–83).

The London Array wind farm is situated in the area of Long Sand and Knock Deep. Foulger's Gat is a buoyed channel through the SW end of the wind farm; it may be used subject to the usual restriction of an advisory 50m exclusion zone round wind turbines and possible extra exclusion zones round maintenance works. For latest information see www.londonarray.com Monitor VHF16 for calls from guard vessels.

England, East Coast distances (miles)

	N Foreland,1M E	Harwich	Orfordness	Southwold	Lowestoft	Wells	Grimsby	Flamborough Hd	Scarborough	Whitby	Hartlepool	Sunderland	Blyth	Amble	Holy Island	Eyemouth	Stonehaven
N Foreland,1M E	0																
Harwich	44	0															
Orfordness	45	16	0														
Southwold	58	32	15	0													
Lowestoft	68	43	25	12	0												
Wells	124	101	81	68	56	0											
Grimsby	170	145	127	115	102	54	0										
Flamborough Hd	190	165	147	133	122	77	47	0									
Scarborough	205	180	162	148	137	92	62	15	0								
Whitby	222	197	179	165	154	117	94	31	18	0							
Hartlepool	245	220	202	188	177	141	119	55	42	24	0						
Sunderland	258	233	215	201	190	153	130	67	53	36	17	0					
Blyth	269	244	226	212	202	165	166	78	65	48	29	11	0				
Amble	283	258	240	226	216	179	193	92	79	62	43	26	15	0			
Holy Island	302	277	259	245	235	198	247	111	98	81	61	44	33	23	0		
Eyemouth	320	294	276	262	252	215	291	129	115	98	79	62	51	40	18	0	
Stonehaven	385	359	341	327	317	280	356	194	180	163	144	127	116	105	82	66	0

The Cruising Almanac

Thames Estuary distances (miles)

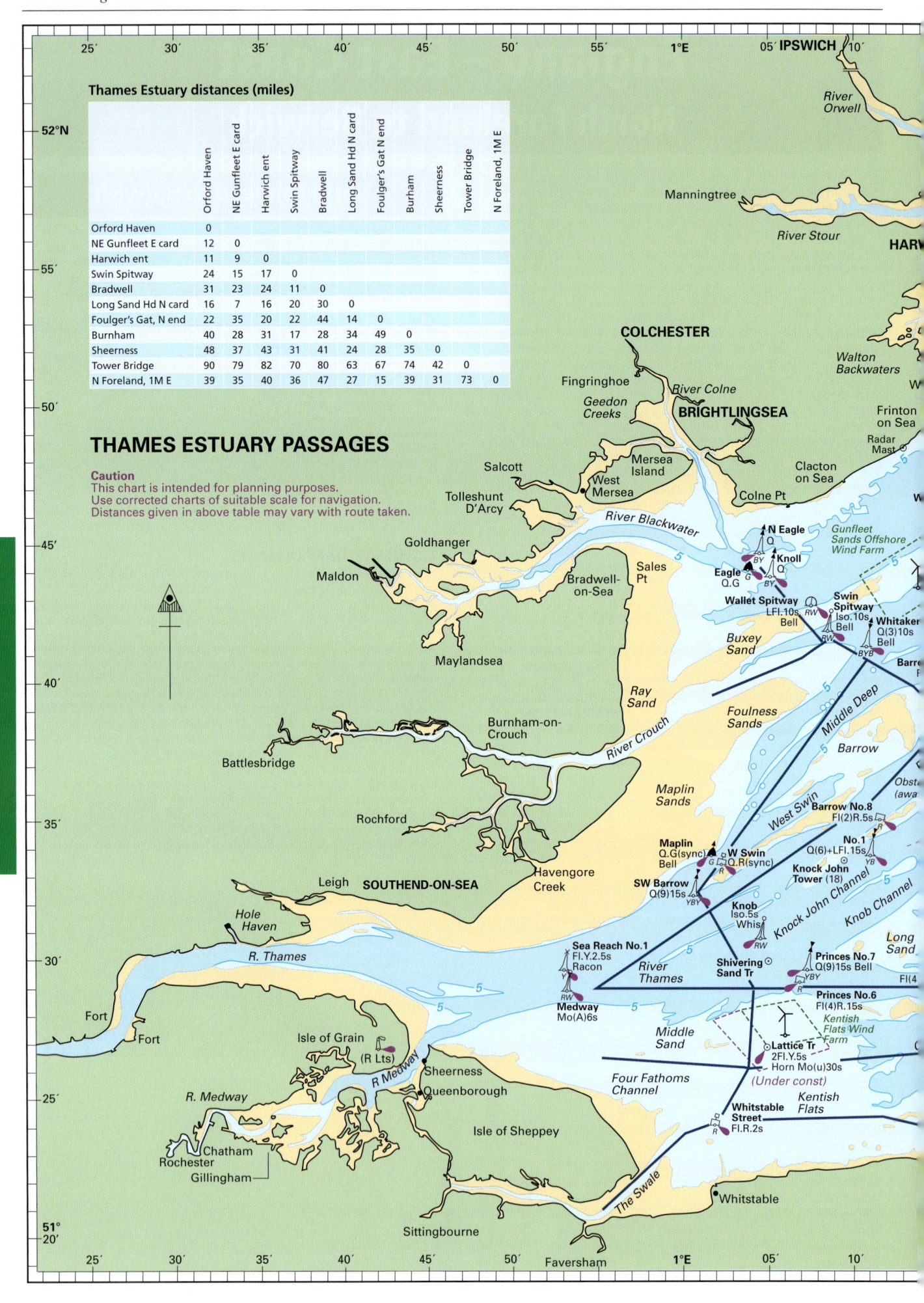

	Orford Haven	NE Gunfleet E card	Harwich ent	Swin Spitway	Bradwell	Long Sand Hd N card	Foulger's Gat N end	Burnham	Sheerness	Tower Bridge	N Foreland, 1M E
Orford Haven	0										
NE Gunfleet E card	12	0									
Harwich ent	11	9	0								
Swin Spitway	24	15	17	0							
Bradwell	31	23	24	11	0						
Long Sand Hd N card	16	7	16	20	30	0					
Foulger's Gat, N end	22	35	20	22	44	14	0				
Burnham	40	28	31	17	28	34	49	0			
Sheerness	48	37	43	31	41	24	28	35	0		
Tower Bridge	90	79	82	70	80	63	67	74	42	0	
N Foreland, 1M E	39	35	40	36	47	27	15	39	31	73	0

THAMES ESTUARY PASSAGES

Caution
This chart is intended for planning purposes.
Use corrected charts of suitable scale for navigation.
Distances given in above table may vary with route taken.

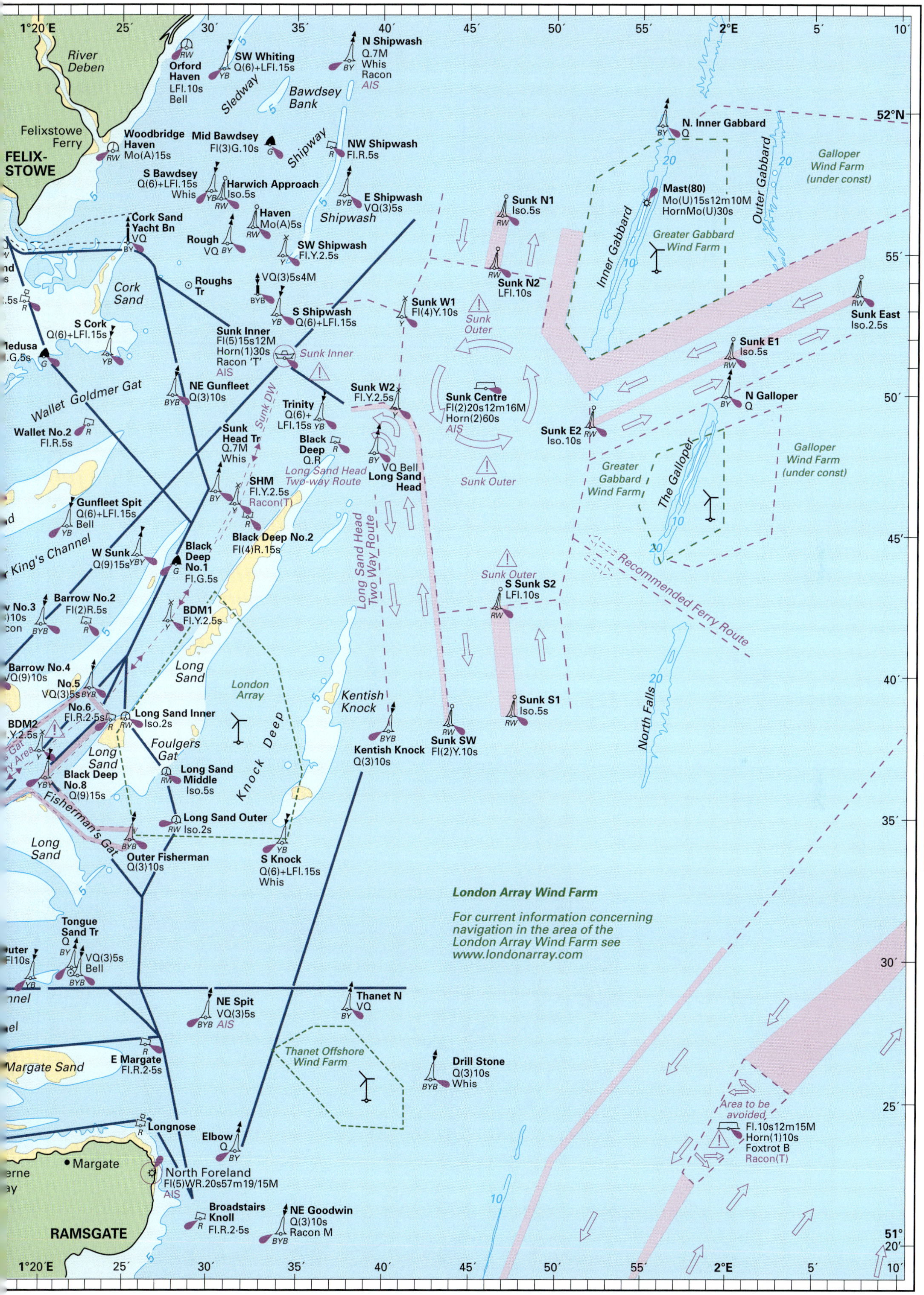

ENGLAND – EAST COAST

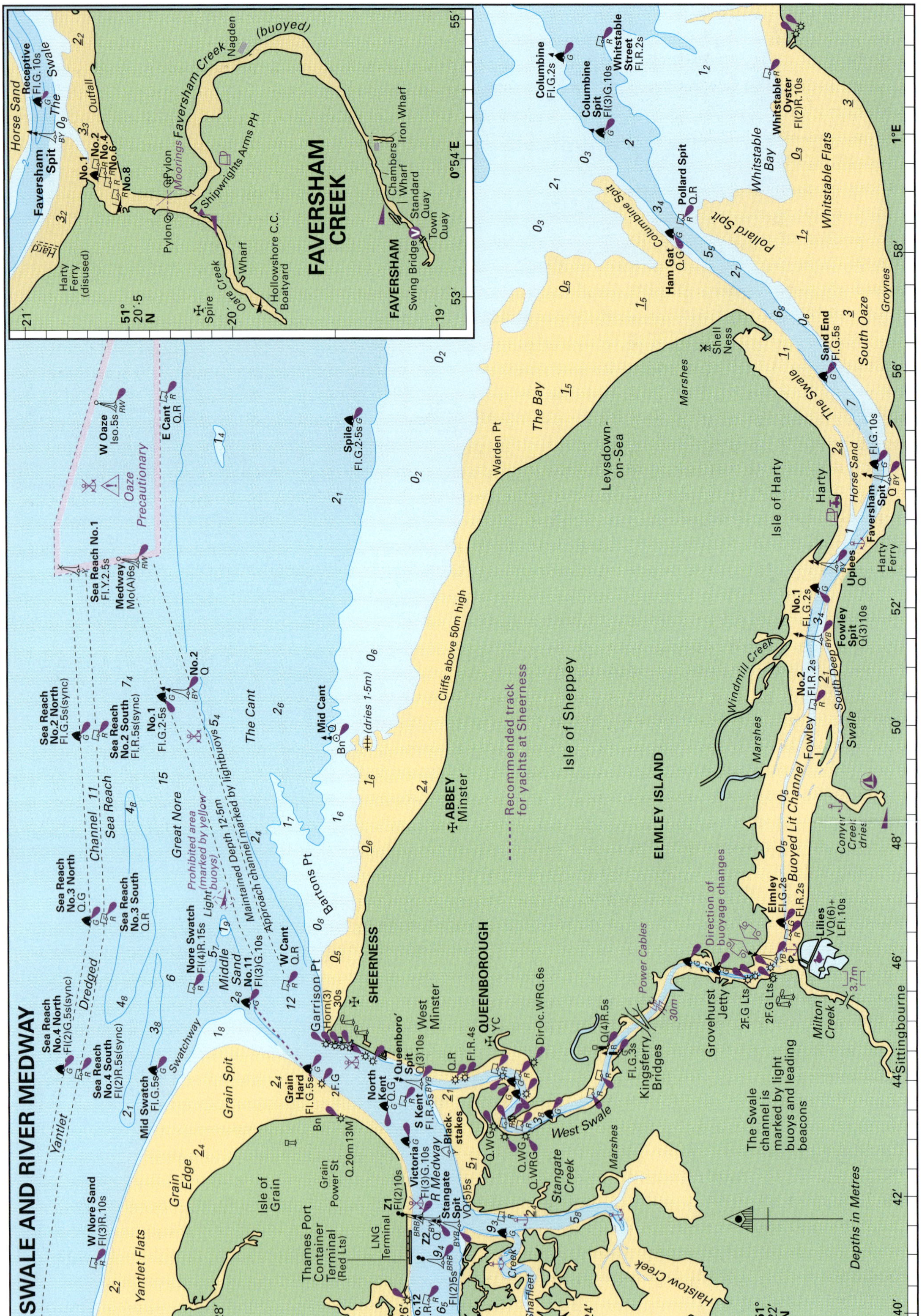
SWALE AND RIVER MEDWAY
FAVERSHAM CREEK
Isle of Sheppey
ELMLEY ISLAND
Isle of Harty
Isle of Grain
SHEERNESS
QUEENBOROUGH
Leysdown-on-Sea
Whitstable Bay
Whitstable Flats
Columbine Spit
Pollard Spit
South Oaze
The Swale
West Swale
Grain Spit
Yantlet Flats
Great Nore
The Cant
Cliffs above 50m high
Recommended track for yachts at Sheerness
Prohibited area (marked by yellow buoys)
Maintained Depth 12·5m Approach channel marked by lightbuoys
Oaze Precautionary
The Swale channel is marked by light buoys and leading beacons
Direction of buoyage changes
Buoyed Lit Channel
Depths in Metres
Faversham Spit
Harty Ferry
Sittingbourne
Milton Creek
Conyer Creek dries
Halstow Creek
Stangate Creek
Kingsferry Bridges
Power Cables
Windmill Creek
Thames Port Container Terminal (Red Lts)
LNG Terminal
Grain Power St
Hollowshore C.C. Boatyard
Shipwrights Arms PH
Oare Creek
Swing Bridge
Standard Quay
Town Quay
Chambers Wharf
Iron Wharf
Nagden
0°54´E
1°E
51°22´N

THAMES ESTUARY PASSAGES continued

- **N Foreland to the Swale, River Medway and River Thames** Through the Gore and Copperas channels, S of Margate sands. They have few lit buoys and there are unmarked shallows and drying patches. Probably better E of Margate Sand through the Queens or Princes Channels. The latter has lit buoys but considerable commercial traffic. In onshore winds the only secure anchorages are the E Swale and River Medway. Anchored ships will frequently be encountered in Medway Roads. Mariners are particularly warned to avoid the shallow obstructions caused by cables from the wind farms, marked by the South Card buoy and three unlit Y buoys due N of Herne Bay.

- **N Foreland to River Crouch, River Blackwater and River Colne** From N Foreland pass E of Margate Sand and through Fisherman's Gat or Foulger's Gat using the buoyed channel through the wind farm to Black Deep. With sufficient height of tide and good conditions Sunk Sand can be crossed close to Barrow No.2 Fl(2)R.5s. Proceed N round E Barrow and N Middle Sands to the Whitaker E card buoy. Be aware that the drying sands in this area have been increasing in recent years. If in doubt take the Knock John Channel SW, pass W of West Barrow Sand into the West Swin and East Swin Channels to the Whitaker Channel for the Crouch or across the Swin Spitway to the Blackwater and the Colne.

- **N Foreland to Harwich** Pass E of Margate Sands and 2M E of the Tongue Sand Tower through Fisherman's Gat or Foulger's Gat using the buoyed channel through the wind farm and Black Deep. In either case leave the Black Deep at Sunk Head Tower N card Lt buoy Q and take the Medusa Channel to Harwich. Alternatively enter Barrow Deep as above following deep water E of the Gunfleet Spit S card Lt buoy until clear of Gunfleet Sand before turning to port for the Medusa channel. There is also the offshore route either through the Knock Deep or outside Kentish Knock to Long Sand Head N card VQ. If passing outside the Kentish Knock be careful to avoid the TSSs and Sunk Outer Precautionary Area by following the recommended two way route from the Kentish Knock E card buoy to Long Sand Head N card buoy. This route may be used by any vessel less than 20m, or if sailing or fishing. Then make for the Roughs Tower and the Cork Sand N card yacht beacon.

- **Sunk Inner to Rivers Medway and Thames** The main routes are Barrow and Black Deeps but E and W Swins avoid shipping. A few buoys mark the passages.

- **Sunk Inner to River Crouch** Pass SW along the Kings Channel to the Whitaker E card Lt buoy and then into the Whitaker channel.

- **Sunk Inner to Rivers Colne and Blackwater** Pass N of the NE Gunfleet E card Q(3)10s into the Wallet, then SW to the Knoll N card Q and the buoyed channel to Colne Bar G con Fl(2)G.5s for the River Colne or to the Bench Head G con Fl(3)G.10s to enter the River Blackwater.

- **Harwich to the River Crouch** Leave Harwich by the recommended yacht track preferably about LW -0200. Pass close W of Stone Banks R. can buoy towards Medusa buoy. Turn to stb up the Wallet to the Wallet Spitway buoy and then through the Spitway which has least depth of 1.6m. Turn SW up the well buoyed channel to the Crouch. Tides run strongly in both the Wallet and in the approaches to the Crouch, so time of departure is all important.

- **Whitaker Channel to E Swale** From the Whitaker E card Q(3)10s pass through the E and W Swins to the SW Barrow S card Lt buoy Q(9)15s Sand, then given sufficient depth, go to the Whitstable Street R can buoy at the entrance to the E Swale. If there is need to avoid the Red and Middle Sands, from the SW Barrow go first to the Princes No.8 and then around Kentish Flats Wind Farm to Whitstable Street.

- **Thames Estuary to the near Continent** Bound for France head for North Foreland (see above). Bound for Belgium see p.244 or for the Netherlands p.249.

WHITSTABLE

Standard Port Sheerness
HW (sp) +0014 (np) +0001
LW (sp) +0003 (np) +0017

MHWS	MHWN	MLWN	MLWS
–0.2m	–0.2m	0.0m	–0.1m

Small hbr, controlled by Canterbury Council, mainly used commercially. Temporary shelter for yachts seeking shelter from strong W or SW winds at discretion of HM. Access HW ±0300.

Anchorages Good anchorage in the bay for up to 1·5m draught close by the yacht moorings W of the hbr entrance and clear of fairway, also in Tankerton Bay 1M E of hbr, in suitable winds.

☎/VHF HM VHF 9, 01227 274086 Monday–Friday 0800–1700; Whitstable YC 01227 272942
www.whitstableharbour.org

SWALE AND HARTY FERRY

Standard Port Sheerness
Grovehurst Jetty
HW (sp) –0007 (np) +0000
LW (sp) +0000 (np) +0016

MHWS	MHWN	MLWN	MLWS
0.0m	0.0m	0.0m	–0.1m

Harty Ferry to Queenborough through the Swale

Least depth at MLWS 1m. All times relate to Dover.
DS –0430 to –0400: slack everywhere.
Harty Ferry +0130 E, –0400 W.
Fowley Is –0400 to +0130 streams run in at both ends and meet here. From +0130 to +0500 the stream is E-going. From +0500 to –0430 streams separate here and run out at both ends.
Kingsferry –0400 SE, +0330 NW. (i.e. in from Medway for 7·5h, out towards Medway for 4·5h).
Streams are strongest soon after they begin and the greatest rates, about 4kn at springs, occur near Kingsferry. It is easier to carry a fair tide when bound E.
Queenborough –0400 S, +0230 N.
Buoyage Inward from Shellness to Milton Creek. Inward from Queenborough to Milton Creek. The Swale is well buoyed and has Ldg lines for large vessels at the W end. It is essential to keep to the marked channels and to be aware of depth at all times.
From Harty Ferry, where there are moorings and good holding, steer to clear No.1 G con Lt buoy Fl.G.2s well to S, then to No.2 R can Lt buoy Fl.R.2s near Fowley Island. Least water, nearly dries, near Fowley I and just before Elmley Ferry, where a causeway stands ½m above the river bed. Marked by four posts. Best water on N (island) side. At LW, channel only a few metres wide bounded by large areas of mud.
Kingsferry Bridge lifts on request, rly traffic permitting. Contact Bridge Keeper well in advance before committing to passage as opening times can be erratic. Clearance at MHWS: closed 3·3m; lifted, up to 27m. Traffic signals are shown only when bridge is about to open or close.

Fl.G+R	Br about to be lifted
F.G	Br open for passage
Fl.R	Br closing
Fl.Or	Br not working – keep clear
No lights	Opening not imminent

Use of Lts variable. Be prepared to move as soon as bridge rises even if no Lts showing.
VHF 10 Bridge keeper.
VHF 74 Message may be passed through Medway Radio.
Beware very bright sectored lights.

Approach and Entrance From the Columbine G con buoy Fl.G.2s on 234° to close N of the Pollard Spit R can Lt buoy, thence 227° leaving the Sand End G con Lt buoy to stb. Thence 237° towards Faversham Spit N card buoy which should be left to port if proceeding up Swale but to stb if entering Faversham Creek, (access HW±0130), keep to mid channel. For Faversham Creek, continue to port at the fork, leaving the pub to stb. Detailed navigation information is given on guide from Faversham Town Council ☎ 01795 594442 or www.faversham.org.uk.

Faversham Creek
Berthing
- **Hollowshore Services** at Oare Creek. Alongside mooring. Access HW±0045. Limited facilities. Uncomfortable in strong NE winds. ☎ 01795 532317.
- **Iron Wharf Boatyard**, Abbeyfields, Faversham. Access HW±0200. Limited facilities. ☎ 537122. VHF 8 Iron Wharf.
- **Front Brents Jetty**, Upper Brents, Faversham. Access HW±0200. Limited facilities. ☎ 591140
- **Youngboats**, Oare Creek, Faversham. Access HW±0130. Limited facilities, diesel. ☎ 536176.
- **Swale Marina**, Conyer Wharf, Sittingbourne. Pontoon mud berths, access HW±0100. Diesel. ☎ 521562.
- **Conyer Creek Marina**, Conyer Quay, Sittingbourne. Access HW±0200 ☎ 521384.

Anchorages
- Good holding ground (mud) between Fowley Spit buoy and Faversham Creek, avoiding moorings and shellfish beds by Horseshoe Sands. More comfortable shallow-draught anchorages may be found in South Deep. Oare and Faversham are accessible from the hard on the S side. Boatyard and Inn at junction of Faversham and Oare Creeks.
- In the South Deep between Fowley Is and the S shore in 1m. To approach follow the S bank for approx 1M from Harty Ferry hard leaving a small Island marked by a E card buoy to stb.

Facilities Faversham is a medieval market town, 10 miles from Canterbury. Rly to London, Canterbury and Ramsgate. Oare and S Swale Nature Reserves.

QUEENBOROUGH

Tidal data as Sheerness
DS Dover –0400 S; +0230N

A convenient port, easily accessible by day and night. Sheltered except in strong N/NE winds.

Approach and Entrance From the R Medway leave the Queenborough Spit E card Lt buoy close to stb. A course of 178° leads up the fairway; at night keep in the narrow W

The Cruising Almanac

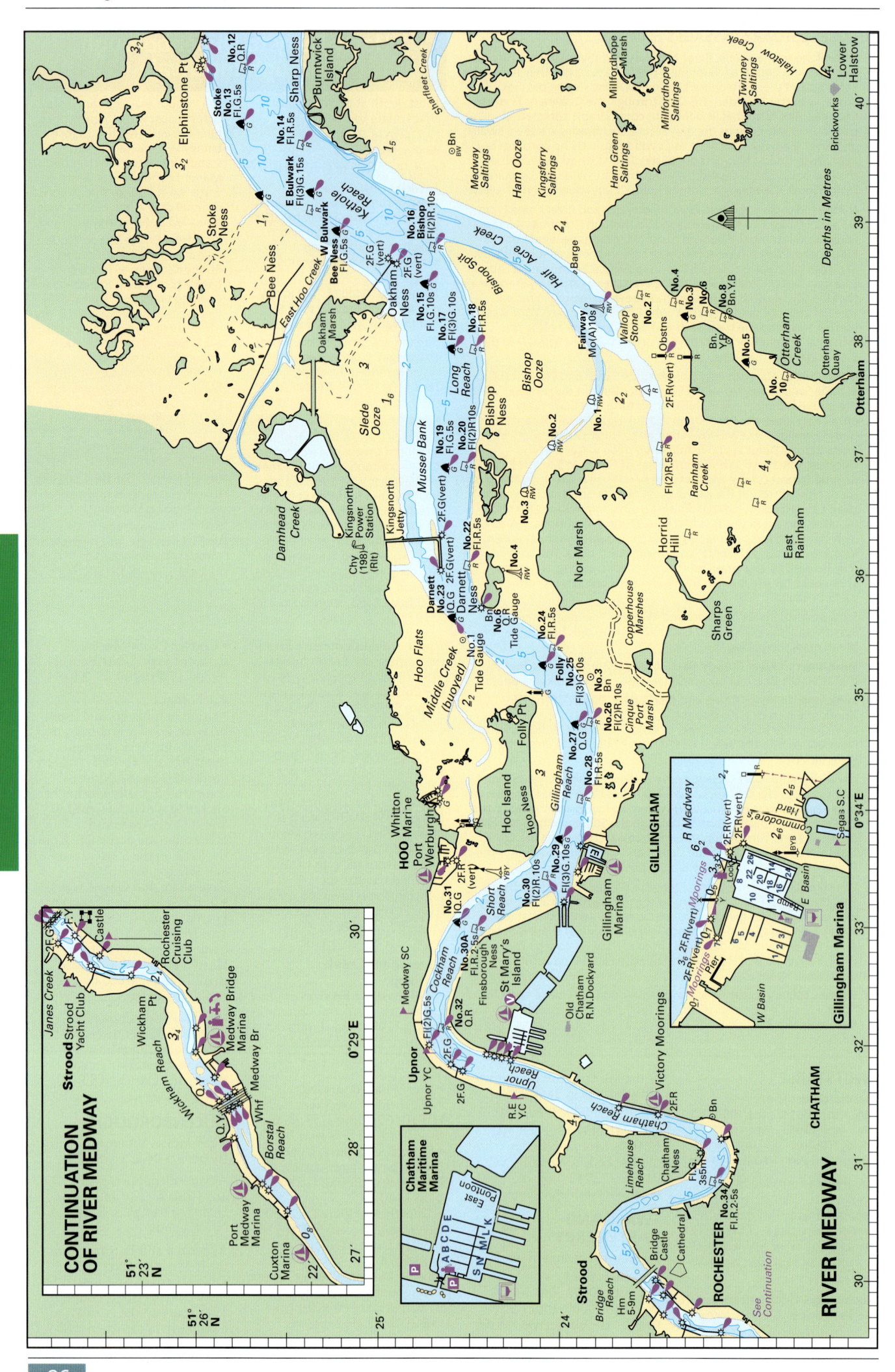

QUEENBOROUGH

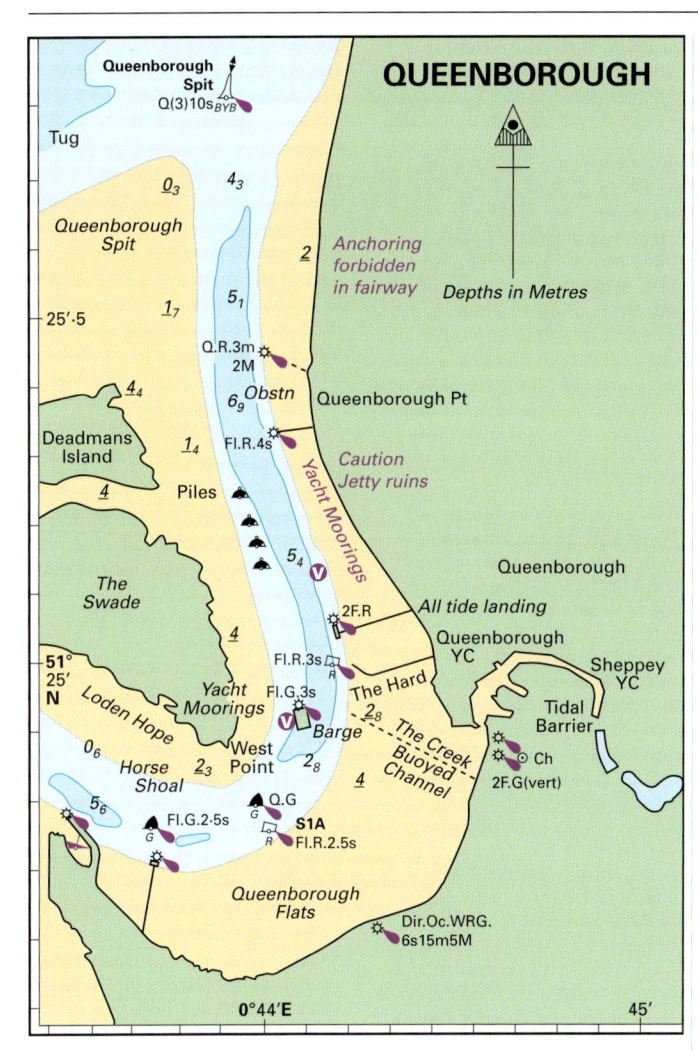

sector of the Dir.Oc.WRG.6s light. Further into the creek leave to port the ruins of the rly pier; the area of the derelict pier is dangerous and stumps are exposed at half-tide.

Berthing
- Two yellow visitors' buoys N and two grey visitors' buoys S of the all tide landing, all with strops. Rafting may be necessary
- Concrete lighter on W side of Swale opposite all tide landing. Do not moor on E/fairway side overnight
- Small yellow buoys E of the fairway to N of the all tide landing may be available to visitors. Consult HM. VHF 08
- All tide landing. Vessels may moor temporarily to take on water. For longer periods visitors may moor alongside with permission from the HM. Access gate needs code available from HM. Landing by dinghy is allowed. Visitors should read the instructions on the notice board.

Facilities Rly to London. Showers ashore. Scrubbing berth.

☎/**VHF** Queenborough Harbour 01795 662051. HM, Trot boat and water taxi VHF 08.
www.queenborough-harbour.co.uk

RIVER MEDWAY

Standard Port Sheerness

Upnor
HW (sp) +0015 (np) +0015
LW (sp) +0025 (np) +0015
MHWS MHWN MLWN MLWS
+0·2m 0·2m –0·1m –0·1m

DS (Sheerness Narrows)
Dover–0430S;+0145N

Sheltered sailing and mooring are available in all winds. The main fairway is clearly marked by lit buoys and is suitable for yachts at all states of tide. At high water, wide areas of ooze and saltings cover deceptively. Three marinas on the Medway welcome visitors, there are numerous buoys and anchoring is possible in Stangate and Half Acre creeks and outside the fairway in the river.

Traffic is controlled by Medway Ports Authority and a listening watch should be kept on VHF 74 for VTS information. There is extensive commercial traffic to the Swale wharves, Sheerness Docks, Thamesport, Chatham Docks, Kingsnorth Power Station and several timber and aggregate wharves, together with LASH operations and the exercises of Royal Engineers afloat.

The river is tidal up to Allington, but is effectively divided by the bridges at Rochester, which prevent most masted yachts from proceeding upstream.

East Coast Pilot has a chapter on the lower reaches of the Medway with *The River Medway* covering Gillingham to Tonbridge. Both are published by Imray. For local information on the Medway and Swale see www.msba.org.uk.

Approach
- From the E, an inshore passage from Spile G.2·5s to No.6 Q.R of the Medway Approach Channel may be taken on a rising tide, leaving the Mid Cant pile and Cheyney Tripod (N card) posts marking inshore hazards well to port. There is deep water at Garrison Point by the disused ferry terminal.
- From Sea Reach on the Thames, the Nore Swatchway may be taken, leaving Nore Swatch R to stb, then join Medway Approach Channel at No.11 G. Fl(3)10s. The recommended track for leisure craft should be followed to Grain Hard G con Lt buoy Fl.G.5s.
- From N and E, follow the Medway Approach Channel, which runs SW for six miles from Medway safe water buoy, Mo(A)6s to Garrison Point. There is a Medway Secondary Channel, S of the main shipping channel, marked by buoys Fl(2)Y.5s. There is plenty of water outside the marked channel, except to the NW after No.7 Fl.G.10s. where the wreck of the second world war ammunition ship *Richard Montgomery* is still fully loaded. The wreck is extensively buoyed. There are strong tides across the approach channel.

The E side of the Medway is marked by a fort at Garrison Point, from which a bright W light Fl.7s is displayed (both to sea and up river) when big ship movements are in progress. Yachts may proceed with caution.

The W side has Grain tr, marked by a buoy Fl.G.10s. A wide berth should be given to large ships containing Liquefied Natural Gas using Sheerness Docks and berthing at LNG terminal at 51°25'·9N 0°42'·55E where there is a 150m exclusion zone.

Entrance Stream may run up to 3kn. On the ebb considerable advantage may be gained from an inflowing eddy that runs close in by the seaward side of Garrison Point, or the main strength of stream avoided by keeping to the W.

From Garrison Point to Rochester the channel is marked by lit buoys. Beware numerous large unlit buoys outside channel. The entrance to the West Swale is marked by the Queenborough Spit E card Lt buoy Q(3)10s. A further 1½M on in Saltpan Reach the entrance to Stangate Creek on the S side of the river is marked by the Stangate Spit E card Lt buoy VQ(3)5s which lies S of the conspic five container cranes on the N side of the Reach. These wharves extend from Victoria to Elphinstone Pt. Large vessel movements take place in this area and small craft must keep well clear. The hbr authority prohibits any unauthorised vessel from coming within 30m of the jetties or the vessels moored there.

From Kethole Reach inwards the river appears deceptively wide towards HW, but the buoyed deep-water channel is only about 2ca wide. Speed limit of 6kn from Gillingham Reach inwards. Large vessels including tugs and lighters use the river below Rochester. Take particular care at bends. Navigation for vessels with high fixed masts stops at Rochester Br. Headroom under the middle span 5·96m above MHWS giving 11·36m at MLWS but with depths of less than 1m in places. For motor cruisers the other key br is the stone br at Aylesford 8·4M upstream from Rochester Br. This has 2·87m clear at MHWS. Passage under Rochester Br is safest at HW±0300. Centre arch has least water, is subject to difficult tidal eddies and leads directly on to shoal patch. When depth is critical take Strood arch obliquely. Line up with end of pier on Rochester bank above br and straighten up into channel along outside line of RCC moorings. If heading for MPA visitors buoy on Strood side, follow same approach, cross river when above these moorings and fall back onto them. Progress beyond this point to Allington Lock 12M, the end of the tidal part of the river, is inadvisable before half flood. The lock is operated from HW–0300 to HW+0200 and manned at all times. Craft proceeding upriver against the stream give way to craft going downriver. ☎ Allington Lock 01622 752864.

Berthing
- **Gillingham Marina** Access HW±0430 to locked basin. Access lock manned 0600–2200 April to October, 0800–1700 otherwise. Once through the lock be ready to manoeuvre in a confined space and maybe to moor between posts. Fuel pontoon (diesel and petrol) outside but no foot access from these into the Marina. There are also holding moorings and a tidal basin with access HW±0130. ☎ 01634 280022, VHF 80.

Facilities Supermarket. Heliport.
- **Chatham Maritime Marina** Access 24 hrs by lock. Waiting pontoon. Strong cross currents in the approach. Restaurants and pubs, many located in historic buildings. Historic Dockyard with museum. RNLI Museum with 15 lifeboats on show. Diesel. Launderette. Regular bus to Rly and shops in Chatham. ☎ 899200, VHF 80.
- **Medway Ports Ltd** maintains six visitors' buoys above Rochester Br on the Strood side. VHF 80.
- **Medway Bridge Marina** Access all tides.

Facilities Shops in Borstal nearby; Rochester Castle and Cathedral are a 15 minute walk. ☎ 01634 843576, VHF 80.

Anchorages
- **Stangate Creek** and off lying creeks afford a quiet sheltered anchorage clear of traffic, in among the marshes. To enter the creek leave the Stangate Spit E card VQ(3)5s buoy to stb. Proceed in centre of creek keeping large mooring buoy (reserved for vessels carrying explosives) to stb and between port and stb unlit buoys ½M from entrance. Good anchorage on either side beyond this point. Riding Lt essential as creek is used by barges etc. Entrance at night not advisable for strangers.
- **Sharfleet Creek** leads off on the stb hand ½M from the entrance of Stangate. Good anchorage, probably the best on the Medway, on the S side just inside, or on either shore further in, clear of any oyster beds.
- There are many moorings suitable for yachts between Gillingham and Rochester, mostly controlled by yacht clubs or privately owned. Some commercially available. None are intended for visitors but may be available from Medway Cruising Club, REYC, Upnor SC ☎ 07092 197923 or commercial operators at Gillingham Wharf. Beware fore-and-aft moorings with fixed lines between buoys.

Facilities Diesel from Marinas at Gillingham, Chatham and Medway Br.

RIVER THAMES
Standard Port Sheerness
Gravesend
HW +0005   LW+0005
MHWS MHWN MLWN MLWS
+0·7m +0·6m +0·1m –0·1m
Standard Port London Bridge
Erith
HW (sp) -0057   (np) -0045
LW (sp) -0007   (np) -0050
MHWS MHWN MLWN MLWS
–0·6m –0·6m +0·2m –0·2m
Hammersmith Bridge
HW (sp) +0040   (np) +0035
LW (sp) +0205   (np) + 0155
MHWS MHWN MLWN MLWS
–1·4m –1·3m –1·0m –0·5m
Richmond Lock
HW (sp) +0105   (np) +0055
LW (sp) +0325   (np) + 0305
MHWS MHWN MLWN MLWS
–2·2m –2·7m –0·9m –0·5m
DS London Br -0055E +0500W

The River Thames is the gateway to London and provides an interesting sail to marinas in the centre of the capital. The Port of London Authority (PLA) controls the river downstream from Teddington. Their website (www.pla.co.uk) gives much useful information and they publish annually *The River Thames Recreational Users Guide* (laminated fold-out chartlet) and *Handbook of Tide Tables and Port Information*. These, together with PLA published charts and NM can be purchased from www.pla.co.uk. They are also available from London River House, Royal Pier Road, Gravesend, Kent DA12 2BG ☎ 01474 562200. Imray publish *The River Thames Book* which covers the area upriver from the Thames Barrier and *East Coast Pilot* which covers down river from Tower Br.

Vessels navigating any part of the River Thames must comply with sound signals. Failure to do so may lead to proceedings and a substantial fine. It is advisable to monitor *London VTS*.

VHF 69 Seaward limit to Sea Reach No.4 buoy: VHF 68 Sea Reach No.4 buoy to Crayford Ness: VHF 14 Crayford Ness to Teddington.

The RNLI run a lifeboat service on the Thames. In emergency ☎ 999 and ask for London Coastguard, use VHF 16/67 or the appropriate London VTS working channel.

Tides Tides can run at 3–4kn and it is essential to use them to best advantage. Since the tide off the entrance to R. Medway turns approx 1h before that at London Bridge, up-river one can usually carry a fair tide for 7h but down-river for only 5h.

Sea Reach to Margaret Ness Inward bound, begin the upriver passage at LW in Sea Reach. Queenborough, on the River Medway, is a convenient stopover point to await the tide in all conditions. From there start using the last hour of ebb. Outward bound, e.g. from Limehouse, leave 1h before HW, with average speed one should be in Sea Reach by LW. The Sea Reach deep-water channel is well marked. Keep well clear of commercial vessels by using the N and S navigable margins. It is best to keep to the S side between Southend and Lower Hope Pt.

Margaret Ness to Blackwall Point and Thames Barrier When planning a passage on the Thames, routine closures for maintenance of the Thames Barrier can be found on www.gov.uk/the-thames-barrier#upcoming-scheduled-closures. A control zone exists between Margaret Ness and Blackwall Point for regulating traffic; passage of all craft is strictly controlled. Contact *London VTS* on VHF 14 or ☎ 020 8855 0315 for permission to proceed when passing Margaret Ness inward or Blackwall Point outward. London VTS will then allocate a span which will be indicated as being available by the lit green arrows and red crosses. Green arrows will be exhibited from the ends of piers either side of the span(s) open to navigation. The arrows point inwards towards the span open to navigation from a particular direction. Red crosses will be exhibited from the ends of the piers either side of span(s) closed to navigation from one or both directions. Keep a watch on traffic from astern. Spans A, H, J and K are permanently closed to navigation. Maintain a listening watch on VHF 14. London VTS makes regular broadcasts at 15 min before and 15 min after the hour. You may be asked to call again when the barrier is in sight. There are illuminated notice boards indicating Barrier closure at Barking or False Pt, Blackwall Pt, and Blackwall Stairs. Closed spans may be open to navigation in the opposite direction. Before you reach the barrier, keep a close look out for the Woolwich cross river ferries which leave their berths very quickly. Vessels proceeding under sail between the Woolwich Ferry Terminal and Hookness must keep to the stb side of the fairway and are not to impede any other vessels. Whenever possible, such vessels should take in their sails and use the engine to navigate through the Barrier. The tide runs hard through the open spans. No stopping, turning or anchoring within 100m of the Barrier.

Blackwall Point to Tower Bridge There are no special problems here. Sailing is difficult. Beware of high speed ferries.

Berthing and anchorages
- **Gravesend** Entrance to Embankment Marina, ☎ 01474 535700, VHF 80, is at the E end of the promenade. Access HW–0100 to HW through a narrow gut between drying banks to the lock. Diesel and gas. Gravesend SC, ☎ 07538 326623, have a visitors' mooring – eastern end of outer trot, landing at wooden causeway. PLA have yellow small craft moorings upriver of Gravesend Sailing Club which may be available. Anchor in Higham Bight, near Shornmead Lighthouse Fl(2)WR.10s. Tripping line essential. Wash uncomfortable.
- **Thurrock YC** welcomes visitors. A member's mooring may be available for vessels less than 10m. ☎ 01375 373720.
- **Erith YC** has moorings for yachts up to 10m. Larger vessels should anchor above moorings. Smaller, shallow draught vessels below moorings. Water at HW by arrangement. Supermarket. ☎ 01322 332943.
- **Greenwich YC** has deep water moorings for yachts up to 12m. Contact HM ☎ 0844 736 5846 prior to arrival.
- **Gallions Point Marina** Access HW±0500. Lock Monday–Friday 0630–1830, weekend 0930–1830. DLR London City Airport ☎ 020 7476 7054. VHF 37/M, 80. Diesel.
- **South Dock Marina** Access HW-0230/+0130. National Maritime Museum, Royal Naval College, Royal Observatory and Cutty Sark. Crane: 20 tonnes. ☎ 020 7252 2244. VHF 37/M.
- **Limehouse Dock Marina** Access HW±0300 approx. 0800–1800 April–September; 0800–1600 October–March. ☎ 020 7308 9930, VHF 80, when passing the Cutty Sark. Out of hours locking available from 0500 or until 2200 at any time of year if prebooked at least 24h in advance. Waiting pontoons may dry at LW. Beware cross tide. Headquarters of the Cruising Association which, with its renowned library, overlooks the basin and welcomes visitors. Cruising Association ☎ 020 7537 2828, www.theca.org.uk. Docklands Light Railway nearby.
- **Hermitage Moorings** Visitors' mooring may be available on N bank downstream of St Katharine's Docks ☎ 020 7481 2122, VHF 80, 37/M www.hcmoorings.org.
- **St Katharine's Docks** Access HW–0200 to +0130, lock working hours 0600–2030

April–October, 0800–1800 November–March. ☎ 020 7264 5312, VHF 80, www.skdocks.co.uk. Six Y waiting buoys just downstream. A tranquil place within the City of London. Supermarket and Tower of London nearby. Pump out facility.

Fuel Diesel (not petrol) available from fuel barge *Heiko*, usually moored outside St Katharine's Dock, but advisable to ☎ 020 7481 1774 (Westminster Petroleum) to confirm current position. Usually open Monday–Friday 0630–1430; closed Saturday and Sunday. VHF 14. Petrol is not available anywhere on the river in central London.

Canals Canal and River Trust (formerly British Waterways) control the canals which connect to the Thames. Information may be obtained from CRT ☎ 0303 040 4040 www.canalrivertrust.org.uk has details of tidal locks, marinas and inland waterways. Limehouse Dock ☎ 020 73089930; Bow Locks ☎ 020 75175570; Thames Lock (Brentford) and Brentford Locks ☎ 0208568 2779. The Grand Union Canal is in Syon Reach and is normally open HW±0200.

LEIGH AND SOUTHEND

Standard Port Sheerness
HW +0005   LW +0005

MHWS	MHWN	MLWN	MLWS
+0·1m	0·0m	–0·1m	–0·1m

An exposed shore. Visitors should ask local advice. The only reasonable moorings are in the Ray Gut which leads to Benfleet. This gives sheltered anchorage except in Force 5 SW to E winds. Safe water HW±0200. Comfortable in SW winds, not so in strong E winds with wind over tide. There are drying moorings in Hadleigh Ray. In strong winds best go to Queenborough.

Approach Either make for the moorings E or W of Southend Pier if able to take the ground or enter the Ray Gut channel 8ca WNW of Southend Pier for Leigh, Canvey Is and Benfleet. This has 2·4–4m. Silting occurs. Approach with caution.

Entrance Leave the Leigh G con buoy close to stb. A pair of unlit G con and R can buoys mark the channel. Then head for moored fishing boats leaving them close to stb for best water. Benfleet Creek continues W to S Benfleet after ½M marked by stb then numbered port hand marks. Canvey Road Bridge blocks navigation.

Berthing Only for craft able to take the ground.
• **Leigh** Alongside Bell or Victoria Wharf. Both free.
• **Chalkwell** Anchor close in for crew changes etc. Close to stn.
• **Canvey Is E** Island YC and Halcon Marine. Drying mud berths, access HW±0200 from Ray Gut. Limited facilities, diesel, repairs. Maximum 30m length, 1·2m draught.

☎ YC 01268 510360; Halcon Marine 511611.
• **Benfleet YC and boatyard** Access as Canvey Is E but further in. A drying mooring may be available. Apply to moorings manager ☎ 01268 792278.

Anchorages
• **Ray Gut** Suitable in good weather whilst waiting for the tide.
• **Southend** Anchor off Pier end for a short period. Land by dinghy on to Pier. Area is patrolled April–October by Southend BC Launches *Alec White II*, *Sidney Bates* and *Low Way*.

Facilities
• **Leigh** Water Leigh SC or Essex YC. Telephone outside Smack PH, all facilities in town 2M, Rly. Southend Airport.
• **Southend** Water from YCs, all facilities in town. Rly.
• **Canvey Is** Water Island YC, Halcon Marine Boatyard.
• **Benfleet** Water Benfleet YC, Dauntless Boatyard. Rly.

HAVENGORE CREEK

This creek runs between the Rivers Thames and Crouch/Roach. Vessels with less than 1·5m draught may use it near HW when the tides are higher than mean springs. Navigate only in daylight. At the S end start between HW–0130 to –0030 by crossing the raised causeway, the Roman Broomway, ½M from the Creek entrance. In calm conditions the route has 2m at MHWS, 0·9m at MHWN, reduced by up to 1m by S winds or high barometric pressure.

The Maplin Sand is a very active MoD firing range. The passage of vessels through the area is strictly controlled. Do not enter when red flags fly on the sea wall, hoisted 1hr before firing commences. For latest information on firing VHF 16 or 72 *Shoe Radar* or ☎ 01702 383211.

Entrance Approaching from the Thames, make for S Shoebury G con Lt by Fl.G.5s at HW–0100. Leave the isolated danger mark to port. Make for two unlit MoD radar reflectors on wire stayed posts on the Broomway. Steer towards the Havengore Br, where, once between the sea walls, there is better water on the N side. The br keeper is on duty HW±0200 from sunrise to sunset, less in winter. In the entrance the bottom is mud to the SW and sand to the NE. All dries HW+0230. The ebb and flood meet about ½M inside and, as the Broomway covers, the flood reverses to run from seaward. There is a wreck 1M off the entrance and off the two approaches above, marked with bn with two ball top mark. Once through the br either turning goes to the Middleway and thence to the River Roach. Heading north after the bridge take the right-hand channel, the Narrow Cuts and then join the Middleway. Heading south from the Roach, passing the two dammed creeks, take the Narrow Cuts down to the bridge. There are unmarked saltings that cover in the Narrow Cuts. Potton Island swing bridge is available on all tides (night & day) and provides an alternative route to the Roach, passing south of Rushley Island and west of Potton Island.

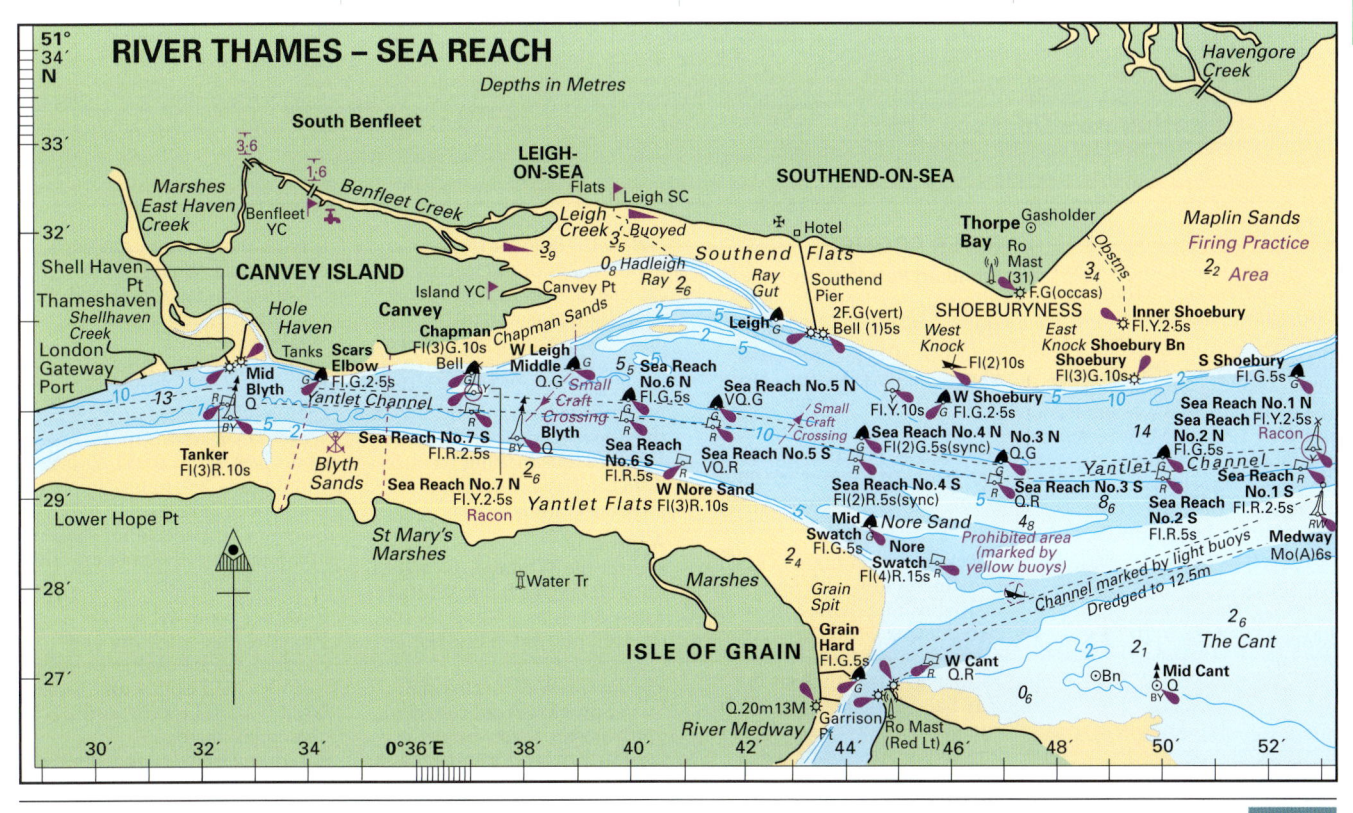

The Cruising Almanac

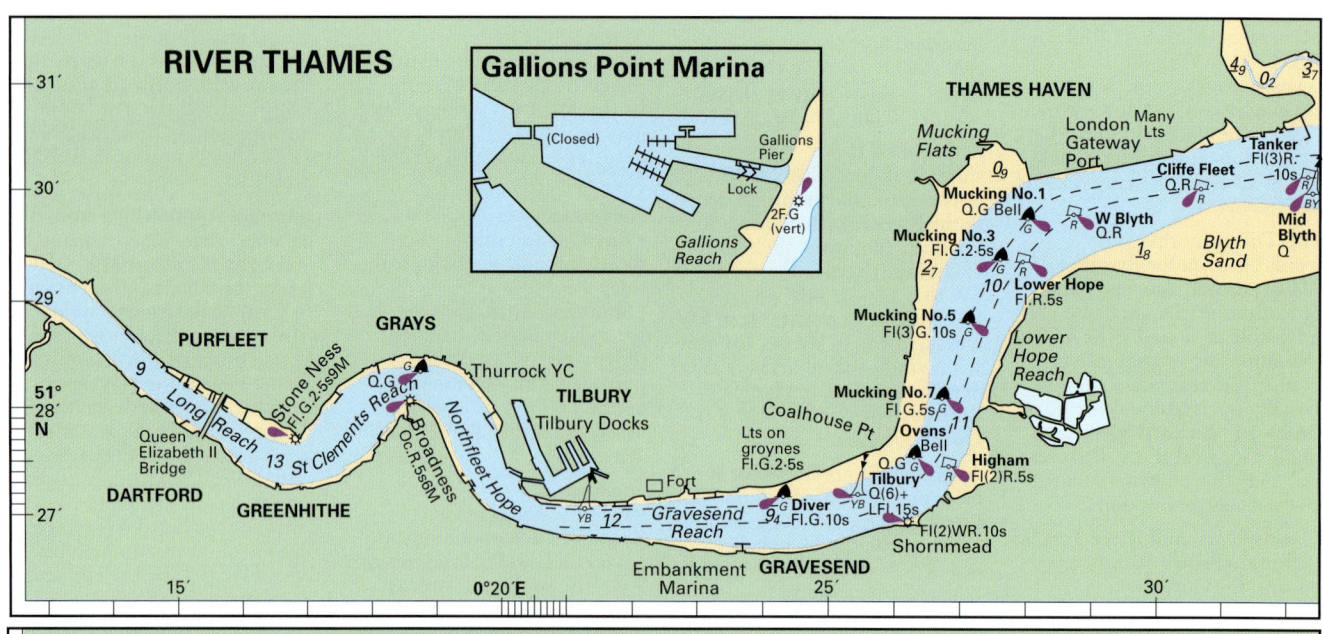

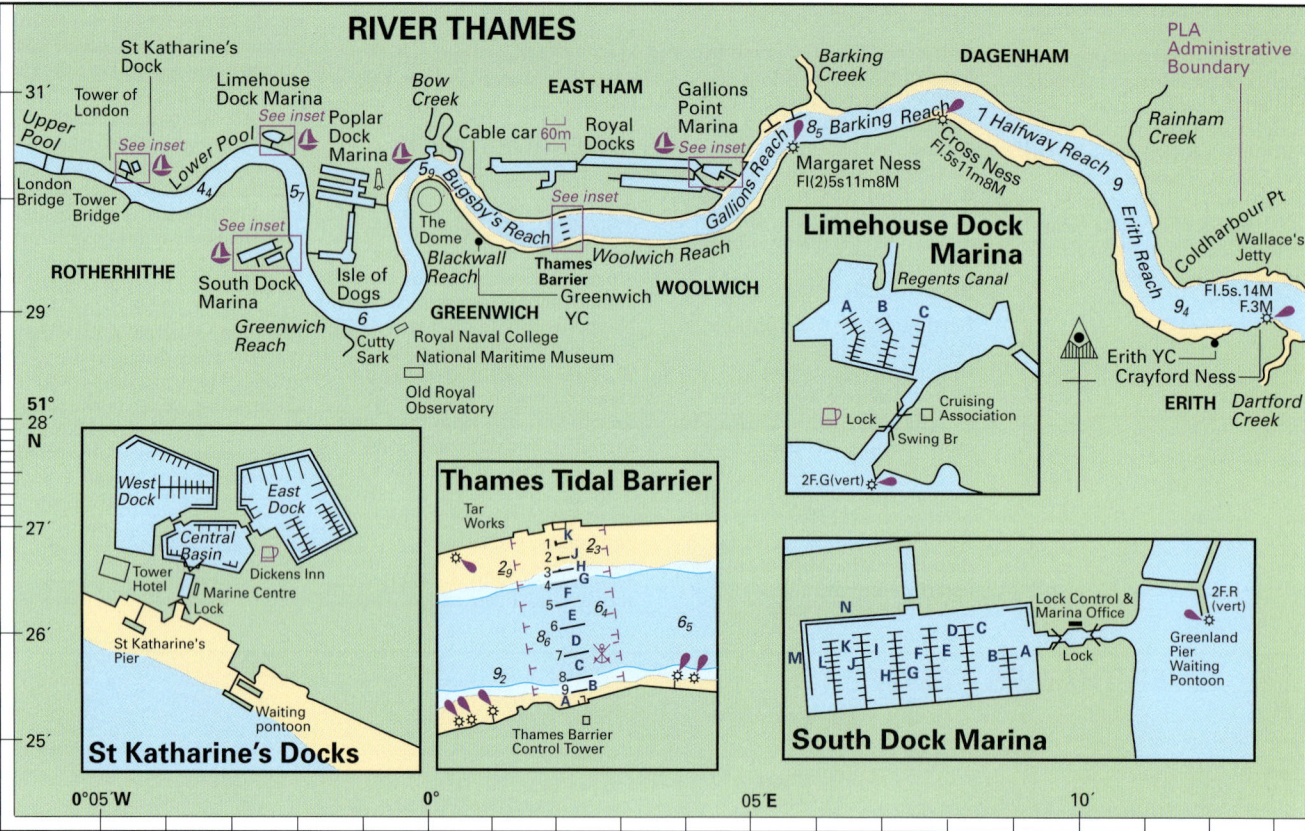

To go S from Burnham take first creek to port in the River Roach and then the third to port again missing the two dammed creeks. The nearest to the br where a vessel can lie afloat is in the Middleway off the dammed creeks where there is 1·2 to 1·5m at MLWS. When the mud on the bank of the channel at this point is covered there is 1m of water at the entrance to the Ahaven.

☎/**VHF** Firing information: 01702 383211, VHF 16, 72 Call sign *Shoe Radar*. Bridge keeper 383436, VHF 72 *Shoe Bridge*.

RIVER CROUCH

Standard Port Walton

Burnham

| HW | (sp) +0050 | (np) +0036 |
| LW | (sp) +0115 | (np) +0050 |

MHWS	MHWN	MLWN	MLWS
+1·0m	+0·8m	−0·1m	−0·2m

Fambridge

| HW | (sp) +0115 | (np) +0050 |
| LW | (sp) +0130 | (np) +0100 |

MHWS	MHWN	MLWN	MLWS
+1·1m	+0·8m	0·0m	−0·1m

Accessible at all times. The coastline is low with few distinguishing marks; there are two conspic lattice towers well to the S on Foulness. These form a near transit with the Ray Sand Channel. The tides run up to 3kn on a spring ebb and follow the line of the channel. The river has a least depth of 2m in or close by the channel at the Sunken Buxey. The channel is narrow in places and shoals rapidly at the edges. Vessels drawing up to 2m can reach Battlesbridge, the upper limit of the river at MHWS, but the upper reaches are crowded and tortuous making passage difficult. Beware streams crossing channels.

Approach

• From the Whitaker E card Lt buoy Bell leave Inner Whitaker S card buoy to stb and follow the well buoyed Whitaker Channel.
• From the Wallet cross the Swin Spitway. From the Swin Spitway safe water buoy Iso.10s Bell steer approx 245° leaving the Y can buoys with cross topmarks close to port. Shoaling has been reported towards the west end of the Swallowtail bank.
• From the Wallet through the Ray Sand Channel. This channel dries 1·2m at the S end; seasonal variations in the line of deepest water occur. Passage should only be attempted on a rising tide. Take care to avoid Bachelor Spit and other shallow areas and sound across into the Crouch channel.

Entrance From Whitaker Channel follow the buoyed channel, taking care at Buxey No.1 S card Lt buoy and Buxey No.2 N card Lt buoy as the channel is narrow. Alternatively, coming from the

90

Swin Spitway, after Swallowtail W card buoy pass N of Sunken Buxey N card Lt buoy. At the entrance to the Roach there is a RGR buoy, Branklet, leave to stb if entering the Roach, otherwise leave to port.

Continue up the buoyed channel, leaving the moorings to stb. To port, W of Fairway No.1 buoy, keep well clear of the breaches in the sea wall, into the Wallasea wetlands which are marked by steel tubular piles carrying red port hand topmarks. Burnham Yacht Harbour is at the west end of the town. After Burnham, Essex Marina is situated on the S bank closely followed by Baltic Wharf at which timber ships berth. At the NW end of Cliff Reach, Althorne Creek leads to Bridgemarsh Marina. Between Creeksea and Fambridge, Bridgemarsh Is is completely covered at HW making identification of the channel difficult. Keep to the centre of the channel and do not enter bights in the river bank; the line of the S bank indicates the channel. About ½M E of Fambridge on the N bank there is a sunken sea wall, which is deceptive at HW owing to a bight in the sea wall at this position. At Fambridge moorings line both sides of the river.

Berthing
- **Burnham Yacht Harbour** 350 berths; access 24hrs. Entrance ½M W of Town Quay on N bank marked by a buoy Fl.Y.5s and entrance Lt bns to port Fl.R.10s and stb Fl.G.10s.

Facilities Travel-lift to 35-tonnes. Slip to 100-tonnes. Supermarket within walking distance. VHF 80. ☎ 01621 786832. WiFi.
- **Essex Marina** 500 berths; access 24hrs. On S side of river. Ferry to Burnham, Easter to 31 October. ☎ 01702 258531, VHF 80, 37(M).
- **Burnham** Two blue visitors' buoys marked RCYC off RCYC clubhouse, otherwise on mooring buoy, by arrangement with Burnham Yacht Harbour or one of the yards or YCs. Do not leave boat unattended on buoy without permission.
- **Bridgemarsh Marina** Althorne Creek 120 berths; access HW±0400. Hoist, repairs. ☎ 01621 740414.
- **Fambridge Yacht Station** Visitors' pontoon at Fambridge Yacht Station on N bank at North Fambridge. Ferry Boat Inn. ☎ 01621 742911 Mobile 07917 390005
- **Fambridge Yacht Haven** In Stow Creek, on N bank, marked by bn and ldg Lts. Leave Stow Post, Q.Fl(4)8s, to port on entering, follow buoyed channel. Access HW±0500.

Facilities at both sites. Diesel at marina.
☎ 01621 740370 Mobile 07917 390005, VHF 80.

Anchorages
- Burnham, ½M below the town, clear of the fairway and power cables marked by bns on banks and buoys in midstream.
- Cliff Reach. Keep well over to the S bank abeam of the Baltic Wharf to avoid a spit which extends from the N bank a quarter of the way across the river. Anchor in the bay of the S bank beyond the moorings in 5·5m if the wind is W, and off the red cliff further upriver on the N bank in 3·5m if the wind is E.

Anchorage notes
Do not anchor among moorings as the ground is foul. Crouch Harbour Authority Bye-laws prohibit anchoring to obstruct any fairway.

Facilities Burnham, all facilities; rly to London.

☎/VHF HM 01621 783602
www.crouchharbour.uk/authority

RIVER ROACH

Entrance From seaward do not cut the corner at Nase Point as the mud is extensive and unmarked. From Burnham do not pass inside the RGR Branklet buoy near LW. 1½M beyond the entrance the river turns W; on the port hand in this reach is Yokefleet Creek leading to Havengore. ½M further on the river bears away SW and leads to moorings at Paglesham. Beyond Paglesham the river shoals rapidly.

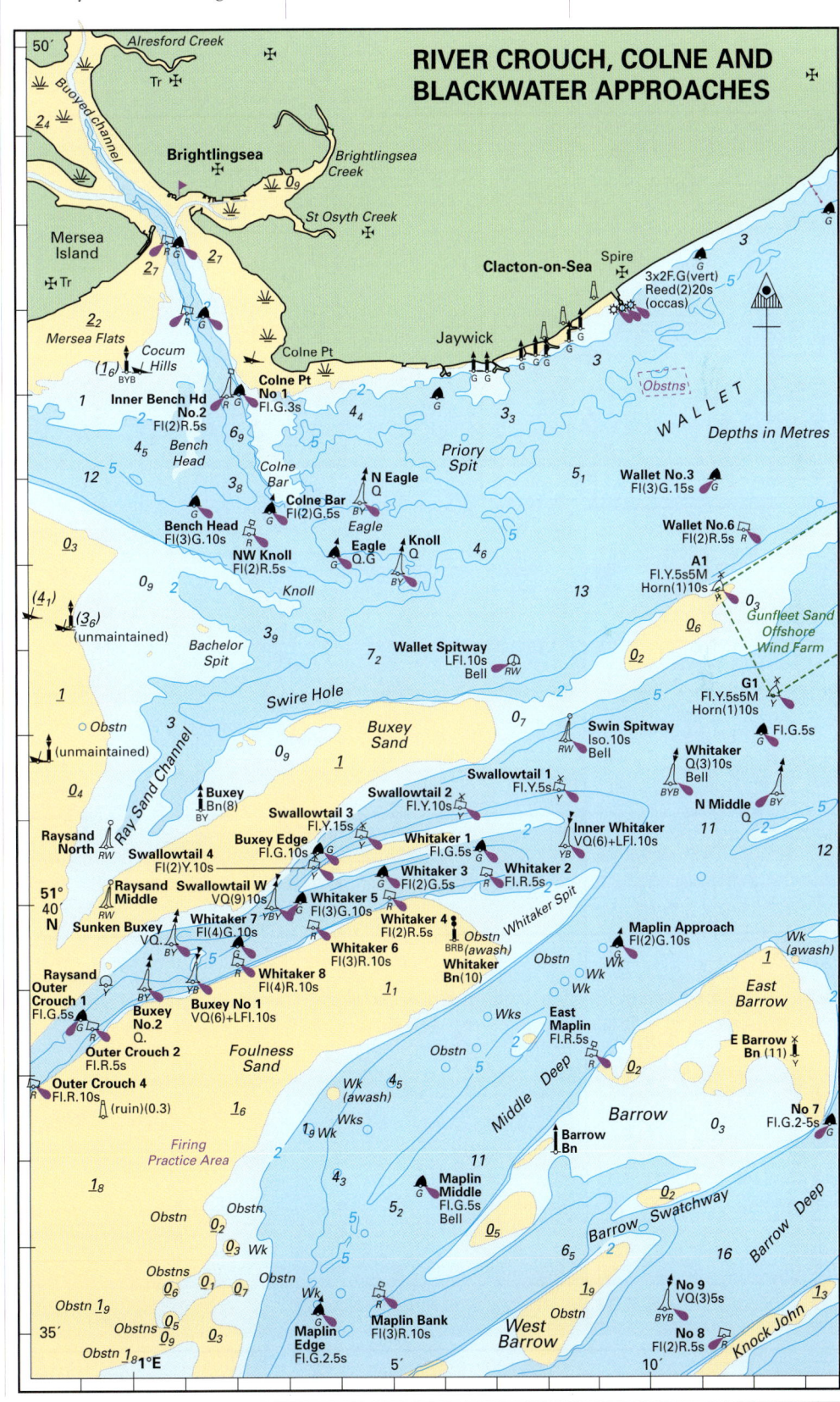

RIVER CROUCH, COLNE AND BLACKWATER APPROACHES

ENGLAND – EAST COAST

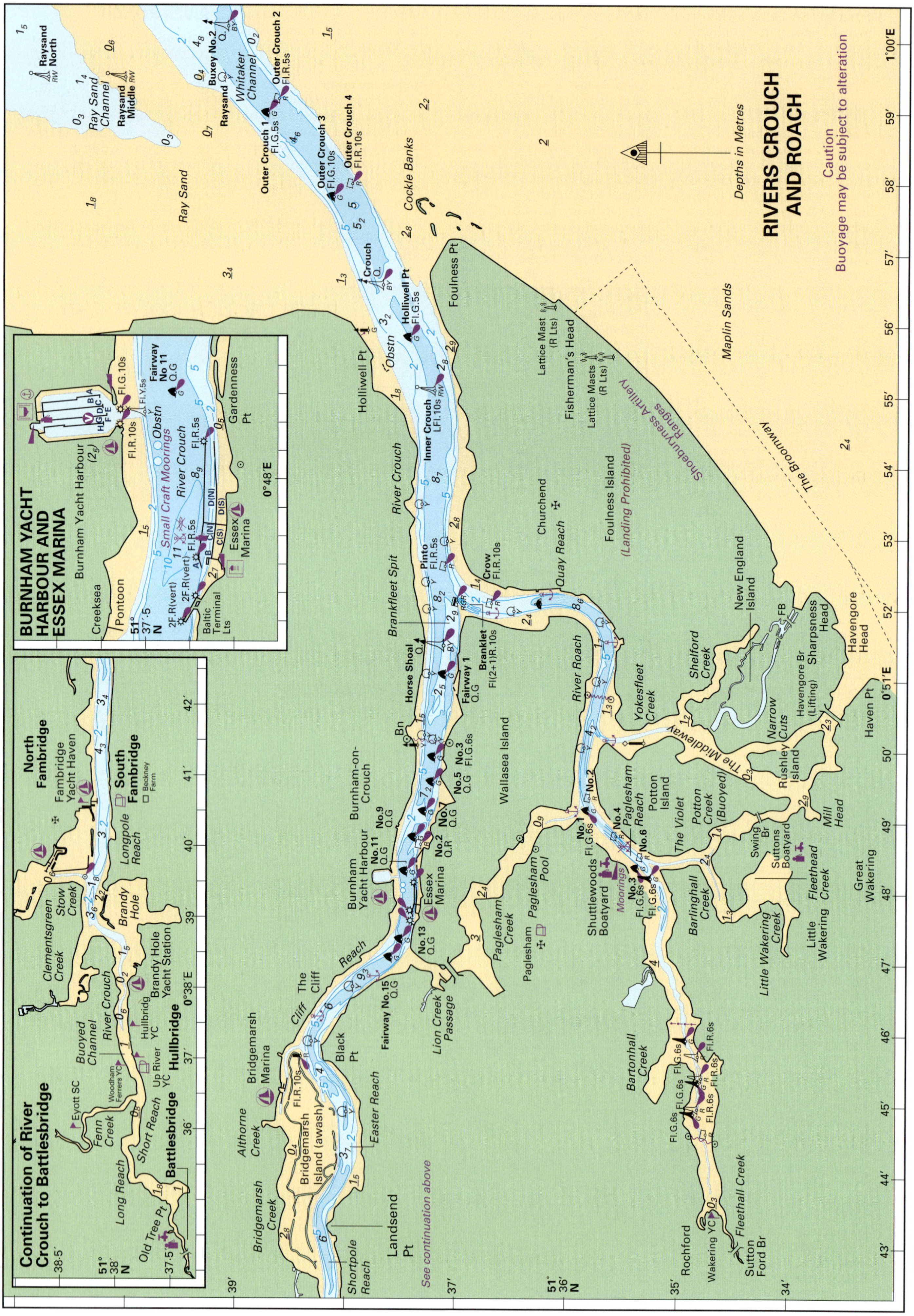
RIVERS CROUCH AND ROACH
Caution
Buoyage may be subject to alteration
Depths in Metres
BURNHAM YACHT HARBOUR AND ESSEX MARINA
Continuation of River Crouch to Battlesbridge
See continuation above
Ray Sand
Ray Sand Channel
Raysand North
Raysand Middle
Whitaker Channel
Buxey No.2
Outer Crouch 1
Outer Crouch 2
Outer Crouch 3
Outer Crouch 4
Cockle Banks
Crouch
Holliwell Pt
Foulness Pt
Inner Crouch
River Crouch
Brankfleet Spit
Pinto
Crow
Branklet
Horse Shoal
Fairway 1
Burnham-on-Crouch
Burnham Yacht Harbour
Essex Marina
Wallasea Island
Lion Creek Passage
The Cliff
Cliff Reach
Black Pt
Easter Reach
Bridgemarsh Marina
Bridgemarsh Island (awash)
Bridgemarsh Creek
Althorne Creek
Landsend Pt
Shortpole Reach
Paglesham Creek
Paglesham Pool
Paglesham
Churchend
Quay Reach
Foulness Island
(Landing Prohibited)
Shoeburyness Artillery Ranges
Fisherman's Head
Lattice Masts (R Lts)
Lattice Mast (R Lts)
The Broomway
Maplin Sands
New England Island
River Roach
Yokesfleet Creek
Shelford Creek
The Middleway
Narrow Cuts
Rushley Island
Havengore Br (Lifting)
Havengore Head
Sharpsness Head
Haven Pt
Mill Head
Great Wakering
Paglesham Reach
Potton Island
The Violet
Potton Creek (Buoyed)
Swing Br
Suttons Boatyard
Fleethead Creek
Little Wakering Creek
Little Wakering
Barlinghall Creek
Shuttlewoods Boatyard
Moorings
Bartonhall Creek
Fleethall Creek
Rochford
Wakering YC
Sutton Ford Br
Small Craft Moorings
Creeksea
Pontoon
Baltic Terminal Lts
Gardenness Pt
Burnham Yacht Harbour
North Fambridge
Fambridge Yacht Haven
South Fambridge
Longpole Reach
Stow Creek
Clementsgreen Creek
Brandy Hole
Brandy Hole Yacht Station
Buoyed Channel
Hullbridge YC
Up River YC
Hullbridge
Woodham Ferrers YC
Eyott SC
Fenn Creek
Short Reach
Long Reach
Old Tree Pt
Battlesbridge
1°00′E
0°51′E
0°48′E
0°38′E
51° 36′ N

Landing on Foulness is prohibited.

Anchorages
- In W winds close under the W Bank under the high sea wall in the bay. In E winds off the quay on the E side ½M further up.
- Inside the entrance to Yokesfleet Creek in 2m.
- Off Paglesham clear of the moorings and S of the fairway marked by G con and R can buoys. Land at muddy hard. Water and fuel from boatyard. Reputed last resting place of *HMS Bounty*.

RIVER BLACKWATER
Standard Port Walton

Osea Island
HW (sp) +0057 (np) +0045
LW (sp) +0050 (np) +0007
MHWS MHWN MLWN MLWS
+1·1m +0·9m +0·1m 0·0m

Maldon
HW (sp) +0107 (np) +0055
MHWS MHWN
−1·3m −1·1m

The river is navigable as far as Osea Pier at all times and to Maldon at HW.

Approach From the Wallet approach from Knoll N card Lt buoy or North Eagle N card Lt buoy. Both channels clearly marked and have a least depth of 3·8m.

Entrance From Benchhead G con Lt buoy maintain a course of 290° until Bradwell Power Station barrier stands well clear of land. After passing the barrier and Bradwell Marina to port keep to midstream, leaving Thirslet G con Lt buoy to stb and Stone Point and Marconi Yacht Club to port, both of which have numerous moorings. Leaving Marconi R can Lt buoy to port, follow the buoyed channel with Doctor G con Lt buoy and Osea Island to stb. Lawling Creek, the channel to Maylandsea, is accessed by leaving No.2 R can Lt buoy to stb – it is a port hand mark for the river, not the creek. Keep closely to channel marked by moorings.

On turning to port rounding Northey Island, Heybridge Basin is on the stb side, marked by G con buoy Lock Approach.

Berthing (see also Bradwell and Mersea Quarters)
- **Blackwater Marina**, Maylandsea in Lawling Creek Pontoon mud berths, drying, access HW±0300. Floating moorings. ☎ 01621 740264. VHF 37(M).
- **Heybridge Basin** For access there is a depth of 4m in the approach channel at MHWS. The lock opens at times varying from HW−0100 to HW for any boat visible in the approach channel. Wait until out-going boats are clear of the channel and the green light is showing. Leave Lock Approach G. con buoy close to stb and proceed towards the lock, leaving the withies to port.

Facilities Launderette. Supermarket, by dinghy up the canal to Maldon. Lock ☎ 853506, *Mobile* 07712 079764. VHF 80.
- **Maldon** A drying pontoon berth may be obtained on soft mud. There is 2·5m at MHWS and 1·0m at MHWN at Hythe Quay. ☎ 01621 875837. River Bailiff *Mobile* 07818 013723 for mooring.

Anchorages
- In Latchingdon Hole in 2m. Leave No.4 R can Southey Creek buoy to stb and follow the channel by sounding.
- E of Osea pier-head. Strong tidal stream.
- Thirslet Creek in 3·3m or less.
- Goldhanger Creek in 2m. Goldhanger Spit is marked by No.1 G con buoy. Leave well to port to enter creek.
- Lawling Creek, opposite Osea Pier; good anchorage in 2m, within 2ca of the entrance.
- Off the Stone. Clean landing on shingle.
- Visitor's mooring off Marconi SC.

Supplies All facilities at Maldon.

BRADWELL
Standard Port Walton
HW (sp) +0035 (np) +0023
LW (sp) +0047 (np) +0004
MHWS MHWN MLWN MLWS
+1·0m +0·8m +0·2m 0·0m

A small inlet on the S side of the River Blackwater inside Pewit Is with the approach channel to Bradwell Marina. The creek is full of small craft moorings with approx 0·6m at MLWS.

Approach Approach from the N then steer to leave the prominent square pile entrance N card Lt Bn Q 'Tidepole' approx 3m to stb. Tide gauge on bn gives available depth in channel to Marina.

Entrance The narrow entrance channel is marked by withies and R can buoys. Leave withies about 3m to stb. At last withy steer for G con buoy. At G con buoy turn sharply to stb and pass between shore and lines of moorings. Then head for R can buoy marking marina entrance channel and follow marked channel into marina.

Berthing
- **Bradwell Marina** Access HW±0400. Regular dredging aims to maintain 1½m at MLWS but less depth at some berths. Visitors moor to end of 'A' or 'B' pontoon on arrival. ☎ 01621 776235. VHF 37(M) and 80.

Facilities Marina club with restaurant and bar; inn in village; Bradwell Quay YC nearby, open at weekends.

WEST MERSEA
Standard Port Walton
HW (sp) +0035 (np) +0015
LW (sp) +0055 (np) +0010
MHWS MHWN MLWN MLWS
+0·9m +0·4m +0·1m +0·1m

Mersea Quarters has a depth of up to 6m. It is on the N side of the River Blackwater N of the Nass Spit. This is marked by an E card Lt bn VQ(3)5s6m2M. The bn has a tide gauge showing height of water over the sill at Tollesbury Marina. Over the whole area the simplistic advice is where there are no moorings there is no water.

Approach From the NW Knoll R can Fl(2)R.5s steer 288° 4½M to the Nass E card Lt bn.

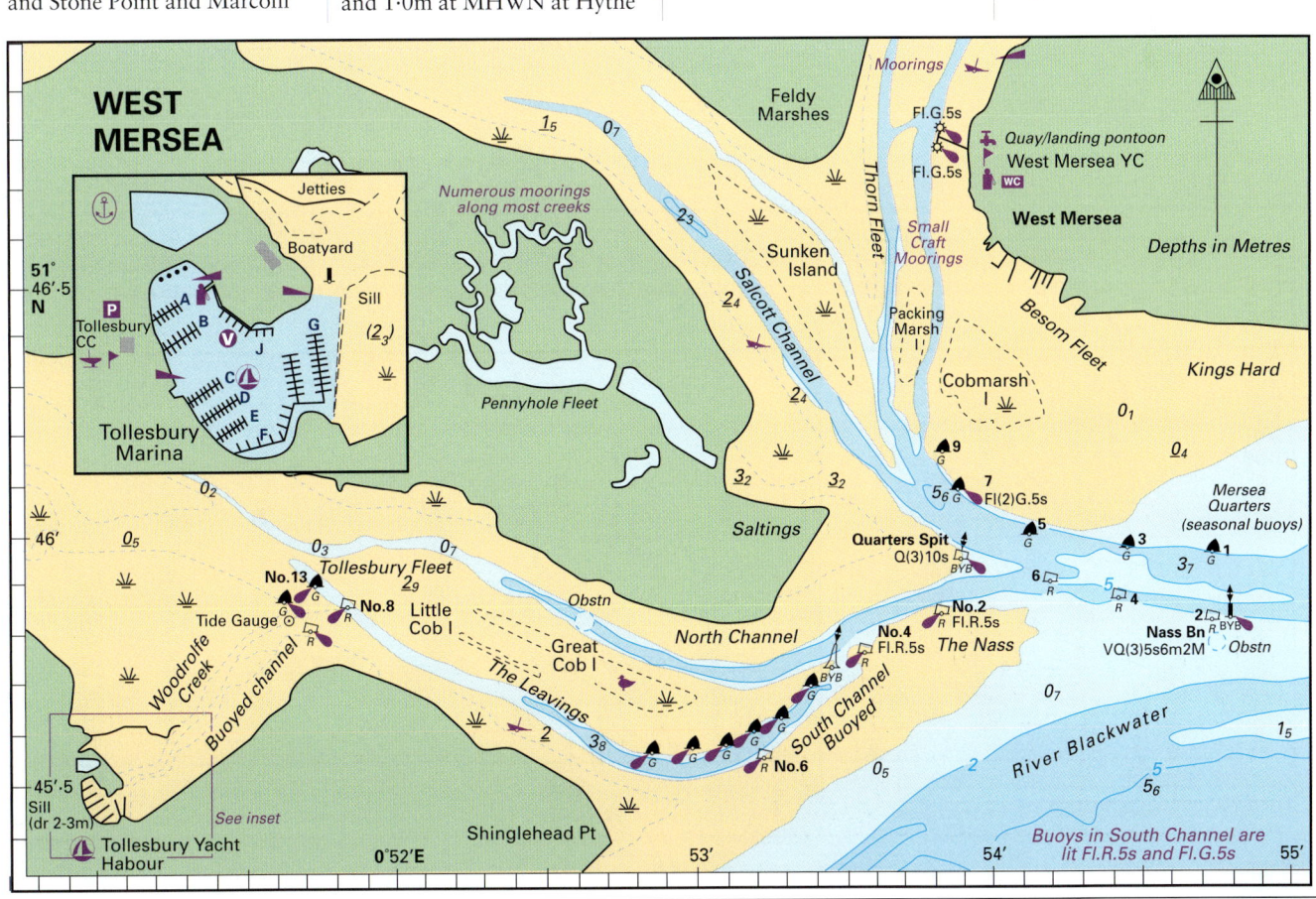

93

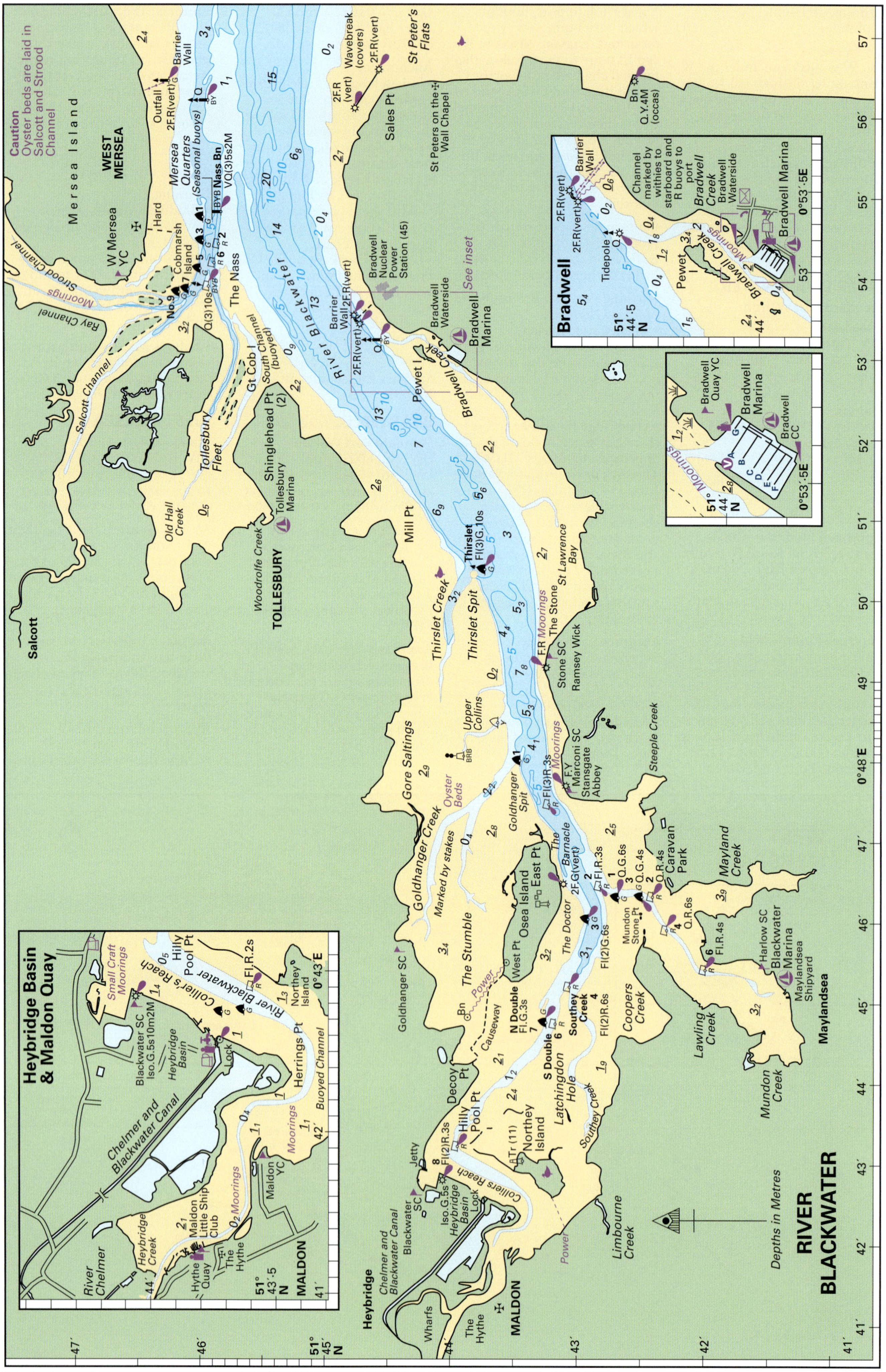
RIVER BLACKWATER
Depths in Metres
Heybridge Basin & Maldon Quay
Bradwell
Caution
Oyster beds are laid in Salcott and Strood Channel
Mersea Island
WEST MERSEA
W Mersea YC
Strood Channel
Ray Channel
Salcott Channel
Mersea Quarters (Seasonal buoys)
Cobmarsh Island
The Nass
Nass Bn
Tollesbury Fleet
Old Hall Creek
Woodrolfe Creek
TOLLESBURY
Tollesbury Marina
Shinglehead Pt
South Channel (buoyed)
Gt Cob I
Salcott
River Blackwater
Bradwell Nuclear Power Station (45)
Bradwell Waterside
Bradwell Marina
Bradwell Creek
Pewet I
See inset
Sales Pt
St Peters on the Wall Chapel
St Peter's Flats
Wavebreak (covers)
Mill Pt
Thirslet Creek
Thirslet Spit
St Lawrence Bay
The Stone
Stone SC
Ramsey Wick
Marconi SC
Stansgate Abbey
Steeple Creek
Gore Saltings
Goldhanger Creek
Oyster Beds
Upper Collins
Goldhanger Spit
Goldhanger SC
Marked by stakes
The Stumble
Osea Island
East Pt
West Pt
The Barnacle
The Doctor
N Double
S Double
Southey Creek
Mundon Stone Pt
Caravan Park
Mayland Creek
Harlow SC
Blackwater Marina
Maylandsea Shipyard
Maylandsea
Lawling Creek
Mundon Creek
Coopers Creek
Latchingdon Hole
Northey Island
Decoy Pt
Causeway
Hilly Pool Pt
Colliers Reach
Limbourne Creek
Heybridge
Chelmer and Blackwater Canal
Blackwater SC
Heybridge Basin
Lock
Jetty
Wharfs
The Hythe
MALDON
River Chelmer
Heybridge Creek
Hythe Quay
Maldon Little Ship Club
Maldon YC
Herrings Pt
Northey Island
Buoyed Channel
Small Craft Moorings
Moorings
Power
Bradwell Quay YC
Bradwell CC
Tidepole
Channel marked by withies to starboard and R buoys to port
Bradwell Creek
Bradwell Waterside
Bradwell Marina
0°48'E

This is difficult to pick up from a distance but the church tr and RH end of large grey block of flats in West Mersea give a good line. Outer approach from E or W is across shallows of 0·6–1·0m depending on line taken. After passing through the buoyed channel in Mersea Quarters, the black shed on Packing Marsh Island is then a guide to Thorn Fleet to which visitors are usually directed. Coming from the River Colne, keep the shed well open of the W end of Mersea Is to clear the Cocum Hills shoal, leaving Molliette E card bn to stb and ensure there is sufficient rise of tide for your draught.

Entrance Pass at least 2ca to the NE of the Nass Bn particularly at LW, as the spit dries W of the bn and only 1·2m will be found close E. Then follow buoyed channel. After some 4ca from the Nass Bn the channel divides:
- Thorn Fleet, W of Packingmarsh Is, identified by its conspic black shed, has 1·7m. Mersea Fleet, the channel between Cobmarsh Is and Packingmarsh Is and extending N to the Gut, locally called the Creek has 1·5m, but 1m on bar abreast shed. Thorn Fleet is the best channel but care should be taken to follow the line of deep keeled moored craft as many moorings on the E and W edges are half drying. Keep to a general N/S line past Packingmarsh Is to avoid grounding. Salcott Channel is to the W of Thornfleet, bear to port after No.7 G con buoy; there is 1·8m to Sunken Island.
- For Tollesbury Marina bear to port and follow the buoyed S channel on a SW course into Tollesbury Fleet. This has about 2m for 2M. The S channel leads to Woodrolfe Creek. A small E card buoy, marking the E end of Gt Cob Is, should be left to stb on entering South Channel. The entrance channel to Tollesbury Marina has a tide gauge to indicate depth of water on the Marina sill.

Berthing
- **Tollesbury Marina** Access HW±0200 sp; HW±0100 np Depth over sill 2·9m MHWS, 1·8m MHWN, Cruising Club, restaurant, swimming pool, tennis. Laundry. Scrubbing posts, repair yard. The marina is at the head of the ½M Woodrolfe Creek. Inside hbr is dredged to about 2m below sill level. Waiting buoys marked Tollesbury Marina in Tollesbury Fleet near Woodrolfe Creek. Tide gauge in creek. ☎ 01621 869202, VHF 37(M), 80.
- **W Mersea** No marina with pontoons but otherwise the full facilities of a major yachting centre. The creeks are narrow and too full of moorings to anchor. Beware extensive oyster beds where anchoring prohibited. For best water keep close to moorings. A vacant buoy can usually be found, for which a charge is made – enquire from West Mersea Yacht Club launches and water taxi on VHF 37/M, call sign YC1, or Mobile 07752 309435.
- Scrubbing posts: apply to WMYC.
- Mooring piles with pontoon in Thorn Fleet – contact WMYC launch.
- There are some deep water moorings in Mersea Quarters – exposed from NE to SW.

☎ WMYC 01206 382947; West Mersea Marine 382244.

Facilities Renowned fish restaurant. Store at end of causeway and more extensive shopping facilities in Mersea town, 1M. Shops and pubs in Tollesbury village.

RIVER COLNE
See plan, p.96
Standard Port Walton
Rowhedge
HW (sp) +0032 (np) +0023
MHWS MHWN
+0·2m −0·2m

Approach
- From seaward at any state of tide, by day or night from Knoll N card Q to Eagle G con Q.G; then to Colne Bar G con Fl(2)G.5s and to Inner Bench Head R pillar.
- From N. Eagle N card Q to Colne Bar buoy.
- If sufficient depth on a rising tide, from N. Eagle direct to Inner Bench Head. Beware that, between the Colne Bar and Inner Bench Head buoys the tide sets strongly E or W up to 1½kn on spring ebb and flood tides respectively.
- From the River Blackwater at any state of tide, from Bench Head buoy to Inner Bench Head buoy gives least depth of 2·3m. Or, if sufficient rise of tide to clear Cocum Hills, from Nass Bn to ½M S of Molliette E card Bn on Mersea Flats, then enter channel south of No.8 R can Fl.R.3s buoy. This has a least depth of 0·5m.

Entrance From Inner Bench Head buoy follow the buoyed channel. Bateman's Tr Fl(3)20s has a conical roof and is visible from seaward.

Anchorages In Pyefleet Channel, E of Pewit Is beyond the moorings and clear of oyster beds marked by withies or at entrance to Pyefleet Creek, clear of moorings.

Berthing A W mooring buoy marked by W disc with G 'V', now with strops, may be available (call Colchester Oyster Fishery ☎ 01206 384141 who collect fees). Watch depth on N trot at LWS in S'ly winds. Land at Mersea Stone Point from where a foot ferry runs to Brightlingsea in summer. Alternatively, after half flood, land either at E Mersea hard or on the beach at Bateman's Tr ½M from Brightlingsea.

At Rowhedge, alongside pontoon or quay for short stay near HW. Nearby shop and pub.

Facilities Shops, all facilities at Brightlingsea. Foot ferry ☎ 07981 450169, VHF 68

BRIGHTLINGSEA
Standard Port Walton
Brightlingsea
HW (sp) +0025 (np) +0021
LW (sp) +0046 (np) +0004
MHWS MHWN MLWN MLWS
+0·8m +0·4m +0·1m 0·0m

Entrance From No.13 G con Lt buoy Q.G. stand out in mid channel until abeam of G stb hand post with tide gauge showing depth in entrance channel. Pass between Brightlingsea Spit S card Lt buoy and the post, keeping ldg bns, rectangular white boards with red vertical lines, on a bearing of 041°. Pass between R can Lt buoy and G con Lt buoy then approach the hbr, leaving N card Lt bn Q to stb and pass to moorings area. By night there are F.R Ldg Lts; two F.R(vert) mark the end of Brightlingsea hard on the N side of the channel; 2F.R(vert) at either end of Colne YC hammer head jetty and 2F.R(vert) at SW corner of Olivers Wharf close E of Colne YC. Watch out for commercial vessels in entrance channel and also manoeuvring in the vicinity of the quay at Olivers Wharf.

Berthing Call HM on VHF 68 when approaching S Card Lt buoy Brightlingsea Spit for berth on floating pontoons. Waterside Marina (maximum LOA 12m; minimum depth 2m) has some berths – apply to Waterside Marina VHF 80 ☎ 308709 in advance. Sill 1m above CD.

Facilities Landing at town pontoon. Mooring allowed for 20 minutes. Water at Colne YC pontoon and at up river facility, where diesel and pump-out is now available by request from HM. Showers in YC and laundry in Wreck House (apply to HM for tokens). Chandleries, boatyard with hoist, scrubbing posts (apply HM). Convenience store near marina.

☎/VHF HM 01206 302200; Brightlingsea Harbour VHF 68. Water taxi VHF 68; Mobile 07535 508537.

www.brightlingseaharbour.org

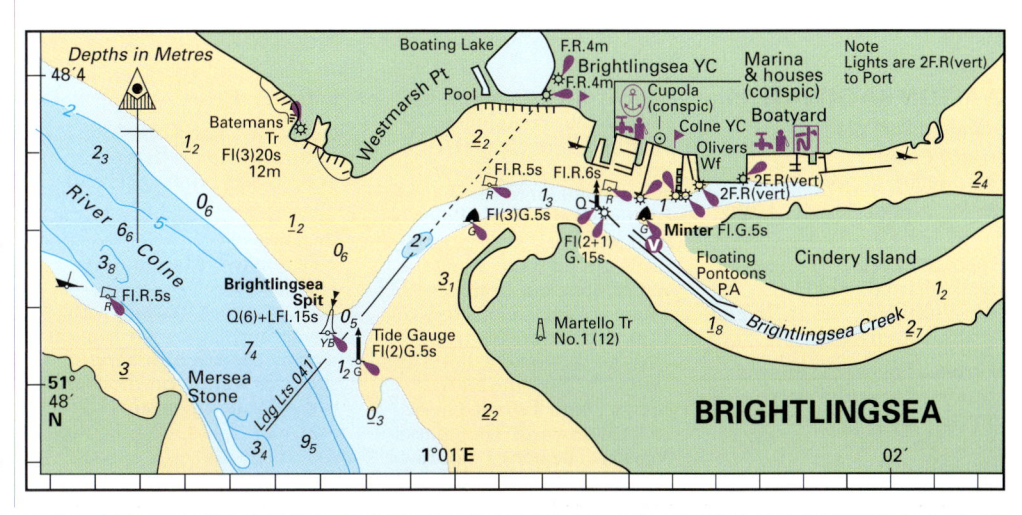

ENGLAND – EAST COAST

95

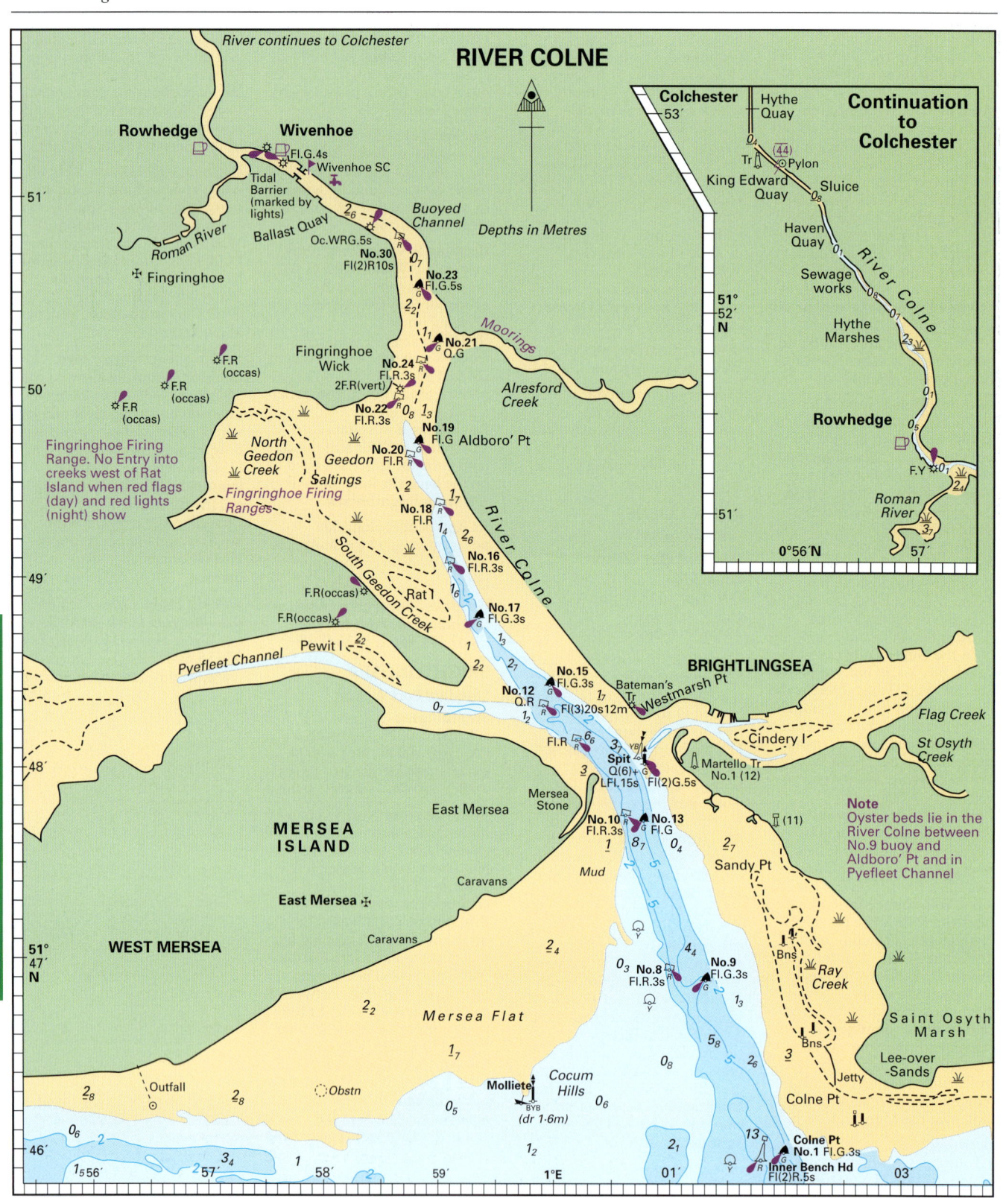

WALTON BACKWATERS
Standard Port Walton

Oakley Creek
HW +0008   LW −0002
MHWS MHWN MLWN MLWS
+0·3m +0·3m +0·3m +0·3m

Approach Locate *Pye End* RW small pillar buoy LFl.10s at 51°55'·0N 1°17'·9E at NE end of entrance channel.

Entrance Follow the buoyed channel in a southwesterly direction from Pye End RW buoy. After No.9 G con buoy the channel becomes very narrow, 2017 survey gives depth 0·2m. Bound into Hamford Water leave Island Point N card buoy to port. When bound into the Walton Channel, keep Island Point N card to stb and keep close to the R can buoys to avoid the spit running out from Island Pt where the channel narrows to 17m, but beware of strong cross current on late flood and early ebb. Take the buoyed channel until Twizzle Creek bears W towards Titchmarsh Marina. The line of moorings indicates the best water.

Continue S into Foundry Reach, which dries, for the Walton and Frinton YC and boatyards.

Berthing
• **Titchmarsh Marina** Access HW±0500.
Well-equipped marina, with restaurant. Basic provisions at marina chandlery, otherwise shops at Walton-on-the-Naze 1M. Marine engineer.

☎/VHF 01255 672185, 851899, VHF 80.
• **Walton Yacht Basin** located near YC. Craft up to 2m draught can lie afloat. 60 berths, access HW±0200 most tides. May be no access at low neaps. Berthing by prior arrangement. ☎ 01255 675873 Bedwell & Co.
• **Walton and Frinton Yacht Club** Drying quay. Visitors limited to 2hrs. Open seven days a week in season.
☎ 678161.

WALTON BACKWATERS

Anchorages Off Stone Point, leaving a fairway to the W side of the channel. If landing on Stone Point respect Nature Reserve. Hamford Water is uncomfortable in NE winds. Heavy pipe reed may impede anchoring. In Kirkby Creek anchor clear of all moorings and oyster beds. Oakley Creek is not a recommended anchorage due to movement of ships carrying explosives. Land at the WFYC hard or quay at head of Kirby Creek approx HW±0200.

Facilities Shops and Rly in Walton-on-the-Naze.

HARWICH AND FELIXSTOWE

Standard Port Walton
HW (sp) +0005 (np) +0003
LW (sp) –0020 (np) –0005
MHWS MHWN MLWN MLWS
+ 0·2m 0·0m –0·1m –0·1m
DS Landguard Point
Dover +0530 flood, –0030 ebb

Accessible at all times. Harwich and Felixstowe are major ports for both ferry traffic and large container vessels. Small craft must at all times keep clear of commercial vessels in the approaches, anchorages and hbr area. The Harwich Haven Authority (HHA) publish an annual Yachting Guide obtainable from Harbour House, The Quay, Harwich CO12 3HH ☎ 01255 243030. See also
www.hha.co.uk/leisure.html
HHA patrol the hbr throughout the year.

Harwich VTS VHF 71 is extremely busy with commercial operations. Yachts should monitor but not make calls on this channel, except in an emergency.

Yachts should use the recommended yacht channels and cross the deep water channels at right angles and at the designated crossing points.

Approach Well marked. From the S by night 355° from the Medusa G con Lt buoy Fl.G.5s to join the recommended yacht track S of the Inner Ridge R can Lt buoy Q.R passing Stone Banks R can Lt buoy Fl.R.5s and avoiding unlit Outer Ridge R can buoy. From the E keep S of the deep water channel to pass S of the Inner Ridge R can Lt buoy Q.R. From the N at or near LW, stand out from shore to pass seaward of the Wadgate Ledge G con Lt bn Fl(4)G.15s before crossing the deep water channel W of the Platters S card Lt buoy to join the recommended yacht track.

Entrance From S of the Inner Ridge R can Lt buoy Q.R follow the recommended yacht track by leaving all channel marker buoys close to stb but the small Harwich Shelf E card Lt buoy (seasonal) to port. At the Guard R can Lt buoy leave the buoy to stb and cross the deep water channel to the Shotley Spit S card Lt buoy. Then take either the N route into the River Orwell, or turn due W for either Shotley Marina, or, staying N of the deep water channel, continue into the River Stour keeping well clear of commercial ships and unlit mooring buoys.

Berthing
• **Shotley Marina** Access 24hrs through lock. Call *Lockmaster* VHF 80 before starting approach. From the Shotley Spit buoy take a course to pass close N of the Ganges G con Lt

The Cruising Almanac

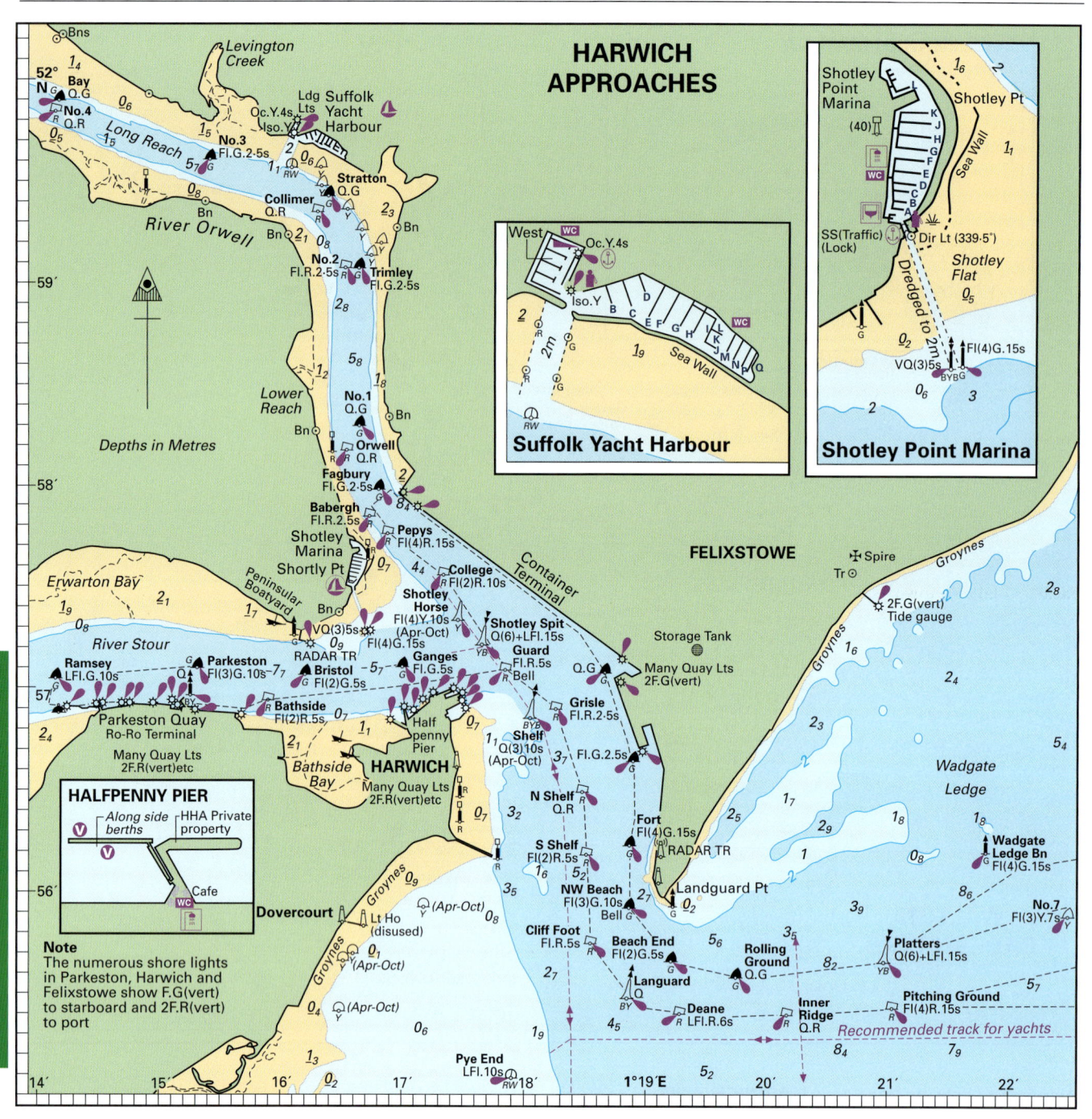

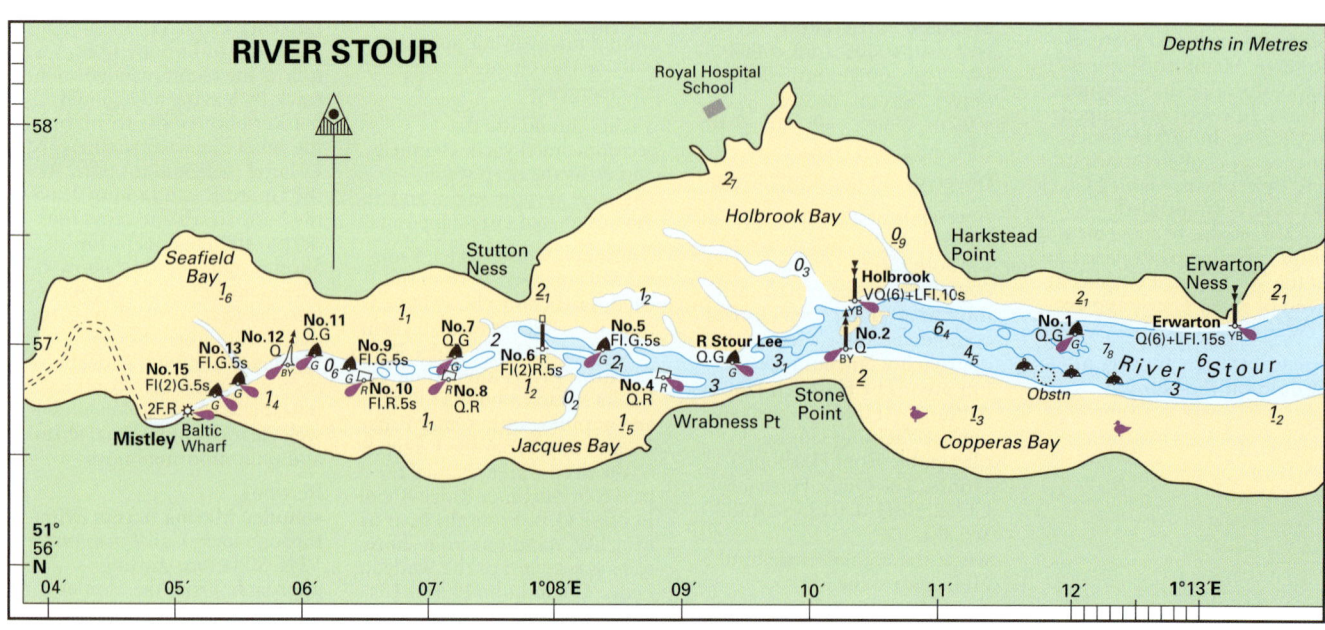

buoy and round to enter approach marked by Lt bns, E card VQ(3)5s to port; Fl(4)G.15s to stb. Traffic lights at lock entrance plus Inogon directional lights (arrows show direction to steer). Channel dredged to 2m MLWS. Lock can be turbulent, good fenders essential.
Facilities Chandler with limited supplies. Foot ferry to Harwich and Felixstowe. Marina restaurant; farm shop next to pub on way to village; some provisions in marina chandlery.
☏ 01473 788982 or *Mobile* 07748 154039, VHF 80.
• **Halfpenny Pier, Harwich** At the SW end of the quay. Berth either side of the pontoon, the E end of the N side is reserved for a ferry. Maximum stay 72 hours. Free mooring 0900–1600 hours. Avoid in strong winds. Take advice from HM ☏ 07748 154039. Depth 2·5m.
Facilities Harwich town. Rly.
Anchorages Well inshore immediately to seaward of the moorings on the Shelf, otherwise upstream of Parkeston Quay in the River Stour.

RIVER STOUR

Standard Port Walton
Mistley
HW (sp) +0028 (np) +0019
LW (sp) +0007 (np) 0020
MHWS MHWN MLWN MLWS
+0·2m +0·1m −0·1m n/a

Entrance Leaving Parkeston Quay to port proceed upriver in a W direction. The river is broad and straight for a distance of 2½M until approaching Wrabness; the channel is buoyed and lit as far as Mistley. The River Stour is navigable as far as Manningtree, 5M upriver of Wrabness, for 1·2m draught at HW. Frequent commercial traffic to Mistley Quay. Riding light advised, even when on moorings.

Berthing
• **Shotley Marina** *see Harwich*.
• **Wrabness** A vacant mooring buoy may be used for a short period but, for many yachts, only the outer row is deep enough at LWS. Yachts should not be left unattended.
• **Mistley Quay** No access to shore.
• **Manningtree Stour SC** has a quay which visitors may use. Access HW±0020 HWS only. Not easy to reach.
Anchorages In the River Stour, clear of the channel.

RIVER ORWELL

Entrance From close Shotley Spit S card Lt buoy enter the River Orwell in 8m leaving close to stb the R can Lt buoys College, Pepys and Babergh. The channel is dredged to 5·8m as far as Ipswich, the navigable limit 9M from Harwich. It is well marked with Lt buoys. The river narrows above Collimer Point with extensive mud banks on both shores. Pleasure craft must keep clear of the frequent commercial shipping. Anchoring in the channel is prohibited.

Berthing
• **Suffolk Yacht Harbour** Access 24hr. Entrance marked by sph RW buoy. Channel, 2·5m, marked by port and stb bns. Ldg Lts Y shown at night. Contact HM for berth.
Facilities Extensive yachting facilities including sailmaker, rigger, electronic and marine engineers. ☏ 01473 659465. VHF 80.
• **Pin Mill** All services, swinging moorings only. Landing at concrete hard at all states of tide except low springs. Muddy.
Facilities Shop, by bus, from Chelmondiston to Food Hall near Orwell Br. Famous pub Butt and Oyster.
• **Royal Harwich Yacht Club** Visitors berths on hammerheads and contact berthing master. *Mobile* 07742 145994, VHF 77.
Facilities Yacht club welcomes visitors to their bar and restaurant. Pump out. ☏ 01473 780319.

• **Woolverstone Marina** Sailmaker, electronic engineers, marine engineers, diesel, chandlery, restaurant.
☏ 780206, VHF 80.
Anchorages All occupied vessels should show a riding light, whether anchored or on a mooring. There is much commercial traffic.
• Above Shotley Point on W side above Orwell QR and R bn, clear of channel. Shore is steep-to, beware tel cable. Landing on beach at HW. Good shelter in W winds.
• In Long Reach on S side, well clear of main channel.
• In Buttermans Bay below moorings.

IPSWICH

Standard Port Walton
HW (sp) +0015 (np) +0025
LW (sp) +0010 (np) +0000
MHWS MHWN MLWN MLWS
+0·2m 0·0m −0·1m −0·1m

Ipswich is a large town with a historic waterfront benefiting from a regeneration programme. The town centre has many historic buildings, art galleries and museums within walking distance from Ipswich Dock. Rly to London, Cambridge and Norwich. Coach to Stansted Airport.
• **Fox's Marina** At the W side in Ostrich Creek. Access 24hrs. Enter channel S of No.12 buoy, through dredged and buoyed channel with approx 2m MLWS. Visitors' berth by arrangement.
☏ 01473 689111, VHF 80.

• **Ipswich Dock** Inward bound craft, on passing Orwell Br, must contact *Ipswich Lock* VHF 68 for details of lock opening. Waiting pontoon. Access 24hrs. Before leaving berth call the lock for next opening. Floating pontoon on E side of lock; ropes to W. Pontoon removed when ship expected.
• **Neptune Marina** At the NE end of Ipswich Dock. 150 berths. No chandlery. Berth depths vary 5·8m to 3·5m. Berths alongside quay available for very large craft.
Facilities Close to town centre shops. ☏ 01473 215204, VHF 80.
• **Ipswich Haven Marina** On south side of Ipswich Dock. Call on VHF 80 when in the lock. Visitors normally berth on pontoon K, or alongside on L. 270 berths, 30 visitors. Can accommodate vessels up to 6m draft and 20m in length.
Facilities All marine services on site and restaurants close by.
☏ 01473 236644, VHF 80.

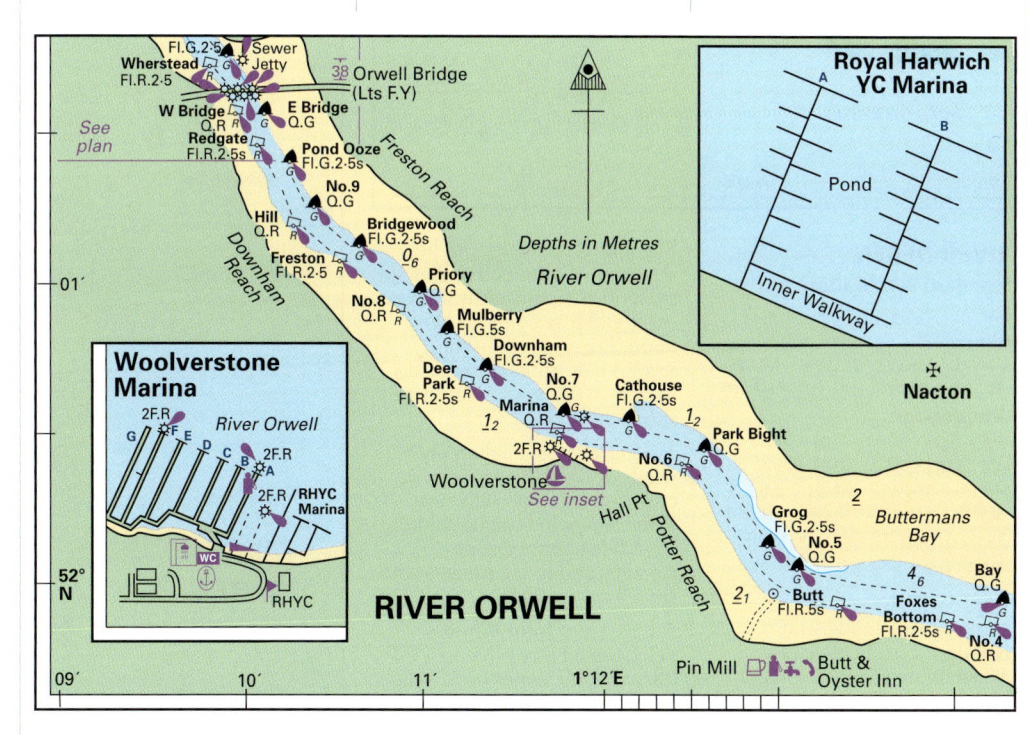

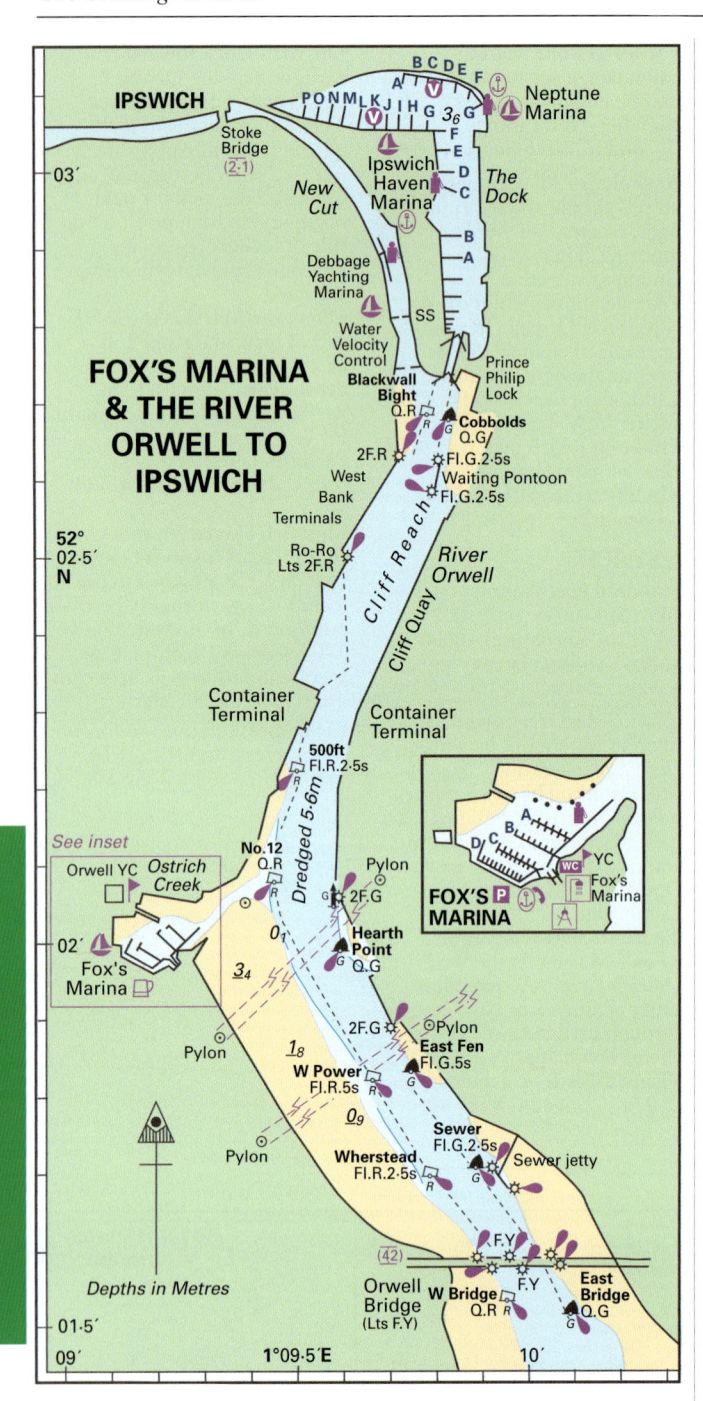

RIVER DEBEN

Standard Port Walton

Bar
HW –0003   LW –0022
MHWS MHWN MLWN MLWS
–0·5m –0·5m –0·1m +0·1m

Woodbridge
HW (sp) +0045 (np) +0025
LW (sp) +0020 (np) +0025
MHWS MHWN MLWN MLWS
–0·2m –0·3m 0·2m 0·0m

DS in offing: Dover +0015NE;
–0605SW

Approach The entrance lies between Felixstowe and Bawdsey Cliff between two Martello trs (T and U on the plan) to the W and a radio tr to the N. Make for the Woodbridge Haven safe water buoy from which the W Knoll R can buoy can usually be seen. Least depth on the bar is 0·2m in the narrow channel between Knoll Spit and Mid Knoll (Apr 2017).

Entrance The banks and lie of the channel alter every winter, sometimes significantly. Advise enter and leave only on the flood. Entry is best in the second half of the flood or up to HW+0100 with caution and sufficient power.

The entrance is rough in onshore winds or swell. Beware strong cross currents especially near Knoll Spit, wind can be fickle; advisable to have engine running, and to use transits with shore background.

Advice from John White, Felixstowe Ferry HM on VHF 08, call *Odd Times* or *Mobile* 07803 476621. Free download of latest plan from www.eastcoastpilot.com

From Woodbridge Haven RW buoy steer approx 325° to the R can W Knoll buoy. On the flood beware of being set to the west.

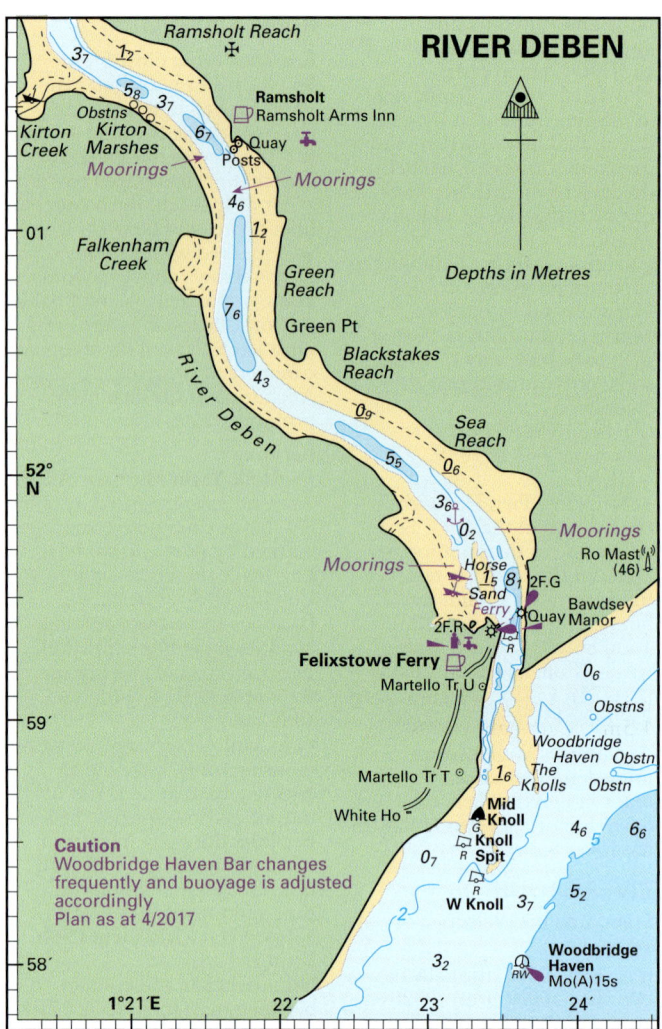

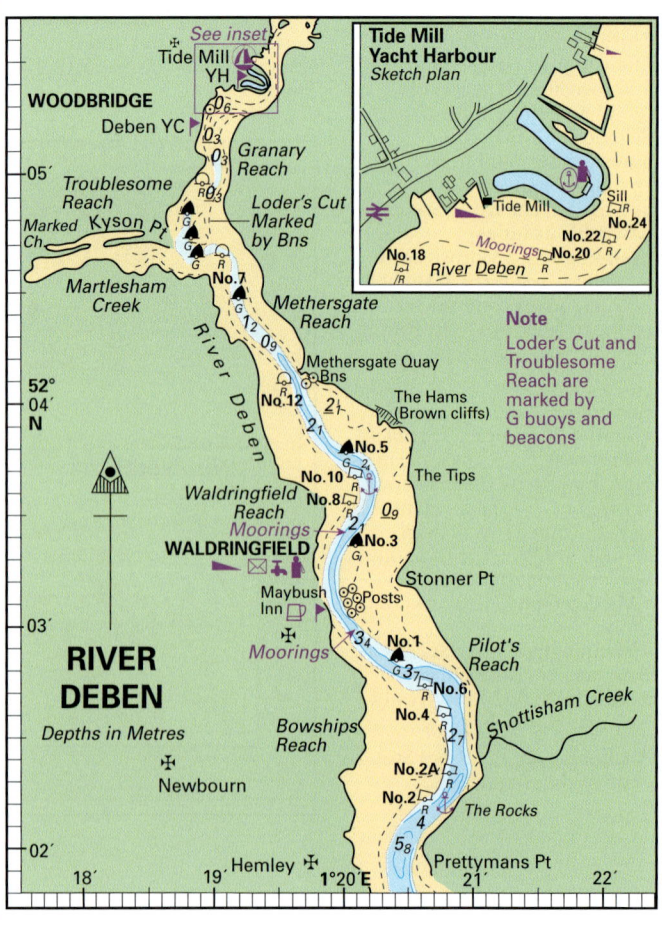

After leaving the Horse Sand R can buoy close to port follow the channel near mid stream as far as The Rocks. Above this the channel is buoyed.

Berthing
- **Felixstowe Ferry Boatyard** 20-ton slip. A mooring may be available. Limited facilities. ☎ 01394 282173.
- **Ramsholt** a mooring sometimes may be obtained. Pub, phone, no other facilities. HM George Collins, ☎ 334318 (evenings). *Mobile* 07930 304061.
- **Waldringfield Boatyard** 3 moorings with orange dinghy, marked visitor. ☎ 01473 736260. HM ☎ 07925 081062 or 01473 736291.
- **Tide Mill Yacht Harbour Woodbridge** On port hand just beyond the Tide Mill. Access for 1·5m draught HW–0230 to +0100 approx at springs. www.tidemillyachtharbour.co.uk has tide tables giving predicted heights over the sill which dries 1·5m. 2m draught yachts may not be able to pass at neaps. Waiting buoys, dredged entrance channel. If a yacht has enough water to reach Woodbridge, there is usually enough water to enter the yacht hbr. Tide gauge. All facilities, including repairs and laying-up. 12-tonne crane. Diesel. Visitors welcome but advisable to contact in advance. VHF 80, ☎ 01394 385745.

Anchorages
- Off the west bank above moorings at Felixstowe Ferry.
- Ramsholt, clear of moorings.
- Above Ramsholt at The Rocks.

Facilities Woodbridge all, sailmaker, rly to London.

ORFORD HAVEN

Standard Port Walton

Bar
HW –0028	LW –0037
MHWS	MHWN	MLWN	MLWS
–1·0m	–0·8m	–0·1m	0·0m

Orford
HW +0040	LW +0055
MHWS	MHWN	MLWN	MLWS
–1·4m	–1·1m	0·0m	+0·2m

Slaughden Quay
HW +0105	LW +0125
MHWS	MHWN	MLWN	MLWS
–1·3m	–0·8m	–0·1m	+0·2m

DS in offing: Dover +0030NE; –0530SW

There is a shingle bar at the entrance over which the depth at CD is about 0·8m. The bar frequently shifts, especially in the winter. It is essential to obtain up to date information, free download of latest plan from www.eastcoastpilot.com. Streams run fast, the ebb reaching 5kn at springs. The flood and ebb streams run for about 0115 after local HW and LW respectively. The rivers Ore, Alde, and the Butley River are attractive unspoilt rivers with mainly muddy banks and a few landing places, but many safe anchorages.

Approach The entrance to Orford Haven may be located by a cluster of small white cottages known as Shingle Street and an old CG station about ⅓M to the N. Keep at least ½M offshore to avoid the shingle banks and make for the Orford Haven RW safe water buoy.

Entrance Entry or exit best local HW –0330 to HW+0130. It is not advisable during the ebb or with onshore winds over Force 5. Wind against tide or an onshore swell can set up a heavy sea at or near the bar. Unlit buoys, R can Oxley and G con Weir are laid April to October. Once past Weir, gradually turn up river. Just before North Weir Point comes abeam, beware of being set onto the W bank where there are many semi-submerged old stakes and shallow hard clay banks. Thereafter the best water is on the seaward side until past the Narrows. Water-skiing areas in Long Reach. The W side of Havergate Is has more room for beating up river. Above Westrow Point the channel is marked by withies, R topmarks to port (unreliable), explore only above half tide and rising.

Moorings At Orford there are six marked visitors' moorings on E side of river below the quay and at Aldeburgh there are three visitors' moorings on E side of river opposite Martello tr where rafting may be necessary, max 25-tonnes. Other temporary moorings may be possible by application to:
- New Orford Town Trust, Orford Quay. VHF 8, call sign *Chantry* or ☎ 01394 459950 *Mobile* 07528 092635
- RF Upson & co, Slaughden Boatyard ☎ 01728 453047
- D Cable, Slaughden ☎ 01728 452569.

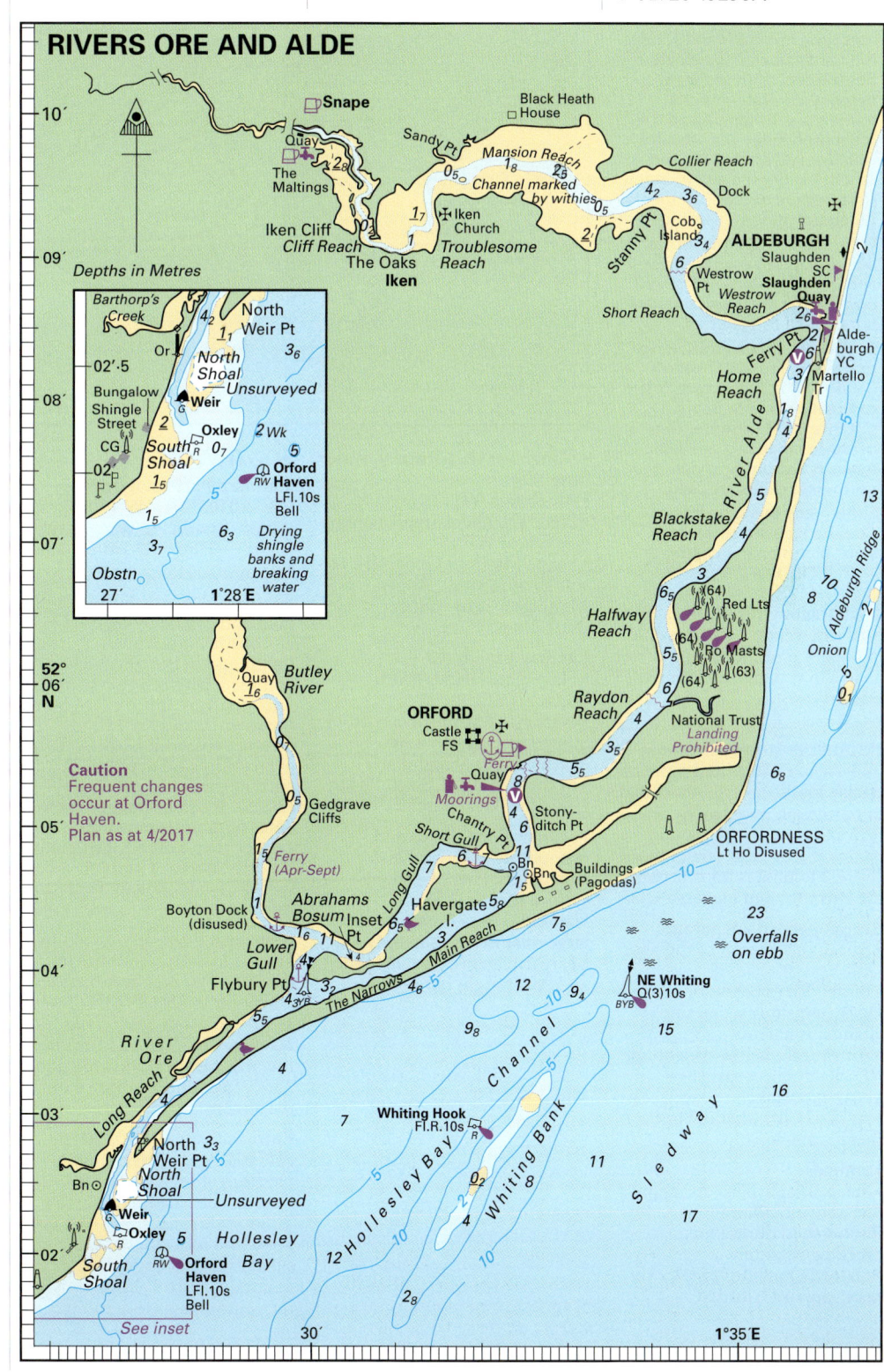

HARWICH TO GREAT YARMOUTH

DS Dover –0600SW +0015NE

Passage lights	BA No
Southwold	2272
Fl.10s37m24M AIS	
Lowestoft	2280
Fl.15s37m23M	

Leave Harwich on the recommended yacht track; round Landguard Point S of the buoyed deep water channel; cross W of the Platters S card Lt buoy and proceed NE leaving the Wadgate Ledge G bn close to stb to avoid wreck on the Wadgate Ledge. Then a least offshore distance of ½M will clear outlying dangers as far as Orfordness.

Orfordness is steep-to. An eddy runs close inshore N and S. Tides run hard and with wind over tide a steep, confused sea is raised. Calm water may be found close inshore. Avoid the Aldeburgh Ridge 7ca offshore which nearly dries at LW and cannot be ignored at HW. Stand close inshore or pass E of the Aldeburgh Ridge R can buoy.

Orfordness to Southwold has off-lying sand banks at Sizewell and Dunwich. Conspic Sizewell power stn is the main landmark but beware of its outfall.

Southwold to Lowestoft: keep to the E of Barnard Shoal off Benacre Ness. From Lowestoft to Great Yarmouth a safe distance is ½M offshore. The offshore sandbanks are liable to move, it is strongly advised that up-to-date charts are used.

Fishermen's buoys on long floating lines are a hazard in some places on this coast.

Anchorages Outside, in calm offshore weather, it is possible to anchor S of the Shingle Street Martello tr whilst awaiting the tide.

Inside, one may anchor anywhere clear of the fairway avoiding underwater cables and pipelines clearly marked on the shore and, in particular, avoid anywhere near moorings since ground chains run at right angles to the shore. Holding is poor between the entrance and Havergate Is.

Recommended anchorages
• Abrahams Bosom or the Short Gull
• Butley River below Boyton Dock, use short scope since channel is narrow
• Aldeburgh, below Aldeburgh YC in suitable weather or above moorings
• At Iken Cliff, shallow but there is a hole.

Landings
• Steep shingle bank for approx 3M above N Weir Point, discouraged during the breeding season
• Orford Quay (0·5m LW) 1hr max, slip or Orford SC
• Slaughden Quay (dries), water hose, slip
• Aldeburgh YC
• Iken, The Oaks, small sandy beach near HW
• Snape Maltings Quay (dries to soft sloping mud). Apply Maltings Marine Office ☎ 01728 699303.

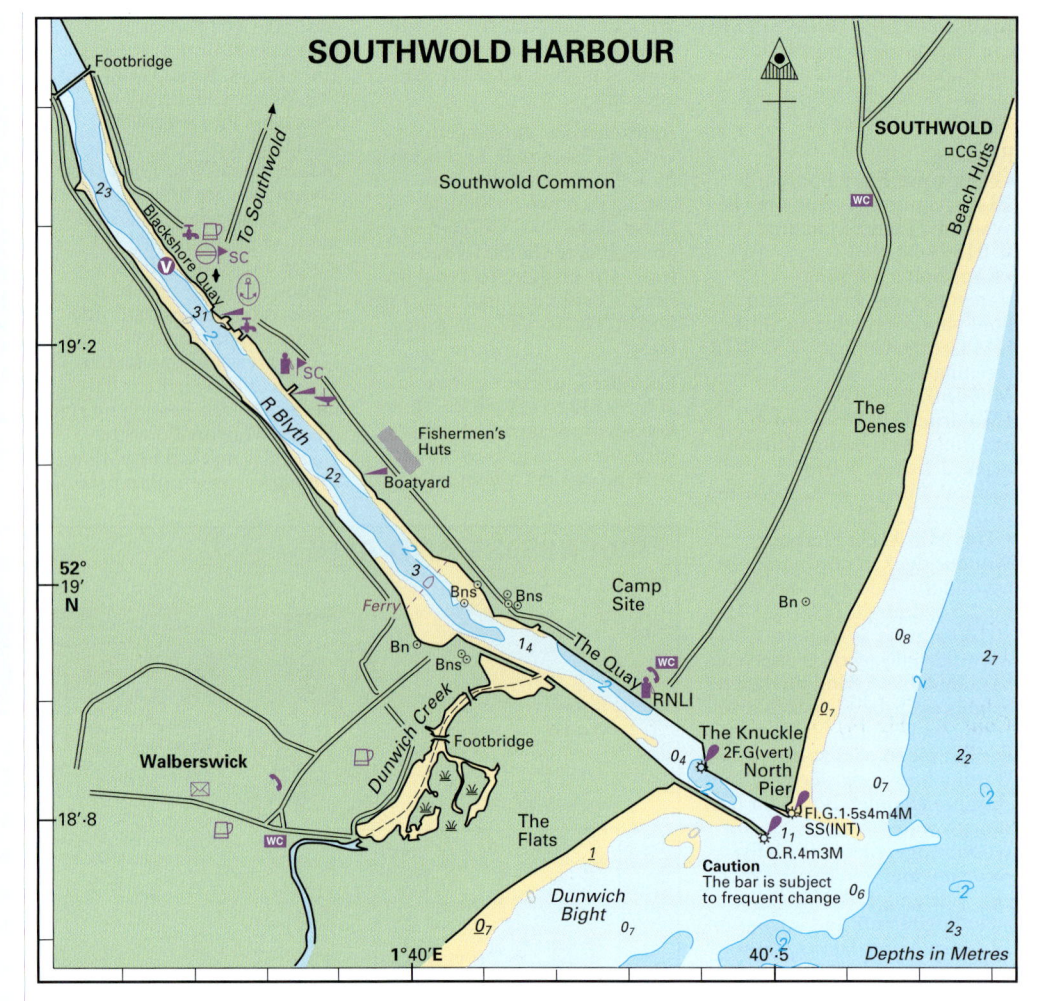

Landing prohibited
• Havergate Island, RSPB sanctuary
• National Trust property from Stony Ditch to 1M S of Martello tr at Slaughden.
• In the vicinity of Black Heath House or Iken church.

Facilities Pubs, shops and restaurants at Orford and Aldeburgh. Fuel by can, at Orford garage (½M) or Slaughden Quay (by pipe if large quantity, Upsons). Good boatyard facilities at Slaughden and Aldeburgh, but no petrol.

SOUTHWOLD

Standard Port Lowestoft
HW +0105   LW +0055

MHWS	MHWN	MLWN	MLWS
0·0m	0·0m	–0·1m	0·0m

DS Dover +0015N; –0600S

Southwold is on relatively high land and can be recognised by its conspicuous white lighthouse in the town. The hbr entrance, between two piers 36m apart, is approx ¾M S of the town. Call HM 24h in advance to check berth availability and depth in entrance. Least depth 1m (2016). It can be dangerous to enter with onshore winds greater than Force 5, especially if northeasterly. Go to www.waveney.gov.uk for latest information.

Approach From any direction keep at least 4ca offshore for the last mile. Best approach waypoint is 52°18′·78N 1°40′·54E. Call *Southwold Harbour* on VHF 12. Turn in towards the piers, making good 330°. Take due allowance for the stream.

Entrance Best HW–0330 to HW+0130. 3.F.R.(vert) on N pierhead show that hbr is closed. The channel is narrow. Tides are strong, up to 4kn on flood and 6kn on ebb. Go slowly but fast enough to maintain control. Enter down the centre; pass close to the Knuckle, turn to stb towards the N wall following it within 2–3m, leave the G bn with triangular topmark about 8m to starboard, then head towards the black huts on the SW shore until in the centre of the river, then head directly up the middle of the river. The Ferry is a rowing boat and has right of way over all vessels.

Berthing At busy times it is essential to book in advance. On visitors' staging, as directed, 2m alongside at LWS at W end reducing to 0·5m at E end. Rafting is usual, as many as six deep. Come alongside stemming the tide. Turning can be difficult: if you have suitable stem, put the bow into the mud on the S side and let the current swing you round. Long shore lines (up to 20m) and good springs are essential. Moor parallel to the tide, secure tiller amidships. Call *Southwold Harbour* before departure.

Facilities Pub with food. Fresh fish. Electricity. Showers at Harbour Office, Sailing Club (when open) or caravan site. Good boatyards. No petrol. Shops, restaurants etc in town 1M.

☎/VHF HM 01502 724712. *Southwold Harbour* VHF 12.

LOWESTOFT

Standard Port Lowestoft
DS Dover −0020N; +0540S

This is a valuable passage port available at all times.

Approach From the S make E Barnard E card Lt buoy, then follow buoyed Stanford Channel E of Newcome Sand to N Newcome R can Lt buoy before turning W to hbr. From the E enter the Stanford Channel S of S Holm S Card Lt buoy and then as from S. From the N follow the buoyed Roads to the W of the sandbanks.

With fresh wind against tide a heavy sea gets up off the hbr. Vessels should remain inside the buoyed channels since the banks are continuously changing. Buoys may well have been moved since the last correction applied to the chart.

The ebb runs strongly across the entrance. When about 2ca off, call *Lowestoft Harbour Control* (VHF 14) for permission to enter. Make the final approach from the ENE, keeping closer to the S pier on entry.

Entrance IPTS are shown on the S pierhead. Call *Lowestoft Harbour Control* (VHF 14) for permission to enter. It is also essential to obtain permission to leave the RN & SYC Marina, since vessels leaving cannot see those about to enter.

If waiting for the br opening, yachts must use the waiting pontoon in the Trawl Dock. Maintain a listening watch on VHF 14.

A free lifting road br gives access to inner harbour, opening times are: 0300, 0500, 0700, 0945, 1115, 1430, 1600, 1900, 2100, 2400 LT. On Saturday, Sunday and Bank Holidays there is an additional opening at 1800. Call on VHF 14 at least 20 minutes before desired opening. Other openings may occur for commercial traffic, yachts may only use these with prior permission. Whilst waiting, all vessels must listen on VHF 14. Navigation through the br is controlled by R and G lights. Wait for 3 G lights.

Access to the Broads is via Mutford Lock, max beam 6·4m, (a £10 charge is made) about 1½M from the br. Operates 0800–1200, 1300–1700 (Sat, Sun until 1930). Advise 24hrs in advance, the lock gets congested at weekends. Lock-keeper arranges opening of the nearby Carlton rail br. When making for the sea ask to enter the lock 2–3hrs before the desired road br opening time. If draught >1·7m seek advice from lock.

Berthing

• **RN & SYC Marina**, immediately to port on entering narrow channel to br. Visitors should secure to outside of pontoons, rafting if necessary, but not enter the fingered area. The YC is friendly and makes facilities available to visitors. 24hr toilets for visitors, free internet access to weather forecasts, electricity by card from office.

• **Lowestoft Cruising Club** has berths on the N shore at the W end of Lake Lothing. Welcoming and sheltered. Contact moorings officer before arrival if possible. No VHF.

• **Lowestoft Haven Marina** at School Road Quay has 30 visitors' berths with full marina facilities.

Facilities As expected of a major port and town.

☎/VHF Lowestoft Port Control VHF 14, ☎ 01502 572286. Mutford Lock VHF 73 (occas), ☎ 01502 531778 / 574946. RN&SYC VHF 80, ☎ 01502 566726. Lowestoft Cruising Club Moorings Officer ☎ 01502 732970, *Mobile* 07810 522515; Club ☎ 01502 574376. Lowestoft Haven Marina VHF 80, ☎ 01502 580300.

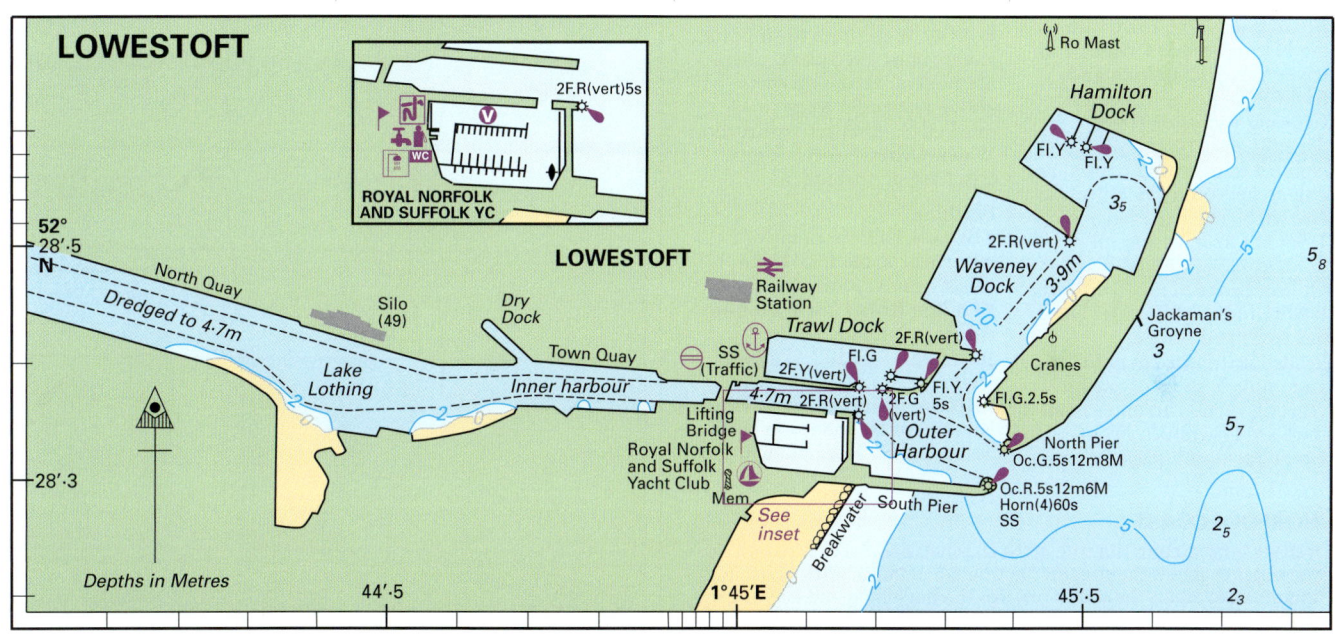

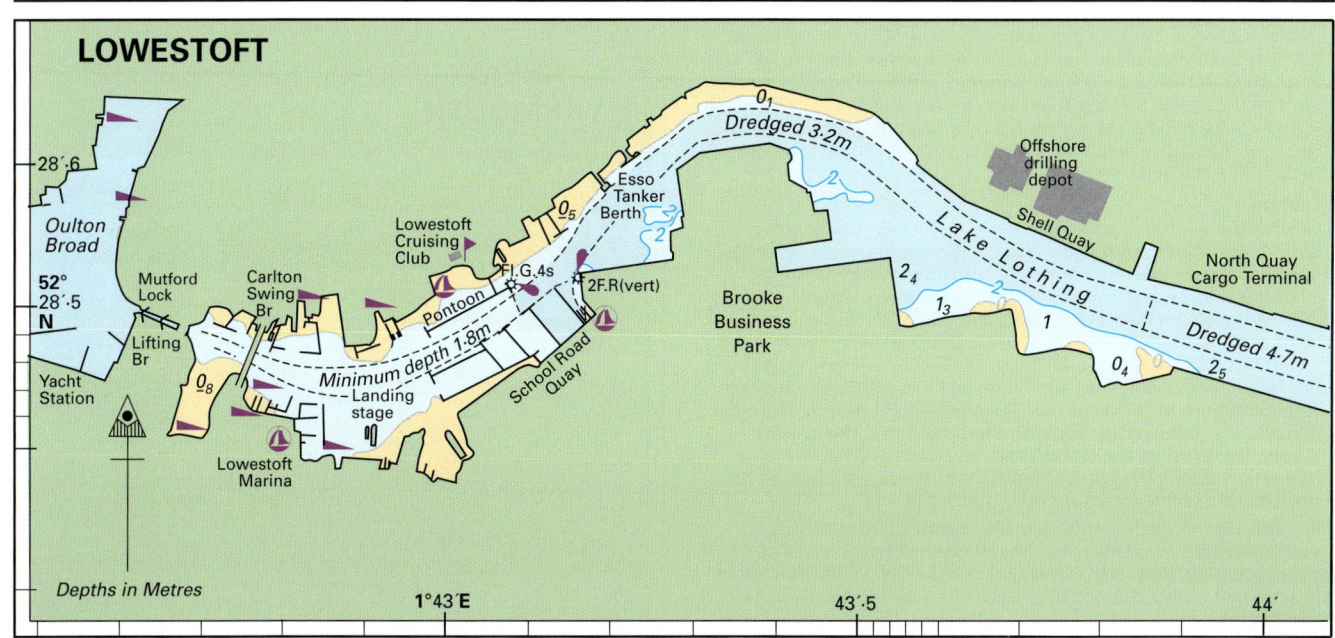

NORTH SEA PASSAGE NOTES

Lowestoft to IJmuiden
Leave Lowestoft by the Stanford Channel, preferably avoiding the worst of the N-going tide since the tides are strong along the English coast. Pass to the south of the Brown Ridge which lies just over halfway on this 100M passage. It is marked near its S end by a W card Lt buoy Q(9)15s. The best time to arrive at IJmuiden is soon after dawn so that shore lights can have been identified. The rear Ldg Lt Fl.5s29M is the most powerful light. By day, the tall steelworks chimneys (166m) to the N of the hbr are a useful landmark. It is a busy commercial port. Aim to make the final approach to one side or other of the harbour avoiding the main shipping channel, the Ij-Geul, track 100°, which is well marked by Y Lt buoys for the final 18M to the harbour entrance.

NORFOLK BROADS

There are two entrances, Lowestoft to the S into Oulton Broad and Great Yarmouth to the N into Breydon Water and River Yare to Norwich and River Waveney to Lowestoft. Cruising yachts of 1·5m draught and 10m air draught (subject to overhead cables) are able to get to Lowestoft or Norwich. The tidal range is 1·5m at Great Yarmouth to 0·3m at Norwich and 0·6m at Oulton Broad. There is also the R Bure to the N Broads. This has two fixed bridges, headroom about 2m at HW, and unlikely to be of use for cruising yachts. To enter from the S see Lowestoft. From Great Yarmouth pass the lifting Haven Br at E end of Breydon Water (air draught when closed 4·2m at MLWS, 2·4m at MHWS), preferably at slack water. For Breydon Water also pass the Breydon Br (air draught when closed 4·5m MHWS) which lifts in conjunction with the Haven Br. Yachts must book opening of the bridges, preferably before entry to hbr, by calling the Harbour Office on ☏ 01493 335522 before 1645 on the previous day. Booking for Saturday, Sunday and Bank Holidays must be made by 1600 or the previous Friday afternoon. The bridges normally open between 0900–1200 and 1300–1600. If waiting for an opening, moor alongside Town Hall Quay. Traffic lts turned on 10 min before opening. 3F.R(vert) Lts indicates passage is from the other side.

Norfolk Broads temporary licences from The Haven Commissioners, 21 South Quay, Gt Yarmouth ☏ 01603 610734 or from a patrol.

Priority at all times to shipping, yachts must keep clear. There are boatyards and marinas above Haven Br. Keep to marked channel across Breydon Water. Observe speed limits. Discharging forbidden.

Berthing
• **Broads** There are many moorings, some free, some offset against food etc.
• **Oulton Broad Yacht Station.** Advance booking advised July/Aug. ☏ 01502 574946; VHF 73.
• **Broom Boats Ltd,** Brundall on River Yare 100 pontoon berths, access 24hrs. Normal facilities, full repairs, restaurant, no chandlery or launderette. No VHF, ☏ 01603 712334.
• **Burgh Castle Marina** on River Waveney ½M from S end of Breydon water. 93 berths max draught 1·5m, access HW±0300. Full facilities. 32-tonne hoist. One visitor's pontoon. No VHF, ☏ 01493 780331. Book in advance.
• **Riverside moorings** many but use only with local permission. When in doubt tie up but be prepared to move.

NORFOLK COAST

Inshore tidal streams run true in the channels parallel to the coast. In the outer channels the streams run true when they are strongest, but there is a set across the shoals towards the beginning and end of each stream. The SE stream changes through SW to NW, and the NW stream changes through NE to SE. On this coast generally the NW stream is strongest at LW by the shore, and the SE stream strongest at HW. The sea breeze often comes from the SE rather than the NE. This helps going N but causes difficulty going S. Offshore, there is a wind farm on the Scroby Sands marked at its extremities by Lt Fl.Y.5s13m Horn Mo(U)30s and an abundance of oil and gas rigs. Beware of frequent changes of depth between Gt Yarmouth and Winterton Ness. Follow buoyed channel.

Caution
Only Wells-next-the-Sea harbour on the N Norfolk coast is accessible during fresh winds appreciably N of E or W and then only near HW. Most become dangerous before that. Also all harbours along this coast dry at low water. In poor conditions the outer entrances are a mass of broken water making marks and buoys very difficult to see, some being small or substandard. Grounding can easily result in the loss of the vessel. Conditions in entrances rapidly worsen when the ebb begins or if there is any swell running from offshore. Under these conditions entrances may be unsafe even in a light breeze. The most dangerous conditions are at spring and surge tides. The nearest alternative safe hbrs are 30M or more away and need accurate navigation among the sands to reach them. Passage should not be started, even in fine weather, without recognising this.

It is difficult to assess conditions in the entrances from outside. In poor conditions avoid Blakeney. The choice is between Wells or staying outside. Wells is lit but only accessible HW ± 0200 If in doubt it is prudent not to attempt. Wells-next-the-Sea HM will assist. See Wells details.

GREAT YARMOUTH

Standard Port Lowestoft

River Entrance
HW –0035   LW –0030

MHWS	MHWN	MLWN	MLWS
0·0m	0·0m	0·0m	0·0m

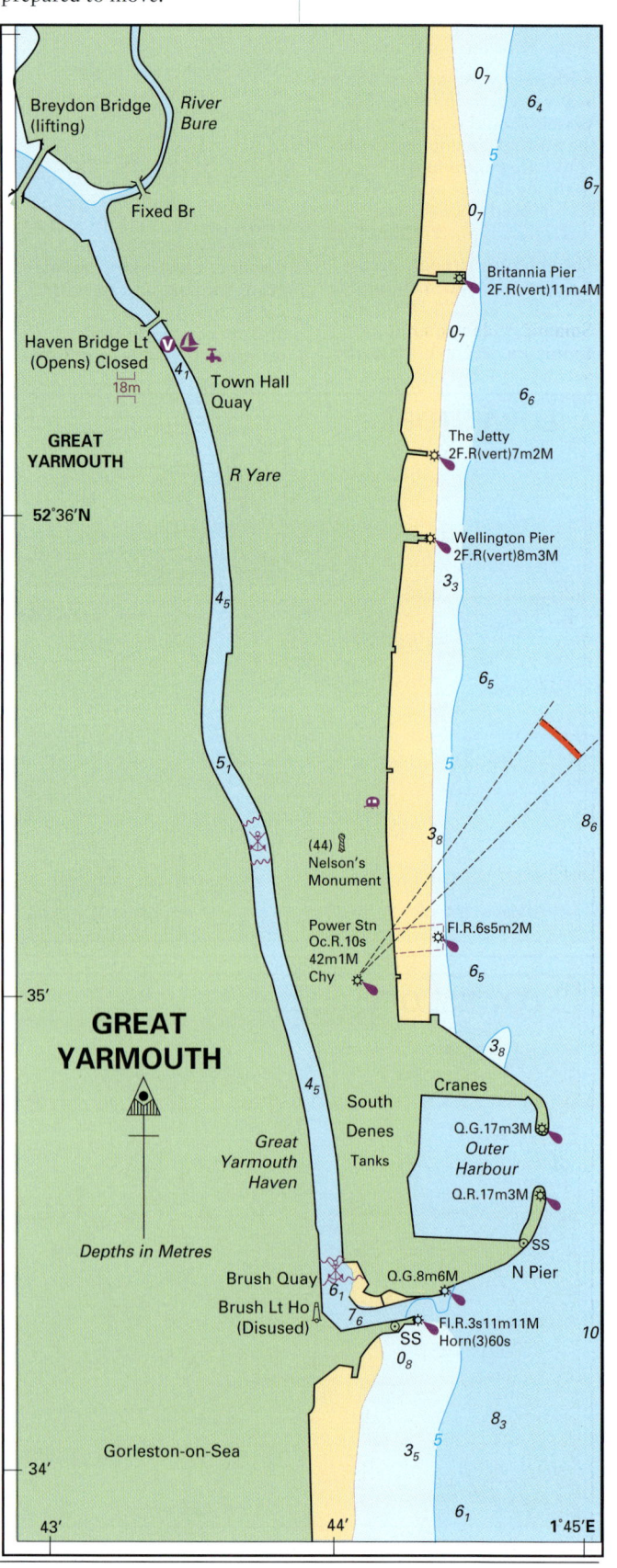

There are two harbours, the new Outer Harbour where yachts are forbidden and the River Harbour. The latter remains busy mainly as an offshore industry support base. No special yacht facilities exist but it does provide a gateway to the Broads, with a mast-up route towards Norwich.

Approach and Entrance From the N avoid passing too close to the Outer Harbour. Call *Yarmouth Radio* before entry or departure and maintain a listening watch. The one-way traffic system at the hbr entrance must be strictly observed. The white rectangular building on the E end of the S pier is illuminated at night.

On its roof there are three vert Lts Oc.12s:
- 3R(vert) entry prohibited
- 3G(vert) enter, if safe
- GWG enter if given permission

At Brush Quay similar lights control vessels leaving the hbr downstream of the lifeboat house.

Q amber tidal signal is displayed from S pier head indicating tide flooding.

Small craft can enter at most times, but preferably at slack water; the stream runs up to 5kn or more. Slack water at the entrance is approx 90 mins after local HW/LW, but this may vary with weather conditions. Seas near the entrance are confused. Entrance should not be attempted in strong SE winds, when a dangerous sea occurs especially on the ebb tide. Passage under sail within the port limits is not normally permitted. Anchoring in the hbr prohibited except in emergency. Vessels are strongly advised to keep an anchor cleared ready to drop especially if navigating up-tide of the br.

Berthing Visitors should berth on the east side of the river close to the S side of Haven Br against a ladder. There are vertical wooden piles, large fenders or a fender board desirable.

The streams runs strongly; a spring is essential and it helps to tie the helm to hold the vessel off the piles. Beware of vandalism.

Facilities None on quay, but near town centre.

☎/VHF *Yarmouth Radio* VHF 12. Port Control ☎ 01493 335511.

BLAKENEY

Standard Port Immingham
Bar
HW (sp) +0025 (np) +0035
LW (sp) +0030 (np) +0040
MHWS MHWN MLWN MLWS
−1·6m −1·3m n/a n/a
DS Dover −0100NW & W; +0600E and SE

A stunning, well sheltered hbr adjacent to National Trust bird sanctuary and large seal colony on Blakeney Point. Great walks at LW on flat sand. Abundant wildlife. Very exposed to winds from a N'ly direction when conditions in the entrance can be treacherous and deteriorate quickly. Only suitable for shoal draft craft or ones that can dry out. First time entry should only be undertaken on spring tides HW±0200 in offshore winds. Local pilotage advice recommended; contact Charlie Ward on ☎ 01263 740377 or 07771 597985 (free of charge by phone or for a small charge by following a pilot boat).

Approach From the E, conspic mark is Blakeney church with large and small towers, Langham church tr, and turret above trees on skyline 3M inland. Follow 5m contour to Blakeney Point (grass topped sand dunes). Then steer due W to the RW Fairway buoy. The conspic isolated danger beacon marks the west end of the *Hjordis* wreck. From the W, stand off 1M from the Bink, the low sandy point with a clump of fir trees ½M E of Wells and steer due E to RW Fairway buoy.

Entrance From Fairway buoy, follow the conspic G and R buoys all the way into Blakeney harbour (known as Blakeney Pit). In June 2017 the marked channel was to the east of the wreck. Buoys are well lit at night all the way to the W end of Blakeney Pit. For detailed info on buoy positions (constantly changing due to shifting sands), lights, and Navigation Warnings, refer to www.blakeneyharbourassociation.co.uk

Moorings Contact Charlie Ward as above; drying on flat sand £5/night, deep water (shoal draft only) £10/night. Alternatively contact Neil Thompson on ☎ 01263 741172 for drying moorings. Berthing, free of charge at Blakeney quay, but very congested. No moorings or berths in the creek to Morston, but access by tender HW±0230, beware numerous seal trip boats operating.

Facilities Supermarket, garage and pubs at Blakeney. Good pub with food at Morston Water and fuel by can only from Charlie Ward's boatyard at Morston. Water, by can only, from Old Lifeboat House on Blakeney Point (large blue building).

WELLS-NEXT-THE-SEA

Standard Port Immingham
Bar
HW +0020   LW +0020
MHWS MHWN MLWN MLWS
−1·3m −1·0m n/a n/a
DS Dover −0030NW and W; +0600E and SE

Wells is a working hbr busy with wind farm service vessels which use the dredged Outer Hbr. Otherwise the hbr mainly dries but there is 1·5m at MLWS alongside the visitors' pontoon in the Inner Hbr. With onshore winds over F4 or heavy N'ly swell it should not be attempted by strangers.

Approach Make for the W card Wells Harbour buoy, known locally as the 'Leading Buoy'. Previous to, or on arrival there, call *Wells Harbour* on VHF 12 for advice on entry and berthing instructions. The best time for entry is HW−0200 to +0100.

Entrance The channel is dredged from the entrance to the LB house (conspic W building with R roof) to allow entry HW±0300 for 1·5m draft. The entrance channel across the bar into the hbr is subject to change from time to time, however, the buoyage system is relatively stable. From the W card buoy make good approx 165° to leave the West End Bar buoy to port. Beware of strong tidal set to E for 2h before HW. Leave the East Bar buoy to port then make good a course to pass between buoys No.1 and No.2. The smaller buoys of the channel should become visible. From the G buoy No.9 the channel bends away towards the SE into quieter waters. The wide sweep to the SE past the LB Ho must be made with the R buoys quite close to port as the channel is narrow. The Outer Hbr (dredged) just S of the LB Ho may only be used by yachts with specific instruction from the HM. On passing the G buoy (named the Pool) sweep round to the SW and follow the buoys until the last R buoy then back to the SE, close to the marsh edge, and follow the R buoys all the way to the quay. Waiting buoys for yachts are laid in The Pool for use whilst waiting to proceed to the visitors' pontoons.

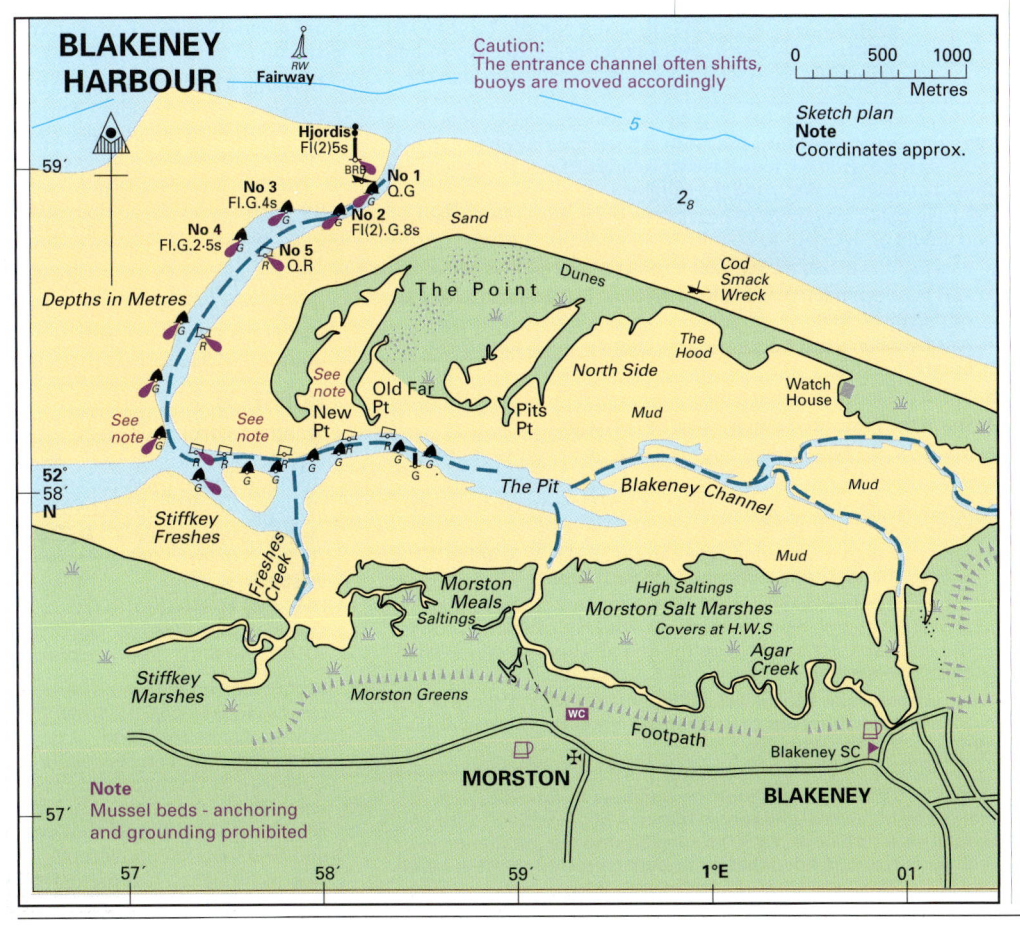

WELLS-NEXT-THE-SEA

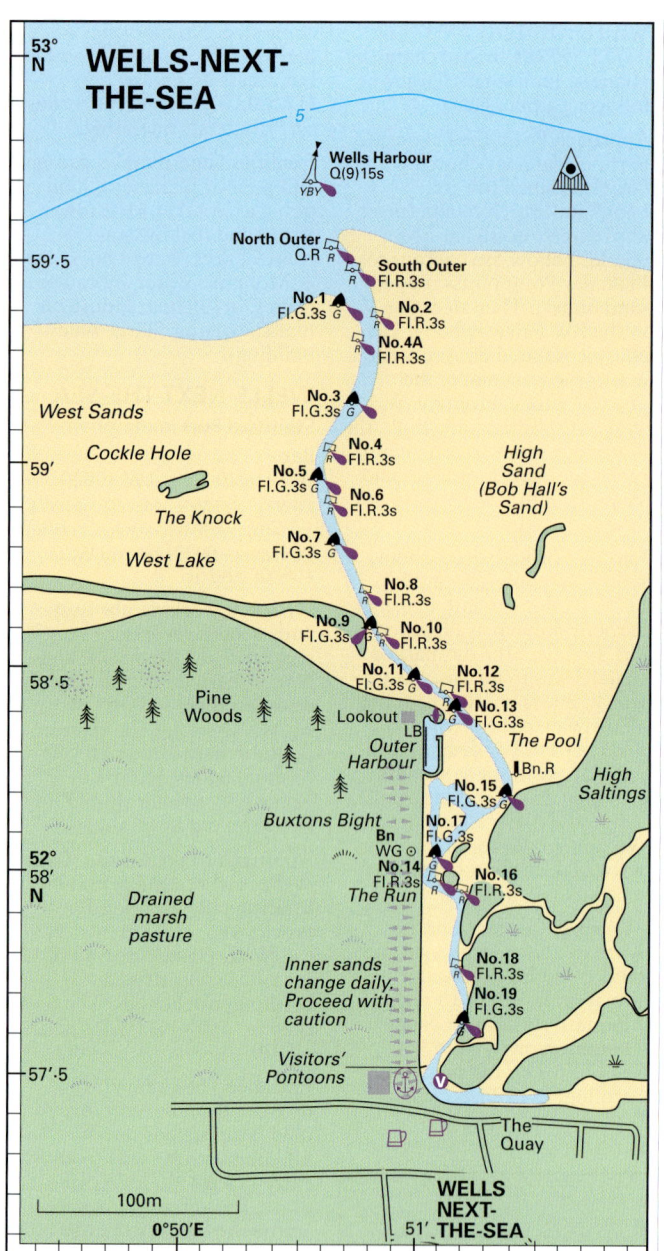

Berthing There is over 200m of alongside visitors' pontoons with shore access. You will normally be directed to a berth, rafting may be necessary. *Caution* At times, the tide runs strongly and perhaps not quite parallel to the pontoons. Good springs desirable.

Facilities Electricity, water, diesel, 7·5 tonne hoist, chandlery. Shops nearby.

☏/VHF *Wells Harbour* VHF 12 Office 01328 711646; HM 07775 507284, or 07881 824912.

www.wellsharbour.co.uk

THE WASH

In main channels DS Dover +0130 in, –0445 out

In main channels the tide range is about 7m springs and 2·7m neaps, so that it is possible to find 2m more than charted at MLWN.

Approach The Wash is not easy once out of the main channels and the latest corrected charts are advised. It is best to wait until half flood before entering any of the rivers. Buoys may be moved to conform with frequent depth changes.

From the E
- Docking Channel, well buoyed ship route, to N Docking N card Lt buoy, then SW to the Roaring Middle LtF LFl.10s.
- From Bridgirdle R can buoy off Brancaster to Woolpack R can Lt buoy Fl.R.10s, N of Middle bank. Narrow passage and seas break on both sides in NE winds. Then SW to the Roaring Middle LtF LFl.10s
- From Bridgirdle R can buoy off Brancaster through the Bays, between Middle Bank and Sunk Sand. There is approx 5m at LW between the banks but less than 2m in the approach from the E. The channel is not buoyed and is difficult to follow.

www.sailthewash.com

KINGS LYNN

Standard Port Immingham
HW (sp) +0030 (np) +0030
LW (sp) +0305 (np) +0140

MHWS	MHWN	MLWN	MLWS
–0·5m	–0·8m	–0·8m	+0·1m

A mainly commercial port with some facilities for yachts. Useful for vessels heading to Denver Sluice and the inland waterways.

Approach Head towards the *Sunk* W card buoy, then make for Daseley's Sled channel arriving at *No1* con lightbuoy Fl.G.3s. Gauge not more than 3½h before HW. Follow the buoyed channel. It is highly desirable to have the latest plan available from www.kingslynnport.co.uk. Listen on VHF 14 for commercial shipping movements.

Entrance From No.26 R buoy it is 3½M to the commercial docks; the channel becomes more confined, with the ebb running at up to 5kn. It is advisable to contact *Lynn Pilots* or *Lynn Docks* VHF 14.

www.portauthoritykingslynn.fsnet.co.uk has details of latest surveys and local Notices to Mariners.

In the Lynn Cut and the river 9–10hrs ebb and 2–3hrs flood are usual. Ebb in the river may run up to 5kn.

Berthing There is a visitors' pontoon, max draught 1·5m, in 52°45'·06N, on the E side beyond the commercial docks. There are no berths on the quays or with the fishing boats. It is essential to make contact 24h in advance.

☏/VHF Port and nav info: 01553 773411 or 07784 548842, VHF 14; Visitor pontoon 01553 763044.

WISBECH

Standard Port Immingham
Wisbech Cut
HW (sp) +0010 (np) +0020
LW (sp) +0120 (np) +0055

MHWS	MHWN	MLWN	MLWS
–0·3m	–0·7m	–0·4m	n/a

Wisbech
HW (sp) +0040 (np) +0055

MHWS	MHWN	MLWN	MLWS
–0·2m	–0·6m	n/a	n/a

Secure marina with pontoon berths close to historic town centre. Access to inland waterways and Peterborough. Vessels of 2·5m draught can reach Wisbech at neaps. Monitor VHF 09 at all times and be aware of commercial ship movements. It is preferable

CROMER TO RIVER HUMBER

Along Lincolnshire coast
DS Dover
+0200 S and SW, –0500 NE and N
Off N Norfolk
DS Dover
+0300 W turning S, –0300 E turning N

Passage lights	BA No
Newarp Lt buoy LFl.10s7M AIS Racon O (– – –)	2332
Happisburgh LtHo Fl(3)30s41m14M	2336
Cromer Lt Ho AIS Fl.5s84m21M, Racon O (– – –)	2342
Inner Dowsing Lt buoy Q(3)10s7M Racon T(–)	2351
Dowsing B1D Fl(2)10s28m22M Mo(U) (··–)R 15s Horn(2)60s Racon T(–)	2420
Spurn LtF Q(3)10s10m8M Racon M (– –)	2422

With the exception of the sandy cliffs from Happisburgh to Cromer much of the coastline is low. It is particularly difficult to identify the shore between the Wash and the Humber.

Off-lying banks may produce heavily breaking seas in bad weather and should be avoided. To do this:
- Pass E of the Blakeney Overfalls R can Lt buoy Fl(2)R.5s Bell;
- Pass between the E Docking R can Lt buoy Fl.R.2·5s and S Race S card Lt buoy, Bell;
- Pass between the N Docking N card Lt buoy and N Race G con Lt buoy Fl.G.5s Bell;
- Leave the Inner Dowsing E card Lt buoy Q(3)10s approx 1M to port;
- Leave the Protector Lt buoy Fl.R.2·5s 1M to port;
- Make for the Rosse Spit Lt buoy Fl(2)R.5s marking the approach to the R Humber;
- Make for and leave R can DZ No3 Fl.Y.2·5s close to port, thereby keeping clear of the TSS.
- Alter course to NW making for R can No 2B Fl.R.4s to enter Humber buoyed channel using recommended yacht tracks.
- The Tetney Monobuoy is used by large tankers discharging oil via an underwater pipeline to the shore. They are often held on station by one or more tugs on the end of a long hawser. A wide berth is requested.

There are many gas and oil installations mainly well offshore which must be passed at not less than 500m. At night, these are lit Fl.15s Mo(U) (··–); in fog Horn 30s.

Closer inshore beware of wind farms. The Race Bank wind farm in the vicinity of 53°17'N 0°50'E should be complete by late 2017; it is marked by lit cardinal and special buoys. A 50m exclusion zone exists around each turbine and a 500m zone around the installation vessel. It is highly recommended that up-to-date corrected charts are used.

APPROACHES TO KING'S LYNN AND WISBECH

to call *Wisbech Yacht Harbour* 24hr in advance.

Approach Make for *E Knock* E card buoy. Report to *Swing Bridge* which opens HW±0300, then follow the buoyed channel to *Lake* S card buoy and then *MAC* E card buoy. Maintain a watch on VHF 09; you may meet commercial vessels of up to 5,000T, of length considerably greater than the channel width, keep reasonably close to the stb bank, but if in doubt call on VHF 09. The buoys may often be moved to follow the changing channel.

Entrance Once past Big Tom bn report to *Crosskeys Swing Bridge* with ETA and air draught. Maintain watch on VHF 09 since you may be asked to stop at the waiting pontoon on the E side of the river 500m north of the br. The channel is marked by lit bns, G on W bank, R on E bank.

Bridge signals:
- Red   closed
- Orange   preparing to open
- Green   open, proceed.

Spring tides run at up to 4kn.

Berthing When 1M away from Wisbech Yacht Harbour which is 8M beyond the br, call on VHF 09 for instructions. If no berth has been allocated go to any outside vacant berth. HW is best time to arrive, i.e. Immingham +0155.

Facilities as expected of a modern marina, incl. laundry. 75-tonne travel hoist.

☎/VHF Swing Bridge ☎ 01406 350364 VHF 09: Wisbech Yacht Harbour ☎ 01945 588059 VHF 09, out of hours call Duty Officer on ☎ 07860 576685 (24hrs).

FOSDYKE

HW Immingham +0005

Approach From the north via Boston Deep; from the east via Roaring Middle and the Freeman channel: thence to Clay Hole, anchor and await tide if necessary.

Entrance By the Welland Cut which runs SW from the Welland Cut bn QR. It is marked by lighted bns on top of stone banks on either hand, at approx 64m intervals. Tides may reach 4kn at springs. Best to enter HW–0100 so as to arrive at Fosdyke at HW.

Berthing At Fosdyke Yacht Haven which is just to seaward of the Fosdyke Br (clearance 4·5m). Max draught 1·8m, preferable to phone 24h in advance to secure a berth.

Facilities As usual for a small yacht hbr, including travel hoists and repairs. No diesel. Nearby pub with food, but little else.
Fosdyke Yacht Haven ☎ 01205 260240.

BOSTON

Standard Port Immingham
HW (sp) +0010 (np) +0000
LW (sp) +0140 (np) +0050

MHWS	MHWN	MLWN	MLWS
–0·5m	–1·0m	–0·9m	–0·5m

An active small commercial port. Yachts, which can lower their masts, can enter the inland waterways through the Grand Sluice. Contact the Sluice Keeper, giving 24h notice (☎ 01205 364864).

Approach is best through the Freeman Channel, subject to silting however it is well buoyed.

Entrance at half flood is best. Temporary anchorage to await the tide 5ca SW of No.9 buoy in Clay Hole. After No.9 buoy call *Boston Port Control* on VHF 12. Lower masts near the dock. The dock is only available in an emergency. Entry at the Grand Sluice is twice each tide, approx HW±0230, this varies due to variability of levels.

Berthing in Boston Marina, above the Sluice.

☎/VHF Port/Dock 365571, *Boston Port Control* VHF 12; Grand Sluice 364864, VHF 74; Marina 364420, VHF 06.

RIVER HUMBER

Approaches The Humber is a busy commercial river. While in the Humber monitor VTS Humber VHF 12 or 14 if below Clee Ness or in the approaches for shipping movements and weather reports. From S see passage notes. From the N steer for the Spurn LtF and follow recommended yacht track. From seaward leave Spurn LtF between LW and half flood to carry favourable stream to Hull.

Spring tides run at 4·5kn at Immingham, 5kn at Hull. Wind against tide can be very unpleasant and best avoided. In the Humber fairway pass between the Bull N card Lt float VQ.8m6M Horn(2)20s and Spurn Head Fl.G.3s11m on the stb side of the channel. Then follow the well lit and buoyed channels, Bull to Grimsby and Hawke to Hull taking care NW of Immingham to avoid Foulholme Spit and Skitter Sand. Shoaling occurs frequently, buoys are moved as necessary.

Anchorages

- **Spurn Head** at river entrance in N channel a good anchorage inside Spurn Pt sheltered in N and E winds, uncomfortable in strong NW winds particularly on spring ebb. Anchor in 2–3·5m opposite the LtHo off brickyard chimney N of pilot boat station. Clay bottom gives good holding but strong ebb.
- **Killingholme**, in S or W winds off brickyard chimney.
- **Hawkins Point**, opposite Grimsby, sheltered in N'ly winds.
- **Cleethorpes**, about 1M offshore near Haile Sand Fort, in fine SW'ly weather.
- **Humber Mouth Yacht Club** Drying moorings are reached by a channel which runs roughly N–S. The channel is marked by B stb barrel buoys. It is essential to identify them before attempting to reach the moorings. The best approach is on line from the Haile Sand Fort to the Cleethorpes sewer outfall. Following this course will result in crossing the line of marker buoys between Nos.2 and 3. The anchorage is safe for boats which can take the ground though it is uncomfortable at HW springs when the Haile Sand Bank covers.

GRIMSBY

Standard Port Immingham
HW -0012   LW -0015

MHWS	MHWN	MLWN	MLWS
–0·2m	–0·1m	0·0m	+0·2m

Entrance Approx 60m E of conspic square brick tr (94m). The western part, Alexandra Dock, is commercial with no facilities for visiting cruising yachts who should enter the Fish Dock by the easterly lock. Call *Fish Dock Island* on VHF 74 for permission to enter or leave. The lock is on free flow HW±0200, beware of strong currents. Access may be possible HW±0400 with a charge of £10. Keep a sharp lookout for shipping entering or leaving Alexandra Dock or Ro Ro piers, immediately to the west. When entry not possible wait in tidal basin, can be difficult, or anchor outside. Uncomfortable in fresh E winds.

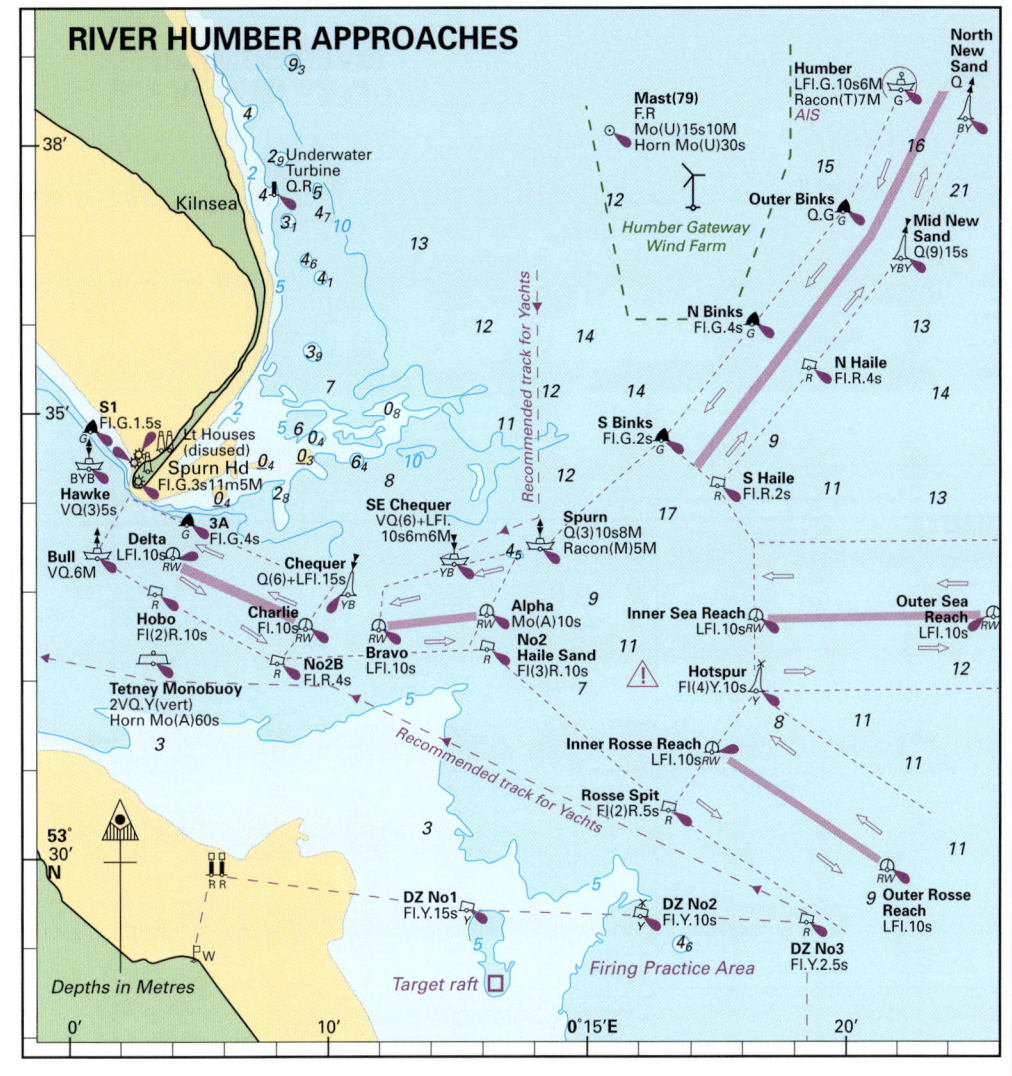

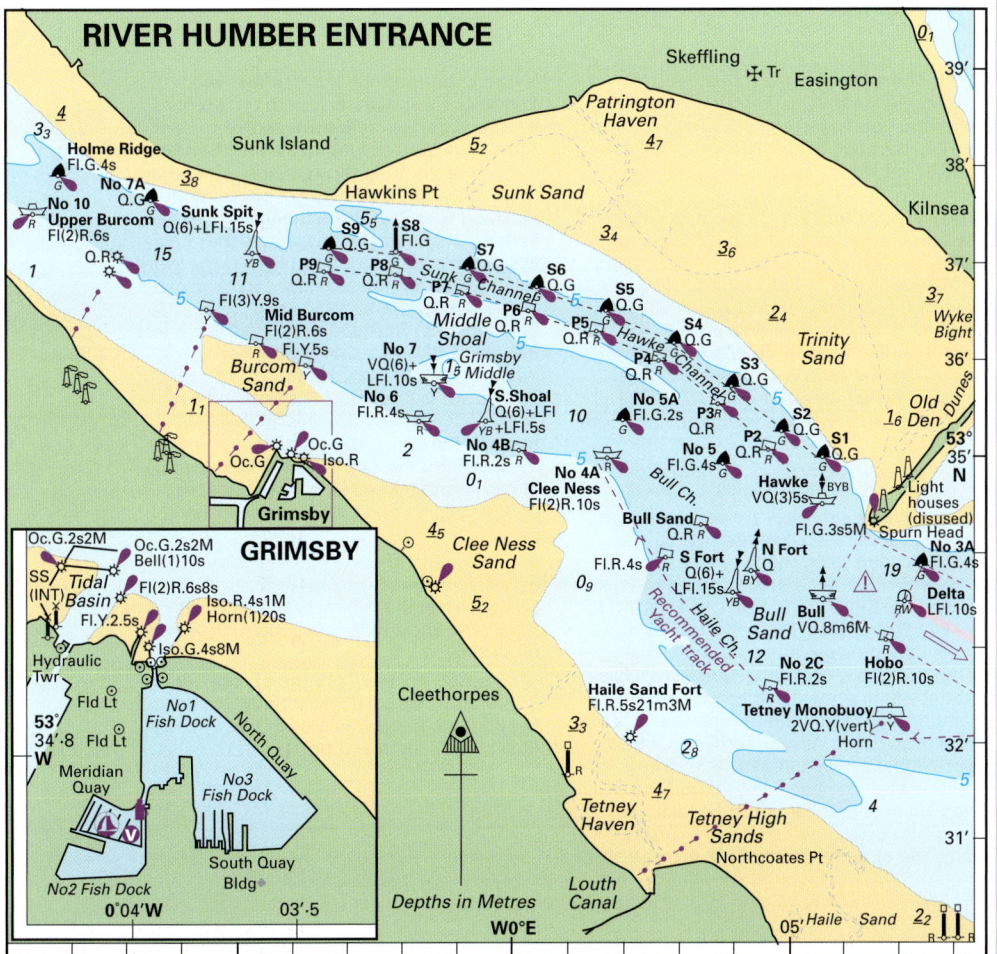

Berthing Berth holder marina run by the Humber Cruising Association at Meridian Quay in SW corner of Fish Dock. Visitors' pontoon and finger berths to port beyond the travel-hoist.

Facilities Diesel, showers, a welcoming club, supplies ¾M in town.

☎/VHF Marina 01472 268424, berthing master 07415 209659. No VHF; Lock *Fish Dock Island* 01472 267240, VHF 74 (24h).

HULL

Standard Port Immingham
HW +0022   LW +0030

MHWS	MHWN	MLWN	MLWS
−0·2m	−0·1m	0·0m	+0·2m

A modern marina with excellent access to city and rly.

Entrance Lock operates HW±0300. Call 15 mins before arrival. Full facilities, diesel, 50-ton travel-hoist and storage ashore. If waiting better to moor to stb on inside of outer basin wall, dries to soft mud. Shore access by steps and vert ladder. Alternatively anchor outside avoiding prohibited areas. Lock gates operate 24h when depth over cill >2m. Lts, 2G over W to enter. Allow for strong set past outer entrance.

☎/VHF VHF 80 or 01482 609960. Lock VHF 80 or *Mobile* 07789 178501 (24h).

UPPER REACHES

Standard Port Immingham
Goole
HW (sp) +0115 (np) +0130
LW (sp) +0355 (np) +0350

MHWS	MHWN	MLWN	MLWS
−1·6m	−2·1m	−1·9m	−0·6m

For the most up-to-date information on navigation above Hull, contact Associated British Ports ☎ 01482 327171 who have responsibility for Humber estuary, as the channel and its buoyage (light floats) are constantly changing. Above the Humber br, VTS works VHF 15. There can be severe standing waves above Humber Br in wind over tide conditions.

• **South Ferriby Marina**
HW Immingham +0035
S bank, 3M upstream of Humber Br. 120 berths, access HW±0300. Normal facilities, diesel, chandlery, sailmaker, shore storage, repairs. Visitors advised to phone in advance. VHF 80, ☎01652 635620. Lock keeper (48hrs notice required in winter) VHF 74, ☎ 635219.

ENGLAND – EAST COAST

109

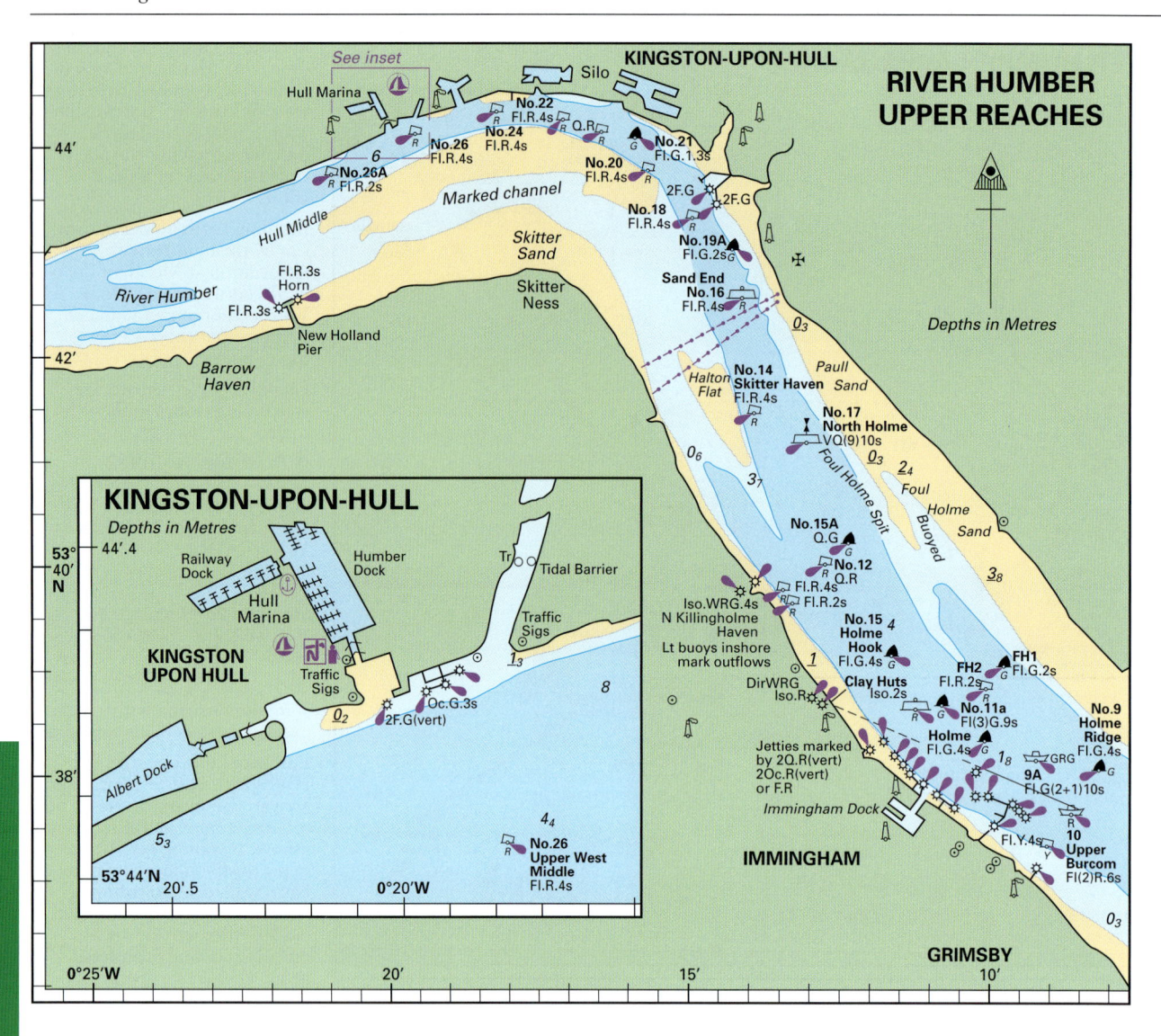

SPURN HEAD TO BERWICK

Passage lights	BA No
Flamborough Head	2582
Fl(4)15s65m24M Horn(2)90s	
Whitby High	2596
Fl.WR.5s73m18/16M	
South Gare – Tees	2626
Fl.WR.12s16m20/17M	
The Heugh – Hartlepool	2663
Fl(2)10s19m19M	
Roker Pier, Sunderland	2681
Fl.5s25m18M Siren 20s	
Tynemouth, N pier Hd	2700
Fl(3)10s26m26M Horn 10s	
Blyth, E Pier Head	2754
Fl(4)10s19m21M+	
F.R.13m13M Horn(3)30s	
Coquet	2780
Fl(3)WR.20s25m19/15M	
Horn 30s	
Bamburgh Black Rocks	2810
Oc(2)WRG.8s12m14-11M	
Longstone – Farne Is	2814
Fl.20s23m18M AIS	

Tidal streams
Spurn Point to Bridlington
DS Dover +0130S, –0445N
Flamborough Head
DS Dover +0015S, –0600N
Tees Bay to Farnes
DS Dover HW S, –0555N
Farnes, Inner Sound
DS Dover –0010 SE, +0600 NW

North of the Humber the *Royal Northumberland YC Sailing Directions* is excellent. Copies and corrections (s.a.e) from RNYC, S Harbour, Blyth NE24 3PB ☎ 01670 353636 or from Imray who also publish Henry Irving's *Forth, Tyne, Dogger, Humber, Blakeney to St Abbs*. For most of its length the passage from Spurn Head to Tees Bay offers no particular navigational difficulties or offshore hazards. But in strong NE'ly winds or with a heavy NE'ly swell keep at least 2M offshore. Many harbour entrances become unsafe under these conditions, when Whitby should only be approached with extreme caution and certainly not near LW. However Hartlepool and Blyth are well protected from the NE.

There are well used bombing ranges off the Humber estuary which should be avoided. The Humber approaches are very busy with commercial shipping. See plan of TSS and recommended yacht channel, monitor VTS Humber VHF Ch 14. Dangerous seas can be set up over the Binks shoal which extends 4M to the E of Spurn Head. 6M North of Spurn Head, Easington gas and oil terminal is conspicuous in an otherwise bleak, low lying coastline with some crumbling cliffs. Flamborough Head with its high chalk cliffs is very conspicuous. Around it there is a tidal overfall that can be dangerous in strong winds against the tide. In such conditions keep 3M offshore. Care must be taken to avoid Filey Brigg, marked by an E card Lt buoy, and also the Whitby Rock marked by a N card Lt buoy about 1M offshore. The Yorkshire coast with its superb cliff scenery, bays, and ports is delightful in offshore winds. Along this coast the inshore tides often seem to be stronger than those predicted, turning 1½ to ½h earlier than those offshore, until reaching Tees Bay where the tides are weak. In many of the smaller bays there may be an appreciable in-draught. In Tees Bay there are usually several ships at anchor, some may be manoeuvring, waiting for a pilot to board. Once north of Hartlepool the coastline is less industrial. Blyth is a safe port in heavy weather, except from the SE. Do not attempt to pass inside Coquet Is. The Northumberland coast with its sandy beaches and views towards the Cheviots is attractive. Approaching the Farne Is, tides run strongly; in bad weather keep at least 1M E of the Longstone and don't attempt the inshore passage.

In summer months one may encounter the occasional salmon drift net laid across the tide between the fishing boat and usually a large pink buoy; maintain a listening watch on VHF 16.

On passage there are pontoon berths at Bridlington Scarborough, Whitby, Hartlepool, Sunderland, Newcastle, Royal Quays marina (River Tyne), Blyth and Amble.

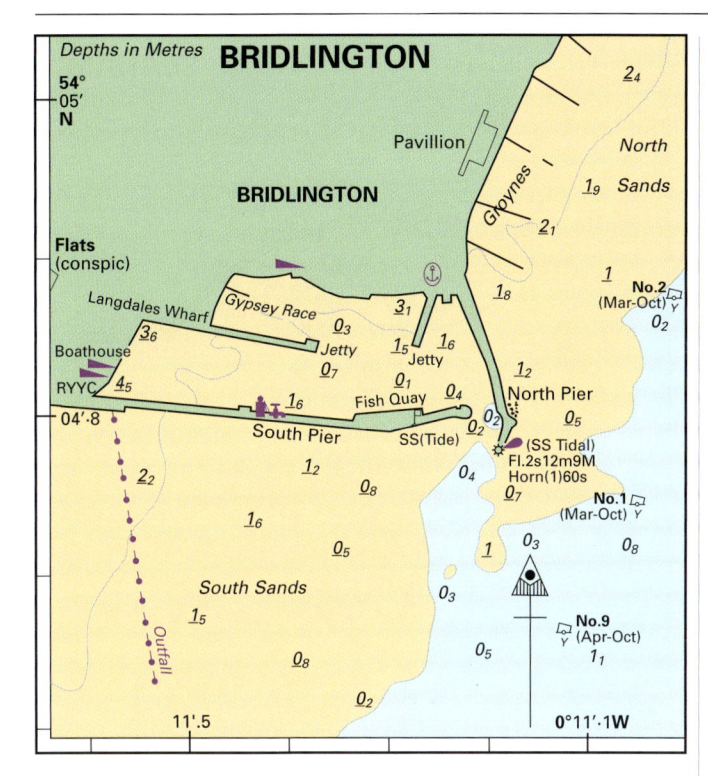

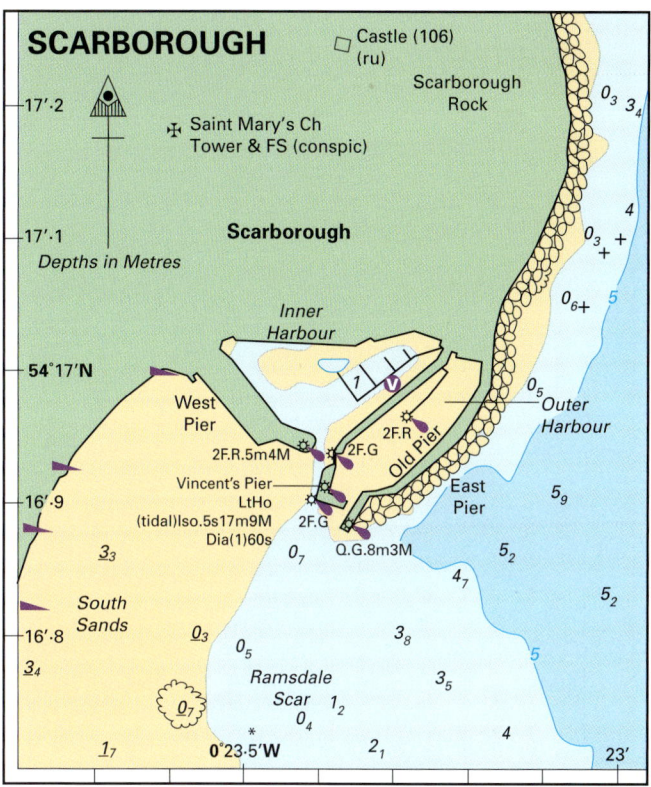

- **Winteringham Haven** (S bank) Humber Yawl Club. Buoyed entrance with R port spars to channel, useable for 1·5m draught ±0130 HW neaps to ±0230 MHWS. Drying mud creek with pontoons. Toilets. Beware of submerged saltings downstream of entrance at HWS. ☎ 01724 733458.
- **Rivers Trent and Ouse** These rivers provide access to the extensive inland waterways network. York Marina is accessible to yachts 1·2m draught and 13m air draught. Useful information can be obtained from
www.canalrivertrust.org.uk
www.waterscape.com

BRIDLINGTON

Standard Port River Tyne
HW (sp) +0115 (np) +0102
LW (sp) +0101 (np) +0110
MHWS MHWN MLWN MLWS
+1·1m +0·8m +0·5m +0·4m

Access HW±0300 for 2·7m draught. Sand bar across hbr entrance, minimum 0·6m approx. Hbr dries. Call *Bridlington Harbour* VHF 12 before making an approach.

Approach from S so that hbr entrance is open. N pier head Fl.2s12m9M Horn 60s. Depth of water in hbr – signals are by day >2·7m R flag, by night Fl.R. >2·7m, Fl.G. <2·7m. Day signal station 50m W from head of S pier. Light signals at head of N pier.

Berthing There are 2 visitors' pontoon berths, drying soft mud, with water and electricity, accessible HW±0230 for 1·5m draught, otherwise enquire of HM VHF 12.
☎ 01262 670148, *Mobile* 07860 275150 before entry.

Anchorage With the wind from NNW to SSW, anchor approx ¼M off the pier end. Winds from NNW round to NE, bring up under Danes' Dyke or near the S landing.

Facilities All supplies, repairs, crane, shipwright. Diesel fuel from tank/hose. Petrol from town in cans. Water from S pier.

☎ /**VHF** *Bridlington Harbour Watchkeeper* 07860 275150 VHF 12; Hbr Office 01262 670148; Royal Yorks YC 672041.

SCARBOROUGH

Standard Port River Tyne
HW +0054 LW +0043
MHWS MHWN MLWN MLWS
+0·7m +0·7m +0·5m +0·2m
DS Dover +0200SE –0400NW

Just to the north of the hbr there is a conspic rocky promontory, Scarborough Rock, on which there are castle ruins. Scarborough is a vibrant holiday town. Shops near the hbr are mainly fast food outlets and amusements.

Approach E of the hbr, close inshore, there is a NE going eddy from quarter flood to HW. From the S make for 54°16'·6N 0°22'·0E then make good a course of 290° for the entrance. Call Scarborough Harbour Watchkeeper on VHF 12 (24H) before entry for advice and berthing instructions.

Entrance Access for 1·5m draught is H24 at neaps and HW±0400 at springs. Enter the Inner Harbour leaving Vincent's Pier LtHo to stb. Beware of trip boats and speedboats. No vessel should attempt to enter in strong onshore winds (NE through E to SSE). When by night a Lt Iso.5s is shown from LtHo, there is at least 3·7m available in the inner harbour. R flag indicates entry forbidden.

Berthing Unless directed otherwise, on SE side of long pontoon in Inner Harbour. Near LW keep close to pontoon, where there is a narrow channel dredged to 1.8m. No rafting is allowed, or even desirable. The two end berths nearest the gangway are reserved for local trip speedboats. Do not go to the north of the small RW horizontal banded bn which marks the SW end of a scrubbing grid adjacent to the harbour wall. Turning can be difficult below half tide. If wishing to make a LW departure make sure you have turned to head outwards when there is sufficient water. In season, usually met by berthing master who supplies a key to the marina gate. Showers, toilets, laundry and berthing master's office are below the LtHo. Entry code provided by the berthing master who normally comes to direct you to your berth.

Anchorage 1–3ca from outer pier, keeping E of a line Scarborough Castle-Vincent Pier Lt Ho. Sand over blue clay, good holding. Open to E.

Facilities Shops, 10 minute walk up the hill. There is a well stocked chandler, facing the hbr, 50m from the marina gate, who also supplies diesel by can.

WHITBY

Standard Port River Tyne
HW +0034 LW +0030
MHWS MHWN MLWN MLWS
+0·6m +0·5m +0·4m +0·3m
DS Dover –0430 NW +0130SE

Picturesque port of interesting old town. Whitby Abbey, Captain Cook museum, etc.

Approach Avoid entrance in strong onshore winds. Otherwise approach directly except, from SE keep 1M offshore to avoid breaking seas off the Whitby Rock. Make for the Whitby N card Lt buoy Q Bell about ¾M from hbr mouth (where the tide turns approx HW and LW+0200). Leave it to port. Then approach on 169° to Ldg Bns (W ▲ below a W circle with B stripe) and both Fl.Y.4s (sync) on the SE side of the lower hbr.

Entrance Depth 0·9m min, access HW±0500. Concrete ledge awash on piers gives depth 4m minimum in channel. Entrance can be rough. A strong tidal set may occur across entrance, to E on flood, W on ebb. The ebb stream between piers can reach 5kn when River Esk in flood. On entrance, when abeam of bend in E pier, turn onto 209° with two ldg Lts Fl.Y.2s (sync) astern on the E pier. Proceed to fish quay then turn onto 160° and follow 1·5m channel to upper hbr through swing br. Br control Lts F.G open, F.R closed.

Call *Whitby Bridge* VHF 11, ☎ 01947 602354. Swing br opens HW±0200 on hrs and ½hrs. First and last openings may not be exactly on the hr or

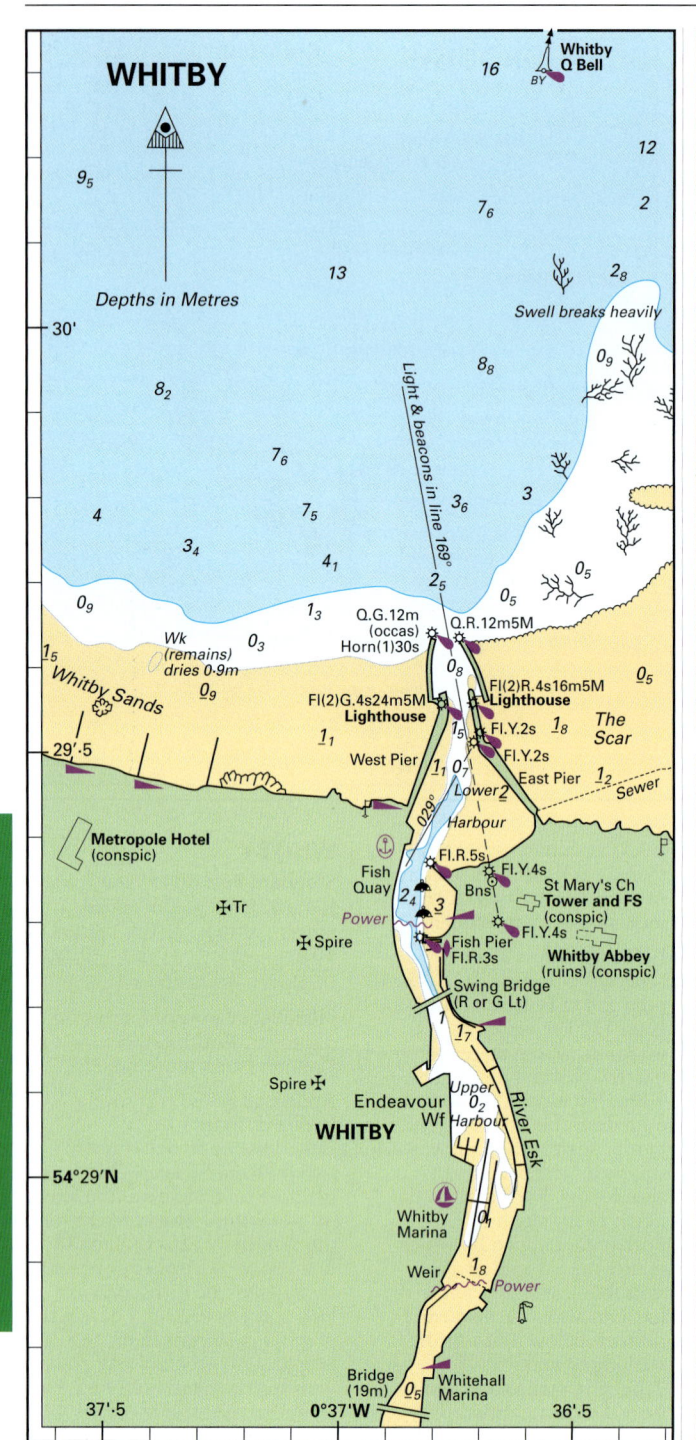

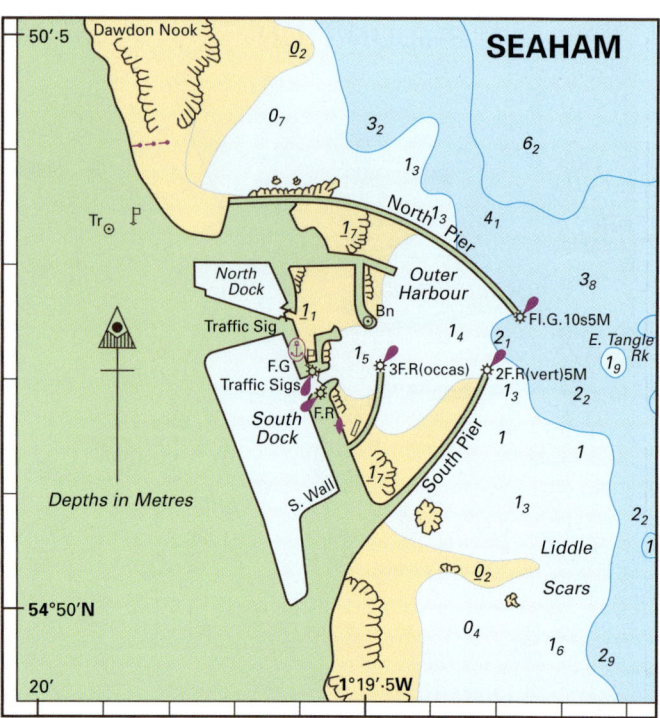

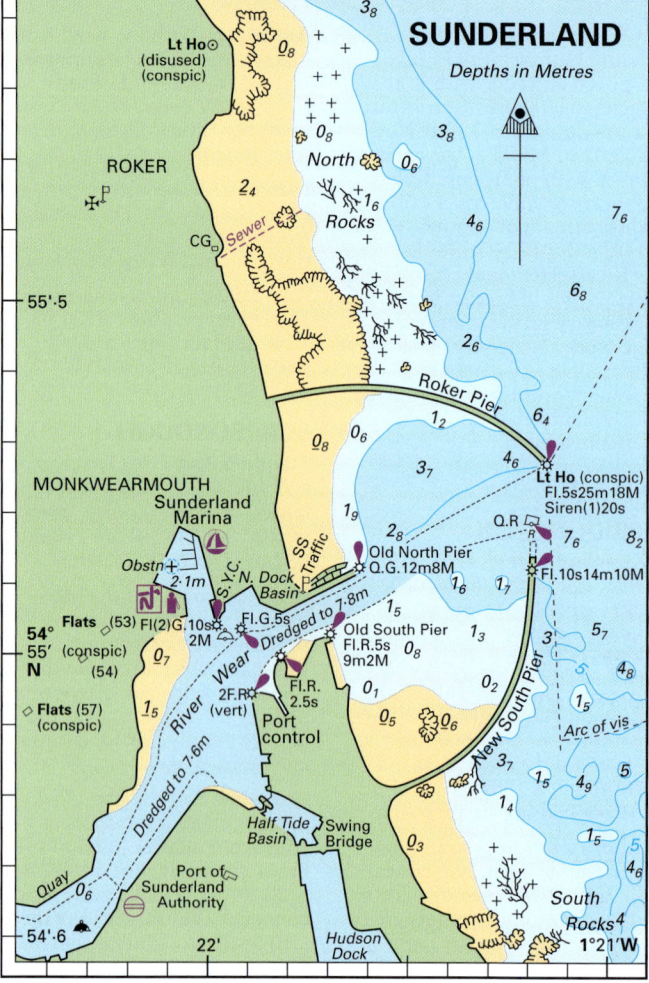

½hr. Some additional openings Saturday and Sunday in summer 0830–1730 regardless of tide. Outside the br opening times wait in the lower hbr alongside the Fish Quay/fishing vessels or the waiting pontoon on E side. Boats on the quay must remain manned at all times.

Berthing
- **Whitby Marina** 12 visitors' berths on N end of W pontoon. Call *Whitby Marina* VHF 11 for allocation of berth. ☎ 600165. Normal facilities. Depths maintained at 1·5m minimum as far as possible but subject to rapid shoaling.
- **Fish Quay** with fishing boats. Short stay only with HM permission.

Anchorage Outside ¼–½M NNW of W pier opposite hotel buildings in 5m, sand.

Facilities Nearby supermarket. Diesel by can from marina.

OFFSHORE ANCHORAGES
- **Filey Bay.** Keep the Flamborough Head Lt open above the cliff tops and stand off the Filey Brigg card Lt buoy. The bottom is clay covered with sand, with foul ground beginning with Scarborough Rock appearing outside Car Naze. Do not remain in the bay with the wind E of NNE. In winds from W of S anchor 4M S of Filey under Speeton Cliffs.
- **Whitby Bay and Sandsend Bay.** Beware of Up Gang Rocks lying ¾M offshore mid-way between Whitby and Sandsend with 0·5m over them and 11m close by.
- **Runswick Bay.** When entering to anchor, give Kettleness a wide berth.

RIVER TEES
The River Tees is heavily industrialised and is not recommended. If requiring refuge, Hartlepool is much to be preferred. In heavy E'ly weather seek a temporary berth in Victoria Harbour.

The Cruising Almanac

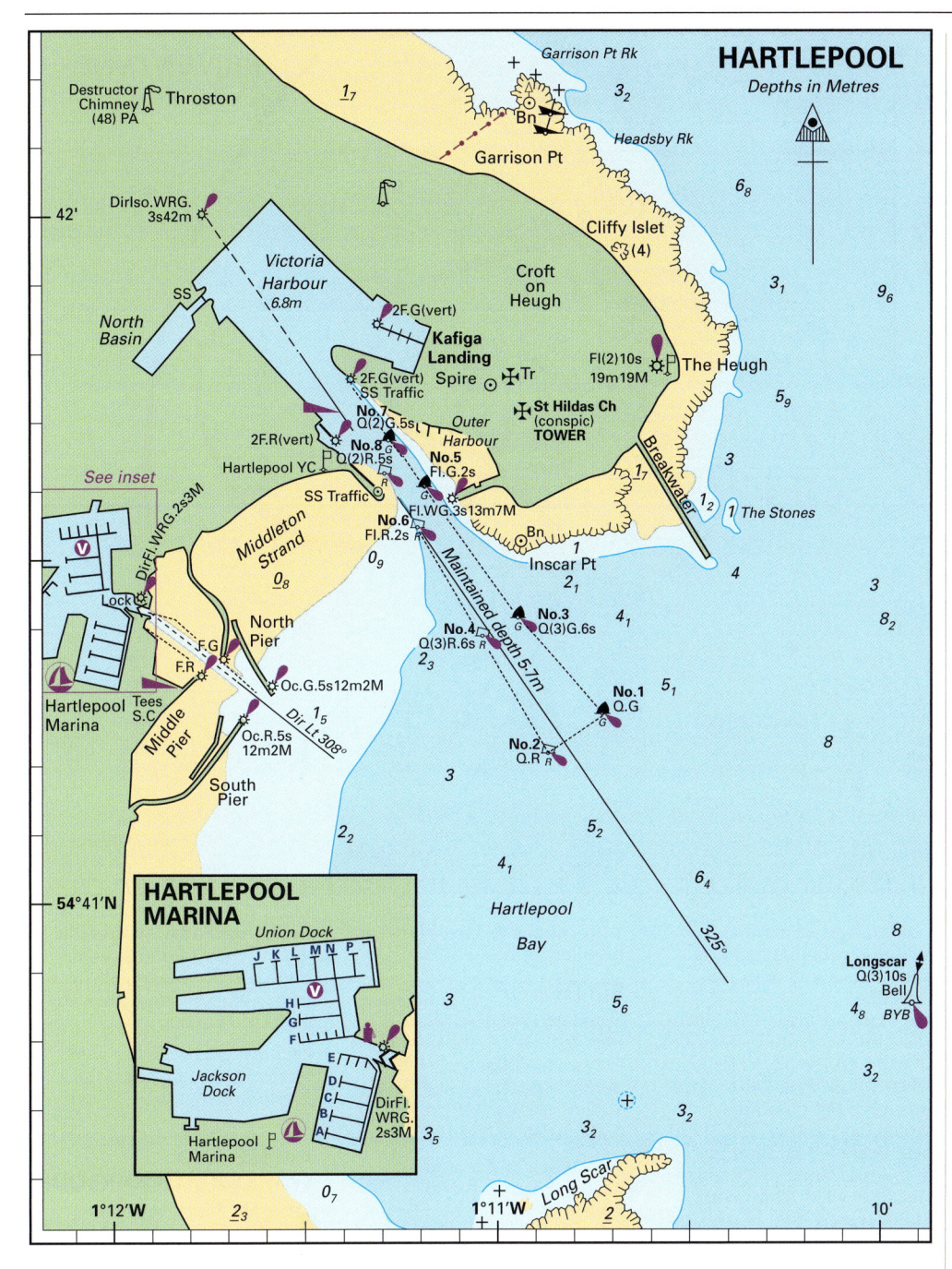

A mainly commercial hbr with marina and leisure facilities in N Dock.

In severe NE and E winds the hbr may be closed but otherwise entrance is normally easy.

Approach and Entrance Keep ½M offshore until E of hbr entrance. FS at NE corner of S Dock in line with N LtHo (W with B bands) Fl.G.10s leads in 256° clear of E Tangle Rock 1·9m. Then head directly for N Dock (276°).

Berthing N dock has been dredged. Automatic gate opens when height of tide >2·5m, approx HW±0300. Lts near gate; 3 vert G two-way traffic, 3 vert R stop. Four visitors' berths immediately to stb, max length 10m draught 1·5m. Elsewhere, 1·5–1·0m.

Larger craft may lock into S Dock HW–0200 to +0100.

Facilities Supermarkets 300m.

☎/VHF Marina: 0191 5818998; Seaham Marina VHF 80 (daytime only), at weekends 0785 5778836; Commercial port: HM 0191 5161700; VHF 12 (HW –0230 to +0130).

SUNDERLAND

Standard Port River Tyne
HW –0004   LW –0004

MHWS	MHWN	MLWN	MLWS
+0·2m	+0·3m	+0·2m	+0·1m

DS Dover –0500N; +0100S

Approach On approach to the hbr, call *Sunderland Marina*. If from the S beware of White Stones and Hendon Rock which lie 1·5M offshore to the SE of Roker Pier LtHo. The entrance to the River Wear is made between two crescent shaped piers, the N'most Roker Pier has LtHo conspic at its head Fl.5s25m23M Siren 20s. The S pier Fl.10s14m10M has a R can buoy just N of it which must be left to port to avoid underwater pier end.

Entry signal on old N pier; three Fl.R(vert) = Danger in hbr – no entry or departure. There are no yacht facilities in S Dock and beware commercial traffic. Signal Station VHF 14, 16 or ☎ 0191 567 0161.
On approach to the hbr, call *Sunderland Marina*.

Berthing
• **Sunderland Marina** in N Dock, 200 moorings and pontoons, access 24hrs. Max LOA 40ft, in season advisable to contact in advance. VHF 37(M)/80 or ☎ 0191 514 4721.

Anchorage Clear of fairway inside Roker Pier in 3m.

Facilities Limited. Fuel berth immediately to port on entering marina, call marina before use. Town 1M.

ENGLAND – EAST COAST

HARTLEPOOL

Standard Port River Tyne
HW +0015   LW +0014

MHWS	MHWN	MLWN	MLWS
+0·5m	+0·4m	+0·2m	+0·2m

Hartlepool Marina is a modern development with full facilities. An historic quay with museums and the *Trincomalee*, a fully restored 18th-century warship, are nearby. The marina has 500 berths, with 100 for visitors, up to 50m LOA and 5m draught. Access for 1·5m draught approx HW±0400: it can be difficult in strong easterly weather, especially near LW, in which case, call *Tees Port Control* VHF 14 for permission to use Victoria Harbour as a temporary refuge.

Approach Conspic landmarks are St Hilda's church 2·5ca WSW of Heugh LtHo. The LtHo lies NE of the hbr entrance. From either N or S make for the Longscar E card Lt buoy, bell. From the N, in heavy weather, give the Heugh a good clearance to avoid the backwash which upsets the swell for some distance E and S of it. From the S avoid the Long Scar shoal lying 6ca SW of the buoy. Fifteen minutes before arrival Call *Hartlepool Marina* VHF 37/M or 80, or ☎ 01429 865774.

Entrance
Marina by channel dredged to chart datum with Lts Oc.G.5s on N pier and similar R on S. Pass through into W inner harbour through fixed R&G. DirFl.WRG.2s sector Lt on lock N side shows 308°. Enter lock with port side fenders and lines to pontoon. Control Lts; G enter; R keep clear, vessel departing; 2R lock closed. Lock cill is 0·8m below chart datum.

Victoria Harbour by channel marked by sector Lt Iso.WRG.3s42m on ldg line 325° and buoyed channel.

Berthing
• **Hartlepool Marina** 100 visitors' berths up to 50m LOA and 5m draught. Berths allocated when in the lock. Usually on S side of the long pontoon marked with V symbol; a variety of finger berths.

Facilities Diesel and Calor Gas are available 24h near the Lock Office. Boatyard and chandlery. There are many shops and services in the adjoining development. A 24h hypermarket and retail park is a 10 minute walk.
• **Victoria Harbour** Private moorings. Call *Tees VTS* VHF 14 for temporary berthing.

SEAHAM

Standard Port River Tyne
HW –0002   LW –0001

MHWS	MHWN	MLWN	MLWS
+0·2m	+0·2m	+0·2m	+0·0m

DS Dover –0500N; +0100S

113

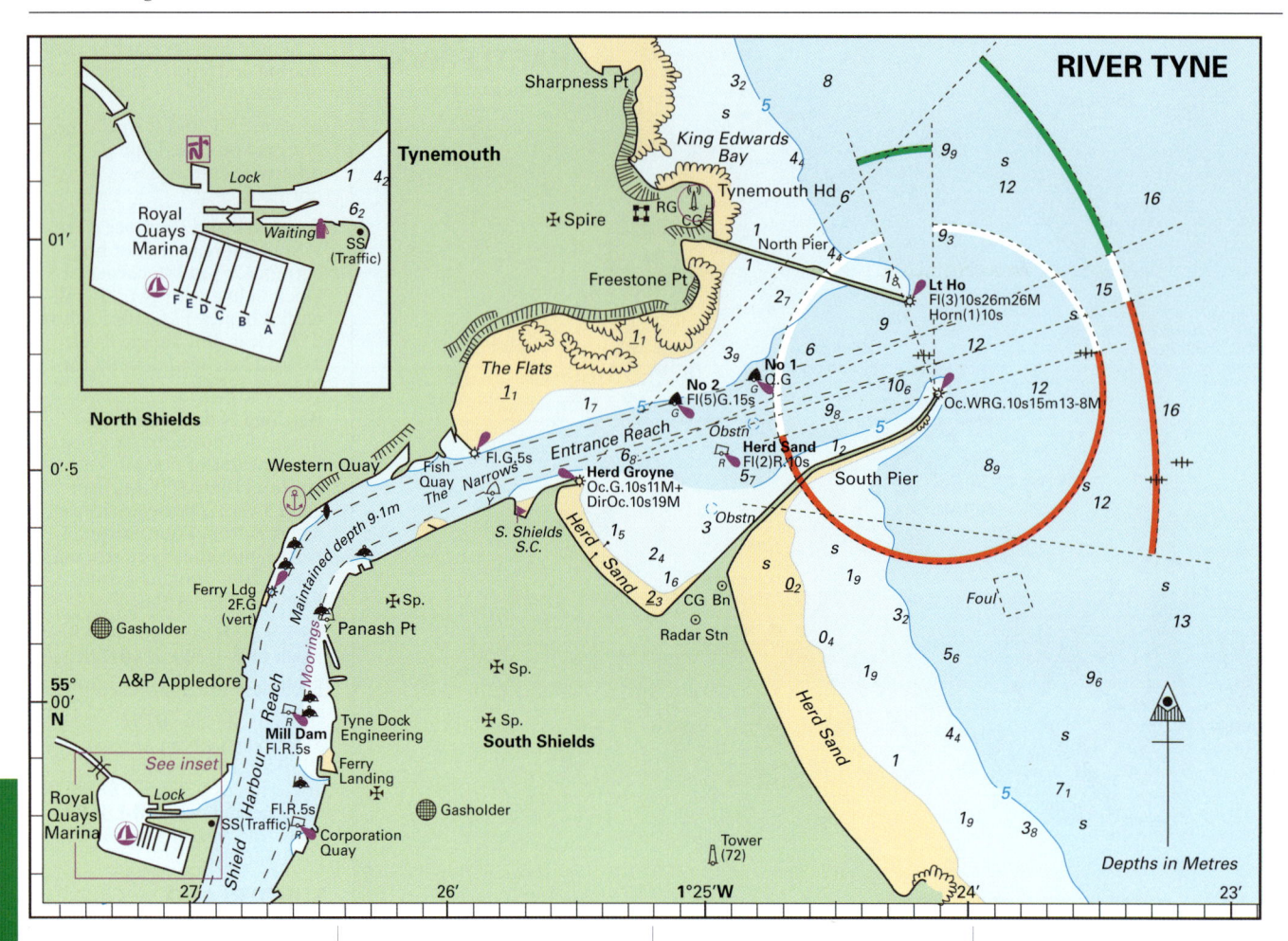

RIVER TYNE

Standard Port River Tyne
Newcastle upon Tyne
HW +0003   LW +0008
MHWS MHWN MLWN MLWS
+0·3m +0·2m +0·1m +0·1m
DS Dover –0500 N; +0100S

The channel of the River Tyne from the sea to the hbr in Newcastle city centre (Jarrow Quay Corner) is dredged to a minimum depth of 8m. Can be difficult in strong winds from E through N to NE. Inform *Tyne VTS* ☎ 0191 257 2080 VHF 12 before entering the pierheads and on departure from the marina.

Approach On 258° pass between LtHo conspic on N pier head Fl(3)10s Horn 10s and S pier head Oc.WRG.10s Bell 10s. Inner light on Herd Groyne Oc.RG.10s+DirOc.10s, (W sector 005°).

Entrance After clearance from Tyne VTS pass between the piers. Keep to N inward except in strong flood or E winds when mid-channel avoids steep seas beyond N pier. Leaving, keep to S side.

Berthing
• **Royal Quays Marina** 170 berths in Albert Edward Dock 2M upriver. Call *Royal Quays Marina* 15 min before arrival ☎ 0191 272 8282, VHF 80 (24/7). Lock in quarter past and quarter to the hour. Max beam 8·0m. Use outer pontoon unless otherwise directed. Comprehensive marina facilities including fuel berth outside lock and 30-tonne travel-hoist.
• **St Peter's Marina** 150 berths. 7½M upriver from Tynemouth. ☎ 0191 265 4472, VHF 37, 80 when within 3M. 24hr all tide waiting pontoons and attendance, access HW±0400, max beam 5·3m, 2m min depth in marina. Good place to visit city, about 1M from centre. Full facilities, boat hoist, small chandlery. Nearby bar/restaurant but no shops.
• **Friars Goose** berths (S side of river) minimum facilities.
• **Newcastle Motor Boat Club** Ouseburn. (N bank within walking distance of town centre) Welcomes yachts on short or overnight stay. ☎ 0191 224 3832, VHF 77 occasionally. Club house.
• **Newcastle City Marina** A security controlled pontoon in the heart of the city. *Mobile* 07435 788426 or ☎ 0191 2211348, preferably 24h in advance to book berth and opening of the Millennium Bridge.

Anchorage
Tynemouth In settled weather, 200m N of the G con No.1 buoy W of the N pier head or off Herd Sand S of dredged channel.

Upriver Vessels with air draught <4·5m MHWS can proceed upriver through bridges and when raised, <20m. 24hrs notice to Tyne Harbour required.

BLYTH

Standard Port River Tyne
HW (sp) +0005 (np) –0007
LW (sp) +0009 (np) –0001
MHWS MHWN MLWN MLWS
+0·0m +0·0m –0·1m +0·01m
DS Dover –0500N +0100S

A commercial hbr and headquarters of Royal Northumberland YC.

Approach Two conspic wind turbines ½M offshore. The entrance opens to the S with sands to W and rocks to E abreast of breakwaters. There are Ldg Lts 2F.Bu in line 324° on lattice towers with Or diamond topmarks. From S, Blyth Bay is clear. After passing St Mary's Is head for the pier. From N, clear the Sow, Pigs and Seaton Sea Rocks to stb and proceed towards the entrance. Seas may break on the bar in heavy weather from SE especially at LW.

Entrance Call *Blyth Harbour Control* VHF 12 or ☎ 01670 352678 before entry or departure. Enter between the piers, turn hard to port round the N end of the inner W pier Fl.R.6s into S hbr.

Berthing Visiting yachts may be accommodated by the Royal Northumberland YC ☎ 353636. Use N side of outer pontoon unless otherwise directed. Apply direct to RNYC and pay dues at bar after 1900.

Anchorage In fair weather in 4m in centre of bay to N of Blyth off Newbiggin. Shelter from SW to N winds. Beware rocks to N and S.

Facilities Showers, bar with weekend food at Royal Northumberland YC. Town 1½M.

AMBLE AND WARKWORTH HARBOUR

Standard Port River Tyne
HW –0013   LW –0018
MHWS MHWN MLWN MLWS
+0·0m +0·0m +0·1m –0·1m
DS Dover –0500N +0100 S

Amble is the town adjacent to Warkworth Harbour, with all usual facilities. Warkworth Harbour is at the mouth of the R Coquet which runs down from the historic town of Warkworth.

Avoid in strong NE to E winds when Blyth is a port of refuge.

Approach Pass sufficiently to the north of Coquet Island to clear its rocky ledges. Beware of Pan Bush rocks 4ca ENE of hbr entrance. The passage between the SE corner of Coquet Island and the shore should not be attempted except in calmest conditions and at HW.

Entrance Best HW±0400 midway between piers, 68m apart, marked by LtHo with RW horizontal stripes, Fl.R.5s, on S pierhead, and tall G bn on N pierhead, Fl.G.6s. After about 150m move to the S side

ENGLAND – EAST COAST

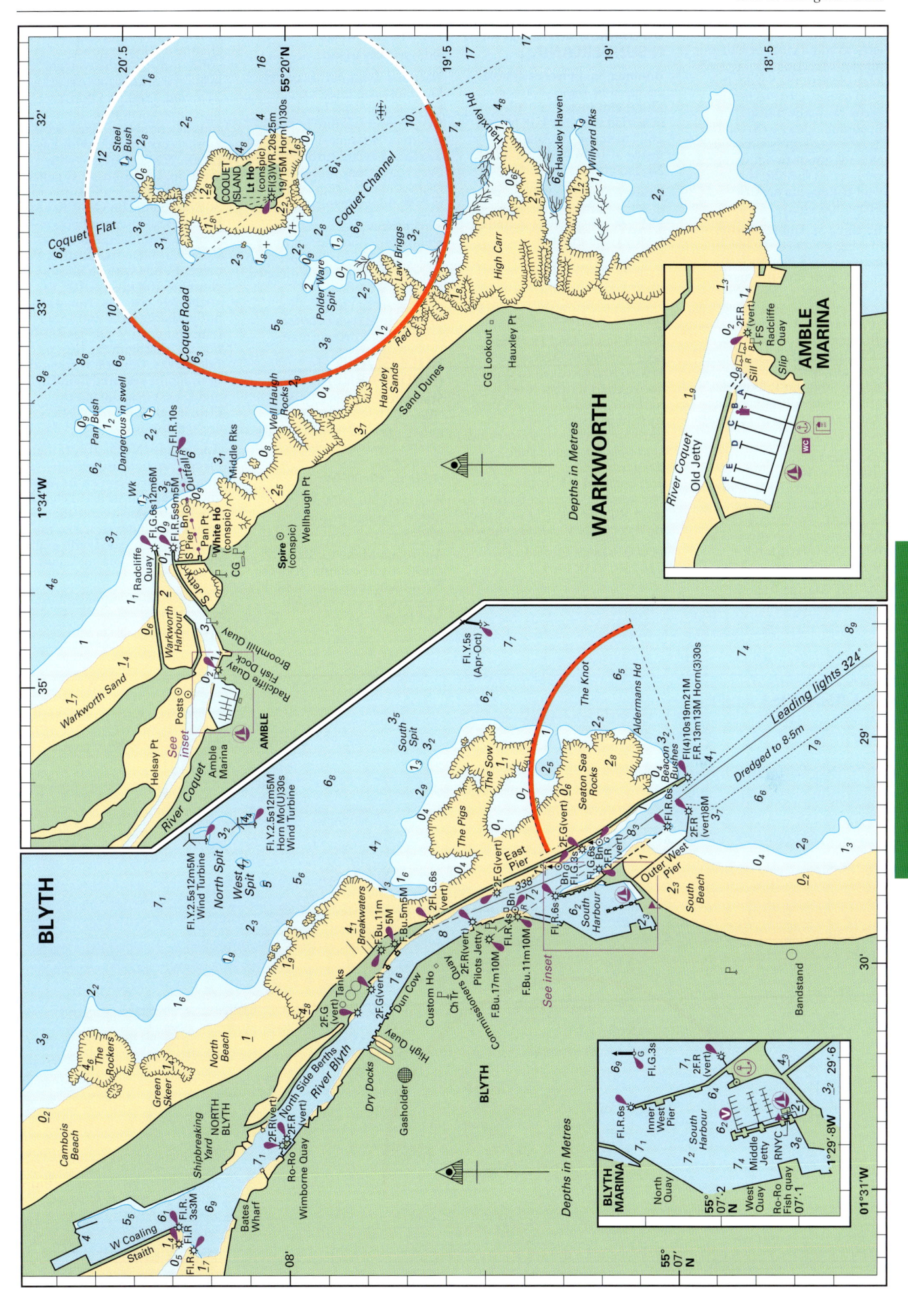

but keep approx 10m N of S jetty to stand clear of half-tide piled obstruction. Continue to keep close to the S side. It is vital to pass close to fishing boats normally moored on Broomhill Quay to avoid the drying shoal on N side which extends about two thirds of the way across the hbr. If necessary, wait for marina against Broomhill Quay.

Berthing at Amble Marina Having followed the line of quays, pass R can buoy and turn to port into the marina. Depth over sill, which dries 0·8m at CD, is on a tide gauge at entrance. Access for 1·5m draught HW±0300 MHWS; HW±0400 MHWN. Visitors normally berth alongside east side of pontoon F. Outside office hours collect berthing instructions from reception/fuel pontoon.

Facilities Laundry, limited chandlery. 40t travel-hoist expected (late 2017) in marina. Most repairs at adjacent boatyard. Provisions and good hardware shop in town ¼M. Bus to Newcastle and Warkworth.

☏/VHF Marina 01665 712168, VHF 80

BOULMER, CRASTER AND N SUNDERLAND

Boulmer Small haven almost enclosed by rocks. Narrow (30m) entrance. Only advisable in settled weather. Ldg bns on 262° to entrance. Anchor just inside in 1·5m or dry on sand. No facilities.

Craster Tiny drying hbr for use in settled offshore weather only. 1M S of conspic Dunstanburgh Castle ruins. Anchor just inshore of 40m wide entrance between Muckle Carr (to N), Little Carr (to S) or, if able to take the ground, berth at E pier on sand over rock.

North Sunderland Harbour near Seahouses. Access HW±0300. Dredged to 0·7m above chart datum. Inner harbour, good shelter but used by fishing boats. Outer harbour, swell in onshore winds very uncomfortable and dangerous. Beware rks to W of entrance and NE from breakwater. When dangerous to enter R Lt over F.G Lt or R over Bu flags on NW pier are shown.

HM ☏ 01665 720033 or 721558, VHF 14, 12.

FARNE ISLANDS

Tides as Holy Island.

National Trust nature reserve. Landing prohibited except on Farne, Staple and Longstone. Magnificent wildlife but no facilities. Attempt only in good weather. Beware turbulence over Knivestone and Whirl rocks and eddy S of Longstone in NW tidal stream.

Anchorages
• The Kettle, NE side of Inner Farne near the bridges between Knocks Reef and W Wideopen.
• S of W Wideopen.
• S of Knocks reef.
• Pinnacle Haven between Staple Is and Brownsman.

HOLY ISLAND (LINDISFARNE)

Standard Port River Tyne
HW –0041   LW –0108
MHWS MHWN MLWN MLWS
–0·2m –0·2m –0·3m –0·1m
DS in offing:
HWD SE; +0600NW

A natural hbr with 3–7m inside. Strong streams and eddies.

Approach Make for Ridge E card buoy. If coming from the N, at night or in poor visibility, pass to the east of Plough Seat Reef.

Entrance The long and narrow channel is easy in good conditions once the conspic leading marks (stone obelisks 21m and 25m) on Old Law have been identified. The ebb runs at up to 4kn. Least depth 1·3m. Steer on 262° with East Bn Oc.WRG.6s in line with West Bn. Leave Triton G con buoy Q.G. to stb and turn onto 309° when the bn Oc.WRG 6s on the Heugh (caution: do not confuse with the tall narrow stone war memorial further W) comes in line with St Mary's church belfry giving 309° to anchorage. The ebb runs at 4kn in the channel, the entrance is long and narrow but easy in fine weather with the help of Ldg marks. Caution is advised in using the sectored lights by night. East Beacon and the Heugh lights, both Oc.WRG are synchronised.

Anchorages Normally off the Heugh bn. In W gales boats should lie to two anchors. Buoy anchors as many buried chains. Small craft able to take the ground are more secure in the Ooze, very crowded with many mooring lines, soft mud, but avoid in S and SE winds.

Facilities Water tap in square, stores at PO, PH.

HM ☏ 01289 89217.

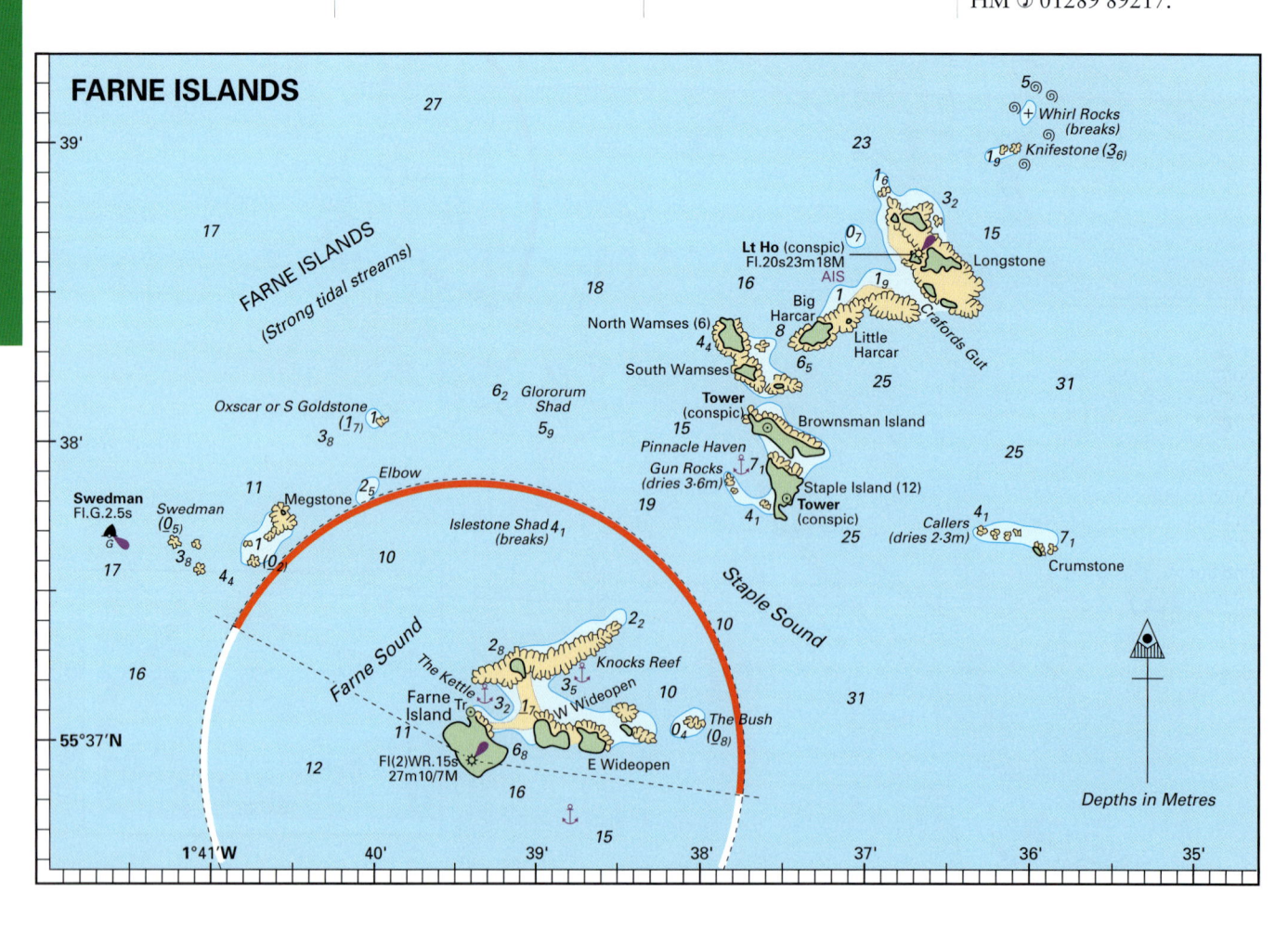

BERWICK

Standard Port River Tyne
HW –0053   LW –0108
MHWS   MHWN   MLWN   MLWS
–0·2m   –0·2m   –0·3m   –0·1m

A commercial hbr with few facilities for yachts but attractive with good shelter and worth a visit.

Approach From SE, keep sufficiently offshore to clear Park Dkye shoals. There are many fishing floats in this area. From N stand off ¾M from the shore. On the seaward end of the breakwater there is a conspicuous W LtHo. The Bar and the shoals in the entrance vary in position and the depth which may be only 0·3m at CD. Approach on 294° on a transit of LtHo and Town Hall spire. Call *Berwick Habour* VHF 12 or ☎ 01289 307404 before entry for advice and berthing instructions. Entry is best HW±0300, not advisable in strong onshore winds, especially on the ebb.

Entrance Bar 0·6 to 1·8m very variable. Enter parallel with breakwater approx 10m off and head for bn Q.G W of breakwater. When Spittal Ldg marks (Lt bns F.R with triangular topmarks) come in line turn onto 207° until S of 2nd G con Lt buoy Q.G. Beware, ldg bns may not show best water. Then steer for NW end of fish jetty. Do not keep too close to G buoys which are laid in shoal water outside the channel. From here steer for the end of the pier at Tweed Dock. Enter 5m off, well clear of E card bn.

Berthing Tweed Dock is tidal and yachts may enter or leave at most states of the tide. Berth alongside E wall which has one ladder or against fishing boats, then as directed. Do not leave boats unattended without permission from HM. Depth approx 1m at MLWS, 0·6m in entrance, bottom soft mud. 3-tonne mobile crane.

Anchorage In river clear of traffic or may pick up one of few mooring buoys.

Facilities Water on quay. Town 1M, small local shops nearby. Good rail and road transport.

☎/VHF ☎ 01289 307404, *Berwick Harbour* VHF 12

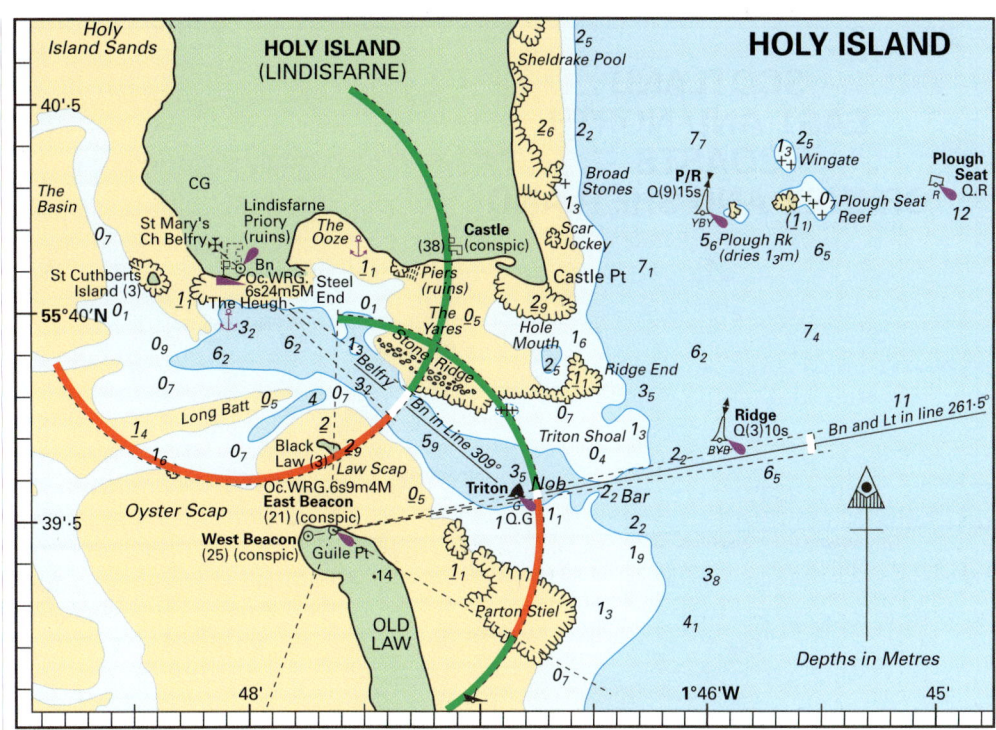

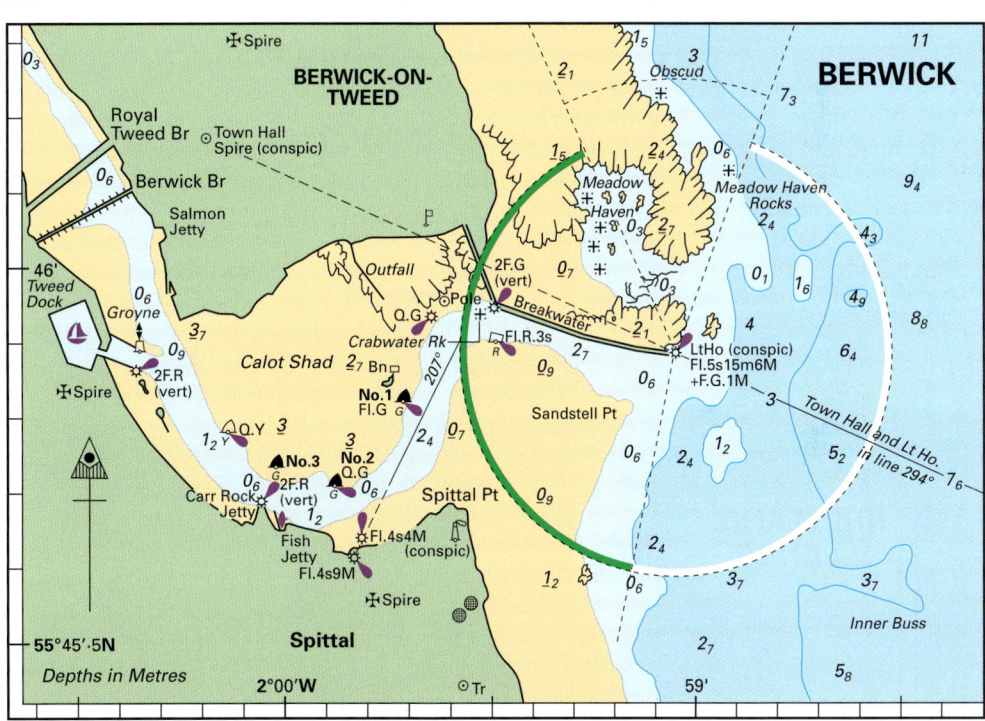

The Cruising Almanac

HOLY ISLAND

BERWICK

ENGLAND – EAST COAST

117

The Cruising Almanac

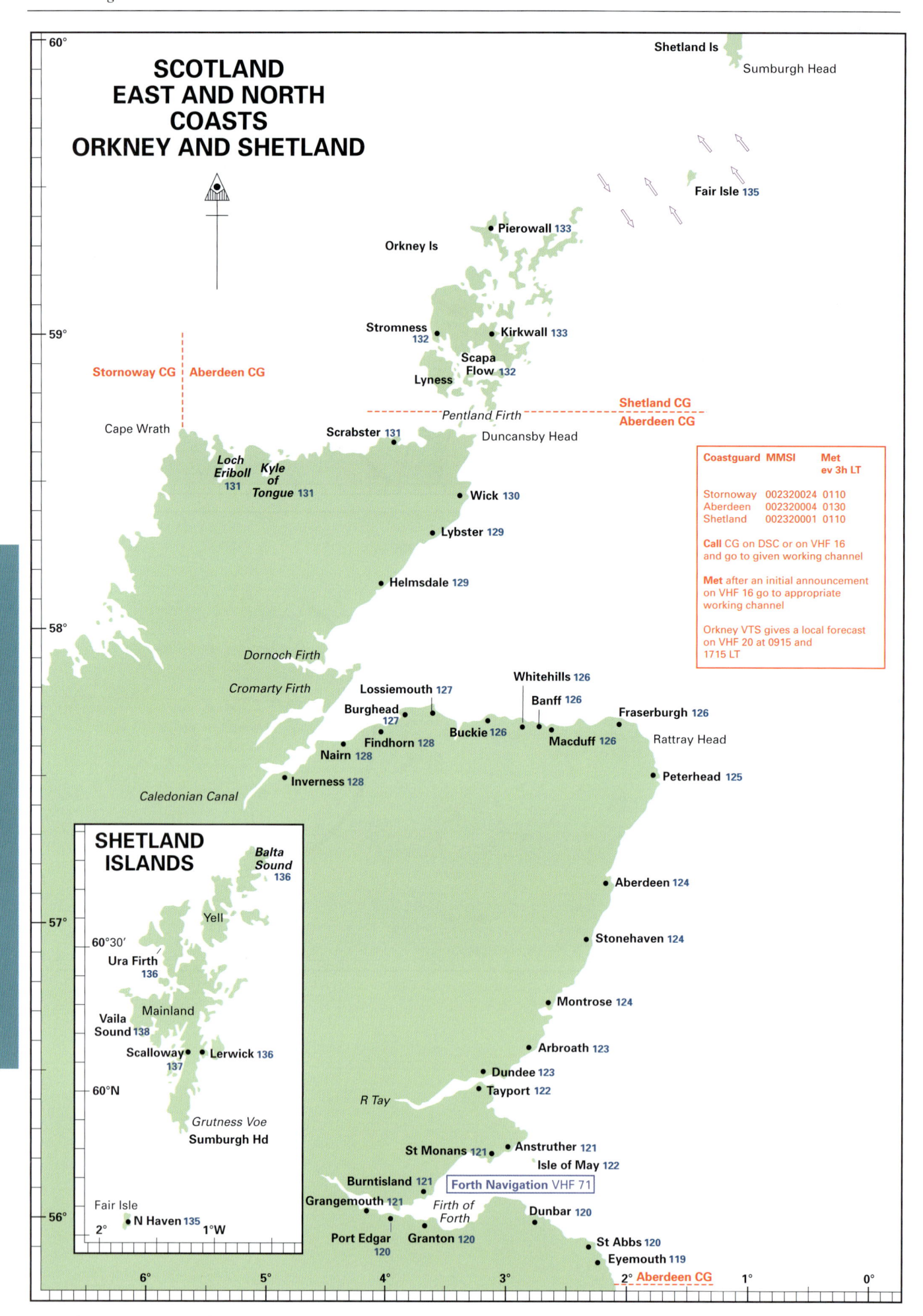

SCOTLAND EAST AND NORTH COASTS ORKNEY AND SHETLAND

Shetland Is
Sumburgh Head

Fair Isle 135

Pierowall 133
Orkney Is
Stromness 132
Kirkwall 133
Scapa Flow 132
Lyness

Stornoway CG | Aberdeen CG
Pentland Firth
Shetland CG
Aberdeen CG

Cape Wrath
Scrabster 131
Duncansby Head

Loch Eriboll 131
Kyle of Tongue 131
Wick 130

Coastguard	MMSI	Met ev 3h LT
Stornoway	002320024	0110
Aberdeen	002320004	0130
Shetland	002320001	0110

Call CG on DSC or on VHF 16 and go to given working channel

Met after an initial announcement on VHF 16 go to appropriate working channel

Orkney VTS gives a local forecast on VHF 20 at 0915 and 1715 LT

Lybster 129

Helmsdale 129

Dornoch Firth
Cromarty Firth
Whitehills 126
Lossiemouth 127
Banff 126
Fraserburgh 126
Burghead 127
Buckie 126
Macduff 126
Findhorn 128
Rattray Head
Nairn 128
Inverness 128
Peterhead 125
Caledonian Canal

SHETLAND ISLANDS

Balta Sound 136
Yell
60°30′
Ura Firth 136
Mainland
Vaila Sound 138
Scalloway
Lerwick 136
137
60°N

Aberdeen 124

Stonehaven 124

Montrose 124

Arbroath 123
Dundee 123
Tayport 122
R Tay

Grutness Voe
Sumburgh Hd

Fair Isle
N Haven 135
2° 1°W

St Monans 121
Anstruther 121
Isle of May 122
Burntisland 121
Forth Navigation VHF 71
Grangemouth 121
Firth of Forth
Dunbar 120
Port Edgar 120
Granton 120
St Abbs 120
Eyemouth 119

2° Aberdeen CG

Page references are shown after locations, for example:
Peterhead 124. Bold type indicates that it is accompanied by a plan. *Italics* are used for rivers, lochs, bays, seas etc.

118

Scotland – East and North Coasts

The Border to Duncansby Head

A yacht cruising this coast needs to be able to make off-shore passages of 100 miles and to keep at sea in adverse conditions. Many of the harbours are unavailable in strong on-shore winds; and a large swell, which may make entrances dangerous, persists for some days after heavy northerly or northeasterly winds have died down.

Nevertheless, with the prevailing offshore wind, it is an interesting cruising area with a coastline varying from spectacular high rocky cliffs, abounding in bird life, to low-lying farming land and sand dunes. The main yachting centres are Port Edgar and Granton in the Firth of Forth, the River Tay and also in the Moray Firth at Lossiemouth and Findhorn. Many harbours on this coast are working harbours, busy with fishing and the oil industry. However with the decline in fishing, yacht facilities are increasing. For yachts on passage, Peterhead, with its good marina facilities, is available in virtually all conditions. Wick, with its marina, is a good port of departure for the Northern Isles.

For more details refer to:

CCC Orkney and Shetland Islands Including North and Northeast Scotland Clyde Cruising Club Sailing Directions (Imray, 2016)

The Yachtsman's Pilot – North and East Scotland. Martin Lawrence (Imray)

Berwick to Fraserburgh Forth Yacht Clubs Association Pilot Handbook

Humber to Rattray Head R Northumberland YC Sailing Directions:.

Map of the Inland Waterways of Scotland (Imray).

BERWICK TO ARBROATH

On a direct passage, the crossings of the Forth and Tay estuaries pose no great problems; but bad seas can be experienced off the Forth, particularly in E winds against the tide. The Tay is shoal for several miles out and should be given a wide berth especially with wind or onshore swell against the tide. St Abbs Head (90m) has the appearance of an island from NW and SE.

Passage lights	BA No
St Abbs Head Fl.10s68m26M	2850
Bass Rock Fl(3)20s46m10M	2864
Isle of May Fl(2)15s73m22M	3090
Fife Ness Iso.WR.10s12m15/12M AIS	3102
Bell Rock Fl.5s28m18M AIS	3108

North and East Scotland and the Orkney Islands distances (miles)

	Eyemouth	Granton	Fife Ness	Stonehaven	Peterhead	Whitehills	Lossiemouth	Chanonry Point	Helmsdale	Duncansby Head	Scrabster	Cape Wrath, 2M N	Stromness	Kirkwall	Whitehall, Stronsay
Eyemouth	0														
Granton	43	0													
Fife Ness	30	29	0												
Stonehaven	66	71	43	0											
Peterhead	99	105	77	35	0										
Whitehills	137	140	113	71	35	0									
Lossiemouth	158	163	135	93	58	23	0								
Chanonry Point	188	191	163	122	89	52	30	0							
Helmsdale	181	180	151	110	75	43	26	36	0						
Duncansby Head	180	185	158	116	81	60	56	75	42	0					
Scrabster	202	207	181	139	103	82	79	97	64	22	0				
Cape Wrath, 2M N	267	288	223	181	166	145	144	128	107	65	48	0			
Stromness	202	207	180	139	103	82	79	97	67	23	28	56	0		
Kirkwall	213	210	182	141	107	89	91	111	78	34	49	78	37	0	
Whitehall, Stronsay	205	212	185	143	107	95	96	115	82	43	55	87	39	21	0

EYEMOUTH

Standard Port Leith
HW (sp) –0005 (np) +0007
LW (sp) +0012 (np) +0008

MHWS	MHWN	MLWN	MLWS
–0·4m	–0·3m	0·0m	+0·1m

A busy fishing hbr, safe in any weather but not to be approached in strong winds from between N and E or near LW with N'ly swell. Bar and entrance varies but normally dredged to 2m MLWS, subject to silting. Yachts welcome.

Signals R flag by day, F.R Lt by night: hbr closed.

Approach Keep ½M offshore until Ldg marks orange poles (F.G) come in line on 174°. E pier head lit Iso.R.2s. If any sea, approach after half flood. Passage S of Hurkar Rocks is unmarked, keep mid-channel, borrowing slightly towards Hurkars.

Entrance 16m wide. Keep to Ldg line until hbr is well open, then round E pier fairly close.

Be prepared to stand off for fishing vessels leaving hbr.

Berthing Usually alongside pontoon on SE side of inner hbr.

Facilities Shops, pubs. Diesel from HM.

☎/**VHF** HM 01890 750223, *Mobile* 07885 742505, VHF 12.

ST ABBS HARBOUR

Standard Port Leith
HW –0025 approx

MHWS	MHWN	MLWN	MLWS
–0·8m	–0·7m	n/a	n/a

Small attractive hbr 1M S of St Abbs Head. Inner harbour dries; outer harbour has about 1m LWS. Not to be attempted in strong on-shore wind/seas.

Bar 1m.

Approach From S identify by cliff top village and high SE-facing cliffs whitened by birds; from N round St Abbs Head which is steep-to. Make for Maw Carr, a prominent steep-sided reddish rock (15m) about 120m NNW of entrance. Conspic Y LB Ho identifies hbr.

Entrance Bring E edges of NW pier and centre pier in line and steer exactly on this line. Channel through rocks is narrow but all dangers show. Ldg line lit F.R.

Berthing As directed; best alongside towards S end of NE pier (diagonally across corner).

☎ HM 07881 767587

DUNBAR

Standard Port Leith
HW (sp) –0005 (np) +0003
LW (sp) –0003 (np) +0003

MHWS	MHWN	MLWN	MLWS
–0·3m	–0·3m	0·0m	+0·1m

A pleasant resort town with picturesque hbr. 0·5m MLWS in entrance. Good anchorage outside, sheltered from W through S to E, clean sand, good holding.

Do not approach with winds between NW and E greater than Force 5 or if there is an appreciable onshore swell.

Approach On Ldg line 198°, orange triangles on white posts on grassy slope (Lts Oc.G.6s).

Entrance Enter HW ±0300. 10m cleft cut through rock to port, invisible until open.

HM should be contacted prior to entry.

Berthing In 1·2m alongside S quay as near to castle as possible, sand. N quay dries, uneven, sand at E end. Uncomfortable surge with onshore swell. In bad weather HM will open br admitting to old hbr, dries out, mud.

Facilities Showers at Dunbar SC. Stores. Rly.

☎/**VHF** HM (office) 01368 865404, *Mobile* 07958 754 858, VHF 12.

GRANTON

Standard Port Leith
Tidal data as Leith

Headquarters of River Forth and Forth Corinthian YCs. Hbr divided by central pier; yachts use E arm. Much of hbr dries.

Entrance 3m. Beware pilot boats.

Signals Tide signals on middle pier. Red flag W cross (F.G Lt) = No Entry. Yachts drawing less than 3m can ignore these signals with caution.

Berthing Visitors' pontoons (1·5 to 2·0m at LWS) on east side of Middle Pier. Security gate; key fob on payment of dues to RFYC. Information sheets at head of ramp.

Facilities Buses to Edinburgh and Leith. No fuel. No power on pontoon. Welcome to use club.

☎/**VHF** RFYC: Office 0131 552 8560, Bar 07551 426 8130, VHF 80/M (occas). Port: 523385, VHF 20. *Forth Navigation Service* VHF 71.

PORT EDGAR

Standard Port Leith
HW +0100 approx

MHWS	MHWN	MLWN	MLWS
0·0m	0·0m	0·0m	+0·1m

Large yachting centre on S shore immediately above the two iconic rail and road bridges and below the new Queensferry crossing. Active sailing school. Considerable recent development of shore facilities.

Approach Follow the buoyed shipping channel N or S of Inchkeith as convenient and pass through centre of rail and first road bridge.

Entrance Pass W of floating breakwater of lorry tyres (lit 4x Q.Y) leaving W breakwater (Fl.R.4s) to stb. Keep close to the pontoons.

Berthing Call by VHF/☎ prior to arrival for berth.

Facilities Include laundry, boatyard, rigger, engineer, electronics and chandlery. WiFi. Restaurant, shops, etc. in S Queensferry, ½M E, bus and Rly to Edinburgh.

☎/**VHF** HM 01313 313330, VHF 80 (0900–1730). Up to 2030 call 07960 258523.

DUNBAR TO GRANGEMOUTH

Between Dunbar and Granton there are a number of anchorages and harbours which dry. Most significant are North Berwick and Fisherrow – both are restricted and subject to surge. Yachts are not normally allowed into Leith Docks. Dunbar entrance can be dangerous even in light winds if any swell. From Dunbar a direct course to Bass Rock, a very conspicuous cone island ht 115m with large gannetry, clears all dangers. If proceeding up the Firth pass at least ¼M outside Fidra, thereafter the coast falls away and becomes low lying. Monitor Forth Navigation Service VHF 71. For Granton make for the South Channel passing at least 1M south of the island of Inchkeith to avoid off-lying drying rocks. For Port Edgar or Grangemouth it is preferable after dark or in poor weather to take the well buoyed North Channel passing to the north of Inchkeith. From Hound Point westwards, on the north side, when large craft are manoeuvring, yachts must keep clear of the navigation channel. On the south side from a point 200m to the north of the unlit bn off Hound Point, keep north of a line between it and the base of the south cantilever of the rail bridge, clearance 44m. Pass at least 30m away from either side of the oil terminal. Pass anywhere between the main N and S towers of the road bridge, clearance 45m. Tides may reach 4kn. Thereafter there are extensive mud flats.

Tankers entering or leaving Mortimer's Deep shall have an exclusion zone of 1M.

A replacement Forth road bridge has been constructed W of existing bridge. There are exclusion zones, marked by Y buoys, round the sites of two new columns. Monitor VHF 71.

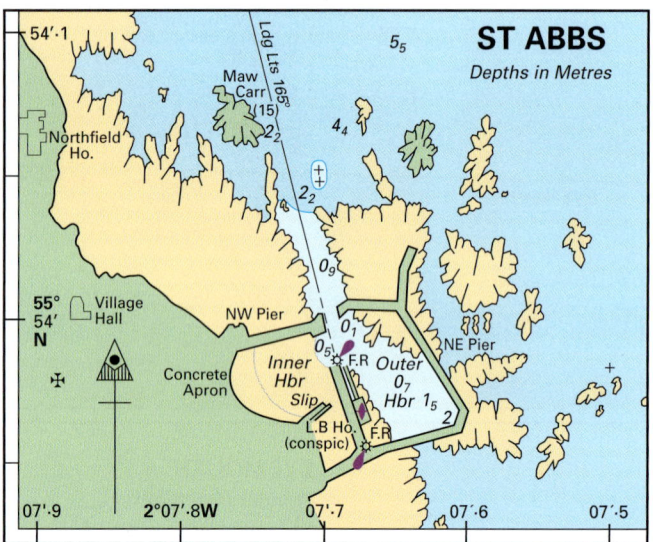

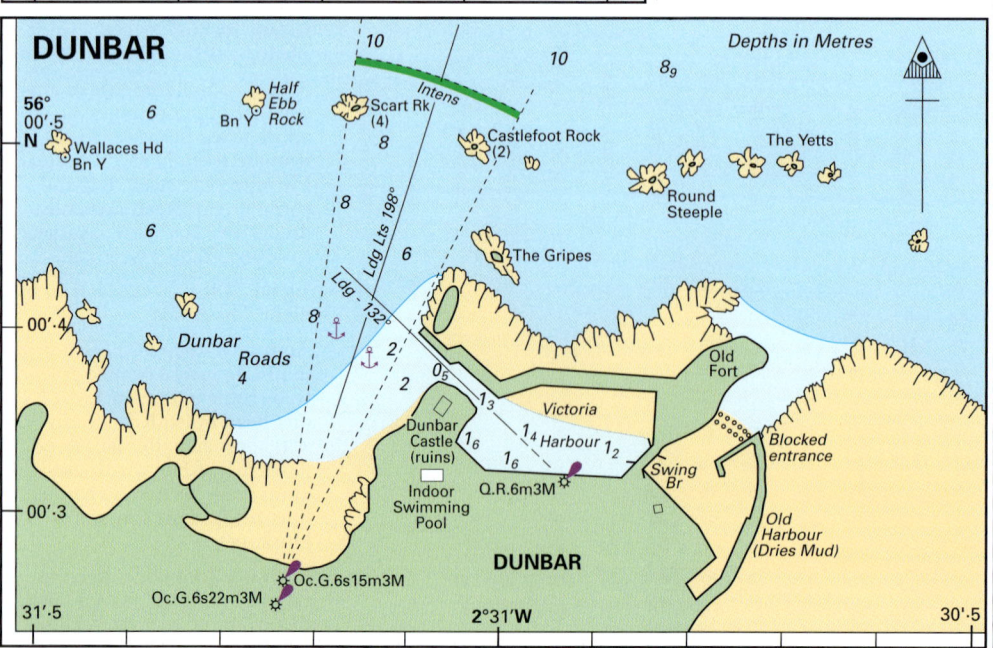

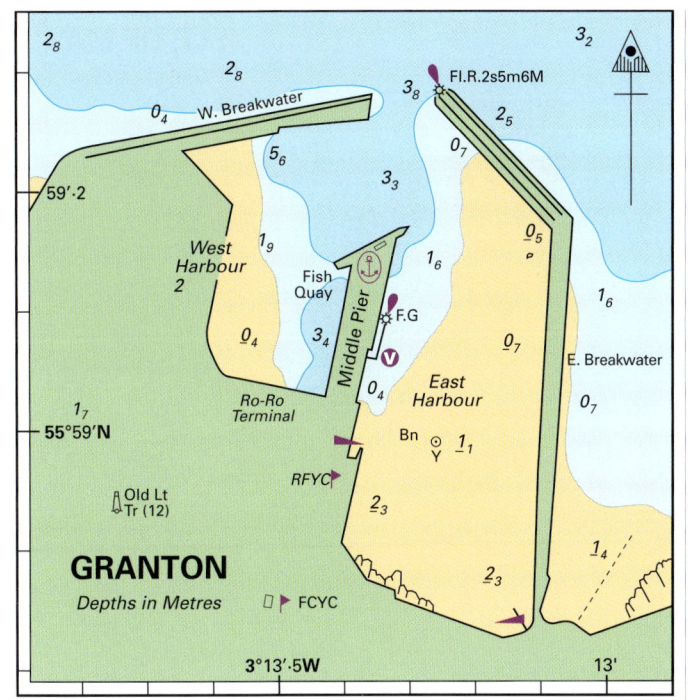

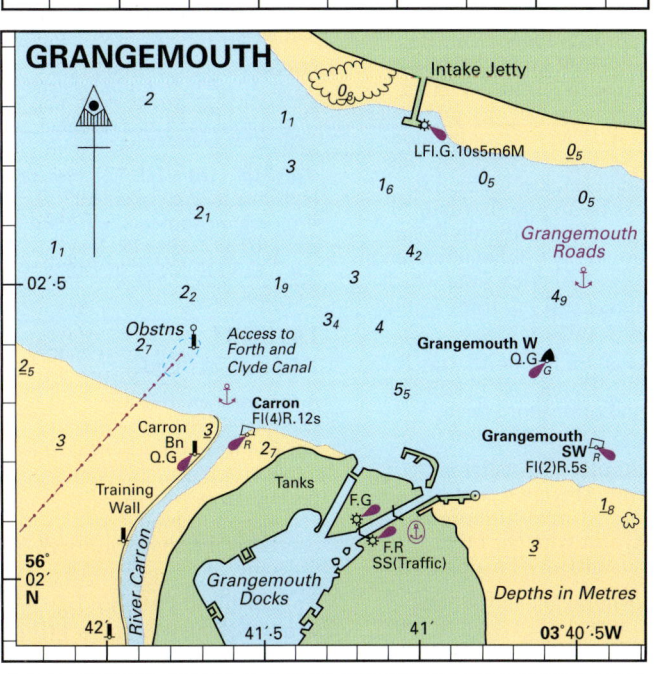

FORTH-CLYDE CANAL AND RIVER CARRON

Standard Port Leith

Entrance

HW (sp) +0025 (np) +0010
LW (sp) −0015 (np) −0052

MHWS	MHWN	MLWN	MLWS
−0·1m	−0·2m	−0·3m	−0·3m

Passage must be booked in advance (☏ 0845 67766000). Max depth 1·83m, max beam 5·0m. It is advisable to study the *Skipper's Guide*, download from www.scottishcanals.co.uk. Single handed passage is possible but not recommended.

The entrance to the Forth-Clyde Canal is 2·5M from the mouth of the River Carron; it is immediately to the west of the busy commercial port of Grangemouth, which is not available to yachts. Monitor VHF 14 for shipping movements. As air draft is 3m, masts should previously have been unstepped at Port Edgar, or in River Carron, phone in advance ☏ 07833 953288 (before 1600 on Friday for weekends). Be prepared to handle the lowered mast and set up on deck (assistance given at Port Edgar).

Approach From seaward hold to the north side of the main channel. Prior to arrival at the Carron R can Lt buoy Fl(4)R.12s contact Carron Sea Lock VHF 74 ☏ 07810 794468.

Entrance Navigation is constrained by the Kerse Road Br. When the rise of tide is 4·5m there is 1·8m depth and 3·0m air draught. All depth and air draught gauges are calibrated to this br. It is best to enter at HW−0200, but possible up to HW+0100. Leave Carron bn Fl.G.5s, marking the end of the training wall, close to stb and follow the buoyed channel keeping towards the centre or outside of the curves.

Transit See Scotland – West Coast section. Exit and step mast at Bowling. The canal office ☏ 01324 671217 should be contacted for times of opening.

N SHORE FIRTH OF FORTH

Of the harbours on the N shore of the Forth, Pittenweem is a restricted and very busy fishing harbour, yachts unwelcome except weekends. Many of the harbours dry, most are inaccessible in strong E–SE winds but then Methil is available. Burntisland may be convenient for yachts on passage.

BURNTISLAND

Standard Port Leith

HW (sp) +0013 (np) +0004
LW (sp) +0007 (np) −0002

MHWS	MHWN	MLWN	MLWS
−0·1m	0·0m	+0·1m	+0·2m

Commercial hbr with oil rig fabrication yard. Outer tidal hbr and two wet docks. Accessible at all states of tide and in most weather, heavy surge in winds SE to SW. Keep clear of pilot boats. Useful for yachts on passage.

Berthing Report to HM. Yachts may sometimes lock into E dock HW−0200 to HW. Outer harbour unsuitable for yachts in strong winds and E dock wide open to W wind. W side of outer harbour shoals to less than 1·5m.

Facilities Water, stores, trains to Edinburgh and Dundee.

☏/VHF HM 01592 87373, VHF 20, 71 *Forth Navigation Service*.

ST MONANS

Standard Port Leith

HW −0015 LW −0005 approx

MHWS	MHWN	MLWN	MLWS
−0·1m	−0·1m	n/a	n/a

Small pleasant fishing hbr, dries completely, sand and mud. Conspicuous church close W of hbr.

Approach After half tide; avoid in bad weather.

Entrance Between E breakwater (Oc.WRG.6s) and pole bn on rocks to W.

Berthing In E hbr on outer pier. Dries, hard sand. Two reserved visitor berths, contact HM.

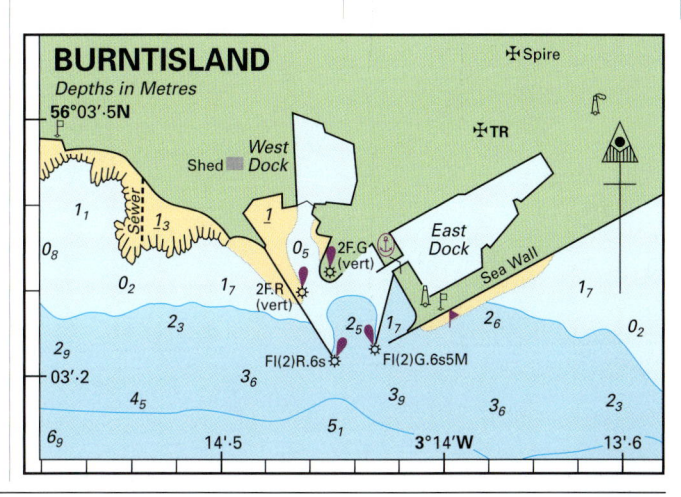

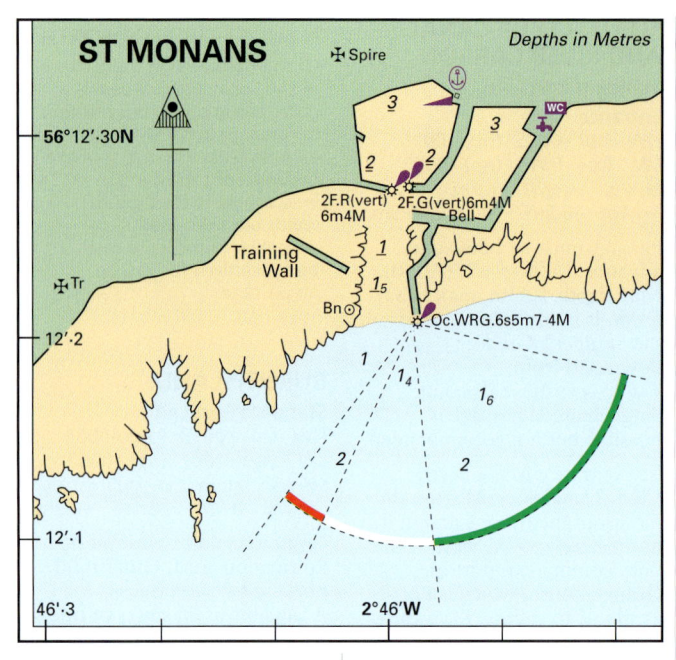

Facilities Water, stores, local buses, boatbuilder. Windmill and saltpans worth a visit.

✆ HM (part-time) 07930 869358.

ANSTRUTHER

Standard Port Leith
HW (sp) –0018 (np) +0012
LW (sp) –0008 (np) –0006
MHWS MHWN MLWN MLWS
 –0·3m –0·2m 0·0m 0·0m

A busy holiday town with usual facilities. Admirable fisheries museum. Hbr dries, inner to soft mud, used by leisure and small fishing vessels. Advisable to call HM 24h in advance.

Approach HW±0300. Conspic. white light tr on W breakwater. Enter on line of Ldg Lts, F.G. on 019°.

Berthing As directed. Pontoons for bilge keelers <10·5 m, otherwise alongside W pier in inner harbour just above first knuckle. Shore-side access from the pontoons requires a key provided by HM.

✆/VHF HM 01333 310836, VHF 11 (Office hours only).

OFFSHORE ANCHORAGES

Isle of May Shore is bold except NW end, bottom rocky, holding poor.

Shelter from E winds at W Tarbert and Altar Stones; from W winds at E Tarbert. Kirkhaven small boat hbr requires detailed knowledge; enter on 216° on white Ldg marks just south of the Pillow. The island is a nature reserve, landing restricted.

Largo Bay On N shore of Firth of Forth. Good anchorage in N and E winds.

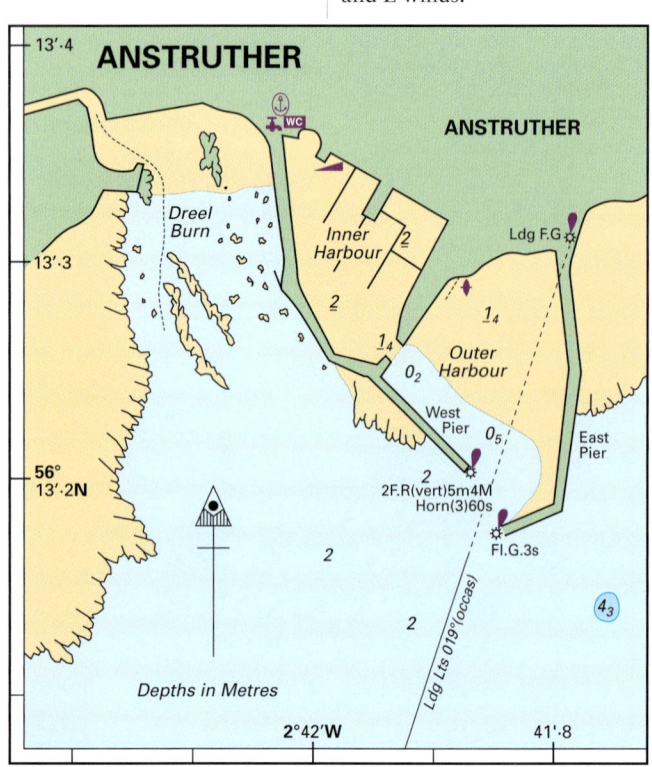

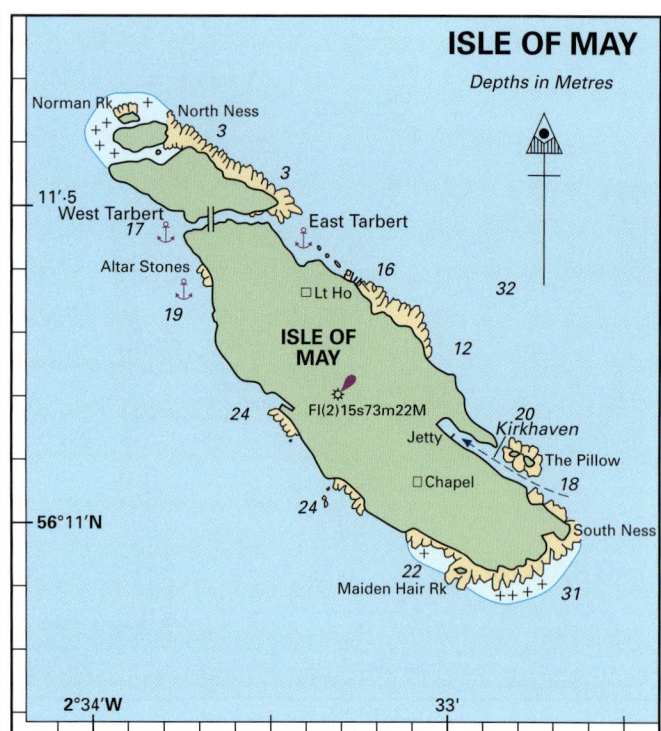

St Andrew's Bay (N of Fife Ness) Good in S winds through W to NW. Anchor about ½M E of St Andrew's harbour pier in suitable depth, sand. Beware of rocks beyond pier head.

RIVER TAY

Standard Port Aberdeen
Bar
HW (sp) +0100 (np) +0100
LW (sp) +0110 (np) +0050
MHWS MHWN MLWN MLWS
+0·9m +0·8m 0·3m 0·1m
Dundee
HW (sp) +0140 (np) +0120
LW (sp) +0145 (np) +0055
MHWS MHWN MLWN MLWS
+1·2m +1·0m +0·5m +0·2m

A major river leading to port of Dundee and navigable on tide to the deep-water hbr of Perth. Approaches are shoal a long way offshore. Once in the river ebb stream is stronger on N shore, flood on S.

Approach Enter channel between R and G Middle Lt buoys. In onshore weather enter from Fairway safe water buoy 3½M ENE of Buddon Ness. From S, after half tide and in smooth water, it is possible to join the main channel near Abertay R can buoy (Fl.R.6s). Do not attempt to cross Abertay Sand which extends 5M out from S shore – submerged stakes.

Bar 3·2m NE of Abertay R can buoy. Dangerous in strong E wind or onshore swell, especially on the ebb.

Entrance Channel is buoyed. From Abertay E card Lt buoy steer on steep-to shore at Tayport with Dir LtHo (Iso.WRG.3s) bearing 269°.

Anchorages and Berthing
• Tayport – see separate entry.
• Temporary anchorage on S side just N of Lucky Scalp E of Tayport. On N side close inshore SW of Buddon Ness, out of main ebb stream.
• Good anchorage clear to W of Tayport entrance, to N of line of high and low lights (low Lt disused). Exposed.
• In W Ferry Bay 8ca WNW from Broughty Castle by River Tay YC moorings, use trip. Yellow YC visitor's buoy at E end of moorings. Stream runs strongly.
• Broughty Harbour dries; available ±0300hrs, keep to W wall. Slip, crane. Exposed.
• Dundee Docks: Entrance 4ca E of Road Br. Anchoring off not recommended. Yachts can enter wet docks by prior arrangement; perfect safety but commercial port. Lock HW–0200 to HW. Strictly no smoking.
• Pleasant anchorages above bridges off Balmerino and further W.

For upper reaches and **Perth** leave rly br 2–2½h before HW Dundee. HW Perth approx 1½h after Dundee.

✆/VHF HM VHF 12 *Dundee Harbour Radio* covers all shipping movements, weather etc ✆ 01382 224121. Royal Tay YC VHF M, ✆ 01382 477516.

TAYPORT

Tidal data as Dundee

A pleasant small town. Completely sheltered private hbr 7M from the Abertay BYB buoy, offering an excellent passage stop. Mostly dries to very deep soft mud. No commercial activity, visitors welcome.

Approach and Entrance Just W of Larick Bn (conspic pile Lt) head for fairway buoy about

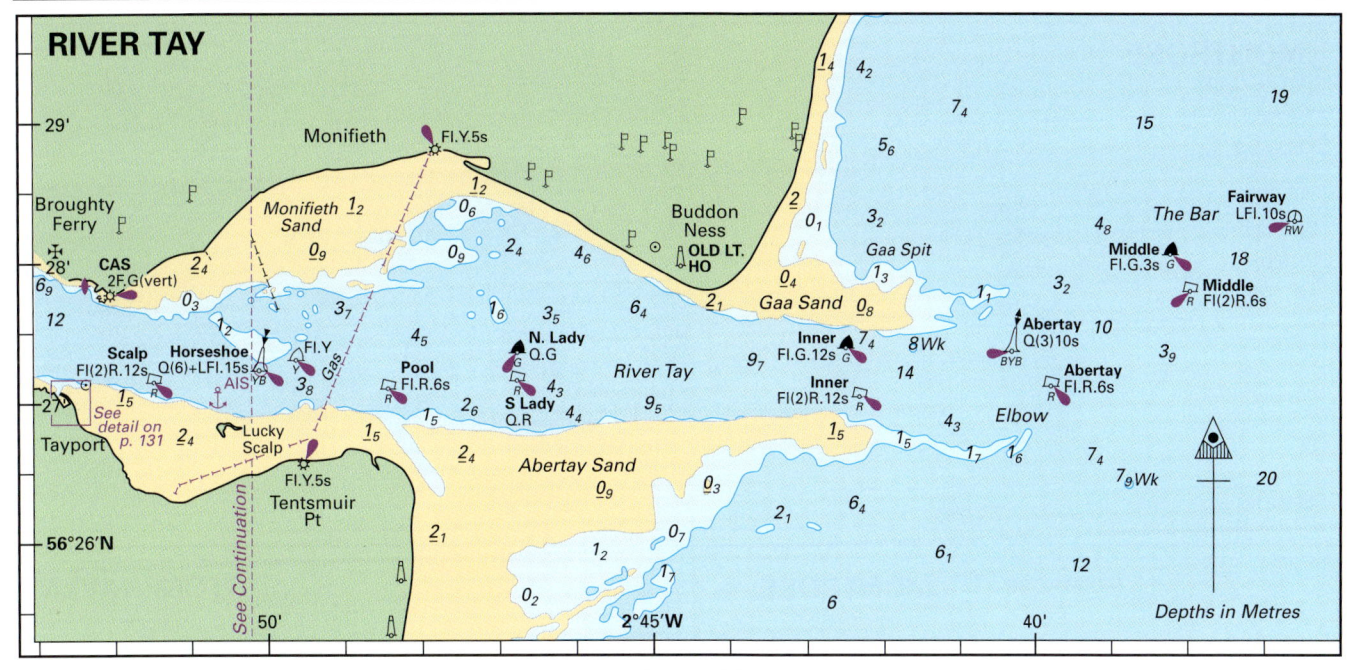

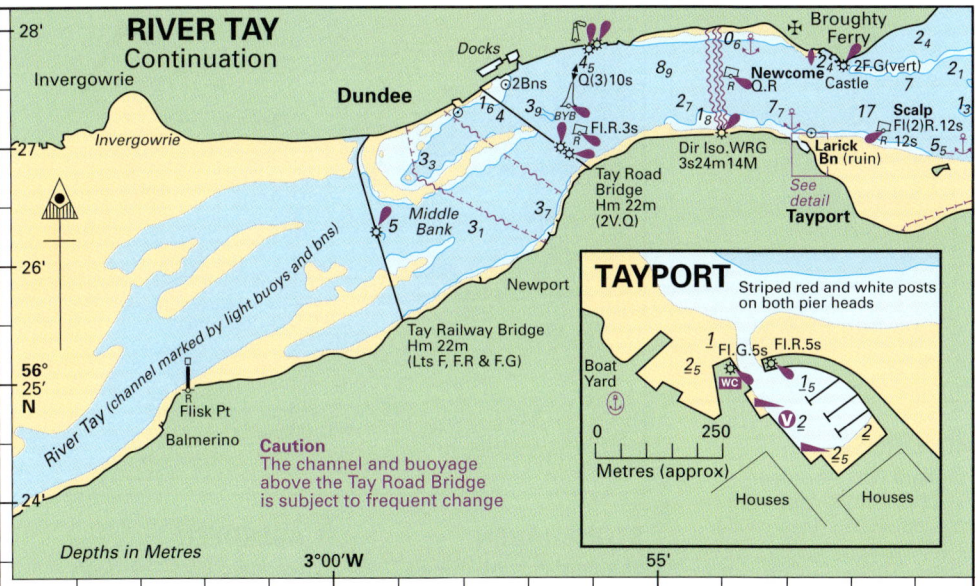

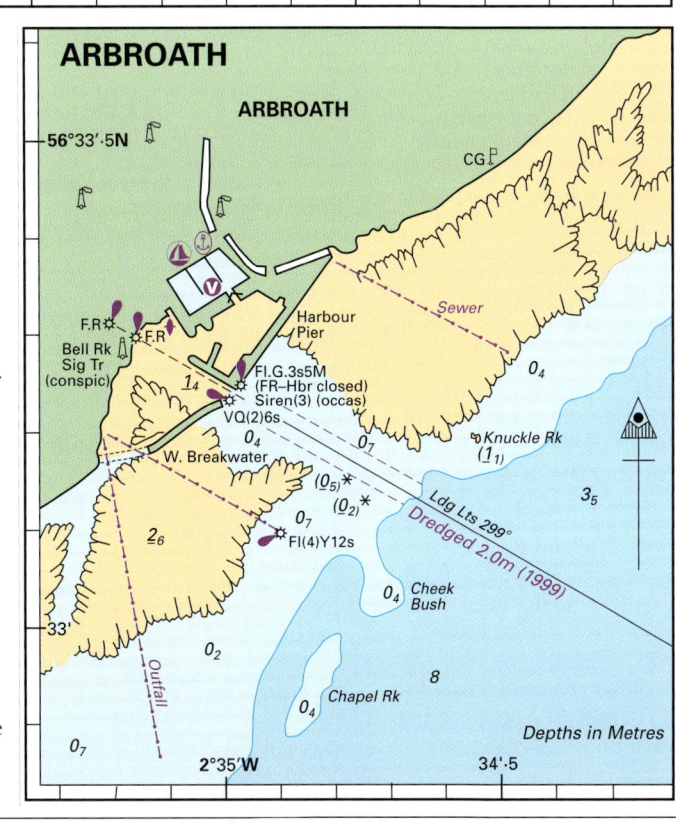

ARBROATH TO RATTRAY HEAD

Not a stretch of coast to be trifled with in on-shore weather. Advise passing to seaward of large offshore anchorage approx 1M NE of Aberdeen. All vessels, including recreational craft, must call Aberdeen VTS (VHF Ch 12) when 3M from Fairway buoy to obtain permission to enter Aberdeen VTS area which is within 2M of Aberdeen N pier and north of 57°07'·7N. An offing of ¾–1M (but 2M in on-shore weather) is sufficient as far as 57°20'N. S of Cruden Bay a reef, 'The Scares', runs 1M to seaward, buoyed Fl.R.10s AIS. In thick weather the 30m contour gives clearance of all dangers, closing the coast at Buchan Ness just S of Peterhead. Peterhead alone offers safe entry in almost any conditions.

Tidal Stream Close inshore, the streams tend to change earlier than that shown in the *Admiralty Tidal Atlas*. Going north the difference increases by up to 2h off Rattray Head.

Rattray Head Seas can be dangerous in heavy weather. Best rounded at slack water, 2M off (this clears inshore dangers and leaves area of steepest seas to seaward). In bad conditions pass five miles off and if necessary more.

Passage lights	BA No
Scurdie Ness Fl(3)20s38m23M Racon(T) (–)	3220
Girdle Ness Fl(2)20s56m22M Racon(G) (– – ·)	3246
Buchan Ness Fl.5s40m18M Racon(O) (– – –)	3280
Rattray Head Fl(3)30s28m18M Racon(M) (– –)	3304

100m N or hbr mouth. Make good 185° on the ldg ln marked by bns with triangular Y topmarks. Beware strong cross-stream. Keep close to E quay wall for best water. Enter HW±0300.

Berthing On SW wall, fender board desireable, or with permission at private pontoon berth. Check with Berthing Master. Top of hbr dries very early on ebb.

Facilities Water on quay. Shops. Bus to Dundee.

☎ Berthing Master 07811 328955.

ARBROATH

Standard Port Aberdeen
HW (sp) +0056 (np) +0037
LW (sp) +0055 (np) +0034

MHWS	MHWN	MLWN	MLWS
+0·9m	+0·8m	+0·3m	+0·1m

Fishing and recreational hbr. Outer harbour dries; wet dock gates open approx HW±0300 between 0715 and 1945, phone HM for accurate times. Identified by conspic white swimming pool ½M W of entrance and white signal tr W of entrance.

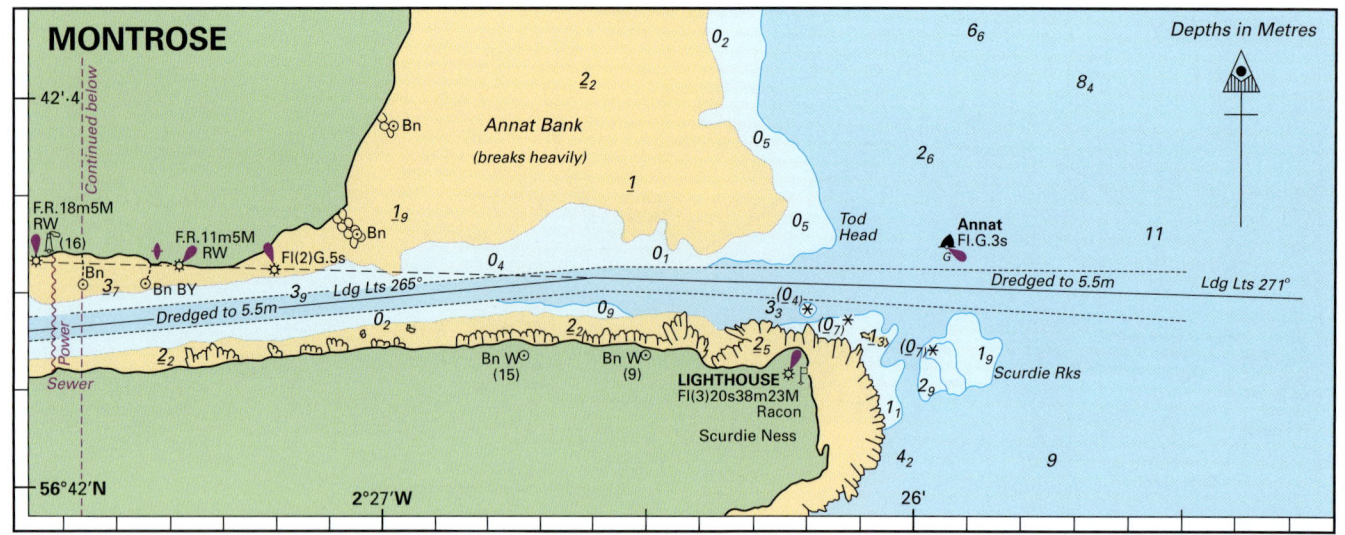

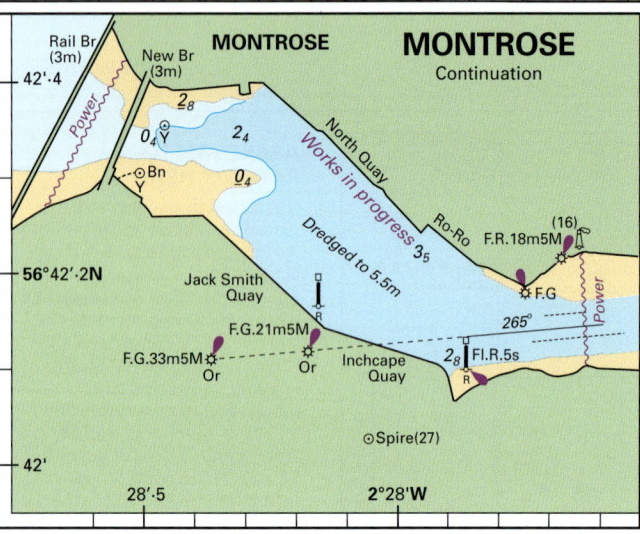

Approach Channel bounded by drying rock ledges for ½M from a bar (0·5m). Outlying dangers Knuckle Rock (stb), Cheek Bush and Chapel Rock (port). Enter HW±0330.

Entrance and Berthing Steer with twin towers of church between the gap in piers until white pole Ldg marks (F.R) located, 299°. Keep strictly to line. Moderate SE swell causes very awkward swell in entrance. Berth at pontoon hammerheads in inner harbour, minimum depth 2·5m.

Signals F.R on E pier when hbr closed.

Facilities Water and electricity on pontoons, showers, stores, fuel at garage. EC Wednesday. Rly.

☎/VHF HM 01241 872166, VHF 11.

OFFSHORE ANCHORAGE

Lunan Bay offers temporary anchorage in off-shore winds, either close to S shore (no further W than Ethie village) or under Boddin Point at N end. Subject to swell.

MONTROSE

Standard Port Aberdeen
HW (sp) +0056 (np) +0037
LW (sp) +0055 (np) +0034
MHWS MHWN MLWN MLWS
+0·9m +0·8m +0·3m +0·1m

A busy commercial and oil port with ship movements round the clock. Not recommended except in an emergency. No special facilities for yachts. Very strong tides in channel and entrance.

Approach From S or N keep minimum ½M offshore. Enter on Ldg line 271°. 50m-wide channel dredged to a minimum of 4m. Hold Ldg line until abeam inner of two W unlit stone bns on S shore; then alter to 265° on inner Ldg line. Call VHF 12 Montrose Port Control 1hr before entry for permission and berthing instructions.

Entrance Best at slack water or first hour of flood. Avoid in strong on-shore weather; seas break in channel.

Berthing As instructed. Fender board essential; risk of damage from effect of tide especially on ebb.

Facilities of a commercial port.

☎/VHF HM 01674 672302, VHF 12.

STONEHAVEN

Standard Port Aberdeen
HW +0010   LW +0011
MHWS MHWN MLWN MLWS
+0·2m +0·2m +0·1m 0·0m

A good small fishing boat and holiday hbr 9ca N of Dunottar Castle (ruins). Outer harbour dredged 1·5m along piers but subject to silting. Inner harbour dries, sand and mud. Inner harbour closed with booms in bad weather.

Avoid in heavy onshore weather. Outer harbour subject to surge with onshore swell.

Approach Steer just S of W, giving good clearance to Downie Point and Bellman's Head. Pierhead lit DirWGR. F.G Lt (B Ball) on S Pier 'unsafe to enter'.

Entrance Keep up to stb after passing outer pier head.

Berthing In offshore weather alongside pier in outer harbour. Otherwise enter inner harbour and dry out against quays as directed.

Facilities Stores, water, showers. EC Wednesday.

☎/VHF HM 01569 762741 or 07741 050210, VHF 11 (occas).

ABERDEEN

Standard Port Aberdeen

Very busy oil and commercial port; not recommended except as a port of refuge/emergency. Well protected from S but open to NE; do not attempt on ebb in strong NE wind. The F.R Ldg Lts are changed to F.G when it is unsafe to enter.

Approach Ldg line 236° from Fairway RW Lt buoy. Keep S face of N pier just open.

Entrance Call Aberdeen VTS for permission to enter or leave. Traffic signals from control tr:
• F.G. no entry
• F.R. no departure
• F.R. & F.G. Port closed

N pier and S breakwater floodlit.

Berthing As directed.

Facilities Large town. Rly. Coaches. Dyce Airport 7M.

☎/VHF Aberdeen VTS 01224 597000, VHF 12.

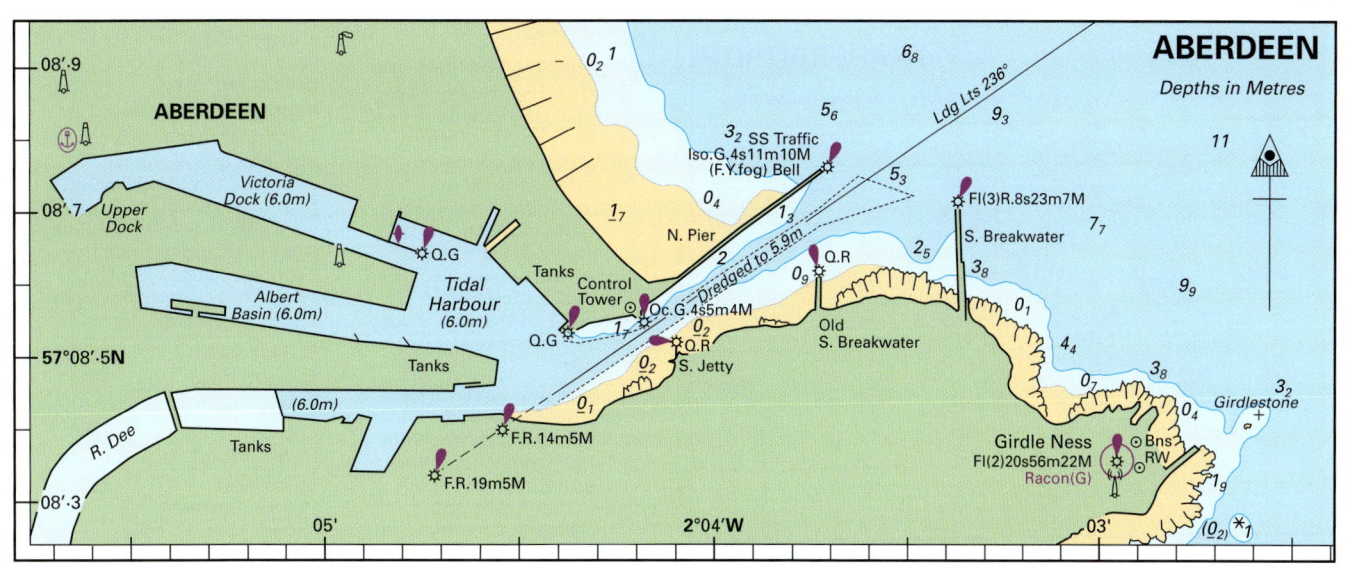

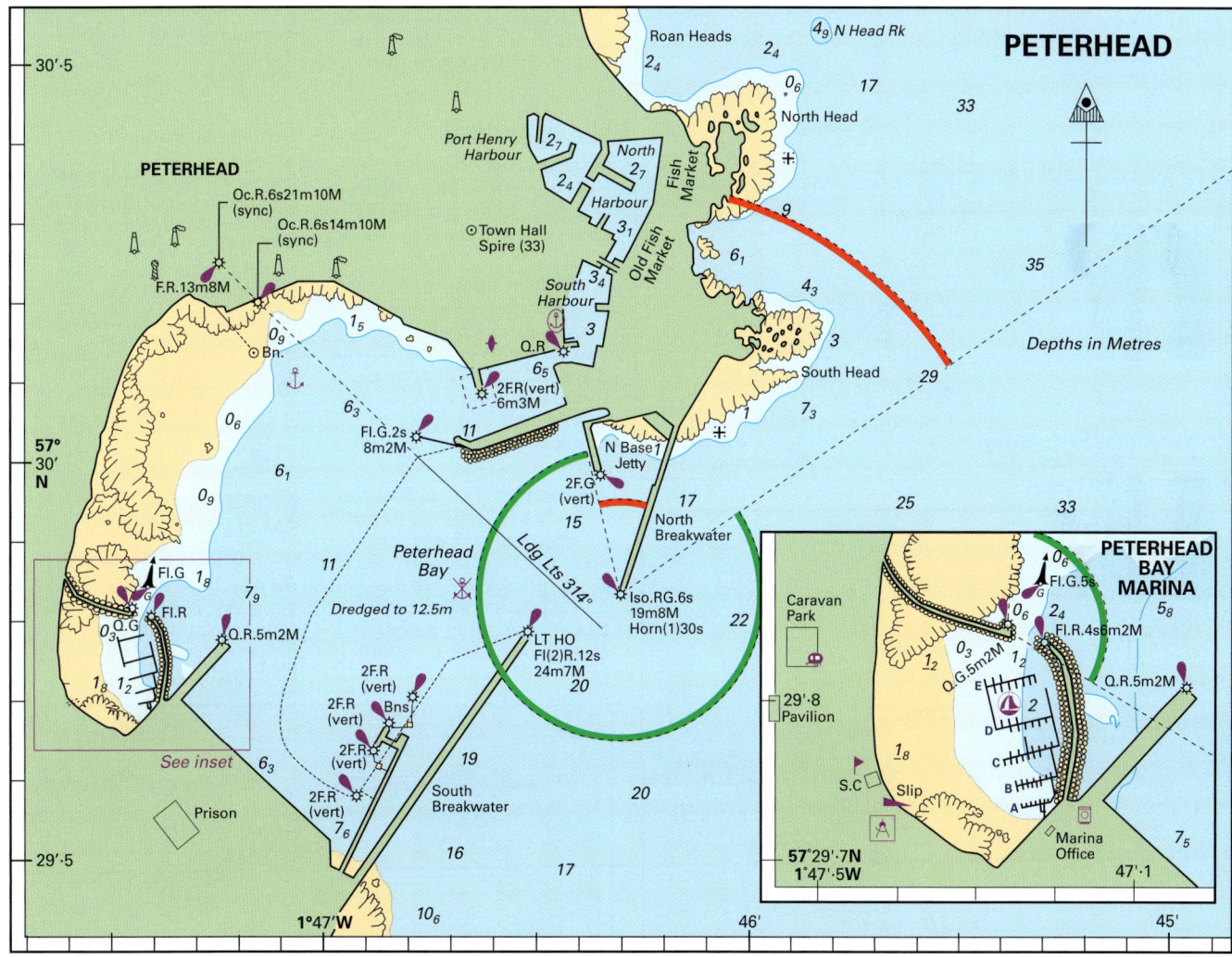

PETERHEAD

Standard Port Aberdeen
HW −0035   LW −0037

MHWS	MHWN	MLWN	MLWS
−0·5m	−0·3m	−0·1m	−0·1m

An invaluable all-weather hbr with modern marina. Much fishing and oil traffic. Power station chimney S of bay makes conspic landmark. Long breakwaters turn whole bay into hbr of refuge available in almost any weather.

Approach Headlands to N and S are foul for ¼M; then approach between SE and NE (Ldg Lts 314°). Call *Peterhead Harbour* VHF 14 when 1M from the outer breakwater.

Anchorage In NW corner of bay 150m offshore below Ldg marks.

Berthing Marina in W corner of the Bay. Approach from the E, beware of shallow rocky ledge to NE of G buoy, lower sails before entering marina. Silting reported. Visitors normally berth on pontoon E. Marina office usually open 0800–1900. Outside these hours contact *Peterhead Port Control* for instructions on obtaining security key. Yachts may not use the main fishing hbr except with special permission. Call VHF 14 before leaving marina. Bound N leave at local HW +0100 and bound S local LW +0100.

Facilities All stores in town 1M. Enquire at marina office for fuel by bowser (in main hbr) by can (office), also for gas and laundry. Regular bus service (½M) to Aberdeen.

☎/VHF HM (Port) 01779 483630

Marina 01779 477868; (mob) 07803 264617.

VHF 14 (port control and marina).

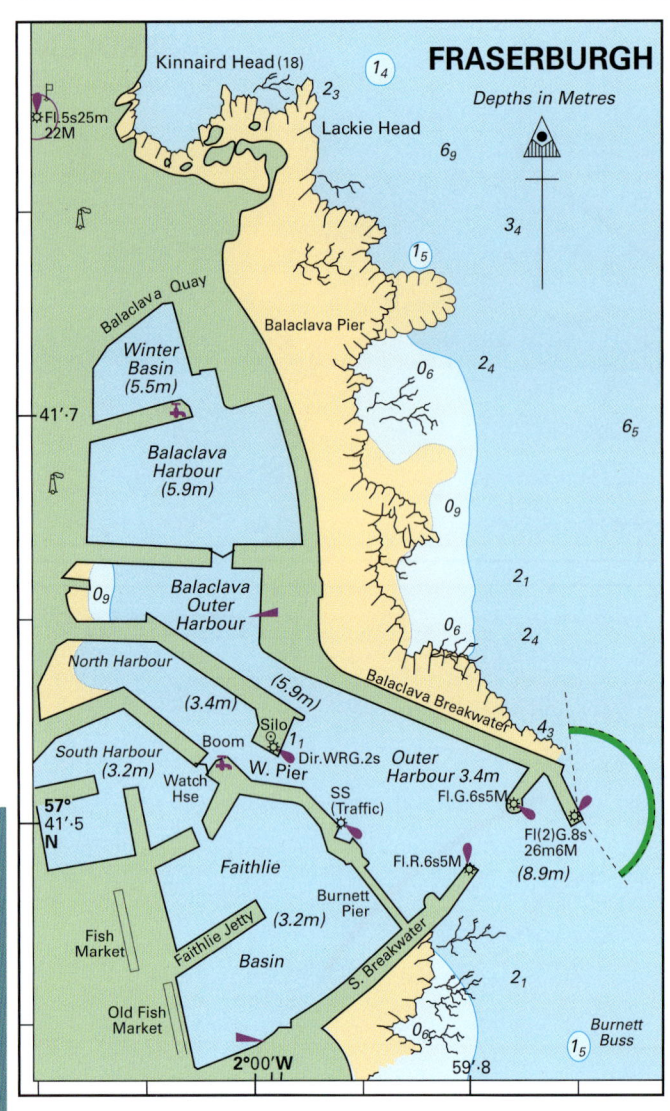

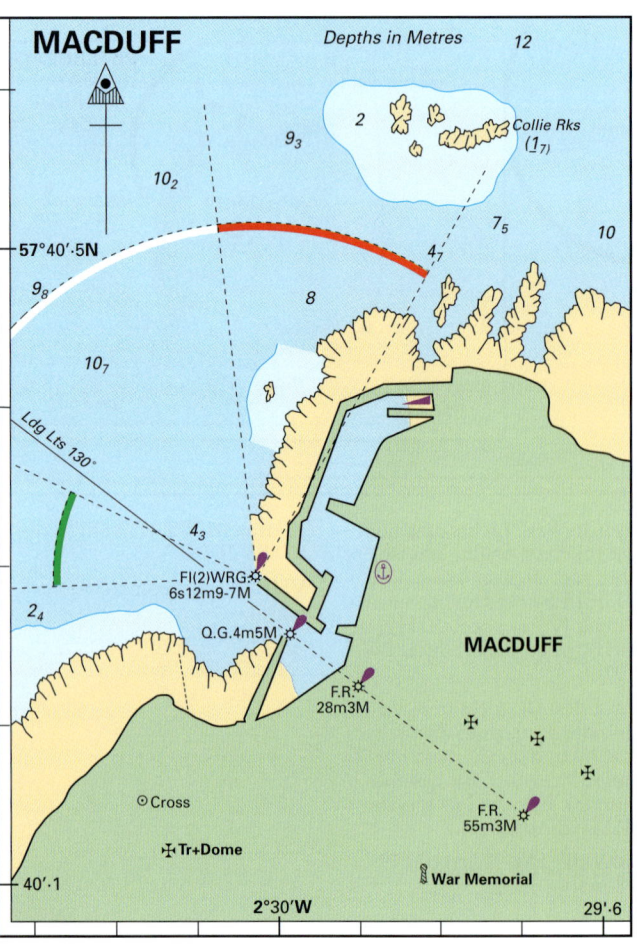

MORAY FIRTH
Rattray Head to Inverness Firth

In heavy onshore weather keep 2M off the coast otherwise keep ½M off R Lt bn (Fl.10s10M) marking reef off Cairnbulg Point and at least 1M off Kinnaird Head in wind against tide conditions. W of Lossiemouth, beware of the Halliman Skerries, marked by an unlit beacon; these lie 1M offshore, NE of the conspicuous disused Covesea Skerries white lighthouse.

Tides, once past Kinnaird Head, are relatively weak and complex, except off headlands and in the approaches to the Inverness Firth. Close inshore between Rosehearty and Portknockie the flood tide runs east, not as shown in the *Tidal Stream Atlas*. With strong N'ly winds or large N'ly swell most of the harbours on this coast are dangerous. Large scale charts are needed for the approach to Inverness Firth and the Caledonian Canal.

Rattray Head to Wick

Surprisingly heavy seas can be met in W or NW winds, otherwise this 65M passage presents no problem. Once 10M clear of Kinnard Head, tides are weak until approaching the Caithness coast where they reach 2kn at springs between Clyth Ness and Noss Head.

Passage lights	BA No
Kinnaird Head Fl.5s25m22M	3332
Chanonry Point Oc.6s12m12M	3440
Tarbat Ness Fl(4)30s53m24M Racon(T) (–)	3506
Noss Head Fl.WR.20s53m25/21M	3544
Duncansby Head Fl.12s67m22M Racon(T) (–)	3558

FRASERBURGH

Standard Port Aberdeen
HW (sp) –0105 (np) –0115
LW (sp) –0110 (np) –0120
MHWS MHWN MLWN MLWS
–0·6m –0·5m –0·2m 0·0m

A very busy fishing port, especially Sunday evenings. It has some pontoon berths for visiting yachts in S hbr. Advisable to call in advance. Useful if waiting for a fair tide. Can be dirty and noisy. Entrance dangerous in onshore gales.

Approach on 291° in W sector of Iso.WRG.2s, or old parish church spire (to S of dome) just open S of Balaclava Pier. Keep W silo on N Pier open S of Lt on Balaclava breakwater. Essential to call *Fraserburgh Harbour* on VHF 12 before entry or departure.

Berthing directions from watch-tower on VHF 12; usually on pontoon in S hbr. Security key either from hbr office or watch-tower (long walk). For departure south round Rattray Head, leave harbour at local LW.

Signals R flag/R Lt – entrance dangerous.
2B Balls/2R Lts vert – port closed.

☎/**VHF** Hbr office 01346 515858; Watch-tr 515858, VHF 12 (24hrs).

MORAY FIRTH SMALL HARBOURS

In good weather these hbrs on the Moray Firth are available, many dry, Portsoy, Portknockie (good shelter from E, berth just inside entrance, beware of broken quay), Findochty,

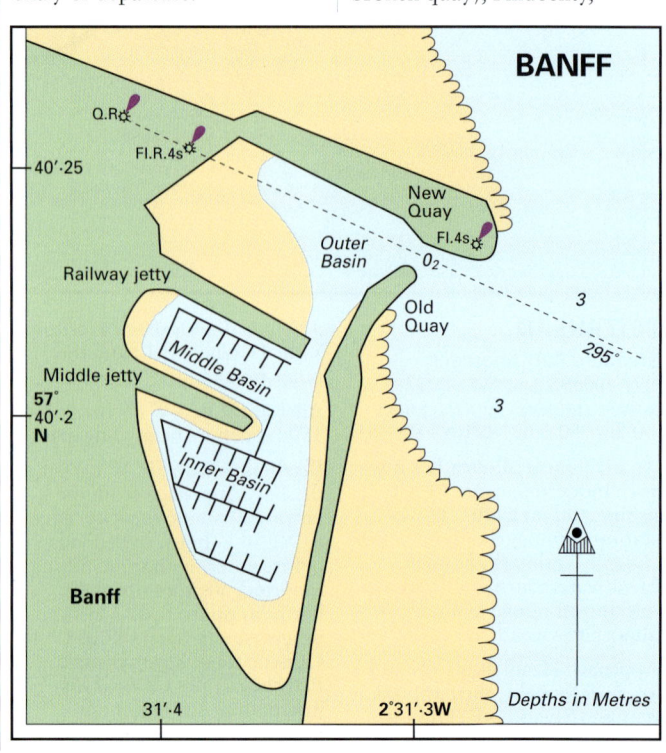

Hopeman (popular and crowded in season), Nairn (bars at river mouth and in channel). Portmahomack on S side of entrance to Dornoch Firth, where there is also good anchorage in 2m, sand, in winds from SE to SW. Beware stake nets and pot markers.

MACDUFF
Tidal data as Banff

Fishing hbr with three basins, least depth 2m; generally crowded. Good shelter but entrance very rough in winds from W to N. Not to be attempted in onshore gales or in heavy swell.

Signals Ldg Lts October–March only. B ball/G Lt – hbr closed.

Berthing Turn to port after entry. As instructed. No electricity, no showers.

☎/**VHF** HM 01261 833962. VHF 12 (24hrs).

BANFF
Standard Port Aberdeen
HW (sp) –0100 (np) –0150
LW (sp) –0050 (np) –0150
MHWS MHWN MLWN MLWS
–0·4m –0·2m –0·1m 0·0m

A flourishing historic town with a recreational hbr and small marina for vessels <10m, though larger vessels can dry out alongside New Quay on clean sand. Access HW±0200. Do not attempt in strong N/NE winds or with heavy onshore swell. A useful hbr if W or NW winds make Macduff dangerous. Silting reported.

Entrance Approach on 295°, ldg Lts Q.R and Fl.R4s on two posts near the building above the beach. Depth at entrance is at CD (2017).

Berthing Six visitors' berths. Middle basin, depths up to 1·8m at 10m berths. Inner basin 0·7m or less. As directed by HM.

Facilities Shops, library, hospital.

☎/**VHF** HM (part time) VHF 12, 01261 815544 or 07770 646115.

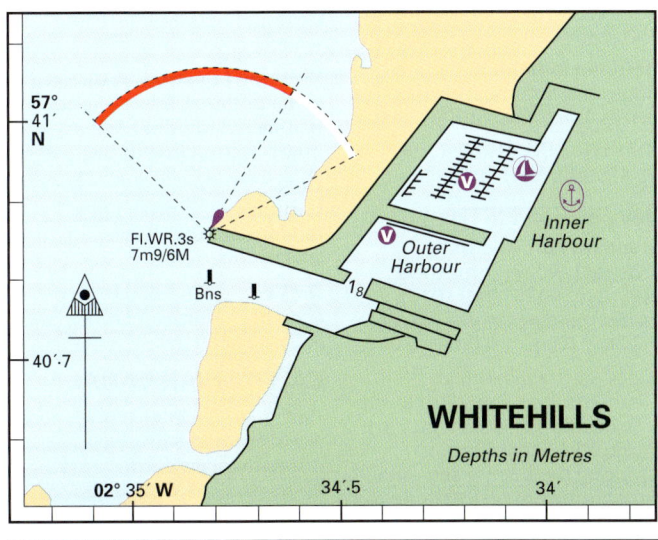

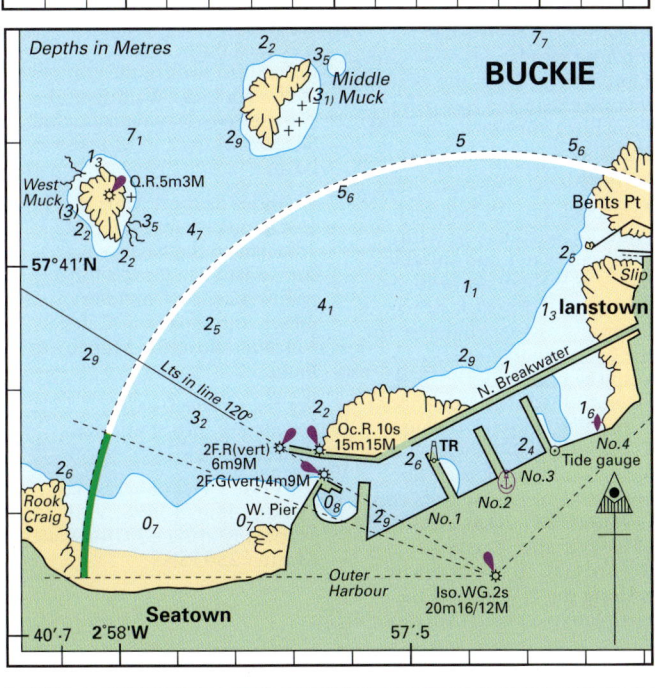

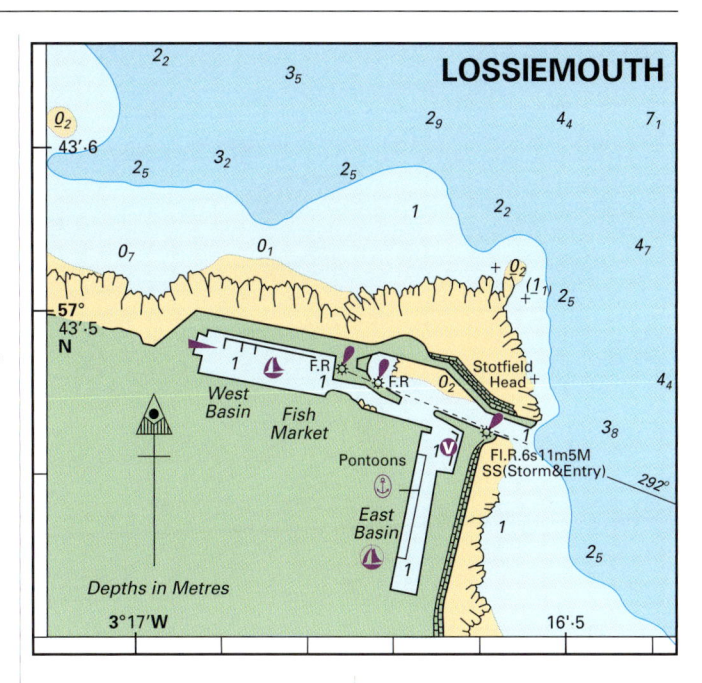

WHITEHILLS
Standard Port Aberdeen
HW (sp) –0122 (np) –0137
LW (sp) –0127 (np) –0117
MHWS MHWN MLWN MLWS
–0·4m –0·3m +0·1m +0·1m

A small recreational hbr. Entrance dangerous with strong onshore winds or heavy swell.

Approach from the N or NW. Head for end of N pier, Fl.WR.3s.

Entrance is narrow, keep close to N pier, leaving bns, which mark drying rocks, to stb. At MLWS min depth is 1·3m. Beware of surge. There is a very sharp turn to port into outer hbr.

Berthing Alongside pontoon in outer harbour.

Facilities Stores, fuel, laundry, WiFi, toilets.

☎/**VHF** HM 01261 861291, Mobile 07906 135786, VHF 14.

BUCKIE
Standard Port Aberdeen
HW (sp) –0130 (np) –0145
LW (sp) –0140 (np) –0125
MHWS MHWN MLWN MLWS
–0·2m –0·2m 0·0m 0·0m

A fishing and commercial harbour with increasing offshore renewable traffic. Yachts made welcome, limited facilities. Essential to obtain permission to enter (VHF12). Safe entry in virtually all weathers. 2·2m minimum in entrance and 3m alongside. Beware of reflected swell in W winds.

Signals Three B balls/3F.R (vert) – hbr closed.

Berthing As directed, usually No.3 basin.

Facilities Shops, water, showers, fuel.

☎/**VHF** HM 01542 831700. VHF 12 (24h).

LOSSIEMOUTH
Standard Port Aberdeen
HW (sp) –0125 (np) –0200
LW (sp) –0130 (np) –0130
MHWS MHWN MLWN MLWS
–0·2m –0·2m 0·0m 0·0m

Recreational hbr, identified by Covesea Skerries LtHo to W of town. Avoid in winds Force 6 or over from N to SE.

Entrance 1·2m in entrance MLWS but silting possible; best HW±0400. Beware strong current setting N across entrance. Call before entering.

Berthing East Basin, alongside pontoon near entrance.

Facilities Stores. Showers, laundry, key and electricity card from HM or Steam Boat Inn. Diesel by can.

Signals Ldg Lts (F.R 292°) when entrance is safe.

☎/**VHF** HM 01343 813066, VHF 12. Lossiemouth Cruising Club 813767.

BURGHEAD
See plan p.128
Standard Port Aberdeen
HW (sp) –0120 (np) –0150
LW (sp) –0120 (np) –0135
MHWS MHWN MLWN MLWS
–0·2m –0·2m 0·0m 0·0m

A commercial hbr used by local fishing and grain vessels. Access can be difficult in onshore winds or swell.

Entrance 1·5m LWS. Tide gauge. Keep 15m off extension of N pier hd then keep mid-channel; at night identify Lts on N pier spur (Q.R) and S pier (F.G), both vis only from SW, and keep G open S of R.

Berthing Only as directed by HM and may not always be possible.

Facilities Stores, water, fuel, buses.

☎/**VHF** HM 01343 835337, VHF 14.

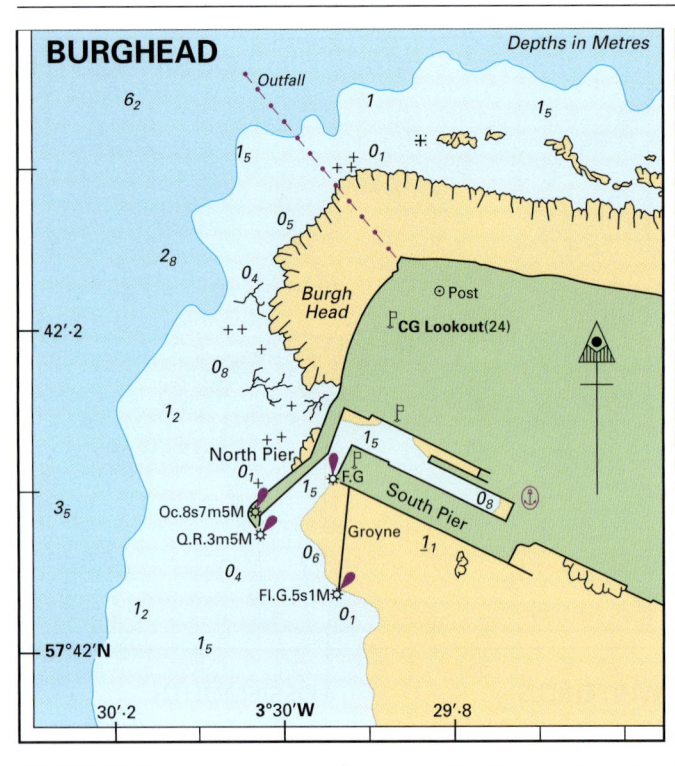

FINDHORN

Standard Port Aberdeen

HW	(sp) −0125	(np) −0155
LW	(sp) −0125	(np) −0140

MHWS	MHWN	MLWN	MLWS
−0·2m	−0·2m	0·0m	0·0m

This is the most sheltered natural hbr in the Moray Firth and is a main yachting centre, however there is a bar. Entrance is dangerous in strong NE winds or in a heavy NE swell.

Bar There is more than 1·0m at half tide. Strangers are advised to enter HW−0200 to HW+0100. www.rfyc.net has latest information.

Approach The land is low, to the west it is wooded and to the east there is a conspicuous windsock. Keep 1M offshore and make for the RW spherical Landfall buoy, from here it is possible to see the outermost port-hand buoy.

Entrance Make for the outer bar buoy, R can Fl.R. There may be breaking waves on the outer sandbank, these should be left close to port. Thence follow the lateral buoys, leaving the three bns, which are on drying sands, about 50m to port. At the next red buoy turn hard to port and follow the line of moorings.

Anchorage Anchor between the south end of the moorings and the twin stone piers on the east bank. Good holding in sand, but tide may run at up to 4kn. Visitors' moorings or alongside pontoon berths may be available from Findhorn Boatyard, ☎ 01309 690099.

Facilities Water and electricity at N pier (dries). Boatyard with chandlery, slip etc., shop, pubs, showers and restaurant at Royal Findhorn YC
☎ 01309 690247.

NAIRN

Standard Port Aberdeen

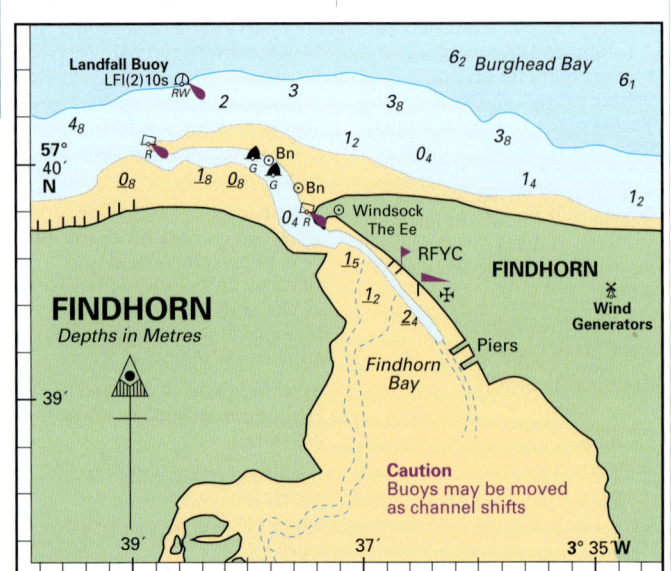

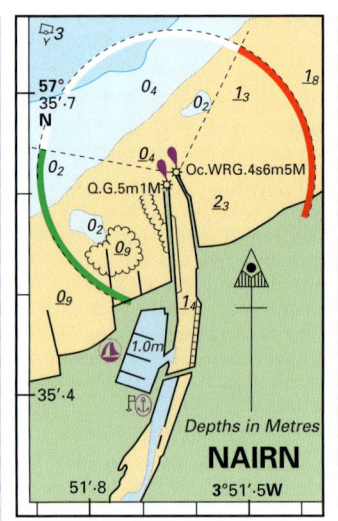

HW	(sp) −0112	(np) −0153
LW	(sp) −0120	(np) −0135

MHWS	MHWN	MLWN	MLWS
−0·2m	−0·2m	0·0m	0·0m

A non-commercial hbr with a drying entrance.

Approach Keep in W sector of Lt Oc.WRG on E pier head. Y waiting buoy 2ca NNW of pier heads.

Entrance HW−0200 to HW+0100, difficult in fresh northerly winds, dangerous with heavy onshore swell.

Berthing In basin, 1m at pontoons, soft mud, three berths 1·8m against E wall.

☎/**VHF** HM 01667 452877 or 456008, VHF 09.

INVERNESS FIRTH

Standard Port Aberdeen

HW	(sp) −0050	(np) −0150
LW	(sp) −0120	(np) −0135

MHWS	MHWN	MLWN	MLWS
−0·2m	0·0m	0·0m	0·0m

Tides may reach 4kn at Chanonry Point and also at the Kessock Br. Elsewhere they are weak. Within the Firth, if awaiting the tide for the canal, suitable anchorage/berthing can be had:
• Anchor off Fortrose in offshore winds
• Enter River Ness and berth at Inverness Marina (see below)
• Anchor temporarily 2ca NW of sea lock entrance, good holding.

Approach From Chanonry Point Oc.6s12m15M with sufficient water and suitable rise of tide there are two passages via Kessock Br to Inverness or Clachnaharry for the Caledonian Canal.
• Up the middle of the Firth Steer 220° for Munlochy Safe Water RW buoy(Fl 10s) at 57°32'·9N 4°07'·6W, avoiding Skate Bank to stb, then on approx same course to G con Lt buoy (Fl.G.3s) at 57°30'·2N 4°12'·0W and then head towards the centre of the br.
• Along the NW side of the Firth Having passed Chanonry Point turn sharp to stb keeping fairly close to the shore. Leave two red can buoys to port (these mark the NE extremity of Skate Bank) then make for a WP at 57°34'·53N 4°08'·0W which is SW of Fortrose. It may be convenient to anchor near here in offshore winds if awaiting the tide. Follow the NW shore to a WP 57°31'·2N 4°12'·4W which is SW of the ruins of Kilmuir church which can best be detected by a stone wall round the graveyard and some yew trees. Then head 160° to G con Lt buoy Fl.G.3s at 57°30'·3N 4°12'·0W, before heading for the br.

INVERNESS

The capital of the Highlands with a modern marina at entrance of River Ness. Close to the Caledonian Canal. Excellent rail and road connections. City centre ¾M.

Entrance River Ness is narrow but deep. Beware of unmarked spit on W side of entrance; there are strong cross tides. Give way to commercial craft, main activity HW−0200 to HW. Call *Inverness Pilots* on VHF 12 to check channel is clear and maintain listening watch.

Berthing In marina as directed or on pontoon B/C alongside hammerhead or in first two finger berths close to the entrance.

Facilities As expected of a modern marina. WiFi. City centre ¾M.

☎/**VHF** 01463 220501. *Inverness Marina* VHF 12 (office hours).

CALEDONIAN CANAL

Entrance Clachnaharry sea lock is 1M beyond River Ness, normally open during working hours except LW ±0200: beware of extensive shoal to W side of river mouth, marked by a N card buoy. It may be difficult to wait in the entrance to the sea lock. Waiting in the canal before leaving is best at Seaport Marina in Muirtown basin.

Facilities Seaport Marina. Fuel, gas, showers; supermarkets adjacent to the basin, easy transport to Inverness for trains/coaches. Chandlery, diesel, and repairs at Caley Marina, above the Muirtown flight.

See the *Corpach* entry, p.151, for further information on the canal.

☎/**VHF** Clachnaharry Sea Lock 01463 713896, VHF 74; Seaport Marina 233140; Caley Marina 236539.

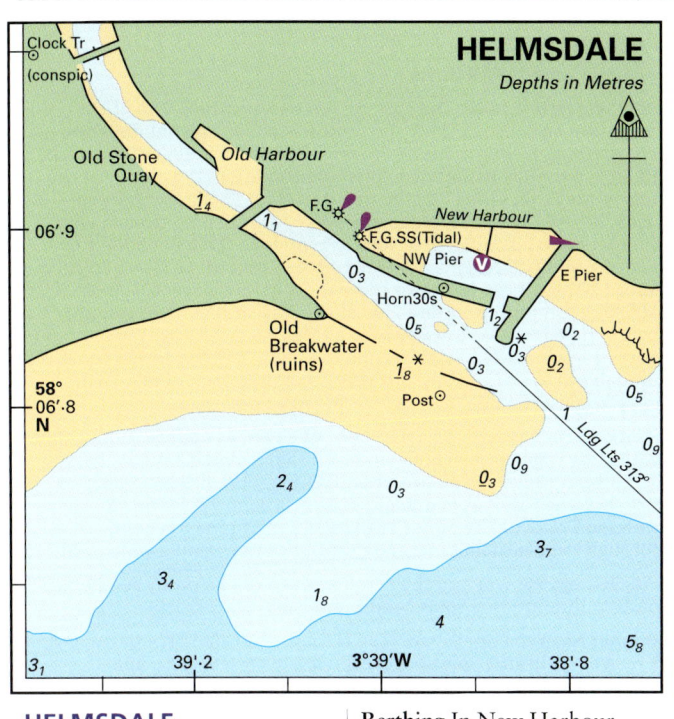

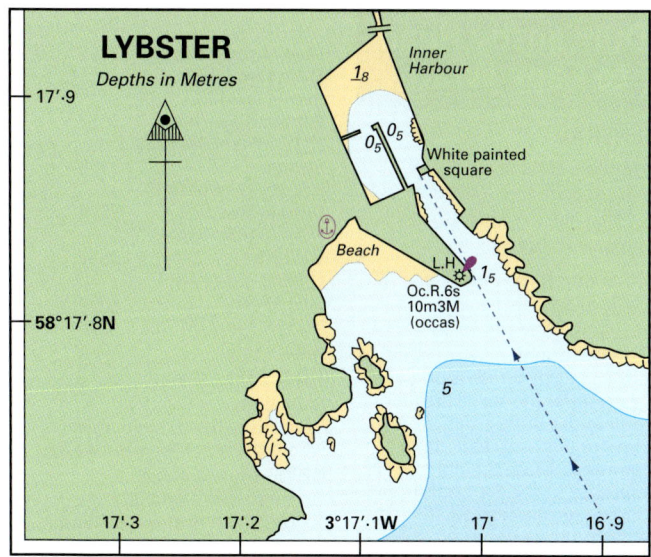

HELMSDALE

Depths in Metres

LYBSTER

Depths in Metres

APPROACHES TO INVERNESS AND CALEDONIAN CANAL

HELMSDALE
Standard Port Wick
HW +0025   LW +0032

MHWS	MHWN	MLWN	MLWS
+0·5m	+0·3m	+0·1m	−0·1m

A good small hbr; avoid in strong easterlies.

Approach Keep 0·5M offshore for 1M southwestwards of the hbr and to seaward of the R can buoy.

Bar About 2·0m on sand bar at entrance at half tide.

Entrance Ldg marks 313° (F.G) two grey poles with long fluorescent red rectangular topmarks near base of NW pier.

Berthing In New Harbour alongside or at pontoon.

Facilities Showers, shops and restaurant in town.

☎/VHF HM 01431 821692, VHF 12.

LYBSTER
Standard Port Wick
HW +0010   LW n/a

MHWS	MHWN	MLWN	MLWS
+0·2m	+0·2m	+0·1m	0·0m

Small hbr 2½M WSW of Clyth Ness. Good refuge; entrance needs to be accurate, and difficult in strong easterlies.

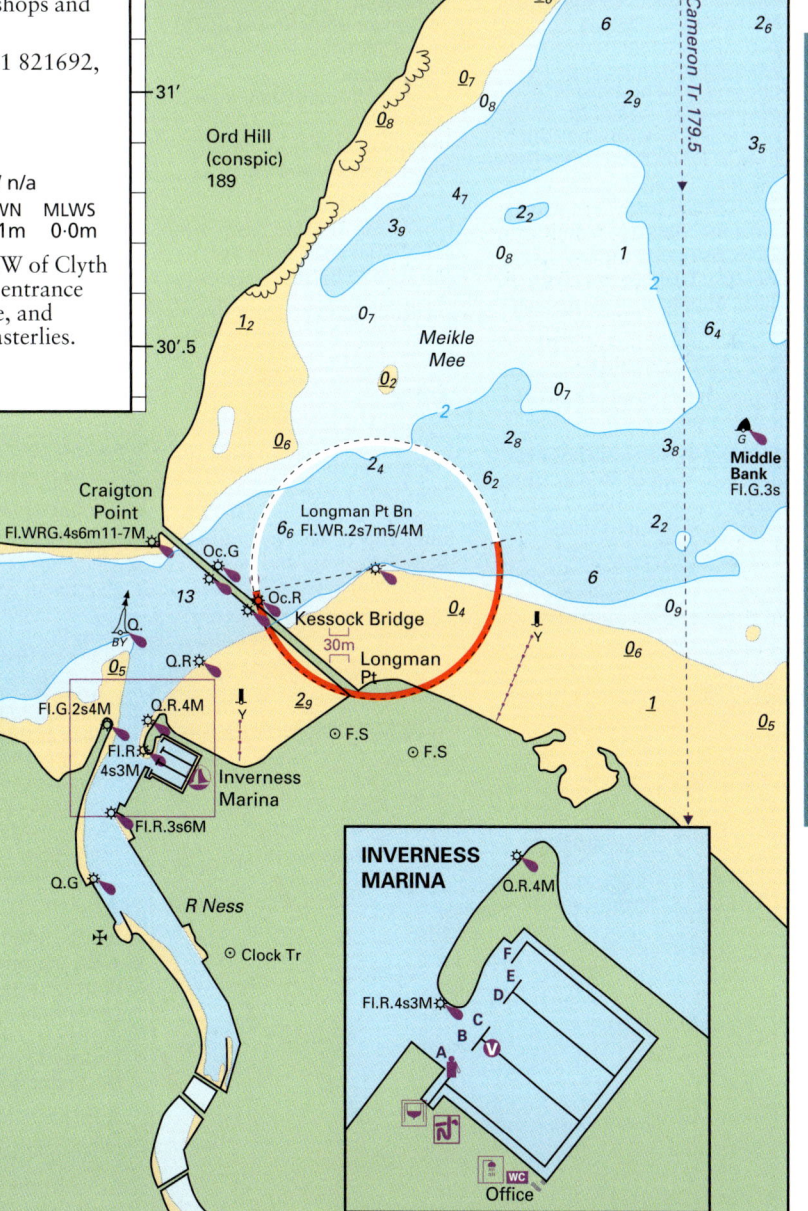

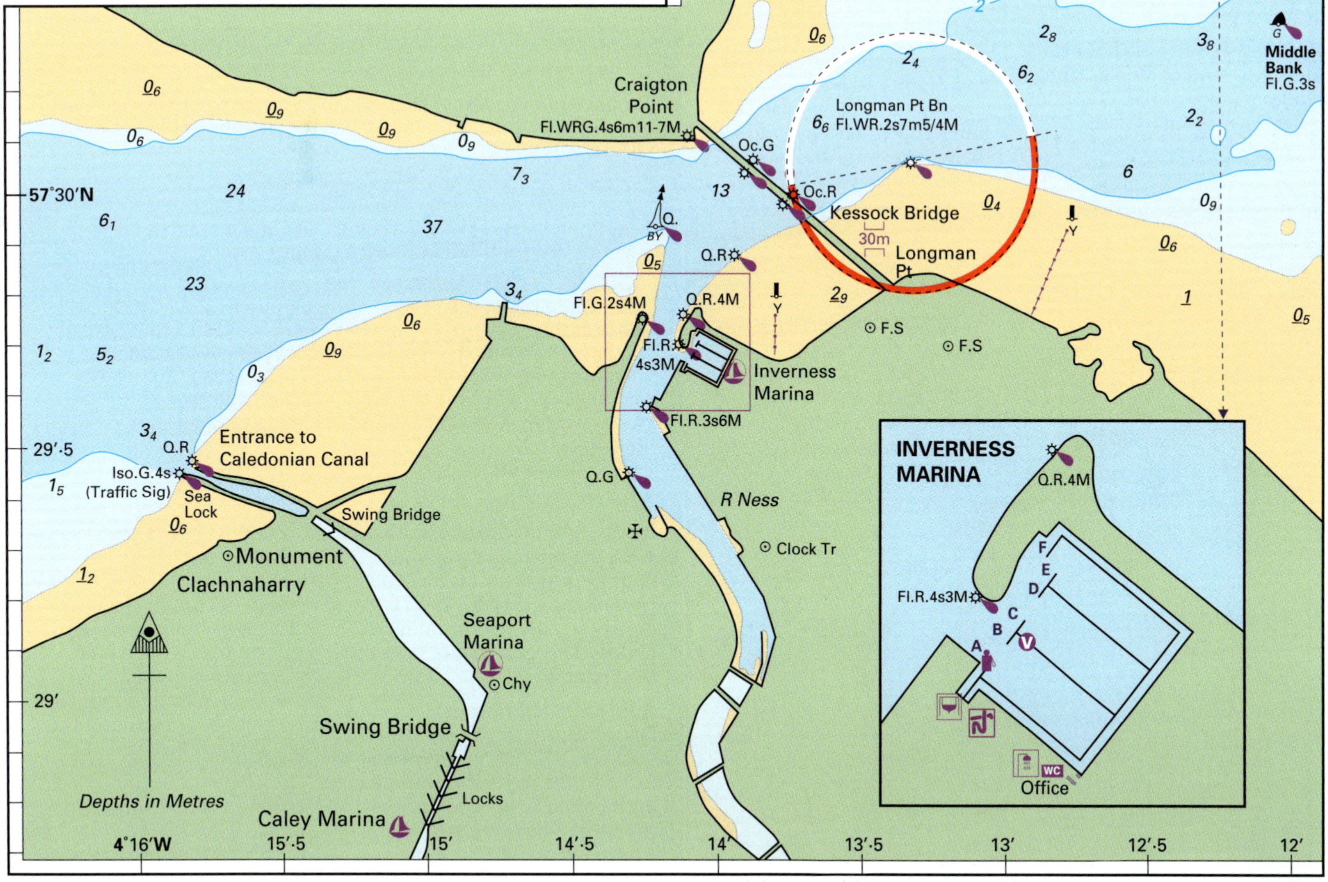

SCOTLAND – EAST AND NORTH COASTS

129

Duncansby Head to Cape Wrath

GENERAL

BA Sailing Directions, *North Coast of Scotland* – NP52

BA *Tidal Atlas Orkney and Shetland Is* – NP209

CCC Sailing Directions, N and NE Coasts of Scotland and Orkney (including Pentland Firth)

Passage through or across the Pentland Firth, which is one of the most dangerous stretches of water in the British Isles, where tidal streams may reach 16kn, requires accurate timing. Reference to the BA *Tidal Atlas* is highly recommended. It should not be attempted at spring tides, wind over Force 4, wind against the tide or swell, or in poor visibility. Flotta in Scapa Flow is an important oil terminal and very large oil tankers use the Firth. However calm it may seem, all yachts should be thoroughly secured, safety harnesses worn etc. A reliable engine is desirable. The Merry Men of Mey is a particularly dangerous race which forms on the W going tide and must be avoided; it consists of an area of breaking seas reaching across the Firth from St John's Point to Tor Ness.

Passage lights	BA No
Duncansby Head Fl.12s67m22M Racon(T) (–)	3558
Pentland Skerries Fl(3)30s52m23M AIS	3562
Stroma Fl(2)20s32m20M AIS	3568
Dunnet Head Fl(4)30s105m23M	3574
C Wrath Fl(4)30s122m22M	3880
Sule Skerry Fl(2)15s34m21M AIS Racon(T) (–)	3868

TIDAL STREAMS

From Freswick Bay (S of Duncansby Head) keep inshore where there is 10hr slack water.

Off Duncansby Head
Dover +0100W –0545E
To Westward of Dunnet Head
Dover +0030W –0600E but close inshore W until –0430

Gill's Bay
Stream sets towards St John's Point for 9hr from Dover –0300

Brough Bay
HW Dover NW for 4hrs. Eddy continues to run NW on main E-going stream.

Brims Ness
HW Dover W for 6hrs at up to 8kn at springs

Cape Wrath
Inshore of Duslic (Stag) Rock always W

2M seaward of Duslic Rock
Dover –0145W +0415E

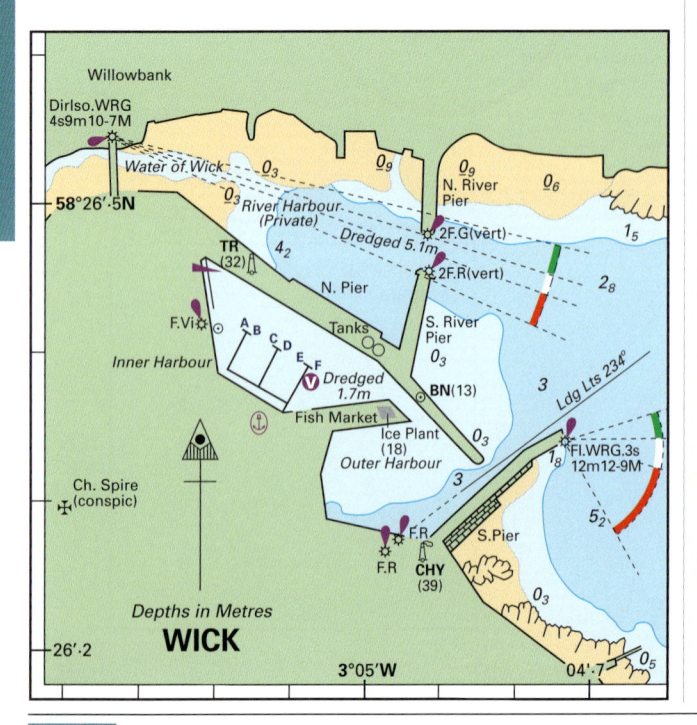

PASSAGE NOTES

All times refer to HW Dover

Pentland Firth E to W The passage can be hazardous. The RNLI coxswains and HMs at Wick and Scrabster are always helpful. If approaching from the South, Freswick Bay, 3·5M south of Duncansby Head, is a useful anchorage in offshore conditions if waiting for the tide in the Firth. In the bay the tide runs N for 9hrs starting Dover–0545. Round Duncansby Head at Dover +0100 keeping close in with Dunnet Head just open of St John's Point: take the Inner Sound about ½M offshore. Pass the Men of Mey Rocks off St John's Point about 100m off. Do NOT pass these rocks before Dover+0300 or +0500 at springs (i.e. before 2hrs of ebb have run or 4h at springs): by this time the severe Merry Men of Mey Race will have moved north allowing safe passage round the point. If early, anchorage is available in W of Gill's Bay, but beware of fishermen's lines. With wind against the tide, give Dunnet Head a good clearance.

Pentland Firth W to E This is somewhat easier, as no race forms while tide is favourable and wind with tide is more common. Leave Scrabster at Dover+0430 to arrive off Dunnet Hd at Dover +0530 as stream turns E'ly. Pass mid-way between St John's Point and Stroma steering S to avoid being set onto rocks S of Stroma (bn unlit). Then through middle of Inner Sd and give Duncansby Head a wide berth.

Via Orkneys the worst of the Pentland Firth can be partly avoided by passing through Hoy Sound and Scapa Flow.

Dunnet Head to Cape Wrath The N coast of Scotland stretches 50M E to W. E of Strathy Point the coast is relatively low-lying and agricultural, beyond this the cliff scenery becomes more spectacular with the Sutherland mountains in the background. In NE winds anchorage can be had in Dunnet Bay behind Dunnet Head, Scrabster provides the only perfect shelter in virtually all conditions. In offshore winds, temporary anchorage may be had in numerous sandy bays but these are very dangerous if the wind changes N'ly and wind changes are often sudden. There are several anchorages in Loch Eriboll but they may be subject to severe squalls. Advantage can be taken of the continuous N going eddy to E of Strathy Point, off which, the W going tide starts at Dover +0030. But beware of turbulent seas off the point in wind against tide conditions. E of Cape Wrath there is a live firing range extending 4M out to sea: contact Stornoway coastguard for firing times. Duslic Rock lies ¾M NE of Cape Wrath Lt Ho; it covers at half tide though it can usually be seen in the swell. In calm conditions it is possible to pass inside the rock where the tide is nearly always W'ly, keeping well towards the steep-to headland, otherwise give it and Cape Wrath a wide berth, especially if a heavy swell is running or if the wind is against swell or tide.

Wick to E coast of Orkney No special problems – keep at least 6M E of Pentland Skerries.

Wick to Scapa Flow Reach a point 1M NE of Duncansby Head at Dover +0300 (nearly slack water) then make good a course of 001° to the W coast of S Ronaldsay. This goes across the tidal streams. If wind is in the W the passage can be safely made if less than Force 4.

Scrabster to W coast of Orkney and Stromness This passage avoids the Firth. Time departure to arrive at Sound of Hoy at slack water (Dover +0530).

Scrabster to Scapa Flow Time departure to arrive off Dunnet Hd at Dover –0600. Make good a course for a point about 1M S of Tor Ness – a strong favourable tide will then take you past Brims Point, round Cantick Head and E of Switha into Scapa Flow.

Scrabster to E coast of Orkney This is a fast passage, do not attempt with E'ly winds over Force 3. Time departure to arrive off Dunnet Head at Dover +0530. Pass between Swona and Stroma. Constant updating of position is required to avoid being swept onto the islands or the Pentland Skerries. One should round Old Head by Dover –0330, when the tide turns and overfalls occur.

For more details and other possible passages consult the *CCC Sailing Directions*.

Entrance Steer for W pier-head (Oc.R.6s occas) on 330°. Do not stray E of ldg line, rear mark W pole with W topmark above white painted square, front mark R pole with R topmark near LH. Keep up to W pier; beware set onto rocks and first pier to stb.

Berthing In outer harbour on innermost end of W pier using fender plank or in SE corner of inner basin (W part dries).

E or S side of inner basin 1·8m MLWS but only 1·0m at entrance to basin.

Facilities Showers, laundry, key from café. Hotel, stores ½M. EC Thursday.

WICK

Standard Port Wick

The hbr, at the head of Wick Bay 2½M S of Noss Head, consists of three basins. The Inner and Outer Harbours are the main fishing and leisure berths, and the River Harbour is the commercial area which must be avoided. It is an ideal port of departure for the Northern Isles or for timing a passage through strong tides of the Pentland Firth.

Approach and Entrance
Dangerous in strong winds between NE and S; heavy seas run into the bay. Hbr obscured until bay fully opened up. Both shores of Wick Bay are foul. Approach on 289°, DirIso.WRG.4s. Then steer for LtHo on S pier (W tr, Fl.WRG.3s) on 270°–285°, i.e. in the W sector. Port Closed Signal: a black ball is hoisted by day, or a fixed Green light shown by night, on a prominent mast at South Head. Pass close N of pierhead and keep along N face (Ldg Lts F.R.234°).

Berthing Visitors should contact *Wick Harbour* by VHF (office hours) or telephone before arrival. Berth as directed, normally on pontoon F. Outside office hours you will be given the security code by telephone.

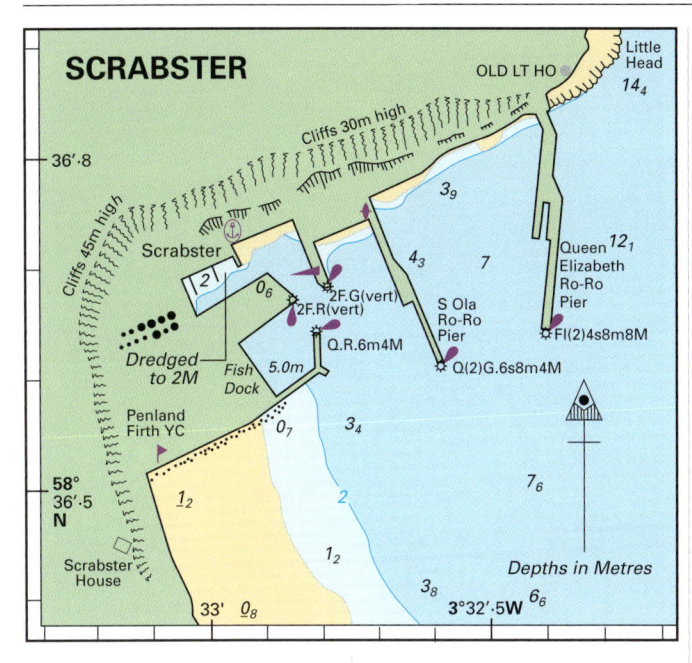

Facilities Electricity and water on pontoons. Showers. Launderette. WiFi. Nearby supermarket. Rly to Inverness. Airport.

☎/VHF HM 01955 602030 VHF 14/16 (office hours or when vessel expected).

SCRABSTER

Standard Port Wick
HW (sp) –0255 (np) –0225
LW (sp) –0230 (np) –0240
MHWS MHWN MLWN MLWS
+1·5m +1·2m +0·8m +0·3m

Hbr can be entered at all states of tide; complete shelter. It is used by Orkney Ro-Ro ferry, coasters and fishing vessels, and increasingly by service vessels to the oil and renewable energy industry. It is essential to call *Scrabster Harbour* VHF 12 for berthing instructions before entry. Berthing usually in the Inner Harbour, either pontoon berths may be available or moor against south wall. www.scrabster.co.uk has the latest information.

Facilities Restaurant. No provisions. Water, diesel. Shops in Thurso, two miles. Bus.

☎/VHF HM 01847 892779. VHF 12/16 (24hr); radio contact poor from N and W until clear of Holborn Head.

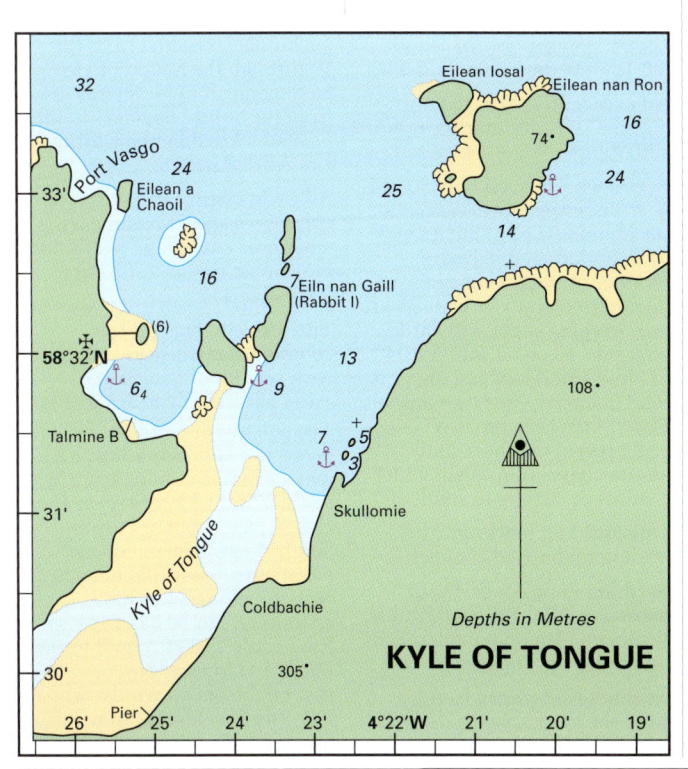

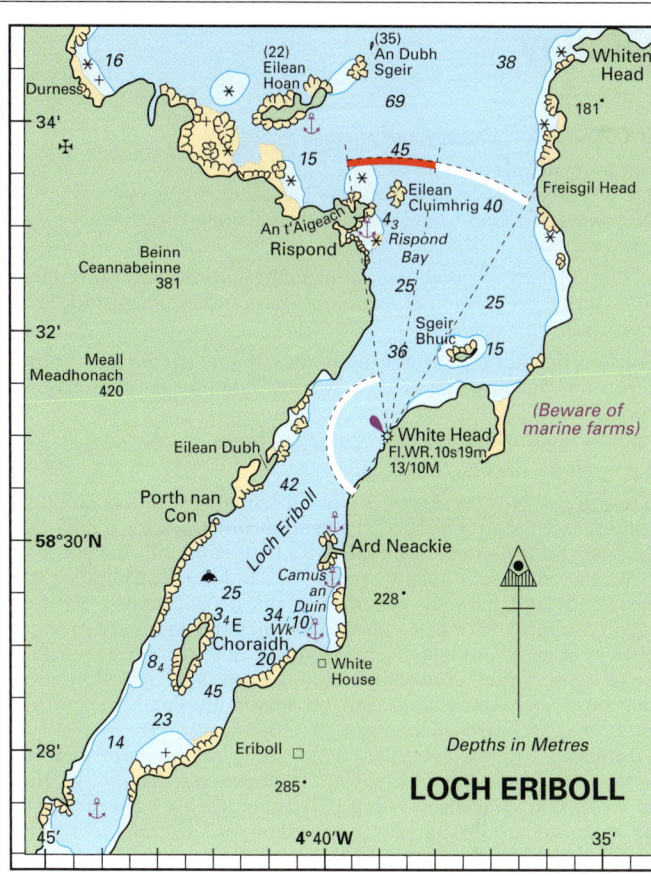

KYLE OF TONGUE

Standard Port Wick
HW –0350   LW –0315
MHWS MHWN MLWN MLWS
+1·1m +0·7m +0·4m –0·1m

The Kyle of Tongue contains a number of sheltered anchorages but entry during gales or strong N'lies is not recommended.

Anchorages
• Talmine, good protection except from N and E winds. Approach from N, but do not turn S until the W edge of the largest islet of Eiln nan Gaill (i.e. the westernmost) bears no less than 200°. Anchor in 5m S of small islet connected to shore by jetty. Sand. Shop 10 mins. Shelter from W and N in 5m off beach at S side of Eiln nan Gaill.
• Shelter from W and NW off Mol na Coinnle, a small bight on E of Eiln nan Ron. Anchorage is recognised by tin-roofed hut near foreshore. Uninhabited. Landing possible.
• On E side of Kyle just off small hbr of Skullomie. Entrance directly below house on hillside, best seen looking SE from Eiln nan Gaill. Keep well clear of broken wall to stb and towards E shore. Limited supplies at Coldbachie ½M.

LOCH ERIBOLL

Standard Port Wick
Portnancon
HW (sp) –0340 (np) –0255
LW (sp) –0255 (np) –0315
MHWS MHWN MLWN MLWS
+1·6m +1·3m +0·8m +0·4m

Loch Eriboll lies on W side of the high cliffs of Whiten Head. Funnelling produces extremely strong winds in SW'ly weather, when the entrance can be very rough; but good sheltered anchorages are available.

Anchorages
On E side
• In bays N and S of Ard Neackie, good shelter. N bay, pebbles and weed, holding reported as poor. S bay firm sand, good holding.
• In 7m off white house 1M to S. Fish farm cages extend S of Ard Neackie across whole of Camus an Duin. Pass N of cages and anchor inshore. (Fish Farm, VHF 14, helpful).
On W side
• Excellent anchorage in Rispond Bay, sand, but congested by fishing boat moorings.
• Admiralty buoy 4ca NNW of E Choraidh.
• In S of loch. Beware mussel farming; large buoys, long ropes.

Orkney

GENERAL

BA Tidal Atlas, Orkney and Shetland – NP209

For more details refer to:
CCC Orkney and Shetland Islands Including North and Northeast Scotland Clyde Cruising Club Sailing Directions (Imray 2016)

A vast amount of good passage planning information is available at www.orkneycommunities.co.uk/westraysc/documents/tide%20book.pdf

Anyone intending to cruise the islands should carry these sailing directions. Information given here is intended for passage-making boats.

Approaching from the E, Whitehall Harbour, (Stronsay) and Kirkwall are the best 'target' ports.

Though the Northern Isles provide fascinating cruising grounds, sailing here calls for particular attention to barometer trends and weather information. Essentially the flood runs SE and the ebb NW but there are many anomalies and back eddies round headlands and between the isles. In the main channels the tide changes approx Kirkwall +0100. Both tides and winds are stronger than in other UK waters: the avoidance of both wind-over-tide and swell-against-tide conditions take on special importance in entrances, between islands and off major headlands. There are numerous secluded anchorages. In Orkney there are marinas at Stromness, Kirkwall and Pierowall. Many islands have piers or jetties which may be used subject to commercial traffic, visitors mooring buoys are also available. Berthing fees are valid for use in all marinas/harbours, it may be advantageous to pay for a week rather than individual days.

All yachts within Scapa Flow should monitor *Orkney VTS* on VHF 11.

See www.orkneymarinas.co.uk for latest details. This site has a link which provides very useful Sailing Notes.

Lobster pot markers are numerous. Mussel rafts and salmon farms abound in sheltered waters. Salmon farms are marked with Y buoys and flashing lights.

Orkney has probably the highest concentration of archaeological sites anywhere in NW Europe. It is famous for its settlements dating from the 4th or 3rd millennia BC, e.g. Skara Brae, its chambered tombs demonstrating engineering skill and ingenuity, many open to the casual visitor, and its standing stones such as the Ring of Brodgar. Many of these can be visited by sailing to a suitable anchorage and walking or hiring a bicycle.

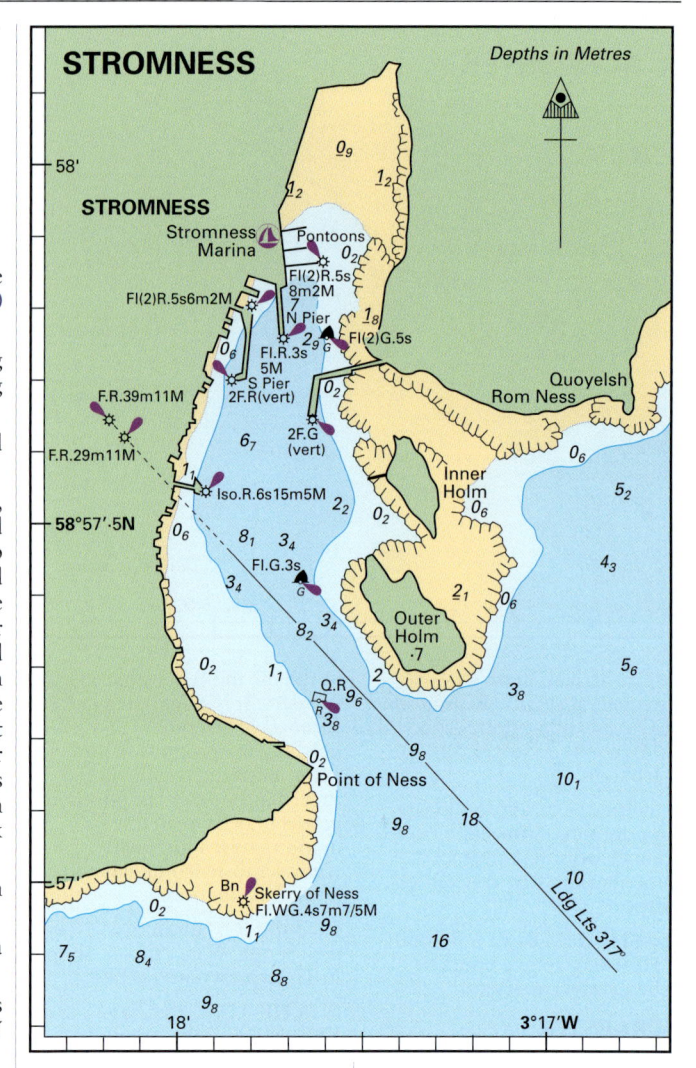

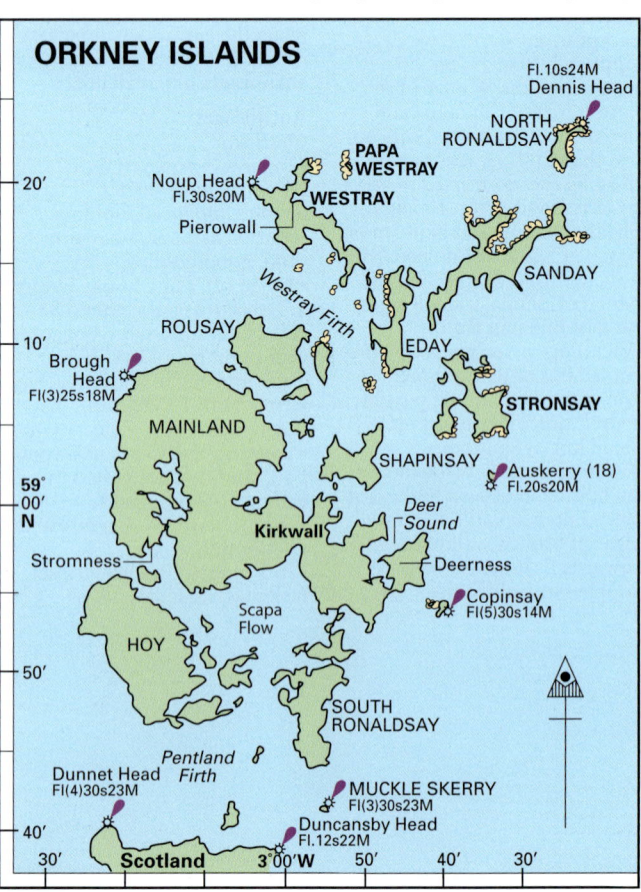

STROMNESS

Standard Port Wick
HW (sp) –0225 (np) –0135
LW (sp) –0205 (np) –0205

MHWS	MHWN	MLWN	MLWS
+0·1m	–0·1m	0·0m	0·0m

An excellently sheltered port; no tidal streams, marina at N end of bay.

Approach Through Hoy Sound or from Scapa Flow. Very strong tides in approaches, not to be undertaken in bad weather or with wind against tide. Easiest from W with flood tide, keeping slightly towards Hoy side. Keep on transit 104° of Hoy Sound low and high Lts (on Graemsay – *see plan Scapa Flow*), then keep bn Fl.WG.4s well open of the shore until abeam chapel ruins, then mid-channel or slightly to south.

Entrance Ldg marks lit 317° leading up buoyed channel.

Berthing Pontoon berths in marina to N of Ro-Ro terminal. Visitors >14m on hammerheads otherwise on S fingers.

Facilities Fuel, water, laundry, good shopping, cycle hire. WiFi.

☎/VHF Piermaster 01856 871313. Marina *Mobile* 07810 465825, VHF 14. *Stromness Harbour* VHF 14. *Orkney VTS* VHF 20 gives local weather forecast and *Notices to Mariners* at 0915 and 1715. *Orkney VTS* VHF 11.

SCAPA FLOW

An inland sea with many good anchorages, entered from the W through the Sound of Hoy, passing north of Graemsay, or from the South. Passages to the East are closed by the wartime Churchill Barriers.

All yachts with LOA>12m, on entering Scapa Flow or leaving a berth or anchorage within the Flow must report to *Orkney VTS* VHF 11.

The whole of Scapa Flow contains many historic wrecks with surrounding restricted areas particularly near Cava Is. The ebb out of Sound of Hoy is fierce; if conditions allow, it may be better, coming from W, to enter from S keeping very close to the shore of Hoy and South Walls. Lyness, former naval base, has 120m quay with 8m alongside. Good anchorage can be had between Rysa Little and Hoy, and to the north, in Howton Bay, sheltered from all winds. Scapa Pier (tug base) has 80m with 6m depth, but very exposed to the SW. St Mary's (small shop) is convenient for a visit to the Italian chapel on Lamb Holm. Long Hope, to the east of the narrows, is useful in order to ensure accurate timing for the Pentland Firth.

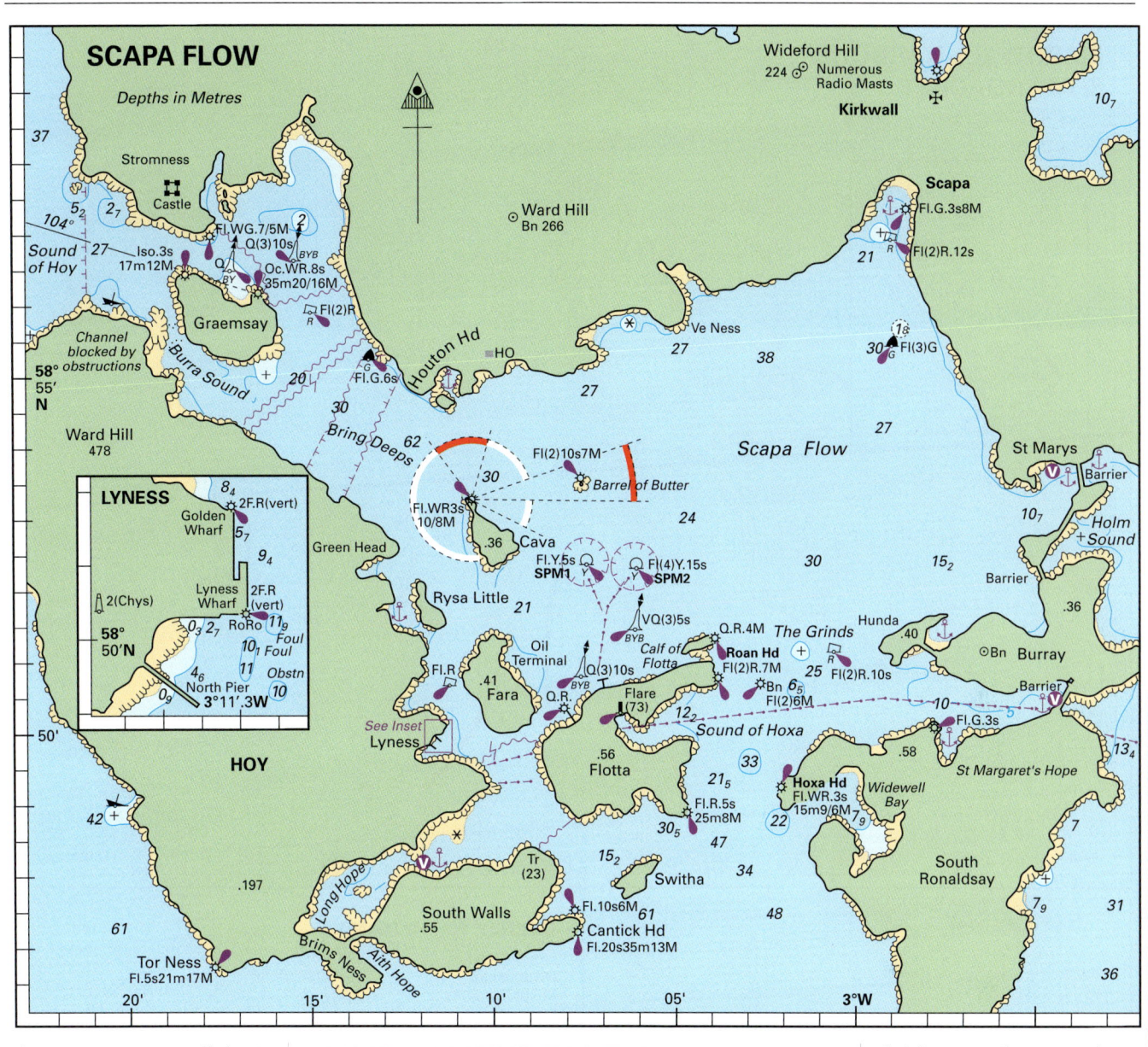

KIRKWALL
Standard Port Wick
HW −0042   LW −0041

MHWS	MHWN	MLWN	MLWS
−0·5m	−0·4m	−0·1m	−0·1m

Principal town of Orkney. Spire of cathedral conspic.

Approach Easiest from E through Shapinsay Sound, turning S when cathedral bears 190°. By night keep in W sectors of WRG Lts on Helliar Holm and outer pier-head. Tide negligible in Kirkwall Bay.

Berthing In marina to E of Ice Plant. Anchoring possible between W pier-head and Crow Ness Point to W but holding reported poor.

Facilities Most, fuel, no chandler. Showers at SC. WiFi.

☎/VHF Piermaster 01856 871313. Marina *Mobile* 07810 465835, VHF 14. HM 01856 873636, VHF 14 (office hours).

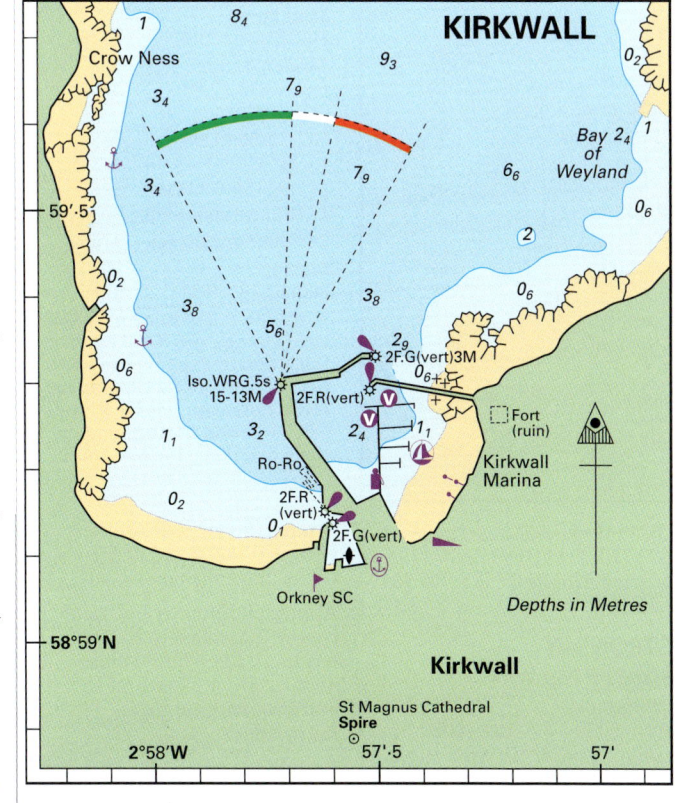

Elwick Bay on Shapinsay, clean sand but weed round edges, offers a peaceful alternative. Approach S and W of Helliar Holm LtHo and anchor in 2½ to 3m off village or use visitors' mooring. E side obstructed by fish farm.

PIEROWALL, WESTRAY
See plan p.134
Standard Port Wick
HW −0150   LW −0145

MHWS	MHWN	MLWN	MLWS
+0·2m	0·0m	0·0m	−0·1m

Pierowall Harbour at S end of Papa Sound between Westray and Papa Westray comprises a ferry pier with a marina at Gill Pt and anchorages at the head of the bay.

Approach From W and N via Papa Sound keep towards the Papa Westray shore. This entrance requires caution. A tide race forms rapidly at N end of Papa Sound as soon as ebb sets in. From S and E note that Skerry of Skelwick (off our plan) extends 6ca N from shore. White sector of Lt on Gill Pt leads in, 280°, but Lt is weak compared with nearby shore lights.

133

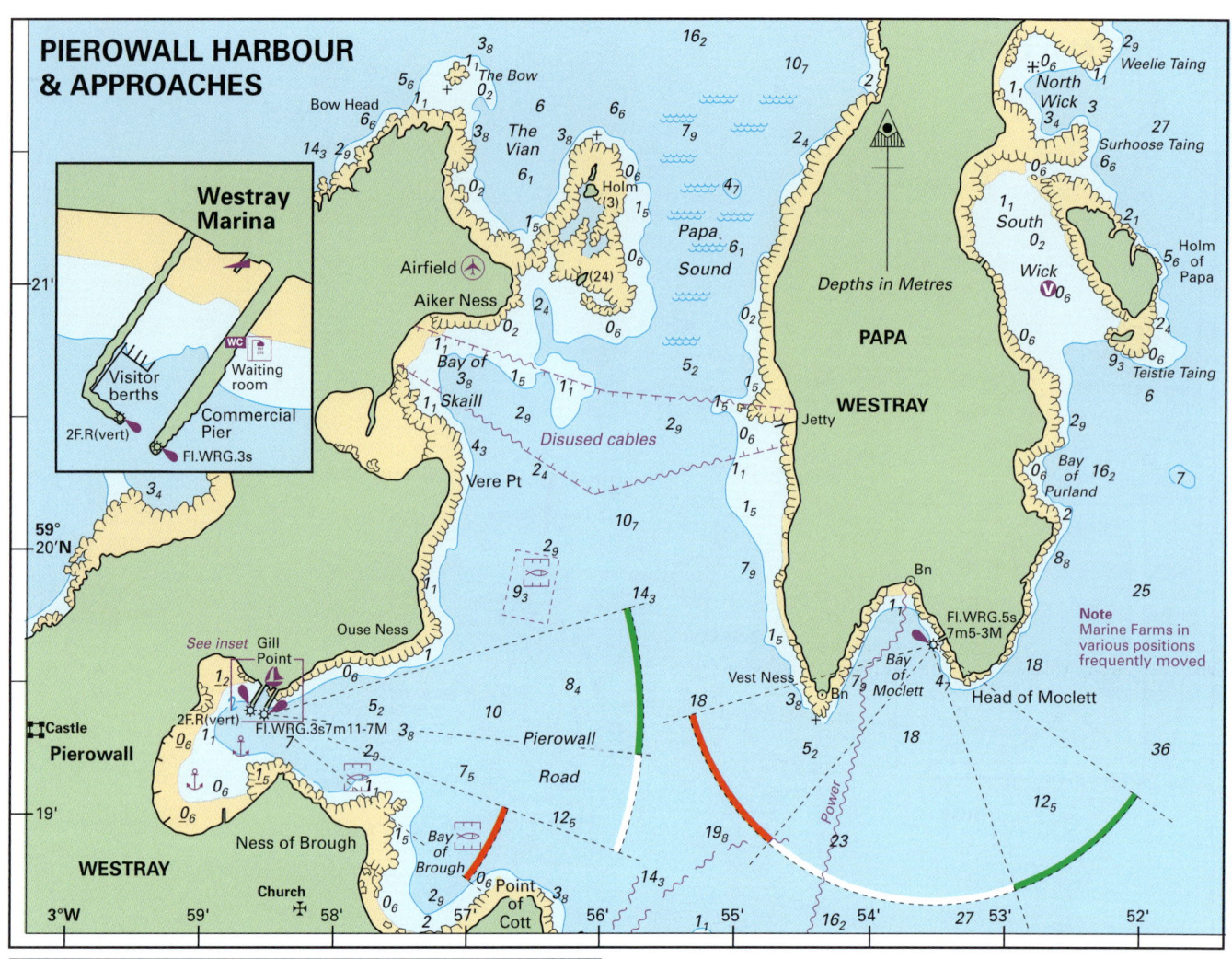

PIEROWALL HARBOUR & APPROACHES

STRONSAY

ORKNEY TO SHETLAND

Passage lights	BA No
Noup Head Fl.30s79m20M	3736
N Ronaldsay Fl.10s43m24M	3722
Start Point Fl(2)20s24m18M	3718
Skaden, Fair Is Fl(4)30s32m22M	3750
Skroo, Fair Is Fl(2)30s80m22M	3756
Foula Fl(3)W.15s36m18M	3860
Sumburgh Head Fl(3)30s91m23M AIS	3766
Bressay Fl(2)10s18m10M	3776

If making the passage from the W of Orkney, give Mull Head at the N end of Papa Westray a berth of 5M since a violent race forms here with tides reaching 6kn. From the North Sound or the E of Orkney the passage is much easier, with Fair Isle making a convenient port of call.

A traffic routing scheme specifies a westbound lane only to the north of Fair Isle, but both eastbound and westbound lanes between Fair Isle and N Ronaldsay.

The tides run generally NW and SE at up to 2kn apart from a race off the S end of Fair Isle and the notorious race off Sumburgh Head which should be given a berth of 3M. If proceeding round the heads from Lerwick to Scalloway the latter can be avoided by keeping close in to Sumburgh Head.

In poorer weather the best route from Westray, once clear of Orkney, is to make for Scalloway. This avoids the worst of the turbulence.

Berthing Pontoon berths (April–October) in small marina at Gill Pier.

Anchorage 50m off Gill Pier close to moorings in least depths 3·7m or on W side of bay in 1·8m.

Facilities Village on W shore of bay, shops, hotel. Diesel from ferry pier. Flights and ferry to Kirkwall.

☎/VHF Piermaster 01856 871313. HM 01857 677273. Marina *Mobile* 07515 397561. VHF 14.

STRONSAY

Standard Port Wick
Whitehall
HW –0030   LW –0028
MHWS MHWN MLWN MLWS
–0·1m 0·0m +0·2m +0·2m

Whitehall Harbour off the village at the N end of Stronsay offers good shelter.

Approach Enter by buoyed N channel, dredged to Ro-Ro terminal. Keep buoys close aboard. Do not attempt E entrance without local knowledge.

Berthing Secure along seaward end of W pier or on W side of E pier, clear of Ro-Ro berth and consult HM; or anchor in 3m between pier ends or elsewhere in bay.

Facilities Provisions. Showers in hostel. Hotel. Flights and ferry to Kirkwall.

☎ HM 01856 873636.

Shetland

For more details refer to: CCC *Orkney and Shetland Islands* or *Shetland Islands Pilot* Gordon Buchanan (Imray). It is useful to carry BA Tidal Atlas, Orkney and Shetland – NP209. There is useful information on www.shetlandmarinas.com and www.lerwick-harbour.co.uk/yachts. The passage ports covered here comprise Fair Isle; on the east Lerwick, the main port, and Balta Sound, Unst; on the west, Ura Firth (Hillswick), Vaila Sound (Walls) and Gruting Voe, and Scalloway. Grutness Voe on the E coast just N of Sumburgh provides a convenient first anchorage coming from the S. (Beware of two rocks awash at LW in entrance: enter with head of bay on 225° or less, or round S headland very close). Many small boat marinas have been built. Generally they are occupied by local boats but some have one or two visitors' berths, watch out for depth. Some have showers. Charge usually £10/day. Recommended are: Skeld 60°09′N 1°27′W, sheltered. Aith 60°17′N 1°22′W, good facilities, if too shallow use pier. Voe (Olna Firth) 60°21′N 1°16′W. Brae 60°24′N 1°22′W Delta Boating Club, laundry, small chandlery. Burra Voe (Yell), if too shallow use pier or anchor. Vidlin 60°22′N 1°08′W. In addition many piers may be used but don't obstruct ferries or local fishermen. There is a plentiful choice of anchorages, but beware of heavy loose weed; however, the water is usually clear enough to avoid this. Tides are strong around headlands where races, or 'rosts' occur; also, Yell Sound should be avoided in wind over tide conditions.

It is best to stock up with provisions and fuel at either Lerwick or Scalloway. The islands are rich in archaeology, notably near Grutness Voe, the Iron Age village at Old Scratness, and Jarlshof, believed to have been inhabited for more than 4,200 years; also the best broch to be found anywhere is on the island of Mousa. The Shetland Isles are one of the last wilderness areas in Europe and are noted for their wildlife; the coastline is probably more dramatic than that of Orkney.

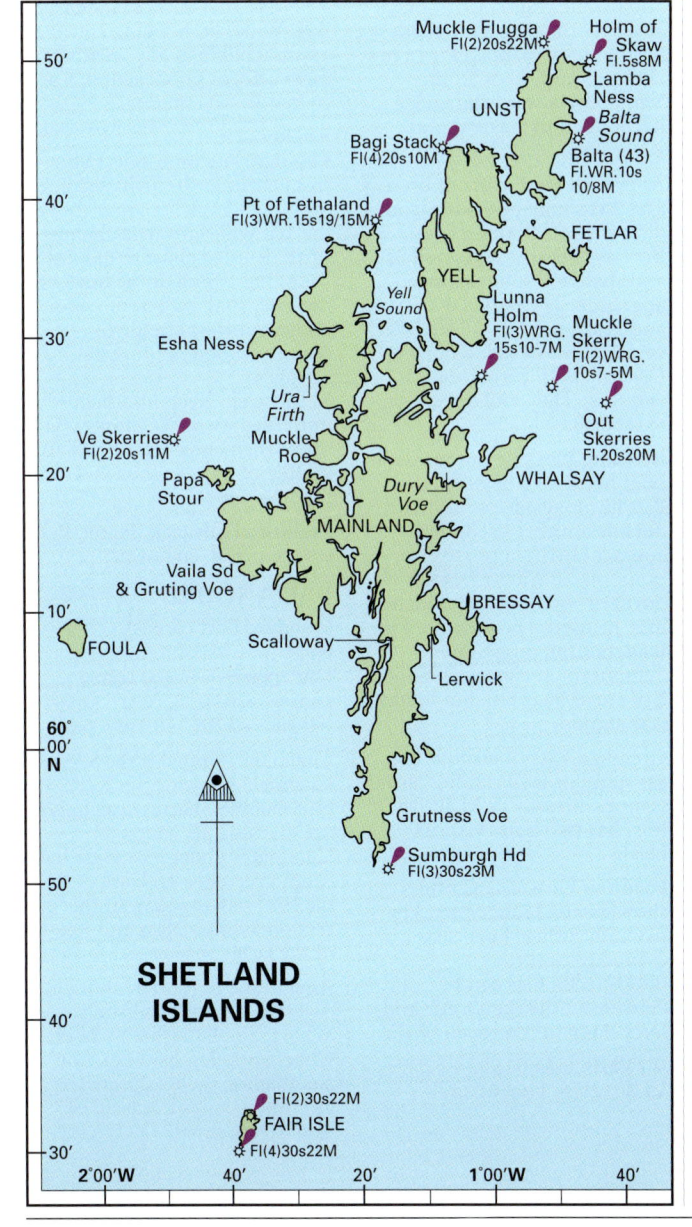

FAIR ISLE

Standard Port Lerwick

HW (sp) –0006 (np) –0015
LW (sp) –0037 (np) –0031

MHWS	MHWN	MLWN	MLWS
+0·1m	0·0m	+0·1m	+0·1m

The secure anchorage of North Haven on the NE side offers a useful half-way stop between Orkney and the main islands of Shetland, apart from its particular charm and ornithological interest.

Both South Haven and South Harbour are full of rocks and should be avoided except with detailed local knowledge.

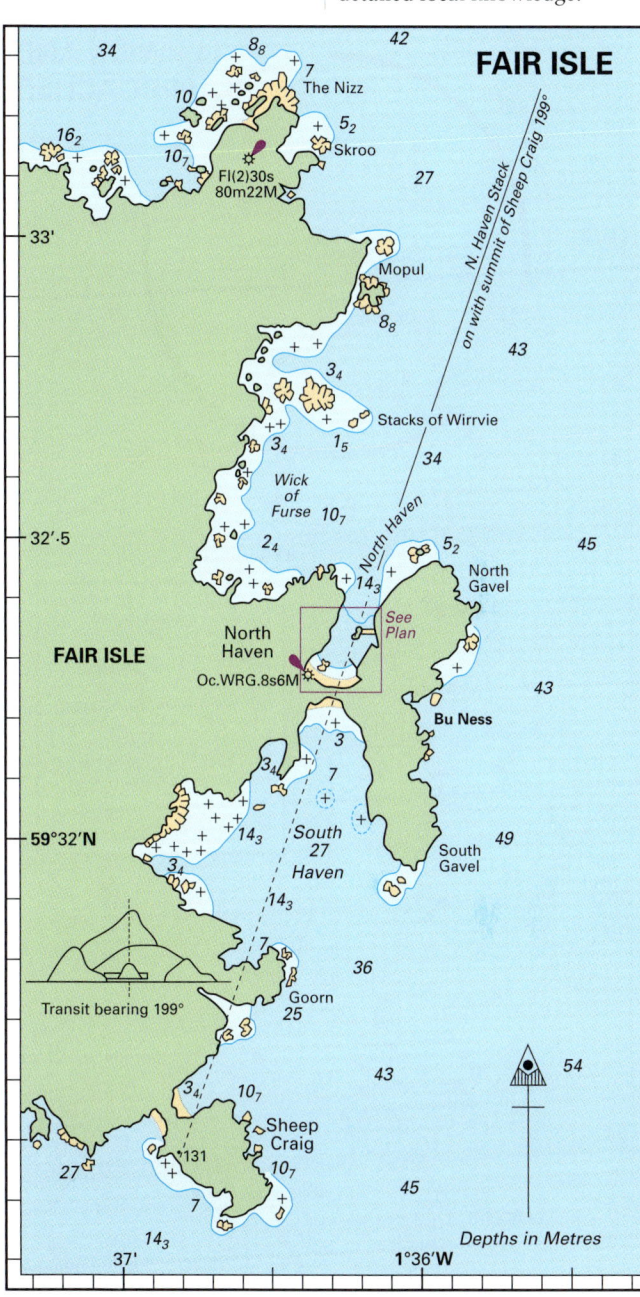

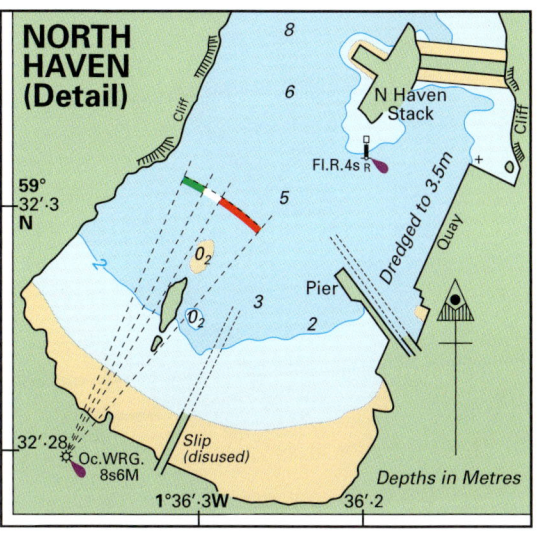

The Cruising Almanac

N Haven is uncomfortable in strong NE winds but usually tenable in summer. Enter on 199° keeping N Haven Stack on with summit of Sheep Craig behind. Keep W of Stack now incorporated in rock breakwater. Night entry in white sector of Oc light.

Berthing at quay on port hand inside (N end is used by ferry) or S side of pier.

Facilities Showers and meals at Bird Observatory. Shop 1½M. Water on quay. Large fenders are available on the quay for use by visitors.

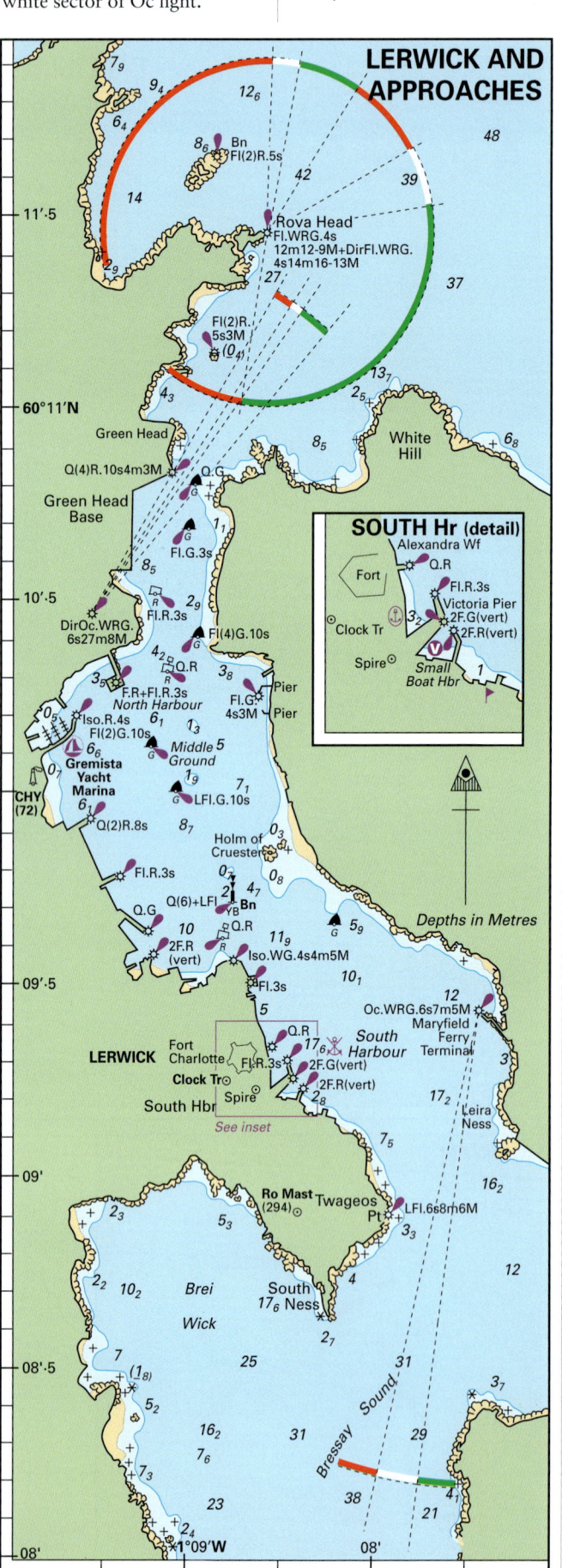

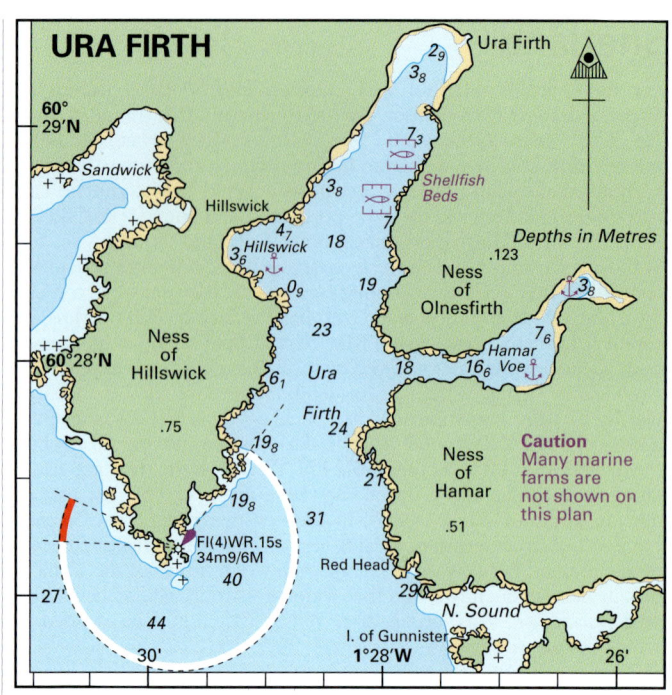

LERWICK

Standard Port Lerwick

The capital of the Shetland Isles. A busy hbr with considerable oil, commercial and fishing traffic. Convenient and easy to enter with good berthing for yachts. Hbr of first choice bound to or from Scandinavia. www.lerwick-harbour.co.uk has a useful yacht pack.

Approach High cliffs in Bressay and Noss may be visible from a long way off. Entry S of Bressay is easier, with well lit and sheltered funnel-shaped approach. N channel is narrow and much used by oil rig vessels. Call *Lerwick Port Control* VHF 12 before entering. They will direct you to a berth.

Berthing Variable but in small boat hbr on S side of Victoria Pier lie alongside pontoon or outside another yacht and contact HM. There are also pontoons in Albert Dock, north of Victoria Pier, which may be used if not required by tenders from cruise liners. Temporary anchorage possible S of small boat hbr, but holding is not good.

Gremista Yacht Harbour has NO space or facilities for casual visitors. Bressay (½M across hbr) has two quiet visitors' berths.

Facilities Lerwick BC offers showers and launderette, key from hbr office. Fuel (Monday–Saturday) 0900–1630. Gas can be delivered. All repairs. Air and ferry daily to Aberdeen. WiFi.

☎/**VHF** HM 01595 692991, VHF 12/16. Fuel 692379.

URA FIRTH

Standard Port Lerwick
HW –0220 (approx)

MHWS	MHWN	MLWN	MLWS
–0·1m	–0·1m	–0·1m	–0·1m

At NE corner of St Magnus Bay. Wide, lit, S-facing entrance approachable in any weather. Firth affords good shelter. Keep to middle on entering.

Anchorages
- Hamar Voe on E side 1M in from entrance to firth. Anchor in 4–10m anywhere just above the 1ca wide entrance channel. With detailed chart or careful sounding a pool at the head of the Voe, shallow but no hidden dangers, offers complete security. Good holding but no supplies.
- Hillswick. Keep mid-firth until the bay on W shore is well open, then enter steering W for middle of bay. Anchor in 4–6m, holding poor.

Facilities Hillswick. Hotel, PO, stores, diesel, engineer.

BALTA SOUND

Standard Port Lerwick
Pier
HW –0043   LW –0043

MHWS	MLWN	MLWN	MLWS
+0·3m	+0·2m	+0·1m	0·0m

The main channel is the S Channel, 3ca wide, lit. Keep in mid-channel. Heavy seas build up in strong SE winds. N Channel is under ½ca wide but deep: keep close to Unst shore on 209° passing ½ca off the reef on Swinna Ness and ½ca E of the G bn.

Anchorage Best off N shore in 4–8m just W of Sandison's Wharf. Small marina to W of wharf with depths 0·6m, not suitable for yachts. Elsewhere as wind dictates but head of Voe is very shoal.

BALTA SOUND

(chart of Balta Sound, Unst, Shetland)

SCALLOWAY APPROACHES

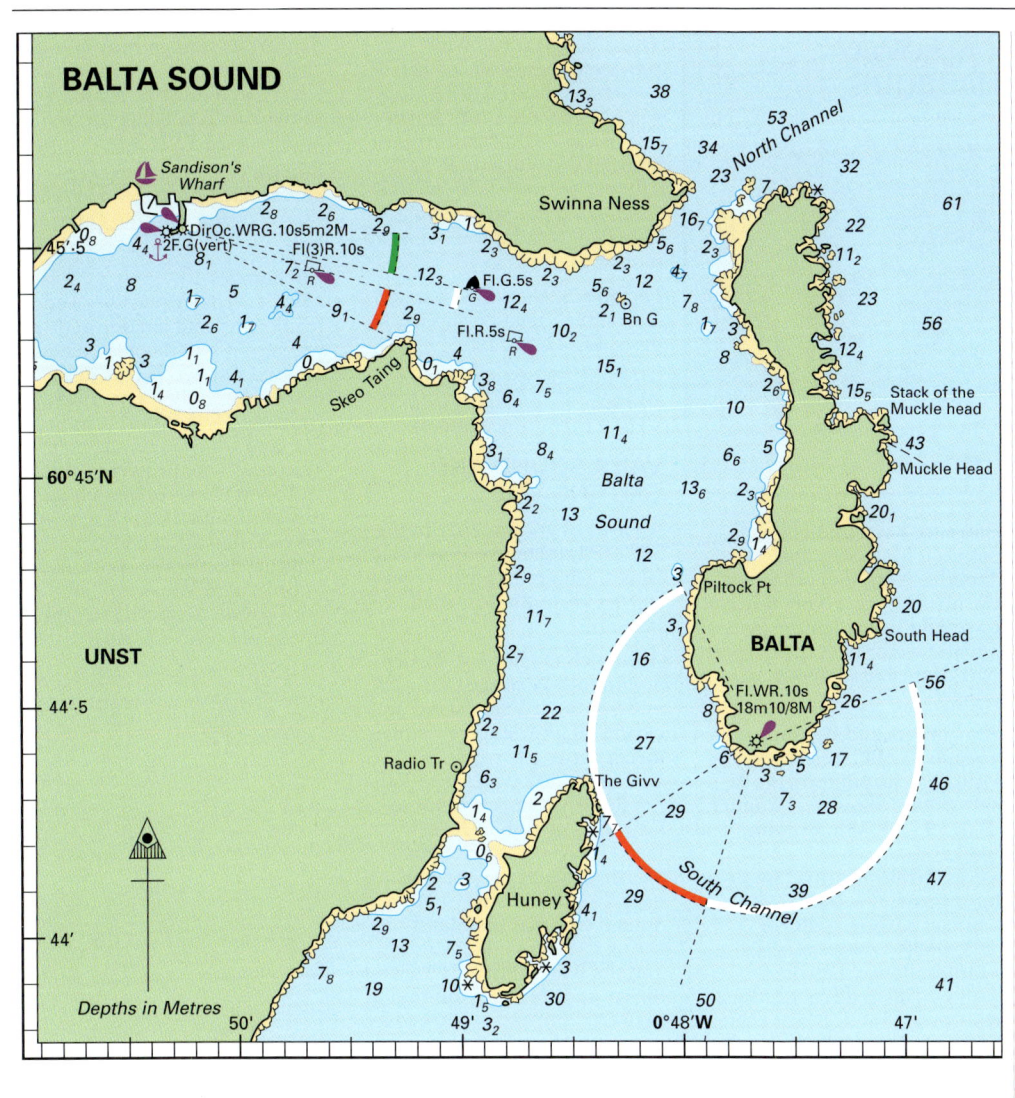

(chart of Scalloway approaches with Hogg of Hildasay, Linga, Langa, Papa, Oxna, Trondra, Fugla Ness, etc.)

Facilities Water, diesel, boatyard, hotel, shop. PO ¼M. Boat museum.

SCALLOWAY

Standard Port Lerwick

Pier

HW −0150	LW −0150
MHWS	MHWN	MLWN	MLWS
−0·5m	−0·4m	−0·3m	0·0m

A convenient port of arrival from S and W with sheltered anchorage on W coast of mainland. Hbr protected by numerous islands. Entry should be possible in all weathers, but great care needed in strong SW winds.

Approach Of the two approaches, the North Channel is the easier and safer.

North Channel Enter between Hildasay Island and Sanda Stour keeping in mid-channel to avoid the dangerous rock close north of Hildasay. Pass between Burwick Holm and Langa keeping 2ca off Langa to avoid the fish farm on the island's E side, and then keep 1ca off Point of the Pund to clear the drying Whaleback Skerry to stb.

South Channel Enter between Fugla Ness and Bulia Skerry. Keep the Fugla Ness light between 032° and 082° in the W sector.

Note the two dangers, Bulia Skerry and Helia Baa, which can cause heavy breaking seas across the entrance during

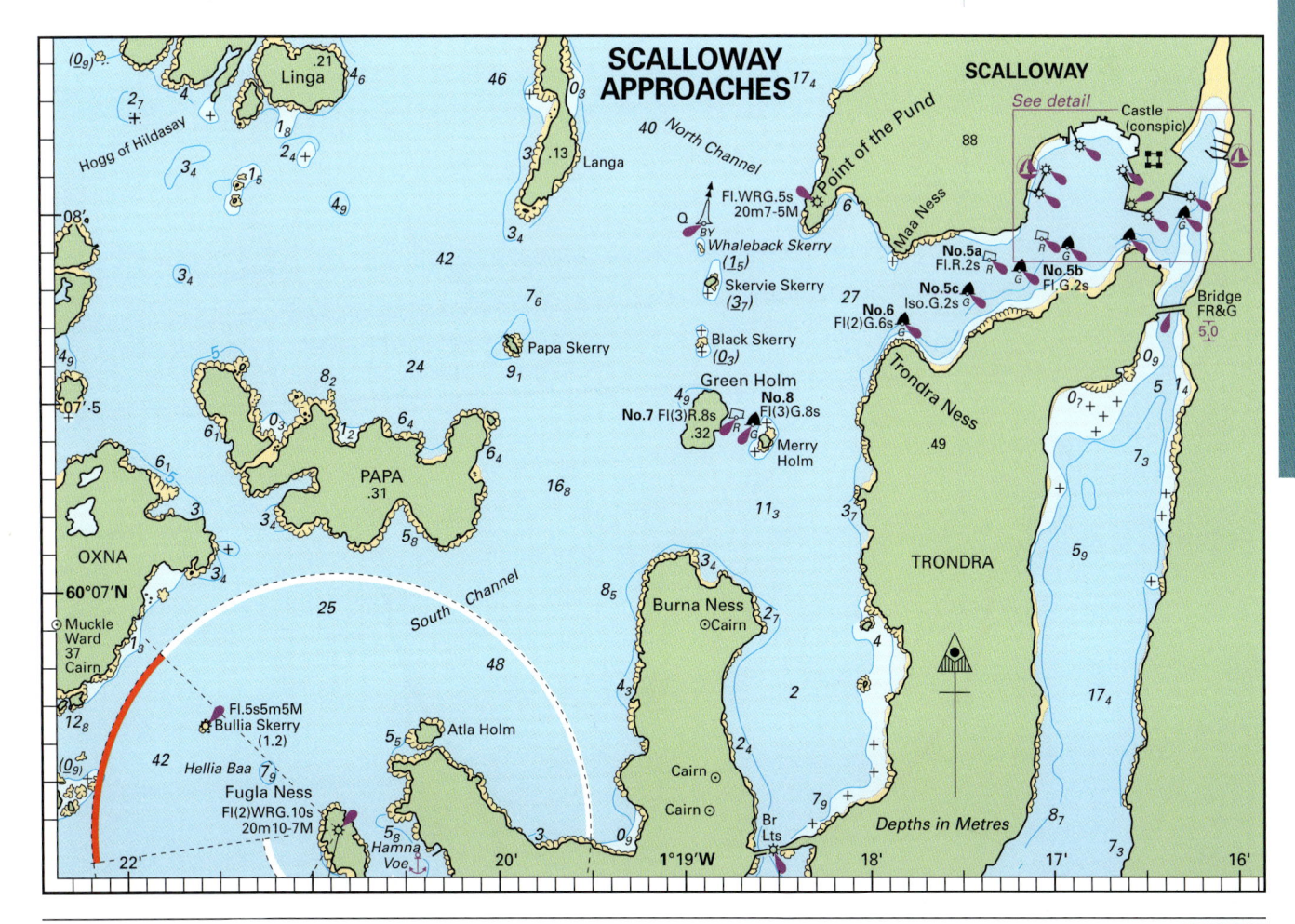

SCOTLAND – EAST AND NORTH COASTS

137

The Cruising Almanac

SCALLOWAY HARBOUR

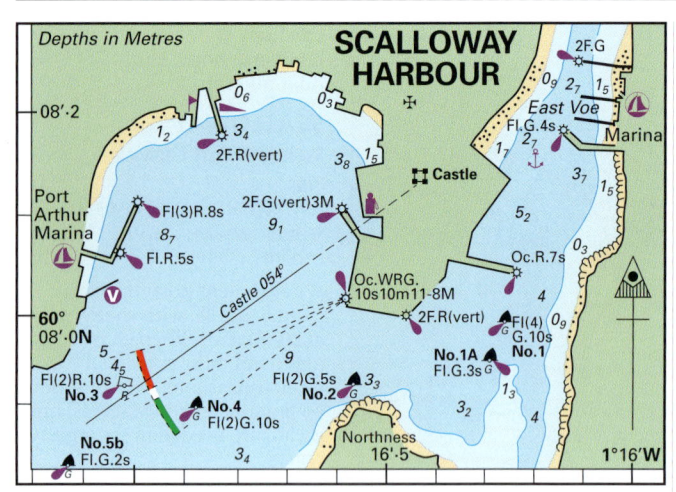

southwesterly gales. At such times the South Channel is not recommended.

From a position between the two dangers bring Scalloway Castle just open N of Trondra Ness on 054° and pass either between Green Holm and Merry Holm, leaving Green Holm close to port, or turn N to enter N of Whaleback Skerry.

At night LtHos on N Havra Fl(3)WRG.12s and Point of Pund (Fl.WRG.5s) provide easy night-time access via North Channel. For South Channel approach Fugla Ness light in SW'ly white sector to 1½ca and round the point northwards to anchor in Hamna Voe and wait for daylight.

Entrance Keep mid-channel between Maa Ness and Trondra Ness, thence follow the hbr buoyage. Note that a day/night sector light provides a white sector over the deepest part of the bar in depths of 6·6m.

Anchorages and Berthing
- Scalloway BC welcomes visitors to its pontoon on W side of hbr. Showers, Laundry. ☎ 01595 880388 (evenings and weekends).
- Port Arthur Marina. Small local boats, few free berths. Contact Scalloway BC or ☎ 880649.
- Off Scalloway between Gallow Hill and Blacks Ness, 6–10m soft mud. Better shelter in W winds E of the castle.
- East Voe Marina. Well protected. Few visitors' berths by arrangement. ☎ 880476.
- In Hamna Voe on W Burra just inside Fugla Ness. Almost land-locked and safe in bad summer weather (*also night – see above*); but busy fishing hbr, crowded, bottom foul with old moorings.

Facilities Scalloway – water, stores, fuel, repairs, slip, crane, diver. EC Thursday.

☎/VHF Piermaster 01595 744221, *Scalloway Harbour* VHF 12, 16 (office hours).

VAILA SOUND AND GRUTING VOE

An area of good shelter to the SW of Mainland behind Vaila Island. Choice of anchorages to suit wind conditions, mud bottom.

Approach Do not use Wester Sound to NW of the island. W and S sides of Vaila Island are clean and any dangers visible; give E shore a berth of ½ca. Easter Sound divides into Vaila Sound to W, and entrance to Gruting Voe to E of Ram's Head (WRG sectored light). Northwards of the narrows keep 1½ca off E side of Vaila Sound, towards the island shore, to clear Galta Skerry, and the Baa of Linga. The Skerry runs NNW from the eastern shore and is marked by a concrete bn; the Baa, a dangerous sunken rock in mid-channel, lies 2ca NW of the Skerry, and must be passed well to the East if heading for Walls at the top of Vaila Voe.

Entering Gruting Voe keep course 055° or less and favour the West shore. Callie Taing is foul.

Anchorages
- Walls. From Vaila Voe head for the pier and anchor midway between it and the post. There are two visitors' berths in the marina but only for small craft; contact 01595 809311. Shop, PO, and showers on the pier.
- Gruting Voe. Browland, Seli and Scutta Voes offer a choice of anchorages. (Olas Voe is very shallow.) Keep to N entering Scutta Voe. Entrance to Browland Voe is foul on both hands, keep mid-stream but rather nearer N side.

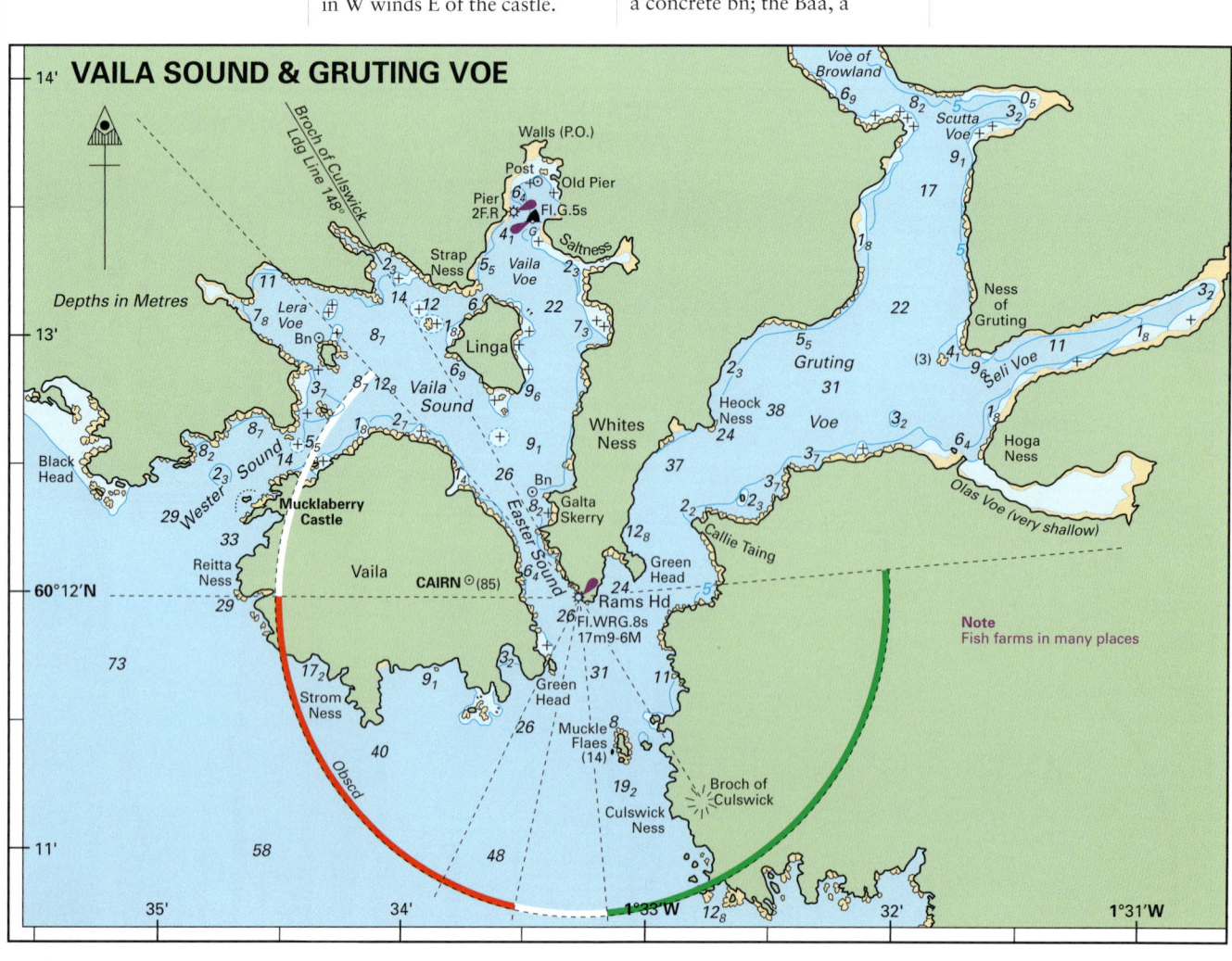

VAILA SOUND & GRUTING VOE

SCOTLAND – EAST AND NORTH COASTS

138

15 reasons why you should be part of the Cruising Association

— as well as the fact that we work with Imray to produce this Cruising Almanac:
we do the words, they do the pictures

A wealth of information – the world's best cruising library and a member-only web site wiith thousands of web pages

Friends afloat and ashore – 20 local and sea-area groups meeting regularly

The chance to learn – lectures, seminars, training around the UK

Make your budget go further – a long list of suppliers offer you significant discounts: many members save more than the cost of membership every year

A London home – affordable guest cabins at CA House when you're visiting the UK capital

Crew finding – our crewing service puts skippers in touch with crew, and crew in touch with skippers

In-port help – you'll be able to call on almost 250 CA special representatives in ports around the UK, Europe and the world

Rallies – from in-port meets to extended cruises in company

Exclusive publications – things like cruising area guides, lay-up directories and a quarterly magazine

Online advice – general, specialist and geographical forums, with help offered by known, named and trusted contributors

Influence – we're invited by the authorities to consult widely on matters ranging from windfarms to colregs

Classified advertising – buy and sell between members: everything from charts to boats

Paperwork – advice on what you need to take when you go foreign

Cruise planning – all the latest planning and navigation software available on PCs in our library

Don't just join, join in – we're volunteer-run; there's always the opportunity for you to contribute to the wider cruising community

CAptain's Mate – that's the app you see below. Absolutely up-to-date member-generated information from just about anywhere you can take a small boat

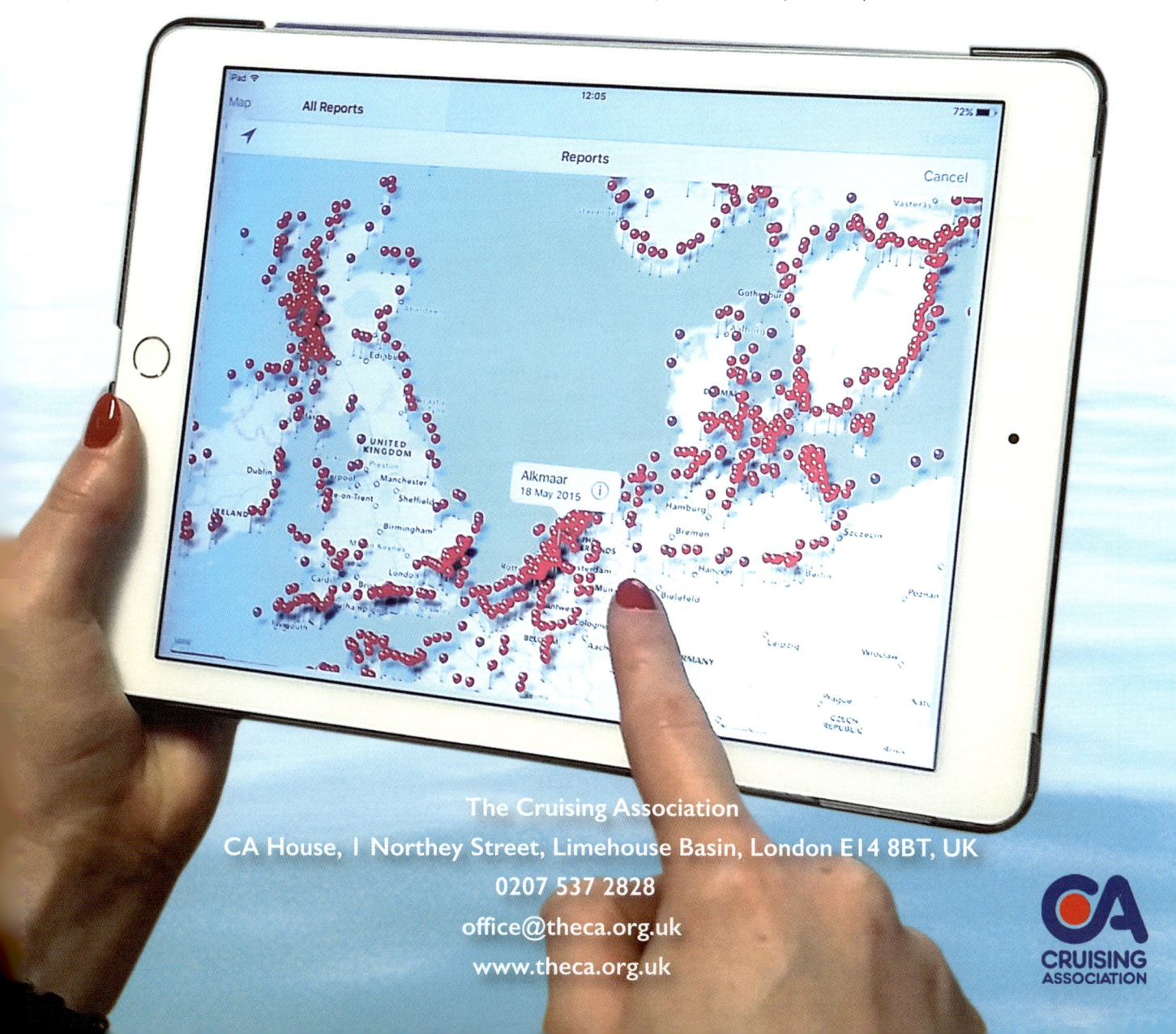

The Cruising Association
CA House, 1 Northey Street, Limehouse Basin, London E14 8BT, UK
0207 537 2828
office@theca.org.uk
www.theca.org.uk

CRUISING ASSOCIATION

The Cruising Almanac

SCOTLAND WEST COAST

Map locations (with page references):

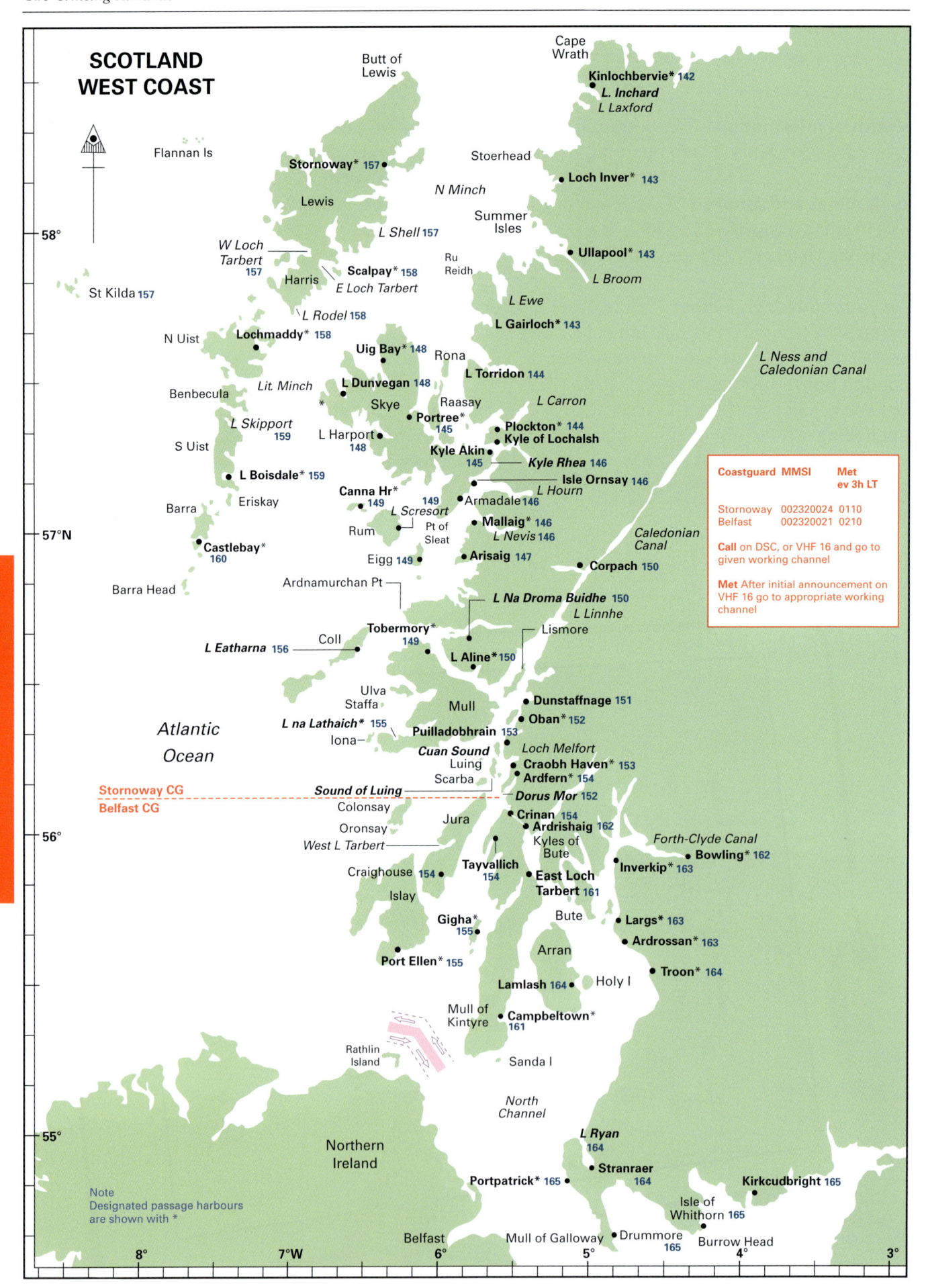

- Kinlochbervie* 142
- *L. Inchard*
- *L Laxford*
- Cape Wrath
- Butt of Lewis
- Flannan Is
- Stoerhead
- **Stornoway*** 157
- Lewis
- *N Minch*
- **Loch Inver*** 143
- *L Shell* 157
- Summer Isles
- *W Loch Tarbert* 157
- Harris
- **Scalpay*** 158
- *E Loch Tarbert*
- Ru Reidh
- **Ullapool*** 143
- *L Broom*
- St Kilda 157
- *L Rodel* 158
- *L Ewe*
- **Lochmaddy*** 158
- **L Gairloch*** 143
- N Uist
- **Uig Bay*** 148
- Rona
- *L Torridon* 144
- *L Ness and Caledonian Canal*
- Benbecula
- *Lit. Minch*
- **L Dunvegan** 148
- Skye
- Raasay
- *L Carron*
- **Portree*** 145
- **Plockton*** 144
- **Kyle of Lochalsh**
- *L Skipport* 159
- S Uist
- *L Harport* 148
- **Kyle Akin** 145
- ***Kyle Rhea*** 146
- **L Boisdale*** 159
- **Isle Ornsay** 146
- *L Hourn*
- **Canna Hr*** 149
- Armadale
- *L Sresort*
- **Mallaig*** 146
- Barra
- Eriskay
- Rum
- *L Nevis* 146
- **Castlebay*** 160
- Pt of Sleat
- **Arisaig** 147
- Eigg 149
- **Corpach** 150
- *Caledonian Canal*
- Barra Head
- Ardnamurchan Pt
- **L Na Droma Buidhe** 150
- *L Linnhe*
- **Tobermory*** 149
- Lismore
- Coll
- *L Eatharna* 156
- **L Aline*** 150
- Ulva
- Staffa
- Mull
- **Dunstaffnage** 151
- *Atlantic Ocean*
- **L na Lathaich*** 155
- **Oban*** 152
- Iona
- **Puilladobhrain** 153
- *Loch Melfort*
- *Cuan Sound*
- **Craobh Haven*** 153
- Luing
- **Ardfern*** 154
- Scarba
- Stornoway CG
- Belfast CG
- *Sound of Luing*
- **Dorus Mor** 152
- Colonsay
- **Crinan** 154
- Jura
- **Ardrishaig** 162
- *Forth-Clyde Canal*
- Oronsay
- *Kyles of Bute*
- **Bowling*** 162
- *West L Tarbert*
- **Tayvallich** 154
- **Inverkip*** 163
- Craighouse 154
- **East Loch Tarbert** 161
- Islay
- Bute
- **Largs*** 163
- **Gigha*** 155
- Arran
- **Ardrossan*** 163
- **Port Ellen*** 155
- **Troon*** 164
- **Lamlash** 164
- Holy I
- Mull of Kintyre
- **Campbeltown*** 161
- Rathlin Island
- Sanda I
- *North Channel*
- Northern Ireland
- *L Ryan* 164
- **Portpatrick*** 165
- **Stranraer** 164
- **Kirkcudbright** 165
- Belfast
- Mull of Galloway
- Isle of Whithorn 165
- **Drummore** 165
- Burrow Head

Coastguard	MMSI	Met ev 3h LT
Stornoway	002320024	0110
Belfast	002320021	0210

Call on DSC, or VHF 16 and go to given working channel

Met After initial announcement on VHF 16 go to appropriate working channel

Note: Designated passage harbours are shown with *

Page references are shown after locations, for example: **Oban** 152. Bold type indicates that it is accompanied by a plan. *Italics* are used for rivers, lochs, bays, seas etc.

Scotland – West Coast

The West Coast of Scotland offers yachtsmen possibly the finest cruising area in Europe, with thousands of miles of highly scenic coastline, hundreds of secluded anchorages and extensive protected sailing waters. Some of the coast exposed to the W and N may suffer severe conditions with strong onshore winds and yachts sailing in these waters must be well found and crewed. However much of the more popular cruising is either protected by offshore islands or in sea lochs that extend many miles inland.

During the summer months the average wind strength is about the same as in the English Channel and there are marginally fewer gales. However the weather can change quickly and yachts must be prepared to clear out from some anchorages at short notice if the wind becomes on-shore. In the lee of high hills and mountains squally katabatic winds may be at least two forces greater than those prevailing in open waters. Fog is rare but misty conditions with visibility down to 1·0M is not uncommon. The best weather can usually be had from mid May to mid July. During this period there is the added bonus of few hours of darkness so that night sailing is seldom necessary.

The flood tide flows mainly N and W. The streams may be strong with associated overfalls off prominent headlands and in some of the sounds between the islands. Details are given in each section. Elsewhere the tidal streams are relatively weak. The tidal range varies from 0·3m at Islay to 4·9m at N Uist and is still more varied S of the Mull of Galloway.

Navigational aids are thinly spread and many harbours are unlit. GPS navigational system operates well in the area but with strong tides transits can be useful. Many large scale charts in this area are still on the old datum but give the correction to be applied to plot a satellite derived position (less than 0'·08).

The Navy notifies the sea areas in which submarines will be operating (*Subfacts*) by giving names which roughly correspond with a geographical name in the area. Details of *Subfacts/Gunfacts* are available twice daily at the end of the MSI (met) broadcast by Stornoway Coastguard at 0710 and 1910 LT and by Belfast Coastguard at 0810 and 2010 LT. Guard ships fly International Code flags NESS. Submarines monitor VHF 16 and may hear engines and depth sounders. Low-level lights are more easily seen by periscopes at night.

It would be impractical to give details in this almanac of all the numerous harbours and anchorages available. Some 34 harbours have been selected as Passage Harbours and are marked by *. These offer good access, secure anchorages, some facilities and are usually lit. Plans and pilotage information are provided for each. In addition a further 30 secondary harbours, suggested by members of the CA, are listed with pilotage information, 11 of which have plans. There are also plans of three passages with strong tides. As the West Coast of Scotland does not neatly fit into a coastline this information together with passage and tidal notes is given in the four separate sections listed below:

A. Mainland coast from Cape Wrath to Ardnamurchan Point together with Skye, Canna and Rhum

B. Mainland coast from Ardnamurchan Point to Mull of Kintyre including Inner Hebrides S of Ardnamurchan

C. The Outer Hebrides

D. The Firth of Clyde and the S Galloway coast

Any yacht cruising on the W coast of Scotland should carry the relevant volumes of the Clyde Cruising Club *Sailing Directions* (CCCSD) incorporating Martin Lawrence's *The Yachtsman's Pilots to the West Coast of Scotland* (Imray). These with the

A. Cape Wrath to Ardnamurchan Point

CAPE WRATH TO KYLE AKIN

Passage lights	BA No
Cape Wrath	3880
Fl(4)30s122m22M AIS	
Stoer Head	3882
Fl.15s59m24M	
Ru Reidh (Re)	3900
Fl(4)15s37m24M AIS	
Rona (NE Point)	3904
Fl.12s69m19M	

The coast from Cape Wrath to Ru Reidh (Re) is exposed to the W and in heavy weather big and dangerous seas build up particularly off the headlands of Stoerhead and Ru Re. There are many offshore rks and islets which make running for shelter hazardous. S of Ru Re some shelter is provided by Skye and the passage through the Inner Sound E of Rona and Raasay is free from hidden dangers. The passage down the E coast of Skye through the Sounds of Raasay, Scalpay and Pabay presents a number of hazards. Drying and submerged rocks extend nearly 1M N of Rona. The Sound of Raasay is clear as far as its S end where it narrows and the channel is marked by buoys. Caolas Scalpay is obstructed by narrows which are shoal and is not recommended without a large-scale chart.

Tidal streams.
All related to Dover
Cape Wrath
–0530 N –0045S
Stoerhead
+0015N HWD S (2½kn)
Ru Reidh
+0430NE –0115SW (3kn)
Raasay Narrows
–0500N +0200 S (2kn)
Kyle Akin
–0015W +0345E (sp 3kn)
+0145W –0415E (np 1½kn)

West coast of Scotland distances (miles)

	Bangor	Canna Harbour	Cape Wrath	Castle Bay	Corpach	Crinan	Croabh Haven	Kinlochbervie	Kyle of Lochalsh	Loch Boisdale	Lochinver	Loch Maddy	Mull of Kintyre	Oban	Plockton	Port Ellen	Portree	Stornoway	Tobermory	Ullapool
Bangor	0																			
Canna Harbour	153	0																		
Cape Wrath	266	119	0																	
Castle Bay	162	36	135	0																
Corpach	138	75	185	96	0															
Crinan	89	72	182	92	52	0														
Croabh Haven	95	66	175	89	46	9	0													
Kinlochbervie	257	111	15	124	177	174	167	0												
Kyle of Lochalsh	178	40	91	75	94	91	85	82	0											
Loch Boisdale	170	28	119	21	96	93	88	108	67	0										
Lochinver	238	94	37	107	158	154	148	29	64	92	0									
Loch Maddy	193	41	93	48	115	113	107	86	64	31	70	0								
Mull of Kintyre	39	113	228	122	98	50	56	220	137	140	201	160	0							
Oban	109	54	164	91	30	23	17	155	73	75	137	96	69	0						
Plockton	185	48	92	83	102	99	93	83	8	76	64	64	146	81	0					
Port Ellen	64	100	218	109	89	40	46	210	126	122	191	150	24	59	134	0				
Portree	195	59	84	94	114	111	104	75	20	87	56	50	157	93	22	147	0			
Stornoway	230	77	53	90	152	153	146	47	61	74	37	49	191	135	62	178	50	0		
Tobermory	128	32	142	52	45	42	35	133	51	53	114	73	88	24	59	81	70	109	0	
Ullapool	236	92	54	106	155	152	146	48	61	90	28	69	198	134	62	189	54	44	112	0

appropriate medium-scale Admiralty charts will provide a basic minimum but large scale-charts where available are required in many areas, especially to gain access to the smaller anchorages. About 200 'unofficial' very large scale electronic charts are available at www.antarescharts.co.uk. If space on the bookshelf allows, the *Admiralty Pilot* contains a wealth of information.

The spelling of Gaelic names varies widely and may cause confusion. The following abbreviations are used in this section of the Cruising Almanac.

Ru = Rubha or rudha   A headland
En = Eilean   An island
Bo = Bogha   A dangerous rock

Many villages have a PO/shop for provisions. Early closing days are often ignored in the summer months especially in places where there is a supermarket. Calor Gas is generally obtainable but not in all areas. It is prudent to carry a spare cylinder. Camping Gaz is not readily available. Diesel can be obtained at marinas and at most fishing harbours but not always by hose.

Many anchorages are remote with no facilities. Yachts contemplating crew changes may need to use public transport. Scotrail runs regularly to some ports e.g. Kyle of Lochalsh/Plockton; Mallaig; Oban and ports in the Firth of Clyde. There is a wide ranging bus network. The Scottish Tourist Board at Edinburgh, ☎ 0131 332 2433 is very helpful. Yachts may be chartered from a number of centres.

Yacht marinas, though increasing in number, are still comparatively few except in the Clyde area. Apart from Dunstaffnage, there are none N of Oban. There are pontoons with some shoreside facilities at Loch Aline, Tobermory, Mallaig, Kyle Akin, Kyle of Lochalsh, Flowerdale, Loch Boisdale, Loch Maddy, Stornoway, Kinlochbervie and Loch Inver. Repair facilities and chandlers are concentrated in these areas and at some fishing harbours. *Welcome Anchorages* published by a consortium including The Crown Estate lists visitors' moorings and berths, it is available from many marine outlets. www.welcome-anchorages.co.uk is a useful website.

Visitors' buoys are usually large, blue and labelled to give the safe gross weight or length.

Owing to the presence of heavy weed in some areas, anchoring with a CQR or a Danforth may present difficulties and yachts are advised to carry a Fisherman, Bruce or modern high holding power anchor and chain of sufficient weight. Shallow draught yachts, and especially those that can take the ground, can often find a clean sandy bottom (visible at 7m) as well as added protection, by going well up into an anchorage. An extra scope of chain may also be advisable for deep water anchoring.

Caution In recent years there has been a huge growth in marine farming. Many popular anchorages are now partially occupied by fish farms, these are moved regularly and debris may be left on the seabed. Not all are shown on either Admiralty charts or plans in this Almanac. Basically there are two types of marine farm:

1. Those for fin fish e.g. salmon, consisting of large floating cages.
2. Those for shellfish, consisting of a series of long cables suspended from buoys, sometimes in a radial manner to which the shellfish attach themselves.

Both types of farm are usually marked by special yellow can buoys, occasionally lit.

KINLOCHBERVIE*, Loch Inchard

Standard Port Ullapool
HW +0019   LW +0015
MHWS MHWN MLWN MLWS
–0·4m –0·2m –0·1m +0·1m

A useful passage hbr for yachts rounding Cape Wrath.

Approach Entrance may be difficult to identify. Ru na Leacaig to N is bold and reddish with a W concrete Lt bn Fl(2)10s30m8M. There is a group of rocky islets to SW of entrance to Loch Inchard.

Entrance Contact harbourmaster before entry. Keep close to N shore to avoid Bo Ceann na Saile (3m). Kinlochbervie harbour is in a small inlet on N shore 1M E of Ru na Leacaig marked by DirWRG Lt. Narrow W sector 327° leads in. Dayglow Y framework tr and port and stb Lt bns, Fl.R.4s and Fl.G.4s, respectively. A back Lt at Creag Mhor DirIso.WRG.2s W sector 146·5°-147·5°.

Anchorages / Berthing
• Kinlochbervie. Berth on visitors' pontoon SE of ice factory.
• Rhiconich at head of loch. Shoals. Anchor according to depth. Fish farms may restrict anchoring.

Facilities Kinlochbervie: Diesel and water at pier. Water on pontoon. Chandlery. PO/shop, hotel. Rhiconich: PO, hotel. Bus to Lairg and rly to Inverness.

☎/VHF HM 01971 521235, *Mobile* 07901 514350; VHF 14.

LOCH LAXFORD

Standard Port Ullapool
HW +0015   LW +0005
MHWS MHWN MLWN MLWS
–0·3m –0·4m –0·2m 0·0m

A remote loch of easy access offering good shelter but no facilities.

Approach and Entrance Ru Ruadh the SW point of entrance is reddish. Keep N of islands off S shore of loch.

Anchorages
• Loch a Chadh-Fi. Beyond moorings of Adventure School. Pass W of En a Chadh-Fi.
• In bays behind islands off S shore. Beware fish farms.

Facilities None.

LOCH NEDD

Standard Port Ullapool
Tide times as Ullapool
MHWS MHWN MLWN MLWS
–0·3m –0·2m –0·2m 0·0m

A very attractive safe anchorage in wooded surroundings.

Approach and Entrance From the S side of Eddrachillis Bay. Identify Ru na Maoile Point and approach down the coast on the E side of the entrance. Beware a reef which dries on the W half of the entrance. Keep closer to E shore.

Anchorage Anchor in mud, good holding in SW corner of loch in 3·7m. Trip line advisable owing to many empty moorings.

Facilities PO/shop, hotel at Drumbeg 1½M.

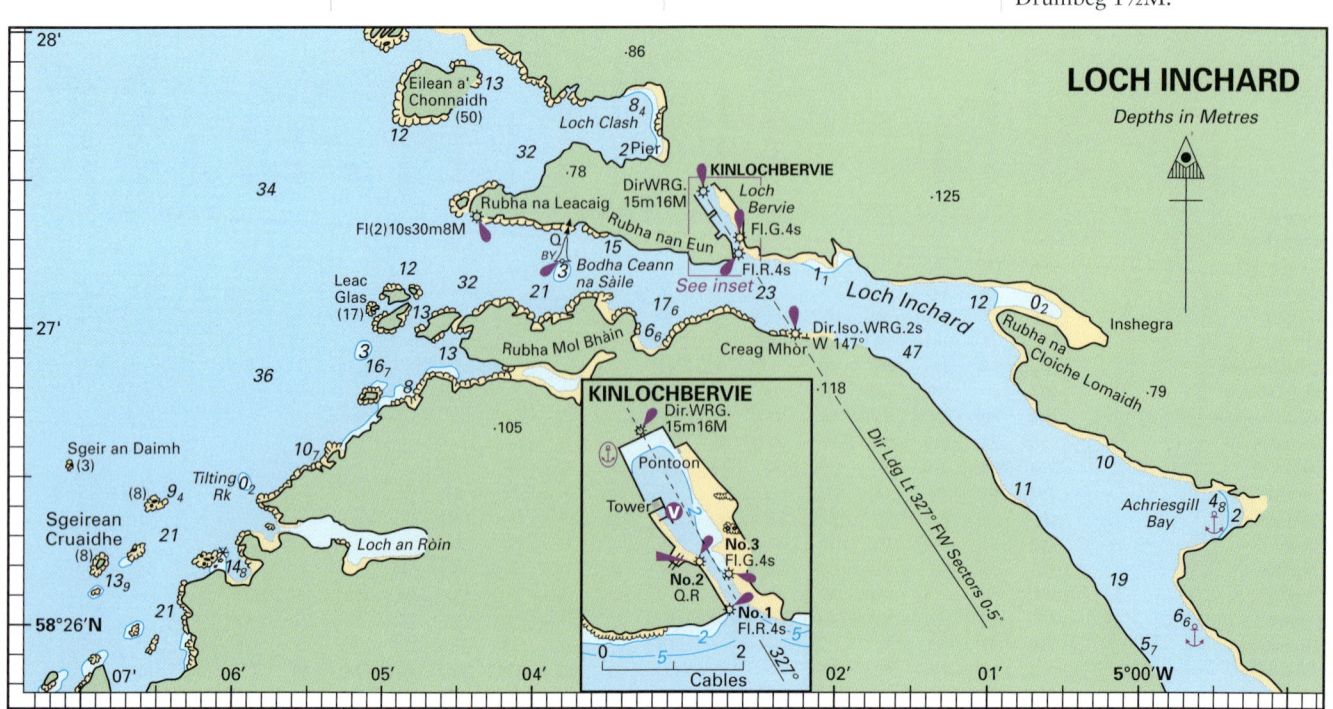

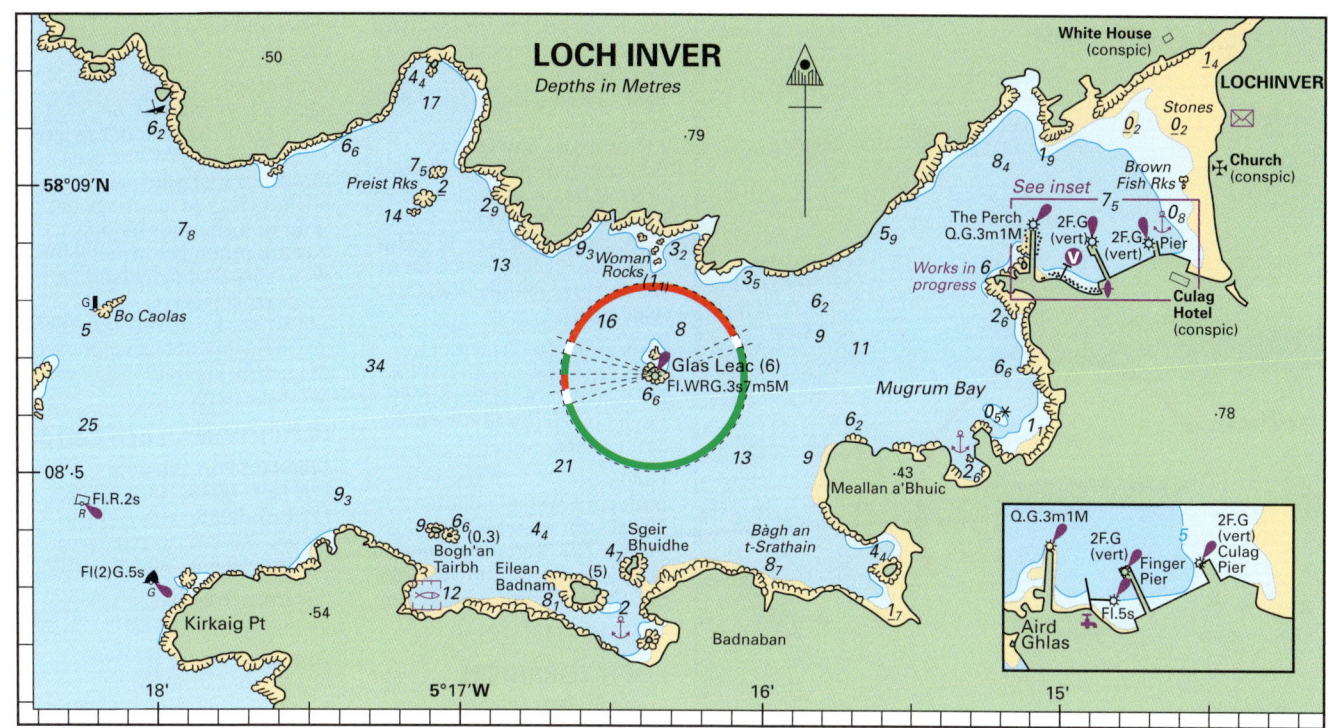

LOCH INVER*

Standard Port Ullapool
HW −0005   LW −0005
MHWS MHWN MLWN MLWS
−0·2m 0·0m 0·0m +0·1m

Approach In clear weather sugar loaf mountain, Suilven, 4M SE is a good landmark for entrance. From S give A'Chleit Is a wide berth to the W and pass close S of Soyea Is, Lt Fl(2)10s34m6M, and steer 075°.

Entrance Leave Glas Leac Lt Fl.WRG.3s to port. At night use W sector 243°–247° as a guide. Leave G bn Q.G to stb.

Berthing and Anchorages
• Visitors' pontoon between breakwater and main pier.
• Anchor off Culag Pier as directed by HM.

Facilities Water and diesel at pier. PO, bank, shops EC Tuesday, chandlery, showers in Harbour Office or at Leisure Centre. Laundry at Mission. Bus to Ullapool and rly to Inverness at Lairg.

☎/VHF HM 01571 844247, Mobile 07787 151498; VHF 12.

SUMMER ISLES

Standard Port Ullapool
HW (sp) −0005 (np) −0005
LW (sp) −0010 (np) −0010
MHWS MHWN MLWN MLWS
−0·1m +0·1m 0·0m +0·1m

An attractive group of islands with several good anchorages. Large-scale chart desirable.

Approach From NW keep towards N of Dorney Sound to avoid drying rocks N of Tanera Beg but beware Iolla a Mealan (dr 0·8m) 2ca off mainland shore opposite N end of Tanera More. From S leave islands stretching 4½M SW of Tanera More to port.

Anchorages
• Tanera More. In bay to E either close to stone pier or possible mooring in 'Cabbage Garden' S of two islands and enter between them. Uncomfortable in swell from NNE.
• Tanera Beg. In bight to S of En Fada Mor or NE of Tanera Beg. If approaching from N keep close to En Fada Mor. Beware of 1·5m patch off SW corner of En fada Mor.
• Caolas En Ristol. To E of Is. Lt Fl.G.3s on mainland shore towards N end.

Facilities Tanera More: Water and diesel at new pier in SE corner of bay. Achiltibuie: Badentarbet Bay on mainland: PO/shop and Calor.

ULLAPOOL*, Loch Broom

Standard Port Ullapool

A busy ferry and fishing port. Easy access. Good protection.

Approach and Entrance Straightforward. Ru Cadail (Fl.WRG.6s) marks the port hand entrance to Loch Broom 3·7M NW of Ullapool. Leave R can buoy Q.R and Ullapool Point Iso.R.4s8m6M to port.

Anchorages and Berthing
• 8 visitors' buoys ENE of pier.
• If you wish to come alongside, contact the hbr office. On the inside of the pier there is a 40m landing pontoon which is available by prior arrangement for taking on provisions, water, and fuel.
• Altnaharrie on SW shore of loch opposite Ullapool Point. Ferry to Ullapool.
• Loggie Bay on SW shore just beyond Narrows.

Facilities Water and diesel at fish pier. Showers at swimming pool and at shower block near ferry berth. Chandlers, charts, some repairs, PO, shops, EC Tuesday, banks, hotel, laundry near supermarket. Ferry to Stornoway. Bus to rly at Inverness.

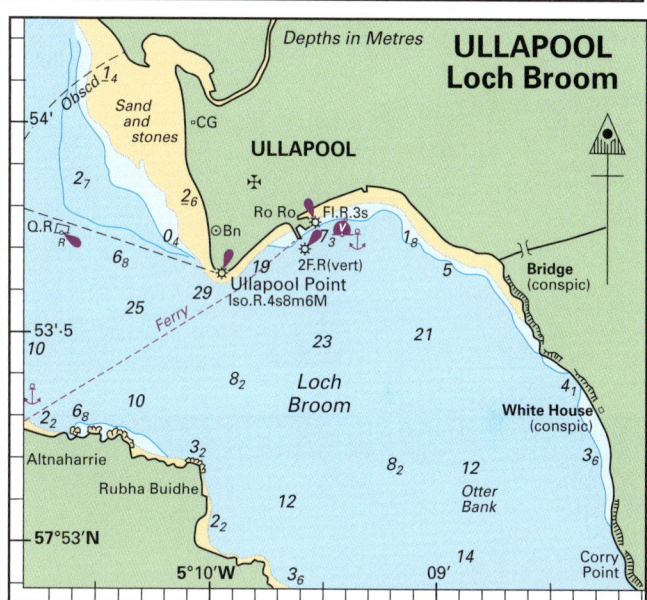

☎/VHF Harbour Office 01854 612091; VHF 16, 14.

LOCH EWE

Standard Port Ullapool
HW −0008   LW −0005
MHWS MHWN MLWN MLWS
−0·1m −0·1m −0·1m +0·1m

A large loch open to the N. The sound E of Is Ewe has a number of large unlit mooring buoys. There are some Naval establishments at Aultbea.

Approach and Entrance Straightforward.

Anchorages
• At head of loch off Poolewe, according to depth. Beware of Boor Rocks 2ca off W shore. If visiting gardens, anchor off small pier SW of Inverewe Ho, or in Loch Thuraig.
• Aultbea To E of pier.

Facilities
Poolewe Water at pier SW of Inverewe Ho, PO, shops EC Thursday, garage, hotel.
Inverewe Gardens are outstanding.
Aultbea Water at pier, PO, shops EC Wednesday, garage, hotel, Calor.

LOCH GAIRLOCH*

Standard Port Ullapool
Gairloch
HW −0012   LW −0011
MHWS MHWN MLWN MLWS
−0·2m +0·1m −0·2m +0·2m

Approach Pass S of Longa Is 3M NW of Glas En Fl.WRG.6s4M.

Anchorages
• Badachro SW of Horrisdale Is. A beautiful well-sheltered anchorage, crowded with many moorings. Keep to E side of channel. Anchor N or S of islets to SW. Note submerged wreck (dr 1·6m) ½ca E of rock

The Cruising Almanac

LOCH GAIRLOCH

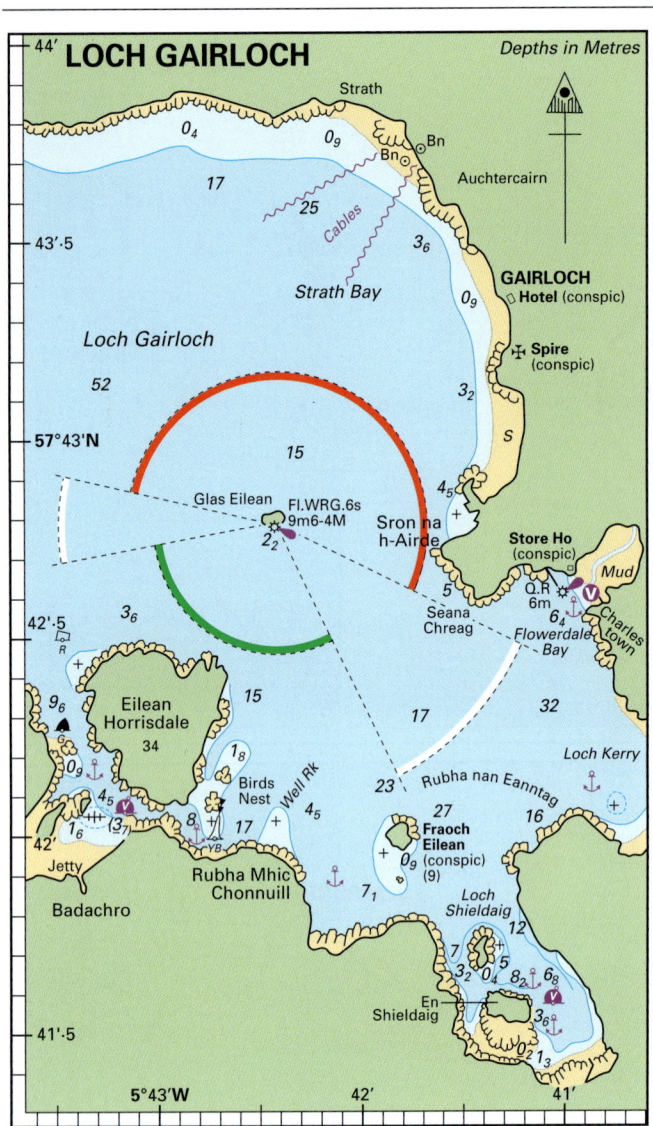

(dr 3·7m) 1ca SE of islet. Two visitors' moorings may be marked 'Inn'.
• SSE of Eilean Horrisdale, limited space.
• Flowerdale Bay visitors' pontoon E of pier, usually full of local boats, or anchor SE of pier, subject to swell.
• Loch Sheildaig E or W of En Shieldaig. Leave Fraoch En to stb and give middle island a wide berth.

Underwater rocks with less than 2m in the vicinity of En Horrisdale, SW of Fraoch En in Loch Shieldaig and off Rubha nan Eanntag.

Facilities
Badachro Water, laundrette, Hotel with showers.
Flowerdale Water and diesel, hotel/restaurant, showers at SC.
Strath Bank, shops, laundrette.
☎ HM 01445 712140.

LOCH TORRIDON
Standard Port Ullapool
Shieldaig
HW −0020   LW −0015
MHWS MHWN MLWN MLWS
−0·4m −0·4m −0·1m 0·0m

This loch comprises three lochs joined by narrows. Loch Torridon, Loch Shieldaig and Upper Loch Torridon.

Entrance 3M wide between Red Point and Ru na Fearn. Sgeir na Trian (2m) lies 1¼M SSE of Red Point. Entrance to L Shieldaig under ½M wide and narrows into Upper Loch Torridon only 2ca between N shore and En a Chaoil. Tide here runs at 2·3kn.

Anchorage
• In Loch a Chracaich off Kenmore in 5m clear of fish farm.
• In L Shieldaig two visitors' moorings E of Shieldaig Is or anchor clear of moorings or head of loch, poor holding. New pontoon below hotel for short stay or dinghy landing, no overnight stays.
• In Upper Loch Torridon there are many possible anchorages, the best being in the SE corner W of the jetty.

PLOCKTON*, Loch Carron
Standard Port Ullapool
HW (sp) −0025   (np) +0005
LW (sp) −0005   (np) −0010
MHWS MHWN MLWN MLWS
+0·5m +0·5m +0·5m +0·2m

An attractive hbr with many facilities.

Approach There are two approaches from SW.
• S of Sgeir a Chinn and Sgeir Bhuidhe (*not on plan*) then N of Golach and High Stone rocks giving them a clearance of 2ca and steering 065° on white bn (*see plan*). When Duncraig Castle conspic bears 164° alter course and steer towards castle to clear Hawk Rock (depth 0·1m) leaving Dubh Sgeir bn 2½ca to port.
• Mid-channel between the port bn marking High Stone rocks and the old LtHo on a heading to Bogha Dubh Sgeir bn.

Entrance Steer 164° towards castle conspic until hbr opens

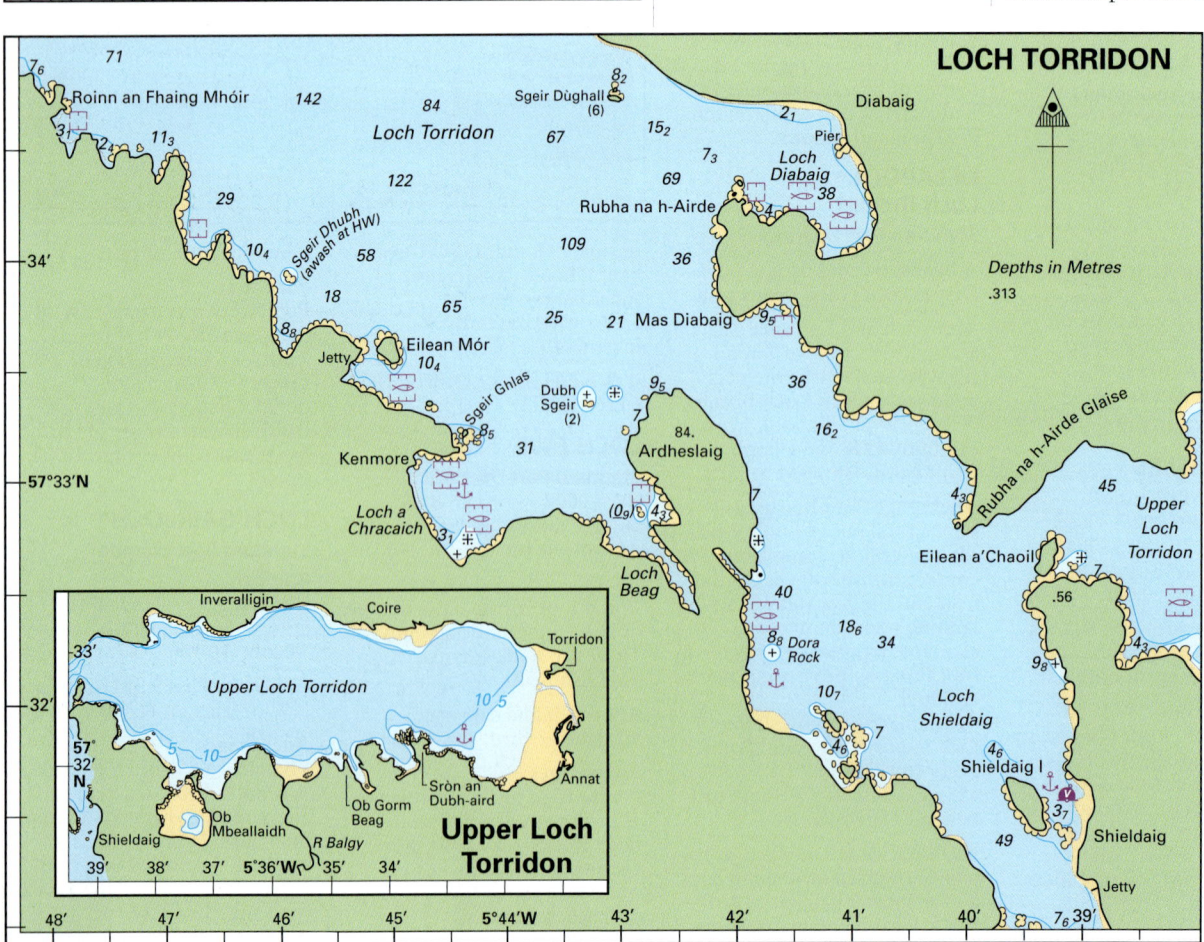

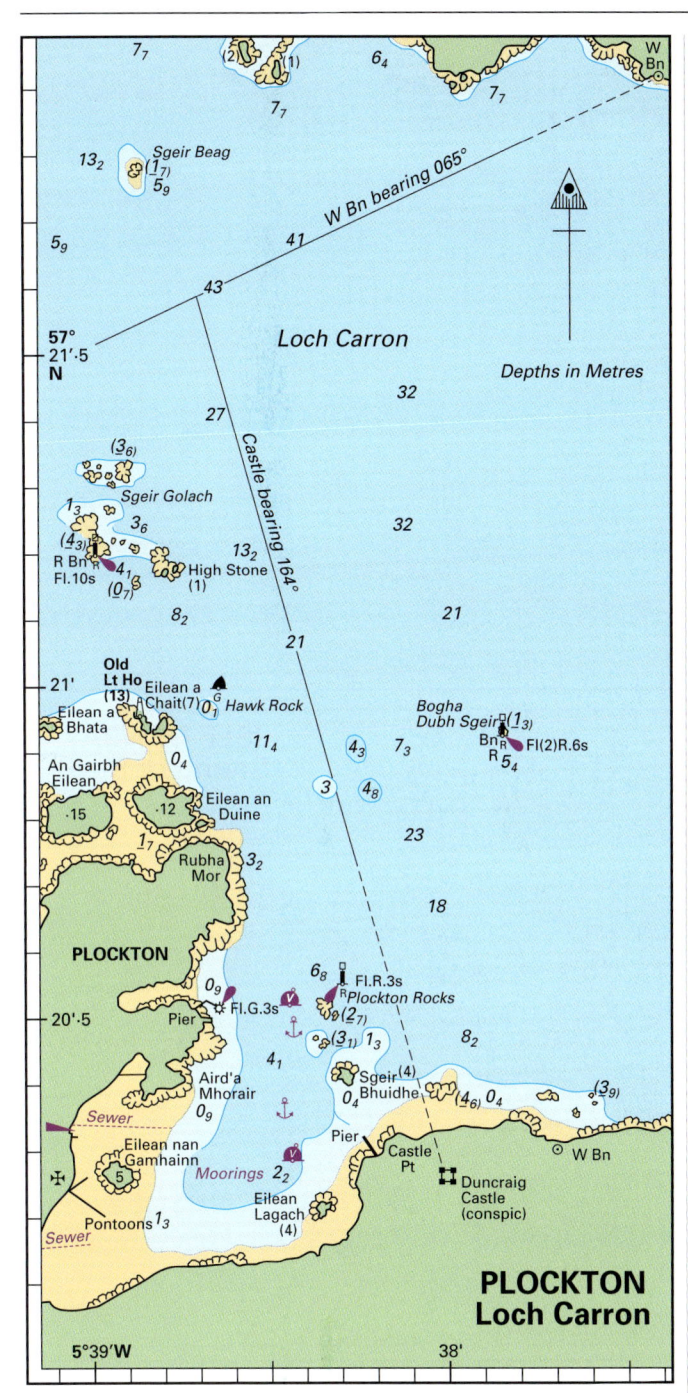

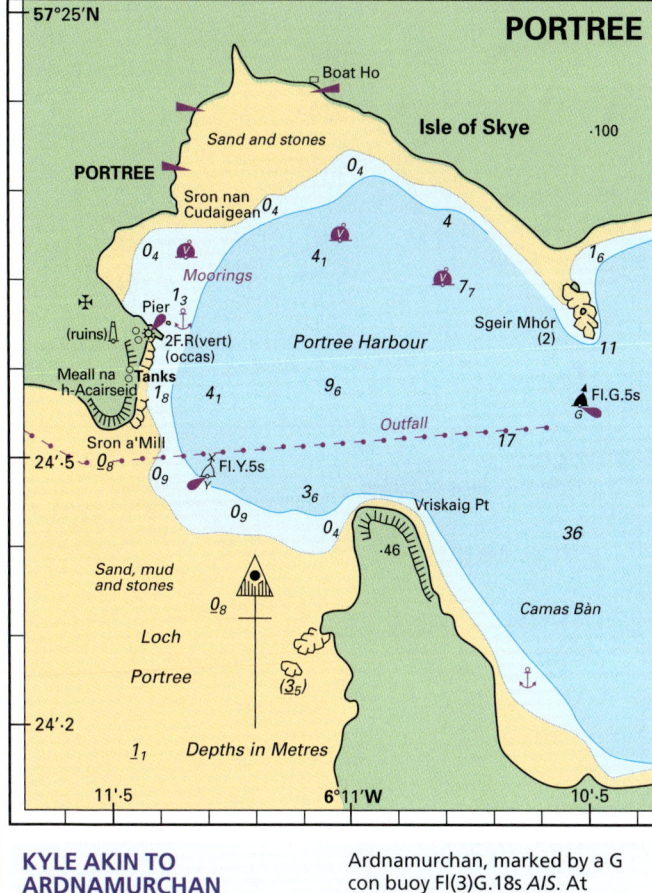

The Cruising Almanac

KYLE AKIN TO ARDNAMURCHAN

Passage lights	BA No
Isle Ornsay Oc.8s.18m12M	3944
Pt of Sleat Fl.3s20m9M	3952
Ardnamurchan Point Fl(2)20s55m22M AIS	4082

The tides are strong in Kyle Akin and Kyle Rhea, but the channel is well marked and lit. It is essential to go with the tide in Kyle Rhea. Overfalls may be encountered at Glenelg on the ebb with a S'ly wind. From here the passage to Ardnamurchan is straightforward, though pass N of a dangerous rock, Bo Faskadale, 6M NE of Ardnamurchan, marked by a G con buoy Fl(3)G.18s *AIS*. At Ardnamurchan Point a big sea can build up with strong onshore winds and one is well advised to stand off at least 1M.

Tidal streams
All related to Dover
Kyle Akin
−0015W +0345E (sp 3kn)
+0145W −0415E (np 1½kn)
These can be significantly affected by climatic conditions
Kyle Rhea
+0145N −0415S (6–8kn)
Sound of Sleat
+0130NE −0430SW (1kn)
Ardnamurchan Point
+0130N −0430S (1½kn)

---

to SW. Beware Plockton Rks (dr 2·7m) extending 3ca NNW of Castle Point.

Anchorage In bay as marked on plan and clear of moorings. Large patches of kelp reported. 15 visitors' moorings with orange pick up buoys. Mooring fees can be paid using an envelope system on the pontoons.

Facilities Short-stay pontoons for loading stores. PO, shop, EC Wednesday, water, diesel in cans, hotel with showers, restaurant, launderette. Rly to Inverness and to Kyle of Lochalsh.

PORTREE, SKYE*

Standard Port Ullapool
HW −0025   LW −0025
MHWS MHWN MLWN MLWS
+0·1m −0·2m −0·2m 0·0m

The principal town on Skye. Anchorage subject to squalls.

Approach and Entrance
Straightforward. 2F.R(vert) occas on pier.

Anchorages and Berthing
• Visiting yachts may use the landing pontoon attached to the main pier, max stay 2 hours. During cruise liner activities this is a restricted area and is closed to public use.
• 12 visitors' moorings in N of bay, but subject to swell in S'lies. Weight limit 8 tonnes. Pay at honesty box in doorway of RNLI station.
• To NE of pier clear of moorings. Avoid mouth of burn to N where holding poor. Exposed to SW winds. Patches of kelp reported in anchorage.
• Camas Ban to SE. Protected from S.

Facilities Water and diesel at quay, engineer, Calor. Showers at swimming pool. PO, shops, launderette, EC Wednesday, hotels. Bus to Inverness. Rly to Inverness at Kyle of Lochalsh on mainland.

☎ HM 01478 612926.

KYLE AKIN

Standard Port Ullapool
HW (sp) −0025 (np) −0055
LW (sp) −0005 (np) −0025
MHWS MHWN MLWN MLWS
+0·1m 0·0m 0·0m −0·1m

A temporary stopping place for stores and crew changing.

Approach There are numerous hazards in Kyle Akin (*see plan*), but these are well marked and lit. Tides run strongly. The channel under the br is 80m wide and has a clearance of 29m. There is a secondary passage (lit) to the N of the main channel with a clearance of 4·5m.

Berthing
• **Kyle of Lochalsh** Alongside pontoon, about 10 berths, poor shelter in strong winds. Beware of dangerous rocky outcrop immediately W of pontoon.
• **Kyleakin** Alongside pontoon, can be crowded, good shelter. Three visitors' buoys on S shore between hbr and Skye br.

Facilities
• **Kyle of Lochalsh** Water on pontoon, diesel at pier. Showers at tourist office. Supermarket, shops, bank, PO, chandler, calor. GRP repairs, engineer. Rly to Inverness.
• **Kyleakin** Small shop, hotel.

☎ HM 01599 534167,
Mobile 07748 105730

ISLE ORNSAY, Sound of Sleat, Skye

Standard Port Oban
HW +0017 (approx)
MHWS MHWN MLWN MLWS
+1·0m +0·9m +0·2m +0·1m

Easy access. Convenient if awaiting a favourable tide to pass through Kyle Rhea going N.

SCOTLAND – WEST COAST

145

The Cruising Almanac

SCOTLAND – WEST COAST

KYLE AKIN

KYLE RHEA

ISLE ORNSAY
Sound of Sleat

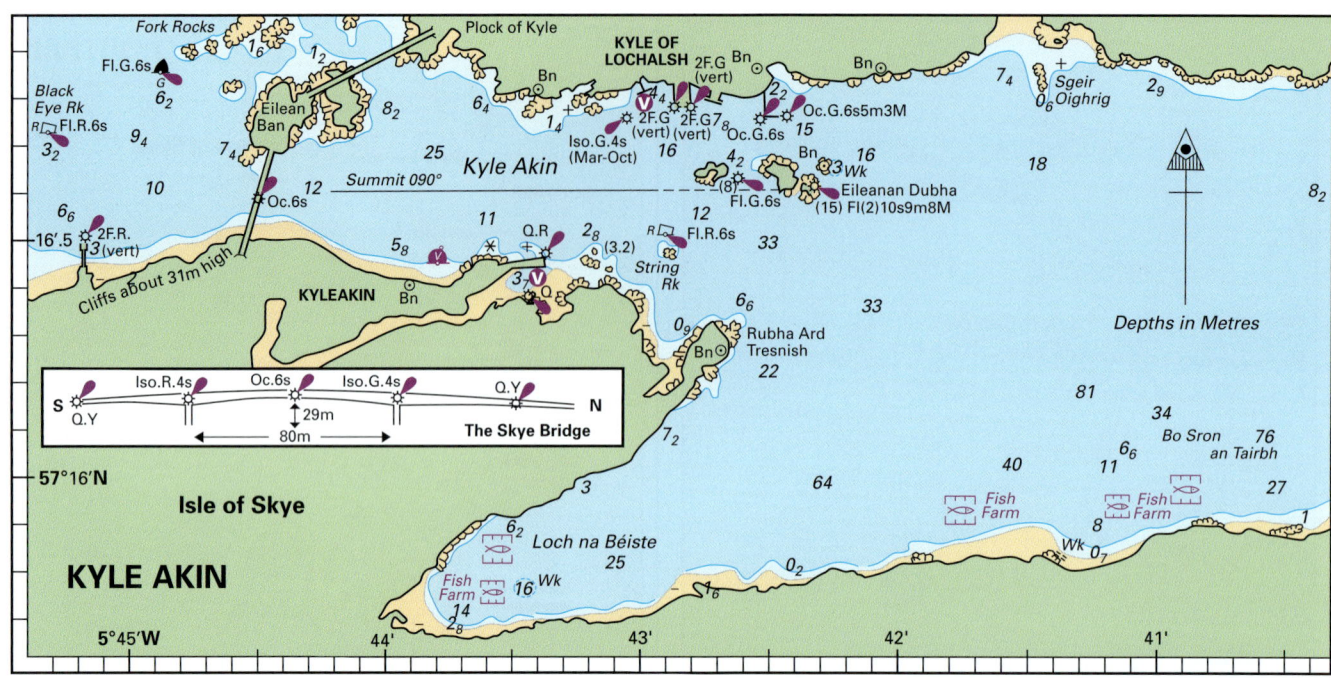

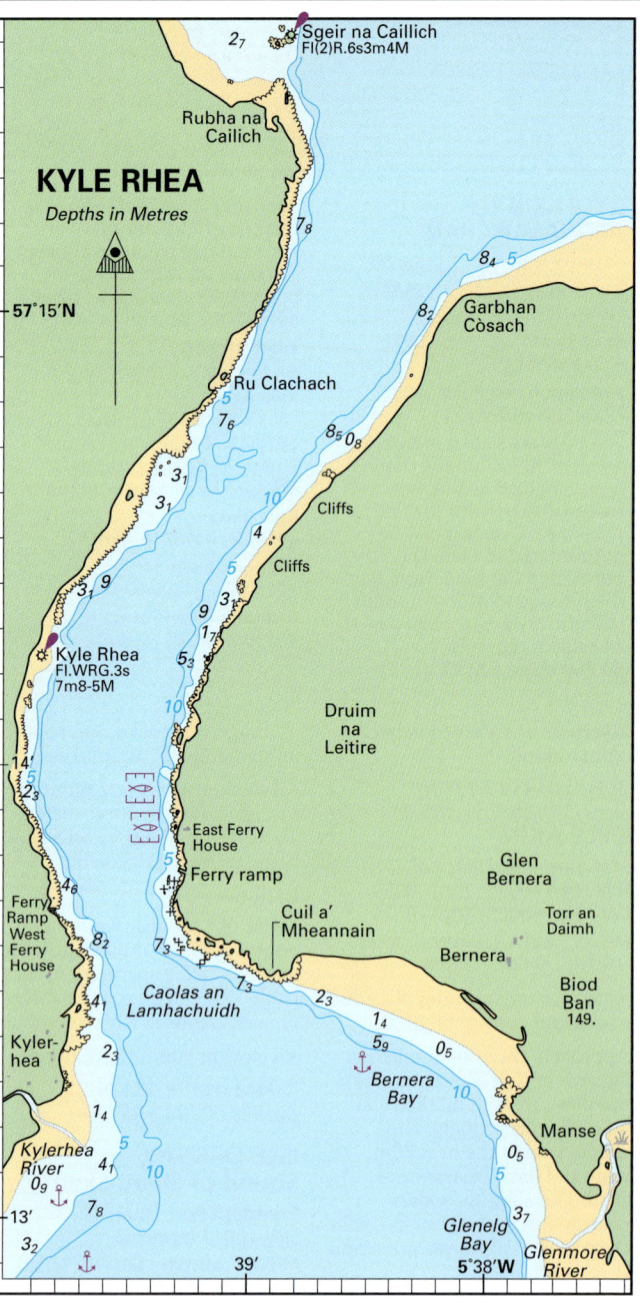

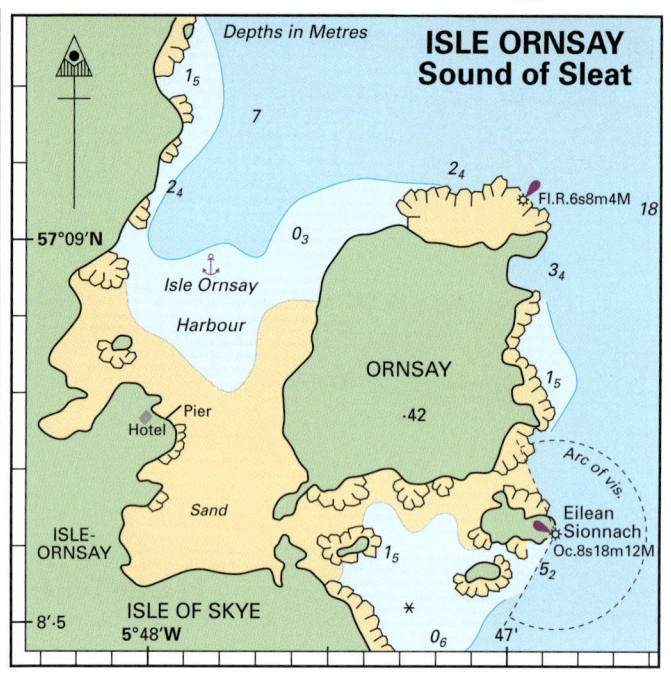

Approach Enter to N of island.

Anchorages
- Towards head of bay according to depth and clear of moorings.
- 5 visitors' moorings off Duisdale Hotel (just N of plan).

Facilities PO, store 1M, hotel, showers (Duisdale).

ARMADALE
Tidal data as Isle Ornsay

On the W side of the Sound of Sleat a useful passage hbr open to NE.

Entrance Straightforward from the NE. From the S rocks off Ru Phoil. Give a wide berth until hbr opens up. At night give Oc.R.6s Lt on end of pier a wide berth.

Anchorage
- Visitors' moorings subject to swell; distinguish from yacht charter moorings. Little room for anchoring further out in sand. Good holding.
- Alongside ferry pier.

Facilities Diesel and water from Isle of Skye Yachts workboat, general repairs. Showers, laundrette, PO/shop ¾M. Ferry to Mallaig; bus to Portree.

Isle of Skye Yachts administer moorings, ☏ 01471 844216.

LOCH NEVIS
Sound of Sleat
Standard Port Oban
Inverie Bay
HW +0028   LW +0027

MHWS	MHWN	MLWN	MLWS
+1·0m	+0·9m	+0·2m	0·0m

A useful and beautiful anchorage if Mallaig full. Subject to severe squalls.

Entrance Along the coast E of Mallaig keeping about 3ca out from S shore.

Anchorage
- En na Glasehoille in the NW corner of the loch gives

146

The Cruising Almanac

Entrance Leave Sgeir Dhearg Fl(2)WG.8s to stb. At night in G sector and then W sector of pier head Lt Iso.WRG.4s and Fl.G.3s. Three vert R Lts mean a ferry is about to leave or enter, no other craft may leave or enter without HM permission.

Berthing
- On pontoons S of Fish Pier, as directed.
- There are 12 visitors' moorings in the inner harbour.

Facilities Water and electricity on pontoons. New marina reception building contains, toilets, showers, and laundry. Diesel at Fish Quay. Chandler, charts, slip, repairs. PO, shops EC Wednesday, hotels, launderette and showers at Seaman's Mission, banks. Ferry to islands. Beautiful rly to Glasgow. Minibus link to Oban. Bus to Fort William.

☎/VHF HM 01687 462154 (office hours); Mallaig Marina *Mobile* 07824 331 031, VHF 16, 09 call sign *Mallaig Harbour Radio*.

ARISAIG, Loch Nan Ceall

Standard Port Oban
HW +0016   LW +0027
MHWS MHWN MLWN MLWS
+0·7m +0·1m +0·2m +0·2m

Approach this beautiful hbr with caution in clear weather as it is not easy to identify. The marked channel is winding with rocks (dr 0·2m) and has a fast tidal stream particularly towards LW. Enter HW±0400.

Approach Identify Rubh Arisaig, with W paint mark, S of channel, keeping ½M to W to avoid Meallan Odhar rocks, 1m high, *see plan*. Luinga Mor, 15m high, lies to the N of the channel with drying rocks extending ½M SE. A stone cottage known as the 'Waiting Room' lies 1M ENE of Ru Arisaig and to S of Torr Mor, 79m high, inside entrance.

Entrance Enter on a heading of 080°. Leave the first, second and third bns ½ca to port, avoiding Cave Rock to stb. Follow the curving channel leaving bns on appropriate side. Do not follow a straight course from one bn to the next. Then pass between R & G buoys and head ESE leaving the last R bn ½ca to N. Make E to village 1M away.

Anchorages
- Above Cave Rock 1M inside entrance.
- There are 50 visitors' moorings in various depths in Loch Nan Ceall.
- In bay SE of village at Camas an t-Salainn, crowded with moorings.

Facilities Water at pontoon and diesel at pier. Showers, laundry, chandlery. Calor gas at shop, PO, hotels, restaurants. Repairs, 210-tonne crane. Rly to Glasgow. Bus to Fort William.

☎/VHF *Arisaig Marine* VHF 37, 01687 450224.

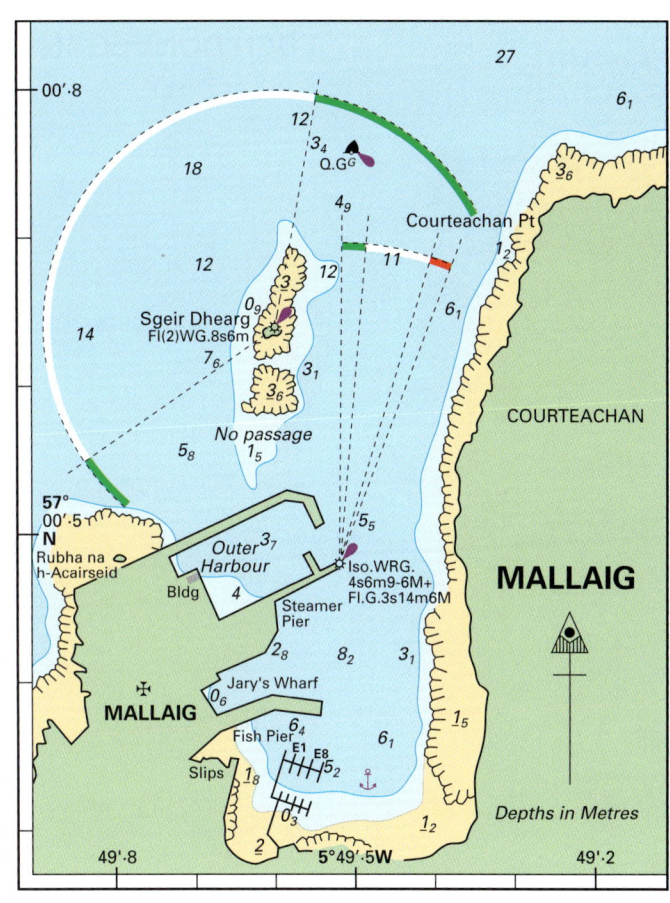

protection from the W/SW.
- Inverie Bay 1M to the E, anchor off village. Restaurant/pub, visitors' moorings ☎ 01687 462267, VHF 12.
- Tarbert in the SE corner before the narrows into the second part of the loch.

MALLAIG*

Standard Port Oban
HW +0017   LW +0027
MHWS MHWN MLWN MLWS
+1·0m +0·7m +0·3m +0·1m

A busy fishing and ferry port with good facilities. Open to N.

Approach Straightforward.

SCOTLAND – WEST COAST

147

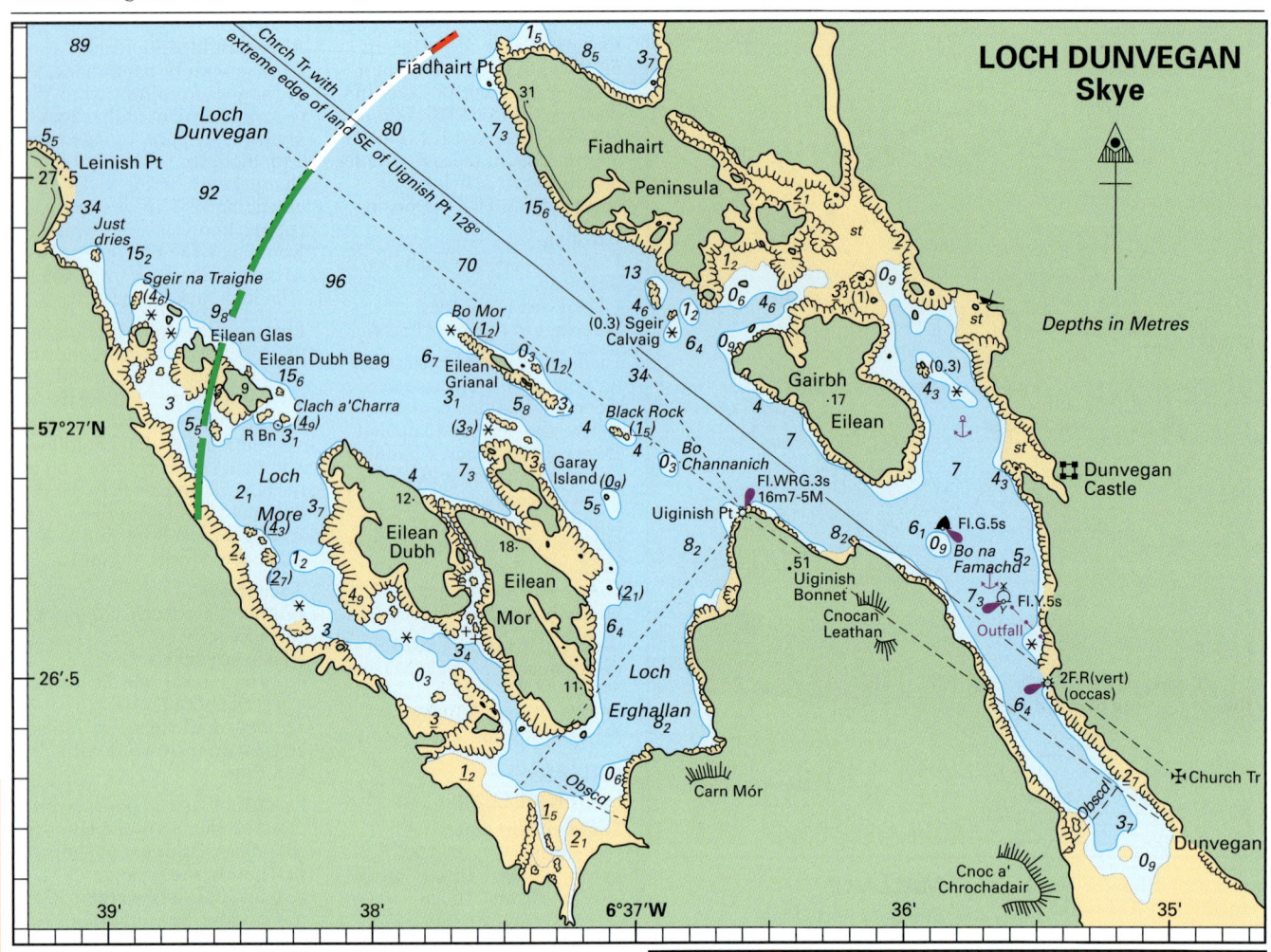

The Cruising Almanac

N AND W COASTS OF SKYE TO ARDNAMURCHAN

Passage lights	BA No
Neist Point Fl.5s43m16M AIS	4064
Oigh Sgeir, Hyskeir Fl(3)30s41m24M AIS	4076

The N and W coasts of Skye present a series of prominent headlands with strong tides and overfalls, in the bays and lochs there may be back eddies. SW of Canna there are dangerous rks for over 7M and in bad weather the seas can be bad here. Around the Small Isles there are severe magnetic anomalies in places, particularly S of Muck.

Tidal streams
All related to Dover. Sp.Rates

Ru Hunish
+0415NE –0215SW   2½kn

Neist Point
+0400N –0200S   1½kn

UIG BAY*, Loch Snizort, Skye

Standard Port Ullapool

HW (sp) –0020 (np) –0045
LW (sp) –0005 (np) –0025

MHWS	MHWN	MLWN	MLWS
+0.1m	–0.4m	–0.2m	0.0m

Bay on E side of Loch Snizort in the N of Skye. Easy access. Rather exposed to W.

Approach and Entrance Note spit extending 1ca S from Ru Idrigill (dr 2·6m).

Anchorage NNE of pier, Iso.WRG.4s, in 5m. Bottom reported foul, advisable to buoy anchor.

Facilities Water and diesel at pier. PO, shops, hotels. Launderette at caravan park. Bus to Glasgow. Ferry to Harris.

☎ HM 01470 542381, *Mobile* 07771 958102, VHF 8.

LOCH DUNVEGAN*, Skye

Standard Port Ullapool

HW (sp) –0030 (np) –0105
LW (sp) –0020 (np) –0040

MHWS	MHWN	MLWN	MLWS
0·0m	–0.1m	0·0m	0·0m

Large loch in NW Skye. 2½ca between the Fiadairt peninsula to E and En Grianal to W. Note drying and submerged rocks extending 4ca SE of En to Bo Channanich (0·3m). (*See plan*).

Entrance The shore SE of Uiginish Point in line with Dunvegan Church tr 128°, leads mid-channel. Leave Uiginish Point Lt (Fl.WRG.3s) and Bo na Famachd G con buoy to stb.

Anchorage
• Head of loch beyond pier. Leave Bo na Famachd buoy well to stb.
• E of Gairbh Eilean opposite the Castle. Note submerged and (dries 0·3) rocks to N. Poor shelter in strong SW'lies.
• L Erghallan, to S of En Mor obstructed by mussel beds.
• Loch More.

Facilities PO, shops, garage. Water and diesel at hotel jetty. Bus to Portree.

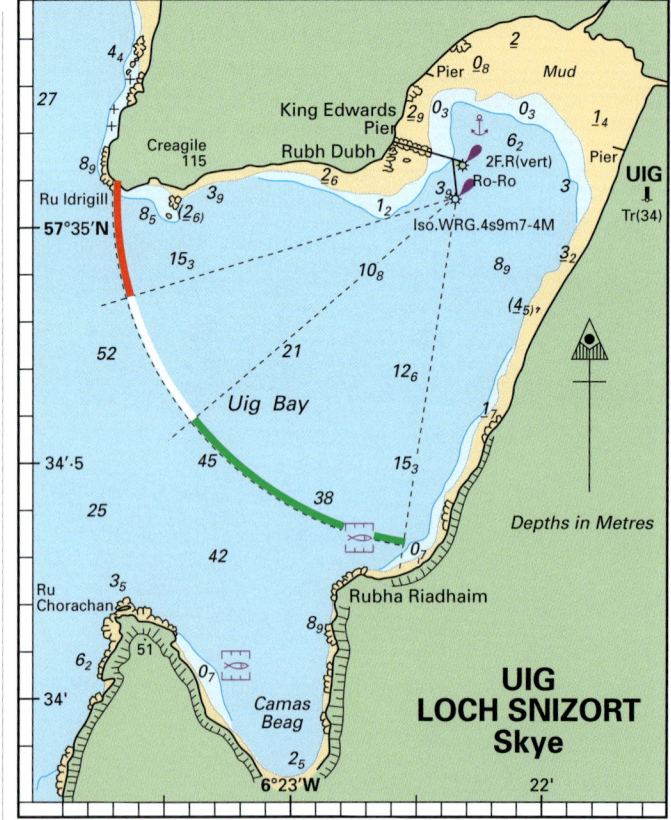

LOCH HARPORT, Skye

Standard Port Ullapool

HW (sp) –0035 (np) –0115
LW (sp) –0020 (np) –0100

MHWS	MHWN	MLWN	MLWS
–0.1m	–0.1m	0·0m	+0.1m

Situated in the SE arm of Loch Bracadale in the S of Skye.

Approach and Entrance From NW note dangerous Dubh Sgeir (5m) 1½M S of Ru Ruadh. Enter between Oronsay and Ru nan Clach. Give the SW and E shore of Oronsay a berth of ¼M. Leave Ardtrech Point, Fl.6s18m9M, to stb.

Anchorages
• Portnalong. Space limited by fish farm. Useful if storm bound. Bottom reported foul.

• Carbost 1½M from head of loch. Good holding opposite Talisker Distillery, also 5 visitors' moorings. Dinghy landing pontoon. Sheltered except from the SE.

Facilities PO, shop, showers, drying room and excellent food at the Inn. EC Wednesday.

B. Ardnamurchan to Mull of Kintyre and Inner Hebrides S of Ardnamurchan

ARDNAMURCHAN TO OBAN	
Passage lights	BA No
Ardnamurchan Point	4082
Fl(2)20s55m22M AIS	
Ru nan Gall	4112
Fl.3s17m10M	
Lismore	4170
Fl.10s31m17M	

Entering the Sound of Mull from the N shore keep close to the Mull shore leaving the New Rocks G con buoy to port to avoid dangerous drying reefs towards entrance of Loch Sunart. All dangers in the Sound of Mull and the Firth of Lorne are well marked. Strong tides and overfalls may be encountered off Duart Point.

Tidal Streams.
All related to Dover. Sp rates
Ardnamurchan
+0130N –0430S 1½kn
Lismore Lt Ho
+0115N –0500S 2kn
Corran Narrows (L. Linnhe)
+0600 NE –0530SW 5kn
Firth of Lorne
–0100NE +0500 SW 1½kn

CANNA IS*

Standard Port Ullapool
HW (sp) –0037   (np) –0130
MHWS MHWN MLWN MLWS
–0·4m –0·2m n/a n/a

A very beautiful hbr and useful passage port when bound for the Outer Hebrides. Easy access and sheltered except from E.

Approach from N and E is straightforward. Lt at E end of Sanday Is, Fl.10s32m9M. Steer to pass close S of Ru Carrinis. From S beware of drying reef to N of Sanday marked by R can buoy Fl.R.2s. Magnetic anomalies reported.

Entrance Beware of drying reef ¾ca SW of pier.

Anchorage Best in line between two churches. Much kelp, poor holding reported. Shoals. Hard sand suitable for bilge keelers. 10 visitors' moorings have been established, pay at community shop. Showers and toilets at the farm.

Facilities PO opens as required. Tiny restaurant. Ferry to Mallaig.

LOCH SCRESORT
Isle of Rum

Standard Port Oban
HW +0018   LW +0023
MHWS MHWN MLWN MLWS
+0·6m +0·6m +0·1m 0·0m

Protection from all winds except the E and squalls from the W.

Entrance Straightforward, keep to middle or N side. Reef on S side of entrance is marked by N Card buoy Q.

Anchorage Bay shallows towards the shore. Anchor according to depth and clear of ferry. Moderate holding.

Facilities PO, Stores, water from pier. Hotel. Ferry to Mallaig. Showers in youth hostel.

EIGG

Standard Port Oban
HW +0017   LW +0024
MHWS MHWN MLWN MLWS
+0·7m +0·8m +0·2m +0·2m

The Island of Eigg is a pleasant and convenient anchorage about half way between Mallaig and Ardnamurchan. Exposed to swell from N to E and S. Strong tides can be uncomfortable.

Approach Identify Sgurr(391m) conspic and En Chathastail Lt bn Fl.6s24m8M.

Entrance From NE identify two perches – circular topmark to N and triangular to S – and pass between them. Then head for stone pier. From S keep at least 1ca W of En Chathastail. Note rks extending 1½ca SW of En.

Anchorages
• To N of pier according to depth and clear of moorings. Sandy bottom shoals rapidly to W.
• S of Galmisdale Pt as close to shore as possible to avoid tide.

Facilities Water and café at pier, diesel, Calor. PO/store 2M. Hotel. Ferry to Arisaig and Mallaig.

TOBERMORY*, Mull

Standard Port Oban
HW +0017   LW+0020
MHWS MHWN MLWN MLWS
+0·5m +0·6 m +0·1m +0·2m

Sheltered, pretty town in the NE of Mull.

Approach From N keep close to Mull shore between Ru nan Gall LtHo Fl.3s17m9M, 1M to N and New Rocks G con buoy Fl.6s 1¾M N.

Entrance Main entrance N of Calve Is. No hazards. The S

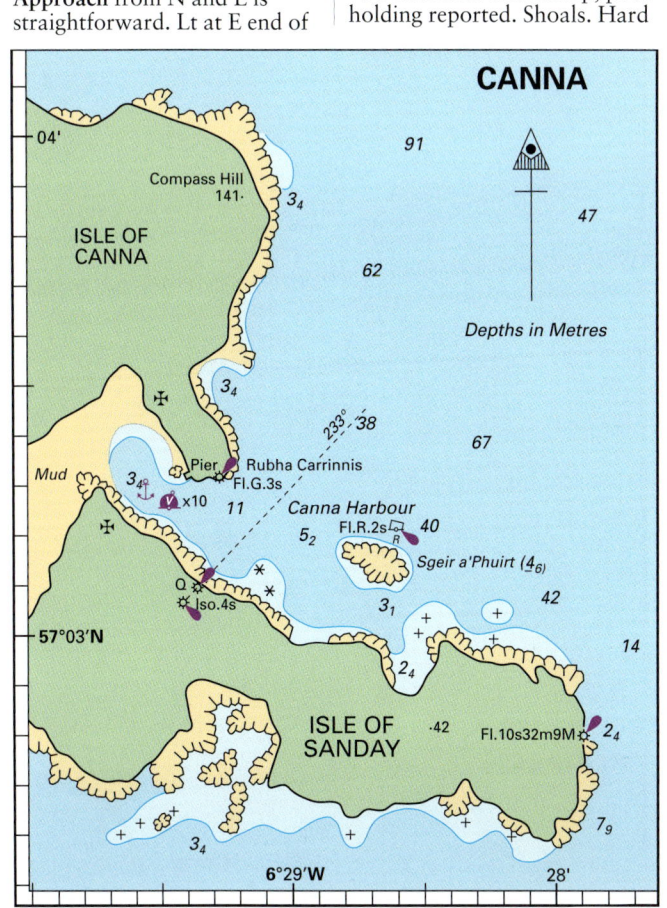

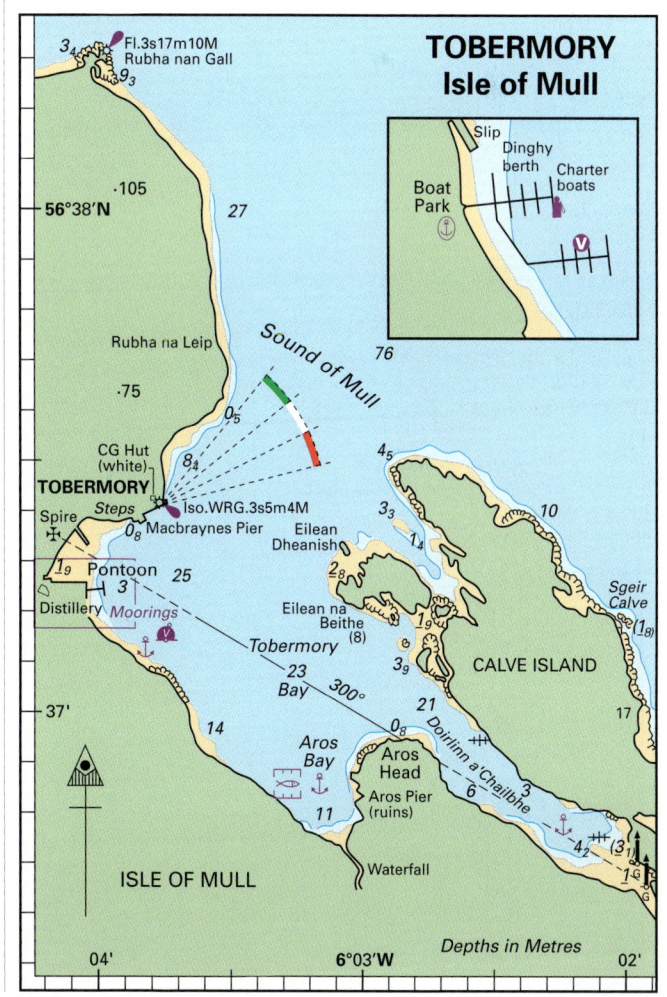

entrance is a narrow drying channel with a sandy bottom passable at HW. Church spire on Aros Head 300°.

Anchorages/Berthing
- 50 pontoon berths near distillery. Free short stay for shopping by day.
- Off town as far S as furthest W mark on shore. Be prepared to anchor in up to 20m. Often crowded. Many visitors' moorings, marked THA.
- Aros Bay according to depth.
- Doirlinn Narrows (S entrance); fishing boats may use this at night.

Facilities Water and diesel (Diesel is supplied by Mackays Garage ☎ 01688 302103) at pontoons, showers and launderette in Harbour Office building. Chandlery, charts, engineer, shops, free electricity and WiFi, bank, hotels. Ferry to Kilchoan, Ardnamurchan.

☎/**VHF** HM 01688 302876 Mobile 07917 832497, VHF 12.

LOCH NA DROMA BUIDHE, SUNART

Standard Port Oban
HW +0020   LW +0020
MHWS MHWN MLWN MLWS
+0·4m +0·3m 0·0m −0·1m

Popular anchorage S of the Is of Oronsay sheltered in all winds.

Approach Beware of New and Red Rocks if coming from the W. From N beware rocks W of Oronsay.

Entrance Steep to, ½ca wide. Keep to N shore to avoid rock (0·3m) to S of E end of entrance.

Anchorages Suitable anchorages can be found in many parts of the loch.

Facilities None.

LOCH ALINE*, Sound of Mull

Standard Port Oban
HW +0012   LW +0020
MHWS MHWN MLWN MLWS
+0·5m +0·3m n/a   n/a

A useful and protected loch on mainland side of Sound of Mull. Frequent ferries use the channel.

Entrance Avoid reef off Bolorkle Point to E of entrance by keeping 2ca off-shore then keep in mid-channel. The channel is marked by two port and one stb Lt buoys. The Ldg Ln into Loch Aline has been discontinued and replaced by a directional light on the concrete front mark of the old leading line. The front mark is painted orange and a new directional light mounted on it DirOc. WRG.6s; R 358°-002°; W 356°-358°; G 353°-356°. The tide runs at 2½kn in the entrance. Keep a look out for the Loch Aline to Fishnish ferry.

Anchorages and Berthing
- 24 visitors' pontoon berths with min depth of 2·9m on the W side of the loch just N of the old jetty for the silica mine. Water and electricity, toilets, showers, washing machine and tumble driers. Short walk to the village. VHF 80 call sign *Lochaline Harbour* ☎ 07583 800500.
- 10 moorings, 1 South of pontoons and 9 North of pontoons.
- In SE corner of loch, partially obstructed by fish farm and moorings. Subject to squalls in SE winds.
- Head of loch: moorings or anchor according to depth.
- Moor to stone pier on W side of entrance. Short stay only.

Facilities PO/Store, water. Diesel, Petrol and Calor in village, launderette, restaurant. Bus to Fort William.

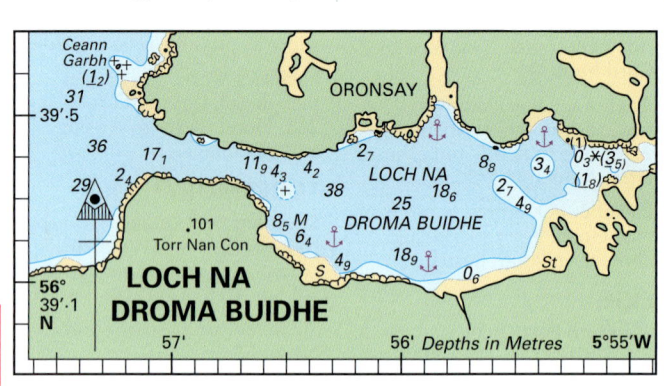

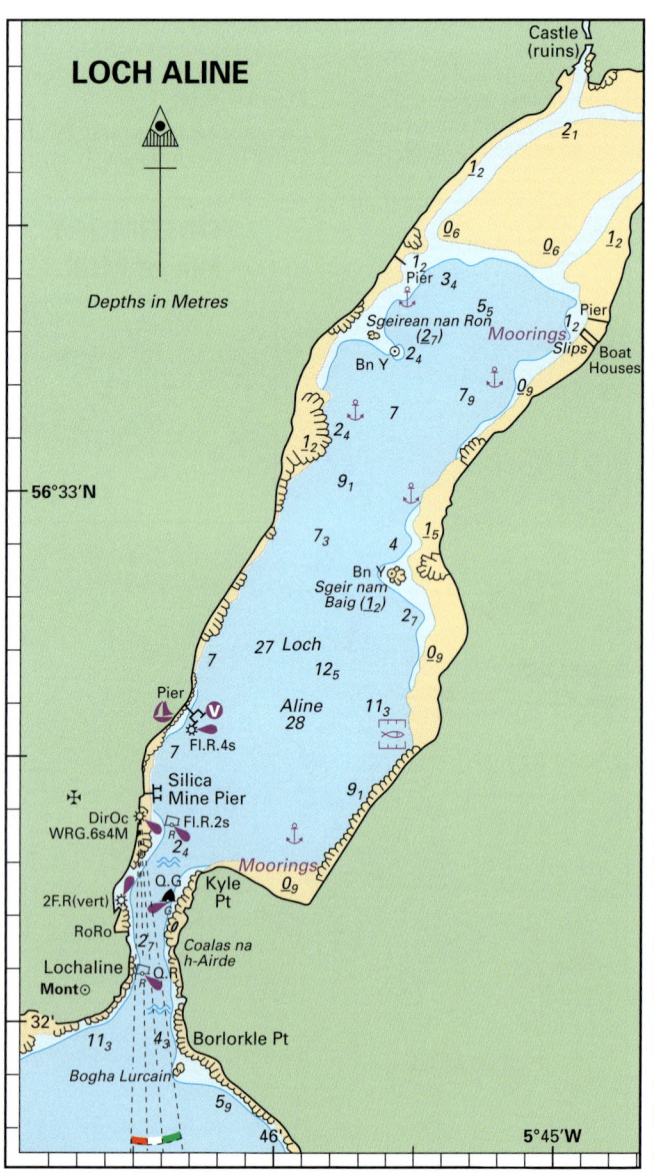

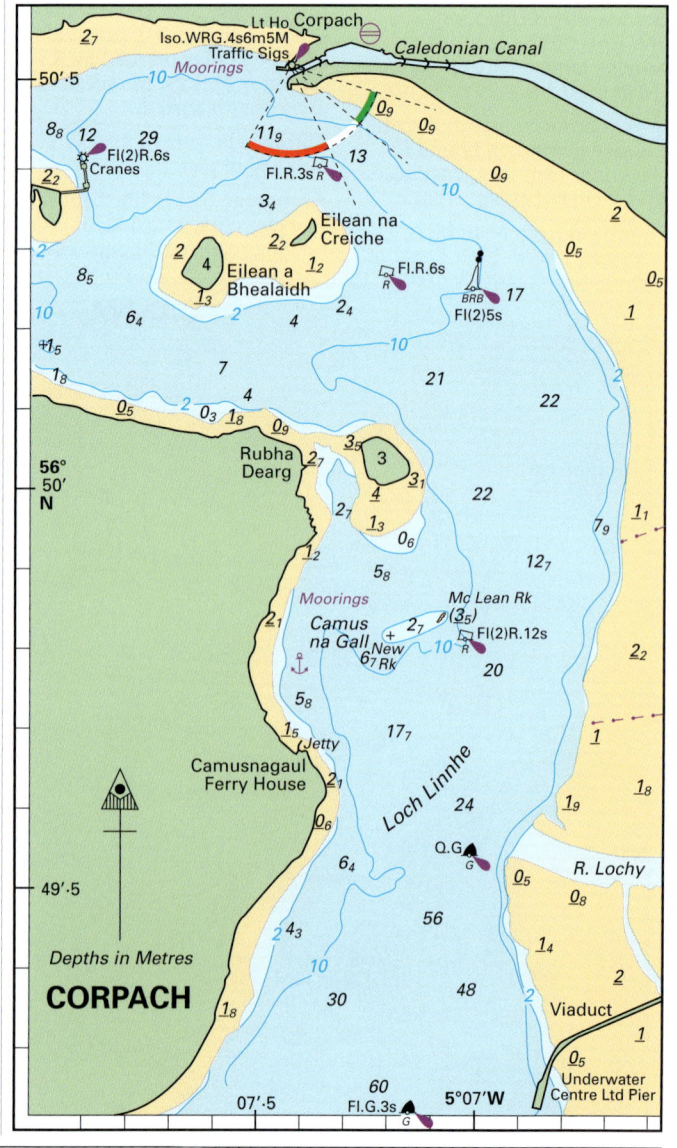

150

CORPACH

Standard Port Oban
HW (sp) +0020 (np) +0000
LW (sp) +0040 (np) +0000
MHWS MHWN MLWN MLWS
0·0m 0·0m −0·2m −0·2m

Corpach is just beyond the SW entrance to the Caledonian canal. The approach through Loch Linnhe gives an impressive view of Ben Nevis.

Approach Through Loch Linnhe which is divided between the S and N parts of the loch by the Corran Narrows where the tide runs at up to 5kn at sp the in-going stream beginning at LW Oban and the outgoing stream at HW. After the Narrows leave the Corran shoal to port and continue up the loch which is buoyed towards Corpach. Leave En na Creiche to port and R can Lt buoy before turning W and coming round to canal entrance.

Anchorage If waiting to enter canal anchor W of entrance in 4·6m out of the way of canal traffic or at waiting pontoon. Or in Camus na Gall. One visitors' mooring off Lochaber Y.C., Fort William.

CALEDONIAN CANAL

The Caledonian Canal runs 60M NE from Corpach to Clachnaharry, near Inverness, via Lochs Lochy, Oich and Ness with 29 locks. Vessels up to 45m LOA, 10m beam and 4m draught can use the canal. The *Skipper's Guide* from www.scottishcanals.co.uk or Seaport Marina, Muirtown Wharf, Inverness IV3 5LS is invaluable.

Entrance Sea locks at Corpach at SW end and Clachnaharry at NW end normally operate HW±0400 within the operating hours 0800–1730 daily in summer, less at other periods. Waiting in the canal before transitting the canal is possible at Corpach or at Seaport Marina (NE end).

Transit All locks and bridges are manned with the same operating hours as above, but there may be a lunch break. Minimum passage time 2½ days. Eight days transit time allowed. There are random spot checks, usually at sea lock, for boat safety, e.g. gas, electricity, fuel. There may be delays at Neptune's Staircase, a spectacular flight of seven locks at Banavie (near Corpach), and also at the Fort Augustus flight.

Facilities Shops at Corpach, Fort Augustus, and Muirtown. Diesel at Corpach and at Muirtown from Seaport or Caley Marinas. Showers, water, and pump out facilities.

☎/**VHF** Sea locks, and most locks and bridges VHF 74; Corpach Sea Lock 01397 772249; Clachnaharry Sea Lock 01463 713896; Seaport Marina 01463 233140.

DUNSTAFFNAGE

Standard Port Oban
HW +0003 LW +0003
MHWS MHWN MLWN MLWS
+0·1m +0·1m +0·1m +0·1m

A marina just N of Oban.

Entrance Channel between En Mor to stb and Rubha Garbh with castle ruins on headland.

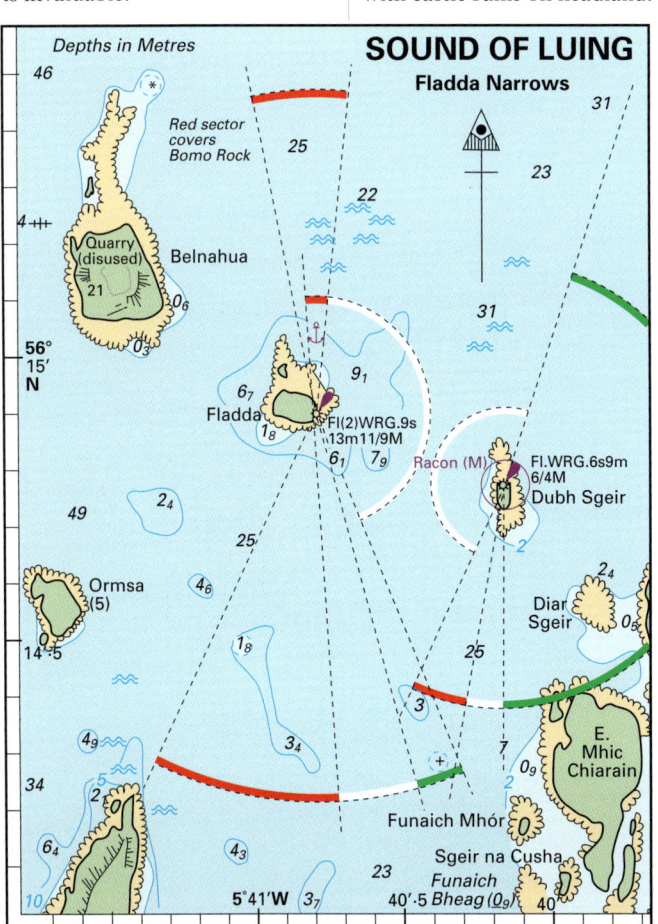

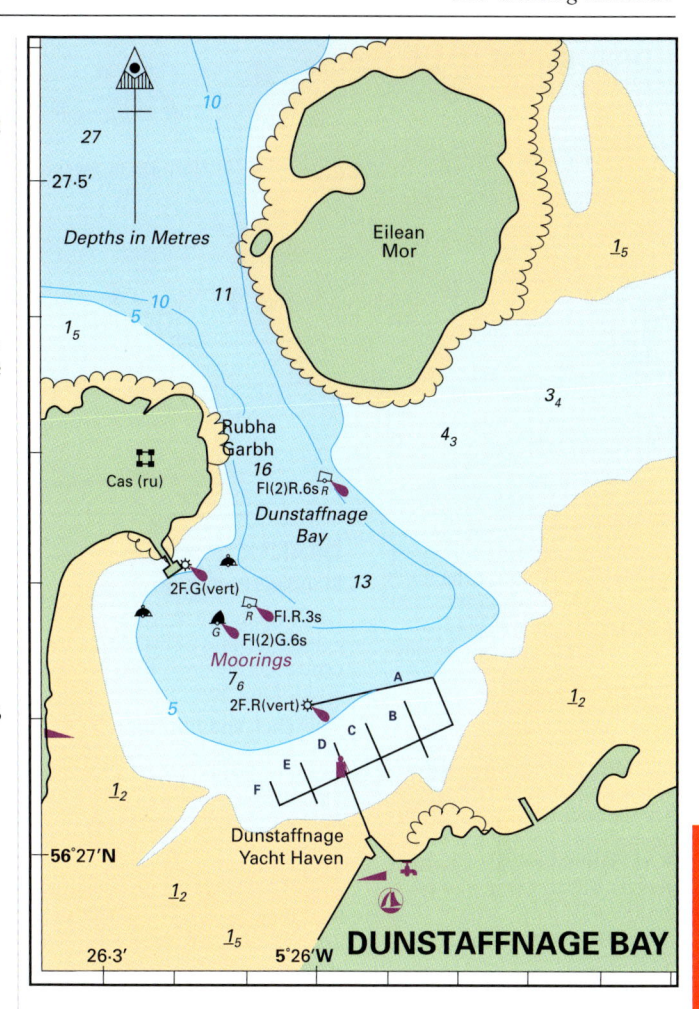

OBAN TO MULL OF KINTYRE

Passage lights	BA No
Fladda	4190
Fl(2)WRG.9s13m11-9M	
Skervuile	4230
Fl.15s22m9M	
McArthur's Head	4240
Fl(2)WR.10s39m13/10M	
Mull of Kintyre	4272
Fl(2)20s91m24M	

Strong tides will be experienced through the Fladda Narrows in Luing Sound, Cuan Sound and Dorus Mor, often with overfalls.

In the **Sound of Luing** pass midway between Fladda LtHo Fl(2)WRG.9s13m11-9M (sectors 169°-R-186°-W-337°-G-344°-W-356°-R-026°-obscd-169°) and Dubh Sgeir Fl.WRG.6s9m6-4M (sectors 000°-W-010°-R-025°-W-199°-G-000°) into the Sound of Luing.

Alternatively, **Cuan Sound** (see plan on p.152) provides a challenging passage, even at slack water, between the Firth of Lorne and Seil Sound and Loch Melfort. The tides run at 7kn springs, 5kn at neaps and there are numerous off-shore hazards. The NW entrance can be identified by overhead cables (clearance 35m) and their pylons. Overfalls may be experienced here in fresh W winds when coming through the Sound with the tide from the E. Coming from the W, beware Cullanach rks (dries 1·2m) (not on plan) SW of Cuan Point entrance. Keep in mid-channel until An Cleiteadh (Cleit Rk) bn is identified and pass ¼ to ½ca N of bn. Note rock awash ¾ca from S point of Seil. Keep in mid-channel and pass either ¼ca or 3ca NE of Torsa. Good anchorages clear of the tidal stream S of An Cleiteadh and at Ardinamar Bay. Leave G posts close to stb on entry.

In the Sound of Jura there are numerous islets and submerged rocks W and S of Craignish Peninsula terminating in Ruadh Sgeir Lt Fl.6s. If proceeding to Crinan or Ardfern pass S of Coiresa and Craignish Point through **Dorus Mor** (see plan on p.152). If keeping W on the flood beware of being swept into the very dangerous Gulf of Corryvreckan between Jura and Scarba.

Large-scale charts are advisable if approaching Gigha or the SE of Islay, owing to numerous off-lying rocks. Strong tides and heavy seas possible between the Mull of Kintyre, Rathlin Is and the S coast of Islay.

Tidal Streams.
All related to Dover. Sp rates

Fladda Narrows
−0100N +0500S 7kn

Cuan Sound
−0100 NW +0530SE 7kn

Gulf of Corryvreckan
−0115W +0430E 8½kn

Dorus Mor
−0200NW +0445SE 8kn

The Cruising Almanac

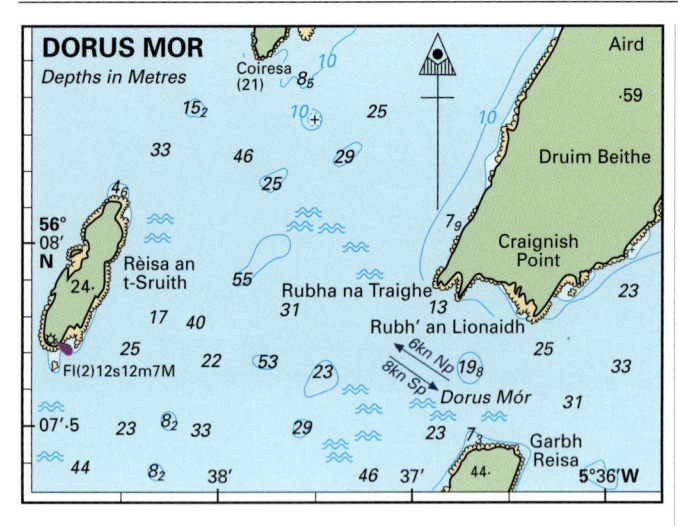

DORUS MOR
Depths in Metres

To enter the marina follow the fairway (150°), after the 2nd G stb hand buoy turn on to 270° and the entrance should become apparent, but do not pass through moorings.

Berthing 200+ berth marina with some moorings.

Facilities Full marina facilities, restaurant and accommodation. Shop (will deliver) and garage in Dunbeg ½M. Sailmaker 5M. Charter centre. Bus to Oban and Fort William.

☎/VHF 01631 566555, VHF 37.

OBAN*

Standard Port Oban

Large open bay. Rather exposed. Main hbr and tourist centre for the area. Busy ferry and fishing port.

Approach and Entrance From N keep SW of Maiden Is in W sector of Dunollie LtHo Fl(2)WRG.6s. From S by Kerrera Sound. Note Sgeir Rathaid marked by N and S card Lt buoys. A Voluntary Code of Practice is operated in the Oban Bay area. Vessels over 20m have right of way over smaller vessels when entering or leaving the bay. Listen on VHF 16/12 for vessel movements.

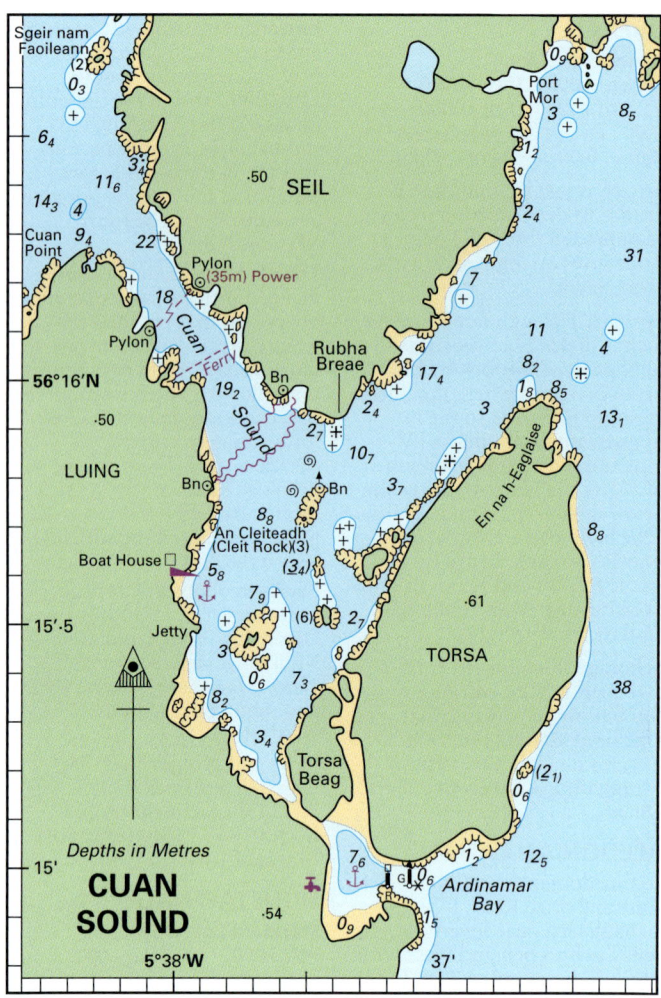

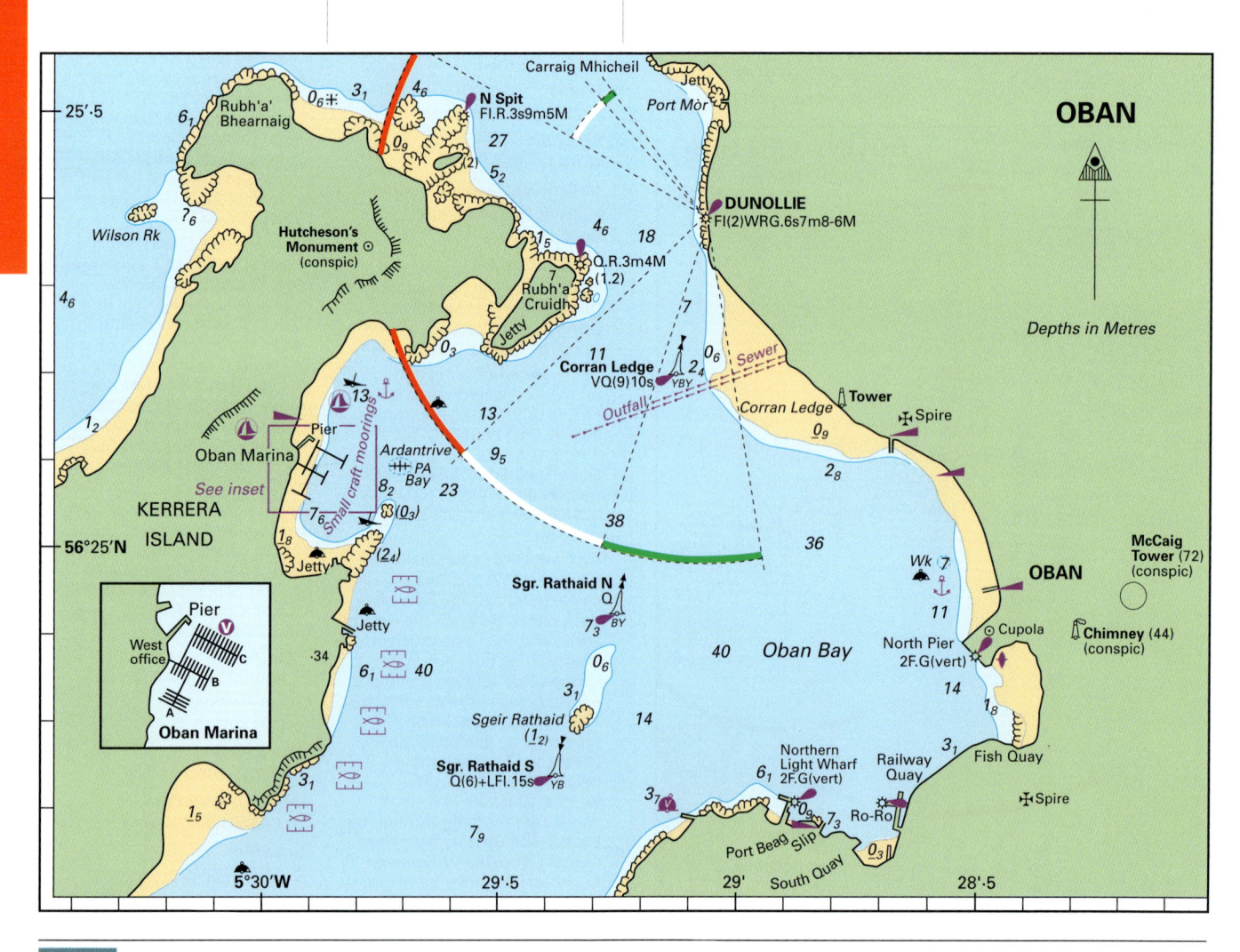

SCOTLAND – WEST COAST

CUAN SOUND

OBAN

152

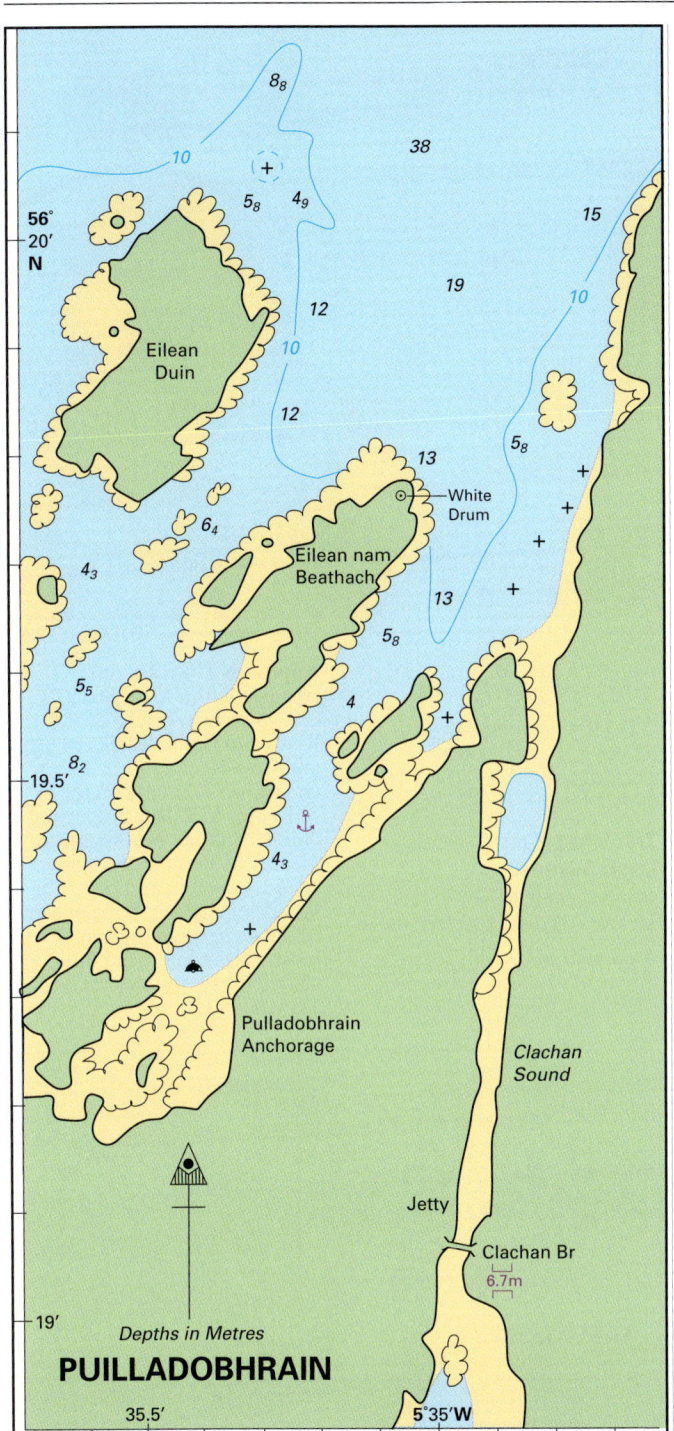

Approach and Entrance From the W and N avoid rocks awash N of En Duin. Entrance is close to En nam Beathach (W Drum on N end) avoiding rock which dries 2·7m off the mainland shore to the E. About 100m beyond the W Drum turn on to 215° down the anchorage.

Anchorage Anchor in 4m where room. A popular anchorage in summer. Holding has recently been reported as poor. If full, alternative anchorage to the SW in Ardencaple Bay, exposed to NW.

Facilities Inn at Clachan Br which is 18th century known as 'Bridge over the Atlantic'.

LOCH MELFORT
Standard Port Oban
HW (sp) –0025 (np) –0055
LW (sp) –0040 (np) –0035
MHWS MHWN MLWN MLWS
–1·2m –0·8m –0·5m –0·1m

A very attractive and popular loch with many moorings and fish farms.

Entrance Note Campbell Rock 1·8m ¾M NE of Ru Chnaip. Also beware of covering rock marked by bn N of pontoon in L na Cille.

Anchorages
• Moorings in L na Cille at head of L Melfort. Apply Kilmelford Yacht Haven.
• Fearnach Bay. Moorings. Limited space for anchoring.

Facilities Kilmelford Yacht Haven ☎ 01852 200248. Full facilities. Shop/PO, hotel at Kilmelford 1½M. Bus to Oban. Fearnach Bay: water at pier.

CRAOBH HAVEN*, Loch Shuna
Standard Port Oban
HW –0045 (approx)
MHWS MHWN MLWN MLWS
+1·1m +1·1m +0·5m +0·1m

Craobh Haven, pronounced 'Creuve', is a modern 250 berth marina 7M N of Crinan formed by the construction of breakwaters between off-shore islands and the mainland.

Approach Beware extensive reef (dries 1·5m) ¼M N of Eilean Buidhe.

Entrance From N leave G con buoy to stb. Inside to port R buoys mark a shoal patch between the entrance and the pontoons. On the W side of the Haven a perch marks a submerged spit, the rest of the Haven has sufficient depth.

Berthing Visitors' berths on pontoon C. Four visitors' moorings off Loch Melfort Hotel in Asknish Bay.

Facilities Full facilities. Shop, Chandlery, and pub/restaurant. Bus to Oban.

☎/VHF 01852 500222, VHF 80, 37.

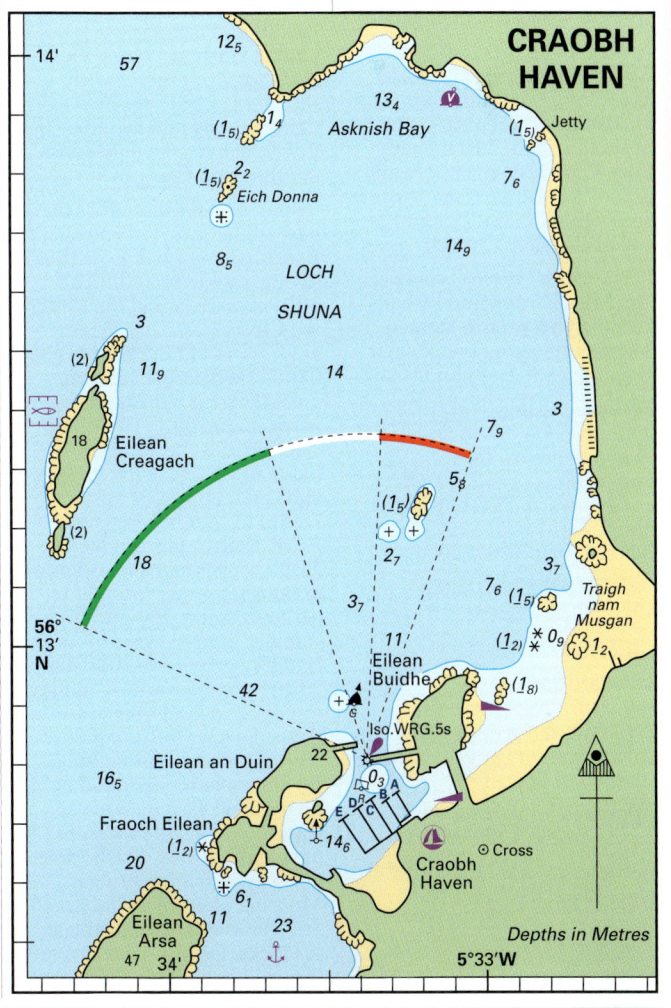

PUILLADOBHRAIN

Berthing
• Oban Marina, Ardantrive Bay, Kerrera opposite Oban. 115 pontoon berths, 33 moorings capacity 20 tonnes, limited facilities, boatyard, no diesel available. Free ferry to Oban, check with reception for timetable and booking. VHF 80, ☎ 01631 565333, www.obanmarina.com.
• Visitors' buoys W of Port Beag, with short stay pontoon, water and garbage disposal available on pontoon.
• Anchor N of N pier
• Temporarily alongside at N pier or Fish Quay, by negotiation with harbourmaster. Diesel can be obtained alongside the Railway pier near the CalMac terminal. Berth by arrangement with harbourmaster VHF 16/12, ☎ 01631 562892. For fuel contact T. Barbour ☎ 01631 562849, delivery is by road tanker.
• A 36 berth transit marina is proposed on the North side of the North pier.

Facilities Busy town, chandlery, charts. Water at N pier, Fish quay and short stay pontoon. Rly and coaches to Glasgow. Ferries to Inner Hebrides, S Uist and Barra.

PUILLADOBHRAIN
Standard Port Oban
HW –0015 (approx)
Heights as Oban

Pronounced 'Pulldochran', this anchorage provides excellent shelter from winds of all directions but in a severe W gale the low-lying rocks on its W side may be overwhelmed.

SCOTLAND – WEST COAST

153

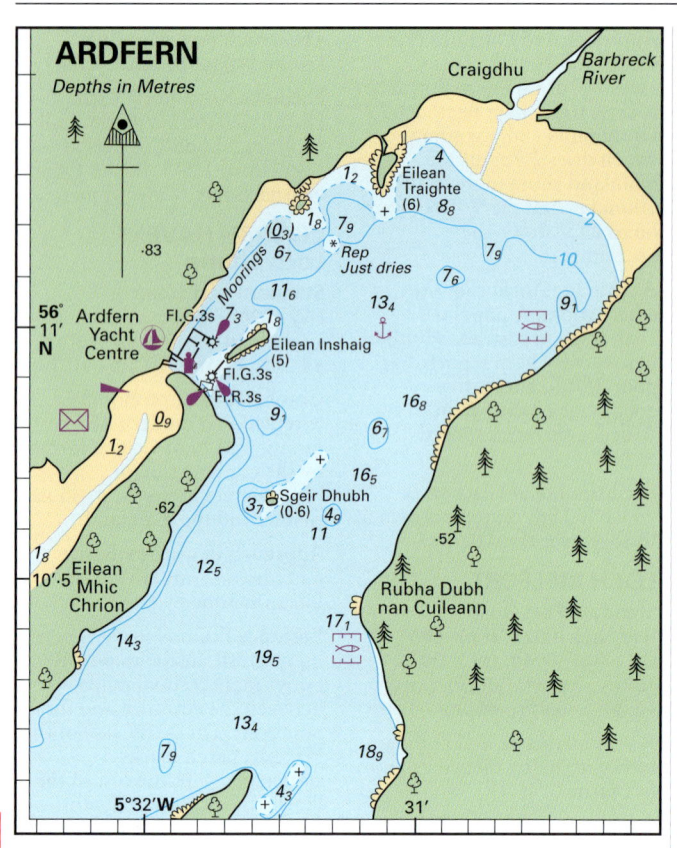

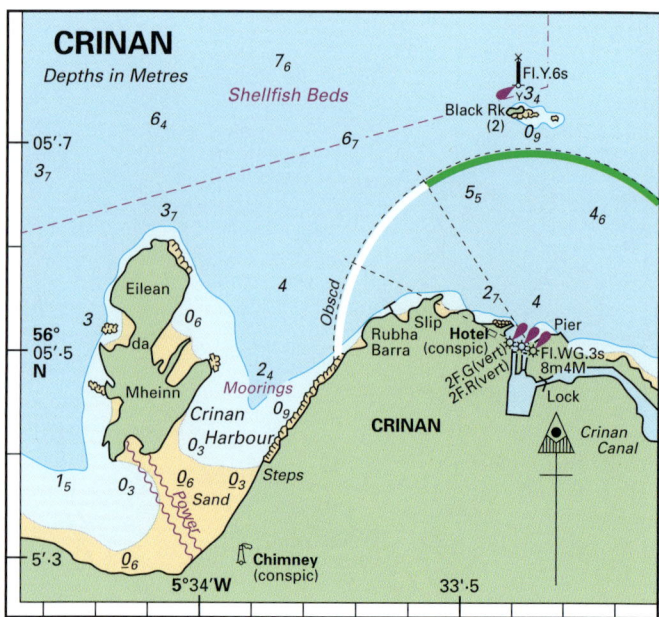

SCOTLAND – WEST COAST

ARDFERN*, Loch Craignish

Standard Port Oban
HW –0045 (approx)

MHWS	MHWN	MLWN	MLWS
+1·6m	+1·2m	+0·8m	–0·4m

May be squally in strong N and NE winds. Barometric pressure and SW winds can alter tidal height up to 1m.

Approach From N via Dorus Mor S of Craignish Point. (Tide 8kn at springs). From S keep E of Ruadh Sgeir Fl.6s then in Loch Craignish give shore and islands a berth of 1½ca. Note Sgeir Dubh (0·6m) 2ca E of N end of En Mhic Chrion.

Entrance to Ardfern is between Ens Mhic Chrion and Inshaig keeping well over to former. There is a floating breakwater extending SW from En Inshaig.

Facilities Ardfern Yacht Centre with pontoon berths and swinging moorings. Full facilities, good chandlery and boatyard. PO/shop and hotel.
Bus to Oban.

☎/VHF 01852 500247, VHF 80.

CRINAN*

Standard Port Oban
HW (sp) –0025 (np) –0055
LW (sp) –0040 (np) +0035

MHWS	MHWN	MLWN	MLWS
–1·2m	–0·8m	–0·5m	–0·1m

Approach Straightforward. W hotel conspic. LtHo Fl.WG.3s.

Entrance to canal E of hotel. Note Black Rock 2ca N.

Anchorages
- Crinan Harbour: VHF 74. For moorings Crinan Boats ☎ 01546 830232, VHF 12.
- Anchor off hotel in 4m. Exposed to NW.
- Moor in canal basin.
- Alongside concrete pier to E of Lt Ho.

Facilities
Crinan Harbour Water, diesel, café, hotel/restaurant with showers.
Crinan Boats Full facilities. Bus to Lochgilphead, connections to Oban and Glasgow.
Crinan Canal runs across the base of the Kintyre Peninsula to Ardrishaig on Loch Fyne thus saving a sometimes difficult 80M passage round the Mull to the Clyde. Canal can be entered at all states of tide from 0800–2100 daily in season, unless there is a drought, when entry confined to HW±0300. The Canal is 9M long with 15 locks and seven swing bridges and can take vessels up to 26·8m LOA, 6m beam and 2·7m draught in fresh water. *Note:* you should add 100mm to your sea water draught to get fresh water draught. In summer, June–August locks and bridges open 0830–2000 daily, 2100 Friday, Saturday, Sunday. Other periods shorter opening times. Further information see www.scottishcanals.co.uk. Inland locks are operated by boat's crew. Passage time at least 6hrs. Yachts proceeding W have right of way. Use horn when approaching bridges. Mooring pontoons established at Bellanoch. Dues payable at sea locks. Details from Crinan Canal, Pier Square, Ardrishaig, Argyll PA30 8DZ
☎ 01546 603210.

☎/VHF Crinan Sea Lock 01546 830285, Ardrishaig Sea Lock 01546 602458 or 07917 374678; VHF 16/74.

TAYVALLICH, Loch Sween

Standard Port Oban
1st HW –0330   2nd HW –0030

A popular and well protected hbr at head of Loch Sween. Many moorings.

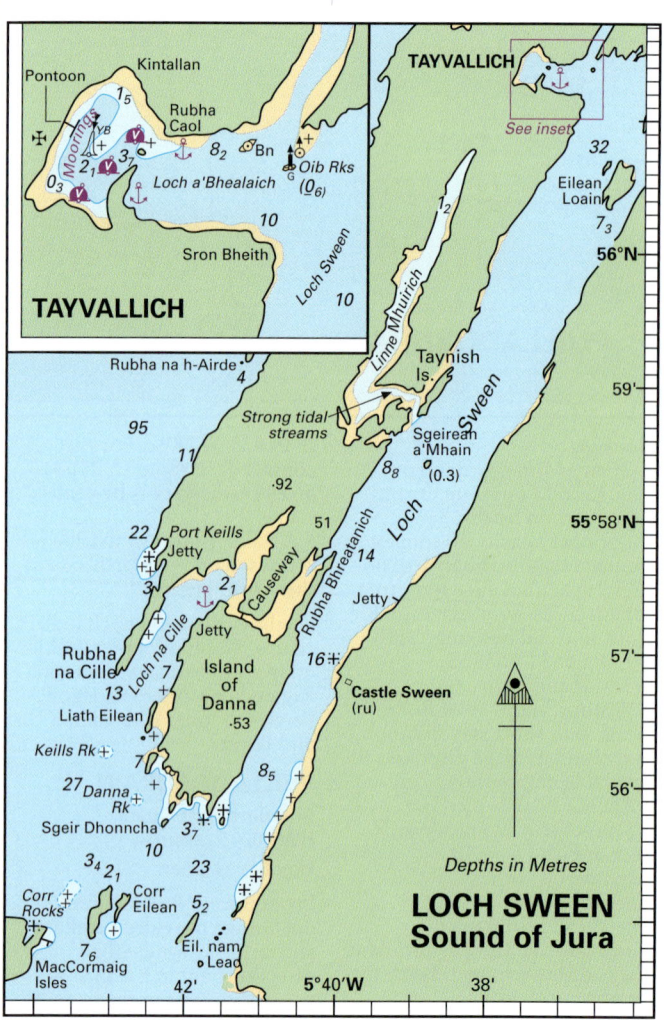

Approach The tides run strongly in this area. From N care must be taken to avoid Keills and Danna Rocks to port and Corr Rocks to stb. The N end of En Ghamhna on the Pt of Knapp 155° leads clear but landmarks may be difficult to identify as Point is 2M away. Avoid Sgeir Bun an Locha on W side of entrance to L Sween. In the loch, the shores are mostly clean but avoid mid-channel rock awash at HW 1½M N of Castle Sween, (see *plan).* At head of loch keep close to Sron Bheith.

Entrance Enter hbr through narrow passage S of mid-channel islet.

Anchorages
- Anchor W of central reef between reef and moorings. Space limited.
- In Loch a' Bhealaich SE of entrance reef.
- 3 visitors' moorings may be found in the NE, central and S parts of the hbr.

Facilities Water on pontoon, short-stay only, shop, restaurant. Calor and showers in Caravan Park. Ferry to Craighouse, Jura. Bus to Lochgilphead.

CRAIGHOUSE, Loch Na Mile, Jura

Standard Port Oban

HW (sp) –0250 (np) –0230
LW (sp) –0150 (np) –0230

MHWS MHWN MLWN MLWS
–3·0m –2·4m –1·3m –0·6m

A useful alternative to Gigha. Good shelter but subject to swell.

Approach and Entrance Na Cuiltean Fl.10s9M lies 1½M SW of entrance. Enter between En nan Gabhar Lt bn Fl.5s to stb and perch to port.

Anchorages
- 16 visitors' moorings, dinghy landing pontoon.
- Anchor clear of moorings off stone pier. Holding reported poor, kelp.
- In sandy cove at SW entrance of Lowlandmans Bay N of L na Mile.

Facilities PO/Shop, restaurant, water, fuel, Calor, hotel.

GIGHA*

Standard Port Oban

HW (sp) –0210 (np) –0450
LW (sp) –0130 (np) +0410

MHWS MHWN MLWN MLWS
–2·5m –1·6m –1·0m –0·1m

A convenient, useful passage hbr for yachts proceeding to or from the Mull of Kintyre. Exposed from NE to SE.

Approach From S, keep about 2ca E of Gigalum, leave W card buoy Q(9)15s to stb. From N, keep 1M offshore to avoid Sgeir Nuadh (dr 1·3m), marked by R can buoy Fl.R.6s.

Entrance When jetty bears 270° head in, but beware of Kiln Rock (dr 1·5m) 1ca ENE of jetty.

Anchorage and Berthing in Ardminish Bay, 11 visitors' moorings. Plenty of room to anchor, hard sand. Moor alongside pontoon.

Facilities PO/shop, cycle hire, showers at hotel (½M), diesel at shop (300m), launderette and water at café. Ferry to Tayinloan connects with bus to Glasgow. Pontoons are planned.

PORT ELLEN, Islay*

Standard Port Oban

HW (sp) –0050 (np) –0530
LW (sp) –0045 (np) –0530

MHWS MHWN MLWN MLWS
–3·1m –2·1m –1·3m –0·4m

A useful passage hbr on the S coast of Islay, if proceeding S to Mull of Kintyre or N Ireland. Exposed to swell from S. Note very small tidal range.

Approach From E keep 1½M off Islay shore and ¾M S of Texa to avoid offlying rks. From W beware of tide races and overfalls off the Oa. From S avoid breakers over Otter Rocks marked by S card buoy Q(6)+LFl.15s. Keep Carraig Fhada Lt Fl.WRG.3s in line with Ro masts 330° leaving G con buoy to stb.

Anchorages and Berthing
- Pontoons in hbr behind ferry terminal, uncomfortable in strong SW winds. Take care in final approach to pontoons, depth reduces rapidly outside channel buoys.
- Kilnaughton Bay provides some shelter from the W, good holding.

Facilities PO, shops, hotels, water at pier head, diesel. Ferry with link to Glasgow.

RUM TO ISLAY

Passage lights	BA No
Skerryvore Fl.10s46m23M Racon (M) (--) AIS	4096
Dubh Artach Fl(2)30s44m20M	4098
Orsay Fl.5s18M	

SW of both Tiree and Mull dangerous rks and an uneven bottom extend 10M causing a bad sea. Great care must be taken to avoid the Torran Rocks extending 5M SW of the Ross of Mull. The passage N of Colonsay to the Sound of Islay is clear.

Tidal Streams
All related to Dover. Sp rates.

Passage of Tiree	
+0100N –0515S	1½kn
Ross of Mull	
–0115N +0445S	1½kn
W of Islay	
–0030NE +0600SW	2kn
Sound of Islay	
–0100N +0515S	5kn
Race off Onsay, Sound of Islay	
HW NW –0615SE	8kn
Mull of Oa (S. Islay)	
HW NW –0615SE	5kn

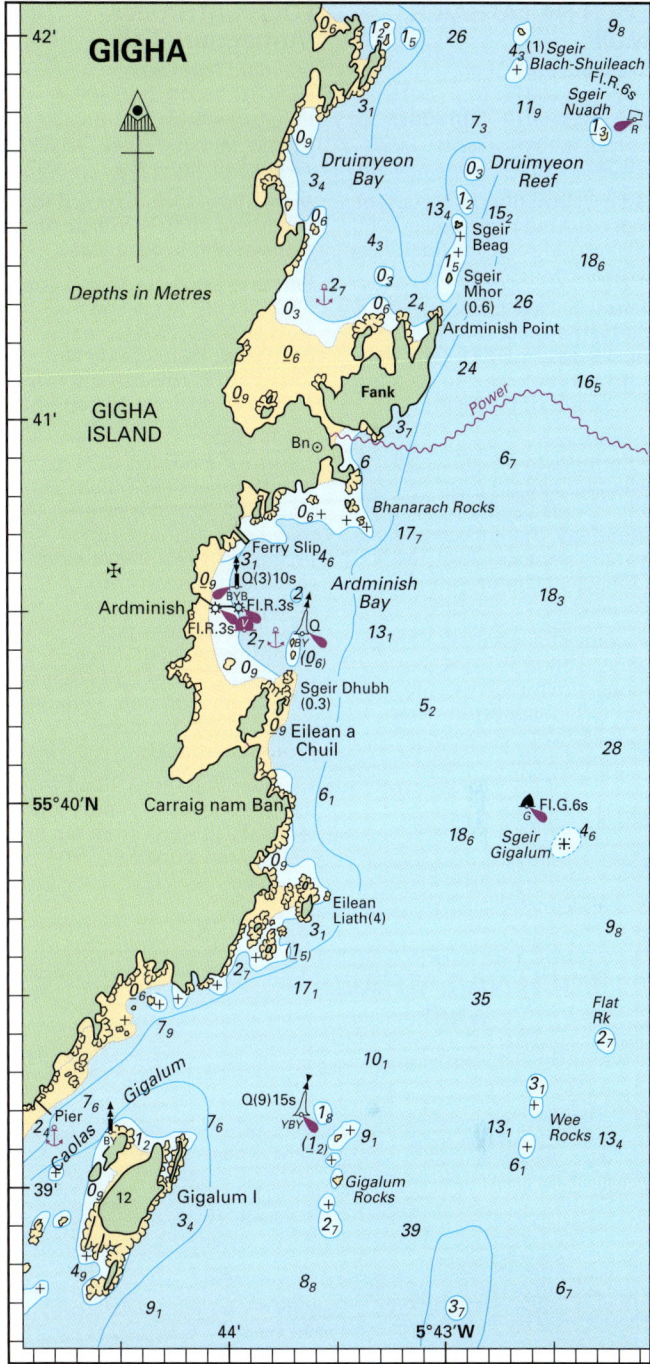

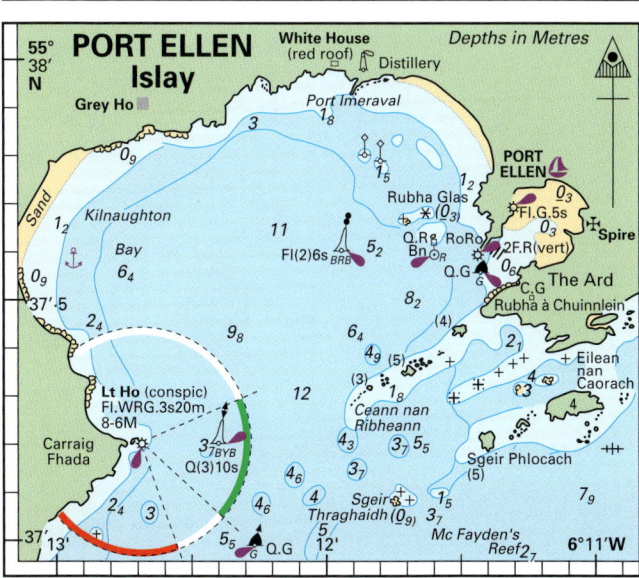

The Cruising Almanac

LOCH NA LATHAICH, Mull*

Standard Port Oban
HW (sp) –0015 (np) –0015
LW (sp) –0010 (np) –0015
MHWS MHWN MLWN MLWS
+0·3m +0·1m 0·0m –0·1m

An excellent hbr on N coast of Ross of Mull providing good shelter and some facilities. Easy access.

Entrance Pass either side of En na Liathanaich, Fl.WR.6s12m8/6M. Give the En a berth of 2ca and keep to the W side of the loch.

Anchorages
• Entrance to L Caol to W.
• S of En Ban off pier.
• In bay off Bendorran, many moorings, trip line advised.
• Staffa (Fingals Cave) 5M N. Difficult anchorage off SE corner.

Facilities Bunessan: PO, shops, garage, hotel at 1½M. Bus to Craignure for ferry to Oban. Bus to Fionnphort for ferry to Iona.

LOCH EATHARNA (Arinagour), Coll

Standard Port Oban
HW (sp) +0010 (np) +0025
LW (sp) +0015 (np) +0025
MHWS MHWN MLWN MLWS
+0·4m +0·3m n/a n/a

Main hbr of Coll. Exposed to winds from E to S. Village of Arinagour at head of loch.

Entrance Leave Bo Mor G con buoy Fl.G.6s to stb and make for pier DirOc.WRG.7s and 2F.R(vert), then ½ca off W shore turn N towards old stone pier where loch shoals rapidly.

Anchorages
• Visitors' moorings to N of pier 10 tonnes GRT max. Untenable in winds greater than Force 4 from E to S because of swell. Pay at ferry terminal or honesty box at hotel.
• Anchor off stone pier according to depth. Note drying rks NW of En Eatharna.
• NE of En Eatharna. Swinging space limited but more protected from SE.

Facilities PO, shops, hotel offering showers, laundry and meals. Fuel, water from tap in field behind stone pier. Ferry to Oban.

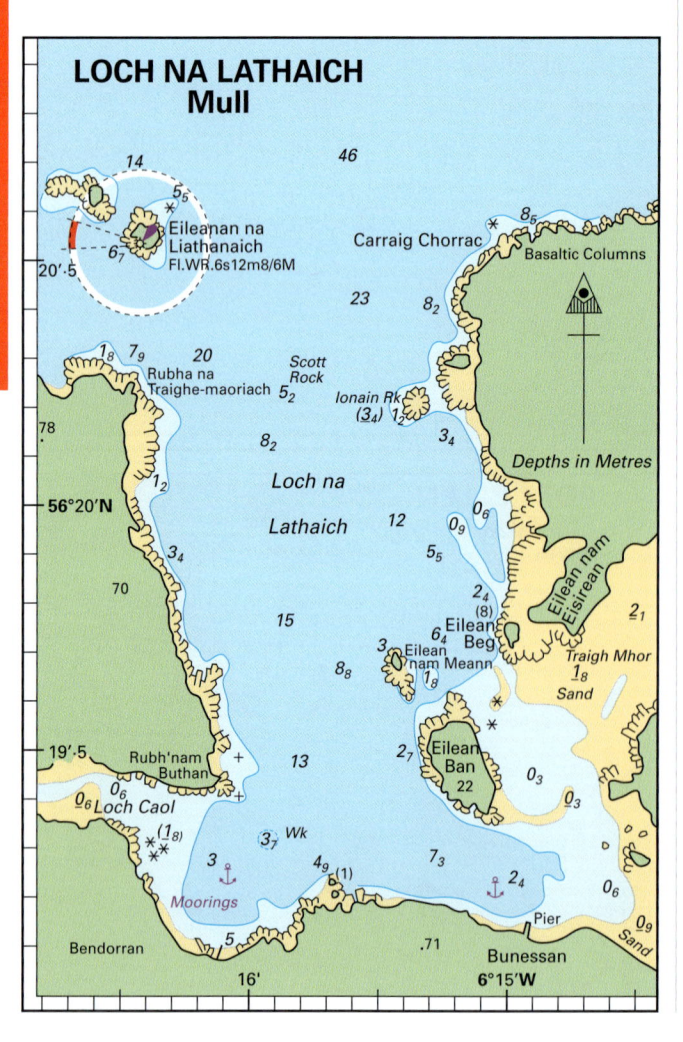

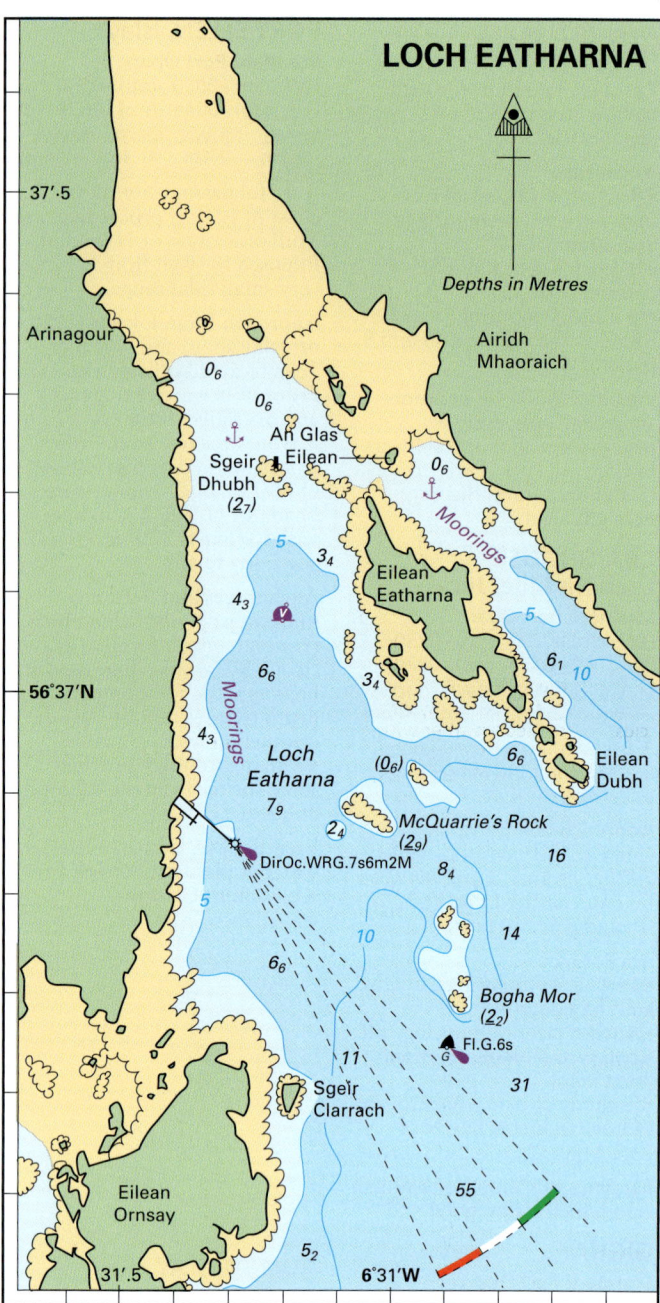

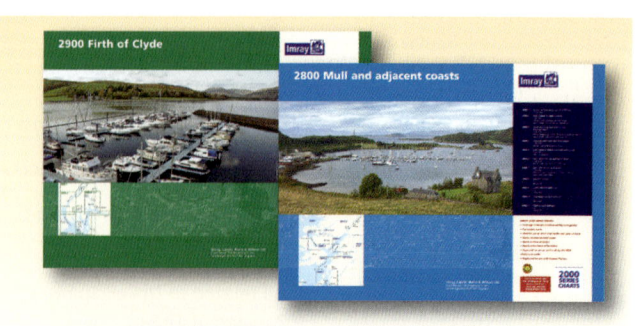

SCOTLAND – WEST COAST

• Folios of charts in a plastic wallet
• Small format A2 size sheets – 594mm x 420mm
• Yeoman plotter points
• All WGS 84 Datum
• Corrected to date of issue with free updating service from www.imray.com

156

C. The Outer Hebrides

Passage lights	BA No
Flannan Is Fl(2)30s101m20M AIS	4028
Butt of Lewis Fl.5s52m25M AIS	3968
Tiumpan Head Fl(2)15s55m25M	3972
En Glas E L Tarbert Fl(3)20s43m23M Racon AIS	3990
Ushenish Fl.20s54m19M	4004
Barra Head Fl.15s208m18M AIS	4020
Ru A'Mhail Fl(3)15s45m19M	4236

The navigation of the W side of the outer Hebrides should not be attempted without a crew capable of handling the yacht in severe conditions. Heavy seas are common along the whole 100M of the western seaboard and the coast should only be closed in settled weather with large-scale charts aboard. Shelter can be found by sailing either N or S of the chain into the lee of the islands. Off Harris, Benbecula and N and S Uist a vessel should stand off several miles. The land on the W is so low that an accurate visual fix may be difficult to obtain.

In order to make a passage to the W side of the Outer Hebrides the three possible passages are:

- Round the Butt of Lewis and passing down the W side between the coast and the Flannan Is.
- Through the Sound of Harris. This passage requires strict attention to the tides and the channel taken for which BA chart *2802* is absolutely essential. CCC Directions *Outer Hebrides*.
- From Castlebay at the S end through either the Sound of Barra or the Sound of Berneray for which BA charts *2770* or *2769* are required. Again CCC Directions are detailed.

The E coast of Lewis and Harris is clear from the Butt of Lewis to the Shiant Is. There are numerous dangerous rocks and islets with strong tides and overfalls extending from the Shiants to Ru Hunish (N Skye). Heavy seas may be experienced S of the Shiants. Between the Sound of Harris and the S end of N Uist the coast is clear beyond ½M off-shore but Benbecula and its islets should be given a berth of at least 1M. Dangerous rocks exist up to 2M S of Barra.

Tidal Streams
All related to Dover Sp rates

Ru Uisenish to Shiant Is
+0500NE −0100SW 3-4kn

En Glas (Harris) to Sgeir Inoc
+0500NE −0100SW 2½kn

Ru Hunish (Skye)
+0400NE −0200SW 2½kn

ST KILDA

Standard Port Stornoway

HW −0040	LW −0045
MHWS	MHWN	MLWN	MLWS
−1·4m	−1·1m	−0·8m	−0·3m

A small group of islands. The main island is owned by National Trust for Scotland and leased to the Scottish National Heritage and the Army. As a courtesy, visitors should call *Kilda Warden* on VHF 12/16 on arrival. Excellent information can be found at www.kilda.org.uk.

Approach Fine, settled weather is particularly desirable when undertaking the 35M+ journey to St Kilda. Rip tides form between the Islands of the group when wind and tide are opposed.

Anchorages
In Village Bay off concrete pier. Ldg Lts Oc.5s 270°. Subject to swell. Untenable in winds from ENE to SSW when Glen Bay to NW may be possible with line ashore, but subject to extreme squalls.

Facilities Water from well near landing. Seek assistance from warden.

WEST LOCH TARBERT, Harris

Standard Port Stornoway

HW −0015	LW −0046
MHWS	MHWN	MLWN	MLWS
−1·1m	−0·9m	−0·5m	−0·0m

One of the few harbours on the W coast of the outer Hebrides offering protection from all winds except those from the W.

Approach Either side of Taransay, the N being clearer. From S keep Toe Head and summit of Coppay Is in line. Once past Bo Ushig (dr 2m), ½M S of Taransay, keep to mid-channel to avoid sand spits on either side of the Sound.

Anchorages
- Head of loch at Tarbert.
- Taransay N of Corran Raah spit.
- Loch Leosavay: Beware drying rocks SW of jetty.
- Loch Bun Abhainn-eader: N of Ardhasaig. Anchor SW of chimney of old whaling station (swell) or off E bay. Telephone, store, garage (marine diesel) on main road. Land with permission, at fish farm in SE corner of bay.

Facilities Tarbert: Shops, PO, hotel. Ferry to Skye.

STORNOWAY, Lewis*

Standard Port Stornoway

Busy ferry and fishing port. Excellent website with marina information and plan at www.stornowayportauthority.com.

Entrance Between Holm Point and Arnish Point. Beware of the Beasts of Holm, drying rocks marked by unlit G bn off Holm Point and Reef Rock off Arnish Point marked by port hand R can buoy Q.R. At night use the sectored lights shown on plan. Call *Stornoway Harbour* VHF 12 before entering, they will allocate a berth.

Anchorages
- In bay NW of En na Gobhail. Shoals.
- 77 pontoon berths at inner harbour beyond lifeboat. Beware shallow water marked by port hand pillars just west of the pontoons.
- Glumaig Harbour, 3M S of town. Advisable to buoy anchor.

Facilities PO, Launderette, shops closed all day Wednesday, charts, water, diesel, slip. Showers at Leisure Centre. Ferry to Ullapool.

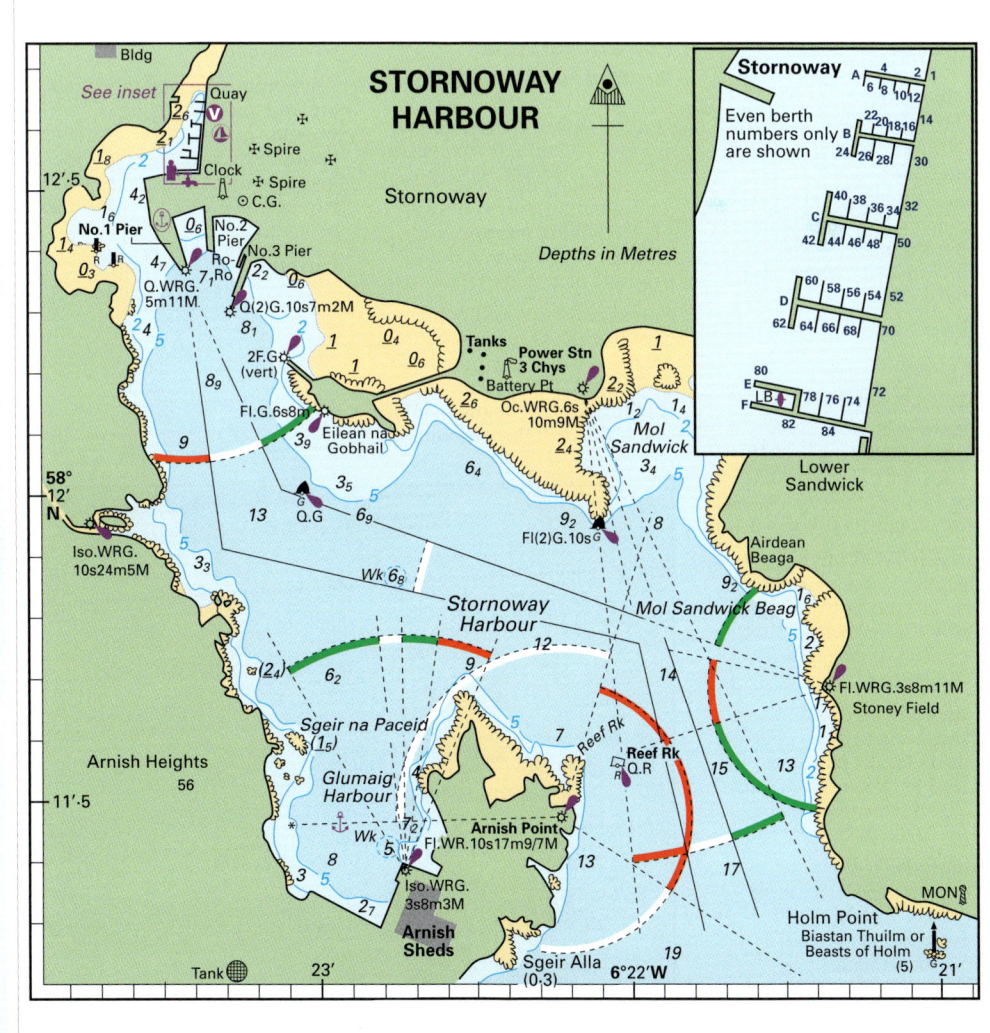

SCOTLAND – WEST COAST

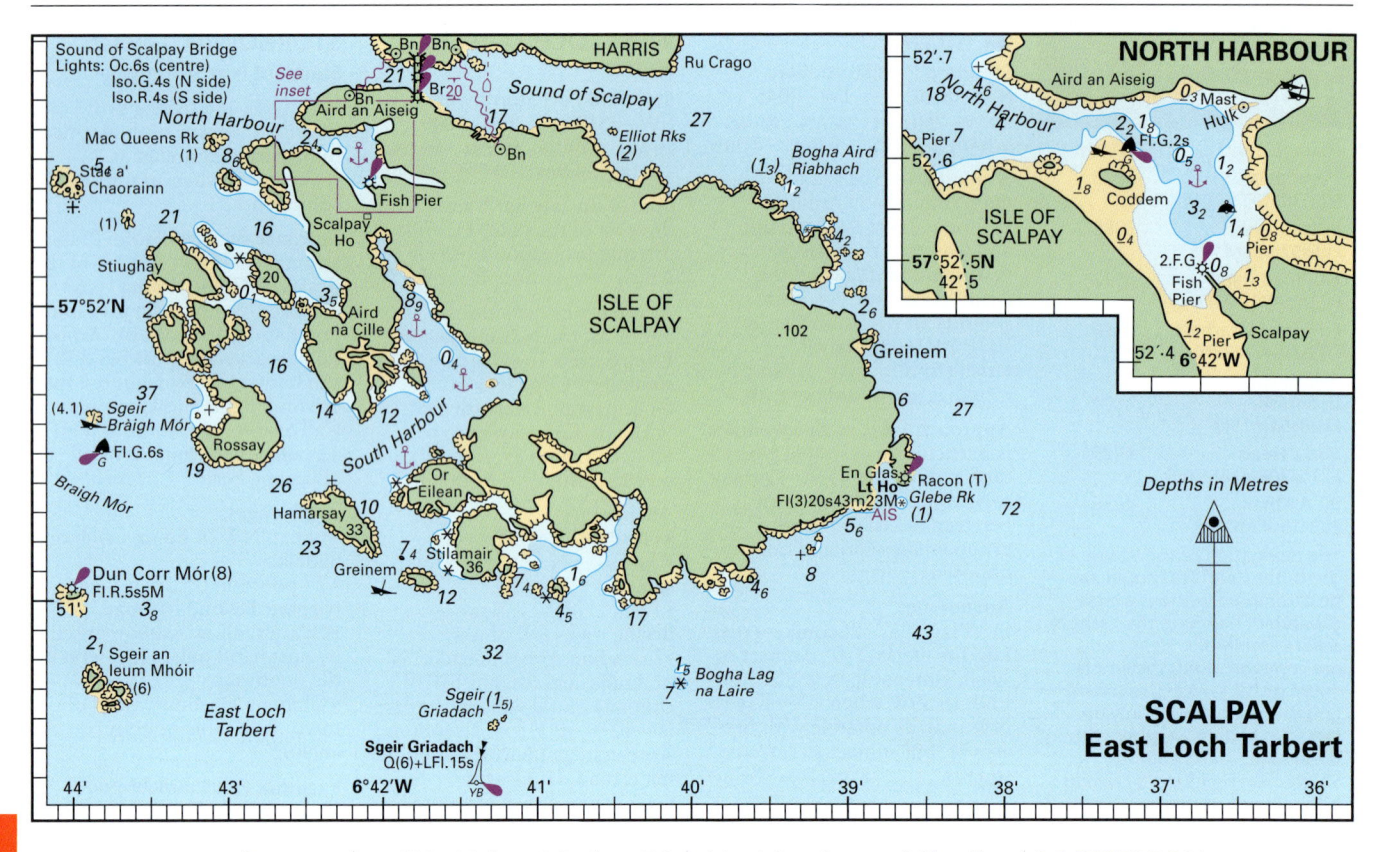

LOCH SHELL, Lewis

Standard Port Stornoway
HW (sp) +0000 (np) −0013
LW (sp) +0000 (np) −0017
MHWS MHWN MLWN MLWS
0·0m   −0·1m −0·1m 0·0m

Entrance Enter S of En Lubhard. Note drying rocks to NW of En.

Anchorages
• Head of loch. Shoals. Exposed to E. Fish farms developing.
• Tob Eisken.
• Tob Lemreway leaving En Lubbard to port.

Facilities None.

SCALPAY, East Loch Tarbert*

Standard Port Stornoway
HW (sp) −0010 (np) −0025
LW (sp) −0010 (np) −0020
MHWS MHWN MLWN MLWS
+0·2m   0·0m +0·1m +0·1m

Approach The Sound of Scalpay is clearer than the passage to the S of the island, the only danger being Elliot Rocks (2m) off the S shore. Pass under br (20m).

Entrance to Scalpay N hbr give Aird an Aiseg to NW a berth of ½ca. Ldg marks two W ▲s in line lead between G con buoy Fl.G.2s to stb and submerged rock 1·1m to port.

Anchorages
• N hbr off pier (2F.G(vert) Lts). Good shelter.
• S hbr, not easy to identify rocks off entrance.
• Tarbert 3M WNW of Scalpay. WSW of Ferry pier, not much room. Exposed to E.
• Pontoons are planned.

Facilities Tarbert: PO, shops EC Thursday, hotel, diesel, water at pier. Ferry to Skye.

LOCH RODEL
Poll an Tighmhail

Standard Port Stornoway
HW −0015 (approx)
MHWS MHWN MLWN MLWS
+0·6m +0·2m −0·1m −0·1m

The unusual anchorage at Poll an Tighmhail offers complete protection but entrance only at HW±0100. Nearby, a fine example of a medieval church.

Entrance By way of Loch Rodel avoiding the Duncan rock 0·3m off the W shore. Although Tighmhail appears to have three entrances the only viable one is through Bay channel dries 1·9m, the most N'ly off Loch Rodel and to the N of Corr-eilean. Enter HW±0100 according to draught. Do not attempt to enter via the other two channels.

Anchorage Visitors' moorings are laid and anchoring is possible outside these although depth in parts deep, requiring kedge to avoid swinging. Use a trip line as bottom has fishing nets and gear.

Facilities None but hotel.

LOCHMADDY, North Uist*

Standard Port Stornoway
HW (sp) −0014 (np) −0044
LW (sp) −0016 (np) −0030
MHWS MHWN MLWN MLWS
0·0m   −0·1m −0·1m 0·0m

Approach From S pass either side of Madadh Mor (26m high). Note submerged rocks ½ca N of Leac nan Madah. From N pass between Weavers Point and Madadh Beag (6m). Thence by channel between Glas En Mor, Fl(2)G.4s and Ru Nam Pleac, Fl.R.4s and S of Ruig Liath Q.G to W sector of Lt Fl(3)WRG.8s. Follow Ldg Lts front 2F.G(vert), rear Oc.G.8s on 298° to pier.

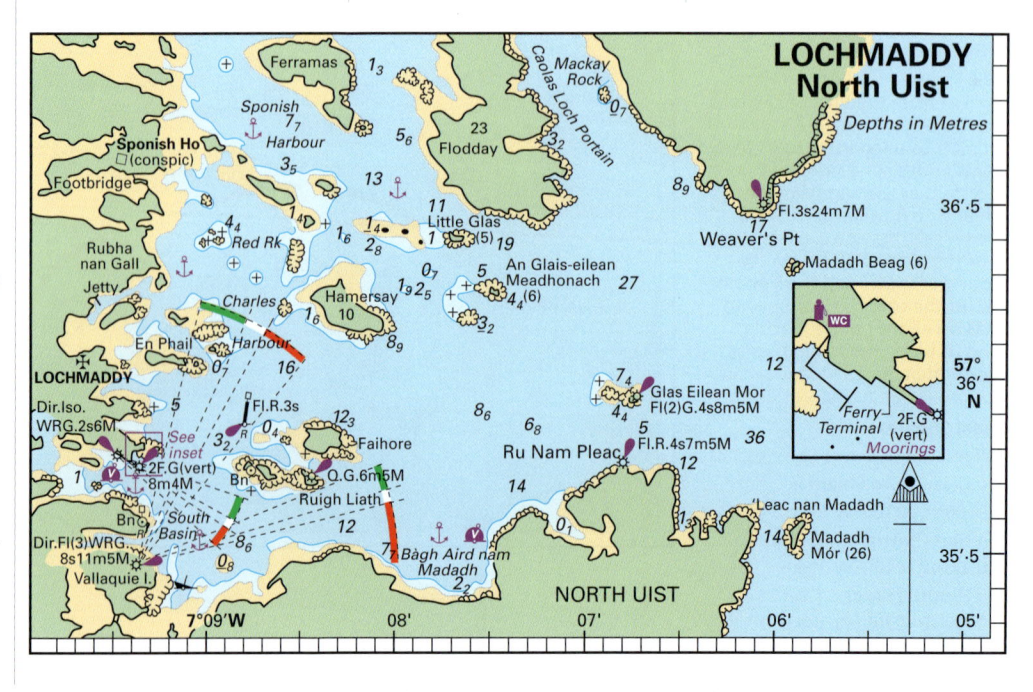

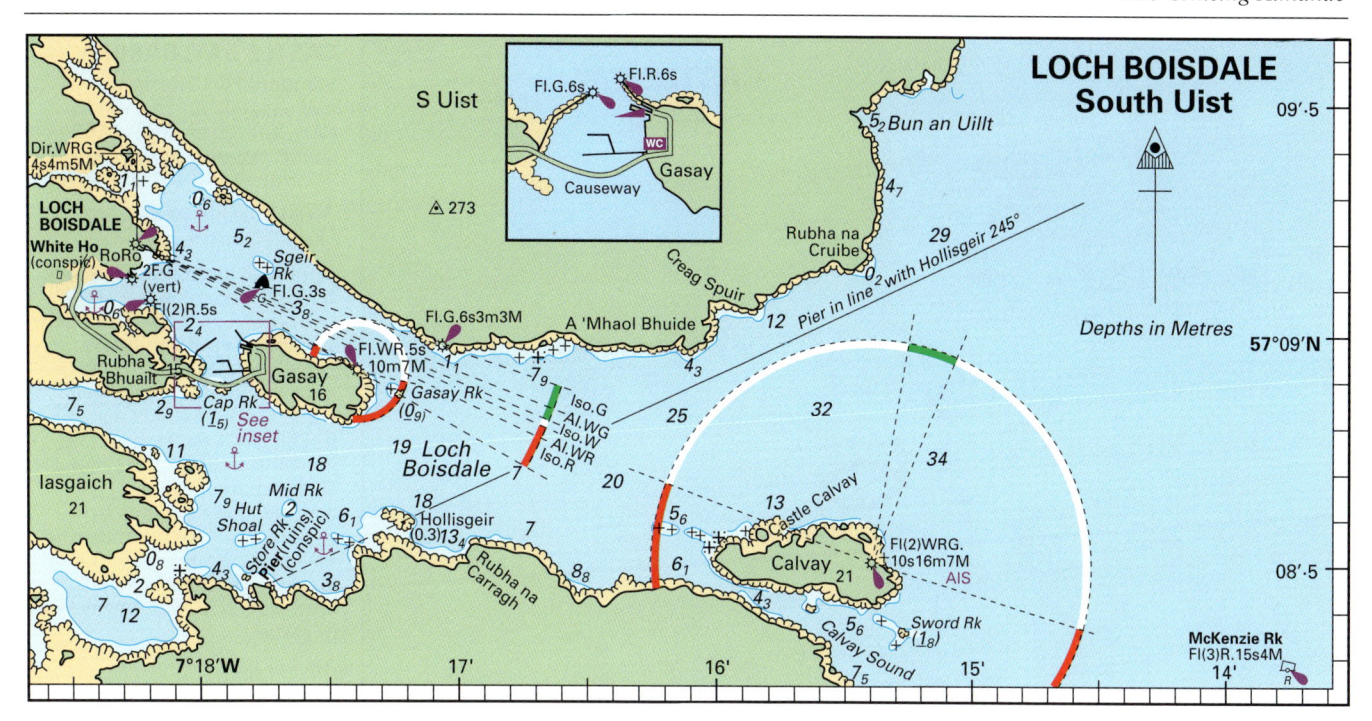

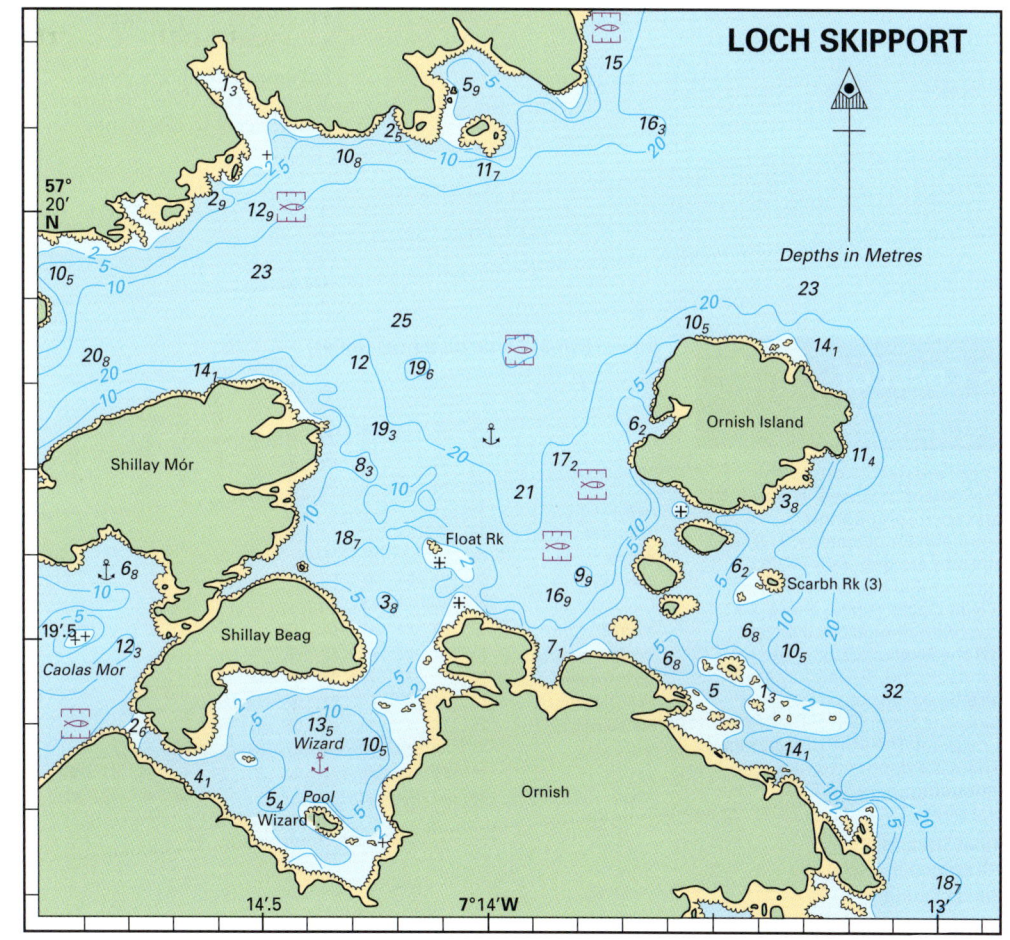

2·3m) thence mid-channel keeping Wizard Is just open of Skillay Beg. Note drying rock (0·3m) 1¼ca NW of Wizard Is.
• Bagh Charmaig: (NNW of Shillay Mor) Note reef ½ca off middle of W shore. Anchor at head of bay or just within E arm which shoals. Good holding.

Facilities None.

LOCH BOISDALE*

Standard Port Stornoway
HW (sp) –0030 (np) –0055
LW (sp) –0020 (np) –0040
MHWS MHWN MLWN MLWS
–0·7m –0·7m –0·3m –0·2m

Approach and Entrance Pass between Ru na Cruibe and Calvay Is Lt Fl(2)WRG.10s then N of Gasay Lt bn Fl.WR.5s at NE pt of island. Beware Gasay Rocks (dr 0·9m) and an obstruction extending 2½ca to E of end of Is. Follow marked channel to pier 2F.G.

Anchorages and Berthing
• New marina and fishery pier has 51 berths for local and visiting yachts.
• Good anchorage is available NE of ferry pier. Prone to strong gusts when wind in N.
• S of loch NE of ruined pier. Note rocks 2ca NNW of pier and many marine farms in this area.

Facilities Very limited supplies. Hotel. Water and electric on pontoons at pier, fuel at garage. Shops at Daliburgh 3M. Ferry to mainland.

Anchorages and Berthing
• Pontoons, with water, electricity, and WiFi, SW of the ferry terminal with 15 berths. Laundry, toilets, showers. Berthing master ☎ 07453 606899. Beware, only the outer 3rd of the pontoon has 2·0m at LW.
• Visitors' moorings SW of pier in soft mud.
• SW corner of S Basin.
• Bagh Aird nan Madadh. (Heavy moorings for visitors).

• Loch Portain 2M NNE. Keep in mid-channel NE of Flodday and 1ca off Ru nam Gall. Good holding and protection.
• Tie up to pier if no ferry due but beware of surge.

Facilities PO, shop, water at pier, diesel, calor, showers at hotel. Ferry to Skye and Harris.

LOCH SKIPPORT, South Uist

Standard Port Stornoway
HW (sp) –0025 (np) –0100
LW (sp) –0024 (np) –0024
MHWS MHWN MLWN MLWS
–0·2m –0·4m –0·3m –0·2m

Easy access N of Ornish Is. Several remote anchorages.

Anchorages
• Wizard Pool: Keep well over towards the Shillays Mor and Beg to avoid Float Rock (dr

SCOTLAND – WEST COAST

159

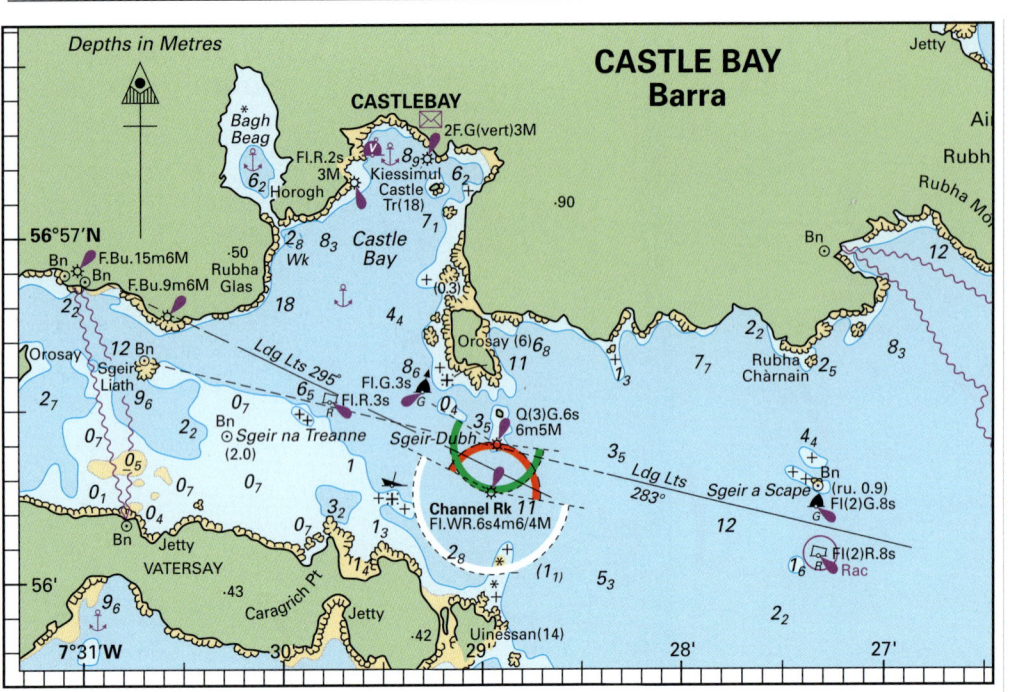

CASTLE BAY, BARRA*

Standard Port Stornoway
HW (sp) −0040 (np) −0115
LW (sp) −0045 (np) −0100

MHWS	MHWN	MLWN	MLWS
−0·5m	−0·6m	−0·3m	−0·1m

A valuable hbr at S end of Outer Hebrides.

Approach and Entrance From Bo Vich Chuan buoy, Q(6)+LFl.15s, 2·2M E of Sgeir a Scape, keep R can buoy, Fl(2)R.8s, close to port and head midway between Sgeir Dubh Q(3)G.6s and Channel Rock Fl.WR.6s. Pick up Ldg line on Ru Glas 295°, Or and W day marks, F.Bu Lts, between these two bns by steering 270° for not more than ½M from Sgeir a Scape. Leave G con buoy, Fl.G.3s, to stb until pier, 2F.G vert, opens W of castle.

Anchorages
- 12 visitors' moorings.
- NW of castle in 6–10m.
- Pontoons are planned.
- Vatersay Bay.

Facilities PO, shops, hotel. Water at pier, diesel at garage, Calor. Ferry to mainland.

SCOTLAND – WEST COAST

D. Firth of Clyde and S Coast of Galloway

CAMPBELTOWN TO PORT PATRICK

Passage lights	BA No
Mull of Kintyre Fl(2)20s91m24M	4272
Sanda Is Fl.10s50m15M AIS	4274
Davaar Fl(2)10s37m15M	4276
Toward Point Fl.10s21m22M	4362
Little Cumbrae Fl.6s28m14M	4346
Holy Is, Pillar Rock Fl(2)20s38m18M	4330
Pladda Fl(3)30s40m17M	4326
Turnberry Point Fl.15s29m12M	4580
Ailsa Craig Fl.4s18m17M	4582
Corsewall Point Fl(5)30s34m22M AIS	4604

The waters of the Clyde Estuary are very popular with many yachts and consequently there are more facilities for yachtsmen. The passages are protected and well marked.

There are restrictions to the movement of vessels in Gareloch and Loch Long during submarine movements. The tidal streams are generally weak turning N'ly at HW Dover and S'ly at Dover +0600. There is a race with dangerous overfalls off the Mull of Kintyre and in Sanda Sound. Strong tides will also be encountered between Bennane Head (8M SSE of Ailsa Craig) and the Mull of Galloway. There is a dangerous race extending some 3M S of the Mull.

Tidal Streams
All related to Dover Sp rates
Sanda Sound
+0500E −0100W 5kn
Davaar Is
HWD N +0600S 4kn
Black Head
−0130N −0430S 5kn

Inner Firth of Clyde distances (miles)

	Ardrishaig	Ardrossan	Bangor	Bowling	Campbeltown	Inverkip	Lamlash	Largs Marina	Mull of Kintyre	Portpatrick	Stranraer	Tarbert	Troon
Ardrishaig	0												
Ardrossan	33	0											
Bangor	84	66	0										
Bowling	54	37	97	0									
Campbeltown	40	35	49	65	0								
Inverkip	39	20	81	17	46	0							
Lamlash	33	12	57	41	25	25	0						
Largs Marina	33	11	72	25	41	9	18	0					
Mull of Kintyre	55	44	39	74	21	59	35	51	0				
Portpatrick	75	53	23	83	41	68	45	59	37	0			
Stranraer	71	46	39	78	39	62	40	54	38	22	0		
Tarbert	10	25	75	46	32	30	25	24	47	66	63	0	
Troon	39	8	64	43	34	26	15	18	44	49	43	31	0

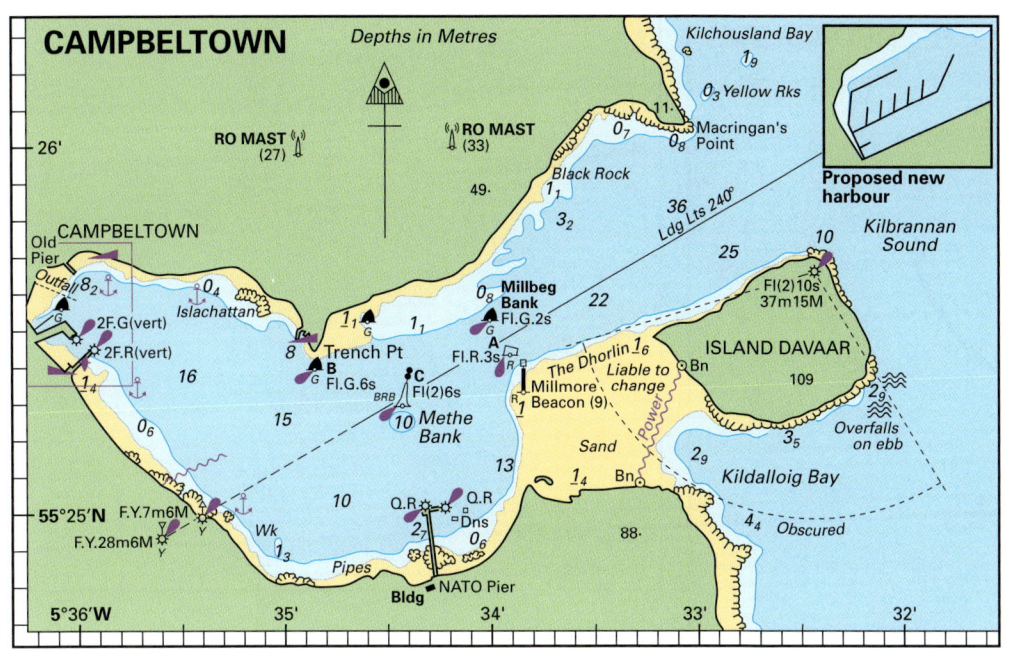

CAMPBELTOWN

Standard Port Greenock
HW (sp) −0025 (np) −0005
LW (sp) +0005 (np) −0015
MHWS   MHWN   MLWN   MLWS
−0·5m   −0·3m   +0·1m   +0·2m

A well sheltered loch. Useful if waiting to round the Mull.

Approach and Entrance From N avoid Otterard Rock marked by E card Lt buoy, 1M N of entrance. From S pass to N of Davaar Is, Lt Fl(2)10s, then enter loch on 240° Ldg Lts F.Y. Thence to hbr entrance. Lts 2F.G(vert) and 2F.R(vert).

Anchorages
- Berth at new pontoons just NW of N quay. Beware shallow water to NW of pontoons.
- Anchor S of hbr.

Facilities PO, shops. Usual facilities at pontoon. Showers and payment facilities at N quay, next to lifeboat shop.

☏/VHF HM 01586 522522, VHF 16, 12, 13; Pontoon Berthing Master *Mobile* 07798 524821.

EAST LOCH TARBERT*, Loch Fyne

Standard Port Greenock
HW −0005   LW −0003
MHWS   MHWN   MLWN   MLWS
+0·2m   +0·1m   0·0m   0·0m

An excellent, sheltered and popular hbr.

Entrance Pass N of bn, Fl.R.2·5s, and S of bn, Q.G, off En a Choic (ignoring buoys marking passage N of Choic). Leave stb bn VQ.G. S of Sgeir Bhuidhe to stb before turning NW towards visitors' pontoon and finger berths (row A). Call Tarbert Harbour on VHF Ch 14 before entering.

Berths
- Pontoon and finger berths on NW side of hbr.
- Alongside fish quay, for taking on fuel only.

There is no anchoring space within hbr.

Facilities Shops, PO, chandlers, charts. Slip, sailmaker, some marine and electronic repairs. Fuel, diesel on fish quay (weekdays only). Bus to Glasgow.

☏/VHF HM 01880 820344, VHF 14.

PORTAVADIE

Standard Port Greenock
HW (sp) −0005 (np) −0005
LW (sp) −0005 (np) +0000
MHWS   MHWN   MLWN   MLWS
+0·2m   +0·1m   +0·1m   0·0m

A fully serviced modern marina with excellent facilities. Access at all states of the tide.

Entrance From the south be aware of a fish farm just to the north of Rubah Stillaig, otherwise no problems identifying the entrance. Lit for easy access at night. Enter between breakwaters Fl.R.2s and Fl(2)G.8s.

Berths 230 fully serviced berths accommodating all sizes up to 70ft LOA with no restriction on draft. Diesel and petrol available from fuel berth.

Facilities Shop, selling basic provisions and gifts, limited Chandlery, Yard services, Bar/Restaurant, Range of self catering accommodation, Bike hire.

☏/VHF 01700 811075; VHF 80
www.portavadiemarina.com

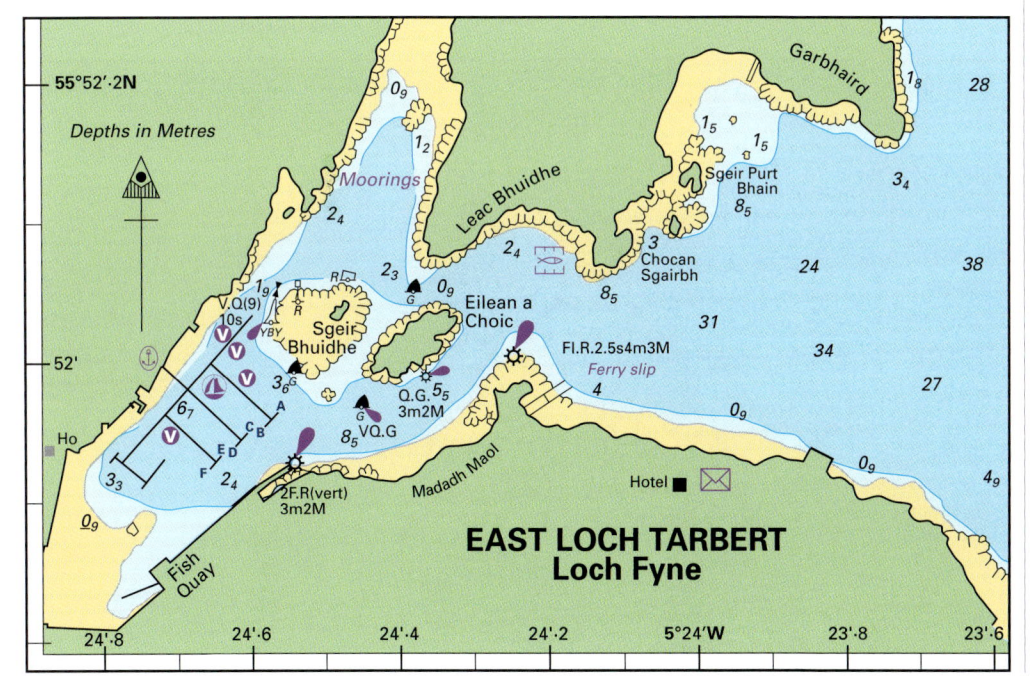

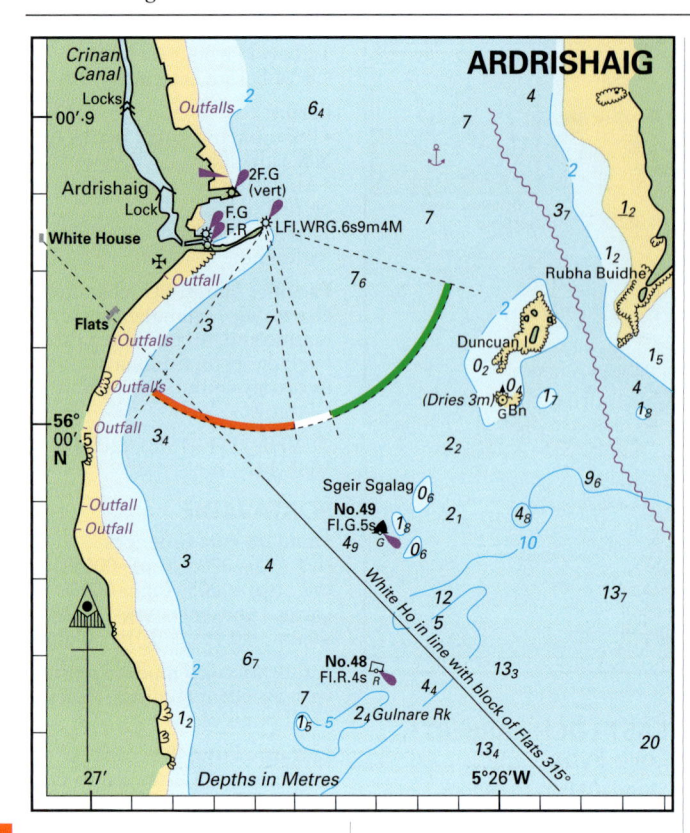

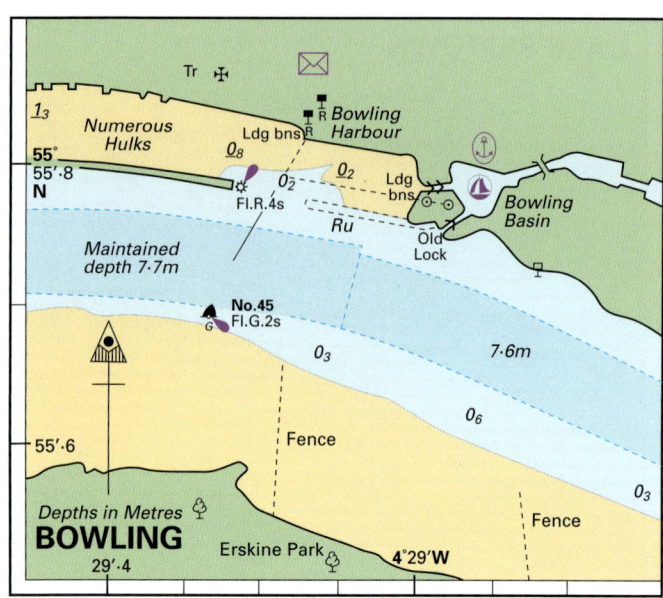

The Cruising Almanac

SCOTLAND – WEST COAST

ARDRISHAIG*

Standard Port Greenock
HW +0005

MHWS	MHWN	MLWN	MLWS
+0·2m	0·0m	+0·1m	–0·1m

This is the hbr at the entrance to the S end of the Crinan canal in Loch Gilp. *For Canal Directions see p.154.*

Approach 3M from the hbr pass either side of Big Rock 2·1m. Pass between Nos.48 and 49 R & G buoys, Ldg line conspic W house and block of flats, 315°.

Entrance Give the S breakwater a wide berth and wait on pontoon until lock gate opens.

☎/VHF Canal Office 01546 603210, Sea Lock 01546 602458 or 07919 374678, VHF 16/74.

BOWLING*

Standard Port Greenock
HW (sp) +0020 (np) +0010
LW (sp) +0055 (np) +0030

MHWS	MHWN	MLWN	MLWS
+0·6m	+0·5m	+0·3m	+0·1m

In the canal the air draft is 3m; there are facilities for masts to be unstepped at Bowling. Locking HW±0200.

Approach From seaward contact estuary control tower VHF 12 or ☎ 01475 726221 prior to arrival at No.1 buoy off Greenock container terminal.

Entrance To port off the River Clyde opposite G con Lt buoy Fl.G.2s No.45 turn on to Ldg line 030° marked by R posts with topmarks. Once inside ruined breakwater marked by posts turn on to Ldg line 100° marked by R posts and topmarks. Follow lock keeper's instructions when entering lock mooring on port side.

Transit Allow three days. 39 locks including sea locks. To pass the Dumbarton road br a drop lock enables boats to pass under. Some locks are operated by BW staff, some by the boats crew with assistance and some entirely by the boats crew. Exit at Grangemouth into River Carron, step mast at Port Edgar. *See Scotland – E Coast section on p.120.* Bowling Basin operates 0830–2100 June–August daily but shorter opening hours other periods. Transit time five days allowed. Further information www.scottishcanals.co.uk.

☎/VHF 01389 877969, VHF 16, 74 Call sign. *Bowling Basin* (only manned during sealock opening hours).

INVERKIP*

Standard Port Greenock
HW –0015 (approx)

MHWS	MHWN	MLWN	MLWS
–0·1m	0·0m	+0·1m	+0·1m

A large well-founded marina and convenient stopover before entering the Clyde.

Approach and Entrance ½M N of power station (conspic) head for G con buoy Fl.G.5s and follow buoyed channel into marina.

Berthing Kip marina with 600 berths and all facilities and chandlery.

Facilities Rly to Glasgow

☎/VHF 01475 521485, VHF 80.

www.kipmarina.co.uk

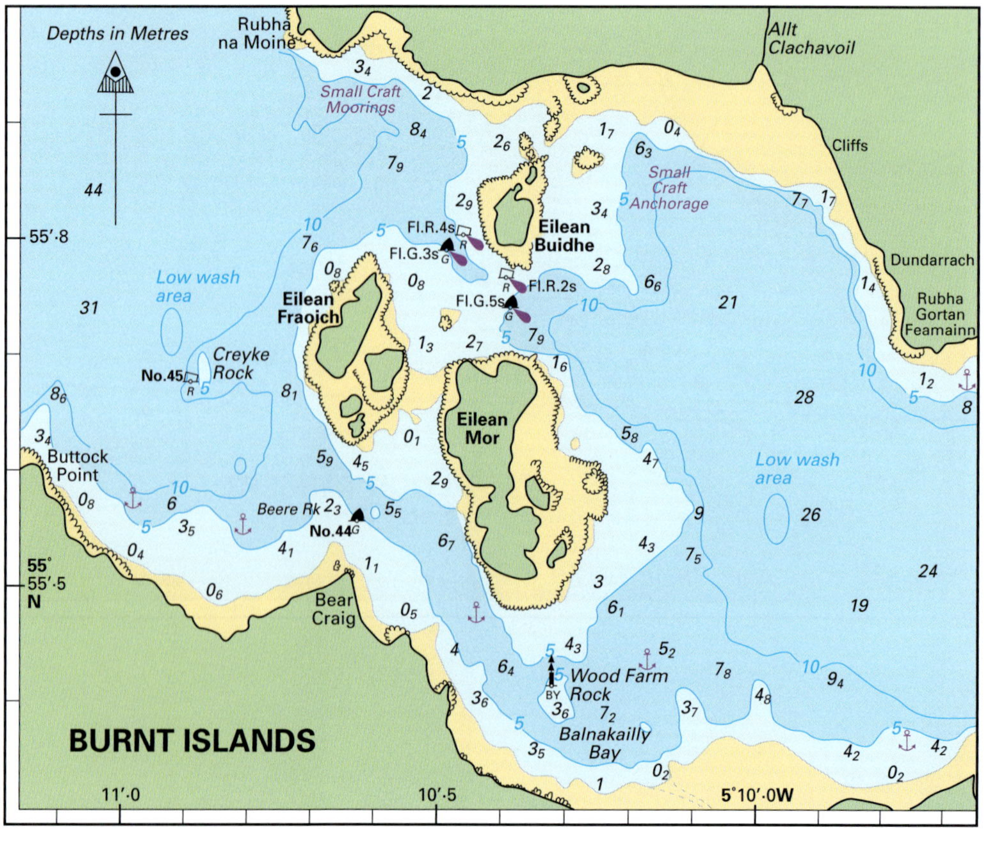

162

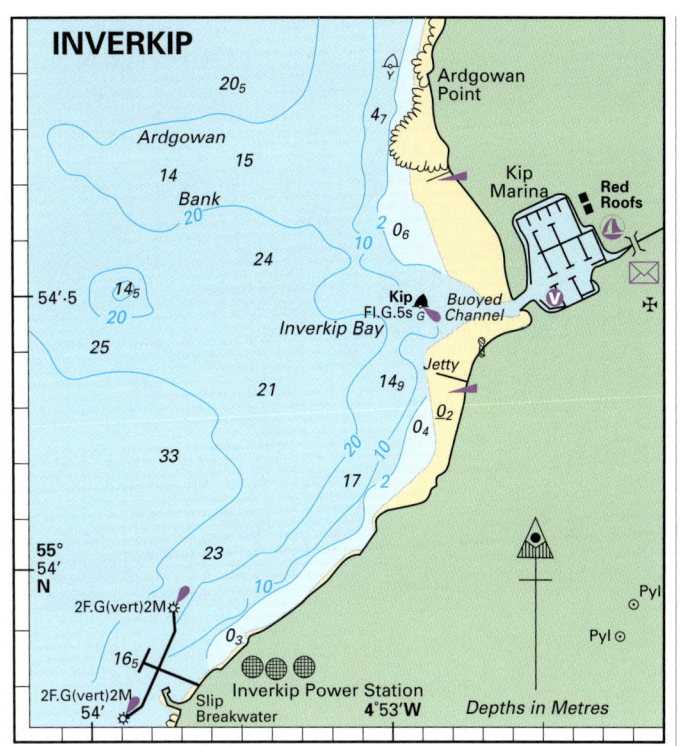

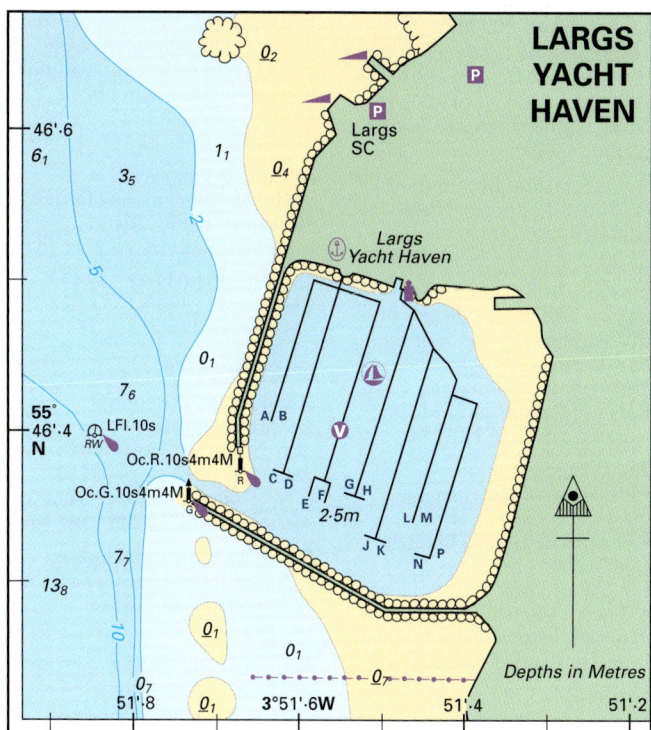

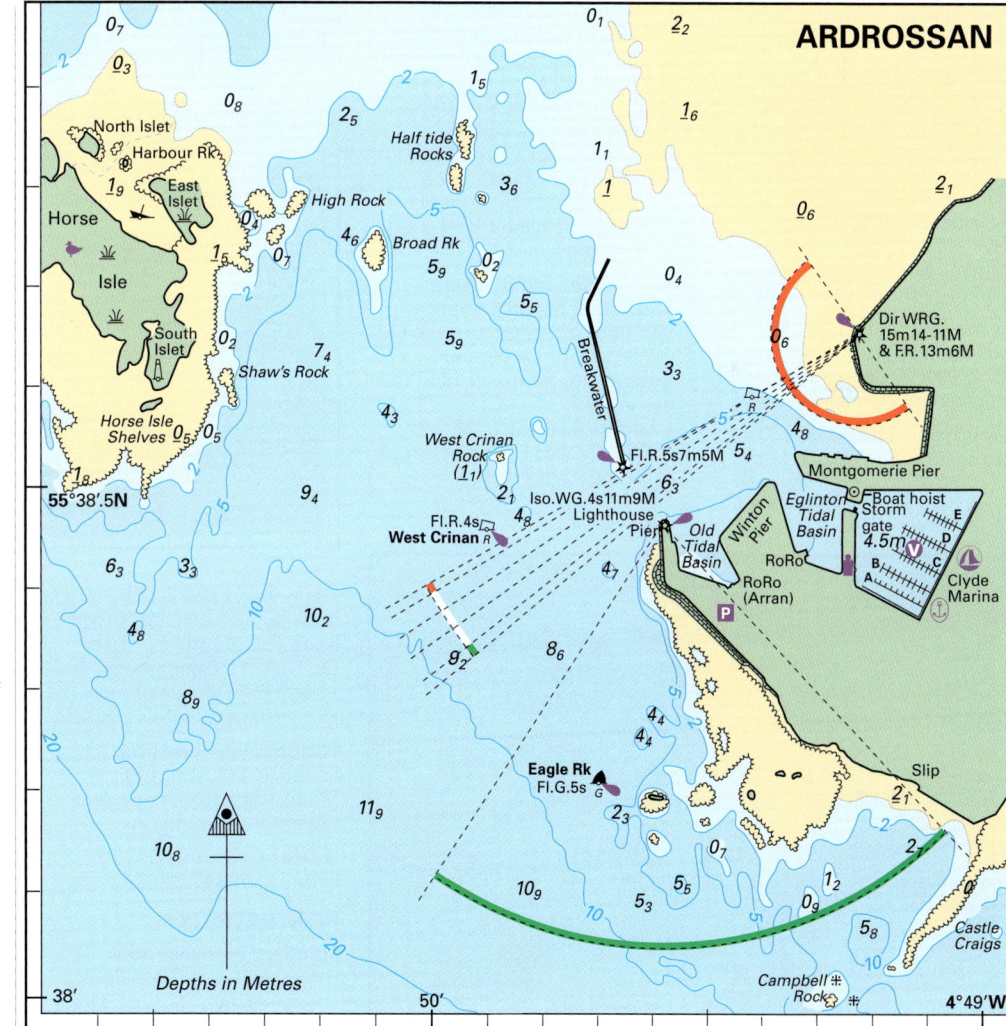

LARGS YACHT HAVEN*

Tidal data as Inverkip

A convenient modern marina on the Firth of Clyde 1M S of Largs.

Approach Easy access. Pass close to RW sph buoy LFl.10s and enter between breakwaters (Oc.G.10s and Oc.R.10s) painted W.

Facilities Full marina facilities, including chandlery, PO, Shops EC Wednesday, hotels 1M, Rly to Glasgow.

☏/VHF Marina 01475 675333, VHF 37, 80.
www.yachthavens.com/largs

ARDROSSAN*

Standard Port Greenock
HW −0015   LW −0010

MHWS	MHWN	MLWN	MLWS
−0·2m	−0·2m	+0·1m	+0·1m

A well-protected deep water marina with 20 visitors' berths. Entrance closed by a storm gate in extreme weather. The outer harbour is the Cal Mac ferry port for Arran.

Approach From the W or NW keep clear of low-lying Horse Isle, conspic tr on S end, ringed by drying ledges. The passage between Horse Isle and the mainland should not be attempted. From S or SE make for 55°38′·0N 4°50′·2W. Head for entrance leaving G con buoy Eagle Rock Fl.G.5s to stb and R can buoy West Crinan Rock Fl.R.4s to port. Inside the hbr entrance, engines must be used, keep clear of commercial craft, monitor VHF 12/16.

Traffic Signals shown from control tr at entrance to marina.

• 3F.R.(vert) Hbr and Marina closed.
• 3F.G.(vert) Hbr closed, Marina open; pleasure craft may enter/leave marina.
• 2F.R. over 1F.G. Hbr open, Marina closed.

Entrance DirWRG.15m14–11M, W sector, 055° leads to hbr entrance between the breakwaters.

Berthing As instructed by Clyde Marina or on the third pontoon from N.

Facilities as expected of a modern marina. Boatyard, chandlery, sail repairs. Large supermarket nearby. WiFi. Rly to Glasgow.

☏/VHF 01294 607077, VHF 80, Call sign *Clyde Marina* (office hours seven days).
www.clydemarina.com

SCOTLAND – WEST COAST

LAMLASH, Arran

Standard Port Greenock
HW (sp) −0016 (np) −0036
LW (sp) −0004 (np) −0024

MHWS	MHWN	MLWN	MLWS
−0·2m	−0·2m	n/a	n/a

A large natural hbr on the E of Is of Arran opposite Holy Island, limited shelter.

Approach by either N or S passages lit by port and stb marks. The flood tide sets into the S and out of the N of the bay. In strong NW winds the S channel may be difficult. Pillar Rk Lt Fl(2)20s38m25M, is situated on SE of Holy Is.

Anchorages
• Off Lamlash. 25 visitors' buoys. Exposed to SE.
• W of Holy Island (Budhist sanctuary).
• In SW of hbr.
• When Lamlash Bay is exposed, better shelter may be found in Brodick 3M to the N.

Facilities PO, shops EC Wednesday, hotels. Water near pier. Showers at Pier Head Café. Diesel in cans. Bus to Brodick for ferry to Ardrossan.

☏/VHF Holy Isle Ferry 07970 771 960 (During ferry hours) 01770 700 463 (Evenings). VHF 37.

TROON*

Standard Port Greenock
HW −0025 LW −0020

MHWS	MHWN	MLWN	MLWS
−0·2m	−0·2m	0·0m	0·0m

A useful hbr and marina at southern approach to Clyde. Easy access. Before arrival call marina on VHF 37/80.

Approach and Entrance Give shore an offing of 2ca. Leave G con buoy Fl.G.4s to stb and pass between pierheads. Lts Fl(2)WG.5s11m9M (shore-W-036°-G-090°-shore) on west and Q.R on E Port entry signals not applicable to yachts. Proceed through outer harbour to marina.

Facilities PO shops EC Wednesday. Full marina facilities. 50 visitors' berths. Rly to Glasgow. Prestwick Airport 4M.

☏/VHF HM 01292 313412, VHF 14; Marina 315553, VHF 37/M, 80.

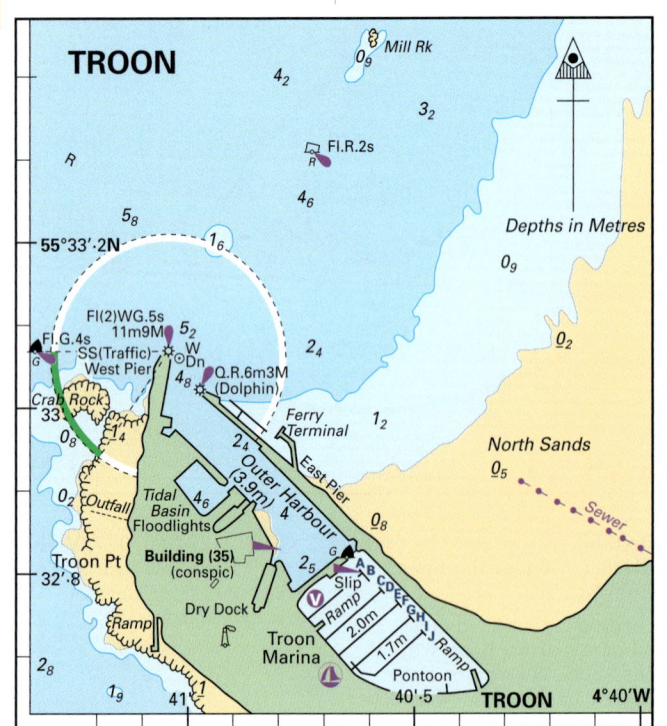

LOCH RYAN*

Standard Port Greenock
Stranraer Marina
HW (sp)−0030 (np) −0025
LW (sp) −0010 (np) −0010

MHWS	MHWN	MLWN	MLWS
−0·2m	−0·1m	0·0m	+0·1m

A busy ferry port, including HSS and superferries, operating from Loch Ryan Port or Cairnryan.

Approach and Entrance From S give N shore of Rhins of Galloway a good berth. The new ferry terminal, Loch Ryan Port, is in operation at Old House Point to the NW of Cairn Point. Pass the new ferry terminal and leave the S card buoy (VQ(6)+LFl.10s) to port, then head for the Spit buoy (Fl.G.6s). Keep a good lookout for ferries using both Loch Ryan Port and Cairnryan Ferry Terminal. Listen on VHF 14 for all ferry movements.

Anchorages and Berthing
• Stranraer Marina. South of Spit buoy, three G Lt bns mark the W side of the channel leading into Stranraer Hbr and marina.
• Anchor 3ca NW of W pier. Holding good, Uncomfortable in strong northerlies. 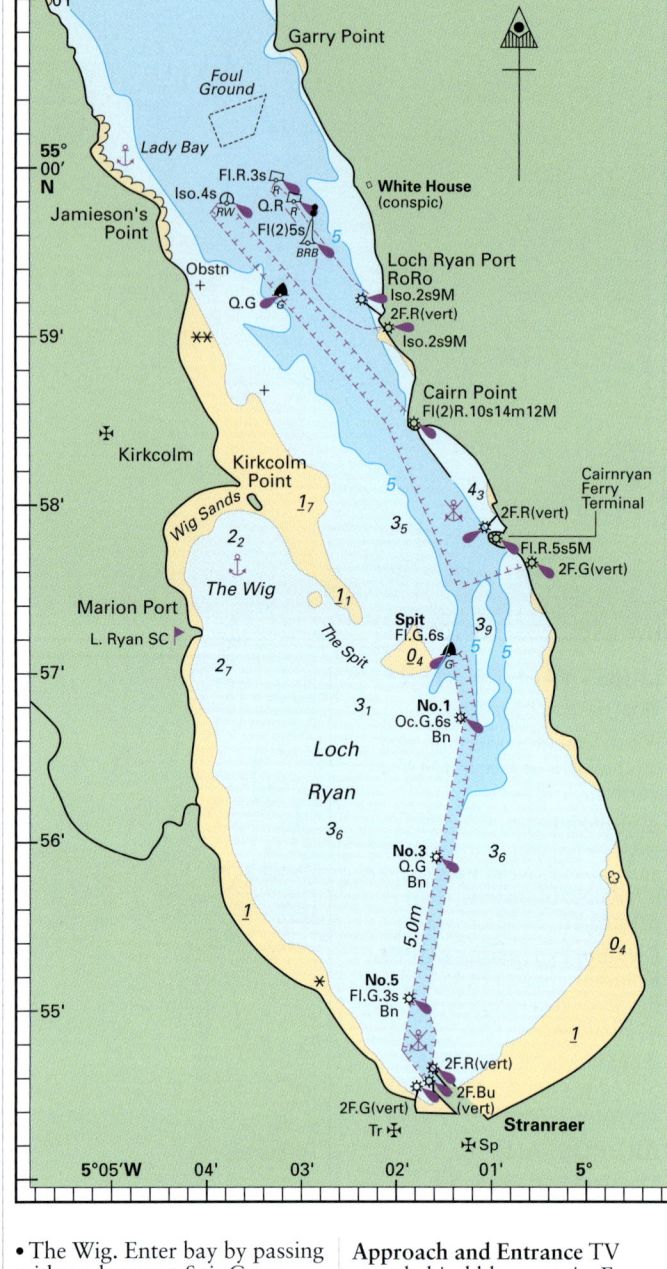
• The Wig. Enter bay by passing midway between Spit G con buoy Fl.G.6s and No.1 bn Oc.G.6s. Holding poor.
• Lady Bay. W side of loch 1M S of entrance. Holding good.

Facilities Small marina, basic facilities. PO, shops EC Wednesday. Rly or coach to Glasgow and London.

☏ Marina *Mobile* 07734 073421, 07827 277247.

PORTPATRICK*

Standard Port Liverpool
HW +0035 LW +0002

MHWS	MHWN	MLWN	MLWS
−5·5m	−4·4m	−2·0m	−0·6m

This small hbr 15M N of the Mull of Galloway provides good shelter. Strong tides across entrance. Do not approach in strong onshore winds. Busy at weekends in season with yachts from N Ireland 21M away.

Approach and Entrance TV mast behind hbr conspic. From N keep 1ca off. Narrow entrance opens suddenly. Ldg Lts 2F.G.(occas), two orange lines by day bearing 050°, on wall and building behind, lead between ruined piers. Beware Half Tide Rock marked by a buoy, to port and enter inner hbr.

Berthing Alongside NE and NW walls of inner harbour. Fender plank desirable. HM will advise. Subject to swell from SW. Harbour has recently been dredged to give 2·0m at low water.

Facilities PO, shops EC Thursday, hotel/restaurants, water, fuel. Bus to Stranraer.

☏ HM 07565 102096.

PORTPATRICK

PORTPATRICK TO KIRKCUDBRIGHT

Passage lights	BA No
Crammag Head Fl.10s35m18M	4608
Mull of Galloway Fl.20s99m28M	4610
Little Ross Fl.5s50m12M	4634
Hestan Is Fl(2)10s42m9M	4640

There are strong tides between Portpatrick and the Mull of Galloway off which there is a dangerous race extending some 3M S of the Mull. The Galloway coast is frequented by increasing commercial traffic. The few harbours are small and drying and there is limited refuge if caught out in a SW–SE blow. There are dangerous sand banks at the entrance to the Solway Firth. The tidal range is over 6m sp and there is a dangerous race in strong winds extending 3M S of the Mull. Note Scares Rocks 6M E of the Mull. Shelter for deep keeled yachts may best be found in Kirkcudbright.

Tidal Streams
All related to Dover sp rates
Black Head (Portpatrick)
–0110NNW +0500SSE 1·8kn
Mull of Galloway
+0040WSW –0535ESE 4·5kn

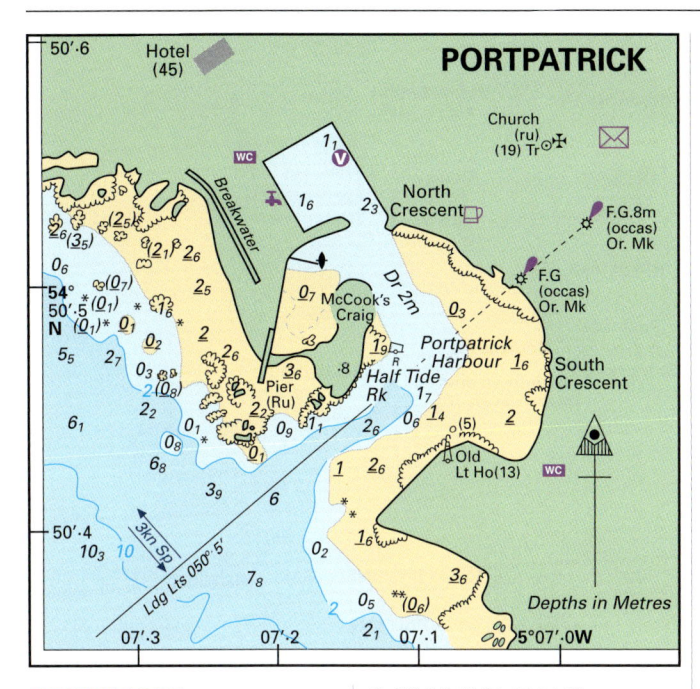

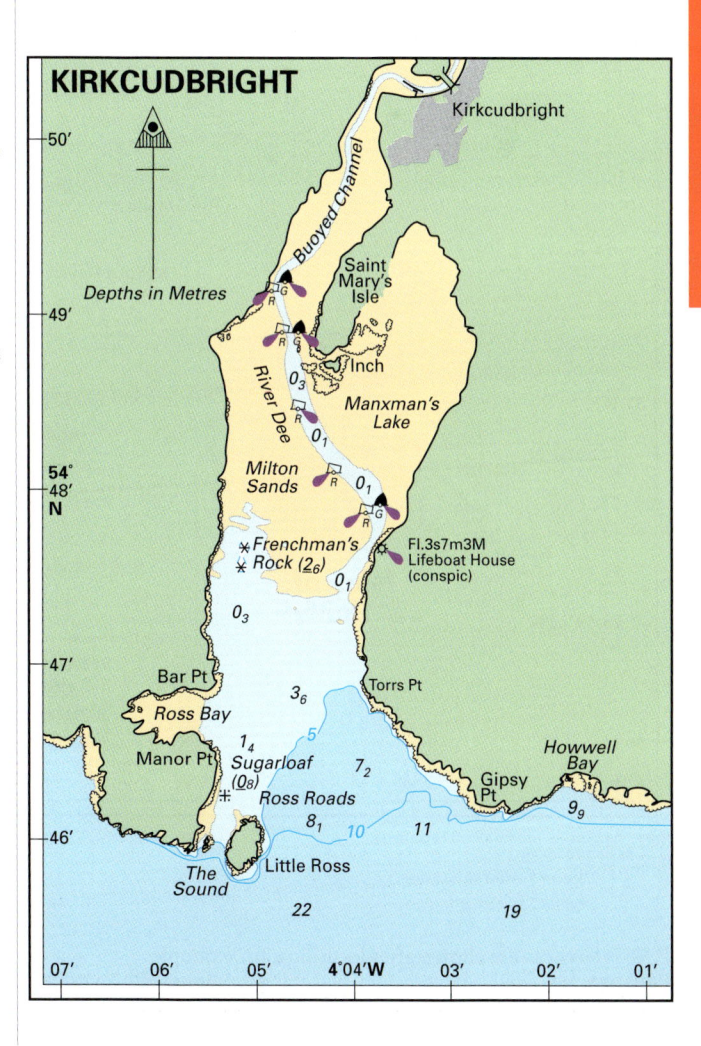

DRUMMORE

Standard Port Liverpool
HW +0040   LW +0013
MHWS MHWN MLWN MLWS
–3·5m –2·6m –1·2m –0·5m

Small drying hbr 4M N of Mull of Galloway.

Approach and Entrance Enter after half tide, unmarked shingle bank extends W from pier head. The entrance can be very difficult to see through the mudbanks.

Berth Alongside pier. N end reserved for MoD range boat. Very limited space.

Facilities Water on pier. PO, shops, hotel.

ISLE OF WHITHORN

Standard Port Liverpool
HW +0028   LW +0010
MHWS MHWN MLWN MLWS
–2·5m –2·1m –1·1m –0·4m

A drying hbr with 2½m at half flood.

Entrance On the E side of the bay there is a conspic W low square tr. An isolated unmarked rock lies off shore. From the W side of the bay the Skerries reef extends E to R bn. The stream sets very strongly SW across entrance at all times when there is 2m or more in the hbr. Keep to the apparent middle third of the channel on entry. Conspic Ldg marks (Or diamonds) lie on a bearing 335° in the W of the hbr. At night these are replaced by Lts Oc.R.8s7M.

Anchorages
• Alongside quay in SE corner, HM will advise. Space limited.
• Anchor in entrance S of the slip on E side to lie well afloat. Subject to big swell in S'ly winds.

Facilities Water at pier. Showers, PO, shops, garage, hotel, chandlers.

☎ HM 01988 500468, *Mobile* 07734 073420.

Offshore Anchorage

Portyerrock Bay 1·5M north of Whithorn provides a safe anchorage in W and SW winds. Perhaps useful on passage to Whitehaven or Maryport while awaiting the tide.

KIRKCUDBRIGHT

Standard Port Liverpool
HW +0020   LW +0005
MHWS MHWN MLWN MLWS
–1·9m –1·6m –0·8m –0·3m

A 4M long narrow channel between sandbanks forming estuary of River Dee.

Approach and Entrance Beware of firing range at entrance, no restrictions on passage, safety boat always present when in use. Bar (0·5m) 5ca N of Torr Point. Ldg marks astern on Little Ross 201°. Channel (dries) is buoyed and lit.

Several substantial fishing boats moor to the quay which is between the marina pontoon and the bridge: keep a careful lookout when using the buoyed channel.

Anchorages and Berthing
• At marina, alongside outside of floating pontoons. Often very busy, access HW±0230.
• N end of Little Ross in position giving most shelter. Stream runs fast. Beware of Sugarloaf Rock.
• Flint Bay. N of Torrs Point sheltered in E'lys.

Facilities PO, shops, EC Thursday. Diesel, chandlers.

☎/VHF HM 01557 331135, VHF 12. Range Safety Officer 0141 2248520, Range Safety Boat VHF 73.

KIRKCUDBRIGHT

SCOTLAND – WEST COAST

165

ENGLAND WEST COAST AND WALES

Map of the west coast of England, Wales, Isle of Man, and east coast of Ireland with page references to harbours and features.

Locations and page references

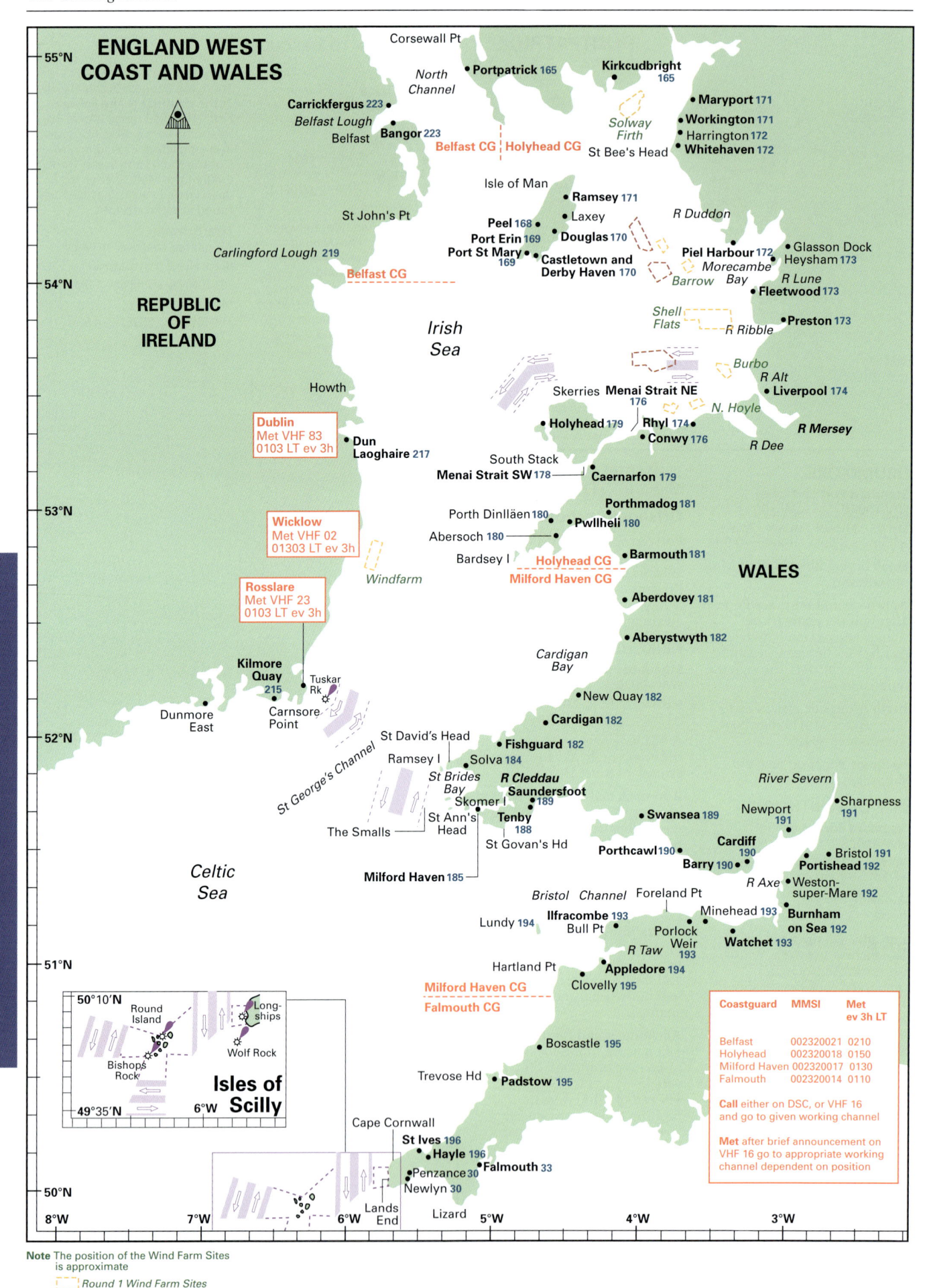

Scotland/Northern England (north coast):
- Corsewall Pt
- Portpatrick 165
- Kirkcudbright 165
- Carrickfergus 223
- *Belfast Lough*
- Belfast
- Bangor 223
- *Solway Firth*
- St Bee's Head
- Maryport 171
- Workington 171
- Harrington 172
- Whitehaven 172

Isle of Man:
- St John's Pt
- Ramsey 171
- Laxey
- Peel 168
- Port Erin 169
- Port St Mary 169
- Douglas 170
- Castletown and Derby Haven 170

North West England:
- *R Duddon*
- Piel Harbour 172
- *Morecambe Bay*
- Glasson Dock
- Heysham 173
- *R Lune*
- *Barrow*
- Fleetwood 173
- *Shell Flats*
- *R Ribble*
- Preston 173
- *Burbo*
- *R Alt*
- Liverpool 174
- *N. Hoyle*
- *R Mersey*
- *R Dee*

Ireland east coast:
- REPUBLIC OF IRELAND
- *Carlingford Lough* 219
- Howth
- Dublin — Met VHF 83, 0103 LT ev 3h
- Dun Laoghaire 217
- Wicklow — Met VHF 02, 01303 LT ev 3h
- Rosslare — Met VHF 23, 0103 LT ev 3h
- Kilmore Quay 215
- Tuskar Rk
- Carnsore Point
- Dunmore East

North Wales:
- Skerries
- Menai Strait NE 176
- Holyhead 179
- Rhyl 174
- Conwy 176
- South Stack
- Menai Strait SW 178
- Caernarfon 179
- Porth Dinllaen 180
- Porthmadog 181
- Pwllheli 180
- Abersoch 180
- Bardsey I
- Barmouth 181
- Aberdovey 181
- Aberystwyth 182
- *Cardigan Bay*

South Wales:
- New Quay 182
- Cardigan 182
- Fishguard 182
- St David's Head
- Ramsey I
- Solva 184
- *St Brides Bay*
- Skomer I
- St Ann's Head
- The Smalls
- *R Cleddau*
- Saundersfoot
- Tenby 188
- St Govan's Hd
- Milford Haven 185
- Swansea 189
- Porthcawl 190
- Cardiff 190
- Barry 190
- *River Severn*
- Newport 191
- Sharpness
- Bristol 191
- Portishead 192
- *R Axe*
- Weston-super-Mare 192
- Burnham on Sea 192

South West England:
- *Bristol Channel*
- Foreland Pt
- Lundy 194
- Ilfracombe 193
- Bull Pt
- Minehead 193
- Porlock Weir 193
- Watchet 193
- *R Taw*
- Hartland Pt
- Appledore 194
- Clovelly 195
- Boscastle 195
- Trevose Hd
- Padstow 195
- Cape Cornwall
- St Ives 196
- Hayle 196
- Penzance 30
- Falmouth 33
- Newlyn 30
- Lands End
- Lizard

Isles of Scilly:
- Round Island
- Longships
- Bishops Rock
- Wolf Rock

Seas/Channels:
- North Channel
- Irish Sea
- St George's Channel
- Celtic Sea

Coastguard

Coastguard	MMSI	Met ev 3h LT
Belfast	002320021	0210
Holyhead	002320018	0150
Milford Haven	002320017	0130
Falmouth	002320014	0110

Call either on DSC, or VHF 16 and go to given working channel

Met after brief announcement on VHF 16 go to appropriate working channel dependent on position

Coastguard areas shown: Belfast CG, Holyhead CG, Milford Haven CG, Falmouth CG

Note The position of the Wind Farm Sites is approximate
- Round 1 Wind Farm Sites
- Round 2 Wind Farm Sites

Page references are shown after locations, for example:
Padstow 195. Bold type indicates that it is accompanied by a plan. *Italics* are used for rivers, lochs, bays, seas etc.

England West Coast and Wales

This coast, along with the Irish east coast, provides some beautiful cruising areas as well as being the main through route to and from West Scotland. The most direct passage route to/ from Scotland is from Lands End via Milford Haven, Pwllheli, Holyhead, Peel (IOM), Portpatrick and on to the Clyde or round Kintyre, or along the East Irish Coast from Lands End via Kilmore Quay, Arklow, Dublin Bay, Ardglass, Belfast Lough, Glenarm and then to the Clyde or round Kintyre. If the outlook is for strong W'lies, vessels on passage to/from Scotland will find more refuge on the Irish East Coast (see p.215).

Tidal strategy plays a key role in these waters. Tides reach 3kn in St George's Channel and 5kn in North Channel at springs. Tidal streams flood north to Liverpool/Dublin Bay, and flood south through the North Channel, with a slack area to the west of the Isle of Man, so it is possible to carry a fair tide for many miles and hours with judicious planning. Key tidal gates are the whole of the North Channel, Point of Ayre, Calf of Man, South Stack (Holyhead), Bardsey Island, Milford Haven to Strumble Head, and Land's End.

Most harbours on the West Coast of England and Wales are tidal, with entrance bars or strong currents restricting access to a window either side of local high water, and with a prevailing onshore wind. On the entire coast from the Solway Firth to Lands End, only Holyhead, Fishguard and Milford Haven provide all tide, all weather access. Fishguard is only secure in winds from W through S to SE.

Douglas and Peel on the Isle of Man have marinas, accessible HW±2, which offer some shelter outside the marinas whilst waiting for tide but Douglas and Peel waiting areas are both exposed to NE. Although a major commercial port, Liverpool has strong currents and no sheltered waiting area. Pwllheli is secure in all winds but the entrance is dredged to 0·6m below datum.

The route down the English coast has a number of well-found marinas at Maryport, Whitehaven, Fleetwood and others in estuaries at Glasson Dock, Preston and Liverpool. The coast is a lee shore with extensive shoals, with wind farms, either completed or under construction. These should pose few problems except in poor visibility. There are exclusion zones during construction. In North and West Wales there are marinas at Conwy, Holyhead, Port Dinorwic, Caernarfon, Pwllheli and Aberystwyth.

From Conwy there is a choice of going N of Anglesey, carrying the tide to Holyhead then taking the tide south past South Stack, or going through the Menai Strait, a beautiful route through The Swellies to Port Dinorwic, Caernarfon and out over Caernarfon Bar. Tides are critical to this passage.

Porth Dinllaen provides a sheltered anchorage in winds from S to W winds in settled weather, en route to Bardsey Sound and Cardigan Bay, where Abersoch and Pwllheli are major yachting centres.

Three well buoyed major shoals project west from the coast in Cardigan Bay – Sarn Padraig (St Patricks Causeway) running SW from Harlech, Sarn y Bwch running SW from S of Barmouth, and Cynfelyn Patches running SW from S of Aberdovey.

Porthmadog, Barmouth, Aberdovey, Aberystwyth and Fishguard are all good cruising destinations within day-sail of each other and Abersoch and Pwllheli.

From Fishguard south the next major harbour is Milford Haven, easily reached by taking the tide round Strumble Head then west of S Bishop light and via Skokholm/Skomer round St Ann's Head.

Ramsey and Jack Sounds provide a slightly shorter route, albeit with challenging navigation in strong tidal streams.

In the Bristol Channel, Pembrokeshire, Gower peninsula, Devon and Cornwall have beautiful coastlines. Lundy Island is beautiful and interesting. Clovelly is unique. Except for Milford Haven, which is very scenic and provides a large sheltered area for cruising (useful in bad weather), there are no all-weather, all-tide hbrs. The area is exposed to frequent Atlantic swells, and being on W side of UK, receives its fair share of rain and poor visibility. Strong winds are usually from W'ly sector. In strong N winds, no safe approach to anywhere on S side of Bristol Channel. Twin keels are advantageous because many hbrs are small and dry. Many have entrance bars that are difficult or dangerous under wrong conditions. Cardiff Bay has a barrage and offers good facilities. Marinas at Milford Haven, Swansea, Porthcawl, Cardiff, Bristol, Portishead, Watchet and Padstow. For crew changes, road and rail connections to Milford, Swansea, Cardiff and Bristol are good, but poor along N coast of Somerset, Devon and Cornwall.

The north Cornish coast is mainly beautiful but with rugged cliffs. The long distances between ports often enforce night sailing, particularly out of season in shorter days. Many popular tourist towns, like Ilfracombe, Clovelly, Boscastle, Newquay and St Ives have drying hbrs vulnerable to a surge (scend) when a heavy ground swell is running, usually off season. Many lobster pot markers off N Cornish coast, including well offshore and not always very visible. Lundy's SE anchorage provides good holding and protection in strong winds from S to W, but there are tidal races to N and S of the island. Clovelly Roads has good holding and is sheltered from strong SE to W winds.

Useful references for greater detail are *Irish Sea Pilot* by David Rainsbury, *Cruising Anglesey and Adjoining Waters* by Ralph Morris, *Blue Book (Guide to the Bristol Channel)* by and from BCYA.org.uk, and *Bristol Channel and Severn Cruising Guide* by Peter Cumberlidge, most from Imray.

Irish Sea to St George's Channel distances (miles)

	Bangor (N.I.)	S. Rock	Whitehaven	Peel	Douglas	Carlingford	Liverpool Bar	Conwy Fairway	Holyhead Pier	Howth	Caernarfon Bar	Pwllheli	Aberystwyth	Fishguard	S Bishop 1M W	Arklow	Tuskar Rk 1M E
Bangor (N.I.)	0																
S. Rock	23	0															
Whitehaven	74	62	0														
Peel	47	26	46	0													
Douglas	69	47	39	27	0												
Carlingford	62	39	97	54	64	0											
Liverpool Bar	113	90	64	75	56	106	0										
Conwy Fairway	109	84	77	70	54	93	25	0									
Holyhead Pier	98	74	83	60	58	112	50	37	0								
Howth	88	66	112	100	74	42	99	80	53	0							
Caernarfon Bar	101	88	103	93	77	86	70	53	21	62	0						
Pwllheli	146	123	133	107	108	110	104	85	56	79	40	0					
Aberystwyth	181	137	148	122	106	126	119	99	70	93	55	33	0				
Fishguard	168	146	165	136	139	130	132	112	83	93	71	57	40	0			
S Bishop Lt Ho 1M W	175	153	160	146	143	137	136	124	95	96	86	73	60	23	0		
Arklow	124	102	142	99	102	81	114	93	64	40	66	72	80	64	62	0	
Tuskar Rk 1M E	159	137	171	135	133	115	139	126	90	74	86	80	79	47	36	36	0

North Channel to Milford Haven

Passage lights:	BA No
Mull of Galloway Fl.20s99m28M	4610
S Rock R pillar Fl(3)R.30s9M Racon (T) (–)	5966
South Stack Fl.10s60m24M Horn 30s	5204
Codling E card AIS Q(3)10s	5861
Bardsey Is Fl.R.10s39m18M	5234
Wicklow Head Fl(3)15s37m23M	5850
Tuskar Rock Q(2)7·5s33m24M Racon (T) (–) AIS	5838
Strumble Head Fl(4)15s45m26M	5274
S Bishop Fl.5s44m16M Horn(3)45sRacon (O) (– – –)	5276
The Smalls Fl(3)15s36m18M+ Iso.R.4s13M Horn(2)60s Racon (T) (–) AIS	5278

There are two main routes from N Channel to Milford Haven and reverse. One can either take the English/Welsh side or the Irish side. If wishing to cut out night passages, the first route is possible going N, stopping at Fishguard, Holyhead, Isle of Man, Portpatrick, and Loch Ryan. Going N from the IoM it is not possible to get through the N Channel on one tide hence the stop at Port Patrick. Going S and leaving Corsewall Point (off Loch Ryan) at Dover +0600 one can get into the slack water off the W coast of the IoM for Peel or Port Erin on one tide. Then make for Holyhead, Fishguard and from there work the tides round Strumble Head, Ramsey and Jack Sounds to Milford Haven. This takes five days N and four days S. The other route is to leave Milford Haven to suit the tides through the Sounds (*see Passage Note Strumble Head to St Ann's Head*) and head straight for Belfast Lough (Bangor) which is 200M and can be accomplished with one night at sea. Leave Bangor at Dover +0500 on the last of the ebb for the S'ly passage. Ports of refuge on the Irish side are Ardglass, Howth or Dun Laoghaire and if needed Wicklow or Arklow.

PEEL

Standard Port Liverpool
HW +0010   LW –0025

MHWS	MHWN	MLWN	MLWS
–4·2m	–3·2m	–1·7m	–0·7m

This is a picturesque hbr with a conspic castle on the W coast. It makes a pleasant port of call for supplies when on passage from one end of the Irish Sea to the other. The hbr has 3·3m at MHWN. It has a sill and a flapgate.

The new 120 berth marina also has 15 visitors' berths. A call on VHF 12 1h before entry smoothes the approach.

Approach The breakwater should be given good clearance and vessels should not stand in too far towards the shore as a shoal lies between the breakwater and the shore and depths on it are variable. Strong NW'ly to NE'ly winds may cause heavy seas at the entrance.

Entrance There are Ldg marks. The training wall to the Fl.R Lt covers at half tide.

Entry to the Inner Hbr and Marina is through a flapgate, retaining a depth of 2·5m (but silting may make it less), and a swing foot br. Access HW±0200. Call *Peel Harbour* on VHF 12 upon approach to request an opening of the bridge. Outwith office hours (0800–1630), Douglas Harbour Control will answer and open the bridge for you. IPTS signals for entry and Fl amber Lts when gate or br are about to move. VHF 12, ☎ 01624 842338 or 07624 495036 or Douglas Harbour Control.

There are three Or Vs buoys SE of the Fl.R.5s Lt in 2m. All stores, fuel outside entrance to marina, card obtained from Manx Fishing Producers

Isle of Man

Passage lights	BA No
Point of Ayre Fl(4)20s32m19M Racon (M) (– –)	4720
Douglas Head Fl.10s32m24M	4770

Tidal Streams related to Dover (0015 before Liverpool)

Langness to Point of Ayre
–0330NE for 0900 +0530S for 0315

Point of Ayre
+0500S –0015W, race.

Contrary Head to Calf Sound
–0115N +0445S

S of Niarbyl Point stream nearly continuously N in an eddy close inshore.

Calf Sound
+0400S –0130N

Note the tidal races off Chicken Rock: Eddies and a race both E and W of Langness Lt Ho. Ayre Point has a race and a dangerous 2m shoal, the Whitestone Bank over which the sea breaks, 5ca E marked by a W card buoy. The inshore channel is ¾M wide. With SW winds and low barometer the rise of tide is increased by up to 1m. With high pressure and E and N winds the tides are lowered to the same extent. None of the harbours where yachts can lie afloat is safe in all winds unless locked into a marina e.g. Douglas or Peel. Douglas is safe in all but NE gales. Douglas is a busy commercial and ferry port. If HMs are warned in advance of a yacht's probable time of arrival they take a lot of trouble to allot a suitable berth. Except at Douglas where a continuous service is maintained, it is the practice of HMs to be on duty 2hrs either side of HW and to meet incoming vessels and direct them to their berths. Harbour staff are extremely helpful. Hbr dues are moderate. In good weather vessels coming from the W can find shelter in Peel Hbr when there is sufficient rise. From the S make first for Port St Mary. From the N find a temporary anchorage at Ramsey at all states of the tide. These anchorages are all exposed to winds from certain directions. At the time of writing yachts may not be left unattended unless in the charge of an IOM resident.

www.gov.im/about-the-government/departments/infrastructure/harbours/ gives much useful information on harbours and marinas.

Passage through **Calf Sound** should only be undertaken in quiet conditions as there are overfalls. There may be a distinct step in the water opposite Thousla Rock. Tide through the sound runs at about 3·5kn, the N going stream starts at Liverpool –0145 and the S-going stream at Liverpool +0345. The stream runs at 4kn sp (2kn np) and is maximal near HW and LW Liverpool. The main sound between Kitterland and Thousla Rk with Lt bn Fl.R.3s is just over ½ca wide; beware the Clett rks extending 1ca from the Calf near S entrance. Little Sound should not be attempted except with local knowledge. BA chart *2696* essential.

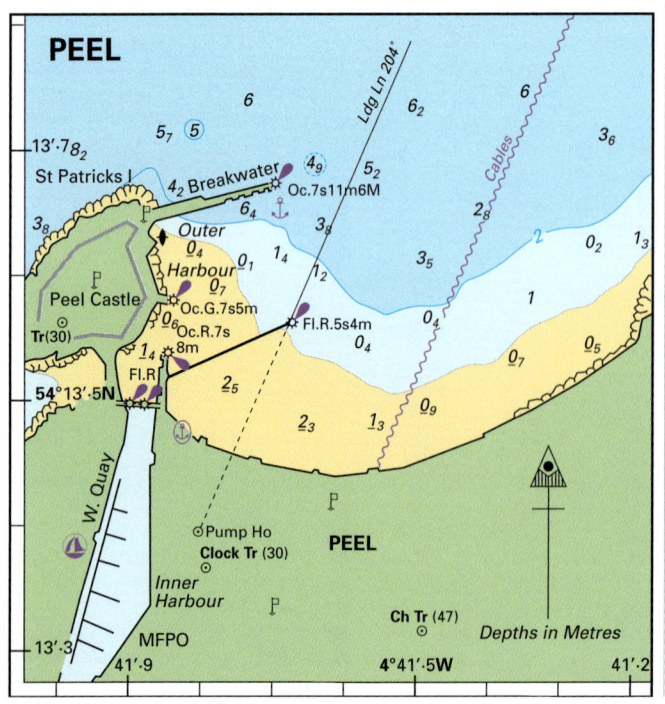

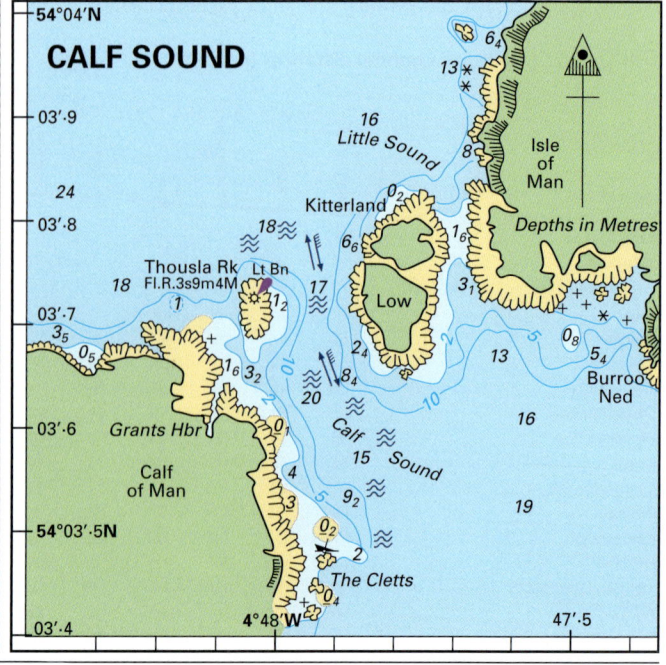

Organisation (MFPO) in marina. On the waterfront, the Peel Sailing and Cruising Club welcomes visitors, nearby there is a launderette. Buses to Ramsey and Douglas.

☎ HM 01624 842338.

PORT ERIN

Standard Port Liverpool
HW +0014   LW +0020
MHWS   MHWN   MLWN   MLWS
–4·2m   –3·3m   –1·6m   –0·6m

This inlet affords secure anchorage in 4–9m and shelter in winds from N through E to SW. Raglan Pier (Oc.G.5s) on S side of bay forms a drying hbr with sandy bottom having 3·6m MHWN alongside.

Approach In the middle of the head of the bay are Ldg Lts F.R 099° W columns, R bands which lead into the middle of the bay.

Entrance A demolished breakwater, covered at HW, runs out N from the SW arm of the bay and is marked by an unlit G con buoy.

Berthing Anchor in 3–5m N off Raglan pier or use one of the two Y visitors' buoys W of this. A telegraph cable runs roughly E–W across S side of bay so care is necessary when anchoring. Good landing at jetty shown on plan. All stores. Buses to Castletown and Douglas.

☎ HM 01624 833206.

PORT ST MARY

Standard Port Liverpool
HW +0015   LW +0025
MHWS   MHWN   MLWN   MLWS
–3·5m   –2·7m   –1·5m   –0·6m

The hbr dries to sand and mud. It has 3m at MHWN, 2m when the Carrick covers; good shelter off the entrance in 2–3·5m from NE through NW to SW winds. The bay should not be approached in strong S winds. Note that the Carrick should be given 1ca clearance from its bn in all directions but 2ca to the E.

Approach To clear The Carrick (Lt bn Q(2)5s) which dries 4·3m keep Langness Lt Ho well open of Scarlett Point Stack or at night when nearing the bay bring the Lts of the hbr in line 303°. Approaching from the E during the first of the ebb, from Stack of Scarlett to S of The Carrick, small craft should avoid standing inshore until The Carrick shows when the sea steadies. From SW give the shore a berth of 2ca and round in to N of the Alfred Pierhead (Lt Oc.R.10s).

Berthing Anchor 50–100m NW of Alfred Pier outside the line of the two Lts (one on Alfred Pier and the other on the inner pier). Take care to avoid reef NE of Alfred Pier marked by a G bn with con topmark. The outer part of Alfred Pier is often occupied by fishing vessels, but yachts may raft up afloat near its root. Inner harbour dries to channel, hard sand: centre is full of local moorings but yachts taking the ground can lie alongside. Four W visitors' buoys off Chapel Bay in a line between ends of Alfred and Little Carrick (the rock with the G bn near the small inner pier). There is a landing below the clubhouse of the IoM YC which has excellent facilities and is welcoming to visitors many of whom come over from Ireland for Saturday night.

Facilities All stores. Bus to Castletown and Douglas.

☎/VHF HM 01624 833205, 07624 460096, VHF 12 (if the Harbour Office is closed, HM Douglas will reply); YC 842088. IoM YC 932 088.

CASTLETOWN

HW Liverpool +0010 (approx)

It is difficult to imagine a more romantic little hbr with its castle, quays and ancient buildings. Behind the sea-front is a busy modern town. The bay affords good shelter in NW through NE to E winds. The bottom is not good and the tidal streams are felt. The hbr dries.

Approach To avoid the race off Langness Pt give it a good berth in all winds. Approaching from E in heavy weather keep Clay Head well open of Douglas Head to clear rough ground 8ca SE of St Michael's Is where a race causes heavy overfalls.

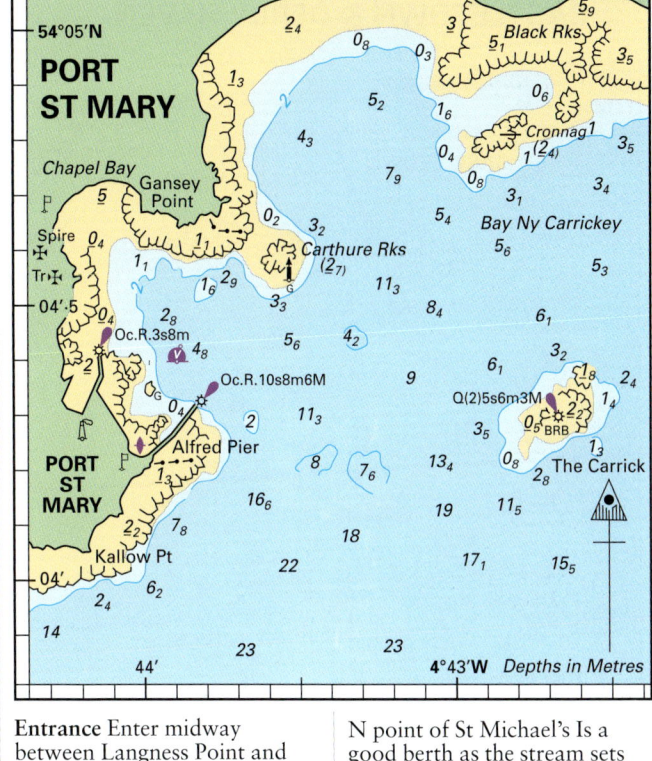

Entrance Enter midway between Langness Point and the R can buoy Fl.R.3s which marks the Lheeah-Rio Rocks which should be left to port. From abreast the buoy steer 022° until the light house on the inner jetty comes open N of the pier head LtHo. Then steer 317° for the entrance to the hbr. At the end of the breakwater the ground consists of rocky ledges and large boulders. Beware of confusing the hbr bns with Ronaldsway airport landing Lts.

Berthing Anchor in 5·5m off the entrance to the hbr, King William College tr bearing 022°. One W can buoy 3ca SE of breakwater. The hbr has 2·7m MHWN; there is a basin between the outer swing and inner fixed bridges. Berth alongside the vertical NE face of the inner quay (Irish Quay). Bollards, ladders, water and electricity. Bottom is flat, hard sand.

Facilities All stores. Bus to Port Erin and Douglas. Steam train in the summer.

☎/VHF HM 01624 823549, VHF 12 (usually answered from Douglas).

DERBY HAVEN

HW Liverpool +0010 (approx)

The bay affords shelter on a good bottom of sand and mud in 2–5m inside St Michaels Is and is available in N through W to S winds. Inside the breakwater the hbr which dries affords complete shelter in all winds. Bottom mud and sand, 2m MHWN. It is very close to Ronaldsway Airport which is busy and noisy.

Entrance With the S going stream which runs for 9hrs give N point of St Michael's Is a good berth as the stream sets hard across a shelving rock at the entrance point. For the hbr bring the Lt Iso.G.2s on SW end of breakwater to bear 262° and pass between it and the R perch marking a rk to S of it to enter the drying hbr.

Anchorage Two or 3ca from the S end of the breakwater. The bottom is foul 1ca out from it. Stores at Castletown 2M. No supplies at Derby Haven.

DOUGLAS

Standard Port Liverpool
HW +0015   LW –0025
MHWS   MHWN   MLWN   MLWS
–2·5m   –2·1m   –0·8m   –0·3m

The outer harbour has 4–7m and a heavy sea runs in during NE gales.

Approach Request entry from Harbour Control. Come in on 229° along approach channel with Ldg marks front W ▲ and back W ▼ with both in R borders (Lts Oc.Bu.10s) past G con Lt buoys. Watch out for IPTS entry signals on Victoria Pier. Beware ferries and HSS and keep S of Ldg line. The only hazard is a dolphin 2F.R.

Berthing
• Inner harbour marina. Call *Douglas Inner Harbour* VHF 12 to book a bridge opening and request a berth (preferably 1h before arrival, there is no earlier pre-booking of berths). Access through flap-gate, which holds 2m water in the hbr, is approx HW±0200. Due to silting this depth is not guaranteed. If the gate is not open, berth temporarily alongside inner end of Battery Pier.
• Outer harbour. Alongside pontoon near steps at inner end of Battery Pier, subject to wash and exposed in N and E winds.

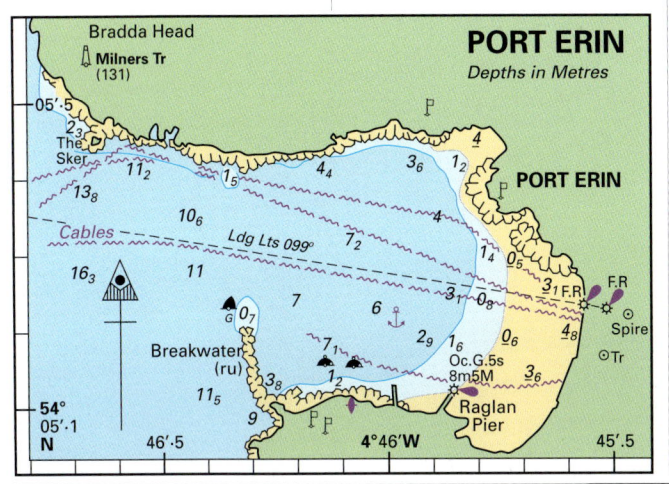

169

The Cruising Almanac

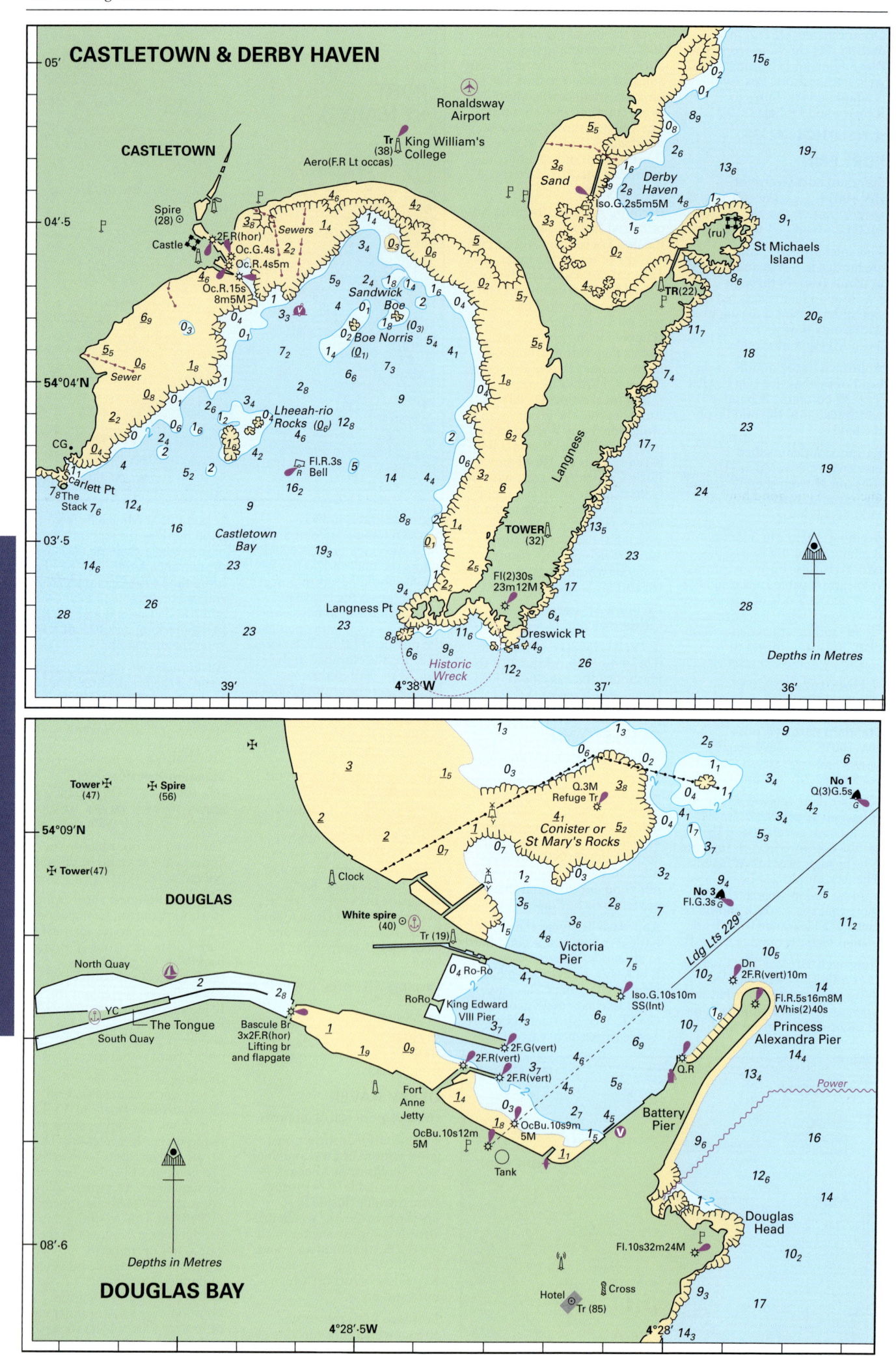

CASTLETOWN & DERBY HAVEN

DOUGLAS BAY

ENGLAND – WEST COAST AND WALES

170

• Anchor in bay, preferably N end, sheltered from N through W to S.

Facilities As expected, shops nearby. Fuel pump on Battery Pier, card from Manx YC.

☎/**VHF** Harbour Control 01624 686628 (24hrs), VHF 12, also broadcasts nav warnings every 4hrs from 0133; YC 673965.

LAXEY

Laxey Bay offers good anchorage in N to SW winds through W. The hbr dries and has about 2m MHWN. Care is needed in entering the hbr which is very crowded. There are seasonal visitors' buoys in Garwick Bay (1 mile S).

RAMSEY

Standard Port Liverpool
HW +0015   LW −0015
MHWS MHWN MLWN MLWS
−2·0m −1·6m −0·9m −0·2m

The bay affords secure anchorage and good holding ground, and is sheltered with winds from NW through W to S. The Queen's Pier extends 685m from the shore to the S of the hbr. Landing is prohibited on this pier which is partly derelict. Vessels waiting to enter should anchor between this pier and S pier clear of any moorings. There are two summer only waiting buoys. S and N piers are 90m inside LW mark. The hbr dries and has up to 5·5m at MHWS, 4m at MHWN. Vessels are advised not to attempt the entrance earlier than HW−0230 or later than HW+0200. The swing br operates 0700–1600 daily.

Approach From N rounding Point of Ayre (N point of Is) Fl(4)20s keep close inshore to avoid Whitestone Bank (7ca E of Ayre Point). The stream sets round the pt into Ramsey Bay at about LW Douglas, and runs for 3hrs. Watch for lobster pots.

Berthing Berth as instructed by HM, the seaward side of the swing br is for commercial vessels only. When entering, watch the stream which sets N across the entrance for 9hrs from half flood to LW approx. Most facilities. Buses to Peel and Douglas, tram to Douglas in summer.

☎/**VHF** HM VHF 12, 01624 812245 (24h).

MARYPORT

Standard Port Liverpool
HW (sp) +0021 (np) +0036
LW (sp) +0002 (np) +0017
MHWS MHWN MLWN MLWS
−0·8m −0·9m −0·7m −0·2m

The Senhouse Basin to seaward is a secure marina. Contact marina on VHF 12 before entry.

Bar It dries for some distance W of S pier and is liable to change. There was a channel dredged to 1m and 2·5m wide from the end of the S pier, this has not been maintained. Beware the tidal set 2kn sp which starts at Dover − 0400 and runs N for 5hrs.

Approach Keep at least 1M off coast until in the offing because the shelving bottom is clay, foul with large rocks. Open work pier is conspicuous.

Entrance Lt Fl.1·5s10m, W tr on S pier head. Keep closer to S pier head on entry. Leading line is old LtHo in transit with the third window of the house close S of church spire. When square on to lock gate turn to stb. There are extensive quays outside the docks. These all dry and have a bank of silt. Entry to the marina is through a flap-gate which folds down into the lock and forms a sill at 3·5m above CD. Access is 2hrs either side of HW and the water level is maintained at 1·5m above the sill.

Facilities 25 tonne boat lift. MP Marine have extensive workshops and use of slipway with 100-tonne cradle and up to 8m beam.

☎/**VHF** Marina 01900 814431, VHF 12; MP Marine 01900 810299.

Solway Firth to Holyhead

This coast tends to be low but with high ground inland. The ports and harbours of N Lancashire are relics of the industrial revolution as many of the towns were connected with coal and iron. Their harbours have well constructed stone basins and quays. In some cases these have been converted to marinas. The strong tides carry much silt and the harbours mostly dry at low water. Further south are the shallow estuaries forming Morecambe Bay, the Ribble, the Mersey, the Dee and the N entrance to the Menai Strait. It is interesting for a boat which easily takes the ground as there is a lot of shallow water. It is a lee-shore for W and SW winds; rough seas and breakers easily occur.

SOLWAY FIRTH TO ST BEES HEAD

Passage light   BA No
St Bees Head   4710
Fl(2)20s102m18M

The Solway Firth is difficult and dangerous without recent local knowledge as the streams run at 6kn between shifting sandbanks. In the upper estuary, the length of the flood stream shortens to about 2hrs and is associated with a bore wave at spring tides. There are Solway Sailing

WORKINGTON

Standard Port Liverpool
HW (sp) +0029 (np) +0027
LW (sp) +0004 (np) +0014
MHWS MHWN MLWN MLWS
−1·1m −1·1m −0·5m −0·1m

Directions produced by the SW Scotland SC which may be obtained from Matheson Kidsdale, Whithorn, Newton Stewart DG8 8HZ. It is not possible to make the direct passage from Hestan Is to Maryport, nor should any attempt be made higher up the Firth where streams are strong, the shifting sands are hard and seas can be steep. When leaving Hestan Is for the English shore keep off Barnhourie Sand, Dumroof Bank and Robin Rigg by making 170° over the ground until S of the 'Two Feet Bank' W card buoy before turning E. Workington is the only port of refuge which can be entered at all states of the tide. Wind can raise a difficult sea over Workington Bank but the passage inside the Bank is safe. Going further S, the ebb will help to St Bees Head: aim to get there 1hr after LW and pick up the S-going flood from the head onwards. The streams run at 4kn round the point.

Ranges Firing of various weapons takes place at Eskmeals and Ravenglass about 10M S usually on weekdays with variable danger areas off St Bees Head. You are advised to call *Eskmeals Gun Range* on VHF 13 or ☎ 01229 712246.

This is a commercial hbr for coasters at the mouth of the River Derwent. It is easily identified by the large wind farm 1M NE. There is a considerable current after heavy rain as well as a 2kn tidal set across the entrance. The only attraction to

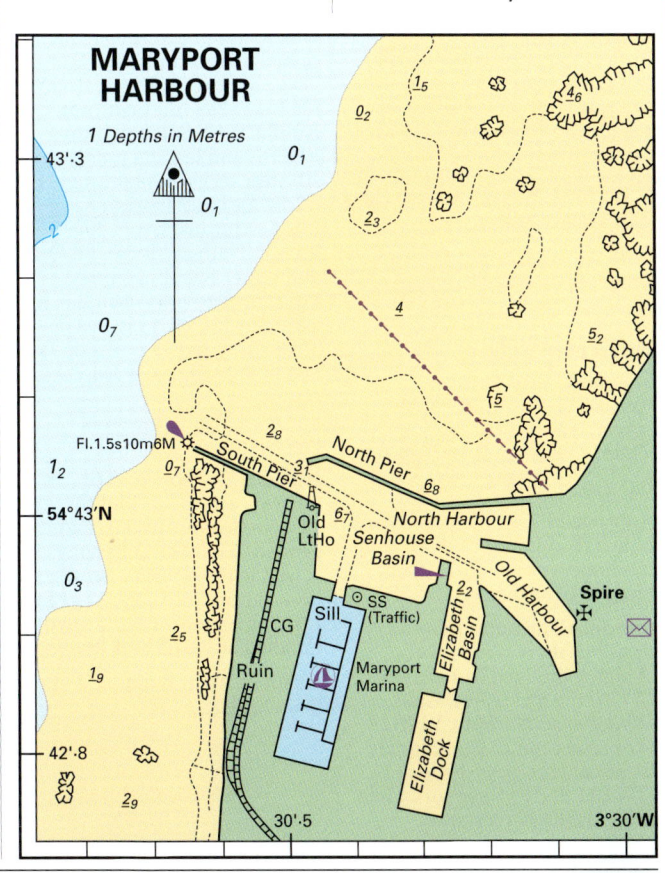

ENGLAND – WEST COAST AND WALES

171

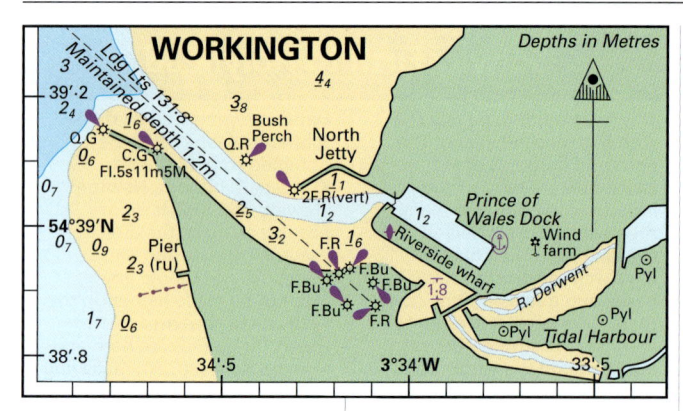

the yachtsman is that this is a safe hbr deep enough to enter at any state of the tide.

Bar Extends for 3ca N of R brick disused CG Lt Fl.5s near end of S pier. Localised steep seas occasionally.

Approach Clear when S pier head bears between 010° and 180°. From the S and W pick out Q.G Lt on end of S pier and head N until the Ldg Lts F.R on W pyramids are in line 132° clearly framed between two pairs of F.Bu Lts which mark the edge of the channel to the Turning Basin, dredged to 1·2m.

Entrance Marked by Q.R Lt on 'Bush' perch N of dredged channel. When 2F.R(vert) on end of N jetty abeam round up to port N into turning basin.

Berthing
• In offshore winds anchor 2ca NE or SE of CG.
• In Turning Basin sheltered from all winds but must not be left unattended as large ships pass through. Good shelter.
• Vanguard SC may have a half tide mooring free in the tidal dock S of Riverside Wharf. Trawlers, Pilot and Fishery Protection vessels take up all this dock's quay berths but try to negotiate a berth alongside.
• With short or lowering masts, drying moorings may be found on berths in tidal hbr inside rly br which no longer opens. Air draught 1·8m.

☏/VHF HM 01900 602301, VHF 16, 11, 14 *Workington Harbour Radio*.

WHITEHAVEN

Standard Port Liverpool
HW +0015   LW +0002
MHWS MHWN MLWN MLWS
−1·4m −1·2m −0·8m −0·1m

Bar 1ca N of W pier head.

Approach Easily identified from N by tall chimney and tall monuments on cliffs just S of hbr. No obstructions.

Entrance The outer harbour dries but there is a buoyed channel, dredged to 1m above CD, to the lock gates. Call *Whitehaven Harbour* VHF 12 for permission to enter. It may be possible to pass the lock at HW±0400 (IPTS shown). Hold towards the N pier head, Fl.R.5s, until lined up with the lock, do not pass too close to the W pier head, Fl.G.5s, since a bar is building up there. Beware being set to port by an anticlockwise rotation in the hbr. In rough westerly weather wait for more water and keep close to the W pier head. Near HW there may be a period of free flow, but in exceptional tidal surges the lock may remain closed at HW to prevent flooding.

Berthing as instructed on entry. Max length of 13m on finger pontoons.

Facilities as expected of a modern marina. 45-tonne boat lift. Boatyard. WiFi. Town nearby.

☏/VHF HM and Marina 01946 692435 (24hrs); HM and Sealock VHF 12.

PIEL HARBOUR AND BARROW-IN-FURNESS

Standard Port Liverpool
HW +0015   LW +0020
MHWS MHWN MLWN MLWS
−0·1m −0·4m −0·2m 0·0m

Approach Strangers should take the entrance at half flood which, in the sea, runs from NW. The ebb runs from S. There are extensive shoals 5M offshore. Pick up Lightning Knoll RWVS Sph bell buoy LFl.10s and leaving it close to stb steer 041° on first Ldg Lts (No.1 Q, No.2 Iso.2s). Keep on this line for just over 3M leaving Halfway R can bn Q.R and Outer Bar R can buoy Fl(4)R.10s to port until Bar R can buoy Fl(2)R.5s is reached. Then bring Nos.3 & 4 Ldg Lts 005° (No.3 Q, No.4 Iso.2s) in transit and follow line for 1M till abreast of Piel Island.

Berthing Anchor clear of fairway, off or south of the castle unless preared to take the ground. Channel to Barrow 3M is well marked with lateral buoyage and further sets of Ldg Lts. Some moorings off town. Landing at Piel Is and Roa Is.

Facilities All at Barrow. Water from HM.

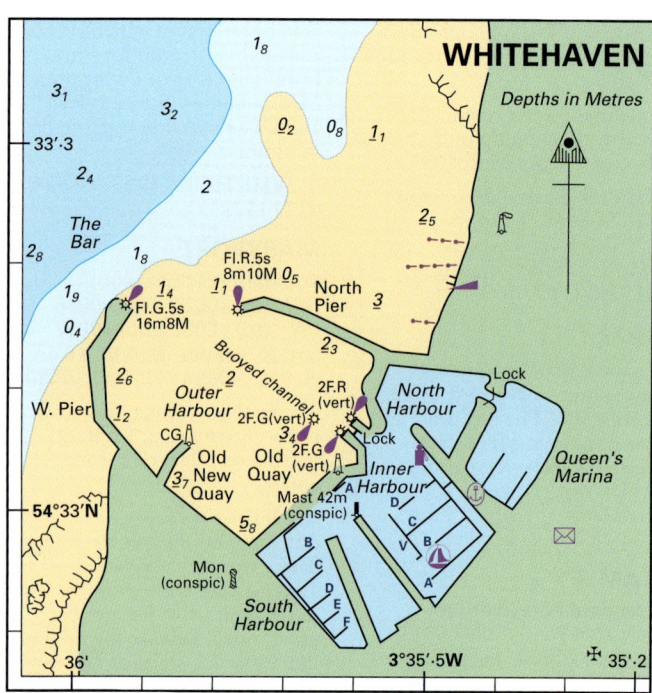

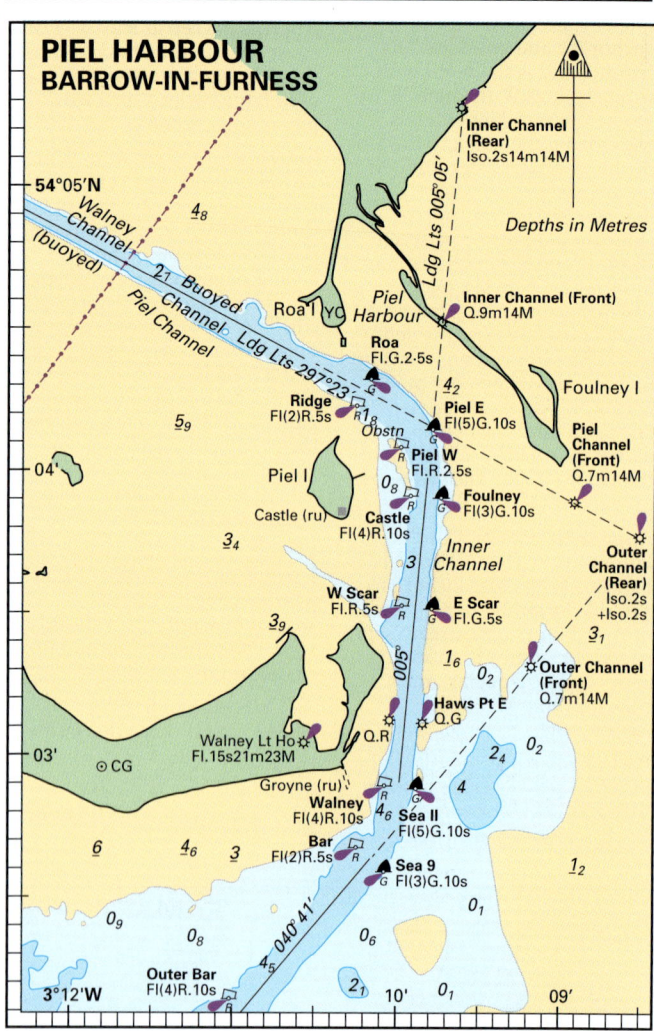

RIVER LUNE AND GLASSON DOCK

Standard Port Liverpool
Glasson Dock
HW +0030   LW +0225
MHWS MHWN MLWN MLWS
−2·8m −3·1m n/a n/a

Approach As for Fleetwood then continue to River Lune W card Lt buoy. Advisable to contact marina 24h in advance.

Entrance Much of the river dries so plan to arrive at River Lune No.1 W card Lt buoy 0115 before HW and proceed up channel at 4kn to be at Glasson Dock 45 minutes before HW Liverpool when gates open until HW. Lock only opens during daylight. Channel marked by lateral buoys, course 084° but channel varies until Plover Scar W bn which has tide gauge for sill at Glasson.

The Cruising Almanac

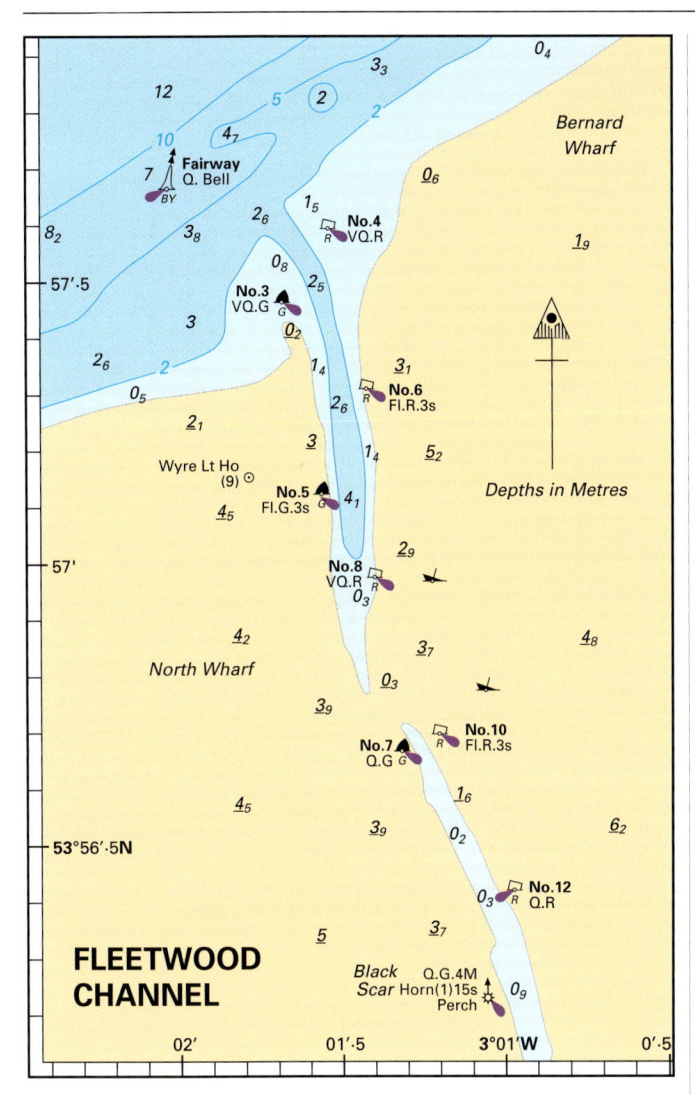

Call *Glasson Dock Radio* (VHF 69) to confirm the gate opening time: the flood sets SE onto Plover Scar. It turns N past Chapel Hill; then follow river round with training wall to port until No.18 R can Q.R buoy whence make for lock with short length of training wall to stb.

Berthing Glasson Dock has good laying up berths and a boatyard with all facilities including electricity on quays, showers, boat storage under cover and chandlery. Glasson Basin Yacht Harbour lies E of swing br and has pontoons (Canal and River Trust). Lancaster lies 5M above Glasson can be reached by small craft near HW. The channel is narrow and local knowledge advisable. The river has 1·5m at the town at HW.

☎/VHF HM 01524 751724, VHF 69; Marina 751491.

HEYSHAM

Standard Port Liverpool
HW (sp) +0005 (np) +0005
LW (sp) 0000   (np) +0015
MHWS MHWN MLWN MLWS
−0·0m −0·2m −0·1m +0·1m

Although the hbr affords good shelter it is unavailable to yachts except in emergency.

MORECAMBE BAY

Passage lights   BA No
Lune Deep   4870
S card Q(6)+LFl.15s5M
Fleetwood Fairway
No.1 N card Q Bell
River Lune
W card Q(9)15s
Heysham Breakwater   4860
2F.G(vert)9m5M Siren 30s
(Streams run hard, 5kn max, and raise a short steep sea on the ebb with W winds).
N Hoyle wind farm marked by four turbines 61m F.R and Fl.Y.2·5s11m5M Horn Mo(U) centred at 53°25'·0N 3°25'·5W.

Approach As for Fleetwood until past the Fairway buoy which is left to stb. Make No.1 Heysham buoy and then make good 045° to No.5 G con buoy Q.G and thence to hbr entrance. Beware ferries and HSS.

Entrance Or Ldg marks on S quay (not jetty) on a line 102° show the entry in middle of dredged channel. Front Lt F.Bu.11m, rear F.Bu.14m.

Berthing Berth as directed.

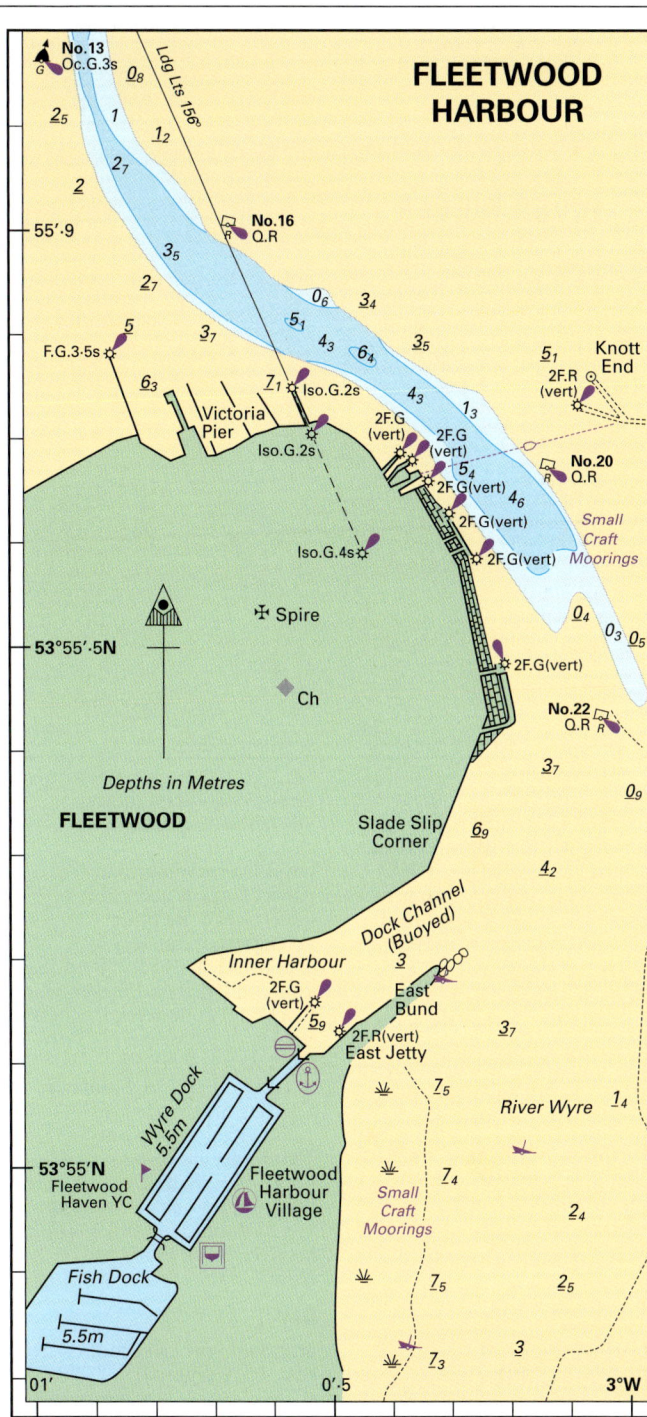

FLEETWOOD

Standard Port Liverpool
HW (sp) −0004 (np) −0004
LW (sp) −0006 (np) −0006
MHWS MHWN MLWN MLWS
−0·0m −0·2m −0·1m +0·1m

Bar 2·7m to 3·7m in main channel to Isle of Man quay.

Approach and Entrance Arrival at N card Fairway buoy, Q. Bell, at HW −0100 is ideal for a stranger bound for the marina. Steer SE for G con buoy No.3, VQ.G, then follow the well buoyed channel, which is subject to silting. Beware of the flood tide which sets E across the channel. If bound for the marina call *Fleetwood Dock Radio* VHF 12 after passing R can buoy, No.20.

Berthing
• Fleetwood Haven Marina in Wyre Dock. Max length 17m. Dredged to 5m. Gates operate HW±0130 (approx). Usual marina facilities including diesel, calor gas and laundry. Tram and bus to Blackpool.
• Anchor, using trip line since many mooring chains, out of channel at Knott End or at jetty (53°55'·70N 2°59'·73W) or at landing stage used by local yachts ½M S of Knott End. Land ferry slip, also on beach opposite No.2 IoM berth.

☎/VHF HM and Marina 01253 872323 *Fleetwood Dock Radio* VHF 12 (both Harbour Control and Marina).
www.fleetwoodhavenmarina.co.uk

PRESTON/RIVER RIBBLE

Approach and Entrance should not be attempted in strong W winds or heavy swell. Aim to arrive at fairway RW buoy, Gut,

ENGLAND – WEST COAST AND WALES

173

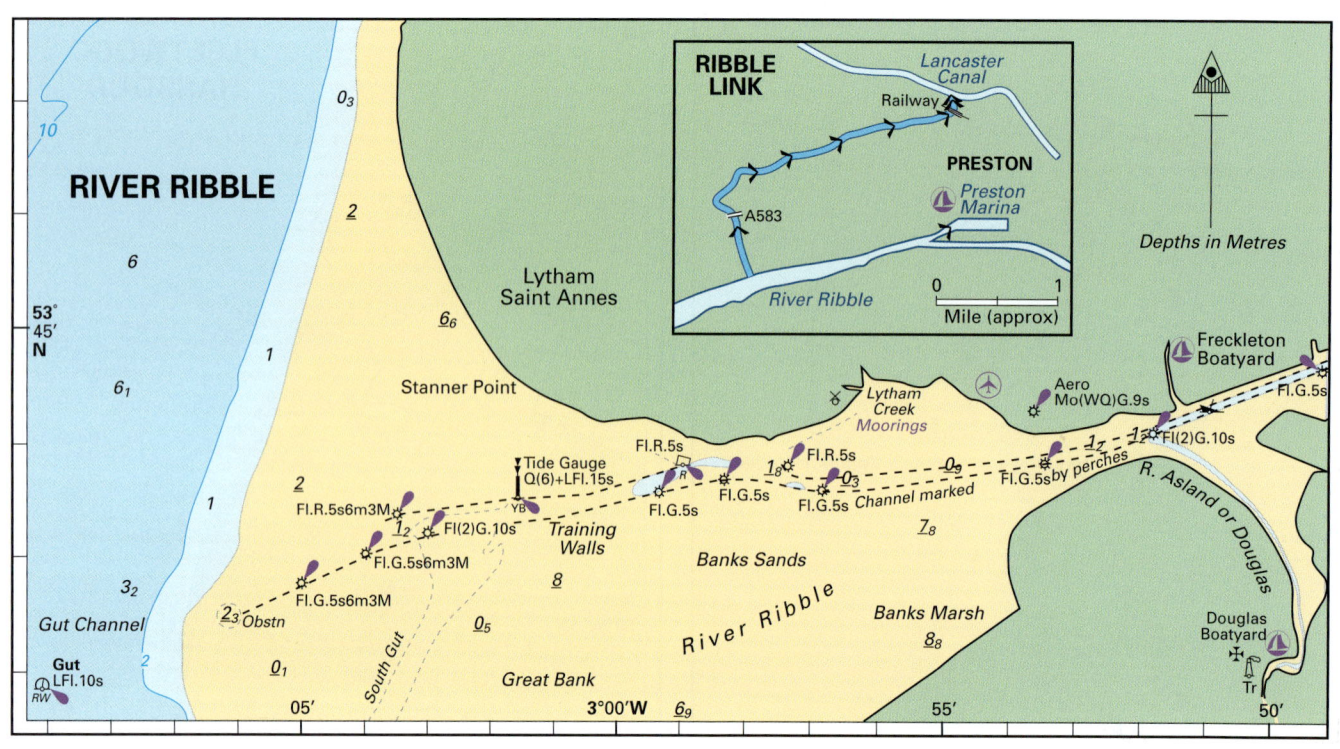

LFl.10s at HW Liverpool –0200. With boat speed of 5kn one should be at Preston within ½hr of HW. Make good 068° leaving the first three stb perches approx 25m to stb. Follow the perches up to Preston (14M).

Berthing It may be possible to pick up a mooring at Lytham between LB and W windmill. Preston Marina lock gates open HW Liverpool –0100 to +0200. There is a deep water waiting pontoon outside the gates.

Facilities include pump-out, chandlery, boatyard. Nearby supermarket. Good rail and road connections.

☎/VHF Marina 01772 733595; Preston Lock *Riversway* VHF 14.

LIVERPOOL/ RIVER MERSEY

Standard Port Liverpool

Liverpool is a busy commercial port and was European Capital of Culture 2008. It has much to offer visitors.

Approach The Anglican Cathedral is a land mark visible from 40 miles. The Bar light float (Fl.5s11m12M) marks the entry to the 10 mile long, well buoyed Queens/Crosby Channel. Be aware of tidal streams up to 5kn; training walls either side of channel; HS ferries; ships limited by draught; Rock Channel not recommended for use by visitors.

Berthing Liverpool Marina, at Coburg Dock is accessible HW±0200, call on VHF 37/M or ☎ 0151 707 6777. NB for arrival between 2200 and 0600 necessary to arrange in advance. 450 berths with full club facilities and limited on site chandlery, rigger, mechanical repairs, straddle carrier.

www.liverpoolmarina.com. Albert Dock is accessible HW –0200 to HW by prior arrangement but very expensive. ☎ 0151 709 6558. Langton Dock and Birkenhead Docks are commercial, access only with permission of Port Operations, VHF 12 ☎ 0151 949 6136. Similarly, Landing Stages are for commercial vessels only. Temporary mooring possible opposite Canada Dock at New Brighton but, more usefully, 1M SSW of Liverpool Marina, between Rock Ferry and New Ferry.

RHYL

Standard Port Liverpool
HW –0019 (approx)

MHWS	MHWN	MLWN	MLWS
–1·5m	–1·3m	n/a	n/a

Rhyl Harbour is the mouth of the River Clwyd and is at the western end of Rhyl. The harbour has a drying height of 4m above CD and vessels wishing to stay at the harbour over low water must be capable of drying out and taking the ground. Access to inner harbour pontoons is via the lifting pedestrian/cycle bridge. Lifting is on demand, subject to wind strength and whenever the harbour and approaches are navigable. Entry and exit to the harbour by a 1·5m draft vessel should only be undertaken HW±0200.

Approach Make for the RW Fairway buoy Mo(A)10s in 53°19'·60N 3°32'·00W, contact the Harbour Office to arrange berth and br opening. Then make good 094° for 1M towards the seaward perch.

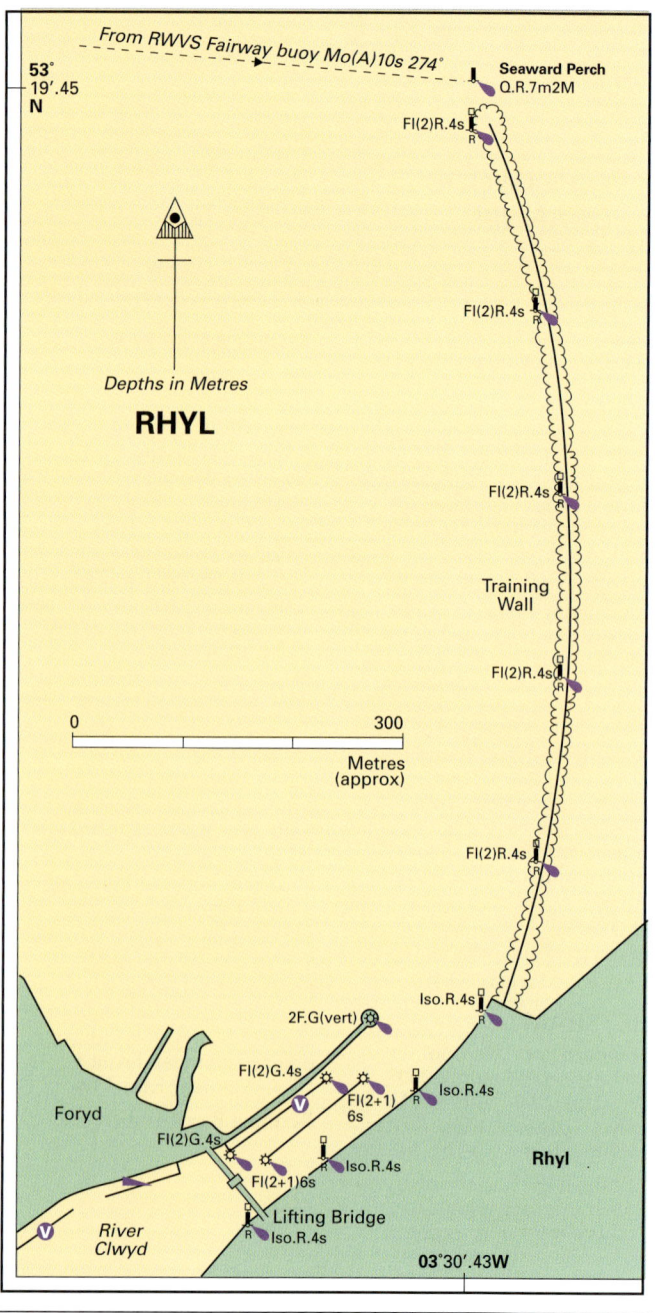

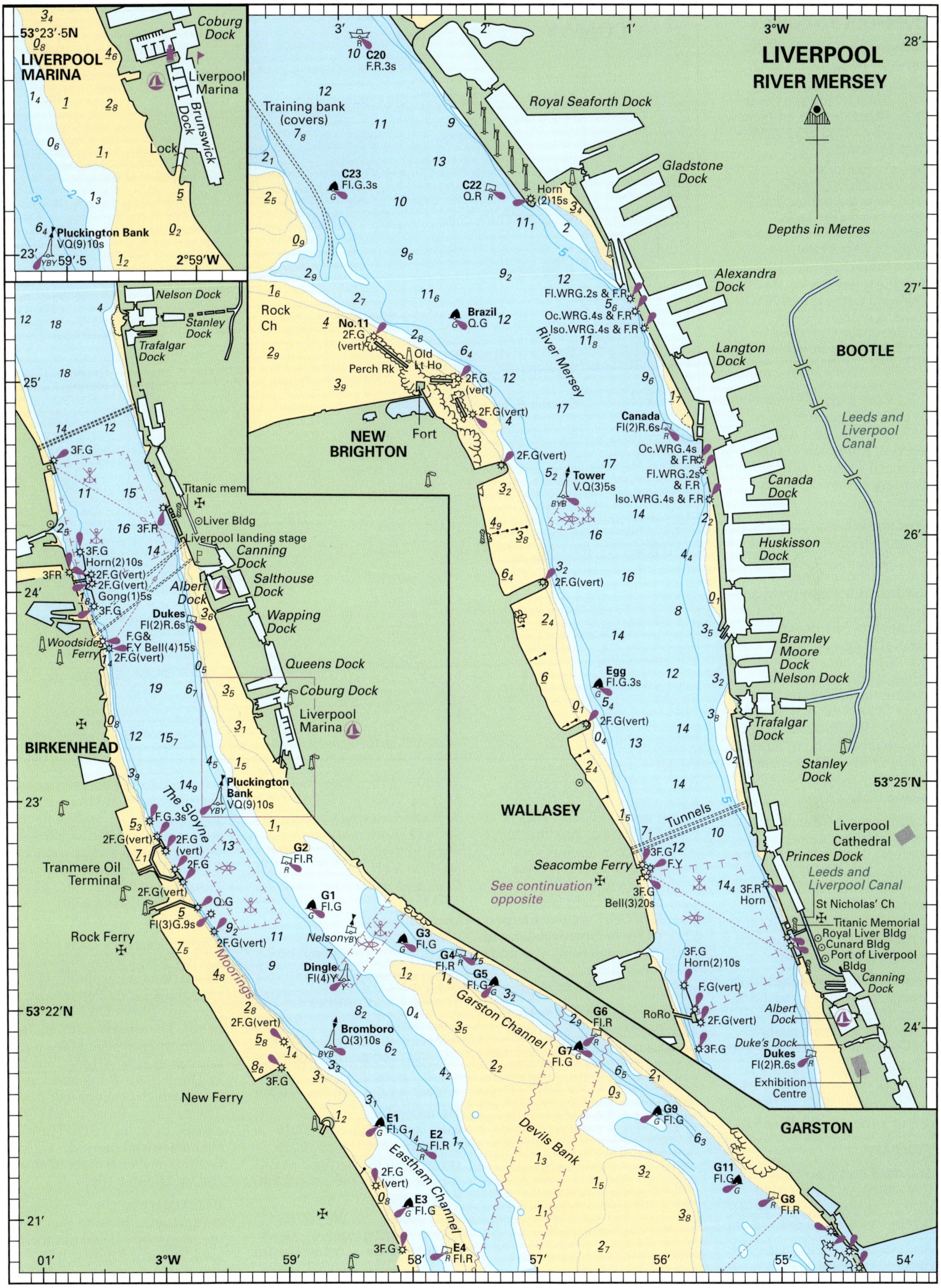
LIVERPOOL
RIVER MERSEY
Depths in Metres
LIVERPOOL MARINA
53°23′·5N
Coburg Dock
Liverpool Marina
Brunswick Dock
Lock
Pluckington Bank
VQ(9)10s
59′·5
2°59′W
Royal Seaforth Dock
Gladstone Dock
Alexandra Dock
Langton Dock
Canada Dock
Huskisson Dock
Bramley Moore Dock
Nelson Dock
Trafalgar Dock
Stanley Dock
BOOTLE
Leeds and Liverpool Canal
Training bank (covers)
Rock Ch
C20
F.R.3s
C23
Fl.G.3s
C22
Q.R
Horn (2)15s
No.11
2F.G (vert)
Perch Rk
Old Lt Ho
Brazil
Q.G
Fl.WRG.2s & F.R
Oc.WRG.4s & F.R
Iso.WRG.4s & F.R
River Mersey
Canada
Fl(2)R.6s
Oc.WRG.4s & F.R
Fl.WRG.2s & F.R
Iso.WRG.4s & F.R
NEW BRIGHTON
Fort
2F.G(vert)
Tower
V.Q(3)5s
Egg
Fl.G.3s
WALLASEY
Tunnels
Seacombe Ferry
See continuation opposite
3F.G
Bell(3)20s
3F.G
F.Y
3F.R
Horn
Liverpool Cathedral
Princes Dock
Leeds and Liverpool Canal
St Nicholas' Ch
Titanic Memorial
Royal Liver Bldg
Cunard Bldg
Port of Liverpool Bldg
Canning Dock
Albert Dock
Duke's Dock
Dukes
Fl(2)R.6s
Exhibition Centre
RoRo
3F.G
Horn(2)10s
F.G(vert)
2F.G(vert)
3°W
53°25′N
24′
GARSTON
Nelson Dock
Stanley Dock
Trafalgar Dock
25′
3F.G
Titanic mem
Liver Bldg
Liverpool landing stage
Canning Dock
Salthouse Dock
Albert Dock
Wapping Dock
Dukes
Fl(2)R.6s
Queens Dock
Coburg Dock
Liverpool Marina
3F.R
3FR
3F.G
Horn(2)10s
2F.G(vert)
Gong(1)5s
Woodside Ferry
F.G& F.Y Bell(4)15s
BIRKENHEAD
Pluckington Bank
VQ(9)10s
The Sloyne
F.G.3s
2F.G (vert)
2F.G
Tranmere Oil Terminal
Q.G
Fl(3)G.9s
Rock Ferry
Moorings
G2
Fl.R
G1
Fl.G
Nelson
G3
Fl.G
Dingle
Fl(4)Y
G4
Fl.R
G5
Fl.G
Garston Channel
G6
Fl.R
G7
Fl.G
Bromboro
Q(3)10s
53°22′N
New Ferry
3F.G
E1
Fl.G
E2
Fl.R
Eastham Channel
Devils Bank
E3
Fl.G
E4
Fl.R
G9
Fl.G
G11
Fl.G
G8
Fl.R
23′
21′
01′
3°W
59′
58′
57′
56′
55′
54′
28′
27′
26′

LIVERPOOL TO CONWY

Passage lights	BA No
RW Pillar Buoy	4942
Bar Fl.5s12M	

Tidal Streams between Great Orme Head and Formby Point run Dover +0100 to +0500W, –0500 to –0100E.

Do not attempt short cuts as the seaward edges of some sandbanks are not buoyed. Do not cut across the sands between Great Orme Head and Conwy without local knowledge.

Pass the N Hoyle buoy 1M off. The wind farm extends 20M W to NE, N of this line. The turbines have Lts F.R and Fl.Y.2·5s11m5M Horn Mo(U)30s.

Follow the marked channel, the best water is approx 5m to 20m off each of the port hand beacons. Tidal flows in the approach channel and harbour areas are strong (>5kn) at times.

Entrance When proceeding to the inner harbour leave No.14 and No.16 bns to port, and the centre harbour pontoon to stb (marked at both seaward and landward ends with a Preferred Channel to Port Bn, Green Conical Topmark and G(2+1)6s Light). Pass under the Bridge southern span. On passing the bridge the best water lays to the N (stb) side of the inner hbr. Proceed to your allocated berth. If remaining in the outer hbr take up your berth after passing No.12 bn when safe to do so.

Berthing For overnight stay use Outer Harbour Drying Pontoon, longer stays at drying pontoon on stb side Inner Harbour, both have electricity and water. Contact the Harbour Office before leaving a berth or exiting the inner hbr to arrange bridge opening.

Facilities Slipway, 12-ton Boat Mover for vessels up to 2·5m draft. Boat park with power, water and wash off facilities. Toilets, showers, café, Rly and all stores.

☏/**VHF** Harbour Office VHF 14, 01824 708400; Mobile and out of hours 07920 203851.

CONWY

Standard Port Holyhead
HW +0020   LW +0112

MHWS	MHWN	MLWN	MLWS
+2·3m	+1·8m	+0·6m	+0·4m

An historic town in an area of outstanding natural beauty. 13th-century castle. Two modern marinas. Access HW –0200 to HW+0200.

Bar About 0·6m at MLWS. Flood runs for 5hrs, ebb 7hrs. Vessels drawing 1·8m enter at HW –0230. The channel shifts.

Entrance Make the Fairway RWVS sph buoy and turn on to 094° for 9ca to pass between C2 R can buoy Fl.R.10s and C1 G con buoy Fl.G.10s. Follow lit buoyed channel. Pass the buoys within 10 to 20m. It is very shallow to seaward of No.6 buoy less than 1m LWS. After passing Perch Light (steel tower) LFl.G.15s carry on for about 45m before turning on to 139° which will bring you into the Conwy River.

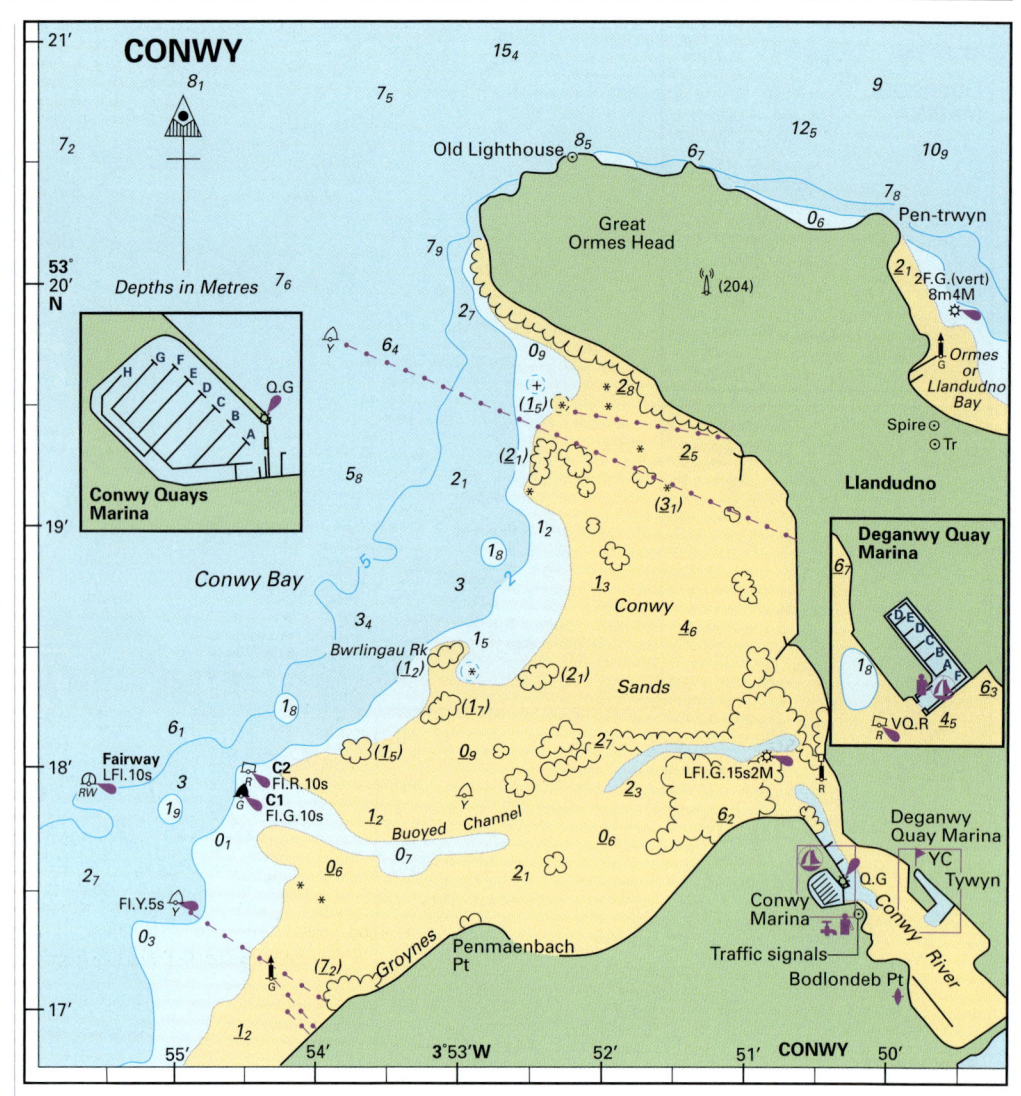

Berthing
• **Conwy Marina** 520 berths, access HW±0330, flap gate opens when tide height >3·5m. Waiting pontoon, request berth before entering, RG traffic lights.
• **Deganwy Quay Marina** 200 berths, access HW±0315 flap gate opens when tide height >4·0m, request berth before entering.
• SE of Bodlondeb Pt there is a long pontoon. No shore access. Obtain permission from HM.
• Pick up vacant mooring and inform HM.
• Floating pontoon at town quay, only accessible HW±0200. Nearby shops.

Facilities As expected in the marinas. WiFi at both marinas. Boat lift. N Wales Cruising Club in Lower High Street.

☏/**VHF** Conwy Marina 01492 593000 (24hr), Deganwy Marina 576888, HM 596253, N Wales Cruising Club 593481. Both marinas www.quaymarinas.com VHF 80, HM VHF 14, NW Cruising Club and Water Taxi VHF 37/M.
Useful information from www.conwy.gov.uk (Enter 'harbours' in the Search box.)

MENAI STRAIT

Standard Port Holyhead
Beaumaris
HW (sp) +0025 (np) +0010
LW (sp) +0055 (np) +0035

MHWS	MHWN	MLWN	MLWS
+2·0m	+1·6m	+0·5m	+0·1m

Menai Bridge
HW (sp) +0030 (np) +0010
LW (sp) +0100 (np) +0035

MHWS	MHWN	MLWN	MLWS
+1·7m	+1·4m	+0·3m	0·0m

Caernarfon
HW –0030   LW –0010

MHWS	MHWN	MLWN	MLWS
–0·4m	–0·4m	–0·1m	–0·1m

The Menai Strait between Anglesey and the mainland offers good shelter, except in strong NE or SW winds, excellent facilities and fine scenery. It runs NE/SW and can be entered at either end. There are two bridges, the Menai Suspension Br (NE) and the Britannia rly br (SW) and an overhead cable, min vertical clearance 22m at HAT. Between the two bridges lie the rocks known as the Swellies where the tides run at speeds up to 8kn. The direction of buoyage changes at the S Card buoy called 'Change' off Caernarfon.

The NE Entrance leads in from Conwy Bay, leaving Puffin Island (landing prohibited) with the R bn on Perch Rock to port and Trwyn Du LtHo Fl.5s to stb. The stream starts to flow in here at Holyhead HW +0530 and out at HW –0145. To the S lie Dutchman's Bank and Lavan Sands which cover at half tide. The Anglesey shore should be cleared by at least 3ca. The channel is well buoyed, Beaumaris Pier is marked at its end by 2Fl(3)G.10s.

Beaumaris castle is conspicuous. Most of the moorings are private but there are 2Y visitors' buoys. It is possible to lie alongside the SW side of the pier to take on provisions. The Royal Anglesey YC is near the pier and the NW Venturers YC are at Gallows Point which dries 3ca offshore. There is a boat yard with 14t boat lift and chandlery at Gallows Point. ABC Powermarine ☏ 01248 811412

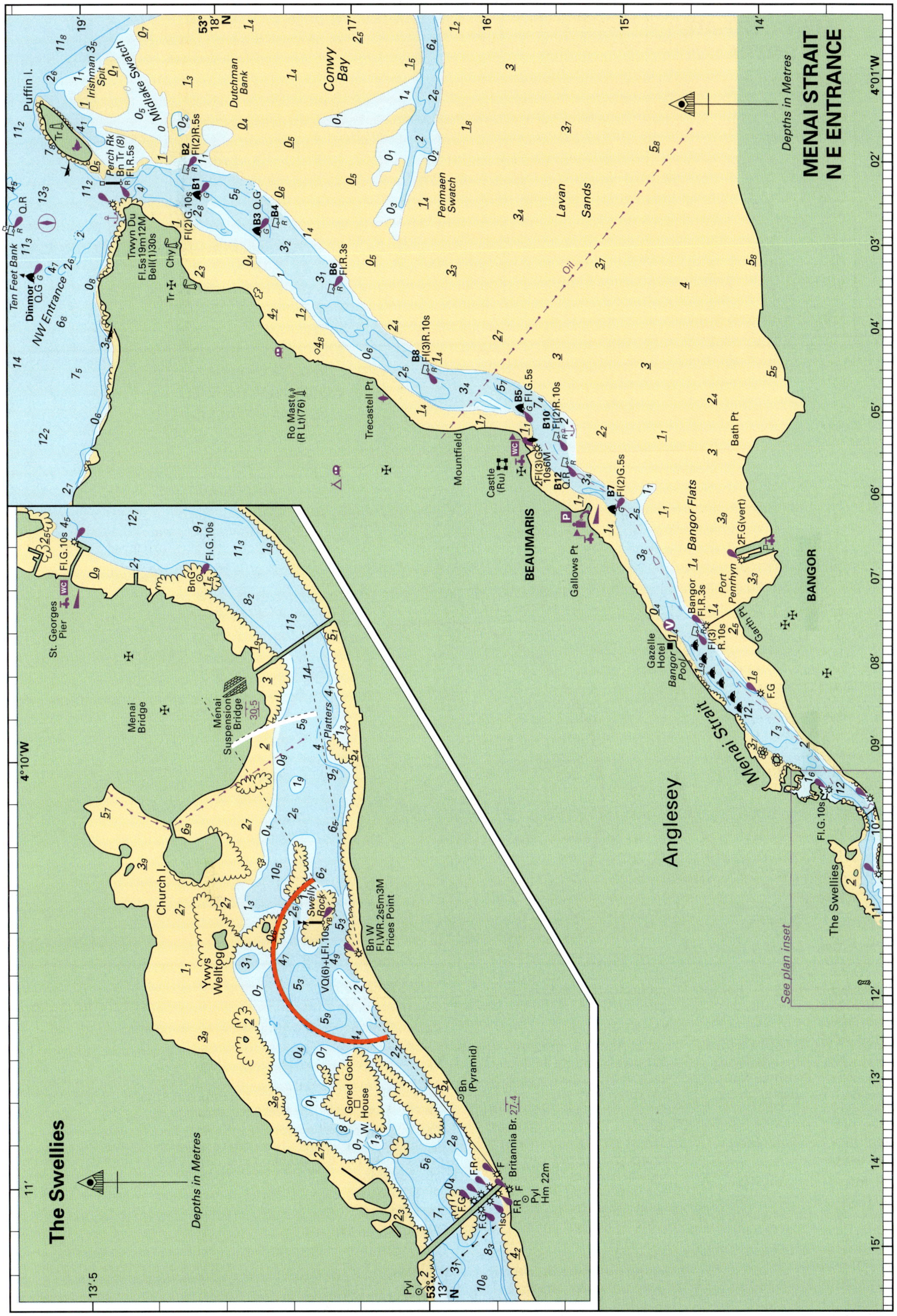

ENGLAND – WEST COAST AND WALES

The Cruising Almanac

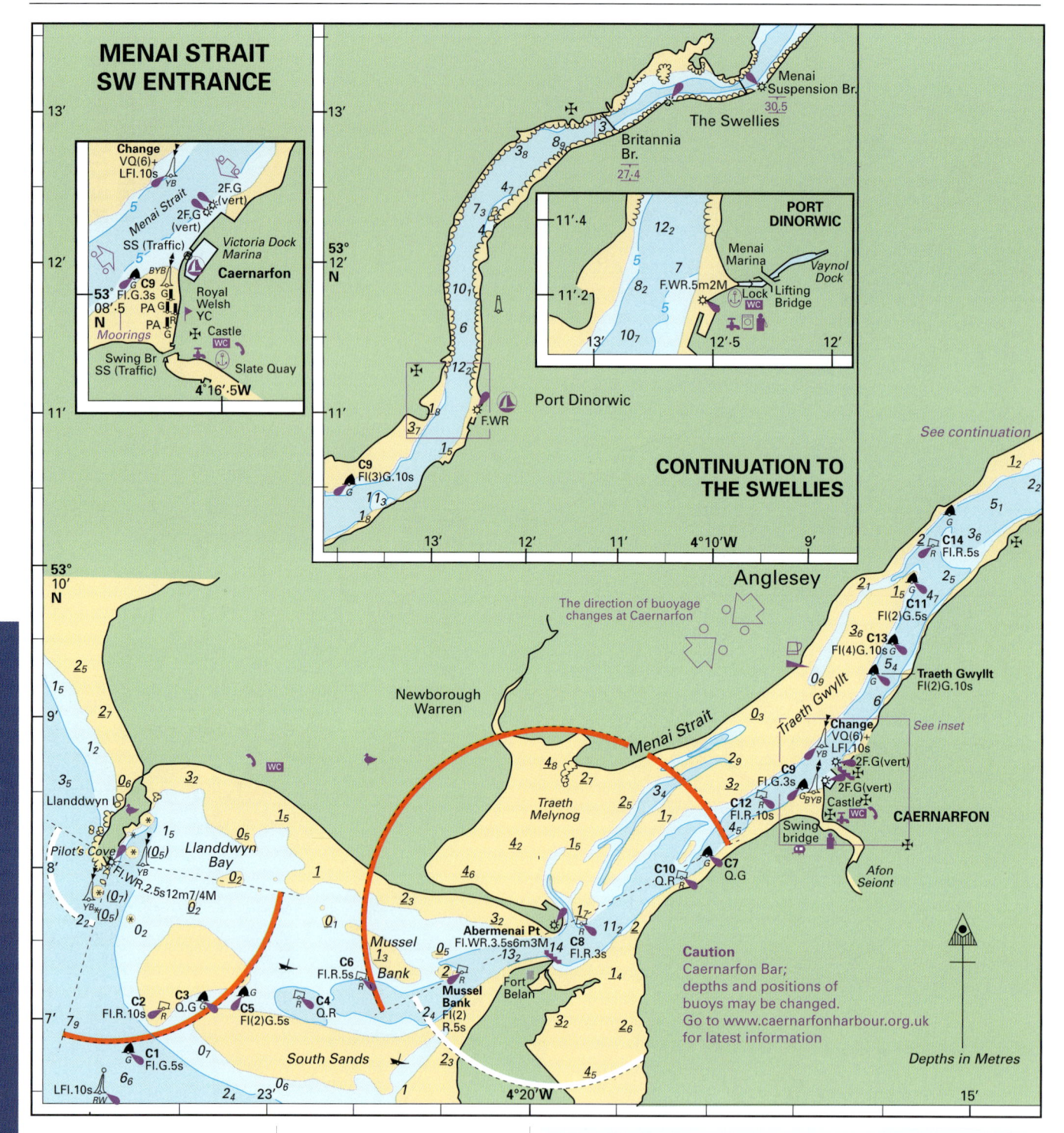

www.abcpm.co.uk Anchorage SE of B10 buoy or outside moorings.

Bangor has a long pier with a bn Fl.R.3s. There is a drying dock at Port Penrhyn, for allocation of a berth/drying mooring contact Dickies boatyard ☎ 01248 363400 www.dickies.co.uk/office-info/bangor.

Facilities Toilets, showers, boatyard, no diesel or gas. Opposite on the Anglesey shore, there is the Gazelle Hotel. There are two Y visitors' moorings here.

Menai Bridge Temporary swinging moorings, 2Y visitors' buoys or berth alongside St George's Pier which is the mooring of Bangor University's research ship. Only water and a public toilet. Pier Masters office. ☎ 01248 712312.

The Swellies The tides run round Anglesey and into both entrances creating an area of slack water at the Swellies at Liverpool HW –0200 and LW –0200 lasting between 10–20 minutes. The tide is an hour later at the NE entrance of the Straits and the tide can be 1·8m higher. Timing is crucial to a safe passage and if the tide sets against your craft it is safer to abort the passage than to fight it as there is a risk of being set sideways onto the rocks. There is plenty of water between the rocks as coasters drawing 4·6m use it but the channel past the Swelly Rock is only 30m wide at LW and without local knowledge the HW passage is recommended. Advice from

THE SWELLIES

Passage from NE

Pass St Georges pier Fl.G.10s and the G bn on the rock to stb and move into midstream.

Pass under centre of Suspension Bridge.

Keep Swelly Rock S card Lt bn open on port bow to clear the Platters until Price's Point bn is on with the centre of Britannia Bridge. Steer on Price's Pt until Swelly Rock bn is abeam to stb.

Pass midway between Price's Pt and Swelly Rock bn with bow on Gored Goch Island which has a White house on it. When Price's Point is past, steer on Lts at port end of Britannia Bridge until W pyramid is abeam to port.

Pass under centre span of Britannia Bridge and favour the N shore to Port Dinorwic.

Passage from SW

Pass under the middle of the S span of Britannia Bridge and steer on W pyramid on stb shore until F.G Lts at base of S tower of bridge are in transit. Keep Swelly Rock Lt bn fine on stb bow until Price's Point bn is close abeam to stb. Pass midway between Price's Point bn and Swelly Rock bn until Price's Point shuts out centre tower of Britannia Bridge.

Steer on NW tower of Suspension Bridge until on a line between Swelly Rock and the middle of the Suspension Bridge to clear the Platters.

Finally turn to pass under the centre of the Suspension Bridge.

Menai Bridge piermaster ☏ 01248 712312 (Menai Pier), VHF 16, 69 or Victoria Dock ☏ 01286 672346, VHF 80. See Caernarfon Harbour Trust website for local pilotage notes www.caernarfonharbour.org.uk

HW Menai Br is Holyhead +0030 at sps and HW +0010 at nps.

HW Caernarfon is Holyhead HW –0030 at sps and HW –0030 at nps.

Times for Westward passage
Dover HW –0240
Liverpool HW –0230
Holyhead HW –0140

Times for Eastward passage
Dover HW –0215
Liverpool –0235
Holyhead HW –0145

The slack at the Swellies is at Liverpool HW –0200, Holyhead HW –0115. These times allow for boats to carry the flood tide from the NE. If you are late you will be swept through very fast. If you are early you may find the end of the contrary tide. It would be prudent not to attempt the Caernarfon Bar on a falling tide so plan to stop at Port Dinorwic, Caernarfon or anchor.

From the SW the times are deliberately early because it helps to carry the flood through the Swellies and then the ebb past Bangor. Do not be late if travelling NE as the tide will set strongly against you before you pass the Swellies.

SW winds make the times of HW earlier and NE winds make it later.

On the N bank 2ca beyond the Britannia Br you will see Nelson's statue and a little further on you will catch glimpses of Plas Newydd, the home of the Marquis of Anglesey now in the care of the National Trust.

Port Dinorwic This old dock which was used to export slate is now a marina. 2m available through the lock HW±0230. Lock operates all tides, berthing alongside in freshwater. All facilities. The tidal basin outside dries HW±0300 at springs but has pontoons. Moorings available outside, free first 24h. Boatyard, engineer, rigger. Contact on VHF 80 before arrival. ☏ 01248 671500.

Caernarfon This spectacular town is dominated by its castle. The old hbr in the River Seiont dries and is crowded with moorings under the swing br (opening signal is three short blasts. The br is left open between 2300 and 0700). Lie against wall or raft up and contact hbr office, ☏ 01286 672118. The Victoria Dock marina 2m entered through a flap gate which opens at half tide (October–March during daylight hours only). Port entry signals. There are two waiting buoys SW of C9 G buoy. At half-tide there is a strong set across the Victoria Dock entrance. Chandlery, toilets, showers, diesel. VHF 80 (0700–2300 summer), ☏ 01286 672346.

Leaving to the SW, remember to leave C9 and C7 G buoys to port. C10 and C8 R can buoys keep boats off shoals to starboard. Pass midway between Abermenai Point and Fort Belan. The R Mussel Bank buoy Fl(2)R.5s lies 5ca ahead on 260°. On the same bearing the first of the bar buoys should be 1M ahead. This is between the R and W sectors of the Abermenai Lt.

Caernarfon Bar This is an area extending 3M out to sea where the charted depths are mostly less than 1m. The Fairway buoy, RWVS LFl.10s, lies 0·5M to SW of the outer bar buoys. There is a shifting buoyed channel winding across it. The Lt buoys are numbered C1 to C6. It is unsafe to cross the bar except in the top half of the tide, depending on sea state. Follow the buoys in sequence and do not pay much attention to chart. www.caernarfonharbour.org.uk gives latest positions of buoys. It is dangerous in SW winds more than Force 4 or in poor visibility. Advice about Caernarfon Bar at Harbour Office ☏ 01286 672118 or VHF 14, 16. As the channel narrows at Abermenai Pt the stream gets stronger, 3–4 knots, it starts to run NE at Holyhead HW +0430 and SW –0130.

Anchorages around Anglesey (see chart 1971)
• SW Menai Straits; **Llanddwyn Island** at 53°08'·0N 4°24'·6W. Shelter from W to NE wind, Uncomfortable in SW. Fair to good holding. Approach with care from small S Card buoy 600m S of Llanddwyn Lt, anchor E of Lt in 2m or more. Beware sub rocks 150m NE and 400m E of Lt (latter marked by small S Card).
• **Abermenai Point** at 53°07'·6N 4°19'·6W in 2m or more 250m NE of Point Lt. Shelter from W. **Fort Belan** This lies on the S side and close E of the fort. Sound in carefully as the water shoals rapidly in this bay.
• NE Menai Straits; **Puffin Island** at 53°18'·9N 4°01'·60W. Shelter from N wind, impossible in E. Good holding. Approach with care from N of B2 600m S of Perch Rock entrance bn, arcing right to left towards tr on Island. Anchor 200m off in 1·5–4m when CG Station and Perch Rock bn in line.
• E Coast; **Moelfre** at 53°21'·0N 4°13'·5W. Shelter from all but NE–SE wind. Good holding. Approach easy, anchor 200m off in 3m SE of RNLI slipway.
• N Coast; **Porth Eilian** at 53°24'·9N 4°17'·6W. Shelter from E–SW wind. Strong tidal stream off Point Lynas. Easy approach. Anchor in 2–5m, ½ cable off, SSW of Lynas LtHo, holding fair to good.
Amlwch Dock at 53°25'·0N 4°19'·9W. Shelter from all winds but swell if from N. Small confined, rough/tall dock sides with ladders, plank/fenders in outer dock in 2m. Approach with care (possible overfalls and strong current) from NNE, entrance unclear until near to end of RH mole marked 2FRvert. No facilities.
Cemaes Bay at 53°25'·2N 4°27'·6W. Shelter from all wind depending on anchorage. Large swell possible in strong N wind. Good holding. Approach from Middle Mouse only when fully open. Shoals 500m off E entrance. Rocks 200m off W entrance. No marks or buoys in bay.
Cemlyn at 53°25'·0N 4°30'·0W. Shelter from E through S to W, N winds deny access. Swell possible, holding varies in 2m. Approach on 180° from 250m E of Harry Furlong buoy.

HOLYHEAD
Standard Port Holyhead

The hbr of Holyhead lies between Holyhead Mountain a conspic landmark 213m and Carmel Head. Holyhead is the only Harbour of Refuge accessible at all states of tide and all weather conditions, on the UK coast between the Clyde and Milford Haven. The town has excellent facilities for provisioning with 4 Supermarkets, (2 within 20 minutes walk) Petrol 1.5M. Good rail and motorway links. Ferry service to Dublin. A good port for crew changes and base for exploring Anglesey, Snowdonia. The large commercial harbour of Holyhead is used by High Speed (40kn) and large traditional ferries, cruise ships and other large commercial vessels. The focus of these vessels is the Old Harbour (south of Salt Island) and Jetties on and north of Salt Island. Yachts should keep clear of commercial traffic and monitor VHF 14 Holyhead Port Radio. Be aware of traffic separation zone at the port entrance. The depth inside the new hbr is generally 5–15m, shoaling to 2m or under near the shore, and to just under 1m over the Platters on the E side of the hbr.

Approach From N give the Skerries a berth of at least 1M and keep S Stack well open of N Stack till breakwater LtHo bears SSE to avoid race over Langdon Ridge. Thence steer

SKERRIES/CARMEL HEAD AND STACKS PASSAGE

Passage lights:	BA No
Skerries	5168

Fl(2)15s36m20M & Iso.R.4s26m10M Horn(2)60s AIS

S Stack 5204
Fl.10s60m24M Horn 30s

DS between Skerries and Carmel Head

Dover +0005NE –0100SW 5·6kn

DS N and S Stacks

Dover +0530NNE –0030SSW 5kn

Race up to 1½M NW of S Stack and ½M W of N Stack on NNE stream.

Race up to 5ca W of S Stack with SSW stream.

for breakwater. From SW give the Stacks a berth of at least 1M. Conspic chimney (the former Anglesey Aluminium Smelter) is a good mark. Holyhead race extending 1½M offshore is worst N of the Stacks in NW winds. At the breakwater the W going stream runs for 9hrs from half flood to LW by the shore.

Entrance Between the breakwater and Clipera Rocks R can bell buoy Fl(4)R.15s. The breakwater and the Aluminium jetty mark the entrance to New Harbour. Give breakwater ½ca clearance.

Berthing In New Harbour only where a strong NE wind can make it very uncomfortable.

The conspic new apartment buildings at the W end of the Harbour are adjacent to the Marina and the Sailing Club.

• **Holyhead Sailing Club** has visitors' moorings: call Holyhead Club Launch on VHF 37 or HSC Bosun Mobile 07933 701150 for allocation of an available swinging mooring. Launch usually operates from 0900–2100 (later at weekends) summer only. Holyhead Sailing Club is very welcoming to visiting yachts. Good value catering is available; ☏ 01407 764072 to check availability/book.

• **Holyhead Marina** In the west end of the harbour, the 320 berth marina has full facilities and min. depth of 2m throughout. Contact Holyhead Marina on VHF 37 for allocation of berth. Visitors normally berth on pontoon B or outside of the north/south pontoon E, which can be very uncomfortable in NE winds. Boatyard, chandlery, WiFi at reception, mechanical/electrical/rigging services, restaurant and small shop/café.

• **Holyhead Marine** at Mackenzie Pier 500m E of HSC (where RNLI craft are serviced) with 30-tonne crane and boatyard facilities.

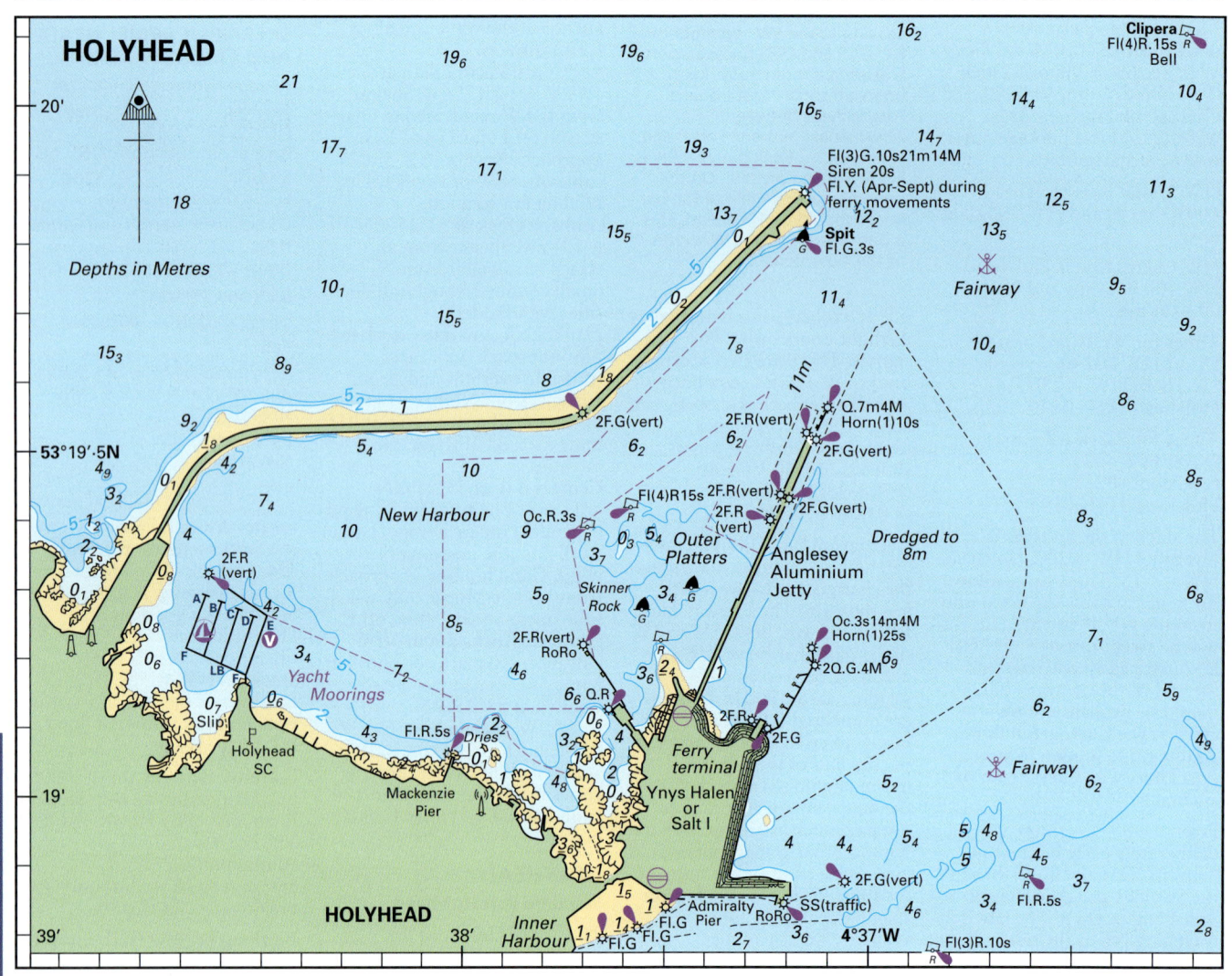

PORTH DINLLÄEN

This fine bay on the N side of the Lleyn peninsula 15M SW of Caernarvon affords the only safe anchorage between there and Pwllheli in S to W winds and settled weather. With strong NW winds some shelter may be found by shallow draught boats close to the point but strong winds from NNW to NNE send in a heavy sea.

Approach From W keep Yr Eifl (twin conspic peaks 561m) open of Porth Dinllaen Point to clear Careg-y-Chad dries 2m ¾M W of Point. Give the rocks off the point a fair berth. Chwislen Rock, BRB bn, extends ½ca to W. From seaward steer for Boduan a rounded wooded mountain 275m high 1M S of Nevin.

Anchorage About 1ca S of lifeboat station in 1·5 to 3m. Better holding further out in the bay but less shelter. Groceries at Morfa Nevin, Ty Coch pub on beach. For petrol and general stores Nevin 2M or in Nevin Bay 1M to E. Anchorage in Nevin Bay not recommended.

BARDSEY SOUND

Tidal streams in the vicinity of Bardsey Island are strong and run at up to 7kn in the Sound. Slack water occurs, turning NW at HWD +0500 and SE at HWD –0100 approx. The sound can be extremely dangerous in strong wind over tide situations with severe overfalls. There are two shallow ridges SE of Bardsey, Bastram Shoal and the Devil's Tail, where severe overfalls may also be encountered in adverse conditions. There are also overfalls to the N of Braich-Y-Pwll at the north end of Bardsey Sound. Aberdaron offers an anchorage to await slack water for passage North through Bardsey or overnight under suitable conditions, shelter from W through N to NE.

Without local knowledge Bardsey Sound should only be taken at slack water and in winds Force 4 or less.

ABERSOCH AND ST TUDWAL'S ROAD

Standard Port Milford Haven
HW (sp) +0145 (np) +0155
LW (sp) +0240 (np) +0310
MHWS MHWN MLWN MLWS
–2·2m –1·9m –0·7m –0·2m

This sandy bay with fine beaches is a very popular summer yachting centre with many moorings in St Tudwal's Road. The village has a vibrant beach/café culture with many trendy shops and is well worth a visit.

The anchorage offshore in St Tudwal's Road offers protection from S through W to NE. Better shelter from the South can be obtained at Chapel Bay on the north side of St Tudwal's Island East.

A heavy sea comes in with strong winds from the E or SE South Caernarfon YC on Penbennar has three visitors' moorings and a launch service during the summer months. Contact SCYC on VHF 37. www.scyc.co.uk. SCYC offers catering facilities; contact club for details.

Landing slip, water, small boatyard and chandlery. All stores and many restaurants in Abersoch.

PWLLHELI

Standard Port Milford Haven
HW (sp) +0150 (np) +0210
LW (sp) +0245 (np) +0320
MHWS MHWN MLWN MLWS
–1·9m –1·6m –0·6m –0·1m

The only 'all-weather' harbour on the Welsh coast between Holyhead and Milford Haven, Pwllheli, in Tremadoc Bay is home to the Welsh National Sailing Academy and events centre and welcomes visitors to its safe and secure 420 berth marina.

A popular yachting and holiday centre with safe sandy beaches. Pwllheli hosts many major Dinghy Sailing Championships.

Bar The entrance channel has been dredged to 0·6m below CD. If awaiting the tide, shelter from NE through N to W is available off Abererch, to the E of the harbour entrance, from W through SW at Abersoch, from S off St Tudwal's Islands, 6M SW of Pwllheli.

Approach Gimblet Rock (30m, quarried) lies E of conspic row of white houses on the promenade. From the Fairway Buoy, RW Iso.2s, (52°52'·98N 4°22'·93W) make good approx 294° towards the end of the training arm, Q.G 3m3M.

Entrance Buoyed with tide gauge on N of entrance channel controlled by training wall on N side which covers around half-tide. Follow the channel marked by buoys and bns to the marina.

Berthing In Hafan Pwllheli Marina. Pile and drying moorings may also be available, contact the marina who control all berthing in Pwllheli hbr.

Facilities Fuel, gas, boatyards, 50-tonne hoist, chandlers, sailmaker, sailing club (bar food may be available).

All stores and restaurants in Pwllheli town. Rly.

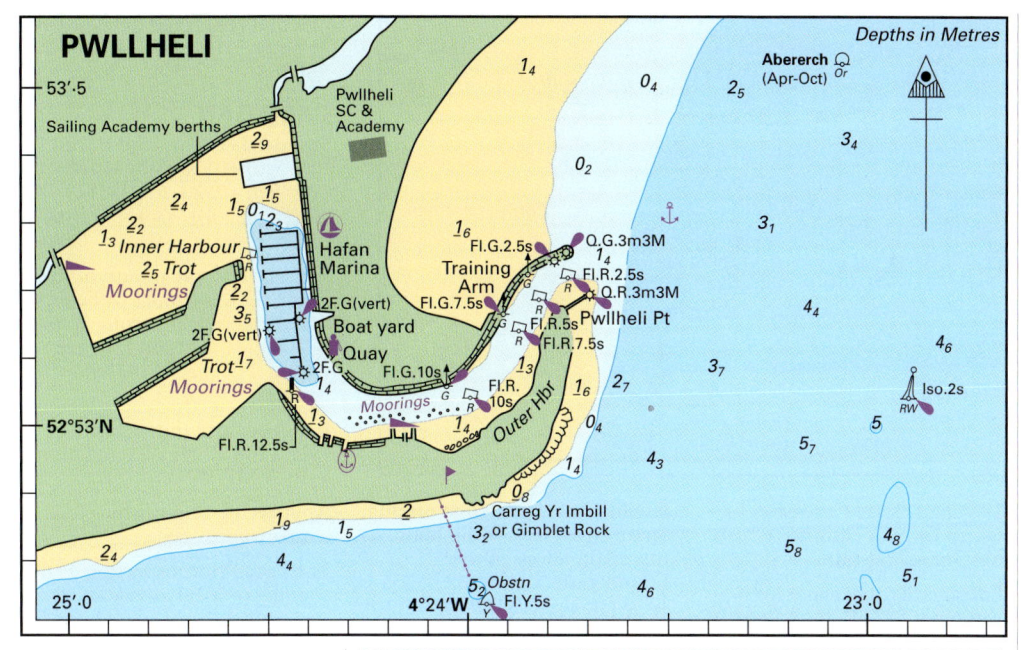

☎/VHF Hafan Pwllheli (24 hrs) 01758 701219, VHF 80; Pwllheli Sailing Club 01758 614 442.
www.hafanpwllheli.co.uk;
www.pwllhelisailingclub.co.uk

PORTHMADOG

Standard Port Milford Haven
HW (sp) +0210 (np) +0235
MHWS MHWN MLWN MLWS
−1·9m −1·8m n/a n/a

A beautiful walled hbr in the middle of a bustling holiday town. Suitable for vessels up to 50ft, maximum draught 2m. Good shelter in inner hbr, outer exposed to S and SE'lies.

Bar with least depth about 0·5m lies across the entrance. Caution: seas break on the bar when winds from S to SW exceed Force 4. Access should only be attempted HW ±0200. Entry is not hazardous in up to Force 5–6 from E (Seek advice from HM before entry).

Approach Fairway Buoy RWVS LFl.10s, at 52°52'·35N 4°10'·01W

Entrance Follow the buoyed channel from Fairway buoy. The channel is well marked by small lit buoys, which may be moved without prior notice throughout the year to meet frequent changes in the channel.

A sketch of the channel is available from the HM, by email if possible. If in doubt contact HM before entry, direct or via the CG.

Berthing Visitors who can take the ground should go alongside the N wall of inner hbr or at Madoc YC on Outer Drying Pontoon. Contact MYC for berth. At night, or boats which cannot take the ground, pick up a vacant mooring in main stream and await instructions or double up on boats berthed on wall to seaward of MYC.

HM Office on N Wall of inner hbr (Oakley Wharf).

Facilities Madoc Yacht Club – bar and food. Chandlery. Boatyard. Diesel (cans) and Waste Facilities at HM Office. All stores and restaurants in town. Rly.

Interest Narrow gauge Festiniog & Welsh Highland Railways. Closest hbr to Portmerion.

☎/VHF HM 01766 512927, Mobile 07879 433147, VHF 12/16; Madoc YC 01766 512976
www.madocyc.co.uk

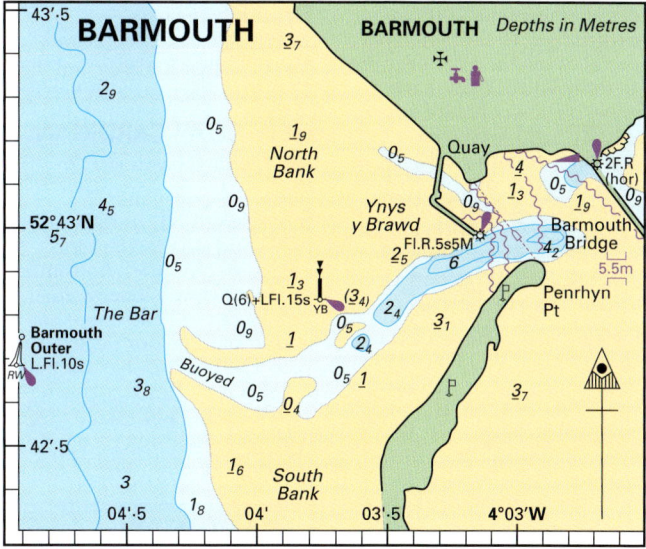

BARMOUTH

Standard Port Milford Haven
HW (sp) +0200 (np) +0207
LW (sp) +0300 (np) +0233
MHWS MHWN MLWN MLWS
−2·0m −1·5m −0·6m 0·0m

A very beautiful estuary and interesting town with cafés, pubs and restaurants overlooking the harbour.

Bar About 0·5m, 1M off the town, harbour is unapproachable in strong SW winds, advice should be sought from HM before entry in onshore winds over F4.

Approach Identify the large RW Barmouth Outer pillar buoy, LFl.10s, and leave the G Bar Buoy to stb then follow the buoyed lit channel into the hbr.

Berthing Good shelter is available in the hbr in winds between W and N. Contact HM for berthing advice on VHF 12/16 before entry. Alongside drying berths and five deep water visitors' moorings available. A small pontoon (dries, no electricity) max length 9m. Strict booking of berths in advance. Anchoring in the hbr is NOT advised due to poor holding ground.

Facilities Water, electricity and diesel on quayside, WiFi, bar and showers from Merioneth YC. Rly and all stores. Resident mechanic and launching/recovery for trailable boats.

☎ HM 01341 280671
Mobile 07795 012747
barmouthtowncouncil.gov.uk/harbour includes weather site.

Cardigan Bay

Aberporth Range

An active firing area covering a large part of Cardigan Bay, with target floats, some unlit. The range is normally operational Monday–Friday 0900–1630, and occasionally at weekends. Contact Aberporth Marine Control on VHF Ch 13 or 16, or ☎ 01239 813760, or Aberporth Range Control on ☎ 01239 813480.

St Patricks Causeway
Sarn Badrig

This rocky ridge extends 14M SW from just N of Barmouth. It includes many drying heights up to 1·5m above CD and is a major hazard for vessels sailing S from Pwllheli and St Tudwals. It is marked at its W end by a W card called Causeway. There is an unmarked twisting passage, East Passage, at the E end of St Patricks Causeway. This is used by local boats and local knowledge is required.

ABERDOVEY

See plan on next page
Standard Port Milford Haven
HW (sp) +0200 (np) +0215
LW (sp) +0230 (np) +0305
MHWS MHWN MLWN MLWS
−2·0m −1·7m −0·5m 0·0m

This hbr is the first major inlet south of Cader Idris, it is a beautiful estuary with a lively town and well worth a visit.

Bar About 0·25m shifts continually. Entry HW±0300. In stronger W winds a bad sea gets up on the ebb and advice should be sought from HM on VHF 12/16 prior to proposed entry. If entry is inadvisable, shelter can be found in St Tudwal's Roads or Pwllheli (over 30 miles to the NW).

Approach Identify the large spherical fairway buoy RWVS Iso.4s. At the fairway buoy turn due E and identify the G/R gate proceed through the gate and follow the buoyed channel (all stb marks) to the wooden jetty. Leave Y Special Mark (denotes hbr 4 kn speed limit) to stb on entry.

Berthing Advice on berthing/mooring should be sought prior to entry. Berths available on jetty 1·5m LW and three visitors' moorings in >3m, other free moorings may be made available. Advice should be sought from HM before anchoring.

Facilities Water, diesel and electric alongside wall at Harbour Office. All stores, pubs, restaurants, cafés, rly.

☎ HM 01654 767626, Mobile 07879 433148
www.aberdyfi.com.

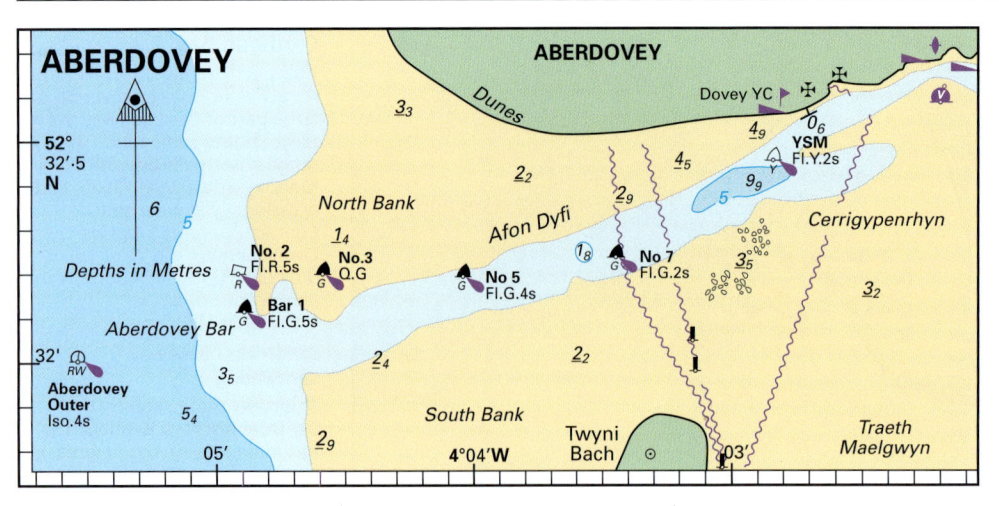

ABERYSTWYTH

Standard Port Milford Haven
HW (sp) +0130 (np) +0145
LW (sp) +0210 (np) +0245
MHWS MHWN MLWN MLWS
−2·0m −1·7m −0·7m 0·0m

The hbr may be located by Pendinas, a conspic 120m hill with Wellington monument, S of entrance.

Bar 0·7m off the head of S pier. Can be dangerous in onshore winds access HW±0230. The hbr mostly dries but affords good shelter at marina 2m LWS. Narrow entrance with right-angle turn inside the pier head.

Approach The approaches are dangerous in strong onshore winds. Beware of strong cross tides and boulders around the head of S pier and the Trap to the N of the N breakwater. The head of the N breakwater on Wellington's monument leads 140° and clears Castle Rocks which lie N of entrance which has 3m at half-tide.

Entrance By day make for a waypoint 52°24′·5N 4°06′·0W about 3ca W of the entrance. Identify the ldg ln, 100°, marked by a W card bn (front) seen between the piers near the far shore and a Y daymark (rear), the lower half of a lamp post. By night keep within the W sectors of both pierhead lights (R sector of Lt on N pier marking hazards to N and G sector on S pier marking hazard to S). When abeam of the N pierhead turn 90° to port to head up river to the marina.

Berthing In marina as directed. About 2m at LWS. Outside office hours, on the fuel berth. Marina office at NE end of marina. The long, most W'ly pontoon does not have visitors' berths.

Facilities as expected in marina. Small chandlery. WiFi. Boat hoist 10t. Shops in town. Launderette 5 mins.

☏/VHF Marina 01970 611422, VHF 80; Abermarina HM VHF 16, 14
www.themarinegroup.co.uk
Visit Talyllyn Railway and the Centre for Alternative Technology.

NEW QUAY CARDIGAN

HW Milford Haven +0132

Sheltered from winds W through S to NE; with N or NW wind a dangerous sea comes in. Hbr dries, bottom sand and clay. In fine weather vessels can lie head to anchor and stern to pier or outside the pier. The E side of bay off Ina Point is foul. Pier head has Fl.WG.3s Lt, 135°-W-252°-G-295°. An extension runs out 80m SSE from the end of the pier and is marked by a E card Lt bn Q(3)10s. HM ☏ 01545 560368.

CARDIGAN

Standard Port Milford Haven
HW (sp) +0120 (np) +0140
LW (sp) +0220 (np) +0130
MHWS MHWN MLWN MLWS
−2·3m −1·8m −0·5m 0·0m

The hbr is at the mouth of the River Teifi. Entrance difficult, and dangerous in strong W to NW winds, but good shelter within. No special outlying dangers.

Bar Dries and shifts. There is over 2·5m at MHWS and about 1·5m a MHWN.

Approach Straightforward on a course approx SSE.

Entrance Prior inspection of the channel or local advice is desirable. Leave isolated danger Lt bn to stb, passing it about 6m off.

Berthing
• Good anchorage in soft mud with sufficient depth in several pools between St Dogmaels and Cardigan.
• Take ground on muddy sand alongside Spillers Quay on right bank, good shelter. Land on the beach below br.

Facilities Chandlery, provisions, hotels, PO and launderette in town, mainly on N side of river. EC Wednesday.

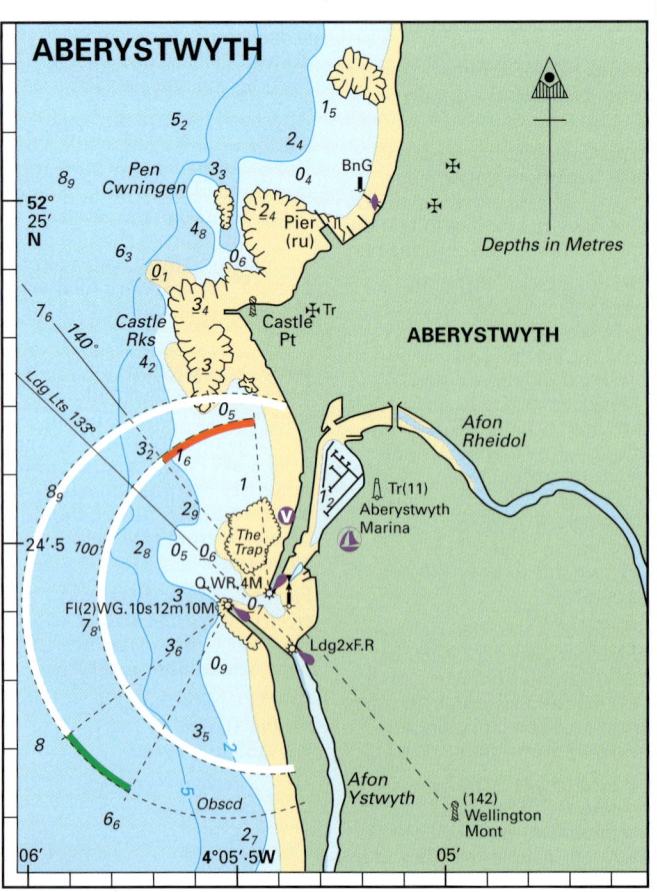

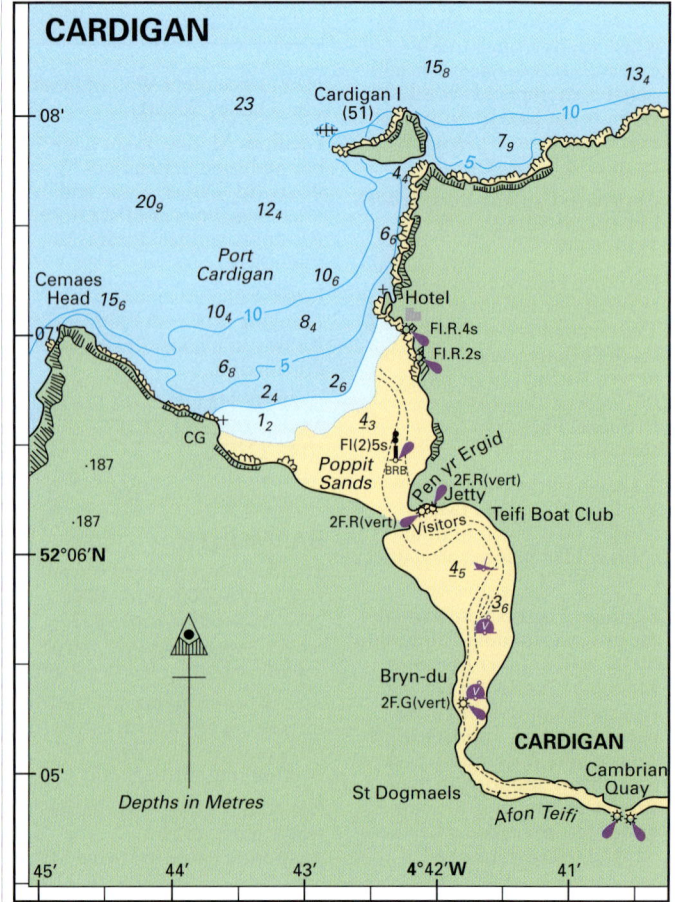

FISHGUARD TO ST ANN'S HEAD

Strumble Head to St Ann's Head

Passage lights	BA No
Strumble Head	5274
Fl(4)15s45m26M	
South Bishop	5276
Fl.5s44m16M Horn(3)45s	
The Smalls	5278
Fl(3)15s36m18M+	
Iso.R.4s33m13M Horn(2)60s AIS	
Skokholm Is	5282
Fl.WR.10s54m8M	
St Ann's Head	5284
Fl.WR.5s48m18/14M,	
R(intens)17M Horn(3)60s	

This is an area of strong tides and turbulent seas. The streams run at 5kn near the Bishops, 4kn between Skomer and Grassholm and up to 6 or 7kn in the narrow parts of the inner sounds. 2–3M W of the Bishops and Smalls the streams are much weaker (2–3kn). Eddies and races form off the rks and islands, the Wild Goose Race W and SW of Skokholm being particularly dangerous.

Four routes are available:
1. Outside the Smalls but staying between 1–2 M W of the Smalls LtHo to avoid the N going traffic separation lane and well S of Wild Goose Race. It clears all dangers and avoids the worst of the tidal stream. It is much the longest and is really more suitable for a passage from the middle of the Irish Sea.
2. Outside the Bishops and between Skomer and Grassholm.
3. Inside the Bishops along the W coast of Ramsay and between Skomer and Grassholm.
4. Inshore through Ramsay and Jack Sounds.

FISHGUARD

Standard Port Milford Haven

HW (sp) +0100 (np) +0115
LW (sp) +0110 (np) +0135

MHWS	MHWN	MLWN	MLWS
–2·2m	–1·8m	–0·5m	+0·1m

Although this is the only harbour between Holyhead and Milford Haven that can be entered in any weather at any state of the tide, it is only secure in winds from W through S to SE. A considerable swell exists in winds above Force 5 in winds from NNW through N to E. In E gales Pwll Gwaelod ¾M E inside Dinas Hd offers some shelter to small craft.

Approach Avoid the shoals off Strumble Head particularly in NW to NE winds. From NW after passing Pen Anglas on coast steer to leave the N breakwater Lt Fl.G.4·5s 200m to stb. This will clear the rocks, dry 1·7m, off Pen Cw near the root of the breakwater. Hold course until E breakwater Lt Fl.R.3s is well open then proceed to anchorage watching out for fishing nets.

For the second: pass N of N Bishop but do not turn S for S Bishop until at least 1¼M W of N Bishop to clear heavy overfalls. Then steer to pass midway between Skomer and Grassholm. One should take Broad Sound between Skomer and Skokholm to avoid the Wild Goose Race. Then steer to clear St Ann's Head.

The third route: From N pass between St David's Head and Carreg-trae (dries 4m) and steer to leave Gwahan to port. Pass down W coast of Ramsay Is leaving Lech Uchaf to stb and continue S across entrance to St Bride's Bay to pass W of Skomer Is. Continue as for the second. Do not attempt at night. Tides are weaker than in sounds.

The fourth route is a valuable short cut but should only be used by strangers in good visibility. Always go through at slack water or with a fair tide and avoid with wind over tide in Force 4 or over. Chart BA *1482* is absolutely essential. See separate entries for Ramsey Sound and Jack Sound on pages 188 and 189.

Bound S from Fishguard leave the harbour 1hr before local HW. This will take you past the dangerous overfalls of Strumble Hd near slack water. Advantage can be taken of an inshore eddy by keeping fairly close to the land until Porthgain. Keep clear of rk awash off Penbwchdy Head. After Porthgain the coast must be left 7ca to clear outlying rocks. This helps to get through Ramsey Sound before the full strength of the tide develops and causes overfalls at the S end.

Anchorage and Berthing

• **The Commercial Port and Goodwick** Access to the commercial port is controlled by the Commercial Port HM. Entry to the quay for Fuel (own arrangements with tanker), water or shelter must be agreed with the HM. The quay has no facilities for yachts. Anchoring is prohibited N of the line from the RoRo pier to a large yellow buoy.

Anchorage is available to the S of the line from the RoRo Pier to a large yellow buoy, good holding, no stream. If draught permits anchorage is possible inside the E breakwater and between the breakwater and Saddle Pt. Any mooring buoys in this area cannot be trusted as no formal maintenance has been carried out.

• **Old Harbour** This sits between Saddle Pt and Castle Pt and is exposed to strong winds from the N and NE which cause dangerous seas. It has six visitors' buoys, without bridles, amongst the outer mooring buoys; they are free of charge and may also be used to await tide to enter the old harbour. These buoys are unsafe in N winds of Force 5 or over. The Old Harbour has six visitors' berths (drying, mud and clay) behind the main quay with water and free electricity. A charge is made. For advice on entry and mooring/berthing enquiries contact Old Harbour HM.

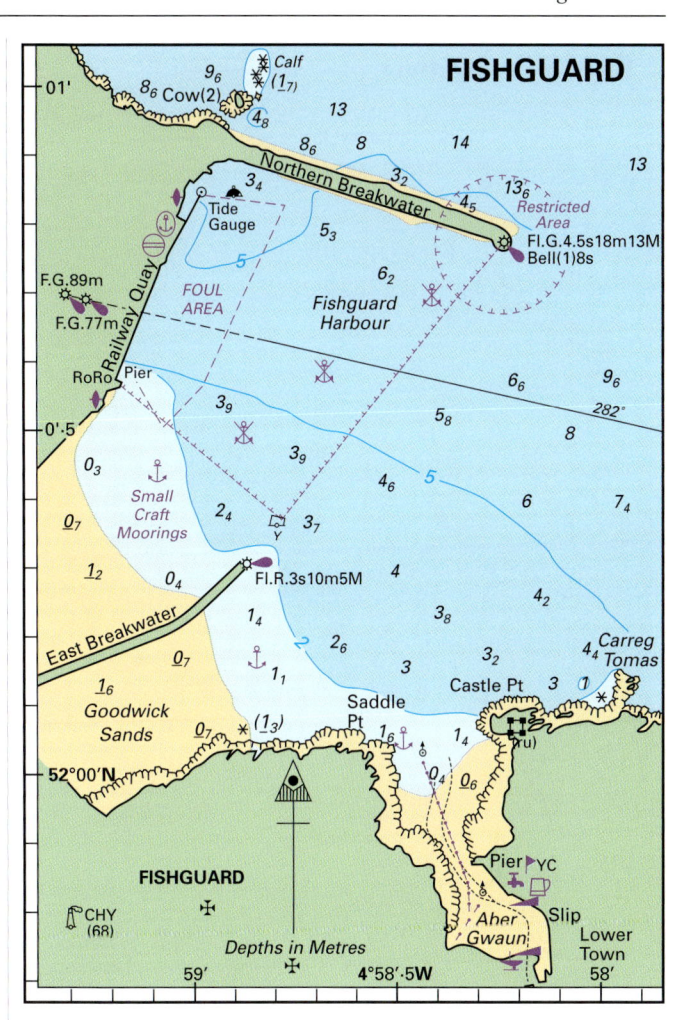

Facilities Fishguard Bay Yacht Club has showers and toilets. Shops, launderette, fuel and Rly in Fishguard town.

✆/VHF Commercial Port; HM 01348 404425 VHF 14: Old Harbour; HM 01348 873389, *Mobile* 07812 559482.

RAMSEY SOUND

See plan on next page

Tides
Milford Haven (Dover)
DS +0300 (–0200) S 6kn
   –0325 (+0400) N 8kn

Careful timing is essential. One should arrive at slack water. The N going stream, east of the Bitches can reach 8 kn with white water and a water level difference of 1·5m over the Bitches. The S going stream is less dramatic. From N pass close to St David's Hd and steer to leave Carreg Gafeilog off the S end of Whitesand Bay 3ca to port. Leave Horse Rock (dr 1m) well to port. When Pen Dal-aderyn is abeam keep St David's Head in sight astern to avoid Shoe Rock (dr 2·7m).

From S leave Sylvia Rock to the W and when clear of it open St David's Head of Pen Dal-aderyn to clear Shoe Rock. Steer midway between E end of Bitches and the mainland and continue due N being careful to leave the Horse Rock 1ca to stb. Steer midway between Gwahan to port and Carreg Gafeilog to stb.

Ramsey Island Anchorage lies just N of the Bitches off a white farmhouse and the little hut, close in to the steep to cliffs. It is open to the N but sheltered from other directions. The tidal stream is weak (<1½kn at springs). The holding is good but an anchor buoy is essential due to the presence of old chains. Landing on this RSPB Sanctuary is permitted 1 Apr-31 Oct, 1000–1600 max 6 persons; pay fee to warden on arrival. To anchor, if N bound, stay in N going current until 3ca past the Bitches then turn to port into a S-going eddy that will carry you into the anchorage. If you turn too soon the eddy will carry you into the Bitches. If bound S sail over to the island shore and anchor off the farmhouse and its little hbr.

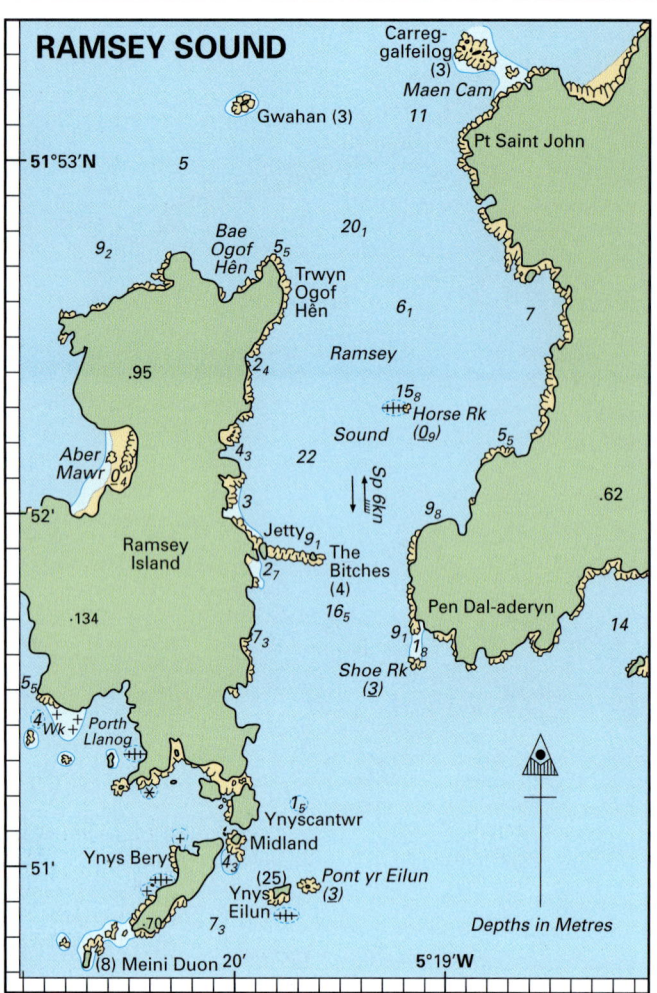

SOLVA

Standard Port Milford Haven
HW +0013 LW +0025
MHWS MHWN MLWN MLWS
−1·5m −1·0m −0·2m +0·1m

A charming village with small creek on the N side of St Brides Bay, 5M E of Ramsey Sound. Difficult to locate from seaward. Hbr dries to hard sand 100m inside entrance rock. Complete shelter for craft that can take the ground, though swell in extreme weather. Hbr crowded.

Entrance 50m wide. Black Rock 4m showing at HW lies in centre; it is steep-to on its E side, so leave close to port. Beware spit of stones just inside entrance on W side at Trwyn Caws. S winds render the entrance impassable. Leave a central orange buoy to stb. This has light ground tackle and is unsuitable for mooring. Immediately past this buoy there are 8 Y visitors' moorings marked 'V', (each having two bow lines and a single stern line). Do not use other moorings, even if vacant. Alternatively proceed keeping to outside of bend and lie against wall on shingle at Trinity Quay or Sand Quay, both to port further on.

Enter HW±0300. Book ahead especially if wanting a long stay or a berth alongside quay (available HW±0200 for 1·4m draft). Showers, stores. Diesel 3M.
☎ HM 01437 721725 or *Mobile* 07974 020139.

Anchorage Temporary anchorage in calm weather may be found in 3m just behind Black Rock but there is little room. In N winds it is better to anchor outside or behind Dinas Fach 1M E.

ST BRIDE'S BAY

Standard Port Milford Haven
HW +0010 LW +0020
MHWS MHWN MLWN MLWS
−1·1m −0·8m −0·2m 0·0m

It is possible to anchor in fine weather at various places in St Bride's Bay, especially in offshore winds. Avoid if any possibility of strong winds from the W, as although the tides in the bay are weak, to get out one has to go through the sounds or round Skomer Is or Ramsey Is, either way encountering strong tides.

Anchorages In N or E winds anchor between Solva and Dinas Fach.

Dinas Fach An inlet 1·5M ESE of Solva. Anchor in 3m on sand abeam of the middle of the headland.

Goultrop Roads 51°46'·20N 5°07'·50W, lies just E of Borough Head off Little Haven. It gives shelter from the E and S and, surprisingly, even from the W if one anchors close in. Unfortunately, the best places are taken up with small boat moorings. A tripping line is essential because of old mooring chains.

SKOMER ISLAND

Standard Port Milford Haven
HW −0005 LW +0005
MHWS MHWN MLWN MLWS
−0·4m −0·1m 0·0m 0·0m

Skomer Is is a Marine Nature Reserve and the waters around it are protected. Care should be taken on the Is to respect wildlife particularly where nests are marked. No facilities.

North Haven is the only place where landing is permitted with a small charge. Beware of the reef on the E side on entry, keep well to the W of the bay. It is open to the N and NE. Visitors' mooring buoys are provided and you are expected to use them. Anchoring is not permitted shoreward of them because of a bed of rare seagrass. Land on the slip out of the way of the ferry. Close inshore beware of rock, the Loaf, 10m from the cliff, which shows at LW.

South Haven A small bay on the SE side of Skomer giving shelter in winds from W through N to E. This is a beautiful anchorage and although exposed to winds from the S it is normally an easy beat or fetch down to Milford Haven should winds come from this direction.

Entrance If coming from Milford Haven aim for the Mewstone a prominent rock 48m high off the S tip of Skomer. Beware of rocks extending SW from the Neck on the E side of entrance.

Anchorage Right up towards the head of the bay in about 6m, sand. Do not go further in at neaps as the ground becomes rocky. Landing is not permitted here.

JACK SOUND

Tidal streams related to HW Milford Haven

Slack, turning S, +0200
Slack, turning N −0425
Max rate may reach 7kn

It is a cable wide and at slack water, on a neap tide and in calm weather it presents no difficulty. It should be avoided in heavy weather, particularly with spring tides and especially if wind is against tide.

It is advisable to have to the engine running because even in fair weather, there are both wind eddies and strong tidal stream eddies. Timing is essential. Go through at slack water or with the stream very newly turned with you. You may await slack water in N or S Haven of Skomer Island, which lies immediately to W of Midland Isle.

From N identify Tuskar Rock (1·5m) ¾ca W of Wooltack Point and the Blackstones 2ca S of Midland Is before entering the sound. Pass W of Tuskar Rock and immediately bring the Blackstones on with the W end of Skokholm. Approach the Blackstones to pass 100m E of them. Rough water will be encountered on leaving the sound with a moderate S wind against tide. There are dangerous eddies around Tuskar Rock and S of Midland Is on the S going tide.

From S identify the Blackstones (1·5m) while still S of them and also Tuskar Rock. Leaving the Blackstones 100m to port steer for Tuskar Rock keeping the Blackstones on with the W end of Skokholm as a back bearing. When Garland Stone (29m) off the N point of Skomer opens N of Midland Is you are free of all dangers W of Tuskar Rock. Except, maybe, when bound N on a spring tide it is not possible to pass both Jack and Ramsay Sounds at slack water on the same tide.

Little Sound between Skomer and Middle Is used by some locals but should not be attempted without BA *1482*.

MILFORD HAVEN

Standard Port Milford Haven

Picturesque and one of the finest harbours in the British Isles. May be entered in any weather and any state of tide. From Dale to Lawrenny in the E is about 12M with width varying from 1½M to ½M. It is a major commercial, oil and LNG port with four terminals for very large tankers. In the entrance there are two deep-water channels and yachts must keep out of the way of deep-draught vessels, which are restricted to these channels and must maintain steerage-way. However, there is plenty of room to manoeuvre and tack inshore of these channels or between them.

Small craft must not impede large vessels. It is particularly important not to cross the channel ahead of a tanker under way. No yachts may approach within 100m of any tanker or terminal.

Maintain a listening watch on VHF 12, *Milford Haven Port Control*. Shipping movements broadcast 0800–0830 and 2200–2230. The *Leisure User Guide* on
www.mhpa.co.uk/downloads/
is recommended. NB do not secure to private moorings without permission. The Authority's launches have green hulls and white upperworks. They are helpful, but their instructions must be obeyed.

☎ Port of Milford Haven 01646 696100.

Caution Tugs and pilot boats may travel at 10kn escorting vessels in the W Channel, producing a considerable wash in the bays between St Ann's Head and Dale Fort.

Approach The Turbot Bank 4M S of St Ann's Head, marked at its W end by a W card buoy, causes a heavy sea in bad weather. There is also a confused and sometimes dangerous sea close to St Ann's Head especially with a strong southwesterly against the ebb. Large yachts have capsized there. In these conditions quieter water and less traffic will be found in the E Channel near Sheep Is. At night the first Lt to be seen from 30M is likely to be from the Valero oil refinery stack where gas is burned off.

Entrance The entrance offers no obstructions to yachts but Middle Channel Rocks 5m and Chapel Rocks 3m in the centre should be avoided in heavy weather.

Both E and W Channels are well buoyed and lit, W Channel being the deeper with two sets of leading lights before the channels combine. Yachts should not follow these but keep out of the channels. If the lights come on in the daytime it is warning that large vessels are moving. In poor visibility, at night, the Ldg Lts on W Blockhouse Point may be seen before St Ann's Head Lt.

The most noticeable mark in the entrance is the bn Fl(3)G.7s18m8M on Middle Channel Rocks.

Although there is never any necessity to go between Thorn Is and the shore the channel has 3m and an overhead cable clearance of 14m.

W of the line Dale Fort to Thorn Is the shores, on both sides are clean and steep to and can be safely approached within ½ca but note that Thorn Rock has only 3·3m at LAT.

For vessels going up to Neyland the channel is well buoyed. The water is very shallow off Chapel Bay, between Thorn Is and Angle Bay and it is obstructed by fishing buoys. Angle Bay is also shallow but it is possible to navigate outside the main channel as far as the gap between the Murco and Valero terminals. Thereafter one can skirt the Milford Shelf. Then it is wise to cross the channel and skirt Pwlcrochan Flats. These are very shallow and near LW do not stray S of the N card LtF. Beware of Wear Spit (marked), Carr Rocks (marked), over which the tide sets strongly, and Neyland Spit (marked). When navigating the Haven it is best to keep out of the fairway or, failing that, keep to the side with an escape route should a large vessel appear.

If proceeding beyond the Cleddau Br (36m) pass under the arch marked by 2F.G and 2F.R Lts. The channel is remarkably deep but beware of unmarked spits on the inside of bends. Above Lawrenny do not approach Benton Castle closer than midstream to avoid rocks. The river shoals rapidly above Llangwm. The Cockle Ground (sand and mud) extends almost to the rocky E shore. The river divides into the E and W Cleddau at Picton Point off which there is ample water on neap tides. This is a beautiful, peaceful river in complete contrast to the industry lower down. There is a firm landing slip near Landshipping just inside the entrance to the E Cleddau. Shallow draught vessels can sail up the E Cleddau to Slebech on the tide and dinghies to Blackpool Mill. Shallow draught vessels with an air-draught of less than 6m can get to Haverfordwest on the tide. The br below the town is fixed. From Lawrenny, Carew Mill and Creswell Quay can be reached by dinghy.

Berthing

• **Milford Marina** is approached from Milford Dock Lt buoy RGR Fl(2+1)R.6s Ldg Lts F. Bu. 348°, muddy bottom dredged to 1·8m. Lock opens every 30 mins starting:

Entry HW–0400 , Exit –0330
Entry & Exit (free flow) HW–0210 to HW–0010 and then
Entry HW+0030, Exit HW+0100

At neaps locks work 24h. Times are latest times to enter the lock. Freeflow times are approximate.

www.milfordmarina.com or *Pierhead* VHF 14 gives more exact lock times.

Call *Pierhead* before entry. Waiting only pontoon (Apr–Oct) 1·5m, E side of entrance, very exposed to S wind and wash of many passing vessels. Yachts should not be left unattended here. Metal pontoon immediately to W is reserved for fishing vessels. Outer lock gates are often left open so wait at floating pontoon to port or stb in the leisure lock (sheltered). Book exit with Marina Control Office at least 1h before departure. Remain on berth until directed.

Facilities Fuel, gas, free WiFi, chandlery, boat repairs, restaurants. Internet available at HM and Martha's Vineyard. Supermarket with cashpoint. Rly five min walk.

☎/VHF *Milford Marina* 696312, VHF 37; *Pierhead* 696310, VHF 14.

• **Neyland Yacht Haven** Normally has room for visitors. It is dredged to 2m. Call on VHF 80, 37 when past Wear spit bn ☎ 01646 601601. WiFi, café, restaurant and three chandlers. Dale Sailing Company ☎ 601636 can undertake all repairs including engine and have a fibreglass paint workshop. Stephen Ratsey Sailmakers ☎ 601561 have an extensive loft and can undertake repairs at short notice.

Anchorages from W to E

• **Dale** Clear of moorings. Comfortable in winds S to W. In strong N winds anchor off N shore or in Castlebeach Bay. In strong E winds very exposed and landing difficult. There is a detached pontoon outside the moorings to which one can moor and stay afloat. Damage may occur in strong winds or large wash; rigging of rafted boats could tangle. There is also a landing pontoon (Apr–Sept) dries 1m. These and four other free MHPA seasonal moorings (Mar-Oct) are shown on the plan. Most dry, or partially dry at MLWS. Only very basic provisions in village. Restaurant. Showers and WiFi at welcoming YC. Water on pontoon but no fuel, limited chandlery, PO has internet. Bus to Milford and Haverfordwest.

• **Longoar Bay** (behind Great Castle Head) has two mooring buoys (daytime only) for vessels less than 40ft and 10t. No anchoring in this area of sensitive habitats.

• **Sandy Haven** is sheltered from N and E but beware of Bull Rock on W side.

• **Off Ellen's Well** and **Angle Pt** both on S shore sheltered from S.

• **Angle Bay** may be entered with sufficient rise of tide. Useful for boats that can take the ground.

• At Milford off Hakin Point.

• **Pennar Gut** on S side 1M W of Pembroke Dock, entrance marked by red can buoy. Sheltered anchorage in 4m, buoy anchor.

• **Pembroke Dock** no anchoring. Watch out for Irish ferry, which enters and leaves by channel E of Dockyard Bank. Grid for drying inside slipway. Rly. Diesel from nearby E. Llanion Marine (☎ 686021) HW±0130, telephone first.

• **Burton** E of Cleddau Br, moorings, no anchoring. Rudders Boatyard has moorings, lifting and comprehensive engineering and repairs. ☎ 01646 600288. www.ruddersboatyard.co.uk

• **Williamston Pill** opposite Lawrenny.

• **Lawrenny** moorings may be available off the jetty. Large yachts should select moorings with sufficient room to swing as space is tight. Visitors' buoy at entrance to creek, pontoon but phone ahead of visit. Chandlery, fuel, restaurant and supplies available.

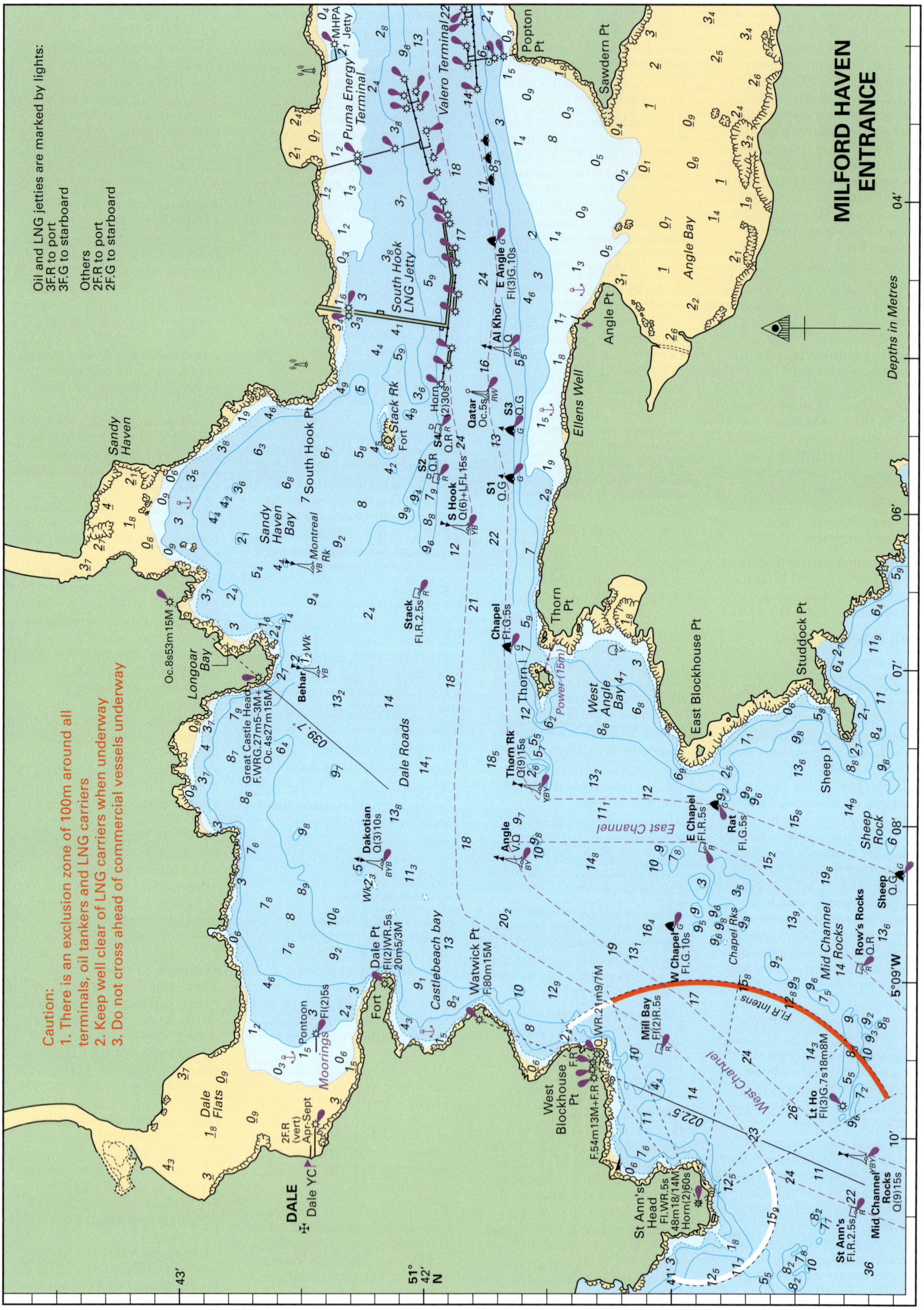
MILFORD HAVEN ENTRANCE
Depths in Metres
Caution:
1. There is an exclusion zone of 100m around all terminals, oil tankers and LNG carriers
2. Keep well clear of LNG carriers when underway
3. Do not cross ahead of commercial vessels underway
Oil and LNG jetties are marked by lights:
3F.R to port
3F.G to starboard
Others
2F.R to port
2F.G to starboard
DALE
Dale YC
Dale Flats
Moorings
Pontoon
Dale Pt
Fl(2)WR.5s 20m5/3M
Fort
Castlebeach bay
Watwick Pt
F.80m15M
West Blockhouse Pt
F.54m13M+F.R
WR.21m9/7M
St Ann's Head
Fl.WR.5s 48m18/14M Horn(2)60s
Mill Bay
Fl(2)R.5s
W Chapel
Fl.G.10s
Chapel Rks
Mid Channel 14 Rocks
Row's Rocks
Q.R
Sheep
Q.G
Sheep Rock
Sheep I
Lt Ho
Fl(3)G.7s18m8M
Mid Channel Rocks
Q(9)15s
St Ann's
Fl.R.2.5s
West Channel
East Channel
Fl.R Intens
Dakotian
Q(3)10s
Angle
V.Q
Thorn Rk
Q(9)15s
Thorn I
Power (15m)
West Angle Bay
East Blockhouse Pt
Studdock Pt
Rat
Fl.G.5s
E Chapel
Fl.R.5s
Dale Roads
Great Castle Head
F.WRG.27m5-3M+
Oc.4s27m15M
Oc.8s53m15M
Longoar Bay
Behar
Wk
039.7°
022.5°
Stack
Fl.R.2.5s
Chapel
Fl.G.5s
Thorn Pt
Sandy Haven
Sandy Haven Bay
Montreal Rk
South Hook Pt
Stack Rk
Fort
S Hook
Q(6)+LFl.15s
S1
Q.G
S2
Q.R
S3
Q.G
S4
Q.R
Horn (2)30s
Qatar
Oc.5s
Al Khor
Q
E Angle
Fl(3)G.10s
South Hook LNG Jetty
Puma Energy Terminal
Valero Terminal
MHPA
Jetty
Ellens Well
Angle Pt
Angle Bay
Popton Pt
Sawdern Pt
51° 42' N
43'
41'
5°09'W
04'
06'
07'
08'
10'

The Cruising Almanac

☎ Lawrenny Quay 01646 651212.
• Upper end of Beggars Reach (below moorings) very sheltered in W gales.

Yachts on passage requiring a night's shelter use Dale or Ellen's Well, otherwise any anchorage of choice, Pennar Gut and off Williamston Pill being the most peaceful. Neyland Marina is probably most convenient if fuel and water is required, unless Milford Marina is on free-flow.

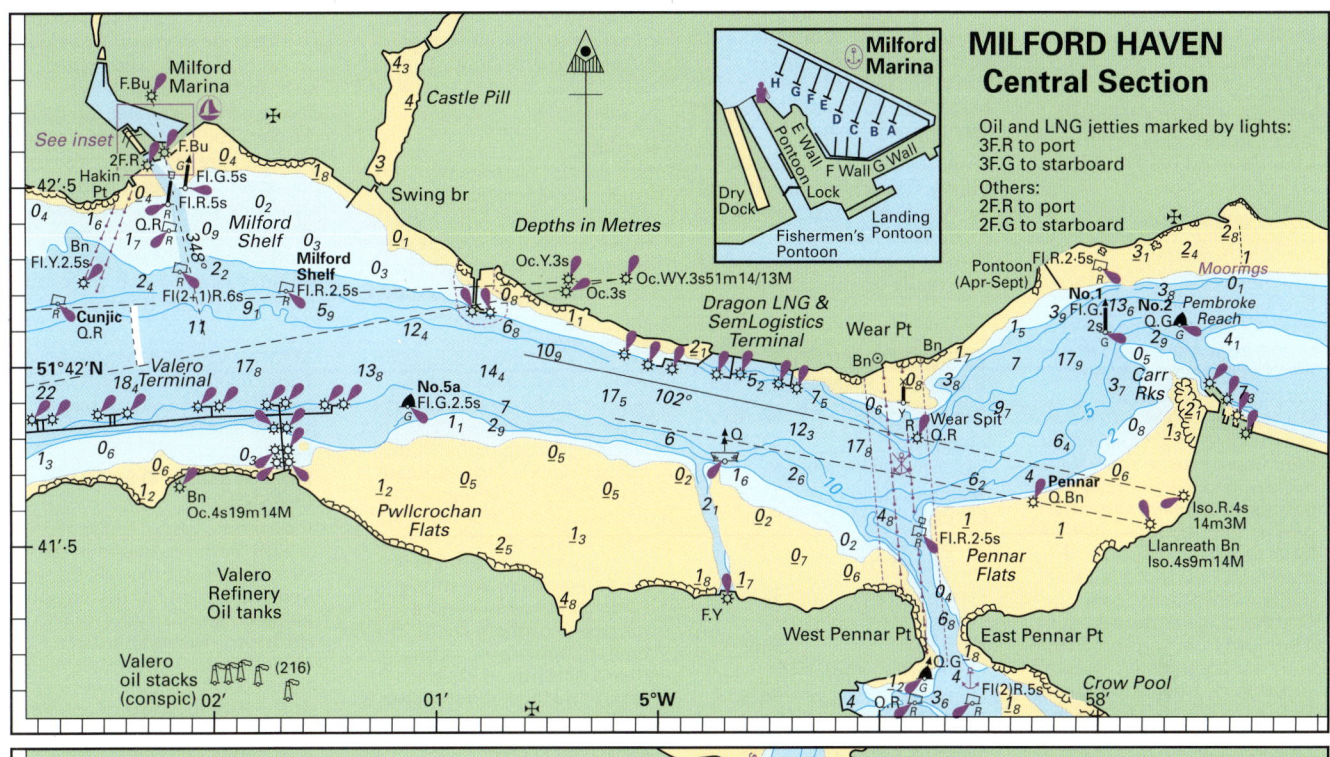

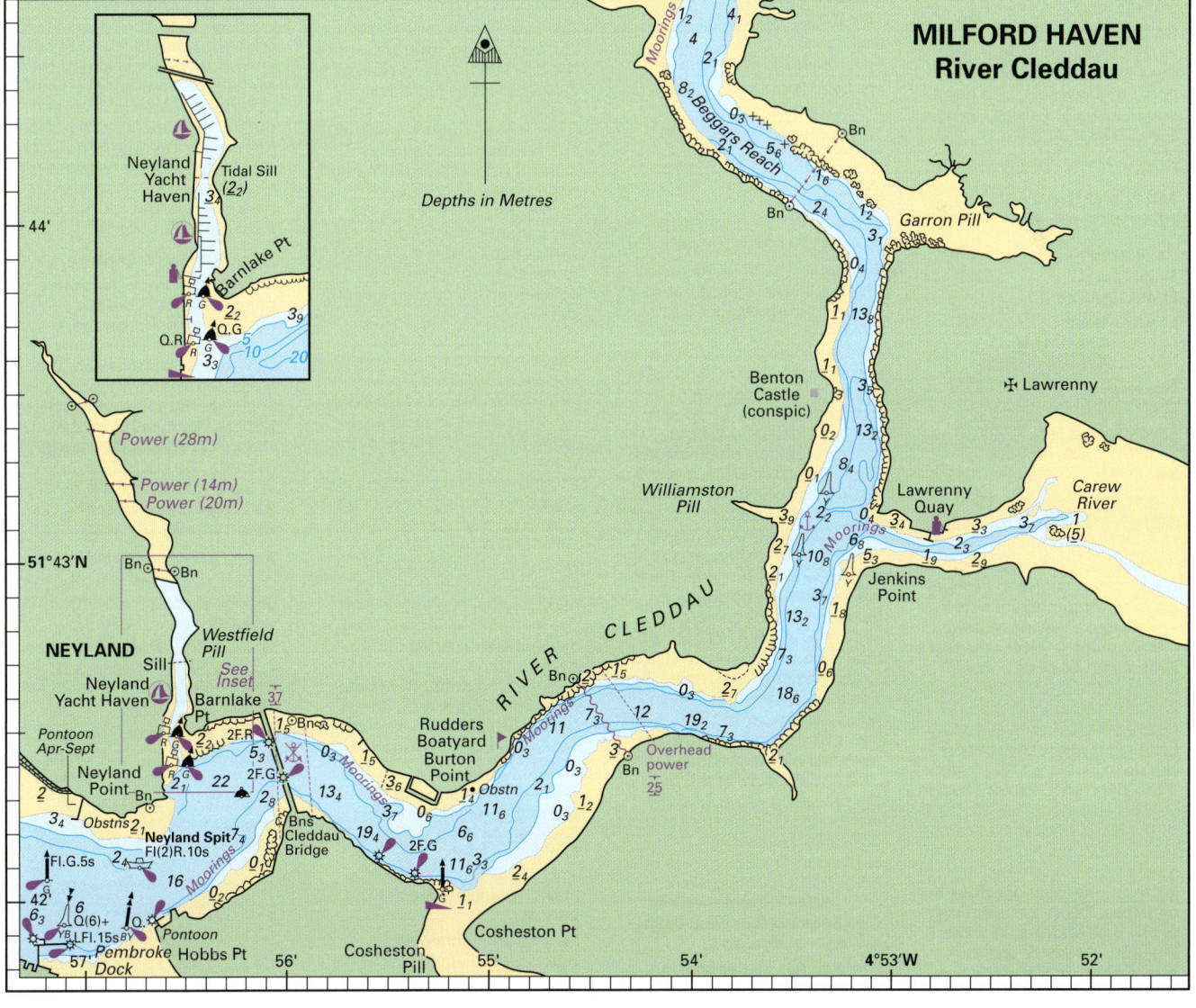

MILFORD HAVEN Central Section

Oil and LNG jetties marked by lights:
3F.R to port
3F.G to starboard
Others:
2F.R to port
2F.G to starboard

MILFORD HAVEN River Cleddau

ENGLAND – WEST COAST AND WALES

187

TENBY

Standard Port Milford Haven
HW –0012   LW –0017
MHWS MHWN MLWN MLWS
+1·4m +1·1m +0·5m +0·2m

Delightful old tourist town. Hbr dries 1m at pier head to hard sand.

Approach
From the W by day through Caldey sound. Pass between Giltar Spit and Eel Point buoys. Then make for N Highcliff buoy before turning N and avoiding Sker Rk off St Catherine's Isle. The stream runs hard in Caldey Sound. A weather going ebb stream causes overfalls at the W end of the sound. The Whitebank off S Beach extends seaward of the direct line Giltar Pt to Sker Rock. By night pass S of Caldey keeping ½M offshore.

From the S and E by day. St Mary's Church steeple on with the N side of St Catherine's Is, 275°, leads ½M N of Woolhouse Rocks. DZ2 Y buoy is virtually on this transit. A vessel approaching from S at night could steer for DZ2 buoy, Fl.2·5s, keeping in the W sector of Caldey LtHo. From DZ2 track 290° for Tenby Roads allowing for any cross tide. Alternatively, by day, a yacht can steer to pass close E of North Highcliff buoy. There is normally no need to pass E of E Spaniel buoy.

Berthing
- Off the hbr, there are two trots of strong non–drying visitors' moorings (no pick–up strops).
- Anchor NNE of old LB slip. Beware of rk awash off First Pt. Good holding, sand over mud. Safe except in strong E winds.
- To enter hbr, accessible HW±0230, steer well towards iron post on shore S of Gosker Rock (in middle of North Beach) and when nearly on line joining rock and pier head round up and go alongside pier; apply to HM for berth. The hbr is crowded, busy and there are only two drying berths available alongside the pier. The wooden stairs at the pier head are in constant use by passenger launches. There are also stone steps and ladders. It is smooth except in strong E winds. Beware of being neaped.
- **Caldey Island** Small craft can anchor in Priory Bay outside of 51°40'N and active Monday–Friday 0800–1800. Call CG prior to departure on day, or range safety vessel on VHF Ch 16 before approach.

MILFORD HAVEN TO KILMORE QUAY
Distance 60M

Best time to leave Milford Haven is at HW taking the ebb tide. Give St Ann's Head a wide berth as there is a dangerous sea near the head in strong SW'lies. Best course is to leave Skokholm to port avoiding the Wild Goose race on the SW side of the island. Either break the passage at Skomer N hbr after passing through Jack Sound or leave Grassholm to port and preferably pass N of the TSS to the W of the Smalls. From Grassholm to Carnsore Point is 43M. 13M from Carnsore Point you cross the shipping lanes off Tuskar Rock. Alternatively, keep S of all the islands. Streams 3kn. Do not pass between Grassholm and the Smalls.

On the Irish side BA SC5621 or Imray C57 recommended. Use the tides to best advantage, pass S of Black Rock card buoy, and head for St Patrick's Bridge. See p.212 for details.

MILFORD HAVEN TO LAND'S END

Passage lights	BA No
Skokholm Is	5282
Fl.WR.10s54m8M	
St Ann's Head	5284
Fl.WR.5s48m18/14M	
R(intens)17M Horn(2)60s	
Pendeen	5670
Fl(4)15s59m16M	
Seven Stones LtV	0020
Fl(3)30s15M Horn(3)60s	
Racon O (– – –) AIS	
Longships	0028
Fl(2)WR.10s35m15/11M	
Horn 10s	

The tidal stream runs at right angles to the course to be made good although there is a slight advantage in leaving Milford Haven on the flood for the first 10M. As the coast of Cornwall is closed so the tide will be more in line with the course especially between Cape Cornwall and Land's End where the streams run up to 2kn. It is 110M from Milford Haven to Land's End and very little shelter offers. To the E of the direct track shelter can be found under the lee of Lundy in S to W winds otherwise Padstow is the only harbour of refuge but entry over Doom Bar is difficult at any time in strong W winds or big ground swell. St Ives Bay offers shelter in SW winds only but any swell (e.g. SW) will turn into the Bay.

NAVIGATION IN THE BRISTOL CHANNEL

Passage lights	BA No
Caldey Is	5328
Fl(3)WR.20s65m13/9M	
Mumbles Head	5358
Fl(1)30s35m15M Horn(1)30s	
Lundy N Point	5616
Fl.15s48m17M	
Lundy S Point	5618
Fl.5s53m15M	
Nash Point	5406
Fl(2)WR.15s56m21/16M	
Flatholm	5426
Fl(3)WR.10s50m15/12M	
Foreland Point	5590
Fl(4)15s67m18M	
Bull Point	5600
Fl(3)10s54m20M+F.R.48m12M	
Hartland Point	5621
Fl(6)15s30m8M	
Trevose Head	5638
Fl.7·5s62m21M	
Godrevy	
Fl.WR.10s8M	
Pendeen	5670
Fl(4)15s59m16M Horn 20s	

The funnel shape of the Bristol Channel causes a larger range of tide, and thus stronger tidal streams as one goes further east. The change of tidal stream occurs within about 10 minutes of the time of local HW, except that in many bays the stream inshore turns up to ½ hour earlier, especially on the new flood tide. If the tide turns against a strong wind, a short, steep sea soon builds up, which can be uncomfortable or even dangerous to small craft. With a strong wind against tide there will be overfalls off some headlands. Boats on passage will need to make full use of the tidal stream, particularly in the east of the Bristol Channel. The tide may be carried for seven hours eastbound, but only five hours westbound, because of the difference in the time of local HW. Because of this and the prevailing winds, passage westbound is usually more difficult than passage eastbound. Owing to large tidal range, most harbours are only open HW±0200 and then not with large swell or wind from the 'wrong' direction.

There is little shelter on the N Cornish coast if it blows up from any direction except from SE. In SW gales if Padstow cannot be entered then Milford Haven may be the best port of refuge. St Ives Bay is subject to swell but will afford some shelter from offshore winds. Clovelly Roads and Lundy's anchorage are sheltered in S to W winds but beware overfalls off both ends of Lundy and off Hartland Pt. Here the streams are strong. Hartland Pt has an inshore passage in offshore winds. The tidal streams are less strong clear S of Hartland Pt. After Land's End the nearest shelter is Newlyn or Isles of Scilly.

MILFORD TO TENBY
Tides inshore on the W side of Carmarthen Bay from St Govan's Head to Pendine are strong at 2–3kn especially in Caldey Sound; the SW going stream starts HW Milford Haven –0200. This means that a yacht on passage from **Milford to Tenby** has only 4h of fair tide. Fortunately there is a permanent E going eddy inside Turbot Bank and if the firing range allows one can compensate by making an early start.

There is a firing range at **Castlemartin** to the E of the entrance to Milford Haven. Firing extends up to 12M WNW from Linney Head in an arc to 12M S off St Gowan's on most weekdays 0900–1700. Night firing is usually on Tuesdays and Thursdays. During these times it is necessary to proceed S of the Turbot Bank buoy before passage E. If shorter-range weapons are used it may be necessary to keep only 3M off. ☎ 01646 662367 for recorded message about firing during next few days. Before approaching during times of firing call Castlemartin Range Officer on this number or VHF 16. Range launch is usually on guard.

There is a rocket range at **Manorbier** where it may be necessary to keep 12M off. Enquire on VHF Ch 16, 73 or ☎ 01834 871282 ext 209. You may be guided through close inshore.

Penally rifle range seldom causes a problem.

Pendine range sea danger area in Carmarthen Bay is normally N of 51°40'N and active Monday–Friday 0800–1800. Call CG prior to departure on day, or range safety vessel on VHF Ch 16 before approach.

ISLES OF SCILLY TO BRISTOL CHANNEL
If departing Isles of Scilly off season, better to depart in the dark than to approach Padstow at night, because of fishing pot markers. Avoid an adverse tide off Trevose Hd and Hartland Point. Depart Padstow hbr before HW–0200 but could wait at The Pool for worst of ebb tide to ease. Beware overfalls off Hartland Pt and Lundy with wind against a strong stream. In offshore winds Hartland Pt has an inshore passage, almost clear of the race. Consider overnight at Lundy or Clovelly. If caught out in SW gales, Clovelly Roads offers an anchorage or possibly a mooring. Beware overfalls off Morte Pt and Bull Pt. The max stream is stronger further E; you must use it, not fight it.

ILFRACOMBE TO BARRY
Depart Ilfracombe hbr before going aground. Consider anchoring off Ilfracombe or Watermouth (¾M to E) and setting sail on last of ebb. The scenic route is to follow Devon-Somerset shoreline with Exmoor National Park and cross the channel at Foreland Pt avoiding overfalls. Do not plan to arrive at Barry much after HW because a strong stream will soon strengthen against you.

BARRY TO ILFRACOMBE
Leave Barry at HW–0100 and initially keep to the Welsh shore; but near LW avoid unmarked Castle Rock (dries 0·7m) 1M E of Rhose Pt. East of Ilfracombe beware of unmarked Hangmans Rock'.

BARRY TO PORTISHEAD OR BRISTOL
Leave Barry at LW–0100. On neap tides you may only get enough tidal help to reach Portishead. There is no advantage in sailing via Cardiff and certainly not Newport.

BRISTOL TO SHARPNESS
See port notes.

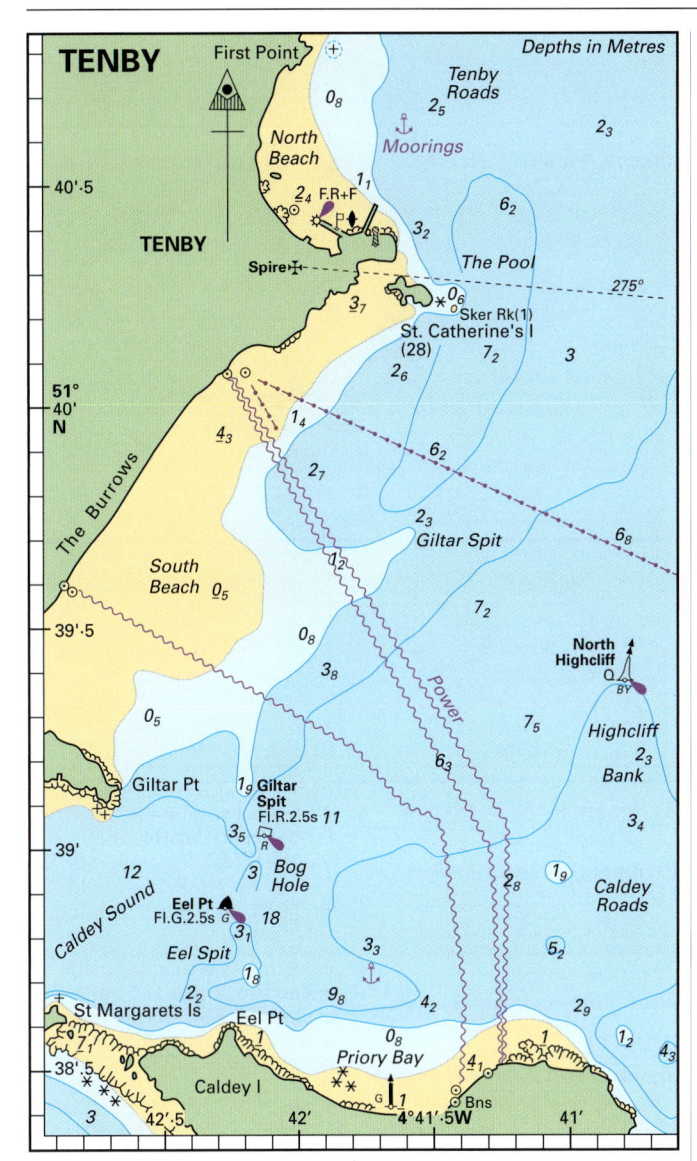

moorings but as close inshore as draught permits to avoid the tidal stream. Uncomfortable in any wind, it gives reasonable shelter from SE through S to WSW. In E winds shelter may be found in Sandtop Bay on the W side of the Is. Close in there is little swinging room between rocks but in moderate winds shelter extends offshore although there might be a swell.

Unusually, the Caldey foreshore belongs to the monks rather than the Crown. Landing is permitted only at Priory Bay and never on Sunday. A landing fee is payable at the post office.

Facilities at Tenby limited. Stores, water from tap below SC, diesel from garages in town, showers and bar in SC, rly. EC Wednesday. HM ☏ 01834 842717.

SAUNDERSFOOT

Tidal data as Tenby

A quiet hbr dries at 4hrs ebb but there is at least 3·5m at MHWS and 1·5m at MHWN. Yachts drawing 1m can enter at half tide. There is a good anchorage in 2·5m 5ca SE of hbr Lt, about 3ca offshore keeping the glasshouses on the W shore of the bay well open. Well sheltered from winds from NNE through W to SW good holding. Send in W and SW gales.

Approach At night, once clear of Monkstone Pt (unlit) keep S pier head Lt Fl.R.5s due W. Keep about 100m NE of entrance until N pier head is abeam to stb. A variable sandbank (about 3m at MHWS) extends about 50m from S pier head.

Berthing There may be room alongside against the NE pier, sharp to stb inside the entrance, or alongside the SW wall with ladders. A few moorings are available in the centre of the hbr. Enquire from HM whose office is next to SC at NW of hbr. Bottom level, sand and mud. Pontoon on SW wall in hbr for drop-off only. Pontoons outside, max 10m LOA in −1m sand which does shift.

Yacht yard and laying up facilities, provisions. Concrete slip for vessels up to 15m, buses to Tenby and Haverfordwest, rly 1M.

☏ /VHF HM 01834 812094, VHF 11.

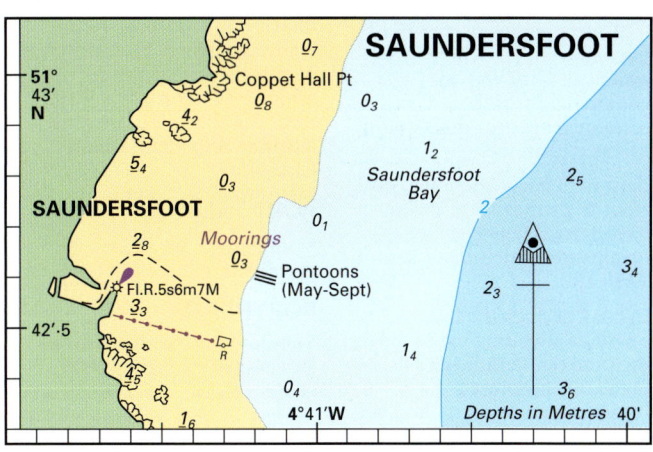

OFFSHORE ANCHORAGES

Pwll Du and **Oxwich Bay** provide anchorages with good holding in sand to stay overnight or await the change of tide. Both are sheltered from SW to NE but unusable in S to E winds. The W side of Pwll Du has rocks that are not obvious at HW. At Oxwich avoid the moorings and a drying wreck, shown by BA and Imray, 200m off W shore and indicated by a white arrow painted on the rocks.

The Mumbles One can anchor in hard sand N of the pier off the village, limited shelter from NW through W to S. Abandoned moorings, so use trip line. A long row ashore. In Swansea Bay the tide flows anti-clockwise for 9½h (from Swansea HW −0330 to HW+0600) often with a race near Mumbles Hd. From HW−0600 to HW−0300 the stream is clockwise, flowing N from Mumbles Hd.

SWANSEA

Standard Port Milford Haven
HW (sp) +0006 (np) −0001
LW (sp) −0007 (np) −0017
MHWS MHWN MLWN MLWS
+2·5m +2·0m +0·6m +0·3m

There is a barrage across the River Tawe and to reach the marina, which is in the city centre, there are two locks to negotiate.

Approach Do not approach in S'ly gale, especially not near LW due to surfing on sea swell. Make for the SW Inner Green Grounds S card buoy and track

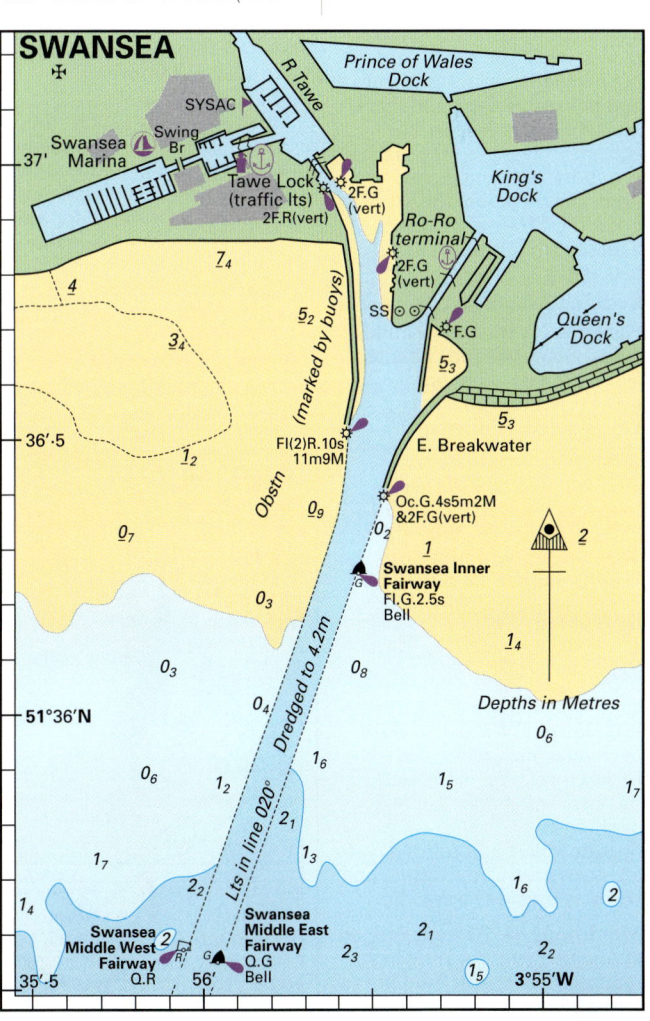

020° keeping just to the W of buoyed channel, where practical. Give way to commercial vessels manoeuvring near docks or in dredged channel.

Beware of bank extending SSW from W pierhead. Once you have entered between the breakwaters call *Tawe Lock* on VHF 18.

In busy periods the lock operates a waiting list based on the time that a radio call was made on entering the breakwaters. Boats are to keep in the lower part of the river, or on a waiting buoy, until they are called forward. Initial calls made from boats outside the breakwaters (covered by a camera) will be ignored.

Entrance The locks operate 0700–2200 (1900 weekdays in winter). Tawe Lock times: Entry on the half hour, exit on the hour. Last entry is half an hour before close of business. Waiting buoys outside barrage lock have depths near CD.

2R or no Lts – Lock not operating or freeflow. Do not proceed.
1R – Wait.
1G – Enter as directed.
R and G – Free Flow in operation, vessels proceeding against the stream give way to those proceeding with it.

Call *Swansea Marina* VHF 80, on leaving Tawe Lock.

There is a large lagoon above the barrage. The pontoons here are owned by Swansea Yacht and Sub-Aqua Club and there are no visitors' berths. The entrance channel to the marina is to port, between quays, immediately before the first pontoon. Moor to chains hanging from walls to await lock entry.

Berthing As directed.

Facilities 20t travel-hoist and crane. Boatyard and chandlery. WiFi. No petrol but garage nearby. Rly and coach to London and Midlands

☎/VHF *Swansea marina* VHF 80, 01792 470310; Swansea Dock Radio VHF 14; SYSAC (Mon–Fri 0900–1500) 469084; Wray Marine (engineering) 07903 963947.

RIVER NEATH

About 3M E of Swansea breakwater. Do not enter in gales from SE to SW even at HW. Entry HW±0200 to HW in channel dredged to 2m between training walls marked by posts and buoys, but less depth in river. Dredger may operate above half tide. May do a U-turn near Club Marina and berth upriver just below br.

Monkstone YC Marina with an automatic gate and sill which retains 1m over soft mud lies to port Fl.R on W pier just before motorway br (30m). Two waiting buoys in river upstream of entrance. If stream too strong to enter marina wait until near HW. YC operates marina, ☎ 01792 812229 (occas).

PORT TALBOT

Commercial, no yachts permitted.

PORTHCAWL

Standard Port Milford Haven
HW +0008   LW –0008
MHWS MHWN MLWN MLWS
+2·9m +2·3m +0·8m +0·3m

New gated marina. Essential to phone ahead.

Approach Avoid entry in SE winds >F4. Keep to W of Tuskar and Fairy Rocks. From 1ca W of Fairy Rk track 010° to LtHo at end of pier. At night stay in the G sector. At springs tidal stream runs 6 kn near breakwater and any swell may break here. Beware rks to SW of LtHo. Leave LtHo to port and track parallel to pier, leaving it 10m to port. Stb bn marks end of submerged breakwater on E side of entrance. Entry signals: Red = no access, Green = enter only upon verbal instruction.

Berthing Retained water suitable for 1.75m draught, and 2m on the two long hammerheads. Sill, dries 3·45m, is shallowest point of approach. Gate opens and closes when ht of tide is 4·95m above CD (approx half tide). Gate open in summer 0700–2200 (in winter 0700–1900), only HW±0300, closes in bad swell. Gate might open on request in bad weather, and by request at any time with 24h notice. On rising tide, wait in front of gate alongside E wall which has 3 ladders with vertical chains: beware step at base of wall of same height as sill. Avoid W wall, used by fishermen. Unless otherwise directed, berth alongside a hammerhead.

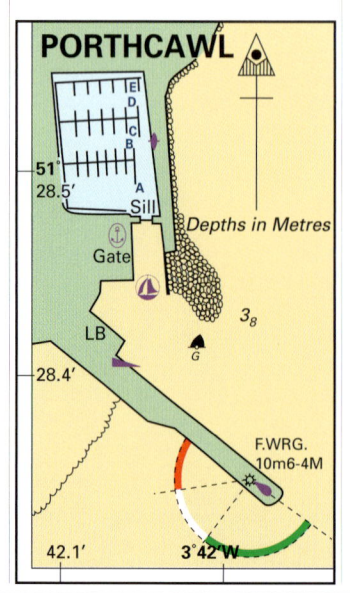

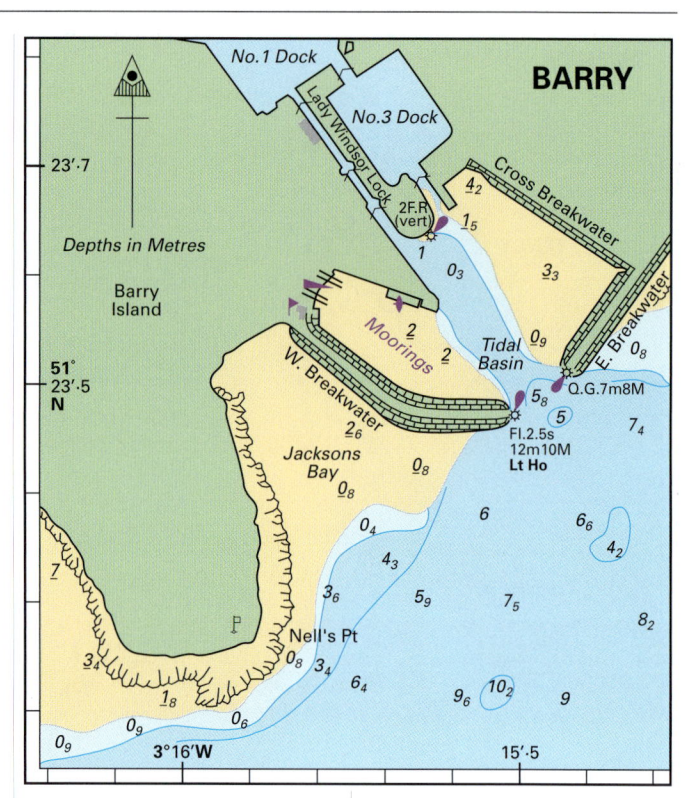

Anchorage In 7m 3ca SSE of LtHo, poor holding.

Facilities Fuel and chandlery 1M.

☎/VHF *Porthcawl Marina* VHF 80; 01656 815715 or 07580 947347.
www.porthcawlmarina.co.uk/

BARRY

Standard Port Avonmouth
HW (sp) –0025   (np) –0025
LW (sp) –0130   (np) –0045
MHWS MHWN MLWN MLWS
–1·5m –1·1m 0·0m +0·2m

The hbr is available at any state of the tide, but do not enter in SE gales. Yachts over 11m and multihulls not easily accommodated. Do not approach if ship approaching or departing. At LW craft may anchor in fairway but must move into the yacht area as soon as the tide serves. Keep clear of pilot launches, LB, and pontoon N of the moorings. The Bristol pilot boats' swinging mooring may be used with permission to await rise of tide.

Approach Beware Bendrick rocks to E of ent, and overfalls on the ebb stream off Nell's Pt to W.

Entrance Beware cross-setting W-going stream off entrance at all times. Once inside, dredged channel initially has 3m but steep-sided.

Berthing Hbr is crowded but a berth can always be found. Tie up alongside moored boats in centre of hbr and enquire at YC for berth. Most moorings dry to soft mud below half tide. Some moorings suitable for fin keel vessels. Yachts must not be left unattended overnight. No charges. Do not drop anchor on W side of hbr due to mooring chains and in any case a tripping line is advisable. Diesel 1M. WiFi, water and showers at YC. Water at old LB slip HW±0200 (flush standing water first).

Shore access available at slip HW±0300. Town 1M but YC grounds locked. Drying out area. In emergency 12-tonne marine trolley and hoist.

☎ YC 01446 735511.
www.barryyachtclub.co.uk.

Sailmaker ☎ 07736 1128420.
GRP repairer ☎ 07789725002.

CARDIFF AND PENARTH

Standard Port Avonmouth
Outside Barrage:
HW –0020   LW –0032
MHWS MHWN MLWN MLWS
–0·9m –0·7m +0·2m +0·2m

Cardiff Bay Barrage has changed Cardiff Bay into a large, freshwater lagoon with a group of three entry locks, protected by an outer harbour, at the SW end of the barrage. All marinas and berths inside are well sheltered. If draught >2.0m contact Barrage Control well in advance.

Approach From Cardiff and Penarth Roads locate Outer Wrach W card buoy, 3ca ENE of Penarth pleasure pier head. Maintain a listening watch on VHF 68 *South Wales Radio* for shipping movements. At the Outer Wrach call *Cardiff Bay Barrage Control* on VHF 18 for permission to enter the outer harbour. Do not enter without permission. If clear of ships, steer 349° up the Wrach Channel keeping clear of commercial vessels, preferably on the Penarth side just W clear of the dredged channel.

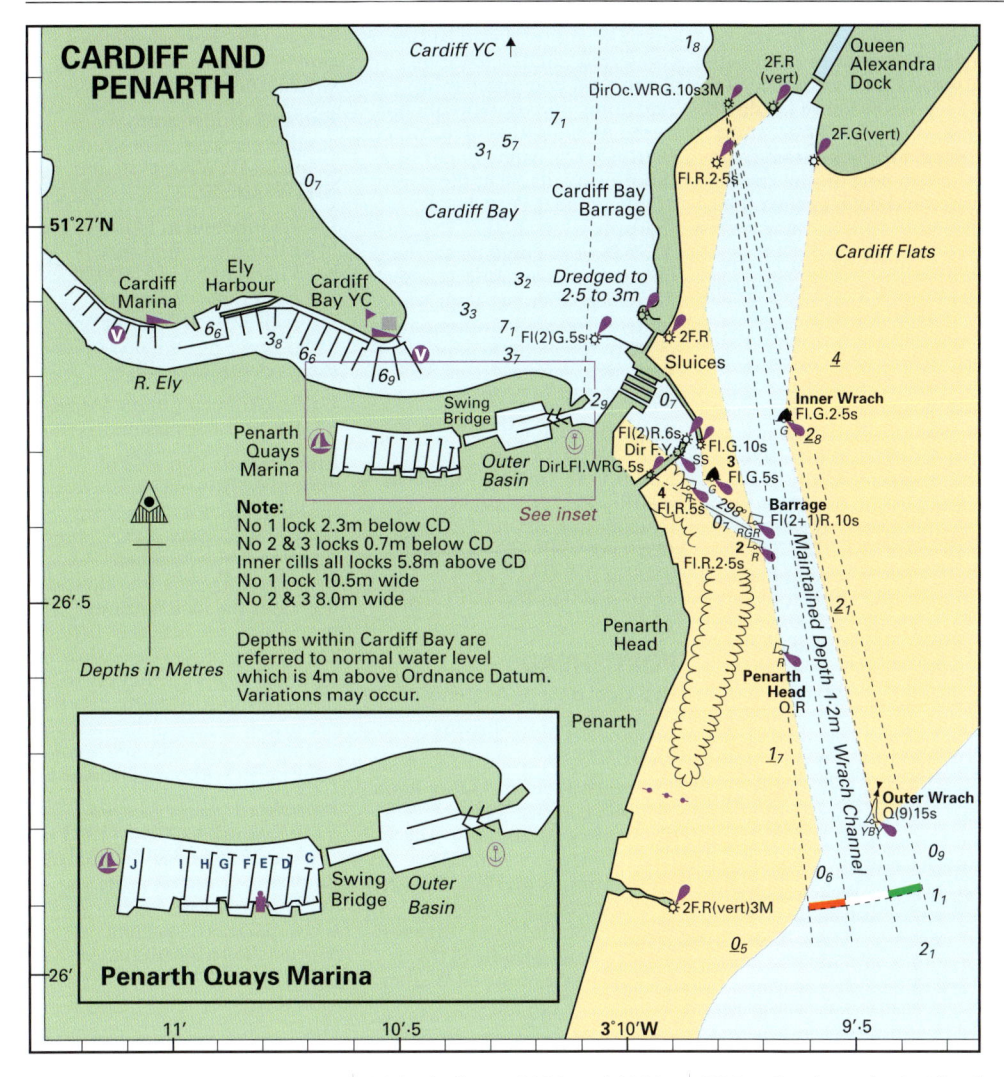

Entrance

• **By night** in Wrach Channel keep in W sector of DirOc.RWG Lt situated on barrage just outside entrance to Queen Alexandra Dock. At buoy Fl.R.2·5s turn to port onto 298°, keeping in W sector of DirRWG Lt at root of S outer harbour breakwater. Immediately look out to stb for W chevron Ldg Lt which will guide you into the outer hbr.
• **By day** Turn to port between No 2 R can and Barrage RGR can.

Traffic signals are displayed on the N pier head:
3R(vert) Flashing – Emergency; Stop and contact *Barrage Control*.
3R(vert) – Do not proceed.
3G(vert) – Enter
GWG – Proceed on instruction from *Barrage Control*.

In outer harbour, which is dredged to 0·7m below chart datum, moor to a barge and listen on VHF 18 for permission to enter one of the three parallel locks. The locks operate throughout the 24hrs except at the highest spring tides. The outer sill of No.1 (E'most) lock is 2·3m below CD, the other two 0·7m above CD. Entry signals with same characteristics as that on pier head displayed on each lock. Lock-in times are 0015 and 0045, lock-out 0000 and 0030. Enter lock dead slow, moor securely, in emergency inform *Barrage Control*.
www.cardiffharbour.com

Berthing

• **Penarth Quays Marina** immediately to port on leaving barrage lock, very sheltered. Marina lock normally open, inner gate closed to provide footpath. Call *Penarth Quays Marina* VHF 80; ☎ 01725 84118. Entry signals from N pier:
Double R – Keep clear of lock: danger.
Single R – Lock in use.
G – Proceed only on instructions from marina staff.
If swing br is closed call the marina. Berth as instructed. Usual marina facilities, pubs and restaurants nearby. Diesel, petrol. Supermarket. Engine mechanic, chandlery. 20t hoist. ☎ 02930 709985.
• **Cardiff Marina** on N side of River. Ely, 50m beyond Cardiff Bay YC pontoons. Unless otherwise instructed, moor in a vacant berth and report to office at head of pontoons C and D. Usual facilities, diesel but no petrol. Rigger ☎ 07897 252736.
• **Cardiff Bay YC** As you leave the barrage locks, the clubhouse is visible dead ahead. Visitor berth on the inside of the wave break pontoon. Bar and meals.
• **Cardiff YC** near entrance to R. Taff.

Facilities Regular bus service to Cardiff. Rly. Airport 12M by road.

☎/VHF *Barrage Control* VHF 18, 02920 700234; *Penarth Quays Marina* VHF 80, 705071, WiFi; Cardiff Marina 343459, WiFi; Cardiff Bay YC VHF 37, 66627 (office); 226575 (club), WiFi in bar; Cardiff YC 463697.

NEWPORT

Standard Port Avonmouth
HW –0008   LW –0015
MHWS   MHWN   MLWN   MLWS
–0·9m   –0·9m   –0·2m   –0·2m

Bar There is a least depth of 0·2m on the bar between Newport Deep and No.1 buoys.

Approach Make for Newport Deep G con buoy Fl(3)G.10s and leave it about ½M to stb steering 021° to pass between No.1 Q.G and West Usk Q.R buoys at mouth of River Usk. Ldg Lts on E Usk Tr Fl(2)WRG+Oc.WRG.10s on same tr.

Entrance Possible within 1hr of LW but tide is strong 4–5kn. Follow buoyed channel (dredged 0·7m) to South Lock (entrance to Alexandra Dock) after which there is no buoyage but keep slightly to stb of centre of river.

Berthing Moorings on S side between jetty in front of power stn and SC which dry HW+0330. Anchoring possible in 1m outside line of moorings, essential to display anchor Lt.

Departure If bound E leave on last of ebb tide to pass W of Middle Grounds.

SHARPNESS

HW Avonmouth +0042

BA 1166 or SC5608 is essential. Sharpness lock and bridges must be booked inbound and outbound at least 24 h in advance. ☎ Sharpness Pierhead (HW–0500 to +0100). Canal & River Trust short term licence (apply online or on arrival), and Boat Safety Certificate or equivalent required.

Approach The channel is well marked and lit, but do not attempt first at night or if fog is likely or wind above F4 from NE sector, especially on springs. Because of sandbanks and obstructions, keep to marked channel. (If your vessel grounds she may be rolled over.) However, do not impede big ships in these confined waters. During spring tides beware floating debris, e.g. trees. Sharpness is 20M from Portishead. With about 4kn boat speed depart Portishead at Avonmouth HW –0300, (or –0400 at neaps).

Listen on *Bristol VTS* VHF12 until 1st motorway bridge (Second Severn Crossing) (35m) then listen on *Sharpness Radio* VHF 13. At 2nd motorway bridge (old Severn Bridge) (34m) (9·5M to go) call *Sharpness Radio* giving your position and ETA Sharpness. Do not arrive before HW – 0100 (due to strength of stream and outbound traffic), nor after HW Sharpness (gates shut to conserve water). Plan to arrive at HW Sharpness –0030 or slightly earlier at neaps. Within 2M, if necessary to delay ETA, reduce ground speed by turning into the stream. If fog descends advise your position on radio.

Entrance Sharpness Pierhead entry signals: Either single R or 2R.(vert) Do not enter.
2G.(vert) Entry only for commercial vessels.
Single G Enter.

Beware of being swept above Sharpness by the stream (the channel is uncharted and unmarked). Enter under engine with good boat speed by turning sharply to stb close to end of S pier. (The differential tide may catch your stern and accelerate the turn.) The tidal stream may be strong between the piers, which are not solid, and may set the boat towards the N pier. Go through the large tidal basin into the lock, unless requested to wait at the pontoon on the south side of the tidal basin. If asked to share the lock with a commercial vessel, moor alongside her. After two bridges, turn to port for yacht hbr: straight ahead the canal leads to Gloucester Docks. On sp tides, River Severn bore forms slightly upstream of Sharpness. See www.gloucesterharbour trustees.org.uk and https://canalrivertrust.org.uk/notices

Departure Book lock; see above. You will be notified when to be at the bridges, e.g. HW–0230. After locking out, clear the lock for inbound traffic. Either enter the river (but beware being swept upstream) or wait in the tidal basin. Suggest depart: neaps at HW–0100, and springs at HW–0015. If making for Bristol (unlikely on one tide) stay N of channel and cross just E of Firefly G buoy to await the flood at Portishead Marina or anchor in Portishead Pool.

☎/VHF *Bristol VTS* VHF 12, 0117 9802638. *Sharpness Radio* VHF 13, Sharpness Pierhead 01453 511968. If anxious, Gloucester Pilots 07774 226143 are available for leisure craft.

RIVER AVON AND BRISTOL

Standard Port Avonmouth
Cumberland Basin Entrance
HW +0010 (approx)

Bristol's Historic 'Floating' harbour is situated 8 miles up the River Avon. Chart BA1859 or SC 5608 or Imray 2600 is essential. The entrance to the Avon is flanked by two busy docks, Avonmouth and Royal Portbury. A booklet Bristol Harbour Information for Boaters is available from Bristol Harbour Office, Underfall Yard, Cumberland Road, Bristol BS1 6XG, ☎ 0117 9031484. HM ☎ 9273633 for berth availability.

Approach In the offing, beware high tidal range and strong tides. A strong wind against tide will make short steep seas. Do not impede commercial traffic in narrow (for them) channels. *Bristol VTS* area is approx from Flatholm to the Second Severn Crossing. Keep a listen watch to learn whereabouts and actions of big vessels. Do not call VTS (except see below or if fog descends, or if crossing the channel in fog). If wishing to cross the channel, do so just E of Firefly buoy. When approaching from the W, beware of wash from tugs meeting their ships at EW Grounds. After passing Avon buoy keep S of the buoyed channel. At and after Portishead Pt, which is steep to, also keep well inshore (as depth allows). (On a flood tide, ships may enter the docks directly or may turn to port off the river entrance and dock against the tide.)

Entrance Keep just S of Firefly and Outer buoy, before heading for the S pier at Avonmouth. When entering Avon at Swash channel (just S of South Pier at Avonmouth Docks), just dries at MLWS, beware possible 5kn cross-tide, setting NE. There are two bridges, M5 br (29m) and Clifton suspension br (71m). Plan to arrive at Cumberland Basin for locking in at HW–0235, –0125 or –0015. After passing Black Rock inbound (1M below lock) call *City Docks Radio* on VHF 14 (on low power). Signal Lts 1½ca and 2½ca above Clifton Suspension Br, at Hotwells Pontoon on E bank before dock entrance indicate that the lock is open. If they are R you must tie up to the ladder on the tongue head just upstream of the entrance to the lock approach channel.

If too late to be locked in take the ground in soft mud opposite Survey Mark No.4 and certainly not any closer to the lock or against any other ladder as the bottom there will be foul as it is off Hotwells Pontoon. Plimsoll Br opens in conjunction with the inner lock gate but not 0800–0900 and 1700–1800. Once in the lock check your air draught for the swing bridges exiting the Cumberland Lock System. If the height of tide over the sill is over 9·4m you may be held in the Cumberland Basin until the river level has fallen.

Bristol City Docks (Bristol Floating Harbour) Locking during BST from HW–0305 to HW on all tides. During GMT, for arrival or departure outside of 0900-1700, 48 hours' notice is required.

Berthing At Bristol Marina ☎ 0117 921 3198 on the S side of Floating Harbour W of *SS Great Britain* or at E end of Floating Harbour or at Arnolfini pontoons (coded access) or serviced pontoon berthing at Harbour Inlet (opposite SS Great Britain) for vessels with draught <1.5m. No WiFi in Bristol City Docks. See www.bristolport.co.uk

Departure 12h notice is required, but see above. Locking outs are at HW–0250, –0140, –0030, but attend 1 hour earlier. When passing Nelson Point outbound, call *Bristol VTS*, who will advise when to exit the river.

Bristol to Cardiff is 20M. Bristol to Sharpness is only 24M but you will need to wait over LW at Portishead Marina (preferred), or at anchor in Portishead Pool (preferably remaining afloat), or at anchor in the Avon (not advised by *Bristol VTS*). There might be a mooring available in the river at Pill; contact Portishead Cruising Club ☎ 01275 373988. You could go aground in soft mud, either alongside Portishead Pier, or at anchor (outside the no-anchoring area) close to the pier and gain shelter from winds from SE through SW to NW.

☎/VHF *Bristol VTS* VHF 12, 0117 9802638. *City Docks Radio* VHF 14 (HW –0300 to +0100) 0117 927 3633. Dockmaster, *Bristol Floating Harbour* VHF 73 (Mon–Sun 0800–1700 GMT, or 1000–1500 in BST) 0117 903 1484.

PORTISHEAD

HW Tidal data as Avonmouth

Ideal if bound for Bristol or Sharpness.

Approach Read the *River Avon Approach* above. Beware Firefly rock (0·9m). Portishead Pier submerges when tide is above approx MHWS. Beware a reverse eddy near the Pierhead on the flood. Between Pierhead and Middle SHM to the E, the stream turns W 2hrs before HW. Portishead Pool can be dangerous with strong winds from NW to E.

Entrance Under normal conditions, access for draft 1·5m is MHWN±0430 and MHWS±0330.

Locks: Inbound at H+0045 and H+0015; Outbound (needs booking) at H and H+0030; but both reduce to hourly intervals near HW and LW. Tidal gauge at each end of lock shows depth over sill.

Call *Portishead Quays Marina* VHF 80 for permission to enter.

Entry signals Port side of entrance. 3R(vert) or 3R(vert) flashing: Do not enter, keep clear of lock gates. GWG(vert): Enter lock slowly when instructed. During free-flow, do not enter the lock without permission because the current can be violent. Go dead slow in lock and moor adequately to pontoons, port-side-to preferred. When outbound during free-flow, do not leave your berth without permission.

Portishead Quays Marina VHF 80 or ☎ 01275 841941 or Mobile 07764 635877. Fuel at pontoon A (first on port). WiFi. Boat hoist.
www.quaymarinas.com/Marinas/PortisheadQuays/

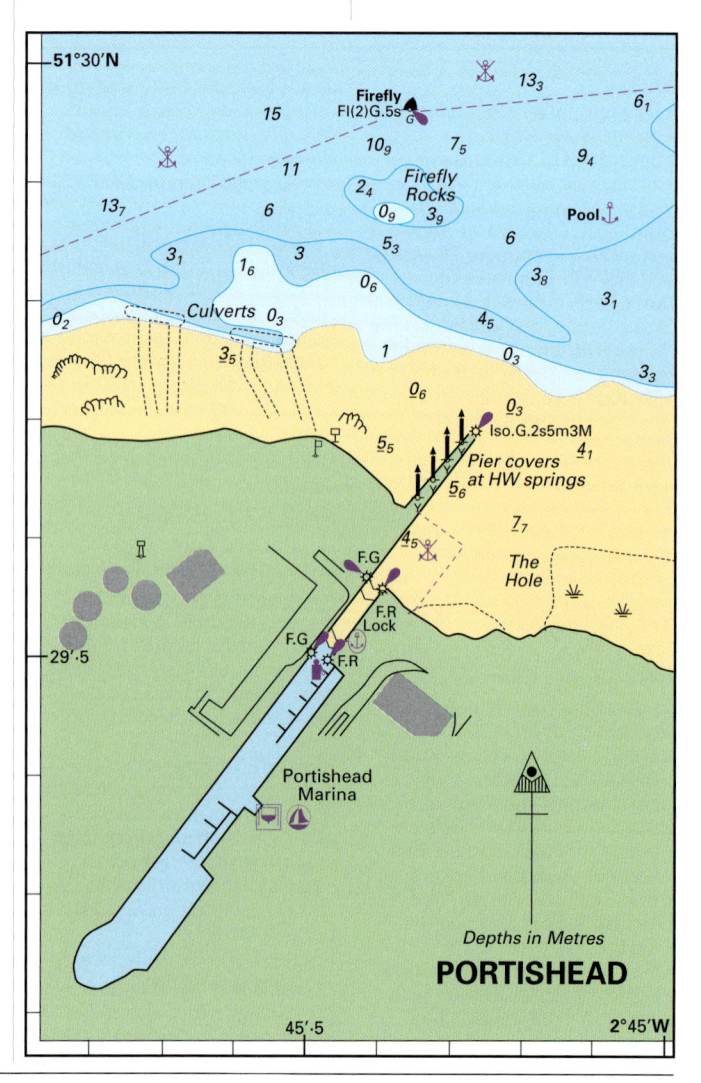

WESTON-SUPER-MARE

Standard Port Avonmouth
HW (sp) –0030 (np) –0020
LW (sp) –0130 (np) –0030

MHWS	MHWN	MLWN	MLWS
–1·2m	–1·0m	–0·8m	–0·2m

Approach The causeway at the hbr entrance is marked by a bn and there are 2F.G(vert) Lts on the Grand Pier.

Berthing Anchorage is available from HW±0200 except at dead neaps but Knightstone harbour dries out and yachts normally use legs or make fast alongside two wooden dolphins. Shelter from all winds except S. Small yachts anchor S of old pier near the LB Ho in what is called the Cut or Sound; mainly dry at MLWS. Boatman will indicate the best berth. All stores, engine repairs, rly. EC Thursday.

RIVER AXE

This drying muddy river flows into the S of Weston Bay. In moderate winds anchor in shallow bay under Brean Down. Fresh N'lies make the entrance difficult. To enter bring Black Rock into line with W mark on Uphill Hill. Approach the rk to within 1ca and leave it to port, then keep in mid channel. Weston Bay YC buoy 'Juicy' (pink and white) indicates the bar 4ca from Brean Down about halfway along. Approaching Black Rock, R buoys mark winding channel. After Black Rock pass between R and G buoys, then port bns.

Berthing No room to anchor. Take vacant mooring or go alongside single pontoon and enquire ashore. In moderate winds anchor in shallow bay under Brean Down. Boatyard at the top of Uphill Pill can handle craft up to 8m and 3 tonnes. Chandlery.

Anchorage under Brean Down, secure but turbulent.

BURNHAM-ON-SEA

Standard Port Avonmouth
HW (sp) –0025 (np) –0020
LW (sp) –0030 (np) +0000

MHWS	MHWN	MLWN	MLWS
–2·3m	–1·9m	–1·4m	–1·1m

Shoals 5M out from the land which is flat and featureless except for Brent Knoll, a conspic hill.

Bar Dries about 1·3m.

Approach and entrance Best approach is at HW–0200 when riverbanks are clearly distinguishable: vessels drawing 2m have enough water for Burnham in moderate weather. In strong winds against tide the sea around Gore buoy is very rough.

Keep just S of Gore RW buoy and No.1 R buoy. Then track 076° keeping in W sector of Burnham Lower Lt, a W structure on the beach with R vert stripe on piles, which indicates the channel. R sector indicates Gore sands, G sector the N edge of Stert Flats. Upper light disused. Continue until 2 R Ldg Lts are in transit bearing 112°, back Lt on St Andrew's Church, front Lt in street. Daymarks are painted W rectangles with R vert stripe on sea wall and SW corner of St Andrew's Church. Continue on this transit until 4ca from sea wall, when No.2 buoy Fl.G.2s bears 265° and steer middle of River Parrett.

Berthing 3 visitor pontoon berths to port in River Brue, access HW±0200, dry to soft mud. Contact Pontoon Officer before arrival. See
http://myweb.tiscali.co.uk/burnhamsailingclub/contacts.html

Marineer Engineer ☎ 01278 794988. Stores, Fuel, ½M.

In the River Parrett in quiet weather there are a few holes where yachts may lie afloat. It is possible to go up the River Parrett at HW–0100 to Combwich, a drying inlet, and to Dunball, although commercial shipping possible here e.g. on sp tides. Beware shipping (e.g. restricted in ability) associated with building Hinkley C power station off Hinkley Pt and in River Parrett. Hinkley HM ☎ 0800 096 9650 (24hr). SC ☎ 01278 781689 (occas).

WATCHET

Standard Port Avonmouth
HW (sp) –0050 (np) –0035
LW (sp) –0145 (np) –0040

MHWS	MHWN	MLWN	MLWS
–1·9m	–1·5m	+0·1m	+0·1m

A quaint old village. Outer hbr dries completely. Marina retains water using an automatic rising gate. It is subject to silting, but dredged.

Approach Call *Watchet Harbour Marina* on VHF 80 (0730–1730), ☎ 01984 631264 or *Mobile* 07969 138938 at 1M off to request berth. Beware Culver Sand in mid channel NNE of hbr. Lilstock firing range extends in a semicircle offshore to Hinkley Point nuclear power station, 7·3M E. Hbr entrance lies 210° 3·2M from DZ No.2 buoy Fl.Y.10s. Two radio masts with R lights bear 208° 1·6M from hbr. The rocky shore dries ½M out.

An obstruction dries 2·8m on the foreshore NW of the pierhead and fishing stakes N of the hbr entrance.

Entrance On first visit do not approach hbr before HW–0130, and never in strong onshore winds. Usually W'ly tidal set across entrance. No anchorage or mooring available in outer drying hbr. On entry leave R tr with G light on W pier to stb. Tidal gate with gauge showing depth over sill is sharp to port behind E pier head. The gate opens when there is 2½m in the entrance and up to 3m inside. Entry sigs:
3G(vert) – proceed.
3R(vert) – stop.

Facilities 15t boat hoist. Limited chandlery. WiFi. EC Wed. West Somerset Steam Rly.

MINEHEAD

Standard Port Avonmouth
HW (sp) –0052 (np) –0037
LW (sp) –0155 (np) –0045

MHWS	MHWN	MLWN	MLWS
–2·6m	–1·9m	–0·2m	0·0m

Hbr is formed by a single pier curving E to SE and dries. Shingle bank off entrance (2015). It should not be approached earlier than HW–0230 when there is 2·1m of water at the hbr steps alongside the quay.

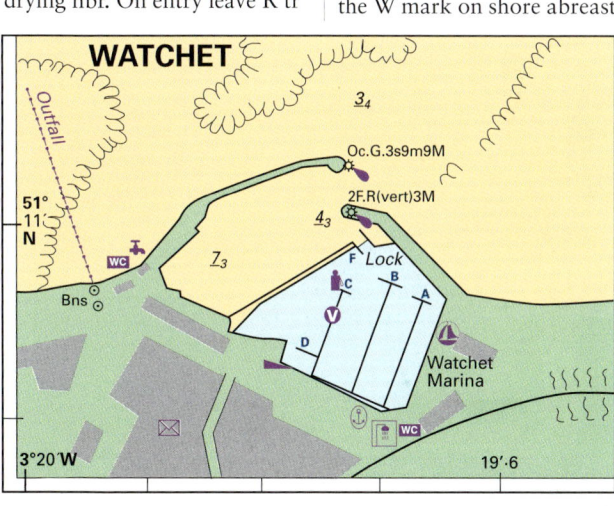

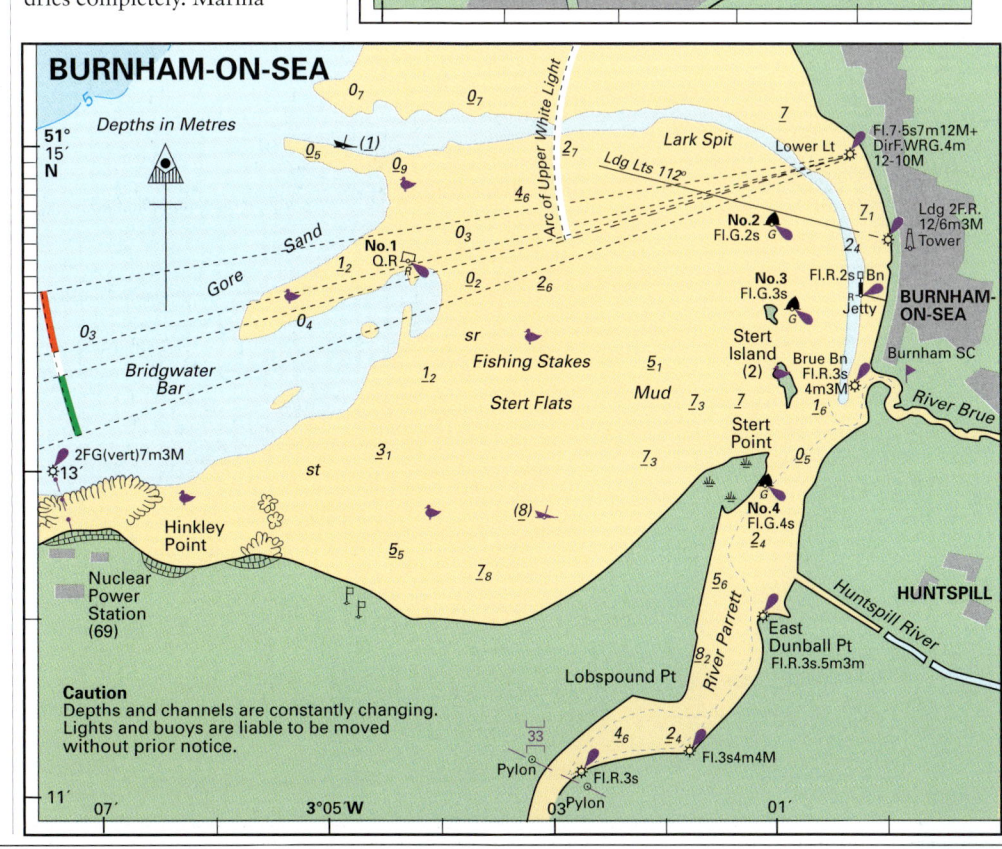

Approach From seaward, if the tide too low to enter, approach the W mark on shore abreast the hilltop 5ca E of Greenaleigh Point and 5ca NW of the column on the foundations of the old pier and anchor abreast the mark 2ca offshore in about 3½m. The column shows 3m above HW. If approaching from E beware of Gables ridge extending 1M to NW of Warren Point.

Entrance From W round G stb hand bn with cone topmark Q.G and then round the pier head Fl(2)G.5s at least 10m off. Go slow as hbr is crowded.

Berthing As directed or as space allows, alongside pier or other vessels. The bottom is an easy slope upwards from entrance. HM ☎ 01643 702566. All supplies. EC Wed.

PORLOCK WEIR

Standard Port Avonmouth
HW (sp) −0055 (np) −0045
LW (sp) −0205 (np) −0050
MHWS MHWN MLWN MLWS
−3·0m −2·2m −0·1m −0·1m

A delightful privately-owned, small, crowded hbr in rural surroundings. Difficult and narrow entrance channel but safe once inside. Not lit. Hbr dries HW−0300 but moorings for twin keelers and 1 or 2 yachts <10m in pool 1·5m. Beware terraced shorings round basin. Exposed to N–NE winds near HW. Moorings in inner harbour by prior arrangement, HM ☎ 01643 863187, no VHF.

Entrance At the W end of Porlock Bay. The bar dries. The channel is about 10m wide and the entrance is marked by a pair of withies. Thereafter keep about 3m off the remaining two port-hand withies marking a timber-piled wall below water. There is a pebble bank to stb. Channel available HW−0130 to HW+0100 for 1·8m draught.

Berthing Anchor in Porlock Bay only in very settled conditions; holding poor on pebbles except in patch of sand off thatched cottages to the W of entrance channel. Reverse stream on flood tide against W winds makes for uncomfortable anchorage.

Pub, hotel and small village store at hbr side, otherwise 1½M to village of Porlock where good shops, fuel and gas.

ILFRACOMBE

Standard Port Milford Haven
HW −0016 LW −0036
MHWS MHWN MLWN MLWS
+2·2m +1·7m +0·6m +0·3m

An interesting tourist town, crowded in summer, good shops, and a busy harbour.

Approach Beware of overfalls at Buggy Pit ¾M NE of entrance, where the stream turns 1h after local LW and HW. Ferry plies between hbr and Lundy Is and may return at HW day or night. Beware of fishing pot buoys to E of approach to ent. If arriving near LW springs in strong N or NE winds, there will be no sheltered anchorage to await rise of tide to enter hbr.

Berthing Inner hbr is full of fore and aft moorings which dry to flat firm sand after half tide. A mooring may be available but do not anchor here. N and possibly S wall are for visitors. Outer hbr dries to flat sand at LW springs and has one row of fore and aft moorings for visitors, or anchor in outer hbr, with anchor light, but avoid commercial pier to N and fairway to inner hbr e.g for LB. Shallow draught boats can remain afloat at neaps. Water on pier and S side of inner harbour. Chandlery, diesel, marine engineer. Stores five minutes, petrol 20 minutes each way. ☎ 01271 862108, VHF 12 (office hours only). WiFi. Shower at YC.

LUNDY ISLAND

Standard Port Milford Haven
HW (sp) −0025 (np) −0025
LW (sp) −0035 (np) −0030
MHWS MHWN MLWN MLWS
+1·0m +0·8m +0·2m +0·1m
DS clear of the land:
Dover +0030 ENE −0500 WSW

Lundy (meaning 'Puffin' in Viking) is beautiful and an interesting place to explore. It is surrounded by the UK's first marine nature reserve. Lundy is a MCZ owned by the National Trust and administered by the Landmark Trust. No Take Zone (fishing) on E coast. No dogs ashore. Landing fee payable at Mariso Tavern, but free to NT members. Guided walks, snorkelling and evening talks.

Approach Beware of tidal races. On E-going stream a heavy race extends 1M N from the N end of the Is and 1½M E of Rat Is in the S. The White Horses race over Stanley Bank NE of the Is is severe and should be avoided. Similar races form during the W-going stream extending 1M SW of Shutter Point but that over Stanley Bank is less violent.

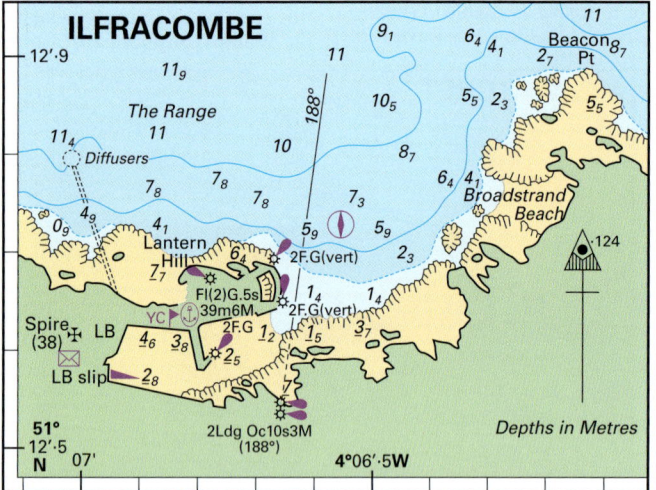

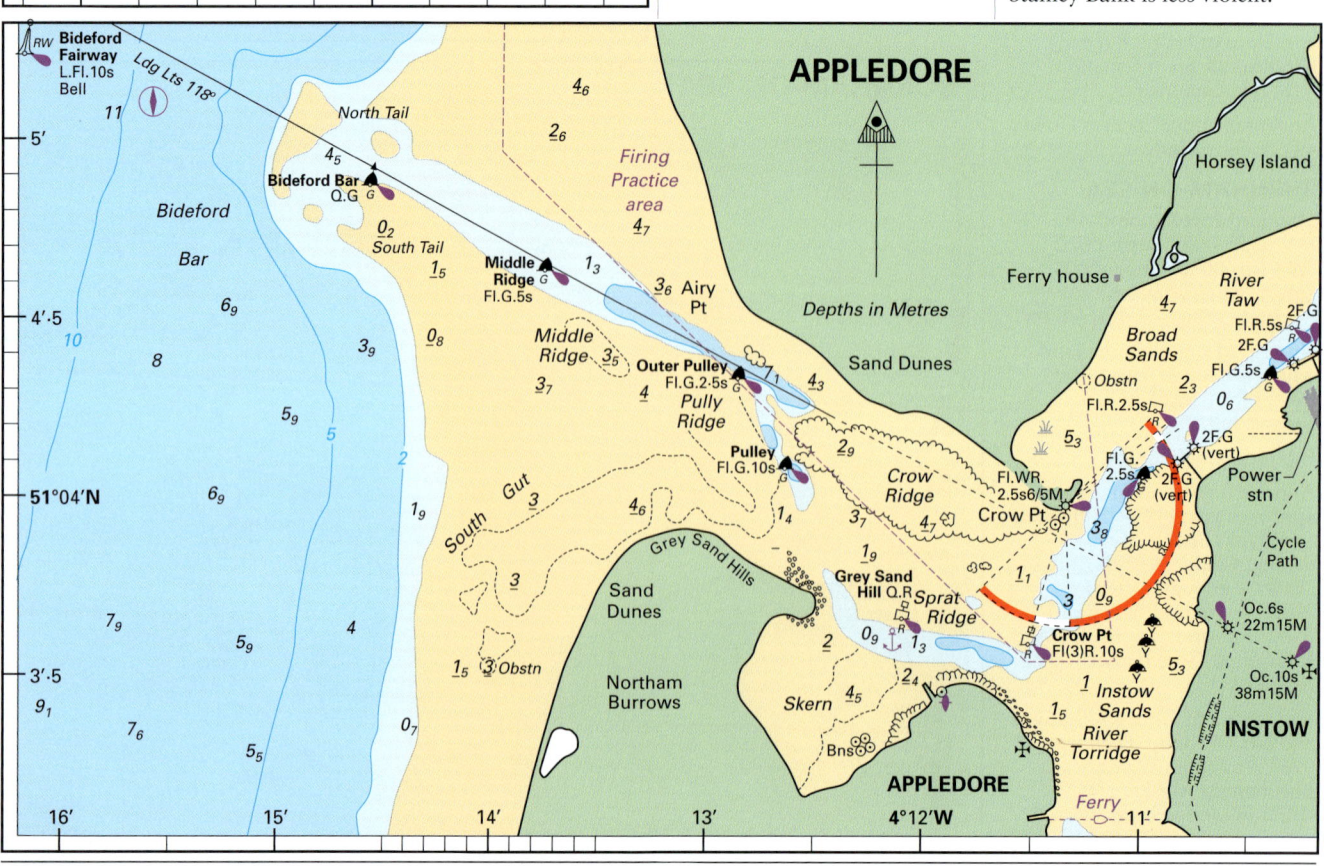

Anchorage If caught out in gales from SSW to W, Lundy offers an anchorage of refuge with good holding and shelter. The anchorage is at the Landing Beach, just N of the SE point of Is, as far in as draft and tidal range permit. Keep clear of the commercial jetty (Fl.R.3s) used by *MS Oldenburg*, the island's supply ship, that sails to Lundy up to four times a week from either Ilfracombe or Bideford. Dinghy may land at slipway S of jetty, or at Landing Beach, but this latter is exposed to winds of any strength from NE to SE, which will make launching the dinghy difficult. In NW gales a swell enters the anchorage, which is also completely exposed to any wind with E in it. If preferred, a privately-laid mooring might be available. Contact the *Lundy Warden* VHF 16, but do not leave your boat if mooring owner might return. Inn and shop (limited supplies) available at top of track from Landing Beach. In strong and persistent winds from E sector, shelter for a few boats in 10m at Jenny's Cove on middle of W side of Is, provided no remaining swell from W. Dinghy access ashore by landing on Pyramid Rock to N of anchorage, is possible but not easy. In persistent N winds perhaps try The Rattles anchorage off S of Is.

APPLEDORE

Standard Port Milford Haven
HW (sp) −0025   (np) −0020
LW (sp) −0015   (np) −0045

MHWS MHWN MLWN MLWS
+1·0m +0·8m +0·2m +0·1m

Has a maritime history.

Bar Bideford Bar, sands and channel are continuously shifting. Buoys and Oc Ldg Lts are moved to suit the fairway. Entrance is dangerous if a heavy ground sea is running, especially against an ebb tide. The best time to enter (or depart) is usually on the last of the flood. Avoid entering (or leaving) on the ebb tide, especially if there is a strong W wind or a large ground swell against the ebb stream. Under normal conditions expect breakers on the sands to port and stb just outside the channel. The tide may be awaited in Clovelly Bay.

Approach After passing Outer Pulley buoy turn on to 160° to leave Pulley G con buoy to stb and continue to SE end of Grey Sand Hills. Then steer 102° through Appledore Pool. After passing slip on stb, watch out for three mooring buoys which may be partly submerged near HW.

Berthing The stream runs strongly through this pool which is uncomfortable in N winds during early ebb. LB buoy in pool available with permission. Better to anchor in the River Taw to NE of Crow Point Lt bearing 240° and Appledore church about 197° but holding is only moderate. Instow sands and R. Torridge offer many drying moorings, but there are sand waves in places because of the strong streams. North Devon Yacht Club, Instow, may offer vacant mooring.

BRAUNTON

Anchor close inshore abreast the Ferry House on Broad Sands; a boat of 1·8m draught can berth in very soft sand. The vessel will make its own berth but care should be taken not to be neaped. The position is excellent if a few days stay is desired but the berth should be located beforehand. Near midstream the sand is hard and anchor likely to drag.

BIDEFORD

Regularly handles large ships, best not to anchor. The passage from Appledore to Bideford is easy for 1·8m draught at HW−0200. At Bideford, with permission, dry out alongside boat already alongside quay, but avoid quay near the bridge (too deep).

CLOVELLY

Extremely picturesque village with one cobbled street (without cars) tumbling down 400ft to a tiny small drying hbr drying to firm sand. Only suitable for twin keelers <12m. Only two visitors' berths, each with ladder alongside hbr wall. Enter HW±0200. Enter and stay only with no ground swell. On approach, to avoid protruding groin NE of pier head and single shingle bank to SE, keep RNLI boathouse and slip just open off the pierhead on track of 240°. When inside turn immediately to starboard and follow harbour wall to berth. Do not dry out near pier steps, these are used by tripper boats. Alternatively, anchor in Clovelly Roads with good holding and protection from W through S to E, and row ashore, but remember the strength of the tidal stream.
HM *Mobile* 07975501830.

BOSCASTLE

Standard Port Milford Haven
HW (sp) −0010   (np) −0045
LW (sp) −0110   (np) −0100

MHWS MHWN MLWN MLWS
+0·3m +0·4m +0·2m +0·2m

A picturesque medieval fishing village. Lies within the Cornwall AONB. King Arthur's Tintagel is 3M away by land.

Approach HW±0200 and stay only in fine settled weather. Difficult to locate from seaward. Beware lobster pot markers in approach. Unlit. Night entry dangerous. Essential to identify Meachard Rock before attempting to enter. Narrow entrance with very sharp bend to stb. Berth against wall and dry out on hard sand over rock. Heavy bumping in any slight ground swell.

PADSTOW

Standard Port Milford Haven
HW −0052   LW −0045

MHWS MHWN MLWN MLWS
+0·3m +0·4m +0·1m +0·1m

DS off Trevose Hd Dover HW
NE, +0600 SW

An interesting tourist town, crowded in summer, with a secure floating harbour and all facilities.

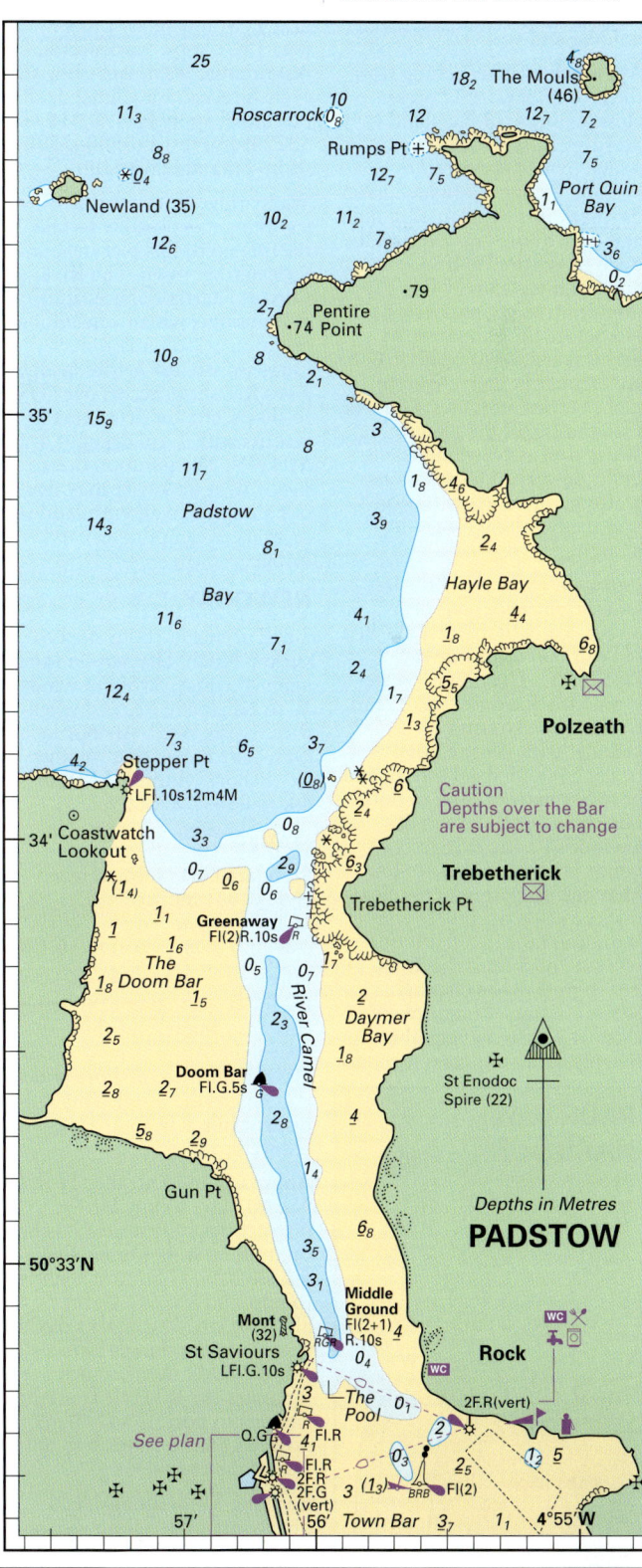

Bar Under normal conditions the entrance is perfectly safe and is best approached HW−0230 to HW+0200. Depth over bar likely to change. For latest survey and other useful information, including navigation with a drone's eye view, see www.padstow-harbour.co.uk. Do not attempt entry across the bar at any state of tide (even HW) when seas are breaking on the bar, e.g. near LW, in strong winds from W to N, or when there is a significant ground swell causing seas to break periodically especially below half tide. It will be difficult to tell from upwind if the waves are breaking. Be extra cautious at night. The breaking seas are usually worse on the ebb rather than the flood stream, and worse on spring rather than neap tides. To await the rise of tide: in good weather, anchor as close inshore as depth allows just inside Stepper Point, but beware of fishing gear. In strong winds from S to W, anchor in Polventon (or Mother Ivey's) Bay just SE of lifeboat slip in 3m on sand, or anchor in the W corner of Port Quin Bay, south of The Mouls (island), as close inshore as depth and tidal height allow to get clear of the tidal stream, but stay clear of rocks at LW. Here there is good holding and shelter.

Approach If approaching from the E or N beware of rocks close W and E of Newland Is and also Roscarrock 0·8m, which by day is cleared by keeping Stepper Pt (which has a daymark just off plan 12m high and 83m above sea level) well open of Pentire Pt. If approaching from W it is important to get past Trevose Hd before the ebb starts; at night, you need to be N of W to see Stepper Pt light. Also, by night beware of Quies, Gull Rk, Gulland Is (off the plan to the W) as well as Newland Is, all unlit. Beware of lobster pots scattered in Padstow Bay on approach to hbr, dangerous at night.

Entrance The start of the bar and the entrance channel is about 2ca N of the first mark, a red can buoy, **Greenaway**, Fl(2)R.10s. The deepest water is on a track from Pentire Pt to **Greenaway**, so enter the channel with Pentire point bearing 000°T dead astern, and pass **Greenaway** close to port. Later pass very close to St Saviour's Pt, the extremity of which is marked by a stb bn. Here the deepest water is close inshore (20m off bn). If you stand too far off, a flood tide will set you S onto the Town Bar to port of the channel. When passing N outer pier and clear of vessels leaving hbr, turn sharply to stb and pass through dock ent between second set of 2F.R(vert) and 2F.G(vert).

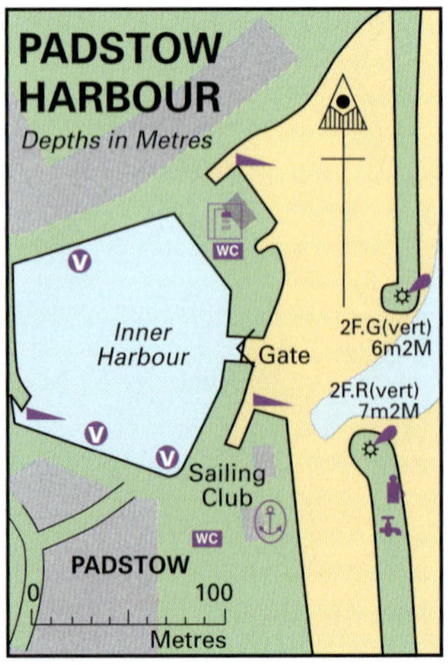

Berthing Dock gate is open, i.e. lowered, HW±0200 approx, but if waiting to enter or to set sail outside gate opening times, pick up a mooring in The Pool (charged same rate as hbr). Beware that The Pool shallows to the S and some moorings dry. The most N'ly buoy belongs to LB. OK to use if staying aboard. The Pool and much of the river is subject to strong tidal streams and scouring, so do not anchor. In narrow channels avoid obstructing vessels constrained by their size and draught. The Padstow-Rock ferry uses hbr near HW and St Saviour's Pt near LW. Shops, launderette, restaurants, WiFi, webcam, and cycle hire, e.g. for Camel Trail. For diesel apply HM ☎ 01841 532239, VHF 12 (0900–1700 Mon–Fri and HW±0200).

Wadebridge With careful sounding it is possible to take the tide up to this picturesque little market town. The River Camel is partially buoyed to Wadebridge, where a new long pontoon at Commissioners' Quay (to stb just before bridge) gives free shore access over HW to shops, etc, for occasional visitors with 1·2m draught at MHWN. The pontoon dries over LW. A fin keeler may dry out alongside wall with ladders, to stb between pontoon and bridge.

NEWQUAY

Small drying harbour next to surfing beach. Dry out on sand against S quay. Avoid in winds W to NE above F3, and when there is any swell. Anchor in Newquay Bay in fine weather or offshore winds. HM VHF 14, ☎ 01637 872809.

HAYLE

Standard Port Milford Haven
HW −0100 (approx)

MHWS	MHWN	MLWN	MLWS
−0·4m	−0·3m	−0·1m	+0·1m

Hbr dries to ½M offshore. Essential to contact HM before entry as channel can shift overnight. Approach HW±0200 with offshore wind and no ground swell. This historic hbr is being redeveloped.

Approach and Entrance From N card buoy follow HM's instructions to first Oc.G.4s bn on training wall. On passing 5th stb hand G bn turn slightly to port and leave Q.G. bn ahead to stb. This marks the N end of a steep shingle bank, called Middle Wear, which separates the R.Hayle from the channel to port. Cockle Bank now lies ahead, so keep to port side of the channel.

Berthing Moor alongside N quay with ladder. If no vacant berth, moor there alongside another boat. All stores, Rly.

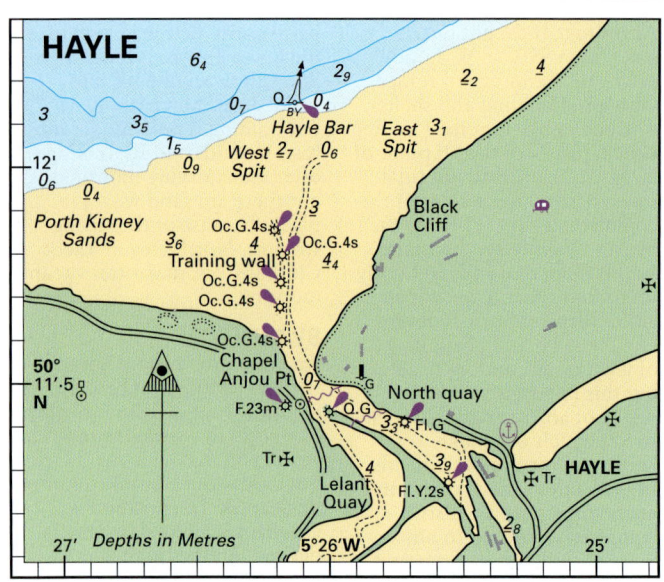

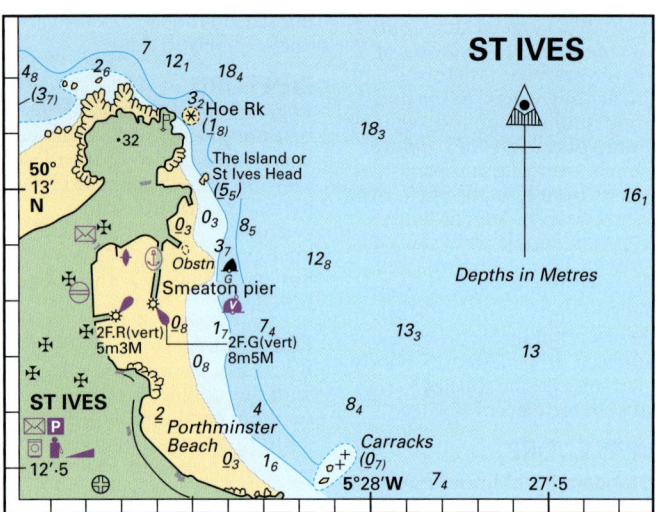

☎/VHF HM 01736 754 043 Emergency only 07500993867; VHF 18,14 (0900–1700).

ST IVES

Standard Port Milford Haven
HW (sp) −0115 (np) −0050
LW (sp) −0105 (np) −0040

MHWS	MHWN	MLWN	MLWS
−0·4m	−0·3m	−0·1m	+0·1m

A tourist town overcrowded in August but otherwise idyllic with a drying hbr and an anchorage with very limited protection. Boats moored here do not always show lights.

Approach and Entrance Hoe and Merran rks are cleared by keeping Knill's monument on with Tregenna Castle Hotel. The G buoy marks the remains of an old submerged breakwater. 2 visitors' Y moorings (Mar–Oct) S of G buoy in 3m but a long row to hbr. Enter ±0200 approx. 5 visitors' drying moorings inside hbr for bilge or long keel boats. Smeaton Pier is for the fishing fleet. Hbr and entrance subject to sea swell from local winds NW to NE and particularly from N–NE F3 and above. Also subject to unpleasant ground swell which turns easily into the bay at any time, even if no wind. Off St Ives the stream sweeps N for much of the time. Alternatively, in offshore winds anchor in 3m between hbr and the Carracks or in Carbis Bay S of the Carracks. All stores. Rly.

HM ☎ 01736 795018, VHF 12.

SW England and S Wales to Ireland distances (miles)

	Baltimore Ent	Old Hd Kinsale	Kilmore Quay	Arklow	Padstow Bar	Milford Haven ent.
Longships LtHo	163	143	131	166	47	100
Hugh Town	151	133	138	178	75	121
Padstow Bar	178	150	115	142	0	68
Swansea	210	175	113	129	74	51
Milford Haven ent.	159	126	62	79	68	0
S. Bishop Lt Ho	151	117	48	63	78	14

Ireland

This section of the almanac covers the whole of the coast of Ireland and gives directions for entering over 60 anchorages together with their facilities. The Irish Cruising Club *Sailing Directions* are published in two volumes, one for the South and West Coasts and one for the East and North. They are obtainable from: www.iccsailingbooks.com, or from Imray, www.imray.com, who are agents for the UK and the rest of the world. They publish *Cruising Cork and Kerry* by Graham Swanson. These publications are recommended for those wishing to cover the area in greater detail and mention all anchorages known to yachtsmen, many of which are remote, secluded and sometimes difficult to find but very rewarding. BA Sailing Directions *Irish Coast Pilot* NP 40 is also useful.

Weather forecasts Forecasts for Irish coastal waters are broadcast five times daily by Radio Eireann (RTE1) on 567 and 729kHz at 0602, 0755, 1253, 1755 and 2355 hours LT, but times may be changed by as much as five minutes. Forecasts are for 24hrs with a 48hrs outlook and gale warnings. The forecasts go round the coast in a clockwise direction between various headlands. These are shown distinctively marked on the accompanying introductory plans of Ireland. Coast radio stations broadcast a weather forecast for shipping at 0103 and thence every three hours updated every sixth. Gale warnings are preceded by an announcement on VHF 16. The BBC shipping forecasts on 198kHz are easily picked up on the W coast and are essential for tracking incoming weather.

continued on page 200

Ireland, Howth to Slyne Head north-about, distances (miles)

	Howth	Carlingford ent.	Strangford ent.	Bangor	Glenarm	Fairhead	Port Rush	Malin Head	Mullroy Bay ent.	Bloody Foreland	Aranmore Island	Rathlin O'Birne	Sligo entrance	Broadhaven ent.	Erris Head	Blacksod Bay ent.	Achill Head	Westport ent.	Inishbofin Island Hbr	Slyne Head
Howth	0																			
Carlingford ent.	37	0																		
Strangford ent.	58	27	0																	
Bangor	87	57	26	0																
Glenarm	107	76	47	23	0															
Fairhead	124	93	64	46	23	0														
Port Rush	144	113	84	66	43	20	0													
Malin Head	189	138	109	91	68	45	29	0												
Mullroy Bay ent.	203	152	123	105	82	59	43	14	0											
Bloody Foreland	213	162	133	115	92	69	53	24	19	0										
Aran More Island	226	175	146	128	105	82	66	37	32	13	0									
Rathlin O'Birne	253	215	173	155	132	109	93	64	59	40	24	0								
Sligo entrance	279	241	199	186	158	135	119	90	85	66	50	26	0							
Broadhaven ent.	291	240	211	193	170	146	131	102	97	78	68	47	48	0						
Erris Head	294	243	214	196	173	150	134	103	100	81	71	49	50	6	0					
Blacksod Bay ent.	314	263	234	216	193	170	154	123	120	101	91	69	70	26	20	0				
Achill Head	318	287	238	220	197	174	158	127	124	105	95	73	74	30	24	12	0			
Westport ent.	342	312	262	244	221	198	182	151	148	129	119	97	98	54	48	36	24	0		
Inishbofin Island Harbour	342	312	262	244	221	198	182	151	148	129	119	97	98	54	48	36	24	25	0	
Slyne Head	355	325	275	257	234	211	195	164	161	142	132	111	112	67	61	49	37	38	13	0

Ireland, Howth to Slyne Head south-about, distances (miles)

	Howth	Dun Laoghaire	Wicklow Head	Arklow	Carnsore Point	Kilmore Quay ent.	Dunmore East ent.	Cork Harbour ent.	Old Head of Kinsale	Mizen Head	Lawrence Cove ent.	Dursey Head	Bray Head	Dingle ent.	Blasket Sound	Loop Head	Kilrush	Kilronan ent.	Roundstone	Slyne Head
Howth	0																			
Dun Laoghaire	8	0																		
Wicklow Head	28	22	0																	
Arklow	40	34	12	0																
Carnsore Point	77	71	49	39	0															
Kilmore Quay ent.	87	81	59	49	10	0														
Dunmore East ent.	102	96	74	64	25	16	0													
Cork Harbour ent.	152	146	124	114	75	68	54	0												
Old Head of Kinsale	166	160	138	128	89	81	66	15	0											
Mizen Head	217	211	189	179	140	132	117	66	51	0										
Lawrence Cove ent.	233	227	205	195	156	148	133	82	67	16	0									
Dursey Head	235	229	207	197	158	150	135	84	69	18	16	0								
Bray Head	255	249	227	217	178	170	155	104	89	38	36	20	0							
Dingle Ent.	271	265	243	233	194	186	171	120	105	54	52	36	16	0						
Blasket Sound	268	262	240	230	191	183	168	117	102	51	49	33	13	9	0					
Loop Head	302	296	264	254	225	217	202	151	136	85	83	67	47	43	34	0				
Kilrush	314	308	286	276	237	229	214	163	148	97	95	79	59	55	46	18	0			
Kilronan ent.	336	330	308	298	259	251	236	185	170	119	117	101	81	77	68	48	56	0		
Roundstone	348	342	320	310	271	263	248	197	182	131	129	113	93	89	80	36	67	22	0	
Slyne Head	346	340	318	308	269	261	246	195	180	129	127	111	91	87	78	42	69	27	13	0

The Cruising Almanac

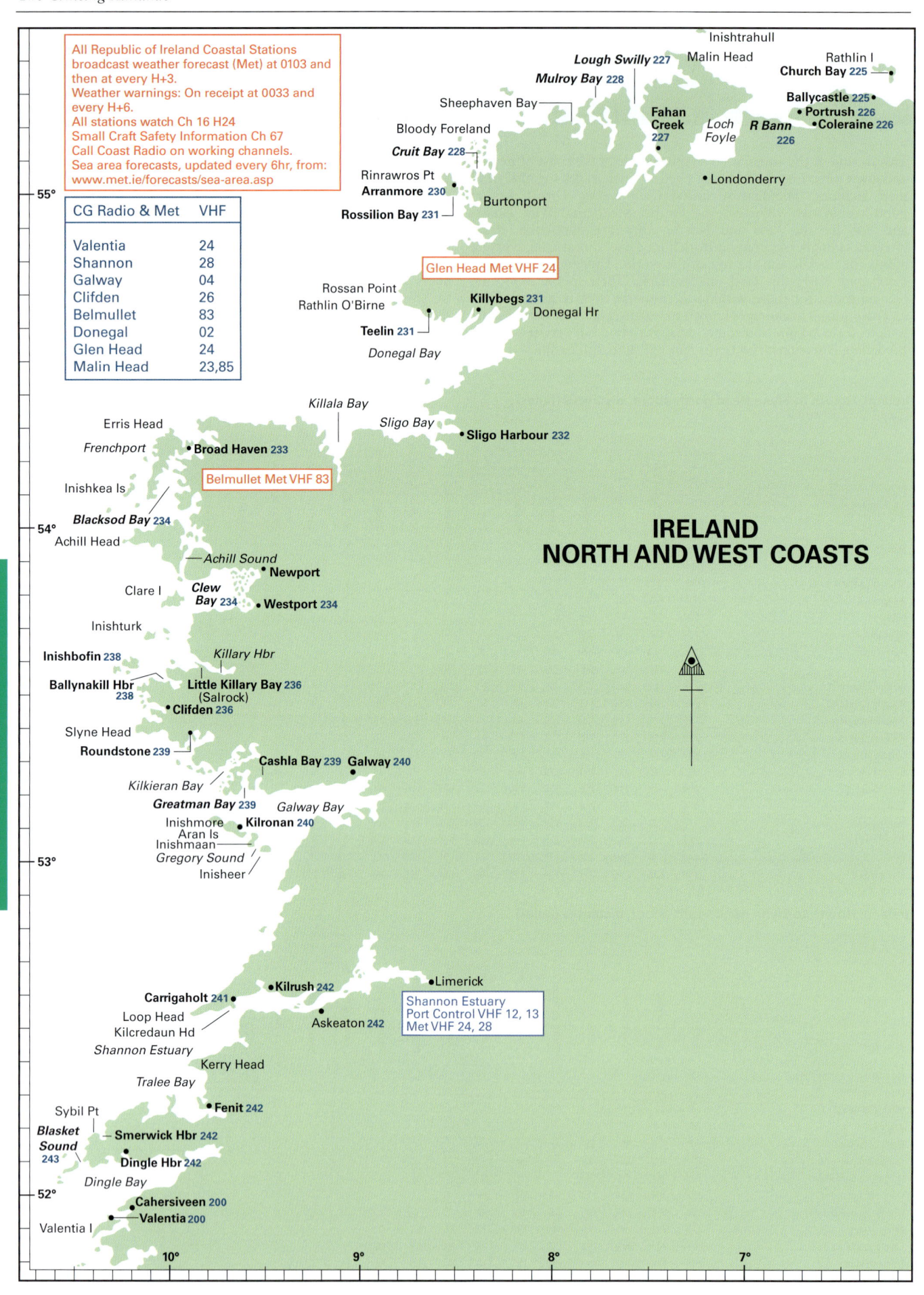

IRELAND NORTH AND WEST COASTS

All Republic of Ireland Coastal Stations broadcast weather forecast (Met) at 0103 and then at every H+3.
Weather warnings: On receipt at 0033 and every H+6.
All stations watch Ch 16 H24
Small Craft Safety Information Ch 67
Call Coast Radio on working channels.
Sea area forecasts, updated every 6hr, from: www.met.ie/forecasts/sea-area.asp

CG Radio & Met	VHF
Valentia	24
Shannon	28
Galway	04
Clifden	26
Belmullet	83
Donegal	02
Glen Head	24
Malin Head	23,85

Glen Head Met VHF 24

Belmullet Met VHF 83

Shannon Estuary
Port Control VHF 12, 13
Met VHF 24, 28

Inishtrahull
Lough Swilly 227 Malin Head   Rathlin I
Mulroy Bay 228   **Church Bay** 225
Sheephaven Bay   **Fahan**   **Ballycastle** 225
Bloody Foreland   **Creek**   • **Portrush** 226
                          227   *R Bann* • **Coleraine** 226
Cruit Bay 228   *Loch*
Rinrawros Pt   *Foyle*
Arranmore 230 Burtonport
Rossilion Bay 231   • Londonderry

Rossan Point   **Killybegs** 231
Rathlin O'Birne   Donegal Hr
Teelin 231
Donegal Bay

Killala Bay
Erris Head   *Sligo Bay*
Frenchport • **Broad Haven** 233   • **Sligo Harbour** 232
Inishkea Is
Blacksod Bay 234
Achill Head
         Achill Sound
Clare I • **Newport**
         Clew Bay 234
         • **Westport** 234
Inishturk
         Killary Hbr
Inishbofin 238
Ballynakill Hbr **Little Killary Bay** 236
         238   (Salrock)
         • **Clifden** 236
Slyne Head
Roundstone 239
                 Cashla Bay 239 **Galway** 240
Kilkieran Bay
Greatman Bay 239 *Galway Bay*
Inishmore **Kilronan** 240
Aran Is
Inishmaan
Gregory Sound
Inisheer

                              • Limerick
         • **Kilrush** 242
Carrigaholt 241 •
Loop Head   Askeaton 242
Kilcredaun Hd
Shannon Estuary
         Kerry Head
Tralee Bay
Sybil Pt • **Fenit** 242
Blasket **Smerwick Hbr** 242
Sound
243   **Dingle Hbr** 242
         Dingle Bay
         Cahersiveen 200
         Valentia 200
Valentia I

Page references are shown after locations, for example:
Valentia 200. Bold type indicates that it is accompanied by a plan. *Italics* are used for rivers, lochs, bays, seas etc

The Cruising Almanac

IRELAND
SOUTH WEST, SOUTH AND EAST COASTS

All Republic of Ireland Coast Stations normally broadcast weather forecast (Met) at 0103 and every H+3. Belfast Coastguard covers Carlingford Lough to Lough Foyle broadcasts weather forecast at 0810 and every 3hr after initial announcement on VHF16, then go to appropriate channel.
Small Craft Safety: Ch 67
Weather warnings on receipt and with forecasts.
Sea area forecasts, updated every 6hr, from: www.met.ie/forecasts/sea-area.asp

CG Radio & Met	VHF
Carlingford	04
Dublin	83
Wicklow	02
Rosslare	23
Minehead	83
Cork	26
Mizen Head	04
Bantry	23
Valentia	24

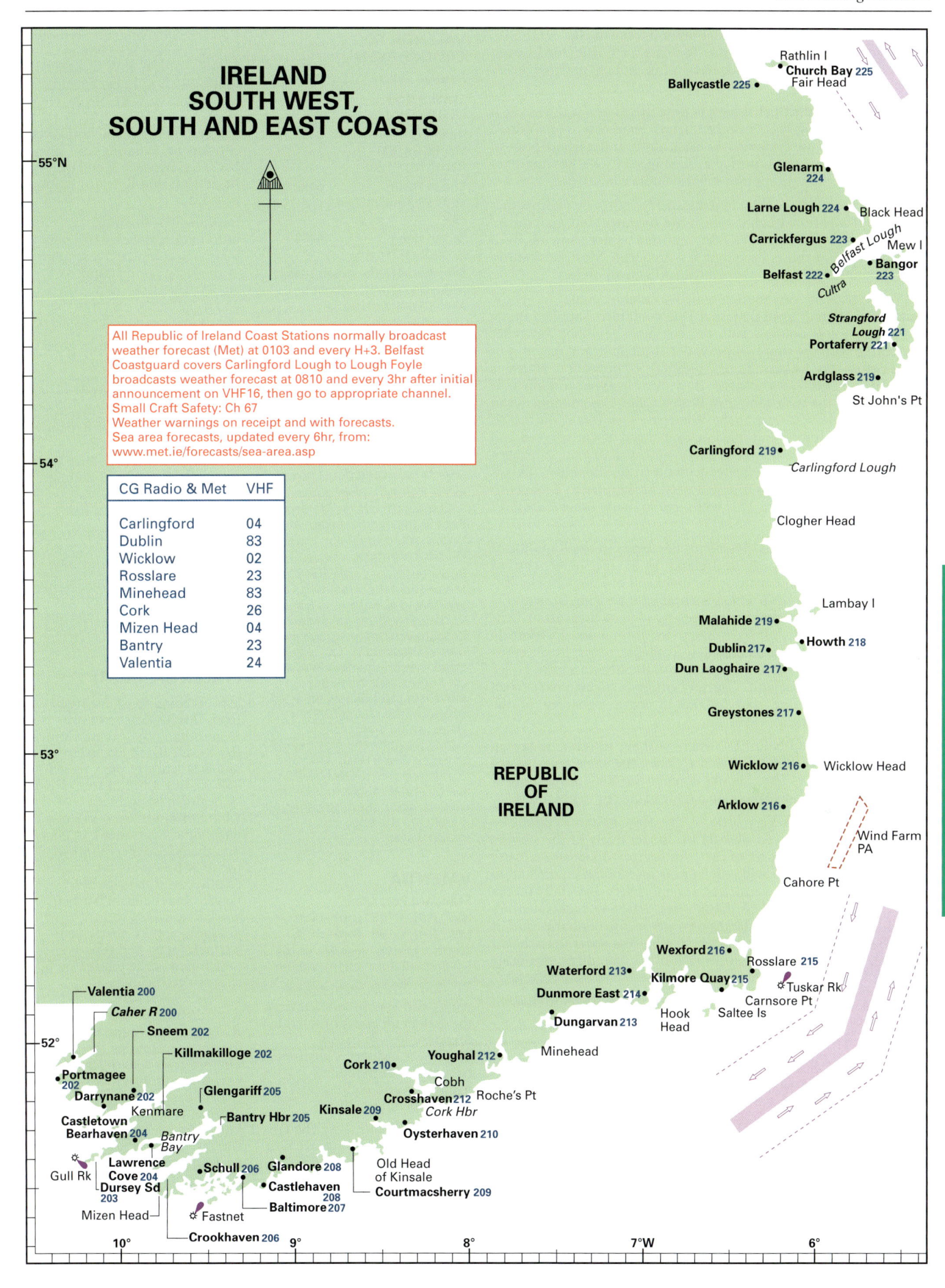

REPUBLIC OF IRELAND

IRELAND

Locations (with page references):

- Rathlin I
- **Church Bay** 225
- **Ballycastle** 225
- Fair Head
- **Glenarm** 224
- **Larne Lough** 224
- Black Head
- **Carrickfergus** 223
- *Belfast Lough*
- Mew I
- **Belfast** 222
- **Bangor** 223
- Cultra
- *Strangford Lough* 221
- **Portaferry** 221
- **Ardglass** 219
- St John's Pt
- **Carlingford** 219
- *Carlingford Lough*
- Clogher Head
- Lambay I
- **Malahide** 219
- **Dublin** 217
- **Howth** 218
- **Dun Laoghaire** 217
- **Greystones** 217
- **Wicklow** 216
- Wicklow Head
- **Arklow** 216
- Wind Farm PA
- Cahore Pt
- **Wexford** 216
- **Rosslare** 215
- **Waterford** 213
- **Kilmore Quay** 215
- **Dunmore East** 214
- Tuskar Rk
- Carnsore Pt
- **Dungarvan** 213
- Hook Head
- Saltee Is
- Minehead
- **Youghal** 212
- **Cork** 210
- Cobh
- **Crosshaven** 212
- Roche's Pt
- *Cork Hbr*
- **Kinsale** 209
- **Oysterhaven** 210
- Old Head of Kinsale
- **Courtmacsherry** 209
- **Glandore** 208
- **Castlehaven** 208
- **Schull** 206
- **Baltimore** 207
- Fastnet
- **Crookhaven** 206
- **Valentia** 200
- *Caher R* 200
- **Sneem** 202
- **Killmakilloge** 202
- **Glengariff** 205
- **Portmagee** 202
- **Darrynane** 202
- Kenmare
- **Bantry Hbr** 205
- **Castletown Bearhaven** 204
- *Bantry Bay*
- **Lawrence Cove** 204
- Gull Rk
- Dursey Sd 203
- Mizen Head

Page references are shown after locations, for example:
Dublin 217. Bold type indicates that it is accompanied by a plan. *Italics* are used for rivers, lochs, bays, seas etc

The Cruising Almanac

IRELAND

Belfast Coastguard, after initial announcement on VHF 16, broadcasts MSI including weather forecast for Carlingford Lough to Lough Foyle at 0810 and every three hours, updated every six hours.

Warning Salmon drift net fishing is now illegal at sea, however it has been reported at night near headlands. Snap nets are permitted in some rivers and estuaries. Lobster, crab and shrimp pots in many places have been reported as having very long floating lines that can foul props, prompting a marine notice in 2016.

Lights A reason for avoiding making smaller ports by night is that the lesser navigational lights, which are operated and maintained by the local authorities, have been reported as not showing from time to time. But this is becoming less frequent. Most lighthouses in the Republic are now equipped with AIS transponders.

Gas Calor (Kosan) gas, though widely available, comes in yellow containers different from the usual 10lb containers supplied in the UK. Though still holding 10lb the container is about 5in taller when fitted with the supply tube, wider at the base and may not fit into existing gas lockers. It has a different connection which is provided for no extra charge if a British type container is exchanged for the Irish container. British Calor Gas containers can be refilled while you wait at the Whitegate Gas Depot on the SE side of Cork Harbour and filled or exchanged at Crosshaven and Killbegs. Standard Calor containers are available in Northern Ireland. Camping Gaz is widely available in the Republic. This is the same gas as Calor but one will need an adapter to connect to the Calor reducing valve. This will serve in many other European countries.

Customs The international boundary line between the Republic of Ireland (Eire) and Northern Ireland is at the inner end of Carlingford Lough and again at the inner end of Lough Foyle. It is marked on the charts. No action is required if arriving from an EU port unless you have anything to declare, such as firearms or non-EU nationals on board. If so or if arriving from a non-EU port fly Q flag. If no customs are immediately available, report by phone to the nearest police station – Garda in the Republic and the police service of Northern Ireland. Courtesy ensigns are customary when in the Republic. Note that Ireland is not a signatory of the Schengen Agreement.

Long term laying up Non-EU owners wishing to leave or lay up their vessels in the Republic need to obey the same rules as for other EU countries. They should contact the VAT authorities in Dublin Castle, Dublin 1 to obtain a copy of current regulations.

Hydrographic surveys Very little of the coast of the Republic of Ireland has been surveyed since 1914. In fact many of the surveys date back to the latter part of the 19th century. Extensive surveys are now in progress but will only appear on modern charts and in *Notices to Mariners*. Nevertheless, several charts, especially on the west coast, are still on OSI datum, not WGS84. Yachtsmen are particularly warned about depths of water in river estuaries and of sandy bays where there may be considerably less water than shown on the charts. Tidal information is readily available (www.sailing.ie).

Fish farms These have been noted on plans where currently known but they are liable to movement without notice.

Imports To protect Irish agriculture; avoid importing any raw or cooked meats. Certainly never take any ashore. At prsent there is great anxiety about potato ring rot. Do not take potatoes ashore, not even the peelings.

Safety Regulations have been introduced to require that a lifejacket is carried for every person aboard. The regulation also requires that lifejackets will be worn outside the cockpit at all times on board a craft less than 7m (23ft) in length and by children less than 16 years of age.

Visitors' Moorings can be found, especially in the S and W. They are usually large Y buoys, up to 15t. A charge of €5 may be made. Moorings may not be serviced annually. The Irish Sailing Association maintains a web page with information.
www.sailing.ie/cruising/visitor-mooring/

Aircoach Dublin Airport operates a fleet of coaches that radiate to many harbours around the coast. See www.aircoach.ie.

VALENTIA TO CROOKHAVEN

Passage lights	BA No
Skelligs Rock	6422
Fl(3)15s53m12M AIS	
Bull Rock	6430
Fl.15s91m18M	
Racon (N) (–) AIS	
Sheep Head	6432
Fl(3)WR.15s83m15/9M AIS	
Mizen Head	6448
Iso.4s55m12M AIS	

Direction of tidal streams (all related to Dover) between Skelligs and the shores
+0530S –0015N
between Bull Rock and Dursey Head
+0245S –0315N.
Dursey Sound is a useful channel between Dursey Is and the mainland, but be aware tides run up to 4kn.
DS Dover +0145S –0415N. See later for plan and directions.
In the Kenmare River above Sneem watch out for Maiden Rock in the middle, awash at LWS, marked by G con Lt buoy Fl.5s 3ca N of rock.
Between Three Castle Head and Mizen Head the streams run S and NW to N, becoming E and W between Mizen Head and Crookhaven Dover +0130S and E and –0430N and W. Off Mizen Head the spring rate is 4kn, and off Three Castle Head 3kn decreasing to 1·5kn when 4–5M offshore. The race off Mizen Head can be dangerous in windy weather and may extend to Three Castle Head. On S and E going stream it extends SE in a crescent. If caught in the race steer straight out to sea, then parallel to the edge of rough water.

VALENTIA

Standard Port Cobh
HW (sp) –0118 (np) –0038
LW (sp) –0136 (np) –0056

MHWS	MHWN	MLWN	MLWS
–0·6m	–0·4m	–0·1m	0·0m

The hbr affords shelter in all winds and may be entered from the NW at all states of the tide (exposed in NW gales). Portmagee channel is obstructed by a bridge with limited headroom and permanently closed opening span.

Bars By NW entrance: The Fort (Cromwell) Point entrance has 7m on the Ldg line.
By SW entrance: Until inside Reencaheragh Point there is 8m. Then there is down to 1·5m through the Portmagee Channel.

Approach NW entrance: make Doulus Head, avoiding the CG patch in severe conditions. Make toward Fort Point. Sectored Lt
Fl.WR.2s16m17/15M 104°-W-304°-R-351°.

Entrance For Valentia Harbour, having located Fort Point, Fl.WR.2s keep in W sector (140°-142°) of Lt on Valentia Island Dir.Oc.WRG.4s, leaving Harbour Rock bn Q(3)10s to stb, and thence to anchorage as convenient, avoiding the Caher bar 0·6m between E end of Beginish Is and Reenard Point near LW.

Berthing The floating pontoon/breakwater to a new marina is completed just south of the ferry ramp at approx 51°55′·2N 10°17′·1W. Mooring on the inside of the pontoon gives excellent shelter.

Anchorages In N winds, good anchorage off SE bight of Beginish Is, in 2–8m; or, according to wind, off Knightstown to S of jetty, in Glanleam Bay, or S of Reenard Point. As convenient in Portmagee channel. There is a pier at Reenard Point with 3m on the SE side. 6 visitors' moorings off Knight's Town.

Caution Do not anchor close to the pecked lines E of Knightstown owing to submarine cables. Buoy anchor if near the lifeboat. Silting of the channel has been reported. Frequent ferry to Cahersiveen.

CAHER RIVER (VALENTIA RIVER)

If proceeding to Cahersiveen from Doulus Bay enter over Doulus bar, 3m, leaving Doulus Rocks (Or Black Rocks) to stb and Kay Rock to port, thence SSE passing a full ca from E end of Beginish Isl and ½ca E of Church Island. From Valentia harbour, cross Caher bar, 0·6 to 1m, then close the S shore of the river following the buoyed channel until Ballycarberry Castle comes abeam N, then work towards N shore gradually until Cahersiveen barracks open and proceed in midstream to the marina on S shore or to the quay at Cahersiveen. There is a series of five Ldg lines up the Caher River, F.G Lts on rather inconspic telephone type poles One set gives a stern lead. It is very important to follow closely these Ldg marks as the channel is not wide, but the buoys are adequate. Streams run fast at springs. If anchoring off Cahersiveen it is not possible to lie clear of the current. Welcoming marina.

Supplies at Knightstown, limited to some general stores and fuel. Water on pontoon and quay at Reenard Pt, hotel and restaurants. Beginish Is uninhabited. Cahersiveen, all requirements and a heritage museum.

☎/VHF Cahersiveen Marina 066 9472777, VHF M, 37.

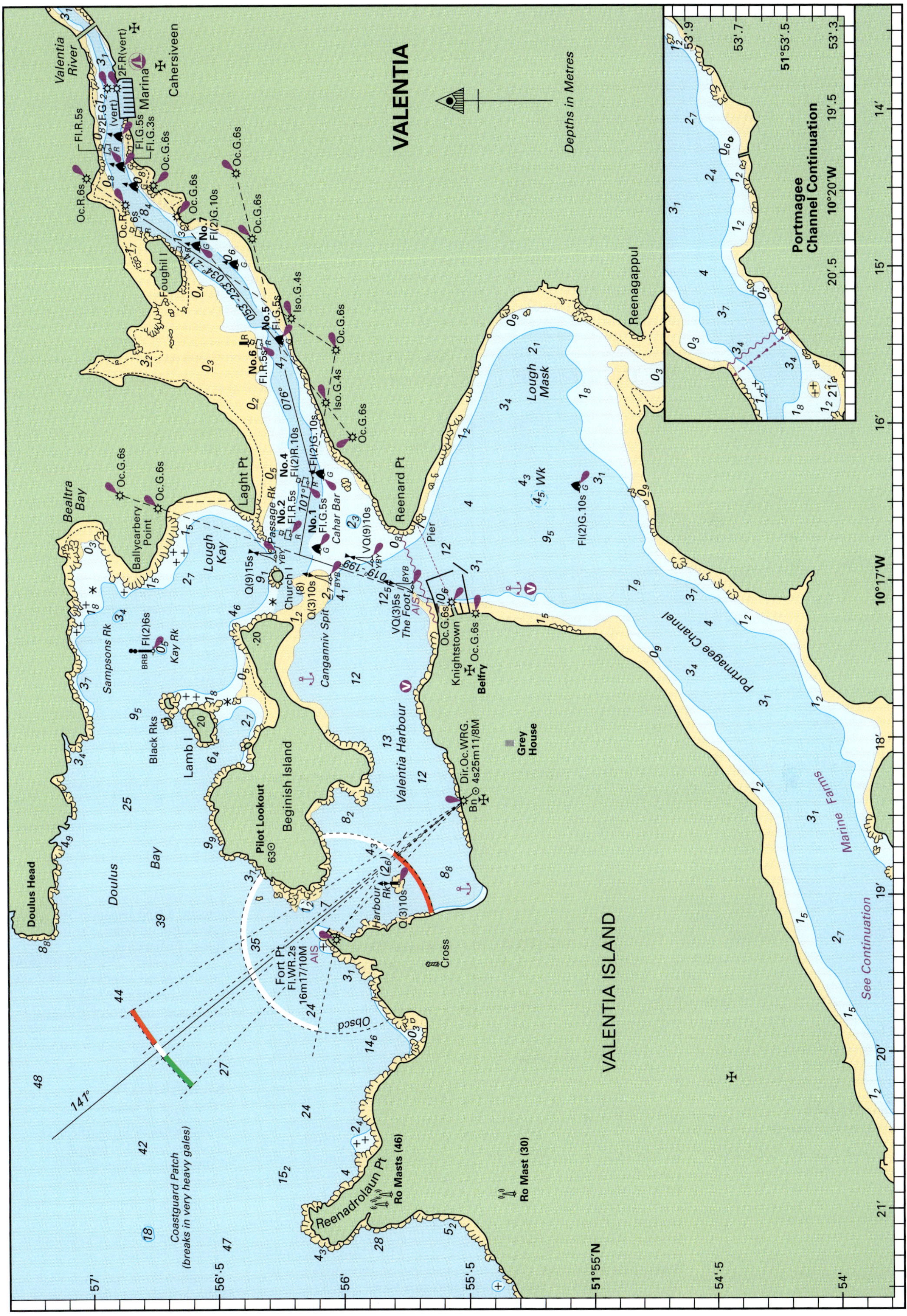
VALENTIA
VALENTIA ISLAND
Depths in Metres
Valentia River
Cahersiveen
Marina
Foughil I
Valentia Harbour
Doulus Head
Doulus Bay
Bealtra Bay
Ballycarbery Point
Laght Pt
Lough Kay
Sampsons Rk
Kay Rk
Black Rks
Lamb I
Beginish Island
Pilot Lookout
Church I
Passage Rk
Canganniv Spit
Cahar Bar
Reenard Pt
Pier
The Foot
Knightstown
Belfry
Grey House
Harbour Rk
Fort Pt
Fl.WR.2s
16m17/10M
Dir.Oc.WRG.
4s25m11/8M
Cross
Obscd
Reenadrolaun Pt
Ro Masts (46)
Ro Mast (30)
Coastguard Patch
(breaks in very heavy gales)
Lough Mask
Wk
Reenagappul
Portmagee Channel
Marine Farms
See Continuation
Portmagee
Channel Continuation
10°20'W
10°17'W
51°55'N

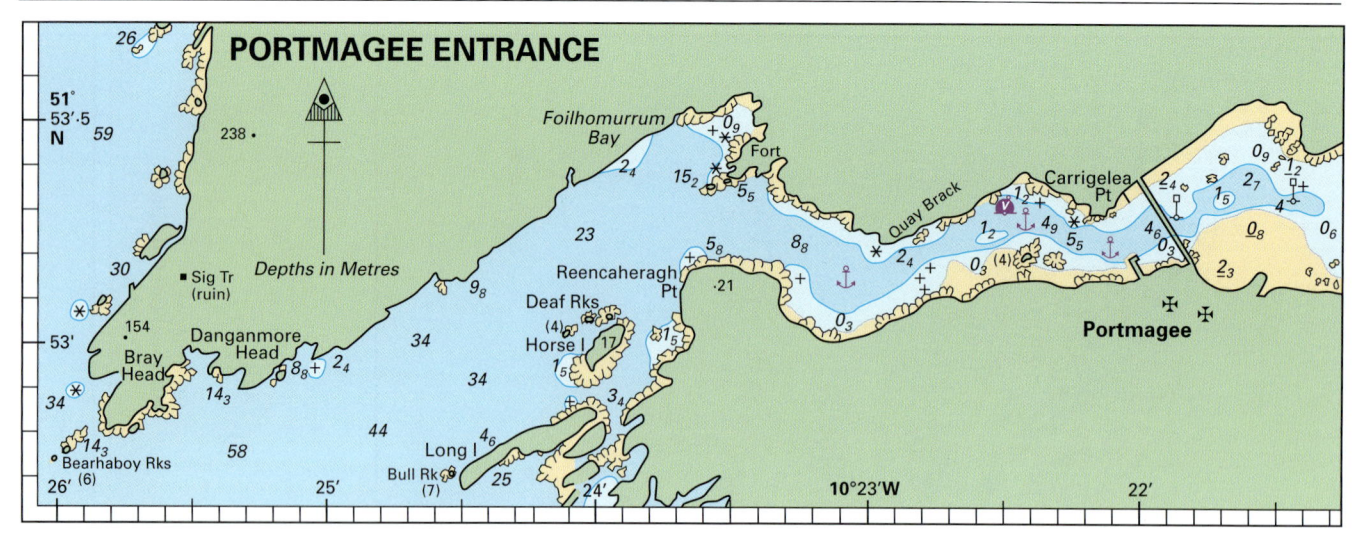

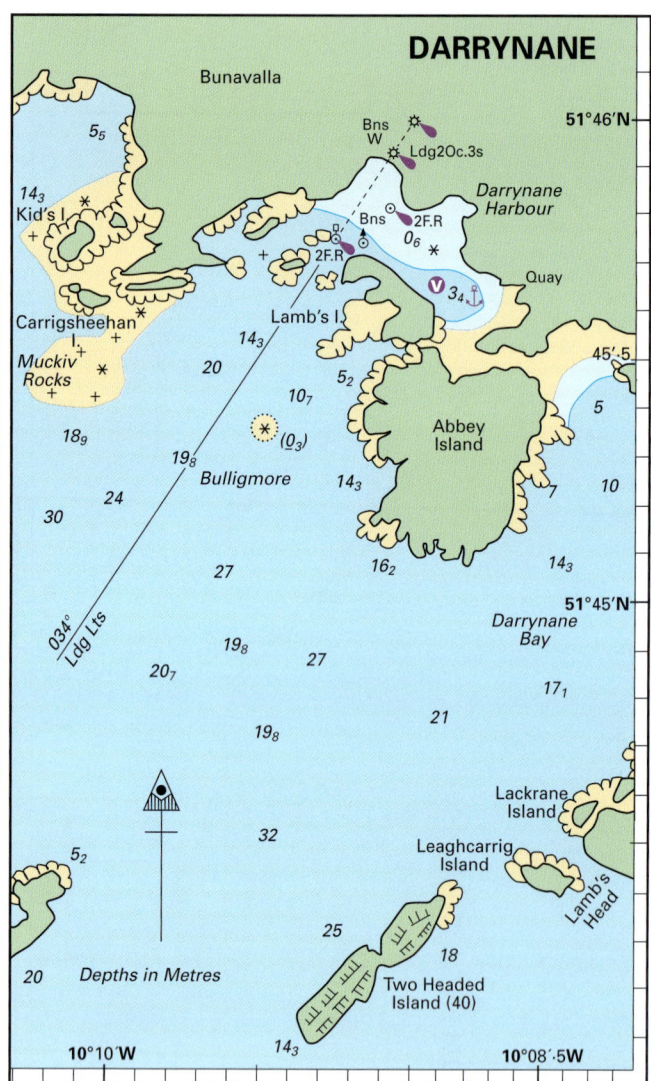

DARRYNANE

Standard Port Cobh
HW (sp) –0119 (np) –0039
LW (sp) –0134 (np) –0054

MHWS	MHWN	MLWN	MLWS
–0·5m	–0·5m	–0·1m	0·0m

A beautiful, natural hbr 1½M NW of Lamb's Head, well sheltered in all weathers.

Avoid entering in heavy W'ly or SW'ly weather when the narrow entrance between rocks may be dangerous. Even impossible in bad weather.

Approach From S pass between Two Headed Is and Moylaun Is. Make north approx 1M and sight two conspicuous white Lt bns Oc.3s bearing 034°.

From SW pass between Moylaun Is and Deenish Is then steer ENE to sight the bns. From W or NW make to position 5ca N of Deenish Is then steer E to sight the bns. Steer carefully on the transit to avoid rocks close either side. When ½ca past Middle Rock (always shows) to stb alter course 030° to stb to pass between a lit R bn 2F.R. to port and a B topped bn to stb on Lamb's Rock to the N of Lamb's Is.

Entrance When past Lamb's Rock some ½ca, pass between it and Odd Rock bn 2F.R to the NE of it.

Anchorage Steer SE down into the hbr some 2ca to come to anchor clear of moorings in 3m. One visitors' mooring.

Facilities Land at the quay in the SE corner or on the sandy beach. There are no shops nearby but, some 150m along the road from the quay, there is a friendly bar where they can direct you to shops some 2M distant. There are fine sandy beaches in Darrynane bay to the SE of the hbr and Daniel O'Connell's House some 600m walk beyond the quay is well worth a visit.

SNEEM

Standard Port Cobh
HW (sp) –0113 (np) –0033
LW (sp) –0129 (np) –0049

MHWS	MHWN	MLWN	MLWS
–0·6m	–0·5m	–0·1m	0·0m

A small hbr on N side of the Kenmare River opposite Kilmakilloge. Affords sheltered anchorage for small craft in 3–6m and upwards in very beautiful surroundings.

Approach Close with the SE side of Sherky Is. To pass inside Sherky Is and avoid Cottoner Rock (dries 0·3m), keep nearer to Pigeon Is to port than to Sherky Is.

Entrance Thence steer 047° on the hotel. When well past the third Is, Inishkeragh, steer 318° on the NE extreme of Garinish Is, leaving it close to port.

Visitors' moorings Three Y visitors' moorings established 51°48'·65N 09°53'·75W.

Anchorage In 6m between Goat Is and the pier, or in 3m inside the bay at the NE end of Garinish known as 'The Bag'.

Facilities All necessities from Sneem, 1½M by water but only accessible by dinghy at half flood. Otherwise approximately 2M walk up the lane from the Oysterbed Ho pier. Water at pier NW of anchorage symbol. Parknasilla Hotel, with restaurant, can be approached on foot from Goat Island.

KILMAKILLOGE

Tidal data as Sneem

Inside Kilmakilloge, there are three separate harbours: Kilmakilloge, Bunaw and Collorus.

Approach From E give Laughan Point a berth of over 2½ca give W side of entrance a berth of 1½ca.

Entrance Book Rocks, awash at LW, extends 3ca off E shore, R can Fl(2)R.10s, near a grassy precipice 53m high. Off Collorus Point on W side dangers extend 1½ca. Enter on mid-channel course steering

PORTMAGEE

Tidal data as Valentia

Approach Entrance inadvisable in heavy weather owing to violence of sea under Bray Head and baffling winds. No dangers in approach.

Entrance N entrance via Knightstown is not accessible as br is permanently closed. Approaching from SW for 1¼M inside Reencaheragh Pt, navigation requires caution and the chart should be studied carefully.

Anchorage Below the br off the pier in 5m. There are visitors' moorings 3ca west of the fixed br. Alongside mooring may be possible on the pier for short periods and longer at pontoon on the N shore between Carrigalea Point and the br. Good restaurant and shop with some provisions on S shore. Tour boats to Skelligs.

Pontoon connected to land but no water or electricity yet.

DURSEY SOUND

Tidal Stream
Dover –0430 N-going, +0145 S-going. Spring rate 4kn with overfalls. It can be even swifter close to the shore on the spring stream. There are eddies on both sides of the S entrance during S-going stream. This is a narrow and useful channel between Dursey Island and the mainland. It is advisable to go through with a favourable tide or at least before it reaches its maximum rate. Entering the sound from the S a peculiarity about which strangers should be forewarned is that having rounded Crow Head the bay presents the appearance of a cul-de-sac as the similarity of colour of the island and the mainland shores prevents contrast where they overlap. There is a temporary anchorage off the pier on the E side of Dursey Is while waiting for the tide.

Having cleared the Bull's Forehead off Crow Head steer for Illanebeg on the island shore. Look out for lobster pots SW of the entrance. Keep very close to the island shore going through the narrows which are only 1ca wide. Flag Rock with only 0·3m over it at LW lies almost in mid-channel in the narrowest part of the sound, thus limiting the navigable part to 90m. The N-going tide sets directly on to the rock. There is deep water close to the shore of the island so a yacht should keep very close in. The E extremity of Scariff Is in line with the E shore of the island, 339°, leads W of the 0·3m rock. Note that Scariff Is, 252m, and Deenish Is, 141m, are the same shape viewed from the S. There is a cable car across the sound also a telephone wire; the least clearance at HWS is 21m under the car itself with 24m under the cables and 26m under the telephone wires. There is usually a disturbed sea at the N entrance which can become dangerous in strong to gale force N/NW winds. The sea rebounds from the cliffs of Glasfeactula Rock, 9m high, at the E side of the N entrance. Quite frequently a different wind is met on either side of the sound. Be prepared for sudden changes in wind direction going through the sound especially near the N entrance where heavy squalls from the high ground may be met. Salmon nets may be just N of the N entrance and it would be very dangerous to foul one here.

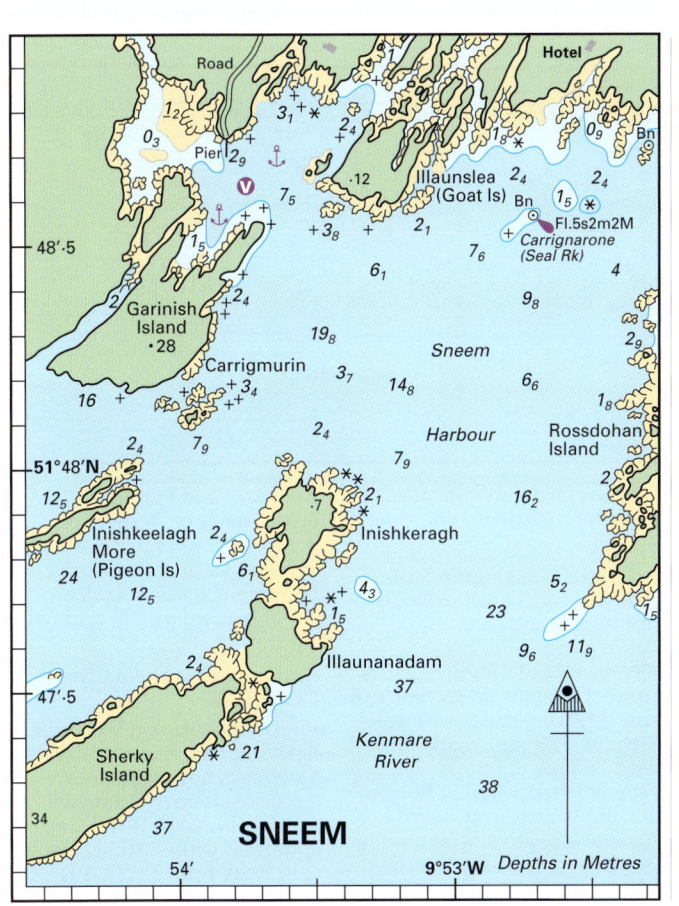

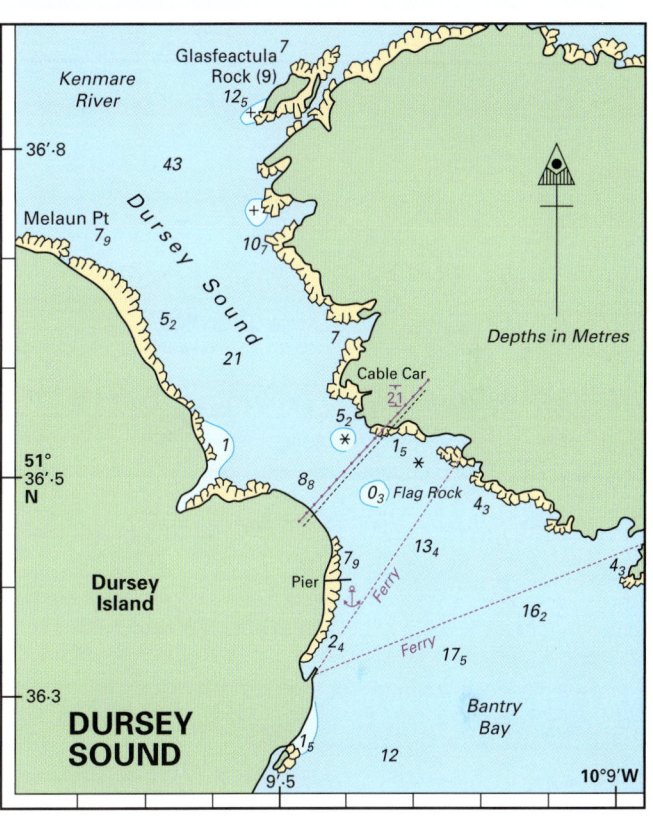

slightly W of Spanish Is. Thence according to anchorage.

Anchorages
- For Kilmakilloge harbour, once past Collorus Point alter course to 102° for the woods near Dereen Ho. Anchor in 4m SW of Yellow Rock, (Bn missing) awash at HW. Landing at Dereen, shop 1½M E at Lauragh. Good pub lunches.
- For Collorus harbour, round Collorus Pt keeping a good ca off, and passing between the Pt and Spanish Is slightly nearer the former. Anchorage in middle of hbr in 5m, holding soft with kelp and unreliable. Look out for oyster fishing rafts. No shops.
- For Bunaw harbour, on NE side of entrance, enter through channel 1ca wide between unmarked rocks, with pier-head bearing 041°. There are B & Y Ldg poles with Lts: Oc.R.3s9m (front) Iso.R.2s11m (back) on this bearing: front Lt on pier-

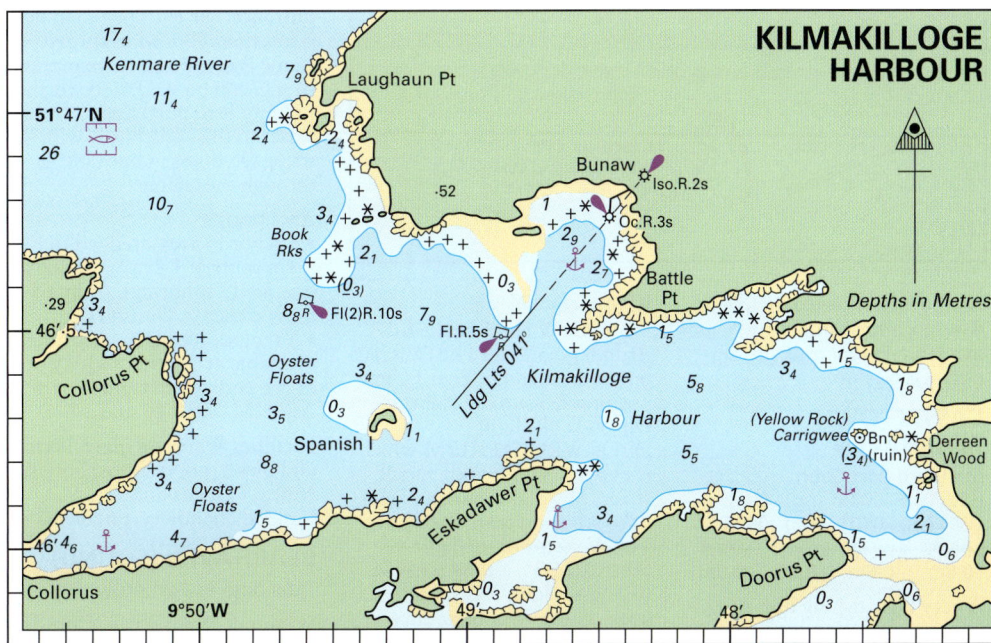

CASTLETOWN AND BEARHAVEN

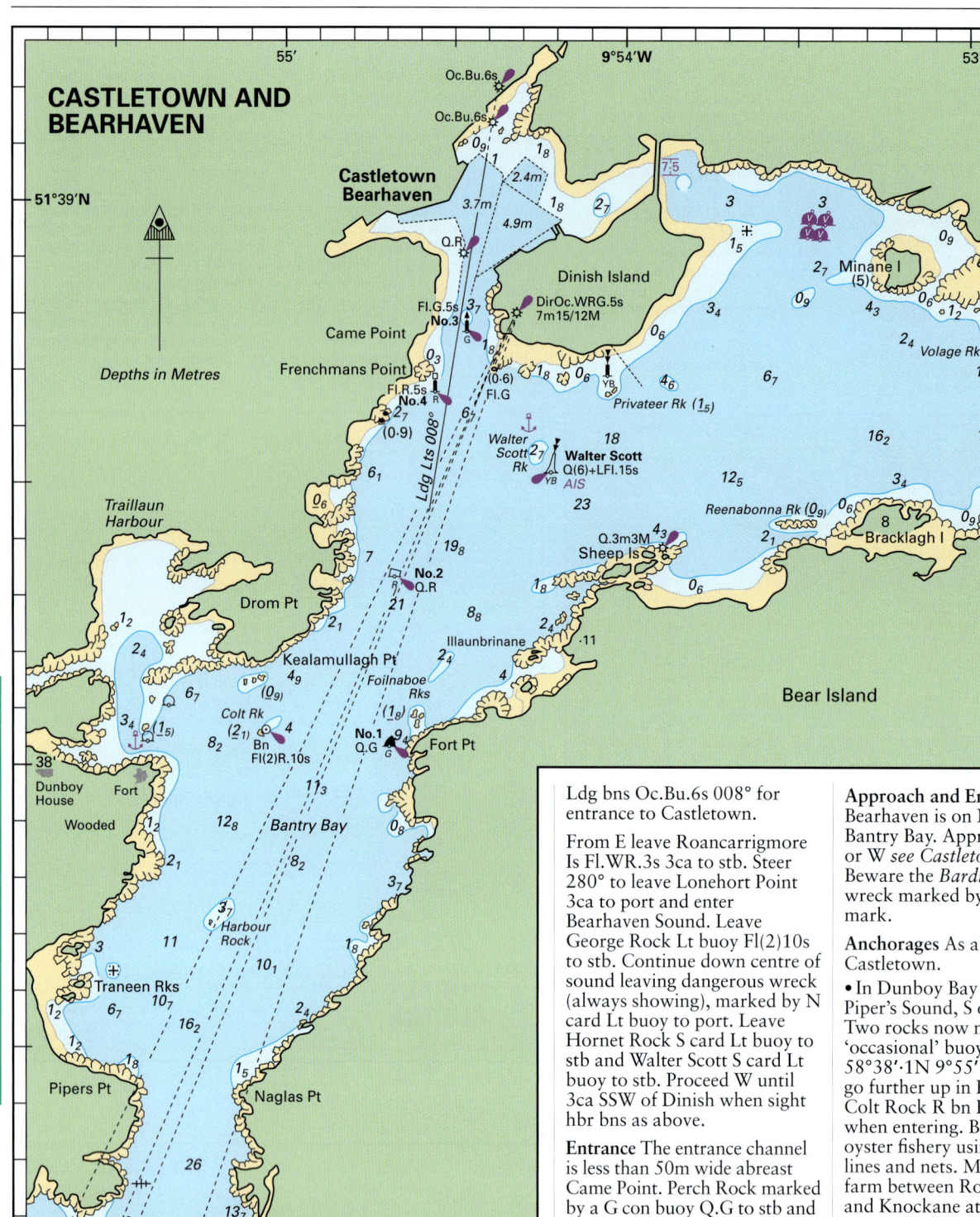

head. Anchor near Ldg line in 4–6m. Limited stores and water available. Numerous shrimp pots. Good pub.

CASTLETOWN BEARHAVEN

Standard Port Cobh
HW (sp) –0048 (np) –0012
LW (sp) –0101 (np) –0025
MHWS   MHWN   MLWN   MLWS
–0·8m   –0·6m   –0·2m   0·0m

A very busy fishing hbr. Also known as Castletownbere.

Bar 3m W of Dinish Is.

Approach
From the W and S make for Ardnakinna Point Fl(2)WR.10s on the west end of Bear Is. In a position 2·5ca to W sight, on Dinish Is, the light DirOc.WRG.5s15/12M which is above a W hut with vert R stripe. Head in between Naglas Pt to stb and Pipers Pt to port. The W sector of the light, centre 023·3°, is very narrow (0·5°); at night, it is safest to keep on the W/G boundary through Piper's Sound. When 4½ca short of Dinish Is sight Ldg bns Oc.Bu.6s 008° for entrance to Castletown.

From E leave Roancarrigmore Is Fl.WR.3s 3ca to stb. Steer 280° to leave Lonehort Point 3ca to port and enter Bearhaven Sound. Leave George Rock Lt buoy Fl(2)10s to stb. Continue down centre of sound leaving dangerous wreck (always showing), marked by N card Lt buoy to port. Leave Hornet Rock S card Lt buoy to stb and Walter Scott S card Lt buoy to stb. Proceed W until 3ca SSW of Dinish when sight hbr bns as above.

Entrance
The entrance channel is less than 50m wide abreast Came Point. Perch Rock marked by a G con buoy Q.G to stb and Lt bn Q.R to port. Keep a little closer to this. Ldg bns R with W stripe Oc.Bu.6s in line 008° lead through the channel.

Anchorages
- Anchor in area dredged to 2·4m centred 1·2ca W of quay (see RNLI mooring), or in a S blow closer to Dinish Is.
- A temporary berth may be available at W end of Quay or at NE end: avoid central part. Ask HM, VHF 16 and 14.

Facilities
Water on quay. Petrol and diesel, good shops, hotels, banks, PO, gas and fuel. Limited chandlery. Engineer.

BEARHAVEN (SOUND)
Tidal data as Castletown

Stream in offing is negligible. In entrance at HWD tide floods, from +0615 ebbs, max rate 2kn.

Approach and Entrance
Bearhaven is on N shore of Bantry Bay. Approach from E or W see *Castletown, above*. Beware the *Bardini Reefer* wreck marked by a N cardinal mark.

Anchorages
As alternatives to Castletown.
- In Dunboy Bay on W side of Piper's Sound, S of rock drying. Two rocks now marked by 'occasional' buoy. Approach 58°38'·1N 9°55'·38W 1·5m; or go further up in E winds. Avoid Colt Rock R bn Fl(2)R.10s when entering. Beware of an oyster fishery using floating lines and nets. Massive fish farm between Roancarrigbeg and Knockane at E entrance.
- Picturesque anchorage in Adrigole Hbr behind Orthons Is just beyond east entrance to the Sound.
- Visitors' moorings 1½ca NW of Minane Island
- See Lawrence Cove 7ca SSE of George Rock.

LAWRENCE COVE
Tidal data as Castletown

A secluded, picturesque haven in the north shore of Bear Island 8ca S by E of George Rock buoy offering good shelter in all weather except strong north winds. Further into the cove is a small, well run, marina that offers good shelter in all weathers.

Approach
From E or W, in Bearhaven make for Ardnagh point (NNW of the Cove). From E keep 2½ca off shore to

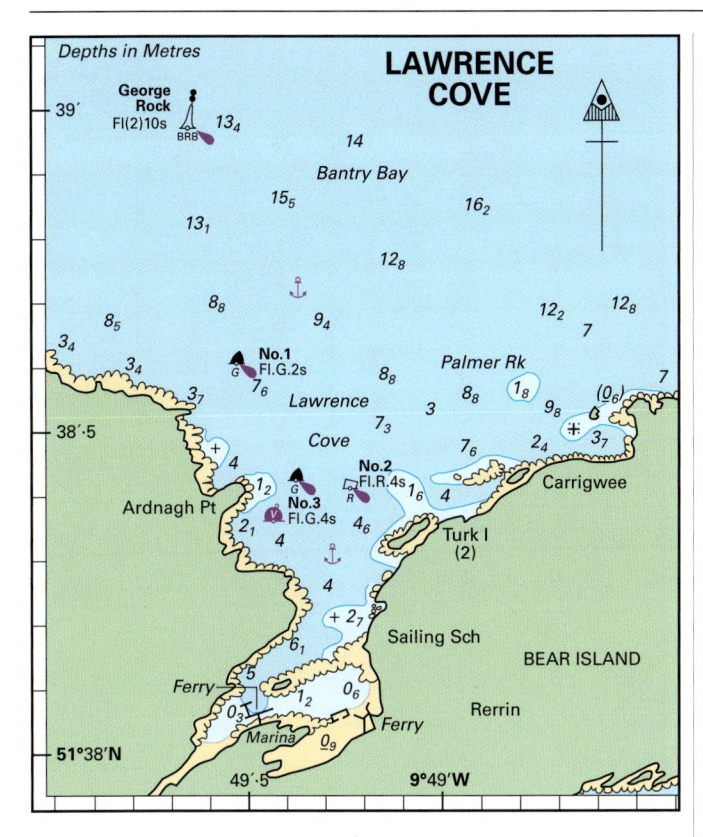

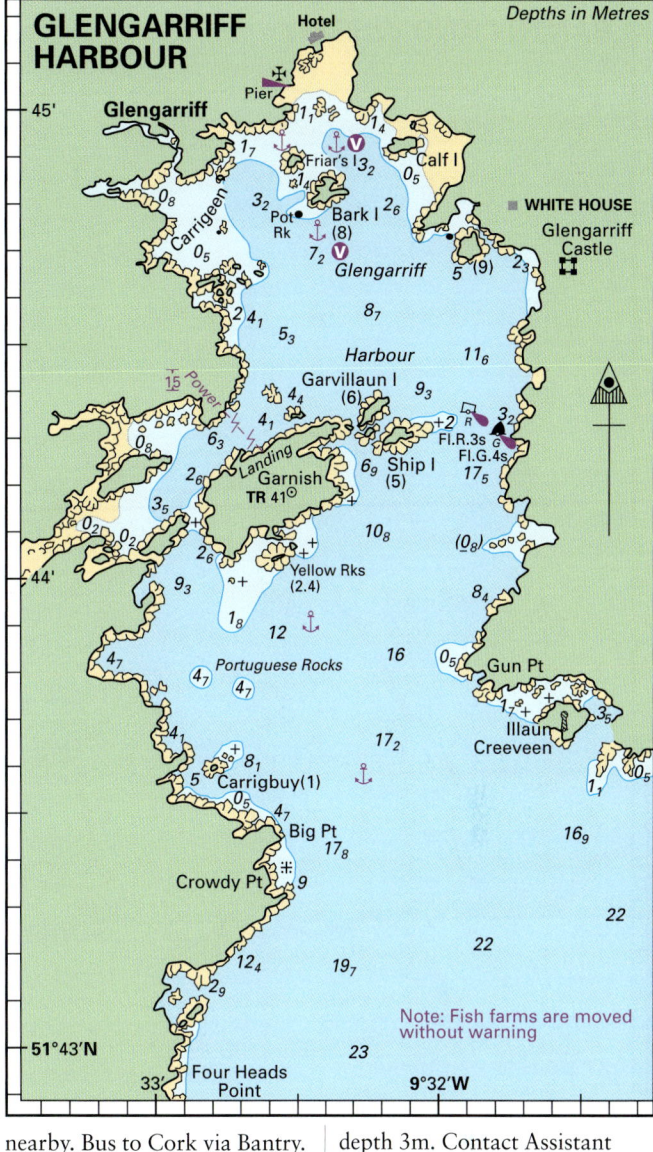

avoid Palmer Rock. From W keep 1ca off shore.

Entrance From Ardnagh point head SSE closing toward the next headland. There is a rock in the centre of the cove entrance. To keep clear of this stay within ½ca of the shore to stb. Come round this headland which forms the west side of the entrance keeping within 50m. There is a rocky island in the centre of the cove with a large cylindrical tank on it. The marina lies beyond this island some ½ca to SW. The channel to the marina is now buoyed. Seek instruction from the marina management where to berth.

Moorings and anchorage There are four visitors' buoys to the SSE of Ardnagh point. One may anchor near this.

Anchor within the entrance N or NE of the tank island in 5–6m but leave room for the small car ferry to enter to the N of you.

Facilities Marina has fuel, laundry, showers, toilets and electricity. Travel-lift crane. Below waterline repairs undertaken and secure over-wintering, storage ashore.

Payphone (no mobile cover) and Craft-Shop with many boat needs.

Provision can be made for leaving the boat in care and the ferry can connect with buses to Cork enabling crew change. The nearby village shop PO has necessity provisions. There are two restaurants and a pub. Large charge for rubbish disposal. Hiking and cycle trails on Bere Is.

☎ Marina 027 750 444.

GLENGARRIFF

Standard Port Cobh
HW (sp) –0045 (np) –0025
LW (sp) –0105 (np) –0040

MHWS	MHWN	MLWN	MLWS
–0·7m	–0·6m	–0·2m	+0·1m

The hbr is situated at the E end of Bantry Bay and affords complete shelter in beautiful surroundings.

Approach Leave Corrid Point (Four Heads Point) about 3ca to W and steer 010°, leaving Gun Point 2ca to E.

Entrance From position off Gun Point head 015° toward a conspic house on shore NW of Glengariff castle. Beware of extensive mussel farms. Keep 1½ca E of Ship Is and ½ca clear of the eastern shore. There is an uncharted patch of rock, having 3m at MLWS, 30m E of Ship Rocks. When 1ca or so to the N of Ship Is and Garvillaun Is the hbr is clear of submerged rocks.

Anchorages
• S of Bark Is This anchorage may have oyster rafts in it.
• NE or N of Bark Is in about 3m. Easy access to a new concrete slip and steps available all tides, near symbol for church.
• For yachts of less than 1·8m draught, close to wooden pier N of Carrigeen Is or at floating pontoon a ca W of pier. Pier has 1m LWS. There is a wide choice of other anchorages and six visitors' moorings have been laid.

Facilities Water at public toilets near Blue Pool, PO, telephone, convenience store, pubs, excellent restaurants, petrol and good small shops in Glengariff village. Large hotel at head of hbr. Recycling nearby. Bus to Cork via Bantry. Restored formal gardens at Garinish Is. Forest walks.

BANTRY HARBOUR

See plan on next page
Tidal data as Glengarriff

Entrance from N On approach beware of ruined, badly lit oil terminal jetty 2·5ca N of Whiddy Is oil terminal. Whiddy East Point may be rounded close in, but islands in hbr are generally foul all round. Leave Horse Lt buoy Fl.G.6s to stb, Gurteenroe Lt buoy Fl.R.3s to port and Chapel Lt buoy Fl.G.3s to stb. In the area E of Whiddy Is beware of mussel rafts or lines of barrels with long floating mooring lines which are hard to see.

Entrance from W Use only in good conditions. Bar has only 1·7m and sometimes breaks. Outside bar, Cracker Rock has only 1·7m. On an easterly course steer towards Relane Point, keeping approximately 150m off shore. Turn on to about 063° when the S side of Reenbeg Point is in line with the HW mark on South Beach, passing S of Cracker Rock.

Anchorages and Berthing
• Bantry Marina, just inside the main town pier, has 40 berths, depth 3m. Contact Assistant HM.
• 7 visitors' pay per night moorings, contact AHM for details.
• 1ca NW of town pier; keep over 1ca from pier on N side (foul), but clear of fairway.
• About 3ca W of above, outside local yachts in 3·5m.
• 1ca SW of Rabbit Is in 2–3·5m; oyster fisheries inside Rabbit Is.

The first and second anchorages are subject to wash from Whiddy Is launches. With permission from AHM it may be possible to moor, for short periods in good weather, on outside of town pier. Beware of unlit oyster rafts in hbr and (Sept/Oct) shrimp pots. It is unsafe to pick up moorings without permission.

Facilities Water and electricity in marina. Petrol, diesel, engineers, some repairs. Good pubs, restaurants and hotels. Best shopping and transport centre on this coast. Bus to Cork, Glengariff, Castletownbere and (summer only) Kenmare, Killarney, Clonakilty.

☎ Assistant HM 027 53277, (mob) 087 9532777.

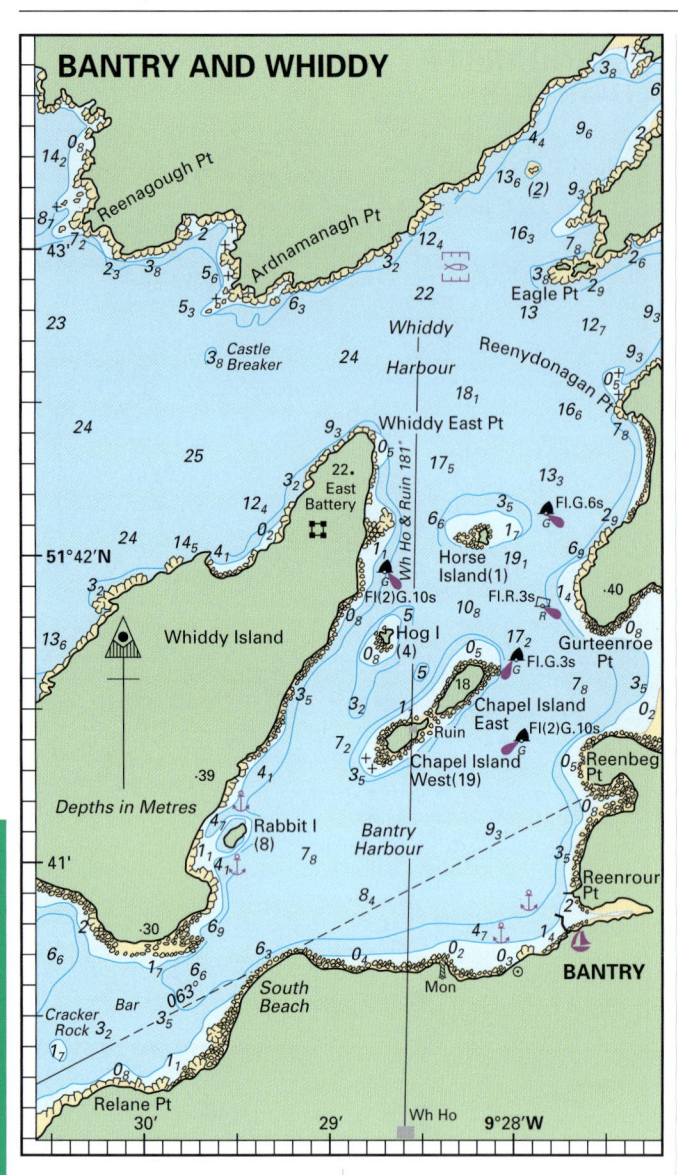

CROOKHAVEN

Standard Port Cobh
HW (sp) −0057 (np) −0033
LW (sp) −0112 (np) −0048

MHWS	MHWN	MLWN	MLWS
−0·8m	−0·6m	−0·4m	−0·1m

An excellent hbr which may be entered at all states of the tide and in all weathers. 2M long, 2ca wide, 10m depth at entrance, 3m off Crookhaven village, shoaling thence gradually to its head. Busy holiday town in summer.

Approach From the Fastnet Rock steer N to fetch the entrance. Beware salmon nets. Give Alderman Rocks and Black Horse Rocks, which extend ½M to E of Streek Head (the latter marked by N card QFl. bn), give both a good berth. Otherwise both shores are steep-to. Silting of the channel has been reported. Beware tidal set through Alderman Sound. Uncharted racing buoys in channel.

Entrance At night do not steer for the LtHo Fl.WR.8s at N point of entrance until R sector covering Alderman Rocks turns to W, then enter along N shore.

Anchorage Anchor abreast village in 3m. There is kelp in parts of this anchorage; holding otherwise good in sand and mud. In a SW blow some shelter can be found behind Granny Is. In E blow shelter to be found N of W point of Rock Is. Eight visitors' moorings.

Facilities Water from tap on pier, large dinghy pontoons, PO. Good pub with small shop and restaurant.

SCHULL

Standard Port Cobh
HW (sp) −0040 (np) −0015
LW (sp) −0110 (np) −0015

MHWS	MHWN	MLWN	MLWS
−0·9m	−0·6m	−0·2m	0·0m

The hbr is situated between Schull Pt and Cosheen Pt and is protected by Long Is and other islands from S. It affords good shelter and may be preferred to Crookhaven in W'ly or E'ly winds. However, it is untenable in a S gale and then shelter should be sought behind Long Is. Dig the anchor in well with engine to ensure that it is clear of kelp both in the hbr and Long Is channel. Heavy fishing boat traffic. Calves Regatta brings many boats.

Approach From S, when about 3ca S of Amelia Rock G Lt

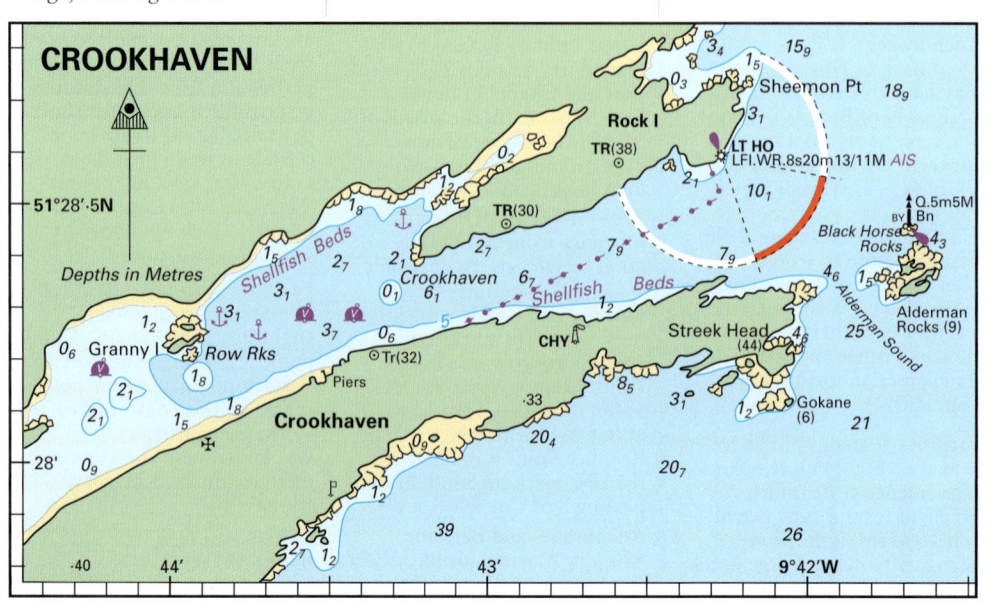

buoy Fl.G.3s marking the rocks W of Castle Is, steer 346° for entrance. From W, leave Cush Spit N card Lt buoy to stb, thence for entrance.

Entrance By day pass Bull Rock, dries at half-ebb, Lt bn Fl(2)R.6s. Pass on either side. W shore is then clear apart from Baker Rock 4·5ca N of Schull Point but E shore must be given a berth of at least 1ca. By night Ldg Lts Oc.5s lead 346° to E of Bull Rock. In season, beware salmon nets in approaches and fairway.

Anchorage To E and NE of pier but holding generally poor. Better clear of moorings to S of pier. But avoid track SSE of pier – fishing boat approach channel. Twelve visitors' moorings NNE of pier and S of pier.

Facilities Good shops, hotels, pubs and restaurants. Water from tap on pier. For fuel see HM. Chandlery and sail repairs.

BALTIMORE

Standard Port Cobh
HW (sp) –0025 (np) –0005
LW (sp) –0050 (np) –0010
MHWS MHWN MLWN MLWS
–0·6m –0·3m +0·1m +0·2m

Baltimore is a popular holiday village with a wide expanse of water providing a safe haven under virtually all conditions. The main entrance is open to the S, the other entrance through The Sound at the NW corner provides an alternative passage to Schull and Roaring Waters Bay.

Main Approach and Entrance
The position of hbr may be recognised by a conspic W tr called Lot's Wife on E Point of entrance, Beacon Point, and by the W LtHo Fl(2)WR.6s on Barrack Point, the W pt of entrance. S of the LtHo, give the W shore a berth of fully ¾ca to clear Wilson Rock, awash at HW.

Steer in 340° between entrance points and give the inner E entrance point, Loo Point, a berth of ¾ca, leaving Lt buoy Fl.G.3s marking Loo Rock, 0·2m, to stb. Steer N, leaving Quarry Rock, 2·1m, to stb until the North Pier comes open N of Connor Pt, 060° Leave G. con buoy Q.G. to stb.

Alternative Approach and Entrance to The Sound from N and W. There are two options, both need careful pilotage between islands and rocks. Charts SC 5623 or BA 2129 are recommended, the latter at the time of writing is still on OSI datum.

• Southerly passage between Hare Is and Sherkin Is. Aim to pass 1 ca N of Drowlaun Pt. Then keep SE of the transit Drowlaun Pt and Mt Lahan on E end of Cape Clear. This will lead to the SE of the isolated rock (1m at CD) shown on the plan about 2ca WSW of the Catalogue Is. Pass to the E of Two Women's Rock. Follow round the deep water channel until past Sanday Is when The Sound will open up leading into Baltimore hbr.

If heading for Baltimore village head SE leaving Lousy Rks (S card bn) clear to stb to join the main channel at Wallis Rk R can buoy.

If heading for the Platform and nearby pub/restaurant on the E side of Sherkin Is head S keeping at least 1½ca clear of the shore.

• The northerly option requires sufficient rise of tide, is shorter and more sheltered. From a position about 2ca south of the Amelia buoy, off Skull, steer approximately 070° leaving Castle Is to port and Horse Is no more than 1½ca to port. When the E end of East Skeam Is is abeam turn to approx 145° to pass E of Goose Is. Round Frolic Pt leaving the N card buoy, Taylor, close to stb. Steer to pass between Hare Is and the mainland keeping closer to the latter until S card buoy off Turks Hd is seen. Leave to port and join the channel as above written.

Anchorages
- N or W of North Pier.
- In Church Strand Bay beyond the RNLI slip, the safest place in gales – 'a hurricane hole'.
- Yachts can also berth alongside NW face of North Pier, 1·3m, for short periods in fine weather or at pontoon off S pier for a fee at pub.
- Off Skerkin Is under Dunalong Castle ruins. Yachts can berth alongside pontoon S of this point for a fee at pub.

Rocks Quarry Rock, 2·1m, lies 1¾ca 004° from Loo Point. Lousy Rocks, situated in the W centre of the hbr, dry, and are marked by a S card bn on the SE rock. Wallis Rock, 1·6m, in centre of the hbr, has a R can buoy SSE of the rock. Many rocks obstruct the NW shore of the hbr.

Facilities Water on N Pier. Chandler and small yard, PO, hotels, showers at Baltimore YC, general store, fuel, bus to Skibbereen, 8M. Good pub and restaurant on Sherkin Island.

CASTLEHAVEN

Standard Port Cobh
HW (sp) −0020 (np) −0030
LW (sp) −0050 (np) −0020

MHWS	MHWN	MLWN	MLWS
−0·4m	−0·2m	+0·1m	+0·3m

River inlet that can be entered at all states of tide and affords a protected and excellent anchorage in most weathers, with some swell in strong S or SW winds.

Approach Hbr lies 3M NE of Stag Rocks. Black Rock SE of Horse Island is clean but sea can be turbulent in strong winds. Give a clearance of 1ca.

Entrance Steer in midway between Horse Is to port and Skiddy Is to stb. A Lt Fl.WRG.10s9m5–3M is shown from W tr on Reen Point, and at night the W sector leads in. Continue heading for NE shore until the Stags open through Flea Sound, to port, which line clears Colonel Rock, 1m, on SE shore. In hazy weather keep in mid-channel.

Anchorages Anchor abreast of Castletownshend in 3m or lower down clear of fishing boats, which enter at night along SE shore. In SW winds excellent shelter will be found upstream just above the ruined fort and Cat Is. Slip at Castletownsend renovated. Dinghy access at all tides. Jetty on opposite shore repaired and vessels may be able to berth alongside for FW hose.

Facilities Water from hose on pier. One small shop. Good pubs and one excellent restaurant. Interesting church. The Castle Townsend right on the harbour is a B&B and café. Skibbereen, where all stores may be obtained, is 5M.

GLANDORE

Tidal data as Castlehaven

A picturesque haven with an active yacht club. Well sheltered from all except winds from SE when shelter may be found at Union Hall.

Approach The entrance lies between Goats Head on E and Sheela Point on W and is divided into two channels by Adam Is. From SW give High Is a berth of 1ca. From E there are no dangers on the direct course from a position S of Doolic Rock off Galley Head.

Entrance Between Adam Is and Goats Head giving Adam Is a wide berth, or between Adam Is and Sheela Point; then steer to

CROOKHAVEN TO CORK

Passage lights	BA No
Fastnet	5702
Fl.5s.49m27M	
Racon (G) (−−·) AIS	
Galley Head	5708
Fl(5)20s53m23M	
Old Hd Kinsale	5710
Fl(2)10s72m20M AIS	
Roche's Point	5718
Fl.WR.3s30m18/14M	

Tidal Streams All related to Dover. In general the streams up to 5M offshore change at nearly the same time from Crookhaven to Old Head of Kinsale: +0215 E-going stream −0400 W-going; spring rate 1 to 1·5kn, but 2–2·5kn off the Fastnet Rock and the main headlands. In Gascanane Sound: 0030SE; −0545NW. spring rate 3kn. Old Head of Kinsale to Cork Harbour: +0045E; −0500W.

The channel between Fastnet Rock and Cape Clear is free of dangers apart from a rock with 3m ¼M NE of Fastnet. Galley Head is fairly steep-to, but ½M WSW is Dhulic Rock, dries 3·4m, with Sunk Rock, less than 1·8m, 1·5ca to SSW of it. Tides set across Dhulic Rock and it must be given a wide berth.

With wind against tide there can be a bad sea close to Galley Head and to Seven Heads.

Off Old Head of Kinsale a potentially dangerous tide-race extends over 1M to SW on W-going stream, to SE on E-going stream. The race can be avoided by rounding the hd close up except in S winds or any strong winds; in these conditions give it a berth of over 2M.

pass close to E of Eve Is. Avoid Adam, hug Eve. Turn to port a little to pass midway between W shore and the Dangers, three separate rocks in the middle of the channel. The Outer Danger is marked by a bn Fl(2)G on its W side, and a R port perch, can topmark, on its E side. The Middle Danger and the Inner Danger are each marked by one perch G, con topmark. Sunk Rock, about 1ca N of the Inner Danger, is marked by a lit G con buoy Fl.G.5s. Strangers should not attempt to sail between the Dangers and should particularly note that the perches on the Outer Danger mark the ends of what is in effect one rock.

Anchorages
- In SW through N to E winds off Glandore pier in 2·5m; or secure to a visitors' buoy.
- In S or SE winds off Union Hall in 2·5m; give Coosaneigh Point a good berth to avoid mudbank extending 1ca from it.

There is a new, large fishing boat pier at Keelbeg, Union Hall, with a dredged channel to it. Yachts may berth for short periods and use the water hose.

Facilities Water at both piers. Provisions, small supermarket, fish store, and fuel at Union Hall. Good pubs with food in Glandore high up overlooking the hbr.

COURTMACSHERRY

Standard Port Cobh
HW −0016   LW −0012
MHWS   MHWN   MLWN   MLWS
−0·1m   −0·1m   0·0m   +0·1m

The entrance lies in the NW corner of the bay about 6M from Old Head of Kinsale. The Bar has only about 2m at LWS with constantly shifting sands. In strong to gale southerly to south-easterly winds seas break and the entrance should not be attempted. Otherwise, after half tide it is straightforward and, once inside, the hbr affords excellent shelter, has a picturesque charm and the unspoiled village is very welcoming.

Approach Hazards to avoid: Horse Rock, visible except HWS; Black Tom, marked by G con Lt buoy Fl.G.5s; Barrel Rock marked by unlit S card bn. Aim to leave Black Tom G con Lt buoy close to stb (*see appropriate chart*). At night enter on W sector of Wood Point Fl(2)WR.5s.

Entrance Make for close S of bar buoy, *Courtmacsherry*, Fl.G.3s, then steer approx due W for 5ca leaving the three lit G buoys close to stb. Turn to port at the lit R can buoy, stay close to the line of moored boats on the village side of the channel toward the quay at the village. For advice phone the 'Sea Anglers' ℡ 023 46427. HM ℡ +353 86 104 0812.

Anchorage Either just north of the moored boats, leaving room for the lifeboat to pass, or 100m WNW of the pontoon at the quay. Caution: The tide runs hard here and there is a range of 3·4m at springs.

Moorings Secure to the pontoon just west of the pier. There is ample depth at the pontoon all tides. One may be charged a berthing fee. Leave the down-stream end of the pontoon free for angling boats.

Facilities Cosy bars in close proximity to pier.

Fresh water tap and diesel on the quay by arrangement. Some stores. Other supplies from Timoleague 2M to the west.

KINSALE
See plan on next page

Standard Port Cobh
HW −0012   LW −0016
MHWS   MHWN   MLWN   MLWS
−0·2m   0·0m   +0·1m   +0·2m

Bar 3m, 2–3ca S of Charles Fort.

Approach From E keep outside the Bulman Rock S card Lt buoy off Preghane Point.

The hbr will then open up to N and when Charles Fort is visible between Money Pt and Preghane Pt, steer for it. At night the W sector of Charles Fort Lt Fl.WRG.5s leads in.

Entrance Keep in mid-channel and cross the bar S of Charles Fort. At night enter on the White sector 358°–004° Lt Fl.WRG.5s. The W side of the channel from the bar round Blockhouse Point to the town is marked by three R can Lt buoys (Fl(2)R.6s, Q.R & Fl(3)R.10s) which must be left to port.

Berthing
- At Kinsale YC marina N of Town Quay; visitors' berths on outer pontoon, but a finger berth inside marina may be available. Berthing controlled by marina supervisor.
- Anchor on bank N of James Fort, 2–4m.
- Anchor in river between Town Quay and br outside prohibited area.
- At Castlepark Marina on opposite bank.

Facilities Sailmaker, mechanic, boat repairs, chandlery in Skiberreen. Landing at Town Quay or on SE shore from Castlepark Marina. All stores, bus to Cork. EC Thurs. Cork airport 12M. Diesel available at Gibbons Quay and Castlepark marina, water at marina and pier head, electricity at marina. Showers, laundry, restaurant/bar and WiFi in YC. Many good restaurants. 'The Gourmet Capital of Ireland'. Interesting maritime museum. Museum of wine. Charles Fort is an exceptional star fort, via off-road walk along the hbr.

℡/VHF HM 021 4772503, VHF 14. Kinsale YC Marina 4773433, VHF 37. Castle Park Marina 4774959, VHF 06.

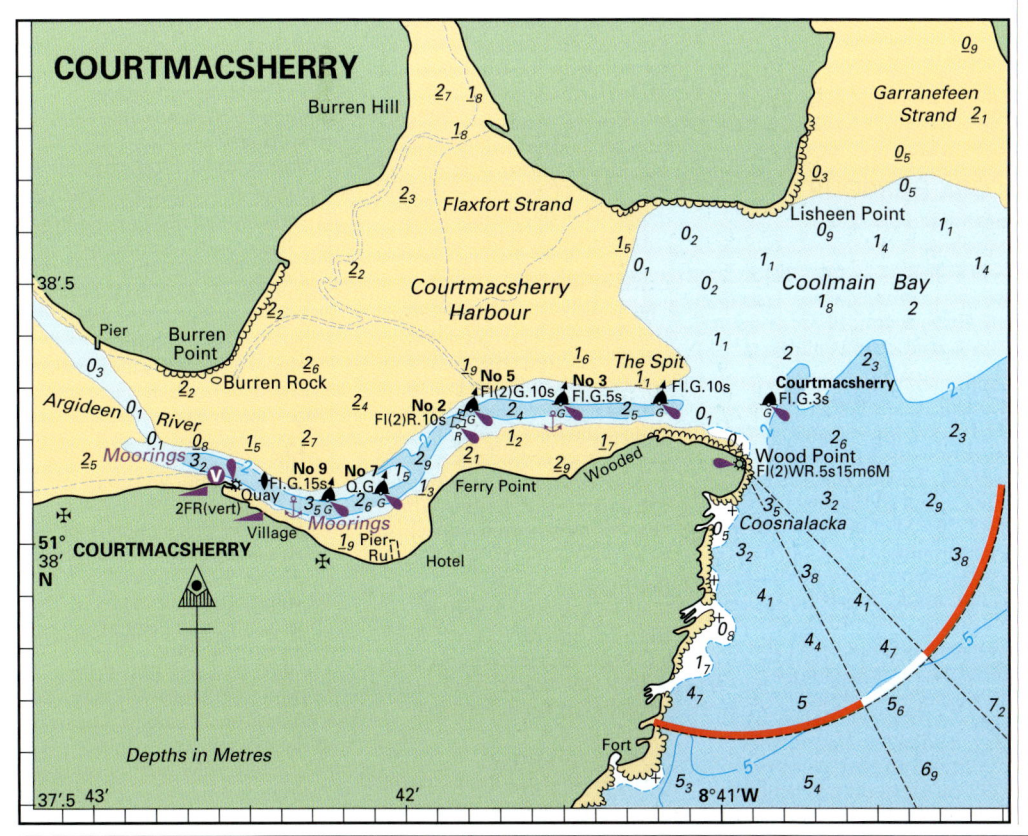

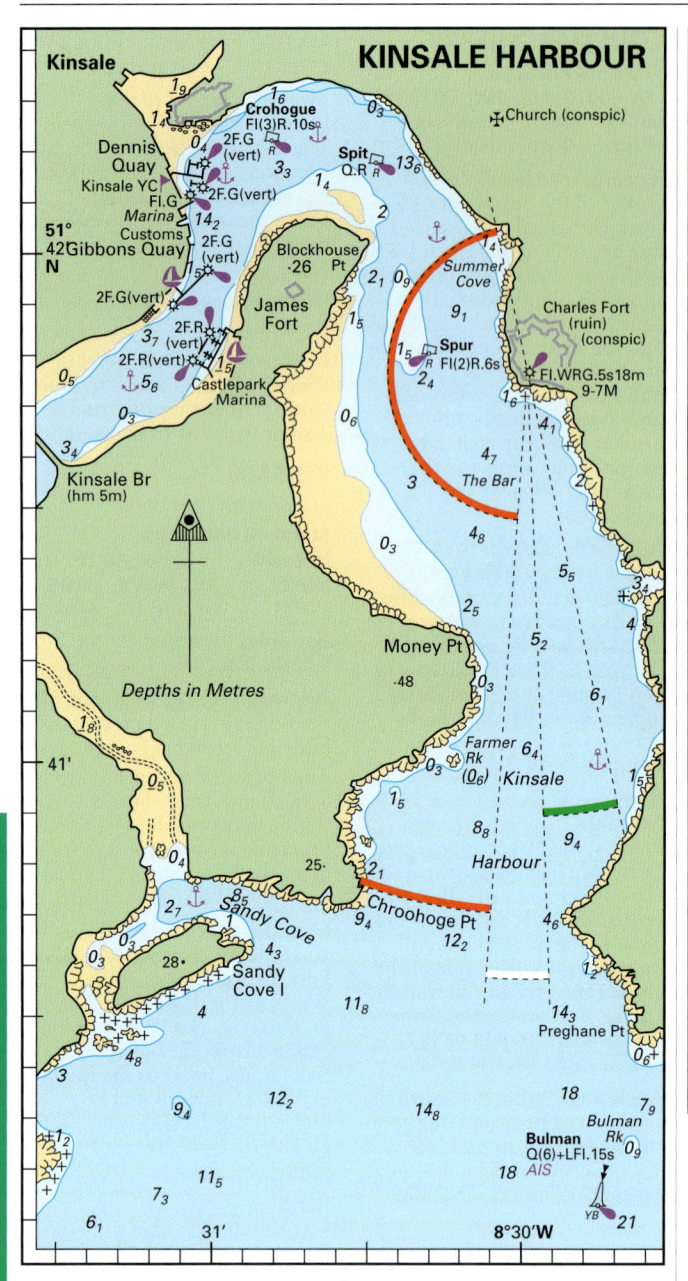

OYSTER HAVEN
Tidal data as Kinsale

A picturesque, quiet, safe hbr 2M E of Kinsale, where shelter can be found from all weathers bar the strongest of south winds.

Entrance Approach either side of Big Sovereign. In quiet weather or above half tide there is safe passage between Little Sovereign and the shore. Make for centre of entrance. Give Ballymacus Point on W of entrance a berth of at least ¾ca. Inside the haven Harbour Rock, 0·9m, is 1·5ca E of Ferry Point and must be passed on its W side. To clear, keep 'Big Sovereign' open of Kinure Point.

Anchorages
• N of Ferry Point midway between N and S shore in 4–6m, soft mud and weed. Keep Kinure Point on E side of entrance open of Ferry Point.
• In stronger southerly weather, clear of spring tides, better shelter can be found midstream in 2m 1½ca further up the W branch.
• In stronger SE'ly weather, in N branch of haven 5ca N by E of Kinure Point in 3m sand close to eastern shore. Scenery but no facilities.

CORK HARBOUR
Standard Port Cobh
Cork City
HW +0008   LW +0015
MHWS MHWN MLWN MLWS
+0·4m +0·4m +0·3m +0·2m
Hbr is accessible at all times.

Approach From Old Head of Kinsale, Cork RWVS buoy, Fl.10s, off the entrance to the port of Cork bears 058°, 12½M. Thence Roche's Point, the E point of the entrance, 001°, 4¾M. The approach is clear of obstruction for small craft excepting Daunt Rock, 3·5m, marked by R buoy Fl(2)R.6s, 7ca 140° from Roberts Head: to leave this to W bring the high tr E of Roche's Point LtHo on with tree clump in rear, 018°. By day, having left Daunt Rock about 4ca to port, a course 009° made good will lead into the entrance between Weaver Point and the LtHo. By night, a R sector from Roche's Point LtHo Fl.WR.3s covers Daunt Rock, and this sector should be shut in after passing Daunt Rock R can Lt buoy before rounding up for Roche's Point LtHo 016°.

In offshore winds, awaiting tide, anchorage will be found outside the entrance in Ringabella Bay. There are no dangers for small craft in the entrance to Cork Harbour.

Crosshaven
This is the main yachting centre. Round Rams Head at a distance of fully 2ca and steer for the G con Lt buoy Fl.G.10s C1 at entrance of Owenboy River. Follow the buoyed channel. In the entrance the tidal streams follow the bends, the flood and ebb streams setting into White bay. Silting reported, stay close to the buoys marking channel.

Berthing
Royal Cork YC W end of Marina. (Interest: Royal Cork YC is the oldest in the world). ✆ 021 483 1023.
Crosshaven Boat Yard In marina or ask for a mooring. ✆ 021 483 1161.
Salve Marine at long pontoon E of RCYC. Visitors' berths marked on upstream portion. Diesel by hose. ✆ 021 4831145.
• Anchor below Town Quay clear of telephone cables and out of busy fairway.
• Anchor beyond the bend ¾M up stream of the town in 3–5m. Good holding and peace, landing to road possible toward HW.
• Anchor above Drake's Pool.

Facilities Good supplies, all facilities. Small market and PO in village, pubs/restaurants (close early), sailmaker McWilliam Sails ✆ 021 4831505. Bus to Cork Airport. Ferry Port Ringaskiddy. Walking/cycle path along river to Carrigaline where there is a large supermarket.

Cobh
Follow main buoyed channel up the hbr.
• Anchor W of town clear of Fairway. Garage, shops, hotels, PO, bank. EC Wednesday.
Warning No yacht may approach within 50m of Whitegate oil jetty.
• In East Passage: **East Ferry Marina** S of Belgrove Quay.
• Anchor on W side to S or to E of Belgrove quay, 2–3m.
• On E side ½M further up East Passage 3–4m.

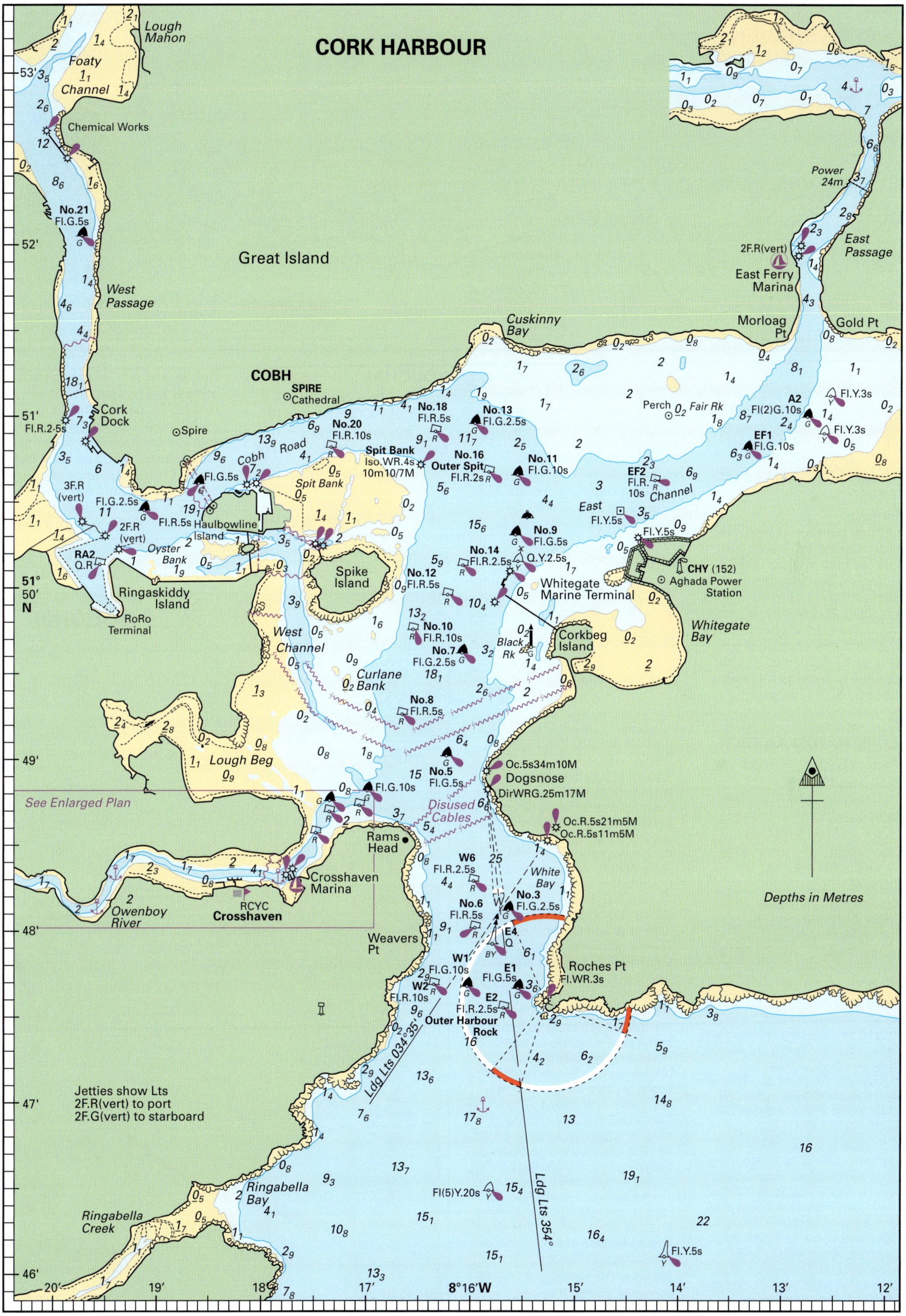
CORK HARBOUR
Great Island
Lough Mahon
Foaty Channel
Chemical Works
West Passage
COBH
SPIRE Cathedral
Spire
Cork Dock
Cobh Road
Spit Bank
Haulbowline Island
Oyster Bank
Ringaskiddy Island
RoRo Terminal
Spike Island
West Channel
Curlane Bank
Lough Beg
See Enlarged Plan
Crosshaven Marina
RCYC
Crosshaven
Owenboy River
Rams Head
Weavers Pt
Disused Cables
Dogsnose
Oc.5s34m10M
DirWRG.25m17M
Oc.R.5s21m5M
Oc.R.5s11m5M
White Bay
Roches Pt
Fl.WR.3s
Outer Harbour Rock
Ldg Lts 034·35°
Ldg Lts 354°
Ringabella Bay
Ringabella Creek
Jetties show Lts
2F.R(vert) to port
2F.G(vert) to starboard
Whitegate Marine Terminal
Corkbeg Island
Whitegate Bay
Black Rk
CHY (152)
Aghada Power Station
East Channel
Perch
Fair Rk
Cuskinny Bay
Morloag Pt
Gold Pt
East Ferry Marina
East Passage
Power 24m
Depths in Metres
No.21 Fl.G.5s
No.18 Fl.R.5s
No.20 Fl.R.10s
No.13 Fl.G.2.5s
No.16 Outer Spit Fl.R.2s
Spit Bank Iso.WR.4s 10m10/7M
No.11 Fl.G.10s
No.9 Fl.G.5s
No.14 Fl.R.2.5s
No.12 Fl.R.5s
No.10 Fl.R.10s
No.7 Fl.G.2.5s
No.8 Fl.R.5s
No.5 Fl.G.5s
No.6 Fl.R.5s
No.3 Fl.G.2.5s
W6 Fl.R.2.5s
W1 Fl.G.10s
W2 Fl.R.10s
E1 Fl.G.5s
E2 Fl.R.2.5s
E4 Q
A2 Fl(2)G.10s
EF1 Fl.G.10s
EF2 Fl.R.10s
RA2 Q.R
Fl(5)Y.20s
53'
52'
51'
51° 50' N
49'
48'
47'
46'
20'
19'
18'
17'
8°16'W
15'
14'
13'
12'

IRELAND

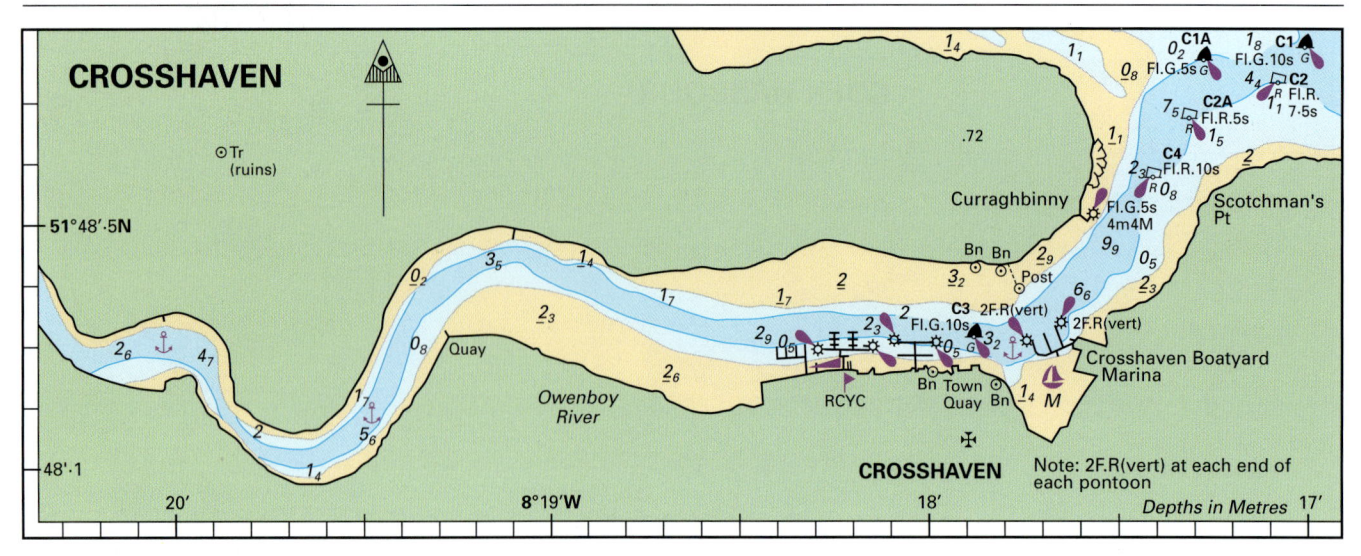

Cork

Cork is the second largest city in the Republic of Ireland and has all facilities including customs, rail to Dublin, international airport and ferry (from Ringaskiddy) to Swansea and France.

Berthing

- A large pontoon (150m) has been installed for leisure craft at Custom House Quay in the centre of Cork City. It is for day visits and short term stays (max 6 nights). Access is by security-coded locks. Inside berths for draft of 2.5m. Outside berths have up to 4m depth. Double banking is permitted. Contact HM 021 427 3125 M-F 0900–1700. Outside hrs contact Tivoli Security 021 453 0466. Water, power available for fee on request. Waste bin and recycling.
- Cork Hbr Marina (Monkstown) 90 berths, all facilities, chandlery, repair. Max. 17m. ☎ 087 366 9009. Restaurants, pubs nearby. Bus service.

Facilities

- Cork Int. Airport is 10 minutes from Crosshaven, 20 minutes from Cork. All rental cars there.
- Irish Rail hub. Ferries to France.
- Cork Hbr Radio, VHF 12, ☎ 021 4811380

CORK TO TUSKAR ROCK

Passage lights	BA No.
Mine Head Fl(4)30s87m12M AIS	5778
Ballycotton Fl.WR.10s59m18/14M AIS	5774
Hook Head Fl.3s46m18M AIS Racon(K) (-·-)	5798
Coningbeg S card buoy Q(6)+LFl.15s9M Racon(M) (--) AIS	5832
Tuskar Rock Q(2)7·5s33m24M Racon(T) (-) AIS	5838

Tidal Streams All related to Dover. Cork to Waterford less than 0·5kn starting progressively later towards Waterford where they begin +0530ENE; –0100WSW. Between the Saltees and Carnsore Point +0515ENE, spring rate 2·4kn; –0045WSW, spring rate 2·6kn.

Off Hook Head there is a dangerous tidal race extending 1M S of the Head, especially in strong westerlies. To avoid this race keep outside the 20m line. The passage between the Tuskar Rock and Carnsore Point can become very rough in bad weather. Dangerously so in strong SW wind against tide and should be avoided.

E of Hook Head, Baginbun and Bannow Bays though exposed to SE give good shelter from W'lies. The recommended offshore anchorage is at the SW end of Bannow Bay just N of Ingard Point.

A yacht proceeding from Waterford to the E coast has the choice of the offshore or inshore passage. Using the offshore passage keep well clear of the dangerous rocks extending some 4M SW through S to E of Great Saltee, marked by the Conningbeg S card buoy (52°03'·12N 6°38'·57W) together with lit W and E card buoys. Thence go to a position S of South Rock Lt buoy, S card, and pass E of the Tuskar Rock giving it a good berth as the tide sets on to it, but avoiding the TSS.

For the inshore passage, pass between the Saltees or north of them through St Patrick's Bridge marked by G & R Lt buoys Fl.6s. There are two dangerous rocks and a wreck some 2M SW of Carnsore Point. In anything other than fair weather it would be wise to pass S of the buoys guarding them. Black Rock S card Lt and Barrels E card Lt. Then either S of South Rock, S card Lt and ½M E of Tuskar Rock Lt. Or in fair weather 1½M W of Tuskar. Beware of poorly marked fishing gear in this area.

Warning The sea area off the SE corner of Ireland is to be avoided in bad weather especially wind against tide in the channel between the Tuskar Rock and Carnsore Point.

YOUGHAL

Standard Port Cobh
HW (sp) +0000 (np) +0010
LW (sp) +0000 (np) +0010

MHWS	MHWN	MLWN	MLWS
–0·2m	–0·1m	–0·1m	–0·1m

Youghal is an historic town just inside the Blackwater River estuary. Well protected, careful navigation required. Tidal stream in entrance can reach 3kn at springs.

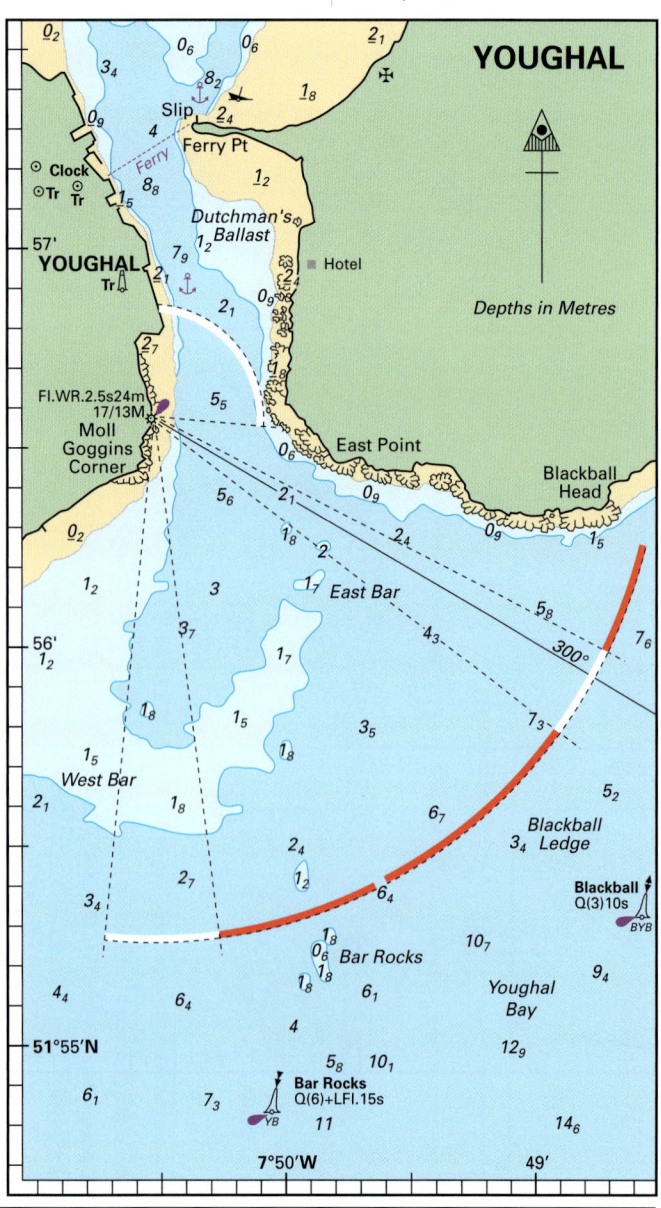

Bar Should not be attempted in a big sea. The approach is divided by Bar Rocks, 0·6m and Blackball Ledge, 3·4m, into two channels, East Bar having least depth 2·8m, and West Bar, 1·8m. Over E Bar one may expect less sea and less stream. Strong E and S winds cause a heavy and dangerous sea in the bay. N winds reduce the tidal rise, and SW gales cause a swell inside; the ebb sets on to the W bar. Best approach is round Black Ball E card Lt buoy.

Approach From W, using the W bar channel, leave Bar Rocks S card Lt buoy marking Bar Rocks 0·6m about 2ca to stb, then steer direct for the entrance, about N.

Using E Bar channel, coming from S, leave Blackball Ledge E card Lt buoy to port.

From E, steer for LtHo Fl.WR.2·5s when it comes well open of Blackball Head and bears about 300°. Give East Point 1½ca offing before bearing round into the hbr.

Entrance Having passed the LtHo, keep in towards the W shore. The E side of entrance on a transit between East Point and Ferry Point is shoal. Streams run hard between LtHo and Ferry Point.

Anchorages
• On a 3m bank off the most N'ly warehouse.
• In 2–4m N of Ferry Point.
• Off market clock.
• ENE of clock, abeam of a building with conspic circular balconies, outside moorings in 2m LWS.
• N of LB slip off small landing beach.

Caution Depths continually changing in hbr.

Facilities Shops, PO, banks, pubs, hotels, restaurants. Boat yard for repairs to hull and machinery. Chandlery, electronics. Bus to Cork.

DUNGARVAN

Standard Port Cobh
HW (sp) +0004 (np) +0012
LW (sp) −0001 (np) +0007
MHWS MHWN MLWN MLWS
0·0m +0·1m −0·2m 0·0m

A large and attractive expanse of open water, much of it drying, sheltered from winds from N through W to S.

Approach between Helvick head to the S and Ballynacourty Point to the N. Between these lie three hazards: midway *Carrickpane*, always showing at least 2m, 5ca to its SSW, Helvick Rk guarded by *Helvick E Card* buoy Q(3)10s, and 2½ca W of the buoy a foul rocky area *The Gainers*.

Entrance
• Dungarvan Harbour. Give *Carrickpane* a good berth to port and make for a position 2½ca south of Ballynacourty Light. At night enter in the W sector (274°–302°), but move to south when closing the light. Then steer 300° until identifying the buoyed channel which leads to Dungarvan town hbr. In the channel from Wyse's Point to Abbey Point at half tide there should be at least 1·8m between the buoys. Follow round Abbey point to stb to reach the town quay.
• Helvick Harbour. Go to Helvick Head then west along the coast for ½M.

Mooring and Anchorage
• Dungarvan town: Port side to, as the ebb runs strongly, alongside the club pontoon or alongside the quay but take soundings and be prepared to take the ground at LWS. Anchor in a deep hole NW of Cunnigar Point (at the N end of the long sand spit) but caution, sp tide runs at 2·5kn.
• Helvick: There are eight Y visitors' moorings NW of the hbr or inside the N pier if it is not occupied by fishing vessels. Anchor anywhere convenient N or NW of the hbr in more than 2m.

Facilities Dungarvan all supplies. Water on pontoon. Fuel from garage. Good pubs, hotels and restaurants. Showers at SC.

WATERFORD

Standard Port Cobh
Dunmore East
HW (sp) +0008 (np) +0003
LW (sp) +0000 (np) +0000
MHWS MHWN MLWN MLWS
+0·1m 0·0m +0·1m +0·2m

Cheek Pt
HW (sp) +0026 (np) +0021
LW (sp) +0022 (np) +0019
MHWS MHWN MLWN MLWS
+0·5m +0·4m +0·3m +0·2m

Waterford
HW (sp) +0053 (np) +0032
LW (sp) +0100 (np) +0015
MHWS MHWN MLWN MLWS
+0·6m +0·6m +0·4m +0·2m

The Port of Waterford, up the River Suir, is a busy commercial port 15M from Dunmore East. Waterford is a significant city with visitors' pontoons at its centre. Tides can be a major factor in the transit up river.

Approach The entrance, some 2M wide, lies between Swines Head (ht 60m) and Hook Head, long and low lying, with conspic squat LtHo Fl.3s.

Coming from the west in hazy weather, don't confuse it with Tramore Bay, which has three white towers at its W end and two on the E end. Beware of the drying Falskirt Rk (covers at flood) which lies 2ca S of Swines Hd.

From the E, give Hook Head a wide berth, especially in strong W'ly weather. In wind over tide conditions, a dangerous race can extend for 1M to the S. This race can be violent when the outgoing stream meets the west-going tide.

Dunmore East

A picturesque village on W side of the entrance with artificial fishing hbr, entrance facing NNW. With strong SE'ly winds a swell can set into the hbr. Pontoon berthing at N end of East Pier, electricity, showers, laundry, diesel if tanker is supplying a fishing boat. Private moorings may be available (YC ☎ 051 83230); alternatively anchor to N of the moorings.

Prior to arrival, contact HM ☎ 087 7931705 or VHF 12.

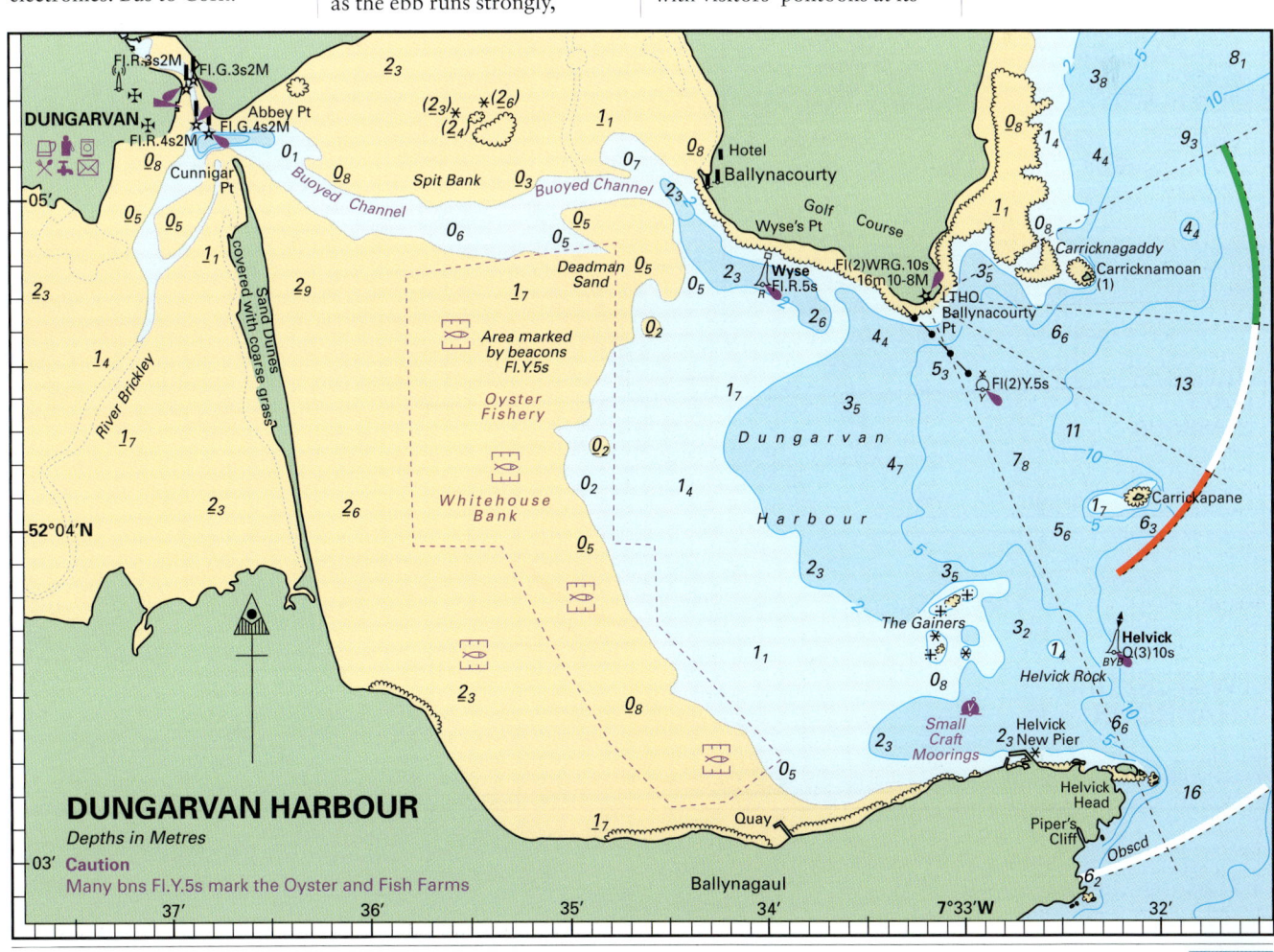

IRELAND

DUNGARVAN HARBOUR
Depths in Metres
Caution
Many bns Fl.Y.5s mark the Oyster and Fish Farms

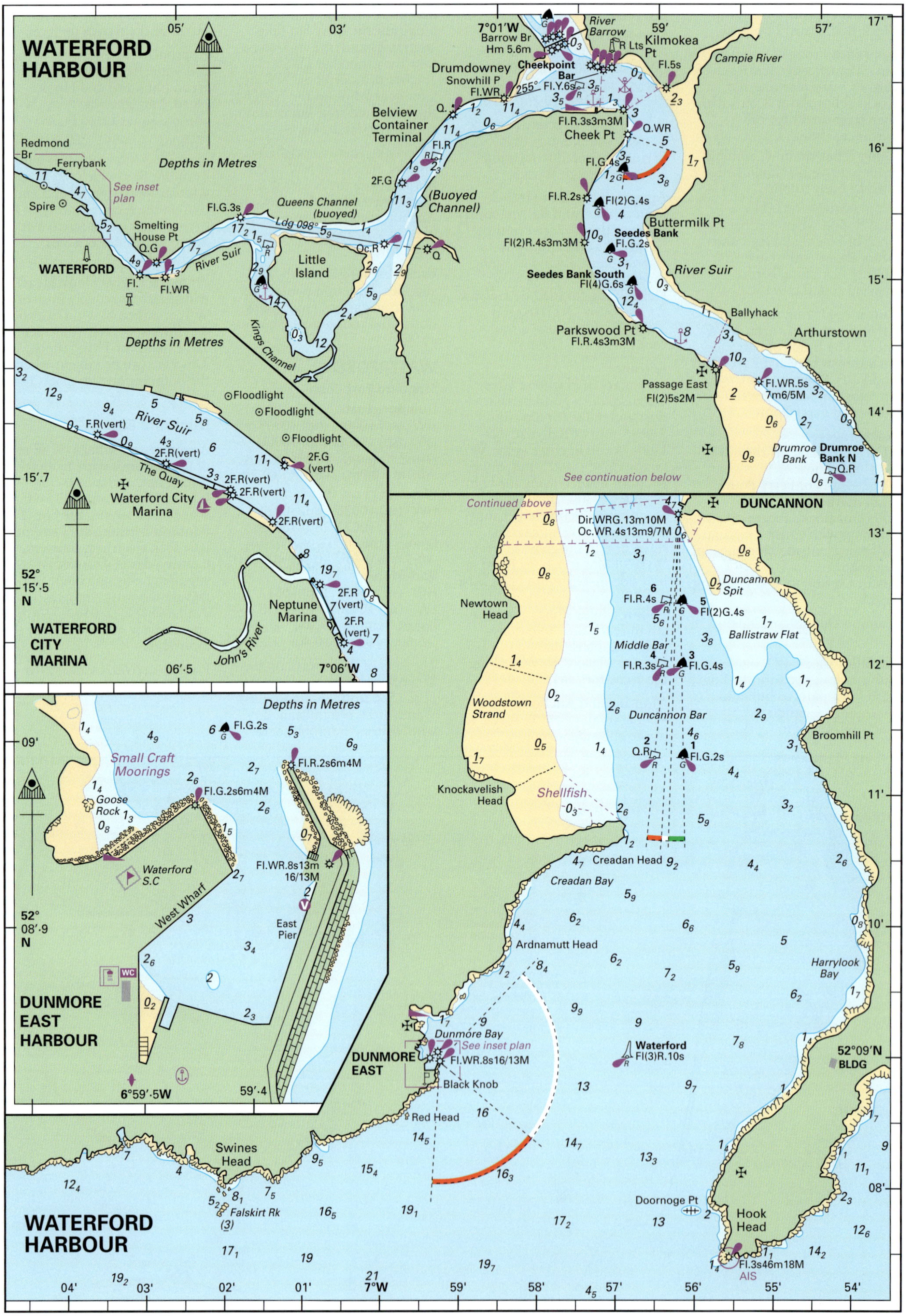
WATERFORD HARBOUR
Depths in Metres
Redmond Br
Ferrybank
See inset plan
Spire
Smelting House Pt
Q.G
WATERFORD
Fl.
Fl.WR
River Suir
Fl.G.3s
Queens Channel (buoyed)
Ldg 098°
Oc.R
Q
Little Island
Kings Channel
2F.G
Fl.R
Belview Container Terminal
(Buoyed Channel)
Q.
Drumdowney
Snowhill P
Fl.WR.
255°
7°01'W
Barrow Br Hm 5.6m
Cheekpoint Bar
Fl.Y.6s
River Barrow
R Lts
Kilmokea Pt
Fl.5s
Campie River
Fl.R.3s3m3M
Q.WR
Cheek Pt
Fl.G.4s
Fl.R.2s
Fl(2)G.4s
Buttermilk Pt
Seedes Bank
Fl.G.2s
Fl(2)R.4s3m3M
River Suir
Seedes Bank South
Fl(4)G.6s
Ballyhack
Arthurstown
Parkswood Pt
Fl.R.4s3m3M
Passage East
Fl(2)5s2M
Fl.WR.5s 7m6/5M
Drumroe Bank
Drumroe Bank N
Q.R
See continuation below
05'
03'
59'
57'
17'
16'
15'
14'
Depths in Metres
Floodlight
Floodlight
Floodlight
River Suir
F.R(vert)
2F.R(vert)
2F.G (vert)
The Quay
2F.R(vert)
2F.R(vert)
Waterford City Marina
2F.R(vert)
15'.7
52° 15'.5 N
Neptune Marina
2F.R (vert)
2F.R (vert)
John's River
WATERFORD CITY MARINA
06'.5
7°06'W
Depths in Metres
Fl.G.2s
Small Craft Moorings
Goose Rock
Fl.G.2s6m4M
Fl.R.2s6m4M
Waterford S.C
Fl.WR.8s13m 16/13M
West Wharf
East Pier
WC
09'
52° 08'.9 N
DUNMORE EAST HARBOUR
6°59'.5W
59'.4
Continued above
DUNCANNON
Dir.WRG.13m10M
Oc.WR.4s13m9/7M
13'
Newtown Head
Fl.R.4s
Fl(2)G.4s
Duncannon Spit
Ballistraw Flat
Middle Bar
Fl.R.3s
Fl.G.4s
12'
Woodstown Strand
Duncannon Bar
Q.R
Fl.G.2s
Broomhill Pt
11'
Knockavelish Head
Shellfish
Creadan Head
Creadan Bay
Ardnamutt Head
10'
Harrylook Bay
Dunmore Bay
See inset plan
DUNMORE EAST
Fl.WR.8s16/13M
Waterford
Fl(3)R.10s
52°09'N
BLDG
Black Knob
Red Head
Swines Head
Falskirt Rk
Doornoge Pt
Hook Head
Fl.3s46m18M
AIS
08'
WATERFORD HARBOUR
04'
03'
02'
01'
7°W
59'
58'
57'
56'
55'
54'

IRELAND

Duncannon Bar and R.Suir

Below the Bar the ebb follows the E side and the flood the W side. The bar is well marked by lit lateral buoys and a Dir.WRG sectored light. The R Suir up to Waterford and the Barrow to New Ross both have 4m. After Cheek Point keep towards the N side, heading towards Snowhill Pt; by night pick up the R Suir Ldg Lts over Cheek Pt bar. The N side is industrial with several wharves. At the junction of the Queen's and King's Channels, take the buoyed, northerly Queen's channel.

Anchorages
- Just above Ballyhack Ferry ramp in 5m, close in and out of the stream.
- In the W side of the King's Channel just N of the W bank ferry ramp. Approach only from the N as there is no passage through the ferry wires. Silting has been reported.

Waterford City Marina

Convenient for visiting city. Secure 370m pontoon 5ca below lifting bridge. Visiting yachts are advised to call in advance for berthing arrangements, usually Pontoon C. Beware strong tide. Moor both sides. Minimum depth outside 2m. Access gate by mobile phone system; contact the Marina Superintendent on ☎ 087 2384944 (available 24h) in order to be set up on the security gate access system. Water, electricity, showers and laundry. Diesel from garage.

New Ross & River Barrow

The Barrow swing bridge has 7m clearance, opens as required. After passing the Ballyhack ferry, call ☎ 086 816 7826 to confirm your ETA at the bridge. Enter E side, leave W side. When 6M upstream from the br, the channel is very narrow & buoyed. Steer mid way between the W bank and the G buoys.

Berthing The Three Sisters marina on the E bank at New Ross, 9M from the Barrow Br offers 10 fully serviced visitors' berths, showers etc at Marina Office, nearby boat lift-out, diesel from adjacent local garage. Visitors should initially berth on the hammerheads. Marina ☎ 086 3889652 or 087 1474158.

Anchorage S of town on E side or at Marsh Pt 2M downstream.

KILMORE QUAY

Standard Port Cobh
HW (sp) +0019 (np) +0009
LW (sp) +0006 (np) −0004

MHWS	MHWN	MLWN	MLWS
−0·3m	−0·4m	+0·2m	+0·2m

Visiting yachts are welcome. Kilmore Quay is a pleasant village, the small fishing hbr providing excellent shelter to a 55 berth marina (20 visitors') in the north of the hbr. Dredged 3m. A good arrival port from Lands End, Scillies or S Wales.

Approach Large scale chart such as BA2049, SC5261; Imray C57, 2700 recommended. Keep a sharp lookout for fishermen's buoys on long floating lines. Hbr entrance exposed to SE and approach could be dangerous in strong SE'ly winds, particularly toward HW. Approach from RW safewater buoy 4ca west of St Patrick's Br, marked by port and stb Lt buoys Fl.R & G.6s. Sight Ldg marks, white with red stripe, on foreshore (Oc.4s by night) bearing 008°. Follow ldg line, tide sets strongly east local HW±0300.

Entrance Approaching hbr entrance depth is 1·1m CD, reported to be silting, shoaling steeply either side, keep within 30m of western breakwater then turn to port to leave it and the south quay to port. Once past the east pierhead bear round to stb towards the marina. By night the breakwater light shows sectored Lt. Q 269°-R-354°-G-003°-R-077°.

Ireland – East Coast

CARNSORE POINT TO DUBLIN BAY

Passage lights	BA No
Arklow S Superbuoy	5845
Q(6)+LFl.15s AIS	
Racon(O) (– – –)	
Wicklow Head	5850
Fl(3)15s37m23M	
Kish Bank Lt Tower	5865
Fl(2)20s29m21M	
Racon(T) (–) AIS	
Dun Laoghaire	5872
Fl(2)R.8s16m17M	
(E breakwater)	

Tidal Streams DS (related to Dover) in middle of St George's Channel – +0600NE; HWD SW. Outside Tuskar Rock −0530 NE; HWD SW, 2·5kn; there is a strong set onto the rock. Streams change about 1½hrs earlier between the Irish banks and the shore. They set across these banks. From Land's End it can be dangerous to come in W of the Tuskar Rock, but coming from the W yachts need not leave this rock to port in settled weather.

At night, the passage from Carnsore Point to Rosslare should only be attempted with care and competent navigation. Rosslare is not a comfortable harbour for yachts but, if need be, a berth may be found alongside a fishing boat at the quay west of the ferry terminals. From Tuskar to Dublin Bay the normal route is outside the Blackwater bank, inside the Arklow Superbuoy, thence past Wicklow Head and through Dalkey Sound, quite clean except close to island side, or through Muglins Sound, but this has rocks with under 2m on each side. By night go outside Muglins Lt Fl.5s14m11M. A good lookout should be kept for fishing gear on the passage inside the Kish banks.

Keep away from **Arklow Bank**, a dangerous shallow ridge with seven windfarm turbines Fl.Y.5s14m10M. Approaching Dublin Bay from E make Kish Bank Lt F, thence to S Burford S card Lt buoy, leaving N Kish N card Lt buoy to port. In Dublin Bay, yachts are required to yield clear channel to commercial shipping.

Berthing On the hammerheads, unless allocated a finger berth by HM.

Facilities Fuel – low sulphur gas-oil at 24/7 self-service pump with card payment, gas, good chandlery and hardware store. Two mini-supermarkets. Restaurants and pubs. Toilets and showers at Harbour Office.

☎/VHF HM +353 53 9129955 mob +353 87 9001037; VHF 09.

(Kilmore Quay HM is also HM for Rosslare and Wexford.)

For passage notes Milford Haven to Kilmore Quay see p.188.

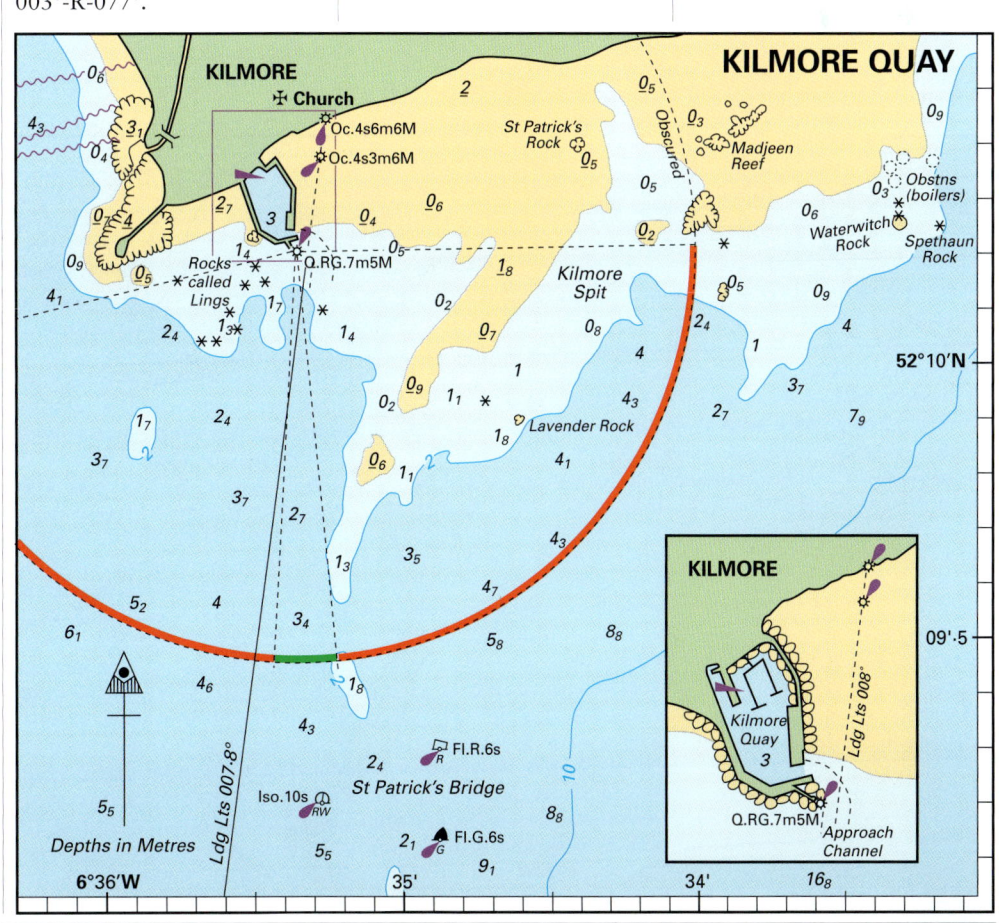

ROSSLARE

Not suitable for yachts and should only be used in emergency.

The only place to moor is at the quay furthest west from the ferry terminal. This is used by fishing boats and small commercial vessels so yachts should not be left un-attended. Uncomfortable in strong NE'lies.

☎ As Kilmore Quay, HM 053 9129955.

WEXFORD HARBOUR

Standard Port Cobh
HW +0126 (approx)

MHWS	MHWN	MLWN	MLWS
–2·1m	–1·8m	–0·4m	+0·1m

Once entered, this hbr is completely safe, sheltered and charming but route in is circuitous. The approach and entry channel are well marked, but subject to change. Before entry, contact Wexford Boating Club or HM for latest information on depths.
A Harbour Navigation App is available at
www.wexfordharbour.com.
This provides the latest positions of the buoyage. The one printed below should not be relied on in detail.

Approach Dangerous in strong winds between S and E. Otherwise make for Wexford Bar, a RW safewater Lt buoy LFl.10s, approx position 52°19'·2N 6°19'·4W. From the N keep outside the 5m contour to avoid the Dogger Bank and the unmarked dangerous Slaney wreck which lies 8ca NW of Bar Buoy.

Entrance It is essential to find the bar buoy. The channel is marked with lateral lit buoys; head for No.2 (R can) about 7ca to the WNW, then follow the R and G buoys which may not agree with the plan, to 52°20'·13N 6°26'·8W to the S of the Black Man, a lit stb bn marking the end of the training wall which covers. Thereafter the water is deep to the quay. Buoys No.2 to No.8 are removed in the winter.

Berthing Four visitors' moorings marked 'Bank of Ireland' opposite Town Quay. Berthing against town quay not recommended; anchoring the other side of the channel is comfortable.

Facilities Good shops, restaurants, boatyard, YC, fuel and water along the quays. Free WiFi broadband throughout the town.

☎/VHF HM 053 9122300 (occas), alternative 053 912995 or VHF 16 (occas): Wexford Boating Club 053 9147504 (office hrs), 053 9122039 (evening or weekend) VHF 16, 69: John Sherwood, Rosslare 053 9122875 (shop hrs) or 9122713 (home).

ARKLOW

Standard Port Dublin
HW (sp) –0315 (np) –0242
LW (sp) –0138 (np) –0158

MHWS	MHWN	MLWN	MLWS
–2·8m	–2·4m	–0·5m	0·0m

Bar and river to marina dredged to not less than 3·5m. Note very small tidal range.

Entrance Narrow and difficult under sail. Dangerous in gales from N through E to SE. S pierhead has 10m steel Tr, Fl.WR.6s11m13M. N pierhead Lt Fl.G.7s. Beware of small breakwater groynes on inside of S Pier to stop swell running up the hbr. Each is marked by a lit bn F.R.

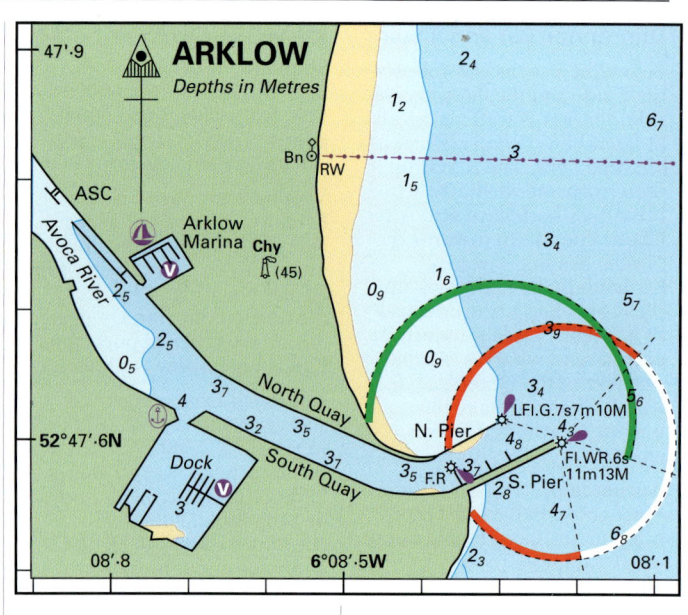

Berthing The dock on S side with 10m wide entrance provides perfect shelter. There is a T shaped pontoon with 20 finger berths for yachts up to 12m LOA. Average depth is 3m. Wheelchair accessible gangway. Security gate on gangway. Water and electricity (with a card) but as yet no toilets or showers.

1ca NW of the dock entrance through a gap in the NE quay there is access to a small marina with visitors' berths, toilets and showers. Beyond this, on the NE side there is a long visitors' pontoon. Depth is approx 2·5m on the NE side of the river as far as ASC premises. River subject to silting.

Facilities include engineers, shops in town, showers at marina. Good pubs and restaurants.

☎ Harbour Office 0402 32466; Marina 087 2588078

WICKLOW

Standard Port Dublin
HW –0019   LW –0137

MHWS	MHWN	MLWN	MLWS
–2·7m	–2·2m	–0·6m	–0·1m

The hbr faces N and is exposed in NE winds; inner part offers complete shelter. In very strong NE to E winds port may be closed.

Approach Pass between West pier head Iso.G.4s and East pier head Fl.WR.5s.

Entrance For inner harbour steer SSE between outer piers towards W boathouse; when face of ferry quay opens turn sharp to stb. Keep front of

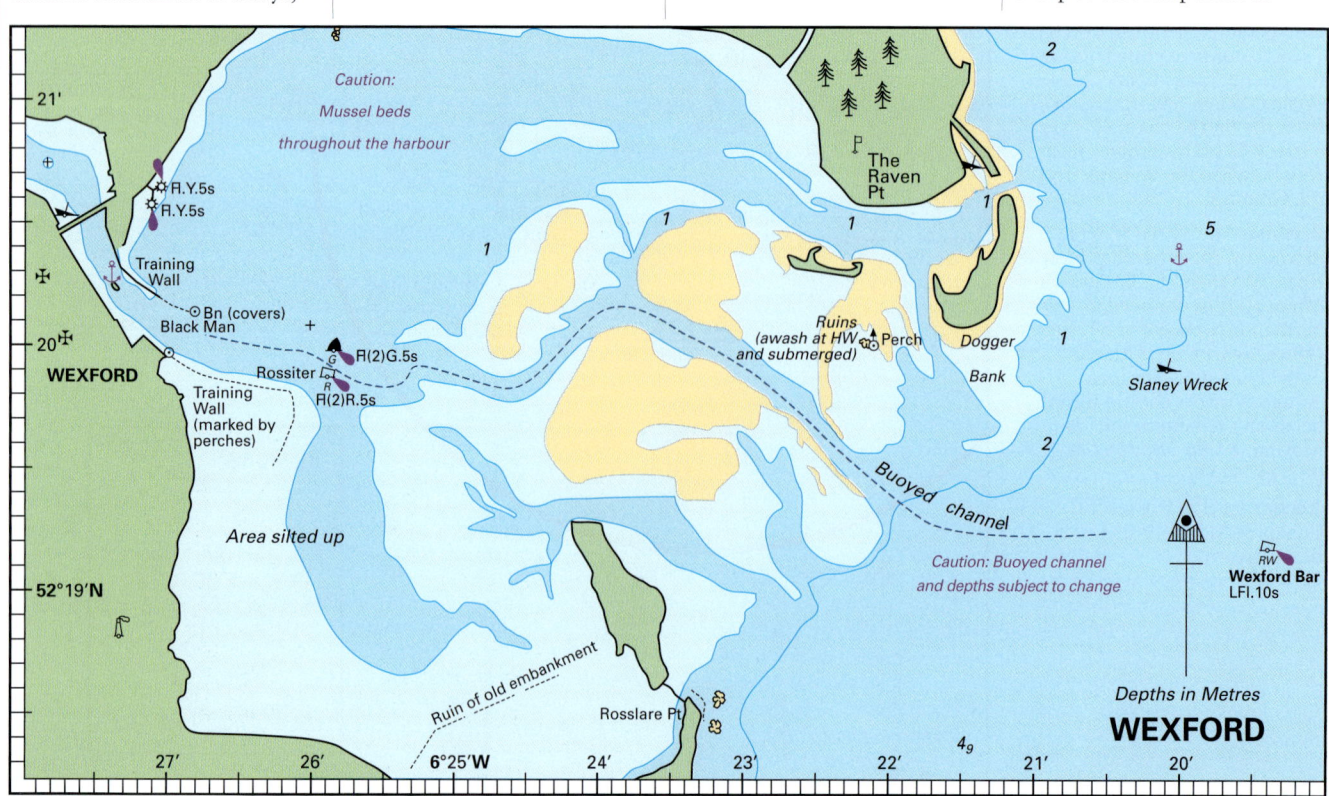

216

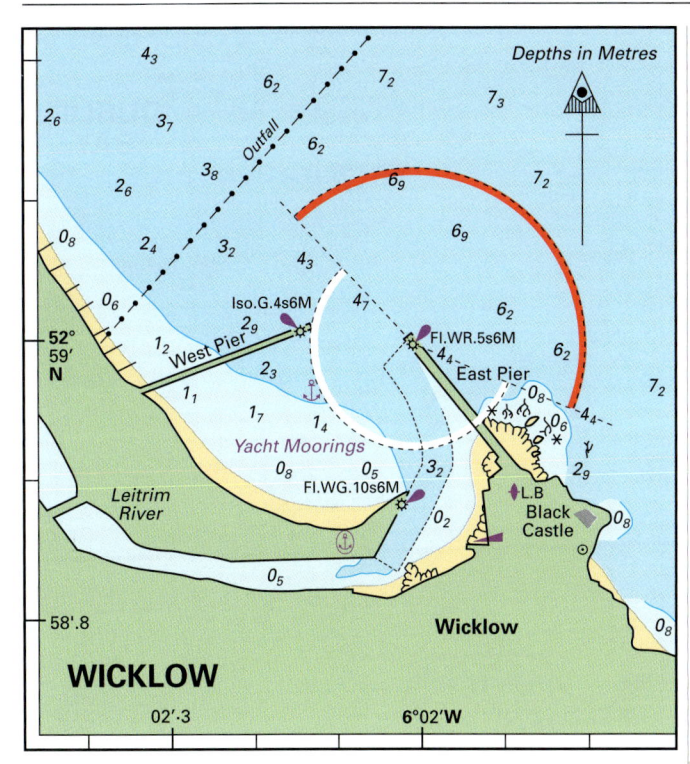

RNLI boathouse open to avoid shallows on SE side.

Berthing
- Anchorage in outer harbour midway between ends of W pier and quay in 2–3m outside YC moorings.
- In inner harbour the S side is being developed for use by fishing boats and yachts; if the quays there are not available a yacht may go alongside the steamer quay, beyond knuckle, with permission from HM – office in middle of pier. VHF 14.
- Moor against climbing frames on inside of East pier.

Facilities Fuel and water on S quay. All stores and facilities except sailmaker. EC Thursday.

GREYSTONES

Standard Port Dublin
HW (sp) –0008 (np) –0008
LW (sp) –0008 (np) –0008
MHWS MHWN MLWN MLWS
–0·5m –0·4m n/a n/a

This new, harbour marina is within the larger, formerly commercial, harbour, 11M N of Wicklow Hd. It offers perfect shelter from all disturbance of the open sea and is under the lee of the spectacular Wicklow Mountains. A comfortable berth for vessels between 6m and 30m is assured.

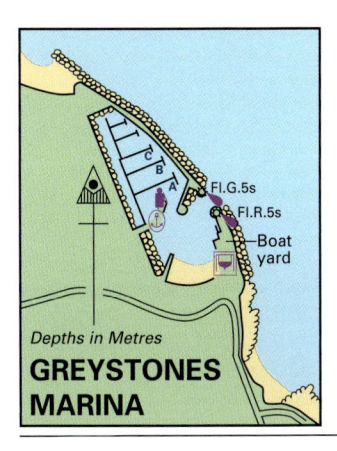

Approach The marina harbour entrance is at 53°09'·10N 6°03'·85W. From north along the clean coast from Bray Head. From south it lies some 2M NW from the offshore Moulditch Bank R can buoy, Fl.R.10s. When 1M distant call the marina office for berthing instruction.

Entrance Marked by beacons either side, Fl.G.5s and Fl.R.5s.

Berthing On entry give the breakwater a clearance as you bear round to stb. Pontoon 'A' will be seen ahead. Proceed as instructed to your allocated berth.

Facilities 25t travel hoist. The small town offers all that may be needed. Shops, supermarkets, cafés, inns and excellent restaurants. Fast road and rail connection to Dublin and to southward. Tours of the magnificent Wicklow mountains and walks along the spectacular coast.

☎/VHF Marina VHF 80, 37/M and 16; +353 (0)1 2873131, Mobile +353 (0)86 2718161; www.greystonesharbourmarina.ie

DUN LAOGHAIRE

Tidal data as **Standard Port** Dublin

A large artificial hbr on S side of Dublin Bay, always available. Major yachting centre. Exposed to NE and E gales when the outer and eastern part of the hbr may become untenable to moored and anchored small craft. Outer harbour being developed for cruise liner berthing.

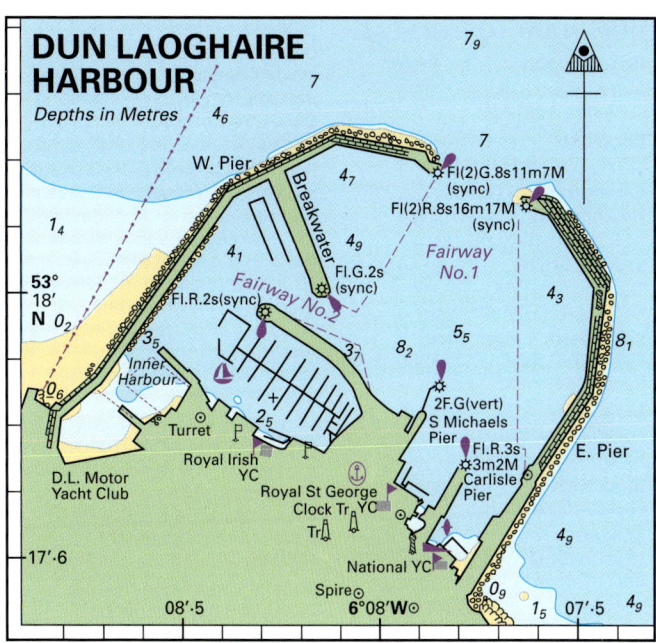

Two breakwaters within the hbr enclose a marina in complete shelter.

Entrance Allow for tide across hbr mouth. Keep well clear of commercial vessels. When through the main entrance make SSW to leave the end of the outer inner breakwater, Fl.G.2s to stb and thence to the marina.

Berthing Call marina control VHF 80 for advice.

Facilities All supplies. EC Wednesday. Chandlery and boatyard. Boat hoist. Hotels and restaurants. Frequent DART rly to Dublin. Maritime Museum within a few hundred yards.

☎/VHF Port 01 280 1130, VHF 14; Marina 01 202 0040 VHF 80, 37/M.

HOLYHEAD TO DUBLIN

A passage of some 55M. The tides ebb and flood on the Irish and Welsh coasts at much the same time. Thus, all other things being equal, the north and south sets will more or less balance.

However, leaving Holyhead, there is a westerly, helpful, component in the tide flow from about +0300 to +0600 HW Holyhead. So there is a benefit in starting between these times. Additionally the tide will carry you away from the concentration of shipping at the southern end of the Holyhead traffic separation zone. But avoid allowing your vessel to be swept south of the North Stack as there are overfalls between that headland and the South Stack.

Once clear of the land set a tide corrected course to leave the Kish Bank Light tower to port. The waters to its south, over the Kish Bank, can be turbulent.

On reaching the Kish Tower one must decide whether one is to pass, dependent upon conditions, to the north or south of the Burford Bank. This is marked with the 'North' and with the 'South' Burford cardinal buoys.

Dublin Port Authority operates traffic separation schemes between these buoys and the Dublin Bay RW buoy. Yachts are strongly requested to keep well clear of the triangle formed by the three marks.

When a position is reached, either a mile to the north or to the south of the Dublin Bay buoy, head for the Poolbeg Light house. But keep outside the 'maintained channel' and enter Dublin port in accordance with the guidance to be found in the Dublin entry.

If ones arrival at the port is likely to be in darkness the recommendation is to divert either to Howth, to the north of, or to Dun Laoghaire, on the south side of, Dublin Bay then to enter Dublin Port in daylight.

DUBLIN BAY TO FAIR HEAD

Passage lights	BA No.
Ben of Howth–Baily Fl.15s41m18M AIS	5898
Rockabill Fl.WR.12s45m17/13M AIS	5904
Carlingford-Haulbowline Fl(3)10s32m10M AIS	5928
St John's Point Q(2)7·5s37m25M Fl.WR.3s15/11M AIS	5958
South Rock R pillar buoy Fl(R).30s7m9M Racon(T) (–) AIS	5966
Mew Is Fl(4)30s35m18M Racon(O) (– – –) AIS	5976
Black Head Fl.3s45m27M AIS	6028
Maidens Fl(3)15s29m23M+Fl.R.5s8M Racon(M) (– –) AIS	6042

Tidal streams All related to HW Dover. Between Ben of Howth and St John's Point –0600N; HWD S; strong S of Rockabill Point, weak further N and negligible S of St John's Point. Between St John's Point and Fair Head – HWD N and NW; +0600 S and SE; weak near St John's Point, strong N of Belfast Lough, reaching 4·5kn in entrance to North Channel. There is an inshore eddy on the SE stream between Torr Hd and Fair Hd, –0400NW for 10hrs.

TSS orientated NE to SW 1·3M SE of Bailey.

Ballyquintin Point, E of the entrance to Strangford Lough, should be given a berth of ½M. There are extensive rocks off Kearney Point 3¼M NE of Ballyquintin Point. South Rock R pillar buoy is moored 2M E of South Rock, marked by a disused LtHo 18m high. North Rocks, 1½M E of Ringboy Point, must be passed at least 1½ca to E. Donaghadee Sound, see plan, inside Copeland Is is the normal passage for yachts sailing along the coast; S entrance marked by buoys.

Bound north from Belfast Lough it pays to leave early and have a foul tide in the lough: tides are far weaker in the lough than those in the North Channel. From Black Head to the Isle of Muck, close inshore, there will be a back eddy running north. Aim to be off the Isle of Muck at about HWD –0100 when the tide will be weak.

SE of Muck Is there is a race which should be taken with the stream. The Maidens are two dangerous groups of rocks within 4M of Ballygalley Head separated by a channel 1M wide.

Rogerstown Inlet in the bay facing Lambay Is provides sheltered anchorage for up to 1·7m draught. Drogheda, on River Boyne, provides good shelter for a night but has no special berths for yachts. Portavogie, some 8M N of Strangford Lough, is at present so congested that yachts should use it only in emergency.

Carnlough Harbour, some 11M N of Larne, provides shelter for yachts drawing less than 1·5m, and for these is a useful port for a passage to or from the Scottish coast.

Similarly Red Bay, some 10 miles south of Fair Head can make a useful anchorage in its SW corner, S of Cushendall, when awaiting the tide on passage north or south. The tide swilling past outside the bay seems to shut out the swell. But it should not be used in strong onshore winds.

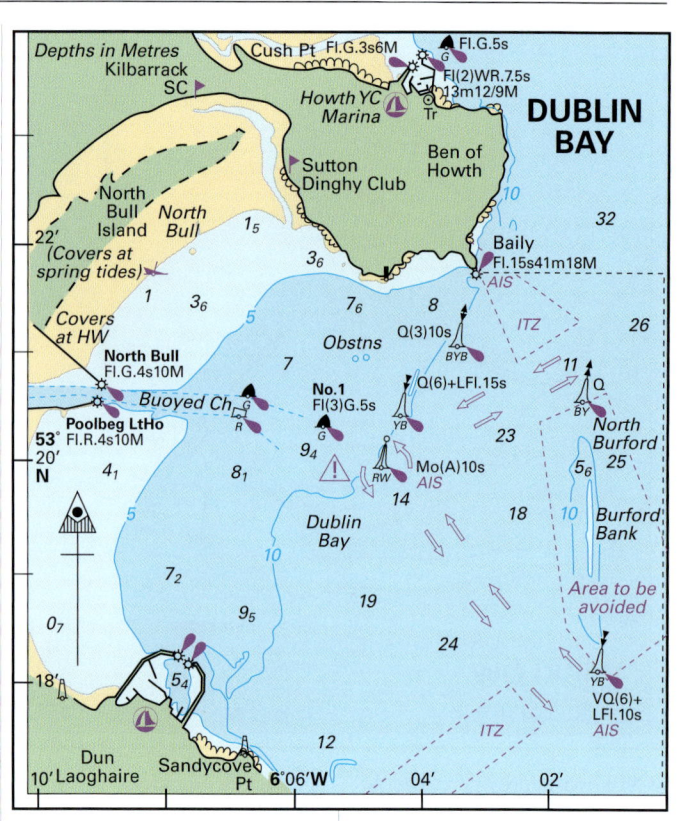

DUBLIN
Standard Port

A major hbr in the River Liffey and its estuary. Deep water, all weather entrance with channel dredged to 7·8m through the bar. A capital city well worth a visit.

Approach Avoid the area surrounding the Burford Bank and neighbouring TSS, keep at least 0·5M from the Dublin Bay RW buoy. Ships, especially ferries, may be moving fast in the approaches. Monitor *VTS Dublin* on VHF 12 at all times. Cross TSS or Fairway channels on a heading at 90°. Yachts are required to give large vessels the freedom to manoeuvre at all times (Colregs Rule 9). Conspic land marks are the two tall chimneys on the S side of the river and the lighthouses on the ends of the outer piers, Poolbeg (red) on the end of the Great S Wall and N Bull (green) on the end of the semi-submerged NE pier.

Entrance Keep out of the fairway and proceed under power, but probably best to lower sails once in the shelter of the piers. From the South, make for the waiting area to the south of port hand buoy No 8. From the North, make for the waiting area N of stb hand buoy No.7. In both cases call *VTS Dublin* VHF 12 with position and intentions. You will normally be instructed to follow the recommended yacht track/safe water passage, close S of the red buoys. If instructed to keep to the N side of the channel, only cross the channel at 90° to the S side when abeam the two tall power station chimneys if proceeding upstream to Poolbeg Marina.

Dublin is a busy commercial hbr, keep a sharp lookout for Ro Ro and other commercial vessels which normally berth on the N side of the river. Vessels may swing during berthing, occupying most of the river. Before departure, call VTS for permission to use the recommended safe water passage.

Poolbeg Marina This is a private marina run by the Poolbeg Yacht and Boating Club. Very welcoming. Bar or Office usually open 1000–2000, if no response on tel or VHF, berth on the outside of the long pontoon. Do not go to an inner finger unless instructed – there are some shallow patches. Shops 1km; a 20 min walk to city centre.

☎/VHF Marina 01 6689983; VHF 37/80.
Dublin Port 01 8876000; VHF 12.

Leisure Craft Guidelines is with plan of port available from www.dublinport.ie/information-centre

Alternatively the marinas at both Dun Loaghaire and Howth offer a ready welcome, with quick and frequent access to Dublin City by the 'Dublin Light Railway' (The DART).

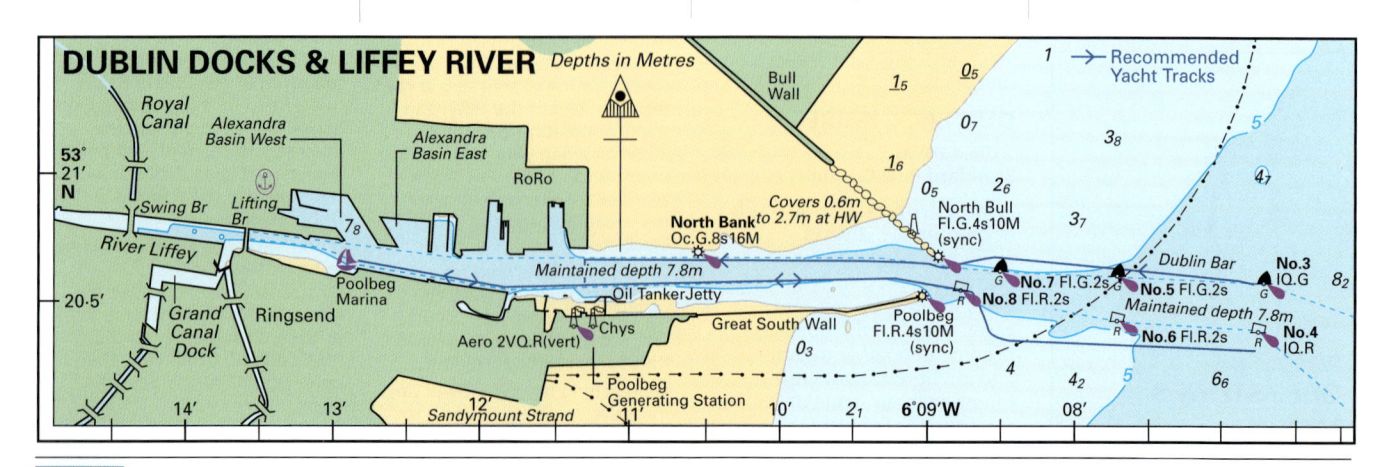

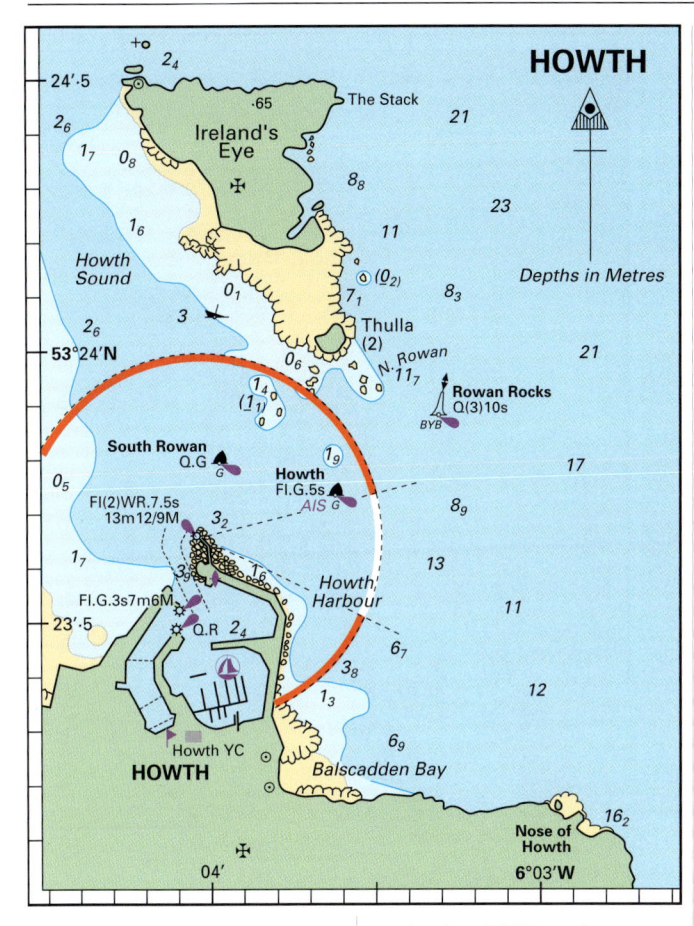

HOWTH

Standard Port Dublin
HW −0006   LW +0003

MHWS	MHWN	MLWN	MLWS
0·0m	−0·1m	−0·2m	−0·2m

This hbr, fishing port to W, separate marina to E, affords excellent shelter and facilities.

Approach and Entrance From E leave to stb Rowan Rocks E card Lt buoy, Howth G con Lt buoy Fl.G.5s and South Rowan G con Lt buoy Q.G. Give E pier head Lt Fl(2)WR.7·5s a berth of at least 50m; do not turn into the hbr until it is well open; enter nearer W pier-head Lt Fl.G.3s. Keep watch for fishing boats leaving. Inside hbr is the Trawler Breakwater Head Q.R.

Berthing In marina operated by Howth YC. Yachts are advised to call on VHF 37(M) or 80 before entering the hbr. Follow the port and stb-hand spar buoys marking the dredged channel toward the marina. A gabionade 30m long and 2m wide is positioned to shelter the marina. Leave this to port then follow berthing instructions received on VHF to take you to allocated mooring or secure at waiting berth, first pontoon.

Facilities Water, diesel, WiFi, showers, clubhouse in hbr area. Grid and boat lift. Shops, hotels, restaurants and pubs within walking distance. Frequent 'DART' rly to Dublin.

☎ Marina 01 839 2777.

MALAHIDE

Standard Port Dublin
HW (sp) +0002 (np) +0003
LW (sp) +0009 (np) +0009

MHWS	MHWN	MLWN	MLWS
+0·1m	−0·2m	−0·4m	−0·2m

Approach Entry not advised in strong onshore winds. A frequently shifting bar. Otherwise enter on adequate rise of tide. Make for small pillar RW safe water Lt buoy LFl.10s. The least depth over the bar is approx 2.3m less than that at the RW buoy. Bar is liable to silting.

Entrance Enter at HW±0300. Flood 3kn, ebb 3½kn. Follow the lit buoyed channel. Call the marina for berthing instructions before reaching the moorings. Once between the moorings gradually bear round to stb. The marina entrance will be seen to port.

Facilities A well appointed marina with full boat repairs. Shops in the town.

☎/VHF 01 8454129, VHF 37/M.

CARLINGFORD LOUGH

See plan on next page
Standard Port Dublin
Cranfield Point
HW (sp) −0027 (np) −0011
LW (sp) −0010 (np) +0005

MHWS	MHWN	MLWN	MLWS
+0·7m	+0·9m	+0·2m	0·0m

Carlingford Lough lies 39M N of Dublin, 28M S of Strangford, and may be located by Carlingford Mt, 585m, some 5M NW of entrance and by the Mourne mountains to the N. There are shoals E and W of the approach within 1M of the entrance points, Ballagan on W and Cranfield on E. The whole entrance is blocked inside at LW by the Limestone Rocks, except the Cut, a narrow channel 1M long on NE side. Beware areas of shellfish beds.

Approach
Tidal streams weak outside, 3·5kn in buoyed approach channel, 4·5kn just E of LtHo, 1·5kn between entrance and Greenore, 5kn off Greenore, 2·5kn between Stalka and Watson rks, 1·5kn off Carlingford, quiet above Killowen Point. Between LtHo and No.5 buoy the flood tends to N; there is a S-going eddy on flood along E side of Block House Is. Otherwise the streams follow channels. Small yachts cannot enter or leave against the tide and should have reliable power or leading wind even with fair tide. A heavy and disturbed sea occurs with a southerly wind against the ebb immediately outside the entrance. In onshore gales the entrance is impassable.

From NE or SE, leave to stb Hellyhunter S card Lt buoy, From S, keep a mile or more off Ballagan Point. Cranfield Point (not conspic) with houses bearing 016° or No.2 R can Lt buoy bearing N will lead to entrance.

Entrance Steer on Vidal Ldg Lts, Oc.3s on RW piles 1M inside the Point, 310°, along buoyed and lit channel, leaving Haulbowline LtHo ¼M to port, till Greenore Lt, Fl.R7·5s, bears 287°, when steer for it. Proceed between further lighted lateral Lt buoys till abreast Killowen Pt, hence 355° to anchor off Wood House, or off Rostrevor quay, 1–4m. Alternatively turn to port at No.18 R can Lt buoy steer 185° to Carlingford marina or just beyond same to anchor off Carlingford village.

Anchorages In S wind the lough is disturbed by squalls from the hills.
- ½M N of Carlingford Harbour in 3m, or berth alongside either pier in hbr, which dries.
- Between Killowen Point and Rostrevor.
- Carlingford Sailing Club have laid four complimentary visitors' moorings 4ca north of the hbr for deep draught vessels and four similar for shallow draught at about half the distance.

Berthing In Carlingford marina. Do not turn until No.18 port-hand buoy. Depth 3·5m, 30 visitors' berths, usually on pontoon ahead as you enter.

Facilities at marina include launderette, restaurant and boat lift. Shopping in village, ten minutes' walk.

Landing is impossible at Rostrevor pier at LW, but Carlingford Lough YC just N of Killowen Point has a slip where one can always land, though caution needed at LW. Water Warrenpoint; stores at Carlingford, best at Warrenpoint, there are also reasonable stores at Rostrevor.

Note The NE shore of the lough is Northern Ireland, the SW the Republic.

☎/VHF Marina 042 937 3072, VHF 37/M

ARDGLASS

See plan on next page
Standard Port Belfast
HW +0012   LW +0008

MHWS	MHWN	MLWN	MLWS
+1·7m	+1·2m	+0·6m	+0·3m

Pier Harbour 1M N of Ringfad Point, a conical hill with tr. Always available, has 2–3m. Used by fishing vessels. SE winds send in heavy swell. There is an inner basin with 3m at HW, bottom deep mud, affording perfect shelter at all times. A marina (20 visitors') has been dredged in the bay west of Churn Rock. Rocks extend from both sides of the shore outside the hbr entrance.

Approach Give shore on either side a fair berth. At night, approach in the W sector of

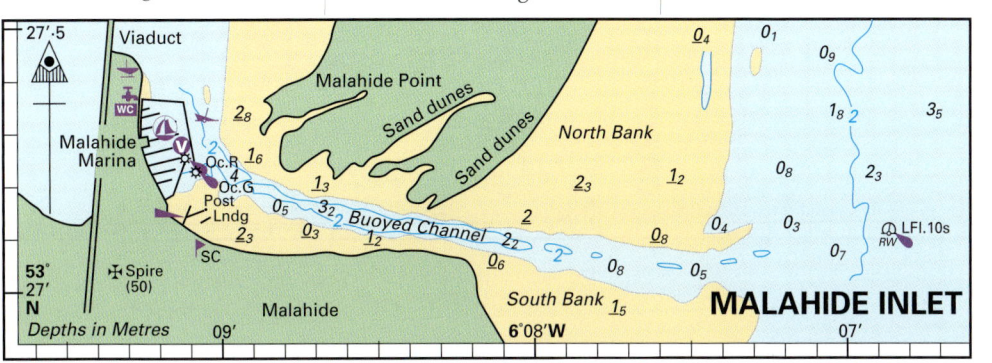

ARDGLASS HARBOUR

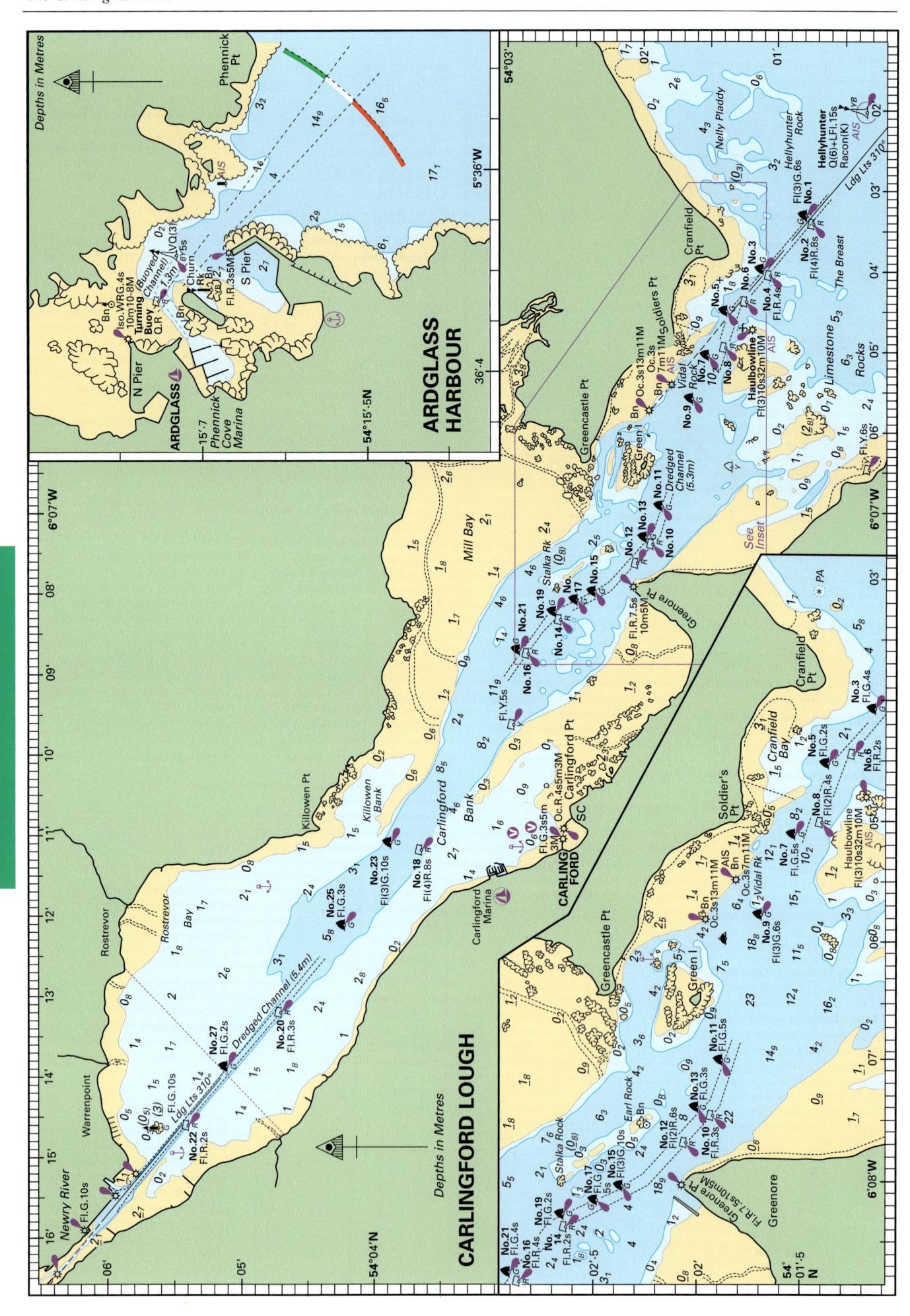

CARLINGFORD LOUGH

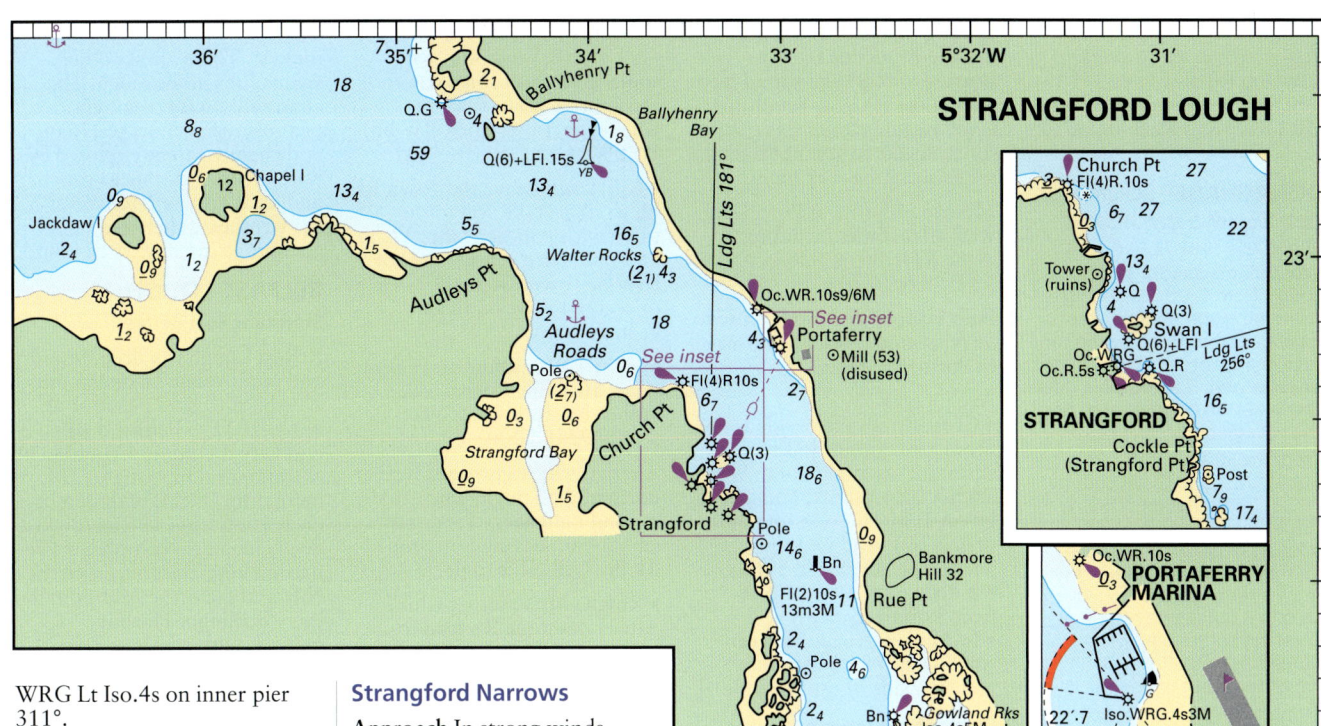

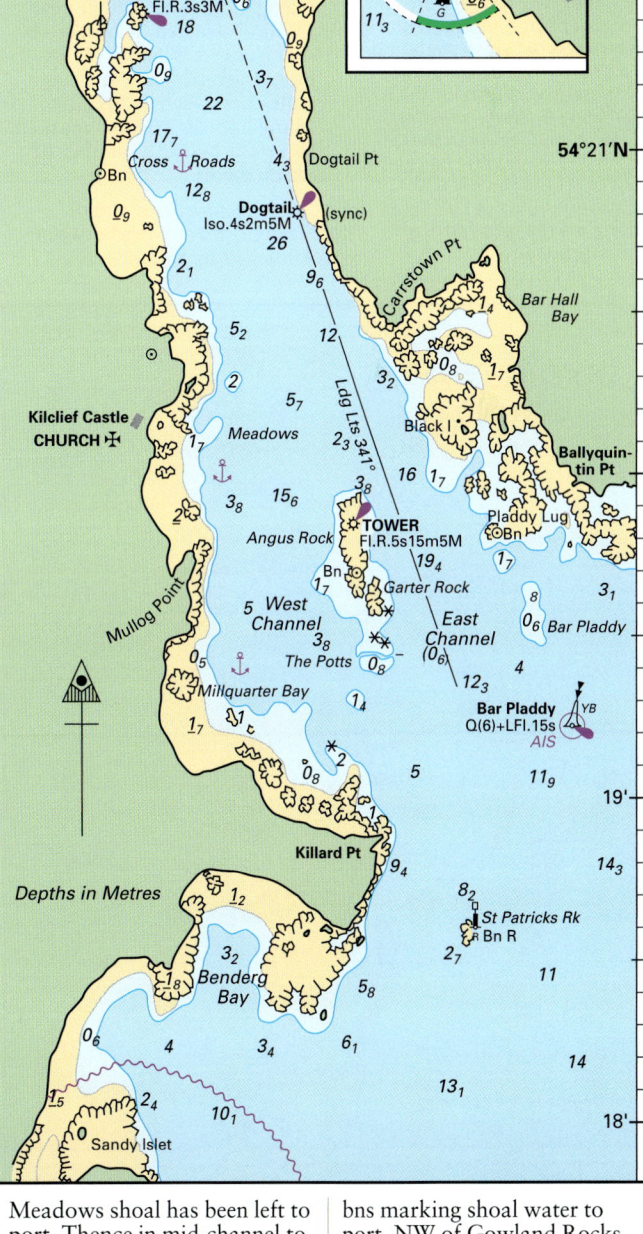

The Cruising Almanac

WRG Lt Iso.4s on inner pier 311°.

Entrance Leave quay pier head Lt Fl.R.3s to port. For the fishing hbr turn to port leaving S card bn to stb. This bn marks rocks to the W of the pier head and W of fairway.

For the marina leave the S card bn well to port, leave a R bn to port, head for the R can Turning Buoy, Fl(2)R. Turn to port; the approach channel to the marina is marked with port and stb hand buoys channel to marina. Foul outside channel. Call VHF 80 or listen for verbal instructions, not 24hr.

Berthing In marina or, if no room, berth alongside and contact HM.

Anchorage In quiet weather, for overnight stop, space to anchor in 4m can be found 100m N of the pier head.

Facilities Shops nearby, calor gas. Pubs, restaurant. Bus to Downpatrick.

☎/VHF Marina 028 44 842332, VHF 37/80 (occas).

STRANGFORD LOUGH
Standard Port Belfast
Killard Point
HW (sp) +0011 (np) +0021
LW (sp) +0025 (np) +0005
MHWS MHWN MLWN MLWS
+1·0m +0·8m +0·1m +0·1m

Strangford
HW (sp) +0147 (np) +0157
LW (sp) +0208 (np) +0148
MHWS MHWN MLWN MLWS
+0·1m +0·1m –0·2m 0·0m

Killyeagh
HW (sp) +0157 (np) +0207
LW (sp) +0231 (np) +0211
MHWS MHWN MLWN MLWS
+0·3m +0·3m n/a n/a

Beyond Strangford Narrows lies Strangford Lough, a picturesque area of some 100km² of navigable water, magnificent for small craft.

Strangford Narrows
Approach In strong winds between SSW and E no yacht should approach or leave the entrance on the ebb, when the sea breaks heavily outside. In such conditions departure should be timed for the young flood. Otherwise enter with the flood and leave with the ebb. The stream runs true, out of the Narrows at HW+0230 and in at LW+0200 (Belfast) except that immediately N of Angus Rock, flood and ebb run NW and SE respectively. At Rue Point springs run at up to 7kn. Guns Is, 30m high with W obelisk bn, is SW of entrance.

Angus Tr, (R&W) Fl.R.5s, is visible in the centre of the entrance, Angus bn, a truncated obelisk, immediately to the S of the Tr. N of the entrance there is a conspic windmill above Portaferry.

From the S: give St Patrick's Rock bn, 3ca off Killard Pt, a good berth.

From the N: give Butter Pladdy, E card Q(3)10s, off Kearney Pt, a berth of 8ca to stb. Then keep Guns Is bearing no less than 230° until Bar Pladdy, S card buoy, is brought abeam. Thence turn to west to leave Bar Pladdy to stb. Stand on 2ca then turn to 324° to enter the Narrows.

From seaward the RWVS Strangford buoy, Fl.10s, at 54°18'·6N 5°28'·6W may be a useful guide. Thence make good approx 300°, allowing for cross-set tide, to leave Bar Pladdy S card buoy to stb. Continue as above.

Entrance By E channel, when N end of Portaferry town comes open W of Bankmore Hill and Rue Point steer 341°, leaving Bar Pladdy buoy to stb and Pladdy Lug W pile bn at least 1ca to stb and Angus bn to port, into the Narrows until Kilclief castle bears 265°, then Meadows shoal has been left to port. Thence in mid-channel to pass between Gowland Rocks bn Fl.8s to stb, and poles and bns marking shoal water to port. NW of Gowland Rocks strong eddies in midstream. Then anchor as required.

STRANGFORD LOUGH

PORTAFERRY MARINA

Depths in Metres

IRELAND

221

By night keep Dog Tail Point Oc(4)G.10s in transit with Gowland Rocks LFl.8s 341° until Salt Rock bn Fl.R.3s bears 330°. Keep Salt Rock bn on this bearing till Dog Tail Point is abeam. Bring this Lt on a bearing of 098° and sound into anchorage at Cross Roads (see Anchorages below). It is risky for strangers to attempt to make other anchorages by night.

DONAGHADEE SOUND
DS Dover HWD NW; +0600SE. The sp tide runs up to 4½kn

Whether making for Belfast Lough from South or coming from the lough bound south, passage through this sound can save nearly three miles in distance and, if favourable tides are taken, an hour or more on the voyage time.

From the SE identify R can Lt buoy Fl.R.3s and G con Lt buoy Fl.G.3s (Governor and Deputy respectively) passing obliquely midway between on a course of about 290°. When abreast the G buoy alter on to 340° to leave second R can Lt buoy Fl(2)R.6s Foreland Spit to port. When abreast of that alter to 310° which leads out of Sound.

From the NW enter Sound midway between Copeland Is and the coast and identify Foreland Spit R can Lt buoy which will be left to starboard. Pass within 1ca of it and when abreast alter course for the R can buoy Governor leaving the G con buoy Deputy to port. With a SE-going tide be careful not to let the Deputy and Governor buoys get in line as there is a reef close NNE of Deputy buoy.

Mooring Marina at Portaferry with all facilities including WiFi. VHF 80, ☎ 02842 729598 or 07703 209780.

Four visitors' moorings close to ferry terminal, black, courtesy of Portaferry Hotel.

Anchorages
• Cross Roads on W side is the nearest anchorage to the entrance, but no landing. W anchor bn on shore, and a W bn on Tully Hill (not on plan) in line 260° lead into the anchorage; anchor in 3·5m.
• Ballyhenry Bay, ¾M NW from Portaferry town
• In Audleys Roads between small stone pier and perch. S and W inside of this is all shoal.

Strangford Lough
Navigation in the Lough near LW is obstructed by numerous shoals, called Pladdies. It is highly advisable to use a large scale chart, such as BA2156. Many hazards are now marked by bns or buoys, a number of which are lit.

Leave the northern end of Strangford Narrows between Audley Pt to port and Ballyhenry Pt, marked with bn, Q.G, to stb; head 305° for some ½M, this brings you to the approach line 270° to Killyleagh Town Rock RW bn, Fl(2)WRG 5s.

• **Killyleagh** Leave the Town Rk bn to stb to take you to the town with pontoon, slip, YC and sail board centre. Anchor SSW of Town Rk bn in 2–4m, or secure to one on the Y visitors' buoys.

Facilities Water, fuel and gas at quay, available HW±0200. Stores, bus to Belfast. YC ☎ 028 9258 7200.

Alternatively, to proceed further north in the Lough, when ½M beyond Ballyhenry Pt turn to stb to 350° leaving Limestone Rk bn, Q.R., 2ca to port.

• **Ringhaddy** Cruising Club. After Limestone Rk turn to port and head for conspic White House keeping it on bearing 317°. Leave Prawle Island to stb then Warren Pt to port and Eagle Hill Pt (Islandmore) to stb. Follow Eagle Pt round at about ½ca distance into the enclosed, sheltered and attractive waters off Rinhaddy pontoon with Fl.R.5s end light. Deep water to anchor and the tide runs at 2kn. Secure temporarily to club pontoon and seek advice to secure to a vacant mooring. No facilities. ☎ 028 4483 0520 or 078 1285 6060.

• **Kircubbin** Sailing Club and Village. From about 2ca E of Limestone Rk head approx 005° to leave Long Sheelagh shoal, E card bn Q(3)10s to port. Then turn to 045° to leave Tip Reef S card Q(6) + LFl.15s to port. Follow the buoyed channel between Hoskyns Shoal and Sand Pladdy. Alter course to 005°, passing between Woman's Rk and Black Neb. Continue ¾M to anchor in 2–8m off the slip in Kircubbin Bay. This anchorage is completely exposed to the W.

Facilities Water at SC. Stores in village. Bus to Belfast with connections to both airports. SC ☎ 028 4277 1707.

• **Ballydorn** on the W side of the lough is the location of the Down Cruising Club. At Long Sheelagh bn turn to port and head 348° towards Mahee Pt on the extreme E tip of Mahee Is sectored Lt. When some 6ca beyond Dead Man's Rk E card bn and some mile short of Mahee Pt turn W across Mahee Roads. (Caution: many racing buoys). Head for the channel between Rainey Is and Sketrick Is, only 1·5m at LW. Inside the sheltered and picturesque sound off the LtV clubhouse there is 3–4m. There are four visitors' moorings. Berth temporarily at the LtV for advice, water and fuel. ☎ 028 9754 1663.

These are but four places of interest. There are six other yacht clubs in the lough. The chart will reveal countless picturesque anchorages, islands and channels to be explored by both the long-distance cruiser and local potterer! Whatever the weather, a sheltered anchorage can always be found.

BELFAST LOUGH
Standard Port Belfast

Belfast Lough is a deep, broad and picturesque incursion into Northern Ireland penetrating about 10M to **Belfast docks and City** it is some 6M broad at entrance and tapering to 2M before the Docks, with depths decreasing from 12–3m. Belfast docks include a comprehensive marina with close access to the City and facilities. Additionally there is **Bangor Harbour marina**, with adjacent YC, beside the town on the south shore and **Carrickfergus harbour and marina** with all facilities on the north shore.

Approach Tidal streams run strongly in the offing reaching 4kn at springs and may raise a big lop. From the south, when rounding Orlock Pt avoid Briggs Rocks ¾M offshore, N cardinal buoy Q. Thence give the shores a reasonable offing. The navigable area is considerably reduced by shoal banks towards the head of the lough.

BELFAST HARBOUR
This is at the head of the Lough, with a marina 10 min walk from city centre.

Approach The RW Fairway buoy, Iso.4s6M AIS, in 54°42'·32N 5°42'·30W some 1·5M SE of Carrickfergus is at the entrance to the main channel, marked by two pairs of lateral buoys, followed by a narrow dredged channel marked by lit beacons. Before entering the beaconed channel call Harbour Control VHF 12 to state position and intention to berth in the marina. There is no requirement to follow the marked channel until the water shoals either side of the beacons, but after bns 11 and 12 keep to the channel, the south side dries.

Entrance In the hbr take the centre of three channels. When approaching the first bridge the marina is to port in Abercorn Basin. It has finger berths and, alongside pontoons, berths for vessels up to 40m and 4m draft. Security gate access code will be given by mooring ticket machines on main pontoon at base of entry bridge. Payment by credit or debit card. Adjacent there is a plan showing route to city and facilities such as chandlery.

Facilities Electricity included. No fuel.

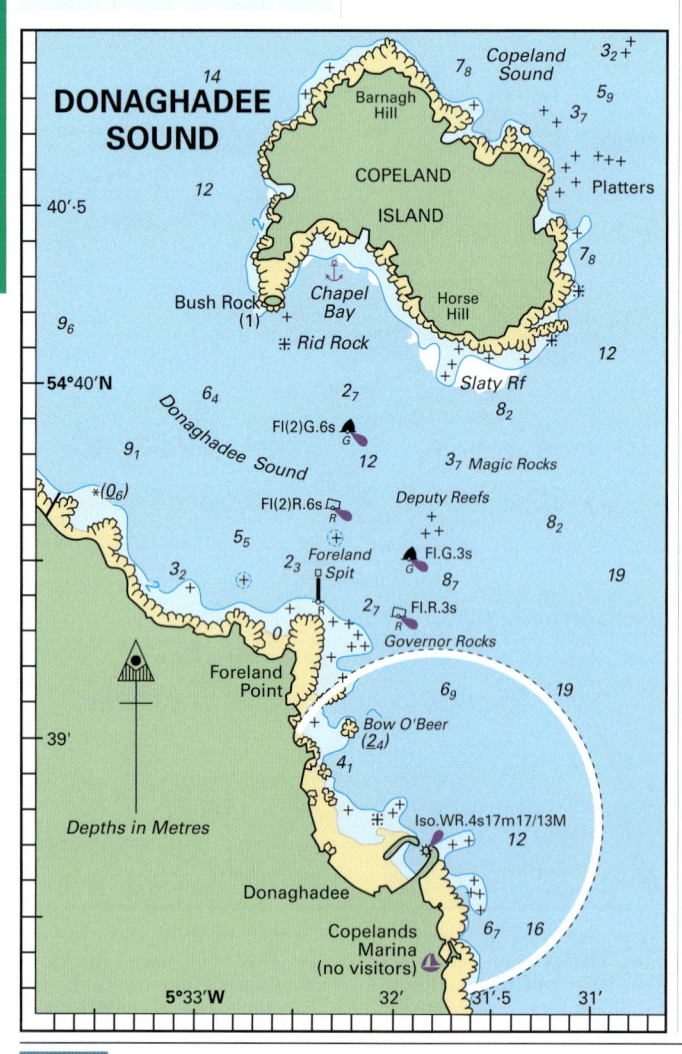

The Cruising Almanac

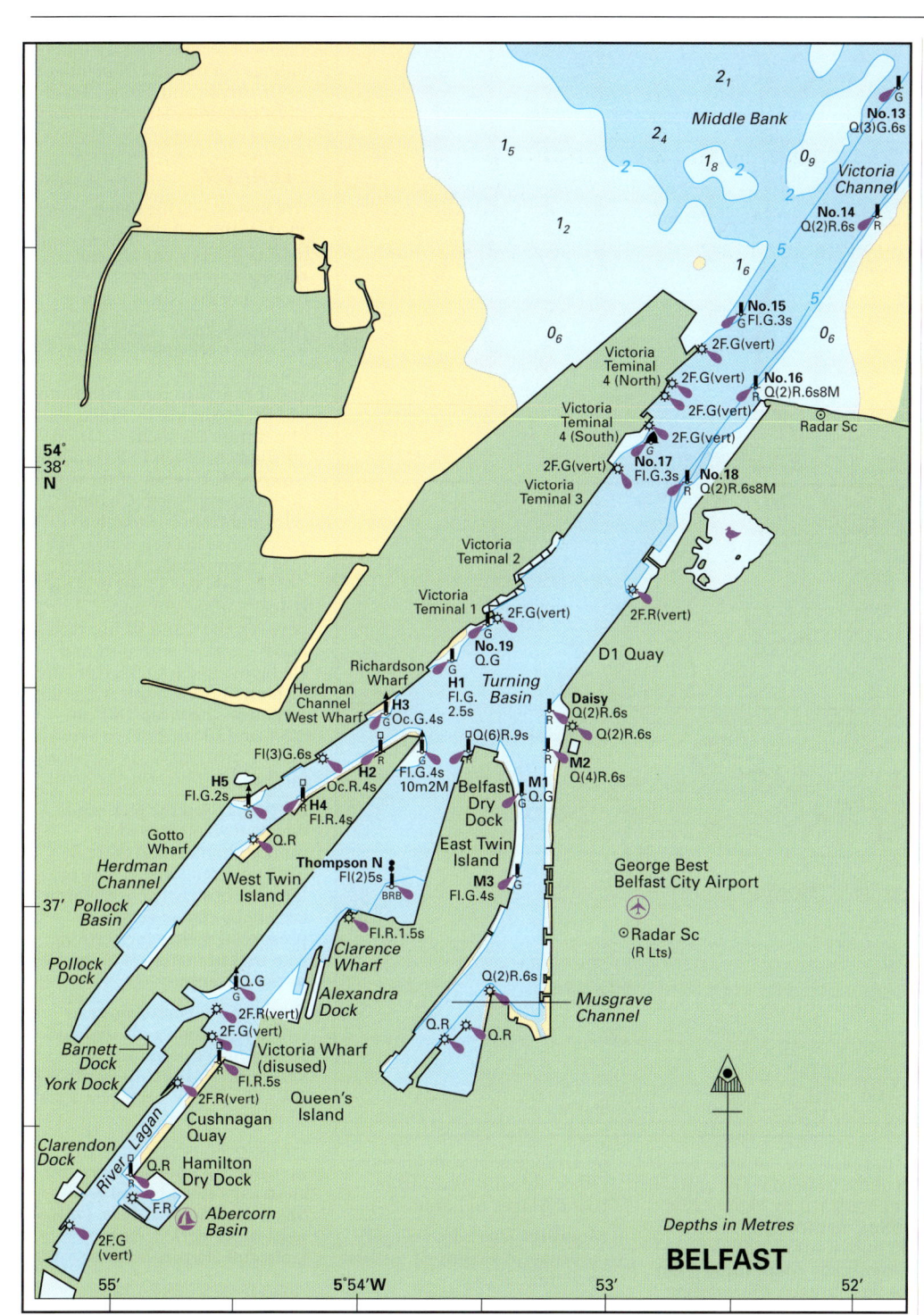

☏/VHF 02890 553013, VHF 12.
Marina 02890 553504.

BANGOR MARINA

Marina with all facilities and services. Before approach call on VHF 80 for a berth, giving an ETA. You will be too busy later. Visitors' berths are normally on the south pointing fingers of pontoon E.
On approach the entrance is obscured; from the north, leave the end of the North Breakwater, Iso.R.12s9M, some 100m to port. At night, it is vital to identify this light amongst the many shore lights before making an approach. When to W of the pierhead turn to port to a position 75m S of it. The entrance will be visible; leave the dolphin 2F.G(vert) on the end of the Pickie Breakwater some 30m to stb, likewise the dolphin Fl.G.3s. There is then a very sharp turn to stb following round the S side of the breakwater to enter a well-lit marina. Leave the pontoons H, G, and F to port. Turn to port leaving all the Fl.G. marks to stb; the first opening to port is the access lane to pontoon E. Bangor is a prosperous town where all requirements can be obtained. Fuel on W side Central Pier. ☏ 02891 453297.

Anchorages

• Anchor in Ballyholme Bay in 3·5 to 5·5m exposed to winds from NW to NE.
• Cultra, 5M W of Bangor. Anchor in offshore winds in 3·5 to 4m outside yacht moorings. Water, diesel from RNIYC, stores at Holywood 1M. Boatyard and slipping facilities. Contact Secretary on ☏ 02890 428041 for visitors' mooring and launch service.

CARRICKFERGUS

Carrickfergus Marina about 330m W of Carrickfergus harbour. Approach on 320° to marina retaining wall which has Ldg bns with top marks.

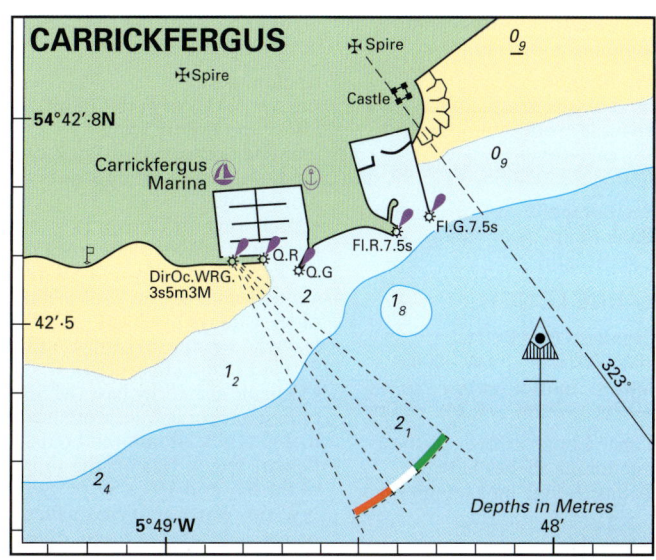

IRELAND

223

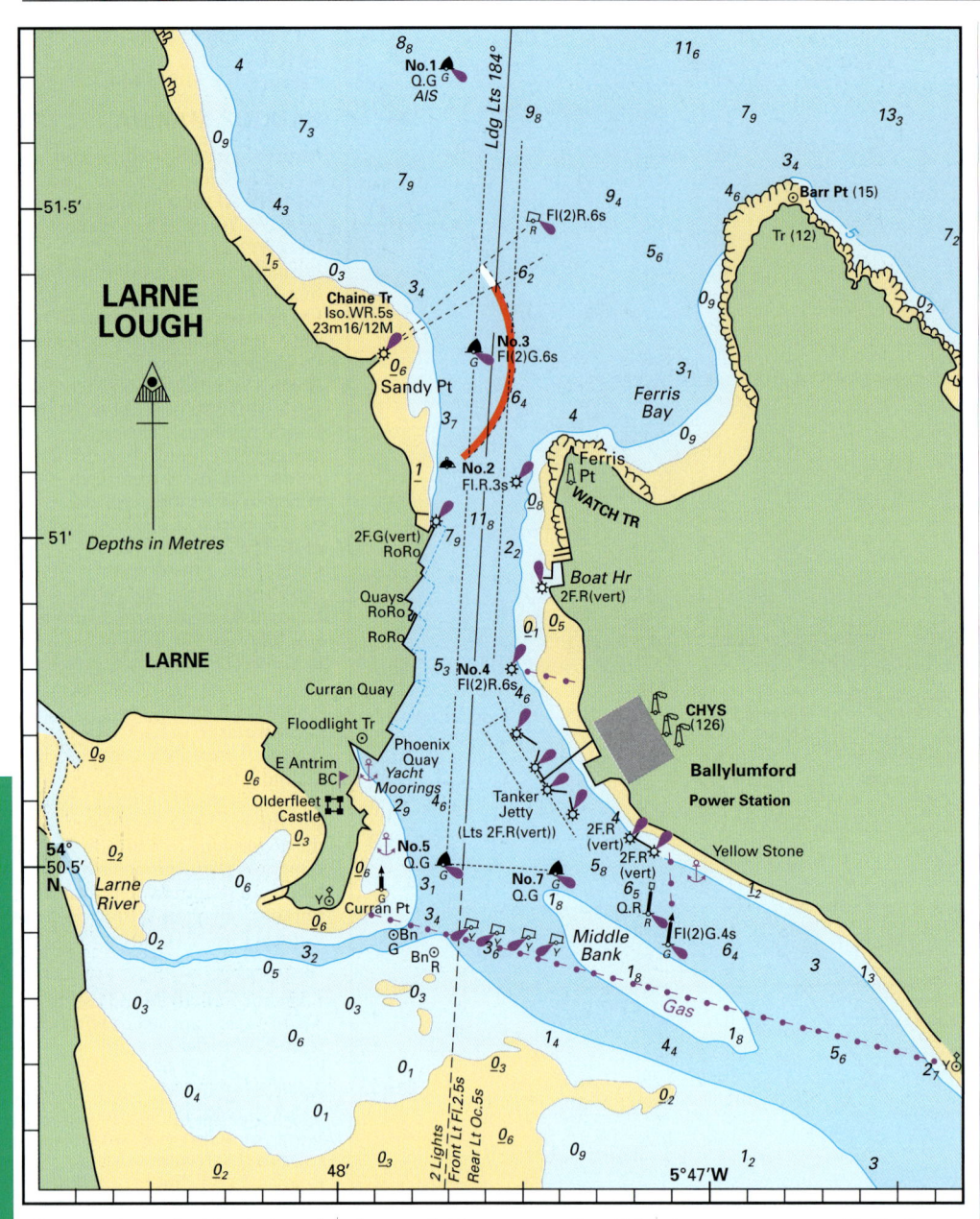

Entrance is marked by Q.G and Q.R bns but the R is obscured by the breakwater from 205°-305°. Thus when using the Ldg bns entrance will not open up until you are nearly opposite the stb mole. By night; the west wall has a sectored light Oc.WRG.3s near the pier head. Approach in W sector 320°. Turn sharply to stb to enter and, when in, to port.

Facilities as expected of a modern marina including chandlery and sailmaker. All stores in town.
☎ 028 9336 6666, VHF 37, 80.

Anchorage W of Carrickfergus Bank in 2m 2ca offshore at Greenisland.

LARNE LOUGH

Standard Port Belfast
HW −0019   LW −0003
MHWS	MHWN	MLWN	MLWS
+0·7m	+0·9m	+0·2m	0·0m

Larne Lough affords the best anchorage shelter between Belfast Lough and Lough Foyle.

Approach The entrance lies 4M S of the Maidens. The approach is obstructed by Hunter Rock, 0·8m, marked by N and S card Lt buoys, situated 2½M 036° from Ferris Point, the E point of the entrance. On entering steer between quays to stb and two pile bns to port, Fl.R.3s and Fl(2)R.6s respectively. By night Ldg Lts, Oc.4s 184°, lead in through the entrance.

Anchorages
• In 5m ¾M S of Ferris Point, SW of the Yellow Stone (painted occasionally) 1ca E of the L-shaped wharf opposite No.7 buoy.
• Anchoring off Curran Pt is permitted NW of a line from the Pt to No.5 buoy and SW of a line from No.5 buoy to S end of ferry quays but local yachts leave no room for visitors; VHF 37 for berthing instructions.
• Outside a shallow bay 1M SE of first anchorage, ½ca offshore in 2–3m NW of moored boats. Beware wreck ¾ca off the shore of the bay and 1¼ca SE of its NW tip. Water at Wymers Pier, petrol and stores in town, diesel by arrangement with Harbour Office. Repairs. Ferry from Island Magee to Larne.

Moorings There are visitors' moorings in vicinity of the first anchorage above.

Caution This is a busy ferry port and it is advisable to call Larne Port Control VHF 14 before approaching.

Frequent ferry service up to 24 sailings per day to UK mainland at Cairnryan and Troon. Train to Belfast. International airport 20M.

GLENARM

HW Belfast −0010±10min
This small, well sheltered marina offers a convenient staging post for yachts traversing the North Channel.

Approach Entry is safe in all but severe NE gales. Tucked into the root of Glenarm Bay about 8ca W of Rath Head and 1M SE of Straidkilly Point, the hbr entrance is sheltered from all winds between ESE through S to NNW. It is out of the run of the strong North Channel tides and from N though to E; approach is in deep water. The HM recommends entry from 54°58′·33N 05°57′·02W. This is 1ca N of the entrance between the E and W hbr pier heads, marked with port and stb lights. In darkness, from 1M distant, approach this waypoint on courses between 180° to 200° or 230° to 270° to avoid a marine farm that may be poorly marked.

Entry Between the pier heads which are constructed of random boulders so there is little reflected swell. There is a large, unobstructed area within the hbr to enable vessels to prepare in shelter for berthing. The well-lit marina is to the SW of the entrance.

Berthing Two hammer-head ended pontoons with well spaced finger pontoons for vessels up to 14m. 4m depth LW. 30 Visitors' berths near end of pontoon.

Facilities Security coded gate access to pontoons. Water and electricity. (Fuel by can 3M). Shower at marina office. One mini-supermarket. Bus to Coleraine, Larne, Belfast.

☎/VHF 028 2884 1285, Mobile 07703 606763; VHF 80/37. Very poor VHF reception in some positions.

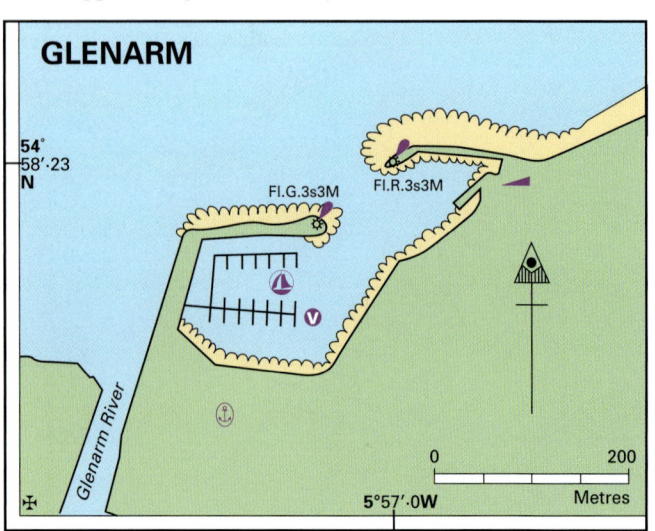

FAIR HEAD TO BLOODY FORELAND

Passage lights   BA No

Altacarry Head
(Rathlin East)   6062
Fl(4)20s74m26M Racon(G) (– – ·)

Rathlin West   6064
Fl.R.5s62m22M AIS

Inishtrahull   6164
Fl(3)15s59m19M Racon (T) (–)
AIS

Fanad Head   6168
Fl(5)WR.20s39m18/14M AIS

Tory Island   6200
Fl(4)30s40m18M Racon(M) (– –)
AIS

Note A sharp lookout should be kept for salmon nets and lobster pots when navigating this coast.

Tidal steams DS (all related to Dover): Fair Head to Malin Head, +0100WNW, –0500ESE. Malin Hd to Bloody Foreland, inshore, –0230WSW, +0300ENE. Malin Hd to Horn Hd, offshore, –0530ENE, becoming E and SE; –0130SW, becoming W, slack –0230 and from +0300 to +0600. Streams are strong near Fair Hd but get progressively weaker to W; 6kn in Rathlin Sound, 4kn in Inishtrahull Sound, 2kn in Tory Sound. Rathlin Sound, 2–3M wide, is the normal approach to the N coast. A fair tide is essential; the NW-going tide commences HWD and the SE-going –0500. The overfalls SW of Rue Pt must be avoided from HW+0100 to +0300. Beware Carrickmannanon Rock 3ca NE of Kinbane Point, across which the tidal streams set. Skerries Sound is convenient in moderate conditions but keep outside in swell or strong offshore winds.

Inishtrahull Sound should not be attempted if there is a big sea running; in bad weather it is advisable to pass 3M N of Torr Rocks.

Between Lough Swilly and Mulroy Bay the coast should be given a wide berth using the clearing marks on chart BA 2699. An area of abnormal magnetic variation has been reported 1M 250° from Malin Head.

• Portstewart is a small harbour 2½M SW of Portrush which in quiet weather is convenient for a temporary visit. Advice may be obtained about entering the Bann and a berth arranged at Coleraine Marina.

• Culdaff Bay provides good anchorage in winds between SE and NNW, and is useful if awaiting favourable conditions for Inishtrahull Sound. Sheephaven anchorage offers a reasonable anchorage.

The N coast of Ireland is most beautiful, with many interesting geological formations, including the famous Giant's Causeway, and in ideal conditions it can be an idyllic cruising ground. However, it must never be forgotten that the whole length of the coast is completely exposed to the full weight of the Atlantic swell when the wind is from between W and N, and in established strong winds from this quarter, conditions can be such as to test even the most seaworthy and strongly crewed yacht. If conditions deteriorate suddenly, the most satisfactory refuge is Lough Swilly; it is easy to enter and there are a number of anchorages. Nevertheless, boats cruising the coast should be prepared to keep to sea for some time before shelter can be reached. Indeed, if a strong SW'ly wind begins to show any sign of veering, it is wise to consider putting in to shelter straightaway, to avoid the danger of being caught on a lee shore.

RATHLIN ISLAND – CHURCH BAY

Standard Port Belfast
HW (sp) –0450 (np) –0155
LW (sp) –0452 (np) –0136

MHWS   MHWN   MLWN   MLWS
–2·2m   –2·0m   –0·4m   0·0m

DS Dover

Church Bay has two substantial breakwaters. It is a sheltered ferry port for the island for ferries from Ballycastle. Yachts are welcomed.

Approach
By day from SW clear of dangers to the hbr entrance.
By night the W sector of Oc.WRG.4s leads to the hbr entrance 023°–026°.

Entrance Pass between the pier heads, West Lt Fl.R.2s, East Lt Fl(2)G.6s.

Berthing
• Alongside pontoon, preferably N side of long pontoon, or on middle pontoon. Do not go east of the pontoons.
• Anchor in NW of hbr if enough depth; do not obstruct Ferry.
• Temporarily, in Inner hbr with HM's approval.

Facilities Limited, a small island, but a warm welcome. Showers and toilets. Ferry to Ballycastle.

BALLYCASTLE

Tidal data as Rathlin

DS Dover. Along the near shore. –0300W +0200E

Ballycastle Harbour The hbr has been substantially improved to provide shelter for the Campbeltown and Rathlin Island ferry terminals. At the same time it encloses an area of complete shelter for a significant marina. The North Quay, ferry berths, is protected by a large, random stone, breakwater against the strongest N'lies and carries a Lt Fl(3)G.6s. The S quay has a Lt Fl(2)R.4s at its head. Obscured north of bearing 261°.

Approach From E, Fair Head, along the coast keeping some 4ca offshore. Outside the 10m line it is clean. Keep south pier head open of north pier.
From N and W shape a course to leave the N quay a clearance of some ½ca. Turn to stb when the S quay is well open of the north. By night when it bears 275°.

Entrance Between the pier heads then bear round to port to leave the Old quay to stb and enter the marina. Berth as directed or in vacant berth to await instruction.

Facilities Diesel. Gas. Supplies in the town. Ferry to Church Bay, Rathlin.

☏/VHF Marina 028 2076 8525, *Mobile* 078 0350 5084, VHF 80.

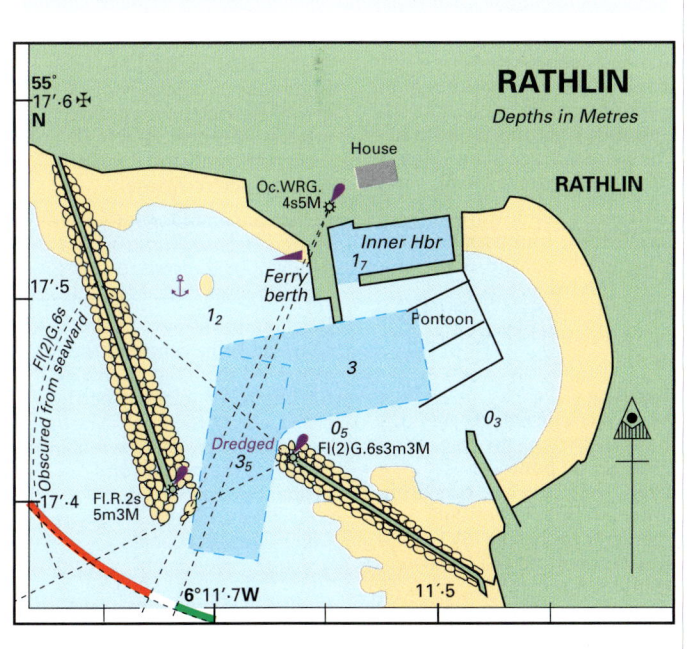

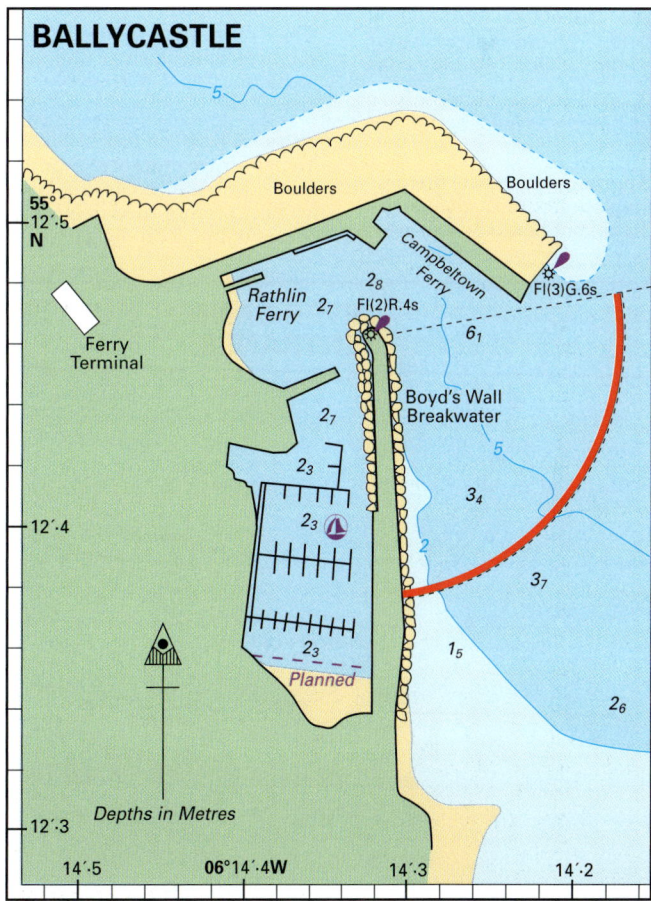

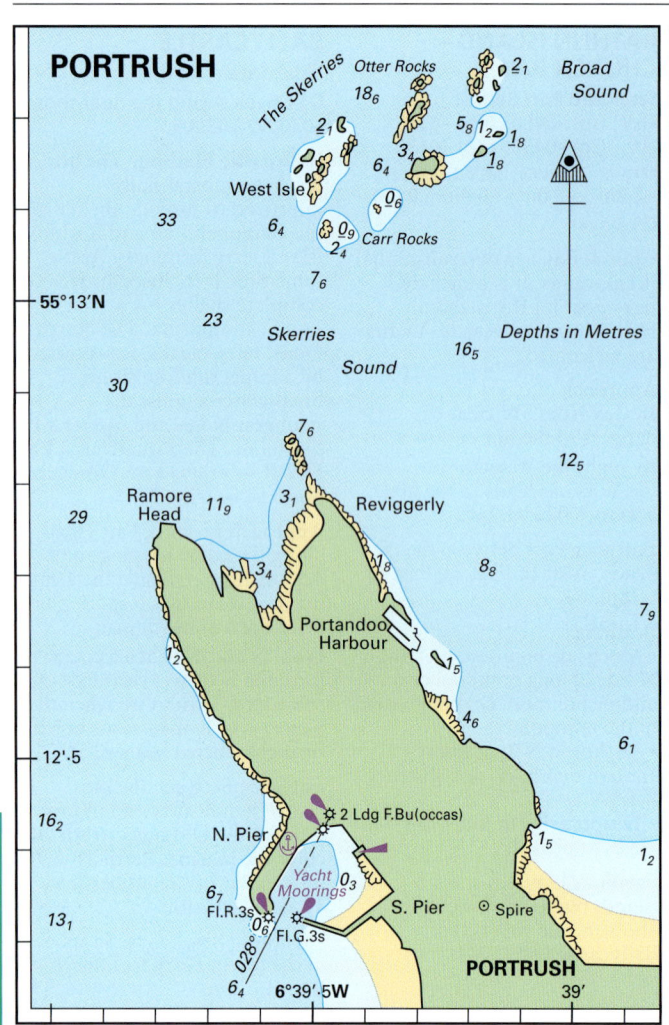

PORTRUSH

Standard Port Belfast
HW (sp) –0410 (np) –0210
LW (sp) –0010 (np) +0005

MHWS	MHWN	MLWN	MLWS
–1·4m	–1·4m	–0·3m	0·0m

A small crowded hbr on W side of Ramore Head, good shelter. RNLI Station.

Approach From East there is ample water through Skerries Sound but beware small area of tidal disturbance. In poor weather approach from outside The Skerries. Swell can make entrance difficult in onshore winds over Force 4. Beware submerged breakwater (0·6m) projecting 20m SW from N pier.

Entrance Between pier heads hbr has 2m in entrance, 3–5m inside. By night (occas) ldg Lts for hbr entrance sited in NE corner of hbr, F.Bu. By day the ldg Lts have good orange triangular daymarks.

Berthing Berth alongside N quay and seek directions from Harbour Office, also temporary pontoon berthing in NW corner. Mooring may be available but congested.

Facilities FW and diesel on the quay. A busy and friendly little town. Rly to Belfast and Derry. All supplies including gas. EC Wednesday. Hotels, restaurants and pubs.

☎/VHF HM 028 7082 2307, VHF 12.

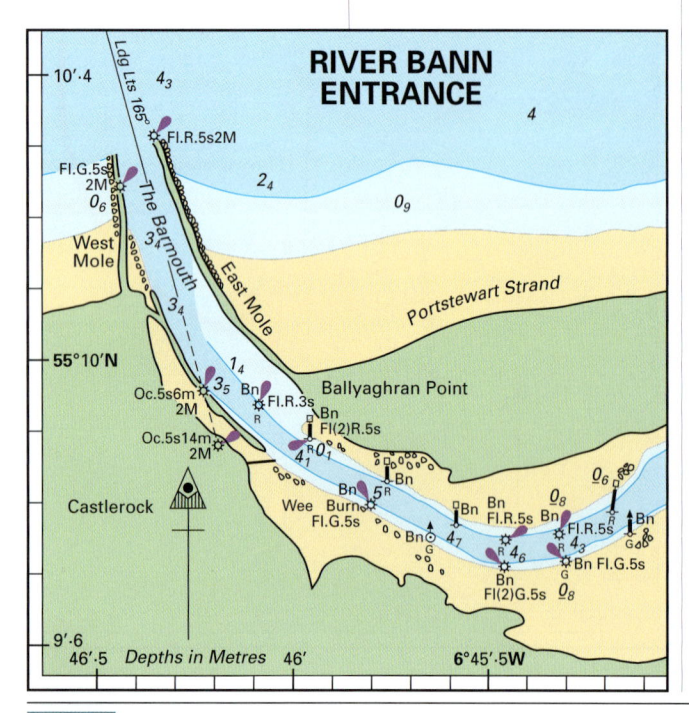

RIVER BANN

Standard Port Belfast
Coleraine
HW (sp) –0440 (np) –0219

MHWS	MHWN	MLWN	MLWS
+0·7m	+0·9m	+0·2m	0·0m

Approach River mouth is between stone training walls projecting 2ca N from beaches. It must not be attempted in strong onshore winds or if swell is breaking noticeably on ends of training walls. The stb entrance Lt is approx 40m from the pierhead, see plan. Ldg Lts 165° Oc.5s.6m & Oc.5s.14m.

Entrance Keep towards E wall as W side is foul with boulders. Channel 45m wide, dredged to 3·4m but subject to shoaling, is marked with lights (which may be weak) and bns. Ebb runs at 4kn.

Berthing
• In Coleraine marina on NE bank 4M from entrance. Water and fuel on pontoons, chandlery, 15-tonne travel-lift crane. ☎ 028 7034 4768.
• Anchor on N side ½M upstream of old CG, clear of channel. Use trip line.

Facilities Shops ½M away in thriving town all supplies. EC Thursday. A possible place to leave a boat. Rly to Antrim for airport and Belfast.

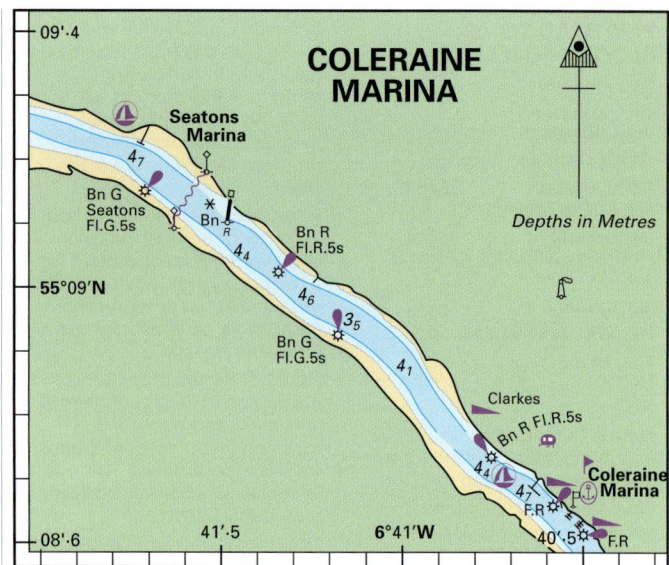

LOUGH FOYLE AND LONDONDERRY

Standard Port Belfast
HW (sp) –0330 (np) –0300

MHWS	MHWN	MLWN	MLWS
–0·8m	–0·9m	+0·1m	+0·2m

Greencastle on the NW of the entrance is a large commercial hbr with no specific facilities for yachts. It is a port of refuge in foul weather. Berth at single pontoon to S of main harbour. Many local boats but enough space for a few visitors. Pontoon is subject to strong tidal eddies, and exposed to the NE to SE. In strong winds from these quarters the crowded inner hbr is preferable. ☎ HM for advice: 086 816 6151. A small town, usual supplies, also a ferry across the lough to Magilligan which has busses to Colraine.

Lough Foyle Using appropriate coastal charts make your approach, taking care not to hamper large vessels, up the well buoyed channel to Londonderry which is a city of great historic and architectural interest. It is now largely free of sectarian conflict and visitors will feel perfectly safe.

Before passing Quigley's Pt call *Foyle Harbour Radio* VHF 14. You will be directed to Londonderry Port, Lisahally.

Berthing In the new Foyle Marina, in the centre of the city, 17M from the mouth of the lough. Vessels may berth either side of the Foyle Marina pontoon where there is a depth of 7m on the outside and 5m inside. Pay harbour dues, collect security access keys and tokens for electricity.

Anchorage Either side of the approach channel, well clear of the approach channel, preferably on the more sheltered side near village of Carrowkeel. Seek advice from *Harbour Radio*.

Facilities Nearby chandlery. Launderette. City centre easy walking distance, shops, etc as expected of a large city.

☎/VHF +44(0)28 7186 0113, VHF 14 (24h),
www.londonderryport.com/marina.htm

LOUGH SWILLY

Standard Port Galway
Rathmullan
HW (sp) +0125 (np) +0050
LW (sp) +0118 (np) +0126

MHWS	MHWN	MLWN	MLWS
–0·8m	–0·7m	–0·1m	–0·3m

The lough is entered between Fanad Head Lt Fl(5)WR.20s and the bold Head of Dunaff. It is 26M long, 3½M wide at entrance, and has 15 to 20m up to Fort Stewart; bottom sand and mud.

Approach From E care should be taken to carry tide through Inishtrahull Sound, NE of Malin Head, where the W-going stream runs 4hrs only. Dover +0100 to +0400.
From W give Fanad Head a berth of ½M and leave Swilly Rocks G con Lt buoy Fl.G.3s to stb. By night, keep out of the R sector of Fanad Lt.

Entrance Off Dunree Head up to Buncrana Bay, keep at least ½M clear to W, or keep Dunree Head Lt Fl(2)WR.5s and Fanad Lt in line.

Anchorages
• Pincher Bay, just south of Fanad Head. Exposed to E'lies.
• Ballymastocker Bay 4 ½M inside Fanad Head on W shore, anchor off the pier in 2–5m, small shop and pub. Exposed to E.
• Fahan Creek is the most sheltered anchorage although uncomfortable in NW winds. The bar is subject to silting and alteration; care should be taken on entry and exit which, except in very smooth conditions, should be between HW–0300 and HW+0200 when a least depth of 3m should be found. With a NW sea running extreme caution should be applied, particularly on the ebb. Anchor near moored yachts in 2–5·5m. Bus to Buncrana and Londonderry.

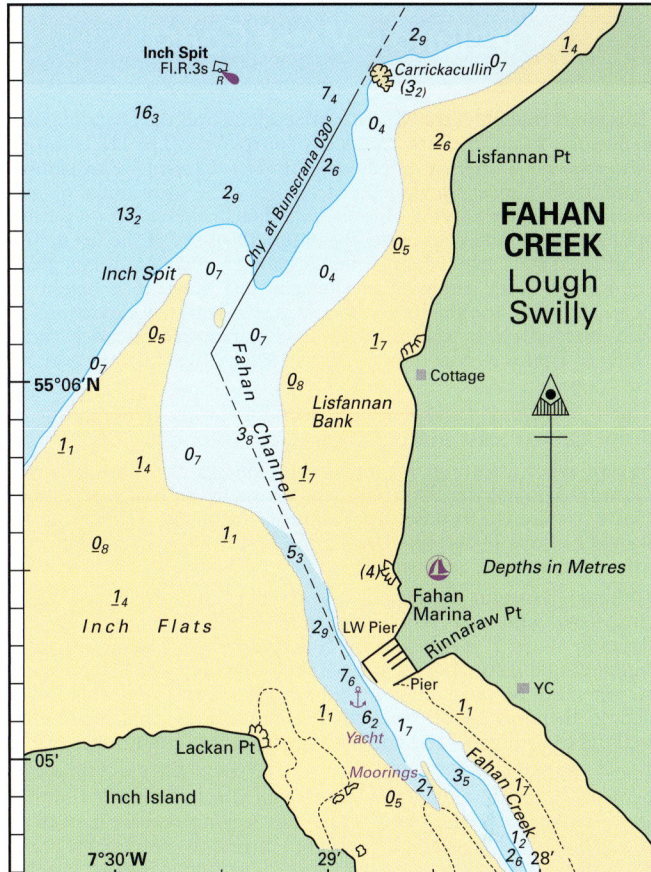

Sometimes the entrance is buoyed by the local YC.
• W of Macamish Point sheltered from SW to N through W, 3–5m, sand.
• Rathmullan Road, N of pier off the town. The best place for visiting yachts; water at pier-head. Pontoon on south side of pier. Small grocery, petrol, good local hotels.
• This large lough offers many other anchorages and much exploration in beautiful scenery further inland.
Guest moorings at Portsalon. FW hose on pontoon at Rathmullan and Calor Gas at the pub.

Ireland – West Coast

This coast resembles the W coast of Scotland and the Scandinavian peninsula. In an uncharacteristically 'purple' passage HJ Hanson, who compiled the early editions of *The Cruising Association Handbook* almost single-handed, wrote 'The splendour of the mountains, their varying colours, whether in the rising or setting sunlight, by noonday or under the moon, the glory of the sea in fine weather at sundown, when it often resembles a lake of molten gold, the mighty cliffs, attaining in Donegal and Mayo to a height of nearly 2,000ft, and the secure hbrs scattered with few exceptions at easy intervals, will well repay the efforts required to reach these waters.' That is as true today as it was when it was written over 80 years ago.

The *ICC Sailing Directions* are essential for those exploring in detail the west coast and its many smaller anchorages.

Except when crossing the mouth of Donegal Bay and between Galway Bay and the Blaskets, there is usually an easily accessible harbour close by. In unsettled weather a yacht may be held up to leeward of one of the headlands, but on such occasions most hbrs afford facilities for excursions.

Although a careful and experienced skipper can in general navigate this coast with ease and confidence, it is fully exposed to the Atlantic swell. If overtaken by bad weather and poor visibility, unless a familiar anchorage is close at hand it may well be necessary to get clear of the land until the weather improves. This coast should therefore be cruised only by seaworthy yachts capable of making to windward and remaining at sea in any conditions.

Local opinion is that the sailing season starts in May and closes in September, on account of the heavy swell which is usually running in the Atlantic at other times of the year. So long as there is swell in the offing, only a moderate onshore breeze is needed to bring it quickly into the coast, but from June the coast is usually subject only to such seas as may be caused by local breezes or a summer gale.

The coastline is rocky and great care must be given to navigation as many hazards are not marked. The datum on chart plotters can be significantly off. The anchorages along the west coast vary from sandy on many islands to muddy on the mainland, or a mix of sand and mud with occasional seaweed, rock or shell. The CQR can clog and drag under those conditions. Newer generation scoop type anchors (Rocna, Ultra, Manson, Vulcan, etc) when well set have proven reliable in most bottom types found here and under challenging conditions. Gale force winds can be encountered unexpectedly and should be anticipated. Visitors' moorings (yellow) are available in many places but are not always serviced annually; the Irish Sailing Association maintains a listing of visitor moorings with maintenance dates (www.sailing.ie/cruising/visitor-mooring/).

Marinas are few and far between. On the west coast, marinas (S to N) include Lawrence Cove (Bere Island) Cahersiveen (93 berths), Dingle (80 berths), Fenit (130 berths), Kilrush (170 berths), Rossaveal (35 berths), Galway (31 berths) and Killybegs (63 berths). There are no marinas north of Killybegs until Loch Swilly on the north coast. Self-sufficiency is essential around the NW quadrant. New marinas are planned for the west coast.

Streams are not extensively charted, but are apt to be considerably stronger off headlands giving rise to confused and possibly breaking seas with any weight of wind. Headlands such as Bloody Foreland, Erris, Achill, Slyne and Loop Heads should be treated with the greatest respect and an offing of two to three miles lessens the chances of a shaking-up when rounding. Avoid, in all but calm periods, those areas in which the symbol for overfalls is indicated on the chart. Useful information about tidal streams and currents can be found at www.inyourfootsteps.com.

The ensuing pages of this almanac, between Bloody Foreland and Valentia provide brief general notes followed by sailing directions on a selection of harbours. They indicate possible harbours of refuge although very bad weather may make it unsafe to approach any harbour.

The Rosses, extending 15M from the Bloody Foreland to Arranmore, afford a fascinating cruising area on the direct route for a yacht sailing round Ireland, sheltered by a string of islands and with several good anchorages. The Stag Rocks and more particularly the Bullogconnell shoals must be given a good berth.

The direct course between Rinrawros Pt on Arranmore and Rathlin O'Birne some 20M to S leads clear of dangers, but there is a strong set into Boylagh Bay.

Yachts proceeding S with insufficient time to explore Donegal Bay should make for Erris Head (47M from Rathlin O'Birne) with the option of putting into Broadhaven or carrying on.

Proceeding N on the direct passage, Rathlin O'Birne is the best landfall, with the options of making for Killybegs (or Teelin in favourable weather) or for Arranmore.

Between Killala and Broadhaven there is a 24M stretch of inhospitable, but spectacularly scenic, cliffs of the N Mayo coast but these should be given a wide berth if unsettled weather between WSW and N is forecast. The best harbours of refuge are Killybegs, Aran Road in W winds and Rutland harbour inside Arranmore in S or E winds although passage into the latter is intricate.

For those with more time, Clew Bay in county Mayo provides a delightful stopover with safe anchorage at Clare Island and in Rosmoney near Westport. Galway Bay, with the Aran Islands and Galway town, a locked hbr, is a must visit. Dingle and Bantry Bays provide fine cruising grounds that could delight for weeks.

MULROY BAY

Standard Port Galway

Bar

HW	(sp) +0052	(np) +0108	
LW	(sp) +0102	(np) +0118	
MHWS	MHWN	MLWN	MLWS
–1·2m	–1·0m	n/a	n/a

Mulroy Bay affords 12M of navigable channel. A power cable across Moross channel, clearance 6m, bars North Water to most yachts. Some of the finest scenery in Ireland.

Approach The coast both east and west of the entrance to the bay is foul and must be given an offing.

From West From a position some 4ca or more N of Frenchman's Rk (always visible) make for 55°16'·05N 7°47'·15W about ½M N of Melmore Hd, (to make sure that you are clearing the dangerous, submerged rocks keep Horn Hd well open to the N of Frenchman's Rk). Thence alter course to 150° to a position 55°15'·12N 7°46'·40W, 3ca E of the light on Ravedy Island, Fl.3s.

From East Keep the highest part of Dunaff Hd open of Fanad Hd, bearing 91°, steer 271° until the light on Ravedy Island bears 220° (55°17'·05N 7°45'·15W) then steer for it until some 4ca distant at which point alter course to 180° to the position 3ca to its east.

Entrance and Bar Least water is likely to be 2·8m at datum over the east bar, when seas break in onshore winds and/or there is a big swell running. Inspect before entry and watch your echo sounder. The best time of entry is from half tide to HW–0100 when most of the rocks are well visible and the flood can be carried far inland. From the position 3ca E of the Ravendy Island Lt steer 165° to leave the square concrete G bn Fl.G.2s about ½ca to stb. High Rk and Sessiagh Rks only cover at HW springs. At this point turn to 210° toward the First Narrows. When 2ca off the Glinsk Pt shore gradually turn to stb and pass through the middle of the Narrows. Thereafter keep in mid channel until past the Dundooan rocks, Bn Q.G., then work toward the west shore. The Low Rock Bar 'beacon' has no topmark or light on it at present, and is almost covered at HW. Apart from the green weed on it, and its rectangular shape, there is no way of identifying it, other than by its GPS coordinates. Mulroy Bay is especially important in shellfish harvesting and fish farming. Beware of marine farms throughout.

Anchorages

- N of Dundooan Rocks in 3·5–5·5m, sand.
- Fanny's Bay on W side about 3M inside the bar in 2m affords complete shelter out of the stream at all times and is probably the best anchorage on the NW coast of Ireland. PO and shop at Downings village, 1M across the peninsula dividing Sheep Haven from Mulroy. Excellent hotel at Rosapenna, ¾M. Bus to Londonderry.
- In Bullogfemule, a land-locked basin on E side just above the second narrows, where there is a road br vert clearance 19m. The third narrows or Hassans Pass has 8kn stream and should be taken at slack water. Flood begins at Galway –0230, ebb at +0325.
- There are two useful passage anchorages in relatively settled weather just inside the mouth of the Bay. The first is just S of Ballyhoorisky Island off Portnalong which provides

BLOODY FORELAND TO ERRIS HEAD

Passage lights	BA No.
Tory Island	6200
Fl(4)30s40m18M	
Racon(M) (– –) AIS	
Bloody Foreland	6203
Fl.WG.7·5s14m6/4M	
Arranmore	
Rinrawros Point	6208
Fl(2)20s71m18M+Fl.R.3s13M AIS	
Rathlin O'Birne Is	6216
Fl.WR.15s35m12/10M AIS	
Mullaghmore Head	6231
Fl.G.3s5m3M	
Eagle Is	6268
Fl(3)20s67m18M AIS	

228

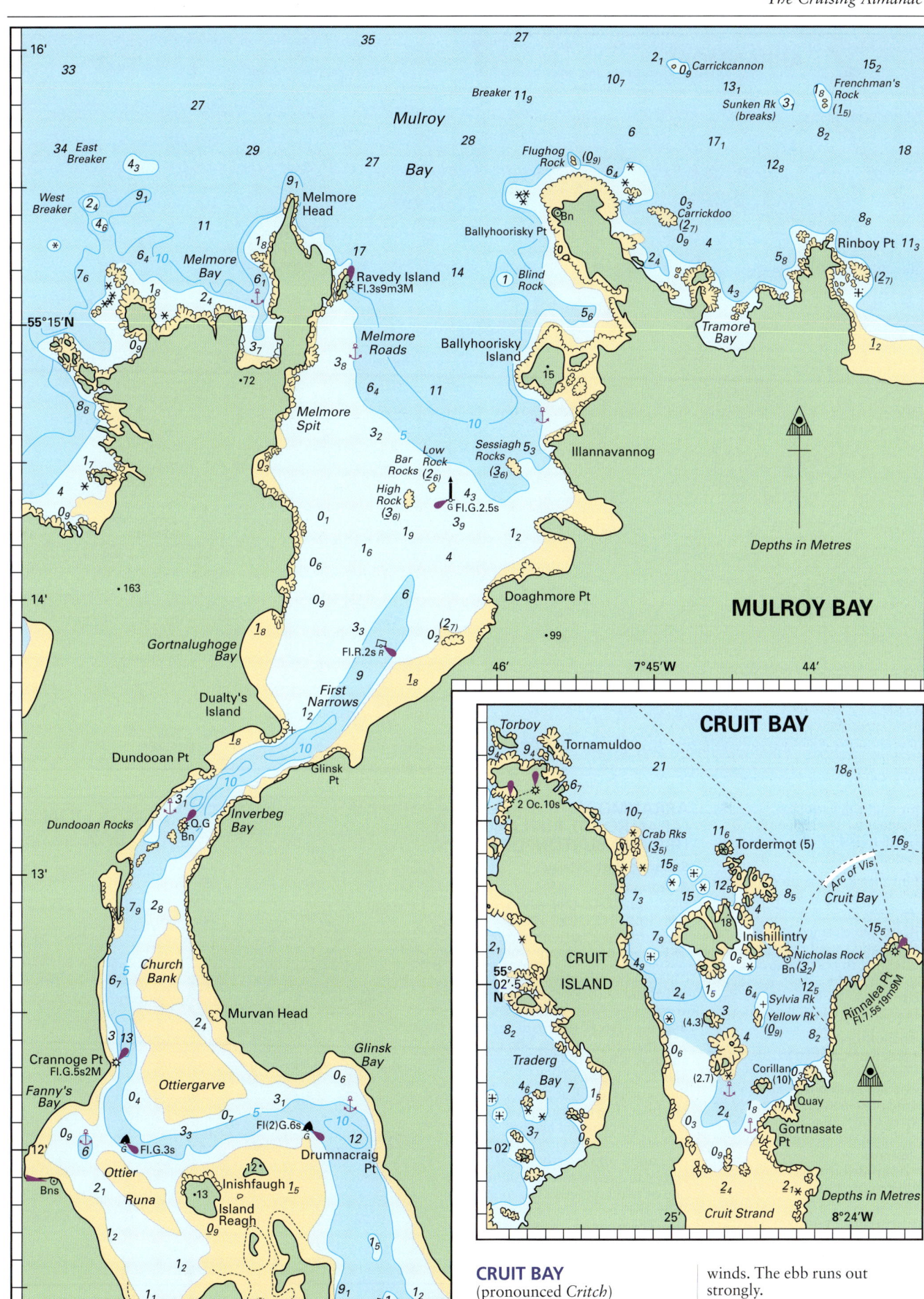

shelter from the south and east. The other is just N of Ravedy Island providing shelter from the south and west. Neither is suitable in a northerly wind or swell.

CRUIT BAY
(pronounced *Critch*)
Standard Port Galway
HW (sp) +0042 (np) +0055

MHWS	MHWN	MLWN	MLWS
–1·2m	–1·0m	–0·6m	–0·3m

A good anchorage in summer winds, and easy to enter, but can be subject to swell in N'ly winds. The ebb runs out strongly.

Approach from N. Leave Gola Island which has Knockaculleen 69m at the N end to port with a fair offing ½M and head due S to leave Inishfree also to port. This takes a yacht clear of all possible breakers. The transit for entering Cruit Bay is Gortnasate Point open E of Corillan Is 195°. The Is is well into the bay.

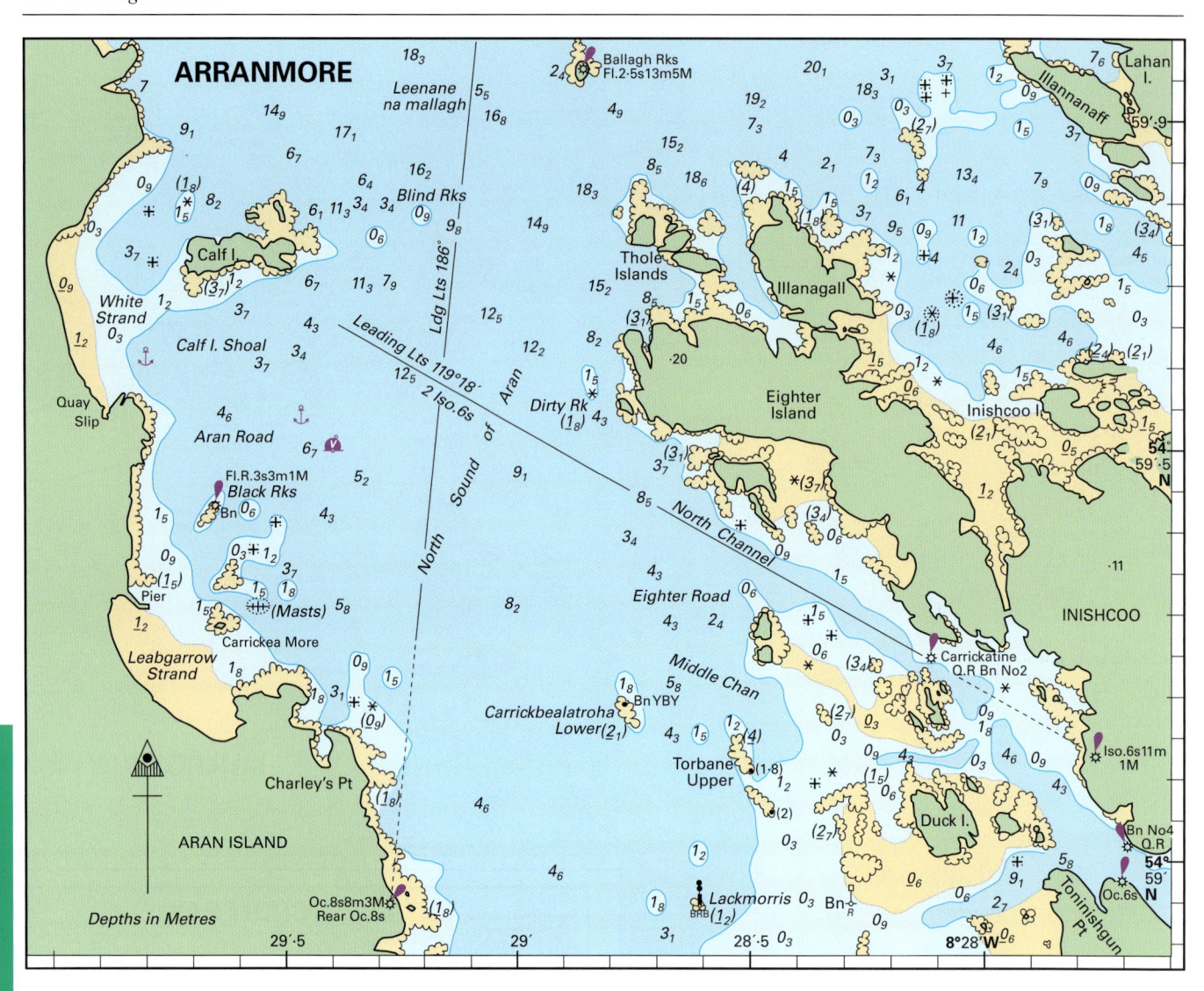

Entrance Keeping on the transit leave Nicholas Rock with bn to stb. This also clears the Yellow Rock. On closing Corillan turn to stb and round the islet close leaving it to port. Take care not to mistake the entrance with the bay to the W of Tordermot and Inishillintry which is very foul.

Anchorages
- Just S of Corillan in 2m sand.
- To W of the above and N of existing local boats, also in sand. Take care not to get N by W of Corillan as there is a bad rock just off an unmarked Is in this area.
- It is possible to go alongside Gortnasate Quay while getting stores.
- Town quay pontoon. HM ℡ 071 9111237 or 086 0890767 for gate code.

Facilities Water at quay. PO and limited stores at Kincaslough ½M. Fuel 2M. Enquire from the locals who may be able to help with transport.

ARRANMORE (ARAN ROAD), RUTLAND HBR AND BURTONPORT

Standard Port Galway

Burtonport
HW (sp) +0042 (np) +0055
LW (sp) +0115 (np) +0055

MHWS	MHWN	MLWN	MLWS
–1·2m	–1·0m	–0·6m	–0·3m

This is a popular area of the W of Ireland with good, sheltered anchorages. Most of the difficult parts of the roads are well marked by buoys, Ldg Lts and bns. Chart 1883 is essential and 2792 is essential for Burtonport and Rutland Harbour. The easiest passage in is through N Sound leaving Ballagh Rocks bn Fl.2·5s to port and Calf Is to stb. At, or before this point one can sight one of two Ldg lines: The more W'ly 161° is the line of two bns. The front on Carrickbealatroha Rock and the rear on Lackmorris Rock. The E'ly lead line 186° on two lighted bns Oc.8s on the SE shore of Arranmore. Each line is safe water into North Sound of Aran. They cross just east of Calf Island. For the best anchorage off the E shore turn to stb at this point to 241° on the transit of an obelisk on the shore with the summit of Moylecorragh 162m. When S or SW-by-S of Calf Is come to anchor in 3–4m some 2ca N of the Black Rock Fl.R.3s. Further S than this and you may hamper the Island ferry fairway which berths at a pier 2ca SSW of Black Rock. Good landing at the slip beside the small obelisk.

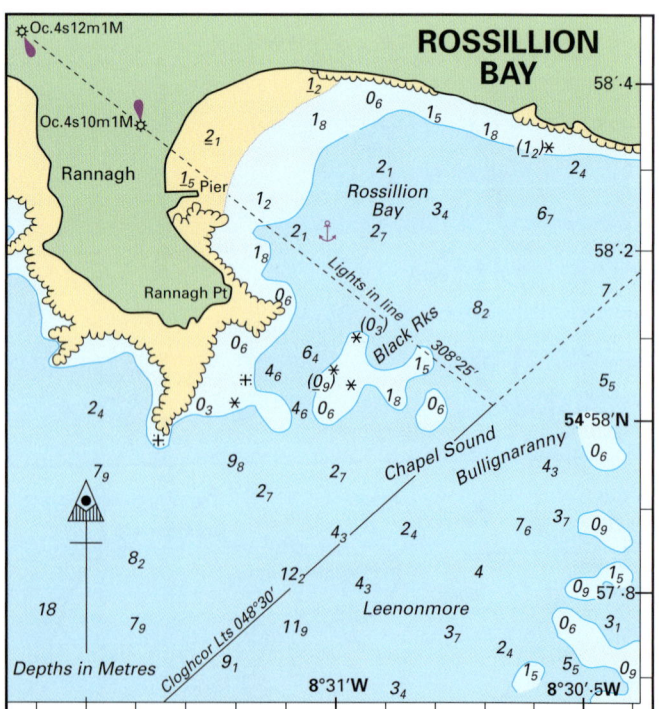

Visitors' moorings may be found in this vicinity.

Facilities General store, two small hotels, well water, restaurant/pub, fuel by can.

TEELIN HARBOUR

Depths in Metres

To make for Rutland Harbour or Burtonport, both well sheltered, continue on the N entry transit (161° or 186°) until two bns Iso.6s come in transit 119°. The channel is narrow with rks each side and busy with fishing vessels and ferries coming to and from Burtonport. Follow this lead until Carrickatine bn Q.R. abeam to port, when turn gently to 137° on the transit of two bns Oc.6s on Rutland Island. Half way past Duck Is come to anchor in the wider part of the channel in 5–7m but avoid the centre line of the fairway for the ferry and fishing boats. Alternatively continue toward Inishcoo to come to anchor in 4–5m some 75m WNW of the ruined quay, put a line ashore abreast the anchor to hold boat out of the fairway where the tide runs hard. Anchor lights essential here as fishing boats use the channel day and night. A further anchorage is Black Hole, just beyond the inner of Rutland Is Ldg Lts. A little bay some 55m across and 35m deep with a depth of 4m where one can anchor. A secure and sheltered S to NW gale hole. For Burtonport continue up marked channel on sufficient rise (half tide) to reach the quay. It is possible to secure here alongside the pier or a fishing boat, with permission, in a least depth of 1·7m. Yachts now welcome. HM VHF 14, 16, ☏ 086 8310121.

Facilities FW hose, diesel, petrol in cans. Shops, hotel and bar. Hull and engine repairs. Electronics. Bus to Donegal.

Approach from south Some 3ca S of Ranagh Pt on transit 048° two Lt bns Iso.8s at head of Chapel Bay through Chapel Sound. Either turn to port on transit 308° of two bns Oc.4s but beware of Black Rocks, 0·3ca, to port of line. Come to anchor in 2m 1½ca ESE of pier in Rossillion Bay, or continue toward the first bns, toward Chapel Bay, keeping clear of rocky foreshore to port to come to anchor in 4m 1ca SSW of the quay.

Both these anchorages are good in northerly breezes but may be troubled by westerly swell.

TEELIN

Standard Port Galway
HW (sp) +0040   (np) +0050
LW (sp) +0055   (np) +0035
MHWS MHWN MLWN MLWS
–1·0m –0·9m –0·5m –0·2m

A naturally beautiful haven. Other than in strong S or SE winds, it offers a quiet anchorage or mooring. Access to Slieve League sea cliffs 2·5M from the village.

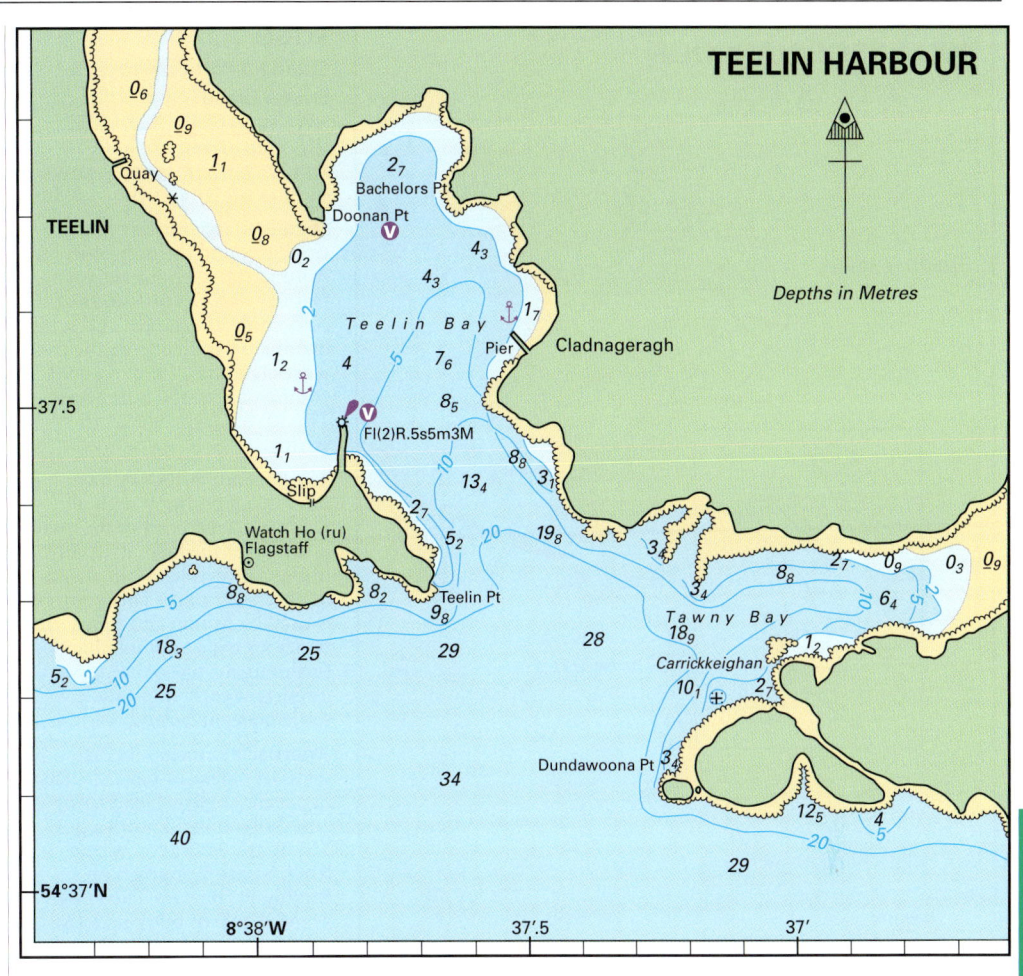

Approach From the W make for Carrigan Head, which has a conspicuous tr (101m) then easterly along the coast keeping 3ca offshore. After 2M the entrance will open up to port. From SW or S approach the coast 1½M east of the conspicuous tr on Carrigan Hd. From the E from Muckross Head shape a course for Dunawoona Point 1·3M. Close to this point Teelin will be seen ½M ahead to the NW.

Entrance is straightforward by day. There is no longer a light on Teelin Point. Pier head lit Fl(2)R.5s5m3M. Avoid making a first entry at night.

Anchorage Quiet anchorage can usually be found 100m NW of the pier. If a swell is chasing in, there may be quieter water on the eastern side of the bay close N of the old pier at Cladnageragh.

Moorings There are four yellow visitors' moorings between Teelin pier and Bachelors point, but these are exposed to the S.

Facilities The nearest shops are at Carrick, 3M, friendly pub ½M from Teelin pier. New café/craft shop in town. Water on the pier, but it can be busy with fishermen. Electricity on pier head, cards Paddy Byrne ☏ 0876284688, 0749739365. Taxi ☏ 0749739145.

KILLYBEGS

Standard Port Galway
HW +0045   LW +0045
MHWS MHWN MLWN MLWS
–1·0m –0·9m –0·5m –0·2m

A very busy fishing port providing very good shelter and can be entered day or night. New quays recently built. New marina in 2016.

Approach

From the W Pass two miles S of Muckross Head and head E until the E side of Drumanoo Head bears NE, then turn in to pass SE of it, passing midway between Ellamore Shoal and the 14·3m shoal 1½M to the W. In heavy westerly weather it can break heavily on these shoals.

From the S Leave Inishmurray 2M to port and head for Bullockmore buoy which lies 3M W of St John's Point, then alter course for Drumanoo Head to leave Ellamore shoal to stb and follow the directions above.

Entrance Keep in the mid channel leaving Rotten Island Fl.WR.4s to stb. Keeping mid-channel locate R Lt buoys Fl.R.3s and Fl.R.7s. Head for the S card Lt buoy on the Harbour Shoal and when ½ca S of this buoy turn in towards the quays. There is sectored Lt WRG.6s bearing 338° to lead to the quay.

Anchorages
- To the E of the town in 2·5–3·5m in mud, thus avoiding heavy fishing boat traffic. Sometimes poor in SW'ly weather.
- To the SW of W end of the town in 4–7m. Subject to fishing boat traffic.
- In Walkers Bay (SE of Rough Point) if the wind is S'ly. Off the slip to NW in 5–8m, avoiding local moorings.

Warning Do not anchor in Port Roshin, (½M NW of Rotten Is) holding poor and an uncharted rock. Beware of lost ground tackle in all anchorages.

Facilities Mooney Boats on the W side of the inner harbour has 75t travel hoist and all services, including chandlery, but no sailmaker. Second chandlery in town, usual shops etc. Bus to Donegal Town, Sligo from Tara Hotel. Small hospital. Marina new in 2016 (63 berths), 3 visitors' moorings W of the fish quay or yachts can lie at the town pier with small fishing boats. Killybegs Sailing Club maintains several guest moorings off the fish processing plant. HM VHF 14, 16 ☏ 074 973 1032.

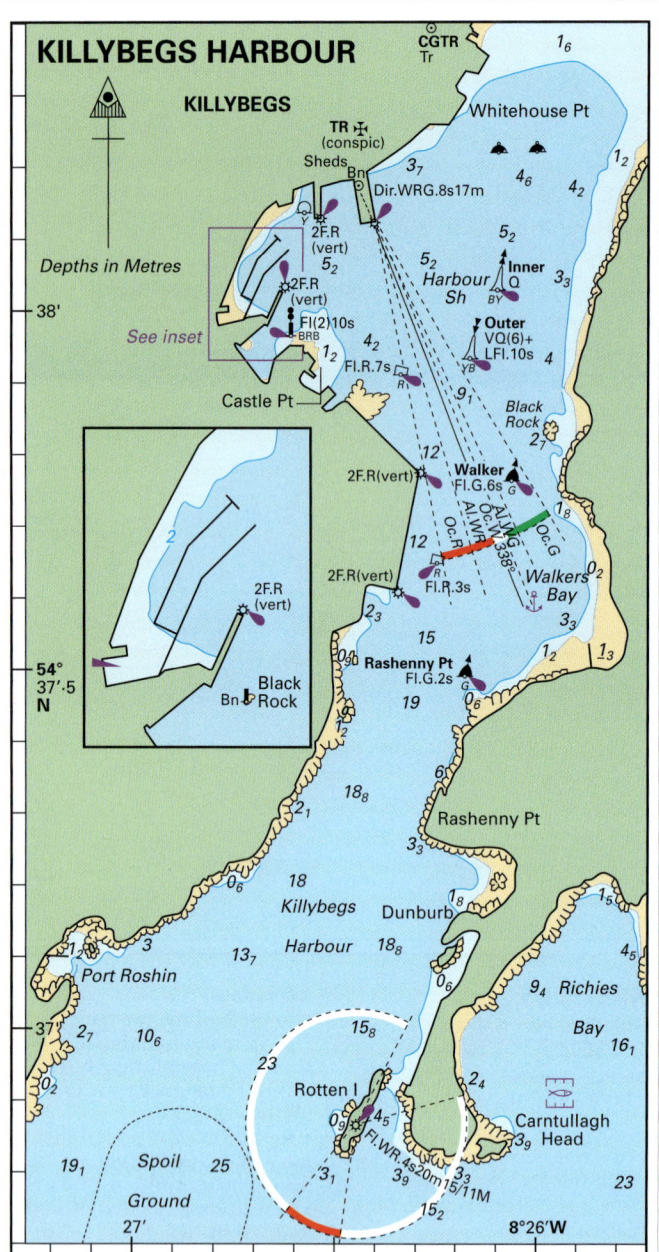

SLIGO

Standard Port Galway
Oyster Island
HW (sp) +0043 (np) +0055
LW (sp) +0042 (np) +0054

MHWS	MHWN	MLWN	MLWS
−1·0m	−0·9m	−0·5m	−0·3m

Sligo is a large estuary hbr in a small city and the only working commercial harbour between Galway and Derry. Cargoes of coal, timber, fish meal and scrap metal are handled from the two working jetties. Care to avoid commercial traffic is imperative. The River Garavogue runs swiftly.

The harbour authority have provided a pontoon with all facilities at the head of the quays just NW of the first city road bridge, advisable to call ahead to check on space. This pontoon is used by fishing and sightseeing boats for trips to uninhabited Inishmurray, one of the most important early monastic settlements in Ireland.

Approach Donegal Bay is relatively clear of hazards. Pass between Anghris Head to stb and Ballyconnel Point to port 5M apart. Make for Wheat Rock S card Lt buoy S of Raghly Pt. Beware The Ledge 2½M WSW of buoy and 1M off Anghris Point (Breaks in heavy weather). From 2½ca S of the card buoy sight 068° for Lower Rosses Lt bn Fl(2)WRG.10s.

Entrance Maintain this heading for 1·4M to N card buoy, Bungar Bank, then turn to stb on 125° transit Metal Man Rock bn Fl(3)6s (Metal Man actually is a metal statue of a sailor) and Oyster Is bn Fl(3)6s. Hold this course to Metal Man then leave the statue bn to stb and two perches to port. Turn to port round the south of Deadman's Point into the channel between Oyster Island and Deadman's Point keeping closer to the N shore.

Beware The passage between Oyster Island and Coney Island is dangerous.

Anchorage Vessels can anchor anywhere suitable in Sligo Bay as the bottom is mostly sand. The mouth of the river is protected by sandy islands, and at low water the sand stretches for miles. Yachts should anchor to the north side of Oyster Island to await the tide or daylight when approaching or proceed up the channel to the town quays. Sligo Bay Y C, off Deadman's Point, has bar/showers/visitor's moorings. Rosses village has shops and bus to Sligo. One can anchor in this vicinity. Either 1ca to the SW of the pier in 2–3m but the holding is poor and the tide runs hard. Safer and more comfortable, in similar depth ¾ca WNW of the first port-hand Lt bn Fl.R.1·5s.

Continuing to Sligo The channel is marked with port and stb bns. After about 1M one reaches the bn marking the end of the training wall Fl.1·5s. Leave it to stb and continue keeping training wall 30m to stb until a port training wall appears when keep closer to it in 2m dredged channel. When first jetty to stb is seen some 2½ca ahead cross toward it and keep close to stb-hand bns. Beware: There is a mid-channel middle ground/rock marked by

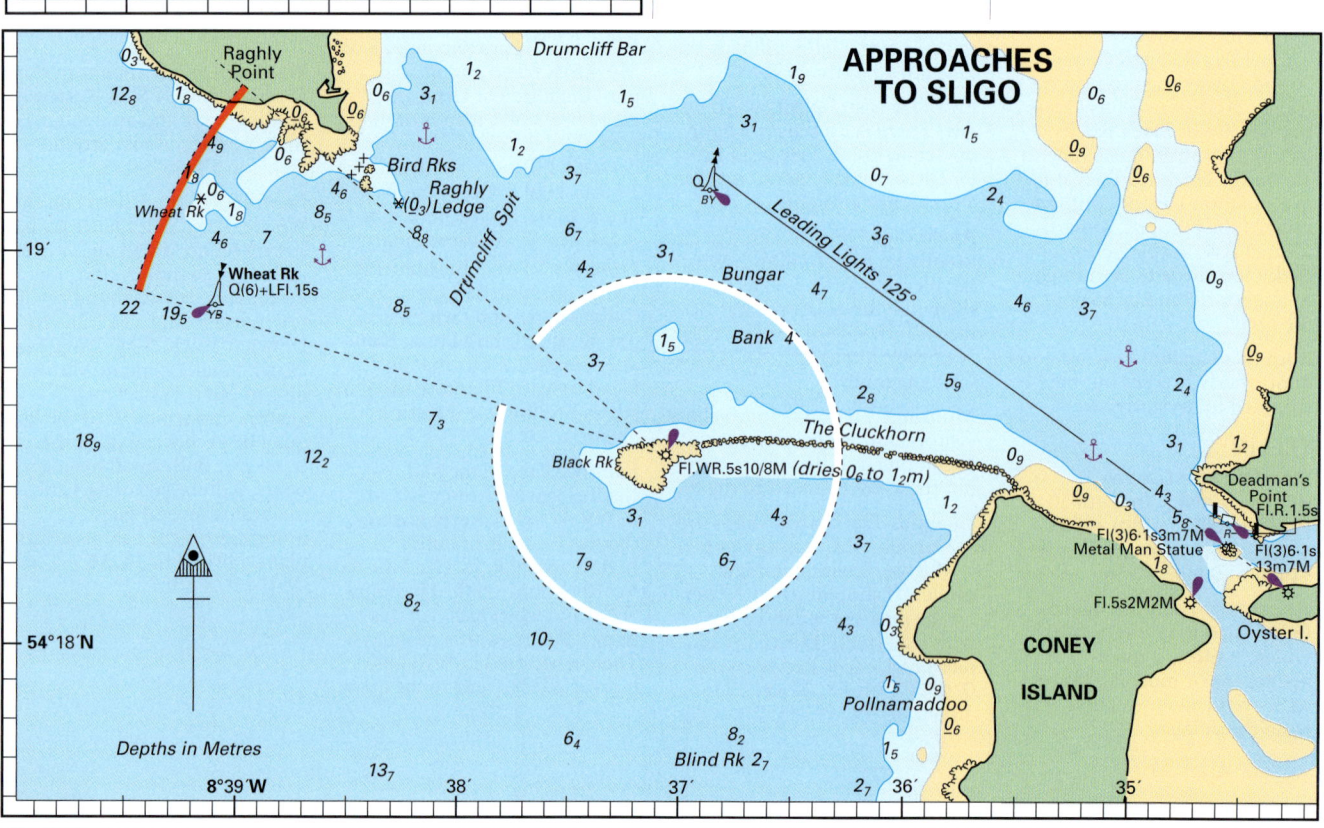

The Cruising Almanac

SLIGO HARBOUR

BROAD HAVEN

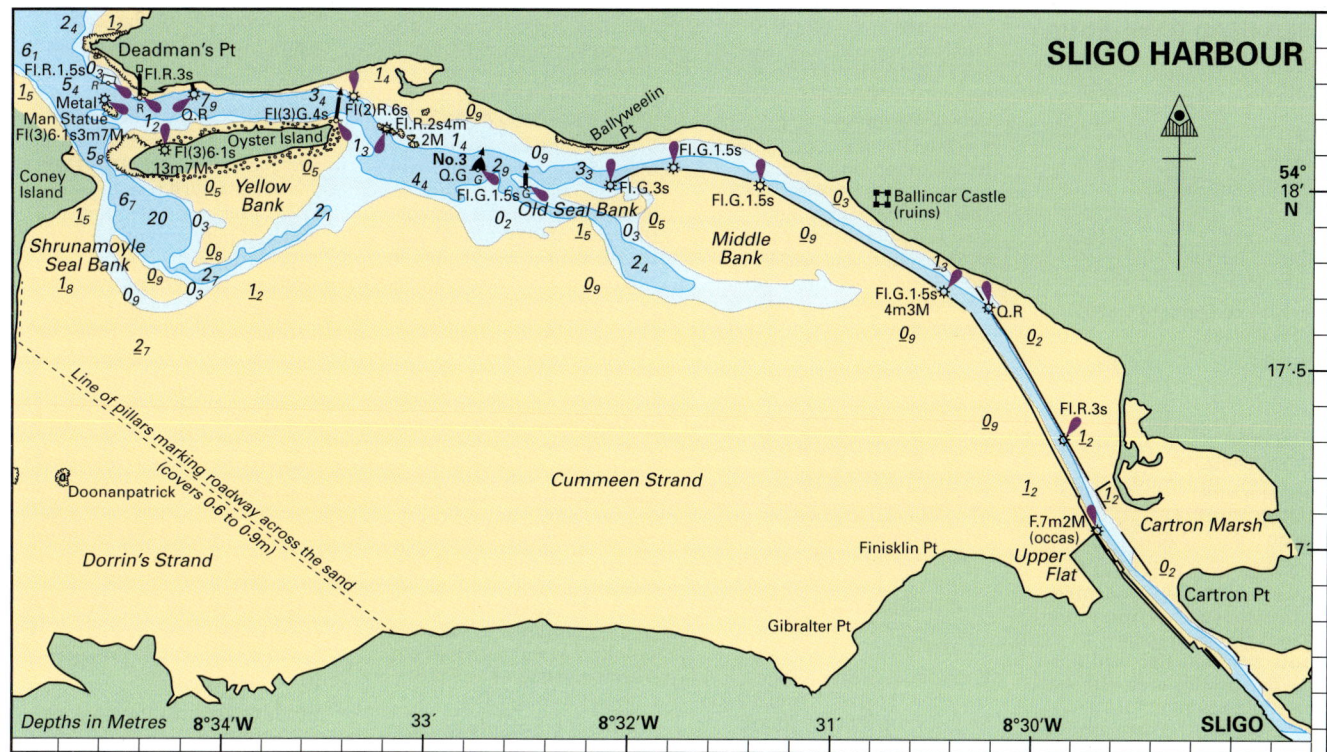

two stb bns. Do not pass between this and the SW quay. Beyond the second of these bns proceed up the channel parallel with the SW quays. The first city bridge will come into sight. At the head of the quays there is a 60m pontoon with depths; MHWS 4·0m MHWN 3·0m MLWN 2·0m MLWS 1·5m. Moor securely since the ebb can run quite quickly.

Facilities Water, fuel and electricity on the pontoon. Security by coded gate. All services in town, good hospital, shopping centres, restaurants, pubs/bars, hotels, and places of entertainment. High concentration of prehistoric (megalithic) archaeological sites. Frequent festivals. Bus station hub, Ireland West Knock Airport, Rly to Dublin.

☎/**VHF** Hbr Office 0719111237 VHF16/12 HM Mobile 0860890767.

BROADHAVEN

Standard Port Galway
HW (sp) +0035 (np) +0035
LW (sp) +0040 (np) +0040

MHWS	MHWN	MLWN	MLWS
–1·4m	–1·0m	–0·6m	–0·2m

A good safe hbr in all summer weather. It is 5M long and 1M wide in places. In bad NW and N gales the entrance breaks and should not be attempted.

Approach From N: Pass outside the Stags and give Kidd Island a 1M berth to avoid the race. Alter course for Gubacashel Lt Iso.WR.4s. This takes you clear of the rk off Doonanierin Point. From S: Leave Eagle Is light Fl(3)10s to stb and head for a point 1M N of Erris Head – again to avoid the race. Turn into Broadhaven Bay and head for Gubacashel Lt. Do not get inside a line between this point and Duvell Point as Monastery Rock is nasty.

Entrance The entrance is clear for 1M. After that there are shallow patches on each side.

Anchorages
• In bay N of Ballyglass in 3·5m. The line is Gubacashel Point in line with the W side of Kidd Is. Shelter from SW to NW.
• Off the pier in the next bay to stb in 3m with Ballyglass Lt bearing 035°. The pier has 2m alongside and it is sometimes possible to lie alongside a trawler there. Bellmulet 6M. PO. Showers at LB station. Telephone. Friendly local transport.
• On port side ½M S of Inver Point in 3·5m off the hamlet. Best in E winds. Telephone 2M at Barnatra. The rest of the bay can be explored on a rising tide in a dinghy.

FRENCHPORT (PORTNAFRANKAGH)

A small inlet providing a port of call on the direct route for yachts sailing round Ireland, especially in an E'ly. Not recommended if W'ly swell is running high. Give the southern shore a wide berth to avoid the rocky promontory extending from Annagh Head. Beware of rock at 7m depth in the middle of the entrance that breaks in heavy weather and Parson's Rock inside the harbour. No facilities, no water. Good pub and shop at Corclogh (2M) and more in Belmullet (4M). Head of hbr is foul with shingle. Eagle Island Lighthouse to the North.

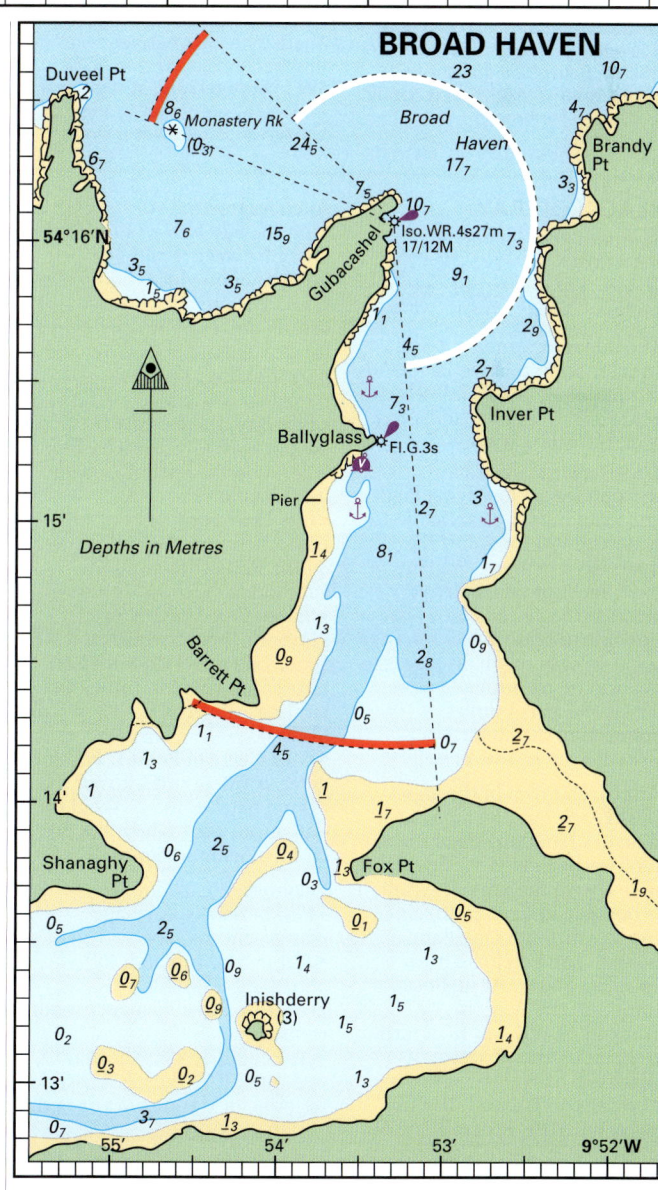

IRELAND

233

ERRIS HEAD TO VALENTIA

Passage lights	BA No.
Black Rk Fl.WR.12s86m18/14M AIS	6270
Achillbeg Is Fl.WR.5s56m16/9M AIS	6276
Slyne Head Fl(2)15s35m19M Racon (T) (–) AIS	6288
Rock Island (Earagh) Fl.15s35m18M	6296
Inisheer Iso.WR.12s34m16/11M AIS	6334
Loop Head Fl(4)20s84m23M	6338
Inishtearaght Fl(2)20s84m18M Racon (O) (–––) AIS	6408

The coast from Erris Head to Slyne Head is deeply indented, with long stretches fronted by islands affording some protection from the swell. It is a fine day-cruising area, although not well enough lit for sailing inshore at night. There are many sheltered bays, the pick of the anchorages being Blacksod Bay, Clew Bay, Killary and Little Killary, Ballynakill, Inishbofin and Clifden. Frenchport is handy if pressed for time.

BLACKSOD BAY

Standard Port Galway
HW +0030   LW +0040

MHWS	MHWN	MLWN	MLWS
–1·2m	–1·0m	–0·6m	–0·4m

The tide runs strongly 2·5kn straight on to the two headlands Turduvillaun and Achill which guard the outer bay. In the bay itself the tide is weak.

This is a large open bay surrounded by low-lying land and sand hills. It is about 3M wide and 9M long. Off the main bay are many smaller bays, most of which are very shoal at their heads. It is always possible to select a bay for any wind so only the main places to anchor are mentioned below. The canal at Belmullet connecting through to Broadhaven is now closed.

Approach From N through Inishkea Sound, leading mark to avoid Pluddany Rocks to the E of Inishkea N is Turduvillaun in line with the Ears of Achill. It is possible in daylight to enter the bay through Duvillaun Sound. The Ldg bns are on Inishkea South. At night sail S until into the W sector of Black Rock Lt Fl.WR.12s then turn in to open up the W sector of Blacksod Lt Fl(2)7·5s. 3½ca abeam is an E card pillar Lt buoy Q(3)10s. Proceed due N until clear of the E Card bn VQ(3)5s with topmark on Carrigeenmore and anchor until daylight.

When, and if, the bridge is repaired, Mayo CC will require 2 working days notice to open the bridge. ✆ 097 81004 or email Belmullet@mayococo.ie

Blacksod Bay is a good refuge in bad weather, with quite a number of anchorages. The South Connemara coast between Roundstone Bay, 15M E of Slyne Head, and Cashla, 32M from Slyne Head, affords a fascinating cruising ground with a wide choice of anchorages among several bays.

For 20M between Cashla and Galway the N shore of Galway Bay is exposed with no safe hbrs. The S side has a number of anchorages between Galway and Black Head. Thence the 45M of coast to Loop Head has no safe anchorage and should be given a good offing. Passages to or from the S can be shortened by spending a night at Kilronan, Aran Is, in most weather conditions.

If making a direct passage between the Aran Is and Blasket Sound, note that the course from the Gregory Sound to Sybil Pt passes 7M W of Loop Head. There is no light between Inisheer and Loop Head (33M SW of Inisheer) and at night it is important not to get to the E of the direct course. Nor is there any major light between Loop Hd and Inishtearaght (39M). In the prevailing swell there is a pronounced set to the E for which it is wise to allow 5°.

Yachts bound between the Mayo, Sligo or Donegal coasts and the S might consider a direct Inishbofin – Valentia passage, thus eliminating considerable deviation of course to hbrs on this coast. Direct course takes you within 1M of Slyne Head.

There are, however, possible anchorages between Loop Head and Sybil Point which, apart from Smerwick Harbour, involve varying deviations from the direct course.

If passing through or outside the Blaskets, it is especially important to note and respect those areas where overfalls are indicated on the large-scale chart. The magnetic anomaly to the N of the Blaskets is to be treated seriously: its influence is reported as very localised but extreme enough to spin the compass through 360°!

The best hbrs of refuge are, in the N of the area, Roundstone and Cashla Bays, and S of Loop Hd, Smerwick in S'ly gales and Dingle or Valentia in N'lies. Yachts may also run for shelter in the River Shannon, notably to Carrigaholt or Kilrush.

Anchorages
- On the bay NW of Blacksod Quay between it and Doobeg Point avoiding local boats, 3m sand. The quay itself dries and is foul, and the immediate area for 2ca around is shallow and poor holding. Visitors' moorings available.
- **Elly Bay** is one of the best anchorages. Give Ardelly Point a good berth. Anchor outside local boats.
- **Elly Harbour** just N of Elly Bay. Anchor in the middle in 3–4m. Subject to swell in southerlies. Visitors' moorings.
- **Saleen Bay** 1½M N of Elly Harbour. Tend towards the NE shore Ldg line 319° with Lts Oc.4s5M. There is 3m. Good landing. Subject to swell in S or SE'lies.
- **N of Claggan Point** If possible enter at LW in order to see the drying patches to N. Avoid the dangerous rock which lies 3ca S by E of Ardmore Point.

Facilities
- Pub in Blacksod village convenient to quay.
- About 1½M inland, PO, petrol, diesel and limited groceries. Possible local friendly transport.
- At Belmullet 3M. Shops, PO, fuel, pub, RC Church. Possible friendly local transport or taxi.

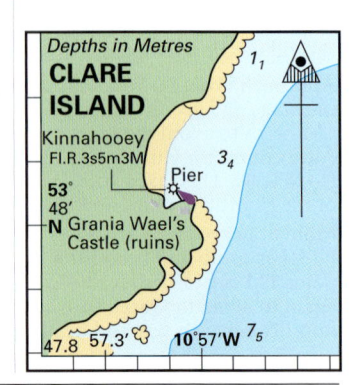

CLEW BAY

Standard Port Galway
Inishgort
HW +0040   LW +0108

MHWS	MHWN	MLWN	MLWS
–0·7m	–0·5m	–0·2m	0·0m

Westport lies in the SE corner of Clew Bay, a very scenic, picturesque part of the Irish west coast. Protected to a large extent by Clare Island to the west, sheltered by the high hills of Achill Head to the north and the mountains of Mayo and Connemara to the south, it is a sheltered sailing area. Westport itself, with railway from Dublin, is excellent for crew changes.

Approach Enter Clew Bay either to the N or S of Clare Is. From the S keep within 1M of Clare Island to avoid isolated rocks. At half tide the following directions should find no less than 4m depth all the way to the 'Entrance' to Westport Quay. Do not attempt without an up to date chart.

Pass between Inishgort LtHo Fl.10s and Dorinish buoy Fl.G. Steer ESE toward Inishlyre some 3ca and when the shore is about 2ca ahead a G buoy should be seen to stb marking the extent of the Dorinish Bar. Steer S toward two small islands; Inishlagen and Inishimmel. The channel between the two is buoyed. Then steer ESE toward Inishraher. There will be a port hand buoy then a stb to take you north of Inishraher on an E'ly course. As Inishgowla South draws close on the port bow the south cliff of Inishlyre will be seen to come in transit with the N end of the white wall at Inishgort LtHo bearing 307°, as shown on plan. Using this as an astern transit steer 127°, after some 6ca port and stb hand perches will be seen. Pass between these into Westport Bay. On reaching a position some 2ca south of Green Isle steer 080° to leave Carricknacally rock with R Lt bn to port and pick up the buoyed channel to Westport Quay.

Entrance Pass between Lt bn Fl.3s.G box on con stone bn and Monkellys Rocks into Westport Channel, marked by G perches to stb. Bear round Roman Island to approach Westport Quay. Keep close to stb side. At HW –0200, mean tides, 2·2m can be found all the way to the quay with sandy bottom.

Berthing Against the quay near the 'Old Derrick Crane'. Prepare to dry out as tide falls. Soft mud on hard underlay.

Facilities At Westport Quay; pubs, restaurants, four-star hotel and medium-sized supermarket. Westport town 1M with all facilities. Clew Bay Boats chandlery and repair ✆ 098 50633. Rly to Dublin. Buses to Ireland West Knock Airport and elsewhere.

Anchorages
- Small anchorage for shallow draft vessels near entrance to Westport House estate.
- **Clare Island** has visitor moorings and is an excellent passage anchorage. PO/shop, pub, restaurant, community centre with showers/laundry, Grace O'Malley's castle and chapel.
- **Achillbeg Is** has protection from northwesterlies. Deserted village. Access to Achill Island by dinghy.
- **Inishgowla Is** Secure anchorage for waiting out heavy weather in the inner Bay. Uninhabited.
- **Dorinish Is** Good holding in bay to E. Once owned by John Lennon and Yoko Ono. Uninhabited.
- **Inishlyre Hbr** To E of island
- **Collanmore Hbr** in bay to E of island.

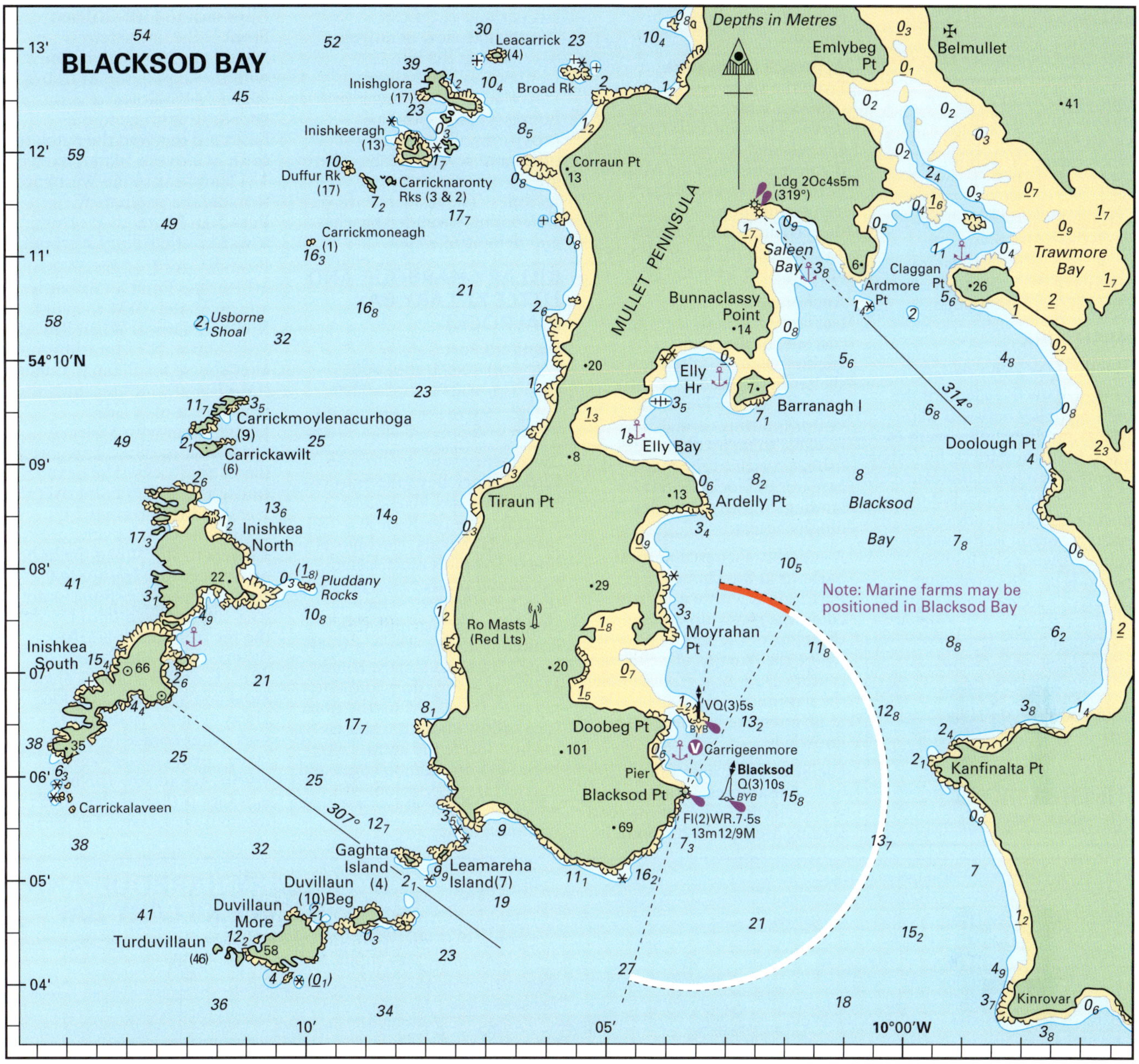
BLACKSOD BAY
Depths in Metres
Leacarrick
Broad Rk
Inishglora
Inishkeeragh
Duffur Rk
Carricknaronty Rks (3 & 2)
Carrickmoneagh
Corraun Pt
MULLET PENINSULA
Emlybeg Pt
Belmullet
Ldg 2Oc4s5m (319°)
Saleen Bay
Claggan
Ardmore Pt
Trawmore Bay
Bunnaclassy Point
Usborne Shoal
Elly Hr
Barranagh I
Elly Bay
Carrickmoylenacurhoga
Carrickawilt
Doolough Pt
Tiraun Pt
Ardelly Pt
Blacksod Bay
Inishkea North
Pluddany Rocks
Ro Masts (Red Lts)
Moyrahan Pt
Note: Marine farms may be positioned in Blacksod Bay
Inishkea South
VQ(3)5s
Doobeg Pt
Carrigeenmore
Kanfinalta Pt
Pier
Blacksod Pt
Blacksod Q(3)10s
Fl(2)WR.7·5s 13m12/9M
Carrickalaveen
Gaghta Island
Leamareha Island(7)
Duvillaun Beg
Duvillaun More
Turduvillaun
Kinrovar
54°10′N
10°00′W

IRELAND

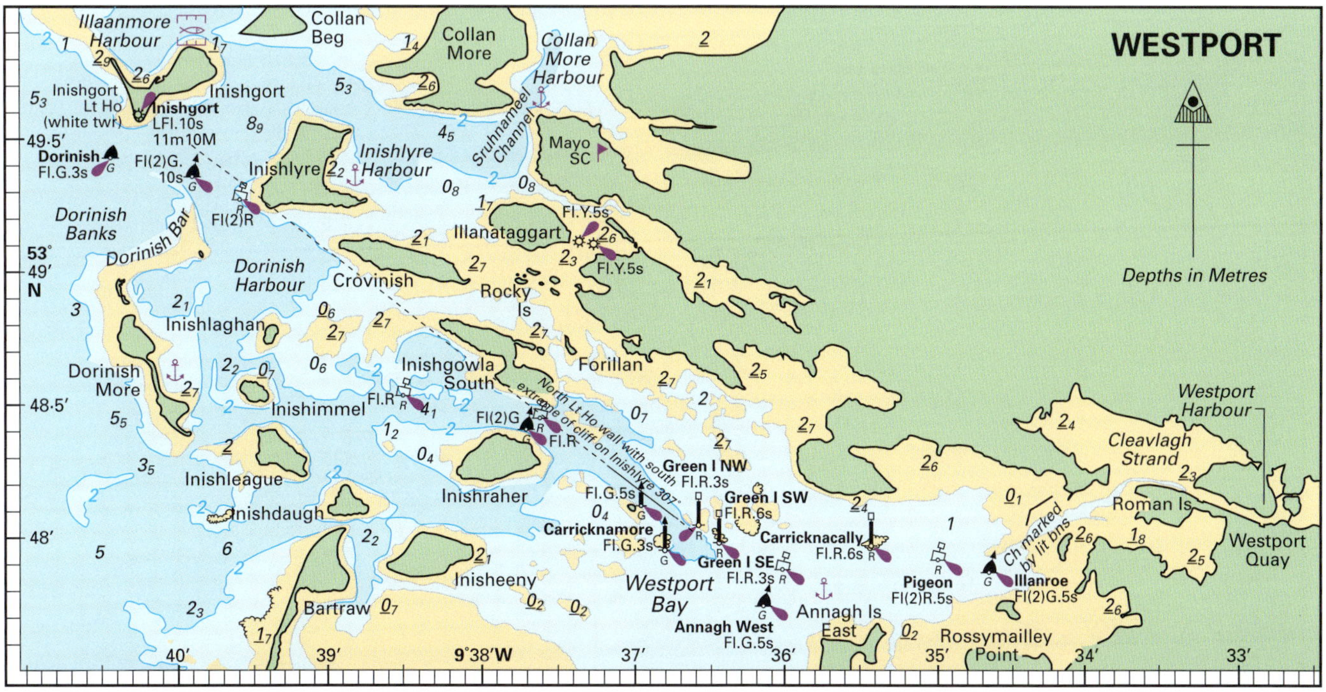
WESTPORT
Depths in Metres
Illaanmore Harbour
Collan Beg
Collan More
Collan More Harbour
Inishgort
Inishgort Lt Ho (white twr)
Inishgort LFl.10s 11m10M
Dorinish Fl.G.3s
Fl(2)G.10s
Fl(2)R
Inishlyre
Inishlyre Harbour
Sruhnameel Channel
Mayo SC
Dorinish Banks
Dorinish Bar
Dorinish Harbour
Crovinish
Illanataggart
Fl.Y.5s
Rocky Is
Inishlaghan
Dorinish More
Inishgowla South
Forillan
Inishimmel
Fl.R
Fl(2)G
North Lt Ho wall with south extremity of cliff on Inishlyre 307°
Inishleague
Inishdaugh
Inishraher
Green I NW Fl.R.3s
Green I SW Fl.R.6s
Carricknamore Fl.G.3s
Carricknacally Fl.R.6s
Green I SE Fl.R.3s
Pigeon Fl(2)R.5s
Illanroe Fl(2)G.5s
Ch marked by lit bns
Westport Harbour
Cleavlagh Strand
Roman Is
Westport Quay
Inisheeny
Westport Bay
Annagh West Fl.G.5s
Annagh Is East
Rossymailley Point
Bartraw
9°38′W
53° 49′ N

- **Mayo Sailing Club** visitors' moorings. Turn to stb on entering Collanmore Hbr. Club has pontoon with water for 10 minute stay and a slip for dinghy landing. Clubhouse has showers and bar open on days when racing or training is taking place. Rosmoney to Westport is 6M.
- **Annagh Island East** To N of island, an all states of tide 'hole' can be found. Useful when awaiting tide to Westport Quay or departing same.

INISHTURK
Standard Port Galway

Inishturk, or the island of the wild boar, lies between Clare Island and Inishbofin south of Clew Bay. It is flanked by Caher Island which has significant early Christian ruins but no anchorage. Inishturk is a rocky, tranquil island with a ruined tower at its highest point. It has 58 permanent residents and almost no tourism.

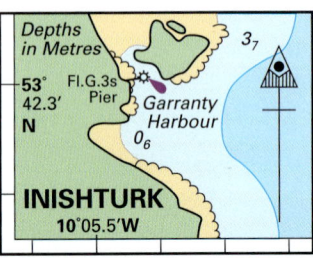

Approach to Inishturk
From the south give Gubnagawny point a wide berth. The approach from Clare Island is straightforward. If coming through the Middle Ground, be aware that a significant chop can develop in the varying shallow depths. Take care in the Floor Shoals if approaching from the W.

Anchorage
Garranty Harbour is on the east side of the island. The anchorage in 5m offers good shelter in the predominantly westerly winds. There are visitor moorings and it is possible to tie up alongside fishing vessels at the quay. Take care not to block the ferry landing. Slipway provides dinghy access.

A superbly sheltered natural harbour at the Dun at Portdoon is within a narrow cut in the rocks along the shoreline of the south coast where the remains of a 9th century Dun, or fort, overlook the natural lagoon. This is not to be attempted without local knowledge.

Facilities The Community Club has a bar and restaurant open weekends at the top of the road leading around the harbour. It has perhaps the most spectacular view of any bar overlooking the hills of Connemara and Killary Harbour. The building also houses a shop with basic provisions. There is a post office and several B&Bs. There are no other services or facilities. The residents are very welcoming. Secluded beaches and delightful walks.

KILLARY HARBOUR AND LITTLE KILLARY BAY (SALROCK)
Standard Port Galway
HW (sp) +0021 (np) +0015
LW (sp) +0035 (np) +0029
MHWS MHWN MLWN MLWS
−1·0m −0·8m −0·4m −0·3m

Two picturesque anchorages, Little Killary Bay (aka Salrock) lies S of Killary Harbour separated by the Rosroe peninsula. Killary Harbour is one of Ireland's most scenic fjords and offers easier access than Little Killary, which should not be attempted in limited visibility. There are off-lying rocks and shoals. Killary Harbour is very deep and one needs to travel 3M up the fjord for shallow enough water to anchor. Inside the entrance to both bays are salmon cages and mussel farms, positions of which are often changed without notice.

Approach to Little Killary
From N the line astern is Mweelaun 19m high in line with the sloping top of Clare Island 341°. However it is necessary to come to the Eastward to avoid the patch to the E of Govern Island, likewise 1M later bear to the Westward to avoid the patch to W of Inishdegil More, then turn in toward Little Killary Harbour. From W give Inishbroon Island off Rinvyle Point a fair berth of approximately ½M to avoid Mweelaunatura. When Rinvyle Point shows N of Innishbroon alter course for Illaunananima (Live Island) until reaching the next transit of N side Freaghillaun with S islet of Shanvallybeg 089°. This clears the Puffin Rocks. The next transit is Cleggan Point over the E end of Inishbroon (051°) taking one clear of various dangers to stb. When the lit bns on Doonee and Inishbarna come in line alter course onto 099° and proceed until Doonee bn, the front mark is ½M distant. Then alter course to 128°, Carrickclass rocks ahead. Hold course until Carricklea, always visible, is abeam 1ca to port. Alter course to 115° to leave Carricklass, always visible, 1ca to stb. The hbr entrance is then visible ahead on stb bow. Leave a fair berth

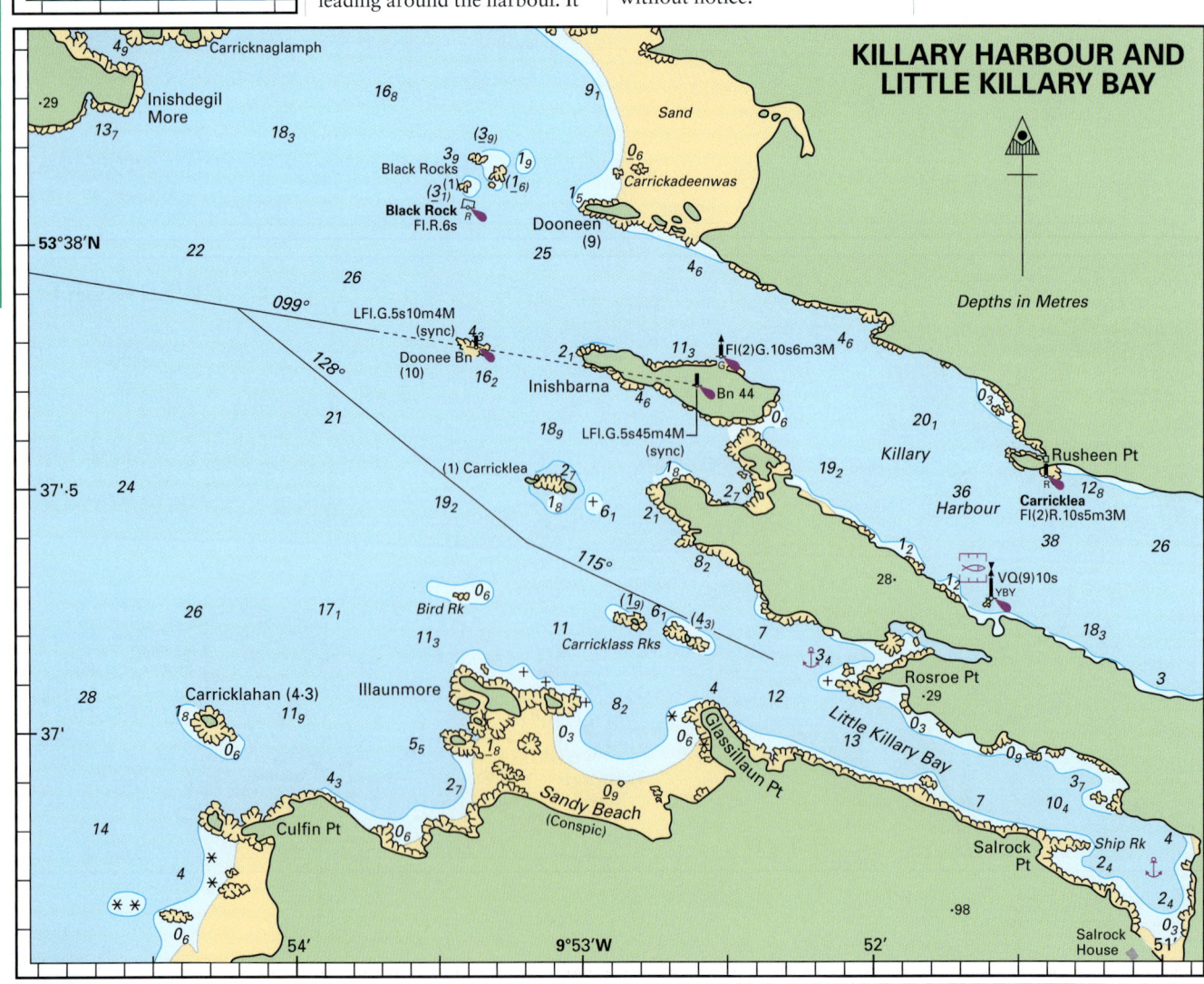

to port off Rosroe Pt, submerged rock, and to stb off Ship Rk, a tapering reef.

Entrance All dangers are above water and should be given a fair berth.

Anchorages
- In 3–4m off Rosroe Point as shown on chart.
- Better still at the head beyond Ship Rock. Turn to stb to anchor as convenient in 2–3m (mud) ½ca SE of Ship rock or in the bay 1½ca NNE of Salrock House; a good berth in perfect shelter. A good anchor is required in strong blows. Water from well with permission of the owner of Salrock House. No other facilities.

Approach to Killary Harbour
Alternatively, leave the bns and Inishbarna to stb to enter this dramatically picturesque 'fjord'. There are eight visitors' moorings near the top of the 7M long hbr close to the village of Leenane (Leenaun). Apart from a few rocks close to shore, there are no hazards in the length of the inlet, with the exception of fish farming. Keep watch for cruise catamaran. Anchor at Derrynasliggan or on the N shore at Bundorraghan. Do not venture too far into the head of the harbour which shallows and is foul with tree limbs in mud. In a W'ly, wind can funnel up inside the high walls of the fjord making the anchorage uncomfortable at best.

Facilities In the heart of Connemara, surrounded by breathtaking mountain scenery and walking trails. Killary Adventure Centre (no moorings) meals, showers, water, day trips by arrangement is about halfway in on stbd shore. Access to village at slip beside Leenane Quay which dries. Meals and showers at Leenane Hotel. Good pub, restaurant, PO, shop, petrol, sheep and wool museum, hostel. Bike hire at The Convent B&B.

Caution Only attempt this area in good visibility during daylight. Chart 2706 essential.

CLIFDEN BAY
Standard Port Galway
HW +0005   LW +0016
MHWS   MHWN   MLWN   MLWS
–0·7m   –0·5m   n/a   n/a

This bay is well sheltered, but now has a number of fish farms with their attendant gear. The town of Clifden (about 2M along coast road) which can be approached by dinghy on a rising tide has all facilities and is the heart of Connemara.

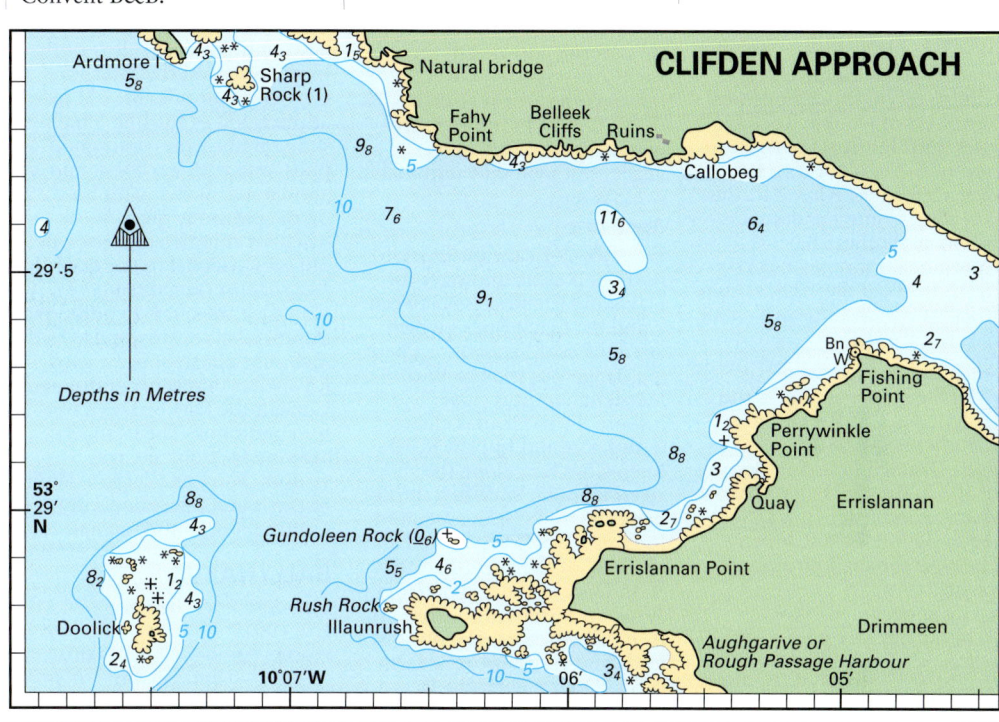

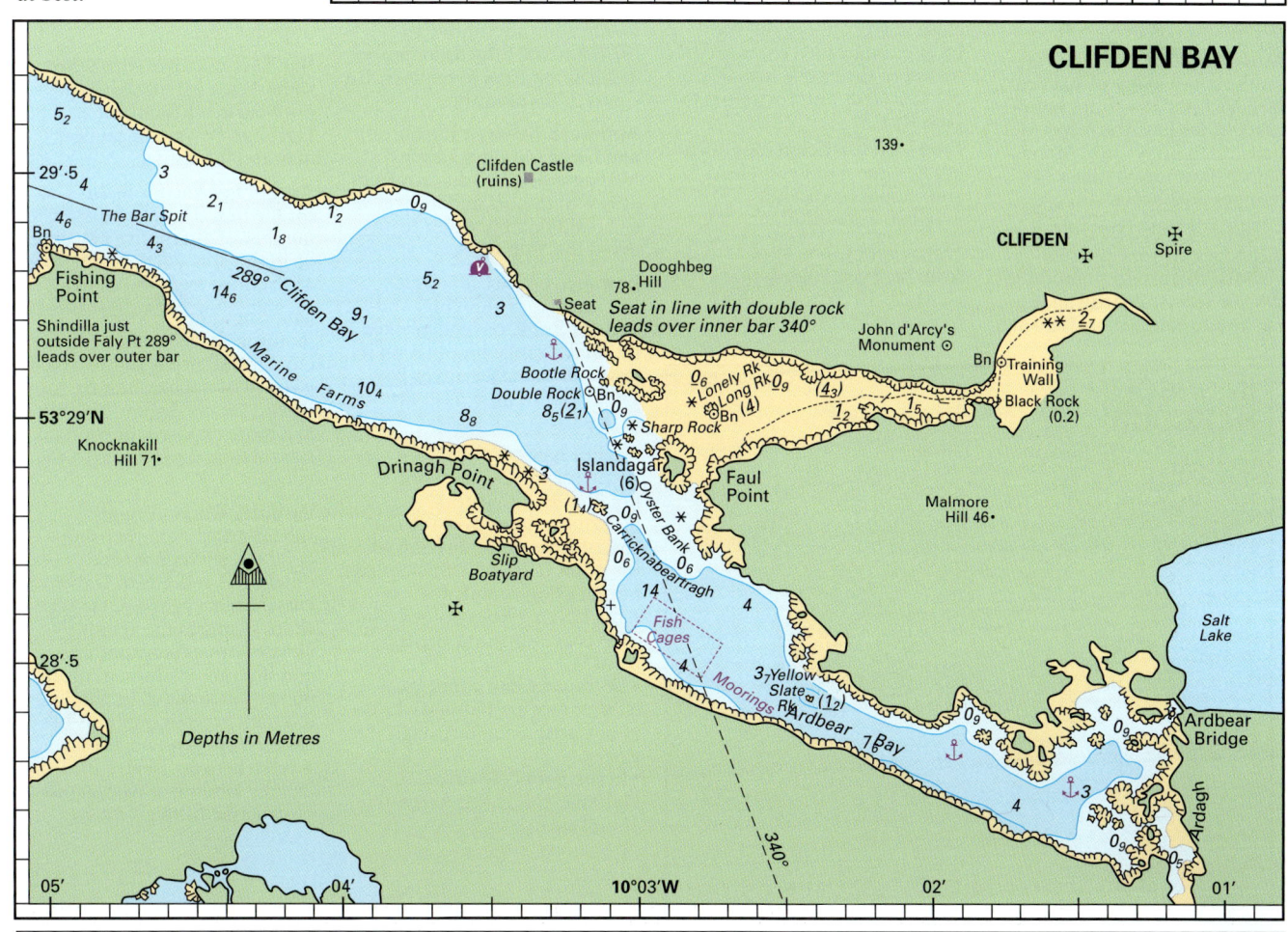

Approach Pick up the conspic bn on Carrickrana Rock. Keep clear of the Corbet Shoal breakers. Approaching the Carrickrana rock alter course to stb to leave the Carrickrana bn at least 4ca to port, continue round the bn at this range until Clifden Castle (ruins) is just open of Fishery Point on a bearing of 080°. Steer this course, leaving the Doolick rocks and ledge well to stb, toward Fishery Point until it is 4ca distant, fine on the stb bow, then alter course to 045°.

Entrance Steer 045° until Fahy Point (to your NW) bears 289°. Turn to stb to 109° and maintain Fahy Point on the stern bearing 289°. This will take you over the Bar. 4m minimum at datum.

Caution Have your echo sounder on as silting is reported from the north.

Thence steer up the bay toward 'Double Rock' bn. There is a second bar, 'The Oyster Bank', (0·9m datum) a little S of the shallow creek that leads to Clifden town. From a position 50m west of Double Rock bn steer 160° for 2ca, then ease to port until the bn bears 340° over your stern. After a further 2ca you are into the deeper waters of Ardbear Bay. Continue up this bay but keep to stb to avoid the 'Yellow Slate Rock' (dr 1·2m) after which all hazards are visible.

Anchorages
• Off the bn which marks the entrance to Clifden Harbour, slightly to NW. Mud.
• Off Drinagh Pt in 5m. Beware of ebb in overfall from Ardbear Bay. A good place to wait for the flood tide up to Clifden Harbour for shallow draught yachts.
• Any unoccupied place in Ardbear Bay (*see above for entrance transit*). Beware of Yellow Slate Rock which dries 1·2m about 5ca above Oyster Bank.

Moorings There are moorings on the south shore of Ardbear Bay. Visitors' moorings below castle ruins in Clifden Bay and by Clifden Boat Club. Many legacy moorings in the area hamper anchoring.

Facilities Clifden Boat Club welcomes visitors and has visitors' moorings, pontoon for dinghy access, Boardwalk Cafe bar/restaurant, water, WiFi and showers. Clifden Harbour is 1½M farther east providing a sheltered tidal harbour with a depth of about 3m at MHW. Quay dries. Walk along waterfront from CBC to town (2M): supermarket, restaurants, pubs, shops, banks. All amenities in town. Buses. Fuel by truck at quay by arrangement.

INISHBOFIN

Standard Port Galway
HW +0011   LW +0019
MHWS   MHWN   MLWN   MLWS
–1·0m   –0·8m   –0·4m   –0·3m

A favourite port of call for yachts on passage N or S, however the area is strewn with rks so it must be approached with caution. Whilst safe inside, exit would be impossible in S/SW gales.

Approach
From the N Leave Inishturk to port – it is clear, and steer for Davillaun Island. Pass between it and the Black Rocks which lie to the E of Inishbofin. There is a dangerous rock to W of Davillaun but it is close inshore. Lyon Head is clean with a sectored Lt Fl.WR.7·5s. Keep close ½ca along the shore steering to the W. When the hbr opens up look for the sectored Lt DirOc.WRG.6s, about 130m to WSW of the nearest conspic W tr. Once in the very narrow W sector turn hard to stb onto 021°. As you enter the hbr this leads you very close to a 1.2m patch. Do not enter the R sector. Leave Gun Rk Fl(2)6s close to stb. Should the sectored Lt be extinguished enter on the transit of the two W trs (032°) but this leads you very close to Gun Rk.

From east Carrickmahoy rock lies 8ca due S of Lyon Head and should be carefully avoided. Then similar to above.

From south Good approach is from between High Is and Friar Is. Make 10° toward Gun Rock to pick up transit as above.

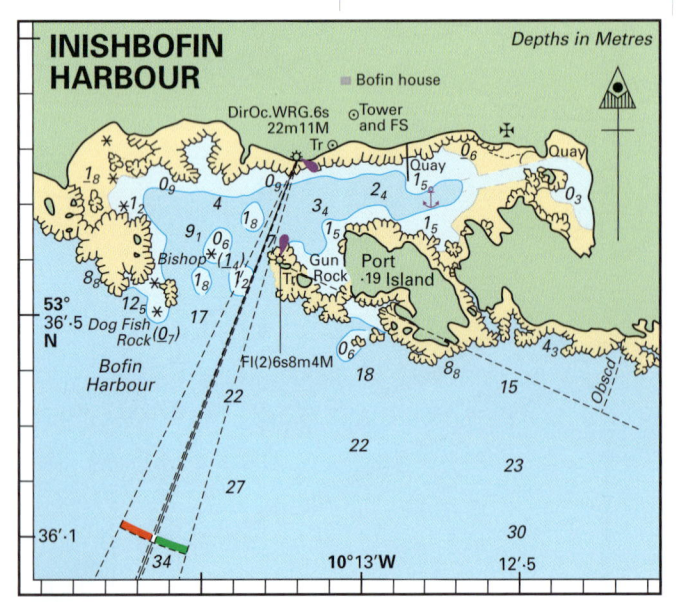

At night Enter on 021° in the narrow W sector of the Dir.Oc.WRG.6s light.

Anchorage Having passed the fort on Port Is turn to E and anchor in the pool in 2–4m. Leave fairway clear for access of ferries to the new pier. Do not go further E than abreast of the building with three chimneys, as the bay shelves rapidly. Fishing boats moored here have heavy ground tackle running E–W. Holding good in sand. Can be gusty.

Facilities Dinghy landing at the new quay, but keep clear of the ferry berths, on the foreshore or, above half tide, the old pier at the E end of the hbr. Small shop on hbr front. Two good pubs, one with bar food, and a good hotel. Water, with hose, on the old stone quay. Work has been completed to provide 2m LAT channel to the quay and short-term mooring alongside the quay. In addition improved access to the dredged inner hbr allows it to be used for shelter in severe conditions. Consult the HM or Day's Inn for conditions. The islanders are very friendly towards visitors. Ferry to Cleggan. WiFi at Day's and the community Centre. Poor mobile signal.

BALLYNAKILL

Standard Port Galway
HW +0018
MHWS   MHWN   MLWN   MLWS
–1·0m   –0·8m   –0·4m   –0·3m

This bay is a good and picturesque alternative to Inisbofin and affords a number of sheltered bays to explore. BA Chart 2706 desirable.

Approach Between Inishbroon and Cleggan Point. Leave Mullaghadrina rocks (covered at HWS) to port and keep close to Freaglillaun in order to avoid the Ship Rock.

Entrance Leave Carrigeen Rocks, always showing, and Ardagh Rock, covers, marked by small orange bn tr, to stb if proceeding to Deryinver Bay. Otherwise to port. Fish farming in the area.

Anchorages
• Fahy Bay in 2–3m. Good holding. Eight visitors' moorings. Enter over the bar SSE of Ross point 2ca SSE of the point 0·2m on sufficient rise of tide using sounder.
• 1ca ENE of Ross Point 2–3m. Tide rode, but good shelter from W.
• Derryinver Bay about ½ca SSW of pier in 2m (mud). Entry N of Carrigeen and Ardagh Rocks.
• In the pool NW of Doleengarve 3–4m. Accessible at half tide.

• Barnaderg Bay. Sound your way in with care on a rising tide. Utter shelter. Very narrow entrance.

Facilities Tullycross 1.5M from Derryinver Quay has small market and pub. The village of Letterfrack lies 2.5M up the road at Barnaderg Bay and has a shop, pubs, PO, petrol and museum. Connemara National Park begins at Letterfrack. Walking trail to the top of Diamond Hill.

Cleggan Bay, the next Bay south, is a busy ferry and fishing port with a small village.

ROUNDSTONE

Standard Port Galway
HW +0003   LW +0008
MHWS   MHWN   MLWN   MLWS
–0·7m   –0·5m   –0·3m   –0·3m

A well-sheltered anchorage in shallow water exposed only to strong SSE winds when shelter could be found in Bertraghboy Bay. A good base from which to explore the nearby bays: Bertraghboy and Cashel. The appropriate chart is recommended.

Approach From the W steer E to avoid Murvey and Caulty Rocks to be left to port. The Wild Billows Rock with Illunacroagh More and its outlying dangers to be left to stb.

When SE of Inishlackan alter course for Inishnee Pt sectored Lt Fl(2)WRG.10s, enter the bay giving a fair berth to both sides but tend towards the W side to avoid rock which lies 3½ca SE of pier.

Bar There is a bar with 0·9m some 1½ca SSE of the 2·4m pool outside Roundstone Harbour. Beware of salmon nets and fish farms.

Anchorage Anchor in 2m just off the pier. There are quite a number of alternative places to lie in the area which can best be ascertained from the chart.

Moorings Four visitors' moorings have been laid in the bay ½M SE of the hbr to avoid passage of the bar. Beware the Rock 1½ca NW. But these are in a more exposed location and leave a long dinghy ride to the village.

Facilities Water. A mini supermarket and other shops, good pubs with bar food, hotels, PO and bus to Galway. Diesel at local garage. Gas in shops. Picturesque artisans' village with gallery, pottery, and Bodran (traditional drum) maker, surrounded by the dramatic steep mountains of Connemara (known as the Twelve Bens or Twelve Pins). Dinghy landing at pier; avoid obstructing fishing vessels.

The Cruising Almanac

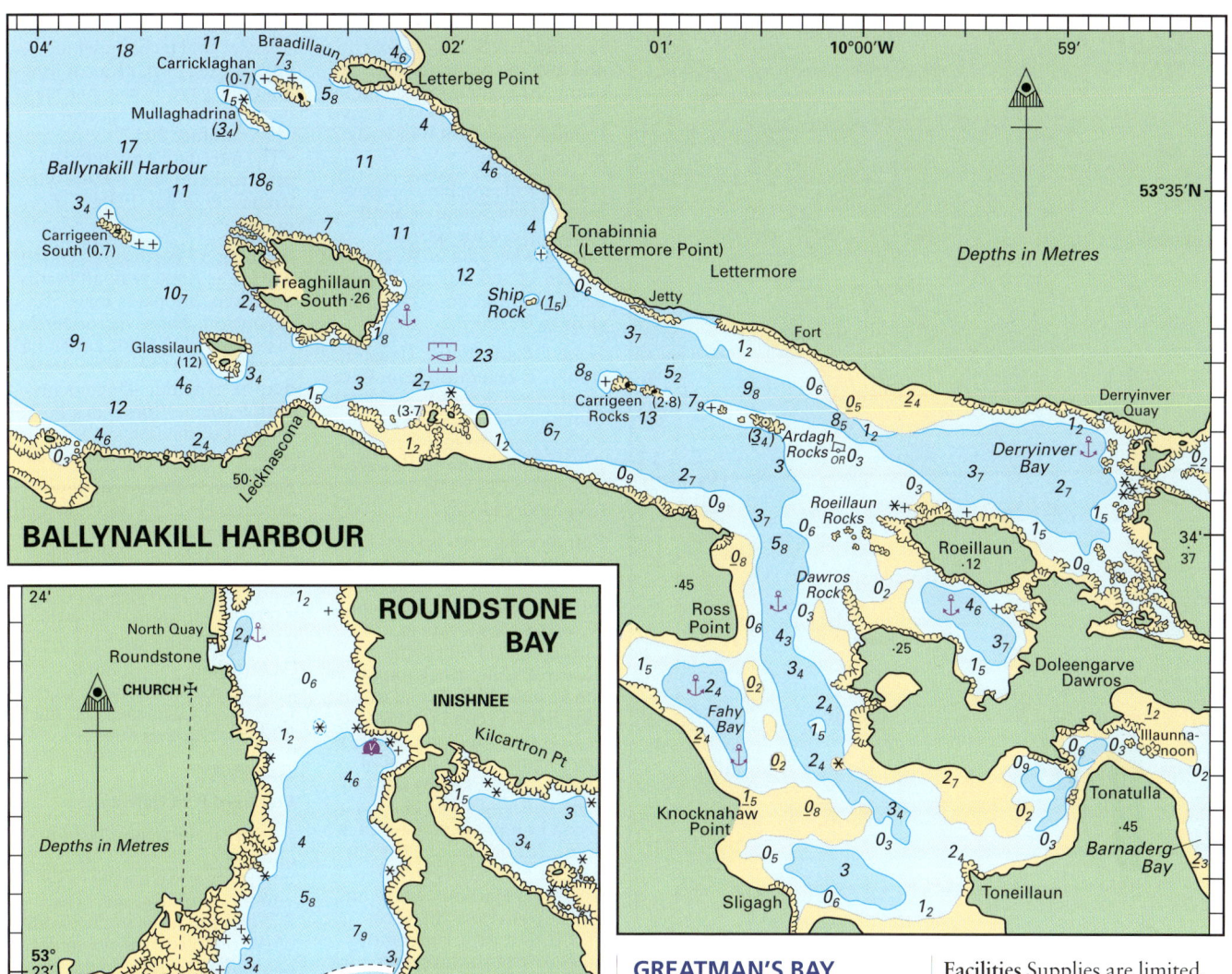

BALLYNAKILL HARBOUR

ROUNDSTONE BAY

GREATMAN'S BAY

Standard Port Galway
HW +0008

MHWS	MHWN	MLWN	MLWS
–0·4m	–0·3m	–0·2m	–0·3m

This bay lies between Gorumna Island and the mainland. It is immediately to the W of Cashla and can be confused with Cashla if care is not taken.

Entrance Its entrance, which has no lights, is relatively simple provided chart 2096 is on hand.

Anchorages There is an anchorage off the quay at Natawnay in approx 3m but it is a 2M walk to the village of Carrowe for the simplest of supplies. The best anchorage is off Maurmeen Quay approx 1½M further up the bay on the Gorumma side. It is guarded by a number of unmarked rocks. The best place to lay your anchor is 4ca NW of the quay in 3m.

Moorings Four visitors' moorings have been laid off Maurmeen.

Facilities Supplies are limited, but there are groceries, telephone, church, bus to Galway and a pub about 1M where petrol can be obtained.

There is a further anchorage up the bay at Bealadangan which can be approached with great care on a rising tide. Again limited stores and pub. If time permits, the rest of this bay and the inlet to westward, Kilkieran, can be explored with care and a dinghy.

IRELAND

239

CASHLA BAY

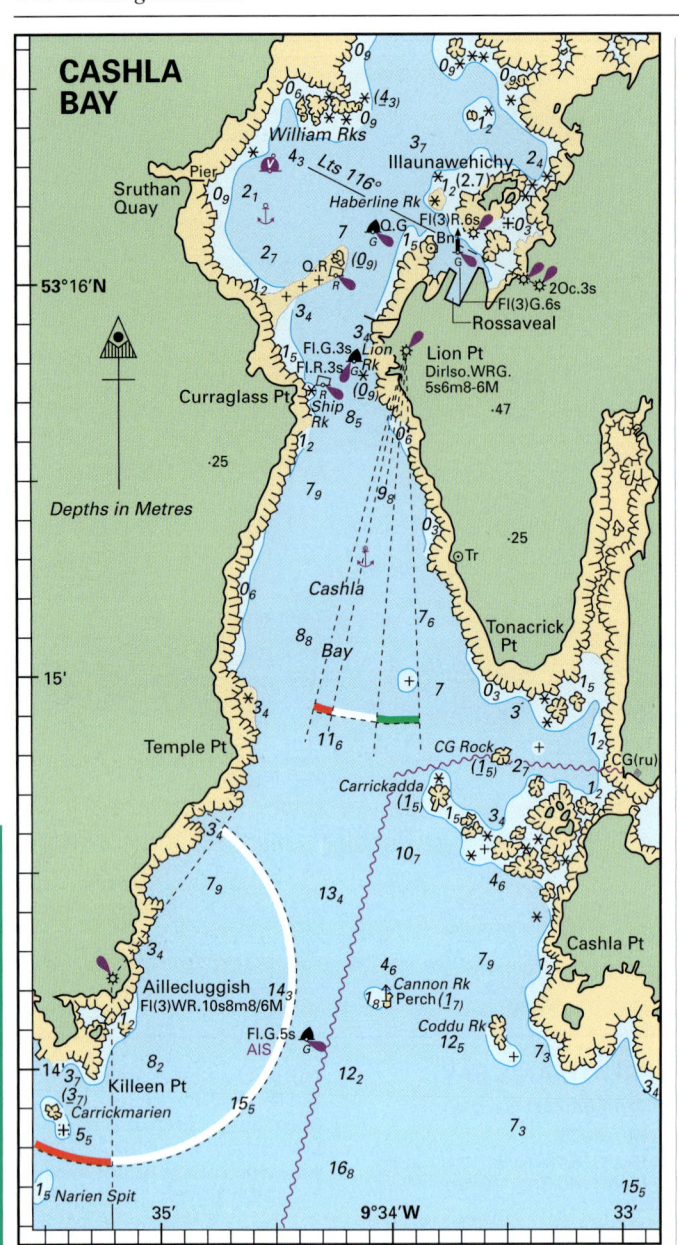

toward Cashla keeping Killeen Point Fl(3)WR.10s on port bow and give the point at least 7ca offing. At night approach in the W sector bearing <360°. Leave Cannon Rock G con Lt buoy Fl.G.5s to stb.

From S Killeany Bay, Gregory Sound, Foul Sound or South Sound. Head for Cashla Entrance keeping in W sector of Killeen Lt and leaving Cannon Rock G con Lt buoy Fl.G.5s close to starbord.

From E Galway Bay. Coast to stb (N) is generally clean. Give an offing of 5ca. When abreast Cloghmore Point steer for Killeen Point to find Cannon Rock G con Lt buoy. Beware off-lying rocks to W of Cloghmore Head.

Entrance Between Killeen Point with its outlying Narien Spit and Cannon Rock. Lion Point bn, DirIso.WRG.5s, by night in W sector, shows way in. Off Curraghglass Point is the dangerous Ship Rock to port R can Lt buoy Fl.R.3s and to stb Lion Rock G con Lt buoy Fl.G.3s off Lion Point. There is a drying patch 3ca due N of Lion Rock marked by a R can buoy Q.R and 1·5ca beyond it a G con Lt buoy Q.G. Give each a berth. 1ca beyond the G sight the Ldg Lts Oc.3s 116° to Rossaveal Harbour. Leave bn Fl(3)R.6s to port and G bn Fl(3)G.6s to stb. The transit takes care of the bn on the rock to W of the pier head and Haberline Rock 1ca due N of it. New 100 berth marina and other associated works centred on; 53°16'·1N, 9°33'·5W expected to be completed by time of publication.

Anchorages
- Rossaveal Harbour, which is a busy fishing port, clear of fishing boat fairways. A new marina is being developed, expected to open summer 2017.
- The alternative anchorage is off Struthan Quay to WNW of Rossaveal in 3m. Eight visitors' moorings.

Berthing 35-berth small craft marina at Rossaveal, all berths are taken, but plans for expansion. Three visitor berths, max 15m LOA draft 2m and a fourth ,16m LOA, 3·7m draft may be available. Documents with fees/rules/forms in a box at the foot of the link span walkway. Rafting is permitted.

Facilities At **Rossaveal**: few services. HM 091 560506, VHF 16 when manned. Fuel by tanker and from local co-op tanks at No.1 Pier. Fresh water. Ice at No.2 Pier. Fish auctions M/Th. Small shop ½M, pub 1M, bus to Galway.

At **Struthan**: shops, hotel, church, telephone, and bus to Galway at Carraroe, 1M. Fuel 200yds. Water at quay.

GALWAY
Standard Port Galway

Galway is the major harbour and city on the west coast. It is a university town and so has a vibrant cultural scene. The locked harbour is in the middle of the old medieval city and convenient to all services. It is a commercial harbour and accommodates large ship traffic.

Approaches From between the fairway buoys, Fl.R.3s and Fl.G.3s to the S of Black Rock. Head 054° for Hare Island or Levrets bn sectored light Q.WRG.9m10M. Stay within the W sector until within 2ca

CASHLA
Standard Port Galway
HW +0008

MHWS	MHWN	MLWN	MLWS
–0·4m	–0·3m	–0·2m	–0·3m

One of the most sheltered anchorages on this part of the coast. It has the added advantage of being lit with two fixed lights and a number of lit and unlit buoys. Entry is possible in practically all weather. But it is the ferry port for the Aran Isles and with the growing tourist activity plus many fishing boats is becoming noisy and busy. If seclusion and scenery are sought Greatman's Bay, though lacking facilities, may be preferred.

Approach
From W The North Sound, between Inishmore and Gorumna Is. 1M or more S of Golam tr steer 090°. Keep Golam tr open of Loughcarrick Is (S Point of Gorumna) 283° clears English Rock (dries 1m). When Greatman's Bay (do not mistake this bay for Cashla) is clear open to N, alter to port

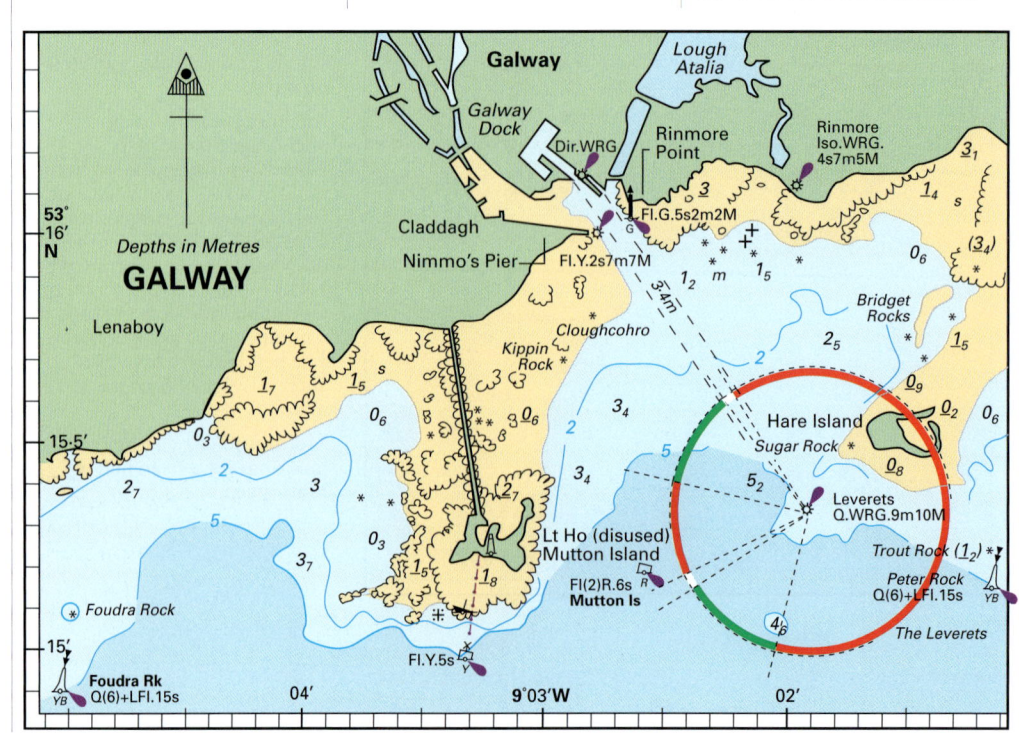

The Cruising Almanac

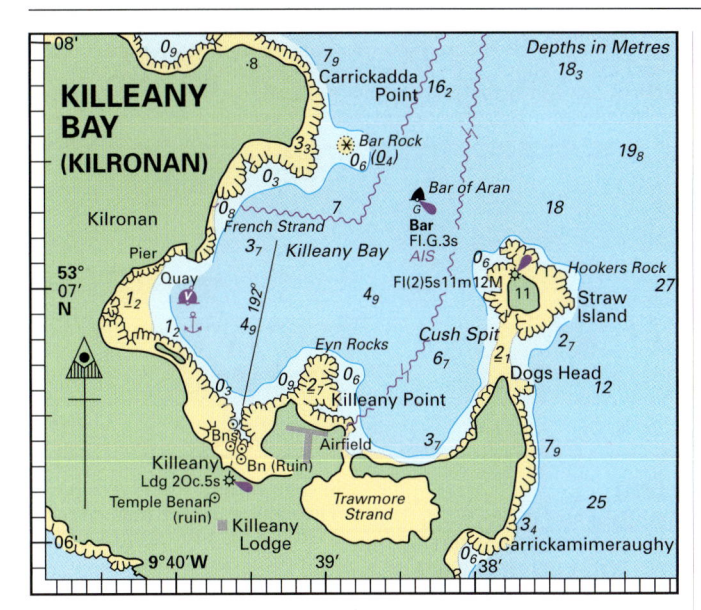

then head N until into the NW W sector of the same light. Turn to 325° toward the hbr entrance staying in the W sector.

Entrance Between Nimmo's Pier head Fl.Y.2s7m7M and Rinmore Point G bn Fl.G.5s, in the W sector of a fixed sectored light on the end of the dock pier. The narrow W sector has Alt.WG immediately to stb then F.G. To port there is Alt.WR immediately then F.R. The lock opens from HW−0200 to HW. Lie alongside the SW side of the pier to the E of the lock or to the NE of this pier in the 'layby'. Yachts must not be left unattended as the fishing fleet uses these berths and it becomes crowded. Enter through the lock to the Inner Dock then turn to port and moor in the SW basin, reserved for small craft.

Anchorage Swing moorings are located outside the inner harbour. It is inadvisable to anchor anywhere outside the city. Dinghy access to city via steps at stone pier, but care must be taken to navigate across the mouth of the River Corrib which runs swiftly.

Facilities Locked marina, gates open HW −0200 to maintain depth; 31 pontoon berths and 60m pontoon walkway along wall, with water/elec. Pump out facility. Fuel by can or truck. Visiting yachts may be accommodated with advance reservation. Harbour Office, New Docks. ✆ 091 561874 or 091 562329, VHF 16/12. Hbr can be noisy and polluted. Fishing and very large commercial vessels offload. Boat repairs, sailmakers, chandlery, bus. Many fine restaurants/shops. Excellent medical facilities. Airport only for private traffic. Last marina before Killybegs if heading N. Plans for massive development of new commercial harbour are underway, which would open up the current city harbour for a marina.

KILRONAN HARBOUR, KILLEANY BAY, ARAN IS

Standard Port Galway
HW nd LW as Galway

MHWS	MHWN	MLWN	MLWS
−0·1m	+0·1m	+0·1m	+0·2m

Kilronan Hbr on Inishmore is the most sheltered anchorage in the Aran Islands. Convenient passage anchorage but worth a longer stay. Dramatic landscape, prehistoric ruins, magnificent stone structures, distinctive knitwear patterns and warm welcoming people. Exposed to the fetch of Galway Bay in easterly winds.

Approach
From W through to N North Sd. Between Inishmore and Goruma Island. Keep at least 1M clear of the Inishmore shore line. A shoal extends N from Carrickadda Point over which swell may break. When Killeany Lodge opens clear of Carrickadda Point >192° shape course for Straw Is Lt Fl(2)5s leaving Killeany G con Lt buoy Fl.G.3s 1ca to stb.

From N through to ESE make for position 3ca N of Straw Is Lt then for G con buoy.

From S Gregory Sound. Keep 2ca clear of Inishmore shore and 3ca off Straw Is. Steer for G con buoy.

Entrance For best water 1ca E of Killeany G con buoy on transit of Temple Benan (ruin) in line with N edge of sand patch 226° on S shore of the bay. When 1ca S of the buoy turn to stb WSW for 1ca S of the pier.

Anchorage 1–2ca S of the pier in 3m. There are also several visitors' moorings. Well sheltered.

Facilities The inner pier is used by multiple ferries and fishing vessels. The outer pier inside the new breakwater accommodates the lifeboat and is suitable for visiting yachts. Ferry to Rossaveal, Inisheer and Inishmaan. Water on pier. Fuel at co-op on quay. Mini-supermarket, restaurants, pubs, shops, bicycle hire. Excellent walking trails. Outstanding promontory fort at Dun Aengus.

CARRIGAHOLT

Standard Port Galway
HW −0035 LW −0030

MHWS	MHWN	MLWN	MLWS
−0·1m	−0·1m	+0·2m	+0·2m

This is a wide bay about 1½M N of Kilcredaun Point in the entrance to the River Shannon. Well sheltered from SSW through W to NNW. If going well into the bay to anchor off Old Quay, shallow draught only, take care regarding the soundings which date from 1842.

Approach The mouth of the Shannon is approx 11M wide lying between Loop Head and Kerry Head. It is well lit and all dangers are marked. In strong winds S through W to NW there are bad races during the ebb. Give both heads a good berth.

Entrance The inner entrance to the River is between Kilcredaun Head and Kilconly Point. Approx 1¾M wide. The main channel is marked by buoys. The coast to port is clear of dangers if given a cable offing to pass Ladder Rock under the light and the wreck which shows 1·2m at LW under the battery.

Anchorages
• E of the New Quay in 6m, sand. It is possible to lay alongside, but it is occupied by lobster boats most of the time.
• About 2ca SSW of above in 4m if the wind is NW.
• About 3ca E of the Old Quay in 2m, or use one of the visitors' buoys.

Facilities 10 minutes' walk from the New Quay to the village of Carrigaholt. Groceries, fuel, meat, doctor, PO and telephone, restaurant in summer.

IRELAND

241

The Cruising Almanac

KILRUSH

Standard Port Galway
HW +0020   LW +0035
MHWS   MHWN   MLWN   MLWS
−0·1m   −0·2m   −0·3m   −0·3m

Good place to leave a boat or for a crew change on the W coast. Excellent marina accessible at all states.

Approach About 5M up the Shannon from Kilcreadaun Point on a course of 068° to Kilrush Channel. Leave Scattery Is and Hogg Is to stb. N of Hogg Is turn to port at a RW sph Lt buoy LFl.10s to enter the buoyed Kilrush marina channel.

Entrance Channel, subject to silting, is dredged 1·5m and buoyed port and stb. Ldg Lts Oc.3s by night 355°. Then turn to stb to 070° in G sector of lock approach Lt Fl.G.3s to reach the lock. Lock available at all states of tide and free-flow if height sufficient. Major works have been undertaken. The locks are automated. Visitors should call ☏ 065 9052072 or VHF 80 24hrs in advance to ensure outer gate is open. There is a pontoon inside the lock on the port side with self-service controls on it. Berth holders can automatically operate the gates for access to the lock.

New 36m floating breakwater inside marina to west of outer pontoons, all round R Lt at S end of marina channel.

Facilities As expected of a modern marina, including 24h self-service credit/debit card diesel pump on boatyard pontoon, boatyard and travel hoist 40t, indoor and outdoor storage, shipwright and all boatyard services. Manager Kim Roberts, is CA HLR ☏ 086 2313870. Taxi service to Shannon Airport. Shops, hardware, banks, supermarkets within walking distance.

Anchorages
• Temporary or fair weather anchorage to the NE of Hogg Island. Tide runs hard.
• In the bays to the E and SE of Scattery Island. Check depths carefully on the shoaling shore.

ASKEATON

Some 18 miles further up the well-marked Shannon, beyond Foynes Island on south shore is the River Deel tributary. RW pillar buoy at entrance to channel, marked by port hand perches, to pontoon berths with 1·7m LWS. But channel is only accessible HW −0100 through HW. Fully equipped boatyard, ☏ 061 392198, with specialist services, including GRP repairs and crane.

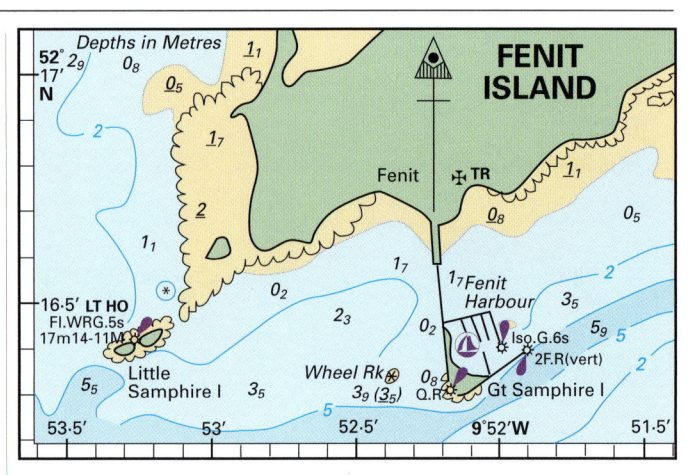

FENIT

Standard Port Cobh
HW (sp) −0057 (np) −0017
LW (sp) −0109 (np) −0029
MHWS   MHWN   MLWN   MLWS
+0·5m   +0·2m   +0·3m   +0·1m

The hbr is formed by a long breakwater connecting Great Samphire Island northward to the shore and a short breakwater projecting NE from the island for 1½ca. Within the enclosed angle an L-shaped breakwater with a short overlapping pier enclose a custom built marina.

Approach From seaward about midway between Mucklaghbeg and Mucklaghmore rocks. Keep in the W sector of a light on Little Samphire Island Fl.WRG.5s 17m16-13M. Head for the island 147° until within ½M then turn S to leave it comfortably to port. When Great Samphire Lt Q.R comes in sight turn to round it to port. Then along the NE aligned pier to round the pier head to a reciprocal course toward the marina. Watch depth carefully.

Entrance Between the pier heads Iso.G.6s6m and Iso.R.6s6m. Berth as directed. VHF 80 or ☏ 097460516.

Anchorages Clear of the fairway to the marina or further east under the lee of the hbr. The bottom shoals rapidly northward.

Facilities Electricity and water on pontoons. Tralee Bay Sailing Club has showers and bar. Fuelling berth. Village: one general store/PO with limited supplies. Bar restaurant.

☏/VHF VHF 16, 14. HM +353 66 713 6231 Marina & SC +353 66 713 6119.

SMERWICK HARBOUR

Standard Port Cobh
HW (sp) −0107 (np) −0027
LW (sp) −0121 (np) −0041
MHWS   MHWN   MLWN   MLWS
−0·3m   −0·4m   n/a   n/a

Tide sets N across the entrance at Dover −0100 at 1kn. This wide bay is open to NW to NE and subject to swell in N winds, but some protection will be found close in on the W side in NW winds and tucked up in the NE corner in northeasterlies.

Approach The approach is clear from the N, but there are no lights in the area. From the S coming from Sybil Point a rk about 3ca due N of middle of the Three Sisters must be avoided. These cliffs are about 150m high.

Entrance Between Dunacapple Island and the northern most of the Three Sisters about 1M wide. Do not pass between Duncacapple Is and the mainland. There is a rock just to W of the island.

Anchorage
• In Smerwick Road just N of the Boat Harbour marked on the chart in good holding.

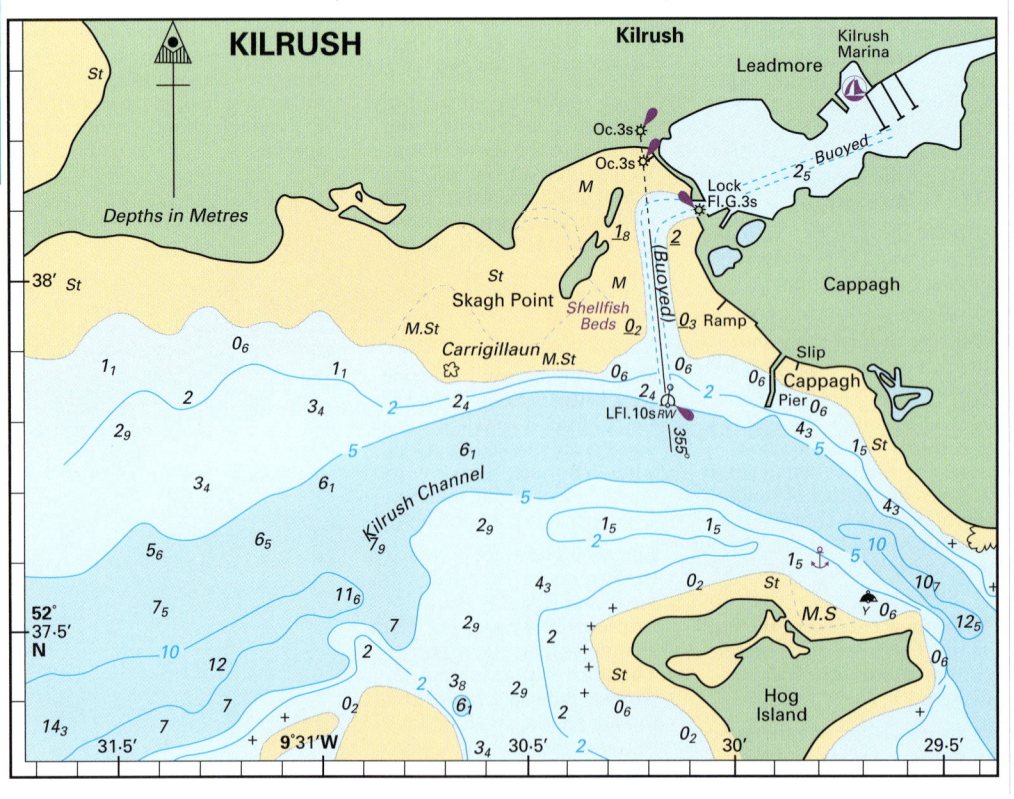

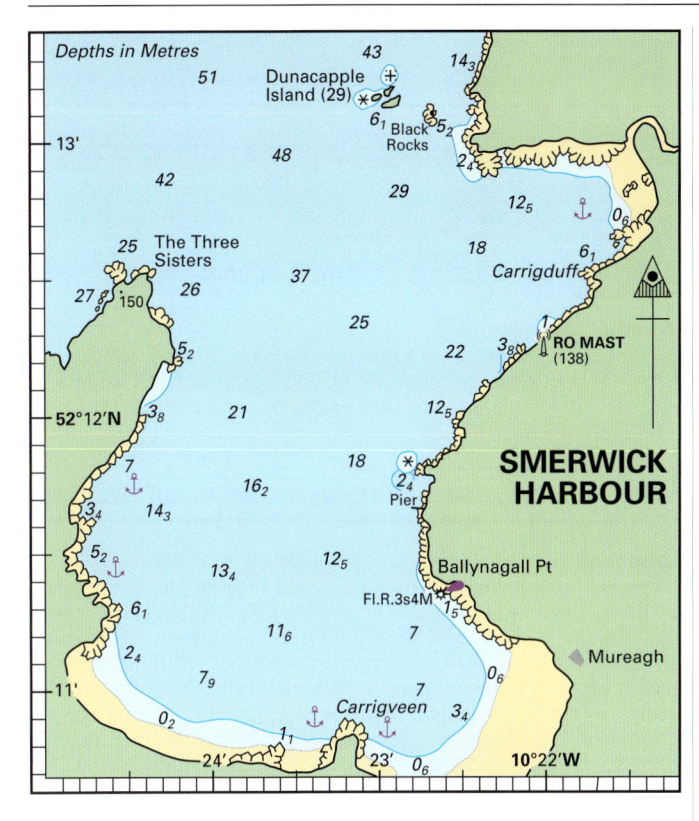

- In the bay to the NE corner of the hbr. Gives shelter in N winds. Do not go in beyond the 2m line as there are boulders. Beware of pots and nets. Pier on Ballynagall Point beware rocks at inshore end.
- In the bay just S of Ballynagall Point in order to get stores at Bulitsnitty. The bottom is rock just off the pier. Further to the SW in this bay is good holding in sand, in 2m just W of Carrigveen Point.

Facilities At Ballynagall (known locally as Ballydavid) there are limited shops, pub, and tel. At Carrigveen there is petrol beyond the sandhills.

BLASKET SOUND

DS Dover –0115 N +0445 S, 2–3kn

From the N steer 195° keeping the Tr on Sybil Point in line with Clogher Rock off Clogher Head making sure not to deviate to the W when passing the rocks off Youngs Is and Beginnish Is. South of Clogher Head and around Stromboli Rock off Dunmore Head there are overfalls which should be avoided.

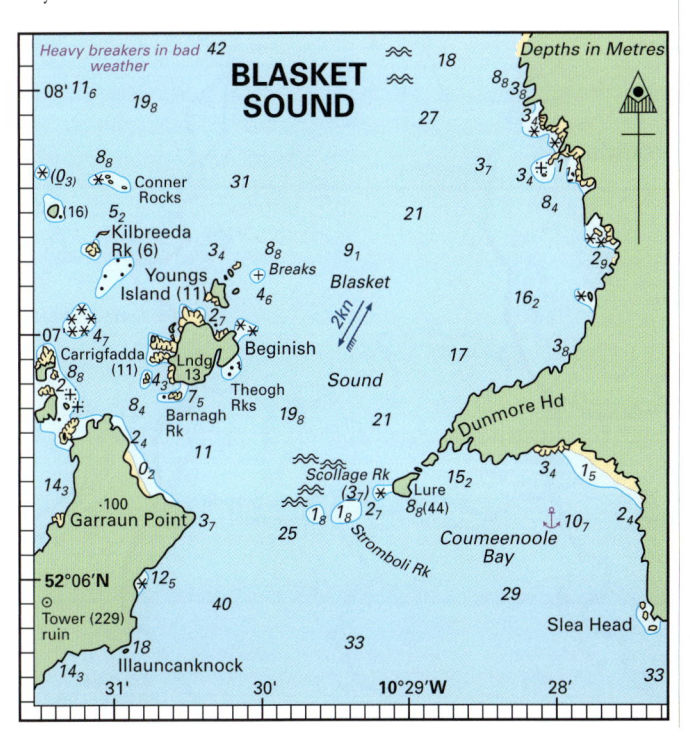

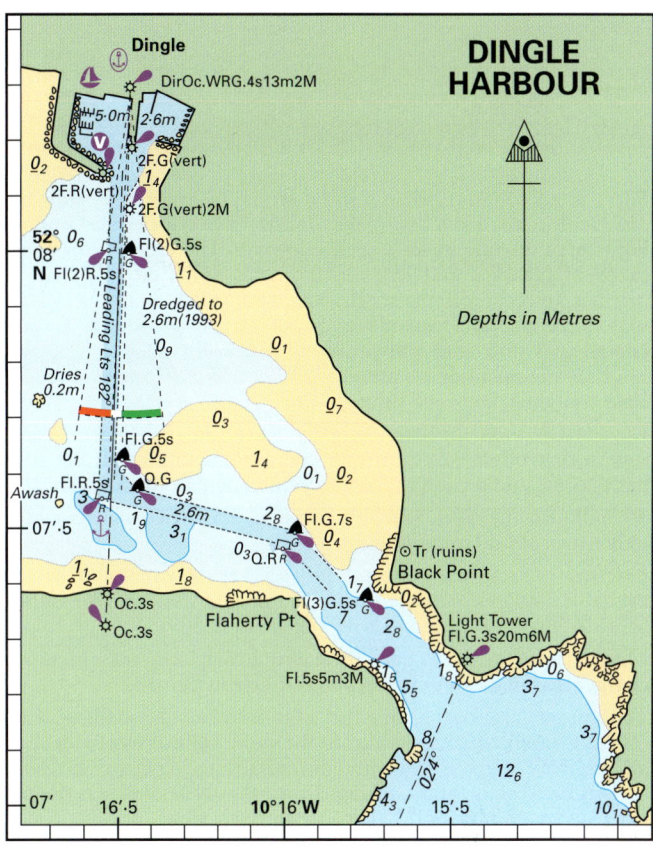

DINGLE HARBOUR

Standard Port Cobh
HW (sp) –0111 (np) –0041
LW (sp) –0119 (np) –0049
MHWS MHWN MLWN MLWS
–0·1m 0·0m +0·3m +0·4m

Dingle is a large natural hbr with a fishing port on its N shore just to the W of which is a well sheltered marina with close access to the town. Well buoyed, transit marked channel dredged to 2·6m.

Approach Identify Eask tr 195m conspic about 8ca W of entrance. Do not pass north of Crow Rock dries 3·7m 3ca off shore to W of entrance. A pinnacle rock, known locally as 'Rod of Iron' with datum depth of 0·8m has been surveyed at 52°05'·88N 10°00'·85W. A course of 024° with Lt tr Fl.G.3.s on NE side of entrance open of Reenbeg Point clears Crow Rock.

If approaching from the east keep at least 2ca off north shore. Rock has been surveyed at 52°06'·68N 10°16'·20W also with datum depth of 0·8m. Do not approach the shore until the hbr entrance is open of Beenbane point.

Entrance At the entrance you are likely to be met by the friendly local dolphin, Fungie, that has brought tourist fame to Dingle. Keep slightly to port of centre of channel to avoid rocky foreshore of Black Point. Then follow a narrow buoyed channel round the S coast of hbr until Ldg Lts Oc.3s come abeam to port. Turn sharply to stb to observe sectored light (Oc.WRG.4s bearing 002°) visible day and night. Keep in White sector N up a narrow, straight, dredged channel toward the pier head 2F.G(vert). When ½ca from the pier turn to port into the marina.

Anchorage There is safe anchorage to be found at 52°07'·50N 10°16'·55W just south of the red can buoy. But keep clear of pot markers.

Berthing Marina master keeps a sharp lookout at all likely times. Berth as directed.

Facilities Dedicated marine sports building beside the marina with restaurant/café, WiFi and showers. Marina master can supply petrol by can, diesel by truck. Locked skip for rubbish and recycling (ask MM). Busy tourist-orientated town for all supplies. Hotels, good pubs and restaurants. Gas at Foxy John's Bar. Bus to trains at Tralee. Large supermarket (delivers to marina), shops, laundry in town. Some marine services.

✆/**VHF** HM +353 66 915 1629, *Mobile* +353 87 232 5844, VHF 14. Marina Manager +353 87 925 4115.

243

Belgium

For a small country, Belgium has a strong pleasure boat industry and facilities to match that make for attractive cruising conditions. Four large all tide havens, well known to UK cruisers for their excellent facilities and ease of approach, offer no less than 3 marinas apiece. From the south, **Nieuwpoort** is a charming village with atmosphere; **Oostende** is a well-established beach resort, commercial port and railway hub; **Blankenberge** is a popular resort of innumerable restaurants; and nearby **Zeebrugge**, a world class container, ferry and fishing port.

All coastal ports are connected by Kusttram, the coastal tram service that offers easy transport connections to all that Belgium has to offer, and a boon to the port-bound on bad weather days!

45 miles up the river Schelde, **Antwerp** offers two marinas and unlimited cultural opportunities.

Practical cruising routes to the interior via the canal system are available via Zeebrugge, Oostende, Terneuzen (NL) and the upper Schelde, but mast up access is restricted (see p.309)

Marine services are good throughout Belgium and berthing charges reasonable, but fuel is not available in Oostende.

The coastal approach from the west is relatively shallow with offshore banks running parallel to the shore west of Oostende, but all are well marked and straightforward to navigate in most conditions.Vessels approaching from the NW will encounter extensive wind farms off Zeebrugge through which passage is not permitted.

Concerns that Belgian officials may pursue UK registered vessels over red marked diesel in their tanks are overdone; in reality free passage is permitted as elsewhere in the Schengen area, subject to the vessel being able to show UK tax paid provenance for the marked fuel in its tanks.

Entry requirements and regulations

Belgium is part of the Schengen system of countries having no internal borders, and vessels from the UK, which is not party to this scheme, must register their presence at the first port encountered. Schengen forms should be downloaded in advance free from the RYA site – they are rarely available from HMs abroad – and deposited in the marked boxes on first landing, retaining a copy on board. Compliance is mandatory, if rarely checked. All ports are recognised ports of entry. See www.rya.org.uk and also p.15 for other necessary documents and fuel regulations.

Weather forecasts

Navtex is broadcast from Oostende on VHF M and T. Weather forecasts in English are broadcast on VHF 27 at 0720 LT and 0820 and 1720 UT. Gale warnings are issued on receipt and at H+55 on VHF 24.

Search and rescue

There is an MRCC based at Oostende VHF 16, for boats with DSC the MMSI No. is 002050480. ☏ 059 701100.

Language

Belgium is divided into two monolingual regions plus the capital, Brussels, which is bi-lingual. The northern Flemish speaking region includes the provences of West and Oost-Vlaanderen, Antwerpen, Vlaams-Brabant and Limburg; the southern Walloon district makes up most of the remainder. Although Flemish is officially the same as common Dutch, dialects account for a number of differences in spelling and pronunciation. In the Walloon region, French is easily understood. English is widely used by harbourmasters and lock operators on the coast and in large cities, but less so in the remoter areas.

Charts

BA and Imray charts provide coverage of the passages to Belgium and along the coast. If intending to continue to the Netherlands, the Dutch Hydrographic Folio *1801* also covers the Belgian coast from Nieuwpoort. Imray offer similar covcerage wih their 2120 North Sea Chart Atlas.

Other sources of information

The following guides may be found useful:

North Sea Passage Pilot by Brian Navin (Imray)
Inland Waterways of Belgium Jacqueline Jones (Imray)
Cruising the Inland Waterways of France & Belgium edited by Margaret Harwood, Brenda Davison & Roger Edgar (18th edition, Cruising Association 2015)

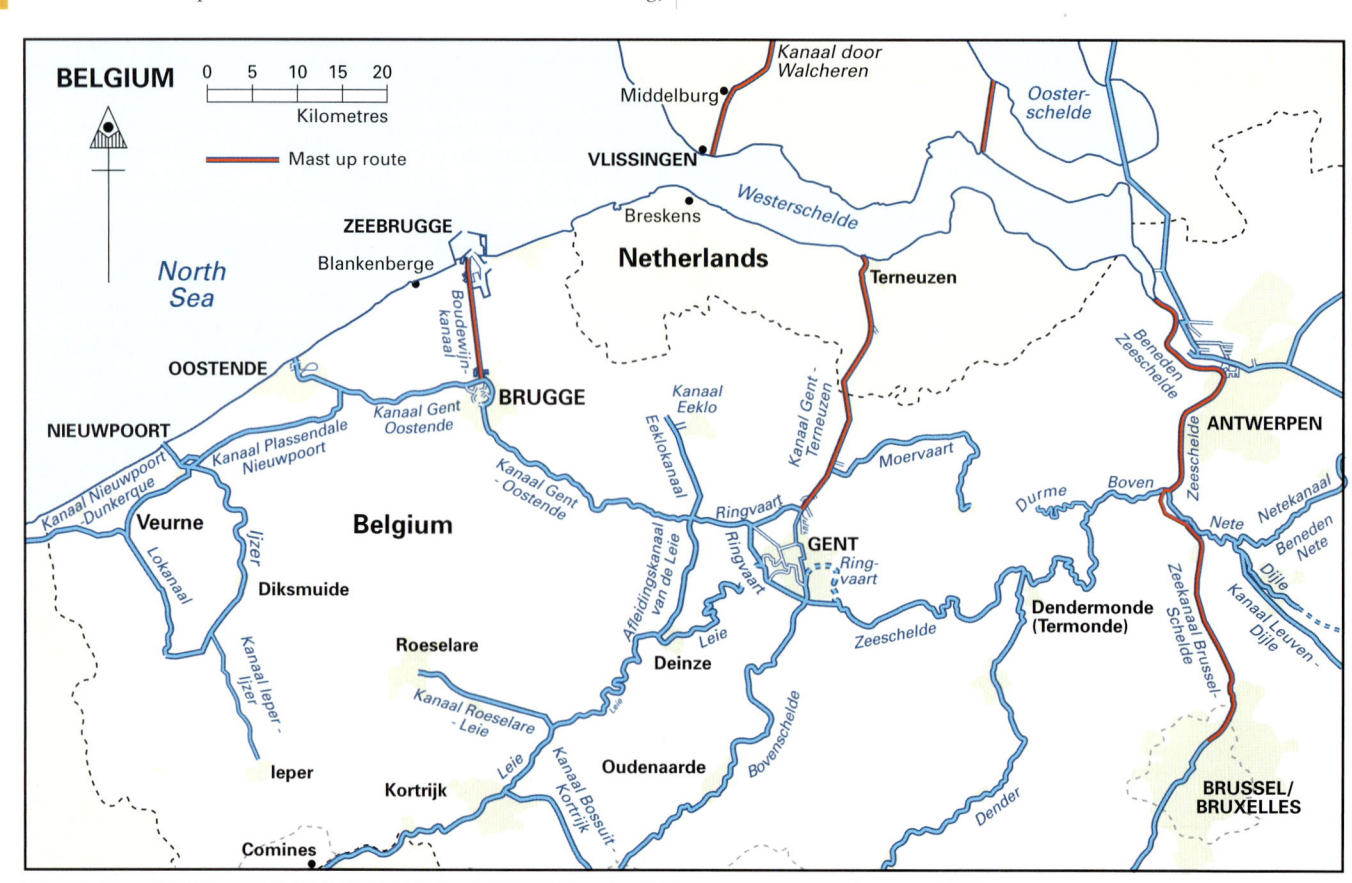

CROSSING THE SOUTHERN NORTH SEA TO BELGIUM

The Belgian coast is mainly sand. The approach is strewn with shallows and banks, but buoyage and lights are excellent, so the approach from UK should be straightforward.

For further navigational guidance see Crossing the N Sea in the Netherlands section (p.249) and the passage planning chart, pp.252 and 253.

Nieuwpoort, Oostende, Zeebrugge and Blankenberge offer excellent shelter and facilities 24/7 but Blankenberge's entrance (see p.246) has depth restrictions. From the UK east coast, Oostende and Zeebrugge/Blankenberge can be approached directly, the channels being well marked. But the approach to Nieuwpoort requires more careful navigation to avoid the off-lying banks.

From the Dover Strait the typical approach is via Dunkerque East, using the buoyed Chenal Intermediare. East of Dunkerque, divert through the Pass de la Zuydcoote (buoyed) into the Westdiep to avoid the Trapegeer sands. Thereafter the inshore channel to Oostende is buoyed. Further passage up the coast holds no major threats beyond navigating the huge moles at Zeebrugge at sufficient distance to avoid reflected waves in rough weather, and commercial traffic.

Shipping movements into Zeebrugge and along the coast to the Westerschelde River are heavy. East of Zeebrugge the Scheur/Wielingen deep water channel runs into the Westerschelde and small vessels should keep S on closing the coast at Vlissingen. North of this waterway lies the Raan bank, to be avoided.

Approaches to Oostende and Zeebrugge are well marked, but at night the number of lit buoys in the area plus vessel movements can be distracting. Offshore wind farms on this route can be an obstacle since passage through them is not permitted.

Many resorts along the coast present a similar appearance but Oostende can be distinguished by its very high Europa Centrum tower right next to the port entrance.

Tides run SW–NE along the coast, starting to the E at Dover -0015, and Dover +0445 to the W; the average rate is 2kn.

Note that E-going tides offer only 4hr 'lift' on this coast, W-going at least 7h; useful for the return trip to UK.

Working the tides along this coast and into the interior is best planned with the *Waterstanden/Stromen HP33* published by the Dutch Hydrographic Office, guide notes in English.

Smoothing the way

Transport facilities in Belgium are very good. The coastal tramway connects all ports along the Belgian coast and is valuable for the ferry ports (Zeebrugge to Hull services) plus rail at Oostende (direct connection to Brussels) The motorway runs along the coast from Dunkerque to Oostende then inland to Brussels, Brugge and Gent. Except Blankenberge, all ports offer canal access to the interior.

NIEUWPOORT

Standard Port Zeebrugge
HW –0031   LW –0010
MHWS MHWN MLWN MLWS
+0·7m +0·5m +0·3m +0·1m
DS Dover –0130E +0545W

A small historic port town, formerly a military base, now housing major marina facilities – arguably the premier small vessel facility in Belgium.

Approach and Entrance The Banc Smal and Nieuwpoort banks lie three miles off and should be skirted in rough conditions at LW when seas break over them. The approach from Dunkerque will be along the Chenal Intermediare, diverting through the Pass de la Zuydcoote (buoyed 3m min depth) into the Westdiep to avoid the Trapegeer sands. A firing range in Lombardsijde close E of the Entrance is in use from 15 September to 15 June. Firing is preceded by a W parachute flare. *Radio Lombardsijde* VHF 67. The harbour entrance between two lattice piers is dredged to more than 3·0m but is subject to silting particularly on the E side. The main LtHo Fl(2)R.14s26m16M is a R tower with W horizontal bands and is situated just E of the root of the E pier. Keep lit pole channel markers to port on entry. Beware cross-set off entrance. VHF 09.

Berthing The entrance channel divides after 1M. The Royal Nieuwpoort YC on the W branch has large premises with a good restaurant. Shops are more than 20 minutes walk away. Entering the narrow entrance close to stb wall, visitors should contact the HM on fuel pontoon to Pt just inside. HM ☎ 058 23 44 13. The second, much larger, yacht basin on the E branch (Novus Portus) houses the 2400-berth VVW Nieuwpoort marina. The town is reached by road and a bridge ½M away. However, bicycles are made available free of charge for shopping trips and can be hired for extended journeys. VHF 8. HM ☎ 058 23 52 32. In the NE corner of the basin, and directly ahead on entering, is the Royal Belgian Air Force YC which is a 10 minutes walk from shops in the village of Lombaerdsijde, VHF 23. HM ☎ 058 23 36 41. There are restaurants in both marinas. Fuel can be obtained from Royal Nieuwpoort YC and from a grey-painted barge belonging to VVW Nieuwpoort on the port side as you enter the fishing harbour which is 200m up-river from the yacht basin. Self service with credit card, but not all types accepted.

There is a frequent service to Oostende, Blankenberge and Zeebrugge on the coastal tramway which also gives access close to Oostende airport.

Inland connections There is access to the Kanaal Plassendale–Nieuwpoort and the Kanaal Nieuwpoort–Duinkerken via the locks and bridges of the Achterhaven that operate HW±0300 during the day. Onward passage on the River Yzer to the Kanaal Ieper–Yzer is via the Kanaal Plassendale–Nieuwpoort. All canals have fixed bridges restricting headroom (4m–5·5m).

OOSTENDE

Standard Port Zeebrugge
HW –0019   LW –0008
MHWS MHWN MLWN MLWS
+0·4m +0·2m +0·2m +0·1m
DS Dover –0045E +0445W

A leading 24h port, less busy now than in earlier times but offering the cruiser all facilities except fuel. A resort town with broad beaches and numerous restaurants, fish market, hotels, a casino, and excellent rail plus air connections. All justify Oostende's claim to serious consideration by the cruising sailor.

Three marinas offer some 1500 berths - two are open at all states of the tide, and the third via locks.

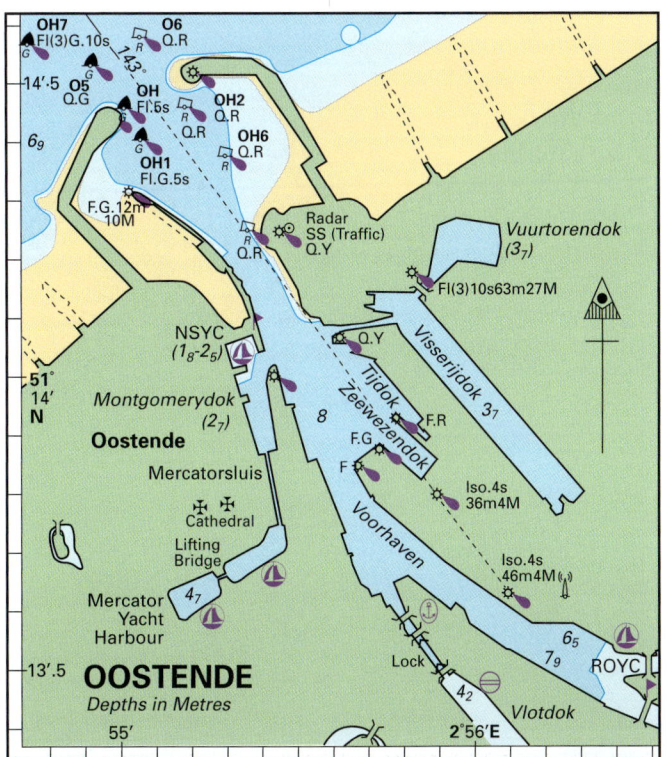

BELGIUM

245

Approach and Entrance
The Approach is straightforward but the Stroombank 1M SW of the entrance is to be avoided in rough weather. Approaches from the W are inshore by the Kleine Rede channel or, further out via the Grote Rede. Approaching from the E offers no obstructions. The very tall Europa building stands 300m W of the port entrance.

A lit approach channel gives entrance via two moles extending 4ca to sea and enclosing the old wooden W pier - a tall lit port marker stands on the E mole; leading lights and port control lights. Port control VHF 09.

Small vessel lights stand at the entrance to the Montgomery Dock and N Sea marina basin and prohibit exit when large vessels are moving in the main channel.

Berthing Three marinas offer convenient short and longer term mooring facilities. The Royal Yacht Club at the far end of the Voorhaven is quieter with pontoons, better security (gate with code lock) and a friendly clubhouse, but ship movements nearby can disturb sleep; shops close by, otherwise a 15 minute walk or a short tram ride back to town. The Mercator harbour (VHF 14 for berth reservation) in the centre of town is close to the action but access through the lock with its twin bridges is time consuming (daylight hours service): best for a longer stay. The Royal North Sea YC Harbour immediately to stb on entering is smaller; part alongside, and part bow to pontoon with an aft buoy; it is right alongside the pricier restaurants and suffers some disturbance from passing vessels.

Inland connections There is access to the Kanaal Gent–Oostende via the Demey lock, on the SW side of the Voorhaven. Operated at all times in conjunction with the brs either side. Canal has fixed bridges restricting headroom (7m).

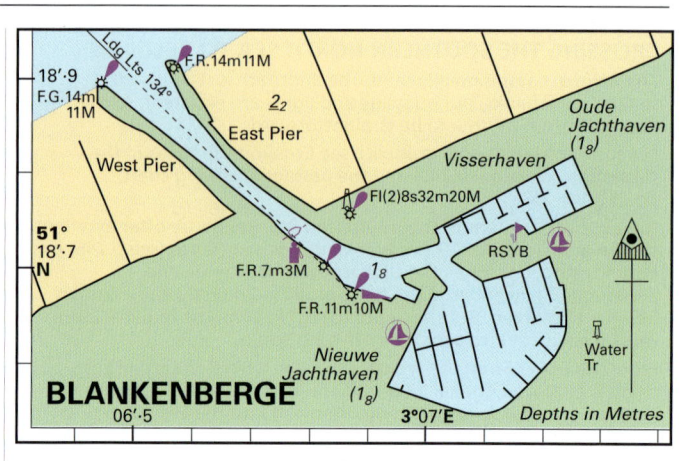

BLANKENBERGE

Standard Port Vlissengen
HW –0040

MHWS	MHWN	MLWN	MLWS
+0·1m	+0·1m	0·0m	0·0m

DS HW Dover –0100E +0500W

An important yachting centre, with customs facilities available all year round.

Approach and Entrance The approaches to this harbour are relatively shallow and uncomfortable, possibly even dangerous in strong onshore winds. The entrance is narrow, between two piers (F.R and F.G), neither of which should be confused with the Casino pier at the E end of the town. The LtHo Fl(2)8s30m20M is near the root of the E pier. The channel is dredged to 1·5m in June each year but is subject to silting, especially after onshore gales. Ldg Lts (F.R) on 134° assist at night and are marked with red crosses for visibility during daylight. If in doubt about conditions or depth, contact Traffic Centre Zeebrugge on VHF 69. All three yacht clubs listen on VHF 23 in season. VHF 8 is local rescue and emergency channel.

Berthing There is a marina in the old harbour which lies to port. Another large marina is reached through a narrow passage to stb marked by dolphins, just after the main channel turns to port. HM's office and visitors' pontoon to port. Security gates with coded entry. Water, electricity and fuel available on pontoons. The three YCs which administer the marina all have good facilities in their own premises. Shops and restaurants are close at hand. Good bathing from the beaches. HM ① VVW Blankenberge YC 050 41 75 36. Royal Scarphout YC 050 42 89 52, *Mobile* 0476 97 16 92. Free N Sea Sailers *Mobile* 0497 565565. Diesel and petrol available from stage in entrance channel.

ZEEBRUGGE

Standard Port Zeebrugge
DS HW Dover E +0500W

A major facility with two massive moles extending 2M to sea surmounted by wind turbines. Entrance lit with two high visibility arrays, leading lights and port entry signals. The leading Belgian fishing port and a fast growing centre for bulk, container and cruiser traffic. Ferry service to Hull, train connections via Knocke, and tram service to all other Belgian coast ports. Canal connection to the interior and Brugge.

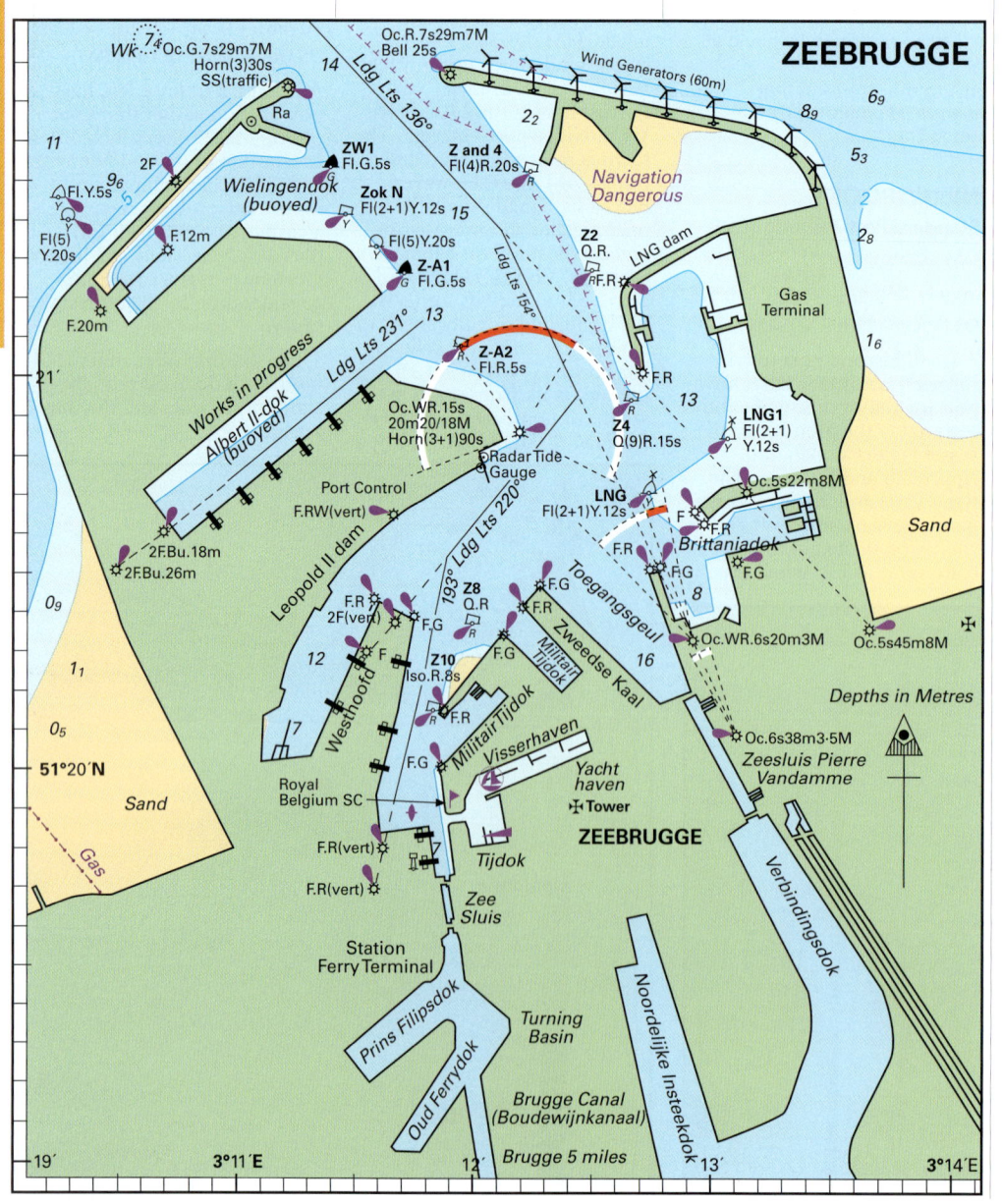

Three excellent all tide marinas lying deep within the old port, offering all facilities, and longer term mooring.

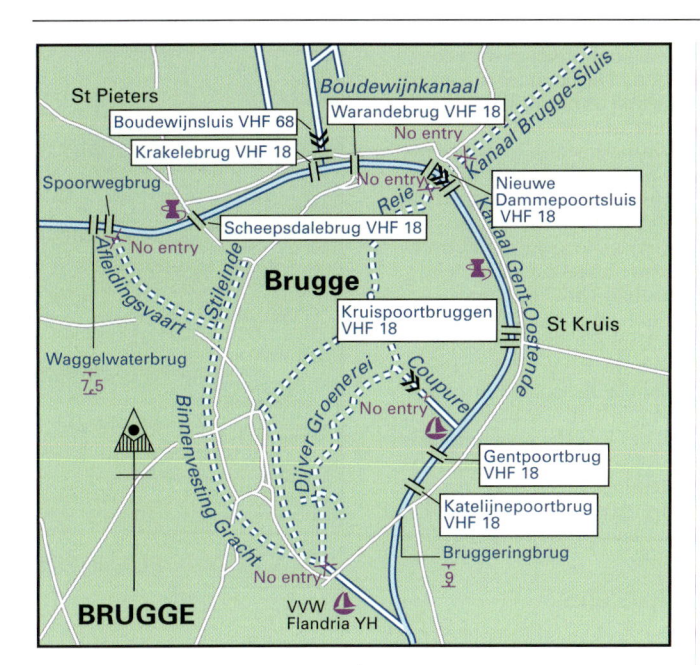

Approach Tide across the entrance can reach 4 kn and throw up a heavy sea in windy conditions. On approaching, beware reflected waves from the harbour wall and steer clear, keep to buoyed channel within – shoaling is severe. Call port control on VHF 71 for clearance to enter; traffic may be curtailed during movements of methane tankers.

Berthing Three marinas lie approx. 2M from the entrance in the old Visserhaven. The route from the entrance is not immediately obvious. On entering the outer harbour, maintain a distance from the wall and pass SSE in the marked channel, leaving two major docks to stb. Approach old harbour wall (lit) dead slow in case of issuing traffic from beyond. With container quays to stb press on SSW past two R cans to port and 3 large posts. Pass the waving base and make sharp turn to port via narrow entrance, revealing marinas.

The newest marina, BZYC, stands opposite the entrance.

The RBSC to port has a visitors' pontoon and HM's office close by. Gated entry, code required. Club house 400m to left of gate, well recommended. Other cafes nearby. Facilities opposite entrance gate.

The Westhinder Club marina is smaller and is situated beyond the RBSC in the old dock but lies closer to shops and the main road.

On leaving the inner harbour, port control will show stop lights when a large vessel is under way in the outer harbour.

Inland connections Entrance to the Boudewijn kanaal is usually through the very large Pierre Vandamme sea lock approached from the Toegangsgeul. The Zee Sluis is an alternative (to port after the marina). Check on VHF 68 for information about operating times and charges. Boats with fixed masts can reach the centre of Brugge from Zeebrugge along this route through two lifting bridges which can be contacted on VHF 68. See Inland Waterways section on p.309 for futher advice.

BRUGGE

The Boudewijnkanaal joins the Kanaal Gent-Ostende (12km from Zeebrugge) at the Boudewijn lock which is operated Monday–Saturday 0800–1200 and 1300–1700. No service on Sunday and holidays. Bridges around the city are operated throughout the day subject to road traffic flow and normally in convoys starting at 1000 from Katelijnepoortbrug on the SE side, and 1430 from the Nieuwegebrug between Oostende and Brugge. Nieuwe Dammepoortsluis operates throughout the day but transit is normally in convoy or with a commercial vessel. Limited moorings without facilities available on the canal S of the Nieuwe Dammepoort lock (mast-up); in the Coupure (depth 1·5m) between Kruispoortbrug and Gentpoortbrug which have water and electricity and are convenient for the town centre, access restricted to 6m headroom; in Flandria YH (depth 1·6m) S of Brugge ringbrug, with all facilities and convenient for the rly station. HM ☎ 050 38 08 66. Water available at the Nieuwe Dammepoort lock.

GENT

Access from W is 40km along Kanaal Gent-Ostende with fixed bridges (7m). Speed limit 12km/hr (6·5kn). There are also two lifting bridges which do not operate 0750–0820, 1155–1225 and 1700–1730. The Beernem flood lock normally stands open. Moorings half way at Beernem YC (maximum depth 2m) HM ☎ 0472 394593. Canal joins the Gent ringvaart west of the city (fixed bridges 7m). Turn N for the Kanaal Gent–Terneuzen and Westerschelde via Evergem lock (operates Monday–Saturday 0600–2200, Sunday and holidays 1000–1800) or S for city centre moorings, Brussels and Antwerp.

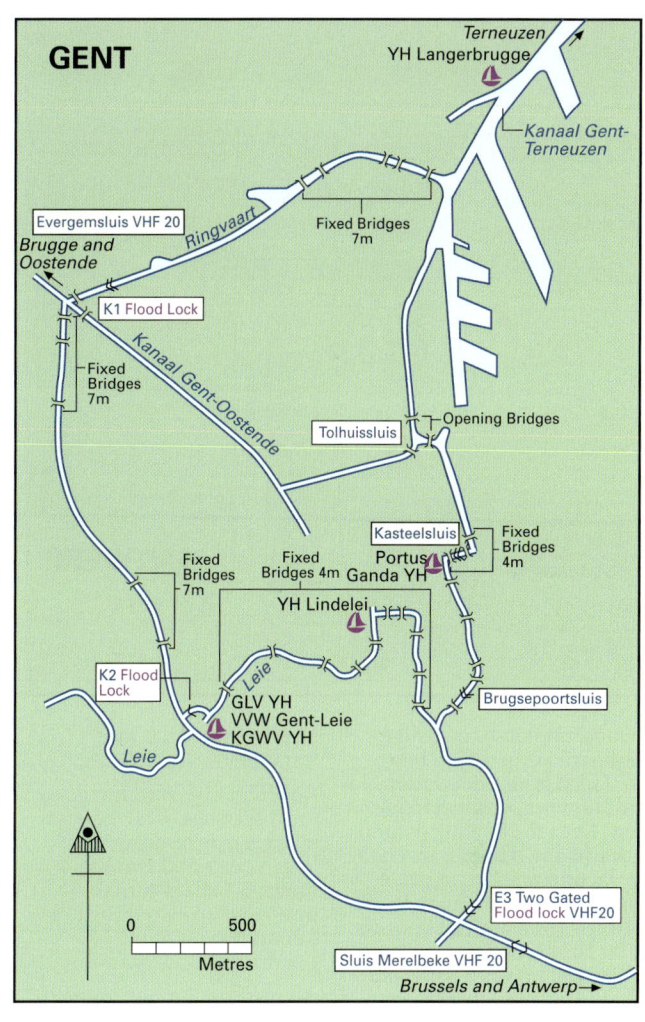

Access from the N is 32km along the Kanaal Gent-Terneuzen and all brs to the ringvaart, N of the city, are opening. Speed limit 16km/h (8·6kn). From E ringvaart can be reached via the Schelde from Antwerp. Moorings with all facilities off the Kanaal Gent-Terneuzen at Royal Gent YC, Langerbrugge (mast-up) HM ☎ 09 253 7920; in the River Leie at YCs south of town (maximum depth 2·1m) HM ☎ 09 220 4424 or in the centre at Lindelei (fixed bridges 4m, max depth 2·1m) HM ☎ 0479 246388 or Portus Ganda (fixed bridges 4m, max depth 2m) HM ☎ 0472 417843.

Yachting Merelbeke is convenient if entering or leaving the Zeeschelde via Sluis Merelbeke, but is a long way from the city centre. ☎ 09 245 16 57.

ANTWERP

Standard Port Vlissingen
Royersluis
HW (sp) +0148 (np)+0140
LW (sp) +0226 (np) +0208
MHWS MHWN MLWN MLWS
+1·1m + 0·8m –0·1m –0·1m

Approach via the Westerschelde some 45M from Vlissingen and 33M from Terneuzen. At the mouth of the Westerschelde spring tidal streams can exceed 4kn and rates are almost as high between sandbanks further into the estuary. Tidal timing is therefore critical and it may be desirable to break the passage at Terneuzen. At Nieuwe Sluis the in-going stream starts at HW Vlissingen –0500 and there is then 8hrs of favourable tide for the passage up river. There is between 4½ and 5hrs of favourable tide for the return passage. The river is well-buoyed and lit, but there is heavy commercial traffic, particularly between Terneuzen and Hansweert. Maintain listening watch on VTS radio channels shown on Dutch charts. Keep to starboard side of channel. Give way to commercial craft. Have engine ready for immediate use and hoist a cone if motor-sailing.

Antwerp Linkerover Yacht Hbr Entrance Keep N of the Stroomleidam, the N end of which is marked by an 82m pylon, and follow the winding channel until a sharp bend to starboard at the 107 G buoy (Iso.G.8s) brings the waterfront and churches of Antwerp into view. Keep the floating pontoon to starboard. The entrance to the Jachthaven Antwerpen is marked by a Y can buoy to starboard and a Y can buoy to port. The gate operates approx HW±0100 between 0800 and 2200 (April–October) as long as the level does not exceed 5·3m. Yachts may moor to the Y waiting buoy opposite the entrance, or moor at the floating pontoon about 1M downstream. All moored yachts must keep at least one crew member on board at all times. HM ☎ 03 219 08 95 There are 350 well-sheltered berths, 70 of which are reserved for visitors. On the return journey, yachts should leave the marina at the first opening of the hbr gate.

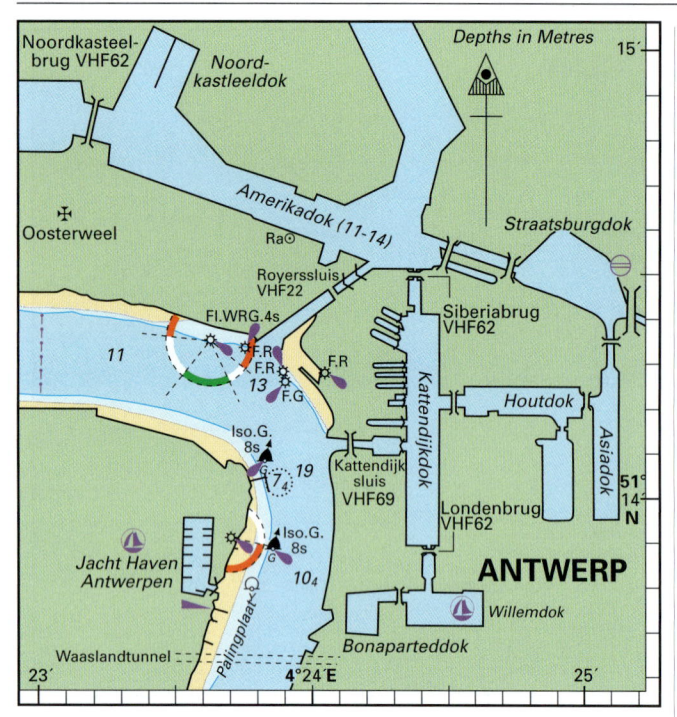

The marina offers good sheltered facilities and restaurants nearby. To reach Antwerp by foot, turn left out of the marina and proceed 800m to the Waaslandtunnel entrance building: the free lift descends to the 1km long foot tunnel under the Schelde. You emerge right in the centre of the ancient town. A large supermarket stands 400m opposite the west bank tunnel entrance.

Marina Willemdok
Entrance This is the mast-up marina of choice for easy foot access to the city centre. The most direct entrance is via the Kattendijksluis (VHF 69) and dock passing S into the marina via the lifting Londenbrug (VHF 62, operates Mon-Sat 0600–2200 but Sun and holidays between Easter and end Sept 0900-1900). Access HW ±0300 - restricted locking possible at spring HW. Good facilities and dock-side restaurants.

An alternative entrance is via the Royersluis (VHF 22) but passage may be delayed by large vessels and two lifting bridges. A sharp turn to stb through the Siberiabrug (VHF 62) brings you to the Londenbrug.

All vessels entering require to be issued with a FD number, obtainable in advance with much other useful information at www.jachthaven-antwerpen.be . Requesting the FD number on arrival in the lock will delay progress.

The Siberiabrug opens 24h except on working days between 0700–0815; 1315–1345 and 1550–1715. The Londenbrug opens at 0630, 0830, 1000, 1130, 1400, 1500, 1730, 1845, 2015, 2145 and 2245. Additional openings at 1245 and 1615 weekends and holidays. The Willemdok is contacted on VHF 23. HM ☎ +0 3231 5066.

Entry to the docks can also be made through the Kruisschans lock further down river. This involves passage through an additional bridge, the Noordkasteelbrug, which opens 24hrs. VHF 62. Both locks open 24hrs a day. It is usually quicker to use the Kruisschans but both can be time-consuming.

Fuel is available in both harbours.

Inland connections Continuing up the Schelde river leads after 80km to Gent with fixed brs (minimum 5m at HW) beyond Rupelmonde. Speed limit upstream of Dendermonde, 12km/hr (6·5kn) for vessels of 1–2m draught. A strong tide of up to 4kn runs and it is wise to time your passage with the flood. The channel is partially buoyed as far as Temse br. S of Rupelmonde is the very large Wintham sealock up into the non-tidal Zeekanaal Brussel-Schelde. The lock operates 24hrs, though access may not be possible around LW, and leisure boats normally lock through with commercial vessels. It is also possible to lock up into the Zeekanaal from the River Rupel at Sluis Klein Willebroek, but only from HW±0300 during the day. SE of Gent the waterway joins the Gent ringvaart where the Merelbeke lock operates Monday–Saturday 0600–1930, Sunday and holidays 0600–1800.

BRUSSELS

The Zeekanaal Brussel–Schelde connects the Schelde river at Rupelmonde to Brussels (27km). Speed limit on the canal is 18km/hr (9·7kn) for vessels up to 1·5m draught. All bridges as far as the Brussels Royal YC N of the city are opening (maximum air draught when open of 32m) and operate Monday–Saturday 0600–2200. Duties are levied for passage on Sunday or holidays except in July and August 0800–1800. Leisure boats are normally bridged with commercial vessels or in convoys. All facilities including diesel and launderette available at BRYC HM ☎ 022 41 48 48. Nearby tram service to city centre attractions.

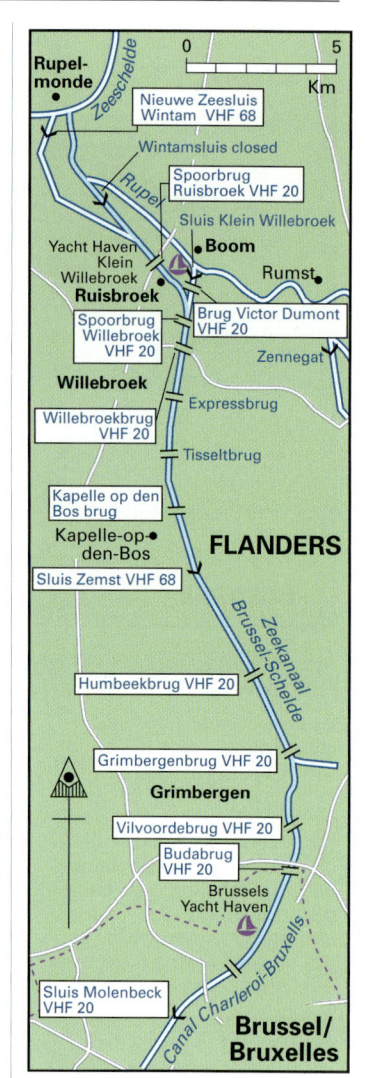

SCHELDE TIDAL DATA
Standard Port Vlissingen
Time differences

	HW		LW	
	0300	0900	0400	1000
	&	&	&	&
	1500	2100	1600	2200

Rupelmonde
+0235 +0225 +0215 +0225
Dendermonde
+0350 +0340 +0405 +0415
Gent (Merelbeke)
+0600 +0545 +0810 +0800
Lier
+0345 +0330 +0505 +0555
Height differences n/a

See Netherlands Section on p.257 for data on Hansweert and Terneuzen.

INLAND WATERWAYS OF BELGIUM
Jacqueline Jones
Jacqueline Jones's waterway-by-waterway guide provides all the essential information for navigation, as well as details about things to do and places to see in Belgium's historic cities. Fully illustrated with clear maps and the author's photography. It comes with a folded map of the Belgian Waterways system.

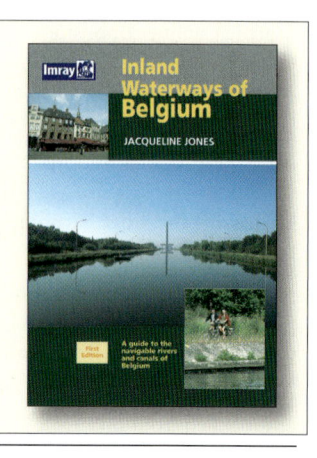

Netherlands

Outstanding cruising opportunities

Holland has a long and rich tradition of water transport, especially sail, and a great legacy of cruising facilities stretching from the major rivers of the south to the Frisian Islands of the north. Hundreds of miles of canals and waterways cross the country, with several hundred marinas, bustling in the summer months with Dutch families, so facilities are generally of a high calibre. Numerous small villages and old fishing ports provide a background of colour and entertainment that sustain all types of cruising.

Although only a few hours sail from Britain, the weather is noticeably more continental in type – warmer and drier in the summer than much of UK. Comfortable sailing is possible on more days on average, than on much of the UK coastline.

Dutch waters are manicured with buoyage and navigational landmarks. Approach from the UK requires careful planning. Off-lying sandbanks are well marked, and the tides running NE–SW along the coast can be used to good advantage. A large volume of heavy shipping passes along the coast and up the rivers: the Westerschelde and Maas are world class waterways and strict observance of procedures is absolutely essential.

The interior waterways are a unique system, intensively used for pleasure and commerce, much of it free for the visitor. The west of the country has a recognised system permitting boats with a draft of some 2m and an air draft of 18m to pass freely, called the Staande Mastroute. Bridges lift either on demand in quiet places, or to a controlled opening schedule. Passing though locks requires preparation with fenders and lines, but represents no challenge to the well tempered crew. In some towns, a small bridge fee is collected via a clog swung by the bridge master; watch for the signs. With a few words of Dutch, the visitor can take advantage of warning signs and advance service notices along the way, although almost all facilities respond in English.

CEVNI signage is ubiquitous; it is important to observe directions in waterways, especially those carrying commercial traffic.

Passanten (visitors) is the helpful sign denoting a facility open for passing cruisers. But *geen* in front of any word negatives what follows; *frei* means open; a berth so marked is open for use; one marked *bezet* is not. *Toegestaan* means permitted.

Hier melden (contact point) is often signposted on the outer pontoon of a marina – the required procedure to ensure the berth taken is indeed free for the night. Other marinas use green and red flags on each berth to signal free or occupied, and can usually be taken as a good guide to availability.

High season considerations

In the summer a huge range of old sailing barges (the brown armada) sets forth on the inland waterways, with parties of young people aboard. The boats make a fine picture and are very well sailed.

From mid July throughout August the Dutch set out in their boats with families and camp for days on end in certain attractive ports, the Frisian Isles being a prime example; entry to these marinas after midday is often impossible. Rafting in such hotspots and major attractions (Amsterdam etc) is to be expected; be prepared to shuffle the raft at about 0900 when departures normally begin. The

CROSSING THE NORTH SEA TO THE NETHERLANDS

Favourite destinations are: Breskens on the river Westerschelde; the Roompot & Stellendam which lock in to the Oosterschelde and Haringvliet waterways; Scheveningen – the port for den Hague; IJmuiden for the North Sea Canal to Amsterdam; Den Helder – gateway to the Waddenzee and IJsselmeer. All are 24/7 ports, well lit and buoyed, and navigable with confidence, with the usual caveat of extra care on approaching a lee shore.

Departure from the east coast of England requires planning to take into account the Thames banks, the tides, the gyratory system off Harwich and the North Sea TSS. From the Thames the optimum course is to head NE with the ebb tide, remaining west of the main North Sea TSS (see below) before striking east to the chosen destination.

From Essex and South Suffolk ports, the favoured course is, again employing the ebb tide, to clear the Long Sand Head and head E to clear the Galloper wind farm – taking care in crossing the Sunk Outer traffic system. But departing from mid Suffolk rivers, it is more usual to make for S Shipwash then navigate N or S of the Galloper depending on destination.

Many cruisers approach Holland via ports from the south. Departing Kent, Dunkerque Est is the first port of call, using the buoyed Chenal Intermediare on the approach. Proceeding to Nieuwpoort in Belgium by the coast route requires a diversion via the Passe de Zuydcoote (buoyed) to avoid the Trapegeer sands. Thereafter the inshore channel to Oostende is buoyed, and passage onwards holds no major threats beyond passing the huge moles at Zeebrugge at sufficient distance to avoid reflected waves in rough weather, and commercial traffic. Note that east going tides offer only four hours 'lift' on this coast.

The Dutch coast is low sand dunes and shallow on the approach, throwing up short seas in breezy conditions, but approach channels are well marked. The Westerschelde estuary is not advisable in strong wind over tide conditions when a large sea builds, likewise the approach to Den Helder. A night approach to Dutch ports is helped by powerful lights, many visible over quite a distance to sea. Buoyage is exemplary. In any approach, vessels are required to maintain a listening watch on Vessel Traffic System (VTS) channels. These channels are indicated on the Dutch 1800 series charts.

Wind farms are continuing to be established on several sites on both sides of the North Sea, some surprisingly far from shore. There is no right of passage through Dutch and Belgian wind farms, as in the UK. Numerous gas well-heads off IJmuiden and the Frisian islands are clearly charted and lit.

The Harwich Gyratory – Sunk Outer

Lying some seven miles E of the old Sunk Inner Lightship, the Sunk Centre light is the focus of this gyratory system where very large vessels enter at the four points of the compass and circle anticlockwise en route to and from Felixstowe, Harwich and the Thames Estuary. TSS rules apply in part and passage by small vessels is otherwise permitted but minimal time should be spent in any part of the system.

The North Sea TSS

A major system for the many commercial vessels passing through the North Sea (p.252-253). On 1 June 2017 extensive revisions and additions were implemented to segregate traffic bound for Zeebrugge, the Westerschelde estuary and Maas approach, and to route vessels safely round the large Thornton and Bligh wind farms. A new Schouwenbank junction is established N of the Scheldt estuary and a number of precautionary areas introduced throughout. But the inshore route, favoured by smaller vessels, remains largely unaffected.

Navigating through this extensive system is permitted, subject to TSS rules where appropriate, but wind farms may not be traversed. Passage in poor visibility entails significant risk.

Approaching from the UK, the best course remains to shape a passage north or south of the complex: passing north of the North Hinder junction avoids the main shipping lane branching east to serve the River Maas, where vessels make major course changes and traffic converges from the Scheldt.

The southern approach is best made close to the West Hinder junction.

The Maas approach

Ships move in the Maas approach at speed, often overtaking. When transiting the Maas approach, small vessels should use the yacht track just off the port entrance, but clearance must first be obtained from Maas control on VHF 03.

IJmuiden is approached via a TSS and heavy traffic can be expected.

Frisian Isles / TSS

From just SW of Den Helder stretching north and east, a complex of TSS zones runs along the Dutch coast into German waters, leading to the river Elbe. Considerable traffic can be expected in this area.

The W Friesland TSS and Texel TSS protect the well heads of the very large offshore Vlieland / Groningen gas fields. Approaching from the UK, a course may be shaped through the fields and across the TSS zones providing regulations are observed, and a 500m range is maintained from any well head.

Typically, a course for the Frisian Islands from Suffolk / Norfolk would head towards Den Helder keeping west of the offlying Noorderhaaks bank, to join the inshore traffic zone northwards. Allow for the shallows that reach out some way from SW of Terschelling and Ameland – all well buoyed and lit. Entrance to any of the gats between the islands requires special planning owing to tide and depth restrictions (see detail below). Passage in wind over tide conditions can be hazardous.

Dutch are masters at this, and very helpful to strangers. Otherwise finding a berth is rarely impossible, given the huge number of boats and berths throughout Holland. A number of websites give up to date information on marina facilities eg. www.marina-guide.net

Charts
The *1800 Series* of sheet charts published by the Dutch Hydrographic service in eight folios, covers in detail all main waterways in the west of Holland including the IJsselmeer. Folio 1801 is especially useful covering the coastal approaches to Belgium and mainland Holland. Available in the UK and everywhere in Holland. Imray's Folio series 2120 (Nieuwpoort to Den Helder) and 2150 (Den Helder to Norderney) cover the area comprehensively - strongly recommended.

Imray C30 offers detailed pilotage between Kent and S Suffolk to Holland as far N as the Maas, with useful port chartlets. C25 and C26 extend coverage N of the Maas.

ANWB sector sheets (*Waterkaart*) are published for 14 areas in west Holland, giving buoyage, lights, depths, locks (Sluis) and movable bridge (Beweegbar Brug/BB) details. Available at chandlers and sports shops. Very desirable.

The *Wateratlas Staande Mastroute* gives details of the route passable for sailing boats from Willemstad in the mid-south all the way to Delfzijl on the northern coast. Detailed information on marinas en route, plus bridge and lock service times, makes this a valuable guide, and value for money. Stocked in chandlers.

Technically, all vessels are required to carry the *ANWB Wateralmanak* written totally in Dutch: *Volume 2* contains much useful data on waterway services to help smooth your passage, which can be understood by careful reading, but is in no way essential. The Wateratlas Staande Mastroute will suffice for many travellers in western Holland, except those going way off the beaten track in smaller vessels.

The combined tidal atlas and tide tables booklet published by the Dutch Hydrographic Office gives information on all tidal waters in and near Holland and is highly recommended. Look for *Waterstanden/Stromen HP33* in chandlers, guide notes in English.

Other sources of pilotage information:
North Sea Passage Pilot by Brian Navin (Imray)
Cruising Guide to the Netherlands by Brian Navin (Imray)
Inland waterways of the Netherlands by Louise Busby & David Broad (Imray)

Official checks on crews, their boats and contents have increased in recent times and visiting vessels are strongly recommended to be prepared with documentation. See the Customs paragraph on p.15, note that vessels and crew from the UK, which is not party to the Schengen scheme, must register their presence at the first border port encountered. Schengen forms should be downloaded in advance free from the RYA site, www.rya.org.uk, and deposited in the marked boxes on first landing, retaining a copy on board. Compliance is mandatory.

If carrying duty-free goods, be prepared to demonstrate the on board stock does not exceed EU allowances. In the event of having a large quantity of dutiable goods on board, or crew without qualifying papers, it is a requirement to seek immigration on entry and gain clearance to the Schengen area before proceeding. Larger ports have Immigration/ Douane Offices: HMs are the best source of up to date info on office hours.

CEVNI – vessels under 15m and capable of not more than 10 knots are exempt from having a CEVNI qualified helmsman on board. However, many waterways employ CEVNI signage and familiarity with the meaning of the symbols is very much to the advantage of the navigator.

Radio communications
Dutch law does not stipulate that vessels must have VHF radio fitted but, where in use it is a requirement to listen in to the channel appropriate for every section of Dutch waterways as shown on navigation charts: this is especially important where commercial shipping is in motion.

VHF radios are required to be ATIS compliant, a facility that tags each broadcast with an individual identifying code based on the MMSI number. The ATIS code can be obtained free from the UK radio licensing authority. Many UK radios do not have ATIS capability, and ATIS is not actually legal in UK waters: if fitted it must be disabled before using the set on returning home. The Dutch authorities do not appear to be pursuing UK vessels that do not have ATIS compliant VHF radios, but this could change. In official communications expect to use your call sign rather than boat name.

VHF M or 37 must not be used in Dutch waters, as it is a commercial frequency. VHF 31 is sometimes specified but many UK radios do not offer this frequency. VHF 16 and high power are only used for emergencies and should be avoided for casual traffic.

Emergency services are obtainable on VHF 16. KNRM is the official lifeboat rescue service; other services responding to a call, including salvage services, will mostly make a charge for assistance.

Smoothing the way
Holding tanks are not yet mandatory for visiting vessels, but strict pollution controls are being introduced throughout Holland, and no sewage discharges in marinas or inland waters is the rule. Most marinas now offer pay pump-out services, and all larger units can be expected to have one.

Holland's railway system is famously efficient, and is well connected with local bus services so putting most marinas in easy touch with airports and ferry terminals. Very fast inter-city rail service now available between Amsterdam / Rotterdam and Brussels, connecting with Eurostar to St Pancras (booking essential). Check out local routes and services in English via– www.9292.nl or, for buses www.connexxion.nl or, Dutch railways www.ns.nl. Ticket offices are now limited to major stations, otherwise machines issue tickets and accept major credit cards. Tickets issued by onboard inspectors attract a €50 penalty: inspectors are ubiquitous and speak excellent English.

Ferry services operate between Harwich and Hoek van Holland, Newcastle and IJmuiden, Hull and Rotterdam.

Intercity buses ply between London and major Dutch and Belgian towns – competitive, and easier on the luggage allowance. See www.eurolines.co.uk.

Telephone kiosks have been removed from many sites in Holland in response to the spread of mobile communications: be prepared. But more marinas now offer WiFi connections, many free.

VAT at 21% is applied to most transactions in Holland, and a tourist tax of up to € 2.00 per head per night may be levied.

Most towns have a tourist bureau; look for the VVV sign in blue.

Weather forecasts
Dutch Coastguard broadcasts in English on Chs 23 or 83 at 0805, 1305, 1905 and 2305 daily, with short and medium term forecasts. Strongly recommended. Most marinas post a very useful synopsis.

IJmuiden Navtex station P broadcasts at 0230 and every four hours, local time. Navtex station T operates from Oostende at 0310 and same intervals.

Gas supplies
Calor gas is not used on the Continent but Camping Gaz is widely available in hardware stores, supermarkets, and chandlers.

Language
Dutch people are generally very appreciative of foreign visitors attempts to speak their language and a little effort goes a long way towards making new friendships. It does not take long to discover that the town of Goes is pronounced 'hoose' or that IJmuiden is pronounced 'Ay-mowd-en'. The following translations may be found useful when trying to interpret notes in the almanacs or on Dutch charts:

aanlegplaatsen	= temporary berthing places	*brug*	= bridge
		douane	= customs
		gat	= channel
afval	= rubbish	*geen*	= no, none
ankerplaats	= anchorage	*gesloten*	= shut
bakboord	= port	*havengeld*	= harbour dues
bediening	= opening times of bridges and locks	*havenmeester*	= hbrmaster
		ligplaatsen	= overnight berths
ma. t/m zat	= Monday–Saturday	*oost (abbr. O)*	= east
		sluis	= lock
zo. en fd	= Sundays and public holidays	*spoorbrug*	= rly bridge
		vast	= fixed (bridge)
di, wo, do, vr	= Tues., Wed., Thurs., Fri.	*veer*	= ferry
		verboden	= forbidden
betonning	= buoyage	*wassalon*	= launderette
beweegbare	= opening (bridge)	*zuid (abbr. Z)*	= south

The Cruising Almanac

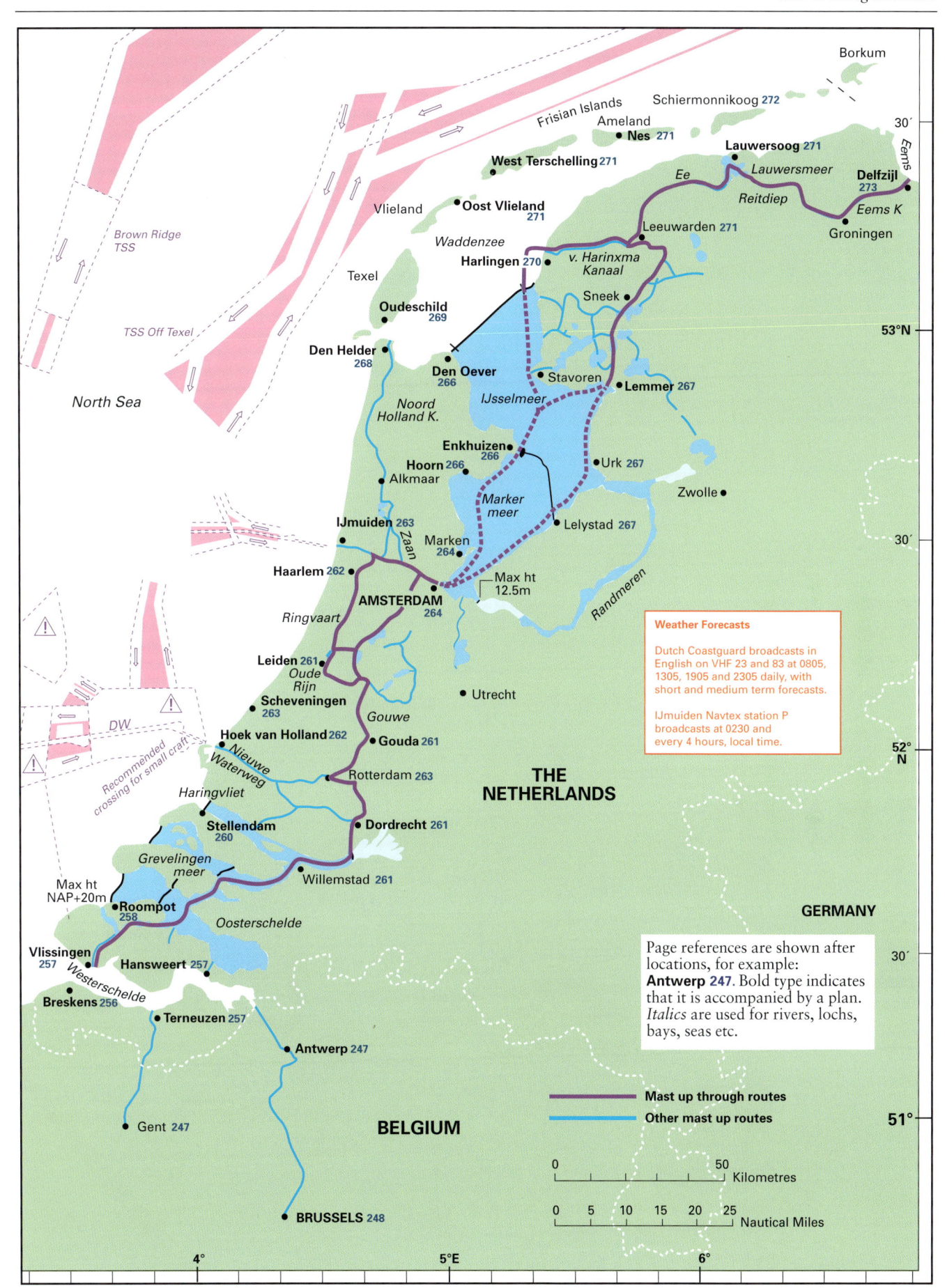

NETHERLANDS

OOSTENDE TO DEN HELDER

Passage lights
Oostende
Fl(3)10s27M
Westkapelle
Fl.3s48m28M
West Schouwen
Fl(2+1)15s57m30M
Westhoofd
Fl(3)15s55m30M
IJmuiden
Fl.5s52m29M
Kijkduin - Den Helder Approach
Fl(4)20s56m30M

251

Dudgeon
Q(9)15s
Racon (O) YBY
Race Bank Windfarm
Under constr 2017-2018
Dudgeon Windfarm
Under constr 2016-2017
Lincs
Windfarm
Docking
Shoal
Sheringham Shoal
Windfarm
Inner Bank
Leman Bank
DR1
LFl
Q(9)
Racon
53°
The
Wash
Wells
Cromer
Haisborough
Sand
Jim Howe Bank
Smiths
Knoll
Happisburgh
Newarp
LFl.10s
RW Racon (O)
Smiths Knoll
Q(6)+LFl.15s
YB Racon (T)
Kings Lynn
Cross Sand
LFl.10s
RW Racon (T)
Great Yarmouth
Scroby Sands
Windfarm
30′
Lowestoft
Southwold
Aldeburgh
Orfordness
Woodbridge
R Deben
Ipswich
N Shipwash
Q
Bell AIS
BY Racon (M)
Greater Gabbard
Offshore Wind
Farm
R Orwell
52°N
R Stour
Outer Gabbard
Q(3)10s
BYB Racon (O)
Felixstowe
Harwich
Sunk E
Iso.2.5s
RW Racon (T)
Colchester
Walton
Backwaters
Sunk Inner
Fl(5)15s12M
Horn(1)30s
Racon (T)
Noord
Hinder
TSS
West
Mersea
Brightlingsea
Sunk Centre
Fl(2)20s16M
Horn(2)60s
Racon (C)
NHR-S
Fl.Y.10s
Gunfleet
Sands
Offshore
Wind Farm
Greater Gabbard
Wind Farm
R Blackwater
King's Channel
S Galloper
Q(6)+LFl.15s
YB Racon (T)
Maldon
Burnham-
on-Crocuh
Black Deep
Southend
London
Array
Thames
Estuary
30′
River Thames
Tilbury
Falls Head
Q
BY
Gravesend
Kentish
Flats Wind
Farm
Thanet Offshore
Wind Farm
West Hind
Fl(4)30s12
Horn Mo(
Racon (W)
Chatham
Isle of
Sheppey
N Foreland
Fl(5)WR.20s57m19/15M
AIS
Foxtrot 3
Fl.10s15M
Horn10s
Racon (T)
TSS West
Hinder
Whitstable
Ramsgate
30′
1°E
30′
2°
30′

The Cruising Almanac

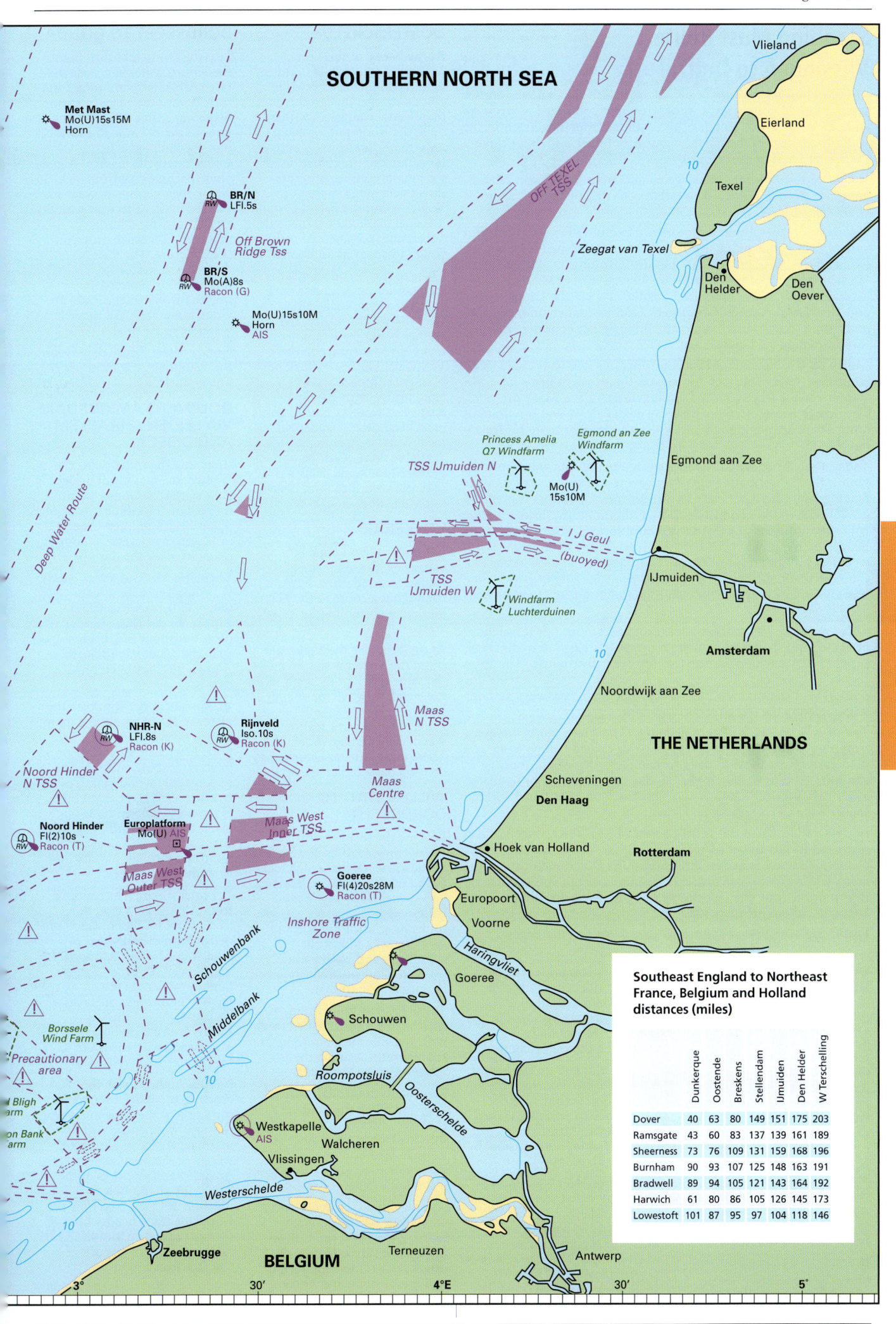

Southeast England to Northeast France, Belgium and Holland distances (miles)

	Dunkerque	Oostende	Breskens	Stellendam	IJmuiden	Den Helder	W Terschelling
Dover	40	63	80	149	151	175	203
Ramsgate	43	60	83	137	139	161	189
Sheerness	73	76	109	131	159	168	196
Burnham	90	93	107	125	148	163	191
Bradwell	89	84	105	121	143	164	192
Harwich	61	80	86	105	126	145	173
Lowestoft	101	87	95	97	104	118	146

NETHERLANDS

253

Standing Mast Route
Vlissingen to Delfzijl

The standing mast route is one of Holland's best known cruiser attractions. It comprises a variety of interconnected waterways stretching the whole length of the country from Vlissingen in the south to Delfzijl in the north, a journey of over 200 miles though the western half of the country.

It also permits sheltered passage to and from the Frisian Islands, gateway to the Baltic, if weather on the open sea route is challenging.

The route is generally straight forward except in Friesland where it suffers a time consuming diversion via Leeuwarden. This is caused by a fixed bridge (6·7m) before Groningen on the van Starkenborgh canal passable to commercial traffic. Mast up traffic diverts at least 20M round Leeuwarden and via the Lauwersmeer and Reit Diep to reach Groningen. Cruisers under time pressure and using the inland route are advised to consider using a foreshortening via Lauwersoog.

Much of the Staande Mastroute operates on waterways with controlled levels: but the waters of the Oosterschelde and the system enclosed between the Haringvliet and the Maas are tidal. The whole route offers at least 2m water draft and air draft of 18m. There are a minimum of 14 locks and rather more bridges to navigate.

Today, more bridges and some locks are remote controlled; moving with a flotilla normally helps to promote earlier opening as does making yourself visible close to the cameras. Operators respond to a VHF call – the channel is shown alongside the bridge name. Mooring positions at most bridges and locks reduce the stress of boat handling in windy or crowded high season conditions (last 2 weeks of July and most of August). Making fast in locks requires a calm calculation: better to stop short then edge forward. Stern line first almost always pays off, then edge slowly ahead. Tending lines at all times.

There are over 700 marinas and recognised moorings throughout Holland, and the standing mast route passes close to many. Fuel, supplies and engineering services are well distributed. The train service connecting all towns of any size is a useful feature for cruisers and their crews; bus services operate to railways stations so completing the public service network.

The plan on p.251 will help planning. The route can be accessed from the North Sea at various points, described below. Even at a moderate pace, allow 7 days to complete the whole journey in comfort. A shorter but useful (5 day) passage can be made to advantage between Lauwersoog and the Roompot when seeking shelter from the North Sea.

Bridges and locks on this route operate all year but service is much restricted in less travelled places during the winter months, often closed all day on Sundays: reference to the Dutch publication, the Staande Mastroute, will give specifics and assist planning. General information on the working of Dutch locks, lights and communications are on p.309.

Further details of ports and services are given on later pages.

VLISSINGEN TO VEERSE MEER

The Vlissingen locks stand just 1M above the town up the R Scheldte; the entrance is shared with the fast ferry to Breskens. Operating 24/7 the small Sports lock lies to stb: fenders should be lowered to counter the heavy baulks at water level. Occasionally the large commercial lock is offered – beware the wall bollards which are widely spaced. The Walcheren canal is a commercial waterway and surprisingly large shallow draft vessels may be encountered.

Beyond the lock is a pool for military and fishing vessels; keeping to stb past the small marina (useful for overnight stops and fuel) brings the first bascule bridge into view. The 5 bridges on the canal to Middelburg are operated in sequence, all remotely controlled through cameras.

Beyond Middelburg the N part of the Walcheren canal ends at picturesque Veere where the Sports lock to port gives entry to the Veerse Meer. The commercial lock is occasionally offered at busy times.

The Veerse Meer is a rural waterway with extensive nature reserves. There are 7 marinas along its 12M length and plenty of staging for free overnighting. The main channel is well buoyed and lit, with small stick buoys marking the 2m contour.

OOSTERSCHELDE

At the N end of the Veerse Meer the large Zandkrieksluis with its double road bridges gives onto the Oosterschelde, a major tidal waterway with a lock, the Roompot, opening onto the N Sea at its W end. A large bank in the centre, used for mussel culture, prevents direct passage N to the Volkerak but the passage round it is well marked on either side. Substantial commercial traffic passes this way at all hours.

Close to the N end stands the lock adjoining Bruinisse – the entrance to the enclosed Grevelingen Meer. Just 1M further N are the Krammersluis locks at the entrance to the Volkerak. The Sports lock lies N of the complex and has a fixed bridge with 18·4m air draft. For vessels exceeding this mast height the commercial locks offer an opening bridge available on request: be prepared for some delay as operators work to limit delays to road traffic.

VOLKERAK

Entering the Volkerak waterway, the main channel swings S round Noorderplaat Island, but a route to the N is marked and suitable for small craft.

At the N end of the Volkerak stand the Volkeraksluisen and the same restrictions apply as at the S end; very tall masts may be told to moor beyond the bridge to ensure clearance when levels change in the lock. There is mooring at Dintelmond on the S bank before the locks.

WILLEMSTAD TO DORDRECHT

Leaving the lock, to port lies the opening road bridge leading to the Haaringvliet which locks out to the N Sea at Stellendam, 15M away. This whole tidal waterway system gives access to the interior of Europe and neighbouring industrial complexes and is very heavily trafficked but surprisingly green in outlook for all that.

To stb lies old Willemstad, a most picturesque fortified town with two marinas, but there are simpler refuges along the waterways to Dordrecht.

Passing up the Hollandsch Diep, avoiding the marked shallows, turn N at Moerdijk into the Dordtse Kil, since passage further inland under the major road and rail bridges is limited to 9m air draft.

Approaching Dordrecht, at the confluence of 2 waterways, the massive road and rail bridges open at set times. Dordrecht offers several mooring facilities and is a bustling and historic centre with full services.

DORDRECHT TO GOUDA

Leaving Dordrecht turn N into the Noord waterway, pass the large Alblasserdam bridge, and turn W into the Maas, a major waterway; after 3M cross the river to the N bank and turn N into the Hollandse Ijssel. Immediately the massive Algera Sluis (barrage) confronts which when open permits passage for smaller craft, otherwise wait on the W bank for a bridge opening. Clearance gauge on the structure. The trail N through the industrial hinterland of Rotterdam eventually brings the locks at Gouda into view. All these waterways are tidal.

Gouda offers plenty of reasons for a stopover, but mooring is not sophisticated.

GOUDA TO AMSTERDAM VIA LEIDEN / HAARLEM AND DIRECT

Rejoining the route N via the Gouwe, the major rail bridge (spoorbrug) at Gouda is an immediate impediment – it only opens briefly at intervals and, in season many vessels moor ready to make the dash past.

Thereafter the waterway winds N through rural landscapes with smaller towns such as **Alphen an der Rijn** offering a pleasant stopover. 7 bridges span the waterway to north Alphen but they open on approach.

At Alphen an der Rijn past the Hefbrug is a crossing: the main course takes a sharp turn to port. After 2 miles is a major junction leading either N direct to Amsterdam and Haarlem or, straight on W via Leiden then Haarlem to Amsterdam. The faster direct route to Amsterdam involves overnight motoring through the city and its numerous bridges.

1. Leiden circuit The route W from Alphen via Leiderdorp leads, via 3 bridges opening on demand, to the outskirts of Leiden itself where a stopover will be well rewarded by the famous university town. Passing N through the lakes and moorings of the Kagerplassen reunites at Buitenkaag with the route to Haarlem.

N from Alphen From the crossing at Alphen take the N turning past the Molenaarsbrug through Woubrugge with its marinas, and cross the broad waters of the Braassemermeer. A narrower channel N of the lake leads after a mile to a T-junction at Oude Wetering where the track heads either W towards Haarlem, or NE skirting Schiphol airport towards Amsterdam.

2. Amsterdam Direct: The route N from Oude Wetering via the Ringvaart waterway and Aalsmeer leads to the Nieuwe Meer where controlled entry to the Amsterdam canal system is permitted. One mile before the Nieuwe Meer stands another barrier – a major bridge serving Schiphol airport that opens up to 3 times a day: planning is essential.

To pass N through the city and all its bridges to reach the North Sea Canal is only possible with the daily convoy operated from about midnight, when bridges open in sequence in both directions. The convoy assembles at the waiting platform at the N end of the Nieuwe Meer where directions are given (not Sundays) Keeping up with the convoy through the city is essential. Toll payable. The route exits at the Hout Haven right on the North Sea Canal, where convoys setting off S also congregate each evening. The trip takes up to 2 hours

3. Via Haarlem to Amsterdam
From the Oude Wetering T-junction head W to Buitenkaag where the Leiden circuit rejoins the route to Haarlem. Proceeding N the next immediate obstacle is the Sassenheim railway bridge with its narrow opening, and lifting only at set times: it pays to plan the best time to pass this bottleneck which can get very congested in season. Thereafter the route is open and pleasant countryside, the canal standing some way above the surrounding fields.

Approaching Haarlem be prepared for intensive bridgework – 9 in all – worked in convoy and rather close together on the narrow and twisting town waterway. The rail bridge towards the N of the centre is busy and reluctant to open: a town toll is payable at the collection office signposted to port nearby. There is some alongside town mooring but facilities are simple: a marina just N of the town next to the Spaarndam lock offers better accommodation.

The town itself is a treasure house of architecture, museums, churches and restaurants – and only a short train ride to the heart of Amsterdam.

N of Haarlem lies the toll lock at Spaarndam with a useful marina just beyond to port. A major obstruction lies at the A9 motorway bridge which opens briefly 3 times a day. Missing an opening could delay progress for hours.

Beyond the motorway, a further local road bridge opens on approach and gives directly onto the North Sea Canal, a major waterway with very large sea going vessels including passenger liners. Turn to stb and make for Amsterdam; sailing is permitted but shipping has priority.

IJmuiden at the sea end of the North Sea Canal is another entry point to the standing mast system. Progress N from Amsterdam to Lauwersoog can be reasonably rapid, 2–3 days, given the open waters and fewer obstacles. The route S to Vlissingen is somewhat slower, 4–5 days, owing to the many bridges, plus lock congestion in the season.

AMSTERDAM
3 marinas now serve Amsterdam, the newest and largest is the Amsterdam Marina on the N canal bank 1M W of the central station. All marinas have free ferry connections to the station wharf.

AMSTERDAM TO FRIESLAND
Passage E into the Markermeer is via the Oranjesluis, a very busy set of locks. The Sports lock lies N of the complex accessed through a signed waiting gate, but be prepared for commercials to join in or even displace pleasure traffic. Beyond the lock a large road bridge opens in conjunction with the lock. The course to N passes one of Holland's most famous landmarks, the lighthouse on Marken Island.

The Markermeer is very shallow but the bed is even, and mostly with 2·5–3·5m depth; shipping channels are well marked. Attractive ports lie on every point of the wind and most cruising vessels will be able to take the breeze N by whatever tack. But in Force 5+ short seas develop that make progress slow and wet.

The Markermeer is separated from the IJsselmeer by the 15M long Houtribdijk carrying a road from Enkhuisen at its west end, to Lelystad at its east; capacious 24/7 locks at each end open on to two alternative routes N through Friesland. Alternatively exit the Ijsselmeer at Den Oever and take the buoyed route S of Texel out to the N Sea.

1. Friesland via Lemmer
Lemmer is a bustling port town offering several marinas, and gives entrance to the Princses Margriet canal, the main route into Friesland. Lemmer has two locking systems – the major commercial lock to the W, skirting the town, and the small town lock to the E. The town system is for pleasure craft, charges a toll, and is a narrow, congested but attractive waterway with alongside moorings close to restaurants and shops.

Past Lemmer the canal strikes N through connected lakes past Sneek, a pleasant and characterful alongside mooring opportunity, and several bridges to Grou before making a W turn on the approach to Leeuwarden, the regional capital. There is no route for standing mast vessels direct to Groningen owing to a fixed railway bridge (6·7m). So masted traffic makes the 20M detour W round Leeuwarden, passing two road bridges opening outside of rush hours, and two railways bridges restricted to 3 openings per day. Transiting Leeuwarden can be time consuming: planning is essential. A pleasant club lies to stb 1M before the first road bridge – pass a small swinging rail bridge opening on demand; a medium walk into town.

1M beyond the second railway bridge, the canal forks: a sharp turn to stb leads back through the 6 lifting bridges in the town centre. A toll is collected via clog at the fifth bridge. Alongside mooring in attractive settings, but shallow along the banks, and simple facilities: ready access to the town and shops.

2. Friesland via Harlingen This route to Leeuwarden has the advantage of less traffic in season and fewer obstructions, and takes 2 full days to the Lauwersmeer.

Make N up the IJsselmeer to the lock through the Afsluitsdijk at Kornwerderzand, observing the marked approach channel. Beyond the lock the channel becomes narrower and more shallow (3m max) through the Boonjes where safe passage to Harlingen is only recommended at HW.

Harlingen offers all services, shops, a historic centre and rail connections.

For onward passage, make to port from the outer harbour past the ferry loading bays, locking in to the van Harinxma Canal, a commercial waterway maintained to 3·5m depth to Leeuwarden. A small yacht club 1M W of Franneker is welcoming and gives easy access to town facilities.

LEEUWARDEN TO GRONINGEN & DELFZIJL
Exiting Leeuwarden the Dokkumer Je is a canalised river wandering across attractive country through Burdaard (clog toll at second bridge) to Dokkum a characterful town with windmills and shops, where staging beyond the third bridge offers 2m draft, otherwise alongside mooring around the town is usually good for only 1·5m. Toll charged.

Beyond Dokkum the lock at Dokkumer Nieuwe Zijlen issues into the reedbeds and nature reserves of the Lauwersmeer, formed by damming the former waterway. A large marina to stb on leaving the lock. Pushing N to the dam permits exit to the N Sea via the Robbengat Sluis where passage to the German Frisians is straight forward.

From the Lauwersmeer making for Groningen, turn E into the Slenk and head E through a narrowing channel, the Reitdiep, to the lock at Zoutkamp: a good marina close by. Thereafter the route passes across the fields and crosses the van Starkenborgh canal, continuing SE via a lock. Approaching Groningen, vessels progress in convoy through 8 remote controlled bridges to skirt S of the town centre, an interesting if slow ride to reach the small marina just beyond the station.

Groningen is a major university town with all facilities including good rail connections. The ride NE to Delfzijl is straightforward along the Ems canal, a commercial waterway with 3·5m min depth.

Approaching Delfzijl the canal forks left to the small marina before the town, and right to the sea lock with another marina just outside to port. The channel out to the Eems River and the N Sea is straight forward and lit. Borkum Island (G) offers useful moorings for passing cruisers.

Zeeland

WESTERSCHELDE RIVER

A major river and waterway serving docks for 45M upstream to Antwerp. Its estuary has two large banks that are a hazard to navigation – the Raan on the seaward side, and the Hooge Platen upstream from Breskens – four navigable channels are buoyed to permit safe passage past them.

The NW approach channel (Oostgat) runs close along the Walcheren coast, the SW (Wielingen) along the Belgium coast. In the river, the Honte passes to the N side, and the lesser Waarwater Langs Hoofdplaat channel along the S of the river.

Approaching along the Belgian coast, stay S of the Wielingen channel until off Breskens. Coming in from the NW, stay close to the boundary of the narrow Oostgat or, take the less used Duerloo that runs in parallel until off Vlissingen where the two meet in a narrow chicane frequented by large vessels. Within the river, heavy traffic uses the Honte channel, but substantial barges can be expected in the shallower Hoofdplat.

Heavy shipping converges in the estuary where pilots are taken on board, and ships can change direction and speed at any time. Tides flow up to 4kns, and strong wind over tide is something to behold.

Fast passenger ferries operate from a dock 500m W of Breskens to the locks entrance lying 1M E of Vlissingen.

The whole river is intensively buoyed to deal with the large areas of sandbanks. Chart number 1803 in the Dutch 1800 Hydrographic Series lays it out nicely.

BRESKENS
Tidal data as for Vlissingen

A favoured port with a large marina accessible 24/7, with all facilities and pontoon berths capable of taking larger vessels, plus a well-known clubhouse and restaurant. More cafés and restaurants 300m away in town, a useful supermarket, and excellent seafood markets, a superior stopover to Vlissingen.

Expect strong streams right up to the entrance with shallows W of the mole. Inside, a barge to port acts as a wave break; turn to port round the barge and enter the reception pen where the HM can be contacted via phone at seaward end of pontoon to allocate a berth. Clubhouse and facilities are on the other side of the marina. Note: seaport marinas in Holland are noticeably more expensive than inland facilities.

Passage upstream towards Antwerp is best made from Breskens using the S (Hoofdplaat) channel which joins the main river 5M upstream and is well marked. Departing just before LW and maintaining a steady speed it is possible to reach Antwerp on one tide. Terneuzen is otherwise a good stopping off port 12M up from Breskens.

Passage westwards from Breskens benefits from 7+ hours favourable tide so is a popular departure port for the UK.

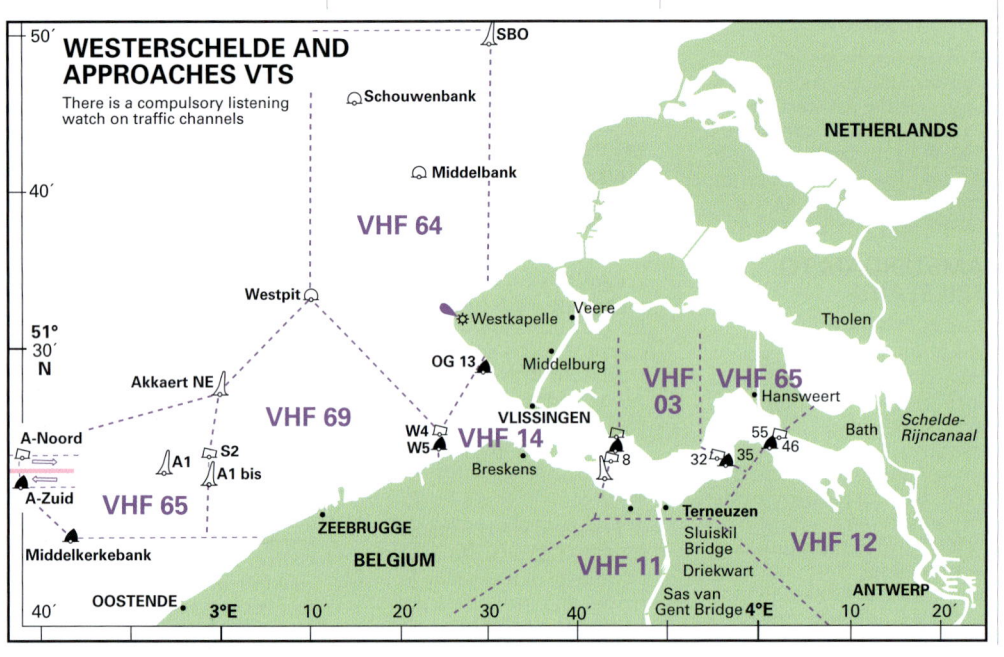

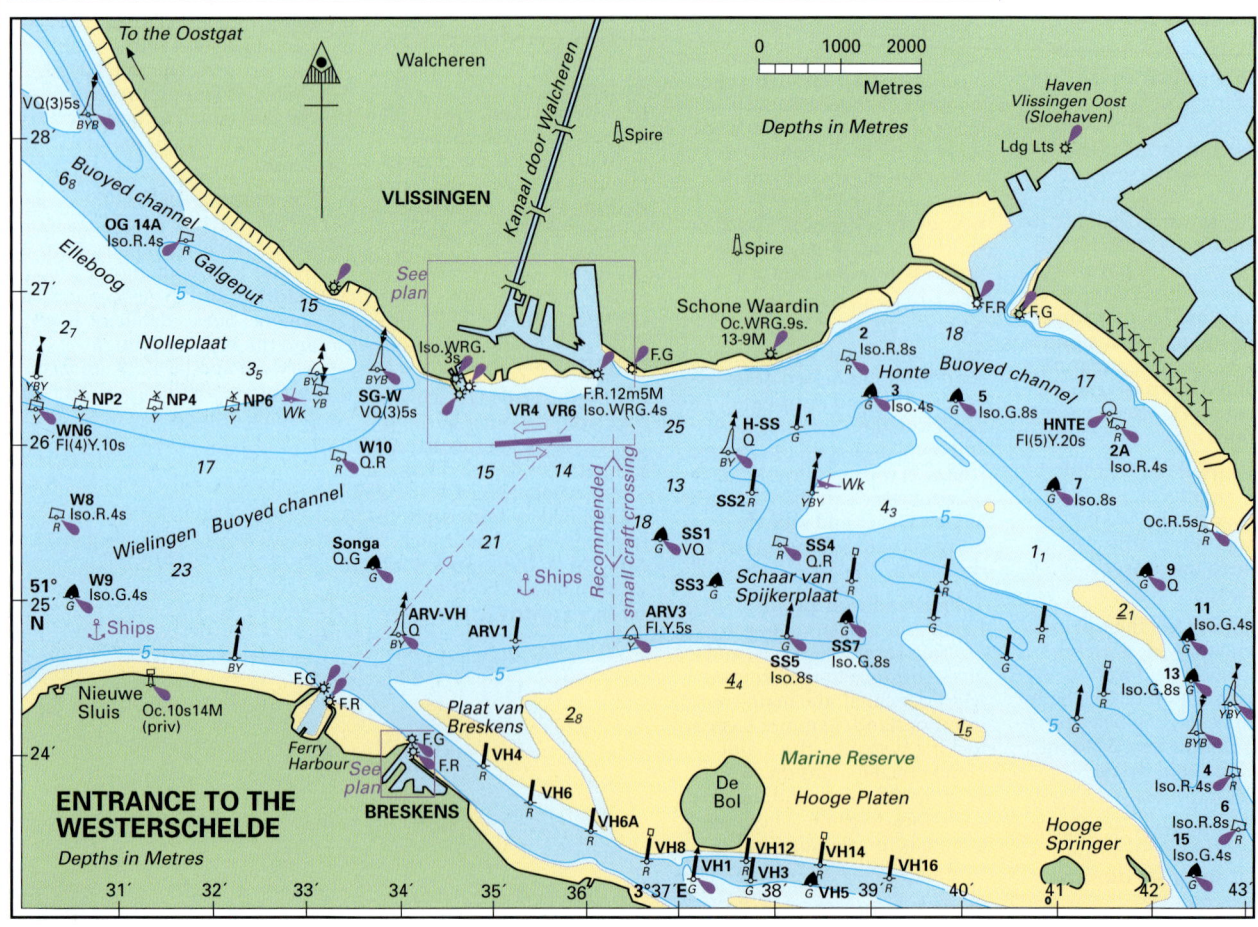

VLISSINGEN

Standard Port Vlissingen
DS Dover −0315E +0300W, up to 4kn

Crossing the river between Breskens and Vlissingen, observe the traffic scheme, and be alert that the flood tide does not press you onto the banks upstream of Breskens. Beware heavy shipping and keep the required radio watch on VHF 14. Small vessels must maintain a minimum speed of 3·5kn, cross lanes at 90° and not obstruct shipping.

Entrance The Michiel de Ruyter Marina in the former Visserhaven shares an entrance with the pilot launch hbr, just W of the conspic public observation tr. The marina is tidal but there is normally a minimum depth of 1m over the sill at the entrance (0·7m at LAT). There is a footbridge over the entrance (min. air draught 6m when closed) which can be opened throughout the day by the HM, and stands open at night. There is no VHF but traffic lights indicate when the br will open. The flood lock may be closed between 1 November and 1 April and the marina is then not accessible.

Vlissingen Marina has over 100 berths and the HM allocates space on passing though the entrance. Showers and launderette but no fuel. Vlissingen town is close to hand with shops and restaurants.

HANSWEERT

Standard Port Vlissingen
HW +0055 LW +0050

MHWS	MHWN	MLWN	MLWS
+0·7m	+0·6m	+0·1m	0·0m

20M upstream on the N bank of the river is the entrance to the S Beveland canal, giving easy access to the Oosterschelde via large locks. Lock control VHF 22 to ask for passage. Limited waiting pontoons at lifting bridges along the canal; mooring only possible at Wemeldinge. Expect heavy barge traffic.

No yacht facilities at Hansweert but customs post manned May–October.

Wemeldinge A pleasant resort village with small beach, lies at N end of the Beveland canal. Inner and outer marinas. Visitors' pontoon at outer marina; HM's office on promontory near old locks for pontoon allocation. Code locked gates. Vessels >12m restricted to outer marina. Good facilities.

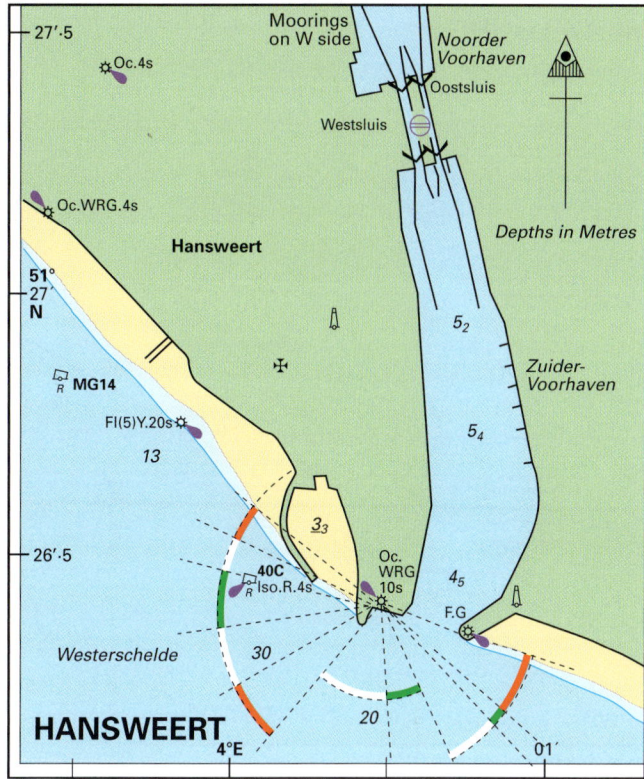

TERNEUZEN

Standard Port Vlissingen
HW +0020 LW +0025

MHWS	MHWN	MLWN	MLWS
+0·4m	+0·3m	+0·1m	0·0m

DS Dover −0130ENE −0030W

An historic town 12M up river from Breskens on the Westerschelde; useful stopover facilities – a good range of shops and market. Also access to Gent, 18M distant, via locks and a canal; three lifting bridges make passage with mast up possible. (Detail Dutch Hydrographic chart 1803.)

On the approach, beware heavy traffic issuing from the W harbour (Westbuitenhaven).

The E lock (Oostsluis accessed through the Oostebuitenhaven) is designated for yachts staying over or moving on to Gent. Contact locks on VHF 18, operates 24/7 at HW ±0100. Through the locks, make a 180° turn to port after 800m for moorings at the YC at the N end of the Zijkanaal A.

Alternatively, the Yacht Harbour, the most easterly facility, is for cruising vessels seeking ready access to town and river. Two marinas are sited in this basin, Yachthaven WV Neusen, and Jachthaven Terneuzen, with regular facilities, but some disturbance can be expected from tugs and ferries using the W side.

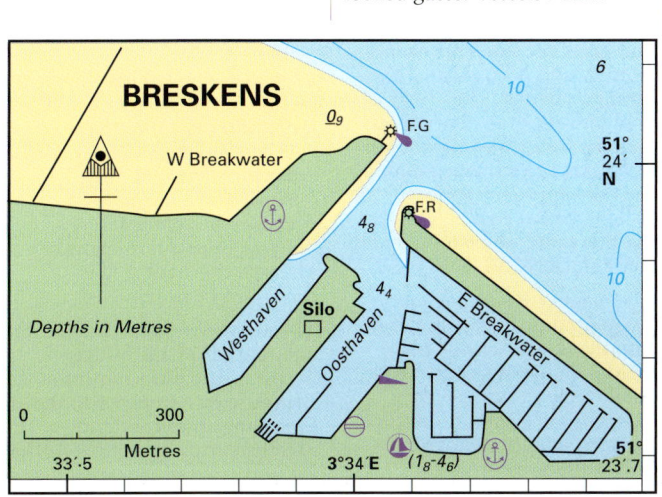

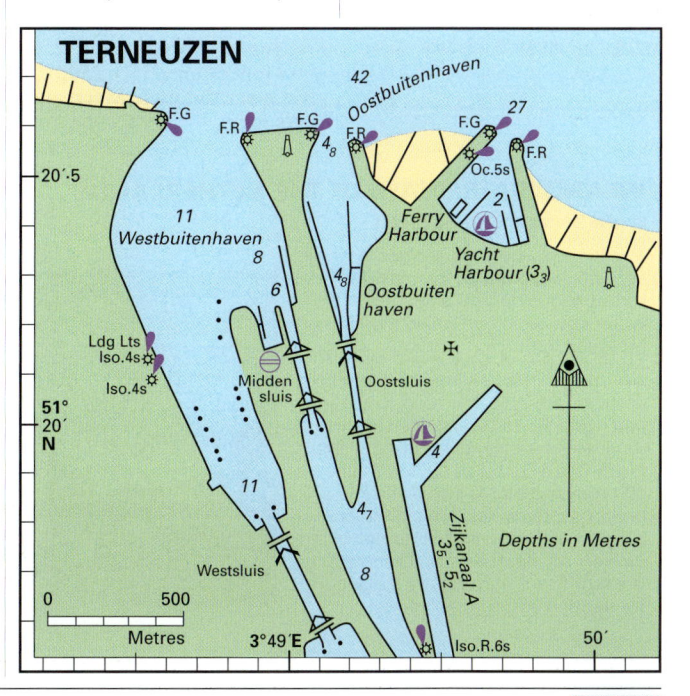

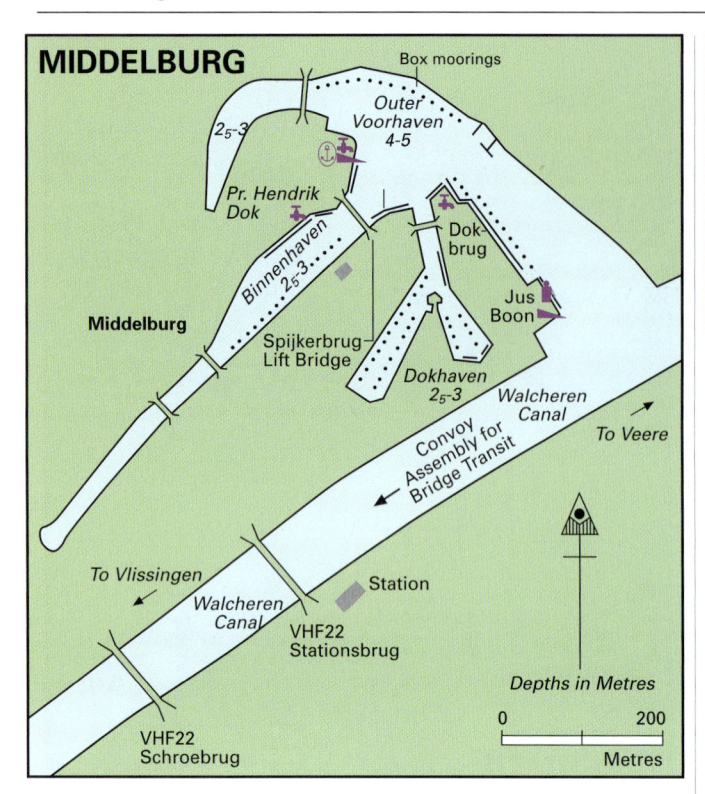

ANTWERP
See Belgium section on p.247.

WALCHEREN CANAL – VLISSINGEN TO VEERE
Travelling N via the Walcheren canal system (max depth 3·5m) make for the lock entrance 1M upstream from Vlissingen town, keeping watch for passenger ferries. Locks (VHF 18) operate 24/7. Proceed through the RH small vessel lock, setting fenders low for the timber baulks on either side. Then bear to stb towards the remote controlled bridge into the canal.

To stb, the **Schelde Yacht Club**: all facilities including diesel, and just 10 minutes' walk to Vlissingen town, and five minutes' walk to the rail terminal serving all Holland: trains every 30 minutes. A good refuge when arriving late.

MIDDELBURG
Three remote controlled bridges lie between Vlissingen and **Middelburg**, where two town bridges operate alternately. Service hours 0900–2100 Sunday and holidays, otherwise 0600–2200.

The popular and capacious town marina lies to port 400m N of the swing bridge: register with the HM at reception pontoon, adjacent the bridge. Fuel and chandlery on barge to port at entry. Well known clubhouse and all facilities in historic town. With its handy (every 30 minutes) train connections, Middelburg is a natural for crew changes. Very busy in July and August; aim to arrive before noon for box berth otherwise late comers face rafting up.

Free run N of Middelburg to locks (operating 0530–2300) gives entry to **Veerse Meer**, and **Veere** town, formerly open to the sea, with its small alongside berthing marina 90° to port on leaving locks: very limited services, but excellent clubhouse and picturesque setting.

VEERSE MEER
An extensive if somewhat shallow waterway formed by damming the sea entrance: numerous attractive (many free) mooring opportunities throughout, and 7 marinas along its length with extensive facilities for the holiday trade.

A commercial waterway linking the Oosterschelde to the Westerschelde, the main channel is fully buoyed throughout; also note the small port and stb stick markers signifying the 2m contour. Nature reserves are marked and must be respected.

At the north end, a lock (Zandkreeksluis) issues into tidal Oosterschelde; many shellfish farms marked by withies, strictly to be avoided.

Oosterschelde
Standard Port Vlissengen
Roompot Buiten
HW −0010 LW −0005
MHWS MHWN MLWN MLWS
−1·2m −1·1m −0·3m −0·1m

Roompotsluis approach With tidal streams running at up to 2½kn it is worth planning to arrive at the Middelbank buoy between HW Zierikzee +0300 and +0600 to carry the tidal stream towards the lock and into the Oosterschelde. Both the Roompot and Oude Roompot channels are well buoyed from over 6M to sea and mark the safe approaches from W and NW, skirting the Hompels banks. The no-go area in front of the barrage is well marked with yellow buoys and is kept to stb when making the final approach to the locking basin. Fishing vessels ply this route, so be prepared to share the lock (VHF 18).

The massive **Roompotsluis** barrage controls the tidal flow into the Oosterschelde but creates dangerous currents and shallows in the approaches. Hazards are clearly buoyed off on both sides of the barrage, and cruisers are strongly advised to stay within the marked, relatively shallow, approach channels.

One mile inside the locks to stb is a marina, otherwise the mooring options are at **Zierikzee** on the N bank or **Colijnsplaat marina**, just 6M distant on the S bank.

ZIERIKZEE
A famous old fishing town, now a centre of mussel culture, reached via a shallow canal (2·4m max depth) passing through old lock gates. Strong tides and very deep water at the seaward entrance. Very busy in season with very few box moorings available, visiting vessels are directed by the HM to turn and moor alongside, often in rafts. Power available.

Excellent eating and shopping opportunities amongst buildings of splendour and quality. Good chandlery on quay.

COLIJNSPLAAT
Subject to strong tides on the narrow approach, a large modern marina with a small characterful village nearby offering a range of eating possibilities. Good facilities.

ZEELANDBRUG
Beyond Zieriksee and Colijnsplaat this elegant bridge, some 2M long spans the Oosterschelde. The marked traffic spans offer air draughts between 13 and 16m – actual clearance shown by gauge on the approach. Otherwise, at the N end of the bridge is an opening span (VHF 18) operating usually on the hour 0700–2130 (0900 start at weekends and holidays). Note the marked shallows in the vicinity of the bridge.

Beyond the bridge lies the main section of the Oosterschelde, a large waterway offering excellent sailing and busy with commercial vessels. An extensive area of shallows occupies the centre and is buoyed: mussel farming takes place on this bank and is forbidden territory.

The marked channels split north and south from the bridge: To the north, locks to port at **Bruinisse** give entrance to the **Grevelingenmeer**, offering excellent cruising waters. At the far north end of the

INLAND WATERWAYS OF THE NETHERLANDS
Louise Busby and David Broad

This book is a user's guide to the whole network, covering all the mast-up routes and excluding only those waterways which offer less than 3·5m bridge height.

Navigational details are provided for each waterway; comprising dimensions and obstacles to be expected, including service arrangements for bridges and locks. This is followed by details of over 300 stopping places across all 12 provinces; some which are large or popular harbours, and others which are well off the beaten track. Comments on the significant features are expanded for nearly 100 'principal venues'.

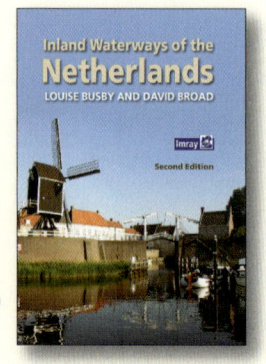

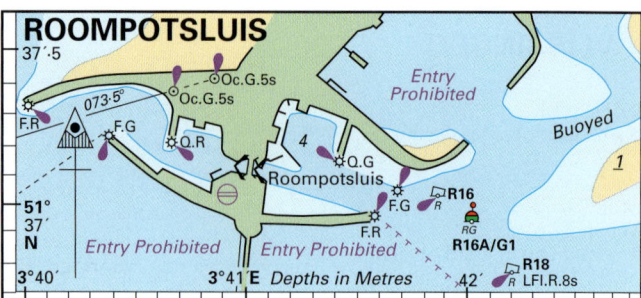

Oosterschelde the Krammer locks open onto the **Volkerak** waterway and central Holland.

Along the S shore of the Oosterschelde, the route passes the N entrance to the **Veerse Meer**, then the lock entrance leading to Goes; close by is **Wemeldinge** at the N end of the Beveland canal, finally reaching the small fishing town of **Yerseke**. Opposite lies the village and marina of **Tholen** reached through the small Bergsediepsluis (VHF 18) and a winding channel. Across the main Schelde-Rhein canal lies a narrow channel leading to the attractive town of Bergen op Zoom but mooring facilities are limited.

GOES

A fine town with two marinas and facilities, good train connections, and markets on the square. Goes is reached via a locked shallow canal (2·4m max) running through picturesque countryside. Lock hours 0600–2100 summer months (VHF 18); small marina inside lock is useful for a short break. Lifting bridge at Wilheminadorp operates on approach. At Goes, take right fork towards town; the HM operates the major road bridge (Ringbrug) at the edge of town opening on the hour 0900–1100 and 1600–2000 in summer, with high season/weekend variations: quayside waiting moorings before bridge.

Inside the bridge to port, an unusual garden-style marina (WV de Werf) for 12m max vessels with less than 2.2m draught. Straight ahead and beyond a hand drawn footbridge lies the alongside berth and box marina, right in the centre of town. All facilities except fuel; useful DIY supermarket right next to Ringbrug.

WEMELDINGE

South side of Oosterschelde, at head of S Beveland canal (24/7) leading to Westerschelde.

Two large sheltered marinas, restaurants and shops with most facilities, plus a small beach.

SOUTH BEVELAND CANAL

Very useful means of accessing the Westerschelde quickly from the Oosterschelde. Heavy commercial use 24/7. Waiting pontoons at two bridges leading to locks at Hansweert; call control on VHF 22 for service. Departure from Hansweert at HW Vlissingen +0100 gives 5h run downriver; departure upriver at HW Vlissingen −0400 should put Antwerp within reach on one tide.

GREVELINGEN MEER

Accessed via lock operating daylight hours, at Bruinisse. This enclosed waterway is a delight for cruisers, lying away from the main commercial traffic. Navigable channels are well marked throughout, with extensive shallows against the N shore. Mooring is permitted in selected island sites, for which there may be a fee.

Bruinisse A resort town with modern developments and a large modern marina on the port bank just outside the lock basin, with facilities, chandlery and restaurants. Visitors pull in immediately to HM office on entering marina for berth allocation.

Also, in the lock basin a smaller marina lies to port.

Brouwershaven is at the W end of the waterway with its marina and alongside berths in quiet and historic settings. Approach the entrance with care; observe buoyage to avoid stranding, and HM signal controlling the narrow entrance. Go alongside pontoon before the old lock gate and report to HM for berthing. Chandlery, fuel and most facilities.

Port Zelande at the far W end of the Grevelingen Meer, is a large resort marina and holiday village giving pedestrian access over the Brouwersdam to the N Sea and beach attractions, plus an exhibition of local conservation activities. All facilities.

Herkingen on the N shore offers two marinas approached through a narrow shallow (2m) channel, with good facilities; a

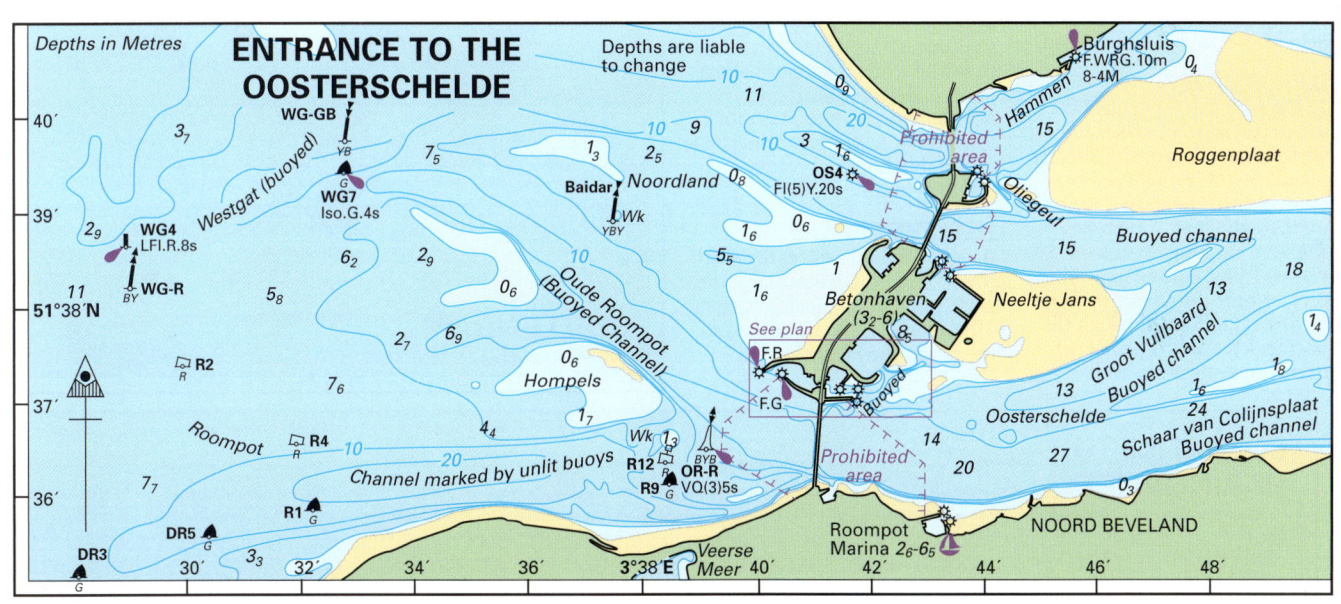

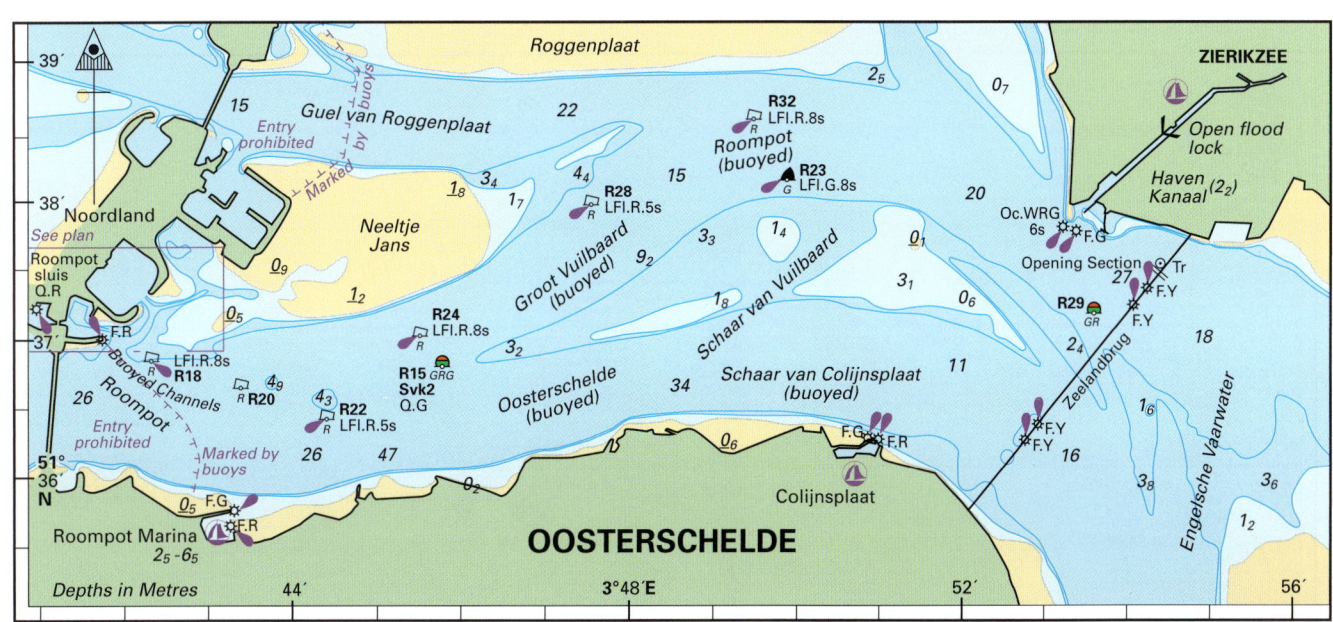

The Cruising Almanac

pretty, small town offering shopping and cafés.

On leaving the Grevelingen meer, the locks to the Volkerak lie to port past a large mussel farm. The 'Sport' sign directs to the smaller yacht lock on the left, north of the complex.

VOLKERAK
The Krammersluis locks (24/7) are often busy; an electric sign shows the max air draft (approx 18·4m) under the fixed bridge. The opening bridge in the commercial lock can be requested by vessels having greater air draft.

In the Volkerak, the channel forks past Noorderplaat island, the lesser north track is bounded on either side by 2m contour markers – most cruising vessels use this track. Otherwise to the south lies the main channel.

At the north end, the (Volkeraksluisen) locks, again with c.18·4m posted max air draft, give onto the Hollandsch Diep, a major artery into East Holland. To port under the long Haringvliet bridge lies the Haringvliet, and to stb the delightful town of Willemstad.

HARINGVLIET
Another major controlled waterway, formed when the Stellendam barrage was erected in the '50s. The main sea approach is a by a long well marked channel, sometimes shallow, running W–E from SG Haven Buoy, ending in a sharp turn to port into outer harbour. Strong tidal flows through the barrage create turbulence – hazardous zones are well marked; staying in channel is strongly recommended. Waiting pontoon before the locks in the outer harbour (Buitenhaven) where fishing boats use the quays to the south.

The shallower approach route from the N (Rak van Scheelhoek) is hazardous owing to movements in the Hinderplaat sands.

Locks operate 24h weekdays April–November, but 0800–2000 at weekends (VHF 20). Twin opening road bridges straddle the locks but the seaward br offers just 14m clearance when closed, so yachts with higher masts must contact control for bridge service on entry. In high winds bridge movements may be suspended.

STELLENDAM
Standard Port Vlissengen HW +0015

MHWS	MHWN	MLWN	MLWS
–1·9m	–1·8m	–0·6m	–0·2m

After the locks, a marina lies on the S bank with most facilities. Ahead lie some 15M of water with excellent cruising opportunities; numerous shallows all well marked, and two well-known former fishing ports – Hellevoetsluis and Middelharnis. The river Spui leads off N towards Dordrecht – a valuable but tidal route towards middle Holland.

HELLEVOETSLUIS
A major sailing centre, the small town offers three marinas – the large full facility marina is some 20 minutes' walk away west of the town, the Heliushaven. Many visiting yachtsmen moor in the approach canal right in the centre of everything with basic alongside facilities, or pass through the swing bridge (daylight hourly service only, on the hour except 1200 and 1600) to quieter pontoon facilities in the Hellevoetsluis YC or Arie de Boom marinas beyond in the Groote Dok.

East of town lies the Voornekanaal, the entrance of which has mooring facilities in the outer Tramhaven, and beyond the lock alongside berths.

Small selection of restaurants and cafés, plus bus connections to Rotterdam – useful for crew changes.

MIDDELHARNIS
Entry via a lock, open daylight hours (VHF 12) over which an extendable pedestrian walkway operates. Town is 1M distant along narrow canal lined with quays and moorings to the attractive village. All facilities, shops and a range of interesting restaurants.

Mooring in boxes on the east side and alongside on the west, just before the town proper.

RIVER SPUI
Tidal waterway departing N bank of Haringvliet to join Oude Maas beyond Beyerland (small town and marina with restricted (1·8m min) sill clearance, suitable for

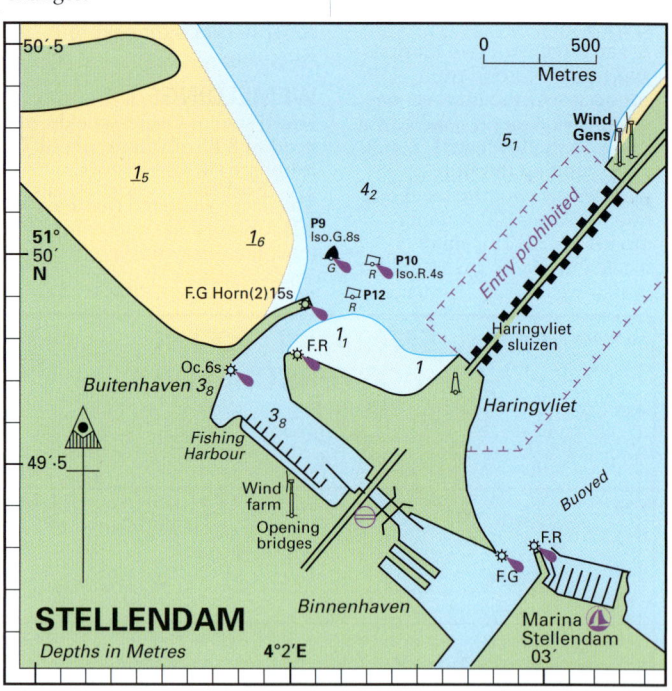

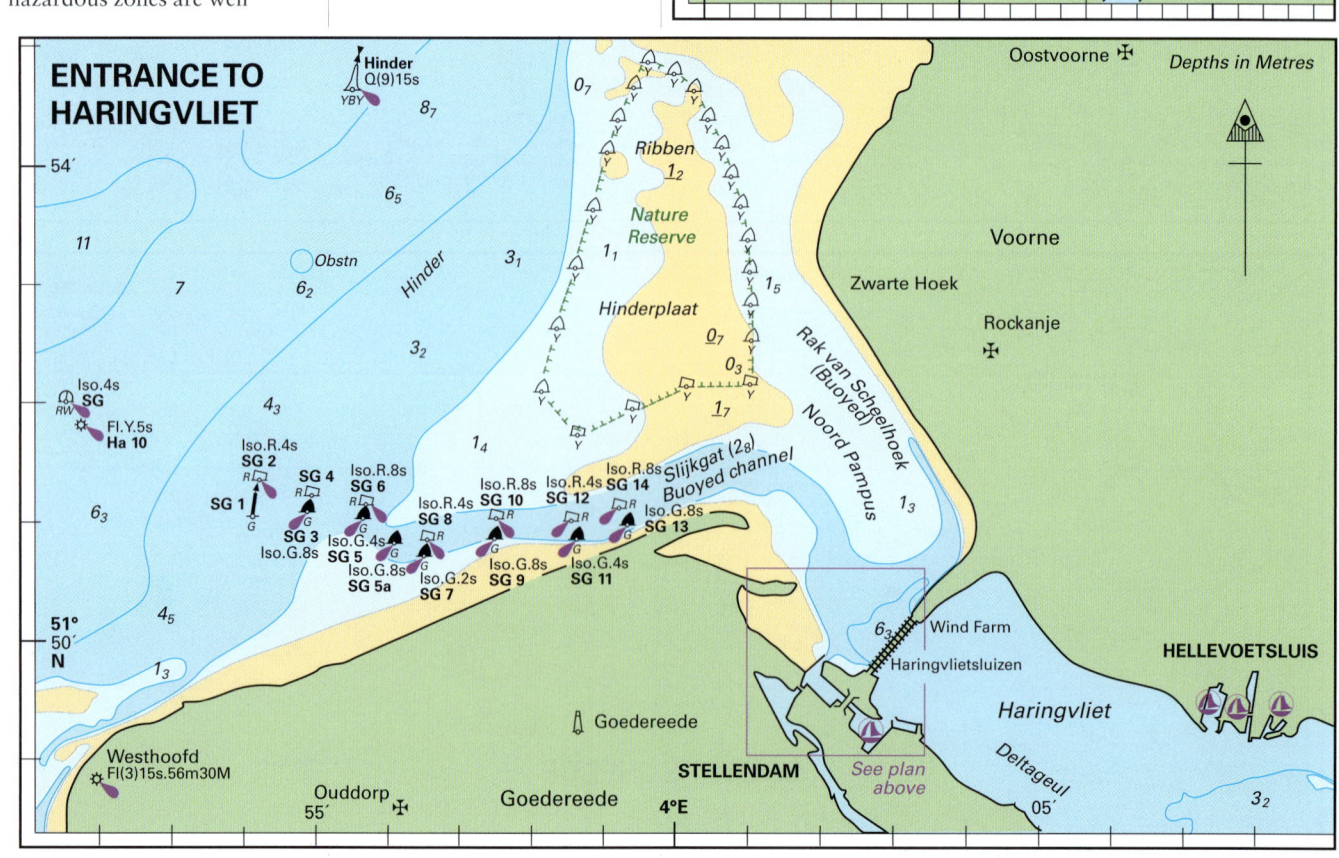

overnight and supplies) en route to Dordrecht. Pleasant country vista but caution required – heavy river traffic.

Note: E-going tide in Spui starts Hoek v Holland HW+0500, but E-going tide in Oude Maas begins HW Hoek v Holland.

Hollandsch Diep to Amsterdam

Leaving the Volkeraksluis, the cruiser has two routes to Amsterdam, to port through the Haringvliet out to sea to IJmuiden and along the N Sea Canal (2–3 days) or straight ahead through the canals via Dordrecht, Gouda, Haarlem / Aalsmeer to the N Sea Canal (4–5 days) The sea route entails two locks and one bridge, the inland route is slower because of the numerous bridges and locks, but has otherwise much of the essence of Holland to offer.

HOLLANDSCH DIEP AND DORDTSE KILL

Hollandsch Diep is tidal and carries heavy traffic from the interior; passable in its entire length only to yachts with up to 9m air draft, it opens up areas of special interest – the Biesbosch, leading to the R Maas, Venlo, Maastrict, and the canals of Belgium and France.

The Staande Maastroute going N takes in the first section of **Hollandsch Diep**, bearing N into the **Dordtse Kil**, where N flowing tides begin Hoek v Holland HW+0600.

WILLEMSTAD

To stb on entering Hollandsch Diep, a very attractive, formerly fortified, town with most facilities including diesel. HM in glasshouse to port on entering, allocates berths either alongside in town harbour ahead or in marina to port.

Also, 400m W of narrow harbour entrance, another marina.

NEUMANSDORP

Small village opposite Willemstad with two marinas; quiet with shops and cafés. An alternative to Willemstad at height of the season. Bus service to Rotterdam and Dordrecht.

DORDRECHT

A major centre of commerce with a long history, standing at the confluence of three waterways, the old town is a delight of warehouses, shops and restaurants. Approached from the S via the impressive twin lifting road and rail bridges which operate to a fixed schedule, 0616 and every two hours from 0916, more often weekends and holidays (VHF 79). Waiting pontoon 800m S to stb in side water.

Several marinas in Dordrecht. One popular choice, the **Kon. Dordrechtsche R & Z.V**, lies 600m N of bridges on stb side, narrow entrance next to fire tug leads under lifting Engelenburgerbrug (summon via button on woodwork next bridge) into reception area, where HM allocates pontoon berths. All facilities. Chandlery on nearby quayside. Diesel from bunker boats on riverfront.

Moving N, take the Noord channel under the lifting **Alblasserdam bridge** (opens 08, 28, 48 minutes in each hour between 0700–1900) Small marina just beyond br to stb for o/night and provisions.

Heavy traffic in **Noord**; bear to port into **Nieuwe Maas** for 3M then take sharp turn to stb into **Hollandsche Ijssel**. Massive **Algera Flood barrier** passable for low air draft boats, otherwise wait on pontoon for bridge opening to port side (VHF 22).

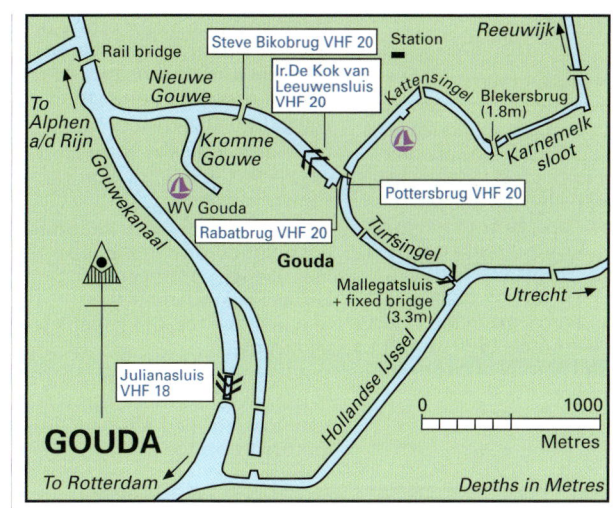

Beyond the barrier, river runs through industrial hinterland of Rotterdam to **Julianasluis** 1M before Gouda. Operates daylight hours on demand.

GOUDA

1M after the lock, one of the difficult railway bridges, only opening briefly 0559, 1012, 1312, 1612, 2112. Waiting pontoon. For entry to outer Gouda moorings turn stb immediately before bridge into Nieuwe Gouwe through lock and opening bridges: opening daylight hours on demand. Few facilities.

Alternate YC marina found in Kromme Gouwe, a small cut to stb 300m before town lock, past industrial site. Alongside and box moorings: HM lives in facilities block close to entry. Short walk to town and historic sights, shops and restaurants.

Continuing N, a further five bridges open on demand, arriving in Alphen A/D Rijn. Passing the town bridges leads to the main junction heading either W along the Oude Rijn to Leiden or, N via Woubrugge and Brassemermeer (moorings, and marinas) to Oude Wetering. Here a T junction leads W to Kaag and the route to Haarlem, or N via the Westeinder Plas for the direct route (overnight passage only) to Amsterdam.

LEIDEN

The city, famous for historic buildings, and university life is accessible on foot from outer moorings. Can be approached via the Kager Plassen lake to the north or, the Oude Rijn from the SE. All bridges operate throughout the day, although some are closed in the rush hour. From the Oude Rijn continue on under two bridges for central moorings offering facilities. Or turn N on the Zijl for a comfortable marina to the N of the city at YC Zijlzicht.

Lakes and waterways N of Leiden, the Kager Plassen, mostly passable with care, are home to much sailing activity in green surroundings.

Heading onwards to Haarlem plan carefully to pass the Sassenheim rly and road bridges which present another pinch point, heavily congested at peak times. Opening briefly at 0558, 0628, 0658, 1228, 1258, 1328, 1828, 1858, 1928 weekdays, and fewer services at weekends April–November only. Good marina to port just before right turn to bridges. All facilities.

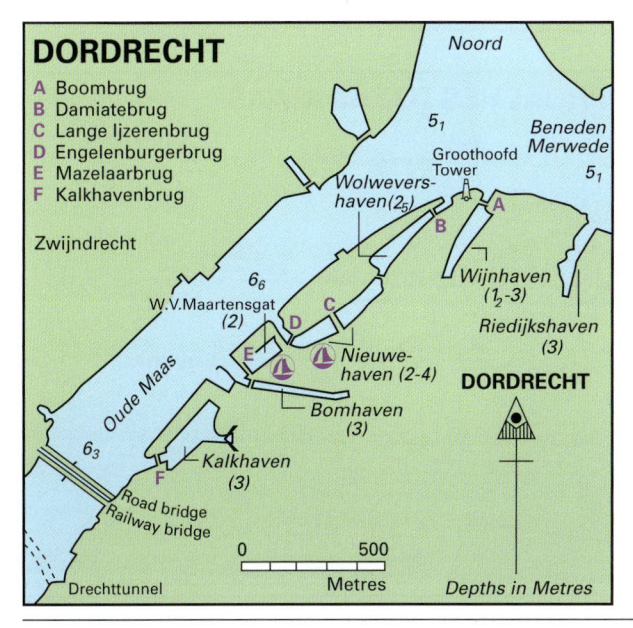

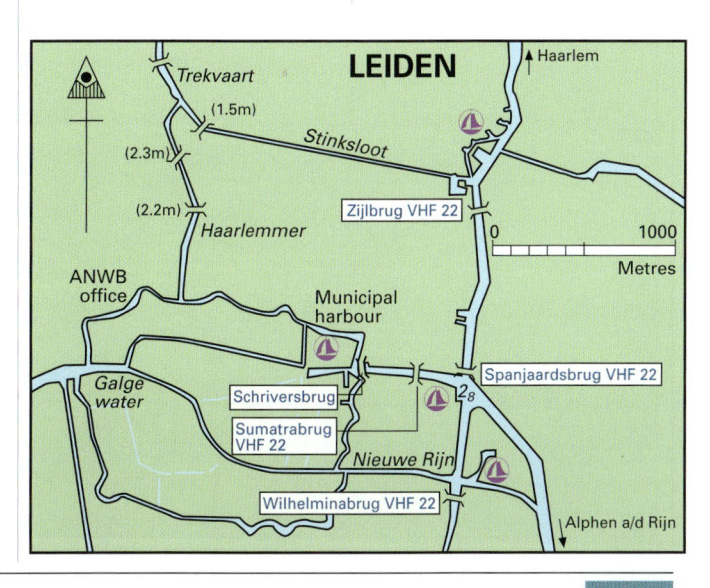

HAARLEM

The Spaarne through Haarlem turns N just E of the Cruquiusbrug and an interesting visit can be made to this steam pump museum. There are nine bridges through Haarlem which are worked by one or more mobile br operators in a convoy system. A transit toll is collected at an office port side N of the rail br. First convoy departs 0900 and on demand thereafter. No service 1600–1800 in rush hour. Rail br in N of city opens reluctantly.

Haarlem city, a major centre of culture, restaurants and cafés: excellent atmosphere and famous cathedral dominating scene from all parts.

Moorings alongside through city; power and limited toilet / shower facilities.

As canal widens, some mooring possibilities to be found, also at Haarlemsche YC to port, before Spaarndam lock (daylight service, toll payable) all facilities.

1M beyond lock, another barrier to the cruiser – the remote controlled A9 motorway bridge which operates only between 0500–0600, 1200–1300, 1930–2030; air daft 6·9m closed. Limited waiting pontoon facilities.

Marina, WV Wymond, to port. Good facilities. Popular place to o/night before Amsterdam.

One lesser road bridge (Zijkanaal C), opening on demand (0500–2300) gives entry to the impressive N Sea Canal.

BRAASSEMERMEER TO AMSTERDAM

The route travels anti-clockwise on the Ringvaart van de Haarlemmermeerpolder across the Westeinderplassen to the Nieuwe Meer S of Amsterdam. Brs on this section operate throughout the day except the final br at Schiphol which opens early morning, lunchtime and evening. The harbours on the Nieuwe Meer are within a short bus ride of the city and make a convenient alternative for those intending to return S, avoiding the difficult route through 14 opening bridges, two of which are rly bridges which open only between 0100 and 0430.

Vessels over 5m air draught take this route in convoy during the night. It is an interesting experience, but keep a watch for plastic debris on the water to avoid propeller problems. Vessels travelling N towards Amsterdam must gather at the Nieuwemeersluis at 2300. If you are travelling S from Amsterdam, go into the SE corner of the Oude Houthaven where there is a pontoon, pay dues at the br office and pass into the Westerkanaal to await the opening of the rly br. The Authorities prefer yachts to enter the Westerkanaal not later than approx 2200 so that they can determine the size of the convoy and make arrangements for all the bridges to be opened by the mobile team of br keepers. Contact the Nieuwemeersluis or Westerkeersluis on VHF 22 for instructions. Vessels must keep pace with the convoy but, after crossing the Nieuwe Meer at dawn and passing under the Schiphol motorway br at its early morning opening, you could anchor in the Westeinder plassen to recover.

Craft with less than 9m air-draught may use the Amsterdam-Rijn canal as an alternative route. Entrance is through a buoyed channel opening to the S from the IJ just W of the Oranjesluizen.

HOEK VAN HOLLAND & NIEUWE WATERWEG

Standard Port Hoek van Holland

Heavy traffic in the Maas has lead to increased restrictions and prohibitions for small craft both in the approaches and the waterway itself. The Nieuwe Waterweg is relatively narrow and carries very large vessels – their wash can combine with swells and strong tides to make passage here dangerous for small craft. Europoort is prohibited to small vessels and shelter, eg. in the Berghaven is very restricted.

Small vessels passing along the coast must clear the Maas TSS at best speed, and keep to the designated track W of MV and MVC cardinals. Clearance is required from Maas control on VHF 03 before proceeding. At night or in bad visibility crossing the Maas can be extremely hazardous owing to the speed and frequency of heavy traffic.

Inland connections The Nieuwe Waterweg, which becomes the Nieuwe Maas east of Vlaardingen, serves the harbours of Maassluis, Vlaardingen, Schiedam and Rotterdam. Vessels entering the Nieuwe Waterweg are required to maintain a listening watch on VHF 65 from km1030. Heading E, the following VHF

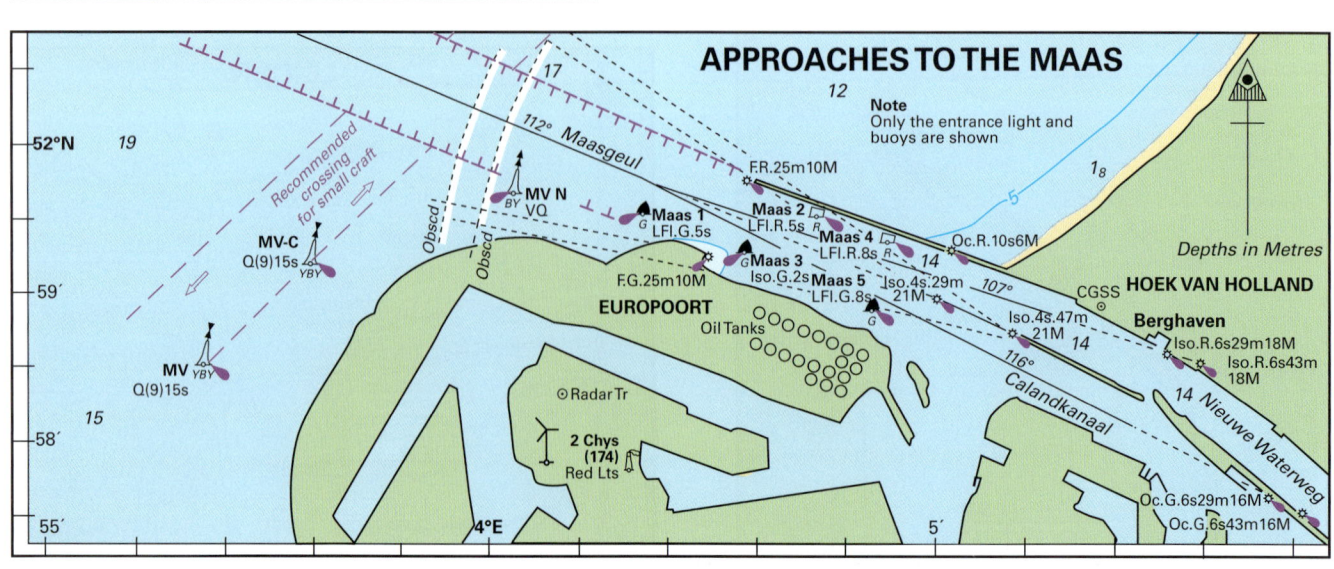

channels must be monitored between the relevant km posts:
1028 and 1017 – VHF 80
1017 and 1011 – VHF 61
1011 and 1007 – VHF 63
1007 and 1003 – VHF 60
1003 and 993 – VHF 81

MAASSLUIS
Entrance on N bank just E of km post 1019. Enter Binnenhaven from Buitenhaven through a road br and rly br. Water and fuel are available. HM ☎ 0105 93 19 82.

VLAARDINGEN
Entrance on N bank just after km post 1011 – E of Delta Hotel. Buitenhaven is uncomfortable; continue through Keersluis, railway br and Prinses Julianabrug to Oude Haven. HM ☎ 0620 83 35 46.

SCHIEDAM
Entrance to Spuihaven at km post 1007 on N bank. Yacht Haven of WV Nieuwe Waterweg and Jachtclub Schiedam. Toilets and showers. Launderette at 750m. Close to shops, restaurants, rly station. 10 minutes by taxi to airport. HM ☎ 0104 26 39 05.

ROTTERDAM
Two bridges cross the Nieuwe Maas at Rotterdam, the Erasmus lifting br (air draught 12·5m when closed) which opens on the hour at 1000, 1100, 1400 and 1500 (VHF 20), and the fixed Nieuwe Willemsbrug which restricts headroom to 10·5m at HW. Moorings downstream of Erasmus br on the N bank at the Veerhaven HM ☎ 010 436 5446 or upstream at City Marina in Binnenhaven via lifting br which opens on request (VHF 20). All facilities. HM ☎ 010 485 40 96.

SCHEVENINGEN
Standard Port Vlissengen
HW +0102   LW +0232
MHWS MHWN MLWN MLWS
−2·7m −2·3m −0·7m −0·2m
DS Dover −0500SW +0100NE

A busy fishing port. There is no access to the inland waterways but it is a lively seaside resort and convenient for visiting Den Hague. Customs post. The outer harbour entrance faces NW, is uncomfortable in strong N to E winds and dangerous in NW winds of Force 6 or more when swell can run in through the entrance. Tidal streams, especially the N-going stream near the time of HW, run strongly across the entrance.

Approach Scheveningen LtHo Fl(2)10s48m29M lies ½M E of the entrance. The area between the N hbr wall and the pier shallows sharply so be sure to round the safe water buoy (Iso.4s2M) 2M NW of the hbr and then follow a course of 156° on Ldg Lts (Iso.4s) into the outer harbour.

Entrance Call *Scheveningen port* on VHF 21 to ensure clear passage. On entering the Voorhaven, Basin No.1 to NE is mostly for commercial vessels. Proceed hard stb through narrow cut to No.2 basin: marina HM and facilities to stb – visitors mainly alongside. Basin to NE available for mooring in busy periods.

Restaurants and all facilities close to hand. Fine beach, entertainment and shops a few minutes' walk N of marina. Supermarket and chandlery on E side of No.2 Basin where tram service runs direct to Den Hague with major rail connections, including Schiphol airport.

☎ HM 0703 52 00 17.

North Sea Canal
A major waterway, 15m deep and 15M long from massive locks at **IJmuiden** to Amsterdam, with huge quays and alongside ship repair services en route. Major cargo and cruise shipping frequently seen. Several ferry services cross the canal, and high speed hydrofoils operate along its length. Sailing permitted but commercial shipping has priority.

IJMUIDEN
Standard Port Vlissengen
HW +0142   LW +0315
MHWS MHWN MLWN MLWS
−2·8m −2·4m −0·7m −0·3m
DS Dover −0400S +0200N, max 2kn

Useful entry port for Amsterdam along the Noordzee Kanaal, and then through to the Markermeer and IJsselmeer.

VTS Monitor VHF 61 from 5M off.

Approach There are steel works N of the town and the coloured smoke often provides the first positive identification by day. Keep a good look-out for fishing vessels entering and leaving. Vessels fitted with VHF should report to IJmuiden Traffic Control (VHF 61) on approach when 5M from the hbr. The S arm of the hbr extends 1M offshore. Strong tidal streams run across the entrance.

Entrance From the IJmuiden IJM racon buoy Morse(A)8s a course of 100·5° on the Ldg Lts for 5M leads through the outermost pierheads and the Buitenhaven towards the Zuider Buitenkanaal. IJmuiden Port Control should be contacted on VHF 61 when approaching from seaward. The approach and outer harbour and even the Buitenhaven can be rough in onshore winds. The Customs office ☎ 020 25 81 36 14 is situated on the ground floor of a grey tr block between the Zuider Buiten Kanaal and the Visserhaven, W of the Kleine Sluis (☎ 0255 52 33 09). Take care before leaving that conditions are suitable outside.

Berthing The Seaport Marina IJmuiden is on the seaward side of the locks and has a capacity of 600 boats. Entrance is from the S side of the Buitenhaven between IJM3 (Iso.G.4s) and IJM5 R/G buoys and then along a buoyed channel, to the marina entrance which is marked by F.R and F.G lights. VHF 74.

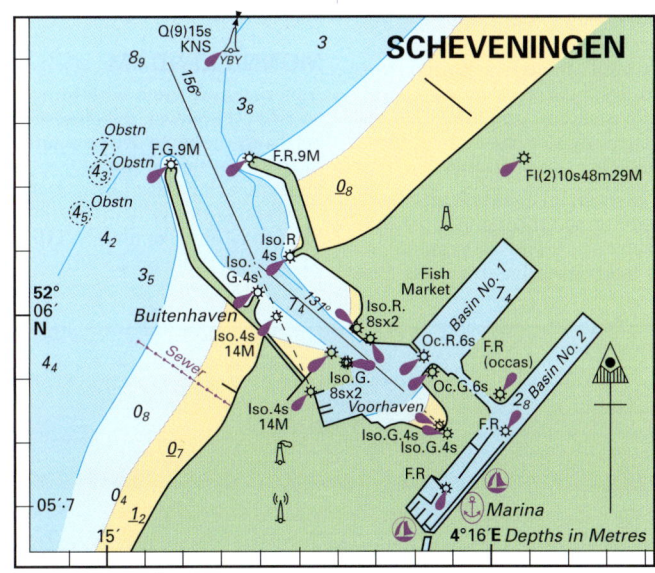

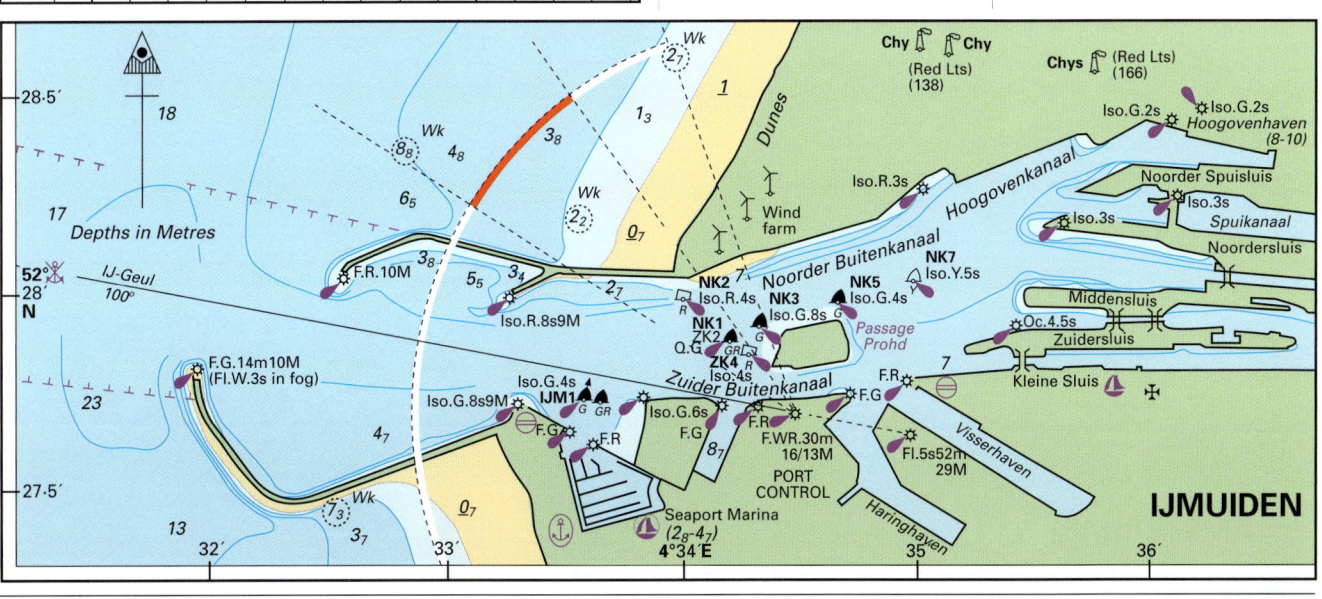

HM ☎ 0255 56 03 00. Diesel and petrol available.

Marina has restaurants and chandlery / services and good beach, but is 1M from IJmuiden town and few shops. Berthing charges above average. Bus connection to Schiphol via Haarlem.

North Sea Canal From sea, enter by sports lock (Kleine Sluis) to S side (24/7). Vessels monitor VHF 22 in the locks and VHF 03 to 10km inland, then VHF 04 to Amsterdam.

After locks, limited waiting alongside on quay to stb.

5M from IJmuiden, **Zijkanaal C** enters from S and route to Haarlem. Buitenrust road br opens on demand (0500–2300) giving access to marina, **WV Wymond**, to stb. Good facilities. Popular place to overnight before Amsterdam / N Sea voyage.

Further 10M to Amsterdam, passing major docks and port installations / traffic.

Hout harbour on S side close to town is gathering point for daily (not Sunday) night convoy S through Amsterdam canals and lifting bridges heading S via Gouda.

AMSTERDAM

This principal city of The Netherlands is a natural mecca for all visitors to Holland. Among many other attractions the Maritime Museum, the Rijksmuseum, the Vincent van Gogh Museum, the Rembrandthuis and Anne Frank House are worth a visit. The Noordzee Kanaal continues through the city as the R Het IJ.

Locks on N bank lead to **Noord-Hollands Kanaal** which runs to den Helder through historic landscapes and Alkmaar. An alternative connection to this canal for mast-up vessels starts at Km18, the Zijkanaal G routing through Zaandam, and connecting at the Alkmaarder Meer.

Approaching Amsterdam the long low rounded roof of the central railway station comes into view. Amsterdam has 3 marinas, all on N bank, connected to the station quay by free ferry:

New Amsterdam Marina located opposite Hout Haven, the newest and largest facility with over 300 berths and some local services.

Sixhaven, opposite the station behind a green screen and wave barrier, a popular site but very crowded in season – be prepared to raft. Occasionally closed from noon at busy times.

Supermarket five minutes right out of gates. For Amsterdam town and onward transport, walk left, over N Holland canal lock gates and take (free) ferry to Centraal Station – excellent point for train service to Schiphol airport (20 minutes) and pedestrian access to downtown Amsterdam.

Aeolus marina, 300m beyond Sixhaven, is alternative overnight alongside and pontoon berthing, good facilities, but small. Supermarket outside gates.

E of Amsterdam the waterway splits, bearing stb to the RijnKanaal, or straight ahead to the **Markermeer** via the **Oranjesluis** (VHF 18). For the lock, hold to port and enter 'sport' waiting area for the N lock. Beware: commercial traffic has priority. Often a busy lock, be prepared.

Beyond lock wait for road bridge (Schellingwouderbrug VHF 18) opening on demand, and stay in dredged channel.

The small hbr of Durgerdam is reached through a narrow buoyed channel to the N. HM ☎ 020 4904 717. It is only a short bus ride from the city centre. Anchoring is possible in the bay if the hbr is full.

Markermeer and IJsselmeer

Originally open to the sea, until the outer Afsluitdijk was built in 1932 forming an inland sea: 1975 this was cut in two by the Houtribdijk, linking Enkhuisen in the W with Lelystadt in the E. The inner Markermeer is semi-fresh, and the outer Ijsselmeer is partly open to the sea through small sluices. Previous sea-going ports all around are now protected from surges but keep their locks and infrastructure, offering charming settings and excellent mooring opportunities.

Commercial channels are maintained throughout the two waterways, and the remainder is freely passable to vessels drawing no more than 2·0m, and 2·5m with careful navigation. In winds over Force 5 the shallow conditions throw up a short sea that makes progress wet and slow, but a port is always near to hand. Polderisation, or land recovery, ceased some years ago, but straight sea walls indicate where land was recovered, especially (as in Flevoland) where it lies some metres below the level of the lake.

A circuit of the waterways has much to offer, but taking the quiet and peaceful route round Flevoland has limitations – the 12·7m max clearance under the fixed Hollandse Brug near Naarden, prevents a full circuit of the polder to larger vessels.

MARKEN

Between 1164 and 1957 Marken was an Is but is now joined to the mainland by a causeway. From the N end of the Is there is a wall stretching 1M NNW to the 2m contour, and on the E tip there is a prominent white LtHo. Enter the Gouwzee from N of Marken and follow the buoyed channel (2·2m) into any of the three hbrs, avoiding the busy ferry quay.

HM ☎ 0299 60 13 82.

MONNICKENDAM

A picturesque town with four marinas. However, the closest berths to the town are beyond the marinas in the Town Harbour which has toilets and showers. Diesel is available in Marina Monnickendam. VHF 31. HM ☎ 0299 65 25 95.

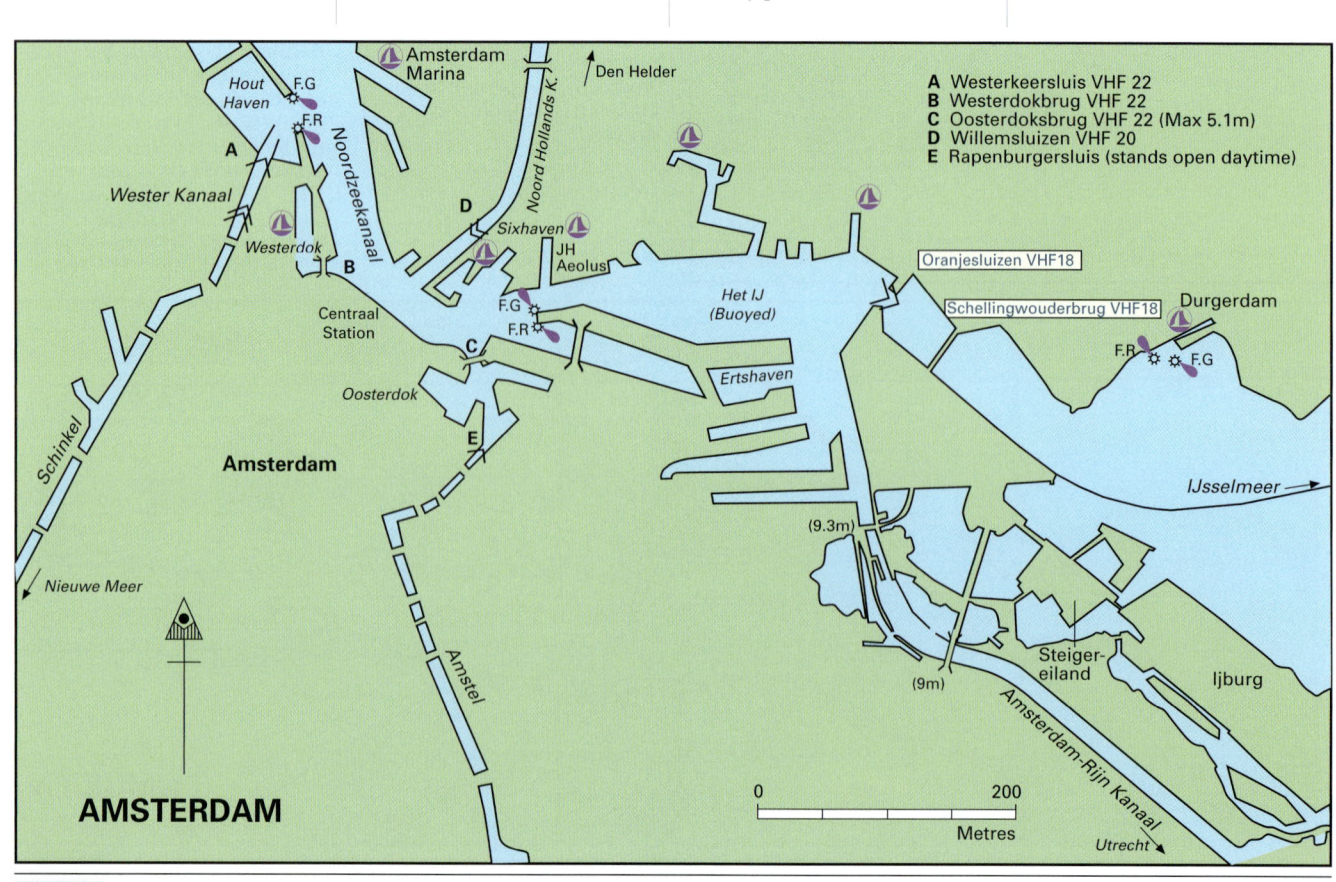

A Westerkeersluis VHF 22
B Westerdokbrug VHF 22
C Oosterdoksbrug VHF 22 (Max 5.1m)
D Willemsluizen VHF 20
E Rapenburgersluis (stands open daytime)

AMSTERDAM

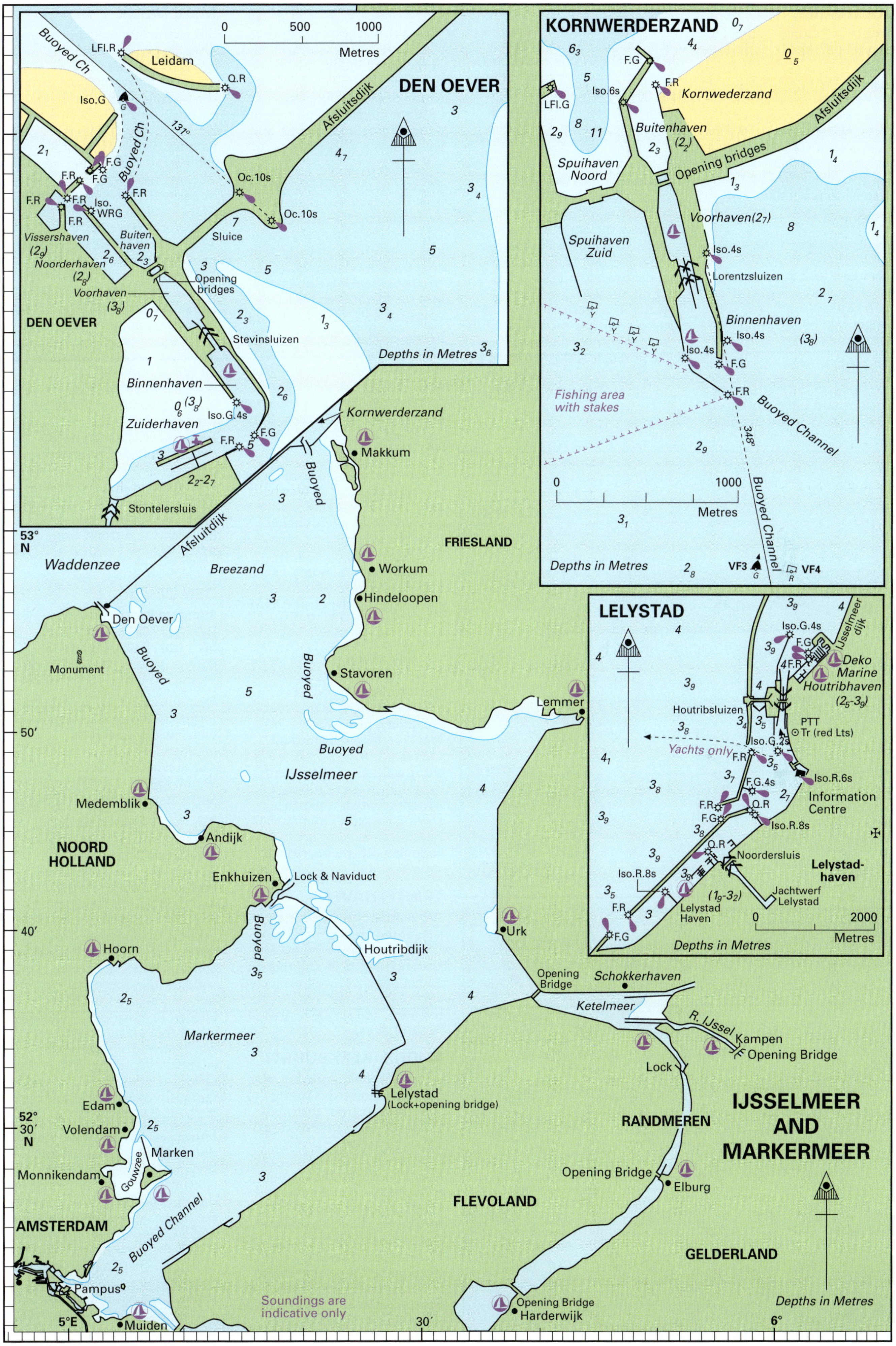

NETHERLANDS

VOLENDAM

Visitors' moorings on the quayside in the NE half of the hbr. HM ☎ 0299 36 96 20. A new marina to SW of the town has excellent facilities for visitors, or as a longer term berth. Harbourmaster ☎ 06 1276 2921, VHF 31. Town and eel market worth a visit and can also be reached by bike from Monnickendam.

EDAM

Small, quiet town. Narrow entrance, max depth 2m, through a lock and br to a canal with mooring space on both banks; Jachthaven Galgenveld on the port side before the lock.

HOORN

The home of the first European to sail round Cape Horn has many signs of its former glory as a Hanseatic town. The streets are brimming with history and the Westfries Museum is worth a visit. The former warehouses now serve as private dwellings or restaurants, and the bronze statues of the 'Boys from the Bontekoe' still look out for a suitable ship on which to stow away.

Entrance From the S on 352° from a R can buoy 1ca to the S of the rough stone walls forming the outer harbour walls. You may anchor in the outer harbour (2m) or raft out in the town hbr. HM ☎ 0229 21 40 12. VHF 74. Diesel available. Alternatively, there are quieter box moorings available in the Grashaven on the port side (HM ☎ 0229 21 52 08) or to stb in the Hoorn YC (HM ☎ 0229 21 35 40).

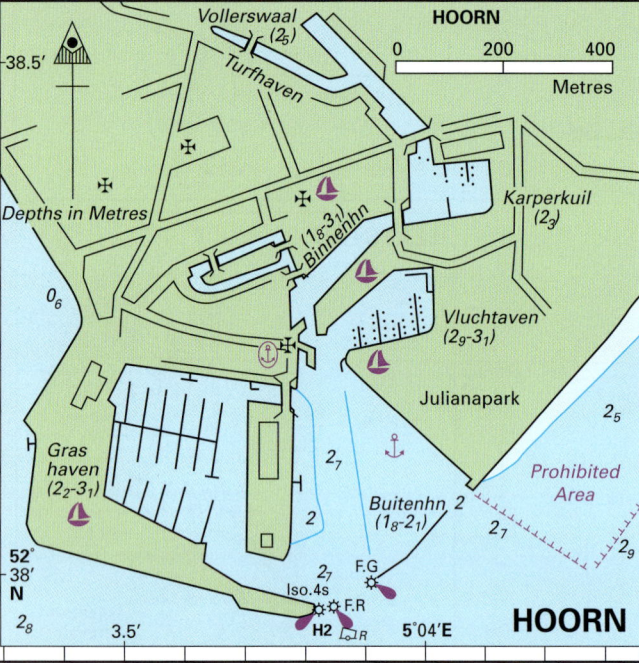

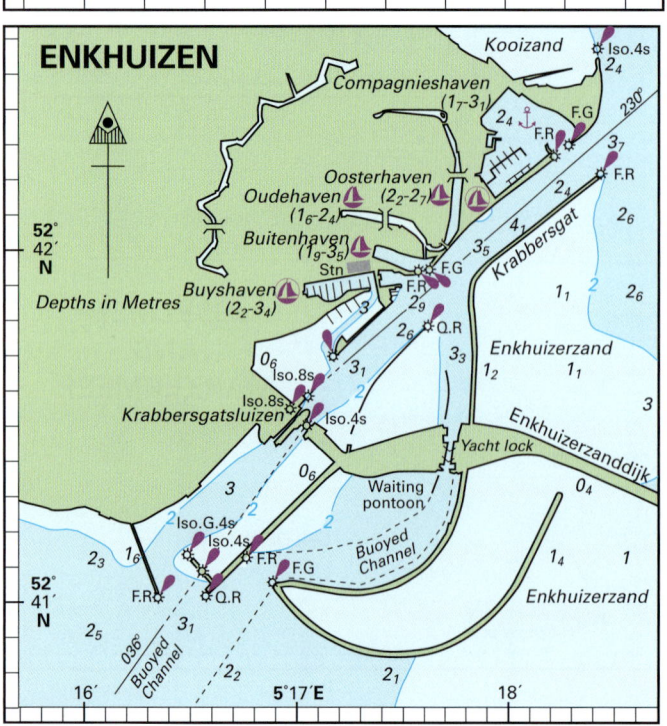

ENKHUIZEN

This is the largest port of the Zuiderzee and lies at the N end of the Houtribdijk. It is also a busy ferry port. The Zuiderzee Museum consisting of an outdoor village and an indoor marine museum is superb and well worth a whole day's visit.

Approach from the S, the channel to the Krabbersgatsluis is well buoyed and the course to the entrance is marked by Ldg Lts. The two new yacht locks operate on VHF 22. The N approach is from the EZ1/KG2 (Iso.RGR.2s) buoy into the Krabbersgat on a course of 230° (Ldg Lts Iso.8s).

Entrance There are three yacht hbrs. The first to port is the Buyshaven which has a marina at the S side. There is a good toilet/shower block but the box moorings are the furthest from the town. HM ☎ 0228 31 56 60. VHF 31.

The second is the Buitenhaven which is adjacent to the rly station and is therefore convenient for crew changes. This hbr is often very crowded and you may have to raft alongside several boats. Toilets and showers are next to the HM office on the N side. HM ☎ 0228 31 24 44. VHF 12.

The third hbr, the Compagnieshaven, houses the largest marina. It is beyond the town to the NE and has showers, toilets, water, fuel, chandlery, provisions, launderette and restaurant. HM ☎ 0228 31 33 53. It is a short walk to the town and next door to the Zuiderzee Museum which is worth staying an extra day for. Enkhuizen has a good shopping centre, boatyards, sailmaker and engine repairs.

TRINTELHAVEN

A free 'hbr of refuge' on the N side of the Houtribdyk between Enkhuizen and Lelystad. The entrance is well lit and there is a long quay and well-protected anchorage within, but no other facilities, and stay is restricted to three days.

ANDIJK (KERKBUURT)

A large, well equipped marina but fairly isolated (visiting shop). Apart from the small village of Andijk there are no other attractions nearby. Entrance is obtained by following the sea wall round from the N tip at Andijk and continuing along the W of the breakwater before turning its S end and heading N through the hbr entrance between breakwaters. A sharp turn to stb brings one to the end of the first pontoon where a reporting telephone is provided. Chandlery and restaurant. HM ☎ 0228 59 30 75. VHF 31. Diesel available.

MEDEMBLIK

3M to the NW is identified at a distance by its collection of spires and the large white pumping house building just to the N. Approach the narrow entrance on 232° (Oc.5s Lt between F.R and F.G on wooden piers). There are submerged rocks either side. The first turning to port, almost opposite the ferry berth, leads to the modern marina in the Pekelharinghaven HM ☎ 0227 54 21 75; VHF 31. Diesel and petrol available. The Middenhaven has no facilities but yachts can lie alongside on either side of the hbr. Access to the marina in the Westerhaven is through an opening road br. The HM office and facilities are all in one building. HM ☎ 0227 54 18 61. VHF 09. The Noordhollands canal can be entered here via the Westerhavensluis at the SW of the hbr, but there are fixed bridges.

A large yacht hbr, the Regatta Centre Medemblik, is 2ca S of the main hbr entrance. It is, however the furthest from the town. VHF 31. HM ☎ 0227 54 77 81.

DEN OEVER

Standard Port Helgoland
HW (sp) –0245 (np) –0410
LW (sp) –0305 (np) –0400

MHWS	MHWN	MLWN	MLWS
–1·2m	–1·0m	–0·5m	–0·2m

One of four old villages on the former island of Wieringen which was joined to the mainland by a dyke in 1924. The Stevinsluis links the Waddenzee and the IJsselmeer at the W end of the Afsluitdijk.

Approach There is no deep water approach from the E on the seaward side of the Afsluitdijk. This area is well-buoyed but the streams run fast and the edges of the channels dry out. The mean spring rates off Den Helder reach 3½kn. Strong winds create difficult and sometimes dangerous conditions in these shallow waters. Passage from Den Helder/Texelstroom to Den Oever locks is by buoyed Malzwin and Visjagergatje channels, departing HW Helder –0400. Visibility here is famously variable and staying in channel is essential.

Entrance Turn to stb just before the O12 buoy (Iso.R.4s) and keep in the W sector of the Iso.GWR.2s Lt on the end of the inner harbour wall, entering the outer harbour between F.R and F.G Lts. The outer harbour is well sheltered by moles on each side. Turn to port, keeping between the port and stb buoys, towards the Afsluitdijk where it may be necessary to tie up to the piles while waiting for the two bridges to open. Enter the Voorhaven and the lock (VHF

20). The channels are lit, but a first-time passage at night is inadvisable. The fishing hbr N of the locks has limited facilities for yachts. After passing through the locks a temporary berth may be found on the W side of Binnenhaven. For overnight stays the Jachthaven Den Oever, with all facilities, is at the S end of the Zuiderhaven. HM ☏ 0227 51 17 89. Diesel available.

KORNWERDERZAND

Standard Port Helgoland
HW (sp) –0210 (np) –0315
LW (sp) –0215 (np) –0300
MHWS MHWN MLWN MLWS
–1·0m –0·8m –0·4m –0·2m

The NE entry point for the IJsselmeer.

Approach From the E by the Boontjes channel from Harlingen with a minimum depth of 1·8m at LW. The channel is well marked at regular intervals, but very narrow. From the N by the Inschot and Zuidoostrak with a turn to the E at the KWZ W card buoy, 12ca W of the entrance. The sea-dyke is featureless with the occasional ch spire showing above.
Entrance There are two apparent entrances but only the smaller one to the E leads to the locks. The W or Spuihaven is not used for navigation. The Buitenhaven piers have F.R and F.G Lts. Enter on a course of 225° taking care to avoid the shoal to port. Before the swing bridges there are waiting pontoons to stb if it is necessary to wait for a lock opening. The Lorentzsluizen operate 24hrs VHF 18. On the S side are mooring posts with good shelter which may be used for a few hours or overnight. No facilities. HM ☏ 0517 57 81 70. Customs ☏ 0582 94 94 44.

MAKKUM

Only 2M SE from Kornwerderzand locks.

Entrance From the Kornwerderzand lock there is a buoyed channel leading between shoals to the start of the entrance channel proper which has Ldg Lts on 090·5°. Several marinas to stb, first YC Makkum, HM ☏ 0515 23 14 08. Small marina, but supermarket, chandler, sailmaker and beach nearby. Then marina Makkum, ½M along the entrance channel to stb, has 500 residents berths plus 100 for visitors. HM ☏ 0515 23 23 55. There are also marina berths at the Prins YC HM ☏ 0515 23 29 30. Vessels may continue to the end of the entrance canal where there are box moorings in the town hbr (closest to town). For craft drawing less than 1·5m it is possible to enter the Friesland canal system here and join the fixed mast route to Leeuwarden and beyond. There is a chandler, a supermarket and fried fish take-away in the town. Diesel available from several outlets.

WORKUM

5M further S is entered from the Workum-Hindeloopen middle-ground buoy H2/W1 Iso.RGR.2s through a narrow buoyed channel and 1M long entrance canal with Ldg Lts on 081·5° Oc.6s. The steam rising from the tall chimney of a crop-drying plant often makes a good landmark. This is another entrance to the Frisian canals and lakes. A large marina on the N bank (It Soal) has all facilities. HM ☏ 0515 54 29 37. Between It Soal and the lock are a number of additional moorings. The entrance canal, Het Zool, has a min depth of 1·7m and ends in a quaint circular basin before the lock where it is possible to moor overnight. The basin has a toilet block and it is just a short walk into the town. It is hardly worth entering the lock unless proceeding to the lakes.

HINDELOOPEN

This beautiful town is famous for its enamelled woodware. No access to the inland waterways, but the small canals and tiny bridges are very attractive.

Entrance Enter from the H2/W1 buoy (Iso.RGR.2s) on a general SE course, keeping to the buoyed but unlit channel. Enter between high wooden piers and turn to port immediately for the large Jachthaven Hindeloopen, which has all facilities including fuel, launderette, 20-tonne travel-lift, swimming pool and engineers. HM ☏ 0514 52 45 54. Moorings can also be found in the old hbr to the S of the entrance. VHF 10. HM ☏ 0514 52 20 09. Stores from the town close by. The Church with its leaning tr and graves of servicemen from both sides from the 1939–45 war should not be missed. Although there is full shelter from the seas in the marina, strong winds from the N blow right across.

STAVOREN

4M S of Hindeloopen offers access to the Friesland canals for craft not over 2m draught. There are several harbours, two of which do not involve passing through the locks into the canal system. The one to the N is the Oude haven where a small ferry to Enkhuizen operates every two hours. The S side of the Oude haven is suitable for yachts; it is close to town and the rly station but can be very crowded. HM ☏ 0514 68 12 16 VHF 74. The S hbr is the 500-berth Marina Stavoren Buitenhaven which has its entrance just S of the E end of the entrance to the Nieuwe Voorhaven. HM ☏ 0514 68 46 74. VHF 74. Diesel available. Access to the canal system is via the Johan Frisosluis at the NE end of the Nieuwe Voorhaven. From off-shore, the distinctive concave roof of the pumping station provides a useful steering mark. Inside the lock, a turning almost immediately to port leads to the Jachthaven Stavoren, while the entrance to the 425-berth Marina Stavoren is on the stb side of the canal (HM ☏ 0514 68 46 86) and the 170-berth Jachthaven de Roggebroek about 150m further up on the port side. HM ☏ 0514 68 14 69. Stores from shops in the town. Fuel alongside.

LEMMER

The Prinses Margriet canal, 1M W of the town harbours, provides access to the Friesland canals for craft not exceeding 3m draught via the Prinses Margrietsluis (VHF 20 no fee, open all days). However, there is also a route via the town which is well worth visiting.

Approach is E between Friesland and the Nordoost Polder with a buoyed channel close to the S shore. The small Friese Hoek LtHo on the NW corner of the Noordoost polder provides a steering mark until the channel buoys, less than 2ca from the steep-to shore, can be identified. Lemmer is a large yachting centre and there are ten yacht harbours, plus mooring places both outside and inside the locks through the town. Full facilities. Fuel is available at the Marine Center in the Industrie haven on the N shore outside the locks and at the marinas on either side of the canal after the Zijlroedebrug. Opening times for the locks are: Monday–Friday 0700–2100, Saturday 0700–2000, Sunday, holidays 0830–1200, 1400– 1730, 1800–2000. VHF 11. All the town brs open on approach. A fee for the lock and town bridges is collected by the HM in the lock.

Lemmer leads inland to the many delights of Friesland and Groningen via the canal system. Sneek, Leeuwarden, Dokkum and Lauwersoog, Groningen are rewarding destinations; bridges opening along the way (small bridge tolls in Leeuwarden and Dokkum and Burdaard) during daylight hours, often closed for an hour midday and evening rush hour – so timing is important, especially in busy Leeuwarden with its railway bridge on the S approach.

URK

A former island, now linked by dykes to the polders, Urk retains its individuality – which includes steep streets! A large fishing fleet operates mainly from coastal ports, but some boats still work from here. The entrance, which is only possible from the S, requires care. There are more mooring places than the single marina symbol on the chart indicates. Visiting yachts can moor on the N, S and W sides of the Nieuwe Haven, all three walls of the Westhaven and the S wall of the Oosthaven. VHF 12. HM ☏ 0527 68 99 70. Fuel is available in the Westhaven. Small shopping centre and an interesting memorial to fishermen lost at sea.

LELYSTAD

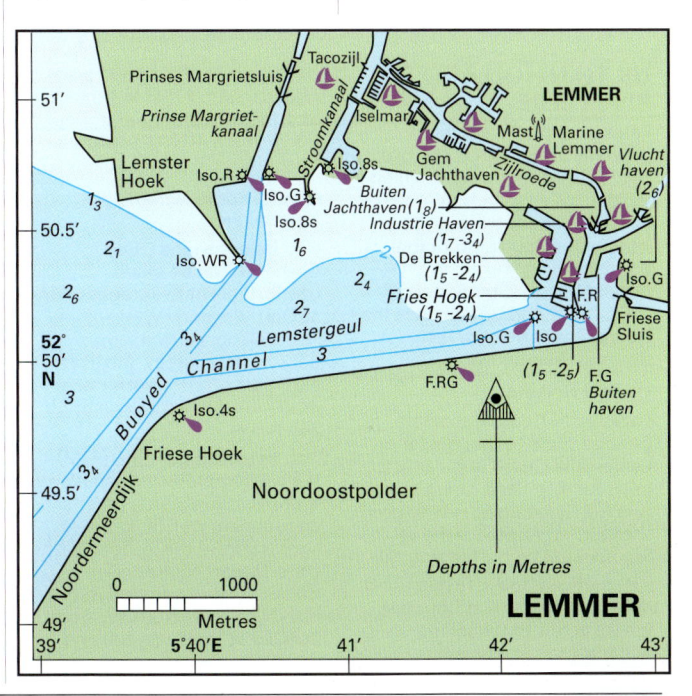

This port has a lock, the Houtribsluis (VHF 20), through the dyke separating the IJsselmeer from the Markermeer. There are large marinas both N and S of the lock. Jachthaven Lelystad HM ℡ 0320 26 03 26, WV Lelystad HM ℡ 0320 26 01 98. VHF 31. Deko Marine HM ℡ 0320 26 02 48. VHF 31. IJsselmeer museum close by.

Approach This is clearly defined by the dyke and the seawall whilst the two very conspic chimneys of the electricity generating station are passed close to port. These chimneys provide an excellent navigating mark for the whole of the S part of the IJsselmeer. The S exit from the locks is between the sea-wall and offshore training dykes. There is a yacht hbr 1½M further S by the Noordersluis.

MUIDEN

At the S end of the IJsselmeer, Muiden is approached from the main shipping channel leading to Amsterdam by leaving the channel at the P8/IJM27 RG buoy, 11ca N of the old fort of Pampus Is. The narrow buoyed channel is then followed on 142° until the Pampus is abeam to stb. A course of 202° for a further 12ca leads to the spar buoys marking the channel into Muiden. The E mole (port hand on entry) is submerged for the first 2ca and considerable caution should be exercised in keeping on 181° in the entrance and close to the W training wall. Even greater care is needed on leaving if other vessels are entering. There are several yacht hbrs including the Royal Netherlands Sailing and Rowing Club. HM ℡ 0294 26 14 50. Fuel available in the hbr. N of the Pampus the buoyed channel leads SW to the Buiten IJ. Through the Muiden lock (small fee payable) a motorway bridge (limited openings) and railway bridge, the Vecht provides a short route to the very pretty town of Weesp. Marina and services.

UK TO N HOLLAND & RIVER ELBE

Passage to the River Elbe, gateway to the Baltic, can take only a few days from E England via the Frisian Islands. A satisfying journey offering a variety of colourful stopping points, and not taxing in reasonable conditions; part of the passage can be taken via the Dutch canal system or less exposed Waddenzee.

UK to N Holland

Lowestoft offers the shortest passage 104M to **Den Helder / Oudeschild** (Texel) popular first ports for N Holland. Using at least two full NE going tides will speed the journey. Approach the lit Schulpengat on the ingoing tide. Alternatively, make first landfall 40M further south at IJmuiden where access to the inland waterways is also possible.

THE RANDMEREN

3M SE from Urk, the Ketelbrug – clearance 12·9m, but with a lifting span – separates the IJsselmeer from the Ketelmeer and Randmeren. VHF 18. The Randmeren is all that is left of the SE part of the Zuiderzee after reclamation of the Noordoost and Flevoland polders. It provides a continuous navigable waterway, with a buoyed channel 3m deep, between the Flevoland polder and the original Zuiderzee coast. However, yachts with more than 12·5m air-draught will not be able to pass under the fixed Hollandse br at Muiderberg and so would have to retrace their track to the Ketelmeer.

KAMPEN

This interesting medieval town, about 6M up the R IJssel from the Ketelmeer, has four yacht marinas and a good shopping centre. The channel has a minimum depth of 3·2m and is well marked. The Eilandbrug, completed in 2003, has a clearance of 15·8m, and an opening span.

ELBURG, HARDERWIJK, SPAKENBURG & HUIZEN

Elburg is a 13th-century town with impressive ramparts and a moat. Moorings alongside the S bank of the canal and in the town hbr. Harderwijk is an old Zuiderzee trading port with several 13th and 14th-century buildings and a choice of three hbrs. Spakenburg has a very picturesque old hbr with many traditional Dutch sailing barges. The townsfolk are noted for their wearing of traditional dress. Huizen has two buoyed entrance channels, the W one leading to three marinas while the E leads through an opening br to the old fishing hbr. The town has suffered considerable development.

Harwich is another good point of departure, 125M to **IJmuiden** and 140M to **Den Helder**. Depart Harwich HW-0100 to optimise tidal lift.

Coastal Route N from Den Helder

Den Helder to the Elbe / Cuxhaven can be made comfortably in five stages calling at Oost Vlieland / West Terschelling, Lauwersoog, Borkum, Norderney, Cuxhaven, each port offering scenic or practical advantages and lit for 24h access.

Den Helder to Borkum, (93M) the westernmost German island, is also feasible direct; the islands en route are well lit, with only light traffic in the inshore traffic zone. Depart NE from Den Helder at Hoek van Holland HW+0055 and return SW from Borkum at Hoek van Holland

Frisian Islands and the Waddenzee

The Waddenzee, an area of sandbanks and shallow channels, is the tidal remnant of the former Zuider Zee. The non-tidal S section became the IJsselmeer with the completion of the Afsluitdijk in 1932. It is an inhospitable expanse of wild seascape and frequently-changing channels which, although buoyed, can be difficult to follow. It requires particularly careful concentration in the reduced visibility to which this area is liable during the summer. For yachts with fixed keels, the only area for reasonable sailing until one has acquired some local knowledge, is the area between Terschelling, Texel (pronounced 'Tessel') and the mainland from Harlingen to Den Helder. From Terschelling or Vlieland the Vliestroom leads S and after 4M divides into the Blauwe Slenk, leading to Harlingen, and the Inschot which leads via the Verversaat to Kornwerderzand and the locks into the IJsselmeer. On the flood tide either route may be taken, but in the reverse direction proceeding N from Kornwerderzand, departure must either be made 1–2 hours before HW, or a diversion taken through the Boontjes close to the dykes to join the channel from Harlingen. This avoids the Zuidoostrak which at one point dries at LW.

It is slow but interesting to pass close inside the Frisian Islands. Every island has a drying height where the HW depth is about 2m at neaps extending for a mile or more and marked by withies. There are buoyed channels into the small drying hbrs and the islands have beautiful sands.

HW-0400. Spring rate up to 1·5kn.

Alternative Sheltered Routes:

Waddenzee route: Den Helder to Oost Vlieland is accessible by careful use of the Scheurrak channel (max 2m draft at HW) to the Inschot; otherwise route via Harlingen and the Blauwe Slenk channel – a longer but less restrictive passage.

Canal Route: the Friesland canal system connects Harlingen to Lauwersoog, or further N still via Groningen to Delfzijl, exiting on the R Eems to Borkum. All passable for mast up vessels drawing no more than 2m. (See p.255.)

Return Passage from R Elbe

Departing Cuxhaven at Helgoland HW+0220 taking maximum advantage of the tide, turn SW at the Elbe No.1 buoy from which in favourable

You must not stray outside the marked channels because if you ground, you may be fined, as the Waddenzee is a conservation area.

DEN HELDER

Standard Port Helgoland
HW (sp) –0410 (np) –0520
LW (sp) –0430 (np) –0520
MHWS MHWN MLWN MLWS
–1·0m –0·8m 0·0m +0·2m
DS Dover +0315E –0300W

This is the principal naval hbr of Holland: there is also a large fishing fleet and a Customs office (℡ 0223 65 75 15).

VTS Monitor VHF 62 from 5M seawards to M13 buoy about 2M E.

Approach From the N the Molengat buoyed channel lies between 1M and ½M W off the coast of Texel and has at least 6m. From the S the Schulpengat buoyage commences at the SG buoy situated 3M W of the Grote Kaap Oc.RWG.10s LtHo and is within the narrow W sector. There is a Dir.WRG. Lt on Texel (026·5°). The channel runs NE through the Breewijd for 7M to join the Marsdiep between Texel and the mainland. The Noorderhaaks is an uninhabited area of sand with off-lying banks to the W of Marsdiep and presents a major hazard in the approach. There is a S card Lt buoy off the E end of Noorderhaaks from which an E course for 2M leads to the entrance. The North Sea coasts of both Texel and the mainland are low-lying and fringed by dunes with few landmarks. This area is now covered by a Vessel Traffic System (VTS) and all vessels in the Schulpengat, Molengat and Marsdiep are required to monitor VHF 62. This rule also applies when leaving hbr. Keep a look-out for busy ferry traffic as you cross between the ferry harbours of Den Helder and Texel.

conditions Norderney (50M) can be made direct. A passage break can also be taken at Spiekeroog Island. Alternatively, make for Helgoland and head S from there on following tide. Great care has to be exercised in German waters to stay well clear of shipping lanes (at least one mile) whenever possible, making meticulous log entries to present a convincing defence should a German coastguard cutter challenge your navigation.

Passage lights

Eierland (Texel)
Fl(2)10s52m29M

Brandaris
Fl.5s54m29M

Schiermonnikoog
Fl(4)20s44m28M

Grosser (Borkum)
Fl(2)12s63m24M

APPROACHES TO DEN HELDER

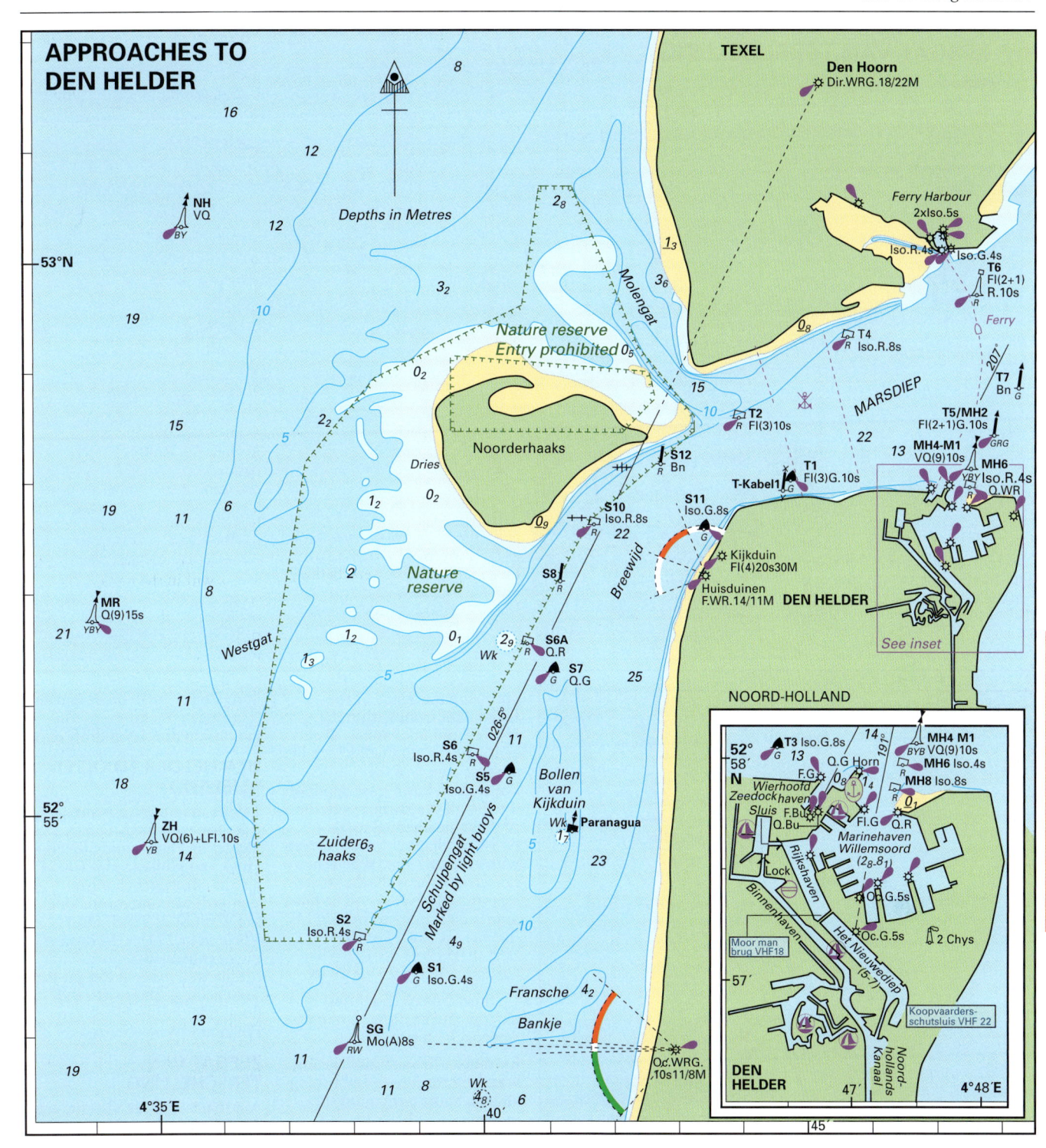

Entrance There are two sets of Ldg Lts, one on 207° (Iso.2s) for the ferry hbr to the W of the main hbr and the other on 191° (Oc.G.5s) for the Marinehaven. Signals apply to all vessels and permission to enter should be requested on VHF 62, call sign *Den Helder Traffic Centre*. Tidal streams run fast across the Marinehaven entrance and reference to Dutch *Waterstanden/Stromen HP33* is recommended. There are two successive sets of port and stb Lts marking the hbr entrance.

Berthing The KMJC yacht hbr is to stb after entering the main hbr piers and has water and electricity to the pontoons. Diesel available. The Koninklijke Marine Jachtclub is part of the Dutch Navy and toilets and showers are in the Officers' Mess. HM ☎ 0223 65 26 45. VHF 31. Customs office in the YH. ☎ 0205 81 36 14. Bicycles available for hire from the HM. At the north end of the Rijkshaven, the Zeedock Sluis gives access to the Passantenhaven Willemsoord. All facilities including diesel. HM ☎ 06 51181879. Alternatively pass through the Vice-Admiral H.V. Moorman Bridge (VHF 18) into the Nieuwe Diep and lock through the Koopvaardersschutsluis (VHF 22) into the Noord-Hollands canal. There are three YCs to the N in the Binnenhaven. Going N they are: WSOV Breewijd (☎ 0223 61 55 00); WV Marine (☎ 0223 65 21 73) and WV Helder-Willemsoord-N (☎ 0223 62 44 22). The Noord-Hollands canal connects with Alkmaar and Amsterdam to the S (opening bridges throughout).

OUDESCHILD (TEXEL)

Standard Port Helgoland
HW (sp) –0310 (np) –0420
LW (sp) –0400 (np) –0445
MHWS MHWN MLWN MLWS
–1·4m –1·1m –0·4m –0·2m
DS Dover +0400NE –0145SW up to 3kn

The only harbour available to cruisers – the car ferry harbour with service to Den Helder, to the SW, is prohibited. Good bus services and bikes for hire. Den Bourg is the pretty capital of the island, busy in summer with tourist trade, but never overwhelmed. N side beaches are magnificent sand, and much of the island is farmed / nature reserve behind massive dykes.

Approach
Flood tide begins Den Helder LW +0200
From seaward through the Molengat or the Schulpengat leading to the wide and deep Marsdiep. From SE and the Den Oever locks at the NW corner of the IJsselmeer. From the E from Kornwerderzand or from the ENE via an intricate channel from Terschelling. All routes lead into the Texelstroom. This is a naval exercise area and submarines may be encountered on the surface.

ZEEGAT VAN TERSCHELLING

Caution
The depths shown on this plan are very generalised and changes occur frequently. Only the current Dutch charts should be used for navigation.

OUDESCHILD

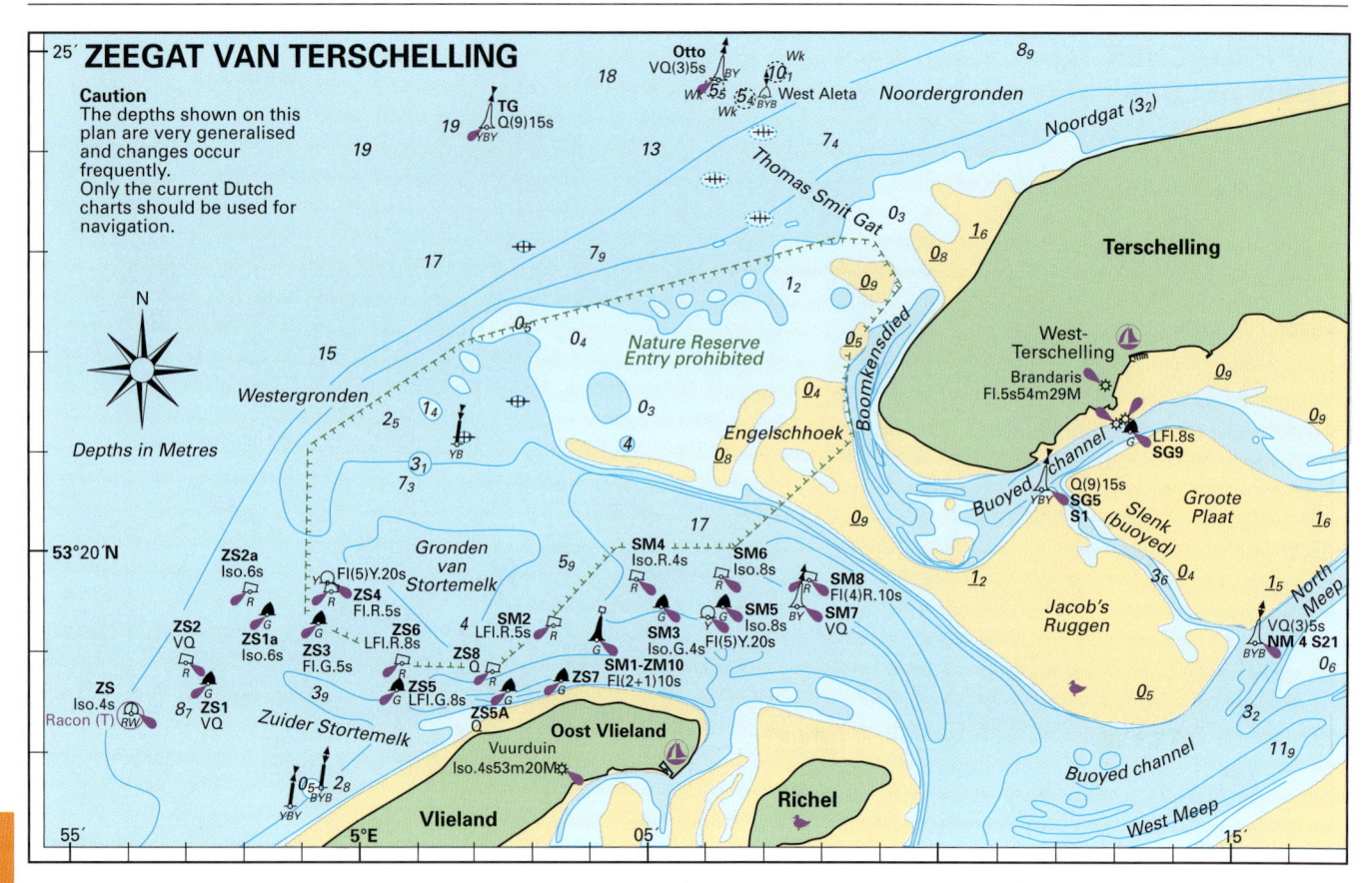

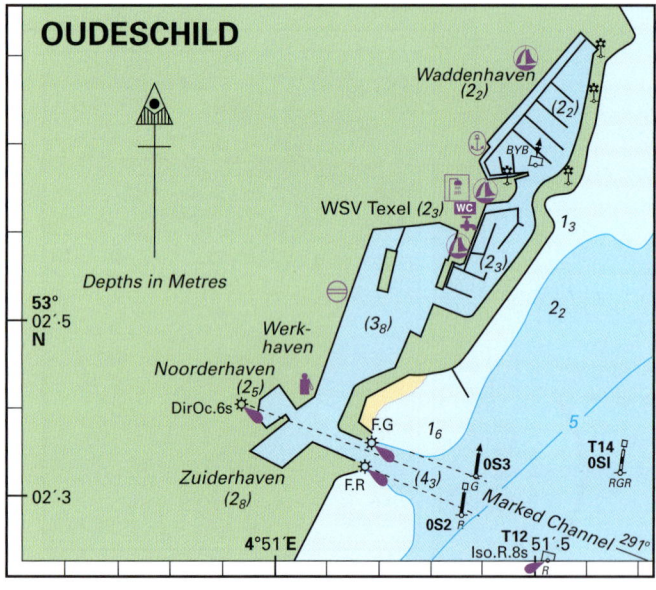

Entrance is from between a R Lt buoy (T12) and a RGR buoy (T14/OS1) followed by R and G spar buoys on the NW side of the Texelstroom. Keep the Oc.6s Lt between the 2F.R and 2F.G pier head Lts for approach of 291° through the moles. Strong currents across the entrance. On entering harbour, area to port is for ferries and 'brown armada'. To stb is pool for fishing vessels with large chandlery. 100m to stb is entry to small channel leading through sharp 90° turn N to large visitors' pontoon marina with all facilities; locals moor in first section. Buy electronic key at HM to access facilities. Bike hire and small shops to hand. Several rather good restaurants around small village.

Note: Mid July– end August is very busy in the visitors' moorings, leaving newcomers to raft against fishing boats in main pool.

HARLINGEN

Standard Port Helgoland
HW (sp) –0155 (np) –0245
LW (sp) –0130 (np) –0210
MHWS MHWN MLWN MLWS
–0·8m –0·7m –0·4m –0·2m
DS Dover –0115S –0600N

An important ship-building and repairing port.

Approach The Blauwe Slenk continues into the main approach channel which runs along the S side of the Pollendam. This training wall is awash at half-tide and the row of R topped bns mark the top of the wall. It is critical to approach the S side of the Pollendam from within the buoyed and lit channel. The centre of the channel, which lies approx 50m S of the Pollendam, has a least depth of 6m. Small Y spar buoys to the S of the main channel mark a two-way channel for small craft with at least 1·8m. When the tide covers the wall, the stream sets strongly across it. The final approach is marked by Ldg Lts (Iso.6s) on 112°. Port VHF 11. HM ☎ 0517 41 25 12. Customs ☎ 058 29 49 49 44.

Channel from S (Boontjes) is narrow and shallow (2m) max. Approach on rising tide.

Entrance Through mole heads, watching for ferries and fishing vessels. Short term alongside moorings to stb in exposed outer harbour.

N Harbour reached through lock gates (Keersluis) and split swing bridge (service on demand, but closed at HW springs for one hour) Note moorings to port for 'brown armada'. Under lifting bridge to N harbour, some pontoons, mostly alongside; normal facilities. Otherwise, S Harbour reached over stb lifting bridge, AB and small quiet marina. Electricity and water only. Supermarket on RH side of S Harbour.

From outer harbour, waterway to port leads to large commercial facility. Hold to stb in Oude Buitenhaven past ferry loading positions towards lock for van Harinxma canal (daylight hours) and route to Leeuwarden. Just beyond lock, hard stb for small quiet marina (Harlingen Yachthaven) 4m max beam and 1·9m draft max.

DEN HELDER TO OOST VLIELAND

Taking maximum advantage of tides for each stage, depart Den Helder or Oudeschild (Texel) at Hoek van Holland HW+0055 via the Molengat channel (buoyed) running close along the W coast of Texel. Oost Vlieland (p.271) 35M distant is the next accessible port, lying off the well marked Zeegat van Terschelling. Enter with the flood tide (begins Hoek van Holland HW +0055)

ZEEGAT VAN TERSCHELLING

Approach to Oost Vlieland and West Terschelling, whether coming from N or W is via the Zuider Stortemelk; from the Iso.4s ZS safe water buoy (53°19'·75N 4°55'·80E) a course of 110° leads into the buoyed channel, uncomfortable in strong winds from W to NW. Channels are constantly shifting and buoyage changes are made frequently and should be followed.

Call VHF 02 for the latest navigational information. Call sign *Verkeerscentrale Brandaris*. VHF 04 for the Dutch Waddenzee.

The Eierlandsche Gat between Vlieland and Texel is sparsely marked and should not be attempted without local knowledge. No facilities.

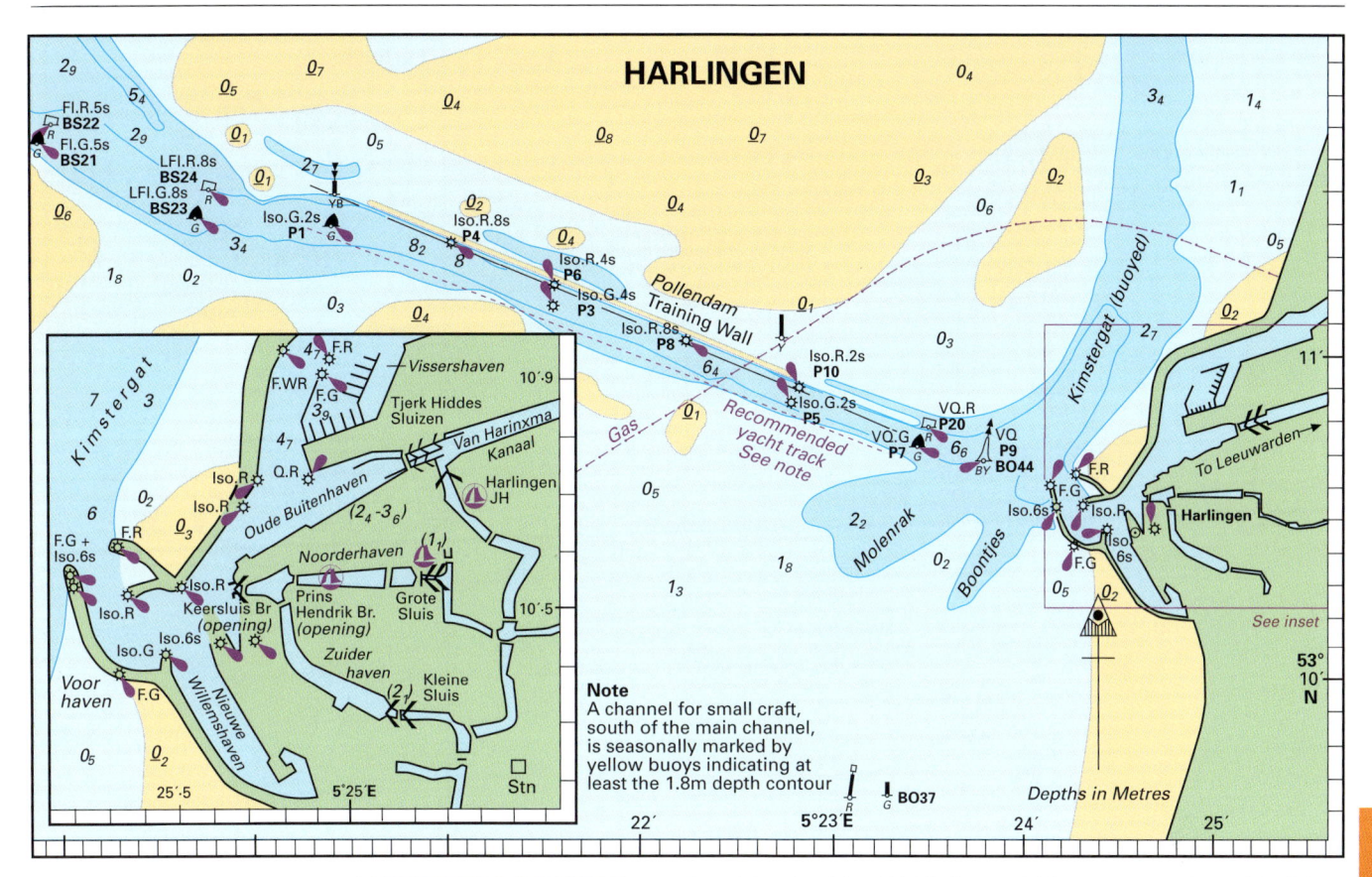

OOST VLIELAND

Standard Port Helgoland
HW (sp) –0250 (np) –0320
LW (sp) –0330 (np) –0355
MHWS MHWN MLWN MLWS
–0·8m –0·7m –0·3m –0·3m

Approach From the Zuider Stortemelk, the ZS11–VS2 N card Lt marks the entrance to the Vliesloot buoyed and partly lit channel. Keep to the middle of the channel until approaching VS14 R buoy Iso.R.4s before making for the hbr entrance avoiding shallows E of the E mole. HM ☎ 0562 45 1729; VHF 12.

Entrance is lit. HM office only opens for short periods morning and evening. Very busy late July and all of August. Anchoring off is feasible W of harbour entrance. Beware not to leave the vessel unattended until satisfied it will remain afloat at LW! The sand is hard.

Facilities. Superb beaches, excellent walks, wonderful views from LtHo, and the scent of the pines on a summer evening make this the pearl of the Frisian Islands. Small shops and restaurants in the town, 15 minutes' walk away. Bicycles and trailers may be hired from HM. Fuel may be ordered from the HM for delivery by tanker. Visitors' cars prohibited. Ferries ply to Harlingen. Customs office (1 May– 1 November) is at the NW end of the yacht hbr ☎ 058 294 94 44.

WEST TERSCHELLING

Standard Port Helgoland
HW (sp) –0220 (np) –0250
LW (sp) –0310 (np) –0335
MHWS MHWN MLWN MLWS
–0·8m –0·7m –0·3m –0·2m
DS Dover –0100E +0500W

VTS VHF 02 for 20M out to sea and 10M in the Waddenzee.

Approach from the S (Vliestroom), turn E into the W Meep and make for narrow buoyed and lit Slenk channel. Beware ferries. No safe route across the sands from the SW into the Schuitengat. The Boomkensdiep channel leading round the SW end of Terschelling is unreliable: take local advice.

Entrance between lit piers. E mole covers at HW. Yacht hbr with pontoons for visitors at N end of hbr. Good facilities, including launderette. Diesel available. Stagings near entrance are for ferries and large commercial sailing vessels. Berth alongside by arrangement. HM ☎ 0562 44 33 37. VHF 31. HM is also authorised Customs Officer. Good selection of shops and restaurants in the town. Very picturesque landscape and magnificent beaches. Bicycles are available for hire from HM.

OOST VLIELAND TO LAUWERSOOG

From Oost Vlieland, back track along the Stortemelk for four miles to avoid the Westergronden shallows; departing Helgoland HW +0320, the turn of the tide will then carry NE past Terschelling and Ameland for 40M before turning S into the Westgat for Lauwersoog harbour and marina; note the yellow small craft channel markers giving passage S of the Plaatgat shallows into the Westgat entrance.

AMELAND (NES)

Standard Port Helgoland
HW (sp) –0135 (np) –0150
LW (sp) –0225 (np) –0245
MHWS MHWN MLWN MLWS
–0·3m –0·2m –0·2m 0·0m

Approach a stopover in Nes is possible on the flood tide, but access is not straightforward, and facilities are limited. The marked approach into the Zeegat van Ameland leads in a loop to the Borndiep channel, with two routes (Dantziggat and Molengat) leading off NE to Nes hbr entrance in the mid-S of the Is. Yachts settle on the firm bottom against the N end of E hbr wall with permission of HM. Shelter except in strong S winds. HM ☎ 0519 54 21 59. Diesel and petrol available from nearby garage.

LAUWERSOOG

Standard Port Helgoland
HW –0138   LW –0228
MHWS MHWN MLWN MLWS
–0·3m –0·2m –0·2m 0·0m

Approach from the W for small craft is possible via the yellow cans marking a channel ESE past the Plaatgat to the Westgat. Otherwise enter via the Westgat heading SE into the Zoutkamperlaag for 7m, turning stbd at the R Z18 buoy through the lit piers to the large commercial harbour. Ahead lies

LAUWERSOOG TO BORKUM (G)

From Lauwersoog return N via the Westgat, departing near the tail end of the ebb, about Helgoland +0300, then head NE to clear Rottumerplaat island (no landing permitted). Join the marked Huibertgat E–W channel for 7m before turning into the R Eems.

Cross the R Eems for the harbour on **Borkum** (Germany, p.280) or carry on SE for 13M to **Delfzijl** via the well marked Doekegat channel: stay close to the marks to avoid the Randzelgat shallows and other banks.

ONWARD PASSAGE TO R ELBE (G)

Departing Borkum on passage E, stay with the Riffgat channel markings for at least 5m before rounding the Borkum Riff shallows. **Norderney** is an easy one tide ride past Juist island.

From Norderney the **R Elbe** entrance, or a detour to **Helgoland**, are one long tidal ride away. The flood tide will make light of the trip up the Elbe to Cuxhaven, taking precautions against the wash of large ships passing at full speed. Great care should be exercised when navigating close to or crossing shipping lanes: keep a detailed log. German patrol cutters are known to levy large fines for perceived deviations from regulations. For more detail see the next section 'Approaches to the Baltic'.

The Cruising Almanac

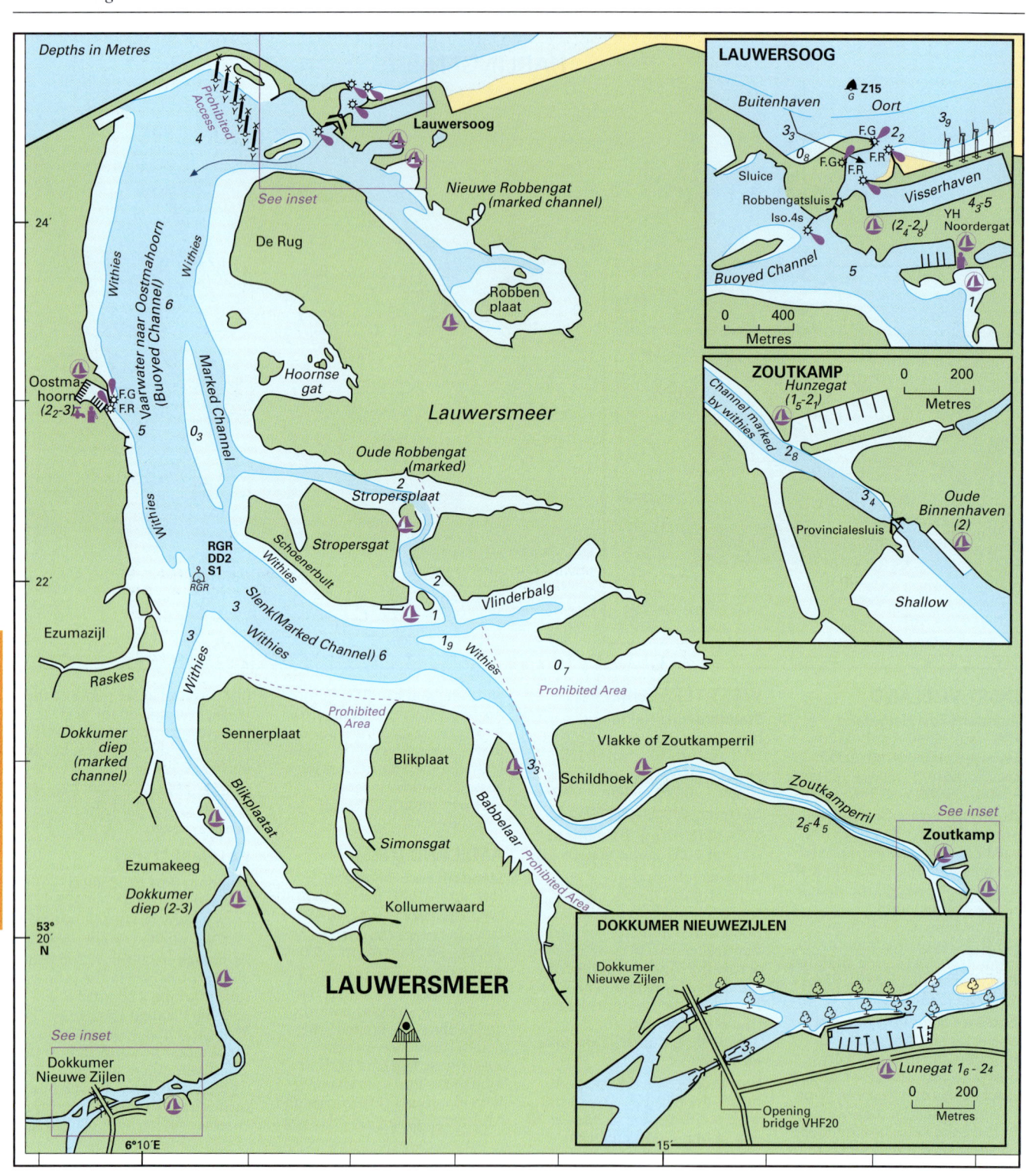

a small marina close to the Robbengatsluis lock (VHF 84). Through the lock (open Monday–Saturday 0700–1900, and Sunday 0900–2000, April–October) to the pastoral delights of the Lauwersmeer for berths and good facilities at the Noordergat YH (HM ☎ 0519 349040) and YH Het Booze Wijf (HM ☎ 0519349133). Diesel available at YH Noordergat.

Immediately to the W of the lock is a Customs office (☎ 0598 69 6560). On the N side of the sea wall, E of the lock, are a restaurant, fish cafés, chandlers and a small supermarket. Bus connections to Groningen.

Onward cruising routes to the interior – Groningen via Zoutkamp, or Leeuwarden and Harlingen via the Dokkumer ei.

SCHIERMONNIKOOG ISLAND

Standard Port Helgoland
HW –0125   LW –0230
MHWS MHWN MLWN MLWS
–0·3m –0·2m –0·2m –0·2m

Hbr lies in the SW of the island at the end of the causeway across the sands. From the Zoutkamperlaag follow the buoyed Gat van Schiermonnikoog to the RGR GVS/R1 buoy. Head N to leave R3 G buoy to stb and follow withies across the 'Siege wal' drying area. It is advisable to approach and leave on a rising tide within 2hrs of HW. No entrance Lts. The hbr has min depth of 1·3m and max 1·5m. Necessary to reserve a berth in busy summer months. HM ☎ 0519 53 15 44 or VHF 31 from 3hr before to 2hr after HW.

Friesland

HARLINGEN TO DELFZIJL

From **Harlingen** (see p.270) to **Lauwersoog** takes two days via the canal systems of Friesland and Groningen – a unique panorama of town and country life in N Holland, and a delightful contrast to the modernity and industry of SW Holland.

Take the van Harinxma canal, maintained to 3·8m depth to busy Leeuwarden, pass through town and exit on shallower (2·2m) Dokkumer Ei to rustic Dokkum. Onwards via the Dokkumer Grutdjip; wander through the fields to the open waters, reed beds and country peace of Lauwersmeer. All bridges en route open on demand, daylight hours, some closed for lunch break. Diesel at several points along canal. Whole route passable for 2m draught, but some moorings may offer less. Note: canal gates at Harlingen operate free flow at LW to purge canal – care required on entering.

Franeker Small club marina to port 1M before town centre. Shops and banks 15 minutes' walk in pleasant setting. Alongside mooring in town centre.

Leeuwarden The van Harinxma canal swings S on approach to town, leading to Sneek and Lemmer, well signed. Ahead into Leeuwarden, marvel at ingenuity of first lifting bridge, and pass six more conventional bridges; toll collected at 5th bridge by swinging clog. Bridge service on demand 0900–1600 and 1800–2000 on summer weekdays but closed 1200–1300 at weekends.

Alongside mooring through picturesque town centre, but variable depth under trees; some facilities.

Van Harinxma route to Sneek and Lemmer – note restricted service at Leeuwarden railway bridges S of town – 0500–0700, 0900–1600, 1800–2100. YC (Leeuwarden yachthaven) to port after railway bridges, via remote-controlled swing bridge. Quiet, but 20 minutes' walk to town: basic facilities.

Leeuwarden to Lauwersmeer via Dokkum is a canalized river, passable for 2m draft with care; many side waters and moorings no more than 1·5m. Toll at pretty village of Burdaard, collected by clog at 2nd bridge.

Dokkum A very pretty town. mooring along canal bank, with most facilities. 2m draft moorings best found on staging beyond 3rd bridge. Bridge toll collected at 2nd bridge. Service hours as for Leeuwarden.

Further box marina beyond 3rd bridge to port. Supermarket and bus services to Groningen / train connection.

Entry to Lauwersmeer is via lock at Dokkumer Nieuwe Zijlen. Large marina to stb on exit, all facilities.

Lauwersmeer formed when dam constructed – now a large shallow nature reserve with much on-water activity. Part of standing mast route to Groningen.

Channel wanders N through reed beds, marked by withies. Several nature reserves – off limits to boats. Buoyage requires close observation to avoid stranding.

Good facilities at Jachthaven Oostmahorn, at NW side of Lauwersmeer, and Yachthaven Noordergat close to the lock. Diesel. Restaurants nearby. Short walk to dam, sea views and village.

Lauwersoog A small fishing village on dike with ferries to Schiermonnikoog island. Exit to Wadden Zee via Robbengatsluis lock (daylight hours VHF 84). Marina on sea side of dam, but rather exposed boxes. Large fishing fleet in industrial harbour. Good facilities. Bus service to Groningen.

Access canal route to Groningen via narrow waterway (Slenk) at S end of Lauwersmeer. Locks at Zoutkamp. Large friendly marina (Yachthaven Hunzegat) before lock to port – suitable for longer term mooring.

Zoutkamp Small marina and restaurants / shops. Onwards via canalized Reitdiep (2·4m max depth) crossing van Staarkenborgh canal, into approaches to Groningen.

Groningen Major regional centre, university town with long history and museums, shops and restaurants. Good onward train connections.

Multiple bridges to navigate round S side of town centre for mast up vessels; bridges work in sequence – service hours 0900–1200, 1300–1600, 1730–1900. Jachthaven Oosterhaven lies E of ring, close to railway station, all facilities and very close to shops / cafés.

Eemskanaal From Groningen to Delfzijl the Eemskanaal (5·4m draft) runs straight, forking at Delfzijl. Town and small marina to port. Bypass S to locks (VHF 26) for R Eems. Immediately past lock to port lies ZV Neptunus marina, chandlery and shops, cafés.

DELFZIJL

Standard Port Helgoland
HW (sp) –0020 (np) –0005
LW (sp) +0000 (np) –0040
MHWS MHWN MLWN MLWS
+0·5m +0·6m –0·1m –0·1m

This is the most important commercial and fishing port in the N of Holland. Customs post. Eems Kanaal leads via Groningen along a fixed mast route to the IJsselmeer. A resort town with a small selection of shops plus rail service via Groningen to S.

Marina boxes and most facilities in the Abel Tasman marina, close to town.

VTS Monitor VHF 20. Going N change to VHF 18 at buoy 35.

Approach The outer part of the Eems estuary is divided by the island of Borkum and large drying areas in the Westereems and Oostereems. From the Oostereems buoy there is a difficult passage across the shoals S of Memmert to join the Westereems 7M N of Delfzijl. A safer approach from the E is to continue to the Riffgat or Westereems, both of which are marked at their seaward ends by safe-water buoys bearing the names of their respective channels. (The Huibertgat channel is now marked by a series of unlit safe water buoys and the fixed W sector Lt which used to guide vessels along this channel has been extinguished). From the W the main approach channel is the Westereems which is well buoyed. After the Noll pillar buoy (Q.G), follow the Ranselgat buoyed channel SE guided by the leading sector Lt of Campen LtHo, keeping just outside the shipping channel. Change course slightly to stb after the No.27 G pillar buoy (Fl.G.4s) to follow the buoyed and lit Doekegat channel into the Oostfriesche Gaatje. After the second R sector of the multi-sector Knock LtHo, the W sector guides you towards the Ldg Lts on a heading of 203°. In any event, keep N of the PS3/BW26 GRG buoy Fl.G(2+1)12s on approach.

Entrance is between F.R and F.G pier head Lts followed by a turn to stb between bns exhibiting G Lts to stb and R to port for 3M. The pontoons of the yacht hbr lie against the W wall of the Handelshaven. The HM office is halfway along the W wall ☎ 0596 61 50 04. Diesel available at the marina.

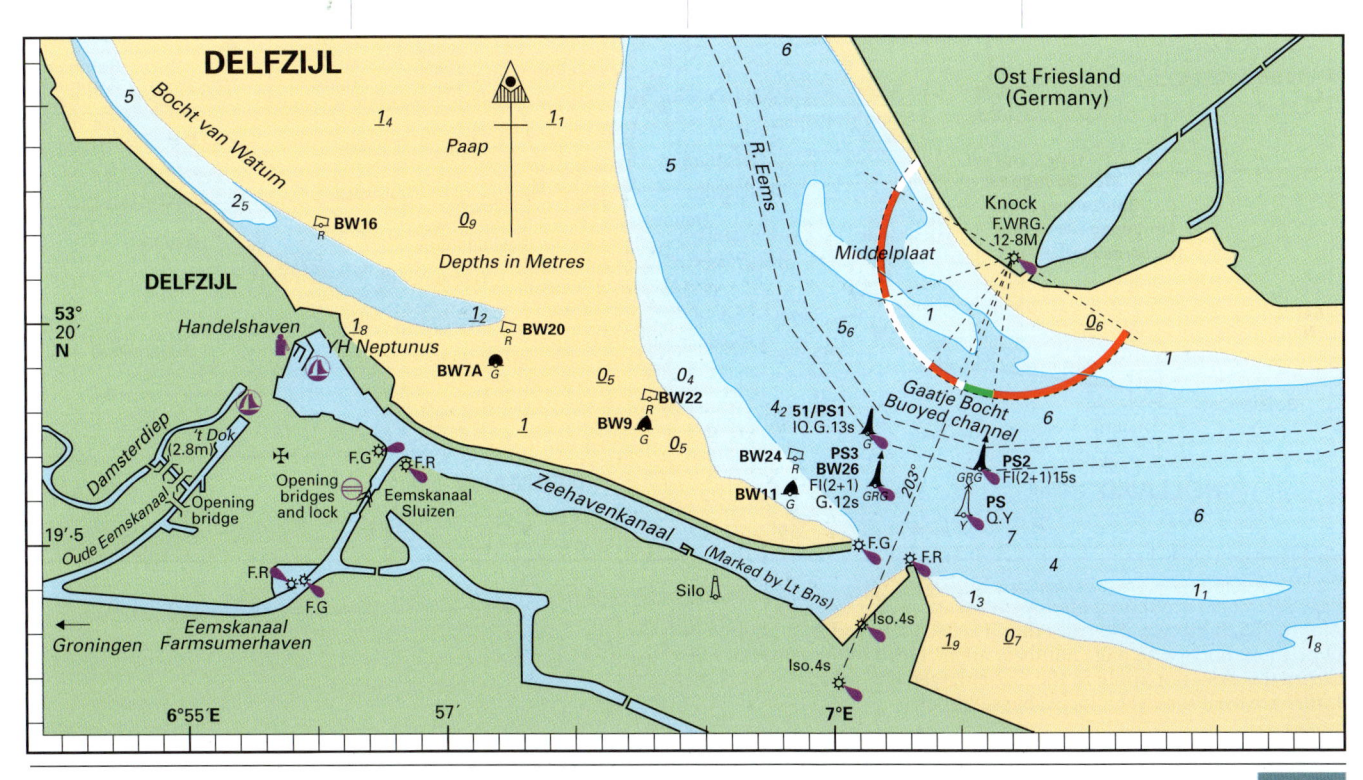

The Cruising Almanac

ROUTES AND PORTS

Map showing Approaches to the Baltic, covering Norway, Denmark, Sweden, Germany, Holland, and Poland with numbered routes (1, 2a, 2b, 3, 3a, 4, 5, 6a, 6b, 6c, 6d, 7) and VHF radio channel information for various ports.

Norway ports with page references:
- Bergen 289
- Haugesund 289
- Skudeneshavn 290
- Stavanger
- Tananger 290
- Egersund 291
- Arendal 292
- Kristiansand 291
- Mandal 291

Rogaland Radio VHF Channels: 01, 07, 20, 21, 27, 28, 60, 66, 78, 79, 81

Tjøme Radio VHF Channels: 01, 07, 20, 21, 22, 27, 81

Swedish VHF Channels: VHF 21, 22, 23, 25, 26, 81, 84

Danish ports:
- Thyborøn 287
- Skagen 288
- Ålborg

Swedish port: Göteborg 293

German/Danish VHF stations (*DP07 members only service, but everyone listens in):
- *Nordfriesland VHF 26
- *Flensburg VHF 27
- *Accumersiel VHF 28
- *Borkum VHF 61
- *Elbe-Weser VHF 24
- *Bremen VHF 25
- *Kiel VHF 23
- *Hamburg VHF 83
- *Lübeck VHF 24
- *Rostock VHF 60

Other:
- Arkona VHF 66
- Bornholm (Denmark) Rønne VHF 04, 07
- Szczecin VHF 12, 16

German ports:
- Helgoland 281
- Wangerooge 281
- Spiekeroog 280
- Langeoog 280
- Norderney 280
- Borkum 280

Note: * These are a DP07 members only service, but everyone listens in

---

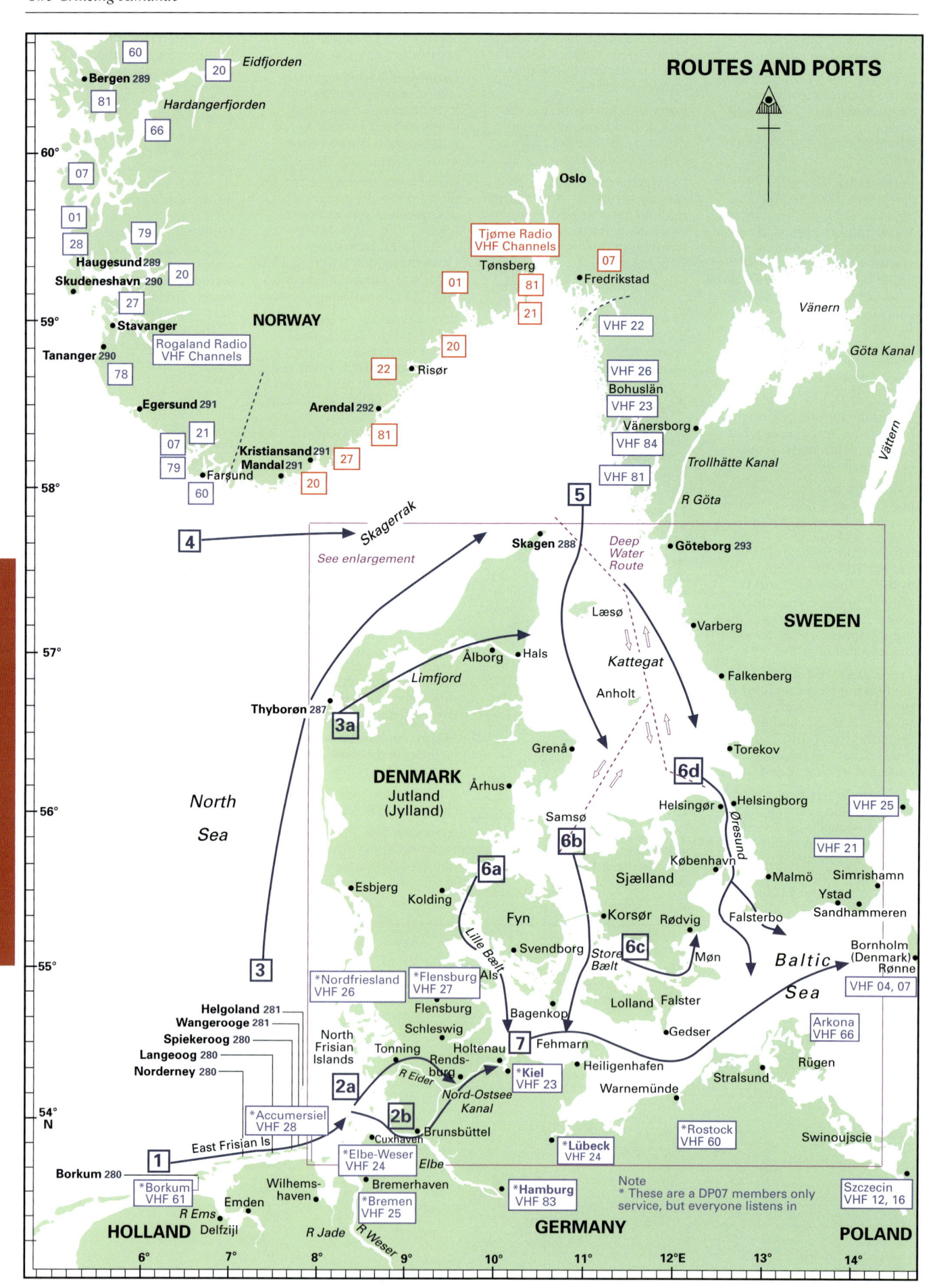

Page references are shown after some locations, for example:
Ålborg 285. Bold type indicates that it is accompanied by a plan. Only those ports with page numbers are included in the text. For clarity this does not apply to the 'See enlargement' area.
Italics are used for rivers, lochs, bays, seas etc.

Approaches to the Baltic

Introduction

The sea area known in English as the Baltic comprises the Skagerrak, the Kattegat, the Sound, the Belts, the Baltic proper (the East Sea in the languages of the littoral states), the Gulf of Bothnia, the Gulf of Finland and the waters of the Baltic States. This is a popular cruising ground with negligible tides and usually warmer summers than in the North Sea. Facilities are good but harbours tend to be crowded in July and August. This section provides suggestions for routes to the Baltic. It does not pretend to be comprehensive – some of the routes described are cruising grounds in their own right. Crews wishing to explore further will want more detailed literature. There is a wide selection of boatyards in the Baltic, and many British boats winter here. The Cruising Association has a very active Baltic Section and members will find much useful and updated information in the Baltic section pages at www.theca.org.uk.

Approaching the Baltic from the N Sea there are two main routes: through the German Bight and the Nord-Ostsee Kanal or through the Skagerrak passing to the N of Jylland (Jutland). There is a variation of the Nord-Ostsee-Kanal route which uses the river Eider for part of the passage or one may pass through the scenic Limfjord in N Jylland. For a crossing of the S part of the N Sea and the mast-up inland route through the Dutch canals see previous section.

1. S approach: through the German Bight

a) Along the E Frisian Islands

The Nord-Ostsee-Kanal route is usually preferred by yachtsmen from the UK S and E coast. Following this route it is feasible to reach the Baltic by day sailing from the English Channel. The Dutch, German and Danish coasts of the N Sea however have few hbrs of refuge and there are extensive offlying shoals and a formidable lee shore to be avoided in strong winds from the W through to the N. The rivers Ems, Jade, Weser and particularly the Elbe have strong tidal streams and detailed passage planning is necessary. The waters are busy with large ships and are closely monitored by authorities. Shallow draft vessels may do part of the passage inshore, passing S of the East Frisian Islands between rivers Ems and Jade. It is worth noting during planning that the prevailing winds being from the W, the return journey may be longer and wetter than the outward trip. Nowhere is this more true than in the Elbe, which becomes so rough in fresh W winds that passage to seaward is not possible.

b) Direct crossing

Yachts from UK E coast may consider a direct passage to Elbe approaches, passing N of the German Bight Western Approach TSS. Call *German Bight VTS* (VHF 79/80) before crossing the TSS. Construction of extensive offshore wind farms is underway in the German Bight. Updated charts should be consulted, listening on VHF 16 and good watch-keeping routines essential. Helgoland is an all-weather all-tide hbr and ideally located for final approach up the Elbe. From Grimsby to Helgoland is 285M, from Whitby 300M. Updated charts should be consulted for position of oil rigs and wind farms under construction. Oil rigs enforce a 500m safety zone. Listen VHF 16 for information from guard vessels. A point-down cone must be shown when motor-sailing in German waters.

2. N approach: through the Skagerrak

This approach avoids the TSS and large tides of the German Bight. The passage from Peterhead to Egersund is 255M, to Mandal 310M. From Lerwick to Tananger is 220M, from Lerwick to Marstein LtHo in the approaches to Bergen 185M. On the crossing a keen lookout is required for fishing boats. Not all have AIS transponders. Updated charts should be consulted for position of oil rigs. With the exception of Danish W coast there are small tides. The Norwegian coast with its many offlying islands has many harbours that can be approached in all weathers. Where the Skagerrak enters the Kattegat lies Skagen hbr which can be entered in all weather conditions. When planning a passage across the North Sea, note that websites such as www.yr.no provide detailed 48hr forecasts for many of the oil installations and the graphic 48hr display on www.dmi.dk (links Hav – Havprognoser – Nordsøen) extends as far N as the passage Orkneys – Tananger.

Tides

Tides in the approaches to the Baltic vary from more than 3m in the German Bight to less than 1m in the Skagerrak. Surges caused by persistent strong winds and changes in barometric pressure lead to marked changes in tidal heights. In the German Bight E'ly winds will generally give less water than indicated in tide tables. See Route 1 for sources of detailed tidal predictions. The Baltic Sea is almost landlocked. Its salinity is variable but is about half that of the ocean. Because it is fed by many rivers there is a tendency for a N-flowing current between the Danish islands and this is accentuated by a tendency for the warmer, lighter Baltic water to run N and for deeper, colder and denser water to run back into the Baltic. There are few true tides in the Baltic but like in the North Sea massive movements of water may take place as the result of changes in barometric pressure and wind. In the W Baltic strong W'lies will cause lower water levels than indicated in tide tables. Danish Met Office www.dmi.dk has a useful graphic display of predicted currents next 48 hrs: follow links to [Hav] [Havprognoser] choose area boxes then click on small circles [strøm] and [strømretning] then run graphic display.

Immigration

For a list of documents that should be carried aboard see Chapter 1 (General Information). Holders of non-EU/EEA passports should establish beforehand whether there are any visa requirements. The countries in this section are all signatories to the Schengen agreement. Any vessel approaching a Schengen member state from offshore (usually 12M) will by definition be crossing a Schengen outer boundary. Such a crossing may formally require border control procedures on entry and exit. Implementation varies and may change at short notice. Enquire about formalities at ☎ +49 0800 6888 000 (Germany); ☎ +46 77 114 14 00 or 114 14 (Sweden). In Denmark enquire with HM about any entry procedures. Norway has plans to require any vessel not registered in a Schengen country to notify the authorities >24h before landfall. In practice, arrive at a Port of Entry (i.e. any port in this

North Sea, southeast part distances (miles)

	Borkum	Norderney	Helgoland	Cuxhaven	Brunsbüttel	Esbjerg	Thyborøn
Borkum	0						
Norderney	34	0					
Helgoland	75	45	0				
Cuxhaven	94	64	35	0			
Brunsbüttel	109	79	52	17	0		
Esbjerg	137	121	85	109	124	0	
Thyborøn	204	188	162	182	203	96	0

(Distance Borkum to Helgoland passing W of the Riffgat RW buoy. Distances from Borkum and Norderney to Helgoland are measured passing E of buoy TG19.)

North Sea, north and Skagerrak distances (miles)

	Bergen	Tananger	Egersund	Mandal	Arendal	Thyborøn	Skagen
Bergen	0						
Tananger	101	0					
Egersund	136	40	0				
Mandal	175	96	60	0			
Arendal	231	151	119	58	0		
Thyborøn	262	166	128	85	109	0	
Skagen	303	206	170	118	80	122	0

Skagerrak, Kattegat distances (miles)

	Skagen	Göteborg	Hals	Grenå	Helsingør	Korsør	Kolding
Skagen	0						
Göteborg	44	0					
Hals	51	72	0				
Grenå	88	87	43	0			
Helsingør	124	107	97	62	0		
Korsør	158	158	112	70	101	0	
Kolding	169	172	126	91	116	66	0

(Distance Göteborg measured to/from Långedrag)

DENMARK AND SWEDEN

TSS Traffic Separation Scheme
DWR Deep Water Route
⬚ Offshore Wind Farm
Denmark All call sign *Lyngby Radio*
Sweden All call sign *Stockholm Radio*

APPROACHES TO THE BALTIC

almanac except Skudenshavn) and phone the authorities on ☎ +4702800. After a direct crossing from a non-Schengen state (e.g. UK) contact should be made with authorities as indicated. If you plan to spend more than 90 days in any of the countries covered, enquire about application/registration formalities. For entry procedures on return passage to UK, see chapter 1 (General Information).

Customs

Germany, Denmark and Sweden are members of the EU. Norway is not a member of the EU but is in the EEA. Helgoland is duty free but in the EU. The import of alcohol and tobacco into the EU countries in this section is restricted to reasonable quantities. If not bringing tobacco, the amount of alcohol allowed into Norway is limited to one litre of spirits, 3 litres of wine and 2 litres of beer per adult crew member. For details see www.toll.no. Leaving a boat behind in Norway for more than six weeks should only be done after arrangement with Customs about VAT exemption; application form can be downloaded from www.toll.no [skjema] [RD 0027].

Health

For First Aid see General Information. Ticks carrying borrelia (Lyme disease) may be found throughout the Baltic and approaches. Tick borne encephalitis (TBE) has been reported in all countries in this region but is uncommon. Vaccination against TBE is available. General advice is to wear long sleeved shirts and long trousers tucked into socks when walking in infested areas. Ticks should be removed intact; special tweezers are available from local pharmacies. Should a red ring develop around a tick bite or any

COAST RADIO STATIONS

Working channels supplied in plan are to relay stations, from where calls are passed on to a central unit.

Denmark Call *Lyngby Radio* (MMSI 002191000) on VHF 16, working channel will be given. Lyngby Radio is operated by Ministry of Defence and has no service to leisure craft other than distress calls.

Germany Search and Rescue VHF16 and 70 (DSC) call sign *Bremen Rescue* (MMSI 002111240). Working channels supplied in plan serviced by DP07 Seefunk, a 'members only' service funded by membership fees (www.dp07.com)

SW Norway Call sign all working channels *Rogaland Radio* (MMSI 002570300).

SE Norway Call sign all working channels *Tjøme Radio* (MMSI 002570100).

Sweden Call sign all working channels *Stockholm Radio* (MMSI 002652000).

For latest information on VHF working channels see www.stockholmradio.se [För abonnenter] [Kartor och kanalplan - VHF] then choose relevant region. For contact information Rescue Coordination Centers see Chapter 1 General Information.

WEATHER FORECASTS

1. VHF (working channels)

DP07 Seefunk weather forecast in German at 0745, 0945, 1245, 1645 and 1945 (local time).

Stockholm Radio inshore weather forecast in Swedish: S coast 0915, 1715 and 2215. W coast 15 minutes later (May–October, local time)

Stockhom radio shipping forecast in English 0600 and 1800 (UTC).

VHF Rogaland and Tjøme radio weather forecast in Norwegian at 0900, 1200, 1500, 1800 and 2100 (local time) and in English at 1200 and 1800 (local time, summer only)

2. Radio frequencies and times

Local language, local time. Many also available as livestream or downloads/podcasts from stations' webpage.

Denmark DMI Kalundborg 243kHz; DRM enabled: 0545, 0845, 1145 and 1745.

Germany Deutschlandfunk/ Deutschlandradio kultur DAB+ 0105, 0640, 1810, from DP07 (commercial): 7310kHz and 9560kHz 0930 and 1400.

Norway Norsk Rikskringkasting P1 DAB 0545 DAB+ NRK Vær (continous coastal forecast)

Sweden Sveriges Radio P1 FM/DAB 0555, 0755, 1255 (1250 Sat & Sun), 1555, 2150.

3. Websites and Apps

Norway www.yr.no type location in searchbox or follow link [Hav og Kyst] then choose relevant area.

Popular weather apps include weatherpro, windguru, windfinder, klart.se and kustväder from sjöraddning.se.

For more comprehensive information see Frank Singleton's website www.weather.mailasail.com/ Franks-Weather.

---

other unexplainable symptom appear, seek medical attention. The common adder (Vipera berus) is found in the Baltic as far north as the Arctic Circle. If bitten keep afflicted body part at rest and seek medical advice. ✆ 112 for emergency services in all countries covered, in Norway ✆ 113 for emergency medical services. All crew should carry a valid European Health Insurance Card (www.ehic.org.uk).

Rescue services

Sea rescue operations in Germany are offered by Deutsche Gesellschaft zur Rettung Schiffbrüchiger (DGzRS) (www.seenotretter.de). This is a charitable organisation, dependent on memberships and private contributions. In Norway Redningsselskapet (www.redningsselskapet.no) is run on similar lines, in Sweden the service is supplied by Sjöräddningsselskapet (www.sjoraddning.se). In Denmark rescue services are offered by Søværnets Operative Kommando (a public service) and Dansk Søredningsselskab (www.dsrs.dk). The charitable sea rescue organisations in the Scandinavian countries offer a membership service, giving a member in one organisation equal benefits in the sister organisations.

Authorities monitor VHF 16 and 70 (DSC), see Chapter 1 (General Information). ✆ 112 is the emergency tel no in the countries covered.

Offshore wind farms

Offshore wind farms are under construction, in operation or projected throughout all the waters of the approaches to the Baltic. For example, such farms exist (or are planned) for the Dogger Bank, the German North Sea coast, west of Jutland, The Sound, east of Fehmarn, the Mecklenburger Bucht, north and east of Rügen and southwest of Gedser. They represent a significant hazard to navigation and mariners should proceed with caution using fully corrected charts.

Charts

Cost-efficient small craft portfolios are available for the areas covered in this section. These are widely available from dealers throughout the region, many also available from UK suppliers such as Imray and ChartCo.

For an index of officially approved printed charts see website of national Hydrographic offices. Note that with the increasing use of Print-On-Demand, charts bought off-the-shelf may not be updated.

Denmark www.eng.gst.dk [Danish Hydrographic Office] [Nautical charts] [Paper charts] [Danish nautical chart index]
Germany www.bsh.de [produkte] [seekarten] then select region
Norway www.kartverket.no has English translation [kart] [navigere til sjøs] [sjøkart på papir] [last ned produktkatalog]
Sweden www.sjofartsverket.se also has an English version of its website [sjöfart] [sjökort och publikationer] [se på sjökort].

Charts for much of the region can be viewed online at sites such as http://webapp.navionics.com; www.nv-pedia.de; http://kartor.eniro.se [Sjökort]; www.norgeskart.no [Sjø] and www.openseamap.org

Pilots and Harbour Guides in English

The British Admiralty publishes pilots, sailing directions, list of radio signals and maritime communications relevant for the region, for details see www.ukho.gov.uk. Other useful literature published in English:

Cruising Guide to Germany and Denmark Brian Navin (Imray)
The Baltic Sea RCC Pilotage Foundation (Imray)
Norway RCC Pilotage Foundation/Judy Lomax (Imray)
The Norwegian Cruising Guide Phyllis Nickel and John Harries (also available as e-book from www.norwegiancruisingguide.com)
Havneguiden vol 10 Scandinavia Hanne and Jørn Engevik
Cruising Guide Booklets from the Cruising Association include publications covering all countries in this section. Some are for sale to non-members from CA house, all are available for members as free downloads from www.theca.org.uk, together with a number of other useful documents such as *Leaving Your Home*, *Routes to the Baltic*, *Formalities* and *Baltic Lay-up Directory*. Information on many hbrs can also be accessed from a mobile device using the Captain's app from the CA.

Pilots and Harbour Guides in local languages

National Hydrographic Offices publish pilots mostly targeting commercial shipping. Some yachtsmen find these useful. Some Danish and all Norwegian official pilots are available as free downloads: www.danskehavnelods.dk and www.kartverket.no (type Den Norske Los in search-box then choose relevant volume). For other official pilots see websites for charts. There is a wide range of harbour guides published locally. Many of these are richly illustrated and may be useful even with no knowledge of German or a Scandinavian language. These are available at local dealers or from websites such as www.weilbach.dk, www.naudi.de, www.nautiskfritid.no and www.nautiska.se.

The comprehensive *Havneguiden* series have a summary in English for their guides to German, Norwegian and Swedish waters. Can be downloaded as individual hbrs, app available (www.havneguiden.no). Free printed hbr guides such as *Sejlerens* (www.sejlerens.com), *Gästhamnsguiden* (www.gasthamnsguiden.se) and *Baltic Sailing* (www.balticsailing.de) are distributed through marinas as well as available online. Baltic sailing also has text in English.

Other useful online resources, mostly local language:
www.wattsegler.de
www.wattenschipper.de
www.skipperguide.de
www.mein-ostseehafen.de
www.havneguide.dk (link in English)
www.marinaguide.dk
www.velihavn.no
www.gjestehavner.no
www.havna.com

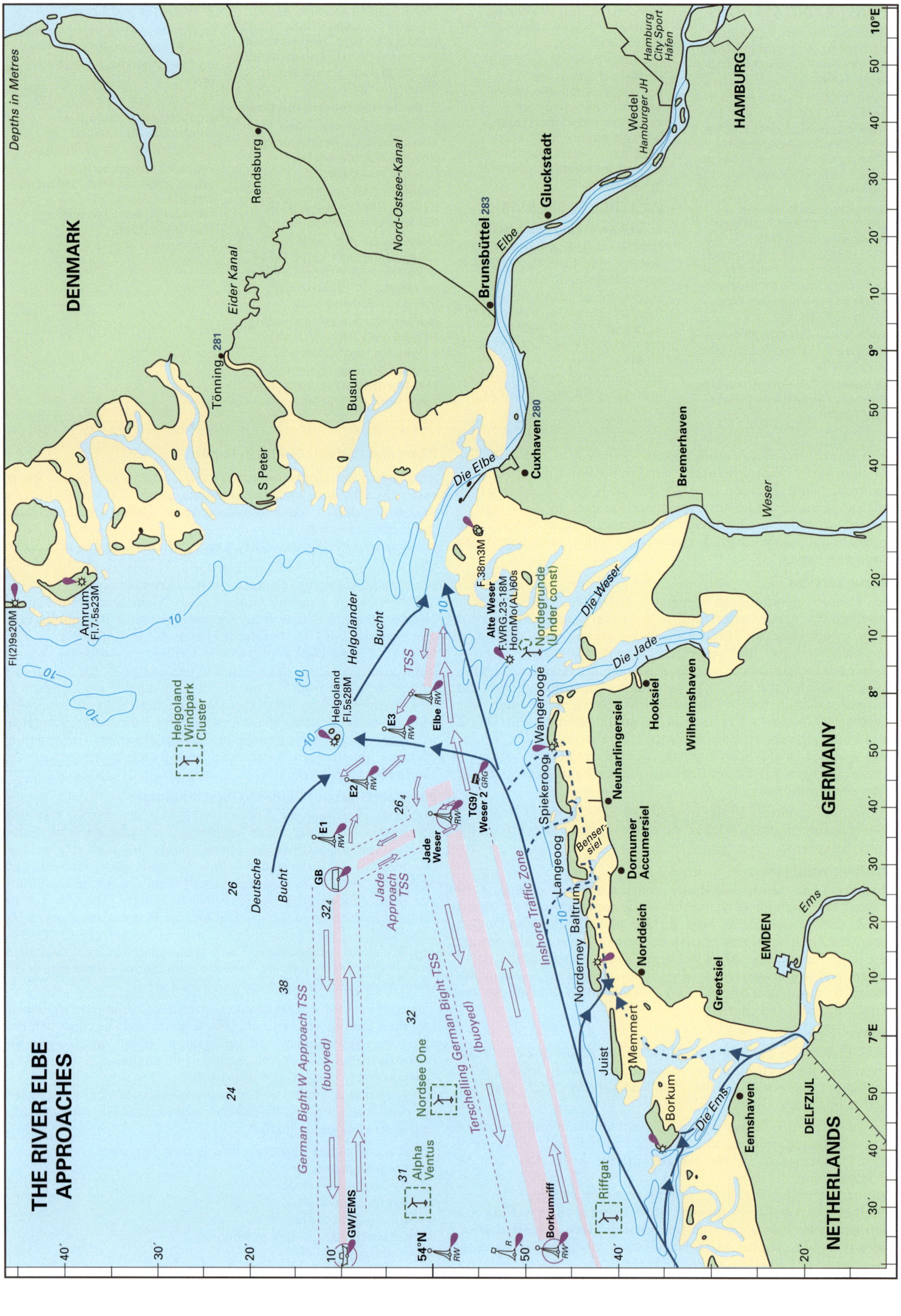
THE RIVER ELBE APPROACHES
Depths in Metres
DENMARK
GERMANY
NETHERLANDS
HAMBURG
Hamburg City Sport Hafen
Wedel Hamburger JH
Gluckstadt
Brunsbüttel 283
Elbe
Nord-Ostsee-Kanal
Rendsburg
Eider Kanal
Tönning 281
Busum
S Peter
Die Elbe
Cuxhaven 280
Bremerhaven
Weser
Die Weser
Die Jade
Hooksiel
Wilhelmshaven
Neuharlingersiel
Dornumer Accumersiel
Bensersiel
Norddeich
EMDEN
Ems
Greetsiel
Eemshaven
DELFZIJL
Die Ems
Borkum
Juist
Memmert
Norderney
Baltrum
Langeoog
Spiekeroog
Wangerooge
Amrum Fl.7.5s23M
Fl(2)9s20M
Helgoland Windpark Cluster
Helgoland Fl.5s28M
Helgolander Bucht
Deutsche Bucht
TSS
Alte Weser F.WRG.23-18M HornMo(AL)60s
Nordergrunde (Under const)
F.38m3M
E1 RW
E2 RW
E3 RW
Elbe RW
GB
Jade Weser RW
TG9/ Weser 2 GRG
Jade Approach TSS
German Bight W Approach TSS (buoyed)
Terschelling German Bight TSS (buoyed)
Inshore Traffic Zone
Nordsee One
Alpha Ventus
Riffgat
GW/EMS
Borkumriff RW
54°N RW
26
24
38
32
31
32_4
26_4
10
40´
30´
20´
10´
50´
20´
30´
40´
50´
7°E
10´
20´
30´
40´
50´
8°
10´
20´
30´
40´
50´
9°
10´
20´
30´
40´
50´
10°E

Accessing internet
WiFi will be found in many marinas, cafés, public libraries and tourist information facilities. GSM and 3G services are widely available in the region, increasingly also 4G. In Scandinavia data traffic is also available through the NSM 450 system (www.ice.no). To minimise charges ensure your subscription is appropriate for the planned cruise, and enable 'data roaming' on your device only when needed. If spending a long time in an area enquire about local sim card/pre-paid dongle. Many network providers only offer their services to residents with national ID number. Bring your passport to supplier and make certain your device is up and running before leaving shop. Regulations that abolish end-user roaming charges in the EU and EEA are planned for 2017, after which installing a local sim card may no longer be worthwhile.

Spelling
There are minor (occasionally major) differences in the spelling of geographical names in the different languages. For example, The Sound is Øresund in Danish and Öresund in Swedish (sometimes Sundet in both languages) and the capital of Denmark could be called København, Köpenhamn, Kopenhagen or Copenhagen. As far as possible the spelling in the local language has been used throughout the text with the English equivalent occasionally given.

Note that there are three additional letters in the Scandinavian languages (Norwegian and Danish: æ, ø, å; Swedish: å, ä, ö). In telephone directories, gazetteers etc these letters appear alphabetically after z. In Danish the letter å is often written aa.

Marina telephone numbers and VHF channels
Information in text is liable to change. Marinas are usually staffed once or twice daily for a few hours. Few marinas in this area listen to VHF and most do not accept berth reservations by telephone. For information about hbrs offering pre-booking of berths and booking online see www.dockspot.com and www.marinabooking.dk .

Fuel
Diesel is widely available throughout this region. Not road-taxed (dyed) diesel is not available to yachts in mainland EU. Yachts entering Germany with tanks containing dyed fuel should retain receipts. Diesel sold from marinas in the EU will contain biodiesel (FAME). Boat owners should consider using appropriate additive, especially if planning winter lay up in the Baltic. Non road-taxed diesel dyed green is, at time of writing, available to yachts in Norway. This is reportedly free of biodiesel.

Gas
All the Baltic countries use propane gas routinely but some butane (Camping Gaz) is found in Germany, Denmark and S Sweden. Calor butane and propane gas are not available and spare bottles should be taken. It may be possible to have propane cylinders refilled at outlets of LPG Norge and Primagaz Sverige, see www.lpgnorge.no and www.primagaz.se for retailers. An adaptor fitting your cylinder should be carried. Calor discourages refilling of their cylinders outside of the UK. For longer stays in the Baltic a change to local cylinder may be necessary. For 5kg composite propane cylinders there is an exchange agreement between AGA and Kosan dealers in the Nordic countries, adaptor required. For further information see Baltic General Cruising Information on the Cruising Association website (www.theca.org.uk members only).

Holding tanks
In Sweden and the Baltic shores of Denmark and Germany, discharging black water to sea may only be done when 12M from shore. Holding tanks with deck pump-out must be installed. There may be exemptions for smaller yachts, older yachts and foreign flagged yachts but regulations and implementation seem to vary. In Norway holding tanks may be emptied 300m from shore in non-congested waters. Crews should use shore-based toilet facilities when available. Popular anchorages in Norway and Sweden often have basic (composting) toilets ashore.

Berthing
In German and Danish hbrs in the Baltic a 'box' mooring is common, bows to pontoon or quay with long warps to piles from the stern. Boats with wide beam may have difficulty fitting between piles, fenders best removed. It is worth preparing two long lines with large bowlines before entering hbr. Locals often cross stern lines to minimise sideways movement: line from stb cleat to port pile. In other areas pontoons with outriggers are the norm. Some hbrs supply lazy lines or mooring buoys for stern lines, few hbrs now require use of stern anchor. Vacant berths are usually indicated by green tag. Some marinas charge more for collecting mooring fees at the boat, so it is worth while visiting the HM or pay at the ticket machine where available. A sticker is sometimes given as receipt to be displayed on the pulpit. Some hbrs have berths that can be pre-booked (www.dockspot.com, www.marinabooking.dk).

Anchorages, moorings
Mooring buoys outside settlements are available in the Scandinavian countries courtesy of local clubs, notably Svenska Kryssarklubben (SXK – Sweden), Kongelig Norsk Båtforbund and Oslo Friluftsråd (Norway) and Dansk Sejlunion (Denmark). This is generally a service to members only. The Cruising Association is affiliated with SXK and members can apply for one of the seasonal stickers. There are many anchorages along Norwegian and Swedish coasts of Skagerrak and Kattegat. These get crowded in season and yachts usually anchor from stern and take lines ashore from bow.

ROUTES

ROUTE 1 GERMAN FRISIAN ISLANDS – RIVER ELBE
Offshore
Borkum can be reached through the Westerems at all states of the tide, but in strong onshore winds approach should be made on the flood. Norderney can most seasons be reached at all states of the tide, but the two approach channels are shallow, they frequently change course and entry is not advisable in onshore winds above Force 4. Helgoland can be entered in all weather conditions. The *Seegats* to Langeoog, Spiekeroog and Wangerooge have shallow bars and should only be attempted in calm weather on last 2hrs of rising tide. The Elbe, with its strong tidal streams, is usually approached from Norderney or Helgoland. Yachts should keep well clear of TSSs in the German Bight. The waters are closely monitored by authorities and on-the-spot fines are issued for infringement of regulations. On passage N of the Frisian Islands yachts should stay in the Inshore Traffic Zone and keep at least 1M S of the TSS. Contact German Bight Traffic VHF 79 (W) or 80 (E) if you need to pass closer than this or want to cross the TSS. On passage from E Frisian Islands to Helgoland passing E of buoy TG 9 will keep you clear of TSS. When motor-sailing point-down cone must be shown.

Inshore
The Wattensee S of the E Frisian Islands is well known to yachtsmen as the scene of Erskine Childers' *Riddle of the Sands* and Sam Llewellyn's follow-up *The Shadow in the Sands*. The channels behind the islands offer an interesting passage for yachts with limited draught. Much of the Wattensee is a Nature Reserve. Passage is generally allowed HW ±3hrs (Zone 1), but there are conservation areas for birds and seals where entry is not permitted in summer months. There is a distinct pattern to the channels, with a watershed towards the E end of each island with a drying height of approx 1m. The channels are marked by buoys except for drying areas which are marked by withies. Boats with draught 1·5m can usually pass S of the islands Langeoog, Spiekeroog and Wangerooge at *mittleren Tide-Hochwasser* (MHW), while even deeper draught boats pass S of the islands between river Ems and Norderney. The passage S of Baltrum, between Norderney and Langeoog, has less water and boats with draught >1.3m will struggle. It is usually not possible to pass more than one watershed on each tide. The channels are constantly changing and charts may be unreliable. Local information should be sought before attempting these passages. There is a canal system connecting the rivers Elbe, Weser/Jade and Ems, with height and depth restrictions.

River Elbe
The Elbe is bounded by shoals and sandbanks that run far out to sea. Very severe seas occur in wind over tide conditions and with W or NW winds the river should not be entered until the flood has begun. Until then keep W of the Elbe RW Lt buoy. A vessel passing the Elbe RW buoy at Helgoland HW -0500 will normally carry the flood up the 25M to Cuxhaven for 7hrs or the 40M to Brunsbüttel for 8hrs. Stay well clear of the Elbe Approach TSS. The channel E of the TSS is well buoyed but traffic is heavy. Keep right over to stb side of channel outside but close to the buoys and if necessary cross the shipping lanes at right angles. Monitor VHF 80 (German Bight Traffic) in approaches, as you pass up the river VHF 71 (Cuxhaven Elbe Traffic) then VHF 68 (Brunsbüttel Elbe Traffic).

Current water depths and tidal predictions
Depths at Seegats at MLW and the watersheds in the Watts at MHW are regularly monitored by surveying vessel *Lütjeoog*. The information is posted at hbr offices in the islands and usually published on local websites such as www.wattsegler.de and

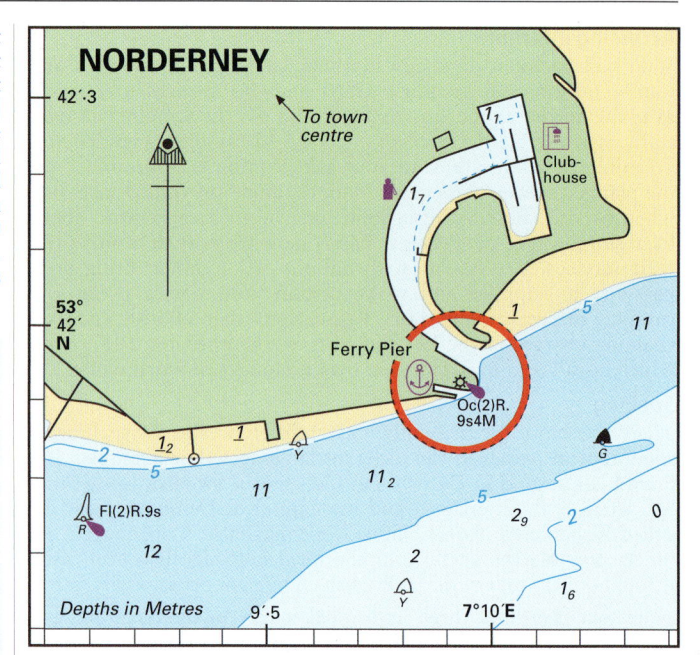

www.wattenschipper.de. Information may also be had from HM at Norderney. For a passage S of the islands information of current tidal heights and 24h predictions essential and usually posted at hbr offices. Also available from www.bsh.de [*Meeresdaten*] [*Vorhersagen*] [*Wasserstand*], and www.nlwkn.niedersachsen.de [*Aktuelles*] [*Warndienste*] [*Aktuelle Pegelstände*] then choose tidal gauge from where you want details. Tidal information transmitted in German on VHF from DP07 Seefunk after weather forecast on working channels as listed in plan, from Jade Traffic VHF 20 (H+10) and EMS Traffic VHF 18/20 (H+50) (limited range). Generally expect less water in winds from E, more in winds from W/NW.

BORKUM

Standard Port Helgoland
HW (sp) –0048   (np) –0052
LW (sp) –0105   (np) –0124
MHWS   MHWN   MLWN   MLWS
0·0m   0·0m   0·0m   0·0m

DS (offshore) Helgoland
+0000ENE +0600ESE

Borkum Island has two areas of high dunes and the W end of the island is distinguished by the Großer Borkum Lt Ho 63m, located in Borkum town.

Approach This hbr can be approached from the W by the buoyed Westerems fairway in onshore gales. Wind over tide conditions should be avoided if possible. From the Fischerbalje Bn Oc(2)16s, a narrow buoyed channel leads along S side of training wall, covered at HW.

Berthing There are two hbrs with three berthing options:

Sporthafen Bahlman 'Port Henry' first hbr to port. Yachts with draught <1·4m can usually enter at all states of tide, but may have to wait inside moles before able to come alongside pontoon. Deeper draught yachts should enter and leave at HW ±0200. Many berths dry to soft mud: yachts sink in and stay upright. Scenic surroundings, some noise from windmills.

Burkana Hafen second hbr to port. Old navy hbr with large pontoons N in hbr. Deep with room for large yachts. Uncomfortable in S'lies and when support vessels for wind farms manoeuvre. Industrial surroundings. Smaller boats will be more comfortable at club pontoons W in hbr, report to Burkana Hafen Café.

Facilities Diesel in Burkana Hafen by can. Restaurants and bars. Bicycle rental. Resort town 7km with shops and restaurants, buses from hbr and train from ferry terminal.

Passage lights	BA No
Borkum (Grosser Lt)	0970
Fl(2)12s63m24M+F.WRG	
Norderney	1054
Fl(3)12s59m23M	
Wangerooge	1112
Fl.R.5s64m23M+F.WR+Dir.WRG	
GB (German Bight) LtF	1052
Iso.8s17M	
Horn 30s (R) (·–·)	
Helgoland	1312
Fl.5s82m28M	
Elbe RW Lt buoy	
Iso.10s Racon (T) (–)	

✆ YC +49 (0) 15154274088
www.borkum-hafen.de
www.borkum-yachthafen.de
www.burkana-hafen.de

NORDERNEY

Standard Port Helgoland
HW –0027   LW –0050
MHWS   MHWN   MLWN   MLWS
+0·1m   0·0m   0·0m   0·0m

DS (offshore) Helgoland –0400E +0200W

Town at W end of island has conspic skyline. The Lt Ho is a R octagonal tr 59m middle of island.

Approach From the NW through the Schluchter and NE through the Dovetief channels. Nov 2016 depth at MHW Schluchter 5·50m (at buoy S4), Dovetief 6·30m. Neither approach should be attempted in onshore winds >F4. On passage from Delfzijl yachts with limited draught may consider the inshore passage through the Dukegat/Osterems and Memmeret Wattfahrwasser. Local advice should be sought for this passage. For information on current tidal predictions see Route 1 above.

Berthing Hbr is on SW corner of island, a 90° turn to port after ferry terminal. Hbr is secure. Moor at vacant finger berth (green tag) or along quay as available. Like in the other E Frisian islands a tourist tax (kur taxe) is charged per crew member, in addition to the regular hbr fee.

Facilities WiFi. Restaurant in YC building. Diesel on N quay. Supermarket by ferry terminal. Bicycle rental. Town 1M worth visiting as imperial spa. Many shops, mostly clothing and accessories.

✆ HM +49 (0) 493 28 35 45
www.norderney-hafen.de

LANGEOOG

Standard Port Helgoland
HW +0001   LW –0026
MHWS   MHWN   MLWN   MLWS
+0·3m   +0·2m   +0·1m   0·0m

DS (offshore) Helgoland –0400E +0100W

From offshore Langeoog water tower is conspicuous.

Approach From the Accumer Ee RW buoy enter the buoyed channel with depths less than 2m. Enter on last two hours of the flood. Entry not advised in strong onshore winds. On the last half of the ebb there are breakers over the bar even in settled weather. Position of buoys changes regularly. Once over the bar enter the deep channel passing around SW end of island.

Berthing A well sheltered hbr at the SW corner of the island has a small marina. Enter between pierheads, final part of approach marked with withies (twigs fanning downwards = stb/green, fanning upwards = port/red). Fairway to marina dredged to 1·5m, but many berths dry to soft mud at LW – yachts sink in and stay upright. Visitors' berths at E fingerberth pontoons or enquire about vacant berths elsewhere.

Facilities Two restaurants in hbr. WiFi. Shops and restaurants in town 2kms from hbr, train, horse carriage or ½hr walk. Langeooge has no cars, hence no fuel available. Peaceful resort island with lovely beaches.

✆ HM +49 (0) 173 8832 567
www.sv-langeoog.de

SPIEKEROOG

Tidal data as Langeoog

Arguably said to be the most beautiful of the E Frisian islands. The town is small and located near the hbr, without the large tourist developments seen on many of the other islands.

Approach Apart from a windmill on E end, the low island is featureless from offshore. From the Ozumer Balje safewater mark follow the marked channel. The channel changes frequently and even the most recent charts may not be correct. There is a bar and the approach should only be made on last half of the flood. Approach should not be attempted in strong onshore winds or in poor visibility. From SW end of island there is a long narrow approach channel to the hbr. Beginning of channel marked with G and R buoys, remainder with withies. Be aware ferry traffic.

Berthing At fingerberths without red tag, or alongside S side of N pontoon. Most berths dry to soft mud – yachts sink in but stay upright. Yachts >12m enquire about mooring at docks W of pontoon SW in hbr. Hbr uncomfortable at HW in strong winds from S.

Facilities Usual marina facilities. Short walk to pretty town with 17th-century church, many restaurants. Swimming pool. Limited supplies, provisioning best done elsewhere. No cars on island, hence no fuel available.

✆ HM +49(0) 4976 9598822
www.spiekerooger-segelclub.de

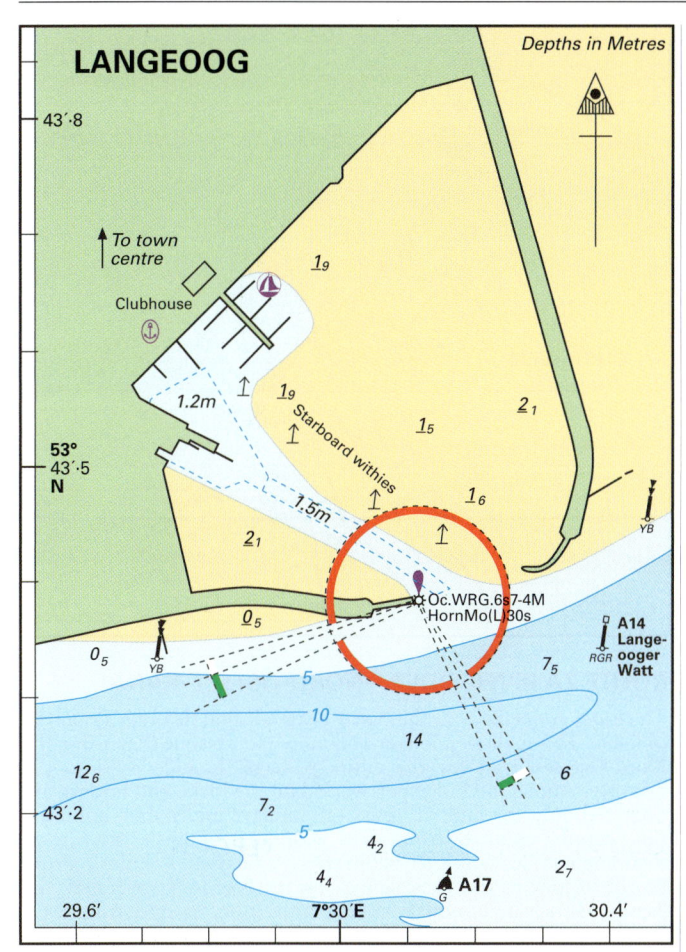

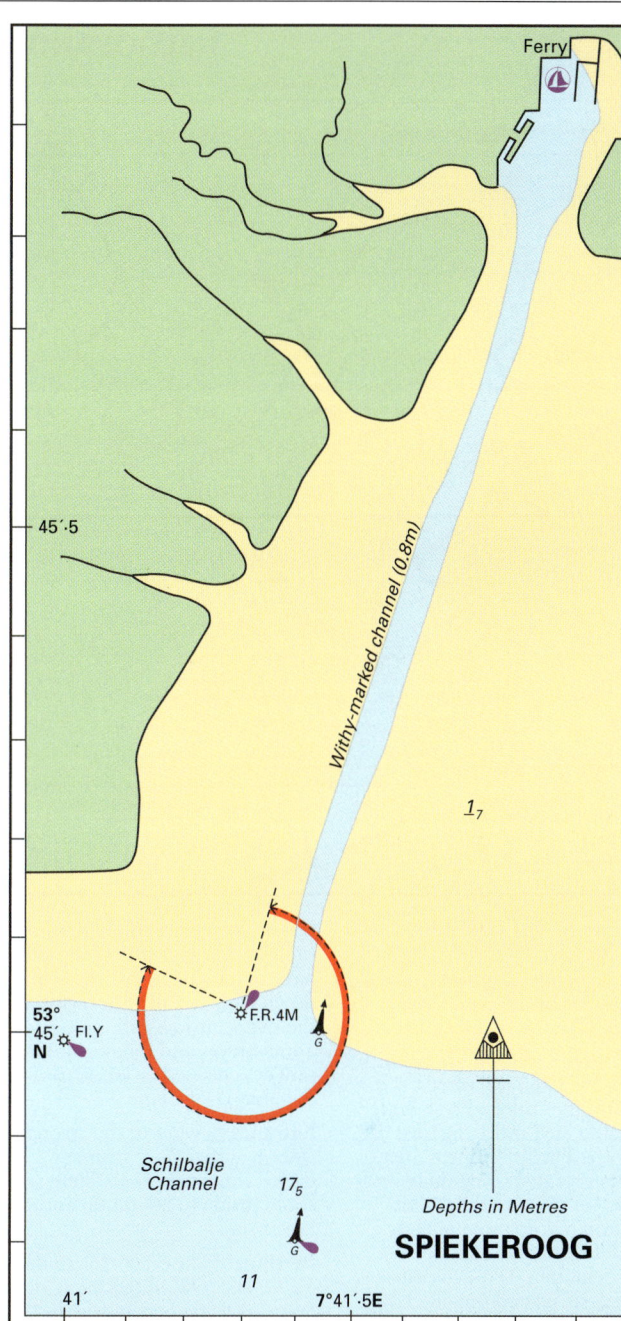

The Cruising Almanac

WANGEROOGE

Standard Port Helgoland
HW +0005   LW n/a

MHWS	MHWN	MLWN	MLWS
+0·6m	+0·4m	0·0m	0·0m

DS (5M N) Helgoland –0500ENE +0100WNW

Approach The tall Wangerooge LtHo and old tr (Westturm) are on W end of the island. From the offshore Harle Lt buoy enter buoyed Harle channel. Position of buoys changes regularly. Enter on last two hours of the flood. Entry not advised in strong onshore winds. Mole ends marked with red and green bns, W 'mole' mostly rocks on a sandy spit. Keep W in final part of approach, near the W2 red buoy and approx ½ ca off W mole. Final approach marked with port-hand withies.

Berthing Marina E of ferry terminal. Moor at vacant fingerberth (G tag) or alongside guest pontoon E in hbr. Large yachts moor alongside piles N in hbr or in main hbr N of ferries. Despite regular dredging depths at guest pontoon at times 1m and yachts touch bottom at LW. Recent extension of moles should improve protection at HW.

Facilities Bar at Wangerooge Yacht Club. Pleasant resort town at centre of island 5km from hbr. Infrequent trains corresponding with ferry arrival/departure at HW±0200. Bicycles for rent at Westturm Youth Hostel 1km from hbr. No cars on island. Basic shopping in village, several restaurants, no fuel.
☎ +49 (0) 151 234 57106
www.wyc-wangerooge.de

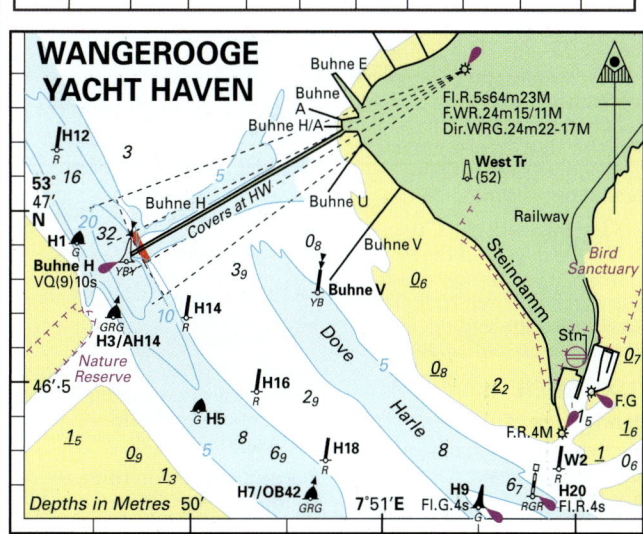

HELGOLAND

Standard Port Helgoland
DS (5M SE) Helgoland –0400ENE +0200W

A conspic red rock with a conspic tall radio mast. Although described as an all-weather hbr, there is an uncomfortable swell in E gales. Strong winds from S also makes hbr uncomfortable, especially during large raft-ups. One or other approach should be sufficiently sheltered and hence a useful port of refuge. Good place from where to begin passage up the Elbe or Eider or to the E Frisian islands. The island is duty free and popular with day trippers. Worthwhile walk on the cliffs giving close-up views of the bird colonies. No bicycles allowed.

Approach On passage from E Frisian islands passing E of buoy TG9/Weser 2 will keep you clear of TSS. Channels from NW and S are well buoyed. It is important to stay in the channels which are narrow, to avoid offlying hazards and the Nature Reserves. Enter Vorhafen between mole heads then turn stb for Südhafen.

Berthing Alongside pontoons in Südhafen. Buoys are to take pressure off during large raft-ups. Yachts <10m may find vacant berth in private YC to NE of projecting pier in Südhafen or enquire about vacant berth in Nordosthafen (Wassersportclub Helgoland). Binnenhafen usually for fuelling only. Hbr very crowded at weekends. Nordseewoche regatta takes place on Pentecostal weekend when hbr best avoided. The Vorhafen is being developed as a service port for offshore windfarms

APPROACHES TO THE BALTIC

281

The Cruising Almanac

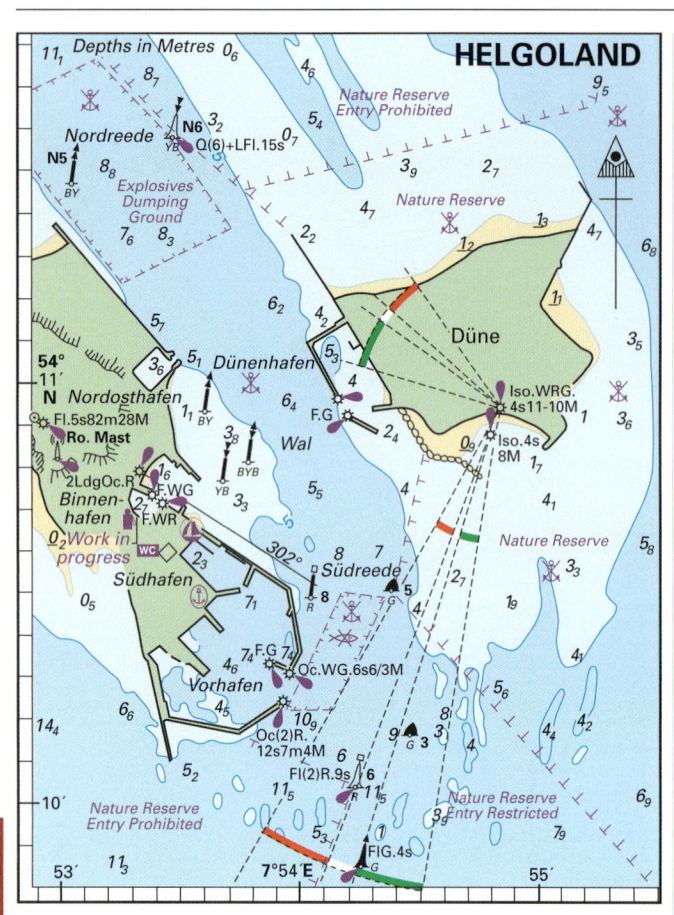

and is not accessible for yachts. Yachts are not allowed into the hbr at Düne (shuttle boat to Düne for beaches and seal colony).

Facilities Service building with laundry. Coin-operated electricity outlets. Fresh water outside HM office, against charge. Fuel in Binnenhafen, deepest water along quay on S side – enquire with bunker station before moving your vessel from Südhafen to Binnenhafen. DWD weather forecasts posted outside HM office. Longer term forecast available from DWD office above HM office but against a fee. Charts and some chandlery at Jörn Rickmers in Hafenstrasse 1105. Goods available duty free, however basic supplies other than alcohol not cheap.

☎/VHF HM +49 (0) 170 7072809 *Helgoland Port* VHF 67. www.wsv/de/wsa-toe [Bauwercke][Hafen Helgoland] www.wsc-helgoland.de www.rickmers-online.de

CUXHAVEN

Standard Port Cuxhaven

DS Cuxhaven –0410 upstream +0130 downstream

This hbr has one of the largest of all the German N Sea yacht fleets.

Approach The channel is well buoyed from both directions, and the yacht hbr entrances lie close to the conspic radar tr in front of the 23m former LtHo. At night the conspic Ro-Ro terminal is easier to see than the radar tr. Upriver traffic should have no problem, but travelling down from Brunsbüttel with the ebb, considerable anticipation and reliable engine power is needed to cut across the busy traffic lane.

Entrance Beware of the strong stream across the entrances which can reach 5kn. There is room inside to round up and lower sails.

Berthing Pontoon berths in the YC (SVC) NW of the radar tr. Some visitors' berths may be available in smaller YC (LCF) in Americahafen. For longer stay consider City-Marina Cuxhaven which is accessed through the Vorhafen and the Alter Hafen.

Facilities All facilities of a major town including chandlery. WiFi in YC. Diesel.

☎/VHF Cuxhaven YC HM SVC +49 (0) 4721 34111; HM LCF +49 (0) 170 187 1495; City Marina HM +49 (0) 175 902 0015; Bridge +49 (0)4721 500 120, VHF 69. www.svconline.de www.lcf-cuxhaven.de www.marina-cux.de

For information on route to Hamburg see p.307.

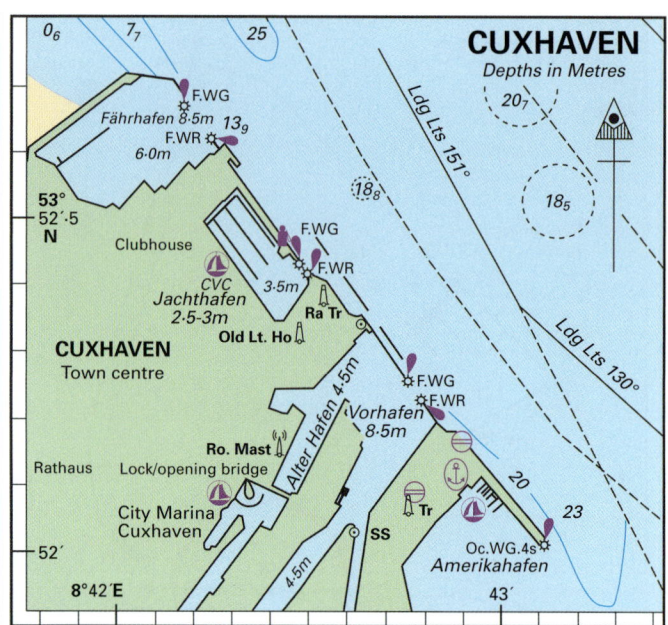

ROUTE 2A RIVER EIDER – NORD-OSTSEE-KANAL

The Eider connects with the Nord-Ostsee-Kanal through a number of locks. This is slower, longer and more picturesque than using the Nord-Ostsee-Kanal for the entire passage. It adds 30M to the distance. Above the Eidersperrwerk dam the locks and bridges are operated only for limited hours on Sundays and public holidays. For details enquire from HM Tönning or visit www.wsa-toenning.wsv.de (links to Schiffart – Schleusen – Eider). From Nordfeld lock to the Gieslau lock on the Nord-Ostsee-Kanal, the canalized river is peaceful with numerous mooring opportunities.

Note Gieselau lock has been closed for repairs.; these are scheduled to be completed by summer 2017, but yachtsmen should confirm lock is operating before committing themselves to this route, see official web site www.de/wsa-bb [Der Nord-Ostsee Kanal][Schleusen][Gieselauschleuse] or relevant *Pilot and Harbour Guides in local languages* above.

TÖNNING

Standard Port Helgoland

HW +0243

MHWS	MHWN	MLWN	MLWS
+0·3m	+0·2m	–0·5m	–0·5m

DS (R Eider approach)
Helgoland –0430 S to E (Flood)
+0125 NE to W (Ebb)

Approach This should only be attempted on a rising tide in calm weather. A course of 078° from Helgoland 23M brings a boat to Eider RW Lt buoy. The winding channel is then clearly buoyed and should be carefully followed. Buoys are moved regularly. Bend in channel N of Linnenplatte may have <1m at LW. The Eidersperrwerk Dam must be passed by a lock on the N side. The dam is for flood relief and is usually open. The river continues to be tidal for a further 16M to the Nordfeld lock (beyond Tönning).

Entrance The Eidersperrwerk lock (VHF 14 or ☎ +49 (0) 4833 4535 – 0) operates 24 hrs. Tönning 5M above the lock has a depth of 3m at MHW. Silting takes place in approaches, usually from W mole so keep well to stb.

For a passage from Tönning to North Sea local advice is to depart Tönning HW–0100. This will leave you fighting the flood initially, but gives sufficient water in approaches to the lock, at the Linnenplatte and over the bar.

Berthing Moor alongside pontoon to port as you enter inner hbr if berths available, or at visitors' pontoon SW in hbr. Much of the hbr dries – soft mud and yachts stay upright.

Facilities Several cafés, restaurants. Coin-operated internet stations at local game shop. Wattenmeer National Park visitors' centre (Multimar Wattforum).

☎ HM +49 (0) 157 782 907 41
www.toenninger-yacht-club.de

Passage light	BA No
Tönning (St Peter)	1624
LFl(2)WR.15s23m16/13M	

APPROACHES TO THE BALTIC

282

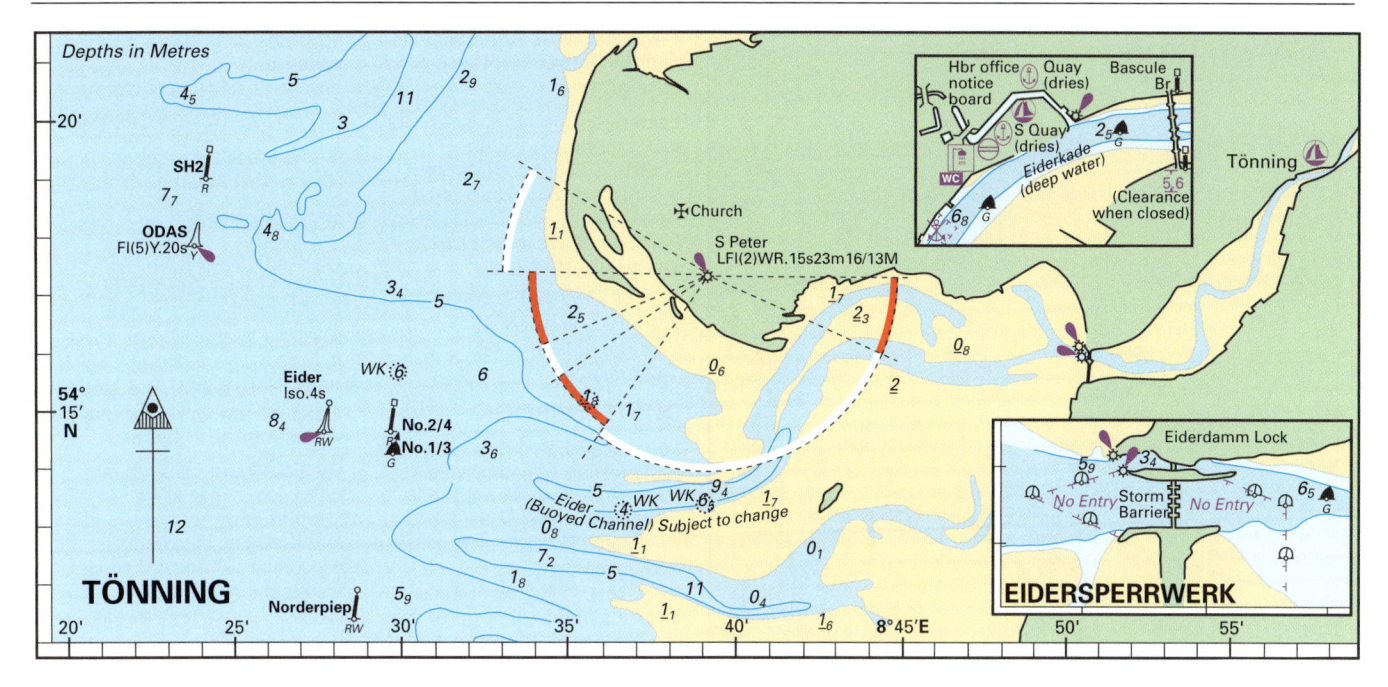

ROUTE 2B RIVER ELBE – NORD-OSTSEE-KANAL

The river is under continuous radar surveillance and police launches enforce strict obedience to the regulations. *German Bight Traffic* transmits information on weather and ship movements on VHF 79 (W) and 80 (E) H+00, *Cuxhaven Elbe Traffic* on VHF 71 H+35 and *Brunsbüttel Elbe Traffic* on VHF 68 H+05. *Kiel kanal II* VHF 02 transmits information on ship movements H+15, H+45, *Kiel kanal III* VHF 03 H+20, H+50.

The Nord-Ostsee-Kanal (Kiel Canal) extends for 54M to Kiel-Holtenau. The only locks are at Brunsbüttel and Holtenau. The canal is a busy commercial waterway. Yachts must have their engines running but may motor sail if the wind is free. A black cone, point down, must be displayed when motor sailing. Yachts may not navigate at night or in limited visibility, except when heading for the hbrs at Brunsbüttel and Holtenau or locking out into the Elbe or Kieler Förde (by arrangement with the lockmaster).

Berthing in the canal
Overnight mooring is permitted only at Brunsbüttel, Dükerswish siding 20·7km, Gieselau lock entrance 40·5km, Rendsburg (Obereidersee) 66km, Borgstedter Enge 70km, Flemhudersee roadstead 85·5km and Holtenau 99km. When visibility is unexpectedly reduced yachts may moor behind the dolphins at the 'sidings'. Yachts may also be asked to wait at sidings when especially large vessels are expected. VHF listening watch compulsory.

Lt signals at sidings
Q.R entrance prohibited, 3Oc.R(vert) exit prohibited, 2Iso(vert) exit prohibited for small vessels. A pdf file of this and other useful information is available at www.kiel-canal.org [Notes for pleasure craft] [Instructions for pleasure craft].

VHF channels on the canal

Brunsbüttel locks	VHF 13 (call *Kiel canal I*)
Brunsbüttel-Breiholz	VHF 02 (call *Kiel canal II*)
Breiholz-Holtenau	VHF 03 (call *Kiel canal III*)
Holtenau locks	VHF 12 (call *Kiel canal IV*)

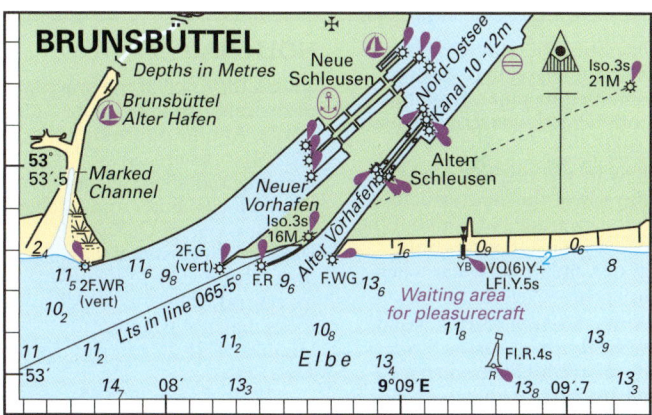

BRUNSBÜTTEL
Standard Port Cuxhaven
HW +0100

MHWS	MHWN	MLWN	MLWS
+0·2m	– 0·2m	–0·2m	0·0m

DS Cuxhaven –0300 upstream +0220 downstream

Approach From the Elbe yachts usually pass through the E locks (Alte Schleussen). This may change when the new 5th lock is completed and renovation of the old locks begins. Lock keeper monitors VHF 13, call sign *Kiel kanal I*. The lock approach is reserved for commercial shipping. There is a waiting area in the Elbe E of the locks but it is unsheltered and the stream runs strongly. Bottom is reported to be foul. Yachts may enter the lock approaches when an Oc.W Lt is shown from mast on lock island, and enter the lock when Oc.W Lt is shown from mast on lock. The locks have narrow floating pontoons.

Berthing Just inside the locks to port is the small Binnenhafen with pontoons. Some noise from big ships passing through locks 24hrs. Mooring also possible N bank ½ M further E. Brunsbüttel Alter Hafen is approached from the Elbe W of the locks. Approach last half of flood. Guest pontoons N end of hbr, dries. Scenic and peaceful.

Facilities Shopping centre 25 min walk from Kanal Yachthafen. Diesel N of Kanal Yachthafen on W bank.

www.wsv.de/wsa-bb [Aktuelles]
www.svb-bru.de

RENDSBURG
This town is N of the canal at km66.

Approach The yacht hbr is in the dammed section of the Upper Eider River and is approached by a buoyed channel from the canal at the E end of the town, passing shipyards.

Berthing The main yacht hbr lies to port, 1½M along this channel and has bows-to moorings with piles. Some alongside berths for larger yachts, signposted. Alternatively in nearby Marina Schreiber, which is close to the canal at the 67·5km mark by a R buoy No4 just NE of the turnoff for Rendsburg. There are no G or R tags; find an empty space. www.marina-guide.de/harbour/gast-marina-schreiber/. Small supermarket and bakery about ½M away.

The Cruising Almanac

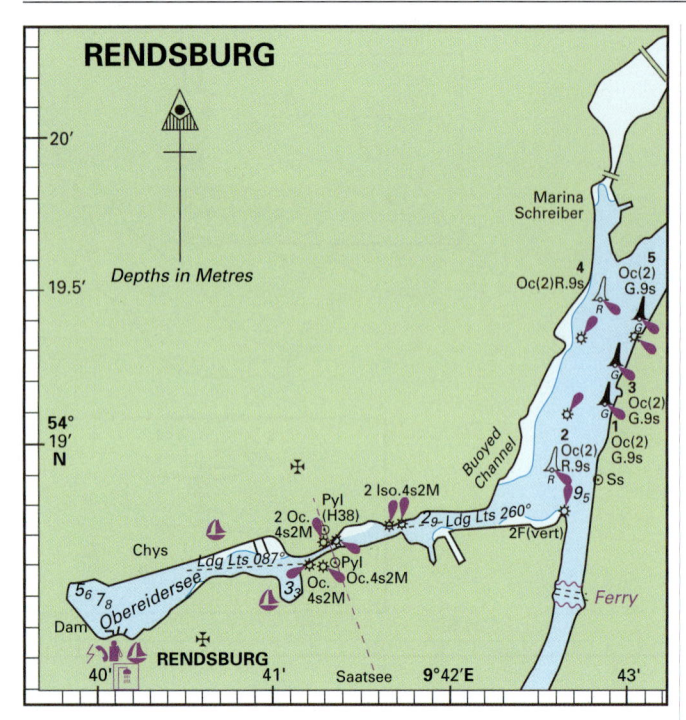

[Chart: RENDSBURG]

Facilities Diesel fuel supply in marina. Diesel may also be obtained by pump from the commercial wharf on the main canal.

Beware a transporter br near this town, the main structure has a clearance of 40m but the conveyer itself passes only about 2m above water when lowered.

At the 85·4km mark beyond some dolphins on the S side is the beautiful Flemhudersee where it is possible to anchor in 2–3m (5m at the N end) overnight.

☎ +49 (0) 433 123 961
www.regatta-verein-rendsburg.de
www.eider-yachtclub.de

HOLTENAU

This is the town at the junction of the canal and the Kieler Förde. At time of printing the old (N) locks are closed for re-building and all vessels use the large S locks. Enter approaches to lock when an Oc.W Lt is shown on lock island, enter lock when Oc.W Lt is shown on central wall of lock. All locks may not be in use (enquire VHF 12 call sign *Kiel kanal IV* or

☎ +49 (0) 431 3603 152).
See also www.wsa-kiel.wsv.de [Schiffart] [Lock availability].

Payment of canal dues for both E and W passage is done here. The entrance to the canal from the sea is often crowded and it is wise to clear the area as soon as practical. Beware large ships manoeuvering.

Berthing Visitors' berths at YC on N bank in Kieler Förde after the locks, W of Holtenau LtHo and the Tiessenkai. Up to 4 days stay.

Facilities Supermarket. Charts may be obtained from Nautische Dienst (Kapitän Stegman) at Mäklerstrasse 8 (www.naudi.de). Shop is inside Holtenau lock security zone and passport needed.

☎ HM +49 (0) 431 36 38 30
www.wsa-kiel.wsv.de
[Schiffart][Tiessenkai, Yachthafen]

DÜSTERNBROOK

Located near Kiel city centre, this is the former Olympic Marina from 1936. Largest marina in inner part of Kiel fjord. Home of Kieler YC. Vacant berths marked with green tags. Northern basin for yachts >13m. Additional moorings for vessels up to 25m available at northern mole. HM at Düstenbrook also operates marinas at Blücherbrüke, Reventlou and Seeburg S of Düsternbrook. Kieler YC organise Kiel Woche usually the last full week of June. During this week hundreds of racing yachts converge on Kiel Fjord and room for visiting yachts will be limited.

☎ +49 (0) 431 2604 8426
Mobile +49 (0) 172 802 4354
www.sporthafen-kiel.de

STICKENHÖRN

Large marina located on W shore of Kieler Förde 1M N of Holtenau. Note that British Kiel Yacht Club previously located W of the breakwater has closed.

Approach From Stickenhörn E card buoy pass E of breakwater for S facing opening in mole.

Berthing Visitors' berths marked with green tag

Facilities Usual marina facilities. Boat yard N of marina. Diesel at Laboe and Strande. Local shops and restaurants ½M walk, regular buses to Kiel city centre.

HM ☎ +49 (0) 431 260484 24
www.sporthafen-kiel.de
[sporthafen Stickenhörn]

MÖLTENORT

Fishing port and yacht hbr on E coast of Kieler Förde opposite Stickenhörn.

Berthing Yachts usually moor bow or stern to piles in S basin (least depth 2·8 m), but larger vessels can moor on the inner side of mole in N basin.

Facilities Most facilities inc sailmaker. Diesel at Laboe or Strande. Ferry service to Laboe and Kiel. The Heikendorfer YC welcomes visitors at their club ship in the N basin.

☎ HM +49 (0) 431 242838,
www.hyc86.de
www.hafen-moeltenort.com

LABOE

Two large marinas 3M from Holtenau and E end of Kiel Canal. Baltic Bay Marina is the large modern marina with all facilities immediately SW of the old harbour.

Entrance Between pierheads, F.G and F.R. For Old Hbr best to enter S of N mole, then turn hard to stb.

Berthing Finger pontoons. G tags on visitors' berths or where instructed by HM. Pile berths in Old Harbour

Facilities Shops and restaurants in town above old hbr. Diesel in old hbr. Ferry or bus to Kiel Rly station and city centre.

☎ HM Baltic Bay +49 (0) 4343 4211 51 or *mob* 0171 785 4327. HM Yachthafen (Old Hbr) +49 (0) 151 15064 563
www.yachthafen-laboe.de
www.schiffswerftlaboe.de/marina

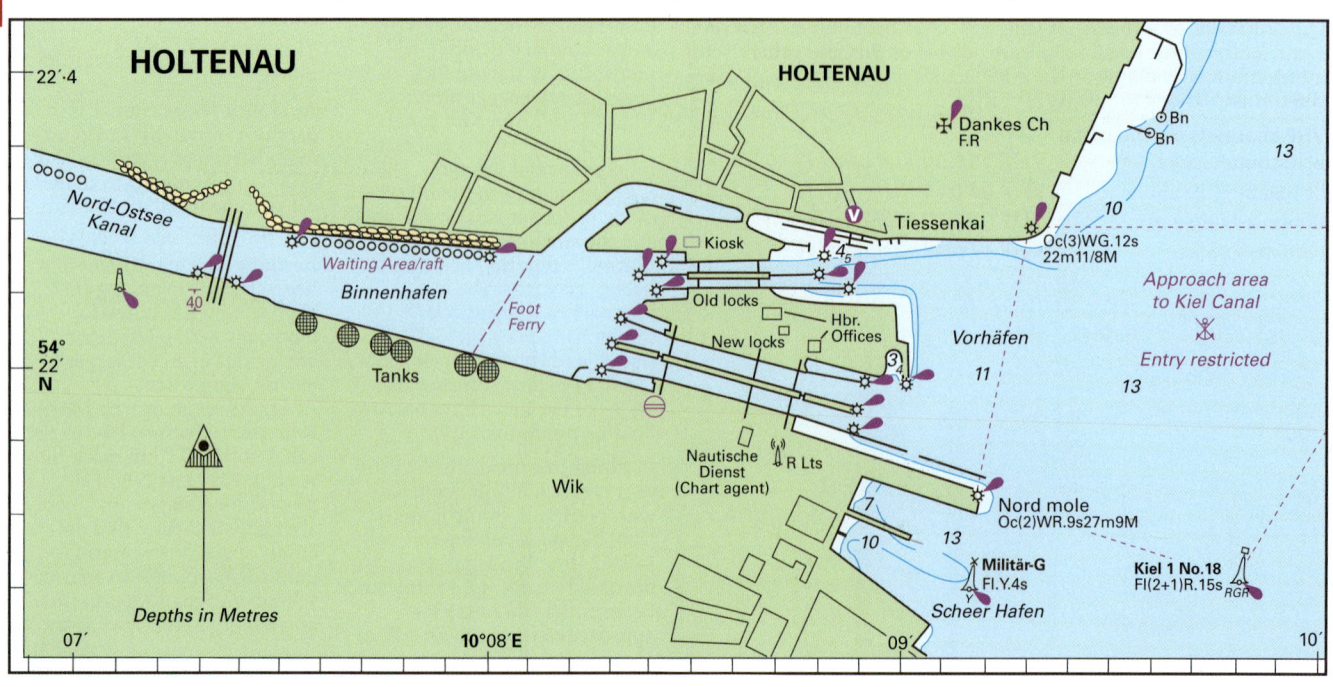

APPROACHES TO THE BALTIC

[Chart: HOLTENAU]

284

The Cruising Almanac

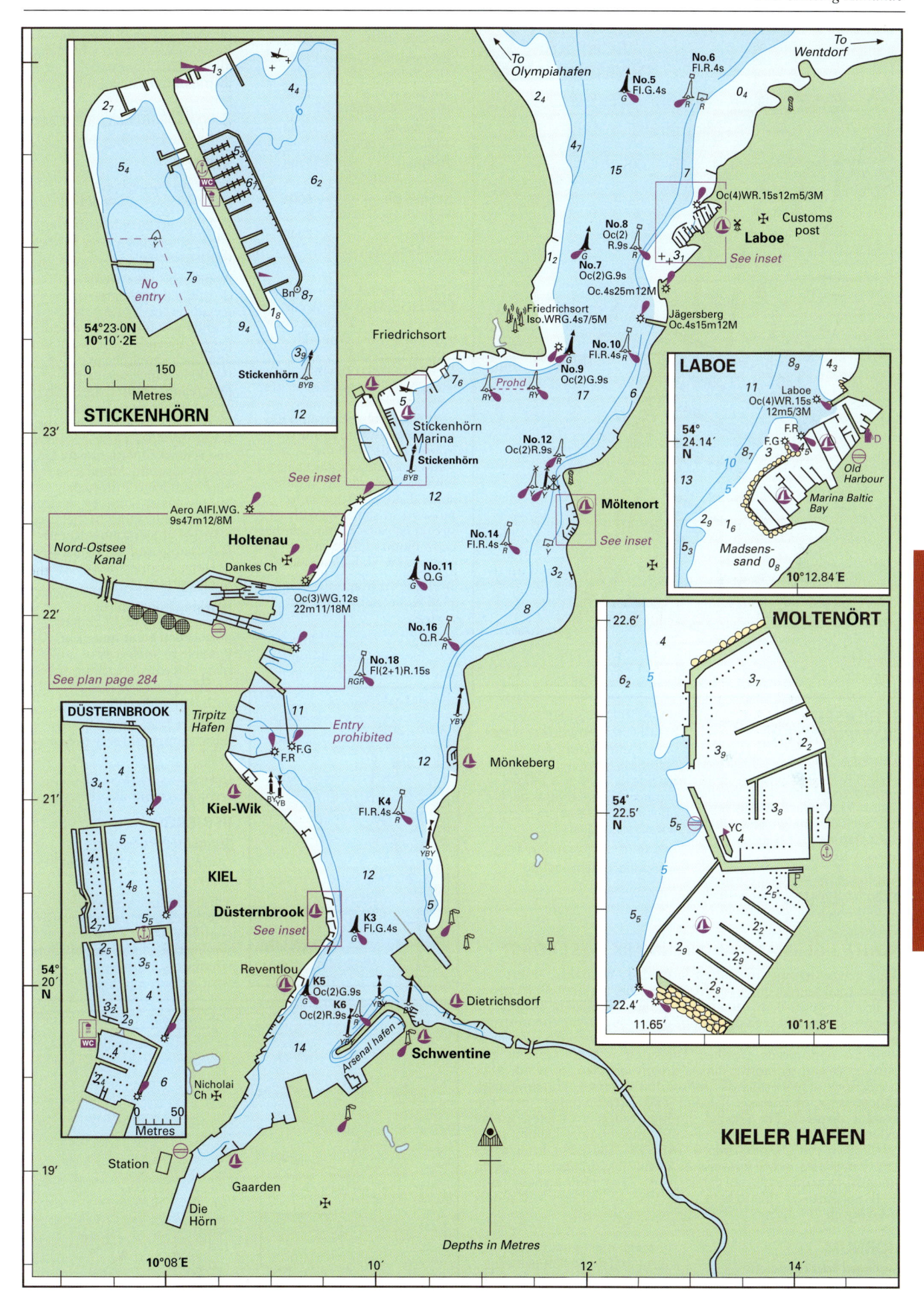

APPROACHES TO THE BALTIC

STICKENHÖRN
54°23·0N
10°10'·2E

LABOE

MOLTENÖRT

DÜSTERNBROOK

KIELER HAFEN

Depths in Metres

285

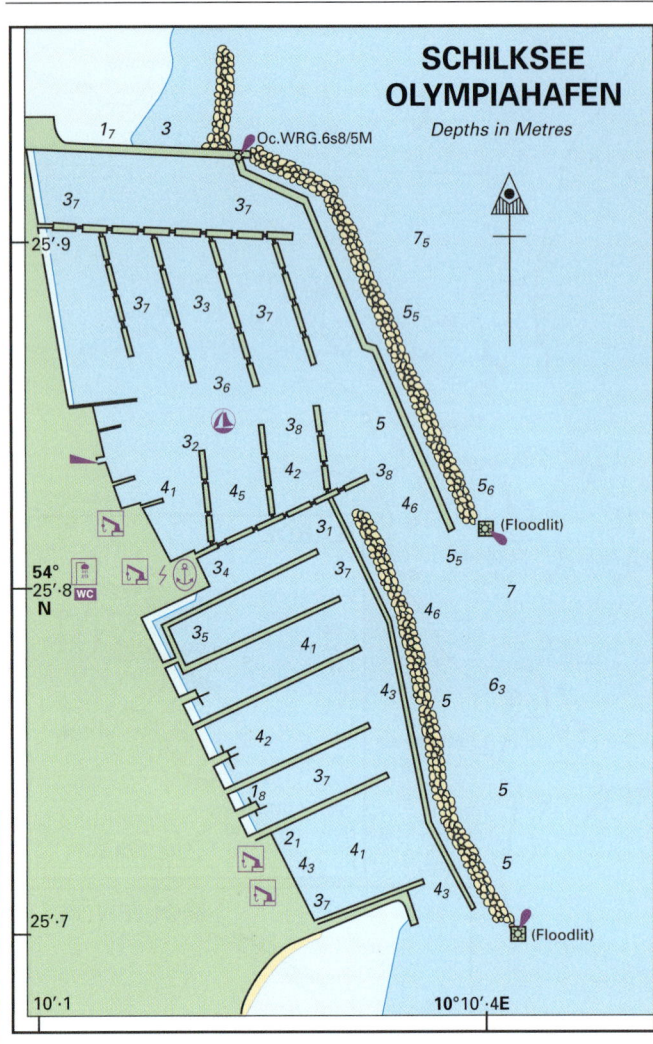

The Cruising Almanac

SCHILKSEE OLYMPIAHAFEN
Depths in Metres

Passage lights	BA No
Blåvandshuk (Esbjerg) Fl(3)20s55m22M	1848
Thyborøn Fl(3)10s24m12M	1890
Hantsholm Fl(3)20s65m24M	2084
Hirtshals FFl.30s57m18/25M	2106
Skagen W Fl(3)WR.10s31m14/11M	0001
Skagen Fl.4s44m20M Racon(G)	0002

in E'lies. Flood at bar begins HW Helgoland –0330, current initially setting E across the approach route. You may wish to wait until HW Helgoland –0100, which leaves three hours for passage to hbr before ebb begins. Final approach S-shape around low outer breakwater. From W approach through the Holtknobsloch seegat, marked with R buoys placed at quite some distance. Approach passes near shallows with breakers, suitable fair weather only. Flood Holtknobsloch begins HW Helgoland -0350.

Berthing At pontoons N in hbr. HM will usually assist on arrival.

Facilities Service building at YC. No fuel. Basic shopping and several restaurants in pleasant village. Bicycle rental. Buses to Westerland which has all the attractions and distractions of a major tourist resort.

☎ HM +49 (0) 4651 8802 74
www.sylter-yachtclub.de

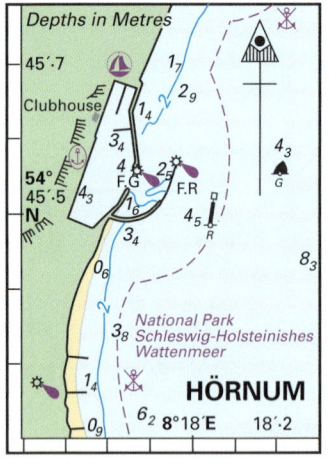

RØMØ
Standard Port Esbjerg
HW –0035   LW n/a

Fishing and ferry hbr offering all-weather protection. Town tourist resort.

Approach Lister Tief is considered among the safest seegats in the North Frisian islands as it is quite wide and deep. Currents in excess of 3kn, approach should be made on the flood which begins HW Helgoland +0300 (barely ½h after LW Esbjerg). From the Lister Tief safe water buoy the waterway does a gentle S-curve and is marked with mostly Gn buoys, some lit. Alternative approach from S through buoyed Lister Landtief, settled weather only. Once in sheltered water N of Sylt follow Romø Dyb (buoys and lit bns) to mole opening. Strong cross current in hbr mouth.

Berthing Pontoons berths courtesy local yacht club to port as you enter inner hbr. Possible to anchor N of mole hbr (alternative berthing at List on Sylt where hbr is small and with limited facilities).

Facilities Boat yard. Diesel. Basic shopping. Ferry to List on Sylt.

☎ HM +45 3136 5245
www.portromo.dk

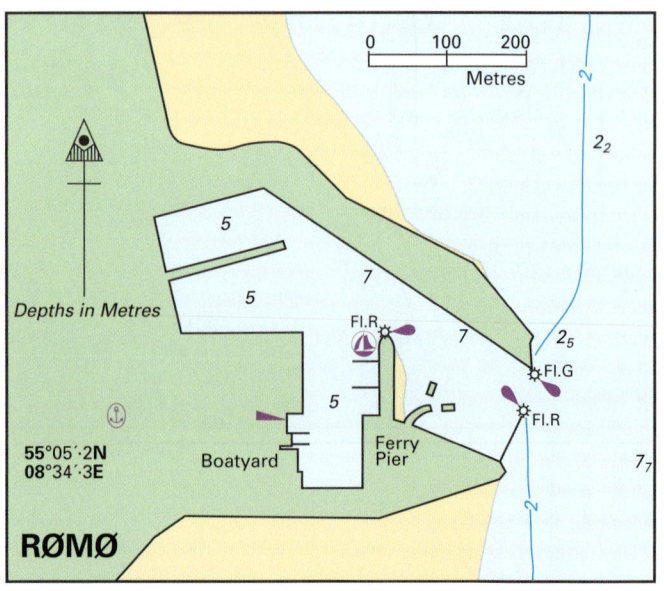

ESBJERG
Standard Port Esbjerg
DS Helgoland –0305 ESE +0315 WSW

This is Denmark's largest North Sea port and a busy commercial hbr with ships serving the oil rigs and offshore windfarms. It is the only all weather port and hbr of refuge

SCHILKSEE – OLYMPIAHAFEN

This large marina lies 4M N of Holtenau on the W side of the Kieler Förde. The Kieler Woche regatta takes place usually last full week of June, during which participating yachts have priority to berths.

Approach from Kieler Förde up Strander Bucht with all hazards well marked, W sector on Lt (Oc.WRG.6s) on NE breakwater shows clear water from main fairway. All facilities. There is also a small marina close N of Schilksee at Strande. Diesel at Strande, for opening hours see www.ytstrande.de

☎ +49 (0) 431 26048421/22
www.sporthafen-kiel.de

ROUTE 3 GERMANY AND DENMARK WEST COAST

This route avoids the often crowded W Baltic. Hbrs are commercial and facilities for cruising sailors are limited. In strong W'lies this coast is a formidable lee shore. The only all-weather hbr is Esbjerg, and even this can be dangerous on the ebb in strong onshore winds. Cruisers considering this route should have time to wait for appropriate weather. The coast is tidal. Current gets weaker as you go north, and is greatly affected by wind, 48hr predictions at www.dmi.dk (follow links –Hav – Havprognoser, choose area, tick boxes [strøm] and [strømretning] then run graphic display). The Oksbøl shooting range N of Esbjerg may extend offshore. For firing times and range enquire Lyngby radio VHF 23 or call Oksbøl camp ☎ +45 7267 1867. For firing times and range see www.forsvaret.dk/oksbl [Skydninger i Oksbøl] [month] or enquire Oksbøl camp ☎ +45 7283 9560. Lyngby radio VHF may also be able to help – call VHF 16 and they will supply working ch.

HÖRNUM
Standard Port Helgoland
HW +0220   LW +0137

MHWS	MHWN	MLWN	MLWS
–0.4m	–0.3m	–0.1m	0.0m

Ferry hbr with friendly YC. All weather protection but there is a bar to cross. The long approach makes it a rather substantial detour on passage to or from the Danish hbrs.

Approach From S through the Vortrapptief seegat. From Vortrapptief deep water buoy find well marked passage across bar with approx 4m, less

HÖRNUM
Depths in Metres
National Park Schleswig-Holsteinishes Wattenmeer

RØMØ
Depths in Metres
55°05'·2N 08°34'·3E
Boatyard   Ferry Pier

APPROACHES TO THE BALTIC

286

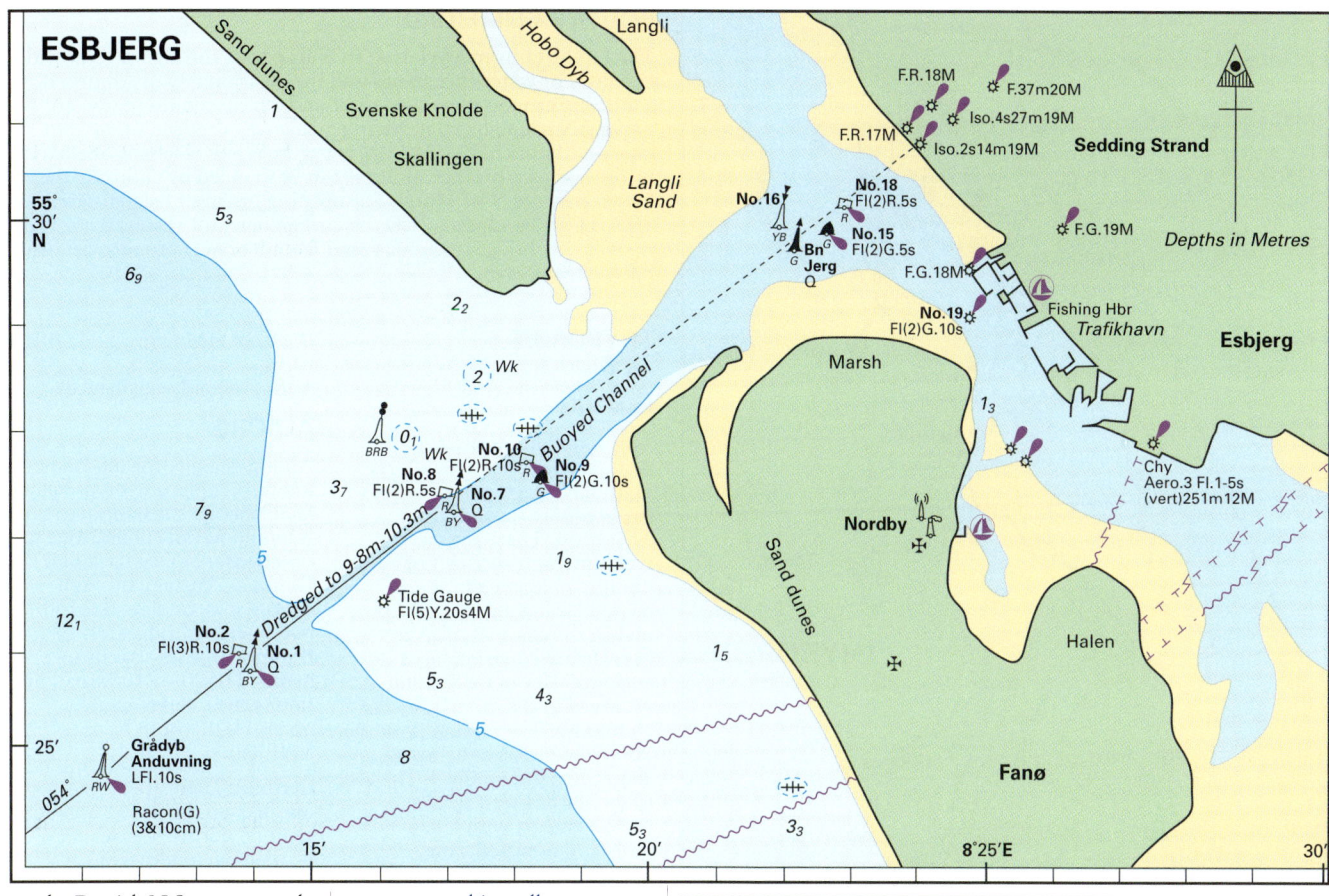

on the Danish N Sea coast and even this hbr has breakers in the channel in a W Force 8 and entry may be dangerous.

Approach The Grådyb approach channel is 200m wide and dredged to 9·5m. It is well marked for approach day and night. In strong onshore winds enter on the flood. Large vessels with limited margins for maneuvering use this channel. Monitor VHF 12 for information on ship movements.

Berthing Pontoon berths at Esbjerg Søsport by the veteran Horns Rev Lt Vessel, N of Trafikhavnen. Enter between mole heads with consp R and G bns, turning sharply to port once inside mole opening. Be aware unlit wavebreaker N of pontoons. Green tag indicates vacant berth. Hbr in industrial surroundings, 1·5km from city centre. There are plans for a new 300 berth marina N of Esbjerg Søsport. Alternative berthing at pretty Nordby on Fanø island: large vessels alongside rough docks in village, smaller boats at boat club pontoons approached through dredged channel (1·8m, prone to silting). Beware frequent ferries.

Facilities Wide range of repair facilities. Diesel by cans from road pump approx 500m from hbr, trollies provided. For large quantities enquire about fuel from barge. Plans for new marina indicate fuel pump. Rly.

☎ /VHF YC +45 2613 1672, *Esbjerg Port* VHF 12
www.esbjergsøsport.dk
www.portesbjerg.dk
www.fanoesejlklub.dk

HVIDE SANDE

Standard Port Esbjerg
HW +0005   LW –0020
MHWS MHWN MLWN MLWS
–1·2m –0·9m –0·4m –0·2m

DS (9M offshore) Dover –0500W –0400SE +0100NE +0200NW

Busy fishing and industrial hbr. Town tourist resort popular with surfers and anglers.

Approach On passage from S note current regularly >2kn in the Slugen channel inside Horns Rev, generally flowing NW from HW Esbjerg +0315. Three conspic wind turbines on shore N of hbr. Approach channel dredged to 4·5m, but may be less after NW gales. Regular dredging carried out throughout the year. Approach dangerous in strong onshore winds – enquire HM about conditions. Signal mast N side of drainage lock indicating current (triangle point down = strong current inflowing, point up = strong current outflowing). HM will advise.

Berthing Visitors' berths at pontoons in S basin. For longer stay enquire about locking into Ringkøbing Fjord and berthing at boat club.

Facilities Service building incl laundry as provided for fishing fleet. Diesel from truck, will also supply small quantities, contact HM. Ship yards, wide range of repair facilities. Chandlery with diesel engineer by small marina on Ringkøbing fjord 15 mins' walk from hbr. Restaurants and shops catering for the many tourists.

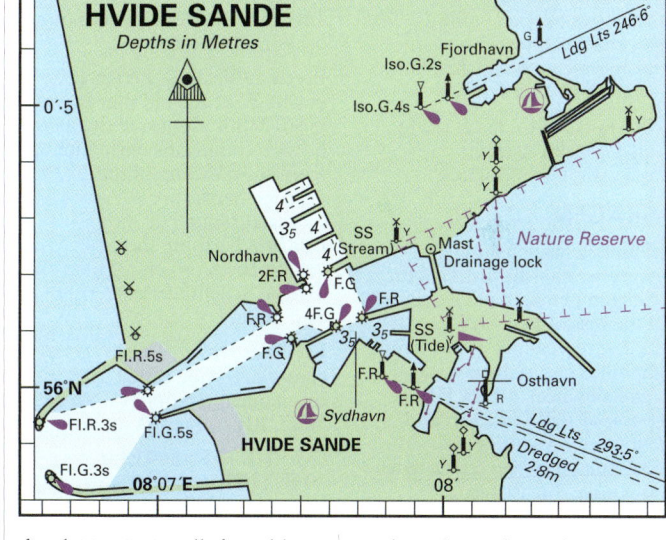

☎ /VHF HM/lock keeper +45 9731 1633 (24hrs); VHF 12, 16. www.hvidesandehavn.dk

THYBORØN

Standard Port Esbjerg
HW (sp) +0120 (np) +0230
LW (sp) +0210 (np) +0410
MHWS MHWN MLWN MLWS
–1·6m –1·3m –0·5m –0·2m

DS Helgoland –0400N +0100S

There is a 2kn tidal stream which can be increased to 6kn by strong winds.

Approach From W find the Lt buoy LFl.10s. There is a church N of entrance and conspic industrial complex and windmills S of entrance. Ldg bns with triangulated top markers, lower bn is the sector Lt – red structure with peaked top. Ldg Lts Oc.WRG.4s & Iso.4s, 082°.

Final part of approach into Søndre Dyb well buoyed with lit Ldg bns Iso.2s 120°. Channel tends to vary according to dredging. Seas break in onshore strong winds especially on the ebb when entry is dangerous.

Berthing Enter hbr by lit entrance, turn to stb and go to northernmost basin. Pile moorings or moor alongside. The hbr is commercial – for longer stay consider Lemvig 10 miles S. (Lystbådehavnen/Thyborøn YC S of commercial hbr with shallow approach and not advisable for first time visitors).

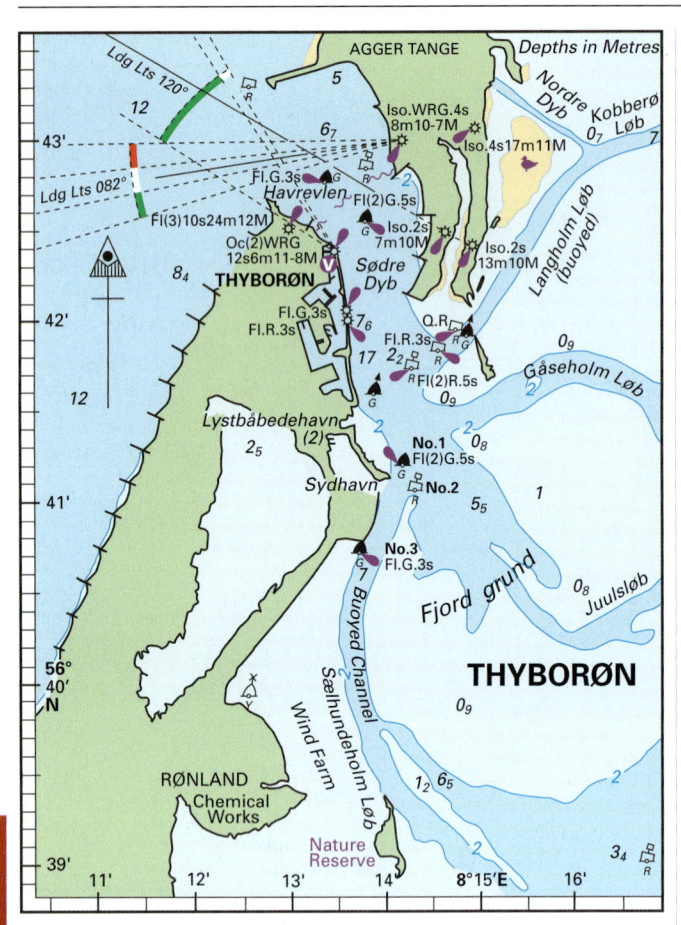

ROUTE 3A LIMFJORD

The Limfjord from Thyborøn to Hals passes through several wide expanses of water (Bredning) and the pleasant city of Ålborg. It is a cruising ground in its own right and a pleasant alternative to passing N round Skagen. Main passageway dredged to 4m, but many harbours have <2m, less water in W'lies. There is one fixed bridge with a clearance of 26m (can be avoided by choosing the longer passage N of Mors). For opening bridges Lt signals are: 1F.R. Lt bridge closed, 2F.R. Lts bridge open for vessels from N or E, 3F.R. Lts bridge open for vessel from S or W. For more detailed pilotage see Navin.

THYBORØN
See Route 3

LEMVIG

This is an interesting and picturesque town with a large marina lying 10 miles S across the bredning (broad) from Thyborøn. There is a clear water mark at the start of a 4m dredged channel and R triangular ldg marks (F.R Lts at night); the channel turns to port. Lemvig marina has a lit entrance. Room for visiting yachts N in the marina, by the clubhouse. The marina is on the W side of the bay, the town, shops, fuel are on the S. The old town hbr has seen recent improvements with a new N mole and new pontoons.

☎/VHF HM Lemvig +45 4010 0116

www.visitnordvestjylland.dk

ÅLBORG

Ålborg is a picturesque and interesting place with all the facilities of a substantial town. It has good rail connections to other parts of Denmark and to Germany. Passage through Ålborg may be slow due to the two opening bridges: rly br (Limfjordsbroen) opens on demand 0500 – 2100, road br same time interval usually opens H+00 (Both bridges VHF 16).

Berthing There are three marinas on the S side, all with visitors' berths. Vestre Baadehavn in pleasant

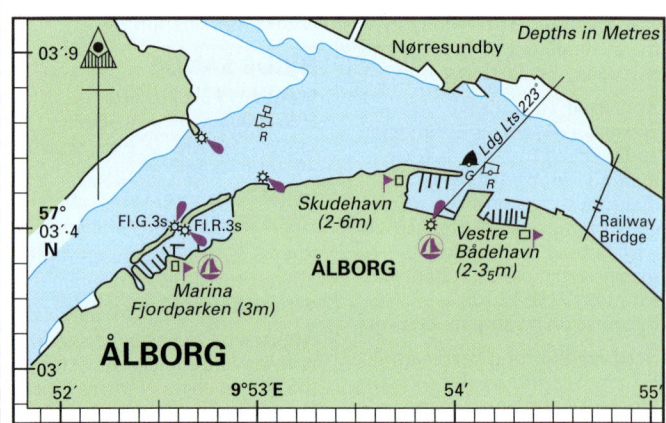

Facilities Service building. WiFi locked to Danish Met Office web forecast for Fisher. Some chandlery, sailmaker.

☎ Marina +45 9783 1288; HM +45 9690 0320

www.thyboronport.dk

SKAGEN

This is a large fishing and commercial hbr just E of the Skagen peninsula (The Skaw). Like rest of Danish E coast, tides are negligible, but strong E winds can reduce water levels by nearly 1 m. Hbr is popular with Swedish and Norwegian sailors and crowded in season. The town is a busy tourist resort.

Approach Hbr is protected by triple moles and can be approached in all weather and any state of tide. Opening in outer mole faces E.

Berthing Visitors' berths in basins W of the old pier (gamle pier). Moor alongside docks or bows to pontoons with anchor from stern. Many of the visitors' berths are overlooked by restaurants. For more peaceful berthing look for vacant berth (green tag) at Skagen Sejlclub to port after 2nd mole.

Facilities Diesel, some chandlery, wide range of mechanical repairs available. WiFi. Rly to Fredrikshavn.

☎/VHF +45 98441346; VHF 12 Skagen port (commercial hbr)

www.skagen-havn.dk
www.skagensejlklub.dk

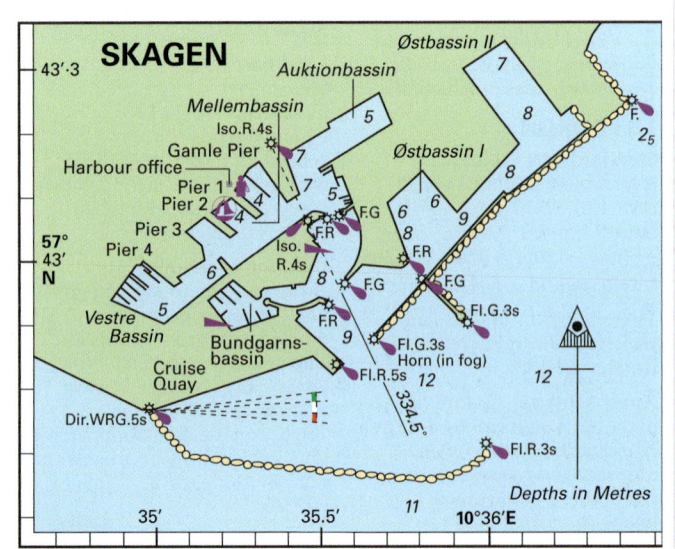

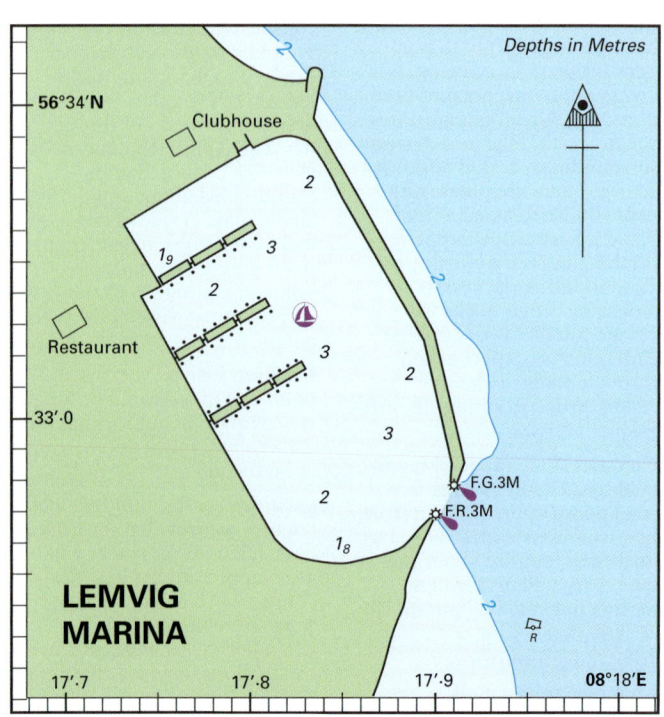

LIMFJORD-EASTERN ENTRANCE

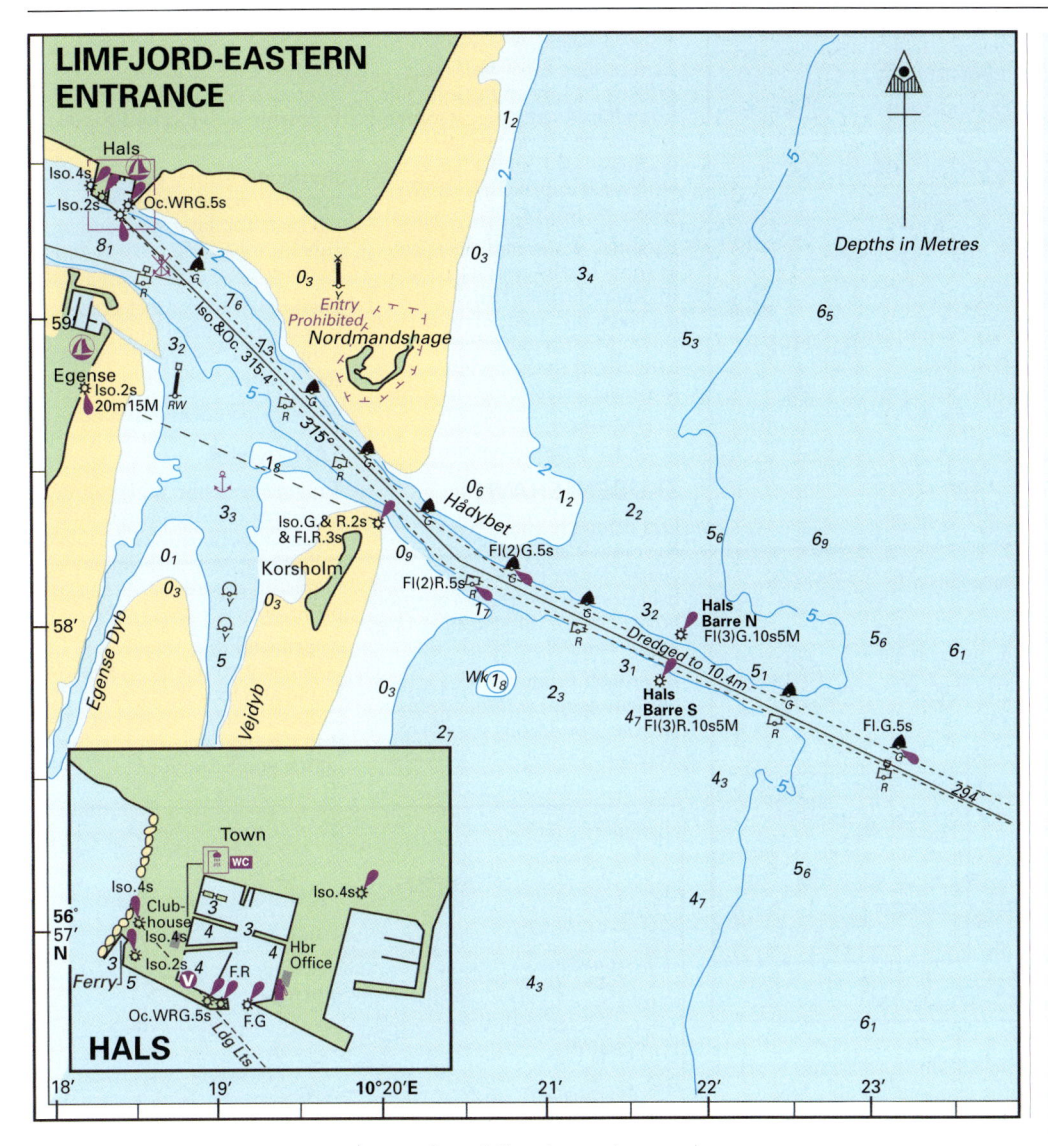

Passage lights	BA No
Denmark	
Thyborøn	1890
Fl(3)10s24m12M	
Hantsholm	2084
Fl(3)20s65m24M	
Hirtshals	2106
FFl.30s57m18/25M	
Skagen W	0001
Fl(3)WR.10s31m14/11M	
Skagen	0002
Fl.4s44m20M Racon (G)	
Norway	
Marstein	3780
Iso.WR.4s37m11M	
Racon (M)	
Slåterøy	3752
Fl(2)30s18M Racon(T)	
Utsira	3540
Fl(3)30s10M	
Kvitsøy	3246
Fl(4)40s18M	
Feistein	3228
FFl(2)20s36m12M	
(Feistein, same structure)	
Iso.RG.6s20m11M	
Racon(T) (–)	
Jærens Rev Lt buoy	N/A
Q(9)15s7M	
Obrestad	3220·1
FFl.30s38m18MRacon(O) (–––)	
Kvassheim	3217
Oc(2)WRG.8s11m6-4M	
Eigerøy	3184
Fl(3)30s46m19M	
Lista	3112
Fl.4s38m17MRacon(G) (– – ·)	
Lindesnes	3058·1
FFl.20s50m18M	
Ryvingen (Mandal)	3014
Fl(4)40s52m19M	
Racon(M) (– –)	
Oksøy (Kristiansand)	2926
Fl(2)10s46m17M	
Racon(O) (–––)	
Store (ytre)	2798
Torungen	
Fl.20s42m18M Racon(T) (–)	

APPROACHES TO THE BALTIC

surroundings with restaurants and short walk to town but limited space, especially for larger boats. Marina Fjordparken, home of Ålborg YC, long-term berthing for visitors available at favourable price (see webpage in English).

Facilities Diesel in marina Fjordparken. Chandlery. Lift-out facilities. In E-most marina Mathis boatyard with extensive repair facilities.

☏/VHF HM Marina Fjordparken (YC) +45 6155 4660; Skudehavn and Vestre Bådehavn +45 40247034; Aalborg port +45 9930 1500, VHF 16.
www.aalborglystbaadehavn.dk
www.anf-adm.dk
www.aalborg-sejklub.dk

HALS

Old fishing port, now a pilot station and yacht hbr, located at E end of Limfjorden.

Approach From E there is a deep water ch marked by buoys and an offshore LtHo (Hals Barre Fl.10s and Iso.WRG.2s). In settled weather, yachts avoid the deep water channel heading straight for R and G lights at Hals Barre S & N (see plan).

From here follow buoyed channel and ldg Lts.

Berthing At vacant berths W in hbr or as indicated by HM. Alternative berthing for smaller boats at Egense across the fjord or anchor at Vejdyb 2M SSE.

Facilities Diesel available but very limited opening hrs. Limited shopping. Shuttle ferry to Egense.

☏ Hals +45 9825 9370;
Egense +45 9831 5700
www.halsbaadelaug.dk
www.egense-sejlklub.dk

ROUTE 4 NORTH SEA – SKAGERRAK

This relatively tideless route to the Baltic takes you from the N Sea into the Skagerrak. The Norwegian SW coast between Egersund and Tananger is exposed, with Sirevåg being the only port of refuge. Between Egersund and Mandal the hbrs at Rekefjord, Flekkefjord and Farsund can be entered in most weather conditions although Rekefjord should be avoided in SW gales. On the Danish coast Thyborøn should not be approached in strong onshore winds. Between Thyborøn and Skagen the commercial hbrs of Hantsholm and Hirtshals are useful ports of refuge. Skagen can be entered in all weather conditions. On a direct crossing of the N Sea note that web sites such as www.yr.no give detailed 48h forecasts for the oil installations.

BERGEN

Bergen is Norway's second biggest city and the west coast capital. Scenic hbr front dating back to the Hansa league.

Approach From offshore enter Korsfjorden passing N of Marstein LtHo, then N through the well marked fjords W or E of Tyssøyna/Bjorøyna. Current in narrows N-going on rising tide, S on falling tide. Pass under bridges to Sotra (49m) and to Askøy (63m). Enter Vågen between G buoy and molehead with sector Lt.

Berthing Yachts moor alongside SE in Vågen, large raft ups common. Wash from express boat traffic, noise as expected with inner city location. Visitors' berths may also be available in Puddefjorden, on N shore past the 26m bridge and opening foot bridge. More peaceful alternatives are Strusshamn 3·5M W, Kvitturspollen (Bergen YC) (60°15'·7N 05°15'·0E) or Lysevågen (60°12'·9N 05°21'·5E). The airport is a 45 minute drive S of Bergen. Several marinas nearby offer

289

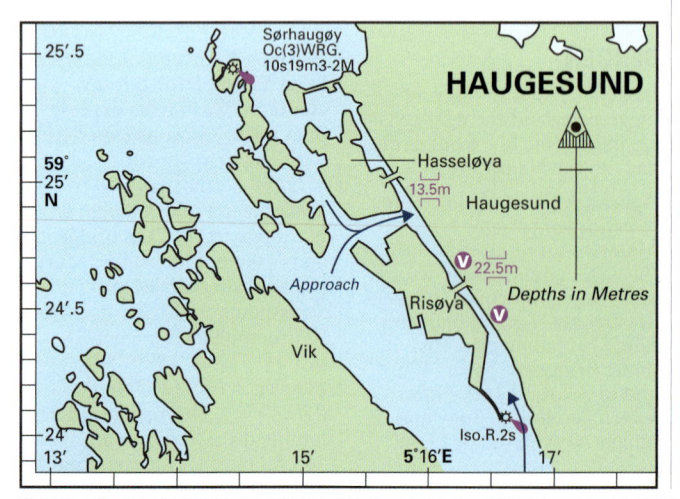

There is berthing N and S of 22m bridge. Busy with large raft-ups in July and during film-festival mid/late August. Some visitors' berths at private marina N of 13m bridge. Boats with mast approach from W where no bridge.

Facilities Water and electricity at some berths. Service rooms by Rica Maritim Hotel. Diesel S on Hasseløy. Some chandlery in town. Most repairs can be carried out in the region but few mechanical shops in town.

☎ HM +47 5270 3750
www.karmsundhavn.no

SKUDENESHAVN

Old fishing harbour S on Karmøy. Well preserved town centre dating from rich herring fisheries. All weather protection but approach difficult in strong winds from S.

Approach From offshore pass S of Geitungen Lt. Depending on weather conditions pass N of Treboen rock or S of Austboen rock, both marked by perches. For first time visit, final approach best made from SE following well marked passage N of Vikeholmane.

Berthing Visitors' berths in inner hbr basin, opening up to stb N in hbr. First weekend in July local boating festival and hbr very crowded.

Facilities Water and electricity in inner hbr, diesel pump in approaches. Several shops and restaurants.

www.visitskudeneshavn.no

TANANGER

Tananger old hbr WNW of the new large oil hbr has retained much of its charm. Mole connecting Melingsholmen to mainland provides all weather protection.

Approach From Jærens Rev Lt buoy lay a course W of Feistein Lt Ho and into W sector at Kolneshl LtHo and sheltered water. Remaining approach taking you S and E of

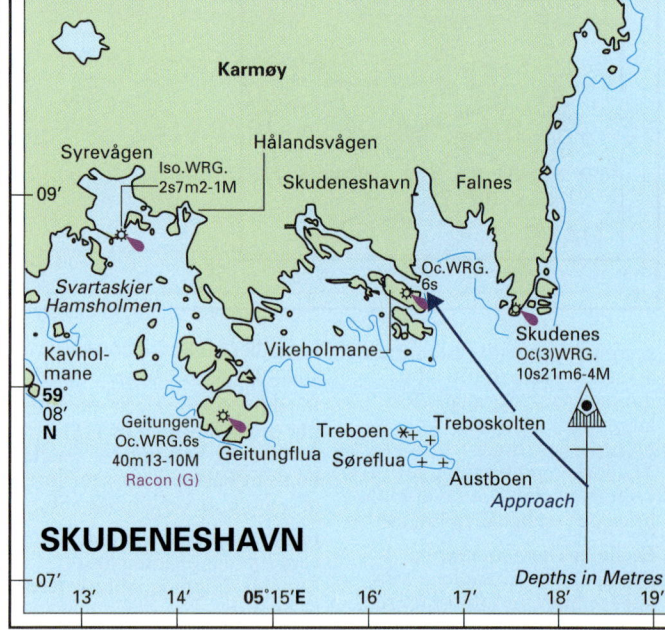

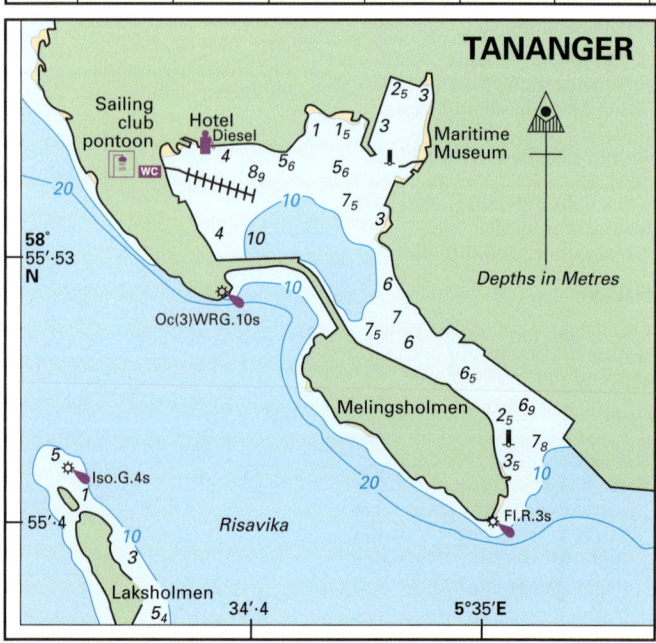

decent rates and basic facilities, including Hjellestad (60°15′·4N 05°14′·3E).

Facilities Water, diesel, some electricity outlets, service building. Chandlery, sailmaker out of town centre. Fish market.

☎ HM +47 5556 8980, +47 95 98 99 80;
www.bergenhavn.no
YC +47 5552 7270;
www.bergens-seilforening.no

HAUGESUND

Town with many facilities supporting fisheries and offshore oil industry. Hbr offers all weather protection. Good place to wait for suitable conditions for passage N across the exposed sea area Sletta.

Approach From N using the main shipping channel passing between NE Karmøy and Vibrandøya or the small craft approach passing E of Sørhaugøy and Gardsøy. From S up Karmsundet under 45m bridge in Salhusstraumen. Current greatly influenced by wind but generally S going current from 3hrs before HW, N going from 3hrs after HW. Final approach from W between Hasseløya and Risøya or from S between Østre Storesundflu and mainland.

Berthing Berth alongside on E side of Smedasundet, the sound between Risøya and mainland.

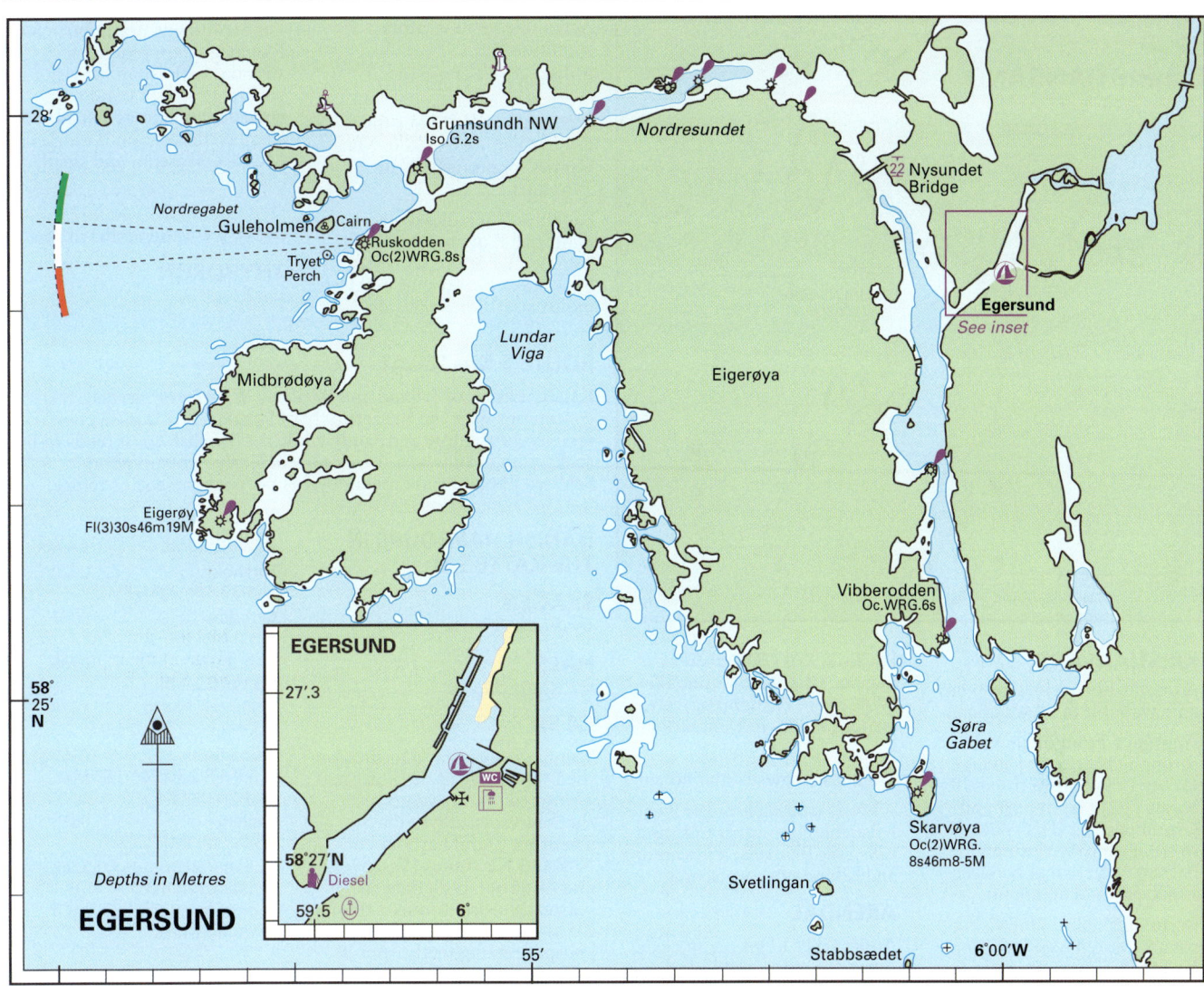

Melingsholmen keeping Melingshl Lt and perch to port.

Berthing Alongside mole S of pilot boat and lifeboat. Alongside wood dock and pontoon by service building NW in hbr. At vacant pontoon berths at local boat club N in hbr. Outside Hummeren Hotel NE in hbr.

Facilities Diesel – key for pump at Hummeren hotel. WiFi in hotel lobby. Shops, restaurant, bus to Sola Airport and Stavanger.

www.tanangerhavn.no
☎ Boat Club +47 911 40 216

EGERSUND

Useful hbr offering all weather protection on an otherwise exposed coast. Ship building and repair facilities serving fishing fleet.

Approaches From W and N through Nordregabet, passing S of cairn on Guleholmen and N of perch on Tryet, in W sector of Ruskodden Lt. Yachts with air draught >22m use S approach due to br. S approach through Søragabet, keeping clear of Stabbsædet and shallows E of this before passing between Skarvøy Lt and mainland. S approach preferable in strong westerlies.

Berthing Pontoons NE in hbr past church, marked 'Gjestebrygge'. Larger yachts moor alongside docks NE of lifeboat and pilot vessel. Anchorage in public recreation area at Gyrahamn in Nordregabet, position 58°28'·0N 05°51'·1E or, for more swinging room, in Kvernavågen 1M to the E of position given.

Facilities Diesel, chandlery, Rly. Customs.

☎ HM +47 4815 2573
www.egersund.gjestehavn.com

MANDAL

A landlocked river hbr, totally protected and available in all weathers. Popular summer resort.

Approach From the seaward, identify Ryvingen LtHo, conspic R metal tr with white band. Steer 350°, with major islands to stb and rocks and skerries to port, altering slightly as necessary. All relevant hazards show above water. Sjøsanden beach W of river mouth conspic.

Entrance Keep mid-channel, beware of outgoing current.

Berthing At pontoons or fendered docks NW in hbr before pedestrian lifting bridge.

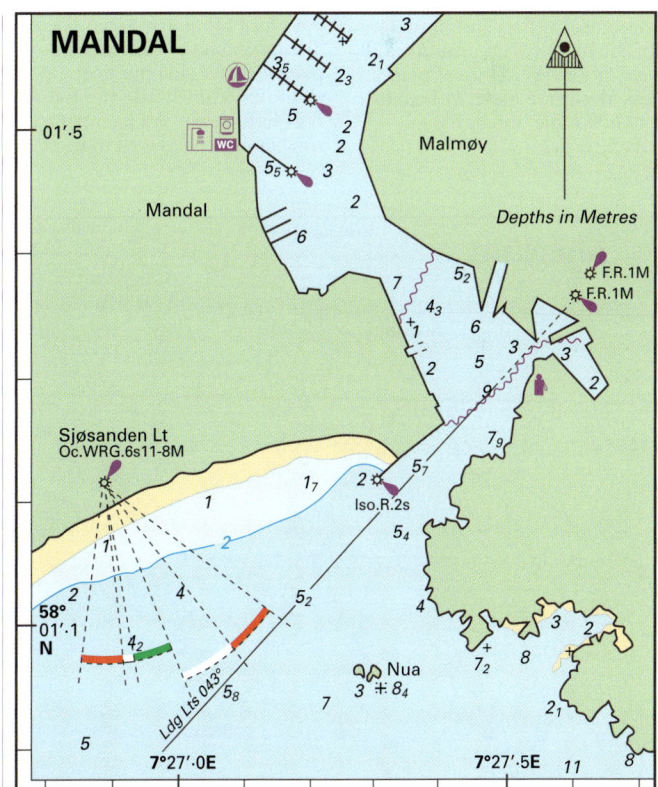

Facilities Ship and yacht repair facilities. Diesel SE in hbr. Buses to Kristiansand.

☎ HM +47 982 47 262/ +47 4000 5152

www.mandal.kommune.no/gjestehavn

291

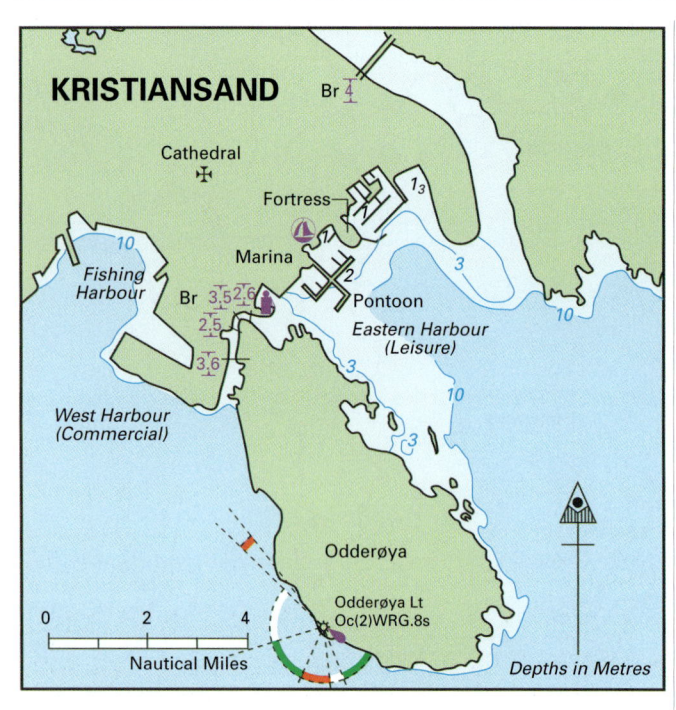

KRISTIANSAND

A double hbr set in a deep bay and available in all weathers.

Approach From offshore through Østergapet leaving Oksøy Lt (W metal tr with R bands Fl(2)45s) to port and Grønningen Lt (Fl(2)WRG.10s) to stb. From SW through the narrow Vestergabet between Flekkerøy and mainland.

Berthing Facilities for visiting yachts located near city centre E of Odderøya. SW of old fort (Christiansholm). Fort floodlit at night. Lt (F.R) end of mole. Inside mole two pontoons and pile moorings 2m most places, less alongside mole. Pontoons outside mole untenable in strong S'lies.

Facilities WiFi. Diesel W of marina. Chandlery. Sailmaker. Wide range of shopping. Rly, airport, ferries to Denmark.

☎ HM +47 3802 0715
kristiansandgjestehavn.no/en/

A lovely cruising area lies E of Kristiansand towards Lillesand called the Blindleia. It lies among and behind offshore islands.

ARENDAL

Approaches LHos on Store (ytre) Torungen and Lille (indre) Torungen both conspic. Pass E of Store Torungen. Lille Torungen sector light can be passed either side but note shallows S of Mærdø if passing E of lighthouse. All hazards in further approach well marked.

Accessible in all weather conditions.

Berthing Best all weather protection in city centre hbr (Pollen), but notorious for noise in summer season. Main visitors' pontoons SW on Tyholmen.

Facilities WiFi, diesel on mainland E of city. Arendal is a commercial centre with several boat builders and ship building industry. Hbr busy in July. YC has facilities at Bratholmen S of Rægevig in approaches to Arendal with room for visiting yachts. In settled conditions consider anchorage outside small settlement on N shore of Mærdø. Museum and small café.

☎ Arendal HM +47 9075 0601, www.arendalhavn.no

THYBORØN
see Route 3

ROUTE 5 KATTEGAT

Kattegat lies E of Jylland and W of the W coast of Sweden. It is continuous with the Skagerrak N of Skagen. The Danish coast tends to be shallow and sandy while the Swedish coast tends to be rocky with islands and skerries particularly N of Göteborg. Selected hbrs only are mentioned as ports of passage or refuge.

DANISH HARBOURS IN THE KATTEGAT

SKAGEN
see Route 3

HALS
see Route 3a

LÆSØ

Popular resort island located on the Danish side of the Kattegat. The surrounding waters are shallow, especially to the S. There are useful harbours on NW and NE shores (Vesterø and Østerby), both busy in season. Nordre Rønner LtHo 3·5M N of Vesterø havn is consp. A reef extends from W of LtHo to Læsø.

Approach
• Vesterø havn from NW bearing 136° to mole opening, keeping clear of ferry traffic.
• Østerby havn from NW to N, keeping W of Engelskmandsbanke (red buoy). Mole opening narrow and should not be attempted in strong winds from N through E.

Berthing
• Vesterø havn in inner S hbr using lazy lines for stern (or bow) line.
• Østerby havn W in hbr, some berths with piles for stern lines otherwise alongside berthing.

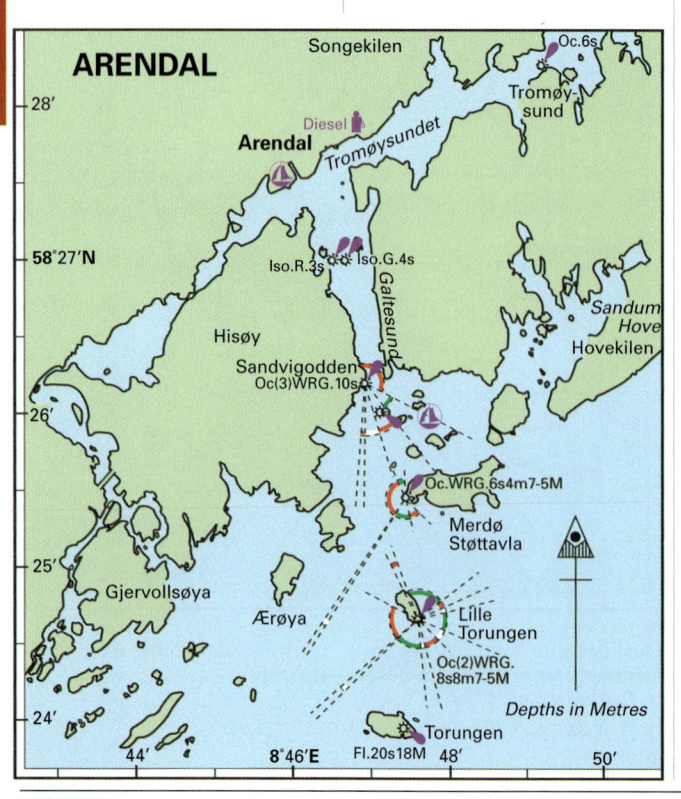

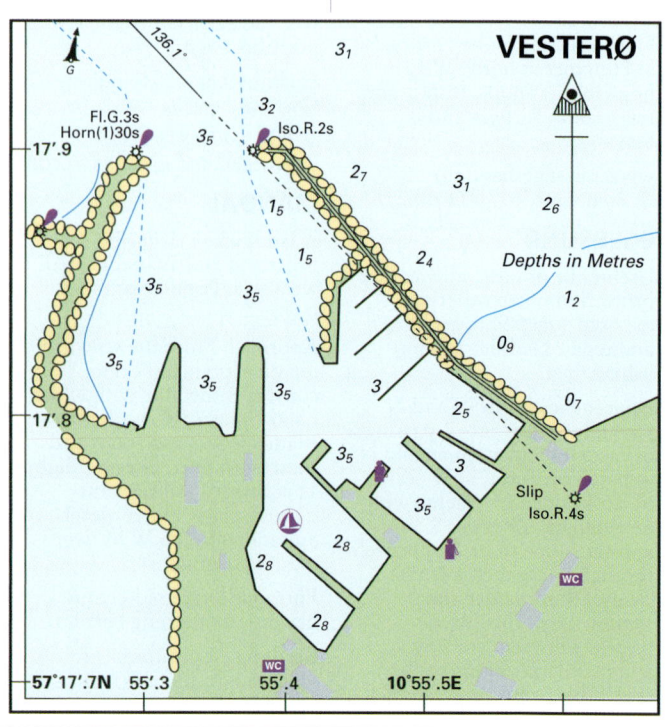

Passage lights	BA No
Hirsholm	0020
Fl(3)30s30m22M+F.WR	
Syrodde	0057
Fl.3s12m13M	
Hals Barre	0066
Iso.WRG.2s8M	
Sjællands Rev N	1478
Iso.WRG.2s25m16-13M	
Trubaduren	0569
LFl(3)WRG.30s24m14-7M+	
Iso.R.4s18m9M	
Fladen	0671
LFl.8s24m9M+Fl.Y.3s	
Kullen Västra	2262
Oc(3)20s12m6M	
Anholt (East)	0164
Fl.15s.40m14M	

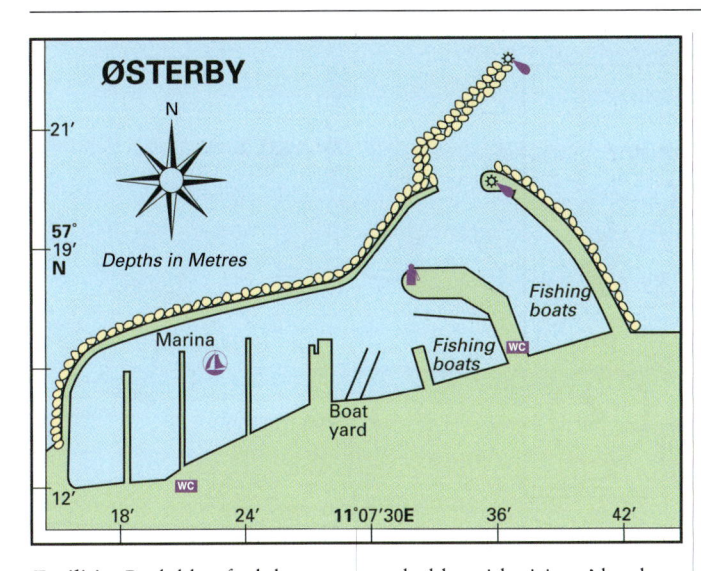

Facilities Both hbrs fuel, boat yard, several restaurants. Beaches. Bicycles can be hired to visit main settlement at Byrum and saltworks for which island famous. From Vesterby havn ferries to Fredrikshavn.
http://havne.laesoe.dk

☎ HM commercial hbrs
Vesterø +45 98499222
Østerby +45 98498027

GRENÅ

The busy fishing and ferry port lies 2M S of the conspic round tr of Fornæs LtHo Fl.20s32m21M but this is exclusively commercial. The yacht hbr with visitors' berths lies 1M S.

Approach and Entrance From the N leave cardinal buoys marking shallows off the commercial hbr to stb. Then steer towards the yacht hbr which is entered between W pyramids with R and G tops Fl.R&G.3s. From S avoid Naveren shallows by keeping well offshore, or in suitable calm conditions following 4 m contour inside shallows.

Berthing Yachts >13m moor alongside pontoon inside E mole, otherwise as indicated by HM.

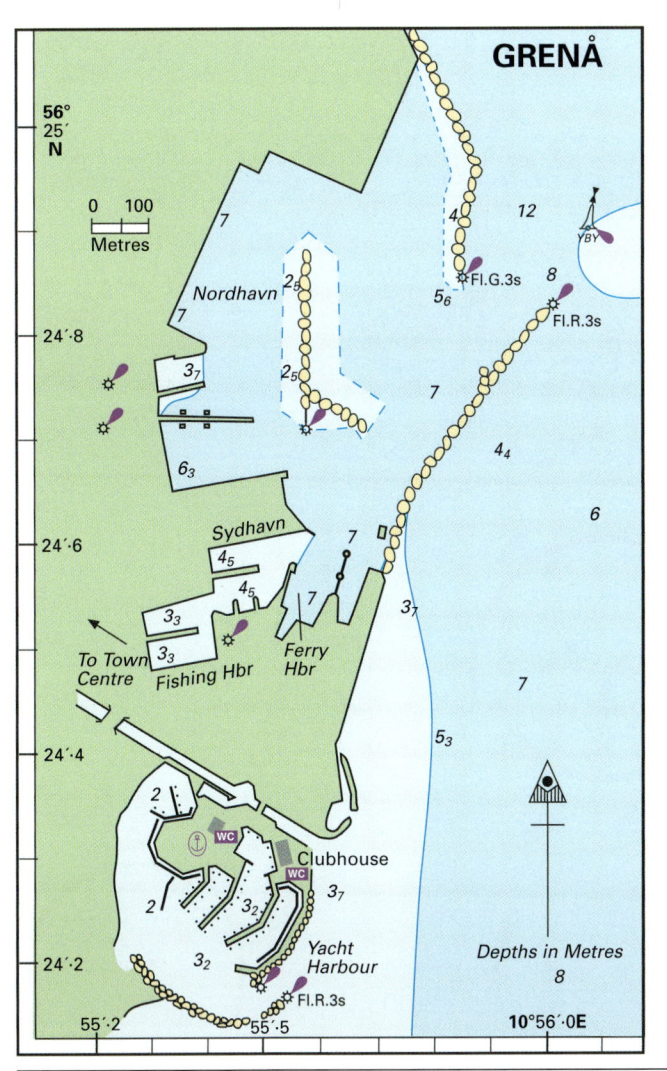

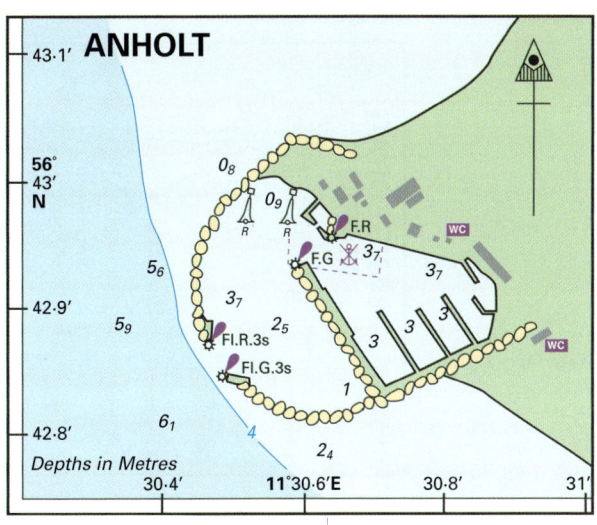

Facilities Shops, chandlery, sailmaker in commercial hbr. Diesel. Kategatcenteret aquarium near marina worth seeing. Old village 2kms.

☎ HM +45 8632 7255
www.grenaamarina.dk

ANHOLT

Popular resort island with well protected mole hbr on W shore. Conspic radar tr above hbr and LtHo on N mole.

Approach From N identify W card buoy marking NW end of Nordvestrevet. Possible approach in good weather through Nordvestrevet at Slussen, unmarked. From S keep clear extensive shallows along SE shore. Breaking seas in approaches in strong W'lies.

Berthing To stb after second mole, room for up to 250 yachts moored fore-aft. 3·5m shallowing to 1·5m towards mole. Buoys for stern lines. Anchor in outer harbour only after agreement with HM. In calm weather yachts anchor off beach S of hbr.

Facilities WiFi. Diesel. Shops, café and PO in village 2·5km from hbr. Large part of island is a nature reserve. Seal colony E part of island. Extensive beaches.

☎ +45 86 31 90 08
www.anholthavn.dk

SWEDISH HARBOURS IN THE KATTEGAT

GÖTEBORG

This is the second largest city in Sweden, situated on the R Göta. There are numerous marinas but not all welcome visitors. There is a major inland waterway via the Göta river, the Trollhättekanal, the lakes Vänern and Vättern and the Götakanal to Mem near Stockholm. For further information on Göta kanal see www.gotakanal.se. Bohuslän is a challenging archipelago with many small fishing harbours

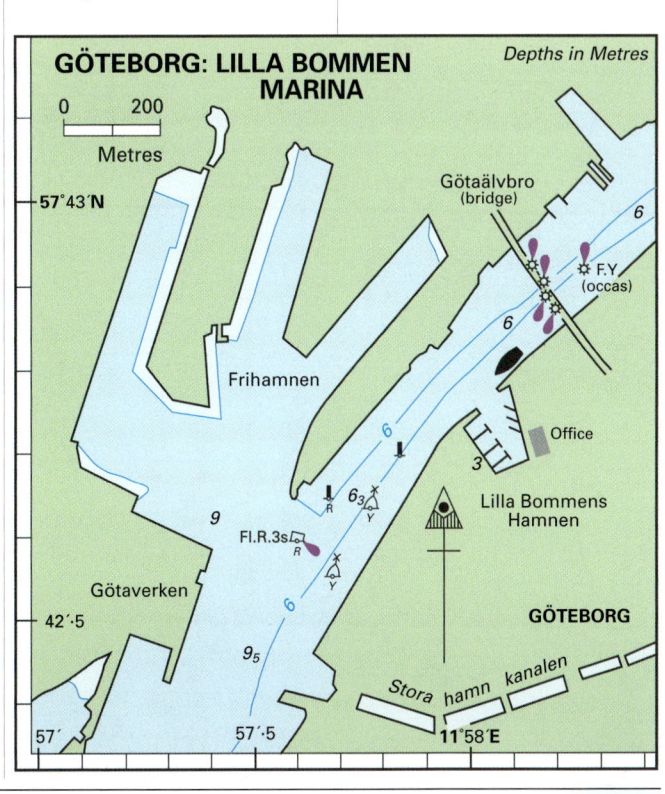

APPROACHES TO THE BALTIC

293

The Cruising Almanac

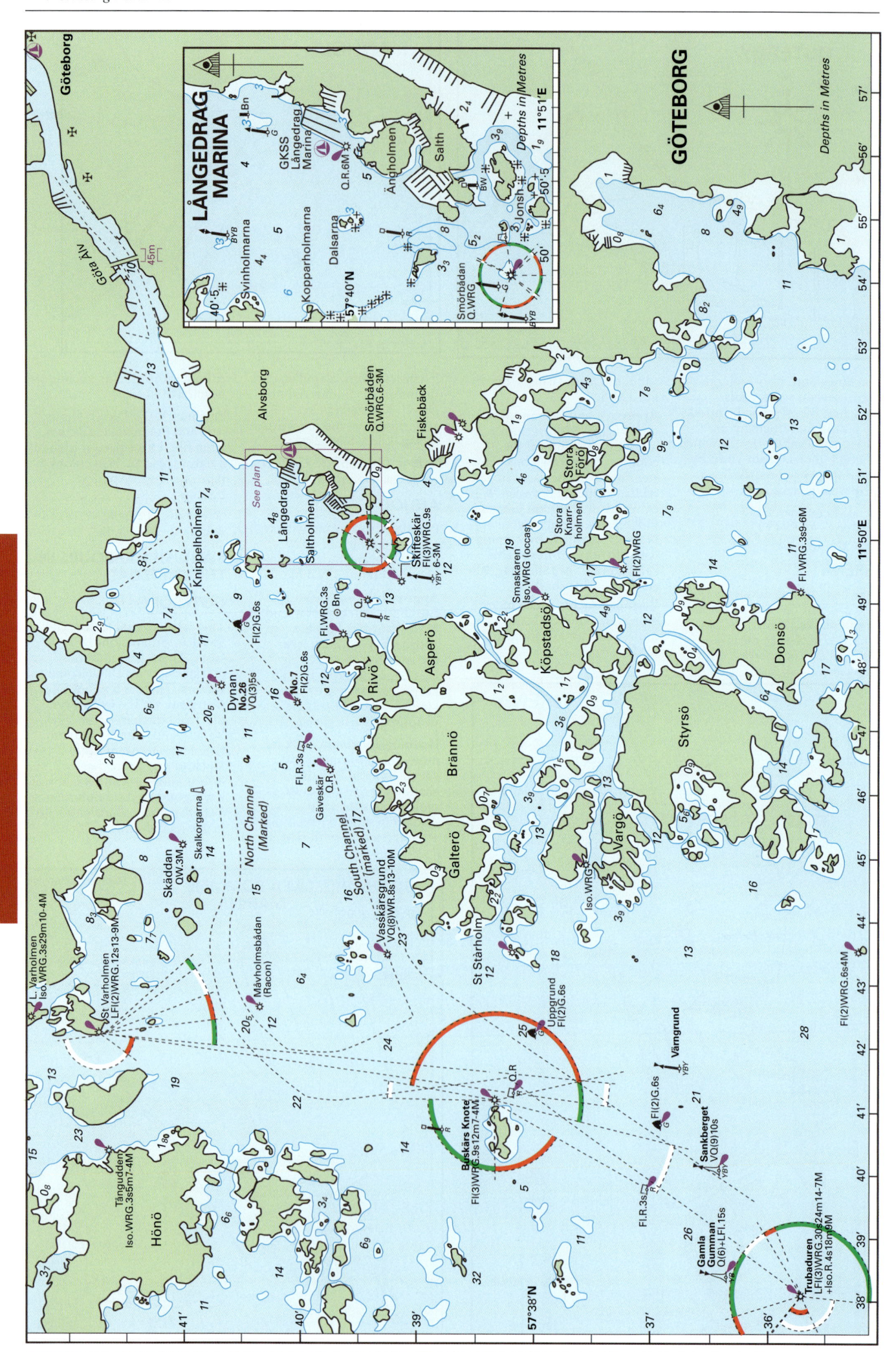

APPROACHES TO THE BALTIC

294

The Cruising Almanac

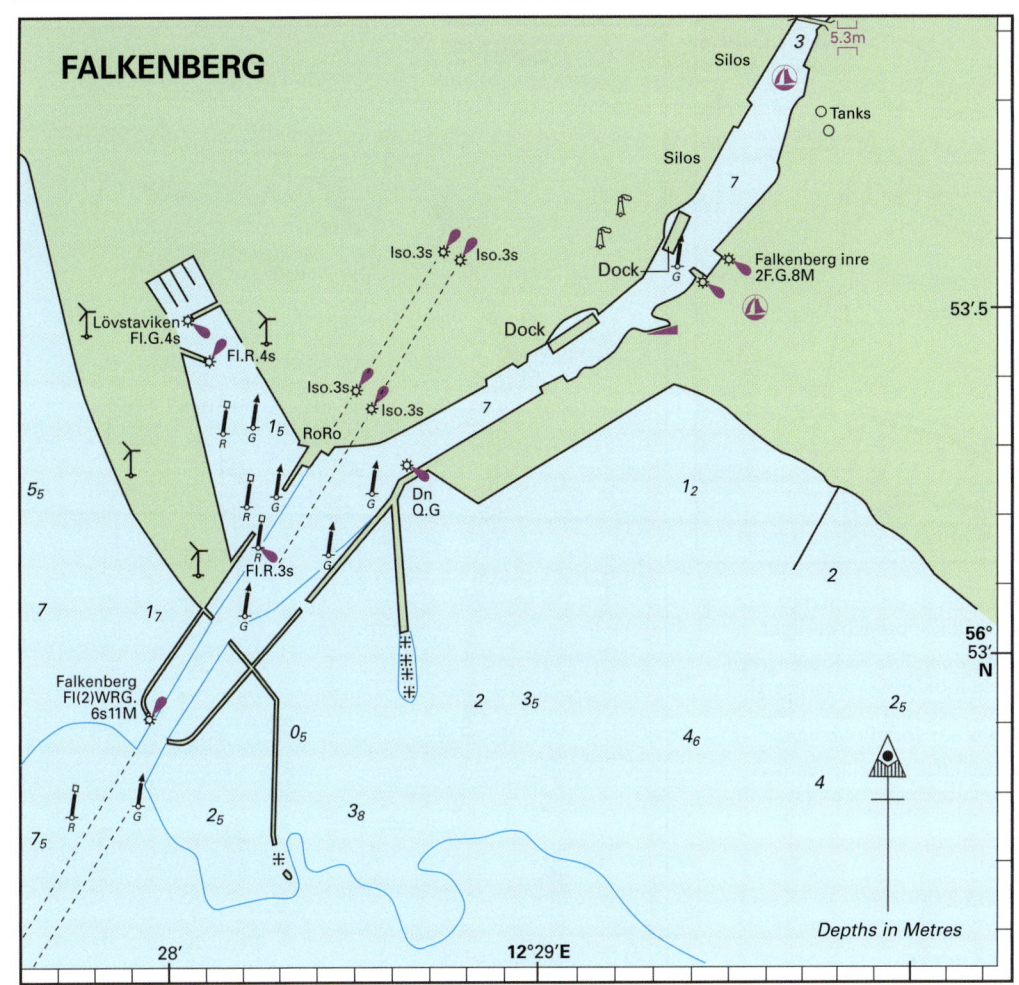

Approach and Entrance
Approach from the SW. Conspic windmills N of hbr entrance. Sector Lt on W mole. Buoyed channel inside mole. The current in the hbr narrows can reach 4kn. Listen VHF 16 for announcement of big ship movements.

Berthing There are visitors' berths at YC on SE side. Green tag indicates vacant finger/pile berth, or moor alongside wood dock upriver of YC.

Facilities Diesel at YC. Shopping and many restaurants in town.

☎ HM +46 (0) 3468 4124
www.falkenbergs-batsallskap.se

TOREKOV
A pretty, well protected hbr in popular resort town. Crowded in season.

Approach From N or S in W sector of Vingaskär LtHo (Fl(3)WRG9s). Ldg Lts until past W mole then stb between G/R buoys and mole ends.

Berthing Alongside in inner hbr, expect to raft up. Inside outer mole with piles for stern lines. In settled weather moor alongside wavebreaker in E of hbr. Yachts >12m should enquire to the HM about vacancy before approaching hbr.

Facilities Diesel. Several restaurants, grocery store. There is a passenger ferry to Hallands Väderö, a nature reserve.

☎ HM +46 (0) 4313 63534
www.torekovshamn.nu

---

and delightful anchorages lying N of Göteborg. Detailed charts are essential to taste the flavour of Swedish skärgård (archipelago) sailing.

Approach From offshore the Trubaduren LtHo (24m) is conspic by day as it stands in clear water. At night it has a wide SW White sector and a narrower NE White sector. From here steer 030° towards Buskärs Knöte LtHo Fl(3)WRG.9s12m 3½M away. Leave this to port. From NE of Buskärs Knöte the two deep water channels (North and South channel) are clearly marked. Both are busy with commercial shipping. Note that some of the lateral markers resemble small cranes and are flood lit in addition to the R and G Lts. To Långedrag marina an approach in darkness should be made from the SW using sector Lts on Skifteskär and Smörbåden.

Berthing Lilla Bommen harbour is located on the S bank in the city centre, between the Göteborg opera and the barque *Viking*. Some wash from ferries and express boats that dock nearby. No anchoring, use provided lazy lines. Just a footbridge away from a large shopping centre. Excellent if preparing for a passage up the Trollhätte and Göta canals. Open year-round. Berths can be pre-booked at www.dockspot.com. For berthing at lower cost and in more peaceful surroundings consider Långedrag, an artificial hbr 5M WSW of the city and HQ of Royal Göteborg YC. Green tag indicates vacant berth.

☎ Långedrag
+46 (0) 3129 1145,
+46 (0) 70339 9398
www.gkss.se

Lilla Bommen
+46 (0) 31154005
www.goteborgsgasthamn.se

FALKENBERG
Major town on the river Ätran. Industrial hbr with extensive docking facilities and ship yard. Old town pretty, nice walks along river above bridge and a large beach 500 m S of YC.

KATTEGAT SOUTHWARDS
From the S end of the Kattegat there are three channels into the Baltic proper: Lillebælt, Storebælt and Øresund (Sundet/the Sound). In the Lillebælt to the W lies Kolding which has a pleasant fjord and is a major town with good communications to Billund for crew changes. Further S are Sønderborg and the German hbr of Maasholm. The Storebælt between Fyn and Sjælland leads past Korsør and Bagenkop. The Øresund to the E is the busy channel between Denmark and Sweden with Helsingør, København and Rødvig on the Danish side and Limhamn and Falsterbo on the Swedish side. In the middle of the Sund is the delightful Swedish island of Ven.

APPROACHES TO THE BALTIC

The Cruising Almanac

ROUTE 6A LILLEBÆLT

The current can run strongly through Lillebælt, especially so in the N end (Snævringen) where it can reach 4 knots. Flow is largely dictated by wind: S flow in winds from N and W, N flowing in winds from E and S. In spring, flow generally N wards out of the Baltic. Detailed graphic predictions found at www.dmi.dk follow links to [Hav] [Havprognoser] choose area, then click boxes [strøm] and [strømretning] then run graphic display.

KOLDING

A major town located 5M up a pleasant fjord from the N end of Lillebælt. Many sites of historic and cultural interest.

Approach A buoyed channel leads up Kolding Fjord. The main hbr has 2.F.R. Lts 267°. Buoyed channel to Sørhavnen leads off SW from main channel ½M before mole.

Berthing There are two marinas, Nordhavnen and Sydhavnen, both nearly 500 berths. Nordhavnen approached from commercial hbr hence deep water in approach and ample room for manœuvering. Sørhavnen approached through channel dredged to 2·5m, but less depth in strong winds from N and W. Sørhavnen located in green surroundings and less noise from road and railway. Both hbrs 1,500m to town centre, from Sørhavnen reasonably pleasant walk along river. Work is underway to expand Sydhavnen. When completed Nordhavnen will be for commercial shipping only.

Facilities Diesel in Sørhavnen. Chandleries. Wide range of shopping in town. Buses to Billund airport. Rly.

✆ Marina +45 7553 2722
www.koldinglystbaadehavn.dk

ASSENS

Assens is SW on island of Fyn, in S end of Lillebælt. Large well protected marina in harbour shared with a shipyard. 10 minutes' walk to picturesque town centre.

Approach From NNW, identify the N card mark at N end of Asnæs Rev. Sectored Lt and ldg Lts for approach at night.

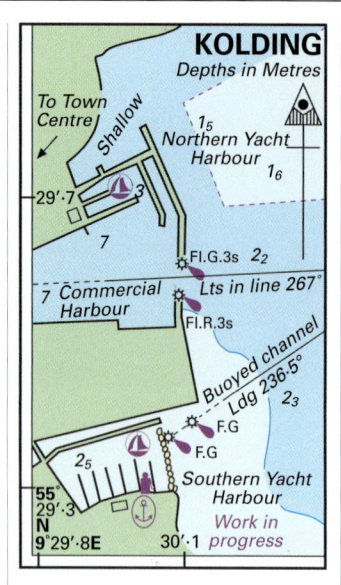

Berthing Pile berthing, green tag indicating vacant berth. For pre-booking of berth see www.marinabooking.dk

Facilities Diesel, chandlery, small restaurant and pub in marina. Usual range of shopping in town.

✆ HM +45 6471 3580,
+45 2169 1567
www.assens-marina.dk

FÅBORG

Fåborg is an attractive town and a busy commercial and ferry port. It is located on the island of Fyn and is a popular starting point for cruising in the archipelago to the S – 'Det Sydfynske Øhav'.

Approach From SE up Fåborg Fjord with all hazards marked.

Berthing at marina NW of commercial hbr or in old inner hbr as available. For pre-booking of berth in inner hbr see www.marinabooking.dk

Facilities All facilities of a major town including ship yard (Fåborg Værft).

✆ HM +45 7253 0260
www.faaborghavn.fmk.dk

SØNDERBORG

Picturesque hbr on SE shore of Als Sund.

Approach From the N leave the Alsfjord into the clearly buoyed Als Sund. Before the town the sound is crossed by the opening King Christian X's Br. From the S leave the Østerhage W card Lt buoy to stb and Vesterhage R can to port.

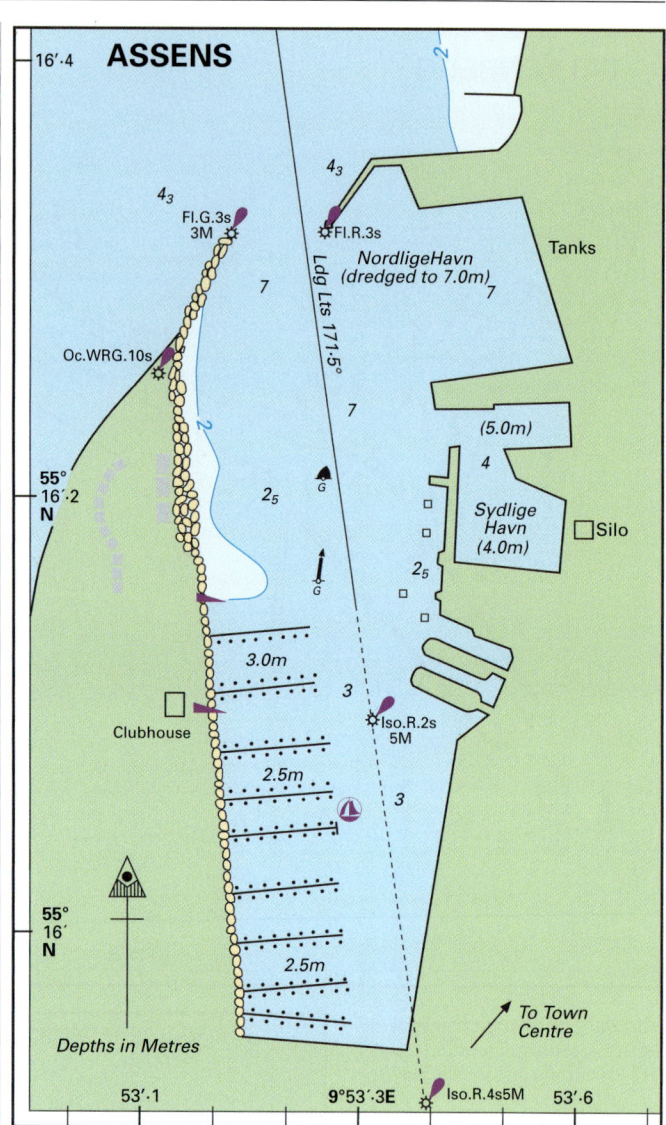

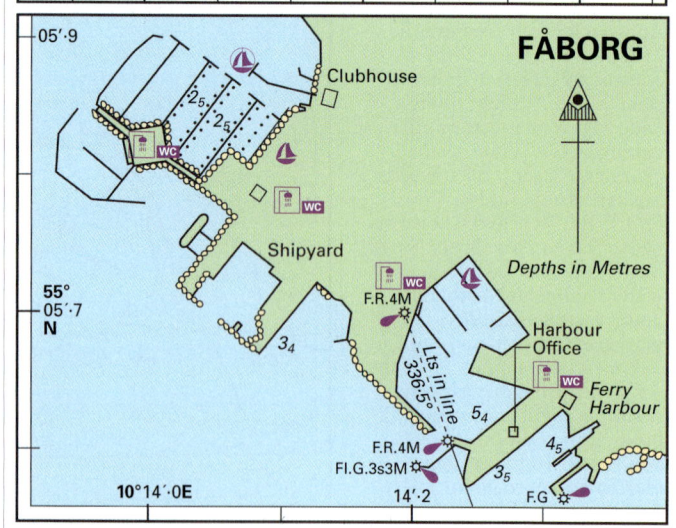

Signals for bridge 1F.R. no passage. 2F.R. Lts pass N to S. 3F.R. Lts pass S to N. 2+3F.R. Lts: pass both directions. Long sound from horn indicates stay clear of br. Time of next opening shown on light board.

NB The br marks the change in the direction of buoyage.

Berthing
• Along city docks S of opening br, E side of sound. Rather rough wooden docks, good fendering essential. Some wash in strong winds from SW through SE. Electricity and water. Large yachts will prefer these docks.
• Sønderborg Lystbådehavn. Marina SE of city with pile moorings for stern lines.

Facilities Marina all facilities including 5-tonne crane, diesel, laundry, WiFi. Usual range of

Passage lights	BA No
Trelde Næs Iso.WRG.2s26m9-6M	0894
Æbelø Fl.15s20m14M	0893·5
Strib Oc.WRG.5s21m13-10M	0922
Assens Oc.WRG.10s5m14-11M	0977
Helnæs Lindehoved Fl.WRG.5s30m13-10M	0988
Nordborg Oc.WRG.5s27m12-9M	1030
Taksensand Oc(2)WRG.12s15m15-12M	1034
Skjoldnæs LFl.30s32m22M	1070
Gammel-Pøl Oc(3)WRG.15s20m11-8M	1100
Vejsnæs Nakke Fl.5s23m12M	1082
Schleimünde LFl(3)WRG.20s14m13/11M Horn Mo(SN)30s (···/−·)	1186

296

The Cruising Almanac

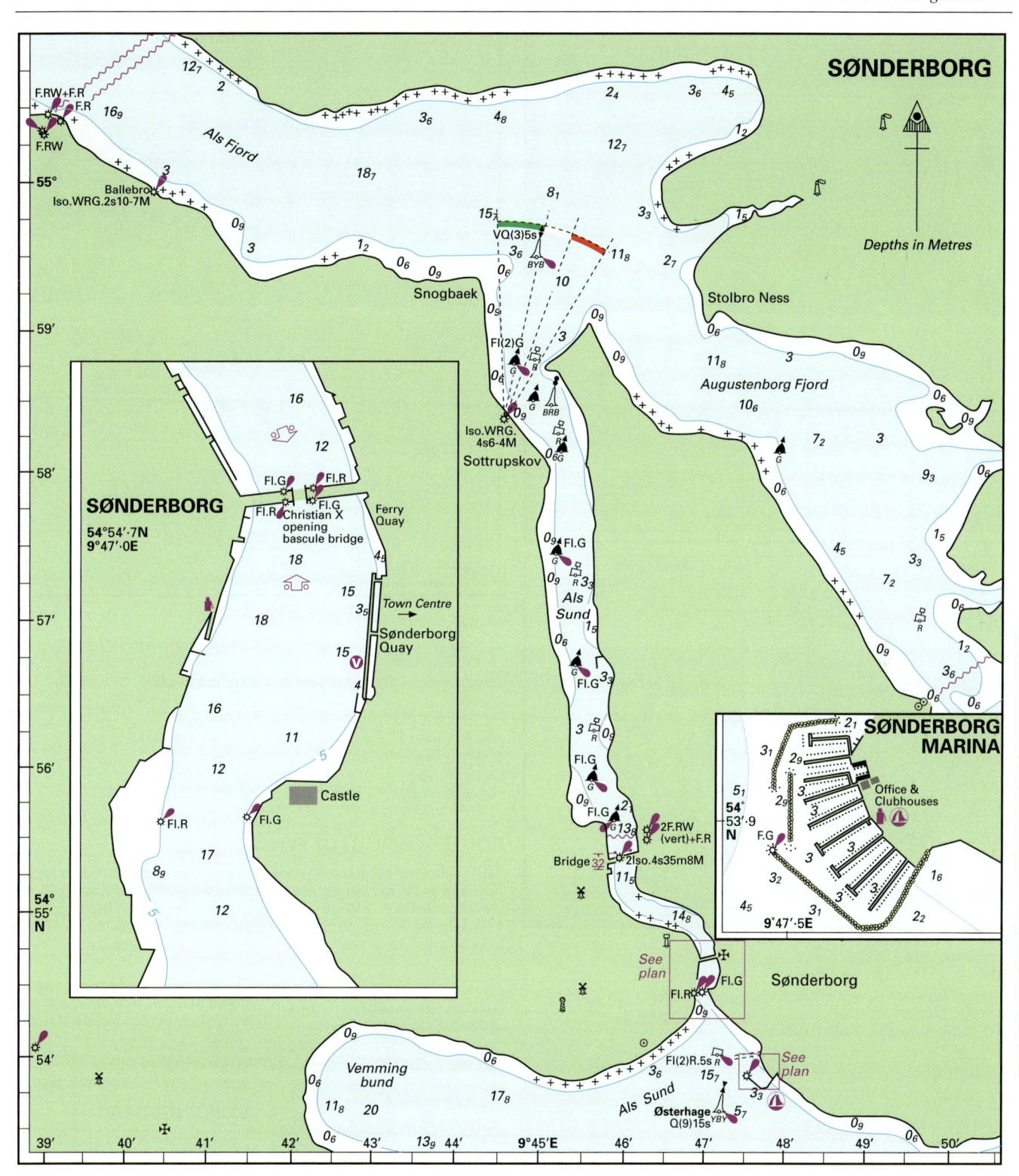

APPROACHES TO THE BALTIC

shopping in town. Sønderborg has many historic sites relating to centuries of strife between the two neighbouring nations Denmark and Germany. Nearby Augustenborg in bottom of Augestenborgfjord two fully serviced boatyards, winter storage under cover. www.augustenborg-yachthavn.dk, www.mj-vaerft.dk

⌕ Marina +45 2784 8525; Port +45 7442 2765, VHF 16, 12. www.soenderborg-lystbaadehavn.dk

BAGENKOP
See plan p.298

This small marina and fishing hbr is situated on the W side of the S end of Langeland, 30M NE of the Kiel LtHo. It is also convenient for vessels on passage through the Storebælt.

Approach Shoals may make the approach rough in W winds. Safest approach from SW staying in deep water until you can steer 102° on the Ldg Lts on N mole to clear the W mole head.

Entrance The hbr faces N. Just inside the N breakwater lies the disused ferry hbr. The yacht hbr is in the NE basin of the inner harbour. Additional moorings in the S basin.

Facilities Customs, water, diesel and shops.

www.langelandhavne.dk [Bagenkop]

MAASHOLM

The river Schlei is a cruising ground in its own right. Maasholm is a small fishing village and tourist resort, 1½M inside the Schleimünde. It is the largest marina on the river.

Approach Schleimünde Seegat is a buoyed channel dredged to 5m. From the safe water buoy follow buoyed channel to the entrance between two moles. N mole has conspic W tower with black band. Approach dangerous in strong E'lies. Pass Schleimünde with small hbr to stb then follow buoyed channel. Hbr subject to considerable tidal surges depending on wind directions, less water in strong W'lies. With decline in commercial use of the river, dredging operations may be less regular; updated charts should be consulted before approaching Schleimünde.

Berthing Vacant pile berths indicated by green tag. Alternative berthing in old hbr NW of village or anchor NW of this or S of passageway in Olpenitzer Noor.

297

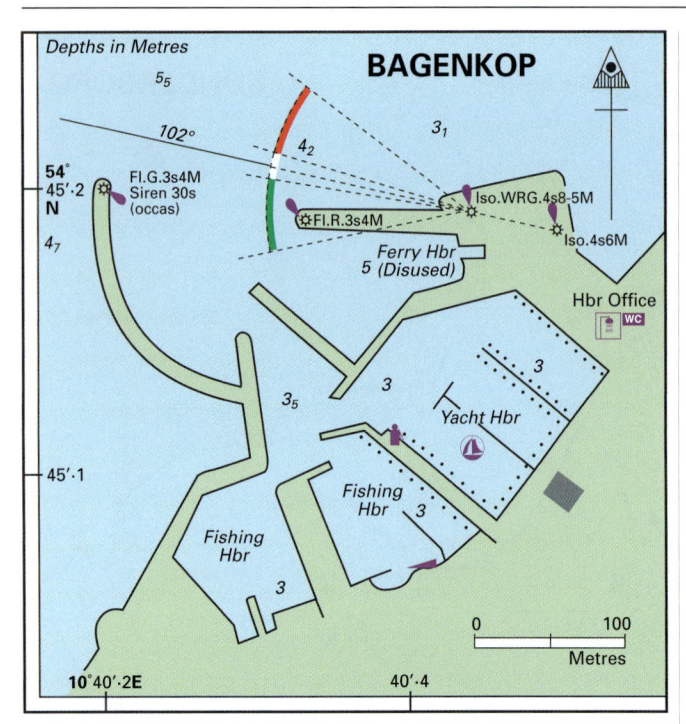

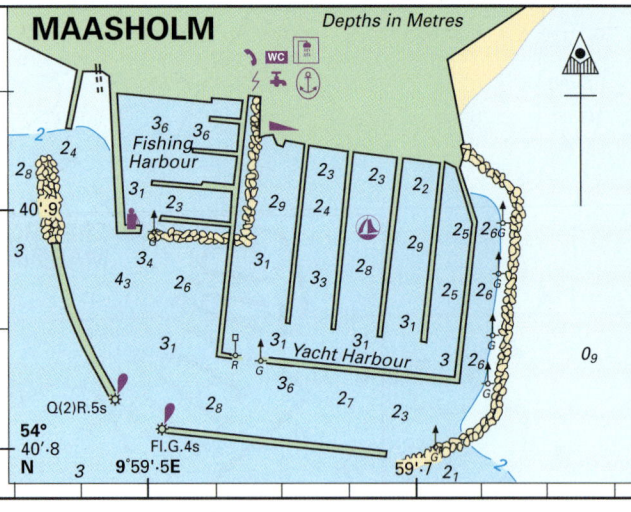

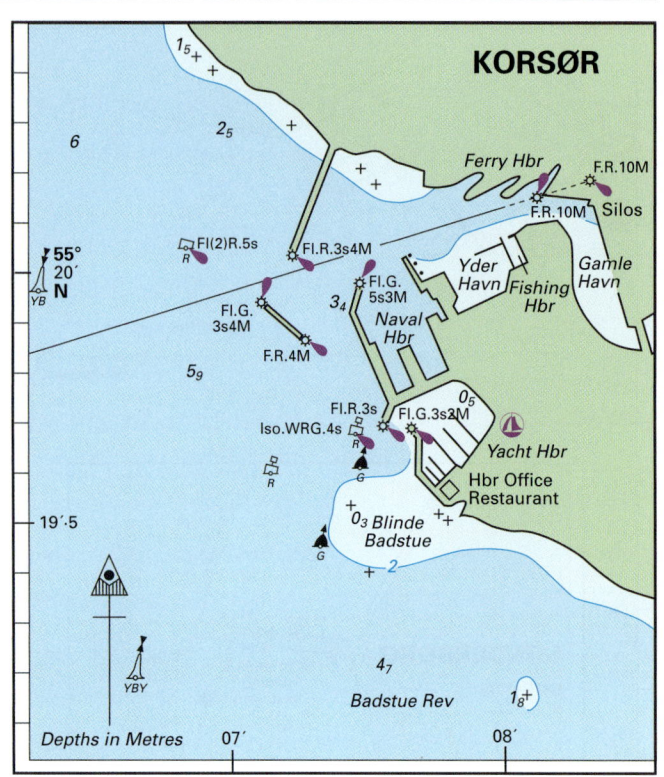

Passage lights	BA No
Romsø Tue Fl.WRG.3s10m9-7M	1526
Østerrenden East Bridge Centre N side Fl.R.3s71m7M	1532.6
Østerrenden S Fl(3)R.10s10m8M	1534
Knudshoved Oc.WRG.10s16m12-10M	1556
Langelandsøre (Omø) Oc(2)WRG.12s21m17-14M	1640
Spodsbjerg SE Fl.WRG.3s10m8-7M	1673
Højbjerg E Fl.RG.5s10m8/7M	1673.3
Keldsnor Fl(2)15s39m17M Oc.WRG.5s22m12-9M	1706

ROUTE 6C SOUTH OF FYN AND SJÆLLAND

This inshore route from Fåborg, through the islands S of Fyn and Sjælland passing N of Langeland to Vordingborg and Rødvig, is a pleasant sheltered alternative to continuing S on the Lille Bælt. Crossing the Storebælt the route leads directly to København. It may also be joined from Route 7 by sailing E of Langeland.

Passage lights	BA No
Helnæs Lindehoved Fl.WRG.5s30m13-10M	0988
Skjoldnæs LFl.30s32m22M	1070
Frankeklint (Langeland) Oc.RG.5s16m8M	1656
Langelandsøre (Omø) Oc(2)WRG.12s21m17-14M	1640

FÅBORG
see Route 6a

SVENDBORG
Major town with a distinguished maritime history and home port of many historic vessels. Good starting point for a sail through the archipelago S of Fyn - "Det Sydfynske Øhav".

Approach From Svendborg Sund passing E of Fredriksø into N hbr.

Berthing At pontoons in N hbr, larger vessels enquire about mooring alongside docks N of these.

Facilities Floating service building in marina. Diesel, chandlery, sailmaker and rigger, diesel mechanic. Wide range of shopping. Ferries to islands.

☎ +45 6223 3080
www.svendborg-havn.dk
www.detsydfynskeoehav.dk

VORDINGBORG
After passing N of Langeland and crossing the Storebælt the wide inlet of Smålandsfarvandet leads S of Sjælland to the narrows at Vordingborg. The town is on the N bank and can be reached either through the Masnedsund opening br (road and rail) or by passing under the Storstrøm Br (clearance 26m) and crossing the Middelgrund (least depth 2·5m). There are two small marinas immediately E of the opening br but yachts usually proceed to the Nordhavn which is convenient for the town.

Facilities WiFi. Chandlery fuel and 42 tonne travelift at Masnedø Marinecenter SE of lifting br.

☎ Vordingborg Nordhavn +45 40 49 44 25

Facilities Diesel in the fishing hbr, several restaurants. The town Kappeln 3M up-river has a wide range of services available to yachts, and several berthing options down-river of the opening bridge.

☎ HM +49 (0) 4642 6571
www.maasholm.de

ROUTE 6B STOREBÆLT

This is a major shipping channel between the Kattegat and Kieler Bucht crossed by the Great Belt br. Direction of buoyage is to the S. When passing the br yachts should if possible use the Vesterrenden channel between Nyborg and Sprogø (clearance 18m). In the Østerenden, pleasure craft should stay clear of TSS. VTS Great Belt Traffic listen VHF 11 (N sector) or 74 (S sector) or 16, call sign *Belt Traffic*, or can be contacted on ☎ +45 58376868. Pleasure craft <15m are exempted from the mandatory ship reporting system.

KORSØR
An old ferry and naval port with interesting streets.

Approach From the Badstue Rev W card buoy steer NE leaving two G con buoys to stb. Enter yacht hbr between mole heads.

Berthing In the yacht hbr (S of the naval hbr) with perfect shelter. Piles for stern lines, large vessels moor alongside on pier 5 or 6, or ask HM.

Supplies Water, fuel, showers, chandler, restaurant and shops.

☎ +45 5837 5930,
+45 2118 5930
www.korsoersejlklub.dk

BAGENKOP
see Route 6a.

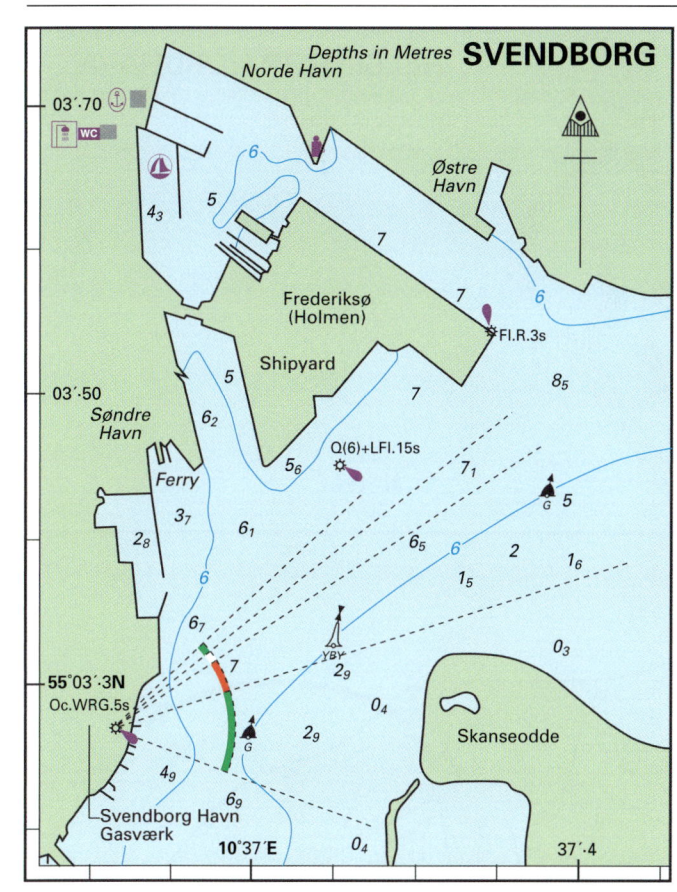

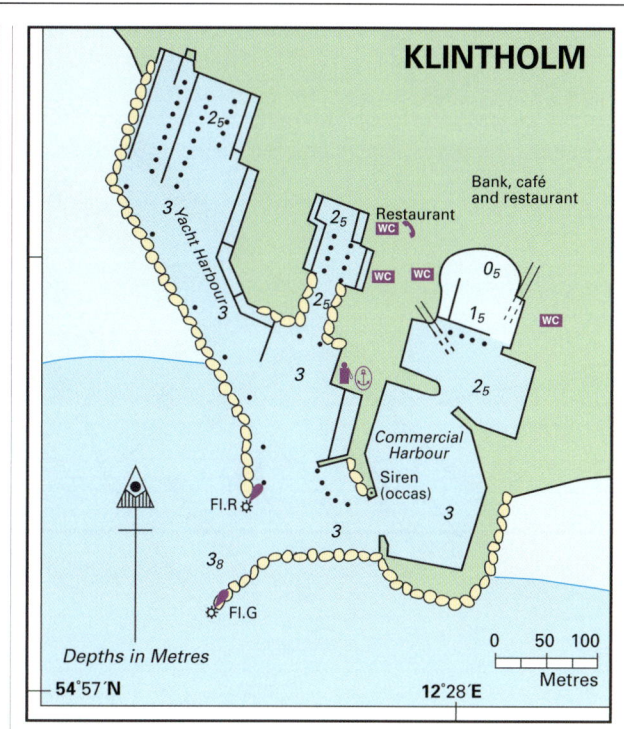

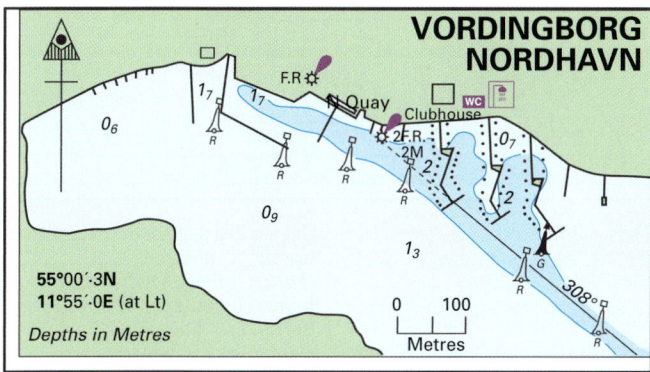

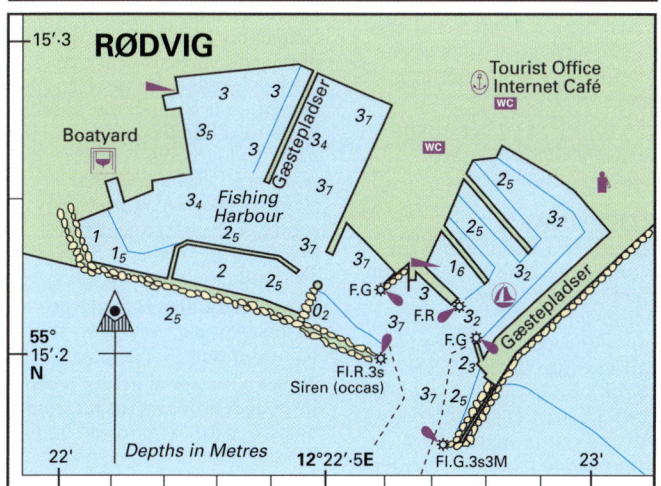

Lts. There are fishing stakes E of approach.

Berthing Yacht hbr to stb on approach, limited room for manœuvering once inside. Piles for stern lines, some alongside berths. When crowded, yachts use the fishing hbr to port. Large yachts will prefer the fishing hbr.

Facilities There is a boatyard and a couple of shops, several restaurants. Regular trains to Copenhagen.

☏ +45 5650 6007.
www.stevns.dk [Borger] [Kultur og Fritid] [Lystbaadehavne]

KLINTHOLM

Located SE on the island of Møn, this is a popular landfall or point of departure for German Baltic hbrs. E side of Møn with conspic white chalk cliffs Møns Klint.

Approach From SW avoiding fish stakes both sides of hbr approach. Approach hazardous in strong winds from SW.

Berthing Large marina to port upon entry. Piles for stern lines. Large vessels enquire about mooring in commercial (east) hbr, usually busy with fishing boats and service vessels for offshore wind farm.

Facilities Diesel. There is a general food store and a fish shop, bicycle rental useful if wishing to visit the geological centre at Møns Klint.

☏ HM +45 2442 2182.
www.vordingborg.dk [Oplev] [Lystbådehavne] [Klintholm Havn]

ROUTE 6D ØRESUND (THE SOUND)

This important deep waterway between Denmark and Sweden has very heavy commercial traffic and ferry-links. The road/railway link between Denmark and Sweden is in way of a tunnel on the Danish side, so there is no headroom restriction in the Øresund. There are many hbrs and marinas on both shores but they tend to be busy in season. The Sound VTS monitors VHF 73 (N), 71 (S), and 16. Callsign *Sound Traffic*. Vessels <300 GRT are exempted from the mandatory ship reporting system.

DANISH PORTS IN THE ØRESUND

HELSINGØR

A large town and communication hub.

Passage lights	BA No
Kronborg (Helsingør) Oc(2)WRG.6s34m15-12M	1908
Helsingborg Oc.WRG.15s17m18-13M	2288
Ven LFl.WRG.10s24m16-12M	1928
Middelgrunds Fort E Iso.WRG.4s11m8M	1965
Middelgrunds Fort W Iso.WRG.8s11m8M	1964
Trekroner Iso.WRG.2s20m17-13M	1978
Nordre Røse Oc(2)WRG.6s14m17-13M	2042
Drogden Oc(3)WRG.15s18m18-13M Horn Mo(U)30s (··−)	2060
Falsterborev Fl(4)WR.12s29m14–12M	2417

Commercial hbr (Port of Elsinore) S of Kronborg castle does not cater for pleasure boats <15m; entry only after

www.sejlklubben-snekken.dk
www.vordingborg.dk [Oplev] [Lystbådehavne] [Vordingborg Nordhavn]

RØDVIG

The route continues N of the island of Møn under two fixed bridges (20 and 26m clearance). The Bøgestrøm channel then leads out to the deeper waters of Fakse Bugt. Navigation of the Bøgestrøm should only be attempted in daylight. Least depth is around 2m. Rødvig lies across the Fakse Bugt on the S side of Sjælland. It is a charming old fishing village and a convenient passage port.

Approach From SW through mole opening with R and G

APPROACHES TO THE BALTIC

299

The Cruising Almanac

HELSINGØR NORDHAVN

THE SOUND N APPROACHES

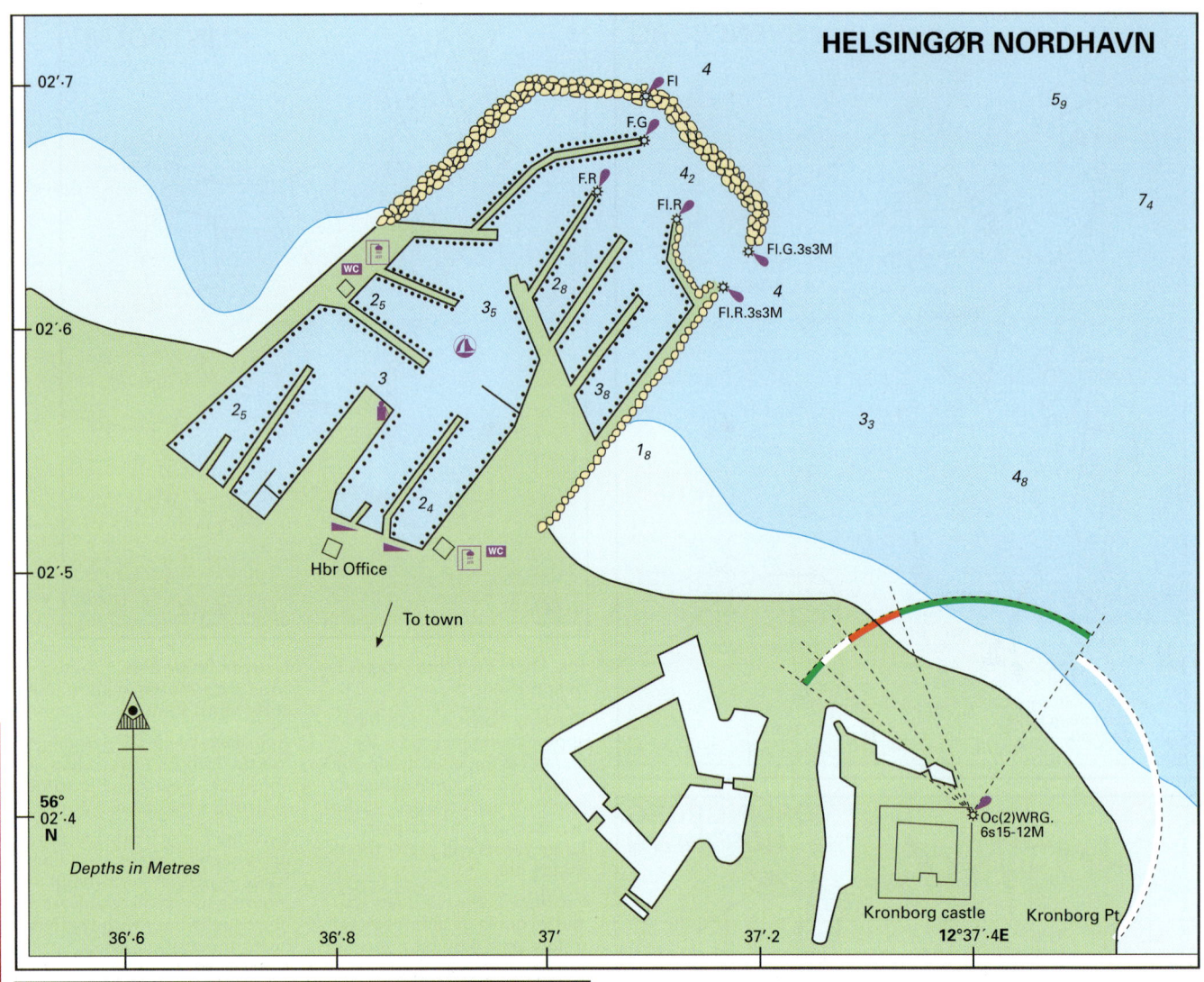

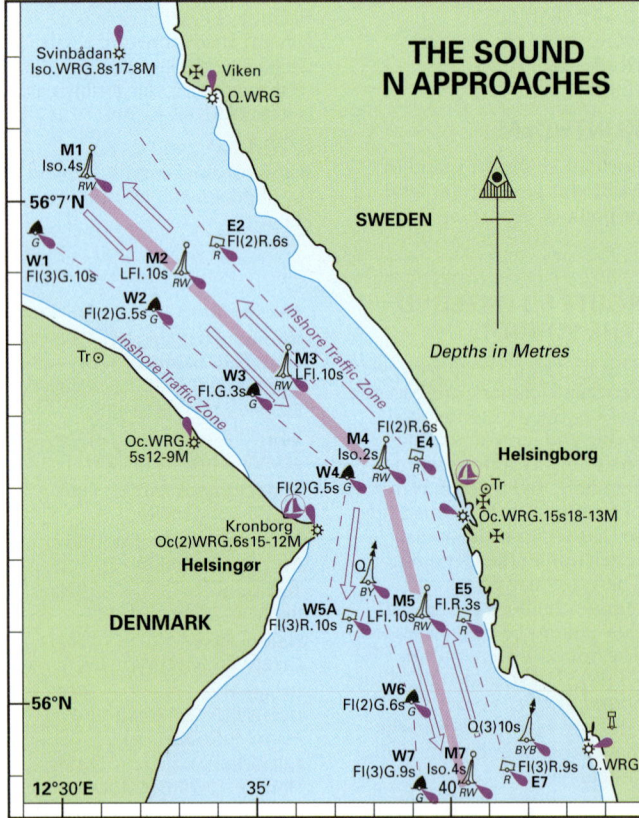

agreement with HM. Helsingør Nordhavn large marina with >1000 berths.

Approach N hbr 3ca NW of conspic Kronborg castle. Deep water to mole opening, but be aware of the heavy ferry traffic between Helsingør and Helsingborg. Note that Kronborg Lt is on the NE tr of the castle.

Berthing Mostly box moorings.

Facilities New service building. Diesel, chandlery, sailmaker, maritime museum. Kronborg castle, setting for Shakespeare's Hamlet, is a world heritage site.

☏ Marina +45 2531 1080
www.helsingor-havne.helsingor.dk

KØBENHAVN

Approach København is on Kongedybet, the W branch of the Øresund S of the Middelgrund island. Yachts are not allowed through the N fairway into the inner hbr (Kronløbet). Yachts must use the S fairway (Lynetteløbet). All city centre marinas are approached from Lynetteløbet. A fairway for pleasure yachts E of Trekroner fort, between Kronløbet and Lynetteløbet, is laid out april – nov and marked with yellow sparbuoys.

Berthing There are numerous marinas in the København area. Those nearest the centre tend to be more expensive and crowded. There is an excellent public transport system and peripheral marinas may be more peaceful. Yachts wishing to visit city centre marinas must use the S entrance (Lynetteløbet). Once inside Lynetteløbet, keep E of yellow buoys, crossing passageway at right angles when required.

Inner Harbour
Langelinie Marina is set in parks and gardens near the Little Mermaid Statue (Den lille Havfrue). It is small; berth with bows to pontoon, stern to buoy. In high season arrival by noon is advised to have a chance of a place. 1km to city centre. The chart agent Iver Weilbach & co is near here at Toldbodgate 35.

Hotel Admiralen is for large yachts. It is exposed to wash from shipping.

Nyhavn is a canal in city centre, surrounded by restaurants and buzzing with life day and night. Visiting yachts berth outside lifting bridge. Exposed to wash from shipping hence smaller vessels tend to moor elsewhere. Expect the usual noise that goes with an inner city berth.

Christianshavns Kanal
Entrance lies opposite Nyhavn. It is picturesque but crowded, with limited facilities. Access is under the new Trangraven (opening) pedestrian bridge.

N of the city lie 4 marinas:
Skovshoved is an artificial basin 3M N of Tuborg. There is a

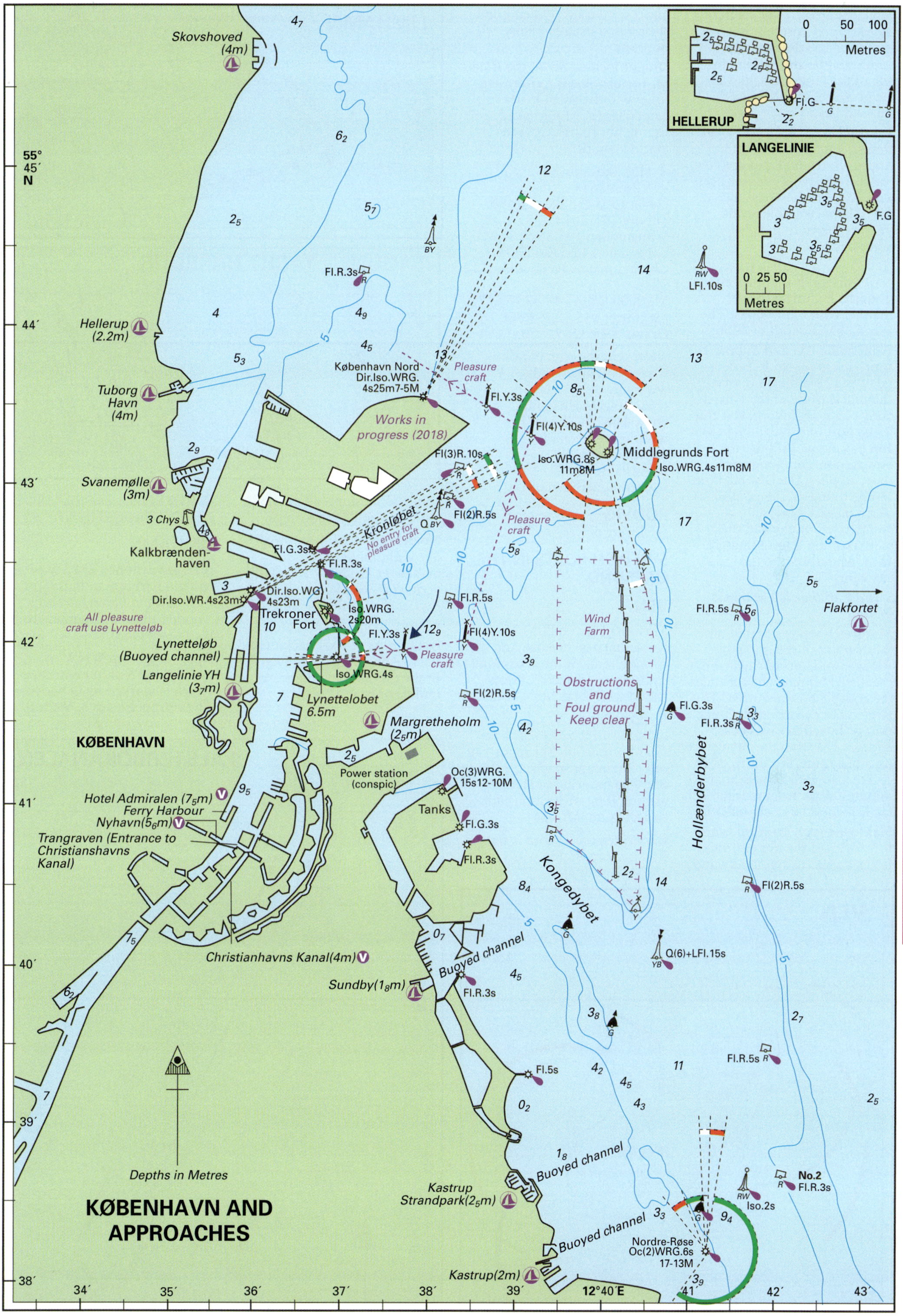
KØBENHAVN AND APPROACHES
Depths in Metres
Skovshoved (4m)
Hellerup (2.2m)
Tuborg Havn (4m)
Svanemølle (3m)
3 Chys
Kalkbrænden-haven
Dir.Iso.WR.4s23m
All pleasure craft use Lynetteløb
Lynetteløb (Buoyed channel)
Langelinie YH (37m)
KØBENHAVN
Hotel Admiralen (75m)
Ferry Harbour
Nyhavn(56m)
Trangraven (Entrance to Christianshavns Kanal)
Christianhavns Kanal(4m)
Sundby(18m)
Kastrup Strandpark(25m)
Kastrup(2m)
København Nord Dir.Iso.WRG. 4s25m7-5M
Pleasure craft
Works in progress (2018)
Fl.R.3s
Fl.Y.3s
Fl(4)Y.10s
Fl(3)R.10s
Fl(2)R.5s
Q BY
Kronløbet
No entry for pleasure craft
Fl.G.3s
Dir.Iso.WG 4s23m
Trekroner Fort
Iso.WRG. 2s20m
Iso.WRG.4s
Lynettelobet 6.5m
Margretheholm (25m)
Power station (conspic)
Oc(3)WRG. 15s12-10M
Tanks
Fl.G.3s
Fl.R.3s
Buoyed channel
Fl.5s
Middelgrunds Fort
Iso.WRG.8s 11m8M
Iso.WRG.4s11m8M
Wind Farm
Obstructions and Foul ground Keep clear
Kongedybet
Hollænderbybet
Q(6)+LFl.15s
Fl.R.5s
Fl(2)R.5s
Fl.R.3s
Flakfortet
LFl.10s
No.2 Fl.R.3s
Iso.2s
Nordre-Røse Oc(2)WRG.6s 17-13M
HELLERUP
Fl.G
Metres
LANGELINIE
F.G
55° 45′ N
44′
43′
42′
41′
40′
39′
38′
34′
35′
36′
37′
38′
39′
12°40′E
41′
42′
43′

The Cruising Almanac

detached breakwater sheltering the entrance. A recent hbr extension has doubled the number of berths making this one of the largest marinas in the greater København area. All facilities.

Tuborg Havn Home of Royal Danish Yacht Club (KDY). Approach from SE passing first between off-lying breakwaters with R/G Lts then passing WSW between mole heads. Visitors' berth to port in outer basin.

Hellerup is a small marina, ½M N of Tuborg. It is approached from the E along a short channel with unlit buoys. The marina has a depth of 2·2m.

Svanemølle ½M S of Tuborg is approached on Iso.R.2s & 4s Ldg Lts 208° along a buoyed channel starting at the E card buoy 5ca E of Tuborg. It is the home port of three sailing clubs and has about 1100 berths, bow to pontoon, long stern ropes to piles, the best facilities can be found on the pontoons to stb. Diesel. Shops, launderette, banks and the metro station approximately 1km. About 4km to the city centre.

S and E of the city, marinas include:

Margreteholm is situated on the N point of the island of Amager and approached from the main shipping channel near the conspic power station. This large quiet marina is the home port of Lynetten sailing club and lies 3M from the city centre on a bus route. Access to city centre also with shuttle boat 10 minutes' walk from marina. All facilities and large chandlery.

Flakfortet is an artificial island fort 4M E of the hbr entrance. It has an encircling breakwater and a restaurant. Quiet, good shelter and usually plenty of room.

Dragør located SE on the island of Amager, this is a charming town with frequent buses to Copenhagen. Moor in old fishing hbr (north) or new marina (south).

✆ HM Skovshoved +45 26302611
Hellerup as for Skovshoved
Tuborg +45 2013 3787
Svanemøllen +45 3920 2221
Langelinie +45 3526 2338
Christianhavns kanal +45 4112 7744
Margreteholm +45 3257 5778
Flakfortet +45 3296 0800
Dragør +45 32891570

www.skovshovedhavn.dk
www.helleruphavn.dk
www.kdy.dk
www.langeliniehavn.dk
www.smhavn.dk
www.trangraven.dk
www.lynetten.dk
www.flakfortet.dk
www.dragoerhavn.dk

RØDVIG
see Route 6c

SWEDISH PORTS IN THE ØRESUND

VEN

This small island 20M N of Köbenhavn is Swedish and the former home of the astronomer Tyco Brahe (d.1597). Pretty island with three hbrs:

Kyrkbacken on W side of island is principal yacht hbr. Good protection but reports of only 2m in approaches, 2·2m in hbr. Pile mooring or stern anchor, if mooring alongside expect large raft-ups.

Bäckviken on E shore is ferry hbr and exposed to wash from commercial shipping passing close to hbr. Pile moorings.

Norreborg on N shore small hbr with limited room to maneuver inside mole, smaller boats may find vacant berth. Box or alongside berthing.

Facilities Diesel in Kyrkbacken, restaurants at Kyrkbackan and Bäckviken. Shops and Tyco Brahe museum in village on middle of island.

✆ Kyrkbacken +46 (0) 418 72400; www.kyrkbacken.se

LIMHAMN

A large yacht hbr 3M SW of Malmö harbour and just S of the main Limhamn harbour. Another marina, Lagunen, to the N (see plan).

Approach From WNW to avoid shoal S of hbr entrance which is marked by G buoys. The entrance faces S. Visitors'

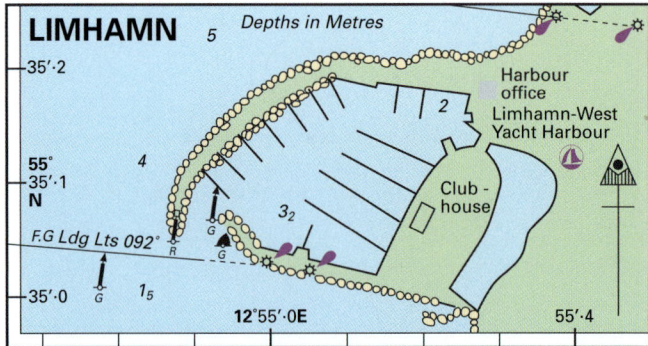

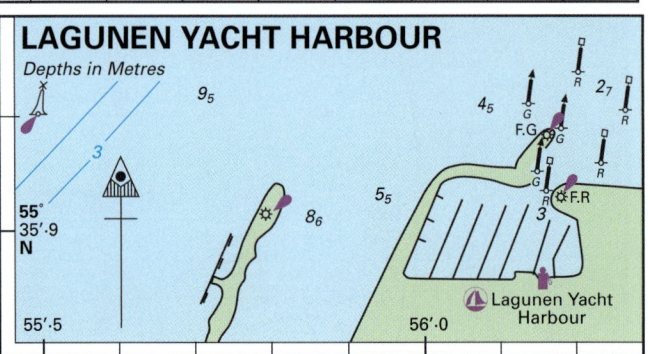

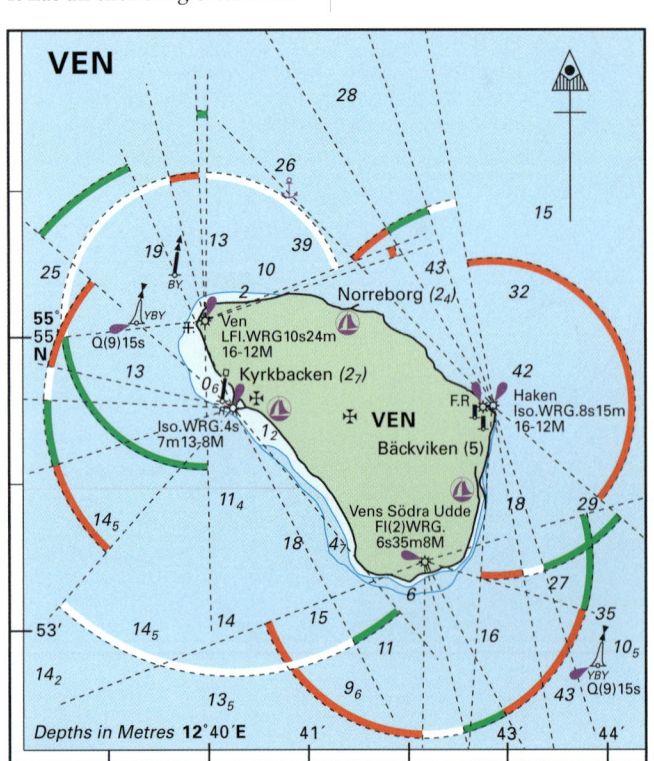

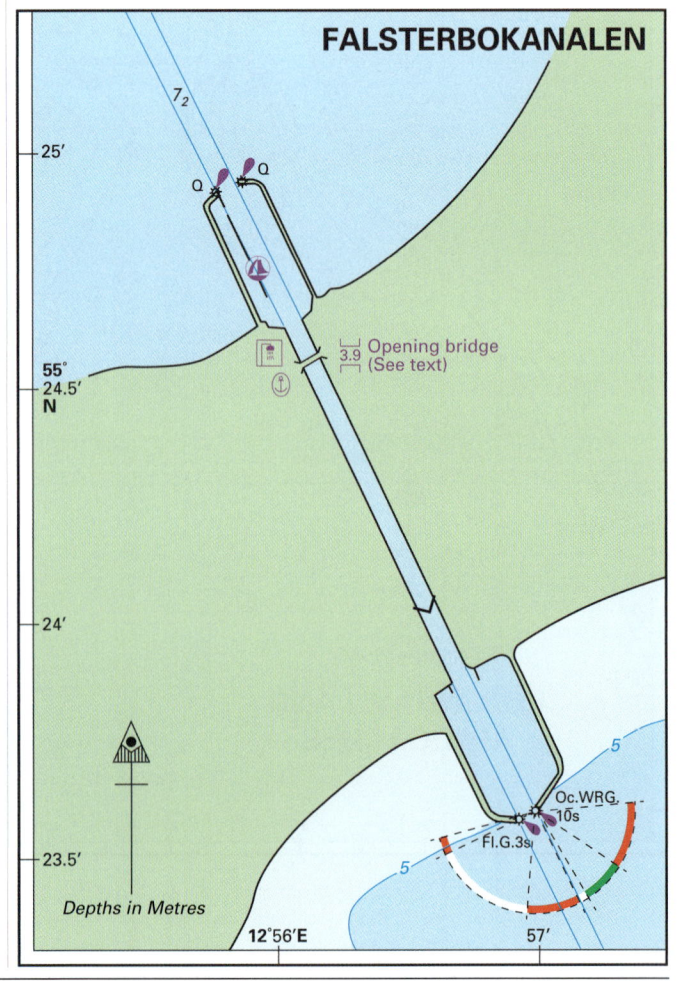

berth on pontoon F. Vacant berths are also indicated by G card.

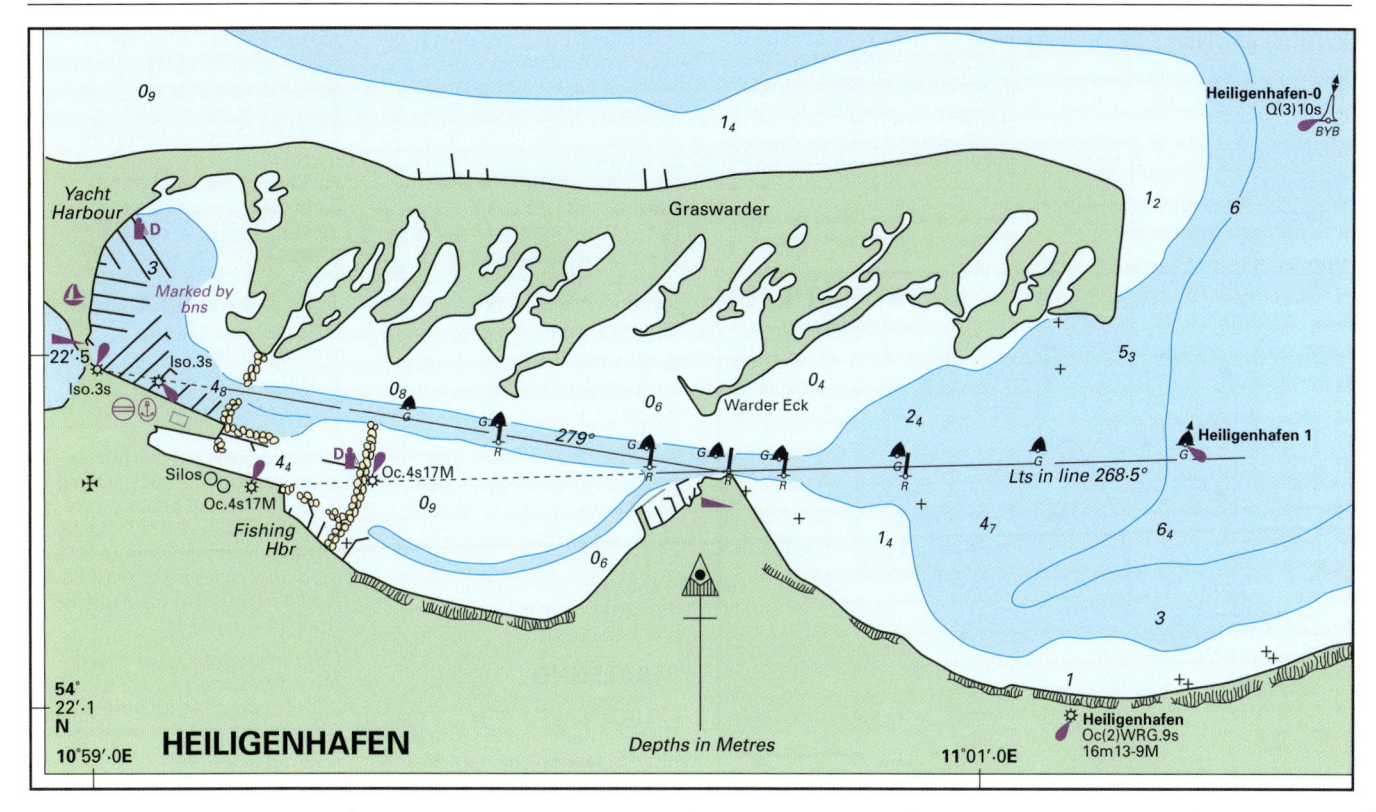

Facilities Fuel and pump-out station both hbrs. Chandlery in S hbr (Limhamn). 3km to Malmø city centre with all facilities of a big city.

☏ HM +46 (0) 4015 2024
www.smabatshamnen.nu
www.lagunen.nu

FALSTERBOKANALEN

On passage from Øresund to the Baltic proper this route avoids the Falsterborev TSS roundabout. The canal sees little commercial traffic. Min depth 4m. Bridge opens every hour on the hour (0600–2200) during summer, except 0800 and 1700. Bridge operated by remote control from a central canal monitoring unit located inland of Göteborg, follow instructions on screen. Lock usually open.

Approach From N or S along buoyed and lit channel.

Berthing At berths with green tags at boatclub N of bridge.

Facilities Diesel, holding tank pump-out. Bicycles available.

VHF (bridge remote control) VHF 11 (call *Falsterbokanalen*)
www.falsterbokanalen.se
www.sjofartsverket.se follow links [Båtliv] [Falsterbokanalen]

ROUTE 7 WEST BALTIC

This route leads from the E end of the Nord-Ostsee-Kanal S of the Danish islands and between Germany and Sweden to the southern parts of the Baltic Sea. The routes through the Lillebælt, Storebælt and Øresund join the northern side of the route.

There are several shooting ranges off the German coast, details from local HMs or official waterways website www.elwis.de . Latter is easiest accessed through links from local websites such as www.mein-ostseehafen.de [Service für Skipper] [Sperr-/Warngebiete].

Construction of a tunnel between Lolland in Denmark and Fehmarn in Germany (Fehmarn Belt Fixed Link) may affect navigation in these waters until expected completion in 2026.

GERMAN PORTS IN THE W BALTIC

STICKENHÖRN & SCHILKSEE – OLYMPIAHAFEN
see Route 2b

HEILIGENHAFEN

Lies 30M E of Kiel on the mainland opposite Fehmarn. W of Heiligenhafen the Todendorf-Putlos shooting range extends up to 7M offshore. Firing announced VHF 16/11. Usually no activity during main holiday season June 20 – August 20, details available from local HMs or online sources (see above).

Passage lights	BA No
Kiel	1215
Iso.WRG.6s29m17-13M	
Horn Mo(KI)30s (–·–/··)	
Bülk	1216
Fl.WRG.3s29m14-10M	
Friedrichsort	1230
Iso.WRG.4s32m7–5M+aux Lts	
Flügge (Fehmarn)	1288.1
F.37m25M+Oc(4)20s38m17M	
Westermarkelsdorf	1280
LFl.WR.10s16m18/14M	
Marienleuchte	1284
Fl(4)WR.15s40m22/18M	
Staberhuk	1286
Oc(2)WG.16s25m18/14M	
Buk	1400
LFl(4)WR.45s95m24/20M	
Warnemünde	1404
Fl(3+1)24s34m20M	
Darsser Ort	1440
Fl(2+4)22s33m23M	

Approach The area has extensive shoals. The Heiligenhafen-O E card Lt buoy marks the NE extremity of these. From this buoy steer towards the Heiligenhafen LtHo before entering buoyed channel with two sets of Ldg Lts.

Berthing Heiligenhafen marina is one of the largest in W Baltic with nearly 1,000 spaces. Many charter companies are based here. YC SE of fishing hbr offers a more intimate atmosphere when berths available.

Facilities Diesel in marina (no loose cans allowed due to Nature Reserve restrictions). Chandlery, sailmaker, mechanical repairs. Usual range of shopping.

☏ HM +49 (0) 174 58 668 71
www.marina-heiligenhafen.de
www.svh-ssch.de

BURGTIEFE

Located S on Fehmarn, 3M E of the 22m bridge. Fehmarn is a popular holiday resort and there are several smaller marinas. Burgtiefe is a large well protected marina that will usually have vacant berths even during high season. Neighbour to a major tourist resort, but 2km to Burg which is an interesting town with buildings dating back to 13th century.

Approach From SE, three conspic large hotel buildings on Fehmarn E of channel. Follow sectored Lts to buoyed channel which divides at Burgtiefe buoys 1 (G) and 2 (GRG). Turn 90° to stb between these for Burgtiefe marina.

Berthing Green tag indicates vacant berth, pile moorings. Large yachts moor alongside concrete wave breakers to E.

Facilities Fuel, chandlery, 20-ton boat lift. Several restaurants and bars. Bicycles for hire. Indoor water sports centre. Beach (access small fee). Basic groceries, buses to Burg with wide range of shopping. Railway station in Burg. Burgstaake hbr ½M NW has boatyard with repair facilities and winter storage.

☏ HM +49 (0) 4371 8888 900
www.yachthafen-burgtiefe.de

WARNEMÜNDE

Old seaside resort on the Mecklingburger Bucht, with large marina (Hohe Düne) E of old port.

Approach For Hohe Düne approach from NE. Note that on approach from N the W mole overlaps E mole, which may cause confusion in darkness when lights appear wrong way around. For Warnemünde between mole heads as charted, keeping clear of commercial traffic to Rostock.

Berthing Hohe Düne usually has many places for visitors, also in season. Ferry or shuttle boat to Warnemünde. In Warnemünde some visitors' berths in Alter Strom (alongside, pile moorings SE in canal) and in YC, E of inner mole. Alter Strom busy with tourist boats and fishing vessels but you are moored right in front of the old captains' houses. Outer berths in Alter Strom exposed to N'lies.

Facilities Höhe Düne is a high quality marina development with modern facilities, in Alte Strum facilities at YC. Warnemünde has many restaurants and bars, large beach. Ferries to Gedser and Trelleborg, Rly to Rostock.

① Marina Hohe Düne +49 (0) 381 5040 8000
www.yachthafen-hohe-duene.de
www.wscev.de

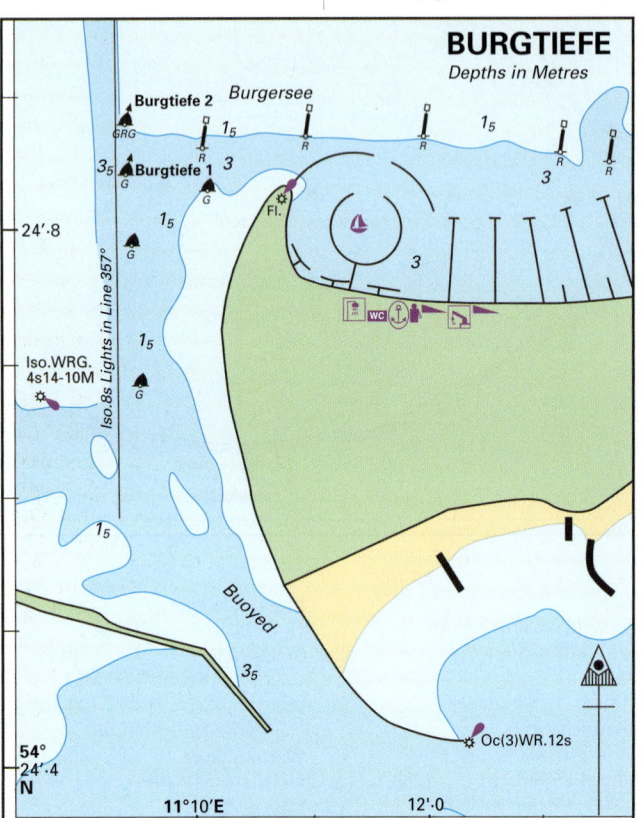

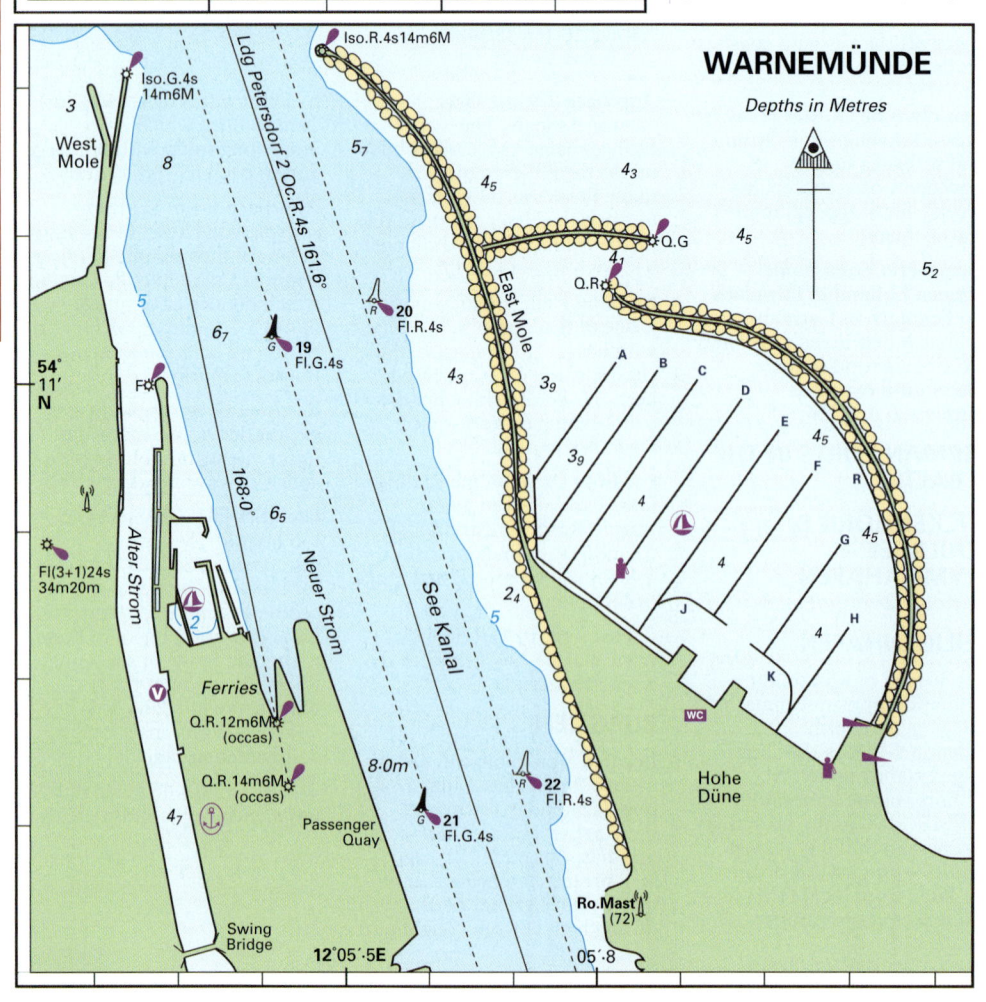

STRALSUND

On passage between Warnemünde and Stralsund the hbr of **Darsser Ort** may be entered in emergencies. A rescue vessel is stationed here. Attempts are made to maintain adequate depths but the approach to Darsser Ort is susceptible to silting and the hbr is at times closed.

Approach From W and N from Gellen safe water buoy, following buoyed channel W of Hiddensee. In settled weather part of the channel can be by-passed by following white sector of Gellen LtHo, depth 3m. Boats on passage from N or E often use the buoyed channel E of Hiddensee, where Vitte is a useful hbr before further passage up the Strelasund. Approach from S passing under opening bridge Ziegelgraben brücke (opening times for yachts: 0520; 0820; 1220; 1520; 1720 and 2120 changes posted at YC website www.ycstr.de .

Berthing
NordMole (Citymarina) fingerberths and some alongside berths, visitors use E most pontoons as sign posted. Near city centre hence popular and often crowded. Docks by tallship *Gorch Foch* may be used after agreement with HM. A few berths also inside lifting bridge by diesel pump.

Ost mole Large marina that often has vacant berths even high season. Rather austere surroundings but friendly club atmosphere. Small restaurant, sailmaker. 3km to city centre.

Dänholmen Approached from SE (after Ziegelgraben bridge on passage eastwards). Visitors' berths at sailing school and at YC. Peaceful hbr in scenic surroundings. Pub in YC. 3kms to city centre.

Facilities Wide range of companies offering services to yachts including several small chandleries and a couple of sailmakers. Many sites of historic interest. The Altstadt (old town) is a UNESCO World Heritage Site.

① Citymarina +49 (0) 3831 444 978
YC +49 (0) 3831 297 300
www.rundtoern-marinas.com
follow link [Citymarina Stralsund]
www.ycstr.de

DANISH AND SWEDISH PORTS IN THE W BALTIC

Passage lights	BA No
Keldsnor	1706
Fl(2)15s39m17M+Oc.WRG.5s	
Møn	2142
Fl(4)30s25m21M	
Falsterborev	2417
Fl(4)WR.12s29m14/12M	
Kullagrund	2445
Iso.WRG.3s18m8-5M	

BAGENKOP

see Route 6a

GEDSER

This is a useful passage hbr. It is situated on the S tip of the Danish island of Falster and has a tall LtHo 26m.

Approach The main hbr is for the ferry to Rostock/Warnemünde in Germany and yachts are not welcome there. The marina lies 1M NW along

The Cruising Almanac

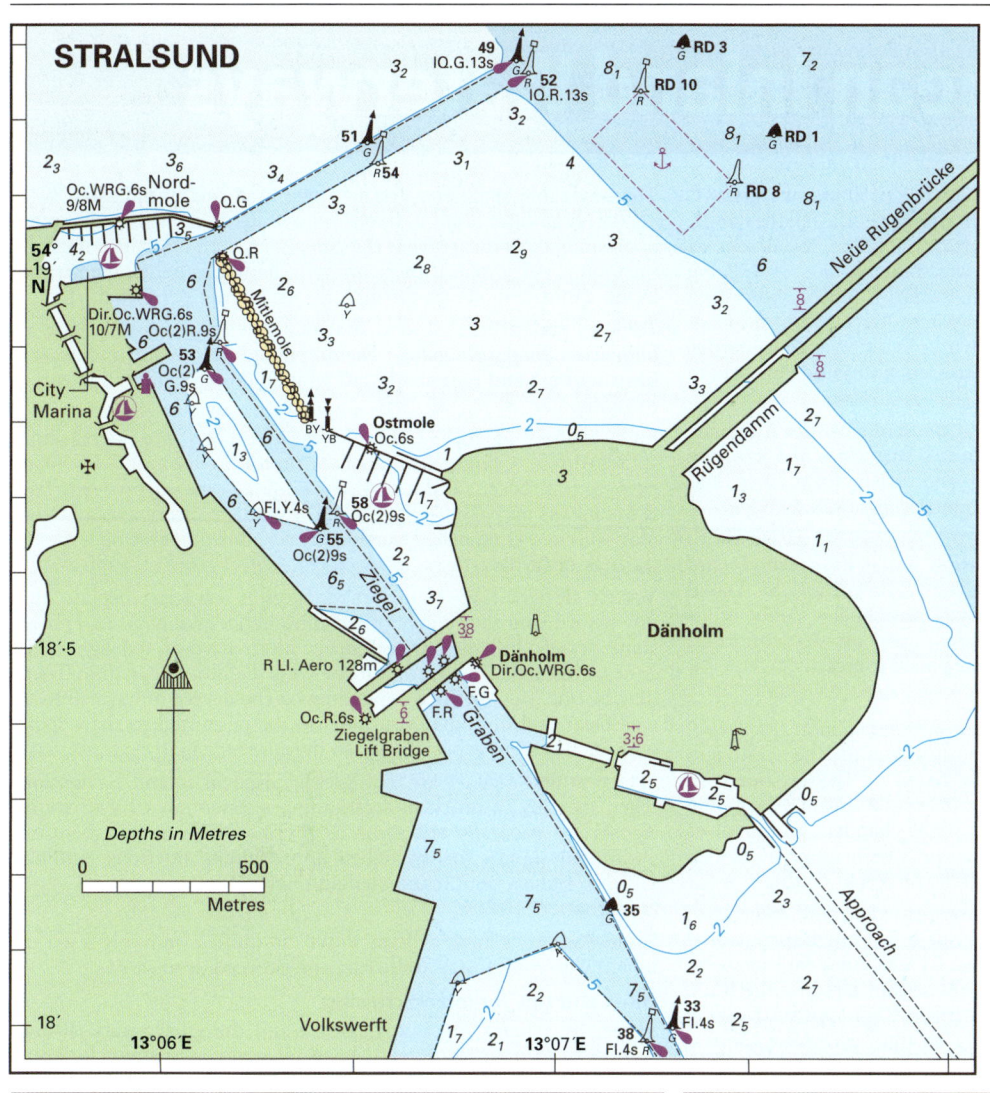

a narrow buoyed channel skirting the coast which starts near the entrance to the main hbr. Depth 2·5–3m. It is sheltered from the E but is rather exposed from the W being protected only by reefs and a hbr wall. Usual marina facilities including fuel but somewhat remote.

☎ HM +45 5417 9245
www.guldborgsund.dk/lystbaadehavne [Gedser Havn]

YSTAD

Hbr on the S Swedish coast in the NW corner of the outer harbour. The ferry port to Bornholm and Poland and a commercial hbr are nearby. There are some old houses and a 13th-century monastery.

Approach From 2nd offshore Q.R. buoy the Ldg Lts F.R. 019° lead to the yacht hbr.

Berthing Visitors moor at most W'ly pontoon or at vacant berth as indicated by HM. Depth 2–4m. Visitors' pontoon can be uncomfortable in strong S winds, but protection has improved with recent extension of mole. Shops and chandlery near hbr. WiFi.

☎ HM +46 (0) 702 55 29 32
www.ystad.se (links Fritid – Småbåtshamnar – Ystads marina).

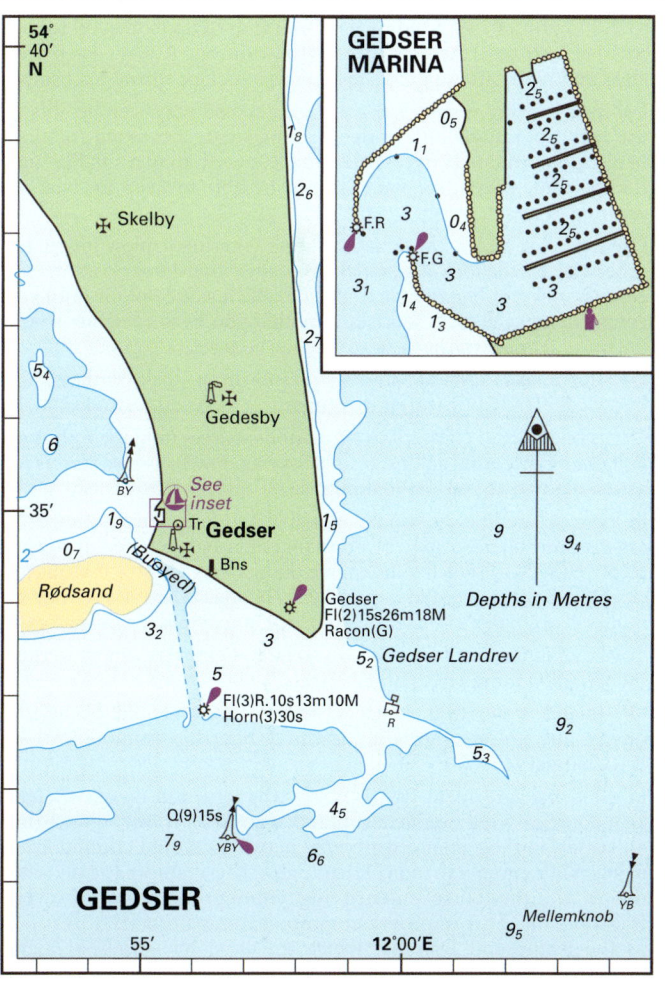

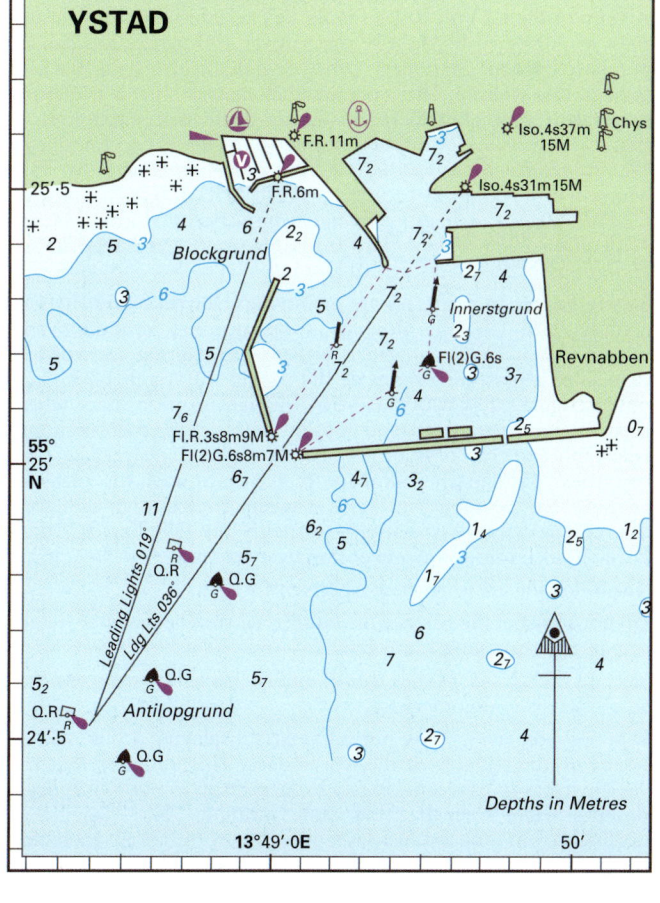

APPROACHES TO THE BALTIC

305

European Inland Waterways

Europe has a vigorous and growing network of inland waterways, which can easily be entered through Germany, the Netherlands, Belgium or France and which connects to the Baltic, the Black Sea and the Mediterranean. Whilst it was built and is still being developed primarily for commercial traffic, it offers interesting cruising into northern, middle and eastern Europe for pleasure craft. The scale of locks and other works is sufficiently generous for use by a majority of both motor cruisers and sailing craft with lowered masts.

Whilst detailed information is beyond the scope of this Almanac, the following country by country notes introduce the cruising potential, ports of entry, licensing and other formalities and sources of information for the four countries mentioned above.

For other countries, from Ireland to the west, as far as Russia to the east, a useful source of information is the *European Inland Waterways Map and Concise Directory*, 5th edition by David Edwards-May, published in 2015 by Transmanche Publications (distributed by Imray). This contains data on 30 countries, including some information on standing mast routes.

CEVNI and other rules

The CEVNI (*Code Européen des Voies de la Navigation Intérieure*) Rules are an inland waterway equivalent of the Collision Regulations (IRPCS).They are closely based on IRPCS, but with important additions to reflect that almost all inland navigation takes place within the constraints of narrow channels, and involves close quarters manoeuvring. They also provide a range of marks, signs and signals intended to be understood internationally.

In most of Europe, it is a requirement that UK helmsmen navigating inland waterways should hold an International Certificate of Competence (ICC) with a CEVNI rules endorsement. In the UK, tests on the CEVNI rules are administered by the RYA, and may be taken as written tests at many RYA approved sailing schools, with a number now offering an option to take the test online. The ICC so issued states that it is in accordance with the relevant (United Nations) resolution on Inland Water Transport.

A copy of the CEVNI Rules should be carried on board. The full rules as published by the UN run to over 190 pages, and can be purchased via the Stationery Office or downloaded from the UN publications website. They contain much material that is irrelevant to pleasure craft, but there are several competent summaries of that which is relevant, published as *The RYA European Waterways Regulations (the CEVNI Rules explained)* by Tam Murrell, 2nd edition 2012, reprinted 2015, *RYA Handy Guide to CEVNI*, 2016, *Euroregs for Inland Waterways* by Marion Martin, 3rd edition 2008 from Adlard Coles Nautical, and *RYA CEVNI Handbook* by Roy Gibson, 2011.

Slowly European countries are modifying their rules and signs to comply with CEVNI, although some regional variations still remain. The CEVNI equivalent of Rule 9, requiring craft of less than 20m length not to impede the passage of vessels which can only navigate safely within a narrow channel is one instance where there are local variations, and in some countries the corresponding rule applies to craft of less than 15m. On some waterways in some countries, particularly Germany, larger craft used for pleasure cruising may be subject to more stringent control than indicated above. The Barge Association – formerly the (UK based) Dutch Barge Association – is aware of the latest position.

The following are important aspects of CEVNI.

Do not obstruct the passage of commercial vessels, whether freight or passenger-carrying at any time.

Keep to the stb side of the channel unless directed by signs or other ship's signals to do otherwise.

Especially on rivers, look out for vessels displaying a blue flag or board on the stb side of the wheelhouse. This indicates that the vessel wishes to pass you stb to stb. At night or in poor visibility a flashing white light has the same meaning. Blue flagging is normally (but not exclusively) initiated by a vessel travelling upstream, to stay out of the way of one travelling downstream, but it may also be used to stay out of, or to take advantage of, the current, or to provide a better alignment on the approach to a quay, a bend, or a bridge or similar obstruction of the channel.

The navigable span of a fixed bridge is normally indicated by a yellow diamond (and a fixed yellow light at night). A single diamond/light indicates that the passage in both directions through the arch is permitted: if there are two diamonds/lights, then traffic in the opposite direction through the arch is not permitted.

Two red and white diamond shapes on a bridge span indicate an obligation to pass between them (possibly to avoid underwater obstructions) and two green and white diamond shapes indicate a recommendation to pass between them.

Light signals at locks and moveable bridges are increasingly standardised. A single R Lt means wait, a R Lt above a G Lt means prepare to proceed, and a single or double G means proceed. Two R Lts means no passage possible. (On smaller waterways, all lights may well be extinguished outside the scheduled operating hours of the lock or bridge.)

Vessels designed to transport dangerous cargoes display blue downward pointing cones (fixed blue lights at night). In France, some vessels still display an earlier alternative of red lights and cones, although most now comply with the blue of CEVNI. There may be one, two or three depending on the degree of hazard. Keep well clear and note that you may not be permitted to share locks with such vessels, especially when they are laden.

Whilst sound signals are not greatly used in inland navigation, when they are, a quick understanding is essential. CEVNI sound signals are generally the same as those of IRPCS, but there are additional signals for use when approaching junctions, and the CEVNI signals for acknowledging intention to overtake differ from those of IRPCS.

Code flag A, 'I have a diver down' is quite commonly used on inland waterways: stay well clear and proceed dead slow.

Hints and tips for inland cruising

Especially on the larger waterways, and the great rivers (Rhine, Schelde, Rhône, Seine etc) keep a good all-round lookout; powerful 'pusher' tugs, propelling four or more barges each of up to 4,000 tonnes are the equivalent of a ship of up to 18,000 tonnes and need to be treated with extreme caution. Always keep well clear and never attempt to race them to a lock or through a bridge.

Following larger vessels is a good idea as you may well be able to use lock operations and bridge openings that are timed for their benefit, but note that they will create less wash than a smaller boat for the same speed, so you may not be able to keep up without creating excessive wash.

On arrival at a lock check astern befor entering. Unless instructed otherwise by the lock-keeper, always enter after larger commercial craft. It may not be possible to decide which side to moor until you actually enter the lock, so make sure that you have adequate length lines and fenders for both sides of your boat.

Do not make fast to another vessel in a lock without the knowledge and approval of its skipper.

Occasionally (and contrary to regulations) barges hold their position in locks by motoring against a single spring, in which case stay as far astern of them as you can to minimise the effect of their wash.

In locks secure lines as soon as possible and keep them secure until after the turbulence caused by departing ships has subsided. If you are secure enough to switch your engine off in a lock, do so – it is quieter, cleaner and cheaper, and especially in regions where there may be numbers of smaller craft sharing the lock, it may well be obligatory.

Towed dinghies in a lock can be a source of embarrassment to their owner and a nuisance to other vessels.

On inland waterways radio communications should be at low power, and unless otherwise indicated, intership communications use Channel 10.

In 2000, an agreement (RAINWAT) was signed in Basel, whereby 16 countries with significant inland waterway traffic agreed that all vessels in their inland waterway networks would communicate using ATIS equipped radio telephones. These automatically send out a unique vessel identifying number as part of every transmission. This improves communications on waterways such as the Rhine and Danube, which are used by vessels of many different countries, since shore based ATIS receivers can

Inland Waterways of Germany

- Large scale waterway (class IV or larger)
- Waterway for 300t barges (class I or II)
- Waterway for small barges (class 0) or Light Craft

automatically recognise the identity and nationality of the transmitting vessel. The time scale for implementation of this was left in the hands of the national navigation authorities, and with the exception of France it had been generally adopted by 2015.

The RAINWAT agreement has been amended several times, most recently in October 2016, and anyone using ATIS capable equipment should now carry a copy of this latest version of the agreement on board. It may be downloaded, in Dutch, English, French or German from www.bipt.be, the website of the BIPT, the Belgian based telecommunications organisation that administers the system and maintains the international database of vessels. A comprehensive if possibly outdated (2010) explanation of ATIS, RAINWAT and the UK licensing procedures that allow UK vessels to comply is available on the Ofcom website.

DSC activated radios must not be used on European Inland Waterways, and ATIS must not be used within 14 miles of the coastline of the UK, the Isle of Man and the Channel Islands.

When navigating in longer tidal estuaries, such as the Scheldte in Belgium, note that the tidal predictions from an almanac, which are necessarily based on average river flow figures, become increasingly unreliable as one moves further upstream. Strong river flows increase the duration of the ebb and delay the time of LW, and thereby reduce the duration of the flood.

GERMANY

Cruising potential

As well as being accessible from the North Sea and the Baltic, German Inland Waterways interconnect to those of Poland, the Czech Republic, Austria, Switzerland, France and the Netherlands.

From the North Sea, the major routes for inland entry are via the Ems, Weser and Elbe estuaries. From its junction with the Nord-Ostsee-Kanal at Brunsbüttel to the city of Hamburg, (Germany's largest port,) is about 40M; this is a busy 'mast-up' route as far as the large City Sporthafen which is on the north bank just east of the extensive trip and tour boat moorings. Shallower draught craft can also cruise several smaller northern canals with entry via Emden or Wilhelmshaven.

	Time differences		Height differences in metres			
	HW	LW	MHW	MHWN	MLWN	MLWS
CUXHAVEN	0200 0800	0200 0900				
	1400 2000	1400 2100				
Gluckstadt	+0205 +0214	+0220 +0213	–0·3	–0·2	–0·2	0·0
Hamburg	+0338 +0346	+0422 +0406	+0·3	+0·4	–0·4	–0·3

From the Baltic, as well as the Nordostsee Kanal (Kiel Canal) and the smaller linked Eider and Gieselaukanal to Tönning, there is a possibility of entry from the sea to the Elbe-Lübeck Kanal at Travemünde, which takes one south to the Elbe.

Emden can be reached by the standing mast route (Vlissingen to Delfzyl) on the Dutch canal system, see section on Netherlands. There are two further connections from the Netherlands to Germany, the minor Haren-Rütenbrock Kanal in the north with a limited depth of 1·5m, and the lower Rhine south east of Arnhem.

The Moselle and its tributary, the Saar, link the French canals to German routes at Schengen and Saarguemines. For about 38km the Moselle is bounded by Luxembourg to the northwest, and Germany to the southeast.

The Rhine forms the boundary between France and Germany for about 184km of its navigable length and between Switzerland and Germany for a further 20km.

Northeastern links are provided by the Elbe which flows down through Prague in the Czech Republic (albeit with variable and limited depth) and the Oder-Spree Canal which runs east from Berlin to join the R Oder in western Poland which then flows north to enter the Baltic at Szczecin (Stettin). Southeast, the Main-Donau Canal links the Rhine to the Danube, and provides a route into Austria, Hungary and eventually to the Black Sea between Romania and Bulgaria.

The key north–south route is of course the Rhine, which in spite of carrying more freight than any road or railway in Europe, offers spectacular scenery and fascinating cruising. Since most of it is free flowing river, downstream cruising is much easier than upstream, and a useful strategy is to travel southeast through the French canals, and enter the Rhine at Strasbourg, upstream of its most dramatic stretch.

Berlin and its surroundings are a diverse and fascinating cruising ground, with the River Spree running right through the historic city centre past the Reichstag and close to the Brandenburg Gate. The former East Germany maintained and extended its canal network, and the Mecklenburg area northeast of Berlin with several hundred km of navigable waterways (which also links to the Elbe upstream of Hamburg) is one of several areas where facilities for cruising are steadily being improved.

Formalities Save for a number of smaller waterways, the German system is administered by regional water and shipping authorities and no licence or other fees are levied on visiting foreign craft. Unlike the Netherlands, most yacht harbours are either privately owned or run by boat clubs. These are normally very welcoming, but since they are required to contribute to the costs of maintaining navigation, they will charge (usually modestly) for moorings.

Particularly on the busier rivers and canals, expect checks by Water Police, which may include ship's and crew's papers, VHF licence. Sobriety of helmsman and active crew is also taken seriously. The permissible blood alcohol level for Rhine navigation is lower than the permissible level for car drivers. Checks may also be made on the usual safety related equipment, lifejackets, lifebuoys, fire extinguishers, anchor and first aid kit.

Sources of information In English a general account of the whole network is given by Barry Sheffield in *Inland Waterways of Germany* published by Imray 1996. In 2016 a revised 1st edition with updates by C & R Best and Rob Thomas was published. Unfortunately a significant part of the cruising information was not updated, although the new edition benefits from an extensively revised introduction.

Delius Klasing, based in Bielefeld, publish a range of chart guides in book and electronic form. Delius Klasing acquired the Edition Maritim range of guides several years ago, and now only the older guides are published under the Edition Maritim label.

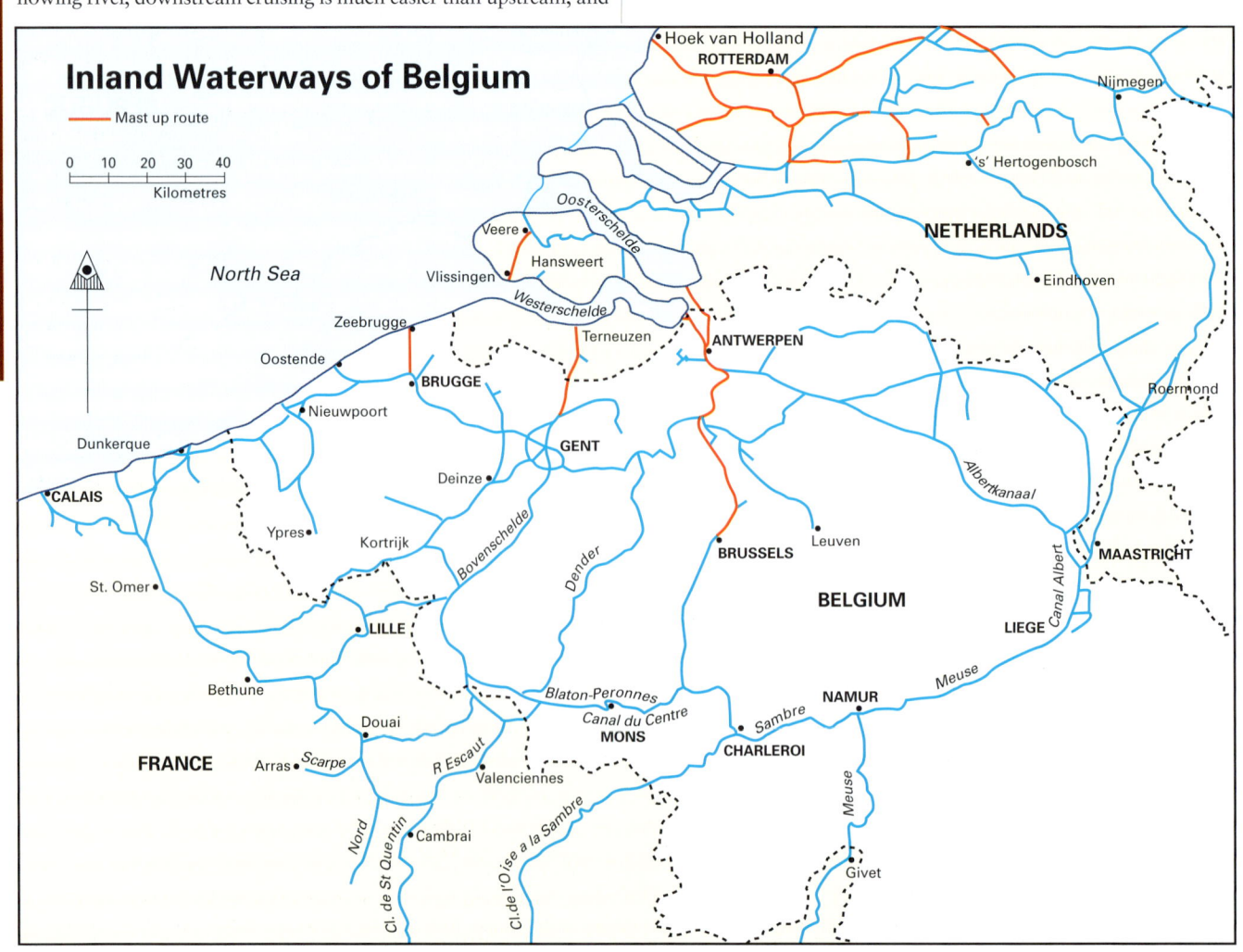

DSV Verlag published a useful set of 20 guides to German Inland Waterways in the 1990s, but these are now out of print and although a few still appear in bookshop lists, they are likely to be out-of-date.

Nautische Veröffentlichung of Eckernförde publish six inland cruising guides covering almost all of the area east of Hamburg and north from Berlin (as well as guides to Poland and the Swedish Göta canal).

Verlag Rheinschiffahrt of Bad Soden (between Mainz and Frankfurt) publish 8 guides, primarily to the Rhine and its tributaries and the Danube.

Binnenschiffahrt-Verlag of Duisburg offer a range of about a dozen guides including some on CD rom also covering the Rhine region and the Danube.

THE NETHERLANDS
Cruising potential
The fixed mast routes are described in the Netherlands section, but there is also a vast network of navigable waterways ranging from major rivers capable of accommodating 2,000-tonne barges, right down to navigable drainage channels barely wide enough to row a dinghy.

In some parts of the country, older mobile bridges on small waterways have been replaced by fixed bridges with headroom of 2·5m, so craft with low air draught have a greater choice of route.

Of the major seaports of the Netherlands, only Scheveningen does not connect into the inland waterway system.

There are three links between the Dutch and German canal systems, and several others to Belgium, from which the French canals and eventually the Mediterranean can be reached.

Formalities
Most of the network is open to navigation without licences or formality. Especially on the busier routes which carry large commercial vessels, police checks may be carried out, as described above for Germany.

In some rural areas, small waterways and areas of water opening off rivers may be designated as nature reserves from which powered craft are excluded. These restrictions are usually well signed and shown on the *Waterkaarten* and should of course be respected.

Smoothing the way – the Dutch canal system
All opening bridges and locks display red and green lights. Double red means the service is closed, either for lunch, the night, or during rush hour. Single red means the service is ready: combined with a green indicates it will operate imminently and you should be prepared to move through smartly. Green is go. If a bridge or lock opens and no green is seen, hold back – a commercial vessel may be given priority by radio. Public address loudspeaker announcements will be more valuable to you if you clearly display your national ensign on approach.

All bridge and lock facilities have a VHF channel: calling the name of the lock or bridge and asking for the next opening will usually provide the guidance you seek. Using the Dutch for 'please' encourages even better responses – phonetically *Als tu blieft* often shortened to AUB on signs. Thank you – *Dank U Vell* – rounds off communications with a nice touch! Most facilities will respond in English.

Many bridges these days are remotely operated: positioning your craft within easy view of the surveillance cameras will produce a faster response when facing a red. Alert the controller to your presence by calling on the posted VHF channel the name of the bridge and AUB eg. "Ruck Brug, Ruck Brug, Als tu Blieft." Within a few minutes the red over green lights will appear and you can line up for clearance. In rural areas a call button is sometimes mounted on a post near the bridge and must be used to initiate the service.

Railway bridges (Spoorbrug) are subject to strict schedules, and may open only three to four times a day, and briefly at that. Close attention to opening times can save hours of waiting. Traffic congregates at these critical openings, so be prepared and move through swiftly or risk the bridge closing in your face.

Waiting before locks and bridges is often encountered at the height of the season. Be prepared with copious fenders on both sides and raft as directed, moving ahead slowly into the lock. Getting one aft or centre mooring line ashore quickly, then fine tuning your position, makes for a more orderly landing.

Major facilities operate 24/7 during the summer months, many others between 0800-2000. In winter much of the non-commercial waterway network closes to pleasure craft or has heavily restricted hours of service – see notices on each facility for up to date details.

Many Dutch marinas moor bow-to in 'boxes', employing poles to secure the aft cleats. Often these poles are set for 3·5m beam, or even less. So, on allocation of a berth, it pays to make your beam known to avoid an untenable berth. And on berthing, have an aft mooring line ready to drop over the upwind pole on entry.

Sources of information
A majority of the system is covered by a series of *Waterkaarten* maps published by the ANWB and usually revised every two years. These show all major navigation features, and also useful detail relating to the surrounding landscape. Most importantly, they show water depths and heights of fixed bridges. Whilst they are in Dutch, with no multilingual glossary, the style and quality of the graphics used makes them easy to understand.

From 2015 the ANWB has offered electronic downloads of its *Waterkaarten* by way of Apps for iPhone and Android. These are significantly less expensive than paper charts, and are updateable online.

The most comprehensive information available is contained in of the *ANWB Wateralmanak 2* which gives water depths, bridge heights, moveable bridge and lock operating times, hbr facilities and much more. It is worth noting that although the *Wateralmanak* gives depths and heights in metres, the *Waterkaarten* maps use decimetres (dm).

For the Netherlands from Rotterdam southwards, see also Nautische Atlas & Gids in the Belgian section below.

Inland Waterways of the Netherlands by Louise Busby and David Broad (Imray, 2016) is a valuable guide to routes with 3·5m air draught.

BELGIUM
Cruising potential
From seaward, the Belgian waterway network can be entered at Nieuwpoort, Zeebrugge, and Oostende. The Scheldte estuary permits access at Terneuzen and Antwerp, and upstream of Antwerp the Scheldte remains tidal as far as Gent. Brugge is accessible from Zeebrugge with a fixed mast and similarly Brussels can be reached by way of the Brussels Maritime Canal which leaves the Scheldte near Rupelmonde and has lifting bridges providing 30m headroom.

With few exceptions, the network is heavily used by commercial craft, and so water depth is rarely an issue. The Albert Canal, running east from Antwerp across the Dutch border to join the Maas near Maastricht is probably the busiest, with lock chambers tripled to handle the volume of 2,000-tonne barges. However, there are quieter and more pleasant alternative routes.

In the south, five Belgian canals link into the French system. Whilst these are on a smaller scale (300-tonne), several of them still handle significant freight, including large tonnages of French grain shipped to the Belgian breweries in summer and autumn. The most westerly link connects to Dunkerque, the most easterly to the Meuse.

Formalities
Boats navigating the Belgian waterways must be licensed. Unfortunately, the Flemish and Walloon regions of the country have different requirements. Roughly speaking, Flanders is the part of the country north of about 50°45′N, (which is just south of Brussels conurbation,) and Wallonia is the remainder.

In Flanders, a licence disc is purchased which must be displayed on the boat. The charge, usually payable at the first lock or lifting bridge, depends on the duration of the licence, boat size and its maximum speed. Fortunately, even for a large boat, a 12 month licence is unlikely to cost more than about €160.

In Wallonia, there is no longer any charge for the use of the system, but it is still necessary to declare the route that you plan to take and be issued with a permit. It is possible to reduce the frequency with which you will need to present this permit, by obtaining a MET Number from one of the lock offices that is described as a *Bureau de Perception*, which are usually at the beginning or end of a waterway, or at a junction. You can quote this number to the lock by VHF, avoiding the need to physically present the permit.

The requirement for vessels underway to fly a red flag with a white rectangle to indicate intention to pass through locks was abolished in 2007, although a few local vessels still fly such a flag.

The Cruising Almanac

Inland Waterways of France

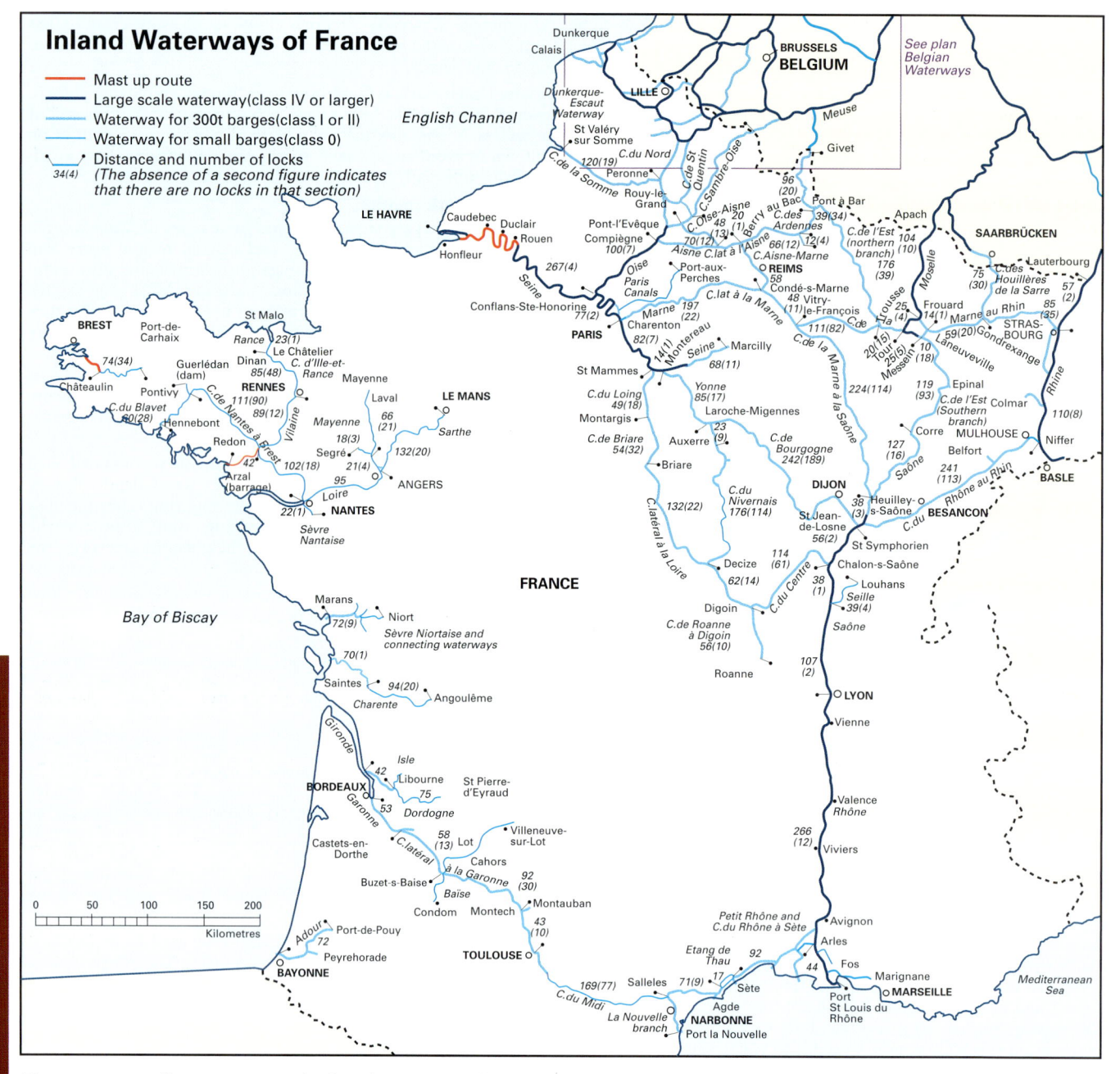

- Mast up route
- Large scale waterway (class IV or larger)
- Waterway for 300t barges (class I or II)
- Waterway for small barges (class 0)
- 34(4) Distance and number of locks (The absence of a second figure indicates that there are no locks in that section)

There are normally no customs checks when crossing between Belgium and its neighbours, except in the Schelde Estuary, where you might have arrived from seaward rather than another Schengen country.

Since 2005 it has been illegal for yachts to use untaxed (red) diesel in Belgium. Since 2008 the UK has permitted yachts to refuel with red diesel in UK harbours and marinas on condition that they pay duty on it, or at least that fraction of the diesel that was used for propulsion.

The Belgian authorities contend that even if duty is paid in this way, the use of red diesel remains illegal in Belgium, and there have been instances of checks on UK craft by the Belgian authorities, resulting in financial penalties being imposed of their owners. Both Belgium and the UK have complained about each other's interpretation of the European law. Until such time as this dispute is resolved, you are advised not to cruise in Belgium with any significant level of red diesel in your tanks.

Also note that in Belgium there are only a limited number of waterside refuelling points that offer white duty paid diesel. (These include Antwerp, Antoing, Bocholt, Brussels, Comines, Dijksmuide, Liège and Nieuwpoort.)

Sources of information

Inland Waterways of Belgium by Jacqueline Jones, Imray 2006, is an excellent and very comprehensive guide to the Belgian network.

Cruising the Inland Waterways of France and Belgium 20th edition, published by the Cruising Association (CA) in 2017, contains a wealth of information not published elsewhere on boatyards, moorings and other facilities.

Belgische Vaarwegen – Navigatie Atlas & Gids / Voies Navigables Belges – Atlas & Guide de Navigation Substantial (360 pages) guide, bilingual in French & Flemish, published by De Rouck Geocarte of St-Niklaas in Belgium in 2010. Excellent maps but no place name index.

Nautische Atlas & Gids published by De Rouck Geocarte in Brussels 2015-2016. Two substantial volumes, bilingual in French & Flemish. Volume 1 covers Northern France (as far south as Reims, Wallonia and the Brussels region. Volume 2 covers the Brussels region, Flanders and the Southern Netherlands as far north as Rotterdam. Good maps but no place name index.

The Dutch *ANWB Wateralmanak* contains a chapter with information about the Belgian waterways, in a similar format to the Dutch data noted above.

Fluviacarte No. 23, Belgium, new edition in 2013 of a useful route planning map published by Editions Fluviale.

The earlier section of this Almanac covering Belgium includes information and chartlets for the ports of Antwerp, Brugge and Gent which although inland are accessible by 'mast-up' routes.

FRANCE

Cruising potential

For more detailed information than this brief summary, see the CA publication *Cruising the Inland Waterways of France and Belgium* and the other sources of information given below.

From a yachtsman's point of view, France has a twofold attraction, offering routes between sea cruising areas, and as an interesting cruising area in its own right.

From seawards, the northern and central parts of the network can be entered from Dunkerque, Gravelines, Calais, the Somme estuary or by way of the Seine estuary.

All inland routes south converge on the Saône, and in turn the Rhône, which enters the Mediterranean at Port St Louis, some 40km west of Marseille.

The waterways of Brittany, which do not connect to the main routes, offer interesting cruising for smaller craft, however restricted headroom (2·5m) and water depth (between 1·2m and 1·0m or less at times of drought) prevent most seagoing craft from using them.

In the southwest, the Midi route provides a link from Atlantic to Mediterranean, albeit with limited depth.

The canal links between France and Belgium to the north, and Germany to the east have already been noted; crossing these borders involves no more formality than a change of courtesy ensign.

Formalities

The main navigable waterways in France are under the management of Voies Navigables de France, (VNF), who issue licenses and a *vignette*, that must be displayed on the boat. Charges are based on the length of the boat; licences are available for the full year, for 30 or 3 consecutive days and for a single day, all at reasonable cost. They are sold at VNF offices including the main ports of entry from sea or by canal, but many only open for limited hours. Thus it may be easier to apply well in advance by post. Internet payment is now possible, via the VNF website www.vnf.fr.

Licences are not needed for the Brittany waterways and the navigable part of the R Somme, both of which are under local control.

Boat safety checks are not common in France, but fire safety checks may be made, with an emphasis on ensuring that fire extinguishers are in working order and are in date. It is expected that they will be checked every 2 years.

When planning to use an inland route through France, note that stretches of canal or locks are sometimes closed for maintenance or repair. A list of the scheduled stoppages or *chomages* is available from the offices that issue licences and on the VNF website, which also lists the prices of the various *vignette* options, the addresses of the VNF offices and other information about navigation conditions, moorings etc. The list is normally published in March for the following 12 months, and is usually fairly reliable. Nonetheless unscheduled stoppages can occur, and it is a good idea to check when passing any VNF office.

Dimensions

The maximum dimensions for a yacht going from the UK to the Mediterranean via the main canals are: length 38·5m, beam 5·00m, draught 1·80m and air draught 3·50m. On the Burgundy route the maximum depth is only 1·40m, beam 4·50 and air draught 3·10m. The alternative Canal du Nivernais only offers 1·20m depth and 2·70m air draught.

For the Canal du Midi between Atlantic and Mediterranean maximum dimensions are: length 30m, beam 5·45m, water draught 1·40m and height 3·10m at the centre of bridge arches, reducing to 2·10m over 5·0m of beam.

Do not place too much reliance on published depths. On many canals dredging has not kept pace with silting up. Thus the nominal depth may only be available in the centre of the cut, and there are few mooring places with full depth alongside.

Through routes (see map)

The popular routes southwards through France pass through Paris, either entering the canal system at Dunkerque, Calais or via the Somme and selecting one of several possible routes; joining the Oise at Compiègne, and then south to Paris, or alternatively travelling up the tidal Seine from Le Havre or Honfleur to Rouen and then to Paris.

Navigation of the Seine is described in outline in Imray *Map of the Inland Waterways of France* or CA *Cruising the Inland Waterways of France and Belgium* and also in Fluviacarte No.1 *La Seine Aval du Havre à Paris*. Note that yachts are prohibited from navigating the tidal Seine upstream of buoys 27 and 28 (about 6km upstream of Honfleur) during the hours of darkness, and there are very few satisfactory moorings or anchorages.

Yachts travelling between Honfleur and Rouen must log in and out to the Port de Rouen at Honfleur, and Port Fluvial de Rouen, both on VHF 73, giving estimated time of arrival and confirming arrival.

Between Le Havre and Rouen, three spectacular bridges provide headroom of over 50m, so the route is navigable with masts stepped as far as Bassin St Gervais, where a new marina was opened in 2012 with all facilities including haul-out, repairs and lowering and storage of masts available. Alternatively masts may be unstepped and stored at the yacht hbr at Le Havre. Several French transport companies offer a service that transports masts between the Channel or Seine ports, and those of the French Mediterranean. This can be a useful alternative to transporting a mast on deck, which can be a stressful experience in locks, especially if there is considerable overhang.

After Rouen, the Seine offers good depth and 6m of headroom all the way to Paris. Once through Paris there is a choice of three main routes to the Saône.

The Bourbonnais (western) route Paris to Lyon via Canal de Briare, 643km and 158 locks, with moderate commercial and pleasure traffic. This is the easiest and quickest route, but check before starting, since in several recent years, problems with water supply to the southern end restricted passage to shallow draught boats, especially in late summer.

The Burgundy route Paris to Lyon via Dijon, 629km and 219 locks. Beautiful but slow, with little commercial traffic but many hire boats in summer season.

The Marne (eastern) route Paris to Lyon via Vitry-le-François, 713km and 155 locks. This carries a fair amount of commercial traffic, especially between Paris and Vitry, and is probably the best route if draught is close to the limit.

All three routes converge by Chalon-sur-Saône, and join the Rhône at Lyon. From Lyon, south to the Mediterranean is 310km with 13 locks. Whilst the Rhône is canalised, there is still a considerable current in some stretches, up to 3kns in normal times, but exceeding 6kns at times of flood. Coupled with strong winds that funnel along the river valley, dangerous conditions can be created, so unlike most inland cruising, it is important to heed weather forecasts. Do not try to enter the Mediterranean by way of the Rhône delta, which is shallow and also has restricted headroom. Either lock out at Port St Louis, or if west bound take the Petit Rhône and then enter the Canal du Rhône à Sète, from which there are several ways to the sea, including a recently opened cut at Frontignan.

The Midi route from the Gironde estuary through Bordeaux and Toulouse to Port la Nouvelle, Agde or Sète, is about 480km long with about 135 locks. This direct route from the Atlantic to Mediterranean offers some magnificent scenery and fascinating industrial and other architecture. The disadvantages are that parts of it are shallow and have limited headroom, and that especially in the months of July and August the Canal du Midi is overcrowded with hire boats.

Sources of information

Carte-Guides Fluviacarte More than 20 published, with English, French & German text and clear maps. *No.21* is a good route planning chart.

Carte-Guides Chagnon Limited range that appears to be no longer updated.

Editions du Breil Waterway Guides A series of 21 trilingual guides plus a good but unnumbered route planner, covering the whole of the French network save the north (pas de Calais.) For the Rhone, either Fluviacarte No. 16 or Breil No. 18 is essential.

For France from Reims northwards, see also *Nautische Atlas & Gids* listed in the Belgian section above.

Cruising the Inland Waterways of France and Belgium published annually by the CA. 20th edition January 2017.

Inland Waterways of France, 8th edition David Edwards-May. (Imray 2010).

Cruising French Waterways by Hugh McKnight (Adlard Coles Nautical 2005) gives water depth figures which barely take into account over 20 years of silting up and little dredging.

Waterway Routes through France. Map by Jane Cumberlidge (Imray 2005).

The VNF website www.vnf.fr contains a good deal of useful information in French, particularly the *Horaires* pages giving operating times for locks, moving bridges etc and the *Chomages* pages which provide information about closures of waterways or restrictions on navigation, both scheduled and unscheduled. Unfortunately there are only a limited number of pages in English and they are rarely updated.

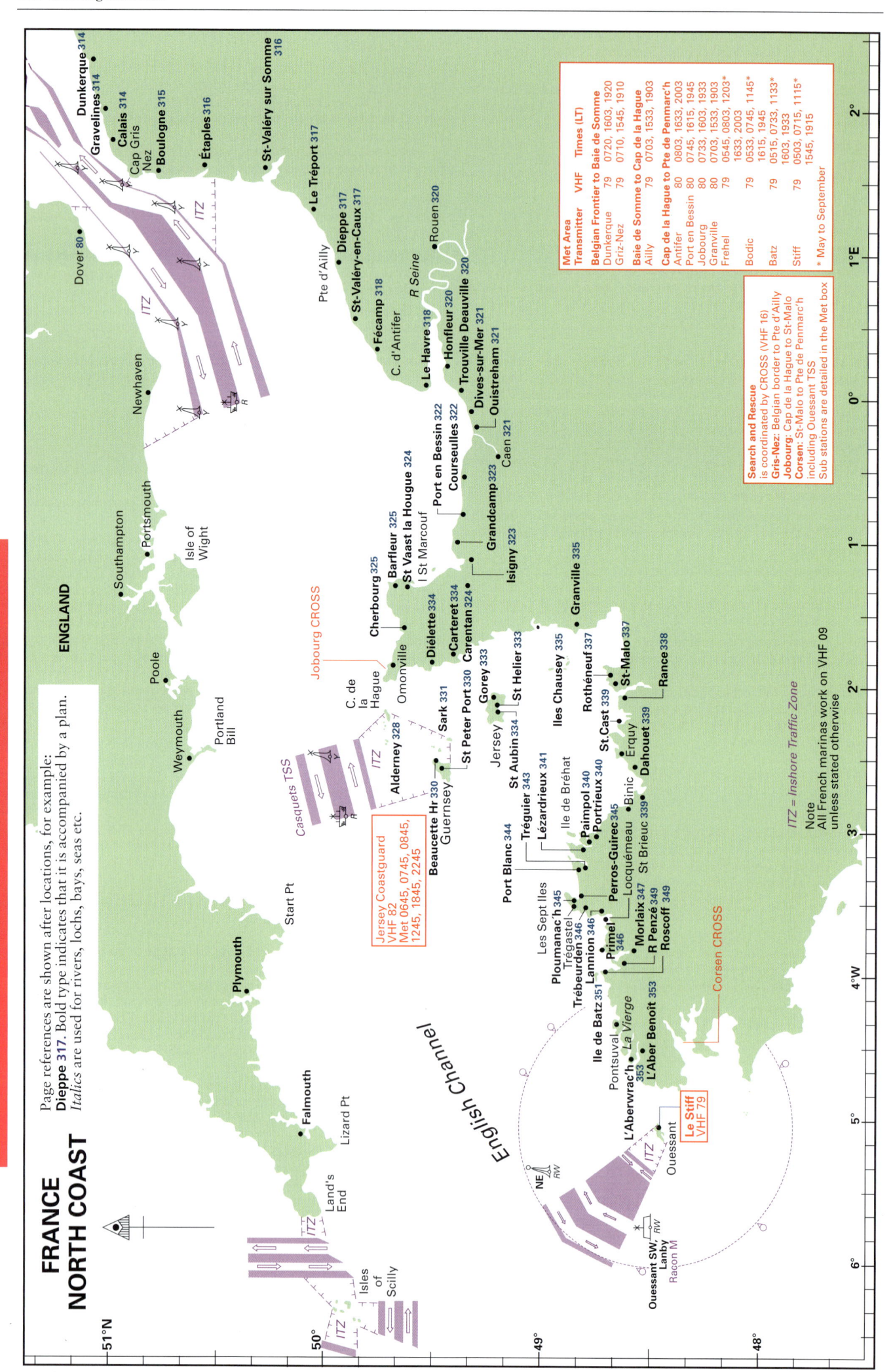

FRANCE – NORTH COAST AND CHANNEL ISLANDS

FRANCE NORTH COAST

Page references are shown after locations, for example: **Dieppe 317**. Bold type indicates that it is accompanied by a plan. *Italics* are used for rivers, lochs, bays, seas etc.

Locations

- **Dunkerque** 314
- **Gravelines** 314
- Cap Gris Nez
- **Calais** 314
- **Boulogne** 315
- **Étaples** 316
- **St-Valéry sur Somme** 316
- **Le Tréport** 317
- **Dieppe** 317
- **St-Valéry-en-Caux** 317
- Pte d'Ailly
- **Fécamp** 318
- C. d'Antifer
- **Le Havre** 318
- **Honfleur** 320
- Rouen 320
- *R Seine*
- **Trouville Deauville** 320
- **Dives-sur-Mer** 321
- **Ouistreham** 321
- **Caen** 321
- **Port en Bessin** 322
- **Courseulles** 322
- **Grandcamp** 323
- **Isigny** 323
- **Barfleur** 325
- **St Vaast la Hougue** 324
- I St Marcoup
- **Cherbourg** 325
- C. de la Hague
- Omonville
- **Diélette** 334
- **Carteret** 334
- **Carentan** 324
- **Alderney** 328
- **Sark** 331
- **Beaucette Hr** 330
- **St Peter Port** 330
- Guernsey
- Jersey
- **Gorey** 333
- **St Aubin** 334
- **St Helier** 333
- **Iles Chausey** 335
- **Granville** 335
- **Rothéneuf** 337
- **St-Malo** 337
- **St.Cast** 339
- **Rance** 338
- **Erquy** 339
- **Dahouet** 339
- St Brieuc 339
- **Binic** 340
- **Portrieux** 340
- **Paimpol** 340
- Locquémeau
- Ile de Bréhat
- **Lézardrieux** 341
- **Tréguier** 343
- Port Blanc 344
- Les Sept Iles
- **Ploumanac'h** 345
- **Perros-Guirec** 345
- Trégastel
- **Trébeurden** 346
- **Lannion** 346
- **Primel** 346
- **Morlaix** 347
- *R Penzé* 349
- **Roscoff** 349
- **Ile de Batz** 351
- *La Vierge*
- Pontsuval
- **L'Aberwrac'h** 353
- **L'Aber Benoît** 353
- **Le Stiff** VHF 79
- Ouessant
- Ouessant SW Lanby *Racon M*

England locations
- Dover 80
- Newhaven
- Portsmouth
- Southampton
- Isle of Wight
- Poole
- Weymouth
- Portland Bill
- Start Pt
- Plymouth
- Falmouth
- Lizard Pt
- Land's End
- Isles of Scilly

Key boxes

Jersey Coastguard VHF 82
Met 0645, 0745, 0845, 1245, 1845, 2245

Jobourg CROSS
Corsen CROSS

ITZ = Inshore Traffic Zone

Note
All French marinas work on VHF 09 unless stated otherwise

Met Area

Transmitter	VHF	Times (LT)
Belgian Frontier to Baie de Somme		
Dunkerque	79	0720, 1603, 1920
Griz-Nez	79	0710, 1545, 1910
Baie de Somme to Cap de la Hague		
Ailly	79	0703, 1533, 1903
Cap de la Hague to Pte de Penmarc'h		
Antifer	80	0803, 1633, 2003
Port en Bessin	80	0745, 1615, 1945
Jobourg	80	0733, 1603, 1933
Granville	80	0703, 1533, 1903
Frehel	79	0545, 0803, 1203* 1633, 2003
Bodic	79	0533, 0745, 1145* 1615, 1945
Batz	79	0515, 0733, 1133* 1603, 1933
Stiff	79	0503, 0715, 1115* 1545, 1915

* May to September

Search and Rescue

is coordinated by CROSS (VHF 16)
Gris-Nez: Belgian border to Pte d'Ailly
Jobourg: Cap de la Hague to St-Malo
Corsen: St-Malo to Pte de Penmarc'h including Ouessant TSS
Sub stations are detailed in the Met box

France – North Coast and Channel Islands

This cruising ground covers the French coast from Dunkerque in the NE to Brest in the west and includes the Channel Islands. The varied landscape and culture are a delight. The cliffs from Calais to Boulogne give way to low land across the Bay of the Somme. Once past Boulogne there is much less cross-channel traffic and also the tides are less strong. From Le Tréport to Le Havre, high land with harbours such Dieppe, St-Valery-en-Caux, and Fécamp nestling in gaps in the chalk cliffs give way to low cliffs and sandy beaches south of the Seine estuary starting in Honfleur through to Barfleur. The fascinating and thought-provoking history of the D-Day landings makes this particular part of Normandy memorable.

For many people, Cherbourg, with a harbour accessible in virtually all weathers, is the first port of call having crossed the Channel. It is a convenient place to start cruising the coast to the east or to the west towards the Channel Islands. The Channel Islands and adjacent coast of France combine superb sailing with excellent opportunities to use the tides to advantage and to hone your pilotage skills.

The rocky coastline of North Brittany is stunning, with plenty of options: rocks and islands extend well offshore; there are many attractive harbours, secluded anchorages, and rivers. Tides are strong and as you go west the Atlantic swell becomes more noticeable.

Formalities

For craft registered in EU countries and whose last port of call was in an EU country there is no requirement to clear in. France does not operate Schengen declarations. However, boats may be subject to random inspection by French Customs at any time both at sea and in hbr. NB The Channel Islands are not part of the EU. For documents to be carried, see *Customs* p.16.

Crossing to France E of the Greenwich meridian the Dover Strait Traffic Separation lanes must be crossed and the rules observed. Similarly there is the Casquets TSS to the E of the Channel LtV. Lanes must be crossed at right angles as defined by the course steered, not the course made good. In the Dover Strait listen on VHF 16 or 11 for broadcasts from the Channel Information service. Avoid the voluntary separation scheme used by cross-channel ferries. High speed ferries demand extra vigilance especially when approaching from astern. Where International Port Signals are in use it is vital to obey them even though some fishing vessels or local craft may be ignoring them. A listening watch on VHF is advised at all commercial ports.

Boats may be scrubbed only in approved areas with the proper facilities for collecting the residue. It is an offence to have out of date flares on board.

France, Dunkerque to Cherbourg and cross Channel to England distances (miles)

	Dunkerque	Calais	Boulogne	Dieppe	Fécamp	Le Havre	Ouistreham	St Vaast	Cherbourg	Dover	Sovereign Hbr	Brighton	Nab Tr
Dunkerque	0												
Calais	28	0											
Boulogne	43	21	0										
Dieppe	95	74	53	0									
Fécamp	117	97	77	33	0								
Le Havre	142	124	101	57	26	0							
Ouistreham	156	134	114	71	40	21	0						
St Vaast	174	154	133	94	66	54	47	0					
Cherbourg	184	161	142	107	79	70	65	29	0				
Dover	42	22	27	89	98	125	140	139	143	0			
Sovereign Hbr	85	65	48	59	63	83	93	125	101	44	0		
Brighton	109	90	73	74	71	83	92	86	87	68	25	0	
Nab Tr	135	115	113	65	74	83	75	72	65	95	52	29	0

Marinas and Pilotage

French marinas use VHF 09 unless stated otherwise, many do not provide hoses from taps on pontoons. Diesel (*gazole*) is widely available, in some ports by self-service only, requiring a credit or debit card. Marinas do not normally pre-allocate berths. Enquire at the *capitainerie* on arrival. Pump-out facilities are being installed in many marinas.

The following pilots may be of value supplementing the information in this *Almanac*:
The Shell Channel Pilot Tom Cunliffe (Imray)
The Channel Islands, Cherbourg Peninsula, North Brittany RCC Pilotage Foundation (Imray)
Votre Livre de Bord; Atlantique Manche – Mer du Nord published annually by Bloc Marine, *Almanach du Marin Breton*
Bloc – Côtier Manche-Atlantique is a much smaller version but with all the necessary information for the Channel and Brittany coasts.

www.guide-du-port.com contains information on 15 ports between Granville and Perros Guirec.

Tidal information, with curves, is easily available from http://maree.info

Both British Admiralty and Imray charts cover this area, but more detail may be found on the French SHOM (www.shom.fr) charts available from British chart agents, often only to order, or in France from most chandlers.

The datum on some old charts may still be ED 50. Position derived from a GPS must be adjusted otherwise it may be up to 100m out.

Telephone

When in France calling a French number with a UK mobile, use the international dialling code +33 and drop the leading zero e.g. +33 (0)1 23 45 67 89.

BELGIUM TO CALAIS

Passage lights	BA No
W Hinder LtV	0145
Fl(4)30s21m12M	
Horn Mo(U)30s (··–)	
Dunkerque	1114
Fl(2)10s 59m26M	
Calais Main	1144
Fl(4)15s59m22M	
Calais Approche Lt buoy	1162
VQ(9)10s8m6M AIS	

STREAMS RELATED TO DOVER
Mainly parallel to banks; generally 1½–2kn.
HW Dover –0100 E to NE. HW +0500 W-going.

A series of sandbanks running roughly SW to NE, on which the sea breaks heavily with wind against tide, lies off this section of the coast. The banks shelve gently on the seaward side but are steep-to on the land side. Cross in the gaps between the banks rather than crossing the banks themselves, except possibly at HW in light winds. The coast is low-lying with few readily identifiable features. On the approach, course should be set for buoys marking the banks rather than attempting to pick up a shore landmark.

The inshore approach from Belgium is via Passe de Zuydcoote (2°30′E), entering between E12 S card buoy and E11 buoy, Fl.G.4s, to port then steering SW, leaving E10, 8 and 6 Lt buoys to N and E9 to S, to the inshore buoyed channel to Dunkerque.

From the N take the Banc de Flandre route (9m). Cross the West Hinder traffic lanes to enter it W of Oost Dyck N Card Lt buoy at N end of Oost Dyck bank. Some six miles SW steer W between Bergues-S S card and Ruytingen-E N card buoy. Thence SW to leave Ruytingen-SE E card buoy and Dyck-E E card buoy to stb and the W card buoy off Haut-Fond de Gravelines to port to enter the buoyed and lighted Calais-Dunkerque channel.

Alternatively the Banc de Flandre route can be approached further W and entered between Ruytingen-N and Ruytingen-E N card buoys.

The inshore channel W from Dunkerque is clearly marked and lit.

France – Channel Ports

DUNKERQUE

Standard Port Dunkerque
DS Dover −0200E; +0400W

A commercial hbr, good shelter for yachts and good facilities at two tidal marinas. Two locked marinas for large vessels rather than short-term visiting yachts. A possible entry to the canal system.

Approach from E or W along one of the inshore buoyed channels. The offshore banks dry in places at LAT and should only be crossed having verified water depth available, and in light winds.

Signals Three pairs of Lts are shown in Avant Port, the top pair for the large W lock, the middle for the S (Wattier) lock, and the bottom for Trystram. A listening watch on VHF 73 is advised. Small craft movements may be halted in fog or poor visibility.

Entrance Straightforward except for strong cross-set across entrance. At night enter between two ldg lines 179° and 185° (both F.Vi.4M) and then keep along E breakwater on Ldg Lts both Q, 137°, through Avant Port and continue to tidal marinas.

Locks The W lock out of Avant Port leads into W hbr – yachts not allowed. Trystram lock, just past LtHo on stb, leads into inner basins, canal system and non-tidal marinas. For times call *Dunkerque VTS* VHF 73.

Berthing Tidal
• **Port du Grand Large** tidal marina to port. Pontoons will take large and multi-hull yachts, 3m draught, 25 visitors'. Moor anywhere on visitors' pontoon.
• **Yacht Club de la Mer du Nord** tidal marina. About 50 visitors' berths. Depth 2–2·5m. HM monitors VHF 09 when on duty. Moor at visitors' pontoon initially and enquire at *Capitainerie*.

Non-tidal
Enter via Trystram lock, then make for the lifting br (opening co-ordinated with locking). About 1½ cables before the far lock turn to port under a second lifting br (opens a few minutes after the first). Now turn to stb for Bassin de la Marine, or to port under a third br into Bassin du Commerce. Moor at first pontoon. Advisable to book in first week in June when racers congregate. Office opens only 1700–1900 Monday–Friday and 1000–1700 Saturday–Sunday.

Facilities Engineers, chandlers and sailmakers. Fuel at YCMN on inner end of visitors' pontoon and Port du Grand Large. Long walk to shops from Port du Grand Large.

☎ /VHF Port Control 03 28 28 75 96, VHF 73; Port du Grand Large 03 28 63 23 00, both non-tidal marinas 03 28 24 58 80; YCMN 03 28 66 79 90.

Items of interest *Duchesse Anne* square-rigger, maritime museum, lighthouse, St Eloi church, town hall, numerous war memorials.

DUNKERQUE OUEST

7M W of Dunkerque is a tanker and ferry terminal; yachts are forbidden to enter.

GRAVELINES

Standard Port Dunkerque
HW (sp) −0010 (np) −0015
LW (sp) −0005 (np) −0010
MHWS MHWN MLWN MLWS
+0·5m +0·3m +0·1m 0·0m
DS Dover +0600W; −0100E

A small fishing port on the mouth of River Aa with long drying entrance, a non-tidal small marina and access to canal system.

Approach Six conspicuous 60m buildings 1·5M to the east and the spire of Petit-Fort-Phillipe identify the entrance.

Entrance Dries with variable sandbanks. On no account attempt to pass between the N card bn and E pierhead due to a submerged training wall. Beware strong E going tidal stream off entrance near local HW. On entry, for the first 100m keep nearer to the E pier. Without local knowledge access is only possible from HW−0200 to HW, is difficult in fresh onshore winds and should not be attempted in such winds over Force 5. Entrance to marina in Bassin Vauban has single pair of lock gates which open approx HW±0300, when the depth, over the lock sill is about 2·0m. Max beam in lock 6m. Possible to lock into canal system at far end of the basin but requires 48h notice and only if free flow is possible; ☎ 03 59 73 42 42.

Berthing Visitors' berths are on the first pontoon to stb; most dry to very soft mud. Single keel boats remain upright. HM may direct you to a berth.

Facilities. Fuel from garage. Large supermarket 1km, small supermarket on site. Good restaurants in town.

☎ *Capitainerie* 03 28 65 45 24; Lock 03 28 23 19 45.

Items of interest Vauban fortifications, arsenal museum.

CALAIS

Standard Port Calais
DS Dover −0200E +0330W

A very busy ferry port geared to British visitors, with a non-tidal basin for yachts and access to the canal system.

Approach To the N of the entrance is the bank Ridens de la Rade which at MLWS has only ½m in places. In winds of Force 6 or more from NW to NE it is wiser to make for Boulogne; otherwise the bank

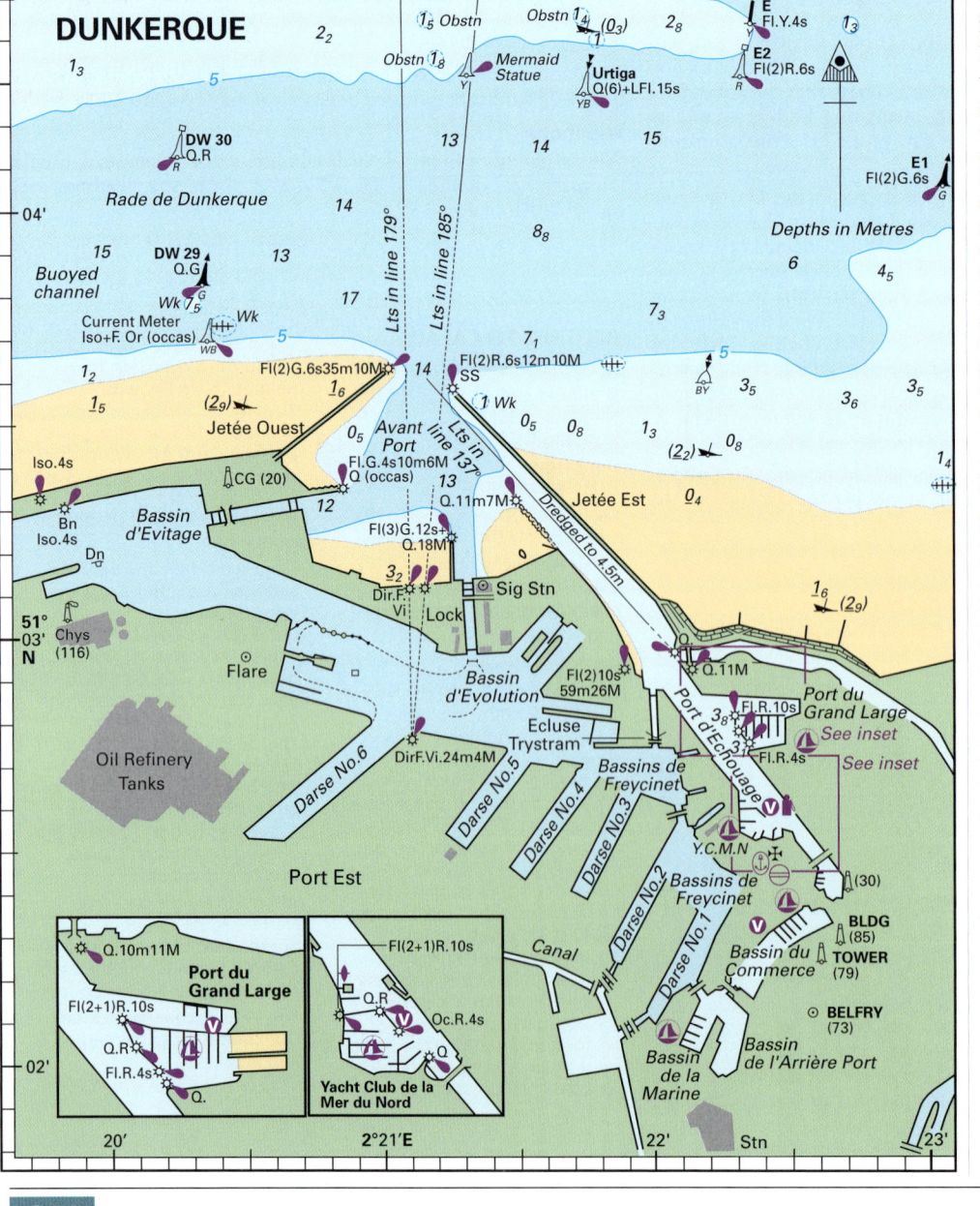

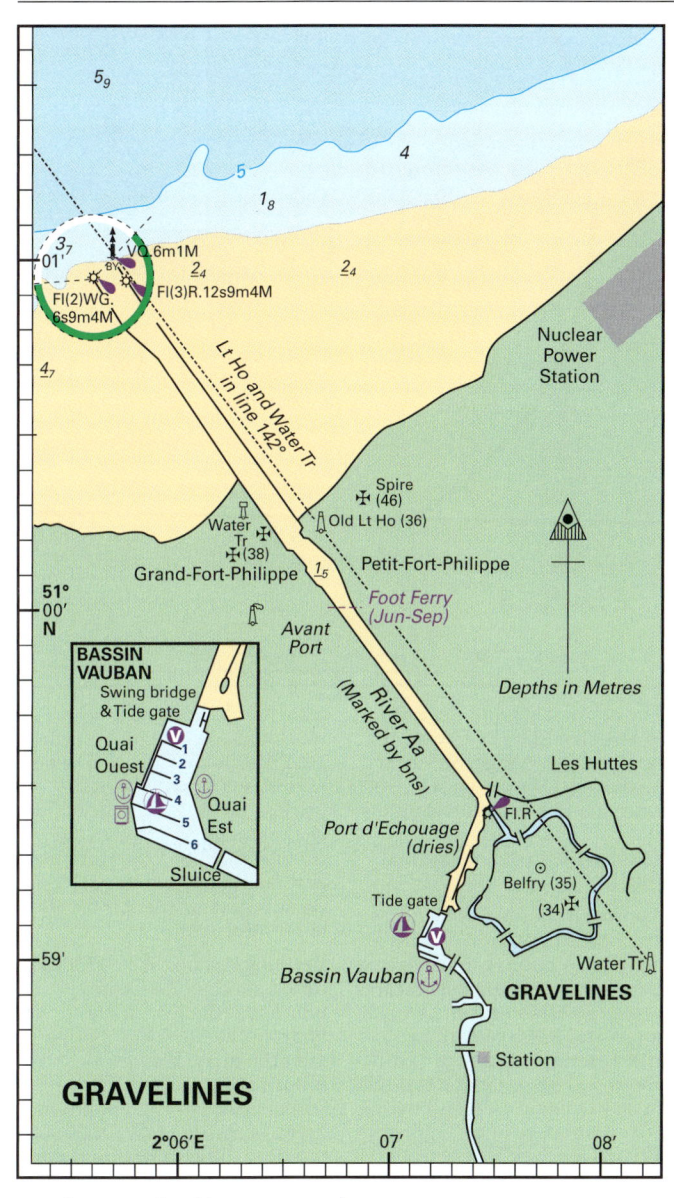

The Cruising Almanac

may be crossed safely at HW±0300. With less water keep S of the R buoys S of the shoal when coming from W; from E keep at least 2M offshore and do not make for the entrance until the W jetty head bears about 100° – in bad weather keep on round SW end of the bank. The banks 1M to the NE of the outer end of the Jetée Est continue to move.

Signals IPTS shown to seaward from E jetty for entry to Avant Port, and at foot of W jetty for entry to Arrière Port. Signals are also shown for exit to stb on leaving Bassin de l'Ouest as well as foregoing. These signals must be obeyed, with no exemptions for small craft. Attempts to transgress receive loudspeaker-amplified rebukes. Call *Calaisport* on VHF 17 to request permission and monitor. Enter at best speed with engine assistance.

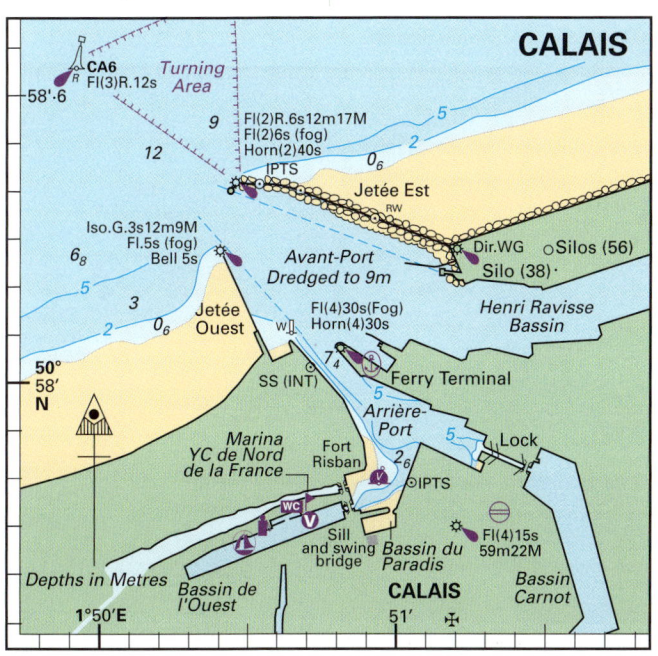

Entrance If asked by Port Control to wait outside, avoid the fairway. Some protection on the ebb may be found behind tip of W jetty. Beware strong current past E jetty; on entry, keep W jetty close to stb and bear to stb round Fort Risban (beware shallows) for entrance to yacht basin. For the canals lock into Bassin Carnot, then through a second lock into Bassin de la Batellerie and thence under br to port.

Berthing Waiting buoys in Arrière Port. Concrete blocks reported at foot of wall opposite Fort Risban, dangerous at less than half tide. Berth in marina through lifting br depth maintained at 3m by gate. Tide gauges indicate depth in entrance. Red and orange lights are shown 15mins before br opening which is HW-0200 HW-0100 HW HW+0100 HW+0200 HW+0300 but opening may be delayed by harbour traffic. Vessels intending to leave should contact Calais Port VHF 17 otherwise the br may not open. Once inside, the visitors' pontoon is immediately to starboard. You will be required to produce your ship's papers, and possibly passport and proof of insurance.

Facilities Diesel. Crane for demasting, and chandlery at Calais Nautic 03 21 96 07 57. Wide range of bars and restaurants. Rly to Paris, ferries to Dover. WiFi.

☎/**VHF** *Calaisport* VHF 17; Port de Plaisance 03 21 34 55 23; Yacht Club de Calais 03 21 97 02 34.

Items of interest Town hall, lighthouse, belfry.

BOULOGNE

Standard Port Calais
HW -0025   LW -0022
MHWS MHWN MLWN MLWS
+1·6m +1·3m +0·5m +0·2m
DS Dover +0330S -0200N

A fishing and commercial port with tidal marina. Accessible at all times except in very strong W–NW winds.

Approach The sea breaks heavily on the Bassure de Baas shoals, N and S of the entrance in gales from SW to NW, when it is best to keep 3M offshore until entrance bears E; otherwise from S keep about 1½M offshore inside the shoal. From W make for ZC1 Y buoy, Fl(4)Y.15s, and head E. The church tr is prominent behind the town as is the tall Colonne de la Grande Armeé (145m).

Signals Yachts must obey the IPTS shown from SW pierhead of inner harbour for entry to the latter and from signal mast at Darse Sarraz Bournet for exit to outer harbour. Call *Boulogne Port* VHF 12 for permission to enter or leave.

Entrance The N breakwater is submerged for its outer ½M with the outer end marked by a tr, Fl(2)R.6s (Ldg Lts F.G and F.R, 197°, lead to Ro Ro berth). 1ca inside S pier steer S until inner piers open (Ldg Lts front F.G with neon ▲, rear DirF.R, 123°), then steer for inner harbour. Follow round the N side for the marina.

Berthing Avant Port all tide marina on S bank before lock and bridge. 70 visitors' berths, some extra wide where fingers have been removed; beware of metal projections from the pontoon in these. Fuel berth and scrubbing grid beyond last pontoon. The locked Bassin Napoleon, access ±0300HW, is used for long stay visitors.

Facilities Fish market. Diesel. Scrubbing grid. Laundry. Boat lift in Bassin Napoleon. WiFi.

DOVER TO CALAIS
See p.78

CALAIS TO LE HAVRE

Passage lights	BA No
Cap Gris Nez Fl.5s72m29M	1166
Cap d'Alprech Fl(3)15s62m23M	1190
Pointe d'Ailly Fl(3)20s95m31M	1234
Cap d'Antifer Fl.20s128m29M	1250
Cap de la Hève Fl.5s123m24M	1256

The approach to Boulogne is impeded to the NW by the Bassure de Bas, marked by N and S cardinals over which steep seas develop in wind.

The features of concern outside the 10m contour after Boulogne are the Vergoyer, Bassure de Baas and Ridens de Dieppe banks which throw up breaking big seas with wind. The latter two are not buoyed. Inshore, drying banks are found until Ault after which the coast is more steep-to until Le Havre.

The approach channel to Cap d'Antifer must be crossed at right angles and not inshore of buoys A21 and A22. The approach channels to Le Havre and the Seine should be crossed with care.

The Fécamp Offshore Wind Farm is being developed (2017) in the vicinity of 49°53'·00N 0°14'·00E, with a planned 83 wind turbines. A metmast has been established in position 49°50'·85N 0°13'14E.

FRANCE – NORTH COAST AND CHANNEL ISLANDS

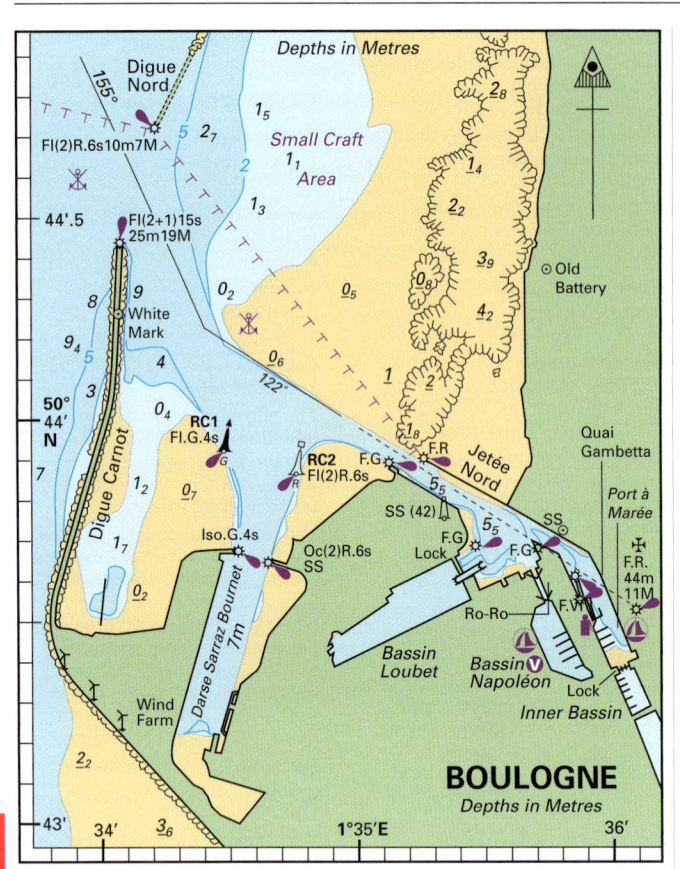

☎ /VHF Port control VHF 12; Marina 03 21 99 66 50.

Items of interest Interesting old town, church, Nausicaa Aquarium.

ÉTAPLES

Standard Port Dieppe
HW +0012   **LW** +0030
MHWS MHWN MLWN MLWS
+0·2m +0·2m +0·3m +0·4m
DS Dover −0245N +0315 S

The drying estuary of the River Canche. Le Touquet is a popular holiday resort: beware sailboards, dinghies and swimmers.

Approach The approach is impracticable with strong winds from SW through W to NE because of breakers. It should be attempted only in daylight, in settled weather between HW±0200 according to tide and preferably before springs to avoid the risk of being neaped. (There is 3m at springs but only 1m at neaps.) Identify La Canche Lt tr (Or oct with brown band) at Le Touquet, S of entrance, and the heights of Terres de Tourmont, 175m, to N.

Entrance Channel is marked by buoys and bns, altered to meet changes. The first pair is usually about ½M W of Pte de Lornel, whence the course is on the N side of the estuary. After the buoys, currently seven pairs, the channel to Étaples is marked by port bns.

Berthing Small drying basin at Le Touquet is no longer used. At Étaples, there is a marina for yachts up to 13m but only 1·3m draught; some moorings for visitors. Current makes mooring difficult except at slack HW. Accessible HW±0200, open to NW.

Facilities Pump-out. Fuel from garages. Good shops at Le Touquet. Shipyard.

☎ /VHF *Capitainerie* 03 21 84 54 33. VHF 09 (HW±0200).

Items of interest Le Touquet-Paris-Plage has much human interest during high season.

SOMME ESTUARY

Standard Port Dieppe
Le Hourdel HW+0020
MHWS MHWN
+0·8m +0·6m
St Valery HW+0035
DS Dover −0215NNE +0315SW

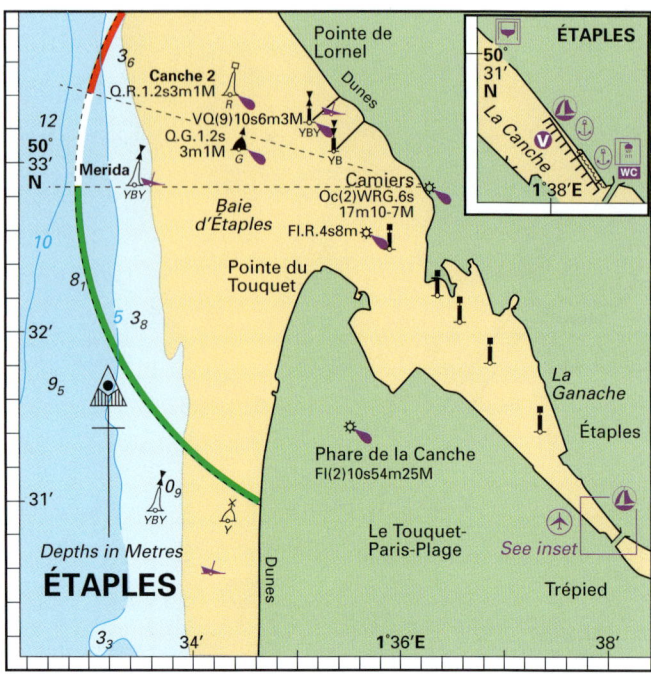

The approaches and the estuary to St-Valéry dry; Le Crotoy is a small fishing village. St-Valéry is somewhat larger with a marina and a lock giving access via the Canal Maritime d'Abbeville to the main canal system.

Approach should not be attempted in onshore winds, at night or in poor visibility. Coast is low-lying, prominent features being the LtHo of Ault (W tr, R top, 95m) 8M S of entrance and Toran (W tr, R top, 32m) about 3M SE of landfall buoy. Accurate navigation and timing are essential, to allow 2hrs (at 4kn) to reach St Valéry from the entrance. Approach S1 at HW−0100 suggested.

Entrance Make for the Baie de Somme RW buoy AT-SO, Mo(A)12s, about 3M 325° from Toran LtHo. The positions of the channel buoys vary from year to year. The first pair (S1 and S2) at time of publication are SE of the card buoy. The channel winds – it is easy to mistake which pair to make for. It approaches the blockhouse on Pte du Hourdel, after which the Crotoy channel (1m MHWS), with buoys marked C, runs NE. The major channel runs SE towards the training wall, St Valery marina, and canal lock. Go to www.portsaintvalery.fr for latest information.

Berthing Anchor at Le Hourdel (dries, sand) or Le Crotoy pontoons (shallow draught boats only). St-Valéry marina is after the quay. Visitors' moorings (maximum 12m) on hammerhead of each pontoon, 2·1m, accessible HW±0100; mooring difficult when stream running. If waiting for lock it is sometimes possible to tie alongside a work boat opposite the marina. Enquire at the *bureau du port* because the canal is frequently closed due to lack of water.

Facilities Water and petrol at marina. Diesel at garage. Shops at St-Valéry and Crotoy; nothing at Le Hourdel.

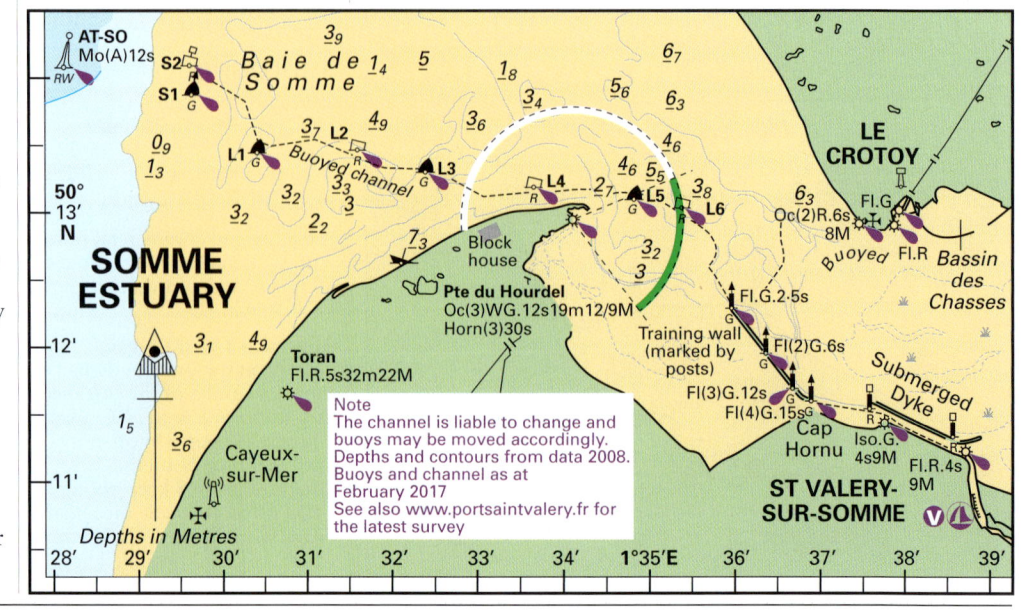

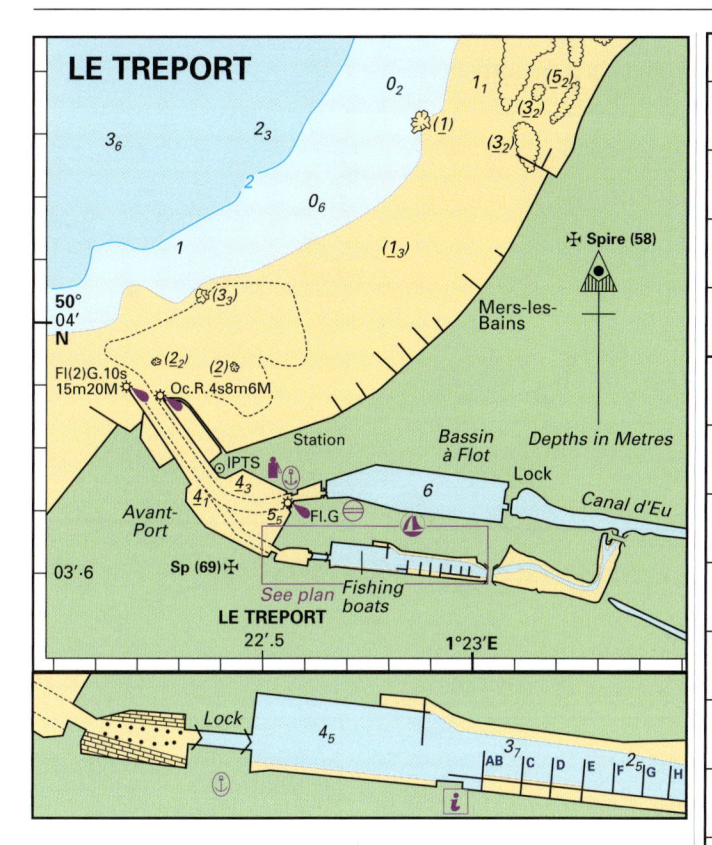

◑ St-Valéry-sur-Somme Marina 03 22 60 24 80.

Items of interest Steam railway.

LE TRÉPORT
Standard Port Dieppe
HW +0003   LW +0010
MHWS MHWN MLWN MLWS
+0·3m +0·2m +0·1m +0·1m
DS Dover +0200 SW –0430NE

A small drying commercial port and holiday resort with wet basins and yacht berths.

Approach Difficult to identify by day. Distinguishable from adjacent towns by two clock towers or at night by west jetty Lt Fl(2)G.10s15m20M Horn(2)30s. Difficult in strong onshore winds; severe scend in outer harbour in such conditions.

Entrance dries 2m, Avant Port dries 4·3m in centre, 2m in lock approaches. From W keep E pierhead, Lt Oc.R.4s, open of W pierhead, Fl(2)G, to clear off-lying rocks. Allow for NE set, and squalls in entrance. Call on VHF 12 before entry.

Berthing Enquire at *capitainerie*. Yacht berths at far end of S basin (Port de Pêche), 2·2m. Crowded and difficult for more than 12m. Strong current at times through the pontoons. Gates open approx HW±0400, entry lights. If full may have to use Bassin du Commerce, N basin.

Facilities Water on pontoons and on quay; stores; fuel from garage.

◑/VHF HM 02 35 50 63 06, VHF 12.

Items of interest Funicular railway, Mont Huon military cemetery.

DIEPPE
Standard Port Dieppe
DS Dover –0515ENE +0015WSW

A commercial, fishing, and ferry hbr with a large tidal marina which welcomes visitors. Accessible at all states of the tide though there can be a large swell in the entrance with strong N'ly winds.

Approach is straightforward, but the entrance is exposed to winds from NW to NE, causing a heavy scend. Entrance channel and Avant Port are dredged to 5m. Beware strong tidal stream across entrance. The east jetty has a W tr with R top, Iso.R.4s12m8M while the west has W tr with G top Iso.G.4s11m8M.

Signals IPTS signals control entry/exit during ferry movements. Yachts are required to request entry before entering hbr on VHF 12 and to request permission to exit before leaving marina. Signals displayed on W jetty ½ca from seaward; for leaving, display is on W bank at N end of Port de Plaisance, opposite signal mast; additional Lts may be shown above normal signals; R or G for ferry entering or leaving, W for dock gates open, 2R dredger in channel. Simplified code at entry to inner basins.

Entrance Listen on VHF 12; do not attempt when a ferry is entering or leaving. On the flood make for the up-tide jetty at entrance, passing the ferry terminal at the E side of port entrance, and then follow W wall around fixed wavebreak close W of entrance to Arrière-Port (prohibited to yachts) into marina Jehan Ango at Quai Henri IV.

Berthing Port de Plaisance at the Quai Henri IV (50 berths for visitors). Call on VHF 09 because pontoons are access controlled from shore. In high season there are pontoons alongside entrance to Ango lock; some scend in winds NW to NE. You will be required to produce your ships papers.

Facilities Fuel, shops, good restaurants. Saturday market. Rly to Paris. Ferry to Newhaven. WiFi.

◑/VHF Port de Commerce 02 35 84 10 55; Harbour Control (*Dieppe Port*) VHF 12. Marina Jehan Ango 02 35 40 19 79, VHF 09.

Items of interest Maritime museum, museum in castle.

ST-VALÉRY-EN-CAUX
Standard Port Dieppe
HW –0005   LW –0015
MHWS MHWN MLWN MLWS
–0·5m –0·4m –0·1m –0·1m
DS Dover –0500ENE +0030WSW

A holiday resort with locked marina.

Approach Dangerous in strong winds from NW to NE. From NE keep 1½M off to avoid shoals (0·6m) ENE of entrance which can be identified by the four dome-roofed buildings of Paluel nuclear power station 3M to the W and six conspic wind turbines immediately to the E. The west jetty has G tr and the E a W mast.

Entrance dries 2·5m. Leave R posts marking wave-break ramp close to port to avoid shingle bank off W pier, then keep to mid-channel. On the flood there is an eddy across the entrance from E to W until HW+0030.

Berthing Avant Port accessible HW±0300, moor on buoys to wait for gates to inner harbour to open. Gate, 9m wide, operates HW±0215 (day), ±0030 (night, April–October only). Inside tie to pontoon on stb and report to hbr office. 40 visitors' berths.

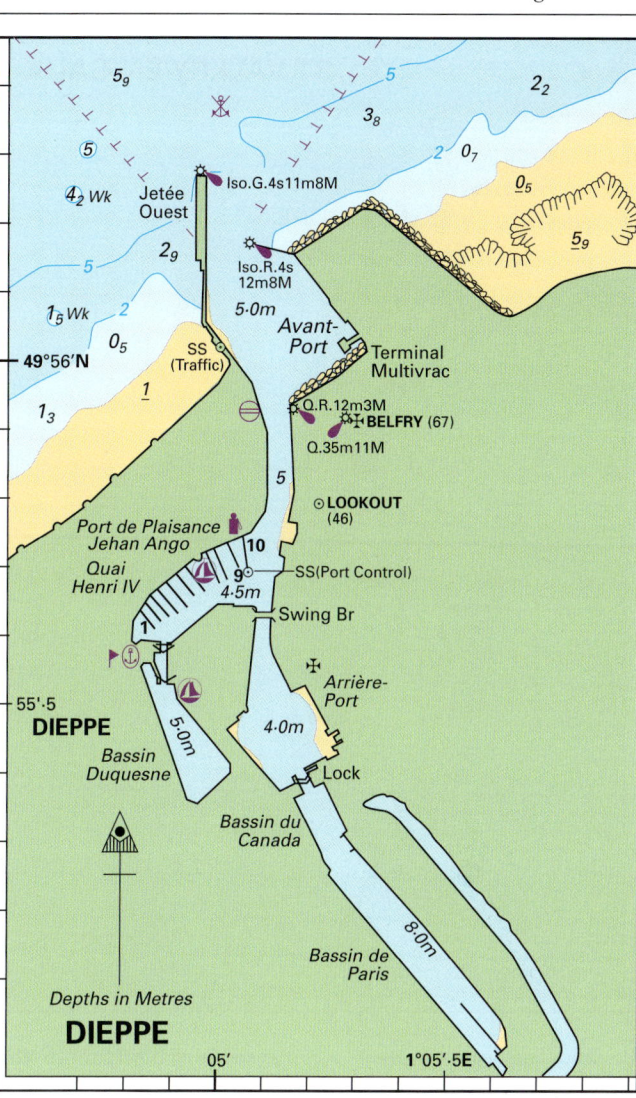

The Cruising Almanac

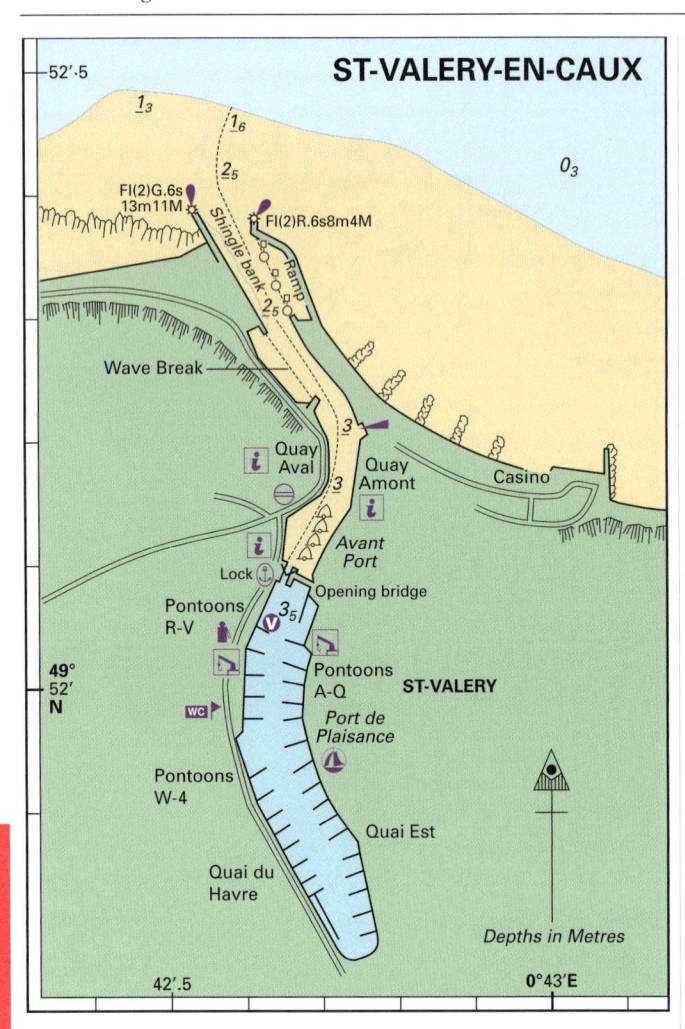

ST-VALERY-EN-CAUX

Facilities Fuel from service station, shops, especially fish. Choice of restaurants.

☎ Marina 02 35 97 01 30.

Items of interest Henry IV house, cliffs.

FÉCAMP

Standard Port Dieppe
HW −0013   LW −0035
MHWS MHWN MLWN MLWS
−1·0m −0·6m +0·3m +0·4m
DS Dover +0015SW −0500NE

A fishing port with good tidal yacht marina and locked basin.

Approach Dangerous in strong onshore winds. SW of hbr are two square church towers (one with sloping top) and a water tr (conspic). Give wide berth to rocks N of entrance: Pte Fagnet semaphore in view guarantees 3·7m. Jetty marked by Grey tr with R top Fl(2)10s15m16M Horn(2)30s.

Signals IPTS on tr by Avant-Port show when Bassin Bérigny is open.

Entrance is dredged 1·5m, but is subject to shoaling. Heavy swell frequent: in strong onshore winds attempt only from HW−0200 to +0100. Best approach on ldg ln 082°, Q.R.10m4M (rear) and Q.G. 14m9M on SW jetty head; beware spit running W from latter and cross-set onto rocks during flood which flows strongly (ebb is weak). At end of entrance channel turn to stb for yacht berths.

Berthing 75 visitors' berths at pontoons in Avant Port (Pontoon C, 1·2m, severe scend at times) or in Bassin Bérigny (gates open HW−0200 to HW+0045). If Avant Port berths full, raft on hammerhead and report to *Capitainerie*.

Facilities Fuel with card, chandlery, supermarkets, restaurants.

☎ Marina 02 35 28 13 58; Bérigny lock 02 35 28 23 76.

Items of interest Bénédictine distillery.

LE HAVRE

Standard Port Le Havre
DS off Le Havre is complicated by the flow from the Seine and an eddy close N of the entrance.
DS 3M W of Cap de la Hève:
Dover −0415NE +0045SE;
+0245SW −0515SE
Close inshore of Cap de la Hève:
Dover −0315NE +0045NW +0345S
2M S of entrance:
Dover −0615S −0415E −0215NE −0015 slack +0045W

A busy commercial and ferry port and a major yachting centre, well sheltered tidal marina.

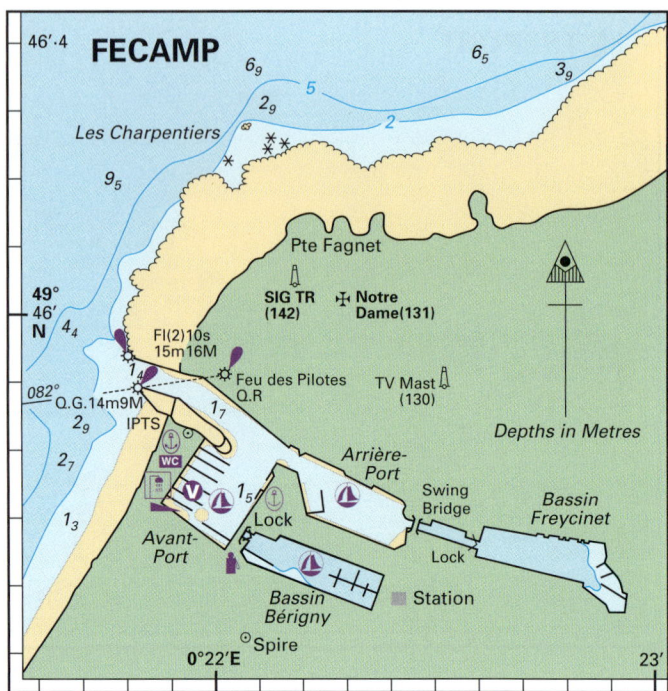

Approach The main hazards are the Banc de l'Éclat, 1m, which lies approx 2M WNW of the entrance, and the shallows at the mouth of the Seine.
From the NE aim to pass 1½M off Cap de la Hève and enter the main channel W of LH12.
From the S or the Seine pass to the W of Duncan L. Clinch W card buoy and proceed with caution to the main channel.
From the W make for LHA safewater mark Mo(A)12s AIS at 49°31'·4N 0°09'·8W and follow the main channel.
In all cases leave LH 2000 W card buoy to stb; give way to commercial traffic by keeping just outside the main channel, crossing it if necessary at right angles, and monitoring VHF 12.

Entrance and Berthing For the marina, pass the end of Digue Nord and leave the short spur breakwater Fl(2)R.6s to port, but do not leave the main channel until W end of Digue Augustin-Normand becomes visible. Unless directed otherwise find a berth (often rafting) on the marked visitors' pontoons and report to the *capitainerie*. If making for Le Havre from the Seine when conditions in the outer estuary are bad, it is better to enter the Canal at Tancarville: locks open HW (Le Havre) −0400 to +0315. An inner basin, Port Vauban, is available for long stay visitors (3 nights or more). Make arrangements with the Capitainerie in the main marina the day before by 1730LT. The lock opens twice daily during April to October and once daily otherwise.

Facilities Fuel at SE corner of outer basin of yacht hbr; grid, and crane for unstepping masts. Good shopping near Les Halles Centrales to E of marina. Rly and bus connections, ferry to UK and Ireland.

☎/VHF Port control VHF 12, 20 callsign *Le Havre Port*; Port de Plaisance 02 35 21 23 95.

Items of interest Maritime museums, fine arts museum (includes local boy Monet), amazing concrete church by Auguste Perret.

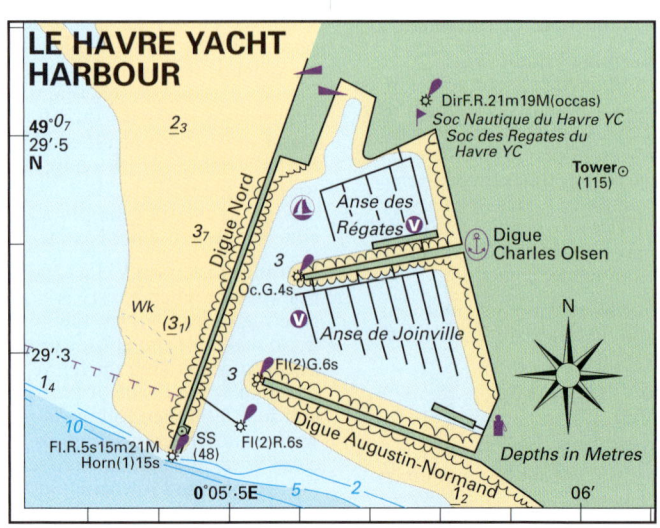

318

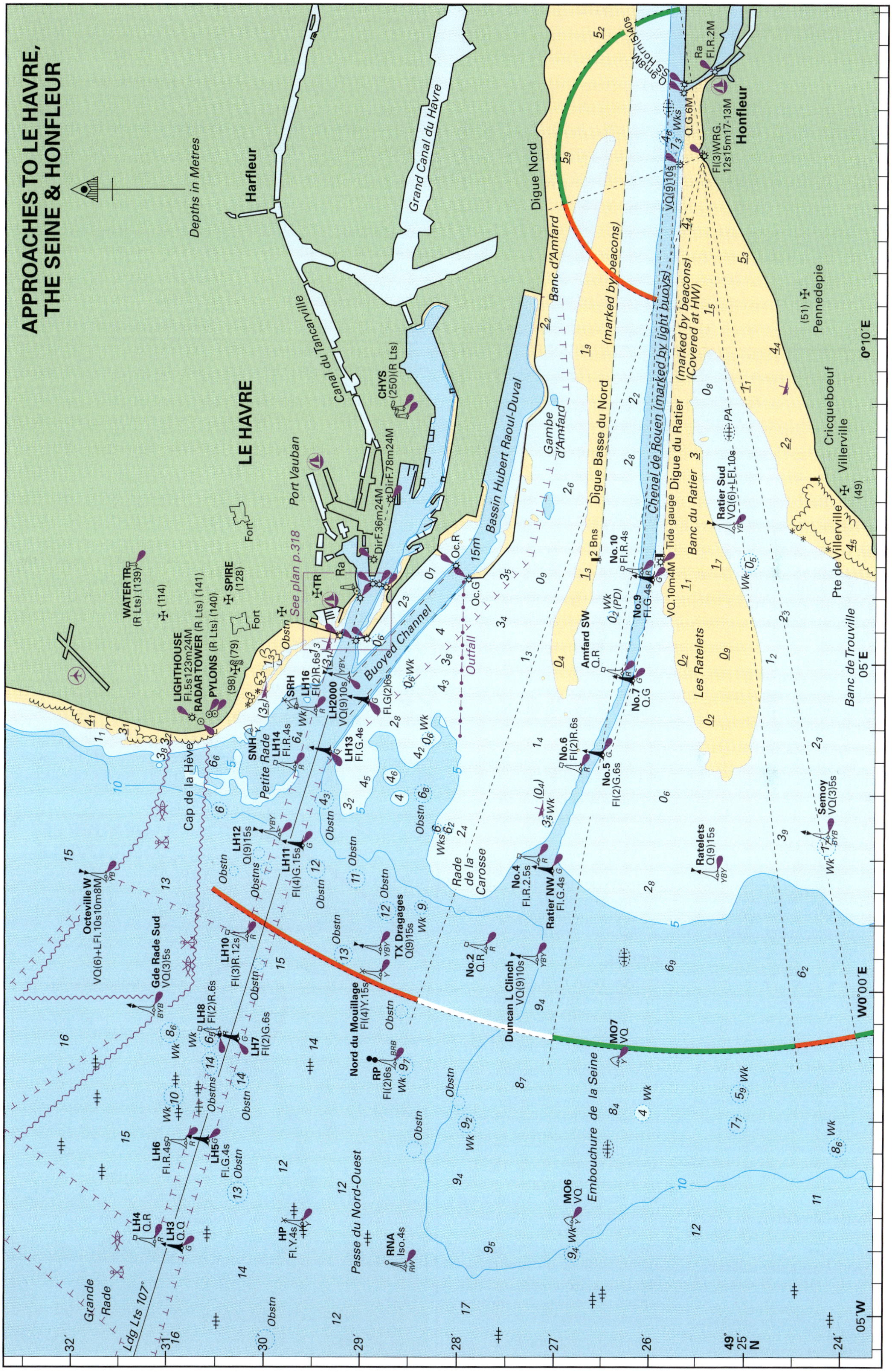
APPROACHES TO LE HAVRE, THE SEINE & HONFLEUR
Depths in Metres
LE HAVRE
Harfleur
Honfleur
Grand Canal du Havre
Canal du Tancarville
Port Vauban
See plan p.318
Bassin Hubert Raoul-Duval
Buoyed Channel
Outfall
Digue Nord
Banc d'Amfard
Gambe d'Amfard
Digue Basse du Nord
Chenal de Rouen (marked by light buoys)
Digue du Ratier
Banc du Ratier
Les Ratelets
Banc de Trouville
Pte de Villerville
Villerville
Cricqueboeuf
Pennedepie
Cap de la Hève
Petite Rade
Grande Rade
Rade de la Carosse
Passe du Nord-Ouest
Embouchure de la Seine
Ldg Lts 107°
LIGHTHOUSE Fl.5s123m24M
RADAR TOWER (R Lts) (141)
PYLONS (R Lts) (140)
WATER TR (R Lts) (139)
SPIRE (128)
CHYS (250) (R Lts)
DirF.36m24M
DirF.78m24M
Octeville W VQ(6)+LFl.10s10m8M
Gde Rade Sud VQ(3)5s
LH4 Q.R
LH3 Q.G
LH6 Fl.R.4s
LH5 Fl.G.4s
LH8 Fl(2)R.6s
LH7 Fl(2)G.6s
LH10 Fl(3)R.12s
LH12 Q(9)15s
LH11 Fl(4)G.15s
LH14 Fl.R.4s
LH13 Fl.G.4s
LH16 Fl(2)R.6s
LH2000 VQ(9)10s
HP Fl.Y.4s
RNA Iso.4s
RP Fl(2)6s
Nord du Mouillage Fl(4)Y.15s
TX Dragages Q(9)15s
No.2 Q.R
Duncan L Clinch VQ(9)10s
MO7 VQ
MO6 VQ
No.4 Fl.R.2.5s
Ratier NW Fl.G.4s
No.6 Fl(2)R.6s
No.5 Fl(2)G.6s
Amfard SW Q.R
No.7 Q.G
No.10 Fl.R.4s
No.9 Fl.G.4s
VQ.10m4M
Tide gauge
Ratier Sud VQ(6)+LFl.10s
Ratelets Q(9)15s
Semoy VQ(3)5s
Fl(3)WRG. 12s15m17-13M
Q.G.6M
Fl.R.2M
(marked by beacons)
(Covered at HW)
49° 25' N
0°10'E
05'E
0°00'E
05'W

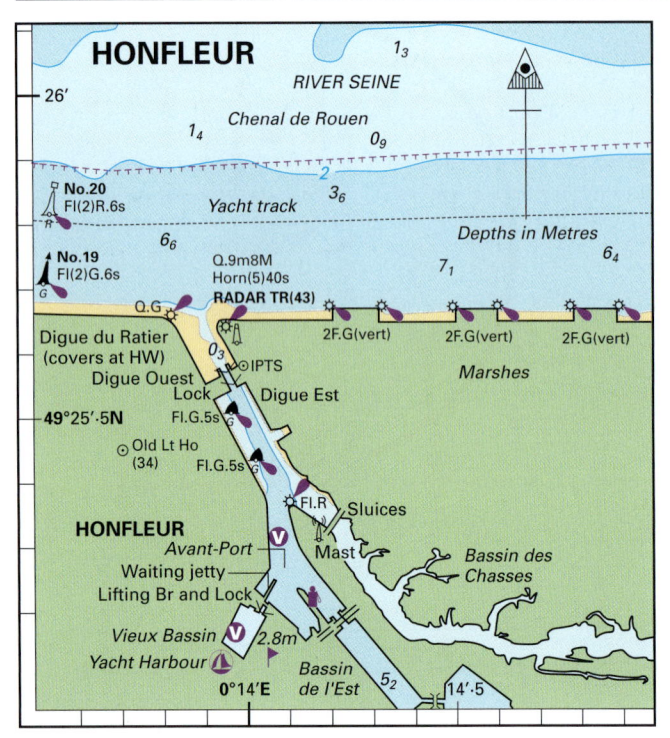

LE HAVRE TO CHERBOURG

Passage lights	BA No
Pointe de Ver	1396
Fl(3)15s42m26M	
(obscured when bearing >275°)	
Iles St Marcouf	1424
VQ(3)5s18m8M	
Pointe de Saire	1442
Oc(2+1)10s11m10M	
Cap Barfleur	1454
Fl(2)10s72m25M	
Cap Lévi	1462
Fl.R.5s36m17M	

STREAMS RELATED TO HW DOVER

9M WSW of Cap de la Hève – 0515E +0045W, 1½kn

9M NE of Grandcamp –0515SE; +0045NW; 2kn

Inshore W of Iles St Marcouf: – 0515 S-going to SE –0015 NE-going to NW, 1kn

Between Pte de Saire and Pte de Barfleur +0415SSE –0315 NNW, 2¾kn

3M N of Pte de Barfleur –0515SE +0045 WNW, 5¼kn

Pte de Barfleur: slack water. +0430 and –0200.

In strong onshore winds there is no easily accessible port of refuge between the Seine and St Vaast. Tidal streams can run at up to 4kns in the Seine approaches. With onshore winds against ebb seas are steep and break. The streams in Baie de la Seine are weak until rounding Pte de Barfleur. Approaching Iles St Marcouf keep clear of Banc du Cardonnet, extending 6M to SE, marked by E card buoy, VQ(3)5s at SE end, with another E card (wreck) buoy Q(3)10s halfway along N edge; and of Banc de St Marcouf extending 2½M NW, marked at NW end by W card buoy VQ(9)10s.

In the Barfleur race the sea breaks heavily, especially at Springs with wind against tide. It extends 3–4M E and NE from the point and should be given a wide berth. From Basse de Rénier buoy to Cherbourg, keep well N of Pierre Noire W card buoy, Q(9)15s to clear the shoals off Cap Lévi. (Leaving Cherbourg with the E-going tide, the stream sets hard onto the shoals).

HONFLEUR

Standard Port Le Havre
HW (sp) –0150 (np) +0135
LW (sp) +0040 (np) +0025
MHWS MHWN MLWN MLWS
0·0m 0·0m +0·1m +0·4m
DS in Seine: LW Le Havre +0130E +0700W (approx HWD –0500 at sps +0530nps)

A locked fishing port with several non-tidal basins, one for yachts. A picturesque town and popular tourist attraction. Very busy in high season.

Approach Via Chenal de Rouen, buoyed and lit with submerged training banks either side marked by bns. Yachts are required to keep outside the buoyed channel, close N of R buoys (2m). Coming from W, round Ratier NW G buoy, Fl.G.2·5s to clear Banc du Ratier.

Signals IPTS code shown to E of entrance. Locks 2R(vert) or 2G(vert).

Entrance Conspic Radar Tr on E side. Wait N of Chenal de Rouen until entry permitted, no waiting facilities in entrance. Pass E of buoys 19 and 20. Beware of strong current across the entrance channel, very strong around half tide. In strong NW–N winds water in lock rough when seaward gates are open. Lock opens on the hour for ingoing traffic and on the half hour for exit. Free flow approximately HW ± 0200.

Berthing
- **Avant Port** raft up to pontoons on west side, best for large yachts
- **Vieux Bassin** controlled by Cercle Nautique Honfleur YC (max. 20m)

There is a lifting br across the entrance which opens in season at 0830, 0930, 1030, 1130, 1630, 1730, 1830, 1930. Be ready to enter or leave on time – it does not wait for ditherers. While waiting for the br, make fast to one of three metal ladders on the W side. The moorings to port and at far end are for local boats only; immediately to stb is an area reserved for fishing boats. Visitors raft up alongside pontoon about a third of the way down the SW (stb) quay. Wait afloat in outer harbour; beware rush of boats leaving as br opens.

Larger boats may lie in Bassin de l'Est – consult HM.

Facilities Water on pontoons; fuel only at garages. Good shops; boatyard.

☎/VHF Capitainerie 02 31 98 87 13; Honfleur Sea Lock 02 31 98 72 82, VHF 17; Radar Tr, Honfleur Radar VHF 73. See www.cnh-honfleur.net for details.

ROUEN

Standard Port Le Havre
HW (sp) +0305 (np) +0240
LW (sp) +0525 (np) +0525
MHWS MHWN MLWN MLWS
 –0·2m –0·1m +1·6m +3·6m

60M upstream of Honfleur on N bank in the basin St Gervais is a large marina, Port de Plaisance La Crea downstream of the historic centre of Rouen, with all facilities. ☎ 02 3508 3059 or 06 07125241. This is the last possible stop for yachts with mast stepped. An adjacent boat yard has travel lift with crane and can unstep and store masts for anyone planning to venture further upstream.

Rouen is a major port, and this stretch of the Seine can be busy round the clock.

Note that navigation by pleasure craft is forbidden E of buoys 27 and 28 (about 3M upstream of Honfleur) between 30 min after sunset and 30 min before sunrise.

DEAUVILLE / TROUVILLE

Standard Port Le Havre
HW (sp)–0100 (np) –0010
LW (sp) +0005 (np) +0000
MHWS MHWN MLWN MLWS
 +0·4m +0·3m +0·3m +0·1m
DS Dover +0530NE –0215SW

Deauville is a sophisticated and expensive holiday resort with a private marina. Trouville offers a municipal hbr with basic facilities, but a practical town.

Approach dries for 6ca. In good weather, approach can be made after half-tide; in strong onshore winds, from HW–0200 to HW or avoid altogether. From N keep W of the town to avoid Banc du Ratier (S side of Seine estuary) and inshore shoals. From W keep 1½M offing to Trouville SW buoy, W card VQ(9)10s 49°22'·6N 0°2'·6E, then steer about 100° for the entrance. At

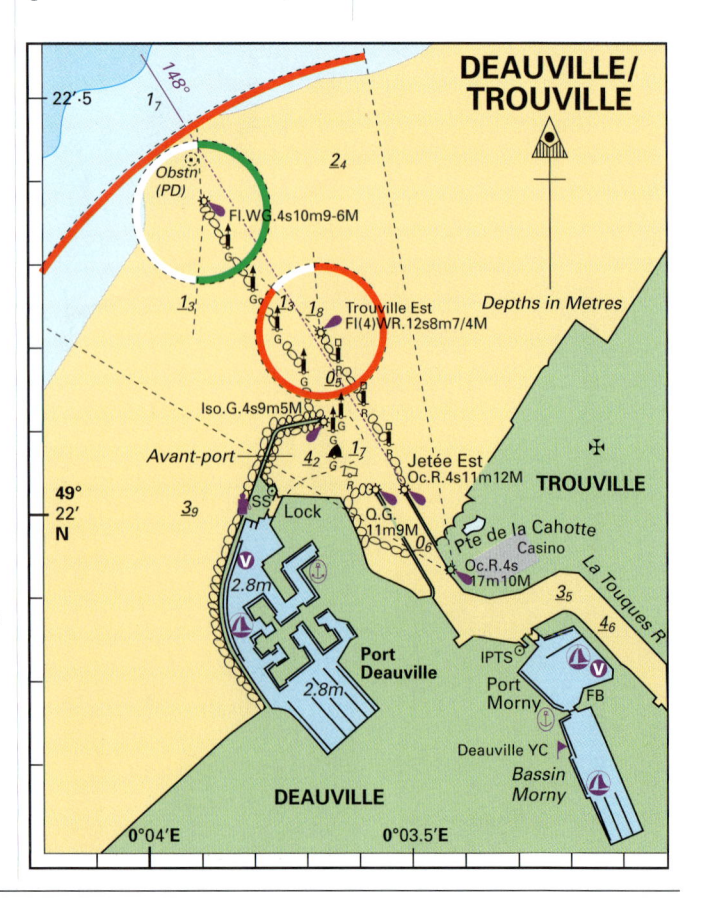

DIVES-SUR-MER

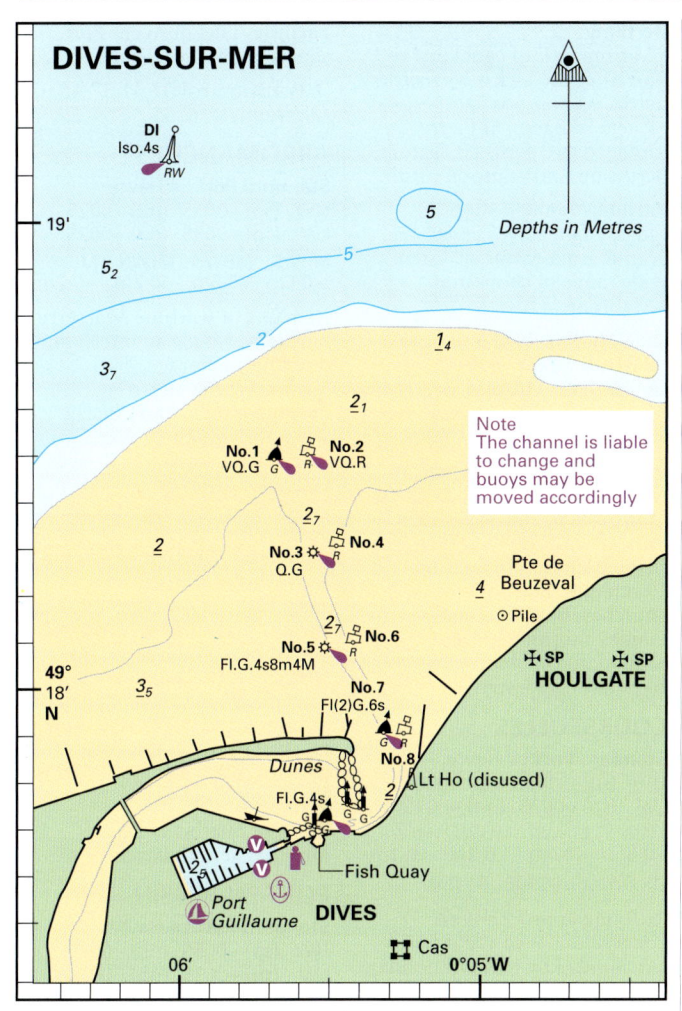

night keep in W sectors of two outer Lts until on ldg line 148° Oc.R.4s. The front Ldg Lt is obscured NE of the line of the E outer breakwater; coming from N it will not be seen until close in.

Entrance At night keep on the ldg line, 148°; by day clear the posts on E and W training walls, and obstruction ½ ca NW of W training wall. Turn to stb round end of Digue du Large, Iso.G, use buoyed channel for lock to Port-Deauville, or straight on for gate to Trouville basin, avoiding shoals at the sides. (Do not continue up-river past the Trouville entrance).

Signals at municipal hbr: 3F.R(vert) closed; 2G/1W two-way traffic; 3G(vert) proceed, one-way traffic.

Berthing
- **Port-Deauville** lies to stb on entry, seaward of a modern housing development. There is accommodation for 100 visitors at pontoons alongside the outer breakwater. 3m depth in basin. Approach through Avant Port (dries) where there are two waiting buoys for the lock which functions when there is 3·50m depth, approx HW±0400. Free flow when water 7m.
- **Port Morny** is the municipal hbr with 2 basins. The first is for residents. In the second, Bassin Morny, there are 60 alongside/rafting visitors' berths on the E side. Gate opens and closes when depth is 5·50m, approx HW±0230.

Facilities Fuel, water at both harbours (Bassin Morny fuel point closes Tuesdays). Deauville is Paris-on-Sea in season, market. High quality bars and restaurants. Trouville has supermarkets and more practical items. Airport 7km.

☎ Port-Deauville 02 31 98 30 01. Port Morny (municipal hbr) 02 31 98 50 40, Lock 02 31 98 95 66.

Items of interest Casino, boardwalk, horse racing, bars, Deauville market.

DIVES SUR MER

Standard Port Le Havre
HW (sp) −0100 (np) −0010
LW (sp) +0000 (np) +0000
MHWS MHWN MLWN MLWS
+0·3m +0·2m +0·2m +0·1m

Port Guillaume is a large recently built marina, surrounded by holiday homes. The estuary of River Dives dries 3m but is accessible to small craft HW±0230. Should not be approached in strong onshore winds. Make for RW safewater Lt buoy, Iso.4s, DI then make good 170° for entrance channel marked by buoys and bns. The estuary quays are occupied by fishing boats; the drying area is almost fully taken up by moorings. Up-river at Cabourg it is possible to anchor in soft mud but landing is impossible below half-tide.

Port Guillaume Marina lies to port after entering estuary.

Entrance Lock opening according to tidal range, roughly HW±0300, but for 2m+ enter HW±0230.

Berthing on pontoons for 25 visitors, 17m x 2m draught max in locked basin.

Facilities Fuel, water, electricity. Shops Dives 1M.

☎ Marina 02 31 24 48 00.

Items of interest Grand Hotel in Cabourg (Proust's Balbec).

OUISTREHAM AND CAEN

Standard Port Le Havre
HW (sp) −0045 (np) −0010
LW (sp) +0000 (np) −0005
MHWS MHWN MLWN MLWS
−0·3m −0·3m −0·2m −0·3m

DS Dover −0600ESE; HWD WNW

A ferry hbr accessible all states of the tide with access to rural marina after locks. Canal to Caen marina. The only hbr between Le Havre and Cherbourg with deep water access at all times. Useful for crew changes. Estuary of River Orne non-navigable.

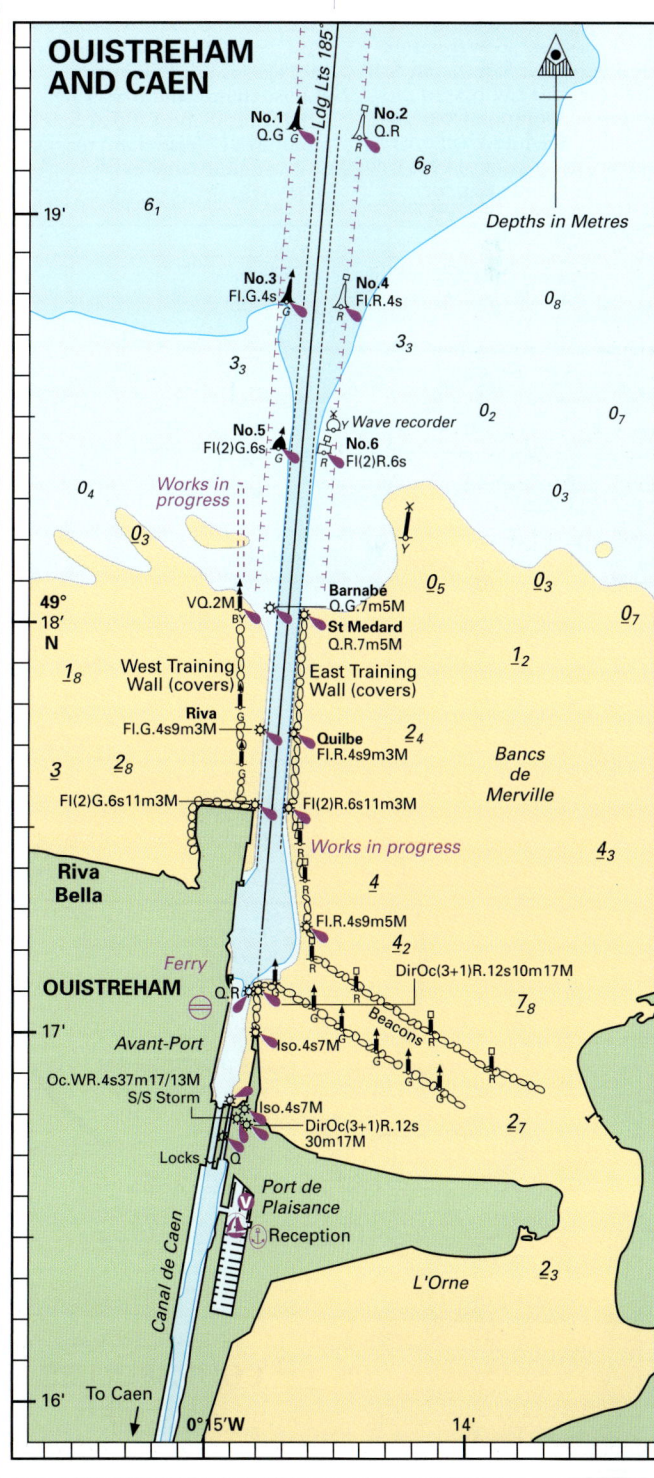

Approach Prominent LtHo: W tr, R top, WR.4s37m17/13M (115°-R-151°, W elsewhere). Sands dry for 2M but approach channel is dredged 3m; make for E card pillar buoy Ouistreham, VQ(3)5s 49°20'·4N 0°14'·7W, and make good 175° 1·2M to G pillar buoy No1 Q.G then follow buoyed channel. Strong cross current on flood.

Signals IPTS code for locks; small craft enter when 3F.G(vert) displayed with W alongside. (W left or right of G indicates which lock to use). W alone means lock will open 1hr before usual time.

Entrance Channel buoyed, Ldg Lts DirOc(3+1)R.12s, 185°. E training wall covers, with Lt Q.R at head on pylon, nearly 1M N of head of main jetty. W training wall also covers and has Lt Q.G offset to E at head and Fl(2)G.6s at root.

Locks A waiting pontoon connected to the shore, lies to port, beyond and opposite the ferry terminal. Beware of the drying banks close N and S. If arriving near LW best to approach pontoon from mid channel. See notice ashore or www.caen-plaisance.com/web/horaires-des-sas.php for planned lock opening times. Upstream lock opens HW–0200; last downstream exit HW+0215; small craft generally use smaller E lock, entrance dredged to CD. From 15 June to 15 September, and at weekends in April to October incl, lock opens upstream at HW–0215, –0115, +0030 +0215, and +0315; and downstream at HW –0245 – 0145, HW, +0145 and +0245. Congested on summer Sunday evenings. Lock openings may vary according to tidal conditions. Lock turbulent near low water. Vertical cables along the sides.

Canal de Caen is 7½M long, dredged to 7·8m and has three moveable bridges and a viaduct with over 22m clearance. Yachts go free in convoy at 5kn. Usual departure times are to Caen 1010, 1330 and 1630 at Pegasus Br (4·5km from Ouistreham), and from Caen 0845, 1200 and 1500 at first br. Enquire at Ouistreham marina for variations and extra convoys.

Berthing
• Marina to E of canal just to port after the locks: 16 visitors' berths on pontoon D.
• Caen: in Bassin St Pierre (dredged to 3·8m). 20 visitors' berths on 2nd pontoon to stb.

Facilities Limited shops in Ouistreham across canal: fuel N of marina entrance. Caen: wide range of shops and restaurants.

☏ /VHF Port HM and Locks 02 31 36 22 00 VHF74. Ouistreham Marina 02 31 96 91 37 VHF 09 (day only). Caen Port HM 02 31 95 24 47.

Items of interest Museums of landings and Grand Bunker in Ouistreham; Pegasus Bridge museum at Ranville; Caen has a castle built by William the Conqueror, many interesting churches, museums and a Sunday morning market around marina basin. Train to Bayeux for tapestry.

COURSEULLES
Standard Port Le Havre
HW (sp)–0100 (np) –0005
LW (sp)–0025 (np) –0015
MHWS MHWN MLWN MLWS
–0·6m –0·6m –0·3m –0·1m

DS Dover +0530E –0115W

A drying approach with congested locked yacht basin surrounded by modern holiday flats; entrance dangerous in strong onshore winds.

Approach Courseulles lies 2½M E of Pte de Ver LtHo, W square tr, Fl(3)15s42m26M, and 1½M W of Bernières church spire. Calvados Plateau shoals extend 2M off shore and dry to ½M off pier-heads. From W steer with Bernières spire on with twin towers of Délivrandes, 134° to Fosse de Courseulles RW pillar buoy, Iso.4s. If necessary anchor there (6m) to await rise in tide for entry.

Entrance Dries 3·5m. Enter between HW–0200 and +0100. There are training walls either side of entrance marked by bns, leading to a jetty on E and a spur on W. W side has a wooden tr, brown with G top, Iso.WG.4s (135°-W-235°) on dolphin at head of W training wall; E side has brown pylon, R top, Oc(2)R.6s at head of E jetty. Keep to E side until the end of the wooden part of the E pier, then continue in mid channel.

Berthing
• Yacht basin in River La Seulles for shallow draught local boats only.
• Bassin Joinville marina at end of Avant Port. Gates, 9·6m wide, open HW ±0200. Depth in basin reduced by silting to <1·5m in 2015. Max LOA 11m. Visitors' berth on hammerheads if vacant, raft if space allows.

Facilities Fuel in Avant Port, shops, restaurants, boat yard.

☏ Port Control 02 31 37 46 03, *Capitainerie* 02 31 37 51 69.

ARROMANCHES
Standard Port Le Havre
HW (sp) –0055 (np) –0025
LW (sp) –0035 (np) –0025
MHWS MHWN MLWN MLWS
–0·6m –0·6m –0·2m –0·2m

Remains of wartime Mulberry harbour provide an interesting daytime anchorage, uncomfortable in strong onshore winds, particularly when the caissons cover. Approach from E has Roche du Calvados, dries 5m, ½M to NNE. Keep 2M offshore until near approach because of fishing pot chains. Make for E card BY wreck buoy Harpagas then steer 160° for entrance marked by port and stb buoys near W end of N side of hbr. Avoid wrecks on E side and anchor near the W end, sand, gradually shoaling, clear of obstruction marked by W buoys. Foul patches, buoy anchor. E part is foul with wrecks.

Items of interest D-Day museum next to beach.

PORT-EN-BESSIN
Standard Port Le Havre
HW (sp) –0055 (np) –0030
LW (sp) –0035 (np) –0030
MHWS MHWN MLWN MLWS
–0·7m –0·7 –0·2m –0·1m

DS Dover +0200W –0400E

A drying fishing port with very limited accommodation for visiting yachts in wet basin.

Approach should not be attempted in winds from NW to NE over Force 5; otherwise approach at over half-tide. Anchor off in 3m, good holding, subject to swell, while waiting.

Entrance Pier heads are painted white, visible a long way off. Ldg Lts Oc(3)12s 204°. Channel through Avant Port dries 2m; at end is a long passage, 10m wide, leading through a lock into wet basins. Beware the rock breakwater (covers) to port between entrance and lock.

Signals R over G lock gates closed. Signal station ½M W of entrance shows traffic signals on simplified code.

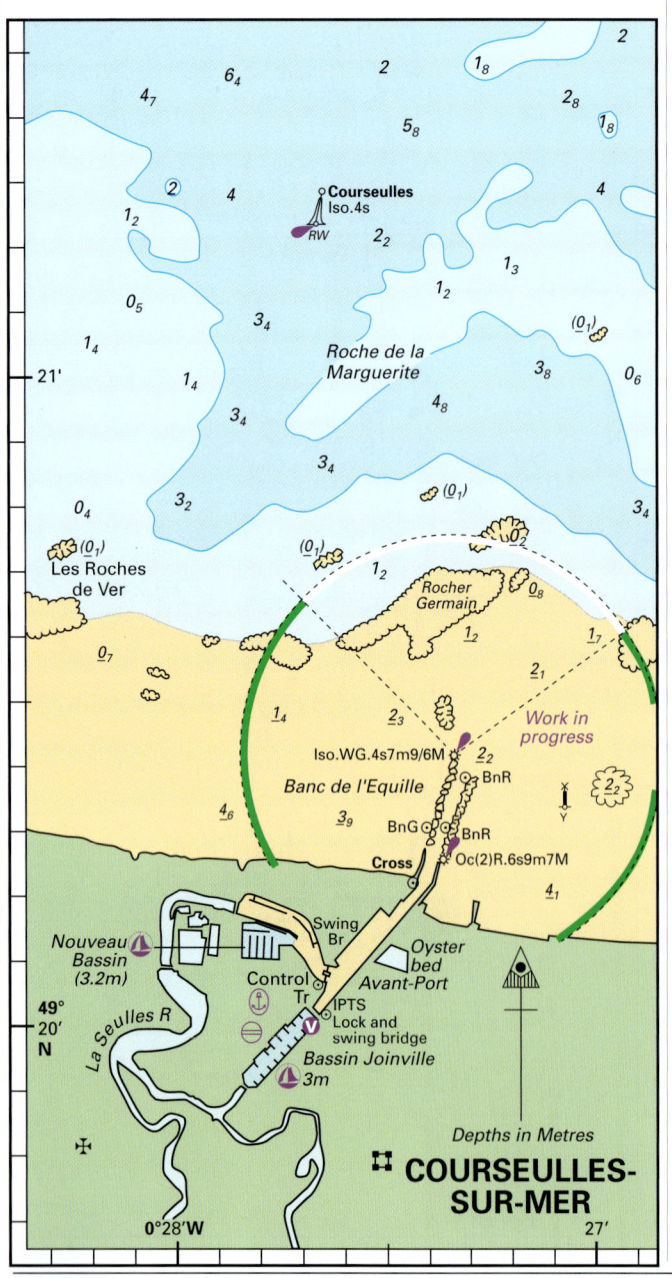

Berthing There are buoys in the outer harbour (dries). Wet basin is crowded with fishing boats but in principle there are berths for six visitors in the NW corner of the first basin. May have to raft up to fishing vessel in practice. Locks open HW±0200 but swing br only opens on demand. Call on VHF 18. After gates close, level may fall by 1m if sluices are opened to scour outer harbour (24hrs warning is given by blue flag at lock gates). Yachts may be limited to 48hrs stay.

Facilities Water on quay; fuel at garage. Shops, fish, scallops.

☏/**VHF** Lock 02 31 21 71 77, VHF 18.

Items of interest Fish market.

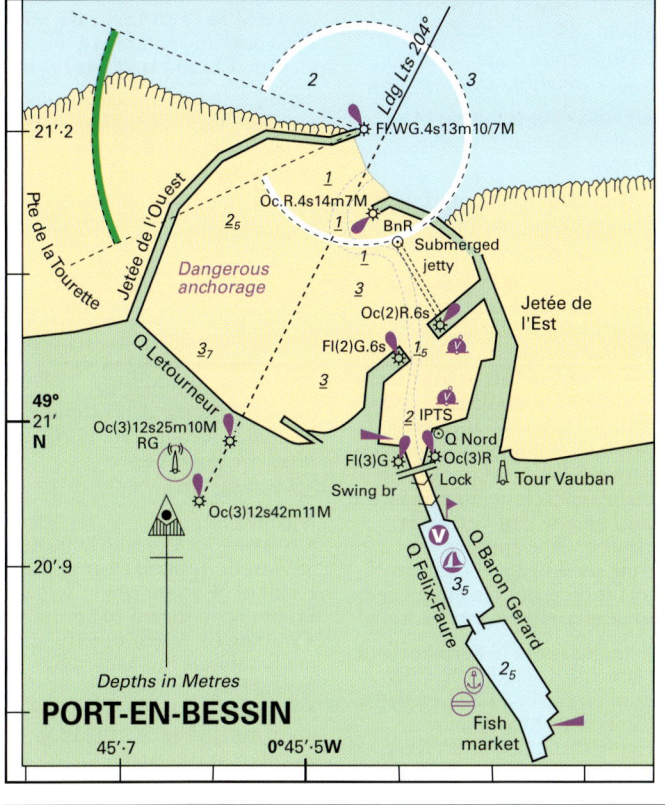

GRANDCAMP-MAISY
Standard Port Cherbourg
HW (sp) +0053 (np) +0118
LW (sp) +0129 (np) +0107
MHWS MHWN MLWN MLWS
+0·7m +0·7m +0·1m +0·1m

A fishing port with a wet basin, which welcomes yachts.

Approach Roches de Grandcamp dry 1·6m for 1M. N limit marked by three BY N card unlighted buoys marked Nos.1, 3, 5 from E to W. Approach from any of these at HW±0200.

Signals IPTS shown from control tr on E side of lock. These apply to entrance to hbr as well as inner basin.

Entrance is exposed to winds from NW to NE, has Lts Fl.G.4s6M and Oc(2)R.6s9M on towers 50m beyond the jetty heads with obstruction between. Two sets of Ldg Lts DirQ.15M 146°. Much Japanese seaweed reported.

Berthing Do not wait in front of the gates: considerable surge. Berths for 12 visitors at pontoon C in wet basin. Gates open HW±0230. If coeff <40 gates may close HW+0130 or earlier. Sill dries 2m; basin has 2m. Mass exodus when gates open, so hang back.

Facilities Fuel at garage, shops, restaurants. Bus to Bayeux.

☏ Port de Plaisance 02 31 22 63 16. Lock 02 31 22 19 17.

Items of interest Pointe du Hoc memorial and museum.

ISIGNY
Standard Port Cherbourg
Rade de la Capelle
HW (sp) +0055 (np) +0125
LW (sp) +0125 (np) +0110
MHWS MHWN MLWN MLWS
+0·7m +0·7m 0·0m +0·1m

At Isigny, LW is at HW −0245; the tide comes in with a rush

DS in Rade de la Capelle, off the entrance: Dover +0500SSW −0130NNE

In Chenal d'Isigny: Dover +0500S −0130NNE

E-going stream begins S and quickly changes to E; W-going stream begins SW and quickly changes to W.

Small town famous for cream and cheese, with drying quays on River Aure.

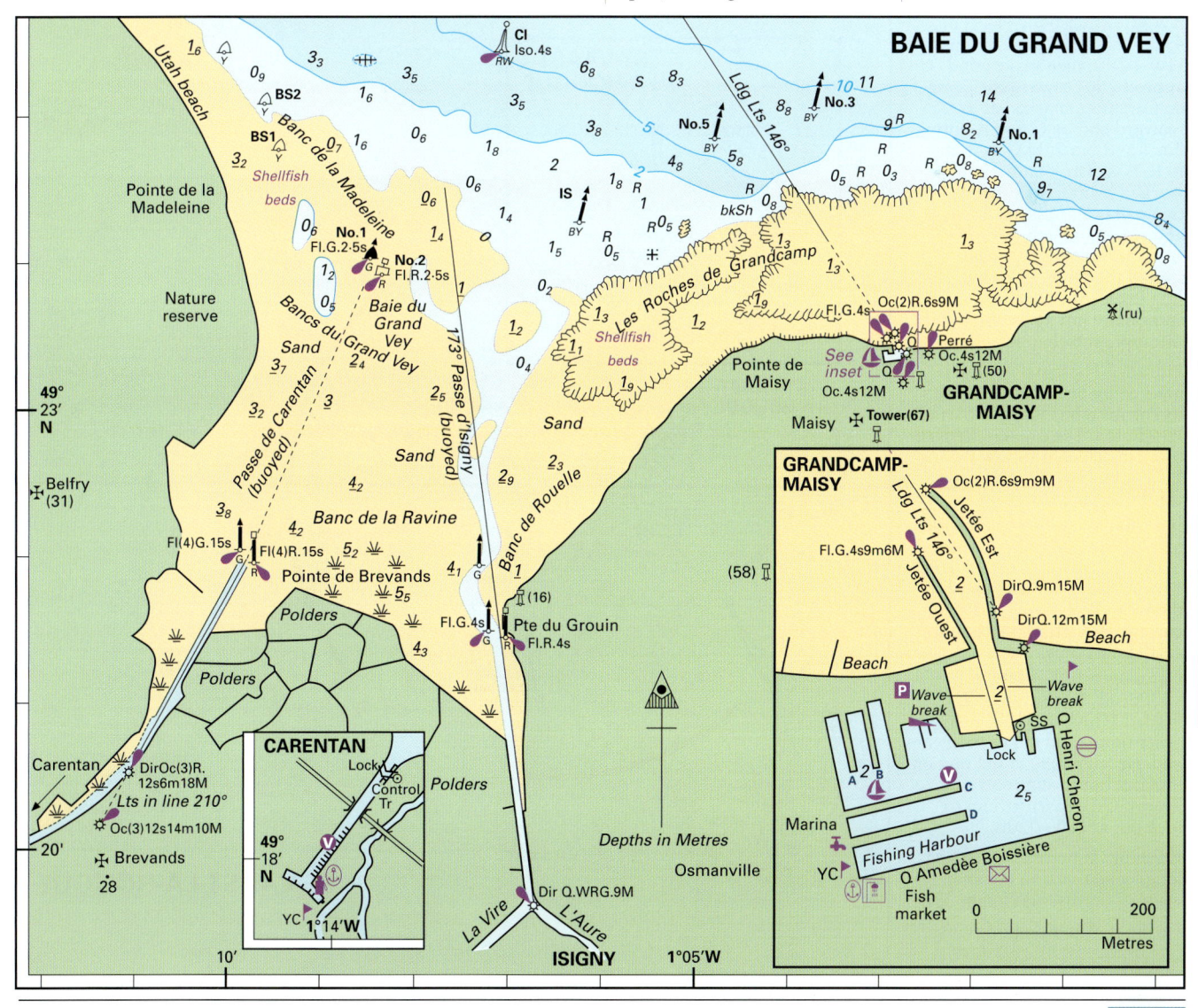

Approach should not be attempted in winds of Force 5 or more; otherwise approach HW+0300. From E make for the three BY N card buoys N of Grandcamp (marked 1, 3, 5); from No.5 (W-most) bear SW

for N card buoy IS 1M N of W end of Roches de Grandcamp. From NW make for CI RW pillar buoy, Iso.4s and then steer SE for the IS buoy.

Entrance dries in parts, but more water than Carentan approach; passable for 2·7m at half-tide. From IS buoy the channel is marked by buoys and bns. At G tripod, channel follows S shape and then enters canal. At junction with River Vire turn to port for Isigny but beware mud bank off left bank just short of the division.

Berthing Five visitors' berths (soft mud; dries 4m) at pontoon on W bank. Quai Neuf, near Spar warehouse. E bank quay slopes, hard bottom, and spaces mostly taken by work boats.

Facilities Water and fuel on quay. Shops, restaurants.

☏ Mairie 02 31 51 24 01.

CARENTAN

Tidal data, see Isigny
DS in Rade de la Capelle:
Dover +0500SSW −0130NNE
Flood lasts for 2hrs sp, 3hrs np.

A small town with pleasant marina of rural aspect at end of long canal with good rail connections.

Approach Aim to be at the C1 RW safewater buoy Iso.4s at 49°25'·5N 1°07'·1W by HW−0200, then make good approx 200° toward the Passe de Carentan, marked at its seaward end by G and R buoys, No.1 and No.2, Fl.G.2·5s and Fl.R.2·5s. The channel is marked by at least a further two pairs of lit buoys. There is about 1·2m at half tide. All these buoys may be moved should the sands shift. NB The Ldg Lts for the canalised section are not appropriate for the approach channel.

Entrance The canal section is marked by bns or perches with its entrance bns Fl(4)G.15s and Fl(4)R.15s. The canal is dredged to 3·2m, at night follow the ldg Lts Dir.Oc(3)R.12s and Oc(3)12s on 210°.

Immediately in front of the lock gates (8M from the safewater buoy) River Douve enters from stb and River Taute from port: there can be a strong cross current. A waiting pontoon for small boats only.

Gates open HW−0200 to +0300; sill 1·8m above CD. Staffed 1 June to 31 August. At other times land at pontoon and use telephone in red box on lookout hut to summon lock keeper. On departure aim to lock out at HW−0200.

Berthing At pontoon K in ¾M long locked section of canal; 50 visitors' berths, maximum 37m.

Facilities Water on pontoons; fuel (0900–1000 weekdays); shops.

☏ Marina 02 33 42 24 44; Lock 02 33 71 10 85.

Items of interest Boat trips through marshes. Cheese.

ILES SAINT-MARCOUF

Standard Port Cherbourg
HW (sp) +0055 (np) +0130
LW   (sp) +0120 (np) +0110
MHWS MHWN MLWN MLWS
+0·5m +0·5m 0·0m 0·0m

Two uninhabited fortified islands, which sea birds dominate. Avoid in bad weather, especially from SW.

Approach Keep clear of Banc de Saint-Marcouf, extending 2½M to NW, on which there are breakers with fresh winds from N to NE; and of Banc du Cardonnet running 6M SE.

Anchorage 3–4m, to SE of S card bn, on rocks 1ca WSW of larger Is, Ile du Large, and SW of LtHo. Buoy anchor, stream strong. Land between HW+0200 at boat hbr on W side of Is; when rocks to bn are awash there is 1·3m in entrance. Expect gull attacks. Ile de Terre, smaller Is, is a bird sanctuary; landing forbidden without permission.

Facilities None.

Items of interest Birds.

SAINT-VAAST-LA HOUGUE

Standard Port Cherbourg
HW (sp) +0045 (np) +0115
LW   (sp) +0120 (np) +0110
MHWS MHWN MLWN MLWS
+0·3m +0·3m −0·2m −0·1m

DS in Grande Rade:
Dover +0530SW −0200NE, 1kn

An eddy runs N during the English Channel E-going stream.

A delightful fishing port with marina in wet basin; wide range of restaurants, bars and shops.

Approach From N leave Pte de Saire 1M to stb and continue for 1¾M W of S past Ile Tatihou (broad tr on S end with low detached fort to S); steer W round one lit and one unlit S card pillar buoys, then bear NW for end of jetty. From S go between Iles St-Marcouf and mainland to leave to port two E card buoys, E of Fort de la Hougue. The approach, Le Run, used by local boats to N of Tatiou is not recommended since it crosses oyster beds.

By night From N keep Barfleur-Gatteville Lt, Fl(2)10s, open until on the line La Hougue Lt Oc.4s with Morsalines Oc(4)WRG.12s, 267°. Keep on the latter until in W sector of St Vaast Lt Oc(2)WRG.6s10–7M bearing NW. From S leave Quinéville W card Lt buoy, well to stb; do not cross La Houge-Morsalines line until in W sector of St Vaast Lt. Leave this Lt to port and enter between Oc(4)R.12s and Iso.G.4s Lts to lock.

Entrance Port side of approach to the jetty head from S is marked by buoys and bns; exposed to strong winds from NE and SE. Dries 1½m but sandbank outside the gates covers at half flood – draught over 1·6m will touch; stay within 15m of wall until just past first (stone) bollard. Lock opens from HW−0215 to HW+0300, but may be extended during depressions or decreased if coeff <50. Lock times are published at
www.ports-manche.fr

Berthing
• To await lock opening, anchor SSW of Ile Tatihou clear of the E half of W sector of Oc.WRG Lt, but open from S to SE.
• Waiting on N side of jetty inadvisable as this is used by fishing boats to unload.
• Marina. 100 visitors' on pontoon B >14m, C 12–14m, E <12m or as directed.

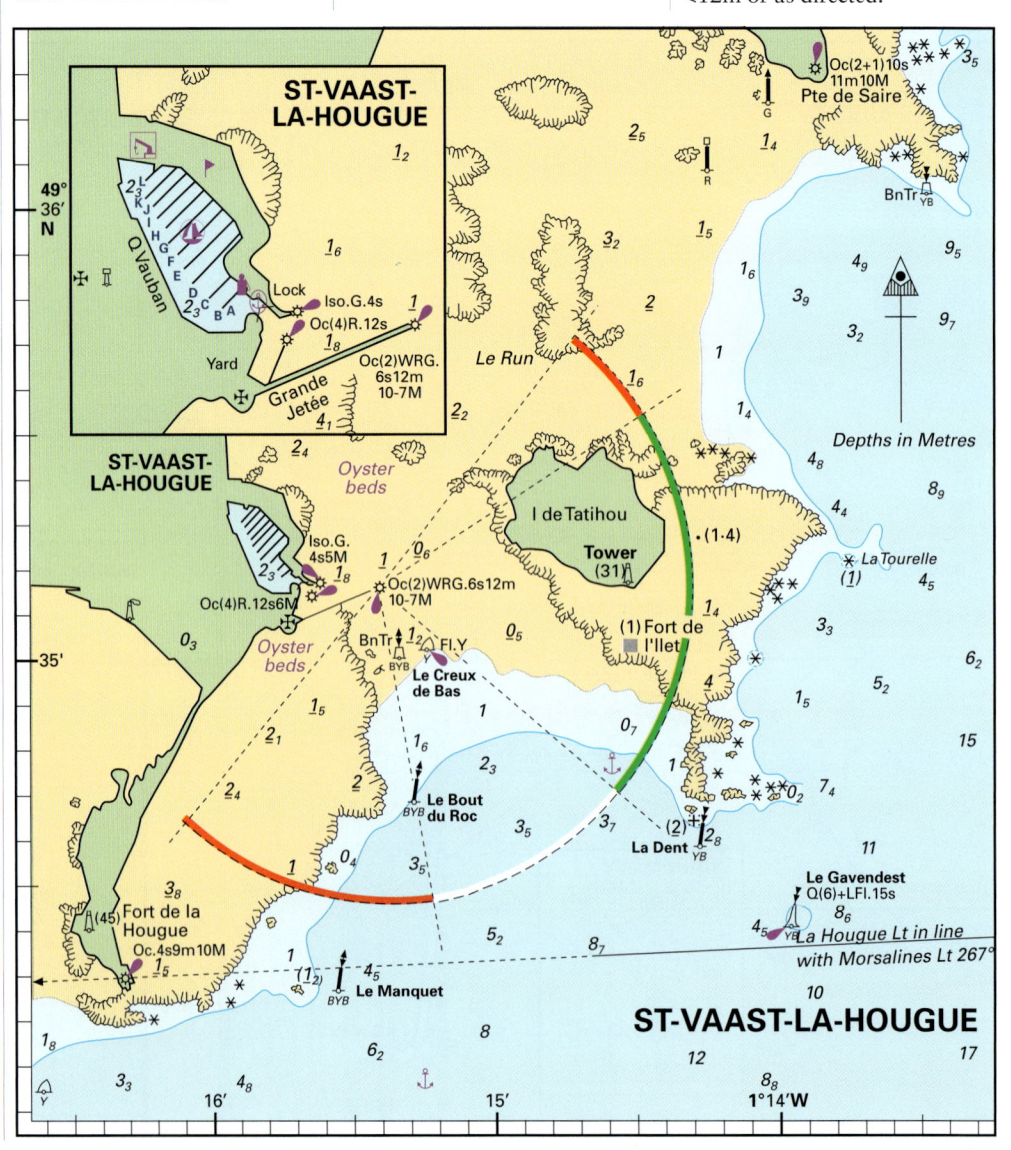

Facilities Fuel. Good shops. Restaurants at all price levels, shellfish a speciality. Mkt Sat.

☎ *Capitainerie* 02 33 23 61 00.

Items of interest Île de Tatiou maritime museum, Gosselin shop, coastal walks.

BARFLEUR

Standard Port Cherbourg
HW (sp) +0050 (np) +0115
LW (sp) +0045 (np) +0050

MHWS	MHWN	MLWN	MLWS
+0·2m	+0·1m	0·0m	+0·1m

DS Dover −0445N +0430S

A small picturesque drying hbr. Access HW±0200.

Approach See Passage Notes re Barfleur Race. From a position about 1¼M ESE of Pte de Barfleur, steer 219° on the 7m W square Lt tr (Ldg Lts Oc(3)12s). Do not confuse this tr with the squat W tr at end of S breakwater: ldg line passes about 50m S of the latter.

Entrance Ldg line is 219°, front W square tr Oc(3)12s7m; rear Grey and W square tr, G top, Oc(3)12s13m, synchronised. Channel is marked by buoys and bns and has a strong cross-current. Near HW adjacent rocks are awash and it is most important to keep on the ldg line and not steer direct for the entrance. When two or 3ca off the entrance the Ldg Lts will be hidden by the hbr wall; at this point, about abreast of the last port bn, head for the entrance. There is a tide gauge on concrete base close SW of lifeboat slip: when the base is covered there is 1·6m along the quay.

When leaving at night have compass course prepared as Ldg Lts are not visible for first 250m.

Anchoring Waiting to enter, near the ldg line, 5–6m, sand and mud, poor holding. Also in bay N of town, except with winds E to NE. Approach 256° from La Roche à l'Anglais G con buoy.

Berthing along SW part of NW quay, dries 2–3m, level mud, sand and gravel. Room for 10 visitors, in principle but may have to moor alongside fishing boats which use space allocated for yachts. E side is rocky. There is a strong surge with fresh winds E to NE.

Facilities Water on quay; fuel delivered; shops. Hôtel Moderne has restaurant.

☎ *Capitainerie* 02 33 54 08 29. No VHF.

Items of interest Charming village, church, Gatteville 1hr, coastal walks.

CHERBOURG

See plan on next page
Standard Port Cherbourg
DS Dover +0600E −0100W

Tidal streams change 2–3hrs later in mid-channel than along the shore.

An enormous commercial, ferry, naval and yachting hbr, which is a true port of refuge and can be entered at all times. Tides outside the hbr are very strong and so they are in the Grande Rade.

Approach To E and W keep at least 2½M off the land; and keep well clear of Raz de Lévi in E, end of which is marked by W card YBY Lt buoy. Cherbourg can be located by atomic power station on high ground to W, a cliff behind the town, a long low breakwater with prominent circular forts, and Cap Lévi LtHo (36m) to the E. Note that the entrances are 3M apart and large vessels tend to prefer the W.

West Entrance Follow leading Lts Dir.2Q through the entrance which is marked on its E side by Fort de l'Ouest Fl(3)WR.15s, and on the W side by Querqueville Lt Fl(2)G.6s. There is a R port buoy Fl.R.4s close inside the entrance. Keep well to stb on entry to avoid emerging craft. From here the Ldg line for Petite Rade is 124°, front Q.G, rear Iso.G.4s leaving front Lt on Digue du Homet to stb.

East Entrance Ldg line, twin spires of Notre Dame and small tr of Ste Trinité, 212°, clear the shoals near Ile Pelée. At night Fort des Flamandes Dir.Q and Jetée des Flamands Q.,189°, serves the same purpose. The shoals are marked by two R buoys Fl.R.2.5s and Fl(4)R.15s. Enter between these buoys and Fort de l'Est Iso.G.4s. Steer 220° for the Petite Rade.

Passe Cabart-Danneville at E end of Grande Rade is narrow with strong streams; not recommended.

Petite Rade The NE breakwater, Jetée des Flamands, covers. Its W end is marked by R pillar buoy, Q.R. Once clear of breakwater, steer 196° for marina and entrance to inner harbour (at night marked by Fl(3)G.12s and Fl(3)R.12s).

Departing If heading for Passe de l'Est it is imperative to leave to stb the R pillar buoy VQ.R in the entrance to clear Jetée des Flamands.

Berthing At Port Chantereyne marina, tidal, 250 visitors' berths: take any space available according to length, pontoons N, P and Q are marked with length, east side of H and J max 25m, K <9m. If arriving at night and outer berths are full, raft up on waiting pontoon (30 spaces). In high season, a waterborne HM will direct boats. Anchoring is possible in Petite Rade close N of marina breakwater (wash and uncomfortable in N winds) or at W end of Grande Rade (isolated and considerable swell).

Facilities Fuel with card, boatyard, chandlery, sailmakers. Hypermarket within walking distance. Market Tuesday, Thursday, Saturday. Restaurants. Ferry. WiFi.

☎/VHF Port Chantereyne 02 33 87 65 70; Port control VHF 12.

Items of interest Fort, maritime museum, Park Liais.

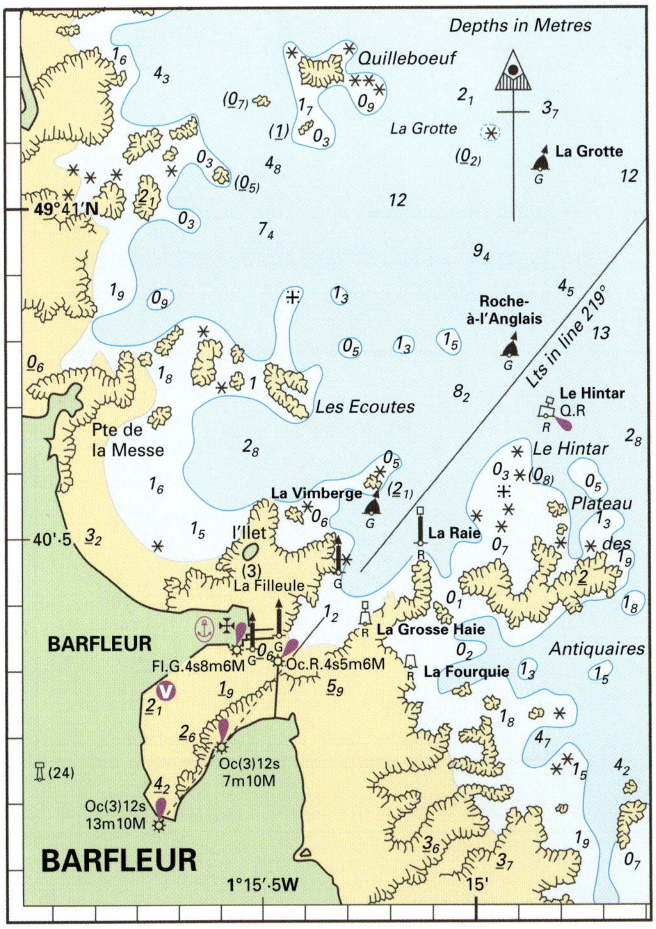

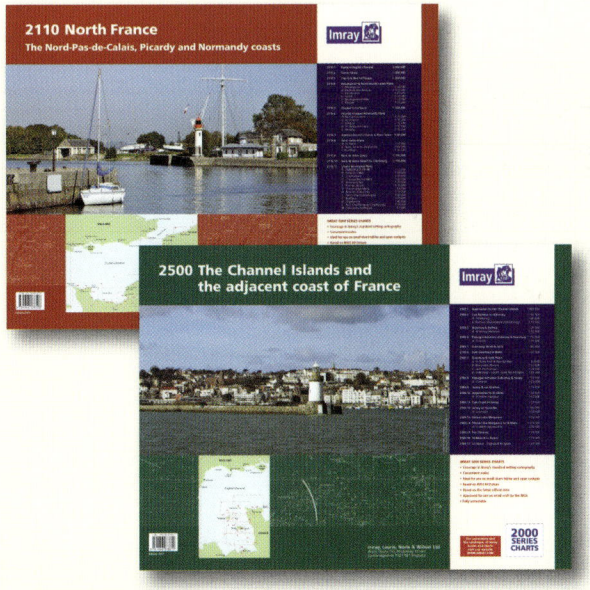

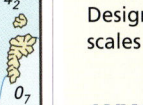

FRANCE – NORTH COAST AND CHANNEL ISLANDS

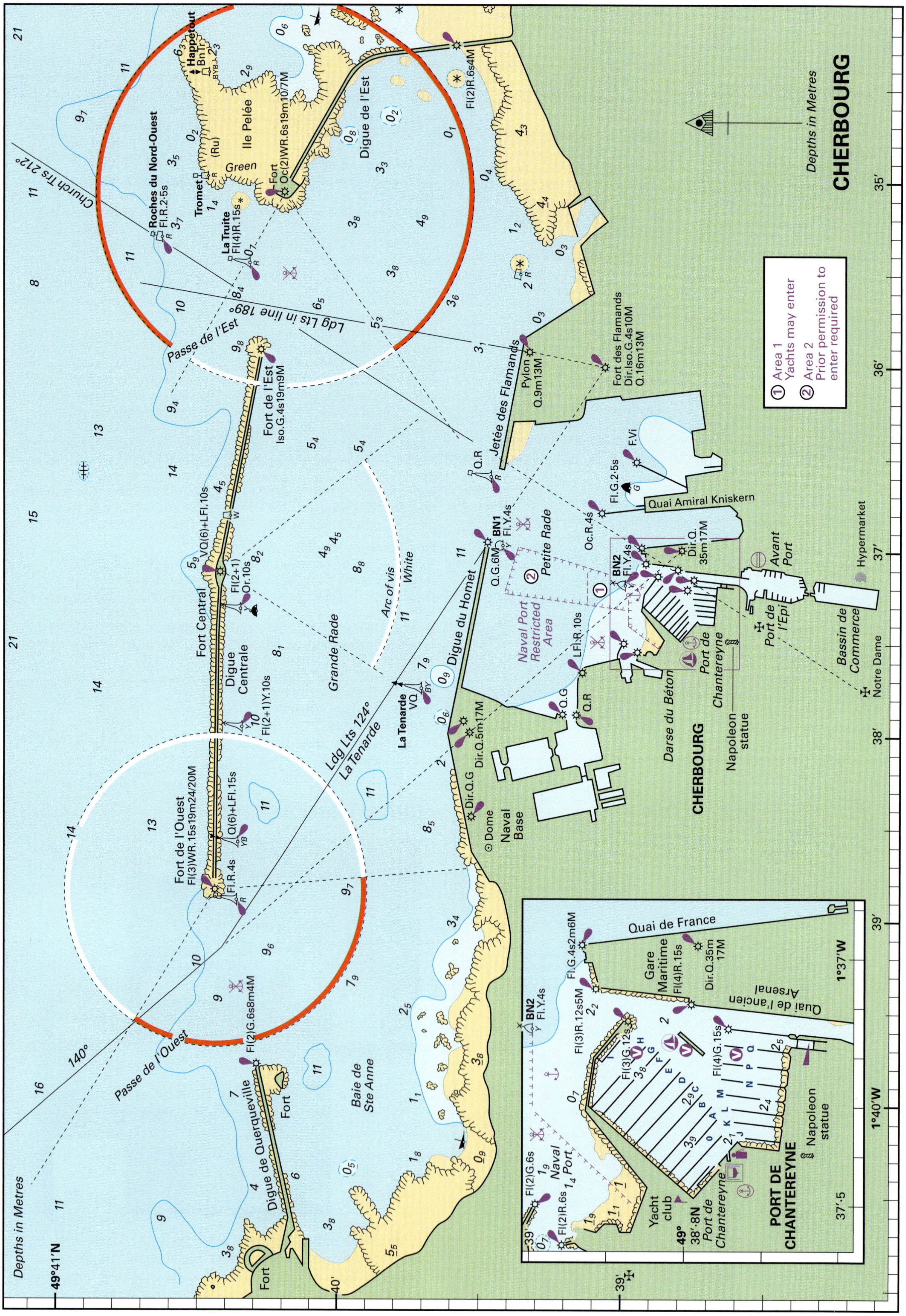

Channel Islands

These islands afford fascinating sailing for the well-equipped yacht with an experienced navigator. The hazards are concealed rocks, strong tidal streams and poor visibility. Good up-to-date charts are essential. BA 2669 gives the outlines of the Channel Islands and is adequate if passing round them; but for inter-island navigation larger scales are needed. Recommended folios containing charts of convenient size (A2) and scale are the British Admiralty Small Craft Folio SC 5604 and Imray Chart Atlas 2500. A good pilot guide is also highly desirable because of the importance of transit lines when navigating in these waters; in some places the difference between a course steered and the course made good can be as much as 60°. *The Admiralty Channel Pilot* is a mine of detailed information. For those wishing to make the most of inshore routes and anchorages the RCC Pilotage Foundation's *Channel Islands, Cherbourg Peninusula & North Brittany* (Imray) is exceptionally well provided with sketches of transit lines and marks.

The *Admiralty Tidal Atlas for Channel Islands and Adjacent Coasts of France* (NP 264) or a good equivalent is also essential. The range of mean spring tides shows a remarkable variation from 5·5m to 11·5m within the area of the Islands and the adjacent French coast; within the islands the range varies from 9·8m at springs to only 2·1m at neaps. Tides make and take off rapidly; streams run rapidly even at neaps; and there may be considerable variation from predictions due to weather. There may also be many local variations in streams, particularly eddies, not shown on the tidal atlas. Of the 25 harbours with quays for berthing alongside, only five do not dry.

Information is also obtainable at:
www.alderney.gov.gg   www.sailalderney.com
www.harbours.gg   www.ports.je

The Admiralty Pilot shows an incidence of fog on only two days a month in the summer: this is deceptive because there are also many days of morning mist when poor visibility makes it impossible to pick up some leading marks. Radar and a GPS are most helpful if caught by mist or fog when at sea; but neither is sufficiently reliable to keep on transit lines and their possession does not justify leaving hbr in poor visibility.

There is complete shelter at all times at St Peter Port or Beaucette in Guernsey and at St Helier in Jersey. Elsewhere there are very many anchorages which provide shelter in settled weather or offshore winds, but all are subject to swell.

Search and Rescue
VHF 16 or DSC will connect to Jersey Coastguard (MMSI 002320060), Guernsey Coastguard (MMSI 002320064) or Joburg CROSS (MMSI 002275200). Lifeboats operate from Braye, St Peter Port and St Helier.

Weather
Jersey Coastguard VHF 82 at 0645, 0745, 0845 (all LT); and 1245,1845, 2245 (all UTC).
BBC Radio Guernsey 1116kHz, 93·2mHz at 0630 (weekdays only) 0730 and 0830 LT.
BBC Radio Jersey 1026 kHz, 88.8 MHz at 0725, 0825 and 1725 weekdays, 0725 and 0825 weekends. Channel Islands shipping forecast at 0625 daily and 1825 Mon –Sat. All LT.
Island FM 93·7mHz (Alderney) on the half hour.
St Helier Pierheads gives current conditions on VHF 18 every two minutes.
Channel Islands Shipping Forecast ☏ 0900 6690022 (recorded message) Updates 0000 0600 1200 1800LT (premium rate call).

Navtex
This area is covered from Niton Areas S and K also by Corsen Area A. It is probably sufficient to use Area K alone. This will give two forecasts at 0840 and 2040 UTC. Gale and Navigational warnings are updated every 4hrs.

Customs
The Channel Islands are Crown Dependencies but they are not part of UK nor of EU. Customs requirements for yachts are more rigorous than in France: Q flags must be flown and it is necessary to report to customs (usually by depositing a form) not only when arriving from France but also from UK and when moving from one Island administration to another (e.g. from Guernsey to Jersey). Clearance can be given at Braye in Alderney; St Peter Port, St Sampson or Beaucette marina in Guernsey; and St Helier or Gorey in Jersey. Normal EU duty-free limits apply.

In practice the French customs are not very interested in the arrival and departure of yachts provided that the yacht has evidence of having paid VAT in the EU and is not carrying non-European nationals, animals, drugs, firearms or duty-free stores. Duty-free includes alcohol and tobacco purchased in the Channel Islands in excess of personal allowances. It is really only in these circumstances that it is necessary to fly a yellow flag and report. Evidence is the VAT receipt, not a photocopy.

On return to UK from the CI it is necessary to fly the yellow flag from the 12M limit. You must then attempt to contact a customs officer by telephone and follow any instructions on the pre-recorded message. Use the National Yachtline ☏ 0845 723 1110 (24hr). Customs notice No.8 gives full details and this may be found in all hbrs and marinas together with Form C1331 which should be completed and posted in the special customs boxes. The customs are usually very helpful provided you comply with the regulations and do not attempt to smuggle drugs, animals, firearms or foreign nationals into the country. It is helpful to have receipts for dutiable goods, fuel and an original VAT certificate for the boat.

Island airports shut in fog which makes crew changes unreliable.

Health Insurance
Since the United Kingdom NHS no longer has a reciprocal agreement with the Channel Islands, do not expect free health care even if carrying an EHIC. Medical Insurance is strongly recommended. The same applies to CI residents visiting the UK.

Diesel
Diesel fuel is available at a low rate of duty. Keep receipts and do not carry duty-free fuel in loose containers.

CHERBOURG AND THE CHANNEL ISLANDS

Passage lights	BA No
Cap de la Hague Fl.5s48m23M Horn30s	1512
ALDERNEY	
Quénard Point Fl(4)15s37m12M	1536
Casquets Fl(5)30s37m18M AIS	1532
C.de Carteret Fl(2+1)15s81m26M	1638
SARK	
Pt Robert Fl.15s65m20M Horn(2)30s	1544
GUERNSEY	
Platte Fougère Fl.WR.10s15m16M Horn 45s Racon(P)(· — — ·) R sector over rks to NW	1548
Les Hanois Fl(2)13s33m20M Horn(2)60s	1580
St Martin's Point Fl(3)WR.10s15m14M Horn(3)30s R sector over rks to SW	1574
JERSEY	
Grosnez Point Fl(2)WR.15s50m19/17M R sector over rks to NE.	1622
Corbière Iso.WR.10s36m18/16M R sectors over rks to N and SE	1620
Roches Douvres Fl.5s60m24M AIS	1734

STREAMS RELATED TO DOVER
Alderney Race HWD -0020 SW; +0540 NE.

Between Guernsey and Jersey the stream is rotatory anti-clockwise, HWD W; +0300 S; +0600 E; –0300 N.

The Alderney Race is 7M wide and presents no difficulty in reasonable weather although there are overfalls, marked on the chart, which should be avoided, especially with wind against tide. Tidal streams can reach 10kn and it is essential to time a passage carefully taking advantage where necessary of the inshore eddies round Alderney.

From Cherbourg to Channel Islands, leave Cherbourg at about HWD –0300 to catch the start of the inshore W-bound eddy. If bound for Alderney or the Casquets, a generous allowance must be made for tidal set. If bound through the Race for Jersey or Guernsey, the most comfortable passage will be made at HWD before the overfalls have built up.

Southbound from Alderney, the shortest route to Guernsey is through the Swinge. Depart Braye Hbr at local HW+0200 to 0230 (Dover –0200 to –0130) to avoid the overfalls S of Burhou. Leave Corbet Rk about 100m to port and then change course to keep Great Nannel just open E of Burhou, 003°, until Les Etacs are on the port beam.

Northbound from St Peter Port Leave as soon as the stream in the Little Russel turns N at about HWD+0430. This should give a favourable tide through the Swinge or the Alderney Race. If bound for Alderney note that the tide runs NE in the Race longer than in the Swinge and change course if you run out of tide before entering the Swinge. Approaching the Swinge keep Great Nannel just open E of Burhou, 003°, to clear Pierre au Vraic (dries 1·2m) and to clear Les Etacs at SW end of Alderney. Keep to E side of Swinge to avoid the overfalls, about 100m W of Corbet Rock.

To Cherbourg from Alderney leave at about HWD+0500 to catch the start of the NE-going stream. If coming from Guernsey note that the early W-going stream along N coast of Cherbourg Peninsula is stronger than suggested in *Tidal Atlas*. Avoid it by keeping well offshore.

Alderney

Alderney is an unspoilt island with reasonable facilities. No animals may be landed. Air connections to Southampton and Guernsey.

Anchorages There are a number of possible anchorages around Alderney. None of these provide any facilities and should only be considered in calm weather or with offshore winds.
- **Saye Bay** Close E of Braye in 3m sand.
- **Longis Bay** SW of Quenard Pt in 3m sand. Useful to wait for a fair tide in the race. Beware the drying patch 200m SW of Raz Island.
- **Hannaine Bay** On the NW coast immediately S of Fort Clonque in 4m sand. Useful to await the N going tide in the Swinge.
- **Burhou** SW end of the island in 3m sand. Below half-tide on the SW stream only. Landing on Burhou prohibited 15 Mar–27 Jul.

BRAYE

Standard Port St Helier
HW (sp) +0040 (np) +0050
LW (sp) +0025 (np) +0105
MHWS MHWN MLWN MLWS
–4·8m –3·4m –1·5m –0·5m
DS (Race):HWD SW+0600NE

The artificial hbr is exposed to NE. Also subject to swell in strong W to NW winds.

Approach is best from NE at HWD+0500 when the stream off the entrance is least. From NW either pass N of the Casquets and Burhou Is or, if the SW stream is running, leave them to N, pass S of Alderney and go NE through the Race with flood tide.

From S see Passage Notes; but at night it is prudent to use the Race approach rather than the Swinge because in the latter it is difficult to establish the clearance off rocks to the side.

Entrance Beware sunken continuation of the breakwater running NE for 3ca. The W-going stream sets strongly onto it for 0930hrs. When rounding it, if coming from SW, keep E of Ldg line of two bns: front W with W globe on islet on W side of Saye Bay, rear BW ▲, 142°; then bring W cone near head of Old Harbour pier on with St Anne's spire, 210° (this transit leads 1ca E of the submerged breakwater).

At night to clear the breakwater extension keep in W sector of Château à L'Etoc Lt Iso.WR (071°-R-111°-W-151°) the R sector covers the shoals W of Saye Bay. Then sight the Ldg Lts into the hbr (215°) which are both Q., visible 210° to 220°. The port radar can assist vessels in poor visibility.

Berthing There are 70 Y visitors' buoys max LOA 15m or anchor clear of moorings with a riding Lt, 8m. There are some patches of rock and weed with poor holding. Little Crabby Harbour is used for local boats except for visitors when re-fuelling, HW±0200. Land at pontoon below HM office (keep it clear), not on the slip.

Facilities Fuel, water, showers, laundry, gas, chandler. Restaurants, small supermarket at hbr, otherwise 1M up the hill at St Anne.

☎/**VHF** HM 01481 822620. VHF 16, 74, call sign *Alderney Coastguard* (0800–2000 June–September). Call *Guernsey Coastguard* when closed. Water taxi *Mainbrayce* VHF 37 and *Mobile* 07781 415420 or 01481 822772. Runs 0800–2359.

NB **Burhou** Landing prohibited 15 March–27 July.

In distress call VHF 16, 74 for Radio Direction Finding Service and radar VTS.

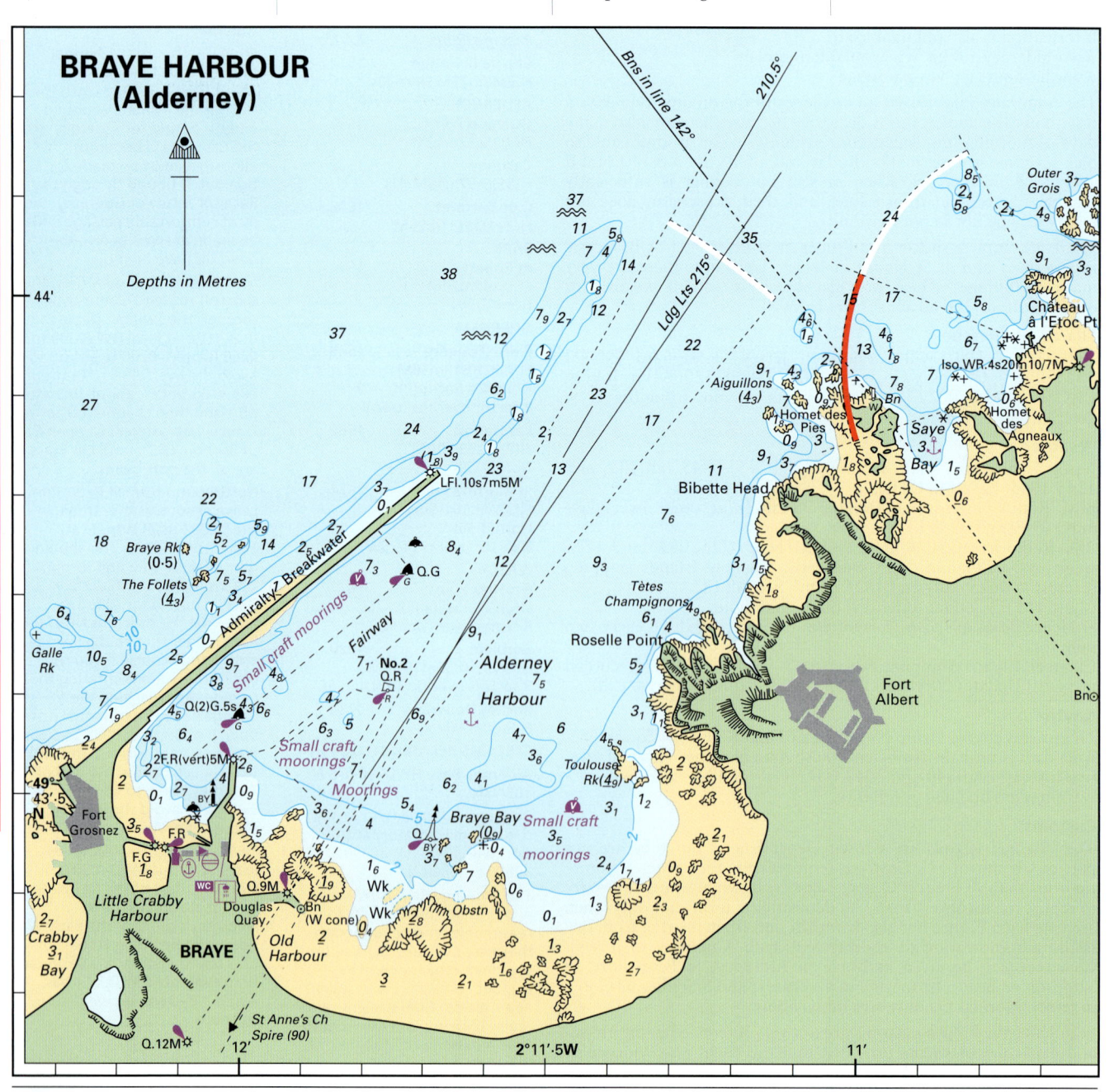

Guernsey

HW St Peter Port HW
DS off E side:
Dover −0100SW +0500NE
off W side: HWD SW;+0600NE

The W coast is rocky and inhospitable; the E coast offers better shelter and facilities.

Approach There are three main lines of approach to the E coast and St Peter Port:
• by Little Russel channel;
• by Great Russel channel;
• from W and S.

Approaching from N, as from the Solent, the traditional pilotage is to make for the Casquets, then make good 224° down W coast to Les Hanois LtHo and follow S coast 1M off to pick up approach from W and S. In bad visibility this route is strongly to be preferred. Warning: with the SW-going tide there is a considerable set SE across the N end of Guernsey.

• Little Russel Channel entrance is marked on W by Platte Fougère W octagonal tr with B hor band, Fl.WR.10s (085°-R-155°) and on E by Tautenay Lt tr, BW vert stripes Q(3)WR.6s (R over area to E, 215° to 050°). It provides the most direct route from N, and can be used at LW with good visibility, but the streams run at up to 6kn and it can be very rough, with overfalls, with wind against tide. At NE end of channel, between the Braye Rocks and Amfroque, the stream sets directly towards the N end of Herm from Dover +0100 to +0345. Do not approach Platte Fougère octagonal tr with B and W hor bands, from W on a bearing less than 165° or from E on a bearing greater than 255°. Make for a position about 2M NE of Platte Fougère and then bring Brehon tr (low, squat) just to the E of St Martin's Point, 208°. Keep on this line until Roustel tr, BW, is 1¼ca to stb, then get on transit of Belvedere House, W, on with Castle Breakwater Lt tr, white on NE side, 220°. If these latter marks are difficult to pick out against the sun or in poor visibility, steer 220° from Tautenay, adjusting as necessary to clear Roustel tr, BW chequered stone, to port; Platte tr, G con stone, to stb; and Brehon tr, squat circular fort, ½M to port.

At night from a position NE of Platte Fougère Fl.WR.10s, pick up Ldg Lts front Castle Breakwater Al.WR.10s16M, rear Belvedere Ho Oc.10s14M, 220°. When St Sampson front Ldg Lt F.R is obscured, bear to E of line to open Castle Breakwater and Belvedere Lts by about 2° to clear Agenor shoal, 1·8m.

• Great Russel Channel is 2M wide, easy of access, and has weaker streams than Little Russel. In rough weather or poor visibility it is safer. Enter it with W edge of Little Sark open E of the E side of Brecqhou. When St Martin's Point comes well open S of Goubinière Rock (½M SE of Jethou) 243°, make good 230°, allowing for tide, round Lower Heads S card buoy to make for St Peter Port. At night keep in the W sector of Noire Pute Lt, Fl(2)WR.15s (W 220°–040°) as far as Lower Heads S card buoy. Leave this close to stb and make directly for the Castle Breakwater Lt, Al.WR.10s16M.

• From W and S give the NW shore of Guernsey a berth of 3½M, Les Hanois Lt 1½M and the S shore about 1M. At night do not let Les Hanois Lt bear more than 164° until Casquet Lt bears 051°. Round St Martin's Point about a mile off and bring E side of Castle Cornet in line with White Rock LtHo (round, 11m) 350° and make good this line to clear the drying rocks to port. If beating, keep Brehon tr E of N to avoid being set E into the Great Russell. Remember that the E-going tide does not set N round St Martin's Point till about Dover +0300.

At night, from a position off St Martin's Lt, Fl(3)WR.10s, keep the Victoria Marina Lt Oc.R.5s, just open of Terres Point, 342°. When St Martin's Lt bears 215°, steer 015° until White Rock Pier Lt, Oc.G.5s, comes on with Castle Breakwater Lt, Al.WR.10s,

Marks in the Little Russel

| Corbette d'Amont Bn Tr | Roustel Lt | Platte Fougère |
| Tautenay Bn Tr | Vivian Bn Tr | Brehon Tr |

ST PETER PORT APPROACHES

Depths in Metres

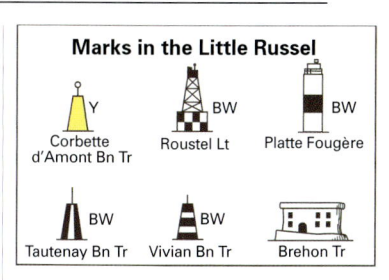

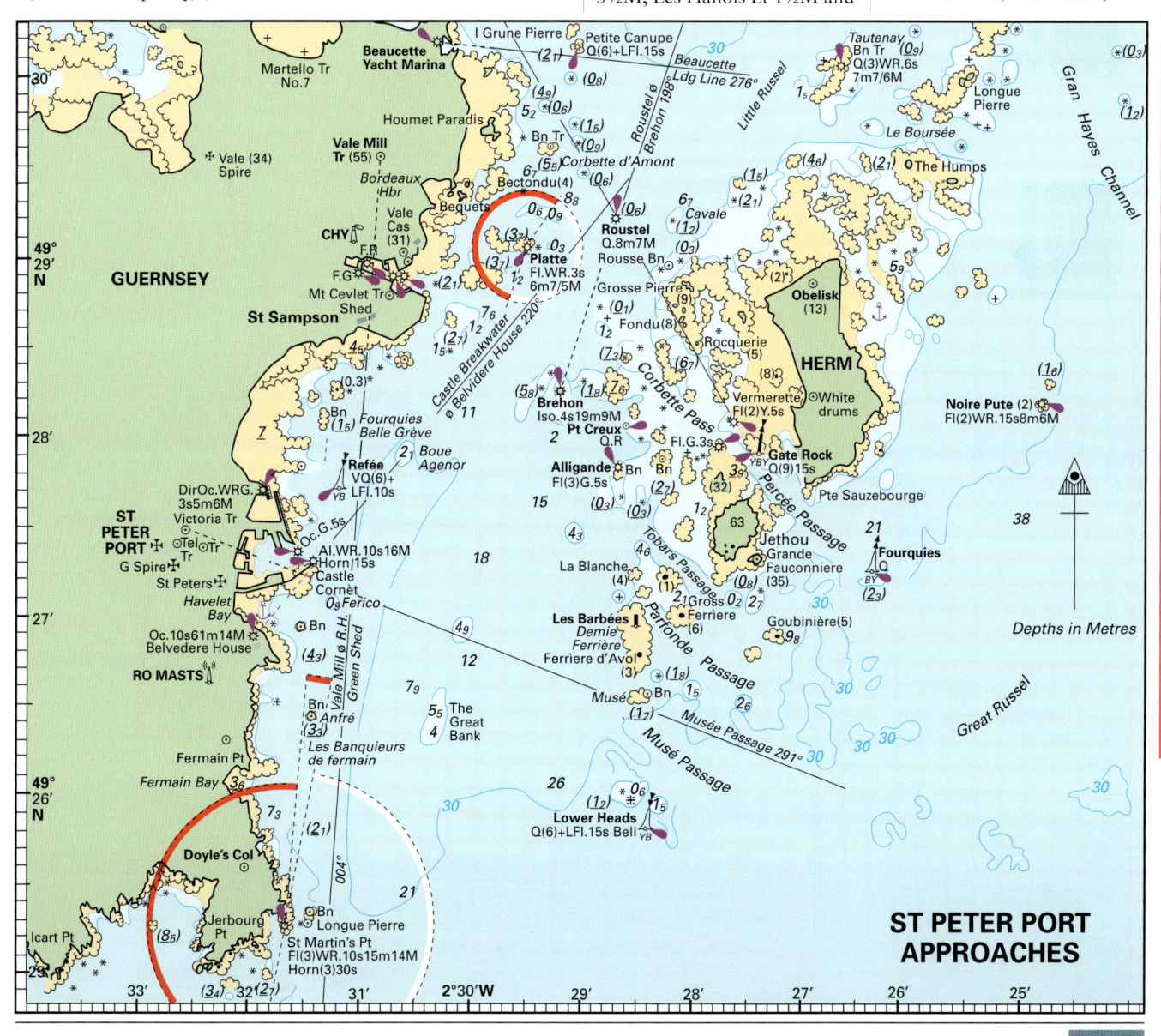

The Cruising Almanac

308°, when steer 330° until the Victoria Marina Lt bears 265°, thence enter.

Anchorages There are several anchorages suitable for use in offshore winds:
• **Icart Bay and Petit Port** on SE (each has drying rocks and is subject to swell);
• **Havelet Bay** adjacent and S of St Peter Port is useful when the latter is crowded, but swell can be a problem;
• **Grande Havre and L'Ancress Bay** on N side, the latter being more protected from SW winds. Clearance at St Peter Port or Beaucette is required before anchoring in any of these places.

ST PETER PORT

Standard Port St Peter Port
DS Dover −0200S +0400N

A good centre with all facilities.
Entrance Monitor Port Control on VHF 12. When inside pier head follow buoyed small craft fairway leaving the boats in the pool to stb and around towards Victoria Marina. In high season the Harbour Control dory will meet you.
R Lts on White Rock Pier, facing E and W indicate entry and exit prohibited except small boats of 15m or less under power with care. R Lts with strobe on S ends of New Jetty and Inter Island Quay facing W also indicate large vessel movements. R Lt on S Pier of Victoria Marina indicates no entry / exit. If closed, moor on waiting pontoon immediately E of marina entrance.

Berthing Victoria Marina, VHF 80 call sign *St Peter Port Marina*, is for visitors (max 12·8m LOA, 1·8m draught) sill dries 4·2m access approx HW ±0230. Entry controlled by marina staff using Lts on S pier head at entrance, entry/exit commences when there is 2m on sill. Larger craft or those wishing to depart before half tide may be directed to moor on the Swan Pontoons in the Pool. These are linked at W end, gangway ashore to Victoria Pier.

It may be possible to obtain a berth in one of the other marinas, contact Victoria Marina for assistance.

Regulations Do not use marine toilets in marina, hbr or Havelet Bay; nor use outboards on tenders. Fly a Q flag on approach unless coming from Alderney, Herm or Sark.

Facilities Fuel point on S side of hbr, dries 2·5m; water in marina, at fuel pt and at root of Victoria Pier. All supplies and services. WiFi at Ship & Crown and Visitor Information Centre.

☎/VHF Harbour office 01481 720229; Marina 725987, VHF 80. Port control VHF 12; Customs 726911. CG (Guernsey Coastguard) call direct on VHF 20.

ST SAMPSON

Entrance dries 3·6m. Marina behind gate (1·8m depth). For local boats, visitors may only enter by prior arrangement for commercial services.

BEAUCETTE MARINA

Approach from the NW in daylight by the Doyle Passage from 1M W of Platte Fougère tr get Corbette Amont Y con bn midway between Herm and Jethou 146° depth 15m.

From the Little Russel leaving Tautenay astern, on 276° pass S of Petite Canupe S card lit bn to find R and W approach buoy LFl.10s, 1ca SE of Grune Pierre. There are two lit porthand buoys and one lit stb buoy. Ldg Lts are both F.R. on W column with R arrow and R column with W arrow rear near windsock. Call *Beaucette Marina* before entry.

Entrance This is narrow (15m at half tide) and the rocks are painted white. Boats leaving have right of way. The sill dries 2·4m and has about 2·7m at half tide. Y waiting buoys N of entrance. Inside, turn to port.

Note this entrance is dangerous in NE or E winds.

Berthing It is advisable to call ahead to reserve a berth.

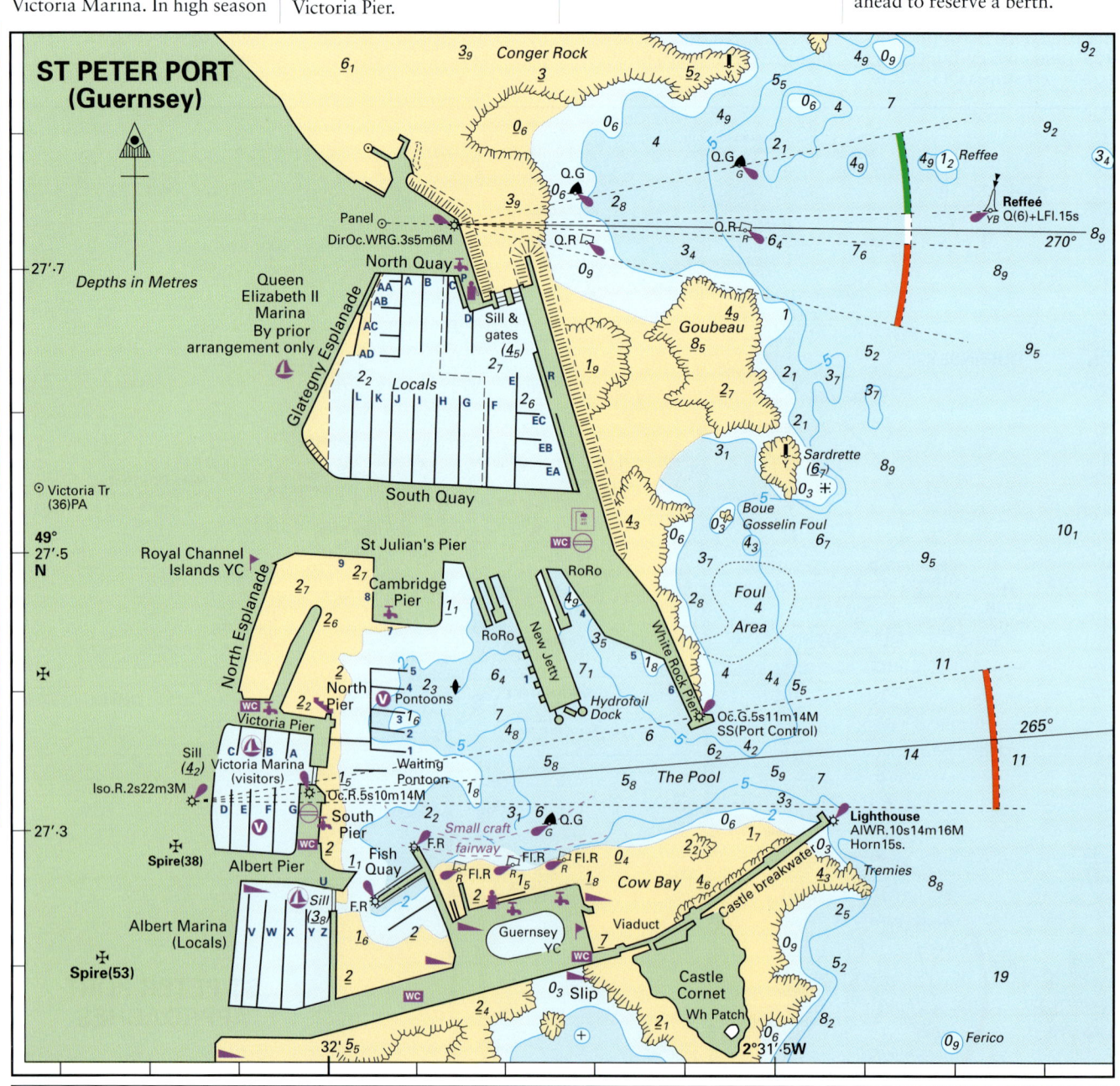

330

The Cruising Almanac

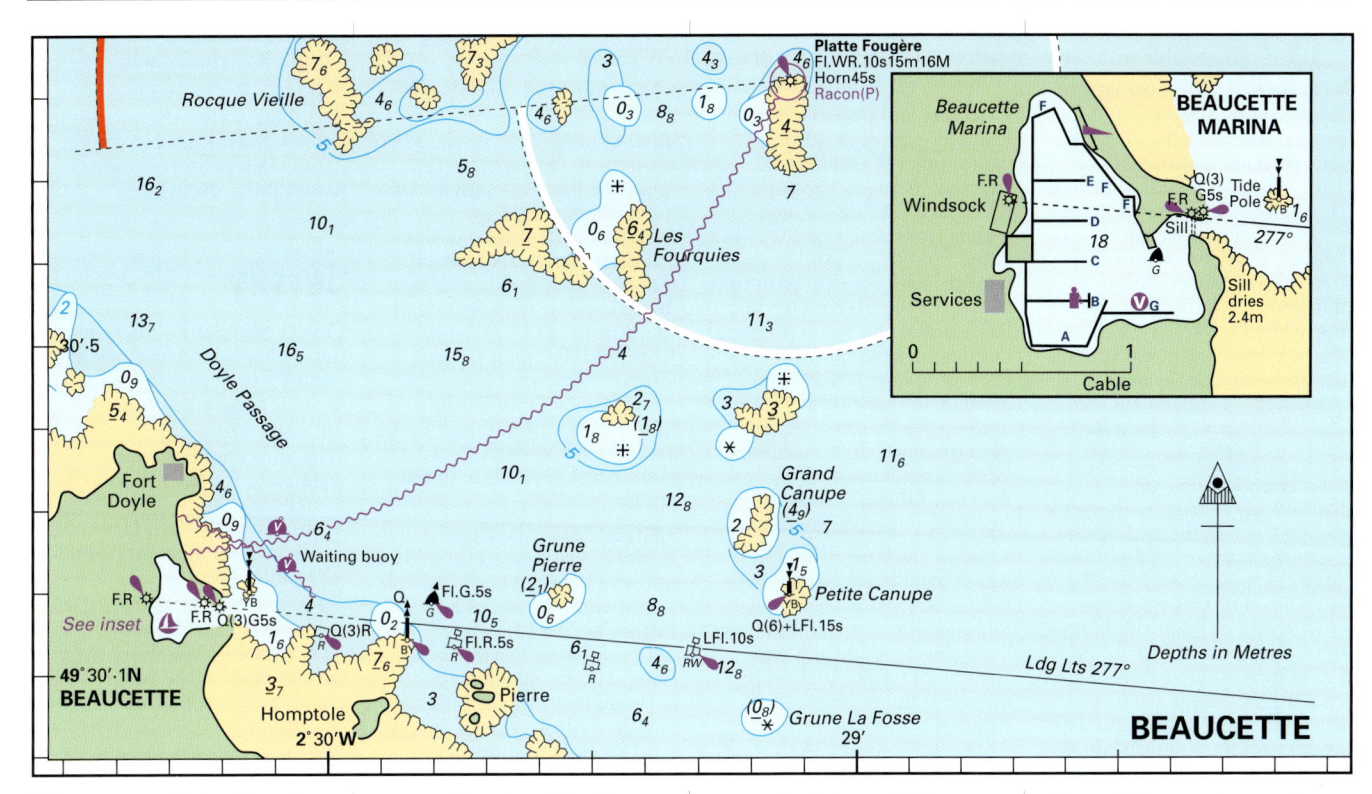

Visitors generally berth on long pontoon to port after entrance.

Facilities All. Restaurant on site. Bus stop ½M. Free WiFi.

☎/VHF Marina 01481 245 000, 07781 102302, VHF 80
www.beaucettemarina.com

Sark

Standard Port St Helier
Maseline Pier
HW +0010   LW +0008
MHWS MHWN MLWN MLWS
−2·1m −1·5m −0·6m −0·3m

DS NE coast is slack at half-tide and HW; SW coast is slack at half-tide and LW

Off W coast:
Dover +0500NE −0100SW
Off E coast:
+0600NE; −0100SW

An island with basic facilities and good anchorages, sometimes subject to swell.

Approach Should not be attempted by night. The safest, but longest route from St Peter Port is to go S, round Lower Heads S card buoy. Bound for La Grande Grève, Musé Passage (29m), Victoria Tr in line with N face of Castle Cornet 291°, is more direct; but if going N of Sark, use the mailboat route, Tobars passage. The transits are:

• **Grande Fauconnière** bn (or, better, Bec du Nez of Sark) seen just over the S slope of Jethou, 090° (or 093°).

• 2ca short of Jethou, get Vale Mill in line with W edge of Brehon tr, 321°; hold this course for 2ca.

• **Noire Pute** just SE of Grande Fauconnière, 061°, leaving Quarter rocks of Jethou ½ca to port, and bearing off to leave Grande Fauconnière (steep-to) also ½ca to port. Beware cross tides; these shorter routes are best taken near slack water.

Anchorages All may be subject to swell. None should be considered in onshore winds except the lightest. Slack water around the island is at half-tide. There are moorings in several bays, most of which are private. Visitor's buoys have been laid in Havre Gosselin and La Grève de la Ville, no charge but donations welcome.

• **Port a la Jument** Approach from N with Moie de la Bretagne (17m) off Little Sark seen through Gouliot Passage 186° until Noire Pute (off E coast of Herm) bears 320°. Alter course to 140° into bay. Anchor

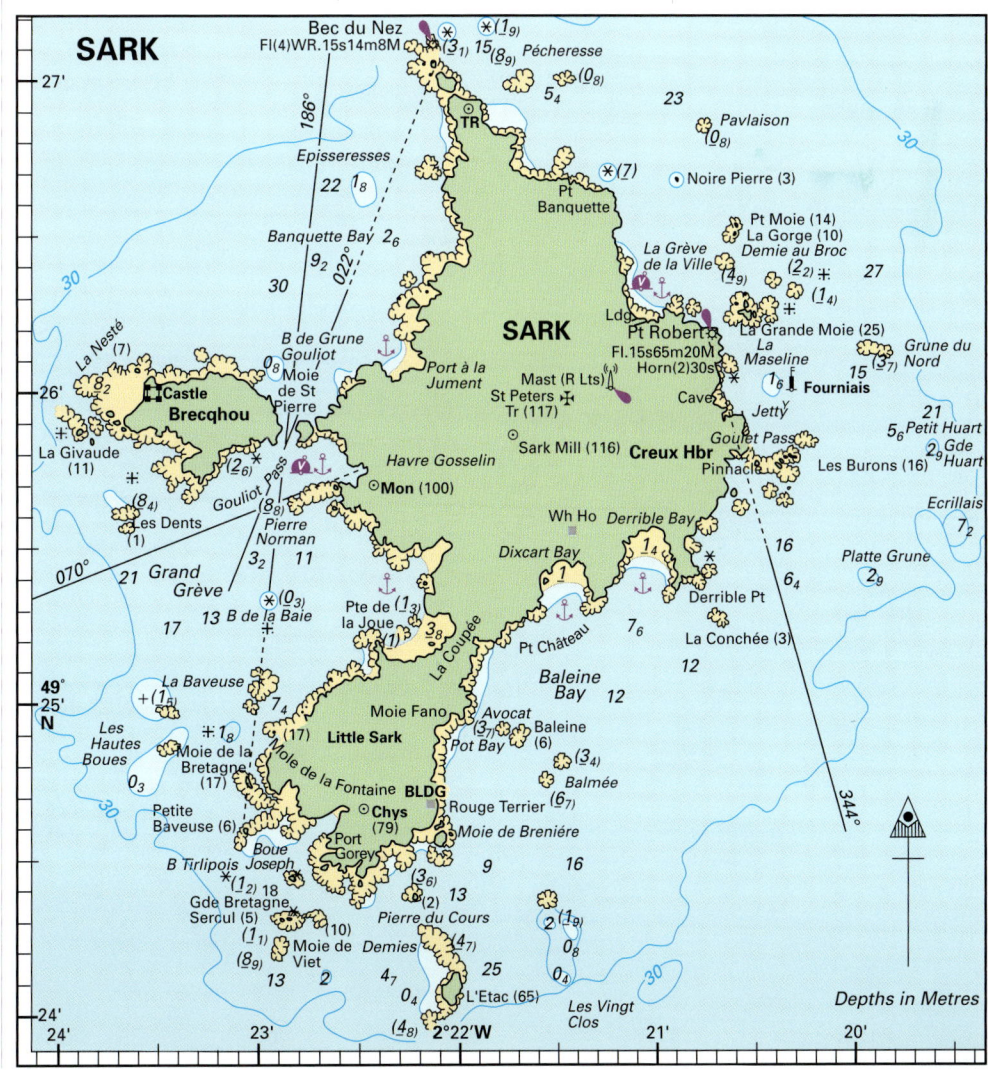

FRANCE – NORTH COAST AND CHANNEL ISLANDS

331

in 5m sand and shingle. Access to top of cliff possible with care.

• **Havre Gosselin** Approach from N with Moie de la Bretagne (17m) off Little Sark seen through Gouliot Passage 186°. Through Gouliot, head E leaving Moie de Gouliot 50m to port. From W Monument in line with Sark Mill (no vanes) 070° clears dangers. Alter to 030° when Gouliot Passage opens then E into bay. Yellow visitors' buoys. Anchor in 5m, sand and shingle, as near to stone jetty as convenient well clear of moorings. Steep steps (300) up to the Monument.

• **La Grande Grève** on W coast has a sandy bottom with a rock drying 0·3m in the middle and a group of drying rocks in the south. Approaching from W keep S end of La Coupeé on with N end of Pointe de la Joue, 090°. From the S, first round Les Hautes Boues by keeping W end of La Givaude bearing at least 355° or, if visible, on with middle of Grande Amfroque, 355°. Anchor 1ca NE of Pointe de la Joue. Access via steep path to La Coupeé. Risk of surf on the beach around HW.

• **Dixcart and Derrible Bays** From SE with Sark Mill (no vanes) open W of Point Chateau, between the bays, 337°. Dixcart Bay – stony incline from about half way in. Good holding on sand at the seaward end. An easy path to the top of the island. Derrible Bay – a shelving bay with good holding on sand. Avoid anchoring near to the large permanent mooring as this is used by the HS Ferry. A long path to the top of the island. Leave dinghies near the steps as the top of this bay is cut off from the steps near high water.

• **Creux Harbour** dries and is full of local boats. With HM's permission visiting boats may moor against the wall but must leave the steps and slip way clear at all times. Anchoring outside is not permitted. Approach from SE until Pt. Robert LtHo bears 344°. Follow that bearing towards hbr wall. Narrow entrance at SW end of wall.

• **Maseline Harbour** is the main arrival place for ferries and other commercial vessels. There is no room for yachts at the quay, the bay has many private moorings and it is not permissible to anchor within 100m of the pier. Approach from NE with E side of L'Etac de Sark in line with W side of Les Burons, 211°. When Pt. Robert LtHo opens to S of Grande Moie alter course to pass close by Grande Moie (30m) and N of Founiais Bn be aware that Grune du Nord (awash at LW) is close to the track.

• **Grève de la Ville** Approach from N until Noire Pierre (3m) midway between Grande Moie (30m) and NE face of Les Burons (22m) 153°. Pass between Noire Pierre and Banquette Pt into steeply shelving bay with cliff path to village. Yellow visitors' buoys. Anchor clear of moorings in 11m sand. Access to shore difficult around HW due to steeply shelving beach.

Supplies At Creux Hbr: Drinking water. Up the hill from Creux: Diesel in cans from Gallery Stores, shops, bank, pubs, cycle hire.

Jersey

A very popular holiday island, Jersey has a large marina, a number of drying harbours and several good anchorages for offshore winds.

The SE corner has reefs extending for over 3M but the Is may be readily approached from SW to NW, and from N between the Paternosters and Dirouilles groups.

At N and S of Jersey it is slack water at local HW and HW+0500 by the shore. At E and W ends of the Is, it is slack water at about half-tide by the shore.

Yachts arriving from outside the Bailiwick, unless from the

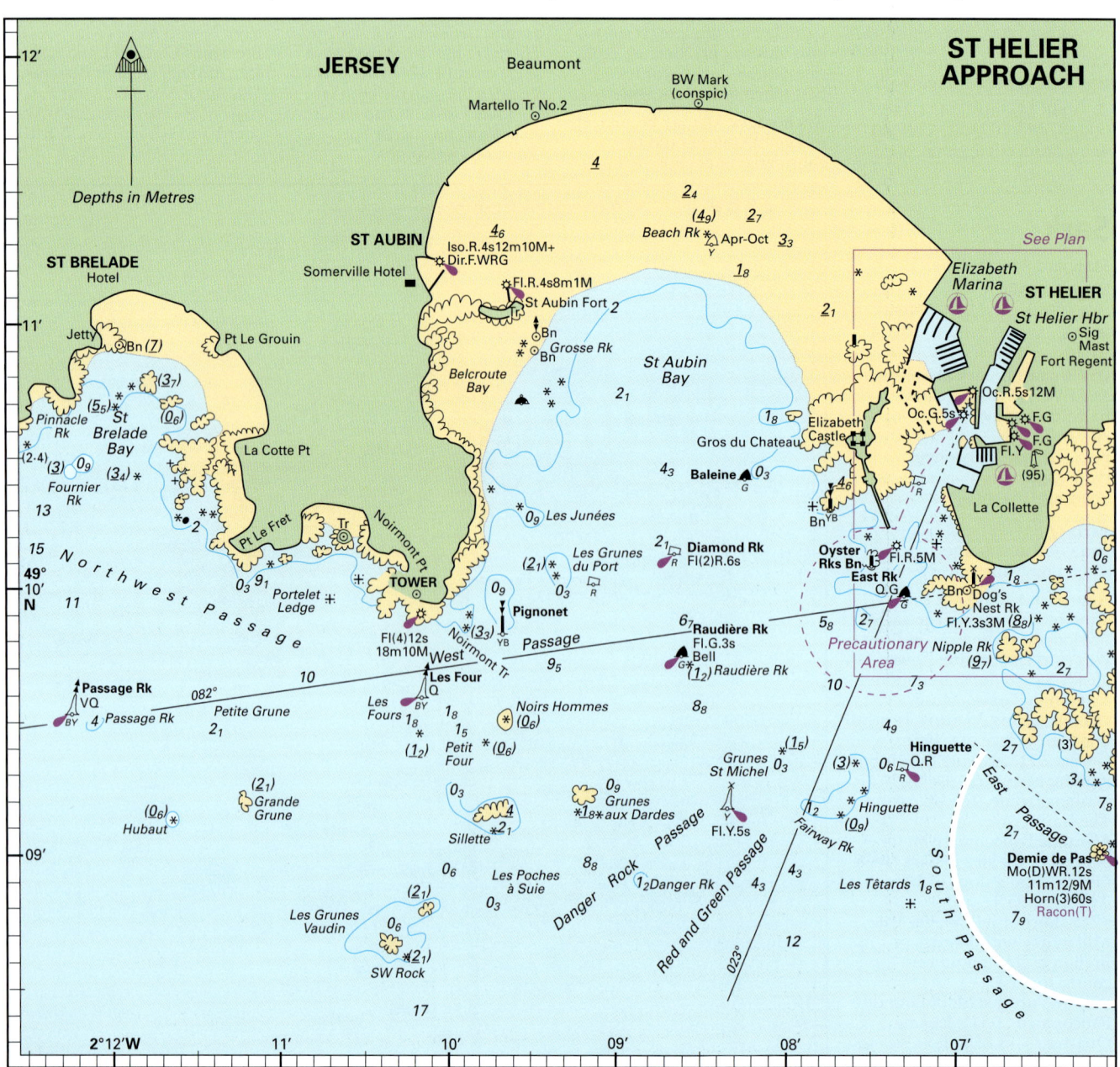

332

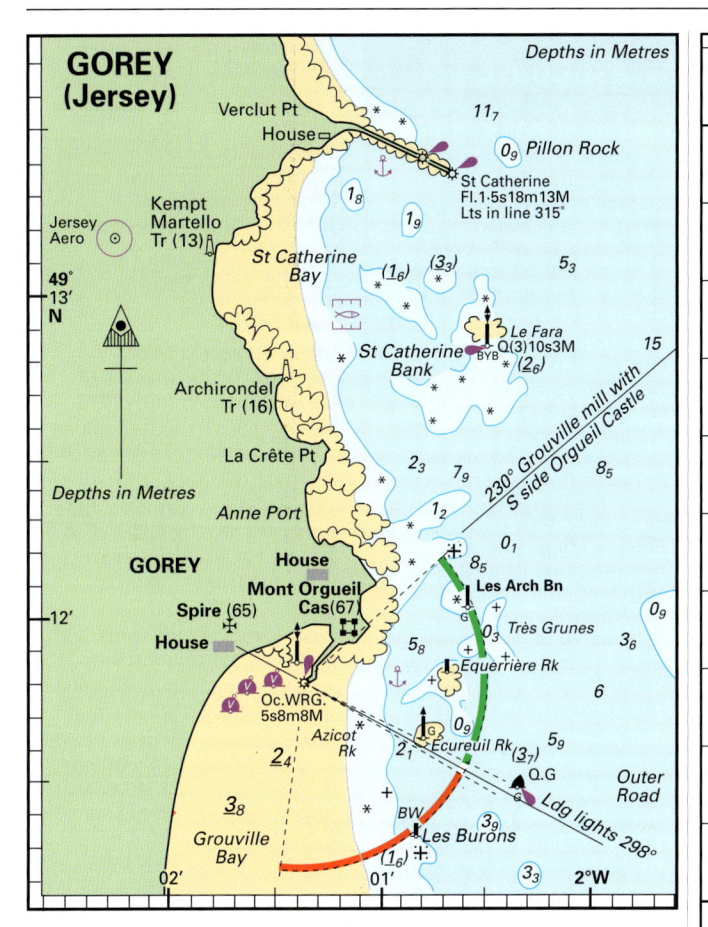

Minquiers or Ecrehous, must fly a Q flag and clear at either St Helier or Gorey.

Coastguard: for routine traffic, passage reports etc, call direct on VHF 82.

GOREY

An attractive drying (3–5m) hbr but generally very crowded.

Approach From NE, the Ldg line is Grouville white mill (rear) over SE slope of Mont Orgeuil Castle (front), 230°. At night use the Ldg Lts (see *Entrance*). From SE, at a position 1M E of Grande Anquette W card bn, steer on line pierhead with Gorey ch spire, 305°. When abeam of Le Giffard R can buoy, alter course to N for leading line.

Entrance Ldg line 298°, front W frame tr Oc.WRG.5s8M, rear WOr patch on stone wall of house. When leaving, if bound N go at half flood with N-going inshore eddy.

Anchorage There are some drying visitors' moorings. Otherwise anchor E of pier, stream runs fast; or take the ground inside, hard sand, mooring bow and stern; or lie alongside pier inside staging at pierhead. Also at St Catherine's Bay inside breakwater off Verclut Point, sand and weed, 3–9m, moderate holding.

Supplies Fuel and Water at end of pier. Shops.

☎/VHF 01534 853616, VHF 74.

ST HELIER

Standard Port St Helier
DS (2M S):
Dover –0400W +0200E

Approach from NW, rounding La Corbière, keep the summit of Jersey high land in line with or above the lantern of the LtHo, but in bad NW weather keep 1½M off; at night keep the F.R Lt to the NE at the level of Corbière lantern. Once round keep ½M off S coast until just E of Noirmont Point it is possible to get on the Western Passage Ldg line, front Dog's Nest Y bn, × top; rear Grève d'Azette Y daymark, 082°.

At night
- Keep Noirmont Point LtHo bearing 095° until La Corbière LtHo is touching La Moye Point, 290°.
- Then steer 110° on that back bearing to pass about 2ca S of Noirmont Point.
- When Noirmont Point is abeam, steer 082° on Western Passage Ldg Lts: front La Grève d'Azette; rear Mont Ubé Lt tr Oc.R.5s. This passage passes N of Les Fours N card buoy; N of Ruaudière G bell buoy, Fl.G.3s; and S of RW Oyster Rock bn.
- Soon after passing Oyster Rock bn, and before reaching East Rock G con buoy Q.G, alter course to port round Platte bn, Fl.R.1·5s to bring Ldg Lts in transit: front Oc.G.5s, rear Oc.R.5s synchronised (R daymarks), 023°. Port side of entrance is well marked by BW diagonal bands visible by day before Ldg marks in haze.

From Gorey come down E coast on line La Coupé Turret open E of Verclut Pt 332° until about ½M N of Violet pillar buoy, RWVS Fl.10s. Steer about 240° to leave this buoy close to port and continue to pick up the line Icho BW tr, 14m, open S of Conchière S card bn, 2m. After about ½M on this line steer W to pass midway between Conchière S card bn and Canger W card Lt buoy, and continue so as to pick up line Noirmont LtHo B tr W band, Fl(4)12s open S of Demie de Pas YB tr 11m Mo(D) (– · ·) WR.12s, (R 130° to 303°), Racon, 290°. Follow this line until ½M from Demie de Pas, then pass 2ca to the S to get St Aubin Fort bearing 314°. Keep on this bearing, leaving Hinguette R can buoy, Q.R to port and East Rock G con buoy, Q.G, to stb until on hbr Ldg line, 023°.

IPTS at Victoria Pier Head: Q amber in addition: power craft under 25m may proceed contrary to signals, keeping to stb.

Entrance Yachts exceeding 14m LOA or 1·8m draught should call St Helier VTS on VHF 14 to confirm there is berthing space. All should watch on this channel. Keep on Ldg marks until entrance opens: two G Lts in line 078°. Beware strong cross-set. Speed 5kn. IPTS on W arm of Elizabeth ferry terminal and E side of St Helier hbr entrance, if Lts R wait in W side of Small Roads well clear of La Collette dolphin and await signal to proceed.

Berthing Visitors are directed by port control to St Helier marina in N part of hbr. Depth gauges and an electric indicator board show when entry and exit are possible, approx HW±0300. There is a fixed sill 3·6m above CD; on this a hinged gate rises 1·4m to maintain a depth of 2·5m inside. The flap is lowered/raised when there is 2·0m of tide above the sill. The

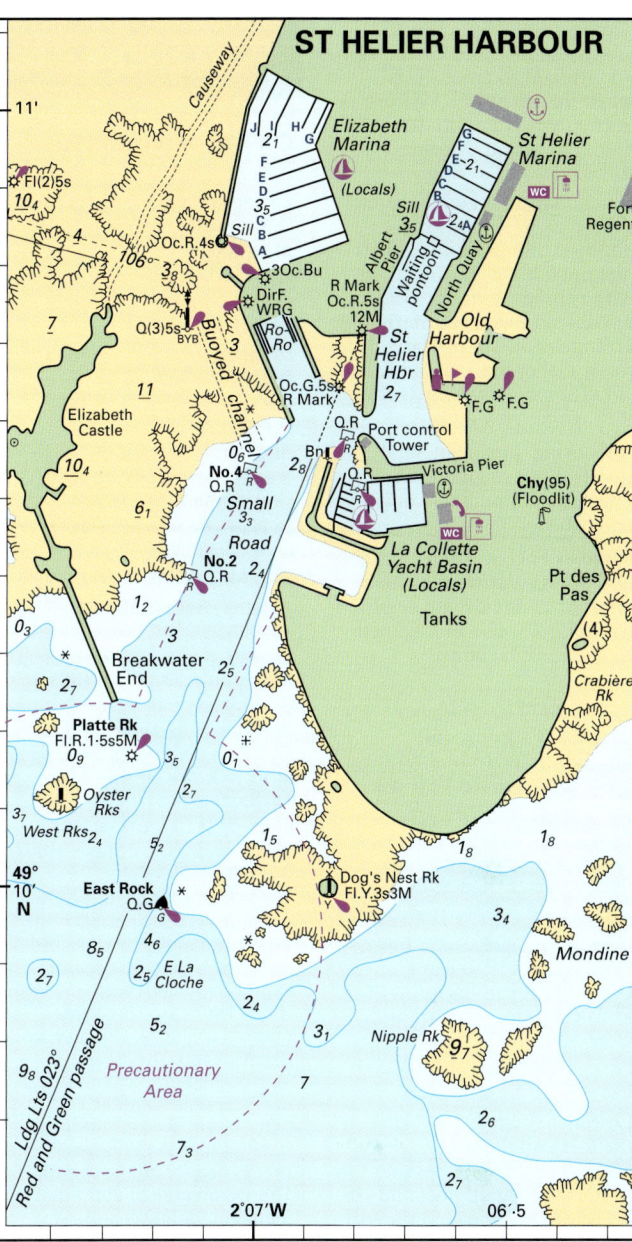

333

depth gauges Fl at 2·5m indicating the sill is closing. Do not attempt to cross the sill when the Lts are Fl. Visitors normally berth at pontoons E, F or G at N end. Marina sometimes full in August. When marina is closed yachts should go to the waiting pontoon alongside the Albert pier outside the marina with rafting. A visitor berth is possible in Elizabeth marina by arrangement. Sill operates as for St Helier marina and R and G Lts control one way traffic through narrow entrance.

Anchoring outside in Small Roads is not recommended owing to shipping movements and fish storage boxes.

Supplies Fuel at E side of main hbr, opposite entrance, no pontoon. Note drying height at base of quay also in Elizabeth Marina. All facilities.

☎/**VHF** Jersey marina office 01534 447730. St Helier VTS VHF 14. Customs and Immigration 01534 448000. Jersey Coastguard VHF 82.

ST AUBIN

A pleasant but drying hbr, much quieter than St Helier.

Approach as for St Helier but from Ruaudière G con buoy, Fl.G.3s, turn N to leave Diamond R can buoy, Fl(2)R.6s, close to port and steer 332° for 1·3M leaving two bns SSE of fort well to port.

Entrance A causeway between the fort and the shore dries 5·1m. The channel, leaving fort to port, has small port and stb buoys. At night round the fort pierhead, Fl.R.4s, and steer 254° in W sector of Lt Dir.F.WRG on N pier head (with Lt Iso.R.4s on same structure). Tide gauge on N pierhead; enter HW±0130.

Berthing There are berths for about 10 visiting yachts (with rafting) alongside N quay: dries, mud.

Anchorage E of Platte Rock bn SE of fort, 2m. RCIYC has three moorings for visitors in Belcroute Bay, 3½ca S of fort, 0·9m.

Supplies Water on quay; fuel; shops; boatyard.

☎ RCIYC 01534 745783.

France – Northwest Coast

W COAST OF THE CHERBOURG PENINSULA

Passage lights	BA No
Cap de la Hague	1512
Fl.5s48m23M Horn 30s	
Alderney	1536
Fl(4)15s37m12M	
Cap de Carteret	1638
Fl(2+1)15s81m26M	
Le Sénéquet	1648
Fl(3)WR.12s18m9/6M	
Iles Chausey	1654
Fl.5s39m23M	
Horn 30s	
Pte du Roc	1660
Fl(4)15s49m23M	
La Pierre de Herpin	1670
Iso.4s20m13M	

STREAMS RELATED TO DOVER
Alderney Race HWD SW; +0600NE

5M NW of Cap de Carteret: Rotary anti-clockwise, +0530N – 0100S, each 3¾kn.

Between Les Écrehou and Chaussée des Boeufs: rotary anti-clockwise –0445N 1·2kn, +0145S 0·5kn.

Entré de la Déroute –0500NE, 1·2kn; –0300NW, 2·1kn; –0100W 0·5kn; +0200S 1·0kn.

The W side of the Cherbourg Peninsula is inhospitable, with shoals and mussel and oyster parks extending far offshore, exposed to winds with any W in them. There are now three marinas (Diélette, Carteret, and Granville) but these can be approached only after half tide in reasonable weather. Fog may occur at any season. Tides run strongly and the W'ly swell breaks heavily on the shoals. There is an area of abnormal magnetic variation around Cap Flamanville.

DIÉLETTE

Standard Port St Malo
HW +0040   LW +0028
MHWS MHWN MLWN MLWS
–2·5m –1·9m –0·7m –0·3m

Diélette is a hbr about 11M S of Cap de la Hague, sheltered between ENE and S. Entrance dredged to –0·5m. It has a marina (2·5m) with a flap gate sill at +3·5m and 70 berths for visitors. Gate opens when there is 1·5m over the sill. There is a waiting pontoon, a tide gauge showing height over sill and IPTS entrance Lts for the marina. Dangerous to approach and uncomfortable in strong W or SW winds.

Approach The approach is without hazard but keep outside the W card lying 1½M WSW which marks the prohibited zone off the conspic nuclear power station. W card buoy unlit close W of Rocher Piernier.

Entrance On entering give the inner pier to port a wide berth as silting takes place at the end. The small commercial hbr opens up and the marina entrance is to stb. Dredging in progress. –2m in Bassin de Commerce. –1·5m in approach channel. 70 visitors' berths.

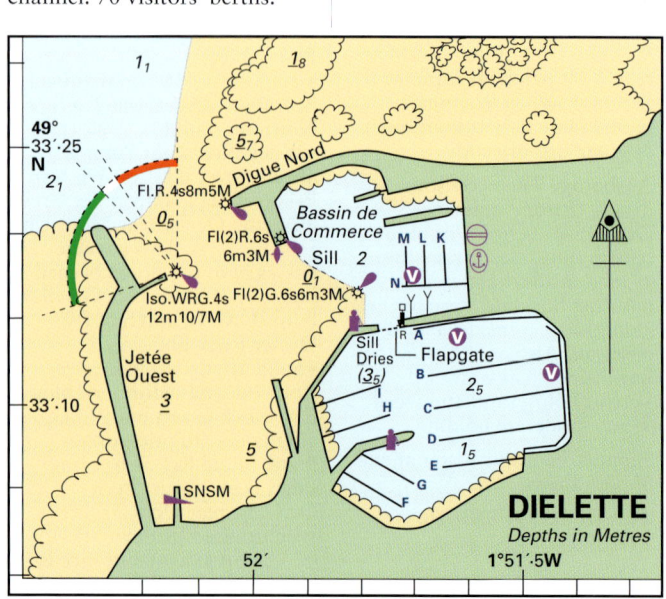

Nevertheless, although it is simpler to go W of Jersey and Les Minquiers, this inshore passage provides the most direct route between Cherbourg, Granville and St-Malo, for which there are two channels: Passage de la Déroute and Déroute de Terre. Only the latter is possible by night.

Passage de la Déroute leads from Cap de la Hague between Les Ecrehou and Basses de Taillepied; between Basse Occidentale des Boeufs and S Anquette (beware dangerous wreck position (doubtful) 49°05'·00N, 1°50'·00W); W of Basse Le Marié; E of Les Ardentes; over Banc de la Corbière and through Entrée de la Déroute between Les Minquiers and Iles Chausey. In the narrows the flood runs at 4–5kn, the ebb at 3½–4kn. Fishing buoys are common on this passage and some of these are linked by stout rope lying just beneath the surface.

Déroute de Terre should be attempted only near HW there being only 0·9m at the S end. It passes inshore between Trois Grunes and Cap Carteret; between Bancs Félés and Basses de Portbail; between Basse Jourdan Lt buoy and the W card buoy NW of Le Sénéquet; close E of special buoy, Internationale F, marking outer edge of oyster beds, 4M SW of Sénéquet Lt; E of La Catheue buoy; E of a wreck buoy to 1M W of Pte du Roc at Granville.

The night passage involves eight transits on shore lights: details in *Admiralty Pilot*.

Extra moorings on waiting pontoons. May ground.

Facilities Chandler, sailmaker, laundry, pump out. Restaurants. Free shuttle bus to Flamanville (6km) and Le Pieux for supermarkets, etc. July/August, not Sundays.

☎ HM 02 33 53 68 78.
Taxi 02 33 52 53 53.

CARTERET

Standard Port St Malo
HW (sp)+0020 (np)+0030
LW (sp) +0015 (np)+0030
MHWS MHWN MLWN MLWS
–1·6m –1·2m –0·7m –0·3m

Carteret, 10M S of Cap de Flamanville, is a small fishing port used also by vedettes to Jersey. The hbr dries apart from a marina with 60 visitors' berths.

Near local HW tide runs NW across the entrance at 4kn.

Approach Do not approach from N as there are rks 1M offshore. From W dries 5ca off-shore. Steer for a W building with R roof on the shore at Barneville, 1½M E of Cap Carteret LtHo until it is possible to see inside the estuary, with the white head of W breakwater to port. Steer N for the entrance.

Entrance Dries. Dangerous in S to W winds. It is best to enter HW–0100. Port breakwater has Lt bn Oc.R.4s at head. Keep 50m off. To stb is a training wall, Fl.G.2·5s. This and a parallel training wall inside it both cover. The entrance channel dries 4m. Move to centre of channel just before the bn on E training wall. Inside the hbr the deeper water is to port, near the quays leading to basin. There are R and G piles where the channel turns E. The entrance to the marina is dangerous at opening time as there are often boats waiting and a very fast current runs out.

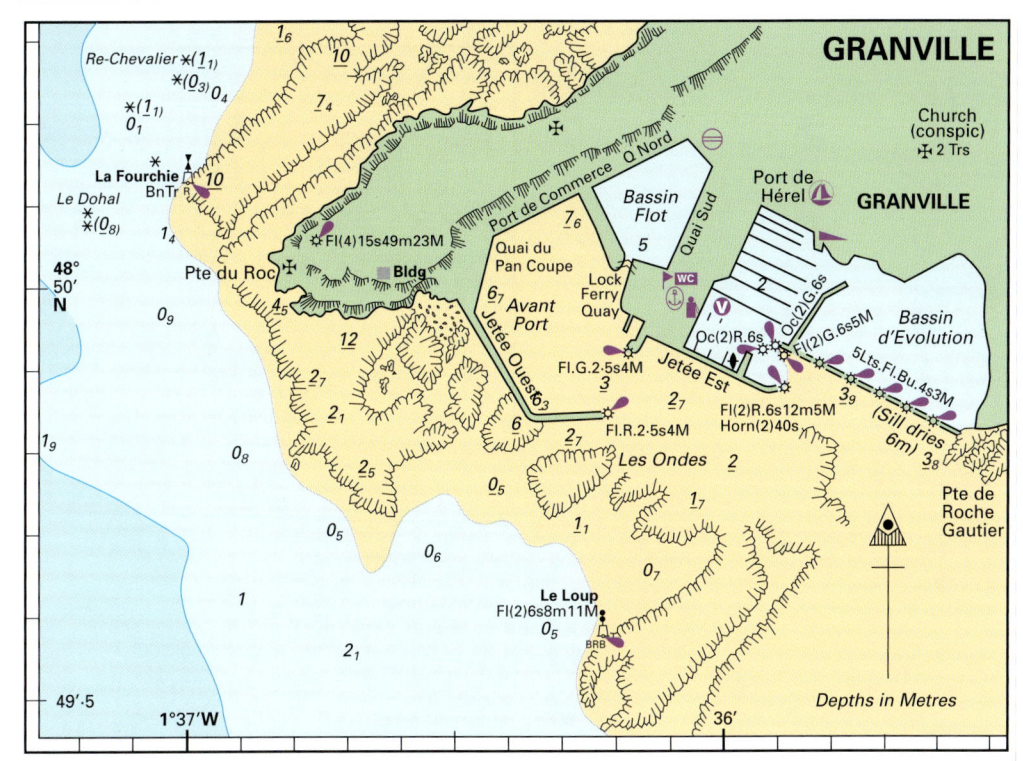

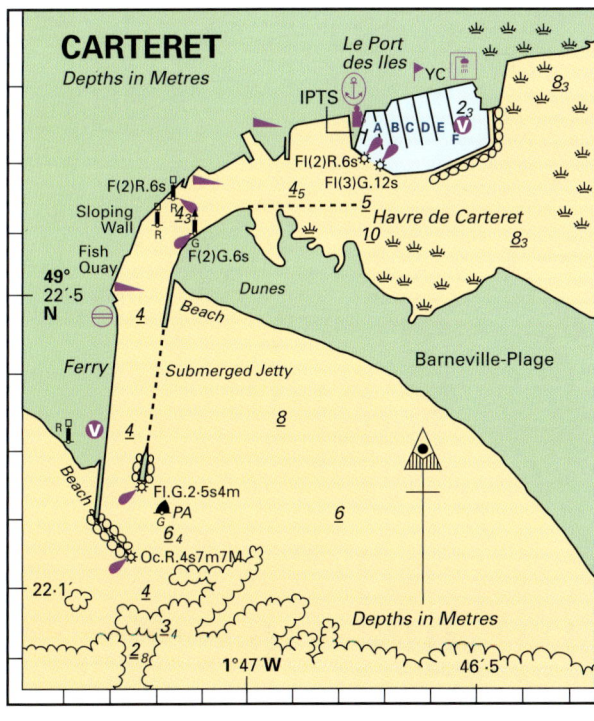

the sill. An illuminated panel on the breakwater shows the depth of water on the sill. If the panel shows 'O', entry is forbidden as the gate is closed. Moor to ends of first two pontoons, in front of office, 2·5m (but only 1·3m in N end of basin). Maximum 15m by 2·5m draught. 150 visitors. Pontoons are marked in alphabetical order, with A at north side of basin. Vessels >15m should use the Port de Commerce.

Supplies Fuel on quay; water on pontoons. All facilities. Railway.

☏ Marina 02 33 50 20 06; Port de Commerce 02 33 91 18 62.

ÎLES CHAUSEY

Standard Port St Malo
HW +0005   LW +0015
MHWS MHWN MLWN MLWS
+0·8m +0·7m +0·6m +0·4m

DS 1M N and S:
Dover +0130E −0500W

1M E and W:
Dover +0415N −0230S
Up to 3·7kn

A beautiful archipelago of islets and rocks. Grande Ile, the largest island, with anchorage and moorings in the Sound on its NE side. Much frequented in summer.

Note If coming from the Channel Islands, customs must

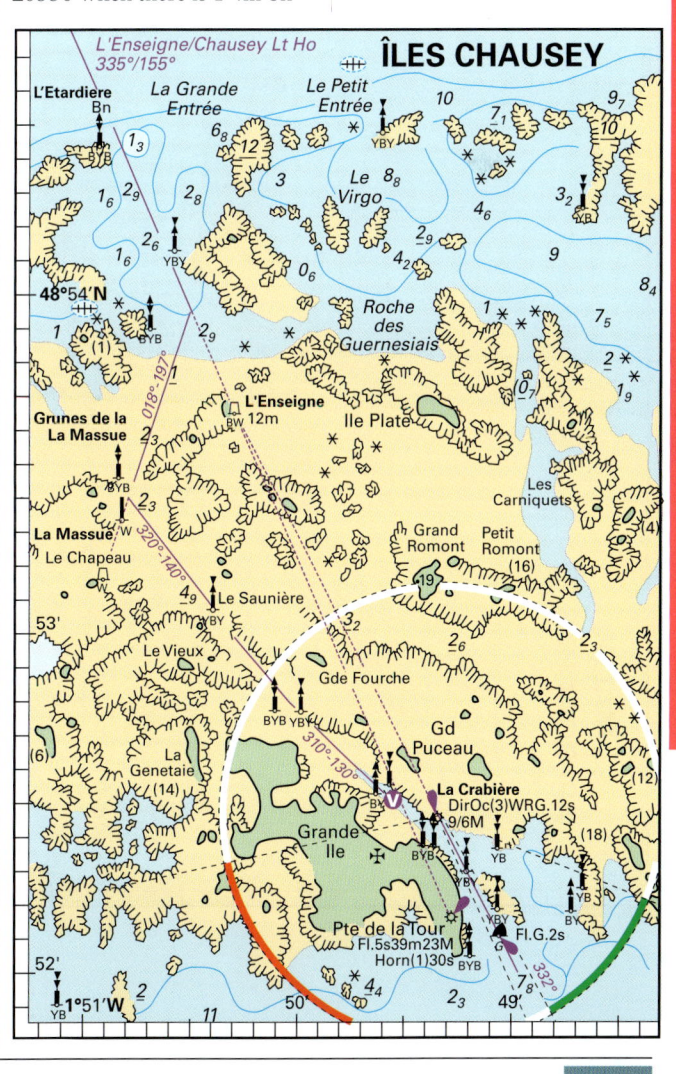

of R posts, Fl.Bu.4s, marking the submersible breakwater of the dinghy basin.

Berthing Access to the Hérel marina is over a hinged gate, 16m wide, sill dries 4·5m, between R and G bns, Oc(2)R or Oc(2)G.6s. The gate opens and closes at HW±0300 to ±0330 when there is 1·4m on

Berthing Marina (2·3m) is on port side beyond town. Sill +5m between R & G Lt bns. The gate opens when there is +1·3m over it. Fl.R or G Lts indicate whether the gate is up or down. Depth inside from 2·3 to 8m according to tide. Visitors at far end on pontoon 'F' often with rafting.

Facilities All. Small town.

☏ Port de Plaisance 02 33 04 70 84.

GRANVILLE

Standard Port St Malo
HW +0008   LW +0020
MHWS MHWN MLWN MLWS
+0·7m +0·4m +0·3m 0·0m

DS (1½M offshore):
Dover −0500NE HW SW

A commercial and fishing port; also a popular holiday resort and yachting centre. Accessible only after half-flood. Note the huge range of tide.

Approach is rough in strong winds between W and NW. Pte du Roc has a steep cliff under grey, circular Lt tr with R top, Fl(4)15s. 3½M to W is a W card Lt buoy marking Videcoq Rk (dries 1m).

Entrance Best to arrive at HW−0130. From Videcoq buoy steer 090° to leave Le Loup BR Lt tr, Fl(2)6s to stb and W jetty head, Fl.R.2·5s, to port. Continue easterly past Avant Port and double back round the southern breakwater, Fl(2)R.6s, leading to the Port de Hérel marina basin. Keep clear of line

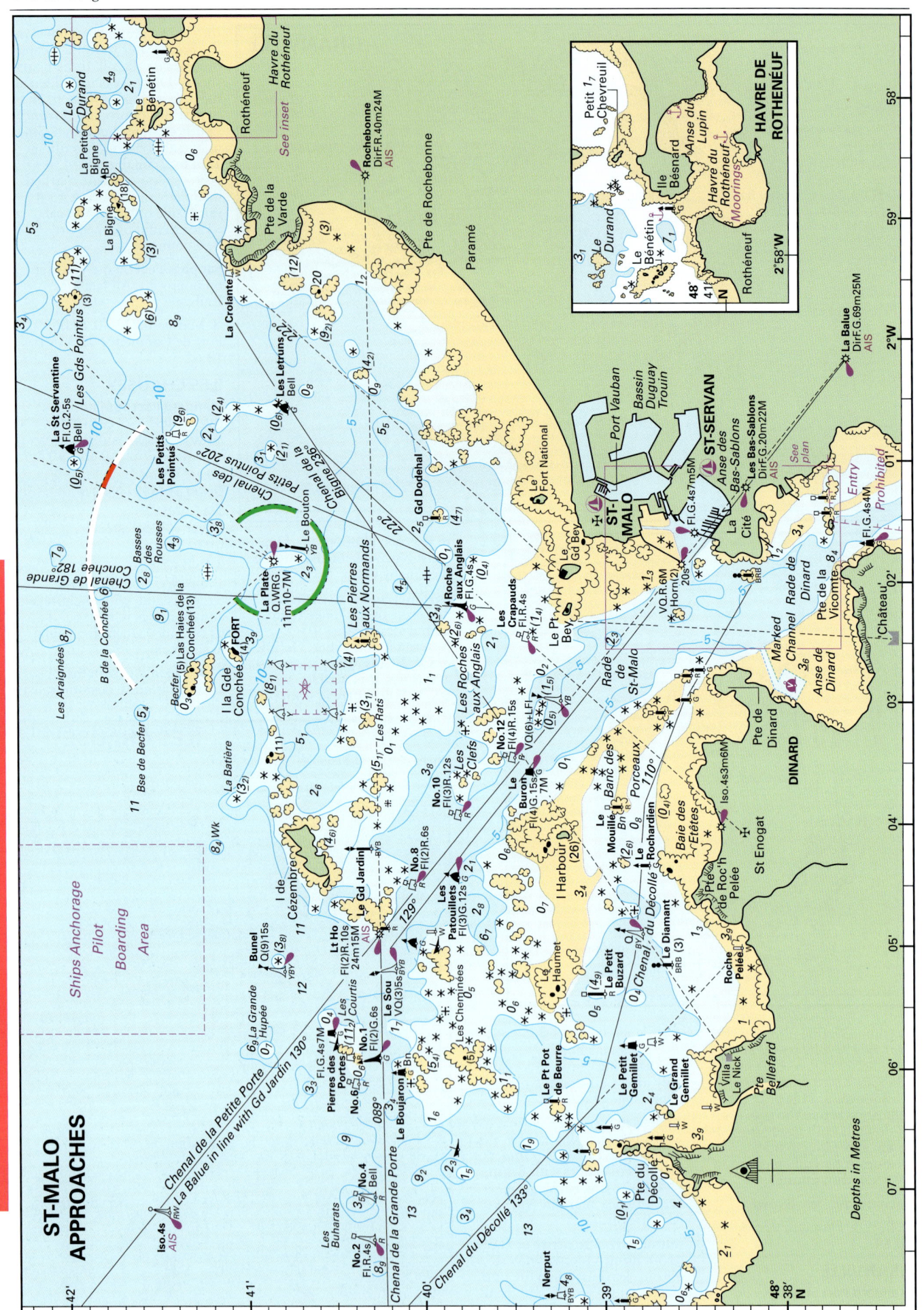

ST-MALO APPROACHES

FRANCE – NORTH COAST AND CHANNEL ISLANDS

be cleared at Granville or St-Malo.

Approach is straightforward from the S. The N is more difficult: marks are harder to distinguish and the approach dries.

Entrance from a position SE of the grey square LtHo, Fl.5s39m Horn 30s, on SE tip of Grande Ile, steer 332° with La Crabière Est bn, Dir.Oc(3)RWG.12s (329°-W-335°) in line with L'Enseigne W tr, to leave Epiettes G con bell buoy, Fl.G.2s, to stb. Keep La Crabière close to stb, and bear 030° to port to leave next RW bn to stb.

Berthing Moorings are normally available in the Sound, sheltered at LW, apart from swell from SE winds; but exposed at HW and uncomfortable with wind against tide. Take care with soundings to avoid grounding near Springs. Anchorage is restricted by moorings but craft that dry out can find large stretches of flat sand, but beware rocky outcrops and poor holding with strong streams. The N part dries at springs but there is 2m in S. Anchorage is also possible in the bay to the W of the LtHo, sheltered from NW to E.

ST-MALO TO LES HÉAUX DE BRÉHAT

Passage lights	BA No
Cap Fréhel Fl(2)10s85m29M	1698
Le Grand Léjon Fl(5)WR.20s17m18/14M AIS	1716
Barnouic VQ(3)5s15m7M	1730
Roches Douvres Fl.5s60m24M AIS	1734
Les Héaux Fl(4)WRG.15s48m15-11M AIS	1738

STREAMS RELATED TO DOVER
1½M N of Cap Fréhel HW Dover +0200ESE −0530WNW, both 3¾kn

Near La Horaine +0130 ESE 4kn −0445WNW 3¾kn

Near Les Héaux +0115E −0500W both 3¾kn

Keeping well offshore this passage presents no particular difficulties, apart from the strength of streams. Further inshore Cap Fréhel can be uncomfortable with wind against tide, which approaches 4kn at springs.

An area of magnetic anomaly is reported SE of Grand Léjon.

Going to Trieux river or further W, keep N of Grand Léjon.

Anchorages in offshore winds can be found in several places, including Erquy, Rade de Portrieux and W of Le Taureau bn tower (2°55'W).

ROTHÉNEUF
Tidal data as St Malo
DS (Chenal de la Bigne): Dover +0145NE −0500SW

A drying hbr about 3M E of St-Malo, offering good shelter.

Approach and Entrance The approach is dangerous near HW when the rks are covered; and the flood, crossing the approach, is at its strongest just after half-tide. It is best to approach before then and if necessary anchor outside to await more water.

Leave St-Malo by Chenal de la Bigne; after passing La Petite Bigne G bn 50m to port, continue on that line (042°) to leave Le Durand (dr 10m) and le Roger (dr 4·7m) to stb, until the entrance bn, G cone up, is about 7ca off bearing 162°. Steer on that course to leave the bn close to stb. If too early to enter, anchor to await the tide about 50m N of this bn, 3–4m.

Anchorage The whole hbr dries about 8m, good flat sand. Supplies, shops in village.

ST-MALO
Standard Port St Malo
For DS see various approach channels.

St-Malo is an attractive old town with good shops and yacht moorings in the locked docks and a tidal marina.

Approach There are six approach channels, of which only the second and third are lit. Beware strong cross-streams. From E to W they are as follows:

Chenal de la Bigne
0·5m. DS Dover +0200ENE − 0500SW
A useful short cut bound for Granville or Cancale. Start about ¾M E of Rochefort bn tr and steer 222° with La Crolante W bn tr in line with N edge of Grand Bey. Be careful to be on this line when passing the narrow gap E of La Bigne stb bn. ¼M after La Bigne bn, steer 236° with Le Buron G Lt tr in line with W stripe under a villa on Pte Bellefard (if the latter not visible, keep Buron just left of Ile Harbour fort behind Buron). In rounding La Crolante keep at least 200m to NW to clear unmarked drying rock (3·2m) to SW of it. When La Plate tr comes on with Conchée fort, bear to port, 222°, to S of Roche aux Anglais buoy to join Chenal des Petits Pointus.

Chenal des Petits Pointus
DS Dover +0145E −0500WSW
This is another day channel for good visibility, with 0·3m but is the most direct from Iles Chausey. From a position 1¼M W of Rochefort bn tr steer 202° on line of W edge of small fort on Petit Bey with either high W house with four chimneys or with bell tr of Dinard ch to join Chenal de la Bigne E of Roche aux Anglais.

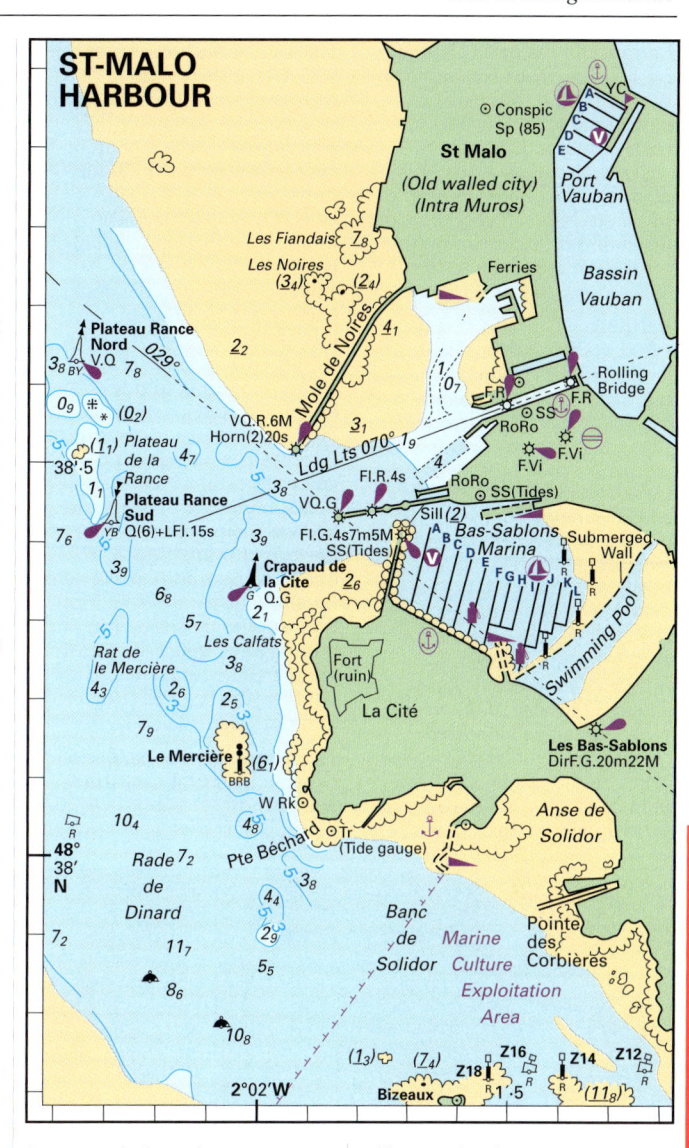

Chenal de la Grande Conchée
DS as for Chenal des Petits Pointus
Can be taken by day at all times save LWS; least depth 0·5m. Identify La Grande Conchée, a rock with round ruined fort on top, 5m, 1M E of Ile Cézembre. From a position 3ca E, steer 182° to leave La Plate N card Lt tr, Y with B top, Q.WRG, to port. At night keep in W sector; R sector covers La Servantine Rock. Beware strong cross-stream and alter course if necessary to leave Roche aux Anglais G con, Fl.G.4s, clear to stb and bear SW to leave Les Crapauds R can buoy to port to join Chenal de la Petite Porte. Shallows are E and SE of Roche aux Anglais and W of Les Crapauds – about 0·5m, but easily passable after half-tide.

Chenal de la Petite Porte
7·2m. DS Dover +0215E −0430W
Is the approach from NW. From the RW safewater buoy, Iso.4s, get Le Jardin Lt tr in line with La Balue grey square Lt tr (on high ground behind town), DirF.G, 129°. Beware strong cross-streams. When about 4ca off Le Jardin, bear S to get Bas-Sablons W square Lt tr, B top, DirF.G (intense 127°−130°) 20m, in line with La Balue, 129°. Beware ferries.

Chenal de la Grande Porte
7·2m. DS Dover: +0215E −0430W
Is the main approach from W. Le Grand Jardin grey tr, R top, Fl(2)R.10s24m, in line with Rochebonne W square tr, R top, DirF.R.40m 088°-intens-090°, 089°. The latter is difficult to distinguish by day: the buoyed channel can be followed. Finally No.3 Le Sou E card buoy VQ(3)5s marks the turn into Chenal de la Petite Porte.

Chenal du Décollé (regard as drying 1·2m) is the shortest approach from the W but is unlit. Tidal streams as in Chenal de la Grande Porte. Starting about 3½ca SW of No.2 R buoy, get W pyramid on Roche Pelée in line with W bn tr Grand Genillet, 134°. From this line steer with Pte de Dinard bn on with Rochardien bn 105°, altering course to N to round the latter to get on line of Ste-Croix ch round belfry with Pourceaux bn, 110° to round Pte de Dinard, marked by two stb bns.

FRANCE – NORTH COAST AND CHANNEL ISLANDS

337

The Cruising Almanac

Entrance In the main channel get Ldg Lts, front Bas-Sablons W square tr, B top; rear La Balue grey square tr, both DirF.G, in line 129°; channel is well marked. This leads N of N card Rance Lt buoy, to head of Môle des Noirs, VQ.R. Port des Bas-Sablons (St Servan marina) is to stb of approach to the locks (dredged 2m).

Berthing

• **Port des Bas-Sablons** Pontoon berths (70 for visitors) max 12m. Entrance via narrow channel S of ferry catwalk. A sill, drying 2m, runs SW–NE across entrance to marina. Entry is possible at LW+0100 to –0130 with tidal coefficient over 70. Passage is possible at all times at neaps (coefficient 40). There are two 'Sablons' waiting buoys, 2m depth, at S edge of dredged channel. All other outside anchoring or mooring is forbidden or reserved. A tide gauge at the head of the ferry pier, with large illuminated repeater on W breakwater, shows depth on the sill, which is unmarked when covered. Three vert F.R light means 'no exit'. The head of the breakwater is lit, Fl.G.4s, but there is no corresponding R Lt at the far end of the sill. Visitors moor to pontoon A in season, pontoon B out of it. Sheltered at LW but surge when sill is covered, especially with strong NW winds. Note that fuel can only be bought with card.

• **Bassin Vauban** in the docks, reached via L'écluse du Naye, Ldg line 070°, Lts F.R. Gates work between HW±0230, varied according to tide. Simplified code of signals. Possible to wait for opening in Port des Bas-Sablons. Yachts enter after ships and fishing boats; high lock sides require keepers' help with mooring lines. Yachts are moored to quay and pontoons at N end of Bassin Vauban; when full it is necessary to pass the lifting br into bassin Duguay-Trouin and moor to quay immediately to left after the br. Well protected and near old town.

Facilities All at Bas-Sablons marina. Visit Old City (Intra Muros).

☏/**VHF** Les Bas-Sablons 02 99 81 71 34. Bassin Vauban 02 99 20 55 00. Commercial Port *Saint-Malo Port* VHF 12.

DINARD

Berthing sometimes available in basin S of Pte de Dinard, dredged 1–2m with approach channel (1m) from Rade de Dinard. 150 berths, buoys sometimes available in bay (NR5 & 7).

Facilities Convenient water and fuel on quay. Nearby shops and restaurants. Mkt: Tues, Thur, Sat. Ferry to/from St Malo.

☏ HM 02 99 46 65 55.

RIVER RANCE

The Rance is dammed by a hydro-electric barrage 1M above St Servan. A lock at the W end gives access to the river which with a reasonable engine and less than 1·6m draught and 16m head height is navigable to Dinan, above Le Châtelier lock, and thence to Brittany canal system. Above Dinan the canal has max 1·2m draught and 2·5m headroom. Do not go above Plouër (½M S of Pont St Hubert) when sea HW less than 9m. Remember that you need an ICC endorsed for Inland Waterways and a CEVNI rule book.

Approach, dredged 2m, is along W shore by La Jument G Lt tr, Fl(5)G.20s, leaving to port an exclusion safety zone below the barrage, marked by R conical buoys, cylinder topmarks, lettered ZI with a number. ZI12 is lit, Fl.R.4s.

Signals at the lock
3R Lts: No entry. 3G Lts vessels may pass. 2G 1 W act as instructed.

Signals near the centre of the barrage
W cone over B cone, pts up or G over W Lts:
Flood stream through sluices.
B cone over W cone, points down ebb stream through sluices.

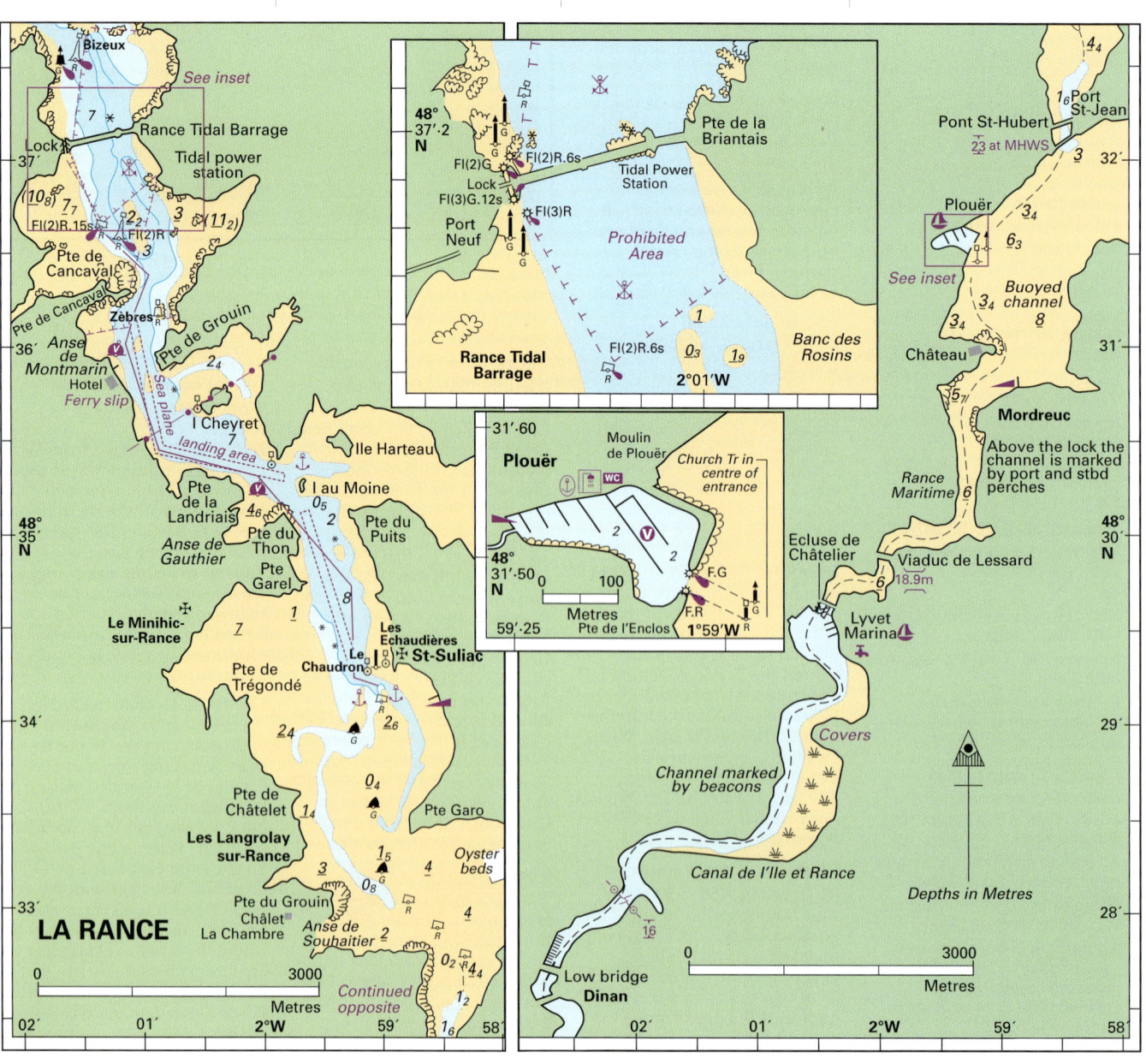

Entrance The lock is 65m by 13m with 2m depth on the sill. It works from 0430–2030 and opens on the hour when height of tide on each side of it exceeds 4m. Yachts should arrive 20 minutes before opening (30 minutes if leaving). Locks open on the hour from seaward and on the half hour from the river. There are three mooring buoys to port in the approach from seaward. Boats with no masts enter last (first when descending) as they may otherwise be berthed under the lowered br. Enter as soon as there is room or gates may close. Ropes in lock.

Water levels do not follow the tide times. They are given 48hrs in advance at St-Malo office and at the locks at the barrage and at Châtelier. The channel dries at LW between St Suliac and Le Châtelier. Do not go above Plouër (½M S of Pont St Hubert) when sea HW is less than 9m. Le Châtelier lock, 3M below Dinan, opens when the river depth exceeds 8·5m, giving about 5hrs working per tide. When the lock is working there is 2m in the approach. Boats with 1·8m draught can lock through and berth to stb, but cannot get to Dinan. To Châtelier from seaward, leave HW−0300 to have the best conditions above Mordreuc. From Châtelier to the sea, leave at HW.

Headroom: Pont St Hubert 23m; De Lessard viaduct 18·9m. Headroom under power cable above Châtelier lock reported as 15m.

Anchorage anywhere up to St Suliac clear of main channel; holding variable.

Moorings
- Off St Suliac (1·5m).
- Small marina at Plouër on W bank just above Pont St Hubert. Enter between R and G Lts (lit when entry possible) on 284° with church midway between Lts. Sill gives 2m depth. 10 visitors' berths max 13m; two outside waiting buoys and visitors' buoys in approach.
- **Port de Lynet** 25 visitors' berths. 2m depth. Capitainerie ☎ 02 96 83 35 57.
- Boats with 1·4m draught may proceed to Dinan where visitors' berths are available in small marina on stb side. Local shops. HM and showers in half-timbered building.

☎/VHF Lock La Pointe de la Brebis 02 99 46 21 87. VHF 13; Plouër Port de Plaisance 02 96 86 83 15. Chatelier lock 02 96 39 55 66.

ST-CAST (LE GUILDO)
Standard Port St Malo
HW +0000   LW −0005
MHWS MHWN MLWN MLWS
−0·2m −0·2m −0·1m −0·1m

The 800 berth marina is situated inside the east mole which runs in a WSW direction for approximately 350m, the end of which, is marked by a light Fl.G. It has been dredged to 2m. 24h access. There is a substantial tidal range similar to St Malo. The main shops are in the town, pleasant walk 1M. Extensive sandy beach.

Approach By day, either side of Les Bourdinots, drying rocks 1M E of Pointe de St-Cast, marked by E cardinal buoy. At night, approach in either W sector of the hbr light Iso.WG.4s. Beware west mole, submerged at HW and marked by a cardinal S marker pole.

Entrance Follow round to the south of the mole. The access channel is marked by small lit R and G buoys.

Berthing 40 visitors' berths. As directed by HM RIB (red); otherwise call VHF 09 and proceed to holding pontoon A.

Facilities Fuel by credit card on pontoon G. *Capitainerie*, showers etc. near visitors' berths. Slip, boat hoist, pump out, chandler. Shops, 10 mins' walk to town. Bread etc can be ordered from marina office. Cycles for hire. Ferry to St Malo and Dinard in summer months.

☎ Marina Office 02 96 81 04 43.

BAIE DE SAINT BRIEUC
The hbrs dry except Dahouet, Le Légué and Binic which have wet basins. The best anchorage in westerly winds is in the Anse de Bréhec, 48°43′N, 2°56′W.

ERQUY
Standard Port St Malo
HW +0003   LW −0015
MHWS MHWN MLWN MLWS
−0·8m −0·6m −0·2m −0·2m
DS (Chenal d'Erquy):
Dover +0145ENE 3kn, −0500WSW 2½kn

A drying hbr whose roadstead provides a useful passage anchorage open SW.

Approach From E, steer 229° through Chenal d'Erquy (dangerous with strong wind against tide) with Cap d'Erquy in line with Le Verdelet Rock, leaving two S card Lt buoys to stb, La Justière 15s and Basse de Courant 10s. When Rohein YBY W card Lt tr is behind La Basse de Courant S card buoy, bear to stb to round the headland about 2ca off. From W, from 1ca S of Rohein Lt tr make good 100° until the jetty W Lt tr, R top, Fl(2)WRG.6s, bears 090°. Enter in W sector (081°-094°); beware lobster pots in R sector.

Anchorage Good holding ½M W of jetty. Not recommended with W or SW winds. Berths at or in lee of jetty are taken by fishing boats. Drying anchorage for visitors to E of the two moles. Anchoring in the W sector of the jetty Lt is forbidden.

Supplies Fuel.

☎ HM 02 96 72 19 32.

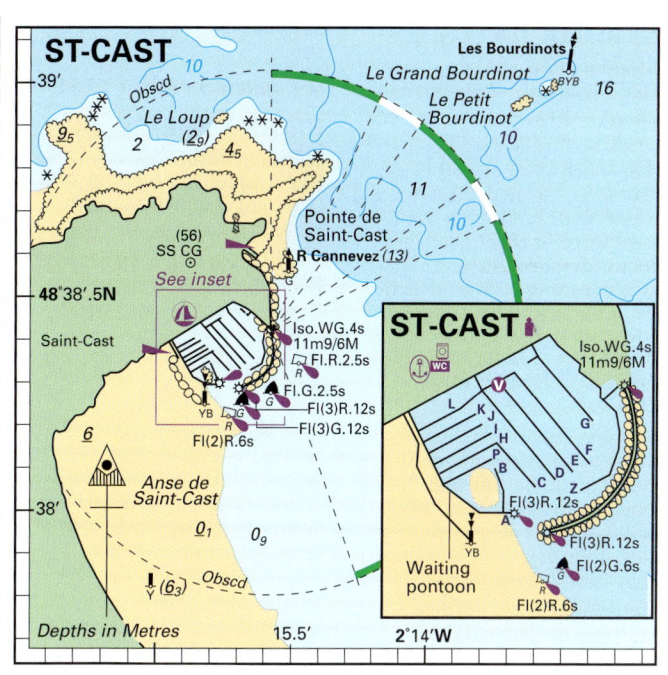

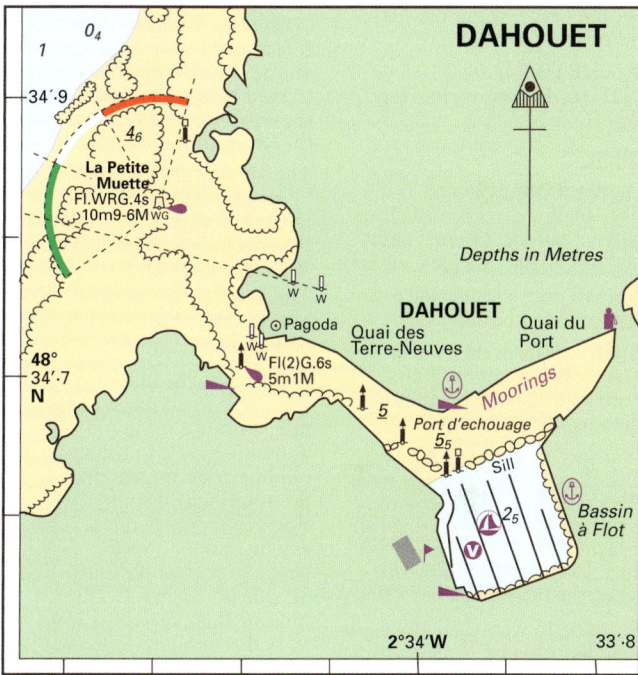

DAHOUET
Standard Port St Malo
HW +0003   LW −0018
MHWS MHWN MLWN MLWS
−0·8m −0·7m −0·2m −0·1m
DS Plateau des Jaunes: Dover +0130ESE 3kn, −0500W 2½kn

A small fishing port with drying anchorage and wet basin open to the NW.

Approach from NW leaving Rohein W card bn tr, VQ(9)WRG.10s8M, and Plateau des Jaunes W card bn tr both to port and Dahouet N card buoy to stb. At night keep in W sector, 114°−146°, of Petite Muette Lt Fl.WRG.4s9–6M.

Entrance lies in a gap in the cliffs 1M SW of Pte Pléneuf. Bar is dangerous with strong NW winds and on the ebb with any sea. Await HW for entry, otherwise accessible at half-tide with 1m draught. La Petite Muette Lt tr may be passed on either side but locals use Ldg line 133°, pagoda just open N of tr, leaving it to stb, then steering S between tr and port bn at edge of shore, then to SE as entrance opens. The S approach with tr to port is on line of two Ldg bns, 100°. La Muette tr stands on a rocky platform and should be given 100m clearance.

Berthing Avant Port reserved for fishing boats. NE branch of inner harbour has 180 drying moorings on buoys. On the S side the wet basin has pontoons with 20 visitors' berths up to 12m o.a. and 2·4m draught at neaps. Sill passable HW±0200, dries 5·5m. Fair weather anchorage W of Petite Muette 2m.

Supplies Water, fuel (only at HW), gas. provisions.

☎/VHF HM 02 96 72 82 85, VHF 16.

ST BRIEUC (LE LÉGUÉ)

Standard Port St Malo
HW –0008   LW –0018

MHWS	MHWN	MLWN	MLWS
–0·8m	–0·5m	–0·2m	–0·1m

Approach W of Grand Léjon RW Lt tr, Fl(5)RW.20s17m, and 1½M W of Le Rohein YB W card Lt tr. At night keep in W sector of Grand Léjon (350°-015°) leading between Roches de St Quay and Le Rohein, to the landfall RW buoy, Mo(A)10s (·–); thence make good 210° for the entrance channel.

Entrance Channel which has some bends, dries about 5m, buoyed and lit. Entrance lock opening times between HW–0200 and +0130 according to tide. Blue flag from lock indicates sluicing of channel.

Berthing at end of W basin (turning br) beyond the swinging bay. Maximum 15m.

Supplies Fuel, water on quay; shops.

☎/VHF HM 02 96 33 35 41, VHF 16, 12 (during locking times).

BINIC

Standard Port St Malo
HW –0005   LW –0020

MHWS	MHWN	MLWN	MLWS
–0·8m	–0·6m	–0·2m	–0·1m

A small port with drying avant port and wet basin.

Approach from the NW is easier offshore of St Quay Portrieux rocky plateau rather than by the inshore passage.

Entrance to Avant Port dries 5m; W tr, Oc(3)12s on N mole. Wet basin has an underwater gate that opens on a rising tide when the height reaches 8·5m and closes on the falling tide when the height reaches 9·0m.

Berthing In wet basin alongside long pontoon on N side of hbr, rafting as necessary or as directed at entrance. Maximum 16m LOA. Space for 50 visitors dependent on length. Outer harbour, hard flat sand, space limited. S jetty has rocky base.

Supplies Fuel in town, water, shops.

☎ Capitainerie 02 96 73 61 86.

ST-QUAY-PORTRIEUX

Standard Port St Malo
HW (sp)–0010   (np)–0010
LW (sp)–0030   (np)–0010

MHWS	MHWN	MLWN	MLWS
–0·9m	–0·7m	–0·2m	–0·1m

DS W of Roches St Quay:
Dover +0100SSE; –0515NNW, 2kn.

The 1,000 berth marina is sheltered, lit and available at all states of the tide. The entrance faces SE.

Approach Drying rocks lie 6ca off-shore and the channel inside these can be approached from N or SE.

From the N, 5ca W of Madeaux W card tr in the W sector of the DirIso Lt on the elbow of the hbr wall steer 153° towards Les Noires W card buoy. When La Moulière tr is abeam, (at night alter course on entering the G sector of the Herflux Lt) steer 185° for the entrance Fl(3)G.12s giving the hbr wall 1ca clearance.

The SE approach is from 3ca SE of La Roselière W card Lt buoy. A course of 317° leads to the entrance Fl(3)G.12s in the W sector of the DirIso.WRG. Lt. This approach is narrow and is bounded by shoals and oyster beds. It needs good visibility.

Entrance to the marina accessible at all states of the tide; entrance Lts are Fl(3)G and Fl(3)R.12s. Entrance to the old hbr dries 3m. Berthing to pontoons max 18m LOA. Reception pontoon No.7. In season, a dory directs. Anchorage possible in the Rade SE side of marina. Good holding but exposed at HW to N through E to S. Avoid oyster beds.

☎ Marina 02 96 70 81 30 or 06 63 67 71 77 after hours. Old Harbour 02 96 70 95 31.

PAIMPOL

Standard Port St Malo
HW –0008   LW –0030

MHWS	MHWN	MLWN	MLWS
–1·4m	–0·9m	–0·4m	–0·1m

DS La Jument channel:
Dover +0100SSE 2¾kn,
–0530NNW 2½kn

In Chenal du Denou
Dover +0045SE –0545NW both 2¾kn.

A pleasant small town with marina in wet basins.

Approach From the E by Chenal de la Jument. At 1¾M NE of L'Ost Pic Lt, 2 W towers R tops, Fl(4)WR.15s (105°-W-116°-R-221°-W-253-R-291°-W-329°), follow line of Paimpol spire over wooded Pte de Brividic, 260°, but N of La Jument R tr steer 262° on Ldg line, front W hut R top, Q.R.5m7M; rear W pylon R top, Q.R12m14M (260°-264°). By night keep in W sector of Porz Don, Oc(2)WR.6s, past R sector of Lost Pic until the latter changes to W when the Ldg Lts can be followed.

From N by Chenal du Denou (2.8m). At ¾M E of Men-Gam BYB E card tr, make good 193°, allowing for cross-set, with W Denou tr in line with Plouézec church spire. ¾M N of Denou tr it is essential near LW to keep on this line which passes E of Garap stb bn and only 50m E of a rock drying 1m close E of Garap, and W of Rohan-Hier port bn. Pass about ½ca W of Denou bn.

From the N the Chenal de La Trinité is well marked by bns but start from position at least 1ca E of Les Piliers BY bn (see plan) to avoid drying rks E of bn.

Anchor to await at least half tide 1ca SW of La Jument.

Entrance Continue on Ldg line to the buoys marking last 800m. Front Ldg mark is small Lt bn W with R top. Channel very narrow between buoys. Banks dry 6m. Lock gates open between HW±0230 (less at neaps) with sometimes free flow around HW, with a current up to 2kn. Channel dries 6m in places and should not be attempted before half tide.

Berthing Boats under 10m moor in NW No.2 basin, immediately after the lock;

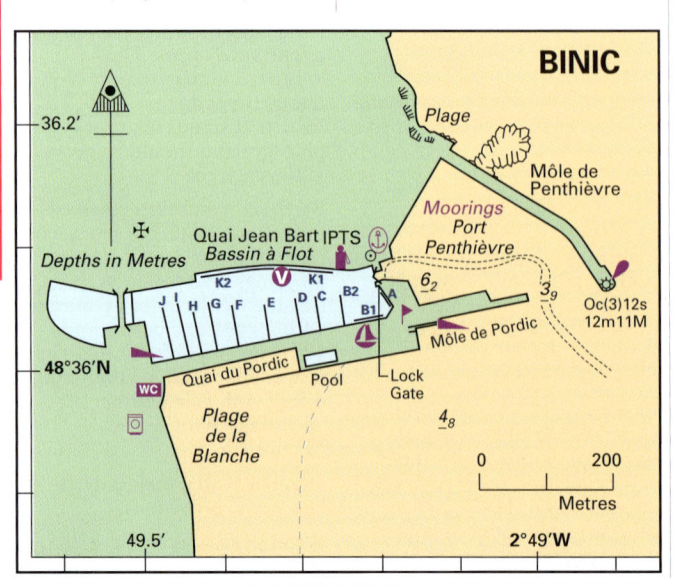

APPROACHES TO PAIMPOL AND LEZARDRIEUX

Depths in Metres

The Cruising Almanac

FRANCE – NORTH COAST AND CHANNEL ISLANDS

larger ones (max 20m) go through the narrow passage to port into SE No.1 basin and moor at pontoons at the far end. If in doubt enquire at office on central mole between the two basins.

Supplies Water at entrance jetty and in No.2 basin; fuel. Good shops.

☎/VHF Port office 02 96 20 47 65; Lock 02 96 20 90 02, VHF 09.

ILE DE BRÉHAT

Approach From the E take the Ferlas Channel, DS Dover +0100E -0545W both 3½kn

Transit lines are Bréhat chapel to the left of Quistillic W pyramid 296°; La Croix LtHo (two trs joined) in line with S side of Raguenez-Bras (small islet off SW tip of Bréhat) 277° and into well-marked Ferlas channel. At night, steer for Paon Lt, Oc.WRG (307°-W-316°) in its W sector until in W sector of Men-Joliguet Lt, Fl(2)WRG.6s (279°-W-283°). Steer in this sector past unlit Piliers tr and pick up the narrow W sector of Quinonec Lt, DirQ.WRG, (257°-W-257·7°). Near Rompa tr pick up the W sector of a third dir Lt on W bank of Trieux River – Kermouster DirFl.WRG.2s (270°-W-272°) which comes onto Coatmer Ldg line.

If rounding the N end of Ile de Bréhat keep at least 100m N of the N card tr, Pt-Pen-Azen, since a drying reef extends 110m to the NE.

Anchorages
- **La Chambre**, off Ferlas channel, E of Men Joliguet tr. Very congested with moorings and uncomfortable at HW with a NE to SE wind. Anchor as far in as tide height allows.
- **La Corderie**, off the N end of the Kerpont channel which dries 1·5m and leads off Ferlas channel past SW tip of the island; it is passable only after 2hrs of flood. The tide runs at up to 5kn. Enter leaving Pierres Noires bn to port. (Note: There is no passage between Pierres Noires bn and Pierre Jaune bn to SW). Steer 352° for 2ca and then slightly W of N between visible rocks and bns (leave cones to W, cans to E). La Corderie is well marked with bns. At springs it is impossible to stay afloat out of the strong tide in the Kerpont, but at neaps a quiet berth can be found. Yachts can take the ground on hard flat sand. Four W visitors' buoys, the inner two nearly dry at springs.
- **Port Clos** at the SW tip of Bréhat is the main landing place for tripper launches and room to anchor is limited. Not recommended. There is much anchoring space off and immediately W of the entrance to La Chambre, off Port du Guerzido, but the tide runs strongly.

TRIEUX RIVER, LÉZARDRIEUX
Standard Port St Malo

Lézardrieux
HW –0018 LW –0050
MHWS MHWN MLWN MLWS
–1·7m –1·3m –0·5m –0·2m

DS (near La Horaine):
Dover +0130ESE, 4kn
–0345WNW, 3¾kn

A beautiful river with many anchorages and good shelter.

Approaches The coastline is low-lying and the marks are not easily distinguished against the sun or in a haze.

The main approach channels are the Grand Chenal (6m) from NE; the Chenal du Ferlas (2·4m) from the E and Chenal de la Moisie (less than 2m), unlit, from NW.

From the N, if W of Roches Douvres, get in the W sector of Le Paon square Lt tr, Oc.WRG.4s22m11–8M (181°-W-196°) and head S until on Ldg Lts of Grand Chenal, 225°.

Coming from N, E of Roches Douvres, or coming offshore from E, get in W sector of Les Héaux grey Lt tr, Fl(4)WRG.15s48m15–11M (247°-W-270°) until on Grand Chenal Ldg line. Both of these approaches leave to port La Horaine grey octagonal Lt tr, B diagonal stripes, Fl(3)12s.

By day make for a position 9ca NW of Nord Horaine N card buoy, 1M N of La Horaine, thence make good SW to Grand Chenal.

From NW, there is a more direct daytime approach via the Moisie Passage, dangerous in strong onshore winds and LW±0100.

DS Dover +0015S –0600N both 3¾kn.

At 1¾M E of Les Héaux Lt tr, steer 159° with Rosédo W pyramid in line with the chapel, both on Ile de Bréhat. Keep exactly on this line when passing close NE of La Moisie bn tr and Noguejou bn, both E card, to clear drying rocks to port, until in the Grand Chenal.

Le Grand Chenal
DS Dover +0100 inward; –0515 outward, both 3¾kn.
From Les Sirlots G con whistle buoy the Channel is clearly marked by day. At night the Ldg Lts are front La Croix (two towers joined) Q15m18M (215°-intens-235°); rear Bodic W ho with gable, DirQ.55m22M (221°-intens-229°). When Bodic dips behind La Croix, bear slightly W to keep it at the W edge of the tr. When Men-Grenn Lt Q(9)15s is abeam to stb, steer 235° until on Coatmer Ldg line, front Q.RG (220°-R-250° to seaward; 250°-G-053° up-river); rear Q.R.7M (219°). When Olenoyère unlit R tr is abeam to port head for W sector of Perdrix Lt

LEZARDRIEUX

Depths in Metres

LES HEAUX TO ILE DE BATZ

Passage lights	BA No.
Les Heaux Fl(4)WRG.15s48m15–11M AIS	1738
Perros Guirec Kerjean DirOc(2+1)WRG.12s78m 10-8M	1770
Les Sept-Iles Fl(3)20s59m23M	1786
Mean Ruz Oc.WR.4s26m12/9M	1784
Les Triagoz Fl(2)WR.6s31m14–11M AIS	1790
Le Lande Fl.5s85m23M	1800
Ile Louet Oc(3)WG.12s17m12/8M	1800.1
Ile de Batz Fl(4)25s69m23M+F.R AIS	1816

STREAMS RELATED TO DOVER
Plateau de Triagoz and Canal des Sept-Iles Dover+0145 ENE, –0430 WSW, both 3¾kn

Baie de Lannion (centre) Dover +0130S-E-S 1kn, –0530 S-W-S 1½kn

Plateau des Duons (to E of Roscoff) Dover+0600 SSE, –0530 NNW, both 2¾kn

This is the most difficult section of the N Brittany coast, especially at night or in poor visibility. Inshore the coast has off-lying rocks which although buoyed are often not lit. Offshore are three main hazards: Les Sept-Iles, LtHo but off-lying rocks for 3M to NE; Plateau des Triagoz, LtHo but rocks and shoals to W; Plateau de la Méloine, rocks and shoals extending for 5M, unlit and only a W card buoy at one end. Between these the streams run strongly.

Bound for Chenal du Four it may be wiser, apart from settled weather and good visibility, to go N of these hazards. For Chenal de Batz go N or S of Les Sept-Iles, S of Triagoz, continuing W to pick up the main approach for Batz. For Baie de Lannion it is possible to go inshore by the Canal des Sept-Iles, in which there are 'high seas with wind against tide' (Channel Pilot).

At night approach from E in W sector of Méan Ruz Lt; when in the W sector of Kerjean Dir Lt (near Perros Guirec) steer 270°, leading S of Triagoz.

Anchorages are to be found with suitable winds E of Ile Tomé; Trégastel; off the slipway E of Sept-Iles LtHo; N of Ile Milliau; between Pte de Bihit and Rivière de Lannion.

Search and rescue From Les Heaux westwards the CROSS is based at Corsen. In distress call VHF 16 or DSC (MMSI No 002275300). There are six repeater substations.

Weather Navtex Area A is also based here.

RIVIERE DE TRÉGUIER

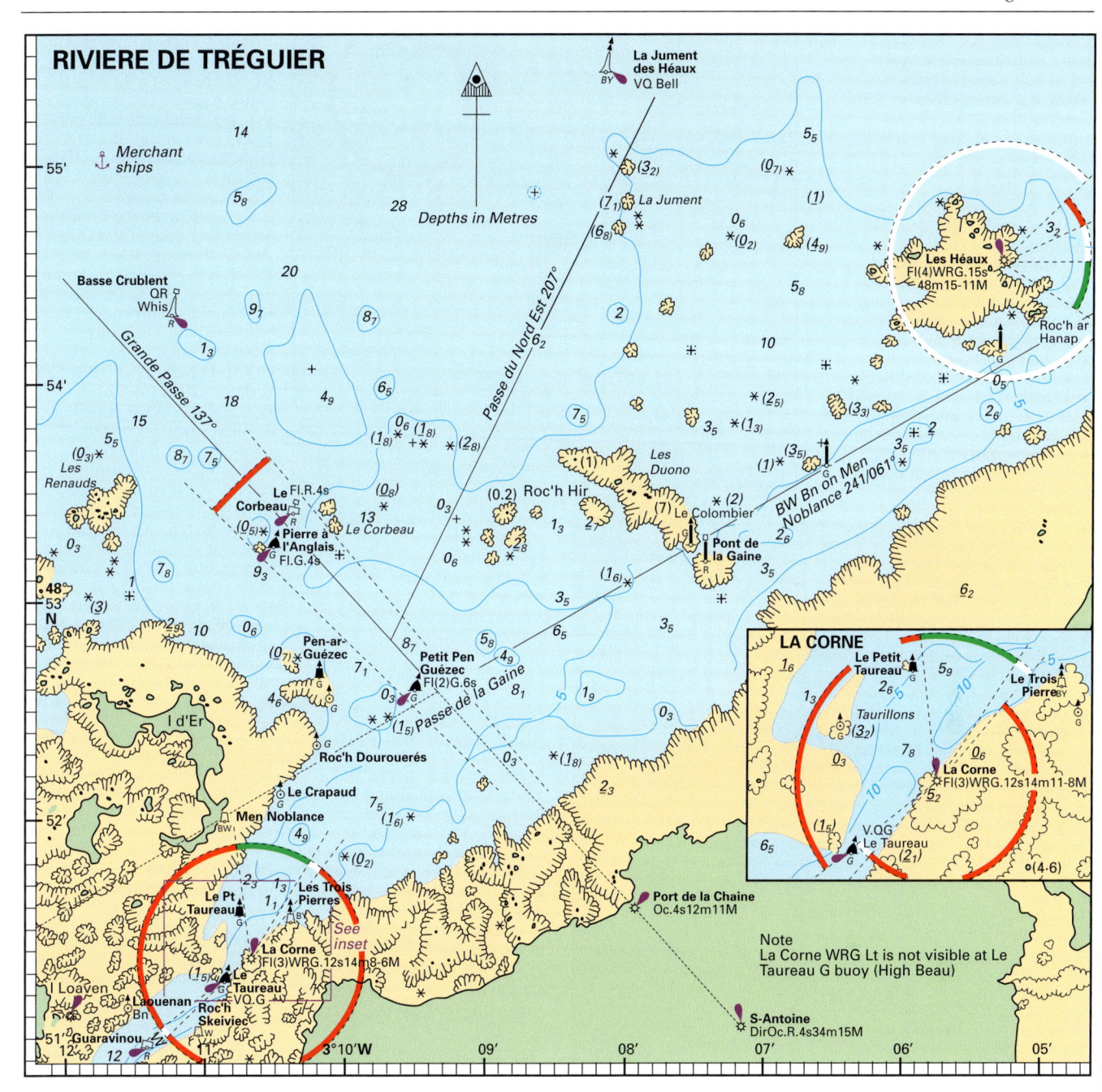

Fl(2)WG.6s, (197°–W–203°). Leave Perdrix about 60m to stb; F Bu Lts ahead mark marina pontoons.

Berthing pontoons at Lézardrieux marinas maximum 15m. N marina has strong tides on outer berths. S marina has drying entrance. There are W visitors' buoys on west edge of channel N of Perdrix and fore and aft buoys off Lézardrieux marina. With care it is possible to anchor in the estuary between Ferlas channel and Perdrix (although the best places are taken by buoys); above the suspension br (17·7m above MHWS, 28m above CD) at Lézardrieux; and in the Ferlas Channel off Loguivy.
Rivière de Pontrieux is navigable at HW to Pontrieux lock and quays above it. Very rewarding. The channel is straightforward (keep to outside of bends) and is navigable, except at LWS, to Roche Jagu chateau, visitors' buoys, 4M above Lézardrieux. Beware of bulk sand barges. Above that, passage best attempted after HW St-Malo – 0230. Keep to stb at the next two branches to Pontrieux lock (sill 3·5m above CD): gates open by day nominally HW±0215. Waiting buoy. Lock is open by day and night with a free flow when tide exceeds 8·8m. Moor to town quay (100 boats, rafting), port side ¾M above the lock, as directed by HM. Clearance under cable at Pontrieux lock reported as 25m.

Supplies Fuel and water at N marina. Water and fuel at Pontrieux. Shops at Lézardrieux, Pontrieux and Loguivy and some small ones on Ile Bréhat. Good chandlery and sailmaker at Lézardrieux.

☏ **/VHF** Lézardrieux HM 02 96 20 14 22; Lock Ecluse de Pontrieux 02 96 95 60 70, VHF 12.

TRÉGUIER RIVER

Standard Port St Malo

Tréguier

HW (sp) –0020 (np) –0020
LW (sp) –0100 (np) –0045

MHWS	MHWN	MLWN	MLWS
–2·3m	–1·6m	–0·6m	–0·2m

TIDAL STREAMS
5M N of Les Héaux:
Dover +0145 E –0430 W, 4kn
La Jument buoy:
Dover +0115 E –0500 W, 4kn

A pleasant sheltered river leading to the old cathedral town of Tréguier and marina.

Approach From the N and E the dominant feature is Les Héaux grey LtHo, Fl(4)WRG.15s44m15-11M. From W get 7M WNW and enter by Grande Passe. From E, either pass N of the LtHo and La Jument des Héaux N card bell buoy VQ to enter by Grande Passe or by day and in good visibility, get 2M ENE of Les Héaux and enter by Passe de la Gaine. The latter is shorter and may seem more attractive if conditions round Les Héaux are uncomfortable, but the marks are difficult to see and the line must be strictly followed. From Trieux River, in good weather leave by the Moisie Passage (*details under Trieux*) for Passe de la Gaine.

Entrance There are two main entrances, only one lit, and a third more difficult.

La Grande Passe (4·4m)
DS N of Les Renauds:
Dover +0030 E, –0545 W, 4kn.
It can be taken at any time with reasonable visibility. From Basse Crublent R buoy, Q.R Whis, the Ldg line is 137°: front, Port de la Chaine W ho Oc.4s12m, and rear, Ste Antoine W ho, R roof, DirOc.R.4s34m. It can be hard to identify by day, in which case pick up the entrance buoys (Pierre à l'Anglais G con and Corbeau R can) and steer 137°,

343

The Cruising Almanac

to Petit Pen ar Guezec G con buoy and alter course to stb when La Corne bears 217°. There is a strong cross-set from Crublent buoy to well past Corbeau, dangerous at springs, 3¾kn, Dover +0030E, −0545W.

Passe de la Gaine (0·3m)
DS Dover +0015 ENE; +0445 WSW, 3kn
It is not easy and is unlit; the Ldg marks require 8M good visibility, but if there is enough, about 1M, to see the first bn before starting the passage, after half flood there are few difficulties. At 1¾ca S of Roche ar Hanap (7m), which is 3ca SE of the LtHo, get Men Noblance BW pyramid in line with Plougrescant mark (W wall with B vert band, 1¾M behind

it), 242°. Pass two stb bns into the Duono narrows between port and stb bns to Petit Pen ar Guezec G con buoy.
Chenal du Nord-Est (0·8m) is to the E of Corbeau rocks. W and NW seas break across it; the Ldg marks are often not visible and with a strong cross-tide this entrance can be dangerous. At a position SW of

La Jument N card Lt buoy, Ldg line is Roc'h Skeiviec W tr in line with Tréguier cathedral spire, 207°. When the latter disappears, follow buoys and bns. Not recommended.

River
DS N of La Corne Lt tower: Dover +0030 SW, −0545 NE, 3kn.
From La Corne the channel is clearly buoyed. At night on the Grande Passe line, when G sector of La Corne light, Fl(3)WRG.12s, changes to W, steer in that sector 217°. The W sector Lt is focussed high, so not seen near Le Taureau buoy. Leave La Corne on junction of RW sectors 239° leaving VQ.G con buoy Le Taureau 40m to stb. Proceed to Guarivinou Lt buoy, Fl.R.4s (each of these two buoys is near E edge of the white sector of Corne Lt), whence come S into the lit channel. Approaching the marina, the channel follows the E bank on outside of the bend: do not aim straight for the marina Lts. The br has 3m headroom at HW, when river is navigable for 3M above it.
On leaving remember that from S La Corne has R sectors on either side of W sector.

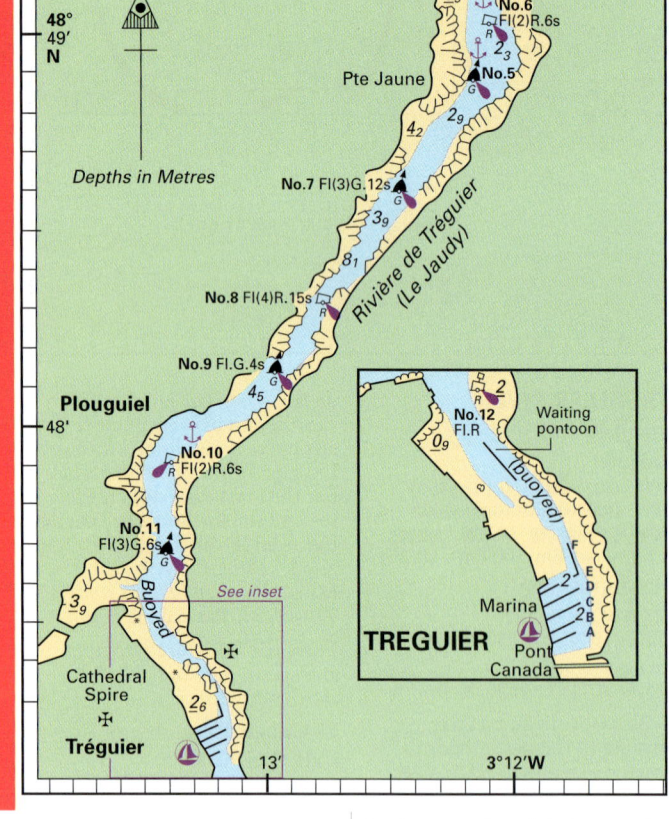

Berthing There is a marina at Tréguier (maximum 30m) on stb side before the br over the main channel. The stream is strong around half-tide: only enter between the lines of pontoons at slack water. If the stream is too strong, go alongside the first pontoon (F). It is equally important not to leave other than at slack water. At LWS there may only be 1·5m between the waiting pontoon and the marina. Shallow berths near bank. Visitors normally berth on pontoon E (first pontoon) outer half for LOA <15M, D outermost berths, and C outer half, S side only. Pontoon F if LOA<30m, but call first since it is often over-crowded. Temporary anchoring only is permitted in sight of the town but is otherwise possible in the river, out of the fairway, especially off Roche Jaune village (off small shingle beach 1½ca S of ramp); at Pen Paluc on W bank 1½M to the N; or anchor close inshore under the château 1ca to seaward of No.10 buoy, 5m (crowded in season; charge). Strong stream, dig in anchor.

Supplies Water at marina and Roche Jaune; diesel at marina. Shops at Tréguier and Roche Jaune. Well-stocked chandlery over the br. Wednesday market. Launderette.

☏ HM 02 96 92 42 37.

PORT BLANC

Standard Port St Malo
HW −0035   LW n/a

MHWS	MHWN	MLWN	MLWS
−2·9m	−1·9m	−0·8m	−0·2m

DS Dover +0015E −0600W, 2½kn

Beautiful and unspoilt small village, open NW to NE.

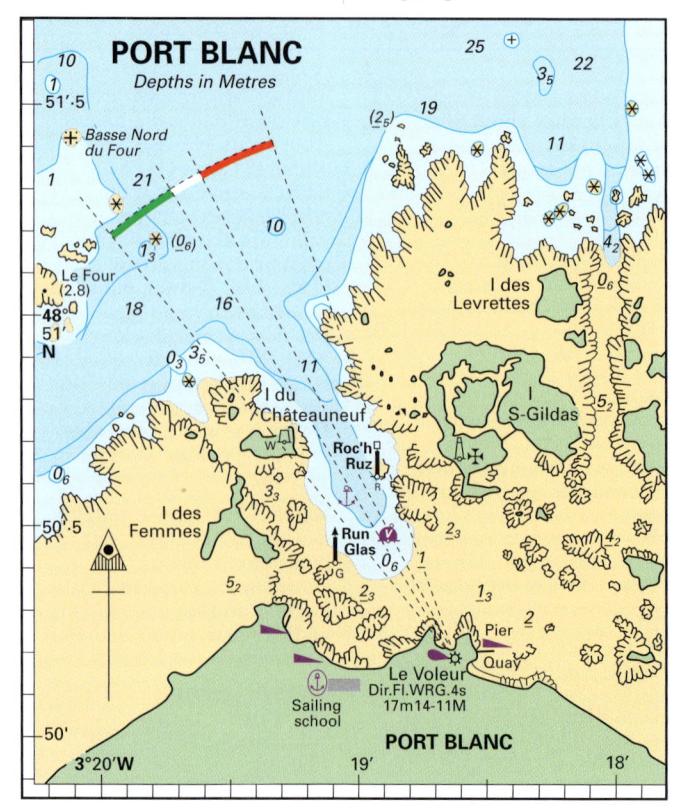

Approach To the E are rks extending 1½M offshore as far as Pte du Château, and Ile Ziliec with a large house. To NW the Plateau du Four has a R can whistle buoy on its NW side.

Entrance (7m) lies between Ile du Château Neuf to W and Ile St Gildas to E, both with conspic W pyramids. Enter with Le Voleur W tr DirFl.WRG.4s17m14–11M, 150°. Marks in gap in trees are difficult to see until on the line. Best line is with Ile St Gildas twice as far to port as Ile du Château Neuf is to stb.

Berthing Available space is being taken up by buoys; subject to this anchor SW of Ldg line, SW of Roc'h Ruz R bn, 7m, or closer in, sand and shell. There are 10 W visitors' buoys in the W part of the hbr, offshore of small craft moorings. Anchoring is officially forbidden. Very uncomfortable at HW with a W or NW sea. If taking the ground in shallower area, beware of some deep holes.

Supplies Water from tap on drying ramp E of the Lt tr. Small shop in village.

⌕ Capitainerie (Sailing School) 02 96 92 64 96.

PERROS-GUIREC

Standard Port St Malo
HW (sp) –0035 (np) –0035
LW (sp) –0115 (np) –0100
MHWS MHWN MLWN MLWS
–2·8m –2·0m –0·7m –0·1m
DS NW of Ile Tomé:
Dover +0100E –0430W, both 3¼kn

A popular holiday resort with a marina and drying approach.

Approach Ile Tomé with its surrounding plateau separate the E and W channels.

Passe de l'Est
DS Dover +0030ENE –0430WSW, both 3kn

From Guazer R whistle buoy, 2½M NE of Ile Tomé, pick up Ldg line 224°: front Le Colombier W ho DirQ.28m14M (217°-intens-233°); rear Kerprigent W tr, DirQ.79m21M (221°-228°).

Passe de l'Ouest
(0·9m) DS Dover +0030SE, –0430NW, both 2¾kn

Enter between Bilzic R tr and La Fronde G con buoy with Kerjean W tr, B top, DirOc(2+1)WRG.12s78m15-13M (143°-W-144°), bearing 144°. By day have it in line with Nantouar W disused LtHo on the shore, 143°. When ¼M SW of Pierre du Chenal BR bn tr, turn SW into Passe de l'Est. Moorings cross Ldg line, lights may be lost once past R. de Perros.

Entrance The Passe de l'Est leads to the hbr to stb. Entry is possible after half-flood with 1·5m draught. There are some waiting buoys. The basin has a sill on the SE side, drying 7m, marked by R and G perches and a gate 6m usable width, at E end. The gate is open by day at springs between HW–0200 and +0130; at neaps between HW–0030 and HW. At night it is open only at HW. At low neaps, coefficient less than 40, it may not open at all. Sometimes shorter opening at weekends. Beware of strong current as the gate opens.

Berthing On entry turn to port for pontoons. Depth 2·4m decreasing to NW and towards the shore. Or anchor to NE of port according to height of tide; on E side of peninsula, S of Roche Bernard (swell with NE winds); or on E side of Ile Tomé (beware Platier du Tomé, 0·6m, 1ca off middle of Is). Trots of W buoys have been laid N of the marina many of these dry at spring tides.

Facilities Water on pontoons. Fuel station at E end of basin serves when gate is open. French bank cards needed. Shops on quay and up hill to town where there is a fine church.

⌕ Marina 02 96 49 80 50.

PLOUMANAC'H

Standard Port St Malo
HW –0038   LW –0110
MHWS MHWN MLWN MLWS
–2·9m –2·0m –0·7m –0·2m
DS Dover +0030E –0615W 2¾kn

A village with wet inner harbour with sill and drying outer harbour. There are fantastic shapes in the wind eroded rose pink granite in the entrance.

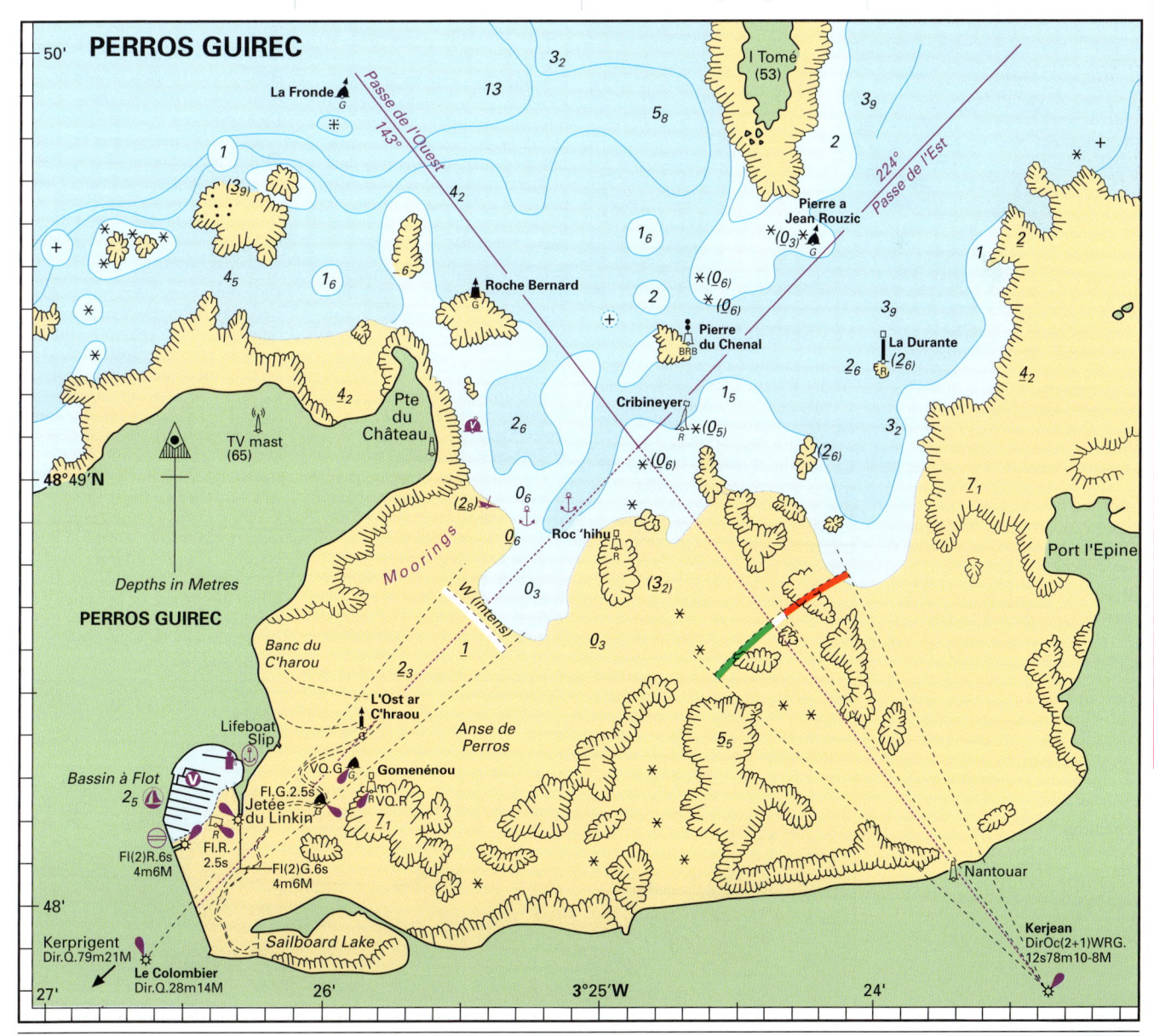

FRANCE – NORTH COAST AND CHANNEL ISLANDS

The Cruising Almanac

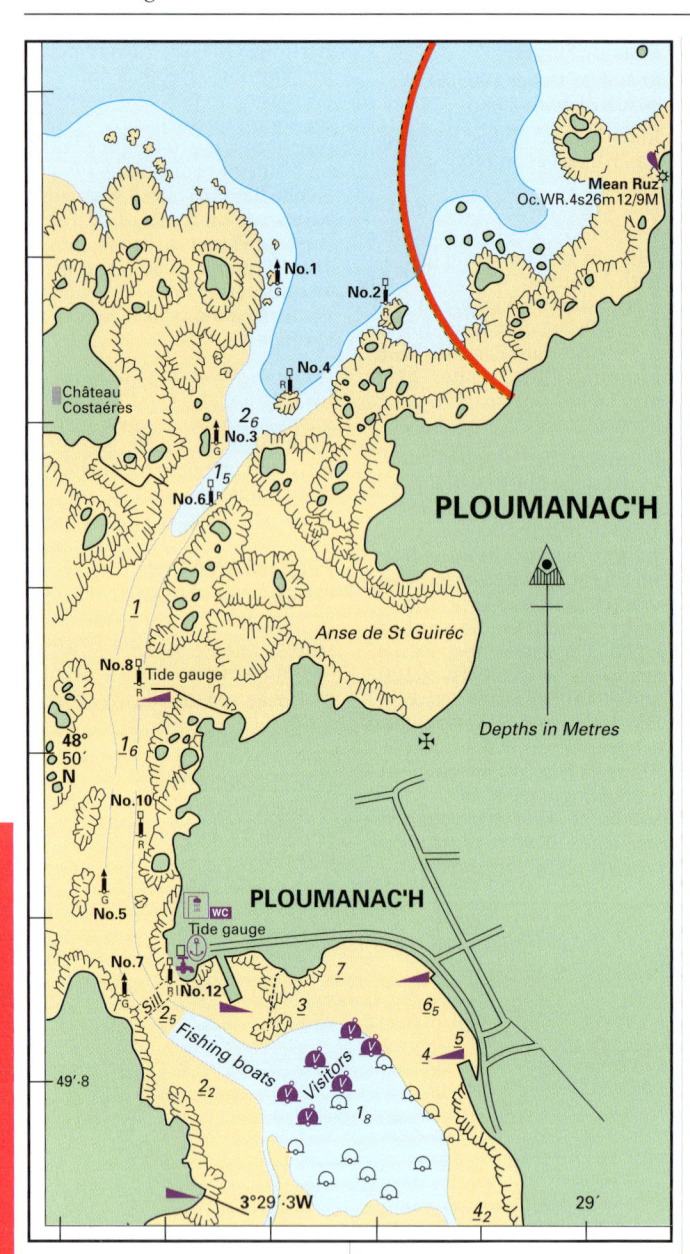

Approach By day make for W side of peninsula on which is Ploumanac'h Mean Ruz pink square Lt tr, not conspic, Oc.WR.4s26m12/9M.

Entrance between the LtHo and Ile Costaeres (towered château, conspic) is well marked by bns. S end dries 1·6m. At LW keep No.2 and No.4 in transit to avoid rocks near No.1.

Berthing Anchoring in outer harbour is not permitted. Two W waiting buoys. Inner harbour has sill drying 2·5m. There is a large digital gauge to port just before the sill showing depth of water over the sill. There are two lines of moorings for visitors, 1·3 to 2·2m. Shore access at slipway save at LWS.

Facilities Apart from a boulangerie the nearest food shops are at Trégastel.

LES SEPT ILES

A fair weather open anchorage. Approach on 285° towards the E end of Ile aux Moines from Les Dervinis S card buoy, avoiding isolated rocks. When Ile de Bono bears 345° steer on this bearing into anchorage Anchor E of LtHo on Is. Landing on steps at end of slip; this is the only landing place allowed. Path to LtHo and old fort at W end of Is. Bird sanctuary.

TRÉGASTEL

About a mile W of Ploumanac'h, this hbr provides moorings afloat. Rock La Pierre Pendue conspic E of entrance which is marked by bns. Inner buoys dry but outer ones have 2m; 10 are for visitors. Uncomfortable in winds between W and N, especially near HW when outer rocks cover. Some shops.

TRÉBEURDEN

Standard Port Brest
HW +0105   LW +0110
MHWS MHWN MLWN MLWS
+2·2m +1·8m +0·8m +0·3m
DS at Basse Blanche buoy:
Dover +0100 SE–E +0500 SW–W, both 2kn

A popular holiday resort with marina, and good anchorages except in W and NW winds.

Approach on the W side of Le Crapaud shoal. The marks for the passage to the E are difficult to identify and it cannot be recommended. By night keep W of R sector of Triagoz Lt Fl(2)WR.6s and steer 064° on junction of W and G sectors of Lan Kerellec Lt Iso.WRG.4s8-5M (48°46·8N 3°35·0W). Warning: the flood sets strongly from S onto the rocks near Ar Gouredec buoy.

Entrance Steer 064° on Lan Kerellec Lt (grey tr) to pick up buoyed and lit channel to entrance on N side of marina. Enter over sill between G and R lit bns with signal Lts: GGW Lts (vert): entry permitted, >1·5m over the sill; 3R(vert): entry prohibited.

Berthing at pontoons in marina (maximum 16m, 1·5 to 3·4m depth) or to W visitors' buoys outside, uncomfortable around HW with W swell. There are anchorages
• N of Ile de Milliau, W of a line joining the Is slipway to the white high-rise apartment block at Trébeurden, 2m.
• NW of that, as close in as tide allows to the edge of the beach SE of Ile Molène. Exposed at HW.
• 1½M N of the marina is a neap tide anchorage for deep draught boats or for bilge keelers. Large-scale charts SHOM 7124, 7125 are needed for the interesting approach to this anchorage which is free of swell.

Facilities All. Shops. WiFi.
☎ HM 02 96 23 64 00.

LANNION RIVER

Standard Port Brest
HW +0102   LW n/a
MHWS MHWN MLWN MLWS
+2·0m +1·6m +0·7m +0·2m
DS at Le Crapeau:
Dover +0100ESE +0500WSW

A mainly drying river in a wooded valley leading to Lannion about 4½M from the entrance.

Le Taureau rock, 2m, 2M offshore is a good guide.

Approach should not be attempted with winds from WNW to NW, when shelter can be sought under Pte de Locquirec, 3M to SW. From W keep Ben Leguer W LtHo, R top, Oc(4)WRG.12s60m12–9M, bearing 090° (at night keep in the W sector, 084°-098°), leaving Kinierbel G bell buoy to stb. From NW the two G towers in the entrance in line, 123°, lead N of Le Taureau rocks (11m), but the line leaves close to stb the Ar Boulier rock, 4·9m, 4ca N of Le Taureau. When Ben Léguier LtHo bears 095° make for it and follow instructions for entrance.

By night keep W of R sector (339°-010°) of Triagoz Lt, Fl(2)WR.6s, leaving Le Crapaud W card Lt buoy, Q(9)15s, to port, to pick up Locquémeau Ldg Lts 121°, Q.R.7M, and then follow W sector of Ben Leguer.

Entrance dries 0·4m and the sea bed may be marked by dredgers digging gravel. Do not come S of Ben Leguer, or into its G sector, until Locquémeau Q.R Lt is just W of S to miss rk drying 0·1m ¾M to its N; then bear SE to leave two G towers close to stb. If waiting for the tide to rise, anchor in the bay N of Locquémeau front Lt, keeping E of N of it. River is clearly marked to Lannion but is unlit. There is a br at Lannion, headroom 2·5m. If going above the br by dinghy, beware large masonry blocks in the channel which are used as a canoe slalom.

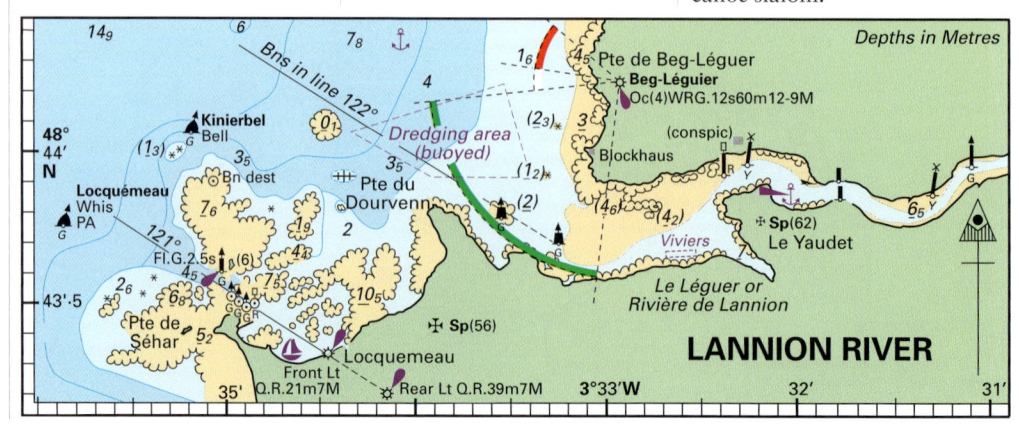

The Cruising Almanac

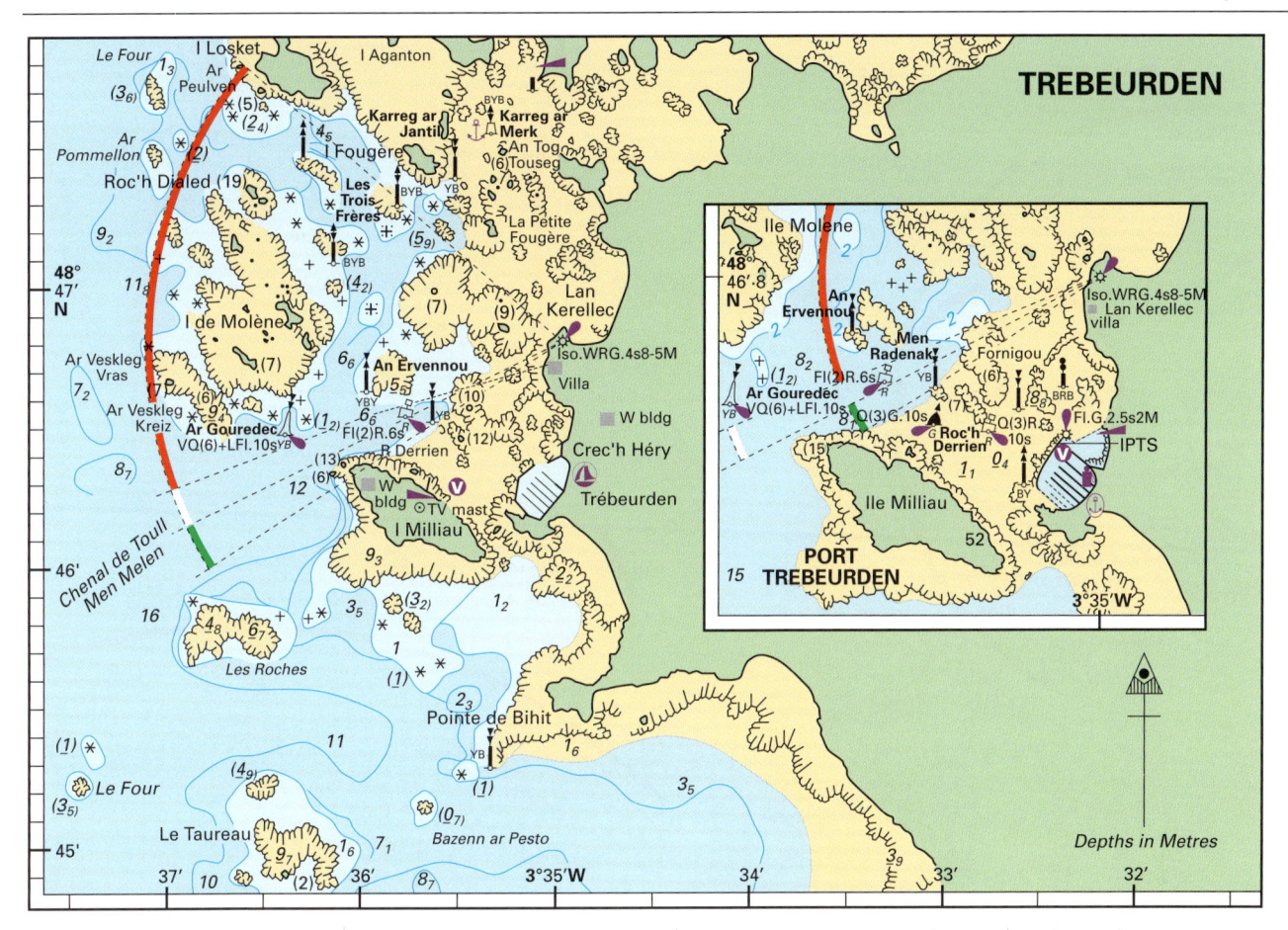

Berthing There is room for two boats to anchor in a pool not used by local boats which has 2m. The pools just upstream of it, 1–3m, have many moorings leaving little swinging room, two anchors necessary. At Lannion moor to short quay on S bank by the first houses, dries 5m. There is a wrecked fishing boat at the W end.

Supplies Water on quay, fuel from garage, shops at Lannion.

LOCQUÉMEAU

A drying hbr with anchorage open to winds W to NW.

Approach At ¾M S of Le Crapaud W card buoy, steer 121° on Ldg line: W frame, R top, Q.R (068°-228°) 21m front; W gabled ho Q.R.39m7M (016°-232°).

Entrance Leave Locquémeau G con whistle buoy close to stb and enter N of G Séhar bn.

Berthing Anchor E of bn off end of slipway, 1·5m; or dry further in E of second, short, slipway.

LOCQUIREC

Drying hbr at head of bay (3°38'·5W) with deep water moorings, including visitors. Report to Mairie. Considerable surf in onshore winds.

Supplies Water on quay. Shops.
☎ HM 02 96 91 44 31.

PRIMEL
Standard Port Brest
HW +0105   LW +0113
MHWS	MHWN	MLWN	MLWS
+2·0m	+1·8m	+0·8m	+0·2m

A small fishing village in a rocky bay exposed to NW.

Approach At ½M NW of Pte de Primel pick up Ldg marks, three W rectangles with vert R stripes, two lit Q.R, 35 and 56m, (134°-vis-168°), 152°.

Entrance Leave Zamégue rk (painted bright GW on seaward side with con top mark) to stb and enter between two conspic rocks marked by bns. Gap is 27m wide, 7m depth.

Berthing Some visitors' buoys, 10 in deep water. Reported rolling in SW Force 4/5+. Anchor in channel, 2–9m, but not more than 2ca inside the entrance, or dry out clear of the outcrops. The dredged area behind the jetty is used by fishing boats; the rest of the jetty is rocky.

Supplies Water on quay. No shops at Primel.
☎ HM 02 98 62 28 40.

MORLAIX ROADSTEAD AND RIVER
Standard Port Brest
Chateau du Taureau
HW (sp)+0105 (np)+0055
LW (sp)+0115 (np)+0055
MHWS	MHWN	MLWN	MLWS
+1·9m	+1·6m	+0·7m	+0·2m

A wide estuary, available at all times except by night in strong onshore winds, leading by a drying channel to Morlaix, where there is a wet basin with marina.

Approach Prominent marks are: Ile de Callot with chapel, 18m, and small W tr off Carantec peninsula; Château de Taureau, a large square fort; Ile Noire W Lt tr, R top, Oc(2)WRG.6s15m11–8M, 4ca ESE of Le Taureau; and Ile Louet W Lt tr, Oc(3)WG.12s17m15/10M.

From Roscoff keep Piguet W bn tr in line with steeple of Notre Dâme among trees on Ile de

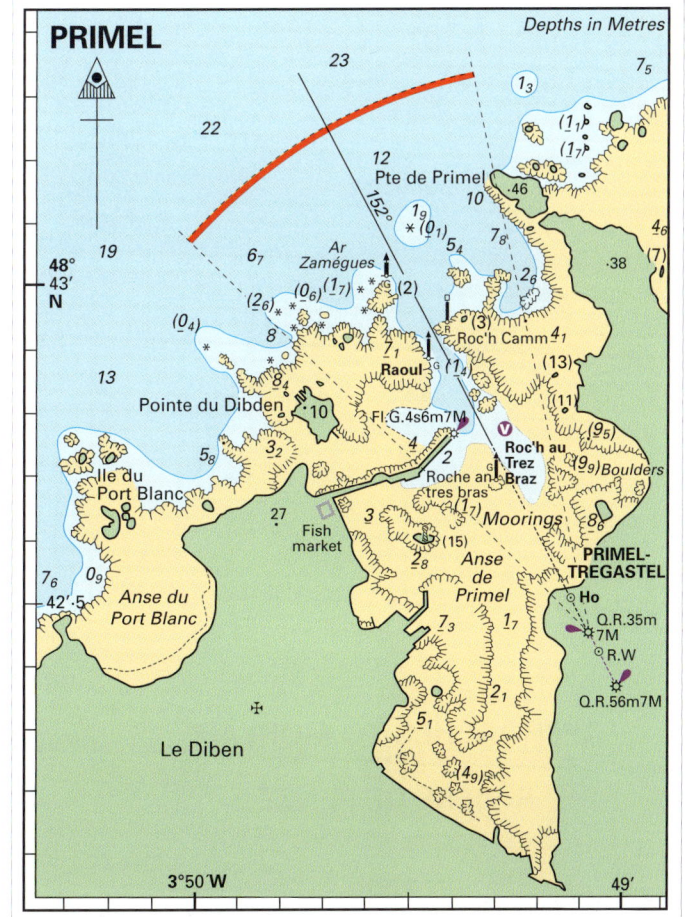

FRANCE – NORTH COAST AND CHANNEL ISLANDS

347

APPROACHES TO MORLAIX AND RIVIÈRE DE PENZÉ

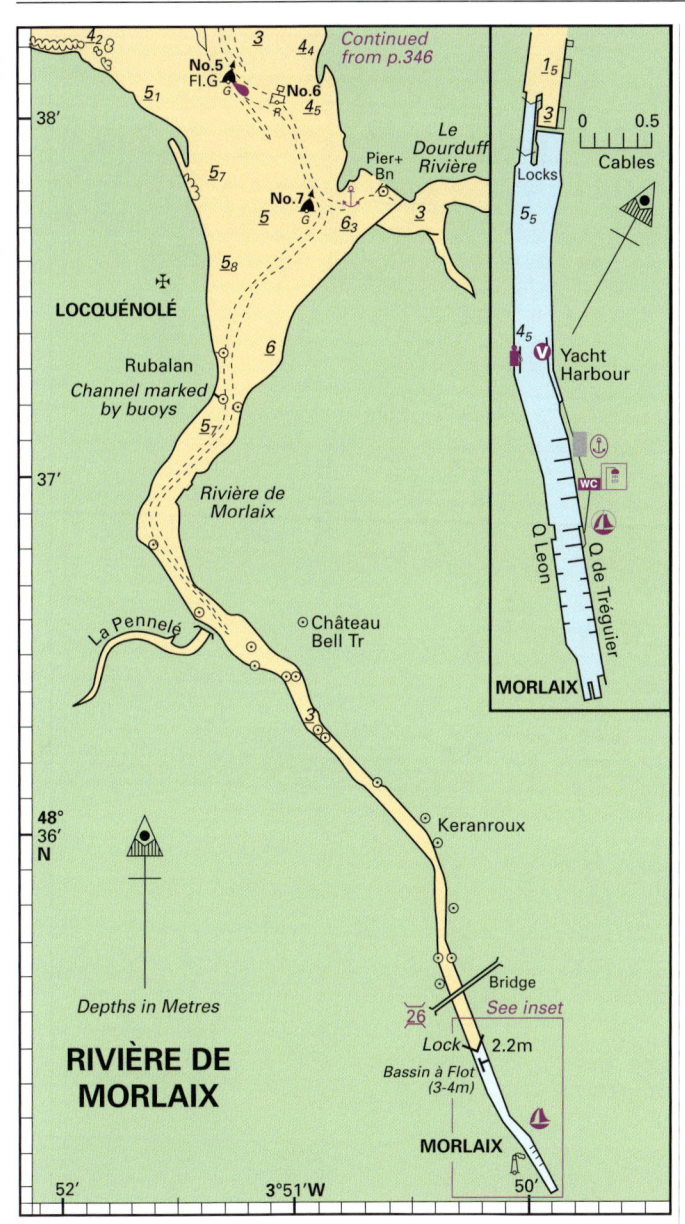

Batz 293° (at night in W sector of Charden Lt Q(6)+LFl.WR.15s (289°-W-294°) until on Ldg line of Grand Chenal, just W of Stolvezen R buoy. From the N pass between Plateau des Duons, grey bn tr 10m, and Plateau de la Méloine, W card whistle buoy, for any of the three entrance channels.

From NE pass between La Méloine and Pte de Primel. At night from the E keep in W sector of Triagoz Lt Fl(2)WR.6s, bearing at least 063° astern to pass N of Méloine bank.

Entrance There are three main entrance channels, of which only the first is available at all times, and even that is difficult at night, especially with strong onshore winds.

• **Grand Chenal E of Ile Ricard** 2m
DS: Dover +0015 in-going; –0615 out-going, 2½kn
Get Ile Louet Lt tr in line with La Lande rear W Lt tr, B top, Fl.5s85m23M, behind it, 176°. On this line, abreast Calhic G bn tr, steer 160°, leaving Corbeau G tr to stb and pass between Château de Taureau and Ile Louet. Hence keep edge of the Château on with W edge of Ile Ricard astern steering 153° past La Barre de Flot stb buoy into the estuary. At night get the two Ldg Lts, front Ile Louet Oc(3)WG.12s15M, rear La Lande Fl.5s23M, in line 176°, leaving Ile Ricard G tr close to stb. When Ile Noire Lt, Oc(2)WRG.6s, changes from R to G, steer 160°, leaving Taureau fort and bn to port and entering G sector of Louet. It is then prudent to round the Lt at just over 1ca off, leaving unlit Barre de Flot buoy well clear to port and anchor or pick up W buoy off Pen Lann until daylight.

• **Chenal de Ricard**, 5·8m, is a wider variant of Grand Chenal going W of Ile Ricard. It is a safer choice when an onshore swell is breaking on the rks bordering Grand Chenal but it is unlit. From a position on the Grand Chenal Ldg line, N of Stolvezen R buoy, bring La Pierre de Carantec, an isolated double rk, in line with a W mark, Kergrist, 4ca E of Carantec church tr, 188°. The channel is well marked by G stb bns. After La Noire stb bn bear round to SSE with a back bearing of L'Enfer W bn tr in line with Paradis W bn tr, 319° to join Grand Chenal NE of Calhic bn.

• **Chenal de Tréguier** dries 0·8m and should not be attempted before half-tide. DS as for Grand Chenal. Steer with Ile Noire W Lt tr, R top, in line with La Lande W Lt tr, B top, 190°. Having passed between La Chambre G tr and Ile Blanche R tr, steer SW until E edge of Château de Taureau comes on with W edge of Ile Ricard and with this line astern continue past Barre de Flot buoy into the estuary. By night keep Ile Noire Lt Oc(2)WRG and La Lande Lt Fl.5s in line 190° until Ile Louet Lt Oc(3)WG changes from W to G, 244°, then steer for it until Ile Noire Lt, Oc(2)WRG.6s, turns from R to G, 135°, then round to 180°. Leaving Barre de Flot to stb, Ile Noire will change from G to W. 051°; continue for 1ca. The channel continues 153°: find a berth as convenient either side.

MORLAIX RIVER
HW Morlaix Lock: Brest+0110

From Barre de Flot the river is marked by buoys and stakes, including two G and two R Lt buoys, Fl(2)G.2s/Fl(2)R.2s. The channel dries about 1M NNW of Dourduff. It is 5½M from Pen Lann anchorage to Morlaix lock. Leaving at half-tide or HW–0200 will give sufficient time. The narrow part is entered at Dourduff and is clearly buoyed; unlit but many of the buoys have reflectors. As the river narrows there are Ldg marks, with St Andrew crosses, showing the deeper water; also marked by G withies with G tops. Below Morlaix are an overhead cable (32m) and a viaduct (30m).

Anchorages
• Between **Barre de Flot** and **Pen Lann**. Land near NE corner or at fish quay on S side of Pen Lann. Do not pick up buoys marking oyster beds.

• **Mouillage des Herbiers**, a creek between mud banks, ½M S of Barre de Flot, on W side of channel, 4m.

• Between **Barre de Flot** and **Dourduff**, just outside the channel clear of oyster beds; exposed to NW.

• At neaps, in the entrance to **Dourduff** river; br has 3m headroom.

• Off **Locquénolé**, on W side, if space allows among the moorings. Sand barges pass close and good anchor Lt is essential. Anchoring is forbidden above this point.

• **Morlaix** The wet basin, 2·50m, is formed by a weir with lock at W side; the inner sill is 3·1m above CD, the lock 63m by 16m. The gates operate only by day at HW–0130, HW and HW+0100. Moor to quay on E side (dries 3m) while waiting. N part of the basin is for commercial use; yachts moor to pontoons in S part, max 12m, run by Morlaix YC; larger craft moor on W quay. If leaving after HW, clear the river before ebb sets hard.

Facilities Fuel from HM. Large town. Rly to Paris. Rly and bus to Roscoff.

☏/**VHF** Locks 06 77 50 15 90; Marina 02 98 62 13 14, VHF 9, 16 (HW±0200); YC 02 98 88 38 00.

PENZÉ RIVER
Tidal data as Morlaix Roadstead and River
DS Dover –0015 ingoing; +0515 outgoing, 1kn

A wide estuary, approached through a maze of rocks. The narrow channel has good depths but is open to N and the banks dry. Small drying hbr of Penpoul is convenient for St Pol-de-Léon.

Approach With the aid of a large-scale chart various lines of approach can be followed.

Entrance From Bloscon N card Lt buoy, the transits are Guerheon G tr with Trébunnec G tr, 169°; Benven W tr with Mazarine W tr, 137°; La Tortue R port perch with Caspari isolated danger bn 171°, to pass midway between Trousken R tr and La Petite Fourche G tr. For **Penpoul** leave Trébunnec tr 2ca to stb and when about 3ca S of it with enough water make for the trumpet-shaped bn off the end of the breakwater at Penpoul.

For **St Yves**, having cleared Caspari isolated danger bn, make good 168° towards the small WB pyramid, Amer de Stum, seen against the green shore.

The river dries below La Corde br (10m) with 1m at the first of the St Yves slipways. At HW it is navigable above the br as far as Penzé; small quay dries 5m.

Anchorages Swell in N–NE winds unless well up the river.
• Off Penpoul, drying hbr is full of moorings.
• Mouillage de Carantec, S of Figuier isolated danger bn, 4m sand; difficult to land at low water.
• At the side of the channel before the moorings, land at muddy hard on W bank below St Yves.
• Off St Yves in 1–2m, little room, no visitors' moorings.

Supplies Fuel from garage at Carantec. Shops at St Pol-de-Léon, 2M.

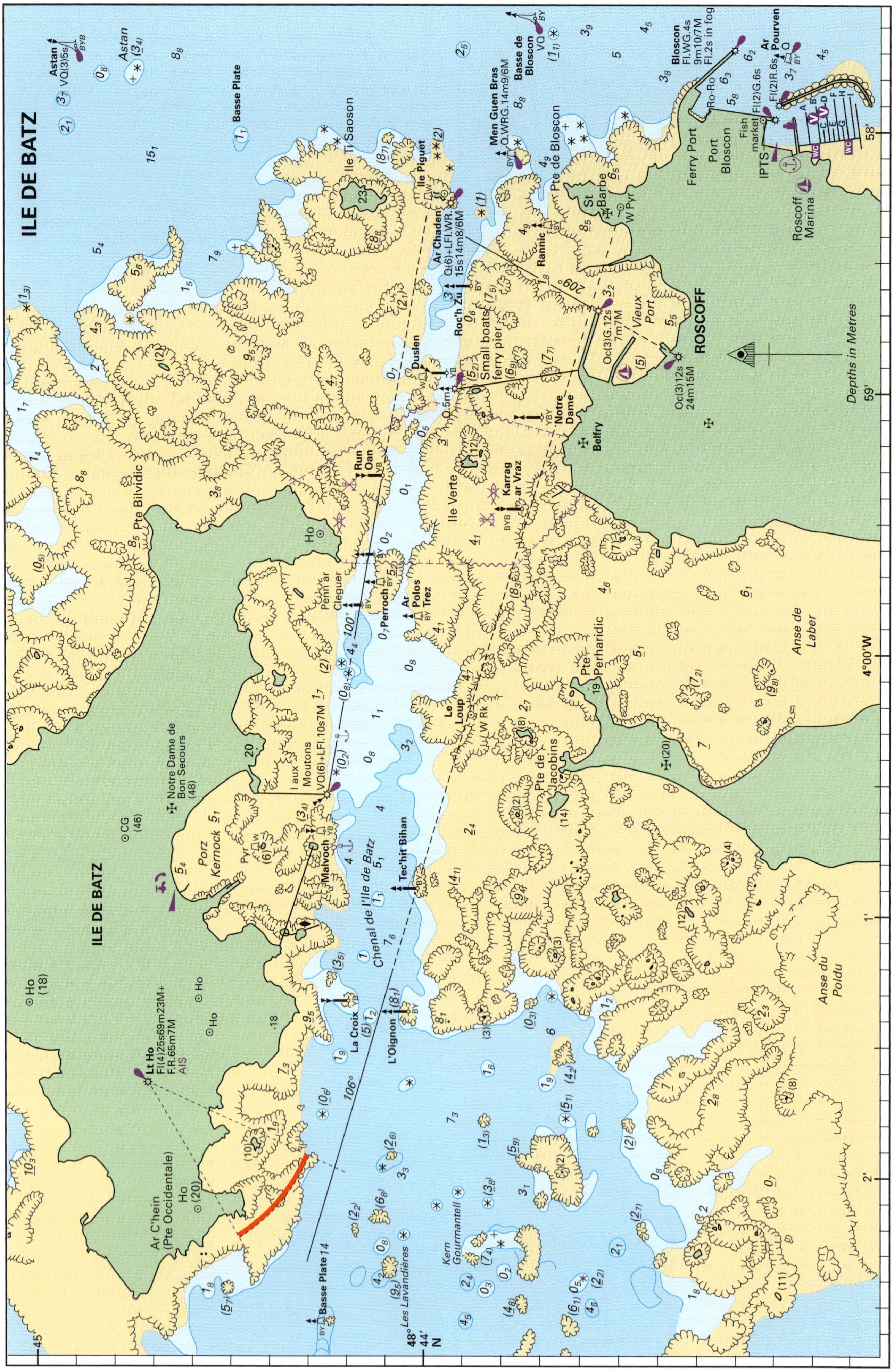
ILE DE BATZ
ROSCOFF
Chenal de l'Ile de Batz
Roscoff Marina
Ferry Port
Port Bloscon
Vieux Port
Anse de Laber
Anse du Poldu
Ar C'hein (Pte Occidentale)
Lt Ho
Fl(4)25s69m23M+
F.R.65m7M
AIS
Porz Kernock
Notre Dame de Bon Secours (48)
I aux Moutons
VQ(6)+LFl.10s7M
Malvoch
Tec'hit Bihan
La Croix
L'Oignon
Le Loup
Pte de Jacobins
Pte Perharidic
Ile Verte
Karrag ar Vraz
Notre Dame
Belfry
Run Oan
Perroch
Ar Polos
Penn ar Cleguer
Duslen
Roc'h Zu
Small boats ferry pier
Ar Chaden
Q(6)+LFl.WR.15s14m8/6M
Ile Piguet
Ile Ti Saoson
Men Guen Bras
Q.WRG.14m9/6M
Basse de Bloscon
VQ
Pte de Bloscon
Rannic
St Barbe
Oc(3)G.12s 7m7M
Oc(3)12s 24m15M
Bloscon
Fl.WG.4s 9m10/7M
Fl.2s in fog
Ar Pourven
Fl(2)R.6s
Fl(2)G.6s
Fish market
IPTS
Ro-Ro
Astan
VQ(3)5s
Basse Plate
Pte Bilvidic
Basse Plate 14
Les Lavandières
Kern Gourmantell
106°
100°
209°
48°44'N
4°00'W
Depths in Metres

ROSCOFF MARINA (PORT DE BLOSCON)

Tidal data as Roscoff (Old Port)

A hbr on the NE side of the Roscoff peninsula built primarily for car ferries and commercial shipping but with a new 625 berth marina, with 50 visitors' berths, approx 2ca S of the ferry terminal. Anchoring is now prohibited in the vicinity of the commercial port and marina. Accessible at all states of the tide and weather.

Approach Like most of this coast there are many drying rocky areas, however in good visibility, using suitable charts, it should present no problems except in strong onshore weather. From seaward, the grey 69m LtHo at the W end of the Ile de Batz is a prominent landmark. From the N make for 48°44′N 3°57′W, leaving Astan N card buoy well clear to stb. Monitor VHF 12 for ferry movements.

Entrance From N leave Basse de Bloscon N card Lt buoy to stb. The ferry port entrance, ½M south of it has a pier with a light Fl.GW.4s on a W column with G top at its east end. The ferry terminal is on the S side of this pier. At night enter in the W sector, 200–210°. The marina entrance is between the fishing port pierhead, Fl(2)G.6s, and the northern end of the marina outer breakwater, Fl(2)R.6s. Call marina on VHF 9 before entry/exit, controlled by IPTS lights.

Berthing In the marina, as directed, strong through current at times.

Facilities include laundry, chandlery, bike hire. Roscoff town 15 min walk; Mkt Wed.

☎ /VHF Marina 02 98 79 79 49; VHF 09, Ferry Port VHF 12.

ROSCOFF (OLD PORT)

Standard Port Brest
HW (sp) +0105 (np) +0055
LW (sp) +0110 (np) +0055
MHWS MHWN MLWN MLWS
+1·9m +1·6m +0·7m +0·2m

DS in Chenal de Batz:
Dover +0030E; –0600W, 3¾kn

An interesting old town and popular holiday resort, with drying hbr.

Approach From W by Chenal de Batz. From N leave Astan E card buoy, VQ(3)5s8M, clear to stb and then approach in W sector (197°–257°) of Men-Guen Bras BY N card Lt tr, Q.WRG. Align it with Roscoff rear Ldg Lt Oc(3)12s (grey tr, W on NE side) and when Ar Chaden R Lt appears, Q(6)+LFl.WR.15s, steer to leave that close to stb. Continue for a short distance to W for the Ldg Lts 209°. From Baie de Morlaix follow directions for Chenal de l'Ile de Batz; by night approach in W sector of Ar Chaden Q(6)+LFl.WR, 291°.

Entrance dries 3·2m and should not be attempted until after half-tide. Six W waiting buoys available west of Ar Chaden bn NE of entrance. Steer on the Ldg Lts 209°, front W rectangle with B stripe on W column with G top at head of NW mole, Oc(3)G.12s7m; rear grey tr, W on NE side, Oc(3)12s (synchronised with front), 2ca to SW. This line leaves rks drying 7m close to port. Nearing the front Lt, bear away to leave it to stb and round second pierhead to Vieux Port.

Berthing in outer harbour (Port Neuf) is discouraged as quays are for fishing vessels. Inner harbour, drying 3–5m, is available for yachts. Moor alongside rough jetty or anchor in centre. Jetty to E has rocks at base. Surge in strong NE winds.

Anchoring outside possible while awaiting tide on line between Roch Zhu N perch and Ar Chaden Lt tr, 2–3m, but uncomfortable with weather-going tide. Buoys sometimes available.

Supplies Water on quay. Fuel from tanker. Shops.

☎ /VHF Old Port (Port de Plaisance) 02 98 69 76 37, VHF 09.

CHENAL DE L'ILE DE BATZ

Standard Port Cherbourg
HW (sp) +0050 (np) +0055
LW (sp) +0105 (np) +0055
MHWS MHWN MLWN MLWS
+2·0m +1·6m +0·8m +0·3m

DS W entrance, Basse Platte:
Dover –0415SSW; +0015NE, 1–2½kn, reaching 3kn on ebb

The channel is unlit W of Roscoff. The transits pass close to shoals and one almost dries in the area of Per Roc'h, ½M NW of Roscoff landing stage. It should not be attempted 2hrs either side of LWS. Only E entrance is practicable at night.

Directions From E to W the transits are as follows, with E-most mark of each pair quoted first:
• Duslen W tr with Malvoc'h S card tr 282°. Passes close S of Ar Chaden S card YB Lt tr, Q(6)+LFl.WR.15s, and N of Men Guen Bras N card BY Lt tr, Q.WRG. Before coming abreast of Roc'h Zu N card bn steer 270° to clear rocks from Duslen W tr to mid-stream N of long Roscoff landing stage, conspic. Keep close to the former to:
• W pyramid in Kernoc'h harbour in line with E-most of the two mills (named Moulin de l'Ouest) SE of Batz LtHo, 291°. This leaves Per Roc'h N card BW bn to port.
• About 1ca past Per Roc'h, steer on rear bearing 078° with Pte Pen Ar Cléguer in line with Horville rock (dr 15m) to just N of Tehi Bihan N card bn.
• At Tehi Bihan bn steer W to get on rear bearing 106° with Le Loup W rock in line with W pyramid at Ste Barbe to clear the entrance.

From W to E the transits are reversed.

Anchorages
• While awaiting the tide to enter at the W end, off Ar Skeul W card YBY bn tr SW of Ile de Siec; beware drying rock to its SW.
• Porz Kernoch on Ile de Batz. Level ground N and NW of W Kernoch pyramid, dries 5m. Ferry wash. Area S of pyramid has rocks. Slipway to E used by passenger boats.
• W of Roscoff entrance on line joining Roc'h Zu bn and Ar-Chaden tr. W visitors' mooring buoys.

Supplies Small shops in Kernoch village on Ile de Batz.

PONTUSVAL (BRIGNOGAN)

Standard Port Brest
HW (sp) +0045 (np) +0040
LW (sp) +0100 (np) +0040
MHWS MHWN MLWN MLWS
+1·4m +1·1m +0·5m +0·1m

Dries 2–5m

Useful day harbour. Open to N and accessible only by day after half-tide. Lies 1M to E of Pontusval Lt tr with conspic W lookout tr to W of entrance. From a position 48°41′·43N 4°19′·20W, about 1ca E of Port de Pontusval E card buoy, approach on 178° with Coat Tanguy W tr in line with Plounéour-Trez spire passing G con buoy and R An Neudden tr. Anchor SW of the latter, 4m, or dry further in. Six W visitors' buoys, some in deep water, rather exposed. Stores at Brignogan.

www.imray.com

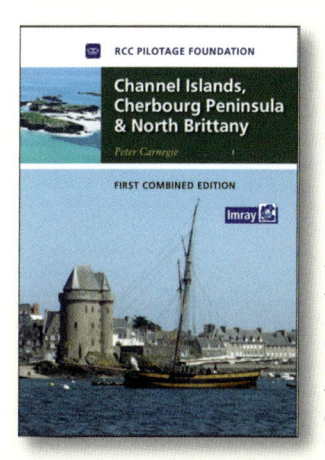

RCC PILOTAGE FOUNDATION

CHANNEL ISLANDS, CHERBOURG PENINSULA & NORTH BRITTANY

First combined edition

Peter Carnegie

The RCC PF's detailed pilot for the *Channel Islands* is now part of this new pilot for the North Coast of Brittany and Cherbourg Peninsula. It is the definitve pilot for anyone interested in exploring the less frequently used inshore passages and anchorages.

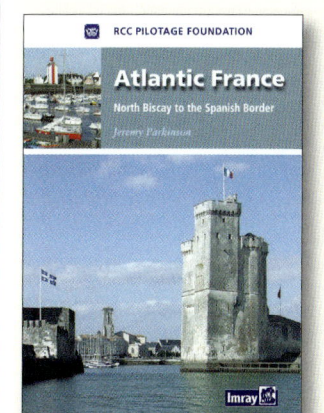

RCC PILOTAGE FOUNDATION

ATLANTIC FRANCE

North Biscay to the Spanish border

Jeremy Parkinson

North Biscay has been renamed *Atlantic France* to reflect the extended coverage to the Spanish border. The Brittany harbour of L'Aberwrac'h, the key to entering the Chenal du Four, is now included. At the south end the guide now covers Arcachon, Cap Breton, Bayonne, St Jean de Luz and the Rada de Higuer up to the Spanish border.

Atlantic France is the authoritative cruising guide for this long and varied coastline, and its revision will be welcomed by both first time visitors and old west coast of France hands.

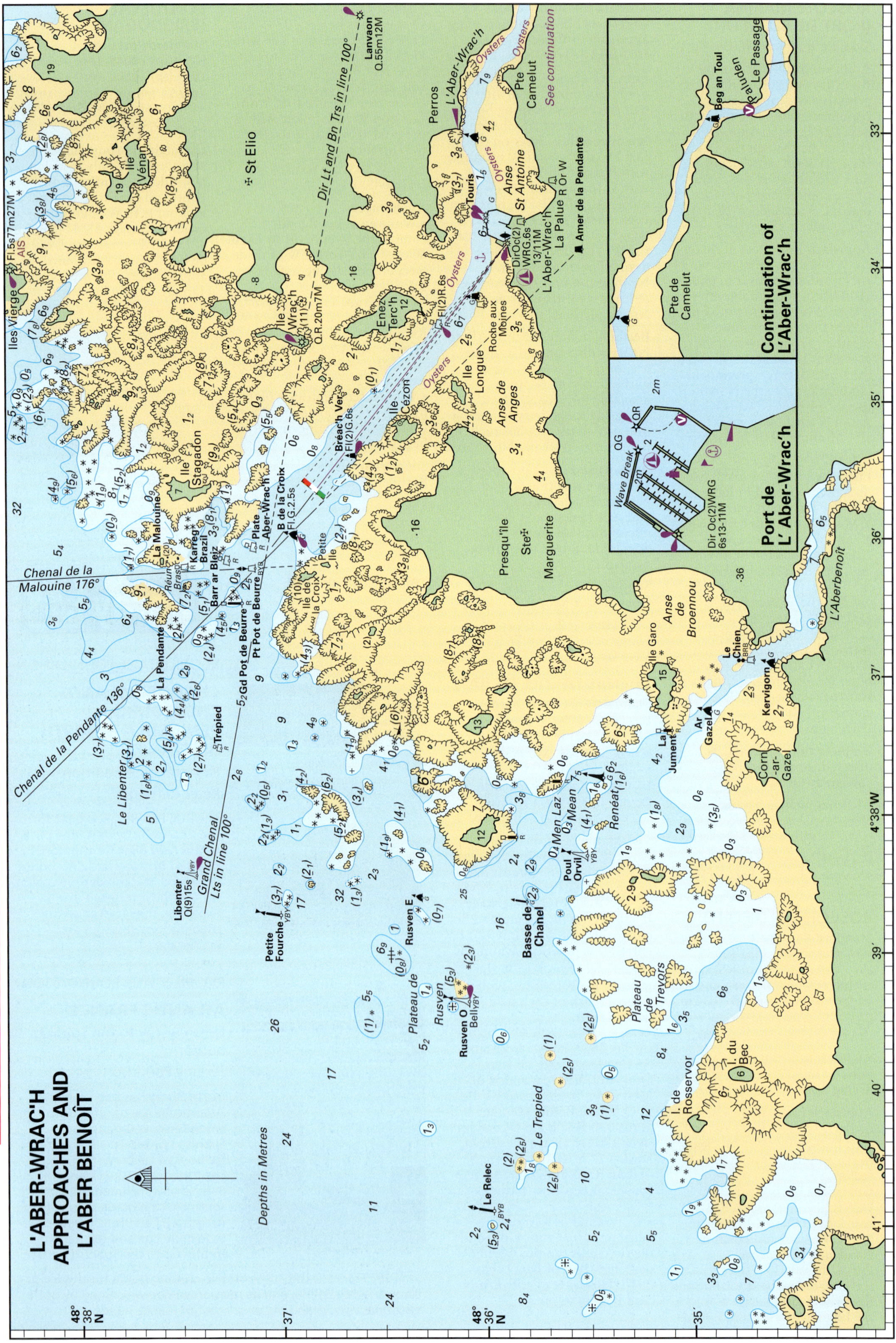
L'ABER-WRAC'H APPROACHES AND L'ABER BENOÎT
Depths in Metres
Port de L' Aber-Wrac'h
Continuation of L'Aber-Wrac'h
Chenal de la Pendante 136°
Chenal de la Malouine 176°
Grand Chenal Lts in line 100°
Dir Lt and Bn Trs in line 100°
Iles Vierge Fl.5s77m27M AIS
Ile Vénan
St Elio
Ile Stagadon
La Malouine
La Pendante
Le Libenter
Libenter Q(9)15s
Petite Fourche
Trépied
Barr ar Bleiz
Karreg Brazil
Gd Pot de Beurre
Pt Pot de Beurre
Plate Aber-Wrac'h
B de la Croix Fl.G.2.5s
Ile de la Croix
Petite Ile
Ile Wrac'h Q.R.20m7M
Lanvaon Q.55m12M
Breac'h Ver Fl(2)G.6s
Ile Cézon
Enez Terc'h
Ile Longue
Roche aux Moines
Anse de Anges
Presqu'île Ste Marguerite
Touris
Anse St Antoine
La Palue R Or W
Amer de la Pendante
Dir Oc(2) WRG.6s 13/11M
L'Aber-Wrac'h
Perros
Pte Camelut
See continuation
Oysters
Rusven E
Plateau de Rusven
Rusven O Bell
Basse de Chanel
Poul Orvil
Men Laz
Mean
Renéat
La Jument
Ar Gazel
Corn-ar-Gazel
Kervigorn
Le Chien
Ile Garo
Anse de Broennou
L'Aberbenoît
Plateau de Trevors
I. du Bec
I. de Rosservor
Le Trepied
Le Relec
Wave Break
Dir Oc(2)WRG 6s13-11M
Pte de Camelut
Beg an Toul
Paluden
Le Passage
48° 38′ N
37′
48° 36′ N
35′
41′
40′
39′
4°38′W
37′
36′
35′
34′
33′

L'ABER-WRAC'H

Standard Port Brest
HW +0030   LW +0038
MHWS   MHWN   MLWN   MLWS
+0·7m   +0·6m   +0·1m   −0·1m
DS at entrance to Grand Chenal: Dover HW SE; +0600NW, 1½kn

An estuary accessible at all times, open to NW but with shelter in the upper reaches.

CHENAL DE BATZ TO L'ABER-WRAC'H

Passage lights	BA No
Ile de Batz Fl(4)25s69m23M+ F.R.65m7M (024°-059°) AIS	1816
Pontusval Oc(3)WR.12s16m10/7M (R over rks to SW)	1820
Amann Ar Rouz N card Lt buoy Q.7M Whis	
Lizen van Ouest W card Lt buoy VQ(9)10s5M	1821·3
Ile Vierge Fl.5s77m27M AIS	1822
Libenter buoy W card Lt buoy Q(9)15s8m6M	
Le Four Fl(5)15s28m22M	1854

STREAMS RELATED TO HW DOVER
2M N of Ile de Batz +0115E – 0515W, 3¾kn. Off Le Libenter +0015E; –0600 W, 2½kn

Allowance must be made for the tidal streams which are stronger nearer the coast. There are no sheltered harbours or anchorages in this 26M stretch; such harbours as there are, dry, the best being:

Mogueriec SW of Ile de Siec. Rocks to NE are in Ile de Batz R sector. Ldg Lts 162° front W tower G top Iso.WG.4s9m11/6M, rear W column G top F.G.22m7M. Shelter by quay taken by fishing boats. Entrance impossible LW±0200 or with fresh N winds. There is a shoal in the middle of the harbour.

THE WEST COUNTRY TO L'ABER-WRAC'H

From Plymouth the overall distance is 107M, bearing 189°.

The streams run strongly on the headlands outside the Eddystone and the Lizard. Streams run W from HW Dover −2 and E from HW Dover +4. Max stream 2kn sp and 1kn np and run E/W.

Tidal streams increase near the French coast to 2·5kn sp and 1·2kn np and run SW from HW Dover -0400 and NE from HW Dover +0200.

Shipping will be encountered throughout the passage. Naval vessels exercise off Plymouth and coastal shipping heading for Lands End TSS will be encountered S of Eddystone. The recommended traffic route between Casquets TSS and Ouessant TSS lies 50M out, with the W going ships in the N lane. Fishing boats are found near the Brittany coast.

Do not close the French coast in poor visibility as rocky shoals extend 3M out.

The Ile Vierge Lt Ho is one of the tallest in the world and lies 3M NNE of the Libenter W card Lt buoy. Libenter Shoal lies NE of the buoy, approach from N.

In good weather La Malouine is an easy passage. At night or in poor visibility use the Grand Chenal starting 2ca S of the Libenter buoy. L'Aber-wrac'h is available in any weather at any state of the tide.

Approach From W or N make for a position ½M W of Libenter W card Lt buoy, whistle, 3M WSW of Ile Vierge Lt. From NE, with good visibility and reasonable sea, make a position 1½M W of the light for the Malouine channel.

Entrance There are three entrance channels of which only the first is usable at all times.

• **Grand Chenal** (3m) From 1ca SW of Libenter buoy pick up the Ldg line, 100°, of front, Ile Vrac W LtHo, R top, Q.R.20m7M; rear Lanvaon W Lt tr with Or ▲, Q.55m 12M (090°-110°); and also on this line, Plouguerneau belfry. Beware of cross tide in entrance. The flood sets hard on Libenter. After Petit Pot de Beurre E card bn tr, steer 128° following the line of buoys and towers; at night change course from 100° at La Croix Lt buoy, Fl.G.2·5s, and follow W sector of La Palue molehead Lt, DirOc(2)WRG.6s (127°-W-129°). This leads past Breac'h Ver G stb tr, Fl(2)G.6s, Fort Cézon and Roche aux Moines G tr (ignore the W tr to SW of it) all to stb; and then bear E for marina and moorings.

• **Chenal de la Malouine** (3m, ½ca wide at entrance). Coming from E this saves the distance round Libenter. 4M visibility is needed. It passes between La Pendante rock (6m) to W and La Malouine (17m) to the E. At 1½M W of Ile Vierge Lt pick up the Ldg marks 176°: front BY E card tr, 5m, and rear Petite Ile de la Croix W tr, 6m and 4ca to its S. Beware strong cross tide, up to 3kn, in entrance and pass ¼ca W of Karreg Brazil R tr. At Bar-ar-Bleiz R buoy bear SSE between Plate Aber-Wrac'h and Petit Pot de Beurre, at which steer 128° as in Grand Chenal.

• **Chenal de la Pendante** (0·3m) can be used only by day with good visibility. At 2½M W of Ile Vierge, leave La Pendante 1½ca to port, making good 136° (cross-set 2½kn) on line of front W mark on Fort Cézon, rear Amer de la Pendante B tr 1¼M SE. When 1½ca off Grand Pot de Beurre R bn, 2m, come to port and make for Bar-ar-Bleiz R buoy; when close, steer SSE past Plate Aber-Wrac'h R buoy into the main channel.

The river is navigable (2·7m) to Paluden which is more sheltered with winds from W to NW. When past Touris R tr, steer for the quay upriver on N shore. Nearing it turn to stb up centre of river, with stakes on the edges. Give Beg-an-Toul a wide berth and keep to W side of channel until near the quays.

Berthing In the marina for boats under 12m at La Palue; otherwise there are 30 visitors' buoys on which rafting is permitted. Anchoring is allowed only to W of life-boat slip (not in NE winds); otherwise it is prohibited within hbr limits, including Beg an Toul. In bad weather, especially from W to N, it is more comfortable to moor up the river at Paluden where there are dumbbell moorings for visitors, good shelter.

Facilities Fuel (self service with card). Water at the quay and pontoons, chandlery. Small shop in the village; more at Landéda, 1M. Restaurant at Paluden.

☎/VHF *capitainerie* 02 98 04 91 62, VHF 16, 09. Customs 02 98 85 07 40; Harbour launch VHF 09. Paluden 02980 46312. Bus to Brest.

L'ABER BENOIT

Standard Port Brest
HW +0024   LW +0028
MHWS   MHWN   MLWN   MLWS
+0·9m   +0·8m   +0·3m   +0·1m
DS Dover +0030 in-going; +0615 out-going, 3kn

A wide estuary, less developed than L'Aber-Wrac'h. Unlit but providing good shelter.

Approach by the W of Le Libenter W card buoy, which is 3M WSW of Ile Vierge Lt.

Entrance should not be attempted in strong NW winds. From close W of Petite Fourche W card buoy, ½M SSW of Libenter buoy, make good 170°. From about 2ca S of Rusven Est G con buoy, at Basse du Chenal G con buoy (Rusven Sud on some charts), steer 141° on line of Le Chien BRB bn tr just open to right of white topped La Jument rock west of Ile Garo (4m). Bear to port to clear stb buoy marking Mean Renéat rocks, then steer for Le Chien, leaving La Jument to port.

Alternatively from Rusven Est G buoy steer 190° on line of front Ven Bihan rock (19m) in line with Lampaul-Ploudalmezeau spire (W-most of two). When Orvil W card buoy is in line with Jument de Garo alter course to leave the buoy close to port, 130°. Bear to port to clear Ar Gazel G buoy SE of La Jument de Garo and leave Le Chien BR isolated danger tr to port. Thereafter follow the channel.

Berthing Anchor clear of moorings by Le Passage (old ferry site) about 6ca past Le Chien, or round the bend to S. Depths greater than shown due to sand dredging. The inter-tidal zone has extensive oyster beds. It may be best to pick up a buoy.

Supplies Small shops up the hill on S side of the ferry. Water on S quay. Large oyster centre on S side.

NW France, Channel Islands and cross Channel to England

	Cherbourg	Alderney	St Peter Port	St Helier	St Malo	Lezardrieux	Roscoff	L'Aberwrac'h	Longships 1M W	Falmouth	Plymouth BW	Dartmouth	Portland Bill 2M S
Cherbourg	0												
Alderney	23	0											
St Peter Port	42	22	0										
St Helier	60	37	32	0									
St Malo	89	68	54	39	0								
Lezardrieux	88	75	47	46	48	0							
Roscoff	119	84	73	79	83	51	0						
L'Aberwrac'h	149	124	103	109	114	83	36	0					
Longships 1M W	164	145	139	154	212	139	108	101	0				
Falmouth	141	133	112	129	150	119	93	97	41	0			
Plymouth BW	111	88	87	107	139	106	98	108	72	38	0		
Dartmouth	85	70	70	94	131	98	99	117	96	63	35	0	
Portland Bill 2M S	58	47	63	88	132	112	122	146	135	102	72	44	0

The Cruising Almanac

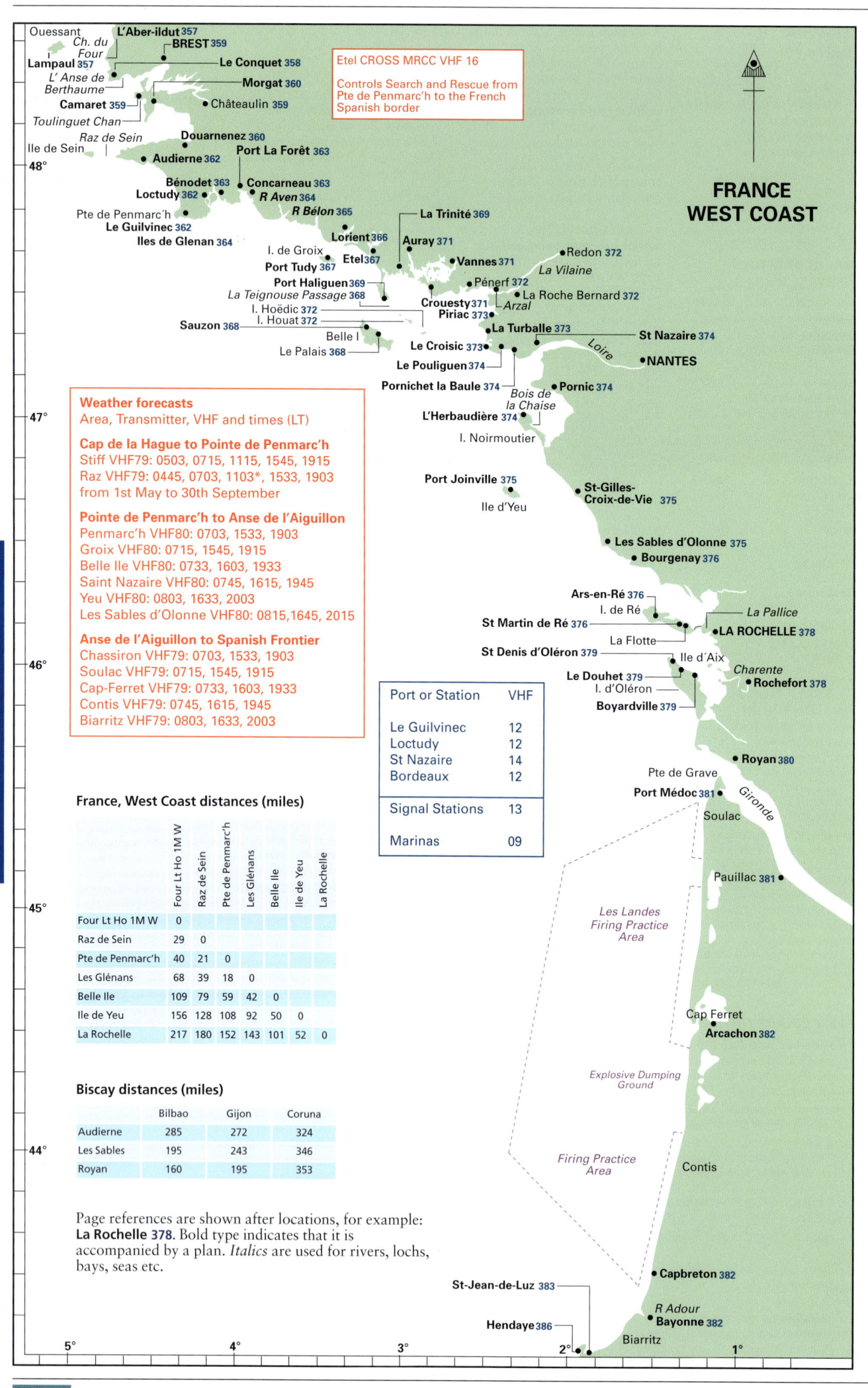

FRANCE WEST COAST

Etel CROSS MRCC VHF 16
Controls Search and Rescue from Pte de Penmarc'h to the French Spanish border

Locations (with page references):

- Ouessant
- *Ch. du Four*
- L'Aber-ildut 357
- **BREST** 359
- Lampaul 357
- Le Conquet 358
- *L' Anse de Berthaume*
- Morgat 360
- Camaret 359
- Châteaulin 359
- *Toulinguet Chan*
- *Raz de Sein*
- Ile de Sein
- Douarnenez 360
- Audierne 362
- Port La Forêt 363
- Bénodet 363
- Concarneau 363
- Loctudy 362
- *R Aven* 364
- Pte de Penmarc'h
- *R Bélon* 365
- La Trinité 369
- Le Guilvinec 362
- Iles de Glenan 364
- Lorient 366
- Auray 371
- *I. de Groix*
- Etel 367
- Vannes 371
- Port Tudy 367
- *Redon* 372
- Port Haliguen 369
- Crouesty 371
- Pénerf 372
- *La Vilaine*
- *La Teignouse Passage* 368
- La Roche Bernard 372
- *I. Hoëdic* 372
- Piriac 373
- *Arzal*
- *I. Houat* 372
- La Turballe 373
- St Nazaire 374
- Sauzon 368
- Belle I
- Le Croisic 373
- *Loire*
- Le Palais 368
- Le Pouliguen 374
- **NANTES**
- Pornichet la Baule 374
- Pornic 374
- *Bois de la Chaise*
- L'Herbaudière 374
- *I. Noirmoutier*
- Port Joinville 375
- St-Gilles-Croix-de-Vie 375
- *Ile d'Yeu*
- Les Sables d'Olonne 375
- Bourgenay 376
- Ars-en-Ré 376
- *I. de Ré*
- La Pallice
- St Martin de Ré 376
- La Flotte
- **LA ROCHELLE** 378
- St Denis d'Oléron 379
- *Ile d'Aix*
- Le Douhet 379
- *Charente*
- *I. d'Oléron*
- Rochefort 378
- Boyardville 379
- Royan 380
- Pte de Grave
- Port Médoc 381
- *Gironde*
- Soulac
- Pauillac 381
- *Les Landes Firing Practice Area*
- Cap Ferret
- Arcachon 382
- *Explosive Dumping Ground*
- *Firing Practice Area*
- Contis
- St-Jean-de-Luz 383
- Capbreton 382
- *R Adour*
- Bayonne 382
- Hendaye 386
- Biarritz

Weather forecasts
Area, Transmitter, VHF and times (LT)

Cap de la Hague to Pointe de Penmarc'h
Stiff VHF79: 0503, 0715, 1115, 1545, 1915
Raz VHF79: 0445, 0703, 1103*, 1533, 1903
from 1st May to 30th September

Pointe de Penmarc'h to Anse de l'Aiguillon
Penmarc'h VHF80: 0703, 1533, 1903
Groix VHF80: 0715, 1545, 1915
Belle Ile VHF80: 0733, 1603, 1933
Saint Nazaire VHF80: 0745, 1615, 1945
Yeu VHF80: 0803, 1633, 2003
Les Sables d'Olonne VHF80: 0815, 1645, 2015

Anse de l'Aiguillon to Spanish Frontier
Chassiron VHF79: 0703, 1533, 1903
Soulac VHF79: 0715, 1545, 1915
Cap-Ferret VHF79: 0733, 1603, 1933
Contis VHF79: 0745, 1615, 1945
Biarritz VHF79: 0803, 1633, 2003

Port or Station	VHF
Le Guilvinec	12
Loctudy	12
St Nazaire	14
Bordeaux	12
Signal Stations	13
Marinas	09

France, West Coast distances (miles)

	Four Lt Ho 1M W	Raz de Sein	Pte de Penmarc'h	Les Glénans	Belle Ile	Ile de Yeu	La Rochelle
Four Lt Ho 1M W	0						
Raz de Sein	29	0					
Pte de Penmarc'h	40	21	0				
Les Glénans	68	39	18	0			
Belle Ile	109	79	59	42	0		
Ile de Yeu	156	128	108	92	50	0	
La Rochelle	217	180	152	143	101	52	0

Biscay distances (miles)

	Bilbao	Gijon	Coruna
Audierne	285	272	324
Les Sables	195	243	346
Royan	160	195	353

Page references are shown after locations, for example: **La Rochelle** 378. Bold type indicates that it is accompanied by a plan. *Italics* are used for rivers, lochs, bays, seas etc.

France – West Coast

Given a three week cruising period, the harbours of Southern Brittany are within reach of the South and West Coasts of England and Wales. The Rade de Brest together with the Bays of Camaret and Douarnenez and off-shore islands of Ushant, Molène and Sein provide an excellent introduction to the attractions of South Brittany.

South of the Pointe de Penmarc'h, the weather is warmer and sunnier. The jewel of the Breton cruising grounds lies within the shelter of the Quiberon Peninsula. Together with Belle Île, three weeks could easily be spent exploring the islands in the bay, the Morbihan and the ports on the mainland. The marina at Vannes is close to its mediaeval centre and across the bay from the entrance to the Morbihan lies the pretty town of Piriac.

For those able to make a longer cruise, or who decide to sail further south, the Vendée ports can be reached within a four day sail from L'Aber-Wrac'h. The Ile d'Yeu is sufficiently far off shore to have retained its identity and here the bicycle is king. Further south lie the delightful islands of Ré, Oléron and Aix, La Rochelle and the Charente. This cruising ground has the advantage of excellent connections to the UK from the airport at La Rochelle.

The alternative to crossing Biscay is to follow the coast south from the Gironde and conditions may permit entry into Arcachon Bay. Although a shallow draught boat will allow an exploration into the smaller ports and harbours around the Bay, there are also deeper water anchorages.

With rare exceptions, it is very easy to access supplies from all harbours and anchorages; even on small islands like Houat and Hoëdic. The traditional markets continue and sometimes fish can be bought directly from the boats. WiFi and laundry facilities are widely available. French traffic laws and cycle tracks make cycling a pleasure. Marina charges, although they have risen are usually more modest than those on the South coast of the UK. In May and June, charges are lower than high season; anchorages are less crowded, except at weekends on the islands.

Detailed information on lock times may be found on marina websites.

Currents and Tidal Streams

South of the Raz de Sein, apart from few exceptions, tidal streams are relatively weak. South of the Gironde, there is a north-going current 0·5–1kn extending up to five or six miles offshore; prolonged W'ly gales often increase its rate. Inshore of this, a south-going current may be found.

Weather and Swell

Most forecasts give information on swell (*houle*) indicating height in metres and frequency in seconds as well as the effect of wind on sea (*vent du mer*).

In spring and summer prevailing winds between Ouessant (Ushant) and the Gironde are from between W and NE through N, but in the neighbourhood of Brest SW winds are often experienced. Gales are not frequent during June through August, but at no time can freedom from W gales be relied on, and in unsettled weather small craft are well advised not to stray too far from shelter. In the autumn, E winds are slightly more frequent. Fog rarely lasts long on most of this coast but is quite frequent around Ouessant at all times.

Le Vent Solaire

Warm, sunny weather often produces this cycle of sea breezes. Beginning in the early afternoon, the wind goes into the northwest, strengthening to Force 4; after which it veers to the north, dying away towards dusk, to be replaced by a fresh NE wind. The latter may blow with enough force to make anchorages uncomfortable. By morning, this wind dies completely. This phenomenon is particularly noticeable S of Penmarc'h.

Pilots and Charts

Bloc Marine Votre Livre de Bord Atlantique edition (in French)
Bloc Marine French Harbours (in English) Almanach du Marin Breton.
Atlantic France: North Biscay to the Spanish Border RCC Pilotage Foundation (Imray).
SHOM tidal atlases 558, 559, 560.

CHANNELS BETWEEN OUESSANT AND THE MAINLAND

There are three channels between the Is and the mainland; the Fromveur, where the streams run at 9kn at springs, the Helle, the channel of approach from NW and Land's End, and the Chenal du Four from the English Channel. The last two are well buoyed. At the N end of the Chenal du Four, the stream runs at 3·5kn at springs. Where the channels unite near the Grand Vinotière the tidal stream reaches 6–7kn at springs. By using either the Helle or Four, boats may avoid the traffic separation zone to the NW of Ouessant, as well as the heavy swell often found there. Use VHF Ch 13 to report position if crossing the Ouessant TSS. Avoid taking these passages in poor visibility, strong winds, high swell or wind against tide.

CHENAL DU FOUR (FOUR CHANNEL)

HW (Ouessant) Brest +0005

MHWS	MHWN	MLWN	MLWS
6·9m	5·3m	2·5m	1·0m

Approach

From the North At the North end of the Channel, slack water is at HW Brest; the south-going stream running from Brest HW+0100 to Brest HW+0500. Arrival time at Le Four depends on passage plans. If making a passage from L'Aberwrac'h to Camaret or Brest, leave no later than Brest HW+0215 to arrive off Le Four at Brest HW+0445. From L'Aberwrac'h to beyond the Raz de Sein, leave Brest HW–0300 in order to be off Le Four at slack water (HW Brest), thus making the passage through the Raz at slack water.

Coming directly from the UK, it may be difficult to time the arrival at the Chenal du Four to coincide with the tide. As the streams are weaker in the Northern end of the channel in calm conditions, a boat could reach either the Anse de Porsmoguer or Anse des Blancs Sablons and wait for the tide. It may even be possible, in quiet weather and good visibility, to skirt inside the Grande Vinotière.

By night Remain in the white sector of Kermorvan, until in the white sector of Pte de Corsen. Change course to remain in this sector until R pillar buoy, Tournant et Lochrist, has been passed. Then steer a course that will lead between G con buoy, La Fourmi, and R bn tr, Les Vieux Moines.

From the South

If making for L'Aberwrac'h from Brest, be off Les Vieux Moines at Brest HW–0500. A boat bound northwards from south of the Raz, entering the Raz at Brest HW+0530 and with the help of the north-going stream, should be entering the Chenal du Four Brest HW–0400; thus having a fair tide from the N end of the Chenal to L'Aberwrac'h.

The channel is well buoyed and, in good conditions, the marks are easy to follow. It is easier to check progress noting the buoys as they are passed, rather than trying to align lights and marks.

Anchorages

- Anse de Porsmoguer
- Anse des Blancs Sablons

Useful anchorages when on passage through the Chenal du Four. The holding in both is sand. The latter is appropriate in fine weather as it is exposed to the W and N, and has an eddy stream in the S of the bay.

Passage lights	BA No
La Vierge Fl.5s77m27M AIS	1822
Le Stiff Fl(2)R.20s85m22M	1842
Créac'h Fl(2)10s70m30M Horn(2)120s	1844
La Jument Fl(3)R.12s36m10M	1848
Le Four Fl(5)15s28m22M	1854
L'Aber-Ildut DirOc(2)WRG.6s12m10M	1856
Trézien DirOc(2)6s84m20M AIS	1873·9
Kermorvan Fl.5s20m22M AIS	1874
St Mathieu Fl.15s56m24M (Rear) DirF AIS	1874·1
La Grande Vinotière Fl.R.4s12m5M	1872

355

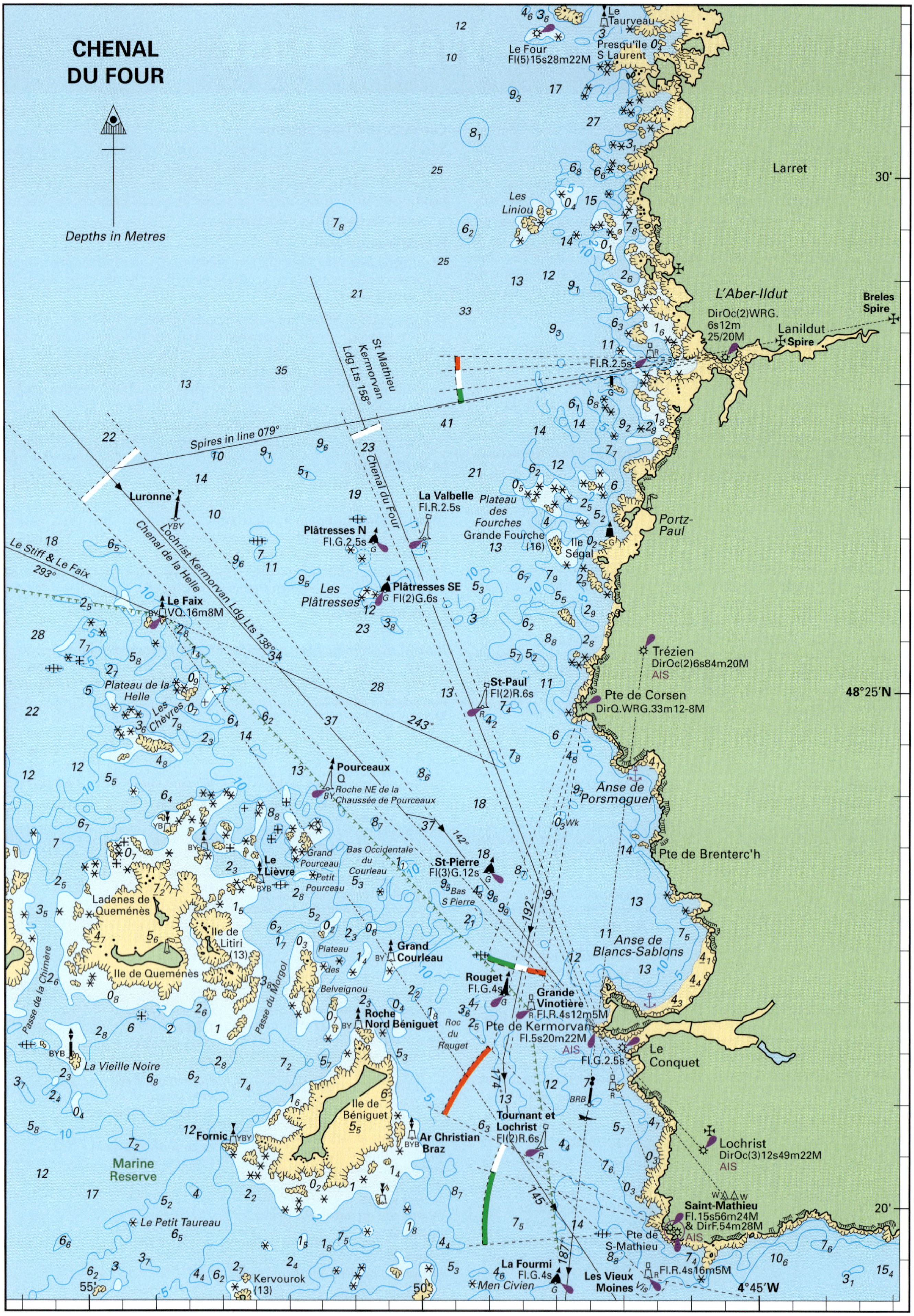
CHENAL DU FOUR
Depths in Metres
Le Four
Fl(5)15s28m22M
Le Taurveau
Presqu'ile
S Laurent
Larret
Les Liniou
L'Aber-Ildut
DirOc(2)WRG.
6s12m
25/20M
Lanildut
Spire
Breles
Spire
Fl.R.2.5s
St Mathieu
Kermorvan
Ldg Lts 158°
Spires in line 079°
Chenal du Four
Luronne
YBY
La Valbelle
Fl.R.2.5s
Plateau des Fourches
Grande Fourche
(16)
Ile Ségal
Portz-Paul
Plâtresses N
Fl.G.2.5s
Plâtresses SE
Fl(2)G.6s
Les Plâtresses
Le Stiff & Le Faix
293°
Chenal de la Helle
Lochrist Kermorvan Ldg Lts 138°
Le Faix
VQ.16m8M
Trézien
DirOc(2)6s84m20M
AIS
Pte de Corsen
DirQ.WRG.33m12-8M
48°25'N
St-Paul
Fl(2)R.6s
Plateau de la Helle
Les Chèvres
243°
Pourceaux
Q
Roche NE de la Chaussée de Pourceaux
Anse de Porsmoguer
Wk
142°
Grand Pourceau
Petit Pourceau
Bas Occidentale du Courleau
St-Pierre
Fl(3)G.12s
Bas S Pierre
Pte de Brenterc'h
Le Lièvre
Ladenes de Queménès
Ile de Litiri
(13)
Ile de Queménès
Passe de la Chimère
Passe du Morgol
Plateau des Belveignou
Grand Courleau
192°
Anse de Blancs-Sablons
Rouget
Fl.G.4s
Grande Vinotière
Fl.R.4s12m5M
Roche Nord Béniguet
Roc du Rouget
Pte de Kermorvan
Fl.5s20m22M
AIS
Fl.G.2.5s
Le Conquet
La Vieille Noire
Ile de Béniguet
174°
BRB
Tournant et Lochrist
Fl(2)R.6s
Fornic
Ar Christian Braz
Lochrist
DirOc(3)12s49m22M
AIS
Marine Reserve
145°
Saint-Mathieu
Fl.15s56m24M
& DirF.54m28M
AIS
20'
Le Petit Taureau
Pte de S-Mathieu
Kervourok
(13)
La Fourmi
Fl.G.4s
187°
Men Civien
Les Vieux Moines
Vis
Fl.R.4s16m5M
4°45'W
55'
50'
30'

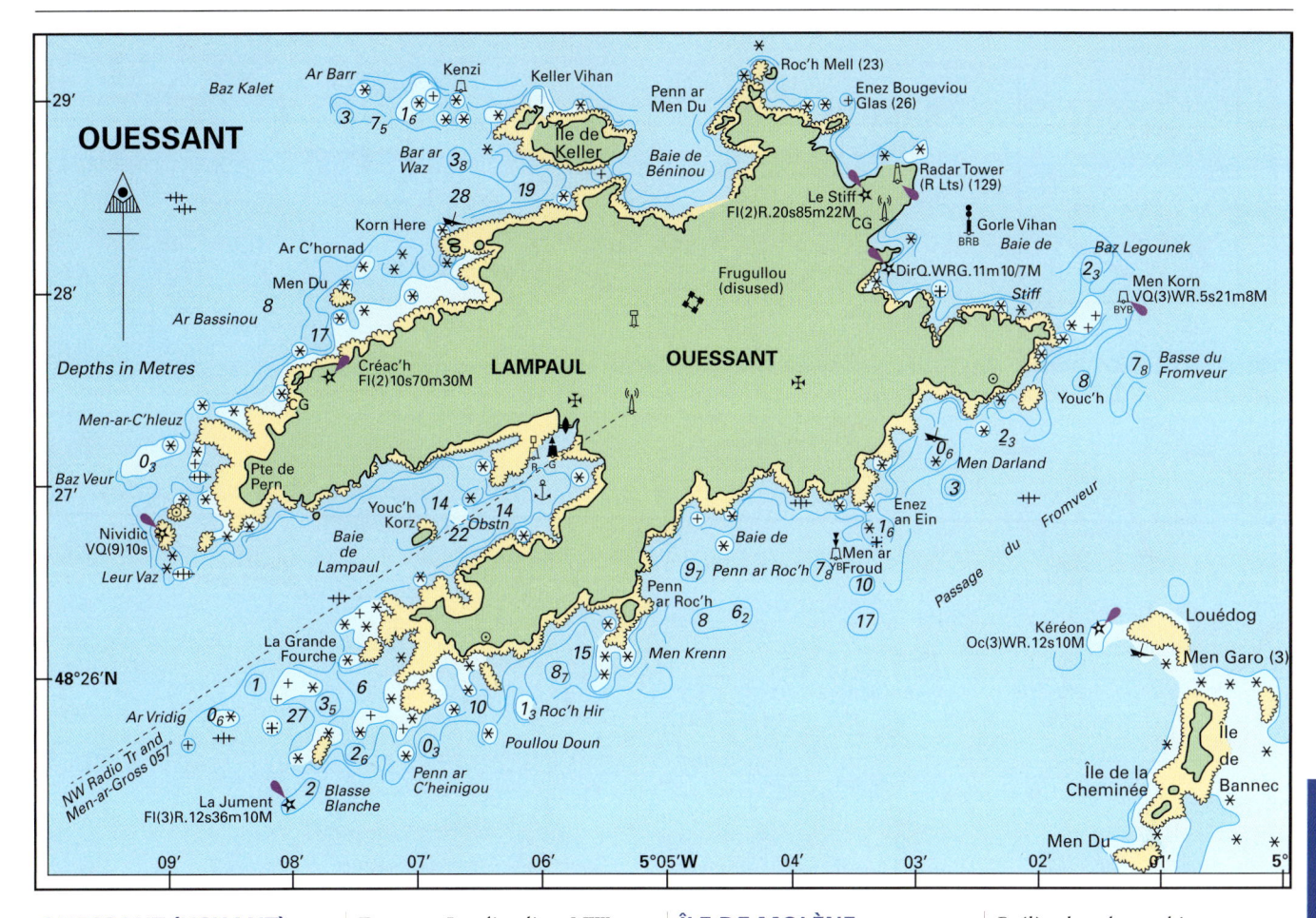

OUESSANT (USHANT)

Standard Port Brest
HW +0010   LW 0000

MHWS	MHWN	MLWN	MLWS
−0·1m	−0·1m	−0·1m	−0·1m

A fascinating place to visit in settled weather, with a picturesque anchorage at Lampaul.

Approach The tidal stream runs very strongly in the Passage du Fromveur; it is best taken at slack water, Brest +0030 or Brest −0530. On rounding La Jument, take care to allow for a southwesterly current.

Entrance Leading line, NW radio tr and Men-ar-Gross G bn tr 057°.

Anchorage Lampaul Bay provides more shelter than might be imagined; there is no current at the head of the bay where there are 24 white, visitors' mooring buoys. When the inner harbour Pors-Pol dries, go alongside either the lifeboat slipway or the end of the wharf to its west.

Facilities Water, fuel in small quantities from garage, PO, hotels, restaurants, shops, supermarkets with ATMs. Cycle hire.

ÎLE DE MOLÈNE

An attractive island whose anchorage is sheltered in winds from E through S to WSW. Navigation is now prohibited within the Molène Archipelago, except for access to Ile Molène through the Chenal des Laz.

L'ABER-ILDUT

Standard Port Brest
HW +0010   LW +0015

MHWS	MHWN	MLWN	MLWS
+0·3m	+0·2m	−0·1m	−0·1m

DS as Chenal du Four

Bar 2m approx at LW.

Approach Transit of 078·5° on the spires of Lanildut and Brelès churches, taking care to avoid the shoals of 1·8m and 2·3m, by leaving Le Lieu R. bn tr 100m to port. Then steer for the small lighthouse on the N side of the L'Aber-ildut shore. Steer to leave Le Lieu R close to port, then follow the buoyed channel. Beware of cross tides.

Anchorage 20 visitors' moorings (<12m) on lines V and G. Contact Harbour Office ☎ 02 98 04 36 40 or 06 31 93 58 71 prior to arrival. July–Aug 0800–1130, 1700–1930. Mid-Season: daily except Sun 0800–1130, 1700–1900. Low Season: Tues-Sat 0915–1200, 1245–1700.

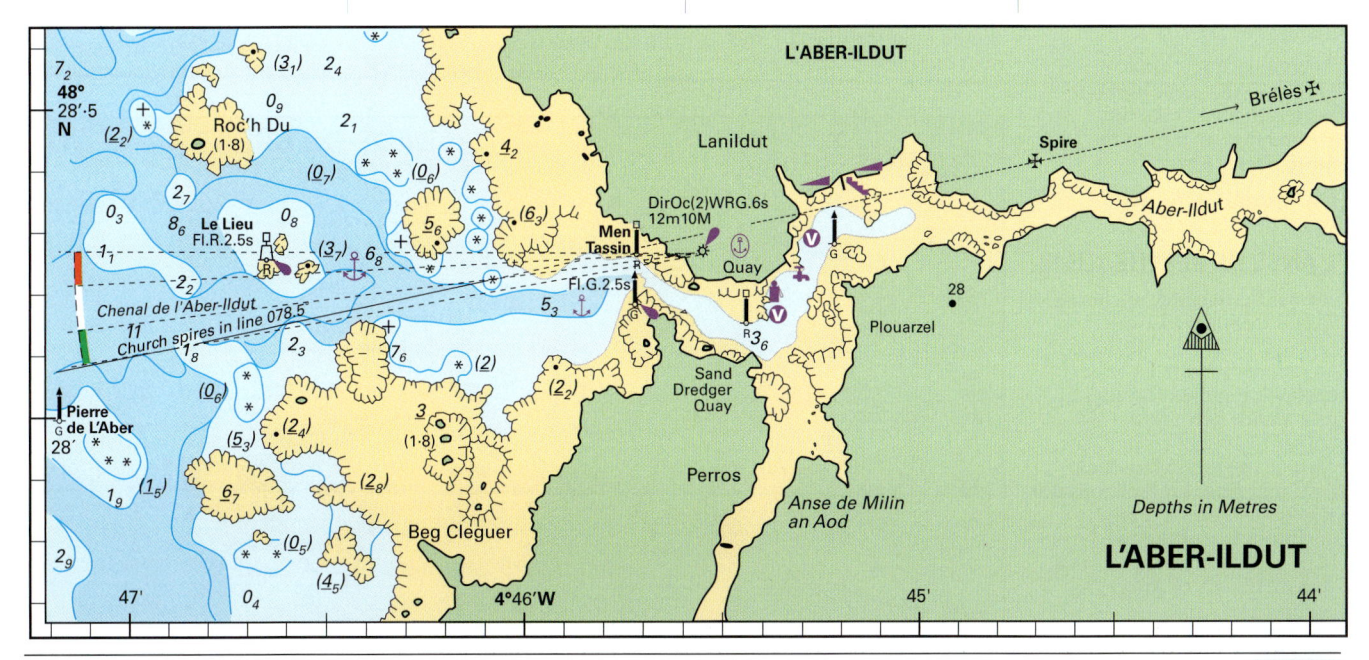

FRANCE – WEST COAST

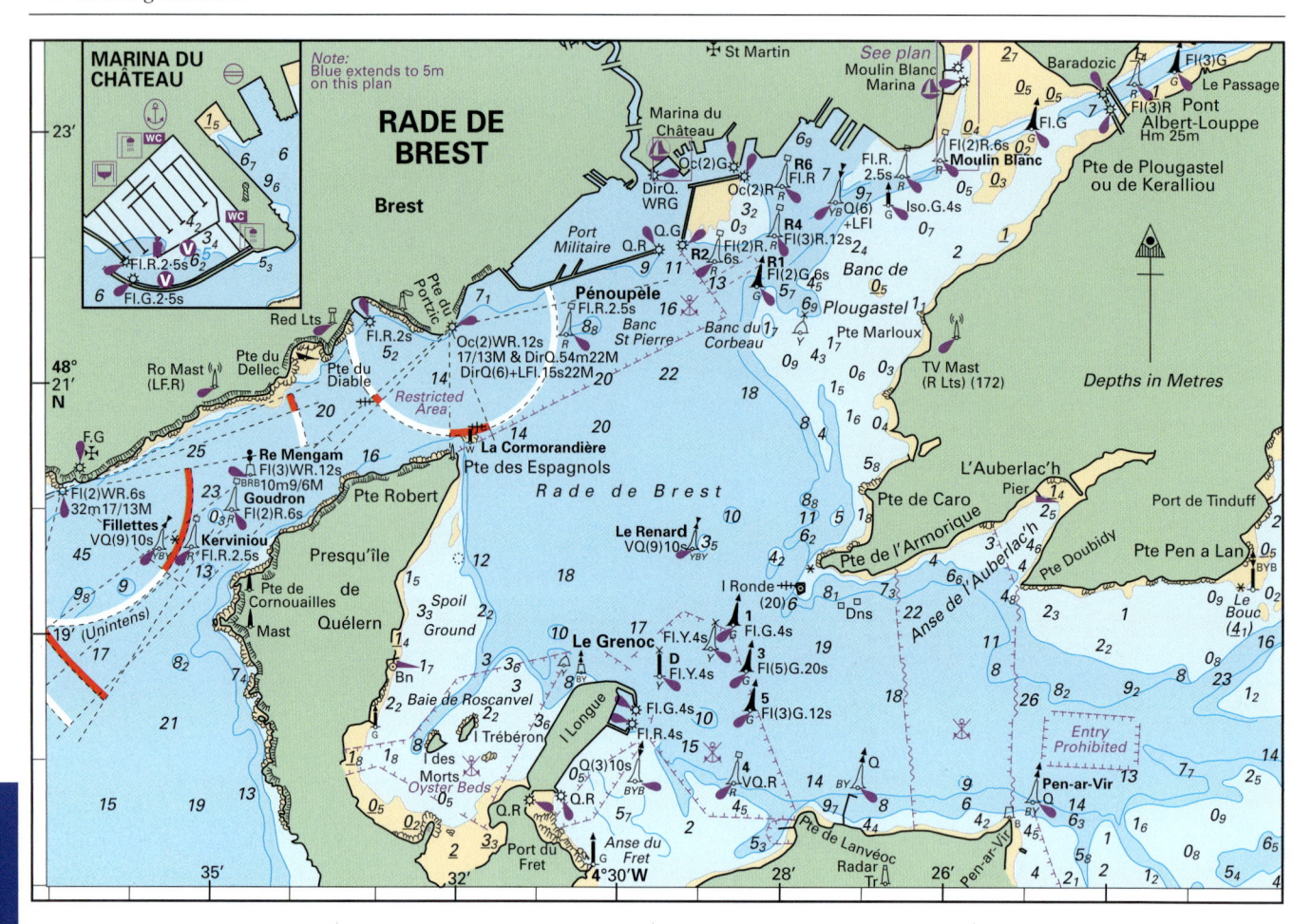

Use of pontoon limited to two hours.

Facilities Water and electricity on pontoon at Combarelle quay. WC, showers, fuel, boatyard, chandlery, supermarket, restaurant.

LE CONQUET
Standard Port Brest
HW +0000   LW +0005
MHWS   MHWN   MLWN   MLWS
−0·2m   −0·2m   −0·1m   0·0m

A picturesque hbr between Kermorvan and Point St Barbe for visiting in settled conditions.

Entrance There are strong cross tides in entrance at springs. Hbr dredged to 2m.

Anchorage Yachts may not anchor in the outer harbour. Vessels that can take the ground may anchor in the inner, drying hbr.

Facilities All stores and restaurants.

L'ANSE DE BERTHEAUME

Anse d'Bertheaume anchorage. Useful stopover to await favourable streams through Goulet de Brest or Le Four channel. Exposed to S and E, give a wide berth to the SW corner to avoid Le Chat rock close to the fort. Many small craft moorings off Plougonvelin with some visitors' buoys, anchor in one of the two bays N of le Chat in 2–3m on sand. Avoid NE part of Anse, foul ground and rocks.

BREST AND THE RADE DE BREST
Standard Port Brest

The Rade de Brest offers an excellent cruising ground with the rivers Élorn and Aulne to explore and many anchorages. Yachts are unwelcome in the Naval and commercial ports.

Approach This is straightforward and well buoyed.

In the Goulet de Brest naval ships and other large vessels have priority. Vessels with a LOA of 25m or greater are not permitted to transit Goulet de Brest without authorization from Brest VTS. Smaller vessels should monitor VHF 24 and obey instructions from patrol boats. Passage through the Goulet may be restricted by military operations.

Brest

• **Marina du Château**
Approach and entrance At night remain in the green sector of the Tour Vige Lt Dir.Q.WRG.24M on shore, by day 344°. Take care to respect the limits of the Military Port to port. Head for conspic G pile at entrance beneath naval signal station on château.

Berthing On pontoon near the outer wall or the most easterly pontoon. Pontoon M reserved for military.

Facilities Fuel, launching and lifting. Some repairs. WiFi. Restaurants, stores and in town centre. Chandleries at Moulin Blanc. Rail and air connections.
☎ HM 02 98 33 12 50.

• **Le Moulin Blanc Marina**
Approach Turn to port after Moulin Blanc R can Fl(2)R.6s and follow buoyed channel.

Berthing On the wave baffles.

Interest Océanopolis-Acquarium close to Moulin Blanc Marina. Ferries to Ouessant and Île Molène.

Facilities All marina and boatyard facilities. Restaurants. Small supermarket. Bus service into Brest. TGV and air connections.
HM ☎ 02 98 02 20 02.

Anchorages There are many delightful anchorages in the

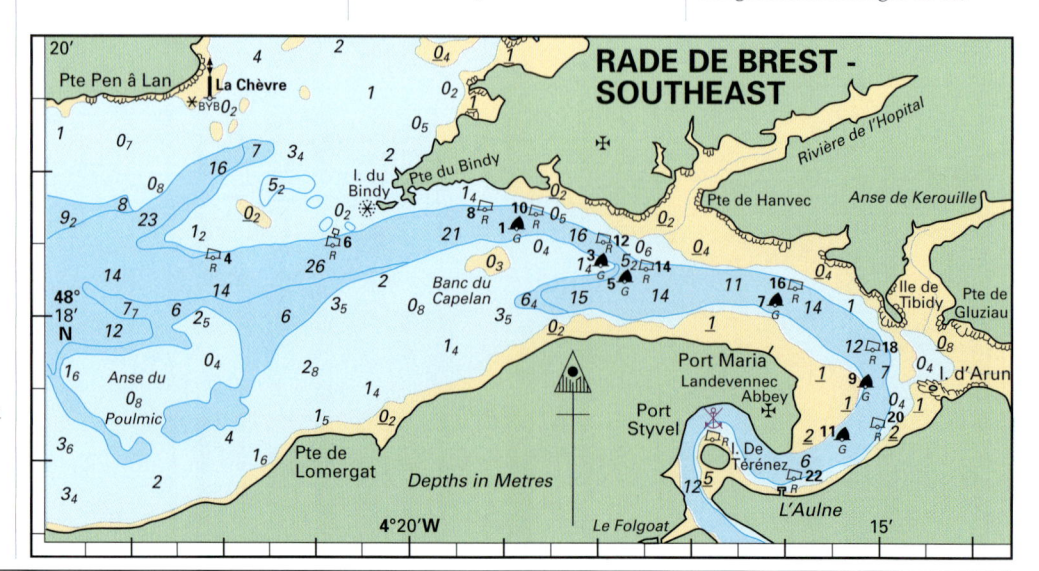

358

Rade de Brest, in some of which there are also moorings.

• **Élorn River** With suitable charts and rise of tide this river may be explored, but only boats that can take the ground will be able to stay at Landerneau 12M. 24m clearance under the br; use the N arch. It is advisable to leave early on the ebb or before HW.

TIDAL STREAMS IN THE GOULET DE BREST

In Passe Sud the flood stream begins ½hr after local LW and flows E; the ebb soon after HW, to W. The ebb sets obliquely between Point des Espagnols and Pt de Dellec. During the ebb an E-running eddy flows inshore along the S side of the Goulet, attaining its greatest strength during the latter half. In the Passe Nord the streams begin about ½hr later. Contrary wind and tide produce a steep sea.

THE TOULINGUET PASSAGE

At Brest +0015 the stream sets S, and at –0550 N. The passage is 3ca wide, but may be made with care by day or night with a fair tide, in clear weather, as the tide sets straight through the fairway at 2–3kn. From N, pass midway between La Louve rock tower and Pohen rock on a course of 156°. Channel has 4·5m.

From the S make W of Les Tas de Pois allowing for the inset into Douarnenez Bay. Hence steer for Toulinguet Lt Oc(3)WR.12s with the Petit Minou LtHo Fl(2)WR.6s a little open to W of Toulinguet Point, 011°. Abreast of Toulinguet rocks at night when St Mathieu Lt is hidden behind them, steer about 335° to pass between Pohen and La Louve tower. When clear to the N of them, round up to E as soon as Portzic LtHo Oc(2)WR.12s comes open from the S side of the Goulet, but if bound for the N channel (Goulet de Brest) hold on for the Minou Lt till well clear to N of the Fillettes, onto which the flood tide sets. There are fair weather anchorages in the Anse de Penhir and Anse de Dinan sheltered NW to E through N after rounding Les Tas de Pois heading S.

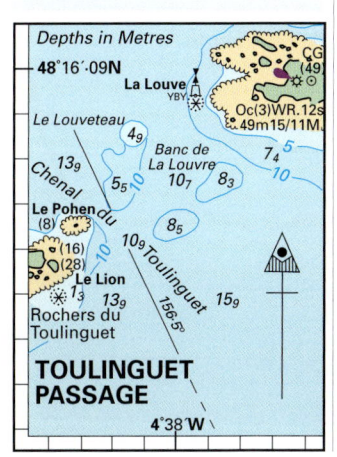

There is much mud exposed at LW and a permanent barrier which covers at half tide between the sand quays and the main town quay.

Anchorages

Sheltered anchorages at Le Passage and St Jean. Lie alongside the quay at Landerneau.

• **Anse de L'Auberlac'h** Excellent anchorage at the end of the bay in 3–5m, equidistant from the shores. Jetty on W bank, dries 1·3m at end of jetty and 2·7m at end of slip. No supplies in village, only a bar.

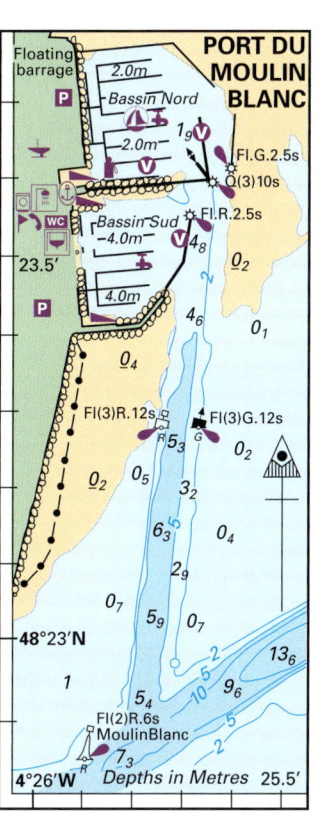

• **Daoulas River** Vessels of 2·7m draught can reach Daoulas at HWS.

• **Anse de Poulimic** Good holding to the E of the Pen-ar-Vir Point, marked by N Card bn of the same name. Avoid oyster beds.

• **Baie de Roscanvel** On W side about half way down prominent headland in 2m (mud) exposed from N through E. Southeast area of bay prohibited anchorage due to French naval activity.

• **River Aulne** Probably the prettiest river running into the Rade with abundant wildlife. The lower reaches of the river are buoyed and there is a good depth of water at all states of the tide to just above the br at Terenez. Air-draught below bridges 21m, that under the electricity cables given as 15m at highest HW on French charts. Above the lock at Guily-Glaz, there is 3m of water to Port Launay, and rather less to Châteaulin. Best water above the lock nearer to port bank. About 1km above Port Launay, unlit stb hand bn, marking underwater mid-channel obstruction, reported as unreliable.

Anchorages Port Styval and on S bank near the creek to Le Folgoat.

Lock Opens local HW–0200 to HW+0130, (HW Brest –0130 to +0200).

Facilities Restaurants at lock, Port Launay, and Châteaulin. Water and bread at Port Launay. Water, electricity and all shops including large supermarket near to pontoon on stb bank as you approach at Châteaulin.

CAMARET-SUR-MER

Standard Port Brest
HW +0010   LW +0015
MHWS MHWN MLWN MLWS
+0·3m +0·2m –0·1m –0·1m

Exceedingly popular with British yachts because of its convenient position. Weak tidal streams within the bay, good beaches. Megaliths.

Approach and Entrance Easy by day; at night remain in white sector of Lt Iso.WG.4s, on N Mole. Avoid fish farms.

Marina Visitors' berths in Port Vauban, the outer marina. Exposed to E winds. Large vessels berth on the wave baffle. By arrangement, visitors may berth on the outer pontoons in Port de Notic.

Anchoring No anchoring in either the hbr or channels. Visitors' buoys to SE of Port Vauban.

Facilities Fuel, WiFi, shops and restaurants in town. Good beaches. HM Port Vauban ☎ 02 98 27 89 31.

MORGAT

Standard Port Brest
HW (sp) –0010 (np) –0005
LW (sp) –0020 (np) –0005
MHWS MHWN MLWN MLWS
–0·5m –0·4m –0·2m 0·0m

Typical French seaside town set in a wide, sandy bay.

Entrance After passing Pte de Morgat make for the Morgat R can Lt buoy.

Anchorage To the N of the Morgat buoy in 2m sheltered except from S and E.

Berthing Leave Morgat buoy to port and enter marina dredged to 2m. Visitors use pontoon extending from a point adjacent to crane and fuel berth

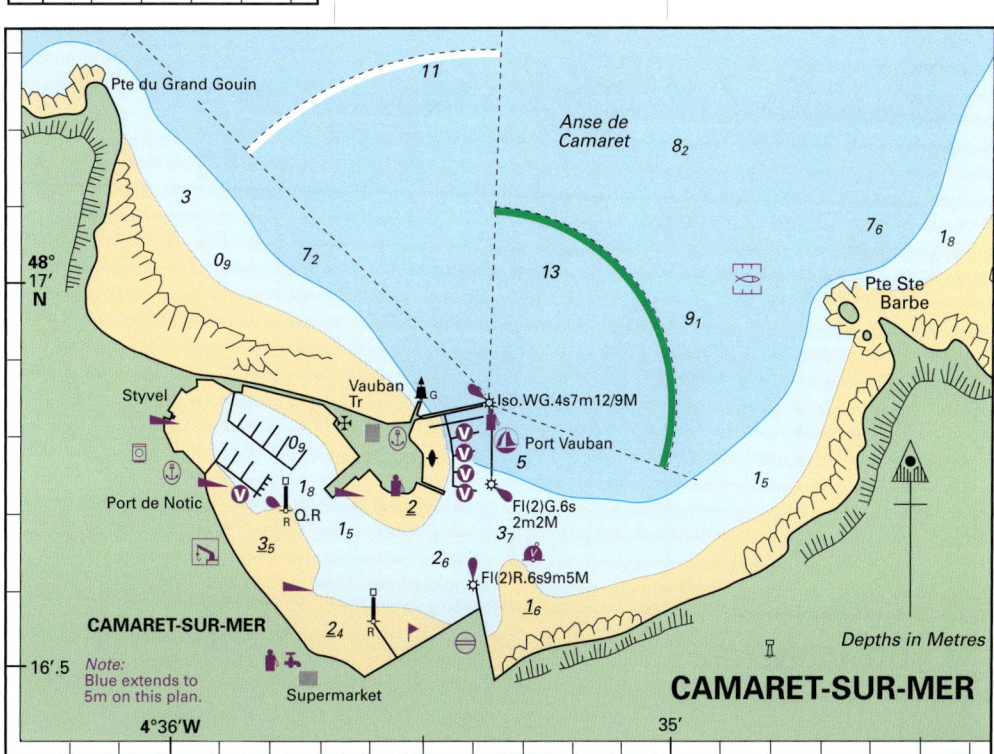

CAP DE LA CHÈVRE
Rounding Cap de la Chèvre beware of uneven bottom as far as Basse Vieille BRB Lt buoy Fl(2)6s.

at right angles to other pontoons. Marina is small and often full.

Facilities All supplies in town.
☎ HM 02 98 27 01 97.

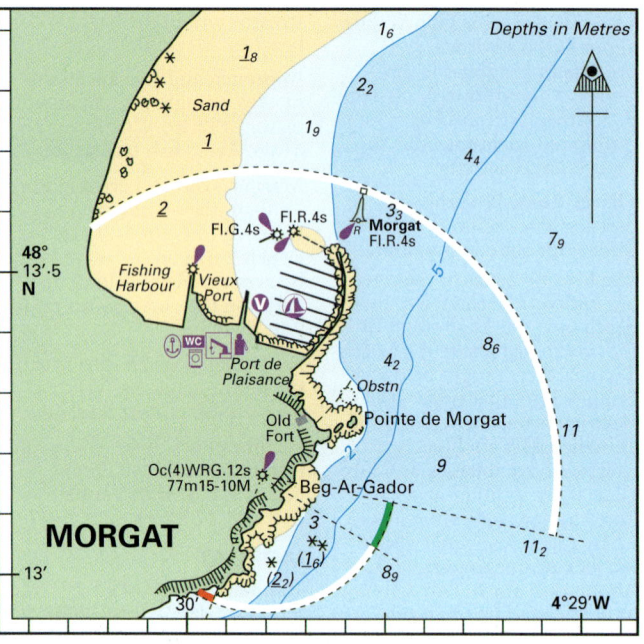

DOUARNENEZ – TRÉBOUL
Standard Port Brest
HW –0010   LW –0015
MHWS MHWN MLWN MLWS
–0·4m –0·4m –0·2m –0·1m

A fascinating spot, 17M E of Pte du Raz. Marina at Tréboul. Maritime museum ashore and afloat at Port Rhu. Megaliths. Beaches.

Approach At night, avoid the two shallow patches Basses Neuve and Basse Veur which are in the red sector of the Tristan Lt Fl(3)WR.12s.

Entrance At all states of the tide.

Berthing Visitors' pontoon to stb before entrance to marina at Tréboul, may be affected by swell.

Facilities 15-tonne travel lift, chandleries, shops, daily market.
☎ HM 02 98 74 02 56.

• **Port Rhu**
30 visitors' berths at Port Rhu. Sill 1·1m above CD. 16·5m headroom at coeff 80. HM ☎ 02 98 92 00 67 for lock times.

Anchorage Yachts are not allowed in fishing hbr. Rade de Guet anchorage is not recommended in north and easterly winds. Anchoring in Port de Rosmeur may be possible by arrangement with HM ☎ 02 98 92 14 85, VHF 12.

ÎLE DE SEIN
An interesting port of call if the weather is settled but chart BA 2351 or SHOM 7423 essential. Approach is best made by the N channel guarded by a lateral buoy, Fl.G.4s. Anchor in 4–6m, sand and rock, 3ca N of Men Brial Lt Ho, or take the ground in SW of hbr or alongside quay on S side. Better visited at neaps and with winds other than from the N. Entrance channel may be buoyed in season.

AUDIERNE AND STE–EVETTE ANCHORAGE
Standard Port Brest
HW –0032   LW –0032
MHWS MHWN MLWN MLWS
–1·8m –1·4m –0·7m –0·3m

A charming, friendly town with a small marina. Also moorings at Ste-Evette. A useful place to

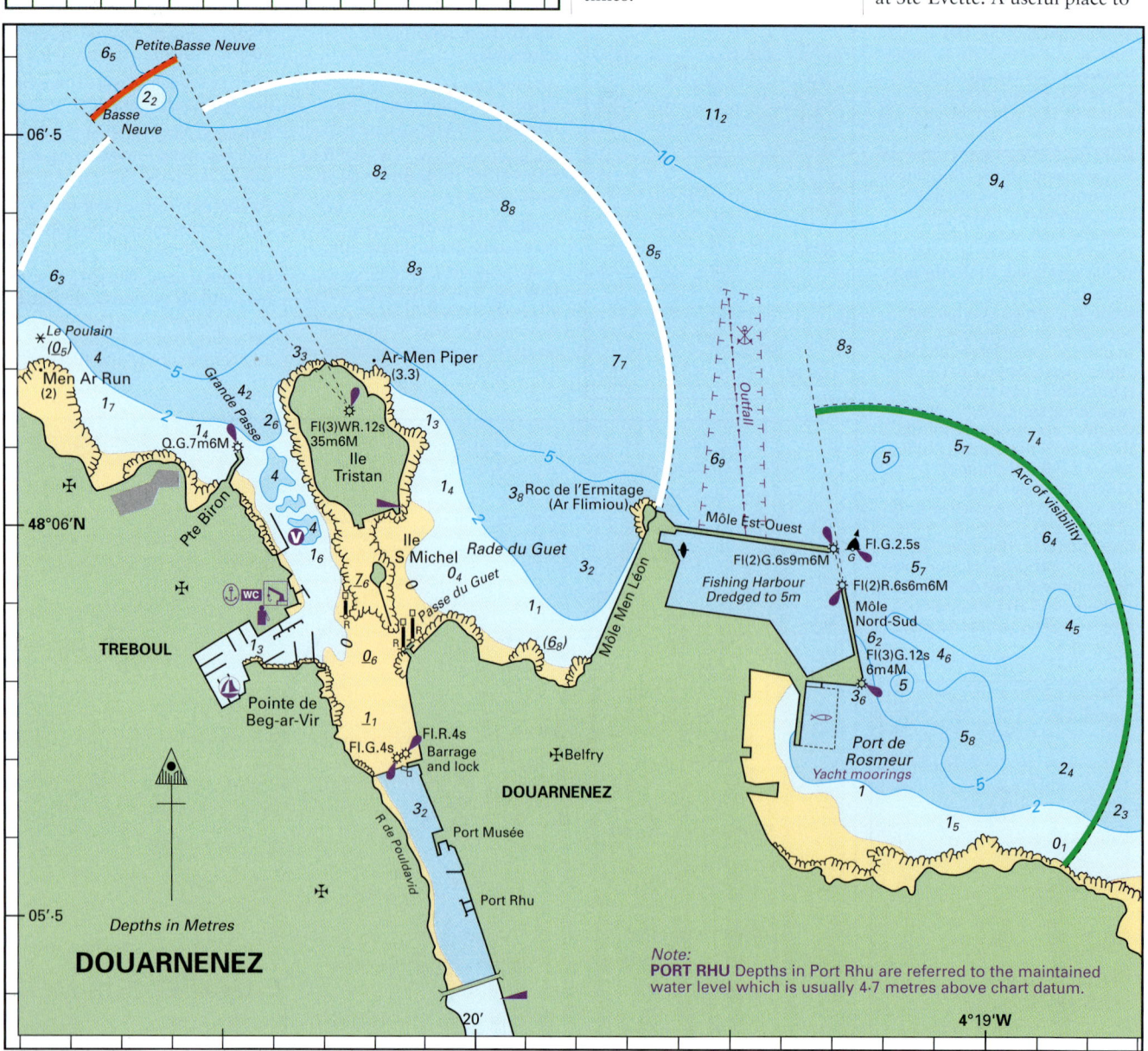

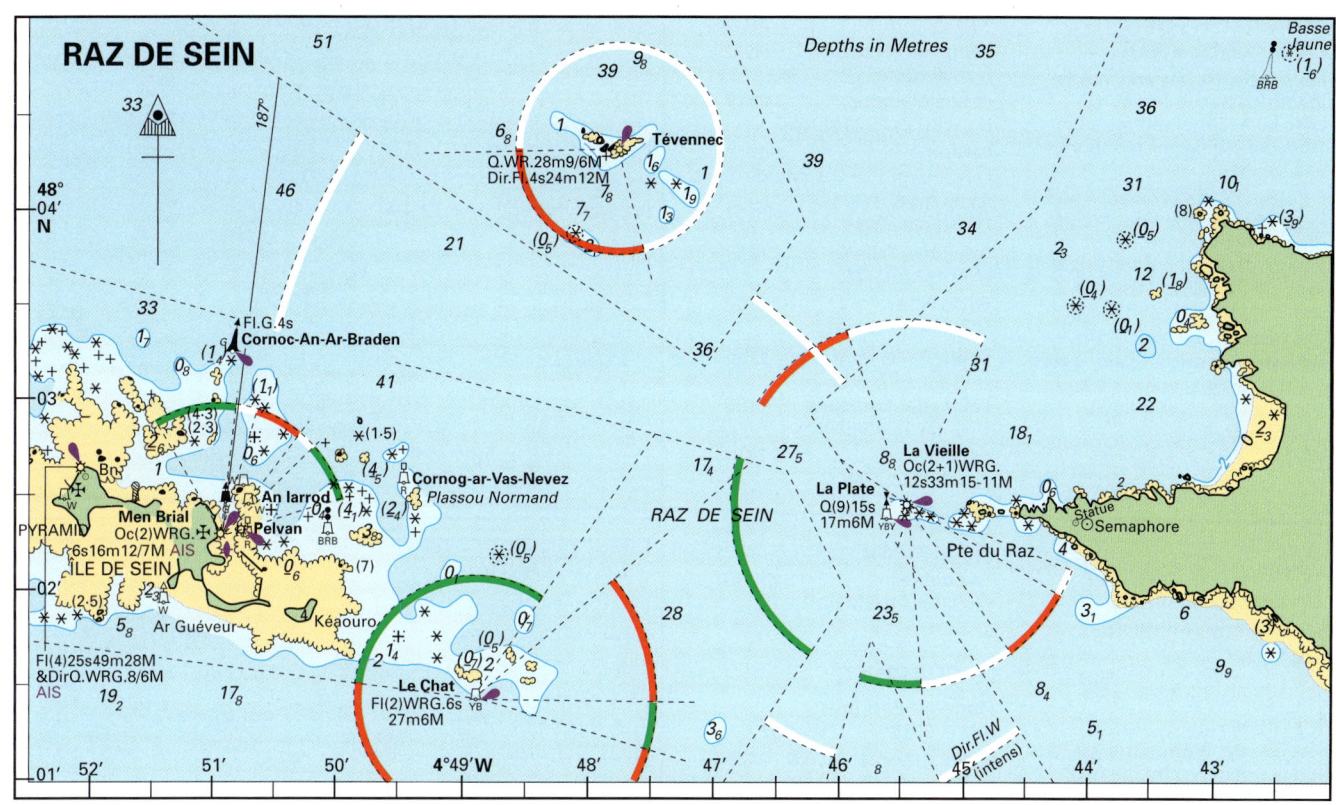

RAZ DE SEIN

Slack water, which lasts for about 30 minutes, is Brest −0100 and Brest +0530. The Raz presents few problems if it is taken at these times and when conditions are calm and visibility is good. Quite moderate winds can produce rough conditions, as can wind against tide or swell. Even when conditions are calm and windless, fighting the tide is time consuming because of the strength of the streams. Keep at least 6ca off Tévennec and a respectable distance off La Platte W Card bn tower.

If coming from the North, a yacht may wait for slack water in the Baie des Trépassés: from the South, use Ste-Evette.

Passage lights	BA No
Île de Sein Main Lt Fl(4)25s28M and DirQ.WRG	0856
Tévennec Q.WR.28m9/6M+ DirFl.4s24m12M	0866
La Vieille Oc(2+1)WRG.12s33m15-11M	0870
La Plate Q(9)15s17m6M	0872
Le Chat Fl(2)WRG.6s27m6M	0862

wait for a fair tide through the Raz.

Approach From N, leave Plateau de Gamelle, marked by two Cardinal buoys, W and S to stb, keeping a safe distance off Le Sillon de Galets. Keep at least ½ca from the mole of Ste-Evette.

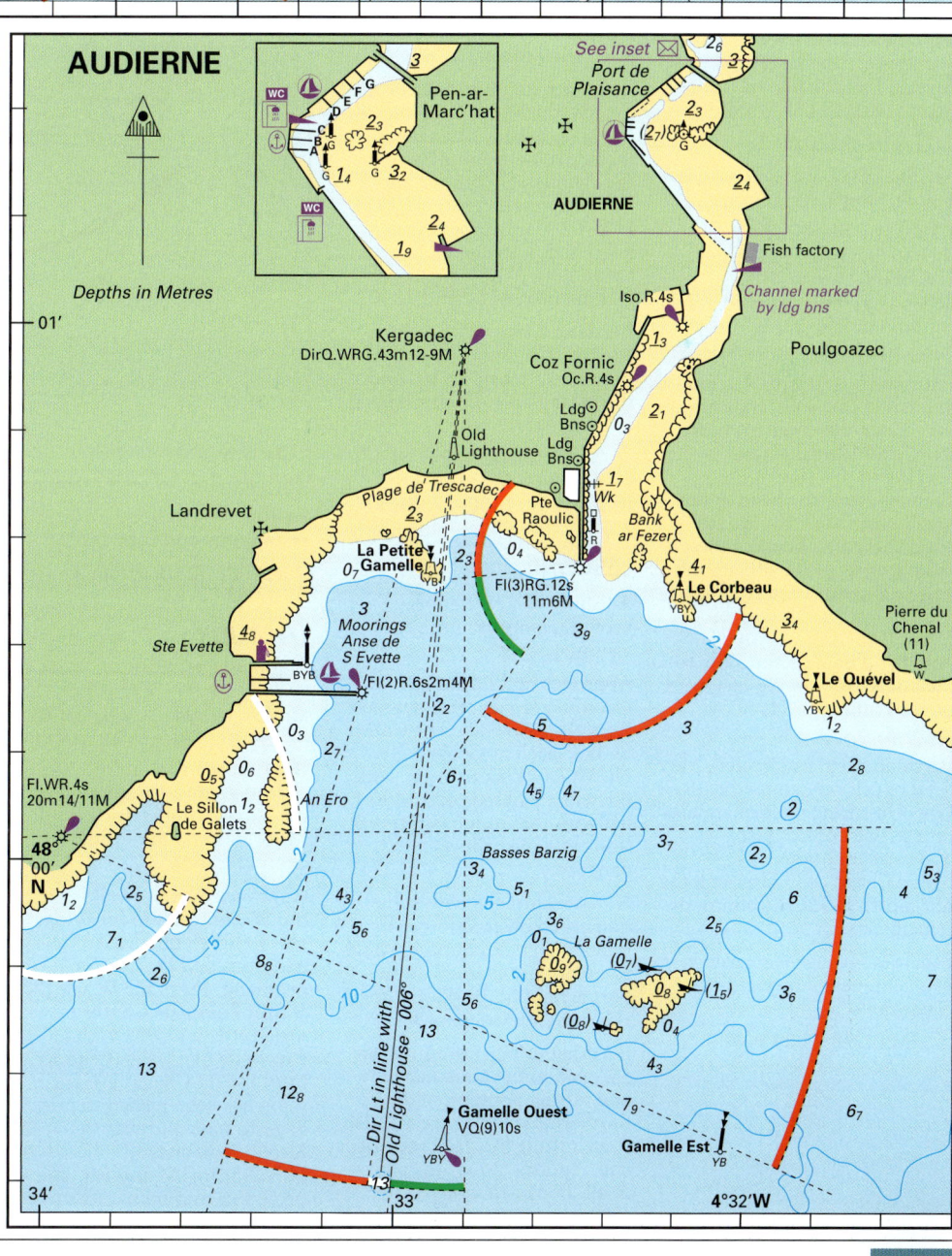

PENMARC'H POINT TO LA GIRONDE RIVER

Penmarc'h lies low and may be identified by the octagonal LtHo 60m high standing 120m from the old tr, which is shorter and smaller.

Between Pte de Penmarc'h and Îles de Glénan the tidal streams are rotary clockwise. SW of Penmarc'h Pte the flood sets N changing to NE and the ebb SE changing to SW Max 1½–2kn. The general direction of the tidal streams offshore along the coast between Penmarc'h and the R Gironde is as follows:

Time and direction

Brest	Brest
HW Slack/S	–0600NW
+0100SW/SE	–0500NE/NW
+0200SW	–0400NNE
+0300SW by W	–0300NE/E
+0400SW by W	–0200E
+0500NW by W	–0100ESE
+0600NW	

Anchorage

- **Ste-Evette** White visitors' buoys, sheltered by the Mole. Those closer to the LB slip are less exposed to the swell. Vedettes use the landing slips. Anchor E of the buoys. Safe, except in strong SE winds.

☎ HM 02 98 70 00 28

Facilities Fuel, water from tap ashore. Shops, restaurants

- **Audierne Marina** Very sheltered marina. Accessible HW–0300 to HW+0100, depending on draught, in good conditions. The bar is dangerous in strong winds.

Entrance Leading marks, red and white chevrons, indicate safe water. On entering, keep 25m off the breakwater, keeping to this side of the channel. After the bend in the breakwater, steer for the stb hand chevrons. Keeping these in line, cross to the other bank and follow this until reaching the fish factory. Now steer towards the slipway on the port-hand bank. Keep close to the boats (3m) on the quay and on the hammerheads of the marina.

Berthing Berth as directed. May need to raft on hammerheads of G+F. On spring tides, there may be a strong current just downstream of the hammerhead of F. Although the hbr mostly dries, the pontoons remain afloat.

Facilities Fuel (at Audierne from garage). Shops and restaurants.

☎ HM 02 98 75 04 93, 06 72 91 70 52

Passage lights	BA No
Pointe de Penmarc'h Fl.5s60m23M	0890
Ils aux Moutons Iso.WRG.2s15–11M AIS	0918
Penfret Fl.R.5s36m21M+Q.11M AIS	0922
Ile de Groix, Pen Men Fl(4)25s60m29M	0962
Goulphar, Belle Ile Fl(2)10s87m27M	1032
Ile du Pillier Fl(3)20s33m29M+Q.R AIS	1152
Petite Foule, Ile D'Yeu Fl.5s56m24M AIS	1176
Pointe des Corbeaux Fl(2+1)R.15s25m20M	1186
Les Baleines Fl(4)15s53m27M	1218
Chassiron, Ile d'Oléron Fl.10s50m28M	1270
La Coubre Fl(2)10s64m28M+Q.R	1290

LE GUILVINEC

Standard Port Brest
HW –0018   LW –0020

MHWS	MHWN	MLWN	MLWS
–1·8m	–1·5m	–0·7m	–0·2m

A crowded fishing hbr and interesting town.

Approach and Entrance From the SW, the buoyed channel is easily identified. Mooring is forbidden in the approach and the channel. Do not use the E or SE channels before HW–0200 unless sea-state is good and in strong SE winds. Speed limit 2kn. No entry or exit between 1600 and 1830.

Berthing 8 places for visiting yachts, four on buoys and 4 on pontoons in the port beyond the fishing port. Limited space to manoeuvre.

☎ /VHF HM 02 98 58 14 47, 06 63 39 14 47 (Mon–Fri 0830–1200, 1330–1730); VHF 12.

LESCONIL

A fishing village that now provides more facilities for visiting yachts.

Approach and Entrance Not recommended in strong winds from the SW to SE. The transit of 355° Men ar Groas Fl(3)WRG.12s or by day with the white painted rock on its left with the church bell tr will lead clear of shallows and dangers.

Narrow entrance with some unmarked obstructions will require close attention in rough weather. The channel to the port is buoyed. Beware of the fish farm SE Mes-Cas (R).

Berthing A finger pontoon on SW wall of the main harbour and rafting pontoon in the northern corner. There are also some rafting buoys in the north end. Approx. 35 visitor places in all. Buoys 3m quay 1·5m.

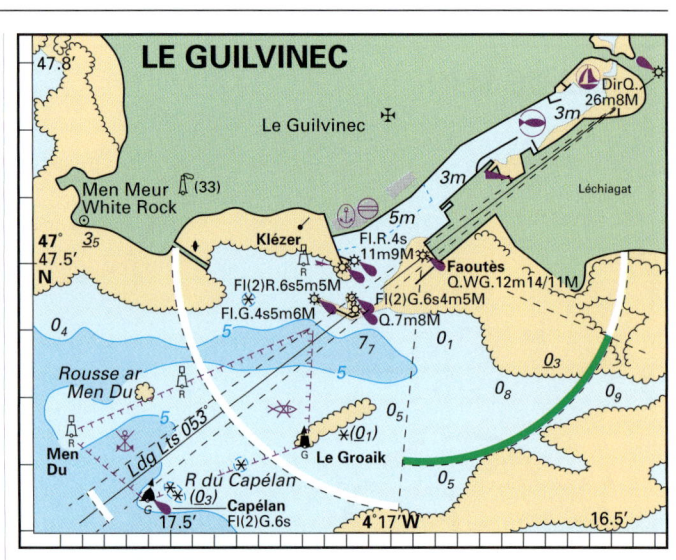

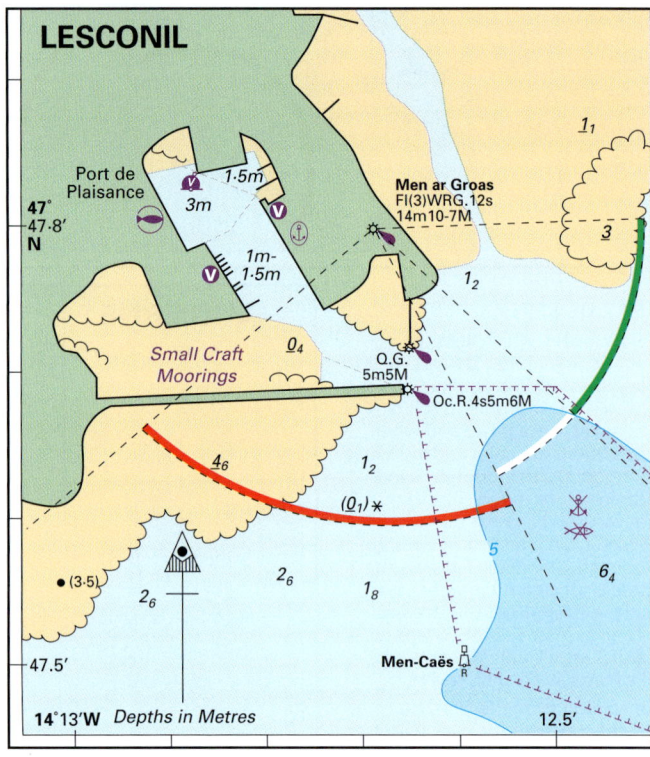

Facilities Chandlery, restaurants and supplies.

☎ HM 06 72 04 55 80, 06 47 82 77 12

LOCTUDY

Standard Port Brest
HW –0020   LW –0025

MHWS	MHWN	MLWN	MLWS
–2·1m	–1·7m	–0·9m	–0·4m

Bar Outside the entrance the S part of the bar has about 1½m; the N part almost dries. Moorings in 3·5m inside; a charming spot.

Approach Strong swell from the W can result in breaking seas between the Îles Aux Moutons and the Lesconil headland. From the W, use the transit Pointe de Combrit Oc(2)WR.6s12/9M with La Pyramide Oc(3)12s (Benodet), until Bse du Chenal E Card buoy has been passed to port. Steer to pass mid-way between Karek-Saoz bn tr Fl.R.2·5s3m1M and Ru unlit G bn tr, to avoid rocks close to these two marks. The port is easily identified by the black and white chequered Le Perdrix Tr.

Entrance Leave No.2 R can buoy Fl(2)R.6s that marks the entrance to Loctudy close to port. At No.3 G con buoy, Fl(3)G.12s, steer towards the fish quay to port, then alter course to NW for the marina. When the fishing fleet returns, between 1630 and 1830, engines must be used in the channel and the hbr.

Berthing Ebb runs at 3kn. Visitors' berths on A pontoon and inside the wave-baffle. Hbr dory usually allocates a berth. Visitors' buoys N of the marina. Marina dredged 2013.

Facilities Good marina. WiFi. Boatyard. Bicycles for the use of visitors. Shops and restaurants. Important port for langoustines. Rail and bus connections for Pont L'Abbé.

☎ HM 02 98 87 51 36.

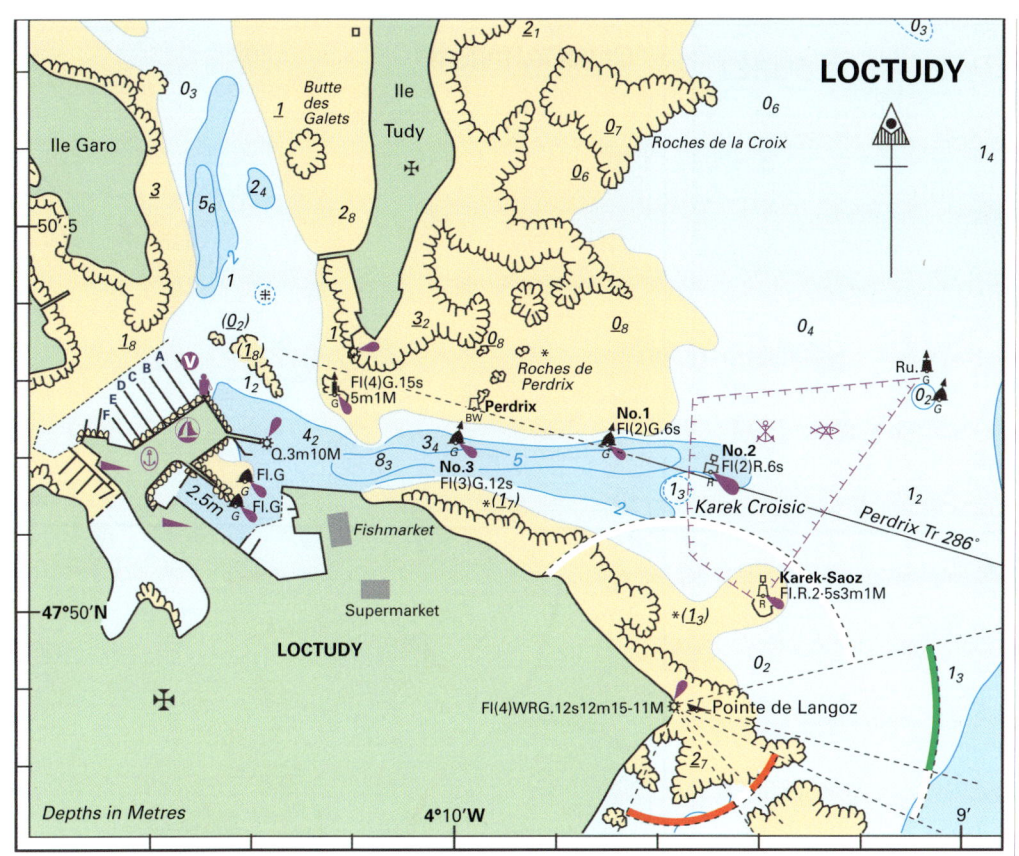

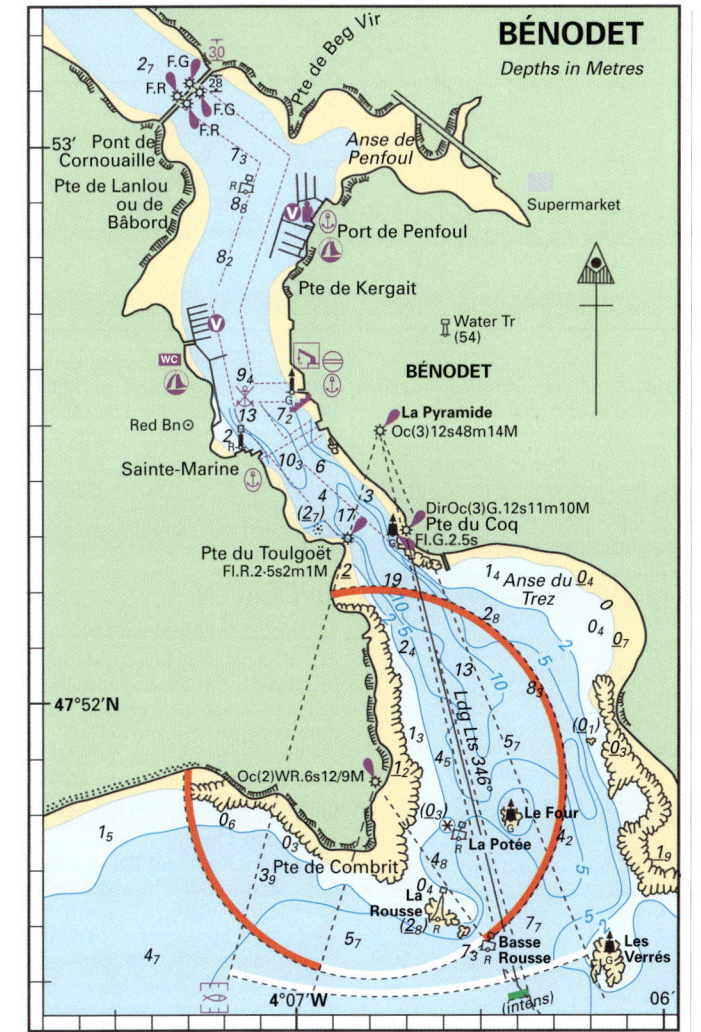

① HM Ste Marine 02 98 56 38 72; Penfoul 02 98 57 05 78.

PORT LA FORÊT
See plan on next page
Standard Port Brest
HW −0020   LW n/a
MHWS MHWN MLWN MLWS
−2·0m −1·6m −0·8m −0·3m

A picturesque village with a large marina.

Approach Beware many rocks off Beg Meil on W point of La Fôret Bay. Keep to W of centre line of bay leaving (difficult to identify) Le Score stb bn to stb. Identify Cap Coz. There are four conspic W waiting buoys S of it.

Note shoal patch 0·9m between waiting buoys and Cap. No entry at LWS.

Entrance Round Cap Coz following the channel marked by R and B buoys or bns. Leave long pontoon to port and near inner end turn to stb to enter marina. Visitors' pontoon facing.

Facilities Excellent. Fuel, boatyard, sailmaker, mechanical and electrical repairs, WiFi and chandlery. Shops, restaurants, bar and small grocers. Bus services to Quimper and Concarneau.

① HM 02 98 56 98 45.

CONCARNEAU
See plan on next page
Standard Port Brest
HW −0020   LW −0025
MHWS MHWN MLWN MLWS
−1·9m −1·5m −0·7m −0·2m

A splendid walled town built by Vauban enclosing the fishing hbr and yacht marina.

Approach From S, to clear the Corven de Trévignon and Soldats do not let Point de la Jumet W pyramid bear less than 005°; at night keep in the intensified sector of the Ldg Lts. When Point de la Jumet is abeam bring the Ldg Lts (front Q.14m13M, rear Q) in line, 029°. By day the front Ldg mark is a W tr on the quay outside a small chapel with a dark roof. The rear mark will be seen over the top of a large block of flats. This leads between Basse du Chenal bn to port and Le Cochon tr, Fl(3)WRG.12s, to stb. Continue until past Men Fall buoy, Fl(2)G.6s until Maison Feu de Lanriec Lt Q.G becomes visible.

Entrance Steer towards Maison Feu de Lanriec Lt Q.G. until channel to the marina, marked by Le Médée Fl(3)R.12s opens to port.

Berthing Visitors on D pontoon or inside the wave break. Berths nearer the hammerhead exposed to wash from fishing vessels. Many berths occupied by boats of Glénans sailing

---

BÉNODET AND ODET RIVER
Standard Port Brest
HW −0020   LW −0025
MHWS MHWN MLWN MLWS
−1·7m −1·4m −0·6m −0·1m

An attractive river with marinas on both banks near the entrance. The river upstream of Bénodet deserves exploration. At Pte de Kersabiec the current can run at 4–6kn. Sound signals are required from boats at these bends in the river. Buoyage extends to Quimper, with a minimum depth in the channel of 2m up to Lanroz, above which it is too shallow for most yachts. Low br just downstream of Quimper.

Approach and Entrance The transit 346° on the Pte du Coq DirOc(3)G.12s11m10M and La Pyramide Oc(3)12s48m14M leads clear of all dangers. Beware, sea can break off the Pointe de Mousterin in SW winds.

Anchorage Outside the channel in Anse de Trez. Anchoring forbidden in the fairway between Pte de Coq and Anse de Penfoul. Private moorings downstream of both marinas and above the br (clearance 30m). Anchorages upstream of the br: Anse de Kérandraon (stb), Anses de Combrit and Kérautren (port). Narrow inlet to stb, just downstream of Lanroz. There are a few moorings on W bank by Lanroz.

Berthing Tidal flows can be very strong through both marinas. If necessary, wait on a mooring for slack water. Ste-Marine, visitors on pontoon A and the hammerheads of other pontoons. Penfoul, visitors on the wave baffle.

Interest Quimper upstream. Moorings downstream of Baie de Kerogan, continue by dinghy.

Facilities All facilities expected of a modern marina. Shops and restaurants. Fuel at Penfoul.

363

The Cruising Almanac

PORT LA FORÊT

CONCARNEAU

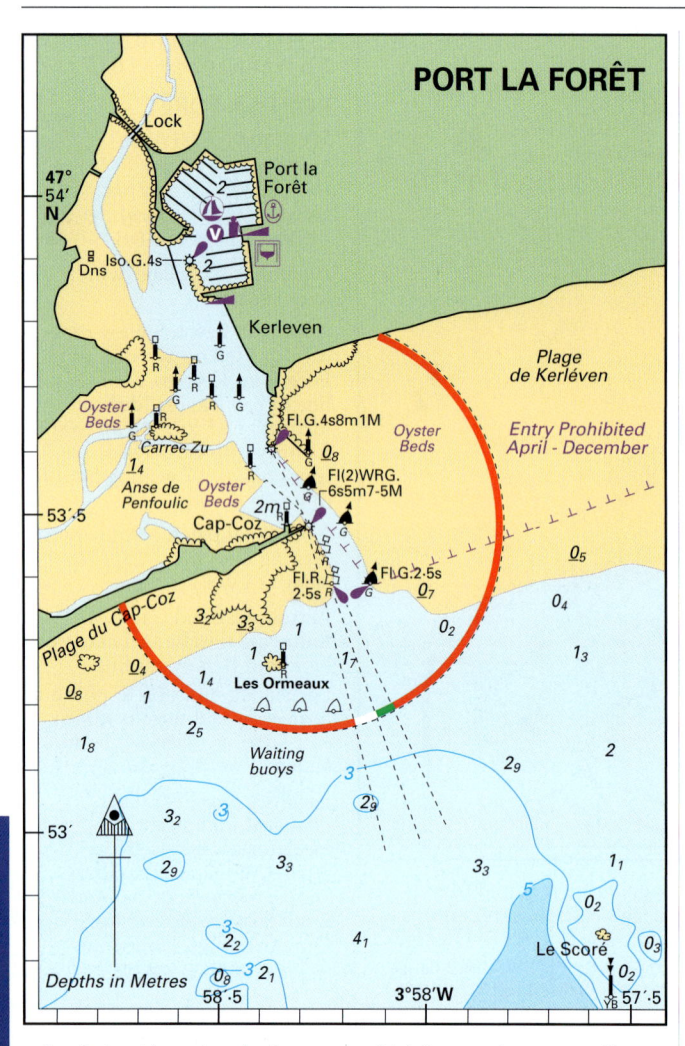

FRANCE – WEST COAST

school. Avoid marina during strong onshore winds.

Anchorage Anchoring within the limits of the port authority is no longer permitted. The quays within the inner harbour are reserved for fishing and commercial vessels.

Facilities Fuel, shops, restaurants. Rail and bus connections. Mkt daily (am), outdoors Monday and Friday.

☎ HM 02 98 97 57 96.

ÎLES DE GLÉNAN

Standard Port Brest

Penfret

HW (sp) –0030 (np) –0005
LW (sp) –0030 (np) –0020

MHWS	MHWN	MLWN	MLWS
–2·0m	–1·6m	–0·8m	–0·3m

A picturesque archipelago, well sheltered in summer, that has the only coral beach in Europe. It is the home of the famous Centre Nautique de Glénans Sailing School, whose boats are in evidence everywhere among the Is. To explore the interior of the archipelago, a large-scale chart is essential. Between the islands there are rocks and drying patches. With care, and suitable conditions of weather and tide, an exploration can be very rewarding.

Approach A safe approach can be made from the N to Île de Penfret, the eastern Is, recognised by the LtHo Fl.R.5s, which has no dangers until within ½ mile.

Anchorages Anchoring is permitted off all the islands. Often crowded, especially at weekends. Fenced nature area on St-Nicolas to protect rare narcissus.

• **St-Nicolas** The easiest, but exposed to the N, is N of the bay formed by St Nicolas and Ile de Bananec. La Pie, isolated danger bn Fl(2)6s3M, marks a drying rock to the W side of the entrance to the bay. W visitors' mooring buoys.

• **La Chambre** (South of St-Nicolas) The most sheltered of all anchorages, but exposed to swell in southerlies.

From the E, follow the W coast of Île de Penfret until off the coral beach about halfway down the W shore. From here, above half tide, steer for houses on Île St-Nicolas, about 260°.

From the N, leaving Le Pie isolated danger bn Fl(2)6s3M, follow a course of 135° until abeam of the E card bn on the SE corner of Île de Bananec.

From the SE, the leading line 311°, gable end of large Ho on Île St-Nicolas with the NE edge of fort on Île Cigogne.

From the W, after half flood, as part of the channel dries, the Chenal des Bluiniers, Penfret LtHo in line with le Broc'h N Card bn tr 088°. With a sufficient rise of tide, this transit may be followed into the W end of the anchorage, depending on draught.

W visitors' buoys closer to the Is. Anchoring permitted outside fairway.

Facilities In season, two restaurants on St Nicolas, reservations advised. Weather forecast. No water or supplies.

Cruising eastwards from Concarneau there are six small hbrs which may be visited in settled weather. They are all protected by bars which vary in position and should only be entered with the help of the RCC Pilotage Foundation's *Atlantic France* or *Pilote Cotier 5A* by Alain Rondeau. The best known of these harbours to cruising yachtsmen are the Aven and Bélon rivers, details of which are given below.

The other four harbours are:

• **Brigneau** a half tide port for 5/6 visitors, entry on 329°–339°. Not in strong W and SW winds.

• **Merrien** very pretty. Outer pool on six buoys (<9m) but limited shelter.

• **Doëlan** In outer harbour, eight fore and aft moorings, marked P1–4 <12m. Allocated by HM in season, 1630–2100. Inner harbour dries. Access dangerous in strong SW winds.

• **Le Pouldu** bar shifts and strong streams. Small marina on E bank.

RIVER AVEN

Tidal data as Îles de Glénan

The River is very beautiful and in calm conditions offers shelter at Port Manec'h. Access is dangerous in SE winds. The 3½M channel to Pont Aven is marked with unlit buoys. All quays on the river dry at LW.

Approach The bay into which the Rivers Aven and Bélon flow is marked to p by Port Manec'h Lt Ho Oc(4)WRG.12s and to stb G unlit buoy on E shore. At night remain in W sector to clear lying dangers to SE.

Anchorages

• **Port Manec'h** Five visitors' moorings at Port Manec'h 1ca off breakwater or anchor to E of moorings in greater depths. Small shop up hill. ☎ 06 82 44 28 33.

364

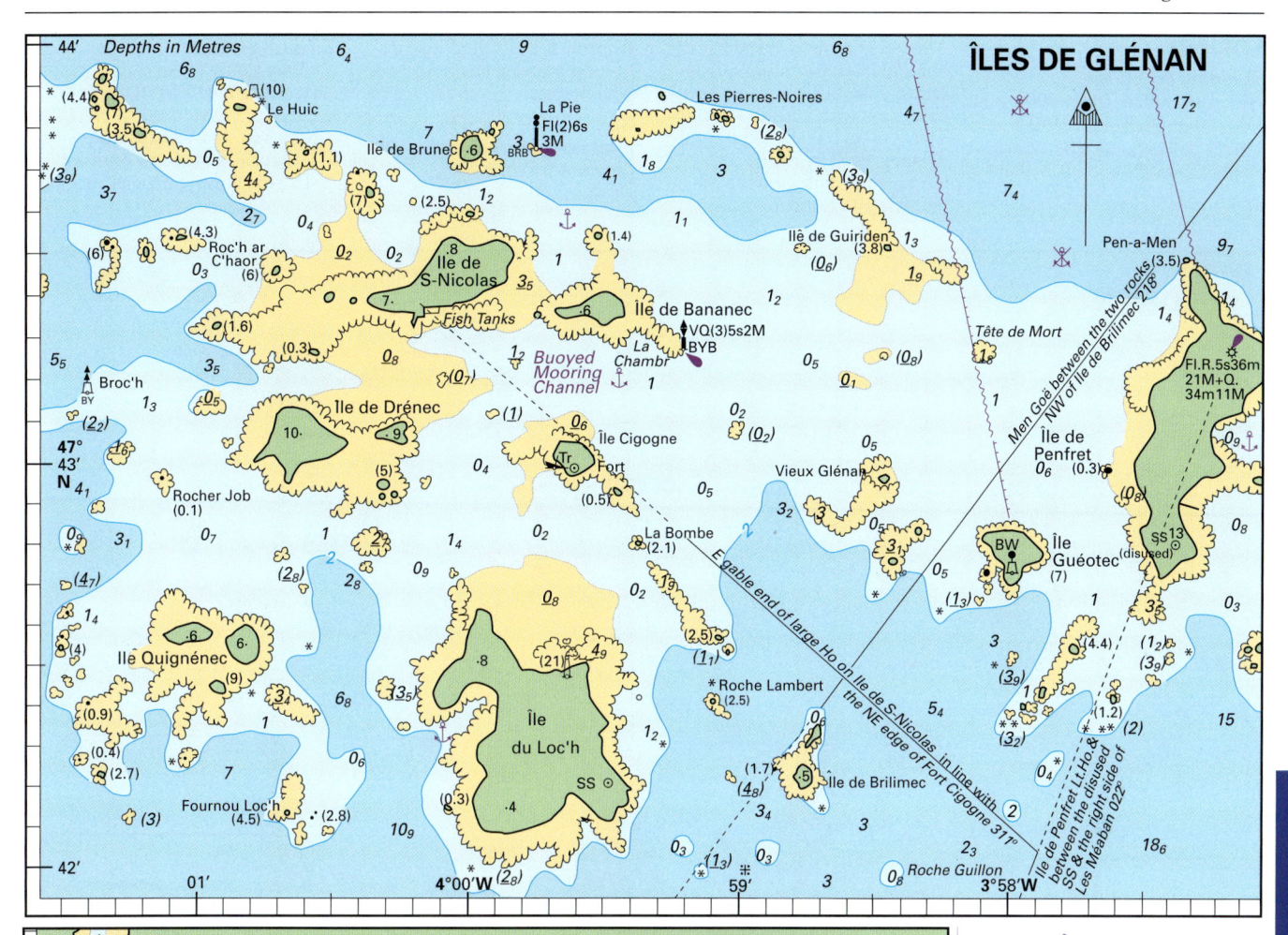

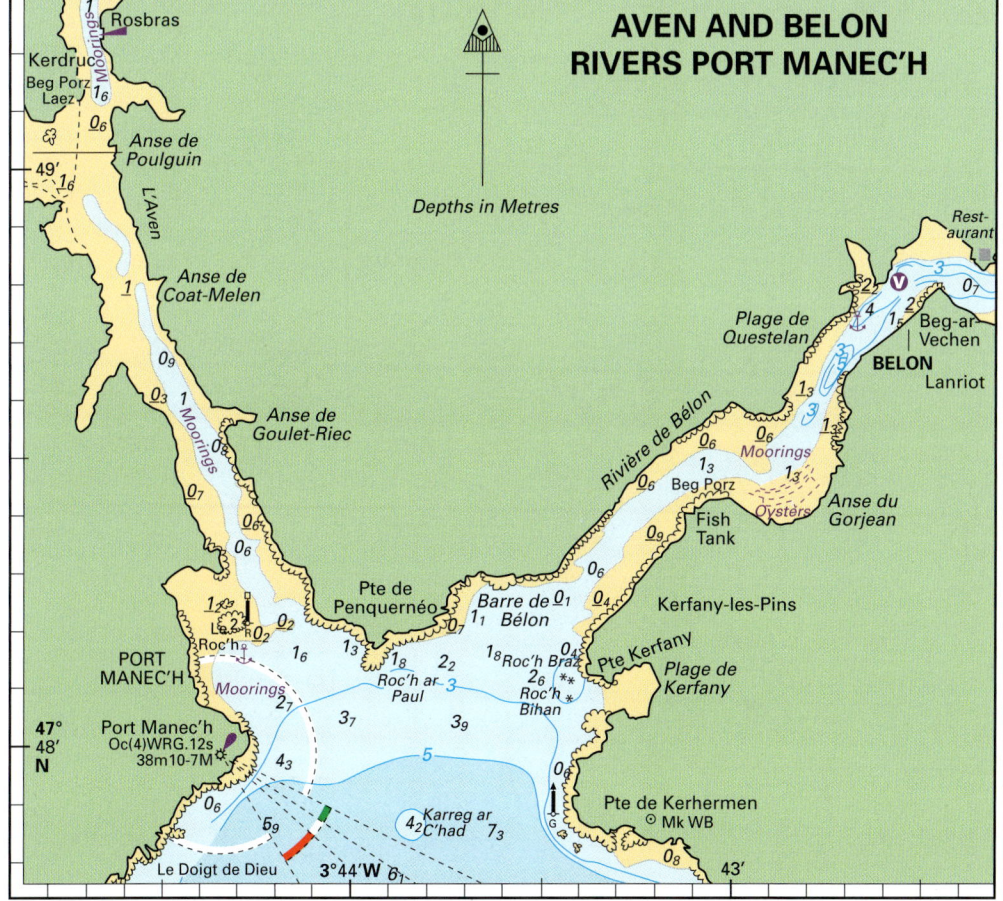

ÎLES DE GLÉNAN

RIVER BÉLON

Tidal data as Îles de Glénan

The entrance is open to SW, and the bar which dries 1·5m is much more exposed than that of the River Aven and impassable in bad weather. There is an inner bar, same depth, abreast the first bend in the river, ½M inside the entrance. Beautiful scenery and Bélon oysters.

Approach Leave the bn on Bec-Lerzou rock off Point Kerhermen to stb, and steer to pass ½ca off the next point, Point Kerfany, on the stb side (caution off-lying rocks).

Entrance The channel then crosses to the N shore, whence bring Port Manec'h Lt to bear 240° astern until abreast next point to stb, where the channel turns somewhat S of E and then 030°; when the next bend comes open to stb, round the point, keeping close to moorings and proceed thereafter in mid-stream.

Anchorage Moor fore and aft to either dumb-buoys to port on entry downstream of Bélon, or to smaller fore and aft buoys at Bélon Lanriot in 2–3·5m rafting if necessary. No marked fairway through anchorage at Lanriot. Some room to anchor at neaps below moorings. Quay dries 1·7m. Oyster beds above Bélon. Stream runs 2kn on the flood and 3kn on the ebb. Restaurant at Lanriot. Bélon oysters.

- **Kerdruc** Further fore and aft moorings (rafting) in varying depths may be available upstream of the bar ☏ 06 32 21 68 01.

- **Rosbras en Riec sur Bélon** Fore and aft moorings. No official visitors' moorings, rafting alongside for one night may be possible. Flood 2kn, ebb 3kn ☏ 02 98 06 91 04.

- **Pont Aven** Drying berths on quays; best is on last straight below footbridge.

Interest Pont Aven where Gaugin painted.

The Cruising Almanac

FRANCE – WEST COAST

365

The Cruising Almanac

LORIENT

Standard Port Brest
HW (sp) −0024 (np) −0000
LW (sp) −0028 (np) −0015

MHWS	MHWN	MLWN	MLWS
−1·9m	−1·5m	−0·7m	−0·3m

A major commercial and fishing hbr and an outstanding sailing centre. Previously a major naval base, now with laid-up warships. The approach is sheltered from Atlantic swell by the Ile de Groix. Ferry link between all marinas and Lorient.

Approach Both the Passe de l'Ouest and the Passe Sud are well marked.

Berthing There are four marinas in the hbr with facilities for visitors.

To stb on entry:
- **Port Louis** In Anse de Driasker 0·4M to stb after Citadel. Leave three G con buoys to stb. Visitors and reception on second pontoon to stb after fishing boat pontoons.

FRANCE – WEST COAST

366

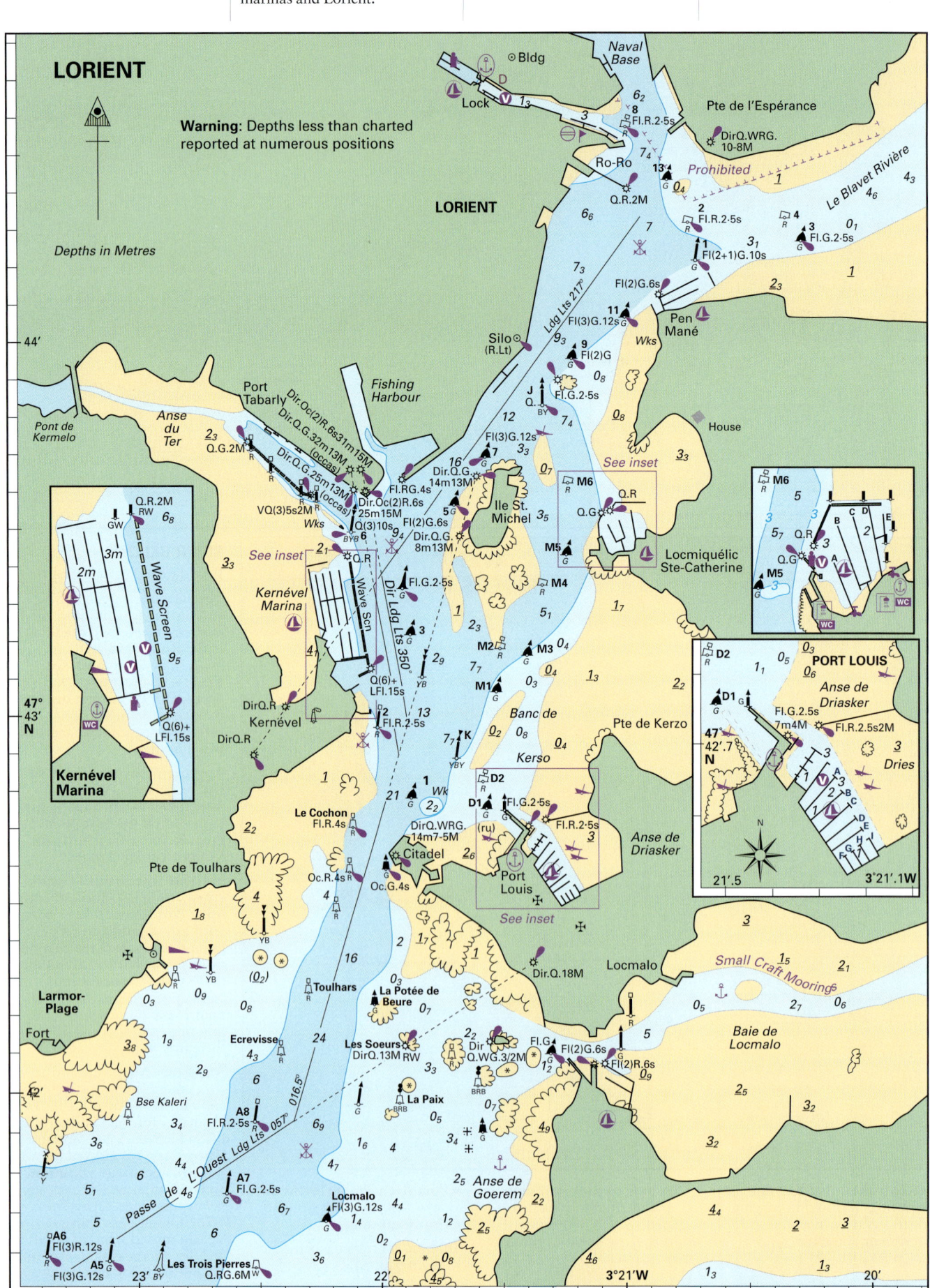

Facilities Shops and restaurants in Port Louis. Supermarket between Port Louis and Locmiquélic. Bicycles available for visitors' use. Fuel at Kernével. WiFi. Mkt Sat.

Interest Port Louis Citadel and its Museums.

✆ HM 02 97 82 59 55.

• **Locmiquélic Ste-Catherine** Channel to stb of Île St-Michel. Entrance NE of M5 G con buoy. Visitors on pontoon A.

Facilities Fuel, WiFi, shops, supermarket towards Port Louis. Mkt Fri. Some bars and restaurants near marina.

✆ HM 02 97 33 59 51.

To port on entry:
• **Kernével** The largest marina in the river, 0·7M to port beyond the Citadel. The entrance is at the N end of the marina. Visitors' berth in the northern section of the marina. On entry, the first section of the inside of the wave baffle is reserved for catamarans, visiting yachts may also berth beyond this and on the pontoon to stb.

Facilities Fuel. 45-tonne lift. Restaurant. Some shops at Larmor-Plage. Bus service to Larmor Plage. Chandlery. WiFi.

✆ HM 02 97 65 48 25.

• **Lorient** After passing Kernével Marina leave Île St-Michel to stb. The entrance to Lorient is to port after Pen Mané marina to stb. Beware of ferries. Max speed in outer harbour 3kn. Contact capitainerie on arrival. Visitors' pontoon at head of the inlet, to port below the br. (Dredged to 2·5m.) Access to inner basin; HW±0030, depending on coefficient, only during the day. Depth in basin, 2·5m. Sill dries 1m. Contact capitainerie on arrival.

Facilities Mobile crane. Chandleries, boatyards. Shops and restaurants. Rly. HM and lock ✆ 02 97 21 10 14.

Interest Cité de Voile Eric Tabarly, Musée Sous Marin and Sous Marin Flore. Ferries to Groix.

PORT TUDY ÎLE DE GROIX

Standard Port Brest
HW (sp) –0025 (np) –0000
LW (sp) –0025 (np) –0015
MHWS MHWN MLWN MLWS
–1·8m –1·4m –0·6m –0·2m

A small hbr affording shelter in 3m, but some swell in NE winds in avant port

Entrance Available in all weathers; use the transit of the LtHo on the N and E jetties of the hbr. Rocky promontories to the E of the entrance marked by N and E Card buoys. Mooring buoy reserved for the French Navy in the N of the hbr. Ferries have priority.

Berthing Lie to buoys in outer harbour, on fingers on the first two pontoons in the inner harbour, or raft on hammerheads. Charges from midday. Locked inner basin, HW±0200 unless coefficient very low.

Facilities Showers. WiFi. Restaurants near hbr, shops up the hill in town.

✆ HM 02 97 86 54 62 (No reservations).

ÉTEL RIVER

Standard Port Brest
HW (sp) –0010 (np) +0020
LW (sp) +0030 (np) +0010
MHWS MHWN MLWN MLWS
–2·1m –1·6m –0·6m –0·2m

The entrance is a few miles SE of Lorient, with moving sandbanks and drying bar which varies in depth and position. Entrance is forbidden at night and inadvisable on the ebb.

Approach Not before Brest HW–0300; from a position to the south of the entrance call *Étel Signal Station* VHF 13 or ✆ 02 97 55 35 59 for entry instructions. Entrance not advised in strong on-shore winds or swell. Semaphore signals; Cross-bar. No vessels may enter or leave. Black Ball: Vessels <8m may not enter or leave. Red flag: No entry or exit due to lack of water. Do not use leading marks until over the bar.

Entrance After crossing the bar, follow the buoyed channel. Then keep to middle or river. Marina to stb.

Berthing Yachts usually met by dory and directed to berth. Tidal flows weaker in marina.

Anchorage Above marina or off Magouer, not recommended because of strong tidal streams, 4–5kn. Anchoring prohibited offshore within ½M centred on LtHo near SS, Oc(2)WRG.6s.

Facilities Shops and restaurants. Chandleries. Fuel.

✆/VHF HM 02 97 55 46 62, *Mobile* 06 83 99 92 39, VHF 13 – according to tide. Out of season Tuesday–Friday and Saturday mornings.

PORT MARIA

Standard Port Brest
HW (sp) –0025 (np) +0010
LW (sp) –0025 (np) –0015
MHWS MHWN MLWN MLWS
–1·7m –1·4m –0·7m –0·2m

Drying hbr. Except in an emergency, forbidden to yachts. Entrance dangerous in high swell from SW to SE.

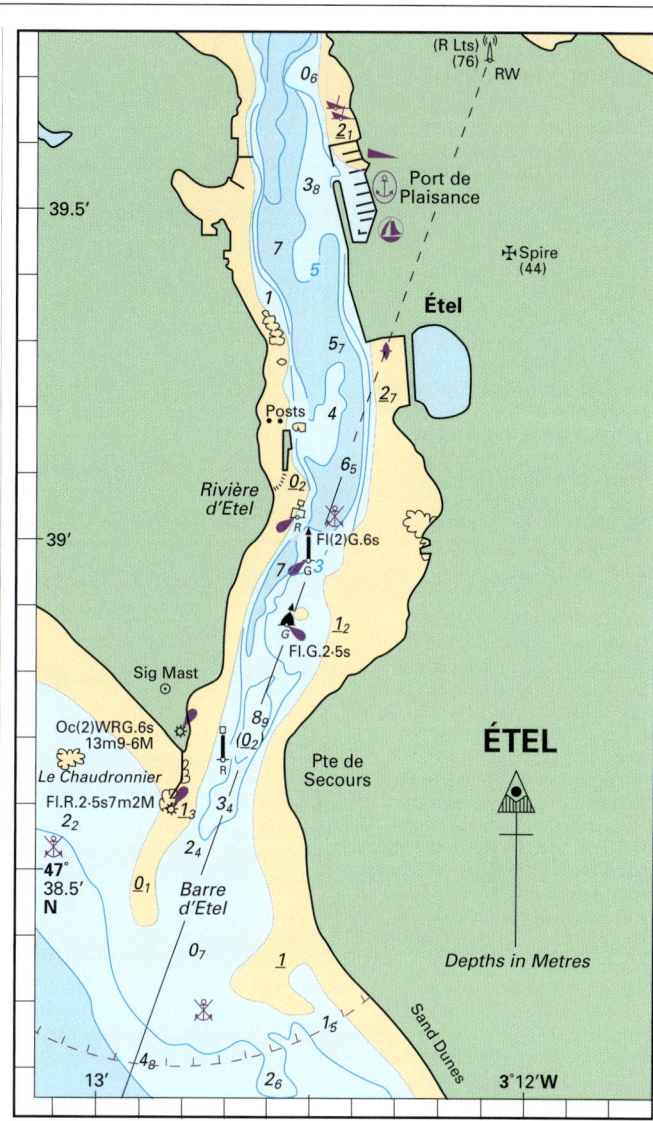

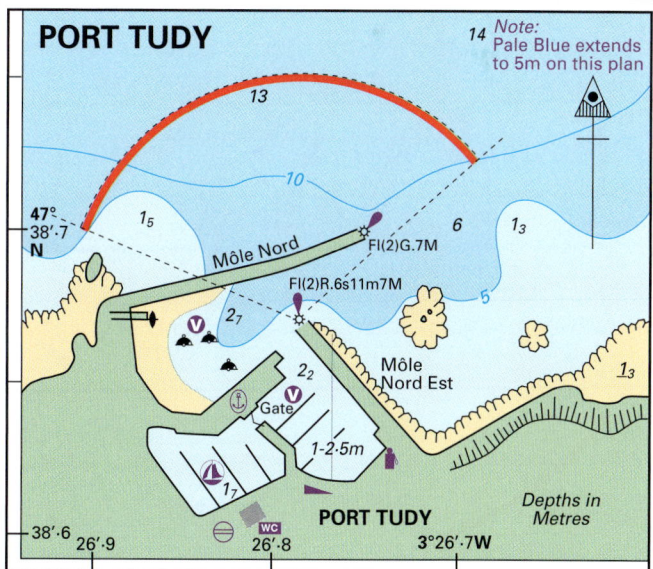

SAUZON, BELLE ÎLE

See plan on next page
Tidal data as Le Palais

A delightful place with good restaurants. Open to the N/NE.

Anchorage 22 white visitors' moorings in W side of bay, Port Bellec, outside the hbr. Two ropes to buoy. Anchoring forbidden here. 40 berths for monohulls <12m and draught <2m, rafting on fore and aft buoys in outer harbour. Visitors' buoys to port in drying, inner harbour. Moor fore and aft. Anchoring possible clear of these buoys, ground hard mud.

Facilities Some shops and a good range of restaurants. Showers and WCs near HM Office ✆ 02 97 31 63 40.

ARCHIPELAGO SE OF QUIBERON PENINSULA

There are several passages through the many islands and rocks which string out for 15M SE from the Quiberon peninsula:

- La Teignouse passage
- Passage du Béniguet
- Passage de L'Île aux Chevaux
- Er Toul Bras

Of these the La Teignouse is the most N'ly, lit and probably the easiest; the Béniguet is the shortest, narrow and all right in good visibilty in daylight; the Chevaux is the longest but a useful passage in fine weather from Belle Isle to Hoëdic. In good conditions of sea-state and visibility Er Toul Bras is a shorter passage around the south of the peninsula. Directions below are given only for the Teignouse passage.

From the SW identify the Guoé Vaz Sud S card Lt buoy and the Básse du Milieu G pillar Lt buoy Fl(2)G.6s and pass between on a course of 036° until past the Goué Vas Est pillar buoy Fl(3)R.12s. Alter course to 068° to pass in 1½M between the Basse Nouvelle R pillar buoy Fl.R.2·5s and the NE Teignouse G pillar buoy Fl(3)G.12s. NE stream commences HW Brest –0600 1·7kn max and SW stream at HW Brest +0100. 2kn maximum.

LE PALAIS, BELLE ÎLE

Standard Port Brest

HW –0015 LW –0018

MHWS	MHWN	MLWN	MLWS
–1·9m	–1·4m	–0·8m	–0·3m

A popular town, often crowded as it is a convenient port when passage-making and an excellent base from which to explore the island. Citadel dominates the entrance to the hbr.

Entrance Five unlit buoys to NE of Mole Bourdelle. Beware of the frequent ferries entering and leaving the hbr from 0600 to 2200.

Anchorage The anchorage to the E of Mole Bourdelle restricted by large buoys laid for commercial craft. Anchoring not advised in winds from SE/E/NE. These conditions produce swell in the outer harbour. On entry to outer harbour, boats are usually directed to the fore and aft buoys, where rafting is the norm. Boats lie either between two buoys or between buoy and chains down hbr wall. In season, hbr staff assist with mooring.

Berthing Lock to the inner harbour opens HW–0130 to +0100 between 0600 and 2200. Berth, or more normally, raft, as directed on pontoons in Bassin à Flot. If requested, a berth may be available in the marina, Bassin de la Saline. The br between the two basins opens at the same time as that over the lock. White stripes indicate that a berth is reserved for commercial boats only.

Facilities Water, power. Shops, chandleries and restaurants. Daily morning market. Ferries to mainland. Cycle and car hire. WiFi.

Interest Citadel.

☎ HM 02 97 31 42 90.

PORT HALIGUEN

Standard Port Brest

HW –0018 LW +0012

MHWS	MHWN	MLWN	MLWS
–1·7m	–1·3m	–0·6m	–0·3m

Pleasant yacht hbr with moorings and marina, 3·5m in entrance, to E of old drying hbr and village on E side of Quiberon peninsula. Complete shelter. Adjacent beach. Ferries to Belle Île.

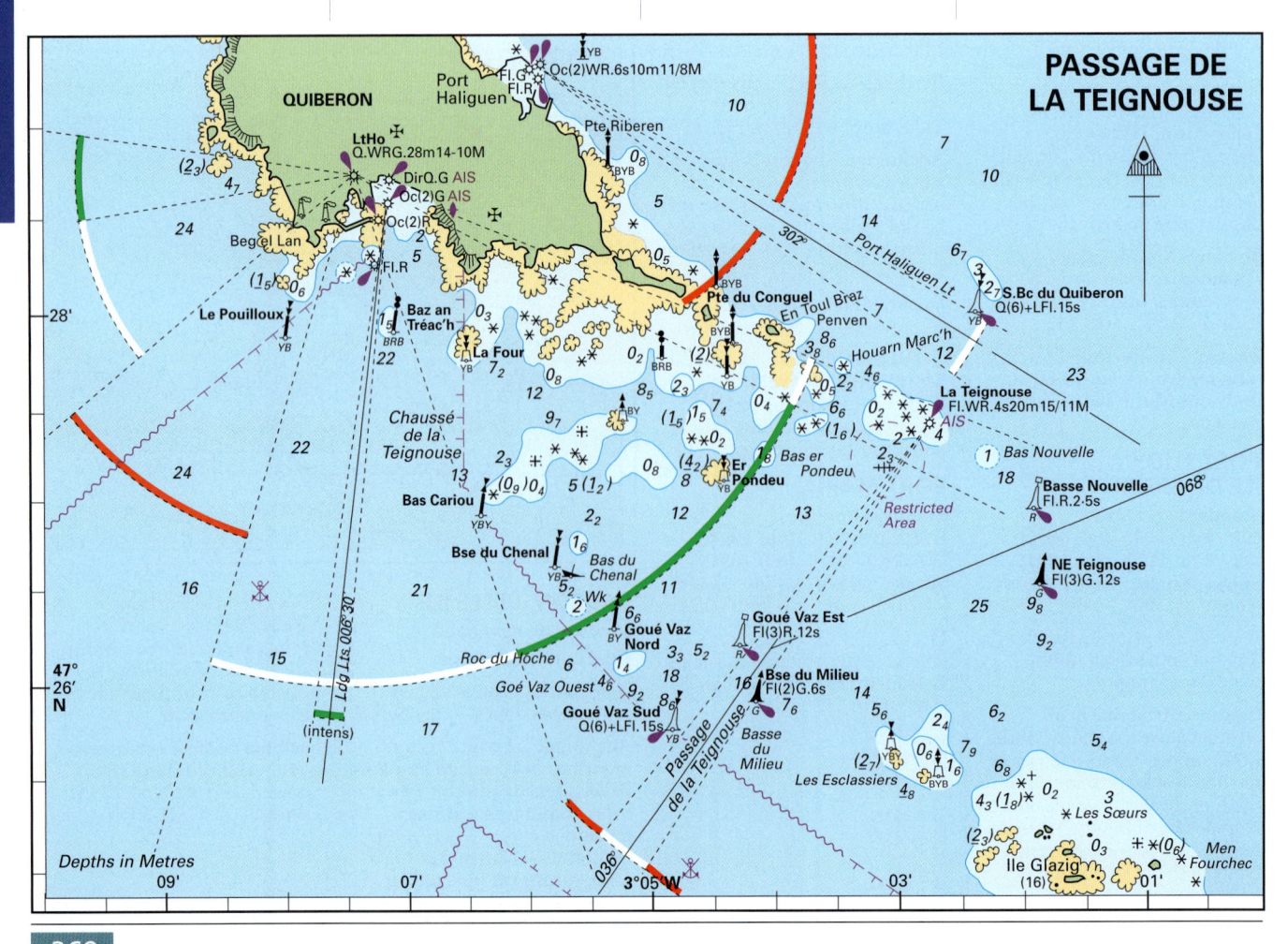

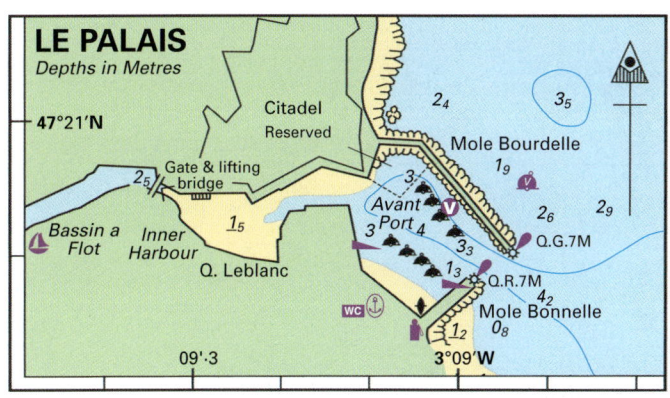

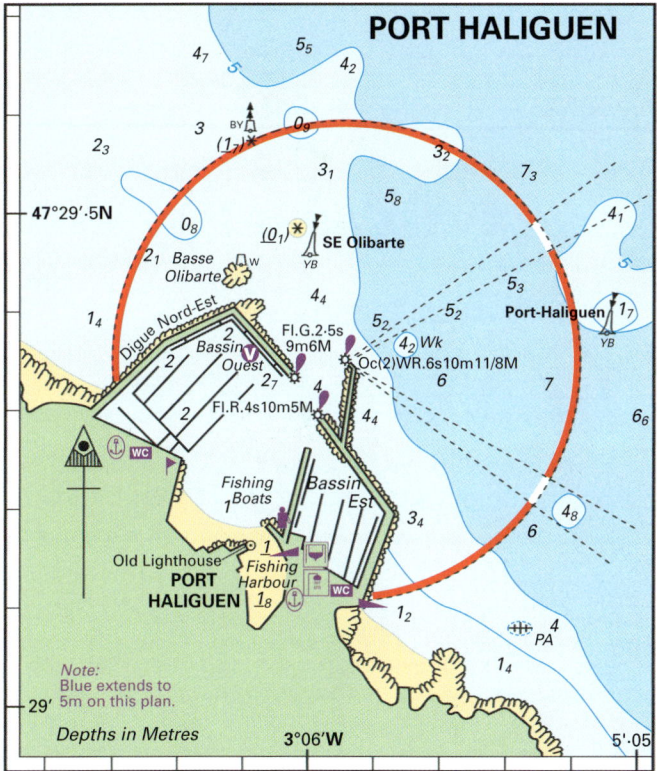

off N end of Grand Mouton reaches 8kn at sp on the ebb and 6kn on the flood. Off Point de Navalo, the ingoing stream begins at HW Brest –0445 4½kn on E side and 3½kn on W side and the outgoing stream at HW+0115. 5¾kn sp on E side and 4¼kn on W side. In Auray R, the flood stream begins at Brest –0455, the ebb at +0020; both attain about 3kn at springs.

Approach Identified by the two hillocks on Île Méaban to port and, if it is visible through the trees, the white Port Navalo lighthouse.

Entrance Easier after local HW –0400 and very difficult when the ebb is running. The official leading line of the white pyramid, Petit Vezid, with the Church spire of Baden is not easy to see as the spire is 5M inland. The port hand side of the entrance channel is marked by three large towers, the E Card Bagen Hir, the R Kerpenhir tr and R Goémorent tr. Keeping to mid-channel as they are passed, the stb Grand Mouton buoy, QG and the S Card Grégan will come into view. The flood sets strongly onto the latter. If entering the Morbihan, pass between these. The S Card buoys marking the shallows to the W of the Île Aux Moines are small. If going to Auray, leave Grégan and the pyramid to stb.

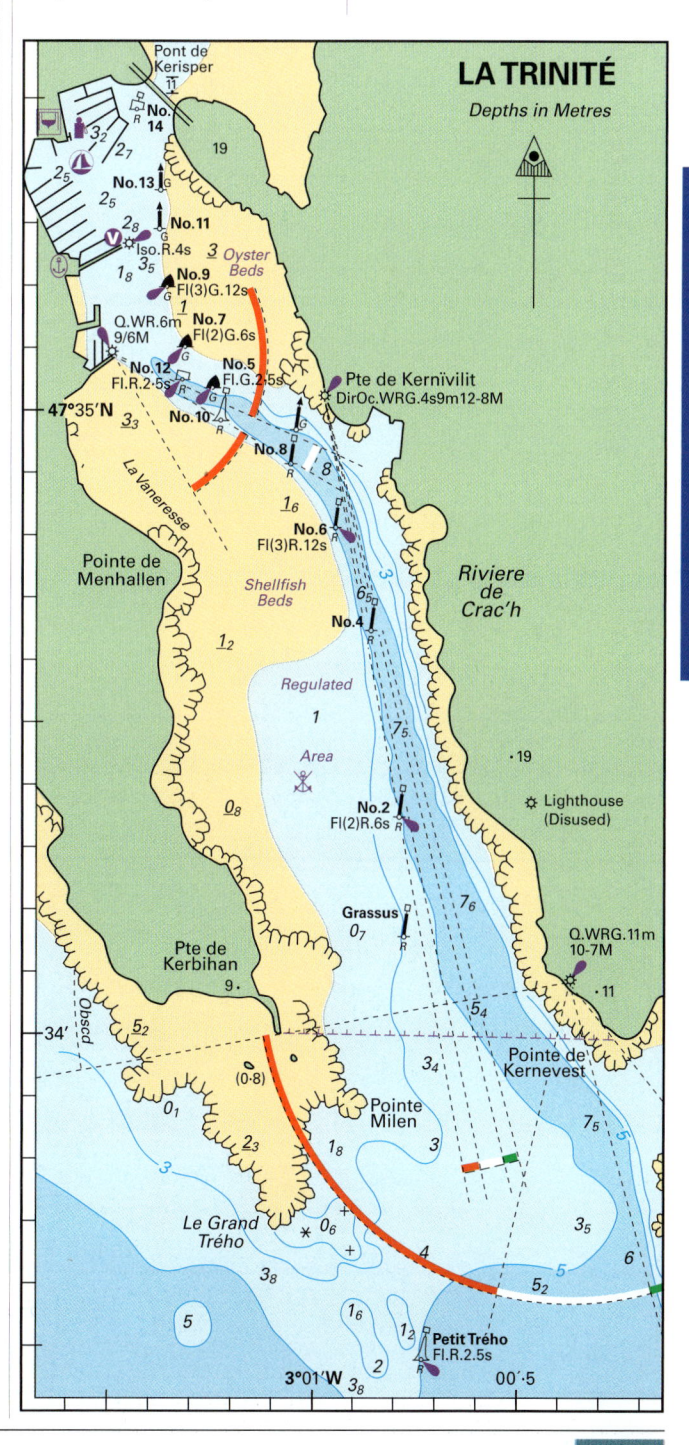

Approach Hazards: unlit buoys, E of entrance S Card buoy Port-Haliguen, N of entrance S Card buoy SE Olibarte. At night keep in W sectors of LtHo on outer mole Oc(2)WR.6s.

Entrance Accessible in all weathers and all states of the tide. No anchoring within the hbr.

Berthing Visitors' pontoon inside harbour wall in West Basin. Visitors usually met by a dory.

Facilities Shops in Quiberon and small épicerie near marina in season. Restaurants and bars nr marina and in town. WiFi. Chandleries. Rly connection from Quiberon to Auray.
☎ HM 02 97 50 20 56.

LA TRINITÉ SUR MER CRAC'H RIVER

Standard Port Brest
HW –0022   LW –0012
MHWS MHWN MLWN MLWS
–1·7m –1·2m –0·6m –0·3m

Large marina, an ocean racing centre with good support facilities. Marina sheltered in all conditions except when certain high tides produce a large swell. Very busy in season. Megaliths at Carnac.

Entrance In all weathers and states of tide. Beware of oyster beds. Even at high tide, remain within the buoyed channel.

Berthing Visitors' pontoon next to S mole and on R pontoon.

Facilities Chandleries, WiFi, boatyards, shops, Mkt Fri, restaurants. Rly connection to Auray. ☎ 02 97 55 71 49.

GOLFE DU MORBIHAN (THE MORBIHAN)

See plan on next page
Standard Port Brest
Port Navalo
HW (sp) –0005 (np) +0030
LW (sp) –0010 (np) –0005
MHWS MHWN MLWN MLWS
–2·1m –1·6m –0·9m –0·4m

The Morbihan is a large inland sea with two main rivers, the Auray and the Vannes, together with many islands, some inhabited, and numerous anchorages. A large scale chart is essential.

Tides These are very strong, particularly near and just inside the entrance, where the stream

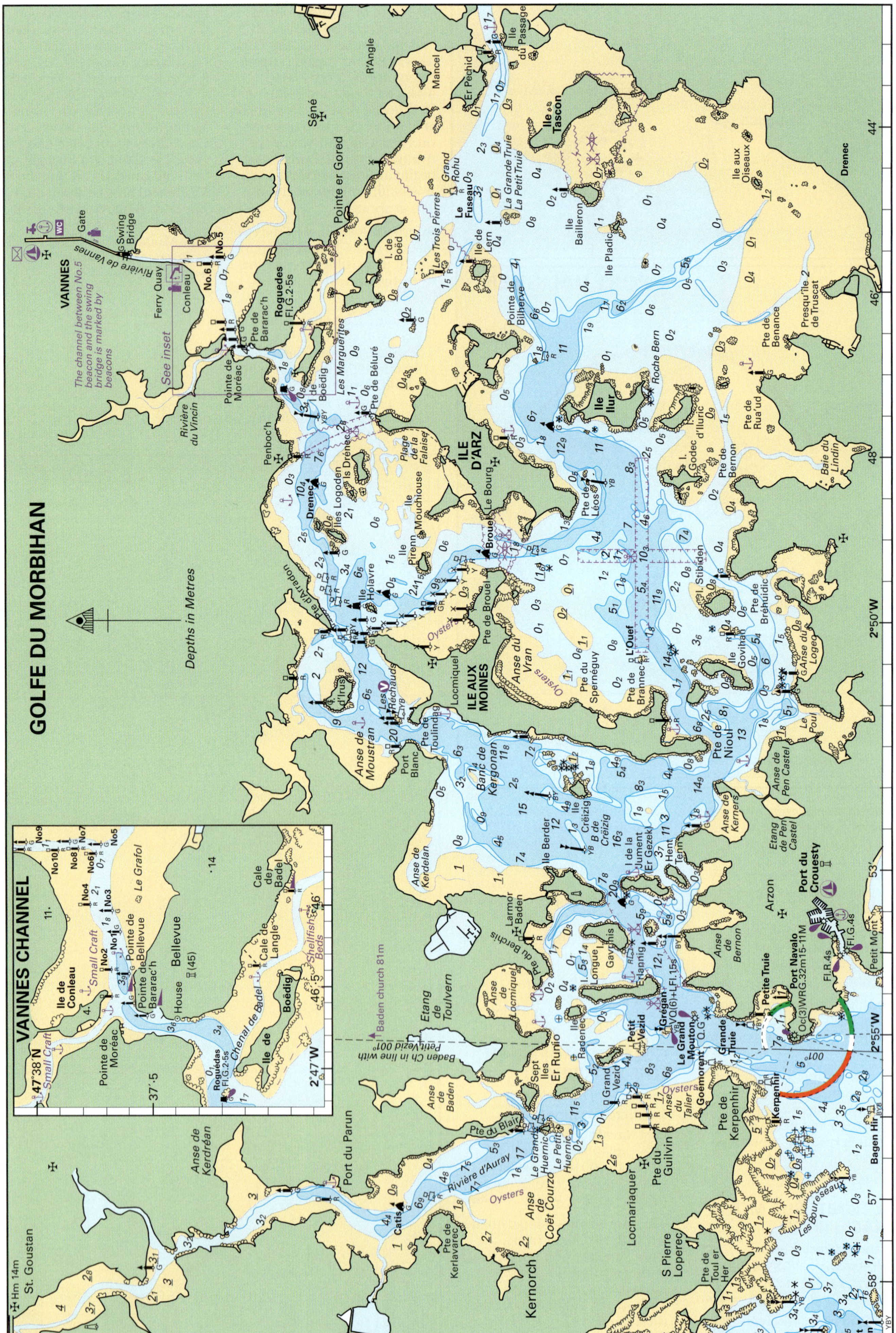
GOLFE DU MORBIHAN
Depths in Metres
VANNES CHANNEL
VANNES
The channel between No.5 beacon and the swing bridge is marked by beacons
See inset
Ferry Quay
Swing Bridge
Gate
Rivière de Vannes
Conleau
Pointe de Moréac
Pte de Bararac'h
Roguedas Fl.G.2·5s
Rivière du Vincin
Penboc'h
Pointe er Gored
Séné
R'Angle
Mancel
Er Pechid
Ile du Passage
Ile Tascon
Le Fuseau
Grand Rohu
Les Trois Pierres
La Grande Truie
La Petit Truie
Ile Bailleron
Ile Pladic
Ile aux Oiseaux
Drenec
Presqu'ile de Truscat
Pte de Benance
Pte de Rua'ud
Baie du Lindin
Ile Ilur
Roche Bern
I. Godec d'Illuric
Pte de Bernon
Pointe de Bilherve
ILE D'ARZ
Le Bourg
Plage de la Falaise
Ile Mouchiouse
Ile Pirenn
Iles Logoden
Drenec
Pte de Béluré
Pte de Boëdig
Les Marguerites
Pte d'Arradon
Ile Holavre
Pte de Brouel
Broue
Pte de Léos
Pte de Brannec
L'Ouef
I. Stibiden
Pte de Brehuidic
Ile Govihan
Anse du Logeo
Le Pouli
Anse de Pen Castel
Etang de Pen Castel
Port du Crouesty
Arzon
Anse de Kerners
Pte de Nioul
ILE AUX MOINES
Locmiquel
Pte du Toulindag
Port Blanc
Anse de Moustran
Les Réchauds
Ile d'Irus
Anse du Vran
Pte du Sperneguy
Oysters
Anse de Kerdelan
Banc de Kergonan
Ile Berder
B de Creizig
I de la Jument (Er Gezek)
Hent Tenn
Larmor Baden
Pte du Berchis
Etang de Toulvern
Baden church 81m
Baden Ch in line with Petit Vezid 001°
Anse de Locmiquel
Ile Longue
Gavrinis
Hapnig
Ile Radenec
Er Runio
Sept Iles
Petit Vezid
Grand Vezid
Grégan Q(6)+LFl.15s
Le Grand Mouton Q.G
Goëmorent
Grande Truie
Petite Truie
Port Navalo Oc(3)WRG.32m15-11M
Fl.R.4s
Fl.G.4s
Petit Mont
Anse de Bernon
Anse du Taller
Pte de Kerpenhir
Kerpenhir
Bagen Hir
Les Boureseaux
Le Petit Buisson
Pte du Gulvin
Locmariaquer
S Pierre Loperec
Pte de Toul er Her
Kernorch
Anse de Coët Courzo
Le Grand Huenic
Le Petit Huenic
Pte du Blair
Rivière d'Auray
Anse de Baden
Pte de Kerlavarec
Catis
Port du Parun
Anse de Kerdréan
St. Goustan
Auray Br
Hm 14m
47° 39' N
47° 36' N
2°55'W
2°50'W
53'
57'
58'
48'
46'
44'
Ile de Conleau
Small Craft
Pointe de Bellevue
Bellevue
House
Chenal de Badel
Ile de Boëdig
Cale de Langle
Cale de Badel
Le Grafol
Shellfish Beds
Roguedas Fl.G.2·5s
47°38'N
37'·5
2°47'W
46'·5
46'

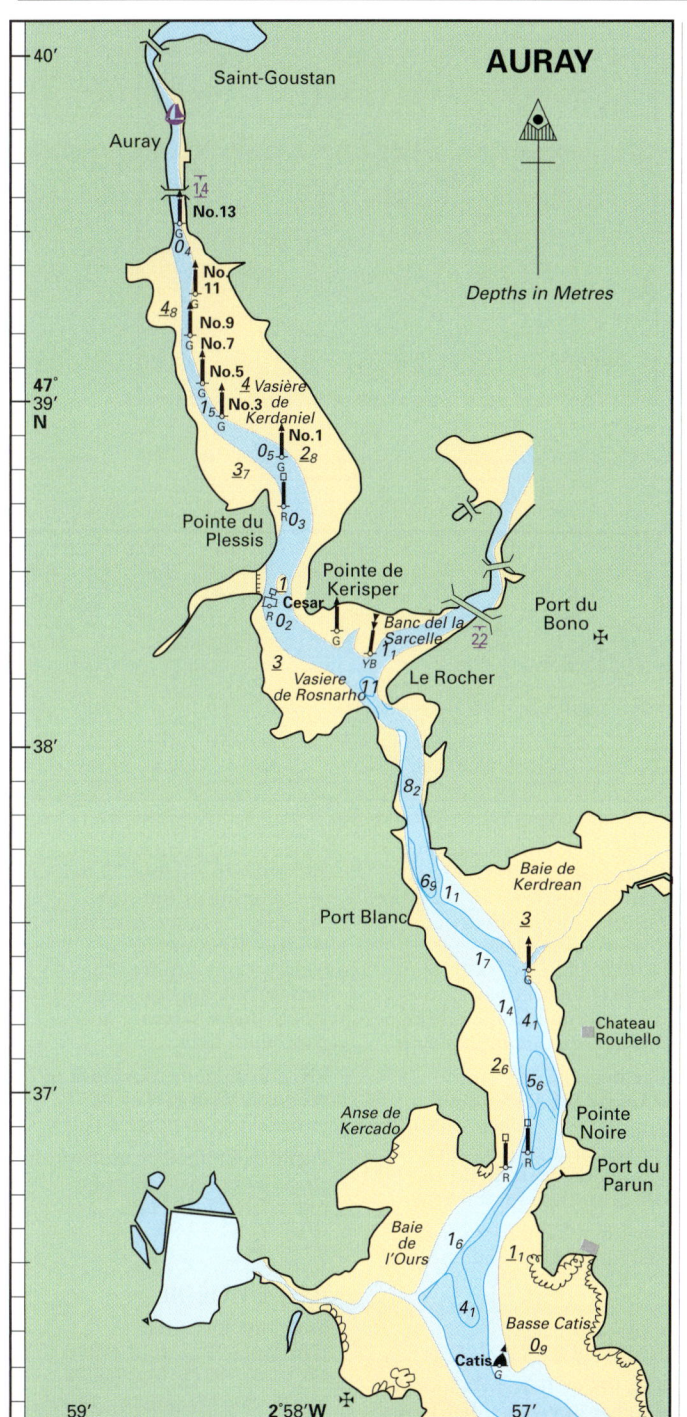

ANCHORAGES WITHIN THE GOLFE DU MORBIHAN

Fewer anchorages are now available to visiting yachts, and many that are marked on the chart will be full of moorings; especially those close to the mainland. Take care to avoid bathing areas which are marked by yellow buoys.

- **Île Longue** E of island in 2–5m. Sheltered from the west.
- **Île de la Jument** East of the island in 2–3m.
- **Île aux Moines** SE of the island between Pointe du Nioul and Pointe de Brannec, in 2–5m.
- **Île Pirenn** In 3–5m, mud, 0·2M S of the island. Slip accessible from half tide on the E point of Île aux Moines; and another which also dries on W side of Île d'Arz.
- **Île d'Arz** S of the island but N of the G con buoy and R can buoy Bilhervé in 2–5m of water. Moorings closer in.

Moorings

- **Île aux Moines** A few visitors' moorings and two visitors' pontoons which are not connected to the shore, better depth of water on the western pontoon. Service to shore provided by port. Only licensed dinghies permitted to tie to landing pontoon. ☏ 02 97 26 30 57.
- **Arradon** 10 visitors' buoys for craft <18m and some berths on a pontoon for shallow-drafted craft. ☏ 02 97 44 01 23.

Facilities Small supermarkets, restaurants and créperies on Île Aux Moines and Île d'Arz. Fuel is not available at any marina or hbr within the Golfe du Morbihan. It is available at Le Crouesty, where there is also a large supermarket.

VANNES

Standard Port Brest
HW (sp)+0150 (np)+0200
LW (sp)+0140 (np)–0120

MHWS	MHWN	MLWN	MLWS
–3·8m	–3·0m	–2·1m	–0·9m

A delightful, historic town, worth a visit of several days. For most boats, the channel up to Vannes may be taken only on the flood. HW at Vannes is approx. 2hrs after that at Port Navalo. The area around the marina has been redeveloped. Capitainerie to stb on entry.

Approach Usually enough water at HW–0300 in channel beyond Conleau. At the sharp port turn (by the pink cottage) better water is towards the stb bank.

Entrance Waiting pontoons upstream and downstream of the lock. Road traffic now uses a tunnel under the river, so the Kérino bridge and lock remain open for a given period around HW. Timings are published on the Vannes Marie website www.mairie-vannes.fr/port-de-plaisance/

Berthing Berth as directed. Visitors may have to raft unless they have pre-booked a berth. Depths less than given for berths closer to the town.

Facilities Indoor market daily each morning except Mon. Market days Wednesday and Saturday. Good shore facilities, chandlery at ZA St Léonard N. Shops, restaurants, museums. Rly, TGV. ☏ HM 02 97 01 55 20 (not Sundays or lunch-time).

Port Navalo Hbr exposed to W and NW. Five visitors' moorings for boats <10m. ☏ 02 97 53 82 12.

PORT DU CROUESTY

Standard Port Brest
HW (sp) –0025 (np) +0010
LW (sp) –0015 (np) –0010

MHWS	MHWN	MLWN	MLWS
–1·6m	–1·2m	–0·7m	–0·3m

RIVER AURAY WESTERN ARM

Standard Port Brest

Auray
HW (sp) +0000 (np) +0035
LW (sp) +0015 (np) –0005

MHWS	MHWN	MLWN	MLWS
–2·3m	–1·9m	–1·2m	–0·5m

The river is buoyed to Auray, which may be reached on the flood if draught and air-draught permit, the br below St Goustan has a clearance of 14m. Pass E of the island, Le Grand Huernic, and its two R can buoys; here in the narrows tidal streams can reach 4kn. Much of the river further upstream is lined with moorings. In the reach below Baie de Kerdréan, deeper water is to be found towards the W bank. At Auray at HW, there is a stand, after which the ebb runs quickly. It is advisable not to wait for the ebb when leaving Auray.

- **Le Rocher** Shallow draught boats may be able to anchor above moorings. **Facilities** Restaurants and a few shops at Bono.
- **Auray – St-Goustan** Only 1·5m CD between Le Rocher and Auray. Good shelter at St-Goustan/Auray, on fore and aft buoys in 3·6m <12m, 200m upstream of br, clearances LW 16·5m HW 14m. Height indicated on scale to stb before br. Crowded in season. Alongside quay at St-Goustan, dries. ☏ HM 02 97 29 46 39, 06 08 42 18 62.

Facilities Restaurants, shops. Market in Auray, open mornings only. Rly TGV.

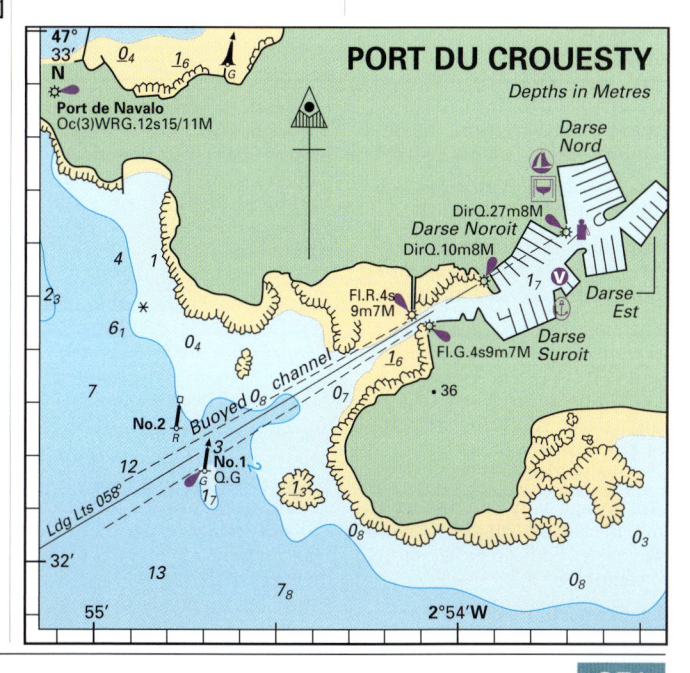

The Cruising Almanac

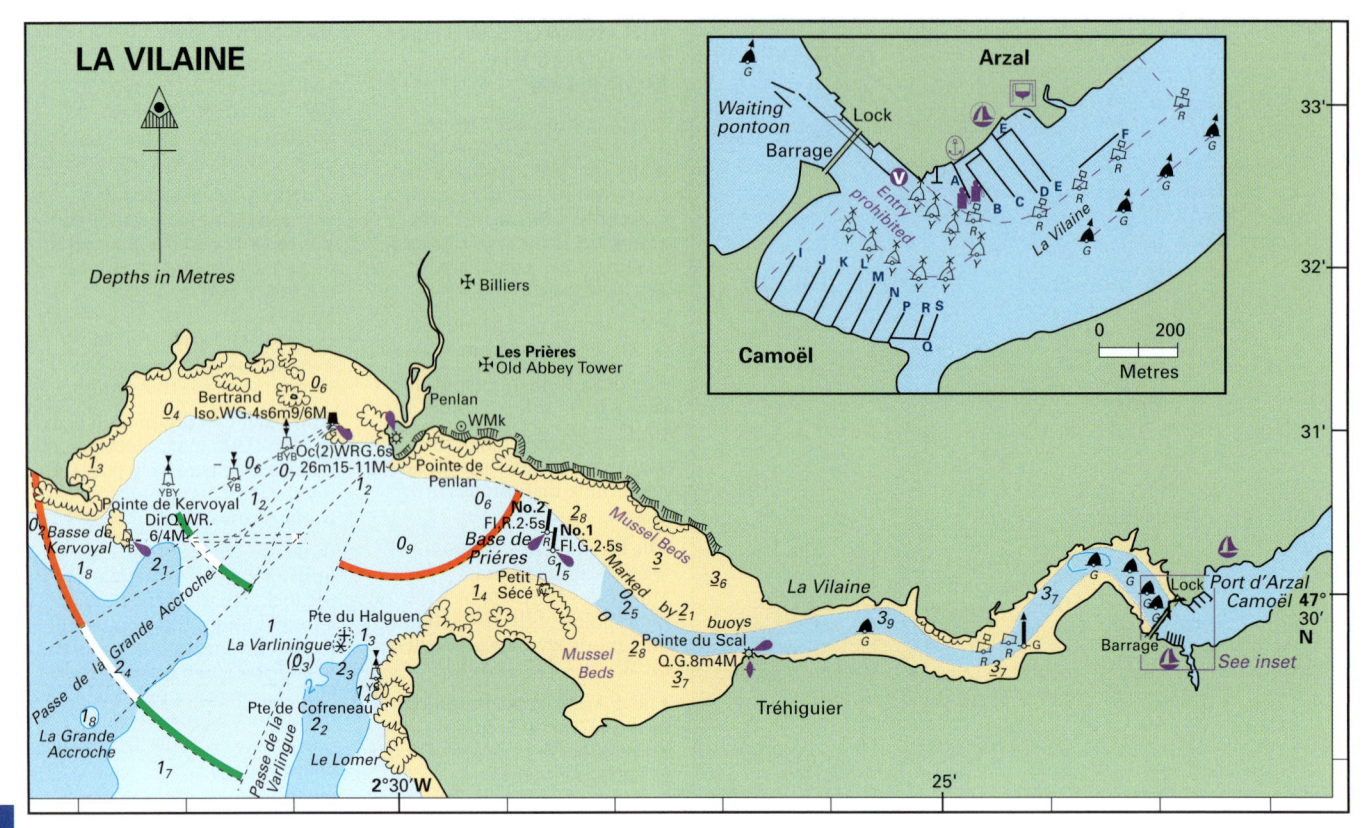

A large marina to the E of the entrance to the Morbihan. Useful if waiting for flood to set into the Morbihan. Short stays for shopping etc, are permitted without charge.

Approach. *See entrance to Golfe du Morbihan p.369.*

Entrance Buoyed channel into the hbr 1·8m. Pass between the breakwaters and watch for G and R bns marking ends of obstacles.

Berthing Visitors' berths in third bay to stb.

Facilities Excellent marina facilities, sailmaker and all repairs. Fuel, chandleries, supermarket, restaurants. WiFi. Pontoon close to supermarket to berth dinghy while shopping.

☏ HM 02 97 53 73 33.

PÉNERF

Standard Port Brest

HW (sp) –0025 (np) +0015
LW (sp) –0015 (np) –0015

MHWS	MHWN	MLWN	MLWS
–1·6m	–1·2m	–0·7m	–0·4m

The river enters Quiberon Bay 3M W of Vilaine River.

Approach The mouth of the river is marked by Le Penvin R can and Borénis G con buoys.

Entrance The buoyage of the E entrance has been improved. R and G bns precede Pignon R tr. Do not pass too close to the first stb bn. After the last pair of bns has been passed, the channel widens.

Anchorage May find a space outside the moorings but avoid the oyster beds on either shore. 2 visitors' buoys.

Facilities Minimal. Hotel.

LA VILAINE

Standard Port Brest

Trehiguer

HW (sp) –0020 (np) +0035
LW (sp) –0005 (np) –0010

MHWS	MHWN	MLWN	MLWS
–1·5m	–1·1m	–0·6m	–0·4m

The river is 135M long, and is dammed at Arzal where one can lock into a non-tidal river as far as Redon. Entry to the Brittany canal system can be made at Bellions Lock, a little below Redon.

Entrance Seas can break on the bar, which has 1m, in W'ly winds. Usually sufficient water at half flood. By day there are two entrance passages:

• **La Grande Accroche** The Tr of Les Prières with the Penlan LtHo 052°. Maintain this bearing until abeam of Bse Kervoyal S Card tr, then turn steer 090° to reach the buoyed channel.

• **Passe de la Varlingue** W of the Varlingue rock, Ldg ln 025° Billiers Church Spire with Penlan Lt Ho. E of the Varlingue, Ldg ln Tr of Les Prières with WMk (a white painted rock).

At night keep in the white sector of the Penlan LtHo, until in the white sector of Bse Kervoyal S Card tr. Keep the latter astern until the buoyed channel has been reached.

Anchorage At Tréhiguier, beyond the moorings, visitors' buoys to stb, or in greater shelter just below the lock. Outside the moorings there is a waiting pontoon on port bank on entry with access to the shore, but no power or water.

Arzal Lock Hourly opening times from 0700–2200 (July/August). 0800–2000 the rest of the year, times not always adhered to.
☏ 09 69 32 2297 (24hrs).
More comprehensive information including bridge timings www.eptb-vilaine.fr.

Berthing

• **Arzal-Camoël** Visitors' pontoon on downstream side of the pontoon to port after leaving the lock. Report to HM office at Arzal for a berth.

Facilities WiFi. Best range of boatyard and chandleries on the River. Fuel. Restaurant and bars near marina, limited shops in Arzal village.
HM ☏ 02 97 45 02 97.

• **La Roche Bernard** Limited number of visitors' berths on downstream side of first pontoon.

Facilities Chandlery. WiFi. Good range of shops and restaurants.
HM ☏ 02 99 90 62 17.

• **Foleux** Visitors' berth/raft on N bank. WiFi.

Facilities Créperie. No shops
☏ 02 99 91 80 87.

• **Béganne** Single pontoon without power or water. Stay limited to 24hrs. Shops, bar and restaurant in village. Above Pont de Cran Br, which lifts 1st Apr to 30th Sep daily at 0930, 1030, 1130, 1400, 1600, 1800 and 1900, two waiting buoys downstream or moor alongside quay. Restaurant. Waiting pontoon upstream with no access ashore.

• **Rieux** Two pontoons, water and power available. Contact the campsite or Mairie to organise the latter. Modest charges. Restaurant, (reservations required for dinner) boulangerie, bars in village and restaurant near pontoons. WiFi.

• **Redon** Take the port fork of the river. Visitors' berths immediately to port on entry.

Facilities Limited chandlery, all shops and restaurants of a town. Rly TGV. HM
☏ 02 99 71 22 96,
07 77 88 23 22.

ÎLE DE HOËDIC

Standard Port Brest

HW (sp) –0035 (np) +0010
LW (sp) –0025 (np) –0020

MHWS	MHWN	MLWN	MLWS
–1·9m	–1·5m	–0·8m	–0·4m

Anchorage

• On the N coast, Port Angol, often crowded, moor to communal buoys if no room on pontoon. Not in N'ly winds.

• Off the Plage du Canot, to W of the port avoiding underwater cables. Exposed to N.

Facilities Shop, restaurants, ferry to mainland.
☏ 02 92 57 45 39.

ÎLE DE HOUAT

Standard Port Brest

HW (sp) –0025 (np) +0005
LW (sp) –0025 (np) –0010

MHWS	MHWN	MLWN	MLWS
–1·8m	–1·4m	–0·7m	–0·4m

Anchorages

• **St-Gildas** If approaching from the N, avoid the mussel park to the N of La Vieille and the zone of aquaculture to the S. Do not get too close to the breakwater when rounding it to enter the hbr. Raft to fore and aft buoys. S end of hbr dries. Few places for visitors. Alternatively, anchor or take a buoy outside the hbr. Mairie ☎ 02 97 30 68 04, 06 32 83 08 87.

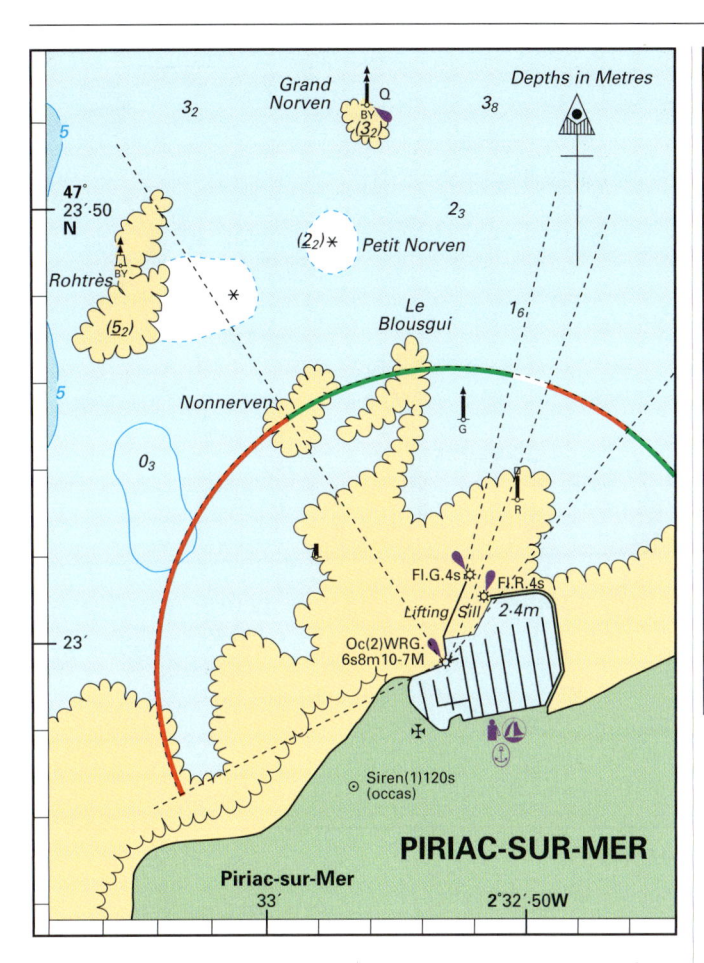

• **Treac'h er Béniguet** Very uncomfortable in W winds but sheltered from E. Leave le Roulou S Card tr to stb. Anchor in 3–4m sand.

• **Treac'h an Gouret** Popular anchorage in fine, settled weather; the NE part of this bay is a bird reserve and anchoring here is forbidden, avoid submarine cables. Exposed to E. Bathing area marked by yellow buoys in season.

Facilities Hotels, restaurants and shops in the small town. Ferry to mainland.

PIRIAC-SUR-MER

Standard Port Brest
HW (sp) –0030 (np) +0015
MHWS MHWN MLWN MLWS
–1·6m –1·2m   n/a   n/a

About 6M S of the Vilaine River; a fishing hbr with a marina built on to the east with lifting sill. 2·4m inside sill. Very attractive town.

Approach only after half tide. From the west there are many rocks, Grand Norven rock marked by N card bn dries 1·8m.

Entrance From a position 3·5ca E of Grand Norven turn on to 197°, at night W sector 194°–210°. Enter between R and G bns. Turn sharply to port after E–W mole and enter over sill. R flashing lights indicate sill is closed. Usually met by harbour dory. Visitors normally berth at northern ends of D and E, or raft on C.

Facilities Chandleries, shops, WiFi, restaurants. Market Mon, Wed, Sat, early June to mid Sept. Beaches.

☎ HM 02 40 23 52 32.

LA TURBALLE

Standard Port Brest
HW (sp) –0040 (np) +0015
LW (sp) –0020 (np) –0015
MHWS MHWN MLWN MLWS
–1·6m –1·2m –0·7m –0·4m

Two miles N of Le Croisic, a fishing hbr with a pleasant town worth a visit. Strong swell in S/SW winds.

Approach Easily identified by Trescalan large water tr. Rocky shoals to N. Ldg marks, Pierhead Lts 060°. In season, the approach channel is marked by the yellow buoys that define the bathing area.

Entrance 006° R bn Iso.R.4s11m3M to W of fish market, with the Lt behind it, Iso.R.4s19m3M. This will lead clear of the rocks to stb.

Berthing In season, usually met by harbour dory. Visitors' berth in box S off B pontoon.

Facilities Fuel, chandlery, shops, restaurants, market Wed, Sat, Sun am. WiFi.

☎ HM 02 40 23 41 65 or mobile 06 65 93 03 15.

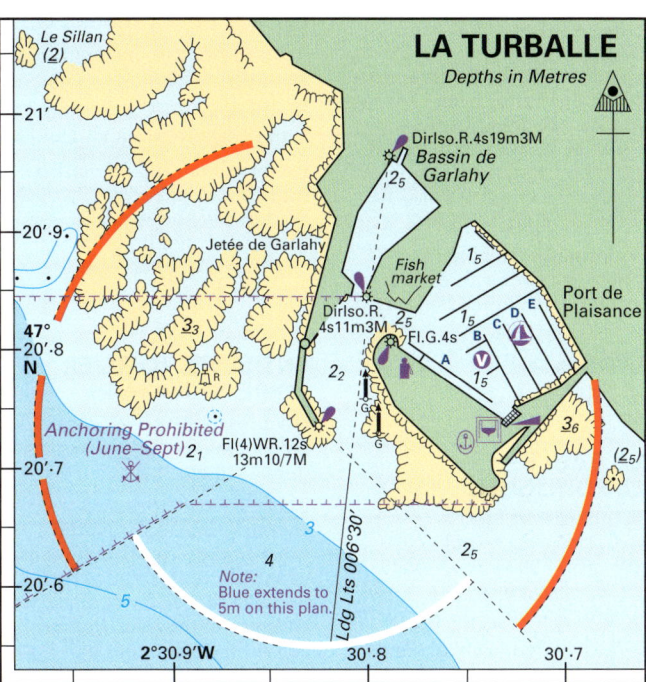

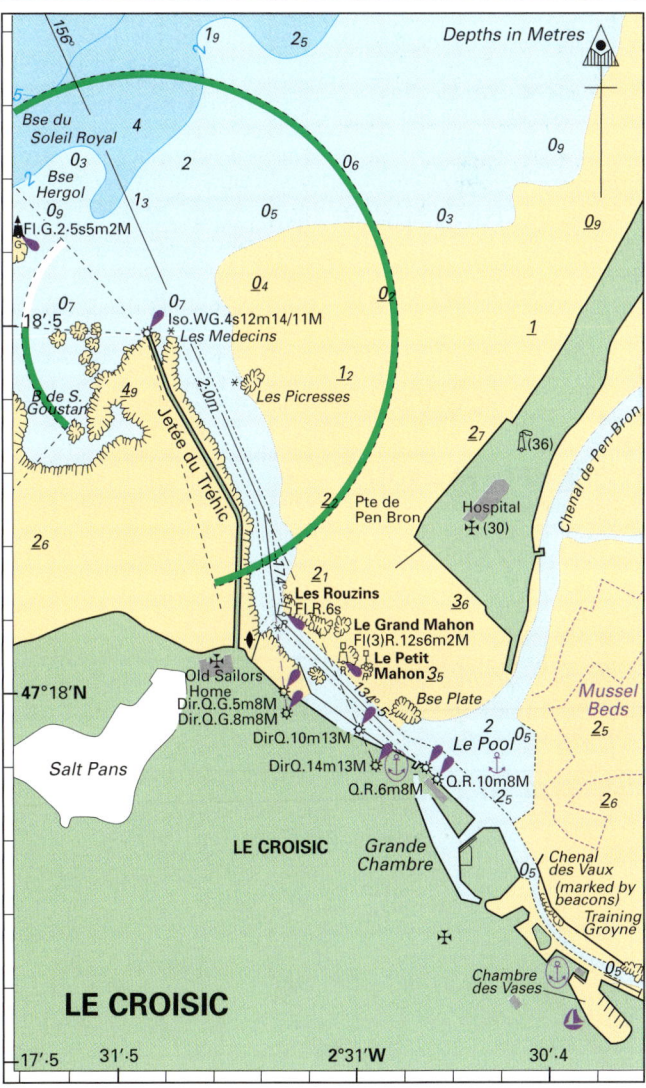

LE CROISIC
Tidal data as La Turballe

A popular holiday resort and fishing hbr which dries. Limited provision for yachts that can take the ground. Anchoring in the pool only permitted with prior agreement from HM. The entrance channel is dredged to 1·2m but the tides are strong, exceeding 4kn at springs, when entry should be made 1hr before HW. At neaps, entry possible at any time. There is a gauge (difficult to read) at the head of the Tréhic jetty indicating depth of water at quayside.

Approach and Entrance Keep on the bearing 156°, until it is possible to identify the ldg Lts

DirQ.13M on the W bank marked with orange dayglo chevrons. At the bend on the Jettée du Tréhic, bear 174°, ldg marks, two DirQ.G.8M on shore. Abeam Les Rouzins R can buoy, bear 135°, leading line on the two Lts. DirQ.R. until reaching the pool.

Mooring In the hbr, on pontoons with legs, or anchor as previously agreed with HM.

Facilities Fuel in town. Chandleries. Rly.

☏ HM 09 81 12 75 92, 06 65 93 34 05.

LA BAULE – LE POULIGUEN

Standard Port Brest
HW (sp) –0025 (np) +0020
LW (sp) –0020 (np) –0025

MHWS	MHWN	MLWN	MLWS
–1·6m	–1·2m	–0·7m	–0·4m

Hbr sheltered from all winds except SE, access after half-tide. Depth 1·2m at LW±0230. Possibility of grounding with a swell.

Approach Marked by Penchâteau Fl.R.2.5s and Martineau R can buoys.

Entrance The entrance to the channel is marked by R bn and la Vieille G bn. The position of the channel changes. Marked by bns.

Berthing Contact HM on arrival. VHF 09,
☏ 02 40 11 97 97.

Facilities Fuel. Shops and restaurants. Daily market in season. Rly.

PORNICHET – LA BAULE

Standard Port Brest
HW (sp) –0045 (np) +0020
LW (sp) –0022 (np) –0022

MHWS	MHWN	MLWN	MLWS
–1·5m	–1·1m	–0·8m	–0·3m

Deepwater, large yacht hbr, protected from all winds and accessible at all states of the tide except at LW Springs. Crowded in season.

Entrance Easy by day, but hbr lights difficult to distinguish against shore lights.

Berthing Visitors' berths on hammerheads except H, J and K.

Facilities Fuel and all marina facilities. Market days Wednesday and Saturday. Les Halles daily am in summer. Shops, restaurants. Good beaches. Rly.

☏ HM 02 40 61 03 20.

ENTRANCE TO RIVER LOIRE, ST NAZAIRE

HW Brest –0040sp +0020np

MHWS	MHWN	MLWN	MLWS
5·8m	4·6m	2·2m	0·8m

There are two approach channels, one to the N, the other to the S. In strong winds, especially westerly, seas can break in the relatively shallow entrance to the river. In these conditions, wait until half flood before entering. Some of the marks difficult to distinguish in poor visibility. There are some facilities for yachts. Yachts may make a brief stay in the St Nazaire Lock Basin, but salvage insurance is required. Unless in emergency, there are no facilities for visiting yachts at Trentemoult. The entrance to the Inland Waterway System at Nantes can be reached within the flood.

Approach and Entrance Off-lying dangers, rocks and shallows off the coast between Pornichet and the Pte du Chémoulin, marked by cardinal buoys, the Plateau de la Lambarde to the SW, and a shallow bank SW of Pte de St-Gildas. Channel buoyed.

Anchorages Bonne Anse in 3m 2M S of St-Nazaire.

Facilities Minimal yachting facilities.

☏ St-Nazaire: Lock 02 40 00 45 89, HM Plaisance 02 40 45 39 00.

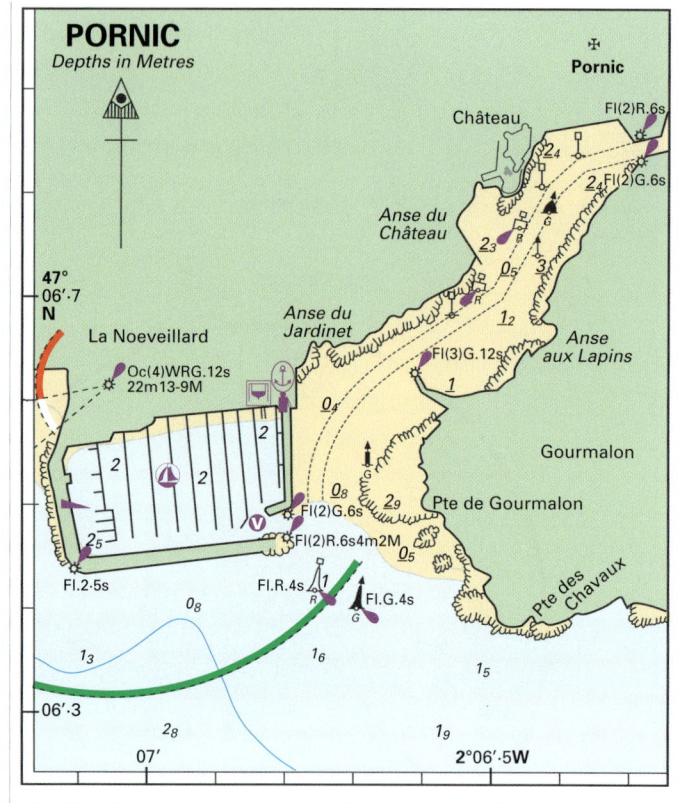

NANTES

Pontoon Belem (formally known as Anne de Bretagne).

On N bank upstream of Anne de Bretagne br, stays of <72h.

☏ 02 40 37 04 62 for entry system. Water and electricity on request.

Facilities An interesting town to visit. Rly and Airport.

PORNIC

Standard Port Brest
HW (sp) –0050 (np) +0030
LW (sp) –0010 (np) –0010

MHWS	MHWN	MLWN	MLWS
–1·2m	–0·9m	–0·5m	–0·3m

The marina is a short walk from the cobbled streets of the town centre. The old port dries 1·8m, sand and mud. The N side is rocky and there is a breakwater off Gourmalon Point which covers at HW. The end is marked by a bn. The extended breakwater off Noëveillard encloses a large marina.

Entrance Access possible at most states of the tide, except ±0200 MLWS.

Berthing Visitors' pontoons P1, P2, P3 to stb on entry and PA at W end of marina. Berth allocated at Reception.

Facilities Chandleries, WiFi, restaurants, shops in town. Beaches nearby.

☏ HM 02 40 82 01 40.

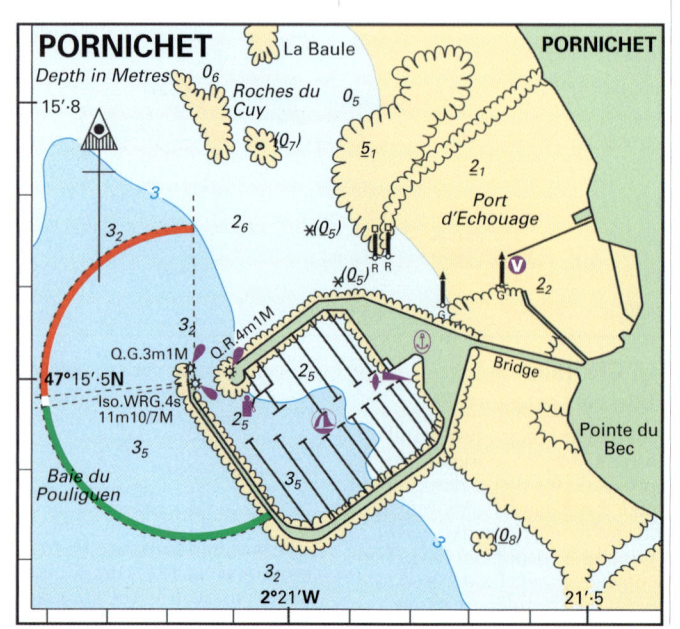

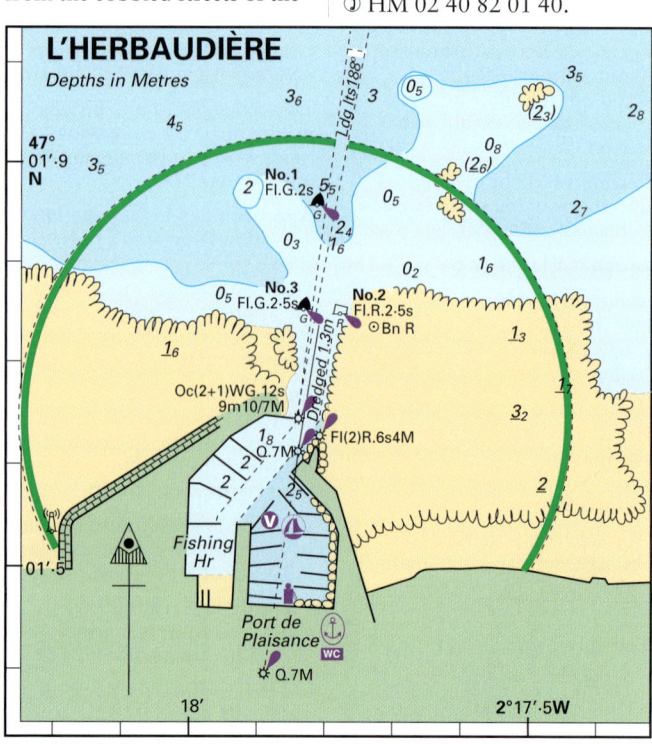

PORT-JOINVILLE

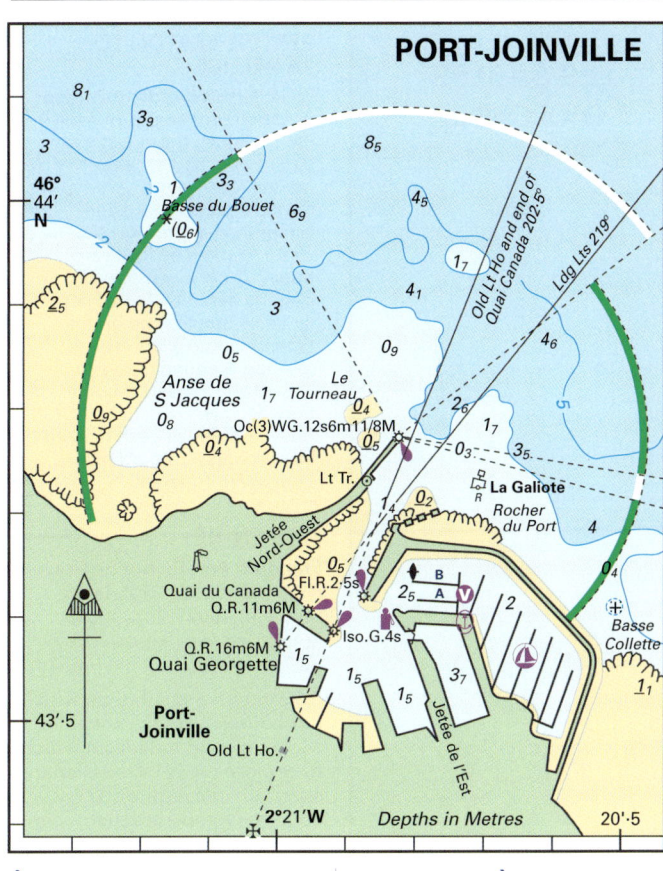

ÎLE DE NOIRMOUTIER
Standard Port Brest
L'Herbaudiere
HW (sp) −0045 (np) +0025
LW (sp) −0020 (np) −0020
MHWS MHWN MLWN MLWS
−1·5m −1·1m −0·6m −0·3m

BOIS DE LA CHAISE
Anchor outside local moorings as close as possible. Uncomfortable in easterlies.

L'HERBAUDIÈRE
An excellent passage hbr modern marina, depth 2–3m. Berths close to entrance exposed to swell and N'ly winds.

Approach and Entrance Least depth 1·3m marked by R and G buoys and bns. Ldg Lts 188°. Idenify Basse du Martroger N card Lt bn tr and come in from about 4ca W of this tr. Keep close to stb-hand buoys with E end of breakwater in line with L'Herbaudiere church clock tr (if not obscured by trees).

Berthing On visitors' pontoon, ahead on entry and adjacent to the fairway or, with permission, on hammerheads.

Facilities WiFi, chandlery, caretaking. Shops, PO and restaurants. Mkt Monday in season.

☎ HM 02 51 39 05 05.

ÎLE D'YEU, JOINVILLE
Standard Port Brest
HW (sp) −0040 (np) +0015
LW (sp) −0035 (np) −0030
MHWS MHWN MLWN MLWS
−2·0m −1·5m −0·8m −0·4m

An attractive island, very busy in high season. Joinville is the only town of any significance on the island. There are some excellent beaches, especially on the S coast. The high water tr just W of the town is more conspic than the LtHo. The marina has 2·5m.

Approach Leading line 202·5° of Ch, former Lt Ho and end of Quai du Canada. At night, Ldg Lts Q.R 219°.

Entrance Marina entrance immediately to port at end of mole. Beware of ferries and vessels leaving marina.

Berthing Anchoring forbidden in outer harbour which is exposed to wind and swell from NW to NE, except to wait for tide. Visitors berth on the A, B and Accueil pontoons; in season often met by hbr dory. May need to raft. In exceptional circumstances, yachts may be directed into inner basin, usually reserved for fishing vessels. Lock opens HW±0200.

Facilities Fuel, chandleries, WiFi, shop, restaurants, small market daily. Ferry and helicopter connections to mainland. No hospital.

☎ HM 02 51 58 38 11.

Anchorages Anse de Ker Chalon in 3·5m, 6ca SE of entrance to Port Joinville. To the S of the island, La Vieille and La Meule. The latter is a drying hbr but there are a few visitors' buoys outside.

ST-GILLES-CROIX-DE-VIE
Standard Port Brest
HW (sp) −0030 (np) +0015
LW (sp) −0030 (np) −0030
MHWS MHWN MLWN MLWS
−1·9m −1·4m −0·7m −0·4m

A sheltered marina accessible at most states of the tide and in most conditions. Swell breaks in S/SW winds Force 7, when great care is needed. Boats drawing more than 1·5m should not attempt to enter ±0200 LWS when the coefficient is high. Current in the channel runs hard, 4–6kn reported. Care need when berthing mid-tide. There have been reports of silting in the entrance channel. Identified by the Pointe de Grosse Terre LtHo, and white water tr.

Approach From the W, leave Pilours S card to port. Leading marks on shore, two white towers with red topmarks, 43·5°. (Not easily distinguished). By night, DirQ.7m15M with DirQ.28m12M.

Entrance Keep mid-channel to avoid rocks and shallows on the edge of the marked channel.

Berthing Visitors' pontoon, (rafting in season) to port on entrance past pontoon 6. Extra berths in season.

Anchoring Only possible offshore in fine weather, not in strong S/SW winds.

Facilities Chandleries, shops, WiFi, restaurants in town. Rly.

☎ HM 02 51 55 30 83.

LES SABLES D'OLONNE
Standard Port Brest
HW (sp) −0030 (np) +0015
LW (sp) −0035 (np) −0035
MHWS MHWN MLWN MLWS
−1·8m −1·3m −0·7m −0·4m

An important fishing port; major yacht hbr and popular holiday resort. The hbr has 1·5m throughout.

Approach From the N and W, leave the Nouch Sud S card buoy and Nouch Nord, N card buoy to port. In strong onshore winds, follow the ldg ln 032·5°, La Potence Iso.4s33m16M and Iso.4s12m16M, and then

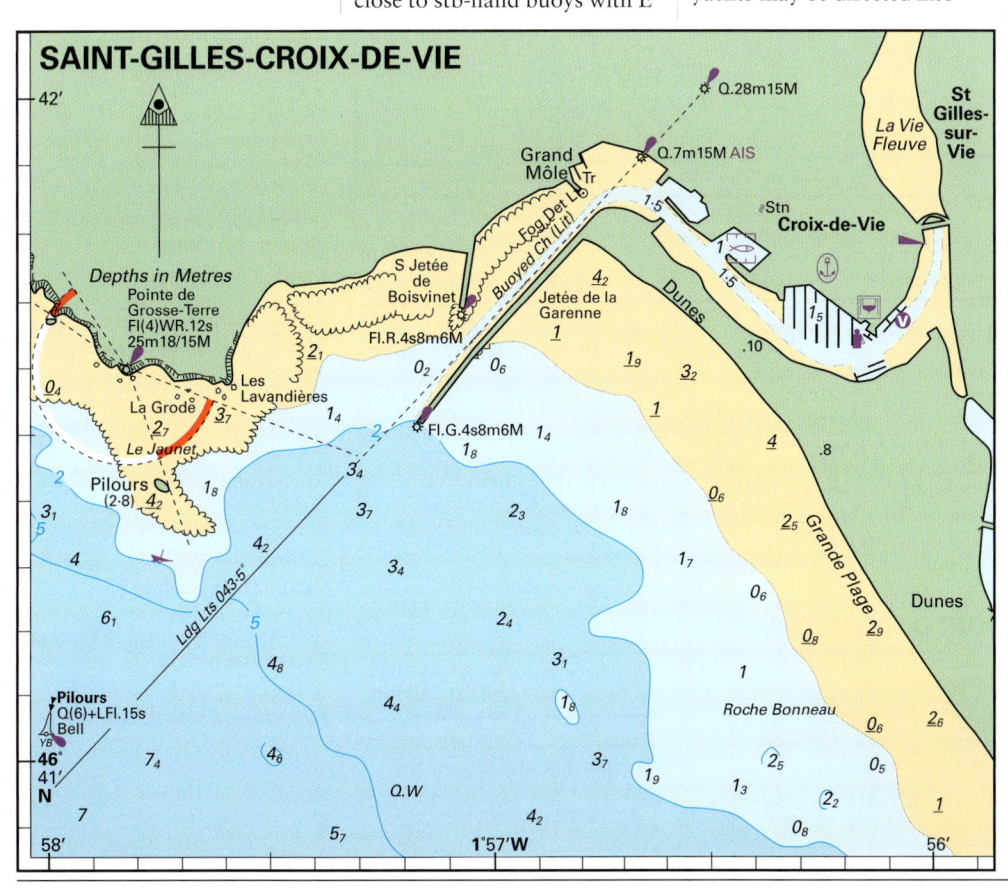

LES SABLES D'OLONNE

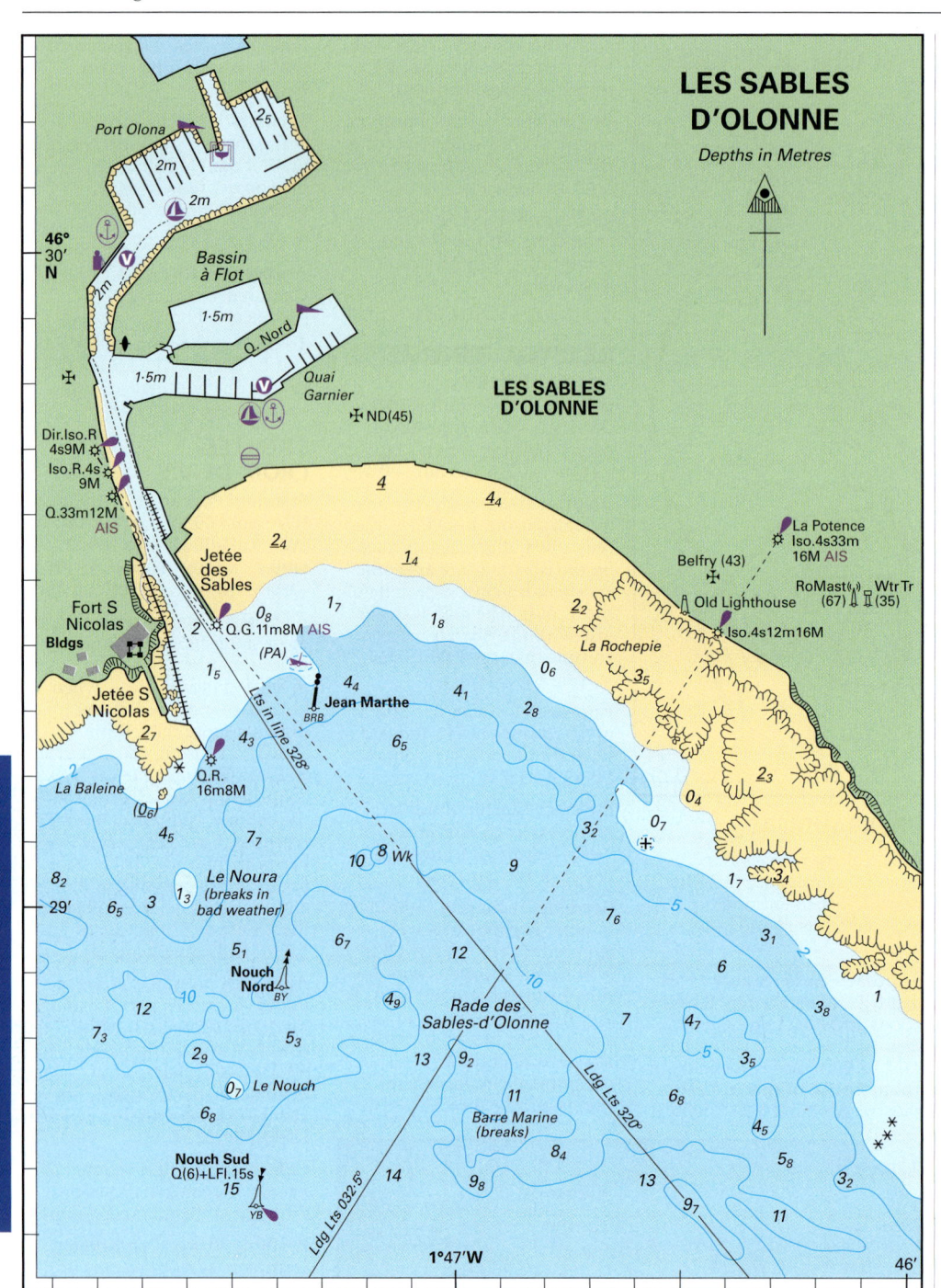

follow the E approach. From the E and S, follow ldg ln 320°, the head of the Jetée des Sables, Q.G., with the Tour Arundel, Q., large tr with castellated top.

Entrance When Jean Marthe, BRB buoy is abeam, bear a little to port, and follow leading line of 328°. Day marks, two white towers with red topmarks, difficult to distinguish. Do not get too close to either jetty. Beware of foot ferries running between banks.

Berthing
- **Quai Garnier** First basin to stb on the approach. Marina on the S bank, convenient for Les Sables. Visitors' pontoon by Capitainerie.

☏ HM 02 51 96 43 34 or Mobile 06 73 76 94 65.

- **Port Olona** Continue past the two basins to stb, reception pontoon, to port. Berth here, and report to HM office, where a finger berth will probably be allocated.

☏ HM 02 51 32 51 16.

Facilities A major yachting centre with a good range of chandleries and repair facilities. Fuel at Port Olona. Restaurants and bars near to marinas. Shops and market in La Chaume, Tuesday, Thursday and Sunday, and Les Sables d'Olonne daily except Monday. Rly. WiFi.

PORT DE BOURGENAY

Tidal data as Les Sables d'Olonne

Purpose built marina and holiday resort 6m SE of Les Sables d'Olonne.

Approach Safe water buoy 46°25'·33N 1°41'·83W immediately SW of marina entrance. Ldg Lts Q.G.7M, 040°, not easy to see. Left-hand corner of conspic large W building to E of marina, easier to see and 040° on this appoximates to ldg bearing.

Entrance Stb edge of channel marked by G can and G bn. Entry channel dredged to 1m below CD. Entry and exit not recommended in swell or in on-shore winds. Keep to mid-channel to avoid rocks near hbr moles.

Berthing Reception pontoon to stb on entry inside Jetée Est.

Facilities Fuel, chandlery, WiFi. In Season, shops up the hill beyond the holiday village. Swimming pool in holiday village. Bars and restaurants. Supermarket at Talmont St-Hilaire.

☏ HM 02 51 22 20 36.

PERTUIS BRETON TO LA PALLICE

DS in Pertuis Breton: the flood or ESE stream begins HW–0600 Pte de Grave; the ebb stream begins at or shortly after HW. A marine farm, length 2½M in NW/SE direction has been established approx 4M N of Ile de Ré, marked by four card buoys. There is restricted passage between La Pallice and Ile de Ré due to road bridge (30m clearance). Controlled passage, S bound between piers Nos.10 and 11, and N-bound between piers Nos.13 and 14, buoyed channels each marked by port and starboard pillar buoys with topmarks.

ARS-EN-RÉ

Standard Port Pointe de Grave
HW (sp)–0030 (np)+0005
LW (sp)–0025 (np)–0030

MHWS	MHWN	MLWN	MLWS
+0·7m	+0·5m	+0·3m	+0·1m

An attractive small town which has become very fashionable. Makes a good base from which to explore the N of the island, especially the nature reserve. Some very good beaches within cycling distance.

Approach and Entrance Best on a rising tide, from HW–0230, according to draft and tidal coefficient. Good visibility recommended and a night entry to be avoided. From a position to the N of Les Islette N Card tr, make good a course to pass S of the Bûcheron buoys. Continue on this course past the stb bn for ½M until the buoyed channel can be seen to port. The black and white spire of the church is a useful landmark at this point. The leading marks, red trellis in front of a rectangle 232°, difficult to see. Channel well buoyed and reputed to be dredged. Check with HM. Tidal streams can reach over 4kn near Bûcheron buoys and at the entrance to the Fiers D'Ars.

Berthing In both basins as directed by HMs.

Basin de la Criée to stb. Visitors' pontoons to port immediately after crossing sill. Berths for larger vessels farthest away from the entrance.

Basin de la Prée, at the head of the entrance channel. Visitors berth on D.

Anchoring Some moorings, outside marina, shallow draught vessels may find a space to anchor.

Facilities Small chandlery. Shops, restaurants and excellent daily morning market. Cycle hire, beaches.

☏ HM (Criée) 05 46 29 25 10;
HM (Prée) 05 46 29 08 52.

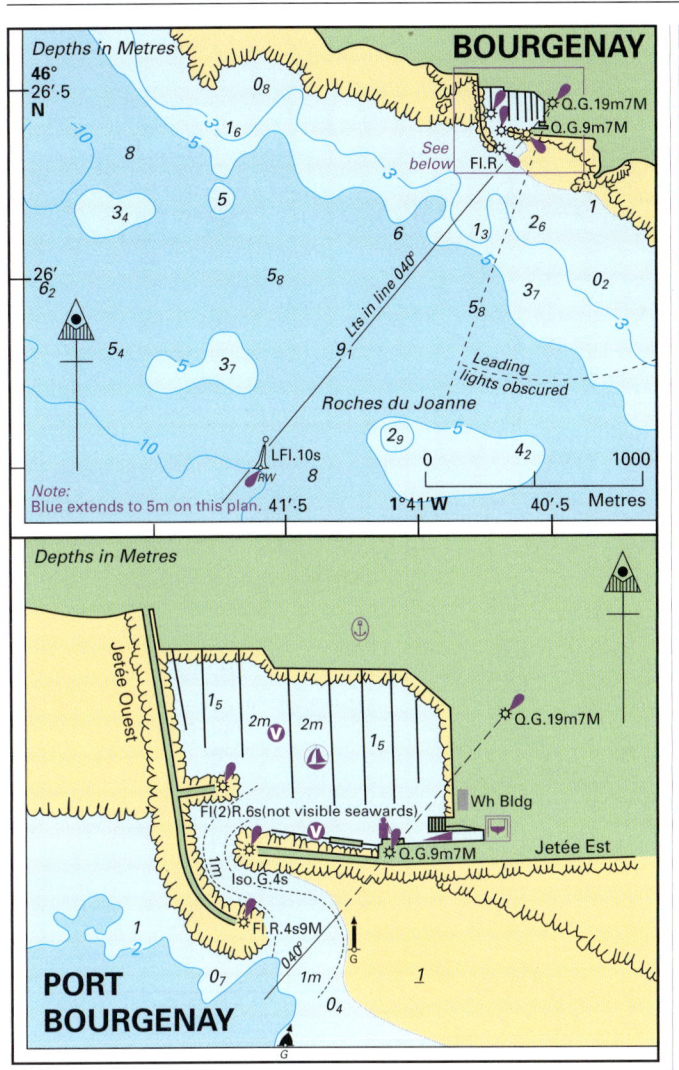

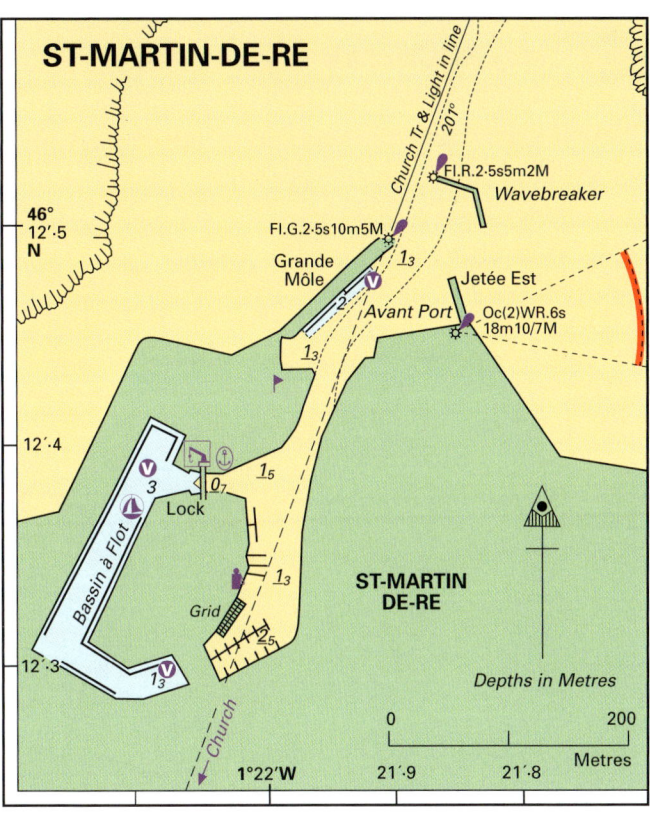

ST-MARTIN-DE-RÉ

Tidal data as Ars–en–Re

One of the most picturesque harbours in W France. Very sheltered in inner harbour. Space is at a premium, but HM accommodates a large number of vessels in the small space available. Multihulls not allowed in marina.

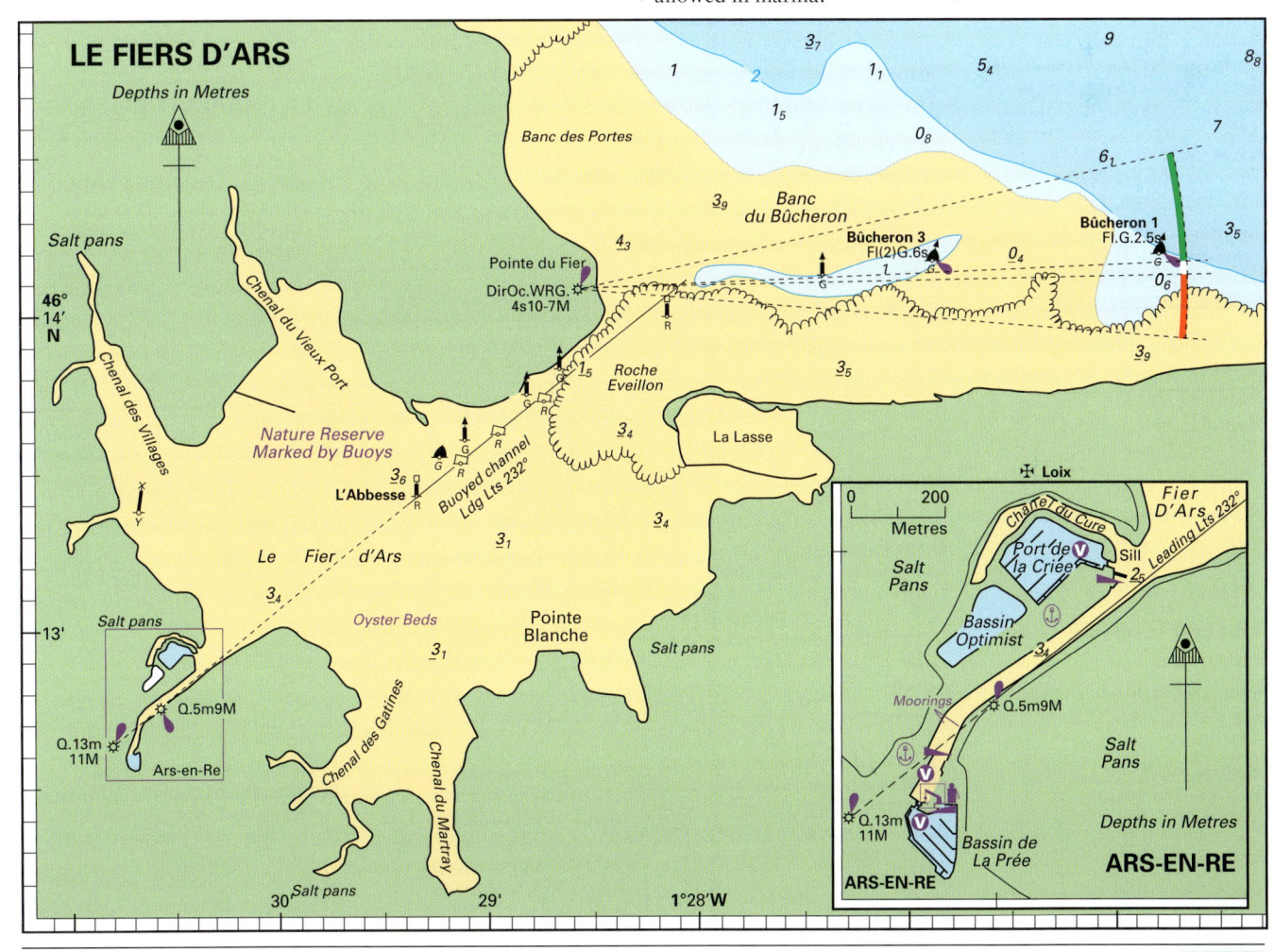

Approach Four W buoys for waiting vessels. Lock opens HW−0300 to HW+0230: July/August within 0500–2300; May, June and September 0630–2200; March/October 0800–1900 (2000 at weekend). Entry difficult in strong NW winds, which produce swell in outer harbour. Leading marks, Fl.G.2·5s on Grande Môle with the square church tr 201·5° to N end of the outer breakwater.

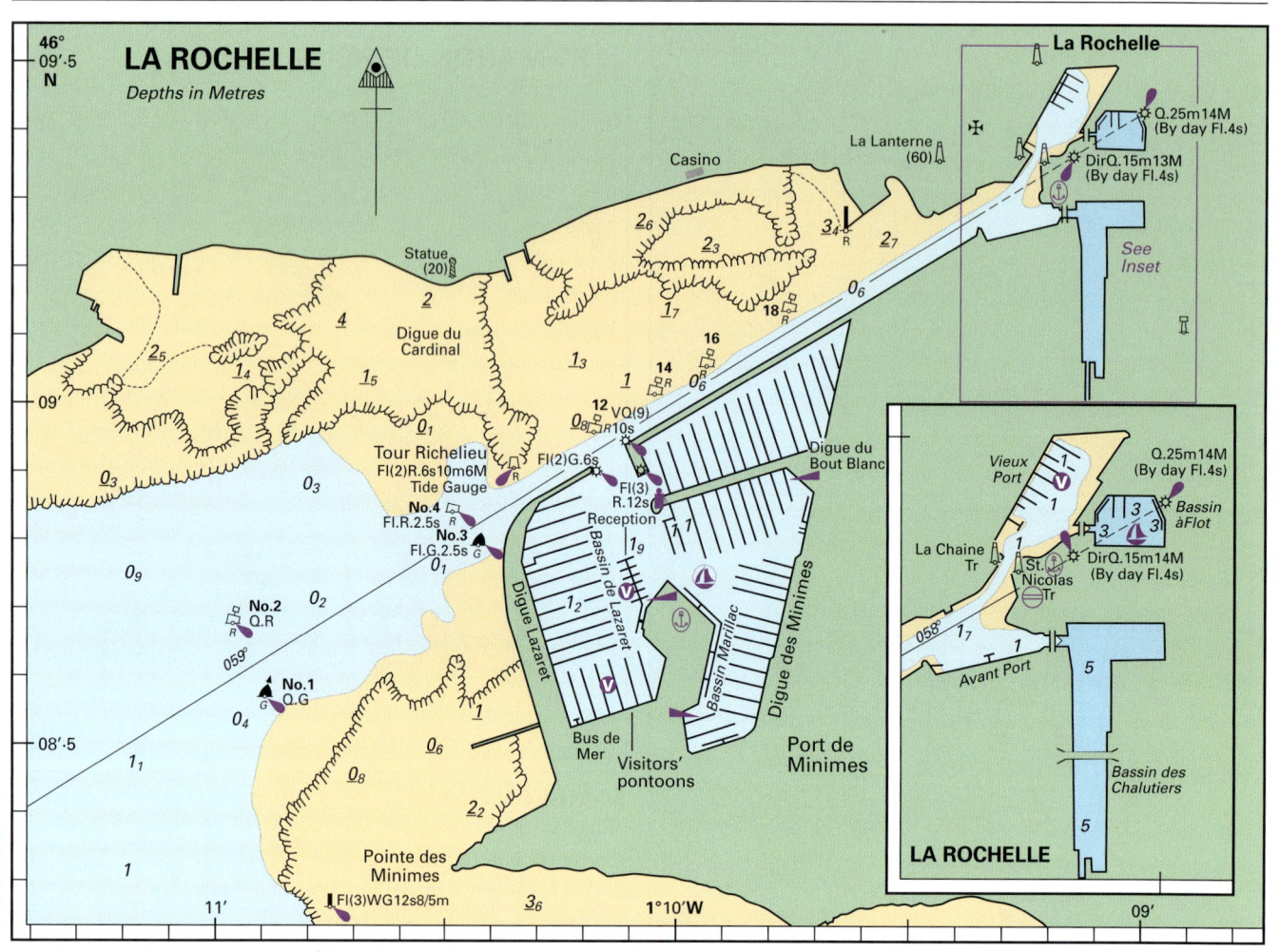

Entrance Turn into outer harbour, and pass between the Grande Môle and Jetée Est. Follow the line of the Grande Môle, to the entrance to inner harbour. Steer so stb on entering inner harbour to pass into inner basin. Entry Lts.

Berthing On Grande Môle in outer harbour (exposed to swell) or in locked marina. Follow directions of HM. Visitors' pontoon, boats >10m immediately ahead of entrance, expect to raft. Further berths at head of basin.

Facilities Restaurants, WiFi, daily morning market. Supermarkets towards La Flotte. Beaches (nearest beyond the prison), museum, cycle hire. Buses to mainland and around island. Excellent cycle tracks.

☏ HM 05 46 09 26 69.

LA FLOTTE-EN-RÉ

Tidal data as Ars–en-Re

Small drying hbr. Delightful town but smaller than St Martin.

Entrance 212° on La Flotte LtHo FlWG.4s10m12/9M. Chevrons indicate final line of approach. Limits of oyster park indicated by bns.

Berthing Visitors berth on the hammerheads immediately to stb on entry on either side of the Jetée Nord.

Anchorage Five W visitors' buoys in good depth of water outside hbr. Exposed to N.

Facilities Shops, restaurants.

☏ HM 05 46 09 67 66.

LA ROCHELLE

Standard Port Pointe de Grave
HW (sp) –0030 (np) +0015
LW (sp) –0020 (np) –0025
MHWS MHWN MLWN MLWS
+0·8m +0·5m +0·3m –0·1m

An important historic town renowned for its architecture and arcades. Yachts may berth in either Minimes, the large marina that may be entered in most states of the tide, or in the Vieux Port if <11m. Larger vessels may arrange berthing in the Bassin des Chalutiers. The marinas provide excellent shelter. However, during the grand Pavois, usually in September, and the weeks before and after it, visiting yachts are not permitted in the Vieux Port and may find it difficult to find a berth in Minimes.

Approach Tour Richelieu (R tr), is easy to identify; the W bn Fl(3)WG.12s8M, near S edge of plan, looks like a Chinese bandstand. Ldg Lts, 059°, by day two white towers, (not easy to distinguish) Fl.4s; by night DirQ. and Q.

Entrance At LWS there may be insufficient depth of water to proceed to either Minimes or the Vieux Port.

• **Minimes** Shortly after passing the Richelieu, R tr, the buoys marking the entrance to Minimes, W Card Buoy, and two R can buoys, will be seen. Leave these to port.

• **Vieux Port** The channel from Minimes to Vieux Port is clearly buoyed. Beware of ferries.

Berthing

• **Minimes** Visitors should report to the reception pontoon which is straight ahead on entry. A berth should be allocated. Failing this, report to the Capitainerie as soon as possible.

• **Bassin de Chalutiers** Entrance to stb downstream of the Towers. Lock opens HW–0200 to HW +0130.

• **Vieux Port** After passing between the towers, find a berth on the N side of the first pontoon, or either side of the second pontoon. For a longer stay, it may be possible to berth by arrangement in either the Bassin à Flot or the Ancien Basin des Chalutiers.

Facilities Bus and ferry service between Minimes and Vieux Port. Daily morning indoor mkt in La Rochelle. Excellent yachting support services. Good rail and air connections. Network of cycle tracks. Beaches close to both marinas. Ferries to offshore islands. Cycle hire. WiFi.

☏ HMs:
Minimes 05 46 44 41 20.
Vieux Port 05 46 41 32 05.

LA CHARENTE RIVER

Standard Port Pointe de Grave
Ile d'Aix
HW (sp) –0040 (np) +0015
LW (sp) –0025 (np) –0030
MHWS MHWN MLWN MLWS
+0·8m +0·5m +0·3m –0·1m

Sheltered river in which the streams can be strong, especially on a spring ebb. Navigation in the river is forbidden at night when the banks cannot be seen.

Bar The bar can be crossed at HW–0300, which will allow sufficient time to arrive at Rochefort to lock into the marina at approximately HW–0030.

Approach From either E or W of L'Île d'Aix where boats may anchor to await the tide.

Entrance Marked by three G con buoys. The white leading towers, with red tops, on the north bank are easily identified, (115°) but the next pair on the southern shore are more difficult. A course of 135° from the second stb buoy will bring the deep-water channel marked by the moorings at Port des Barques to port. Beyond here, the channel is indicated by pairs of lettered bns on shore. Downstream of Rochefort there is the Transponder which now takes only tourists across the river.

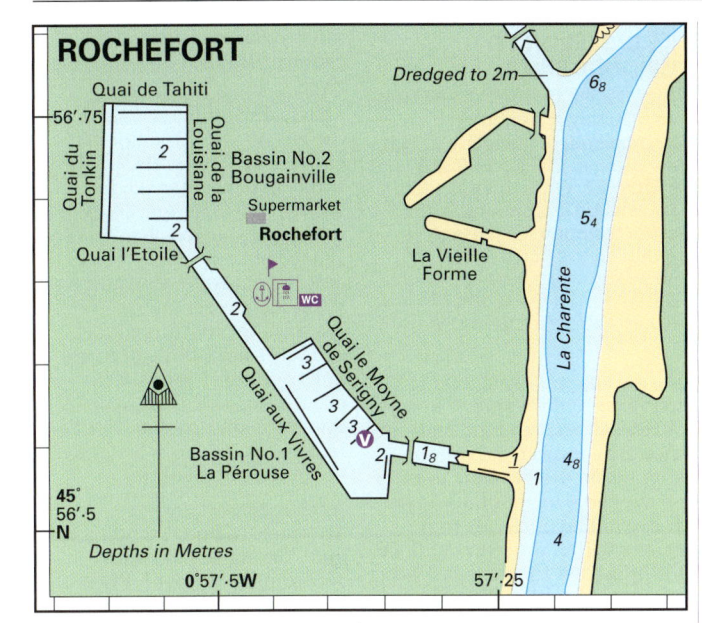

Anchorages Mooring areas are marked by yellow buoys. Boats may anchor outside the designated mooring areas but the river is used by commercial craft which have priority, monitor VHF 12. The stream runs very strongly in the upper reaches of the river (4kn) and it might be prudent to take a vacant mooring. White visitors' buoy above the landing pontoon at Port des Barques, and pontoons at Soubise, where boats may ground at LWS.

ROCHEFORT

Standard Port Pointe de Grave
HW (sp) −0015 (np) +0035
LW (sp) +0125 (np) +0030

MHWS	MHWN	MLWN	MLWS
+1·2m	+0·9m	+0·1m	−0·2m

This historic town, well worth visiting, was where France built her navy. Europe's longest building, La Corderie, is now home to a museum, library and other organisations. Interesting architecture and range of museums. Protected marina with very helpful staff.

Entrance To port just beyond the pontoon of La Corderie Hotel is the entrance to the marina. Waiting pontoon to port. Take care to keep close to the port side as metal poles protrude to stb. Boats may also wait on the Corderie Royale pontoon; avoid berth reserved for the Vedette, no rafting.

Berthing Lock opens May to August 0500 to 2300, April and September 0630–2100, October to March by prior arrangement 24 hrs in advance, at approximately local HW −0030 to HW, unless the coefficient is exceptionally low. Berths allocated prior to entering marina.

Facilities Most marina facilities, 16-ton crane, WiFi, chandleries, but no fuel or garage within a sensible distance. Market days, Tuesday, Thursday and Saturday. Rly. Airport at La Rochelle.

☏ HM 05 46 83 99 96 or *Mobile* 06 86 01 64 29 open high season 0800–1200, 1400–1900; low season 0900–1200, 1400–1700.

ST-DENIS D'OLÉRON

Standard Port Pointe de Grave
HW (sp) −0040 (np) +0015

MHWS	MHWN	MLWN	MLWS
+0·7m	+0·6m	+0·4m	+0·2m

Sheltered marina behind a sill, 1·5m CD. At half-tide 1·9m on sill. White waiting buoys outside the hbr. At springs may be necessary to anchor further out.

Approach and Entrance Entrance dries and the approach is over shallows. Keep to mid-channel. Tide gauge by fuel pontoon.

Berthing Visitors' pontoon to port on entry, <11m on fingers, >11m, alongside or on hammerhead. Usually a reception dory on duty.

Facilities Fuel (cards), WiFi, cycle hire, beaches, bars and restaurants near marina, shops and daily morning market in town. Buses. Ferry service to mainland in season.

☏ HM 05 46 47 97 97.

LE DOUHET

Tidal data as St–Denis d'Oléron

Marina behind a sill, (1·8m in S basin, 2·9m in N basin). Sheltered from W winds. Entry difficult in NE winds, channel subject to silting in winter. Night entry not advised. Waiting buoys outside.

Approach The 300m entrance channel is marked by R and G buoys with reflective bands. Water level gauge to port before sill to S basin.

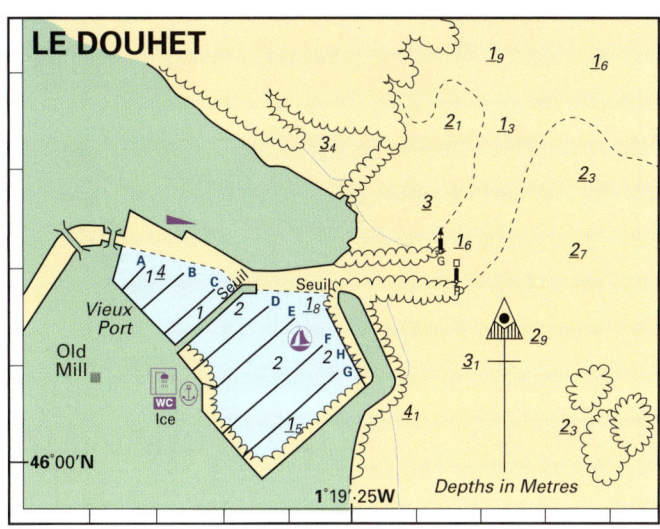

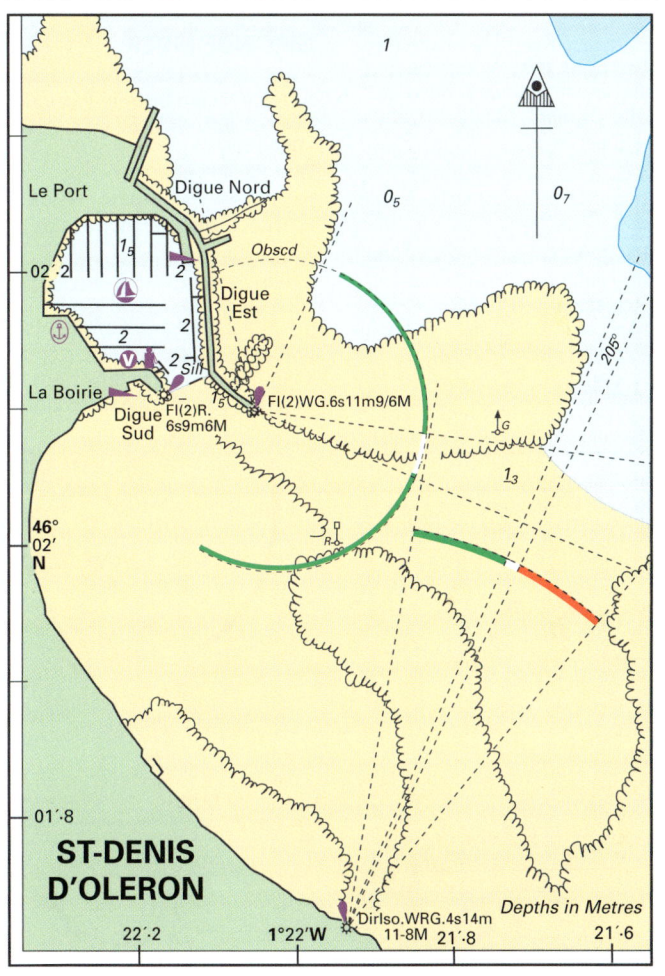

Access Tidal coefficient 80:

Draught 1·0m HW−0345 to HW+0330

Draught 1·50m HW−0315 to HW+0300

Draught 2·0m m HW−0240 to HW+0200

Berthing On visitors' pontoon and report to Capitainerie.

Facilities No fuel. Chandlery. Bakery and cycle hire. Shops at St-Georges-d'Oléron, and Le Brée les Bains. Market days Le Brée Wednesday, Friday and Sunday out of season. In season every morning. Pleasant cycle rides. Restaurant near marina. Beaches.

☏ HM 05 46 76 71 13.

BOYARDVILLE

Tidal data as St-Denis d'Oléron

Sheltered marina behind an automatic gate whose approach is across drying sandbanks. Gate to marina opens at HW±0300 with a coefficient of 100 and from HW−0230 to HW+0130 with a coefficient of 35. Waiting pontoon to stb above the lock.

Approach With a sufficient rise of water, track from La Perrotine G con buoy 0·4M ENE of La Perrotine Jetty to LtHo on La Perrotine Jetty, Fl(2)R.6s8m5M, to avoid the drying banks. Avoid the marine reserve (entry forbidden) to the S of the approach.

BOYARDVILLE

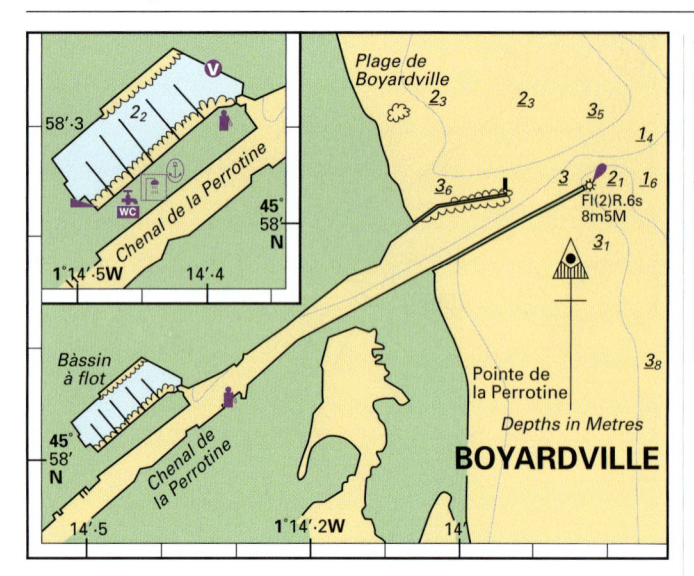

Entrance Keep 10m from the Perrotine Jetty. When the first slip to stb is abeam, move to mid-channel. Marina to stb.

Berthing Visitors' pontoon to stb on entrance. Waiting pontoon outside marina – may dry.

Facilities Some shops and small morning market in season. Restaurants nr marina. Cycle hire, beaches. Buses and ferries to mainland in season.

☎ HM 05 46 47 23 71.

GIRONDE RIVER

HW entrance Pte de Grave HW
At **No.9** N card buoy in Passe de L'Ouest HW –0300 SE 2·5kn HW +0400 NW 4kn
Flood 2·5kn, ebb 4kn

MHWS	MHWN	MLWN	MLWS
5·1m	4·2m	2·1m	1·0m

Approach and Entrance Steep seas occur from swell, strong currents (3–5kn at springs) winds from NW to SW over Force 5 and conditions producing contrary directions of wind, current and or swell.

ÎLE D'OLÉRON TO GIRONDE RIVER

The passage through the Pertuis de Maumusson is not recommended. Complete details are given in the *Bay of Biscay Pilot NP22*. Without local knowledge it is preferable to make the open sea passage rounding the north end of the Île d'Oléron at a suitable distance from the N card bn tower *Antioche* Q.20m11M.

Dangerous seas break on the sandbanks which shift. Current charts essential and the buoyage should be respected. No attempt should be made to enter on the ebb. Height of tide given at five minute intervals from gauges within the river (VHF 16 for broadcast frequency). Two entrance channels, Passe de l'Ouest and Passe Sud. The latter should only be used if coming from the S, and preferably not for the first entry.

• **Passe de l'Ouest** Used by commercial and fishing vessels. The flood may be delayed, entry after LW+0100 or later advised. From the N, leave No.2a Fl.R.2·5s to port, avoiding Banc de la Mauvaise, and follow the stb edge of the channel until after No.11 Iso.G.4s, when yachts may safely navigate between the channel and the N bank of the river.

• **Passe du Sud** Enter only if there is no swell and not before HW Pte de Grave –0430. To avoid all dangers make for Graves RW safewater buoy and follow the buoyed channel. The change of course prior to G3 must be made promptly, or a yacht may be set on the shallows to S of the channel. Leading marks difficult to see unless visibility is good. If proceeding to Royan, keep upstream after passing No.12 Fl(3)R.12s, to avoid being set on Banc de St Georges.

Anchorages

• N shore, in Bonne Anse. Sand, mud, drying area, anchor according to draught. Rade de Royan, only if weather good and no swell, SE of hbr entrance.
• S shore, Verdon-sur-mer, N of Pointe de la Chambrette.

Upstream of Royan, other anchorages may be found in soft mud and strong currents.

ROYAN

Standard Port Pointe de Grave
HW (sp) –0005 (np) +0000
LW (sp) +0000 (np) +0000

MHWS	MHWN	MLWN	MLWS
–0·1m	–0·1m	0·0m	0·0m

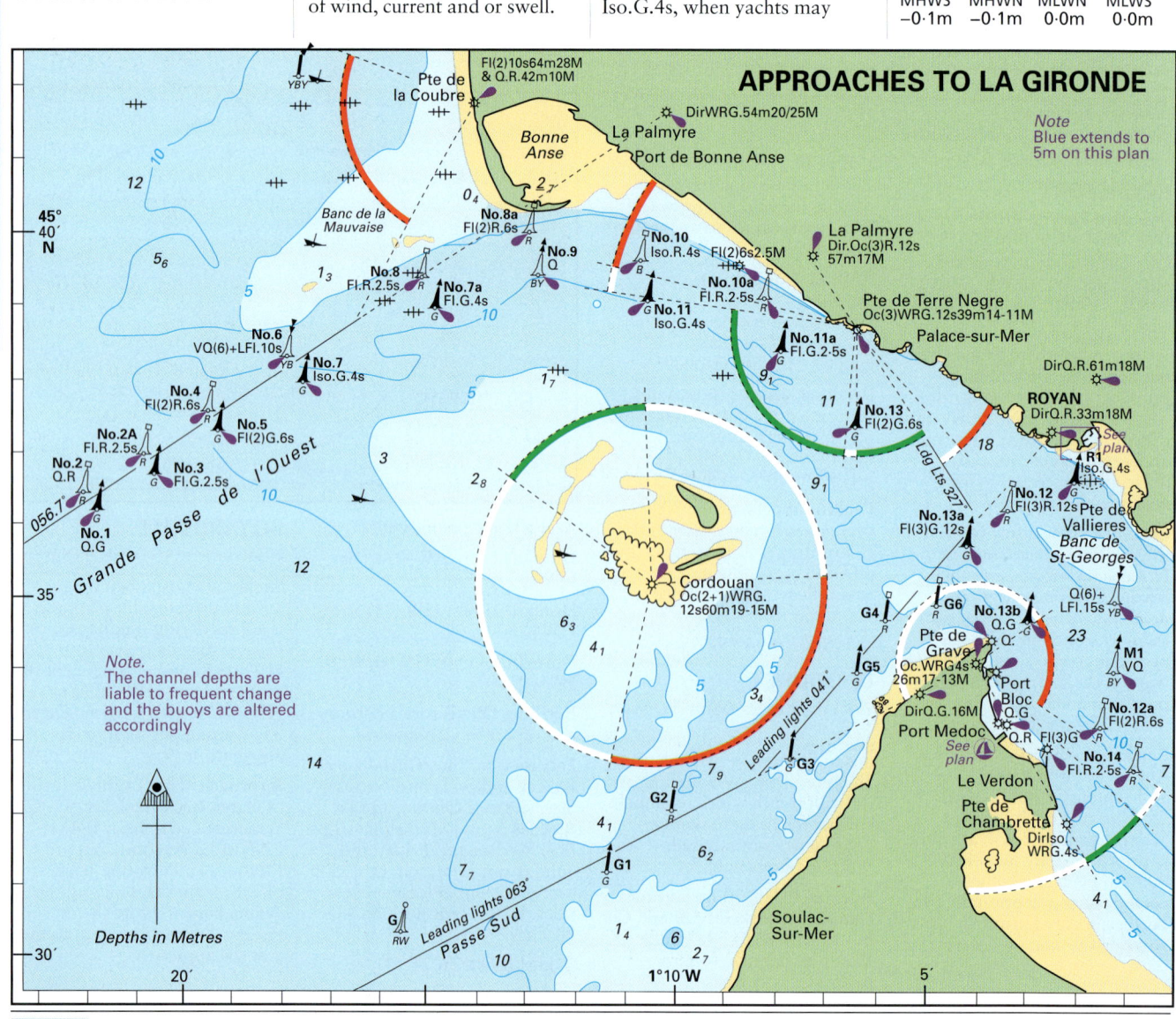

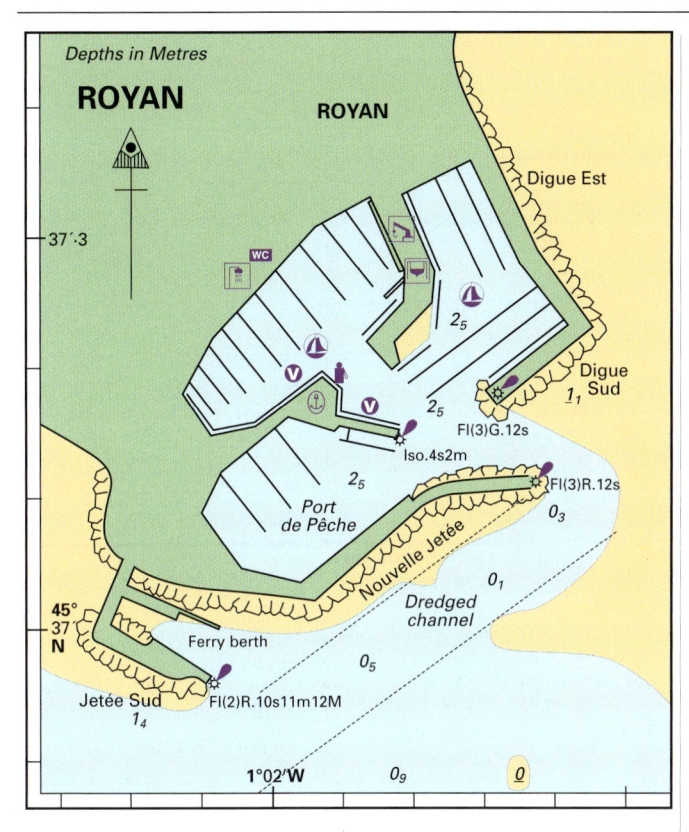

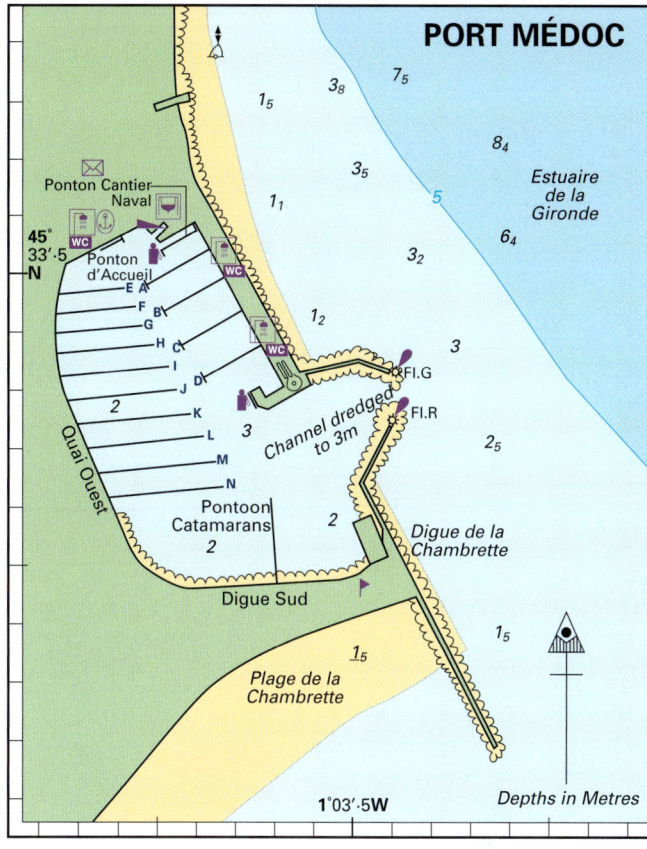

Marina sheltered from all winds.

Entrance Access possible in all conditions and states of the tide, draught permitting. Leave R1 Iso.G.4s to stb. Marina entrance on port side of dredged channel marked by Lts on Jetée Sud Fl(2)R.10s11m12M and Nouvelle Jetée Fl(3)R.12s.

Berthing In season, visiting vessels given berthing instructions from hbr dory. Otherwise, reception pontoon, marked V, is to port on entry.

Facilities Chandleries, boatyard and a good range of support services. Excellent daily indoor mkt. Shops and services of a seaside town.

☎ HM 05 46 38 72 22.

MORTAGNE-SUR-GIRONDE

Small yacht hbr, in attractive town. Lock to inner basin opens from 1 May–31 September HW±0002 from 0600–2300. From October to April lock opens 0800–2000. When the co-efficient is ≤45 these timings are reduced by 1 hour. Phone if in doubt.

Entrance R can Mortagne buoy, close to E Card buoy, narrow channel marked by bns.

Berthing Boats that may take the ground, may berth on the visitors' and reception pontoon on the N bank. If proceeding to inner basin, berth as directed.

Facilities No fuel, restaurants. Stores.

HM ☎ 05 46 90 63 15 or *Mobile* 06 43 48 91 93. HW±0100.

BLAYE

In season 80m pontoon in up to 3m. 24hr stay permitted. Double springs required, moor head to wind. Citadel and resources of a town.

PORT MÉDOC

Tidal data as Royan

Large, well-sheltered marina accessible in all weathers and states of the tide, 2–3m depth, situated on S bank of River Gironde, S of Pte de Grave.

Entrance By a dredged channel, jetty heads painted white, Q.G. and Q.R. Turn to stb after passing the fuel pontoon.

Berthing Reception pontoon for monohulls at far N end of marina. Pontoon for multihulls extends from S side of marina.

Facilities Chandleries, boatyard and restaurants. No supplies. Ferries to Royan from Port Bloc.

☎ HM 05 56 09 69 75.

PAUILLAC

Standard Port Pointe de Grave
HW (sp) +0100 (np) +0100
LW (sp) +0205 (np) +0135
MHWS   MHWN   MLWN   MLWS
+0·2m   0·0m   −1·0m −0·5m

Town renowned for its wine rather than yachting facilities. Marina staff very helpful. Eddies and a strong current run through the marina.

Approach and Entrance Port jetty marked by a large wine bottle with red top. W buoys upstream of entrance for vessels waiting for slack water.

Berthing The two upstream pontoons reserved for visitors. Care is needed when berthing.

BORDEAUX TO CASTETS

At Castets is the first lock into the Canal Latéral à la Garonne which joins the Canal du Midi at Toulouse.

The R Garonne to Castets, 35M, is unbuoyed with extensive mudbanks, and rocky ledges. Garonne pilots do not operate above Bordeaux. Without a detailed chart or a pilot, a barge should be followed; barges moor just above the Bordeaux bridge. Castets can generally be reached on one tide. The flood comes up at over 5kn, the water suddenly rising 0·3m with a 1·5m wave; the last of the ebb goes down at 2kn.

The lock at Castets is to starboard. With the Garonne in spate and the upstream current therefore weakened, it could prove impossible to make Castets on one tide. Ask permission to tie to a barge (they do not move overnight) or to moor alongside the pontoon at Cadillac.

Facilities No fuel (2011). No chandleries but vineyards, restaurants and supplies, Rly. Mast lifting for boats heading for Canal du Midi.

☎ HM 05 56 09 69 75.

BORDEAUX

Standard Port Pointe de Grave
HW (sp) +0225 (np) +0200
LW (sp) +0405 (np) +0330
MHWS   MHWN   MLWN   MLWS
0·0m   −0·2m −1·7m −1·0m

• Marina, Pont du Jour (suspension br) 4M outside city on W bank opposite Lormont. Contact HM when br comes into view. Berth on outer pontoon preferably inside to avoid strong current, quite secure and landing easy; Rly (10 minutes). Shower, toilets and restaurant in YC. Water by hose. Crane on jetty head operated very efficiently by HM for masts. To organise access call HM at least 24hrs or preferably 2–3 days in advance. Lock opens, Tues, Thurs, Sat and Sun, once per day. The new bridge, just upstream of the basins has the same air draught as the Pont de Pierre.

☎ / VHF HM 06 64 49 92 84, VHF 12.
si-plaisance@bordeaux-port.fr

• Dock basin, No.2 at Bordeaux is dirty and charges

Garonne Tidal Data
Standard Port Pointe de Grave

Portets
HW (sp) +0315 (np) +0230
LW (sp) +0525 (np) +0525
MHWS   MHWN   MLWN   MLWS
−0·3m −0·3m −1·9m −1·0m

Cadillac
HW (sp) +0345 (np) +0250
LW (sp) +0645 (np) +0600
MHWS   MHWN   MLWN   MLWS
−1·3m −1·0m −2·0m −1·3m

Langon
HW (sp) +0415 (np) +0310
LW (sp) +0745 (np) +0710
MHWS   MHWN   MLWN   MLWS
−3·0m −2·9m −1·8m −1·0m

Castets
HW (sp) +0435 (np) n/a
LW (sp) +0840 (np) n/a
MHWS   MHWN   MLWN   MLWS
−4·0m   n/a   n/a   −1·0m

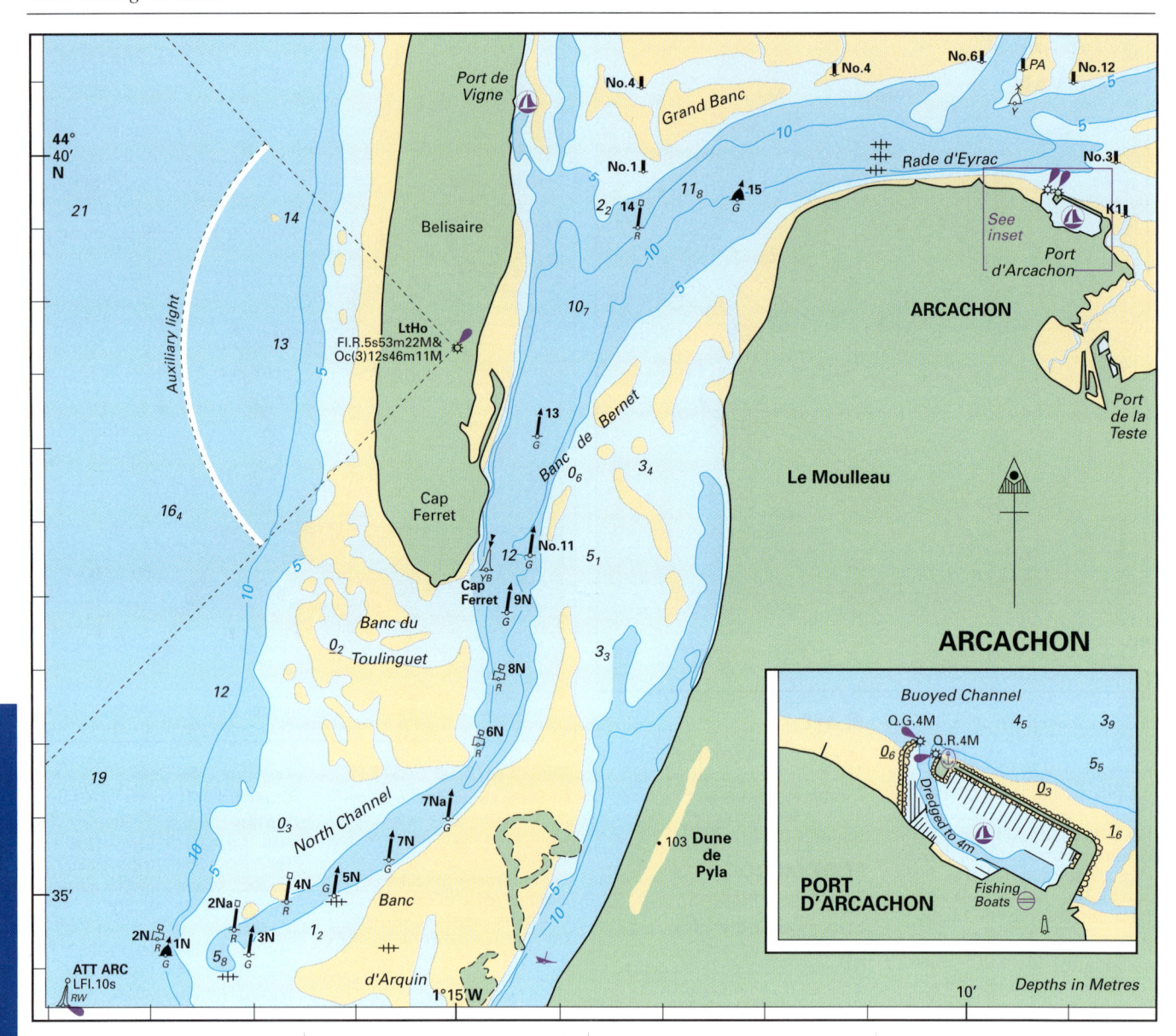

are high. Lock opens HW–0200 to +0030. Canal pilot book available from HM office.

BASSIN D'ARCACHON

Standard Port Pointe de Grave
HW (sp) +0020 (np) +0005
LW (sp) +0030 (np) +0005

MHWS	MHWN	MLWN	MLWS
–1·1m	–1·1m	–0·8m	–0·6m

GIRONDE TO CAPBRETON WARNING

The firing range (CELM) with limits of:
45°28'N 1°14'W,
45°11'N 2°04'W,
43°56'N 2°17'W and
43°41'N 1°31'W
operates from Monday to Friday from 0800. Within this area, there is a forbidden zone:
44°23'·57N 1°26'·22W,
44°23'·57N 1°24'·72W,
44°21'·97N 1°24'·72W and
44°21'·97N 1°26'·22W.
Navigation is forbidden in or near any sector where firing is taking place. Information on firing activity is broadcast on VHF Ch 06 and VHF Ch 10 at 0703, 0715, 0733, 0745, 0803, 0815 and 1615. (This last being

Approach and Entrance
Fairway entrance is about 2½M S of Cap Ferret at the ATT ARC pillar buoy LFl.10s. The position of the channel frequently changes and the buoyage must be observed. Enter in calm conditions, as swell and onshore winds produce breaking seas on the banks, during daylight as the buoys are not lit.

for the following day). Information on firing times and GPS positions of the extent of the areas to be used may also be obtained from the Semaphore stations, Chassiron, Pointe de Grave, Cap Ferret, Messanges, Socoa or Cross Etel or ☎ 02 97 55 35 35. Firing may occur anywhere within the zone and yachtsmen transiting the firing range should ignore any previous information regarding safety channels.

Passage lights	BA No
Cap Ferret	1378
Fl.R.5s53m22M+Oc(3)12s	
Contis	1382
Fl(4)25s50m23M	
Pointe Saint-Martin	1410
Fl(2)10s73m27M	

Enter no later than Pte de Grave HW–0245. Currents in the Bassin d'Arcachon are strong, 3·5kn on a spring ebb. The effect of the flood may be delayed by an hour. Channel dredged to 4m. Information on sea state and conditions on bar Cap Ferrat Semaphore VHF 16: buoyage, depths and positions of sand banks, Le Service Maritime.
☎ 05 56 83 32 97.

Anchorages N of Port de Vigne. There are a number of small ports and other anchorages which may be accessible to vessels, depending on draught. Large scale charts essential. Channels marked by numbered and lettered bns.

Berthing Port d'Arcachon for vessels <20m. Possibility of grounding. A modern marina in a very smart seaside town. Can be entered at all hours and state of the tide. Telephone to reserve berth. Do not take a mooring close to marina entrance without permission.

Facilities All marine support facilities and those of a town. Rly.

☎ HM 08 90 71 17 33.

CAPBRETON

Standard Port Pointe de Grave
HW –0035

MHWS	MHWN	MLWN	MLWS
–1·1m	–1·1m	–0·4m	–0·3m

Large marina, divided into three basins. Entrance after half-flood, but not in strong on-shore winds or swell. From June to September, a foot ferry may operate between basins.

Entrance The very narrow entrance lies between a stone jetty to the N and a wooden jetty to the S. The latter has a 30m extension which is underwater after half-tide. Beware of strong currents and surf. Keep closer to N breakwater until level with the statue. Then cross to just S of mid-stream. When entering marina, beware of cross current from Canal d'Hossegor; this is more noticeable on the ebb.

Berthing Reception on first pontoon to stb on entry, report to Capitainerie. May ground at LWS on visitors' berth.

Facilities Chandleries, WiFi. No fuel Wed in low season. Seaside town, beaches. Rly Bayonne 10M, Airport Biarritz 16M.

☎ HM 05 58 72 21 23.

CAPBRETON

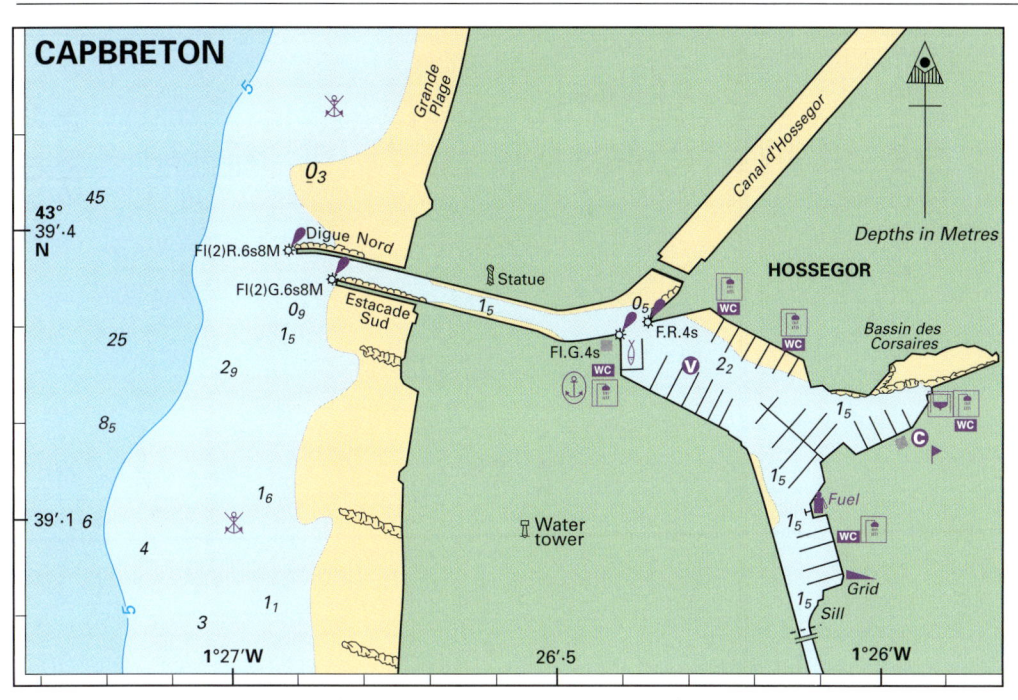

ST-JEAN-DE-LUZ

Standard Port Pointe de Grave
HW –0042   LW –0038
MHWS MHWN MLWN MLWS
–1·0m –1·0m –0·5m –0·4m

A delightful historic town in a sheltered bay. Superb beaches and scenery.

Approach and Entrance Enter the bay between the Digue des Criques and Digue D'Artha. The entrance to Larraldenia Marina at Ciboure is buoyed.

Berthing Marina directly ahead after passing into the inner harbour at Ciboure. Do not enter fishing port to port. Marina is small, crowded but friendly. Use anchorage at Socoa if no berths are available.

Facilities Rail connections, all facilities of a town. Chandlery. Airport at Biarritz

☎ HM 05 59 47 26 81 (not lunchtime).

ANGLET, BAYONNE AND RIVER ADOUR

Standard Port Pointe de Grave
Boucau
HW –0032   LW –0032
MHWS MHWN MLWN MLWS
–1·1m –1·1m –0·4m –0·3m

Approach RW safewater buoy Fl.10s approx. 1M NNW of entrance.

Entrance Digue Jean Lesbordes extends to N of entrance channel. River entrance marked by N and S jetties; the S jetty marked by a W square tr with a G top and ADOUR S in black. Beware of fishing boats that extend their nets across the entrance channel. If proceeding upriver to Bayonne, above Port d'Anglet, best water to stb. Commercial vessels have priority.

Berthing

• **Port d'Anglet** on S bank. Port de Plaisance Brise-Lames. Opposite an industrial area but cleaner than might be expected. Reception on pontoon E.
Facilities Chandleries, travel-lift. Shops and Rly at Bayonne. Buses to Bayonne and Biarritz (airport).
HM ☎ 08 10 10 01 35.

• **Bayonne** Historic town within easy cycling distance of Port Anglet. Good art gallery at Musée Bonnat.
Facilities Good rail and bus connections. Airport at Biarritz.

Anchorage Upstream of Port d'Anglet off N bank opposite G con Iso.4s. Out of the channel at Bouclou. Holding good but may be noisy. A mooring may be available, consult Capitainerie or Yacht Club.

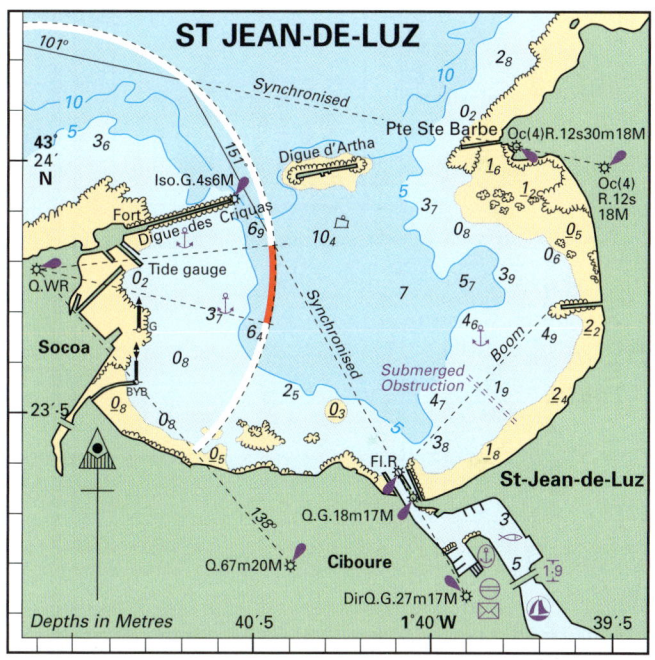

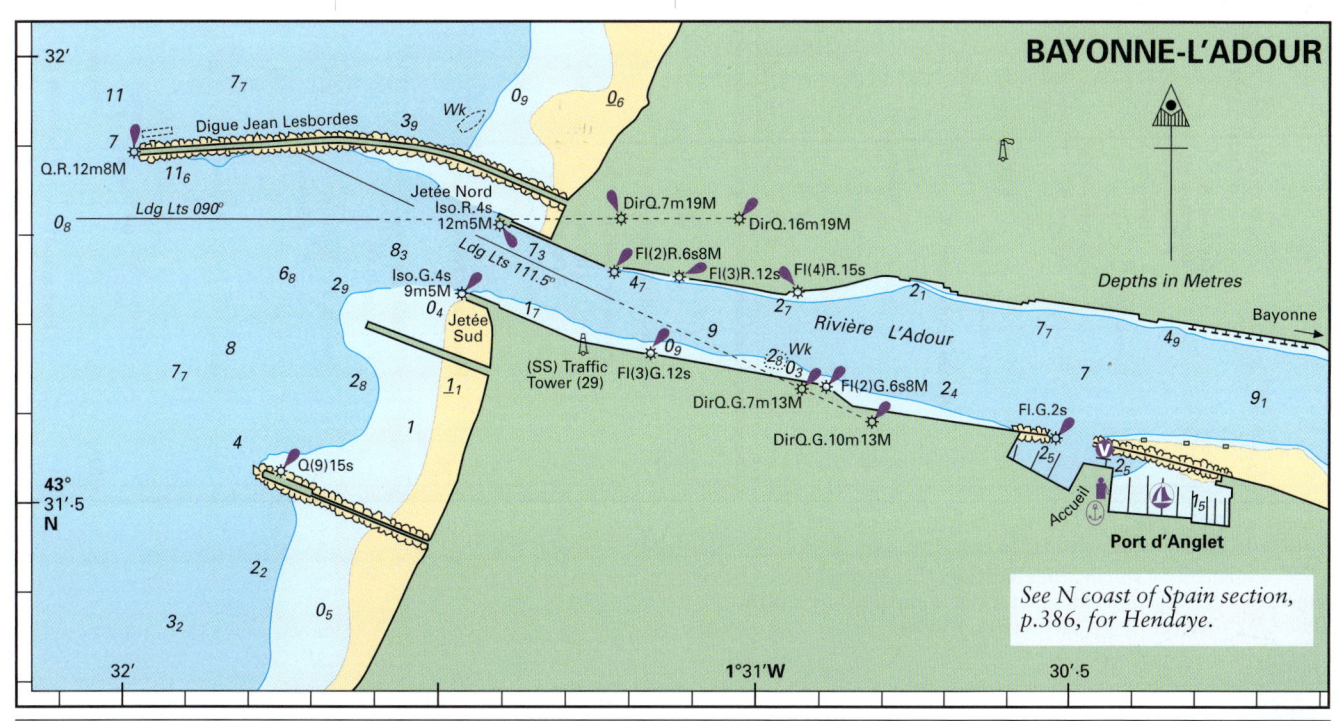

ST JEAN-DE-LUZ

BAYONNE-L'ADOUR

See N coast of Spain section, p.386, for Hendaye.

FRANCE – WEST COAST

383

The Cruising Almanac

SPAIN AND PORTUGAL

SPAIN N & NW COASTS

Note: Spanish marinas work on VHF 09 unless stated otherwise.

Met (Inshore) 0840, 1240, 2010

Station	VHF
Pasajes	27
Bilbao	26
Santander	24
Cabo Peñas	26
Navia	60
Cabo Ortegal	02
A Coruña	26
Finisterre	22
Vigo	65

Navia Radio VHF 60
Met 0840, 1240, 2010

Cortegal Radio VHF 02
Met 0840, 1240, 2010

Locations (Spain N & NW):
- Puerto de Pasajes 386
- Hondarribia 386
- San Sebastián 387
- Getaria 387
- Zumaia 387
- Bermeo 388
- Lequeitio 388
- Bilbao 388
- Laredo 389
- Santander 389
- Castro Urdiales 387
- San Vicente de la Barquera 391
- Llanes 391
- Ribadesella 391
- Gijón 391
- Luanco 392
- Cudillero 392
- Aviles 392
- Luarca 392
- Ribadeo 392
- Vivero 393
- S. Marta & Cariño 394
- Cedeira 395
- *Rias Ares & Betanzos* 395
- A Coruña 397
- *Corme & Laxe* 397
- Corcubión 397
- *Camariñas* 397
- C Finisterre
- Muros 399
- *Ria de Arousa* 400
- Vilagarcia 399
- Combarro 399
- *Ria de Pontevedra* 403
- Vigo 405
- Baiona 405

SPAIN SW COAST

Note: Spanish marinas work on VHF 09

Met (Inshore) 0833, 1133, 2033

Station	VHF
Cádiz	26
Tarifa	21

Locations (Spain SW):
- Vila Real de San Antonio & Ayamonte 412
- Isla Cristina 412
- Punta Umbria 413
- Mazagón 413
- Chipiona 413
- Cádiz 413
- Sancti-Petri 415
- Barbate 415
- Alcaidesa Marina La Línea 416
- Gibraltar 416
- Tangier
- Granada
- Málaga
- Sevilla
- *Rio Guadalquivir*
- *Atlantic Ocean*
- *Mediterranean Sea*

PORTUGAL

Met 1030, 1700

Station	VHF
Lisbon MRCC	11

Locations (Portugal):
- Viana do Castelo 405
- Povoa de Varzim 406
- Leixões 406
- R Douro 406
- *R de Aveiro* 407
- Figueira da Foz 407
- Nazaré 407
- Peniche 407
- Cascais 408
- Lisboa 408
- Seixal
- Sines 409
- Cabo de São Vicente
- Lagos 409
- Portimão 410
- Albufeira 410
- Vilamoura 411
- Faro 411
- Tavira 411

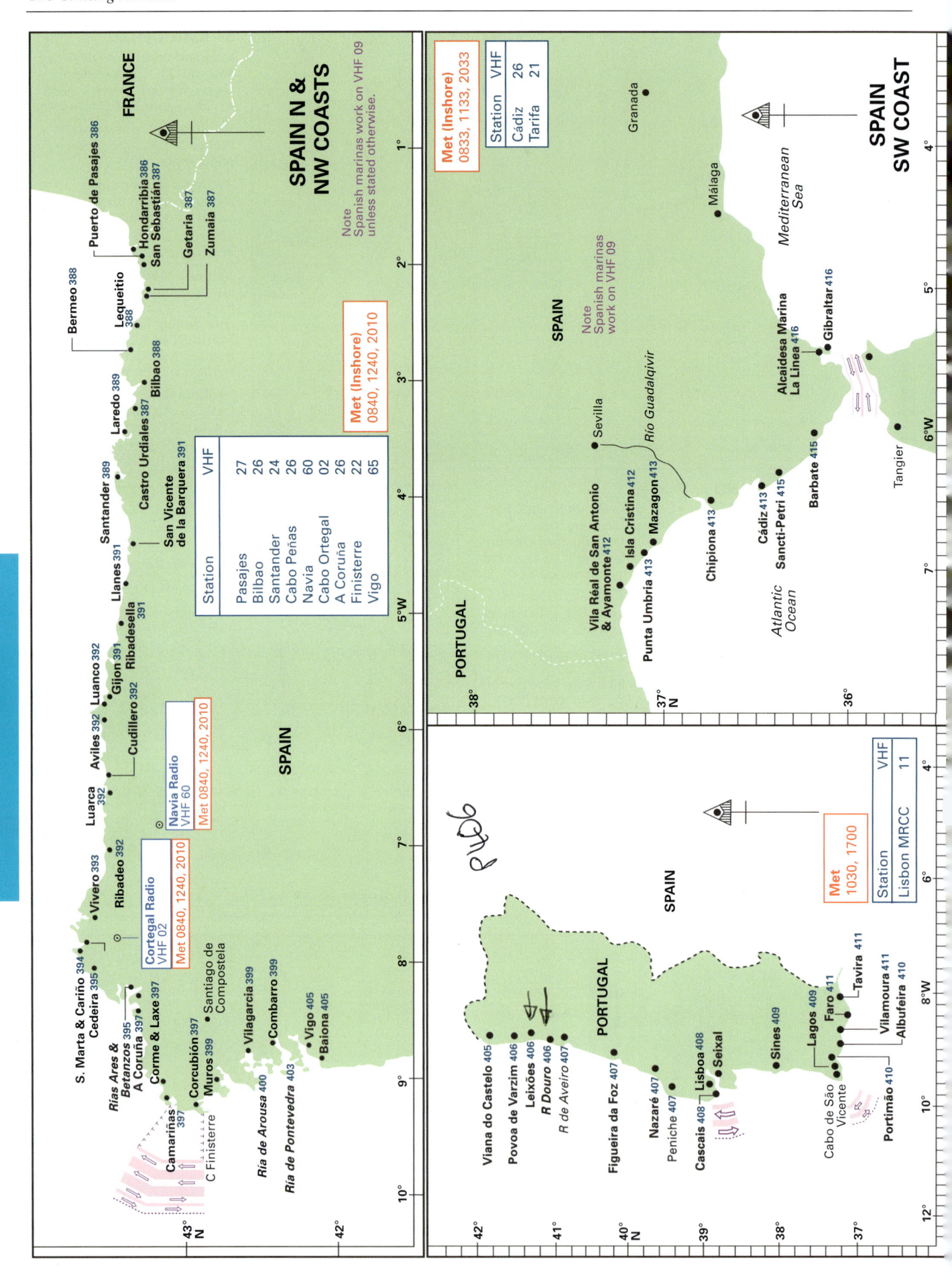

Page references are shown after locations, for example:
Vigo 398. Bold type indicates that it is accompanied by a plan.
Italics are used for rivers, lochs, bays, seas etc.

Spain and Portugal

Routes from the UK to Spain and Portugal
• Outside the shipping lanes, directly from Cornwall to the Ría de Vigo or further south; this may be the fastest route, but it is an ocean voyage, taking too long for forecasts to be dependable, and requires a yacht to be equipped and crewed for both storms and calms; the distance from the Lizard to Cabo Finisterre is about 450 miles

• To a point around the Rade de Brest, then to NW Spain, maybe Cedeira or A Coruña; this voyage is shorter, and can be made in two or three days, within the scope of reliable forecasts; if the winds are contrary, the yacht can cruise down the French coast until they become favourable; Pointe du Raz to Cabo Ortegal is about 290 miles, and La Rochelle to Santander 190 miles

• Coast hopping all the way, with only the passage between the Gironde and Capbreton providing a challenge with no safe harbours and the Landes firing range; this route is delightful, but takes a long time, especially as one is tempted to linger along the way; from the mouth of the Gironde to Capbreton is about 120 miles.

The destinations The coast of Atlantic Spain and Portugal can conveniently be divided into six stretches, each with its own characteristics:

• The north coast, from Hondarribia, on the Spanish/French border to Vivero, the most easterly ría alta. This has glorious mountain scenery, especially at the eastern end, numerous small ports where you moor alongside or anchor at no charge, and very little provision for visiting yachts (significant marinas only at Hondarribia, Laredo, Santander and Gijon). In summer, winds are mainly limited to gentle sea breezes, air temperatures are higher than the UK, but you do get some rain and fog. Highlights are the bay of San Sebastián and the snow covered Picos de Europa between Santander and Ribadesella

• The Rías Altas and Costa da Morte, from Vivero to Fisterra, with more stunning scenery, though not mountainous, ample free anchorages and plenty of good marinas. The summer weather is similar to the north coast, except that, in July and August, the north easterly sea breezes in the afternoons are incessant and often strong, making passages up the coast a challenge. The sea water is freezing, even at the height of summer! The Costa da Morte is dangerous in winter – hence its name

• The Rías Baixas, from Muros to Baiona. This is one of the great cruising areas, offering as much as, say, Devon and Cornwall, or the south coast of Brittany. All the rías have numerous anchorages, all have useful marinas. The scenery is gentler than further north, but still beautiful. The afternoon sea breezes are a bit gentler as well, and the lie of the coast gives shelter and means that the seas are comparatively flat. Many cruisers heading for the Mediterranean linger here for a season or two, and some go no further. Winter cruising here is a possibility, as there is plenty of sailing to be had in sheltered waters. Highlights are the Atlantic islands of Cies and Ons

• The Portuguese west coast, which, frankly, is not an area to linger in. Many of the port towns, if not the ports themselves are attractive, but there are few places to anchor, and the incessant north wind from June to September makes a voyage north a bit of a trial. From October to April, there are fairly frequent fierce south-westerly gales

• The Algarve, from Cabo São Vicente to, say, Sancti Petri, just south of Cádiz in Andalucía. As you round Cabo São Vicente from the north, both the air and sea temperatures jump 5°, the fog lifts, the wind moderates, and suddenly you have a foretaste of Mediterranean weather. Much of this stretch of coast is attractive, with deeply indented cliffs hiding tiny beaches, but much is also despoiled by high-rise holiday apartments and hotels. There are sufficient anchorages to avoid marinas altogether, which is fortunate, because the marinas are very pricey in high season. Most days in summer, the sea breeze starts late morning from the north east, and veers steadily, reaching Force 4 or so, until it dies away in the evening as a northwesterly. From time to time an easterly Levanter sets in, giving fairly strong east winds in the morning and calms in the afternoon, when the sea breeze opposes it. From November to the end of April there are usually several gales – westerly, southerly and easterly. Highlights are the Río Formosa, a 30-mile long lagoon behind sand dunes running east from Faro, and the Río Guadiana, between Portugal and Spain

• From Sancti Petri to Gibraltar. The scenery becomes more dramatic until you reach the stunning straights of Gibraltar. But the cruising is also more challenging, with nowhere sheltered to anchor, stronger winds, and only Barbate as a port of refuge. A strong headwind here brings a contrary current and fierce seas, and makes progress difficult for a small cruiser.

In general, there are fewer tourists and lower prices further north. In the Algarve and Andalucia anyone who works with tourists speaks some English, whereas in smaller places in northern Spain it certainly helps to have some Spanish. The best regional dishes are to be found further north, as are the best wines. Some people argue that the friendliest reception is also to be found further north, but the writer has found the people of both Spain and Portugal to be welcoming and totally honest throughout. For some reason, notwithstanding the EU, big chandlery items such as inflatables are stupidly expensive, and it usually pays to ship from the UK.

Formalities in Spain Yachts should be prepared to provide the normal ship's papers, insurance certificates (with a Spanish translation), passports for skipper and crew, and RYA certificate of competence for the skipper. The Spanish courtesy flag should be flown but in the area E of Bilbao to the French border a Basque courtesy flag is appreciated. If long-term cruising, be aware that the Spanish authorities deem anyone (not any boat) spending more than six months cumulatively in a calendar year in Spain as a resident, possibly with expensive consequences.

Supplies Only diesel *Gasoleo A,* which is taxed, is available for yachts. This can generally be found in marinas or hbrs with yacht facilities. Water is plentiful, piped to most jetties and is safe. A charge is seldom made.

Calor gas is not available but cylinders can be refilled with butane. The Spanish alternative and Camping Gaz are universally available and cheap.

Repairs can be undertaken in most hbrs as can diesel engines. The price of spares is often less than in the UK.

Books If you wish to visit smaller ports, volumes to have on board are:
South Biscay: La Gironde to A Coruña RCC Pilotage Foundation (Imray)
Atlantic Spain and Portugal: El Ferrol to Gibraltar RCC Pilotage Foundation (Imray)
Cruising Galicia Carlos Rojas & Robert Bailey (Imray).

Spain N & NW distances (miles)

	Hondarribia	Bilbao	Gijon	Cabo Prior	A Coruña	C Vilano	C. Finisterre
Hondarribia	0						
Bilbao	60	0					
Gijon	157	115	0				
Cabo Prior	291	282	124	0			
A Coruña	305	295	138	14	0		
C Vilano	353	344	187	62	45	0	
C. Finisterre	371	362	204	80	63	17	0

W and S Spain & Portugal distances (miles)

	C. Finisterre	Baiona	Viana Castelo	C. Roca	C. Vicente	Cádiz	Gibraltar
C. Finisterre	0						
Baiona	53	0					
Viana Castelo	76	33	0				
C. Roca	210	208	176	0			
C. Vicente	320	318	286	110	0		
Cádiz	453	450	419	242	132	0	
Gibraltar	515	512	481	305	194	71	0

The Cruising Almanac

Good helpful brochures are available for every region from:
Spanish National Tourist Office, 64 North Row, London W1K 7DE ☎ 020 7317 2011
The Portuguese National Tourist Office, 11 Belgrave Sq, London SW1X 8PP ☎ 0845 355 1212

Paper charts Official charts for Spain are published by the Armada Española. They offer 'paper charts', covering the whole coast of Spain and principal ports, and 'sports charts', covering the most popular cruising areas. Their catalogue is at www.armada.mde.es (go to the 'IHM Hidrography' tab on the right hand of the home page). The charts can be bought online from www.fragata-librosnauticos.com/seccion/cartas-nauticas-ihm/. The following stores stock the charts: Librería Cartamar, Paseo de Ronda 39, 15011 La Coruña, ☎ 981 255 228 and Suisca, Avda. Blas Infante, Centro Blas Infante Local 1, 11201 Algeciras.

Official charts, both commercial and recreational, for Portugal are published by the Portuguese Instituto Hidrográfico. You can browse their catalogue and buy charts online from http://ln.hidrografico.pt/en/.

The British Admiralty, French SHOM and Imray also publish charts for these coasts. Since the coasts are fairly free from hidden dangers, the yachtsman may well choose to buy relatively small-scale charts, such as those from Imray, supplemented by harbour plans from a book such as this, and large scale charts of any rias that he may wish to explore away from the main channels. The Ría de Arousa is particularly rewarding in this respect. Such local charts can be obtained locally.

Spanish charts online The official Spanish charts are now available, experimentally, from the Spanish hydrographic office at http://ideihm.covam.es/visor.html . The site requires a fairly high bandwidth connection, and light characteristics are not shown, but is otherwise a most useful resource.

Telephone numbers Numbers have been checked before the almanac went to print, but Spanish numbers seem to change very frequently, so they may be out of date. All current numbers are available on the internet.

Plans Deep water is coloured blue. In some parts of this coast it is not possible to include a 2m contour line. Where this is so, the light blue will extend to the 5m line.

Order Text and plans on this coast are sometimes out of the natural sequence E to W in order to achieve maximum correlation between text and plans.

Place names in Spain Many parts of Spain, in particular the Basque region and Galicia, and others in the Mediterranean, have their own language, distinct from Castillian Spanish. In these areas, some places have different names in their local language and Spanish. Often the difference is only in the spelling, and in these cases the editors have arbitrarily chosen whichever seems to be more frequently used. Two places covered by the Almanac have completely different names - Hondarribia/Fuentarribia and Donastia/San Sebastián. These are often written with both names separated by a '/', and we have followed this practice.

Passage lights	
Principal lights	BA No
Igueldo San Sebastián	1483
Fl(2+1)15s132m26M	
Cabo Machichaco	1520
Fl.7s120m24M	
Siren Mo(M)60s (– –)	
Pta Estaca de Bares	1686
Fl(2)7·5s99m25M AIS	
Cabo Prior	1692
Fl(1+2)15s105m22M AIS	
Torre de Hércules,	1704
Fl(4)20s104m23M AIS	
Cabo Villano	1736
Fl(2)15s102m28M AIS	
Racon M (– –)	
Cabo Toriñana	1740
Fl(2+1)15s63m24M	
Cabo Finisterre	1742
Fl.5s142m23M	
Siren(2)60s AIS	
Cabo Silleiro	1916
Fl(2+1)15s83m24M AIS	

HONDARRIBIA/ FUENTARRIBIA – HENDAYE

Standard Port Pointe de Grave
HW –0042   LW n/a

MHWS	MHWN	MLWN	MLWS
–1·0m	–1·2m	–0·6m	–0·4m

An old fortified Spanish town on E side of Rio de Bidasoa opposite the sophisticated resort of Hendaye on the French side. Customs officials may be very active. Strong ebb tide at springs at mouth of Rio de Bidasoa.

Approach Conspic LtHo Fl(2)10s on Cabo Higuer at W end of bay. Give wide berth to Les Briquets in E of bay.

Entrance Enter river on top half of tide, no difficulties except in heavy swell from N, sp ebb is very strong. Enter between breakwater heads Fl(3)G and LFl.R.10s. Keep close to stb training wall until its root at Roca Punta where turn to port and follow dredged channel 3m with mooring buoys.

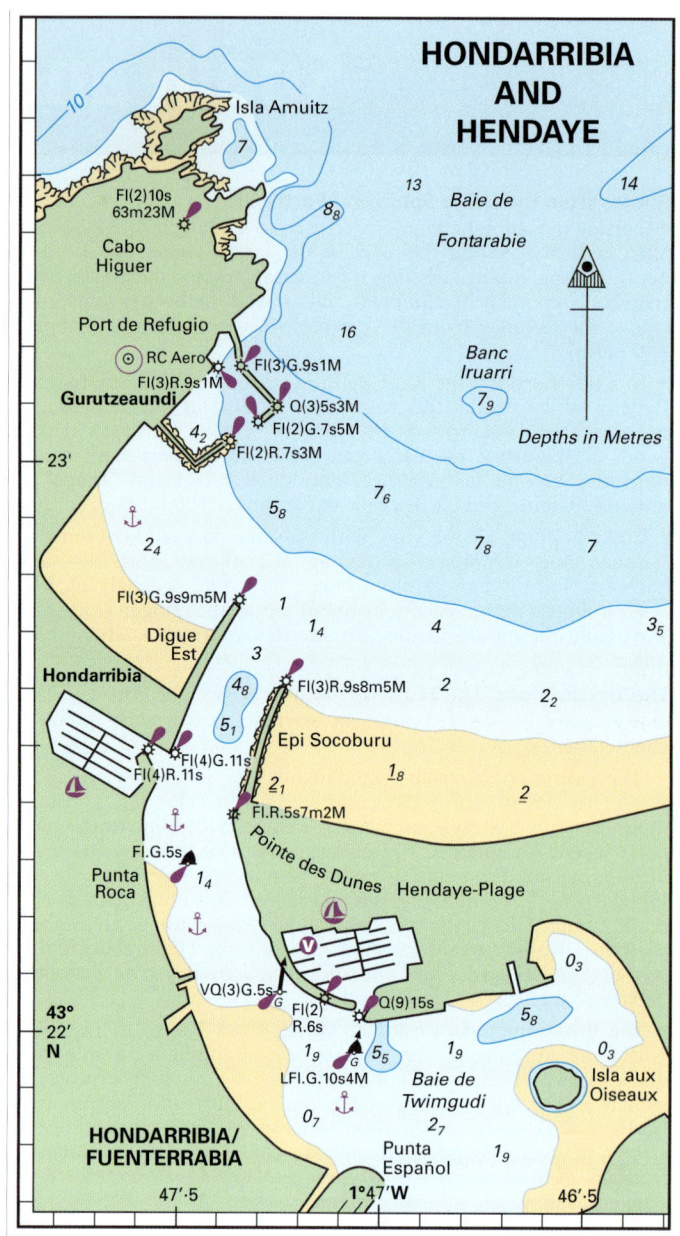

Anchorage
• 1ca SW of landing place at Hendaye Plage near YC in 3·5m clear of buoys.
• 1–2ca S of Puerto Gurutzeaundi (½M S of Cabo Higuer) W of extended breakwater Fl.G.3s in 2·5m clear of buoys (or inside hbr if room, F.G & F.R at entrance).
• In the river 2ca S of entrance to Hendaye Marina (most sheltered).

A first time night entry to the Rio de Bidasoa is not recommended. Use last anchorage given.

Berthing Two marinas – the E side French, the W side Spanish, visitors welcome. The fishing port of Gurutzeaundi does not welcome yachts, but would be the only safe mooring in heavy weather.

☎/VHF Hendaye 05 5948 0600; Hondarribia 943 641 711; both VHF 09.

PUERTO DE PASAJES

Standard Port Pointe de Grave
Boucau
HW (sp) –0030 (np) –0050
LW (sp) –0045 (np) –0015

MHWS	MHWN	MLWN	MLWS
–1·2m	–1·3m	–0·5m	–0·5m

A busy commercial hbr which can be entered in all conditions. In heavy swell enter in the last quarter of flood. Well-sheltered but subject to wash from large vessels.

Approach There is a LtHo (conspic from E) on Cabo La Plata Oc.4s above Pta de Arando Chico, and on opposite E headland a conspic rock El Fraile. IPTS. There is a new fairway buoy, RW Mo(A)7s7M AIS in 43°21'·32N 1°56'·29W, approx 1M NNW of the entrance.

Entrance is straightforward once identified, however, it is narrow. It is marked just off shore by a tower, Fl.R.5s, and a buoy

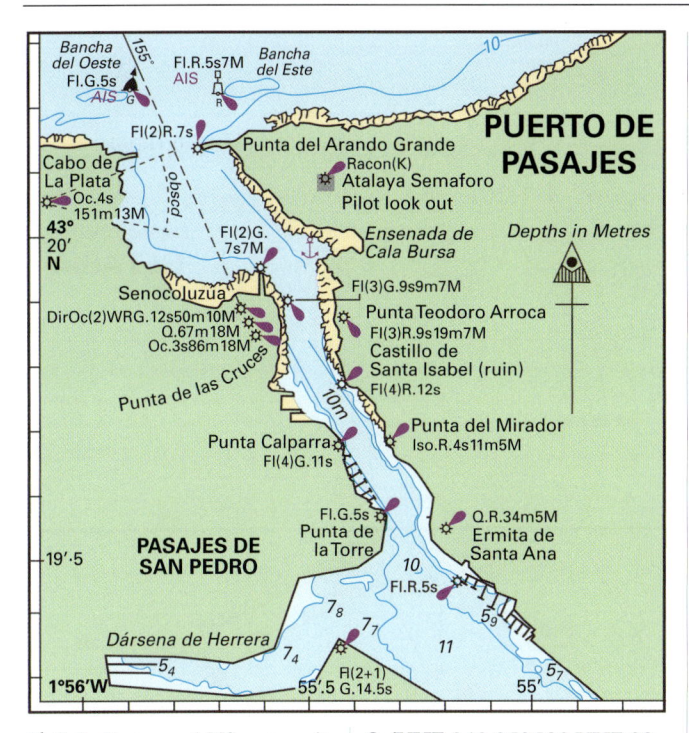

Avoid La Bancha shoal in heavy swell.

Entrance From a position ½M off, follow centre of passage between Mte Urgull and Is de Santa Clara on 158°. By night, intensified ldg Lts Oc.R.4s and front Q.R on 158°.

Anchorage S of Is de Santa Clara on sand 4m, clear of local moorings, close in to avoid swell. Buoy anchor. YC provides visitors' moorings in summer and water taxi.

Berthing The port authority (EKP) has installed new pontoons for visitors on the S wall of the fishing harbour.

☏ Club 943 423 575, EKP 943 000464 VHF 09 for both.

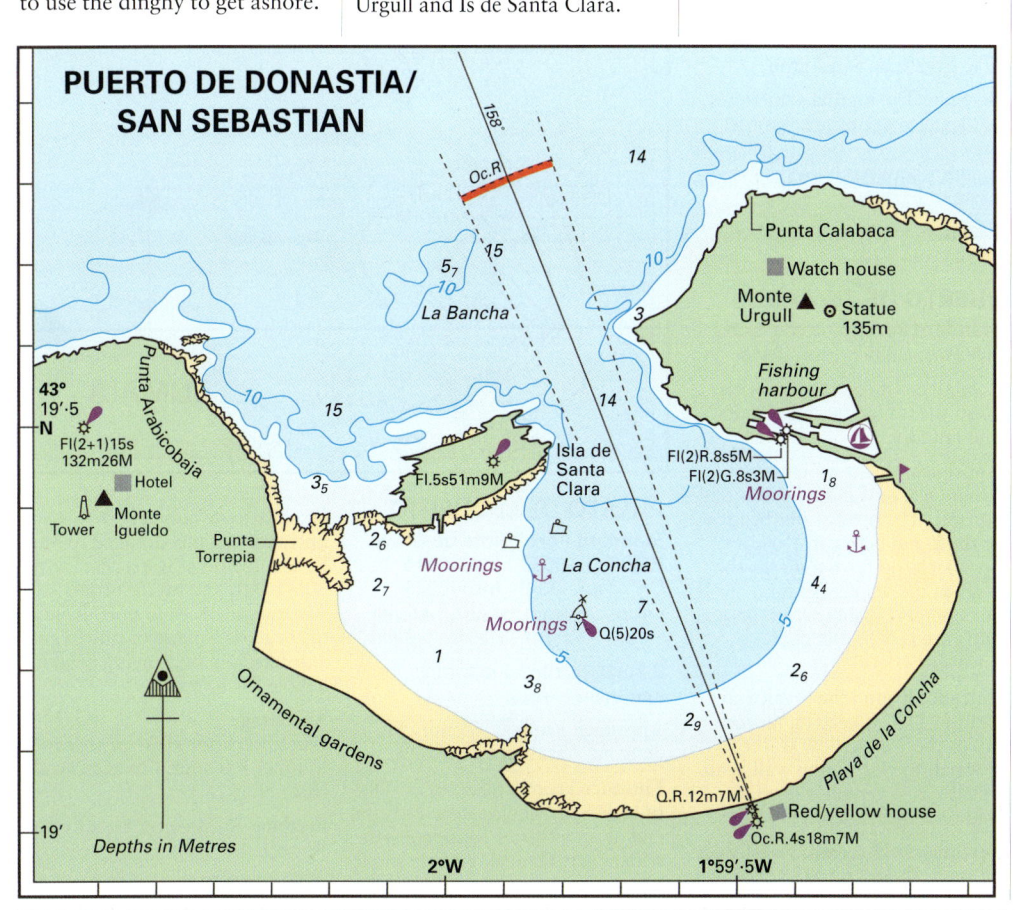

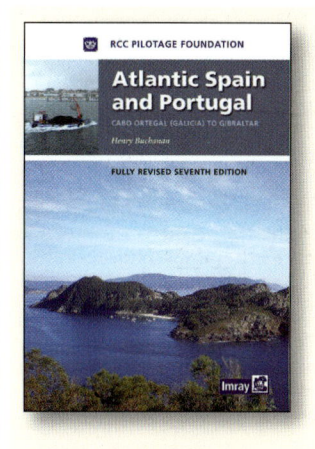

Fl.G.5s. Enter on 155° on transit of Dir Lt Oc(2)WRG.12s. After entry the channel is well marked.

Anchorages
• Off village of Pasajes the San Juan, on both sides of the river, outside moorings in 4m mud. Very crowded.
• In cove opposite Pta de las Cruces (Ensenada de Cala Bursa) in quiet weather only.
• On W side of dunes off Pta del Puntal del Pasajes, moorings.

Berthing There are new pontoons in Santa Ana. Reported that yachts have used them freely, but you may have to use the dinghy to get ashore.

☏ /VHF 943 352580 VHF 09.

DONASTIA/ SAN SEBASTIÁN

Standard Port Pointe de Grave
HW (sp) −0030 (np) −0110
LW (sp) −0040 (np) −0020
MHWS MHWN MLWN MLWS
−1·2m −1·2m −0·5m −0·4m

An elegant city around a beautiful bay. Crowded in summer.

Approach Identify Mte Urgull with large statue, Mte Igueldo Fl(2+1)15s and Isla de Santa Clara Fl.5s. In poor visibility take care not to confuse Mte Urgull and Is de Santa Clara.

ATLANTIC SPAIN AND PORTUGAL

The seventh edition of this RCC Pilotage Foundation has been completely updated from visits to the area by Henry Buchanan who has taken over the editorship of the entire volume. He has completely overhauled the initial section on Galicia and this new edition now commences at Cabo Ortegal, taking in Ría Cedeira. The arrangement of text and plans as been reorganized particularly at Ría de Arousa where an improved whole page approaches plan has been included.

There are new photos and most of the plans incorporate changes accumulated over the four years or so since the last edition was published.

Imray

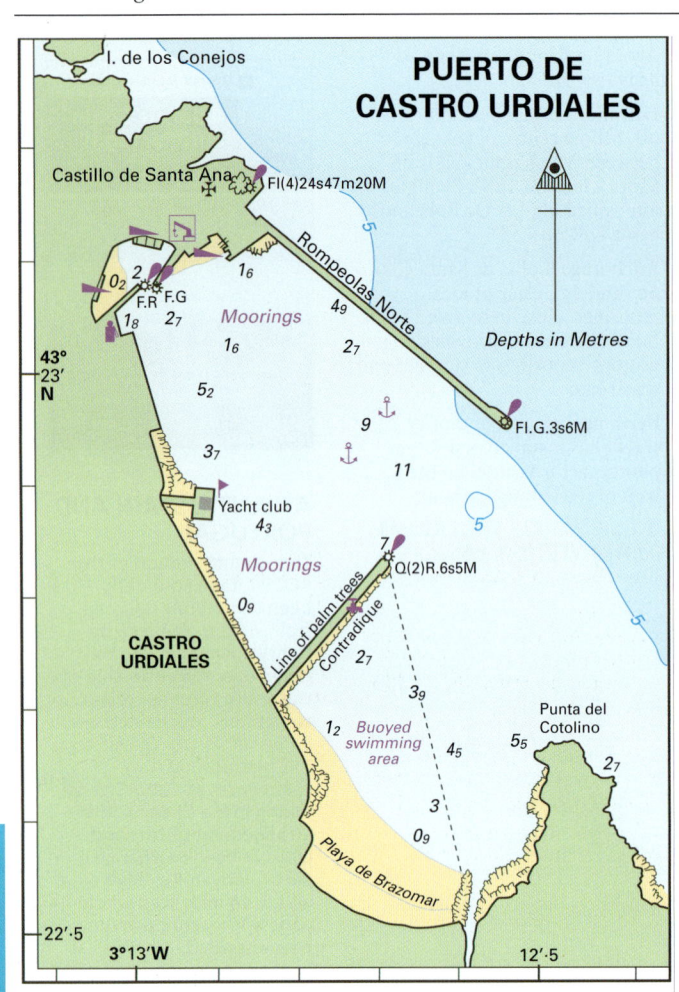

PUERTO DE CASTRO URDIALES

Standard Port Pointe de Grave
HW (sp) −0120 (np) −0040
LW (sp) −0110 (np) −0020

MHWS	MHWN	MLWN	MLWS
−1·4m	−1·5m	−0·6m	−0·6m

A picturesque and interesting old town.

Approach From W Castro Urdiales is not seen until Pta del Rabanal is rounded. From E the buildings, castle and church are conspic. By night use the LtHo of Castillo de Santa Ana Fl(4)24s.
Entrance From a position where LtHo on Castillo de Santa Ana bears W ½M steer 230° and pass between mole heads Fl.G.3s to stb and Q(2)R.6s to port. Give a clearance of 25m.

Anchorage In entrance of outer harbour E of moorings in 11m. Buoy anchor. YC water taxi VHF 09 (summer 0800–2100). Not recommended in strong easterlies. NW swell refracts in.

Berthing
- Alongside moles of inner harbour much of which dries.
- Inside N breakwater Rompeolas Norte of outer harbour in very calm weather.

PUERTO DE GETARIA

Standard Port Pointe de Grave
HW (sp) −0030 (np) −0110
LW (sp) −0040 (np) −0020

MHWS	MHWN	MLWN	MLWS
−1·0m	−1·0m	−0·5m	−0·4m

A small fishing port with easy entrance.

Approach Mte Igueldo Fl(2+1)15s is 9M to E. Conspic LtHo Zumaya Oc(1+3)12s is 2¼M to W.
Entrance Identify conspic Is de San Anton, Fl(4)15s and leave to stb.
Anchorage Behind Dique Exterior F.G in up to 8m. Affected by strong gusts from NW over Is de San Anton.
Berthing The marina sometimes has space on pontoon G, or it may be possible to get permission to moor between buoys in NE basin of harbour.
Facilities YC.
☎ 943 896 129.

PUERTO DE ZUMAIA

Standard Port Pointe de Grave
HW (sp) −0035 (np) −0115

A small coast resort town with good yacht facilities inc repairs and laundry.

Approach The grey octagonal LtHo Oc(1+3)12s on its island is conspic. The breakwater head is to the E and below it. Do not approach too far E towards the cliffs as the sea breaks for a considerable distance out. Best entrance HW±0300, depends on swell.
Entrance Round the breakwater head Fl(2)G.7s keeping more to stb as there is shallow water towards the E training wall head Fl(2)R.7s. After entry keep to mid river. Least depth 2·5m.
Berthing As directed, usually on W wall. ☎ 943 860938.

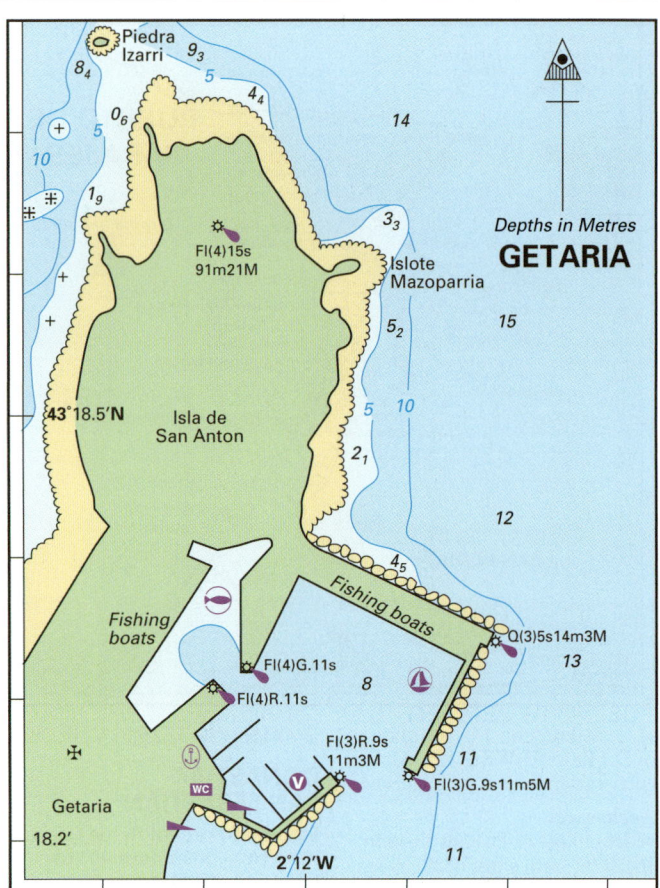

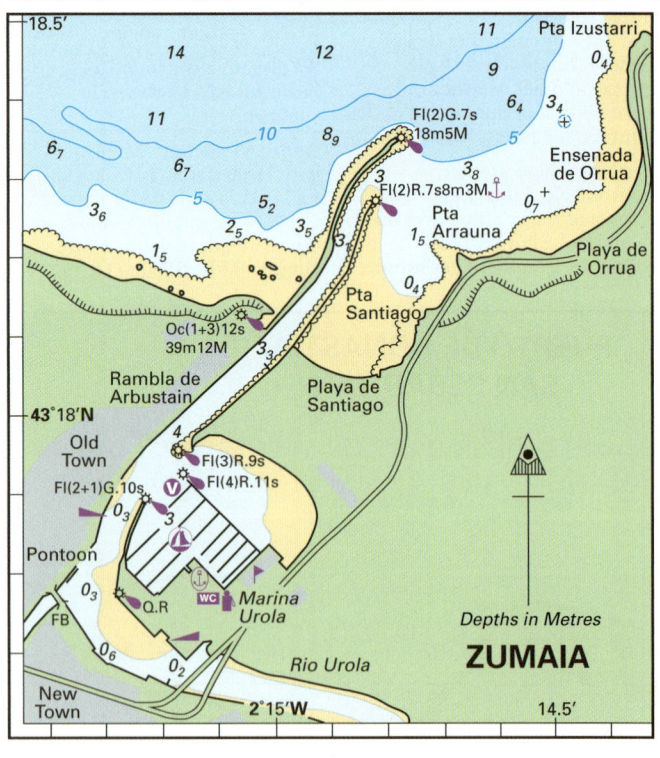

PUERTO DE LEQUEITIO

Standard Port Pointe de Grave
HW (sp) −0033 (np) −0115
LW (sp) −0045 (np) −0025

MHWS	MHWN	MLWN	MLWS
−1·2m	−1·2m	−0·5m	−0·4m

A small picturesque fishing port and holiday resort.

Approach From W, identify Pta de Santa Catalina Fl(1+3)20s.
Entrance From a position 2ca N of Is de San Nicolas steer 212° on end of breakwater Rompeolas de Amandarri Fl.G.4s. Beware shoal patch Bajo de la Barra to port. Entrance channel dredged to 4m. Follow the breakwater leaving it 30m to stb and bn tr Dirque Aislado Fl(2)R.8s to port. Round the head of N mole of hbr F.G at a distance of 3m, leaving head of S mole F.R to port.

Anchorage Outer harbour clear of entrance to inner harbour. Open to swell from N.

Berthing As directed. Usually on W wall.
☎ 946 840 721.

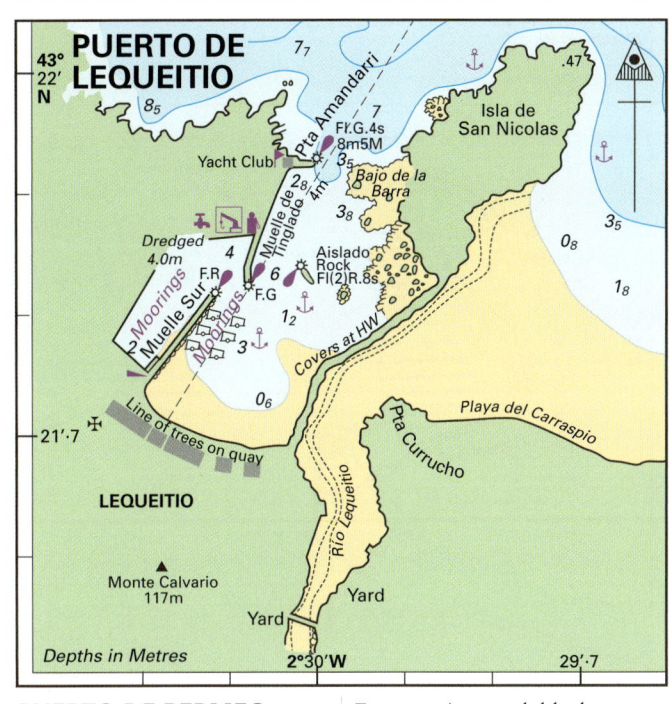

PUERTO DE BERMEO

Standard Port Pointe de Grave
HW (sp) −0015 (np) −0055
LW (sp) −0055 (np) −0035
MHWS MHWN MLWN MLWS
−0·8m −0·7m −0·5m −0·4m

A busy fishing port with a well-protected hbr and easy entrance but swell in E'lies.

Approach Cabo Machichaco Fl.7s is 2M to NW.

Entrance Approach hbr between 150° and 270° and round the end of the new breakwater Fl.G.4·5s, leaving it 50m to stb, into the Antepuerto. By night use white sector of Rosape Pta Lamiaren Fl(2)WR.10s for approach to breakwater Lt. Enter Puerto Mayor between moleheads F.G & F.R. The Puerto Menor is to stb but shallow and crowded with fishing boats.

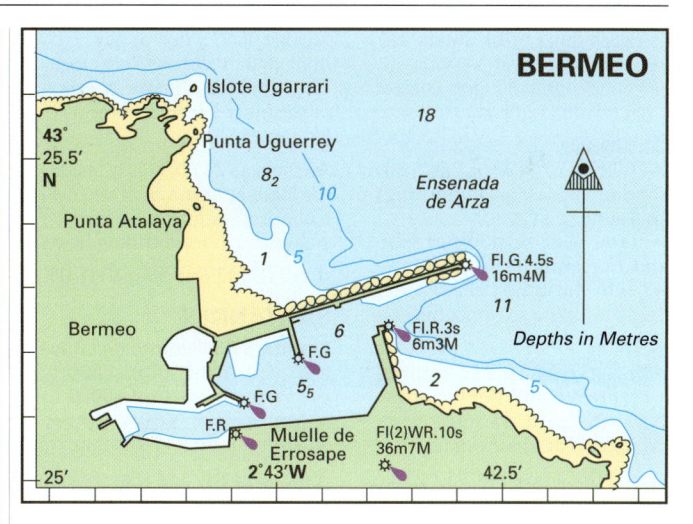

Anchorage N or S side of Antepuerto in 4–6m.

Berthing On new pontoon just before entrance to inner harbour. Showers and toilets, electricity and water promised ☏ 945 226 934.

PUERTO DE BILBAO

Standard Port Pointe de Grave
HW (sp) −0045 (np) −0125
LW (sp) −0055 (np) −0035
MHWS MHWN MLWN MLWS
−1·2m −1·2m −0·5m −0·4m

A large commercial port which can be entered in most conditions for shelter.

Approach Cabo Machichaco Fl.7s is 15M to E. From W identify Pta Lucero and outer breakwater head Fl.G.5s. From E identify Pta Galea with light-coloured cliffs and LtHo Fl(3)8s, and outer breakwater head Fl.R.5s. Dique de Punta Galea is mainly submerged; local boats cross at least 1ca from shore.

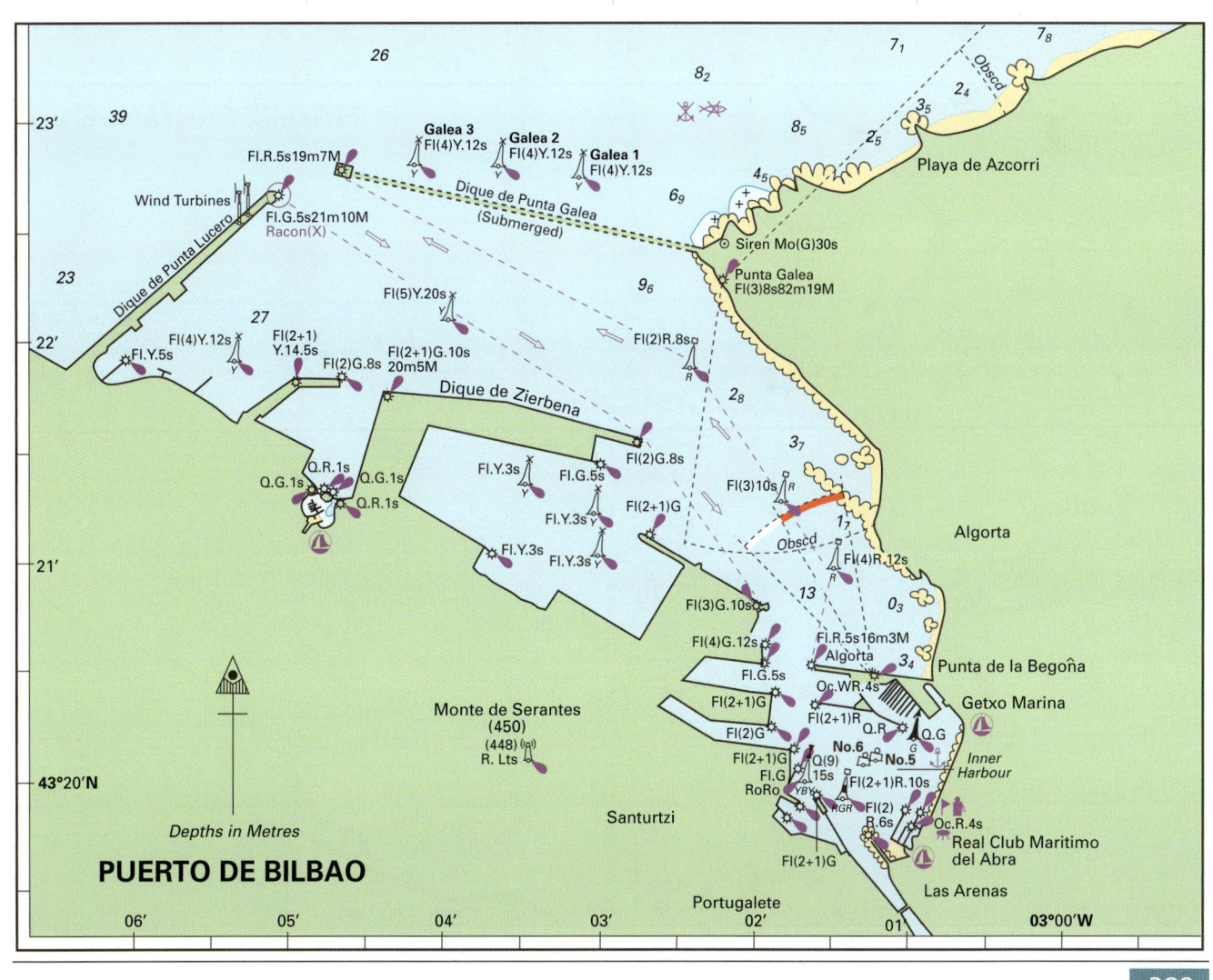

Entrance Between breakwater heads and steer SE down middle of outer harbour. Give inner breakwater heads clearance of 25m leaving Dique de Santurce to stb Fl(3)G.10s and Contramuelle de Algorta to port Fl.R.5s. By night follow the white sector 119° to 135° in middle of E breakwater Oc.WR.4s and pass near R buoy Fl(4)R.12s before entering between inner breakwaters. Do not enter the River Nervion without contacting port control on VHF 06, 12 or 16.

Anchorages
• 100m N or NW of Las Arenas landing pier clear of moorings in 4m near YCs.
• 200m W of boat hbr at root of Contramuelle de Algorta.
• Club Maritimo del Abra stern buoy and line to pontoon.

Berthing
• In Getxo Marina at Algorta, S of E breakwater. All facilities.
• Marina at Real Club Maritimo at Las Arenas.

☎ /VHF Getxo 944 912 2367, Las Arenas 944 637 600; Marinas VHF 09, Port VHF 12.

See pp.387 and 388 for Castro Urdiales and Lequeitio.

LAREDO

The marina at Laredo is accessible at all times and in any weather. It now has all the basic facilities, including fuel.

Approach and Entrance The coast is clean from the E from Punta Sonabia; leave the N breakwater to port. From the W, the N breakwater is conspic to S after rounding the clean Monte de Santoña. The entrance is W of the N breakwater, facing SW. The yacht harbour is to stb. At night, identify the entrance light, Fl.R.5s.17m.5M.

Berthing Telephone or radio for a berth. Otherwise, tie up at the fuel berth on S side of pier immediately opposite entrance. The capitanía is on the N side of the inner harbour in the SE corner.

Anchorage 2M NW just inside the lagoon, or in Canal de Colindres leading S. Beware vicious wash from fishing boats.

☎ /VHF 942 605 592, VHF 09.

SANTANDER

Standard Port Pointe de Grave
HW (sp) –0100 (np) –0020
LW (sp) –0050 (np) +0000
MHWS MHWN MLWN MLWS
–0·7m –1·2m –0·3m –0·7m

A pleasant city and large port on an estuary which can be entered by day or night under all conditions. Ebb stream can reach 3kn at springs.

Approach Cabo Mayor conspic LtHo W round stone tr Fl(2)10s89m21M is 2M NW of entrance to Santander. Cabo Ajo Oc(3)16s is 7M NE.

Entrance Identify Is de Mouro Fl(3)16s.
• From W pass between Is de Mouro and Peninsula de la Magdalena with conspic Palace (now a University).
• From E pass ¼M E of Is de Mouro.

From both entrances pass 1–2ca S of La Cerda LtHo on Pta del Puerto Fl(1+4)20s, then S of Is Horadada Fl(2)7s into lighted buoyed channel. By night enter S of Isla de Mouro on ldg lts 236° front Q, rear Iso.R.4s and when S of Isla Horadada turn on to Lts 260°. Dir WRG.

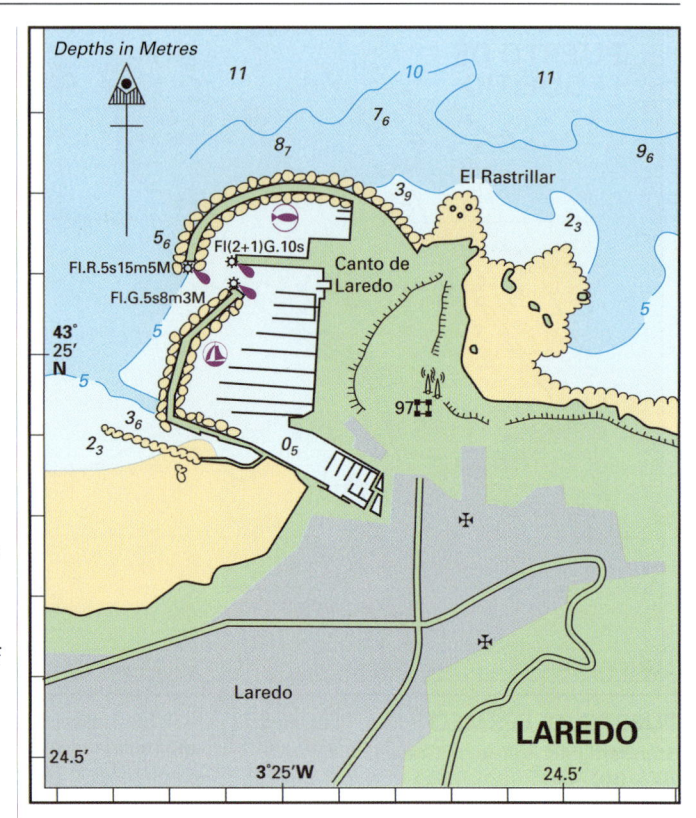

Anchorage Off Pta de San Marcos. 50–100m to SW or SE of YC near Darsena de Molnedo in 3m clear of moorings and race start line. Convenient to town but subject to wash from ferries. Land at YC.

Berthing
• At Marina Puerto Deportivo 2M upriver. Follow buoyed channel as far as conspic head of oil terminal to port then turn SSW, pass between the G and R buoys to avoid sand bank, to marina entrance leaving two G buoys Fl(2)7s to stb. Sheltered. Take taxi, bus to town 2M. Marina has all facilities.

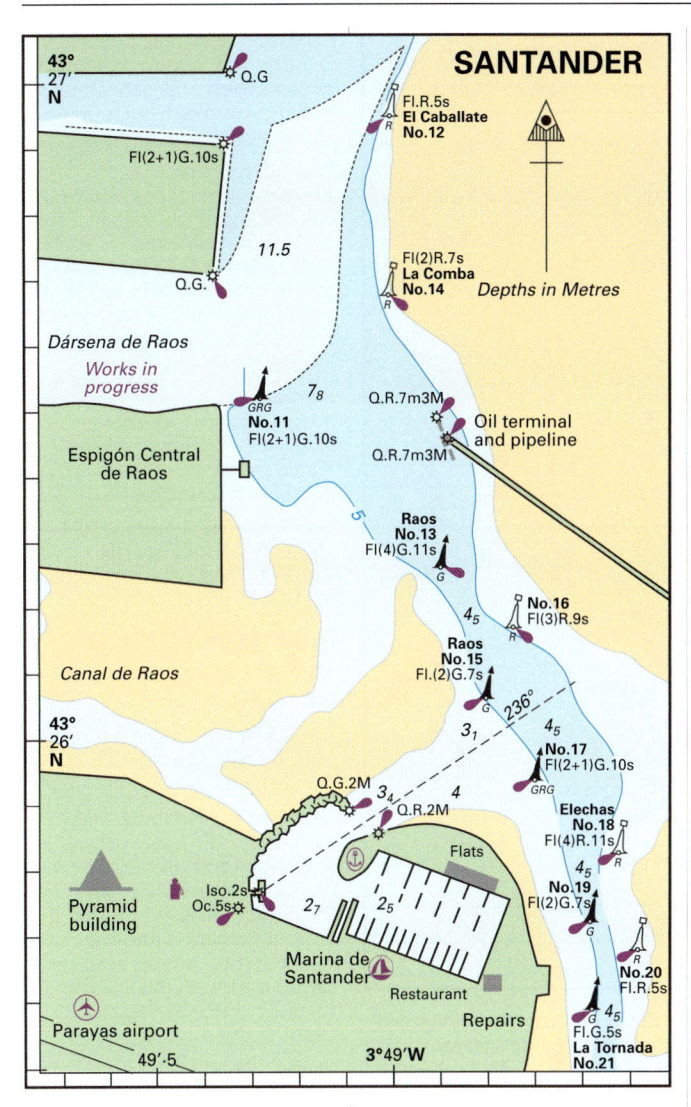

- Dársena de Molnedo, by the yacht club in town, occasionally has space.

Facilities Good English-speaking chandler, 'Yates & Cosas' near E end of Darsena de Molnedo. Brittany Ferries two to three times a week to Plymouth.

☎/VHF Marina Deportivo 942 369 298, VHF 09. Port VHF 12.

PUERTO DE SAN VICENTE DE LA BARQUERA

Standard Port Pointe de Grave
HW (sp) −0100 (np) −0020
LW (sp) −0050 (np) +0000

MHWS MHWN MLWN MLWS
−1·5m −1·5m −0·6m −0·6m

A pleasant town with a Gaudi building at Comillas about 4M and ría in beautiful surroundings. Enter at or near HW by day in the absence of swell. Few inner lights for night entry the first time.

Approach Pta Silla Oc.3·5s is ½M to W and Pta San Emeterio Fl.5s is 6M to W. Both are conspic. Steer to a position where hbr entrance bears SW ½M.

Entrance Enter on 225° halfway between breakwater head Fl.WG.2s to stb and training wall (can be submerged at HW) end Fl(2)R.8s to port. Follow round the small cliffs of Pta de la Espina F.G to stb at a distance of 25m and then steer for fish quay on 237° which is well lit.

Berthing
- Alongside fish quay if room. HM will allocate berth if asked.
- It may be possible to moor alongside a fishing boat on a buoy below the br. It is not recommended to anchor and take bow warps to the br piers. Strong current on spring ebb.

Anchorage
- Deeper draught yachts may find space just inside the entrance, or in the channel leading SE
- Yachts that can take the ground will find firm, clean sand in the channel leading S from the fish quay

LLANES

HW As Ribadesella

Tiny fishing harbour open at all states of the tide, and new inner harbour, available at half-tide except in bad conditions. Attractive town.

Approach Identify the lighthouse and breakwater, surrounded by gayly coloured contrete blocks. Start approach from a point 1ca SE of breakwater, to clear rocks and breakers to E and N.

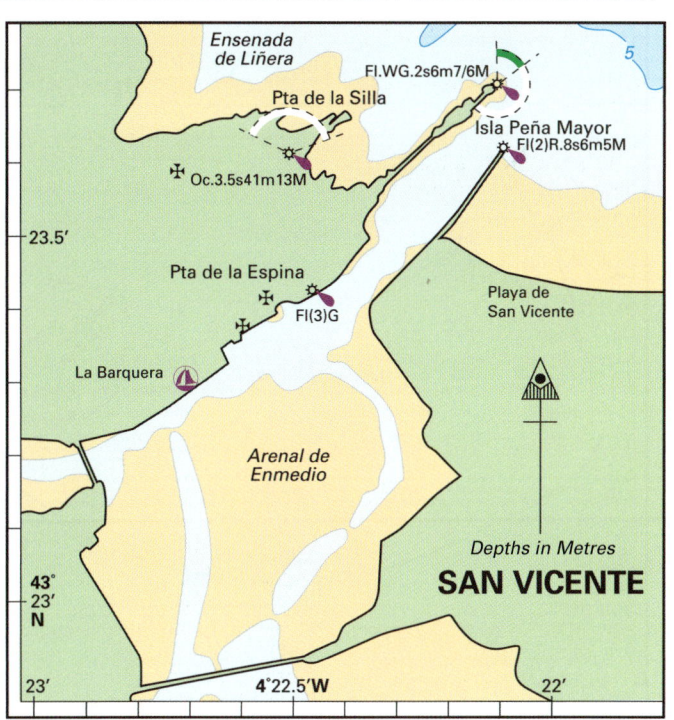

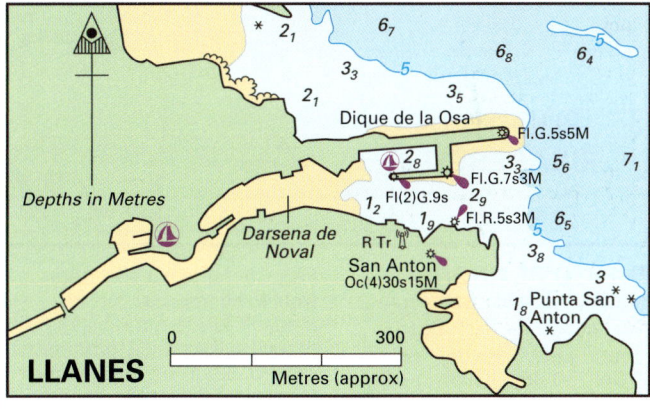

Fishing harbour Head W into bay, leaving breakwater to stb, until harbour entrance opens to stb. Secure to N or E wall, wherever there is room. May need to raft up. Yachts may also berth by the Lonja at weekends and on holidays.

Inner harbour Continue past entrance to fishing harbour to an entrance straight ahead, over a sill with 2m ±0300 HW. There are 3 courtesy berths immediately to port. Water is available, but use of electricity not permitted. Fuel available. Gate at entrance is shut in adverse conditions, leaving the harbour totally secure.

☎ 639 673 516

PUERTO DE RIBADESELLA

See plan p. 392

Standard Port Pointe de Grave
HW (sp) −0020 (np) +0005
LW (sp) −0020 (np) +0020

MHWS MHWN MLWN MLWS
−1·4m −1·3m −0·6m −0·4m

Small fishing port with a bar 1·7m but good shelter inside. Enter HW−0200 to HW. A beautiful mountainous setting.

Approach Conspic LtHo Pta de Somos Fl(2+1)12s is ¾M to W. Conspic flat sloping cliffs off Pta del Caballo with white hermitage on top immediately to E of entrance. Steer to a position where Pta de Somos LtHo is due W and the concrete LtHo Fl(4)R.11s on the breakwater head at Pta del Caballo bears 140° ½M off.

Entrance Approach the breakwater head on 140°, leave it 25m to port and follow the quay round at a distance of 20m for 4ca into the hbr. Do not attempt in a heavy swell.

Berthing The possibilities are:
- Alongside E pontoon of marina on W bank for maximum 3 days. Beware narrow channel
- On the quay to port in space reserved for 'deportivos' downstream of fishing boats
- On quay to port in space reserved for 'deportivos' upstream of fishng boats, reported foul with shoaling and boulders, so check first.

☎ 985 861 331

The Cruising Almanac

PUERTO DE RIBADESELLA

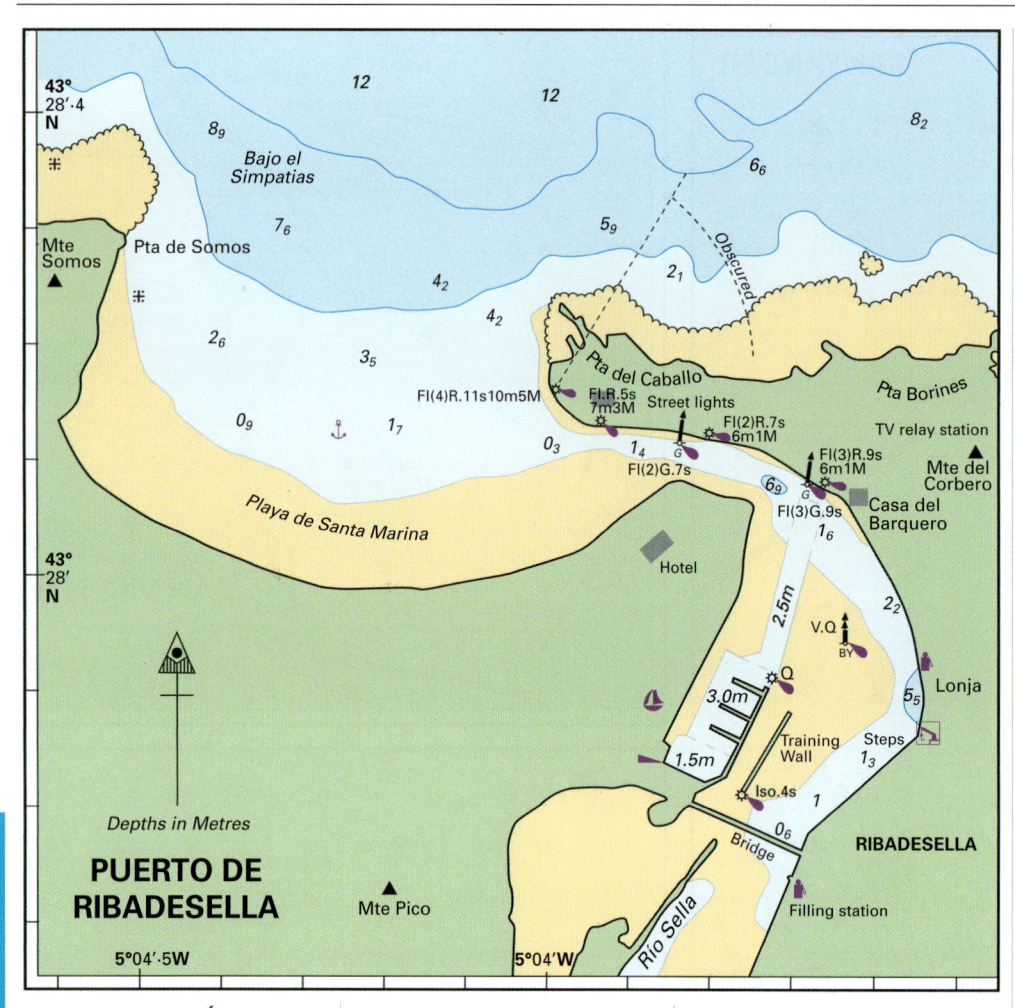

PUERTO DE GIJÓN

Standard Port Pointe de Grave
HW −0018   LW −0010
MHWS MHWN MLWN MLWS
−1·0m −1·4m −0·4m −0·7m

There is a choice of marinas: the original Puerto Deportivo near the Old Town, or the new Marina Yates, situated to the south of the commercial Puerto del Musel, on the Muelle de la Osa. The latter is a bike ride from town (free bike hire available 2011), but is highly praised and reported to be much cheaper. It is also probably easier to enter in adverse conditions.

Approach Cabo Peñas Fl(3)15s115m35M is 9M to NW. Cabo de Torres Fl(2)10s80m18M and the high exterior breakwater Digue Principe de Asturias of Puerto de Musel Fl.G.4s are conspic.

Marina Yates

Entrance From a position near the end of Dique Principe, sail south for a mile for the east corner of Dique de la Osa (Q(3)10s), then follow the wall SW for 0·6M to the end (Fl(4)G.20s). The marina is to stb.

Berthing The waiting pontoon is G, furthest W next to the dique, or on the ends of B, C or D. Usual facilities, inc diesel, but no yard. Cycle hire, 15 mins to town.

Puerto Deportivo

Entrance From a position near end of Digue Principe sail S for 1¼M and then leave Sacramento a G Lt bn Fl(2)G.6s to stb. Enter hbr between Digue de Liquerica Fl(2)R.6s to port and Malecon de Fomento Fl(3)G.10s to stb.

Berthing Marina pontoon berths inside Dique de Liquerica dredged to 3m down to 1·3m. Water, electricity, showers, YC, diesel from near *capitanía*.

☏/VHF Marina Yates ☏ 984 157 171. Puerto Deportivo ☏ 985 34 45 43 Marinas VHF 09, Port VHF 14.

PUERTO DE LUANCO

There is a new harbour to the NE of the town.

Approach From between N, 2ca off coast, and E, with no dangers

Entrance and berthing Make straight for the hammerhead on the larger (first) of the two pontoons on the west (port hand side). There is reported to be an obstruction midway between this hammerhead and the pontoons on the E wall. Friendly club with basic facilities. No fuel.

☏ 699 005 113

RIA DE AVILÉS

Standard Port Pointe de Grave
HW (sp) −0040 (np) −0100
LW (sp) −0050 (np) −0015
MHWS MHWN MLWN MLWS
−1·2m −1·6m −0·5m −0·7m

A commercial hbr surrounded by heavy industry but with an easy approach and entrance, and a useful marina.

On this coast with a strong N'ly a good port of refuge. Picturesque old town.

Approach Cabo Peñas Fl(3)15s 115m35M to NE. Pta de Castillo Oc.WR.5s at entrance to Aviles.

Entrance From a position 2ca W of LtHo on Pta de Castillo enter lighted channel on 099°, in white sector, midway between cliffs to port and training wall and breakwater to stb.

Berthing New marina on W bank at end of channel welcomes visitors on pontoon 11; telephone to get key.

Anchorage At Fondeadero del Monumento 1½M from entrance on port side in 4m, 100m SW of small café. Take dinghy to S end of quay (Muelle de Raices) on stb side of channel. Buses to Avilés.

☏/VHF 607 811 525, Port VHF 06.

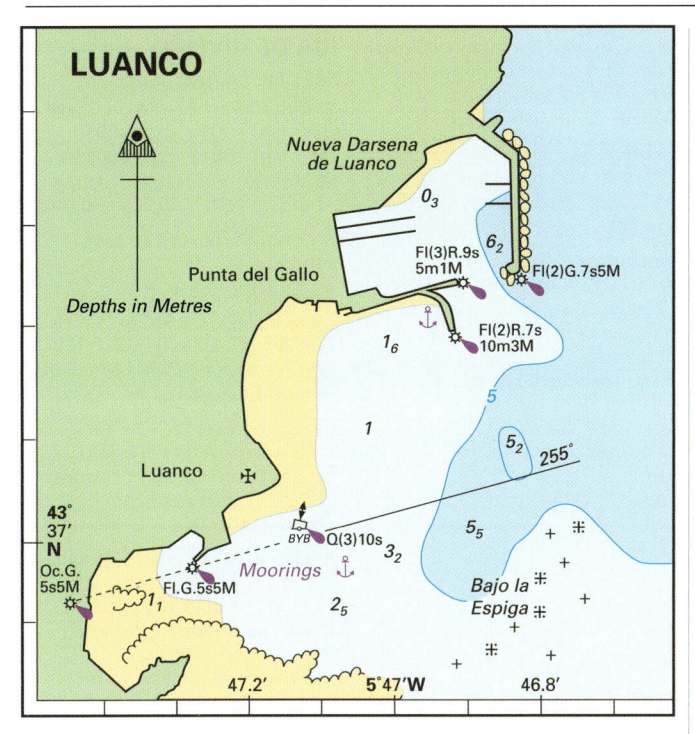

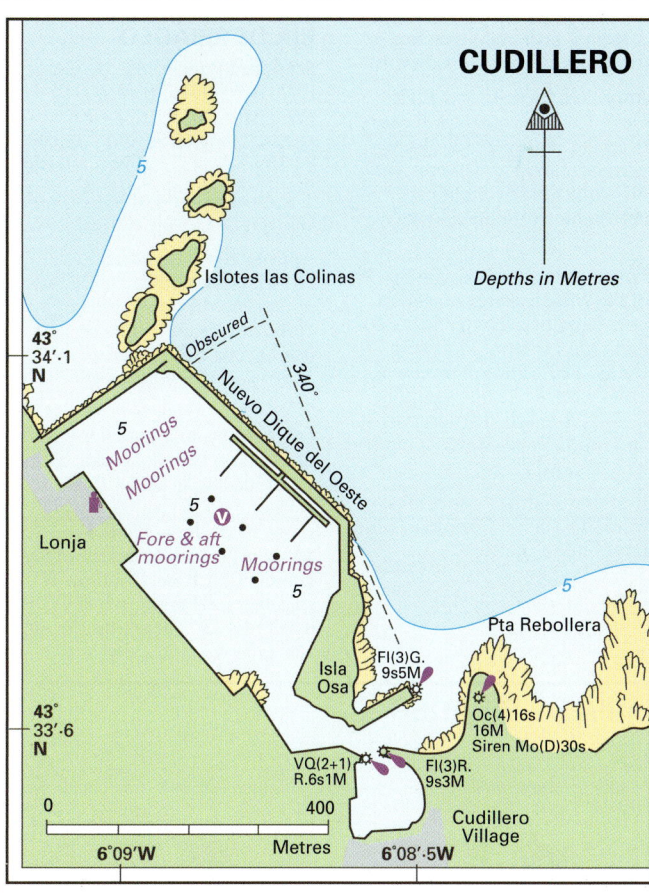

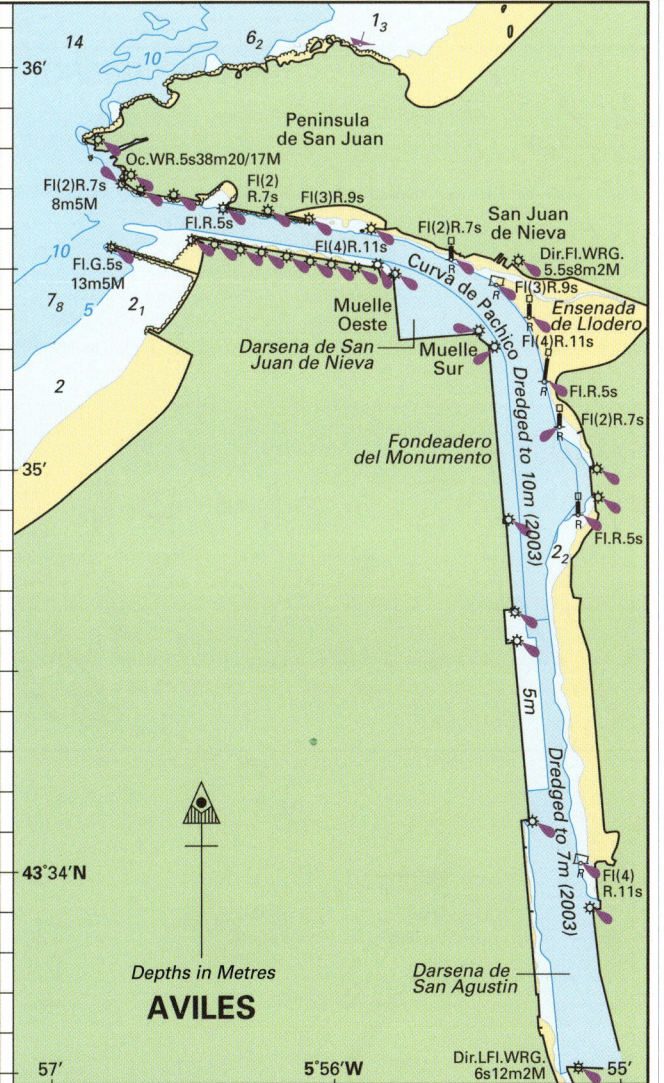

The Cruising Almanac

LUANCO

CUDILLERO

Entrance From a position where Pta Rebollera LtHo bears 200° at ½M steer 200° and leave LtHo to port, E breakwater F.G to stb. For new hbr turn hard to stb through narrow entrance behind Is Osa, swell breaks in the entrance in strong NE wind. Old hbr no longer used.

Berthing Fore and aft visitors' moorings in centre of harbour.

PUERTO DE LUARCA
Standard Port Pointe de Grave
HW (sp) −0015 (np) +0010
LW (sp) −0015 (np) +0025

MHWS	MHWN	MLWN	MLWS
−1·2m	−1·1m	−0·5m	−0·3m

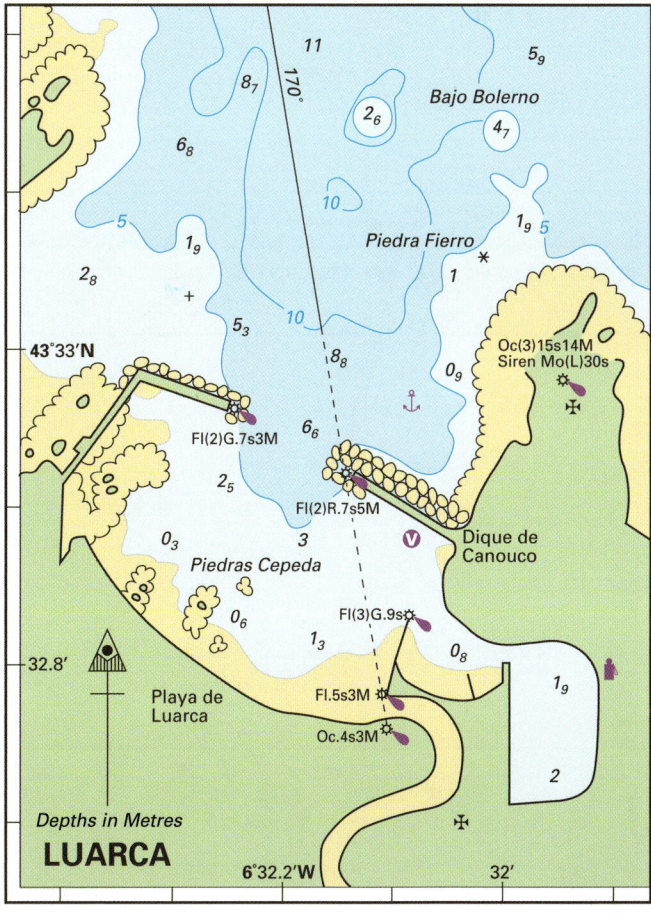

AVILES

LUARCA

PUERTO DE CUDILLERO
Standard Port Pointe de Grave
HW −0035   LW n/a

MHWS	MHWN	MLWN	MLWS
−1·4m	−1·3m	−0·6m	−0·6m

A tiny picturesque old hbr in a gap in cliffs. Huge new fishing hbr 2ca to W. Enter on top half of tide. Swell breaks in entrance in strong NE winds.

Approach Identify Pta Rebollera Oc(4)16s at E of entrance. The new high breakwater Nuevo Dique del Oeste is conspic by day.

SPAIN AND PORTUGAL

393

A fishing port and attractive town in a steep-sided valley.

Approach Identify low LtHo Oc(3)15s and conspic tall church tr on Pta Blanca 2ca E of hbr entrance, and Pta Mujeres 4ca NNW of hbr. By night car headlights around LtHo may confuse.

Entrance From a position 3ca N of Pta Mujeres steer on end of port-hand breakwater 170°. By night ldg Lts front Fl.5s rear Oc.4s, 170°. Enter between breakwaters Fl(3)R.9s to port, Fl(3)G.9s to stb. Turn to port and follow breakwater and port-hand quay 25m off.

Berthing Visitors' moorings inside Dique de Canouco; take bow line to quay.

RIA DE RIBADEO

Standard Port Pointe de Grave
HW (sp) –0015 (np) +0010
LW (sp) –0015 (np) +0025

MHWS	MHWN	MLWN	MLWS
–1·3m	–1·5m	–0·7m	–0·8m

The most easterly of the Rias of Galicia, in a lovely setting.

Approach Is Pancha LtHo Fl(3+1)20s is conspic on W side of entrance to ría. Pta de la Cruz Fl(4)R.11s is on E side. Beware fish havens 2·5m high in approaches. Ebb tide can reach 3kn.

Entrance From a position ½M N of LtHo on Is Pancha follow first set of ldg marks on 140°, R diamond on W towers. By night, Front Iso.R, Rear Oc.R.4s. After 1M, turn on to second set of ldg marks 205°, R diamond on W structures. By night, front VQ.R, rear Oc.R.2s. These lead through the W span of the high-level road br (30m). Leave the quay close to stb and steer for the quay of Muelle de Mirasol Fl(2)R.7s.

Berthing Marina in Dársena de Porcillan has been expanded and refurbished and welcomes visitors.

Anchorage Beware of marine farms which may be unmarked or unlit.
• Figueras in 4m, 250m W of shipyard.
• Off the Muelle de Mirasol 100m W of Castropol, area becoming shallow. Castropol has a pontoon 1·4m for landing.

☏ 982 12 04 28.

RIA DE VIVEIRO

See plan on next page

Standard Port Pointe de Grave
HW (sp) –0015 (np) +0010
LW (sp) –0015 (np) +0025

MHWS	MHWN	MLWN	MLWS
–1·4m	–1·3m	–0·6m	–0·4m

A beautiful ría with an easy entrance.

Approach Pta de la Estaca de Bares Fl(2)7·5s is 6M to NW. Is Coelleira Fl(4)24s is 3M to NW. Conspic high headland Mte Faro Juances on E side of ría.

Entrance Leave Pta de Faro Fl.R.5s to port, Pta Socastro Fl.G.5s to stb and steer towards Celeiro breakwater head Fl(2)R.7s5M to S.

Anchorages All rather exposed, open to N and swell.
• Off Playa del Covas in 5m. Convenient dinghy slip just upstream of marina.
• In Concha d'Area S of the rock Congreiras in up to 6m.

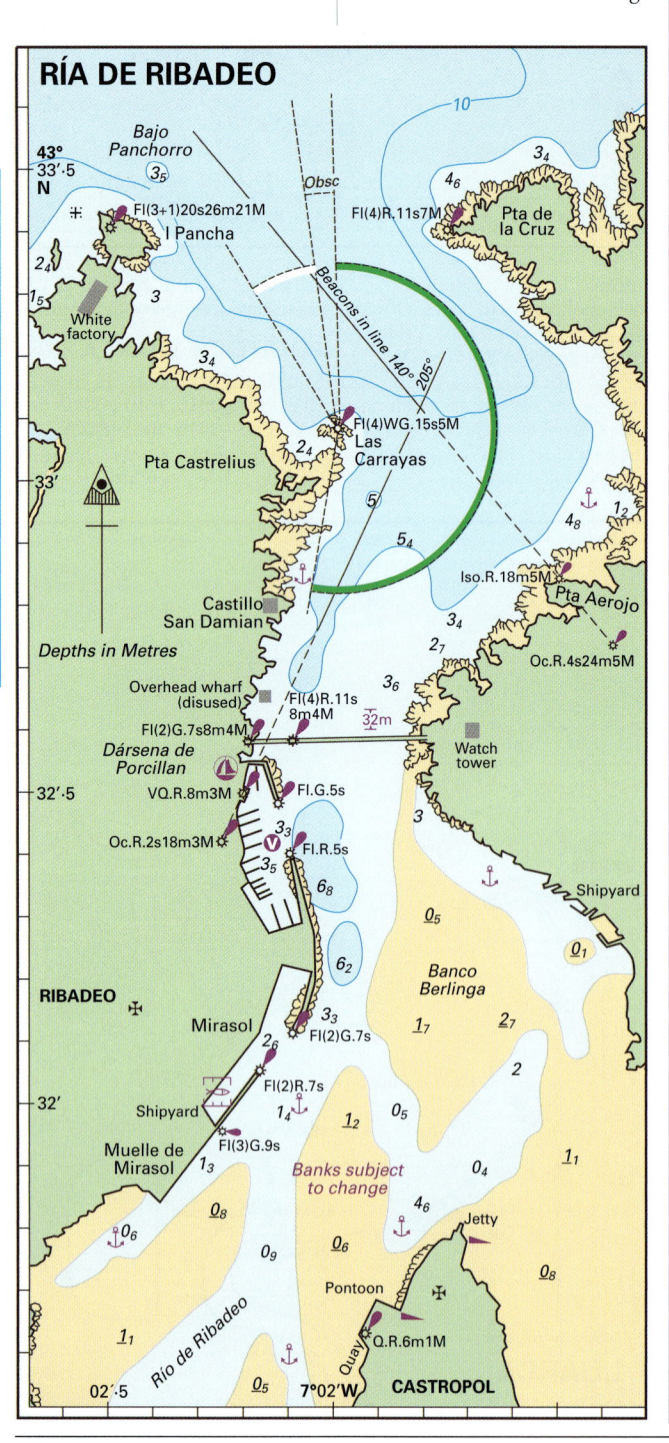

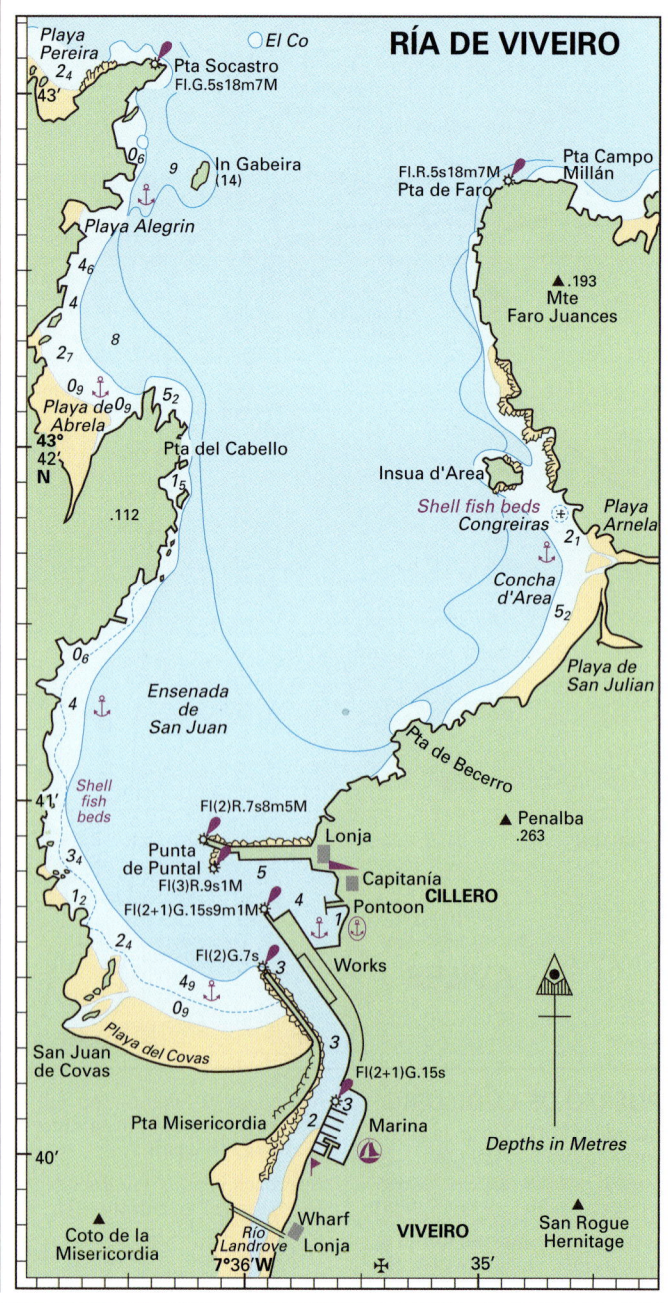

ENSENADA DE SANTA MARTA AND PUERTO CARIÑO

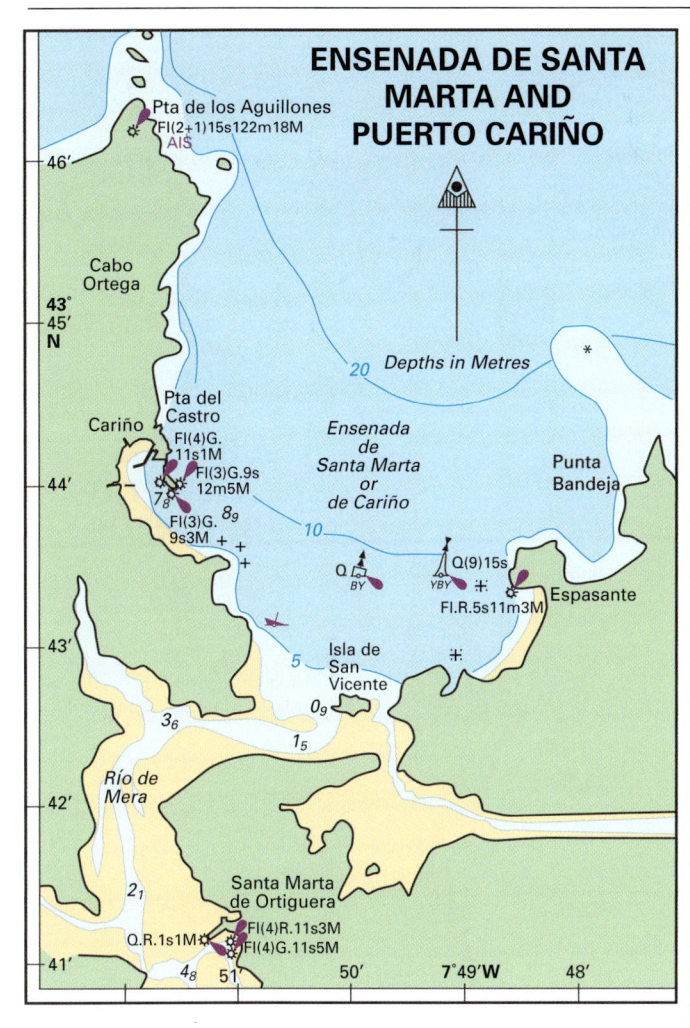

RIA DE CEDEIRA

- Off Playa de Abrela in up to 10m. Open to NE.
- Ensenada de San Julian in up to 8m. Beware of shellfish beds.

Berthing
- The river is dredged to 3m to the marina which is nearly in the centre of town. Usual facilities. Fuel. Visitors welcome.

☎/VHF 690 604 452, VHF 09.

ENSENADA DE SANTA MARTA AND PUERTO DE CARIÑO

Standard Port Pointe de Grave
HW –0005   LW n/a

MHWS	MHWN	MLWN	MLWS
–1·3m	–1·3m	–0·6m	–0·4m

A large bay and ría with wide entrance, and a beautiful Río to Santa Marta.

Approach Pta de la Estaca de Bares Fl(2)7·5s on E side, beware of shallows and rocks off Pta Banjeda, Cabo Ortegal Oc.8s on W side. Conspic line of sharp-pointed rocks Los Aguillones off Cabo Ortegal.

Entrance to Río de Mera has a bar and is not buoyed, so only possible for visitors HW–0200 to HW. Leave Isla de San Vicente close to port, then follow channel to stb behind the line of breakers, along line of yellow buoys. The river is buoyed further up.

Berthing
- Puerto de Cariño is reported full of local boats
- In marina in Santa Marta.
☎ 630 183 901.

Anchorage
- Puerto de Cariño on W side of bay behind extended breakwater Fl(3)G.9s in 6m.
- Ensenada de Espasante in 6m in SE of bay. Open to W or in hbr in N of bay.
- In Río de Mera at Santa Marta de Ortiguera.

RÍA DE CEDEIRA

Standard Port Pointe de Grave
HW –0030   LW n/a

MHWS	MHWN	MLWN	MLWS
–1·0m	–1·4m	–0·5m	–0·7m

Attractive ría with easy access and a small fishing port. Superb secure anchorage makes this a good arrival/departure point for Biscay.

Approach From N leave Pta Candelaria, conspic LtHo Fl(3+1)24s, to port. For 3M keep ¼M offshore until ría opens up. From SW steer 055° towards Pta Candelaria and when 2M from this headland identify to stb Pta Chirlateira and its off-lying rocky shoals. Steer towards Pta Lameda on 070° until the Lt on Pta Promontoiro Oc(4)10s is just clear of Pta del Sarridal Oc.WR.6s, on 160°.

Entrance Pass close to Pta del Sarridal to avoid the rocky shoal Piedras de Media Mar, isolated danger bn Fl(2)5s, to stb in centre of ría, and round the breakwater Fl(2)R.7s to port.

Anchorage E of jetty in 4m, clear of fishing boats. Supplies at Cedeira ½M.

Berthing E side of W jetty. Also at end of the old jetty by the *capitanía* ☎ 981 481 327.

RIA DE BETANZOS AND RIA DE ARES

Standard Port Pointe de Grave
HW −0050   LW n/a

MHWS	MHWN	MLWN	MLWS
−1·4m	−1·6m	−0·6m	−0·2m

Two quiet attractive rías with easy entrance within short distance of El Ferrol and La Coruña.

Approach Cabo Priorño Chico Fl.5s. Torre de Hercules Fl(4)20s.

Entrance Identify Pta Coitelada to port and Pta del Seijo Blanco to stb. Pass between them, clearing coast by 2ca. Leave Is de la Miranda well to port. Beware, unmarked isolated rock 5ca SW of Is de la Miranda.

Anchorages
• Sada, immediately S of marina.
• Ensenada de Ares in 2–3m off hbr on W shore. Pontoon berths may be available.
• Ensenada de Redes, 4ca E of village off beach, sheltered NE.
• Ensenada de Cirno, inshore of mussel rafts.

Berthing
• **Marina Sada**, a modern marina with all facilities. Berth on outer pontoons and report to office. Good transport to Coruña. ☏ 981 619 015.
• **Ares**, friendly marina, VHF or telephone for berth. ☏ 981 46 87 87

A CORUÑA

Standard Port Pointe de Grave
HW (sp) −0050   (np) −0110
LW (sp) −0110   (np) −0030

MHWS	MHWN	MLWN	MLWS
−1·6m	−1·6m	−0·6m	−0·5m

The major port on the NW coast of Spain with an easy entrance by day or night. Subject to swell in strong winds from N and NW. Picturesque old city.

Approach From N leave Cabo Prior Fl(1+2)15s and Cabo Priorño Chico Fl.5s to port 1M off. Enter in mid-ría on S leaving Pta del Seijo Blanco to port and the conspic Torre de Hercules Fl(4)20s to stb. Steer 182°on Ldg marks (W sector) on Pta Fiaiteira front Iso.WRG.2s, rear Oc.R.4s. In heavy weather when the sea breaks across this channel use W approach. From W steer 108° on Pta Mera Ldg marks front Oc.WR.4s rear Fl.4s leaving Pta Herminio with Torre de Hercules 2ca to stb. Turn on to Ldg marks on Pta Fiaiteira 182°.

Entrance Round end of breakwater Dique de Abrigo Fl.G.3s to stb and follow SW side of mole towards new marina 1ca N of Castillo de San Anton Fl(2)G.7s.

Anchorage
• SW of Is de Santa Cristina clear of slip and rocks.
• Ensenada de Mera, clear of rock off head of jetty. Sheltered N through E to SE.

Berthing
• **Marina Coruña**. A modern fully serviced marina at the root of Digue Abrigo. Subject to swell. All repairs. ☏ 981 920 482.

The Cruising Almanac

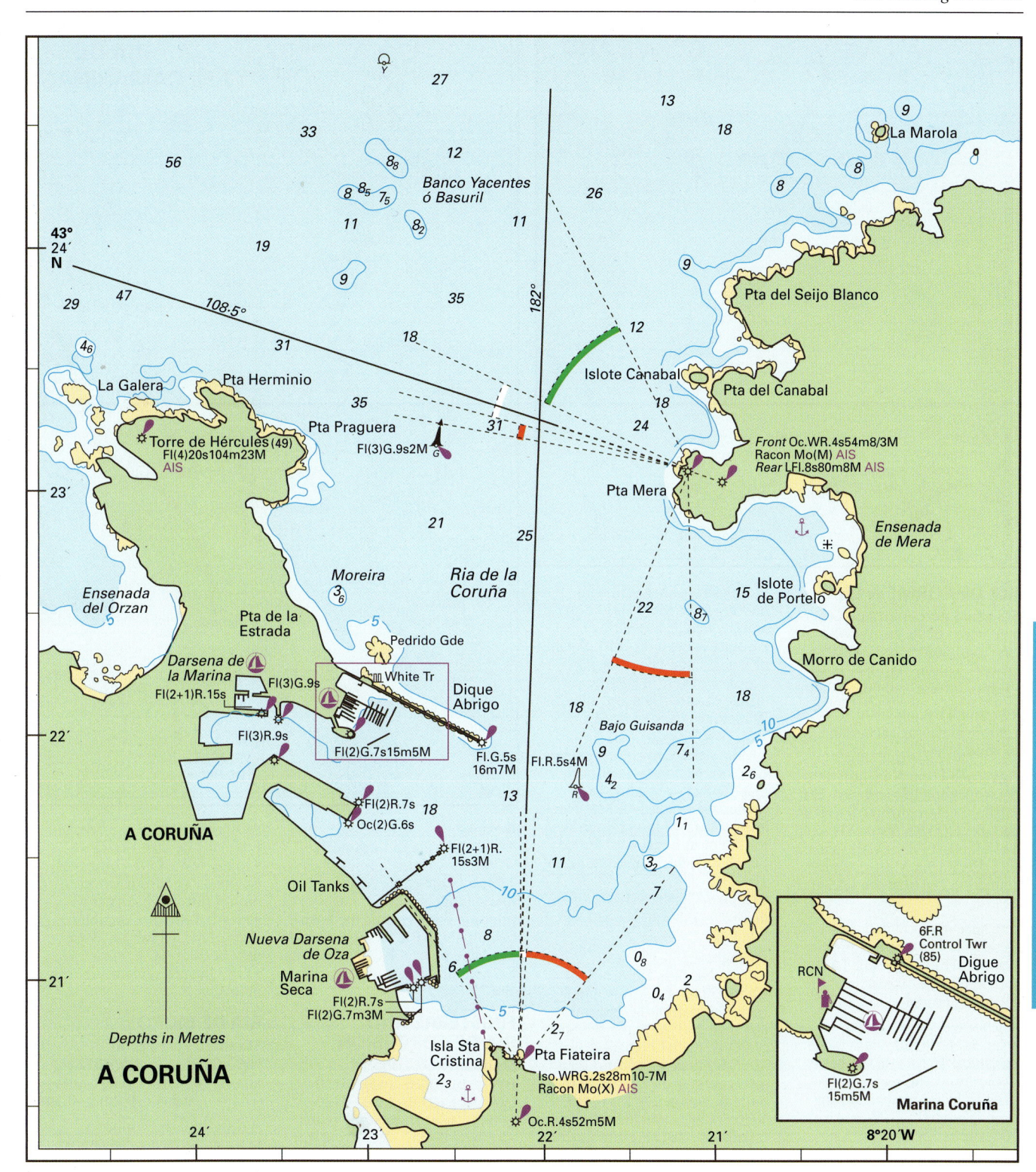

- Real Club Nautico de la Coruña Marina in Darsena Deportiva. In the heart of the city. Reception pontoon 10, near entrance. ☎ 981 226 880.
- Marina Seca in Dársena de Oza. Full facilities. Boatyard. ☎ 881 913 651.

Facilities of a city, market. International airport at Santiago de Compostela, 1hr by bus.

VHF Port VHF 12; Marinas VHF 09.

43° 22N
008° 22W

SPAIN AND PORTUGAL

397

The Cruising Almanac

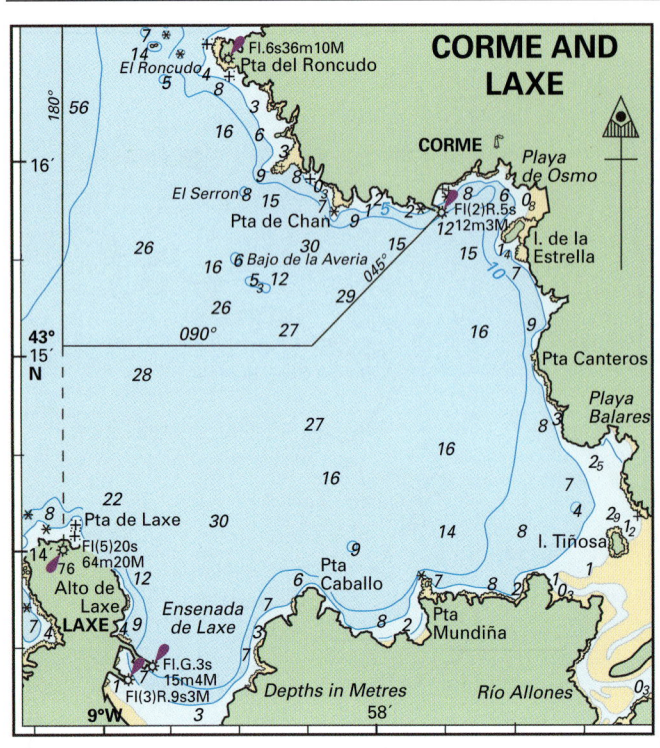

RÍA DE CORME & LAXE
Standard Port Pointe de Grave
HW (sp) −0005 (np) −0025
LW (sp) −0015 (np) +0015
MHWS MHWN MLWN MLWS
−1·3m −1·8m −0·6m −0·7m

Two small fishing villages. Choose anchorage according to wind.

Approach From N identify Pta del Roncudo Fl.6s and pass 1M offshore before turning S to Pta de Laxe Fl(5)20s. From SW keep 1M off coast NE of Cabo Villano Fl(2)15s Racon M (− −), and round Pta Lae between ½M and 1M off.

Entrance Avoid Bajo de la Averia shoal in heavy weather. From a position 1M N of Pta de Laxe steer E until Corme mole Fl(2)R.5s bears less than 045°.

Anchorages
• Corme 100–200m NE–E–SE of molehead 12 to 14m sand clear of moorings and reefs inshore marked by bn. Beware of fish farm. Exposed SW–W and to NW swell.
• Laxe SE end of mole Fl.G.3s clear of hbr entrance in 6–8m sand.

RÍA DE CAMARIÑAS
Standard Port Pointe de Grave
HW (sp) −0055 (np) −0120
LW (sp) −0100 (np) −0030
MHWS MHWN MLWN MLWS
−1·7m −1·6m −0·6m −0·5m

An attractive ría with two villages. Entry by day or night in reasonable visibility. Note Traffic Separation Scheme Cabo Villano to Cabo Finisterre.

Approach Cabo Villano conspic LtHo Fl(2)15s is 2M N of ría. Pass outside or inside El Bufardo, rock awash 3ca off Cabo Villano.

Entrance by day
• From NE round Cabo Villano and steer SW to avoid Las Quebrantas shoal until white hermitage on Mte Farelo bears E and the middle of the ría entrance is open on 108°, the line of Pta de Lago Ldg marks, two concrete towers in line but difficult to see. By night, steer for W sector of Pta de Lago Lt Oc(2)WRG.6s 107°–109°.
• Alternatively, in good weather, from NE pass inshore of Las Quebrantas by heading 135° towards hermitage on Mte Farelo until ¾M from shore. Then steer for Pta de la Barca until Pta de Lago Ldg marks come in line on 108°.
• From SW pass ½M NW of Pta de la Barca to join Pta de Lago Ldg line.

By night
• From NE pass 1½M NW of Cabo Villano to clear isolated rock El Bufardo, then steer not less than 200° until the W sector of Pta de Lago Lt is visible on 108°. If Pta de Lago cannot be seen continue on 200° until the more powerful Ldg Lts of Pta Villueira Fl.5s and Pta del Castillo Iso.4s come into line on 080°. Follow this line until Pta de Lago Ldg Lts are seen.
• From SW steer to pass ½M NW of Pta de la Barca Oc.4s. Follow Ldg Lts on Pta Villueira and Pta Castillo, and Pta de Lago.

Anchorage
• Camariñas (heavy weed reported) From Pta de Lago Ldg line steer for Camariñas molehead Fl.R.5s when it bears 340°. Mole gives good shelter.
• S of Cala de Vila, sheltered N.
• Ensenada de Merexo. Exposed to N and NW.
• Muxía From Pta de Lago Ldg line steer for Muxía molehead Fl(4)G.11s when it bears 220°. Anchor in 3–4m S of end of new breakwater. Beware two rocks off beach to S.

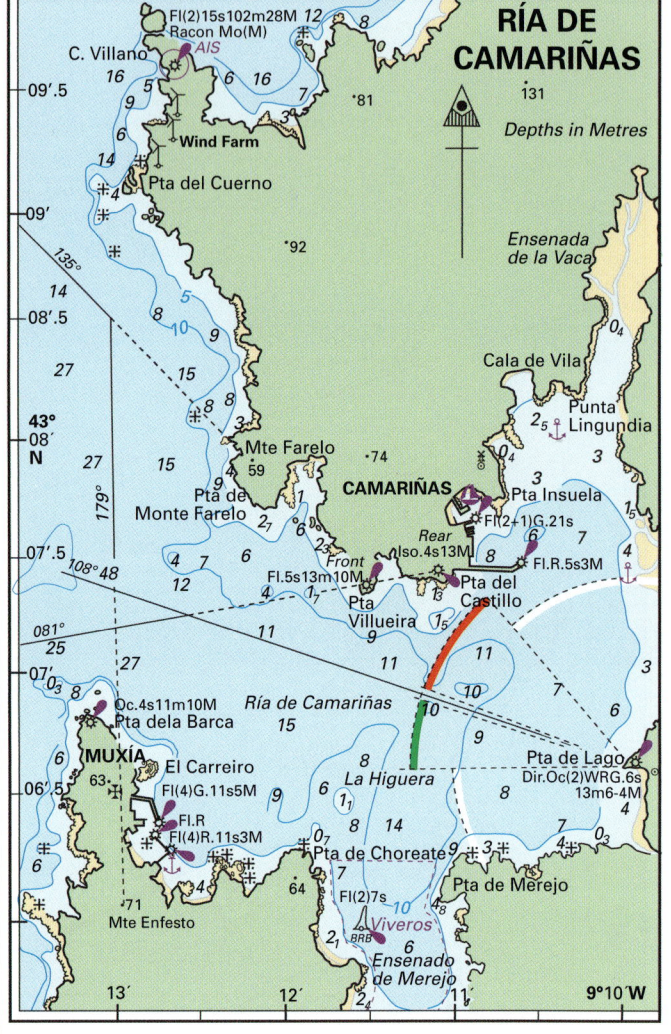

Berthing
• In the marina in Caramiñas ☎ 981 737 130.
• Club Nautico de Muxia marina, opened 2013, finger pontoon berths inside the former fishing hbr. Basic facilities. Fuel available by can. Bar overlooking harbour and restaurant nearby. ☎ 673 168 199.

FINISTERRE AND RÍA DE CORCUBIÓN
Standard Port Lisbon
HW (sp) +0055 (np) +0110
LW (sp) +0135 (np) +0120
MHWS MHWN MLWN MLWS
−0·5m −0·4m −0·3m −0·1m

A large bay, with the rather industrial Ría de Corcubión in the NE corner. All exposed to S, but offering shelter from the predominant summer NE'lies. The walk to the lighthouse of Finisterre is exhilerating.

Approach From the N, pass outside Centola de Finisterra and leave Cabo Finisterre at least ½M to port. There are often sudden squalls off Finisterre. From the S, there are numerous shoals and rocks. With a suitable chart and settled weather, a yacht can thread its way along the shore. Otherwise, approach Cabo Finisterre from a point 8M due S.

Anchorages
• Off Puerto de Finisterre, outside moorings, with some shelter from the mole
• Off the N end of the beach of Ensenada de Llagosteira
• In the NW or NE corners of Ensenada de Sardineiro, clear of mussel raft in NE corner
• Head of Ría de Corcubión, clear of mussel raft on W shore near head of ría
• Off Quenxe, outside moorings in 8m.

RÍA DE MUROS
Standard Port Lisbon
HW +0058 LW +0122
MHWS MHWN MLWN MLWS
−0·3m −0·3m −0·2m −0·1m

A delightful ría, with two marinas and several sheltered anchorages.

Approach From Cabo Finisterre in the N, with a large-scale chart, take a course of 140° leading to the Canal de los Meixidos, between the Piedras las Minarzos and Los Meixidos. Otherwise pass S of Los Meixidos. Give the Islotes de Neixon ¼M offing – there are outliers. From the S, with a large-scale chart, a yacht can thread the rocks up the coast. Otherwise, give Cabo Corrubedo a 2M offing, head N for 6M, then head into the ría on 045°.

Anchorage
• Muros, outside harbour, NW of molehead Fl(4)G.11s. Pontoon for small boats outside N mole. Exposed to NE. Water, diesel on quayside, key holders near fishing shed

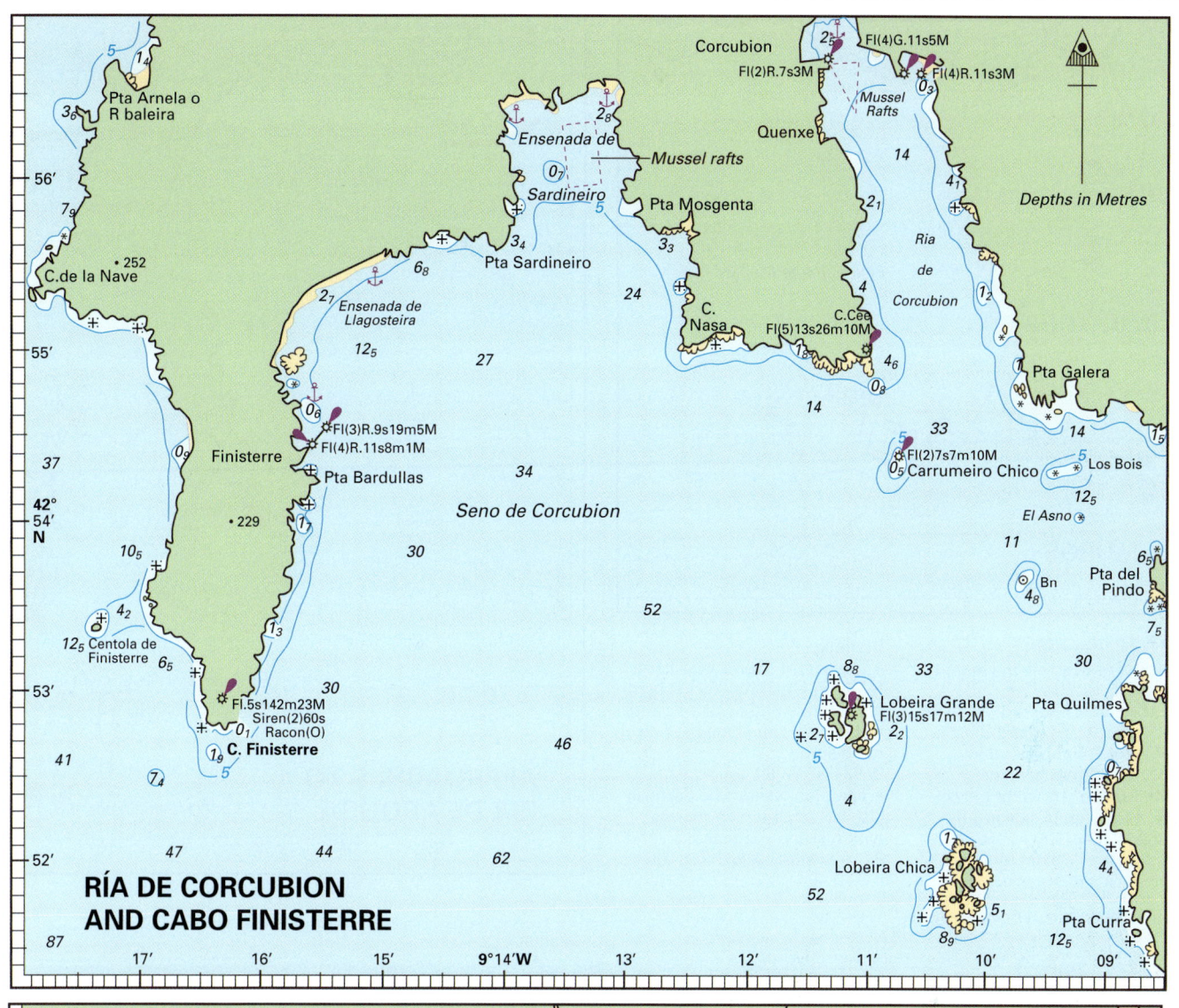

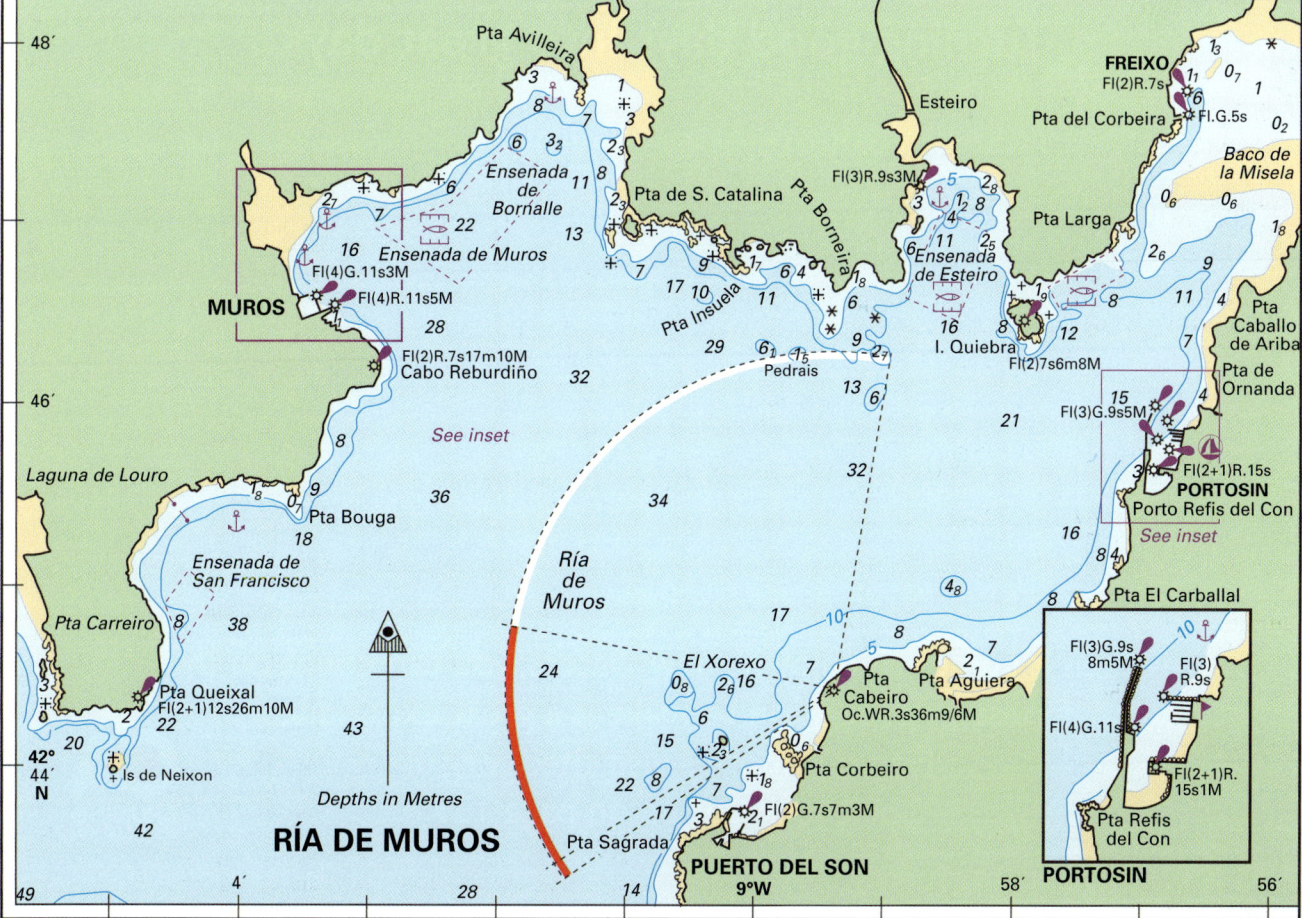

RÍA DE CORCUBION AND CABO FINISTERRE

RÍA DE MUROS

The Cruising Almanac

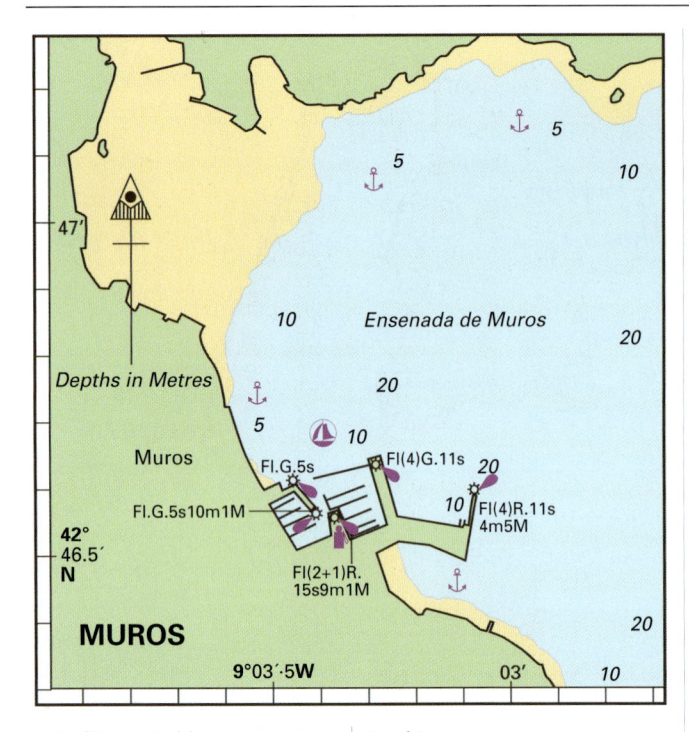

MUROS

APPROACHES TO RÍA DE AROUSA

- N of Portosin hbr
- 5ca N of Muros hbr, close to shore, sheltered N
- Ensenada de Bornalle, clear of rocks. Sheltered from NE
- Freixo, 100m N of mole Fl(2)R.5s. From here the interesting old town of Noya 2½M to E can be reached by dinghy HW±0100
- Ensenada de San Francisco
- Ensenada de Esteiro.

Berthing
- The port of Muros now has a full-service marina. Yachts berth in the E half of the port. Facilities include WiFi and laundry. Best to radio ahead.
☏ 981 82 76 60
- The Club Nautico de Portosin also has a full-service marina, with fuel and a launderette, and a 32t travel-lift. ☏ 981 766 583.

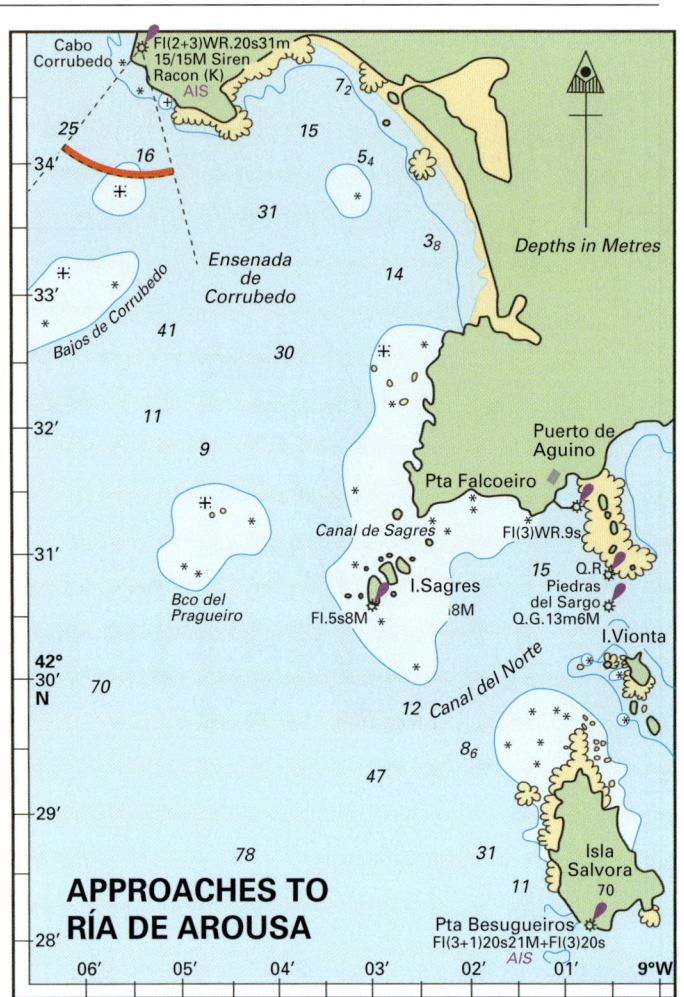

Turning good days into great days

When it comes to enjoying new waters, you can count on the Cruising Association to make it a great experience. Find out more - visit theca.org.uk or check our ad on page 139

CA CRUISING ASSOCIATION

RIA DE AROUSA

Standard Port Lisbon

Vilagarcia
HW +0050   LW +0115
MHWS   MHWN   MLWN   MLWS
−0·3m −0·2m −0·2m −0·1m

A large ría with buoyed channels, sheltered waters for sailing, and a variety of attractive anchorages. Night entry possibly into Vilagarcía and Pobra de Caramiñal. If you want to explore off the main channels, you will need a large-scale chart (Spanish *415*, *BA 1764* or, recommended, *Mapes de Navigació CPP-28*, available locally), as there are numerous isolated rocks.

Approach The Canal Principal between Is Salvora and Pomberiño is the easiest and safest approach.

From N pass 5M offshore from Cabo Corrubedo Fl(2+3)WR.20s Racon K (−·−) to clear rocky shoal patch Bajos de Corrubedo situated within red sector 347°–040°. Leave Is Salvora LtHo Fl(3+1)20s+Fl(3)20s (sectored) to N at a distance of 1M.

Coming from S steer to a position mid-way between Is Salvora and Pombeiriño bn tr Fl(2)G.12s. Two alternatives, Canal de Sagres and Canal del Norte to the NW of Is Salvora and Is Vionta are best explored on leaving the ría and require a large-scale chart, passing N of Piedras del Sargo conspic white con bn tr with G band Q.G.

Entrance Steer for Is Rua LtHo Fl(2)WR.7s on conspic rocky islet and leave to port, passing between Is Rua and Bajo Piedra

Seca W tr Fl(3)G.9s. Continue on 030° for 2M to clear bank Sinal del Maño with R pillar buoy Fl(2)R.7s.

Berthing There are four main, easily accessible marinas with all facilities:

• **Pobra do Caramiñal** Leave bn tr Sinal de Ostreira Fl.R.5s 1ca to port and head for the outer mole Fl(3)G.9s. Leave R can buoy Fl(3)R.9s, marking the end of the mussel bed, to port, and turn in towards the marina. Reception on outer pontoon.
① 981 827 660. Fuel.

• **Cabo de Cruz** Due N from Bajo de Ter buoy, or direct from Pobra do Caramiñal. New marina reported to welcome visitors. Usual facilities. Fuel
① 981 845 358

• **Vilagarcía de Arousa** is an active town with a sheltered marina.

Approach Use Pta Caballo LtHo Fl(4)11s on the N shore of I. de Arousa, steer about 055° past El Seijo G pillar buoy Fl(3)G.10s5M.

Facilities Berthing is mainly on fingers. Good shopping. International airport at Santiago de Compostela. Buses, trains. No fuel. ① 986 511 175.

• **Vilanova de Arousa** Leaving G pillar buoy, El Seijo Fl(3)G.10s5M to port, steer due S to avoid the fish farms. When the commercial hbr entrance is abeam turn in towards this well sheltered relatively new marina. *Note* Bajo el Seijo rocks marked by unlit bn. Fuel. ① 938 561 420.

Anchorages

• **Sta Uxia de Ribiera** A busy fishing port with a small YC marina to the N of the hbr. Anchor outside harbour mole Fl(2)R.7s. Beware Bajo Camouco marked by Bn Q.G.

• **Pobra do Caramiñal** S or SE of marina. Sheltered S to W.

• **Cabo Cruz** To E of rocky peninsula in centre of bay, or N of new hbr on W side of peninsula, exposed to N.

• **Rianxo** A shallow hbr, pontoons for small yachts or anchor about 5ca E off Playa de Quenxo, sheltered N.

• **San Xulian** On I. de Arosa, in bay N of village. There is a sheltered harbour behind a breakwater, but likely to be full.

• **I. de Arousa**, SW of Pta Caballo Fl(4)11s inshore of mussel rafts and inside Pta Barbafeita. Exposed to W. Reported that yellow buoys now take most of the space.

• **Cambados** With deep keel, N hbr only. With shallow draft, there is room to anchor S of pontoons in S hbr.

• **I. Toja Grande** On E side, in 4–6m. Attractive but requires large scale chart and careful pilotage on top half of tide.

• **San Martin del Grove** Approach as above. Anchor S of end of breakwater in fair weather.

• **Puerto Pedro Negras** On S side of Peninsular del Grove. Approach on W sector 305°-315° to Lt Fl(4)WR.11s at root of breakwater. Pontoons.

RÍA DE PONTEVEDRA

Standard Port Lisbon

Marin
HW +0100 LW +0125

MHWS	MHWN	MLWN	MLWS
–0·5m	–0·4m	–0·3m	–0·1m

A ría with several anchorages, and a naval college at Marin. No landing on Is Tambo (military zone).

Approach Identify Is Ons Fl(4)24s.

• N of Is Ons through Paso de la Fagilda, leaving R Lt buoy Q.R to port and Picamillo bn tr Fl.G.5s to stb. Leave Los Camoucos rocky shoal Fl(3)R.18s to stb.

• S of I. Ons. Steer 040° halfway between I. Ons and Pta Couso Fl(3)WG.10·5s.

Entrance Between Pta Cabicastro on N side and Cabo de Udra on S.

Anchorage and Berthing

• **Porto Novo** Moorings may be available see club or anchor E of small bay, clear of fishing boats. ① 986 723 266.

• **Sanxenxo** A large well-equipped marina with room for visitors. All facilities. Possible to overwinter here. All night disco in season.
VHF 09 ① 986 720517.

• **Combarro** A delightful if touristy fishing village. Convenient for visiting Pontevedra. Berth in new marina, or anchor E of harbour.
① 986 778 415.

• **Aguete** Small marina, exposed to the N. ① 986 702 373

• **Bueu** Small pleasant fishing port. E of E jetty Fl(2)R.6s, and N jetty Fl.G.3s clear of fishing boats on buoys, close to beach in 3–4m. Not much room in hbr. Good shelter from SW–W.

• **I. Ons** Pleasant day anchorages on E side. This is a National Park, permission to anchor can be obtained directly from www.iatlanticas.es.

• **Ría de Aldan** Bays on S side.

RÍA DE PONTEVEDRA

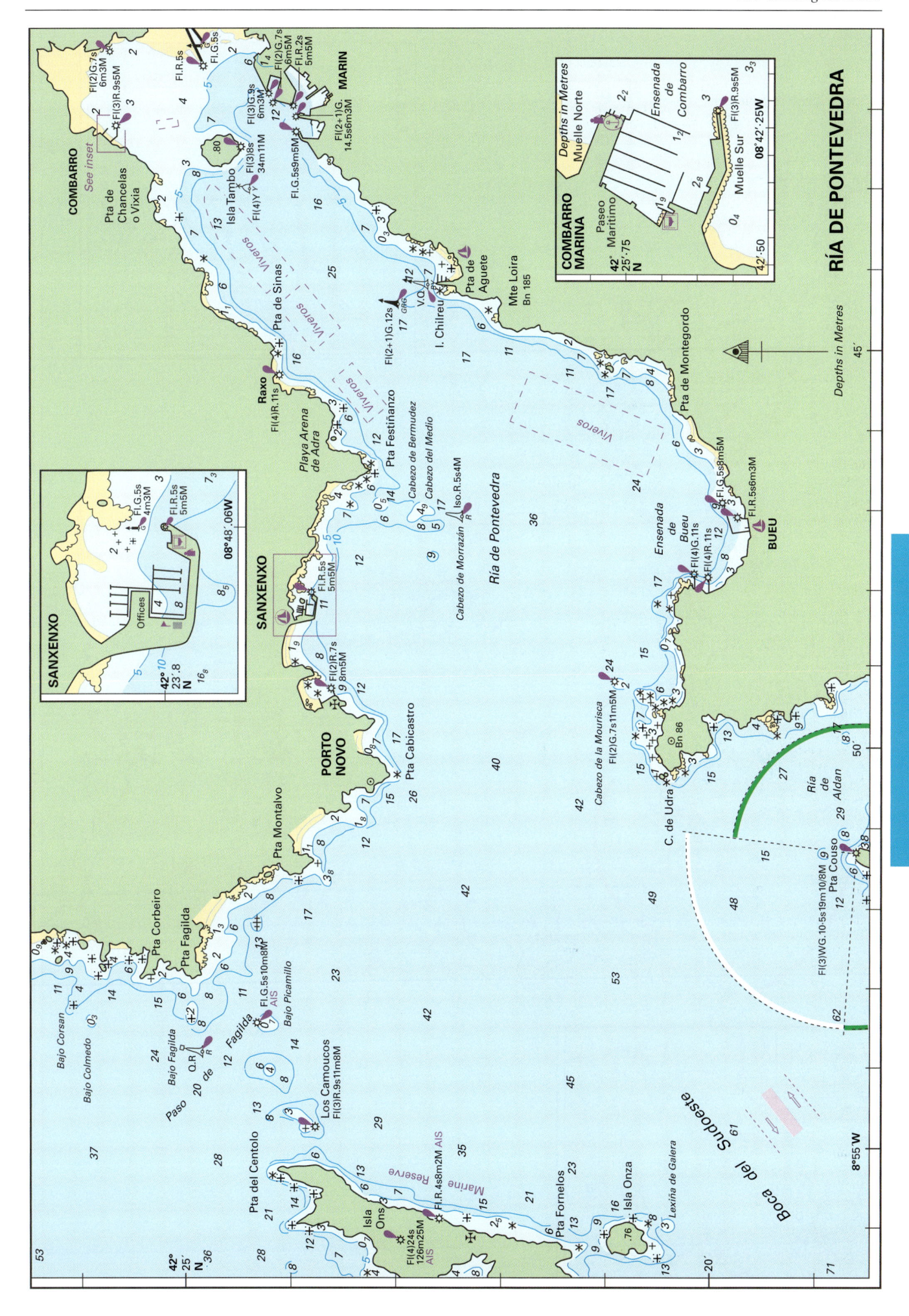

SPAIN AND PORTUGAL

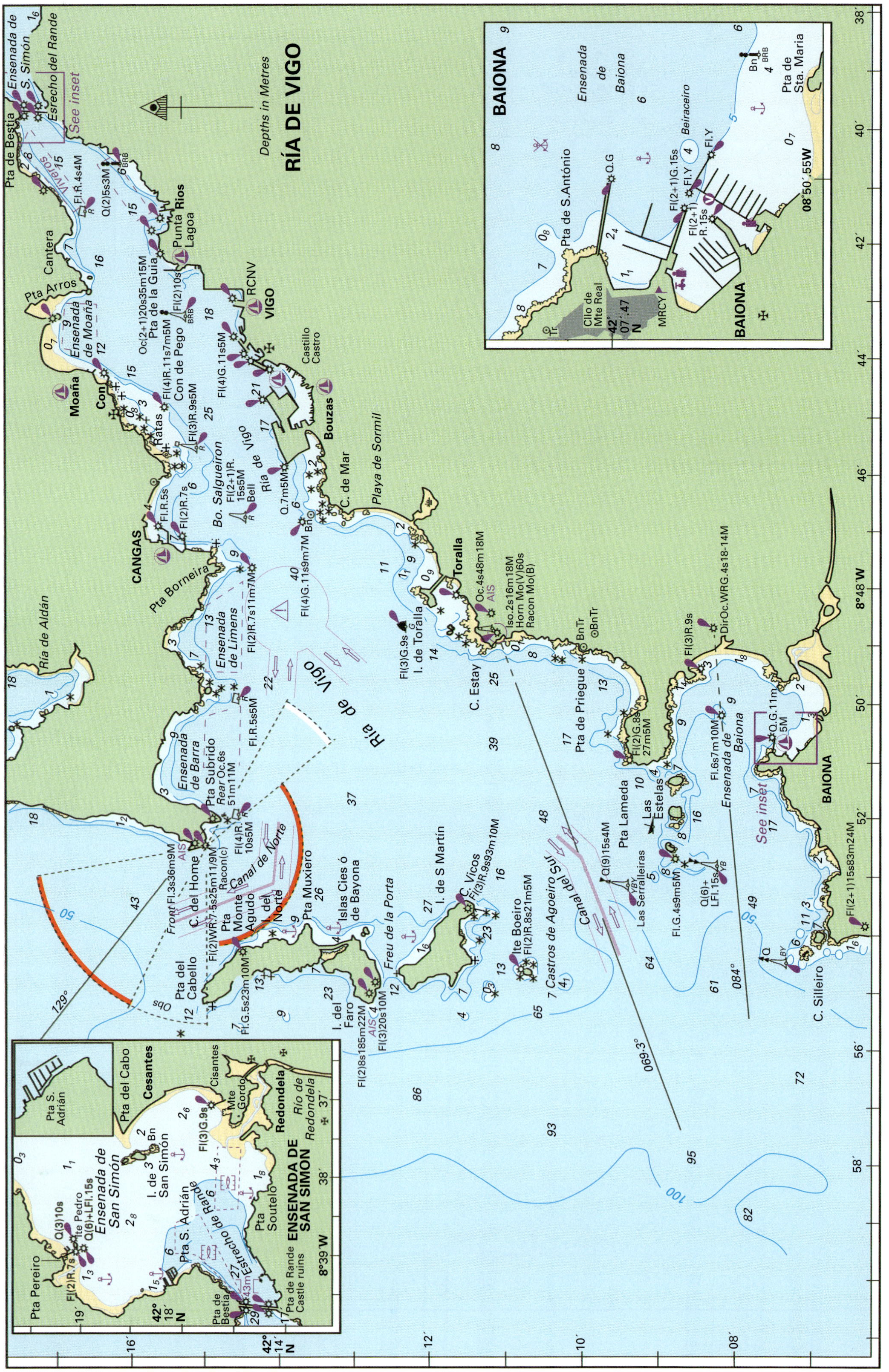

RÍA DE VIGO
Standard Port Lisbon
Vigo
HW (sp) +0040 (np) +0100
LW (sp) +0125 (np) +0105
MHWS MHWN MLWN MLWS
−0·4m −0·3m −0·2m −0·1m

Baiona
HW (sp) +0035 (np) +0050
LW (sp) +0115 (np) +0100
MHWS MHWN MLWN MLWS
−0·3m −0·3m −0·2m −0·1m

The ría is dominated by the large commercial port of Vigo but has attractive anchorages. Baiona is delightful. It is also convenient, with easy access by day or night.

Approach Use Cabo del Horne Fl(2)WR.7·5s from N, Mte Faro Fl(2)8s on conspic Is Cies and Cabo Silleiro Fl(2+1)15s from S.

Entrance Note the TSS in both entrance channels and also the Precautionary Area N of Toralla.
• From the S use the wide deep water entrance, Canal del Sur. Round Cabo Silleiro ¾M off, leave Las Serreillas W card buoy Q(9)15s to stb and make for the G stb hand buoy Fl(3)G.9s off I. de Toralla.
• From the N use the Canal de Norte, avoiding the TSS, giving a good offing to the next four headlands clearly marked by port hand buoys or bns.

Anchorages
• E of Is Cies, N or S of Pta Muxiero or NE of Is de San Martin, off beach. Delightful. Part of the National Park, see web address under Pontevedra, above.
• Ensenada de Barra, sheltered NE.
• Cangas, outer harbour, little room. Pleasant town.
• Ensenada de Cangas, off beach.
• Ensenada de San Simón, beyond the suspension br; beware shellfish beds. Well sheltered.
• Baiona, S of Puerto Deportivo.

Berthing
• **Cangas** A small marina, some room for visitors. Ferry to Vigo. Laundry, Chandlery.
☎ 986 30 42 46, VHF 06.
• **Moaña** Relatively new marina ☎ 986 311 140.
• **Ensenada de San Simón** New marina 1ca N of Pta S Adrián welcomes visitors ☎ 986 673 807
• **Punta Lagoa** Crowded in season. All facilities.
☎986 374 305.
• **Vigo** RCNV in basin immediately beyond conspic former transatlantic terminal buildings. Recently refurbished. ☎986 447 441.
• **Bouzas** Marina Davila Sport is well equipped with good repair facilities.Chandlery. Beware frequent ferries to Cangas from adjacent basin. ☎986 244 612. Major repairs at Astilleros Lago Carsi.
• **Baiona** Enter between Cabo Silleiro and Las Serralleiras on 084°. Sectored Lt Oc.WRG.4s leads in. Steer for molehead Q.G. on not less than 160°. Either berth at YC (Monte Real Club de Yates) at NW side of hbr, crowded. Good YC. ☎986 385 000 VHF 71 or at the larger, modern Puerto Deportivo de Baiona ☎ 986 385 107.

Portugal

From the Rio Miñho southwards to São Vicente the coast flattens progressively and becomes one of sand beaches backed by dunes or low cliffs. The rivers have sand bars and in any swell should only be entered with great care. Some of the fishing harbours have been improved and extended; ports free of a bar include Leixões, Sines, Nazaré and Peniche.

When conditions are not safe for any port, the authorities close the entrance. www.marinha.pt/pt-pt/servicos/informacao-maritima/Paginas/Estado-Barras.aspx gives up-to-date details.

There are TSS off Cabo da Roca and Cabo de São Vicente.

With the exception of Nazaré and Figueira da Foz, where a separate police office needs to be visited, it now appears sufficient to fill out the usual forms in marinas, and not to bother the authorities if anchored. However, there have been numerous reports that the authorities, especially around Faro, have visited yachts and demanded that they be equipped to Portuguese ocean-going standards, pay light dues (a trivial sum), and have proof that all equipment, including fire extinguishers, is in-date. To avoid fines or threats of fines, anchor balls and lights should be used and the boat's name and port of registry (invent one for SSR) must be displayed.

Diesel is available at most ports. Calor Gas not readily obtainable but Camping Gaz is widely available. There may be a charge for water.

Note: Portuguese time is one hour behind Spanish time, i.e. same as UK.

Passage lights

Principal lights	BA No	Principal lights	BA No
Leça Fl(3)14s58m28M	2032	C Espichel Fl.4s167m26M Horn 31s	2139
I Berlenga Fl.10s120m16M Horn 28s	2086	C de Sines Fl(2)15s55m26M	2160
C da Roca Fl(4)17s164m26M	2108	C de São Vicente Fl.5s85m32M Horn Mo(I)30s (··)	2168

VIANA DO CASTELO
Standard Port Lisbon
HW −0010 LW +0012
MHWS MHWN MLWN MLWS
−0·3m −0·4m −0·1m −0·1m

A fishing port and marina with good shelter. Entrance dredged but in heavy swell the sea may break on bar.

Approach Montedor Fl(2)9·5s Horn Mo(S)25s (···) is 5M to N.

Entrance Enter on the stb side of the channel, keep well clear of the W mole. Once abeam of the E mole follow the buoyed channel to Viana Marina before low level br. There is a footbridge across the entrance, call on VHF 62, waiting pontoon in river. Beware cross tide at the entrance.

Berthing Visitors use first pontoon to stb, bow on and pick up stern buoy. Reception pontoon opposite entrance.

Facilities Picturesque old town. Laundry. Rly. Porto International Airport, 30M. No fuel.

☎/VHF Marina 258 359 546, VHF 62; Port VHF 11.

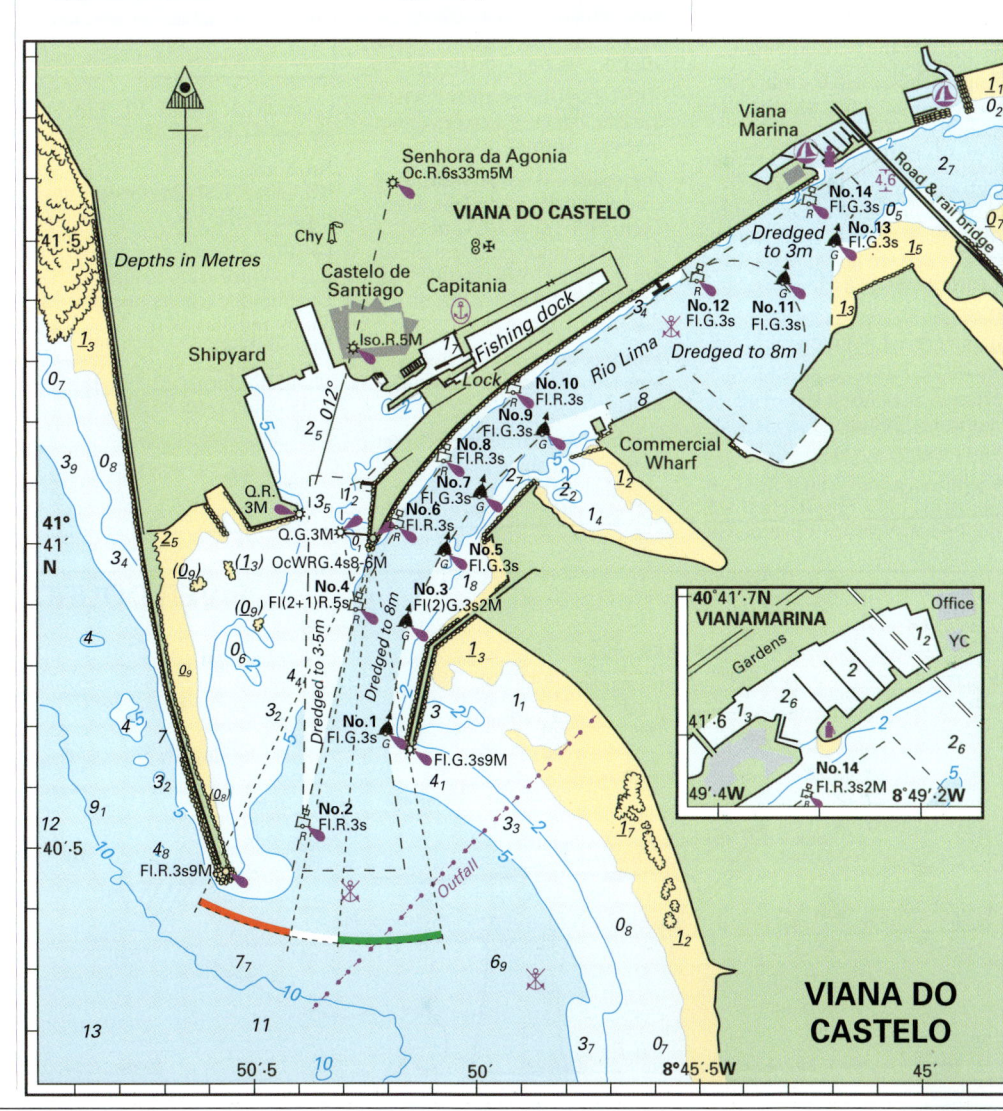

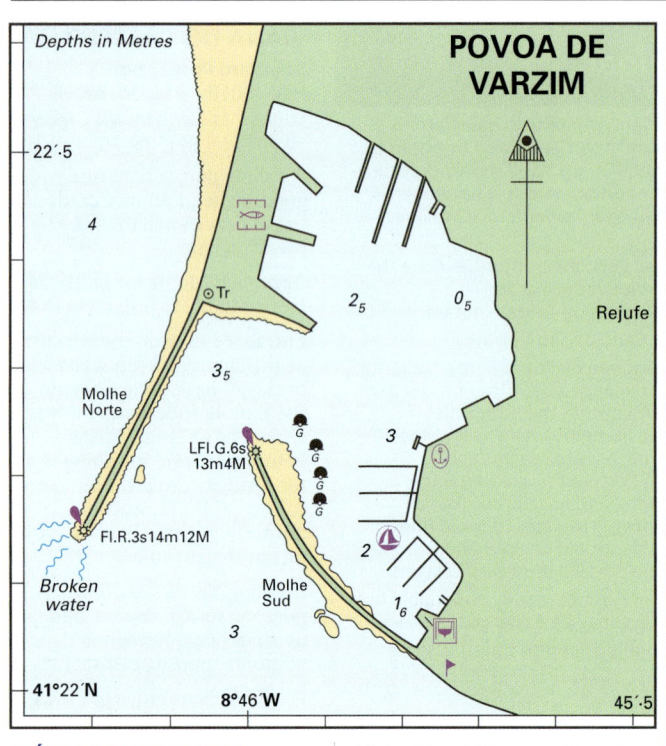

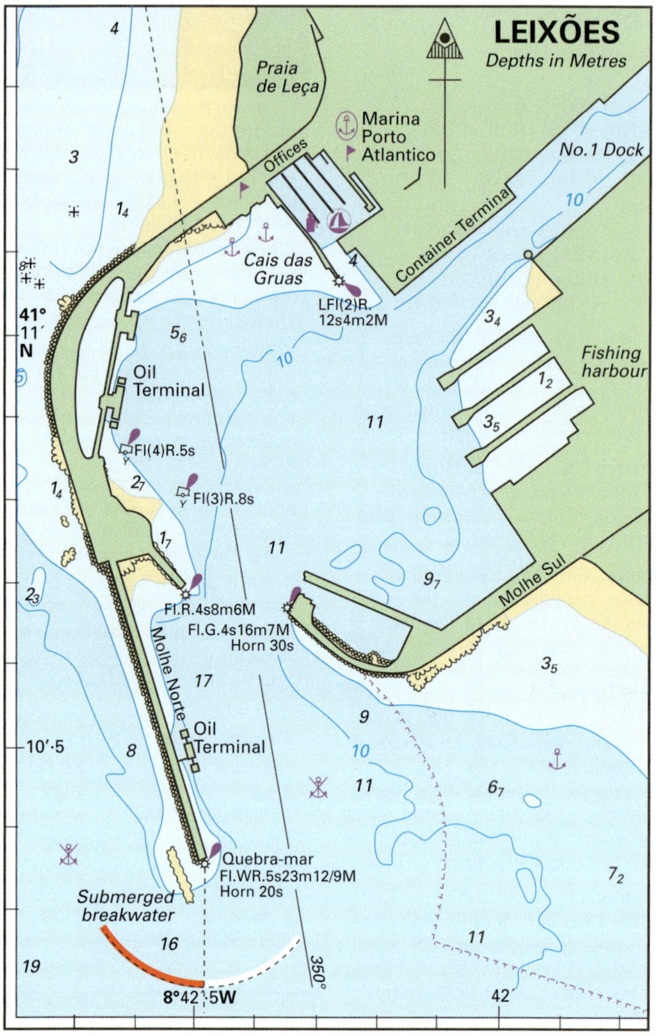

PÓVOA DE VARZIM

Standard Port Lisbon
HW (sp) –0020 (np) +0000
LW (sp) +0015 (np) +0010

MHWS	MHWN	MLWN	MLWS
–0·3m	–0·3m	–0·1m	–0·1m

A reasonably well-sheltered marina, reserving 40 berths for visitors. With heavy onshore swell the entrance can be dangerous and may be closed.

Approach Remain outside 20m contour. Distinctive white tr block stands N of hbr. Leca LtHo Fl(3)14s56m28M is 21M to S.

Entrance Keep well clear of broken water and hazards up to 40m off W mole Fl.R.3s; heading 023°. Turn stb into marina on clearing E mole, LFl.G.6s.

Berthing Reception on short hammerhead pontoon on N side.

Anchorage May be possible in NE corner of hbr, clear of all moorings. Beware of unmarked and possibly rocky shallows.

Facilities Laundry. First Aid Post in marina bldg, hospital in town. Boat hoist. Visitors welcomed by Clube Naval Póvoense, Rua da Ponte 2 (restaurant). Supermarket 2km. Buses and trains to Porto. International airport at Porto 20km.

☎/VHF 252 688 121, VHF 09.

LEIXÕES

Standard Port Lisbon
HW –0018   LW +0005

MHWS	MHWN	MLWN	MLWS
–0·3m	–0·3m	–0·1m	–0·1m

As a refuge, better than Póvoa de Varzim, but even Leixões closes in severe storms.

Approach Oil refinery 2M to N conspic by day and night. Leça LtHo Fl(3)14s is 1½M to N. From N round end of extended breakwater Fl.WR.5s (001°-R-180°-W-001°) Horn 20s, at distance of 200m.

Entrance Steer 350° between inner moleheads, Fl.G.4s and Fl.R.4s.

Berthing At marina in N corner of hbr (old fishing hbr); crowded. Berthing is bows on and stern buoy. Water and electricity at berths. YC and showers ashore.

Anchorage W of marina. No landing on Cais das Gruas – use the marina.

Facilities Launderette, free WiFi. Bus to Porto from behind YC. Facilities for repairs nearby. Shops and market in Matosinhos.

☎/VHF Marina 22 996 4895, VHF 09; Port 995 3000, VHF 12.

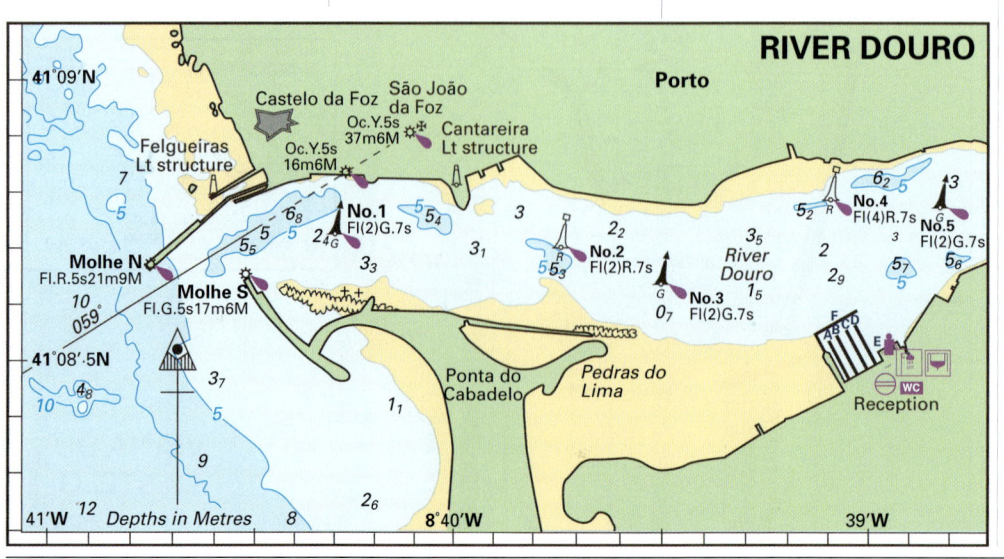

RIO DOURO

Standard Port Lisbon
HW –0008   LW –0020

MHWS	MHWN	MLWN	MLWS
–0·6m	–0·4m	–0·1m	+0·1m

The new Douro Marina offers a more convenient port for exploring Porto than Leixões. There is a new mole across the entrance, to give enhanced shelter inside. In heavy weather Leixōs is a safer destination.

Approach The bar has at least 4m. However, caution is needed on the ebb and/or with significant swell and/or with a strong onshore wind. The (new) leading marks/Lts (Oc.Y.5s) are aligned on a course of 059° through the entrance. Thereafter, there is a dredged and buoyed channel to beyond the marina. At low water, there is a shallow spit between the channel and the marina with its E extremity marked by the G No.5 buoy.

Entrance Leave the mole to stb. The fuel berth, with access to reception, is straight ahead.

Berthing as directed. A dory will escort if you call ahead. Marineros are on-call from 0800 to 2030 in summer.

Facilities include fuel, WiFi, laundry, water taxi to town, bike hire. 10% discount CA members.

☎ 220 907 300

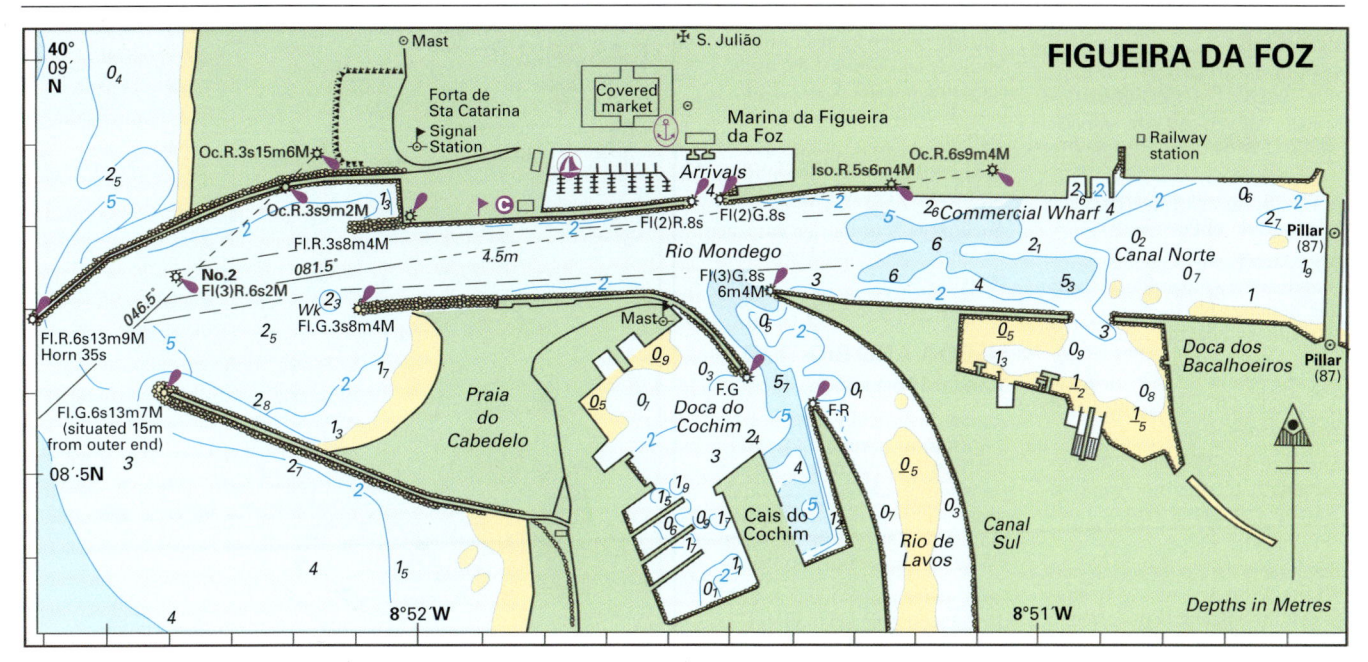

FIGUEIRA DA FOZ

RIA DE AVEIRO

Standard Port Lisbon
HW –0007   LW n/a
MHWS	MHWN	MLWN	MLWS
–0·6m	–0·4m	–0·1m	0·0m

Strong tidal currents. Entrance can be dangerous in the wrong combination of swell, strong onshore winds, ebb tide and-or springs. If in doubt, consult the website given on p.405.

Approach There are few marks along the low sandy coast. Identify Aveiro LtHo Fl(4)13s, R tr, W bands. Keep at least 1M off shore. With S pierhead (W column G bands Fl.G.3s) in transit with Aveiro LtHo, turn onto 086° until inside N pierhead.

Entrance Between extended N mole Fl.R.3s and S mole Fl.G.3s; follow channel for 1½M to Baia de San Jacinto to port.

Anchorage Entry difficult into Baia de San Jacinto, cross currents. Enter between training walls and sph buoys to anchorage in N or S of baia. N end convenient for village, but space restricted due to moorings. S quiet but distant from village.

Berthing It is possible to go up the Canal Principal de Navegação to Aveiro where the yacht club welcomes visitors to its pontoon if there is space.

☎ 234 422 371

FIGUEIRA DA FOZ

Standard Port Lisbon
HW –0008   LW +0015
MHWS	MHWN	MLWN	MLWS
–0·4m	–0·4m	–0·1m	+0·1m

Strong tidal currents. Entrance can be dangerous in the wrong combination of swell, strong onshore winds, ebb tide and-or springs. If in doubt, consult the web site given on p.405. Extended breakwaters and recent dredging of bar to 5m have improved the entrance.

Approach Cabo Mondego Fl.5s is 2½M to N. Conspic suspension br 1½M upriver from entrance.

Entrance Between N mole Fl.R.6s Horn 35s and S mole Fl.G.6s on Ldg Lts front, Iso.R.5s, rear, Oc.R.6s, 082°. Ldg marks difficult to see by day. Keep to N shore. When ¾M inside moleheads turn to port into Marina da Figueira.

Berthing Reception and fuel directly opposite the entrance. Electricity and water at berths and showers ashore. Good security. Diesel from fish hbr to stb on entry. Good covered market alongside.

☎/VHF Marina 233 402 918, VHF 08; Port VHF 11.

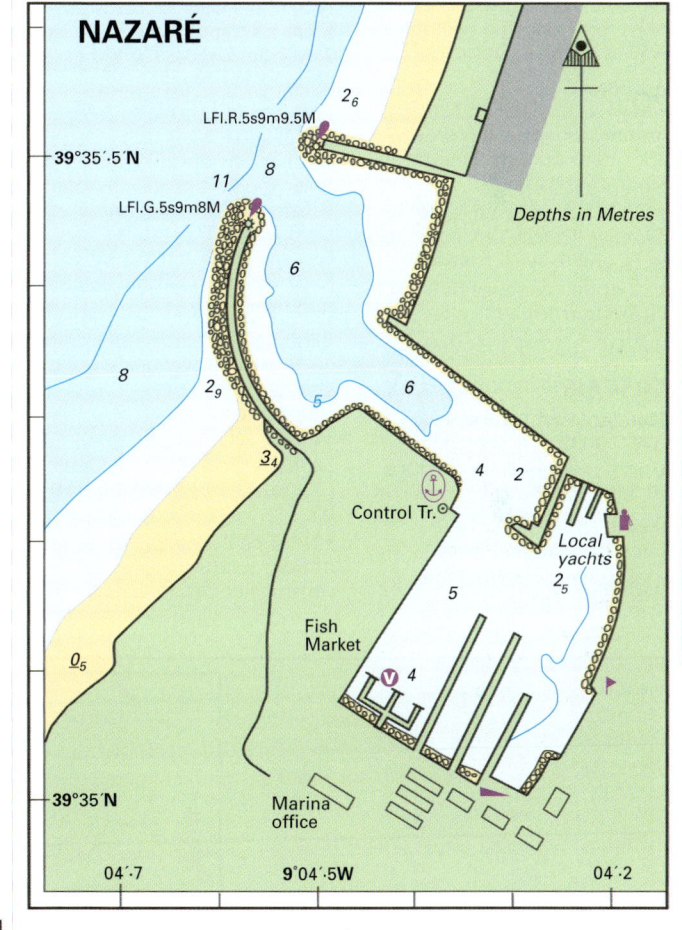

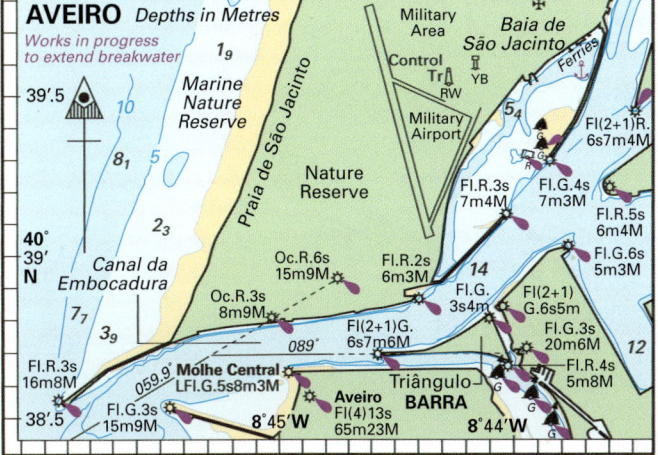

NAZARÉ

Standard Port Lisbon
HW (sp) –0030 (np) +0015
LW (sp) +0005 (np) –0005
MHWS	MHWN	MLWN	MLWS
–0·5m	–0·4m	–0·1m	0·0m

A well-sheltered major fishing port 1M to S of old town and beach. Useful as a port of refuge.

Approach Pontal da Nazaré Oc.3s is 1M to N.

Entrance Straightforward between N mole LFl.R.5s and S mole LFl.G.5s.

Berthing In one of two small marinas. In NE of inner harbour run by YC (best to phone first) or in SW corner for visitors. Diesel and usual facilities.

☎/VHF Marina 262 561 401, VHF 09; Port VHF 11; Club 262 560 422.

PENICHE

Standard Port Lisbon
HW −0025   LW −0002
MHWS MHWN MLWN MLWS
−0·3m −0·4m −0·1m 0·0m

A large, well-sheltered fishing port with easy entrance on S side of peninsula of Peniche.

Approach From N identify two islands, Os Farilhão Fl(2)5s and Ilha Berlenga Fl.10s, 8/5M respectively NW of Peniche and Cabo Carvoeiro Fl(3)R.15s. By day, the peninsula of Peniche can be mistaken for an island. TSS to W of islands.

Entrance The W mole Fl.R.3s extends 1ca S of E mole Fl.G.3s. Narrow entrance 100m, approach on 345°.

Berthing is on a pontoon to port, off the W breakwater. May have to raft up. Fishing boats often cause unpleasant wash. Showers, supermarkets in town. Fuel (cash only) from pump on pontoon NW of berthing pontoon.

Anchorage
- May be possible just N of E breakwater – probably wise to ask authorities first. Foul ground reported in harbours.
- On N side of peninsula in 3–5m at Peniche de Cima. Open to N, and to swell from NW.
- SE of Ilha Berlenga near LtHo Fl(3)20s in 15m.

☎/VHF 262 781 153, VHF 62.

CASCAIS

Standard Port Lisbon
HW −0032   LW −0012
MHWS MHWN MLWN MLWS
−0·3m −0·3m 0·0m +0·1m

Port of refuge. Cheap and frequent trains to Lisbon.

Approach As for Lisboa and Rio Tejo.

Entrance Three S card Lt buoys MC1, 2, and 3 guard the mole enclosing marina. Clear R can buoy Fl.R.4s before entering marina.

Berthing In marina. Reception to stb on entry below marina office.

Anchorage N of marina entrance on 5m contour outside moorings, open to SE.

☎/VHF 214 824 857, VHF 09.

LISBOA AND RIO TEJO

Standard Port Lisbon

A great historically interesting maritime and capital city, with international and national air, rail and bus connections. Tidal streams in river 2–3kn at springs, more after heavy rain. In strong SW winds, enter only on flood.

Approach From N identify Cabo da Roca conspic LtHo Fl(4)17s, 26M NW of Lisbon, Cabo Raso Fl(3)9s and Guia Iso.WR.2s. From S, Cabo Espichel Fl.4s, 26M from Lisboa, TSS 9M to W of Cabo da Roca.

Entrance Steer between conspic Fort Bugio Fl.G.5s on a sandbank to stb and Fort São Julião Oc.R.5s to port. By night Gibalta Oc.R.3s and Esteiro Oc.R.6s give Ldg Lts 047° between Bugio and São Julião. Keep well on to Gibalta before turning upriver.

Berthing There are four harbours on N bank of river of interest to visiting yachts. All have cross currents at entrance.
- Oerias Marina with good facilities. Fuel. Rly to Lisbon (12km). ☎ 214 401 510, VHF 09.
- Doca de Belém, in 3m, 4ca E of Bom Sucesso, just past conspic floodlit Monument to the Discoverers. Reserved for local yachts but some spaces for visitors. Water and diesel on fuelling pontoon. YC, showers, telephone. Travel-lift. Scrubbing grid. ☎ 213 922 203, VHF 12.
- Doca de Alcântara. Lifting br at entrance, currently fixed open for yachts, but if not call VHF 12 for opening times. Water and electricity on pontoons but no fuel (See Doca de Belém earlier). Excellent security but high deposit for magnetic card for entry and exit system ☎ 213 922 048.
- Marina Parque das Naçoes on W bank 1·5M downstream of Ponte Vasco de Gama. All facilities ☎ 218 949 066, VHF 09.

Anchorage
- Canal do Montijo. Round Ponta de Cacilhas 1½M E of suspension br and steer 108° for buoyed Canal da Cuf. After 1M the buoyed Canal do Montijo leads off at 073°. No landing at military airfield.

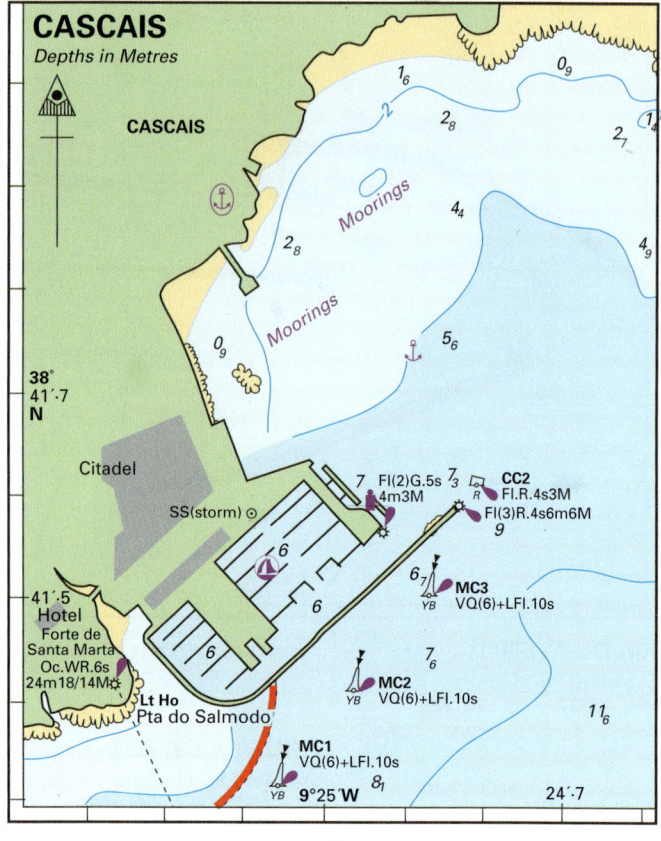

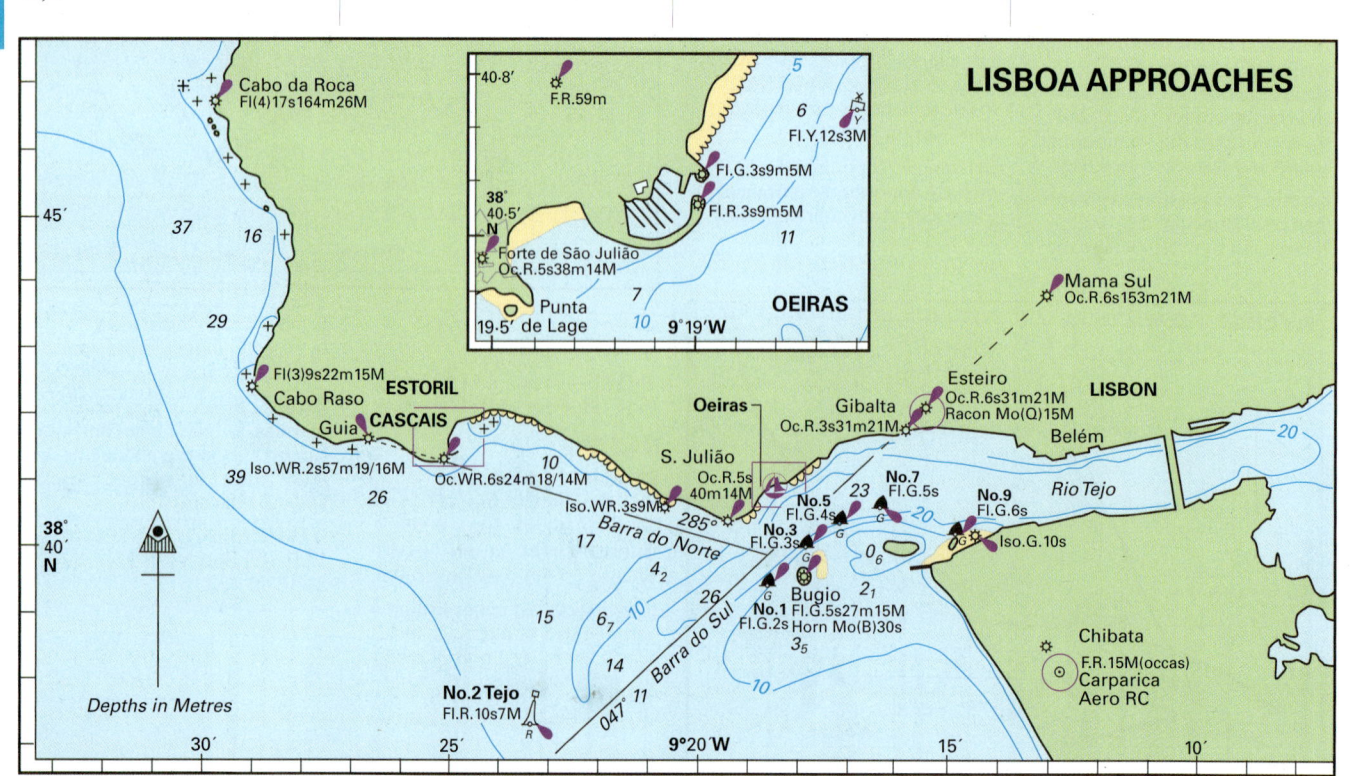

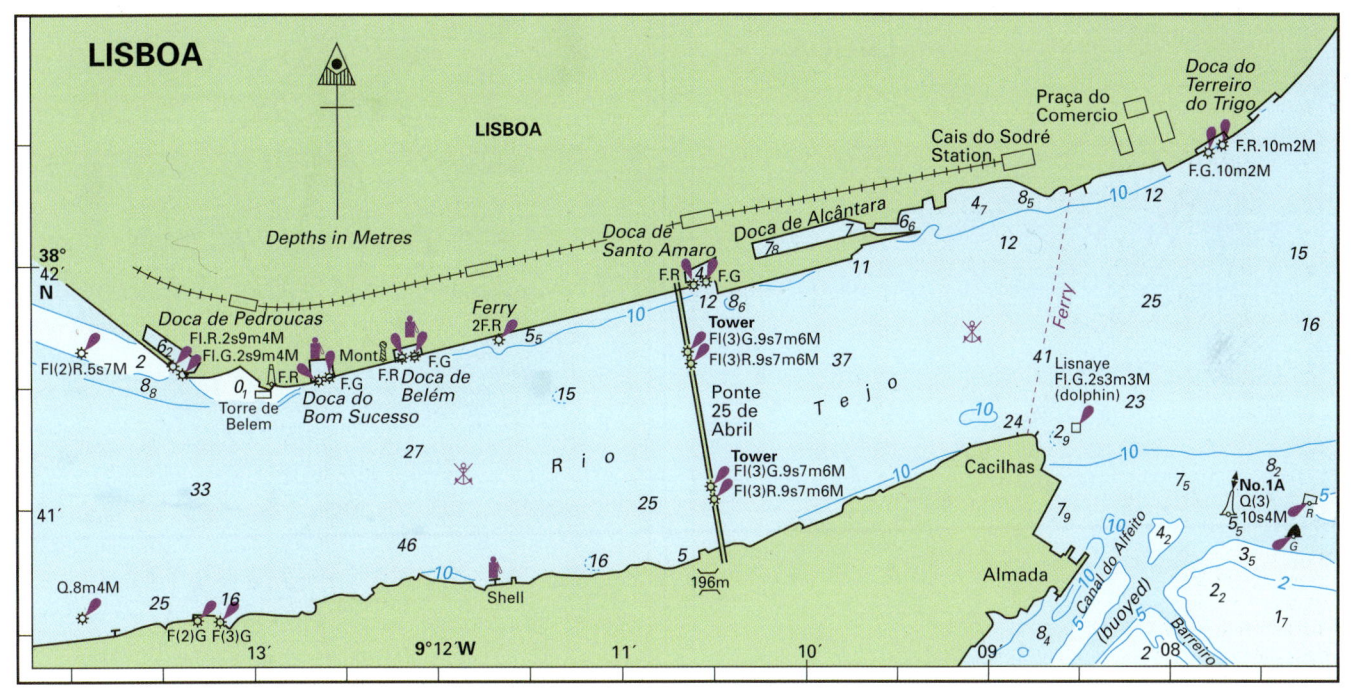

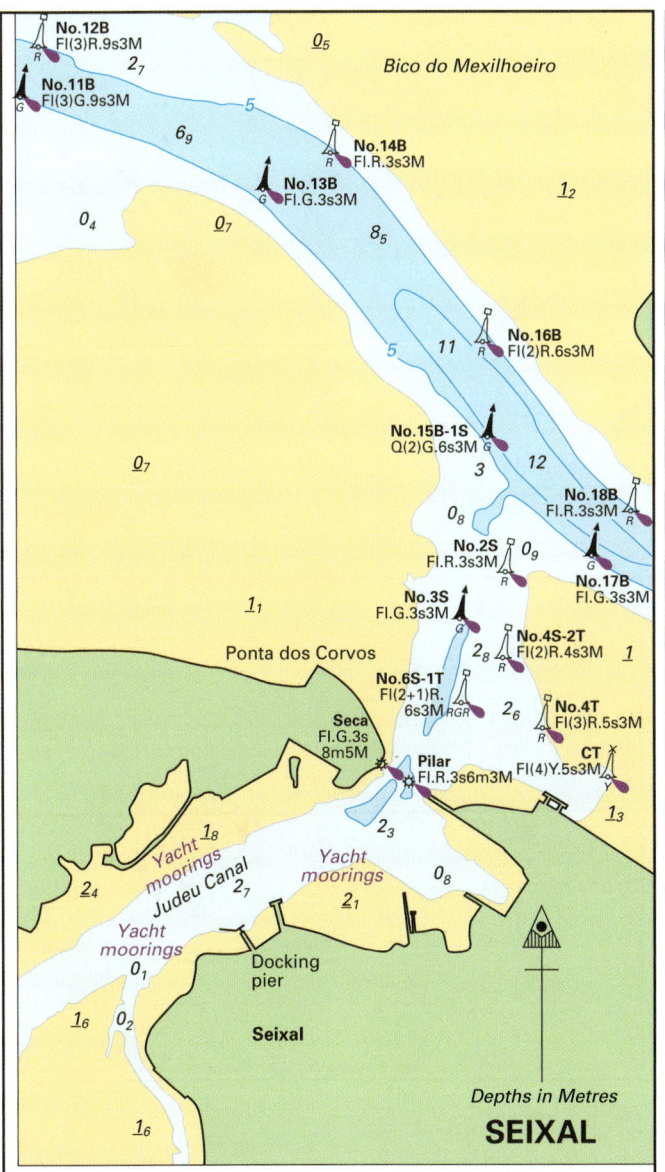

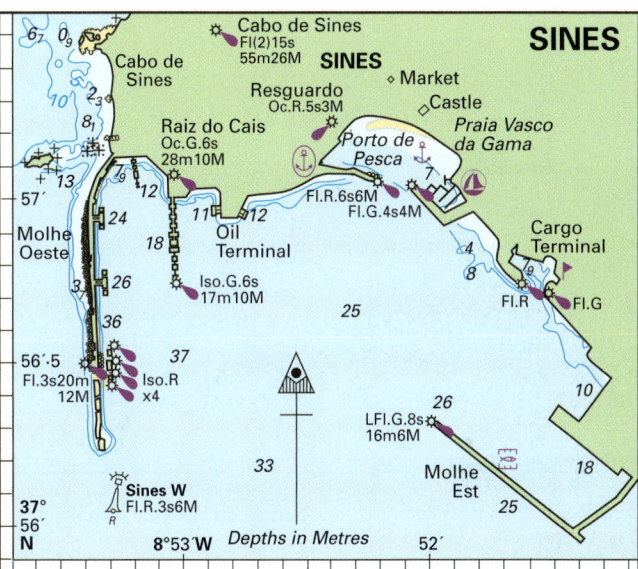

SINES

Standard Port Lisbon
HW +0020 LW n/a

MHWS	MHWN	MLWN	MLWS
–0·4m	–0·6m	–0·1m	0·0m

A port and oil terminal, well protected except from SW, surrounds the old fishing hbr. Interesting old town, birthplace of Vasco da Gama.

Approach 1½M to N is Cabo de Sines Fl(2)15s.

Entrance From N keep 1M offshore and leave to port R pillar buoy Fl.R.3s off unlit end of submerged breakwater. From S the entrance is wide. At night a variety of sectored lights lead into hbr and may confuse. Ldg Lts front Iso.R.6s rear Oc.R.5·6s bearing 358° on inner pier.

Anchorage Off Praia Vasco da Gama, leaving channels to Porto de Pesca and marina free.

Berthing Marina on E side of hbr. Berth at hammerhead of fuel pontoon and report to the office.

Facilities Chandlery and repairs in fish dock. Camping Gaz in town. Groceries some 2km walk from marina, closer by dinghy (land on beach).

☎/VHF Marina 269 860 612, VHF 09; Port VHF 11, 13.

LAGOS

Standard Port Lisbon
HW –0050 LW –0028

MHWS	MHWN	MLWN	MLWS
–0·4m	–0·4m	–0·1m	0·0m

Situated 25M E of C St Vincent, a popular and well-furnished marina, with convenient rail connection to Faro airport.

Approach Find Pta da Piedade which features a Y LtHo tr (Fl.7s) with conspic palm trees either side. Hbr entrance is marked by two moles Fl(2)R.6s & Fl(2)G.6s.

Entrance Straightforward up 3m dredged channel, past fishing hbr, moor to reception pontoon to stb just before lifting br. Little turning room, beware onshore wind with ebb tide. Call VHF 09 to open br.

• **Seixal** As above but turn S into Canal do Alfeite, and Canal do Barreiro and Canal do Seixal. There is now a docking pier available for yachts, and moorings can be rented. Telephone or dock on the pier and enquire locally. Ferry and bus to Lisboa.

☎/VHF 919 306 580 VHF 09.

LAGOS

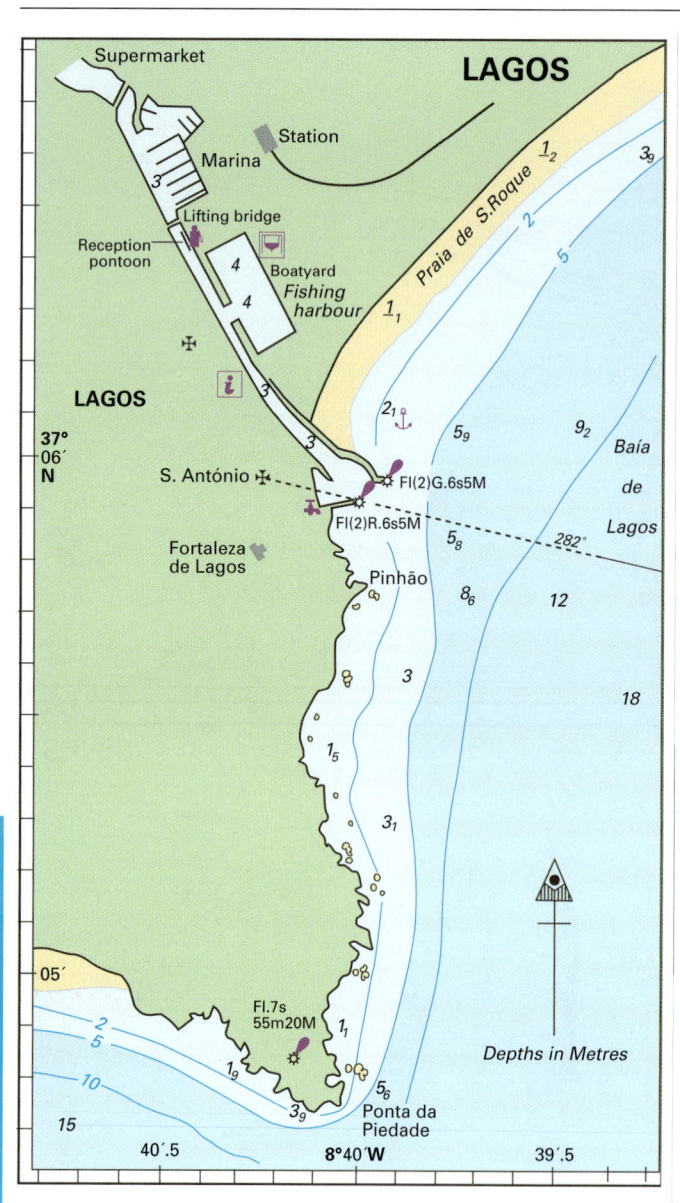

Berthing Report to reception. Finger pontoons. Good facilities. Fuel by reception. Washing machines. Provisioning close. Good yard for storage and all repairs. Free WiFi. Good security. English widely spoken. Weather forecast on notice board, also broadcast on VHF 12, in Portuguese and English, 1000 and 1600 during high season.

☎/VHF Marina 282 770 210, VHF 09; Port VHF 11.

PORTIMÃO

Standard Port Lisbon
HW −0050   LW −0028
MHWS   MHWN   MLWN   MLWS
−0·5m   −0·4m   −0·1m   +0·1m

A busy fishing port and resort town on the Algarve coast.

Approach Ponta da Piedade LtHo Fl.7s is 7½M to W. Alfanzina LtHo Fl(2)15s is 4½M to E.

Entrance Ponta do Altar LtHo LFl.5s is ½M to E of hbr entrance. Conspic communications tr just E of entrance. Pass between W mole Fl.R.5s and E mole Fl.G.5s on Ldg Lts 021°, front Iso.R.6s rear Iso.R.6s Ldg to port-hand buoy Fl.R.4s and buoyed channel. If entering at night anchor at the first anchorage given below until daylight. Strong tidal streams but room to manœuvre in marina.

Berthing Reception on northern breakwater pontoon. Finger pontoons, well sheltered. Good facilities. WiFi (charged), free Ethernet connection. Limited provisioning at marina.

Anchorage
- Inside the E mole, clear of rocks along mole.
- Off Ferragudo on E shore in 3m mud. Supplies at Ferragudo. 1M from town quay for landing at Portimão.

☎/VHF Marina 282 400 680, VHF 09.

ALBUFEIRA

Standard Port Lisbon
HW +0050   LW n/a
MHWS   MHWN   MLWN   MLWS
−0·3m   −0·3m   0·0m   +0·1m

A marina within a purpose built resort. Good shelter and facilities.

Approach Approximately 315° to enter between the sea walls of the hbr.

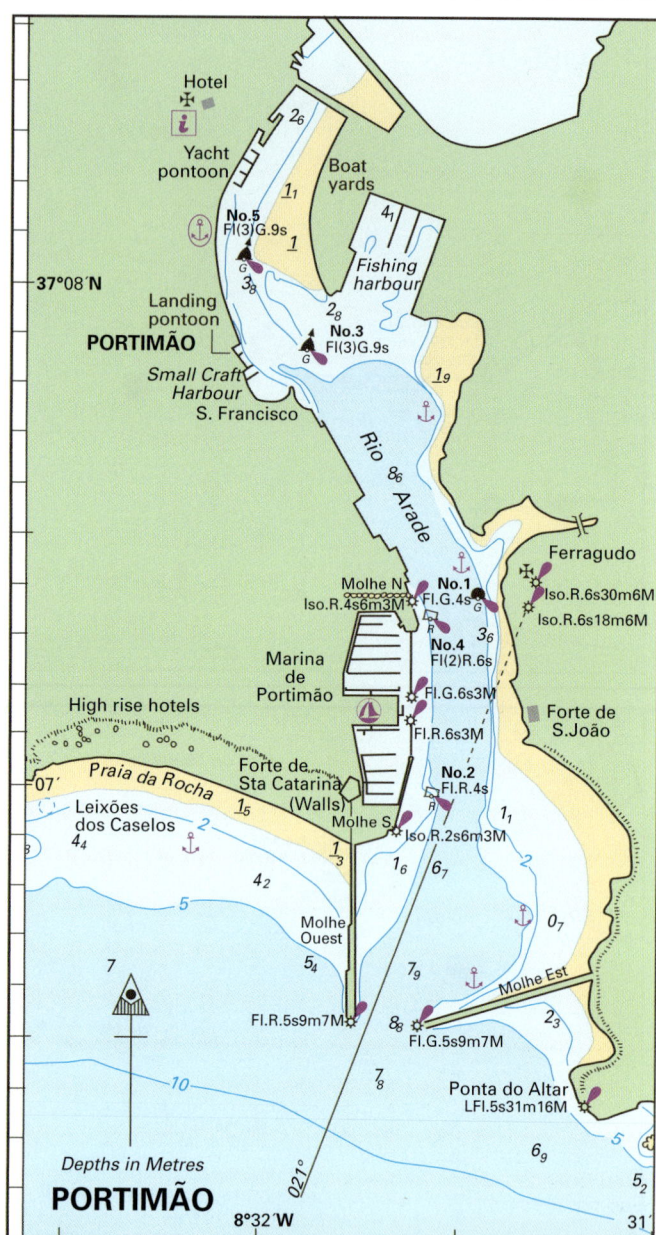

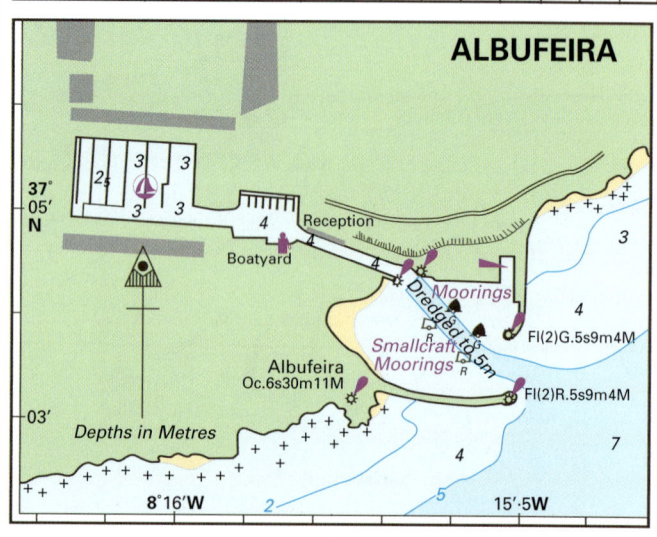

Entrance E mole with tr (hor G and W stripes, Fl(2)G). W mole with tr (hor R and W, Fl(2)R).

After passing through the sea walls, proceed along the navigational channel until the entrance to the marina channel (indicated by two cylindrical tr bns with wide G and W stripes to stb, R and W stripes to port). The channel is dredged to 4m.

Berthing The reception quay is situated at the end of the channel on the stb side. There are 475 berths for vessels up to 26m.

Facilities Water, power, fuel, ice, travel-lift, boatyard, pump out.

☎/VHF 289 514 282, Call *Marina de Albufeira* on VHF 09.

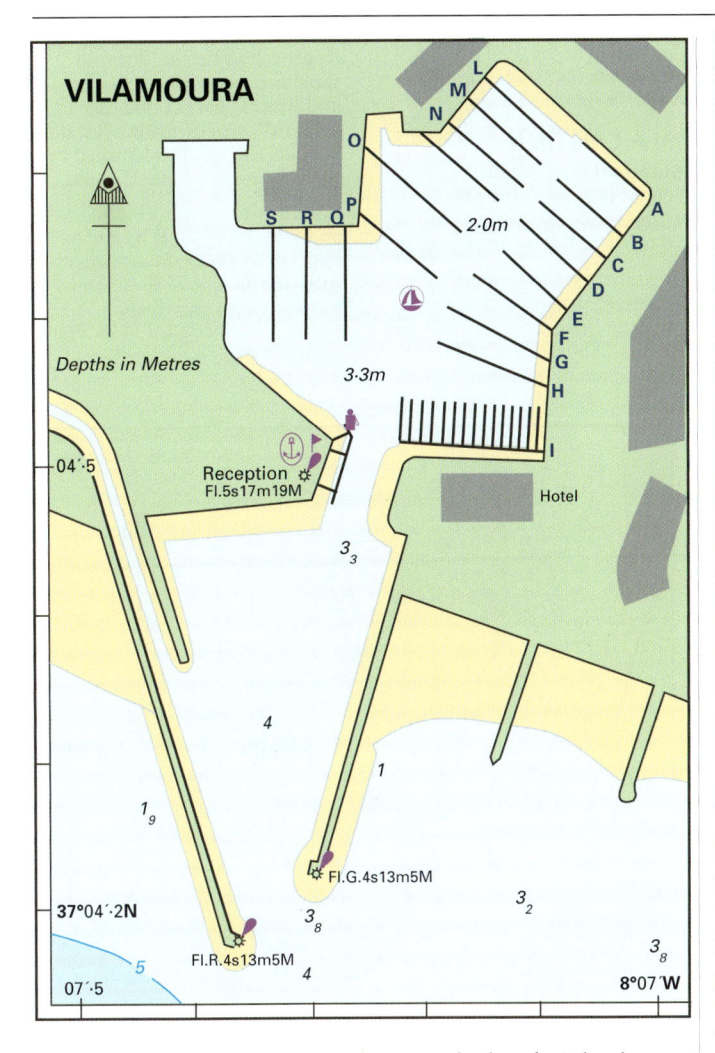

VILAMOURA

Tidal data as Albufiera

A well-developed marina with good facilities, including laying-up. English spoken. Formalities will be observed strictly. Exit at night not possible.

Approach Vilamoura Lt Fl.5s17m19M on control tr of marina.

Entrance Between W molehead Fl.R.4s and E molehead Fl.G.4s. In strong winds and swell seas may break at LW near W molehead. Width between moles 100m. Steer for entrance to inner basin 60m wide and moor to first pontoon to port alongside control tr to obtain clearance.

Facilities Diesel, repairs, chandler, scrubbing grid, hoist, crane, Camping Gaz and butane refills. YC next to marina office. International airport at Faro, ½ to 1hr by taxi/bus.

☎/VHF 289 310 560, VHF 09.

FARO AND OLHÃO

Standard Port Lisbon
HW (sp) –0050 (np) –0030
LW (sp) +0005 (np) –0015
MHWS MHWN MLWN MLWS
–0·4m –0·4m –0·1m 0·0m

The Faro lagoon has extensive and attractive anchorages, access to the regional capital, Faro, and charming Olhão, yards in Faro and Olhão, and two marinas in Olhão.

Approach Identify Cabo de Santa Maria lighthouse Fl(4)17s. Approach from the SE quadrant to avoid the shoals W of entrance, extending nearly 1M offshore.

Entrance Breakwater ends are lit. Access at all states of the tide, although the ebb runs strongly and can be dangerous with onshore wind or swell. Once inside the breakwaters, the channel is buoyed. From No.6 either:

• Anchor about 2ca N of No.1 in the Canal De Faro to await favourable tide or daylight
• Follow the buoyed Canal De Faro W, then NW
• Follow the buoyed Canal De Olhão NE.

Anchorages Numerous, including:

• 2ca N of buoy No.1, as noted above.
• Canal De Faro between buoys No.19 and No.22, for access to Faro.
• N of Culatra, anywhere in the channel N and E of the fishing harbour at Arraiaís.
• Olhão between the two marinas in front of the market, room for four or five yachts.
• Olhão, E of fishing harbour, clear of channel on N side.

Berthing Nothing in Faro. The E marina in Olhão sometimes has space for short visits.

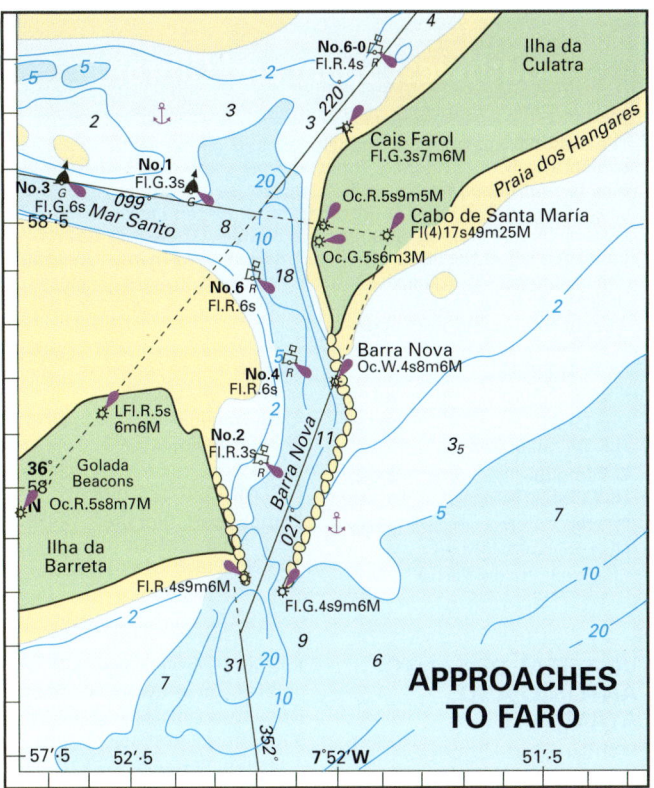

TAVIRA

Standard Port Lisbon
HW –0035   LW n/a
MHWS MHWN MLWN MLWS
–0·7m –0·6m –0·1m –0·2m

Despite development around it, the centre of Tavira and the countryside around are as attractive as any in the Algarve.

Approach and Entrance Identify W breakwater Fl(1)R.2·5s. Enter between breakwaters on 325°, avoiding the shoal E.

Anchorages

• About 4ca into the river, where the main channel turns W. Tide runs hard, and there is much traffic.
• Follow the channel W, past the shallow channel leading N to Tavira itself, to anchor W of moorings. Land and find water at YC.
• Continue about 1·4M beyond YC along the beaconed channel SW then W, to anchor just below Santa Luzia.

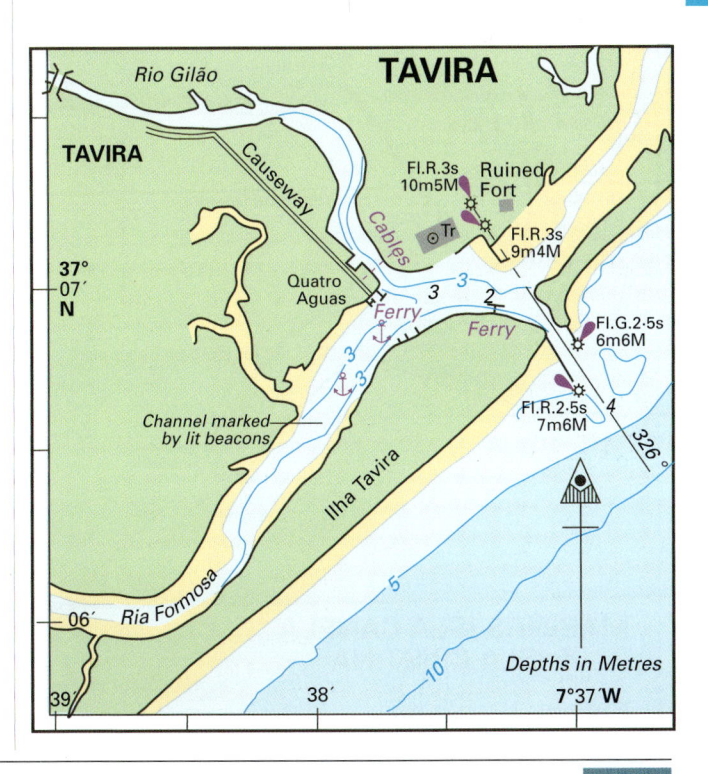

The Cruising Almanac

Southwest Spain and Gibraltar

The coast between the Río Guadalquivir and Tarifa is still comparatively undeveloped. Tunny nets are sometimes laid, from May to September, stretching 6–7M out to sea at right angles to the coast. Towards the Strait of Gibraltar the winds tend to be either easterly (more common in summer) or westerly. There may be an E-going current at the Strait of 2–3kn. Tidal streams can also run up to 3kn at springs. TSS in the Strait: the S limit of the inshore passage is only 1½M off Tarifa Lt. The range of tides at Cádiz is approximately 2·9m at springs and 1·3m at neaps.

Passage lights

Principal lights	BA No
Vila Real Fl.6·5s47m26/19M	2246
El Rompido Fl(2)10s42m24M	2312
Picacho Fl(2+4)30s50m25M AIS	2320
Chipiona (Pta del Perro) Fl.10s67m25M AIS	2351
Castillo de San Sebastián Fl(2)10s37m25M AIS	2362
Cabo Trafalgar Fl(2+1)15s49m22M AIS	2406
Tarifa Fl(3)WR.10s41m26/18M AIS	2414
Europa Point, Gibraltar Iso.10s.49m19M+Oc.R. 10s49m19M+F.R.44m15M	2438

VILA REAL DE SANTO ANTONIO AND AYAMONTE

Standard Port Lisbon
HW (sp) –0050 (np) –0015
LW (sp) +0000 (np) –0010

MHWS	MHWN	MLWN	MLWS
–0·4m	–0·4m	–0·1m	+0·1m

Vila Real (Portugal) and Ayamonte overlook each other across the River Guadiana.

Approach From the W Vila Real can be identified by the LtHo in the town (Fl.6.5s) and by the conspic buildings at Monte Gordo about 2M to the W. From the E the resort at Ilha de Canela can be identified about 2M E of the entrance. Avoid shoals to E of River Guardiana entrance, which extend over 1M from shore.

Entrance The entrance has approx. 2m at LW and can be dangerous when strong onshore winds are against an ebb tide. The outer entrance of the channel is marked by two buoys Fl.R.4s and Fl(3)G.6s either side of which are shoals. The inner entrance is marked by Fl.R.5s at the outer end of the sea wall. There are shoals on the E side.

Berthing and Anchorage Finger pontoons at both marinas. Strong tidal stream through outer Vila Real berths, little turning room inside. Good facilities and provisioning at both. Free WiFi at Vila Real. Good anchoring off both, show anchor light and ball.

Facilities At Vila Real, modern boatyard. No fuel in Ayamonte.

www.marinaguadiana.com

☎/VHF Vila Real 281 541 571 Ayamonte 959 034 498, VHF 09 (both).

ISLA CRISTINA

Standard Port Lisbon
HW as Lisbon   LW n/a

MHWS	MHWN	MLWN	MLWS
–0·6m	–0·6m	–0·1m	–0·2m

Pleasant town and small, well protected marina with the usual facilities (including haul out and repairs). Shops, bars and restaurants in the town.

Approach From the W avoid shoals between River Guadiana and River Carreras that extend over 1M from the shore. Ría de la Higuerita can be identified by the new resort on Isla Canela.

Entrance The entrance is marked by Lt buoys VQ(2)R.5s and Fl.G.6s. Avoid shallows either side. The W side of the channel has a sea wall and the E, a training wall. Ldg lts 313°. The channel in the ria is buoyed.

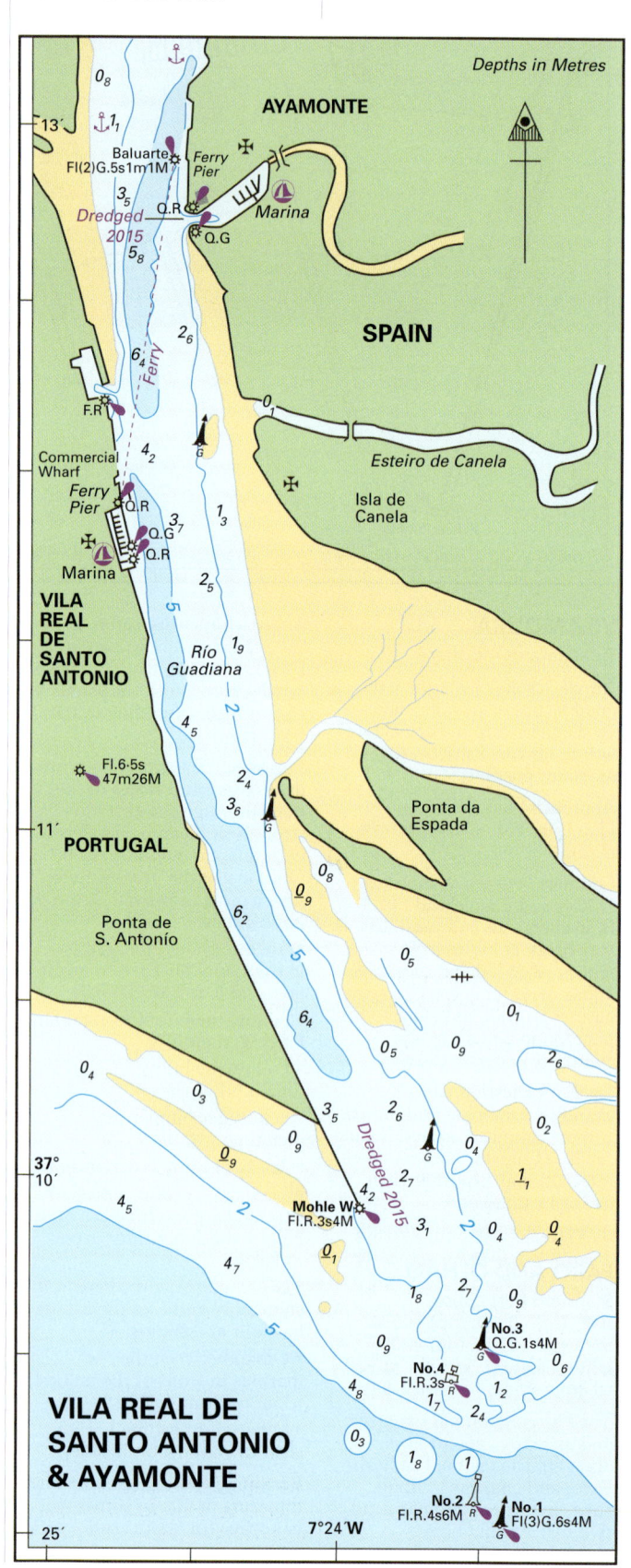

MARINAS ISLA CANELA & ISLA CRISTINA

VILA REAL DE SANTO ANTONIO & AYAMONTE

The Cruising Almanac

PUNTA UMBRIA

Standard Port Lisbon

Bar
HW (sp) +0000 (np) +0015
LW (sp) +0030 (np) +0035

MHWS	MHWN	MLWN	MLWS
–0·1m	–0·6m	–0·1m	–0·4m

A pleasant town, with three marinas and ample space for anchorage. Good general chandlers.

Approach Identify the fairway buoy, whose position varies from time to time, but lies in about 5m. It can be approached safely along the coast from either direction.

Entrance Possible HW ±0300 in good conditions. Follow the buoyed channel.

Anchorage Upstream of the third marina, and the town, on W side, in depth to suit yacht. Convenient landing.

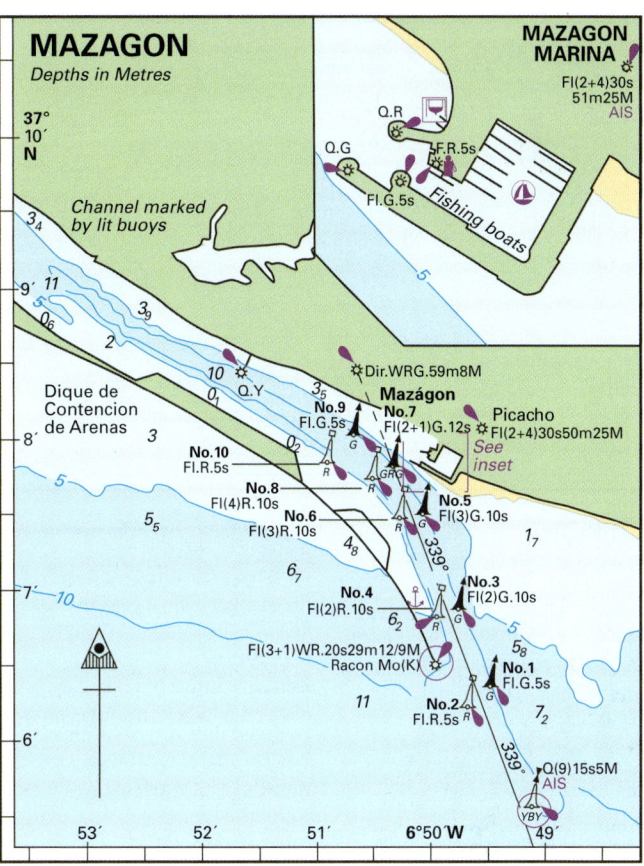

Berthing There are three marinas:
- Real Club Marítimo, reported not to welcome visitors.
- Puerto Deportivo de Punta Umbría – This EPPA marina has been extended.
  ☎ 959 071 081.
- Club Deportivo Náutico Punta Umbria.
  ☎ 959 314 401.

MAZAGON

Standard Port Lisbon
HW +0007   LW n/a

MHWS	MHWN	MLWN	MLWS
–0·1m	–0·6m	–0·1m	–0·4m

Large, well protected marina with usual facilities (including haul out and repairs) and nearby good beaches. Short walk to shops in the town.

Approach The Ria de Huelva can be identified by the Picacho LtHo Fl(2+4)30s.

Entrance The entrance to the ria is well buoyed and protected from the E by a large breakwater. Entry should be possible in nearly all conditions. The marina is on the E side of the ria with its entrance facing NW (marked by Q.R. and Q.G.).

Berthing Reception pontoon below marina office to port, shortly after marina entrance.
☎ 959 070 071.

It is reported that the authorities are now (2016) chasing away yachts that attempt to use the former anchorage NW of the marina.

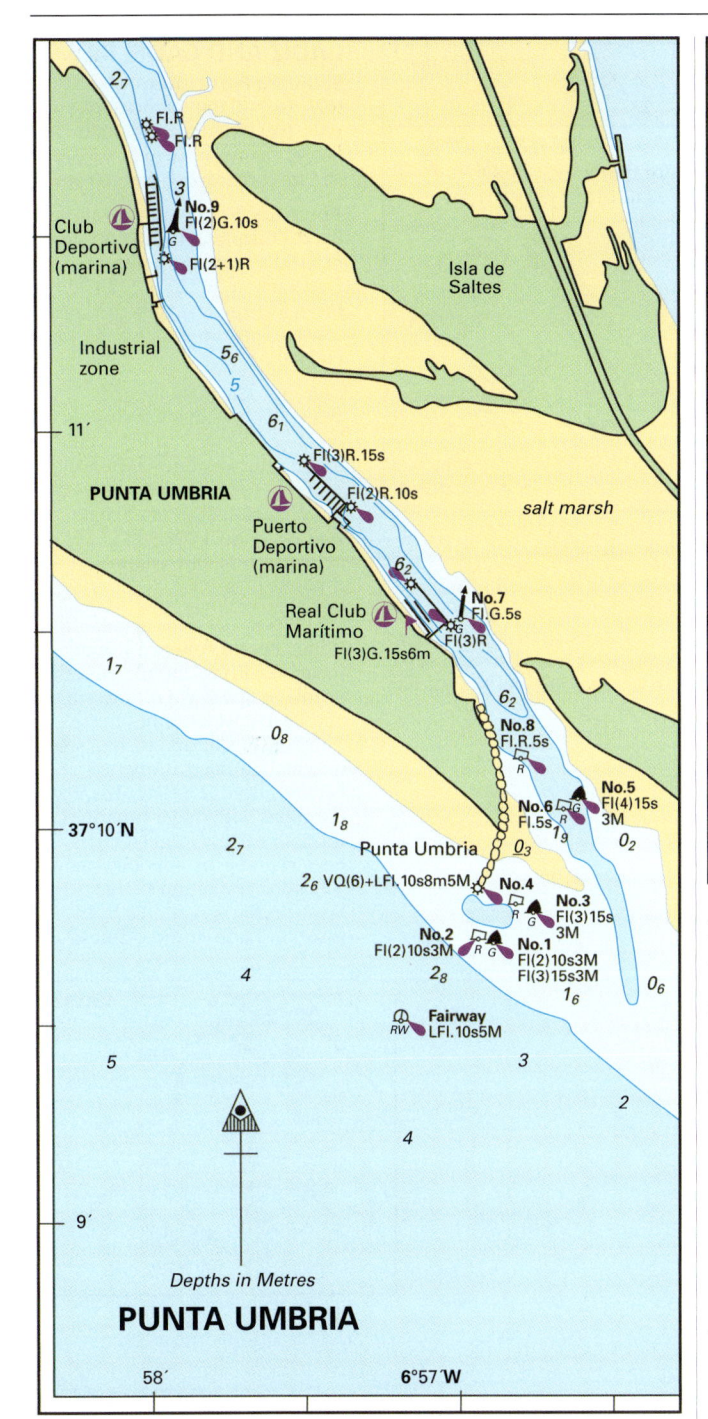

Berthing The marina at Isla Christina has pontoon berths (max LOA 15m). The max. depth in the marina is quoted as 2m. Some swell from fishing vessels. No fuel.
☎ 959 077 613.

There is also a marina at the resort on Isla de Canela. Fuel.
☎ 959 47 90 00.

Anchorage
- With shallow draft, most comfortable and convenient is 2ca NW of entrance to Isla Cristina marina.
- 5ca N of marina in entrance to Cano Canela.

CÁDIZ AND CÁDIZ BAY

Standard Port Lisbon
HW (sp) –0100 (np) –0040
LW (sp) –0035 (np) –0020

MHWS	MHWN	MLWN	MLWS
–0·5m	–0·5m	–0·2m	0·0m

Approach From N pass 2M off Pta del Chipiona Fl.10s. A buoy Fl(2)R.9s marks Bajo El Quemado at 36°36′N 6°24′W. From S keep more than ¾M off conspic Castillo de San Sebastián Fl(2)10s.

Entrance The main lighted channel into Cádiz lies close N of bn tr Las Puercas (unlit). Make for RW fairway buoy L.Fl.10s at 36°34′N 6°20′W and follow buoyed channel. From S make well up to No.1 buoy Fl.G.3s before turning into channel, dredged 13m.

Berthing
Cádiz, Puerto America Round the mole jutting out NE from the headland (2 Lts Fl.G), turn stb and Puerto America lies to stb. Enter on W side and turn to stb into marina Puerto America between heads Fl(4)RG.16s. Five pontoons with finger pontoons for each berth. Good facilities. Fuel available by appointment at YC; good restaurant there. Spanish charts available from Instituto Hidrografico, Tolosa

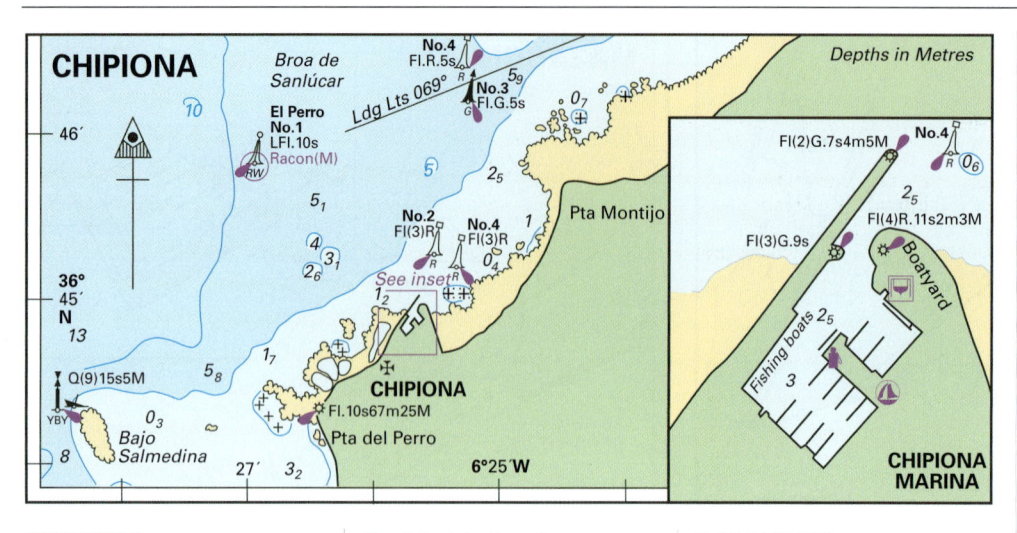

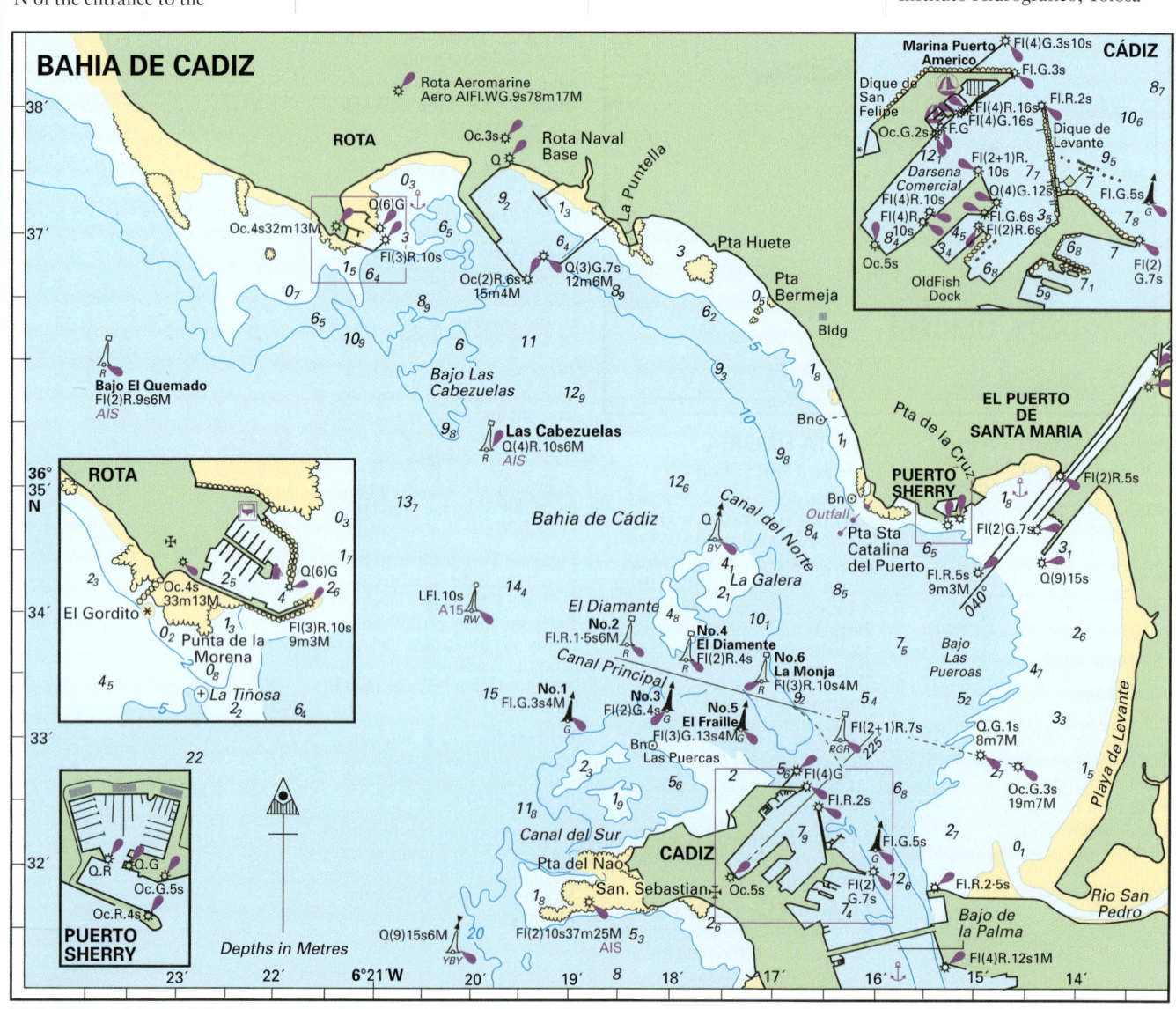

CHIPIONA

Standard Port Lisbon
HW as Lisbon LW n/a

MHWS	MHWN	MLWN	MLWS
–0·6m	–0·5m	–0·2m	–0·2m

Pleasant town with good beaches and marina. All facilities, including haul out, laundry and repairs. Good base to depart for Sevilla (approximately 50M up the River Guadalquivir).

Approach Chipiona is identifiable from the large lighthouse (Fl.10s) in the town. From N keep well clear of shoals N of the entrance to the Guadalquivir river that are marked by W card Lt buoy Q(9)10s and conspic wreck to E. From S keep W of card marker Q(9)15s marking Salmedina drying patch.

Entrance Leave No.2 Fl(2)R.7s and No.4 Fl(3)R.11s buoys to port and then turn 090° to stb into the marina entrance.

Berthing and Anchorage
Reception pontoon below marina office to port, shortly after marina entrance. Fuel at reception. Good facilities.

☎ 856 109 711.

It is possible to anchor in the River Guadalquivir W of Bonanza out of main channel and on the west side. The tidal stream can run strongly but the holding is good.

414

Latour 1, Cadiz. Take passport for entry.
✆/VHF Marina 856 580 002, VHF 09; Port VHF 14, 11, 12.
Rota Marina 1M W of Naval Base. Entrance faces NE and shoals under 2m up to 5ca off. Enter between moles F.G and Fl(3)R.10s. Reception on fuel pontoon opposite entrance. Fuel, boatyard, travel hoist and laundry. Bus to airport. Ferry to Cádiz.
✆ 856 104 011.
Puerto Sherry A large well-founded marina to NW of training walls of Puerto Santa Maria. Conspic W tr at end of S mole Oc.R.4s. Inner lights on N mole reported to be difficult to see. All facilities in marina including petrol and diesel, 50-tonne travel-lift and major repair facilities.
✆ 956 870 103.
Puerto Santa Maria At night Ldg Lts Iso.G.4s back, Q.G front on 040°. Call YC on VHF 09 on approach for possible berth at pontoons on W side about 1M up. Possible anchorage 7ca beyond YC, just below bridge, in 3m. Trains to Jerez and Sevillia. Passenger ferry to Cádiz.
✆ 956 852 527.
Anchorages The following have been reported as good anchorages in suitable weather:
- Bay NE of Rota Marina.
- Bay E of Puerto Sherry.
- Bajo de la Palma, S of Cadiz hbr.
- Up the Rio San Pedro, drying entrance, excellent shelter inside.

SANCTI-PETRI
Standard Port Lisbon
HW −0100   LW n/a
MHWS MHWN MLWN MLWS
−1·0m −0·9m −0·5m −0·2m

Delightful lagoon with beaches, anchorage and 2 small marinas (no haul out but some mechanical repairs). Two or three restaurants. Interesting deserted fishing village. No other facilities. Bus to shops.

Approach Beware onshore swell. Choose settled weather and rising tide to avoid difficulties at the bar in the entrance.

From N pass well clear of reef extending from Punta del Arrecife Q(9)15s to Sancti Petri Castle Fl.3s. Stay at least ½M S of the castle to avoid Los Farallones rocks.

Entrance The buoys have been replaced by beacons. Pick up outer pair, and follow the channel.

Berthing and Anchorage Two small marinas, both crowded. Second marina, belonging to YC has swinging moorings which may be available to visitors. Fuel. Anchor about 5ca N of marinas in main channel or channel branching E, to get clear of moorings.
✆ Club Nautico 956 495 428.

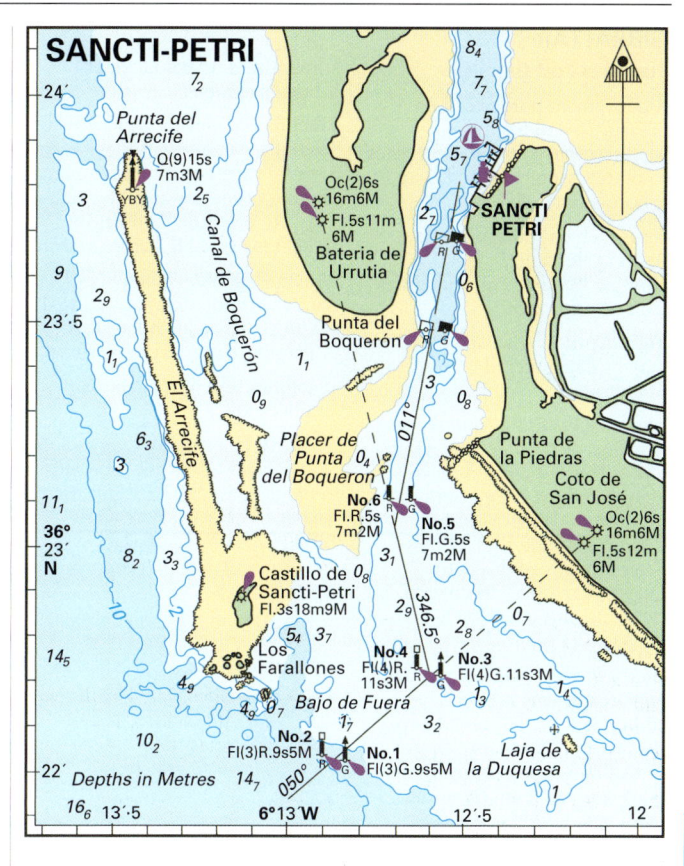

BARBATE
Standard Port Lisbon
HW (sp) −0040 (np) −0044
LW (sp) −0015 (np) −0015
MHWS MHWN MLWN MLWS
−1·9m −1·5m −0·4m +0·1m

A fishing hbr with well protected yacht marina 1M W of shallow Rio de Barbate.

Approach From W keep 3M off Cabo Trafalgar Fl(2+1)15s. From E clear the shoal Los Cabezos with conspic wreck 3M to S of Pta Paloma Oc.WR.5s. Unlit tunny nets May to September.

Entrance Steer on Ldg Lts 298°, both Q on white posts. Turn to port round outer breakwater, and follow into outer hbr to N. The marina is to port (W), between lights Fl.R.3s and Fl(2)G.

Berthing Reception pontoon for marina on S side of entrance. Pontoon berths in two bays further W. Diesel. 30 minutes walk to town.

Anchorage Off the beach in the lee of the harbour in suitable conditions.
✆ 856 108 399.

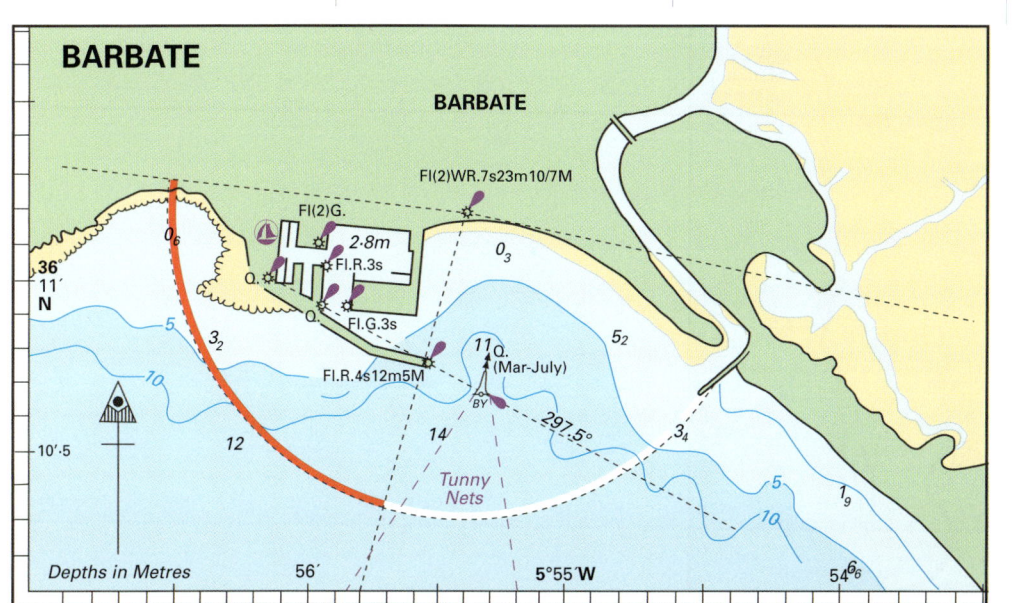

LA LINEA
Tidal data as Gibraltar

A modern marina, now a viable alternative to Gibraltar for mooring, laying up and yard services. Nearby supermarket.

Approach As for Gibraltar.

Entrance Round the outer breakwater, Fl(2)G.7s, then inner mole with control tower.

Berthing No waiting pontoon. Lie alongside mole by fuel point to visit control tower.

Anchorage is not permitted inside outer breakwater, but is apparently tolerated in the N of the bay. Recommended to leave dinghy at the Club Nautico.
✆ 956 02 16 60.

GIBRALTAR

Standard Port Gibraltar

A convenient port of call on passage to and from the Mediterranean, and a good place to fit out, repair and to lay up ashore unattended.

Approach Gibraltar Europa Point LtHo main Lt Iso.10s. Conspic buildings on reclaimed land on approach.

From April to August whales may be encountered in the Strait of Gibraltar.

Entrance Fly Q flag and report to Customs at N end of the Rock, just to the S of airfield runway. Pass round the N end of the N mole or so-called 'E' Head. Customs station flies 'Q' flag. Alternatively, go direct to Queensway Quay where you can clear customs in and out.

Berthing Marina Bay is in the N end of the hbr just S of the airport runway. It has comprehensive boat repair facilities and is close to shops and restaurants. Queensway Quay marina is in the centre of the main hbr N of Gunwharf (former RN base). It is quieter but some swell when big ships move. Queensway Quay is closed with a boom between 2100 and 0800. Probably best to anchor off La Linea if arriving between those times. Usual facilities. Diesel available.

Sheppard's Marina is closed, but chandlery in Ocean Village is still open; lifting out can be arranged. Both Queensway and Marina Bay are very full. Contact by telephone or VHF before arrival.

Anchorage Immediately N of runway is not always permitted. In any case yachts must clear Customs in one of the marinas.

Facilities BA chart agent. Air services to UK.

☎/VHF Queensway Quay +350 2004 47000, Marina Bay/Ocean Village +350 2007 33000. All marinas VHF 71; Port +350 2007 7254, VHF 06, 12.

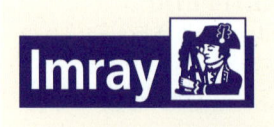

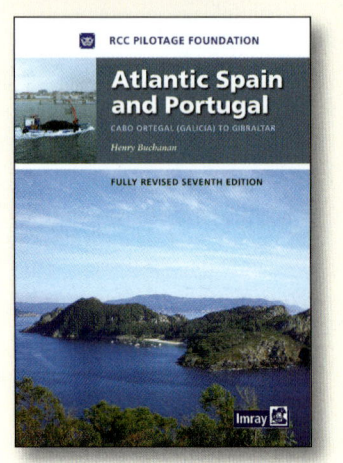

ATLANTIC SPAIN AND PORTUGAL

The seventh edition of this RCC Pilotage Foundation has been completely updated from visits to the area by Henry Buchanan who has taken over the editorship of the entire volume. He has completely overhauled the initial section on Galicia and this new edition now commences at Cabo Ortegal, taking in Ría Cedeira. The arrangement of text and plans as been reorganized particularly at Ría de Arousa where an improved whole page approaches plan has been included.

There are new photos and most of the plans incorporate changes accumulated over the four years or so since the last edition was published.

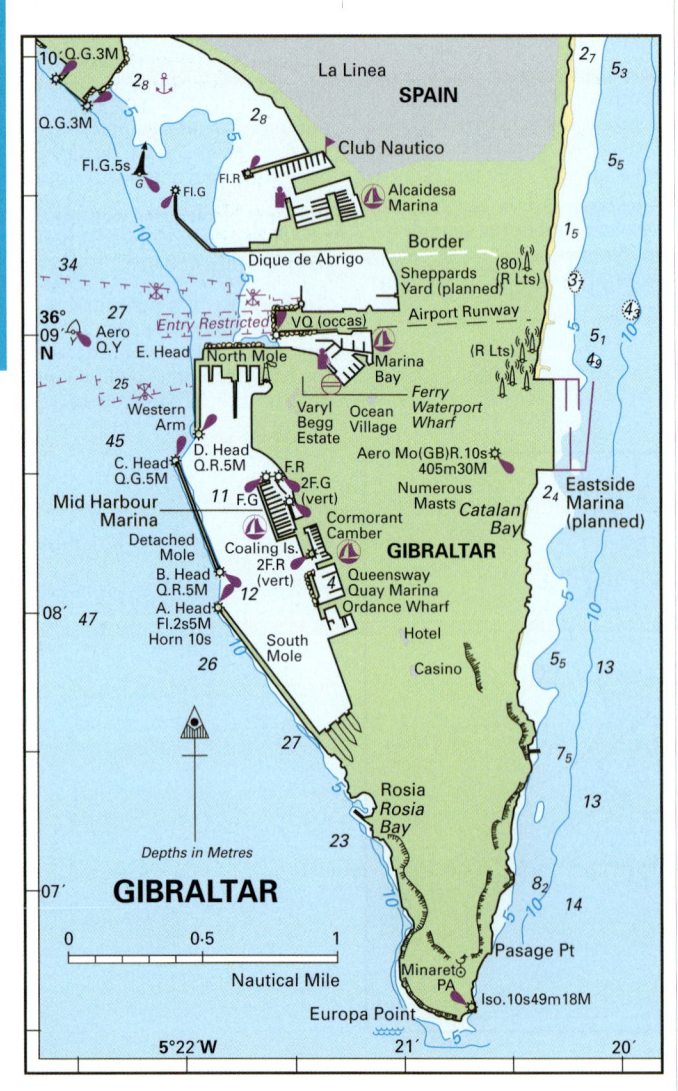

Tides and tidal streams

Tides and tidal streams

Definitions
Chart Datum (CD) is the level from which the depth of water or drying height is measured and is approximately the same as Lowest Astronomical Tide (LAT). BA charts and this almanac use this datum.

Mean High Water Springs (MHWS) is the average height of Spring Tides throughout the year. Spring Tides occur about 36 hours after Full and New Moons. These are higher at the Spring and Autumn Equinoxes and lower in midsummer and winter.

Highest Astronomical Tide (HAT) is the highest level that can be expected to occur under average meteorological conditions and under any combination of astronomical conditions. In practice this is slightly higher than MHWS.

Mean High Water Neaps (MHWN), *Mean Low Water Neaps* (MLWS) and *Mean Low Water Springs* are similar averages.

Variation from the predicted height of tides
Barometric Pressure A rise of 34hPA (millibars) from the average (1013) lowers the predicted height of the tide by 0·3m, a fall in pressure will cause a similar higher tide.

Wind A strong wind blowing on to a coast will cause a higher tide and an offshore wind will cause a lower one. This is very noticeable in the Baltic where tides are minimal.

Seiches The passage of an intense local depression or a line squall may set up a wave having a period from a few minutes to an hour. Some harbours are more prone to this, Fishguard and Wick are examples.

Storm surges occur in the North Sea where a constant Northerly gale causes a surge up to 2·5m. Less marked negative surges may also occur. It is prudent, not only to consider the weather, but also to allow a safe margin when anchoring or making a passage in shallow water.

High Water The time of high and low water at Standard ports may be found in the Tide Tables. It should be noted that most of these are given in Universal Time and will need correction for local time. Most European countries use European Standard Time which is UT+1 in the winter and daylight saving time which is UT+2 from the last Sunday in March to the last Sunday October. Exceptions to this are UK, Ireland and Portugal who use UT in the winter and UT+1 in the summer. It must be noted that the corrections for secondary ports are based on UT.

Tidal range The mean spring range at Dover is 6·0m and the neap range is 3·2m. MHWS springs will take place anywhere in Europe when the Dover range is 6·0m. Larger ranges occur at the Equinoxes.

The French base their tidal calculations on the range at Brest which is converted to tidal coefficients in which the Mean Spring Range at Brest is taken as 100 (*vive eau*) and the Mean Neap Range is 45 (*morte eau*). Be careful not confuse this with HW (*pleine mer*) and LW (*basse mer*). In some French harbours the lock gates do not function when the range is very small.

Depths refer to the depth at chart datum and the height of the tide should be added to this.

Bridges, Cables and Vertical Clearances Vertical clearances are usually measured above HAT, however, on some continental charts the measurement may be from Mean Tidal Level which is about half way between HW and LW.

Anchoring It is customary to use about 5x the depth of chain at HW. More will needed for warp, in swell, high winds, strong tidal streams, depending on the nature of the bottom. The catenary of the anchor chain reduces snatching.

Corrections to tidal height according to barometric pressure

Millibars	Correction	Millibars	Correction
963	+0·50m	1003	+0·10m
968	+0·45m	1008	+0·05m
973	+0·40m	1013	+0·00m
978	+0·35m	1018	–0·05m
983	+0·30m	1023	–0·10m
988	+0·25m	1028	–0·15m
993	+0·20m	1033	–0·20m
998	+0·15m	1038	–0·25m

Tidal heights can in theory be precisely calculated using the tidal curves for the standard ports (*see Index p.453*) corrected when necessary by the secondary port information. Such accuracy is only occasionally required and is only valid at mean atmospheric pressure, little wind and absence of swell. The Rule of 12ths is usually sufficiently accurate for practical purposes. This says that the tide rises or falls by one-twelfth during the first and last hour of the tide, by two-twelfths during the second and fifth hours and by three-twelfths during each of the third and fourth hours. This is very accurate in ports where the curve is near normal but is unsatisfactory when it is not. Le Havre, Poole and the Solent all have a 'stand' at HW or sometimes a double HW.

Tidal Curves From the tidal curves and the tide tables it is possible to calculate the depth of water at any time in any charted position near any standard port and with the use of secondary port corrections the same can be found. (See following page for an example).

Tidal Stream Charts These are copied from BA *Tidal Atlases* most of which are based on Dover and are in the following pages. The speeds are for Spring and Neap tides separated by a comma and give the speed in tenths of a knot. Thus 11, 19 is 1·1 knots at neaps and 1·9 knots at springs. It should be noted that at the equinoxes the tidal streams run faster than the spring rate in proportion to the range of tide. In some places the tides build up to a maximum and then fall off to slack water. In other places flood and ebb alternate reaching their maximum rapidly, this is most likely to take place when a tidal lagoon fills and empties through a narrow entrance.

Example To calculate the times of grounding and refloating:
A craft drawing 2m anchors in Dale Bay in Milford Haven at HW in a depth of 6·4m. The charted depth shows a drying height of 1m. The tide tables show:

HW	0714	7·4m	Range of tide	7·1m
LW	1334	0·3m	Draught of vessel	2m
HW	1932	7·2m		

Drying Height at LAT from the chart is 1m but LW is 0·3 above this so the actual drying height is 0·7m.

The boat will ground when the tide has fallen 4·4m to 3·0m (draught of vessel plus drying height). To find the time when this occurs mark the points HW 7·4m and LW 0·3m on the horizontal scales. Draw a line between these points. From the point at which this line intersects the vertical line representing the grounding height (3·0m) of the tide, draw a horizontal line across to the ebbing (right) side of the curve. Drop a vertical line from this point and read off the time of grounding. It helps if the times of HW, HW +1hr etc have already been written down as shown.

To find the time of refloating the oblique line must be adjusted to the next HW which is 7·2m and the horizontal line drawn to the rising (left hand) part of the curve.

If the boat moves to Solva, the times will be later and the tidal heights less. The details can be found in the Secondary ports list beneath the tidal curve for Milford Haven but need to be extrapolated for the point in the tidal cycle.

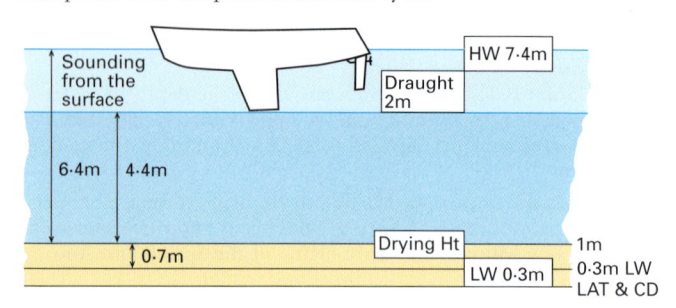

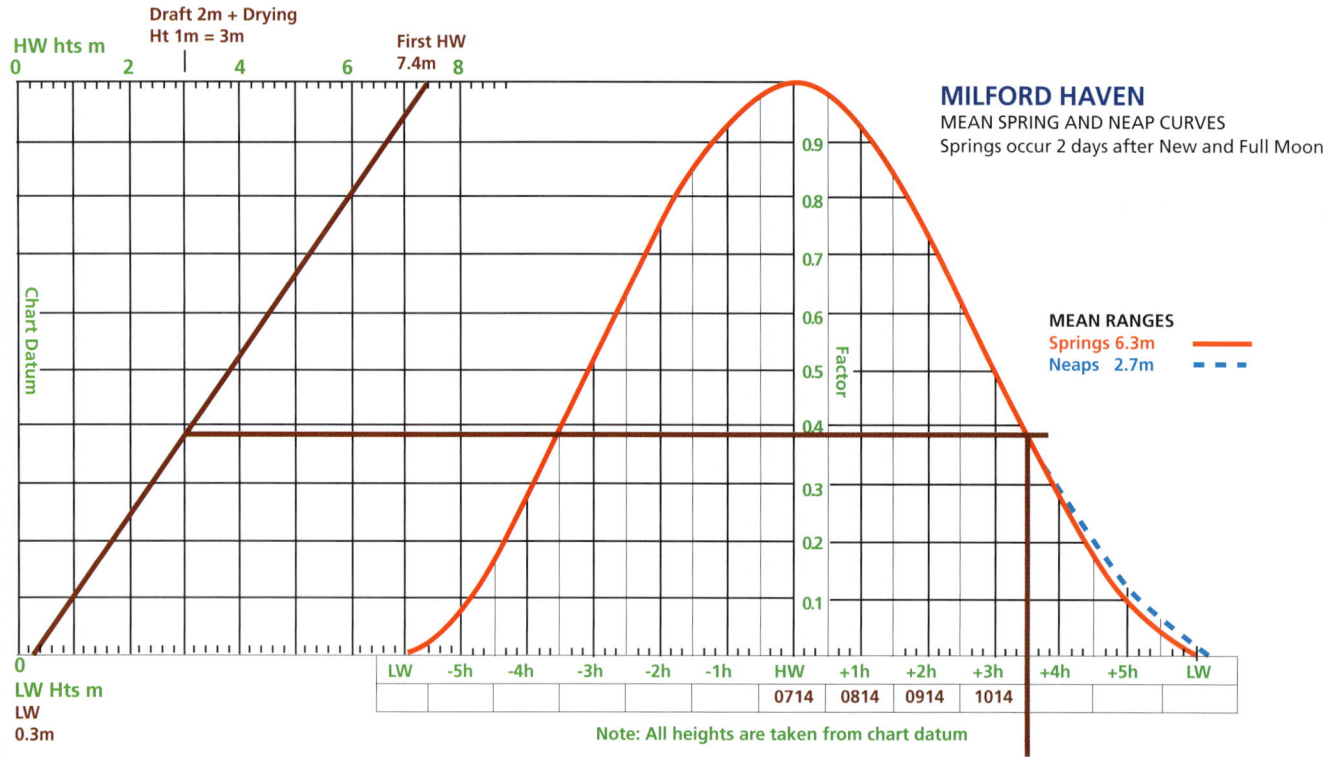

MILFORD HAVEN
MEAN SPRING AND NEAP CURVES
Springs occur 2 days after New and Full Moon

MEAN RANGES
Springs 6·3m
Neaps 2·7m

The boat will ground at 1044 UT

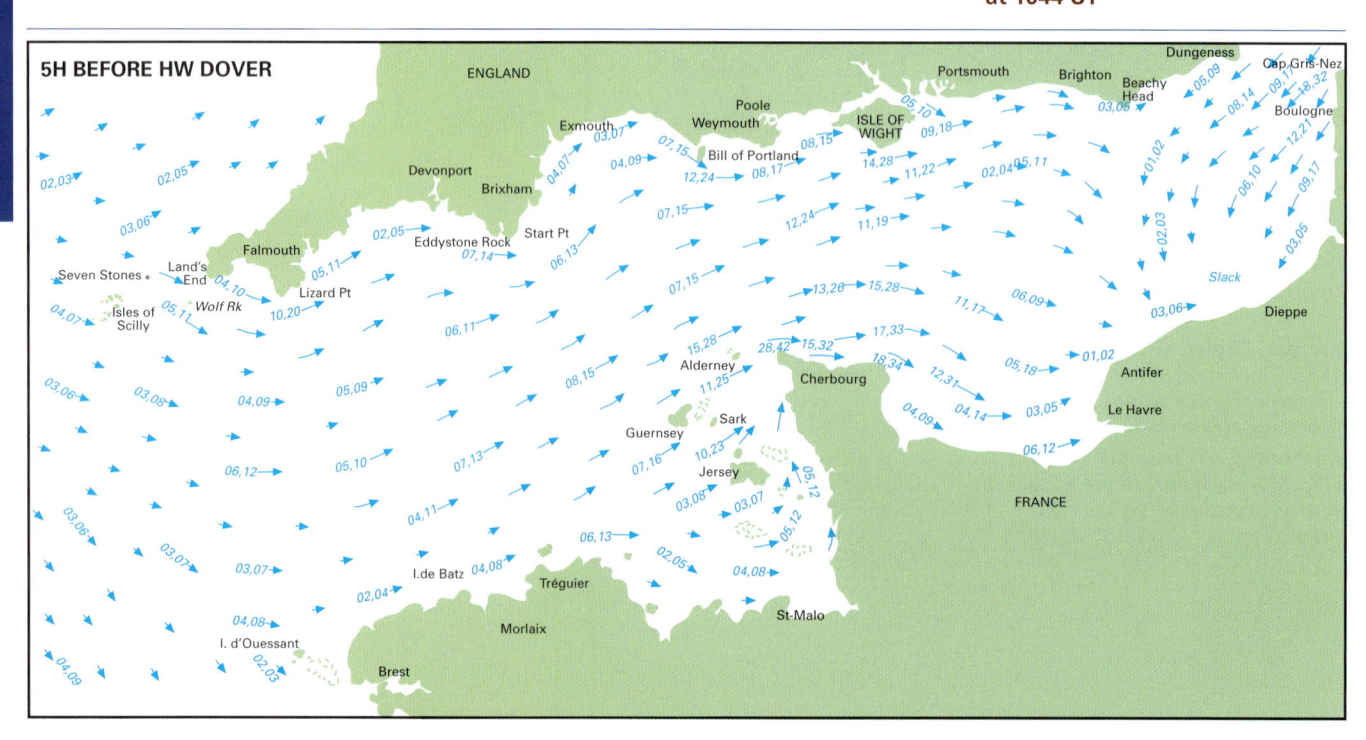

5H BEFORE HW DOVER

The Cruising Almanac

4H BEFORE HW DOVER

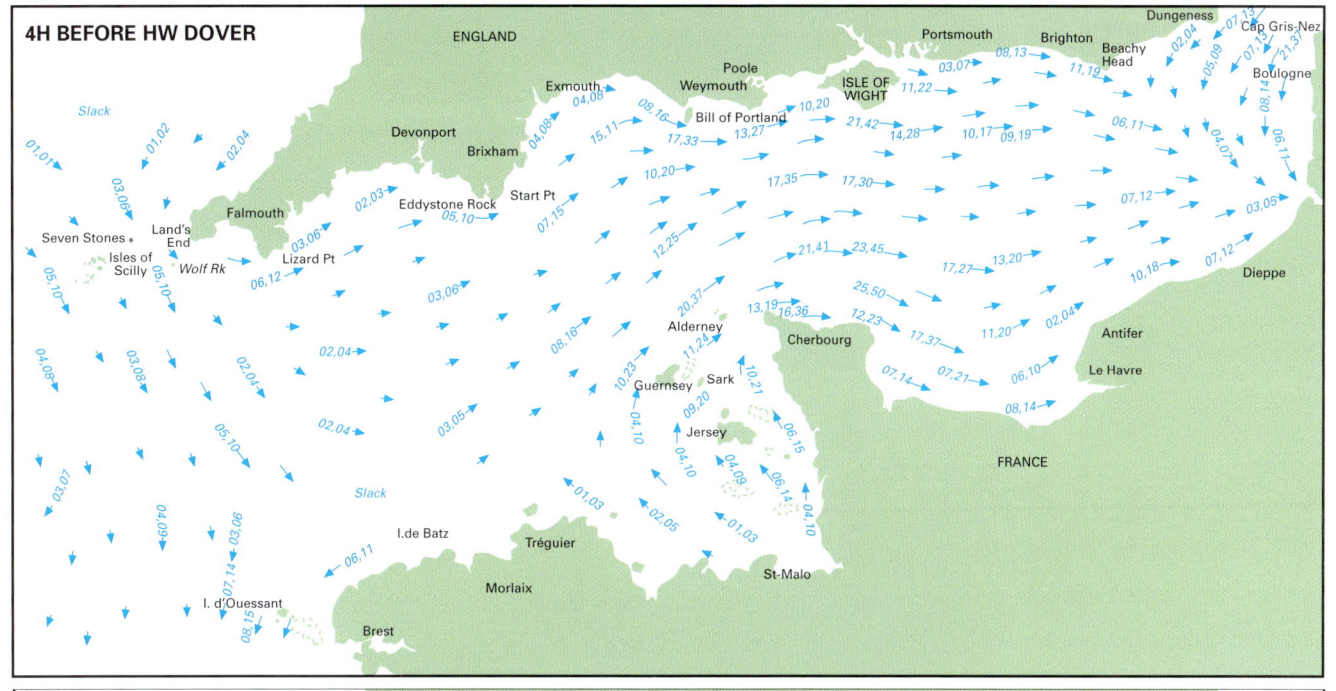

3H BEFORE HW DOVER

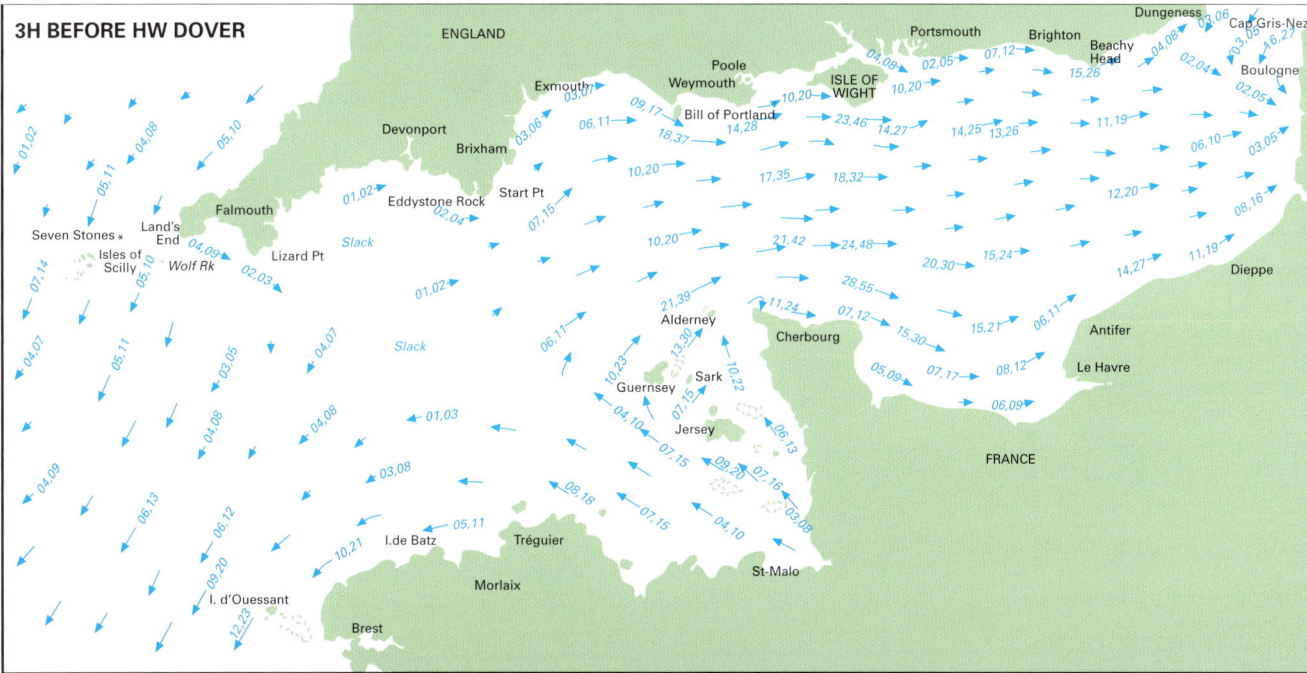

2H BEFORE HW DOVER

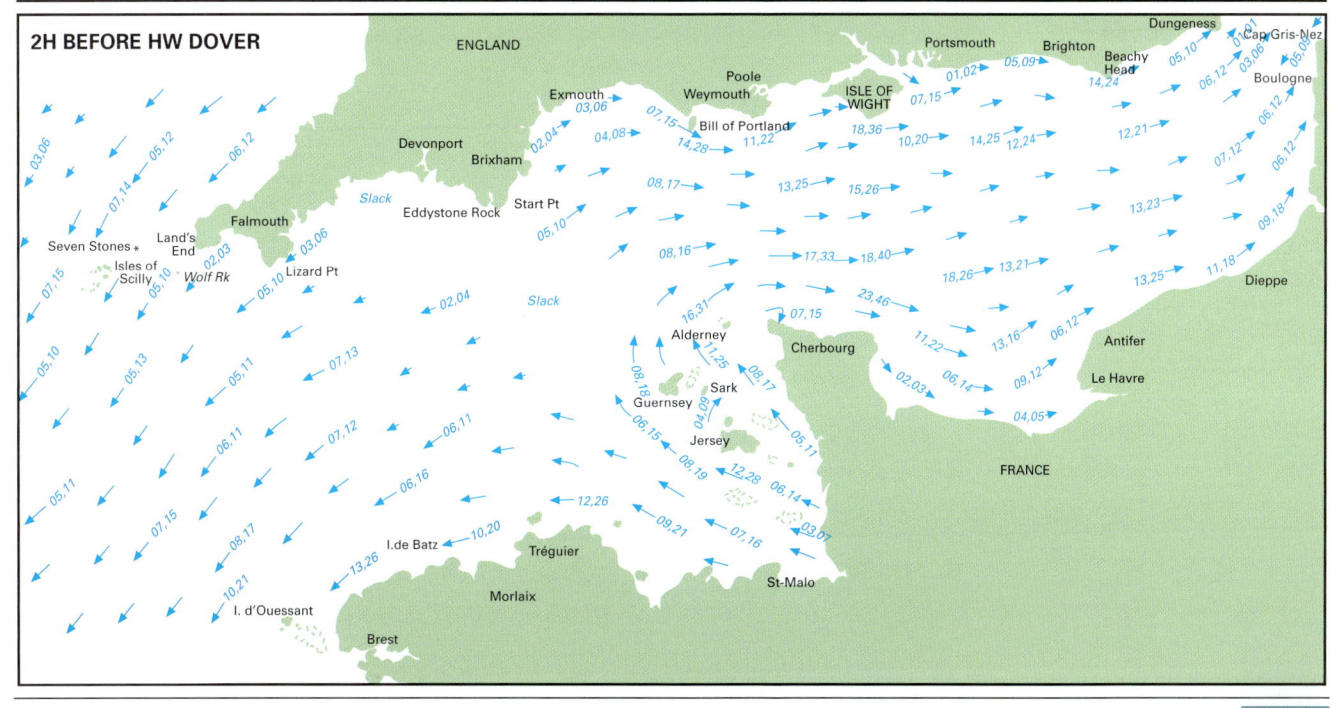

TIDAL STREAMS AND CURVES

TIDAL STREAMS AND CURVES

1H BEFORE HW DOVER

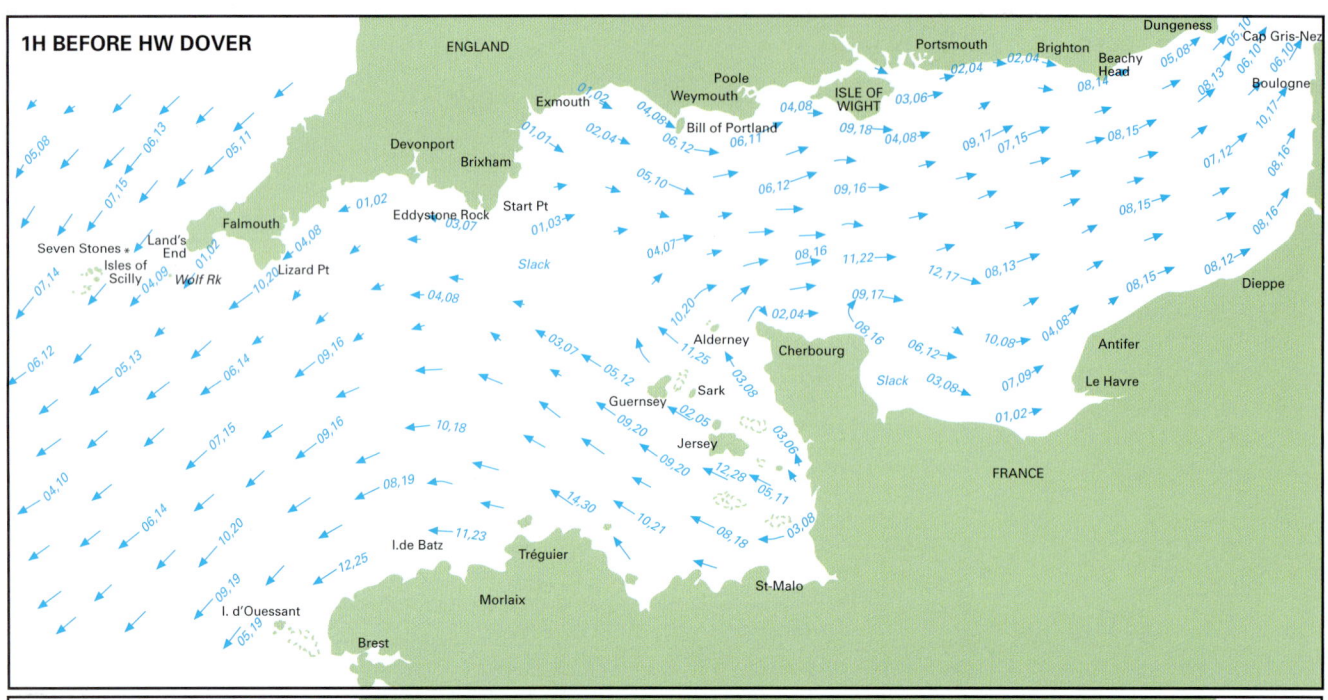

HW DOVER

1H AFTER HW DOVER

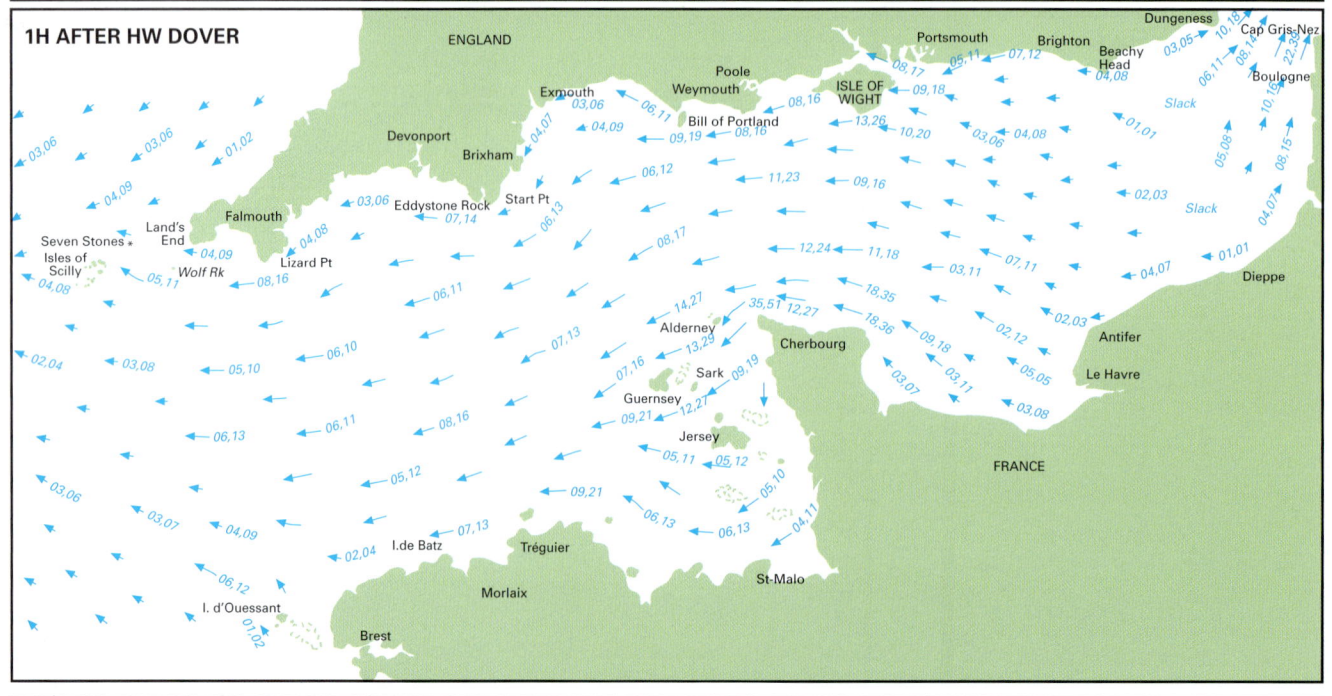

The Cruising Almanac

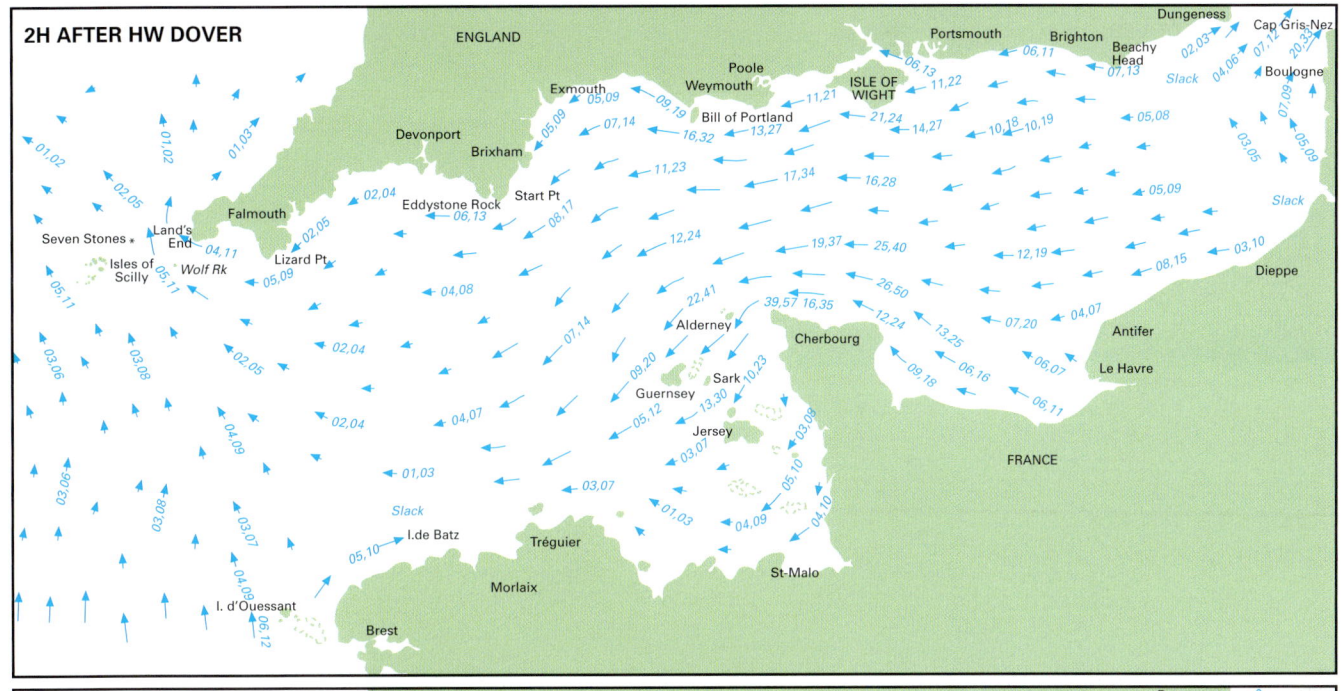

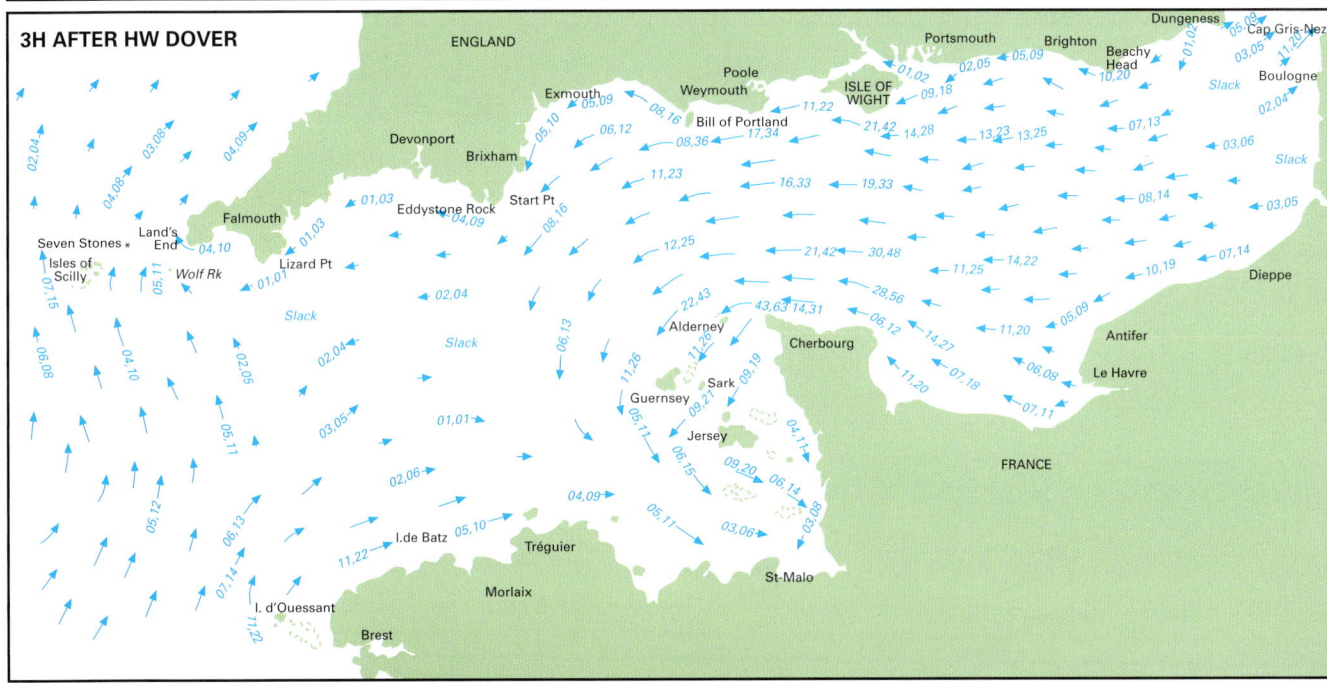

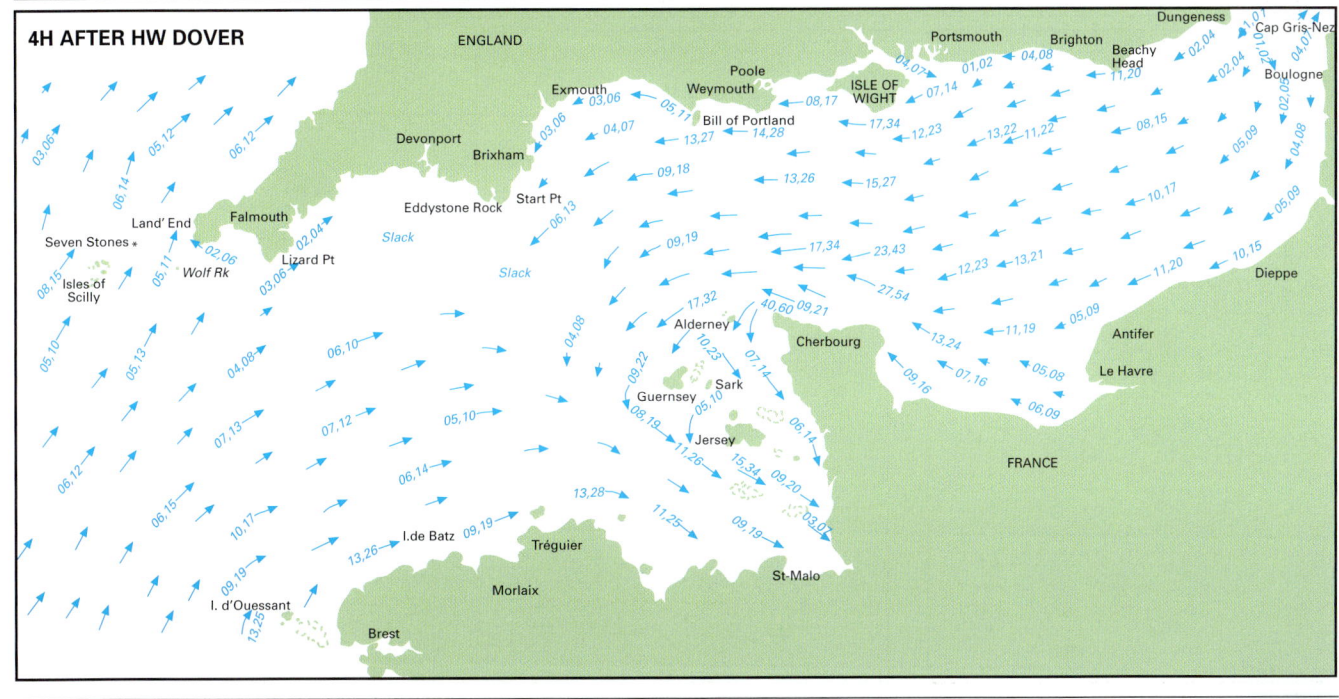

TIDAL STREAMS AND CURVES

421

TIDAL STREAMS AND CURVES

5H AFTER HW DOVER

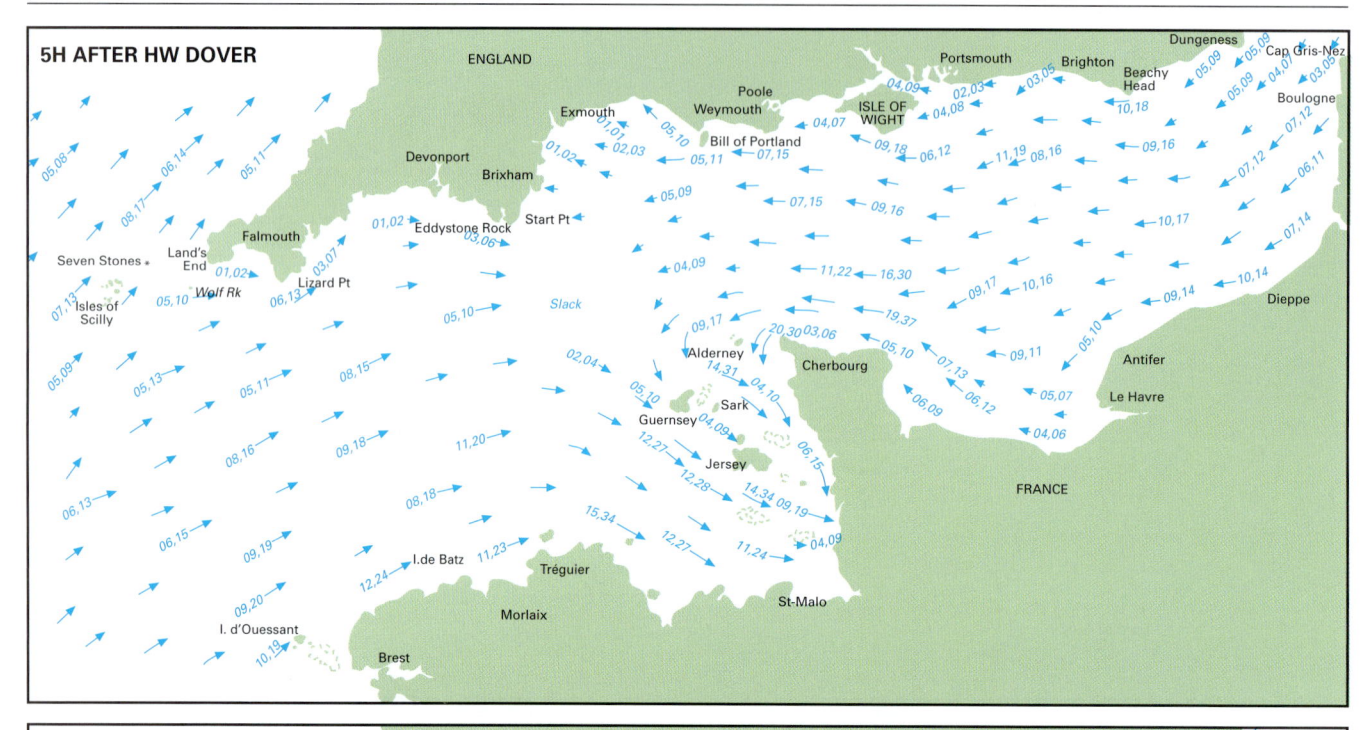

6H AFTER HW DOVER

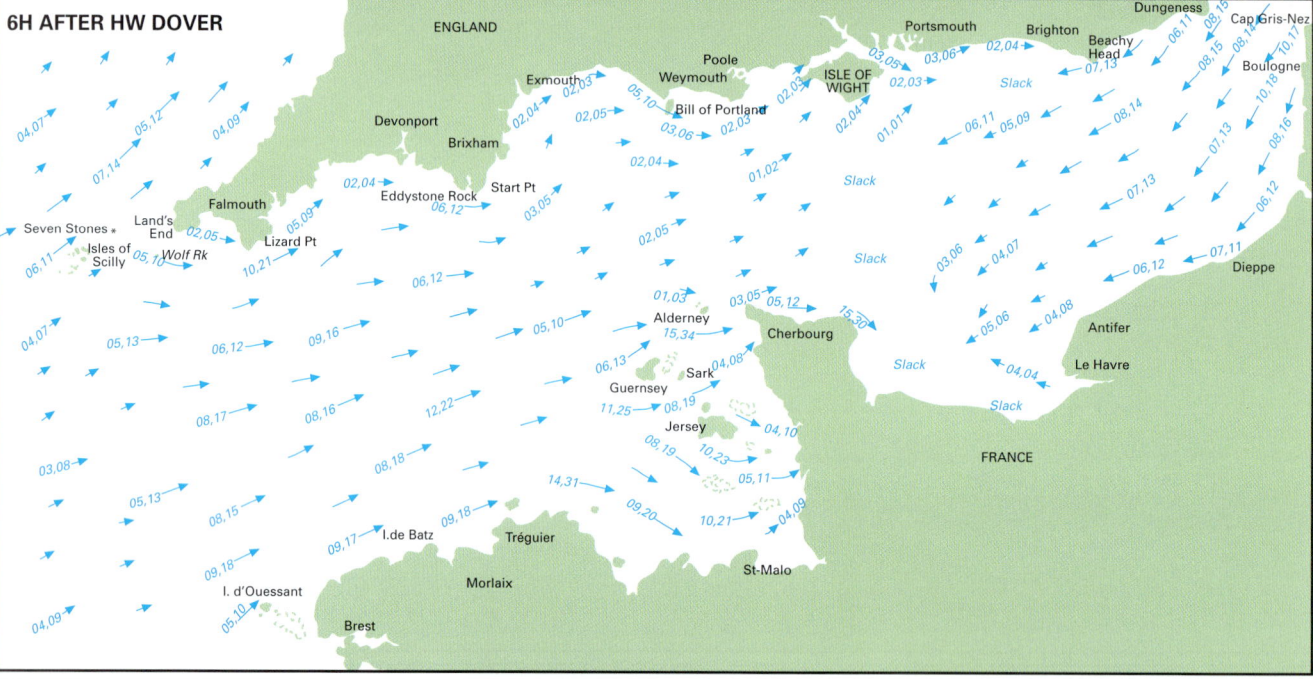

5H BEFORE HW PLYMOUTH
1h 45min after HW Dover

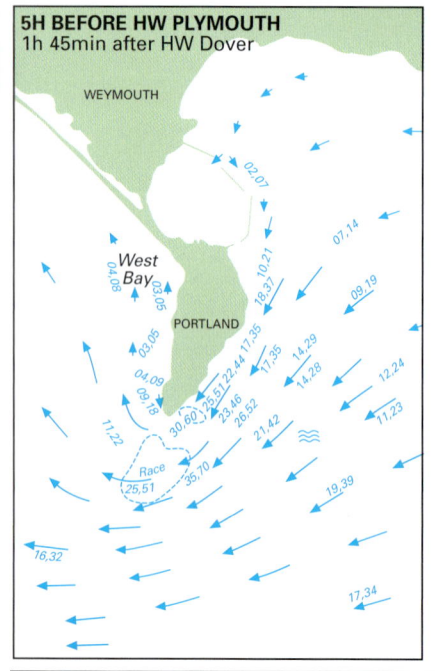

4H BEFORE HW PLYMOUTH
2h 45min after HW Dover

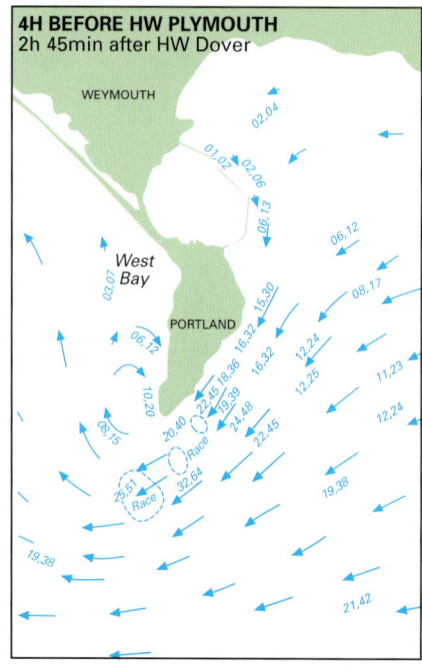

3H BEFORE HW PLYMOUTH
3h 45min after HW Dover

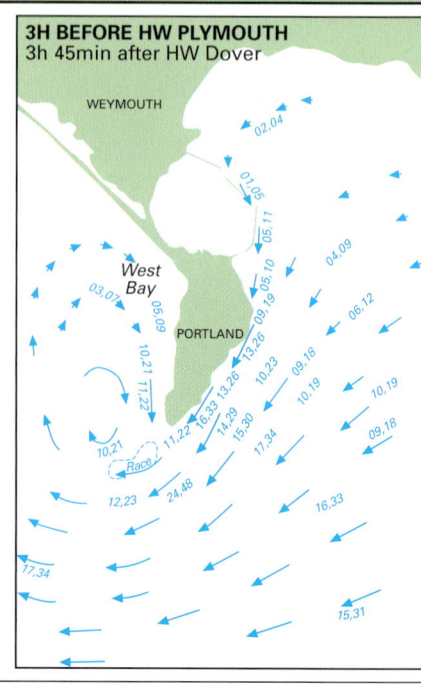

TIDAL STREAMS AND CURVES

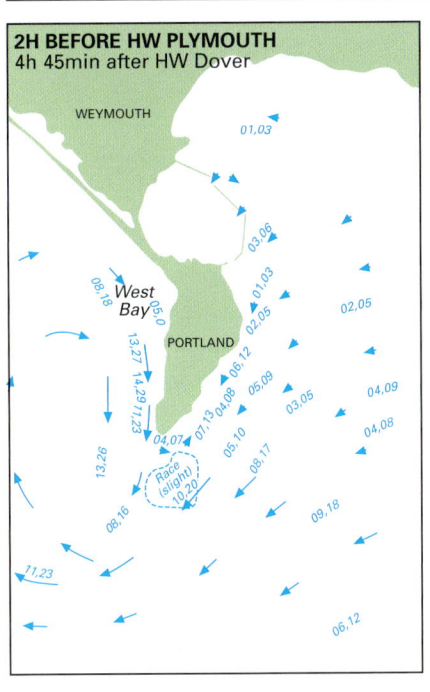

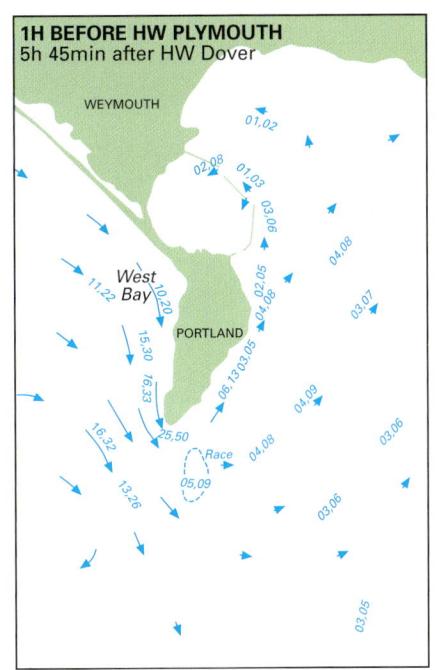

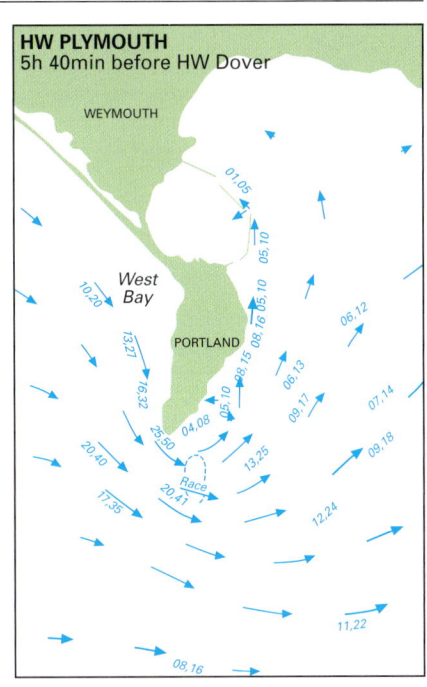

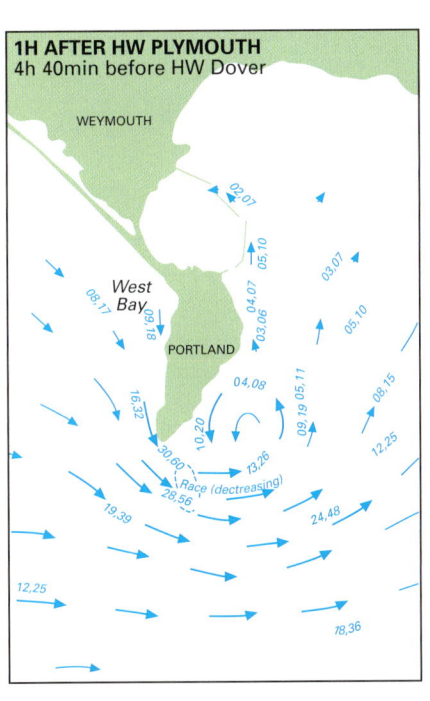

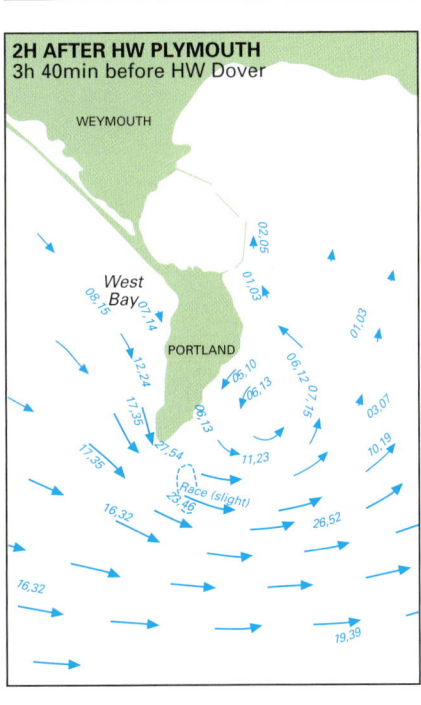

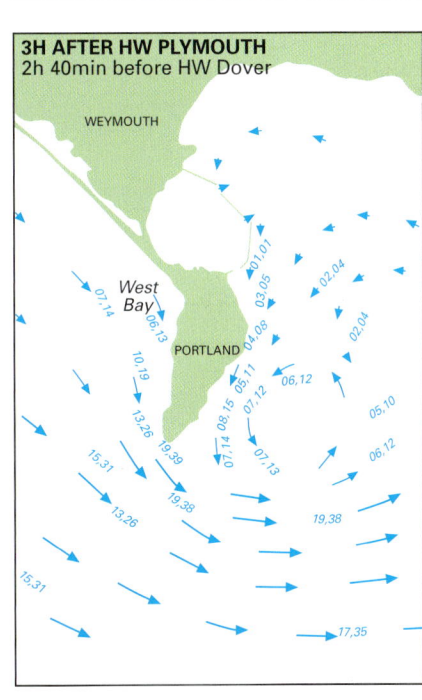

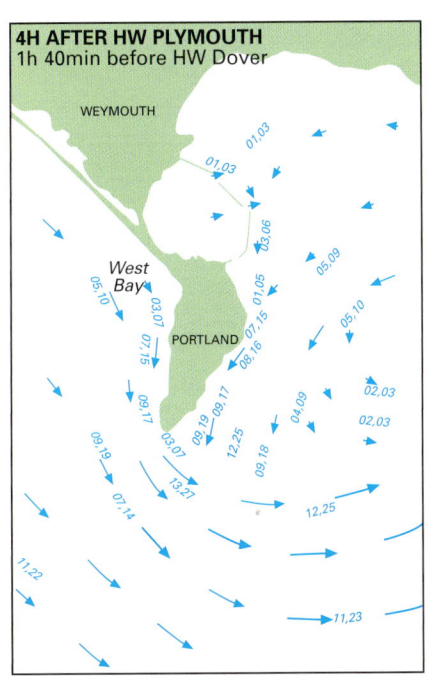

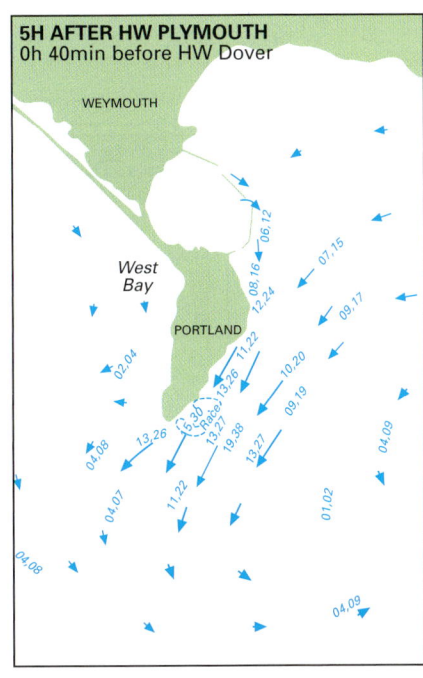

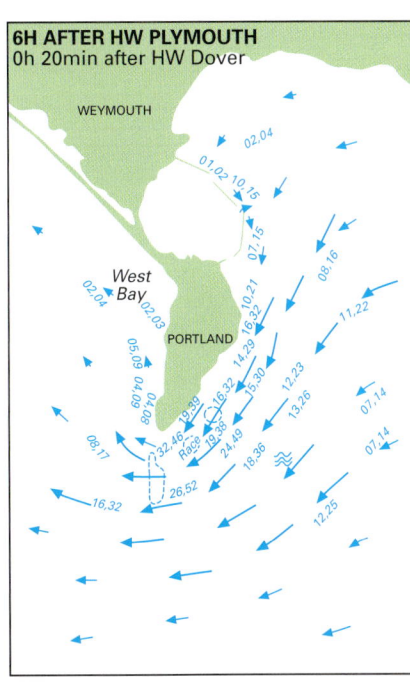

TIDAL STREAMS AND CURVES

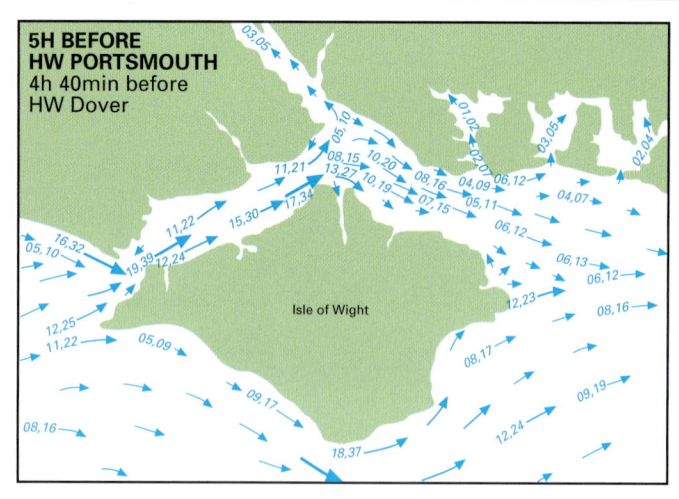

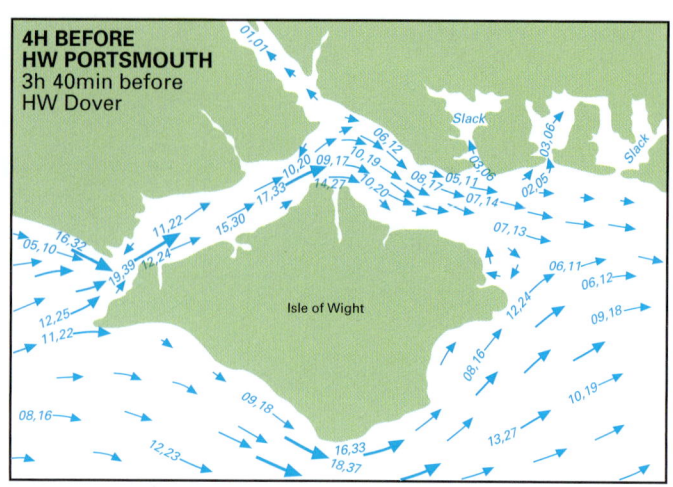

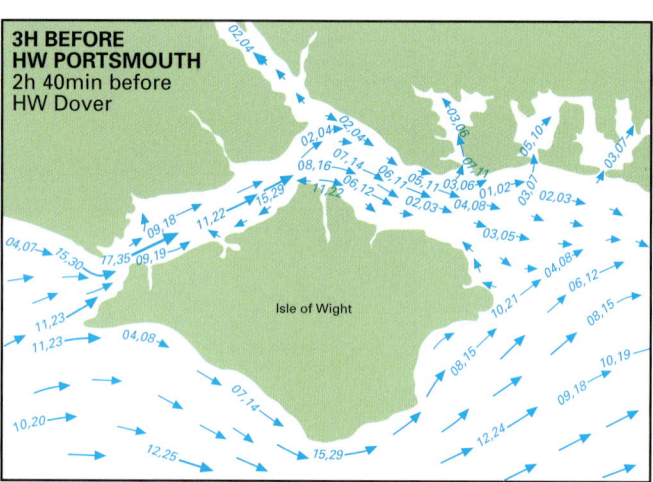

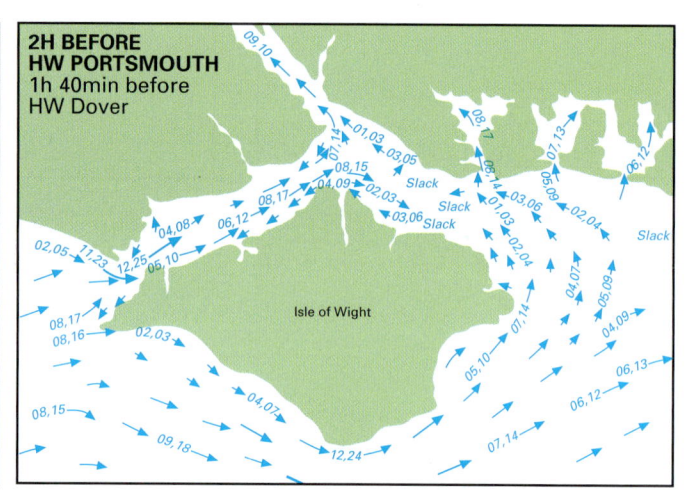

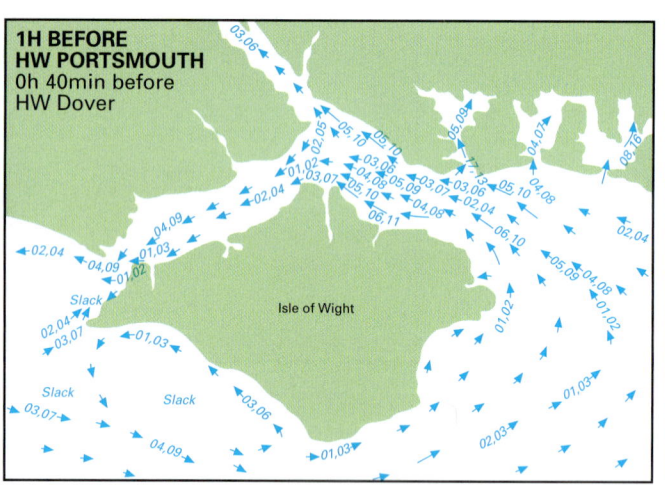

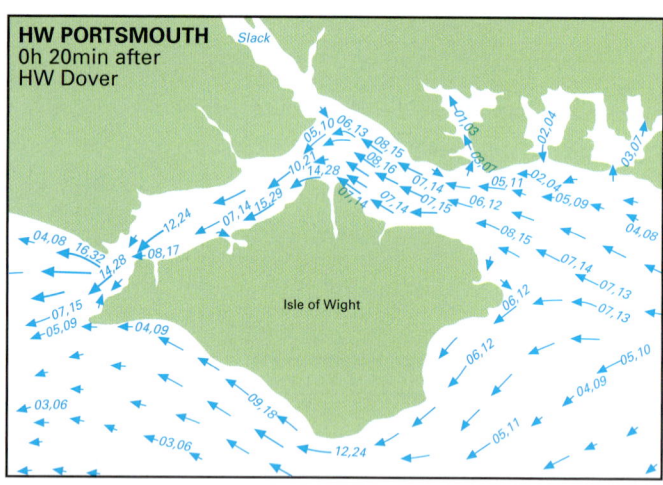

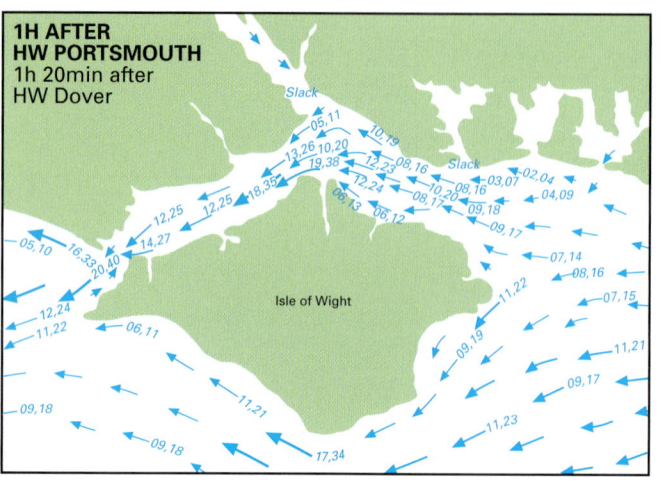

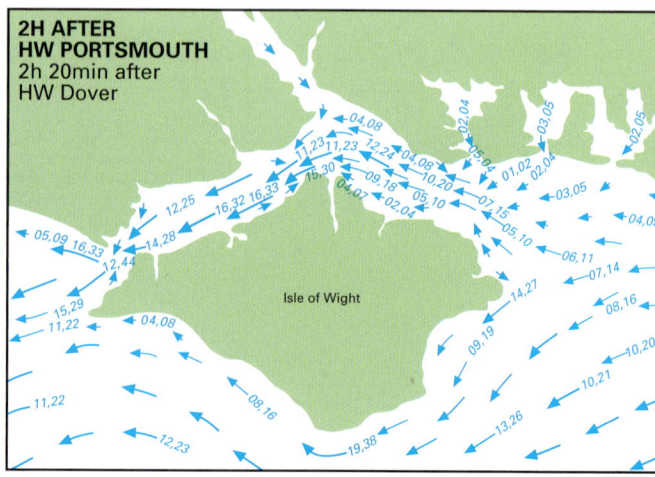

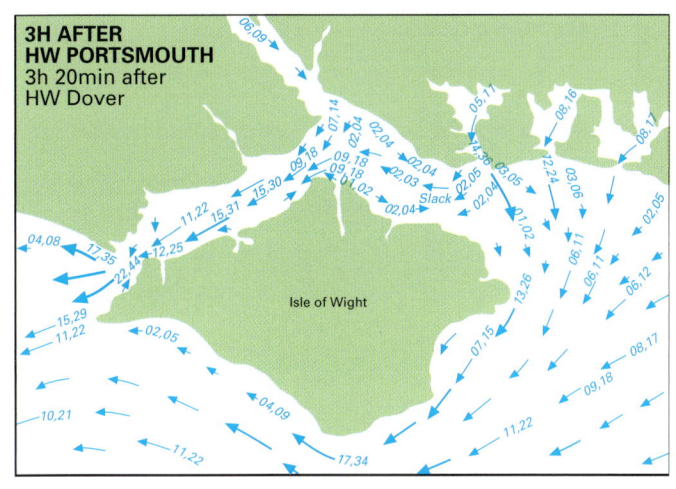

The Cruising Almanac

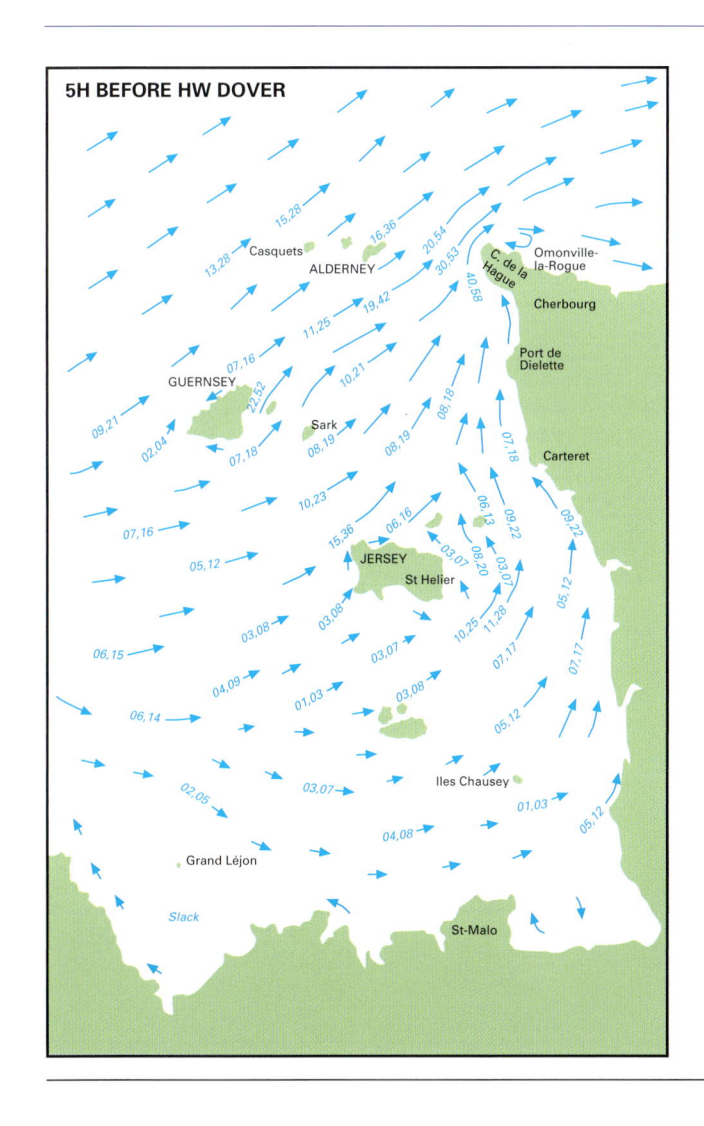

3H AFTER HW PORTSMOUTH
3h 20min after HW Dover

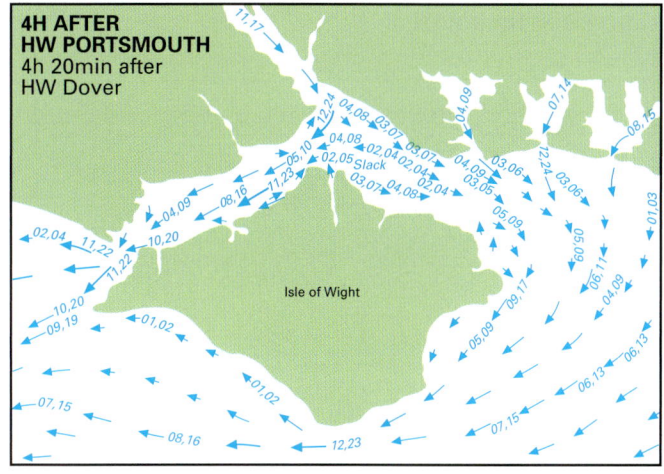

4H AFTER HW PORTSMOUTH
4h 20min after HW Dover

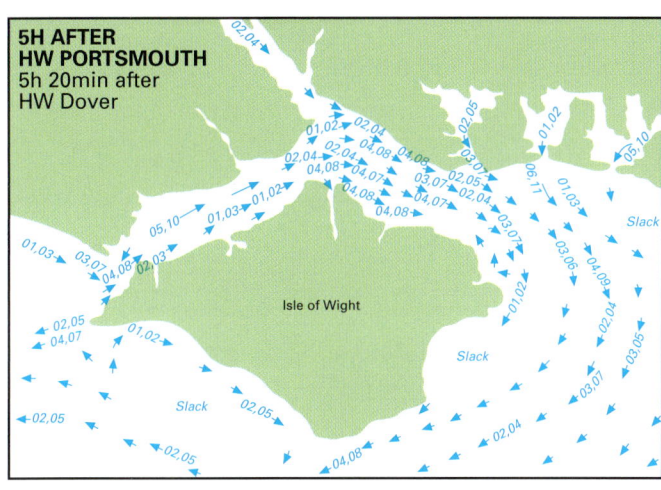

5H AFTER HW PORTSMOUTH
5h 20min after HW Dover

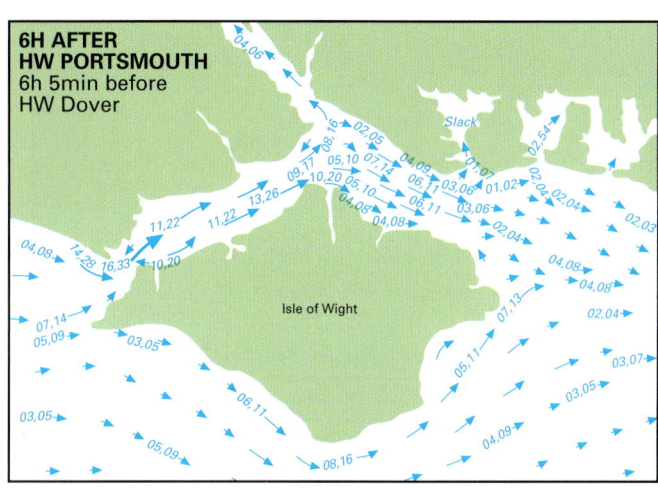

6H AFTER HW PORTSMOUTH
6h 5min before HW Dover

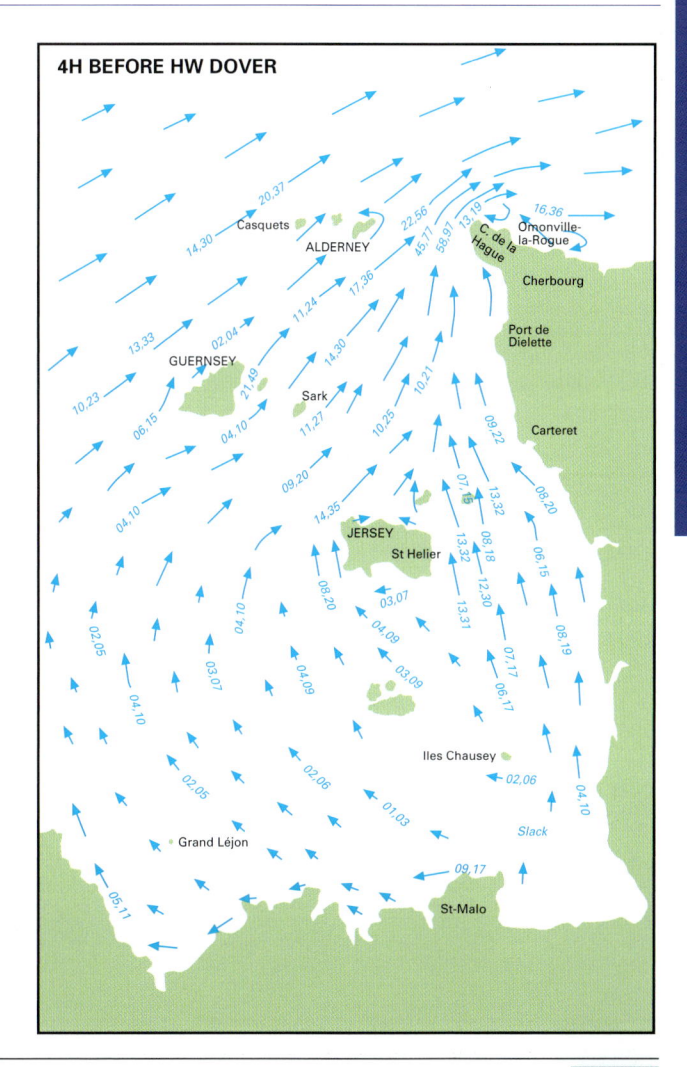

5H BEFORE HW DOVER

4H BEFORE HW DOVER

TIDAL STREAMS AND CURVES

425

TIDAL STREAMS AND CURVES

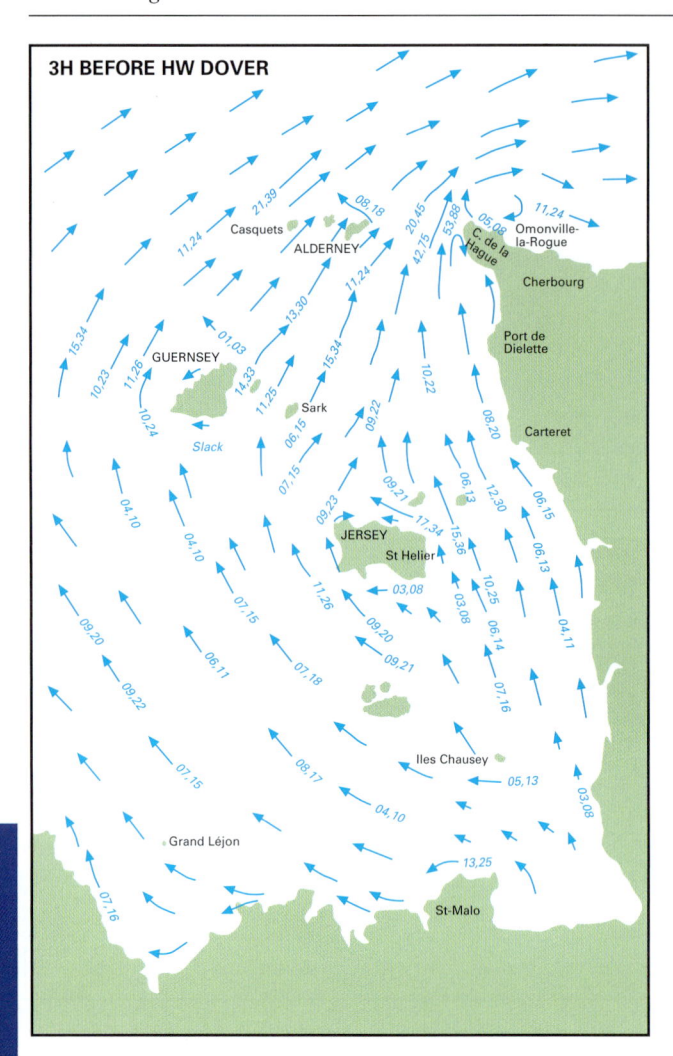

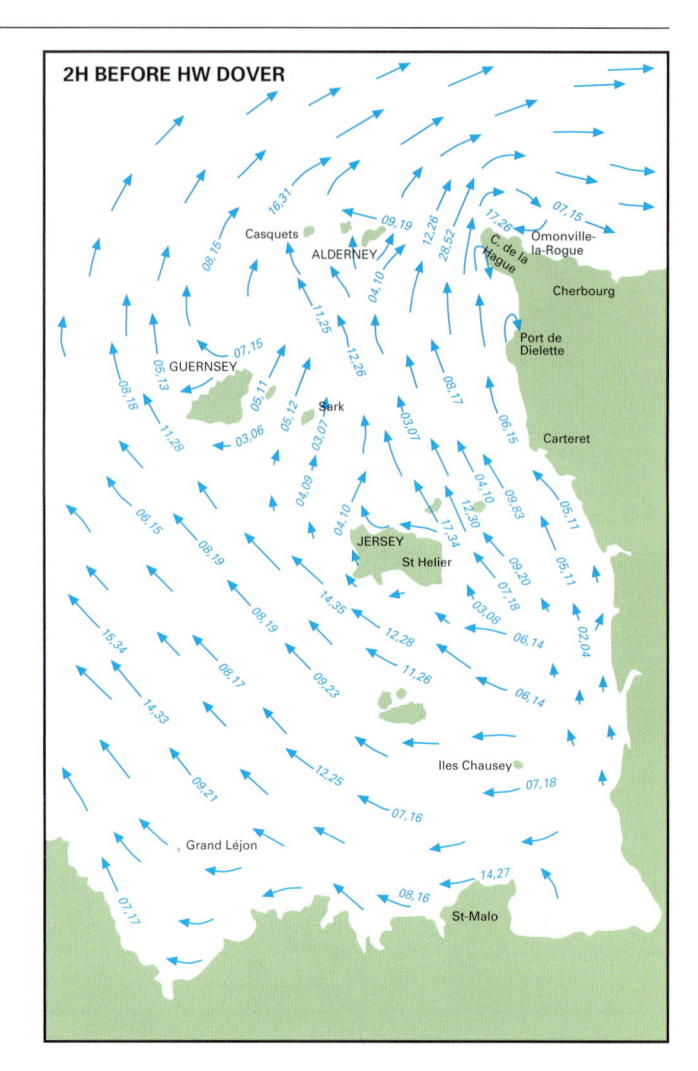

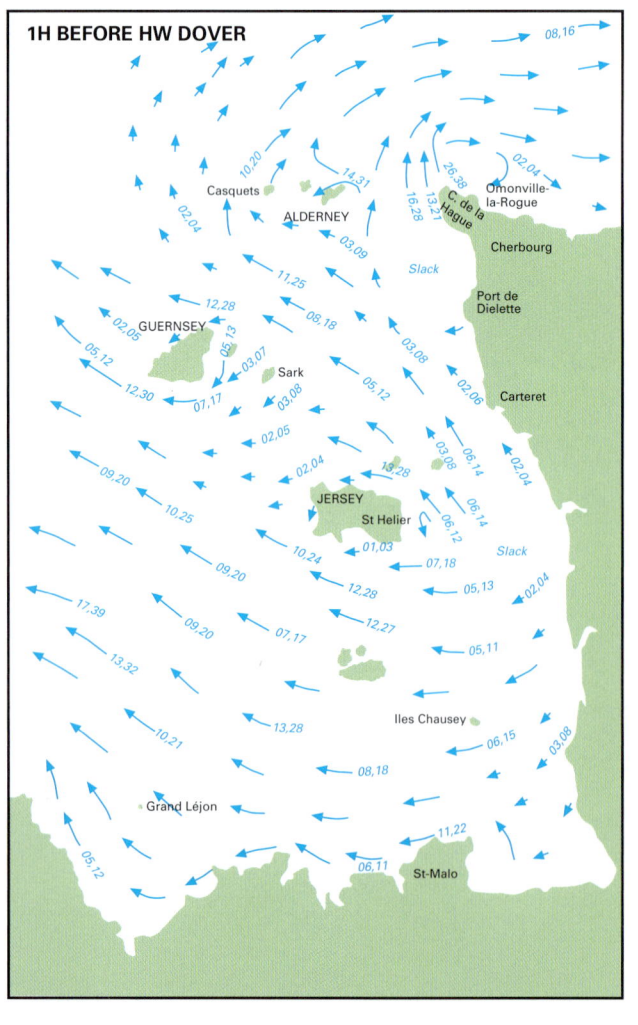

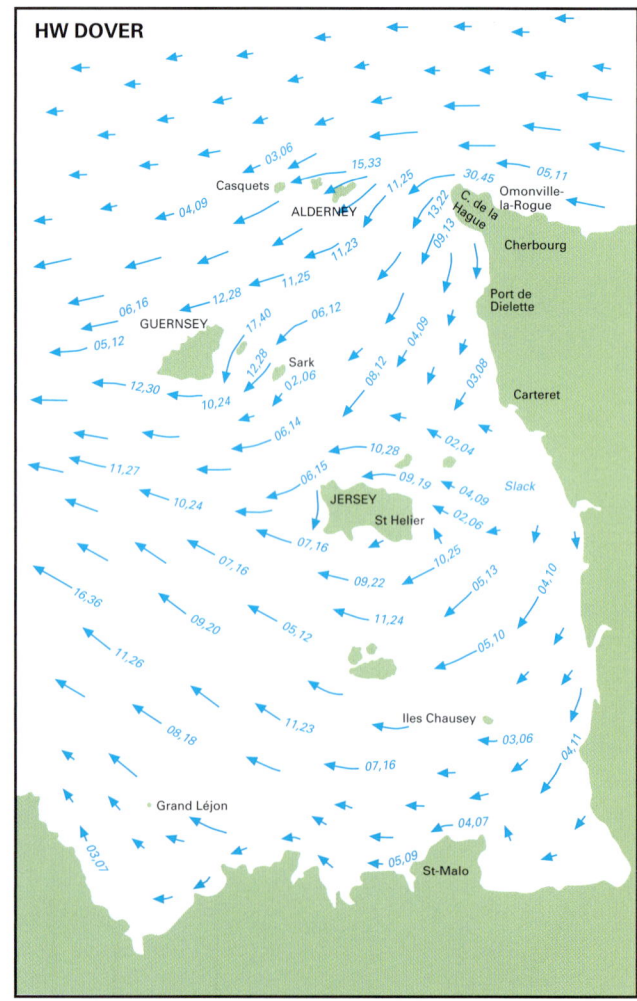

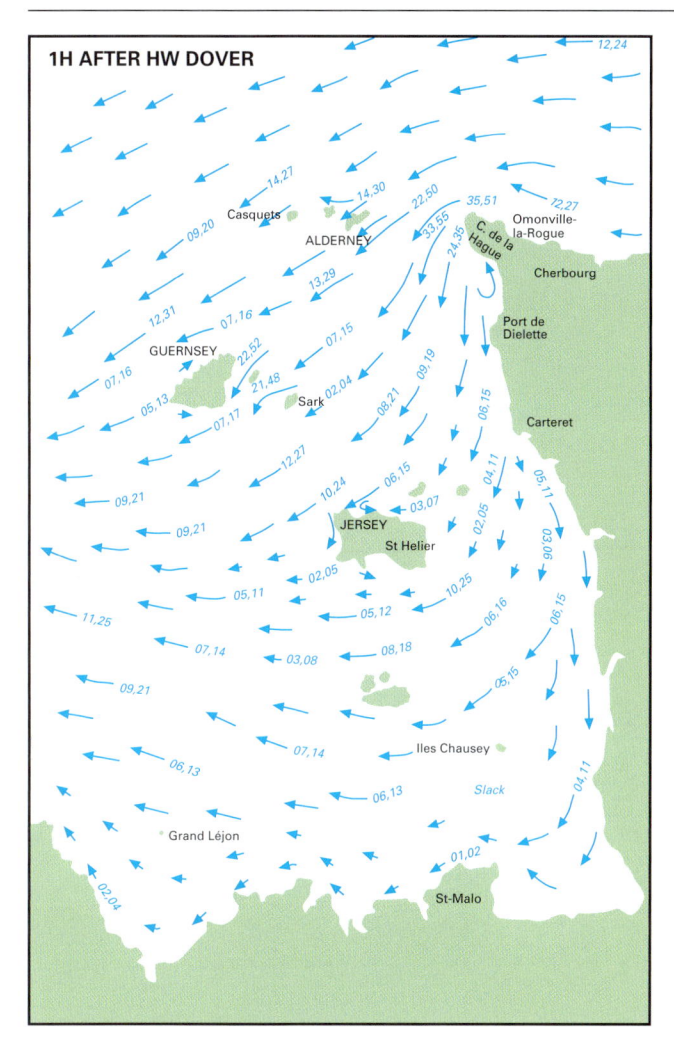

TIDAL STREAMS AND CURVES

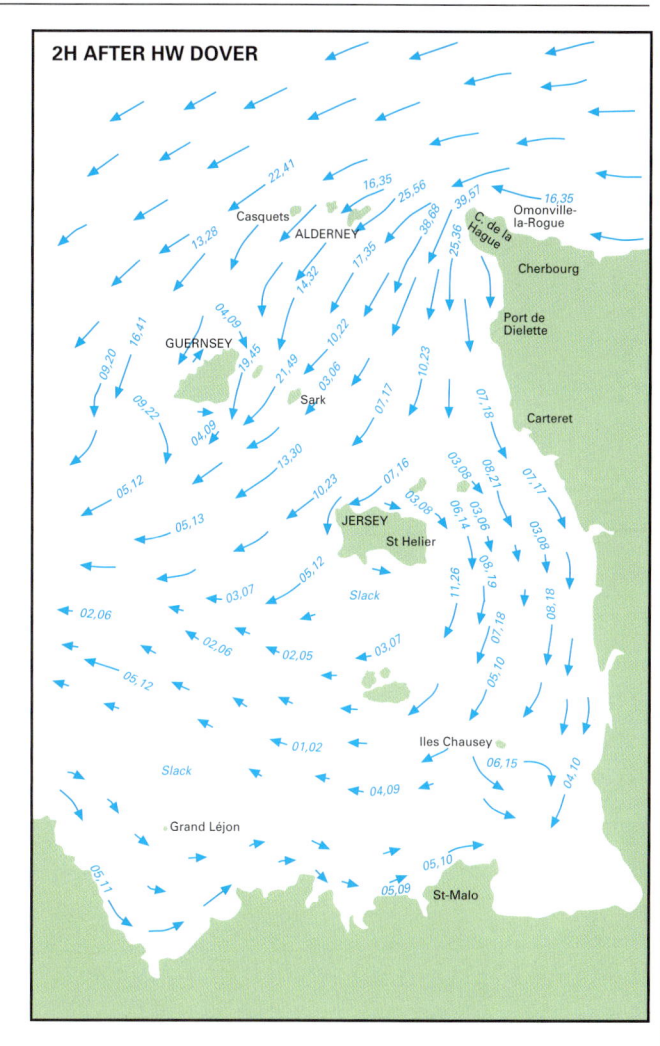

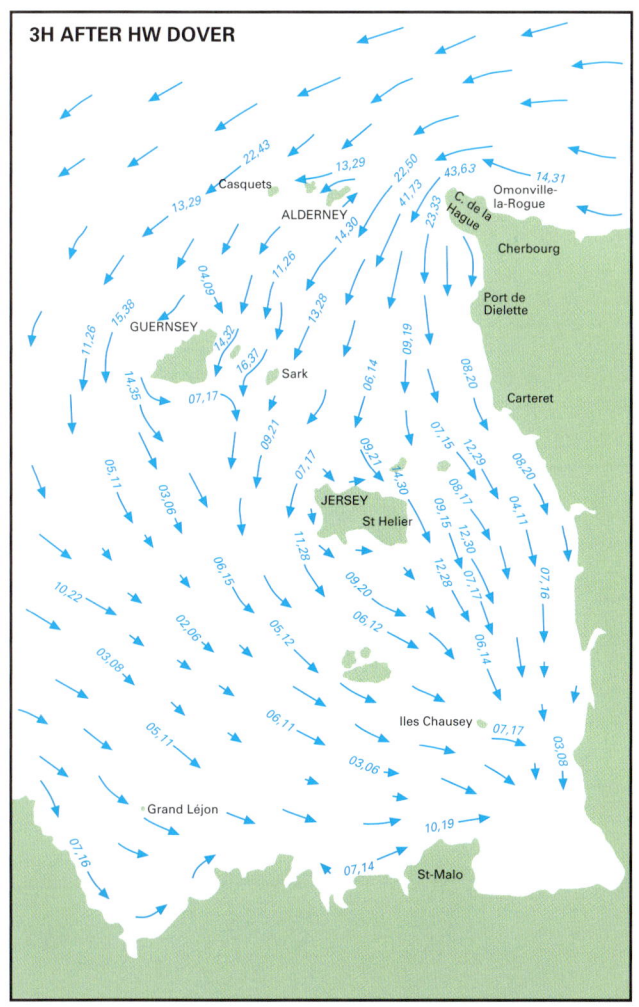

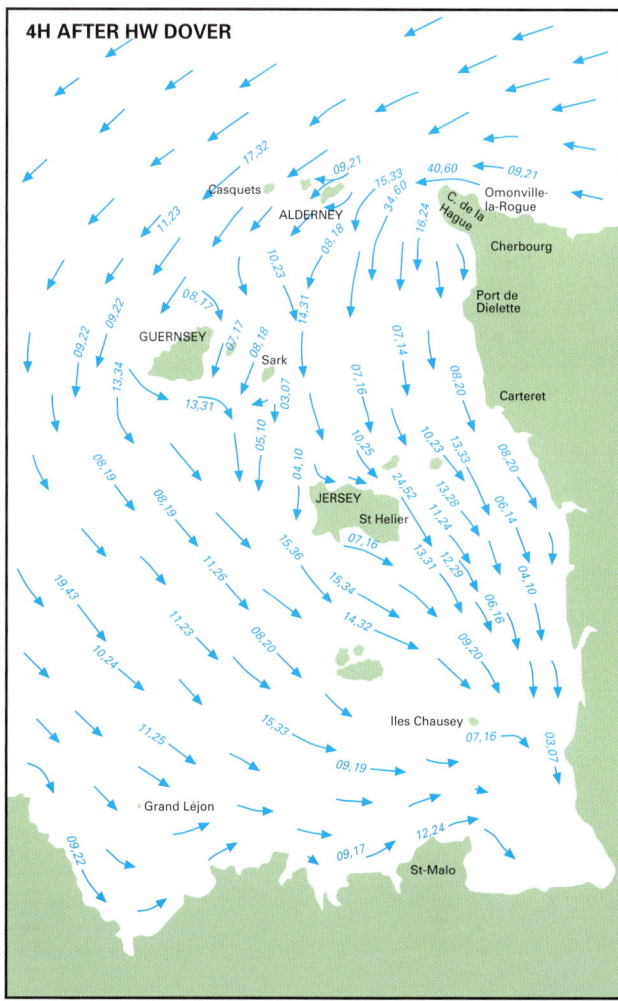

The Cruising Almanac

1H AFTER HW DOVER

2H AFTER HW DOVER

3H AFTER HW DOVER

4H AFTER HW DOVER

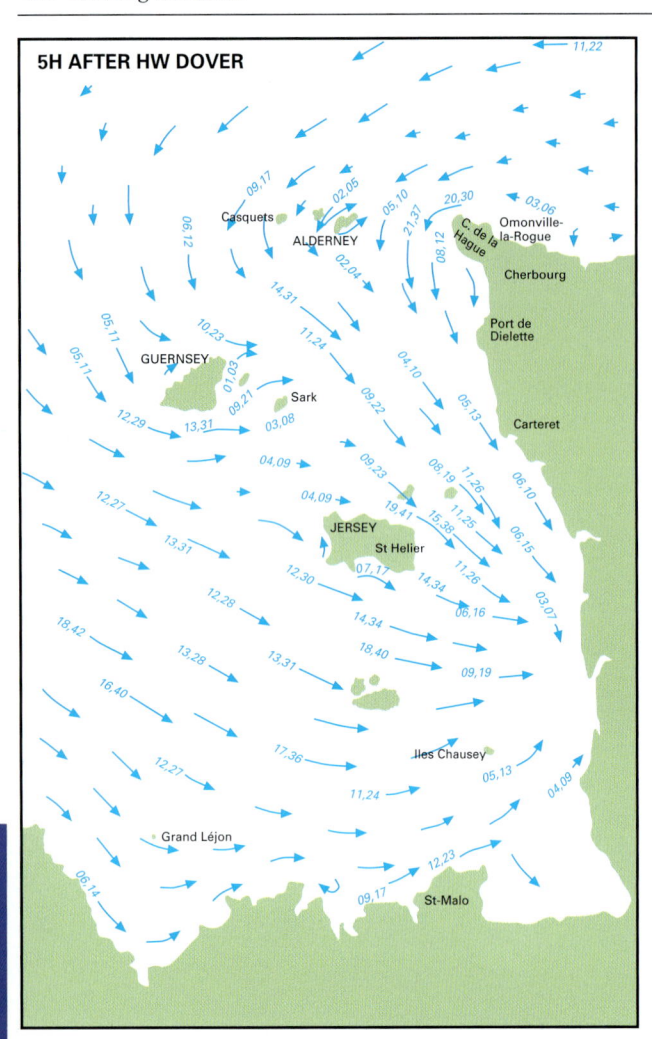

The Cruising Almanac

TIDAL STREAMS AND CURVES

5H AFTER HW DOVER

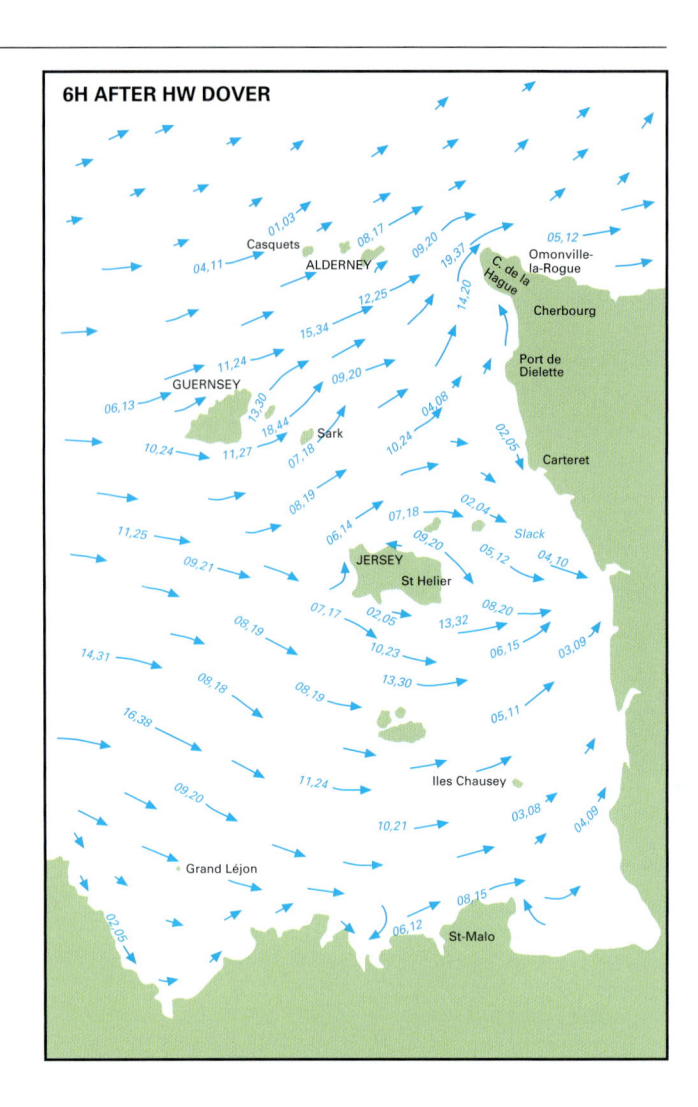

6H AFTER HW DOVER

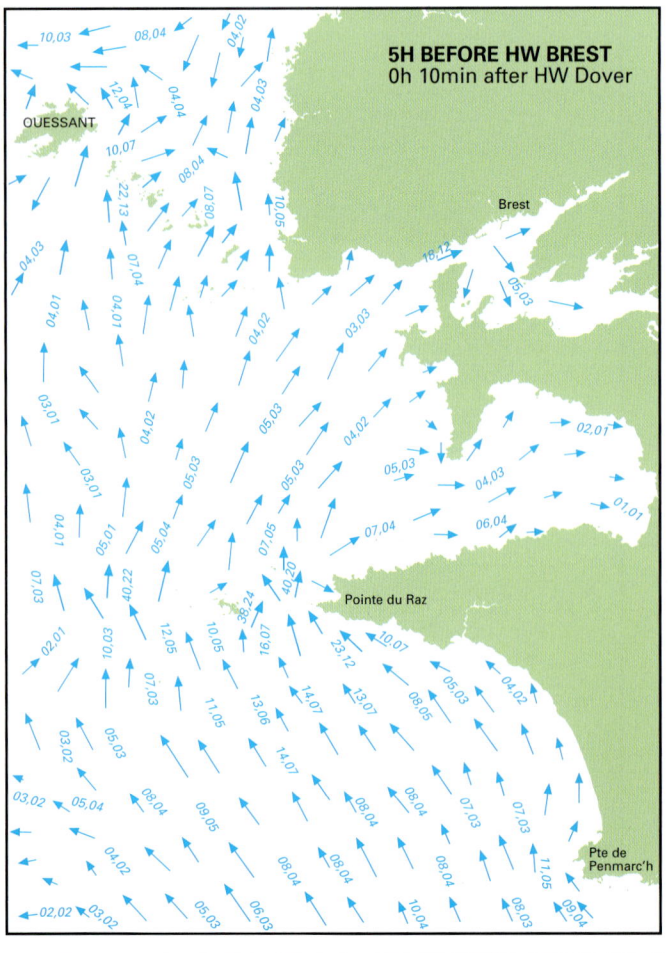

5H BEFORE HW BREST
0h 10min after HW Dover

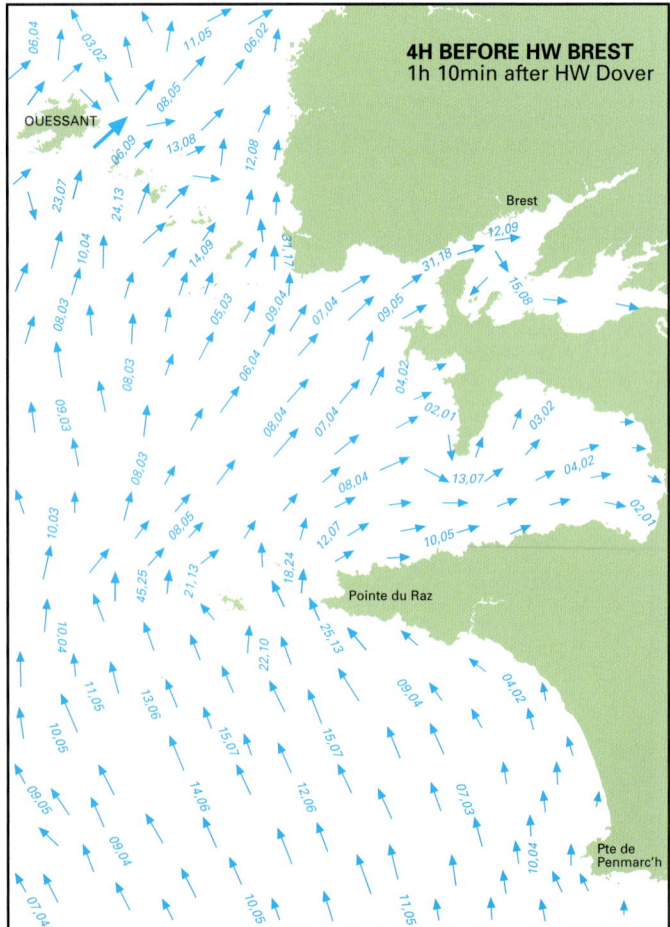

4H BEFORE HW BREST
1h 10min after HW Dover

The Cruising Almanac

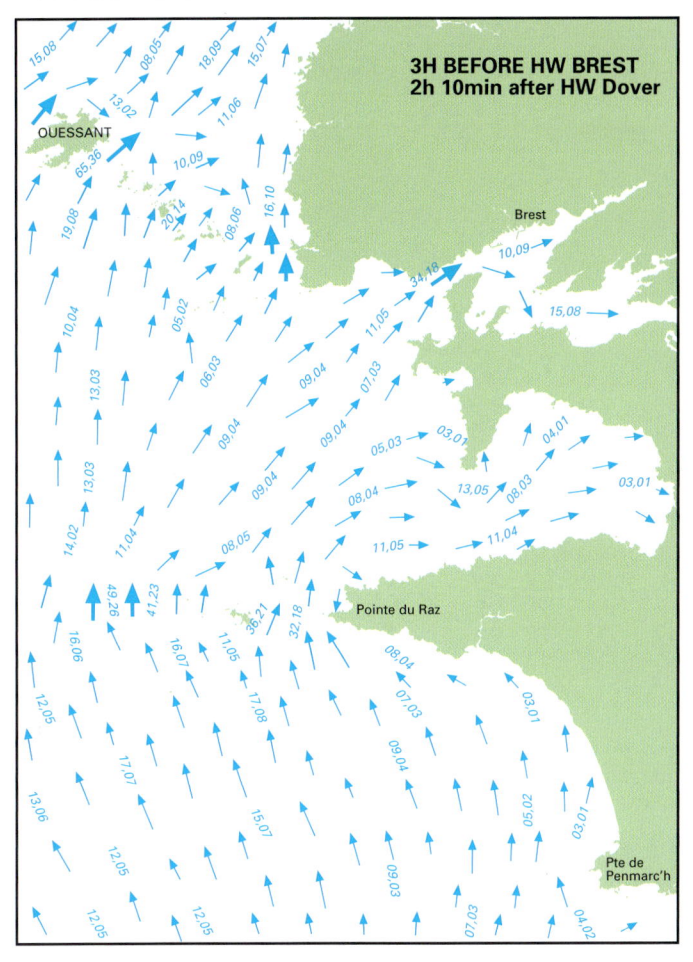

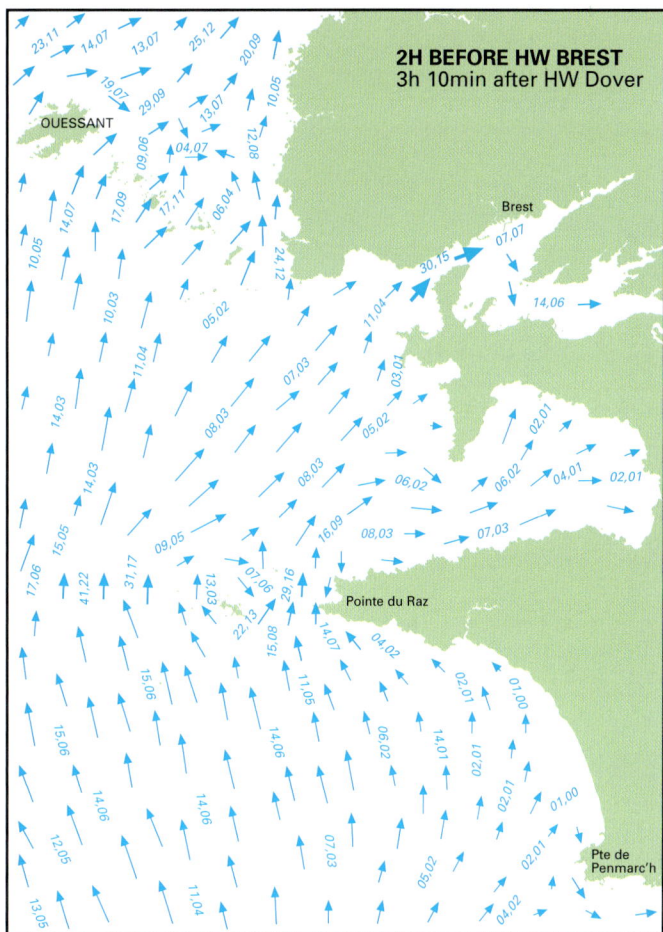

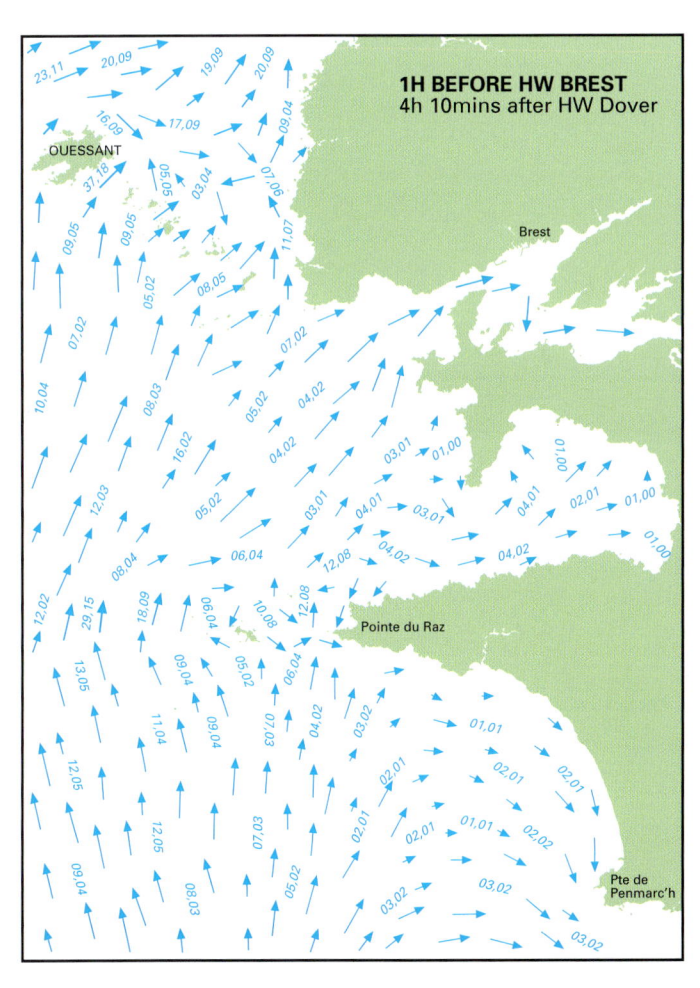

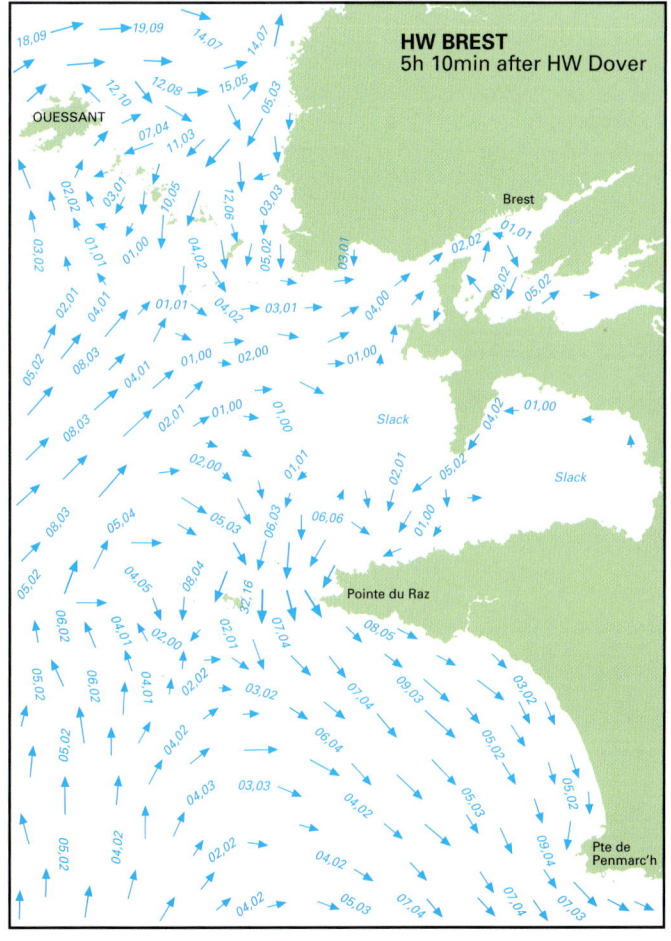

TIDAL STREAMS AND CURVES

429

TIDAL STREAMS AND CURVES

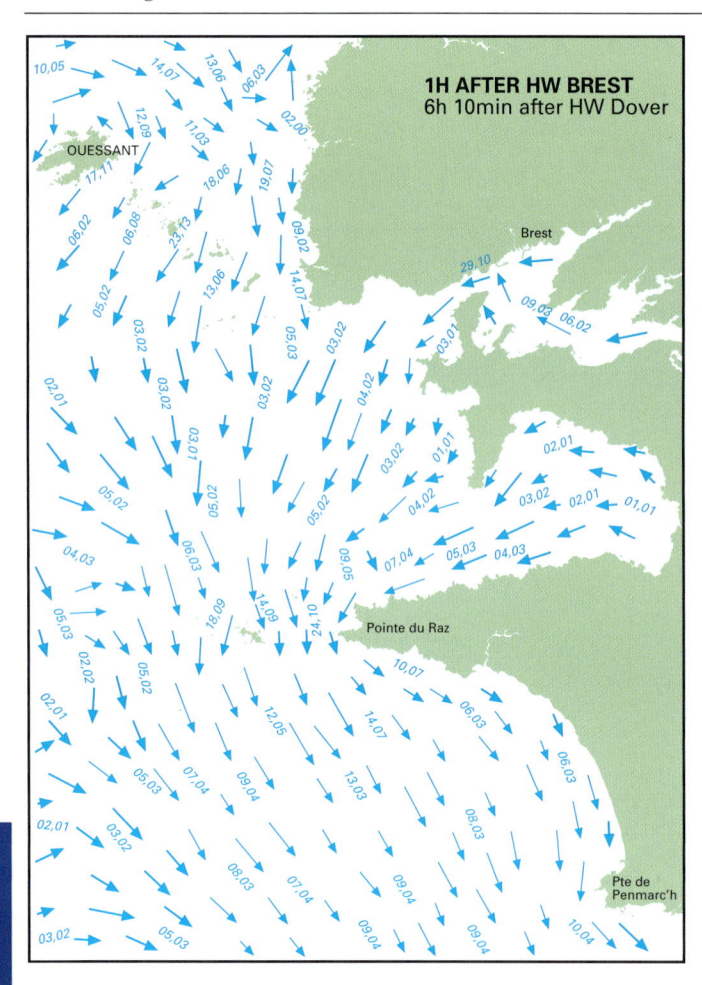

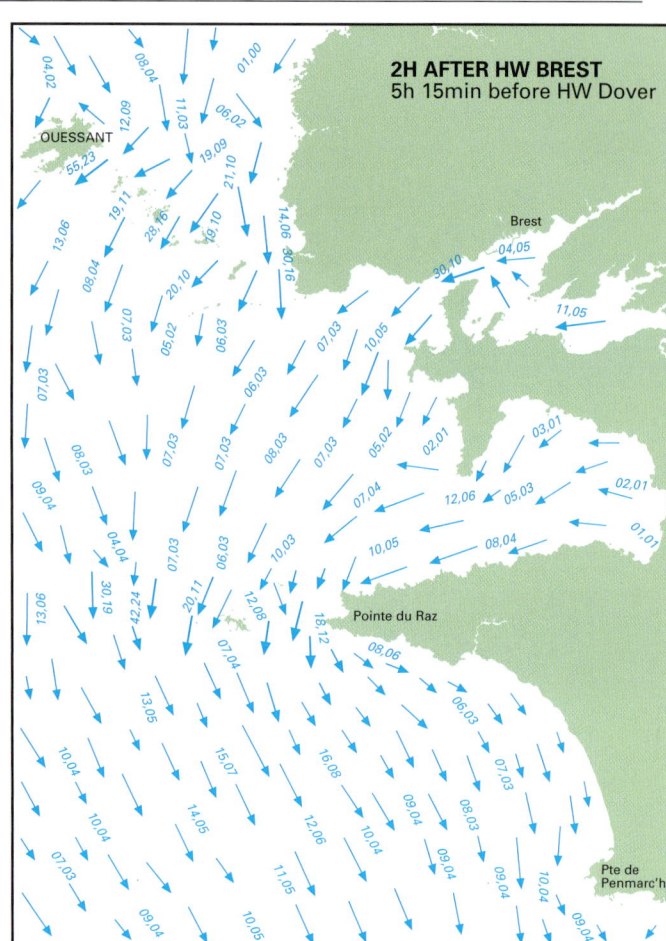

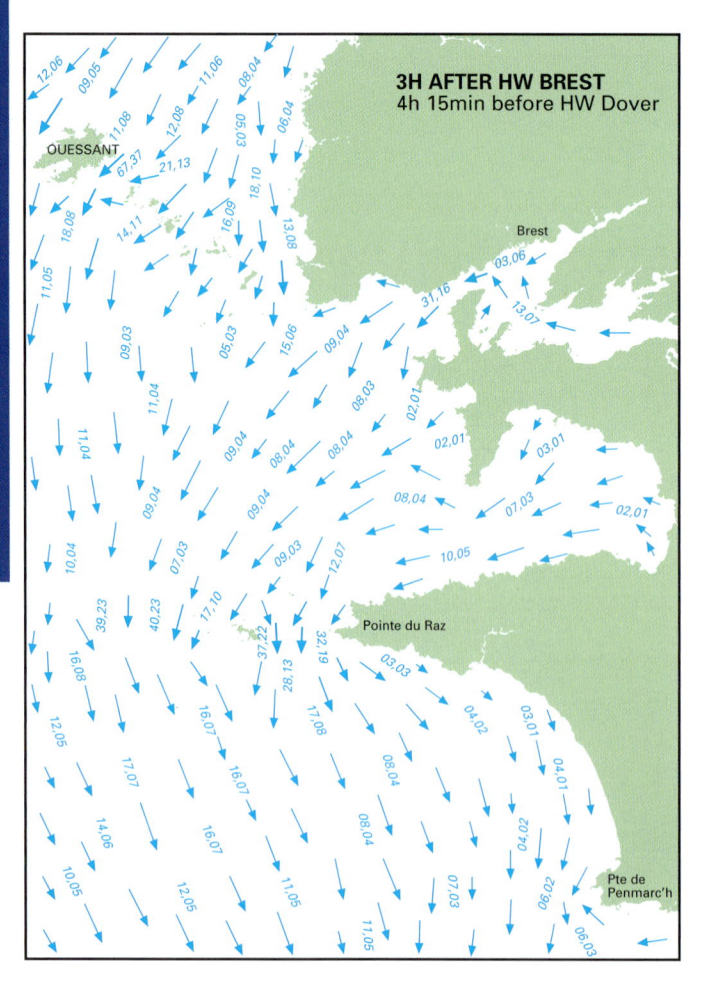

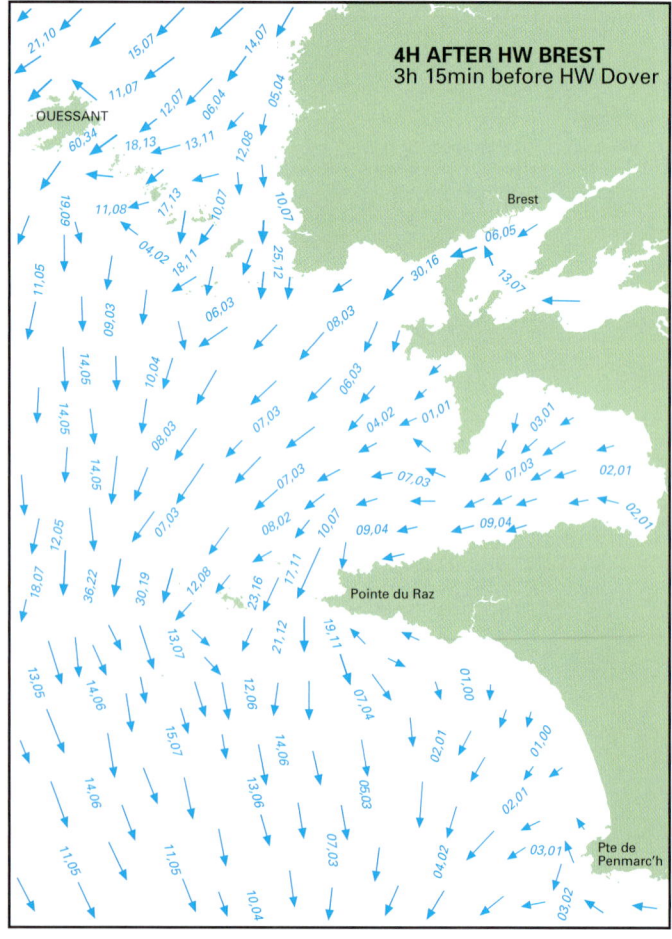

The Cruising Almanac

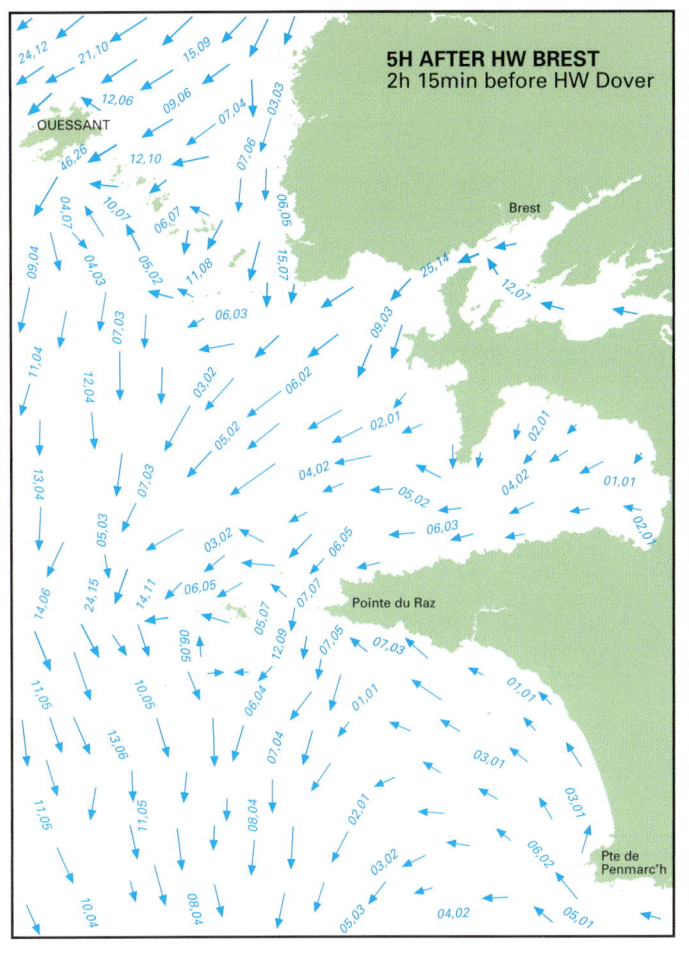

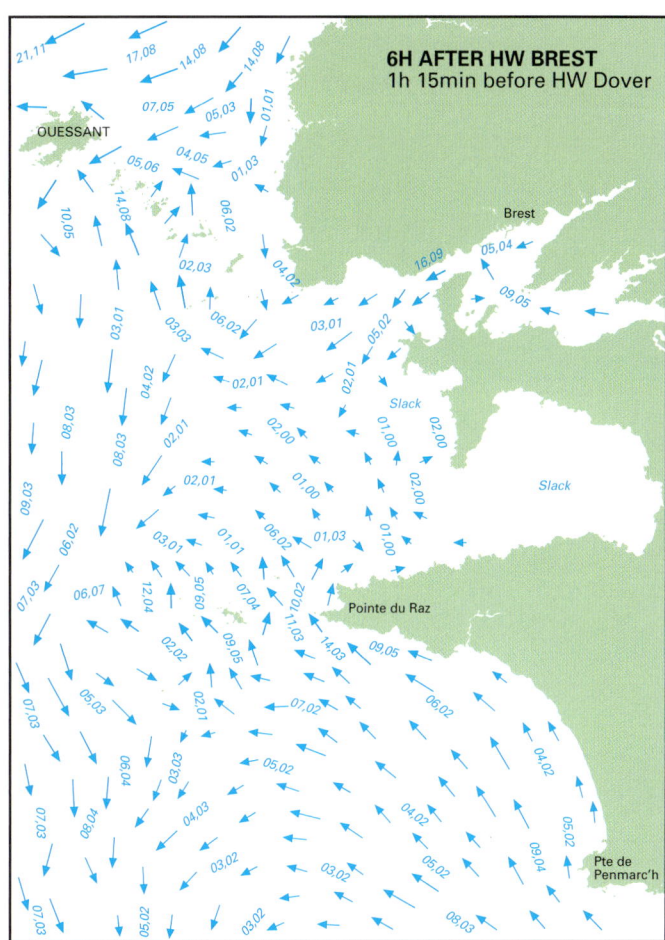

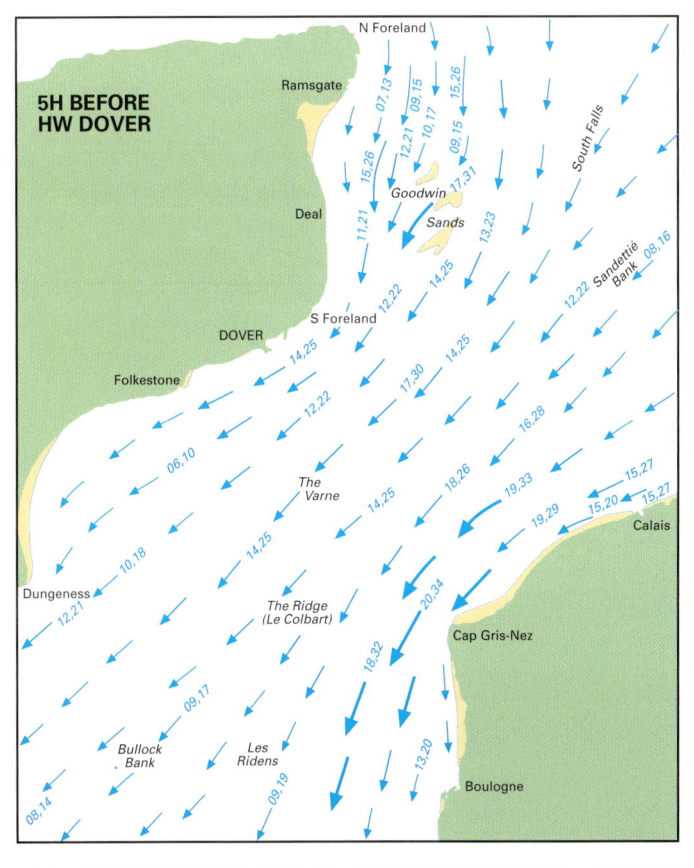

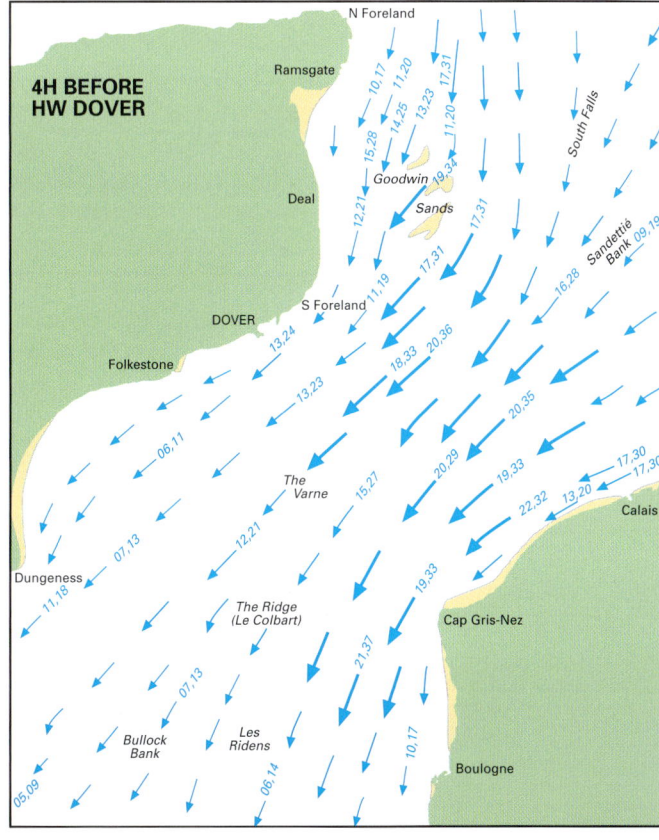

TIDAL STREAMS AND CURVES

431

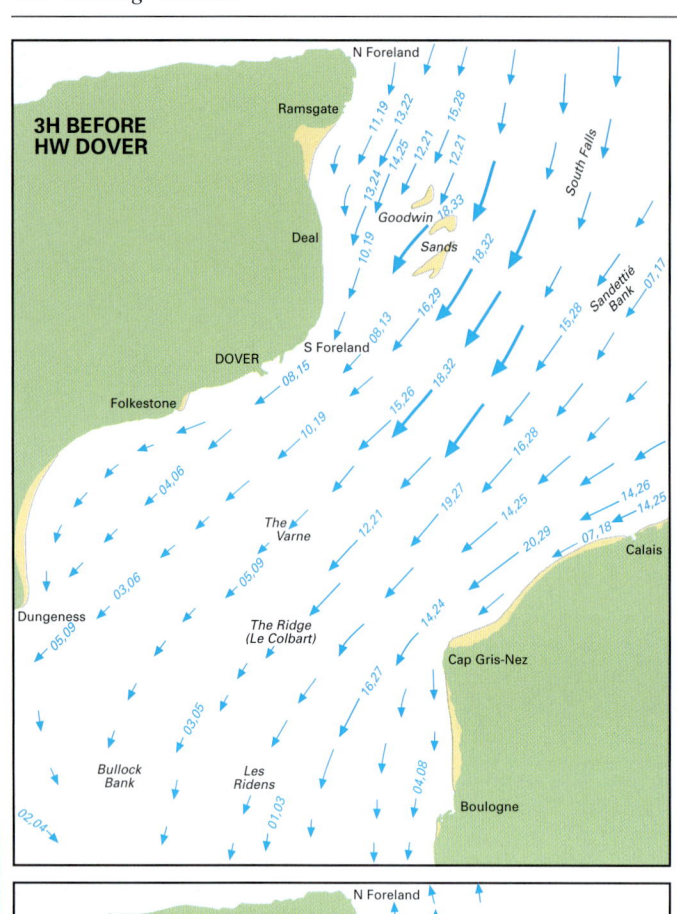

The Cruising Almanac

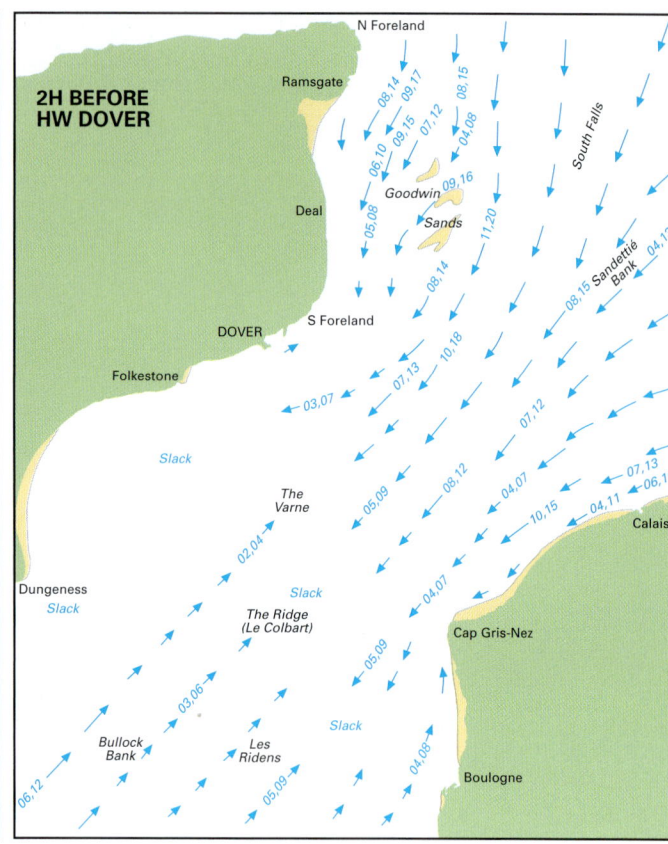

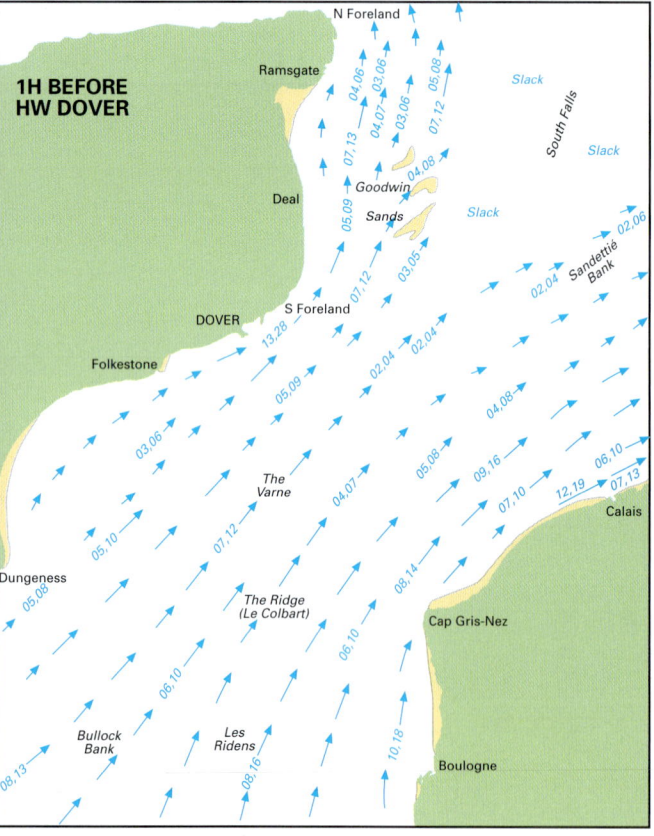

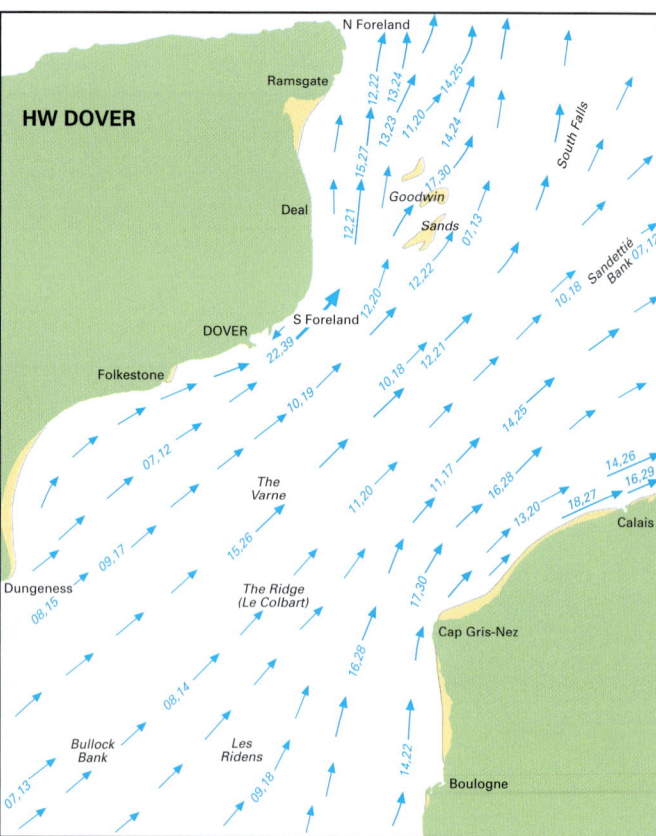

TIDAL STREAMS AND CURVES

3H BEFORE HW DOVER

2H BEFORE HW DOVER

1H BEFORE HW DOVER

HW DOVER

432

The Cruising Almanac

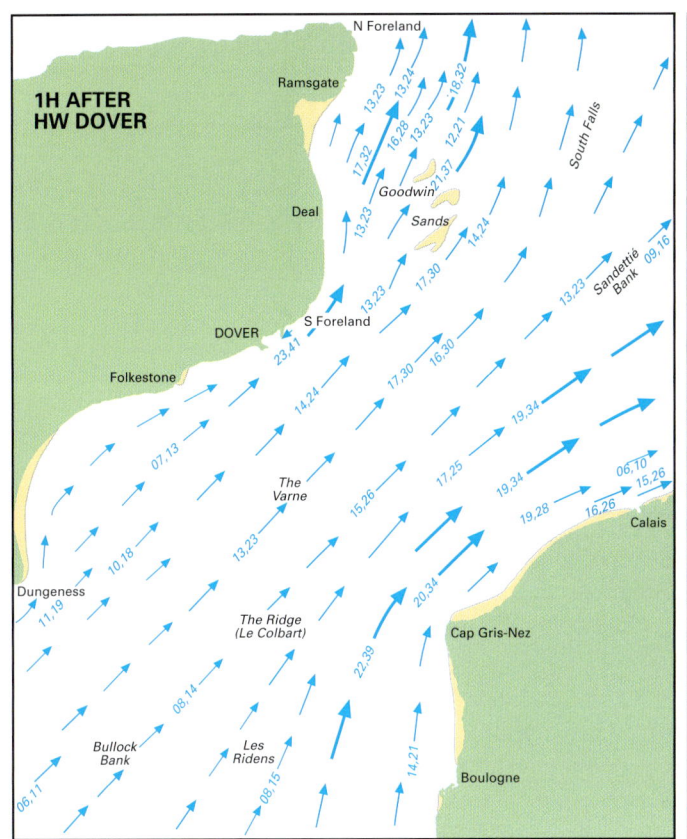

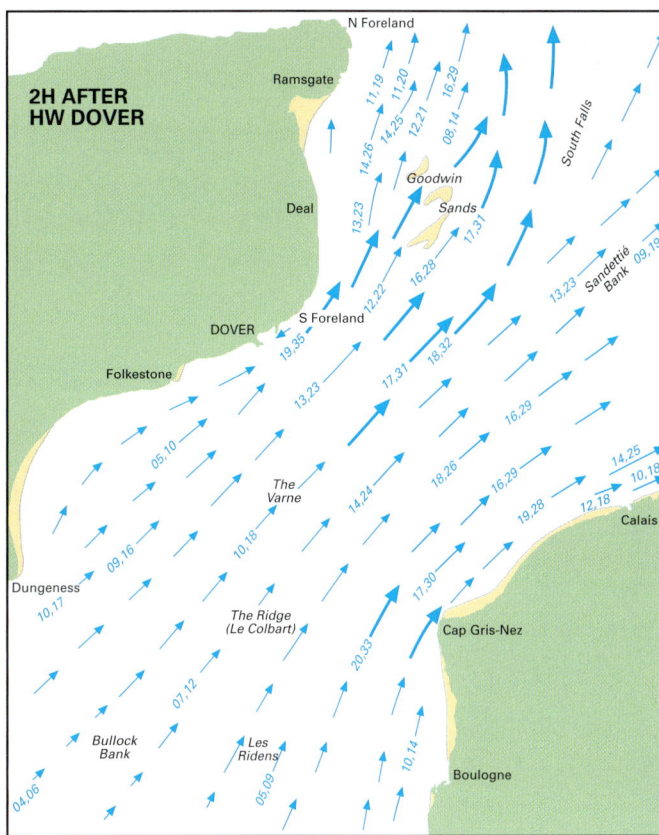

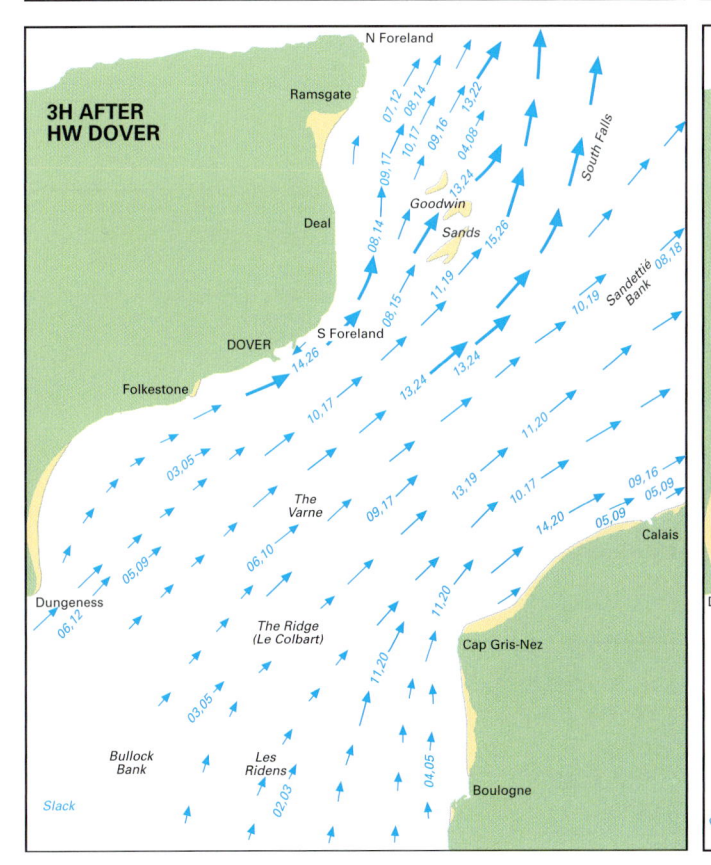

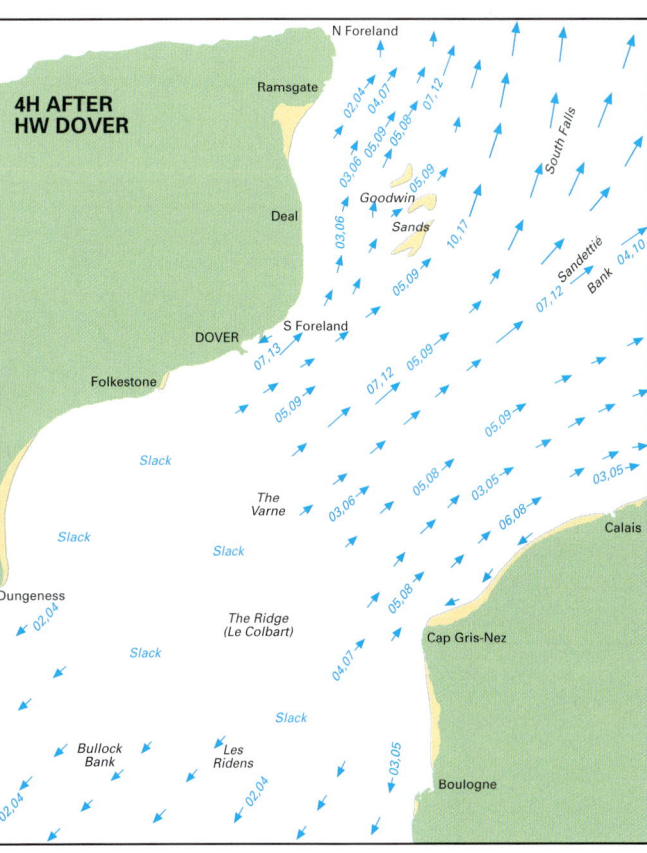

TIDAL STREAMS AND CURVES

The Cruising Almanac

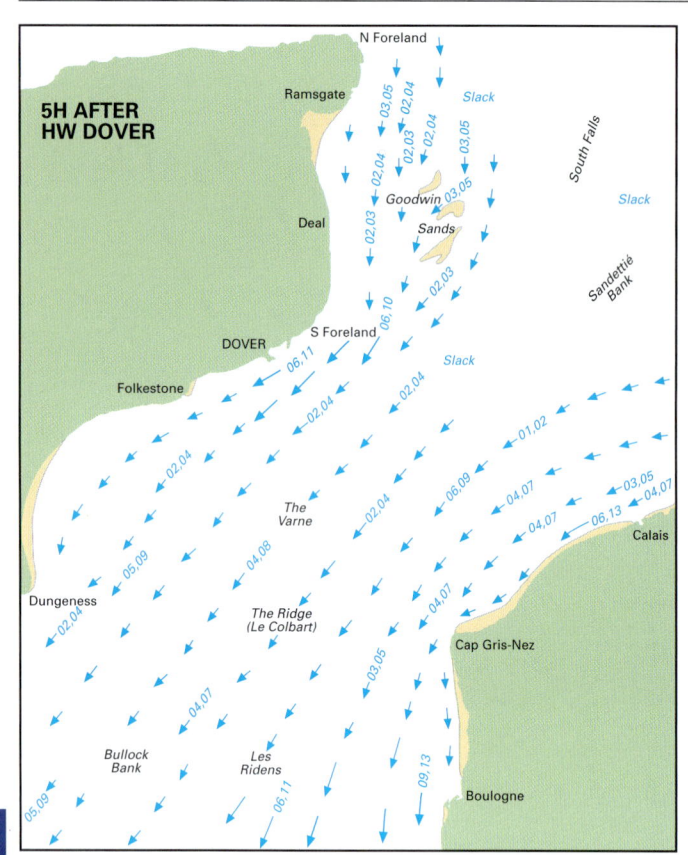

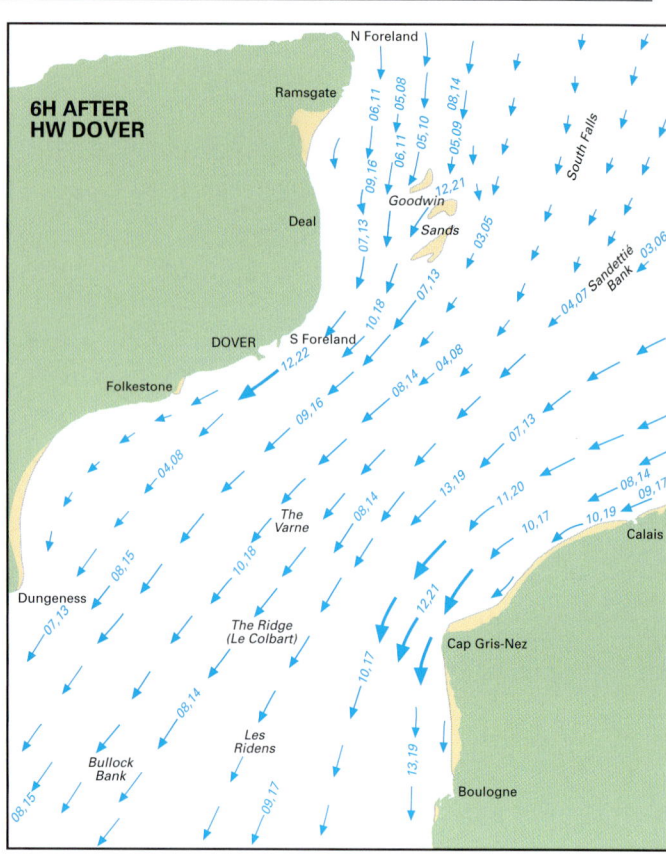

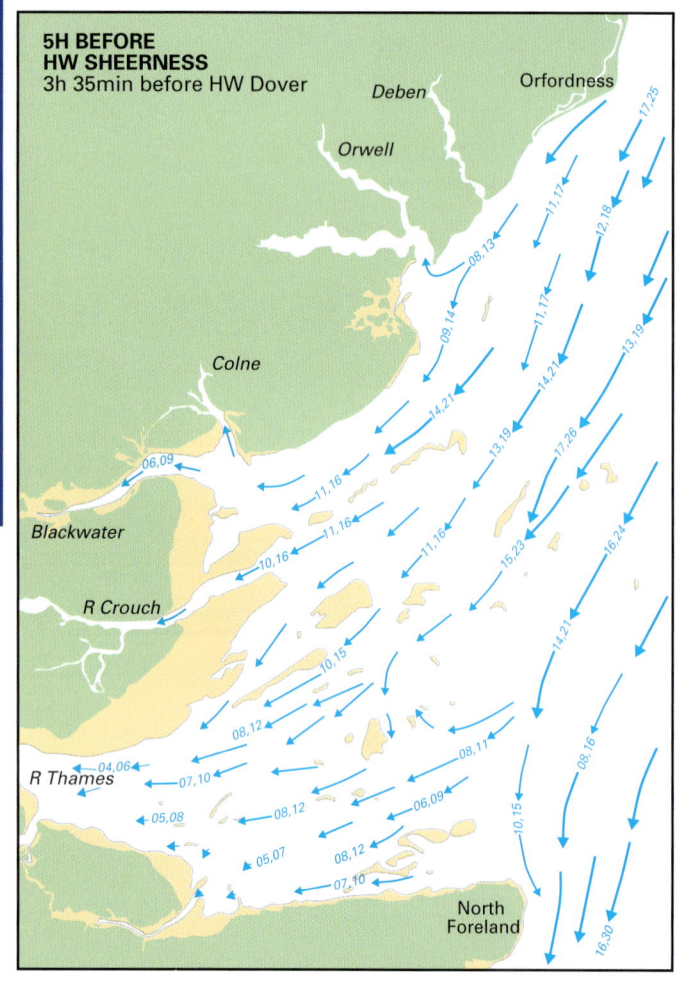

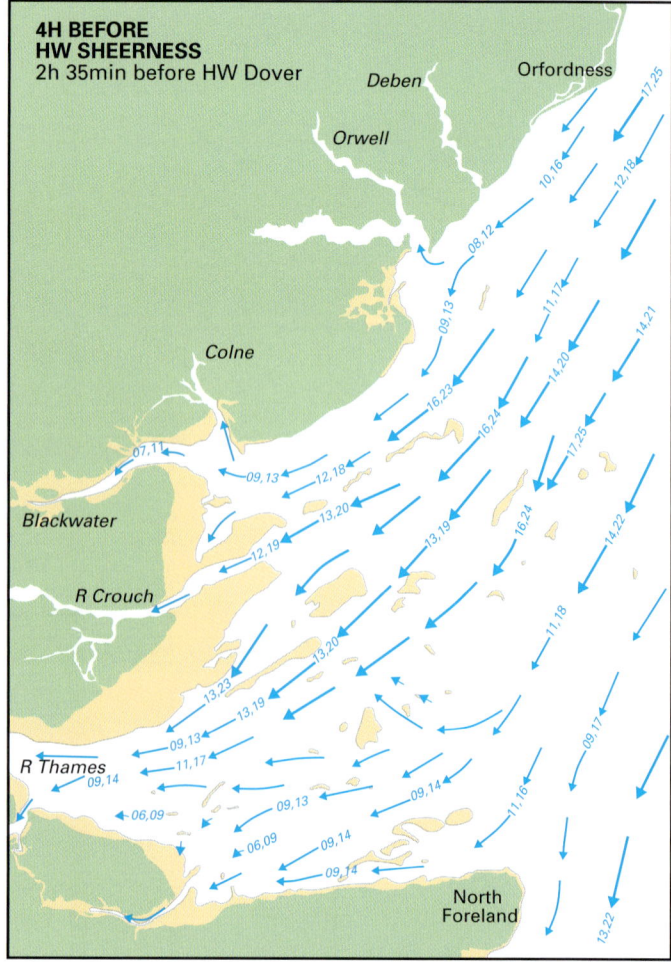

TIDAL STREAMS AND CURVES

434

The Cruising Almanac

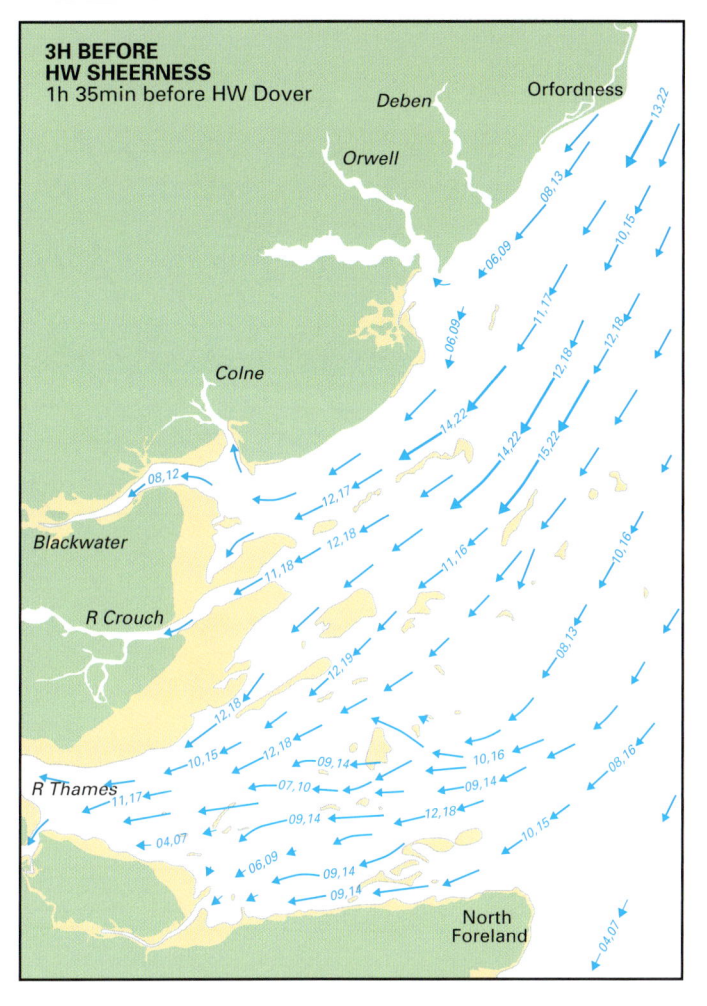

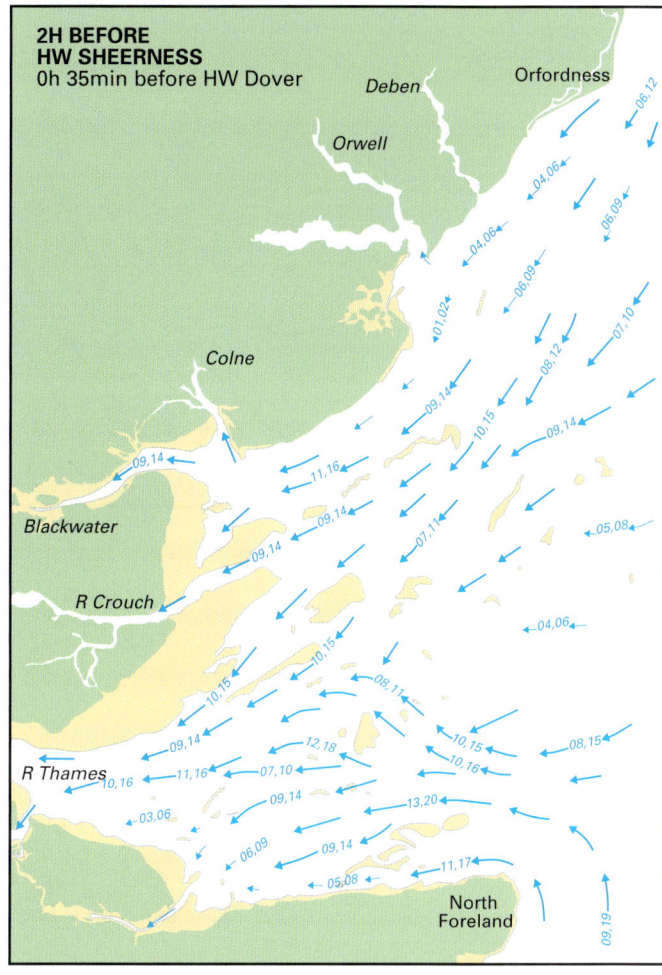

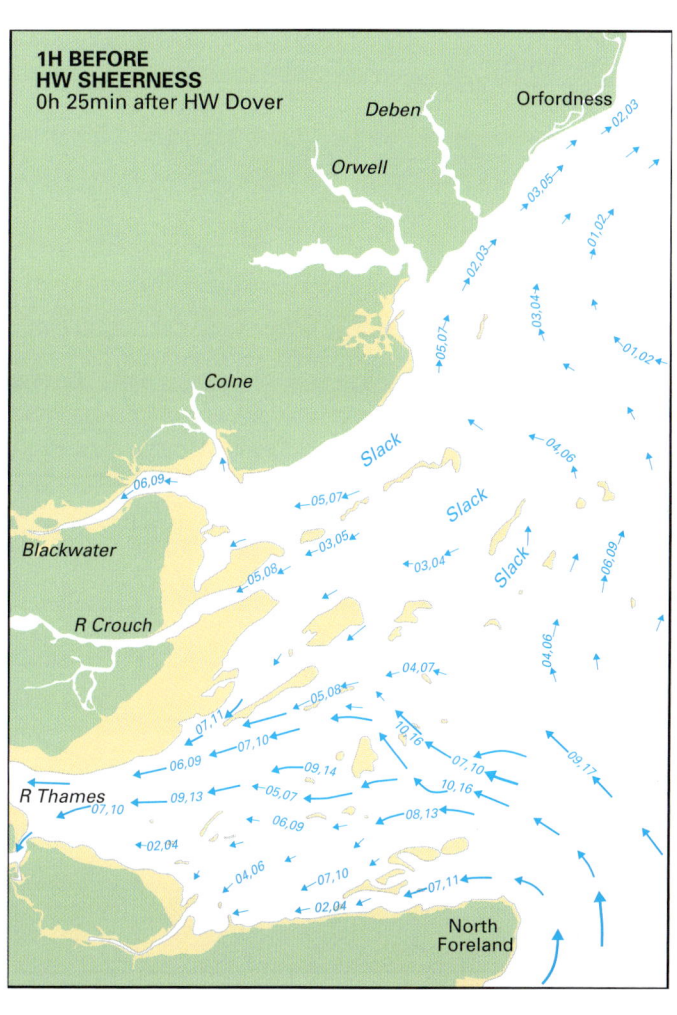

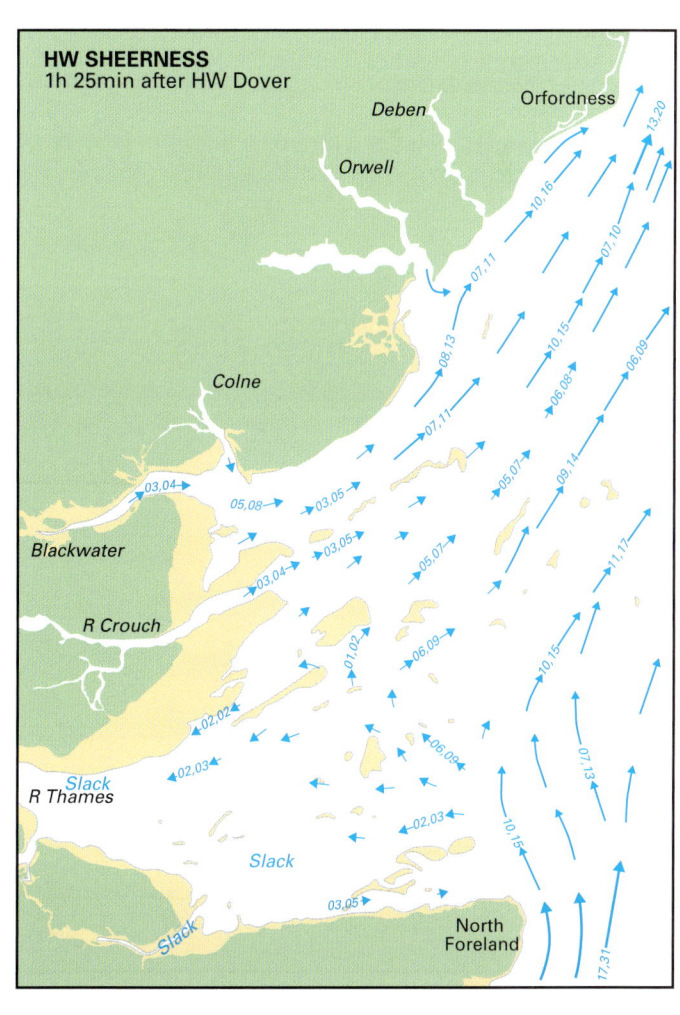

TIDAL STREAMS AND CURVES

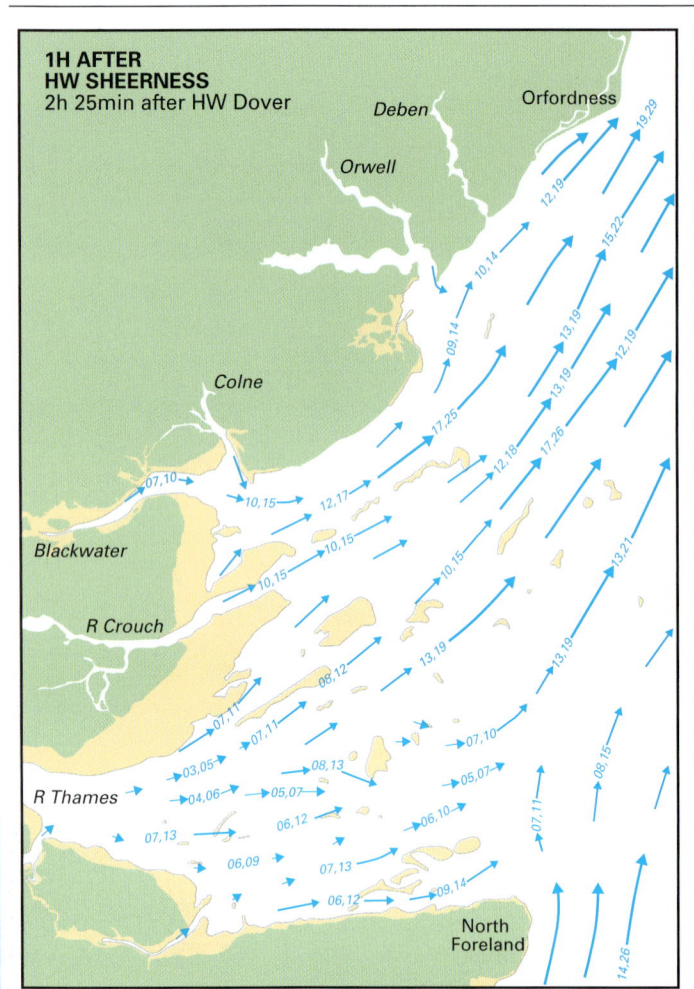

The Cruising Almanac

TIDAL STREAMS AND CURVES

1H AFTER HW SHEERNESS — 2h 25min after HW Dover

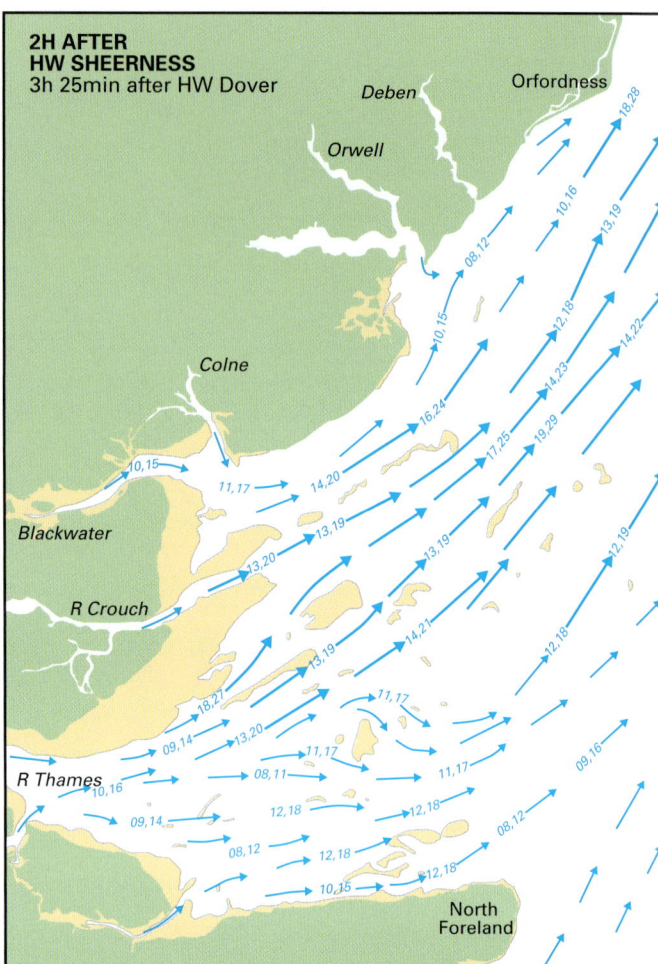

2H AFTER HW SHEERNESS — 3h 25min after HW Dover

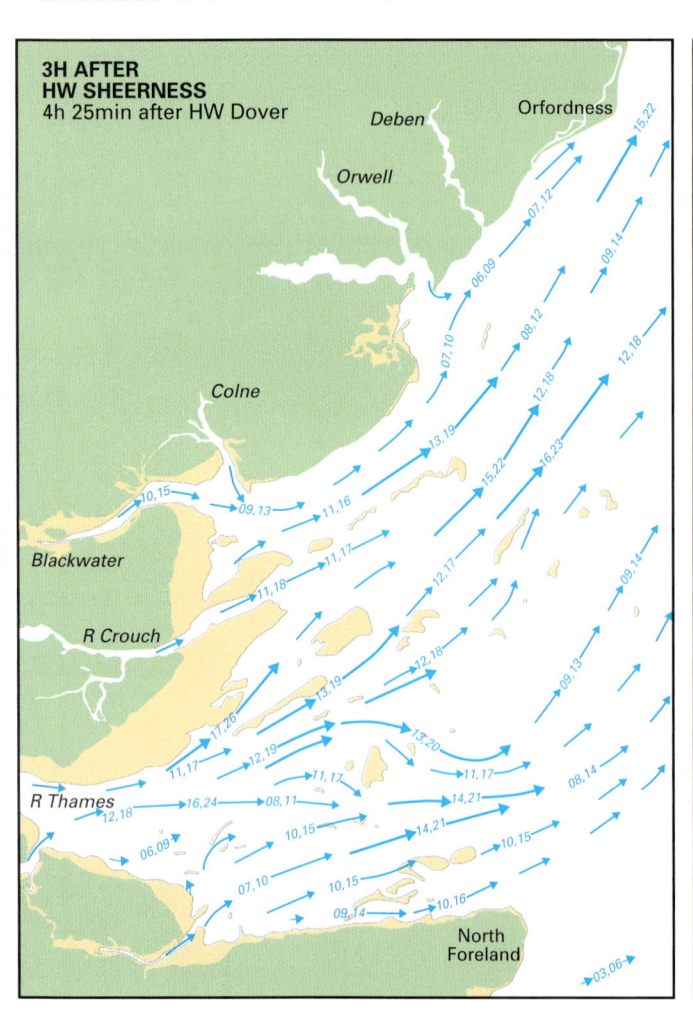

3H AFTER HW SHEERNESS — 4h 25min after HW Dover

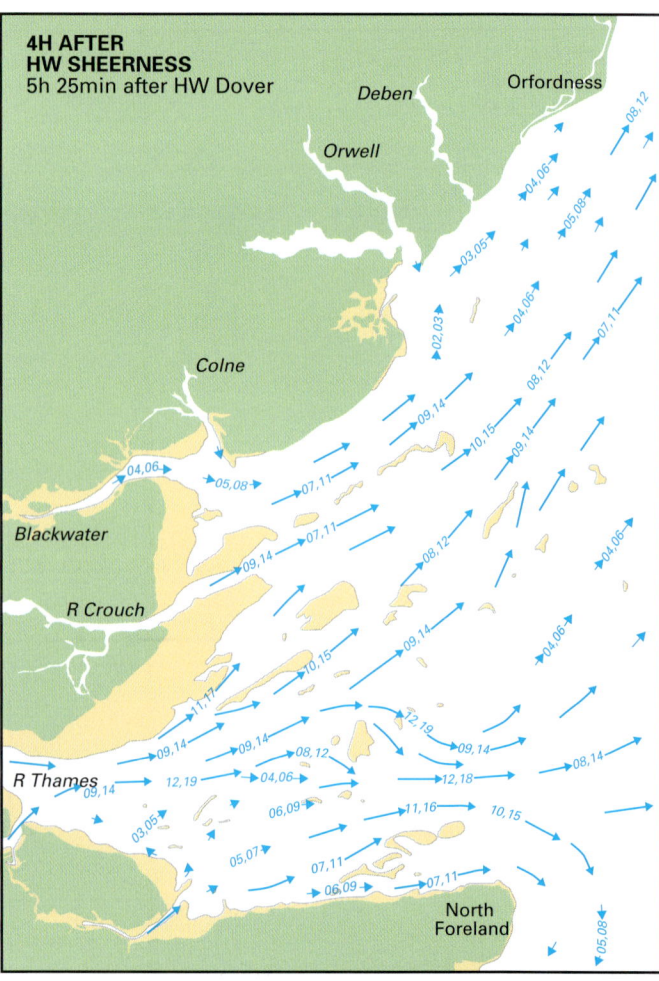

4H AFTER HW SHEERNESS — 5h 25min after HW Dover

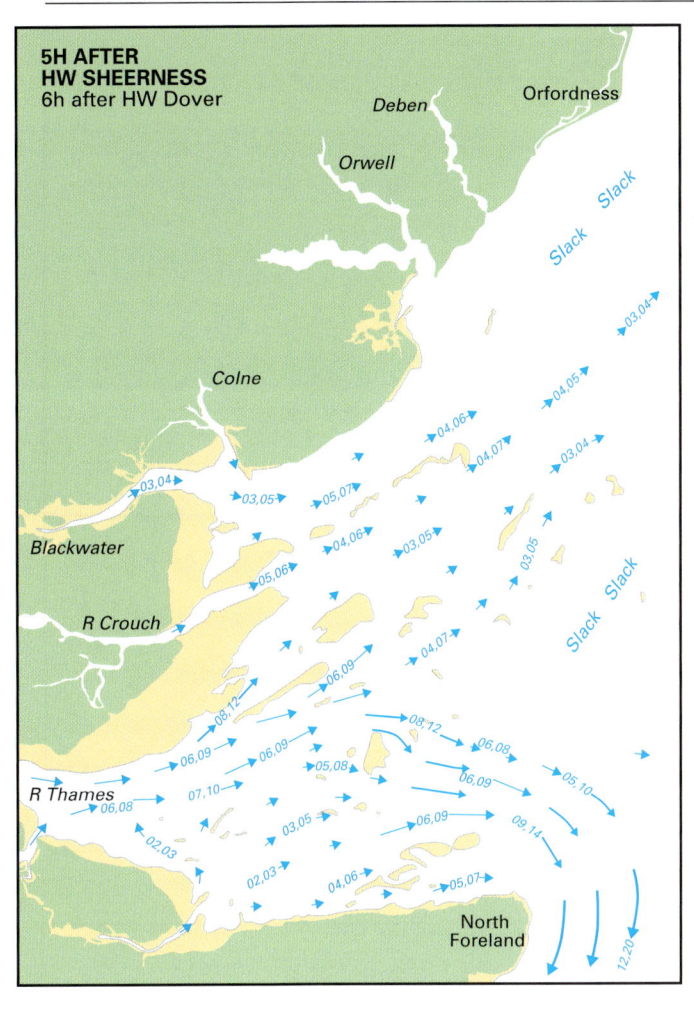

TIDAL STREAMS AND CURVES

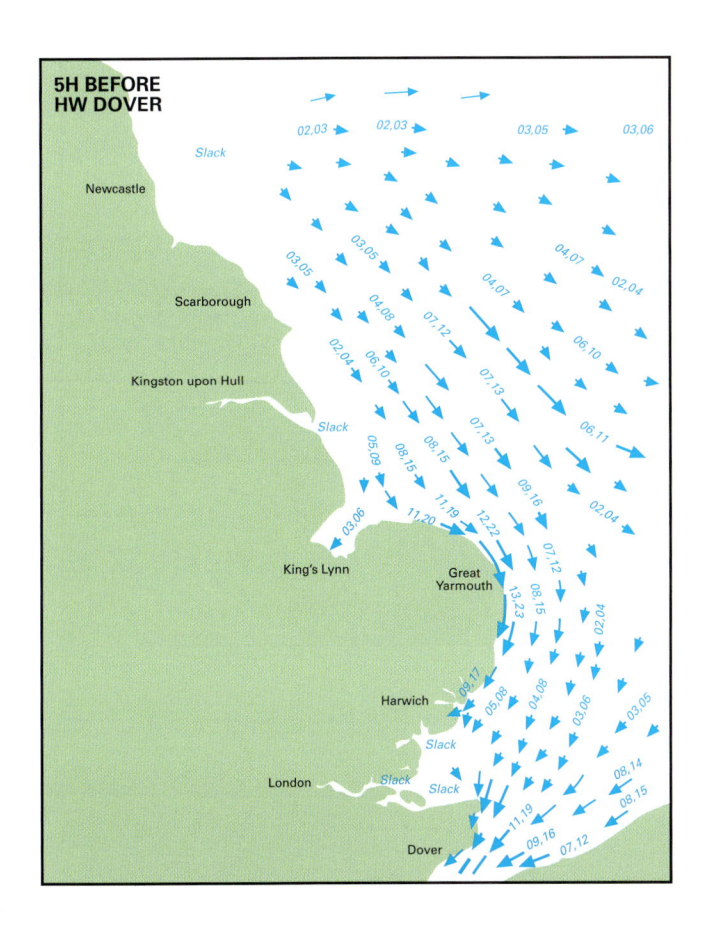

The Cruising Almanac

5H AFTER HW SHEERNESS
6h after HW Dover

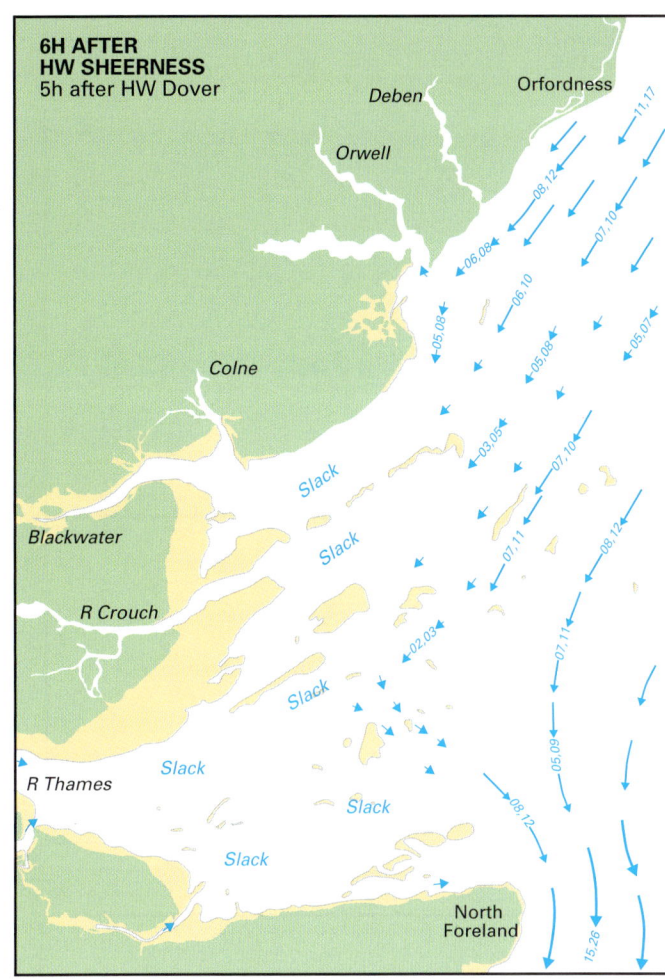

6H AFTER HW SHEERNESS
5h after HW Dover

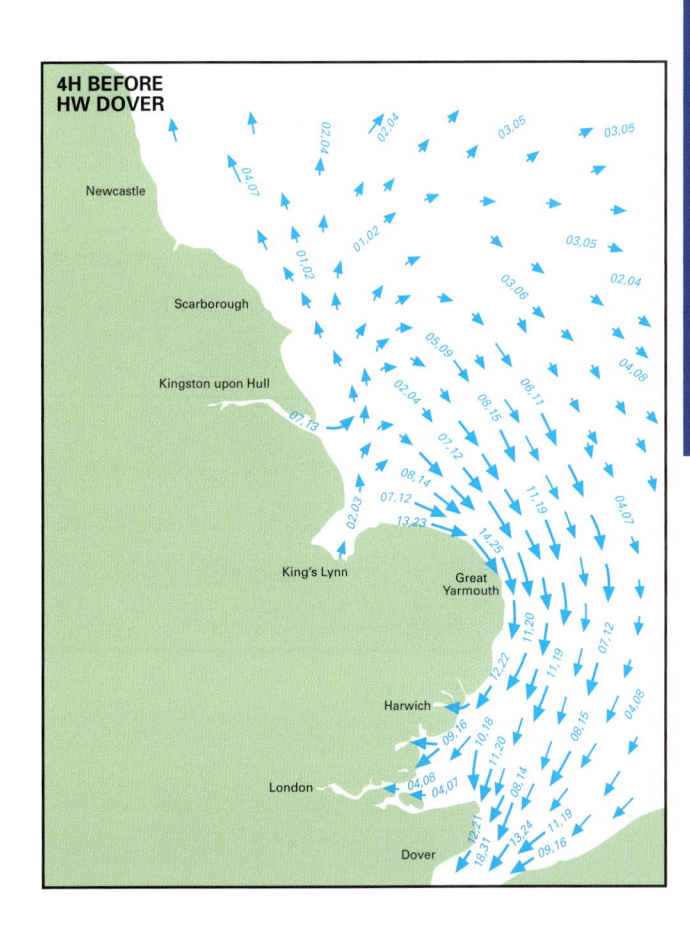

5H BEFORE HW DOVER

4H BEFORE HW DOVER

437

The Cruising Almanac

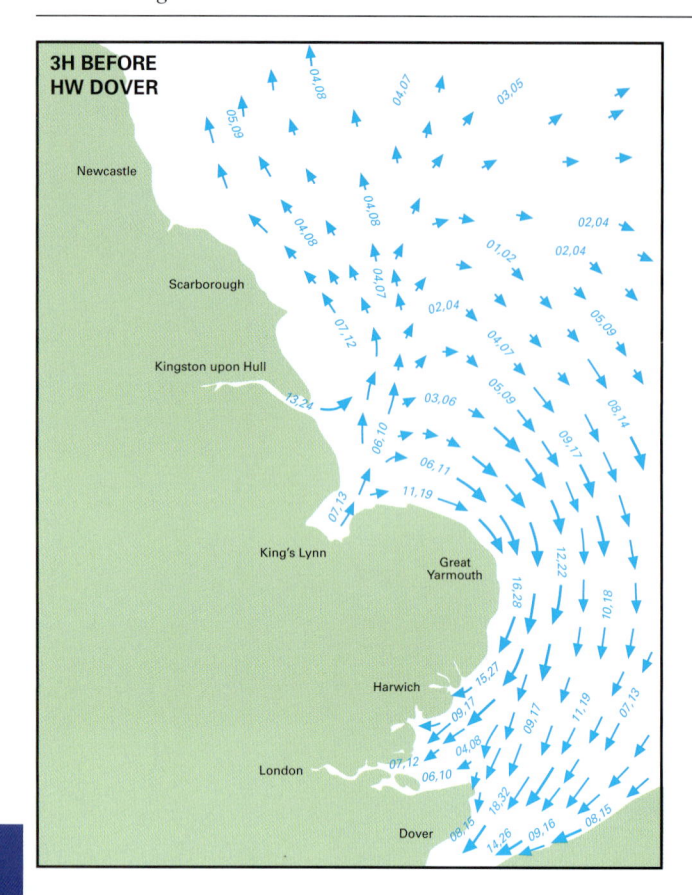

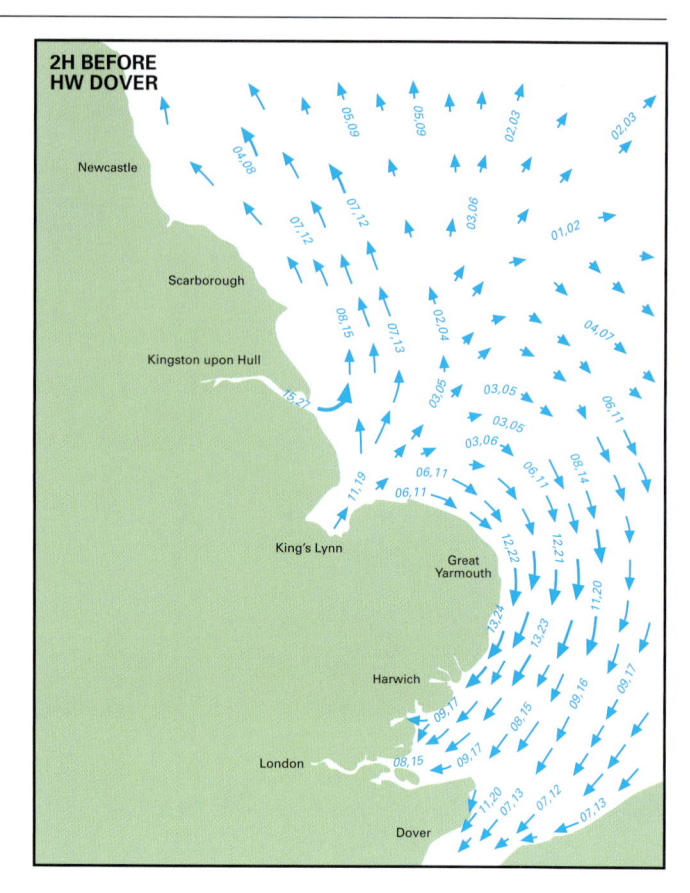

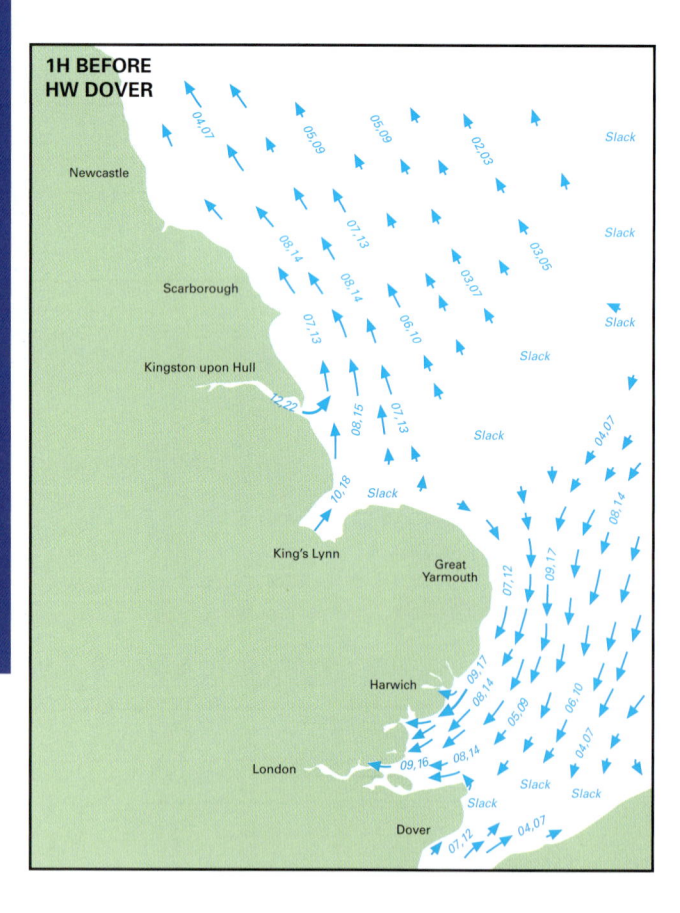

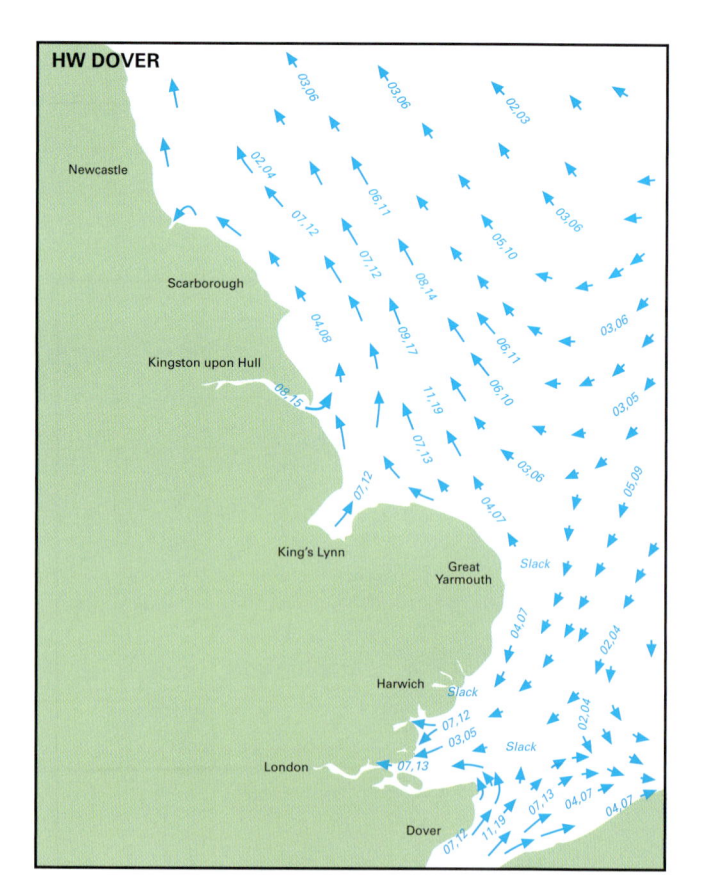

TIDAL STREAMS AND CURVES

438

The Cruising Almanac

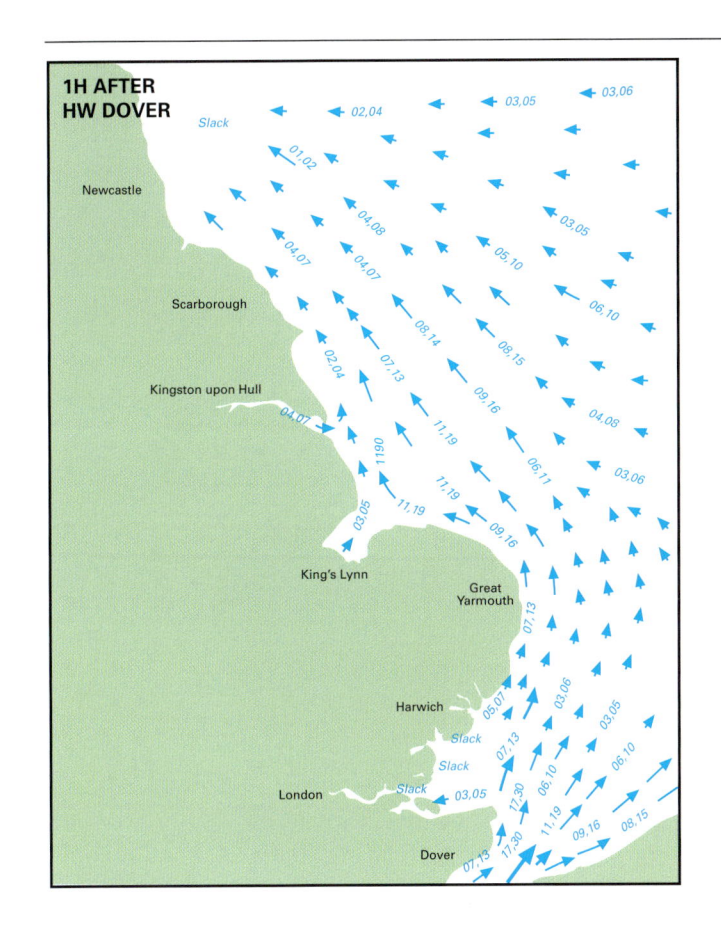

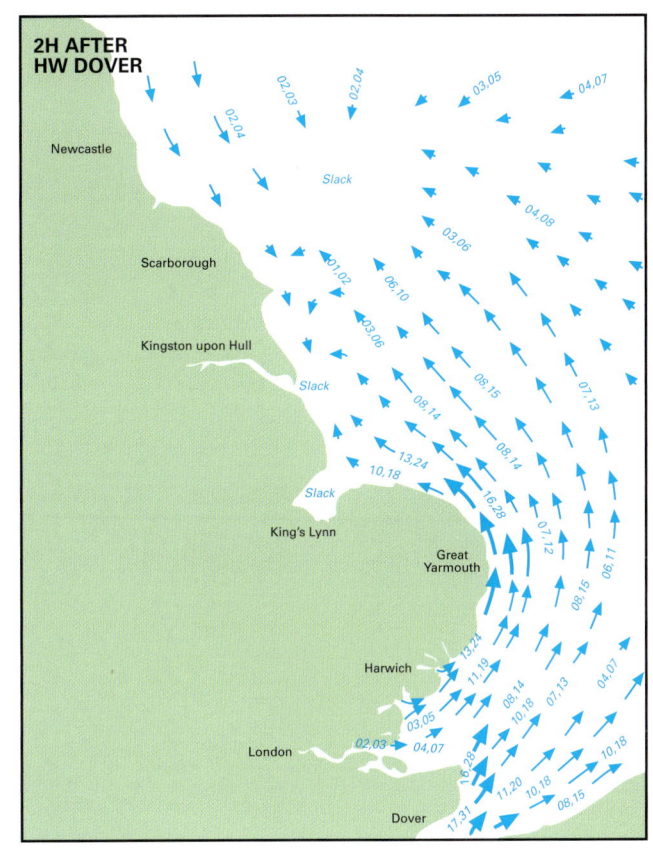

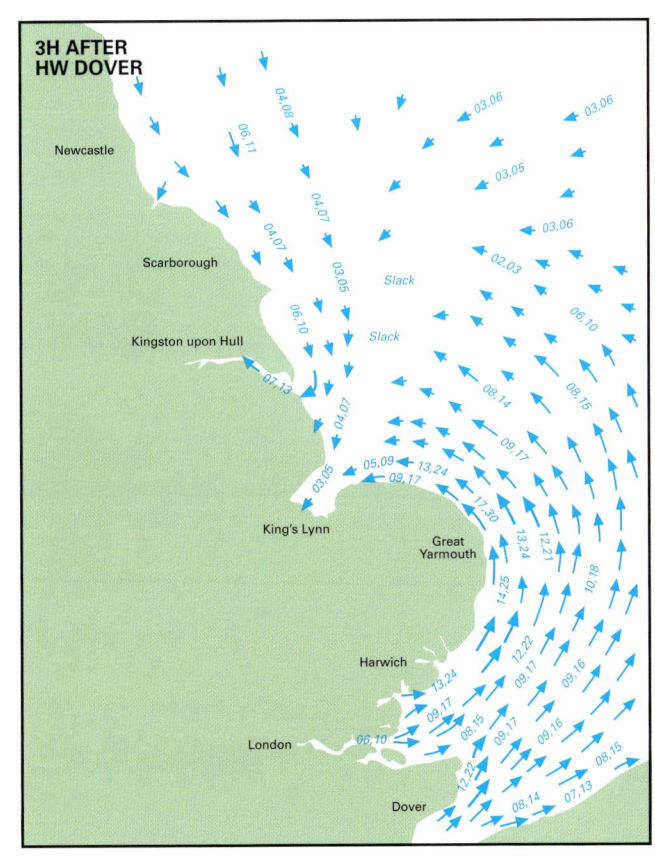

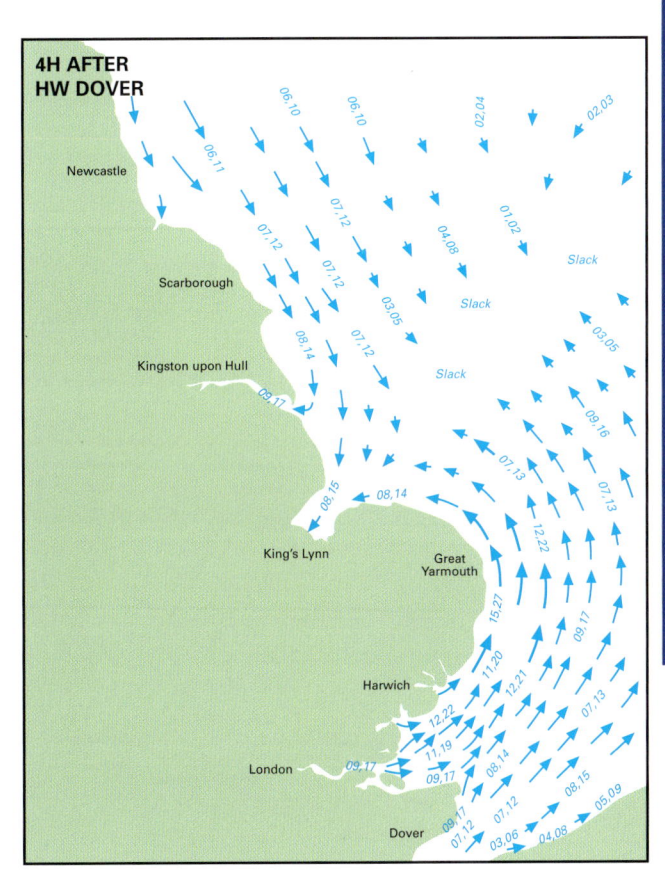

TIDAL STREAMS AND CURVES

439

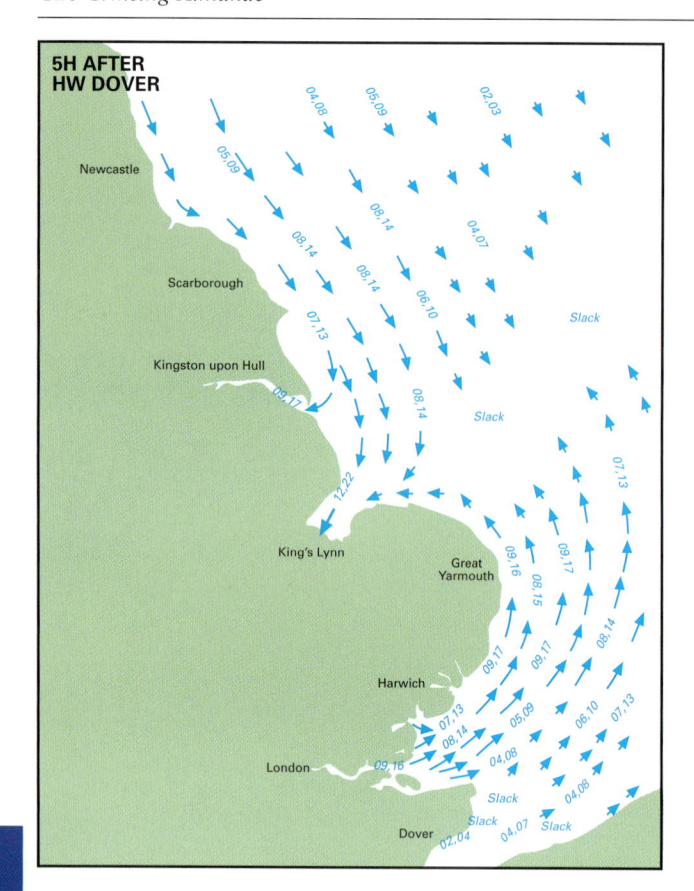

TIDAL STREAMS AND CURVES

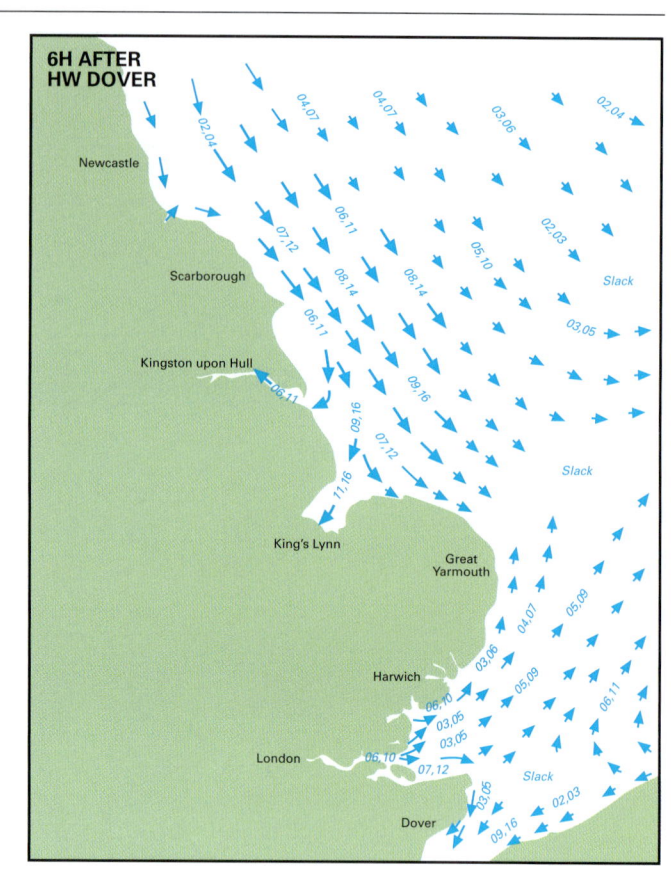

5H AFTER HW DOVER

6H AFTER HW DOVER

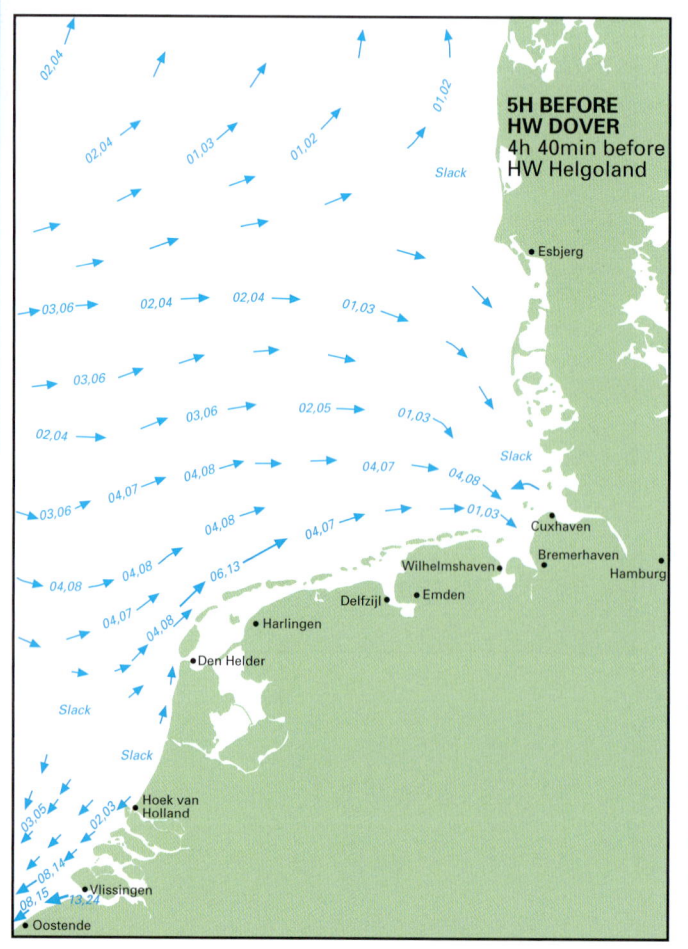

5H BEFORE HW DOVER
4h 40min before HW Helgoland

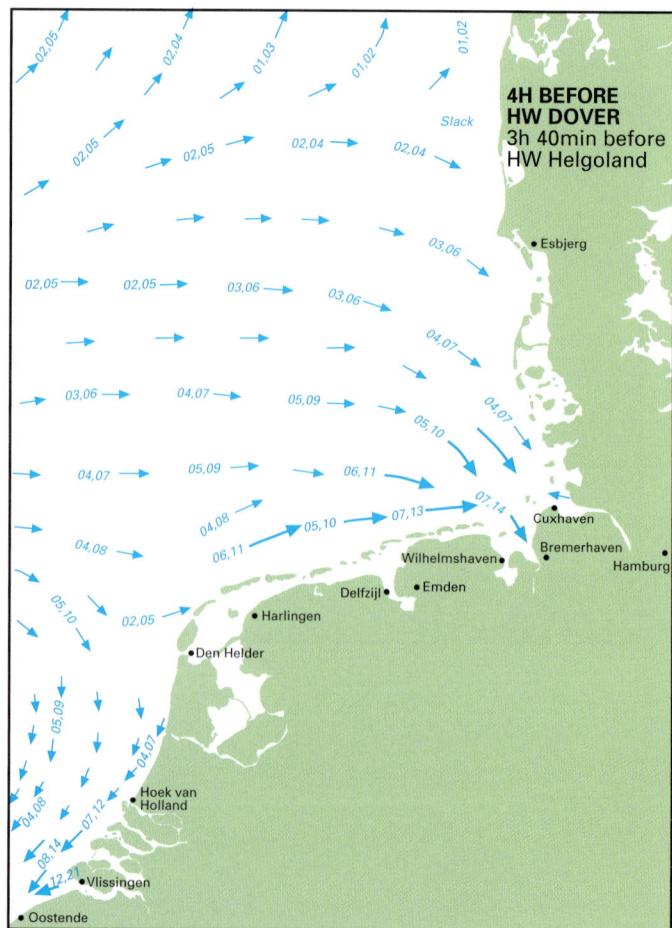

4H BEFORE HW DOVER
3h 40min before HW Helgoland

The Cruising Almanac

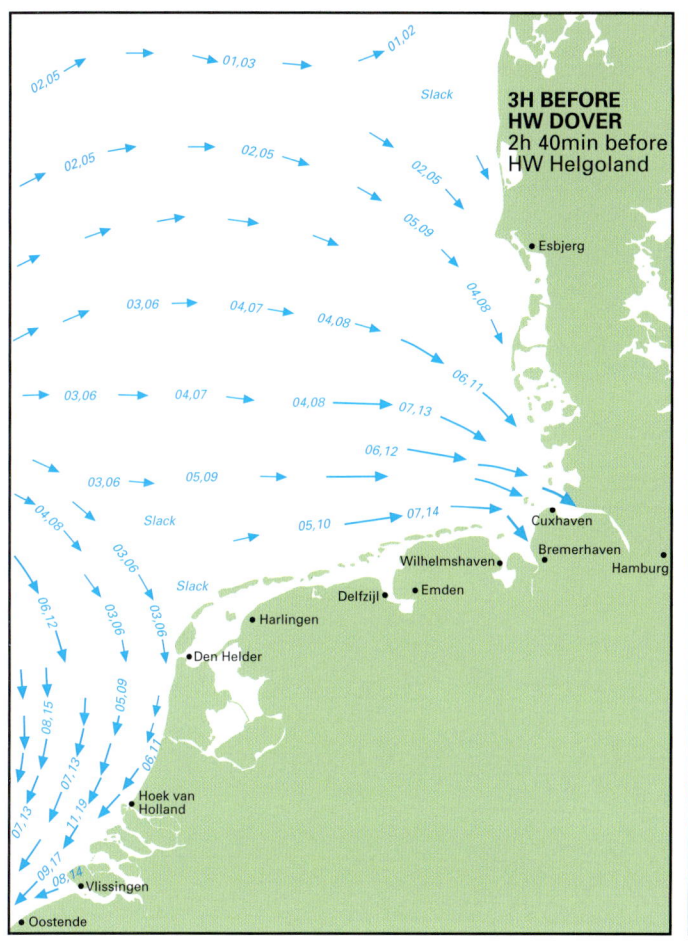

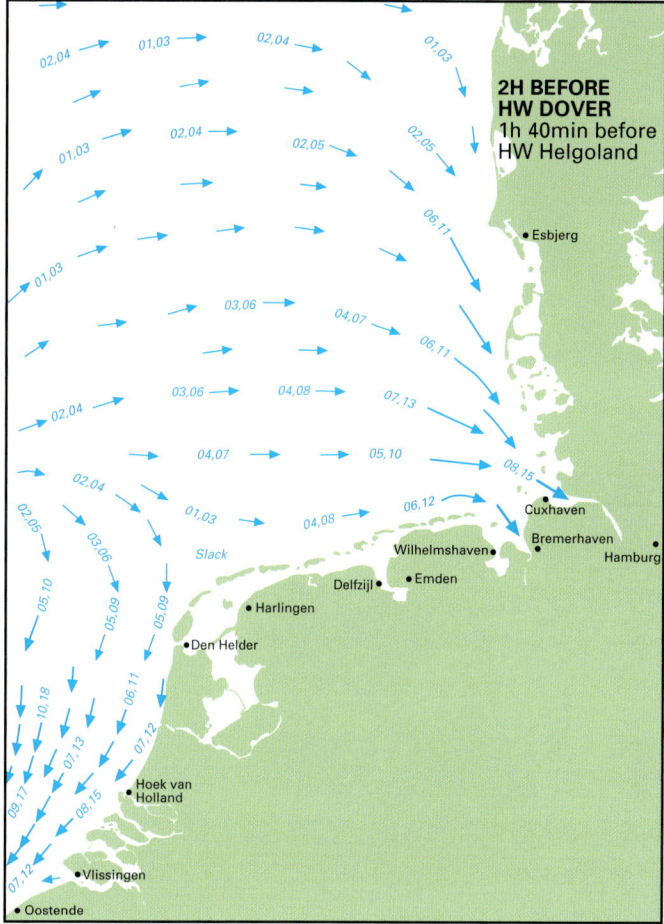

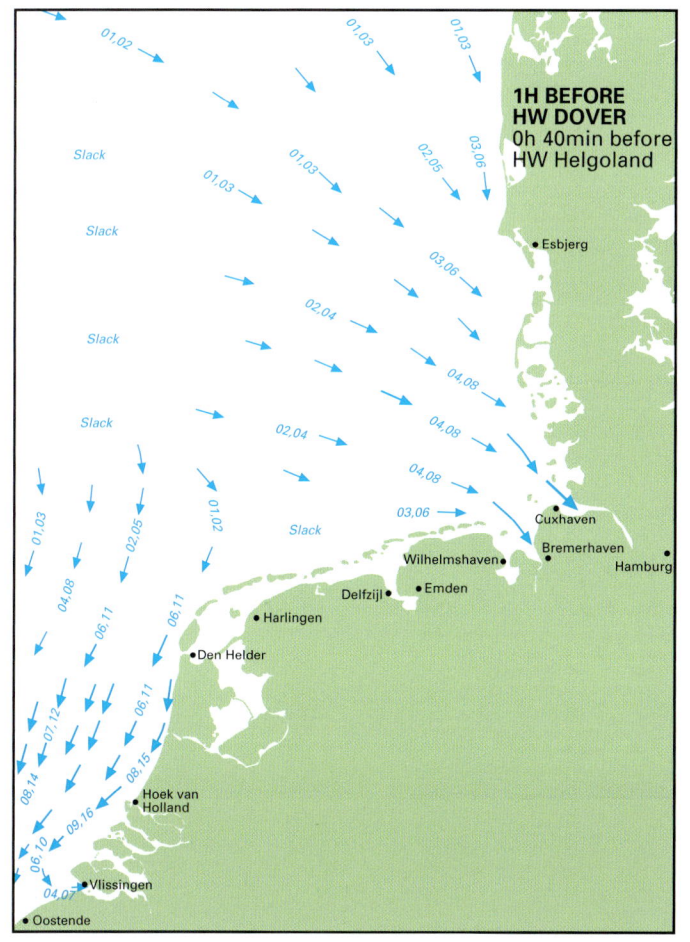

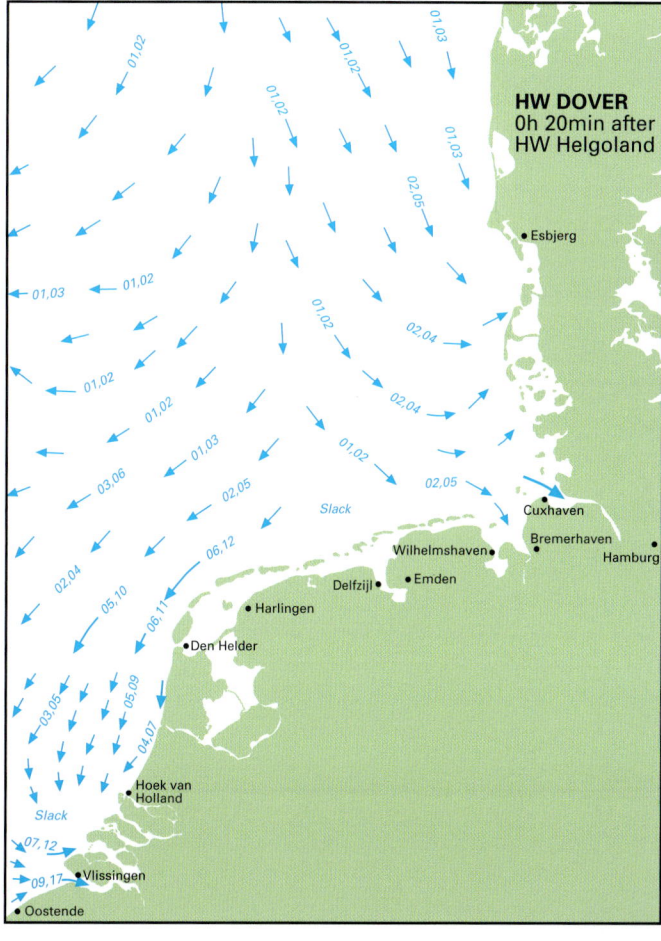

TIDAL STREAMS AND CURVES

441

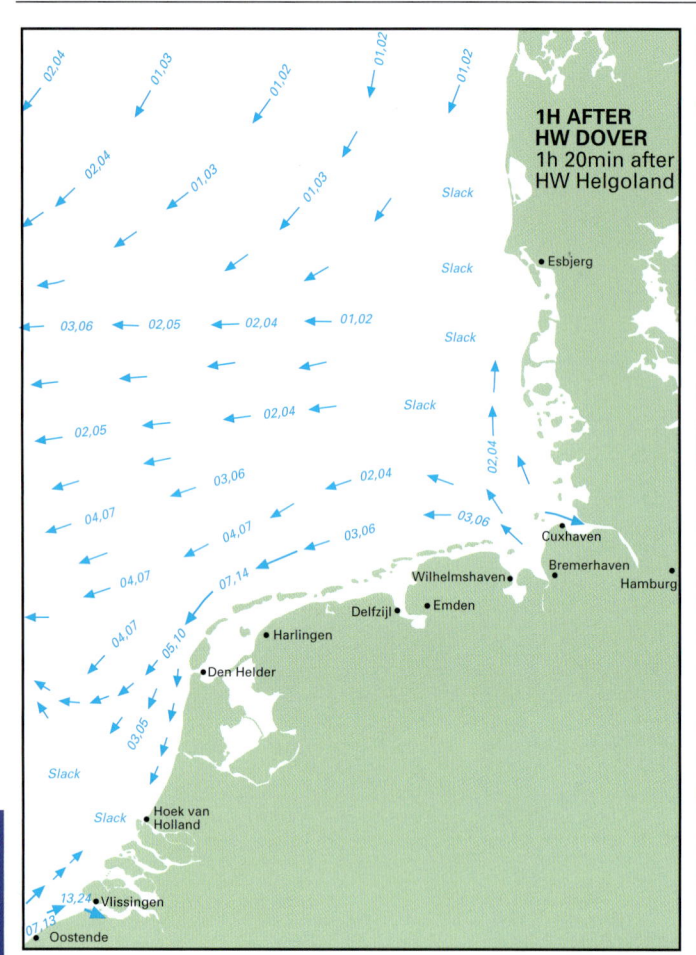

The Cruising Almanac

TIDAL STREAMS AND CURVES

1H AFTER HW DOVER — 1h 20min after HW Helgoland

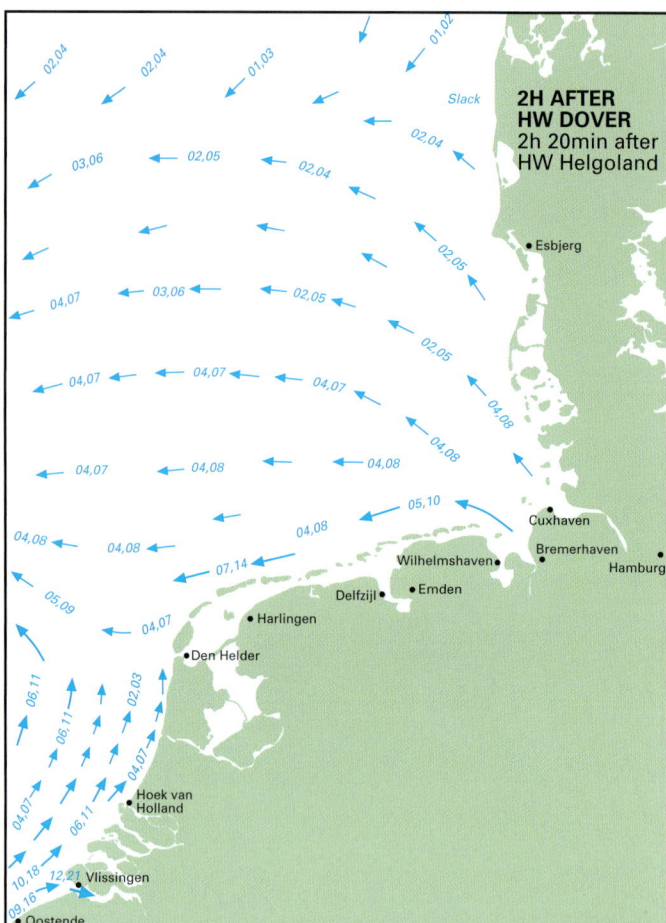

2H AFTER HW DOVER — 2h 20min after HW Helgoland

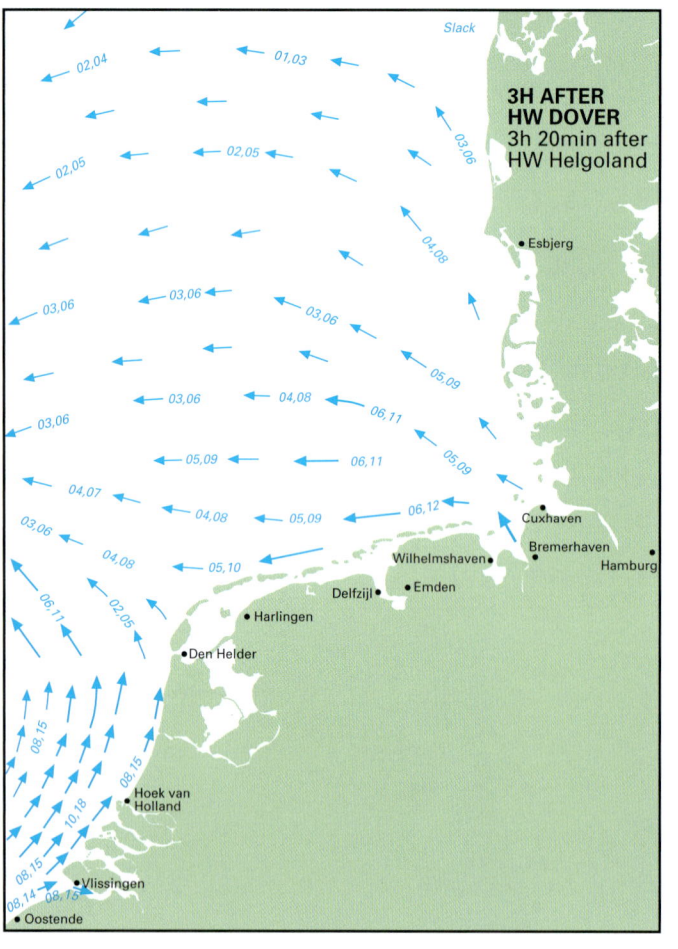

3H AFTER HW DOVER — 3h 20min after HW Helgoland

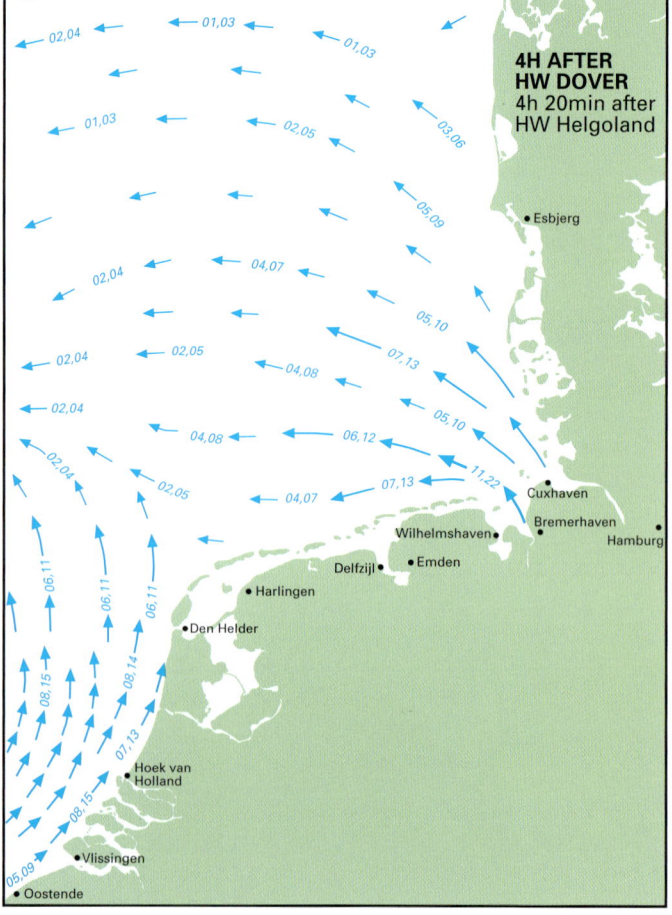

4H AFTER HW DOVER — 4h 20min after HW Helgoland

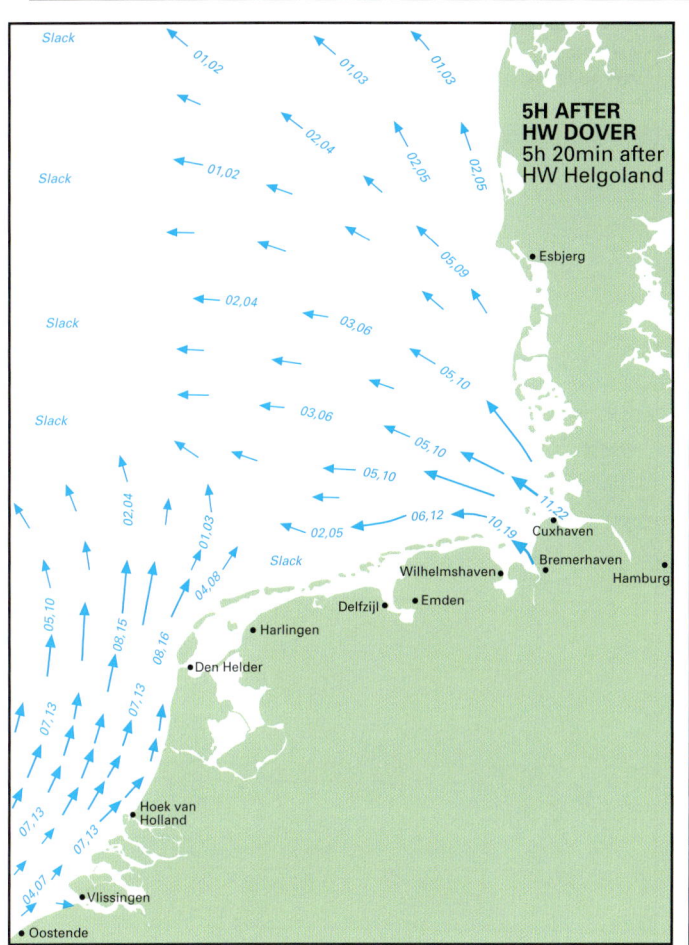

The Cruising Almanac

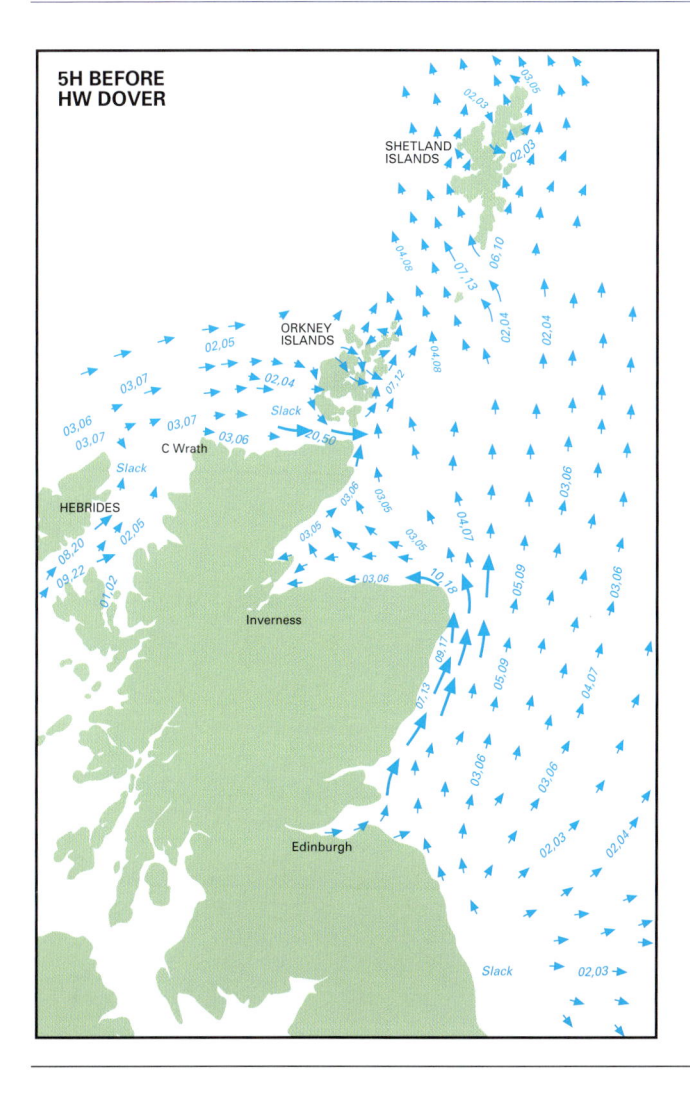

5H AFTER HW DOVER
5h 20min after HW Helgoland

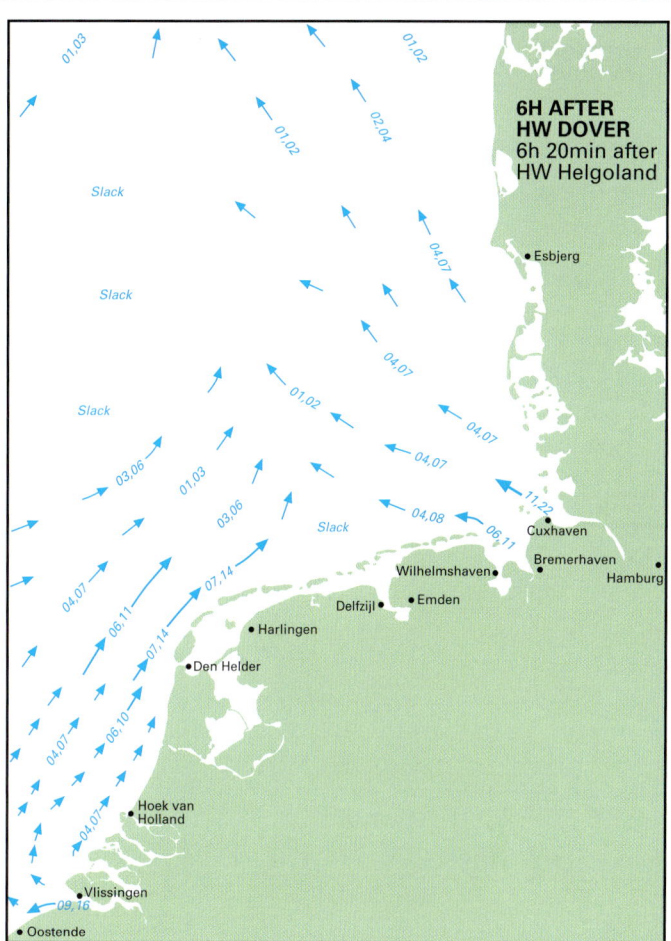

6H AFTER HW DOVER
6h 20min after HW Helgoland

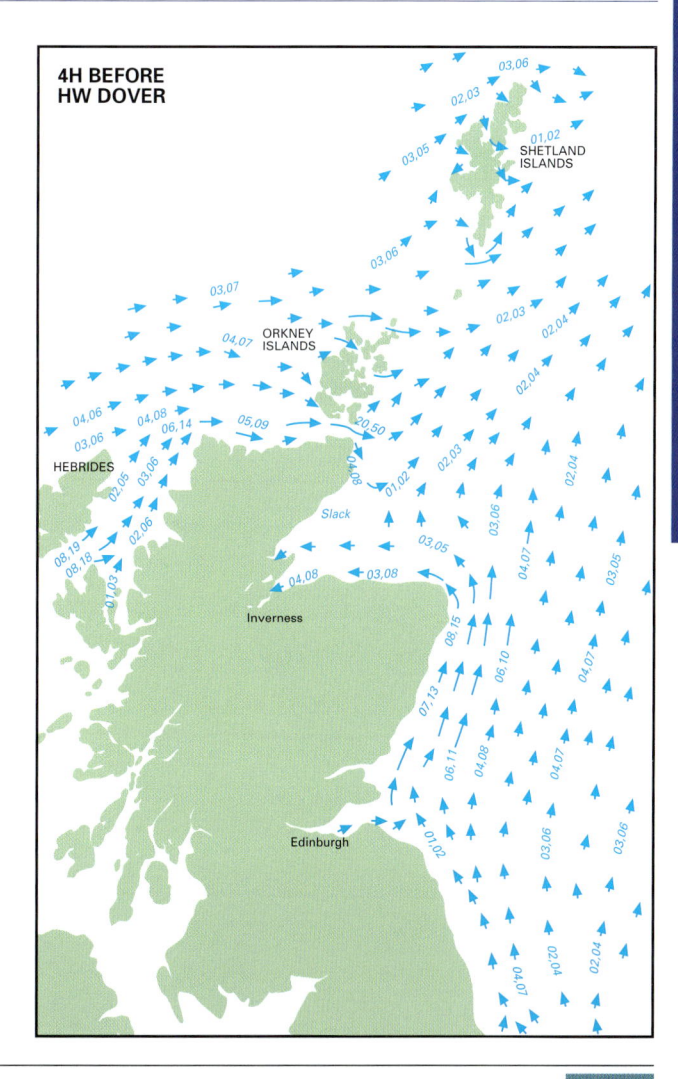

5H BEFORE HW DOVER

4H BEFORE HW DOVER

TIDAL STREAMS AND CURVES

443

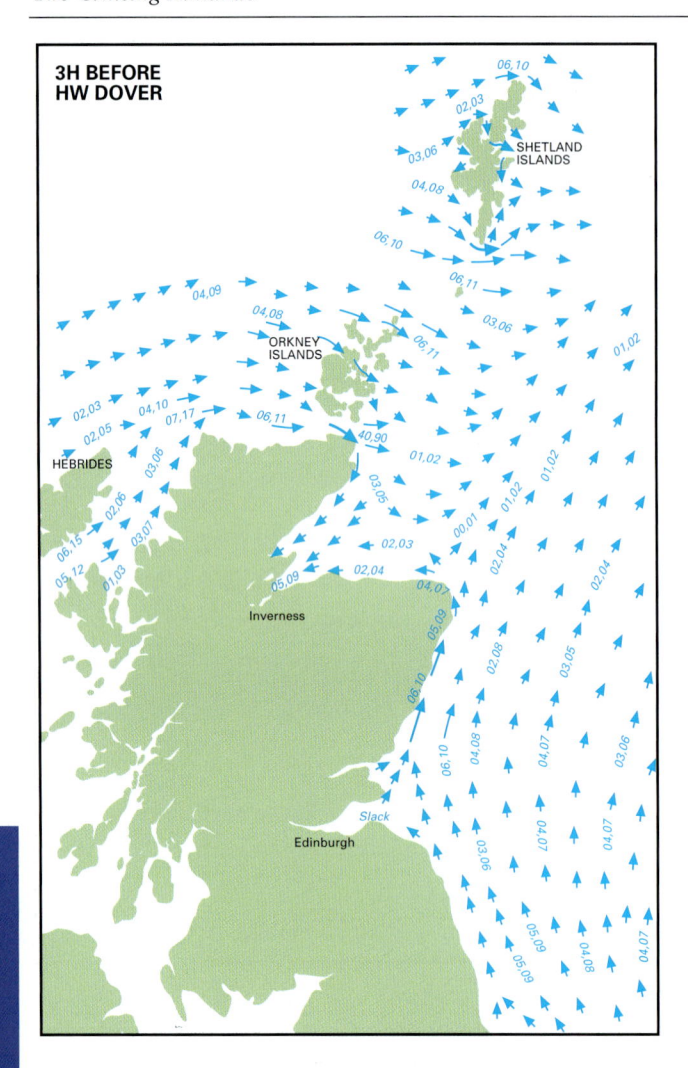

The Cruising Almanac

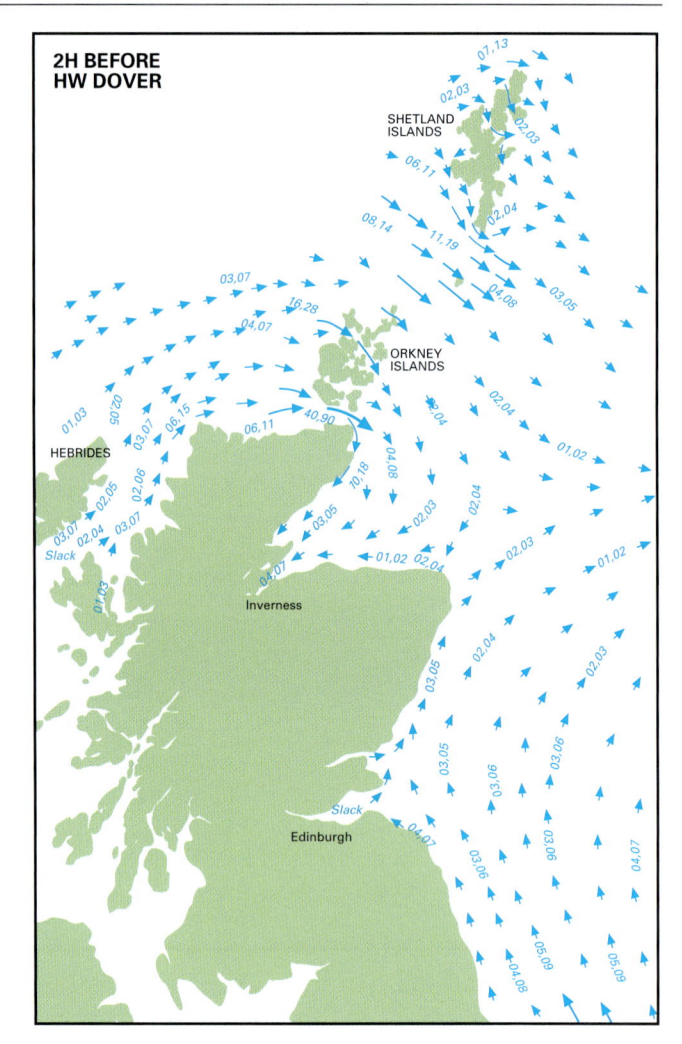

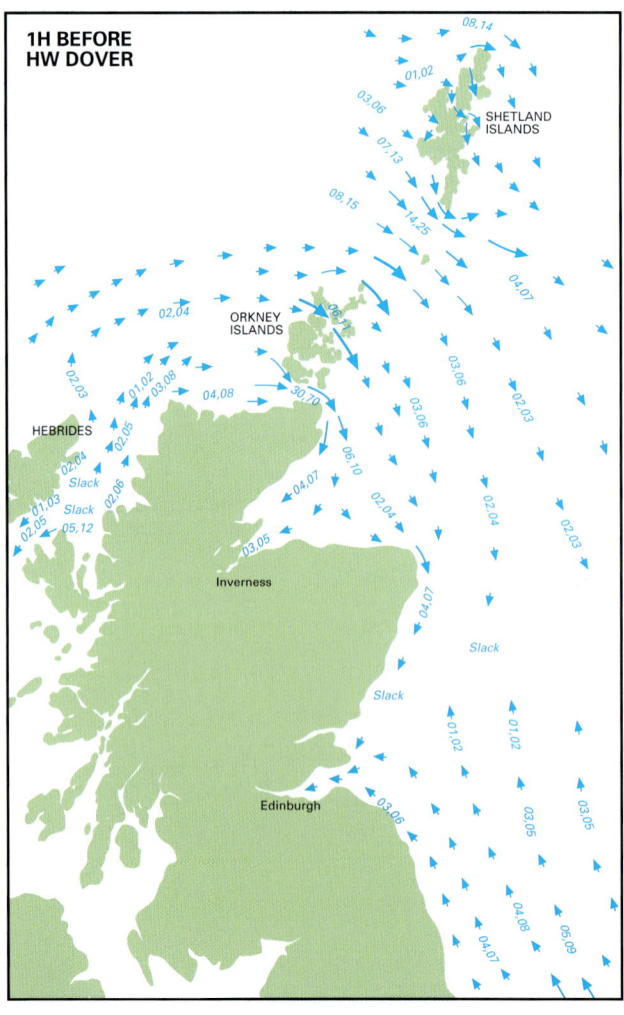

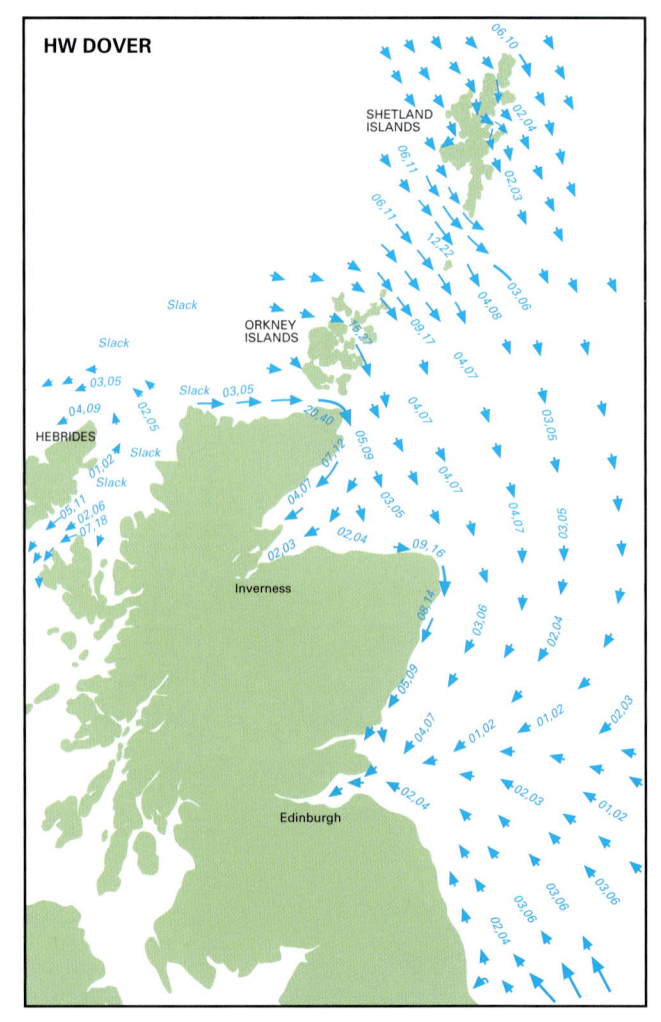

TIDAL STREAMS AND CURVES

3H BEFORE HW DOVER

2H BEFORE HW DOVER

1H BEFORE HW DOVER

HW DOVER

444

The Cruising Almanac

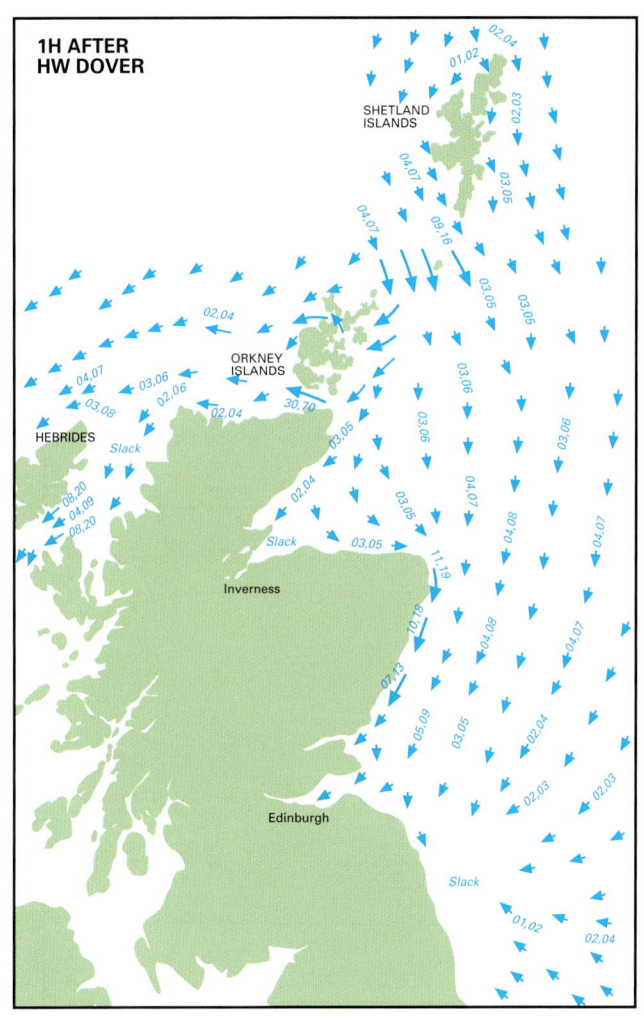

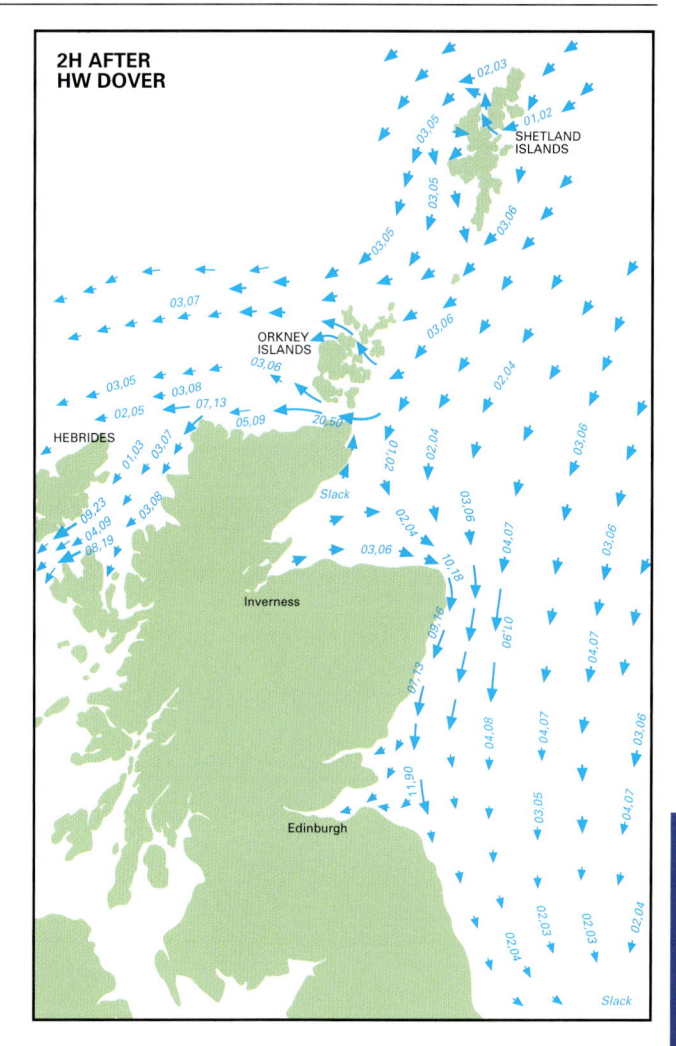

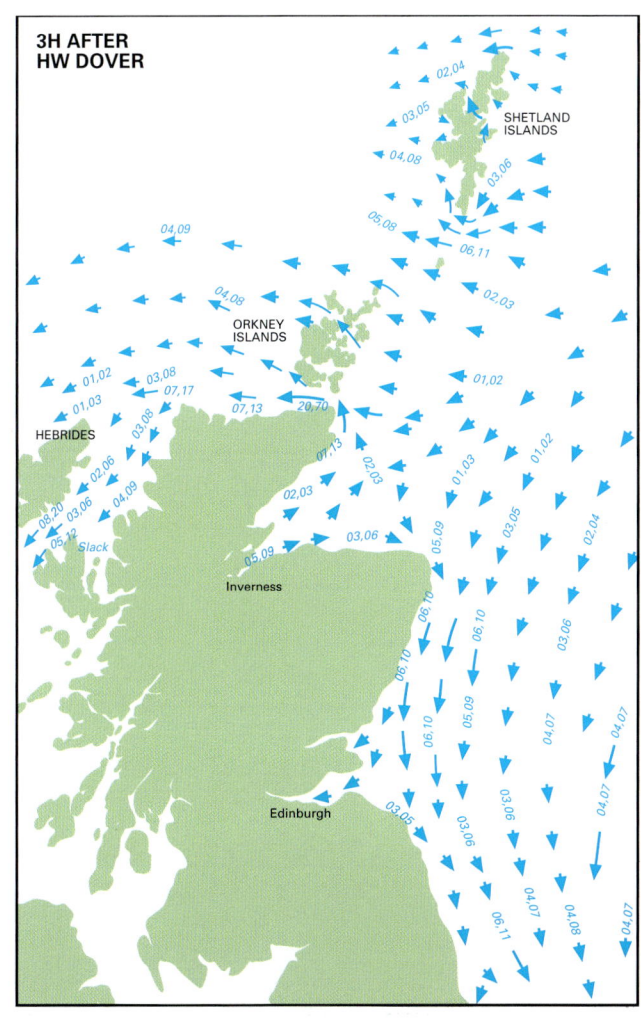

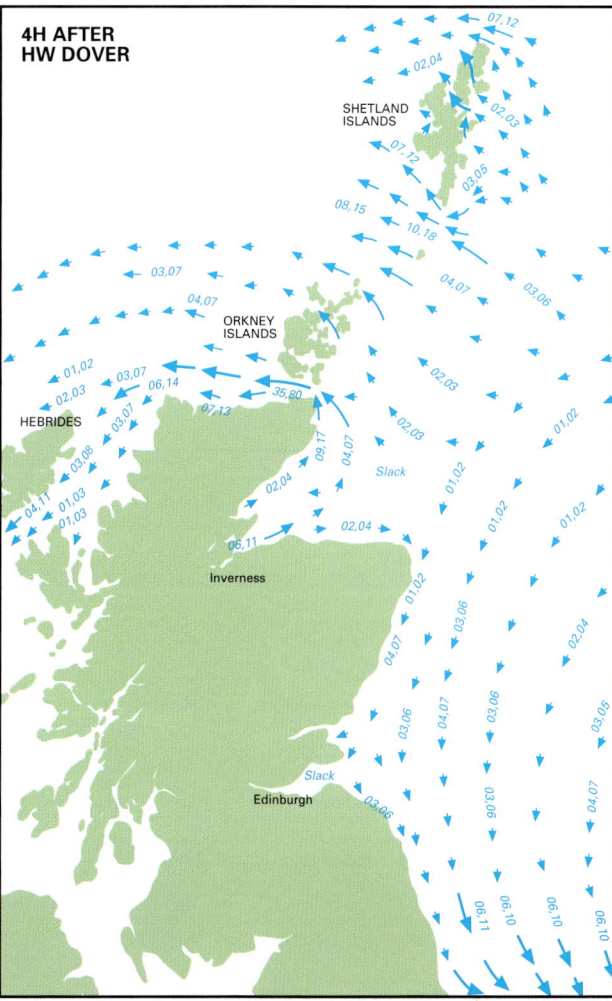

TIDAL STREAMS AND CURVES

The Cruising Almanac

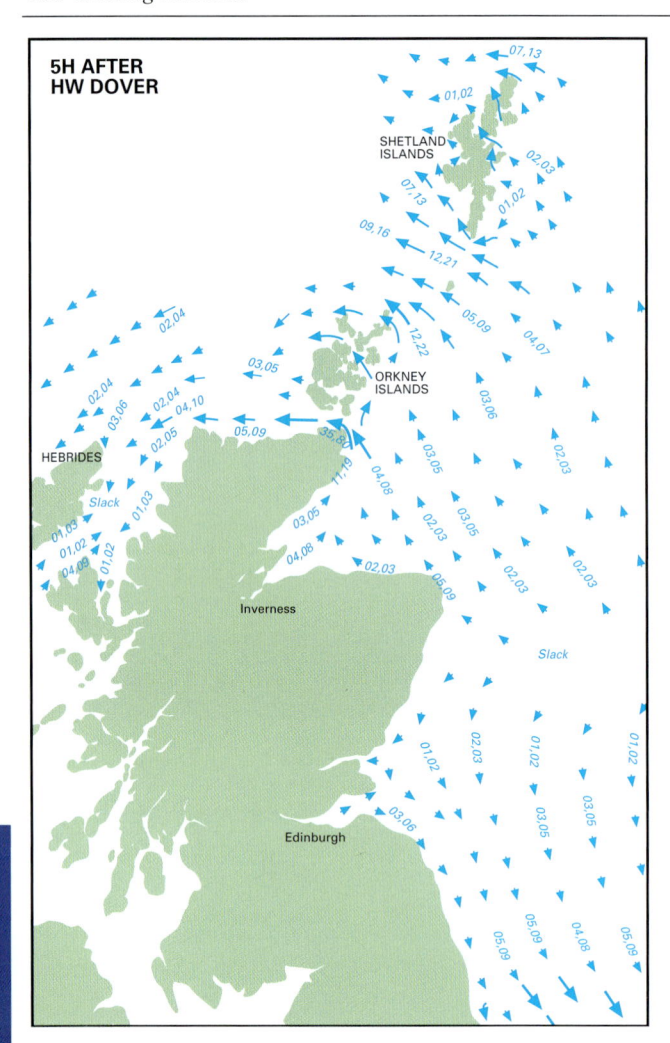

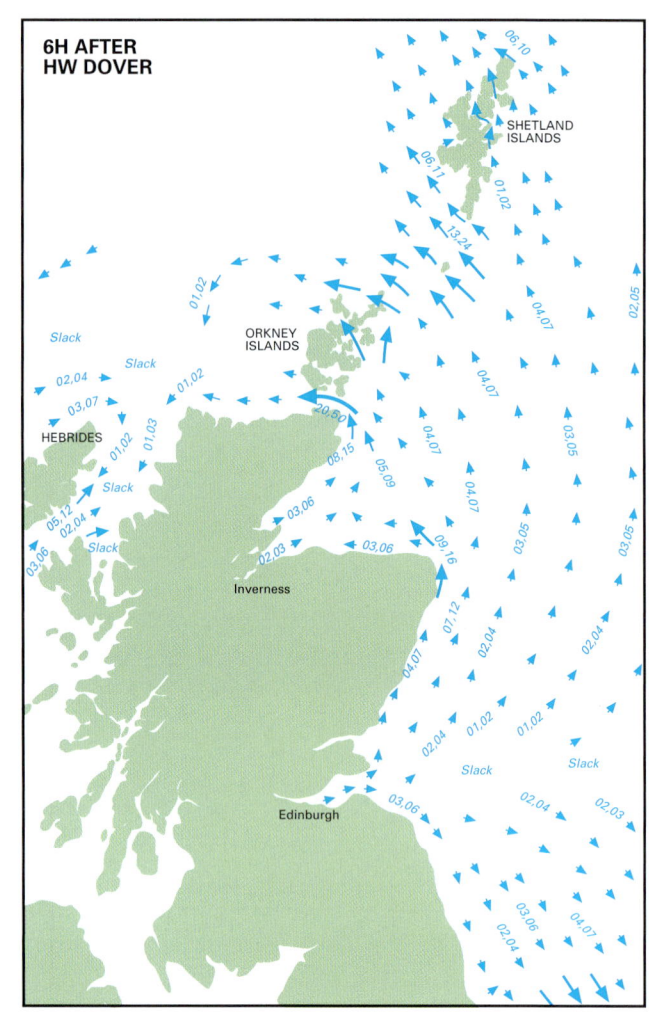

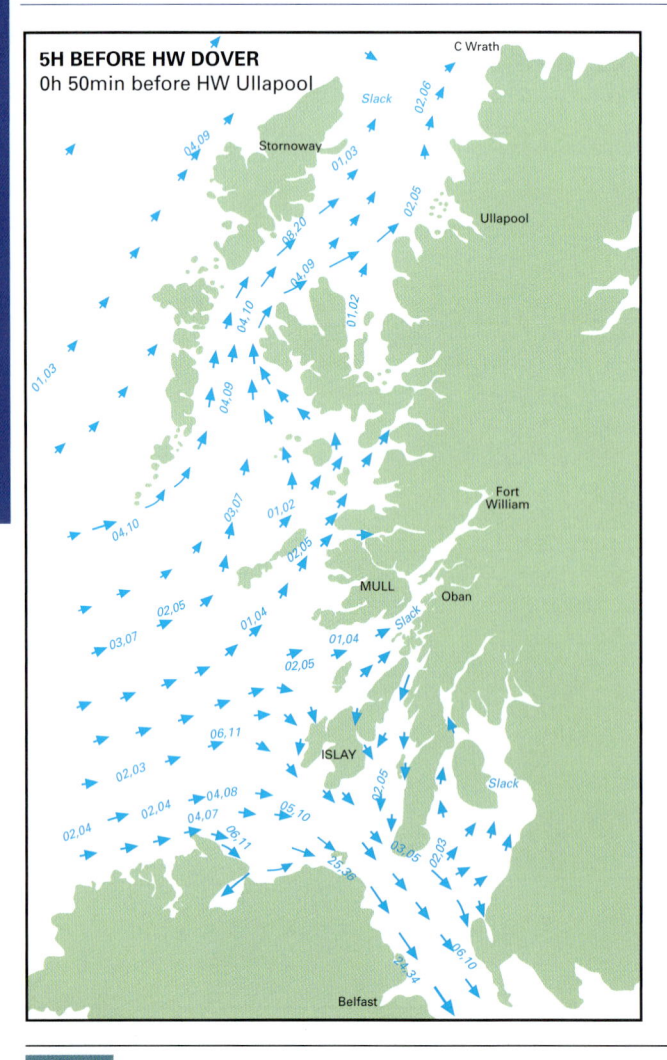

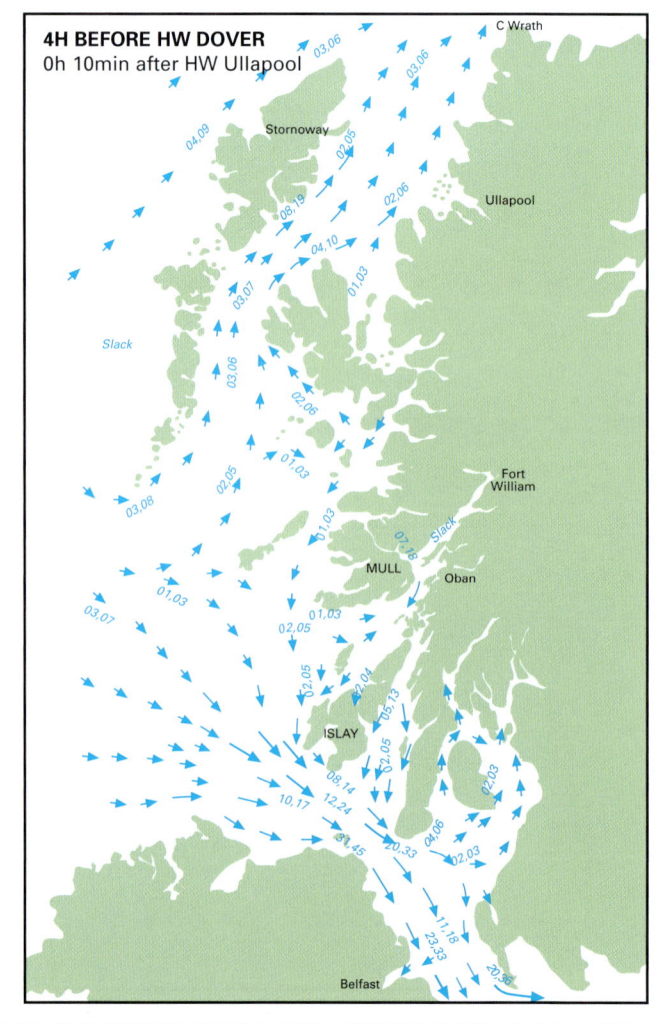

TIDAL STREAMS AND CURVES

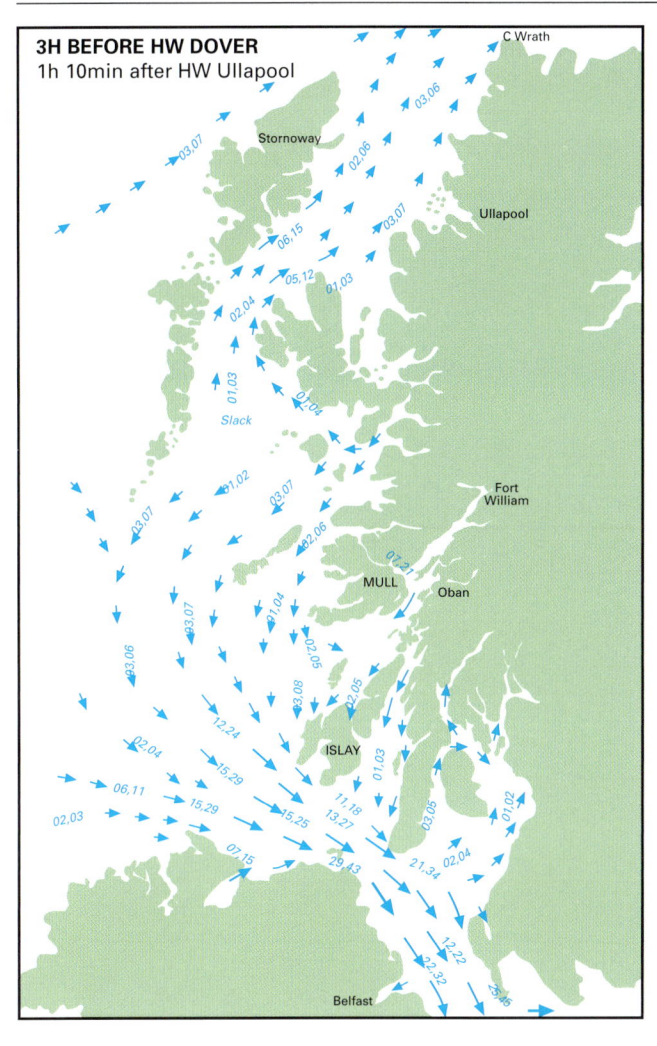

The Cruising Almanac

3H BEFORE HW DOVER
1h 10min after HW Ullapool

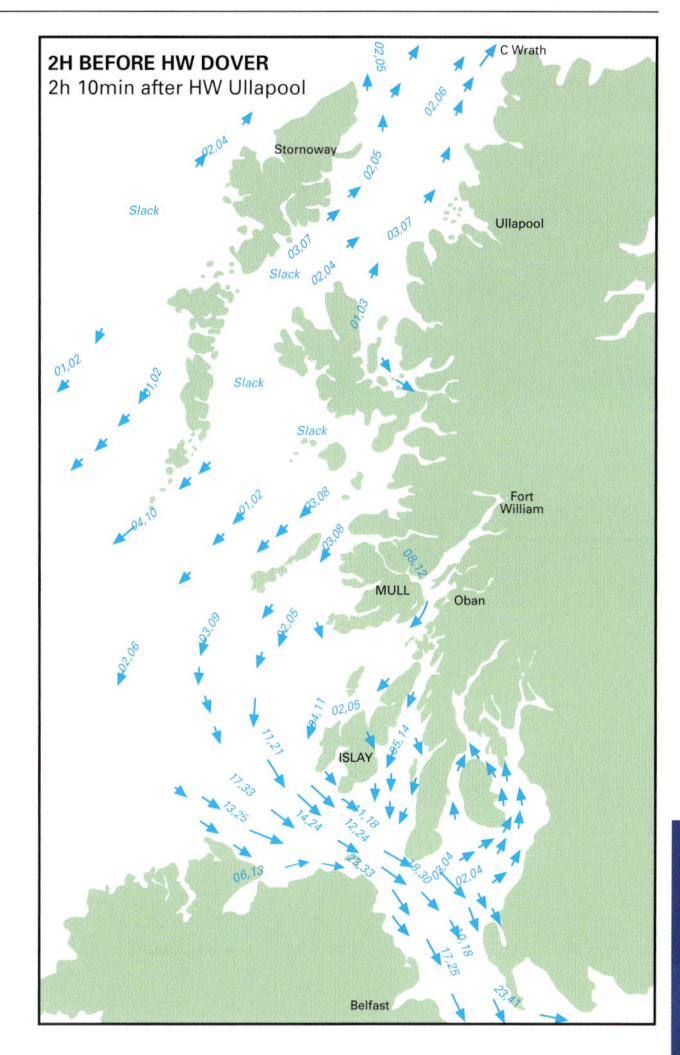

2H BEFORE HW DOVER
2h 10min after HW Ullapool

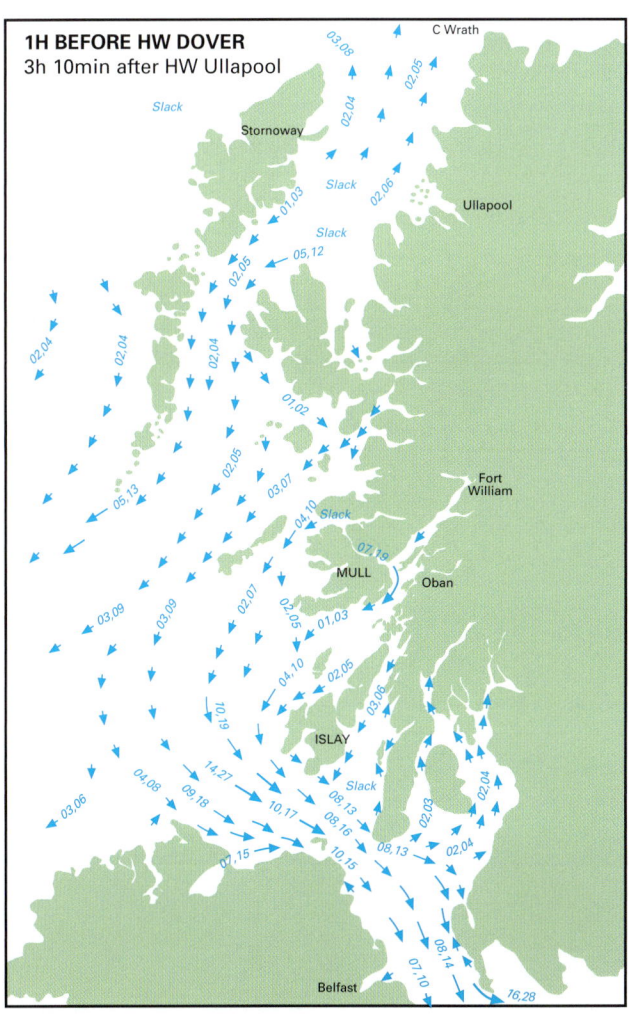

1H BEFORE HW DOVER
3h 10min after HW Ullapool

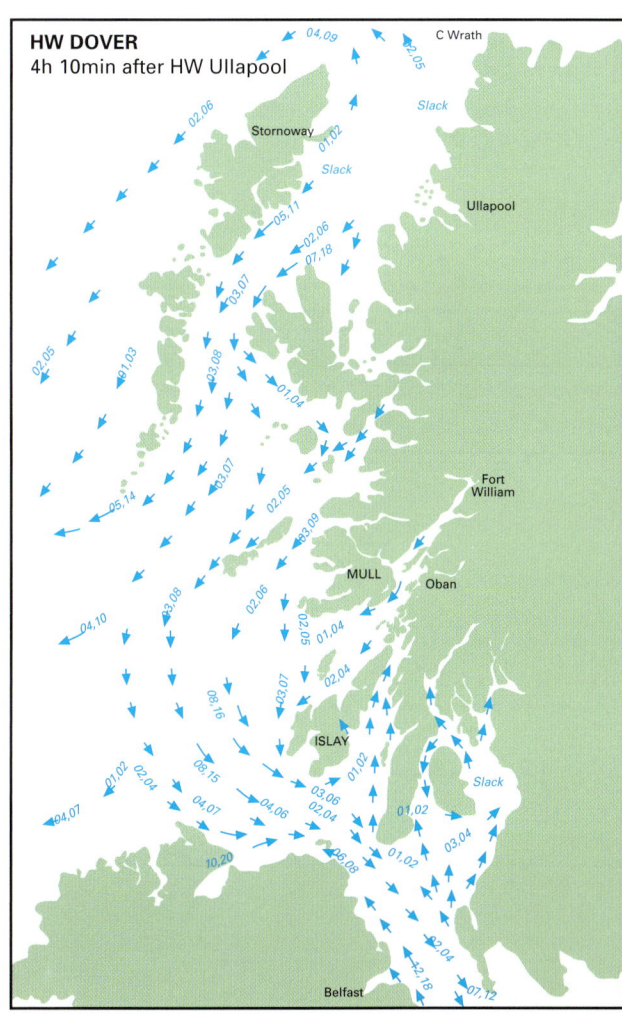

HW DOVER
4h 10min after HW Ullapool

TIDAL STREAMS AND CURVES

447

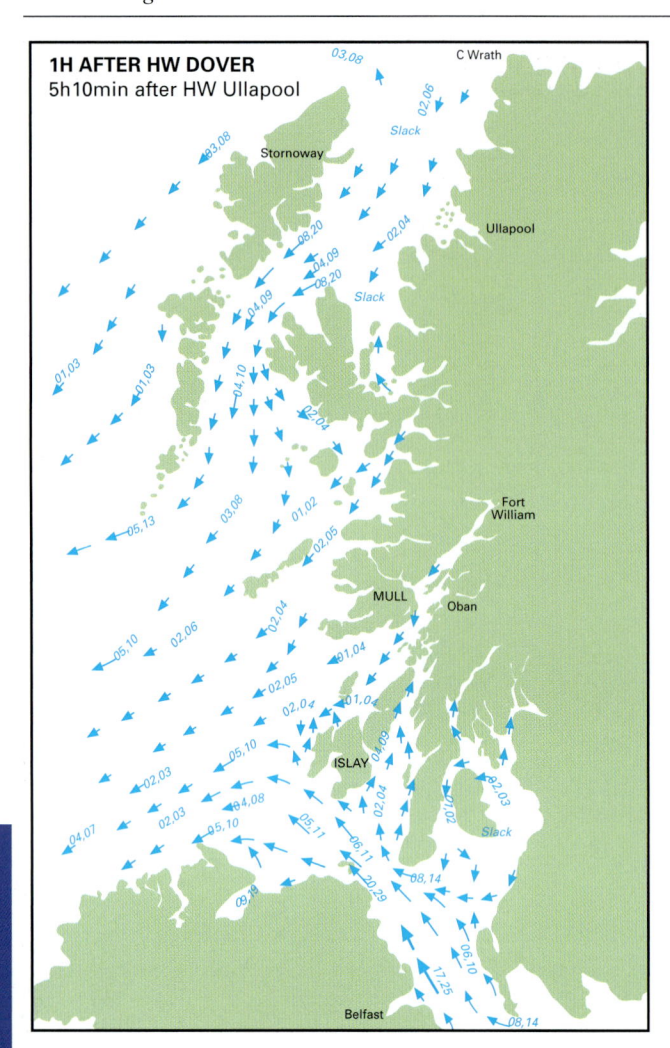

TIDAL STREAMS AND CURVES

1H AFTER HW DOVER
5h 10min after HW Ullapool

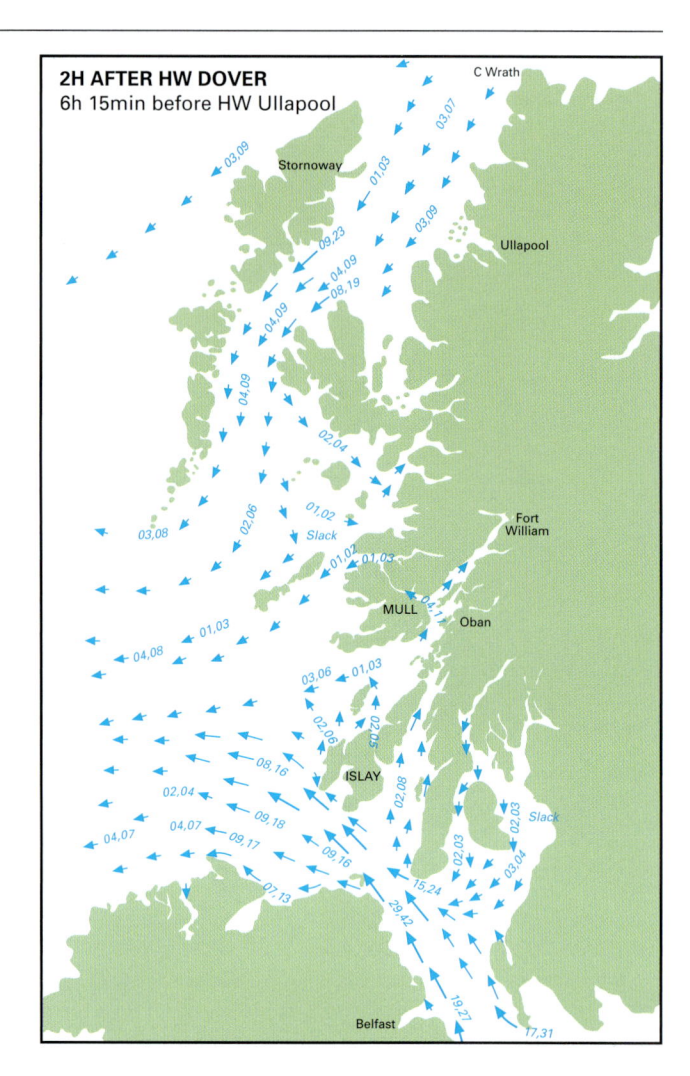

2H AFTER HW DOVER
6h 15min before HW Ullapool

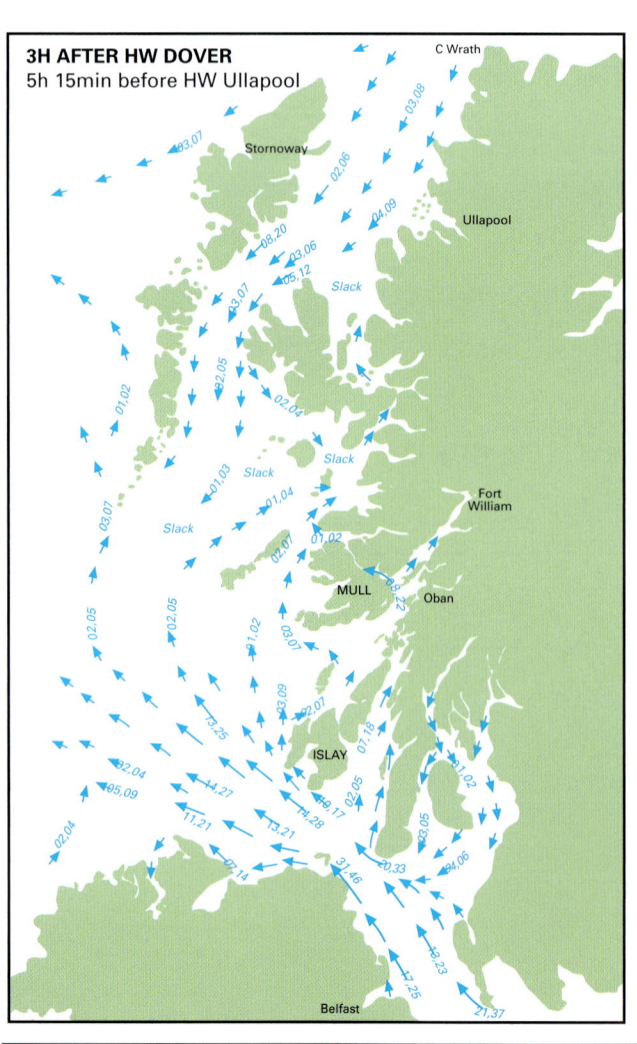

3H AFTER HW DOVER
5h 15min before HW Ullapool

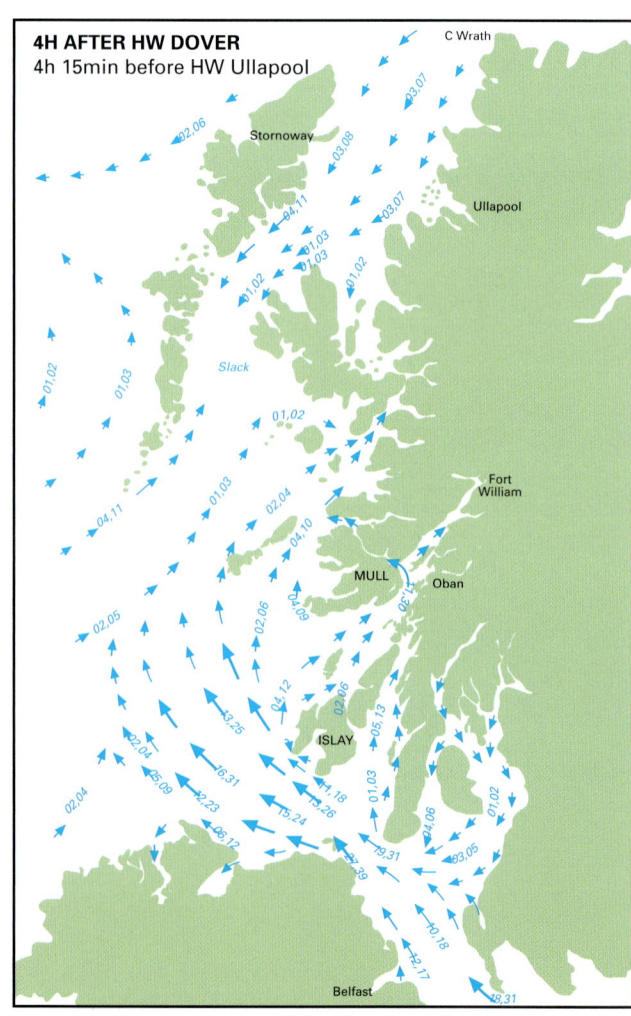

4H AFTER HW DOVER
4h 15min before HW Ullapool

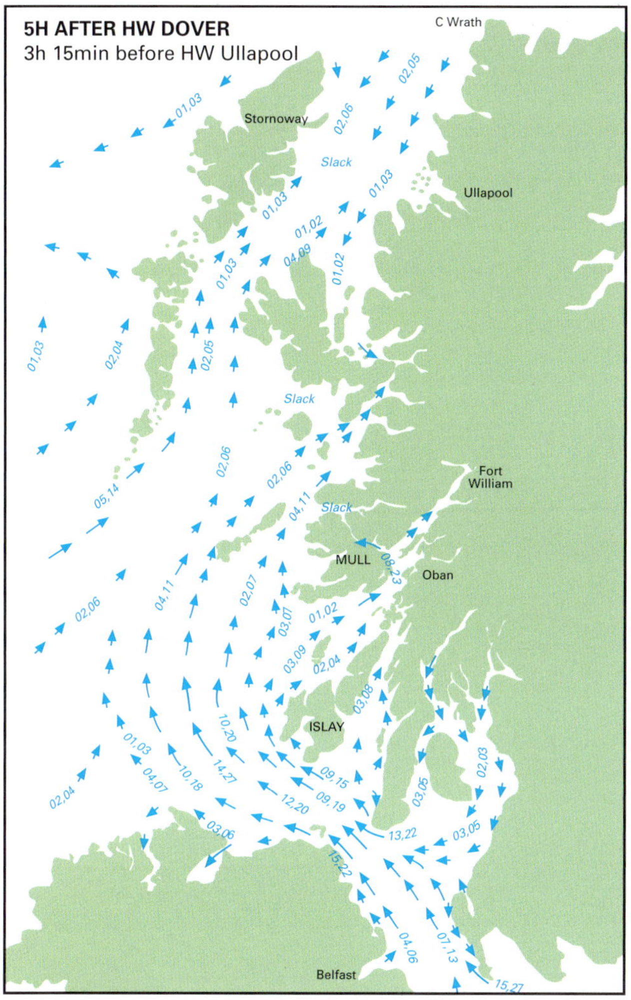
5H AFTER HW DOVER
3h 15min before HW Ullapool
C Wrath
Stornoway
Ullapool
Fort William
MULL
Oban
ISLAY
Belfast

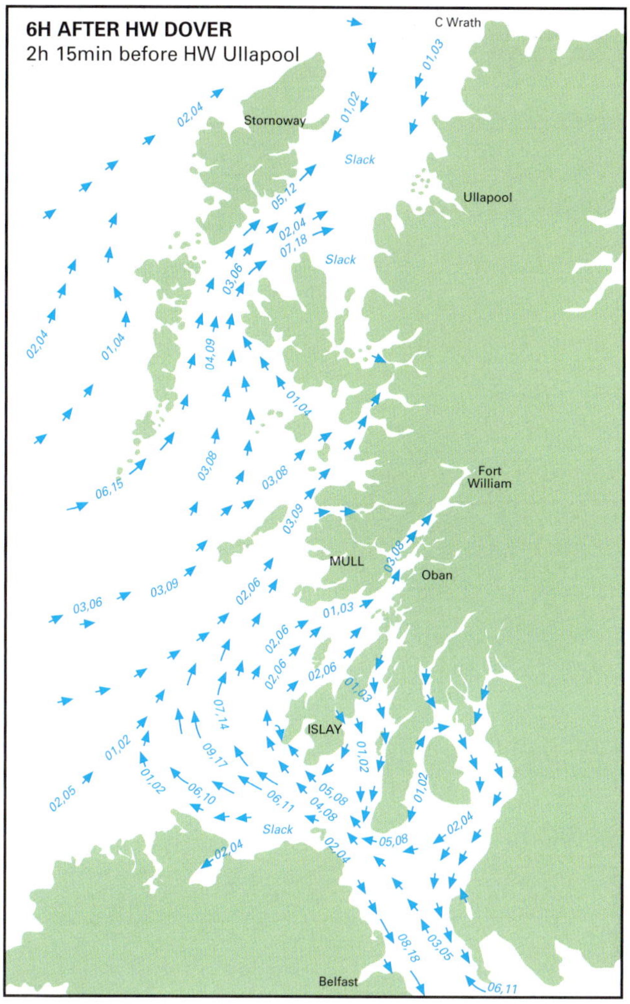
6H AFTER HW DOVER
2h 15min before HW Ullapool
C Wrath
Stornoway
Ullapool
Fort William
MULL
Oban
ISLAY
Belfast

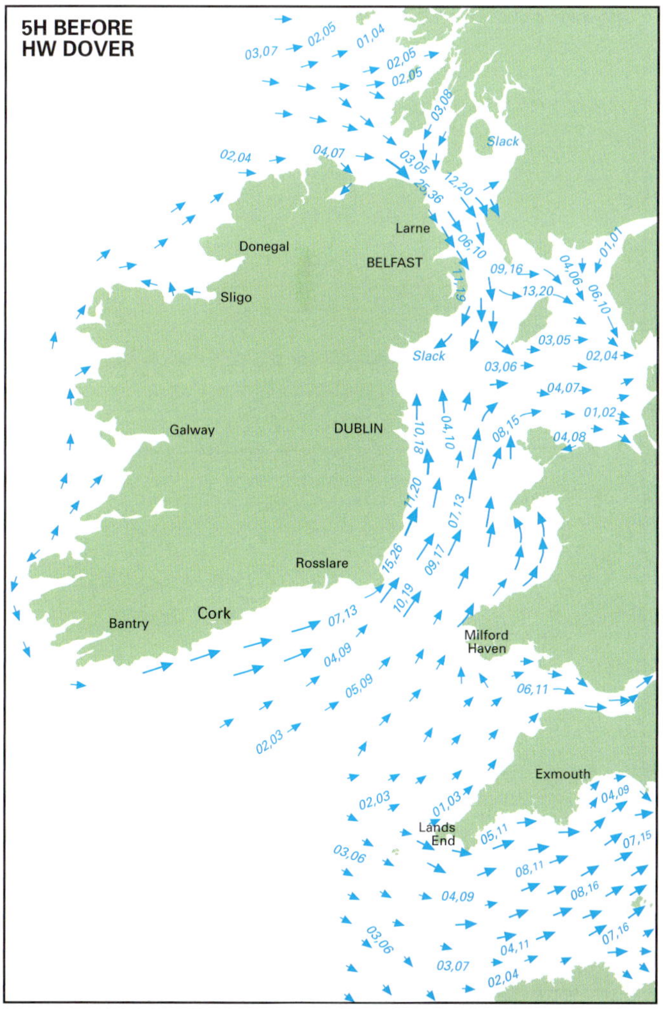
5H BEFORE HW DOVER
Larne
Donegal
BELFAST
Sligo
Galway
DUBLIN
Rosslare
Bantry
Cork
Milford Haven
Exmouth
Lands End

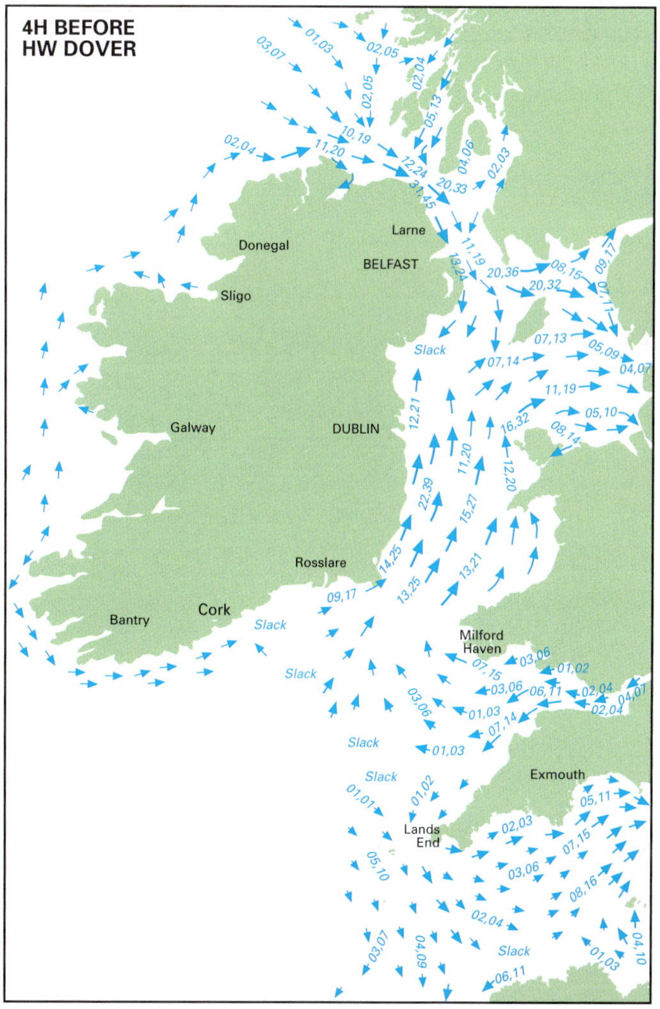
4H BEFORE HW DOVER
Larne
Donegal
BELFAST
Sligo
Galway
DUBLIN
Rosslare
Bantry
Cork
Milford Haven
Exmouth
Lands End

The Cruising Almanac

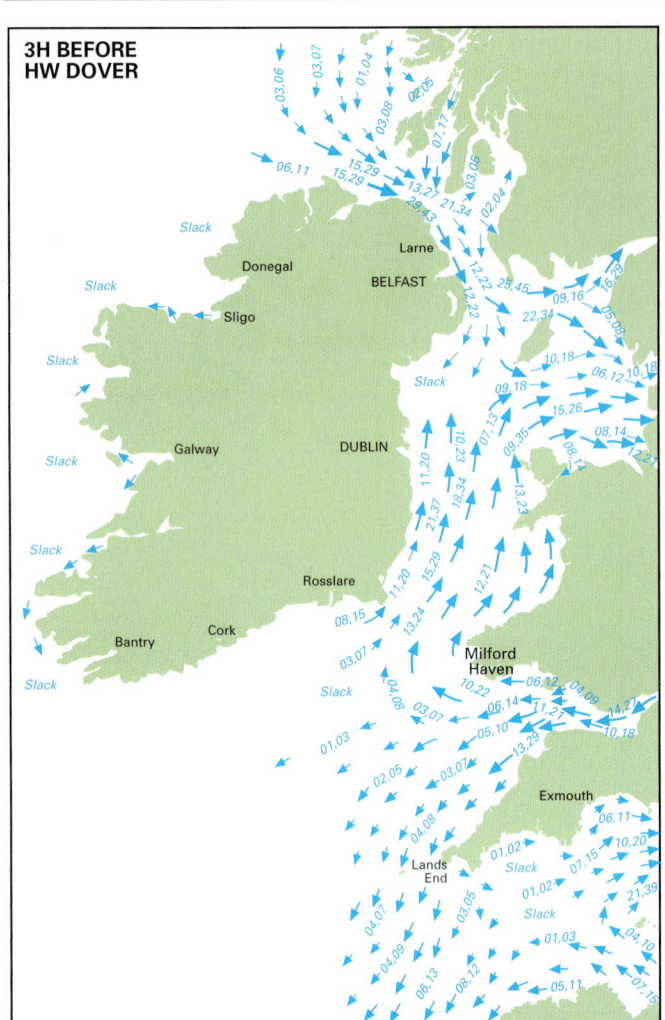

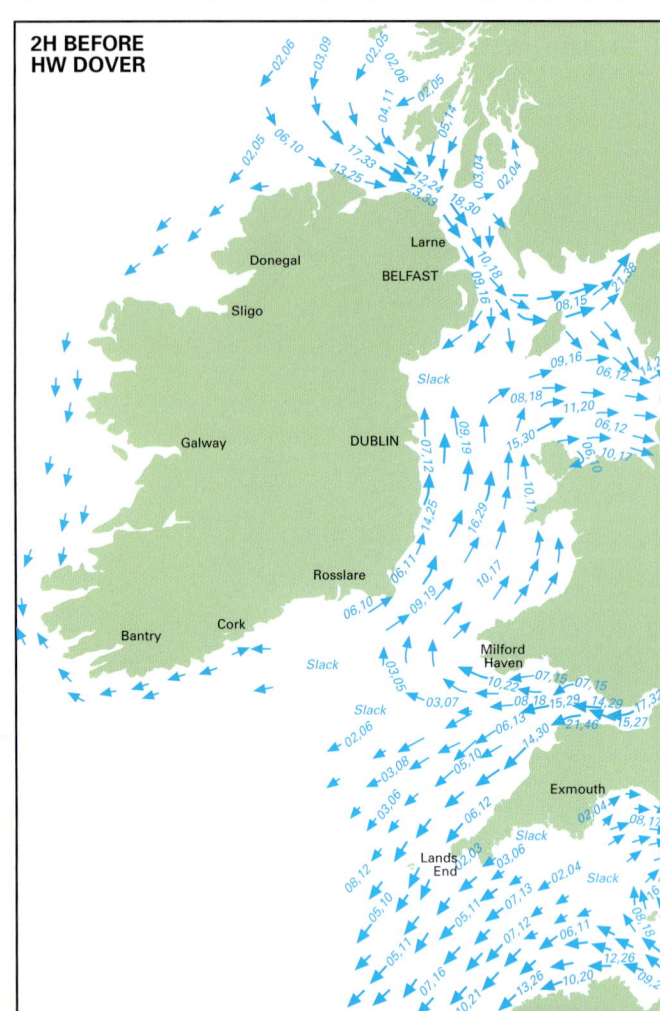

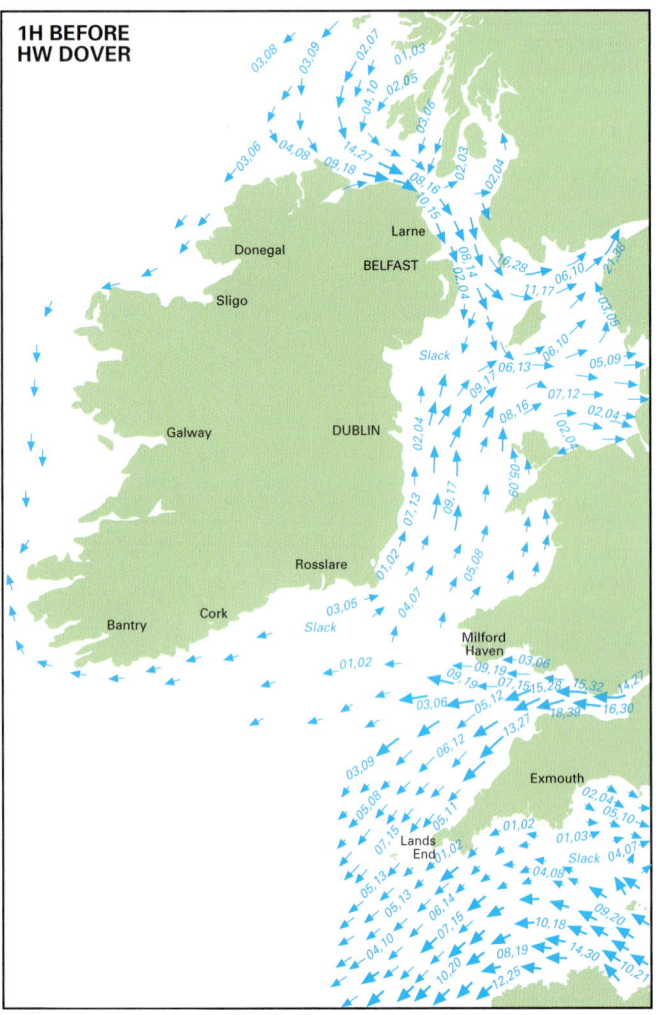

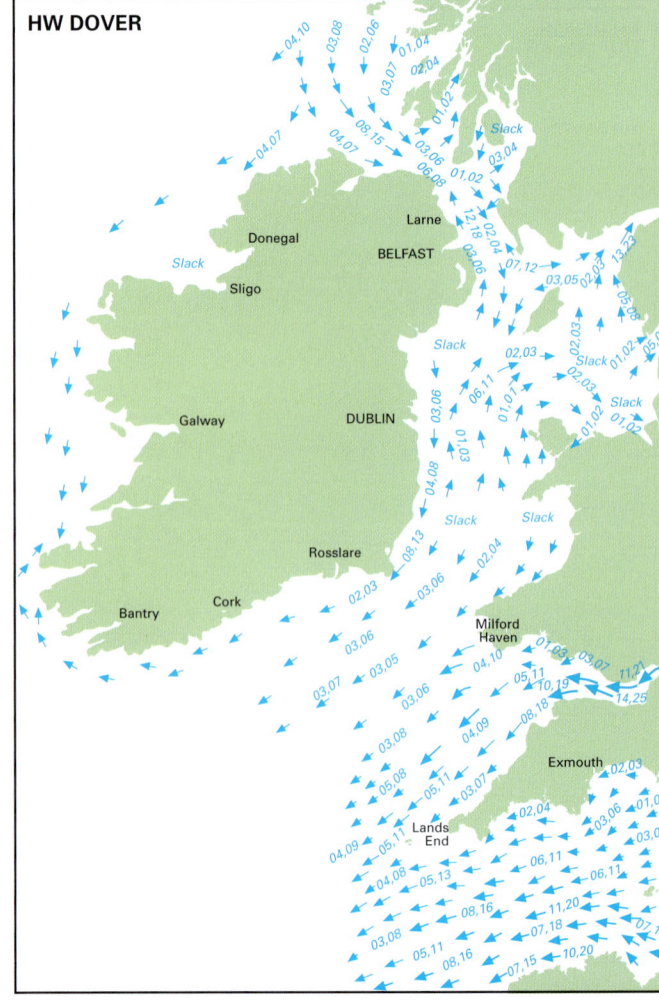

TIDAL STREAMS AND CURVES

TIDAL STREAMS AND CURVES

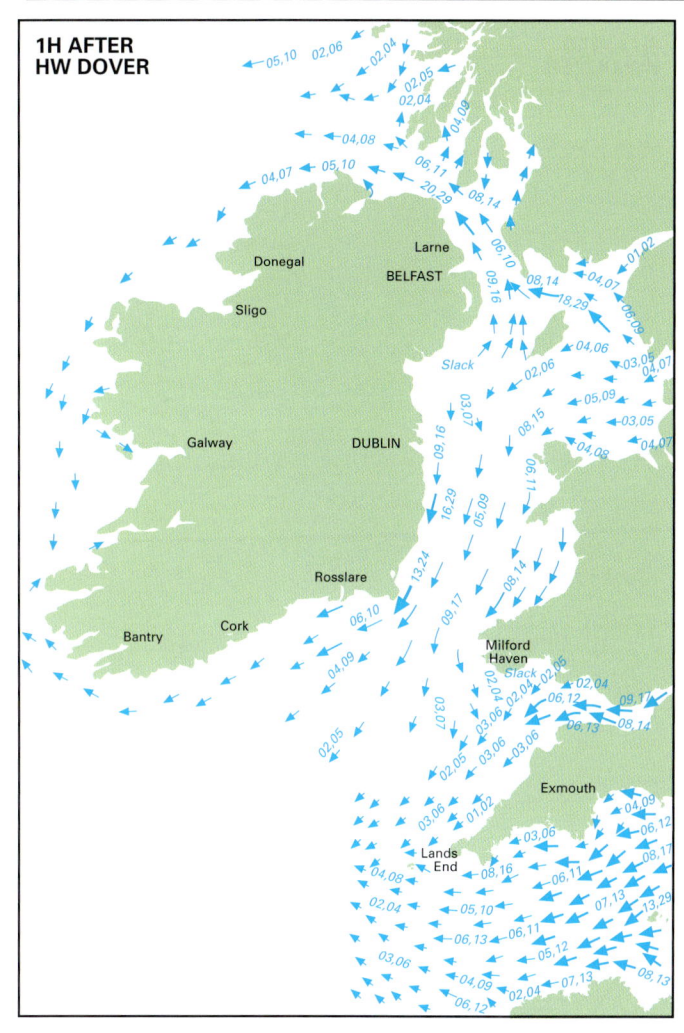

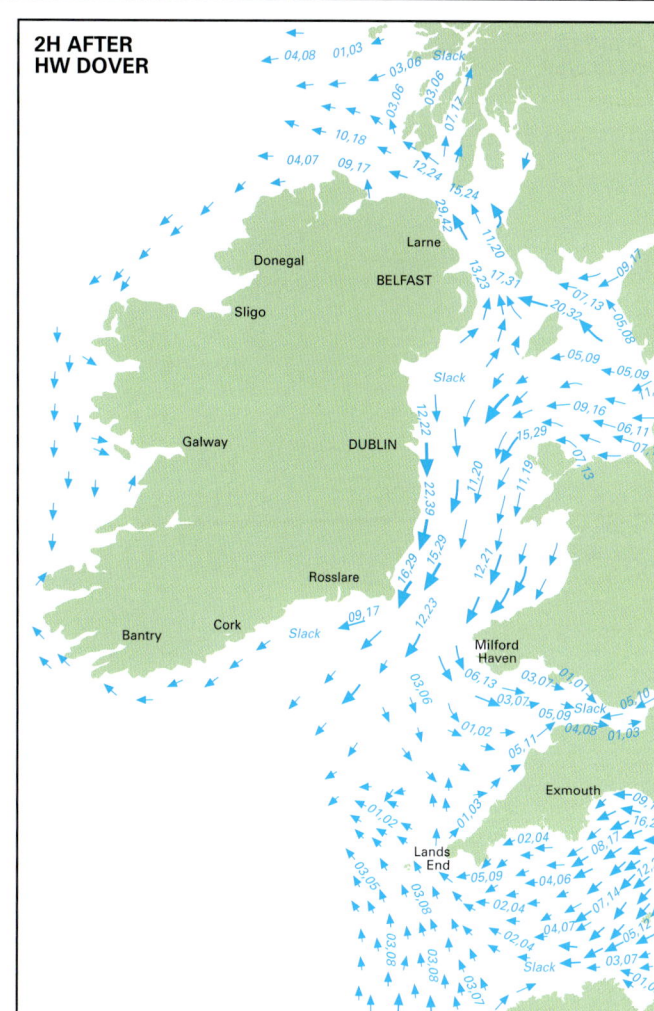

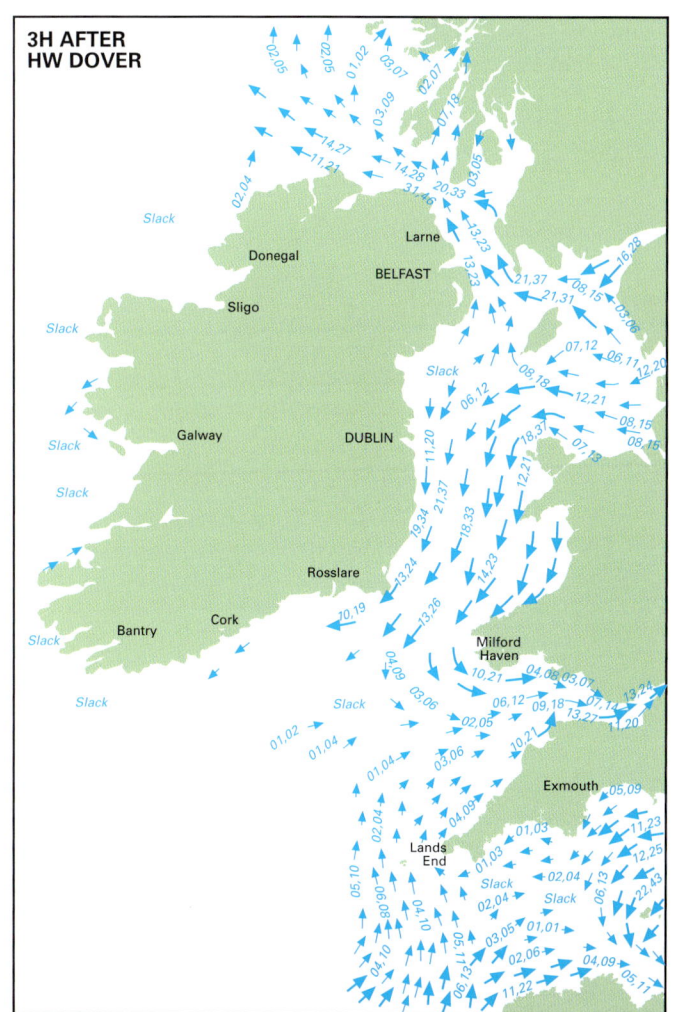

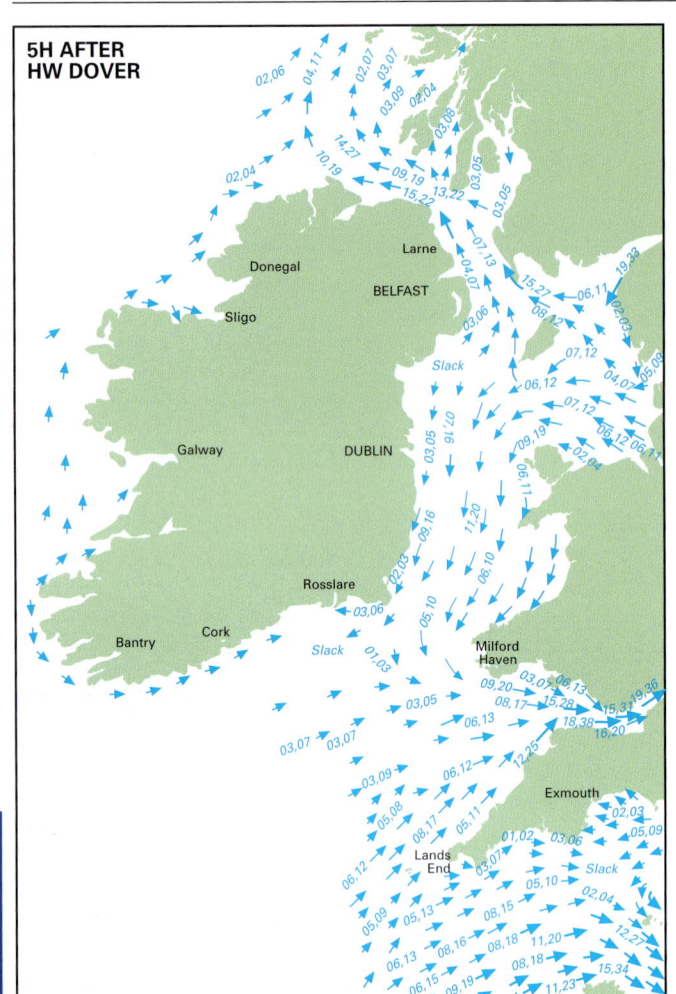

The Cruising Almanac

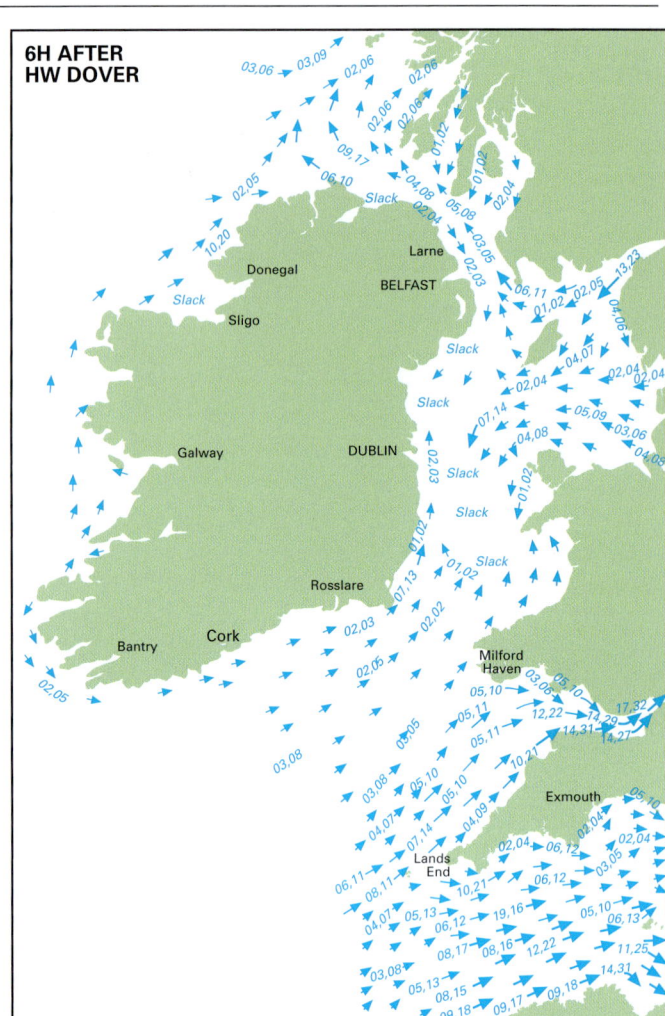

5H AFTER HW DOVER

6H AFTER HW DOVER

TIDAL STREAMS AND CURVES

Index of tidal curves

Aberdeen, 460
Avonmouth, 463
Belfast, 464
Bournemouth to Christchurch, 455
Brest, 470
Calais, 467
Cherbourg, 468
Cobh (Cork), 464
Cuxhaven, 465
Dieppe, 467
Dover, 457
Dublin, 464
Dunkerque, 466
Esbjerg, 465
Galway, 465
Gibraltar, 471
Greenock, 462

Helgoland, 465
Hoek van Holland, 466
Holyhead, 463
Immingham, 459
Le Havre, 468
Leith, 460
Lerwick, 461
Lisbon, 470
Liverpool, 462
London Bridge, 458
Lowestoft, 459
Lymington to Cowes, 455
Milford Haven, 463
Oban, 462
Plymouth, 453
Pointe de Grave, 470
Poole Harbour, 454

Portland Harbour, 454
Portsmouth, 457
Ryde to Selsey, 456
St Helier, 469
St Malo, 469
St Peter Port, 468
Sheerness, 458
Shoreham, 457
Southampton, 456
Stornoway, 461
Tyne River (North Shields), 459
Ullapool, 461
Vlissingen, 466
Walton-on-the-Naze, 458
Wick, 460

PLYMOUTH	Time differences HW 0000 0600 and and 1200 1800	LW 0000 0600 and and 1200 1800	Height differences in metres MHWS 5·5	MHWN 4·4	MLWN 2·2	MLWS 0·8
Isles of Scilly						
St Mary's	−0035 −0100	−0040 −0025	+0·2	−0·1	−0·2	−0·1
Penzance (Newlyn)	−0040 −0110	−0035 −0025	+0·1	0·0	−0·2	0·0
Helford R (Entrance)	−0030 −0035	−0015 −0010	−0·2	−0·2	−0·3	−0·2
River Fal						
Falmouth	−0025 −0045	−0010 −0010	−0·2	−0·2	−0·3	−0·2
Truro	−0020 −0025	− −	−2·0	−2·0	dries	dries
Mevagissey	−0015 −0020	−0010 −0005	−0·1	−0·1	−0·2	−0·1
River Fowey						
Fowey	−0010 −0015	−0010 −0005	−0·1	−0·1	−0·2	−0·2
Looe	−0010 −0010	−0005 −0005	−0·1	−0·2	−0·2	−0·2
River Yealm						
Entrance	+0006 +0006	+0002 +0002	−0·1	−0·1	−0·1	−0·1

PLYMOUTH	Time differences HW 0100 0600 and and 1300 1800	LW 0100 0600 and and 1300 1800	Height differences in metres MHWS 5·5	MHWN 4·4	MLWN 2·2	MLWS 0·8
Salcombe River						
Salcombe	0000 +0010	+0005 −0005	−0·2	−0·3	−0·1	−0·1
River Dart						
Dartmouth	+0015 +0025	0000 −0005	−0·6	−0·6	−0·2	−0·2
Totnes	+0030 +0040	+0115 +0030	−2·1	−2·1	dries	dries
Torquay	+0025 +0045	+0010 0000	−0·6	−0·7	−0·2	−0·1
Teignmouth (Apps)	+0020 +0050	+0025 0000	−0·9	−0·8	−0·2	−0·1
Teignmouth (New Quay)	+0025 +0055	+0040 +0005	−0·8	−0·8	−0·2	+0·1

PLYMOUTH	Time differences HW 0100 0600 and and 1300 1800	LW 0100 0600 and and 1300 1800	Height differences in metres MHWS 5·5	MHWN 4·4	MLWN 2·2	MLWS 0·8
Exmouth (Apps)	+0030 +0050	+0015 +0005	−0·9	−1·0	−0·5	−0·3
Lyme Regis	+0040 +0100	+0005 −0005	−1·2	−1·3	−0·5	−0·2
Bridport (West Bay)	+0025 +0040	0000 0000	−1·4	−1·4	−0·6	−0·2
River Exe						
Exmouth Dock	+0035 +0055	+0050 +0020	−1·5	−1·6	−0·9	−0·6
Topsham	+0045 +0105	− −	−1·5	−1·6	−	−

PLYMOUTH
MEAN SPRING AND NEAP CURVES
Springs occur 2 days after New and Full Moon

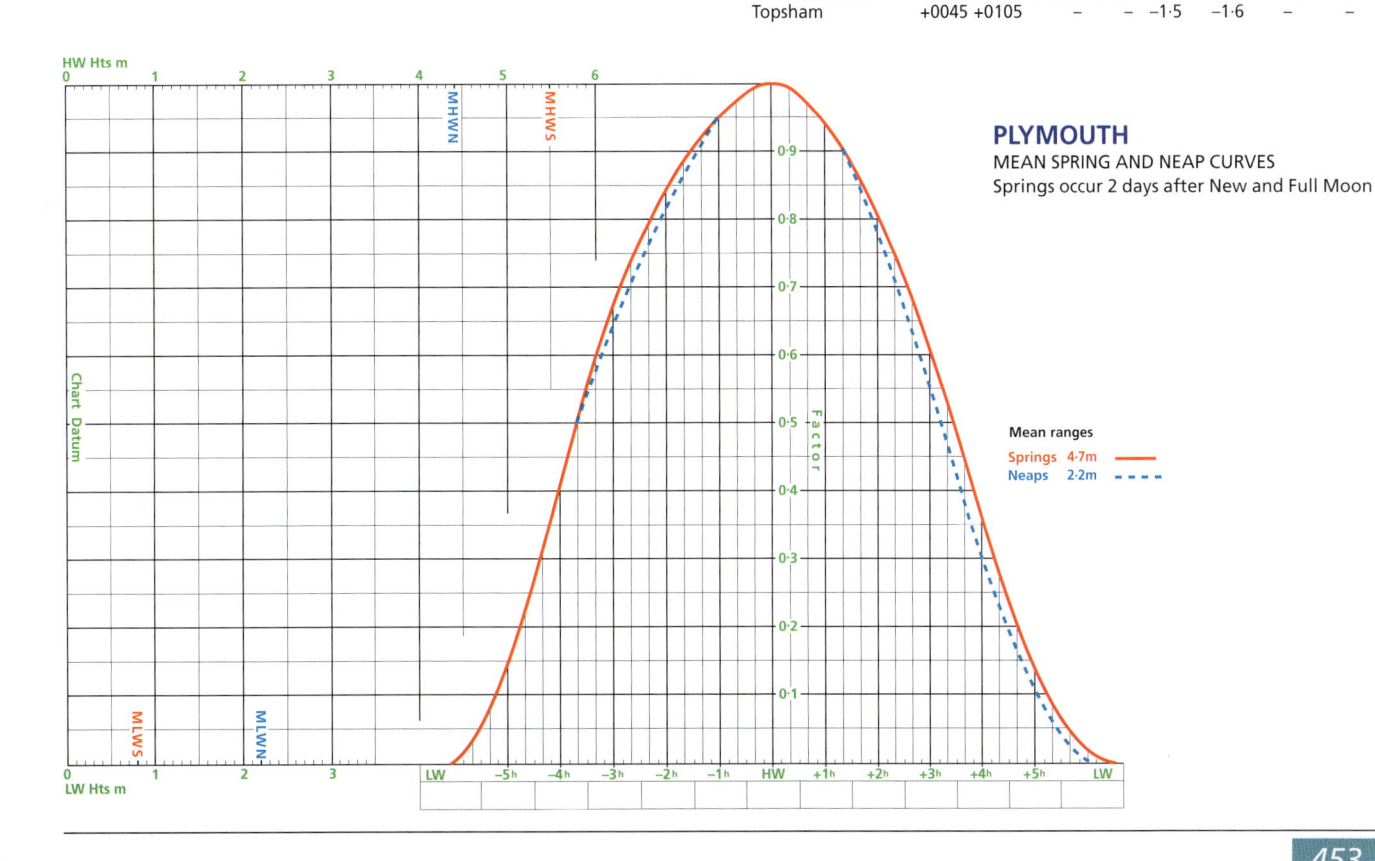

Mean ranges
Springs 4·7m
Neaps 2·2m

PORTLAND HARBOUR
MEAN SPRING AND NEAP CURVES
Springs occur 2 days after New and Full Moon

Mean ranges
Springs 2·0m
Neaps 0·6m

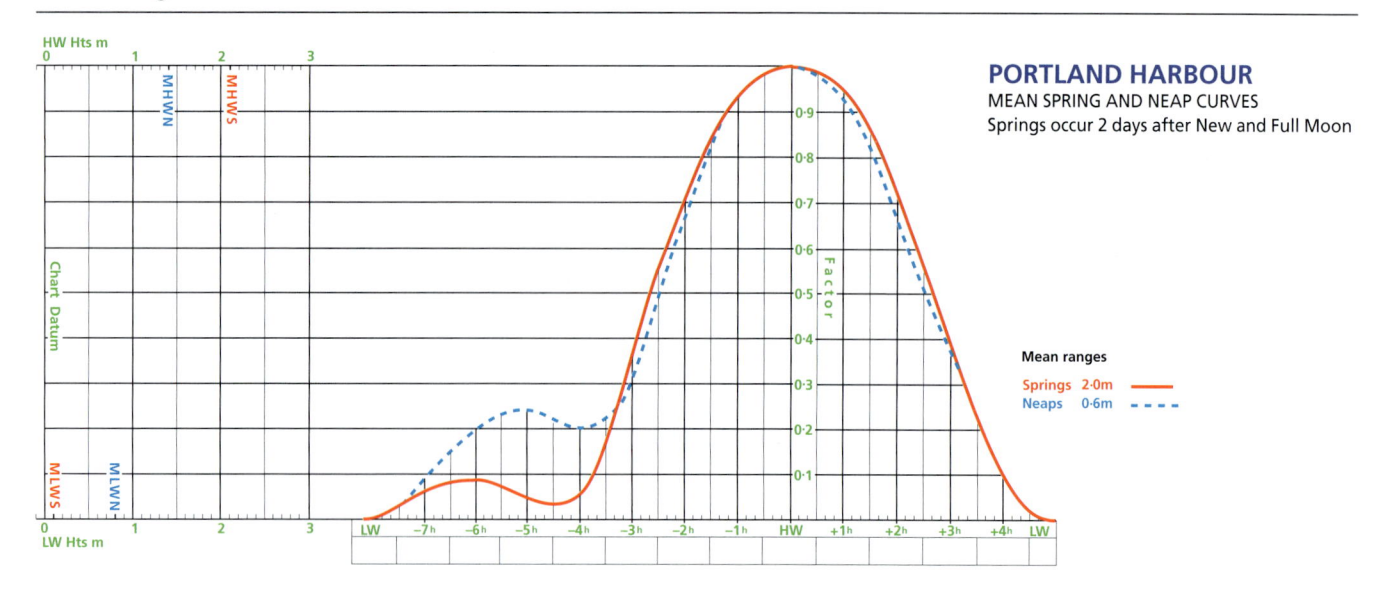

POOLE HARBOUR
MEAN SPRING AND NEAP CURVES
Springs occur 2 days after New and Full Moon

Mean ranges
Springs 1·6m
1·0m
Neaps 0·5m

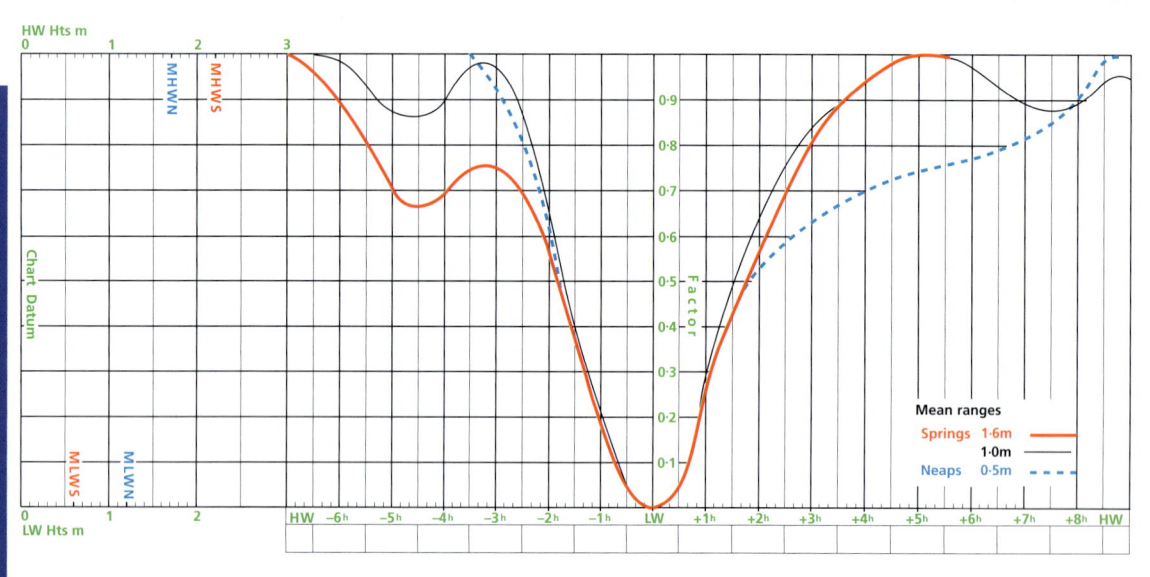

	Time differences				Height differences in metres			
	HW		LW		MHWS	MHWN	MLWN	MLWS
PORTLAND	0100 and 1300	0700 and 1900	0100 and 1300	0700 and 1900	2·1	1·4	0·8	0·1
Lulworth Cove	+0005	+0015	−0005	0000	+0·1	+0·1	+0·2	+0·1
POOLE HARBOUR	–	–	0500 and 1700	1100 and 2300	2·2	1·7	1·2	0·6
(RoRo Terminal)	–	–						
Swanage	–	–	−0045	−0055	−0·2	−0·1	0·0	−0·1
Poole Harbour								
Entrance	–	–	−0025	−0010	0·0	0·0	0·0	0·0
Pottery Pier	–	–	+0010	+0010	−0·2	0·0	+0·1	+0·2
Wareham	–	–	+0130	+0045	0·0	0·0	0·0	+0·3

BOURNEMOUTH TO CHRISTCHURCH

Tides from Poole Harbour to Selsey Bill are based on LW except those related to Portsmouth which uses HW. Ports based on Portsmouth include Christchurch, Lymington, Beaulieu, Cowes, Bembridge and Chichester although some can also be related to the LW curve at Poole.

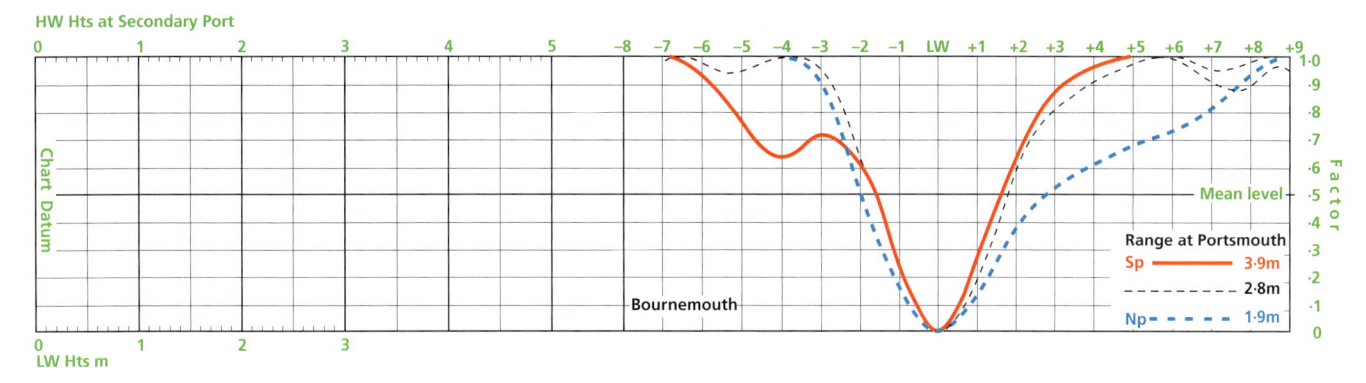

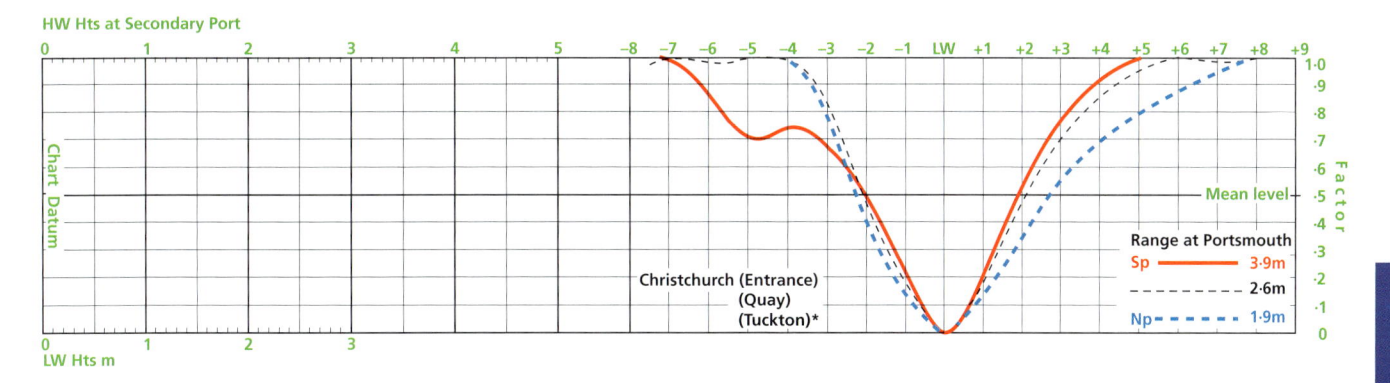

Bournemouth

Range at Portsmouth
Sp — 3·9m
— — 2·8m
Np — — 1·9m

Christchurch (Entrance) (Quay) (Tuckton)*

Range at Portsmouth
Sp — 3·9m
— — 2·6m
Np — — 1·9m

LYMINGTON TO COWES

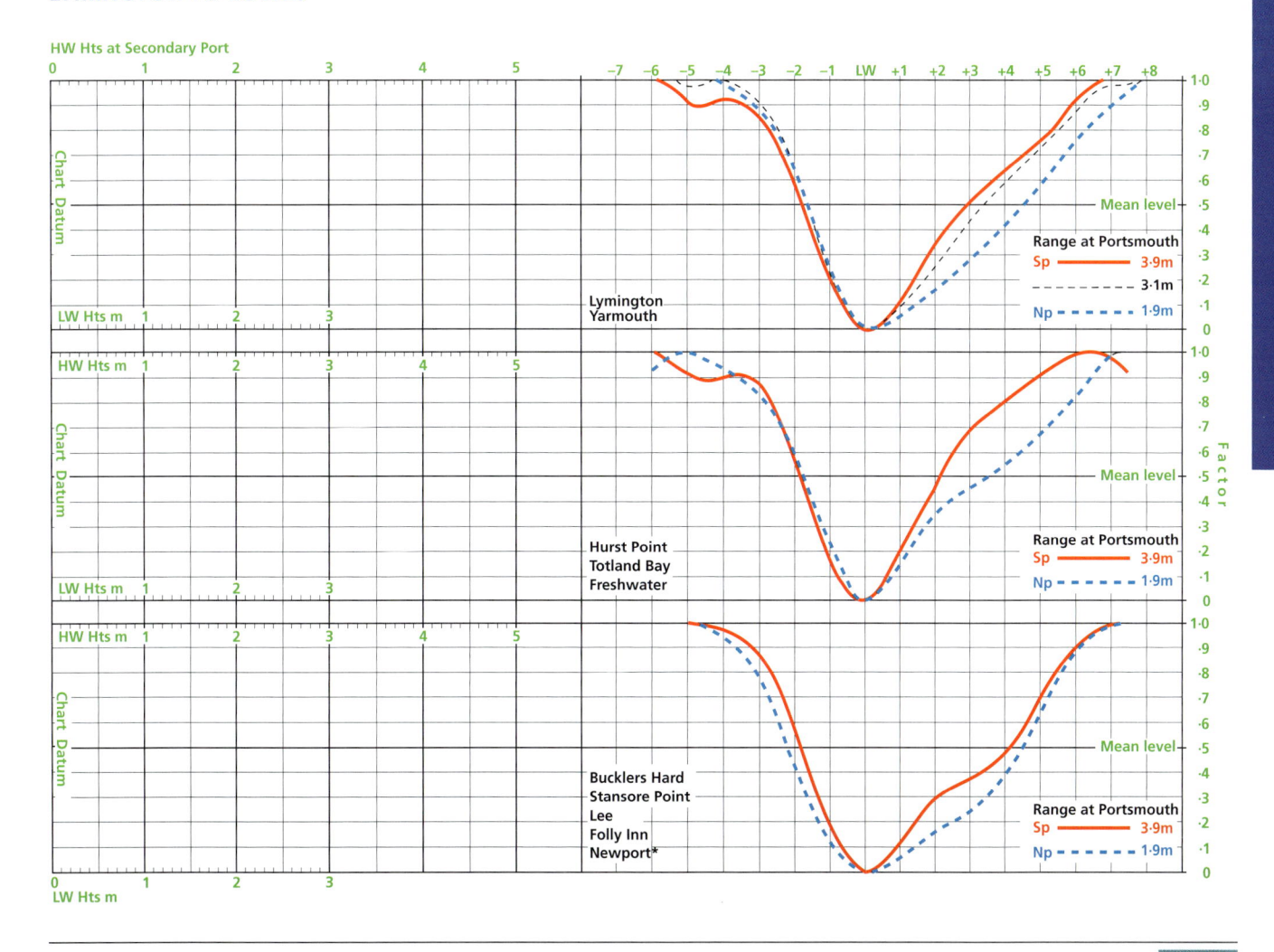

Lymington
Yarmouth

Range at Portsmouth
Sp — 3·9m
— — 3·1m
Np — — 1·9m

Hurst Point
Totland Bay
Freshwater

Range at Portsmouth
Sp — 3·9m
Np — — 1·9m

Bucklers Hard
Stansore Point
Lee
Folly Inn
Newport*

Range at Portsmouth
Sp — 3·9m
Np — — 1·9m

RYDE TO SELSEY

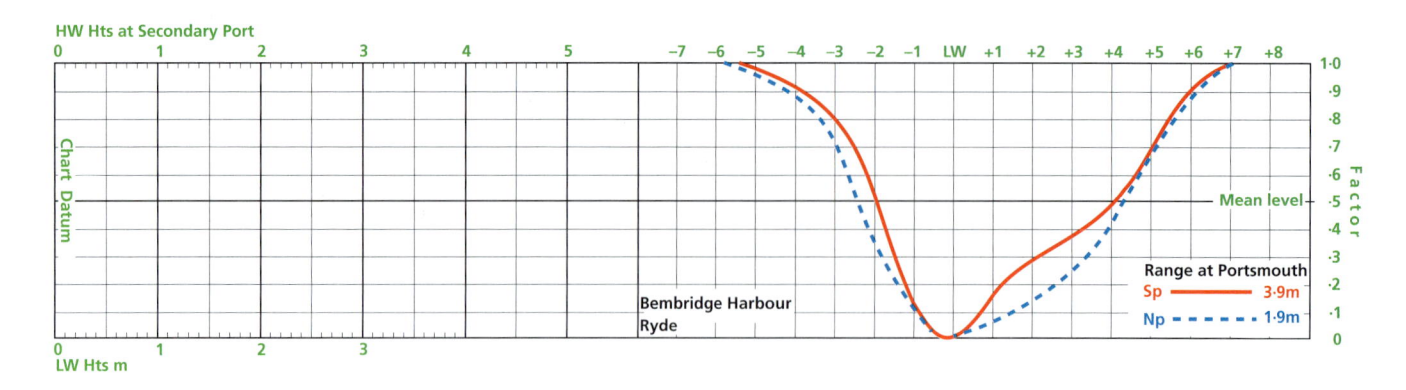

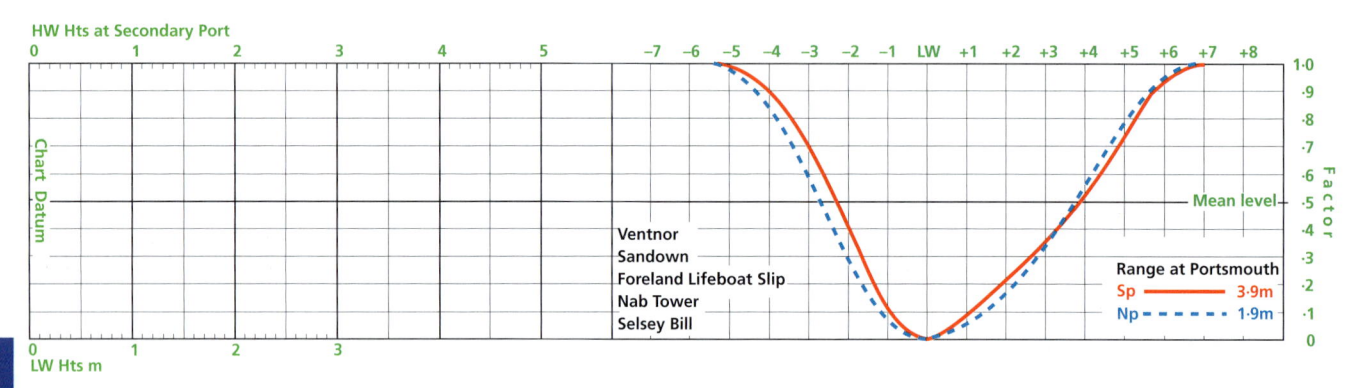

Bembridge Harbour
Ryde

Range at Portsmouth
Sp — 3·9m
Np --- 1·9m

Ventnor
Sandown
Foreland Lifeboat Slip
Nab Tower
Selsey Bill

Range at Portsmouth
Sp — 3·9m
Np --- 1·9m

SOUTHAMPTON
MEAN SPRING AND NEAP CURVES
Springs occur 2 days after New and Full Moon

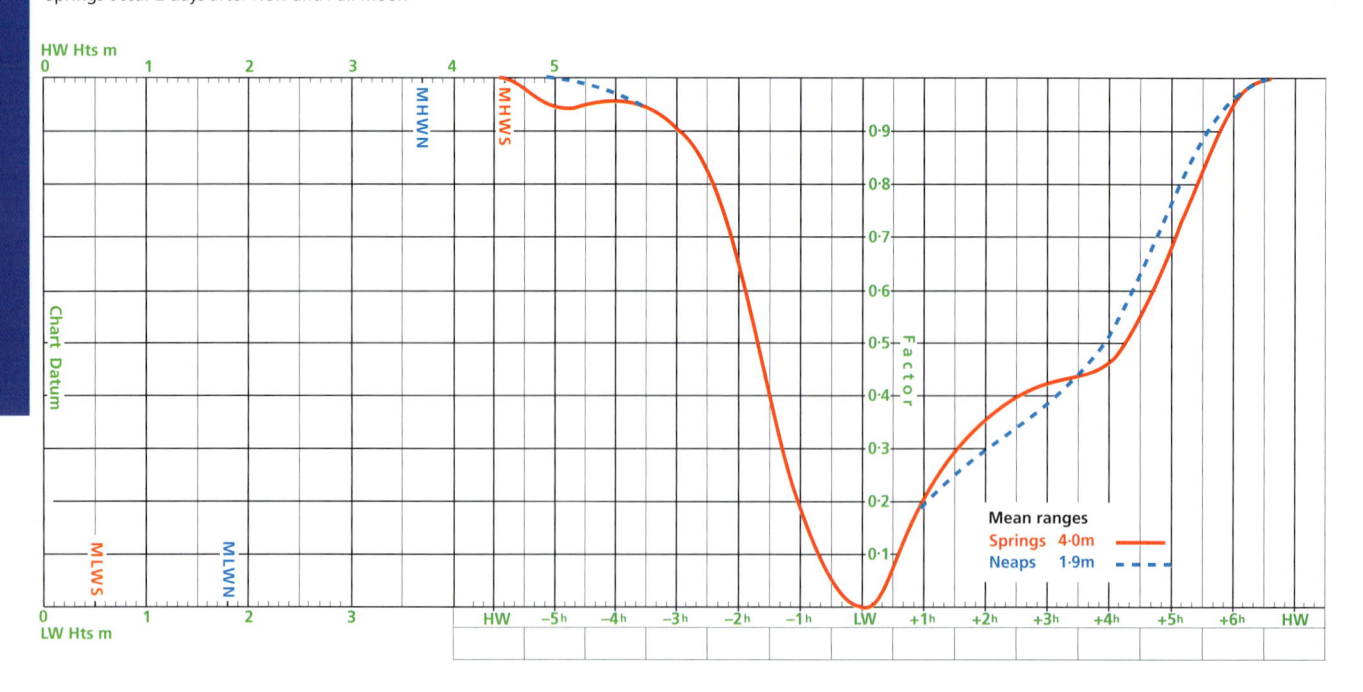

Mean ranges
Springs 4·0m
Neaps 1·9m

The Cruising Almanac

PORTSMOUTH
MEAN SPRING AND NEAP CURVES
Springs occur 2 days after New and Full Moon

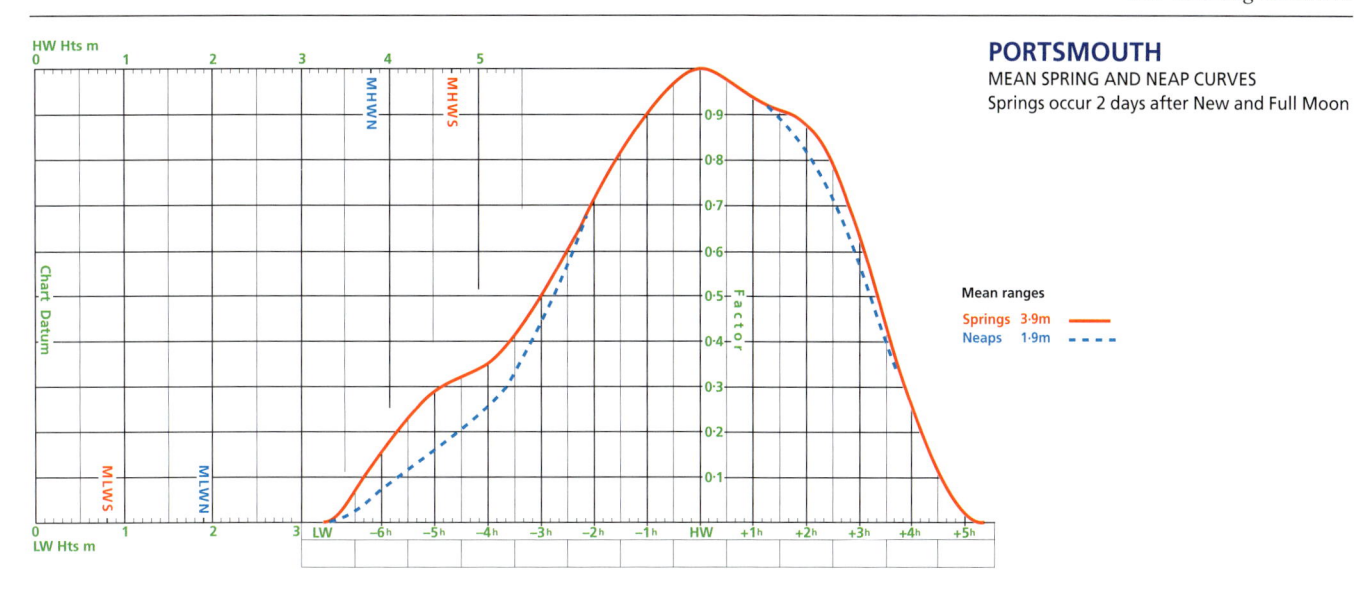

Mean ranges
Springs 3·9m
Neaps 1·9m

SHOREHAM
MEAN SPRING AND NEAP CURVES
Springs occur 2 days after New and Full Moon

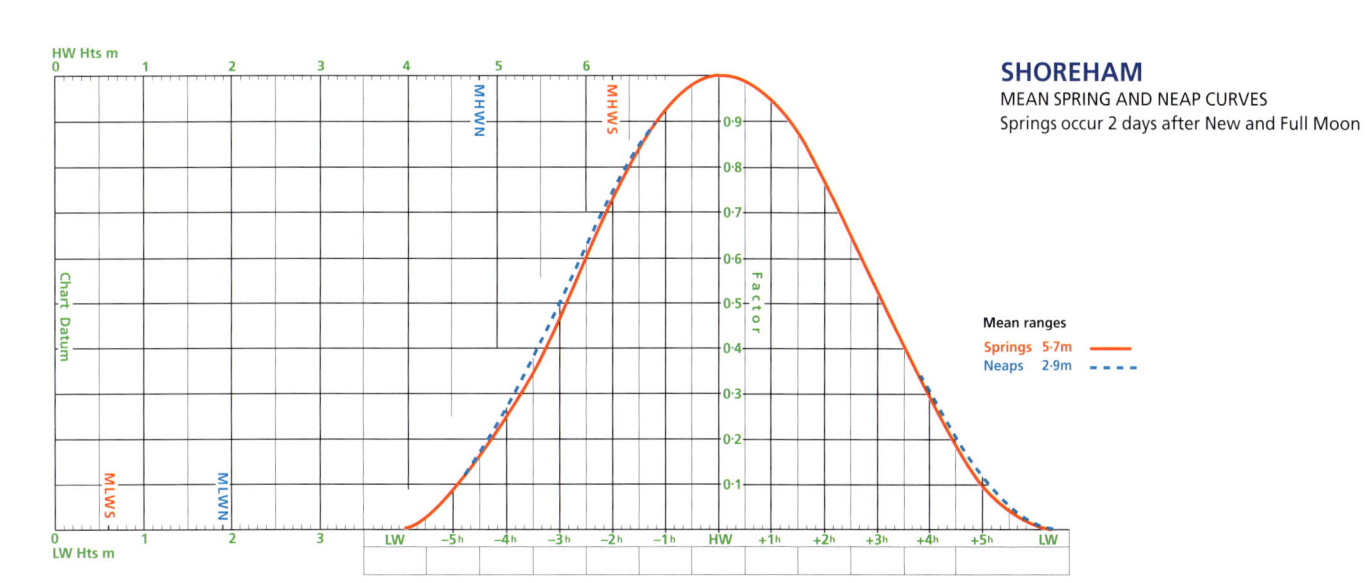

Mean ranges
Springs 5·7m
Neaps 2·9m

DOVER
MEAN SPRING AND NEAP CURVES
Springs occur 2 days after New and Full Moon

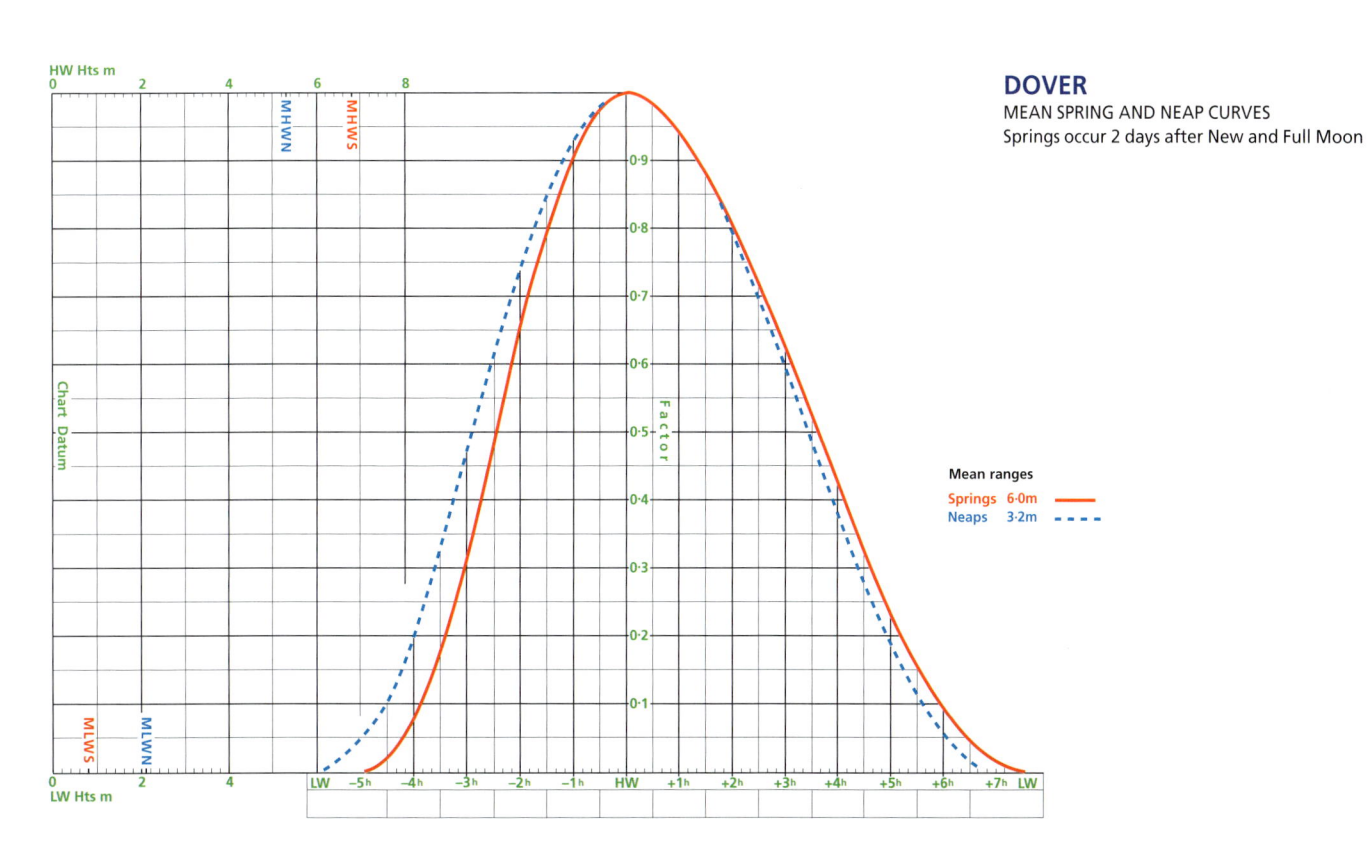

Mean ranges
Springs 6·0m
Neaps 3·2m

TIDAL STREAMS AND CURVES

457

The Cruising Almanac

SHEERNESS
MEAN SPRING AND NEAP CURVES
Springs occur 2 days after New and Full Moon

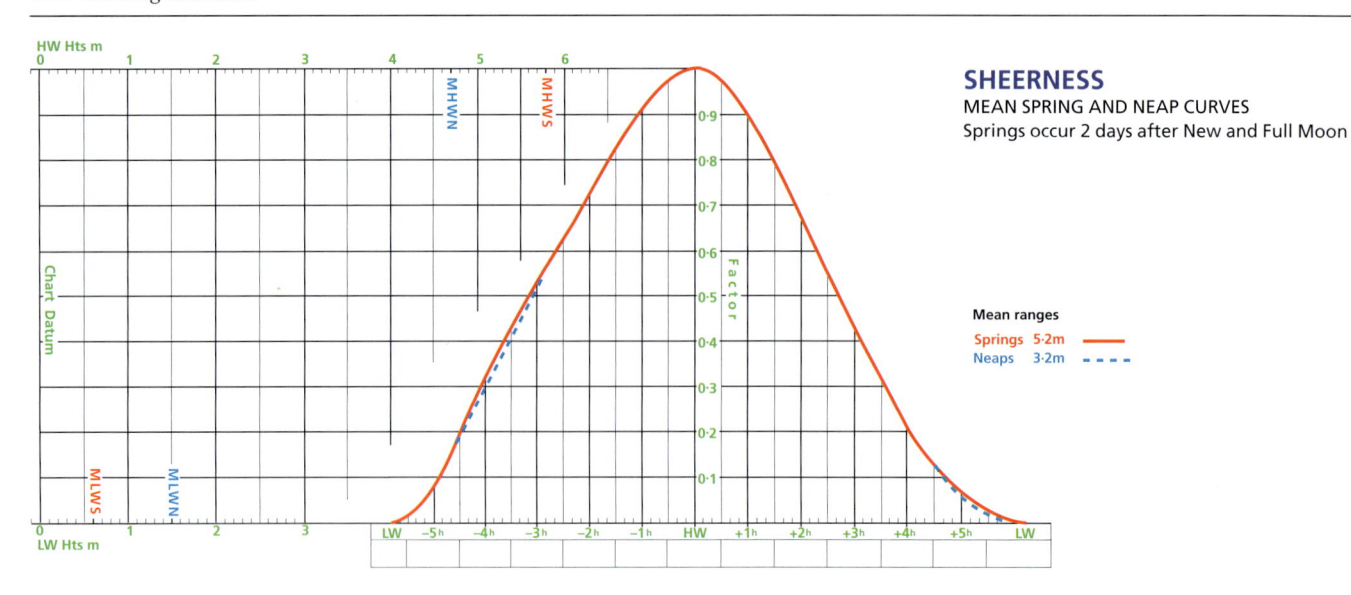

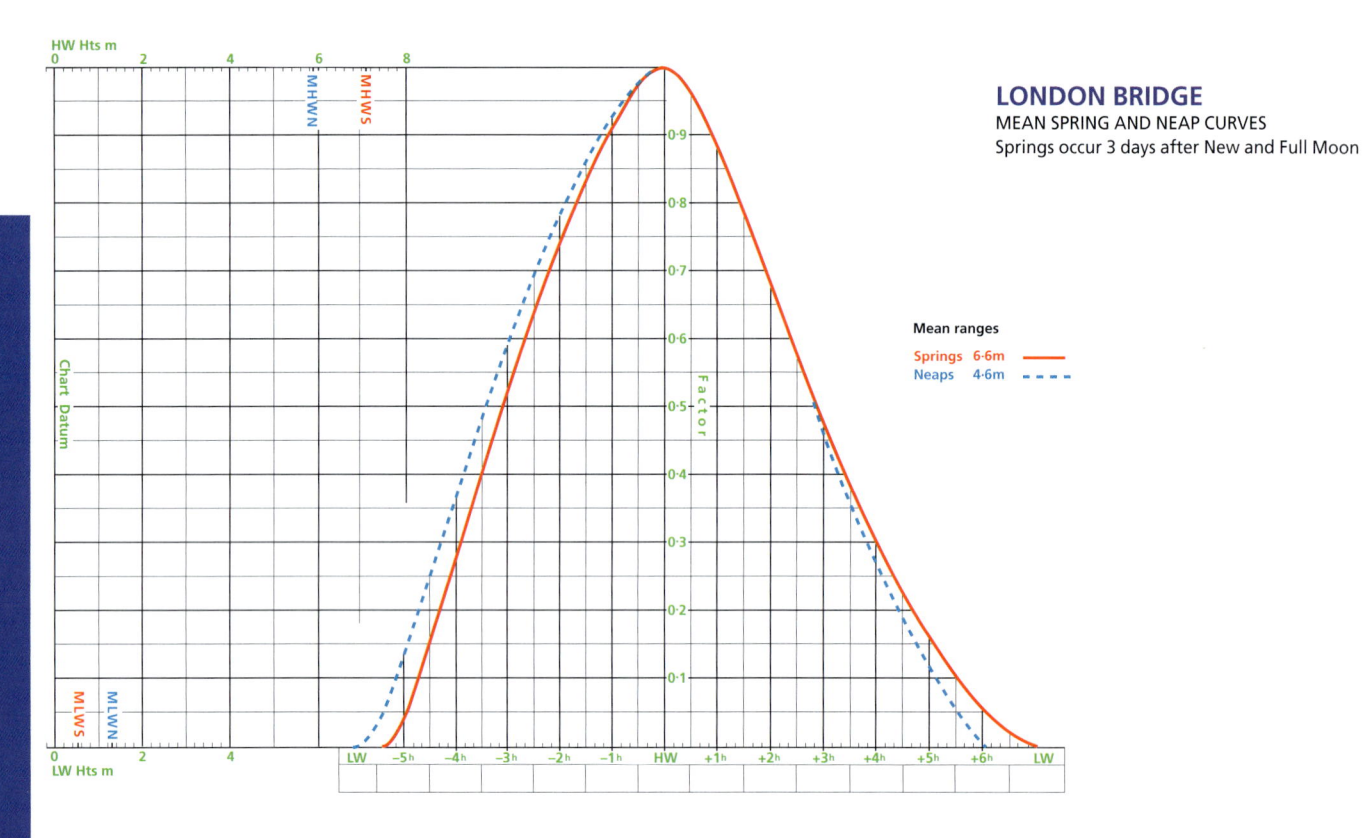

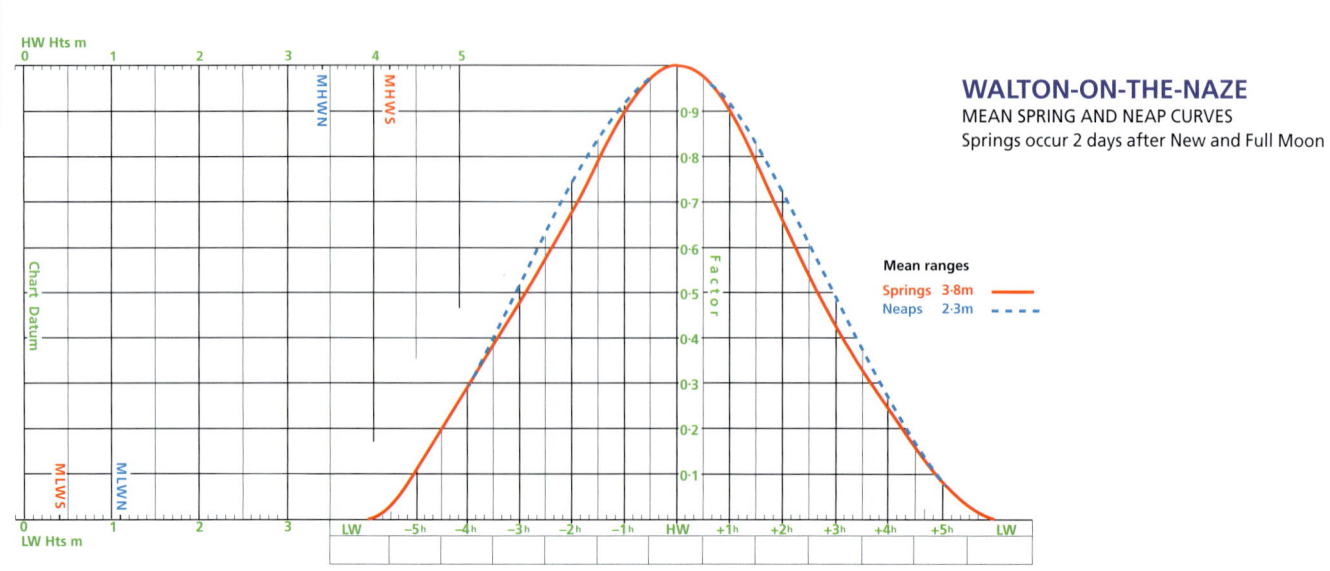

Mean ranges
Springs 5·2m
Neaps 3·2m

LONDON BRIDGE
MEAN SPRING AND NEAP CURVES
Springs occur 3 days after New and Full Moon

Mean ranges
Springs 6·6m
Neaps 4·6m

WALTON-ON-THE-NAZE
MEAN SPRING AND NEAP CURVES
Springs occur 2 days after New and Full Moon

Mean ranges
Springs 3·8m
Neaps 2·3m

TIDAL STREAMS AND CURVES

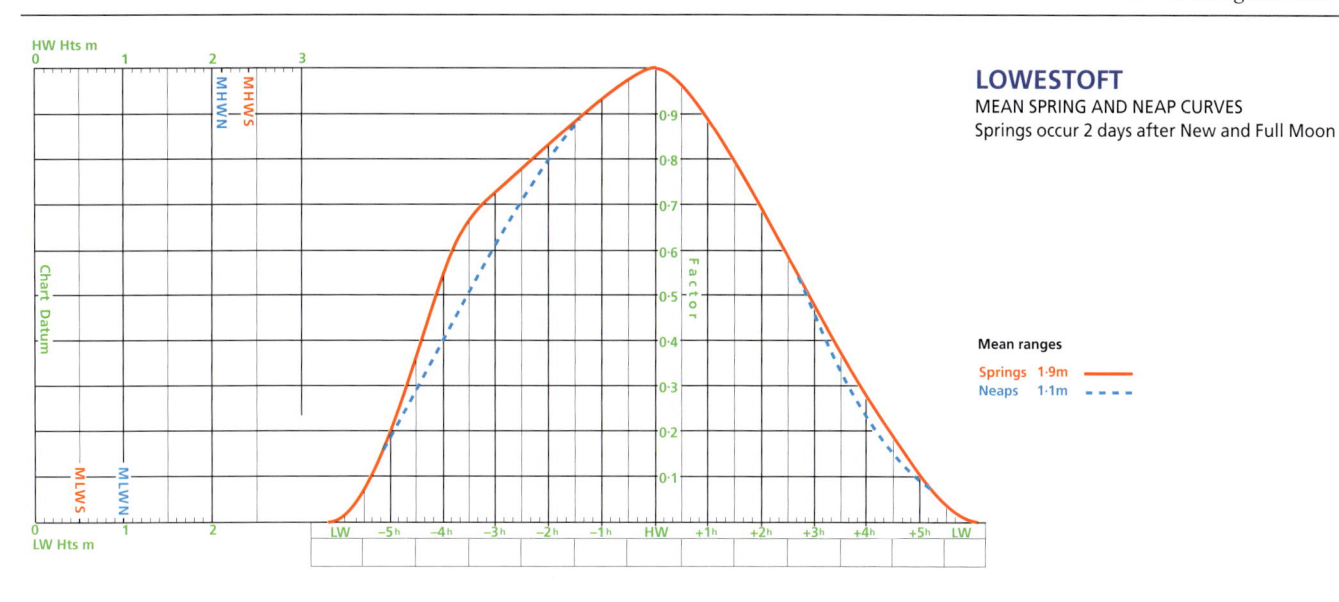

LOWESTOFT
MEAN SPRING AND NEAP CURVES
Springs occur 2 days after New and Full Moon

Mean ranges
Springs 1·9m
Neaps 1·1m

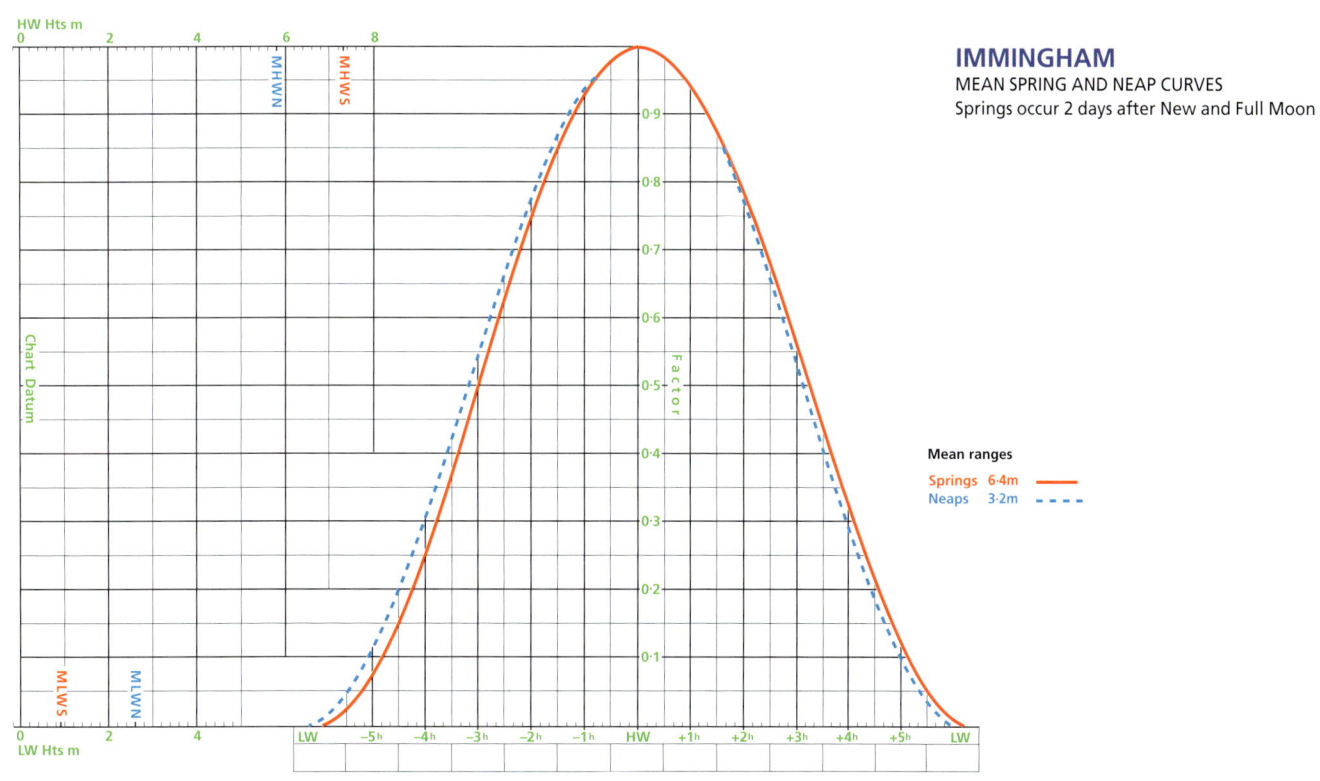

IMMINGHAM
MEAN SPRING AND NEAP CURVES
Springs occur 2 days after New and Full Moon

Mean ranges
Springs 6·4m
Neaps 3·2m

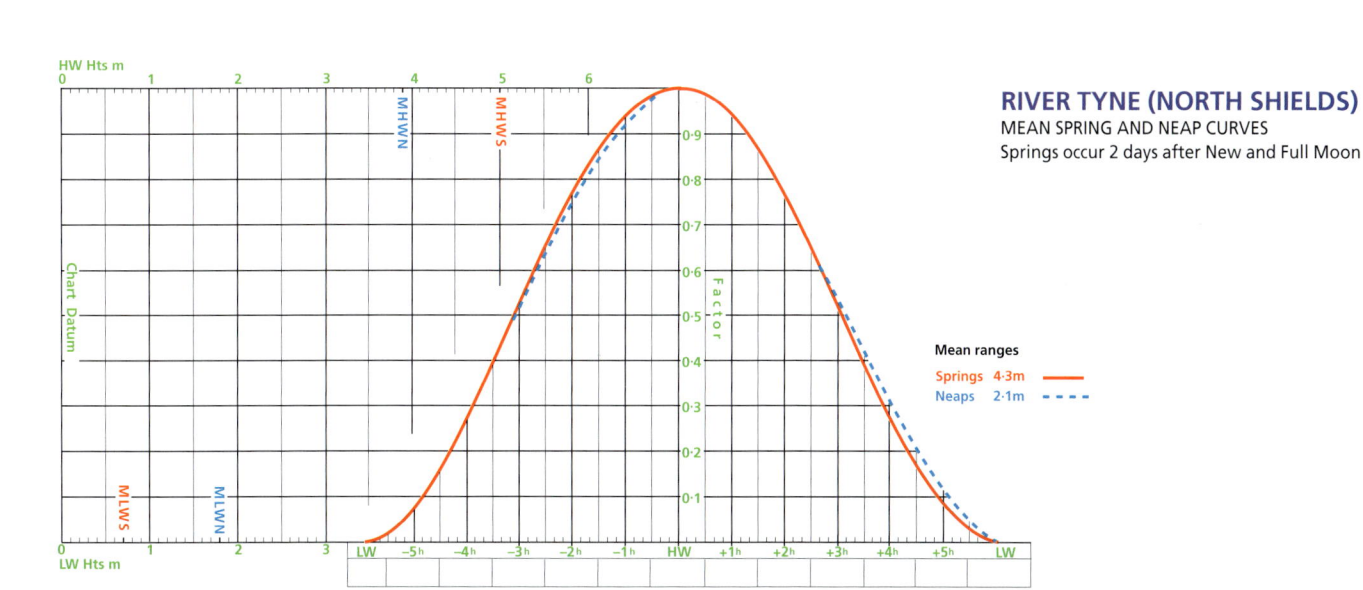

RIVER TYNE (NORTH SHIELDS)
MEAN SPRING AND NEAP CURVES
Springs occur 2 days after New and Full Moon

Mean ranges
Springs 4·3m
Neaps 2·1m

TIDAL STREAMS AND CURVES

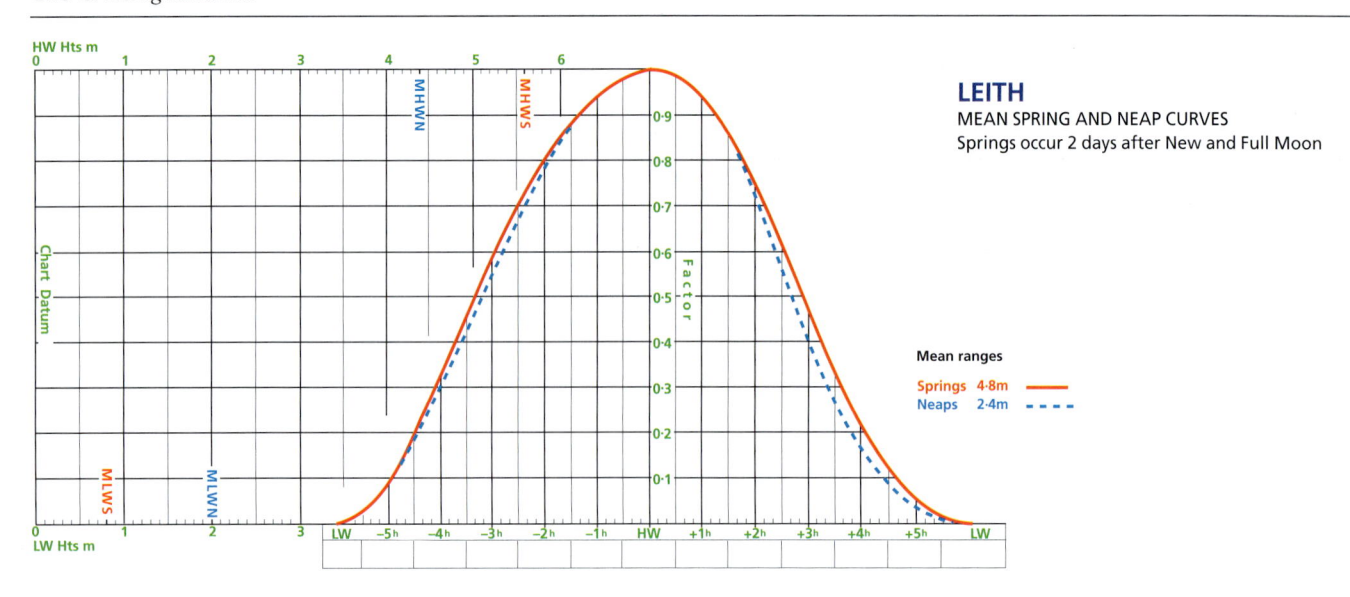

LEITH
MEAN SPRING AND NEAP CURVES
Springs occur 2 days after New and Full Moon

Mean ranges
Springs 4·8m
Neaps 2·4m

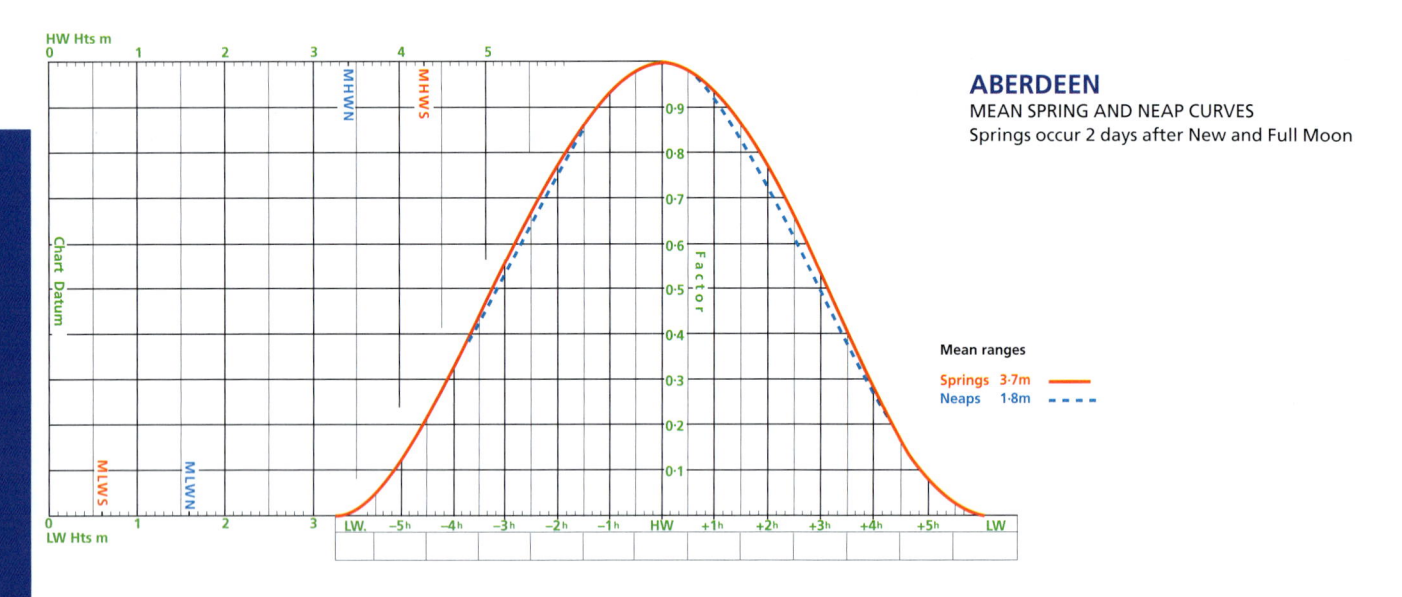

ABERDEEN
MEAN SPRING AND NEAP CURVES
Springs occur 2 days after New and Full Moon

Mean ranges
Springs 3·7m
Neaps 1·8m

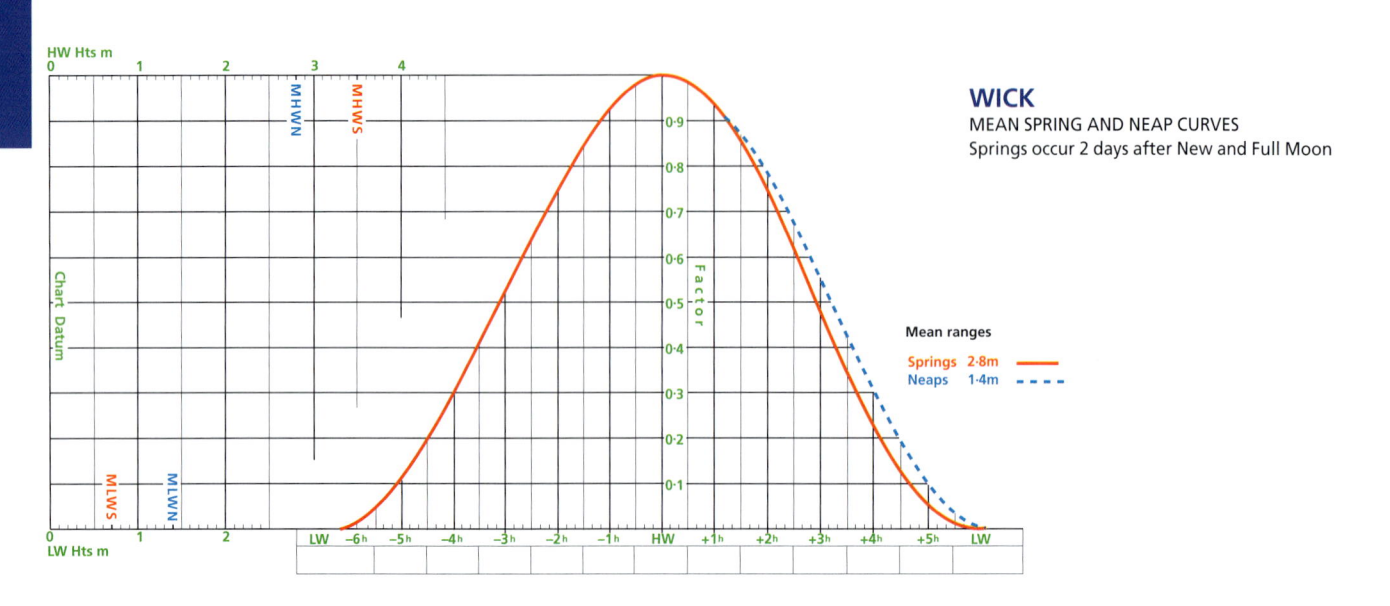

WICK
MEAN SPRING AND NEAP CURVES
Springs occur 2 days after New and Full Moon

Mean ranges
Springs 2·8m
Neaps 1·4m

LERWICK
MEAN SPRING AND NEAP CURVES
Springs occur 1 day after New and Full Moon

Mean ranges
Springs 1·6m
Neaps 0·8m

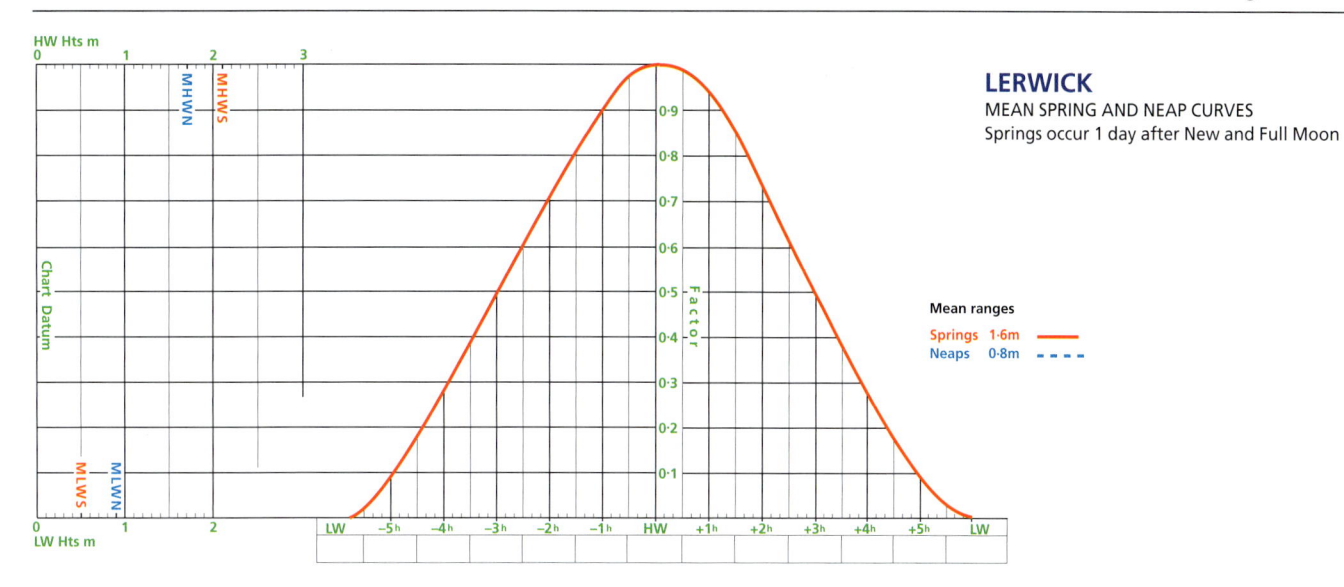

ULLAPOOL
MEAN SPRING AND NEAP CURVES
Springs occur 1 day after New and Full Moon

Mean ranges
Springs 4·5m
Neaps 1·8m

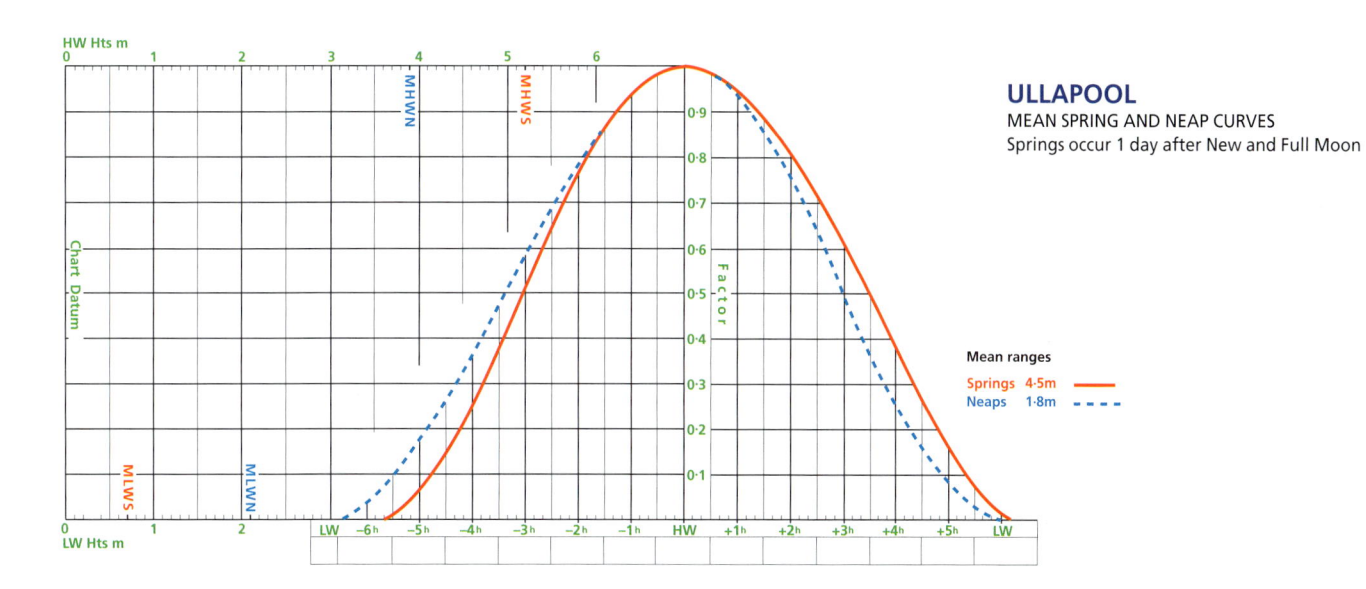

STORNOWAY
MEAN SPRING AND NEAP CURVES
Springs occur 1 day after New and Full Moon

Mean ranges
Springs 4·1m
Neaps 1·7m

TIDAL STREAMS AND CURVES

461

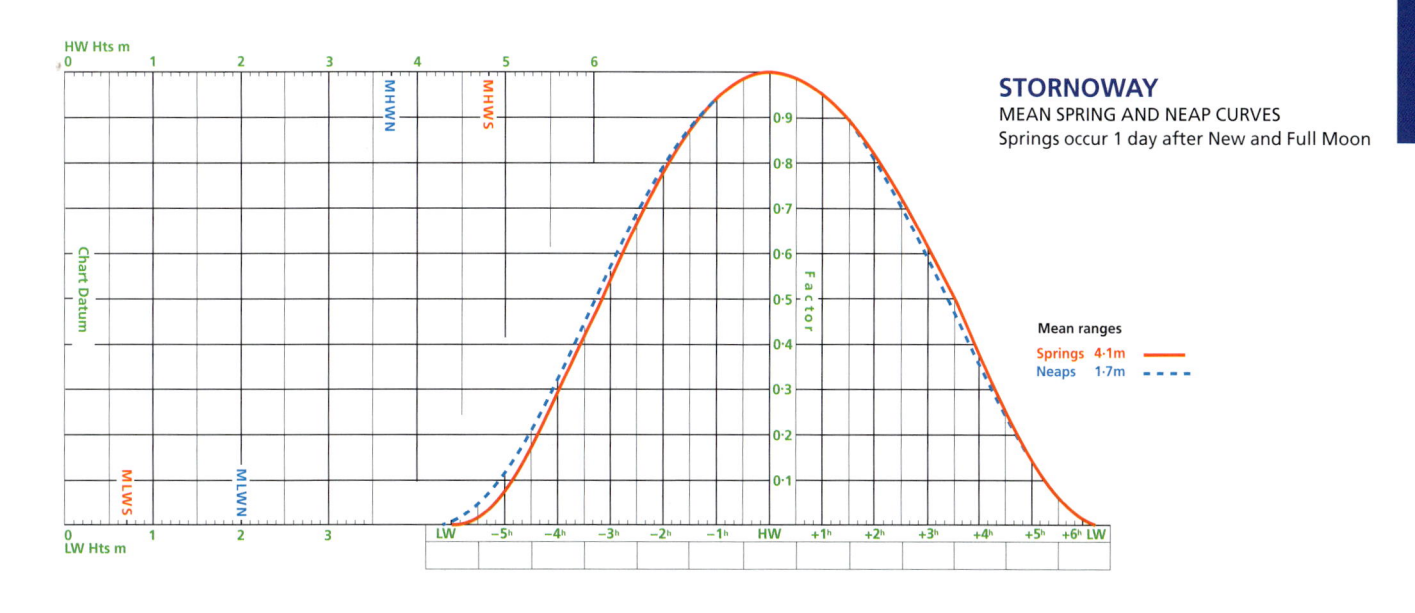

TIDAL STREAMS AND CURVES

OBAN
MEAN SPRING AND NEAP CURVES
Springs occur 2 days after New and Full Moon

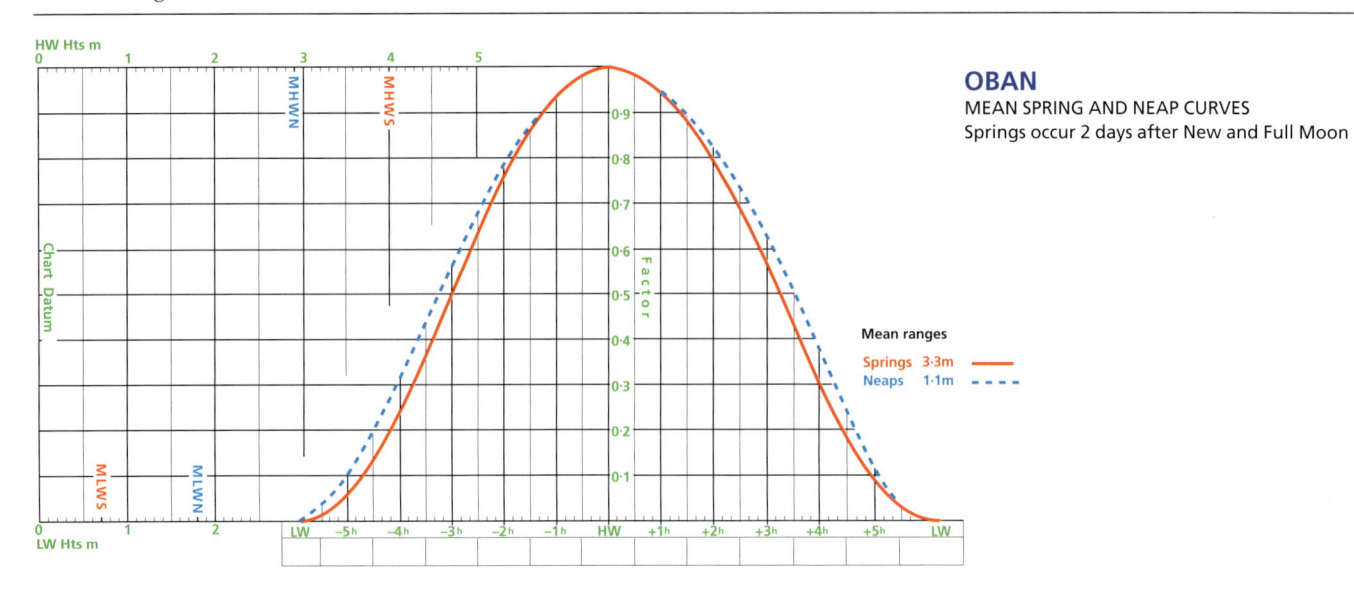

Mean ranges
Springs 3·3m
Neaps 1·1m

GREENOCK
MEAN SPRING AND NEAP CURVES
Springs occur 2 days after New and Full Moon

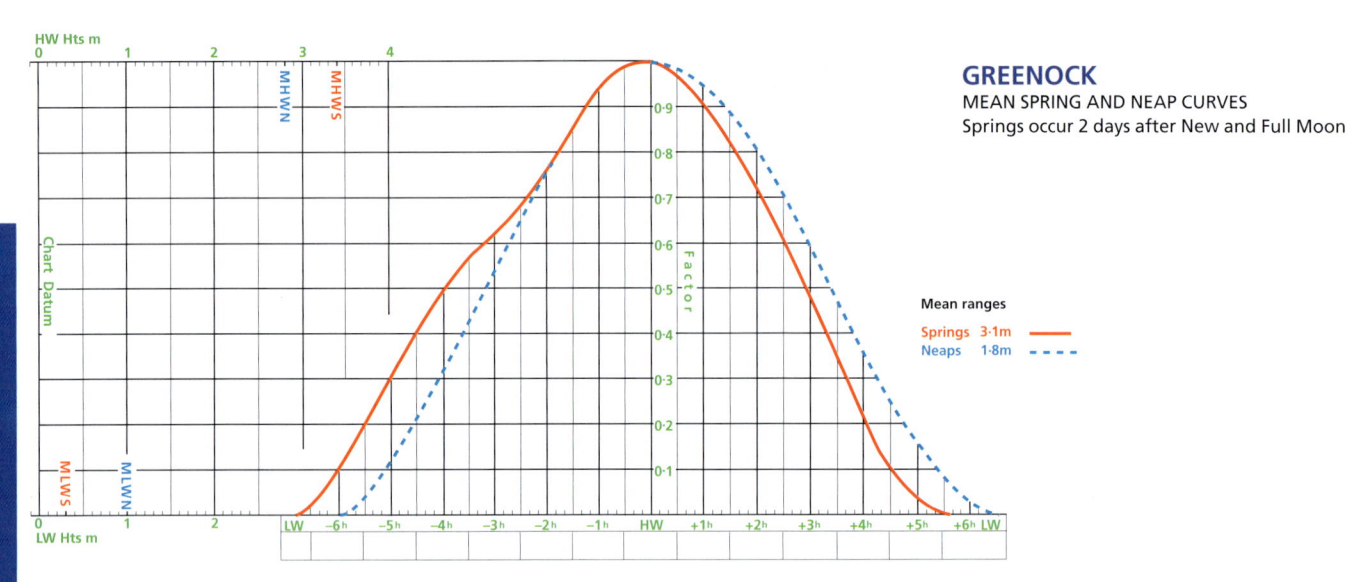

Mean ranges
Springs 3·1m
Neaps 1·8m

LIVERPOOL
MEAN SPRING AND NEAP CURVES
Springs occur 2 days after New and Full Moon

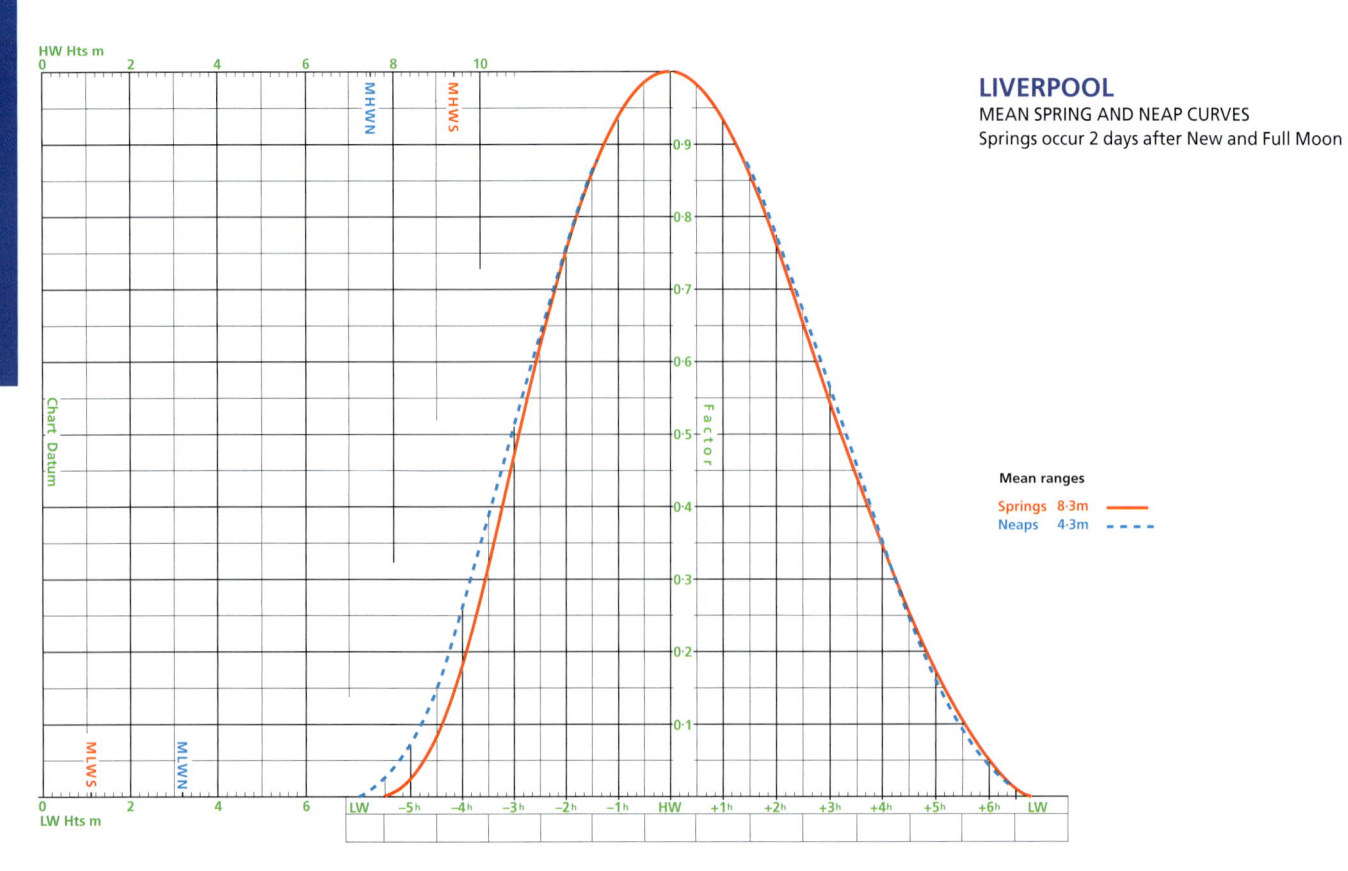

Mean ranges
Springs 8·3m
Neaps 4·3m

The Cruising Almanac

HOLYHEAD
MEAN SPRING AND NEAP CURVES
Springs occur 2 days after New and Full Moon

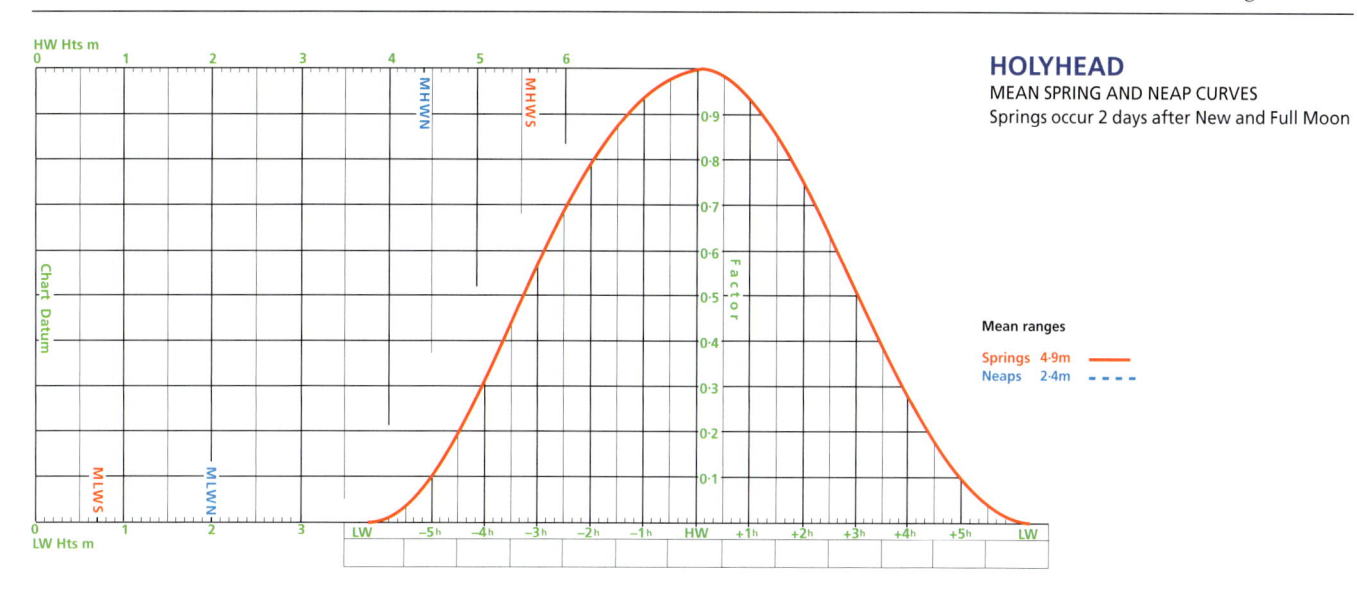

Mean ranges
Springs 4·9m
Neaps 2·4m

MILFORD HAVEN
MEAN SPRING AND NEAP CURVES
Springs occur 2 days after New and Full Moon

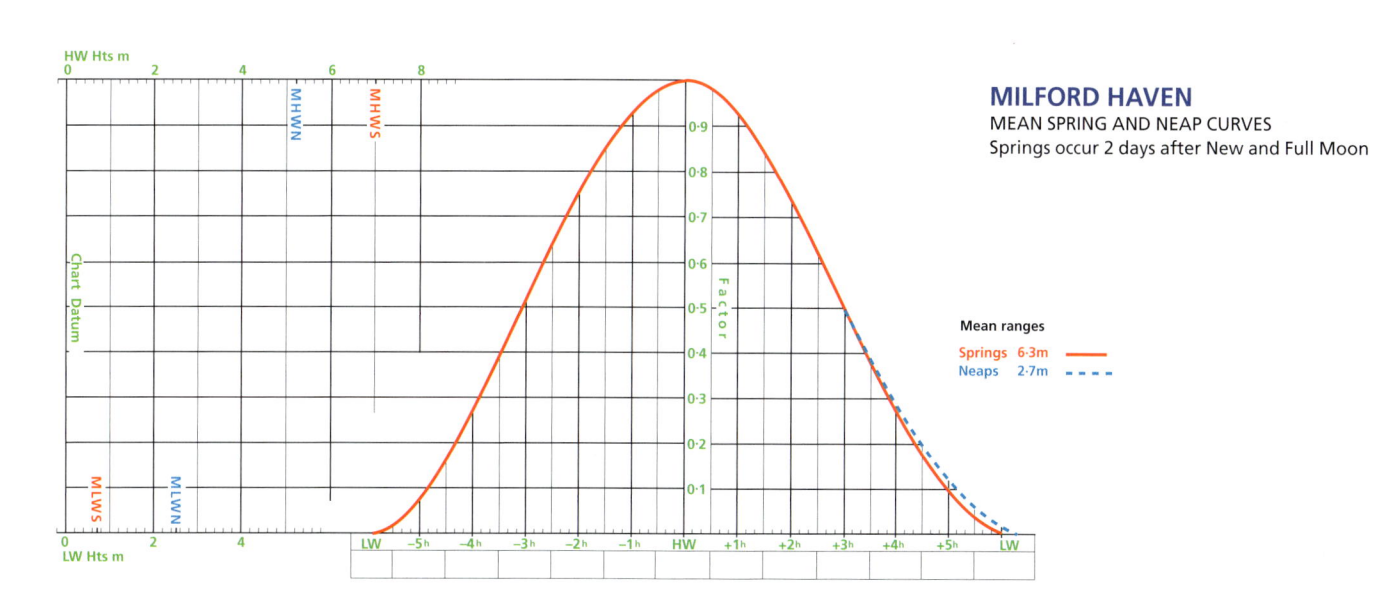

Mean ranges
Springs 6·3m
Neaps 2·7m

AVONMOUTH
MEAN SPRING AND NEAP CURVES
Springs occur 2 days after New and Full Moon

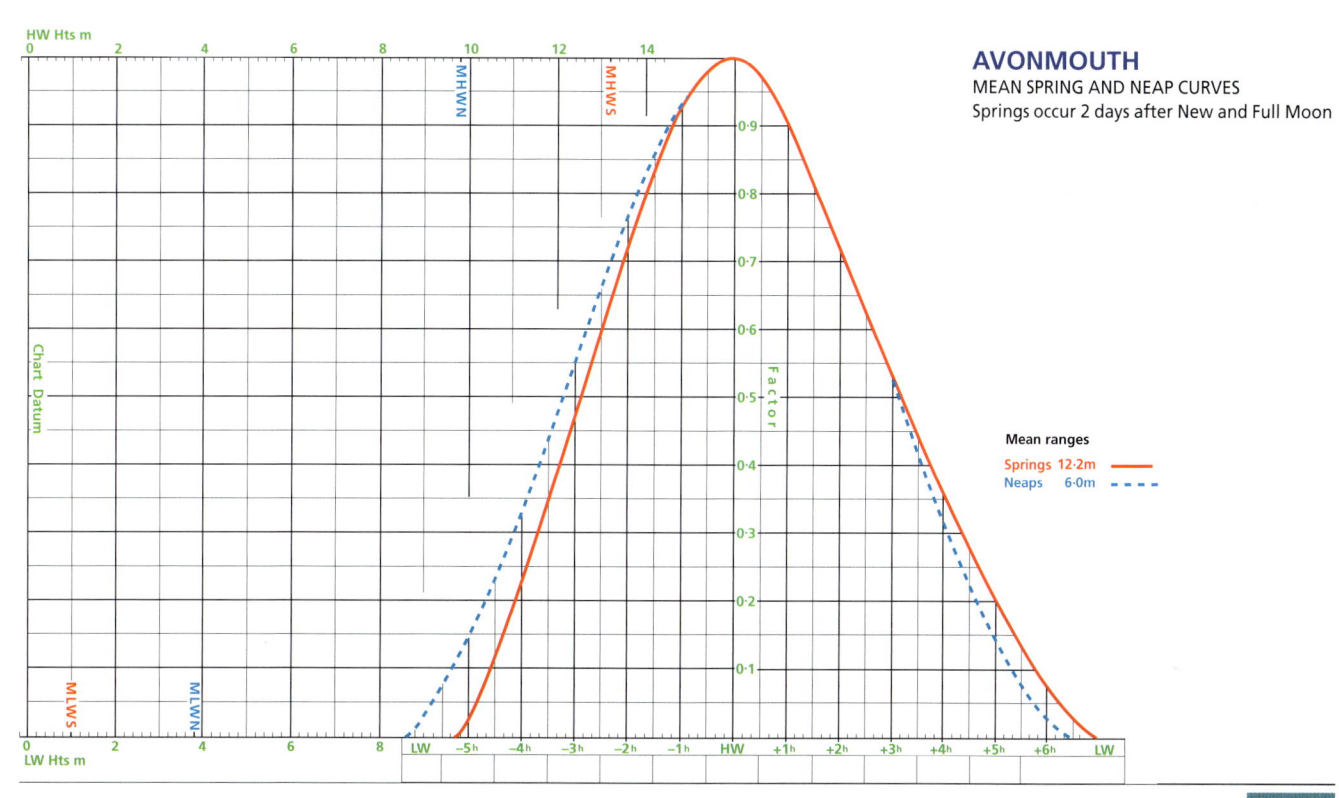

Mean ranges
Springs 12·2m
Neaps 6·0m

TIDAL STREAMS AND CURVES

The Cruising Almanac

COBH
MEAN SPRING AND NEAP CURVES
Springs occur 2 days after New and Full Moon

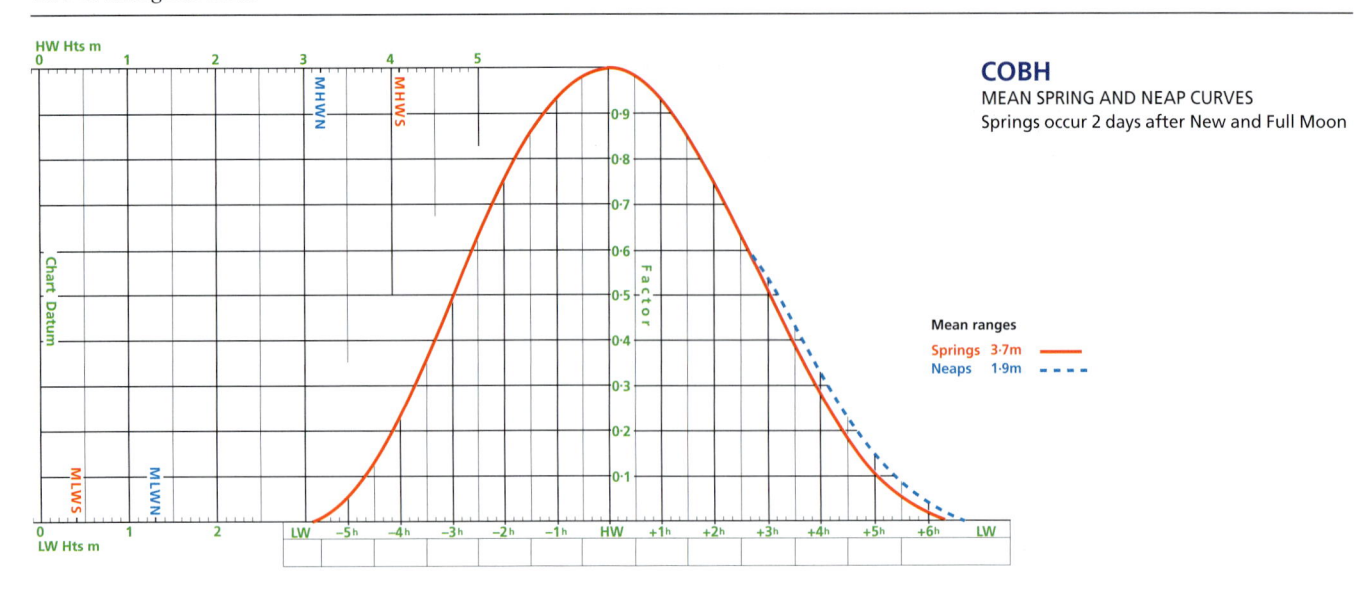

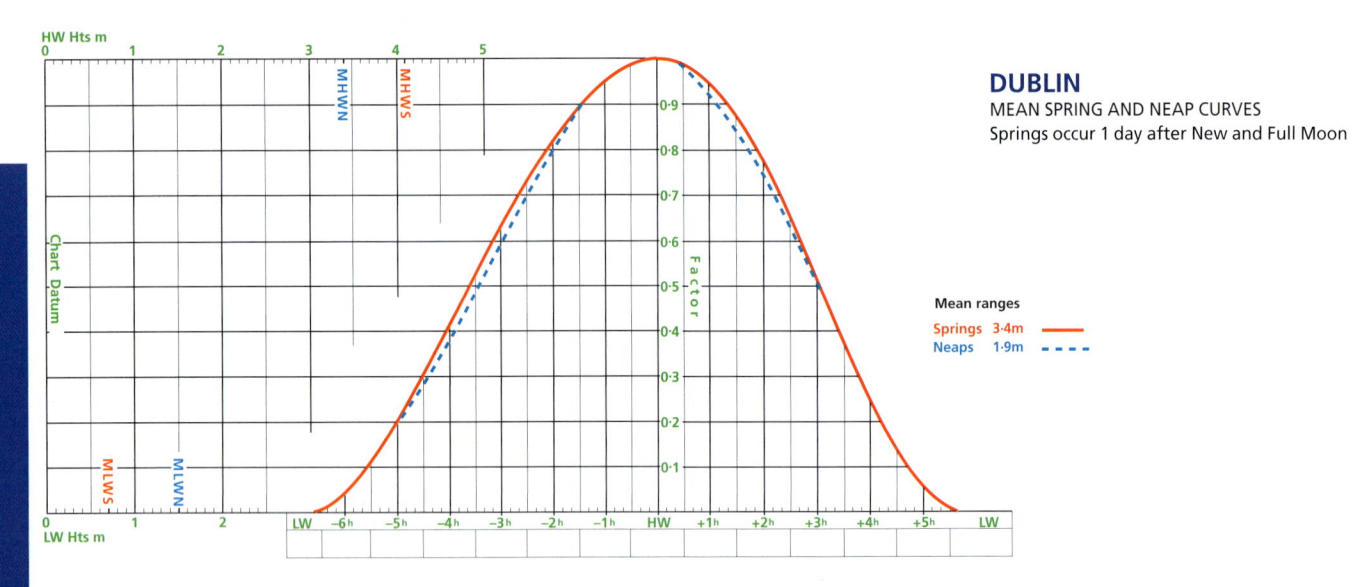

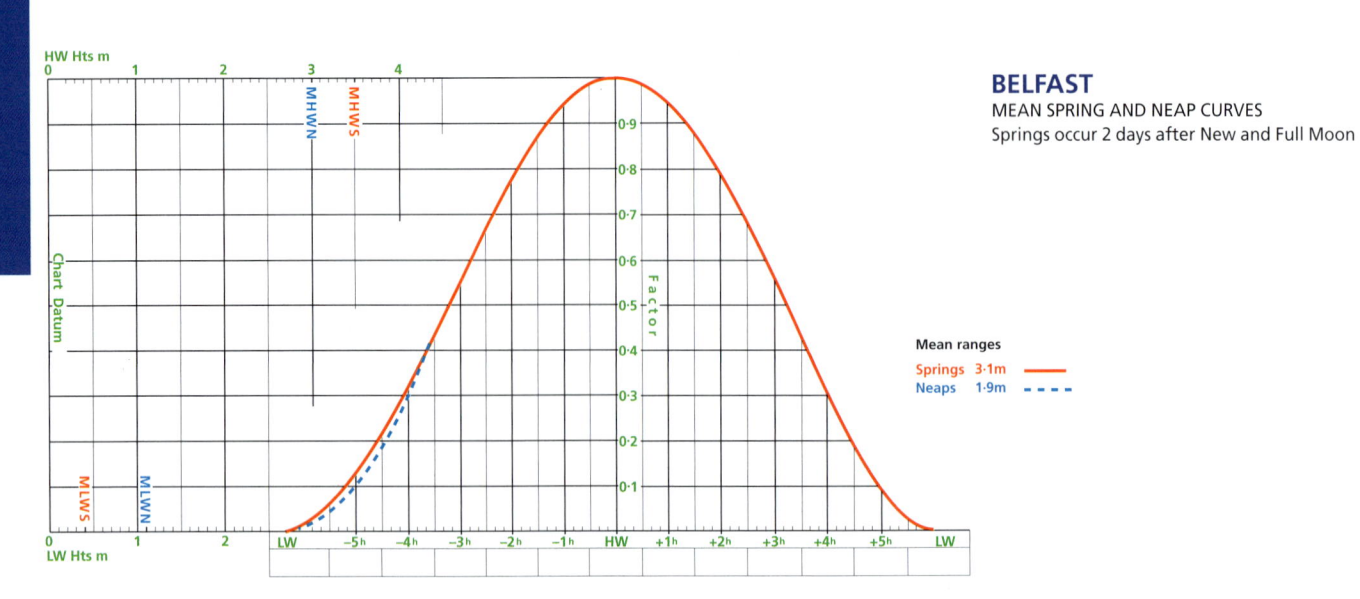

Mean ranges
Springs 3·7m
Neaps 1·9m

DUBLIN
MEAN SPRING AND NEAP CURVES
Springs occur 1 day after New and Full Moon

Mean ranges
Springs 3·4m
Neaps 1·9m

BELFAST
MEAN SPRING AND NEAP CURVES
Springs occur 2 days after New and Full Moon

Mean ranges
Springs 3·1m
Neaps 1·9m

TIDAL STREAMS AND CURVES

GALWAY
MEAN SPRING AND NEAP CURVES
Springs occur 1 day after New and Full Moon

Mean ranges
Springs 4·3m
Neaps 1·9m

ESBJERG
MEAN SPRING AND NEAP CURVES
Springs occur 3 days after New and Full Moon

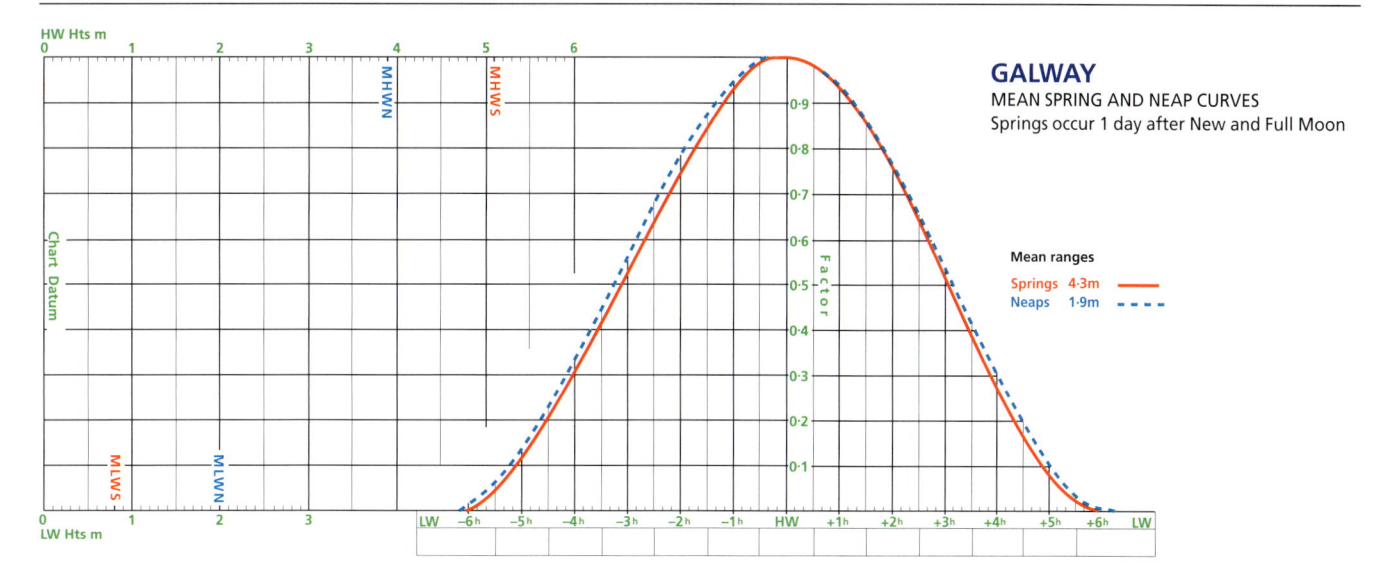

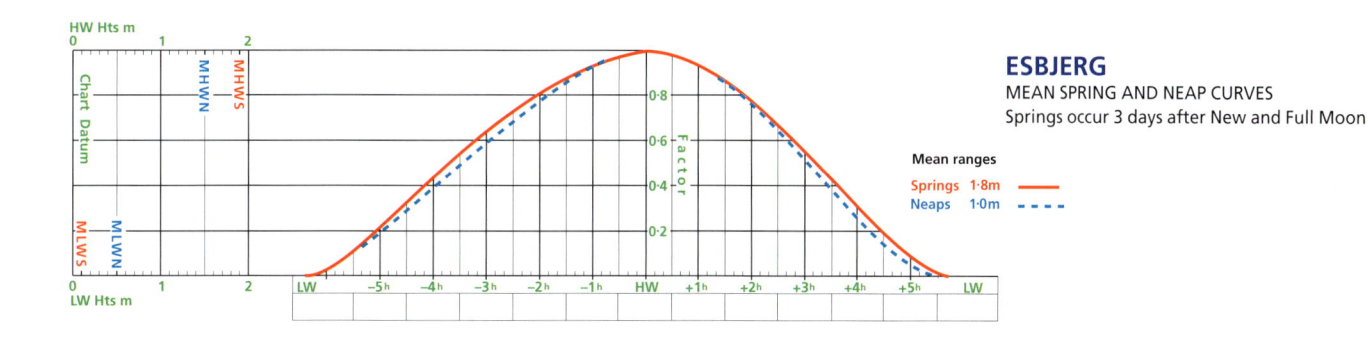

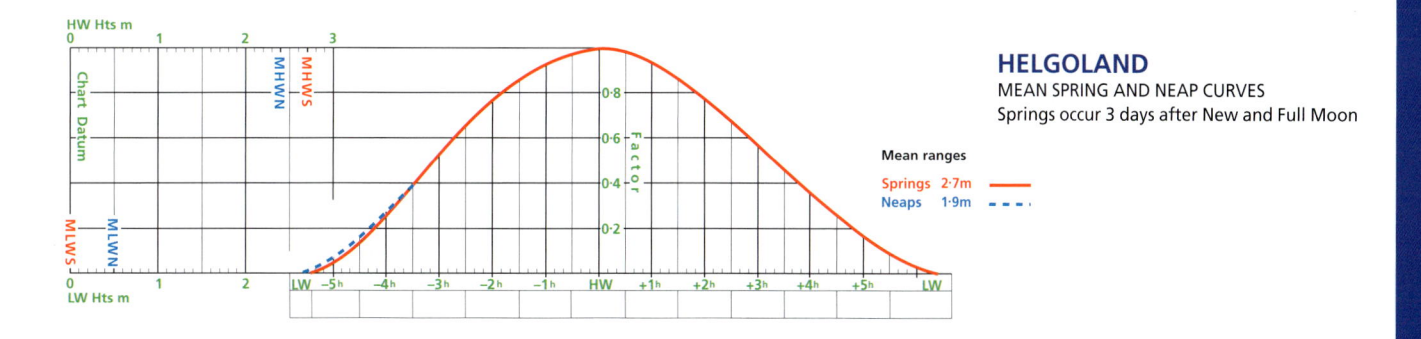

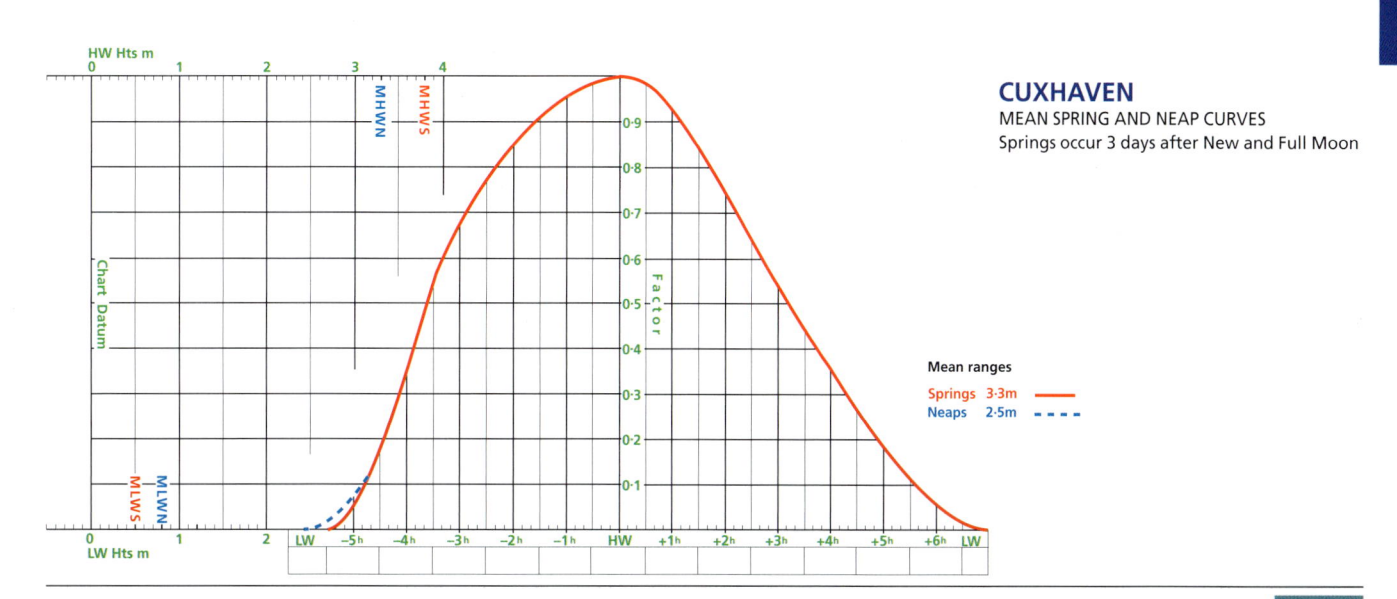

Mean ranges
Springs 1·8m
Neaps 1·0m

HELGOLAND
MEAN SPRING AND NEAP CURVES
Springs occur 3 days after New and Full Moon

Mean ranges
Springs 2·7m
Neaps 1·9m

CUXHAVEN
MEAN SPRING AND NEAP CURVES
Springs occur 3 days after New and Full Moon

Mean ranges
Springs 3·3m
Neaps 2·5m

TIDAL STREAMS AND CURVES

HOEK VAN HOLLAND
MEAN SPRING AND NEAP CURVES
Springs occur 2 days after New and Full Moon

Mean ranges
Springs 1·9m
Neaps 1·5m

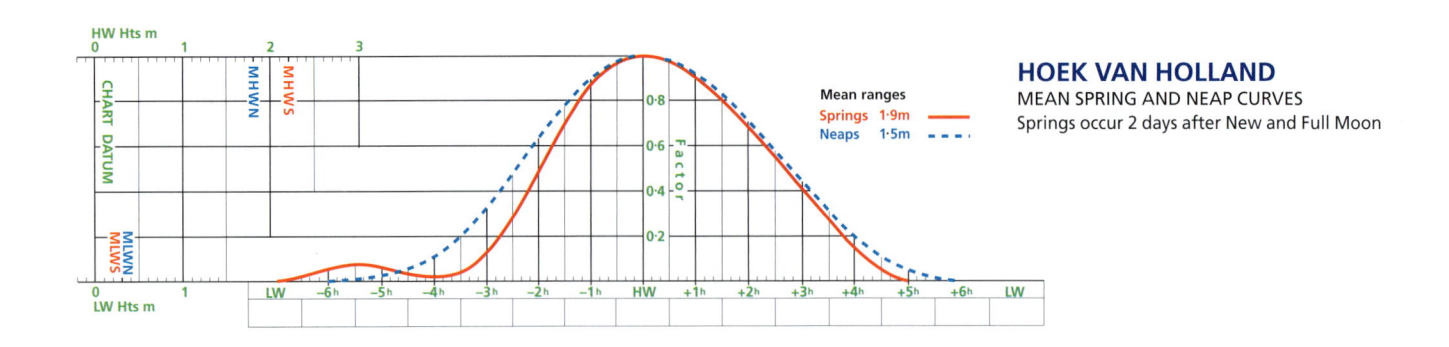

VLISSINGEN
MEAN SPRING AND NEAP CURVES
Springs occur 2 days after New and Full Moon

Mean ranges
Springs 4·4m
Neaps 3·0m

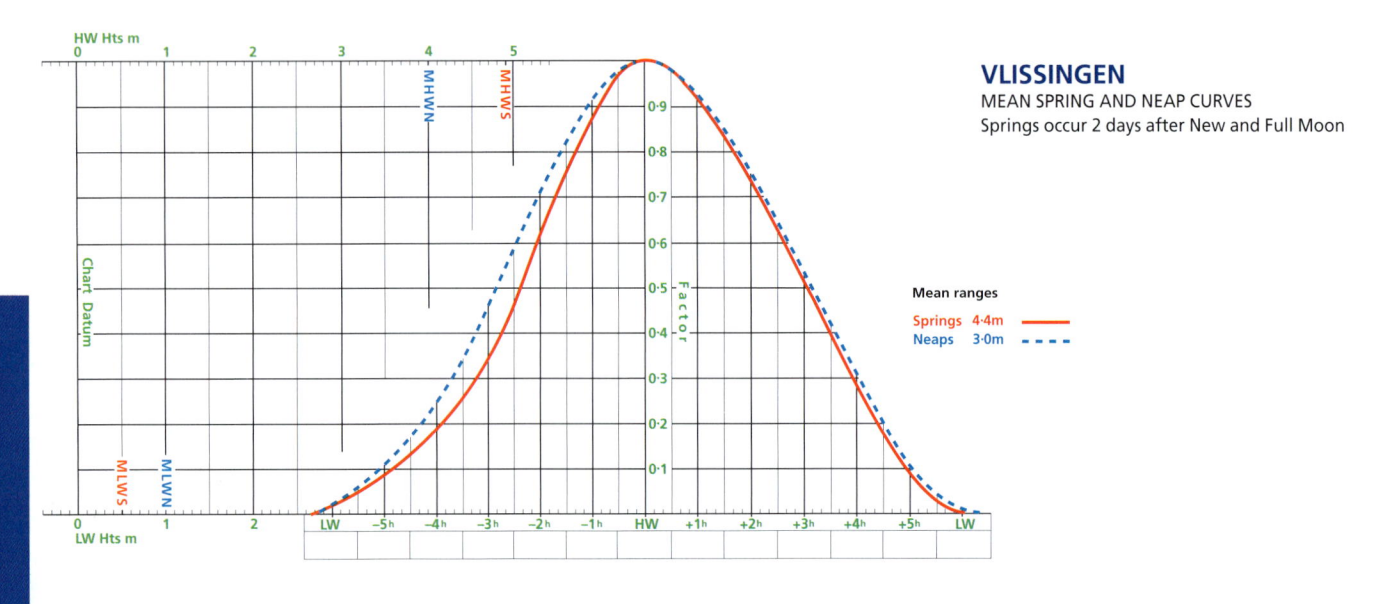

DUNKERQUE
MEAN SPRING AND NEAP CURVES
Springs occur 2 days after New and Full Moon

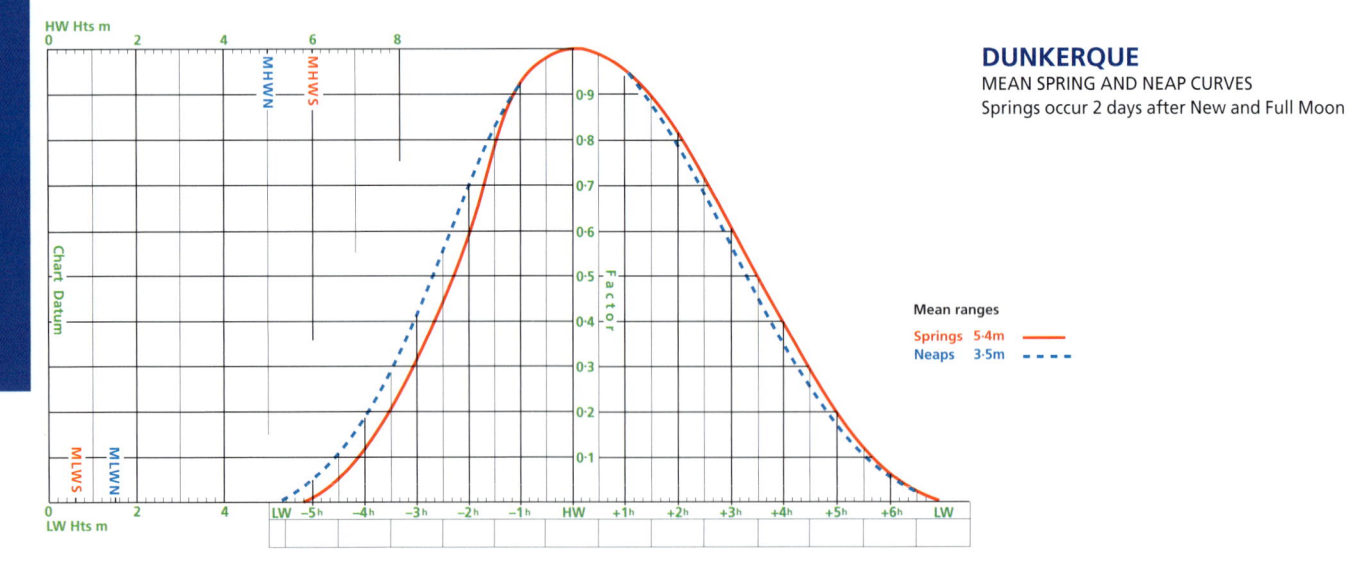

Mean ranges
Springs 5·4m
Neaps 3·5m

CALAIS
MEAN SPRING AND NEAP CURVES
Springs occur 2 days after New and Full Moon

Mean ranges
Springs 6·5m
Neaps 4·0m

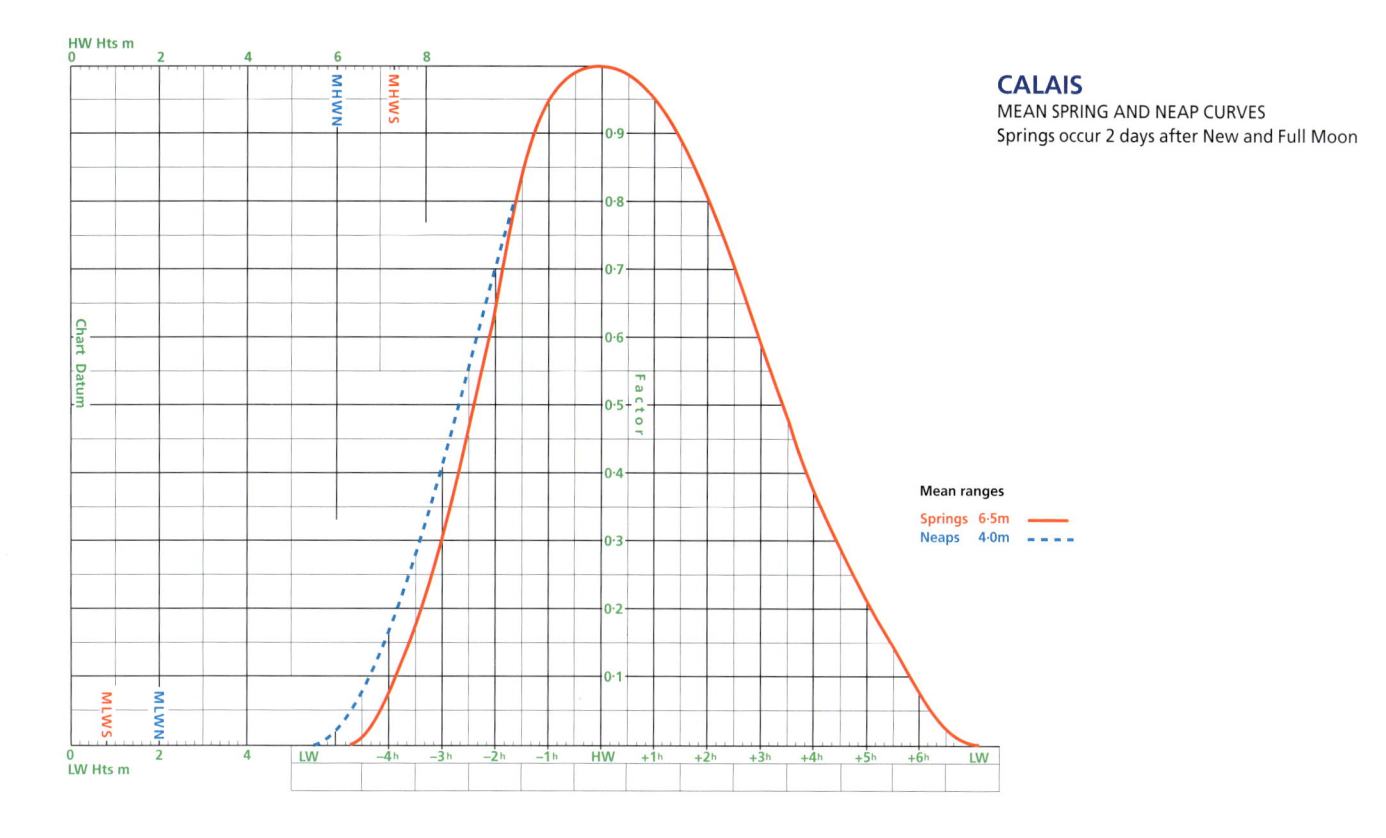

DIEPPE
MEAN SPRING AND NEAP CURVES
Springs occur 2 days after New and Full Moon

Mean ranges
Springs 8·5m
Neaps 4·9m

TIDAL STREAMS AND CURVES

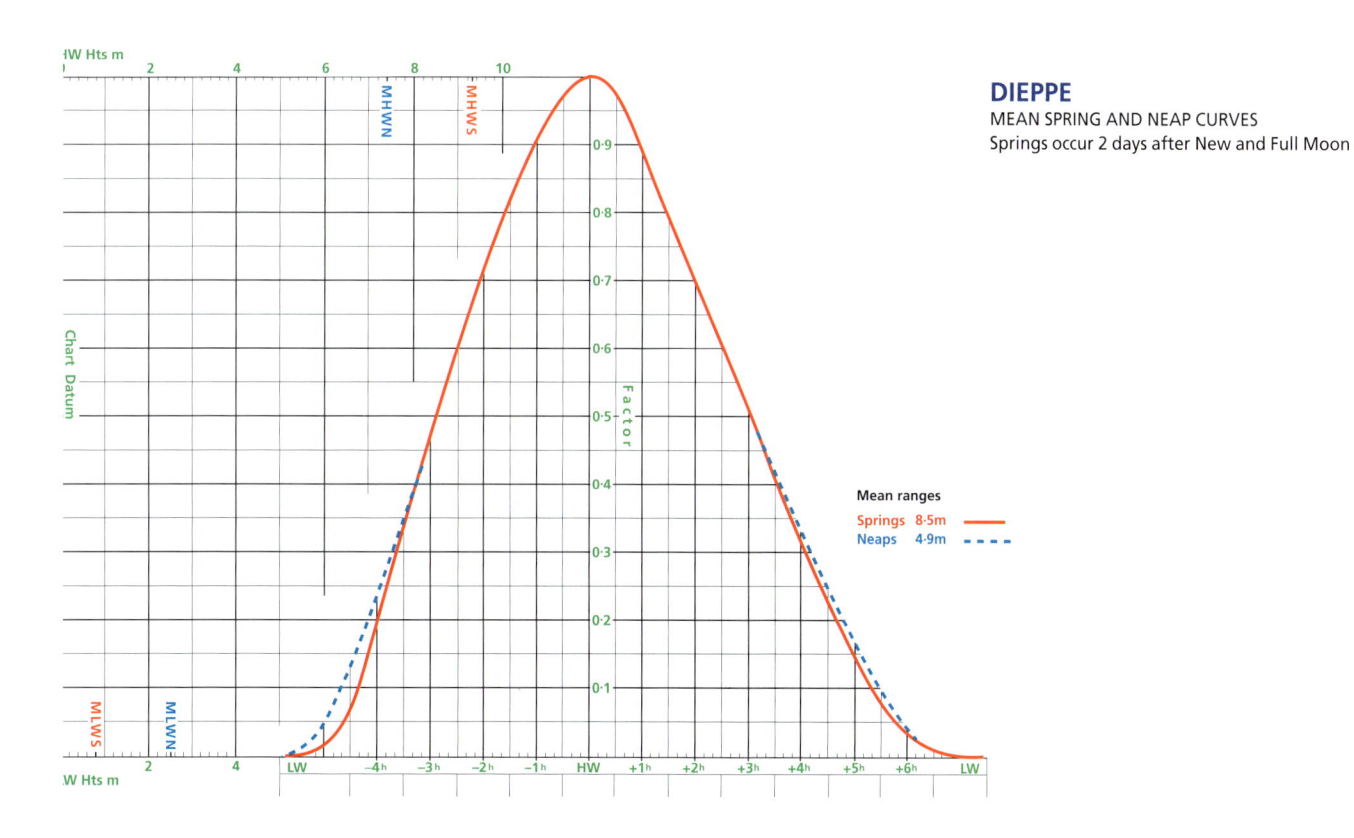

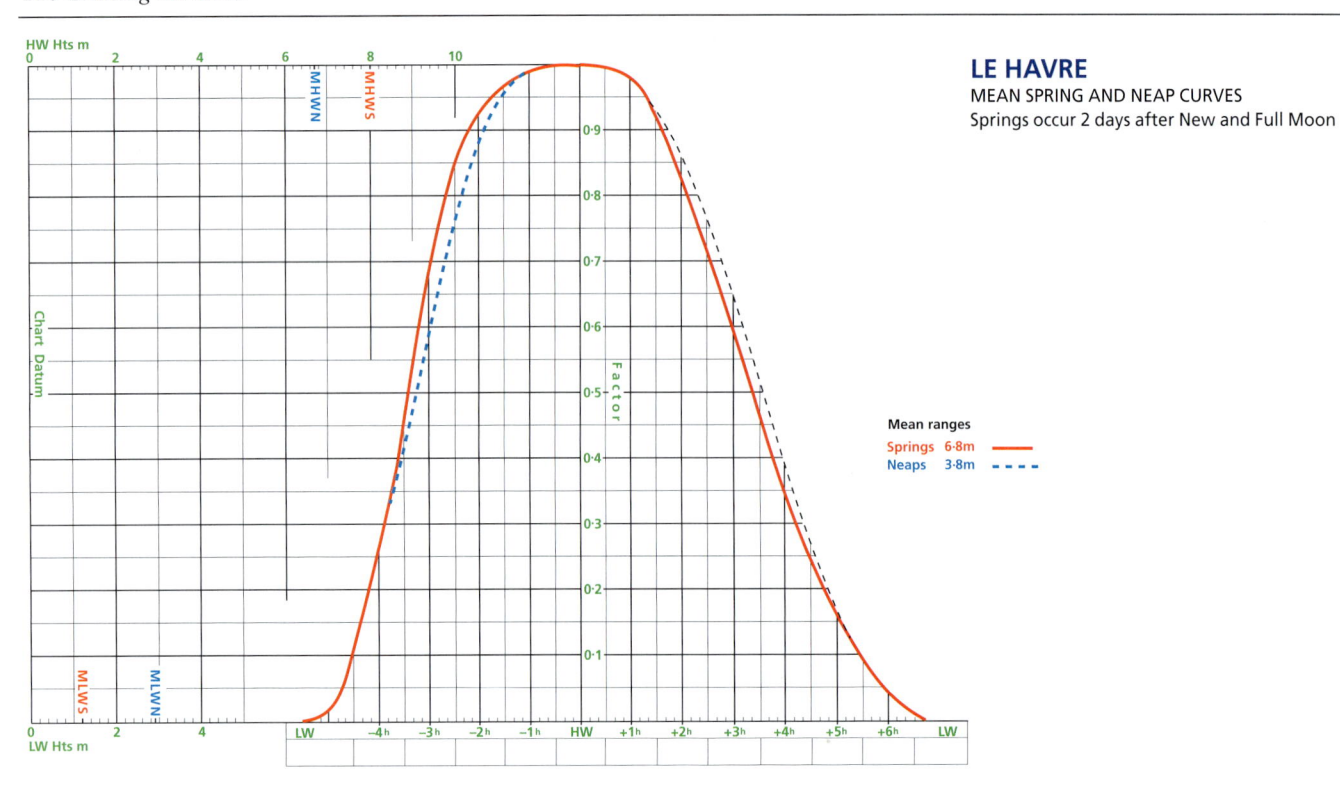

The Cruising Almanac

LE HAVRE
MEAN SPRING AND NEAP CURVES
Springs occur 2 days after New and Full Moon

Mean ranges
Springs 6·8m
Neaps 3·8m

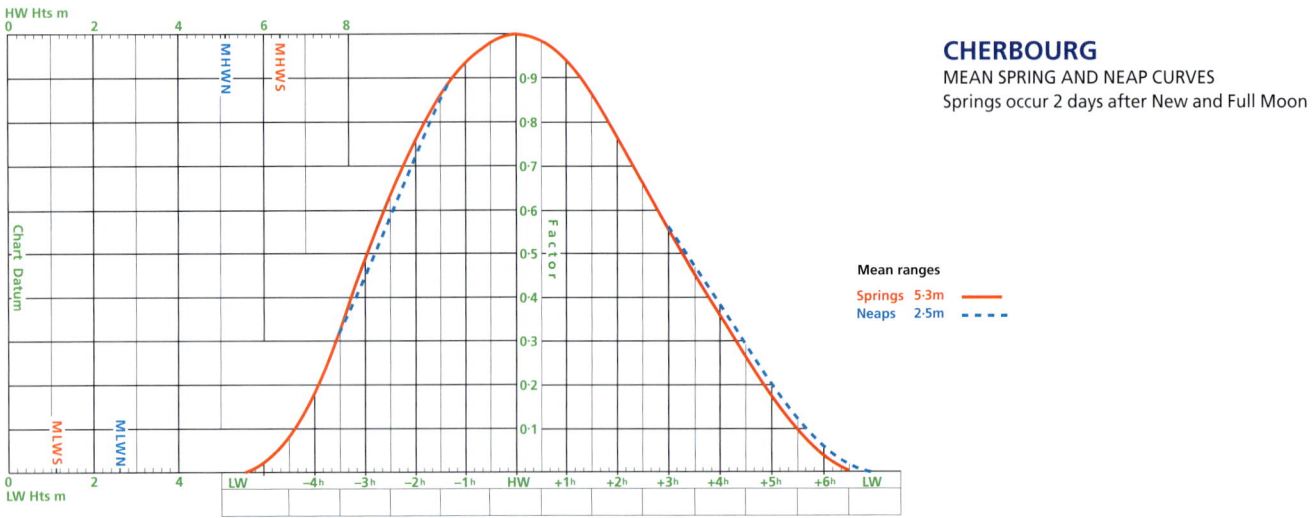

CHERBOURG
MEAN SPRING AND NEAP CURVES
Springs occur 2 days after New and Full Moon

Mean ranges
Springs 5·3m
Neaps 2·5m

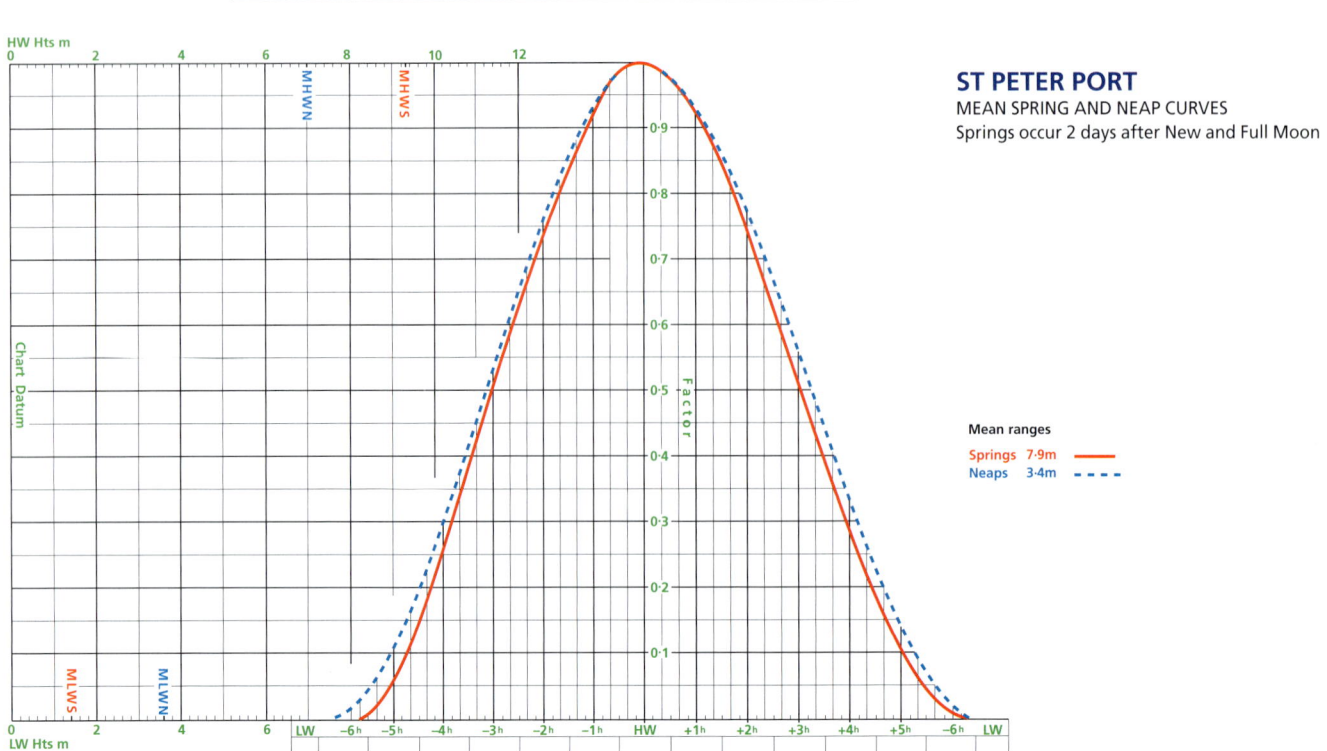

ST PETER PORT
MEAN SPRING AND NEAP CURVES
Springs occur 2 days after New and Full Moon

Mean ranges
Springs 7·9m
Neaps 3·4m

TIDAL STREAMS AND CURVES

ST HELIER
MEAN SPRING AND NEAP CURVES
Springs occur 2 days after New and Full Moon

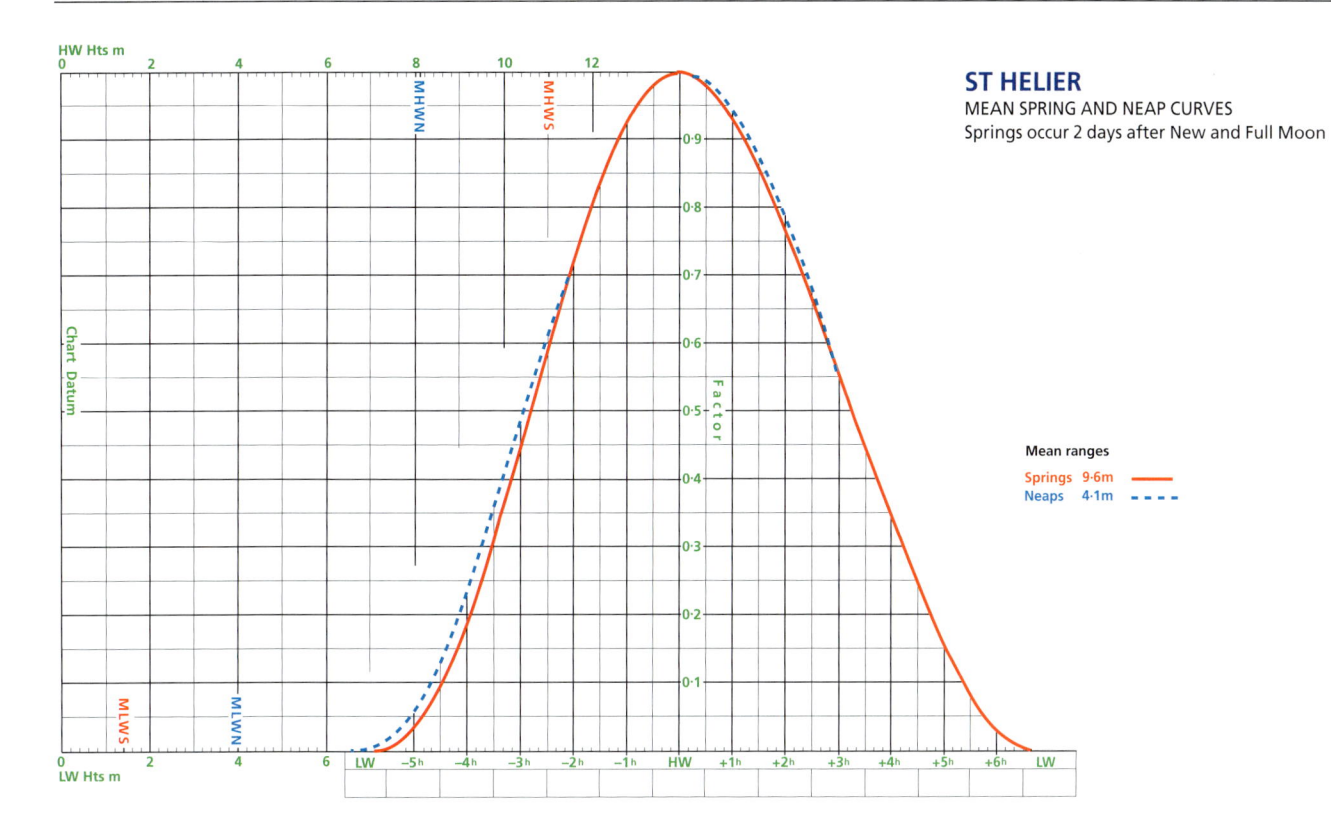

Mean ranges
Springs 9·6m
Neaps 4·1m

ST MALO
MEAN SPRING AND NEAP CURVES
Springs occur 2 days after New and Full Moon

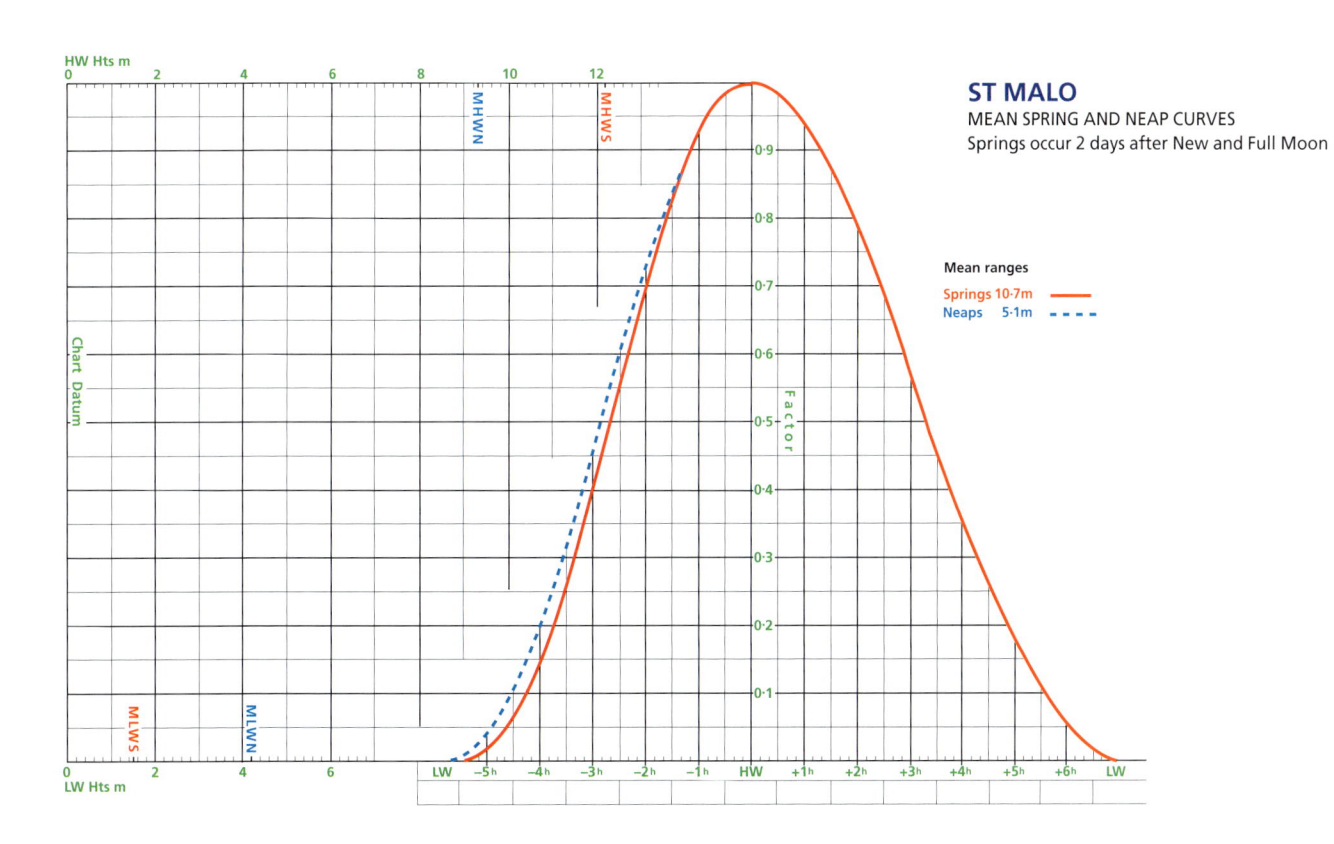

Mean ranges
Springs 10·7m
Neaps 5·1m

BREST
MEAN SPRING AND NEAP CURVES
Springs occur 2 days after New and Full Moon

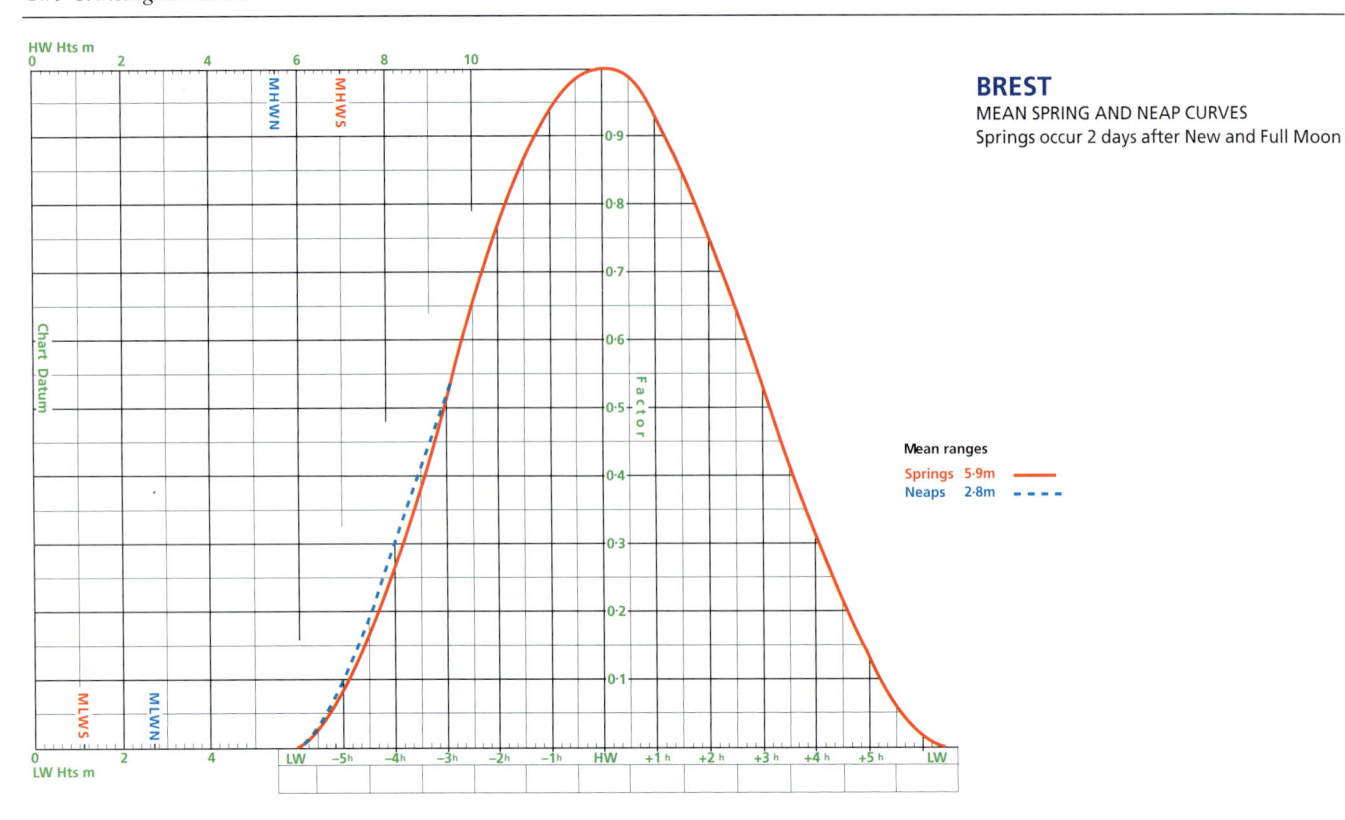

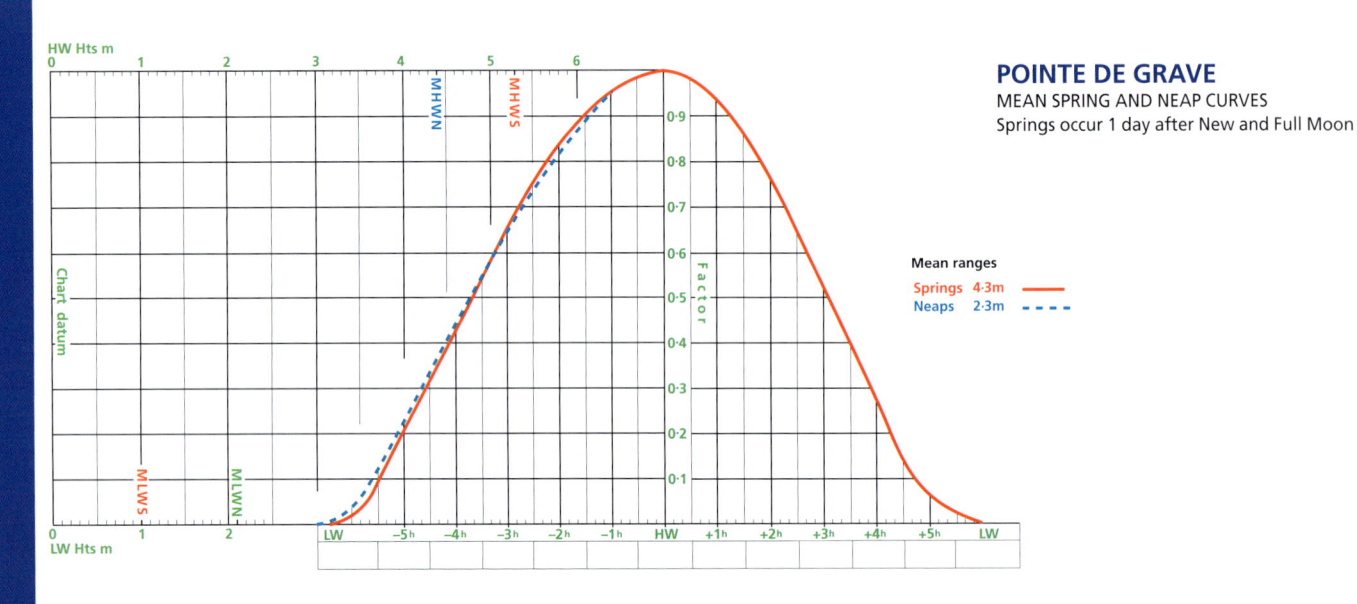

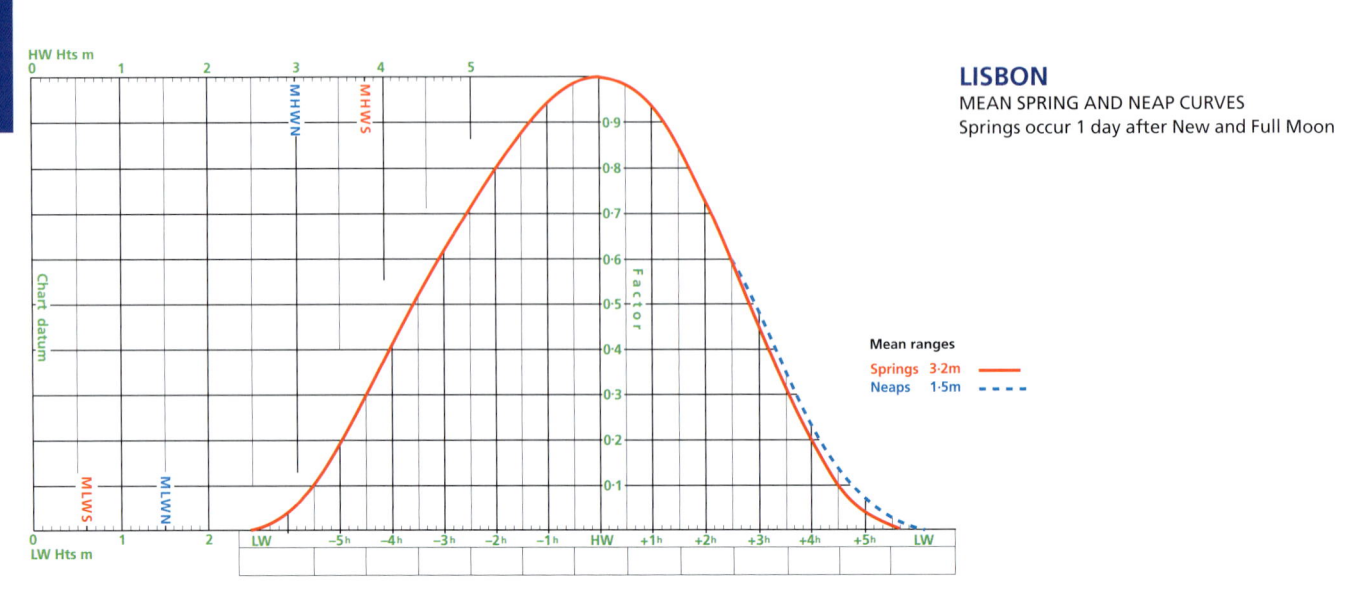

Mean ranges
Springs 5·9m
Neaps 2·8m

POINTE DE GRAVE
MEAN SPRING AND NEAP CURVES
Springs occur 1 day after New and Full Moon

Mean ranges
Springs 4·3m
Neaps 2·3m

LISBON
MEAN SPRING AND NEAP CURVES
Springs occur 1 day after New and Full Moon

Mean ranges
Springs 3·2m
Neaps 1·5m

GIBRALTAR
MEAN SPRING AND NEAP CURVES
Springs occur 1 day after New and Full Moon

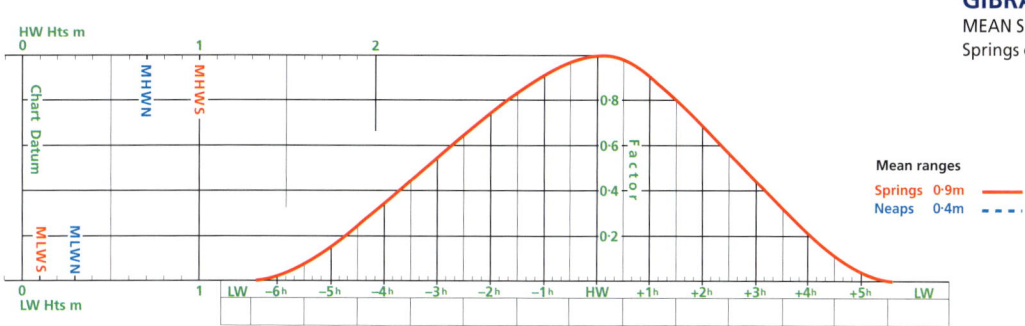

Mean ranges
Springs 0·9m
Neaps   0·4m

Index

A Coruña, 396-7
Aalsmeer, 255
abbreviations, 7
Aberdaron, 180
Aberdeen, 123, 124, 125
  tidal curve, 460
Aberdovey, 167, 181-2
Abermenai Point, 178, 179
Aberporth Range, 181
Abersoch, 167, 180
Aberystwyth, 167, 182
accidents, 12-14, 17-18
Achiltibuie, 143
Adour, River, 383
Afsluitdijk, 268
Aguete, 402
AIS (Automatic Ship
  Identification), 14-15
Aith, 135
Ålborg, 288-9
Albufeira, 410
Aldan, Ría de, 402
Alde, River, 101-2
Aldeburgh, 101, 102
Alderney, 328
Alderney Race, 327
Algera Flood Barrier, 261
Allington, 87
alphabet, phonetic, 10
Alphen an der Rijn, 254, 261
Althorne Creek, 91
Altnaharrie, 143
Alum Bay, 56
Amberley, 73
Amble, 114-16
Ameland, 249, 271
America, Puerto (Cádiz), 414
Amlwch Dock, 179
Amsterdam, 249, 254, 255, 264
  route from Braassemermeer,
    262-3
  route from Hollandsch Diep,
    261-2
  route to Friesland, 255
  routes from Gouda, 254-5
anchoring, 417
L'Ancress Bay, 330
Andijk, 266
Angle Bay, 185
Anglesey, 167, 176-9
Anglet, 383
Anholt, 293
animals, 16
Annagh Is, 234
Anse de L'Auberlac'h, 359
Anse de Bertheaume, 358
Anse de Blancs Sablons, 355
Anse de Dinan, 359
Anse de Penhir, 359
Anse de Porsmoguer, 355
Anse de Poulimic, 359
Anstruther, 122
Antony Village, 40
Antwerp, 247-8
Appledore, 195

Aran Is, 234, 241
Arbroath, 123-4
  passage from Berwick, 119
  passage to Rattray Head, 123
Arcachon, Bassin d', 382
Ardbear Bay, 237
Ardencaple Bay, 153
Ardfern, 154
Ardglass, 219-221
Ardinamar Bay, 153
Ardminish Bay, 155
Ardnamurchan
  passage from Kyle Akin, 145
  passage from Skye, 148
  passage to Oban, 149
Ardrishaig, 154, 162
Ardrossan, 163
Arendal, 292
Ares, Ría de, 396
Arinagour, 156
Arisaig, 147
Arklow, 216
Armadale, 146
Arradon, 371
Arran, 164
Arranmore, 228, 230-31
Arromanches, 322
Ars-en-Ré, 376, 377
Arun, River, 73
Arundel, 73
Arz, Île d'(Morbihan), 371
Arzal, 372
Ashlett Creek, 64
Askeaton, 242
Asknish Bay, 153
Assens, 296
Associated British Ports, 109
Auberlac'h, Anse de l', 359
Audierne, 360-61, 362
Aulne, River, 358, 359
Aultbea, 143
Auray, River, 369, 371
Aure, River, 323-4
Automatic Ship Identification
  (AIS), 15-16
Aveiro, Ría de, 407
Aven, River, 364-5
Avilés, Ría de, 392, 393
Avon, River (Bristol), 192
Avon, River (Devon), 41
Avonmouth, 192
  tidal curve, 463
Axe, River, 192-3
Axmouth, 49
Ayamonte, 412

Babbacombe, 47
Bäckviken, 302
Badachro, 143, 144
Badentarbet Bay, 143
Bagenkop, 297, 298
Bagh Charmaig, 159
Baie du Grand Vey, 323
Baie de Roscanvel, 359
Baie de Saint Brieuc, 339

Baiona, 404, 405
Ballast Pound Yacht Hbr, 40
Ballycastle, 225
Ballydorn, 222
Ballyholme Bay, 223
Ballyhoorisky Is, 228
Ballymastocker Bay, 227
Ballynakill, 234, 238, 239
Balta Sound, 136, 137
Baltic approaches, 20, 268,
  274-305
Baltimore, 207-8
Baltrum, 279
Banavie, 151
Banff, 127
Bangor (N Ireland), 222, 223
Bangor (N Wales), 176, 177-9
Bann, River, 226
Bantry Hbr, 205, 206
Barbate, 415
Bardsey Sound, 180
Barfleur, 325
Barmouth, 167, 181
Barnaderg Bay, 238
Barquero, Ría del, 394
Barra, 157, 160
Barrow, River, 215
Barrow-in-Furness, 172
Barry, 190
  passage to Bristol, 188
  passages to/from Ilfracombe,
    188
Bas-Sablons, Port des, 337
Bass Rock, 120
Bassin d'Arcachon, 382
Battlesbridge, 92
Batz, Île de see Île de Batz
Bayonne, 383
BBC radio forecasts, 18, 19
Beachy Head, 75
Bearhaven, 204
Beaucette Marina, 330-31
Beaufort wind scale, 18-19
Beaulieu River, 59-61
Beaumaris, 176, 177
Beer Roads, 47
Béganne, 372
Belfast Hbr, 222-3
  tidal curve, 464
Belfast Lough, 222
Belgium, 22, 244-8, 251
  inland waterways, 245-8,
    308, 309-310
  passage across North Sea to,
    245
  passage to Calais, 313
Bellanoch, 154
Belle Île, 368-9
Belmullet, 234
Bélon, River, 365-6
Bembridge (IoW), 66
Benbecula, 157
Benfleet Creek, 89
Bennane Head, 160
Bénodet, 363

Bergen, 275, 289
Bergen op Zoom, 259
Bermeo, 388
Berneray, Sound of, 157
Bertheaume, L'Anse de, 358
Berwick-upon-Tweed, 117
  passage from Spurn Head, 110
  passage to Arbroath, 119
Betanzos, Ría de, 396
Bideford, 195
Biesbosch, 261
Bilbao, 388-9
Billund, 295
Binic, 340
Birdham Pool, 70, 73
Birkenhead, 175
Bishops (Wales), 183, 188
Blacksod Bay, 234, 235
Blackwall Point, 88
Blackwater, River, 91-5
  passage from N Foreland, 85
  passage from Sunk Inner, 85
  passage to Netherlands from,
    249
Blakeney, 104, 105
Blancs Sablons, Anse de, 355
Blankenberge, 245, 246
Blasket Is & Sound, 234, 243
Blaye, 381
Blindleia, 291
Bloody Foreland
  passage from Fair Head, 225
  passage to Erris Head, 228
Bloscon, 351
Blyth (Northumberland), 114,
  115
Blyth, River (Southwold), 102
Bois de la Chaise, 375
Bolt Head & Tail, 41
books, pilots & guides, see start of
  each section
Bordeaux, 381-2
  passage to Castets, 381
Borkum, 268, 271
  route from Lauwersoog, 271
  route to Norderney, 271
Borkum Is, 255, 273, 279, 280
Boscastle, 167, 195
Bosham Channel, 70, 73
Boston, 108
Boudewijnkanaal, 247
Boulmer, 116
Boulogne, 316
Bourgenay, Port de, 377
Bournemouth to Christchurch,
  tidal curve, 455
Bouzas, 405
Bowling, 162
Boyardville, 379-80
Boyne, River, 219
Braassemermeer, 254, 261, 262
  route to Amsterdam, 262-3
Bradwell, 93, 94
Brae (Shetland), 135
Braunton, 195

472

Braye Hbr, 328
Bréhat, Île de, 340
Breskens, 249, 256
Brest & Rade de Brest, 355, 358-9
    tidal curve, 470
Breydon Water, 104
Bridgemarsh Marina, 91
Bridlington, 111
Bridport (West Bay), 49
briefing to crew, 12
Brightlingsea, 95
Brighton, 74
Brigneau, 364
Brignogan, 351
Brims Ness, 130
Bristol, 167, 192
    passage from Barry, 188
Bristol Channel, 167, 188
Brixham, 45-6
Broad Sound (Scilly), 26, 29
Broadhaven, 233
Broads (Norfolk), 103, 104
Broom Boats, 104
Brough Bay, 130
Broughty Hbr, 122
Brouwershaven, 259
Browland Voe, 138
Brownsea Is, 52, 55
Brugge, 247
Bruinisse, 254, 258, 259
Brundall, 104
Brunsbüttel, 283
Brussels, 248
Bryher (Scilly), 28, 29
Buckie, 127
Buckler's Hard, 59, 60, 61
Bueu, 402
Buitenkaag, 255
Bunaw, 203-4
Bunessan, 156
buoy reports, 22
buoyage system, 9
Burdaard, 255, 267, 273
Bure, River, 104
Burgh Castle Marina, 104
Burgh Is, 41
Burghead, 127
Burgtiefe, 303, 304
Burhou Is, 328
Burnham-on-Crouch, 91, 92
Burnham-on-Sea, 193
burns, 17
Burnt Islands, 162
Burntisland, 121
Burra Voe (Yell), 135
Bursledon, 64
Burton, 185
Burtonport, 230-31
Butley River, 101, 102
Butt of Lewis, 157
Buttermans Bay, 99

Cabo Cruz (Arousa), 402
Cabo Finisterre, 398
Cadgwith Cove, 31
Cádiz, 414-5
Caen, 321-2
Caernarfon, 167, 179
Caher, River (Valentia River), 200, 201
Cahersiveen, 200, 228
Cairnryan, 164
Calais, 314-15
    passage from Belgium, 313
    passage from Dover, 78
    passage to Le Havre, 315
    tidal curve, 467
Caldey Is & Sound, 188, 189

Caledonian Canal, 127, 128, 129, 151
Caley Marina (Muirtown), 151
Calf Sound (IoM), 168
Calshot Castle, 64
Calstock, 39, 40
Camaret-sur-Mer, 355, 359
Camariñas, Ría de, 398
Cambados, 400
Camel, River, 196
Campbeltown, 161
    passage to Portpatrick, 160
Canal & River Trust, 89
canals see inland waterways
Canche, River, 316
Canela, Isla, 412
Cangas, 405
Canna, 148, 149
Canvey Is, 89
Caolas Scalpay, 141
Cap de la Chèvre, 360
Capbreton, 382, 383
    firing range warning, 383
Cape Clear, 209
Cape Cornwall, 188
Cape Wrath, 130, 142
    passage from Dunnet Head, 130
    passage to Kyle Akin, 141
    passages from Duncansby Head, 130
Carbost, 149
cardiac compression, 17
Cardiff, 167, 190-91
Cardigan, 182
Cardigan Bay, 167, 181-2
Cardio Pulmonary Resuscitation (CPR), 17
Carentan, 324
Cargreen, 39, 40
Cariño, 394-5
Carlingford Lough, 219, 220
Carmarthen Bay, 188
Carmel Head, 179
Carnac, 369
Carnlough Hbr, 219
Carnsore Point, 212
    passage to Dublin Bay, 215
Carrick, 231
Carrickfergus, 222, 223-4
Carrigaholt, 234, 241
Carron, River, 121, 162
Carteret, 334-5
Cascais, 408
Cashla, 234, 240
Castets, passage from Bordeaux, 381
Castle Bay (Barra), 157, 160
Castlehaven, 208
Castlemartin Firing Range, 188
Castletown (IoM), 169, 170
Castletown (Ireland), 204
Castro Urdiales, 387
Cattewater, 37, 38
Cawsand Bay, 37
Cedeira, Ría de, 395
cell phones, 12, 17
Cellar Bay, 41, 43
Celtic Sea, 166
Cemaes Bay, 179
Cemlyn, 179
certificates of competence, 16
CEVNI & other rules, 306-7
Chalkwell, 89
Channals Creek, 32
Channel Is, 22, 312, 313, 327-34
    passage from Cherbourg, 327
    tidal curves, 468-9
Chantereyne, Port, 325, 326

Chapman's Pool, 51
chart datum, 14
charts
    electronic, 15
    weather, 19
    see also start of each section
Château, Marina du, 358
Châteaulin, 359
Chatham Maritime Marina, 86, 88
Chausey, Îles, 335
Chelmondiston, 99
Chenal du Four, 356
    passages, 355
Chenal de L'Île de Batz, 350, 351
    passage to L'Aber-Wrac'h, 353
Cherbourg, 325, 326
    passage from Le Havre, 320
    passage from Solent, 59
    passage to Channel Is, 327
    tidal curve, 468
Cherbourg Peninsula, passages around, 334
Chichester Hbr, 70-73
    passage from Poole, 54
    passage to Newhaven, 70
Chipiona, 414
Christchurch, 54, 55-6
    tidal curve, 455
Church Bay (Rathlin Is), 225
Clachan Bridge, 153
Clachnaharry, 128, 151
Claggan Point, 234
Clamerkin Lake, 61
Clare Is, 234
Cleddau, River, 185, 187
Cleethorpes, 108
Clew Bay, 234-6
Clifden Bay, 234, 237-8
Cliff Reach (Crouch), 91
Clovelly Bay (N Devon), 167, 195
    passage from Padstow, 195
Clovelly Bay (Plymouth), 37-8
Clwyd, River, 174
Clyde Estuary, 160, 162-4
coastal station weather reports/forecasts, 18, 21
coastguard, 11, 12, 13, 21, see also start of each section
Coastguard Operations Centres (CGOC), 18
Cobbler Channel, 37
Cobh (& Cork Hbr), 210-212
    passage from Crookhaven, 209
    passage to Tuskar Rock, 212
    tidal curve, 464
Colchester, 96
Coleraine Marina, 225, 226
Colijnsplaat, 258
Coll, 156
Collanmore, 234
Collorus, 203
Colne River, 91, 95, 96
    passage from N Foreland, 85
    passage from Sunk Inner, 85
Colonsay, 155
COLREGS (International Convention for the Safety of Life at Sea), 13, see also SOLAS V
Combarro, 402, 403
Combwich, 193
communications, 12-14
Concarneau, 363-4
conservation, 16
conventions, 8
Conwy, 167, 176
    passage from Liverpool, 176
Conyer Creek, 85

Coquet Is, 114, 115
Corcubión, Ría de, 398, 399
Corillan, 230
Corme, 398
Corpach, 150, 151
Corryvreckan, Gulf of, 151
A Coruña, 396-7
Cotehele, 40
Courseulles, 322
Courtmacsherry, 209
Coverack Cove, 31
Cowes, 61, 62
    passage to Southampton Water, 59
    tidal curve, 455
Cowlands Creek, 33
CPR (Cardio Pulmonary Resuscitation), 17
Crac'h River, 369
Craighouse, 155
Craobh Haven, 153
Craster, 116
Creeksea, 91
Cremyll, 40
Creux Hbr, 332
Crinan, 154
Crinan Canal, 154, 162
Cristina, Isla, 412-13
Croix-de-Vie, 375
Cromer, passage to Humber, 106
Crookhaven, 206
    passage from Valentia, 200
    passage to Cork, 209
CROSS, 13, 22
Crosshaven, 210, 211, 212
Crouch, River, 90-91
    passage from Harwich, 85
    passage from N Foreland, 85
    passage from Sunk Inner, 85
    passage to Netherlands from, 249
Crouesty, Port du, 371-2
Crow Sound (Scilly), 29
Cruden Bay, 123
Cruising Association, 6, 7, 18, 20, 88, 139
Cruit Bay, 229-30
Cuan Sound, 151, 152
Cudillero, 392, 393
Culdaff Bay, 225
Cultra, 223
Cushendall, 219
customs & immigration, 16, see also start of each section
Cuxhaven, 268, 271, 282
    tidal curve, 465

Dahouet, 339
Dale, 185, 186, 188
Dandy Hole, 40
Daoulas, River, 359
Darrynane, 202
Dart, River, 43-4, 45
Dartmouth, 43-4
Deauville/Trouville, 320-21
Deben, River, 100-101
Deganwy Quay, 176
dehydration, 18
Delfzijl, 255, 268, 271, 273
    route from Harlingen, 272-3
    route from Leeuwarden, 255
Den Bourg, 269
Den Haag, 249
Den Helder, 249, 268-9
    passages & coastal routes, 268
    route to Oost Vlieland, 270
Den Oever, 255, 265, 266-7
Denmark, 22, 274-9, 284-9, 292-3, 295-301, 303, 304-5

INDEX

Denver Sluice, 106
Derby Haven (IoM), 169, 170
Derrible Bay, 332
Derryinver Bay, 238
Devonport, 40
Devoran, 32
diarrhoea & vomiting, 18
Diélette, 334
Dieppe, 317
  tidal curve, 467
Digital Selective Calling (DSC), 11, 12
Dinan, 338
Dinan, Anse de, 359
Dinard, 338
Dinas Fach, 184
Dingle Hbr, 228, 234, 243
Dintelmond, 254
distances see *start of each section*
distress call, 11, 12
Dittisham, 44, 45
Dives-sur-Mer, 321
diving, 16
Dixcart Bay, 332
documentation, 15
Doëlan, 364
Dokkum, 255, 267, 272, 273
Dokkumer Je, 255
Dokkumer Nieuwe Zijlen, 255, 273
Donaghadee Sound, 222
Donastia / San Sebastián, 387
Donegal Bay, 231-3
Dordrecht, 254, 261
  route from Willemstad, 254
  route to Gouda, 254
Dordtse Kill, 254, 261
Dorinish, 234
Dornoch Firth, 126
Dorus Mor, 151, 152
Douarnenez, 360
Douglas (IoM), 167, 168, 169-71
Dourduff, 349
Douro, Rio, 406
Dover, 76-7
  passage to Belgium, 245
  passage to Calais, 78
  tidal curve, 457
Dover Strait, 245
Drogheda, 219
drowning, 14, 17
Drummore, 164-5
DSC (Digital Selective Calling), 11, 12
Dublin, 217-18
  passage from Carnsore Point, 215
  passage from Holyhead, 217
  passage to Fair Head, 218
  tidal curve, 464
Duisdale, 146
Dun Laoghaire, 217
Dunball, 193
Dunbar, 120
  passage to Grangemouth, 120
Duncannon Bar, 215
Duncansby Head, 130
  passages to Cape Wrath, 130
Dundee Docks, 122
Dungarvan, 213
Dungeness, 75
Dunkerque, 249, 314
  tidal curve, 466
Dunmore East, 213, 214
Dunnet Head, 130
  passage to Cape Wrath, 130
Dunstaffnage, 151-2
Dunvegan, 148

Durgerdam, 264
Dursey Sound, 203
Düsternbrook, 284, 285
duty-free, 15
DWD (Hamburg/Pinnenburg) *weather information*, 19

East Loch Tarbert (Harris), 158
East Loch Tarbert (Loch Fyne), 161
East Looe, 37
East Voe Marina (Scalloway), 138
Eastbourne, 75
Eastney, 69
Edam, 266
Eden Project, 35
Eems (Eems), River & Estuary, 255, 271, 273, 275
Eemskanal, 273
Egersund, 275, 291
Eider, River, 275
  passage to Nord-Ostsee-Kanal, 282
Eidersperrwerk, 283
Eierlandsche Gat, 270
Eigg, 149
El Barquero, 394
El Ferrol, Ría de, 395
Elbe, River, 249, 271, 275, 278, 279-80
  coastal passages to & from, 268, 279-80
  passage to Nord-Ostsee-Kanal, 283-6
  passages from UK, 268
Elberry Cove, 41
Elburg, 268
electronic charts, 15
electronic navigation, 15-16
Ellen's Well, 185, 188
Elly Bay & Hbr, 234
Élorn, River, 358, 359
Elwick Bay, 133
email weather forecasts, 20
Embankment Marina (Gravesend), 89
emergencies, 11-13, 16-18
Ems (Eems), River & Estuary, 255, 271, 273, 275
Emsworth, 70, 71, 73
energy generation, 14
Enkhuizen, 255, 266
Ensenada de Llagosteira, 399
Ensenada de San Simón, 404
Ensenada de Santa Marta, 394-5
Ensenada de Sardineiro, 399
Erith, 88
Erme, River, 41
Erquy, 339
Erris Head, 234
  passage from Bloody Foreland, 228
  passage to Valentia, 234
Erth Hill, 40
Esbjerg, 286-7
  tidal curve, 465
Eskmeals, & Gun Range, 171
Essex Marina, 91, 92
Étaples, 316
Étel, River, 367
European Health Insurance Card (EHIC), 15
European Union, 15
Exe, River, 48, 49
Exeter, 49
Exmouth, 47, 48
eye problems, 17-18
Eyemouth, 119-20

Fåborg, 296, 298
Fahan Creek, 227
Fahy Bay, 238
Fair Head
  passage from Dublin, 219
  passage to Bloody Foreland, 225
Fair Isle, 134, 135-6
Falkenberg, 295
Falmouth, 32
  passage from Penzance, 31
  passage to Plymouth, 32
Falsterbo, 295
Falsterbokanalen, 302
Fambridge, 91
Fanad Head, 227
Fareham Lake, 68
Farne Is, 110, 116
Faro, 411
Fastnet Rock, 209
Faversham Creek, 84, 85
Fearnach Bay, 153
Fécamp, 318
Fehmarn, 303-4
Fehmarn Belt Fixed Link, 303
Felixstowe, 97-9, 99, 249
Felixstowe Ferry, 100, 101
Fenit Is, 228, 241
Fiers d'Ars, 377
Figuera de Foz, 407
Filey Bay, 112
Filey Brigg, 110, 112
Findhorn, 128
Findochty, 126
Finisterre, Cabo, 398, 399
Finisterre, Puerto de, 399
firearms, 15
first aid, 16-18
Firth of Clyde, 160, 162-4
Firth of Forth, 119, 120-22
Firth of Lorne, 151
Fisherrow, 120
Fishguard, 167, 183
  passage to St Ann's Head, 183
fishing, 13
Fladda Narrows, 151
flags, 10
Flamborough Head, 110
Flannan Is, 157
flares, 11, 15
Fleetwood, 167, 173
Flotta, 130
Flowerdale Bay, 144
Flushing see Vlissingen
Foleux, 372
Folly Inn, 61, 62
Fort Augustus, 151
Fort Belan, 179
Forth, Firth of, 119, 120-22
Forth-Clyde Canal, 121, 162
Fosdyke, 108
Foulger's Gat, 81, 85
Foulness, 90
Four Channel, 356
  passages, 355
Fowey, 34-5
Fox's Marina, 99, 100
Foyle, Lough & Marina, 226-7
France, 22, 312-26, 334-83
  inland waterways, 310-311
  passage from Thames Estuary, 85
Franeker, 273
Franks-Weather, 20
Franneker, 255
Fraserburgh, 126
Frenchport, 233, 234
Freshwater Bay, 54

Freswick Bay, 130
Friars Goose, 114
Friesland, 255, 265, 266-8, 272-3
  routes from Amsterdam, 255
Frisian Is, 249, 268-72, 275, 279-81
  passage to Elbe, 279-80
  passages from UK, 268
Frogmore Lake & Creek, 43
Frome, River (Poole), 55
Fromveur Channel, 355
Front Brents Jetty, 85
fuel, 15
Fyn, 295-6, 298

gale warnings, 18-19
Gallions Point Marina, 88, 90
Galloway coast, 165
Gallows Point, 176
Galmpton, 44
Galway, 228, 234, 240-1
  tidal curve, 465
Galway Bay, 238-40
Gareloch, 160
Garonne, River, 381
gas rigs & storage, 15, 249, 253
Gedser, 304-5
Gent, 247, 257
German Bight Western Approach TSS, 275, 279
Germany, 22, 274-9, 280-86, 303-5
  inland waterways, 307-9
Getaria, Puerto de, 387, 388
Giant's Causeway, 225
Gibraltar, 412, 416
  tidal curve, 471
Gigha, 151, 155
Gijon, 391-2
Gillan Creek, 32-4
Gillingham Marina, 86, 88
Gill's Bay, 130
Gironde see La Gironde River
Glandore, 208-9
Glasson Dock, 167, 172-3
Glénan, Îles de, 364, 365
Glenarm (Marina), 224
Glengariff, 205
Glumaig Hbr, 157
GMDSS, 11, 13, 19, 20
Goes, 259
Goldhanger Creek, 93
Goodwick, 183
Gorey, 333
Gorran Haven, 32
Gortnasate Quay, 230
Gosport & Marina, 68
Göteborg, 293, 294
Gouda, 254, 261
  route from Dordrecht, 254
  routes to Amsterdam, 254-5
Goulet de Brest, 359
Goultrop Roads, 184
Gouwe, 254
GPS, 14
Grand Vey, Baie du, 323
Grandcamp-Maisy, 323
Grande Havre (Guernsey), 330
Grande Vinotière, 355
Grangemouth, 121, 162
  passage from Dunbar, 120
Granton, 120-21
Granville, 335
Grassholm, 183, 188
Gravelines, 314, 315
Gravesend, 88, 89
Great Belt (Store Bælt), 295, 298-9

Great Ouse, River, 107
Great Yarmouth, 104-5
  passage from Harwich, 102
Greatman Bay, 239
Greencastle, 226
Greenock, tidal curve, 462
Greenwich, 88
Gregory Sound, 234
Gremista Yacht Hbr, 136
Grenå, 293
Grève de la Ville, 332
Grevelingen Meer, 254, 259-60
Grevelingenmeer, 258
Greystones, 217
GRIB files, 20
Grimsby, 108-9
Groix, Île de, 367
Groningen, 255, 267, 268, 272, 273
  gas field, 249
  route from Leeuwarden, 255
Grou, 255
Gruting Voe, 135, 138
Grutness Voe, 135
Guernsey, 329-31
Gugh (Scilly), 29
Gunfacts, 21, 141
Gweek, 31, 32

Haarlem, 254, 255, 262
Hadleigh Ray, 89
Hague, The, 249
Half Acre Creek, 87
Halfpenny Pier (Harwich), 98, 99
Hals, 289
Hamar Voe, 136
Hamble Point Marina, 64, 65
Hamble, River, 64-5
Hamburg weather information, 20
Hamford Water, 96, 97
Hamna Voe, 138
Hamoaze, 38, 39, 40
Hannaine Bay, 328
Hansweert, 257
Harderwijk, 268
Haringvliet, 249, 260
Harlingen, 255, 268, 270, 271
  route to Delfzijl, 272-3
Harris, 157, 158
Hartland Point, passage to Land's End, 195
Hartlepool, 110, 112-13
Harty Ferry, 85
  passage to Queenborough through the Swale, 85
Harwich, 97-9, 99
  Gyratory-Sunk Outer, 249
  passage from N Foreland, 81, 85
  passage to Great Yarmouth, 102
  passage to River Crouch, 85
  passages to Netherlands, 249, 268
Haslar Marina, 68
Haugesund, 290
Havelet Bay, 330
Havengore Creek, 89-90, 91
Havergate Is, 101, 102
Havre Gosselin, 332
Hawkins Point, 108
Hayle, 196
Hayling Is, 69, 73
health matters, 16, 17-18
Héaux de Bréhat, Les, 335, 342
Hebrides, Outer, 157-60
Heiligenhafen, 303
Helcom Convention, 16

Helford River, 31-2
Helgoland, 268, 271, 275, 279, 281-2
  tidal curve, 465
helicopter rescue, 12
Helle Channel, 355
Hellevoetsluis, 260
Helmsdale, 129
Helsingør, 295, 299-300
Helvick, 213
Hendaye, 386-7
L'Herbaudière, 374, 375
Herkingen, 259-60
Hermitage Moorings, 88
Heybridge Basin, 93, 94
Heysham, 173
HF/SSB radio, 11, 19
Hillswick, 135, 136
Hindeloopen, 267
HMCG forecasts, 18, see also Coastguard
Hoëdic, Île de, 372
Hoek van Holland, 262-3
  tidal curve, 466
holding tanks, 16
Holland see Netherlands
Hollandsch Diep, 254, 261
  route to Amsterdam, 261-2
Hollandse IJssel, 254, 261
Holtenau, 283, 284
Holy Is (Lindisfarne), 116, 117
Holyhead, 167, 179, 180
  passage to Dublin, 217
  tidal curve, 463
Hondarribia, 386
Honfleur, 319, 320
Hookness, 88
Hoorn, 266
Hope Cove, 41
Hopeman, 126
Hôrnum, 286
Houat, Île de, 372-3
Housel Bay, 31
Hout Haven, 255
Howth, 219
Howton Bay, 132
Hoy Sound, 130, 132
Hugh Town (Scilly), 26, 27, 29
Huizen, 268
Hull, 109, 110
Humber River, 108, 109, 110
  passage from Cromer, 106
Hurst Point, 54, 56
Hvide Sand, 287
hypothermia, 12
Hythe Marina Village, 63, 64
Hythe Pier, 63

IALA Buoyage System Region A, 8
Icart Bay, 330
IJmuiden, 249, 255, 263-4
  passages from England, 104, 249, 268
IJmuiden TSS, 249
IJsselmeer, 249, 255, 264-8
Iken, 102
Île d'Arz (Morbihan), 371
Île de Batz, 350, 351
  passage from Les Héaux, 342
Île de Bréhat, 341-2
Île de Groix, 367
Île de Hoëdic, 372
Île de Houat, 372-3
Île de la Jument (Morbihan), 371
Île Longue (Morbihan), 371
Île aux Moines (Morbihan), 371
Île de Molène, 357

Île de Noirmoutier, 375
Île d'Oléron, passage to Gironde River, 380
Île Pirenn (Morbihan), 371
Île de Sein, 360
Île d'Yeu, 375
Îles Chausey, 335-7
Îles de Glénan, 364, 365
Îles Saint-Marcouf, 324
Ilfracombe, 167, 188, 194
  passage from Padstow, 195
  passages to/from Barry, 188
immigration & customs, 15, see also start of each section
Immingham, 108, 109
  tidal curve, 459
Inishbofin, 234, 238
Inishgowla, 234
Inishlyre Hbr, 234
Inishtrahull Sound, 225
inland waterways, 306-311
  Belgium, 245-8, 308, 309-310
  France, 310-311
  Germany, 307-9
  Netherlands, 309
  UK, 89, 109, 121, 151, 154, 162, 175
INMARSAT, 11, 12
Inshore Waters forecasts, 18, 19, 21
insurance, 15
International Convention for the Safety of Life at Sea see COLREGS
International Distress Calls, 11-12
International Port Traffic Signals (IPTS), 8
Internet access, 15
Internet weather services, 19, 20
Inverewe, 143
Inverie Bay, 147
Inverkip, 162, 163
Inverness Firth, 128, 129
  passage from Rattray Head, 127
Ipswich, 99, 100
Ireland, 22, 197-243
Irish Sea, passages, 166, 167, 168
Isigny, 323-4
Isla Canela, 412
Isla Cristina, 412-13
Isla Ons, 402
Isla Toja Grande, 400
Island Harbour Marina (IoW), 61, 62
Islay, 151, 155
  passage from Rum, 155
Isle of Man, 166, 167, 168-71
Isle of May, 122
Isle Ornsay, 145-6
Isle of Sheppey, 84
Isle of Whithorn, 165
Isle of Wight, 54, 56, 57-61, 62, 65-6
Isles of Scilly, 24, 25-9, 166, 312
Itchen, River, 64
Itchenor, 73

Jack Sound, 183, 184-5
Jade, River, 275, 279
Jenny Cliff Bay, 37
Jersey, 332-4
Joinville, 375
Jument, Île de la (Morbihan), 371
Jument, Port à La, 332
Jura, 151, 154-5
Jylland, 275

Kaag, 261
Kager Plassen, 261
Kampen, 268
Kappeln, 298
Kattegat, 275, 292-5
Kerdruc, 365
Kerkbuurt, 266
Kernével, 367
Kernoch, 351
Kerrera, 153
Keyhaven, 57
Kiel & Kieler Fjorde, 284, 285
Kiel Canal see Nord-Ostsee-Kanal
Killary Hbr, 234, 236
Killeany Bay (Aran Is), 241
Killingholme, 108
Killowen Point, 219
Killybegs, 228, 231, 232
Killyleagh, 222
Kilmakilloge, 202-4
Kilmelford, 153
Kilmore Quay, 215-16
  passage from Milford Haven, 188
Kilnaughton Bay, 155
Kilronan Hbr, 234, 2441
Kilrush, 228, 234, 242
King Harry Ferry, 32, 34
King Point Marina, 38
King's Lynn, 106, 107
Kingsbridge, 42, 43
Kingsferry Bridge, 85
Kingston-upon-Hull, 109, 110
Kingswear, 44
Kinlochbervie, 142
Kinnaird Head, 127
Kinsale, 209, 210
Kintyre see Mull of Kintyre
Kip Marina, 162, 163
Kircubbin, 222
Kirkby Creek, 97
Kirkcudbright, 165
  passage from Portpatrick, 165
Kirkwall, 132, 133
Klintholm, 299
Knott End, 173
København, 295, 300-302
Kolding, 296
Kornwerderzand, 255, 265, 267
Korsør, 295, 298
Kristiansand, 292
Kyle Akin, 145, 146
  passage from Cape Wrath, 141
  passage to Ardnamurchan, 145
Kyle of Lochalsh, 145
Kyle Rhea, 145, 146
Kyle of Tongue, 131
Kyleakin, 145
Kyrkbacken, 302

La Baule, 374
La Chambre (Bréhat), 340
La Chambre (Glénan), 364
La Charente River, 378-9
La Corderie (Bréhat), 340
La Corne, 343, 344
La Flotte-en-Ré, 378
La Gironde River, 380-81
  firing range warning, 383
  passage from Île d'Oléron, 380
  passage from Penmarc'h Point, 362
La Grande Grève (Sark), 332
La Jument, Port à, 332
La Linea, 415
La Malouine, 353
La Pallice, passage from Pertuis Breton, 376

La Palue, 353
La Pendante, 353
La Roche Bernard, 372
La Rochelle, 378
La Teignouse passage, 368
La Trinité sur Mer, 369
La Turballe, 373
La Vilaine, 372
L'Aber Benoît, 353
L'Aber-Ildut, 357-8
L'Aber-Wrac'h, 353, 355
    passage from Chenal de Batz, 353
    passage from West Country, 353
Laboe, 284, 285
Læsø, 292-3
Lagos, 409-410
Lagunen Yacht Hbr, 302
Lamlash, 164
Lampaul Bay, 357
Lancaster, 172
L'Ancress Bay, 330
Landerneau, 359
Land's End, 166, 167
    passage from Hartland Point, 195
    passage from Milford Haven, 188
    passages around, 24, 25
Landshipping, 185
Långedrag, 294, 295
Langeland, 297, 298
Langeoog, 279, 280, 281
Langstone Hbr, 68-9
Lannion River, 346-7
Lanriot, 365
L'Anse de Bertheaume, 358
Laredo, 390
Largo Bay, 122
Largs Yacht Haven, 163
Larne Lough, 224
Latchingdon Hole, 93
L'Auberlac'h, Anse de, 359
Lauwersmeer, 255, 272, 273
Lauwersoog, 255, 267, 271-2, 273
    route from Oost Vlieland, 271
    route from Vlieland, 268
    route to Borkum, 271
Lawling Creek, 93
Lawrence Cove, 204-5
Lawrenny, 185, 187
Laxe, 398
Laxey (IoM), 171
Le Conquet, 358
Le Croisic, 373-4
Le Douhet, 379
Le Fiers d'Ars, 377
Le Folgoat, 359
Le Guildo (St-Cast), 339
Le Guilvinec, 362
Le Havre, 318, 319
    passage from Calais, 315
    passage to Cherbourg, 320
    tidal curve, 468
Le Légué (St Brieuc), 339
Le Palais (Belle Île), 368, 369
Le Pouldu, 364
Le Pouliguen, 374
Le Rocher, 371
Le Tréport, 317
Leeds & Liverpool Canal, 175
Leenane (Leenaun), 236
Leeuwarden, 255, 267, 273
    route to Groningen & Delfzijl, 255
Leiden, 254, 255, 261

Leigh, 89
Leith, 120
    tidal curve, 460
Leixões, 406
Lelystad, 255, 264, 265, 267-8
Lemmer, 255, 267, 273
Lemvig, 288
Lequeitio, 388
Lerryn, 34, 35
Lerwick, 135, 136
    tidal curve, 461
Les Héaux de Bréhat
    passage from St-Malo, 335
    passage to Île de Batz, 342
Les Sables d'Olonne, 375-6
Les Sept Îles, 346
Lesconil, 362
Lewes, 75
Lewis, 157-8
Lézardrieux, 341-2
L'Herbaudière, 374, 375
lifeboat rescue, 12
lifesaving signals, 11
Liffey River, 217
lights & shapes, 11, see also start of each section
Lille Bælt (Little Belt), 295-6
Lilstock Firing Range, 193
Limehouse Dock Marina, 88, 90
Limfjord, 275, 288-9
Limhamn, 295, 302-3
Lindisfarne (Holy Is), 116, 117
Linney Head, 188
Lisboa, 408, 409
    tidal curve, 470
Little Belt (Lille Bælt), 295-6
Little Killary Hbr, 236
Littleham Cove, 47
Littlehampton, 70, 73
Liverpool, 167, 174, 175
    passage to Conwy, 176
    tidal curve, 462
Llagosteira, Ensenada de, 399
Llanddwyn Is, 179
Llanes, 391
Lleyn Peninsula, 180
Loch Aline, 150
Loch Boisdale, 159
Loch Broom, 143
Loch Carron, 144-5
Loch Craignish, 154
Loch Dunvegan, 148
Loch Eatharna, 156
Loch Eriboll, 130, 131
Loch Ewe, 143
Loch Fyne, 154, 161
Loch Gairloch, 143-4
Loch Gilp, 162
Loch Harport, 148-9
Loch Inchard, 142
Loch Inver, 143
Loch Laxford, 142
Loch Long, 160
Loch Maddy, 158-9
Loch Melfort, 151, 153
Loch Na Droma Buidhe (Sunart), 150
Loch Na Lathaich, 156
Loch Na Mile, 154-5
Loch Nan Ceall, 147
Loch Nedd, 142
Loch Nevis, 146-7
Loch Rodel, 158
Loch Ryan, 164
Loch Scresort, 149
Loch Shell, 158
Loch Shieldaig, 144
Loch Shuna, 153

Loch Skipport, 159
Loch Snizort, 148
Loch Sunart, 149, 150
Loch Sween, 154-5
Loch Thuraig, 143
Loch Torridon, 144
Lochaline, 150
Lochalsh, Kyle of, 145
Lochboisdale, 159
Lochinver, 143
Lochmaddy, 158-9
Locmiquélic Ste-Catherine, 366, 367
Locquémeau, 347
Locquénolé, 349
Locquirec, 347
Loctudy, 362, 363
Loe Beach, 32
Loe Pool, 31
Loggie Bay, 143
Loire, River, 374
Lolland, 303
London Array windfarms, 81, 83
London Bridge, 88
    tidal curve, 458
Londonderry, 226-7
Longis Bay, 328
Longoar Bay, 185
Longships, 25
Looe, 36
Loop Head, 234
Lorient, 366-7
Lorne, Firth of, 151
Lossiemouth, 127
Lostwithiel, 34, 35
Lough Foyle, & Marina, 226-7
Lough Swilly, 225, 227
Lower Hamstead, 61
Lowestoft, 102, 103, 104, 268
    passage to IJmuiden, 104
    passage to Netherlands, 249
    tidal curve, 459
Luanco, 392, 393
Luarca, 393-4
Luing, Sound of, 151
Lulworth Cove & Gunnery Range, 51
Lunan Bay, 124
Lundy Is, 167, 188, 194-195
Lune, River, 172-3
Lybster, 129-30
Lyme Bay, *passage to Weymouth*, 47
Lyme Regis, 49
Lymington, 58-9
Lymington to Cowes, *tidal curve*, 455
Lyness, 132, 133
Lynher River, 39, 40
Lytham, 173

Maas, River, 249, 254
Maas TSS, 249, 262
Maasholm, 295, 297-8
Maassluis, 262, 263
Macduff, 127
MailASail, 20
Makkum, 267
Malahide, 219
Maldon, 93, 94
Mallaig, 147
Malmö, 303
Malpas, 32, 33
Man, Isle of, 166, 167, 168-71
man overboard, 14, 17
Mandal, 275, 291
Manningtree, 99
Manorbier Rocket Range, 188

Maplin Sand Firing Range, 89-90
Marazion, 31
Marchwood, 64
Margaret Ness, 88
marine communications, 12-14
marine conservation, 16
Maritime Mobile Service Identity (MMSI) numbers, 12, 13, 15
Maritime Safety Information, 21
Marken, 255, 264
Markermeer, 255, 264-6
Maryport, 167, 171
Maseline Hbr, 332
Masned Sund, 298
Mawgan, 32
May, Isle of, 122
MAYDAY, 12, 13, 14, 17
Mayflower Marina, 38, 40
Maylandsea, 93
Mazagon, 413
Medemblik, 266
medical matters, 16, 17-18
Medina, River (IoW), 61, 62
Medway, River, 84, 86, 87-8
    passage from N Foreland, 85
    passage from Sunk Inner, 85
Medway Bridge Marina, 88
Menai Bridge, 176, 178
Menai Strait, 167, 176-9
Mengham, 73
Mercury Yacht Hbr (Hamble), 64, 65
Merelbeke, 247
Merrien, 364
Mersea Quarters, 93, 95
Mersey, River, 174, 175
METAREAS, 20
Meteorological Office (UK), 20
meteorology, 18-23
Methil, 121
Mevagissey, 34
MF/SSB radio, 18, 20
Middelburg, 254, 258
Middelharnis, 260
Milford Haven, 167, 185-8
    passage from North Channel, 168
    passage to Kilmore Quay, 188
    passage to Land's End, 188
    passage to Tenby, 188
    tidal curve, 463
Mill Bay, 43
Millbay Docks, 38
Millbrook Lake, 38
Minehead, 193-4
Mistley Quay, 99
MMSI numbers, 12, 13, 15
Moaña, 405
mobile phones, 12, 20
Moelfre, 179
Moerdijk, 254
Moines, Île aux (Morbihan), 371
Molène, Île de, 357
Möltenort, 284, 285
Møn, 298, 299
Monaco Radio, 20
Monkstone YC Marina, 190
Monnickendam, 264
Montrose, 124
Moray Firth, 119, 126-8
Morbihan, 369-72
Morecambe Bay, 171-3
Morgat, 359-60
Morlaix Roadstead & River, 347-9
Morse code, 10
Morston Creek, 105
Mortagne-sur-Gironde, 381
motor-sailing, 14

Mouillage des Herbiers, 349
Moulin Blanc, 358, 359
Mousa, 135
Mousehole, 29, 30
Muck, 148
Mudeford Quay, 55, 56
Muiden, 268
Muirtown, 128, 151
Mull, 149-50, 156
Mull of Galloway, 160, 165
Mull of Kintyre, 160
  passage from Oban, 151
Mullion, 31
Mulroy Bay, 228, 229
Muros, Ría de, 398-400
Mutford Lock, 103
Muxiá, 397
Mylor Yacht Hbr, 32, 33, 34

Nairn, 126, 128
Nantes, 374
National Coastwatch Institution, 14
national flags, 11
Navas Creek, 32
navigation, 15-16
navigational lights & shapes, 11
navigational warnings, 18-19, 23
NAVTEX, 11,12, 18, 19, 23
Nazaré, 407
Neath, River, 190
Needles Channel, 56
Nene, River, 107
Neptune Marina, 99
Nes (Ameland), 271
Ness, River, 128
Netherlands, 22, 249-73, 274, 275, 279-81
  inland waterways, 309
  passages across North Sea to, 249
  Standing Mast Route (Staande Masroute), 249, 250, 254-5
Netley, 64
Neumansdorp, 261
New Brighton, 175
New Grimsby Sound & Hbr (Scilly), 28, 29
New Quay (Cardigan), 182
New Ross, 215
Newcastle-upon-Tyne, 114
Newhaven, 74-5
  passage from Chichester, 70
  passage to Ramsgate, 75
Newlyn, 29-30
Newport (IoW), 61, 62
Newport (S Wales), 191
Newquay (Cornwall), 167, 196
Newtown River (IoW), 61
Neyland, 185, 187, 188
Nieuwe Maas, 261, 262-3
Nieuwe Meer, 255
Nieuwe Waterweg, 262-3
Nieuwpoort, 245, 249
Noirmoutier, Île de, 375
Noord, 261
Noord-Hollands Kanaal, 264
Nord-Ostsee-Kanal (Kiel Canal), 275, 303
  passage from Eider, 282
  passage from Elbe, 283-6
Norderney, 279, 280
  route from Borkum, 268, 271
Norfolk, *coastal passages*, 104, 106
Norfolk Broads, 103, 104
Norreborg, 302
North Berwick, 120

North Channel (Irish Sea), 166, 167
  passage to Milford Haven, 168
North Channel (Scilly), 29
North Foreland
  passage to Crouch, Blackwater & Colne, 85
  passage to Harwich, 81, 85
  passage to Swale, Medway & Thames, 85
North Hinder, 249
North Sea, *passage notes*, 104, 245, 249, 252-3, 268, 275
North Sea Canal, 249, 255, 263
North Sea TSS, 249
North Shields, 114
  tidal curve, 459
North Sunderland, 116
North Uist, 157, 158-9
Northney, 70, 71, 73
Northwood (RN) weather information, 20
Norway, 274-9, 289-91
Norwich, 104
Noss-on-Dart, 44

Oakley Creek, 97
Oare Creek, 85
Oban, 152-3
  passage from Ardnamurchan, 149
  passage to Mull of Kintyre, 151
  tidal curve, 462
Ocean Village Marina, 64
Odet, River, 363
Oerias, 408
oil rigs, 14, 275
Olas Voe, 138
Old Grimsby Sound (Scilly), 28, 29
Old Head of Kinsale, 209
Oléron, Île d', *passage to Gironde River*, 380
Olhão, 411
Olna Firth, 135
Olympiahafen (Schilksee), 286
Ons, Isla, 402
Oost Vlieland, 271
  route from Den Helder, 268, 270
  route to Lauwersoog, 271
Oostende, 245-6, 249
Oostereems, 273
Oosterschelde, 249, 254, 258-9
Oostmahorn, 273
Ore, River, 101-2
Orford Haven, 101-2
Orfordness, 102
Orkney, 132-4
  passage from Wick, 130
  passage to Shetland, 134
  passages from Scrabster, 130
Orwell, River, 99, 100
  passage to Netherlands, 249
Osborne Bay, 54
Osea, 93
Østerby, 293
Oude Rijn, 261
Oude Wetering, 254, 255, 261
Oudeschild, 269-70
  passage from UK, 268
Ouessant TSS, 355
Ouessant (Ushant), 355, 357
  passages from England, 355
Ouistreham, 321-2
Oulton Broad, 104

Ouse, River (Newhaven), 74
Ouse, River (Yorkshire), 109, 111
Outer Hebrides, 157-60
Oyster Haven, 210

Pabay, Sound of, 141
Padstow, 167, 188, 195-6
  passage to Clovelly & Ilfracombe, 195
Pagham Hbr, 70
Paglesham, 91, 93
Paignton, 46
Paimpol, 340, 341
Paluden, 353
Pandora Inn, 32
PANPAN, 13, 17
Papa Westray, 133, 134
Parkeston Quay, 99
Parkstone Haven, 55
Parn, 31
Parrett, River, 193
Pasajes, 387
passage planning, 11, *see also start of each section*
passports, 16
Pauillac, 381
Pedro Negras, Puerto, 400
Peel (IoM), 167, 168-9
Pegwell Bay, 75
Pembroke Dock, 185
Penally Rifle Range, 188
Penarth, 190-91
Pendine Range, 188
Pénerf, 372
Penhir, Anse de, 359
Penmarc'h Point, *passage to La Gironde River*, 362
Pennar Gut, 185, 188
Penrhyn, River, 32
Pentland Firth, *passsage*, 130
Penzance, 30
  passage from Scilly, 29
  passage to Falmouth, 31
Penzé, River, 348, 349
Percuil, 32
Perros-Guirec, 345
Perth, 122
Pertuis Breton, *passage to La Pallice*, 376
Peterborough, 106
Peterhead, 123, 125
Petit Port (Guernsey), 330
pets, 16
phonetic alphabet & numbers, 10
Piel Hbr, 172
Pierowall, 132, 133-4
pilots, books & guides, see start of each section
Pilsey Is, 70, 71, 73
Pin Mill, 99
Pincher Bay, 227
Pirenn, Île (Morbihan), 371
Piriac-sur-Mer, 373
Pittenweem, 121
Plockton, 144-5
Plouër, 338
Ploumanac'h, 345-6
Plymouth, 36-41
  passage from Falmouth, 32
  passage to L'Aber-Wrac'h, 353
  passage to Torbay, 41
  tidal curve, 453
Plymouth Sound, 37
Pobra do Caramiñal, 400, 401
Point Lynas, 179
Pointe de Grave, *tidal curve*, 470
Poll an Tighmhail, 158

pollution, 16
Polperro, 36
Polruan, 34, 35
Polwheveral, 32
Pont Aven, 365
Pontevedra, Ría de, 402, 403
Pontusval, 351
Poolbeg, 218
Poole Hbr, 52, 53-5
  passage from Weymouth, 51
  passage to Chichester, 54
  tidal curve, 454
Poolewe, 143
Porlock Weir, 194
Pornic, 374
Pornichet-La Baule, 374
Porsmoguer, Anse de, 355
Port d'Anglet, 383
Port Angol, 372
Port d'Arcachon, 382
Port Arthur Marina (Scalloway), 138
Port des Bas-Sablons, 337
Port Blanc, 344-5
Port de Bloscon, 351
Port de Bourgenay, 376
Port Chantereyne, 325, 326
Port Clos (Bréhat), 340
Port du Crouesty, 371-2
Port Deauville, 321
Port Dinorwic, 167, 179
Port Edgar, 120
Port Ellen, 155
Port En-Bessin, 322-3
Port Erin (IoM), 169
Port Guillaume, 321
Port Haliguen, 368-9
Port Hamble Marina, 64, 65
Port Joinville, 375
Port La Forêt, 363, 364
Port à La Jument, 331
Port Launay, 359
Port of London Authority, 88
Port Louis (Lorient), 366-7
Port Manec'h, 364-5
Port Maria, 367
Port Médoc, 381
Port Morny, 321
Port du Moulin Blanc, 358, 359
Port Navalo, 371
Port Olona, 376
Port Pendennis, 32, 34
Port Penrhyn, 176
Port Rhu, 360
Port Roshin, 231
Port St Mary (IoM), 169
Port Solent & Marina, 68
Port Styval, 359
port traffic signals, 9
Port Trebeurden, 346, 347
Port Tudy, 367
Port Zelande, 259
Portaferry, 221
Portavadie, 161
Portavogie, 219
Portchester Lake, 68
Porth Cressa (Scilly), 29
Porth Dinllaen, 167, 180
Porth Eilian, 179
Porthcawl, 190
Porthleven, 31
Porthmadog, 167, 181
Porthoustock Cove, 31
Portimão, 410
Portishead, 167, 188, 192
Portknockie, 126, 127
Portland Bill, 47

Portland Hbr, 50
  tidal curve, 454
Portmagee, 201, 202
Portmahomack, 126
Portmellon, 32
Portnalong, 149
Porto Novo (Pontevedra), 402
Portosin, 399
Portpatrick, 164
  passage from Campbeltown, 160
  passage to Kirkcudbright, 165
Portree, 145
Portrieux, 340
Portrush, 226
Portsalon, 227
Portsmouth, 66-8
  tidal curve, 457
Portsoy, 126
Portstewart, 225
Portugal, 22, 384-6, 405-411
  routes from UK, 385
Portyerrock Bay, 165
Porz Kernoch, 351
position, and GPS, 15
Poulimic, Anse de, 359
Póvoa de Varzim, 406
Preston, 167, 173
Primel, 347
Puerto America (Cádiz), 414
Puerto de Bermeo, 389
Puerto de Bilbao, 389-90
Puerto de Cariño, 394-5
Puerto de Castro Urdiales, 388
Puerto de Cudillero, 393
Puerto de Finisterre, 399
Puerto de Getaria, 388
Puerto de Gijon, 392
Puerto de Lequeitio, 388, 389
Puerto de Luarca, 393-4
Puerto de Luanco, 392, 393
Puerto de Pasajes, 387
Puerto Pedro Negras, 400
Puerto de Ribadesella, 391
Puerto de San Vicente de la Barquera, 391
Puerto Santa Maria (Cádiz), 414
Puerto de Santander, 390-91
Puerto Sherry, 414
Puerto de Zumaia, 388
Puffin Is, 179
Puilladobhrain, 153
pumping out, 16
Punta Lagoa, 405
Punta Umbria, 413
Pwllheli, 167, 180-81, 181
Pyefleet Creek, 95
pyrotechnics, 11, 15

Queenborough, 85, 87
Quenxe, 399
Quibéron peninsula, 368
Quimper, 363

Raasay, Sound of, 141
radar, 11, 13, 14, 15, 20
Rade de Brest, 358-9
radio, 11-12
  for inland waterways, 306-7
  weather information, 18-23
  see also start of each section
RAINWAT agreement, 306-7
Ramsey Bay (IoM), 168, 171
Ramsey Is & Sound (Wales), 183, 184
Ramsgate, 79
  passage from Newhaven, 75
Ramsholt, 101

Rance, River & Tidal Barrier, 338-9
Randmeren, 268
Rathlin Is & Sound, 151, 225
Rathlin O'Birne, 228
Rattray Head
  passage from Arbroath, 123
  passage to Inverness Firth, 127
  passage to Wick, 127
Ravedy Is, 228
Ravenglass, 171
Ray Gut, 89
Raz de Sein, 355, 361
Red Bay, 219
Redon, 372
refuse disposal, 16
regulations, 11-15
Rendsburg, 283-4
renewable energy generation, 15
rescue services, 12-14
Restronguet Creek, 32
Rhu, Port, 360
Rhyl, 174-6
Ría de Aldan, 402
Ría de Ares, 396
Ría de Aveiro, 407
Ría de Avilés, 392, 393
Ría del Barquero, 394
Ría de Betanzos, 396
Ría de Camariñas, 398
Ría de Cedeira, 395
Ría de Corcubión, 398, 399
Ría de Corme & Laxe, 398
Ría de El Ferrol, 395
Ría de Muros, 398-400
Ría de Pontevedra, 402, 403
Ría de Ribadeo, 394
Ría de Vigo, 404, 405
Ría de Viveiro, 394-5
Rianxo, 400, 401
Ribadeo, Ría de, 392-3
Ribadesella, 391
Ribble, River & Link, 173, 174
Richborough Quay, 77
Rieux, 372
Ringhaddy, 222
Ringvaart, 255, 262
Rispond Bay, 131
Roach, River, 89, 91-3
Rochefort, 379
Rochester, 87, 88
Rødvig, 295, 299
Rogerstown Inlet, 219
Rømø, 286
Roompot, 249, 254
Roompotssluis, 258
Rosbras en Riec sur Belon, 365
Roscanvel, Baie de, 359
Roscoff, 351
Rosehearty, 127
Rossaveal Hbr, 228, 240
Rossillion Bay, 230, 231
Rosslare, 216
Rostrevor, 219
Rota Marina, 414
Rothéneuf, 337
Rotterdam, 254, 262, 263
Rouen, 320
Roundstone, 234, 239
Rowhedge, 95, 96
Royal Clarence Marina, 68
Royal Harwich YC Marina, 99
Royal Navy, Northwood weather information, 20
Royal Norfolk & Suffolk Marina, 103
Royal Quays (N Shields), 114
Royan, 380-81

Ru Reidh (Re), 141
Ruan Creek, 33
Rum, 149
  passage to Islay, 155
Runswick Bay, 112
Rupel, River, 248
Rutland Hbr, 230-31
Ryde (IoW), 65-6
Ryde to Selsey, *tidal curve*, 456
Rye, 75-6

Sables d'Olonne, 375-6
Sada, Marina, 395, 396
safety, 11-15
Saildocs, 20
sailing vessels, 14
St Abbs Hbr, 120
St Agnes (Scilly), 29
St Alban's Head, 51
St Andrew's Bay, 122
St Ann's Head, 185, 188
  passage from Fishguard, 183
St Aubin, 334
St Austell Bay, 32
St Bees Head, *passage from Solway Firth*, 171
St Bride's Bay, 184
St Brieuc (Le Légué), 340
St Cast (Le Guildo), 339
St Denis d'Oléron, 379
Ste Evette, 360-61, 362
St George's Channel, 167
St German's River, 39, 40
St Gildas, 372-3
St Gilles-Croix-de-Vie, 375
St Goustan, 371
St Govan's Head, 188
St Helen's (Scilly), 28, 29
St Helier, 333-4
  tidal curve, 469
St Ives, 167, 188, 196
St Jean-de-Luz, 383
St John's Lake, 38
St Just Creek, 32
St Katharine's Docks, 88, 90
St Kilda, 157
St Magnus Bay, 136
St Malo, 336, 337
  passage to Les Héaux de Bréhat, 337
  tidal curve, 469
St Marcouf, Îles, 324
St Martin-de-Ré, 377-8
St Martin's (Scilly), 26, 29
St Mary's (Scilly), 26, 27, 28, 29
St Mawes Creek, 32-3
St Michael's Mount, 30-31
St Monans, 121-2
St Nazaire, 374
St Nicolas (Glénan), 364
St Patrick's Causeway, 181
St Peter Port, 329, 330
  tidal curve, 468
St Peter's Marina (Tyne), 114
St Quay-Portrieux, 340
St Sampson, 330
St Suliac, 338
St Tudwal's Road, 180
St Vaast-La Hougue, 324-5
St Valéry-en-Caux, 317-18
St Yves, 349
Salcombe, 42, 43
Salcombe, River, 42, 43-4
Saleen Bay, 234
Salrock, 236
Saltash Bay, 39, 40
Salterns Marina, 54
Salve Marine, 210

Samson (Scilly), 28
San Martin del Grove, 400
San Sebastián / Donastia, 387
San Simón, Ensenada de, 404
San Vicente de la Barquera, 389-91
San Xulian, 400
Sancti-Petri, 415
Sanda Sound, 160
Sandsend Bay, 112
Sandwich, 77
Sandy Haven, 185
Santa Maria, Puerto (Cádiz), 414
Santa Marta, Ensenada de, 395
Santa Uxia de Ribeira, 400
Santander, 389-90
Sanxenxo, 402, 403
Sardineiro, Ensenada de, 399
Sark, 331-2
Sarn Badrig, 181
satellite weather information, 20
Saundersfoot, 188-9
Sauzon (Belle Île), 368
Saye Bay, 328
Scalloway, 134, 135, 137-8
Scalpay, 158
Scalpay, Sound of, 141
Scapa Flow, 130, 132-3, 133
  passage from Scrabster, 130
  passage from Wick, 130
Scarborough, 111
Schelde, River, 247, 248, 254, *see also Oosterschelde; Westerschelde*
Schelde YC, 258
Schengen Agreement, 16, 275
Scheveningen, 249, 263
Schiedam, 262, 263
Schiermonnikoog Is, 272, 273
Schilksee-Olympiahafen, 286
Schlei, River, 297-8
Schull, 206-7
Scilly, 24, 25-9, 166, 312
  passage to Penzance, 29
Scotland, 118-65
Scrabster, 130, 131
  passage to Scapa Flow, 130
  passages to Orkney, 130
Scroby Sands, 104
sea areas, 18-19, 22
Sea Reach (Thames), 88, 89
Seaford Road, 75
Seaham, 112, 113
Seahouses, 116
Seaport Marina (Muirtown), 128, 151
Search & Rescue (SAR), 11-12
seasickness, 18
Sein, Île & Raz de, 361
Seine, River, 319, 320
Seli Voe, 138
Selsey, *tidal curve*, 456
Selsey Bill, 70
Shalfleet Quay, 61
Shambles, The, 47
Shamrock Quay, 64
Shannon, River, 234, 240-41
Shapinsay, 133
Sharfleet Creek, 88
Sharpness, 191-192
Sheephaven, 225
Sheerness, 87
  tidal curve, 458
Sheppey, Isle of, 84
Sherry, Puerto, 414
Shetland, 135-8
  passage from Orkney, 134
Shiant Isles, 157

shipping forecasts (UK), 19, 21
ship's papers, 15
Shoreham, 70, 73-4
  tidal curve, 457
Shotley Marina, 97, 98, 99
Shotley Point, 98, 99
signals
  COLREGS, 13
  distress & lifesaving, 12-13
  inland waterways, 306
  port traffic signals, 8
Sines, 409
Sizewell, 102
Sjælland, 295, 298-302
Skagen, 275, 288
Skagerrak, 275, 289-91
Skeld, 135
Skerries (Anglesey), 179
Skibbereen, 209
Skokholm, 188
Skomer, 183, 184, 188
Skudeneshavn, 290
Skullomie, 131
Skye, 141, 145-6, 148-9, 157
  passage to Ardnamurchan, 148
Slaughden, 101, 102
Sleat, Sound of, 145-6
Slenk, 273
Sligo, 232, 233
Slyne Head, 234
Small Downs, 75
Small Isles, 148, 149
Smalls (S Wales), 183, 188
Smalls Cove (Salcombe), 43
Smerwick Hbr, 234, 242-3
Snape Maltings, 102
Sneek, 255, 267, 273
Sneem, 202, 203
SOLAS V, 11
Solent, 54
  passage through, 59
  passage to Cherbourg, 59
Solva, 184
Solway Firth, 165, 166, 167
  passage to St Bees Head, 171
Somme Estuary, 316-17
Sønderborg, 295, 296-7
Sound, The (Øresund/Sundet), 275, 295, 299-302
Sound of Barra, 157
Sound of Berneray, 157
Sound of Harris, 157
Sound of Jura, 151
Sound of Luing, 151
Sound of Mull, 149, 150
Sound of Pabay, 141
Sound of Raasay, 141
Sound of Scalpay, 141
Sound of Sleat, 145-6
sound signals, 14
South Beveland Canal, 259
South Dock Marina (London), 88, 90
South Ferriby, 109
South Uist, 157, 159
South Voe, 138
Southampton Water, 63, 64
  passage from Cowes, 59
  tidal curve, 456
Southend, 89
Southsea Marina, 69, 70
Southwold, 102
Sovereign Yacht Hbr, 75, 76
Spaarndam, 255
Spain, 22, 384-405, 412-16
  routes from UK, 385
Spakenburg, 268
Sparkes Marina, 70, 73

Spiekeroog Is, 268, 279, 280, 281
Spui, River, 260-61
Spurn Head, 108, 109, 110
  passage to Berwick, 110
St *see under* Saint
Stacks Passage, 179
Staffa, 156
Standing Mast Route (Staande Masroute), 249, 250, 254-5
Stangate Creek, 87, 88
Starehole Bay, 43
Start Bay & Point, 41
Stavoren, 267
Stellendam, 249, 254, 260
Stickenhörn, 284, 285
Stoerhead, 141
Stonehaven, 124
Store Bælt (Great Belt), 295, 298-9
Stornoway, 157
  tidal curve, 461
Stour, River (Dorset), 55
Stour, River (Essex), 98, 99
Stour, River (Kent), 77
Stow Creek, 91
Stralsund, 304, 305
Strangford Lough, 221-2
Stranraer, 164
Strath, 144
Strathy Point, 130
Stroma, 130
Stromness, 132
  passage from Scrabster, 130
Stronsay, 132, 134
Struthan, 240
Studland Bay, 53
Styval, Port, 359
Subfacts, 21, 141
Suffolk Yacht Hbr, 98, 99
Suir, River, 215
Sumburgh Head, 134
Summer Isles, 143
sunburn, 18
Sunderland, 112, 113
Sundet (Øresund/The Sound), 275, 295, 299-302
Sunk Centre, 249
Sunk Inner, *passages*, 85
Sunk Outer, 249
Sunny Cove, 43
Sutton Bridge, 107
Sutton Hbr, 37, 38
Svendborg, 298, 299
Swale, 84, 85-7
  passage from N Foreland, 85
  passage from Whitaker Channel, 85
Swanage, 53
Swansea, 167, 189-90
Swanwick Marina (Hamble), 64, 65
Sweden, 274-9, 293-5, 302-3, 305
Swellies, The, 177-9
  passages, 178
Swilly, Lough, 225, 227
Swinge, The, 327
Sybil Point, 234
symbols, on charts & plans, 8, 9

Talmine, 131
Tamar, River, 39, 40
Tananger, 275, 290
Tanera More & Beg, 143
Taransay, 157
Tarbert (Harris), 157, 158
Tarbert (Loch Nevis), 147
Tarifa, 412
Tavira, 411

Tavy, River, 39, 40
Tawe, River, 189, 190
Tay, Firth & River, 119, 122-3
Tayport, 122-3
Tayvallich, 154-5
Tean (Scilly), 28
Tees Bay & River, 110
Teign, River, 47
Teignmouth, 47
Tejo, Rio, 408
telephone weather information, 21
telephones, 7, 306-7
Tenby, 188
  passage from Milford Haven, 188
Terneuzen, 247, 257
Terschelling, 249, 270-71
Texel, 268, 269-70
Texel TSS, 249, 251
text forecasts, 20
Thames Estuary, 80, 82
  passages, 81-3
  passages to continent, 249
Thames River, 88-9, 90
Thames Tidal Barrier, 88, 90
Thirslet Creek, 93
Tholen, 259
Thorney Channel, 70-73
Thurrock, 88
Thyborøn, 287-8
tidal curves, 453-71
  Aberdeen, 460
  Avonmouth, 463
  Belfast, 464
  Bournemouth to Christchurch, 455
  Brest, 470
  Calais, 467
  Channel Is, 468-9
  Cherbourg, 468
  Cobh (Cork), 464
  Cuxhaven, 465
  Dieppe, 467
  Dover, 457
  Dublin, 464
  Dunkerque, 466
  Esbjerg, 465
  Galway, 465
  Gibraltar, 471
  Greenock, 462
  Helgoland, 465
  Hoek van Holland, 466
  Holyhead, 463
  Immingham, 459
  Le Havre, 468
  Leith, 460
  Lerwick, 461
  Lisbon, 470
  Liverpool, 462
  London Bridge, 458
  Lowestoft, 459
  Lymington to Cowes, 455
  Milford Haven, 463
  North Shields, 459
  Oban, 462
  Plymouth, 453
  Pointe de Grave, 470
  Poole Hbr, 454
  Portland Hbr, 454
  Portsmouth, 457
  Ryde to Selsey, 456
  St Helier, 469
  St Malo, 469
  St Peter Port, 468
  Sheerness, 458
  Shoreham, 457
  Southampton, 456

  Stornoway, 461
  Tyne River (N Shields), 459
  Ullapool, 461
  Vlissingen (Flushing), 466
  Walton-on-the-Naze, 458
  Wick, 460
tidal generators, 14
Tide Mill Yacht Hbr, 100, 101
tides & tidal streams, 417-71
Tiree, 155
Titchmarsh Marina, 96, 97
Tobermory, 149-50
Toja Grande, Isla, 400
Tollesbury Marina, 93, 95
Tolverne, 33
Tongue, Kyle of, 131
Tönning, 282, 283
Topsham, 48, 49
Torbay, 41
  passage from Plymouth, 41
  passage to Weymouth, 47
Torekov, 295
Torpoint, 40
Torquay, 46-7
Totland Bay, 56
Totnes, 44, 45
Toulinguet Passage, 359
Tower Bridge, 88
traffic separation schemes (TSS), 14, *see also start of each section*
traffic signals (ports), 8
Treac'h er Béniguet, 373
Treac'h an Gouret, 373
Trébeurden, 346
Tréboul, 360
Trégastel, 346
Tregothnan, 33
Tréguier, River, 343-4
Tréhiguier, 372
Trent, River, 111
Tresco (Scilly), 28, 29
Trieux, River, 342-3
Trintelhaven, 266
Troia, 409
Troon, 164
Troup Head, 127
Trouville, 320-21
Truro, 33, 34
Truro River, 32, 32-4
Tuckton, 55
Tuskar Rock, *passage from Cork*, 212
Tweed, River, 116-17
Tyne, River, 114
  tidal curve, 459
Tynemouth, 114

Uig Bay, 148
UK Customs Confidential Hotline, 16
UK Customs National Yachtline, 16
UK inland waterways, 89, 109, 121, 151, 154, 162, 175
UK Meteorological Office, 20
Ullapool, 143
  tidal curve, 461
underwater archaeology, 16
Union Hall, 209
Universal Marina (Hamble), 64, 65
Unst, 135, 136, 137
Ura Firth, 136
urgency call, 12
Urk, 267
US NOAA Global Forecast System, 20
Ushant *see* Ouessant

Vaila Sound, 135, 138
Valentia, 200, 201, 234
   passage from Erris Head, 234
   passage to Crookhaven, 200
Van Harinxma Canal, 255, 272-3
Vannes, 369, 371
Vannes Channel, 370
Vannes, River, 369
VAT, 15
Veere, 254, 258
Veerse Meer, 254, 258, 259
   route from Vlissingen, 254
Ven, 295, 302
vent solaire, 355
Ventnor (IoW), 66
VHF radio, 11-12, 13, 18, 21, 22, *see also start of each section*
Viana do Castelo, 405
Vianamarina, 405
Victoria Hbr (Hartlepool), 113
Vidlin, 135
Vigo, Ría de, 404, 405
Vila Real de Santo Antonio, 412
Vilagarcia de Arousa, 401, 402
Vilamoura, 411
Vilanova de Arousa, 401, 402
virtual AIS, 15
visibility, 13, 14-15, 18, 23
Viveiro, Ría de, 393, 394
Vlaardingen, 262, 263
Vlieland gas field, 249
Vlissingen (Flushing), 254, 255, 257, 258
   route to Veerse Meer, 254
   tidal curve, 466
Voe (Olna Firth), 135
Volendam, 266
Volkerak, 254, 259, 260
Vordingborg, 298, 299

Waddenzee, 249, 268, 273, *see also* Wattensee
Wadebridge, 196
Walcheren Canal, 254, 258
Waldringfield, 101
Wales, 166, 167, 174, 176-91
Walkers Bay, 231
Wallasey, 175
Walls, 135, 138
Walton Backwaters, 96-7
Walton-on-the-Naze, *tidal curve*, 458
Wangerooge, 279, 281
Wareham Channel, 54, 55
Warkworth, 114-16
Warnemünde, 304
Warrenpoint, 219
Warsash, 64, 65
Wash, The, 106-8
Watchet, 167, 193
Waterford, 213-15
Watermill Cove (Scilly), 29
Watermouth, 188
Wattensee, 279, *see also* Waddenzee
Waveney, River, 104
waypoint lists, 14
waypoints, and GPS, 14
weather & forecasts, 18-23, *see also start of each section*
Weesp, 268
Welland, River, 108
Wells-next-the-Sea, 104, 105-6
Wemeldinge, 257, 259
Weser, River, 275, 279
West Bay (Bridport), 49
West Friesland TSS, 249

West Loch Tarbert (Harris), 157
West Looe, 37
West Mersea, 93-5, 95
West Terschelling, 268, 271
West Wittering, 73
Westere(e)ms, 273, 279, 280
Westerschelde, 247, 249, 256, 259
Weston-super-Mare, 192
Westport, 234, 235
Westray, 133-4
Wexford Hbr, 216
Weymouth, 50-51
   passage from Lyme Bay (Torbay), 47
   passage to Poole, 51
Whiddy Is, 205, 206
Whitaker Channel, *passage to E Swale*, 85
Whitby, 111-12
Whitehall Hbr, 132, 134
Whitehaven, 167, 172
Whitehills, 127
Whiten Head, 131
Whitesand Bay, 32
Whitstable, 85
WiFi, 15, 20
Wick, 130-31
   passage from Rattray Head, 127
   passages to Orkney, 130
   tidal curve, 460
Wicklow, 216-17
Wight *see* Isle of Wight
Willemstad, 254, 260, 261
   route to Dordrecht, 254
Williamston Pill, 185, 188
wind-farms, 14, 81, 83, 176, 249, 252, 253, 277
winds, 7, 20, *see also start of each section*
Winteringham Haven, 109
Winterton Ness, 104
Wisbech, 106-8
Witham, River, 108
Wizard Pool, 159
Woodbridge, 100, 101
Woodbury Point, 33
Woolverstone Marina, 99
Woolwich, 88
Wootton Creek (IoW), 65
Worbarrow Bay, 51
Workington, 171-2
Workum, 267
Wrabness, 99
wrecks, 16
Wych Channel, 55
Wyre Dock, 173

yacht safety, 11
Yachtline, 16
Yare, River, 104
Yarmouth (IoW), 57-8
Yealm, River, 41-3
Yell, 135
Yerseke, 259
Yeu, Île d', 375
Yokefleet Creek, 91, 93
York Marina, 111
Youghal, 212-13
Ystad, 305
Yzer, River, 245

Zeebrugge, 245, 246-7, 249
Zeegat van Ameland, 271
Zeegat van Terschelling, 270
Zeekanaal Brussel-Schelde, 248
Zeelandbrug, 258-9

Zierikzee, 258
Zoutkamp, 255, 273
Zuider Stortemelk, 270, 271
Zuiderzee, 266, 268
Zumaia, 388